Date	Event	Date	Event
1917	Yerkes (1876–1956), with colleagues, published the Army Alpha and Army Beta tests, which were group-administered intelligence tests used for the assessment of military recruits in the United States.	1938	Gesell (1880–1961) published the Gesell Maturity Scale.
1918	Otis (1886–1964) published the Absolute Point Scale, a group intelligence test.	1939	Wechsler (1896–1981) published the Wechsler-Bellevue Intelligence Scale; revisions were issued in 1955 and 1981 under the titles Wechsler Adult Intelligence Scale and Wechsler Adult Intelligence Scale – Revised.
1919	Monroe (1863–1939) and Buckingham (1899–) published the Illinois Examination, a group achievement test.	1940	P. Cattell (1893–) published the Cattell Infant Intelligence Scale.
1923	Kelly (1884–1961), Ruch (1903–1982), and Terman (1877–1956) published the Stanford Achievement Test.	1949	Wechsler Intelligence Scale for Children was published; a revision was issued in 1974 under the title Wechsler Intelligence Scale for Children – Revised.
1923	Kohs (1890–1984) published the Kohs Block Design Test, a test of nonverbal reasoning.	1959	Guilford (1897–) proposed a Structure of Intellect model of intelligence based on factor analytic methods.
1924	Porteus (1883–1972) published the Porteus Maze Test.	1961	Kirk (1904–) and J. J. McCarthy (1927–) published the Illinois Test of Psycholinguistic Ability.
1926	Goodenough (1886–1959) published the Draw-A-Man Test.	1963	R. B. Cattell (1905–) proposed a theory of fluid and crystallized intelligence.
1928	Arthur (1883–1967) published the Point Scale of Performance Tests.	1969	Bayley (1899–) published the Bayley Scales of Infant Development.
1931	Stutsman (1894–1980) published the Merrill-Palmer Scale of Mental Tests.	1972	D. McCarthy (1906–1974) published the McCarthy Scales of Children's Abilities.
1933	Thurstone (1887–1955) proposed a multiple factor analytic approach to the study of human abilities.	1975	U.S. Public Law 94-142 passed, proclaiming the right to equal education for all handicapped children.
1933	Tiegs (1891–1970) and Clark (1895–1964) published the Progressive Achievement Tests, later renamed the California Achievement Tests.	1979	Judge Peckham in California ruled in *Larry P.* v. *Wilson Riles* that intelligence tests used for the assessment of black children for classes for the educable mentally retarded are culturally biased.
1936	Lindquist (1901–1978), with colleagues, published the Iowa Every-Pupil Tests of Basic Skills, later renamed the Iowa Tests of Basic Skills.	1980	Judge Grady in Illinois ruled in *Parents in Action on Special Education* v. *Joseph P. Hannon* that intelligence tests are not racially or culturally biased and do not discriminate against black children.
1936	Piaget (1896–1980) published *Origins of Intelligence*.	1986	R. L. Thorndike (1910–), Hagen (1915–), and Sattler (1931–) published the Stanford-Binet Intelligence Scale: Fourth Edition, in which a point-scale format replaced the age-scale format of the Stanford-Binet Intelligence Scale: Form L-M.
1936	Doll (1889–1968) published the Vineland Social Maturity Scale; a revision by Sparrow (1933–), Balla (1939–1982), and Cicchetti (1937–) was published in 1985 under the title Vineland Adaptive Behavior Scales.		
1938	Bender (1897–1987) published the Bender Visual Motor Gestalt Test.		
1938	Buros (1905–1978) published the first *Mental Measurements Yearbook*.		

ASSESSMENT OF CHILDREN

———— Revised and Updated Third Edition ————

Jerome M. Sattler
San Diego State University

Jerome M. Sattler, Publisher, Inc.
San Diego

Portions of this book first appeared in *Assessment of Children's Intelligence* by Jerome M. Sattler, copyright © 1974 by Jerome M. Sattler, Publisher, Inc. and in *Assessment of Children's Intelligence and Special Abilities* (2nd edition) by Jerome M. Sattler, copyright 1982 © by Jerome M. Sattler, Publisher, Inc.

Editorial Services: Sally Lifland and Janice Ostock, Lifland et al., Bookmakers
Interior Design: Sally Lifland and Jerome M. Sattler
Interior Design Consultant: Kathi Townes
Cover Designer: Jerome M. Sattler
Proofreaders: Denise Houser, Jerome M. Sattler, and Scott M. Hofer
Production Coordinators: Sally Lifland and Jerome M. Sattler
Compositor: Harrison Typesetting, Portland, Oregon
Cover Printer: New England Book Components
Printer and Binder: Maple Vail Book Manufacturing Group

This text was set in Times Roman and Gill Sans, printed on Somerset matte, Smyth sewn, with Kivar 2 chrome cover stock.

Cover: Tridem-K by Vasarely, © S.P.A.D.E.M., Paris/ V.A.G.A., New York, 1986.

Library of Congress Cataloging-in-Publication Data

Sattler, Jerome M.
    Assessment of children / Jerome M. Sattler. — Rev. and updated.
  3rd ed.
     p. cm.
  Includes bibliographical references and indexes.
  ISBN 0-9618209-2-6
  1. Children — Intelligence testing.   2. Ability — Testing.
  3. Intelligence Tests. I. Title.
  BF432.C48S28 1992
  155.4'1393 — dc20   92-90724
                                   CIP

16 15 14 13 12 11 10 9 8   99 98 97
Printed in the United States of America

To my wife
Bonnie Jeanne Sattler

and my children
Heidi Beth, David Nathan, Deborah Elaine, and Keith Richard

for providing me with the support and love needed
to continue an important part of my life's work

CONTENTS

_ LIST OF TABLES

_ LIST OF FIGURES

_ LIST OF EXHIBITS _____

PREFACE

Children are our nation's most important resource. When questions arise about their growth and development, children are often referred to clinical and school psychologists. When these professionals perform a psychological evaluation, it is to assist in the diagnostic and treatment program. This text is designed to help students and professionals better perform such evaluations.

This text has evolved over a period of 27 years. In 1960 I began working on a manual that would help students learn to administer and interpret individual intelligence tests and to write reports based on their intelligence test findings. This effort culminated in the first edition, published in 1974 under the title *Assessment of Children's Intelligence*. In 1981 a second edition was published under the title *Assessment of Children's Intelligence and Special Abilities*. This edition contained a wider range of assessment procedures, including intelligence tests, achievement tests, perceptual-motor tests, adaptive behavior scales, and behavioral checklists. The third edition, published in 1988 under the title *Assessment of Children*, adds to the coverage of the second edition by including chapters on the Wechsler Adult Intelligence Scale—Revised, the Stanford-Binet Intelligence Scale: Fourth Edition, the interview, and systematic behavioral observation.

The third edition is a thorough revision. There are over 1500 references, approximately 700 of which are new to this edition. Every chapter has been rewritten with one goal in mind: to present as clearly as possible the latest research and theory in the field of assessment of children.

The assessment task will be facilitated by the numerous semistructured interview formats provided. These are designed to help students and clinicians alike obtain relevant information from parents, teachers, children, and their families. Additionally, specific guidelines are included for interviewing parents whose children are recovering from brain injury or who may be developmentally delayed.

Numerous teaching aids are found in the text. They include

• major headings at the beginning of each chapter to help orient the reader
• detailed summaries to aid in mastering material
• key terms, concepts, and names at the end of each chapter to help in reviewing the material
• study questions at the end of each chapter to help in reviewing the issues discussed in the chapter

• test-your-skill exercises to help in sharpening interpretive and writing skills

• detailed analyses of two model psychological reports to help in understanding the construction of reports

• report writing principles to guide in developing assessment findings

• exercises in narrative, interval, event, and ratings types of observational recording to help in learning about systematic observational methods

• technical terms defined throughout the text to help in increasing comprehension level

• guidelines for evaluating test administration techniques, interview techniques, and report writing to help in analyzing assessment skills

The book is designed to teach clinical assessment skills to students in clinical, school, and counseling psychology and to enable students in special education to understand the assessment process. The text also can serve as a reference source for psychologists and other professionals such as teachers, pediatricians, child psychiatrists, social workers, and speech therapists. The text is recommended for courses in assessment of intelligence, assessment in clinical psychology, assessment in school psychology, psychoeducational assessment, assessment of learning disabilities, and assessment in special education. The book also may be used in specialized courses in tests and measurement.

The book can be used in either a one- or a two-semester course in assessment. Various arrangements of chapters will meet the objectives of different courses. For example:

1. The entire text can be used in a comprehensive one-semester course designed for the study of the assessment of intelligence and special abilities.

2. In a two-semester course, the material can be divided as follows. The first semester might cover theory, administration, and evaluation of intelligence tests, using Chapters 1 through 11 and Chapters 23 and 24; the second semester might cover test applications and special ability tests, using Chapters 12 through 22.

The third edition of *Assessment of Children* is accompanied by an Instructor's Manual. The Instructor's Manual contains information on how to organize an individual intelligence testing course; exercises covering clinical, technical, and professional skills; and multiple-choice questions.

The *Revised and Updated Third Edition* contains seven additional appendixes—G, H, I, J, K, L, and M—that cover the Wechsler Preschool and Primary Scale of Intelligence—Revised and the Wechsler Intelligence Scale for Children—III. The seven additional appendixes are also reprinted in a separate publication called *Assessment of Children: WISC-III and WPPSI-R Supplement* (ISBN 0-9618209-3-4).

_ ACKNOWLEDGMENTS _____

I don't believe a committee can write a book. There are all kinds of things a committee can do. It can, oh, govern a country, perhaps, but I don't believe it can write a book. I think a book has to be written by some single mind. But, of course, that's a very large and formidable undertaking, and I think if a writer is wise, he gets all the help he can from other people. The responsibility is on him, it must pass through his mind, but he takes help where he can get it.

—Arnold Toynbee

I have been extremely fortunate in obtaining guidance from some of our nation's outstanding authorities in the field of psychology and measurement. In addition, some of my students and former students gave generously of their time to comment on the manuscript. The following individuals read every chapter of the manuscript and made many invaluable suggestions. Their help is much appreciated.

Ms. Angela Ballantyne, San Diego State University
Dr. Bruce A. Bracken, Memphis State University
Ms. Sandra Delehanty, San Diego State University
Dr. Kathryn C. Gerken, University of Iowa
Dr. Robert Harrington, University of Kansas
Dr. William A. Hillix, San Diego State University
Dr. Thomas J. Kehle, University of Connecticut
Dr. Howard M. Knoff, University of South Florida
Dr. Thomas Oakland, University of Texas, Austin
Dr. Michael C. Roberts, University of Alabama
Dr. Arthur B. Silverstein, University of California, Los Angeles
Dr. William Strein, University of Maryland

A number of individuals made useful comments and suggestions on one or more of the chapters. I wish to express my thanks for their help and advice. They are as follows:

Dr. Galen Alessi, Western Michigan University
Dr. Edward F. Alf, San Diego State University
Dr. Roger Bakeman, Georgia State University
Mr. John Baker, Hewlett-Packard, San Diego
Dr. Richard Berg, West Virginia University
Ms. Amy Bihrle, San Diego State University
Dr. Thomas Bouchard, Jr., University of Minnesota
Dr. Rebecca Bryson, San Diego State University
Ms. Jeannine Feldman, California School of Professional Psychology, San Diego
Dr. Larry Fenson, San Diego State University
Ms. Sara Frampton, San Diego City Schools
Ms. Kristin Gist, Children's Hospital, San Diego
Dr. Gerald Goldstein, Veterans Administration Medical Center, Pittsburgh
Dr. Robert Heaton, University of California, San Diego
Dr. Robert Hoge, Carlton University
Ms. Deanne Johnson, San Diego State University
Dr. Giulio Lancione, University of Leiden
Ms. Sharry LaPage, San Diego State University

Mr. Roy Logan, San Diego City Schools
Dr. Guy Lories, Université Catholique de Louvain
Dr. Sandra Marshall, San Diego State University
Dr. Shay McCordick, San Diego State University
Dr. Charles M. Moore, University of Wisconsin—
   LaCrosse
Ms. Miriam Mott, San Diego State University
Dr. Han Oud, University of Nijmegen
Dr. Nancy Robinson, University of Washington
Dr. Wendy C. Roedell, University of Washington
Dr. Weid Ruijssenaars, University of Nijmegen
Ms. Virginia R. Shabatay, Lewis and Clark College
Dr. Richard Schulte, San Diego State University
Dr. Melvin Schwartz, Private Practice, San Diego
Ms. Paula Shear, San Diego State University
Dr. Jack Smith, San Diego State University
Dr. Keith Stanovich, Oakland University
Dr. Philip Strain, University of Pittsburgh
Ms. Michella Toshima, San Diego State University

Many students at San Diego State University assisted me
in locating references, reviewing test manuals, and performing many other tasks related to the preparation of the
manuscript. I am grateful for their help. They are as
follows:

Ms. Regina Burch
Mr. Daniel J. Christensen
Ms. Eleanor D. Gauker
Ms. Amalie Grabowski
Mr. Scott M. Hofer
Ms. Julie Johnson
Ms. Melissa Kessler
Ms. Eileen Koecher
Ms. Sharon Levy
Ms. Patricia McCabe
Mr. John Meadors
Ms. Janis Paprocki
Mr. Robin Rakosi
Mr. Mark T. Rhea
Ms. Shelly Ruderman
Mr. Christopher Seck
Ms. Bita Vokhshour
Ms. Kim Weiner

I have also benefited from the generosity of many psychologists who willingly shared their cases with me. Their
help enabled me to present some outstanding examples of
psychological evaluations from a clinical or school psychology perspective. These individuals are as follows:

Ms. Jay Bahnsen, Lancaster City Schools
Dr. Elizabeth Bard, Akron, Ohio

Dr. Richard A. Berg, West Virginia University
Ms. Lynda L. Boucugnani, Griffin-Spalding County
   School System
Dr. Susan B. Campbell, University of Pittsburgh
Dr. Frances M. Culbertson, University of Wisconsin—
   Whitewater
Ms. Marilyn Danzig, Montclair, New Jersey
Ms. Ann V. Deaton, University of Texas at Austin
Dr. Sheila Eyberg, University of Oregon
Dr. Antonia Forster, University of Oregon
Dr. Patrick C. Fowler, University of Virginia
Ms. Kristin Gist, Children's Hospital, San Diego
Dr. Charles J. Golden, Nebraska Psychiatric Institute
Mr. Anthony C. Greene, Fairfield, Alabama
Ms. Sara Holland, San Diego City Schools
Dr. John G. Hovater, Florence, Alabama
Dr. Mary Hoy, Iowa State University
Ms. Deanne Johnson, San Diego State University
Mr. T. J. Kenny, Ruxton, Maryland
Mr. John P. Klaber, Yellowstone-West Special Services
   Cooperative
Dr. Shelley B. Kramer, Southwood Mental Health Center,
   Chula Vista, California
Ms. Susan H. Largen, Carlsbad Unified School District
Dr. Harvey S. Levin, University of Texas
Dr. Marc Lewkowicz, Southwood Mental Health Center,
   Chula Vista, California
Ms. Alice Martinez, Regional Program for the Deaf, El
   Paso, Texas
Dr. Michael C. Roberts, University of Alabama
Dr. Carolyn S. Schroeder, University of North Carolina
Ms. Fredye J. Sherr, Regional Special Education Consor-
   tium, Milford, New Hampshire
Dr. Esther Sinclair, University of California, Los Angeles
Dr. Suzanne B. Sobel, Satellite Beach, Florida
Ms. Glenyth A. Turner, San Diego Mesa College
Ms. Judith Wheeler, Texas School for the Deaf

This text could not have been completed without the help
of my two able secretaries, Maria Konczak and Jo Lynn
Mack. Thank you, Maria and Jo Lynn, for your dedication
and your patience. You are both truly professionals in your
craft. At San Diego State University, Doris Townsend and
the late Dorathe Frick typed various chapters. Thank you,
Doris and Dorathe, for your help. Sally Farris and Mike
McCurdy, from the Computer Center at San Diego State
University, gave generously of their time to help us learn
the word processing system provided by the Computer
Center. Your kindness and expert and professional support
are much appreciated. Harry Mack, too, deserves thanks
for his help in setting up a word processing program. The

Interlibrary Loan service at San Diego State University has assisted me in obtaining many books and journals. Their help is gratefully acknowledged. I also wish to thank Anne Brook and Joseph Ferrara from the Media Technology Services at San Diego State University for their help with reproducing various figures needed in the text.

I also wish to recognize the contribution of Joseph J. Ryan to the Wechsler Assessment of Intelligence Scale—Revised chapter. It was a pleasure working with you on this chapter. Michael Geisser is to be thanked for his help in performing the factor analyses on the Wechsler Adult Intelligence Scale—Revised and the Stanford-Binet Intelligence Scale: Fourth Edition.

I also wish to thank the Instituut voor Orthopedagogiek at the University of Nijmegen, The Netherlands for their warm hospitality and support during the 1983–1984 academic year. While I was an exchange professor at the University of Nijmegen, I began my work on the interview and observation chapters. The academic and library staff kindly assisted me in discussing material and obtaining references for these two chapters. I look upon my stay in Holland as one of the highlights of my life.

The staff at Lifland et al., Bookmakers has been outstanding. Thank you, Sally Lifland and Janice Ostock, for making this a truly readable and almost error-free textbook. Both of you represent the highest standards of your profession. Countless readers will appreciate the clarity that both of you have given to my prose and ideas. It has been a pleasure working with both of you and your staff.

Harrison Typesetting, Inc. is to be congratulated for transforming a barely decipherable copyedited manuscript into clear and readable type. Thank you, Richard and Phillipa Harrison and your staff, for turning thousands of manuscript pages into camera-ready copy. Your expertise is most appreciated. I also wish to thank the staff at Maple Vail for their assistance in printing the book.

My family has been a constant source of support during the writing of this text. Thank you, Bonnie, for putting up with me during the many years needed to complete this edition. Debbie, my 11-year-old daughter, assisted in compiling part of the name index. And Keith, my 4-year-old son, has been a delight in our family, waiting for me to finish so that we could go camping. My two older children, Heidi and David, have also been understanding about their father's obsession with writing the definitive text on children's assessment. I also wish to thank Richard, Marjorie, and Paul McIntyre; Paul, Florence, Susan, Robert, and Robin Sattler; and Walter Philips, my son-in-law, for their continual support and interest in my work. Finally, Baxter Venable, my editor at W. B. Saunders, continues to be *my editor*, although my association with W. B. Saunders ended in 1980. His guidance and support since 1971 have been a beacon in my life. Whenever I have an important decision to reach about the book, Baxter is there with his careful advice and suggestions. Thank you, Baxter.

December 1987   Jerome M. Sattler
                                 San Diego State University
                                 Psychology Department
                                 San Diego, CA 92182

FOR THE REVISED AND UPDATED THIRD EDITION

Again, I have been fortunate in obtaining wise counsel from many individuals who generously gave of their time to read the manuscript. I am grateful for their assistance. I wish to thank Ms. Angela Ballantyne, Ms. Valerie Brew, Ms. Beverly Dexter, Dr. Jeannine Feldman, Dr. William A. Hillix, Ms. Tina S. Oprendeck, and Ms. Naomi Singer, all from San Diego State University; Dr. James Gyurke, The Psychological Corporation; Dr. Leslie Atkinson, Surrey Place Centre; Dr. Larry Hilgert, Valdosta State College; Dr. Aurilio Prifitera, The Psychological Corporation; Ms. Bonnie J. Sattler, Kaiser Permanente; Dr. Arthur B. Silverstein, University of California, Los Angeles; Dr. John R. Slate, Arkansas State University; Dr. Lawrence Weiss, The Psychological Corporation; and Dr. Ira Lee Zimmerman, Private Practice in Los Angeles, for making the new appendixes more readable, thorough, and comprehensive.

I wish to thank Dr. Jeff Bryson, Dr. Fred Hornbeck, Mr. James Edwards, Mr. Michael Irwin, and Ms. Rachel Litonjua-Witt, all from San Diego State University, for lending their excellent technical expertise to several different parts of the appendixes.

I wish to thank Ms. Jennifer Mayes and Ms. Deborah Walker, both from San Diego State University, and Colleen Beaudoin, Jerome M. Sattler, Publisher, for their excellent clerical and secretarial help in getting the manuscript ready for production.

I wish to thank Richard and Phillipa Harrison and the staff at Harrison Typesetting, Roy Wallace and the staff at Maple Vail Book Manufacturing, and Ed Corvelli and the staff at New England Book Components, for their professional and technical expertise in getting the text typeset and printed.

And finally, I wish to thank Sally Lifland, Janice Ostock, and the staff at Lifland et al., Bookmakers, for doing a superlative job in editing the manuscript and in helping with the production of the book.

March 1992   Jerome M. Sattler
                                 San Diego State University

ABOUT THE AUTHOR

Ron Ray

Jerome M. Sattler is a Professor of Psychology at San Diego State University, where he has taught since 1965. A diplomate in Clinical Psychology and a fellow of Division 16 (School Psychology) of the American Psychological Association, he served as an expert witness in the *Larry P.* v. *Wilson Riles* case involving the use of intelligence tests for the assessment of Black children in California public schools. He has contributed over 95 publications to the fields of clinical and school psychology and has served as an associate editor for many psychology and psychoeducational journals. Additionally, he has delivered over 155 invited lectures and workshops. In 1972 he was Senior Fulbright lecturer at the Universiti of Kebangsaan in Malaysia.

Jerry completed his undergraduate studies at City College of New York. He obtained his master's and doctorate degrees in psychology at the University of Kansas and spent four years in the Veterans Administration clinical psychology training program. The people who influenced him most at the University of Kansas were Fritz Heider and John Chotlos. When he is not working on *the book*, Jerry enjoys listening to jazz, reading, watching news programs and movies, and walking.

1

CHALLENGES IN ASSESSING CHILDREN

Tests not accompanied by detailed data on their construction, validation, uses, and limitations should be suspect.

—Oscar K. Buros

Exhibit 1-1

Psychological Reports Do Count: The Case of *Daniel Hoffman* v. *the Board of Education of the City of New York*

THE CASE

Introduction

The case of *Daniel Hoffman* v. *the Board of Education of the City of New York* is instructive because it illustrates the important role that testing and psychological reports can play in people's lives. In this case, the report contained a recommendation that was ignored by the school administrators. Years later when the case was tried, the failure to follow the recommendations became a key issue.

Basis of Litigation

Daniel Hoffman, a 26-year-old man, brought suit against the New York City Board of Education in 1978 to recover damages for injuries resulting from his placement in classes for the mentally retarded. The complaint alleged that (a) the Board was negligent in its original testing procedures and placement of Mr. Hoffman, causing or permitting him to be placed in an educational environment for mentally retarded children and consequently depriving him of adequate speech therapy that would have improved his only real handicap, a speech impediment; and (b) the Board was negligent in failing or refusing to follow adequate procedures for the recommended retesting of Mr. Hoffman's intelligence.

Board of Education's Position

The Board of Education took the position that Mr. Hoffman's IQ of 74, obtained on the Stanford-Binet Intelligence Scale when he was 5 years, 9 months old, indicated that his placement in a class for the mentally retarded was appropriate. They contended that the test was proper, that it was administered by a competent and experienced psychologist, and that it was the unanimous professional judgment of Mr. Hoffman's teachers, based on their evaluation and his performance on standardized achievement tests, that a retest was not warranted. The Board made clear that at the time Mr. Hoffman was in school its policy was to retest only when retesting was recommended by teachers or requested by parents.

The psychological report was one of the key documents upon which the entire case rested. The psychologist had recommended that Mr. Hoffman be placed in a class for the mentally retarded on the basis of his IQ of 74. Mr. Hoffman entered special education classes and remained in them throughout his school years. However, the key sentence in the 1957 report was as follows: "*Also, his intelligence should be reevaluated within a two-year period so that a more accurate estimation of his abilities can be made*" (italics added).

The Board of Education argued that the psychologist did not literally mean "retesting" because he did not use this word in the report. Although a minority of the court concurred with this interpretation, the majority supported Mr. Hoffman's position that reevaluation meant only one thing — administration of another intelligence test.

Removal from Training Program

In a curious twist of fate, testing, which resulted in the assignment of Mr. Hoffman to special education, also played an important role in removing him from a special workshop program during his late teenage years. Mr. Hoffman had made poor progress during his school years, and there had been no significant change in his severe speech defect. At the age of 17 years, he entered a sheltered workshop for retarded youths. After a few months in the program, he was given the Wechsler Adult Intelligence Scale and obtained a Verbal Scale IQ of 85, a Performance Scale IQ of 107, and a Full Scale IQ of 94. His overall functioning was in the Normal range. On the basis of these findings, Mr. Hoffman was not permitted to remain at the Occupational Training Center. On learning of this decision, he became depressed, often staying in his room at home with the door closed.

Mr. Hoffman then received assistance from the Division of Vocational Rehabilitation. At the age of 21, he was trained to be a messenger, but he did not like this work. At the time of the trial, he had obtained no further training or education, had not made any advancement in his vocational life, and had not improved his social life.

Inadequate Assessment Procedures

During the trial it was shown that the psychologist who tested Mr. Hoffman in kindergarten had failed (a) to interview Mrs. Hoffman, (b) to obtain a social history, and (c) to discuss the results of the evaluation with her. If a history had been obtained, the psychologist would have learned that Mr. Hoffman had been tested 10 months previously at the National Hospital for Speech Disorders and had obtained an IQ of 90 on the Merrill-Palmer Scale of Mental Tests.

Verdict and Appeals

The case was initially tried before a jury, which returned a verdict in favor of Mr. Hoffman, awarding him damages of $750,000. This decision was appealed to the Appellate Division of the New York State Supreme Court, which affirmed the jury verdict on November 6, 1978 but lowered damages to $500,000. The New York State Appeals Court overturned the Appellate Court's decision, including the original award, on December 17, 1979, finding that the court system was not the proper arena for testing the validity of educational decisions or for second guessing such decisions.

(Exhibit continues next page)

Exhibit 1-1 (cont.)

THE IMPORTANCE OF THE CASE
FOR THE PRACTICE OF
SCHOOL AND CLINICAL PSYCHOLOGY

The case of *Daniel Hoffman* v. *the Board of Education of the City of New York* is one of the first cases in which the courts carefully scrutinized psychological reports and the process of special education placement. The case touches on many important issues involved in the psychoeducational assessment process. Let us consider some of these issues.

1. *Psychological reports do count.* Psychological reports are key documents used by mental health professionals, teachers, administrators, physicians, courts, parents, and children.

2. *Words can be misinterpreted.* A pivotal point in the case was the meaning of the words "reevaluate" and "retest." Some participants in the case, as well as some justices, assigned these words different meanings. Therefore, careful attention must be given to the wording of reports. Reports must be written clearly, with findings and recommendations stated as precisely as possible.

3. *IQs change.* Children's IQs do not remain static. Although there is a certain stability after children reach 6 years of age, their IQs do change.

4. *Different tests may provide different IQs.* The three IQs obtained by Mr. Hoffman at 5, 6, and 18 years of age may reflect differences in the content and standardization of the three tests rather than genuine changes in cognitive performance.

5. *Placement decisions must be based on more than one assessment approach.* A battery of psychological tests and procedures, along with interviews with parents and reports from teachers, should be used in the assessment process. All available information should be reviewed before placement recommendations are made.

6. *The instruments used must be appropriate.* A child who has a speech or language handicap may need to be assessed with performance tests in addition to, or in place of, verbal tests.

7. *Previous findings must be reviewed.* Before the formal assessment is carried out, the assessor must determine whether the child has been previously tested and, if so, review these findings.

Although many issues were involved in the case of Daniel Hoffman, the preceding points are particularly germane to the practice of school and clinical psychology. They illustrate that psychological evaluation, including the formulation of recommendations, requires a high level of competence. The case also demonstrates that it is incumbent on administrators to carry out the psychologist's recommendations.

Note. The citations for this case are 410 N.Y.S.2d 99 and 400 N.E.2d 317-49 N.Y.2d 121.

You are about to begin a study of assessment procedures that affect children, their families, schools, and society. The assessment procedures covered in this text have their roots in century-old traditions of psychological, clinical, and educational measurement. They are used to evaluate children for many different clinical and psychoeducational purposes, including diagnosis, eligibility determination for special programs, and evaluation of progress and change. The tools of assessment are continuously being refined, and this text is intended to help you become aware of new developments in the field.

Those of you who are beginning your study of assessment are likely to be overwhelmed at first by the myriad details that you will encounter in learning how to administer, score, interpret, and report the results of psychological and psychoeducational tests and other assessment procedures. You may be asked to review psychometric theory and to study various theoretical views and models that attempt to explain intelligence and other abilities. Some of you may also be exposed to computer-oriented procedures for interpreting assessment data. And, of course, all of you will be required to write, or at least to generate with the aid of a computer, psychological reports. This text will provide you with tools that will make each of these tasks a little easier and you more competent. The success of this text will be determined by the competency that you develop in meeting these various challenges.

FOUR PILLARS OF ASSESSMENT: NORM-REFERENCED TESTS, INTERVIEWS, OBSERVATIONS, AND INFORMAL ASSESSMENT

Norm-Referenced Tests

This text is based on the premise that norm-referenced tests are indispensable for clinical and psychoeducational assessment. Norm-referenced tests are standardized on a clearly defined group, termed the *norm group*, and scaled so that each individual score reflects a rank within the norm group (see Chapter 2 for further discussion). Norm-referenced tests have been developed to assess many areas, including intelligence; reading, arithmetic, and spelling abilities; visual-motor skills; gross and fine motor skills; and adaptive behavior. We are fortunate to have a choice of well-standardized and psychometrically sound tests with which to evaluate children. Still, there are tests that do not meet acceptable standards. When you have completed your study of this text, you will be in a better position to evaluate the merits of norm-referenced tests.

Green (1981, p. 1001) provides a useful description of what constitutes a test:

A standardized test is a task or a set of tasks given under standard conditions and designed to assess some aspect of a person's knowledge, skill, or personality. A test provides a scale of measurement for consistent individual differences regarding some psychological concept and serves to line up people according to that concept. Tests can be thought of as yardsticks, but they are less efficient and reliable than yardsticks, just as the concept of verbal reasoning ability is more complex and less well understood than the concept of length. A test yields one or more objectively obtained quantitative scores, so that, as nearly as possible, each person is assessed in the same way. The intent is to provide a fair and equitable comparison among test takers.

Norm-referenced tests have several benefits. They provide valuable information about a child's level of functioning in the areas covered by the tests. They take relatively little time to administer, permitting a sampling of behavior within a few hours. Each appraisal can provide a wealth of normative information that would be unavailable to even the most skilled observer who did not use tests.

Norm-referenced tests also provide an index for evaluating change in many different aspects of the child's physical and social world, including developmental changes and the effects of remediation. At present, however, norm-referenced tests provide only limited information about the ways children learn, or about ways to ameliorate learning handicaps. There is much to be learned about tailoring remediation strategies to individual patterns of learning ability. Standardized tests need to be supplemented with new tests and techniques designed for such purposes.

Interviews

Valuable assessment information is gained through interviewing the child, parents, teachers, and other individuals familiar with the child. Interviews are more open and less structured than formal testing and give interviewees an opportunity to convey information in their own words. Chapter 16 provides an in-depth discussion of interviewing techniques.

Observations

Observations of referred children in their natural surroundings provide valuable assessment information. How do they behave in school settings, at home, and in the neighborhood? Does the teacher treat them differently than other children? How do their peers react to them? The answers to these and similar questions will give you a better picture of children and the settings in which they function, and will help you to formulate better remedial and treatment programs. Chapter 17 explains how to conduct observations in a systematic manner.

Informal Assessment

Standardized norm-referenced tests may at times need to be supplemented with informal assessment procedures, such as criterion-referenced tests (which may or may not be standardized and normed) and teacher-made tests. For example, it may be valuable to obtain language samples from children, test children's ability to profit from systematic cues, and evaluate children's reading skills under various conditions. The realm of informal assessment is vast, and you will have many opportunities to develop your own procedures and to use those designed by others. However, because informal assessment procedures have unknown technical adequacy (for example, unknown reliability and validity), they must be used cautiously. Various informal assessment procedures are described in this text.

Comment on the Four Pillars of Assessment

The four pillars of assessment—norm-referenced tests, interviews, observations, and informal assessment—complement one another and form a firm foundation for making decisions about children. Information from the various sources must be woven together so that the final tapestry is integrated and understandable. Recommendations should be based on both assessment results and the resources of the school, family, and community. Major discrepancies among the findings obtained from the various assessment procedures must be resolved before any diagnostic decisions or recommendations are made. For example, if the intelligence test results indicate that the child is currently functioning in the retarded range whereas the interview findings and adaptive behavior results suggest more normal functioning, you are advised not to make a diagnosis of mental retardation. Further inquiry is obviously needed. As another example, before you recommend that a gifted female child receive special class placement, you should consider the feelings and wishes of the child, parents, and teacher. Does the child desire to leave her present classroom? Is she working close to capacity? Will the new setting be more stimulating? Special class placement decisions always call for an understanding of the present setting, the new setting, and how changes may affect children, their families, and the teachers involved.

In clinical and psychoeducational assessment of children, assessment strategies must be selected with developmental processes in mind. Evaluation of children should never be conducted without considering developmental norms. Standardized tests usually provide such norms, but informal assessment procedures should also be based on a developmental perspective. If you use assessment techniques that do not have well-established national norms, it is important to obtain local norms (for example, norms developed for one specific school or community) or to develop informal norms to evaluate the child's performance more accurately.

The use of more than one assessment procedure – the *multiple assessment approach* – provides a wealth of data regarding the child. This approach permits evaluation of the biological, cognitive, social, and interpersonal variables that affect the child's current behavior. It is not always the case, however, that more is better. You must consider carefully whether additional assessment procedures contribute to a better understanding of the child. Certainly, different methods are likely to give additional information, but is the additional information necessary? Is the information obtained worth the extra time, effort, and cost? These questions must be considered when assessment instruments and procedures are being chosen. The nature of the referral questions, as well as personnel and time constraints, will help determine which specific assessment procedures should be used.

In the diagnostic assessment of children, it is important to obtain information from parents and other significant individuals in the child's environment. For school-age children, teachers are an important additional source of information. It is pointless to evaluate only the child without evaluating other factors that may be affecting the child's behavior.

GUIDELINES FOR ASSESSMENT

The assessment process should never focus exclusively on a test score or a number. Each child has a range of competencies that can be evaluated by both quantitative and qualitative means. Your aim is to assess the competencies as well as the limitations of the child; the focus should not be on handicaps solely or on areas of weakness. The

following principles form an important foundation for the clinical and psychoeducational use of tests.

- Tests are samples of behavior.
- Tests do not directly reveal traits or capacities, but may allow inferences to be made about the examinee.
- Tests should have adequate reliability and validity.
- Test scores and other test performances may be adversely affected by temporary states of fatigue, anxiety, or stress; by disturbances in temperament or personality; or by brain damage.
- Test results should be interpreted in light of the child's cultural background, primary language, and any handicapping conditions.
- Test results are dependent on the child's cooperation and motivation.
- Tests purporting to measure the same ability may produce different scores for that ability.
- Test results should be interpreted in relation to other behavioral data and to case history information, never in isolation.

Tests and other assessment procedures are powerful tools, but their effectiveness will depend on your skill and knowledge. When wisely and cautiously used, assessment procedures can assist you in helping children, parents, teachers, and other professionals obtain valuable insights. When used inappropriately, they can mislead those who must make important life decisions, thus causing harm and grief. As we saw in the case of Daniel Hoffman, presented in Exhibit 1-1, assessment results do have an impact on many people, directly affecting the lives of children and their parents. As a result of clinical and psychoeducational evaluations, actions are taken and critical decisions are made. You must be careful about the words you choose when you (a) write reports and (b) communicate with other professionals, the children themselves, and their families. Your work represents a major professional contribution.

LABELS AND CLASSIFICATION

The study of intelligence, which is a primary focus of this text, should leave you with a sense of wonder. We still know relatively little about how information is processed, stored, and retrieved; how differing environments affect learning; and how intellectual growth is best nourished. Consequently, you must be mindful of the labels and classifications that you use to categorize children, recognizing and respecting their resiliency. Do not expect children who receive the same label to perform in the same ways. Mentally retarded children, for example, differ in their abilities, learning styles, and temperaments. You may be surprised at their intelligence and humanity if you view these children without preconceptions. Although labels are important in the assessment process, you must not allow labels to regiment and restrict the ways you observe and work with each individual child.

THE NEED TO CONSIDER ETHNIC AND CULTURAL DIVERSITY

However much we subscribe to the philosophy that well-normed standardized tests provide one of the most important means of assessment, we also must recognize the cultural diversity of children. Children come to us from many different ethnic and cultural backgrounds, and these differing backgrounds must be considered in selection of tests and interpretation of norms. We have, on the one hand, forces that are continuously molding us into a more homogeneous society. On the other hand, subtle and not so subtle differences set apart the various ethnic groups in our country, including differences in language dialects and in patterns of family interaction. Such differences among blacks, whites, Hispanic-Americans, native Americans, and Asian Americans, for example, may affect the kinds of knowledge acquired by children. These ethnic differences must be considered in interpreting test results and in working with children and their families.

RESPONSE TO THE ATTACK ON TESTS

The past 15 years have seen numerous attacks on the use of tests. Accusations have arisen from ethnic minority groups that standardized tests used to allocate limited educational resources penalized children whose family, socioeconomic status, and cultural experiences were different from those of white, middle-class normative groups. The very foundations of assessment practices have been questioned, including the tools that are used and the situations in which they are administered. Some critics maintain that intelligence tests and achievement tests are culturally biased and thus harmful to black children and other ethnic minority children. Others believe that many of the activities of school and clinical child psychologists are not in the best interests of the child. These activities include labeling children, testing children without their permission and without giving them full knowledge of the possible consequences of testing, and moving children from regular classrooms to potentially damaging special classes. Courts have issued decisions limiting the freedom of psy-

chologists to use and select tests for evaluation and placement decisions.

Many critics fail to consider that tests have many valid uses. Tests allow for accountability, for measurement of change, and for evaluation of program effectiveness. As a result of testing, children gain access to special programs, which can contribute to their educational experiences. Tests are a standard for evaluating the extent to which children of all ethnic groups have learned the basic cognitive and academic skills necessary for survival in our culture. Few of the critics have proposed reasonable alternatives to present methods.

Although I believe that fundamentally the criticisms of testing have little merit because they are not based on research evidence and fail to consider current assessment practices, these attacks have uncovered some serious shortcomings in assessment practices. Labeling a Spanish-speaking child who does not speak English as mentally retarded, based on the results of an English-language verbal intelligence test, reflects incompetence on the part of the examiner. To keep poor records of parental permissions authorizing evaluations is shoddy practice, and to administer tests without seeking permission is entirely unethical. These and other such practices must not continue.

We are accountable, as professionals, to the children we serve, to their parents, to the schools, and to the larger community. We must not ignore the many valid criticisms of tests and test practices simply because we do not like them. We must continue to develop procedures and instruments that will better serve our clients. Procedures now available to protect our clients must be adhered to scrupulously. Although none of us like having our shortcomings pointed out, especially in public, we must listen to our critics and make sure that we are following the best scientific and clinical practices. I believe that the discord of the seventies and early eighties has had a cleansing and beneficial effect.

BEHAVIORAL OBJECTIVES OF THIS TEXT

This text is designed to assist you in becoming a skilled clinician. The term *clinician* is used to refer to individuals who have been trained in any of a number of different professional areas such as clinical psychology, school psychology, counseling psychology, educational psychology, special education, social work, and speech therapy. To become a skilled clinician, you will need to master various technical and clinical skills. However, before you begin your study of assessment tools, it is essential to have a background in testing and measurement, statistics, child development, and child psychopathology. Knowledge of each of these areas will assist you in administering and interpreting tests, arriving at conclusions, and formulating recommendations. In addition, those of you who plan to work in school settings will benefit from a study of remedial and educational techniques used to treat and educate special children.

The technical and clinical skills needed to be a competent clinical assessor include the ability to:
- evaluate and select an appropriate assessment battery
- establish and maintain rapport with children
- administer and score tests and other assessment tools by following standardized procedures
- observe behavior
- interview parents, children, and teachers
- perform informal assessments
- interpret assessment results
- translate assessment findings into effective interventions (formulate recommendations)
- communicate assessment findings both in writing and orally
- read and interpret research in the field of clinical and psychoeducational assessment
- understand laws and government regulations concerning the assessment and placement of special children

This text will assist you in obtaining these skills. However, two caveats are in order. First, this text is not a substitute for test manuals or for texts on child psychopathology; it supplements material contained in test manuals and summarizes some major findings in the area of child psychopathology. Second, this text cannot substitute for clinically supervised experiences. Each student in training should receive supervision in all phases of assessment, including test administration, scoring, report writing, and consultation. Ideally every student should examine, in a variety of settings, many different types of children—normal and emotionally disturbed, retarded and gifted, as well as the physically handicapped.

Evaluating and Selecting an Assessment Battery

A prerequisite for effective assessment is the ability to plan assessment strategies and to choose tests to meet specific needs. Table 1-1 presents some useful guidelines for evaluating tests and other assessment procedures. These guidelines indicate that it is important to consider the information contained in test manuals, including reliability, validity, and normative data. An excellent source to consult for information on a vast number of tests and

checklists is the *Ninth Mental Measurements Yearbook* (Mitchell, l985). Started by Buros, this yearbook is now in its ninth edition. The *Standards for Educational and Psychological Testing* (American Psychological Association, l985) is a useful source for information about technical and professional standards for test construction and use.

In deciding whether to administer tests individually or on a group basis, you must consider the nature of the referral question and whether alternative assessment routes are available. How important is it that tests be administered individually? Would group tests be as effective as the individual battery in answering the referral question? Are there any motivational, personality, linguistic, or physically disabling factors that may impair the examinee's performance on group tests? Individual tests should be administered when there is reason to question the validity of the results of group tests or when an extremely careful evaluation of the examinee's performance is needed. You should discuss the reasons for individual assessment with referral sources in order to familiarize them with its values and limitations. Such discussions may lead to a reduction in the number of children unnecessarily referred for individual assessment, making it easier to provide prompt and intensive services to children most in need of individual assessment.

Before beginning the assessment, you may need to confer with the referral source, especially if the referral information is incomplete. In preparation for the formal assessment it is helpful to read background information; interview teachers, parents, or other individuals familiar with the child; and study cumulative records. The tests and other assessment procedures finally selected—the assessment battery—should be geared to the needs of a specific child. The tests selected may be changed from child to child, depending on the referral problem. Additionally, you may want to change or add tests or other assessment procedures as a result of the information you obtain from the initial assessment procedures administered.

Establishing Rapport and Administering and Scoring the Assessment Battery

This text contains information on establishing rapport and administering tests, including sections on working with special children, completion of record booklets (protocols), general administrative procedures and specific test procedures, and examiner-examinee variables. This information should be used in conjunction with test and assessment manuals. Practical administrative suggestions, based on clinical experience and research findings, are also provided for various assessment procedures.

Table 1-1
Guidelines for Evaluating a Test

Information About the Test

1. What is the name of the test?
2. Who are its authors?
3. Who published it?
4. When was it published?
5. Is there an alternative form available?
6. How much does it cost?
7. How long does it take to administer?
8. Is there a test manual?
9. How recently has the test been revised?
10. What was the standardization group?

Aids to Interpreting Test Results

1. Does the manual provide a clear statement of (a) the purposes and applications for which the test is intended and (b) the qualifications needed to administer the test and interpret it properly?
2. Do the test, manual, record forms, and accompanying materials guide users toward sound and correct interpretation of the test results?
3. Are the statements in the manual that express relationships presented in quantitative terms, so that the reader can tell how much precision or confidence to attach to them?

Examinee Considerations

1. What prerequisite skills are needed by the examinee to complete the test?
2. In what languages or modes of communication can the test be administered?

3. Is the vocabulary level of the test's directions appropriate for the examinee?
4. How are the test items presented?
5. How are the test items responded to?
6. What stated and unstated adaptations can be made in presentation and response modes?
7. Is the test free of sex and ethnic biases?
8. Are the test materials interesting to the examinee?
9. Is the test suitable for individual or group administration?

Reliability and Validity

1. How reliable are the test and its component parts?
2. How valid is the test for its stated purposes?

Administration and Scoring

1. Are the directions for administration complete and clear?
2. Are the scoring procedures clear?

Scales and Norms

1. Are the scales used for reporting scores clearly and carefully described?
2. Are norms reported in an appropriate form, usually standard scores or percentile ranks?
3. Are the populations to which the norms refer clearly defined and described?
4. If more than one form is available, are tables available showing equivalent scores on the different forms?
5. Does the manual discuss the possible value of local norms and provide any help in preparing local norms?

Source: Adapted from Salend (1984) and Thorndike and Hagen (1977).

When you administer a test, you must score the child's responses to specific items as you progress. To score tests accurately, you need to be aware of the research findings concerning scoring bias, "halo" effects (the tendency in making a judgment about one characteristic of a person to be influenced by another characteristic or general impression of that person), common errors in test scoring, and use of scoring criteria. These findings are reviewed in this text. Of course it is imperative that you understand fully the scoring principles and criteria described in the test manuals. Similar considerations are involved in interviewing, observing behavior, and informal assessment procedures.

Observing Behavior

An important part of the assessment process is observing the child's behavior during the testing session. Knowing

how the child performs on the various tasks helps in individualizing the clinical evaluation and supplements the more objective evaluation. Behavioral observations focus on such areas as the child's interpersonal relations, attitude, language, motivation, and motor skills. While administering intelligence tests and other types of formal and informal ability tests, you can observe how children solve conventional and novel problems, how well they attend to tasks, and how persistent they are in solving problems. Specific suggestions are made in this text for observing and evaluating the child's behavior during assessment.

Interpreting the Assessment Results

After the tests have been administered and the interview and observation completed, you must interpret the findings. You will find this one of the most challenging of all the assessment activities, as it will draw on your knowledge of children, test theory, developmental psychology, personality theory, and psychopathology. Various parts of this text will assist you with interpreting assessment results.

Formulating Recommendations

In addition to interpreting the assessment findings, you will often be asked to formulate recommendations. Your knowledge of clinical psychology, assessment theory, developmental psychology, psychopathology, and psycho-educational remediation procedures will aid you in performing this task. This text provides some information on the formulation of recommendations. However, it is not designed to systematically cover remediation procedures or intervention strategies. Such knowledge must be gained from texts and journals that cover clinical psychology, rehabilitation, and educational strategies for use with special children, and from clinical experience.

Communicating the Assessment Results

The findings from formal and informal tests, interviews, and observations can make a unique contribution to the study of child development and of exceptional children. The value of the contribution you make, however, will depend on your ability to communicate your findings clearly and meaningfully. The assessment report may be read by any number of professionals (including teachers, psychiatrists, probation officers, pediatricians, neurologists, social workers, and attorneys), by the child's parents, and in some cases by the older child as well. It should be written shortly after the assessment battery has been administered, scored, and interpreted and should contain your findings, interpretations, and recommendations. Chapter 23 provides detailed guidelines for writing reports.

One of the best ways to learn how to write a report is to study reports written by competent clinicians. Several reports are included in this text to demonstrate different styles and approaches to the evaluation task. In spite of their differences they all exhibit clear writing, skillful analysis, and good clinical judgment. However, these reports should be used only as general guides; you should develop your own style and approach to report writing. This text also presents examples of common communication problems encountered in report writing.

After the report has been written, you may want to meet with the child, the child's parents, and the referral source to discuss the results. You may be called on to present your results at a staff conference, which will require skill in

"It's about Benny, doctor. He's just come from school with an IQ of 104! Should I put him right to bed?"

explaining your findings and recommendations. If children or parents are at the conference they may be anxious and defensive, in which case you will need to be able to deal with their reactions. Being thoroughly familiar with the subject matter presented in this text will enable you to present and defend your findings clearly and systematically. The assessment should not stop with the report. Every attempt should be made to work with the child, the parents, and the referral source on a continuous basis. The interventions recommended in the report need to be monitored carefully and modified as necessary.

Conducting Research on Assessment

An understanding of research findings will add greatly to your understanding of assessment procedures and the assessment process; progress in assessment cannot occur without research. Many factors bear investigation—for example, the reliability and validity of tests, interviews, and observations for various populations need to be determined, clinical and educational theories should be evaluated, procedural changes in test administration require further study, and different remediation strategies need to be evaluated. Familiarity with research findings and with the problems involved in such research will provide you with a base from which you can evaluate your own assessment techniques and published research reports. Finally, you may find yourself doing research on intelligence testing, tests of special abilities, interviewing, and observation. Much of the material in this text is relevant to this task. A knowledge of research and research problems may stimulate you to design and conduct your own investigations.

Understanding Laws and Government Regulations

Working with special children requires knowledge of state and federal regulations concerning assessment procedures, particularly if the assessment involves educational programs. Although only a small part of this text addresses regulations such as Public Law 94-142, those of you who plan to work with school systems as psychologists should become thoroughly familiar with relevant state and federal regulations. Regulations currently cover such areas as nonbiased assessment, classification of handicapping conditions, eligibility for special programs, individualized educational programs, rights of parents, and confidentiality of records.

PHILOSOPHY OF THIS TEXT

This text integrates the normative-developmental perspective with the behavioral perspective in the assessment of children. Children change as they grow, and these changes are reflected in the cognitive, affective, and behavioral domains (Edelbrock, 1984). The *normative-developmental perspective* emphasizes the need to evaluate these domains in relationship to (a) the child's age, gender, ethnicity, socioeconomic status (SES), and other potentially important demographic variables and (b) the child's prior development in these domains and its influence on current and future development. Thus, the normative-developmental approach evaluates the child's cognitions, affect, and behavior in relation to a reference group (usually composed of children of the same age as the referred child) and attempts to account for changes as the child grows older.

The *behavioral perspective* focuses on the importance of (a) specifying intraindividual (within-the-individual) changes in behavior, (b) selecting specific target behaviors for change, and (c) accounting for environmental determinants that may shape and control behavior. The careful specification of environmental contingencies that relate to behavior—such as factors associated with the setting, natu-

ral reinforcers, and distractors—is one of the hallmarks of the behavioral approach. The multimethod approach to assessment in this text attempts to wed the best traditions of the normative-developmental and behavioral assessment approaches.

Normative data are useful in various ways (cf. Edelbrock, 1984). First, in epidemiological surveys, normative data help us to determine what constitutes normal or deviant functioning for particular age groups and sexes. Data on the distribution of scores on various tests and on the incidence and prevalence of behavioral problems help set standards for determining significant cognitive, affective, and behavioral deviations. Second, normative data help us to select appropriate target areas and behaviors that need change and remediation. Normative data facilitate the process of identifying the child's areas of strength and weakness and behaviors that are normal or deviant. Third, normative data allow us to make comparisons among different tests and different informants. For example, comparing data from different ability and achievement tests helps us to identify those children who are gifted or retarded across divergent areas, and comparing data from parents and teachers helps us to identify children who are deviant both at home and at school.

CONCLUDING COMMENT ON CHALLENGES IN ASSESSING CHILDREN

An individual assessment is a rare situation in that a highly able and skilled professional devotes his or her exclusive attention to one child for a period ranging from 1 to several hours. This may never have happened before in the child's life, and it may never happen again. As an examiner, you have the opportunity to gather valuable information about the child that will be useful for assessment and intervention purposes.

The assessment procedures covered in this book serve a number of different purposes, including screening, classification/placement, and program planning/remediation. Assessment procedures vary in the extent to which they are useful in meeting one or more of these purposes. As you read about these assessment procedures, keep in mind the different purposes that they may serve and become aware of the purposes for which each procedure is best suited.

This text provides guidelines designed to promote the usefulness and fairness of assessment procedures. I believe that clinical and psychoeducational assessment represents one of the most effective ways of promoting the mental health and educational needs of children from all ethnic backgrounds. Each child represents a separate challenge for the examiner; this book aims to increase your ability to rise effectively to the challenge.

SUMMARY

1. This text introduces important assessment procedures needed to evaluate children.

2. The multiple assessment approach advocated in the text covers four important assessment procedures: norm-referenced tests, interviews, observations, and informal tests.

3. Norm-referenced tests provide valuable information about many areas of development, but should be used only in conjunction with other sources of data.

4. Interviews are a useful way to obtain information in a less structured format.

5. Observations provide valuable information about how the child functions in various settings.

6. Informal assessment procedures may provide additional information about the child's learning ability, language style, and other areas of functioning.

7. Information obtained from all sources used in the assessment should be evaluated and major discrepancies resolved before diagnostic decisions and recommendations are made.

8. Developmental norms are critical in the assessment of children.

9. Parents and significant others must be included in any diagnostic work with children.

10. The assessment process should never focus exclusively on test scores.

11. Tests are powerful tools and must be thoroughly understood before they are used as assessment instruments.

12. The child's competencies as well as deficiencies should be evaluated in any assessment.

13. Much remains to be learned about the assessment of intelligence.

14. Labeling and classifying, although important, must not impair your ability to see the child as a unique individual.

15. Ethnic and cultural differences must be considered in evaluating assessment results.

16. Testing has become a public concern, particularly in relation to the assessment and placement of ethnic minority children. The attacks on testing during the last 15 years should make us doubly vigilant about how we use tests.

17. Competencies needed to become a skilled clinical assessor include the ability to evaluate, select, administer, and interpret assessment tools; the ability to communicate one's findings orally and in writing; and the ability to interpret research findings.

18. This text emphasizes the integration of the normative-developmental and behavioral perspectives in the assessment of children.

KEY TERMS, CONCEPTS, AND NAMES

Daniel Hoffman v. *The Board of Education of the City of New York* (p. 2)
Norm-referenced tests (p. 3)
Norm group (p. 3)
Interviews (p. 4)
Observations (p. 4)
Informal assessment (p. 4)
Multiple assessment approach (p. 5)
Labels and classifications (p. 5)
Cultural diversity (p. 6)
Clinician (p. 6)
Normative-developmental perspective (p. 10)
Behavioral perspective (p. 10)

STUDY QUESTIONS

1. What relevance does the case of Daniel Hoffman have to the practice of school and clinical psychology?

2. What are the four pillars of assessment and how do they complement one another?

3. What are some important guidelines for using intelligence and special ability tests?

4. Why has testing come under attack and how has it been defended?

5. What technical and clinical skills are needed to become a competent clinical assessor?

6. What are the major parts of the assessment process?

7. What are some important guidelines for evaluating tests?

8. Compare and contrast the normative-developmental perspective with the behavioral perspective.

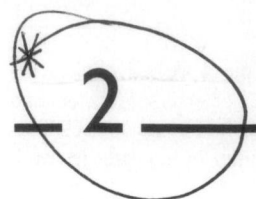

2

USEFUL STATISTICAL AND MEASUREMENT CONCEPTS

We conquer the facts of nature when we observe and experiment upon them. When we measure them we have made them our servants. A little statistical insight trains them for invaluable work.

—Edward L. Thorndike

This chapter covers statistical and measurement concepts that will enable you to evaluate more effectively the psychometric properties of intelligence tests, special ability tests, and interview and observational data. (*Psychometrics* is the quantitative assessment of an individual's psychological traits or attributes.) Additionally, your knowledge of these concepts will enhance your understanding of test manuals and research reports. This chapter reviews basic statistical and measurement concepts; it is not meant to be a substitute for texts in statistics or testing and measurement.

DESCRIPTIVE STATISTICS

Descriptive statistics summarize data obtained on a sample of individuals. Areas covered in a study of descriptive statistics include scales of measurement, measures of central tendency, measures of dispersion, the normal curve, and correlations. The more commonly used symbols in statistics and psychometrics are shown in Table 2-1. These symbols are a shorthand way of describing important characteristics of a test formula or norm group.

Scales of Measurement

Data can be ordered by various methods. In most cases, one of four types of scales is used: nominal, ordinal, interval, or ratio. A scale is a system for assigning values or scores to some measurable trait or characteristic. These values then can be subjected to various mathematical procedures in order to determine relationships between the traits or characteristics of interest and other measured behaviors.

Table 2-1
Some Common Statistical and Psychometric Symbols and Abbreviations

Symbol	Definition	Symbol	Definition
a	Intercept constant in a regression equation	S^2	Variance of the sample
b	Slope constant in a regression equation	SE_{est}	Standard error of estimate
c	Any unspecified constant	SE_m, SEM,	
CA	Chronological age	SE_{meas},	
DQ	Developmental Quotient	S_m, s_m,	
f	Frequency	s_{meas}, or	
F	Test statistic in analysis of variance and covariance	s_{err}	Standard error of measurement
		t	t test
IQ	Intelligence Quotient	T	T score; standard score with a mean of 50 and standard deviation of 10
M	Mean (see also $\bar{X}$)		
MA	Mental age	x	Deviation score $X - \bar{X}$; indicates how far the score falls above or below the mean of the group
Md or Mdn	Median		
n	Number of cases in a subsample		
N	Number of cases in a sample	X	Raw score
p	(a) Probability; (b) Proportion	$\bar{X}$	Mean
P	Percentile	Y	A second raw score
Q	Semi-interquartile range; half the difference between Q_3 and Q_1	z	z score; standard score with a mean of 0 and standard deviation of 1
Q_1	First quartile score (25th percentile score)	σ	Standard deviation of a population
Q_3	Third quartile score (75th percentile score)	σ^2	Variance of a population
r	Pearson correlation coefficient	Σ	"The sum of"; ΣX means add up all the Xs (scores)
r^2	Coefficient of determination; the proportion of variance in Y attributable to X	ϕ	Phi coefficient; a correlation coefficient for a 2×2 contingency table
r_{pb}	Point biserial correlation coefficient		
r_s or ρ	Spearman rank-difference correlation coefficient (also referred to as rho)	χ^2	Chi square
		$<$	Less than
r_{xx}	Reliability coefficient	$>$	Greater than
r_{xy}	Validity coefficient (X represents test score and Y the criterion score)	$\geq$	Greater than or equal to
		$\leq$	Less than or equal to
R	Coefficient of multiple correlation	$\pm$	Plus or minus
S, s, or SD	Standard deviation of the sample	$\sqrt{}$	Square root

Nominal scales.   A nominal measurement scale consists of a set of nonordered categories, one of which is assigned to each item being scaled. The numbers, letters, or names ordinarily represent mutually exclusive categories and thus cannot be arranged in any meaningful order. An example of nominal scaling is the assignment of numbers to baseball players or the designation of examinees as male or female. The scale is of limited usefulness because it allows only for classification.

Ordinal scales.   An ordinal measurement scale has the property of order. The variable being measured is ranked or ordered without regard for differences in the distance between scores. An example of ordinal scaling is the ranking of persons from highest to lowest on the basis of class standing. An ordinal scale tells us who is first, second, and third; it does not tell us whether the distance between the first- and second-ranked scores is the same as the distance between the second- and third-ranked scores.

Interval scales.   An interval measurement scale has an arbitrary zero point and equal units. Examples of interval scales are the Celsius scale, which gives temperature, and the Wechsler Intelligence Scale for Children—Revised (WISC-R), which reports intelligence test scores. On the WISC-R, an increase of 10 IQ points from 100 to 110 means the same amount of change as an increase from 120 to 130 or from any other point to the point 10 points higher on the scale. However, it makes no sense to say that a child with an IQ of 150 is twice as intelligent as a child with an IQ of 75. Interval scaling does not permit such comparative statements.

Ratio scales.   A ratio measurement scale has a true zero point, equal units, and equality of ratios. Because there is a meaningful zero point, a true ratio exists between measurements made on a ratio scale. Weight is one example of a characteristic measured on a ratio scale; an individual who weighs 150 pounds is twice as heavy as one who weighs 75 pounds. Because most psychological characteristics do not permit the measurement of an absolute zero point (such as "zero intelligence"), ratio scales are found infrequently in psychology. In many cases we must be content with interval scales or the weaker ordinal scales.

Measures of Central Tendency

The three most commonly used measures of central tendency—the typical or representative score—are the mean, median, and mode.

Mean.   The mean is the arithmetic average of all the scores in a set of scores. To obtain the mean, divide the sum of all the scores by the total number of scores in the set (N). The formula is as follows:

$$M = \frac{\Sigma X}{N}$$

where M = mean of the scores
 ΣX = sum of the scores
 N = number of scores.

Example: The mean for the four scores 2, 4, 6, 8 is

$$M = \frac{20}{4} = 5$$

The mean is responsive to the exact position of each score in a distribution, but it is also sensitive to a few

MOMMA by Mell Lazarus. Courtesy of Mell Lazarus and Field Newspaper Syndicate.

Table 2-2
Calculation of the Median

X (even number of scores)	X (odd number of scores)
130	130
128	128
125	125
124 ← 123.5 median	124 ← 124 median
123	123
120	120
110	110
108	

relatively extreme scores. Consequently, extreme scores in a set can distort the mean. Overall, the mean is the preferred measure of central tendency. It is appropriate for both interval and ratio scale data.

Median.   The median is defined as the middle point in a set of scores arranged in order of magnitude. Fifty percent of the scores lie at or above the median, and 50 percent of the scores lie at or below the median. If there are an even number of scores, the median is the number halfway between the two middlemost scores and therefore is not any of the actual scores. If there are an odd number of scores, the median is simply the middlemost score.

To calculate the median, arrange the scores in order of magnitude from highest to lowest. Then count up (or down) through half the scores. Table 2-2 illustrates the procedure for both an even number and an odd number of scores in a distribution. In the first column there are eight scores. To obtain the median, count up four scores from the bottom and then determine the number that lies halfway between the fourth and fifth scores (the two middlemost scores). In the second column there are seven scores. To obtain the median, count up four scores from the bottom. The median divides a distribution into two equal halves; the number of scores above the median is the same as the number below.

When distributions are "skewed" (the bulk of the scores are at either the high or the low end of the set), the median is a better measure than the mean of the typical point in the set. The median is less affected by outliers—scores that deviate extremely from the other scores in the set. The median is an appropriate measure of central tendency for ordinal, interval, or ratio scale data.

Mode.   The mode of a set of scores is the score that occurs more often than any other. In some sets two scores occur more often than any other score and with the same frequency; in such cases the distribution is said to be bimodal. When more than two scores occur more frequently than any other score and with the same frequency, the distribution is said to be multimodal.

The mode is greatly affected by chance and has little or no mathematical usefulness. However, it does tell us what score is most likely to occur and hence is useful in analyzing qualitative data (for example, "What was the most frequently occurring classification in the group?"). It is the only appropriate measure of central tendency for nominal scale data.

Measures of Dispersion

The simplest measure of the dispersion, or variability, of a group of scores is the range. More frequently used measures are the variance and standard deviation.

Range.   The range represents the *distance* between the highest and lowest scores in the set. It is obtained by subtracting the lowest score in the set from the highest score. The formula is

$$\boxed{R = H - L}$$

where R = range
         H = highest score
         L = lowest score.
Example: The range for the distribution 50, 80, 97, 99 is

$$R = 99 - 50 = 49$$

The range is easily calculated; however, it is not a sensitive measure of dispersion because it is determined by the location of only two scores. The range tells us nothing about the distribution between the two scores, and a single score can grossly change the result. Still, it provides some information that can be useful in understanding a set of scores.

Variance.   Variance (S^2) is a statistical measure of the amount of spread in a group of scores; the greater the spread, the greater the variance. The fact that two different sets of scores have the same mean but different variances means that one has a larger range, or spread, of scores than the other. The variance is calculated in the following way:

$$S^2 = \frac{N\Sigma X^2 - (\Sigma X)^2}{N(N - 1)}$$

where S^2 = variance of the scores
             N = number of scores
             ΣX^2 = sum of the squared scores
             $(\Sigma X)^2$ = square of the sum of the scores.

Example: The variance for the four scores 2, 4, 6, 8 is

$$S^2 = \frac{4(2^2 + 4^2 + 6^2 + 8^2) - (2 + 4 + 6 + 8)^2}{4(4 - 1)}$$

$$= \frac{4(120) - 400}{4(3)} = \frac{480 - 400}{12} = \frac{80}{12} = 6.67$$

Standard deviation.   The standard deviation (SD), sometimes represented by the Greek letter σ (sigma), is the positive square root of the variance. An important and commonly used measure of the extent to which scores deviate from the mean, the standard deviation is used often in the field of testing and measurement. It is also used in calculating the Deviation IQ, which is discussed later in this chapter. The formula for calculating the standard deviation of a sample is as follows:

$$SD = \sqrt{\frac{N\Sigma X^2 - (\Sigma X)^2}{N(N - 1)}}$$

where SD = standard deviation and N, ΣX^2, and $(\Sigma X)^2$ are as defined for S^2.

Example: The standard deviation for the four scores 2, 4, 6, 8 is given by

$$SD = \sqrt{\frac{4(120) - 400}{4(3)}} = \sqrt{\frac{480 - 400}{12}}$$

$$= \sqrt{\frac{80}{12}} = \sqrt{6.67} = 2.58$$

Normal Curve

The normal (or bell-shaped) curve (see Figure 2-1) is a very common type of distribution. Many psychological traits are distributed roughly along a normal curve. Although a perfect normal curve is rarely achieved, small variations do not appreciably change the relevant statistical interpretations. An important feature of the normal curve is that it enables us to calculate exactly how many cases fall between any two points under the curve.

Figure 2-1 shows the precise relationship between the standard deviation and the proportion of cases under a normal curve. It also shows the percentage of cases that fall within one, two, and three standard deviations above and below the mean. Approximately 68 percent of the cases fall within $+1\,SD$ and $-1\,SD$ of the mean. As we go further away from the mean, the number of cases diminishes. The areas between $+1\,SD$ and $+2\,SD$ and between $-1\,SD$ and $-2\,SD$ each represent approximately 14 percent of the cases. Between $+2\,SD$ and $+3\,SD$ and between $-2\,SD$ and $-3\,SD$ from the mean, there are even fewer cases—in each case approximately 2 percent of the distribution. We will return again to the normal curve when we consider standard scores.

Correlations

Correlations tell us about the degree of association or corelationship between two variables, including the strength and direction of their relationship. The strength of the relationship is determined by the absolute magnitude of the correlation coefficient; the maximum value is 1.00. The direction of the relationship is given by the sign of the coefficient. A positive correlation ($+$) indicates that a high score on one variable is associated with a high score on the second variable. Conversely, a negative correlation ($-$) signifies an inverse relationship—that is, a high score on one variable is associated with a low score on the other variable. Thus correlation coefficients range in value from -1.00 to $+1.00$.

A most important aspect of correlation is its close relationship to prediction. The higher the correlation between two variables, the more accurately one can predict the value of one variable when supplied only with the value of the other variable. A correlation of -1.00 or $+1.00$ means that one can predict perfectly a person's score on one variable if the score on the other variable is known. In contrast, a correlation of .00 indicates that there is no (linear) way of predicting scores on one variable from knowledge of scores on the other variable.

If a nonlinear relationship exists between two variables (that is, the two variables being correlated are related to each other in some curvilinear way), the correlation will underestimate the true degree of association. Similarly, the magnitude of the correlation coefficient will be reduced if one or both variables have a restricted range of scores. This occurs when the group tends to be homogeneous.

The most common correlation is the Pearson correlation, symbolized by r. Pearson's r is not affected by any transformation of the scores. (A transformation is a process by which the original numbers in a sample are altered by some mathematical operation. For example, changing an IQ of 100 to the 50th percentile rank represents a transformation.) When the assumptions of Pearson's r can-

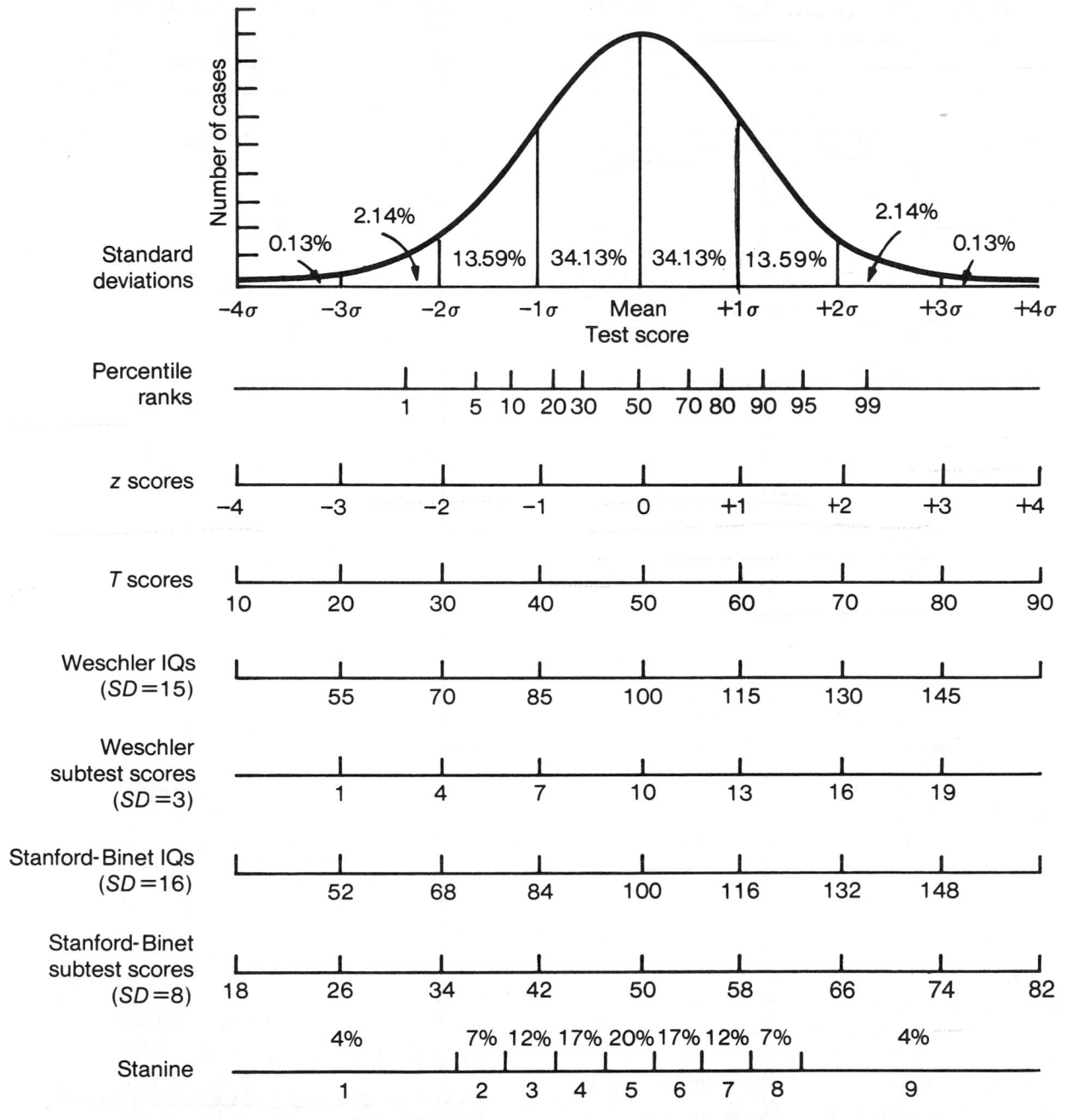

Figure 2-1. Relationship of normal curve to various types of standard scores.

not be met (for example, that the two variables are continuous and normally distributed and that a linear relationship exists between these variables), the Spearman r_s (rank-difference) method can be used (see Table 2-3). This method uses ranks of the scores instead of the scores themselves.

Correlations do *not* provide us with information about whether an observed relationship reflects a simple cause-effect relationship or some more complex relationship. Research indicates, for example, that there is a large, positive correlation between reading speed and IQ. This means that people who read quickly tend to obtain higher scores on intelligence tests than do people who read slowly. We cannot infer, however, that reading speed causes high intelligence or that people will obtain higher intelligence test scores if they increase their reading speed. It may be that fast reading speed and the ability to obtain high scores on intelligence tests are both associated with other factors, such as verbal ability, alertness, or quick reaction time. Formulas for computing a variety of correlation coefficients are shown in Table 2-3.

Correlations used as validity coefficients must be squared (r^2) in order to determine the amount of variance explained by the predictor (or test). Thus, a .60 correlation between IQ and school grades indicates that IQ accounts for 36 percent of the variance in school performance. The value r^2 is known as the *coefficient of determination*.

Regression Equation

The correlation coefficient, together with other information, can be used to construct the best possible linear equation for predicting the score on one variable when the score on another variable is known. (A linear equation is one in which the relationship between the variables can be represented on a graph by a straight line.) This equation, called the regression equation, has the following form:

$$Y_{pred} = bX + a$$

where Y_{pred} = predicted score on Y
b = slope of the regression line
X = known score on X
a = Y intercept of the regression line.

The slope of the regression line is defined as

$$b = r\frac{SD_Y}{SD_X}$$

where r = correlation between the X and Y scores
SD_Y = standard deviation of the Y scores
SD_X = standard deviation of the X scores.

The formula for calculating b directly from raw data is

$$b = \frac{N\Sigma XY - (\Sigma X)(\Sigma Y)}{N\Sigma X^2 - (\Sigma X)^2}$$

The intercept a, or regression constant, is then determined as follows:

$$a = \bar{Y} - b\bar{X}$$

where $\bar{Y}$ = mean of the Y scores
b = slope of the regression line
$\bar{X}$ = mean of the X scores.

Example: To find the regression equation for the following pairs of scores (X, Y), we first calculate X^2, Y^2, and XY.

X	Y	X^2	Y^2	XY
7	9	49	81	63
2	3	4	9	6
6	4	36	16	24
6	5	36	25	30
3	1	9	1	3
$\Sigma = 24$	22	134	132	126
$\bar{X} = 4.8$	$\bar{Y} = 4.4$			

The slope is then given by

$$b = \frac{5(126) - (24)(22)}{5(134) - (24)^2} = \frac{630 - 528}{670 - 576} = \frac{102}{94} = 1.09$$

and the regression constant by

$$a = 4.40 - (1.09)(4.80) = 4.40 - 5.23 = -.83$$

These data can now be substituted into the regression equation:

$$Y_{pred} = 1.09X - .83$$

The correlation coefficient for these data is

$$r = \frac{5(126) - 24(22)}{\sqrt{[5(134) - (24)^2][5(132) - (22)^2]}}$$

$$= \frac{102}{\sqrt{94(176)}} = \frac{102}{\sqrt{16,544}} = \frac{102}{128.62} = .79$$

Standard Error of Estimate

A measure of the accuracy of the predicted Y scores is the standard error of estimate:

$$SE_{est} = SD_Y\sqrt{1 - r^2}$$

where SD_Y = standard deviation of the Y scores
r = correlation between the X and Y scores.

The higher the correlation between X and Y, the smaller the standard error of estimate and hence the greater the average accuracy of predictions will be. A +1.00 correlation coefficient means that perfect predictions can be made; a .00 correlation means that you cannot improve your prediction of Y scores by knowing the associated X scores. (The standard error of estimate will be used later in this chapter in establishing confidence intervals.)

Table 2-3
A Variety of Correlation Coefficients

Name	Description of variables	Formula
Pearson product-moment correlation coefficient (r)	Both variables continuous (on interval or ratio scale)	$$r = \frac{N\Sigma XY - (\Sigma X)(\Sigma Y)}{\sqrt{[N\Sigma X^2 - (\Sigma X)^2][N\Sigma Y^2 - (\Sigma Y)^2]}}$$ where r = correlation coefficient N = number of paired scores ΣXY = sum of the product of the paired X and Y scores ΣX = sum of the X scores ΣY = sum of the Y scores ΣX^2 = sum of the squared X scores $(\Sigma X)^2$ = square of the sum of the X scores ΣY^2 = sum of the squared Y scores $(\Sigma Y)^2$ = square of the sum of the Y scores
Spearman rank-difference correlation coefficient (Spearman r, r_s, or ρ)	Both variables on an ordinal scale (rank-ordered)	$$r_s = 1 - \frac{6\Sigma D^2}{N(N^2 - 1)}$$ where D = difference between ranks for each person N = number of paired scores
Point biserial correlation coefficient (r_{pb})	One variable continuous (on interval or ratio scale), the other genuinely dichotomous (usually on nominal scale)	Formula for r can be used (see above). The dichotomous variable can be coded 0 or 1. For example, if sex is the dichotomous variable, 0 can be used for females and 1 for males (0 = females, 1 = males), or vice versa.
Phi (ϕ) coefficient	Both variables dichotomous (on nominal scales)	1. $$\phi = \frac{BC - AD}{\sqrt{(A + B)(C + D)(A + C)(B + D)}}$$ where A, B, C, and D are the four cell frequencies 2. $$\phi = \sqrt{\frac{\chi^2}{N}}$$ where χ^2 = Chi square N = total number of observations

MULTIPLE CORRELATION

Multiple correlation is a statistical technique for determining the relationship between one variable and several others. The statistic used for this purpose is the coefficient of multiple correlation, R. Predictions based on several variables are likely to be more accurate than those based on a single variable because several different factors relevant to the prediction are considered. A principal drawback to using multiple correlations is that when several variables are used it takes very large samples—usually over 100 subjects—to arrive at a stable prediction equation. A good example of the proper use of multiple correlation is in prediction of performance in college. High school grades, intelligence test scores, and educational attainment of parents have been found to correlate positively with performance in college. By using all of these measures in a multiple correlation analysis, one can predict performance level in college with more accuracy than can be attained through use of any one of these measures alone.

NORM-REFERENCED MEASUREMENT

In norm-referenced testing an examinee's performance is compared with the performance of a specific group of subjects. A norm provides an indication of average or typical performance of the specified group. Norms are needed because a raw test score in itself is not very meaningful. Knowing that a child scored 20 or answered correctly 70 percent of the items on a test is of little use to us unless we also know how other children performed on the same test; we need a relevant normative population. We could compare the child's score with those of a representative population of children in the United States or the children in the child's school or a special population. The comparison is carried out by converting the child's raw score into some relative measure. Such measures are termed *derived scores*, and they indicate the child's standing relative to the norm group. Derived scores also allow us to compare the child's performance on one test with his or her performance on other tests.

Evaluating the Norm Group

Before turning to a discussion of derived scores, let us consider some factors that are important in evaluating a normative group. These include (a) the representativeness of the group, (b) the number of cases in the group, and (c) the relevance of the group.

Representativeness. Representativeness of the norm group refers to the extent to which the group is characteristic of a particular population. The norm sample should match as closely as possible the various demographic characteristics of the population as a whole. For psychoeducational assessment the most salient of these characteristics are age, grade level, gender, geographic region, ethnicity, and socioeconomic status. The date the norms were established is also an important consideration in interpreting the norms.

Size. The number of subjects in the norm group should be large enough to ensure stability of the test scores and inclusion of the various groups that are represented in the population. Usually, the larger the number of subjects used, the more stable the norms are. If the test is to be given to a number of age groups, then the sample should contain at least 100 subjects for each age or grade level in the norm group.

Relevance. It is important to consider how relevant the norms are to the evaluation of the examinee. Proper test interpretation is vitally dependent on the selection of the correct norm group against which to evaluate the examinee's test results. For some purposes national norms may be most appropriate, whereas for others norms of a particular segment of the population may be most relevant. The person interpreting the test must possess the skills and insight needed to select the proper norm group for each individual being evaluated. The examiner's report should clearly state which norm group was used to evaluate the examinee's performance, especially if the norm group is different from the one that is customarily or routinely used by most examiners.

DERIVED SCORES

Derived scores vary in their usefulness. The major types of derived scores used in norm-referenced testing are age- and grade-equivalent scores, ratio IQs, percentile ranks, standard scores, and stanines.

Age-Equivalent and Grade-Equivalent Scores

Age-equivalent and grade-equivalent scores are derived by determining the average score obtained on a test by children of various ages or grade placements. For example, if the average score of 10-year-old children on a test is 15 items correct out of 25, then any child obtaining a score of 15 receives an age-equivalent score of 10. An age-equivalent score is found by computing the mean raw score of a measure for a group of children with a specific age. Similarly, a grade-equivalent score is found by computing the mean raw score obtained by children in each grade. If the mean score of seventh graders on an arithmetic test is 30, then a child obtaining a score of 30 is said to have arithmetical knowledge at the seventh grade level. A grade-equivalent score is expressed in tenths of a grade (for example, 5.5 refers to average performance at the middle of the fifth grade). A grade-equivalent score, therefore, refers to the level of test performance of an average student at that grade level. It does not mean that the student is performing at a level consistent with curricular expectations at his or her particular school.

Other terms for age-equivalent scores. Other terms for age-equivalent scores are *mental age* (MA) and *test age*. In the 1972 norms for the Stanford-Binet: Form L-M, however, the MAs do not refer to scores (or performances) that are associated with children of a certain age; they simply represent certain numbers of points obtained by the child on the test. Chapter 4 discusses more fully the interpretation of MAs. In the WISC-R, Wechsler Preschool and Primary Scale of Intelligence (WPPSI), and Stanford-Binet: Fourth Edition manuals, test ages are presented for raw scores on each subtest.

Interpretation of age- and grade-equivalent scores. Age- and grade-equivalent scores require careful interpretation, for the following reasons (Bennett, 1982; Berk, 1981, 1984; Thorndike & Hagen, 1977):

1. Within an age-equivalent (or grade-equivalent) distribution of scores, the scores may not represent equal units. The difference between second and third grade-equivalent scores may not be the same as the difference between eleventh and twelfth grade–equivalent scores.

2. Many grade equivalents are obtained by means of interpolation and extrapolation. Consequently, the scores may not actually have been obtained by children.

3. Grade equivalents encourage comparison with inappropriate groups. For example, a second grader who obtains a grade equivalent of 4.1 in arithmetic should not be said to be functioning like a fourth grader at the beginning of the school year; this is the wrong comparison group. The second grade student shares with the average fourth grader the number of items right on the test—not other attributes associated with fourth grade mathematical skills. The grade equivalent of 4.1 should be thought of in reference to only the child's second grade group, not any other group.

4. Identical grade-equivalent scores on different tests may mean different things.

5. Grade equivalents assume that growth is constant throughout the school year; this assumption may not be warranted.

6. At upper levels grade or age equivalents have little meaning for school subjects that are not taught at those levels or for skills that reach their peak at an earlier age.

7. Grade equivalents exaggerate small differences in performance—a score slightly below the median may result in a grade level equivalent one or two years below grade level.

8. Grade equivalents vary from test to test, from subtest to subtest within the same battery, and from percentile to percentile, thereby greatly complicating any type of comparison.

9. Grade-equivalent scores depend on promotion practices and on the particular curriculum in different grades.

10. Age- and grade-equivalent scores tend to be based on ordinal scales that are too weak to support the computation of important statistical measures, such as the standard error of measurement.

The preceding discussion indicates that grade- and age-equivalent scores are psychometrically impure; however, they still may be useful on some occasions (Hoover, 1984). Grade- and age-equivalent scores place performance in a developmental context, provide information that is easily understood by parents and the public, and reduce misinterpretations. (Percentile ranks, for example, are often misinterpreted as indicating the percentage of questions that the child answered correctly.) Instead of abandoning grade- and age-equivalent scores, psychometrists should construct better tests that use these scores and educate people in their use (Hoover, 1984).

Ratio Intelligence Quotients

In order to interpret age-equivalent or grade-equivalent scores, we must know the child's chronological age (CA). Knowing the child's MA and CA allows us to make a judgment about the child's relative performance. For example, a child with a CA of 10-0 and an MA of 12-0 has performed at an above average level, whereas a child with a CA of 10-0 and an MA of 8-0 has performed at a below average level.

When IQs were first introduced, they were defined as ratios of mental age to chronological age, multiplied by 100 to eliminate the decimal: $IQ = MA/CA \times 100$. Substituting an MA of 12 and a CA of 10 into the formula yields a ratio IQ of 120 (IQ = 12/10 × 100 = 120). Unfortunately, because the standard deviation of the ratio IQ distribution does not remain constant with age, IQs for different ages are not comparable: The same IQ has different meanings at different ages. The use of the Deviation IQ, which is a standard score (see the section on standard scores), effectively avoids this problem.

Percentile Ranks

Percentile ranks are derived scores that permit us to determine an individual's position relative to the standardization sample (or any other specified sample). A percentile rank is a point in a distribution at or below which the scores of a given percentage of individuals fall. If 63 percent of the scores fall below a given score, then that score is at the 63rd percentile rank. Quartiles are percentile ranks that divide a distribution into four equal parts, with each part containing 25 percent of the norm group. Deciles, a less common percentile rank, contain 10 bands, with each band containing 10 percent of the norm group. Exhibit 2-1 shows some procedures for calculating percentile ranks.

Interpretation of percentile ranks is simple and straightforward. For example, a person who obtains a percentile rank of 35 on an intelligence test has scored as well as or better than 35 percent of the people in the norm sample. However, the psychometric properties of percentile ranks limit their usefulness in data analysis. The primary difficulty is that all points along the percentile distribution do not represent equal units. Raw score differences between percentile ranks are smaller near the mean than at the extremes of the distribution. Thus percentile ranks must be normalized through conversion to another scale before they can be used in statistical tests.

Standard Scores

Standard scores are raw scores that have been transformed to have a given mean and standard deviation. They express how far an examinee's score lies from the mean of the distribution in terms of the standard deviation.

A z score is one type of standard score, with a mean of 0 and a standard deviation of 1. On many standardized tests z scores range from −3.0 to +3.0. Frequently, z scores are transformed into other standard scores in order to eliminate the + and − signs. For example, a T score is a standard score based on a distribution with a mean of 50 and a standard deviation of 10. The Deviation IQ is another standard score; it has a mean of 100 and a standard deviation of 15 or 16, depending on the test used. All of the Wechsler scales (WISC-R, WPPSI, and Wechsler Adult

Intelligence Scale—Revised [WAIS-R]) provide Deviation IQs with a mean of 100 and a standard deviation of 15. The Stanford-Binet (Form L-M and Fourth Edition) provides Deviation IQs with a mean of 100 and a standard deviation of 16.

Table 2-4 shows formulas for computing various standard scores. A general formula for converting standard scores from one system to another is as follows:

$$\text{New standard score} = \left(\frac{X_{old} - M_{old}}{SD_{old}}\right)SD_{new} + M_{new}$$

where
X_{old} = score on old system
M_{old} = mean of old system
SD_{old} = standard deviation of old system
SD_{new} = standard deviation of new system
M_{new} = mean of new system.

Example: A standard score of 60 in a T distribution ($M = 50$, $SD = 10$) is converted to a Deviation IQ ($M = 100$, $SD = 15$) as follows:

$$\text{Deviation IQ} = \frac{60 - 50}{10}(15) + 100$$

$$= \frac{10}{10}(15) + 100 = 1(15) + 100 = 115$$

Stanines

Stanines (a contraction of *sta*ndard *nine*) provide a single-digit scoring system with a mean of 5 and a standard deviation of 2. The scores are expressed as whole numbers from 1 to 9. When scores are converted to stanines, the shape of the original distribution is changed into a normal curve. The percentages of scores at each stanine are 4, 7, 12, 17, 20, 17, 12, 7, and 4, respectively (refer back to Figure 2-1).

Relationship Among Derived Scores

It should be evident from the preceding discussion that the various types of derived scores are all derived from raw scores. The different derived scores are merely different expressions of the child's performance. One type of derived score can be converted to another type. The most frequently used conversion in the area of intelligence testing is from standard scores (for example, scaled scores or Deviation IQs) to percentile ranks. Although standard scores are the preferred derived scores, percentile ranks—and, on occasion, age equivalents—are also useful. The

Exhibit 2-1

Calculating Percentile Ranks

The following formula is used to determine the percentile rank for a score in a distribution:

$$\text{Percentile rank} = \frac{\left(\dfrac{X - \text{lrl}}{i}\right)\text{fw} + \Sigma\text{fb}}{N} \times 100$$

where X = raw score
   lrl = lower real limit of the target interval or score
   i = width of the target interval or score
   fw = frequency within the target interval or score
   Σfb = sum of frequencies (number of scores occurring) below the target interval or score
   N = total number of scores.

   To compute the lower real limit of a whole number, simply subtract .5 from the number; to get the upper real limit, add .5 to the number. The width of the target interval or score (i) is obtained by subtracting the lower real limit from the upper real limit.

Example 1

Let us compute the percentile rank for a score of 110 in the following distribution:

	X	f
	120	5
	119	10
Target interval for a score of 110 →	110	20
	100	40
	90	10
	80	5
		N = 90

where   lrl = 109.5
   i = 1
   fw = 20
   Σfb = 55
   N = 90.

   Substituting these values into the percentile rank formula yields the following:

$$\text{Percentile rank} = \frac{\left(\dfrac{X - \text{lrl}}{i}\right)\text{fw} + \Sigma\text{fb}}{N} \times 100$$

$$= \frac{\left(\dfrac{110 - 109.5}{1}\right)20 + 55}{90} \times 100$$

$$= \frac{\left(\dfrac{.5}{1}\right)20 + 55}{90} \times 100$$

$$= \frac{(.5)20 + 55}{90} \times 100$$

$$= \frac{10 + 55}{90} \times 100$$

$$= \frac{65}{90} \times 100$$

$$= .72 \times 100$$

Percentile rank = 72nd percentile

Thus a score of 110 exceeds 72 percent of the scores in the distribution.

   The formula given here for calculating percentile ranks can be used with both grouped (organized into classes of more than one value) and ungrouped (organized into classes of single values) data. When the distribution is ungrouped and all the intervals are 1, a simplified version of the formula can be used:

$$\begin{array}{l}\text{Percentile rank} \\ \text{(for ungrouped data} = \left(\dfrac{.5\text{fw} + \Sigma\text{fb}}{N}\right) \times 100 \\ \text{with intervals of 1)}\end{array}$$

Example 2

Let us compute the percentile rank for a score of 4 in the following distribution:

	X	f
	5	3
Target interval for a score of 4 →	4	5
	3	4
	2	3
	1	2
		N = 17

where   fw = 5
   Σfb = 9
   N = 17.

(Exhibit continues next page)

Exhibit 2-I (cont.)

Substituting these values into the percentile rank formula for ungrouped data with intervals of 1 yields the following:

$$\text{Percentile rank} = \left(\frac{.5fw + \Sigma fb}{N}\right) \times 100$$

$$= \frac{.5(5) + 9}{17} \times 100$$

$$= \frac{2.5 + 9}{17} \times 100$$

$$= \frac{11.5}{17} \times 100$$

$$= .68 \times 100$$

Percentile rank = 68th percentile

Thus a score of 4 exceeds 68 percent of the scores in the distribution.

latter two scores may be helpful in describing the child's performance to parents or teachers.

Figure 2-1 shows the relationships among various derived scores. If a test has a Deviation IQ of 100, a standard deviation of 15, and scores that are normally distributed, the percentile ranks associated with each IQ can be determined precisely. Let us see how percentile ranks associated with Wechsler IQs at various standard deviation points are computed.

An IQ of 100 represents the 50th percentile rank, because an IQ of 100 has been set as the mean of the distribution. In this example an IQ of 115 represents the point that is +1 SD away from the mean. The percentile rank associated with this IQ—the 84th percentile rank—is obtained by adding 50 to 34 percent. The 50 percent represents the proportion of the population below the mean of 100, and the 34 percent represents the proportion of the population between the mean and +1 SD away from the mean. The key here is to recognize that an IQ of 115 is +1 SD above the mean because 15 is the standard deviation of the distribution.

Using the same rationale, we can readily compute the percentile rank associated with an IQ of 130. An IQ of 130 is +2 SD away from the mean. We know that the area below the mean represents 50 percent of the population, the area from the mean to +1 SD represents approximately 34 percent of the population, and the area from +1 SD to +2 SD represents approximately 14 percent of the population (see Figure 2-1). To arrive at the percentile rank for an IQ of 130, we add the following percentages: 50 + 34 + 14 = 98th percentile rank.

Now try to figure out for yourself the percentile rank associated with an IQ of 85. The answer you should obtain is the 16th percentile rank. You subtract 34 from 50,

because an IQ of 85 corresponds to the point that is −1 SD away from the mean. The percentile rank associated with an IQ of 70 is the 2nd percentile rank (50 − 34 − 14 = 2).

The above examples hold only for tests that have a Deviation IQ with a mean of 100 and an SD of 15 (for example, WISC-R, WPPSI, and WAIS-R). For tests that have a mean of 100 and an SD of 16, such as the Stanford-Binet (Form L-M and Fourth Edition), the percentile ranks associated with the various IQs are slightly different except at the mean. The IQ of 100 is still at the 50th percentile rank, but an IQ of 116 (not 115) is at the 84th percentile rank because the SD is 16.

Since an IQ of 116 is at the 84th percentile rank on the Stanford-Binet: Form L-M and Fourth Edition but at the 85th percentile rank on the WISC-R, the IQs on the two scales are not directly comparable. Although a 1-percentile difference may not appear to be major, it can loom as an important factor when placement decisions are made, especially if the 1-percentile difference places the child into a different classification. A glance at Table BC-1 on the inside back cover will show you the percentile ranks associated with the Deviation IQs found on the Stanford-Binet: Form L-M and Fourth Edition, Wechsler batteries, and other tests.

STATISTICAL SIGNIFICANCE

Statistical results are usually analyzed to determine their statistical significance—the extent to which the findings differ from chance occurrence. Convention has established the .05 level as the minimum significance level indicating that observed differences are real; such results would occur 5 percent of the time by chance. More stringent levels of significance can be reported, such as the (.01) and (.001 levels.) Significance levels are used in evaluating differences between means and differences between a score and the mean of the scale. They are also used to determine whether correlations differ from zero. The expression $p < .05$ means that the results have a probability level of less than .05 (or 5 times in 100), whereas the expression $p > .05$ means that the results have a probability level of greater than .05.

It is important to evaluate not only whether the particular findings probably differ from chance, but also what the magnitude of the difference or the strength of the association is. For example, the mean difference between two groups may be statistically significant and yet have no practical significance. Similarly, if the sample size is large enough, the correlation may be statistically significant and yet suggest only a weak association between the two variables.

RELIABILITY

Reliability refers to the consistency of measurements. Test results need to be dependable—that is, they should be reproducible, stable (reliable), and meaningful (valid). Reliability is expressed by a reliability coefficient or by the standard error of measurement, which is derived from the reliability coefficient. A test should not be trusted if its reliability coefficient is low. High reliabilities are especially needed for tests used for individual assessment. For most tests of cognitive and special abilities, a reliability coefficient of .80 or higher is generally considered to be acceptable.

Table 2-4
Formulas for Computing Various Standard Scores

Score	Example
z score	
$$z = \frac{X - \bar{X}}{S}$$	The z score for an individual with a raw score of 50 in a group having a mean of 30 and standard deviation of 10 is calculated as follows:
where z = z score corresponding to the individual score X X = individual raw score $\bar{X}$ = mean of sample S = standard deviation of sample	$$z = \frac{50 - 30}{10} = 2.00$$ Thus the z score for this individual is 2.00.
T score	
$$T = 10(z) + 50$$	The T score for an individual with a z score of 2 is calculated as follows:
where T = T score corresponding to the individual raw score X 10 = standard deviation of the T distribution z = z score corresponding to the individual raw score X 50 = mean of the T distribution	$$T = 10(2) + 50 = 70$$ Thus the T score for this individual is 70.
Deviation IQ	
$$D\ IQ = 15(z) + 100$$	The Deviation IQ for an individual with a z score of 2 is calculated as follows:
where D IQ = Deviation IQ corresponding to the individual raw score X 15 = standard deviation of the Deviation IQ distribution z = z score corresponding to the individual raw score X 100 = mean of the Deviation IQ distribution	$$D\ IQ = 15(2) + 100 = 130$$ Thus the D IQ for this individual is 130.

The Theory of Reliability of Measurement

When a test is administered to a child on several occasions, the child does not usually achieve exactly the same score on each occasion. Sometimes the score changes in a *systematic* way (regular increase or decrease in scores), and sometimes the score changes in a *random* or *unsystematic* way (Ghiselli, Campbell, & Zedeck, 1981). A test is considered unreliable if scores are subject to random, unsystematic fluctuations; obviously a score is not dependable if readministration of the test is likely to result in a randomly different score. Reliability of measurement refers to the extent to which unsystematic variation affects the measurement of a trait, characteristic, or quality.

According to classical psychometric theory, the score an examinee obtains on a test is composed of two components: *true score* and *error score*. The obtained score is a composite of the amount of the trait the child actually possesses (the true score) and the error of measurement (the error score) (Ghiselli et al., 1981). The child's true score is a hypothetical construct; it cannot be observed. The theory assumes that the child possesses stable traits, that errors are random, and that the obtained score results from the addition of true and error scores. The *reliability coefficient*, then, represents a ratio of the true score variance to the observed score variance.

Reliability Coefficients

The reliability coefficient expresses the degree of consistency in the measurement of test scores. The symbol used to denote a reliability coefficient is the letter r with two identical subscripts (for example, r_{xx} or r_{tt}). Reliability coefficients range from 1.00 (indicating perfect reliability) to .00 (indicating the absence of reliability). There are three types of reliability coefficients: test-retest, alternate form, and internal consistency. The Pearson product-moment correlation procedure is used to determine test-retest and alternate form reliability coefficients, whereas specialized formulas are used to compute internal consistency reliability. Table 2-5 shows some procedures for determining reliability.

Test-retest reliability. Test-retest reliability is an index of stability. The usual procedure for obtaining a test-retest reliability coefficient is to administer the same test to the same group on two different occasions, usually within a short period of time (for example, two weeks to a month). The obtained correlation, sometimes called the coefficient of stability, represents the extent to which the test is consistent over time. This correlation is affected, for example, by factors associated with the specific administrations of the

test or with what the child has remembered or learned in the interim. Generally, the shorter the retest interval, the higher the reliability coefficient, since within a shorter span of time there are fewer reasons for an individual's score to change.

Alternate form reliability. Alternate form reliability, also called equivalent or parallel form reliability, is obtained by administering two equivalent tests to the same group of examinees. If the two forms of the test are equivalent, they should have the same means and variances and a high reliability coefficient. If there is no error in measurement, an individual should earn the same score on both forms of the test.

In order to determine alternate form reliability, two forms of the same test must be given to a large sample. Half of the sample is given form A followed by form B, and the other half of the sample is given form B followed by form A. Scores from the two forms are then correlated, yielding a reliability coefficient. Alternate form reliability coefficients are subject to some of the same influences as test-retest reliability coefficients, such as decreased reliability as the time interval between the tests is lengthened. Because examinees are not tested twice with the same items, however, there is less chance than there is with the test-retest method that memory or specific item content will affect the scores.

Internal consistency reliability. Internal consistency reliability is based on the scores obtained during one test administration. One type of internal consistency coefficient is obtained by dividing the test into two equivalent halves (*split-half reliability*). This division creates two alternate forms of the test. The most common way of dividing the test is to assign odd-numbered items to one form and even-numbered items to the other. This procedure assumes that all items measure the same trait.

Another type of internal consistency reliability coefficient is based on the intercorrelations among all comparable parts of the same test. Special formulas—such as Cronbach's formula for coefficient alpha and the Kuder-Richardson formula 20—measure the uniformity or homogeneity of items throughout the test (see Table 2-5). *Cronbach's coefficient alpha*, a general reliability coefficient that can be used for different scoring systems, is based on the variance of the test scores and the variance of the item scores. The coefficient reflects the extent to which items measure the same characteristic. The *Kuder-Richardson formula 20 coefficient*, a special case of coefficient alpha, is useful for tests that are scored pass/fail. It is obtained by calculating the proportion of people who pass and fail each item and the variance of the test scores. Both coefficients represent the mean of all possible split-half coefficients that could be obtained by various test splittings.

Internal consistency reliability estimates are not appropriate for timed tests and do not take into account changes over time. Generally, the size of the internal consistency coefficient is increased with greater test length.

Factors Affecting Reliability

Several factors affect the reliability of a test:

1. *Test length*. The more items there are on a test and the more homogeneous they are, the greater the reliability is likely to be.

2. *Test-retest interval*. The smaller the time interval between administration of two tests, the smaller the chance of change and hence the higher the reliability is likely to be. Various changes may occur between testings that affect the child's abilities or test-taking skills.

3. *Variability of scores*. The greater the variance of scores on a test, the higher the reliability estimate is likely to be. Small changes in performance have a greater impact on the reliability of a test when the range, or spread, of scores is narrow than when it is wide. Therefore, on a given test, homogeneous samples (those with a small variance) will probably yield lower reliability estimates than heterogeneous samples (those with a large variance).

4. *Guessing*. The less guessing that occurs on a test (that is, the less examinees respond to items randomly),

Table 2-5
Some Procedures Used to Determine Reliability

Procedure	*Description*
Spearman-Brown correction formula $$r_{tt} = \frac{2r_{hh}}{1 + r_{hh}}$$ where r_{tt} = reliability estimate r_{hh} = correlation between halves	An *internal consistency reliability* formula used for the split-half method. It corrects for the reduced number of items (based on the two halves of the test) used to compute the correlation. The formula increases the reliability estimate.
Cronbach's coefficient alpha (α) formula $$r_{tt} = \left(\frac{n}{n-1}\right)\left(\frac{S_t^2 - \Sigma(S_i^2)}{S_t^2}\right)$$ where r_{tt} = coefficient alpha reliability estimate n = number of items in the test S_t^2 = variance of the total test ΣS_i^2 = sum of the variances of individual items	An *internal consistency reliability* formula used when a test has no right or wrong answers. This formula provides a general reliability estimate that simultaneously considers all of the ways of splitting items.
Kuder-Richardson formula 20 (KR$_{20}$) $$r_{tt} = \left(\frac{n}{n-1}\right)\left(\frac{S_t^2 - \Sigma pq}{S_t^2}\right)$$ where r_{tt} = reliability estimate n = number of items on the test S_t^2 = variance of the total test Σpq = sum of the product of p and q for each item p = proportion of people getting an item correct q = proportion of people getting an item incorrect	An *internal consistency reliability* formula used for calculating the reliability of a test in which the items are scored 1 or 0 (or right or wrong). It provides a general method that simultaneously considers all of the ways of splitting items.
Product-moment correlation coefficient formula See Table 2-3 for formula.	A formula used to estimate *test-retest reliability* or *equivalent form* or *parallel form reliability*.

the higher the reliability is likely to be. Even guessing that results in correct answers introduces error into the score.

5. *Variation within the test situation.* The fewer variations there are in the test situation, the higher the reliability is likely to be. Factors such as misleading or misunderstood instructions, scoring errors, illness, and daydreaming introduce an indeterminate amount of error into the testing procedure.

Reliability of an Individual Examinee's Test Score

A test that is reliable for a group may not necessarily be reliable for any subgroup of the population or for any one individual examinee. The reliability of a score obtained on an individually administered test may be affected by idiosyncratic examinee and examiner factors. Unreliable results may be obtained, for example, if examinees are uncooperative or anxious or have difficulty following the instructions, or if examiners are incompetent. Examinees tested under these and other circumstances may perform differently when tested on another occasion by the same or another examiner; thus the initial results may not be reliable. Of course a test that does not have adequate reliability should *never* be used to make decisions about an individual examinee.

Standard Error of Measurement

Because of the presence of measurement error associated with test unreliability, there is always some uncertainty about an individual's true score. The standard error of measurement (SE_m), or standard error of a score, is an estimate of the amount of error usually attached to an examinee's obtained score. It is directly related to the reliability of a test: the larger the standard error of measurement, the lower the reliability (conversely, the smaller the standard error of measurement, the higher the reliability). Large standard errors of measurement mean less precise measurements and larger confidence intervals or bands (see the next section).

The standard error of measurement is the standard deviation of the distribution of error scores. It can be computed from the reliability coefficient of the test by multiplying the standard deviation (SD) of the test by the square root of 1 minus the reliability coefficient (r_{xx}) of the test:

$$SE_m = SD\sqrt{1 - r_{xx}}$$

Let us look at how reliability and the standard error of measurement are related for two popular tests. On the WISC-R ($M = 100$, $SD = 15$), the average internal consis-

tency reliability for the Full Scale IQ is .96, with a standard error of measurement of 3.19. In contrast, on the Bayley Scales of Infant Development ($M = 100$, $SD = 16$) the median internal consistency reliability for the Motor Scale is .84, with a standard error of measurement of 6.40. Thus we can conclude that the WISC-R provides more precise measurements than does the Bayley Motor Scale.

Confidence Intervals for Obtained Scores

Statements about the probability that an examinee's obtained score reflects his or her true score are generally couched in terms of a confidence interval — a band or range of scores that has a high probability of including the examinee's true score. The standard error of measurement provides the basis for forming the confidence interval. The interval may be large or small, depending on the degree of confidence desired. Usually, points selected represent the 68 percent, 95 percent, or 99 percent level of confidence, although the 85 percent and 90 percent levels are also used. A 95 percent confidence interval can be thought of as the range in which a person's true score will be found 95 percent of the time. The chances are only 5 in 100 that a person's true score lies outside this confidence interval. *It is not possible to construct a confidence interval within which a person's true score is absolutely certain to lie.*

Confidence interval formula. The confidence interval is obtained by use of the following formula:

Confidence interval = obtained score $\pm z(SE_m)$

The formula shows that two values are needed in addition to the child's test score: (a) the z score associated with the confidence level chosen and (b) the standard error of measurement. The z score is obtained from a normal curve table, which can be found in almost any statistics book. A normal curve table was used to obtain the following values for the five most common levels of confidence:

68 percent level, $z = 1.00$
85 percent level, $z = 1.44$
90 percent level, $z = 1.65$
95 percent level, $z = 1.96$
99 percent level, $z = 2.58$

The SE_m is found in the test manual or by use of the formula given previously. The upper limit of the confidence interval is obtained by adding the product $(z)(SE_m)$ to the child's score, and the lower limit is obtained by subtracting the product from the child's score (thus the plus/minus symbol [±] in the equation).

Constructing the confidence interval.   Now let us construct a confidence interval, given that the standard error of measurement is 3 and the IQ is 100. First we need to select the degree of confidence desired. Let us say that the 68 percent level is selected.

The z score associated with the 68 percent level, as we have seen, is 1. To obtain the confidence interval, we multiply this value by the standard error of measurement, 3, and add a ± sign to the result to represent the upper and lower limits of the interval. Thus the confidence interval is 100 ± 3. The value 3 is then added to *and* subtracted from the obtained score to determine the specific band or interval associated with the obtained score. The upper limit of the interval is given by

$$\begin{aligned}
\text{Confidence interval (upper limit)} &= 100 + 1(3) \\
&= 100 + 3 \\
&= 103
\end{aligned}$$

and the lower limit of the interval is given by

$$\begin{aligned}
\text{Confidence interval (lower limit)} &= 100 - 1(3) \\
&= 100 - 3 \\
&= 97
\end{aligned}$$

Since the z score we used was associated with the 68 percent level, we can say that the chances that the range of scores from 97 to 103 includes the child's "true" IQ are about 68 out of 100.

For an IQ of 100 (with $SE_m = 3$), the interval would be 100 ± 4 (96 to 104) at the 85 percent confidence level, 100 ± 5 (95 to 105) at the 90 percent confidence level, 100 ± 6 (94 to 106) at the 95 percent confidence level, and 100 ± 8 (92 to 108) at the 99 percent confidence level. The last band indicates that the chances are about 99 out of 100 that the child's "true" IQ falls in the range of 92 to 108. Notice that we must increase the band width in order to increase the confidence level (or degree of certainty).

As another example, let us construct confidence intervals for a child who obtains an IQ of 80 on a test for which $SE_m = 5$. We would complete the equation for the 68 percent level of confidence in the following way:

$$\begin{aligned}
\text{Confidence interval} &= \text{score} \pm z(SE_m) \\
&= 80 \pm 1(5) \\
&= 80 \pm 5 \\
&= 75 \text{ to } 85
\end{aligned}$$

For the 95 percent level of confidence, the equation would be as follows:

$$\begin{aligned}
\text{Confidence interval} &= 80 \pm 1.96(5) \\
&= 80 \pm 10 \text{ (approximately)} \\
&= 70 \text{ to } 90
\end{aligned}$$

In clinical and psychoeducational assessment, it is important to report the confidence interval associated with a child's scores, especially with the IQ. Confidence intervals enable the reader to recognize that a score obtained by a child reflects a range of possible scores. Special tables in Appendix C provide the confidence intervals for various individually administered intelligence tests.

Confidence Intervals for Predicted Scores

An earlier section discussed regression equations and the standard error of estimate associated with the predicted score. The standard error of estimate allows us to associate a confidence interval with a predicted score. This confidence interval is obtained in the following way:

$$\boxed{\text{Confidence interval} = Y_{\text{pred}} \pm z(SE_{\text{est}})}$$

The confidence interval for predicted scores is similar to the confidence interval for obtained test scores. If a z score of 1 is used, then the standard error of estimate tells us that the predicted score can be expected to fall within the range bounded by the standard error of estimate about 68 percent of the time. If we wish to have higher confidence in the prediction, we can use a z score associated with, for example, the 95 percent confidence level ($z = 1.96$) or the 99 percent confidence level ($z = 2.58$). However, increasing the level of confidence means expanding the band (or range) around the predicted score.

The three examples that follow illustrate how various confidence intervals can be established. In each case, we shall assume that $SE_{\text{est}} = 5$ and $Y_{\text{pred}} = 15$.

• For the 68 percent level of confidence, the confidence interval is $15 \pm 1.00(5)$. Thus the confidence interval associated with the predicted score of 15 is 10.00 to 20.00 (there is a 68 percent chance that Y falls within this range).

• For the 95 percent level of confidence, the confidence interval is $15 \pm 1.96(5)$. Thus the confidence interval associated with the predicted score of 15 is 5.20 to 24.80 (there is a 95 percent chance that Y falls within this range).

• For the 99 percent level of confidence, the confidence interval is $15 \pm 2.58(5)$. Thus the confidence interval associated with the predicted score of 15 is 2.10 to 27.90 (there is a 99 percent chance that Y falls within this range).

VALIDITY

The validity of a test refers to the extent to which a test measures what it is supposed to measure, and therefore the appropriateness with which inferences can be made on the basis of the test results. Test results are used for many different purposes, including placement in special training or educational programs, job qualification, and personality assessment. Unless the test is valid for the particular purpose for which it is being used, the results cannot be used with any degree of confidence. Because tests are used for many different purposes, there is no single type of validity appropriate for all testing purposes.

It is important to recognize that no test is valid in general or in the abstract; tests are valid only for a specific purpose. Validity is not a matter of all or nothing, but a matter of degree. Tests are never valid in isolation from the social system in which they are used. Consequently, validity is concerned not only with the proper inferences that can be made from test scores, but also with the potential and actual social consequences of using tests (Messick, 1980). It is the examiner who is responsible for the valid use of test results. Let us now consider the three principal varieties of validity: content, criterion-related, and construct.

Content Validity

Content validity refers to whether the items on a test are representative of the domain that the test purports to measure. In evaluating content validity, one must consider the appropriateness of the type of items, the completeness of the item sample, and the way in which the items assess the content of the domain involved. Issues relevant to these considerations include the following: (a) Are the test questions appropriate and does the test measure the domain of interest? (b) Does the test contain enough information to cover appropriately what it is supposed to measure? (c) What is the level of mastery at which the content is being assessed? If these three questions can be answered satisfactorily, the test is thought to have good content validity.

Content validity can be built into a test by including only those items that measure the trait or behavior of interest. Content validity does not require that all possible elements in a universe be measured, but rather that those measured be representative of the universe in number and kind. Evaluation of such representativeness is a major component in the validation process for any educational or psychological test.

Content validity should not be confused with face validity. *Face validity* refers to what the test appears to measure, not what it actually does measure. Face validity is impor-

tant to examinees in that if the test does not appear to measure what it purports to measure, they may become skeptical and then the results may not accurately reflect their abilities. Although face validity is, in itself, a desirable feature of a test, it is not always necessary for good validity in the technical sense.

Criterion-Related Validity

Criterion-related validity refers to the relationship between test scores and some type of criterion or outcome, such as ratings, classifications, or other test scores. The criterion, like the test, must possess adequate psychometric properties: it should be readily measurable, free from bias, and relevant to the purposes of the test. A complementary relationship between test and criterion is an obvious necessity; otherwise it is impossible to use the criterion to determine whether the test measures the trait or characteristic it was designed to measure. The two types of criterion-related validity are concurrent (or diagnostic) and predictive (or prognostic).

Concurrent validity. Concurrent validity refers to whether test scores are related to some currently available criterion measure. Let us suppose we have a test that we would like to use to place children in a special math class. If we find that the test scores correlate with the teachers' assessment of the children's knowledge of math, the test is said to have concurrent validity. The fact that test scores correlate with the results of a more laborious procedure currently used for a selection process is usually taken to mean that the test may be used to replace the longer procedure.

Predictive validity. Predictive validity refers to the correlation between test scores and performance on a relevant criterion where there is a time interval between the test administration and performance on the criterion. It answers the following question: Is the score obtained on the test an accurate predictor of future performance on the criterion? The accuracy with which an aptitude or readiness test indicates future learning success in school depends on predictive validity. Thus predictive validity is very important in many psychoeducational contexts.

Predictive validity is established by giving a test to a group that has yet to perform on the criterion of interest. The group's performance on the criterion is subsequently measured. The correspondence between the two scores provides a measure of the predictive validity of the test. If the test possesses high predictive validity, persons scoring high on the test will perform well on the criterion measure.

Likewise, those scoring low on the test will perform poorly on the criterion. If the predictive validity of a test is low, there will be an erratic and unpredictable relationship between the test scores and subsequent performance on the criterion.

Construct Validity

Construct validity refers to the extent to which a test measures a psychological construct or trait. Various procedures are used to determine how the items in a test relate to the theoretical constructs that the test purports to measure. The construct validity of an intelligence test can be evaluated by examining how the items relate to a theory of intelligence. Factor analysis also permits an examination of the construct validity of a test. Factor analysis of the Wechsler batteries, for example, usually demonstrates that the batteries have verbal and performance components, thereby supporting the use of separate verbal and performance scores.

Factors Affecting Validity

Since validity coefficients are correlation coefficients, they are affected by such factors as the range of talent being measured and the length of the interval between the administration of the two measures. Predictive validity of the IQ (and other test scores) can be impaired in a number of ways (Deutsch, Fishman, Kogan, North, & Whiteman, 1964). First, test-related factors affect validity. These include test-taking skills, anxiety, motivation, speed, understanding of test instructions, degree of item or format novelty, examiner-examinee rapport, physical handicaps, degree of bilingualism, deficiencies in educational opportunities, unfamiliarity with the test material, and deviation in other ways from the norm of the standardization group. Obviously the test results are not valid for uncooperative or highly distractible examinees or for those who fail to understand the test instructions.

Second, factors related to the criterion may also affect validity. School grades, a commonly used criterion, are affected by motivation, classroom behavior, personal appearance, and study habits. If examinees have problems in any of these areas, the predictive validity of intelligence tests may be lowered.

Third, intervening events and contingencies may also affect predictive validity, especially in testing handicapped children. Consideration should be given to the extent to which an emotionally disturbed examinee's condition is acute or chronic. Acute states of disturbance (that is, sudden occurrences of a disorder) often disrupt intellec-

tual efficiency, thereby leading to nonrepresentative test results. Whenever therapeutic intervention—such as drugs, psychotherapy, foster-home placement, or environmental manipulation—is capable of improving the examinee's performance, the validity or representativeness of the initial test results should be questioned. However, chronic conditions (that is, conditions that have persisted for many years), such as irreversible brain damage or chronic schizophrenia, may not necessarily invalidate the test results, because there may be little that can be done to improve the examinee's performance. If the examinee's performance reflects how he or she is likely to perform during the few weeks after administration of the examination, the examination can be considered to be valid. As Deutsch et al. (1964, pp. 136–137) stated,

If the time interval between the test administration and the criterial assessment is lengthy, a host of situational, motivational, and maturational changes may occur in the interim. An illness, an inspiring teacher, a shift in aspiration level or in direction of interest, remedial training, an economic misfortune, an emotional crisis, a growth spurt or retrogression in the abilities sampled by the test—any of these changes intervening between the testing and the point or points of criterion assessment may decrease the predictive power of the test.

Finally, validity is affected by the test's reliability—reliability is a necessary but not sufficient condition for validity.

In some cases, it may be difficult to determine the validity of the test results on the basis of only one test session, especially when information about previous test results (from, for example, school records) is not available. If there is reason to question the validity of the test results, express any such doubts clearly in the report. If validity is in serious doubt, you might want to destroy the test protocol or mark *invalid* over the face sheet. Deviation from some earlier level of functioning does not necessarily invalidate the results, however, because the current level of functioning may be either lower or higher than the earlier level. In some cases, the earlier level of functioning may be estimated from prior test results, from school grades, or even from parental reports.

FACTOR ANALYSIS

Factor analysis is a mathematical procedure used to analyze the intercorrelations of a group of tests (or other variables) that have been administered to a large number of individuals. Because complex computations are involved, factor analysis is almost always done with the help of a computer. Factor analysis is based on the assumption that intercorrelations can be accounted for by some underlying set of (unobservable) factors that are fewer in number than the tests (or variables) themselves. In the field of intelligence, factor analysis might be used, for example, to determine the number of different mental abilities that account for the pattern of intercorrelations in the tests in the battery. A major purpose of factor analysis is to simplify the description of behavior by reducing the number of variables to the smallest possible number.

The findings from factor analysis tell you the extent to which varying numbers of factors account for the correlations among tests. A factor is defined as that which a cluster of interrelated tests have in common. The results also indicate the extent to which each test loads on, or is correlated with, one or more factors. Factor loadings are simply correlations between factors and tests. The loadings indicate the weight of each factor in determining performance on each test.

Procedures Used in Factor Analysis

Most factor analysis programs work by extracting first the factor that accounts for the largest proportion of variance, then the factor that accounts for the largest proportion of the residual variance, and so on. In some cases (but not all), the first unrotated factor is a *general factor* on which most variables have high loadings. A general factor is found in cases where all subtests have a considerable amount of overlap, such as in an intelligence test. In intelligence testing, this first general factor is considered to reflect general intelligence, or *g*. In other cases, such as in a multidimensional test of personality, there may be two or three important factors but no single factor on which all variables load.

Rather than attempting to interpret the original factors, however, almost all researchers rotate the matrix of factor loadings to make the factor structure clearer. The rotation rearranges the factors so that, ideally, for every factor there are some tests with high loadings on the factor and other tests with low loadings on the factor. The order in which the factors originally were extracted is not always preserved in the rotation; in particular, the first unrotated factor usually cannot be discerned. The factors resulting from the rotation are referred to as *group factors*. It is up to the researcher to name or interpret each factor by looking at the content of the tests that have high loadings on the factor.

After all of the common factor variance has been extracted and the rotation has been completed, there still may be a significant amount of variance that has not been analyzed. This variance, present in one test but not in the other tests under study, may be termed *specific factor variance*, *specific variance*, or *specificity*.

Components of Variance

In a factor analysis, the variance associated with a test or subtest can be divided into three categories:

1. *Communality*. Communality refers to that part of the total variance that can be attributed to common factors (those that appear in more than one test). The formula for obtaining communality is as follows:

$$h_t^2 = a_{t1}^2 + a_{t2}^2 + \cdots + a_{tm}^2$$

where h_t^2 = communality of test t
$a_{t1}^2, \ldots, a_{tm}^2$ = loading of test t on factor $1, \ldots,$ factor m.

For the data in Table 2-7 in the next section, the communality estimate for Similarities is

$$h_t^2 = .64^2 + .34^2 + .28^2 = .60$$

2. *Specificity*. Specificity refers to that part of the total variance that is due to factors that are specific to the particular test, and not to measurement error or common factors. The proportion of specific variance is obtained in the following way:

$$s_t^2 = r_{tt} - h_t^2$$

where s_t^2 = variance specific to test t
r_{tt} = reliability of test t
h_t^2 = communality of test t.

The proportion of specific variance for Similarities is (see Table 2-7 in the next section)

$$s_t^2 = .81 - .60 = .21$$

3. *Error variance*. Error variance refers to that part of the total variance that remains when the reliability of the test is subtracted from the total variance. It is obtained by the following formula:

$$e_t^2 = 1 - r_{tt}$$

where e_t^2 = error variance of test t
r_{tt} = reliability of test t.

Error variance for the Similarities subtest is

$$e_t^2 = 1 - .81 = .19$$

When specific variance exceeds error variance, we can conclude that the test has some subtest specificity.

Illustration of Factor Analysis

Let us examine how factor analysis might be applied to the WISC-R. Table 2-6 shows a partial set of WISC-R subtest intercorrelations (for 4 of the 12 WISC-R subtests). These correlations are based on the entire standardization group ($N = 2,200$). A factor analysis of the complete intercorrelation table would help us to determine, for example, whether intelligence, as measured by the WISC-R, is best viewed as associated with a single general ability or with a number of specific abilities.

If the WISC-R measures general intellectual ability, children with this ability should perform well on all of the subtests and those with a small amount of this ability should do poorly. Applied to the intercorrelations in Table 2-6, this means that children who do well on Similarities should also do well on the other three subtests, whereas those who do poorly on Similarities should also do poorly on the other three subtests. If children's scores on the four subtests are highly correlated, we can reasonably conclude that the subtests have something in common.

Some of the subtests also may correlate highly with other subtests, but to different degrees. Another possibility is that specific abilities are more important than general or group abilities on the four subtests. If so, then the correlations between Similarities, Vocabulary, Picture Arrangement, and Block Design should not be extremely high. Since the correlations in Table 2-6 are high, we might conclude that there is a general ability factor in the WISC-R. More than a general factor may also be present because the correlations are not consistently high—some abilities are important for some subtests but not for others.

The factor analytic findings for the entire WISC-R are shown in Chapter 6. They indicate that both a general factor and group factors are present in the scale. Additionally, a number of subtests have adequate subtest specificity. For the four subtests discussed above, Table 2-7 shows the median general factor and group factor loadings, reliability, communality, specificity, and error variance. Loadings above .70 on the general factor are considered to be substantial, as are loadings above .30 or .40 on the group factors. The loadings indicate that Similarities, Vocabulary, and Block Design are good measures of the general factor, whereas Picture Arrangement is only a fair measure of the general factor. Additionally, Similarities and Vocabulary load highly on the Verbal Comprehension group factor, and Picture Arrangement and Block Design load highly on the Perceptual Organization group factor. None of the four subtests load highly on the Freedom from Distractibility group factor. All four subtests have some specificity, because specific variance (specificity) exceeds error variance.

Other Uses of Factor Analysis

Factor analysis may be used to determine the homogeneity of a test and to develop better tests. Homogeneity is the extent to which the items of a test showed a marked likeness with respect to the quality or attribute under consideration. In investigations of homogeneity, the input data are the scores of each individual on each item of the test. Intercorrelations of the items (not people) are computed and then subjected to a factor analytic procedure. Factor analysis can also be applied to data other than test scores. For example, it can be applied to ratings of personality traits or behaviors of people, thus grouping the variables measured by the rating scales according to their similarities. In addition, it is a useful procedure for studying the underlying constructs associated with a test or tests.

Table 2-6
Average Intercorrelations for Four WISC-R Subtests

Subtest	Similarities	Vocabulary	Picture Arrangement	Block Design
Similarities	—	.67	.41	.50
Vocabulary	.67	—	.44	.48
Picture Arrangement	.41	.44	—	.46
Block Design	.50	.48	.46	—

Source: Adapted from Wechsler (1974).

Table 2-7
General Factor Loadings, Group Factor Loadings, Reliability, Communality, Specific Variance, and Error Variance for Four WISC-R Subtests

| WISC-R subtests | General factor | Group factors | | | Reliability (r_{tt}) | Communality (h_t^2) | Specificity (s_t^2) | Error (e_t^2) |
		Factor A, Verbal Comprehension	Factor B, Perceptual Organization	Factor C, Freedom from Distractibility				
Similarities	.76	.64	.34	.28	.81	.60	.21	.19
Vocabulary	.80	.72	.24	.33	.86	.68	.18	.14
Picture Arrangement	.60	.33	.41	.12	.73	.29	.44	.27
Block Design	.73	.27	.66	.28	.85	.59	.26	.15

Comment on Factor Analysis

Factor analysis is a complex statistical method. The same set of data can yield different results depending on the factor analytic method used, the number of factors retained, and the rotations of the factors. In addition, the naming of factors is a somewhat arbitrary process. Thus, although factor analysis is a useful procedure, the results must be carefully interpreted.

TEST YOUR SKILL

Select a test that is covered in this text. Read the test manual carefully. Before you read any reviews of the test, evaluate the test with respect to the following 20 points. Then compare your review with one in this text, the *Mental Measurements Yearbook*, or another source.

1. Title
2. Author(s)
3. Publisher
4. Purpose of test
5. Ages (or grade levels)
6. Date of publication
7. Cost
8. Time required for administration
9. Number of forms
10. Scoring
11. Types of items
12. Basis for item selection
13. Evidence of validity
14. Evidence of reliability
15. Norms
16. Desirable features
17. Undesirable features
18. Quality of manual
19. General evaluation
20. References

SUMMARY

1. There are four types of scales for recording data: nominal, ordinal, interval, and ratio. Each scale is useful for answering different kinds of questions. Nominal scales simply identify individuals or things. Ordinal scales rank order measured variables. Interval scales contain a unit of measurement and equal intervals, with an arbitrary zero point. Ratio scales contain a unit of measurement as well as a true zero point.

2. The mean, median, and mode are the three principal measures of central tendency. The mean is the arithmetic average of the scores in a distribution. The median is the middle point, with 50 percent of the scores lying above or at the median and 50 percent lying below or at the median. The mode is the score that occurs most frequently.

3. Standard deviation and variance are the two most common measures of dispersion. The range also provides useful information about a distribution of scores.

4. The normal, or bell-shaped, curve reflects the distribution of many psychological traits.

5. Correlations provide an important means of describing the relationship between two (or more) variables or tests. Correlations range from +1.00 to −1.00. A positive correlation indicates that a high score on one variable is associated with a high score on the other, whereas a negative correlation indicates that a high score on one variable is associated with a low score on the other. The square of the correlation coefficient (r^2) tells us the percent of variance in one variable accounted for by the other variable.

6. A regression equation is useful for predicting the score on one variable when the score on another variable is known.

7. The standard error of estimate allows us to determine the accuracy of the predicted score from the regression equation. A

confidence interval can be established around the predicted score.

8. Multiple correlations assist in determining the relationship between one variable and several other variables.

9. Norm-referenced measurement is useful when we wish to compare an examinee's score with those of a known group of subjects. The characteristics of the normative group—such as its representativeness, size, and relevance—should be evaluated carefully.

10. Derived scores are the primary means by which the results of norm-referenced testing are conveyed. Age-equivalent and grade-equivalent scores have poor statistical properties and are potentially misleading. Ratio IQs—the ratio of mental age to chronological age multiplied by 100—also have poor statistical properties, particularly the uneven distribution of IQs at various ages. Percentile ranks are useful in expressing the examinee's position relative to a known sample. Standard scores, such as z scores, T scores, and Deviation IQs, are preferred over other derived scores because they are designed to have a constant mean and standard deviation across all ages of the normative sample. Stanines are based on a nine-category system for grouping scores.

11. It is important to evaluate whether the findings of an investigation differ significantly from chance, as well as whether the results have any practical significance.

12. Reliability refers to consistency of measurement, a vital characteristic of a test. The reliability coefficient represents a ratio of true score variance to obtained score variance. The three types of reliabilities are test-retest, alternate form, and internal consistency. Several factors affect reliability, including test length, test-retest interval, variability of scores, guessing, and situational factors.

13. The standard error of measurement allows us to determine the amount of error associated with an examinee's score. Confidence intervals are developed on the basis of the standard error of measurement.

14. Validity refers to the extent to which a test measures what it is supposed to measure. Tests are only valid for specific purposes. The principal types of validity are content, criterion-related, and construct. They involve, respectively, evaluation of test content, correlations with specific criteria, and evaluation of constructs underlying the development of the test. Predictive validity is affected by test-related factors, criterion-related factors, and intervening factors.

15. Factor analysis is a useful procedure for determining the underlying structure of a test or group of tests. Three types of factors are usually obtained in a factor analysis: *specific* (present in one test only), *group* (found in more than one test), and *general* (found in all of the tests in the battery).

KEY TERMS, CONCEPTS, AND NAMES

Psychometrics (p. 13)
Descriptive statistics (p. 13)

Nominal scale (p. 14)
Ordinal scale (p. 14)
Interval scale (p. 14)
Ratio scale (p. 14)
Measures of central tendency (p. 14)
Mean (p. 14)
Median (p. 15)
Mode (p. 15)
Measures of dispersion (p. 15)
Range (p. 15)
Variance (p. 15)
Standard deviation (p. 16)
Normal curve (p. 16)
Correlations (p. 16)
Correlation coefficient (p. 16)
Pearson correlation (r) (p. 16)
Coefficient of determination (p. 18)
Regression equation (p. 18)
Standard error of estimate (p. 18)
Multiple correlation (R) (p. 20)
Norm-referenced measurement (p. 20)
Derived scores (p. 20)
Age-equivalent score (p. 20)
Grade-equivalent score (p. 20)
Mental age (p. 21)
Test age (p. 21)
Ratio IQ (p. 21)
Percentile rank (p. 22)
Standard score (p. 22)
z score (p. 22)
T score (p. 22)
Deviation IQ (p. 22)
Stanines (p. 22)
Statistical significance (p. 24)
Reliability (p. 25)
True score (p. 26)
Error score (p. 26)
Reliability coefficient (p. 26)
Test-retest reliability (p. 26)
Alternate form reliability (p. 26)
Internal consistency reliability (p. 26)
Split-half reliability (p. 26)
Cronbach's coefficient alpha (p. 26)
Kuder-Richardson formula 20 (p. 26)
Standard error of measurement (p. 28)
Confidence interval (p. 28)
Validity (p. 30)
Content validity (p. 30)
Face validity (p. 30)
Criterion-related validity (p. 30)
Concurrent validity (p. 30)
Predictive validity (p. 30)
Construct validity (p. 31)
Factor analysis (p. 31)
Factor loadings (p. 32)

General factor (p. 32)
Group factors (p. 32)
Specific factor variance (p. 32)
Communality (p. 32)
Specificity (p. 32)
Error variance (p. 32)

STUDY QUESTIONS

1. Compare and contrast nominal, ordinal, interval, and ratio scales.

2. Discuss the three measures of central tendency.

3. Discuss measures of dispersion.

4. Discuss the normal curve.

5. Discuss correlations.

6. Discuss the regression equation.

7. What is the standard error of estimate?

8. What are some important features of norm-referenced testing?

9. Describe and *evaluate* the following derived scores: age- and grade-equivalent scores, ratio intelligence quotients, percentile ranks, standard scores, and stanines.

10. To what does statistical significance refer?

11. Discuss the concept of reliability, the various forms of reliability, and factors affecting reliability.

12. What is the standard error of measurement?

13. Discuss the concept of confidence intervals.

14. Discuss the concept of validity, the various types of validity, and factors affecting validity.

15. What is factor analysis?

3

HISTORICAL SURVEY
AND THEORIES
OF INTELLIGENCE

Only the history of science can clarify adequately the meaning of contemporary science. It alone can attach the fleeting present to man's long march toward the enrichment of mankind.

—Georges Gusdorf

This chapter provides a brief history of developments in the field of intelligence. It describes the contributions of both the pioneer and contemporary theorists and test developers, and it summarizes some of the major definitions of intelligence. The historical survey begins with nineteenth-century developments.

NINETEENTH-CENTURY DEVELOPMENTS

In the nineteenth century, confusion about the differences between so-called idiots and lunatics (both of whom were treated much like criminals) pointed out the need for a practical study of mental ability (Shouksmith, 1970). Jean Esquirol, in 1838, was one of the first to make a clear distinction between mental incapacity and mental illness. He pointed out that idiots never developed their intellectual capacities, whereas mentally deranged persons lost abilities they once possessed. Esquirol also tried to develop methods for differentiating defects from illnesses, focusing first on physical measurements and then on speech patterns as a way of distinguishing the two groups. His descriptions of verbal characteristics at various levels of idiocy may be regarded as the first crude, but effective, mental test.

Interest in intelligence and in intelligence testing, which developed in the latter part of the nineteenth century, was part of the scientific movement that brought psychology into being as a separate discipline. The psychophysical methods developed by E. H. Weber (1795–1878) and G. T. Fechner (1801–1887) and the statistical studies of mental processes initiated by Sir Francis Galton (1822–1911) formed the background for much of the work that would take place in the twentieth century. (See the inside front cover of this textbook for a listing of historical landmarks in cognitive and educational assessment.)

Developments in England

Galton.   Sir Francis Galton is regarded as the father of the testing movement (Shouksmith, 1970). He originated two very important statistical concepts—regression to the mean and correlation—which permitted the psychometric field to flourish and develop. These concepts allowed for the study of intelligence over time, as well as the study of such relationships as that between the intelligence test scores of parents and children.

In 1869 Galton published *Hereditary Genius*, in which

he made a statistical analysis of inherited mental characteristics, estimating the number of geniuses that could be expected in a particular sample of people. In his 1883 publication *Inquiries into Human Faculty*, he considered the problems involved in measuring mental characteristics. In 1884 he set up a psychometric laboratory at the International Health Exhibition, which later was reestablished at University College, London. The laboratory, which was open to the public (see Figure 3-1), provided measures of physical and mental capacities for a small fee. Galton assumed that because our knowledge of the environment reaches us through the senses, those with the highest intelligence should also have the best sensory discrimination abilities. This belief led him to develop tests of sensory discrimination and motor coordination in order to study mental functioning. This assumption generally proved to be invalid, however, and may have been instrumental in limiting the progress of his work. (See Johnson,

ANTHROPOMETRIC
LABORATORY

For the measurement in various ways of **Human Form and Faculty**.

Entered from the Science Collection of the S. Kensington Museum.

This laboratory is established by Mr. Francis Galton for the following purposes:—

1. For the use of those who desire to be accurately measured in many ways, either to obtain timely warning of remediable faults in development, or to learn their powers.

2. For keeping a methodical register of the principal measurements of each person, of which he may at any future time obtain a copy under reasonable restrictions.   His initials and date of birth will be entered in the register, but not his name.   The names are indexed in a separate book.

3. For supplying information on the methods, practice, and uses of human measurement.

4. For anthropometric experiment and research, and for obtaining data for statistical discussion.

Charges for making the principal measurements:
THREEPENCE each, to those who are already on the Register.
FOURPENCE each, to those who are not:— one page of the Register will thenceforward be assigned to them, and a few extra measurements will be made, chiefly for future identification.

The Superintendent is charged with the control of the laboratory and with determining in each case, which, if any, of the extra measurements may be made, and under what conditions.

Figure 3-1.   An announcement for Galton's laboratory. Reproduced by permission of the Photo Science Museum, London, England.

McClearn, Yuen, Nagoshi, Ahern, & Cole, 1985, for a recent analysis of 6,500 individual records obtained from Galton's laboratory.)

Pearson.   Karl Pearson (1857–1936), Galton's close friend and biographer, was a professor of applied mathematics and mechanics at University College, London. Pearson was active in the fields of eugenics, anthropology, and psychology. On the basis of Galton's work, Pearson developed the product-moment correlation formula for linear correlation, the multiple correlation coefficient, the partial correlation coefficient, the phi coefficient, and the chi-square test for determining how well a set of empirical observations conforms to an expected distribution (goodness of fit).

Developments in the United States

James McKeen Cattell.   James McKeen Cattell (1860–1944) studied with Wilhelm Wundt at Leipzig, where the first psychological laboratory was founded in 1879. Wundt believed that the aim of psychology was to analyze the content of consciousness, and thus psychologists should focus on the study of immediate experience, principally by means of self-observation, or introspection. Cattell, however, went on to serve as an assistant in Galton's anthropometric laboratory and to become heavily influenced by Galton's theories. Thus Cattell, instead of becoming a follower of Wundt's introspective approach to psychology, focused on the study of individual differences in behavior. Upon his return to the United States, Cattell established a laboratory at the University of Pennsylvania. In 1890, in an article published in *Mind*, he was the first to use the term *mental test*. He described 50 different measures which, for the most part, assessed sensory and motor abilities and differed little from those designed by Galton. In 1891 Cattell moved to Columbia University to continue his work on measurement.

Cattell stressed that psychology must rest on a foundation of measurement and experimentation. Foreseeing the practical application of tests as tools for the selection of people for training and for diagnostic evaluations, he tried to compile a battery of tests that could be used to evaluate people. Some of the tests he considered included Dynamometer Pressure, Rate of Movement (speed with which an arm was moved a specified distance), Sensation-Areas (two-point discrimination), Least Noticeable Difference in Weight, Reaction-Time for Sound, Time for Naming Colors, Bi-section of a 50-cm Line, Judgment of Ten Seconds' Time, and Number of Letters Remembered on Once Hearing.

We now know that these measures have little predictive validity for educational achievement or for other aspects of intellectual functioning, but Cattell did make a valuable contribution to psychology by taking the assessment of mental ability out of the field of abstract philosophy and showing that mental ability could be studied experimentally and practically.

Other developments in the United States.   Psychological tests made their public debut in the United States at the 1893 Chicago World's Fair, where Hugo Münsterberg and Joseph Jastrow collaborated on a demonstration testing laboratory. For a small fee, visitors to the exhibit could take tests in "mental anthropometry" and learn how their performance compared to that of others.

In the early 1890s Franz Boas at Clark University and J. Gilbert at Yale University studied how children responded to various types of tests. Boas studied the validity of simple sensorimotor tests by using teachers' estimates of children's "intellectual acuteness" as a criterion. Gilbert, also studying simple sensorimotor tests, found only two tests — rate of tapping and judgment of length of distances — that could distinguish bright from dull children.

Clark Wissler (1901), another investigator, sought to determine the validity of some of the tests that were thought to be related to cognitive processes. Most of his tests also measured simple sensory functions. Using the correlational methods of Galton and Pearson to study college-age subjects, he reported low relationships among the test scores themselves and between the test scores and school grades. Stella Sharp (1898) reported that tests similar to those used by Binet and Henri (see the section on Developments in France) were measuring many different functions and were giving unreliable results. Sharp, however, studied only seven graduate students; it is not surprising that there were low correlations among the tests for this small homogeneous sample. Despite their serious methodological shortcomings, these studies by Wissler and Sharp led investigators to believe that the field of mental measurement was not a fruitful field to study.

Developments in Germany

In Germany at the turn of the century, five individuals were making contributions to the field of assessment. Emil Kraepelin (1855–1926), working in the field of psychopathology, was introducing complex tests for measuring mental functioning, including tests of perception, memory, motor functions, and attention. Many of his tests were based on abilities needed in everyday life. Kraepelin, a psychiatrist and one of Wundt's first pupils, recognized the need to examine an individual enough times to reduce chance variation.

H. Münsterberg (1863–1916) was developing various types of perceptual, memory, reading, and information tests for children. H. Ebbinghaus (1850–1909) was working on tests of memory, computation, and sentence completion. He developed a predecessor of the group-administered intelligence test, in which completion tasks were administered using a timed procedure. Passages with missing words were presented, and the examinee's task was to fill as many blanks as possible within a five-minute period. His tests were developed in response to a request from teachers in Breslau, Germany, for help in evaluating the academic aptitude of Breslau's school children.

Carl Wernicke (1848–1905), well known in Poland and Germany for his investigations of brain localization, was developing a set of questions designed to detect mental retardation. The questions—such as "What is the difference between a ladder and a staircase?"—emphasized conceptual thinking. In 1908, T. Ziehen (1862–1950) published a test battery that contained questions requiring generalizations, such as "What have an eagle, a duck, a goose, and a stork in common?"

Developments in France

In France at the end of the nineteenth century, Alfred Binet (1857–1911), Victor Henri (1872–1940), and Theodore Simon (1873–1961) were developing methods for the study of a variety of mental functions. These investigators believed that the key to the measurement of intelligence was to focus on higher mental processes instead of on simple sensory functions. Their work culminated in development of the 1905 Binet-Simon Scale (see Exhibit 3-1). The scale was by no means novel, for many items had been developed earlier and had been reported previously in some of their other papers. But the 1905 scale might be considered the first practical intelligence test, for the items were ranked in order of level of difficulty and accompanied by relatively careful instructions for administration. Unlike previous attempts, the scale reflected some concern with age-based cognitive development. It served the purpose of objectively diagnosing degrees of mental retardation and became the prototype of subsequent scales for the assessment of mental ability. It was revised in 1908 and again in 1911.

Comments on Nineteenth-Century Developments

Developments in the field of intelligence testing proceeded in somewhat different fashions in England, the United

Figure 3-2. Alfred Binet.

States, Germany, and France. The English were concerned with statistical analyses; the Americans focused on implementation of Binet's ideas for developing a scale and statistical methods for treating test data; the Germans emphasized the study of psychopathology and more complex mental functions; and the French focused on clinical experimentation (McConnell, 1930). The early test constructors also had varied reasons for developing tests (Du Bois, 1972). Galton and Pearson devised tests to aid them in their studies of heredity, James McKeen Cattell was interested in the study of individual differences in behavior; and Binet was interested primarily in determining levels of intellectual functioning among people. Further details concerning the intelligence-testing movement may be found in Boring (1950), Linden and Linden (1968), Peterson (1925), and Tuddenham (1962).

From 1880 to 1905 was the "laboratory" period in mental measurement. Various devices enabled psychologists to formulate general psychological principles and study individual differences. The search for a means to measure intelligence focused on such psychological processes as sensation, attention, perception, association, and memory. The work of Binet, Ebbinghaus, and others had a unifying thread—the application of methods used in experimental laboratories to solve practical problems presented by educators from their communities. This interplay of forces

Exhibit 3-1

Description of the 1905 Scale

The 1905 Scale

1. Visual coordination. The degree of coordination of movement of the head and eyes is noted as a lighted match is passed slowly before the subject's eyes.

2. Prehension provoked tactually. A small wooden cube is placed in contact with the palm or back of the subject's hand. He or she must grasp it and carry it to his or her mouth, and coordinated grasping and other movements are noted.

3. Prehension provoked visually. Same as 2, except that the object is placed within the subject's reach, but not in contact with him or her. The experimenter, to catch the child's attention, encourages him or her orally and with appropriate gestures to take the object.

4. Cognizance of food. A small bit of chocolate and a piece of wood of similar dimensions are successively shown to the subject and signs of recognition of the food and attempts to take it are noted carefully.

5. Seeking food when a slight difficulty is interposed. A small piece of the chocolate used in the previous test is wrapped in a piece of paper and given to the subject. Observations are made of the subject's manner of getting the food and separating it from the paper.

6. The execution of simple orders and the imitation of gestures. The orders are mostly such as might be understood from the accompanying gestures alone.
(This is the limit for idiots as experimentally determined.)

7. Verbal knowledge of objects. The child must touch his or her head, nose, ear, etc., and also hand the experimenter on command a particular one of three well-known objects: cup, key, string.

8. Knowledge of objects in a picture as shown by finding them and pointing them out when they are called by name.

9. Naming objects designated in a picture.
(This is the upper limit for 3-year-old normal children. The three preceding tests are not in order of increasing difficulty, for whoever passes 7 usually passes 8 and 9 also.)

10. Immediate comparison of two lines for discrimination as to length.

11. Reproduction of series of three digits immediately after oral presentation.

12. Discriminating between two weights: (a) 3 and 12 grams, (b) 6 and 15 grams, and (c) 3 and 15 grams.

13. Suggestibility. (a) Modification of 7: an object not among the three present is asked for. (b) Modification of 8: "Where [in the picture] is the *patapoum*? the *nitchevo*?" (These words have no meaning.) (c) Modification of 10: the two lines to be compared are of equal length.

(Test 13 is admitted to be a test not of intelligence but of "force of judgment" and "resistance of character.")

14. Definitions of familiar objects—*house*, *horse*, *fork*, *mamma*.
(This is the limit for 5-year-old normal children, except that they fail on Test 13.)

15. Repetition of sentences of 15 words each, immediately after hearing them spoken by the examiner.
(This is the limit for imbeciles.)

16. Giving differences between various pairs of familiar objects recalled in memory: (a) *paper* and *cardboard*, (b) *a fly* and *a butterfly*, and (c) *wood* and *glass*.
(Test 16 alone effectively separated normal children of 5 and 7 years.)

17. Immediate memory of pictures of familiar objects. Thirteen pictures pasted on two pieces of cardboard are presented simultaneously. The subject looks at them for 30 seconds and then gives the names of those recalled.

18. Drawing from memory two different designs shown simultaneously for 10 seconds.

19. Repetition of series of digits after oral presentation. Three series of three digits each, three of four each, three of five, etc., are presented until not one of the three series in a group is repeated correctly. The number of digits in the longest series that the subject repeats is his or her score.

20. Giving from memory the resemblance among familiar objects: (a) *a wild poppy* (red) and *blood*, (b) *an ant, a fly, a butterfly*, and *a flea*, and (c) *a newspaper, a label*, and *a picture*.

21. Rapid discrimination of lines. A line of 30 cm is compared successively with 15 lines varying from 35 to 31 cm. A more difficult set of comparisons is then made of a line of 100 mm with 12 lines varying from 103 to 101 mm.

22. Arranging in order five weights—15, 12, 9, 6, and 3 grams—of equal size.

23. Identification of the missing weight from the series in Test 22 from which one weight has been removed. The remaining weights are not presented in the right order. This test is given only when Test 22 is passed.
(This is given as the most probable limit for morons.)

24. Finding words to rhyme with a given word after the process has been illustrated.

25. Supplying missing words at the end of simple sentences, one for each sentence. This is the Ebbinghaus completion method simplified.

26. Construction of a sentence to embody three given words: *Paris, gutter, fortune*.

27. Replying to 25 questions of graded difficulty, such as "What is the thing to do when you are sleepy?" "Why is it

(Exhibit continues next page)

Exhibit 3-1 (cont.)

better to continue with perseverance what one has started than to abandon it and start something else?"
(Test 27 alone reveals the moron.)

28. Giving the time that it would be if the large and the small hands of the clock were interchanged at 4 minutes to 3 and at 20 minutes after 6. A much more difficult test is given to those who succeed in the inversion—namely,

explaining the impossibility of the precise transposition indicated.

29. Drawing what a quarto-folded paper with a piece cut out of the once-folded edge would look like if unfolded.

30. Giving distinctions between abstract terms, such as *liking* and *respecting* a person, being *sad* and being *bored*.

---

gave birth to applied psychology and ushered in a new period in the field of psychometrics.

TWENTIETH-CENTURY DEVELOPMENTS

The Introduction of the Binet-Simon Scales in the United States

With the introduction of the Binet-Simon Scales, the testing movement began to flourish in the United States. The Binet-Simon Scales were accepted readily by many investigators, but revisions were needed. (For information concerning the scale in other countries, consult Peterson, 1925.)

Goddard (1908), the director of the Psychological Laboratory at the Vineland Training School, introduced the 1905 Scale in the United States in 1908, and two years later he introduced the 1908 Scale (Goddard, 1910). He adapted the 1908 Scale with just a few necessary revisions and standardized it on 2,000 American children. For many years it was the most commonly used version of the Binet-Simon Scale. Early use of the scale was almost entirely restricted to the evaluation of the mentally retarded.

Goddard also altered Binet's conception of intelligence, substituting for

Binet's *idea* of intelligence as a shifting complex of inter-related functions, the concept of a single, underlying function (faculty) of intelligence. Further, he believed that this unitary function was largely determined by heredity, a view much at variance with Binet's optimistic proposals for mental orthopedics. (Tuddenham, 1962, p. 490)

The 1916 Stanford-Binet Scale

Lewis Terman (1911) at Stanford University observed that the 1908 Scale had great practical and theoretical value and

suggested a number of additional tests that could be used to supplement the Binet-Simon Scale. He became interested in the intellectual assessment of school children and, after studying Goddard's work, collaborated with Childs in publishing a tentative revision of the Binet-Simon Scale in 1912 (Terman & Childs, 1912). In 1916, a modified, extended, and standardized form of this revision was published under the name the Stanford Revision and Extension of the Binet-Simon Scale. Although the 1916 Stanford-Binet used the ideas of Binet and Simon, Terman deserves credit for his thorough and accurate implementation of the method suggested by Binet and his co-workers. The standardization of the 1916 Scale was a major contribution.

Terman adopted the concept of *mental quotient* (which is found by dividing mental age by chronological age) from Stern (1914), who originally introduced the concept in a paper delivered at the German Congress of Psychology in Berlin in 1912. Stern also described the concept in his book *The Psychological Methods of Testing Intelligence* (Stern, 1914). Stern's rationale for the development of the mental quotient was, in part, as follows:

It is perfectly clear how valuable the measurement of mental retardation is, particularly in the investigation of abnormal children. It has, however, been shown recently that the simple computation of the absolute difference between the two ages is not entirely adequate for this purpose, because this difference does not mean the same thing at different ages.... Only when children of approximately equal age-levels are under investigation can this value suffice: for all other cases the introduction of the *mental quotient* will be recommended.... This value expresses not the difference, but the ratio of mental to chronological age and is thus partially independent of the absolute magnitude of chronological age. The formula is, then: mental quotient = mental age ÷ chronological age. (pp. 41-42)

Terman and his associates renamed this ratio the intelligence quotient (IQ) when they produced the 1916 version of the Binet-Simon Scale. Although the IQ has become an extremely useful means for classifying persons, Wolf

Figure 3-3. Lewis M. Terman. Courtesy of Stanford University.

(1969, p. 236) noted that it is questionable whether Binet "would have accepted even Terman's elaborate standardizations as a valid basis for calculating IQ's."

Yerkes's Contribution

Soon after the Binet scales were introduced in the United States, discontent with their age-scale format began to appear. The leading spokesman against the age-scale format was Robert M. Yerkes (1876–1956), who, with Bridges and Hardwick, published the Point Scale in 1915. Yerkes (1917) believed that the age-scale format was radically different from the point-scale format.

In an age-scale format, test items are standardized on a group of children at various age levels. Those items passed by a majority of children at a particular age are assigned to that level. For example, an item passed by the majority of 7-year-olds would be assigned to the 7-year-age level. A child's basal age corresponds to the highest level at which he or she can pass all of the tests. Partial credit in months is given for each subtest passed beyond the basal level. The basal age plus the credit in months is the child's mental age.

In a point-scale format, points are assigned on the basis of the correctness and quality of the child's responses, as well as, in some cases, the speed. The raw scores for each subtest are then converted into standard scores, which in turn are converted into an overall score or scores.

The age-scale and point-scale formats also differ with respect to how tests are selected. In age scales tests are selected on the assumption that important forms of behav-

ior appear at various points in development, whereas in point scales tests are selected to measure specific functions. The Terman Revision of the Stanford-Binet (as well as two later revisions) contained a heterogenous collection of tests, with different tests included for different age groups. Point scales—particularly the Wechsler series discussed in the next section—were designed to measure the same aspects of behavior at every age.

Revisions of the Stanford-Binet

The 1916 Stanford-Binet was revised in 1937 and again in 1960 by Lewis Terman and Maud Merrill; in 1972 new norms were published. In 1986 a point-scale format—the Stanford-Binet Intelligence Scale: Fourth Edition—was published by Robert Thorndike, Elizabeth Hagen, and Jerome M. Sattler.

Wechsler's Search for Subtests

Like Yerkes, David Wechsler (1896–1981) was interested in developing a point scale. After studying the standardized tests available during the 1930s, he selected 11 different subtests to form a scale. He called it the Wechsler-Bellevue Intelligence Scale, Form I. This scale was the forerunner of the Wechsler Intelligence Scale for Children—Revised (WISC-R), Wechsler Preschool and Primary Scale of Intelligence (WPPSI), and Wechsler Adult Intelligence Scale—Revised (WAIS-R).

Sources of the subtests in the first Wechsler scale included the Army Alpha (for the Information and Comprehension subtests), 1916 Stanford-Binet (for the Comprehension, Arithmetic, Digit Span, Similarities, and Vocabulary subtests), Healy Picture Completion Tests and other tests having picture completion items (for the Picture Completion subtest), Army Group Examinations (for the Picture Arrangement subtest), Kohs Block Design Test (for the Block Design subtest), and Army Beta (for the Digit Symbol and Coding subtests). Wechsler designed original material for all of the subtests, although in some cases items differed only slightly from those appearing on other scales.

Wechsler's search for subtests was guided by his focus on the global nature of intelligence—he considered intelligence to be a part of the larger whole of personality. The Wechsler scales were designed to take into account factors contributing to the total effective intelligence of the individual; no attempt was made to design a series of subtests to measure "primary abilities" (the basic units that make up general ability or intelligence—see Thurstone later in this chapter) or to order the subtests into a hierarchy of relative importance. The overall IQ obtained from the scale represented an index of general mental ability.

Comments on Early Twentieth-Century Developments

Introduction of the Binet-Simon Scale stimulated the development of clinical psychology in the United States and in other countries. Jenkins and Paterson (1961, p. 81) noted that "probably no psychological innovation has had more impact on the societies of the Western world than the development of the Binet-Simon scales." Tuddenham (1962, p. 494) expressed a similar opinion:

The success of the Stanford-Binet was a triumph of pragmatism, but its importance must not be underestimated, for it demonstrated the feasibility of mental measurement and led to the development of other tests for many special purposes. Equally important, it led to a public acceptance of testing which had important consequences for education and industry, for the military, and for society generally.

Practical demands and interest in the concept of IQ spearheaded the development of the testing movement in spite of a lack of backing from any particular school or system. Although there were many workers in the field of test construction during the first years of the twentieth century, Binet and Simon were the first to have their scale recognized as a practical means of measuring mental ability. Success came to Binet and Simon when they measured intelligence in general terms, abandoning the attempt to

Figure 3-4. David Wechsler. Courtesy of The Psychological Corporation.

analyze intelligence in its component parts. With the introduction of the Binet-Simon Scale, intelligence testing became a popular assessment technique in many types of institutions throughout the country. The 1986 revision of the Stanford-Binet represents the latest step in the evolution of Binet's original idea.

Many other specialized tests have been and continue to be developed to evaluate specific facets of cognitive ability. Testing has become a common practice in schools, clinics, industry, and the military, influencing public policy, business, and scientific psychology. The testing movement, although subject to criticism, continues to thrive in the United States and elsewhere.

We will now examine how intelligence has been defined by various theorists and how factor analysis, specifically, contributes to our understanding of intelligence. Factor analysts have played a powerful role in shaping twentieth-century developments in the field of assessment.

DEFINITIONS OF INTELLIGENCE

Defining intelligence is not an easy task. In a famous symposium conducted in 1921 (reported in the *Journal of Educational Psychology*), 13 psychologists gave 13 different views about the nature of intelligence. (Their definitions had much in common, however.) Terman (1921), one of the participating psychologists, defined intelligence as the ability to carry on "abstract thinking." He was well aware of the danger of placing too much emphasis on the results of one particular test:

We must guard against defining intelligence solely in terms of ability to pass the tests of a given intelligence scale. It should go without saying that no existing scale is capable of adequately measuring the ability to deal with all possible kinds of material on all intelligence levels. (p. 131)

His comments are still appropriate today. Other definitions of intelligence are shown in Exhibit 3-2.

Binet (Binet & Simon, 1905) regarded intelligence as a collection of faculties: judgment, practical sense, initiative, and the ability to adapt oneself to circumstances. His selection of tests, however, was based on an empirical criterion—namely, whether the tests differentiated older from younger children. What he thought the tests were measuring was based only on his opinion or face validity.

Wechsler's (1958) definition (see Exhibit 3-2) states that intelligence is composed of qualitatively different abilities. Wechsler recognized, however, that intelligence is not the mere sum of abilities, because intelligent behavior is also affected by the way the abilities are combined and by the

■ Exhibit 3-2 ▬▬▬▬▬▬▬▬▬▬▬▬▬▬▬▬▬▬▬▬▬▬▬▬▬▬▬▬▬▬▬▬▬▬▬

Some Definitions of Intelligence

Binet (in Terman, 1916)	"The tendency to take and maintain a definite direction; the capacity to make adaptations for the purpose of attaining a desired end; and the power of autocriticism" (p. 45).
Binet & Simon (1916)	". . . judgment, otherwise called good sense, practical sense, initiative, the faculty of adapting one's self to circumstances. To judge well, to comprehend well, to reason well, these are the essential activities of intelligence" (pp. 42–43).
Spearman (1923)	". . . everything intellectual can be reduced to some special case . . . of educing either relations or correlates" (p. 300).
	Eduction of relations – "The mentally presenting of any two or more characters . . . tends to evoke immediately a knowing of relation between them" (p. 63).
	Eduction of correlates – "The presenting of any character together with any relation tends to evoke immediately a knowing of the correlative character" (p. 91).
Stoddard (1943)	". . . the ability to undertake activities that are characterized by (1) difficulty, (2) complexity, (3) abstractness, (4) economy, (5) adaptiveness to a goal, (6) social value, and (7) the emergence of originals, and to maintain such activities under conditions that demand a concentration of energy and a resistance to emotional forces" (p. 4).
Freeman (1955)	". . . *adjustment or adaptation of the individual to his total environment*, or limited aspects thereof. . . . the capacity to reorganize one's behavior patterns so as to act more effectively and more appropriately in novel situations . . . . the *ability to learn* . . . . the extent to which [a person] is educable . . . . the *ability to carry on abstract thinking* . . . the effective use of concepts and symbols in dealing with . . . a problem to be solved" (pp. 60–61).
Wechsler (1958)	"The aggregate or global capacity of the individual to act purposefully, to think rationally and to deal effectively with his environment" (p. 7).
Das (1973)	". . . the ability to plan and structure one's behavior with an end in view" (p. 27).
Humphreys (1979)	". . . the resultant of the processes of acquiring, storing in memory, retrieving, combining, comparing, and using in new contexts information and conceptual skills; it is an abstraction" (p. 115).
Gardner (1983)	". . . a human intellectual competence must entail a set of skills of problem solving – enabling the individual *to resolve genuine problems or difficulties* that he or she encounters, and, when appropriate, to create an effective product – and must also entail the potential for *finding or creating problems* – thereby laying the groundwork for the acquisition of new knowledge" (pp. 60–61).
Sternberg (1986)	". . . *mental activity involved in purposive adaptation to, shaping of, and selection of real-world environments relevant to one's life*" (p. 33).

Note. The first five definitions appeared in Snow (1978, p. 234).

individual's drive and incentive. He took a pragmatic view of intelligence, stating that intelligence is known by what it enables us to do. He recognized that, although the measurement of various aspects of intellectual ability is possible, intelligence test scores are not identical with what is meant by intelligence. He did not, however, supply empirical referents for the definitional terms "aggregate," "global," "purposefully," and "rationally."

The confusion concerning ways of defining and measuring intelligence is linked to the fact that intelligence is an attribute, not an entity, and that it reflects the summation of the learning experiences of the individual (Wesman, 1968). Tests of intelligence, achievement, ability, or aptitude are,

for the most part, measuring similar abilities; the names merely reflect the aspect that has been selected for investigation. All ability tests measure what the examinee has learned. Definitions of intelligence emphasize the ability to adjust or adapt to the environment, the ability to learn, or the ability to perform abstract thinking (to use symbols and concepts).

When 1,020 experts in the fields of psychology, education, sociology, and genetics were recently asked to rate what they believed were important elements of intelligence, their ratings showed a high degree of consensus (Snyderman & Rothman, 1987). Of the 13 behavioral descriptions presented to the raters, (a) three received near unanimous agreement (96% or higher)—*abstract thinking or reasoning, the capacity to acquire knowledge, and problem-solving ability*; (b) seven were checked by a majority of respondents (60%–80%)—*adaptation to one's environment, creativity, general knowledge, linguistic competence, mathematical competence, memory, and mental speed*; and (c) three were rarely checked (less than 25%)—*achievement motivation, goal-directedness, and sensory acuity*. The respondents also stated that intelligence tests adequately measure most of the important elements of intelligence.

FACTOR ANALYTIC THEORIES OF INTELLIGENCE

Historically the factor analytic theorists formed two camps: those who espoused a general-factor theory (*g*) of intelligence and those who favored a multiple-factor theory. Galton first proposed that individuals possess both a general intellectual ability, present in the whole range of their mental abilities, and some special aptitudes. In contrast, theorists such as Thorndike, Kelley, and Thurstone asserted that the intellect is composed of many independent faculties, such as mathematical, mechanical, and verbal faculties. Spearman introduced statistical techniques that allowed for the testing of these rival theories. Factorial methods used by the general-factor theorists (for example, Spearman and Vernon) allow for a large general factor (*g*) to emerge as the first factor. In contrast, the methods used by Guilford, Thurstone, and other faculty theorists yield a number of independent or primary factors, but no large general factor. Each method, however, may be reducible to the other—that is, either method applied to an intercorrelation matrix will produce an analogous set of factors.

Although factor analysts disagree about how intelligence is organized—whether intelligence is a general unitary function or a composite of several somewhat independent abilities—many of them accept the theory of general intelligence (Urbach, 1974), with the belief that intelligent behavior is still multidimensional. Part of the difficulty with factor analytic approaches to the study of intelligence is that the outcomes of the factor analysis vary depending on the nature of the data, the type of statistical procedure, and the proclivities of the investigator in choosing names to designate the factors. Factor names should be viewed as descriptive categories and not as a reflection of underlying entities. Although the factor analysts have made significant contributions to the field, there are pitfalls associated with their methods, just as there are with those of other theorists.

Spearman

Charles E. Spearman (1863–1945) was one of the early proponents of a factor analytic approach to intelligence. Spearman (1927) proposed a two-factor theory of intelligence to account for the patterns of correlations observed among group tests of intelligence. The theory stated that a general factor (*g*) plus one or more specific factors (*s*) per test can account for performance on intelligence tests (see Figure 3-5). Spearman thought of the *g* factor as a general mental energy, with complicated mental activities containing the greatest amount of *g*. This factor is involved in operations of a deductive nature, linked with the skill, speed, intensity, and extent of a person's intellectual output. The cognitive activities associated with *g* are *eduction of relations* (determining the relationship between two or more ideas) and *eduction of correlates* (finding a second idea associated with a previously stated one).

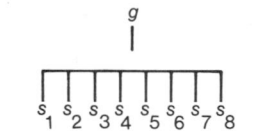

Figure 3-5. Spearman's two-factor theory of intelligence (*g* refers to the general factor, or general ability, and *s* to specific factors).

The *g* factor is an index of general mental ability or intelligence and represents the "inventive" as contrasted with the "reproductive" aspect of mental ability (Jensen, 1979a). Tests with high *g* loadings require conscious and complex mental effort, such as is found in reasoning, comprehension, and hypothesis-testing tasks. The stimuli for these tasks may be either perceived or retrieved from memory. In contrast, tests with low *g* loadings are less complex, emphasizing such processes as recognition, recall, speed, visual-motor abilities, and motor abilities.

Although evidence strongly supports the idea that *g* is important in human ability, this does not necessarily mean that *g* is a thing or an entity. One can accept the evidence for Spearman's *g* without accepting Spearman's explanation of

g as "mental energy, or any other explanation that suggests a unitary something underlying the behavioral phenomena" (Humphreys, Parsons, & Park, 1979, p. 75).

Thorndike

Edward L. Thorndike (1874–1949) conceived of intelligence as the product of a large number of interconnected but distinct intellectual abilities. This view is now known as a multifactor theory. Certain mental activities have elements in common and combine to form clusters. Three such clusters have been identified: *social* (dealing with people), *concrete* (dealing with things), and *abstract intelligence* (dealing with verbal and mathematical symbols) (Thorndike, 1927). Thorndike's conceptions were based on a theoretical perspective, not on factor analytic methods.

Thurstone

The view of human intelligence the most divergent from Spearman's is that of Louis L. Thurstone (1887–1955). Thurstone (1938) maintained that intelligence could not be regarded as a unitary trait. He assumed that human intelligence possesses a certain systematic organization, with a structure that can be inferred from a statistical analysis of the patterns of intercorrelations found in a group of tests. Using a method of factor analysis suitable for analyzing factors at once (centroid method), he identified the following factors as the primary mental abilities: *verbal*, *perceptual speed*, *inductive reasoning*, *number*, *rote memory*, *deductive reasoning*, *word fluency*, and *space* or *visualization*. Thurstone believed that intelligence can be divided into these multiple factors, each of which has equal weight. He went on to develop the Primary Mental Abilities Tests to measure these factors. Although Thurstone's multidimensional theory at first eliminated g as a significant component of mental functioning, the primary factors were found to correlate moderately among themselves, leading Thurstone to postulate the existence of a second-order factor that may be related to g.

Guilford

The most prominent multifactor theorist in the United States is J. P. Guilford (1967). He developed a three-dimensional Structure of Intellect model as a means for organizing intellectual factors into a system. One dimension represents the *operations* involved in processing information, a second dimension represents *contents*, and a third dimension represents *products*. In other words, intellectual activities can be understood in terms of the kind of *mental operation* performed, the type of *content* on which the mental operation is performed, and the resulting *product*. The model posits five different operations (cognition, memory, divergent production, convergent production, and evaluation), four types of content (figural, symbolic, semantic, and behavioral), and six products (units, classes, relations, systems, transformations, and implications). Thus, 120 possible factors—5 operations × 4 contents × 6 products—are postulated in the model (see Figure 3-6). A combination of one element from each of the three dimensions yields a factor, such as Cognition of Semantic Units. *Cognition* refers to the operations dimension, *semantic* to the content dimension, and *units* to the product dimension. In this case, the factor refers to knowing what a word means. (The Structure of Intellect classifications for the WISC-R and the WPPSI are shown in Tables C-12 and C-23, respectively, in Appendix C.)

Vernon

In Philip E. Vernon's (1950) hierarchical theory of intelligence (see Figure 3-7), g, or general ability, is at the highest level. The two major group factors at the next level of generality are skills in the verbal-educational and spatial-mechanical fields. At lower levels of generality are smaller subdivisions of these group factors (or minor group factors). Creative abilities, verbal fluency, and numerical factors are minor group factors under verbal-educational, and spatial, psychomotor, and mechanical information factors are minor group factors under spatial-mechanical. Other more specialized skills (or specific factors) peculiar to certain tests emerge at the next level. Factors low in the hierarchy refer to narrow ranges of behavior, whereas those high in the hierarchy refer to a wide variety of behaviors. Vernon (1965) believes that a general group factor (g) must be considered in any attempt to understand intelligence. This belief is supported by findings of substantial positive intercorrelations among test results when cognitive tests are administered to a fairly representative population.

Cattell and Horn

Raymond B. Cattell and John Horn (Cattell, 1963; Horn, 1967, 1968, 1978a, 1978b, 1985; Horn & Cattell, 1967) have developed an innovative theory on the structure of intelligence. Their theory holds that there are two types of

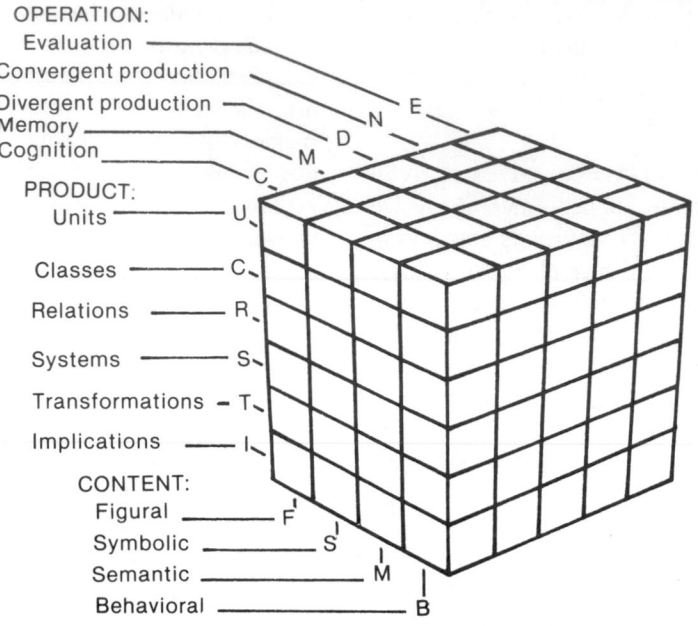

Figure 3-6.   Guilford's Structure of Intellect model.

intelligence—fluid and crystallized. *Fluid intelligence* refers to essentially nonverbal, relatively culture-free mental efficiency, whereas *crystallized intelligence* refers to acquired skills and knowledge that are strongly dependent for their development on exposure to culture. Fluid intelligence involves adaptive and new learning capabilities and is related to mental operations and processes, whereas crystallized intelligence involves overlearned and well-established cognitive functions and is related to mental products and achievements.

Examples of tasks that measure fluid intelligence are figure classifications, figural analyses, number and letter series, matrices, and paired associates. Crystallized intelligence is measured by such tests as vocabulary, general information, abstract word analogies, and mechanics of language. Tests that load equally on both factors include arithmetic reasoning, inductive verbal reasoning, and syllogistic reasoning. The Stanford-Binet: Fourth Edition, WISC-R, WPPSI, and WAIS-R contain measures of both fluid and crystallized intelligence. Tasks that measure fluid intelligence (for example, WISC-R Block Design and Coding) may require more concentration and problem solving than do crystallized tasks (for example, WISC-R Vocabulary and Information), which tap retrieval and application of general knowledge abilities.

Fluid intelligence is more dependent on the physiological structures (for example, cortical and lower cor-

tical regions) that support intellectual behavior than is crystallized intelligence. Fluid intelligence increases until some time during adolescence, when it plateaus; it then begins to decline because of the gradual degeneration of physiological structures. Fluid intelligence is also more sensitive to the effects of brain injury. Crystallized intelligence, which reflects cultural assimilation, is highly influenced by formal and informal educational factors throughout the life span and thus continues to increase through middle adulthood. It is through the exercise of fluid intelligence that crystallized intelligence develops.

Horn (1985) argues against the concept of general intelligence, maintaining that research does not support a unitary theory. Instead, he believes that intellectual ability is composed of several distinct functions that probably have genetic bases. In a recent statement of the theory, Horn (1985) proposed a four-level hierarchical model (see Figure 3-8). At the lowest level are visual and auditory sensory detection functions. The second level involves associational processes, both short and long term. At the third level perceptual organizational processes come into play—broad visualization, clerical speed, and broad auditory thinking. The highest level involves the eduction of relations—fluid ability and crystallized ability. Abilities at the bottom of the hierarchy have low correlations with those near the top.

There are also developmental levels associated with

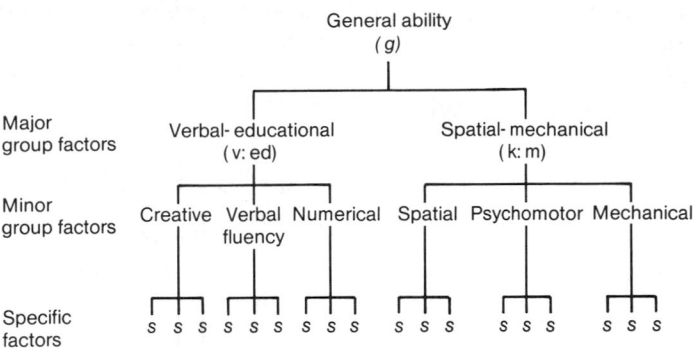

Figure 3-7. Vernon's hierarchical model of intelligence.

Horn's theory (Horn, June 1986, personal communication). Over the period from infancy to adulthood, the sensory detection functions are elaborated first; the associational processes come into prominence next; then the perceptual organizational functions are finely tuned; and finally in adolescence and adulthood the capacities for comprehending relations and drawing implications become most prominent in intellectual functioning. (Horn acknowledges links to Piaget's ideas in his developmental perspective.) Of course, these separate functions at each developmental level represent abstractions from a Gestalt because cognitive functioning in reality cannot be divided. Just as we understand salt in terms of sodium and chloride, so Horn proposes that we understand human cognitive functioning in terms of distinct components.

Gustafsson

Jan-Eric Gustafsson (1984) proposes a three-level model to account for the structure of intellectual abilities (see Figure 3-9). This model integrates a number of models previously discussed in this chapter. At the highest level is g (general intelligence), which represents Spearman's conception of intelligence. At the next level are three broad factors: *crystallized intelligence* (dealing with verbal information), *fluid intelligence* (dealing with adaptive nonverbal abilities), and *general visualization* (dealing with figural information). Fluid intelligence is essentially the same as general intelligence, or g. Although the crystallized and fluid intelligence factors are similar to those in the Cattell and Horn model of intelligence, crystallized intelligence

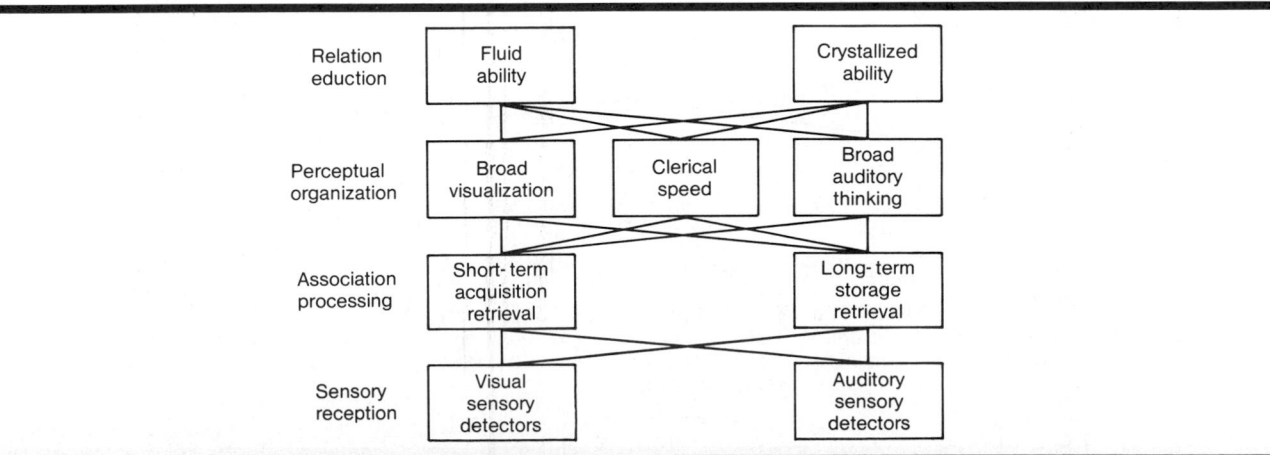

Figure 3-8. Horn's hierarchical model of intelligence (simplified version).

has a somewhat different status. Gustafsson conceives of crystallized intelligence as representing a relatively narrow dimension of knowledge and generalizing less to subsequent problem-solving and learning situations than does fluid intelligence. At the lowest level are the primary factors, similar to those in the Thurstone and Guilford traditions.

INFORMATION-PROCESSING APPROACHES TO INTELLIGENCE

Information-processing conceptions of intelligence focus on ways individuals mentally represent and process information. Information-processing models of cognitive activities categorize mental processes in terms of the different operations performed on the information. In these models, human cognition is conceived of as occurring in a series of discrete stages, with information received being operated on at one stage and then passed on as input to the next stage for further processing. Mental processes, then, are composed of specific covert cognitive behaviors "which transform and manipulate information between the time it enters as a stimulus and the time a response to it is selected" (Torgesen, 1979, p. 516).

The information processing framework assumes that a number of component operations or processing stages occur between a stimulus and a response. It is assumed that all behavior of a human information processing system is the result of combinations of these various processing stages. Typically, two theoretical components are postulated in information processing analysis: a structural component, which defines the constraints of a particular processing stage (e.g., sensory storage, short-term memory,

long-term memory), and a functional component, which describes the operations of the various stages. Of particular interest in the area of intelligence are functional components or strategies that must be performed if a task is to be successfully completed. (Swanson, 1985, pp. 226-227)

Campione, Brown, and Borkowski

Joseph Campione and Ann Brown (1978) used an information-processing framework to develop a general theory of intelligence, which was expanded by John Borkowski (1985). The theory postulates that intelligence has two basic components: an *architectural system*, which represents a structural component, and an *executive system*, which represents a control component (see Figure 3-10). The following summary of this theory is taken from Borkowski (1985).

The architectural system. The *architectural system* refers to biologically/genetically based properties that are necessary for processing information, such as memory span, retention of stimulus traces, and efficiency (or speed of encoding and decoding information). These skills are closely linked to the perceptual skills of individuals and reflect sensory activity and nervous system integrity. The skills are relatively impervious to improvement by the environment and are essential to basic cognitive operations, such as perception and immediate memory. Thus the architectural system corresponds to the major stores, or the system's hardware.

Properties of structures in the architectural system include *capacity*, or the amount of space available in the units (for example, number of slots in short-term memory

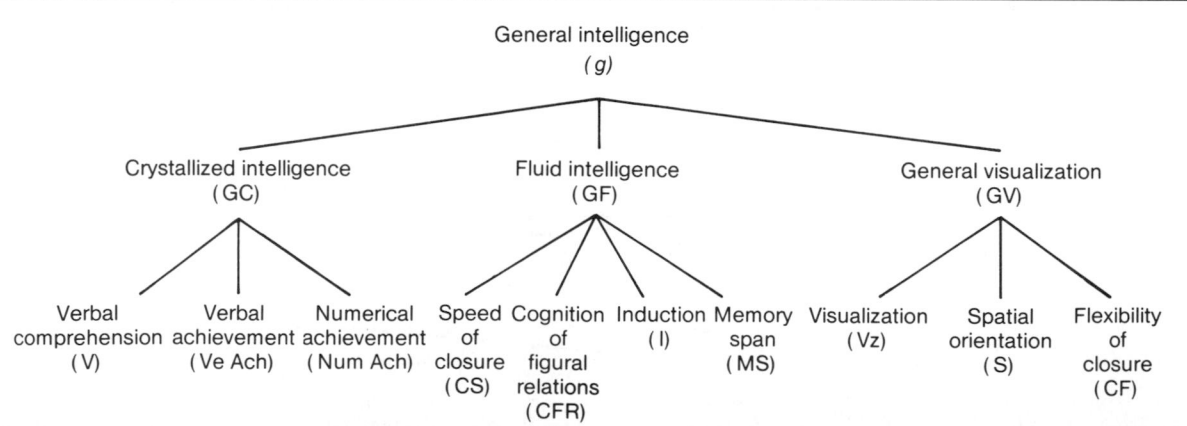

Figure 3-9. Gustafsson's hierarchical model of intelligence.

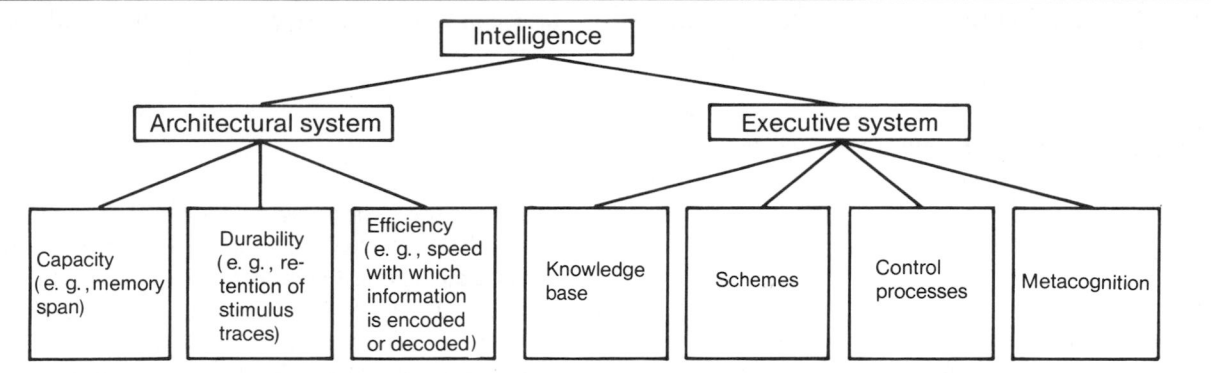

Figure 3-10. Campione, Brown, and Borkowski's model of intelligence.

and amount of filing space in long-term memory); *durability*, or the rate at which information is lost; and *efficiency of operation*, or the temporal characteristics associated with selection and storage of information (for example, speed of encoding, rate of memory search, rapidity with which attention is switched, and duration of alertness). The architectural system registers and responds to sensory input.

The executive system. The *executive system* refers to environmentally learned components that guide problem solving, including (a) a *knowledge base* (retrieval of knowledge from long-term memory), (b) *schemes* (such as those found in Piagetian theory), (c) *control processes* (for example, rehearsal strategies), and (d) *metacognition* (that is, introspective knowledge). These four components are viewed as complementary, overlapping, hypothetical constructs. Although they are assumed to be independent, future research may show them to be interdependent.

The components in the executive system are skills that emerge from experience and from instruction in complex problem-solving tasks. The skills associated with the executive system enable the individual to engage in creative, adaptive learning by initiating and regulating retrieval of knowledge from long-term memory, modifying the knowledge base, and mediating problem solving. These skills allow the individual to rise above rote, nonstrategic learning. They appear to be products of enriched learning experiences and hence are highly modifiable.

Knowledge. Knowledge plays a central role in intelligent behavior because "knowledge informs perceptions, provides a home for new memories amidst the storage of old ones, and informs cognitive routines and strategies in the face of complex problems" (Borkowski, 1985, p. 112).

Schemes. In the Piagetian perspective schemes refer to abstract cognitive structures by means of which individuals assimilate or accommodate new information. Schemes (or rules of thinking) are the active and constructive aspects of human intelligence. In Piagetian theory the major stages of cognitive development—sensorimotor, preoperational, concrete operational, and formal operational (see Table 3-1 ahead)—represent groups of schemes. Passage from one stage to another occurs when there is a major scheme change.

Control processes. Control processes refer to the rules and strategies that aid in memorizing, understanding, problem solving, and other cognitive activities. Strategic behaviors—such as self-checking, rehearsal, and other self-instructional procedures—can be taught to promote greater strategy generalization. Children who possess sophisticated cognitive strategies and skilled routines are likely to become efficient, effective problem solvers who can invent new strategies to meet new cognitive challenges.

Metacognition. Metacognition refers to thoughts about thoughts or awareness of one's own thought processes and strategies of thought. Metacognition helps to inform and regulate cognitive routines and strategies. The integration of metacognitive knowledge with strategic behaviors results in more effective problem solving. Metacognition aids in planning, self-monitoring, and inventiveness and may lead to strategy selection, self-criticism, and even the generation of new strategies.

Examples of metacognition include knowing that a strategy that worked for one task might need to be slightly modified for a new task, knowing that some strategies will work for a variety of different tasks, knowing how to retrieve information from memory, and knowing how to deal with puzzlement when one encounters a logical dilemma. Puzzlement is an experiential aspect of metacognition and may be "both a source of new metacognitive knowledge and a cue for utilizing stored knowledge about appropriate strategies to confront the problem at hand" (Borkowski, 1985, p. 135).

Sternberg

Robert J. Sternberg (1986) divides human intelligence into three dimensions: componential, experiential, and contextual. The *componential dimension* relates intelligence to the internal mental mechanisms of the individual. These mental mechanisms are referred to as information-processing components. A *component* is "a mental process that may translate a sensory input into a mental representation, transform one mental representation into another, or translate a mental representation into a motor output" (Sternberg, 1986, p. 24). There are three basic types of components: metacomponents, performance components, and knowledge acquisition components. *Metacomponents* are higher-order processes used in planning, monitoring, and evaluating the performance of a task. Essentially metacomponents tell other components what to do and when to do it. *Performance components* are processes used in the execution of a task. *Knowledge acquisition components* are processes used in learning new things.

The *experiential dimension* relates intelligence to both the external and the internal worlds of the individual. This part of the theory specifies at what point intelligence is most critically involved in an individual's experience with handling tasks or situations. In particular, intelligence is most involved in dealing with novelty and with the automatization of mental processes. As experience with a task or situation increases, the need to deal with novelty decreases, and automatization skills take over. Thus Sternberg believes that it is difficult—if not impossible—to compare levels of intelligence fairly across sociocultural groups. Even if a test requires members of various groups to exercise the same performance components, because of differences in previous environmental experiences it is unlikely to be equivalent for the groups in terms of novelty and the degree to which performance has been automatized.

The *contextual dimension* relates intelligence to the external world of the individual. It emphasizes adaptation to, selection of, and shaping of the environment. *Environmentally adaptive* requirements can differ widely from one culture to another and thus can only be evaluated in context. When attempts to adapt to a given environment fail and it is not practical or possible to select a new environment, *environmental shaping* may be the best tactic to employ—the individual must attempt to change the environment.

Das

An information-processing model has been proposed by Jagannath Das and his colleagues as a way of categorizing cognitive ability (Das, 1972, 1973a; Das, Kirby, & Jarman, 1975; Das & Molloy, 1975; Jarman & Das, 1977). The model, based in part on Aleksandr Luria's (1966a, 1966b) work in neuropsychology, has two primary modes. In one mode, termed *simultaneous processing*, stimuli are arranged in a simultaneous manner in order to make a decision. Processing is in an integrated, usually semispatial, form. Examples of tasks measuring simultaneous processing are Raven's Progressive Matrices, Figure Copying, and Memory for Designs. In the other mode, termed *successive processing*, stimuli are arranged in a sequence in order to make a decision. Processing is in a sequence-dependent, temporally based series. Examples of successive processing tasks are auditory short-term memory, visual short-term memory, word reading, and color naming.

Which of the two modes of processing individuals will use in a particular situation will depend on their past experiences and the demands of the task. No hierarchy is implied, so equal status is given to simultaneous and successive modes. Complexity is not tied to mode either: The model assumes that a given task can be solved by more than one method, or mode. Intelligence is viewed as the ability to use the information obtained through the simultaneous and successive transformation procedures in order to plan and structure behavior effectively to attain goals.

OTHER APPROACHES TO INTELLIGENCE

Jensen

Arthur Jensen (1970a, 1980) has proposed that mental abilities fall into two major classes: associative (level I) and cognitive (level II). *Associative ability* involves rote learning and short-term memory and is measured by tasks involving digit-span memory, free recall, serial learning, and paired-associate learning. *Cognitive ability* involves reasoning and problem solving and is measured by most tests of general intelligence, particularly those with tasks involving reasoning, problem solving, concept formation, verbal and figural analogies, number series, and matrices. Many tests of intelligence are likely to measure both levels, but to different degrees.

The major difference between level I and level II is that tasks involving level I abilities require little transformation of the input; a high degree of correspondence exists between the form of the stimulus input and the form of the response output. Level II processes, in contrast, involve a transformation of the stimulus input; one must consciously manipulate the input in order to arrive at the correct output. The crucial distinctions between levels I and II are differences in the complexity of the transformation and the mental manipulations that occur between the presentation of a given mental task and the response.

Gardner

Howard Gardner (1983) posits the existence of several relatively autonomous intellectual competencies, or multiple intelligences (see Exhibit 3-2 for Gardner's definition of intelligence). He has identified six competencies, but more may be discovered. They are *linguistic intelligence* (for example, syntactic and pragmatic capacities involved in the use of language for communication), *musical intelligence* (for example, rhythmic and pitch abilities involved in composing, singing, and playing music), *logical-mathematical intelligence* (for example, logical thinking, numerical ability), *spatial intelligence* (for example, perceiving the visual world, transposing and modifying one's initial perceptions, re-creating aspects of one's visual experience), *bodily-kinesthetic intelligence* (for example, dancing, acting, athletics, inventing), and *personal intelligence* (for example, knowledge of self and others, including the ability to identify various feelings in oneself and the ability to discern other individuals' moods, temperaments, motivations, and intentions). The competencies may be viewed as building blocks out of which thought and action develop. They constitute the basis of human symbol-using capacities and interact to produce a diverse mixture of human talents that may be deployed for societal ends.

The multiple intelligence theory may be used as a basis for assessing children; the resulting multiple intelligence profile is useful for guidance and education. Although assessment procedures have not been explicitly designed to develop these profiles, Gardner believes that children's intellectual competencies can be assessed through planned observations. For example, infants can be taught patterns and then tested to see whether they remember the patterns. Preschool children can be given blocks, puzzles, games,

and other tasks. Their block constructions may provide information about spatial and kinesthetic intelligence, their ability to relate a set of stories may reveal information about linguistic capacities, and their ability to operate a simple machine may give information about kinesthetic and logical-mathematical skills. "The future musician may be marked by perfect pitch; the child gifted in personal matters, by his [or her] intuitions about the motives of others; the budding scientist, by his [or her] ability to pose provocative questions and then follow them up with appropriate ones" (Gardner, 1983, p. 386).

Different assessment strategies are required for children of different ages. Testing for spatial ability, for example, might include hiding an object from a 1-year-old, giving a jigsaw puzzle to a 6-year-old, and providing a Rubik's cube to a preadolescent. Developing a reasonably accurate picture of a child's abilities may require 5 to 10 hours of observation of regular classroom activities over the course of a month.

Piaget

Jean Piaget (1896–1980) conceived of intelligence as a form of biological adaptation of the individual to the environment. The individual is constantly interacting with the environment, trying to maintain a balance between his or her own needs and the demands that the environment makes. Cognition extends the scope of biological adaptation by allowing the individual to move from the immediate action level to a symbolic level through the process of internalization. Symbolic trial-and-error thus can eventually replace overt trial-and-error.

According to Piaget, cognitive processes emerge through a process of development that is neither a direct function of biological development nor a direct function of learning; rather, the emergence represents a reorganization of psychological structures resulting from organismic-environmental interactions. Piaget regarded social development, play, and art as having large cognitive-structural components. These views led Piaget to disregard the dichotomy between maturation and learning, and between cognitive and social-emotional components of development.

Piaget proposed that two inherent tendencies govern interactions with the environment: organization and adaptation. *Organization* is the tendency to combine two or more separate schemes into one higher-order, integrated scheme. *Schemes* are individual structures that produce changes in cognitive development—such as those involved in grasping an object or comprehending the concept of time. They are a kind of mini-system forming a framework into which incoming sensory data can fit.

Adaptation contains two complementary processes: assimilation and accommodation. *Assimilation* is a process of taking in information and experiences by fitting them into the schemes or concepts that one has already mastered. *Accommodation*, in turn, is a process whereby existing cognitive structures and behaviors are modified to take into account new information and experiences. Both assimilation and accommodation occur simultaneously whenever children adapt to environmental events, but the particular balance between the two is likely to vary from situation to situation.

An example of assimilation is make-believe play with an object. Special features of the object are ignored, and it is responded to as if it were something else. Accommodation is displayed when a child learns a new scheme by imitating someone else's behavior. Assimilative processes permit intelligence to go beyond a passive coping with reality,

whereas accommodative processes prevent intelligence from constructing representations of reality that have no correspondence with the real world. Intelligence represents the rational processes—the processes that show the greatest independence from environmental and internal regulation.

Piaget's developmental model of intelligence. Piaget's model of intelligence is a hierarchical one, in which intellectual development is divided into four major periods, each characterized by stages and substages. Each period represents a form of cognitive organization that is more complex than the preceding one. Each stage evolves from the preceding one, and none can be skipped in the development of cognition. The stages, representing a form of biological adaptation, emerge from the individual's interaction with the environment.

The four periods of intellectual development are outlined in Table 3-1. As development proceeds, different

Table 3-1
Outline of Piaget's Periods of Intellectual Development

Period	Approximate ages	Characteristic behaviors
I. Sensorimotor period	Birth to 2 years	Child passes through six stages, beginning with the exercise of simple reflexes and ending with the first signs of internal or symbolic representations of actions.
1. Exercising reflexes	Birth to 1 month	Simple reflex activity is exhibited; readymade sensorimotor schemes are exercised.
2. Primary circular reactions	1 to 4 months	Activities involve only the infant's own body and are endlessly repeated. First adaptations are acquired, such as integration and coordination of activities (e.g., finger sucking or watching one's hands).
3. Secondary circular reactions	4 to 8 months	Procedures are developed to make interesting sights last; reactions also involve events or objects in the external world (e.g., shaking a rattle to hear the noise).
4. Coordination of secondary schemes	8 to 12 months	Two or more previously acquired schemes are combined to obtain a goal; acts become clearly intentional (e.g., reaching behind cushion for a ball).
5. Tertiary circular reactions	12 to 18 months	Trial-and-error behavior and goal-seeking activity are designed to produce novel results; movements are purposely varied and the results observed (e.g., pulling pillow nearer in order to get toy resting on it).
6. Invention of new means through mental combinations	18 to 24 months	Mental combinations appear; representational thought begins (e.g., using a stick to reach desired object).
II. Preoperational period	2 to 7 years	Child acquires language and symbolic functions (e.g., ability to search for hidden objects, perform delayed imitation, engage in symbolic play, and use language).
III. Concrete operations period	7 to 11 years	Child develops conservation skills; mental operations are applied to real (concrete) objects or events.
IV. Formal operations period	11 years and upward	Child can think abstractly, formulate hypotheses, use deductive reasoning, and check solutions.

types of organization and adaptation occur. At first, children's thoughts are dominated by their perceptions. By about 2 years of age, language has begun to develop and memory is available concerning actions and prior responses, although the child's thinking is still egocentric. By 7 years of age, thought processes have become more systematic and concrete problem-solving skills have begun to develop. By 11 years of age, the child can construct theories and make logical deductions without the necessity for direct experience.

Piaget's developmental model assumes that mental organization operates as a totality, includes rules of transformation, is self-regulating, changes with age to give rise to new higher levels of organization, and differs at each level in the complexity of the rules of transformation and self-regulation (Elkind, 1981).

Piagetian vs. psychometric approaches. The goal of Piagetian assessment is to disclose the nature of mental organization at successive age levels and to provide information about stages of cognitive development. Although the Piagetian and psychometric approaches to intelligence differ in perspective, they are similar in a number of ways

(see Table 3-2). Neither approach is right or wrong; the two approaches complement each other. For example, the psychometric evaluation of intelligence is valuable in documenting the degree of delay of handicapped children, in predicting school success, and in assessing brain injury and psychopathology, whereas the Piagetian approach is valuable in diagnosing learning difficulties and in designing educational interventions.

There is presently no comprehensive battery of Piagetian tests of intelligence, although some success has been achieved with the development of sensorimotor scales (Uzgiris & Hunt, 1975). Studies have shown that correlations between Piagetian and psychometric scales of intelligence in infant, preschool, and school-age populations are consistently positive and generally moderate in magnitude (Bat-Haee, Mehyrar, & Sabharwal, 1972; Dodwell, 1961; Dudek, Lester, Goldberg, & Dyer, 1969; Elkind, 1961; Goldschmid, 1967; Gottfried & Brody, 1975; Humphreys & Parsons, 1979; Kaufman, 1972b; Keasey & Charles, 1967; Keating, 1975; Lester, Muir, & Dudek, 1970; Orpet, Yoshida, & Meyers, 1976; Rogers, 1977; Wasik & Wasik, 1976). Intelligence, as measured by psychometric testing, is related to such Piagetian measures as

Table 3-2
Comparison of Piagetian and Psychometric Approaches to Intelligence

Similarities	Differences	
	Piagetian	*Psychometric*
1. Both accept genetic determinants of intelligence.	1. Assumes that there are factors which give development a definite, non-random direction. Assumes that mental growth is qualitative and presupposes significant differences in the thinking of younger versus older children. Is concerned with intra-individual changes occurring in the course of development.	1. Assumes that tested intelligence is randomly distributed in a given population, with the distribution following the normal curve. Is concerned with interindividual differences.
2. Both accept maturational determination of intelligence.		
3. Both use nonexperimental methodology.		
4. Both attempt to measure intellectual functions that the child is expected to have developed by a certain age.		
5. Both conceive of intelligence as being essentially rational.	2. Views mental growth as the formation of new mental structures and the emergence of new mental abilities.	2. Views the course of mental growth as a curve, from which the amount of intelligence at some criterion age can be predicted on the basis of intelligence at any preceding age.
6. Both assume that maturation of intellectual processes is complete somewhere during late adolescence.		
7. Both are capable of predicting intellectual behavior outside of the test situation.	3. Assumes genetic and environmental factors interact in a functional and dynamic manner with respect to their regulatory control over mental activity.	3. Assumes that genetic and environmental contributions to intelligence can be measured.

Note. Similarity items 5, 6, and 7 obtained from Dudek, Lester, Goldberg, and Dyer (1969); the remainder of the table adapted from Elkind (1974).

ability to use formal operations, to understand the principle of conservation, and to use sensorimotor operations. There appears to be a general factor common to Piagetian tasks and to standard intelligence tests, although Piagetian tasks have an element of uniqueness and not all studies report a common underlying factor between Piagetian and psychometric measures of intelligence. The significant correlations between Piagetian tests and psychometric tests indicate that children who achieve high scores on psychometric tests of intelligence are not merely "good test-takers"; they have excellent levels of cognitive development in a variety of areas.

COMMENTS ON MODERN VIEWS OF INTELLIGENCE

Current hierarchical theories of intelligence lie somewhere between Spearman's and Thurstone's views. They stress a general factor at the top of the hierarchy, several broad classes of abilities in the middle, and primary factors at the bottom (Stankov, 1983). A widely held view of intelligence is that it is multifaceted and hierarchically organized, with a general factor entering into a large variety of cognitive tasks and narrow group factors and specialized abilities forming the core of abilities. The IQ is viewed as a somewhat arbitrary summary index of many abilities. The hierarchical model, although it may not fit the complexities of the interrelationships of human ability perfectly, is a useful approximation (Humphreys et al., 1979).

The Campione-Brown-Borkowski formulation is an exciting theory of intelligence for those engaged in intellectual assessment. The theory places various cognitive assessment tasks in a broad-based model. It emphasizes that (a) intelligent behavior represents a dynamic interaction of structural and control components, (b) child-rearing practices and quality of education are important determinants of functional components (that is, executive system abilities), (c) environmental enrichments are important for all children who have the requisite ability structure (that is, in the architectural system), and (d) intelligent behavior is dependent on biologically/genetically based components, as well as on culturally based educational-environmental enrichments. The Campione-Brown-Borkowski theory, along with other information-processing approaches, provides valuable guidelines for developing psychometric tests, intervention strategies, and remediation programs.

Guilford's model has been criticized on a number of dimensions. First, it fails to reproduce the essentially hierarchical nature of intelligence test data, with minor factors, major factors, and a general factor (Eysenck, 1967). The one outstanding finding that recurs in studies of intelligence tests is the universality of positive correlations among all relevant tests and between different factors. This fact indicates a basic commonality or central factor in intellectual activity, which Guilford fails to mention in his model. Second, a large number of Guilford's factors of intellect have failed to show any external validity that could not be accounted for by their general or group factors (Vernon, 1965). Third, results from factor analytic studies do not provide convincing support for Guilford's model (Horn & Knapp, 1973). In fact, some factor analytic results provide as much support for randomly determined theories as they do for the Structure of Intellect theory.

Although Gardner's theory is provocative, it is by no means novel. His linguistic intelligence corresponds closely to the concept of crystallized intelligence, and logic-mathematical ability is similar to the concept of fluid intelligence (Bouchard, 1984). Additionally, a spatial or visualization factor and an auditory organization factor (which subsumes musical ability) have been recognized by other theorists. Bouchard believes that neither body-kinesthetic skill nor personal intelligence belongs in the lists of intelligences, the latter more appropriately being assigned to the realm of personality. Additionally, I believe that his assessment approach does not meet acceptable scientific standards. Because observational recordings are particularly susceptible to observer bias, observers must be trained and observations validated (see Chapter 17). Gardner generally overlooks these and related issues involved in the reliability and validity of observational recordings, and he does not provide data about the reliability and validity of components within his assessment approach. Thus further research is needed on both his theory and his assessment recommendations.

An element these modern views of intelligence have in common is an emphasis on both innate and developmental influences (Shouksmith, 1970). Genetically determined mental ability is always seen as being modified by experience. Measures of intelligence sample only a limited spectrum of intellectual ability, and the test responses given by individuals are related to their unique learning histories. Contemporary views suggest that intelligence is a more global concept than was earlier imagined. For projections of what form intelligence tests will take in the year 2000, see Exhibit 3-3. Whatever position you adopt toward conceptions of intelligence, it is important to recognize that the unique learning histories of individuals determine the ways in which they use their intelligence.

■ Exhibit 3-3 ■

Intelligence Tests in the Year 2000: What Form Will They Take and What Purposes Will They Serve?

John Horn

Realistic appraisal, based on historical analysis, suggests that in the year 2000 the tests used to measure intellectual abilities in applied settings will be very similar to the tests used today and 40 years ago. However, if the technology of measurement for applied purposes follows advancements in scientific understanding of human intelligence, then we can expect that intelligence tests of the future:

1. will be architectonically structured to provide for measurements of many separate abilities, ranging from very elementary processes to broad but distinct dimensions of intelligence;
2. will involve, perhaps be focused on, abilities to comprehend and assimilate information that comes to one via the continuous flow of TV-like presentations;
3. will contain subtests designed to indicate features of temporal integration of information, auditory organization, and elementary cognitive processing of information;
4. will derive more from the study of adulthood development than from the study of childhood development.

The mainstreams of cognitive psychology will be diverted more and more into the study of intelligence and thus will influence the shape of practical tests. Tests will be used less and less to measure global intelligence just for the sake of measuring it, or to make invidious distinctions, but more testing will be done to help identify particular ability strengths and weaknesses. Theory about intelligence will improve and more test construction will be based on sound theory.

Lauren B. Resnick

What is the likelihood that IQ tests as we currently know them will still be in use in the schools at the turn of the century? . . . What new kinds of tests of aptitude and intelligence can we reasonably look for? . . . IQ tests, or some very similar kind of assessment instrument, are likely to be functionally necessary in the schools as long as the present form of special education for the mentally handicapped remains with us—or until we are prepared to spend substantially more public resources on education for all children than we are now doing. Further, I have suggested that there is a very real possibility of a *revival* of interest in IQ tests in the educational mainstream as a protective response by school people threatened with legal responsibility for ensuring that all children, even the very hard-to-teach, learn. I believe these two areas—special education and the school's legal responsibility—are the things to watch over the next twenty years for new developments in global IQ measurement. . . .

What new kinds of tests can we expect? I have suggested the possibility of a serious shift in the science and therefore the technology of intelligence testing. Aptitude tests useful for monitoring instruction and adapting it to individual differences are essentially nonexistent today. Current work on the cognitive analysis of intelligence and aptitude tests may be able to provide the basis for much more systematic and refined matching of instructional treatments to aptitudes within two decades. We can particularly look forward to this development as work on the cognitive components of intelligence shifts attention from performance on the tests themselves to the *learning* processes that underlie both skillful test performance and skillful performance in school subject matters.

Ann L. Brown and Lucia A. French

By the year 2000 we would like to see an extension of the predictive power of intelligence tests so that we are able to (a) predict school failure prior to its occurrence and (b) predict potential adult competence by a consideration of performance on tests of everyday reasoning. To achieve these ends we will need to invest considerable energy in ethnographic surveys and experimental testing programs directed at improving our scanty knowledge in two main areas. First we need sensitive indices of early cognitive (in)competence that are related to subsequent academic intelligence. Secondly we need theories and measures of functional literacy, minimal competence, and mundane cognition, so that we can begin to predict life adaptation as well as academic success.

We would also like to see an increased emphasis on the diagnosis and remediation of cognitive deficits, of both the academic and everyday variety.

William W. Turnbull

My view . . . is that over the next 20 years or so we are likely to see evolutionary rather than quantum changes in intelligence tests, at least as they are used in academic settings. We are likely to see tests that provide separate scores on a variety of abilities. They are likely to be standard scores. The ratio defining the IQ may by then have been abandoned everywhere and the term IQ may have disappeared into psychological and educational history.

Norman Frederiksen

Realistic simulations of real-life problem situations might be used to supplement the usual psychological tests and thus to contribute to the database needed to develop a broader con-

(Exhibit continues next page)

Exhibit 3-3 (cont.)

ception of intelligence. It is possible to develop scoring systems that describe intelligent behavior in ways that go far beyond the *number right* score, that make possible the measurement of qualitative variables, such as problem-solving strategies and styles, and that may even provide information about some of the information-processing components of intelligent behavior. Many of the scores based on simulations are reliable, their interrelationships are consistent across different groups of subjects, and some of them predict real-life criteria that are not well predicted by conventional tests. . . .

Our glimpse of a broader picture of human intelligence suggests that the structure of intellect of the future will include a much broader spectrum of intelligent behaviors. Furthermore, it will not be a static model but will be one that recognizes the interactions involving test formats, subject characteristics, and the settings in which the problems are encountered. The structure of intelligence is not necessarily a fixed structure but one that may vary as the subjects learn and as the circumstances are altered.

Earl Hunt and James Pellegrino

Microcomputers can serve as automated testing stations for use in psychometric assessment. There are economic advan-

tages in conducting aptitude and intelligence testing with such stations. Is it possible to improve the quality of cognitive assessment by extending the range of cognitive abilities to be assessed? Two types of extension are considered: modifying and expanding testing procedures for psychological functions that are components of conventional tests, and the extension of testing to psychological functions not generally asssessed by conventional intelligence or aptitude tests. Computerized presentations will make relatively little difference in our ways of testing verbal comprehension. Computer-controlled testing could well extend the ways in which we evaluate spatial-visual reasoning and memory. The impact of testing on the evaluation of reasoning is unclear. Computer-controlled item presentation makes it possible to conceive of tests of learning and attention, neither of which is evaluated in most psychometric programs today.

Source: Frederiksen (1986, p. 451); Horn (1979, p. 239); Hunt and Pellegrino (1985, p. 207); Resnick (1979, p. 252); Brown and French (1979, p. 270); Turnbull (1979, p. 281). Citations from 1979 originally appeared in *Intelligence*, 1979, *3* (3) (Ablex Publishing Corporation, Norwood, New Jersey).

SUMMARY

1. The field of intelligence testing grew from the work of early experimental psychologists such as Weber and Fechner, who developed psychophysical methods, and from the pioneering efforts of Galton in England, Cattell in the United States, Kraepelin in Germany, and Binet and Simon in France. A focus on higher mental processes enabled Binet and Simon to develop useful tests of intelligence.

2. Other early pioneers include Pearson, who developed the product-moment correlation coefficient; Münsterberg and Jastrow, who developed various reaction-time tests; and Ebbinghaus and Wernicke, who worked on various types of cognitive tests.

3. The Binet-Simon Scales were introduced in the United States by Goddard. The scales were extensively revised in 1916 by Terman, who adopted Stern's mental quotient, renaming it the intelligence quotient.

4. Believing that a point-scale arrangement has better psychometric properties than an age-scale format, Yerkes developed one of the first point scales in the twentieth century.

5. Wechsler systematized and organized a series of subtests into a standardized point scale, guided by a conception of intelligence that emphasized its global nature.

6. The success of the Binet-Simon Scales and their derivatives launched the twentieth-century testing movement in the United States and many other countries.

7. Intelligence has been variously defined as a measure of (a)

innate capacity, (b) observed behavior, and (c) performance on specific tests of cognitive ability. Innate capacity, however, cannot be measured directly.

8. The definition of intelligence continues to be a problem. Terman focused on abstract thinking as the essential part of intelligence; Binet focused on a varied set of qualities including judgment, common sense, initiative, and adaptation; and Wechsler stressed the qualities of purposefulness, rationality, and ability to deal effectively with the environment.

9. Factor analytic theories of intelligence arrived on the scene concurrently with statistical methods for the evaluation of large amounts of data. Some theorists (for example, Spearman and Vernon) proposed a general theory of intelligence, whereas others (for example, Thorndike and Thurstone) viewed intelligence as being composed of many independent faculties. Many now accept the theory that general intelligence coexists with separate independent abilities.

10. Spearman proposed a two-factor theory of intelligence, emphasizing a general factor (*g*) and one or more specific factors (*s*).

11. Thorndike described three kinds of intelligence—social, concrete, and abstract.

12. Thurstone described at least eight primary mental factors (verbal, perceptual speed, inductive reasoning, number, rote memory, deductive reasoning, word fluency, and space or visualization). In his later work he postulated a second-order factor which may be similar to *g*.

13. Guilford maintained that three classes of variables must be considered in any account of intellectual abilities: the activities or operations performed (*operations*), the material or content on which the operations are performed (*content*), and the product that is the result of the operations (*products*).

14. Vernon's hierarchical approach to intelligence emphasized the *g* factor, followed by verbal-educational and spatial-mechanical group factors, which can be broken down further into minor group factors.

15. Cattell and Horn postulated two types of intelligence: fluid (capacity independent of experience) and crystallized (learned knowledge). In the latest version of the theory, Horn proposed a four-level hierarchical model. The lowest level contains sensory detection functions; the second, associational processes; the third, perceptual organizational processes; and the fourth and highest, fluid ability and crystallized ability.

16. Gustafsson integrated various approaches to intelligence in a three-level hierarchical model, with *g*, or fluid intelligence, at the top of the hierarchy, followed by three broad factors—crystallized intelligence, fluid intelligence, and general visualization.

17. Information-processing approaches to intelligence attempt to account for the transformation and manipulation of information. They have in common two general components: a structural component and a functional component.

18. The Campione, Brown, and Borkowski information-processing theory of intelligence has two major components. One is the architectural system (the structural component), whose structures differ in such characteristics as capacity, durability, and efficiency of operation. The other is the executive system (functional component), which contains such components as a knowledge base, schemes, control processes, and metacognition. The dynamic interplay of structural and functional components is stressed.

19. Sternberg views intelligence as consisting of three dimensions: the *componential* dimension, which relates to internal mental mechanisms; the *experiential* dimension, which relates to both the external and the internal worlds of the individual; and the *contextual* dimension, which relates to the external world of the individual. All three parts must be considered in the study of intelligence.

20. Das proposed a simultaneous-successive information-processing model as a way of categorizing cognitive ability. In simultaneous processing, processing occurs in an integrated, usually semi-spatial form; in successive processing, processing is sequence dependent and temporally based. No hierarchy is assumed in the model.

21. Jensen's theory of associative ability and cognitive ability is an attempt to demarcate two separate but partially interdependent mental functions. Associative ability is represented by memory and serial learning tasks, whereas cognitive ability is represented by conceptual reasoning tasks.

22. Gardner views intelligence in terms of problem solving and finding or creating problems. At least six intellectual competencies must be considered—linguistic, musical, logical-mathematical, spatial, bodily-kinesthetic, and personal. Unfortunately, no reliable and valid way has been proposed to measure these competencies throughout the developmental period.

23. Piaget viewed intelligence as an extension of biological adaptation, consisting of assimilation (processes responsive to inner promptings—applying existing schemes to the environment) and accommodation (processes responsive to environmental intrusions—changing schemes in response to the environment). Assimilative processes permit intelligence to go beyond a passive coping with reality, whereas accommodative processes prevent intelligence from constructing representations of reality that have no correspondence with the real world. Intelligence represents the rational processes that show the greatest independence of environmental and internal regulation.

24. Piaget viewed intellectual development as consisting of a series of stages that are marked by changes in adaptation. The stages reflect a series of progressively more mature cognitive structures, marked by decreasing dependence on the immediately perceived environment and increasing ability to deal logically with abstract propositions.

25. Piagetian and psychometric approaches to intellectual assessment complement each other. Both approaches accept genetic and maturational determinants and emphasize the rational nature of intelligence. The Piagetian approach emphasizes developmental changes and the emergence of new mental structures, whereas the psychometric approach emphasizes the normal distribution of intelligence and interindividual differences.

26. A resurgence of interest in the study of intelligence is being led by researchers in information-processing laboratories. Their work may soon yield findings that can be applied to the design of remediation programs. Hierarchical theories are also gaining wide acceptance because they provide useful guidelines for understanding the nature of intelligence. These theories stress the importance of a general intellectual factor, several broad factors, and a number of specific factors.

KEY TERMS, CONCEPTS, AND NAMES

Esquirol (p. 38)
Weber (p. 38)
Fechner (p. 38)
Galton (p. 38)
Pearson (p. 39)
Goodness of fit (p. 39)
J. M. Cattell (p. 39)
Münsterberg (p. 39)
Jastrow (p. 39)
Boas (p. 39)
Gilbert (p. 39)
Wissler (p. 39)
Sharp (p. 39)
Kraepelin (p. 39)
Ebbinghaus (p. 40)

STUDY QUESTIONS

1. Compare and contrast work on intelligence assessment in the United States, Germany, France, and England during the nineteenth century and the early years of the twentieth century.

2. Discuss Terman's contribution to the field of intelligence testing.

3. Discuss the contributions of Yerkes and Wechsler to the testing movement.

4. What effect did the Binet-Simon scales have in the United States during the early twentieth century?

5. Give three definitions of intelligence.

6. Compare and contrast the following factor analytic theorists: Spearman, Thorndike, Thurstone, Guilford, Vernon, Cattell and Horn, and Gustafsson.

7. Discuss information-processing approaches to intelligence.

8. Discuss Jensen's and Gardner's approaches to intelligence.

9. Discuss Piaget's approach to the study of intelligence.

10. What are some of the similarities and differences between Piagetian and psychometric approaches to intelligence?

11. What form will intelligence tests take in the year 2000? Discuss the views of Horn, Resnick, Brown and French, Turnbull, Frederiksen, and Hunt and Pellegrino.

4

ISSUES RELATED TO THE MEASUREMENT AND CHANGE OF INTELLIGENCE

It is in connection with intelligence and the tests which measure it that some of the most violent polemics in psychology and in all the behavioral sciences have raged. These polemics have concerned the nature of man's intellectual capacities, how they should be measured, how mutable they are, and what the implication of the decisions on these issues should be for educating and improving the race.

—J. McVicker Hunt

The assessment of intelligence requires not only the ability to administer and interpret tests, but also knowledge of some of the important variables associated with the measurement and change of intelligence and of the social and political implications of the use of intelligence tests. An understanding of the issues discussed in this chapter will aid you in your roles as an evaluator and a consultant. The chapter begins with a discussion of genetic programming, maturational status, and environment and then turns to a consideration of heredity and its relation to intelligence. Also included are a discussion of environmental influences on intelligence and a discussion of the assets and limitations of intelligence testing.

Wilson (1978b, p. 940) succinctly describes the importance of intelligence for the individual:

Among the capabilities of human beings, none is as distinctive nor as central to his or her adaptive potential as intelligence. It is tied to the recently evolved regions of the brain, particularly the association areas of the neocortex. . . . It furnishes an enormous integrative capability by which the experiences of the past can be brought to bear adaptively on the problems of the present and the anticipations of the future. As a species characteristic it progresses from the rudimentary sensorimotor coordinations of infancy to the abstract reasoning of the adult, and the transformation is so drastic that the line of continuity is inferential rather than direct. It is perhaps the most widely studied capability of man, and in recent years by far the most controversial.

GENETIC PROGRAMMING, MATURATIONAL STATUS, AND ENVIRONMENTAL INFLUENCE

Genetic programming, maturational status, and environmental influences interact to affect the course of mental development (Wilson, 1978b). The genetic program for many behaviors reflects a high degree of preorganization and priming laid down in the brain structure by evolution. Gene actions are likely to be associated with patterns of acceleration and lag in the growth of various human behaviors, of precocity, and of deficits in developmental status. Distinctive cycles of gene action operate in conjunction with the maturational state of the child. A prominent feature of the epigenetic process (a process of continuous feedback and modulation which ensures that development proceeds toward specific targets or end states) is individual differences in the rate of development and in the timing of particular phases. Thus intellectual growth for any given child reflects the interaction of many complex factors.

Changes that occur during the first two years of life illustrate how maturational status affects mental development. During the first stages of infancy, primitive sensorimotor functions are the major component of mental development. Between 18 and 24 months, a significant transition occurs in which symbolic functions are enhanced (see the discussion of Piaget in Chapter 3). It is in this period that children become able to draw on internalized memories of past experience as an aid in comprehending the present.

Environmental conditions play a crucial role in fostering enthusiasm for learning and providing the child with an opportunity to develop fully. A supportive and stimulating family environment is needed if each child is to realize his or her maximum potential.

Wilson describes the interaction of the genetic program, maturational status, and the environment between 18 and 24 months as follows:

. . . cognitive functions turn more toward the symbolizing and synthesizing functions that figure so prominently in the growth of intelligence. . . . The efficiency and scope of these symbolizing functions become a predictable attribute of each individual's mental status, and the variations in efficiency become translated into the normal distribution of intelligence. Such variations must ultimately have their roots in epigenetic processes that determine the integrative power of the brain. Within the normal range of environments, these processes unfold in accordance with the intrinsic scheduling of the genetic program, and it is at this level that the synchronies in mental development may be found. (1978b, p. 947)

INTELLECTUAL FUNCTIONING: HEREDITARY INFLUENCES

An estimate of the heritability of a trait describes the proportion of the variation of a trait in a given population that is attributable to genetic differences in that population. The degree of heritability can range from 0 to 100 percent. A value of .60 for the heritability of IQ in a given population means that 60 percent of the observed variation in IQs in that population is attributable to genetic differences among the members of the population and that 40 percent of the observed variation is attributable to other sources. A heritability estimate refers only to *population* variance in a trait; it is not applicable to an individual.

Children do not inherit an IQ. They inherit a collection of genes referred to as a *genotype* for intelligence. The expression of the genotype, called the *phenotype* (the observable performance of individuals), results from the interaction of the genotype with environmental experiences.

Genes set the upper and lower limits of the phenotype, but the environment determines where in this reaction range the final IQ value will fall. The current nature-nurture controversy is reducible to the single issue of how wide the range of reaction is. Those who favor environmental explanations . . . argue for a wide reaction range of 50, 70, or even 100 IQ points. Those who acknowledge genetic determinants assert that the reaction range [within which environmental variables operate] is more narrow, generally around 25 points. . . . (Zigler & Farber, 1985, p. 400)

Polygenic Model

A polygenic model is useful for understanding the heritability of intelligence. This model assumes that intelligence is a result of the combined action and influence of many genes rather than a single gene. Techniques of biometrical genetics clearly indicate that intelligence is under polygenic control (Jinks & Fulker, 1970).

Heritability Estimates of Intelligence

Heritability estimates for human intelligence are obtained by examining the correlations between groups of individuals of different degrees of kinship, such as monozygotic and dizygotic twins. Figures on heritability must remain *estimates* because experimental manipulations of human matings cannot be performed. Although refinements in estimation techniques have taken place recently, heritability estimates differ among researchers. Plomin and DeFries (1980), for example, suggest that heritability accounts for 50 percent of phenotypic variability in intelligence, whereas Vandenberg and Vogler (1985) indicate that heritability accounts for only 30 to 40 percent of the phenotypic variance. Thus estimates indicate that at least 50 percent, and perhaps as much as 70 percent, of the variation in general intellectual ability is *not* related to genetic influences; therefore some degree of external or environmental control over the development of intelligence is possible. Table 4-1 shows that the more similar people are genetically, the more highly related their IQs are.

Genotypic Influence on Intelligence

A study of scores of 142 pairs of monozygotic and dizygotic white twins on the Wechsler Preschool and Primary Scale of Intelligence (WPPSI) over a three-year period (4 to 6 years of age) indicated that the genotype exerts a significant influence on cognitive patterning and development (Wilson, 1975). The correlations of WPPSI Verbal, Performance, and Full Scale IQs were higher for monozygotic twins (.76 to .82) than for dizygotic twins (.49 to .68). Over time, the scores of the monozygotic twins became more closely aligned with respect to the

Table 4-1
Median Correlation Coefficients Between IQs of Persons with Different Degrees of Relationship

Relationship	Number of correlations	Number of pairings	Median correlation
Twins, monozygotic			
reared together	34	4,672	.85
reared apart	3	65	.67
Twins, dizygotic,			
reared together	41	5,546	.58
Siblings			
reared together	69	25,473	.45
reared apart	2	203	.24
Unrelated children,			
reared together	11	714	.30

Source: Adapted from Bouchard and McGue (1981).

direction and magnitude of differences between Verbal and Performance IQs. The monozygotic correlations started out at a relatively high level and increased somewhat with age. Wilson suggested that shared genotype and experience apparently made an equal contribution to the intellectual functions measured by both scales.

The scores of the dizygotic twins displayed moderate correlations, but the pattern of correlations on the two scales differed. The Verbal IQ correlations had a high level initially and then declined (from .73 to .56), whereas the Performance IQ correlations had relatively consistent values around .50. The rate of concordance (agreement) for the difference between Verbal and Performance IQs did not increase for dizygotic twins. Wilson concluded that "within a broad range of home environments, the genetic blueprint made a substantial contribution to cognitive patterning and development" (p. 126).

INTELLECTUAL FUNCTIONING: ENVIRONMENTAL INFLUENCES

Research on the influence of environmental factors on IQ is summarized in Table 4-2. The findings are discussed in greater detail below. (The findings in this section are based primarily on the excellent chapter by Bouchard and Segal, 1985.)

Perinatal and Early Developmental Influences

Interest in the effects of perinatal factors on intellectual functioning in children has led to considerable research.

Table 4-2
Environment and IQ: A Summary of Findings

Area	*Findings*
Prenatal and Early Developmental Influences	
Complications of labor and delivery	Obstetrical complications do not appear to be related to IQ.
Birth weight	Birth weight has a minimal correlation with IQ (e.g., $r = .08$ with 7-year IQ).
Anoxia	Anoxia has a minimal correlation with IQ (e.g., $r = -.05$ to $-.06$) and results in a 4.6 point IQ deficit on average.
Childhood illnesses	Measles, pertussis, rubella, mumps, and scarlet fever show no relationship to test scores; the relationship between these diseases and mental subnormality is inconclusive.
Lead poisoning	The influence of low-level lead exposure on children's IQs remains undetermined.
Malnutrition and Famine	
Vulnerability to malnutrition	Malnutrition, at least at the level experienced in developed economies, does not have a substantial impact on intelligence. For individual children, however, malnutrition may result in stunted mental and physical growth and death.
Family Background and IQ	
Biological families	Background characteristics of biological families (e.g., income, education, occupation, and home atmosphere) correlate significantly with children's IQs (e.g., range from .18 to .58).
Nonbiological families	Family background characteristics influence adoptive children's IQs, but only to a modest extent (e.g., range from .09 to .21).
Specific Home Environmental Factors	
Home environmental variables	Specific home environmental factors—such as press for achievement motivation, press for language development, and provisions for general learning—correlate highly with children's IQs.
Family Configuration and IQ	
Birth order, family size, and sibling birth intervals	The confluence model, which attempts to explain individual differences in IQ, has not been clearly refuted, but there is much evidence that brings into question the adequacy of the model.
Schooling and IQ	
Inequality of schooling and IQ	There is no firm evidence that the quality of primary and secondary education is a major source of individual differences in IQ.
Amount of schooling and IQ	The correlation between adult IQ and schooling completed is about .69.
Preschool enrichment programs	Preschool enrichment programs influence IQ, but long-term effects appear to be small.

Source: Adapted from Bouchard and Segal (1985).

Perinatal factors include *prenatal variables* (for example, abnormal fetus, prenatal stress, or injury); *general birth process variables* (for example, abnormal delivery, instrument delivery, and delivery difficulties); and *neonatal variables* (for example, brain damage, hemorrhage, and other physical malfunctions to the neonate). Related, too, are factors affecting the mother during pregnancy, including illness, weight gain, blood pressure, smoking, drugs, alcohol, anxiety, pelvic difficulties, and difficulties from previous pregnancies.

The weight of an infant at birth is an important developmental milestone and provides a useful index of intrauterine growth. Difficulties occurring during intrauterine life can lead to a reduction in potential for intellectual and physical development. Low birth weight (that is, a weight of less than 2,500 grams or 5½ lb) may be associated with intrauterine difficulties and represents an increased risk factor. Maternal factors associated with low birth weight include low socioeconomic status (SES), extremes of maternal age, short stature, cigarette smoking, the presence of certain pathologic states (for example, hypertension, renal disease, or uncontrolled diabetes), and low maternal weight gain during pregnancy.

Research suggests that the effects of perinatal stress on intellectual functioning are small. Early biological insult may affect subsequent intellectual functioning, but present instruments are not sufficiently sensitive to detect measurable differences in intelligence between normal children and those who earlier experienced prenatal stress.

Malnutrition

Vulnerability to malnutrition is greatest during the nine months of gestation and the first few years of life, the most critical periods in the growth of brain tissue. Nutritional stress can lead to learning difficulties by affecting the central nervous system and creating disturbances in social experiences. Malnutrition may prevent the expression of the full genetic potential for mental development and interfere with learning time, concentration, motivation, and social interaction. Nutritional inadequacy also increases the risk of infection and interferes with immune mechanisms. In spite of the potential adverse consequences associated with malnutrition, the limited amount of evidence available suggests that the relationship between nutrition and intellectual and physical development is not a substantial one.

Family Background and IQ

Family background and IQ are significantly correlated. The correlation between a family's socioeconomic status and children's intelligence test scores is about .33 on average. Table 4-3 summarizes the correlations between four family status variables (father's and mother's education, father's occupation, and income) and children's IQs found in five large-scale studies. The correlations range from .22

Table 4-3
Correlations Between Parental Socioeconomic Status Measures and Child's IQ in Large-Scale Studies of Biological Families

Status variable	Mean r
Father's education	.314
Mother's education	.298
Father's occupation	.278
Income	.223

Note. Based on five studies with samples ranging from 2,700 to 13,695.
Source: Adapted from Bouchard and Segal (1985).

to .31. Pointing out that variables such as the parents' level of education tap parental heredity, not just environmental factors, Bouchard and Segal (1985) estimate that two-thirds to three-fourths of the average IQ differences between children in the various social classes are genetic in origin.

Specific Home Environmental Factors

Several major studies have demonstrated that psychosocial factors in the home environment play an important role in the development of children's intelligence.

Wolf's study. Wolf (1966) sought to discover the relationship between intellectual development and such home variables as quality of language models available to the child, opportunities for enlarging vocabulary, feedback about appropriate language usage, and opportunities for language practice. His sample consisted of 60 mothers of fifth-grade students. He found that the correlation between total ratings of the intellectual environment and general intelligence was extremely high ($r = .69$). Environmental ratings were also highly related ($r = .80$) to achievement test scores. The combination of tested general intelligence and environmental ratings produced a remarkably high correlation of .87 with achievement test scores.

Marjoribanks's study. Marjoribanks (1972) sought to determine the relationship between home environment variables and various types of cognitive abilities in a sample of 185 11-year-old boys. The results (see Table 4-4) indicated that home environmental variables, such as pressures for achievement, activity, intellectuality, and independence, were *highly related* to the verbal, number, and total ability scores of the SRA Primary Mental Abilities Test, *moderately related* to reasoning ability scores, and *minimally related* to spatial ability scores. Other research (McGee, 1982) also indicated that scores on spatial tests have lower correlations with environmental measures than do scores on other ability tests. The environmental variables were also more powerful predictors of mental ability scores than were either social status variables (occupation of father, education of father, and education of mother) or family structure variables (size of family, ordinal position in the family, and crowding ratio in the home).

Hanson's study. A longitudinal study by Hanson (1975) across three time periods (0–3 years, 4–6 years, and 7–10 years), with a sample of 110 predominantly upper-middle-class male and female white children, showed that several home environmental variables were significantly related to

Table 4-4
Correlations Between Mental Ability Test Scores and Environmental Variable Test Scores

Environmental variable	Ability				
	Verbal	Number	Spatial	Reasoning	Total
Environmental Forces					
Press for achievement	.66**	.66**	.28**	.39**	.69**
Press for activeness	.52**	.41**	.22**	.26**	.47**
Press for intellectuality	.61**	.53**	.26**	.31**	.59**
Press for independence	.42**	.34**	.10	.23**	.38**
Press for English	.50**	.27**	.18**	.28**	.40**
Press for ethlanguage[a]	.35**	.24**	.09	.19**	.28**
Father dominance	.16*	.10	.09	.11	.15
Mother dominance	.21**	.16*	.04	.10	.16*
Multiple correlation	.71**	.71**	.26	.40*	.72**
Status variables					
Education of father	.29**	.27**	.26**	.22**	.31**
Education of mother	.39**	.33**	.21**	.16*	.36**
Occupation of father	.43**	.30**	.31**	.29**	.43**
Number of children in family	−.32**	−.33**	−.04	−.03	−.31**
Crowding ratio	−.34**	−.34**	−.07	−.09	−.33**
Ordinal position in family	−.26**	−.25**	−.04	−.04	−.24**
Multiple correlation	.51***	.40***	.28*	.25	.53***
Environmental plus status variables					
Multiple correlation	.71***	.71***	.36*	.42**	.75***

* $p < .05$.   ** $p < .01$.   *** $p < .001$.
[a] Ethlanguage refers to any language spoken in the home other than English.
Source: Reprinted, with a change in notation, from K. Marjoribanks, "Environment, Social Class, and Mental Abilities," *Journal of Educational Psychology, 63*, pp. 106–107. Copyright 1972 by the American Psychological Association. Reprinted by permission.

Stanford-Binet: Form L-M IQs, highly consistent within a given time period, and extremely stable across the childhood years. Variables such as freedom to engage in verbal expression, language teaching, parental involvement, and provision of language development models were found to be related significantly to intelligence in each age period (see Table 4-5).

Wilson's study.   Wilson (1983) studied the relationship between variables in the home environment and mental development at four age periods in a sample of 226 families with twins under 8 years of age. Home environment variables and mental development were weakly related at 6 months of age, more related at 24 months of age, and very significantly related at 3 and 6 years of age (see Table 4-6). Father's and mother's education, socioeconomic status,

and ratings of home adequacy and maternal cognitive skills were most closely related to the child's mental development. Thus when the home was geared to fostering development and when the mother was intellectually alert, positive in mood, and free of tension and frustration, the children tended to have higher IQs. Wilson concluded, however, that genetic factors appeared to be primarily involved in the development of the children's mental ability:

We infer from these relations that the principal link between parental intelligence and offspring intelligence is genetic in origin. Although the comprehensive home assessment clearly added to the prediction of mental development, the elementary demographic variables yielded such strong correlations that the attributes of the parents must be transmitted to offspring primarily by mechanisms other than shared family experiences. The im-

Table 4-5
Concurrent Relationships Between Environmental Variables and Stanford-Binet: Form L-M IQs (N = 110)

	Age		
Environmental variable	*3 years*	*5½ years*	*9½ years*
Freedom to engage in verbal expression	.20*	.45**	.41**
Direct teaching of language behavior	.36**	.36**	.43**
Parental involvement with child	.31**	.36**	.38**
Emphasis on school achievement	.16	.38**	.31**
Emphasis on independent performance	.06	.05	.32**
Models of intellectual interests	.15	.43**	.45**
Models of language development	.25**	.34**	.43**
Emphasis on female sex role development	−.08	−.13	−.12
Freedom to explore the environment	−.10	.13	.12
Models of task orientation	−.02	.04	.04

* $p < .05$.   ** $p < .01$.
Source: Adapted from Hanson (1975).

pact of these family experiences is dependent on the intrinsic biological foundation of the offspring, and that foundation derives chiefly from the genotype supplied by the parents. (p. 311)

Mercy and Steelman's study. Mercy and Steelman (1982) studied the relationship between intelligence, family structure, and childhood experience in a nationally representative sample of 2,994 children, 6 to 11 years of age, from 1963 to 1965. Significant relationships were found between intelligence, as measured by the WISC Vocabulary and Block Design subtests, and familial and social variables (see Table 4-7). The most significant familial and social variables were *father's and mother's education* and *family income*. In all cases in which there were significant correlations, the relationships were higher with Vocabulary than with Block Design. The latter findings suggest that "insofar as language is learned in a social context, verbal ability is probably more amenable to a child's social experiences than nonverbal ability" (Mercy & Steelman, 1982, p. 540). Overall, the results suggest that factors within the family environment differentially influence intellectual development.

McCall, Appelbaum, and Hogarty's study. McCall, Appelbaum, and Hogarty (1973) reported that children who showed *decreases* in IQ in the preschool years tended to come from homes that had minimal stimulation and either a very severe or a very mild punishment regime. In contrast, children who showed *increases* in IQ until approximately 8 years of age came from families that gave their children encouragement in a clear manner and pro-

vided structure and enforcement. Severity of penalties imposed by the parent when the child misbehaved was an important variable related to IQ change. Children with the most depressed IQ records had parents who were most severe in their penalties; children whose parents were lax in their penalties showed some recovery in IQ during the middle school years; and children who gained in IQ points had parents who seemed to adopt a middle-of-the-road policy on the severity of discipline.

Comment on Home Environmental Factors and Family Background Factors

The high correlations between home environmental factors and children's IQs parallel the findings with respect to family background characteristics. Some of the strongest correlations with children's intelligence come from specific home environmental factors. Home environmental factors may not be independent of family background characteristics, however. Measures of pressure for achievement motivation and language development and provisions for general learning, for example, may serve as surrogate measures of parental IQ and education.

Family Configuration and IQ

Zajonc (1976) proposed a *confluence model* to account for the effect of family configuration on intellectual development. It relates intellectual development to a number of family configuration variables, including birth order, family size, and sibling birth intervals. The model postulates

Table 4-6
Correlations Between Home Assessment Variables and Mental Test Scores (N = 226 Families)

Variable	6 months[a]	24 months[a]	3 years[b]	6 years[c]
Father's education	.28	.38	.51	.53
Mother's education	.19	.33	.49	.50
Socioeconomic status	.17	.42	.51	.51
Adequacy of home environment	.23	.45	.54	.55
Maternal cognitive	.24	.40	.41	.52
Maternal temperament	.03	.01	.01	−.08
Maternal social affect	.10	.23	.35	.25
N cases	205	303	321	287

Note. Adequacy of home environment refers to judgments about the adequacy of the interpersonal and physical environment for promoting intellectual and social development plus judgments about play space and features of the home and furnishings. *Maternal cognitive* refers to ratings of the mother's intellectual and verbal facility and home management skills. *Maternal temperament* refers to ratings of the mother's emotional reactivity (e.g., tension, tolerance for frustration, mood, activity level). *Maternal social affect* refers to ratings of the mother's sociability, talkativeness, and interpersonal warmth. Maternal temperament made a significant contribution to the multiple correlation at ages 24 months $(R = .56)$ and 6 years $(R = .66)$.
[a] Bayley Scales of Infant Development.
[b] Stanford-Binet: Form L-M.
[c] Wechsler Preschool and Primary Scale of Intelligence.
Source: Reprinted, with permission of the publisher and author, from R. S. Wilson, "The Louisville Twin Study: Developmental Synchronies in Behavior," *Child Development*, 1983, *54*, p. 308. Copyright 1983 by the Society for Research in Child Development, Inc.

that cognitive development is mediated by the intellectual environment to which the child is exposed. Specifically, it proposes that family size is negatively correlated with IQ, and that later-born children in large families frequently obtain lower intelligence test scores than earlier-born children. The hypothesis is that a large family provides a less stimulating intellectual environment.

At best, the model explains a very small amount of the total variance in IQ. One of the difficulties in interpreting research on birth order is that larger families tend to come from lower socioeconomic classes. Consequently, any comparison involving small and large families may be confounded by variations in socioeconomic status (Bouchard & Segal, 1985).

Schooling and IQ

Inequality of schooling plays a minor role in individual differences in IQ. It is estimated that between 2 and 10 percent of the variance in cognitive functioning may be associated with school quality (Bouchard & Segal, 1985). The high correlation between years of schooling completed and IQ may indicate that bright individuals continue in school; it also may mean that schooling increases IQ. Few studies have addressed these issues. The evidence

suggests, however, that each extra year of education adds about 1 point to the expected adult IQ score of the individual.

Preschool enrichment programs are designed to modify the course of early development in order to better prepare the socially disadvantaged child for public school. Ramey, Bryant, and Suarez (1985) reviewed 18 well-designed compensatory education projects conducted from 1968 to 1985. Twelve of these projects began during infancy, five during the preschool years, and one at kindergarten age. Interventions were conducted with parents, children, or both, at centers, homes, or both. Outcome measures included scores on infant scales, such as the Bayley, Griffiths, and Gesell, and on the Stanford-Binet: Form L-M.

Infant programs were most successful when day care was year-round and when full-day programs were combined with family education training and home visits. At 12 months of age, the differences between experimental groups (range of scores from 103 to 119) and control groups (range of scores from 98 to 113) ranged from 1 to 13 points on the Bayley Mental Developmental Index, in favor of the experimental groups. At 24 months of age, the experimental groups were from 1 to 29 points higher (range of scores from 85 to 125) than the control groups (range of scores from 85 to 102), except for one control group that actually outscored the experimental group by 6 points on the Bayley test. Home visits alone did not alter the children's IQs at this age.

The five preschool programs also raised the children's IQs. Differences between experimental (range of scores from 93 to 126) and control (range of scores from 84 to 104) groups ranged from 3 to 32 points on the Stanford-Binet: Form L-M, in favor of the experimental groups.

Finally, at kindergarten ages, the one study reviewed showed gains of 6 to 10 IQ points on the Stanford-Binet: Form L-M as a result of attending one year of public school kindergarten.

The long-term influences of preschool programs on IQ do not appear to be large. Preschool enrichment programs, however, may change not only children's IQ, but also achievement orientation, school competence, educational attainment, and career accomplishments. Additionally, it is important to keep in mind that small average differences reflect some large differences for given individual children—some children are significantly influenced by such programs. Unfortunately, because the data regarding the effectiveness of preschool enrichment programs are subject to a number of different interpretations, firm conclusions cannot be drawn about their impact on later intellectual development.

COMMENT ON HEREDITARY AND ENVIRONMENTAL INFLUENCES ON INTELLECTUAL FUNCTIONING

Although heredity sets limits on a child's potential, it is the environment that permits that potential to be actualized. Heritability estimates do not set the final limits on human intelligence because intelligence is always expressed in an environment, which may promote or restrict intellectual development. Consequently, our efforts should be geared to investigating which environmental factors—such as nutrition, educational systems, home environments, and personal experiences—nurture or impede intellectual development. Strategies should then be developed that will best enhance children's cognitive functioning. Environmental interventions that can produce significant changes in intelligence, however, are likely to be complex, time consuming, and costly.

No single environmental factor has a large influence on IQ. When maternal IQ was controlled, Longstreth and colleagues found that the highly significant relationships between socioeconomic status and children's IQ and between home environment and children's IQ became nonsignificant (Longstreth, Davis, Carter, Flint, Owen, Rickert, & Taylor, 1981). These results, which have not yet been replicated, suggest that maternal IQ, rather than socioeconomic status or home environment, is the key factor related to the child's IQ.

There is some evidence that the genetic variance in intelligence test scores tends to be proportionately larger in a more stimulating environment (such as is found in middle and upper social classes) and smaller in a less stimulating environment (such as is found in the working class) (Fischbein, 1980). Fischbein hypothesizes that, although it seems paradoxical, "equality of opportunity, with optimal stimulation for everyone, might lead to a greater proportion of genetic variance in intelligence test score differences" (p. 61).

An individual's score on an intelligence test does not permit us to make inferences about either genetic influences (or the biological substrate) or environmental influences (or the psychosocial substrate) (Humphreys, 1971). The independent contributions of these two components

Table 4-7
Correlations Between Familial Factors and WISC Vocabulary and Block Design Scores (N = 2,994)

	WISC subtest	
Familial variable	Vocabulary	Block Design
Family income	.34**	.21**
Mother's working status	−.02	−.03
Father's education	.44**	.27**
Mother's education	.43**	.29**
Number of older siblings	−.09**	−.01
Number of younger siblings	−.21**	−.13**
Preschool education	.20**	.18**
Time spent reading	.24**	.14**
Time spent with friends	−.06	−.03
Time spent alone	.08	.07
Number of activities	.17**	.12**

** p < .01.

Note. *Mother's working status* is the usual activity of the mother: 1 = mother works full-time, 0 = mother does not work full-time. *Preschool education*: 1 = attended kindergarten or nursery school, 0 = did not attend kindergarten or nursery school. *Time spent reading* is the parental estimate (in minutes) of the amount of time the child spends reading either magazines or books on a usual day. *Time spent with friends* is the parental estimate (in minutes) of the amount of time the child spends in the company of friends on a usual day. *Time spent alone* is the parental estimate (in minutes) of the amount of time the child spends playing alone on a usual day. *Number of activities* is the parental estimate of the number of group activities in which the child participates.

The data in this table are based on the National Health Examination Survey. The sample consisted of white children who had not experienced the death of a sibling and who resided in an unbroken home in which no one over 20 years old, other than parents, was present.
Source: Adapted from Mercy and Steelman (1982).

are impossible to assess in the individual case. Intelligence tests measure acquired behavior and yield an estimate of the child's current level of performance (or observed behavior). It is impossible to make inferences from this level of behavior to another level, termed "innate potential." We cannot observe potential—all we can observe is actual behavior. Furthermore, performance on any test reflects the complex and pervasive cumulative effects of education and upbringing. One cannot abstract an index or estimate of innate potential from the child's interactions with the environment or from something measurable in the child's behavior. In the assessment situation, the focus should be on what the child can or cannot do—and not on the child's innate potential.

INTELLECTUAL FUNCTIONING: PERSONALITY, SOCIAL, AND GENDER INFLUENCES

Developmental trends are evident in the personality patterns of children and adults who show increases in IQ. Gains in IQ are associated with independence and competitiveness during the preschool years; with independence, scholastic competitiveness, self-initiation, and problem-solving approaches during elementary school years; and with interpersonal distance, coldness, and introversion during adulthood. "These shifts may reflect the changing sources of educational experiences and motivation for intellectual achievement beginning with the family, then the competition with peers at school, and finally the self-education and intrinsic motivations that characterize maturity" (McCall, Appelbaum, & Hogarty, 1973, p. 71).

In an extensive survey of gender differences in cognitive abilities, Maccoby and Jacklin (1974) concluded that there is ample evidence that girls have somewhat greater verbal ability than boys and that boys excel in visual-spatial ability and mathematical ability during adolescence. There is no evidence that girls are better at rote learning, however, or that boys are better at higher-level cognitive processing tasks or at analytic tasks. Additionally, there is no evidence that girls are more affected by heredity or that boys are more affected by environment.

STABILITY AND CHANGE OF INTELLIGENCE

The stability of IQs obtained during the course of development is a function of measurement factors, genetic factors,

and environmental factors (Ausubel & Sullivan, 1970). We will now consider how each of these factors relates to IQ constancy—the extent to which IQs fluctuate from one age to another.

How Measurement Factors Affect IQ Constancy

The measurement factors that affect a child's initial test performance also affect subsequent test performance. These include types of items, placement of test items, errors of test administration and scoring, situational factors (for example, rapport, fatigue, physical well-being, attitude, motivation, attention span, frustration tolerance, self-confidence, level of aspiration, anxiety, and reaction to failure), variation in the standardization sample over the ranges covered by the test, and test-taking experience (for example, differential exposure to practice and coaching). Additionally, when a different test is used for the retest, any changes in scores may simply be due to the use of different tests. The tendency of extreme scores to regress toward the mean also affects the stability of test scores.

Gains on retest are likely to be larger on performance items than on verbal items because examinees can develop a set of problem-solving strategies that they can apply to the same or similar problems. Puzzles and block designs, for example, may be solved more easily on a repeated administration because the child is familiar with the materials and can re-employ more efficiently problem-solving strategies that proved successful. Another factor contributing to greater changes in performance scores is the importance of speed in determining a child's score. Many tests are timed, and bonus points are awarded for correctly completing the items quickly.

How Genetic Factors Affect IQ Constancy

Changes in IQs may be related to genetically based developmental trends. Some children have a continuous growth pattern, others have spurts and pauses, and still others have a discontinuous curve breaking at puberty and then increasing more gradually thereafter.

How Environmental Factors Affect IQ Constancy

Environmental factors contribute to fluctuations in intelligence test scores in two ways. First, physical and emotional factors (for example, physical illness, emotional trauma, or separation from parents), which are often transitory in nature, may affect a child's test performance. Second, changes in cognitive stimulation or motivation may alter the child's level of performance.

Prediction of IQs from Infant Tests

Tests of young infants assess sensorimotor functions; but at about 18 months of age, more cognitively oriented functions begin to be assessed. Thus infant tests cover a period in which important qualitative changes occur in the child's development. One difficulty in testing infants is their proneness to developmental spurts and lags, which decreases the reliability of the test scores.

To say that developmental tests in infancy bear no relationship to intelligence test scores obtained in childhood is something of an overstatement. Although for normal children correlations are low and not adequate for clinical application, they do attain a level of statistical significance at certain ages, especially after the age of 18 months (see Table 4-8).

Table 4-8
Median Correlations Across Studies Between Infant Test Scores and Childhood IQ

Age at childhood test (years)	Age at infant test (months)				
	1 to 6	7 to 12	13 to 18	19 to 30	
8 to 18	.06	.25	.32	.49	.28
5 to 7	.09	.20	.34	.39	.25
3 to 4	.21	.32	.50	.59	.40
	.12	.26	.39	.49	

Note. Decimal entries indicate median correlation. Marginal values indicate the average of the median *r*'s presented in that row/column. Median *r*'s were based on 3 to 34 different *r*'s and were obtained from 3 to 12 studies.
Source: Adapted from McCall (1979).

A longitudinal study of infants (Wilson, 1978a) tested at 3, 6, 9, 12, 18, and 24 months with the Bayley Scales and at 3 years with the Stanford-Binet: Form L-M showed larger intercorrelations as the infants became older (see Table 4-9), with the highest correlation occurring between 24 and 36 months of age (*r* = .73). The pattern of correlations, Wilson explained, was coherent and orderly. Additionally, the substantial gain in predictive power at 18 months suggested "an emerging dimension of cognitive functioning that becomes more fully operative with age, but that is only modestly related to earlier functions" (Wilson, 1978a, p. 138).

Predictive power of infant tests for developmentally disabled children. Infant Developmental Quotients that fall in the average or superior levels have more limited

Table 4-9
Intercorrelations Between Mental Development Scores at Ages 3 Months to 36 Months

			Months				
Months	3	6	9	12	18	24	36
3		.57	.44	.44	.37	.22	.20
6			.58	.53	.42	.25	.26
9				.57	.43	.30	.34
12					.55	.43	.38
18						.61	.57
24							.73

Note. N is between 177 and 335 for each correlation.
Source: Reprinted, with a change in notation, from R. S. Wilson, "Sensorimotor and Cognitive Development," in F. D. Minifie and L. L. Lloyd (Eds.), *Communicative and Cognitive Abilities—Early Behavioral Assessment* (Baltimore, Md.: University Park Press, 1978), p. 138. Copyright 1978 by University Park Press.

predictive power than do those that are at mentally retarded levels. Willerman and Fiedler (1977), for example, found that infant developmental scores did not predict the unusual intellectual achievements of a group of gifted children tested at 4 and 7 years of age. The picture changes dramatically for developmentally disabled infants. In developmentally disabled children, correlations are much higher between infant test scores and childhood IQs, ranging in some studies from .50 to .97 (Broman & Nichols, 1975; Brooks-Gunn & Lewis, 1983; Fishler, Graliker, & Koch, 1965; Fishman & Palkes, 1974; Illingworth & Birch, 1959; Keogh & Kopp, 1978; Knobloch & Pasamanick, 1960; VanderVeer & Schweid, 1974; Werner, Honzik, & Smith, 1968). For example, infants with serious developmental handicaps (such as Down's Syndrome or a major congenital malformation) who have below-average scores on infant tests during their first 20 months of life, are likely to obtain low IQs at later periods of development. A majority (73 percent) of moderately to profoundly retarded infants, as assessed by the Bayley Scales, were still classified as severely retarded 1 to 3 years after the initial assessment (Brooks-Gunn & Lewis, 1983). Infants who score in mentally retarded ranges on developmental scales during their first year of life have a high probability of obtaining scores in the mentally retarded range during their school years. Infants with Developmental Quotients of 25 are likely to remain severely incapacitated.

The above findings are based on groups. *In individual assessment, it is imperative that a diagnosis of mental retardation never be made on the basis of a single test score in infancy.* Infants who are slow at an early age may gain rapidly at subsequent ages. Assessments of handicapped (or developmentally disabled) infants should always be followed by retesting when the child is older.

Relationship of predictive power of infant tests to ethnic and SES variables.   An extensive investigation of relationships between early, preschool, and school-age mental development and social class indices in black and white children was carried out by the Collaborative Perinatal Project (Broman & Nichols, 1975). The project involved administering tests at three different age levels—the Bayley Mental Scale at 8 months, the Stanford-Binet: Form L-M at 4 years, and the WISC at 7 years—to 14,665 white children and 16,293 black children.

The major findings of this large-scale investigation were as follows: (a) Mental development, measured by correlations of mental test scores at ages 8 months, 4 years, and 7 years, was similar in black and in white children, although the black children obtained lower IQs than did white children at both 4 and 7 years of age. (b) Correlations between social class indices (SES and maternal education) and IQs obtained at 4 and 7 years of age were higher among white children than among black children. (c) Bayley Mental Development scores, although not highly related to IQs obtained at 4 and 7 years of age, were good predictors of severe mental retardation at 7 years of age. (d) A curvilinear relationship was found between social class indices and intellectual level at 7 years of age. That is, families of children with IQs below 50 had higher social class indices than did families of children with IQs between 50 and 90. The curvilinear relationship (see Figure 4-1) probably occurred because profound retardation is usually a result of genetic factors or brain damage and thus is independent of SES, maternal education, and other demographic factors. Mild mental retardation, however, is not independent of these factors.

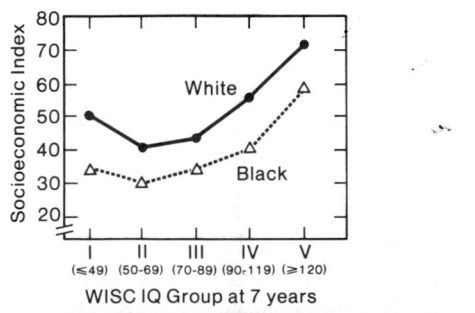

Figure 4-1.   Relationship between socioeconomic status and WISC IQs at 7 years of age. Adapted from Broman and Nichols (1975).

The Relationship of Visual Novelty Preference During Infancy to Later Intelligence

Measures of the visual novelty preference of infants between 3 and 7 months of age have been found to correlate moderately—in the range of .33 to .60—with cognitive measures obtained at 2 to 7 years of age (Fagan, 1984b; Fagan & Singer, 1983). In order to measure visual novelty preference (also referred to as visual recognition memory), researchers expose an infant to a target stimulus until a predetermined amount of fixation time has been accumulated. The target stimulus is then paired with a novel stimulus. The novelty preference score is the time the infant spends looking at the novel stimulus. Brighter infants spend more time with the novel stimulus.

These findings, Fagan (1984a) believes, support the view that intelligence is *continuous over age*, contrary to the prevailing notion that what might be considered intelligent behavior in infancy is discontinuous with later intelligent behavior. He provides the following hypothesis to account for the continuity position:

What is the basis for intellectual continuity over age? My assumption is that the basis of continuity lies in the similarities in the processes underlying early visual novelty preferences and tests of later intelligence. In other words, I assume that the manner in which infants distribute their attention to novel and previously exposed stimuli reveals the operation of processes employed by older children and adults in solving intelligence tests. The ability to detect similarities among otherwise diverse stimuli, for example, is a basic intellectual process. The solution of various tasks such as defining similarities and differences and solving analogies on standard intelligence tests requires the ability to abstract common features. Consider the perceptual learning history of a child required to point to the correct picture when asked to identify a particular object on the Peabody Picture Vocabulary Test. At some time in the past, that child must have noted particular attributes common to different instances of that object. He must have also noted features distinguishing that object from other objects. In addition, features invariant across objects in that set would have to be perceived. The detection of an invariant pattern would be necessary so that the object would be identified as such regardless of distinguishable but non-defining transformations. Detection of invariants would also be necessary for the child to realize that various representations could signify the same object. Information across different sense modalities signifying the same object would be abstracted as well. Finally, abstraction of the features common to objects in the class would lead to the formation of a mental representation such as a prototype which could ultimately be associated with and evoked by a word for the object. (p. 3)

Fagan (1984a) suggests that visual novelty preference provides a valid measure of infant intelligence that can be useful in understanding mental retardation and the origins of cognition. Further work by other investigators will be needed to shed more light on this interesting method of studying possible early manifestations of intelligent behavior.

Childhood IQs as Predictors of Adult Educational and Occupational Success

IQs obtained for a sample of children between 3 and 18 years of age were found to be significant predictors of educational and occupational status at 26 years of age or older (McCall, 1977). The correlations between IQ and attained educational and occupational success rose until 7 to 8 years of age and remained fairly stable thereafter at about .50. IQs obtained by the age of 5 were found to correlate highly with adult IQs (.50 and higher).

Comment on Stability and Change of Intelligence

The constancy of the IQ is greatly influenced by the age of the child at initial testing and by the length of the interval between the test and the retest. *The older the child is when first tested and the shorter the interval is between tests, the greater the constancy of the IQ.* Infant scales have limited predictive power, except for handicapped children, because the items they contain are primarily of a perceptual-motor nature. Preschool intelligence tests have more content reflecting cognitive ability, and therefore they have greater predictive value. Even more stable correlations are found between IQs obtained after 5 years of age and those obtained in adulthood. Generally, whereas IQs obtained prior to 5 years of age must be interpreted cautiously, IQs tend to remain relatively stable from kindergarten on, although individual fluctuations may be great, with children with high IQs showing greater amounts of change than children with low IQs (McCall et al., 1973).

Although there are fluctuations in test scores, most children tend to retain a similar position relative to their age group. The IQ of any given child may change as much as 20 points, but for most children measured intelligence remains relatively stable after 5 years of age (Zigler, Balla, & Hodapp, 1984). *In spite of high test-retest correlations, in assessing individuals it is necessary to conduct frequent and periodic testing if test scores are to be used for guidance or placement decisions.* There is sufficient variability in individual growth patterns to warrant evaluation at the time decisions are to be made.

Much of the constancy of the IQ is related to the invariance of genetic factors; the relative stability of the environment for any particular individual; developmental

irreversibility (current developmental status exerts a strong influence on future development); and the overlap of abilities measured by intelligence tests at different ages (Ausubel, Novak, & Hanesian, 1978). Any long-term predictions must take into account that unassessed traits or unpredictable unusual future circumstances may radically alter the course of an individual's intellectual development. Consequently, caution must be used in the assessment of individuals, especially in predicting future levels of intellectual functioning.

DISTINCTIONS BETWEEN INTELLIGENCE TESTS AND ACHIEVEMENT TESTS

Both intelligence tests and achievement tests sample aptitude, learning, and achievement to some degree, and both sample responses in the child's repertoire at the time of testing. The two types of tests differ on a number of dimensions, however (Humphreys, 1971). Intelligence tests are broader in coverage than achievement tests and sample from a wider range of experiences. Because intelligence tests assess learning that occurs in a wide variety of life experiences, they are more valid measures of future performance than are achievement tests. Achievement tests, such as reading and mathematics tests, are heavily dependent on formal learning acquired in school or at home. They appear to be more culture-bound and to sample more specific skills than do intelligence tests. Intelligence tests stress the ability to apply information in new and different ways, whereas achievement tests stress mastery of factual information. Intelligence tests, consequently, measure less formal achievements than do achievement tests.

CRITERION-REFERENCED VS. NORM-REFERENCED TESTING

Norm-referenced testing, as we saw in Chapter 2, is used to evaluate an individual's performance in relation to the performance of others on the same measure. The individual's performance is compared with that of some normative group. *Criterion-referenced testing,* on the other hand, is used to identify an individual's status with respect to an established standard of performance; it measures levels of mastery. Individuals' performances are compared to some established criterion, rather than to other individuals.

Criterion-referenced tests provide information relevant to instructional decisions, such as whether a child is ready to proceed to the next level of instruction; whether there are certain subskills that require more attention than others; and which curriculum materials might best help the child master the necessary skills.

For instance, a series of tests can be developed with four levels of reading mastery:

I. Ability to read beginning-level basal readers and most of the curriculum materials found in grades one and two.

II. Ability to read all levels of basal readers and most of the curriculum materials found in elementary schools.

III. Ability to read most newspapers and most of the curriculum materials found in high school.

IV. Ability to read college-level material.

The following statements illustrate criterion-referenced interpretations:

• "Jim can read 90 percent of the material at Level II of the reading mastery program."

• "Bill can spell 80 percent of the words in the unit word list."

• "Judith can subtract three-place numbers without error."

These statements refer to performance on a given criterion without reference to the level of performance of other members of the group. A mastery level of performance is set as part of the instructional objective, and the child's test performance is described relative to this level (for example, mastery at the 90 percent level).

Comparison of Criterion-Referenced and Norm-Referenced Measurement

Criterion-referenced measurement differs from norm-referenced measurement primarily in the scale used for measurement. In norm-referenced measurement, the middle of the scale is usually anchored to an average level of performance for a particular norm group, with the units of the scale being a function of the distribution of scores above and below the average level. In criterion-referenced measurement,

. . . the scale is usually anchored at the extremities—a score at the top of the scale indicating complete or perfect mastery of some defined abilities, or at the bottom indicating complete absence of those abilities. The scale units consist of subdivisions of this total scale range. (Ebel, 1971, p. 282)

Criterion-referenced and norm-referenced tests are further compared in Table 4-10.

Difficulties Associated with Criterion-Referenced Testing

Criterion-referenced testing has some limitations, especially when emphasis is placed on specific facts rather than on structures of understanding. Rote learning may take the place of understanding. Additionally,

Criterion-referenced testing has the appeal of novelty and innovation. It may seem to offer more meaningful measures of achievement, as well as escape from some of the problems inherent in norm-referenced measurements. But it creates special problems. There is the problem of first selecting and later defending a unique set of ideas and abilities which each student will be expected to learn. There is the problem of rational definition of a particular level of test performance which will indicate attainment of each objective. There is the problem of repeated testing of those who do not reach the criterion at first, plus the problem of creating multiple parallel test forms for use in the repeated testing. There is the problem of reporting only two levels of an achievement that exists at many different levels, and of treating an achievement ever so slightly above the criterion as completely satisfactory, while an achievement ever so slightly below is treated as completely unsatisfactory. There is the problem of producing, distributing, and using detailed, bulky, and quite ephemeral reports on which objectives a particular student achieved and which he did not. (Ebel, 1975, p. 85)

Although traditional concepts of validity are relevant for criterion-referenced testing, few tests have shown such validity (Nitko, 1980). For example, creators of tests referenced to learning hierarchies need to demonstrate that improved learning occurs when the implied prerequisite sequence is used.

Comment on Criterion-Referenced Measurement

Criterion-referenced tests may diminish the feeling of competition among children because the children are competing with themselves in striving to advance their own skills, regardless of where they stand in relation to other children. But criterion-referenced tests cannot eliminate all competition among children because those performing at lower levels are likely to feel inferior to those who are at more advanced levels. Substituting "levels of ability" for "percentile ranks" may be simply a cosmetic act. It is doubtful whether the replacement of norm-referenced tests with criterion-referenced tests could eliminate invidious comparisons among children.

Table 4-10
Comparison of Criterion-Referenced and Norm-Referenced Tests

Norm-referenced tests	Criterion-referenced tests
1. Test scores are interpreted in relation to established norms.	1. Which, or how many, of a set of specific achievement goals the individual has reached is reported.
2. The domain of a particular achievement area is broadly sampled.	2. A limited number of specifically defined goals are sampled.
3. A concise summary is provided of less clearly defined areas of achievement.	3. Specific and detailed information on pupil achievement is reported.
4. Individual excellence in achievement is encouraged and rewarded.	4. Mastery of specific subject matter by all pupils is emphasized.
5. Learning is treated as the building of a structure of numerous relations among concepts.	5. Learning is treated as the addition of separate, discrete units to the collection of things learned.
6. Relatively high variation in scores is needed to discriminate effectively between individuals.	6. Score variation is relatively low. The test can be useful even if all individuals reach the criterion.
7. Reliability is estimated using test-retest, parallel form, or homogeneity methods (see Chapter 2).	7. Reliability is estimated by the consistency with which a set of items for an objective classifies individuals as "masters" or "non-masters."
8. Validity is established by reference to external criteria (see Chapter 2).	8. Validity is established by comparing the content of each item with the statement of objective.
9. A large number of different items are used to sample a range of skills and concepts.	9. Related to each objective are a number of similar items designed to test a narrowly defined skill or concept.
10. Items are answered correctly by about 50 percent of the group; this difficulty level effectively spreads out the distribution of scores.	10. Items tend to be easy, and the spread of correct responses is relatively small.

Source: Adapted from Ebel (1975) and Satterly (1981).

Both norm-referenced testing and criterion-referenced testing have relatively distinct roles to play, and both contribute to our understanding of a child's abilities. They should be viewed as complementary methods of evaluation. Criterion-referenced procedures are useful for assessing specific skill areas in order to evaluate behavior relative to behavioral objectives and individual teaching programs, whereas norm-referenced procedures are especially useful in measuring individual differences between children in order to determine levels of relative proficiency.

MENTAL AGE

Mental age can be thought of as a developmental measure that indicates a level of cognitive functioning. It can also be conceived of as a level of achievement that may indicate a child's readiness to learn and level of cerebral development (Jensen, 1979b).

MA Defined

$$\frac{MA \times 100}{CA} = IQ$$

Mental age (MA) divided by chronological age (CA) and multiplied by 100 produces the ratio IQ, which was used on the 1916 and 1937 versions of the Stanford-Binet Intelligence Scale and is still used on some tests. The MA provides an age-equivalent for the child's raw score, whereas the IQ indicates a child's performance relative to that of children who are at his or her own chronological age. Mental age is defined as the degree of general mental ability possessed by the average child of a chronological age corresponding to that expressed by the MA score. For example, a child who receives an MA score of 6 is seen as having the general mental ability of an average 6-year-old child.

Limitations of MA Scores

Chapter 2 discussed limitations of MA scores and test-age equivalent scores from a statistical viewpoint; other considerations are discussed in this section.

First, differences between MA units are not the same throughout the developmental period because mental growth is not a linear function. For example, the difference between MAs of 2 and 3 is much greater than that between MAs of 10 and 11. At about 5 years of age the rate of mental growth begins to decrease, and by about the age of 13 the concept of mental age has little meaning.

Second, the same MA may mean different things with respect to different children. Two children with the same MA may have different skills, different interests, different experiences, different academic successes and failures, and different rates of progress in school. All of these factors must be considered when MAs or test-age equivalents are used.

Comment on MA Scores

The mental age (MA) or age-equivalent score obtained on an intelligence test provides useful information about the child's repertoire of knowledge; it reflects a more absolute level of performance than does the IQ, as it is the test-score equivalent of the 50th percentile rank in a given norm group. In contrast, the standard score on an intelligence test (or Deviation IQ, Composite Score, or IQ) provides no information about the size of the individual's repertoire of skills and knowledge. Unlike other writers, Humphreys (1985) believes that the MA concept should be retained because it provides some understanding, albeit coarse, of the individual's absolute level of performance. I support Humphreys's position.

CORTICAL EVOKED POTENTIAL, EEG RECORDINGS, AND INTELLIGENCE

Since the beginning of electroencephalography, a relationship has been sought between brain-wave patterns and level of intelligence (and motor abilities). The cortical evoked potential provides a measure of neural efficiency or spread of neural information processing. The two main sensory modalities that have been investigated are the visual and the auditory, with most research concentrating on the visual modality. When the cortical evoked potential is derived from the visual modality, it is referred to as the *visual evoked response* or *VER*. VER latencies are obtained by placing electrodes over the occipital lobes of the cortex, presenting flashes of light to the child's eyes, and then finding the latency of the response from the brain-wave recordings. The evoked response is obtained by computer analysis of repeated responses to the flashes of light.

The VER is a useful measure of brain activity arising from sensory stimulation.

Overall, the research literature presently indicates that the VER is largely unrelated to intelligence test scores, although it is related to infant test scores (Butler & Engel, 1969; Davis, 1971; Engel & Fay, 1972; Engel & Henderson, 1973; Griesel & Bartel, 1976; Henderson & Engel, 1974; Jensen & Engel, 1971; Perry, McCoy, Cunningham, Falgout, & Street, 1976; Rhodes, Dustman, & Beck, 1969). Because the technical problems associated with standardized recordings have not been completely solved, future research may not support present findings. Even in those instances in which a significant relationship between VER and IQ has been reported, the VER accounts for such a small proportion of the variance that it would be useless for the individual appraisal of intelligence. The VER, however, may be related to intelligence in neurologically impaired children, and there is some evidence that the VER is related to the developmental status of the central nervous system.

Combining electroencephalographic recordings (EEG) obtained during verbal and perceptual tasks with WISC-R, Bender-Gestalt, and other test scores improved identification of children's visuospatial reasoning ability, but not their verbal reasoning ability (Grunau, Purves, McBurney, & Low, 1981). EEG measures thus may be more sensitive indicators of visuospatial ability than of verbal ability. As age increases, the high-frequency content of the EEG also increases; brain damage causes a lowering of the frequency content (John, Ahn, Prichep, Trepetin, Brown, & Kaye, 1980).

REACTION TIME, MOVEMENT TIME, INSPECTION TIME, AND INTELLIGENCE

Early attempts by Galton and Cattell to use reaction time as a measure of intelligence were unsuccessful. Recently there has been a revival of interest in reaction time as a measure of intelligence. Current interest is focused on studying the speed of information processing through a variety of procedures (Vernon, 1983). Measures include *speed of encoding, or inspection time* (the examinee must decide which of two vertical lines, exposed for an extremely short period of time, is longer); *efficiency of short-term memory scanning* (the examinee must decide whether a digit in a string of digits is a new one or one that has been presented previously); *speed of information retrieval from long-term memory* (the examinee must decide whether two words are the same or different); and *simple and choice reaction time* (the examinee must press a button when a light of a particular color appears). Dependent measures include *reaction time*, measured as the interval between stimulus onset and the lifting of the finger from the rest button, and *movement time*, measured as the time required to move the finger from the rest button to the response button.

Theory Behind Inspection Time

Inspection time is thought to reflect rate of perceptual processing. The theory connecting inspection time and intelligence is that individuals who are capable of taking in information rapidly have a learning advantage. A useful measure of inspection time is λ (lambda), which is defined "as the minimum exposure duration at which discrimination in an easy task is virtually error-free" (Nettelbeck, 1985, p. 137). Lambda is weakly associated with IQ in the normal range of intelligence, but more strongly associated with IQ in the range below 80. These findings suggest that there may be differences in the efficiency of certain elementary information-processing skills (such as mental speed involved in inspection time tasks) between mentally retarded and normal children, but not between dull normal and bright normal children (Hulme & Turnbull, 1983). It also may be that (a) mental speed is a component of intelligence only up to some threshold value (the speed of the mental operations tapped by the inspection time task is a limiting factor up to a point, but beyond this point increases in speed have little effect on intellectual performance), or (b) inspection time and intelligence are both related to a third variable, such as neurological functioning. Further research is needed to determine the most appropriate explanation for the pattern of correlations between inspection time and intelligence.

The use of measures of inspection time as a supplement to standard intelligence tests may be premature. Inspection time measures are not valid measures of intelligence in the general population; also, they account for only a small part of what is considered to be intelligence. Additionally, inspection time measures are not highly reliable because of measurement difficulties.

Research on Speed of Information Processing

Speed of information processing is in part dependent on the complexity of the stimuli and the amount of information presented to the individual. An increase in either of these variables increases reaction time. Significant negative correlations have been found between reaction time

and intelligence test scores in a variety of groups, including nonexceptional and retarded children (Carlson, Jensen, & Widaman, 1983). Longstreth (1984), however, questions the validity of reaction-time studies, pointing out problems involving order effects, attention effects, and response bias effects.

Other findings bring into question whether the speed with which complex information is processed is a decisive component of general intelligence. Ruchalla, Schalt, and Vogel (1985) found that in a sample of young adults speed of processing correlated strongly with tests of short-term memory, ability to concentrate, and spatial ability, but only trivially with tests highly loaded with *g*, such as verbal ability, abstract thinking, and mathematical reasoning. Whyte, Curry, and Hale (1985) reported that inspection time was not related to IQ in a small sample of 9- to 11-year-old dyslexic and normal children. Further work is needed before firm conclusions can be drawn about the relationship between speed of information processing and intelligence.

THE TESTING OF INTELLIGENCE: PRO AND CON

Intelligence testing has generated much controversy in recent years. Some maintain that the development of intelligence tests is one of the most significant contributions of the field of psychology; others believe that intelligence tests have many serious shortcomings. Table 4-11 summarizes some of the major assets and limitations of intelligence tests, and Table 4-12 presents some important misconceptions about intelligence tests and intelligence testing.

Intelligence tests have been criticized because IQ does not adequately relate to many measures of everyday functioning. But can any one measure be expected to correlate highly with behaviors that are multidetermined? Individuals with the same IQ vary widely in their social competence, as well as in the expression of their talents (Zigler & Farber, 1985). These divergencies result from personality and motivational factors that arise from each individual's unique socialization history. For example, the retarded child who is restricted and catered to may never develop independence, whereas "the gifted child whose talents are unappreciated or viewed as troublesome may bow to pressures to conform and become an...underachiever" (Zigler & Farber, 1985, p. 398). Because of the many nonintellective determinants of behavior, the IQ should not be expected to be a robust indicator of everyday functioning.

Table 4-11
Intelligence Testing: Pro and Con

Pro	Con
1. The IQ has a larger collection of correlates predictive of success in a wide variety of human endeavors than does any other variable.	1. Intelligence tests limit our understanding of intelligence and sample only a limited number of conditions under which intelligent behavior is revealed.
2. Intelligence testing is the primary leveler preventing the classes from hardening into castes.	2. IQs are used to sort children into stereotyped categories, thereby limiting their freedom to choose fields of study.
3. Intelligence testing has revealed unsuspected talents in many individuals and has improved educational opportunity.	3. Knowledge of their IQs may inhibit children's level of aspiration and affect their self-concept.
4. Intelligence tests provide standardized ways of comparing a child's performance with that of other children observed in the same situations represented by the test items.	4. Intelligence tests fail to measure the processes underlying the child's responses and are limited in the extent to which they reveal the underlying cognitive processes needed for successful test performance.
5. IQs may be regarded as a measure of the child's ability to compete in our society in ways that have economic and social consequences.	5. IQs are misused as measures of innate capacity.
6. Intelligence tests provide a profile of strengths and weaknesses.	6. The single IQ does not do justice to the multidimensional nature of intelligence.
7. IQs are excellent predictors of scholastic achievement.	7. IQs are limited in predicting occupational success.
8. IQs measure the effects of changes associated with special programs, treatment, and training.	8. IQs are limited in predicting nontest or nonacademic intellectual activity; the standard question format cannot capture the complexity and immediacy of real-life situations.
9. Intelligence tests assess individual differences and provide useful reflections of cultural and biological differences among individuals.	9. Intelligence tests are culturally biased against ethnic minorities.
10. Intelligence tests are valuable tools in working with handicapped children.	10. Nonconventional, original, or novel responses are penalized on intelligence tests.

Intelligence is a broad concept that reflects an individual's information-processing capacities and possession of useful knowledge. Intelligence tests measure only a part of a domain that reflects intelligent behavior. Test scores provide a statistical indication of the extent to which a person has critical skills and information, but they should *not* be directly equated with intelligence. Test scores are a useful index of ability, but they may reflect test-taking sophistication and personality and attitudinal characteristics to some extent as well.

Intelligence and the Social Order

Intelligence tests, as presently constituted, cannot be divorced from the social order of our society, which values excellence in judgment, reasoning, and comprehension over other kinds of excellence. Because they measure success in school, intelligence tests are value-laden. They represent such societally valued factors as schooling, verbal abilities, and abstraction and concept formation skills. These are important skills in industrialized societies, but they are not the only important abilities. Attempts are continually being made to find ways to measure and reward intellectual abilities and skills (for example, creativity) other than those currently associated with intelligence tests (also see Gardner's approach in Chapter 3). Such efforts are needed because our tests tap only part of the spectrum of human abilities. Still, intelligence tests generally do their job well. They predict success in school, are extremely useful in neuropsychological assessment, and measure some other important abilities and skills valued in many societies.

The real importance of the IQ is that it has something of a threshold character—below some very low point on the IQ distribution people do not function well in society, nor can any of their other possible latent talents be manifested.

There seems to be no other human defect . . . as severely limiting as a very low intelligence. Deafness, blindness, physical deformity, paralysis—all are not incompatible with achievement, athletic enjoyment, and self-realization. Very low intelligence, on the other hand, seems a different order of misfortune. . . . (Jensen, 1974b, p. 434)

A central criticism, perhaps at the heart of many other criticisms, is that intelligence tests are used to allocate the

Table 4-12
Some Misconceptions About Intelligence Tests and Testing

Misconception	*Comment*
1. Intelligence tests measure innate intelligence.	1. IQs always are based on the individual's interactions with the environment; they never measure innate intelligence exclusively.
2. Intelligence tests measure capacity or potential.	2. Intelligence tests do not measure capacity or potential. They provide information about the individual's repertoire of cognitive skills and knowledge *at a given point in time*.
3. IQs are fixed and immutable and never change.	3. IQs change in the course of development, especially from birth through 5 years of age. Even after 5 years of age, significant changes in intelligence can occur.
4. Intelligence tests provide perfectly reliable scores.	4. No intelligence test has perfect reliability. Test scores are only estimates of a person's ability. Every test score should be reported as a statement of probability (or odds): "There is a 90 percent chance that the child's IQ falls between _____ and _____."
5. Intelligence tests measure all we need to know about a person's intelligence.	5. No one intelligence test measures the entire spectrum of abilities related to intellectual behavior. Some tests measure verbal and nonverbal abilities, but do not adequately measure other areas, such as mechanical skills, creativity, and social intelligence. Other tests measure only verbal and nonverbal ability. Any test only *samples* the individual's repertoire of skills.
6. IQs obtained from a variety of tests are interchangeable.	6. Although there is some overlap among intelligence tests, IQs may not be interchangeable—especially when the standard deviations of the tests are different.
7. A battery of tests can tell us everything that we need to know to make judgments about a person's competence.	7. No battery of tests can give us a complete picture of any person's abilities.

limited resources of our society. Intelligence test results are used to provide rewards or privileges, such as special classes for the gifted, admission to college or advanced study, and employment. Those who do not qualify for these resources may misdirect their anger at the tests, because they see the tests as denying them opportunity for success. For reasons that are still unclear, the IQ has come to be associated not only with an individual's ability to perform certain tasks, but also with his or her essential worth as well: "To have a low IQ is seen as the equivalent of having low caste" (Hudson, 1972, p. 15). This mystique surrounding the IQ must be squelched; it has no constructive place in our society.

Limitations of Assessment Setting

Another important limitation associated with intelligence testing, alluded to in item 8 of Table 4-11, needs further elaboration. Because the intelligence test is administered in a controlled, standardized setting and usually in the examiner's office, there is little or no opportunity for the child to reformulate the problem, develop an original solution, delay the response, use library resources, seek advice, or settle for a less than optimal solution (Frederiksen, 1986). Additionally, (resources)

The cognitive processes that are involved in taking a test may depend not only on the format of the test and thus the mode of responding to a problem but also on such personal characteristics as the level of expertise of the [child] in the area of the problems posed and on the nature of the setting and situation in which the problems are presented. (Frederiksen, 1986, p. 451)

Future work in assessment should deal with these issues.

Value of Intelligence Testing

Intelligence testing is part of the science of human abilities. This science is young and developing. Although there are weaknesses in the technology of the science of human abilities, there is a solid scientific basis for the practice of mental ability testing (Carroll & Horn, 1981). Furthermore, the differential psychology of cognitive abilities can do much to improve the human condition. The robustness of current research on cognitive development augurs well for the future of intelligence testing.

The IQ obtained from standardized intelligence tests is extremely helpful in work with handicapped and nonhandicapped children. As the best available long-range predictor of outcome and adjustment, the IQ provides teachers and parents with a helpful timetable for planning a child's progress. Furthermore, because intelligence tests provide some measure of the child's developmental limitations and impairments, teachers and parents are able to develop individualized curricula within the limits of the child's level of development and developmental expectations.

A summary of major developmental trends associated with intelligence, based on tests and laboratory findings, is shown in Exhibit 4-1. The summary combines work from the fields of psychometric theory, Piagetian theory, and information processing. The findings confirm the importance of viewing intelligence from a multidisciplinary perspective.

Humphreys (1985, pp. 222–223) provides a useful summary of many of the issues addressed in this chapter:

There appears to be continuity in the development of intelligence from 12 months to 17 years. This development is along a single dimension on which children change both absolutely and relatively to each other during this time frame. This hypothesis accounts for the intercorrelations of test scores during the many occasions for which data are available.... Change proceeds smoothly and, apparently, inexorably. One must use different content to measure intelligence at 12 months and at 17 years, but it is not necessary to invoke the difference in content to explain the low correlation between intelligence test scores during this interval of time. The rate of relative change is most rapid early in development, but has become relatively level by the time of school entrance. The rate stabilizes, but change continues.

The construct of general intelligence that emerges *requires* one to infer a multiplicity of causes of individual differences. One subset of these causes is certainly the many genes involved. There is widespread agreement that the inheritance of intelligence is polygenic. Although these genes are largely fixed at the time of conception, there is no reason to consider their resultant an entity. To the extent that there are genetic determinants of instability, individual genes in the complex may be "coming on line" at different times during development. It is also clear that there are environmental determinants of the intellectual repertoire, and there are both genetic and environmental determinants of the many structures within the central nervous system. Both sets of determinants affect how those structures are used in the acquisition of the behaviors sampled by standard intelligence tests.

Du Bois (1972, p. 55) concluded from his study of the testing movement that

Whether measurement leads to an increase in educational opportunity depends on administrators of education programs as well

Cartoon by Tony Hall from *Of Children, an Introduction to Child Development*, Third Edition, by Guy R. LeFrancois. © 1980 by Wadsworth, Inc., Belmont, California 94002. Reprinted by permission of the publisher.

Exhibit 4-1

Developmental Aspects of Intelligence—An Integrated Summary of Findings

---

1. Reliable quantitative measurements of children's general intelligence can be obtained from at least 4 or 5 years onward.

2. For children of these ages, measures of general intelligence possess considerable stability over a period of several years. The stability increases with the children's ages and decreases with the length of the interval between the tests.

3. These quantitative measurements of intelligence quite accurately predict children's future performance in school. Again, predictive accuracy increases with the children's ages and decreases with the length of the interval between the initial test and the eventual outcome measure.

4. Both parental personality and demographic variables predict the intelligence of older children, though the same cannot be said for children below 4 years of age.

5. The factor structure of intelligence, as obtained from IQ tests, is quite stable from 4 or 5 years onward, with the first two factors corresponding to verbal and performance components of the tests. Much greater changes in factor structure are seen in the first few years of life. Perceptual, motor, and recognition skills occupy prominent places in early assessments of intelligence but much lesser roles later on.

6. On many concepts, children progress through a sequence of qualitatively discrete, partially correct knowledge states prior to full understanding.

7. The sequence of partial understandings occurs in an invariant order. Given that two rules appear at some time in development, children progress toward the rule that more often predicts the correct answer in the environments that they encounter.

8. It is possible to teach conceptual understanding at considerably younger ages than those at which the concepts are usually mastered. However, there are also developmental differences in the benefits that children derive from the instruction.

9. Tasks that can be analyzed as being formally similar are often mastered at very different ages. Relative to the Piagetian norms, some tasks are mastered earlier than they should be, whereas others are mastered later. In addition, a wide range of tasks corresponding to a given concept can be devised, and the ages at which these tasks are mastered varies greatly.

10. At present there is little evidence for developmental changes in the capacity of short-term memory that cannot also be explained in terms of changes in strategies or the knowledge base. This statement means not that there are no changes in basic capacities but just that it is exceptionally difficult to provide unambiguous evidence of their existence.

11. There is a large increase between ages 5 and 10 years in the use of general mnemonic strategies, among them rehearsal, elaboration, and organization. The quality of children's implementation of the strategies also improves during this period. Use of such strategies can be taught to children younger than would ordinarily use them, but frequently the children revert to their original approaches when tested later in time or with different material.

12. Children possess considerable knowledge of their own memory limitations and of procedures that can be used to overcome the limitations. As yet, however, no simple links between this knowledge and memorial performance have been demonstrated.

13. Children's knowledge of specific content undergoes enormous development. This growth may account for changes in measures of basic capacities, strategies, and metamemory, rather than the other way around, as has traditionally been believed. Under some circumstances, differences in content knowledge can overwhelm all other age-related differences in memory: more knowledgeable children can remember more than less knowledgeable adults.

14. Children's use of logical reasoning skills is influenced by a variety of factors other than understanding of the logic itself: among them memorial skills, linguistic understanding, and ability to select the appropriate representation for the problem.

15. Developmental differences in problem solving may at times be due less to the particular component operations that are performed than to the resources that are allocated to each component that is performed. Comprehensive encoding may be especially important for efficient problem solving.

16. Concepts that to adults seem to constitute single entities may to children represent many separate concepts. For example, the notion of number conservation may be differentiated by young children according to the particular objects involved, the number of objects, the type of linear transformation, and the type of quantitative operator.

17. Understanding of higher-order principles may guide even very young children's performance in areas with which they have much experience, such as counting.

18. There is a strong relationship between children's initial knowledge and the lessons that they induce from learning experiences. If the learning experience does not discrim-

(Exhibit continues next page)

Exhibit 4-1 (cont.)

inate between their existing rule and the correct solution, they continue to use their existing rule. If the learning experience does indicate that their existing rule is incorrect, they will most often move toward the next higher rule in the typical developmental sequence if this rule is consistent with the learning experience.

19. A younger and an older child with the same initial rule for performing a task may derive quite different lessons from

the identical learning experience. One reason for this variation can be differential encoding; more comprehensive encoding is associated with greater ability to learn.

Source: Reprinted, with changes in notation, with permission of the publisher and authors from R. S. Siegler and D. D. Richards, "The Development of Intelligence." In R. J. Sternberg (Ed.), *Handbook of Human Intelligence*, pp. 959–960, Copyright 1982, Cambridge University Press.

---

as on the psychometricians who devise the tests. In the past 60 years the applications of psychological and educational measurements have increased enormously through the joint efforts of both administrators and test technicians. By and large these applications have improved educational opportunity.

SUMMARY

1. Intelligence plays a central role in the individual's adaptive potential.

2. Mental development is affected by genetic programming, maturational status, and environmental influences.

3. The genotype refers to the underlying genetic structure, whereas the phenotype refers to the observable expression of the genotype.

4. Intelligence appears to be, in part, under polygenic control—that is, under the control of the combined action of many genes.

5. Estimates of the heritability of intelligence—the proportion of variation in the population that is attributable to genetic differences in the population—vary from .30 to .50. There is a strong positive relationship between level of intelligence and degree of kinship, regardless of whether the individuals were reared together or apart.

6. Environmental influences on the development of intelligence indicate that the effects of perinatal stress and malnutrition are small.

7. Correlations between family status variables—such as parents' education, occupation, and income—and children's IQ are in the low .20s to .30s.

8. Specific home environmental factors—such as freedom to engage in verbal expression, language teaching, feedback, press for achievement, positive maternal mood, and time spent reading—are associated with higher IQs in children. Verbal ability appears to be more affected than spatial ability by home environmental factors. Home environmental factors may not be independent of parental IQ and education, however. These factors, in turn, may have a genetic linkage.

9. Children who show *decreases* in IQ during the preschool years tend to come from homes in which there is minimal stimulation and either a very severe or a very mild punishment regime, whereas those who show *increases* tend to come from homes with structure and enforcement, in which encouragement is given in a clear manner.

10. The confluence model, which postulates that family configuration is related to intelligence (for example, family size is negatively correlated with IQ), explains a very small amount of the total variance in IQ; the model remains controversial.

11. Inequality of schooling plays a minor role in individual differences in IQ—about 2 to 10 percent of the variance in IQ is associated with school quality.

12. Well-designed preschool enrichment programs significantly raise children's IQs, but the increase may not be maintained. Firm conclusions about the effectiveness of preschool enrichment programs await further research.

13. The environment influences how much of the genetic potential associated with intelligence is actualized.

14. No single environmental factor has a large influence on IQ.

15. The influences of genetic and environmental factors on an individual IQ (or on any test score) cannot be completely separated.

16. Personality factors associated with gains in IQ change with age; they include independence and competitiveness during preschool and elementary school years, and interpersonal distance, coldness, and introversion during adulthood.

17. Substantial evidence indicates that girls have somewhat greater verbal ability than boys, and that boys excel in visual-spatial ability and mathematical ability during adolescence. There is *no* evidence that girls are better at rote learning, that boys are better at higher-level cognitive processing tasks, that girls are more affected by heredity, or that boys are more affected by environment.

18. Stability of the IQ is affected by errors of measurement, by genetically based developmental trends, and by environmental factors.

19. Correlations between Developmental Quotients obtained

on infant tests and IQs obtained later in childhood tend to be very low for those with average or superior intelligence. For developmentally disabled children, however, correlations tend to be substantial between IQs obtained in infancy and those obtained later in childhood.

20. Correlations between mental development scores in infancy and in early childhood tend to be similar for white children and for black children.

21. Visual novelty preference scores obtained in infancy correlate in the range of .33 to .60 with cognitive measures obtained at 2 to 7 years of age.

22. The correlation of IQs obtained at between 3 and 18 years of age with educational and occupational status at 26 years of age and older is significant (about .50 from age 7 on).

23. IQ constancy is greater when IQ is first measured after 5 years of age and when the interval between test administrations is short.

24. Although intelligence tests and achievement tests both sample learning, intelligence tests assess what has been learned in a wider variety of settings and measure less formal experiences than do achievement tests.

25. Criterion-referenced tests are useful for assessing specific skill areas in order to evaluate behavior relative to behavioral objectives and individual teaching programs, whereas norm-referenced tests are useful for measuring individual differences between children in order to assess levels of proficiency.

26. Mental age (MA) refers to the degree of general mental ability possessed by the average child of a chronological age corresponding to that expressed by the MA score. Limitations associated with the MA score include (a) MA score differences do not mean the same thing throughout the developmental period, (b) MA scores have limited meaning after age 13, and (c) the same MA may be associated with different levels of skill development in different children.

27. The measurement of visual evoked responses (VER) requires sophisticated computer technology. There is little evidence that VER is related to intelligence test scores.

28. Interest in reaction time as a measure of intelligence has been revived. Measures include inspection time, efficiency of short-term memory scanning, speed of information retrieval from long-term memory, efficiency of short-term memory storage and processing, and simple and choice reaction time. Research suggests that inspection time is strongly associated with IQ in ranges below 80, but weakly associated with IQ in the normal range. The study of speed of information processing and intelligence is hampered by methodological problems; thus no firm conclusions can be drawn about the relationship between these two variables.

29. Intelligence testing has generated much controversy in recent years. Opponents argue that intelligence testing restricts children's opportunities, places minorities in an unfavorable position, and sorts children into stereotyped categories. Proponents maintain that intelligence testing facilitates movement between social classes, reveals unsuspected talents in many individuals, and assists in the diagnostic process.

30. It is important to recognize that (a) intelligence tests do not measure innate intelligence or capacity, (b) IQs change, (c) IQs are only estimates of ability, (d) IQs reflect only a part of the spectrum of human abilities, (e) IQs obtained from different tests may not be interchangeable, and (f) a battery of tests cannot tell us everything we need to know about a child.

KEY TERMS, CONCEPTS, AND NAMES

Genetic programming (p. 62)
Epigenetic process (p. 62)
Heritability of a trait (p. 62)
Genotype (p. 62)
Phenotype (p. 62)
Polygenic model (p. 63)
Monozygotic (p. 63)
Dizygotic (p. 63)
Perinatal factors (p. 63)
Low birth weight (p. 64)
SES (p. 64)
Malnutrition (p. 65)
Wolf's study of home environmental variables (p. 65)
Marjoribanks's study of home environmental variables (p. 65)
Hanson's study of home environmental variables (p. 65)
Wilson's study of home environmental variables (p. 66)
Mercy and Steelman's study of familial variables (p. 67)
McCall, Appelbaum, and Hogarty's study of home
    environmental variables (p. 67)
Zajonc (p. 67)
Confluence model (p. 67)
Compensatory education (p. 68)
Gender differences in cognitive abilities (p. 70)
IQ constancy (p. 70)
Prediction of IQs from infant tests (p. 71)
Visual novelty preference during infancy (p. 72)
Distinction between IQ tests and achievement tests (p. 73)
Criterion-referenced tests (p. 73)
Norm-referenced tests (p. 73)
Mental age (p. 75)
Cortical evoked potential (p. 76)
Visual evoked response (VER) (p. 76)
Reaction time (p. 76)
Movement time (p. 76)
Inspection time (p. 76)
Lambda (p. 77)
Developmental trends and intelligence (p. 81)

STUDY QUESTIONS

1. Discuss the interaction of genetic programming, maturational status, and environmental influence.

2. Discuss hereditary influences on intellectual functioning.

3. Discuss environmental influences on intellectual functioning.

4. Compare and contrast hereditary and environmental influences on intellectual functioning.

5. Discuss personality, social, and gender influences on intellectual functioning.

6. Discuss factors that are related to the stability of and changes in intelligence.

7. What are some differences between intelligence and achievement tests?

8. Compare and contrast criterion-referenced and norm-referenced testing.

9. Discuss the concept of mental age.

10. What is known about cortical evoked potential and the measurement of intelligence?

11. Discuss the relationship between reaction time measures and intelligence.

12. Discuss the pros and cons of intelligence testing.

13. Discuss some misconceptions about intelligence tests and testing.

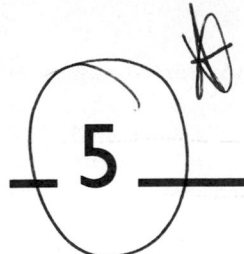

5

TESTING CHILDREN

Tests can enrich the teacher's insight or the therapist's understanding only when the details are looked at in relation to the child's experience in the test situation—what he was coping with and how.

—Lois B. Murphy

Establishing Rapport

Observing Children

Testing Infants and Preschool Children

Testing Ethnic Minority Children

Testing Emotionally Disturbed, Shy, or Delinquent Children

Testing Autistic Children

Testing Brain-Injured Children

Testing Mentally Retarded Children

Testing Physically Handicapped Children: General Suggestions

Testing Visually Impaired Children

Testing Hearing-Impaired Children

Testing Cerebral Palsied Children

Suggestions for Administering Tests

Examiner Characteristics

A Final Thought—Through a Child's Eyes

Summary

When you administer a test, you need to obtain the confidence and cooperation of the child, or else the results may not accurately reflect the child's abilities. The setting should be one that allows the child to demonstrate the best of his or her capabilities. Even before the examination begins, some children will wonder why they are being tested and how the results will affect their future. Children who feel apprehensive about the examination will need reassurance and support. During the examination, difficult questions may produce stress. You should help children through these and other difficult phases of the examination by using various empathic procedures, such as praising their efforts, making understanding comments, and explaining why they are being evaluated. With young children, you might simply begin by saying "We are going to do some things together" or "We are going to work on some fun things together."

Administering tests to handicapped children requires much skill and patience. Emotionally disturbed, autistic, brain-injured, and physically handicapped children present particular problems; such children will test the resources of even the most competent and experienced examiner. The assessment instruments and administrative procedures used must take into account the child's disabilities. Although the general testing procedures used for nonhandicapped children are also used for handicapped children, additional procedures are needed. This chapter describes some of these procedures, alerts you to problems that you may encounter in testing both normal and handicapped children, and provides ways to overcome common testing problems.

ESTABLISHING RAPPORT

When you first meet a child, greet him or her by first name and introduce yourself, telling the child your name. A brief and frank account of the purpose of the examination may be helpful, especially with older children. Opening statements should not be standardized but flexible and adaptable to meet each child's needs. Introductory talk can be kept to a minimum. Be confident and encouraging, making it clear that you want the child to do his or her best. Convey that you are sincerely interested in seeing the child succeed, yet unconditionally accepting and supportive in the event of failure.

Although the introduction is important, the building and maintaining of rapport is a continuous process that must be interwoven throughout the evaluation. While the child is working, observe inconspicuously. Do not stare or do anything that might distract, embarrass, or irritate the child. Try to be discreet when recording observations and scoring responses.

Helping the Child Feel at Ease

The child should be encouraged to respond to each question—to take a chance even when he or she is reluctant. By giving encouragement, you may both reduce the child's anxiety and help to sustain his or her interest level. When fatigue occurs, testing should be discontinued. If you sense that the child has experienced some frustration on a previous test item, you might say something like "That was a bit difficult, but no one is expected to get them all right. Now let's try another one." Because directions cannot cover every situation, be prepared to use tact and common sense when difficulties arise. Stereotyped and routine manners of interacting with children should be avoided.

In most cases it is appropriate to start immediately with the test material, facilitating rapport by giving brief, natural, and casual praise for the child's efforts rather than for answers. Children who are superficially cooperative should be encouraged to participate as fully as possible. Appropriate facial expressions and modulations of voice, in addition to supportive comments, may help. Early experiences of success in answering test questions will help children relax more quickly than almost any other procedure. The following incident illustrates how rapport can be established with a young child in a case in which it seems inappropriate to start with the test materials directly:

The clinician approached the child sitting tensely by her mother in the waiting room. Quietly introducing himself . . . , he extended his hand expectantly to the child and they disappeared into an examining room. We watched through a one-way mirror as the clinician explored the room with the child. He talked softly, almost in a whisper, as he itemized the objects and structures visible in the room. Still talking softly, in short, simple sentences, he opened a small box containing several plastic farm animals. Arraying the creatures on the table top, the clinician named them, purposely confusing the pig and the goat. Sara smiled slightly and shifted her chair closer. The clinician then proposed an animal parade and pranced the horse and the cow closer and closer to Sara. In a short time, the child was playing eagerly with the animals and chatting freely with the therapist. (Emerick & Hatten, 1974, p. 49)

Factors That May Affect Rapport

Examiner characteristics that lead to good rapport include empathy, genuineness, warmth, and respect for children.

Helping children maintain a sense of self-esteem and self-acceptance is a key to ensuring a successful relationship.

Rapport may be affected in a number of ways, some obvious and others not so obvious. For example, do not say "Good answer" or "That's right" or "You're doing great" every time the child responds. If you use excessive praise early in the test, you will be faced with a dilemma when the test questions become more difficult and failures more common. You must then either abandon your previous approach, with the obvious implication that praise is no longer deserved, or continue to use praise in situations where the child is aware that his or her performance is inadequate.

Encouraging children *for their effort* rather than praising them for the *results* of their effort, a subtle but important distinction, may help to reduce some of the problems associated with the use of praise. You can reduce blocking (involuntary inhibition of recall, ideation, or communication, including sudden stoppage of speech) on the part of the child by openly accepting the child's attitudes toward the examination, recognizing that the questions are getting harder, and verbally acknowledging the child's reactions.

Phares (1984, pp. 195–196, with changes in notation) provides the following valuable comments about establishing rapport:

There are many ways to achieve good rapport—perhaps as many as there are clinicians. However, no bag of "rapport tricks" is likely to substitute for an attitude of acceptance, understanding, and respect for the integrity of the client.... Such an attitude does not require that the clinician necessarily like every client. It does not require the clinician to become a friend of every client. It does not require the clinician to master an agreed-upon set of behaviors that is guaranteed to produce instant rapport. It does require that clients not be judged before the invisible sack of rocks that they carry about with them is fully weighed and its effects on their lives completely understood. One can scarcely discuss these matters without seeming to be maudlin. In addition, attitudes of understanding, sincerity, acceptance, and empathy are not techniques. To regard them as such is to miss their true import; to ask to be taught the appearance of sincerity, acceptance, and empathy is to confess their absence. When clients develop an awareness that the clinician is striving to understand their problems in order to help them deal with problems more effectively, then a broad spectrum of interviewer behavior is possible. Probing and even a certain amount of confrontation may be acceptable when rapport has been established. If the client accepts the clinician's ultimate goal in helping, a state of mutual liking is not necessary. The client will recognize that the clinician is not seeking personal satisfaction in the interview. Rapport is not, as is often thought by beginning students, a state wherein the clinician is always liked or always regarded as a great person. It is, rather, a relationship founded upon respect, mutual

confidence, trust, and a certain degree of permissiveness. It is neither a prize bestowed by an awed client nor a popularity contest to be won by the clinician.

Individual Variability Among Children and Examiners

Children are likely to have some idea about the purposes of tests and may react adversely to being tested. Older children usually recognize that they are being judged, and that the test holds the possibility that they may not do well. Such reactions may interfere with the children's performance or influence the responses they give. On such occasions positive reinforcement is particularly useful, along with brief explanations geared to alleviating the perceived apprehensions.

Countless variations preclude giving an examination that is always the same. Because some children react slowly and others quickly, each examination will vary in length of time. The number of follow-up questions that the child is asked will vary depending on the ambiguity of his or her responses. On tests where two trials are allowed, some children may need both trials and others only one. And some children need few, if any, breaks, whereas others may need many. On the examiner's part, variations in temperament, administrative skill, and scoring judgment can diminish the test results' objectivity. However, these examinee and examiner variables may not diminish seriously or significantly the overall reliability or validity of the results, for these sources of variability contribute to the standard error of measurement of the test score and have been taken into account, at least in part, in the standardization of the test.

The Ebb and Flow of the Relationship

Being relatively unprotected by age, experience, skill, and insight, children may attempt to control the test situation in indirect ways, whereas examiners usually try to accomplish their goals in more direct ways. For example, youngsters, who are seldom aware of their explicit role as examinees, may try to control the situation by requesting water frequently or by being silently negativistic; examiners may try to control the situation by never varying the test procedures. You must learn to recognize and understand these and other dynamics involved in the assessment relationship. Such understanding requires an awareness of nonverbal as well as verbal communications; where, when, and why the examination is occurring; and the child's age and background.

Although every attempt should be made to administer a standardized test to handicapped children, there will be occasions when this is not possible. Children who are actively psychotic, severely cerebral palsied, or markedly deficient in attention and motivation may prove to be untestable. In such cases, observations of the child's behavior should be recorded and formal testing rescheduled or abandoned. Overall you must strive to remain in control. When you lose control, the examination should be terminated.

Research Findings on the Examiner-Examinee Relationship

Fuchs and Fuchs (1986) conducted a meta-analysis of 22 studies involving 1,489 children on the effects of examiner familiarity (defined as children's acquaintance with the examiner or prior contact with a rather well-defined class of adults of which the examiner was a member) on children's individual test performance (IQ, speech/language, educational achievement, or similar tasks). The results indicated that examiner familiarity raised test performance by .28 standard deviation. The effect was greater (by about .51 standard deviation—7.6 points when the SD is 15 on the test) when children were of low SES, when they were tested on comparatively difficult tests, and when they knew the examiner for a relatively long duration. These results must be interpreted with caution because the effect may be associated with how the examiners scored the responses, rather than with changes in the examinees' performance (Fuchs & Fuchs, 1986). However, they do suggest that situational factors may affect the performance of children of low SES to a greater extent than they do the performance of children of high SES. More research is needed to determine the effects of situational factors on test performance.

OBSERVING CHILDREN

Important factors to observe about the child during the evaluation include the following:

- appearance (including physical condition, hygiene, and clothing)
- adjustment to the test situation
- degree of cooperation, effort, and attention
- attitudes toward the tests, the examiner (for example, dependence and reaction to authority), and the child's own abilities

- speech (including vocabulary level, fluency, articulation, and irregularities)
- thought patterns
- spontaneity and initiative
- general mood and sociability
- general response style
- responses to failure and success
- anxiety level
- activity level
- flexibility in shifting from one activity to another
- problem-solving approach
- impulse control
- fine and gross motor control
- distractibility

Skill in observing behavior requires training and practice; it does not arise automatically when you find yourself in a situation where observation is required. You must develop various kinds of skills. For example, in order to report accurately you must be alert, perceptive, and attentive to the child's behavior, making notes of observed behavior rather than relying on memory. Try to arrive at a general impression of the child, paying particular attention to the rapport that you have established and your reactions to the child. Then you need to be able to make appropriate inferences from your observations.

List of Behavioral Cues

The behavioral cues presented in Table 5-1 are designed to increase your observational skills. Although the thought of looking for so many cues may overwhelm those of you who are novice examiners, with experience you will learn to do so.

Behavior and Attitude Checklist

The Behavior and Attitude Checklist, shown in Table 5-2, provides a convenient way of recording the child's reactions in the testing situation. Like other checklists in this text, the Behavior and Attitude Checklist is not meant to cover all contingencies that may arise during the course of the examination. Some children may be described easily by the categories found on the checklist; other children may display behaviors that are not covered.

TESTING INFANTS AND PRESCHOOL CHILDREN

Most of us find young children inherently attractive. Young children are spontaneous, open, and direct in expressing

Table 5-1
List of Behavioral Cues

designed to inc. observational skills

Attitudinal Features

Attitude Toward You, the Examiner

1. How does the child relate to you (and how do you relate to the child)?
2. Is the child shy, frightened, aggressive, or friendly?
3. Is the child negativistic, normally compliant, or overeager to please?
4. Does the child's attitude toward you change over the course of the test?
5. Does the child try to induce you to give answers to questions?
6. Does the child watch you closely to discover whether his or her responses are correct?

Attitude Toward Test Situation

1. Is the child relaxed and at ease, tense and inhibited, or restless?
2. Is the child interested or uninvolved?
3. Does the child seem confident of his or her ability?
4. Is the child an eager or reluctant participant?
5. Are the tasks viewed by the child as games, as opportunities to excel, or as threatening sources of failure?
6. How well does the child attend to the test?
7. Is it necessary to repeat instructions or questions? If yes, does this need for repetition suggest a hearing problem, limited understanding of English, attention difficulties, poor comprehension, or an effort on the child's part to obtain more time to think about the question? Asking the child to repeat the question may provide clues about what factors account for the behavior (Zimmerman & Woo-Sam, 1985).
8. Is it easy or difficult to regain the child's attention once you lose it?
9. Does the child appear to be making his or her best effort?
10. Does the child try only when urged by you?
11. Does the child give up easily, or does he or she insist on continuing to work on difficult items?
12. Does the child's interest vary during the examination?
13. How does the child react to probing questions (for example, does the child reconsider the answer, defend the first answer, quickly say "I don't know," or become silent)?

Attitude Toward Self

1. Does the child have poise and confidence?
2. Does the child make frequent self-derogatory or boastful remarks, or is he or she fairly objective about his or her achievement?
3. How aware is the child of the adequacy of his or her answers?

Work Habits

1. Is the child's work tempo fast or slow?
2. Does the child appear to think about and organize answers, or does he or she give them impulsively or carelessly?
3. Does the child revise any answers?
4. Does the child think aloud or only give final answers?

5. Does the child write out answers on the table with a finger, continually ask you for clarification, or use other means to solve the problems?

Reaction to Test Items

1. What type of test item produces reactions such as anxiety, stammering, or blushing?
2. Are there any areas of the test in which the child feels more or less comfortable?
3. Is the child more interested in some types of items than in others?
4. Does the child block on some items ("I know, but I just can't think")? If blocking occurs, is it on easy items, difficult items, or all items?
5. Does the child need to be urged to respond? If yes, does the urging lead to a response? Does the response indicate that the child had the knowledge to respond correctly and merely wanted to be coaxed (Zimmerman & Woo-Sam, 1985)?

Reaction to Failure

1. How does the child react to difficult items? Does the child retreat, become aggressive, work harder, try to cheat, become evasive, or openly admit failure?
2. If the child becomes aggressive, toward whom or what does the child direct the aggression?
3. How does the child react to failure?
4. Does the child apologize, rationalize, brood, accept failure calmly, or become humiliated?
5. If humiliated, does the child express impotence or perplexity, suggesting loss of ability (Zimmerman & Woo-Sam, 1985)?
6. Can the child accept reassurance?

Reaction to Praise

1. How does the child react to praise?
2. Does the child accept praise gracefully or awkwardly?
3. Does praise motivate the child to work harder?

Language

1. How clearly does the child express himself or herself? Is the child's speech fluent, halting, articulate, inexact, or precise?
2. How accurately does the child express himself or herself? Are the child's responses direct and to the point, vague, evasive, free-associative, perseverative, or bizarre?
3. Do the responses reflect personal concerns or egocentrism?
4. Are the responses grossly immature?
5. If the child gives extraneous information, does this information suggest a compulsive need to cover all possibilities or is it completely irrelevant (Zimmerman & Woo-Sam, 1985)?
6. Does the child converse spontaneously or only in response to questions?
7. Does the child's conversation appear to derive from friendliness or from a desire to evade the test situation?

(Table continues next page)

Table 5-1 (cont.)

Visual-Motor

1. Are there any movements the child makes with his or her hands, feet, and face that are worth noting?
2. Is the child right or left handed?
3. Is the child's reaction time fast or slow?
4. Does the child proceed systematically or in a trial-and-error manner?
5. Is the child skillful or awkward?
6. Does the child execute bilateral movements skillfully or awkwardly?
7. Is the child aware of time limits on timed tasks? If yes, how does this awareness affect his or her behavior?

8. Does the child verbalize while performing tasks? If yes, are the verbalizations congruent with his or her actions?

Comparison of Verbal and Nonverbal Tasks

1. Are there differences in the child's reaction to verbal and nonverbal tasks (for example, is the child more anxious or more at ease with one type of task)?
2. Does the child understand the instructions for the verbal and nonverbal tasks equally well?

---

ideas, likes, dislikes, and desires. They are less predictable and may move through many more moods than older children, yet remain more responsive to how you handle the situation. Less restricted by social rules, they will give you feedback about your behavior and feelings. Simultaneously, they permit you to be more spontaneous and joyful than you would be with older children. (Material in this section as well as some material in a later section on suggestions for administering tests was adapted from Robinson and Harris, 1980.)

Compelling clinical considerations make work with young children rewarding. First, you have the opportunity to recognize and arrest potential problems before they mature. (You often can maximize growth even for a child with a central nervous system dysfunction, and you certainly can give significant assistance to family members who are coping with a difficult situation. The young child with developmental handicaps is less likely than the older child to have developed severe self-image problems; therefore, preventive efforts here may be beneficial later.) Second, you are usually working with parents who are highly motivated to do what is best for their child. Such parents would likely have done well with a nonhandicapped child, but probably need assistance in meeting the needs of a special child. In other words, in such situations you have much to do and much worth doing.

Despite the rewards of working with young children, such work is extraordinarily demanding. Fearful or shy children, particularly those who are not accustomed to being with strangers, will need special help. You must guide young children every step of the way, maintaining their attention and cooperation. Often you must not only tell but show the children what you want them to do. Their attention spans are short, and their moods are variable. Hedonism prevails—the younger the child, the more likely it is that he or she will do only what seems attractive at the

moment. Young children also are prone to be overwhelmed by primary physiological needs. Although an attractive task might override mildly unmet needs in an older infant or preschooler, you cannot do much with hungry or sleepy infants other than feed them or give them a nap.

Approach young children with confidence. If you are tense or apprehensive, children may sense these feelings and become resistant or negative, especially if you try too hard and too soon to get their cooperation. At the opposite extreme, prolonging the preliminary getting-acquainted time with overstimulating or entertaining play may interfere with testing. Take into account these considerations in establishing rapport. In any event, try to maintain rapport so as to complete the assessment in one session, if possible.

In talking with a young child, listen carefully to what he or she says (Miller, 1981). Be patient, and do not overpower the child with many requests. Allow some time for pauses, if needed. Follow the child's leads and maintain the child's pace. However, control the pace so as not to prolong the evaluation and cause fatigue. Recognize that the child's comments are important and require your undivided attention. Be warm and friendly in your conversation, consider the child's perspective, and keep in mind the child's age and level of cognitive development.

If you are not accustomed to spending much time with infants or preschoolers, observe several experienced testers. You will eventually develop your own style.

TESTING ETHNIC MINORITY CHILDREN

When you evaluate ethnic minority children, be sure that they understand the test instructions and questions. You

Drawing by Stevenson; © 1976 The New Yorker Magazine, Inc.

may want to repeat the instructions and questions, where permitted by the test manual. Additionally, you may want to ask the children to repeat the instructions or questions (again, where permitted) to ensure that they understand them. Be sensitive to nonstandard dialects. If a response suggests that a child misheard a word (for example, defining *slim* as "something that holds things together" [pin]), be sure to repeat the word.

Establishing rapport may be difficult with some ethnic minority children and with some children from lower socioeconomic backgrounds. Adolescents from these groups may be negativistic or ingratiating in the test situation. The following suggestions will help in dealing with these behaviors. (Also see Chapter 19 for information about testing ethnic minority children.)

Regardless of whether the young person is negativistic or ingratiating, one common characteristic that stands out in the testing situation is the language differences between the middle income examiner and the lower income examinee. Not only are there differences in articulation, vocabulary, and inflection, but there are also more subtle differences in phrasing and emphasis. The communication problem is a very real one that complicates testing and diagnosis.

    . . . a low income youngster may say something like "Humb" that turns out to be Humboldt Avenue, the street on which he

lives. Sometimes the misunderstanding can be amusing, as in the case of the young person who makes a face when he hears "espionage" as "spinach." These language differences are very apparent to the examinee as well as to the examiner, and they pose an additional barrier to effective rapport and valid testing. In my own work I find that it is important to confront the issue directly, to restate words I feel have not been understood, and to have the adolescent repeat words I could not comprehend. If the young person realizes the examiner really wants to understand him and is not making aspersions about his speech, such little confrontations can be most helpful in aiding communication. Minor confrontations are equally effective with negativistic and ingratiating adolescents. (Elkind, 1973, pp. 62–63)

TESTING EMOTIONALLY DISTURBED, SHY, OR DELINQUENT CHILDREN

Although most emotionally disturbed children do not feel threatened by tests, they do require extra patience and effort on your part. When children are difficult to test, you should explore procedures that will help them become less resistant. Beginning the test with performance-type materials may be helpful in cases in which children are reticent about speaking. (This procedure is also recommended for children with expressive language difficulties.) You may

Table 5-2
Behavior and Attitude Checklist

Behavior and Attitude Checklist

Child's name: _____   Examiner: _____
Age: _____   Date of report: _____
Test(s) administered: _____   Date of examination: _____
IQ: _____   Grade: _____

Instructions: Place an *X* on the appropriate line for each scale.

I. *Attitude toward examiner and test situation:*
   1. cooperative   __ : __ : __ : __ : __ : __ : __   uncooperative
   2. passive   __ : __ : __ : __ : __ : __ : __   aggressive
   3. tense   __ : __ : __ : __ : __ : __ : __   relaxed
   4. gives up easily   __ : __ : __ : __ : __ : __ : __   does not give up easily

II. *Attitude toward self:*
   5. confident   __ : __ : __ : __ : __ : __ : __   not confident
   6. critical of own work   __ : __ : __ : __ : __ : __ : __   accepting of own work

III. *Work habits:*
   7. fast   __ : __ : __ : __ : __ : __ : __   slow
   8. deliberate   __ : __ : __ : __ : __ : __ : __   impulsive
   9. thinks aloud   __ : __ : __ : __ : __ : __ : __   thinks silently
   10. careless   __ : __ : __ : __ : __ : __ : __   neat

IV. *Behavior:*
   11. calm   __ : __ : __ : __ : __ : __ : __   hyperactive

V. *Reaction to failure:*
   12. aware of failure   __ : __ : __ : __ : __ : __ : __   unaware of failure
   13. works harder after failure   __ : __ : __ : __ : __ : __ : __   gives up easily after failure
   14. calm after failure   __ : __ : __ : __ : __ : __ : __   agitated after failure
   15. apologetic after failure   __ : __ : __ : __ : __ : __ : __   not apologetic after failure

VI. *Reaction to praise:*
   16. accepts praise gracefully   __ : __ : __ : __ : __ : __ : __   accepts praise awkwardly
   17. works harder after praise   __ : __ : __ : __ : __ : __ : __   retreats after praise

VII. *Speech and language:*
   18. speech poor   __ : __ : __ : __ : __ : __ : __   speech good
   19. articulate language   __ : __ : __ : __ : __ : __ : __   inarticulate language
   20. responses direct   __ : __ : __ : __ : __ : __ : __   responses vague
   21. converses spontaneously   __ : __ : __ : __ : __ : __ : __   only speaks when spoken to
   22. bizarre language   __ : __ : __ : __ : __ : __ : __   reality-oriented language

VIII. *Visual-motor:*
   23. reaction time slow   __ : __ : __ : __ : __ : __ : __   reaction time fast
   24. trial-and-error   __ : __ : __ : __ : __ : __ : __   careful and systematic
   25. skillful movements   __ : __ : __ : __ : __ : __ : __   awkward movements

IX. *Motor:*
   26. defective motor coordination   __ : __ : __ : __ : __ : __ : __   good motor coordination

X. *Overall test results:*
   27. reliable   __ : __ : __ : __ : __ : __ : __   unreliable
   28. valid   __ : __ : __ : __ : __ : __ : __   invalid

---

need to meet with extremely shy children on more than one occasion before they are ready to respond to the test questions.

Delinquent children are likely to experience not only the situational stress induced by the authoritarian setting in which testing usually takes place (such as a juvenile detention center or jail), but also the real and immediate threat posed by the examination itself. Delinquent children may feel that they have everything to lose and nothing to gain by revealing themselves to you. Testing might lead to placement in an institution or foster home, or some other disposition they regard as punishment. As a consequence, they may seek to defend themselves against self-revelation. You must make every attempt to understand and work through these difficulties; if not, a valid picture of the delinquent's abilities will not be obtained.

TESTING AUTISTIC CHILDREN

The inherent handicaps of autistic children—such as their difficulty in establishing social relationships, their impaired communication skills, and their unusual responses to sensory stimuli—are likely to create difficulties in the testing situation and tax your resources as an examiner. These children may show little or no desire to do the tasks or to interact with you. Your normal methods of encouragement, such as smiling, may be ineffective (Baker, 1983). Talk slowly and simply to the autistic child—use short sentences and omit unnecessary words and complex grammatical forms. "Be concrete and specific.... If the child does not respond, repeat your question or direction in the same or a simpler way" (Lord & Baker, 1977, p. 184). Make sure you have the child's visual attention when you speak; visual cues help the child attend to and process your speech.

Learn About the Autistic Child's Communication Skills

Before the assessment begins, find out as much as possible about the child's communication skills from parents, teachers, and your own classroom observations. Consider the following questions (Lord & Baker, 1977):

- Can the child follow simple directions?
- Can the child answer yes or no?
- Does the child understand gestures or pictures or signing?
- Can the child read?
- Does the child have any individual idiosyncrasies, such as using code words or phrases ("bye-bye" for "no" or "look, look" for a favorite toy)?

Also,

Watch how people who know the child talk to him or her. Parents or teachers may assure you that the child understands everything they say. However, they may actually use frequent dramatic gestures or physically guide the child through tasks. When working with the child, experiment . . . with directions or questions of varying complexity. (Lord & Baker, 1977, p. 184)

Consider the Autistic Child's Resources

In conducting the assessment, consider the autistic child's preferences, abilities, handicaps, and individual style (Baker, 1983). Select tests that match the autistic child's developmental level. If necessary, start tests at a point well below the child's chronological age. Because of the autistic child's language problems, select tests that provide separate measures of language and nonlanguage skills or use a battery that contains both language and nonlanguage tests.

Language Deficits of Autistic Children

The language deficits of autistic children tend to manifest themselves in four ways (Baker, 1983).

1. Receptive language skills may be better developed than expressive language skills. A child may understand directions, such as "Give me the pencil," but not be able to say "pencil" when he or she wants it back.
2. Repetition of rote mechanical phrases or delayed echolalia (repetition of what you have said after a short delay) may not constitute meaningful language. A child who repeats the phrase "Go away" may not be able to use it in context. Just the same, immediate and delayed echolalia should not be viewed solely as empty repetition of words, phrases, or sentences with little or no social or communicative function. Research with a group of four autistic boys (Prizant & Duchan, 1981) indicated that many of their echolalic utterances showed evidence of comprehension, and that unfocused echoes were relatively rare, about 4 percent of the total number of utterances. The results suggest that immediate and delayed echolalia may have functional communicative elements and should be evaluated in the context of other communicative elements, such as eye gaze, posture, and gesture.
3. Language skills demonstrated in one setting may not generalize to another setting. For example, an object may be identified correctly only if it is like one the child has at home.
4. The child's language skills may not follow normal or expected developmental patterns. A child who does not talk still may be able to read.

Because of these language problems, you may need to use alternative methods to present stimulus materials to autistic children (Baker, 1983). Visually clear and self-explanatory materials are preferred, with gestures and direct physical guidance used when needed. Alternative modes of communication—such as pointing to pictures, sign language, written words, or other symbols—also may be used with children familiar with these methods. When you interpret test results and formulate recommendations, consider the autistic child's interest in completing tasks, ability to work independently, responses to social and behavioral interventions, strengths, and weaknesses.

TESTING BRAIN-INJURED CHILDREN

Brain-injured children may have a wide range of reactions during testing and show a variety of cognitive deficits (see Chapter 22). Some may react to the evaluation like normal children, whereas others may be more fearful or reticent or show emotional lability (easy arousal and shift from one emotion to another). If you know that a child is likely to be fearful of testing, be prepared to devote additional time prior to the formal testing to helping reduce the child's anxieties. You might try to gain the child's trust and confidence by working with him or her on simple puzzles or game-like materials. In this regard, it is often helpful to ask the parent about the child's reaction to learning that an evaluation was being planned.

With the brain-injured child, praise, encouragement to keep going, and constructive comments should be used more frequently than would be necessary with the normal child. Start the assessment battery with relatively easy tests so that the child will experience an initial success that may help him or her to feel more at ease. Give more difficult tests in the middle of the session, after initial apprehension is dealt with but before fatigue sets in.

On occasion, brain-injured children who know the answer to a problem may require an inordinately long time to organize an appropriate response. They may sit quietly for a long time before responding, or they may make tentative, hesitant responses. If these behaviors occur, permit the children to proceed at their own pace; do not urge them to respond. However, when the delay is excessive (over a minute), the problem should be repeated if standard administration allows, because the children may have forgotten it. You may also wish to repeat the item at a later point in the battery.

Before beginning the examination, minimize all potential sources of distraction in the testing room. The room should be quiet, with objects and toys removed. Some brain-damaged children, when confronted with difficult

material during the examination, may show perseveration (a persistent continuation of a response despite its inappropriateness given a change in test conditions), become emotionally labile, display inappropriate anger and hostility toward the materials or the examiner, withdraw from the situation, or give aberrant responses. These behaviors may represent attempts by the child to cope with a difficult situation. Although these behaviors may interfere with the goals of the examination, such reactions may serve as coping mechanisms to help the child avoid further stress.

Useful Procedures for Handling Perseverative and Avoidance Behaviors

Perseverative and avoidance behaviors can be minimized by using the following procedures:

1. Introduce testing procedures slowly and casually, and permit the child to play with toys similar to the test materials.
2. Avoid any suggestions of inadequacy in the child's performance.
3. Avoid sudden movements or noises.
4. Introduce new materials gradually, reassuring the child that the new activities will be pleasant.
5. When an emotional reaction occurs, do not overstimulate the child by trying to talk him or her into feeling better. Provide a relaxing respite to allow the child to work through his or her moment of anxiety.
6. If perseveration occurs, redirect the child.
7. If the emotional lability becomes too severe, stop testing and then sit quietly or go back to a test that the child has previously passed.
8. Remind the child, as often as necessary, of a specific test instruction, such as "Point to the one that is not alike," when he or she fails to recall the directions.

Useful Procedures for Working with Language-Impaired Brain-Injured Children

Communication will be difficult with brain-injured children who have speech or language difficulties. You may have to experiment with different communication methods, rates of communication, and types of content to find the most effective mode of communication. The following guidelines will promote better communication with language-impaired brain-injured children (Lubinski, 1981):

1. Face the brain-injured child when speaking with

him or her. Eye contact promotes attention and helps the child take advantage of nonverbal cues.

2. Alert the child that communication is about to occur. For example, say the child's name and a few words of greeting before introducing a topic, question, or instruction.

3. Speak slowly and clearly to the child.

4. Talk about concrete topics, such as objects and people in the immediate environment. The child may have difficulty comprehending abstract ideas.

5. Keep related topics together.

6. Use short, syntactically complete utterances. The language-impaired brain-injured child may respond more accurately to individual ideas than to a lengthy string. This concept is particularly important when you are giving the child instructions or asking the child to respond to questions.

7. Pause between utterances to give the child time to comprehend and interpret the message.

8. Check the child's comprehension before proceeding. Ask a question based on the information presented or have the child demonstrate his or her understanding of the information.

9. Repeat important ideas several ways. Redundancy helps comprehension.

10. Use nonverbal cues to augment spoken communication. Combining speech with nonverbal cues (such as gesture, signing, and pictures) may facilitate comprehension.

11. Ask questions that require short responses or that can be responded to nonverbally. This will allow the child to have a sense of active participation even if his or her responses are only single words or gestures.

12. Ask the child to repeat a word when speech is unintelligible or confusing. Although the child may become frustrated if asked to repeat a response many times, one or two repetitions can be helpful.

13. Encourage the child to express ideas in several ways. This may facilitate his or her own thinking and verbal production as well as your comprehension.

14. Encourage the child to use nonverbal cues, such as gesturing and pointing, to supplement attempts to speak about an object verbally.

15. Present the child with a multiple-choice array (if necessary) from which the response can be chosen. For example, in trying to get the child to identify the source of pain, you might ask questions like "Do you have a headache?" and "Do you have pain in your chest?" until the child signals his or her choice. You may want to point or gesture as you provide the alternatives.

16. Repeat what the child has said thus far as a means of focusing the conversation.

17. When the child becomes frustrated by communication failures, discuss the difficulty openly. Recognize that the child is having a difficult time and go on to another topic.

18. Monitor your nonverbal cues for indications of impatience or hostility. When the child has difficulty, try to show a relaxed demeanor. Nonverbal cues may tell the child a great deal about the effectiveness of his or her communication or lack of it.

TESTING MENTALLY RETARDED CHILDREN

In cases where mentally retarded children are uncooperative during the examination, evaluate the possible adaptive significance (as in the case of brain-injured children) of the uncooperative behavior. Negativistic behavior, for example, may enable the retarded child to maintain self-esteem in the face of difficult intellectual or social demands. Aggressive, hyperactive behavior may represent a child's emergency reaction to a novel situation involving difficult tasks. Echolalia may serve as a way of establishing and maintaining a relationship, even though it is maladaptive in other ways. Persistent questioning may represent an effort to ensure stability. Perseveration may help the child to manage the situation. Denial may be used to cover vulnerability.

You can take a number of actions to cope with these behaviors. If mentally retarded children try to reverse roles, you can agree to take turns asking questions and thereby help them become more at ease and diminish their need for control. Aggressive and hyperactive behavior may be reduced by beginning the examination with easy questions. To prevent children from being continually confronted with inadequacy, you can alternate between difficult tasks and easy ones. (Modifying test procedures, however, may produce less reliable results; see the end of this chapter for further discussion of test modifications.) As with all children, development of a warm, accepting relationship will probably reduce unacceptable behavior.

Evaluating Severely and Profoundly Retarded Children

Severely and profoundly retarded children may be difficult to evaluate because of self-stimulating behavior, self-injury, brief attention span, destructive behavior, temper tantrums, seizures, or noncompliance with instructions or requests. Additionally, conventional standardized tests may prove to be of limited usefulness because they have a limited number of appropriate items. If this is the case, you may want to use a functional assessment approach (see Chapter 21), which links assessment directly to instruction.

The challenge of assessing profoundly handicapped children is captured in the following commentary:

One might say that profoundly handicapped children constitute the . . . most challenging group of humans to assess. . . . The profoundly handicapped do not readily respond to one's immediate suggestions, commands, and gestures. They are often immobile, unattentive, disfigured, unpredictable, self-destructive, unresponsive, and lack comprehensible language. They do constitute a challenge to those who elect to interact with them. Sometimes, just when one decides that they are "untestable, unteachable, or hopeless," they respond by displaying the behavior which has been taught them for days or months! One asks what can be so rewarding as witnessing the child's first smile, or word like "milk," or a step forward, or dual response of "yes" or "no," or perhaps the swallowing of a semi-solid food? (Finkle, Hanson, & Hostetler, 1983, pp. 79–80)

Observing Profoundly Handicapped Children

When you observe a profoundly handicapped child, pay close attention to the following (Finkle et al., 1983):

• *Attention*. Does the child attend to things in his or her environment? If so, what things? To what degree? For how long?

• *Movement*. How does the child move from one part of the room to another? To what extent does the child need assistance in moving?

• *Handedness*. Which is the child's preferred hand? Does the child use two hands for activities?

• *Deficits*. What are the child's deficits?

• *Strengths*. What are the child's strengths?

• *Compensatory behaviors*. What compensatory behaviors are present?

• *Reinforcers*. What things in the child's environment serve as reinforcers?

• *Tonicity*. How would you rate the child's general health and physical strength?

• *Endurance*. How long can the child take part in an activity? How readily does fatigue set in?

TESTING PHYSICALLY HANDICAPPED CHILDREN: GENERAL SUGGESTIONS

Many of the techniques used with normal children can be used to test physically handicapped children, but their application is more demanding when the examinees are physically handicapped. Normal children often need little encouragement. They are accustomed to answering test questions and are likely to find the tasks challenging. Physically handicapped children, in contrast, may feel at a disadvantage in the test situation. Their physical limitations may make them appear clumsy and awkward, resulting in feelings of self-consciousness. They must cope not only with specific deficits associated with their disability (such as inadequate sight or hearing), but also with the anxiety and uncertainty of their parents. Anxiety associated with repeated medical examinations, peer difficulties, and related factors may also have influenced their affective development and, indirectly, cognition and learning. Their reactions to the test situation may depend largely on how they perceive themselves outside of the test situation. They may be aware of their handicaps and reluctant to expose their disabilities in the examination. Patience and encouragement will be required to elicit optimal performance.

Potential Sources of Difficulty in Testing Physically Handicapped Children

Testing physically handicapped children poses various problems. First, false impressions of the child's intellectual ability may be induced by communication difficulties, such as speech and hearing deficiencies. Second, because handicapped children may be unaccustomed to concentrated work for long periods of time, they may fatigue easily. Third, it may be difficult to decide whether attention difficulties, when present, are associated with physical deficiencies, with medication (if used), or with cognitive deficiencies. Fourth, it may be difficult to establish rapport with physically handicapped children who have heightened dependency. Fifth, physically handicapped children may feel extreme pressure when a test is timed. Finally, it may require increased effort to ensure that physically handicapped children understand the test directions fully.

In evaluating the cognitive abilities of physically handicapped children, do not confuse sensory deficits (for example, visual, auditory, or tactile deficits) with cognitive deficits. A child may have one or more sensory or motor difficulties and yet have adequate cognitive abilities. If timed tests are used, supplement them with tests that are not timed but that still adequately assess the children's skill repertoire. If children show undue stress when working under time pressure, it may be preferable to discontinue administering the timed test. *It is imperative that physically handicapped children not be penalized because of their sensory or motor deficits when they are administered ability tests.* The tests selected must be such that handicapped children can respond at their optimal level. The tests should assess their cognitive abilities and not the extent of their physical abilities.

Informal Evaluation of Sensory Functioning

Before you test a handicapped child, have the child's vision, hearing, physical condition, and health status screened. Ask the parents of severely handicapped children about signs, signals, or gestures that the child understands or uses and their meaning. Through observation and informal testing, determine the degree to which the child is physically able to respond to the tests. This involves informally evaluating the child's (a) vision, hearing, speech, sitting balance, and arm-hand use, (b) reading and writing skills (for a school-age child), and (c) ability to indicate yes or no by either verbal or nonverbal means. The informal evaluation can be done by observing how the child performs such tasks as describing a picture, putting a puzzle together, reading and then writing a short sentence, and responding to simple questions. During these activities, note how the child responds to your questions, performs motor tasks, and succeeds on the tasks.

Selection of Tests

After you have become familiar with the child's problems and the limitations associated with his or her disabilities, you should select tests that are appropriate and are geared to the child's strengths and limitations. It may be necessary to omit tests or items that require physical or sensory abilities that the child does not have. For example, items that require deftness in object manipulation or drawing may have to be eliminated when children with severe handicaps of the upper extremities are tested.

Other Testing Considerations

Additional valuable suggestions for working with physically handicapped children are as follows (cf. Ramirez, 1978; Shontz, 1977; Wright, 1983):

• Plan to assess physically handicapped children on more than one occasion and, if possible, in at least one setting that is familiar to the child. Blind children, for example, may demonstrate many skilled behaviors in an environment that is familiar to them but not in an unfamiliar setting. Give handicapped children time to acclimate themselves to the surroundings.

• Schedule, if needed, several shorter test sessions spaced over several days to counter the problem of fatigue.

• Position the handicapped child in his or her preferred way. Be sure that the child uses adaptive equipment that was made for him or her.

• Give credit for correct responses given in any form of communication, including sign language, Braille, fingerspelling, and teletouch.

• Converse with a handicapped child as you would with any other child, with the same spirit, content, and approach.

• Simply ask the child who may need assistance, "Do you need help" or "How should I help you?"

• Do not shout at a blind child. The child has a visual problem, not a hearing problem.

• Do not be embarrassed about common expressions that might seem awkward, such as asking a blind child whether he or she has *seen* a specific event. The English language is filled with these terms, and you are likely to be more sensitive to them than is the child with whom you are talking. Moreover, blind children commonly use the term *see* in reference to themselves.

• Use graphic language when directing an older, blind child. Instead of saying "The library is right over there," say "From where you are standing now, walk straight about 20 paces up a ramp, then walk 20 paces to the building, and then enter two sets of double doors that are about two paces apart and swing out."

• Do not "talk over" or provide the words for a child who stutters or has difficulty speaking. Be patient, listen, and let the child speak for himself or herself. You may repeat the thought back to the child to confirm communication of the idea, but it is not appropriate to outguess the child or assume that you know what the child is trying to express.

• Speak directly to a disabled child. Do not direct conversation to an attendant, assistant, or nearby companion as if the child did not exist.

• Always face a child with a hearing impairment. Be sure that the child can see your lips; speak clearly without exaggerating your lip movements.

• Do not call special attention to a disabled child. Approach the child as one who happens to have a handicap — not as a handicap that belongs to a child.

• Do not allow the child's particular disability to bias your perception of the child's functioning in other areas (for example, hearing, general health, or emotional maturity in the case of a blind child).

• Do not overlook behaviors that do not fit in with your expectations.

• Remember that psychological reactions to the disability are not uniformly disturbing or distressing, do not necessarily result in maladjustment, and are not related in a simple way to the physical properties of the disability.

• Recognize that the disability is only one of many factors affecting the total life of a child with a disability, and often its influence may be relatively minor.

TESTING VISUALLY IMPAIRED CHILDREN

Visual Impairment Defined

Before you administer any tests to a visually impaired child, identify the extent of the child's visual impairment, the quality of the usable vision, and the extent of the field of vision. The term *blindness* encompasses a range from total lack of vision to the ability to see at 20 feet what persons of normal vision can see at 200 feet (20/200). In some school districts special programs for visually handicapped children may include those with 20/70 acuity. Individuals may also be classified as legally blind if their acuity is good but their field of vision is so narrow that it subtends an angle no greater than 20 degrees.

Classification Scheme

Visually impaired children can be classified according to three broad groupings (Bauman, 1974):

1. Vision is of no practical use in the test situation. This group includes the totally blind, those who can differentiate only between light and dark, and those who can distinguish shapes, but only when the shapes are held between the eyes and the source of light.

2. Vision can be used in handling large objects, locating test pieces, or following the examiner's hand movements during a demonstration, but cannot be used in reading even enlarged print effectively. These children may be able to use vision and touch in working with form boards, but are at a great disadvantage if they are required to read.

3. Vision can be used to read print efficiently, but only when the type is large, the page is held close to the eyes, or a magnifier or other special visual aid is used.

Assessment Considerations

It is permissible to offer your arm to older blind children, or even to take the hand of young blind children, to lead them to your office. Inform them about the general layout of the room and about other details, such as the presence of a tape recorder, if one is being used. Take into account the amount of useful vision the partially sighted child has, adjusting the testing procedures accordingly. Be sure that partially sighted children wear their glasses when they are tested and that the lighting in the testing room is adequate (bright but without glare). In order to enable the child to form figure-ground discriminations, be sure that the surface of the table is not white or the same color as the objects the child is expected to see.

Signs of visual difficulty.   Signs that are suggestive of visual difficulty include the following:

BEHAVIOR

• Rubs eyes excessively
• Shuts or covers one eye, tilts head, or thrusts head forward
• Has difficulty in reading or in other work requiring close use of the eyes
• Blinks abnormally or is irritable when doing close visual work
• Moves head excessively when reading
• Holds books too close or too far from eyes
• Is unable to see distant things clearly
• Squints eyelids or frowns
• Loses place while reading
• Avoids close visual work
• Has poor sitting posture while reading
• Has difficulty judging distances
• Crossed eyes
• Red-rimmed, encrusted, or swollen eyelids
• Inflamed or watery eyes
• Recurring sties

COMPLAINTS

• Eyes itch, burn, or feel scratchy
• Cannot see well
• Dizziness, headaches, or nausea following close visual work
• Blurred or double vision
• Tires easily after visual work

Lack of these signs should not lead you to assume that the child's vision is adequate. Defects such as slight astigmatism or a binocular visual defect can impede reading without observable symptoms being present. Whenever there is any doubt about the child's vision, referral to an optometrist or ophthalmologist is warranted.

Selecting tests.   If the visual handicap is not too severe, intelligence tests such as the WISC-R, Stanford-Binet: Fourth Edition, WPPSI, and WAIS-R may be used. If the handicap is severe, administer only verbal items. However, keep in mind that the ability to answer even verbal items may be reduced if information required by the items depends in part on visual experiences. The Hays-Binet, Perkins-Binet, and Blind Learning Aptitude Test are also available for evaluating blind children.

TESTING HEARING-IMPAIRED CHILDREN

Hearing Impairment Defined

Hearing impairment is a general term that refers to hearing losses ranging from mild to profound. A *deaf child* is one whose hearing disability precludes successful processing of linguistic information through audition. A *hard-of-hearing child* has residual hearing sufficient for successful processing of linguistic information through audition, generally with the use of a hearing aid. One of the most serious problems of prelingually deaf children (children whose deafness was present at birth or occurred at an age prior to the development of speech and language) is that they cannot acquire speech and language normally.

Classification Scheme

Hearing is represented by a continuum ranging from very acute perception, such as that of a gifted musical conductor who can detect an out-of-tune instrument in an orchestra, to total deafness, such as that of an individual who can detect only strong vibrations through tactile sensations. The following classification scheme is useful in evaluating hard-of-hearing individuals. It is based on the extent to which the individual needs a higher than average level of intensity of sound in order to hear.

1. *Minimal hearing loss (below 15 dB loss).* Children with a loss of less than 15 decibels (dB) are the least hard-

of-hearing. They can be given the same tests administered to normally hearing children.

2. *Mild hearing loss (15–30 dB loss).* Children with a mild hearing loss may not be recognized as having a problem unless communication problems develop, in which case they may be referred for an audiological evaluation. Standard test procedures usually are satisfactory unless communication problems are evident.

3. *Moderate hearing loss (30–50 dB loss).* Children with a moderate hearing loss may hear speech in a one-to-one situation but not in a classroom. Some children in this group may require special testing procedures because of their communication problems. The procedures selected should be based on the individual child's degree of communication.

4. *Severe hearing loss (50–80 dB loss).* Children with a severe hearing loss hear only the loudest speech sounds. Their articulation, vocabulary, and voice quality will differ from that of normally hearing children. Because many will have severe communication problems, special testing procedures will be required.

5. *Profound hearing loss (greater than 80 dB).* Children with a profound hearing loss do not hear speech. They need special testing procedures devised for deaf children or for those with profound hearing losses.

It is important to know if frequency ranges are affected differentially by the hearing loss, in which case particular attention should be given to the ranges that encompass speech sounds.

Assessment Considerations

Before you begin the formal assessment of a hearing-impaired child, consider the type of loss, degree of loss, age of onset, and etiologic components. Hearing-impaired children are not a homogeneous group. If hearing loss was a result of a neurological disorder such as meningitis, there may be other concomitant dysfunctions that you will need to consider in administering the tests. If the child wears a hearing aid, determine when it was last checked, whether the child uses it consistently, and, at the time of the evaluation, whether it is turned on. Try to learn about the child's functioning level—that is, the methods by which the child receives information and how he or she communicates (receptive and expressive skills). Interviewing the parents and teachers and observing in the classroom can help you obtain information about the child's preferred modes of communication. Use these modes, if possible, to present the test items, and encourage children to respond in their preferred modes.

Signs of hearing difficulty.   Some signs of possible hearing difficulty are as follows:

GENERAL SIGNS

- Lack of normal response to sound
- Inattentiveness
- Difficulty in following oral directions
- Failure to respond when spoken to
- Frequent requests to have speaker repeat what was said
- Intent observation of speaker's lips (lipreading, speechreading)
- Habit of turning one ear toward the speaker
- Cupping hand behind ear
- Unusual voice quality (for example, monotonous)
- Speech too loud or too soft
- Faulty pronunciation
- Poor articulation
- Frequent earaches or discharges from ears

EXAMPLES OF POSSIBLE HEARING DIFFICULTIES

- Has difficulty discriminating consonant sounds; for example, hears *mat* for *bat*, *tab* for *tap*
- Has difficulty discriminating and learning short vowel sounds
- Has difficulty sounding out a word, sound by sound; for example, has difficulty saying k-a-t for *cat*
- Has difficulty relating printed letters such as "f," "pl," and "ide" to their sounds
- Has difficulty separating sounds that make up blends; for example, has difficulty determining that "fl" has the sounds f-f . . . l-l
- Spells and reads sight words better than phonetic words

Watch for these signs during all examinations. These signs, coupled with answers to the following questions, will guide you in uncovering possible hearing impairments:

- Are the volume and pitch of the child's voice appropriate to the situation?
- Is the child's pronunciation intelligible, consistent, and age appropriate?
- Is the child's speech fluent or are there unusual pauses?
- Does the child grope for words?
- Are the child's replies timely or are there unusual delays?

- Does the child respond once to a sound and not again?
- Does the child understand speech?
- Does the child confuse similar sounding words?
- If the child does not speak, how is communication carried out (for example, pointing, gesturing, shifting eye gaze)?

In addition, note whether the child becomes frustrated when you do not understand him or her and, if so, how the child then behaves (for example, withdraws or acts out). If you detect any behavior that suggests a possible hearing deficit, refer the child to an audiologist.

Special communication skills needed.   Examiners who work with deaf children need special communication skills. If you have not received special training, prepare for the testing of deaf children by observing classes for the deaf, noting how teachers communicate with their pupils. It is important to use a total communication approach with those deaf children familiar with it. This approach entails the simultaneous use of speech, sign language (a manual system of communication such as American Sign Language or Signed English), and fingerspelling. Generally, in administering tests to deaf children a variety of techniques can be used, including speech, gesture, pantomime, writing, signs, fingerspelling, and drawing.

In one study with severely and profoundly hearing-impaired children, use of the total communication approach resulted in the highest WISC-R Performance Scale IQs (Sullivan, 1982). The total communication approach was found to be superior to pantomime and visual-aid modifications and to verbal statements. These results indicate that if you plan to assess hearing-impaired children, you should be skilled in a manual system of communication. Pantomime and visual aids are poorer administration procedures; they should be used only when you cannot communicate in sign language, or when the hearing-impaired child is not versed in sign language or other special communication modalities. Pantomime and visual aids are, however, preferable to a verbal-only administration. If you cannot administer the test in the child's preferred communication modality, request a psychologist who has the requisite skills to perform the evaluation or hire an interpreter.

Effects of visual cues.   Testing children with impaired hearing requires a high degree of skill and wide range of experiences with deaf children. Because sight is the chief means by which deaf children receive stimuli, they are likely to seek visual clues, such as facial expressions or movements of hands, to gain understanding about their performance. You must realize that any movements you make may furnish cues to deaf children. Facial expressions, rather than tone of voice, will convey your mood, and a frown or a grimace of impatience will be quickly noted and interpreted unfavorably. Smile to reward the children's efforts, but not to reward a correct response. Smiling when a wrong response has been given should be avoided, so that children are not encouraged to make similar responses.

Comprehension problems. Although hearing-impaired children may give the impression of being able to understand directions and test questions, closer inspection may reveal that they are feigning comprehension to obtain your approval. They may have learned how to play a role in order to avoid confronting potentially embarrassing situations. In turn, you may have difficulty understanding the answers of hearing-impaired children, particularly those with expressive difficulties. Responses given in pantomime by the child should be given credit only when you have no doubt about the accuracy of the answer.

Techniques for giving instructions. You must be able to make instructions understood without giving away answers in the process. Pantomime can be used, but it does not always convey to the child what you intend to communicate. A simple demonstration will sometimes suffice, but the demonstration itself may indicate the answer to the problem.

If you use speech, be sure that you are looking at the child while you are reading the test instructions and questions and that the child is watching your face. Speech should be clear, distinct, and natural. Maintain a pleasant face. Be sure that there are no obstructions blocking the child's view of your lips, and that the lighting in the room is appropriate. Children who wear hearing aids should do so during the examination; be sure the hearing aids are in good working order and are turned "on."

In some cases it may be necessary to use an interpreter skilled both in sign language and in English. Anyone who tests hearing-impaired children routinely should learn sign language.

Use of standardized tests. The assessment of hearing-impaired children poses special problems. Arriving at a valid measure of ability is difficult because many tests have large verbal components. Verbally based tests usually do not give an accurate picture of the hearing-impaired child's level of mental ability. They are more likely to measure the extent of the hearing-impaired child's language deficiency.

Verbally oriented tests should be used with extreme caution, if at all.

The performance tests selected for hard-of-hearing children should not depend on verbal directions. Timed tests may be less valid for hard-of-hearing children because the added stress of being timed may interfere with their performance to a greater extent than it does with children with normal hearing. Representative performance tests include the WISC-R, WPPSI, and WAIS-R Performance Scales; the Abstract/Visual Reasoning subtests of the Stanford-Binet: Fourth Edition; the nonverbal subtests of the K-ABC; the Ontario School Ability Examination; the Leiter International Performance Scale; the Hiskey-Nebraska Test of Learning Aptitude; the nonauditory/nonverbal subtests of the Illinois Test of Psycholinguistic Ability; and Raven's Progressive Matrices. These tests differ as to their reliability, validity, and datedness; consequently, your selection of a test should be carefully considered.

Standardized tests designed for hearing children are likely to pose difficulties for hearing-impaired children because such tests do not take into consideration the extraordinary communication requirements of hearing-impaired children. Obviously any test or subtest that is even partially dependent on oral instructions will place the hearing-impaired child at a disadvantage. Therefore, administration and scoring procedures must take into account the child's deficits.

Modification of standard procedures. Modifications in test procedures for deaf children include omitting verbal tests, adding printed or signed words, and using pantomime, demonstration, and manual communication. Modifications that maximize assessment information include testing of limits, reinforcing responses, practicing test-type items, eliminating time limits, and demonstrating task strategies. Appendix D presents special instructions for administering the WISC-R Performance Scale to hearing-impaired children. In examining hard-of-hearing children, select only the most appropriate tests and use at least one performance measure of cognitive ability.

Observation guidelines. Although the audiologist and speech-language pathologist are the specialists in determining the communication skills of hard-of-hearing children, the psychologist also makes observations, both formal and informal, of the child's communication skills. Notes should indicate where the observations occurred (for example, in a quiet one-to-one situation, in a classroom, or in a job or social setting), because the child's communication skills may differ in various settings. Assess the child's skills in reading and writing, speech (intelligibility and pleasantness), and lipreading. Note the extent to which the child is able to understand conversation during the examination. Do not assume that the communication difficulties of hard-of-hearing children indicate that they have limited intelligence. A congenital hearing loss can interfere with the development of many different skills that may or may not be related to cognitive ability.

A primary assessment goal.   A primary goal in evaluating hard-of-hearing children is to determine the extent to which their performance resembles that of a normally hearing child or that of a deaf child. Vernon (1974, p. 209, with changes in notation) explains why this effort is needed:

By interrelating IQ, educational, and other facts about a deaf or hard-of-hearing child it is possible to derive a picture which reveals the role played by his or her hearing loss. If the youth's profile is similar to that of the normally hearing, his or her loss and the way it has been coped with is not particularly disabling. By contrast, if the profile is similar to that of a deaf child, then the loss has had major effects on communication, language development, and education. Appropriate planning for the two kinds of children varies drastically. What would be constructive for one would in certain cases be devastating for the other. An evaluation that does not fully address itself to this issue has failed to serve one of its major functions. The issue cannot be handled without comprehensive information. Shortcuts will not suffice and hasty, inadequately done evaluations are actually unethical and wasteful of human resources.

Vernon and Brown (1964) described the tragic case of a hearing-impaired child who was administered the Stanford-Binet Intelligence Scale: Form L-M for her initial intellectual assessment. Because no one realized that the child was deaf, she received an IQ of 29, which led to her commitment to a hospital for the mentally retarded, where she remained for five years. It was only after she was administered a performance intelligence test and obtained an IQ of 113 that the staff realized that she was not retarded. Upon discharge from the institution, she entered a school for the deaf and made good progress. The case demonstrates what can occur when there has been a failure in the diagnostic process.

TESTING CEREBRAL PALSIED CHILDREN

The testing of cerebral palsied children presents particular difficulties. Their motor, speech, visual, and auditory difficulties may limit the applicability of standardized tests and

make caution mandatory in interpreting test results. Because cerebral palsied children frequently perform motor tasks in a slow and laborious manner, they may be at a particular disadvantage when time limits are imposed. Furthermore, it is sometimes difficult to determine whether their test failures are due to physical disabilities or to cognitive deficits. In spite of the difficulties inherent in using standard tests, however, it is important to compare the cerebral palsied child's performance with that of the normal child, because the latter sets the standards in the world at large.

Many cerebral palsied children talk adequately and have good use of at least one hand; modifications of test administration procedures may not be necessary for these children. However, when serious physical limitations exist, modifications are needed. Tests requiring the least modification should be selected. Use performance tests if the child has good hand usage and poor speech, or use verbal tests if the opposite is true. Tests requiring motor skills are likely to be inappropriate for children with motor handicaps. When subtests are eliminated, scores may be prorated, if prorating is permitted by the test manual.

The following case illustrates the value of employing test modifications.

Tommy, an 8-year-old severely handicapped boy with athetoid-type cerebral palsy, had no speech and communicated only by painstakingly pointing out numbers that corresponded to words or phrases taped to the tray of his wheelchair. Yet Tommy appeared to the examiner to be alert, curious, and eager to participate in the assessment. The examiner attempted to administer the Pictorial Test of Intelligence, a test that requires the child to point to one of four pictures that corresponds to the correct answer to a verbal question. However, Tommy was unable to make the movements necessary to differentiate between the pictures, even though they were printed on a large card. As a modification of the standard procedure, the examiner read each test item and then pointed in turn to each of the four pictures. When the examiner pointed to the choice Tommy wished to make, the child wiggled in his wheelchair. Because of the problem of interpreting Tommy's movements, many of the items had to be administered several times. After an hour and a half of this exhaustive procedure, both examiner and child finished the test with a sense of real accomplishment. Tommy, the boy who at first glance appeared to be mentally retarded, had earned an IQ of 120.

Research studies and follow-up reports indicate that the initial test results obtained by cerebral palsied children have a satisfactory degree of reliability and validity (Crowell & Crowell, 1954; Klapper & Birch, 1966; Kogan, 1957; Portenier, 1942; Taylor, 1961). However, it is still recommended that the first scores not be used as the sole criterion in long-range planning, not only for cerebral palsied children but for all children examined by an intelligence test.

SUGGESTIONS FOR ADMINISTERING TESTS

You are likely to be anxious when you are first learning to administer tests. You must become a juggler in order to successfully carry out a multitude of tasks—establish rapport, administer the appropriate items, keep the materials ready, respond appropriately to the child, precisely record the child's responses, observe the child's behavior, and score the child's responses. In time many of these procedures will become routine, but even the most experienced examiners should review their test procedures periodically. Test manuals usually present valuable suggestions for administering tests; these suggestions should be studied carefully. The following tips are designed to supplement or reemphasize a number of points that are often found in test manuals. These suggestions, coupled with the instructions in the test manuals, will help you to administer tests better. Some tests have specific guidelines that may differ from those presented below; in such cases, the guidelines in the respective manuals should always be followed. Table 5-3 shows an excellent general outline of testing procedures.

General Considerations

1. Know your task well enough that the test flows almost automatically, leaving you maximally free to observe all aspects of the child's behavior. If you stop to read a paragraph in your manual, the child is not likely to wait for you. He or she may be out of the chair, playing games, or wanting to leave. Know your materials so that you can reach for them without looking away from the child; work on perfecting ways to record responses that do not interrupt the relationship.

2. Adhere to test instructions exactly.

3. Be purposeful in what you do and keep control of the situation. Let there be no doubt as to who is in charge. If control becomes an issue, stop the testing until the matter has been settled. You may need to play a game, take a break, enlist the parent's help, retreat to easier items, or use some other tactic, but do not let things get out of hand.

4. Take your time and suit your tempo and decibel level to the child. Some appreciate a boisterous approach, whereas others are quiet and fragile. Use words and a tone of voice that will help the child feel confident and reassured.

5. Give the child a choice only when you intend to leave the situation up to him or her.

6. Do not do or say anything that may diminish the child's self-respect.

7. Avoid motivating the child by making comparisons between the child and another child or by encouraging competition. If the parents are present, discourage them from using such techniques.

8. Try to maintain the child's cooperation at all times. Remember that you need to *earn* the child's attention and cooperation. Keep the situation friendly, interesting, and rewarding. Do not let the relationship degenerate into a power struggle. Sometimes you cannot avoid a modest degree of unpleasantness, especially with unhappy, rebellious children, but it is your responsibility to establish the best rapport you can and to elicit the child's best effort.

9. Establish and maintain rapport with the parents, and enlist their support of the assessment effort.

10. Use your own reaction to the child as a cue. If you find yourself continually trying to improve rapport with an older preschooler, this may suggest excessive manipulation by the child. If the child's behavior makes you feel irritable or angry, then others may feel the same way. (Recognize, however, that a defiant child is an unhappy one who needs help.) Also, watch the complexity of your own language (and that of the mother or father) as a guide to what the child is understanding; you should be adjusting automatically to the cues the child gives you.

11. Do not change the directions because you think the child can do a particular task with the altered directions. *You must follow standard procedures.* Under certain circumstances, if the directions are not part of the task—for example, if you want to see whether a child *can* draw a circle, and not whether he or she *will* draw a circle when given certain directions—then you may be able to change words. These circumstances are unusual, however, and are most often found in informal assessments rather than formal assessments.

12. Be attentive to any signs of visual or hearing difficulties, as noted in earlier sections of this chapter.

Physical Arrangements

1. Use a testing room that has minimal distractions. You and the test materials should be the most salient stimuli. Ideally the examination room should both minimize external sources of distraction and maximize the child's motivation. The many different conditions you will meet on the job will invariably fall short of the ideal. Although you may have to settle for conditions that approximate the

Table 5-3
A General Outline of Testing Procedures

I. *General testing precautions.*
  A. Read, learn, and *reread* instructions.
  B. Always adhere to standardized procedures.
    1. Use exact wording.
    2. Maintain accurate timing.
    3. Present materials in the prescribed manner.
    4. Follow scoring instructions rigidly.
    5. Do not depend solely on reading the printed directions, but do have them available for ready reference.
  C. Be objective.
    1. Give no indication of the correctness or incorrectness of the child's responses.
    2. Give no clues about the answer you expect; watch your verbal intonation; remember you are testing, not teaching.
  D. Be natural.
    1. Be warm but impersonal.
    2. Learn to use standardized wording in a natural and informal manner.
    3. Achieve rapport and verbal give-and-take before the test begins; take a listening attitude.
  E. Prepare the environment.
    1. Avoid distractions.
      a. Visual: Have the child face away from doors and windows where movement and activity are going on. Have him or her face away from large open spaces that have, for example, distracting pictures, colors, or toys. Avoid clutter.
      b. Auditory: Avoid noisy areas.
      c. Emotional: Avoid testing when the child is hurried, troubled, or ill.
    2. Provide optimum conditions for good performance.
      a. See that the child is in a comfortable position and has a clear view of the materials.
      b. Provide a well-lit room with adequate ventilation and comfortable temperature.
      c. Avoid glaring lights, reflections from the pages, and other distractions. Face the child away from the window if possible.
      d. Speak in a clear, audible voice at a moderate rate of speed.
      e. Maintain interest through enthusiasm, attention to the child, and smooth presentation of the material.
      f. Commend and encourage for general performance but never on specific items.
      g. Let the child know you want to see how well he or she can do.
II. *Administering and scoring the test.*
  A. Efficiency.

  1. Provide an efficient arrangement and method of manipulating materials for
    a. Recording.
    b. Viewing the manual *without its becoming a barrier between you and the child.*
    c. Putting away and bringing out materials.
    d. Avoiding delays and distractions for the child.
  2. Make a smooth transition from test to test and from item to item. You must know at each point in the test what your next presentation will be.
  3. Know your materials and scoring well enough that you do not extend the test unnecessarily. Overtesting may create fatigue and disinterest.
    a. Know the scoring standards.
    b. Begin at the appropriate point.
  4. Learn to handle extraneous behavior.
    a. Disregard or redirect irrelevant remarks.
    b. Minimize extraneous movements by developing interest, motivation, and task orientation. If extraneous movements do not interfere with the child's functioning, ignore them. If necessary, provide the child with a positive outlet such as grasping the edges of the desk or folding his or her hands.
    c. Foresee fatigue and distraction.
  B. Scoring.
    1. It is essential that you know the scoring standards well. This requirement applies particularly to the understanding of the *intent* of each test.
    2. Remember that the scoring standards are just what the term says: they are "standards" for scoring rather than all-inclusive right-or-wrong answers. It is often necessary to evaluate equivalent responses in the light of other responses listed in the scoring standards, since not all possible responses are included.
    3. Check all answers with the manual in order to verify any doubtful responses.
    4. Recheck every step in the scoring process.
    5. Double-check all figures and calculations—the chronological age, the number of correct items, additions, and arithmetic calculations.
  C. Care of materials.
    1. Whenever any of the materials presented to the child become marked or defaced in any way that might influence the child's response, replace them.
    2. If you must point to the pictures, be sure not to mark the page. Use the back end of your pen or pencil.
    3. If any materials are lost or damaged, replace them with objects *identical to the original.*

Source: Reprinted, with changes in notation, by permission of the publisher and author from W. D. Kirk, *Aids and Precautions in Administering the Illinois Test of Psycholinguistic Abilities,* pp. 5–7, 13–14. Copyright 1974, University of Illinois Press.

ideal, you must *never* test when the conditions would adversely affect the child's performance.

2. Control your materials. Do not allow the examinee to turn pages in the test manual, to play with the test materials, or to hold pencils, pens, or toys, except when these are needed for a test. Unless specifically prohibited, the child *may* be permitted to turn pages in test booklets that contain items (for example, the pictures in the Wechsler Picture Completion subtest). This permits the child to proceed at his or her own pace and encourages rapport; however, it does not have to be a routine procedure.

With infants up to 6 months, your materials can be in sight, but after that, the only materials visible or accessible should be those needed for the task at hand. Place your test kit on a low chair next to your side such that when the kit is open the back of the lid faces the child. Stay between the kit and the child, keeping the kit out of the child's reach so that the child does not see any answers in the test manual. Check to see that the testing kit contains all necessary materials *before* you begin testing.

3. It is often a good idea to have one attractive object already on the table when you enter the room with the child. This object should not be one you will use for testing.

4. Make sure the child is comfortable. For example, the chair and table should be supportive and at appropriate heights, the lighting should be sufficient, and the ventilation adequate. If the child's feet do not touch the floor, arrange a solid box or block for them. A high chair is optimal for young children who are able to sit upright on their own (usually by about 6 months of age)—they are accustomed to it, it is comfortable, and it provides foot support.

5. Children up to 2 or 3 years of age will usually do better with a parent present. If parents are present, seat them behind the child, out of the child's line of vision. If a parent is to hold a small child on his or her lap, make sure that the chair is low enough so that together their knees can fit underneath the table.

6. Unless the examinee is an infant, no other children should be present. Having another child in the room can be disruptive, and the feelings of the child who is not getting your attention can be hurt. Avoid these problems by requesting, at the time the appointment is made, that the parent make arrangements for siblings.

7. If the examinee is older than 3 years of age, the parent generally should not be in the room, unless the child insists on having a parent there or a parent is needed to facilitate the testing. An observation room with a one-way mirror allows parents to view the testing and facilitates their understanding of the results you obtain.

Making the Child's Acquaintance

1. Keeping in mind that the parent prepares the child for testing, allay parental anxieties as best you can when you arrange the appointment. Tell the parent what you will be doing with the child—such as looking at how the child works with materials, which activities are easy for the child and which are more difficult, and how the child expresses ideas and interests. Avoid words like *test*, *examination*, and *evaluation*. Assure the parent that most children find the activities pleasant and that you are looking forward to meeting the child.

2. Meet the child in the waiting room, and—with a young child especially—spend some time there. When you greet the child, do not overwhelm him or her. If the child is young, you might bring a toy and at first try to keep the parents seated so that you can kneel at the child's level. Initially give most of your attention to the parent and let the child look you over, gradually making friends as the child tolerates your attention. When the child seems comfortable, invite the child and, depending on the child's age, the parent into your room. To a young child you might say something like "I left a book on my table for you to look at; let's go see it" or "Time to do some things now; I'll show you where they are." Do *not* ask "Do you want to come into my room now?" unless you are prepared to accept no as an answer.

3. Do not remove the child abruptly from an interesting activity.

4. Follow the test guidelines for introducing the test. You can set an older child at ease with a few introductory remarks. The following sample may be a useful model for introducing a test:

We will be doing some things together, and most children enjoy doing them. Some of the things that we will be doing will be easy and some will be hard. That's because some of the things are for children younger than you and some of the things are for children older than you. So don't worry if you can't get all of the answers right—I don't expect you to know all of the answers. But I do want you to do the very best you can.

Watch how the child handles the items. Praise with your voice and tone (for example, "You know how to do these things!"). Do *not* let the child play with the test materials to get comfortable. Recognize that it may take a little while for a young child to understand that he or she should do what you ask.

5. You will probably have to teach a young child that, once he or she has worked on one activity, something else interesting will ensue. Children of 1 or 2 years of age need time to understand that you expect them to do something specific with the materials. After a few items, even quite

young infants get this message. It may take a while for some children (particularly those from large families who have learned to defend their toys) to give up one object in exchange for another. Generally you should present the new object as you remove the old one, but you may need to let the child become interested in the new one before requiring that the old one be relinquished. With children who have not yet achieved object permanence (see Chapter 3), covering the old toy with your hand while presenting the new one may facilitate the exchange. A comfortable rhythm will soon develop if you are running the session smoothly.

6. If the parents are present, let them know that you do not expect the child to pass all of the test items; acknowledge from the beginning that some items are simply too difficult. *Never tell a parent that a child "failed" an item.*

Reinforcement

1. Positive reinforcement is your most potent tool; use it. Attend to behavior you like. Nodding, smiling, and appreciative noises may be more effective than words. Be sure to reinforce effort, which may or may not be accompanied by success.

2. Try to ignore or circumvent the behaviors you do not like; in some cases you may have to distract the child. Parents may be able to help you, but some parents interfere. Generally, handle problems by trying to foresee and forestall them.

3. Avoid using tangible reinforcers as motivators, except with autistic or profoundly retarded children who are accustomed to receiving them. In such cases, be sure you have parental permission to use primary reinforcers, such as Cheerios, candy, or raisins. One of the best motivators, in addition to positive reinforcement, is to arrange the activities so that the child experiences successes intermittently.

4. Remember to keep giving positive messages. Build an image as a kindly, fairly exciting but predictably firm adult who likes the child and is (will be) pleased with his or her effort.

5. Clearly define and consistently maintain limits on allowable behavior. Be sure that the child understands the limits of behavior. Although consistency is necessary, do not be inflexible. Accept the child's need to test limits, and try to adapt your limits to the child's needs, giving him or her time to accept them. This approach will demonstrate your respect for his or her feelings.

6. Reinforce parents. Most parents respond positively to kind words about their caretaking and teaching, as well as their patience and effort. Show them that you recognize

their affection, their sense of humor, and the problems with which they are coping. These recommendations are especially important for interactions with anxious or defensive parents.

Management

1. Do not confuse the child. The younger the child, the more important it is that your gestures and use of materials be clear and precise. With babies, it helps to exaggerate your movements a little so that they see what you want (for example, pat the Bayley dolly rather firmly and then motion for the baby to do the same). Through the tone of your voice and your actions (such as handing him or her materials) make clear to the child when you expect a response.

2. Do not ignore any remarks made by the child. Attend and be sensitive to the child's needs, such as for a drink or physical activity. Watch for early signs of boredom, fatigue, physical discomfort, or emotional distress, and take appropriate action before such conditions become acute. The child may prefer that the parent, rather than you, wipe his or her nose or take him or her to the bathroom. But do not take too many breaks, because this will lengthen the overall time and fatigue the child.

3. As an alternative to a formal break in testing, you may administer gross motor items as a break from verbal items.

4. Give the child a chance to get acquainted with the materials if necessary (for example, let an 18-month-old see the "bunny" you are going to hide under the cup on the Bayley), but do not let the child play with the materials. Parents sometimes object to your adherence to structure when the child is attracted to a toy. Explain that if you do not adhere to structure the child will become confused about what the test expectations are and the session will run so long that the child will grow tired.

5. Be sure that the child is ready and expectant when you present a new task. Tapping on the table may help draw a young child's attention to a toy if the child is inattentive. You may need to institute a signal such as "Get ready!" Avoid urging the child to respond before he or she is ready.

6. Redirect activities in a way that is consistent with the child's motives and interests.

7. Recognizing that many of the tasks that you ask the child to perform may be too difficult, make them as pleasant as you can. For example, you might say, with a smile, "Here's another *real* hard one!" or "Here's one for older kids but let's try it!" Learning to encourage effort takes practice.

8. Always be truthful. Do not say that you are almost through if you are not.

9. Finish with some easy items, even if you do not

need to—this leaves both the child and the parent with a good feeling.

10. Particularly with infants and young children, you may have sessions in which testing cannot be completed. The reasons for this outcome are numerous. You may never make friends. The child may remain unhappy or suspicious for the entire session. If things are going badly, reschedule the appointment and reassure the parent that such things occasionally happen.

11. In general, you should accept children as they are, knowing that there are reasons for the ways they feel and act. Help them find acceptable outlets for their feelings, and try to meet their needs. Skills you acquire in handling children can aid you in helping them gain confidence in their abilities. Increased confidence may enhance their cooperativeness and willingness to respond to the tests.

Test Procedures

Arranging materials. A general rule of thumb is to administer items from the child's left to right in the order given in the test manual. Even demonstration items should be so arranged. This rule simply brings some uniformity to the test administration. Stimulus materials should be placed in front of the child one at a time so that the child can see the blocks, cards, or other material clearly. Some beginning examiners have been known to inadvertently cover materials as they placed them on the table. The child should be able to see your complete movements when you rearrange materials in demonstration items, unless the test manual says otherwise. Be sure to record the child's arrangements as soon as the item is completed.

In constructing sample block designs it is a good idea to complete one row at a time, starting each row at the child's left and working to the right. This will tend to ensure that you administer the sample items in the same way to each child. Be sure that the child can easily reach the blocks or other stimulus materials. Do not remove the materials until the child says that he or she has finished the task.

When administering items that appear in booklets, you need not hold the booklet, unless the manual so states. The booklet can be left flat on the table and pages (or cards) turned over for each succeeding item.

Keep the testing table clear of all extraneous materials to avoid needless distractions. Return all materials to the testing kit immediately after they are used.

Giving instructions and asking questions. The instructions for the various tests should be read verbatim, in an even and relaxed manner; avoid a robotic or machine-like approach. Most beginning examiners have a tendency to read the test instructions and questions too quickly or too slowly. Pace your reading and conversation to the child's age and ability level, striving for clarity and a natural quality. Avoid unusual facial expressions or modulations in voice that may give cues regarding performance.

The instructions used for the first trial of a test can be repeated on successive trials or items. It is not permissible to explain any of the words that are used in the directions or in the questions on the various test items unless the manual explicitly permits explanation. Be sure not to add any additional words to the instructions, such as "Now here is . . . ." Memory items should not be repeated. You should know the directions well; ideally, they should be memorized. You should become so familiar with the test materials that you can introduce and remove them without breaking the interaction between you and the child.

Unless specifically prohibited by the test manual, phrasing requests as mild commands (such as "Tell me another reason . . .") is preferable to asking the child if he or she knows the answer. "Can you tell me . . ." and "Do you know . . ." often result in a simple no from a child, whereas a mild command may encourage the child to try to answer the question.

Timing items and encouraging replies. On tests that have time limits, do not tell children how much time is allotted to the task unless the manual says otherwise. If they ask, you might tell them to give their answer as soon as they know it. Timing should begin as soon as the item is shown to the child. Seldom accept the first "I don't know" response given by the child. Ask the child to try to answer, unless the question appears to be too difficult for him or her. It is permissible to say something like "Try to give an answer" or "Try to answer it in some way, if you can."

Clarifying responses. If you are uncertain about what a child has said, ask him or her to repeat the response. To minimize the need for repetition, pay close attention to everything the child says. The purpose of questioning is to clarify ambiguous responses. Obviously incorrect responses should not be probed. When a response contains one part that is correct and one that is incorrect, ask the child for his or her preference and score the response accordingly. Avoid giving the child the impression that a test is being discontinued because of repeated failure. If a child asks to have part of a question repeated, repeat the entire question.

Providing feedback. You should not tell the examinee whether responses are correct. If asked, you can say that it is against the rules to tell the answers, but that you can answer their questions when you have finished.

Recording responses.   Immediately record the child's answers in the appropriate spaces provided in the test record booklet. Be as accurate as possible. Exercise judgment in recording parts of the response that have limited relevance to the test question. In the margin of the record booklet, note behaviors of interest, other observations, hypotheses, and other relevant information.

Scoring responses.   The child's responses should be scored as soon as they are given. Try to shield the scores in the record booklet as unobtrusively as possible. The record booklet should be positioned in such a way that the child does not see answers to questions or get feedback on prior or current responses. You might want to place the record booklet on a clip board and hold it at an angle to the child.

Any doubts about scoring should be resolved by referring to the scoring section of the test manual. On the WISC-R, WPPSI, WAIS-R, Stanford-Binet: Fourth Edition, and other tests that employ entry and discontinuance points, it is absolutely necessary to score the responses immediately at these points so that the correct administration procedures can be followed. As you are administering a test, place a question mark to the left of any responses that were difficult to score. Give special attention to these items on recheck. All scores should be rechecked carefully after the examination.

The scoring examples shown in test manuals are guides. They usually are not meant to represent all possible correct or incorrect answers, except in the case of those items that have only one correct answer or for which the manual lists the only acceptable responses. You should study the scoring criteria for each test so that you know what are correct, questionable, and incorrect answers. Try to discern the kind of response called for by the item. The scoring sections occasionally provide guidelines. When guidelines are not provided, study the sample responses to ascertain the kind of response that should receive credit. Such study will allow you to make appropriate decisions regarding the correctness or incorrectness of a response.

Acknowledging performance.   When the examination has been completed, children should be praised for their efforts. It is *not* necessary to give them trinkets. Unless arrangements have been made with the parents, do not give candy at the completion of the examination.

Informal Observation

It is often helpful to combine informal observation with standardized testing. It is preferable to do the formal testing first because it is easier to move from a structured situation to a nonstructured one than vice versa. Do not overlap them, however, because you may lose the essential structure of the standardized test. The parent (or a sibling) may be especially helpful here. When you have finished testing, you might, for example, bring out some toys and ask the parent to play with the child. Leave the situation unstructured so that you can hear how the child expresses himself or herself when more relaxed. If the parent begins to ask too many questions of the child (in an effort to elicit verbalizations), suggest that the parent just comment on what the child is doing. By noticing nuances in the parent-child interaction you can get an idea of the child's behavior. Watch the child's reactions to parental expectations and control tactics; note contrasts between the child's behavior in this nonstructured situation and in the structured situation required for testing; observe the child's ability to use toys in a constructive/imaginative/appropriate way; and try to get an idea of the child's attention span. (See Chapter 17 for further discussion of systematic observational procedures and Chapter 16 for play interview procedures.)

Talking to Parents

Handling a complex situation involving the parents and the child is not easy. Most of your attention should be focused on the child. You may need to schedule a separate appointment to talk with the parents about their concerns, any information you need, or issues you want to discuss. A young child may be put on the floor to play while you talk after the session, but an older child will be interested in your conversation. Even with a very young child, parents may feel restrained when talking in the child's presence, especially if they are discussing emotionally laden material and feel sad or angry, feelings an infant or toddler may pick up. Such cases need to be handled individually.

Remember that you are the parents' ally in providing the best possible care for the child. Resist the temptation to assign blame, remembering that any behavior you see is a product of a long series of complex interactions. Remain friendly, helpful, warm, objective, and credible. Whatever you discover in the evaluation session will be useless unless your views are (eventually) respected and accepted by the adults who are responsible for the child's welfare.

Finally, be aware of the feelings of the parents. Parents

have limited experience with testing; they may be uninformed about the meaning of test results, anxious about their child's behavior, and defensive about their child's need for testing. By reassuring parents in an honest manner and addressing their concerns whenever possible, you can help to alleviate some of their anxieties.

Pitfalls in Administering Tests

The following examples illustrate test administration procedures that will interfere with establishing rapport (Teglasi & Freeman, 1983).

Example 1. An examiner interacted the "obligatory" few minutes with an 11-year-old girl. Just then, the girl felt comfortable enough to bring up a concern that was directly germane to the referral problem. The examiner's response was, "Well, we've spent enough time talking; shall we get started with the test?" *Comment:* This example violates the principle that *you always need to be attentive to the child's needs and concerns.* Delay beginning the test, if necessary, when there are more pressing matters.

Example 2. The examiner asked, "Do you want to get started?" When the child responded "no!" the examiner said, "Well, we're going to get started." *Comment:* This example violates the principle that *if you offer choices, be prepared to honor them.*

Example 3. The examiner said, "These are getting hard. They are so hard that even I don't know some of the answers. Do you sometimes wonder if your teachers know the answers to tests that they give you? So you're not really expected to know all of them. . . now even I don't know the answers to some of these. I look them up in a book." *Comment:* This example violates the principle that *you should not introduce extraneous material that may increase children's anxiety, perplex them, or reduce their motivation.*

Example 4. The examiner asked, "Can you try to remember any others?" When the child responded "no," the examiner said enthusiastically, "Well, you did very well." *Comment:* This example violates the principle that *you should give praise for children's efforts and not after either an incorrect response or a lack of response.* You can acknowledge the child's statements by saying "Okay" or "Let's try the next one."

Example 5. The child asked, "When can I take a break?" to which the examiner responded, "Any time you want." But when the child said "now," the examiner said, "Well, let's finish this first." *Comment:* This example violates the principle that *if you say something, be prepared to follow it literally.*

Example 6. A child was reading the words on a reading test so quickly that the examiner could not keep up. The examiner frequently said, "Tell me again. . .back up. . . ." *Comment:* This example violates the principle that *you should pace the examination so that you can comfortably and accurately record the information.* The examiner in this example should have provided structure by saying "I'd like you to wait for a little while in between words" or "Say the next word when I say okay."

Departures from Standard Procedures

Departures from standard procedures during test administration may change the meaning of test scores. When standard procedures have been altered, scores based on the test norms may be inappropriate. However, standard test procedures are not applicable to all children, as we saw earlier in this chapter, and on some occasions a more accurate estimate of intellectual ability may be obtained by adaptation of standard procedures, particularly when children with severe physical disabilities or severe brain damage are being tested. For example, you can read to blind children items that they would have had to read for themselves, allow children with major speech problems to use a typewriter or write their answers, and direct children who cannot point or speak to give their answers to multiple-choice items through eye movements.

When do departures violate test norms? In order for the test norms to be used with confidence, the test items must be administered according to standard procedures. This means, for example, that you must use the exact words of the questions, the specific test materials, and the specified time limits. The effects of small deviations in test procedures, however, are not known. Each test has a standard error reflecting deviations caused by the nuances in the examiner-examinee relationship, the conditions of the examination, the time of day, and other similar factors. It is hoped that when small changes occur in rapport or in other aspects of the test situation, the resulting score will remain within the range of the standard error, but this will never be known.

Whether norms are violated when test procedures are modified depends on the extent of the modifications. Most of the procedures suggested in the previous sections do not appear to preclude the use of standardized norms. However, more serious modifications, such as alterations in the wording of questions, changes in the scoring criteria, extensions of time limits, or the use of a multiple-choice procedure for items that call for definitions, are likely to jeopardize the use of test norms.

Although standard administrative procedures should be the rule, occasionally exceptions may be made in order to obtain some estimate of the child's ability without regard for norms. On those occasions when modifications must be used, the resulting scores should be reported as "estimates" obtained by departures from standardized testing procedures and should be interpreted cautiously in light of the modifications. The scores are likely to be less precise and predictions about future levels of functioning cruder than would otherwise be the case.

Incentives and their effects.   The effect of incentives, such as praise, candy, or money—referred to as social or token reinforcement—on children's test performance has been studied extensively. Results of 34 different studies, with normal and handicapped children of various ethnic groups, present a mixed picture:

• Fourteen indicated that incentives or feedback did not affect performance (Busch & Osborne, 1976; Clingman & Fowler, 1975; Cohen, 1970; Cook, 1973; Galdieri, Barcikowski, & Witmer, 1972; Goh & Lund, 1977; Graham, 1971; Jackson, Farley, Zimet, & Gottman, 1979; Lyle & Johnson, 1973; Miller, 1974; Quay, 1971; Sweet & Ringness, 1971; Tiber & Kennedy, 1964; Tufano, 1976).

• Thirteen indicated that the effects were mixed (Bergan, McManis, & Melchert, 1971; Bradley-Johnson, Johnson, Shanahan, Rickert, & Tardona, 1984; Breuning & Zella, 1978; Galbraith, Ott, & Johnson, 1986; Johnson, Bradley-Johnson, McCarthy, & Jamie, 1984; Kieffer & Goh, 1981; Klugman, 1944; Moran, McCullers, & Fabes, 1984; Saigh & Payne, 1976; Sweet & Ringness, 1971; Terrell, Terrell, & Taylor, 1981; Willis & Shibata, 1978; Young, Bradley-Johnson, & Johnson, 1982).

• Seven indicated improvements or decreases (Ali & Costello, 1971; Bradley-Johnson, Graham, & Johnson, 1986; Edlund, 1972; Piersel, Brody, & Kratochwill, 1977; Saigh, 1981a, 1981b; Terrell, Taylor, & Terrell, 1978).

The differences between studies finding significant effects and those finding nonsignificant effects are difficult to

discern. In some studies token reinforcement increased scores on the WISC-R Verbal Scale but not on the Performance Scale. There is no readily available explanation to account for such differential effects. One could hypothesize that incentives are more effective in situations calling for speed and quick reaction time. Yet some findings indicate the opposite effect. Social and token reinforcers appear to operate in similar ways in the various ethnic and social-class groups studied.

The nonsignificant findings suggest that many children view the standard test situation as inherently rewarding. They may enjoy the special attention of and acceptance by an adult examiner. The standard testing condition in all of these experiments that reported nonsignificant findings was apparently one in which the children were motivated to perform at their maximum level; they did not need additional social or token reinforcement or feedback to perform more effectively. The significant findings, in contrast, suggest that for many other children reinforcers do increase motivation. If knowing whether a child can perform better on a specific reinforcement schedule would be helpful in designing remediation programs, you might consider testing limits by evaluating the child under reinforcement conditions *after* you complete the standard administration. This procedure, however, will introduce practice effects, which will make the testing-of-limits findings more difficult to evaluate.

The research on incentives and their effects on intelligence test scores fails in one major respect—there is little information about the validity of the scores obtained under the incentive conditions. It may be that the most valid scores are those obtained under conditions similar to those found in the child's environment. If teachers and parents do not use incentives in teaching children, it is doubtful that the scores obtained using such reinforcement procedures will be more valid than those obtained under standard conditions. Scores obtained using specific reinforcements may be more valid in environments that use reinforcements. These hypotheses need confirmation. At present there is little evidence that scores obtained using tangible or social reinforcement are more valid than those obtained under standard conditions.

Testing-of-limits.   Generally, the only modifications made to standard administrative procedures should be those discussed in the test manuals (for example, changing the order of tests if necessary or eliminating spoiled tests) or those necessary to test handicapped children. However, there may be times when you want to go beyond the standard test procedures in order to gain additional information about the child's abilities. The information from testing-of-limits procedures can occasionally be helpful, especially in clinical or psychoeducational settings. Any successes obtained during testing-of-limits, of course, cannot be credited to the child's scores.

Testing-of-limits techniques should be used only after the entire test has been administered using standard procedures. Otherwise additional cues may facilitate the child's performance on the remaining items of a test. Such score increases have been reported for the Block Design and Picture Arrangement subtests of the WISC and Wechsler-Bellevue Intelligence Scale (Sattler, 1969).

The following procedures may be used in testing-of-limits:

1. *Providing additional cues.* To determine how much help is necessary for the child to solve a problem, you may want to provide a series of cues to the child. One approach is simply to readminister failed items, telling the examinee that there is another solution or arrangement and asking him or her to try to find it. Or you might reproduce the examinee's construction (for example, a block design pattern or picture arrangement layout), tell the examinee that there is an error, and ask him or her to find it and correct it. If this procedure does not lead to a correct solution, you can show the child the first step in solving the problem, after which you can provide a series of additional steps if needed.

A second approach is to begin by asking the child how he or she went about trying to solve the problem (for example, "How did you get that answer?"). Before suggesting that the item be attempted again, you might want to provide the first step in reaching the correct solution or tell the child which part of the original method was incorrect.

Another approach is to provide additional structure (for example, if the child becomes disoriented when asked to throw a ball, you might put a line on the floor to better orient the child). Overall, you can break down and simplify the tasks until it becomes clear to you what the child can and cannot do with help and under what conditions.

The above procedures will help you to determine the extent to which the examinee can benefit from additional cues. The more cues that are needed before success is achieved, the greater the possible degree of learning disorder or cognitive deficit. This information will be helpful in planning remedial efforts.

2. *Changing modality.* To determine the influence of the modality, you may want to change it. For example, if the child fails problems in oral form, you might see if he or she can solve them in written form.

3. *Establishing methods used by the examinee.* There are many different ways of solving the test questions. On Digit Span memory tests, for example, the task can be solved by grouping the digits in sets of two, three, or more digit sequences; by recalling them as a number (4-1-3 as four hundred and thirteen); or by recalling them as distinct digits in sequence. The method used may be related to learning efficiency or to personality features, or it may have no particular import. Learning how the child solved the problem may give you additional insight into how well the task was understood and the particular memory strategy used by the child.

To learn how the child went about solving the problem, you may simply ask what method was used. Some children will be able to verbalize their method, but others will not, even though they have answered correctly.

4. *Eliminating time limits.* When the child does not complete a test because of time limits, you can readminister the test (after the examination) without time limits and delete references to speed or time limits in the directions. This will help you determine whether the child can solve the problem.

5. *Asking probing questions.* Occasionally examinees will give responses or make constructions with blocks or other materials that are vague or idiosyncratic. If you want to, you can go back to these items, repeating the item and response and then saying "Tell me more about what you mean," or reconstructing the design and saying "Tell me about what you assembled (or made); explain it to me." Such probing questions may give you insight into how the examinee approaches tasks.

As a result of the help provided during the testing-of-limits phase, the child may pass tests. During the test proper, too, the child may solve a problem after the time limit has been reached. In such cases, you can include in your report that the child benefited from additional help or time, but do not change the test scores.

One of the problems associated with helping procedures introduced during the testing-of-limits phase is that these procedures may invalidate the results of retesting occurring at a later date. Therefore, you must carefully consider the benefits and costs of testing limits. If retesting with the same test may be needed in the near future, then testing-of-limits procedures probably should not be used. However, if the goal is to evaluate the limits of the child's abilities on the test or determine problem-solving approaches and there is no reason to plan on a retest in the near future (say within the next 12 to 24 months), testing-of-limits may be quite useful.

EXAMINER CHARACTERISTICS

Examiner Skills

A competent examiner must be flexible, vigilant, and self-aware and must genuinely enjoy working with children. Other traits that will prove helpful are a sense of humor and the ability to work under less than favorable conditions. A preschool child who is uncooperative, pushes away toys offered to him or her, and remains silent will test the skills of even the most competent examiner. Realizing that subjective factors—such as your personal style, the child's physical and mental condition, the setting, interruptions during testing, your preparation, and the child's language facility—invariably affect the testing situation and may reduce its objectivity, your task is to obtain cooperation from even the most intractable child under conditions that depart as little as possible from standardized procedures.

Flexibility.   When you test children, you must be prepared to adjust your testing techniques. You may need to have frequent rest breaks, more than one testing session, or additional time for the child to explore and become familiar with the surroundings. Considerable effort may be required to establish and maintain rapport. It is especially important to use tact, diplomacy, and ingenuity, and to have patience and understanding. These procedures will reduce fatigue and help to alleviate the child's anxiety.

Order the battery so as to begin with tests that do not accentuate the child's weakness, particularly in the case of physically disabled children or language-impaired children. Selecting appropriate tests will facilitate rapport and lead to more reliable and valid test results. If a child proves untestable, the child's parents may be able to provide information about the child's language ability, motor ability, social skills, self-sufficiency, mental development, and overall development.

Vigilance.   Test administration should not be routine or automatic. You must become familiar with the test material and procedures so that you are free to exercise constant vigilance, making certain that the child has the necessary physical abilities to proceed with the test, observing when the child is or is not making his or her best effort, and deciding when to offer encouragement and praise. Whenever the child's interest in the tasks wanes, offer encouragement and support. Addressing problem behaviors may be taxing. For example, how do you decide whether a particular behavior reflects true helplessness or is manipulative? And once you decide, what actions should you take? Whatever difficulties you may encounter, keys to successful testing include appropriate timing of supportive comments and actions and maintenance of an appropriate flow of test materials.

Self-awareness.   You should strive to understand your own temperament and attitudes toward handicapped, exceptional, and ethnic minority children. Not all of you will be (or should be expected to be) equally effective in working with all types of exceptional children, every age group, and all ethnic groups. If you are having difficulty establishing rapport with certain children, try to determine why. Whenever you recognize that you are not fully capable of establishing rapport with a child, you should disqualify yourself from testing the child and ask a colleague to complete the evaluation. It is only through encounters with a variety of children and through a willingness to be open to self-evaluation and feedback from others that you will learn the limits of your own abilities. You should continually seek such knowledge by monitoring your own behaviors and reactions and by requesting feedback from colleagues.

Examiner Expectancy Effects

Your test administration should not be influenced by your personal impressions of the examinee—a reaction known as the halo effect. This may occur when you overrate the responses of a child whom you perceive as bright or underrate the responses of a child who appears dull. In the testing of handicapped children, the halo effect may occur in the following way:

Motivated by a feeling of sympathy often reinforced by seeing the physical energy expended by so many palsied children in following instructions, the examiner easily believes his [or her] hope, i.e., that the child knows more than he [or she] can express, and hence overestimates the child's ability. (Burgemeister, 1962, p. 117)

Binet and Wechsler carefully sought to diminish halo effects by their standardization procedures, but examiners too must take precautions to avoid them.

"Mr. Merrill's real strength is his ability to empathize in one-to-one situations."

Cartoon first appeared in *New Era*. Used by permission.

Social-psychological research indicates that an experimenter's hypotheses or expectancies may exert some subtle influence over a subject's performance by affecting how the experimenter behaves with a subject. Early data returns in an experiment may lead to the development of experimenter expectancies that can subtly affect the experimenter's behavior in later interactions with the subject (Rosenthal, 1966). Administering an individual intelligence test is somewhat analogous to conducting an experiment. Background information on the examinee may lead the examiner to formulate a hypothesis, albeit vague, regarding the examinee's level of intelligence, and this hypothesis may affect the examiner-examinee relationship. Consequently, it is imperative that examiners be on guard against the halo effect when administering tests.

Research on expectancy effects. Studies have examined whether information given to examiners affects their scoring of intelligence test responses provided on questionnaires or given by children in actual testing activities. Expectancy has been manipulated by providing various kinds of case history information, such as prior test scores, grades, academic achievement history, socioeconomic status, ethnicity, sex, and behavioral ratings.

Most questionnaire studies indicate that examiners are influenced by pretest information in scoring responses, especially if the responses are ambiguous (Auffrey & Robertson, 1972; Babad, Mann, & Mar-Hayim, 1975; Donahue & Sattler, 1971; Egeland, 1969; Fiscus, 1975; Grossman, 1978; Sattler, Hillix, & Neher, 1970; Sattler & Winget, 1970; Simon, 1969). Generally, examinees described as being bright are likely to receive more credit than examinees described as being dull for the exact same response. No significant scoring differences were found for protocols of black and white children (Mishra, 1983) or in a study where responses were presented in accented or nonaccented speech by means of a tape recorder (Rappaport & McAnulty, 1985).

Findings from studies in which examiners actually tested children are not so clear. In some cases positive expectancies led to children's obtaining higher scores (Hersh, 1971; Larrabee & Kleinsasser, 1967; Schroeder &

Kleinsasser, 1972), but in others they did not (Dangel, 1972; Ekren, 1962; Gillingham, 1970; Saunders & Vitro, 1971; Sneed, 1976). In the latter cases, examiners probably resolved any discrepancies created by the referral information by relying on the children's actual test performance. In actual test situations, the pretest information may color the examiner's attitudes initially, but these attitudes are likely to be less salient than the information the examiner is continually acquiring. The examiner adjusts his or her own judgments as additional information is acquired. For an expectancy effect or self-fulfilling prophecy to occur, the examiner must ignore the child's actual performance.

The studies reviewed indicate that pretest information plays a role in the overall evaluation of the examinee and, on occasion, in the scoring of responses and the administration of the test. The research does not suggest that the existence of expectancies regarding an examinee's probable level of performance means that scoring bias will necessarily occur. Rather, the research confirms that examiners must guard against the occurrence of halo effects when administering intelligence tests. The processes by which pretest information affects the examiner's performance are still unclear.

Awareness of expectancy effects. The elimination of halo effects in administering, scoring, and evaluating intelligence and other ability tests is a difficult goal. It is probably impossible to eliminate completely your positive or negative evaluations of the child; however, it is possible and necessary to minimize the influence of these reactions on your test administration and scoring of the child's test responses. Be sure that you do not smile, nod your head, lean forward, sustain additional eye contact, offer more support, be friendlier, give more praise, repeat questions more frequently, or create a warmer atmosphere with examinees who you believe are bright. You must become aware of your reactions to each child, and be especially alert to possible halo effects in your scoring of a child's ambiguous responses.

Variability Among Examiners

Research conclusively indicates that examiners differ in how they score the same test responses (Bradley, Hanna, & Lucas, 1980; Brannigan, Calnen, Loprete, & Rosenberg, 1976; Brannigan, Rosenberg, Loprete, & Calnen, 1977; Cuenot & Darbes, 1982; Curr & Gourlay, 1956; Davis, Peacock, Fitzpatrick, & Mulhern, 1969; Franklin, Still-

man, Burpeau, & Sabers, 1982; Jordan, 1932; Kaspar, Throne, & Schulman, 1968; LaCrosse, 1964; Mahan, 1963; Masling, 1959; Massey, 1964; Miller & Chansky, 1972; Miller, Chansky, & Gredler, 1970; Plumb & Charles, 1955; Ryan, Prifitera, & Powers, 1983; Sattler, Andres, Squire, Wisely, & Maloy, 1978; Sattler & Ryan, 1973a; Sattler & Squire, 1982; Sattler, Winget, & Roth, 1969; Schwartz, 1966; Scottish Council for Research in Education, 1967; Smith, May, & Lebovitz, 1966; Walker, Hunt, & Schwartz, 1965; Wrightstone, 1941). These reports indicate that the examiner's experience in giving tests probably makes only a minor contribution, if any, to this type of examiner variability (Curr & Gourlay, 1956; Davis et al., 1969; Jordan, 1932; Kaspar et al., 1968; LaCrosse, 1964; Masling, 1959; Plumb & Charles, 1955; Ryan et al., 1983; Sattler & Ryan, 1973a; Schwartz, 1966; Smith et al., 1966). In addition, examiners occasionally differ in the responses they obtain from children (Bennett, 1970; Cattell, 1937; Cieutat, 1965; Cieutat & Flick, 1967; Cohen, 1950, 1965; Curr & Gourlay, 1956; Davis et al., 1969; Di Lorenzo & Nagler, 1968; Green, 1960–62; Kaspar et al., 1968; Krebs, 1969; Nichols, 1959; Oakland, Lee, & Axelrad, 1975; Rothman, 1974; Sattler, 1966, 1969; Sattler & Theye, 1967; Schachter & Apgar, 1958; Schwartz & Flanigan, 1971; Smith & May, 1967; Thomas, Hertzig, Dryman, & Fernandez, 1971). In some studies children performed better for female examiners than for male examiners, but no systematic trends are evident (Back & Dana, 1977; Bradbury, Wright, Walker, & Ross, 1975; Cieutat & Flick, 1967; Pedersen, Shinedling, & Johnson, 1968; Quereshi, 1968; Smith et al., 1966). With ethnic minority children, the examiner's race plays a negligible role (Sattler & Gwynne, 1982b). (See Chapter 19 for further information about the examiner's race as a variable.) Little is known about the temperament variables that are related to examiners' scoring or administration styles (Egeland, 1967; Sattler, 1973b; Sattler & Martin, 1971).

The preceding research confirms clinical impressions that the examination setting has elements of subjectivity. Every attempt should be made to reduce any sources of subjectivity related to the examiner that may affect the validity of the test score. You should become aware of your scoring standards when confronted with ambiguous responses—whether you are lenient or rigorous in your judgments—and always try to be fair and consistent in your application of the scoring criteria. Table 5-4 was designed to assist you in obtaining information about your administrative techniques. During the early phases of your career, you should answer the questions in Table 5-4 after every assessment you complete. The list can also be used as a checklist by an observer. An understanding of child psychology and exceptionality, of test manuals, and of material in this book, coupled with a willingness to evaluate and reflect on your testing skills, will enable you to reach a high level of competence in testing children.

A FINAL THOUGHT—THROUGH A CHILD'S EYES

As repeatedly observed in this chapter, children play an active role in the testing process. They will react to you, just as you react to them. Sometimes you may actually receive feedback from the children you test. Exhibit 5-1 presents a tongue-in-cheek example of such feedback.

SUMMARY

1. Every effort should be made to establish rapport with children. This can be done by using praise, understanding comments, and meaningful explanations. The assessment aims to elicit children's best efforts.

2. Research studies suggest that familiarity with the examiner tends to enhance the performance of low SES children (by about 7.6 points when the test has an *SD* of 15).

3. Observing the child carefully during the evaluation is an important part of the evaluation process. Make notes of the child's behavior, rather than relying on memory. Attend to the child's attitude toward you and the test situation, attitude toward self, work habits, reaction to test items, reaction to failure and praise, language, visual-motor skills, and motor skills.

4. Some of the keys to successful testing of infant and preschool children include listening to the children's communications and timing your communications appropriately.

5. In testing ethnic minority children, openness and frankness in acknowledging miscommunication may help to facilitate rapport.

6. The key to testing emotionally disturbed children is understanding their particular problems and adapting the testing techniques to their needs.

7. Because delinquent children are likely to be defensive, attempts must be made to maximize their cooperative efforts.

8. Autistic children are likely to be extremely difficult to test. Before testing, learn about the child's preferred mode of communication. Flexibility will be needed to obtain an estimate of the autistic child's abilities.

9. In testing brain-injured children (as well as all other children), it is important to reduce any anxiety that is generated by the test situation.

10. Mentally retarded children may try to avoid difficult questions. By showing acceptance and reducing the threatening aspects of the test situation, you can enhance their performance and reduce avoidant behaviors.

11. The administration of standardized tests to physically handicapped children requires patience, understanding, and flexibility. The test items administered to physically handicapped children must be ones to which they can respond. Informally evaluate the child's sensory functions before you begin the evaluation. Be careful not to allow your expectations to bias your judgments.

12. In testing visually impaired children, you must first identify the extent of their impairment and how it may interfere with their ability to take tests. You can then select appropriate tests, or portions of tests, based on your findings.

13. The assessment of hearing-impaired children is particularly difficult because of the unique communication problems associated with their disability. You should recognize your own limitations as an examiner and be prepared to learn the necessary communication skills if you will be working regularly with hearing-impaired children. Although hearing-impaired children differ as to their degree of hearing loss, nonverbal tests usually provide the most valid means of assessing their level of intellectual functioning.

14. Flexibility is needed in the testing of cerebral palsied children. If tests are administered carefully, the results obtained are likely to provide an accurate estimate of the level of cognitive functioning of cerebral palsied children.

15. Skill in the administration of tests develops with experience. An examiner must become adept at developing empathy and understanding, maintaining limits, arranging an appropriate environment, using appropriate reinforcements, and developing a harmonious relationship with parents. Practice is important, especially in learning how to read the directions, handle the test materials, and score the responses. The guidelines presented in this chapter are designed to supplement those that appear in test manuals. Remember that the scoring guidelines in test manuals are just guides, and that in most cases the answers are not meant to be the only correct answers.

16. Departures from standard procedures may be needed when handicapped children are tested. However, the resulting scores may yield less precise estimates of the child's level of ability depending on the extent of the departure.

17. Incentives, such as special praise, candy, or money, *sometimes* lead to higher test scores, but little is known about which specific procedures are effective with which groups of children. There is little evidence to support the position that reinforcers act differentially for different ethnic groups or social classes.

18. On some occasions it is useful to test limits in order to determine whether the child can solve problems when given helping cues or special procedures. Testing-of-limits should be carried out only *after* the standard administration of the entire test. Testing-of-limits should not be used when retesting is planned soon after the initial testing, because it may increase the chances of obtaining invalid scores on the retest.

19. A willingness to be open to self-evaluation and to receive

Table 5-4
Checklist for General Test Administration Practices

General Test Administration Practices Checklist

Examiner: _____   Date: _____

Examinee: _____   Age: _____

Observer: _____   Test administered: _____

Circle one

yes	no	1. Established rapport before beginning the test
yes	no	2. Prepared child for examination
yes	no	3. Arranged test environment to minimize distractions
yes	no	4. Avoided distracting mannerisms
yes	no	5. Showed interest in child
yes	no	6. Gave child ample encouragement and support
yes	no	7. Wore appropriate, nondistracting attire
yes	no	8. Spoke at appropriate volume for the setting
yes	no	9. Appeared open and accepting of child's feelings
yes	no	10. Seemed at ease with child
yes	no	11. Maintained frequent eye contact with child
yes	no	12. Had all necessary materials present
yes	no	13. Arranged materials conveniently
yes	no	14. Placed manual so that child could not read it
yes	no	15. Arranged materials so that child could not view test items other than the one(s) in use
yes	no	16. Manipulated materials with ease and confidence
yes	no	17. Read all directions verbatim
yes	no	18. Used accurate timing procedures
yes	no	19. Used unobtrusive timing procedures
yes	no	20. Recorded responses in record booklet
yes	no	21. Paced examination to suit child's ability
yes	no	22. Explained test procedures adequately
yes	no	23. Used vocabulary suited to child
yes	no	24. Showed awareness of signs of fatigue
yes	no	25. Handled fatigue appropriately
yes	no	26. Showed awareness of emotional upsets
yes	no	27. Handled emotional upsets appropriately
yes	no	28. Took needed breaks
yes	no	29. Handled child's manipulations appropriately
yes	no	30. Gave appropriate explanations or clarifications
yes	no	31. Used additional questions to clarify, not to improve, child's answers
yes	no	32. Made inquiries in a nonthreatening manner
yes	no	33. Praised child appropriately (e.g., did not praise correct answers, praised *effort*)
yes	no	34. Handled disruptions adequately
yes	no	35. Responded honestly and positively to child's questions in ways consistent with the testing

---

feedback from others will help beginning examiners develop clinical skills. A sense of humor can also be helpful.

20. The halo effect is a problem that may arise in the course of conducting an examination. There is substantial evidence that when examiners are provided with information about the examinee's probable level of performance, they may assign better scores to examinees purported to be bright than to examinees purported to be dull. Thus pretest information may play a role in the overall evaluation of the examinee and, on occasion, in the scoring of responses and administration of tests. Recognizing the possibility of their occurrence helps to reduce halo effects.

21. Examiners have been found to differ among themselves in

Exhibit 5-1
". . . On the Other Foot"

My name is Timmy Jones and I am in the third grade. I am as smart as anyone in the Elm Street School, including grown-ups. I even learned their language. Take that woman that tested me last week.

Psychological Report

Name: Audrey O'Neill
Age: Uncertain
Observation of behavior: Mrs. O'Neill is below average height and weight. It was a cold, wet day and she was limping slightly. Her grooming leaves something to be desired. Her clothing was dark and several years behind the style, "comfortable" shoes evidenced lack of concern with the impression made on others, long straight hair would be more appropriate on a younger person, and fingernails were dirty — she looks as if she spends her spare time refinishing furniture. The bag she carried her test equipment in has seen better days. The whole impression she gave was one of mild involutional depression.

Mrs. O'Neill actually lost her way to the supply closet where she had set up makeshift quarters even though she has been using it all semester. This was my first time and I found it right away. Attempts to establish rapport were clumsy and interview techniques emphasized the negative. Of course I don't beat up on my little brother. And what did she mean by asking if everyone in my family has the same last name? She was distracted by the sound of the band practicing in the next room and preoccupied by the three phone calls that interrupted the testing session.

Test performance: Mrs. O'Neill made three errors administering the Stanford-Binet: Form L-M. All the better examiners use the WISC-R anyway. During a 90-minute testing session she managed to misplace her reading glasses once, her glass case twice, and her pen three times. Her handwriting is almost completely illegible, and she dropped three of the blocks. She transposed numbers twice, once administering digits forward and once transcribing a phone message. She definitely became nervous when I went into my hyperactive act, and has a hard time tolerating drumming fingers, tapping feet, etc.

Strengths and weaknesses: She is high in long-term memory and informational background. She remembered my sister and brother, and asked about my grandmother's health. She is low in short-term memory, concentration, and auditory skills: auditory reception and discrimination and auditory figure-ground. She is also low in sequencing, both auditory and visual. She had problems with fine-motor skills and spatial orientations. Her motor coordination is gross.

Social relationships: Both child and peer relationships are in need of improvement. The children who greeted her in the hall are all either failing in school, from broken homes, or from the socioeconomic level that my parents do not allow me to associate with. Nor does she handle peer relationships well. It took us 12 minutes and 48 seconds by the new stopwatch I got for my birthday to get from one end of the hall to the supply closet because every grown-up we passed had to stop and tell her something. No wonder she is not more task-oriented.

Summary: Mrs. O'Neill is of approximately average native endowment for her cultural group membership. However, she is not functioning well because of (a) mild depression and (b) learning disabilities, which are developmental and therefore at her age will get worse. Peer relationships distract her from her work.

Recommendations:

1. Mrs. O'Neill could probably continue to perform her duties adequately in a simpler and more protected setting. Perhaps she could be transferred to the Gilmanton Corners Village School.

2. A program for identifying the gifted would improve her child contacts and broaden her perspective.

3. She should stop eating lunch alone while working on records. Not only did she get three mayonnaise stains on my cumulative folder, but she is heading for a good case of professional burn-out.

Timothy Jones
Grade 3
The Elm Street School

Source: Reprinted, with changes in notation, with permission of the publisher and author from Audrey Myerson O'Neill, ". . .On the Other Foot," *Journal of School Psychology*, 1981, *19*, pp. 71–72. Copyright 1981, Pergamon Journals, Ltd.

---

their scoring of test responses and in the responses that they obtain from examinees. However, the sources of these differences have not been established. The examiner's experience in giving tests does not appear to play a crucial role in the scoring of test responses. The examiner's sex is not usually a critical factor in the child's performance. Examiners' personality variables have not been shown to be associated significantly with either scoring or administration styles.

KEY TERMS, CONCEPTS, AND NAMES

Rapport (p. 86)
Echolalia (p. 93)
Emotional lability (p. 94)
Perseveration (p. 94)
Blindness (p. 98)
Hearing impairment (p. 99)
Deaf child (p. 99)
Hard-of-hearing child (p. 99)
Minimal hearing loss (p. 99)
Mild hearing loss (p. 99)
Moderate hearing loss (p. 99)
Severe hearing loss (p. 99)
Profound hearing loss (p. 99)
Social reinforcement (p. 110)
Token reinforcement (p. 110)
Testing-of-limits (p. 110)
Expectancy effects (p. 112)
Halo effect (p. 112)

STUDY QUESTIONS

1. Explain how an examiner should go about establishing rapport with children. Include a discussion of research studies.

2. What are some useful strategies for testing infant and preschool children?

3. What are some factors to consider in testing ethnic minority, emotionally disturbed, delinquent, autistic, brain-injured, and mentally retarded children? Include in your discussion both unique and common testing principles for these groups.

4. What special adjustments may be needed to test physically handicapped children?

5. What are some useful techniques for testing visually impaired children?

6. What are some factors to consider in testing hearing-impaired children?

7. What are some useful techniques for testing cerebral palsied children?

8. What are some general suggestions for administering tests?

9. Discuss the problems associated with departures from standard procedure. Include relevant research on the use of incentives and feedback.

10. Discuss the concept of testing-of-limits.

11. Discuss the concept of halo effects. Include relevant research.

6

WECHSLER INTELLIGENCE SCALE FOR CHILDREN—REVISED (WISC-R): DESCRIPTION

The concept [of intelligence] has as much scientific status as does the concept of gravity, and the global measures of intelligence, although limited for diagnostic purposes, do help tell us where all our other more experimental measures are located in a general correlational map of human cognitive variations.
—Richard E. Snow

Standardization

Deviation IQs, Scaled Scores, and Test-Age Equivalents

Reliability

Validity

Intercorrelations Between Subtests and Scales

WISC-R IQs and Stratification Variables

Factor Analysis

Administering the WISC-R

Short Forms of the WISC-R

Choosing Between the WISC-R and the WPPSI and Between the WISC-R and the WAIS-R

Administering the WISC-R (and WPPSI and WAIS-R) to Handicapped Children

Assets of the WISC-R

Limitations of the WISC-R

Concluding Comment on the WISC-R

Summary

Exhibit 6-1

WISC-R–Like Items

Information (30 questions)

How many legs do you have?
What must you do to make water freeze?
Who discovered the North Pole?
What is the capital of France?

Similarities (17 questions)

In what way are pencil and crayon alike?
In what way are tea and coffee alike?
In what way are inch and mile alike?
In what way are binoculars and microscope alike?

Arithmetic (18 questions)

If I have one piece of candy and get another one, how many pieces will I have?
At 12 cents each, how much will 4 bars of soap cost?
If a suit sells for ½ of the ticket price, what is the cost of a $120 suit?

Vocabulary (32 words)

ball   poem
summer   obstreperous

Comprehension (17 questions)

Why do we wear shoes?
What is the thing to do if you see someone dropping his packages?
In what two ways is a lamp better than a candle?
Why are we tried by a jury of our peers?

Digit Span

Digits Forward contains seven series of digits, 3 to 9 digits in length (Example: 1-8-9).
Digits Backward contains seven series of digits, 2 to 8 digits in length (Example: 5-8-1-9).

Picture Completion (26 items)

The task is to identify the essential missing part of the picture.
A picture of a car without a wheel.
A picture of a dog without a leg.
A picture of a telephone without numbers on the dial.
An example of a Picture Completion task is shown below.

Courtesy of The Psychological Corporation.

Picture Arrangement (12 items)

The task is to arrange a series of pictures into a meaningful sequence. The photograph of the WISC-R (Figure 6-1) shows a Picture Arrangement item.

Block Design (11 items)

The task is to reproduce stimulus designs using four or nine blocks. An example of a Block Design item is shown below.

Object Assembly (4 items)

The task is to arrange pieces into a meaningful object. An example of an Object Assembly item is shown below.

Courtesy of The Psychological Corporation.

Coding

The task is to copy symbols from a key (see below).

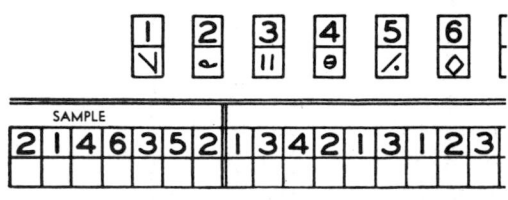

Courtesy of The Psychological Corporation.

Mazes

The task is to complete a series of mazes. The photograph of the WISC-R (Figure 6-1) shows an example of a maze.

Note. The questions resemble those that appear on the WISC-R but are not actually from the test. Chapter 7 describes each subtest in more detail.

The Wechsler Intelligence Scale for Children—Revised (WISC-R) (Wechsler, 1974) was published in 1974, 25 years after the original publication of the WISC. Its predecessor, the WISC (Wechsler, 1949), was developed as a downward extension of the adult intelligence test, the Wechsler-Bellevue Intelligence Scale. To make the original adult scale more suitable for children, easier items were added to the beginning of the subtests. The WISC-R covers an age range from 6-0 to 16-11 years and contains 12 subtests (see Figure 6-1). Six of the tests form the Verbal Scale (Information, Similarities, Arithmetic, Vocabulary, Comprehension, and Digit Span) and the other six form the Performance Scale (Picture Completion, Picture Arrangement, Block Design, Object Assembly, Coding, and Mazes). Items similar to those on the WISC-R are shown in Exhibit 6-1. A total of 72 percent of the WISC items are retained in the WISC-R, either intact (64 percent) or with substantial modification (8 percent); the items in the Coding subtest are the same in the WISC and the WISC-R.

STANDARDIZATION

The WISC-R was standardized on a sample of 2,200 American children selected as representative of the population on the basis of the 1970 U.S. Census. In the standardization sample, there were 11 different age groups, ranging from 6-6 to 16-6 years, with 200 children in each group. Unlike the WISC, which included only whites in the standardization group, the WISC-R included non-whites (blacks, American Indians, Asians, Puerto Ricans, and Mexican Americans). The proportions in the WISC-R sample approximate those in the 1970 Census more closely for whites than for nonwhites. (The discrepancy between the standardization sample and the census data is no greater than 1 percent for whites, but is as high as 4.5 percent for nonwhites.) The extent of the effect of these discrepancies on scaled test scores cannot be assessed. Given the relatively small size of the discrepancy, however, the effects should not be large.

DEVIATION IQS, SCALED SCORES, AND TEST-AGE EQUIVALENTS

The WISC-R, like other Wechsler scales, provides three separate IQs: a Verbal Scale IQ, a Performance Scale IQ, and a Full Scale IQ. All three are Deviation IQs obtained by comparing the examinees' scores with those earned by a representative sample of age peers. Because Deviation IQs

are standard scores, at each age level each of the three IQs has the same mean of 100 and standard deviation of 15.

When the WISC-R is administered, raw scores are obtained on each subtest. The raw scores are then converted to normalized standard scores (or scaled scores) within the examinee's own age group through use of a table in the WISC-R manual. This table is based on four-month age intervals between 6-0-0 (years, months, days), and 16-11-30. The scaled scores for each subtest have a mean of 10 and standard deviation of 3.

Prorating Procedure

The IQ tables in the WISC-R manual are based on only 10 of the 12 subtests. The two supplementary subtests, Digit Span and Mazes, are excluded from the calculation of the IQ even when they have been administered. When fewer than 10 subtests are administered, prorating is necessary to compute the IQ. The WISC-R manual provides a table for prorating the scores when four of the subtests are administered in each scale. When fewer than four subtests are administered in each scale, IQs should be computed using the special short-form procedure described later in this chapter.

Test-Age Equivalents

In developing the WISC-R and the other Wechsler scales, Wechsler did not use mental age to calculate IQs because he believed that the concept was potentially misleading. (See Chapter 4 for criticisms associated with the mental-age concept.) He rejected the notion that mental age represents an absolute level of mental capacity or that the same mental age in different children represents identical intelligence levels. Soon after the initial publication of the WISC, however, he recognized that mental-age or test-age equivalents (average age associated with a score) would be useful. In subsequent publications of the WISC and WISC-R, Wechsler provided a table of test-age equivalents to facilitate interpretation. Test-age equivalents are essentially mental age (MA) scores.

The WISC-R test-age equivalent scores can be compared with scores on other tests that use mental ages or test ages, and reported to parents, teachers, and other individuals. Test ages are obtained directly from raw scores on each subtest. An average test-age equivalent can be obtained by summing the individual subtest age equivalents and dividing by the number of subtests. A median test age can be obtained by rank ordering all of the test ages from high to low and finding the median age. The WISC-R test

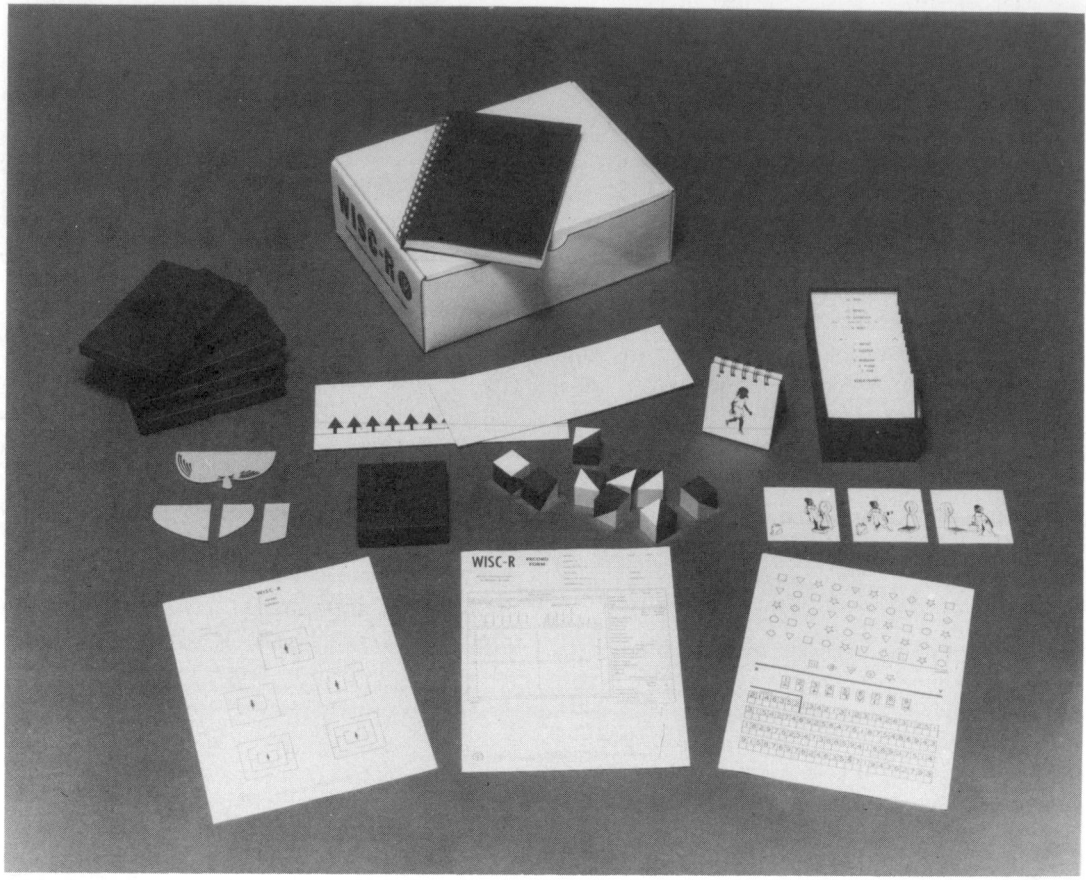

Figure 6-1.   Wechsler Intelligence Scale for Children—Revised. Courtesy of The Psychological Corporation.

ages have adequate validity, as indicated by high correlations with the Stanford-Binet: Form L-M mental age ($r = .88$) (Sutton, Koller, & Christian, 1982) and the Peabody Individual Achievement Test ($r = .82$) (Huberty & Koller, 1984).

RELIABILITY

The WISC-R has outstanding reliability. Each of the three IQ scales has an internal consistency reliability coefficient of .89 or above in the standardization group over the entire age range covered by the scale. Average internal consistency reliability coefficients, based on the 11 age groups, are .96 for the Full Scale IQ, .94 for the Verbal Scale IQ, and .90 for the Performance Scale IQ.

Table 6-1 summarizes average reliabilities and standard errors of measurement for the 12 subtests and three scales. Internal consistency subtest reliabilities, although adequate, are less satisfactory than scale reliabilities. The average subtest reliability coefficients range from a low of .70 for Object Assembly to a high of .86 for Vocabulary. The highest reliabilities are generally found among the Verbal Scale subtests, although one Performance Scale subtest, Block Design, has a reliability coefficient of .85. The average reliability coefficients range from .77 to .86 ($Mdn = .80$) for the Verbal Scale subtests and from .70 to .85 ($Mdn = .72$) for the Performance Scale subtests. When the reliability coefficients are considered for each of the 11 age groups separately, they range from a low of .57 for Mazes at the 16-6 age level to a high of .92 for Vocabulary at the 16-6 age level. The reliability coefficients are similar, for the most part, across the 11 age groups.

Table 6-1
Average Reliability Coefficients and Standard Errors of Measurement for WISC-R Subtests and Scales

Subtest or scale	Average reliability coefficient	Average standard error of measurement
Information	.85	1.19
Similarities	.81	1.34
Arithmetic	.77	1.38
Vocabulary	.86	1.15
Comprehension	.77	1.39
Digit Span	.78	1.44
Picture Completion	.77	1.45
Picture Arrangement	.73	1.57
Block Design	.85	1.17
Object Assembly	.70	1.70
Coding	.72	1.63
Mazes	.72	1.70
Verbal Scale IQ	.94	3.60
Performance Scale IQ	.90	4.66
Full Scale IQ	.96	3.19

Note. Reliability coefficients for 10 of the 12 subtests (except Digit Span and Coding) are split-half correlations. For Digit Span and Coding the reliability coefficients are test-retest coefficients obtained on a sample of about 50 children in six different age groups who were retested after a one-month interval. Verbal, Performance, and Full Scale reliability coefficients are based on a formula for computing the reliability of a composite group of tests.
Source: Adapted from Wechsler (1974).

Standard Errors of Measurement

The standard errors of measurement (SE_m) in IQ points, based on the average of the 11 age groups, are 3.19 for the Full Scale, 3.60 for the Verbal Scale, and 4.66 for the Performance Scale (see Table 6-1). Thus more confidence can be placed in an IQ based on the Full Scale than in an IQ based on either the Verbal or the Performance Scale.

The standard errors of measurement for the subtests in scaled score points, based on the average of the 11 age groups, range from 1.15 to 1.44 for the Verbal Scale subtests and from 1.17 to 1.70 for the Performance Scale subtests. Within the Verbal Scale, Vocabulary and Information have the smallest SE_m (1.15 and 1.19, respectively). Within the Performance Scale, Block Design and Picture Completion have the smallest SE_m (1.17 and 1.45, respectively).

Stability

The WISC-R provides stable IQs for each of the three scales. In the standardization sample the stability of the WISC-R was assessed by retesting a group of 303 children from three age groups after a one-month interval (Wechsler, 1974). For the retest sample, the stability coefficients were .95 for the Full Scale IQ, .93 for the Verbal Scale IQ, and .90 for the Performance Scale IQ; those for the 12 subtests ranged from .65 (Mazes) to .88 (Information) (*Mdn* = .78). The mean test-retest IQs and standard deviations for the Verbal, Performance, and Full Scales for the three groups are shown in Table 6-2. The average increase in IQ from the first to the second testing was about 7 IQ points for the Full Scale, about 4 IQ points for the Verbal Scale, and about 10 IQ points for the Performance Scale. These differences, which can be considered to be the result of practice effects, are much greater for the Performance Scale than for the Verbal Scale. Other studies (Haynes & Howard, 1986; Naglieri & Pfeiffer, 1983a) also report relatively stable WISC-R IQs over a two-year interval (mean Verbal, Performance, and Full Scale IQ changes were less than 3 points).

Precision Range

Table C-1 in Appendix C shows the confidence intervals for the 68, 85, 90, 95, and 99 percent levels for each scale. The confidence intervals are provided for separate age levels as well as for the average of the age levels. *The child's specific age group — not the average of the 11 age groups — should be used to obtain the most accurate confidence interval.* The precision ranges of the WISC-R IQs are similar throughout the age levels covered by the scale. For further discussion of precision range (or confidence intervals), see Chapters 2 and 23.

VALIDITY

A variety of studies have investigated the criterion validity of the WISC-R by correlating the WISC-R with the WPPSI, WAIS-R, WAIS, Stanford-Binet: Fourth Edition, Stanford-Binet: Form L-M, other intelligence tests, and measures of achievement and school grades. Table 6-3 shows the median correlations between the WISC-R Verbal, Performance, and Full Scales and other intelligence tests, achievement tests, and school grades. Although the table is not exhaustive, the representative studies listed show that the WISC-R has satisfactory concurrent validity.

Table 6-2
Test-Retest WISC-R IQs for Three Groups of Children

Age	Scale	First testing		Second testing		Change
		Mean IQ	SD	Mean IQ	SD	
6½–7½	Verbal	98.3	12.3	102.2	12.7	+3.9
(N = 97)	Performance	97.9	14.5	106.5	15.0	+8.6
	Full	97.9	13.2	104.5	14.0	+6.6
10½–11½	Verbal	99.0	13.4	102.4	13.8	+3.4
(N = 102)	Performance	98.5	13.9	109.3	16.3	+10.8
	Full	98.6	13.7	106.2	15.1	+7.6
14½–15½	Verbal	96.8	16.1	100.0	17.1	+3.2
(N = 104)	Performance	96.2	14.4	105.4	18.2	+9.2
	Full	96.1	15.4	103.0	18.0	+6.9

Source: Reprinted, with a change in notation, from the WISC-R manual, pages 32–33. Reproduced by permission. Copyright 1974 by The Psychological Corporation, New York, N.Y. All rights reserved.

Median correlations range from the upper .30s to the low .80s.

WISC-R and WPPSI

Because the WISC-R overlaps with the WPPSI in the age range of 6-0-0 to 6-7-15, either of the two tests can be used to evaluate children in this age range. In one study (Wechsler, 1974), a representative sample of 50 male and female 6-year-olds were given the two tests in counterbalanced order. The correlations were .80 for the Verbal Scales, .80 for the Performance Scales, and .82 for the Full Scales. Although the mean IQs on the Verbal, Performance, and Full Scales were higher on the WPPSI than on the WISC-R, the differences were small (1.5, 2.8, and 2.5 IQ points, respectively).

Another study (Quereshi & McIntire, 1984) of 72 6-year-old normal children, which also used a counterbalanced design, indicated that WISC-R and WPPSI IQs were comparable—WISC-R IQs were slightly higher than WPPSI IQs (differences were .73 on the Verbal Scale, 2.25 on the Performance Scale, and 1.45 on the Full Scale). Correlations were uniformly high for the three IQs (*r*'s = .86, .77, and .85, respectively).

In a study (Rasbury, McCoy, & Perry, 1977) in which 5- to 6-year-old middle-class children were administered both tests, with a one-year test-retest interval, the WISC-R yielded IQs that were 5 points lower on the average than those of the WPPSI. Correlations between the two tests were .81 for the Verbal Scales, .80 for the Performance

Scales, and .94 for the Full Scales. Individual subtest scores on the WISC-R were approximately 1 scaled-score point lower than those on the WPPSI. In 10 percent of the cases, differences between the two tests were larger than 10 IQ points. Consequently, in retest situations where the WISC-R follows the WPPSI or vice versa, differences in the two IQs may reflect errors of measurement rather than any changes in the child's ability.

WISC-R and WAIS-R

Because the WISC-R overlaps with the WAIS-R in the range 16-0-0 to 16-11-30, either of the two tests can be used to test children in this age range. Table 6-4 summarizes the results of studies in which seven different samples were given both the WISC-R and the WAIS-R and one sample was randomly assigned either the WISC-R or the WAIS-R. Firm conclusions about the comparability of the two scales are difficult because some of these studies had retest intervals as long as six years whereas others were conducted within the same day. Populations were also varied, including the mentally retarded, special education students, the hearing impaired, delinquents, and nonreferred children; few studies had representative samples. Still, some trends appear in the findings. The WAIS-R yielded *higher* IQs than the WISC-R in some groups, particularly in groups of mentally retarded or moderately below average students. One sample of mentally retarded children obtained WAIS-R IQs that were, on the average, 11 points higher than their WISC-R IQs (Rubin et al., 1985). The findings

Table 6-3
Criterion Validity Studies for the WISC-R

Criterion	Median correlations		
	Verbal Scale	Performance Scale	Full Scale
Stanford-Binet: Fourth Edition	—	—	.78
Stanford-Binet: Form L-M	.75	.68	.82
Slosson Intelligence Test	.75	.51	.61
McCarthy Scales of Children's Abilities	.68	.62	.72
K-ABC	.50	.65	.70
Woodcock-Johnson Broad Cognitive Ability	.77	.55	.77
Group intelligence tests	.61	.59	.66
Peabody Picture Vocabulary Test—R	.72	.47	.68
Quick Test	.76	.68	.72
Wide Range Achievement Test			
Reading	.57	.34	.56
Spelling	.50	.26	.59
Arithmetic	.62	.46	.52
Peabody Individual Achievement Test	.75	.45	.71
Other achievement tests			
Reading	.66	.47	.65
Arithmetic	.56	.48	.58
School grades	—	—	.39

Source: This table is based on studies cited in Sattler (1982b) and on the following studies: Algozzine and Ysseldyke (1981); Altepeter and Handal (1986); Appelbaum and Tuma (1982); Arinoldo (1982); Bracken, Prasse, and Breen (1984); Breen (1981); Breen and Siewert (1983); Coleman and Harmer (1985); Crofoot and Bennett (1980); Davis and Kramer (1985); Estabrook (1984); Grossman and Johnson (1982); Haddad (1986); Hollinger and Sarvis (1984); Hutton and Davenport (1985); Hynd, Quackenbush, Kramer, Connor, and Weed (1980); Kaufman and Kaufman (1983); Kitson and Vance (1982); Klanderman, Devine, and Mollner (1985); Marshall, Hess, and Lair (1978); Mask and Bowen (1984); McCallum, Karnes, and Edwards (1984); McGrew (1983); Naglieri (1982, 1984, 1985a, 1985b); Naglieri and Anderson (1985); Naglieri and Haddad (1984); Naglieri and Yazzie (1983); Oakland and Dowling (1983); Obrzut, Obrzut, and Shaw (1984); Paramesh (1982); Phelps, Rosso, and Falasco (1985); Pommer (1986); Prasse and Bracken (1981); Reilly, Drudge, Rosen, Loew, and Fischer (1985); Rosso, Falasco, and Koller (1984); Rust and Lose (1980); Smith and Smith (1986); Sutter and Bishop (1986b); Thompson and Brassard (1984); Tramill, Tramill, Thornthwaite, and Anderson (1981); White (1979); Worthing, Phye, and Nunn (1984); Wurtz, Sewell, and Manni (1985); Zins and Barnett (1984).

suggest that some children who are classified as mentally retarded on the WISC-R may not be so classified on the WAIS-R. This hypothesis is based on test-retest intervals of about three or four years.

In studies with nonreferred children, as well as in studies with children who are somewhat below average, delin-

quent, and hard of hearing, the two scales yielded comparable IQs. The Performance Scales may be more comparable than the Verbal Scales, but this hypothesis needs further verification. Little is known about the comparability of the two scales for gifted adolescents.

WISC-R and Stanford-Binet: Fourth Edition

Four studies comparing the WISC-R and the Stanford-Binet: Fourth Edition are reported in the *Technical Manual* of the Fourth Edition (Thorndike, Hagen, & Sattler, 1986b). As Table 6-5 indicates, the WISC-R yielded slightly *higher* IQs than did the Stanford-Binet: Fourth Edition, even though the latter has a larger standard deviation than the WISC-R (16 vs. 15). Correlations ranged from .66 to .83 between the WISC-R Full Scale IQ and the Fourth Edition composite. These results suggest that the two tests yield scores that are approximately equal, but they are not interchangeable. In another study (Carvajal & Weyand, 1986) the correlation between the WISC-R and the six-subtest General Purpose Abbreviated Battery on the Fourth Edition was .78; the Full Scale IQ and Composite Score were very close—115.0 and 113.3, respectively.

INTERCORRELATIONS BETWEEN SUBTESTS AND SCALES

Intercorrelations provide information about the relationships of WISC-R subtests to each other and to the scales. Average intercorrelations between the 12 subtests range from a low of .19 to a high of .69 (*Mdn* = .40). The six *highest* subtest average intercorrelations are between Vocabulary and Information (.69), Vocabulary and Similarities (.67), Vocabulary and Comprehension (.66), Information and Similarities (.62), Block Design and Object Assembly (.60), and Similarities and Comprehension (.59).

The six *lowest* subtest average intercorrelations are between Picture Completion and Coding (.19), Picture Completion and Digit Span (.21), Object Assembly and Digit Span (.21), Coding and Mazes (.21), Picture Arrangement and Digit Span (.22), and Mazes and Digit Span (.22). Thus Verbal Scale subtests are more highly intercorrelated than are the Performance Scale subtests.

Average correlations between the Verbal Scale subtests and the Verbal Scale range from .45 to .78 (*Mdn* = .70); those between the Performance Scale subtests and the Performance Scale range from .33 to .68 (*Mdn* = .53). The intercorrelations between the individual subtests and the Full Scale exhibited a similar trend. Vocabulary has the

Table 6-4
Studies Comparing the WISC-R and the WAIS-R

Study	N	Test-retest interval	Verbal Scale			
			WISC-R	WAIS-R	Diff.[a]	r
Braden & Paquin (1985)	32[b]	1 to 6 years	—	—	—	—
Grace (1986)	55[c]	same day	78.08	81.95	+2.87	—
Meacham (1984)	37[b]	same day	—	—	—	—
Rubin, Goldman, & Rosenfeld (1985)	41[d]	3 to 7 years	58.80	70.05	+11.25	.80
Sattler, Polifka, Polifka, & Hilsen (1984)	30[e]	4 years	81.00	81.30	+.30	.76
Wechsler (1981)	80[f]	1 to 6 weeks	99.40	99.60	+.20	.89
Zimmerman, Covin, & Woo-Sam (1986)	50[e]	4 years	75.80	81.20	+5.4	.84
	40[e]	4 years	70.60	75.30	+4.7	.57

[a] In the difference column (diff.), a plus (+) sign means that WAIS-R IQs were *higher* than WISC-R IQs, and a minus (−) sign means that WAIS-R IQs were *lower* than WISC-R IQs.
[b] Subjects were in a residential school for the deaf.
[c] Subjects were incarcerated male delinquents. This was not a test-retest study. Subjects were randomly assigned to either the WISC-R (*N* = 25) or the WAIS-R (*N* = 30).

highest correlation of any of the subtests with the Full Scale (.74), followed by Information (.70) and Block Design (.68). Digit Span (.43) and Coding (.38) have the lowest correlations with the Full Scale. Within their respective scales, Vocabulary (.78) and Block Design (.68) have the highest correlations with the Verbal and Performance Scale IQs.

WISC-R IQS AND STRATIFICATION VARIABLES

Table 6-6 shows the relationship between WISC-R IQs and the demographic characteristics of the standardization sample. Differences between the boys' and girls' mean IQs on the three scales were less than 3 points. Thus sex differences are not large enough to assume any practical significance on the scale. Mean IQs of white children were about 1 standard deviation higher than those of black children (102 vs. 86). Mean IQs show a clear relation to parental occupation group: for the total group, children of professional and technical workers obtained Full Scale IQs that were 21 points higher, on the average, than those of children of unskilled workers (108.2 vs. 87.3). Urban-rural differences on the three scales were small—less than 3 points. IQs of children from the South were on the average about 6 points lower than those of children from the West (96.6 vs. 102.6).

Table 6-5
Comparison of WISC-R and Stanford-Binet Intelligence Scale: Fourth Edition

Sample	N	WISC-R			Stanford-Binet: Fourth Edition						
		Verbal Scale IQ	Performance Scale IQ	Full Scale IQ	Verbal Reasoning	Abstract Visual Reasoning	Quantitative Reasoning	Short-Term Memory	Composite	Diff.[a]	r
Normal[b]	23	—	—	115.0	—	—	—	—	113.3	+1.7	.78
Normal[c]	205	103.9	105.3	105.2	104.4	98.9	102.1	102.4	102.4	+2.8	.83
Gifted[c]	19	117.6	114.5	117.7	113.5	109.6	117.2	116.1	116.3	+1.4	.69
Learning disabled[c]	90	85.2	92.3	87.8	88.8	87.7	86.3	84.8	84.8	+3.0	.87
Mentally retarded[c]	61	66.2	71.9	67.0	69.4	71.6	73.9	67.5	66.2	+.8	.66

[a] In the difference (diff.) column, the plus (+) sign indicates that WISC-R Full Scale IQs were higher than Fourth Edition composite scores.
[b] Carvajal & Weyand (1986).
[c] Thorndike et al. (1986b).

Performance Scale				Full Scale			
WISC-R	WAIS-R	Diff.[a]	r	WISC-R	WAIS-R	Diff.[a]	r
94.87	97.23	+2.38	.74	—	—	—	—
88.88	83.80	−5.08	—	82.32	82.75	+.43	—
99.08	100.41	+1.33	.75	—	—	—	—
60.66	65.54	+4.88	.82	55.83	66.93	+11.10	.83
84.70	86.47	+1.27	.82	81.13	82.70	+1.57	.86
104.30	102.80	−1.50	.76	101.90	101.00	−.90	.88
79.70	83.30	+3.6	.85	75.90	81.20	+5.2	.88
72.60	72.30	−.30	.75	69.60	73.00	+3.4	.70

[d] Subjects were in a residential school for the mentally retarded.

[e] Subjects were in special education.

[f] Nonreferral sample.

FACTOR ANALYSIS

A factor analysis of the standardization group indicated that three factors could efficiently describe the WISC-R (see Table 6-7) (Kaufman, 1975a). These factors are labeled Verbal Comprehension, Perceptual Organization, and Freedom from Distractibility. The term *Verbal Comprehension* describes the hypothesized ability underlying the factor for both item content (verbal) and mental process (comprehension). This factor appears to measure a variable common to the Verbal Scale subtests. Vocabulary, Information, Comprehension, and Similarities have the highest loadings on the Verbal Comprehension factor, followed by Arithmetic, which has a moderate loading. Two Performance Scale subtests—Picture Completion and Picture Arrangement—also have moderate loadings on the Verbal Comprehension factor, suggesting that these two subtests may require verbal mediation to a greater degree than do the other Performance Scale subtests.

The term *Perceptual Organization* describes the hypothesized ability underlying the factor for both item content (perceptual) and mental process (organization). This factor appears to measure a variable common to the Performance Scale subtests. Block Design, Object Assembly, and Picture Completion have high loadings on the Perceptual Organization factor; Mazes and Picture Arrangement have moderate loadings.

Although researchers had some difficulty naming the third factor, *Freedom from Distractibility* appears to be most appropriate. The name focuses on the ability to concentrate or remain attentive. The Arithmetic and Digit Span subtests have high loadings on the Freedom from Distractibility factor; Information and Coding B have moderate loadings. (Coding A has only a minimal loading on this factor.)

The factor analytic results give strong empirical support to interpretation of the Verbal and Performance IQs as separately functioning entities in the WISC-R. The factor structure of the WISC-R closely agrees with the actual organization of the subtests. As for the measurement of *g*, the WISC-R subtests cluster into three groups (see Table 6-8): those with high loadings (Vocabulary, Information, Similarities, Block Design, and Comprehension), moderate loadings (Arithmetic, Object Assembly, Picture Completion, and Picture Arrangement), and low loadings (Digit Span, Mazes, and Coding).

Other Factor Analytic Studies

Other factor analytic studies of the WISC-R with black children, Mexican-American children, lower-middle-class children, mentally retarded children, adolescent psychiatric patients, epileptic children, children referred for academic difficulties, learning disabled children, slow learners, delinquents, and emotionally disturbed children indicate that the factors found in these groups are generally similar to those found in the standardization group (Blaha & Vance, 1979; Carlson, Reynolds, & Gutkin, 1983; Dean, 1980; DeHorn & Klinge, 1978; Groff & Hubble, 1982; Hodges, 1982; Hubble & Groff, 1981a; Johnston & Bolen, 1984; McMahon & Kunce, 1981; Naglieri, 1981c; Reynolds & Gutkin, 1980b; Richards, Fowler, Berent, & Boll, 1980;

Table 6-6
Relationship of WISC-R IQs to Sex, Race, Occupation of Head of Household, Urban-Rural Residence, and Geographic Residence

	Demographic variables	N	Verbal IQ M	Verbal IQ SD	Performance IQ M	Performance IQ SD	Full Scale IQ M	Full Scale IQ SD
Sex	Boys	1,100	101.2	15.4	100.4	15.1	100.9	15.4
	Girls	1,100	98.8	14.3	99.8	14.9	99.1	14.6
Race	White boys	945	103.3	14.7	102.2	14.3	103.1	14.5
	Black boys	143	87.6	12.4	87.9	13.7	86.7	12.5
	White girls	925	100.7	13.5	102.1	13.9	101.4	13.5
	Black girls	162	88.0	13.7	86.5	13.0	86.2	12.9
Parental occupation group	*Whites*							
	1. Professional and technical	308	109.7	12.8	107.1	13.7	109.4	12.9
	2. Managerial, clerical, sales	538	104.2	14.0	104.0	14.6	104.4	14.1
	3. Skilled	446	100.5	13.2	101.3	13.1	100.9	12.9
	4. Semi-skilled	499	97.9	13.5	99.2	13.4	98.3	13.2
	5. Unskilled	79	92.3	13.3	93.4	13.8	92.1	13.3
	Blacks							
	1. Professional and technical	20	92.0	12.7	90.8	10.4	90.7	11.4
	2. Managerial, clerical, sales	51	91.7	11.5	90.9	12.5	90.5	11.1
	3. Skilled	47	89.6	10.6	87.4	11.1	87.5	10.2
	4. Semi-skilled	129	87.4	13.6	87.0	14.2	86.0	13.6
	5. Unskilled	58	82.6	13.5	82.8	13.3	81.5	12.5
	Total Group							
	1. Professional and technical	329	108.6	13.5	106.1	14.1	108.2	13.6
	2. Managerial, clerical, sales	594	103.1	14.2	102.9	14.8	103.2	14.4
	3. Skilled	495	99.5	13.3	100.1	13.6	99.6	13.3
	4. Semi-skilled	639	95.7	14.3	96.9	14.6	95.9	14.4
	5. Unskilled	143	87.8	14.3	88.8	14.6	87.3	14.1
Urban-rural residence	Urban	1,557	100.6	14.7	100.5	15.1	100.6	14.9
	Rural	643	98.5	15.4	99.0	14.8	98.6	15.2
Geographic residence	Northeast	478	102.8	14.6	101.3	14.4	102.3	14.6
	Northcentral	641	100.0	14.0	101.0	14.6	100.5	14.2
	South	696	96.9	15.7	96.7	15.9	96.6	15.9
	West	385	101.8	14.3	103.1	13.6	102.6	13.8

Source: Adapted from Kaufman and Doppelt (1976).

Schooler, Beebe, & Koepke, 1978; Shiek & Miller, 1978; Sutter & Bishop, 1986a; Snow, Cohen, & Holliman, 1985; Swerdlik & Schweitzer, 1978; Vance & Wallbrown, 1977; Wallbrown, Blaha, Wallbrown, & Engin, 1975).

Subtest Specificity

Subtest specificity refers to the proportion of a subtest's variance that is both reliable (that is, not due to errors of measurement) and distinctive to the subtest (see Chapter 2). Although the subtests overlap in their measurement properties (that is, the majority of the reliable variance for most subtests is common factor variance), many of the subtests also have a relatively high degree of subtest specificity that allows for interpretations of specific subtest functions (see Table 6-9). Although the relatively high degree of subtest specificity provides a firm ground for profile analysis of scaled scores, constraints still must be placed

Table 6-7
Factor Loadings of WISC-R Subtests for 11 Age Groups (Varimax Rotation)

Subtest	6½[a]	7½	8½	9½	10½	11½	12½	13½	14½	15½	16½	Mdn.
Factor A—Verbal Comprehension												
Information	35	49	65	57	63	63	65	77	60	72	57	63
Similarities	44	60	63	64	69	65	67	74	62	65	62	64
Arithmetic	32	38	31	29	41	37	33	53	37	40	32	37
Vocabulary	58	69	74	67	73	72	64	82	75	78	71	72
Comprehension	49	55	67	62	63	64	67	70	69	63	66	64
Digit Span	18	23	04	23	13	17	16	27	27	20	16	18
Picture Completion	39	29	22	27	40	34	35	36	31	35	39	35
Picture Arrangement	38	31	44	44	27	26	34	42	33	25	25	33
Block Design	28	30	27	30	26	22	33	39	23	20	22	27
Object Assembly	19	24	20	34	33	21	22	20	20	14	22	21
Coding	06	12	23	10	14	16	17	23	13	15	31	15
Mazes	21	08	18	06	08	20	15	−06	08	13	12	12
Factor B—Perceptual Organization												
Information	18	33	20	25	22	38	35	19	34	22	32	25
Similarities	23	30	24	38	33	44	35	26	38	34	34	34
Arithmetic	21	20	19	24	19	38	27	23	19	19	16	20
Vocabulary	17	22	24	26	33	31	36	19	24	18	29	24
Comprehension	28	28	30	37	26	33	27	21	31	35	32	30
Digit Span	18	20	14	12	11	07	14	04	07	12	13	12
Picture Completion	27	52	48	63	55	60	62	57	60	57	54	57
Picture Arrangement	38	49	51	49	41	41	61	41	29	49	41	41
Block Design	44	66	58	63	66	73	54	70	70	72	76	66
Object Assembly	57	66	69	65	58	70	61	68	64	64	70	65
Coding	12	23	24	20	17	13	16	22	12	24	20	20
Mazes	60	60	47	49	47	42	47	47	32	48	48	47
Factor C—Freedom from Distractibility												
Information	55	51	31	48	32	41	28	24	47	23	46	41
Similarities	37	27	28	38	32	23	26	23	30	28	31	28
Arithmetic	59	59	51	63	48	44	61	45	58	48	64	58
Vocabulary	36	31	16	53	25	33	44	29	33	39	45	33
Comprehension	33	28	08	28	12	30	28	22	19	15	24	24
Digit Span	54	50	56	52	57	54	59	59	39	56	62	56
Picture Completion	13	06	33	18	01	02	20	05	11	08	12	11
Picture Arrangement	27	28	09	12	19	25	12	07	16	10	09	12
Block Design	25	27	32	36	35	28	50	27	18	33	27	28
Object Assembly	18	25	19	16	12	12	22	05	12	11	09	12
Coding	20	25	46	42	45	53	42	45	15	40	31	42
Mazes	21	23	15	24	22	12	26	30	04	24	18	22

Note. Decimal points omitted.
[a] This row indicates age level.
Source: From A. S. Kaufman, "Factor Analysis of the WISC-R at 11 Age Levels between 6½ and 16½ Years," *Journal of Consulting and Clinical Psychology*, 1975, *43*, pp. 138–140. Copyright 1975 by the American Psychological Association. Reprinted by permission.

Table 6-8
WISC-R Subtests as Measures of *g*

| | Good measure of *g*[a] | | | Fair measure of *g* | | | Poor measure of *g* | |
Subtest	Median loading of *g*	Proportion of variance attributed to *g* (%)	Subtest	Median loading of *g*	Proportion of variance attributed to *g* (%)	Subtest	Median loading of *g*	Proportion of variance attributed to *g* (%)
Vocabulary	.80	64	Arithmetic	.65	42	Digit Span	.49	24
Information	.76	58	Object Assembly	.62	38	Mazes	.45	20
Similarities	.76	58	Picture Completion	.61	37	Coding	.41	17
Block Design	.73	53	Picture Arrangement	.60	36			
Comprehension	.72	52						

Note. The square of the median coefficients provides the proportion of each subtest's variance that may be attributed to *g*.
[a] For children ages 6 to 7 years, there are only three good verbal measures of *g* (Information, Arithmetic, and Vocabulary) and two good nonverbal measures of *g* (Block Design and Picture Arrangement).
Source: Adapted from Kaufman (1975a).

on interpreting subtest functions. These constraints include determining which subtest scaled scores are significantly different from one another and analyzing all relevant subtests before drawing any conclusions about unusual ability or weakness. (See Chapter 8 for a discussion of profile analysis.) For example, low scores on Digit Span, Arithmetic, and Coding and average or high scores on the other subtests may indicate that the child is highly distractible. A low score on Digit Span but not on Arithmetic and Coding, however, may suggest difficulty with auditory memory, or anxiety. Specific interpretations can be given to all subtests, with the exception of (a) Similarities for children above 8½ years of age and (b) Object Assembly for all children; patterns involving these two

subtests probably are attributable to measurement error (Kaufman, 1975a).

Factor Scores

Factor scores also can be obtained from the WISC-R, permitting the identification of meaningful psychological dimensions (Kaufman, 1975a). The Verbal Comprehension factor score measures verbal knowledge and understanding obtained informally and through formal education. It reflects the application of verbal skills to new situations. The Perceptual Organization factor, a nonverbal score, reflects the ability to interpret and organize visually perceived material within a time limit. The Free-

Table 6-9
Specificity for WISC-R Subtests

| Ample specificity | | Adequate specificity | | Inadequate specificity | |
Subtest	Ages	Subtest	Ages	Subtest	Ages
Information	all ages	Vocabulary	all ages	Similarities	9½ to 16½
Similarities	6½ to 8½	Comprehension	all ages	Object Assembly	all ages
Arithmetic	all ages	Picture Completion	9½ to 16½		
Digit Span	all ages				
Picture Completion	6½ to 8½				
Picture Arrangement	all ages				
Block Design	all ages				
Coding	all ages				
Mazes	all ages				

Source: Adapted from Kaufman (1979c).

dom from Distractibility factor score measures the ability to attend or concentrate, but also may involve numerical ability. Short-term memory may be an important component of the Freedom from Distractibility factor. (Chapter 8 provides a more detailed discussion of the Freedom from Distractibility factor.)

The preferred way to obtain the three factor scores is to use the following combination of subtests:

Verbal
Comprehension = Sum of scaled scores on Information, Similarities, Vocabulary, and Comprehension

Perceptual
Organization = Sum of scaled scores on Picture Completion, Picture Arrangement, Block Design, and Object Assembly

Freedom from
Distractibility = Sum of scaled scores on Arithmetic, Digit Span, and Coding.

Use of these combinations ensures against subtests' overlapping in any factors. Table C-4 in Appendix C permits the rapid conversion of the sum of scaled scores for each of these combinations into Deviation IQs. Factor scores should not be reported in a psychological evaluation—they should be used only for evaluating the child's strengths and weaknesses.

ADMINISTERING THE WISC-R

The general procedures discussed in Chapter 5 for administering psychological tests should be helpful in administering the WISC-R. The special procedures developed for the WISC-R must be mastered, however. You must be careful not to confuse procedures for the WAIS-R or the WPPSI with those for the WISC-R—some similar subtests have different instructions and time limits. Specific and detailed suggestions supplementing those in the WISC-R manual are presented in Chapter 7 for each WISC-R subtest. Appendix D presents special procedures for administering the WISC-R Performance subtests to deaf children. Some general administrative issues are discussed below. The suggestions in Exhibit 6-2 should also help you learn to administer the WISC-R.

Before you administer the scale to a child, you should become familiar with the instructions and the materials. Although the Verbal Scale subtests are generally easier to administer than the Performance Scale subtests, they are more difficult to score. You will find a stopwatch (or a

wristwatch with a digital timer) essential for administering the timed WISC-R subtests.

The record booklet (see Figure 6-2) should be clearly and accurately completed; responses must be recorded *verbatim*. The checking of all calculations is an absolute necessity, as is the checking of the conversion of raw scores to scaled scores and of scaled scores to IQs. The correct calculation of the child's chronological age is also important. Try to develop proper administrative procedures early in your testing career.

General Problems in Administering the WISC-R

Beginning examiners as well as professionals have some of the following problems in administering the WISC-R:

1. Reading questions too quickly or too slowly.
2. Failing to enunciate clearly.
3. Failing to clear table of unessential materials.
4. Failing to record all responses.
5. Calculating chronological age incorrectly.
6. Providing more help to the child than the standardized procedures permit.
7. Failing to adhere to directions.
8. Failing to use proper time limits.
9. Failing to question ambiguous or vague responses.
10. Failing to credit all responses.
11. Making errors in converting raw scores to scaled scores.
12. Making prorating errors.
13. Giving time-bonus credits incorrectly.
14. Using inappropriate norms.
15. Crediting an incorrect response.
16. Making errors in adding raw scores.
17. Making errors in adding scaled scores.
18. Failing to check all Coding subtest responses.
19. Failing to credit nonadministered passed items.
20. Failing to score a subtest.
21. Making errors in converting scaled scores to IQs.

It is important that you study your testing practices carefully to ensure that these and other administrative problems do not occur.

The keys to proper test administration are to follow standard test procedures and be an objective, but supporting, examiner. Following are some examples of improper test administration (from Teglasi & Freeman, 1983, pp. 232–234, 239, with changes in wording and comments by the text author).

Example 1. Before administering the WISC-R, the examiner discussed with the child issues connected with the

■ **Exhibit 6-2** ▬▬▬▬▬▬▬▬▬▬▬▬▬▬▬▬▬▬▬▬▬▬▬▬▬▬▬▬▬▬▬▬▬▬▬▬

Supplementary Instructions for Administering the WISC-R

1. Complete the top of the record booklet.
2. Calculate the chronological age (CA) and put it in the box provided. In obtaining the CA, do not drop the days.
3. Administer the subtests in the order presented in the manual, except in rare circumstances. Do not change the wording on any subtest. Read the directions exactly as shown in the manual. Do not ad lib.
4. Start with the appropriate item on each subtest and follow the discontinuance criteria. This means that you must know the scoring criteria before you give the test. Note: The criteria for scoring Similarities, Vocabulary, and Comprehension start on page 154 of the WISC-R manual.
5. Write out all responses completely and legibly. Do not use unusual abbreviations. Record time accurately.
6. Question all ambiguous or unscorable responses. You may need to question responses on Information, Vocabulary, and Comprehension. Use the words suggested in the manual for questioning. Whenever you ask a question, write "(Q)" after the questioned response.
7. On the Information subtests, for #1, "What do you call this finger?" hold out your hand toward the child, make a fist with your fingers, and hold your thumb straight up (the thumbs-up sign). For #7, if the child first says "5" and then says "2" when you ask him or her "How many counting the weekend?" ask "How many altogether, all week?"
8. On Picture Completion, note that the time limit is 20 seconds. If you are not sure whether the child's verbal response is correct, you should say "Show me where you mean." You must know the cautions (top of page 71 in the WISC-R manual) and when to use them.
9. For Similarities, you must follow the directions in the footnote for #16 (page 74 in the WISC-R manual).
10. On Comprehension, you must follow the directions in the footnotes on page 97 exactly. The record booklet is marked to indicate which items require that you ask for a second response.
11. On Digits Forward and Digits Backward, you must always administer both trials of each item.
12. Carefully score each protocol, recheck scoring, and transfer subtest scores to the front of the record booklet under Raw Score. If you have failed to question a response when you should have and the response is obviously not a 0 response, give the child the most appropriate score.
13. If a subtest was spoiled, write *spoiled* by the subtest total

score and on the front cover where the raw and scaled scores appear. If for some reason a subtest was not administered, write *NA* in the margin of the record booklet and on the front cover.

14. Transform raw scores into scaled scores by using Table 19 on page 118 of the WISC-R manual. Be sure to use the page of Table 19 that is appropriate for the child's age. Be sure to use the correct row and column for each transformation.
15. Base the Verbal Score on the total of the scaled scores on the five standard Verbal Scale subtests. Base the Performance Score on the total of the scaled scores on the five standard Performance Scale subtests. Do not use Digit Span to compute the Verbal Score unless you substitute it for another Verbal subtest. Do not use Mazes unless you substitute it for Coding. Add the Verbal Score and the Performance Score together to get the Full Scale Score.
16. If it should be necessary to prorate either the Verbal or Performance section, refer to the directions on page 114 and Table 22 (page 190) of the WISC-R manual.
17. Obtain the IQs from Table 20 on pages 151 and 152 of the WISC-R manual. There is a Verbal section, a Performance section, and a Full Scale section. Be sure to use the correct section of the table for each of the three IQs. Record the IQs. Next, recheck all of your work. If the IQ(s) was (were) prorated, write *PRO* beside the appropriate IQ(s).
18. Make a profile of the examinee's scores on the record booklet.
19. Look up the confidence intervals for the Full Scale IQ, Verbal Scale IQ, and Performance Scale IQ in Table C-1 in Appendix C.
20. Look up the percentile rank and classification for each of the IQs by referring to Tables BC-1 and BC-2 on the inside back cover.
21. If desired, use the material on pages 188 and 189 of the WISC-R manual to obtain test-age equivalents. They can be placed in parentheses in the right-hand margin of the cover page of the record booklet next to the scaled scores. For test-age equivalents above those in the table, use the highest test-age equivalent and a plus sign. For test-age equivalents below those in the table, use the lowest test-age equivalent and a minus sign.

Source: Courtesy of M. L. Lewis.

WISC-R RECORD FORM

Wechsler Intelligence Scale
for Children—Revised

NAME _____ AGE _____ SEX _____

ADDRESS _____

PARENT'S NAME _____

SCHOOL _____ GRADE _____

PLACE OF TESTING _____ TESTED BY _____

REFERRED BY _____

WISC-R PROFILE

Clinicians who wish to draw a profile should first transfer the child's *scaled scores* to the row of boxes below. Then mark an X on the dot corresponding to the scaled score for each test, and draw a line connecting the X's.*

VERBAL TESTS

Information, Similarities, Arithmetic, Vocabulary, Comprehension, Digit Span

PERFORMANCE TESTS

Picture Completion, Picture Arrangement, Block Design, Object Assembly, Coding, Mazes

Scaled Score: 19, 18, 17, 16, 15, 14, 13, 12, 11, 10, 9, 8, 7, 6, 5, 4, 3, 2, 1

*See Chapter 4 in the manual for a discussion of the significance of differences between scores on the tests.

NOTES

	Year	Month	Day
Date Tested	_____	_____	_____
Date of Birth	_____	_____	_____
Age	_____	_____	_____

	Raw Score	Scaled Score
VERBAL TESTS		
Information	_____	_____
Similarities	_____	_____
Arithmetic	_____	_____
Vocabulary	_____	_____
Comprehension	_____	_____
(Digit Span)	(_____)	(_____)
Verbal Score		_____
PERFORMANCE TESTS		
Picture Completion	_____	_____
Picture Arrangement	_____	_____
Block Design	_____	_____
Object Assembly	_____	_____
Coding	_____	_____
(Mazes)	(_____)	(_____)
Performance Score		_____

	Scaled Score	IQ
Verbal Score	_____	*_____
Performance Score	_____	*_____
Full Scale Score	_____	_____

*Prorated from 4 tests, if necessary.

Figure 6-2. Cover page of WISC-R record booklet. Copyright © 1971, 1974 by The Psychological Corporation, San Antonio, TX. All Rights Reserved.

child's stealing. Later, when questioned on the Comprehension subtest about finding a wallet in the street, the child looked distressed, but the examiner failed to recognize the distress. *Comment.* Be sensitive to nonverbal cues as well as verbal ones. An alert examiner would have said something like "Now, this question has nothing to do with our previous discussion. This is one of the questions I ask everyone."

Example 2.   The examiner wanted to say something supportive to the examinee after the Digit Span subtest. *Examiner:* "Are you aware that you have a very good memory?" (Child scored in the below average range on the Digit Span subtest.) *Child:* "No, I have a lousy one. I forget things all the time." *Comment.* It is important that reinforcements be congruent with the examinee's performance and be given at appropriate times.

Example 3.   The examiner watched a 10-year-old assemble the horse on the Object Assembly subtest, leaving one piece out. When the child said "finished," the examiner pointed to the extra piece. The child quickly corrected the error and was given full credit. *Comment.* Nonverbal cues may inappropriately help examinees solve problems.

Example 4.   Only when the child's arrangement on the Picture Arrangement subtest was correct did the examiner ask "finished?" If the child was still checking an incorrect sequence, the examiner was silent. The child soon caught on. *Comment.* Do not give verbal cues that may alert examinees to how well they are doing.

Example 5.   The examiner, noting that a child had misplaced only one block in a complicated design on the Block Design subtest, said, "Be sure to check your answer." *Comment.* It is inappropriate to add directions that are not in the test manual.

These examples illustrate just a few of the ways in which an examiner may inappropriately influence test administration. It behooves each of you to learn about possible sources of error—both overt and covert—in your administration of the WISC-R and other tests, and take appropriate steps to prevent these errors from occurring.

Subtest Sequence

The WISC-R manual states that, although it should be convenient to administer the subtests in the order indicated in the manual, it is permissible to change the order when the needs of a particular child must be met, or when the examiner has a personal preference. *You are strongly urged to administer the subtests in the order specified in the manual unless there is some compelling reason to use another order.* (For instance, children who are extremely bored or frustrated with some subtests may be more motivated if they are given a different subtest or a subtest of their choice.) Because the order in the manual was used in obtaining the standardization data, any other order constitutes a departure from standard procedures, and there is evidence that such departures do affect children's scores (Exner, 1966; Morris, Martin, Johnson, Birch, & Thompson, 1978; Sattler, 1969).

Starting Rules

In some situations, an examiner may have doubts about whether the items at the entry point were passed and thus may decide to administer earlier items in the series. (The entry-point items are those that the child must pass in order for the examiner to administer more difficult items.) Wechsler (1974, p. 59) provided a specific rule for scoring failures on items below the entry point: *"If subsequent scoring of the test reveals that some of the earlier items were administered unnecessarily, the child should be given full credit for these items—even if he [or she] earned partial or no credit"* (italics added). Therefore, when an item below the entry point is failed or partially credited, give *full credit* for the item if further checking indicates that, in fact, the child correctly answered the items at the entry point. This rule applies only to normal children 8 years old and above (because they have entry points above the first item on certain subtests).

Here is an example. After administering words 4 and 5 on the Vocabulary subtest to a normal 8-year-old child, you are uncertain of the scoring of the responses that were given to these two entry items. You therefore decide to administer words 3 and 2, and then word 1 because word 3 was definitely failed. The child passes words 1 and 2, and the subtest is continued with word 6. After the examination, a check of the responses indicates that the child should receive full credit for words 4 and 5. The rule requires that the child receive full credit for defining word 3 (as well as words 1 and 2), even though the definition of word 3 was incorrect, because word 3 occurs *below* the entry words that were defined correctly. This rule favors the child, by ensuring that the child is not penalized for your decision to administer the earlier word that the child subsequently failed. The rule is an attempt to maintain standardized scoring procedures.

Discontinuance Rules

The discontinuance scoring rule applies to situations in which the examiner has some doubts as to whether the items at the discontinuance point were failed and subsequently decides to administer additional items in the series (Wechsler, 1974, p. 59). (The discontinuance-point items are those that the child fails in a consecutive series, indicating, according to the manual, that the subtest should be discontinued.) The rule is as follows: *If subsequent scoring of the items indicates that the additional items were administered unnecessarily, the child should not be given credit for items passed after the discontinuance point.*

Here is an example. After administering the first 15 words of the Vocabulary subtest, you are uncertain of the scoring of some of the responses that the child gave to words 11 through 15. You therefore decide to administer additional words, and the child definitely passes words 16 and 17 but fails words 18 through 22. The subtest is, therefore, discontinued after word 22. After the examination, checking of the responses indicates that the child should not receive credit for definitions of words 11 through 15. The rule requires that the child not receive credit for the definitions of words 16 and 17, even though these definitions were correct, because these words occur *after* the test should have been discontinued. In contrast to the starting rule, this rule does not favor the child. The rule prevents the child from receiving additional points because of your uncertainty in scoring items during the regular administration of the subtests. This rule constitutes another attempt to maintain standardized scoring procedures.

Repetition of Items

The WISC-R manual encourages examiners to use judgment in deciding whether an "I don't know" response reflects lack of knowledge or lack of desire to respond. If you decide that it reflects the latter, repeat the question or ask it again at some later point—especially if the "I don't know" response is given to an easy question. Better yet, the first time a child says "I don't know," say something like "I want you to try your hardest on each of these. Try your best to answer each question." Give credit if the child correctly answers the question. Questions should not be repeated on the Digit Span subtest.

Use of Probing Questions and Queries

The WISC-R manual encourages flexibility in administering test items. Acknowledge, for example, negativistic or mistrustful responses and continue to probe to determine whether the child knows an answer. For example, if the child responds to the Comprehension question "Why are criminals locked up?" with "Society labels people criminals who shouldn't be so labeled," you can say "Well, try to give some answers that other people think are reasonable." You will have to be alert to recognize responses that indicate a need for these kinds of probes. Probes are also required on verbal responses that are incomplete, indefinite, or vague. Queries should be used when you are unsure of how to score the response; they should *not* be used to elicit a higher quality response.

Spoiled Responses

An explicit scoring rule on the WISC-R is that spoiled responses are scored 0. A spoiled response is one that initially was partially right, but was spoiled by the child's incorrect elaboration on his or her initial response. For example, the response "Goes ticktock" (for the Vocabulary word *clock*) would be spoiled by the elaboration "It's the engine on a motorcycle," which reveals the child's misconception about the word *clock*.

Modifying Standard Procedures

Deviations from procedures for administering the subtests are likely to result in scores that differ from those obtained with standard administrative procedures. Studies (Herrell & Golland, 1969; Post, 1970; Sattler, 1969; Schwebel & Bernstein, 1970) indicate that children obtained higher scores on some of the subtests when they were encouraged to talk about their problem-solving procedures, think about their answers before responding, explain their picture arrangements, or solve problems after receiving a series of cues. Such modifications, if used, should be employed only *after* the standard administration. They may be helpful in clinical assessment of the child's potential for learning.

Scoring WISC-R Responses

Arriving at a score for some WISC-R subtests is by no means a simple matter. Judgment is important, especially for handling ambiguous responses that occur on the Vocabulary, Comprehension, and Similarities subtests. To become a skilled examiner, you need to study carefully the scoring criteria, scoring guidelines, and scoring examples in the WISC-R manual. The supplementary WISC-R scoring manual can also assist you in scoring these three subtests (Massey, Sattler, & Andres, 1978).

Even authorities who have published scoring manuals do not always agree on the scoring of responses. Eleven scoring discrepancies (see Table 6-10) were found between the WISC-R manual and two other scoring guides for Vocabulary and Similarities items (Sattler, Squire, & Andres, 1977). Fortunately, however, such differences appear to be relatively few in number.

Some examiners are more lenient than others in giving credit, and at times examiners may not consistently adhere to their own relative standards. For example, examiners may be strict on some occasions and lenient on others. Dramatic differences in the scoring standards of examiners have been illustrated in a number of reports. In one study, 99 school psychologists gave IQs ranging from 63 to 117 to the same WISC protocol (Massey, 1964). In other studies, graduate-student examiners (Miller et al., 1970) and members of the American Psychological Association (Miller & Chansky, 1972) differed by as much as 17 points in scoring the same test protocol.

Extrapolated IQs

When the sum of scaled scores obtained by a child is beyond those shown in the WISC-R manual, Table C-6 in Appendix C can be used to obtain extrapolated IQs. This table extends the IQ table down to the minimum possible sum of scaled scores and up to the maximum possible sum of scaled scores. In using Table C-6, remember that Wechsler recommends that a child's Full Scale IQ not be determined unless he or she obtains raw scores greater than 0 on at least three Verbal and three Performance Scale subtests.

The values presented in Table C-6, which were obtained by using linear regression methods, are helpful in obtaining a specific intelligence quotient. These values, however, are outside the range of the children who were tested in the standardization sample. Therefore *the possibility of error in extrapolations such as these may be disconcertingly large*. Nevertheless, these values may be of some use in reporting results for children who fall in the very low or very high IQ ranges. If possible, use another test (such as the Stanford-Binet Intelligence Scale: Fourth Edition) to evaluate children whose IQs fall outside the range covered by the WISC-R.

SHORT FORMS OF THE WISC-R

Short forms of the WISC-R and other Wechsler scales are occasionally used as screening devices. (Their advantages and disadvantages will be discussed at the end of this section.) The selection of a short form is usually based on such criteria as acceptable reliability and validity, the power of the short form to answer the referral question and provide clinically useful information, the examinee's physical capabilities, and the amount of time available for administering the test.

Table 6-10
Eleven Scoring Discrepancies Between WISC-R Manual and Two Scoring Guides

Subtest	Item and response	WISC-R score	Jastak and Jastak score	Scottish Council score
Vocabulary	8. donkey—"a mule"	1	2	—
	12. diamond—"can cut glass" (or "a rock or an object that can cut glass")	1	2	2
	12. diamond—"mineral"	1 (Q)	2	—
	13. gamble—"a game"	0 (Q)	1	—
	21. stanza—"a phrase"	0	1	—
	22. seclude—"opposite of include"	0	1	—
	25. belfry—"a tower"	1	2	—
Similarities	7. cat—mouse—"both pets"	1	—	2
	13. mountain—lake—"both in country"	0	—	1
	15. first—last—"places"	0 (Q)	—	1
	17. salt—water—"chemicals"	0	—	1

Source: Reprinted with permission of the publisher and authors from J. M. Sattler, L. Squire, and J. Andres, "Scoring Discrepancies between the WISC-R Manual and Two Scoring Guides," *Journal of Clinical Psychology, 33,* p. 1059. Copyright 1977, Clinical Psychology Publishing Co., Inc.

The validity of short forms is usually evaluated by correlating the short form IQ with the Full Scale IQ, evaluating mean differences between the two IQs, and determining the extent of agreement in the intelligence classifications provided by the two IQs. Silverstein (1985a) argued, however, that these three criteria are not useful. First, it is virtually certain that there will be high correlations between short-form and Full Scale IQs. Second, with sufficiently large samples, a significant difference between long and short IQs is likely to occur, making this criterion nearly meaningless. Third, it is virtually certain that the short-form and Full Scale IQs will yield different classifications. [Goh (1978), for example, found that short-form WISC-R IQs misclassified 45 percent of a group of 142 children.] Silverstein suggested that other considerations be used to determine the appropriateness of a short form. If a specific classification must be obtained for the clinical or psychoeducational purpose, then short-form IQs will be inappropriate.

Selecting the Short Form

The 10 best short-form combinations of two, three, four, and five WISC-R subtests, arrived at by using the standardization data and a formula that takes into account subtest unreliability, are shown in Table C-10 of Appendix C. Because the validities of the various short forms are high, clinical considerations should influence short-form selection. For example, when using a tetrad, you may want to select a combination consisting of two Verbal and two Performance Scale subtests in order to obtain some representation of both verbal and performance skills in the short form.

An examinee's physical capabilities may also guide you in selecting a short form. Examinees with marked visual impairment or severe motor dysfunction of the upper extremities will have difficulty with Performance Scale tasks. In such cases, the Verbal Scale can serve as a useful short form. For hearing-impaired examinees, the Performance Scale alone is a useful short form. These short forms should be administered using the child's preferred mode of communication and should be supplemented by other tests designed to accommodate the special physical abilities of these children.

Converting Short-Form Scores into Deviation Quotients

After the specific combination of subtests has been administered, it is necessary to convert the short-form scores to a Full Scale IQ estimate. Simple prorating and regression procedures are not applicable because they do not deal adequately with the problem of subtest reliability (Tellegen & Briggs, 1967). The more acceptable procedure is to transform the short-form scores into the familiar Wechsler-type Deviation Quotient, which has a mean of 100 and a standard deviation of 15. Exhibit 6-3 shows the procedure for converting the short-form scores into a Deviation Quotient. Although this approach does not eliminate the many problems associated with short forms, it does appear to provide fairly reliable IQs.

Yudin's Abbreviated Procedure

In the Yudin (1966) WISC short-form procedure, which also applies to the WISC-R, every other item on most subtests is administered. The specific procedures, modified by Silverstein (1968a), are shown in Table C-11 of Appendix C. After the test has been administered, the scaled scores and IQs are obtained from the manual in the usual way. The Yudin procedure differs from other short-form procedures in that all of the subtests are used. Its advantages are that a representative sample of items is administered, profile analysis can be applied, and approximately 56 percent of the items are used.

Although the Yudin procedure has satisfactory reliability (Reid, Moore, & Alexander, 1968; Yudin, 1966), shortcomings have been noted. These include a moderate loss of validity and reliability, less reliable profile data, and IQs that differ from those obtained on the Full Scale (Dean, 1977f; Erikson, 1967; Finch, Kendall, Spirito, Entin, Montgomery, & Schwartz, 1979; Gayton, Wilson, & Bernstein, 1970; Goh, 1978; Rasbury, Falgout, & Perry, 1978; Satz, Van de Riet, & Mogel, 1967; Tellegen & Briggs, 1967). The assets and liabilities of the Yudin abbreviated procedure should be considered carefully before it is used.

Hobby (1980) described a WISC-R procedure in which only odd items are administered on most subtests. It is similar to the Yudin procedure, but has more specific basal and ceiling procedures and correction factors.

Vocabulary and Block Design Short Form

A popular screening short form consists of Vocabulary and Block Design. These two subtests have excellent reliability, correlate highly with the Full Scale over a wide age range, and are good measures of g. Table C-37 in Appendix C can be used to convert the sum of scaled scores on these two subtests directly to an estimate of the Full Scale IQ.

■ **Exhibit 6-3** ━━━━━━━━━━━━━━━━━━━━━━━━━━━━━━

Obtaining Deviation Quotients for Short Forms

The following formula is used to compute the Deviation Quotient for a short form:

$$\text{Deviation Quotient} = (15/S_c)(X_c - M_c) + 100$$

where $S_c = S_s\sqrt{n + 2\Sigma r_{jk}}$ (standard deviation of composite score)

X_c = composite score (sum of subtest scaled scores in the short form)

M_c = normative mean, which is equal to $10n$

S_s = subtest standard deviation, which is equal to 3

n = number of component subtests

Σr_{jk} = sum of the correlations between component subtests.

This equation considers the number of subtests in the short form, the correlations between the subtests, and the total scaled-score points obtained on the short form.

A more straightforward computational formula for obtaining the Deviation Quotient is as follows:

$$\text{Deviation Quotient} = (\text{composite score} \times a) + b$$

where $a = 15/S_c$

$b = 100 - n(150)/S_c$.

Table C-36 in Appendix C can be used in obtaining the appropriate a and b constants. In using Table C-36, first select the heading corresponding to the number of subtests in the short form. The first column under each heading is Σr_{jk}. This term represents the sum of the correlations between the subtests making up the composite score. To obtain Σr_{jk}, use the WISC-R correlation table of the group closest in age to the examinee (Table 14 on pages 36 through 46 of the WISC-R manual). With two subtests in the short form, only one correlation is needed. With three subtests in the short form, three correlations are summed (1 with 2, 1 with 3, and 2 with 3). With four subtests in the short form, six correlations are summed (1 with 2, 1 wtih 3, 1 with 4, 2 with 3, 2 with 4, and 3 with 4). With five subtests in the short form, 10 correlations are summed (1 with 2, 1 with 3, 1 with 4, 1 with 5, 2 with 3, 2 with 4, 2 with 5, 3 with 4, 3 with 5, and 4 with 5). After Σr_{jk} is calculated, the values for the two constants are obtained under the appropriate heading.

The procedure used to obtain the Deviation Quotient can be summarized as follows:

1. Sum the scaled scores of the subtests in the short form to obtain the composite score.
2. Sum the correlations between the subtests to obtain Σr_{jk}.
3. Find the appropriate a and b constants in Table C-36 in Appendix C after Σr_{jk} has been obtained.
4. Compute the Deviation Quotient by using the composite score and the a and b constants.

Example: A three-subtest short form composed of the Arithmetic, Vocabulary, and Block Design subtests is administered to a 6-year-old child. The child obtains scaled scores of 7, 12, and 13 on the three subtests. The four steps are as follows:

1. The three scaled scores are summed to yield a composite score of 32.
2. The correlations between the three subtests are obtained from Table 14 (page 36) of the WISC-R manual (Arithmetic and Vocabulary, .52; Arithmetic and Block Design, .47; Vocabulary and Block Design, .43). These are summed to yield 1.42 (Σr_{jk}).
3. The appropriate row in Table C-36 in Appendix C is the fourth one under the heading "3 Subtests." The values for the constants a and b are 2.1 and 37, respectively.
4. The formula

$$\text{Deviation Quotient} = (\text{composite score} \times a) + b$$

is used to obtain a Deviation Quotient of 104 [$(32 \times 2.1) + 37$].

Arithmetic, Vocabulary, Picture Arrangement, and Block Design Short Form

Another useful screening short form is Arithmetic, Vocabulary, Picture Arrangement, and Block Design (Kaufman, 1976b). It takes longer to administer than Vocabulary and Block Design, but provides more clinical and diagnostic information.

Other Useful Short Forms

Other short forms discussed in the literature are Similarities and Vocabulary (Fell & Fell, 1982); Similarities and Object Assembly (Fell & Fell, 1982); Similarities, Vocabulary, and Block Design (Karnes & Brown, 1981); Similarities, Vocabulary, Block Design, and Object Assembly (Karnes & Brown, 1981); Similarities, Vocabulary,

Block Design, and Picture Completion (Clarizio & Veres, 1984); Similarities, Object Assembly, and Vocabulary (Dirks, Wessels, Quarfoth, & Quenon, 1980); and Information, Comprehension, Block Design, Picture Arrangement and Coding (Kennedy & Elder, 1982).

Comment on Short Forms of the WISC-R (and Other Tests as Well)

Short forms save time and are useful screening devices, but they have many disadvantages. First, short-form IQs may be less stable than those obtained with the standard form. Second, information about cognitive patterning is lost. Third, opportunity to observe the examinee's problem-solving methods is lost. Fourth, some short forms, such as the Verbal Scale alone, do not allow for the assessment of performance abilities. Fifth, when there is intersubtest variability, the savings in time may be expensive in terms of lost information. Finally, reliability of the obtained IQ is reduced when subtests are eliminated.

Those interested in using short forms must weigh the time saved against the validity lost. In addition, it is important to consider what kind of decision will be made on the basis of the short-form scores. The most efficient testing strategy for a particular situation will depend, in part, on the goal of the evaluation—whether it is for a general assessment of intelligence, classification, selection, or screening.

Even when all of the subtests are administered, the IQ obtained on the WISC-R (and all other intelligence tests) is but an *estimate* of the different kinds of abilities possessed by a child. When a small number of subtests is used, the estimate may be far less adequate than that provided by the Full Scale. *Educational and clinical situations call for more, rather than less, extensive cognitive evaluation. You are encouraged to administer the Full Scale, unless there is some compelling reason to administer a short form.* Included among these reasons would be situations in which the child was ready to quit testing or the physical capabilities of the examinee made some of the subtests inappropriate. *The Full Scale should be administered so as to maximize diagnostic information and minimize placement errors. Short forms are not recommended for any placement, educational, or clinical decision-making purpose.*

CHOOSING BETWEEN THE WISC-R AND THE WPPSI AND BETWEEN THE WISC-R AND THE WAIS-R

The WISC-R overlaps with the WPPSI for the age period 6-0-0 to 6-7-15 and with the WAIS-R for the age period 16-0-0 to 16-11-30. The overlap in ages between the WISC-R and the WPPSI and between the WISC-R and the WAIS-R is especially helpful in retest situations. A child first administered the WISC-R at age 6-0-0 can be retested with the WPPSI at any time during the next seven months. Similarly, a child tested with the WAIS-R at age 16-0-0 can be retested with the WISC-R up until about his or her seventeenth birthday. For these overlapping age periods, the WISC-R manual indicates that "the examiner should choose the Scale that is most appropriate for his [her] purposes" (p. 53).

Unfortunately, it is difficult to see how this statement can guide your choice. In order to select a scale, one needs information about the advantages and disadvantages of each scale. The choice of a test should depend on the validity of the inferences that can be made from scores on it. To this end, it would be helpful to consult validity studies that compare the WISC-R with the WPPSI and the WISC-R with the WAIS-R in their overlapping age ranges, using samples of both normal and exceptional children.

Rather than the personal preferences of the examiner, the choice ought to depend on which test yields the smallest standard errors of measurement for scores at the levels obtained. Because standard errors of measurement are provided in the Wechsler manuals for age but not for ability level, the needed information is not available. In the case of the WISC-R versus the WPPSI, the standard errors of measurement for the Verbal, Performance, and Full Scale IQs are smaller for the WPPSI than for the WISC-R at age 6½ years. In the case of the WISC-R versus the WAIS-R, the standard errors of measurement for the Verbal and Full Scale IQs (but not Performance Scale IQs) are slightly smaller for the WAIS-R than for the WISC-R at 16½ years.

The child's estimated level of intelligence should also be considered in selecting a test. A 6½-year-old child who obtains an IQ that is below the normal level will be administered a greater number of WPPSI items than WISC-R items. (For example, one needs 9 correct WPPSI Information items but only 3 correct WISC-R Information items to obtain a scaled score of 5.) Similarly, a 16-8-year-old child needs many more successes on the WISC-R than on the WAIS-R to obtain the same scaled score. (For example, one needs 13 correct WISC-R Information items but only 4 correct WAIS-R Information items to obtain an age-corrected scaled score of 5.) Consequently, for children with below-normal ability, a more thorough sampling of ability can be obtained from the WPPSI than from the WISC-R and from the WISC-R than from the WAIS-R in their overlapping age ranges. For normal and gifted children, all three tests appear to provide an adequate sampling of ability.

ADMINISTERING THE WISC-R (AND WPPSI AND WAIS-R) TO HANDICAPPED CHILDREN

Various physical abilities are necessary in order for a child to respond to each WISC-R subtest (see Table 6-11). Vision and/or hearing are necessary for most of the Verbal Scale subtests; vision and arm-hand use are necessary for the Performance Scale subtests. In administering the WISC-R (and WPPSI and WAIS-R) to children with physical disabilities, you must attempt to find new ways to give the test without, in the process, providing cues to the child. When needed modifications go beyond simply permitting the child to respond in a different manner, however, it is likely that the results must be reinterpreted in the light of the modifications. The point-scale format of the WISC-R (and WPPSI and WAIS-R) reduces the need to shift continually from one subtest to another, thus making the WISC-R (and WPPSI and WAIS-R) more convenient than the Stanford-Binet: Form L-M (but not the Stanford-Binet: Fourth Edition) for adaptive administration.

Verbal Scale Subtests

All of the Verbal Scale subtests can be administered orally if the child can hear. If the child cannot hear but can read, the Information, Comprehension, Similarities, and Vocabulary questions can be typed on cards and presented one at a time. Visually presenting the Arithmetic and Digit Span items poses more difficulties because of the time limits involved in these subtests and because visual presentation of the items seems drastically different from oral presentation, especially with Digit Span items. Therefore these two subtests may have to be omitted from the battery in testing deaf children. Detailed instructions for administering the Performance Scale subtests to deaf children appear in Appendix D. If the child cannot respond orally, written replies to any of the Verbal Scale subtests can be accepted.

Performance Scale Subtests

WISC-R (and WPPSI and WAIS-R) Performance Scale subtests require the child to have adequate vision. Adaptations center on the child's methods of responding. The Picture Completion subtest can be given only to a child who has adequate vision and who can either describe the missing part orally or in writing or point to it. Block Design, Object Assembly, Coding, Digit Symbol, Mazes, Animal House, and Geometric Design are not easily adaptable for the child whose arm-hand use is severely impaired. Adaptation of the Picture Arrangement subtest is possible when there is impairment of arm-hand use. The cards can be arranged in the order indicated by the child.

Advantages of Two Separate Scales

The testing of handicapped children is facilitated by the division of the subtests into the Verbal and Performance Scales. The Verbal Scale can be administered to blind children and to children with severe motor handicaps, whereas the Performance Scale can be administered to hearing-impaired children and to children who have little or no speech. When the Verbal Scale can also be administered to a hearing-impaired child, a comparison between the two scales may reveal the extent of the child's verbal deficit.

Unknown Effects of Modifications

Without empirical findings, there is no way of knowing how the suggested modifications affect the reliability and validity of the scores. Yet, when standard procedures cannot be used because sensory handicaps prevent the child from comprehending the instructions, such modifications may be needed. *When modifications are used, the resulting score should be considered only as an approximate estimate of the child's test score.*

Timed Subtests

Speed of correct response on the WISC-R Picture Arrangement, Block Design, and Object Assembly subtests is significantly related to chronological age and to problem-solving ability (Kaufman, 1979b). Older children solve the tasks more quickly than younger children, and those who solve the problems quickly also tend to solve more problems than those who solve them slowly. Because speed plays only a limited role in enabling children below 10 years of age to earn bonus points, it is reasonable to administer these subtests to 6- to 10-year-old orthopedically handicapped children who are able to manipulate the materials; these children will not be unduly penalized for failure to earn bonus points (Kaufman, 1979b).

ASSETS OF THE WISC-R

The WISC-R is a well-standardized test, with excellent reliability and adequate concurrent validity. Like the WAIS-R and the WPPSI, it divides the 12 subtests into two sections and provides three IQs—Verbal, Performance,

Table 6-11
Physical Abilities Necessary and Adaptable for WISC-R, WPPSI, and WAIS-R Subtests

Subtest	Vision	Hearing	Oral speech	Arm-hand use
Information	Xr	Xa	Xa	Xw
Comprehension	Xr	Xa	Xa	Xw
Arithmetic	Xr	Xa	Xa	Xw
Similarities	Xr	Xa	Xa	Xw
Vocabulary	Xr	Xa	Xa	Xw
Digit Span	—	X	Xa	Xw
Picture Completion	X	Xa	Xa	Xp or Xw
Picture Arrangement	X	Xa	Xo	Xa
Block Design	X	Xa	—	X
Object Assembly	X	Xa	—	X
Coding, Digit Symbol	X	Xa	—	X
Mazes	X	Xa	—	X
Sentences	Xr	Xa	Xa	Xw
Animal House	X	Xa	Xo	Xa
Geometric Design	X	Xa	—	X

Note. The code is as follows:

X—This ability is required. Adaptation is not feasible if this function is absent or more than mildly impaired.

Xa—This ability is required for standard administration, but the subtest is adaptable.

Xo—Examinees who are able to speak can say their answers.

Xp—Examinees who are able to point can point to their answers.

Xr—Examinees who are able to read can be shown the questions. If the examinee cannot read, hearing is necessary. If neither the ability to read nor the ability to hear is present, the subtest should not be administered.

Xw—Examinees who are able to write can write their answers.

and Full Scale. This division is especially helpful in clinical and psychoeducational work and aids in the assessment of brain-behavior relationships. A valuable feature of the scale is that all children take a comparable battery of subtests. The following are assets of the WISC-R:

1. *Good validity.* The WISC-R has adequate concurrent validity with a variety of ability and achievement measures.

2. *High reliabilities.* The internal consistency reliabilities of the WISC-R Full Scale IQs are extremely high (average $r_{xx} = .96$), with standard errors of measurement of less than 5 points on the three scales. Because the WISC-R manual provides reliability data, standard errors of measurement, and intercorrelations of subtest scores by one-year age intervals as well as for the average of the 11 age groups, the scale's properties can be evaluated throughout its entire age range. Confidence intervals can be established for IQs for each of the 11 separate age groups, thereby providing estimates that are specifically applicable to each child's chronological age.

3. *Excellent standardization.* The standardization procedures were excellent, sampling four geographic regions, both sexes, white and nonwhite populations, urban and rural residents, and the entire range of socioeconomic classes.

4. *Good administration procedures.* The prescribed procedures for administering the WISC-R are excellent. The examiner actively probes the child's responses in order to evaluate the breadth of the child's knowledge and determine whether the child really knows the answer. On items that require two reasons for maximum credit, the child is asked for another reason when only one reason is given. These procedures ensure that the child is not penalized for not understanding the demands of the questions. The emphasis on probing questions and queries is extremely desirable.

5. *Good manual and test materials.* The WISC-R manual is easy to use; it provides clear directions and tables. Reading of the directions is facilitated by the fact that the examiner's instructions are printed in a different color.

Helpful abbreviations are provided for recording the child's responses, such as "Q" for Query, "DK" for Don't Know, "Inc." for Incomplete, and "NR" for No Response. The test materials are interesting to children.

6. *Helpful scoring criteria.* The criteria for scoring replies have been carefully prepared. The Similarities and Vocabulary scoring guidelines, for example, detail the rationale for 2, 1, and 0 scores. A number of examples demonstrate the application of the scoring principles. Many typical responses are scored, and those deemed to need further inquiry are indicated by a "Q."

7. *Extensive research and clinical literature.* There is a vast amount of research and case material on the WISC-R that can be used to aid interpretation.

LIMITATIONS OF THE WISC-R

Although the WISC-R is an excellent instrument, there are a number of difficulties with the test and with the manual that should be recognized.

1. *Limited applicability of norms for children younger than 6-4 years and older than 16-8 years.* One of the major questions about the WISC-R is the applicability of its norms for children between 6-0 and 6-3 years of age and between 16-8 and 16-11 years of age. In the standardization of the WISC-R, the only children tested were those whose birthdates were at mid-year, plus or minus 1.5 months. Consequently, at the 6-year-old age level, no children who were between 6-0 and 6-3 years of age were included. (A footnote on page 48 of the WISC-R manual indicates that there was a small norms group [$N = 50$] at age 6 years, 0 months, which was used as a guide in extrapolating norms for the 6-0 to 6-3 age range.) The same type of gap occurs for children between 16-8 and 16-11 years of age. Nevertheless, the WISC-R manual presents norms for these two three-month age periods. Therefore the standardized normative scores, arrived at by extrapolation, may not yield correct results for these two age groups.

2. *Limited floor and ceiling.* Another difficulty with the WISC-R is that the range of Full Scale IQs (40 to 160) is insufficient for both severely retarded children and extremely gifted children. The test is designed so that a 6-year-old child receives up to 3 scaled-scored points for giving *no* correct answers on some subtests. Throughout the entire age range of the test, children receive at least 1 scaled-score point on every subtest, even if they have a raw score of 0. Wechsler recognized that this can present a problem in computing IQs and therefore recommended that IQs for each scale be computed only when the child

obtains a raw score greater than 0 on at least three of the subtests on each of the scales. Similarly, a Full Scale IQ should not be computed unless raw scores greater than 0 are obtained on three Verbal and three Performance subtests. These are only recommendations, however, and must be considered as such until validity data show that other procedures for computing IQs are not valid.

If Wechsler's recommended procedure is followed, what is the lowest possible IQ that a 6-year-old child can receive? If the child obtained raw scores of 1 on the Information, Vocabulary, Comprehension, Picture Completion, Object Assembly, and Coding subtests and a raw score of 0 on each of the remaining four subtests, the resulting IQs would be as follows: Verbal Scale IQ = 57 (15 scaled-score points), Performance Scale IQ = 48 (11 scaled-score points), and Full Scale IQ = 48 (26 scaled-score points). Six 1-point successes yield an IQ of 48. Therefore the WISC-R may not provide precise IQs for young children who are functioning at 2 or more standard deviations below the mean of the scale. Even for IQs between 70 and 80, only a very small sample of a child's ability is tested because so few items are administered. The WISC-R does not appear to sample a sufficient range of cognitive abilities for low-functioning children. If a child fails all or most of the items on the WISC-R, a different test should be administered to obtain a more accurate estimate of the child's abilities.

The highest IQ that can be obtained by children aged 16-8 years and older is 158, a ceiling score that probably is too low to make the test appropriate for use with extremely gifted children.

3. *Nonuniformity of scaled scores.* The range of scaled scores on all subtests is not uniform throughout the age range covered by the scale. Only in the 6- through 10-year age range can children receive up to 19 scaled-score points on all subtests. At age 11 years, for example, the highest raw score on the Arithmetic subtest (18 points) corresponds to a scaled score of 18. At age 16-8, this same raw score corresponds to a scaled score of 16. On only 5 of the 12 subtests can children aged 16-8 and older receive the highest scaled score.

The nonuniformity of available scaled scores throughout the entire age range makes profile analysis difficult to apply to high-scoring children 11 years of age or older. Profile analysis techniques can be applied appropriately throughout the entire range of scaled scores for five subtests only (Similarities, Vocabulary, Digit Span, Picture Arrangement, and Coding). For older gifted children, profile analysis can be applied only when all scaled scores are 16 or below. *Applying profile analysis uniformly to all subtests would be misleading for individual cases because the same number of scaled-score points cannot be obtained on all subtests.*

4. *Difficulty in scoring responses.* When responses on the Similarities, Comprehension, and Vocabulary subtests differ from those that appear in the WISC-R manual, they may be difficult to score. Such difficulties may lead to halo effects in scoring and contribute to examiner bias (cf. Sattler & Ryan, 1973b).

5. *Difficulty in interpreting norms when a supplementary subtest is substituted for a regular subtest.* With the norms based on only the 10 regular subtests, there is no way to know precisely what the scores mean when one of the supplementary subtests (Digit Span or Mazes) is substituted for a regular subtest. A substitution of this kind, therefore, should be made only in unusual circumstances and the results labeled "tentative" when the scores are reported.

6. *Lack of normative data for raw scores.* The WISC-R manual fails to give means, standard deviations, and frequency distributions for the raw scores.

7. *Failure to describe procedure for establishing cutoff criteria.* The WISC-R manual fails to provide information concerning how the cutoff criteria (the number of items that should be administered before the test is discontinued) were determined (that is, empirically or intuitively).

CONCLUDING COMMENT ON THE WISC-R

The WISC-R has been well received by those who use tests to evaluate children's intellectual ability. It has excellent standardization, reliability, and concurrent validity, and much care has been taken to provide useful administrative and scoring guidelines. Although some minor problems exist in the WISC-R manual, it is, on the whole, excellent. A valuable addition to the manual would have been data about the standard errors of measurement of IQ scores on the Verbal, Performance, and Full Scales at IQ levels of 70, 100, and 130 (if not others). The WISC-R will serve as a valuable instrument in the assessment of children's intelligence for many years to come.

SUMMARY

1. The WISC-R was published in 1974, 25 years after the original WISC. The WISC-R is similar to its predecessor, with 72 percent of the items retained, plus the original Coding subtest.

The WISC-R is applicable to children from 6-0-0 to 16-11-30 years of age. Standardization of the scale was excellent and included both white and nonwhite children.

2. The WISC-R provides Deviation IQs for the Verbal, Performance, and Full Scales ($M = 100$, $SD = 15$) and standard scores for the 12 subtests ($M = 10$, $SD = 3$).

3. Although Wechsler objected to the use of mental ages in the calculation of IQs, the WISC-R manual includes a table of test-age equivalents for the scaled scores; these are essentially mental-age scores.

4. The internal consistency reliabilities of the Verbal, Performance, and Full Scales are excellent (average of .94, .90, and .96, respectively), with a standard error of measurement for the Full Scale of about 3 IQ points. Subtest reliabilities range from .70 to .86.

5. Shifts in IQ due to practice effects (after a one-month test-retest interval) are about 7 IQ points on the Full Scale, 4 IQ points on the Verbal Scale, and 10 IQ points on the Performance Scale. Average changes in Full Scale IQs over a two-year period are about 3 points.

6. The WISC-R has acceptable criterion validity. Median correlations with measures of achievement and school grades range from the upper .30s to the low .80s.

7. The WISC-R has acceptable concurrent validity. Correlations with other Wechsler scales and with the Stanford-Binet: Fourth Edition are in the .70s to .80s.

8. The WISC-R tends to provide lower IQs than do the WPPSI and the WAIS-R. The various Wechsler scales do not appear to provide interchangeable IQs.

9. The relationships between WISC-R IQs and various stratification variables were as follows. Mean differences between girls and boys were less than 3 points. IQs of white children were about 1 standard deviation higher than those of black children (102 vs. 86). Children's mean IQs varied by up to 21 points as a function of their parents' occupational group (108 vs. 87). Urban-rural differences were small, and geographic region differences were largest between the West and the South (103 vs. 96).

10. A factor analysis of the WISC-R standardization data indicated that three factors account for the scale's structure: Verbal Comprehension, Perceptual Organization, and Freedom from Distractibility. The Verbal Scale subtests load primarily on Verbal Comprehension; Performance Scale subtests load primarily on Perceptual Organization; and Arithmetic, Digit Span, and Coding load primarily on Freedom from Distractibility. The best measures of *g* are four Verbal Scale subtests—Vocabulary, Information, Similarities, and Comprehension—and one Performance Scale subtest—Block Design.

11. The WISC-R factor structure found in a variety of ethnic groups and exceptional populations generally is similar to that found in the standardization sample.

12. Because most WISC-R subtests have an adequate degree of subtest specificity, interpretation of profiles of subtest scores generally is on firm ground.

13. The Deviation IQs associated with the Verbal and Perfor-

mance Scale IQs can be used as factor scores. Somewhat purer factor scores can be obtained by using Information, Similarities, Vocabulary, and Comprehension for the Verbal Comprehension factor and Picture Completion, Picture Arrangement, Block Design, and Object Assembly for the Perceptual Organization factor. The three subtests that comprise Freedom from Distractibility—Arithmetic, Digit Span, and Coding—also provide a factor score.

14. It is important to develop proper administrative procedures early in your testing career.

15. Beginning examiners tend to make a variety of administrative errors. They should be especially careful to complete the record booklet properly, adhere to directions, probe ambiguous responses, and follow discontinuance procedures.

16. The standard order of administering the subtests should be followed in all but the most exceptional circumstances.

17. The WISC-R manual describes a number of administrative procedures that must be followed to ensure standardized scoring. When the entry-point items are passed, give credit to items failed below the entry-point items. Conversely, do not give credit to items passed above the discontinuance-point items.

18. The WISC-R requires the use of many probing questions and queries. Spoiled responses are scored 0.

19. Modifications in test procedures have been found to increase children's scores. Use modifications only *after* the standard administration.

20. Scoring WISC-R Vocabulary, Comprehension, and Similarities subtests requires considerable skill. A careful study of the scoring criteria can help to reduce errors in scoring.

21. Extrapolated IQs are difficult to interpret because of errors associated with such scores. If extrapolated IQs are needed, however, Table C-6 in Appendix C can be consulted.

22. Short forms of the WISC-R, although practical, have serious disadvantages. Short-form IQs may be less stable, impede profile analysis, and result in misclassifications. If short forms are needed for screening purposes, the procedures advocated by Tellegen and Briggs should be followed to determine Deviation IQs. Table C-10 in Appendix C shows the best combinations of two, three, four, and five WISC-R subtests. Other tables in Appendix C also provide information about short forms.

23. The WISC-R and the WPPSI can be viewed as alternative forms for children aged 6-0 to 6-7 years, and the WISC-R and WAIS-R for children aged 16-0 to 16-11 years. Although the choice of a test in the overlapping age groups will likely depend on the examiner's personal preference, for children of below-normal ability the WPPSI is slightly preferred to the WISC-R and the WISC-R is slightly preferred to the WAIS-R. In the overlapping age levels, the standard errors of measurement are smaller for WPPSI IQs than for WISC-R IQs and smaller for WAIS-R IQs than for WISC-R Verbal and Full Scale IQs.

24. Children must be able to hear to take most WISC-R (and WPPSI and WAIS-R) Verbal Scale subtests, although vision may be used as a substitute modality for some subtests. Arm-hand use is a prerequisite for almost all of the Performance Scale subtests, although some adaptations are possible. The Verbal and Perfor-

mance Scale arrangement of the subtests facilitates the selection of scales for testing handicapped children. Special procedures, described in Appendix D, are usually needed to administer the Performance Scale to deaf children.

25. The assets of the WISC-R include its excellent reliability, validity, and standardization; good administrative procedures; good manual; and helpful scoring criteria.

26. The limitations of the WISC-R include limited applicability of norms for ages 6-0 to 6-3 years and for ages 16-8 to 16-11 years, limited range of IQs (40 to 160), nonuniformity of scaled scores, difficulty in scoring some subtests, difficulty in interpreting norms when a supplementary subtest is substituted, lack of normative data for raw scores, and failure to describe procedures for establishing cutoff criteria.

27. Overall, the WISC-R represents a major contribution to the field of intelligence testing of children. It serves as one of the most important instruments for this purpose.

KEY TERMS, CONCEPTS, AND NAMES

WISC-R standardization sample (p. 121)
WISC-R Deviation IQ (p. 121)
WISC-R scaled scores (p. 121)
WISC-R test-age equivalents (p. 121)
Reliability of the WISC-R (p. 122)
Standard errors of measurement of the WISC-R (p. 123)
Stability of the WISC-R (p. 123)
Validity of the WISC-R (p. 123)
WISC-R subtest intercorrelations (p. 125)
Stratification variables on the WISC-R (p. 126)
WISC-R Verbal Comprehension factor (p. 127)
WISC-R Perceptual Organization factor (p. 127)
WISC-R Freedom from Distractibility factor (p. 127)
Subtest specificity on the WISC-R (p. 128)
Factor scores on the WISC-R (p. 130)
Entry-point items on the WISC-R (p. 134)
Discontinuance procedure on the WISC-R (p. 135)
Extrapolated IQs for the WISC-R (p. 136)
Short forms of the WISC-R (p. 136)
Yudin's abbreviated procedure for the WISC-R (p. 137)

STUDY QUESTIONS

1. Discuss the WISC-R. Include in your discussion the following issues: standardization, Deviation IQs, test-age equivalents, reliability, and validity.

2. Describe and interpret the intercorrelations between WISC-R subtests and scales.

3. Describe and interpret WISC-R IQs with respect to the stratification variables used in the standardization sample.

4. Describe and interpret WISC-R factor analytic findings.

5. Discuss WISC-R administrative considerations.

6. Discuss WISC-R short forms, including their values and limitations.

7. For overlapping ages how would you go about choosing between the WISC-R and the WPPSI, and between the WISC-R and WAIS-R?

8. Identify the most important factors to consider in administering the WISC-R (and other Wechsler tests) to handicapped children.

9. Discuss the assets and limitations of the WISC-R.

_7

WISC-R SUBTESTS

Wit is brushwood, judgment is timber. The first makes the brightest flame, but the other gives the most lasting heat.

—Hebrew proverb

The knowledge of words is the gate to scholarship.
—Woodrow Wilson

The true art of memory is the art of attention.
—Samuel Johnson

Information

Similarities

Arithmetic

Vocabulary

Comprehension

Digit Span

Picture Completion

Picture Arrangement

Block Design

Object Assembly

Coding

Mazes

Summary

This chapter provides the necessary background for administering, scoring, and interpreting the 12 WISC-R subtests. Included in the description of each subtest is the rationale, factor analytic findings, reliability and correlational highlights, and administrative and interpretive considerations. The factor analytic findings (from Kaufman, 1975a, 1979c) and reliability and correlational data discussed in this chapter are based on the entire standardization sample. Reliabilities for the Digit Span and Coding subtests are test-retest correlations, whereas those for the remaining 10 subtests are split-half correlations corrected by the Spearman-Brown formula.

The abilities measured by each WISC-R subtest, background factors influencing performance, implications of high and low scores, and suggested training activities to improve a child's scores are summarized in Table C-13 in Appendix C. Table C-13 is a useful reference for report writing and deserves careful study and evaluation. Readers interested in the WISC-R Structure-of-Intellect classifications may refer to Table C-12 in Appendix C; a supplementary scoring guide by Massey, Sattler, and Andres (1978) presents additional responses to aid in the scoring of the Similarities, Vocabulary, and Comprehension subtests.

Although many of the subtests have enough subtest specificity (see Chapter 6) to provide reliable estimates of some specific abilities, combinations of individual subtests will produce the most reliable estimates. For example, the Verbal Scale IQ, which is derived from a combination of five subtests, yields more accurate data about a child's verbal skills than does a single subtest score, such as the Vocabulary scaled score.

In the discussions of test administration procedures, a number of questions are posed to aid you in observing children's performance. The answers to these questions will serve as a database for testing clinical hypotheses once the test has been completed. Although you may not have many questions at the beginning of the testing, you should have some specific ones in mind at the end. Precise recording as you proceed will enable you to answer questions that arise later.

INFORMATION

The Information subtest contains 30 questions that sample a broad range of general knowledge. Included are questions concerning names of objects, dates, historical and geographical facts, and other such information. The child's age determines which item is used to start testing: Children 6 to 7 years old start with item 1; 8 to 10 years old, item 5; 11 to 13 years old, item 7; and 14 to 16 years old, item 11. All items are scored 1 or 0 (pass-fail), and the subtest is discontinued after five consecutive failures.

The questions usually can be answered correctly with a brief, simply stated fact. Children need only demonstrate that they know specific facts; they need not find relationships between these facts.

Rationale

The amount of knowledge children possess may depend on their natural endowment, the extent of their education (both formal and informal), and their cultural opportunities and predilections. In general, the Information subtest samples the knowledge that average children with average opportunities should be able to acquire through normal home and school experiences. The child's responses and comments provide clues about the child's general range of information, alertness to the environment, social or cultural background, and attitudes toward school and school-like tasks ("Those questions are hard, just like my teacher asks"). High scores should not be interpreted as indications of mental efficiency and competence, since the fact that individuals have acquired isolated facts does not mean that they know how to use them appropriately or effectively. However, intellectual drive may contribute to higher scores. Successful performance on the Information subtest requires memory for habitual,

HOW WOULD YOU SCORE THIS?

overlearned responses (that is, information that the child has likely been exposed to over and over again), especially in older children. Thus Information provides clues about the child's ability to store and retrieve old data.

Factor Analytic Findings

The Information subtest is tied with Similarities as the second-best measure of g (58 percent of its variance may be attributed to g). It has ample subtest specificity to permit specific interpretation of its functions and contributes substantially to the Verbal Comprehension factor (*Mdn* loading = .63).

Reliability and Correlational Highlights

Information is a reliable subtest (r_{xx} = .85). It correlates more highly with Vocabulary (r = .69) than with any other subtest. It correlates moderately with both the Full Scale (r = .70) and Verbal Scale (r = .74), but to a lesser degree with the Performance Scale (r = .56).

Administrative and Interpretive Considerations

The Information subtest is easy to administer. The questions are simple and direct, and timing is not required. Credit should be given if questions are answered correctly at any time during the course of administering the scale. Scoring is usually straightforward: a correct response receives 1 point; an incorrect response, 0. If two or more answers are given to a question, the examinee should be asked to choose the best answer. Answers should be recorded verbatim. Children who are hesitant to respond should be encouraged to guess or take a chance.

Note the quality of a child's answers. Is the child thinking the questions through or simply guessing? Are answers precise or wordy? Overly long responses or responses filled with extraneous information may suggest an obsessive-compulsive orientation—children with this orientation sometimes feel compelled to prove how much they know. Alternatively, excessive responses may simply reflect the examinee's desire to impress you. The child's entire test protocol plus other relevant information should be considered in interpreting such behavior. Inhibition, too, should be noted, as inability to recall an answer may suggest that the question is associated with conflict-laden material. (For example, a child may not be able to recall the number of legs on a dog because of a traumatic experience with dogs.)

Examine the pattern of successes and failures. Failures on easy items coupled with successes on more difficult

ones may suggest poor motivation, anxiety, temporary inefficiency, or an environment that has not been consistent. Alternatively, this pattern may indicate a problem with retrieval of information from long-term memory. When you suspect such a problem, analyze the content of the failed items—do they deal with numerical information, history, science, or geography? Content analysis may provide clues to areas of interest or suggestions for points of inquiry after the test has been completed.

> Question: What comes in a bottle?
> Answer: Genies.
> (Flumen & Flumen, 1979)

SIMILARITIES

The Similarities subtest contains 17 pairs of words; the child must explain the similarity between the two items in each pair. All children begin with the first item. The first four items are scored 1 or 0 (pass-fail); items 5 through 17 are scored 2, 1, or 0, depending on the conceptual level of the response. The subtest is discontinued after three consecutive failures.

Rationale

In addition to perceiving the common elements of the paired terms, children must bring these common elements together in a concept in order to answer the questions on the Similarities subtest. Thus the Similarities subtest may measure verbal concept formation—the ability to place objects and events together in a meaningful group or groups. Although concept formation can be a voluntary, effortful process, it can also reflect well-automatized verbal conventions (Rapaport, Gill, & Schafer, 1968). Performance on the Similarities subtest may be related to cultural opportunities and interest patterns. Memory may also be involved.

Factor Analytic Findings

The Similarities subtest is tied with Information as the second-best measure of g (58 percent of its variance may be attributed to g). It has ample subtest specificity for children 6½, 7½, and 8½ years old, but not for older children. Thus specific interpretation of the subtest's functions is appropriate only for the three earliest ages. The Similarities subtest contributes substantially to the Verbal

Comprehension factor (*Mdn* loading = .64) and thus is interpretable as a measure of verbal comprehension.

Reliability and Correlational Highlights

Similarities is a reliable subtest (r_{xx} = .81). It correlates more highly with Vocabulary (*r* = .67) and Information (*r* = .62) than with any other subtests. It correlates moderately with the Full Scale (*r* = .71) and the Verbal Scale (*r* = .72), and to a somewhat lesser degree with the Performance Scale (*r* = .58).

Administrative and Interpretive Considerations

Responses to the first four questions are generally easy to score, but scoring of items 5 to 17 is more difficult. On the latter items (5–17), a conceptual response, such as a general classification, receives a 2; a more concrete response, such as a specific property of the item, receives a 1; and an incorrect response receives a 0. This scoring system is designed to take into account whether the responses are essential likenesses or superficial likenesses.

Many Similarities responses are difficult to score, as was shown by a study of the way 110 psychologists and graduate students scored 187 ambiguous WISC-R Similarities, Vocabulary, and Comprehension responses (Sattler, Andres, Squire, Wisely, & Maloy, 1978). A level of 80 percent agreement in scoring was achieved for only 51 percent of the ambiguous Similarities responses (95 out of 187). In practice, however, it is unlikely that any one protocol would include such a large number of ambiguous responses. Scoring difficulties arise in part from the limited number of examples in the manual and the difficulty of establishing precise criteria that apply to all responses, including idiosyncratic ones.

Scoring criteria. A careful study of the scoring guide in the manual will help you become more proficient in scoring. Two parts of Appendix A in the WISC-R manual— "Scoring Criteria" for the Similarities subtest—are especially important. First, you should thoroughly master the general scoring principles, which elucidate the rationale for 2, 1, and 0 scores. Second, you should carefully study the "Sample Responses" section, which lists types of responses that should be queried [as shown by a "(Q)"], so that you can recognize responses that need probing.

Noting children's understanding of the task. Note whether children understand the task. On items 1 and 2, give children the correct responses if they answer incorrectly. Children who state that they do not know the answer

to a question should be encouraged to think about the question, but they should not be pressed unreasonably. When children give multiple acceptable answers to an item, score their best response. When both correct and incorrect responses are given to an item, say "Now which one is it?" The score should be based on the answer to your follow-up question. If the child gives a 1-point answer to item 5 or 6, you should tell the child the 2-point answer, to provide a model response. This procedure may encourage the child to give 2-point responses on later items.

Interpreting responses. Responses to the Similarities subtest may provide insight into the logical character of the child's thinking processes. Observe the child's typical level of conceptualization throughout the subtest. Are the answers on a concrete, functional, or abstract level? Concrete answers typically refer to qualities of the objects (or stimuli) that can be seen or touched (apple-banana: "Both have a skin"). Functional answers typically concern a function or use of the objects (apple-banana: "You eat them"). Finally, abstract answers typically refer to a more universal property or to a common classification of the objects (apple-banana: "Both are fruits").

A 2-point abstract response does not necessarily reflect abstract thinking ability. It may simply be a conventional, overlearned response. For example, there is a difference between the 2-point response "Both fruits" for apple-banana and the 2-point response "Social qualities" for liberty-justice. The former may be a conventional response, whereas the latter likely reflects a more abstract level of conceptualizing ability.

Observe how the examinee handles any frustration induced by the subtest questions. Is the examinee negativistic and uncooperative, or is he or she genuinely unable to see the similarity involved? Responses such as "They are not alike" may be an indication of negativism, an attempt to avoid the task demands, suspiciousness, a coping mechanism, or failure to know the answer. To determine which of these factors may account for a child's responses, compare the child's style of responding on the Similarities subtest with that on other subtests.

Question: In what way are an orange and a pear alike?
Answer: Both give me hives.

ARITHMETIC

The Arithmetic subtest contains 18 problems, 15 of which are presented orally and 3 of which are presented on cards.

The last three Arithmetic items appear in the Picture Completion/Block Design booklet. Many of the problems are similar to those commonly encountered by children. Answers must be given without the use of paper and pencil. Children 6 to 7 years old (and older children suspected of mental retardation) begin the test with item 1; 8 to 10 years old, item 5; 11 to 13 years old, item 8; and 14 to 16 years old, item 10. The problems are timed, with the first 13 items having a 30-second time limit; items 14 and 15, a 45-second time limit; and items 16 to 18, a 75-second time limit. Items are scored 1 or 0, with the exception of items 2 and 3, for which ½ point can be given. The subtest is discontinued after three consecutive failures.

Problems on the Arithmetic subtest test various skills. Problems 1, 2, and 3 require direct counting of concrete quantities. Problems 4, 6, 7, 8, 9, 11, and 12 require simple addition or subtraction. Problems 5, 13, and 15 involve simple division. Problem 10 involves multiplication. Problems 14, 16, 17, and 18 require the use of automatized number facts and subtle operations, such as identifying relevant relationships at a glance. The answers to problems 13 and 15 may come intuitively to children experienced with facts. For those who have not yet automatized simple arithmetic facts, the problems may require reflection and mental operation.

Rationale

The problems on the Arithmetic subtest require the child to follow verbal directions, concentrate on selected parts of questions, and use numerical operations. Children must have knowledge of addition, subtraction, multiplication, and division operations. The emphasis of the problems is not on mathematical knowledge per se, but on mental computation and concentration. Concentration is especially important for the complex problems.

The Arithmetic subtest measures numerical reasoning— the ability to solve arithmetical problems. It requires the use of noncognitive functions (concentration and attention) in conjunction with cognitive functions (knowledge of numerical operations). Success on the subtest is influenced by education, interests, fluctuations of attention, and transient emotional reactions. Like the Vocabulary and Information subtests, Arithmetic taps memory and prior learning; however, it also requires substantial concentration and the active application of select skills to new and unique situations (Blatt & Allison, 1968).

Information-processing strategies as well as mathematical skills may underlie performance on the Arithmetic subtest (Stewart & Moely, 1983). These strategies may include rehearsal (in order to remember the information presented in the task) and recognizing when an appropriate response has been made (in order to change incorrect patterns or strategies). The mathematical skills include the ability to comprehend and integrate verbal information presented in a mathematical context and numerical ability.

Factor Analytic Findings

The Arithmetic subtest is a fair measure of g (42 percent of its variance may be attributed to g). It has ample subtest specificity to permit specific interpretation of its functions. Arithmetic has a high loading on the Freedom from Distractibility factor (Mdn loading = .58) and a moderate loading on the Verbal Comprehension factor (Mdn loading = .37).

Reliability and Correlational Highlights

Arithmetic is a relatively reliable subtest (r_{xx} = .77). It correlates more highly with Information (r = .54) and Vocabulary (r = .52) than with the other subtests. It has a relatively low correlation with the Full Scale (r = .58) and Verbal Scale (r = .58), and an even lower correlation with the Performance Scale (r = .48).

Administrative and Interpretive Considerations

Testing-of-limits procedures can facilitate interpretation of the test results. Examinees should be given additional time to complete the problems when they need it, even though no credit is given for a late response. Any correct late responses should be recorded, along with the amount of time that elapsed between expiration of the time limit and their submission. Such information may help you differentiate between failures due to temporary inefficiency and those due to limited knowledge. Successful delayed performance may indicate temporary inefficiency or a slow, painstaking approach to problem solving.

To determine reasons for children's failure, use inquiry after the test is completed. You might say, for example, "Let's try this one again. Tell me how you solved the problem." Failure may be caused by poor knowledge of arithmetical operations, inadequate conceptualization of the problem, temporary inefficiency or anxiety, poor concentration, or carelessness.

Allowing the child to use paper and pencil is another testing-of-limits procedure that may help you to differentiate inadequate arithmetical knowledge from attentional or concentration difficulties. If the child is able to solve the items with pencil and paper, the failure is not associated with lack of arithmetical knowledge; the errors may be associated with attention or concentration difficulties that inhibit mental computation. If the child fails the items in both situations, the failures more likely reflect difficulties with arithmetical knowledge, although attention and concentration difficulties may be interfering with the examinee's ability to solve written arithmetic problems. Inspect the written work to see whether numbers are misaligned, steps are sequenced incorrectly, or there is evidence of inadequate mastery of basic arithmetical operations.

Question: If I cut a pear in thirds, how many pieces will I have?

Answer: One.

Question: (Testing-of-limits) Are you sure I will have only one piece?

Answer: Yes, and I will have the other two pieces.

VOCABULARY

The Vocabulary subtest contains 32 words arranged in order of increasing difficulty. The child is asked to explain orally the meaning of each word (for example, "What is a _____?" or "What does _____ mean?"). Children 6 to 7 years old (and older children suspected of being mentally retarded) begin with item 1; 8 to 10 years old, item 4; 11 to 14 years old, item 6; and 14 to 16 years old, item 8. All items are scored 2, 1, or 0. The subtest is discontinued after five consecutive failures.

Rationale

The Vocabulary subtest, a test of word knowledge, may tap a variety of cognition-related factors — including learning ability, fund of information, richness of ideas, memory, concept formation, and language development — that may be closely related to children's experiences and educational environments. Because the number of words known by children is correlated with their ability to learn and to accumulate information, the subtest provides an excellent estimate of intellectual ability. Performance on the subtest is stable over time and relatively resistant to neurological deficit and psychological disturbance (Blatt & Allison, 1968). Performance on the Vocabulary subtest is a useful index of the examinee's general mental ability.

Factor Analytic Findings

The Vocabulary subtest is the best measure of g in the scale (64 percent of its variance may be attributed to g). It has adequate subtest specificity to permit specific interpretation of its functions across all ages. It contributes substantially to the Verbal Comprehension factor (Mdn loading = .72).

Reliability and Correlational Highlights

Vocabulary is the most reliable subtest (r_{xx} = .86) in the scale. It correlates more highly with Information (r = .69), Similarities (r = .67), and Comprehension (r = .66) than with the other subtests. It correlates moderately with the Full Scale (r = .74) and the Verbal Scale (r = .68), and to a lesser degree with the Performance Scale (r = .58).

Administrative and Interpretive Considerations

Care should be taken to pronounce each word clearly and correctly. Pronunciation is especially important on the Vocabulary subtest because the test items are single words and you are not allowed to spell them. When you suspect that children have not heard a word correctly, have them repeat it to you. Carefully record the examinees' responses to the words.

Scoring responses. The scoring system (2, 1, or 0 for all items) takes into account the quality of the response. Two points are awarded for good synonyms, major uses, or general classifications, whereas one point is given for vague responses, less pertinent synonyms, or minor uses. Elegance of expression is not taken into account.

Vocabulary is one of the more difficult subtests to score. Often it is not easy to implement Wechsler's scoring criteria. In the study by Sattler et al. (1978), 80 percent of the raters gave the same score to only 38 percent of the 352 ambiguous Vocabulary responses. Probing borderline responses and studying carefully the scoring guidelines in the WISC-R manual and the scoring examples in the Massey et al. (1978) manual will help you resolve some of the scoring problems that arise in the course of administering the subtest. You must try to do the best job possible with the available guides.

Qualitative analysis. A qualitative analysis of a child's responses to the Vocabulary subtest may reveal something about the examinee's background, cultural milieu, social development, life experiences, responses to frustration, and thought processes. The basis for incorrect responses should be determined, since it is important to distinguish among guesses, clang associations, idiosyncratic associations, and bizarre associations. Inquiry is especially

important whenever peculiar responses, mispronunciations, or peculiar inflections are given. Among children
with schizophrenia or other severe forms of mental disorder, language disturbances occasionally can be seen in
word definitions.

Further inquiry.   When young children or older children who may be mentally retarded give a 0- or 1-point
response to the first word of the Vocabulary subtest, tell
them the 2-point answer. This procedure, designed to
encourage 2-point responses, is not followed on subsequent items.

Responses suggestive of regionalism or slang should be
probed further (for example, "Give me another meaning
for _____"). The "Sample Responses" section of Appendix
B of the WISC-R manual lists many responses that should
be queried [as shown by a "(Q)"]; study this section carefully so that you can recognize responses that should be
probed.

The nature of the response should determine whether the
inquiry occurs during or after the standard administration.
For example, if the answer clearly defines a homonym of
the test item, repeat the question by saying "What else does
_____ mean?" However, if the response is possibly indicative of a thinking disorder, further probing should be
delayed until testing has been completed. During the testing-of-limits phase you might say "To the word _____ you
said _____. Tell me more about your answer."

Observing responses.   The following guidelines are
useful for observing and evaluating Vocabulary responses
(Taylor, 1961).

• Write down all responses, whether correct or not.
• Note whether children are definitely familiar with the
word or only vaguely familiar with it. If children explain a
word, do they try to be precise and brief or embark on
lengthy explanations? Are their responses objective or do
they relate to personal experiences?
• Note whether children confuse the word with another
one that sounds like it. If they do not know the meaning of a
word, do they guess? Do they readily say "I don't know"
and shake off further demands, or are they puzzled?
• In testing-of-limits, note whether displaying the
printed word improves recognition.
• Watch for possible hearing difficulties by listening
carefully to how children repeat words. Have the words
been heard correctly or with some distortion?
• Note how the children express themselves. Do they
find it easy or difficult to say what they mean? Do they have
mechanical difficulties pronouncing words properly? Do

they seem uncertain about how best to express what they
think? Do they use gestures to illustrate their statements or
even depend on them exclusively?
• Note the content of definitions. Are the words chosen
synonyms for the stimulus word (thief—"a burglar"), or do
they describe an action (thief—"takes stuff")? Do the children describe some special feature of the object (donkey—
"it has four legs"), or do they try to fit it into some category
(donkey—"a living creature that is kept in a barn")?
• Note any emotional overtones, personal experiences,
or feelings (alphabet—"I hate to write").

Question: What is a chisel?
   Answer: When you are cold you get the chisels.
                    (Flumen & Flumen, 1979)

COMPREHENSION

The Comprehension subtest consists of 17 questions that
deal with problem situations involving knowledge of one's
body, interpersonal relations, and social mores. All children begin the subtest with the first item, and all items are

Courtesy Herman Zielinski.

scored 2, 1, or 0. The subtest is discontinued after four consecutive failures.

Rationale

The Comprehension subtest involves understanding given situations and providing answers to specific problems. Success depends, in part, on possession of practical information plus an ability to draw on past experiences in reaching solutions. Responses may reflect the child's knowledge of conventional standards of behavior, extensiveness of cultural opportunities, and level of development of conscience or moral sense. Success suggests that the child has social judgment, or common sense, and a grasp of social conventionality. These characteristics imply an ability to use facts in a pertinent, meaningful, and emotionally appropriate manner.

Factor Analytic Findings

The Comprehension subtest is a good measure of g (52 percent of its variance may be attributed to g). It has adequate subtest specificity to permit specific interpretation of its functions across the entire age range and has a high loading on the Verbal Comprehension factor (*Mdn* loading = .64).

Reliability and Correlational Highlights

Comprehension is a reasonably reliable subtest (r_{xx} = .77). It correlates more highly with Vocabulary (r = .66) and Similarities (r = .59) than with the other subtests. It correlates moderately with the Full Scale (r = .66) and the Verbal Scale (r = .68), and to a lesser degree with the Performance Scale (r = .53).

Administrative and Interpretive Considerations

The Comprehension subtest is difficult to score because children give many responses that differ from those provided in the manual. In the Sattler et al. (1978) study, 80 percent of the raters gave the same score to only 49 percent of the 187 ambiguous Comprehension responses.

The most complete or best response receives a score of 2; a less adequate response, 1; and an incorrect response, 0. If an inquiry about a response alters the meaning of the initial response, the reply to the inquiry determines the amount of credit given.

On the first item, you are supposed to tell children the correct 2-point response if they give a less adequate response. This procedure is meant to encourage children to give 2-point responses and is allowed only on the first item. On the nine items (3, 4, 7, 8, 9, 12, 14, 16, and 17) that require two ideas for full credit (2 points), you are required to ask for a second idea when only one idea is given, so that children are not automatically penalized for not giving two reasons. However, on the other items, for which an adequate one-idea answer is scored 2 points, obvious 1-point responses should not be probed in an attempt to improve the score.

Scoring criteria. Carefully study the "Sample Responses" section of Appendix C of the WISC-R manual so that you will know which response types need further inquiry [these are labeled "(Q)"]. The examples indicate that many 0- and 1-point responses should be queried. The inclusion of a "Q" with the 2-point responses indicates that the entire response (including the elaboration) is worth 2 points. Additional queries offer you an opportunity to evaluate more thoroughly the extensiveness of the child's knowledge.

Interpreting responses. Responses to the Comprehension questions may provide valuable information about the child's personality style, ethical values, and social and cultural background. Unlike the Information questions, which usually elicit precise answers, the Comprehension questions may elicit more complex and idiosyncratic replies. Because the questions involve judgment of social situations, answers may reflect the child's attitudes. Some responses reveal understanding *and* acceptance of social mores, whereas others reveal understanding *but not* acceptance of social mores. A child may know the right answers but not practice them. Some children may maintain that they do not have to abide by social conventions, believing that such matters do not pertain to them personally.

Initiative, self-reliance, independence, self-confidence, helplessness, and other traits may be revealed in children's replies. For example, children may reveal dependent personality styles by indicating that they would seek help from their mothers or others when confronted with the various problem situations. Replies to questions 6 and 9, which ask the examinee what should be done if a younger child starts a fight with the examinee and why criminals are locked up, may reveal independence, manipulative tendencies, naïve perceptions of problems, cooperative solutions, hostility, or aggression (Robb, Bernardoni, & Johnson, 1972).

Note *how* children respond to the questions (Taylor, 1961):

• Do children's failures indicate misunderstanding of the meaning of a word or the implications of a particular phrase?

• Do the children give complete answers or just part of a phrase?

• Do they respond to the entire question or only to a part of it?

• Do the children seem to be objective, seeing various possibilities and choosing the best way?

• Are they indecisive — unable to come to firm answers?

• Are the children's responses too quick, indicating failure to consider the questions in their entirety?

• Do the children recognize when their answers are sufficient?

Because Comprehension requires considerable verbal expression, the subtest may be sensitive to mild language impairments and to disordered thought processes. Be alert to language deficits, such as word-finding difficulties, circumstantial or tangential speech, or other expressive difficulties.

Further inquiry.   Probe unusual responses by asking children to explain further. Although inquiry may provide insight into the examinee's thought processes, it should not be conducted routinely after every response. Extensive inquiry can be conducted as part of testing-of-limits after the examination has been completed. Record the examinee's responses verbatim during the initial presentation of the items and during the inquiry phase in order to facilitate restudy and qualitative evaluation.

Question: Why should children who are sick stay home?
 Answer: To take their antibionics.
(Flumen & Flumen, 1979)

DIGIT SPAN

On Digit Span, a supplementary subtest, the child listens to a series of digits given orally by the examiner and then repeats the digits. The Digit Span subtest has two parts: Digits Forward, which contains series ranging in length from three to nine digits, and Digits Backward, which contains series ranging in length from two to eight digits. There are two series of digits for each sequence length. Digits Forward is administered first, followed by Digits Backward.

Digit Span is not used in the computation of the IQ when the five standard Verbal Scale subtests are administered. All items are scored 2, 1, or 0. The subtest is discontinued

when the child fails both trials on any one item, both on Digits Forward and on Digits Backward. Separate scaled scores are not provided for Digits Forward and Digits Backward.

Although Digit Span is a supplementary subtest, administering it may make the WISC-R more useful diagnostically and programmatically, especially for obtaining factor scores. Considering the small investment of time and energy required to give this subtest, and the fact that it is used in calculating the Freedom from Distractibility factor, Digit Span should be administered routinely.

Rationale

Digit Span is a measure of short-term auditory memory and attention. Performance may be affected by one's ability to relax. A child who is calm and relaxed may achieve a higher score on the subtest than one who suffers from excessive anxiety. The task assesses the child's ability to retain several elements that have no logical relationship to one another. Because auditory information must be recalled and repeated orally in proper sequence, the task has been described as a sequencing task.

Digits Forward primarily involves rote learning and memory, whereas Digits Backward requires considerably greater transformation of the stimulus input prior to recall. The mental image of the numerical sequence not only must be held longer (usually) than in the Digits Forward sequence, but must be manipulated before it is restated. High scores on Digits Backward may indicate flexibility, good tolerance for stress, and excellent concentration. Digits Backward involves more complex cognitive processing than does Digits Forward and has higher loadings on g than does Digits Forward (Jensen & Osborne, 1979).

Because of differences between the two tasks, it is useful to consider Digits Forward and Digits Backward separately. Digits Forward appears to involve primarily sequential processing, whereas Digits Backward appears to involve both planning ability and sequential processing. Additionally, Digits Backward may involve the ability to form mental images and the ability to scan an internal visual display formed from an auditory stimulus. However, more research is needed to support the hypothesis about the role of visualization in Digits Backward performance. Raw score differences of 3 points between Digits Forward and Digits Backward may be considered noteworthy. Gardner (1981) presents separate means, standard deviations, and percentile ranks for Digits Forward and Digits Backward for children ages 5-0 to 15-11.

Factor Analytic Findings

The Digit Span subtest is a poor measure of *g* (24 percent of its variance may be attributed to *g*). It has ample subtest specificity to permit specific interpretation of its functions across the entire age range. It contributes substantially to the Freedom from Distractibility factor (*Mdn* loading = .56).

Reliability and Correlational Highlights

Digit Span is a relatively reliable subtest (r_{xx} = .78). It correlates more highly with Arithmetic (*r* = .45) than with any other subtest. It has a low correlation with the Full Scale (*r* = .43), the Verbal Scale (*r* = .45), and the Performance Scale (*r* = .34).

Administrative and Interpretive Considerations

Be sure that the examinee cannot see the digits in the manual or on the record blank. The digits should be read clearly at the rate of one per second, with the inflection dropped on the last digit in the series. It is a good idea to practice reading speed with a stopwatch. It is never permissible to repeat any of the digits on either trial of a series.

Both trials of each series are routinely administered. The child receives credit for each trial that he or she passes. On Digits Backward, if the child passes the sample three-digit series (on either the first or the second trial), proceed to the two-digit series. If the child fails the sample series, read the specific directions in the manual that explain how the series should be repeated correctly. Whenever there is any doubt about the child's auditory acuity, an audiological examination should be requested.

Recording performance. The number of digits in each series correctly recalled may be recorded in the record booklet by placing either a mark designating a correct answer above or on each digit correctly recalled or a mark designating an incorrect answer on each digit missed. An even better procedure is to write out the exact sequence given by the child in the available space (whether the digits are right or wrong). These procedures provide qualitative information that can prove valuable when you write your report. An examinee who consistently misses the last digit in the first series and then successfully completes the second series differs from one who fails to recall any of the digits in the first series but successfully completes the

second. Similarly, a child who responds to the sequence 3-4-1-7 with 3-1-4-7 is quite different from the child who says 9-8-5-6.

The scoring system does not distinguish among failure patterns. For example, the same score is given to both the examinee who misses one digit in the eight-digit sequence and the examinee who misses all eight digits, even though the second examinee's performance is more inefficient, perhaps because of lapses in attention associated with anxiety or other factors.

Observing performance. Observe whether failures involve leaving out one or more digits, transposing digits, interjecting incorrect digits, or producing more digits than were given. Children who recall the correct numbers but in an incorrect sequence are more likely to have a deficit in auditory sequential memory than in auditory memory.

Note also whether failures usually occurred on the first trial and successes on the second trial. This pattern may reflect a learning-to-learn process or be indicative of a need for a warm-up in order to achieve success.

Consider the following questions:

• Is performance effortless or is a great deal of concentration used?

• Do the children view the task as interesting, boring, or difficult?

• When errors are made, do the children notice, or do they think that their answers are correct?

• When the Digits Backward series is presented, do the children understand the difference between this task and Digits Forward?

• Are the errors made on Digits Backward similar to or different from those made on Digits Forward?

• As the Digits Backward series proceeds, do the children become stimulated and encouraged, or tense and anxious?

Examinees use various methods of recalling the digits. They may visualize the digits; say the digits to themselves and reproduce them by use of verbal, motor, or auditory techniques; or group the digits. Some grouping techniques introduce meaning into the task so that separate digits become numbers grouped into hundreds, tens, or other units. If grouping occurs, the function underlying the task may be changed from one of attention to one of concentration. After the subtest has been completed, you might ask the examinee how he or she went about remembering the numbers. If you do, be sure to record the response.

Question: Now I am going to say some more numbers, but this time when I stop I want you to say them backwards. For example, if I say 8-4-6, what would you say?

Answer: I'd say, you've got to be kidding!

(Adapted from Flumen & Flumen, 1979)

PICTURE COMPLETION

The Picture Completion subtest consists of 26 drawings of objects from everyday life, each of which lacks a single important element. The pictures are shown one at a time. The child's task is to discover and name (or point to) the missing element within the 20-second time limit. Children 6 to 7 years old (and older children suspected of mental retardation) begin with item 1; those 8 to 16 years old start with item 5. All items are scored 1 or 0 (pass-fail), and the subtest is discontinued after four consecutive failures. Most children enjoy this subtest.

Rationale

The Picture Completion subtest involves recognizing the object depicted, appreciating its incompleteness, and determining the missing part. It is a test of visual discrimination—the ability to differentiate essential from nonessential details. Picture Completion requires concentration, reasoning (or visual alertness), visual organization, and long-term visual memory (as the items require the child to have stored information about the complete figure).

Picture Completion may measure perceptual and conceptual abilities involved in visual recognition and identification of familiar objects. Perception, cognition, judgment, and delay of impulse all may influence performance. The time limit on the subtest places additional demands on the examinee. The richness of children's life experiences also may affect performance on the subtest.

Factor Analytic Findings

The Picture Completion subtest is a fair measure of g (37 percent of its variance may be attributed to g). It has ample to adequate subtest specificity to permit specific interpretation of its functions at different ages and contributes substantially to the Perceptual Organization factor (*Mdn* loading = .57).

Reliability and Correlational Highlights

Picture Completion is a relatively reliable subtest ($r_{xx} = .77$). It correlates more highly with Block Design ($r = .52$) than with any other subtest. It has a somewhat low correlation with the Full Scale ($r = .57$), the Performance Scale ($r = .54$), and the Verbal Scale ($r = .50$).

Administrative and Interpretive Considerations

Picture Completion is easy to administer. Simply leave the booklet flat on the table and turn the cards over to show each succeeding picture. If children have speech difficulties, such as those that occur in aphasia, the subtest can be administered by having examinees point to the place where the part is missing.

As you administer the subtest, consider the following:

• Do the examinees understand the task?

• Do they say anything that comes to mind, or do they search for the right answer?

• When they fail, do they find fault with themselves or with the picture?

• Are they aware of being timed? If so, does the timing make them anxious or prompt them to change the pace of their responding?

If a child's performance leaves any doubt about his or her visual skills, a visual examination should be requested.

Observing perseveration.   Observe whether perseveration occurs. A child who says "mouth" for each picture portraying a person (pictures 2, 12, 15, 17, and 19) is displaying perseveration. "Mouth" is the correct answer for picture 2, but not for the subsequent pictures depicting people.

Recording performance.   Examinees should be aware that they are being timed, because it is important for them to realize that speed is expected. Usually, allowing them to see the stopwatch is all that is necessary.

Record each incorrect response as well as the time taken to make the response. Examinees who usually respond in less than five seconds may be more impulsive, more confident, and, if correct, brighter than those who take more time. Examinees who generally respond correctly after the time limit (for which they do not receive credit) may be brighter than those who respond incorrectly before the time limit is reached. Because the pass-fail scoring makes no provision for such qualitative factors, individual variations should be carefully evaluated in each case and discussed in the report. Delayed correct responses may suggest temporary inefficiency or depression, whereas extremely quick but incorrect responses may reflect impulsivity.

Further inquiry. The WISC-R manual indicates that, if necessary, you may give each of three guiding statements once to help children understand the requirements of this subtest. (a) If children mention a nonessential missing part, you can ask for the most important part that is missing. (b) If children name the object pictured, you can ask what is missing. (c) If children name a part that is off the card, you can ask what is missing.

On five items (6, 14, 22, 23, and 24), children should be asked to point to the missing part on the card if ambiguous responses are given. In other cases, whenever there is any doubt about children's verbal or pointing responses, ask for clarification.

After the subtest has been completed, you may follow up by inquiring about children's perceptions of the task. "How did you go about coming up with the answer?" and "How did you decide when to give an answer?" are possible questions. Any peculiar answers should be queried. Children's behavior during this subtest may provide insight into how they react to time pressure. As a testing-of-limits procedure, children can be asked to look again at those pictures that they missed. You might say "Look at this picture again. Before, you said that _____ was missing. That's not the part that's missing. Look for something else."

PICTURE ARRANGEMENT

In the Picture Arrangement subtest, children must place a series of pictures in logical sequence. The 12 series, or items, are similar to short comic strips. Individual cards, each containing a picture, are placed in a specified disarranged order, and the child is asked to rearrange the pictures in the "right" order to tell a story that makes sense. The number of pictures per set ranges from three to five. One set of cards is presented at a time. Time limits vary from 45 seconds for items 1 through 8 to 60 seconds for items 9 through 12. The only motor action required is to change the position of the pictures.

All children begin with the sample item, after which children 6 to 7 years old (and older children suspected of mental retardation) are given item 1 and children 8 to 16

years old are given item 3. Items 1 to 4 are scored 2, 1, or 0; items 5 to 12 are scored 3 points for the correct arrangement, with up to 2 additional time-bonus points. The subtest is discontinued after three consecutive failures.

Rationale

The Picture Arrangement subtest measures children's ability to comprehend and evaluate a total situation. In order to accomplish the task, children must grasp the general idea of a story. Although trial-and-error experimentation is sometimes involved, an appraisal of the total situation depicted in the cards is necessary for successful completion.

The subtest is primarily a nonverbal reasoning test which may be viewed as a measure of planning ability. Anticipation, visual organization, and temporal sequencing are involved. The ability to anticipate the consequences of initial acts or situations is tested, as well as the ability to interpret social situations. Some children may generate covert, analytical, verbal descriptions of alternative story sequences to guide them in arranging the stimulus cards. In such cases, verbal sequencing processes are measured by the subtest as well. The capacity to anticipate, judge, and understand the possible antecedents and consequences of events is important in lending meaningful continuity to everyday experiences (Blatt & Allison, 1968).

Factor Analytic Findings

The Picture Arrangement subtest is a fair measure of g (36 percent of its variance may be attributed to g). It has ample subtest specificity to permit specific interpretation of its functions across the entire age range and a moderate loading on the Perceptual Organization factor (*Mdn* loading = .41).

Reliability and Correlational Highlights

Picture Arrangement is a relatively reliable subtest (r_{xx} = .73). It correlates more highly with Block Design (r = .46) than with any other subtest. It has a relatively low correlation with the Full Scale (r = .55), the Performance Scale (r = .52), and the Verbal Scale (r = .49).

Administrative and Interpretive Considerations

Arrange the Picture Arrangement items from the examinee's left to right in the order given in the manual. As you present the demonstration items, be sure not to inadvertently cover the pictures with your hand—examinees should be able to see all of the pictures and follow your movements when you are rearranging the pictures. Record the examinees' Picture Arrangement sequence as soon as you pick up the cards. Children should be coached if they fail any of the first four items.

Children can earn bonus points for speed on items 5 through 12. In order to help them understand the importance of speed, encourage them to work quickly. If children do not tell you when they are finished, ask them. If necessary, you can add to the directions "Tell me when you are finished." When children are extremely compulsive, tell them that the cards do not have to be perfectly straight (or aligned) so that they will not be penalized (that is, lose time-bonus points) for their compulsiveness.

Observing performance. The Picture Arrangement subtest gives you the opportunity to observe how children approach performance tasks involving planning ability. Do they examine the cards, come to some decision, and then reassess it while they arrange the cards (Taylor, 1961)? Or do they proceed quickly without stopping to reconsider their decision? Are their failures due to lack of understanding of the task (revealed by their leaving the pictures in their original order)? What types of errors do they make? (For example, are cards placed in a perfunctory manner or is one card always moved to the same position?)

Note persistence, trial-and-error patterns, discouragement, impulsiveness, or rigidity. Compare children's approaches to the Picture Arrangement items with their approaches to the Block Design and Object Assembly items. Are the same patterns consistently employed in searching for solutions? If the same patterns are not employed, what might account for the differences? Consider the extent to which task content, fatigue, and mood changes may have influenced examinees' approaches to the various items.

Note children's response to any coaching on the first four items (Zimmerman & Woo-Sam, 1985): Do they appear to grasp the point of the arrangement or story? Does coaching help them to understand the task requirements?

Further inquiry. Although inquiry into children's arrangements—particularly on those items they have failed—may elicit useful material, such inquiries are best reserved until testing has been completed, so that standardization of test administration is safeguarded. Select for inquiry items that may lend insight into an examinee's thought patterns. The items need not be ones the child failed; the fact that an item was correctly arranged does not

necessarily mean that the child interpreted it correctly. Because the last two items attempted are likely to be the most complex, they may be selected if you have no specific choices. Arrange the Picture Arrangement cards for each item separately, in the order given by the child. Then ask the child to "tell what is happening in the pictures" or to "make up a story" or to "tell what the pictures show."

Consider the following in evaluating the stories (Taylor, 1961):

• Are they logical, fanciful, or bizarre?
• Are they creative or conventional?
• Are attitudes revealed, such as self-oriented or socially oriented themes?
• Are incorrect arrangements a consequence of incorrect perceptions of details in the pictures or of failure to consider some details?
• Did the child consider all of the relationships in the pictures?

Testing-of-limits. Useful testing-of-limits procedures include giving the child additional time to complete the arrangement and arranging one or more pictures on items that were failed. Children who solve the problems with the aid of cues may have greater ability than those who fail in spite of additional guidance. Graded help should be introduced only after the standard examination has been completed, because it has been shown that such help during testing significantly raises Picture Arrangement scores (Sattler, 1969).

BLOCK DESIGN

The Block Design subtest contains 11 items, consisting of two-dimensional, red-and-white pictures of abstract designs. (A model is constructed by the examiner for the first two items.) Examinees must use red and white blocks to assemble a design identical to that in the picture. Children 6 to 7 years old (and older children suspected of being mentally retarded) begin with item 1; children 8 to 16 years old start with item 3. The patterns are arranged in order of increasing difficulty—four blocks are used for the first eight designs, and nine blocks are used for the last three designs.

All items are timed: items 1 to 4 are given a maximum of 45 seconds each; items 5 to 8, 75 seconds; and items 9 to 11, 120 seconds. Items 1 to 3 are scored 2, 1, or 0; items 4 to 11 receive 4 points for a correct completion and up to 3 additional time-bonus points for quick execution. The subtest is discontinued after two consecutive failures.

Rationale

Block design involves the ability to perceive and analyze forms by breaking down a whole (the design) into its component parts and then assembling the components into the identical design, a process referred to as analysis and synthesis. The subtest combines visual organization with the reproductive aspects of visual-motor coordination. Success involves the application of logic and reasoning to spatial relationship problems. Consequently, Block Design can be considered a nonverbal concept formation task requiring perceptual organization, spatial visualization, and abstract conceptualization. It is also a constructional task involving spatial relations and figure-ground separation.

Performance may be affected by rate of motor activity and vision. Inadequate performance should not be interpreted as direct evidence of inadequate visual form and pattern perception, because the ability to discriminate block designs (that is, to perceive the designs accurately at a recognition level) may be intact even though the ability to reproduce them is impaired.

Factor Analytic Findings

The Block Design subtest is the best measure of g among the Performance Scale subtests and is the fourth-best measure of g among all 12 subtests (53 percent of its variance may be attributed to g). It has ample subtest specificity to permit specific interpretation of its functions across the entire age range. It contributes substantially to the Perceptual Organization factor (*Mdn* loading = .66).

Reliability and Correlational Highlights

Block Design is a reliable subtest (r_{xx} = .85). It correlates more highly with Object Assembly (r = .60) and Picture Completion (r = .52) than with the other subtests. It correlates moderately with the Full Scale (r = .68) and the Performance Scale (r = .68) and to a lesser degree with the Verbal Scale (r = .58).

Administrative and Interpretive Considerations

Be sure that the area being used for block arrangement is clear of other blocks and materials. Construct the demonstration design by completing, from the examinee's left to right, first the first row and then the second row. Be careful that your hand does not block the examinee's view. Scramble the blocks before each new design is administered.

Place before the examinee the exact number of blocks needed for the item.

Children should be instructed to tell you when they have completed each item. You might say "Tell me when you have finished." This instruction should be given not only on items 4 through 11, but on items 1, 2, and 3 as well.

Observing performance. Block Design is an excellent subtest for observing children's problem-solving approach. The following issues should be considered:

• Are the examinees hasty and impulsive or deliberate and careful?
• Do they give up easily or become disgusted when faced with possible failure, or do they persist and keep on working even after the time limit has been reached?
• Do children use only one kind of approach, or do they alter their approach as the need arises?
• Do they use trial and error?
• Do they study the designs first?
• Do they have a plan?
• Do they construct units of blocks, or do they work in piecemeal fashion?

Excessive fumbling or failure to check the pattern suggests anxiety. Visual-perceptual difficulties may be indicated if children twist their bodies to improve their perspective on the design or if they leave space between the blocks in the assembled design. Try to differentiate between excessive cautiousness as a personality style and excessive slowness as a possible indication of depression.

Testing-of-limits. If testing-of-limits is indicated or desired, the specific item(s) should be presented *after* the entire examination has been completed. Research has shown that administering a series of cues to children during the standard administration of the Block Design subtest significantly raises subtest scores (Sattler, 1969). A useful procedure to follow in testing-of-limits is to place one block (or one row) in its correct position for those designs that were failed. When you arrange the top row, you might say "Let's try some of these again. I'm going to put together some of the blocks. I will make the top row. Now you go ahead and finish it. Now make one like this. Tell me when you have finished." If examinees still fail, additional blocks can be arranged. The amount of help needed to reproduce the designs accurately should be recorded. Children who need many cues may have less developed spatial reasoning ability than those who need few cues.

Cautionary note.   Prior experience with the commercial game Trac 4, which uses block design patterns, has been reported to increase bright 10-year-old children's WISC-R Block Design scores by about 3 scaled score points (Dirks, 1982). Increases did not occur on other subtests. These results suggest that WISC-R short forms using the Block Design subtest should be avoided if children have played Trac 4, because the scores are likely to be inflated. Standard IQs may also be slightly inflated if children have played this game.

OBJECT ASSEMBLY

The Object Assembly subtest requires that children put jigsaw pieces together to form common objects: a girl (seven pieces), a car (seven pieces), a horse (six pieces), and a face (eight pieces). There is one sample item: an apple (four pieces). Items are given one at a time, with the pieces presented in a specified disarranged pattern. All children receive all items, beginning with the sample and continuing with items 1 through 4.

All items are timed. The first item is given a maximum of 120 seconds; the next two items, 150 seconds each; and the fourth item, 180 seconds. Scores for perfect performance are 6 points each for the girl and the face and 5 points each for the horse and the car. Bonuses of up to 3 points are awarded for quick performance. The girl, horse, and car items each have a maximum score of 8, and the face item, 9. Points are awarded for partially correct performances.

Rationale

The Object Assembly subtest is mainly a test of the examinees' skill at synthesis—putting things together to form familiar objects. It requires visual-motor coordination, with motor activity guided by visual perception and sensorimotor feedback. Object Assembly is also a test of visual organizational ability. Visual organization is needed to produce an object out of parts that may not be immediately recognizable. In order to solve the jigsaw puzzles, examinees must be able to grasp an entire pattern by anticipating the relationships among its individual parts. The tasks require some constructive ability as well as perceptual skill—children must recognize individual parts and place them correctly in the incomplete figure. Performance may also be related to rate and precision of motor activity; persistence, especially when much trial and error

is required; and long-term visual memory (having stored information about the object to be formed).

Factor Analytic Findings

The Object Assembly subtest is a fair measure of g (38 percent of its variance may be attributed to g). Its inadequate subtest specificity prevents interpretation of the specific underlying ability it measures. Since it contributes substantially to the Perceptual Organization factor (*Mdn* loading = .65), however, it may be used as a measure of perceptual organization.

Reliability and Correlational Highlights

Object Assembly is a relatively reliable subtest (r_{xx} = .70). It correlates more highly with Block Design (r = .60) than with any other subtest. It has a somewhat low correlation with the Full Scale (r = .56), a moderate correlation with the Performance Scale (r = .60), and a low correlation with the Verbal Scale (r = .46).

Administrative and Interpretive Considerations

Make sure that children do not see the WISC-R manual, which contains pictures of the correctly assembled objects. The screen used to set up the individual puzzle parts can be used to cover the manual, if desired. If the screen is used, tape, glue, or staple a piece of cardboard or part of a manila folder to the back side in order to prevent the child from seeing the diagrams on the card. Place the pieces close to examinees so that they do not waste time reaching for the pieces. As in other subtests, you may have to ask examinees to tell you when they are finished. Do not give any cues to the examinees that indicate approval or disapproval of their performance.

Observing performance.   Object Assembly is an especially good subtest for observing children's thinking and work habits. Some children envision the complete object almost from the start and either recognize the relations of the individual parts to the whole or have an imperfect understanding of the relations between the parts and the whole. Others merely try to fit the pieces together by trial-and-error methods. Still others may have initial failure, followed by trial-and-error and then sudden insight and recognition of the object.

Observe how children respond to errors and how they handle frustration. Do they demand to know what the object is before they construct it, or insist that pieces are missing, or say that the object doesn't make sense (Zimmerman & Woo-Sam, 1985)? Are low scores due to temporary inefficiency, such as reversal of two parts, which results in loss of time-bonus credits? A child who spends a long time with one piece, trying to position it in an incorrect location, may be revealing anxiety or rigidity.

Testing-of-limits. After the subtest has been completed, inquire about any constructions that appear to be peculiar or unusual (such as pieces placed on top of each other). Testing-of-limits procedures similar to those described for the Picture Arrangement and Block Design subtests can be used after the entire scale has been administered. A series of graduated cues can be introduced, such as placing one or more pieces in the correct location, and then the amount of help children need to complete the task successfully can be noted. Children needing only a few cues to complete the object may have latent perceptual organization skills. Another approach is to see whether asking children to visualize the completed object (for example, a car) mentally first helps them to assemble the puzzle.

Question: What is gasoline?
  Answer: To put on the thing what takes your temperature
       so it don't hurt you.
          (Flumen & Flumen, 1979)

CODING

The Coding subtest requires that children copy symbols that are paired with other symbols. The subtest consists of two separate and distinct parts. Coding A is administered to children under 8 years of age, and Coding B to those 8 years of age and over. Each part uses a sample, or key.

In Coding A, the sample consists of five shapes—star, circle, triangle, cross, and square. Within each shape, a special mark appears (a vertical line, two horizontal lines, a horizontal line, a circle, and two vertical lines, respectively). Children are required to place within each shape the mark that appears within it in the sample. There are 5 practice shapes, followed by 43 shapes in the subtest.

In Coding B, the sample consists of boxes containing the numbers 1 through 9 in the upper part and a symbol in the lower part. The stimuli are boxes containing just a number

in the upper part and an empty space in the lower part. Children must write in the space the symbol that is paired with the number in the sample. There are 7 practice boxes, followed by 93 boxes in the subtest proper. The time limit for each Coding task is 120 seconds.

Rationale

Coding taps the ability to learn an unfamiliar task and involves speed and accuracy of visual-motor coordination, attentional skills, short-term memory, cognitive flexibility (in shifting rapidly from one pair to another), and, possibly, motivation. The subtest also involves speed of mental operation (psychomotor speed) and, to some extent, visual acuity. Success depends not only on comprehending the task, but also on using pencil and paper skillfully.

Coding B may involve a verbal-encoding process if children attach verbal descriptions to the symbols. For example, a "+" symbol may be labeled as a "plus sign" or "cross" and the "V" symbol as the letter "V." Performance may be enhanced when the symbols are recoded in terms of verbal labels. Consequently, Coding B can also be described as measuring the ability to learn combinations of symbols and shapes and the ability to make associations quickly and accurately. Coding A can also involve a verbal-encoding process, but to a lesser degree. Coding A and Coding B thus may involve separate information-processing modes.

The speed and accuracy with which the task is performed are a measure of the child's intellectual ability.

At each step in the task the [child] must inspect the next digit, go to the proper location in the table, code the information distinguishing the symbol found, and carry this information in short-term memory long enough to reproduce the symbol in the proper answer box. (Estes, 1974, p. 745)

Coding thus can be conceptualized as an information-processing task involving the discrimination and memory of visual pattern symbols.

Factor Analytic Findings

The Coding subtest is the poorest measure of g in the scale (17 percent of its variance may be attributed to g). It has ample subtest specificity to permit specific interpretation of its functions across the entire age range and contributes moderately to the Freedom from Distractibility factor (*Mdn* loading = .42).

Reliability and Correlational Highlights

Coding is a relatively reliable subtest (r_{xx} = .72). It correlates more highly with Block Design (r = .33) than with any other subtest. It has a low correlation with the Full Scale (r = .38), the Performance Scale (r = .33), and the Verbal Scale (r = .36).

Administrative and Interpretive Considerations

The Coding subtest appears in a separate booklet (the last page of the Mazes booklet). It should be administered on a smooth drawing surface. Both you and the child should use a pencil with red lead, without an eraser. One point is allotted for each correct item, with up to 5 additional time-bonus points given to children with a perfect score on Coding A. There are no time-bonus points for Coding B.

Children with visual defects or specific motor disabilities may be penalized on this subtest. Generally the subtest should not be given to such children. If it is given, it should not be counted in the final score.

Left-handed children also may be penalized on the Coding subtest. If the way they write causes them to cover the sample immediately above the line of writing, they have to lift their hands repeatedly during the task. Either of two procedures can be used to counteract this difficulty. One method is to show the child the sample from another record booklet. A more satisfactory procedure is to cut the sample from another record booklet, mount it on a strip of cardboard, and then position it for convenient viewing.

Observing performance.   Examinees' methods of proceeding with the task should be observed. Children who stop working after the first line should be told "Continue on the next line." These instructions should be counted as part of the 2-minute time limit. If examinees skip around, filling in symbols for like shapes or like numbers first, tell them to proceed in order.

Useful observational guidelines are as follows:

- Is the child impulsive or meticulous?
- Is tremor evident?
- Does the child's speed increase or decrease as he or she proceeds?
- Are the child's marks well done, just recognizable, or wrong?
- Are there any distortions?
- If distortions are present, do they appear once only, occasionally, or each time the figure appears? How many different figures are affected?
- Is the child being penalized for lack of speed, for inaccuracy, or for both?

- Does the child understand the task?
- Are the child's failures due to inadequate form perception or poor attention?
- Does the child check each figure with the samples or remember the samples?
- Does the child recheck every symbol before moving on to the next one?
- Does the child pick out one figure only and skip others?
- Does the child work smoothly, or does he or she seem confused at times?
- Does the child understand and proceed correctly after explanations have been made?
- Is the child aware of any errors?
- Is the child persistent?
- Does the child need repeated urging?

Answers to the above questions will provide valuable information about various characteristics, including attention span. An increase in speed, coupled with correct copying of symbols, suggests that the child is adjusting to the task well. A decrease in speed, coupled with correct copying of symbols, suggests fatigue. This subtest is particularly useful for evaluating children's attention when attentional difficulties are suspected, such as after a head injury.

Distortion of forms may mean that the child has difficulties with perceptual functioning. Ask about any symbol that is peculiarly written to find out whether it has some symbolic meaning to the child.

MAZES

Mazes is a supplementary test; it is not used in the computation of the IQ when the five standard Performance Scale subtests are administered. Mazes consists of nine maze problems and one sample problem. Children are required to draw a line from the center of each maze to the outside without crossing any of the lines that indicate walls. Each maze is presented separately. Children 6 to 7 years old (and older children suspected of mental retardation) begin with the sample maze, followed by maze 1; children 8 to 16 years old start with maze 4.

All items are timed. The first four mazes are given a maximum of 30 seconds each; the fifth maze, 45 seconds; the sixth maze, 60 seconds; the seventh and eighth mazes, 120 seconds; and the last maze, 150 seconds. The number of errors made determines the child's score. The range of scores is from 0 to 5 points, with mazes 1 to 3 having a maximum score of 2; mazes 4 and 5, a maximum score of 3; mazes 6 and 7, a maximum score of 4; and mazes 8 and

9, a maximum score of 5. The subtest is discontinued after two consecutive failures. Although the subtest does not have to be routinely administered, administering it to children who are either language-impaired or culturally different may generate valuable information.

Rationale

In order to successfully complete the Mazes subtest, children must (a) attend to the directions, which include locating a route from the entrance to the exit, avoiding blind alleys, crossing no lines, and holding pencil on paper; and (b) execute the task, which involves remembering and following the directions, displaying visual-motor coordination, and resisting the disruptive effect of an implied need for speed (Madden, 1974). The Mazes subtest appears to measure planning ability and perceptual organization (following a visual pattern). Success requires visual-motor control and speed combined with accuracy.

Factor Analytic Findings

The Mazes subtest is a poor measure of g (20 percent of its variance may be attributed to g). It has ample subtest specificity to permit specific interpretation of its functions across the entire age range and contributes moderately to the Perceptual Organization factor (*Mdn* loading $= .47$).

Reliability and Correlational Highlights

Mazes is a relatively reliable subtest ($r_{xx} = .72$). It correlates more highly with Block Design ($r = .44$) than with any other subtest. It has a low correlation with the Full Scale ($r = .44$), the Performance Scale ($r = .47$), and the Verbal Scale ($r = .34$).

Administrative and Interpretive Considerations

The subtest should be administered on a smooth drawing surface. A pencil with black lead is used to demonstrate the sample item, but examinees use pencils with red lead, without erasers.

Cues that you should provide after certain errors are made are listed in the manual. When children make these errors for the first time, inform them that an error has been made. The cues should be helpful to children, especially those who do not fully understand the task requirements. A table in the manual clearly shows the number of points allotted for various types of performance. The sample responses, which illustrate the rules regarding the scoring of errors, should help you score children's performance.

Consider the following questions as you observe performance.

- Does the child understand the task?
- Does the child study the mazes and extensively plan a route before proceeding?
- Does the child show signs of tremor, difficulty in controlling the pencil, or difficulty in drawing uniform lines?
- Does the child solve the mazes correctly after the time limit has expired?
- Is crossing of lines related to poor visual-motor coordination or to impulsivity?
- Does the child say anything that suggests anxiety (for example, "The little boy is trapped in the center of the maze")?

Question: Listen, say just what I say: "Eating too much cake and ice cream can give you a stomach ache."

Answer: So you have to take an Alka Seltzer, right?
(Adapted from Flumen & Flumen, 1979)

SUMMARY

1. Information measures the child's available information acquired as a result of native ability and early cultural experience. Memory is an important aspect of performance on the subtest. The subtest ties with Similarities as the second-best measure of g and contributes to the Verbal Comprehension factor. Subtest specificity is ample at all ages. Information is a reliable subtest ($r_{xx} = .85$) and is relatively easy to administer.

2. Similarities measures verbal concept formation and ties with Information as the second-best measure of g. Subtest specificity is adequate only for ages 6½ to 8½ years. Similarities is a reliable subtest ($r_{xx} = .81$), but considerable skill is needed to score some items correctly.

3. Arithmetic measures numerical reasoning ability. It is a fair measure of g, and contributes to the Freedom from Distractibility and Verbal Comprehension factors. Subtest specificity is adequate at all ages. Arithmetic is a reasonably reliable subtest ($r_{xx} = .77$) and is relatively easy to administer.

4. Vocabulary measures language development, learning ability, and fund of information. The subtest is an excellent measure of g and contributes to the Verbal Comprehension factor. Subtest specificity is adequate at all ages. Vocabulary is a reliable subtest ($r_{xx} = .86$), but skill is needed to administer and score it correctly.

5. Comprehension measures social judgment: the ability to use facts in a pertinent, meaningful, and emotionally appropriate manner. The subtest is a moderately good measure of g and

contributes to the Verbal Comprehension factor. Subtest specificity is adequate at all ages. Comprehension is a relatively reliable subtest ($r_{xx} = .77$), but it requires considerable skill to score.

6. Digit Span is a supplementary subtest that measures short-term memory and attention; it forms part of the Freedom from Distractibility factor. It is a poor measure of g. Subtest specificity is ample at all ages. Digit Span is a reasonably reliable subtest ($r_{xx} = .78$) and is relatively easy to administer. It should be administered routinely, even though it is not used in the computation of the IQ when the five standard Verbal subtests are administered.

7. Picture Completion measures the ability to differentiate essential from nonessential details. It requires concentration, visual organization, and visual memory. The subtest is a fair measure of g and contributes to the Perceptual Organization factor. Subtest specificity is ample or adequate at all ages. Picture Completion is a reasonably reliable subtest ($r_{xx} = .77$) and is relatively easy to administer.

8. Picture Arrangement measures nonverbal reasoning ability. It also may be viewed as a measure of planning ability—that is, the ability to comprehend and size up a total situation. The subtest is a fair measure of g and contributes to the Perceptual Organization factor. Subtest specificity is ample at all ages. Picture Arrangement is a relatively reliable subtest ($r_{xx} = .73$) and is easy to administer.

9. Block Design measures visual-motor coordination and perceptual organization. The subtest is the best measure of g among the Performance Scale subtests and contributes to the Perceptual Organization factor. Subtest specificity is ample at all ages. Block Design is a reliable subtest ($r_{xx} = .85$), but skill is needed to administer the subtest correctly.

10. Object Assembly measures perceptual organization ability. The subtest is a fair measure of g and contributes to the Perceptual Organization factor. Because it has an inadequate amount of subtest specificity, its specific underlying ability should not be interpreted. It can be interpreted more generally, however, as a measure of perceptual organization. Object Assembly is a relatively reliable subtest ($r_{xx} = .70$), but skill is needed to administer it correctly.

11. Coding measures visual-motor coordination, speed of mental operation, and short-term memory. The subtest is the poorest measure of g in the scale, but it contributes to the Freedom from Distractibility factor. Subtest specificity is ample at all ages. Coding is a relatively reliable subtest ($r_{xx} = .72$) and is easy to administer.

12. Mazes is a supplementary subtest that measures planning ability and perceptual organization. The subtest is a poor measure of g, but it contributes to the Perceptual Organization factor. Subtest specificity is ample at all ages. Mazes is a relatively reliable subtest ($r_{xx} = .72$) and is easy to administer.

KEY TERMS, CONCEPTS, AND NAMES

WISC-R Information (p. 147)
WISC-R Similarities (p. 148)
WISC-R Arithmetic (p. 149)
WISC-R Vocabulary (p. 151)
WISC-R Comprehension (p. 152)
WISC-R Digit Span (p. 154)
WISC-R Picture Completion (p. 156)
WISC-R Picture Arrangement (p. 157)
WISC-R Block Design (p. 158)
WISC-R Object Assembly (p. 160)
WISC-R Coding (p. 161)
WISC-R Mazes (p. 162)

STUDY QUESTION

Discuss the rationale, factor analytic findings, reliability and correlational highlights, and administrative and interpretive considerations for each of the following WISC-R subtests: Information, Similarities, Arithmetic, Vocabulary, Comprehension, Digit Span, Picture Completion, Picture Arrangement, Block Design, Object Assembly, Coding, and Mazes.

8

INTERPRETING THE WISC-R

The first of our senses which we should take care never to let rust through disuse is that sixth sense, the imagination. . . . I mean the wide-open eye which leads us always to see truth more vividly, to apprehend more broadly, to concern ourselves more deeply, to be, all our life long, sensitive and awake to the powers and responsibilities given to us as human beings.
—Christopher Fry

An understanding of the underlying properties of the WISC-R subtests and scales, how the subtests cluster, Verbal-Performance discrepancies, and patterns of subtest scores will help you in interpreting a child's WISC-R performance. Because the WISC-R and other Wechsler scales have Deviation IQs with a mean of 100 and standard deviation of 15, and subtests with a mean of 10 and standard deviation of 3, statistical approaches to evaluating profiles can be readily applied.

After the Verbal-Performance discrepancy and profiles have been statistically evaluated, you will need to interpret the findings, particularly when significant differences are established between various sets of scores. The information presented in Chapters 6 and 7 forms the basis for such interpretations. The present chapter provides important additional guidelines for interpreting Verbal-Performance differences, making within-scale comparisons, and making between-subtest and among-subtest comparisons. Interpretation of the WISC-R is also facilitated by a knowledge of child psychopathology, exceptional children, and clinical and psychoeducational approaches to test interpretation. This chapter provides an introduction to these approaches, which are discussed in more detail in Chapters 18, 20, 21, 22, and 23. As in all clinical and psychoeducational assessments, a child's performance on any one assessment procedure must be interpreted in light of the child's background and other data obtained during the evaluation.

PROFILE ANALYSIS

Profile analysis, or *scatter analysis*, refers to interpreting or analyzing the pattern of scaled scores and Deviation IQs obtained by an individual examinee. Some profiles show extreme variability (for example, subtest scores that range from 1 to 19), others moderate variability (for example, subtest scores that range from 5 to 15), and still others minimal variability (for example, subtest scores that range from 8 to 12). The pattern of subtest scores within each scale can also be examined, as can the relationship (a) between the Deviation IQs on the two scales and (b) among the three factor deviation scores.

In the early days of the Wechsler and Wechsler-type scales, it was hoped that profile analysis would increase diagnostic precision. Unfortunately, research studies have not provided any firm basis for making diagnostic classification decisions from profile analysis. Using profile analysis with the WISC-R, WPPSI, and WAIS-R is problematic because the subtests are not as reliable as the Deviation IQs and do not measure unique processes. Still, profiles may

point out strengths and weaknesses, and these patterns allow for the development of hypotheses that can contribute to an understanding of the child.

Aim of Profile Analysis

The Deviation IQ does not provide any information about the combination of high and low subtest scores earned by a particular child. The goal of profile analysis is to describe the child's unique ability pattern. Determining which tasks a child handles best may help in describing the child's strengths and in planning programs of instruction that utilize those strengths. A flat and significantly above average profile on an intelligence or special ability test may indicate that the child is gifted and would profit from instruction that capitalized on exceptional intellectual skills. Conversely, a flat and significantly below average profile probably indicates limited intellectual ability. Special instructional programs can be tailored to meet the needs of children with this type of profile as well. Profiles with peaks and valleys may be indicative of special strengths and weaknesses and may provide clues about the child's cognitive style and possible remedial directions.

The goal of profile analysis is not to classify or categorize children; rather, it is to find clues about their abilities. *Ideas generated from profile analysis must be viewed simply as hypotheses to be checked against other information about the examinee.* By clarifying the functional nature of a child's learning problems, profile analysis may assist you in arriving at recommendations for clinical treatment, educational programs, or vocational placement.

Some configurations of subtest scaled scores have great variability. Intersubtest variability may result from temporary inefficiencies, permanent incapacity, or disturbed school experiences. Which, if any, of these interpretations is appropriate must be determined on an individual basis. Psychologists believe that profiles showing high variability indicate more potential ability than do profiles showing limited variability (Sattler & Kuncik, 1976). There is little, if any, research to support this belief, however. In each case, you will have to seek out the best explanation of the child's profile, using all of the test data and the clinical history.

A profile of subtest scores that is within normal limits (scaled scores of 8 through 12) should not be considered diagnostic of any exceptionality. Even variability that is outside of "normal limits" does not necessarily indicate the presence of pathology or exceptionality, however. It may simply reflect the child's cognitive style. *There is no evidence to support the assumption that pathology and subtest variability are necessarily linked.*

Need to Establish Significant Differences

In profile analysis, you cannot simply look at two scores and say that one is meaningfully higher than the other. You must determine whether differences represent chance variation or variation associated with factors other than chance. The procedures used to make such determinations are discussed in the following sections.

Profile analysis is dependent on the presence of statistically significant differences between the scales, factor scores, or subtests that are being compared. Before making any statements about the examinee's cognitive strengths and weaknesses, you must determine whether (a) the IQs on the Verbal and Performance Scales are significantly different from each other; (b) the subtest scaled scores are significantly different from the mean of their respective scales; and (c) the subtest scaled scores (of interest) are significantly different from one another. Differences among factor scores must be determined to be significant before they can be considered to be meaningful.

Primary Methods of Profile Analysis

The methods most commonly used for profile analysis are the following:

1. comparing the Verbal and Performance IQs
2. comparing each Verbal Scale subtest scaled score with the examinee's mean Verbal Scale scaled score
3. comparing each Performance Scale subtest scaled score with the examinee's mean Performance Scale scaled score
4. comparing each subtest scaled score with the mean subtest scaled score based on all subtests administered
5. comparing sets of individual subtest scores
6. comparing the Verbal Comprehension, Perceptual Organization, and Freedom from Distractibility factor scores
7. comparing subtest scaled scores in each factor with their respective mean factor scores

Notice that the first and sixth methods involve comparing IQs, whereas the others involve comparing scaled scores. Now let us examine each of these methods in more detail.

Method 1: Comparing Verbal and Performance Scale
IQs. Table C-2 in Appendix C gives the differences between the Verbal and Performance IQs needed to satisfy the .05 and .01 significance levels. Because the differences required to reach the .05 or .01 significance levels generally are similar throughout the WISC-R age levels, values based on the average of the 11 age groups can be used. The critical values are as follows:

.05	.01
12	15

Thus a 12-point difference between the Verbal and Performance Scale IQs is statistically significant at the .05 level, whereas a 15-point difference is significant at the .01 level. A statistically significant difference reflects a high probability that skill levels in verbal and nonverbal intellectual functioning are different. Exhibit 8-1 describes the procedure used to obtain the critical values shown in Table C-2 in Appendix C. This procedure can be used to determine the needed critical values for any comparison involving two scales, two subtests, or two tests. (Probabilities associated with various Verbal-Performance Scale differences are shown in Table C-8 of Appendix C.)

Methods 2, 3, and 4: Comparing subtest scaled scores with various mean scaled scores.

To compare subtest scaled scores with various mean scaled scores, consult Table C-3 in Appendix C. This table shows the deviations from the Verbal Scale mean, Performance Scale mean, and overall mean that are needed for comparisons involving 5, 6, 10, 11, or 12 subtests to reach the .05 and .01 significance levels.

The procedure for using Table C-3 in Appendix C is as follows:

1. Write the names of the subtests and their respective scaled scores on a sheet of paper.
2. Sum the six (or five) Verbal Scale subtests scaled scores.
3. Compute the mean of the Verbal Scale subtests by dividing the sum of the Verbal Scale subtests by 6 (or 5).
4. Calculate the deviation from the mean for each Verbal subtest by subtracting each Verbal subtest scaled score from the Verbal Scale mean. Enter these deviations, with the appropriate sign (+ or −), opposite the scaled scores.
5. Sum the six (or five) Performance Scale subtests scaled scores.
6. Compute the mean of the Performance Scale subtests by dividing the sum of the Performance Scale subtests by 6 (or 5).
7. Calculate the deviation from the mean for each Performance subtest by subtracting each Performance

---

Exhibit 8-1

Procedure Used to Determine Whether Two Scores in a Profile Are Significantly Different

In order to establish whether differences between scores in a profile are reliable, it is necessary to apply some statistical procedures to the profile. As always, we cannot be 100 percent certain that the differences between any two subtest scores are reliable. A confidence level must therefore be selected, such as a 95 percent level of certainty that the differences are significant. In order to determine whether the difference between two scales or subtests or tests is reliable, the following formula can be used:

$$\text{Difference Score} = z\sqrt{SE_{mA}^2 + SE_{mB}^2}$$

The Difference Score refers to the magnitude of the difference between scales or subtests A and B. The z refers to the normal curve value associated with the desired confidence level. If we select the 95 percent level, the associated z value is 1.96. The terms under the square root sign refer to the standard error of measurement associated with each scale or subtest (or test). Many test manuals provide these standard errors of measurement.

The following example illustrates how to determine whether there is a significant difference between two scaled scores. Let us say that we are interested in determining the value needed to represent a significant difference between the WISC-R Verbal and Performance Scales for children in the standardization group. The average standard errors of measurement associated with these two scales are 3.60 and 4.66, respectively, as indicated in the WISC-R manual. We know from a normal curve table that at the 95 percent confidence level the z value is 1.96. Substituting these values into the formula yields the following:

$$\text{Difference Score} = 1.96\sqrt{3.60^2 + 4.66^2} = 12$$

Differences between these two scales that are at or above this value are significant at the 95 percent level of confidence. A larger difference (15) is needed for the 99 percent confidence level. These values appear in the small rectangle of Table C-2 in Appendix C. All values in Tables C-2, C-15, and C-26 in Appendix C were obtained by following the above procedure. For the 99 percent confidence level, the z value of 2.58 is used in the equation.

---

subtest scaled score from the Performance Scale mean. Enter these deviations, with the appropriate sign ($+$ or $-$), opposite the scaled scores.

8. Compute the mean of the overall subtests by dividing the sum by 10 (or 11 or 12).

9. Calculate the deviation from the overall mean for each subtest scaled score by subtracting each scaled score from the overall mean. Enter these deviations, with the appropriate sign ($+$ or $-$), opposite the scaled scores.

10. Determine whether the deviations from the Verbal and Performance means are significant by using Table C-3 in Appendix C. The values in Table C-3 reflect significant differences at the .05 and .01 levels of probability. Be sure to use the appropriate column in Table C-3 to obtain the significant deviations. Column 1 is used when the five standard Verbal Scale subtests are administered, and column 2 is used when Digit Span is also administered as a sixth Verbal subtest.

11. Place an asterisk next to each subtest deviation that is significantly above or below the mean.

12. After the asterisk write an S to indicate a strength or a W to indicate a weakness.

The above steps are illustrated in Table 8-1, which shows how to determine whether the subtest scaled scores differ significantly from the mean of the Verbal Scale scaled scores, Performance Scale scaled scores, and all the scaled scores. In Table 8-1, none of the Verbal Scale subtest scores differed significantly from the Verbal Scale mean. On the Performance Scale, the Coding score was significantly lower than the Performance Scale mean. With respect to the overall mean, the Information score was significantly lower, whereas Picture Completion and Object Assembly scores were significantly higher. (In determining whether a scaled score is significantly different from the mean, disregard the plus or minus sign in Table 8-1.) You are now in a firm position to infer that the difference between the Coding score and the child's mean Performance Scale scaled score is not a chance difference. A comparison of the subtest scaled scores with the overall scaled score indicates strengths in Picture Completion and Object Assembly and weakness in Information.

The critical values used in the preparation of Table C-3 are based on the assumption that the scores on all subtests in a scale are to be compared with the mean score for that

Table 8-1
An Example of Profile Analysis on the WISC-R—Comparing Each Subtest Scaled Score to Various Mean Scaled Scores

Subtest	Scaled score	Deviation from		
		Verbal average	Performance average	Overall average
Information	4	−2.2	—	−4.3* W
Similarities	7	+.8	—	−1.3
Arithmetic	6	−.2	—	−2.3
Vocabulary	8	+1.8	—	−.3
Comprehension	7	+.8	—	−1.3
Digit Span	5	−1.2	—	−3.3
Picture Completion	13	—	+2.2	+4.7* S
Picture Arrangement	9	—	−1.8	+.6
Block Design	12	—	+1.2	+3.7
Object Assembly	14	—	+3.2	+5.7* S
Coding	6	—	−4.8* W	−2.3
Mazes	—	—	—	—

Mean Verbal scaled score: $\frac{37}{6} = 6.2$

Mean Performance scaled score: $\frac{54}{5} = 10.8$

Mean overall scaled score: $\frac{91}{11} = 8.3$

* Significant at the .01 level.
Note. S = strength, W = weakness. See Table C-3 in Appendix C to obtain deviations that are significant.

scale. Therefore only one significance level (either .05 or .01) should be used to determine the critical values; mixing levels of significance is not recommended (A. B. Silverstein, personal communication, 1980).

Method 5: Comparing sets of individual subtest scores. Table C-2 in Appendix C shows the differences between sets of scaled scores on the 12 WISC-R subtests that are required for the average of the 11 age groups to reach the .05 and .01 significance levels. The table indicates, for example, that a 4-point difference between Information and Similarities is significant. When multiple comparisons are made between the subtests, the values in Table C-2 are overly liberal (that is, lead to many significant differences). The values are more accurate when a priori planned comparisons are made of pairs of subtests, such as Information versus Comprehension or Digit Span versus Arithmetic. The procedure described in Exhibit 8-1 was

followed in obtaining the needed critical values between subtests.

Before multiple subtest comparisons are made (that is, more than one set of subtest scores is compared), the difference between the highest and lowest subtest scores should be determined (A. B. Silverstein, personal communication, 1980). A difference of 7 scaled-score points between the highest and lowest scaled scores is significant at the .05 level. Differences that are 7 scaled-score points or greater can then be interpreted. If the difference between the highest and lowest subtest scaled scores is less than 7 scaled-score points, multiple comparisons between individual subtest scores should not be made.

Method 6: Comparing Verbal Comprehension, Perceptual Organization, and Freedom from Distractibility factor scores. Table C-2 in Appendix C presents the differences between sets of Verbal Comprehension, Perceptual Organization, and Freedom from Distractibility factor scores (in the form of Deviation IQs) that are needed to reach the .05 and .01 significance levels. Chapter 6 discusses how factor scores are obtained. Because the Verbal and Performance Scale IQs contain subtests that are also contained in the Freedom from Distractibility factor, the Freedom from Distractibility factor score should be compared with the Verbal Comprehension and Perceptual Organization factor scores and not with the Verbal Scale and Performance Scale IQs. If the Verbal Scale and Performance Scale IQs were used, the comparison would involve overlapping subtests.

Method 7: Comparing subtest scaled scores in each factor with their respective factor scores.   It is useful to compare each scaled score to the mean of its respective factor score. This procedure allows you to determine whether the subtests that comprise each factor significantly differ from the mean factor scaled score. Consult Table C-5 in Appendix C to obtain the critical values. For Verbal Comprehension, they range from 2.58 to 2.93 at the 5 percent level (3.12 to 3.54 at the 1 percent level). For Perceptual Organization, they range from 2.78 to 3.52 at the 5 percent level (3.36 to 4.26 at the 1 percent level). For Freedom from Distractibility, they range from 2.80 to 3.04 at the 5 percent level (3.43 to 3.72 at the 1 percent level). The steps involved in this procedure are similar to those described in the previous section using the Verbal and Performance subtests (see methods 2 and 3).

Other Approaches to Profile Analysis

Supplementary approaches to profile analysis examine the kinds of variability found in the normative group, allowing features of an individual child's profile to be compared with those of the normative group. The three base rates described below can be used for examining different kinds of variability.

Base rate subtest scaled-score ranges.   In the standardization group, the median scaled-score range—that is, the size of the difference between the highest and lowest WISC-R subtest scaled scores—was 7 points for the Full Scale, 4 points for the Verbal Scale, and 5 points for the Performance Scale (Kaufman, 1976c). These median ranges were similar across age groups, sexes, races, parental occupations, and intelligence levels. The range scaled-score index is not very helpful because it is difficult to interpret and little research is available to guide its interpretation. It deals with only 2 scores, and therefore fails to take into account the variability among all 10 (or 11

or 12) subtest scores. The range index should not be discarded, however, because it provides base rate information about what occurred in the standardization sample.

Base rate differences between each subtest score and an average subtest score in the WISC-R standardization sample.   Table C-7 in Appendix C gives the frequencies with which various differences between subtest scores and average WISC-R Verbal, Performance, or overall scores occurred in the standardization sample. The table shows, for example, that a difference as large as 3.4 points between the scaled score on Information and the Verbal Scale average was obtained by 5 percent of the standardization sample. This table should be used only when differences have been found to be statistically significant. (See numbers 2, 3, and 4 in the preceding section, Primary Methods of Profile Analysis.) Differences of approximately 3 to 5 points between each subtest score and the respective average Verbal Scale or Performance Scale score were obtained by 5 percent of the standardization sample.

Base rate Verbal-Performance differences (the probability-of-occurrence approach).   Determining how frequently a Verbal-Performance IQ difference of a given magnitude occurred in the standardization sample is referred to as the probability-of-occurrence approach. The frequencies with which a variety of Verbal-Performance discrepancies occurred in the normative standardization sample are given in the expectancy table in Table C-9 of Appendix C. The table shows, for example, that a 14.01 difference in either direction between the Verbal and Performance IQs occurred among 25 percent of the children in the standardization sample.

The relationship of Verbal-Performance discrepancies to IQ level and various demographic variables has been determined for the standardization sample. Verbal-Performance IQ differences were not significantly related either to sex or to race, but they were significantly related to intelligence level and parental occupation (Kaufman, 1976d). The median discrepancy for the total group was 8 IQ points (Kaufman, 1976d). Although brighter children (IQs of 110 and above) had higher discrepancies (*Mdn* discrepancy = 9 IQ points) than did less able children (IQs of 89 and below) (*Mdn* discrepancy = 6 to 7 points), neither the Verbal Scale IQ nor the Performance Scale IQ tended to predominate at any level of intelligence. Children of professional parents, however, tended to have higher Verbal than Performance Scale IQs, and children of semiskilled and unskilled workers tended to have higher Performance than Verbal Scale IQs.

Comment on the Verbal-Performance difference approaches. In evaluating Verbal-Performance Scale differences, it is important to determine whether the difference is likely to have occurred solely by chance (referred to as the reliability-of-difference approach). Differences that are not significantly different from those likely to occur by chance should not be interpreted.

Verbal-Performance Scale differences may be significant and yet occur with some frequency in the population. Thus the discrepancy may be reliable but not unusual. Whether a significant difference has practical significance is open to question. Although a statistically significant difference may have less diagnostic relevance if it occurs in a large proportion of the standardization sample (this is where the base rate information about Verbal-Performance Scale differences may be helpful in interpretation), it is still likely to reflect different skill levels in verbal and nonverbal intellectual functioning.

The reliability-of-difference approach is based on the standard error of measurement of each scale, whereas the probability-of-occurrence approach is dependent on the correlation between the two scales. *Both of these approaches are aids to clinical judgment and should not be used in a mechanical fashion or as a replacement for clinical judgment.*

When a reliable (significant) difference occurs between the child's Verbal and Performance Scale scores, hypotheses about the child's cognitive strengths and weaknesses should be formulated. Such discrepancies may provide a meaningful profile of abilities, even though they may occur in a large segment of the population. Any significant discrepancy should be interpreted in light of *all* the data that you have obtained about the examinee.

Comment on Profile Analysis

The assignment of statistical significance to a difference between subtests or scales tells us that the difference is large enough that it cannot be attributed to measurement error. The WISC-R manual recommends using the .15 level of significance as the minimum level for determining whether there are significant differences between scaled scores and between Verbal and Performance Scale IQs. In contrast, I recommend that the .05 level of significance be used in order to reduce the chances of making a Type I error. By using the more stringent confidence level, one can avoid accepting differences between scores as true differences when they are not in fact true differences.

The WISC-R manual also states that a Verbal-Performance difference of 15 points or more calls for "further investigation." No further information is given about how to follow up, however. Should a child be administered additional special tests or be referred for neurological examination? The fact that a Verbal-Performance Scale difference that is significant at the .05 or .01 level is somewhat unusual does not necessarily mean that there is a need for further investigation. A child's entire performance and clinical history should always be evaluated carefully before further investigation is recommended.

The difference between an examinee's subtest score and the mean scaled score is a more stable measure than the difference between pairs of subtest scores. Use of the mean scaled score has the additional advantage of reducing the chance of errors associated with multiple comparisons.

Several factors may account for a profile of scores. These include the child's cognitive skill development, age, sex, racial or ethnic group, socioeconomic status, education, special training, social and physical environment, family background, nationality, temperament, personality, and psychopathology. The possibility also must be considered that the variability of scores is simply a reflection of the unreliability of the individual subtest scores, examiner variability, or situational variability.

Profile analysis is a useful tool for comparing intraindividual differences in various ability and achievement areas. Profile differences may represent only uneven skill development, however; taken alone, they do not constitute a sufficient basis for making decisions about pathological conditions or about possible causes of and cures for the uneven development. Profile analysis should be viewed as a clinical tool to be used in conjunction with other assessment strategies.

A SUCCESSIVE LEVEL APPROACH TO TEST INTERPRETATION

A successive level approach is useful in integrating the various kinds of information obtained from Wechsler scales. The six levels of analysis are as follows:

I. *The Full Scale IQ.* The first level focuses on the Full Scale IQ. In many cases the Full Scale IQ is the most reliable and valid estimate of intellectual ability provided by the scale. It is the primary numerical and quantitative index, providing information about the child's relative standing in the general population, as represented by the standardization group. The Full Scale IQ is a global estimate of the child's level of cognitive ability. The child's classification level is based on the Full Scale IQ (see Table BC-2 on the inside back cover). Converting the Full Scale IQ to a percentile rank (see Table BC-1 on the inside back cover) will help you to interpret this score for personnel who may not be familiar with standard scores.

IIa. *Verbal and Performance IQs.* The second level focuses on the Verbal and Performance IQs and the extent to which there is a significant difference between the two. The Verbal Scale IQ provides information about verbal comprehension skills, whereas the Performance Scale IQ covers perceptual organization skills (see Chapter 6). Table BC-1 can also be used to obtain the percentiles associated with the Verbal and Performance Scale IQs.

IIb. *Factor scores.* An alternative second level procedure is to focus on the factor scores and the extent to which there are significant differences among the three factor scores. The Verbal Comprehension factor (Information, Similarities, Vocabulary, and Comprehension) provides a somewhat purer measure of verbal comprehension than does the Verbal Scale IQ, whereas the Perceptual Organization factor (Picture Completion, Picture Arrangement, Block Design, and Object Assembly) provides a somewhat purer measure of perceptual organization than does the Performance Scale IQ. The Freedom from Distractibility factor (Arithmetic, Digit Span, and Coding) measures a variety of complex processes involving attention, concentration, and problem-solving strategies (see the discussion in a later section on factor scores). When the three subtests comprising Freedom from Distractibility significantly deviate from their scale in the same direction, either positively or negatively, you are on relatively firm ground in comparing the three factor scores.

III. *Subtest variability within scales.* The third level focuses on deviations of the various subtests from the mean of the Verbal Scale or Performance Scale. Hypotheses about strengths and weaknesses can be developed from these analyses.

IV. *Intersubtest variability.* The fourth level focuses on comparisons between sets of subtests or among clusters of subtests. Although these comparisons are open to the errors associated with multiple comparisons, they are valuable for generating hypotheses. (Table C-41 in Appendix C provides the percentile ranks for the subtest scaled scores.)

V. *Intrasubtest variability.* The fifth level focuses on the pattern of performance within each individual subtest. Because the items are arranged in order of difficulty, patterns in which successes and failures are interspersed need to be evaluated carefully. For example, a child who passes the first item, fails the next four, passes the next one, fails the next four, and overall passes a total of four items is showing a different pattern from one who passes the first four items and fails the remainder, although both children receive 4 raw-score points. The child with the markedly uneven pattern may have cognitive or attentional inefficiencies that should be explored further.

VI. *Qualitative analysis.* The sixth level focuses on specific item failures and the content of the responses, or qualitative analysis. Inspecting responses to specific items can aid you in understanding the child's knowledge of specific information, such as knowledge of the concept *half* on the Arithmetic subtest or knowledge of the four seasons of the year on the Information subtest. Careful attention to unique or highly personal responses may be especially informative. Both verbal and nonverbal responses should be evaluated. For example, a child with paranoid tendencies may give querulous, distrustful, or legalistic responses, whereas one who is depressed may give slow, hesitant, and blocked responses, interspersed with self-deprecatory remarks. Qualitative aspects of test interpretation are further discussed toward the end of this chapter and in Chapter 18.

COMPARISONS BETWEEN WISC-R VERBAL AND PERFORMANCE SCALES THAT CAN GUIDE INTERPRETATIONS

The evaluation of the WISC-R Verbal and Performance Scales depends primarily on the hypotheses made about the individual subtests that comprise the respective scales. Some general observations can be made concerning the two scales, however.

Interpretation of Verbal and Performance Scales

The Verbal Scale is dependent on the child's accumulated experience. It usually requires the child to give a response that is in his or her repertoire. The questions (input) are presented verbally, and the responses (output) are given orally. The Verbal Scale might be considered to be an index of verbal ability and crystallized intelligence.

The Performance Scale, in contrast, is more dependent on the child's immediate problem-solving ability. It requires the child to meet new situations and apply past experience and previously acquired skills to a new set of demands. The stimuli (input) are nonverbal, and most are presented visually. Solutions (output) require motor responses and, to a lesser extent, verbal responses. The Performance Scale might be considered to be an index of nonverbal ability and fluid intelligence.

Solving problems on the Verbal and Performance Scales involves both verbal and nonverbal strategies. After examining the extent to which the Verbal Scale subtests involve visualization or other nonverbal processes and the extent to which the Performance Scale subtests involve language activity in the form of overt verbal responses or mediating symbolic activity, Lawson and Inglis (1983) concluded that some Verbal subtests are more verbal than others, and some Performance subtests are more nonverbal than others.

Within the Verbal Scale, some solutions used by examinees on the Arithmetic and Digit Span subtests may involve visualization strategies to a greater extent than do solutions on other verbal subtests. Within the Performance Scale, solutions on the Block Design and Object Assembly subtests may involve the ability to visualize configurations in space and therefore may not depend greatly on verbal processing. In contrast, performance on the Coding, Picture Completion, and Picture Arrangement subtests may depend on both verbal and nonverbal processing. Performance on Coding B depends on the ability to learn associations between digits and symbols that can be encoded verbally. Performance on Picture Completion depends on a knowledge of "the way the world is," and this knowledge may be imparted by verbal means. Consequently, there are no *pure* tests of either verbal or nonverbal ability on the WISC-R and other Wechsler scales. Table C-42 in Appendix C presents a summary of the interpretive rationales, possible implications of high and low scores, and instructional implications for the Verbal, Performance, and Full Scales and for the Freedom from Distractibility factor score.

Formulating Hypotheses About Verbal-Performance Discrepancies

Significant Verbal and Performance Scale differences may indicate the following:

• interest patterns
• cognitive style
• psychopathology (such as emotional disturbance or brain damage)
• deficiencies or strengths in processing information
• deficiencies or strengths in modes of expression
• deficiencies or strengths in the ability to work under time pressure (such as time constraints on the Performance Scale)
• sensory deficiencies

Which interpretations are pertinent must be decided on the basis of the child's entire performance and clinical history.

Hypotheses about Verbal-Performance Scale differences should be formulated in relationship to the child's *absolute* Verbal, Performance, and Full Scale IQs and only when the differences are significant. This means, for ex-

ample, that you would not say that a child with a Verbal Scale IQ of 150 and a Performance Scale IQ of 125 had a performance deficit. In this case both abilities are well developed, with verbal skills even better developed than performance skills. Similarly, a child with a Verbal Scale IQ of 70 and a Performance Scale IQ of 50 should be viewed as having deficits in both verbal and nonverbal areas; the higher Verbal Scale IQ of 70 should not be considered an absolute strength.

1. Illustrative Hypotheses for Verbal > Performance:
a. Verbal skills are better developed than performance skills.
b. Auditory-vocal processing skills are better developed than visual-motor discrimination skills.
c. Knowledge acquired through accumulated experience is better developed than immediate problem-solving ability.
d. The examinee may have difficulty with practical tasks.
e. Performance deficits may exist, including deficits in copying skills.
f. Limitations in visual-motor integration may be influencing performance.
g. Difficulties may be experienced in performing speeded tasks.

2. Illustrative Hypotheses for Performance > Verbal:
a. Performance skills are better developed than verbal skills.
b. Visual-motor discrimination skills are better developed than auditory-vocal processing skills.
c. Immediate problem-solving ability is better developed than knowledge acquired as a result of accumulated experience.
d. The examinee may have difficulty with reading and academic achievement.
e. A language deficit may exist.
f. Limitations in auditory conceptual skills and auditory processing skills may be influencing performance.
g. Difficulties may be experienced in working effectively without time pressure.

COMPARISONS BETWEEN WISC-R FACTOR SCORES THAT CAN GUIDE INTERPRETATIONS

Only when factor scores are significantly different from each other should hypotheses be formulated about a child's strengths and weaknesses (see Table C-2 in Appendix C). The frequencies with which given discrepancies between the WISC-R factor scores occur in the standardization sample are shown in Table 8-2. A summary of interpretive rationales for Wechsler factor scores can be found in Table C-42 in Appendix C.

Interpretations of the Verbal Comprehension and Perceptual Organization factors are similar to those of the Verbal and Performance Scales, respectively. Interpretation of the Freedom from Distractibility factor is based on a number of processes that may underlie performance on this factor. A *high* Freedom from Distractibility score suggests the ability to sustain attention, good short-term memory, numerical ability, encoding ability (such as sequencing ability), use of rehearsal strategies, ability to shift mental operations rapidly on symbolic material, and ability to self-monitor. A *low* Freedom from Distractibility score suggests difficulty in sustaining attention, distractibility, anxiety, short-term retention deficits, encoding deficits, poor rehearsal strategies, difficulty in rapidly shifting mental operations on symbolic material, and inadequate self-monitoring skills. A careful analysis of the examinee's entire performance on the scale, other test scores, and case history information is required to determine the best explanation of the examinee's performance. The list of processes above provides a useful starting point for developing hypotheses about Freedom from Distractibility scores.

The term Freedom from Distractibility may oversimplify the complex processes underlying performance on this factor and therefore may not be appropriate (Ownby & Matthews, 1985). In some cases, distractibility may not be the key factor interfering with performance on the subtests that comprise this factor. Digit Span, Arithmetic, and Coding may involve, to some extent, the use of efficient task strategies to solve problems. These subtests

are not the only ones that may require efficient task strategies, however. Block Design, Picture Arrangement, and Object Assembly are also likely candidates. Further research will be needed to clarify what is measured by the third WISC-R (and WAIS-R) factor.

If Arithmetic, Digit Span, and Coding scores are not consistent (for example, the Digit Span score is high and Arithmetic and Coding scores are low), the Freedom from Distractibility factor score may be especially difficult to interpret. If these three subtest scores are consistently low or high, more confidence can be placed in interpretation of the Freedom from Distractibility factor.

Factor scores should *not* be included in a psychological report. They should simply be used in generating hypotheses about the child's performance.

COMPARISONS BETWEEN WISC-R SUBTESTS THAT CAN GUIDE INTERPRETATIONS

Once differences between subtest scaled scores have been found to be significant (see Table C-2 in Appendix C), the findings must be translated into meaningful descriptions. Interpreting differences between subtest scores is not an easy matter. The material in Chapter 7 and in this chapter will help you in making interpretations. Table 8-3 charts suggested abilities and factors associated with the 12 WISC-R subtests. You should view the interpretations that follow as hypotheses that may prove to be useful in the evaluation of a child's performance. These hypotheses, however, need to be further investigated through a study of the child's entire test performance and clinical history.

The following list of subtest comparisons does not in-

Table 8-2
Percentage of Population Obtaining Discrepancies Between WISC-R Factor Deviation Quotients (DQ)

Percentage obtaining given or greater discrepancy in either direction	Freedom from Distractibility DQ vs. Verbal Comprehension DQ	Freedom from Distractibility DQ vs. Perceptual Organization DQ	Verbal Comprehension DQ vs. Perceptual Organization DQ	Percentage obtaining given or greater discrepancy in a specific direction
50	9.18	10.39	8.38	25
20	17.47	19.77	15.94	10
10	22.41	25.36	20.45	5
5	26.71	30.22	24.36	2.5
2	31.69	35.86	28.91	1
1	35.10	39.72	32.02	0.5

Source: Adapted from Clampit, Adair, and Strenio (1983).

Table 8-3
Suggested Abilities or Factors Associated with the 12 WISC-R Subtests

Information (I)	Similarities (S)	Arithmetic (A)	Vocabulary (V)	Comprehension (C)	Digit Span (DS)	Picture Completion (PC)	Picture Arrangement (PA)	Block Design (BD)	Object Assembly (OA)	Coding (CD)	Mazes (MA)	M	Suggested abilities or factors
		A			DS					CD		___	Attention
		A			DS							___	Auditory memory
		A			DS	PC					MA	___	Concentration
I			V	C			PA					___	Cultural opportunities at home
		A			DS					CD		___	Freedom from distractibility
I	S	A	V			PC						___	Long-term memory
						PC	PA	BD	OA		MA	___	Nonverbal reasoning
		A			DS					CD		___	Numerical ability
						PC	PA	BD	OA		MA	___	Perceptual organization
							PA				MA	___	Perceptual planning ability
								BD		CD		___	Perceptual reproduction
							PA	BD	OA			___	Perceptual synthesis
								BD		CD	MA	___	Perception of abstract stimuli
						PC	PA		OA			___	Perception of meaningful stimuli
								BD	OA	CD		___	Psychomotor speed
					DS		PA			CD		___	Sequencing
		A			DS					CD		___	Short-term memory
				C			PA					___	Social judgment
						PC		BD	OA			___	Spatial perception
I	S		V	C								___	Verbal comprehension
I		A			DS							___	Little verbal expression
	S		V	C								___	Much verbal expression
	S		V									___	Verbal concept formation
I		A		C								___	Long verbal questions
	S		V		DS							___	Short verbal questions
	S	A		C								___	Verbal reasoning
								BD	OA	CD	MA	___	Visual-motor coordination
						PC				CD		___	Visual memory
		A				PC	PA	BD	OA	CD	MA	___	Working under time pressure

Note. M = mean of the subtest scaled scores for the ability or factor. Grossman (1985) provided data for determining significant discrepancies between some of the subtest combinations.

clude all possible comparisons, nor does it reflect all possible interpretations. On the basis of these examples, you should be able to develop other comparisons and formulate other interpretations. *All hypotheses should be treated as tentative. Conclusions derived from profile analysis should never be referred to as definitive findings.* (In Appendix C, see Table C-13 for a summary of interpretive rationales for the WISC-R subtests and Table C-43 for suggestive remediation activities for combinations of subtests.) *All hypotheses must be developed on the basis of both significant differences between subtest scores and the absolute values of the subtest scores.* Thus scaled scores of 10 or higher never reflect absolute weaknesses, and scaled scores of 9 or lower never reflect absolute strengths.

COMPARING SUBTESTS IN VERBAL SCALE

1. *Information (I) and Comprehension (C).* This comparison relates the amount of information retained (Information) to the ability to use information (Comprehension). Information requires factual knowledge, whereas Comprehension requires both factual knowledge and judgment.

I > C: High Information and low Comprehension may suggest adequate general knowledge but difficulty in synthesizing and using information to solve problems involving the social world.

I < C: Low Information and high Comprehension may suggest limited factual knowledge but good ability to use this limited knowledge to make appropriate judgments.

2. *Comprehension (C) and Arithmetic (A).* The Comprehension and Arithmetic subtests both require reasoning ability or, more specifically, the ability to analyze a given set of material and then to recognize the elements that are needed for the solution of the specified problem.

C > A: High Comprehension and low Arithmetic may suggest that reasoning ability is adequate in social situations but not in situations involving numbers.

C < A: Low Comprehension and High Arithmetic may suggest that reasoning ability is better for abstract tasks than for social ones.

3. *Arithmetic (A) and Digit Span (DS).* The Arithmetic and Digit Span subtests both require facility with numbers and ability in immediate recall. Comparing the two subtests may provide an index of the relative balance between short-term attention (Digit Span) and long-term concentration (Arithmetic).

DS > A: High Digit Span and low Arithmetic may suggest that attention is better developed than concentration.

DS < A: Low Digit Span and High Arithmetic may suggest that concentration is better developed than attention.

4. *Similarities (S) and Comprehension (C).* Similarities and Comprehension both involve, in part, conceptualizing skills. Similarities usually requires a single word response, however, whereas Comprehension requires an extended response that interrelates a set of ideas (that is, propositional thinking).

S > C: High Similarities and low Comprehension may suggest good abstract thinking but difficulty in applying conceptualizing ability to solve problems in the social world. This pattern may also suggest a verbal-expressive deficit involving propositional thinking.

S < C: Low Similarities and high Comprehension may suggest a deficit in verbal concept formation relative to real-world conceptualizing ability.

5. *Vocabulary (V) and Similarities (S).* Both Vocabulary and Similarities measure level of abstract thinking and ability to form concepts, but Similarities is a better measure of these abilities.

S > V: High Similarities and low Vocabulary may suggest good ability to do abstract thinking but limited ability to understand the meaning of words.

S < V: Low Similarities and high Vocabulary may suggest difficulty in forming abstract concepts but good ability to understand the meaning of individual words.

6. *Vocabulary (V), Information (I), and Comprehension (C).* All three subtests involve verbal processing, but in somewhat different contexts.

V, I > C: High Vocabulary and Information coupled with low Comprehension may suggest inability to use verbal ability and general knowledge fully in life situations and therefore may indicate impaired judgment.

V, I < C: Low Vocabulary and Information coupled with high Comprehension may suggest limited concept formation, except when conceptualizing ability is applied to solving problems in the social world.

7. *Digit Span—Digits Forward (DS-F) versus Digits Backward (DS-B).* The two components of Digit Span—Digits Forward and Digits Backward—both involve attention. Digits Backward, however, involves more complex attentional processes.

DS-F > DS-B: High Digits Forward and low Digits Backward (differences of 3 or more raw-score points) may indicate that the child did not put forth the extra effort needed to master the more difficult task of recalling digits backward in sequence. Alternatively, it may indicate good auditory memory but poor short-term visual memory based on auditory information (a very tentative hypothesis).

DS-F < DS-B: Low Digits Forward and high Digits Backward may indicate that the child sees Digits Backward as a challenge rather than as a task involving mere repetition of numbers.

8. *Similarities (S) and Digit Span (DS)*. Similarities and Digit Span have little overlap in their measurement properties, although both are in the Verbal Scale.

S > DS: High Similarities and low Digit Span may reflect good conceptualizing ability coupled with poor rote auditory memory for digits.

S < DS: Low Similarities and high Digit Span may suggest poor conceptualizing ability coupled with good rote auditory memory for digits.

COMPARING SUBTESTS IN VERBAL AND PERFORMANCE SCALES

9. *Similarities (S) and Block Design (BD)*. Similarities and Block Design both reflect abstract reasoning ability. They both require the abstraction of relations among stimulus items.

S > BD: High Similarities and low Block Design may suggest that abstract reasoning ability is better with verbal stimuli than with nonverbal materials.

S < BD: Low Similarities and high Block Design may suggest that abstract reasoning ability is better with nonverbal materials than with verbal stimuli.

10. *Comprehension (C) and Picture Arrangement (PA)*. The Comprehension and Picture Arrangement subtests both contain stimuli that are concerned with social interaction. The comparison relates knowledge of social conventions (Comprehension) to the capacity to anticipate and plan in a social context (Picture Arrangement).

PA > C: High Picture Arrangement coupled with low Comprehension may suggest sensitivity to interpersonal nuances, but a disregard for social conventions.

PA < C: Low Picture Arrangement coupled with high Comprehension may suggest an understanding of social situations in the abstract, but difficulty in deciding what the situations mean or what actions to take once the examinee is involved in the situations.

11. *Picture Completion (PC) and Arithmetic (A)*. Picture Completion and Arithmetic both involve concentration. On Picture Completion, however, the concentration is directed to an externalized form—a visual stimulus—whereas on Arithmetic the concentration is directed to an internalized stimulus—a memory trace.

PC > A: High Picture Completion and low Arithmetic may suggest adequate concentration for a visual stimulus, but not for an auditory stimulus.

PC < A: Low Picture Completion and high Arithmetic may suggest adequate concentration for an auditory stimulus, but not for a visual stimulus.

COMPARING SUBTESTS IN PERFORMANCE SCALE

12. *Picture Completion (PC) and Picture Arrangement (PA)*. This comparison provides an estimate of attention to detail versus organization of detail. Both Picture Completion and Picture Arrangement involve perception of details, but Picture Arrangement also requires logical ordering of details, or sequencing.

PC > PA: High Picture Completion and low Picture Arrangement may suggest that perception of details is better developed for nonsequencing tasks than for tasks requiring sequencing and organization.

PC < PA: Low Picture Completion and high Picture Arrangement may suggest that perception of details is less well developed for nonsequencing tasks than for tasks requiring sequencing and organization.

Courtesy Herman Zielinski.

13. *Picture Completion (PC) and Block Design (BD).* This comparison relates visual perception to visual-motor-spatial coordination.

PC > BD: High Picture Completion and low Block Design may suggest adequate nonspatial visual perceptual ability but inadequate spatial visualization ability.

PC < BD: Low Picture Completion and high Block Design may suggest inadequate nonspatial visual perceptual ability but adequate spatial visualization ability.

14. *Object Assembly (OA) and Picture Arrangement (PA).* This comparison relates inductive reasoning (working from parts to a whole) to sequencing. Both tasks require synthesis into wholes without a model, but Picture Arrangement also involves sequencing.

OA > PA: High Object Assembly and low Picture Arrangement may suggest that visual inductive reasoning skills are better developed than visual sequencing skills.

OA < PA: Low Object Assembly and high Picture Arrangement may suggest that visual inductive reasoning skills are less well developed than visual sequencing skills.

15. *Block Design (BD), Object Assembly (OA), and Mazes (MA).* The Block Design, Object Assembly, and Mazes subtests require visual-motor coordination and involve motor activity guided by perceptual organization. The role of visual organization differs in the three subtests. On the Block Design subtest, visual organization is involved in a process of analysis (breaking down the pattern) and synthesis (building the pattern up again out of the blocks). On the Object Assembly subtest, visual organization is used in the arrangement of parts into a meaningful pattern. On Object Assembly, children may develop a mental concept of the whole from parts without the visual representation of the whole, whereas on Block Design the drawing of the whole is provided. On the Mazes subtest, visual organization is involved in planning and foresight. Thus the term *visual organization* refers to different functions on each of these three subtests.

BD > MA: High Block Design and low Mazes may suggest that visual organization skills involving analysis and synthesis are better developed than those involving planning and foresight.

BD < MA: Low Block Design and high Mazes may suggest that visual organization skills involving analysis and synthesis are less well developed than those involving planning and foresight.

OA > BD: High Object Assembly and low Block Design may suggest that nonverbal inductive reasoning skills (working from parts to a whole) are better developed than nonverbal deductive reasoning skills (working from a whole to parts). Additionally, it may suggest difficulty in interpreting figure-ground relationships.

OA < BD: Low Object Assembly and high Block Design may suggest that nonverbal inductive reasoning skills are less well developed than nonverbal deductive reasoning skills, or that a deficit exists in the ideation required to form a visual representation of the objects.

COMPARING THREE OR MORE SUBTESTS

16. *Information (I), Arithmetic (A), and Comprehension (C) versus Similarities (S), Vocabulary (V), and Digit Span (DS).* This comparison contrasts subtests that have relatively long verbal questions (Information, Arithmetic, and Comprehension) with those that have relatively short verbal questions (Similarities, Vocabulary, Digit Span) (Kaufman, 1979a).

I, A, C > S, V, DS: High Information, Arithmetic, and Comprehension coupled with low Similarities, Vocabulary, and Digit Span may suggest that the child performs better when the verbal stimuli are long than when they are short. The child may put forth more effort to attend to verbal material that is of a relatively long duration. The pattern may also reflect the child's ability to benefit from the contextual cues contained in the longer questions.

I, A, C < S, V, DS: Low Information, Arithmetic, and Comprehension coupled with high Similarities, Vocabulary, and Digit Span may suggest that the child performs better when verbal stimuli are short than when they are long. The child may put forth more effort to attend to verbal material that is of a relatively short duration. This pattern also may suggest an auditory reception deficit associated with deriving meaning from spoken language.

17. *Similarities (S), Vocabulary (V), and Comprehension (C) versus Information (I), Arithmetic (A), and Digit Span (DS).* This comparison contrasts subtests that require a fair amount of verbal expression (Similarities, Vocabulary, Comprehension) with those that require relatively little verbal expression (Information, Arithmetic, Digit Span) (Kaufman, 1979a).

S, V, C > I, A, DS: High Similarities, Vocabulary, and Comprehension coupled with low Information, Arithmetic, and Digit Span may suggest that the child performs better when the tasks require a fair amount of verbal expression than when they require relatively little verbal expression. One possibility is that the child may put forth the extra effort in situations that require verbal expression but not in those that require minimal verbal expression.

S, V, C < I, A, DS: Low Similarities, Vocabulary, and Comprehension coupled with high Information, Arithmetic, and Digit Span may suggest that the child performs better when the tasks require relatively little verbal expression than when they require a fair amount of verbal expression. One possibility is that the child may put forth effort only when tasks require minimal verbal effort. Additionally, this pattern may be associated with communication problems or shyness associated with speaking in relatively long sentences.

18. *Picture Completion (PC), Picture Arrangement (PA), and Object Assembly (OA) versus Block Design (BD) and Coding (CD).* This comparison contrasts subtests that contain relatively meaningful perceptual stimuli (Picture Completion, Picture Arrangement, Object Assembly) with those that have relatively abstract perceptual stimuli (Block Design, Coding) (Kaufman, 1979a).

PC, PA, OA > BD, CD: High Picture Completion, Picture Arrangement, and Object Assembly coupled with low Block Design and Coding may suggest that the child performs better when the visual stimuli are meaningful than when they are abstract or nonmeaningful.

PC, PA, OA < BD, CD: Low Picture Completion, Picture Arrangement, and Object Assembly coupled with high Block Design and Coding may suggest that the child performs better when the visual stimuli are abstract than when they are concrete.

19. *Picture Completion (PC) and Picture Arrangement (PA) versus Block Design (BD), Object Assembly (OA), Coding (CD), and Mazes (MA).* Five of the six Performance Scale subtests involve perceptual organization (the exception is Coding). This comparison of the Performance Scale subtests distinguishes those subtests that tap primarily perceptual organization (Picture Completion and Picture Arrangement) from those that involve both perceptual organization and visual-motor coordination (Block Design, Object Assembly, Coding, Mazes).

PC, PA > BD, OA, CD, MA: High Picture Completion and Picture Arrangement coupled with low Block Design, Object Assembly, Coding, and Mazes may suggest that the child performs better when the tasks require only perceptual organization than when they require both perceptual organization and visual-motor coordination.

PC, PA < BD, OA, CD, MA: Low Picture Completion and Picture Arrangement coupled with high Block Design, Object Assembly, Coding, and Mazes may suggest that the child performs better when the tasks require both perceptual organization and visual-motor coordination than when they require only perceptual organization.

ANALYSIS OF THREE WECHSLER SUBTESTS FROM A PIAGETIAN PERSPECTIVE

Piaget's distinction between figurative knowing and operative knowing may be used in analyzing performance on the Wechsler scales and other cognitive tests. *Figurative knowing* refers to knowledge of static states (knowledge of content, such as names of objects), whereas *operative knowing* refers to knowledge of dynamic transformations (knowledge of how to apply content to arrive at a solution, such as putting together three sticks to reach an object). This distinction appears to be similar to the crystallized/fluid distinction in the Cattell/Horn approach (see Chapter 3). Elkind (1979) applied the figurative/operative distinction to three WISC-R subtests: Information, Similarities, and Block Design.

Information

The items on the Information subtest are cognitively quite heterogeneous. Some items assess figurative learning, others operative learning, and still others openness to learning extraneous bits of information. For example, "What do you call this finger?" requires simple figurative knowledge, whereas "How many ears do you have?" may involve "some operative understanding—to the extent that number and counting are involved" (p. 244). Items also tap the preoperational level ("What do you call this finger?"), concrete operational level ("How many pennies make a nickel?"), and formal operational level ("What causes iron to rust?").

To understand the kind of learning shown by a child's responses, we have to study each Information item separately. Ideally, the child's responses should be used to gain some insight into how much of the information was acquired figuratively, how much was acquired operatively, and what was the highest level of operativity involved. A simple construct like "range of information" does not adequately explain tasks found on the Information subtest.

Similarities

The Similarities subtest is far from a homogeneous measure of the processes involved in concept formation. The wheel and ball item is a figurative task, whereas the piano—guitar item involves concrete operations. Early items are preoperational, intermediate ones reflect concrete operations, and later ones reflect formal operations.

Some items even measure divergent thinking (salt—water). Thus the Similarities subtest measures both figurative and operative knowing as well as divergent thinking. It would be simplistic to interpret the Similarities subtest as a straightforward measure of concept attainment ability. Again, each response should be studied to evaluate the type of knowledge shown by the child.

Block Design

Elkind views the Block Design subtest as "almost entirely a test of perceptual regulations—concrete operations in the service of perceptual analysis" (p. 246). It is largely an operative task, measuring primarily concrete operations.

Comment on the Piagetian Perspective

The figurative/operative distinction offers a promising tool for analyzing many different types of content, including those found on cognitive tests and in school curricula. Unfortunately, as Elkind (1979) points out, it is not always possible to determine whether a correct response represents a rote answer (figurative knowing) or genuine problem solving (operative knowing). For example, "How many ears do you have?" can be answered purely by rote or by problem solving. Consequently, the reason for success or failure on some items cannot be known without further inquiry. This is why testing-of-limits is helpful. By asking follow-up questions, you may be able to determine the quality of thinking involved in the child's responses.

ESTIMATED PERCENTILE RANKS AND TEST-AGE EQUIVALENTS FOR RAW SCORES

In some settings and on some occasions it may be useful to convert subtest scaled scores to percentile ranks or to convert raw scores to test-age equivalents. For example, when discussing assessment results with a teacher or parent or physician, you may find it useful to use derived scores. Table C-41 in Appendix C gives the estimated percentile ranks for each WISC-R (and WPPSI and WAIS-R) scaled score and qualitative descriptions for the scaled score. *You should never estimate an IQ on the basis of only one subtest score*, however. Table 21 in the WISC-R manual provides the test-age equivalents of raw scores on each subtest. The test-age equivalents provide approximate developmental levels for achievement on the subtest. For example, a raw score of 6 on the Information subtest is roughly equivalent to a developmental age level of 6-6

years. As noted in Chapter 2, test-age equivalents have many drawbacks; therefore their routine use is not recommended.

ILLUSTRATIONS OF QUALITATIVE ANALYSIS ON THE WISC-R

This section provides a few interpretations based on item content, test responses and behavior, test patterns, and testing-of-limits procedures. An assumption underlying some of the interpretations in this section is that the cognitive variables involved in the WISC-R (and WPPSI and WAIS-R) subtests—such as planning, anticipation, attention, and concentration—are reflective of personality organization. If this assumption holds true, then the pattern of scores may reveal general modes of adaptation. Interpretations should be guided by the consistency present among the various aspects of test performance—profile of scores, content of responses, and style of responses. *All interpretations formulated through these procedures should be viewed as tentative and should be evaluated in light of the child's performance on the entire test, other assessment results, and clinical history.* The examples in this section usually apply only in cases where other information can confirm the hypothesis.

A Variety of Hypotheses About Interpreting the WISC-R

• Some children show a pattern of missing easy items and succeeding on more difficult items. This pattern may occur among bright children who are bored by the easy items and thus give careless or even nonsense replies, only to become challenged by more difficult items that allow them to demonstrate their skills (Palmer, 1983). This pattern may also suggest inconsistent attention or effort resulting from anxiety or other factors.

• Various questions and words may arouse associations with violence or hostility. Two such Vocabulary subtest words are knife and affliction. On Similarities, a response such as "Apple and banana are alike because they both can be used to feed a person poison" may be suggestive of psychological difficulties.

• Reactions to Picture Completion tasks may provide information about a child's difficulties. A child with incapacitating anxiety about separation issues may be unable to answer any item and may ask you why something has to be missing (Brooks, 1979). A child suffering from dysphasia (a form of speech impairment due to central nervous system impairment) may exhibit difficulty in finding words (anomia). For example, the child may point to the missing part instead of naming it, describe the missing part or its use, or indicate the part's function with gestures (Small, 1982).

• Children who continually recheck their work with the Block Design model may be revealing obsessive tendencies.

• The painstaking Coding task may be more difficult for the alert, creative, and intuitive child than for the more pedantic, passive, and slow-moving one (Taylor, 1961).

• Errors on Mazes may be indicative of impulsivity (overshooting alleys and exits); loss of control or poor coordination (walls cut through); or excessive caution, perfectionism, or depression (correct completion after time limits) (Zimmerman & Woo-Sam, 1985).

• In a paranoid individual the content of responses, style of responses, and pattern of scores may be interrelated (Blatt & Allison, 1968). The content of the examinee's responses may reflect suspiciousness regarding the recording of the responses or feelings of being tricked. The style may be cautious, rigid, and legalistic. Scores may be highest in areas related to hyperalertness to details (Picture Completion or Picture Arrangement) and to bringing together and relating disparate things (Similarities).

Interpreting Comprehension Subtest Responses

The following are possible interpretations of Comprehension subtest responses that may reveal characteristics of the child's social judgment.

Question 1. "What is the thing to do if a boy (girl) much smaller than yourself starts to fight with you?" (All examples are from Taylor, 1961.)

Answer: "He should not hit you" (a possible indication of a moralistic response).

Answer: "I should not fight" (a possible indication of a defensive response).

Answer: "I would tell my mother" (a possible indication of dependency).

Question 2. "What is the thing to do when you cut your finger?"

Answer: "You should be more careful and not cut your finger" (a possible indication of a moralistic response, Taylor, 1961).

Answer: "Fingers can fall off or be cut off and maybe they could be sewed on" (a possible indication of preoccupation with aggression and retribution, Brooks, 1979).

Question 3. "What are you supposed to do if you find someone's wallet or pocketbook in a store?" (All examples are from Zimmerman & Woo-Sam, 1985.)

Answer: "Give it back, say you didn't take it" (a possible indication of guilt).

Answer: "Give it to your mother" (a possible indication of passivity).

Answer: "Take the money" (a possible indication of sociopathy).

Answer: "Don't do nothing" (a possible indication of difficulty in coping).

Answer: "I never stole anything" (a possible indication of denial).

Diagnostic Aspects of the Picture Arrangement Subtest

Correct as well as faulty solutions on the Picture Arrangement subtest allow you to evaluate the developmental level of a child's reasoning (Taylor, 1961). Most failures are due to difficulties in logical reasoning. Faulty solutions may also result from inattention (for example, on the SLEEPER item, failure to see the time on the clock).

Reasoning difficulties are suggested when a child who is more than 8 years old regularly makes young child–like arrangements. Reasoning difficulties tend to occur among mentally retarded children and brain-injured children, and sometimes among *severely* emotionally disturbed children. Mildly emotionally disturbed children usually produce logical stories. Their anxieties and preoccupations, however, may be revealed by unusual arrangements, such as neglecting details for the sake of a particular theme.

There are two methods that can be used to obtain thematic material from the Picture Arrangement subtest. These techniques should be used only *after* the entire scale has been administered. Both are screening devices; they are not intended to replace other thematic instruments, such as the Thematic Apperception Test (TAT) or the Children's Apperception Test. These techniques permit the child to project feelings and experiences, however, and may reveal a range of experiences and affect.

One method is to arrange one or more Picture Arrangement items in the order given by the child during the test proper and then ask the examinee to make up a story. Only items that were originally given to the child should be selected. Standard TAT instructions can be used, such as "Make up a story. Tell what is happening, what happened before, what will happen next, and how the people are feeling." The methods usually applied to thematic material can then be used to interpret the stories.

A second method involves randomly placing the FIGHT

sequence of cards before the child and then asking the child to make up a story about *one of the cards*, in standard TAT fashion (Craig, 1969). After the story has been completed and the cards have been removed, the PICNIC sequence of cards is placed randomly before the child and the child is asked to tell a story about one of the cards. This procedure can be followed for any other items that were administered to the child during the test proper.

COMMENT ON INTERPRETING THE WISC-R

The child's performance on the WISC-R should be interpreted in relation to all other sources of data. It is important to verify the validity of the test scores with other information obtained about the child. If the Full Scale IQ does not appear to provide a valid estimate of the child's ability, consider the Verbal Scale and Performance Scale IQs as separate pieces of information that may have greater validity. Any hypotheses about the validity of the Full Scale IQ, Verbal Scale IQ, or Performance Scale IQ should be developed on the basis of all the available information you have about the child.

When a significant Verbal-Performance split occurs, the Full Scale IQ may be a misrepresentation of the individual's functioning level. In this situation, the Full Scale IQ may merely represent some kind of forced average of rather disparate primary skills. What meaning, for example, can we attach to an IQ of 100 that results from a Verbal Scale IQ of 130 and a Performance Scale IQ of 70? Although the IQ of 100 may be the best overall estimate of the child's cognitive level, the child is not likely to be average either in situations calling for verbal reasoning or in those requiring nonverbal reasoning. Unfortunately, there is little research that can help us understand how examinees with large Verbal-Performance discrepancies function outside of the test situation. To a lesser extent, a similar problem exists in interpreting the Verbal and Performance IQs when there is an exceptionally large amount of variability among the subtests within each scale.

Performance on each WISC-R scale and subtest is multidetermined. This means that any one scale or subtest likely measures many different abilities. Consequently, a high score or a low score does not tell you what particular functions are well developed or impaired. This information will come only from a sifting of all WISC-R scores, scores obtained from other tests, qualitative information, testing-of-limits, and clinical history. Good clinical skills constitute the sturdy thread from which the tapestry is woven.

As noted in Chapter 6, the WISC-R may not be the instrument of choice for evaluating the cognitive abilities of children who function at either an extremely low or an extremely high level. In the case of low-functioning children, too few items may be administered. In the case of high-functioning children, there may not be a sufficient number of challenging items. Profile analysis is also hampered by the fact that the highest scaled scores are not available on each subtest throughout all of the age ranges covered by the scale.

In Chapters 20, 21, and 22, brief WISC-R case studies are presented for various groups of exceptional children. A study of these cases will help you in interpreting the WISC-R.

Interpreting the WISC-R is a challenging activity. The WISC-R gives an estimate of the child's level of intellectual functioning. The word *estimate* should be emphasized. The WISC-R provides useful, but limited, information about the range, depth, and real-world applications of a child's intellectual ability.

Many clinicians are not satisfied with merely estimating intellectual ability from the Wechsler scales. They want to use these scales to evaluate personality and temperament, to diagnose various forms of psychopathology, to determine brain lateralization, and so forth. Once one goes beyond the confines of the IQs provided by the Full, Verbal, and Performance Scales, however, the ground becomes loose and wobbly. Interpretations become more impressionistic and may be less reliable and valid. When on this ground, step carefully, continually getting your bearings from research findings and clinical experience.

PSYCHOLOGICAL EVALUATION

The psychological evaluation in Exhibit 8-2 illustrates how the WISC-R can contribute to the assessment of an emotionally disturbed youngster. For illustrative purposes the report focuses on only the WISC-R. A thorough assessment would be based on a battery of assessment procedures.

TEST YOUR SKILL

Exhibit 8-3 presents a series of exercises designed to sharpen your skill in writing reports and in interpreting the WISC-R (and WPPSI and WAIS-R). In each excerpt shown in Exhibit 8-3, some inadequacy of description or interpretation exists. Find the mistakes in the sentences. After you have completed your analysis, check your evaluations with those shown in Appendix A.

Exhibit 8-2

Analysis of and Line-by-Line Commentary on a Psychological Evaluation of an Emotionally Disturbed 7-Year-Old Examined with the WISC-R

INTRODUCTORY REMARKS

Shown on the following pages is a case study of an emotionally disturbed child. Jim, a 7-year-old boy referred for evaluation because of antisocial behavior, was administered the WISC-R. His Full Scale IQ of 113 is classified in the High Average range of intelligence. There was a significant 15-point difference between his Verbal Scale IQ (119) and Performance Scale IQ (104). Most subtest scores were above average, with the exception of those on two performance tasks (Object Assembly and Coding). These results suggest that his nonverbal skills may be more variable than his verbal skills. Notice in the report the several references to Jim's perseverance and need for reassurance during the test session. Also note that several of his answers were related to his antisocial behavior pattern. This case illustrates that emotional disturbance may not necessarily affect cognitive functioning.

ANALYSIS OF THE REPORT

Identifying Data

The report begins with the traditional identification data. In an actual report, the child's last name would be included.

Test Administered

This part of the report cites the test name (or names) and test scores. It is optional because the name of the test and major WISC-R scores (Verbal, Performance, and Full Scale IQs) can be included in the body of the report. Often the subtest scores are not included in the report.

Reason for Referral

This section, which usually begins the narrative portion of the report, explains the reason for the evaluation. It documents what the psychologist sees as the purpose for the evaluation and helps to develop the focus of the recommendations. It also may contain information about the child that is related to the referral question.

Background Information

This section describes portions of Jim's background that might be pertinent to the issues under consideration. The first paragraph sets the stage for a historical understanding of the problem and provides information as to possible resources available within the family for remediation. The second paragraph cites in more detail those behaviors that led to Jim's referral. The third paragraph focuses on school behavior and recent changes in problem behaviors.

Behavioral Observations

This section describes Jim's behavior during the examination, with particular emphasis on his approach to the test and behavior reflective of his unique style.

Assessment Results and Clinical Impressions

This section begins with a description of Jim's overall test performance. Normative data and confidence levels are then reported. The confidence bands for IQs are found in Table C-1 in Appendix C. The percentile ranks for IQs are found in Table BC-1 on the inside back cover of this text.

The second paragraph discusses the discrepancy between his Verbal and Performance Scale IQs. Table C-2 in Appendix C gives values that indicate significant differences between scaled scores and between individual subtest scores. Table C-3 in Appendix C gives values that indicate significant differences between individual subtest scores and their respective mean scaled scores.

The third paragraph describes Jim's strengths and weaknesses based on his subtest scores. Jim's numerical reasoning, range of knowledge, and language usage are well developed, as suggested by his scores on Arithmetic, Information, and Vocabulary, respectively. Less adequate are his visual-motor coordination and psychomotor speed, as indicated by his scores on Object Assembly and Coding. (Table C-13 in Appendix C provides a summary interpretation of skills associated with the individual WISC-R subtests.)

The fourth paragraph describes some idiosyncratic responses that may be reflective of Jim's behavior problem, and the last paragraph provides a brief summary of Jim's overall level of functioning.

Recommendations

Recommendations are made before the final summary. Note that because the evaluation did not include personality tests, the recommendations call for further testing and evaluation.

Summary

The final section of the report summarizes the major findings and recommendations.

(Exhibit continues next page)

Exhibit 8-2 (cont.)

THE REPORT WITH LINE-BY-LINE COMMENTARY

Name: Jim
Date of birth: July 17, 1978
Chronological age: 7-4

Date of examination: November 20, 1985
Date of report: November 21, 1985
Grade: Second

Test Administered

Wechsler Intelligence Scale for Children—Revised (WISC-R):

VERBAL SCALE		PERFORMANCE SCALE	
Information	14	Picture Completion	12
Similarities	12	Picture Arrangement	13
Arithmetic	15	Block Design	14
Vocabulary	13	Object Assembly	8
Comprehension	12	Coding	6

Verbal Scale IQ = 119
Performance Scale IQ = 104
Full Scale IQ = 113 $\pm$ 7 at the 95% confidence level

Reason for Referral

1 Jim, a 7-year, 4-month-old boy, was referred to the
2 clinic for evaluation because of involuntary defeca-
3 tion, fecal smearing, enuresis, and stealing.

1 who was referred
2 to whom he was referred
2–3 specific behaviors leading to referral

Background

4 According to Jim's aunt, Jim was born out of wedlock
5 and never knew his natural father. He was separated
6 from his mother at 6 months of age, when she devel-
7 oped leukemia from which she died a year later. Since
8 that time Jim has lived with a paternal aunt and her
9 three children, who range in age from 8 to 18 years.
10 The aunt has been divorced twice. Jim calls his aunt
11 "mother" and thought of her first husband as his father.
12 This man, who had been in the family as long as Jim,
13 has not been involved with the family since he di-
14 vorced the aunt. Jim was 2½-years-old at the time of
15 the divorce. His aunt described having made in-
16 complete and ineffective attempts at toilet training
17 during this period of turmoil. Last year Jim's aunt
18 remarried. During the six months that the marriage
19 lasted, Jim formed no attachment to his second step-
20 uncle.
21   Jim's aunt reported that he has bowel movements in
22 the bathtub; he smears feces on the walls or leaves
23 them in trash cans around the house. He also soils
24 himself frequently. He wanders around the house at
25 night, and sometimes vanishes for hours while in the
26 park or on his way home from school. His aunt stated
27 that he stole a stopwatch from the principal's office,
28 and food and money from other places. Apparently, he
29 seems to make an effort to be discovered when he
30 steals.

4–7 early infancy and family background

8–10 family constellation

10–11 attachment to parental figures

12–15 time of early separation from parental figure

15–17 past parental behaviors that may relate to Jim's current problems
17–18 recent family changes
18–20 Jim's relationship to new family member

21–24 encopresis

24–26 "wandering" behavior

26–30 stealing behavior

(Exhibit continues next page)

Exhibit 8-2 (cont.)

31 Jim is an excellent student, although he is difficult to	31–32 level of academic achievement and deviant
32 handle because of his opposition and defiance. His	classroom behavior
33 behavior in the past three months has been changing.	33–36 recent changes in behavior
34 There has been a decrease in encopresis and fecal	
35 smearing, and an increase in stealing and aggressive	
36 behavior.	

Behavioral Observations

37 Jim is a small, thinly built, energetic child. He was	37 appearance
38 cooperative and friendly during the testing session.	37–38 overall response to being tested
39 His test behavior was characterized by competitive-	39–42 response to test materials
40 ness, tenacity, and anxiety. He seemed to want to	
41 answer all of the questions correctly and was reluctant	
42 to give up on any question. On the Information sub-	42–48 example of response to a test question
43 test, he responded to "What are the four seasons of the	
44 year?" with "Spring" and "Fall," but could not re-	
45 member the other seasons. He had to be encouraged to	
46 go on to the next question, and three times later he	
47 spontaneously returned to the season question, adding	
48 "Winter" and "Summer." Jim seemed to need continual	48–50 style of relating to examiner
49 assurance from the examiner that he was answering	
50 the items correctly. He often asked, "Have I gotten	50–51 example of test behavior
51 them all right?"	

Assessment Results and Clinical Impressions

52 With a chronological age of 7-4, Jim achieved a Verbal	52 chronological age
53 Scale IQ of 119, a Performance Scale IQ of 104, and a	53 Verbal Scale IQ and Performance Scale IQ
54 Full Scale IQ of 113 $\pm$ 7 on the WISC-R. His overall	54 Full Scale IQ and confidence band
55 performance is classified in the High Average range	55 normative classification based on Full Scale IQ
56 and is ranked at the 81st percentile. The chances that	56 percentile rank
57 the range of scores from 106 to 120 includes his true	56–58 confidence range of IQ
58 IQ are about 95 out of 100. The present measure of his	58–59 validity of test results
59 level of intellectual functioning appears to be valid.	
60 Although there was a 15-point difference between	60–61 discrepancy between IQs
61 the Verbal and Performance Scales, this difference	61–63 variability noted in Performance area
62 was associated primarily with his low scores on two	
63 Performance Scale subtests. Whereas his verbal skills	63–64 description of verbal skills
64 are uniformly well developed, his performance skills	64–66 description of nonverbal skills
65 show more variability, with some abilities well devel-	
66 oped and others less well developed. Overall (with the	66–69 summary of performance on WISC-R
67 exception of two of the Performance subtest scores)	
68 Jim consistently demonstrated above-average skills as	
69 assessed by the test.	
70 Within the verbal area, his numerical reasoning	70–73 verbal skill strengths
71 ability, range of knowledge, and language usage are	
72 excellent. Social comprehension and concept forma-	
73 tion ability are also strong. Within the performance	73–75 nonverbal skill strengths
74 area, his analytic and synthetic ability, planning and	
75 anticipation ability, and ability to differentiate essen-	
76 tial from nonessential details are all well-developed.	
77 Less adequate are skills associated with visual-motor	77–78 nonverbal skill weaknesses
78 coordination and with psychomotor speed. It is diffi-	78–80 relation of weaknesses to overall ability
79 cult to account for his lower scores in these two areas	*(Exhibit continues next page)*

Exhibit 8-2 (cont.)

80 in light of his overall above-average ability. Perhaps	80–83 possible reasons for low scores
81 the scores reflect temporary inefficiency due to fa-	
82 tigue, or perhaps they simply indicate that his abilities	
83 in these areas are not as well developed.	
84 Overall, he approaches problems by giving detailed	84–85 response style
85 answers that are descriptive and meaningful. A	
86 number of Jim's responses were particularly interest-	86–92 examples of unique responses
87 ing. In response to the question "Why are criminals	
88 locked up?" he said, "Because they steal things that are	
89 expensive." In reference to another question asking	
90 why it was better to give money to a charity than to a	
91 beggar, he said, "Because the beggars might be a	
92 burglar." His mention of "stealing" and the specifica-	92–96 relation of responses to current behavior
93 tion of "expensive" and "burglar" are notable re-	
94 sponses in view of his behavior pattern, which in-	
95 cludes stealing. A preoccupation with stealing may be	
96 intruding into his outlook toward life. One response	96–100 instance of unusual response style
97 differed from his general pattern of rather clearcut,	
98 detailed, well-oriented, and direct responses. He said	
99 that apple and banana are alike because they "feel the	
100 same." The above responses were the only ones that	100–101 observation of unusual responses
101 were idiosyncratic.	
102 The test results suggest that Jim's behavioral prob-	102–104 effect of behavior problems on cognitive functioning
103 lems, for the most part, have not interfered with his	
104 intellectual functioning. His psychomotor speed and	104–106 weaknesses
105 visual-motor coordination are less-adequately devel-	
106 oped than his other abilities, but his overall function-	106–107 level of overall functioning
107 ing is better than average. There were suggestions of	107–108 relation of specific responses to behavior problems
108 preoccupation with stealing, but it is difficult to deter-	
109 mine the extensiveness of this preoccupation.	108–109 limits of interpretation

Recommendations

110 On the basis of the present limited evaluation, it is	110 limitations of current testing
111 recommended that a personality evaluation be con-	111–112 recommendation for personality testing
112 ducted. Furthermore, the seriousness of his behav-	112–114 therapeutic interventions
113 ioral disturbance suggests that therapy should be initi-	
114 ated for both Jim and his aunt. Every attempt should	114–117 needed additional information about home environment
115 be made to obtain further information about his home	
116 environment and to determine which factors in the	
117 home may be reinforcing his deviant behavior pattern.	
118 His aunt should be actively engaged in the develop-	118–119 suggested intervention
119 ment of a treatment program.	

Summary

120 Jim, with a chronological age of 7-4, achieved an IQ of	120 chronological age
121 113 ± 7 on the WISC-R. This IQ is at the 81st percen-	121 IQ and name of test
122 tile and in the High Average range. The chances that	121–122 percentile rank and normative classification of IQ
123 the range of scores from 106 to 120 includes his true	122–124 confidence limits associated with IQ
124 IQ are about 95 out of 100. The test results appear to	124–126 validity of test results
125 give a valid indication of his present level of intellec-	
126 tual functioning. Jim's verbal skills were uniformly	126–127 verbal skills
127 well developed, but there was some variability in his	127–128 variability of nonverbal skills
128 performance skills. The findings suggest that his be-	*(Exhibit continues next page)*

Exhibit 8-2 (cont.)

129 havioral problems are not significantly interfering
130 with his cognitive skills. A personality evaluation
131 was recommended, along with a treatment program
132 that would involve Jim and his aunt.

129–130 possible effects of behavior problems on intellectual functioning
130–132 recommendations

(Signature) _____

Jo Lynn Mack, MA

Exhibit 8-3

Test-Your-Skill Exercises for the WISC-R

Read each item to determine where it is inadequate. Check your evaluation with the comments in Appendix A.

Unnecessary Technical Information

1. A difference of 4 points between her Information and Comprehension scores is significant at the 5% level.
2. Mark did not score zero on any Comprehension items. He had 12 2-point responses and 5 1-point responses.
3. On the Comprehension subtest, Bill scored 18; 10 is average and 19 is the ceiling.
4. On Block Design, she failed items 3, 4, and 5.
5. Her Object Assembly score was significantly different from the mean of her other performance scores.
6. Bill scored 5 points on the Similarities subtest.
7. He missed the Picture Arrangement item about rain.
8. The Digit Span is an optional subtest and was not used in computing the IQ.
9. On the WISC-R, the majority of her scores hovered around 12.
10. A total scaled score of 52 yielded a Performance IQ score of 102.
11. On the Information subtest she earned a scaled score of 13, which is 1 standard deviation above the mean of 10.
12. Bannatyne's recategorization system reveals particular strength in the Visuo-Spatial area (prorated IQ = 127).
13. Frank appears to be weak in the areas dealing with Freedom from Distractibility.
14. A review of Glenda's Verbal scores indicates significance at the .05 level in her Vocabulary and Comprehension tests.
15. Her score on Coding was 4 points lower than her score on Block Design and 5 points lower than her score on Object Assembly.
16. There was a significant difference between John's Verbal and Performance IQs at the .05 level.
17. A mean scaled score of 9 was obtained on the 10 subtests.
18. Intersubtest scatter was minimal.

Poor Writing

19. His score on the WISC-R was equivalent to an IQ of approximately 98.
20. Within the Verbal Scale, her abilities ranged from average to very superior when compared to other children in her chronological age group.
21. Average abilities were indicated in Pat's attention and concentration and how well they are used in conjunction with solving basic arithmetic problems, and in her auditory vocal sequencing memory.
22. The examination of the results displayed a significant amount of point discrepancy between the Verbal and Performance IQ scores of 37 points.
23. The Verbal scores were close-knit in the solidly average range from 9 through 11.
24. In the area of math, the regular classroom teacher might make use of concrete situations to add meaning and to reinforce the total experimental background.
25. All of Mary's scores were respectable and adequate, with the exception of Digit Span where she received a 7.
26. Bill has better mental than nonverbal abilities.
27. Statistical factors and the tenor of his test performance indicate excellent chance (95%) that his test performance would fall consistently (other things being equal) within the range of 117 to 129.
28. Jim's high scores on the Performance Scale suggest that he has well developed abilities in the conception of his environment.
29. The following description was written about a 6-year-old's performance on the Block Design subtest: "She gave up easily even after putting the blocks into the design but not recognizing it as it was supposed to be, thus dismantling the design she made."
30. The following sentence was written for Verbal subtest scores between 9 and 11: "Her verbal subtest scores appear to be within the average range."

(Exhibit continues next page)

Exhibit 8-3 (cont.)

31. The accuracy of his intrasubtest scores were intermittent on many of his subtests. He missed items in such proportions that he was able to complete all of the subtests.
32. His other outstanding score that was indicated was his performance in the Picture Completion subtest.
33. In reviewing her Performance Scale subtest scores, there appears to be a significance at the .05 level between her Object Assembly and Block Design.
34. The Verbal test profile showed a peek for the Comprehension subtest.
35. She showed a retarded score on the ability to see spatial relationships.

Technical Errors

36. A lower score on Information (scaled score 9) shows poor range of knowledge.
37. Average to above-average scores were obtained by George in the sequencing area, with a prorated IQ of 103 in the Sequencing I area and a prorated IQ of 120 in the Sequencing II area.
38. Henry scored in the average intellectual range on the WISC-R, with a mental age of 7-2 and a chronological age of 7-6.
39. Five of the 12 WISC-R subtests were 2 standard deviations from the mean, indicating that her performance was in the very superior range.
40. The 10-point difference between Brandon's Verbal and Performance Scale IQs approaches significance at the 5 percent level, suggesting that his verbal skill development is somewhat ahead of his nonverbal development.
41. Her Full Scale IQ of 109 ± 6 just barely reaches the Above Average classification.
42. The range of scores from 6 to 16 indicates good performance.
43. Her scores ranged from a classification of Very Superior to Borderline Mentally Deficient.
44. The Picture Completion score was significantly lower than the Picture Arrangement score. Because these two subtests are somewhat similar in the testing of detail, reasoning ability, and perceptual organization, the Picture Completion subtest may have been spoiled.
45. Bill's IQ of 114 ± 9 classifies him in a range from average, high average, to superior intellectual functioning.
46. On the basis of a range of scores from 12 to 19 (Verbal IQ = 142, Performance IQ = 131, Full Scale IQ = 141), the following statement was made: "His subtest scores show great variability, indicating he has definite strengths and weaknesses."
47. Bill achieved a Verbal Scale score of 65, a Performance Scale score of 60, and a Full Scale IQ of 118.

48. Her scaled score of 3 on Information places her in the Mentally Retarded range.
49. The following statement was made on the basis of a Verbal Scale IQ of 107 and a Performance Scale IQ of 111: "Her Performance Scale IQ is higher than her Verbal Scale IQ."

Inaccurate or Incomplete Interpretations

50. His low Information score reflects potential repressive mechanisms at work.
51. In response to the question "In what way are anger and joy alike?" she said, "telling about something that you do." Clinical interpretation of this statement suggests that it is probably an emotional indication of aggression.
52. Two subtests deviate significantly from his average Verbal subtest score: Vocabulary (high) and Arithmetic (low).
53. A high Picture Completion subtest score and a low Coding subtest score may predict difficulty in reading.
54. Bill's Full Scale IQ was achieved with a 10-point difference between his Verbal and Performance Scale scores, in favor of the latter. This difference suggests an action-oriented person.
55. A high score on Coding reflects a high and sustained energy level.
56. Discrepancies between this WISC-R administration and the one given three years ago may be due to Henry's variable attention and memory span or possibly examiner differences.
57. She scored significantly higher on Information and Vocabulary than on Digit Span.
58. The 13-point difference between Helen's Verbal and Performance Scale scores indicates that her Verbal subtest scores are significantly higher than her Performance subtest scores.
59. Lack of social judgment and immature responses were noted on the Comprehension subtest (scaled score 8).
60. Bill scored high on Object Assembly because he was persistent in his attempt to assemble the objects.
61. The 15-point discrepancy between Mary's Verbal and Performance Scale IQs indicates that she has a learning disability.
62. The consistency of his scores probably indicates that John is functioning at his capacity.
63. His lowest score was on the Picture Completion subtest, where he received a scaled score of 12.
64. A weakness in another modality—i.e., hearing—was evident in the Digit Span subtest score.

(Exhibit continues next page)

Exhibit 8-3 (cont.)

65. Her high Verbal subtest scores indicate that she is able to express herself with little difficulty.

66. Based on his scores, he would be considered a slow learner or a low average student.

67. The following statement was based on a Similarities scaled score of 15 and a Digit Span scaled score of 10: "She has good conceptualizing ability and poor rote memory for digits."

68. The 40-point difference between Greg's Verbal and Performance IQs can probably be accounted for by the fact that at age 6, Greg has not yet developed the visual-motor skills he needs to do his best on the nonverbal part of the WISC-R.

69. Comprehension requires social adaptation, practical judgment, and self-direction.

70. The intrasubtest scatter may indicate a lack of persistence.

71. The following sentence was based on scaled scores of 13 or higher, with the exception of a 10 on Block Design: "His weaknesses seemed to be in visual-motor coordination and spatial orientation. His lowest and only average score was on the Block Design subtest."

72. Another relatively low score occurred in the Performance Scale, indicating attentional skill weakness.

73. Her verbal skills appear significantly better developed than her performance skills, suggesting that her ability to respond automatically with what is already known may be more developed than her ability to use past experiences and previously acquired skills to solve new problems.

74. He scored relatively high on Digit Span and Coding.

75. The fact that her Similarities score was lower than her Comprehension score implies some difficulty involving fear and emotional excesses.

76. The following interpretation was based on scaled scores of 8 on Picture Completion, 7 on Picture Arrangement, 10 on Block Design, 7 on Object Assembly, and 9 on Coding: "On two tests, Picture Arrangement and Object Assembly, she scored in the low average range. Because these tests measure skills similar to those measured by tests on which she scored higher, it appears probable that she did not apply the same effort on these tests or that there is some other intervening factor such as poor visual acuity."

77. The following statement was based on a Verbal IQ of 129, Performance IQ of 100, and Full Scale IQ of 120: "Monica's verbal skills appear to be somewhat more developed than her performance skills."

78. A review of her Verbal tests does not appear to indicate any areas of significance.

79. A third factor on the test generally denotes poor attention, poor concentration, and poor ability to screen out extraneous influences.

80. In the area of acquired knowledge, which assesses life experiences, social-educational exposure, and learning, he obtained an average score.

81. The following sentence was based on a Verbal IQ of 98, a Performance IQ of 131, and a Full Scale IQ of 109: "The discrepancy between her verbal and performance scores is significant and may suggest that she is compensating for her lack of verbal abilities with her superior performance abilities to achieve good grades in school."

82. The following statement was based on a Verbal IQ of 96, a Performance IQ of 131, and a Full Scale IQ of 113: "An examination of the overall results of this WISC-R session indicates that Frank is very strong in areas where using one's hands is important."

83. His low functioning on Coding may relate to his apparently weak background in school-related tasks.

84. On the Coding subtest the child is asked to attach a meaningless symbol to a number.

85. Because she tried hard, she passed many items.

Inappropriate Recommendations

86. The significant difference between his Verbal and Performance IQs indicates a need for further investigation into his intellectual ability.

87. Because of the extreme scatter in her nonverbal abilities, Julie should be examined by a neurologist and given appropriate medical tests to confirm or eliminate the possibility of neurological impairment.

SUMMARY

1. Profile analysis is a method of generating hypotheses about the organization of intellective functions. It is a statistical approach to evaluating differences between various scores. After the significance of such differences has been established, it is necessary to consider a variety of factors that may account for a specific profile. Profile analysis is one form of test interpretation, and it must be employed in relation to the entire test performance and clinical history.

2. The primary approaches to profile analysis include comparing Verbal and Performance Scale IQs, comparing Verbal and

Performance subtest scaled scores with the average scores on the respective scales, comparing sets of individual subtest scaled scores, comparing factor scores, and comparing subtest scaled scores with the average factor scores on each factor.

3. Other approaches to profile analysis—based on frequency of occurrence in the population—include an evaluation of subtest scaled-score ranges, deviations of subtest scores from the child's own average, and Verbal-Performance Scale differences.

4. Profile analysis requires considerable judgment and skill.

5. Scale differences and subtest differences should be interpreted only when the differences are statistically significant. The assignment of statistical significance to a difference means that you can be relatively confident that the difference is due to factors other than chance. The .05 significance level is recommended as a minimum.

6. A successive level approach to test interpretation is helpful in the development of hypotheses. The six levels of the approach are as follows: (a) the Full Scale IQ, (b) Verbal and Performance IQs or factor scores, (c) intersubtest variability, (d) subtest variability within scales, (e) intrasubtest variability, and (f) qualitative analysis.

7. The Verbal Scale is dependent on the child's accumulated experience, whereas the Performance Scale is more dependent on the child's immediate problem-solving ability. Both scales involve verbal and nonverbal strategies in the solution of problems.

8. Verbal-Performance Scale differences may reflect the child's interests or cognitive style, or they may be an indication of some type of deficit. A difference in favor of the Verbal Scale IQ may indicate that verbal and auditory processing skills are better developed than performance and visual discrimination skills. A difference in favor of the Performance Scale IQ may indicate that performance and visual discrimination skills are better developed than verbal and auditory processing skills.

9. Factor scores should be compared with other factor scores and not with IQs.

10. The Freedom from Distractibility factor appears to measure attention, memory, numerical ability, encoding ability, use of rehearsal strategies, ability to shift mental operations rapidly, and self-monitoring ability.

11. Any hypotheses generated from subtest comparisons should be treated as tentative and formulated in relation to the child's *absolute* level of scaled scores.

12. A Piagetian perspective, emphasizing figurative knowing (knowledge of static states) and operative knowing (knowledge of dynamic transformations), may be useful in analyzing the Wechsler scales.

13. It is sometimes helpful to translate scaled scores into percentile ranks or test-age equivalents.

14. Qualitative analysis of WISC-R responses and patterns should be helpful in interpreting performance.

15. A child's performance on the WISC-R should never be interpreted in isolation; it should always be viewed in relation to all other sources of data.

16. The WISC-R provides an *estimate* of a child's level of intellectual functioning; it does not measure the complete domain of intellectual functioning.

17. In cases of large Verbal-Performance discrepancies, the Full Scale IQ may be more difficult to interpret than the separate Verbal and Performance Scale IQs.

KEY TERMS, CONCEPTS, AND NAMES

Profile analysis (p. 166)
Primary methods of profile analysis (p. 167)
Base rate subtest scaled-score ranges (p. 170)
Base rate Verbal-Performance differences (or probability-of-occurrence approach) (p. 170)
Successive level approach to interpreting the Wechsler scales (p. 171)
Intersubtest variability (p. 172)
Intrasubtest variability (p. 172)
Elkind's Piagetian perspective for subtest analysis (p. 179)
Figurative knowing (p. 179)
Operative knowing (p. 179)
Qualitative analysis (p. 180)

STUDY QUESTIONS

1. Discuss the intent of profile analysis, methods of profile analysis, and approaches to profile analysis on the WISC-R.

2. Describe the successive level approach to interpreting the WISC-R.

3. Discuss how to interpret differences between the WISC-R Verbal and Performance Scales and between factor scores.

4. Discuss how to interpret differences between WISC-R subtests. Cite at least seven subtest comparisons in your presentation.

5. Discuss Elkind's Piagetian analysis of Wechsler subtests.

6. Give five illustrations of qualitative analysis on the WISC-R. What precautions must be taken in a qualitative analysis?

7. What are some general considerations in interpreting the WISC-R?

9

WECHSLER PRESCHOOL AND PRIMARY SCALE OF INTELLIGENCE (WPPSI)

From the child of five to myself is but a step. But from the new-born baby to the child of five is an appalling distance.

—Tolstoy

In 1967 the Wechsler Preschool and Primary Scale of Intelligence (WPPSI) was published for use with children between the ages of 4 and 6½ years (Wechsler, 1967) (see Figure 9-1). It is separate and distinct from, although similar in form and content to, the WISC-R. The WPPSI contains 11 subtests (see Exhibit 9-1), 8 of which (Information, Vocabulary, Arithmetic, Similarities, Comprehension, Picture Completion, Mazes, and Block Design) also appear on the WISC-R and 3 of which (Sentences, Animal House, and Geometric Design) are unique to the WPPSI. The WPPSI does not contain the 4 WISC-R subtests: Digit Span, Picture Arrangement, Object Assembly, and Coding. The methods of computing IQs and evaluating scores are similar to those employed on the WISC-R. Thus, the WPPSI can be considered a downward extension of the WISC-R. (The WPPSI-R is discussed in Appendix G.)

STANDARDIZATION

The WPPSI was standardized on 1,200 children, 100 boys and 100 girls in each of six age groups, ranging by half-years from 4 to 6½ years. The 1960 U.S. census data were used to select representative children for the normative sample. Whites and nonwhites were included in the sample, based on the ratios found in the census for four geographic regions in the United States.

DEVIATION IQS, SCALED SCORES, AND TEST-AGE EQUIVALENTS

The WPPSI, like the WISC-R and the WAIS-R, employs the Deviation IQ ($M = 100$, $SD = 15$) for the Verbal, Performance, and Full Scale IQs and scaled scores ($M = 10$, $SD = 3$) for the subtests. The IQs are obtained by comparing the examinee's scores with the scores earned by a representative sample of his or her own age group. A raw score is first obtained on each subtest and then converted to a scaled score within the examinee's own age group through use of a table in the WPPSI manual. Age groups are divided into three-month intervals from 3-10-16 (years, months, days) to 6-7-15. The IQ tables in the WPPSI

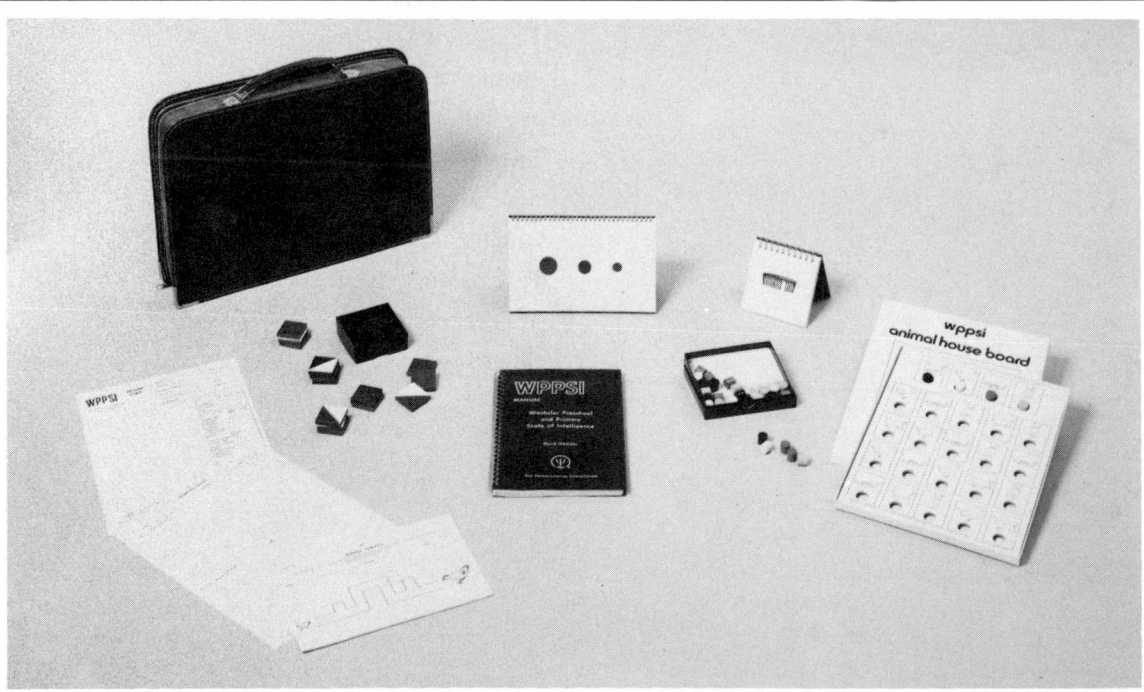

Figure 9-1.   Wechsler Preschool and Primary Scale of Intelligence. Courtesy of The Psychological Corporation.

■ **Exhibit 9-1** ■■■

WPPSI-Like Items

Information (23 questions)

Show me your eyes. Touch them.
How many legs does a cat have?
In what kind of store do we buy meat?
What is the color of an emerald?

Vocabulary (22 words)

boot   nice
book   annoy

Arithmetic (20 problems)

Card with squares of different sizes. Card is placed in front of child. Examiner says, "Here are some squares. Which one is the biggest? Point to it."

Bill had one penny and his mother gave him one more. How many pennies does he now have?

Judy had 4 books. She lost 1. How many books does she have left?

Jimmy had 7 bananas and he bought 8 more. How many bananas does he have altogether?

Similarities (16 questions)

You can read a book and you can also read a _____.
Apple pie and ice cream are both good to _____.
In what way are a quarter and a dollar alike?
In what way are a cow and a pig alike?

Comprehension (15 questions)

Why do you need to take a bath?
Why do we have farms?
What makes a sailboat move?

Sentences (10 sentences)

The task is to repeat sentences given orally by the examiner.

Mother loves me.
Ted likes to eat apples.
Martha likes to visit the museum. She will go there today.

Animal House

The task is to place appropriate colored cylinders in the corresponding holes on a board. The colored cylinders are matched with four different animals. The Animal House task is shown in the photograph of the WPPSI (see Figure 9-1).

Picture Completion (23 items)

The task is to identify the essential missing part of the picture (see Figure 9-1).

A picture of a tricycle without handlebars.
A picture of a doll without a leg.
A picture of a swing without a seat.

Mazes (10 mazes)

The task is to complete a series of mazes. An example of a maze is shown in the lower left-hand corner of the photograph in Figure 9-1.

Geometric Design (10 designs)

The task is to copy geometric designs which are shown on printed cards. The designs include a circle, square, triangle, and diamond.

Block Design (10 designs)

The task is to reproduce stimulus designs using three or four blocks (see Figure 9-1).

Note. The sample questions resemble those that appear on the WPPSI but are not actually from the test. The subtests are described in detail in this chapter.

---

manual are based on 10 of the 11 subtests. The supplementary subtest, Sentences, is excluded from the calculation of the IQ unless another Verbal Scale subtest is skipped. Also excluded from the IQ tables is Animal House Retest.

Prorating Procedure

When fewer than 10 subtests are administered, prorating is necessary. The WPPSI manual provides a table for prorating scores when four of the subtests are administered in each scale. When fewer than four subtests are adminis-

tered in each scale, IQs should be computed by using the special short-form procedure described later in this chapter. This procedure can be used whenever fewer than 10 subtests are administered.

Test-Age Equivalents

The WPPSI manual provides a table of test-age equivalents to facilitate interpretation of a child's performance. Chapters 2 and 4 discuss the assets and limitations associated with their use.

RELIABILITY

The WPPSI has excellent reliability. Internal consistency reliabilities for each of the three IQs range from .91 to .96 over the range covered by the scale. Average internal consistency reliability coefficients, across the six age groups, are as follows: .96 for the Full Scale IQ, .94 for the Verbal Scale IQ, and .93 for the Performance Scale IQ.

Subtest Reliabilities

The reliabilities for the subtests are not so satisfactory as those for the three scales (see Table 9-1). The average subtest reliabilities range from a low of .77 for Animal House to a high of .87 for Mazes. Reliabilities are similar for Verbal and Performance Scale subtests. The reliability coefficients are similar across the six age groups. They range from a low of .62 for Animal House at 4 years of age to a high of .91 for Mazes at 5½ years of age.

Standard Errors of Measurement

Based on the average of the six age groups, the standard errors of measurement (SE_m) in IQ points are 2.88 for the

Table 9-1
Average Reliability Coefficients and Standard Errors of Measurement for WPPSI Subtests and Scales

Subtest or scale	Average reliability coefficient	Average standard error of measurement
Information	.81	1.34
Vocabulary	.84	1.21
Arithmetic	.82	1.23
Similarities	.83	1.24
Comprehension	.81	1.32
Sentences	.85	1.18
Animal House	.77	1.46
Picture Completion	.83	1.20
Mazes	.87	1.08
Geometric Design	.82	1.29
Block Design	.82	1.26
Verbal IQ	.94	3.57
Performance IQ	.93	3.85
Full Scale IQ	.96	2.88

Note. Reliability coefficients for all subtests except Animal House are odd-even correlations corrected by the Spearman-Brown formula. For Animal House the reliability coefficients are test-retest coefficients.
Source: Adapted from Wechsler (1967).

Full Scale, 3.57 for the Verbal Scale, and 3.85 for the Performance Scale (see Table 9-1). Thus more confidence can be placed in the IQ based on the Full Scale than in an IQ based on either the Verbal or the Performance Scale.

The standard errors of measurement for the subtests in scaled score points, again based on the average of the six age groups, range from 1.18 to 1.34 for the Verbal Scale subtests and from 1.08 to 1.46 for the Performance Scale subtests. Within the Verbal Scale, Sentences and Vocabulary have the smallest SE_m (1.18 and 1.21, respectively). Within the Performance Scale, Mazes and Picture Completion have the smallest SE_m (1.08 and 1.20, respectively).

Reliability with Special Populations

Satisfactory split-half Full Scale reliabilities have been reported for a variety of populations, including Mexican-American children ($r = .95$) (Henderson & Rankin, 1973), gifted children ($r = .93$) (Ruschival & Way, 1971), mentally retarded children ($r = .88$) (Richards, 1970), and British children ($r = .97$) (Brittain, 1969). A test-retest study over a one-year time period revealed satisfactory reliability ($r = .89$) for the WPPSI Full Scale IQ for a group of 25 black, lower-socioeconomic-class children (Croake, Keller, & Catlin, 1973).

Test-Retest Reliability

When the test was readministered to 50 children in the standardization group after a period of approximately 11 weeks, average increases of 3.0, 6.6, and 3.6 IQ points were found in Verbal, Performance, and Full Scale scores, respectively (see Table 9-2). Respective test-retest correlations were .86, .89, and .91 for the Verbal, Performance, and Full Scales. The changes in subtest scaled scores, which probably were due for the most part to practice effects, ranged from −.2 (Sentences) to +1.3 (Mazes); changes were significant on the Information (+.7), Similarities (+.7), Animal House (+.4), Picture Completion (+.7), Mazes (+1.3), and Block Design (+1.0) subtests, but not on the others (Wasik & Wasik, 1970). Generally, the Performance Scale subtests showed greater practice effects than did the Verbal Scale subtests.

Precision Range

The precision ranges (or confidence intervals) on the WPPSI are similar throughout the age levels covered by the scale. Table C-14 in Appendix C shows the confidence intervals for the 68, 85, 90, 95, and 99 percent levels for each scale. Confidence intervals are provided for indi-

**Table 9-2
Test-Retest WPPSI IQs for 50 Children Between 5¼ and 5¾ Years of Age**

Scale	First testing		Second testing		Change
	M IQ	SD	M IQ	SD	
Verbal IQ	104.5	14.7	107.5	13.9	+3.0
Performance IQ	103.8	14.1	110.4	13.7	+6.6
Full Scale IQ	105.6	14.8	109.2	13.3	+3.6

Source: Adapted from Wechsler (1967).

vidual age levels as well as for the average of the age levels. *The child's specific age group, and not the average of the six age groups, should be used to obtain the most accurate confidence interval.* For further discussion of precision ranges and how to report them, see Chapters 2 and 23, respectively.

VALIDITY

The WPPSI manual presents minimal information about the validity of the scale. Since the publication of the WPPSI, however, a number of concurrent and predictive validity studies have been reported.

WPPSI and Stanford-Binet: Form L-M

Most of the studies correlating the WPPSI and the Stanford-Binet: Form L-M were done before the 1972 norms became available, so the 1960 Stanford-Binet norms were used. Studies using the 1960 Stanford-Binet: Form L-M norms indicated that the WPPSI had satisfactory concurrent validity (*Mdn r* = .82) (Anthony, 1973; Austin & Carpenter, 1970; Bach, 1968; Barclay & Yater, 1969; Crockett, Rardin, & Pasewark, 1975; Dokecki, Frede, & Gautney, 1969; Fagan, Broughton, Allen, Clark, & Emerson, 1969; Kaufman, 1973b; Oakland, King, White, & Eckman, 1971; Pasewark, Rardin, & Grice, 1971; Plant, 1967; Prosser & Crawford, 1971; Rellas, 1969; Richards, 1968; Ruschival & Way, 1971; Sewell, 1977; Zimmerman & Woo-Sam, 1970). The WPPSI Verbal Scale correlates more highly with the Stanford-Binet: Form L-M than does the Performance Scale (*Mdn r*'s = .81 and .67, respectively).

Before it was renormed in 1972, the Stanford-Binet: Form L-M in many cases yielded substantially higher IQs than did the WPPSI. Therefore IQs provided by the 1960

Stanford-Binet: Form L-M norms were not interchangeable with those of the WPPSI. With the 1972 norms, for children in the 4- to 6-year-old age range the Stanford-Binet: Form L-M yields IQs that are on the average about 7 to 10 IQ points lower than they were with the 1960 norms. Therefore it is likely that the two scales now yield more similar IQs. There are few published research studies comparing the 1972 Stanford-Binet: Form L-M norms with the WPPSI, however. In one study (Sewell, 1977) with 35 black children, the WPPSI yielded somewhat higher Full Scale IQs than did the Stanford-Binet: Form L-M (*M* Full Scale IQ = 96 vs. 91; *r* = .71).

WPPSI and Stanford-Binet Intelligence Scale: Fourth Edition

In a comparison of the WPPSI and the Stanford-Binet Intelligence Scale: Fourth Edition, a sample of 75 children (*M* age = 5 years, 6 months) were administered the two tests in counterbalanced order (52 percent received one order, 48 percent the other) (Thorndike et al., 1986b). On the WPPSI, the three mean IQs were 108.2 (Verbal Scale), 110.3 (Performance Scale), and 110.3 (Full Scale). On the Fourth Edition, the scores were 109.8 (Verbal Reasoning), 100.4 (Abstract/Visual Reasoning), 102.2 (Quantitative Reasoning), 104.5 (Short-Term Memory), and 105.3 (Composite). Correlations between the Fourth Edition composite score and the Verbal, Performance, and Full Scale IQs were .78, .71, and .80, respectively. The Fourth Edition thus yielded a mean composite score that was 5 points *lower* than the WPPSI Full Scale IQ. These two tests do not appear to yield interchangeable scores.

WPPSI and WISC-R: Chronological Ages in Common

As we saw in Chapter 6, the WPPSI and the WISC-R overlap for a six-month period, from 6 to 6½ years. The three studies cited in that chapter (Quereshi & McIntire, 1984; Rasbury et al., 1977; Wechsler, 1974) indicated that the meaning of differences between WPPSI and WISC-R IQs is not clear. WPPSI and WISC-R IQs may or may not be directly interchangeable, depending on the population. Further research is needed to explore the comparability of these two tests.

WPPSI and WISC-R: Predictive Validity Studies

A remarkable longitudinal study (Yule, Gold, & Busch, 1982) examined the relationship of WPPSI scores to WISC-R and achievement test scores obtained 11 years later. Eighty-five normal British children, believed to be representative of their community, were administered the WPPSI at 5½ years of age, and then the WISC-R and achievement tests at 16½ years of age. Correlations between the two intelligence tests were extremely high, ranging from .73 to .86 for the Verbal, Performance, and Full Scales; in addition, IQs on the three scales differed by fewer than 4 points (see Table 9-3). Correlations between the WPPSI and three achievement tests were also extremely high (see Table 9-4). For example, the correlation between the Full Scale IQ and Mathematics was an extremely high $r = .72$, accounting for 50 percent of the variance.

Table 9-3
Means, Standard Deviations, and Correlations Between WPPSI and WISC-R ($N = 85$)

Scale	WPPSI		WISC-R		
	M IQ	SD	M IQ	SD	r
Verbal IQ	103.26	13.91	99.44	16.06	.82
Performance IQ	107.97	14.24	104.78	15.30	.73
Full Scale IQ	106.01	14.18	102.09	15.40	.86

Source: Adapted from Yule, Gold, and Busch (1982).

Another 11-year longitudinal investigation studied a sample of 51 Welsh children with spina bifida (Tew & Laurence, 1983). The children were given the WPPSI at 5 years of age and the WISC-R at 16 years of age. Correlations were extremely high: .88 for the Verbal Scale IQ, .90 for the Performance Scale IQ, and .92 for the Full Scale IQ. Mean IQ differences were less than 6 points (for example, WPPSI *M* Full Scale IQ = 81.3, WISC-R *M* Full Scale IQ = 75.6). These results again attest to the remarkable stability of IQs obtained by children over many years.

In still another longitudinal study of the WPPSI, 139 British children were administered the WPPSI at 4½ years of age and the WISC-R at 8½ years of age (Bishop & Butterworth, 1979). Correlations between the two tests once again were extremely high ($r = .66$ for the Verbal Scale, $r = .70$ for the Performance Scale, $r = .75$ for the Full Scale). The Verbal-Performance discrepancy correlation was weaker ($r = .42$) than the correlations between IQs. The IQs on the three scales differed by 4 or fewer points and were remarkably stable over the four-year period covered in the investigation.

Table 9-4
Correlations Between WPPSI and Scores on Three Achievement Tests

WPPSI subtest or scale	Achievement tests		
	Reading	Spelling	Mathematics
Information	.39	.25	.42
Vocabulary	.62	.49	.57
Arithmetic	.56	.55	.68
Similarities	.48	.47	.52
Comprehension	.43	.22	.48
Animal House	.48	.44	.47
Picture Completion	.39	.29	.43
Mazes	.34	.36	.53
Geometric Design	.34	.44	.56
Block Design	.45	.39	.63
Verbal IQ	.61	.48	.65
Performance IQ	.53	.51	.69
Full Scale IQ	.61	.53	.72

Note. The achievement tests were the Sentence Reading Test NS6, Vernon's Graded Spelling, and Vernon's Graded Arithmetic-Mathematics Test.
Source: Reprinted, with changes in notation, with permission of the publisher and authors, from W. Yule, R. D. Gold, & C. Busch, "Long-Term Predictive Validity of the WPPSI: An 11-Year Follow-Up Study," *Personality and Individual Differences*, 1982, *3*, p. 69. Copyright 1982 by Pergamon Journals, Ltd.

WPPSI and McCarthy Scales

In a study of the WPPSI and McCarthy Scales of Children's Abilities, the WPPSI yielded Full Scale IQs that were on average 7 points *higher* than the McCarthy Scales' General Cognitive Index scores (*M*'s = 107.52 and 100.71, respectively; $r = .86$), a difference that was significant (Schmits & Beckenbaugh, 1979). The sample consisted of 21 predominantly white middle-class children between the ages of 3-10 years and 5-7 years. These results suggest that the two scales do not yield interchangeable standard scores.

WPPSI and Achievement Tests

White middle-class children. WPPSI predictive validity coefficients are satisfactory for white middle-class populations. For example, White and Jacobs (1979) reported a coefficient of .58 between the WPPSI Full Scale and the Gray Oral Reading Test, administered one to three years after the WPPSI, for a group of 28 white middle-class children. Kaufman (1973b) found correlations of .30 and .37 between the WPPSI and the Mathematics and Reading parts of the Metropolitan Achievement Tests, respectively. The achievement tests were administered approximately four months after the WPPSI to a group of 31 white middle-class 6-year-olds. Pasewark, Scherr, and Sawyer (1974) reported a significant correlation between the WPPSI and the Metropolitan Achievement Tests total score ($r = .58$) for a sample of 30 normal 6-year-olds. Reynolds, Wright, and Dappen (1981) reported significant correlations between the WPPSI Full Scale and the Wide Range Achievement Test Reading ($r = .36$), Spelling ($r = .36$), and Arithmetic ($r = .60$) in a sample of 60 6-year-olds (mostly white and middle class) who had been referred for psychological evaluation.

Krebs (1969) investigated the effectiveness of the WPPSI in predicting reading scores. The WPPSI was administered to 70 kindergarten-age children (34 boys and 36 girls), equally divided between lower and upper socioeconomic status groups. One year later, when the children were in first grade, the reading section of the Stanford Achievement Test and the Gilmore Oral Reading Paragraphs Test were administered. As Table 9-5 shows, all of the WPPSI subtest and scale scores were significantly related to reading scores on both tests. When the data were reanalyzed based on socioeconomic class, the WPPSI scores were found to have higher correlations with reading scores of the lower socioeconomic status group than with those of the upper socioeconomic status group. For example, in the lower socioeconomic status group, the correlations between the total reading score on the Stanford Achievement Test and the Verbal, Performance, and Full Scales were .59, .61, and .66, respectively, whereas in the upper socioeconomic status group, the correlations were .32, .35, and .40, respectively. In the total sample, Arithmetic and Geometric Design were the two subtests that best predicted reading achievement on the Stanford Achievement Test ($R = .63$).

The WPPSI, however, was not found to discriminate between good and poor readers in a sample of children initially tested with the WPPSI at 5 years of age and given a reading test 3 years later (Badian, 1984). The children tested were from the lower middle to the middle class in a predominantly white area and were at risk for learning disabilities when initially tested.

Ethnic minority children and low SES children. With ethnic minority children and children of lower socioeconomic status, the predictive validity of the WPPSI is

Table 9-5
Correlations Between WPPSI and Scores on Two Reading Tests

WPPSI subtest or scale	Gilmore Oral Reading Paragraphs Test	Stanford Achievement Test: Reading
Information	.49	.52
Vocabulary	.52	.53
Arithmetic	.54	.58
Similarities	.48	.53
Comprehension	.36	.38
Sentences	.54	.55
Animal House	.41	.46
Picture Completion	.43	.47
Mazes	.42	.47
Geometric Design	.52	.54
Block Design	.44	.49
Verbal IQ	.57	.61
Performance IQ	.58	.63
Full Scale IQ	.62	.68

Note. All correlation coefficients are significant.
Source: Reprinted by permission of the author from E. G. Krebs, "The Wechsler Preschool and Primary Scale of Intelligence and Prediction of Reading Achievement in First Grade" (Doctoral dissertation, Rutgers State University). Ann Arbor, Mich.: University Microfilms, 1969, pp. 73a–73b, No. 70-3361. Copyright 1970, E. G. Krebs.

more variable than it is with white middle-class children. In one study (Crockett, Rardin, & Pasewark, 1976), a sample of Head Start children were administered the Metropolitan Achievement Tests three to four years after administration of the WPPSI. The only significant correlations were between Mathematics and the Full Scale IQ ($r = .43$) and between Mathematics and the Performance Scale IQ ($r = .52$). The investigators indicated that WPPSI Verbal Scale scores must be viewed with caution in the evaluation of Head Start children because many of these children are of lower socioeconomic status, bilingual, and evidence atypical development of language skills during primary school years. In another study with a group of 50 black, 32 white, 4 Hispanic, and 1 Oriental child, all of whom were of lower socioeconomic status and had been referred to a special setting because of personal and social difficulties, the WPPSI Full Scale IQ was significantly correlated with speech development ($r = .61$), motor development ($r = .41$), and perceived improvement in a specialized program ($r = .73$) (Dlugokinski, Weiss, & Johnston, 1976).

Based on their work with Mexican-American 5½-year-old children from economically depressed areas, Henderson and Rankin (1973) suggested that it is ill advised to use the WPPSI routinely in making decisions as to whether to place these children in special classes. They found that there was an 18-point difference between the children's Verbal and Performance Scale IQs (74 vs. 92), and that the predictive validity of the WPPSI, using third-grade Metropolitan Reading Tests scores, was poor ($r = .27$). The WPPSI, therefore, appears to have dubious utility as a predictor of later school performance for this group of children. Unfortunately, there is no way of knowing which of the scales is the more valid predictor of future academic performance, because separate correlations for the Verbal and Performance scales were not reported.

WPPSI and Other Tests

In 11 studies, correlations between the WPPSI and tests other than those previously covered (English Picture Vocabulary Test, Frostig Developmental Test of Visual Perception, Goodenough-Harris Drawing Test, Hiskey-Nebraska Test of Learning Aptitude, Illinois Test of Psycholinguistic Abilities, Metropolitan Readiness Tests, Peabody Picture Vocabulary Test, Pictorial Test of Intelligence, Primary Mental Abilities Test, Progressive Matrices, Stanford Achievement Test, Torrance Tests of Creative Thinking, Vane Kindergarten Test) have ranged from a low of .28 (Metropolitan Readiness Tests) to a high of .82 (Primary Mental Abilities Test) ($Mdn\ r = .64$) (Austin & Carpenter, 1970; Bach, 1968; Dokecki et al., 1969; Kaplan, 1985; Krebs, 1969; McNamara, Porterfield, & Miller, 1969; Plant, 1967; Plant & Southern, 1968; Tsushima & Stoddard, 1986; Yater, Barclay, & Leskosky, 1971; Yule, Berger, Butler, Newham, & Tizard, 1969). In nine of these investigations, lower-class, ethnic minority group, or Head Start children were studied; therefore, it is difficult to know whether the findings are generalizable to other groups of children. WPPSI scores also have been found to be related significantly both to perceptual development and to creativity (Lichtman, 1969; Yule et al., 1969).

Comment on Concurrent and Predictive Validity of the WPPSI

The studies reviewed in this section attest to the concurrent and predictive validity of the WPPSI with most populations. Further work is needed to determine its validity with Mexican American and other ethnic minority children.

The predictive validity of the WPPSI may be related to the specific scale (Verbal, Performance, or Full Scale) and the length of time between administration of the WPPSI and that of the criterion measure. Overall, recent research suggests that the WPPSI administered at kindergarten age may serve as an excellent long-term predictor of intelligence and school performance measured during late adolescence.

INTERCORRELATIONS BETWEEN SUBTESTS AND SCALES

Intercorrelations between subtests and scales permit us to observe the degree of relationship between various parts of the WPPSI. Average intercorrelations between the 11 subtests range from a low of .28 to a high of .60 ($Mdn = .42$). The six *highest* subtest average intercorrelations are between Information and Vocabulary (.60), Information and Comprehension (.60), Information and Arithmetic (.58), Vocabulary and Comprehension (.57), Similarities and Comprehension (.55), and Sentences and Comprehension (.53). The six *lowest* subtest average intercorrelations are between Similarities and Mazes (.28), Similarities and Geometric Design (.30), Sentences and Mazes (.30), Similarities and Animal House (.31), Comprehension and Mazes (.33), and—tied at .34—Animal House and Comprehension and Sentences and Geometric Design.

Average correlations between the Verbal Scale subtests and the Verbal Scale range from .62 to .73 ($Mdn = .65$), whereas those between the Performance Scale subtests and the Performance Scale range from .50 to .60 ($Mdn = .57$). Intercorrelations between the individual subtests and the Full Scale show similar trends. Vocabulary has the highest correlation of any of the subtests with the Full Scale (.70), followed by Arithmetic (.68), and Comprehension (.65). Animal House (.53) and Mazes (.54) have the lowest correlations with the Full Scale. Within their respective scales, Vocabulary (.73) and Geometric Design (.60) have the highest correlations with the Verbal and Performance IQs.

WPPSI IQS AND STRATIFICATION VARIABLES

Geographic and Socioeconomic Differences

A study of the relationship of WPPSI IQs to socioeconomic status (SES) (as determined by father's occupation), urban vs. rural residence, and geographic region of children in the standardization group revealed some important trends (Kaufman, 1973c). With respect to SES, the largest difference, about 18 points, was found between children of unskilled laborers and those of professional men. Differences among SES levels 2, 3, and 4 were not significant (see Table 9-6). Urban-rural residence was not a significant factor, but geographic region was. Children from the West had significantly higher IQs than did children in the other three regions; IQs of children in the other three regions did not differ significantly. There is no readily available explanation to account for the regional difference. SES differences found on the WPPSI corroborate those found on the WISC-R (Kaufman & Doppelt, 1976), WISC (Seashore, Wesman, & Doppelt, 1950), and Stanford-Binet Intelligence Scale: Forms L and M (McNemar, 1942), Stanford-Binet Intelligence Scale: Fourth Edition (Thorndike et al., 1986b), and WAIS-R (Chastain & Reynolds, 1984).

Gender Differences

Gender differences have been found on some WPPSI subtests. In the standardization sample, boys obtained significantly higher scores than did girls on the Mazes subtest, but girls obtained higher scores than did boys on the Animal House, Geometric Design, Block Design, and Sentences subtests (Herman, 1968). Thus, Performance IQs may be achieved in different ways by boys and girls. In a sample of 5½-year-old British children, boys obtained higher WPPSI IQs than did girls (M IQs of 104 vs. 98) (Brittain, 1969). Significant sex differences in IQ were not found by Ruschival and Way (1971) in an American sample, however. Generally, for purposes of individual assessment, sex differences on the WPPSI do not appear to play an important role.

Ethnic Differences

Kaufman (1973a) compared the scores of 132 matched pairs of black children and white children in the WPPSI standardization group. The children were matched on age, sex, geographic region, father's occupation, and urban-rural residence. The white children obtained significantly higher Verbal IQs (99 vs. 88), Performance IQs (97 vs. 88), and Full Scale IQs (98 vs. 87) at all of the age levels studied; differences averaged about 11 IQ points.

On the Verbal Scale, significant differences between the two ethnic groups were found at each age level. On the Performance Scale, however, differences between the two ethnic groups were significant at the 4-year-old level, but not at the 5- and 6-year-old levels. The differences decreased with age, almost in a linear fashion: 16 points at 4

Table 9-6
Means and Standard Deviations of WPPSI IQs for SES, Residence, and Region

Demographic variable	N	Verbal IQ		Performance IQ		Full Scale IQ	
		M	SD	M	SD	M	SD
SES (Father's occupation)							
1. Professional & Technical	78	110	13	108	12	110	12
2. Manager, Clerical, & Sales	78	102	13	102	13	102	12
3. Skilled	78	100	15	100	14	100	15
4. Semiskilled	78	98	14	99	15	99	14
5. Unskilled	78	93	14	93	16	92	15
Residence							
Urban	325	99	14	98	15	98	15
Rural	325	99	14	99	14	99	14
Region							
Northeast	178	101	14	102	14	102	14
North Central	178	101	15	100	15	102	16
South	178	98	15	98	16	98	15
West	178	105	13	104	13	105	13

Source: Reprinted, with a change in notation, by permission of the publisher and author from A. S. Kaufman, "The Relationship of WPPSI IQs to SES and Other Background Variables," *Journal of Clinical Psychology, 29*, p. 356. Copyright 1973, Clinical Psychology Publishing Co., Inc.

years, 11 points at 4½ years, 8 points at 5 years, 7 points at 5½ years and 6 years, and 5 points at 6½ years. This trend suggests that the deficit was not cumulative. It is not easy to explain why the older black children performed at a level so much higher than that of their younger peers.

FACTOR ANALYSIS

A factor analysis of the WPPSI, using the standardization sample, yielded two principal factors: Verbal and Performance (Carlson & Reynolds, 1981). The factor loadings associated with the two factors are shown in Table 9-7. The Verbal factor is best represented by the six Verbal Scale subtests (Information, Vocabulary, Comprehension, Arithmetic, Similarities, and Sentences), whereas the Performance factor is best represented by the five Performance Scale subtests (Block Design, Mazes, Geometric Design, Picture Completion, and Animal House). Although the factor loadings vary across age levels, the general trends noted can be applied to the various age levels covered by the scale. The results support the division of the WPPSI into Verbal and Performance Scales, provide construct validity for the test, and suggest that, for children between the ages of 4 and 6, the WPPSI may be a more sensitive instrument for the purpose of assessing the

structure of intelligence than is the Stanford-Binet: Form L-M, which provides only a global index of intelligence.

WPPSI Subtests as Measures of g

A hierarchical factor analysis, using the WPPSI standardization sample, indicated that all 11 WPPSI subtests have strong loadings on the general intelligence factor (g) (Wallbrown, Blaha, & Wherry, 1973) (see Table 9-8). The loadings are relatively similar across the age levels of the test, suggesting that differentiation of abilities is not apparent during the ages covered by the scale. Although the Verbal subtests tend to have the highest g loadings, the range of median loadings for the 11 subtests is relatively narrow (.55 to .72). The g factor accounts for the largest percentage of subtest variance (39 percent).

WPPSI Subtest Specificity

With the exception of Information and Comprehension, WPPSI subtests have enough specificity to warrant specific clinical interpretation across the age range covered by the scale (Carlson & Reynolds, 1981). Thus most subtests allow for individual interpretation of a child's strengths and weaknesses.

Table 9-7
Factor Loadings of WPPSI Subtests for Six Age Groups (Varimax Rotation)

Subtest	Factor A – Verbal							Factor B – Performance						
	4[a]	4½	5	5½	6	6½	Mdn	4[a]	4½	5	5½	6	6½	Mdn
Information	71	74	66	74	69	74	72	32	29	37	40	34	31	33
Vocabulary	63	70	63	68	70	62	65	31	18	31	31	32	35	31
Arithmetic	50	56	54	61	54	55	54	45	42	51	51	46	54	48
Similarities	75	69	57	66	61	72	67	17	26	13	17	31	23	21
Comprehension	71	77	73	71	75	71	72	29	17	28	31	25	22	27
Sentences	66	66	53	61	55	65	63	27	28	29	30	39	21	28
Animal House	46	40	25	32	25	25	28	29	43	60	56	63	42	49
Picture Completion	43	49	37	37	42	31	40	51	42	50	53	54	49	50
Mazes	15	07	29	30	42	10	22	77	65	57	61	58	65	63
Geometric Design	27	27	24	17	25	20	24	62	57	73	80	75	62	67
Block Design	32	29	22	35	45	34	33	50	56	72	68	55	61	58

Note. Decimals omitted.
[a] This row indicates age level.
Source: Reprinted, with changes in notation, with permission from the publisher and authors, from L. Carlson & C. R. Reynolds, "Factor Structure and Specific Variance of the WPPSI Subtests at Six Age Levels," *Psychology in the Schools*, 1981, *18*, p. 51.

Table 9-8
WPPSI Subtests as Measures of _g_

Subtest	Median loading	Proportion of variance attributed to _g_
Information	.72	52
Vocabulary	.64	41
Arithmetic	.68	46
Similarities	.63	40
Comprehension	.68	46
Sentences	.64	41
Animal House	.55	30
Picture Completion	.60	36
Mazes	.57	32
Geometric Design	.64	41
Block Design	.62	38

Note. The square of the median coefficient provides the proportion of each subtest's variance that may be attributed to _g_.
Source: Adapted from Wallbrown, Blaha, and Wherry (1973).

Factor Analysis of WPPSI Compared to WISC-R

The factor structure of the WPPSI is generally similar to that of the WISC-R, particularly in regard to the Verbal Comprehension and Perceptual Organization factors. The primary difference between WPPSI and WISC-R factor analytic findings is that a Freedom from Distractibility factor emerges on the WISC-R but not on the WPPSI. Conceivably, sustained directed attention, partly measured by the Freedom from Distractibility factor, is a part of every subtest at younger age levels and emerges as a separate factor only at older age levels. Alternatively, it may be that the Freedom from Distractibility factor does not emerge on the WPPSI because the test does not include either Digit Span or Coding; it is these two subtests, along with Arithmetic, that have generally defined Freedom from Distractibility on the WISC-R.

WPPSI Factor Structure for Black Children and White Children

For the black children and white children in the WPPSI standardization sample, the same two factors, Verbal and Performance, were found in each group (Kaufman & Hollenbeck, 1974). Various statistical procedures used to test the similarity of factor loadings also indicated that the WPPSI has virtually the same factor structure for black

children as it does for white children. These results suggest that WPPSI is a fair instrument in the sense that it measures the same dimensions of intellect in both ethnic groups.

Factor Structure for Two White Subcultural Groups

A study (Heil, Barclay, & Endres, 1978) of the WPPSI factor structure of two groups of white preschool children, one labeled "educationally deprived" (educationally handicapped as a result of poverty, neglect, delinquency, or cultural or linguistic isolation from the community at large) and the other normal, found essentially the same three factors in both groups: a Verbal factor, a Performance factor, and a factor limited to the Picture Completion subtest. These results, which generally support those found for samples of black and white children, indicate that sociocultural differences do not produce different intellectual structures on the WPPSI.

Other studies also support the Verbal and Performance dichotomies on the WPPSI (Haynes & Atkinson, 1984; Ramanaiah & Adams, 1979; Silverstein, 1986a).

ADMINISTERING THE WPPSI

The general administrative suggestions described for the WISC-R in Chapter 6 are also appropriate for the WPPSI. The two scales have common problems in administration and scoring. Some subtest names are the same in both scales, so be careful not to substitute WISC-R directions for WPPSI directions or vice versa. The suggestions shown in Exhibit 9-2, which supplement those given in other parts of this chapter, should aid you in learning to administer the WPPSI. Figure 9-2 shows the cover of the WPPSI record booklet.

Physical Abilities Necessary for the WPPSI

The physical abilities children need in order to take the WPPSI are, for the most part, the same as those required for the WISC-R (see Table 6-11 in Chapter 6). Adequate visual-motor skills, in particular, are needed to handle the Performance Scale materials. Alternative ways of administering the WPPSI items are restricted by the fact that young children have limited writing and reading skills. Children who cannot speak usually will not be able to write their answers, and those who cannot hear usually will not be able to read the questions. The specific suggestions for

Exhibit 9-2

Administering the WPPSI

1. Complete the top of the record booklet.
2. Using date of testing and date of birth, calculate the chronological age (CA) and put it in the box provided. On the WPPSI CA must be stated in years, months, and days.
3. Administer the subtests in the order presented in the manual, except in rare circumstances. Do not change the wording on any subtest. Read the directions exactly as shown in the manual. Do not ad lib.
4. Start with the appropriate item on each subtest and follow discontinuance criteria. You must know correct scoring criteria before you give the test.
5. Write out all responses completely and legibly. Do not use unusual abbreviations. Record time accurately.
6. Question all ambiguous or unscorable responses, writing a (Q) after each questioned response.
7. Be patient when working with children in the WPPSI age group. Several breaks may be needed during the testing.
8. On Comprehension, if a child only gives one reason to Questions 7, 8, 9, 10, 14, and 15, request a second reason. These questions are marked with an asterisk (*) in the manual.
9. Carefully score each protocol, recheck the scoring, and transfer subtest scores to the front of the record booklet under Raw Score. If you have failed to question a response when you should have and the response is obviously not a 0 response, give the child the most appropriate score.
10. If a subtest was spoiled, write *spoiled* by the subtest total score and on the front cover where the raw and scaled scores appear. If for some reason a subtest was not administered, write *NA* in the margin in the record booklet and on the front cover.
11. Raw scores are transformed into scaled scores through use of Table 21 on page 90 of the WPPSI manual. Be sure to use the page of the table that is appropriate for the child's age and the correct row and column for each transformation.
12. The Verbal Score is based on the total of the scaled scores on the five standard Verbal Scale subtests. The Perfor-

mance Score is based on the total of the scaled scores on the five Performance Scale subtests. Do not use Sentences to compute the Verbal Score unless you substitute it for another Verbal subtest. Add the Verbal Score and the Performance Score together to get the Full Scale Score.
13. If it should be necessary to prorate either the Verbal or the Performance section, follow the explicit directions given on page 43 of the WPPSI manual. You will also need to use Table 24 on page 106 of the manual.
14. The IQs are obtained from Table 22 of the WPPSI manual. Be sure to use the correct section of the table for each of the three IQs. There is a Verbal section and a Performance section on page 101, and a Full Scale section on page 102. Record the IQs. Next, recheck all of your work. If the IQ(s) was (were) prorated, write *PRO* beside the appropriate IQ(s).
15. Look up the confidence intervals for the Full Scale IQ, Verbal Scale IQ, and Performance Scale IQ in Table C-14 in Appendix C.
16. Look up the percentile rank and classification for each of the IQs in Tables BC-1 and BC-2 on the inside back cover of this text.
17. If desired, use the material on pages 104 and 105 (Table 23) of the WPPSI manual to obtain Test-Age Equivalents. They can be placed (in parentheses) in the right-hand margin of the cover page of the record booklet next to the scaled score. For Test-Age Equivalents above those in the table, use the highest Test-Age Equivalents and a plus sign. For Test-Age Equivalents below those in the table, use the lowest Test-Age Equivalent and a minus sign.
18. In summary, be sure to read directions verbatim, pronounce words clearly, query at the appropriate times, start with the appropriate item, discontinue at the proper place, place items properly before the child, use correct timing, and follow the specific guidelines in the manual for administering the test.

Source: Courtesy of M. L. Lewis

administering the WISC-R to handicapped children are also useful for the WPPSI, however; you should review the material in Chapter 6 carefully before administering the WPPSI to physically handicapped children.

Testing-of-Limits on the WPPSI

The general testing-of-limits suggestions presented in Chapter 5 are also useful with the WPPSI.

WPPSI

RECORD FORM

Wechsler Preschool and Primary
Scale of Intelligence

NAME_____AGE_____SEX_____

ADDRESS_____

PARENT'S NAME_____

SCHOOL_____GRADE_____

PLACE OF TESTING_____TESTED BY_____

REFERRED BY_____

NOTES

	Year	Month	Day
Date Tested	_____	_____	_____
Date of Birth	_____	_____	_____
Age	_____	_____	_____

	Raw Score	Scaled Score
VERBAL TESTS		
Information	_____	_____
Vocabulary	_____	_____
Arithmetic	_____	_____
Similarities	_____	_____
Comprehension	_____	_____
(Sentences)	_____	_____
Verbal Score		_____
PERFORMANCE TESTS		
Animal House	_____	_____
Picture Completion	_____	_____
Mazes	_____	_____
Geometric Design	_____	_____
Block Design	_____	_____
(Animal House Retest)	_____	_____
Performance Score		_____

	Scaled Score	IQ
Verbal Score	_____*	_____
Performance Score	_____*	_____
Full Scale Score	_____	_____
*Prorated if necessary		

Figure 9-2. Cover page of WPPSI record booklet. Copyright 1949, renewed 1976; © 1963, 1967 by The Psychological Corporation, San Antonio, TX. All Rights Reserved.

Extrapolated IQs

Extrapolated IQs are provided in Table C-17 in Appendix C for scaled scores that are either below or above those shown in the WPPSI manual. Extrapolated IQs, however, must be used cautiously, as noted in Chapter 6.

WPPSI Short Forms

Short forms of the WPPSI have the same disadvantages as those of the WISC-R (see Chapter 6) and should never be used for classification or selection purposes. A short form may be useful for screening or research studies, however. The information in Table C-21 in Appendix C can aid you in the selection of a short form. This table, based on the standardization data, shows the best WPPSI short forms for combinations of two, three, four, and five subtests. Because the short forms of a given length are, for all practical purposes, mutually interchangeable, you can use clinical or other considerations to select the short form.

Obtaining a Deviation Quotient from the short form. After the short form has been selected, follow the procedures outlined in Chapter 6 for converting WISC-R composite scores to Deviation Quotients (see Exhibit 6-3). Table C-36 in Appendix C can be used to obtain the appropriate a and b constants. The only difference between the procedure for the WISC-R and the one for the WPPSI is that for the WPPSI the correlation table of the group that is closest in age to the examinee should be used to obtain Σr_{jk} (that is, one of the tables on pages 26 through 31 of the WPPSI manual).

A variety of WPPSI short forms. Dokecki et al. (1969) found that the four subtests that comprised the best short form for middle-class children were Information, Comprehension, Arithmetic, and Geometric Design ($r = .94$ with the Full Scale). The best two-subtest short form for predicting reading achievement in a group of lower-class children consisted of Information and Geometric Design (Plant & Southern, 1968).

Kaufman's short form. Kaufman (1972a) proposed a four-subtest short form composed of the Arithmetic, Comprehension, Picture Completion, and Block Design subtests. This short form was highly related ($r = .96$) to the Full Scale in a sample of 116 outpatient children, with mean IQs showing a difference of less than 3 points (Full Scale IQ = 112.11, four-subtest short form IQ = 109.76) (Haynes & Atkinson, 1983). There was only a 61 percent agreement in IQ classifications between the short form and the Full Scale, however.

Yudin's WPPSI short form. Yudin's (1966) short-form method for the WISC-R, in which the number of items within the subtests is reduced, has been applied to the WPPSI by Silverstein (1968a). Table C-22 in Appendix C shows the specific procedures. Silverstein suggested that Sentences be excluded from the short form because the subtest was omitted in establishing the IQ tables. The following reliabilities were reported for Yudin's short form: .91 for the Verbal Scale, .91 for the Performance Scale, and .94 for the Full Scale.

WPPSI Vocabulary plus Block Design short form. The Vocabulary plus Block Design combination is useful as a two-subtest screening short form. When this combination is used, Table C-37 in Appendix C can be used to convert the sum of scaled scores on the two subtests directly to an estimate of the Full Scale IQ. Correlations of .82 and .89 have been reported between the Vocabulary plus Block Design short form and the Full Scale IQ (Silverstein, 1970b, and Haynes & Atkinson, 1983, respectively). Studies (Haynes & Atkinson, 1983; King & Smith, 1972) also report that the Vocabulary plus Block Design short form agreed with the IQ classifications obtained from the Full Scale in only about 33 to 35 percent of the cases. *These results reinforce my recommendation that short forms never be used for classification or selection purposes.*

WPPSI SUBTESTS

This section describes the 11 WPPSI subtests. The factor analytic findings are from Carlson and Reynolds (1981) and from Wallbrown et al. (1973).

Information

The Information subtest contains 23 questions, 12 of which, with minor changes in wording, come from the WISC. Most questions require the child to give a simply stated fact or facts. All items are scored 1 or 0 (pass-fail), and the subtest is discontinued after five consecutive failures.

Rationale. The rationale presented for the WISC-R Information subtest appears to apply to the WPPSI Information subtest (see Chapter 7). The WPPSI questions, however, appear to assess that part of the child's knowledge of the environment that is gained from experiences rather than from education, especially formal education.

Factor analytic findings. The Information subtest is the best measure of g in the scale (52 percent of its variance may be attributed to g). The subtest contributes substantially to the Verbal factor (Mdn loading = .72).

Reliability and correlational highlights. Information is a reliable subtest (r_{xx} = .81); it correlates more highly with Vocabulary and Comprehension (r's = .60) than with any of the other subtests. It correlates moderately with the Full Scale (r = .70) and Verbal Scale (r = .73) and to a lesser degree with the Performance Scale (r = .56).

Administrative considerations. The administrative considerations presented for the WISC-R Information subtest are also relevant for the WPPSI Information subtest. In addition, some WPPSI items require special scoring considerations. For example, the answers to question 4 ("What comes in a bottle?") do not mention things that come in plastic bottles. Because the term "etc." appears in the scoring criteria appendix of the manual, however, it seems logical to assume that credit should be given for references to substances that come in plastic bottles, such as shampoo and liquid soap. Likewise, the scoring criteria referring to question 9 ("What shines in the sky at night?") do not include "planet," yet a planet shines in the sky at night. It is recommended that credit be given for "planet," "comet," and other astronomical terms.

Question: What do you call a baby goat?
Answer: Matilda would be a nice name.

Vocabulary

The Vocabulary subtest contains 22 words, 14 of which are from the WISC. The child is asked to explain orally the meaning of each word. Each word is scored 2, 1, or 0, and the subtest is discontinued after five consecutive failures.

Rationale. The rationale presented for the WISC-R Vocabulary subtest generally applies to the WPPSI Vocabulary subtest (see Chapter 7). Formal education, however, is less likely to be an influence in vocabulary development for preschool children than for older children. Experiences are likely to be the major contributing factor to vocabulary development of preschool children.

Factor analytic findings. The Vocabulary subtest is a moderately good measure of g (41 percent of its variance may be attributed to g). The subtest contributes substantially to the Verbal factor (Mdn loading = .65).

Reliability and correlational highlights. Vocabulary is a reliable subtest (r_{xx} = .84). It correlates more highly with Information (r = .60) than with any other subtest. It correlates moderately with the Full Scale (r = .65) and Verbal Scale (r = .66) and to a lesser degree with the Performance Scale (r = .51).

Administrative considerations. All examinees start the subtest with the first word. This procedure differs from the one used for the WISC-R, where the starting word depends on the child's age. The general administrative guidelines presented for the WISC-R Vocabulary subtest should be followed for the WPPSI Vocabulary subtest. Scoring requires considerable judgment, and the WPPSI manual provides too few sample responses. Because many of the Vocabulary words have near homonyms (words 1, 13, 14, 15, 16, 17, and 22), you must carefully articulate each word.

Arithmetic

The Arithmetic subtest consists of 20 problems, six of which are from the WISC. For the first 4 items, the child points to the correct answer on a card; for the next 4 items, blocks are used; and for the last 12 items, oral answers are required. The subtest is started at different points, depending on the child's age and possible level of intellectual functioning. Children under 6 years of age (and older children who may be mentally retarded) start with item 1; children 6 years of age and older begin with item 7. The first 8 problems have no time limit, but the last 12 problems have a 30-second time limit. Each item is scored 1 or 0, and the subtest is discontinued after four consecutive failures.

The problems on the Arithmetic subtest reflect various skills. Problems 1 through 4 entail perceptual judgments involving the concepts of biggest, longest, most, and same. Problems 5 through 8 require direct counting of concrete quantities. Problems 9 through 20 involve simple addition or subtraction, although simple division or multiplication also can be used.

Rationale. The rationale described for the WISC-R Arithmetic subtest appears to apply generally to the WPPSI Arithmetic subtest (see Chapter 7). The skills required for the WPPSI Arithmetic subtest, however, are likely to be less dependent on formal education than are those required for the WISC-R Arithmetic subtest. The first four WPPSI questions, which require the child to make comparisons and perceptual discriminations, appear to measure nonverbal reasoning ability; these four problems measure quantitative concepts without involving the explicit use of numbers.

Factor analytic findings.　The Arithmetic subtest is a moderately good measure of g (46 percent of its variance may be attributed to g). The subtest has a high loading on the Verbal factor (*Mdn* loading = .54) and a moderate loading on the Performance factor (*Mdn* loading = .48). Its loading on the Performance factor may be accounted for by the fact that some items employ pictures of sets of objects that must be visually analyzed before verbal comparisons are made.

Reliability and correlational highlights.　Arithmetic is a reliable subtest ($r_{xx} = .82$). It correlates more highly with Information ($r = .58$) than with any other subtest. It correlates moderately with the Full Scale ($r = .68$), Verbal Scale ($r = .62$), and Performance Scale ($r = .60$).

Administrative considerations.　The administrative considerations discussed for the WISC-R Arithmetic subtest generally apply to the WPPSI Arithmetic subtest. Scoring, as in the WISC-R, is for the most part easy — 1 or 0 points. The time taken by the child to solve each problem should be recorded. On problems 9 through 20, correct answers given after the time limit has expired should also be noted.

Similarities

The WPPSI Similarities subtest consists of 16 questions, 7 of which are found in the WISC. The first 10 questions require simple analogies; the remaining questions are similar to those found in the WISC-R Similarities subtest. Items 1 through 10 are scored 1 or 0 (pass-fail), and items 11 through 16 are scored 2, 1, or 0, depending on the conceptual level of the response. The subtest is discontinued after four consecutive failures.

Rationale.　The rationale described for the WISC-R Similarities subtest generally applies to the WPPSI Similarities subtest (see Chapter 7). Because over half of the WPPSI questions (1 to 10) require analogies, however, the subtest may be measuring logical thinking rather than verbal concept formation, especially at the earlier levels (i.e., below 5 years of age).

Factor analytic findings.　The Similarities subtest is a moderately good measure of g (40 percent of its variance may be attributed to g). The subtest contributes substantially to the Verbal factor (*Mdn* loading = .67).

Reliability and correlational highlights.　Similarities is a reliable subtest ($r_{xx} = .83$). It correlates more highly with Comprehension ($r = .55$) than with any other subtest. Correlation is relatively low with the Full Scale ($r = .58$), moderate with the Verbal Scale ($r = .62$), and low with the Performance Scale ($r = .44$).

Administrative considerations.　The administrative considerations discussed for the WISC-R Similarities subtest generally apply to the WPPSI Similarities subtest. Scoring procedures, however, differ. Because responses to the first 10 questions are scored 1 or 0, few scoring problems should be encountered with these questions. As in the WISC-R, however, the questions dealing with similarities (items 11 through 16) are difficult to score. Scoring guidelines should be studied carefully.

Comprehension

The Comprehension subtest contains 15 questions, 6 of which, with minor changes in wording, are from the WISC. Several content areas are covered, including health and hygiene, knowledge of the environment, and knowledge of activities in society. Items are scored 2, 1, or 0. The subtest is discontinued after four consecutive failures.

Rationale.　The rationale presented for the WISC-R Comprehension subtest appears to apply generally to the WPPSI Comprehension subtest (see Chapter 7). Linguistic skill and logical reasoning, however, may play a more important role on the WPPSI Comprehension subtest than on the WISC-R Comprehension subtest.

Factor analytic findings.　The Comprehension subtest is a moderately good measure of g (46 percent of its variance may be attributed to g). The subtest contributes substantially to the Verbal factor (*Mdn* loading = .72).

Reliability and correlational highlights.　Comprehension is a reliable subtest ($r_{xx} = .81$). It correlates more highly with Sentences ($r = .53$) than with any other subtest. It correlates moderately with the Full Scale ($r = .65$) and the Verbal Scale ($r = .69$) and to a lesser degree with the Performance Scale ($r = .44$).

Administrative considerations.　The administrative considerations discussed for the WISC-R Comprehension subtest generally apply to the WPPSI Comprehension subtest. Because Comprehension responses are occasionally difficult to score, judgment is needed to arrive at appropriate scores. As in all decisions on the scoring of WPPSI and

WISC-R responses, the content of the response, not the quality of the verbalization, should be considered.

Sentences

The Sentences subtest, which is a supplementary subtest, contains 13 sentences of increasing length, ranging from 2 to 18 words. The child is required to repeat each sentence verbatim, after listening to the examiner say it. The subtest is discontinued after three consecutive failures. When it is administered as a sixth Verbal Scale subtest, the subtest is not used in calculating the IQ. Items are scored 1, 2, 3, or 4 points, depending on the length of the sentence and the number of errors made. Errors in reproducing the sentences include omissions, transpositions, additions, and substitutions of words.

Rationale. The Sentences subtest is a memory test, measuring immediate recall and attention. Because success may depend on verbal facility, failure may not necessarily reflect poor memory ability. For children 5 years of age and older, scores may be related primarily to memory ability, but for children younger than 5 years of age, scores may reflect verbal knowledge and comprehension, rather than immediate recall ability per se.

Factor analytic findings. The Sentences subtest is a moderately good measure of g (41 percent of its variance may be attributed to g). The subtest contributes substantially to the Verbal factor (*Mdn* loading = .63).

Reliability and correlational highlights. Sentences is a reliable subtest (r_{xx} = .85). It correlates more highly with Comprehension (r = .53) than with any other subtest. It correlates moderately with the Full Scale (r = .61) and the Verbal Scale (r = .64) and to a lesser degree with the Performance Scale (r = .47).

Administrative considerations. Scoring the child's responses on the Sentences subtest is complicated because of the variety of errors that can occur. Responses must be analyzed carefully in order to determine the type of error that has been made. In addition to recording the number of errors, evaluate the quality of the child's responses. For example, were any idiosyncratic or peculiar words added? Did errors occur toward the beginning, middle, or end of sentences? Were sentences completely missed or were only a few errors made in each sentence? The child who misses a few words may be revealing minor temporary inefficiencies, whereas the one who cannot recall any

words in the sentences may have more serious memory problems.

Animal House and Animal House Retest

The Animal House subtest, a replacement for the WISC Coding subtest, requires the child to place a cylinder of the appropriate color in a hole on a board. The subtest's name is derived from the fact that four animals are depicted in various colored cylinders, or "houses." For example, the dog has a black house and the chicken has a white house. Animal House is a liberally timed subtest (maximum time of 5 minutes) in which a premium is placed on speed. A perfect performance in 9 seconds or less is credited with 70 raw-score points, whereas one obtained in 5 minutes is credited with 12 raw-score points.

Animal House Retest is exactly the same test as Animal House. The word "retest" simply indicates that separate normative scaled scores are available for retest performance. Although any subtest can be administered a second time, Animal House is the only one in the scale for which separate retest scores are provided. It is the only subtest in the battery specifically designed to evaluate learning ability.

Rationale. Animal House requires the child to associate signs with symbols. Memory, attention span, goal awareness, concentration, and finger and manual dexterity may all be involved in the child's performance (Herman, 1968; Wechsler, 1967). The subtest may also be a measure of learning ability (Wechsler, 1967).

Animal House has been found to correlate significantly with a measure of learning (r = .71) and a measure of motor skill (r = −.69) in a sample of 36 children 5 to 6 years old (Sherman, Chinsky, & Maffeo, 1974). (The negative correlation results from lower motor skill scores reflect faster reaction times.) The combination of learning and motor scores leads to a better prediction of Animal House scores than do the learning scores by themselves. The results suggest that motor abilities, in addition to learning abilities, may be involved in performance on the Animal House subtest.

Yule et al. (1969) cautioned against accepting Wechsler's statement that performance on the Animal House Retest may differentiate between slow and fast learners. Wechsler's statement is potentially misleading because it is difficult to assess and predict rate of learning and because there are few validation studies to support Wechsler's position. An assessment of learning ability using the Animal House Retest must take into account the child's age and initial score. For example, children who are 4½ years old and who achieve a raw score of 3 on initial testing maintain their initial status on retest by improving their performance by 2 raw score points, whereas children of the same age who achieve a raw score of 18 on the initial subtest need an increase of about 10 raw score points to maintain their position. In addition to the child's age and initial score, motivational factors, the magnitude of the retest change, and the overall level of ability must be considered as factors that may affect learning ability. Yule and his colleagues concluded that empirical work is needed before scores on the Animal House Restest can be meaningfully interpreted.

Factor analytic findings. The Animal House subtest is a moderately good measure of g (30 percent of its variance may be attributed to g). The subtest has a moderate loading on the Performance factor (Mdn loading = .49).

Reliability and correlational highlights. Animal House is a relatively reliable subtest ($r_{xx} = .77$). It correlates more highly with Geometric Design ($r = .43$) than with any other subtest. It has a low correlation with the Full Scale ($r = .53$), the Performance Scale ($r = .50$), and the Verbal Scale ($r = .46$).

Administrative considerations. Note whether the child is right- or left-handed before administering this subtest. Children should be encouraged to use the hand they prefer. As on all timed subtests, do not stop timing once the subtest has begun. If the subtest is spoiled, do not include it in the final calculations. (This is true, of course, for all subtests in the scale.)

The WPPSI manual does not provide adequate guidance about what to do when a child stubbornly reinserts a peg in the wrong hole or refuses to take the examiner's hints during the demonstration items. If a child puts a yellow peg under the same dog for the second time, simply say "No, it should be a black one," insert the peg yourself, and go on to the next sample item.

The Animal House Retest is not used in the calculation of the IQ. Comparing the child's two performances, however, can provide some indication of the child's learning ability or ability to benefit from practice. In the WPPSI manual, Table 20 is used to obtain raw scores for the Animal House and Animal House Retest, but a separate part (last column) of Table 21, "Scaled Score Equivalents of Raw Scores," is used to obtain the Animal House Retest scaled scores.

An inspection of the scaled scores for Animal House and Animal House Retest indicates that the child needs a higher raw score on the Animal House Retest in order to obtain a scaled score equivalent to the one earned on the initial Animal House administration. For example, a raw score of 16 on Animal House is equivalent to a scaled score of 10, but the same raw score on Animal House Retest is equivalent to a scaled score of 9, resulting in a loss of 1 scaled-score point.

Picture Completion

The Picture Completion subtest consists of 23 drawings of common objects (for example, doll, roses, and door), each of which lacks a single important element. Twelve of the drawings appear on the WISC. The child's task is to discover and name or point to the essential missing portion of the incompletely drawn picture. Although there is no exact time limit for each picture, the next picture is shown after 15 seconds if there is no response.

Rationale. The rationale described for the WISC-R Picture Completion subtest appears to hold for the WPPSI Picture Completion subtest (see Chapter 7).

Factor analytic findings. The Picture Completion subtest is a moderately good measure of g (36 percent of its variance may be attributed to g). The subtest has a moderate loading on the Performance factor (Mdn loading = .50) and on the Verbal factor (Mdn loading = .40).

Reliability and correlational highlights. Picture Completion is a reliable subtest ($r_{xx} = .83$). It correlates more highly with Information ($r = .47$) than with any other subtest. It correlates moderately with the Full Scale ($r = .60$) and to a lesser degree with the Verbal Scale ($r = .54$) and the Performance Scale ($r = .55$).

Administrative considerations. The administrative considerations discussed for the WISC-R Picture Completion subtest generally apply to the WPPSI Picture Completion subtest, with the exception of time limits. Unlike the WISC-R Picture Completion subtest, which allows a maximum of 20 seconds per card, the WPPSI Picture Completion subtest has no absolute time limit. Even though the WPPSI Picture Completion subtest is not timed, it may prove to be valuable for qualitative analysis to record the amount of time taken by children to make each response.

In presenting the second card, it is advisable to repeat the directions given for the first card: "Look at this picture. Some important part is missing. Tell me what is missing." Children are given credit if they correctly point to the missing part. If a pointing response is accompanied by a verbal response, however, the verbal response is given precedence over the pointing response. Therefore, an incorrect verbal response (for example, saying "hair" to number 1) accompanied by a correct pointing response (pointing to the missing tooth) receives a score of 0.

Mazes

The Mazes subtest consists of 10 mazes, 7 of which are from the WISC. Three new horizontal mazes intended for younger children appear at the beginning of the subtest. In the WPPSI, Mazes is a standard subtest, whereas in the WISC-R it is a supplementary one. The subtest is discontinued after two consecutive failures.

Rationale. The rationale described for the WISC-R Mazes subtest appears to apply to the WPPSI Mazes subtest (see Chapter 7).

Factor analytic findings. The Mazes subtest is a moderately good measure of g (32 percent of its variance may be attributed to g). The subtest contributes substantially to the Performance factor (*Mdn* loading = .63).

Reliability and correlational highlights. Mazes is a reliable subtest (r_{xx} = .87). It correlates more highly with Geometric Design (r = .48) than with any other subtest. It has a low correlation with the Full Scale (r = .54), the Performance Scale (r = .57), and the Verbal Scale (r = .44).

Administrative considerations. Although the administrative considerations described for the WISC-R Mazes subtest apply to the WPPSI Mazes subtest, the administrative *procedures* differ. Timing, scoring, and other details differ. For example, Mazes 1A, 1B, 2, 4, 5, and 6 are

each allowed a maximum of 45 seconds; mazes 3 and 8, 60 seconds; and maze 10, 135 seconds. Therefore you must be sure to use the procedures appropriate for the scale being administered. Allow the child to finish each maze, regardless of the errors made, because interruptions may generate anxiety and confusion and leave the child with a sense of failure.

Scoring the Mazes subtest requires considerable judgment. You must become familiar with special terms, such as "blind alley," "false exit," "alley wall," and "false start," which designate specific features of the mazes or of the child's performance. Likewise, you must be careful to point out these features of the test to the child in the sample items. Study the child's failures carefully. Note whether there is a pattern to the child's failure, or whether there are signs of tremor or other visual-motor difficulties. After the entire examination has been administered, you may want to return to the Mazes subtest to inquire into the child's performance on any mazes of interest (for example, "Why did you go that way?").

A careful evaluation of the failures that occur on the Mazes subtest may prove to be useful. Two examples are shown in Figure 9-3. In example 1, the girl failed to complete the maze, but made no errors as far as her performance went. In example 2, another girl entered a blind alley, thereby making an error. In the first case one wonders why the girl stopped short before reaching the goal. Perhaps her perseverance is limited, perhaps she takes things for granted and hopes that others will understand her, or perhaps she was distracted. In contrast, the second performance may be that of an impulsive girl who works well until she is about to complete the task and then is unable to do so correctly. These analyses are, of course, only tentative, subject to modification after study of the child's performance on the entire subtest and other subtests on the scale, as well as other sources of data.

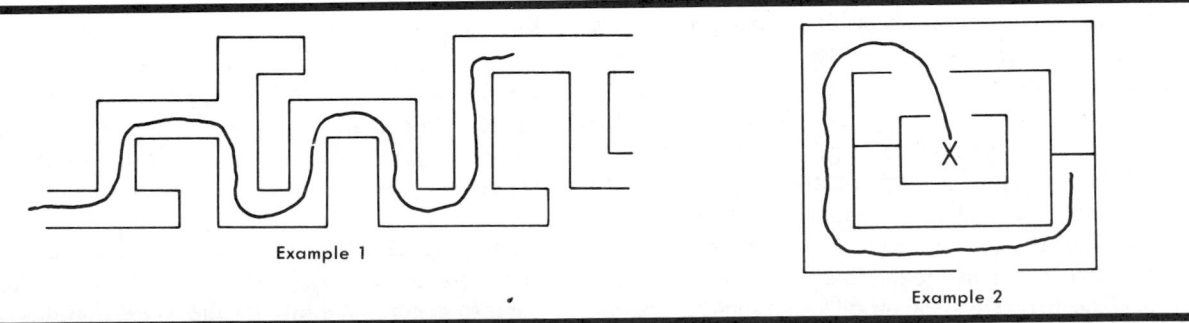

Example 1

Example 2

Figure 9-3.   Two examples of failures on the Mazes subtest. WPPSI Mazes reprinted by permission of the publisher. Copyright 1949; © 1963, 1967, The Psychological Corporation, San Antonio, TX. All Rights Reserved.

Geometric Design

The Geometric Design subtest contains 10 designs—including a circle, a square, and a diamond—that the child is asked to copy. There is no time limit. Scores for items 1 to 5 range from 0 to 2; for items 6 and 7, from 0 to 3; and for items 8 to 10, from 0 to 4.

Rationale.   The Geometric Design subtest is considered to measure perceptual and visual-motor organization abilities. Low scores may indicate lags in the developmental process. Even bright young children may have difficulty obtaining high scores, because the motor ability needed for successful performance (the ability to grasp a pencil appropriately, make contact with paper, and draw appropriate lines) is associated in part with maturational processes that may be independent of the development of cognitive processes.

Factor analytic findings.   The Geometric Design subtest is a moderately good measure of g (41 percent of its variance may be attributed to g). The subtest contributes substantially to the Performance factor (*Mdn* loading = .67).

Reliability and correlational highlights.   Geometric Design is a reliable subtest (r_{xx} = .82). It correlates more highly with Mazes and Block Design (r's = .48) than with any other subtests. It has a low correlation with the Full Scale (r = .58), a moderate correlation with the Performance Scale (r = .60), and a low correlation with the Verbal Scale (r = .48).

Administrative considerations.   The Geometric Design subtest is difficult to score. At least eight different general criteria must be used to score the designs; each design also has special scoring criteria. There is seldom unanimous agreement among examiners on the scores given to the drawings of normal children. Sattler (1976) reported that unanimous agreement occurred among a sample of 18 school psychologists on only 7 out of 50 drawings. Lowering the agreement criterion to 78 percent of the group (14 out of 18) still resulted in agreement on only 23 of the 50 drawings. Similar results were found for a group of 14 inexperienced graduate students. Morsbach, McGoldrick, and Younger (1978) also found that interscorer reliability was inadequate on the Geometric Design subtest, particularly on designs 3, 4, 6, 8, 9, and 10. You will need to study the scoring criteria carefully in order to become proficient in scoring Geometric Design.

The special copyrighted blank paper obtained from the test publisher for the administration of the Geometric Design subtest is not necessary (Yule et al., 1969). You need only fold a sheet of paper in half, writing on each drawing the number of the design and "top" and "bottom" relative to the child's frame of reference. Only half of the paper should be shown to the child at a time to avoid distraction from the design drawn on the other half of the paper.

Block Design

The Block Design subtest contains 10 items. The child is shown a model constructed by the examiner for the first seven items and designs for the last three. Flat blocks are used to reproduce the designs. Children under 6 years of age (and older children who may be mentally retarded) start with item 1; children 6 years of age and older start with item 3.

All of the items are timed. The first four items are given a maximum of 30 seconds; the next two, 45 seconds; the next two, 60 seconds; and the last two, 75 seconds. There are no time-bonus credits as there are on the WISC-R. A score of 2 is given for a successful performance on the first trial, a score of 1 for a successful performance on the second trial, and a score of 0 when both trials are failed.

Rationale.   The rationale described for the WISC-R Block Design subtest appears to apply to the WPPSI Block Design subtest (see Chapter 7).

Factor analytic findings.   The Block Design subtest is a moderately good measure of g (38 percent of its variance may be attributed to g). The subtest contributes substantially to the Performance factor (*Mdn* loading = .58).

Reliability and correlational highlights.   Block Design is a reliable subtest (r_{xx} = .82). It correlates more highly with Arithmetic (r = .50) than with any other subtest. It correlates moderately with the Full Scale (r = .61) and to a lesser degree with the Performance Scale (r = .59) and the Verbal Scale (r = .52).

Administrative considerations.   The administrative considerations described for the WISC-R Block Design subtest generally apply to the WPPSI Block Design subtest.

INTERPRETING THE WPPSI

Much of the material in Chapter 8 pertains to the WPPSI. The successive-level approach to test interpretation, profile analysis, Verbal-Performance Scale comparisons, and subtest comparisons are essentially the same for both the WISC-R and the WPPSI.

The information in Table C-24 in Appendix C can aid you in interpreting the WPPSI subtests, as well as in writing reports. It summarizes the abilities thought to be measured by each WPPSI subtest, background factors that may influence subtest performance, and implications of high and low scores. It deserves careful study.

The classifications associated with WPPSI IQs are shown in Table BC-2 on the inside back cover. Table BC-1 on the inside back cover shows the percentile ranks for the WPPSI Full Scale, Verbal Scale, and Performance Scale IQs. Percentile ranks associated with subtest scaled scores are shown in Table C-41 in Appendix C. The WPPSI Structure-of-Intellect classifications can be obtained from Table C-23 in Appendix C.

The individual subtests should not be viewed as a means of determining specific cognitive skills with precision. Rather, subtest scores should be used as a means of generating hypotheses about the child's abilities. The most reliable estimates of specific abilities are derived from the Verbal Scale IQ (verbal comprehension) and the Performance Scale IQ (perceptual organization), not from individual subtest scores.

Because there is a great deal of overlap between the WPPSI and the WISC-R, especially for the eight subtest types that they share, much of the information in this text on the WISC-R is pertinent to the WPPSI. You are encouraged to review Chapter 7, which discusses the WISC-R subtests, before reading the rest of this chapter.

Profile Analysis

Because profile analysis on the WPPSI is similar to that on the WISC-R, the material in Chapter 8 describing WISC-R profile analysis should be reviewed before a profile analysis is undertaken. Although much less is known about profile analysis on the WPPSI than on other Wechsler scales, the procedure can still be useful in generating hypotheses about a child's strengths and weaknesses.

The five approaches to profile analysis on the WPPSI described here are the same as those described for the WISC-R. The only difference is that different tables in Appendix C must be used. See Chapter 8 for an explanation of each of the approaches. (Factor scores are not included in profile analysis on the WPPSI because the Verbal and Performance Scales adequately describe the organization of the scale.)

1. *Comparing Verbal and Performance Scale IQs.* Table C-15 in Appendix C provides the critical values for comparing the Verbal and Performance IQs: **11** at the .05 level and **14** at the .01 level. (Probabilities associated with various Verbal Performance Scale differences are shown in Table C-19 in Appendix C.)

2. *Comparing each Verbal subtest scaled score to the mean Verbal scaled score.* Table C-16 in Appendix C provides the critical values: they range from 2.83 to 3.05 at the .05 level and from 3.39 to 3.66 at the .01 level for the five standard Verbal subtests.

3. *Comparing each Performance subtest scaled score to the mean Performance scaled score.* Table C-16 in Appendix C provides the critical values: they range from 2.61 to 3.26 at the .05 level and from 3.13 to 3.91 at the .01 level for the five Performance subtests.

4. *Comparing each subtest scaled score to the mean subtest scaled score.* Table C-16 in Appendix C provides the critical values: they range from 2.94 to 3.84 at the .05 level and from 3.78 to 4.50 at the .01 level for the 10 standard subtests.

5. *Comparing sets of individual subtest scores.* Table C-15 in Appendix C provides the critical values: they range from 3 to 4 at the .05 level and from 4 to 5 at the .01 level. The values in Table C-15 are overly liberal (that is, lead to too many significant differences) when more than one comparison is made. They are most accurate when a priori planned comparisons are made, such as Comprehension versus Information or Block Design versus Animal House. (See Chapter 7 for additional information that can guide subtest interpretations.)

Silverstein advises determining the difference between the highest and the lowest subtest scores before making multiple subtest comparisons (personal communication, 1980). If this difference is 6 scaled-score points or more, a significant difference at the .05 level is indicated. Differences between subtests that are 6 scaled-score points or greater can then be interpreted. If the difference between the highest and lowest subtest scaled scores is less than 6 scaled-score points, multiple comparisons between individual subtest scores should not be made.

Other Approaches to Profile Analysis

The supplementary approaches to WPPSI profile analysis described in this section are similar to those discussed for the WISC-R in Chapter 8.

Base rate subtest scaled-score ranges.   In the standard-ization group, the median range between the scaled scores of the highest and lowest subtests was 6 points for the 10 standard subtests, 4 points for the five standard Verbal Scale subtests, and 5 points for the five standard Performance Scale subtests (Reynolds & Gutkin, 1981).

Base rate differences between each subtest score and an average subtest score in the WPPSI standardization sample.   A child's score on each subtest may be compared with his or her average WPPSI Verbal, Performance, or overall score through use of Table C-18 in Appendix C, which gives the frequencies with which various differences occurred in the standardization sample. The table shows, for example, that a difference as large as 3.4 points be-tween the score on Information and the Verbal Scale average was obtained by 5 percent of the standardization sample. This table should be used only for differences that have first been found to be reliable. (See numbers 2, 3, and 4 in the profile analysis section above.) A difference of approximately 4 points between each subtest score and the respective average Verbal or Performance Scale score was obtained by 5 percent of the standardization sample.

Base rate Verbal-Performance differences (or proba-bility-of-occurrence approach).   Table C-20 in Appen-dix C presents the percentage of individuals in the stan-dardization group who obtained a given discrepancy between the Verbal and Performance Scales. The table shows, for example, that between 25 and 50 percent of the population in each WPPSI age group had a 10-point differ-ence (in either direction) between the two IQs.

Clinical and Educational Uses of the WPPSI

The administration of the WPPSI, like the administration of any other psychological or educational test, requires careful observation of the child's performance. For exam-ple, behaviors suggestive of emotional disturbance, lan-guage difficulties, perceptual problems, or visual-motor difficulties should be noted carefully and reported. (See Chapter 18 for further assessment considerations.) There is little published research on the clinically meaningful use of profile variability on the WPPSI; research in this area is needed. The statement by Wechsler (1967) that very poor

performance on the Animal House subtest will at times be associated with organic deficit should be regarded as an unconfirmed hypothesis until research studies become available.

Learning disabilities and the WPPSI.   An interesting contribution by Hagin, Silver, and Corwin (1971) illus-trates how the WPPSI can be used in the assessment of cognitive functioning of children with learning disabilities. These investigators reported on WPPSI profiles for three different subgroups of learning-disabled children: those with specific language disability, brain damage, and devel-opmental immaturity.

Specific language disability.   Children in the specific language disability subgroup have problems in developing body-image concepts, in establishing cerebral dominance for language, and in orienting figures in space and sounds in time (see Chapter 20).

Richard's performance (see Table 9-9) is representative of that of this subgroup. Although a neurological examina-tion did not indicate brain damage, Richard showed some minor soft signs (equivocal signs of brain damage) such as gross errors in right-left orientation and mild difficulties in movement. His visual-motor skills were good, but he had some difficulties with auditory discrimination and se-quencing. On the WPPSI, Richard earned an average Full Scale IQ (98), but showed a 23-point spread between his Verbal and Performance Scale IQs (87 and 110, respec-tively). Within the Verbal Scale, his major difficulties were in areas requiring quantitative reasoning, logical thinking, and social judgment. His range of knowledge and his linguistic skill were adequate, although he sometimes ex-pressed ideas awkwardly. His above-average Performance Scale IQ suggests that he has good potential for learning. It was recommended that educational intervention stress the auditory modality.

Brain damage.   Brain damaged children demonstrate many of the behaviors of the specific language disability group, but in addition show abnormality on the standard neurological examination. Some children are hyperactive, whereas others are hypoactive. Generally the findings do not point to focal brain damage, and specific etiological factors are rarely found in the child's history (see Chapter 22). The children in this subgroup present special educa-tional problems because of poor impulse control, limited attention span, inadequate motor coordination, and anxiety.

Karl (see Table 9-9) is an example of a child in the brain-

Table 9-9
Illustrations of WPPSI Deviations from Mean Scaled Scores for Children with Learning Disabilities in First Grade

Subtest or scale	Richard: Specific Language Disability		Karl: Brain Injured		Rosemary: Developmental Immaturity	
	Score	Deviation[a]	Score	Deviation	Score	Deviation
Information	10	+2	11	− .8	7	+ .3
Vocabulary	11	+3*	14	+2.2	6	− .7
Arithmetic	6	−2	11	− .8	7	+ .3
Similarities	6	−2	15	+3.2*	7	+ .3
Comprehension	7	−1	11	− .8	7	+ .3
Sentences	8	0	9	−2.8	6	− .7
Animal House	10	−1.2	9	−1.8	11	+3.6*
Picture Completion	13	+1.8	11	+ .2	7	− .4
Mazes	12	+ .8	15	+4.2*	6	−1.4
Geometric Design	11	− .2	13	+2.2	7	− .4
Block Design	10	−1.2	11	+ .2	6	−1.4
M Verbal scaled score	8		11.8		6.7	
M Performance scaled score	11.2		10.8		7.4	
Verbal IQ	87		106		80	
Performance IQ	110		112		82	
Full Scale IQ	98		110		79	

[a] The deviations are from the mean of the respective scales.
* These are significant deviations (see Table C-16 in Appendix C).
Source: Adapted from Hagin, Silver, and Corwin (1971).

damaged subgroup. Because there is no typical brain-damaged child, he was selected simply to illustrate how one brain-damaged child performed on the WPPSI. The neurological examination disclosed poor fine and gross motor coordination and severe difficulties in performing skilled movements. Karl exhibited confusion in right-left discrimination, restless motion, tremors, and hyperactivity. His verbal communications were, at times, incoherent and circumstantial. On the WPPSI, he obtained a Full Scale IQ of 110. Conceptual thinking, memory, attention, and concentration were areas in which his performance was below its average level. His motor problems were especially evident in his difficulty in grasping the pegs in the Animal House subtest and in his four-finger, non-oppositional grip on the pencil in the Geometric Design subtest. His best performances were on the Mazes and Vocabulary subtests, subtests that reflect planning ability and word knowledge, respectively. His performance improved when he became familiar with the task require-

ments. It was recommended that educational efforts emphasize visual-motor and organizational skills.

Developmental immaturity. Developmentally immature children exhibit slowness in reaching developmental landmarks, but no clinical or historical evidence of central nervous system damage. In physical appearance, gross and fine motor development, language, and social awareness, these children seem to be younger than their chronological ages. Low birth weight appears frequently in their histories.

Rosemary (see Table 9-9) can be considered to be representative of this subgroup. Neurological difficulties were absent. On the WPPSI, she performed in the Borderline range. The profile of deviations of her subtest scaled scores from the mean of her scaled scores is essentially flat; the only significant variation occurred on the Animal House subtest. Recommendations centered on general enrichment, with particular emphasis on language stimulation.

Reading Disability and the WPPSI

Attempts have been made to determine whether there are differences in patterns of intellectual abilities, as measured by the WPPSI, among preschool and school-age children who differ in their reading skills. The results suggest that the WPPSI profiles for average and poor readers are essentially similar (Barron, 1971; Kavajecz, 1969). This statement holds for both Anglo-American and Mexican-American children. It is difficult to generalize from such research findings, however, because few children in the WPPSI age range are able to read.

ASSETS OF THE WPPSI

The WPPSI has many assets.

1. *It has excellent psychometric properties.* The WPPSI has excellent reliability and validity and has been carefully standardized. The features that are common to other Wechsler tests—such as separate Verbal and Performance Scales, Deviation IQs, and a convenient manual—are also part of the WPPSI.

2. *It provides useful diagnostic information.* The WPPSI provides diagnostic information useful for the assessment of cognitive abilities of preschool children, both normal and mildly mentally retarded. It also furnishes data that are helpful in planning special school programs, perhaps tapping important developmental or maturational factors needed for school success in the lower grades.

3. *The test has a high interest level.* Children enjoy taking the test; the mixture of verbal and performance items maintains their interest.

LIMITATIONS OF THE WPPSI

The WPPSI has a number of limitations.

1. *It takes a long time to administer.* Administration time may be too long for some children, although fatigue is not often a problem. In the standardization sample, approximately 10 percent of the children needed 90 minutes or more to complete the test. The scale often takes over 60 minutes to administer.

With younger children or with handicapped children, two test sessions may be needed. When this procedure is followed, there is no way of determining whether the break between testing sessions affected a child's scores, since the procedure differs from that used in standardizing the scale. Empirical data would be helpful in clarifying the effect of two test sessions on test scores.

2. *It has a limited floor and ceiling.* The WPPSI, like the WISC-R, is limited by the absence of an adequate floor and ceiling (that is, it does not clearly differentiate abilities at the lower and upper ends of the scale). IQ equivalents of the scaled scores range from 45 to 155. This range, however, is not applicable until the 5½-year-old level.

At the 4-year-old level, the lowest Full Scale IQ shown in the manual is 51, the lowest Verbal Scale IQ is 55, and the lowest Performance Scale IQ is 55. A child receives up to 4 scaled-score points for having given *no* correct answers. Wechsler (1967) recognized this problem and recommended that IQs for each scale be computed only when the child obtained a raw score greater than 0 on at least two of the subtests on each of the scales. Similarly, he recommended that a Full Scale IQ not be computed unless raw scores greater than 0 were obtained on at least two Verbal and two Performance subtests.

Following Wechsler's recommended procedure, let us calculate IQs for each of the three scales for a 4-year-old child who obtained raw scores of 1 on the Information, Vocabulary, Animal House, and Picture Completion subtests and a raw score of 0 on each of the remaining six subtests. The resulting IQs are as follows: Verbal Scale IQ = 59 (17 scaled-score points), Performance Scale IQ = 60 (21 scaled-score points) and Full Scale IQ = 55 (38 scaled-score points). Four 1-point successes thus yielded an IQ of 55. This example demonstrates that the WPPSI may not provide precise IQs for children who are functioning two or more standard deviations below the mean of the scale. Further research is needed to determine the validity of the WPPSI for moderately mentally retarded children.

In one study (Rellas, 1969) of a sample of 26 gifted children, the percentages of children who obtained the maximum possible scores on the Arithmetic, Mazes, and Block Design subtests ranged from 11 to 19 percent. In a related study (Hawthorne, Speer, & Buccellato, 1983) of a sample of 306 gifted children, the percentages of children who failed to obtain a ceiling (that is, did not reach the criterion for discontinuance of a particular subtest) were as follows: Arithmetic—8 percent, Geometric Design—17 percent, Block Design—21 percent, Information—50 percent, Mazes—61 percent, Picture Completion—68 percent, Vocabulary—69 percent, Comprehension—95 percent, and Similarities—96 percent. Consequently, the WPPSI appears to be of limited usefulness in assessing the upper limits of the ability of gifted children.

On the basis of the available evidence, the WPPSI does not appear to be appropriate for the assessment of severely retarded or highly superior children. If a child fails (or passes) all or most of the items on the WPPSI, it is advisable to switch to a test that can provide a more accurate estimate of the child's ability.

3. *Scoring of responses is difficult.* Like the WISC-R, the WPPSI is not always easy to score. Scoring is especially difficult on the Geometric Design subtest, in which scores may rely on examiners' subjective decisions, and on the Vocabulary, Similarities, and Comprehension subtests. Consultation with colleagues is recommended when responses are difficult to score.

4. *It may pose special difficulties for disadvantaged children.* Disadvantages of the WPPSI, at least with lower-class children, include the ambiguity and possible emotional loadings of several Comprehension subtest questions and the need to ask for additional reasons on several questions, which may make some children uncomfortable (Fagan et al., 1969).

5. *No information is provided about cutoff criteria.* The WPPSI manual fails to provide information about whether the cutoff criteria were determined empirically or intuitively.

PSYCHOLOGICAL EVALUATION

Exhibit 9-3 illustrates the application of the WPPSI to evaluation of a developmentally immature child. The report summarizes information obtained from the parents and from a kindergarten teacher and cites both qualitative and quantitative information obtained during the evaluation. Profile analysis is used to develop some assessment information, and recommendations are based on the test results and background information.

TEST YOUR SKILL

The WISC-R Test-Your-Skill Exercises in Chapter 8 also pertain to the WPPSI. If you have not reviewed these exercises recently, you are encouraged to do so now. In addition, three exercises that pertain only to the WPPSI follow. In each exercise, there is some inadequacy of description or interpretation. Analyze the mistakes, then check your answers with those shown in Appendix A.

1. "Tom's excellent performance on Block Design and Geometric Design suggests that he has good ability in analyzing social situations and has high moral judgment."

2. "The Geometric Design subtest presented problems for her and she fell in the slow learner category."

3. The following interpretation was given to WPPSI Performance Scale scores on Animal House (12), Picture Completion (15), Mazes (13), Geometric Design (14), and Block Design (12). "While her two lowest scores on the Performance Scale were above average, they may suggest some visual acuity problems."

SUMMARY

1. The WPPSI, designed to be used with children between 4 and 6½ years of age, follows the basic format of the WISC-R, providing Verbal, Performance, and Full Scale IQs.

2. Three WPPSI subtests—Sentences, Animal House, and Geometric Design—do not appear on other Wechsler tests.

3. The standardization sample was representative of the U.S. population, with average reliabilities ranging from .77 to .87 for the individual subtests and from .93 to .96 for the three scales.

4. Like the other Wechsler Scales, the WPPSI employs Deviation IQs for the Verbal, Performance, and Full Scale IQs. Similarly, scaled scores are provided for each subtest. IQs can be prorated when fewer than 10 subtests are administered.

5. The WPPSI has excellent reliability for the three IQs but less satisfactory reliability for the subtest scaled scores. The WPPSI Performance Scale generally shows greater practice effects than does the WPPSI Verbal Scale.

6. Validity studies comparing the WPPSI and the Stanford-Binet: Form L-M and Fourth Edition, indicate that the two scales correlate highly; *Mdn r* = .81 for Form L-M and *Mdn r* = .80 for the Fourth Edition. Scores from the two scales are not interchangeable, however.

7. The WPPSI appears to correlate highly with the WISC-R, but IQs may not be interchangeable. Two 11-year longitudinal studies in Great Britain showed extremely high correlations between the WPPSI and WISC-R, with IQs differing by less than 6 points.

8. WPPSI IQs may not be interchangeable with McCarthy Scale scores.

9. The WPPSI has excellent to adequate predictive validity for both white and black children, using achievement scores as the criterion. More work is needed to establish predictive validity for Mexican-American children, however.

10. The relationship between WPPSI IQs and demographic characteristics indicates that there is an 18-point difference between the highest and lowest socioeconomic status groups (110 vs. 92). Urban-rural differences are not significant. Children from the West obtained significantly higher IQs than did those from other regions of the country.

11. Sex differences are minimal on the WPPSI subtests; when they occur, they are more pronounced on Performance than on Verbal subtests.

12. The IQs obtained by white children in the standardization sample were about 11 points higher on average than those of a matched group of black children (98 vs. 87).

13. Factor analytic studies support the division of the scale into Verbal and Performance sections. All 11 WPPSI subtests have

Exhibit 9-3

Psychological Evaluation: A Child with Developmental Immaturity Evaluated by the WPPSI

Name: Debbie
Date of birth: November 25, 1980
Chronological age: 5-6

Date of examination: June 12, 1986
Date of report: June 15, 1986
Grade: Kindergarten

Test Administered

Wechsler Preschool and Primary Scale of Intelligence (WPPSI):

VERBAL SCALE		PERFORMANCE SCALE	
Information	8	Animal House	5
Vocabulary	13	Picture Completion	6
Arithmetic	10	Mazes	8
Similarities	7	Geometric Design	7
Comprehension	9	Block Design	9

Verbal IQ = 96
Performance IQ = 80
Full Scale IQ = 87 ± 4 at the 85 percent confidence level

Reason for Referral

Debbie's parents requested the evaluation because they were concerned about her rate of development. Her parents described her as being a slow learner and as having a short attention span. Debbie's developmental landmarks were all reached slightly later than is average. The results of a neurological examination were essentially negative. Her parents consider her to be a fairly well adjusted child who is generally happy at home and with other children. There is one other sibling in the family, a boy, who is said by the parents to be gifted.

Debbie's kindergarten teacher described her as being a willing worker when supervised by an adult. When she is on her own, however, her attention often wanders aimlessly. In class, her retention appears to be limited; she is distracted by anything that crosses her vision. She tends to perceive situations as parts, not wholes, and because she fixes her attention on small details she fails to understand many situations. Debbie also has speech problems. In class she speaks slowly and uses phrases that are more characteristic of a 3-year-old than a 5-year-old.

General Observations

Debbie is an attractive youngster, of average height and weight for her age. Although an articulation problem was evident, her speech was understandable. She exhibited some awkwardness in motor coordination. Her walking gait was uneven, and she had some difficulty in turning the pages of a test booklet. At times she was restless during the testing. She was cooperative, however, and attempted to answer the questions and do the tasks asked of her.

Test Results

The WPPSI results were as follows: Verbal Scale IQ of 96, Performance Scale IQ of 80, and Full Scale IQ of 87 ± 4.

Debbie's current level of intellectual functioning is in the Dull Normal range and is ranked at the 20th percentile. The chances that the range of scores from 83 to 91 includes her true IQ are about 85 out of 100. The good rapport that existed between Debbie and the examiner and the child's ability to follow directions and to attempt to respond to the items suggest that the present results are valid.

Debbie's performance skills are not as well developed as are her verbal skills. The 16-point difference between her scores on the verbal and performance parts of the scale suggests that visual-motor ability, perceptual ability, ability to attend to perceptual details, and persistence are at a level of development that is below normal. In contrast, not only do her verbal skills show more variability than do her performance skills, but also the overall level of verbal development is within the normal range. Her outstanding strength was her word knowledge. She was able to define words at a level that was higher than the norm for her age peers and above the average of her verbal scaled scores. For example, she gave satisfactory definitions to such common vocabulary words as "fur," "join," and "diamond." Her arithmetic skills appear to be at an average level.

Debbie's answers were usually short, precise, and direct. Her failures were manifested both by incorrect answers and by her saying "No" when she did not know an answer. She seemed to experience more difficulty on the Similarities subtest, which measures logical thinking, than on most other verbal subtests. Instead of giving analogies, she would repeat part of the question in her answer or give associations. For example, to the question "You ride in a train and you also ride in a _____," she said "Choo-choo." This one verbal subtest, more than any of the other verbal subtests, reflected her difficulty in grasping concepts and suggested some immaturity in reasoning. She at first refused to complete the Animal House subtest, but with encouragement and support finally proceeded with the task. This behavior, too, may suggest immaturity.

Recommendations

The results suggest that Debbie's principal cognitive handicap is a gap between visual-motor skills and verbal skills, in favor of the latter. In school situations she will not likely be perceived as being extremely slow because of her average verbal skills. She will need encouragement and attention, however, because she may tend to remove herself from difficult situations by inattention or by simply refusing to try. Her parents should be helped to accept her present level of development

(Exhibit continues next page)

Exhibit 9-3 (cont.)

and not place unrealistic demands on her. Special programs to improve her muscle coordination and speech are recommended.

Summary

In summary, on the WPPSI, Debbie, with a chronological age of 5-6, obtained a Full Scale IQ of 87 $\pm$ 4, which is in the Dull Normal classification and at the 20th percentile rank. The chances that the range of scores from 83 to 91 includes her true IQ are about 85 out of 100. The results appear to give a valid estimate of her present level of intellectual functioning. Case history material suggested a pattern of developmental immaturity. The examination revealed that she has better verbal skills than performance skills. Visual-motor coordination and other perceptual skills are less well developed than is her vocabulary ability. Immaturity was suggested by some of her responses and behavior patterns. She will need support and encouragement, and her parents should be helped to accept her at her present level of functioning. Special programs were recommended to improve her muscle coordination and speech.

(Examiner's Signature) _____

Examiner

---

strong g loadings. A Freedom from Distractibility factor does not emerge on the WPPSI. The factor structure is similar for both black and white children.

14. The administrative considerations that apply to the WISC-R generally apply to the WPPSI also. Because the WPPSI is used with a younger age group, there are some problems in adapting the subtests to alternative sensory modalities.

15. Table C-21 in Appendix C shows the best combination of two, three, four, and five WPPSI subtests, and Table C-37 in Appendix C shows IQs for the sum of the scaled scores for the Vocabulary plus Block Design short form.

16. The interpretive rationale, factor analytic findings, reliability and subtest correlations, and administrative considerations for each of the 11 WPPSI subtests are presented in the chapter. The proposed interpretive rationales and possible implications of high and low scores are summarized in Table C-24 in Appendix C.

17. The rationale for the WISC-R Information subtest probably applies to the WPPSI Information subtest, although WPPSI questions may be related more to the child's experiences than to formal education. The subtest is the best measure of g in the scale and contributes to the Verbal factor. It is a reliable subtest ($r_{xx} = .81$). Judgment is required in scoring responses.

18. The rationale for the WISC-R Vocabulary subtest probably applies to the WPPSI Vocabulary subtest, although formal education probably has less influence on performance on the WPPSI. The subtest is a moderately good measure of g and contributes to the Verbal factor. It is a reliable subtest ($r_{xx} = .84$). Scoring requires considerable judgment.

19. The rationale for the WISC-R Arithmetic subtest probably applies to the WPPSI Arithmetic subtest, although formal education probably has less influence on performance on the WPPSI. The subtest is a moderately good measure of g and contributes to the Verbal and Performance factors. It is a reliable subtest ($r_{xx} = .82$). Scoring is easy.

20. The WPPSI Similarities subtest appears to measure logical thinking to a greater extent than does the WISC-R Similarities subtest. The subtest is a moderately good measure of g and contributes to the Verbal factor. It is a reliable subtest ($r_{xx} = .83$). Judgment is required in scoring the last six items.

21. The rationale for the WISC-R Comprehension subtest probably applies to the WPPSI Comprehension subtest, although linguistic skill and logical reasoning may play a more significant role on the WPPSI. The subtest is a moderately good measure of g and contributes to the Verbal factor. It is a reliable subtest ($r_{xx} = .81$). Scoring requires considerable judgment.

22. Sentences is the only supplementary subtest in the WPPSI. It is a memory test, measuring immediate recall and attention. The subtest is a moderately good measure of g and contributes to the Verbal factor. It is a reliable subtest ($r_{xx} = .85$). Scoring requires considerable skill.

23. Animal House is considered to measure memory, attention span, goal awareness, concentration, and finger and manual dexterity. It is a moderately good measure of g and contributes to the Performance factor. It is a somewhat reliable subtest ($r_{xx} = .77$). Administration is relatively easy. The abilities measured by the Animal House Retest are not known at this time.

24. The rationale for the WISC-R Picture Completion subtest probably applies to the WPPSI Picture Completion subtest. The subtest is a moderately good measure of g and contributes to the Performance factor. It is a reliable subtest ($r_{xx} = .83$). Administration is relatively easy.

25. The rationale for the WISC-R Mazes subtest probably applies to the WPPSI Mazes subtest. The subtest is a moderately good measure of g and contributes to the Performance factor. It is a reliable subtest ($r_{xx} = .87$). Scoring requires considerable judgment. Administrative procedures differ from those used on the WISC-R.

26. Geometric Design is considered to measure perceptual and visual-motor organization abilities. It is a moderately good measure of g and contributes to the Performance factor. It is a reliable subtest ($r_{xx} = .82$). This subtest may be the most difficult of all WPPSI subtests to score.

27. The rationale for the WISC-R Block Design subtest probably applies to the WPPSI Block Design subtest. The subtest is a moderately good measure of g and contributes to the Performance factor. It is a reliable subtest ($r_{xx} = .82$). The subtest requires skill to administer.

28. Although the same considerations that apply to profile

analysis on the WISC-R apply to profile analysis on the WPPSI, more care should be taken in using profile analysis with the WPPSI because fewer research findings are available.

29. Some WPPSI profiles may be related to specific types of learning disabilities.

30. For the most part, WPPSI profiles of average and poor readers are similar.

31. Although the WPPSI has some limitations—such as long administration time, inadequate floors and ceilings that limit use with severely retarded and highly gifted children, difficult scoring on some subtests, and minor administration problems—it is, overall, a well-standardized, carefully developed instrument that is a valuable tool for the assessment of children's intelligence.

WPPSI Comprehension (p. 206)
WPPSI Sentences (p. 207)
WPPSI Animal House (p. 207)
WPPSI Animal House Retest (p. 207)
WPPSI Picture Completion (p. 208)
WPPSI Mazes (p. 209)
WPPSI Geometric Design (p. 210)
WPPSI Block Design (p. 210)
Profile analysis (p. 211)
Specific language disability (p. 212)
Brain-damaged (p. 212)
Developmental immaturity (p. 213)

KEY TERMS, CONCEPTS, AND NAMES

WPPSI standardization (p. 192)
WPPSI reliability (p. 194)
WPPSI validity (p. 195)
Demographic correlates of WPPSI (p. 199)
Gender differences on the WPPSI (p. 199)
Ethnic differences on the WPPSI (p. 199)
WPPSI factor analysis (p. 200)
WPPSI subtest specificity (p. 200)
Testing-of-limits (p. 202)
Extrapolated IQs (p. 204)
WPPSI short forms (p. 204)
Yudin's WPPSI short form (p. 204)
WPPSI Information (p. 204)
WPPSI Vocabulary (p. 205)
WPPSI Arithmetic (p. 205)
WPPSI Similarities (p. 206)

STUDY QUESTIONS

1. Describe the WPPSI and then discuss its standardization, reliability, and validity.

2. Describe WPPSI factor analytic findings.

3. Discuss WPPSI IQs with respect to the stratification variables used in the standardization sample.

4. Discuss some general administrative considerations for the WPPSI.

5. Discuss WPPSI short forms.

6. Discuss the rationale, factor analytic findings, reliability and correlational highlights, and administrative considerations for each of the following WPPSI subtests: Information, Vocabulary, Arithmetic, Similarities, Comprehension, Sentences, Animal House, Picture Completion, Mazes, Geometric Design, and Block Design.

7. Briefly describe profile analysis on the WPPSI.

8. Discuss the assets and limitations of the WPPSI.

10

WECHSLER ADULT INTELLIGENCE SCALE—REVISED (WAIS-R)

Co-authored by Joseph J. Ryan

When I was a boy of 14, my father was so ignorant I could hardly stand to have the old man around. But when I got to be 21, I was astonished at how much he had learned in seven years.

—Mark Twain

Youth thinks intelligence a good substitute for experience, and his elders think experience a substitute for intelligence.

—Lyman Bryson

Standardization

Deviation IQs and Scaled Scores

Reliability

Validity

Intercorrelations Between Subtests and Scales

WAIS-R IQs and Stratification Variables

Factor Analysis

Administering the WAIS-R

WAIS-R Short Forms

WAIS-R Subtests

Interpreting the WAIS-R

Assets of the WAIS-R

Limitations of the WAIS-R

Test Your Skill

Summary

The Wechsler Adult Intelligence Scale – Revised (WAIS-R; Wechsler, 1981) is the latest edition of an instrument introduced in 1939. In its original version, it was called the Wechsler-Bellevue Intelligence Scale – Form I (Wechsler, 1939), after David Wechsler and Bellevue Hospital in New York City, where Wechsler served as chief psychologist. A second form of the Wechsler-Bellevue, Form II, was published in 1946. Form I was revised in 1955 and again in 1981. The WISC-R and WPPSI are also derivatives of the 1939 adult scale. Because this textbook focuses on testing children, use of the WAIS-R with examinees 16 to 17 years old will be highlighted.

The WAIS-R contains 11 subtests grouped into Verbal and Performance sections. The six Verbal Scale subtests are Information, Digit Span, Vocabulary, Arithmetic, Comprehension, and Similarities; the five Performance Scale subtests are Picture Completion, Picture Arrangement, Block Design, Object Assembly, and Digit Symbol. (Digit Symbol is similar to Coding B on the WISC-R.) The WAIS-R covers an age range from 16 years, 0 months to 74 years, 11 months. It overlaps with the WISC-R from 16 years, 0 months to 16 years, 11 months.

The WAIS-R is similar to the 1955 Wechsler Adult Intelligence Scale (WAIS; Wechsler, 1955). About 80 percent of the items are the same or only slightly modified. Some of the new items and revised procedures were developed on the basis of cultural considerations. For example, two of the WAIS-R Information items make reference to famous black Americans (Louis Armstrong and Martin Luther King). WAIS items that had proved to be either too easy or too hard were eliminated from the WAIS-R. Also, scoring procedures on the WAIS-R Digit Span were altered to increase the variability of scores.

STANDARDIZATION

The WAIS-R was standardized on 1,880 white and nonwhite Americans equally divided with respect to gender, selected to be representative of the U.S. late adolescent and adult population during the 1970s. The demographic characteristics used to obtain a stratified sample were age, sex, race (white = 1,664, black = 192, and Asians plus native Americans = 24), geographic region (Northeast, North Central, South, and West), education, and urban-rural residence. In the standardization sample, there were nine different age groups (16–17, 18–19, 20–24, 25–34, 35–44, 45–54, 55–64, 65–69, and 70–74), with 160 to 300 individuals in each group.

DEVIATION IQS AND SCALED SCORES

The WAIS-R, like the WISC-R and the WPPSI, employs the Deviation IQ ($M = 100$, $SD = 15$) for the Verbal, Performance, and Full Scales and standard scores for the subtests ($M = 10$, $SD = 3$). In order to obtain Deviation IQs, one first converts raw scores into scaled scores, using a table on the front of the WAIS-R record booklet or Table 19 in the WAIS-R manual. These scaled scores are based on a reference group of subjects in the standardization sample who were 20 to 34 years of age. The scaled scores are then summed, and the sum and the examinee's age are used to find Deviation IQs in Table 20 in the WAIS-R manual. Verbal Scale IQs are based on the sum of the six Verbal subtests, Performance Scale IQs on the sum of the five Performance subtests, and Full Scale IQs on all 11 subtests.

Prorating Procedure

The WAIS-R manual provides a table (Table 23) for prorating the scores when five of the Verbal Scale subtests are administered, or when four of the Performance subtests are administered. When even fewer subtests are administered, IQs should be computed by using the specialized short-form procedure described later in this chapter.

Scaled Score Equivalents for Age Groups

The WAIS-R manual (Table 21) also provides scaled score equivalents ($M = 10$, $SD = 3$) of raw scores for each of the nine age groups in the standardization sample. This table is useful in conducting profile analysis and in comparing an individual's performance *directly* with that of age peers; however, *the age-corrected scaled scores should not be used to calculate IQs. Age-corrected subtest scaled scores should be used only to make subtest interpretations and comparisons.* These age-corrected scores, in addition to the reference group scaled scores, should be recorded for every WAIS-R protocol to avoid interpretive errors.

RELIABILITY

The WAIS-R provides highly reliable IQs. Each of the three IQ scales has an internal consistency reliability coefficient of .88 or above in the standardization group over the entire age range covered by the scale. Reliability coefficients, based on a formula for computing the reliability of a composite group of tests, range from .95 to .97 (average

$r_{xx} = .97$) for the Verbal IQ, from .88 to .94 (average $r_{xx} = .93$) for the Performance IQ, and from .96 to .98 (average $r_{xx} = .97$) for the Full Scale IQ. (Similar findings have been reported for a clinical sample by Ryan, Prifitera, and Larsen, 1982.)

The reliabilities for the individual subtests are less satisfactory than those for the IQs. They range from a low of .52 for Object Assembly at ages 16–17 to a high of .96 for Vocabulary at six of the nine age groups. The average reliability coefficients range from .68 for Object Assembly to .96 for Vocabulary (Mdn $r_{xx} = .83$). Similar findings have been reported for a clinical sample (Ryan et al., 1982). Table 10-1 presents the reliability coefficients for each subtest and scale for ages 16 to 17 and for the average of the standardization sample.

The highest reliabilities are found among the Verbal Scale subtests (average reliabilities range from .83 to .96).

Block Design is the most reliable subtest ($r_{xx} = .87$) in the Performance Scale (average reliabilities in the Performance Scale range from .68 to .87). The reliability coefficients for 9 of the 11 subtests are split-half correlations corrected by the Spearman-Brown formula. For Digit Span and Digit Symbol, reliabilities are based on test-retest correlations because the items in these subtests do not lend themselves to the split-half calculation procedure.

Standard Errors of Measurement

The standard errors of measurement (SE_m) in IQ points, based on the average of the nine age groups, are 2.53 for the Full Scale IQ, 2.74 for the Verbal IQ, and 4.14 for the Performance IQ. Thus, more confidence can be placed in the Full Scale IQ than in either the Verbal or the Performance Scale IQ. The Verbal Scale subtests (average SE_m's

Table 10-1
Reliability Coefficients and Standard Errors of Measurement for WAIS-R Subtests and Scales for 16- to 17-Year-Olds and for the Average of the Nine Age Groups in the Standardization Sample

WAIS-R subtest or scale	Reliability coefficient		Standard error of measurement	
	16- to 17-year-olds	Average of standardization group	16- to 17-year-olds	Average of standardization group
Information	.90	.89	.84	.93
Digit Span	.70	.83	1.44	1.23
Vocabulary	.96	.96	.49	.61
Arithmetic	.73	.84	1.20	1.14
Comprehension	.78	.84	1.16	1.20
Similarities	.80	.84	1.29	1.24
Picture Completion	.71	.81	1.43	1.25
Picture Arrangement	.66	.74	1.47	1.41
Block Design	.87	.87	.97	.98
Object Assembly	.52	.68	1.91	1.54
Digit Symbol	.73	.82	1.53	1.27
Verbal IQ	.95	.97	3.30	2.74
Performance IQ	.88	.93	5.18	4.14
Full Scale IQ	.96	.97	2.96	2.53

Note. Reliability coefficients for 9 of the 11 subtests (all but Digit Span and Digit Symbol) are split-half correlations. For Digit Span and Digit Symbol, coefficients are based on test-retest data obtained on subsamples from the standardization group of 48 to 80 individuals in four age groups, who were retested after a 1- to 7-week interval. Verbal, Performance, and Full Scale reliability coefficients are based on a formula for computing the reliability of a composite group of tests.
Source: Adapted from Wechsler (1981).

range from .61 to 1.24 scaled score points) usually have smaller standard errors of measurement than do the Performance Scale subtests (average SE_m's range from .98 to 1.54 scaled score points). Within the Verbal Scale, Vocabulary and Information have the smallest average SE_m's (.61 and .93 scaled score points, respectively); within the Performance Scale, Block Design and Picture Completion have the smallest average SE_m's (.98 and 1.25 scaled score points, respectively).

Stability

The stability of the WAIS-R was assessed by retesting two groups (71 individuals between the ages of 25 and 34 and 48 individuals between the ages of 45 and 54) in the standardization sample after an interval of two to seven weeks (Wechsler, 1981). The stability coefficients for ages 25 to 34 were .95 for the Full Scale IQ, .94 for the Verbal IQ, and .89 for the Performance IQ. For the 11 subtests, the stability coefficients ranged from .69 for Picture Arrangement to .93 for Vocabulary. The stability coefficients for ages 45 to 54 were generally similar to those for the younger group. For the three IQs, the stabilities again were high: .96 for the Full Scale IQ, .97 for the Verbal IQ, and .90 for the Performance IQ. Of the 11 subtests, Object Assembly had the lowest stability coefficient ($r_{xx} = .67$) and Information had the highest ($r_{xx} = .94$). The Verbal, Performance, and Full Scale test-retest IQs, standard deviations, and test-retest score changes for the two groups are shown in Table 10-2.

In the combined sample, the mean changes upon retest after two to seven weeks were 3.3 points on the Verbal IQ, 8.4 points on the Performance IQ, and 6.2 points on the Full Scale IQ (Matarazzo & Herman, 1984a). These differ-

ences likely reflect short-term practice effects. The practice effect was greater for the Performance Scale than for the Verbal Scale. The range of change was −12 to +15 for the Verbal Scale IQ, −12 to +28 for the Performance Scale IQ, and −12 to +20 for the Full Scale IQ. Thus, both gains and losses occurred on retest. Similar findings have been reported with adult clinical groups (Ryan, Georgemiller, Geisser, & Randall, 1985).

The test-retest stability coefficients for the three IQs were all highly significant, yet considerable within-subject variability was demonstrated. These findings underscore the distinction between psychometric and clinical retest stabilities (Matarazzo & Herman, 1984a). High psychometric stability is reflected by a sizable test-retest correlation, whereas high clinical stability is demonstrated by the absence of meaningful score change. For the standardization sample, psychometric stability was satisfactory, but clinical stability was unimpressive; over 80 percent of the subjects showed changes in Full Scale IQ that exceeded the average SE_m. The WAIS-R IQ appears to be less stable than one might infer from the test-retest coefficients alone, and large changes in IQ can occur upon retesting. Additional behavioral or clinical corroborative data are needed for valid interpretation of test-retest changes.

Precision Range

Table C-25 in Appendix C shows the 68, 85, 90, 95, and 99 percent confidence intervals for each scale for all age groups and for the average of the nine age groups in the standardization sample. The examinee's specific age group should be used to obtain the most accurate confidence level.

Table 10-2
Test-Retest WAIS-R IQs for Two Groups

Age	Scale	First testing M IQ	SD	Second testing M IQ	SD	Change
25–34 years	Verbal IQ	102.0	14.0	105.3	14.3	+3.3
(N = 71)	Performance IQ	103.0	15.6	111.9	17.2	+8.9
	Full Scale IQ	102.4	15.0	109.0	16.8	+6.6
45–54 years	Verbal IQ	101.0	14.9	104.1	15.7	+3.1
(N = 48)	Performance IQ	97.3	12.9	105.0	15.6	+7.7
	Full Scale IQ	99.0	13.5	104.7	16.1	+5.7

Source: Adapted from Wechsler (1981).

VALIDITY

The criterion validity of the WAIS-R has been investigated in a variety of studies by correlating the WAIS-R with the WAIS, WISC-R, Stanford-Binet: Fourth Edition, other intelligence tests, measures of achievement, and years of schooling. Evidence of construct validity has been provided by: (a) the level and pattern of intercorrelations between WAIS-R subtests and scales; (b) the observation that scores on the WAIS-R are distributed in a manner consistent with theoretical expectations; and (c) the results of factor analyses applied to the intercorrelations of the 11 subtests.

WAIS-R and WAIS

A sample of 72 individuals in the 35 to 44 age group of the standardization sample were administered the WAIS-R and WAIS in counterbalanced order within a three- to six-week period (Wechsler, 1981). The correlations between the tests were .91 for the Verbal Scale, .79 for the Performance Scale, and .88 for the Full Scale. For the 11 subtests, correlations ranged from a low of .50 for Picture Arrangement to a high of .91 for Vocabulary (*Mdn r* = .79). Subtests on the Verbal Scale have higher correlations (range of .71 to .91, *Mdn r* = .86) than do those on the Performance Scale (range of .50 to .85, *Mdn r* = .66). The high correlations are not surprising, because most items are the same in both tests. What is less clear is why the correlations are relatively low for some Performance Scale subtests. Shifts in scores on the Performance Scale may be due to practice effects.

For each of the three scales, mean IQs were *lower* on the WAIS-R than on the WAIS. The difference was 6.9 points on the Verbal Scale (101.8 vs. 108.7), 8.0 points on the Performance Scale (105.4 vs. 113.4), and 7.5 points on the Full Scale (103.8 vs. 111.3). These results were based on a small sample of the standardization group (those aged 35 to 44) and should not be generalized to other age groups.

Studies that have compared the WAIS-R and the WAIS within a variety of populations almost uniformly indicate that the WAIS-R provides *lower* scores than does the WAIS (*Mdn* differences = −6.6, −6.4, and −6.8 for the Verbal, Performance, and Full Scale IQs, respectively), but correlations between the two scales are *high* (*Mdn r* = .94 for the Verbal Scale, .86 for the Performance Scale, and .94 for the Full Scale) (Edwards & Klein, 1984; Kelly, Montgomery, Felleman, & Webb, 1984; Lewis & Johnson, 1985; Lippold & Claiborn, 1983; Mishra & Brown, 1983; Mitchell, Grandy & Lupo, 1986; Prifitera & Ryan, 1983; Rabourn, 1983; Rogers & Osborne, 1984; Ryan, Rosen-

berg, & Heilbronner, 1984; Simon & Clopton, 1984; Smith, 1983; Urbina, Golden, & Ariel, 1982; Warner, 1983; Wechsler, 1981). Full Scale IQ differences were larger for persons of average and low average ability (*Mdn* = −8.4) than for those of high average (*Mdn* = −5.3) or superior (*Mdn* = −3.7) ability. In contrast, in a study with mentally retarded subjects, the WAIS-R Verbal (+3.9) and Full Scale (+2.1) IQs were found to be higher than corresponding WAIS values. Thus studies suggest that different relationships may exist between the WAIS-R and the WAIS at different points on the intelligence distribution. Overall, WAIS-R and WAIS IQs are not interchangeable.

In assessing individuals who have received an initial evaluation with the WAIS and are later retested with the WAIS-R, it is important to keep in mind that individuals are likely to obtain lower scores on the WAIS-R. *If the WAIS-R IQ equals or exceeds the previously obtained WAIS IQ, the probability is high that an improvement in cognitive efficiency has occurred. If, however, the WAIS-R IQ is lower than the WAIS IQ, do not infer automatically that intellectual deterioration has occurred.* Consider the extent of the difference. A WAIS-R IQ that is *much* lower than the WAIS IQ may suggest some loss of functioning, but this hypothesis must be supported by clinical data.

WAIS-R and WISC-R

The relationship between the WAIS-R and the WISC-R was discussed in Chapter 6. The research suggests that the WAIS-R yields *slightly higher* IQs than does the WISC-R, particularly with low-functioning individuals. More research is needed on the comparability of the two scales, however.

WAIS-R and Stanford-Binet: Fourth Edition

A sample of 47 normal individuals (*M* age = 19-5) were administered the WAIS-R and Stanford-Binet: Fourth Edition (Thorndike et al., 1986b) within a two-week interval. The mean composite score on the Stanford-Binet: Fourth Edition was 98.7, and the WAIS-R Verbal, Performance, and Full Scale IQs were 100.2, 103.7, and 102.2, respectively. Correlations between the Stanford-Binet and WAIS-R scales were .90 for the Verbal IQ, .85 for the Performance IQ, and .91 for the Full Scale IQ.

In another study, 21 mentally retarded individuals (*M* age = 19-6) were administered the WAIS-R followed by the Stanford-Binet: Fourth Edition, with a median interval of three weeks between the two test administrations

(Thorndike et al., 1986b). The mean Stanford-Binet composite score was 63.8, and the WAIS-R Verbal, Performance, and Full Scale IQs were 74.0, 74.2, and 73.1, respectively. Correlations between the composite score and the Verbal, Performance, and Full Scale IQs were .74, .68, and .79, respectively. Like those for normal subjects, results for retarded individuals suggest that the WAIS-R yields *higher* scores than does the Stanford-Binet: Fourth Edition.

Other Concurrent Validity Studies

Table 10-3 summarizes the results of studies that have correlated the WAIS-R with tests of ability, tests of achievement, and years of formal education (*ability*: Edinger, Shipley, Watkins, & Hammett, 1985; Fowles & Tunick, 1986; Gregg & Hoy, 1985; Heinemann, Harper, Friedman, & Whitney, 1985; Hiltonsmith, Hayman, & Kleinman, 1984; Klett, Watson, & Hoffman, 1986; Kling & Kupersmith, 1984; Maxwell & Wise, 1984; Retzlaff, Slicner, & Gibertini, 1986; Zachary, Crumpton, & Spiegel, 1985; *achievement*: Ryan & Rosenberg, 1983; *formal education*: Matarazzo & Herman, 1984b). The studies indicate that the WAIS-R has satisfactory concurrent validity with intelligence tests, picture vocabulary tests, achievement measures, and years of education. Median correlations shown in Table 10-3 between the various measures and the WAIS-R Full Scale IQ range from .43 to .94.

Construct Validity of the WAIS-R

One way to assess construct validity is to determine whether scores from the WAIS-R conform to the expectations or predictions of a viable theory of intelligence. The Cattell-Horn theory (see Chapter 3) postulates that fluid intelligence involves the ability to solve novel problems and process new material, whereas crystallized intelligence involves the retrieval of well-learned facts. Fluid intelligence is believed to decline with advancing age, whereas crystallized intelligence is said to show little or no age-related deterioration.

The age norms for the 11 WAIS-R subtests indicate that with advancing age verbal ability declines much less than perceptual organization and motor skills (Sattler, 1982a). Corrections for age-related decrements are minimal on the Verbal Scale, with the exception of the Similarities subtest (see Table 10-4). Conversely, marked changes are shown on the Performance Scale subtests, for which additional scaled score points are awarded as a function of age. If the Performance Scale is considered a measure of fluid intel-

ligence and the Verbal Scale a measure of crystallized intelligence, then the WAIS-R age norms are consistent with the Cattell-Horn theory: fluid intelligence, but not crystallized intelligence, shows a marked decrement with advancing age.

Factor analysis can also assist in construct validation because it provides a method for determining the structure and components of intelligence measured by a given test. Factor analysis of the WAIS-R standardization sample indicates that all 11 subtests measure general intelligence (*g*) with a moderate to high degree of success (Blaha & Wallbrown, 1982; Gutkin, Reynolds, & Galvin, 1984; O'Grady, 1983; Parker, 1983; Silverstein, 1982a). These results provide support for interpretation of the Full Scale IQ as a global measure of intelligence. Evidence support-

Table 10-3
Concurrent Validity Studies of the WAIS-R

	Correlations		
Criterion	*Verbal IQ*	*Performance IQ*	*Full Scale IQ*
Wechsler Adult Intelligence Scale[a]	.94	.86	.94
Wechsler Intelligence Scale for Children—Revised[a]	.83	.76	.87
Stanford-Binet: Fourth Edition[a]	.82	.77	.85
Wonderlic Personnel Test	—	—	.75
Henmon-Nelson[b]	.77	.62	.79
Slosson Intelligence Test	.83	.51	.78
Revised Beta Examination	.27	.53	.43
Quick Test[c]	—	—	.75
Shipley-Hartford Scale[b]	.80	.68	.76
Peabody Picture Vocabulary Test	.78	.62	.76
Wide Range Achievement Test (1978) Revision			
Reading	.68	.41	.62
Spelling	.67	.42	.60
Arithmetic	.76	.66	.76
Woodcock-Johnson Tests of Cognitive Ability (Broad Cognitive Cluster Score)	.73	.41	.69
Years of education	.56	.41	.54

[a] Median correlations.
[b] Median correlation for Full Scale only.
[c] Median of Forms 1, 2, and 3.

Table 10-4
Additional Scaled Score Points Awarded on WAIS-R Subtests When the Reference Group Receives a Scaled Score of 10

WAIS-R subtest	Age group				
	35–44	45–54	55–64	65–69	70–74
Verbal Scale					
Information	0	0	0	0	1
Digit Span	0	0	1	1	1
Vocabulary	−1	0	0	0	1
Arithmetic	0	0	1	1	1
Comprehension	0	0	0	1	1
Similarities	1	1	1	2	3
Performance Scale					
Picture Completion	1	1	2	2	4
Picture Arrangement	1	1	2	4	5
Block Design	1	1	2	3	4
Object Assembly	0	1	2	4	4
Digit Symbol	1	2	3	5	6

Note. The results in Table 10-4 indicate that raw scores yielding a scaled score of 10 in the WAIS-R reference group yield, in nearly every case, the same or higher scaled scores in the five age groups over 34 years. The greatest change is at ages 70 to 74 years. For example, in the reference group, a raw score of 57 on Digit Symbol yields a scaled score of 10, but at ages 70 to 74 this same raw score yields a scaled score of 16. The 6 additional scaled-score points awarded at ages 70 to 74 change the percentile for a raw score of 57 from the 50th to the 98th. Digit Symbol exhibits the most change of any WAIS-R subtest, showing a steady increment in scaled-score points from ages 35 to 74.

The greatest changes are consistently shown on the Performance Scale subtests. On the Verbal Scale subtests, the increment in scaled-score points is never greater than 1 point, except for Similarities. For this subtest, two additional scaled-score points are awarded at ages 65 to 69, and three additional scaled-score points are awarded at ages 70 to 74 for a performance that is average in the reference group.

The increments in Table 10-4 actually reflect a *decline* in performance ability. The decline is more graphically revealed when we examine the raw-score points needed at the various age groups to obtain an average scaled score. For example, in the reference group, a Digit Symbol raw score of 57 yields a scaled score of 10. At ages 70 to 74, however, a raw score of only 29 is required to obtain a scaled score of 10. Thus, individuals in the oldest age group need 28 fewer raw-score points than do those in the reference group to obtain average status in their age group.
Source: From J. M. Sattler, "Age effects on Wechsler Adult Intelligence Scale – Revised tests," *Journal of Consulting and Clinical Psychology*, 1982, *50*, p. 786. Copyright 1982 by the American Psychological Association. Reprinted by permission.

ing interpretation of the Verbal and Performance IQs as separate entities is also available (Atkinson & Cyr, 1984; Beck, Horwitz, Seidenberg, Parker, & Frank, 1985; Ryan, Rosenberg, & DeWolfe, 1984; Silverstein, 1982a), although some researchers suggest that the Verbal and Performance IQs do not always constitute the most accurate

subdivision of the WAIS-R subtests (see the section on factor analysis later in this chapter). The available research provides substantial support for the construct validity of the WAIS-R.

INTERCORRELATIONS BETWEEN SUBTESTS AND SCALES

The WAIS-R manual provides tables that show the intercorrelations between the 11 subtests and three scales for each of the nine age groups and for the average of the nine age groups. At ages 16 to 17 the subtest intercorrelations range from a low of .21 to a high of .79 (*Mdn* = .43). The six highest subtest intercorrelations are for Vocabulary and Information (.79), Similarities and Vocabulary (.74), Comprehension and Vocabulary (.74), Information and Similarities (.71), Similarities and Comprehension (.66), and Information and Comprehension (.65). The six lowest subtest intercorrelations are for Object Assembly and Digit Symbol (.21), Picture Arrangement and Digit Symbol (.23), Picture Arrangement and Object Assembly (.25), Picture Arrangement and Digit Span (.28), Object Assembly and Arithmetic (.29), and—in a tie—Object Assembly and Information (.30) and Block Design and Picture Arrangement (.30).

The intercorrelations among the six Verbal Scale subtests at ages 16 to 17 range from .36 to .79 (*Mdn* = .61), whereas the intercorrelations among the five Performance Scale subtests range from .21 to .57 (*Mdn* = .36). The Verbal Scale subtests are therefore more highly intercorrelated than are the Performance Scale subtests. Correlations between the 11 subtests and the Full Scale range from a low of .46 (Picture Arrangement and Object Assembly) to a high of .82 (Vocabulary). Five of the six Verbal Scale subtests (Digit Span is the exception) correlate more highly with the Full Scale than do any of the Performance Scale subtests. Of the five Performance Scale subtests, Block Design has the highest correlation with the Full Scale (.67).

The trends observed at ages 16 to 17 are also evident in the intercorrelations based on the average of the nine age groups. Intercorrelations range from .33 to .81 (*Mdn* = .48). The Verbal Scale subtests have higher intercorrelations (.45 to .81, *Mdn* = .61) than do the Performance Scale subtests (.38 to .63, *Mdn* = .47). The Verbal Scale subtests correlate more highly with the Full Scale (.58 to .81, *Mdn* = .75) than do the Performance Scale subtests (.57 to .68, *Mdn* = .61). Vocabulary correlates

Table 10-5
Relationship of WAIS-R IQs to Sex, Race, Occupation, Urban-Rural Residence, Geographic Residence, and Years of Education

	Demographic variables	N	Verbal IQ		Performance IQ		Full Scale IQ	
			M	SD	M	SD	M	SD
Sex	Males	940	100.9	15.1	100.6	15.2	100.9	15.3
	Females	940	98.7	14.7	99.2	15.1	98.7	15.0
Race	White males	836	102.3	14.7	102.0	14.7	102.4	14.8
and sex	Black males	93	88.2	13.1	88.0	14.8	87.3	13.6
	White females	828	100.2	14.3	100.8	14.7	100.4	14.6
	Black females	99	87.5	13.2	86.7	12.4	86.4	12.3
Occupation[a]	*Whites*							
	1. Professional and technical	191	112.4	12.1	109.2	14.0	112.2	13.0
	2. Managerial, clerical, sales	378	105.1	11.9	104.2	12.5	105.0	12.0
	3. Craftsmen and foremen	200	98.6	12.0	101.8	13.6	99.8	12.6
	4. Operatives, service workers, farmers	329	94.4	13.2	96.4	14.8	94.8	13.6
	5. Laborers	51	90.6	15.9	93.4	15.2	91.3	15.4
	6. Not in labor force	515	100.8	15.2	100.2	15.0	100.6	15.3
	Blacks							
	1. Professional and technical	10	92.8	9.8	95.5	9.9	93.2	9.4
	2. Managerial, clerical, sales	29	95.4	13.3	92.1	15.6	93.2	14.6
	3. Craftsmen and foremen	9	95.7	10.2	93.9	13.4	94.4	11.3
	4. Operatives, service workers, farmers	68	85.1	12.7	85.9	13.8	84.6	13.0
	5. Laborers	16	83.8	13.1	83.3	14.5	82.4	13.4
	6. Not in labor force	60	86.5	12.5	85.4	11.5	85.2	11.1
	Total Group							
	1. Professional and technical	206	111.3	12.8	108.4	14.0	111.0	13.4
	2. Managerial, clerical, sales	409	104.3	12.3	103.4	13.1	104.1	12.6
	3. Craftsmen and foremen	213	98.4	11.9	101.3	13.7	99.5	12.6
	4. Operatives, service workers, farmers	404	92.7	13.5	94.5	15.2	93.0	14.1
	5. Laborers	68	88.9	15.3	90.9	15.5	89.0	15.2
	6. Not in labor force	580	99.2	15.5	98.7	15.3	98.9	15.6
Urban-rural	Urban	1421	100.4	15.0	100.0	15.1	100.3	15.2
residence	Rural	459	98.0	14.4	99.4	15.3	98.4	14.9
Geographic	Northeast	465	101.7	14.8	101.4	15.0	101.7	15.0
residence	North Central	497	98.6	14.3	100.2	14.4	99.1	14.2
	South	576	98.6	15.7	97.2	16.2	97.9	16.2
	West	342	101.0	14.3	101.9	14.2	101.5	14.4
Years of	1. 0–7	133	82.2	13.6	84.5	14.9	82.2	13.6
education	2. 8	158	90.2	11.0	93.1	14.3	90.7	12.0
	3. 9–11	472	96.1	13.8	97.8	14.8	96.4	14.3
	4. 12	652	100.1	12.1	100.2	13.5	100.1	12.6
	5. 13–15	251	107.7	10.9	105.7	12.0	107.4	11.1
	6. 16 and up	214	115.7	11.6	111.2	13.0	115.3	12.2

[a] For ages 16–17 and 18–19, stratification of the samples was according to occupation of head of household.
Source: Adapted from Chastain and Reynolds (1984).

more highly (.81) with the Full Scale than does any other subtest. The subtests with the lowest correlations with the Full Scale are Object Assembly (.57) and Digit Symbol (.57).

WAIS-R IQS AND STRATIFICATION VARIABLES

The relationship of WAIS-R IQs to various stratification variables used in the standardization sample is shown in Table 10-5 (Chastain & Reynolds, 1984). Differences between the mean IQs for males and females on the three scales were less than 3 points. Likewise, less than 3 points separated the IQs for the urban and rural subjects of the normative sample. Slightly larger differences emerged when area of geographic residence was considered, the most sizable one being the 3.8 Full Scale IQ points that separated subjects living in the Northeast (*M* Full Scale IQ = 101.7) from those residing in the South (*M* Full Scale IQ = 97.9). Differences attributed to sex, urban versus rural residence, and geographic location are not large enough to assume any practical significance and, in most cases, may be ignored for interpretive purposes.

Mean IQs show a much clearer relation to race, occupation, and education. For example, white subjects in the standardization sample scored about 15 points higher than black subjects on the Full Scale (101.4 vs. 86.8). The IQs of those employed in professional/technical jobs were 22 points higher on average than those of laborers (111 vs. 89). The most striking difference—33 points—was between those with less than 8 years of education and those

with 16 or more years of education (82 vs. 115). Table 10-6 presents a breakdown of IQs on the three scales according to sex and race for 16- to 17-year-olds. As in the total sample, sex differences are minimal. Race differences are similar to those for the total group.

The correlation between years of school completed and the Full Scale IQ was .54 for the total standardization sample (Matarazzo & Herman, 1984b). There was a progressive increase in mean Full Scale IQ as a function of years of school completed: 8 or fewer years of education, *M* IQ = 86.4; 9–11 years, *M* IQ = 96.4; 12 years, *M* IQ = 100.1; 13–15 years, *M* IQ = 107.4; 16 or more years, *M* IQ = 115.3. Matarazzo and Herman recommend that *when you need a crude estimate of an adult examinee's premorbid (before the onset of disease) WAIS-R IQ, you can use the mean IQ values reported above to arrive at an estimate of such a WAIS-R IQ value. This should be done only when no other estimates are available (such as high school transcripts or test scores).*

FACTOR ANALYSIS

Numerous factor analytic investigations of the WAIS-R have been conducted on the standardization sample (Blaha & Wallbrown, 1982; Glass, 1982; Gutkin et al., 1984; O'Grady, 1983; Parker, 1983; Silverstein, 1982a) as well as on various clinical samples (Atkinson & Cyr, 1984; Faulstich, McAnulty, Gresham, Veitia, Moore, Bernard, Waggoner, & Howell, 1986; Ryan, Prifitera, & Rosenberg, 1983; Ryan, Rosenberg, & DeWolfe, 1984; Ryan & Schneider, 1986). Results of these studies indicate that the WAIS-R may be characterized as either a two- or a three-

Table 10-6
Relationship of WAIS-R IQs to Sex and Race for 16- to 17-Year-Olds

Demographic variables		N	Verbal IQ		Performance IQ		Full Scale IQ	
			M	*SD*	*M*	*SD*	*M*	*SD*
Sex	Males	100	100.9	16.0	101.2	15.9	101.1	16.2
	Females	100	99.4	13.6	99.5	14.1	99.2	13.4
Race and sex	White males	85	103.4	14.6	103.8	14.6	103.8	14.8
	Black males	14	86.4	16.9	85.6	15.6	85.4	16.5
	White females	87	100.5	13.2	100.8	13.3	100.4	12.7
	Black females	12	90.5	13.9	88.0	12.8	88.7	13.1

Source: Adapted from Chastain and Reynolds (1984).

factor battery. A three-factor solution is useful for clinical and psychoeducational tasks, but when individual protocols are being interpreted, any hypotheses based on factor analytic findings should be supplemented with clinical judgment.

The three WAIS-R factors are similar to those on the WISC-R—namely, Verbal Comprehension (Information, Vocabulary, Comprehension, and Similarities), Perceptual Organization (Picture Completion [except at 18–19 years], Block Design, and Object Assembly), and Freedom from Distractibility (Digit Span and Arithmetic) (see Table 10-7). The subtests comprising the factors, however, differ somewhat for the two scales. Coding loads on the Freedom from Distractibility factor on the WISC-R, but its counterpart on the WAIS-R, Digit Symbol, does not. Similarly, Picture Arrangement is one of the subtests in the Perceptual Organization factor on the WISC-R, but not on the WAIS-R. There is no simple explanation for these findings. (All factor analytic findings presented in Table 10-7 and below are based on work by the chapter authors.)

WAIS-R Subtests as Measures of *g*

As shown in Table 10-8, all of the WAIS-R subtests are either good or fair measures of *g* (the general intelligence factor). Based on the average of the nine age levels, the subtests with the highest *g* loadings are Vocabulary (.86), Information (.81), Similarities (.79), Comprehension (.78), Arithmetic (.75), and Block Design (.72). The subtests with fair *g* loadings are Picture Completion (.70), Picture Arrangement (.63), Digit Span (.62), Object Assembly (.61), and Digit Symbol (.59). Overall, the Verbal subtests are better measures of *g* than are the Performance subtests.

Subtest Specificity

Subtest specificity refers to the proportion of a subtest's variance that is both reliable (that is, not due to errors of measurement) and distinctive to the subtest. Although individual subtests overlap in their measurement properties (that is, the majority of reliable variance for most subtests is common factor variance), many of them possess a relatively high degree of specificity, which justifies interpretation of specific subtest functions (see Table 10-9). Some subtests have either ample or adequate specificity throughout the entire age range covered by the WAIS-R (Digit Span, Vocabulary, Picture Completion, Block De-

sign, and Digit Symbol), whereas others have inadequate specificity at one or more ages (Information, Arithmetic, Comprehension, Similarities, Picture Arrangement, and Object Assembly). Subtests with inadequate specificity should not be interpreted as measuring specific functions, and cautious interpretation is required for subtests falling within the adequate specificity category. These subtests can be interpreted as measuring *g* and the appropriate principal factor, however (Verbal Comprehension, Perceptual Organization, and Freedom from Distractibility, respectively).

Factor Scores

Factor scores can be obtained from the WAIS-R, permitting the identification of meaningful psychological dimensions. The Verbal Comprehension factor score measures verbal knowledge and understanding obtained by formal and informal education and reflects the ability to apply verbal skills to new situations. The Perceptual Organization factor score reflects the ability to interpret and organize visually perceived material while working against a time limit. The Freedom from Distractibility factor score measures the ability to attend or concentrate, but also may involve numerical proficiency and sequencing skills. These factor scores are discussed more fully in Chapter 8.

The preferred way to obtain the three factor scores is to use the following combinations of subtests:

Verbal Comprehension = Sum of age-corrected scaled scores on Information, Vocabulary, Comprehension, and Similarities at all ages

Perceptual Organization = Sum of age-corrected scaled scores on Block Design, Object Assembly, and Picture Completion at every age level (except 18–19, where the last subtest should be omitted from the factor score)

Freedom from Distractibility = Sum of age-corrected scaled scores on Digit Span and Arithmetic

The sums of the respective age-corrected subtest scaled scores comprising the three factors can be converted into Deviation IQs ($M = 100$, $SD = 15$). Table C-28 in Appen-

Table 10-7
WAIS-R Subtest Loadings on Factor A (Verbal Comprehension), Factor B (Perceptual Organization), and Factor C (Freedom from Distractibility) for Nine Age Levels and the Average Following Varimax Rotation

WAIS-R subtest	Age group									
	16–17	18–19	20–24	25–34	35–44	45–54	55–64	65–69	70–74	Av.
Factor A – Verbal Comprehension										
Information	78	80	77	67	62	70	76	78	76	75
Digit Span	22	46	28	36	36	54	27	30	38	30
Vocabulary	81	83	83	77	80	86	87	75	83	81
Arithmetic	54	58	40	43	41	56	45	45	41	44
Comprehension	69	66	69	71	72	69	71	82	68	71
Similarities	78	67	68	60	68	65	70	67	63	67
Picture Completion	40	26	45	46	45	36	49	38	38	44
Picture Arrangement	37	36	52	48	44	37	45	40	26	42
Block Design	29	19	21	27	31	27	27	31	30	27
Object Assembly	18	16	25	20	23	21	16	17	12	19
Digit Symbol	38	37	11	42	31	44	41	41	24	32
Factor B – Perceptual Organization										
Information	20	21	18	30	28	32	28	31	20	21
Digit Span	23	31	11	19	17	34	37	26	31	22
Vocabulary	31	21	20	28	24	21	14	33	31	26
Arithmetic	25	53	27	30	42	49	44	36	22	34
Comprehension	33	19	31	26	26	20	36	26	33	30
Similarities	25	30	30	38	31	29	46	41	46	36
Picture Completion	46	19	59	64	43	41	57	66	51	56
Picture Arrangement	24	21	33	44	32	33	48	48	54	42
Block Design	79	77	67	67	64	74	72	74	75	69
Object Assembly	60	48	67	78	88	71	65	76	75	73
Digit Symbol	23	52	26	24	25	45	41	55	55	38
Factor C – Freedom from Distractibility										
Information	28	25	26	44	48	38	21	25	33	30
Digit Span	74	09	63	53	63	10	56	68	42	64
Vocabulary	27	31	29	40	40	32	37	41	26	34
Arithmetic	49	15	63	63	55	15	49	53	87	55
Comprehension	22	41	25	32	32	35	27	23	26	27
Similarities	18	27	24	26	33	36	11	31	20	27
Picture Completion	20	67	12	18	35	62	10	25	24	17
Picture Arrangement	18	41	17	22	48	51	20	34	18	23
Block Design	26	25	35	46	42	31	31	19	28	33
Object Assembly	14	47	23	16	18	27	26	21	09	17
Digit Symbol	39	17	49	26	53	14	19	38	09	36

Note. Av. = average. Decimal points omitted. According to Parker (1983), Digit Span and Arithmetic should be included in the Freedom from Distractibility factor at ages 18–19 and 45–54 because these subtests have high loadings on this factor in a four-factor solution.

Table 10-8
WAIS-R Subtests as Measures of *g*

	Good measure of g			Fair measure of g		
Subtest	Median g loading	Proportion of variance attributed to g (%)		Subtest	Median g loading	Proportion of variance attributed to g (%)
Vocabulary	.87	76		Picture Completion	.71	50
Information	.82	67		Picture Arrangement	.67	45
Similarities	.79	62		Object Assembly	.63	40
Comprehension	.78	61		Digit Span	.62	38
Arithmetic	.76	58		Digit Symbol	.60	36
Block Design	.73	53				

Note. These are median loadings based on the nine age groups in the standardization sample. The square of the median coefficients provides the proportion of each subtest's variance that may be attributed to *g*.

dix C provides for a rapid conversion of the three factor scores into Deviation IQs for ages 16 to 17 and for the average of the nine age groups.

ADMINISTERING THE WAIS-R

The general procedures discussed in Chapter 5 for administering psychological tests are also useful in administering the WAIS-R, as are the guidelines in Chapters 6 and 7 for administering the WISC-R. Be careful not to confuse the administration procedures of the WISC-R with those of the WAIS-R, however—different instructions and time limits are used on some subtests of the same name. The general problems in administering the WISC-R also apply to the WAIS-R. The suggestions shown in Exhibit 10-1 should aid you in learning how to administer the WAIS-R. (Figure 10-1 shows the cover of the WAIS-R record booklet.)

Physical Abilities Required for the WAIS-R

Adequate hearing and language functions are required for the Verbal Scale subtests, and adequate vision and visual-motor ability are needed for the Performance Scale subtests. The suggestions presented in Chapters 6 and 7 for administering the WISC-R to handicapped examinees (see particularly Table 6-11) should be carefully studied.

Subtest Sequence

In most situations subtests should be administered in the standard sequence, as specified in the WAIS-R manual. If warranted, however, all of the Verbal subtests can be administered first followed by the Performance subtests. This order may be less stressful for examinees who have minor motor problems that may interfere with the Performance subtests. It is also permissible to adjust the order of administration for examinees who fatigue easily (for example, the elderly or physically ill) or display marked anxiety about the testing situation. Examinees who fatigue easily may be given certain subtests (for example, Arithmetic, Digit Span, or Digit Symbol) early in the session when their energy levels and attention-concentration skills are best. Anxious examinees may be started with subtests that are relatively nonthreatening and do not have strict time limits (for example, Information, Comprehension, or Vocabulary).

Some examinees with psychiatric or neurological disorders may not be able to complete the entire WAIS-R in a single session. In such cases, schedule breaks to coincide with the end of a subtest so that testing can easily be resumed at a later time. In the rare instances where a subtest must be interrupted prior to completion, resume administration of the subtest where you stopped, except on Similarities, Block Design, and Picture Arrangement. On these subtests, the easy items provide some examinees with the practice they need to succeed at more difficult items. Therefore, if Similarities, Block Design, or Picture Arrangement is interrupted, the first few items should be

Table 10-9
Amount of Specificity for WAIS-R Subtests

WAIS-R subtest	Ample specificity Ages	Adequate specificity Ages	Inadequate specificity Ages
Information	—	16–44, 55–74, Average	45–54
Digit Span	16–74, Average	—	—
Vocabulary	—	16–74, Average	—
Arithmetic	20–34, 45–74, Average	18–19, 35–44	16–17
Comprehension	45–54	25–44, 65–74, Average	16–24, 55–64
Similarities	25–34	18–19, 35–74, Average	16–17, 20–24
Picture Completion	16–74, Average	—	—
Picture Arrangement	16–19, 25–64, 70–74, Average	—	20–24, 65–69
Block Design	16–34, 55–69, Average	35–54, 70–74	—
Object Assembly	18–19	—	16–17, 20–74, Average
Digit Symbol	16–64, 70–74, Average	65–69	—

repeated at the next session so that the examinee can reestablish the mental set necessary to succeed on the harder items. Naturally, you must consider how any administrative irregularity will affect the accuracy of the test results.

Starting Rules

Eight of the 11 subtests are started with the first item. The remaining three subtests (Information, Vocabulary, and Arithmetic) are started with the fifth, fourth, and third items, respectively. On these three subtests, score the entry-point items as soon as they are administered. Credit is automatically given for the unadministered early items when the entry-point items (the first two, three, or four items administered) are answered correctly. If the entry-point items are answered incorrectly, it is necessary to administer the earlier items before continuing the subtest.

Discontinuance Rules

Nine of the 11 subtests have discontinuance rules—the subtest is discontinued after a specified number of consecutive items are failed. (Object Assembly and Digit Symbol are the two subtests without discontinuance rules.) If you administer additional items in a subtest because you are not sure whether the items at the discontinuance point were failed, use the following rule to score the additional items (Wechsler, 1981, p. 54): *If subsequent scoring of the items indicates that the additional items were administered unnecessarily, do not give credit for any items passed after the discontinuance point.* This rule, which is also followed in the WISC-R, helps to maintain standardized procedures.

Repetition of Items

Use judgment in deciding when to repeat questions. The Digit Span items are the only verbal items that *cannot* be repeated.

Use of Probing Questions and Queries

Use probing questions when responses are ambiguous, vague, or indefinite, or when probing is indicated by a "(Q)" in the various scoring criteria appendices in the WAIS-R manual.

Testing-of-Limits Procedures

Use modifications in test procedures designed for testing-of-limits only *after* all of the subtests have been administered according to standardized procedures.

Scoring WAIS-R Responses

Arriving at accurate scores for WAIS-R subtests and scales is no simple matter. Scoring errors can have a significant impact on the accuracy of WAIS-R IQs. A study indicated that graduate students and experienced psychologists differed by 4 to 18 IQ points in the scores they gave to two

---

■ Exhibit 10-1 ■

Supplementary Instructions for Administering the WAIS-R

1. Complete the top of the record booklet.

2. Calculate the chronological age (CA) and put it in the box provided.

3. Administer the subtests in the order presented in the WAIS-R manual, except in rare circumstances. Do not change the wording on any subtest. Read the directions and material from the manual. Do not ad lib.

4. Start with the appropriate item on each subtest and follow discontinuance criteria. This means that you must know the scoring criteria before you administer the scale.

5. Write out all responses completely and legibly. Do not use unusual abbreviations. Record time accurately.

6. Question all ambiguous or unscorable responses, using the words suggested in the WAIS-R manual for questioning. You may need to question on Information, Vocabulary, Comprehension, and Similarities. Whenever you ask a question, write (Q) after the questioned response.

7. Carefully score each protocol, recheck scoring, and transfer subtest scores to the front of the record booklet under Raw Score. If you have failed to question a response when you should have and the response is obviously not a 0 response, give the examinee the most appropriate score.

8. If a subtest was spoiled, write *spoiled* by the subtest total score and on the front cover where the raw scores and scaled scores appear. If for some reason a subtest was not administered, write *NA* in the margin in the record booklet and on the front cover.

9. Raw scores are transformed into scaled scores through use of the table on the front of the record booklet (or Table 19

on page 90 of the WAIS-R manual). Be sure to use the correct row and column for each transformation.

10. The Verbal score is based on the total of the scaled scores on the six Verbal Scale subtests. The Performance score is based on the total of the scaled scores on the five Performance Scale subtests. Add the Verbal score and the Performance score to get the Full Scale score.

11. If it should be necessary to prorate either the Verbal or Performance section, follow the explicit directions given on page 88 of the WAIS-R manual.

12. The IQs are obtained from Table 20 (pages 92 through 109) of the WAIS-R manual. There is a Verbal section, a Performance section, and a Full Scale section. Be sure to use the correct section of the table for each of the three IQs. Record the IQs. Next, recheck all of your work. If any IQs were prorated, write *PRO* beside the appropriate IQs.

13. If you want to compare the examinee to the reference group, make a profile of the examinee's scaled scores on the record booklet. A profile of age-corrected scaled scores can also be made.

14. Look up the confidence intervals for the Full Scale IQ, Verbal Scale IQ, and Performance Scale IQ in Table C-25 in Appendix C.

15. Look up the percentile rank and classification for each of the IQs in Tables BC-1 and BC-2 on the inside back cover of this text.

Source: Courtesy of M. L. Lewis.

WAIS-R protocols (Ryan, Prifitera, & Powers, 1983). Additionally, both groups of raters converted scaled scores to IQs incorrectly, gave credit for individual items incorrectly, and added raw scores incorrectly. In another study additional scoring problems included failing to credit responses that appeared in the manual and assigning credit for symbol pairings on Digit Symbol incorrectly (Franklin et al., 1982). Obviously, you should guard against making such errors.

Judgment is important in scoring WAIS-R responses, especially when ambiguous responses are encountered on the Vocabulary, Comprehension, and Similarities subtests. Carefully study the scoring criteria, scoring guidelines, and scoring examples in the WAIS-R manual.

Extrapolated IQs

Because the lowest scaled score is 1 point, the sum of scaled scores cannot be lower than 6 for the Verbal Scale or 5 for the Performance Scale when proration procedures are used. Consequently, the minimum sum of scaled scores is shown in the WAIS-R manual. When the sum of scaled scores is higher than the highest sum shown in Table 20 of the WAIS-R manual, report the IQ as "over 150" (Wechsler, 1981). In some cases, however, you can extrapolate the IQ. Table C-30 in Appendix C extends the sum of scaled scores and IQs up to the maximum possible sum of scaled scores for the Verbal, Performance, and Full Scales separately for each of the nine age groups. As noted in Chapter 6, extrapolated IQs must be used cautiously.

WAIS-R RECORD FORM

WECHSLER ADULT INTELLIGENCE SCALE—REVISED

NAME _____

ADDRESS _____

SEX _____ AGE _____ RACE _____ MARITAL STATUS _____

OCCUPATION _____ EDUCATION _____

PLACE OF TESTING _____ TESTED BY _____

TABLE OF SCALED SCORE EQUIVALENTS*

Scaled Score	Information	Digit Span	Vocabulary	Arithmetic	Comprehension	Similarities	Picture Completion	Picture Arrangement	Block Design	Object Assembly	Digit Symbol	Scaled Score
	VERBAL TESTS						PERFORMANCE TESTS					
19	—	28	70	—	32	—	—	—	51	—	93	19
18	29	27	69	—	31	28	—	—	—	41	91-92	18
17	—	26	68	19	—	—	20	20	50	—	89-90	17
16	28	25	66-67	—	30	27	—	—	49	40	84-88	16
15	27	24	65	18	29	26	—	19	47-48	39	79-83	15
14	26	22-23	63-64	17	27-28	25	19	—	44-46	38	75-78	14
13	25	20-21	60-62	16	26	24	—	18	42-43	37	70-74	13
12	23-24	18-19	55-59	15	25	23	18	17	38-41	35-36	66-69	12
11	22	17	52-54	13-14	23-24	22	17	15-16	35-37	34	62-65	11
10	19-21	15-16	47-51	12	21-22	20-21	16	14	31-34	32-33	57-61	10
9	17-18	14	43-46	11	19-20	18-19	15	13	27-30	30-31	53-56	9
8	15-16	12-13	37-42	10	17-18	16-17	14	11-12	23-26	28-29	48-52	8
7	13-14	11	29-36	8-9	14-16	14-15	13	8-10	20-22	24-27	44-47	7
6	9-12	9-10	20-28	6-7	11-13	11-13	11-12	5-7	14-19	21-23	37-43	6
5	6-8	8	14-19	5	8-10	7-10	8-10	3-4	8-13	16-20	30-36	5
4	5	7	11-13	4	6-7	5-6	5-7	2	3-7	13-15	23-29	4
3	4	6	9-10	3	4-5	2-4	3-4	—	2	9-12	16-22	3
2	3	3-5	6-8	1-2	2-3	1	2	1	1	6-8	8-15	2
1	0-2	0-2	0-5	0	0-1	0	0-1	0	0	0-5	0-7	1

*Clinicians who wish to draw a profile may do so by locating the subject's raw scores on the table above and drawing a line to connect them. See Chapter 4 in the Manual for a discussion of the significance of differences between scores on the tests.

Date Tested ____ ____ ____ (Year Month Day)

Date of Birth ____ ____ ____

Age ____ ____ ____

SUMMARY

	Raw Score	Scaled Score
VERBAL TESTS		
Information	____	____
Digit Span	____	____
Vocabulary	____	____
Arithmetic	____	____
Comprehension	____	____
Similarities	____	____
Verbal Score		____
PERFORMANCE TESTS		
Picture Completion	____	____
Picture Arrangement	____	____
Block Design	____	____
Object Assembly	____	____
Digit Symbol	____	____
Performance Score		____

	Sum of Scaled Scores	IQ
VERBAL	____	____
PERFORMANCE	____	____
FULL SCALE	____	____

(Ψ) **THE PSYCHOLOGICAL CORPORATION**
HARCOURT BRACE JOVANOVICH, PUBLISHERS

9-991829

Figure 10-1. Cover page of WAIS-R record booklet. Copyright © 1981, 1955, 1947 by The Psychological Corporation, San Antonio, TX. All rights reserved.

WAIS-R SHORT FORMS

Short forms of the WAIS-R have the same advantages and disadvantages as do short forms of the WISC-R. Chapter 6 thoroughly discusses the use of short forms; review this material as needed.

Selecting the Short Forms

Table C-34 in Appendix C provides the 10 best short form combinations of two, three, four, and five WAIS-R subtests. For all practical purposes, the short forms of a given length are mutually interchangeable in terms of psychometric properties. The choice of a short form should be based on the considerations discussed in Chapter 6.

After the short form has been selected, follow the procedures outlined in Chapter 6 (see Exhibit 6-3) to convert the composite scores to Deviation Quotients. Use Table C-36 in Appendix C to obtain the appropriate a and b constants. To obtain r_{jk}, use the section of the WAIS-R correlation table (Table 15) that corresponds to the examinee's age group.

Satz-Mogel Abbreviated Procedure

The Yudin short form procedure, which reduces the number of items within subtests, is known as the Satz-Mogel short form when applied to the WAIS-R (Satz & Mogel, 1962). Table C-35 in Appendix C shows the specific procedures for obtaining this WAIS-R short form. Validity coefficients and standard errors of measurement, based on the entire standardization sample, are .94 and ±5.1 for the Verbal IQ, .89 and ±6.8 for the Performance IQ, and .95 and ±4.7 for the Full Scale IQ, respectively (Silverstein, 1982d). Although the Satz-Mogel approach is a useful screening device for estimating the Full Scale IQ, it should not be used to interpret individual subtest scores. Poor correlations have been reported between estimated subtest scaled scores and actual obtained scores. Additionally, estimated scaled scores have been found to exceed the range of ±2 scaled score points from actual obtained scores in over 25 percent of 81 cases studied (Evans, 1985).

Vocabulary plus Block Design Short Form

A two-subtest combination that is popular as a short form screening instrument is Vocabulary plus Block Design. These two subtests have moderate (Block Design) and high (Vocabulary) correlations with the Full Scale, have consis-

tently high reliabilities, and are good measures of g. If this combination is chosen, Table C-37 in Appendix C can be used to convert the sum of *age-corrected scaled scores* directly into an estimated Full Scale IQ (Brooker & Cyr, 1986). The reliability of the composite is impressive (r_{xx} = .94 for the average of nine age groups) with an SE_m in IQ points of 3.58 for 16- to 17-year-olds and 3.64 for the average of all nine age groups (Silverstein, 1985b). The Vocabulary plus Block Design short form consistently overestimates the average Full Scale IQ of clinical samples by approximately 3 points, however (Margolis, Taylor, & Greenlief, 1986; Roth, Hughes, Monkowski, & Crosson, 1984; Ryan, Larsen, & Prifitera, 1983; Thompson, Howard, & Anderson, 1986).

Vocabulary, Block Design, and Information

A useful three-subtest short form is Vocabulary, Block Design, and Information. Table C-38 in Appendix C can be used to convert the sum of the three *age-corrected subtest scaled scores* into an estimated Full Scale IQ.

Vocabulary, Block Design, Arithmetic, and Similarities

A useful four-subtest short form is Vocabulary, Block Design, Arithmetic, and Similarities. Table C-39 in Appendix C can be used to convert the sum of the four *age-corrected subtest scaled scores* into an estimated Full Scale IQ.

Information, Arithmetic, Picture Completion, and Block Design Short Form

Another potentially useful short form combination is Information, Arithmetic, Picture Completion, and Block Design (Reynolds, Willson, & Clark, 1983). Table C-40 in Appendix C can be used to convert the sum of the four *age-corrected subtest scaled scores* into an estimated Full Scale IQ. The reliability of the composite is adequate (r_{xx} = .88 for the average of nine age groups), and estimated stability over time is excellent (.95 for 71 standardization subjects between 25 and 34 years of age; .96 for 48 standardization subjects between 45 and 54 years of age). The SE_m in IQ points is 5.73 for 16- to 17-year-olds, and 5.26 for the average of the nine age groups in the standardization sample. This four-subtest short form is a valid predictor of the Full Scale IQ in normal subjects (Reynolds et al., 1983) and neurologically impaired patients (Ryan, 1985).

WAIS-R SUBTESTS

Information

The Information subtest contains 29 questions which sample a broad range of general knowledge, including literary, historical, and geographical facts and dates. All examinees start with item 5. All items are scored 1 or 0 (pass-fail), and the subtest is discontinued after five consecutive failures. The questions usually can be answered with a simply stated fact. The examinee is not required to find relationships between facts in order to receive credit.

Rationale. The rationale presented for the WISC-R Information subtest applies to the WAIS-R Information subtest (see Chapter 7).

Factor analytic findings. Information is the second-best measure of g in the scale (67 percent of its variance may be attributed to g). It has adequate subtest specificity in every age range with the exception of 45 to 54 years, where its specificity is inadequate. Information contributes substantially to the Verbal Comprehension factor (*Mdn* loading = .76).

Reliability and correlational highlights. Information is a reliable subtest (r_{xx} = .89). It correlates more highly with Vocabulary (r = .81) than with any other subtest. It correlates moderately with the Full Scale IQ (r = .76), the Verbal Scale IQ (r = .79), and the Performance Scale IQ (r = .62).

Administrative and interpretive considerations. The administrative and interpretive considerations presented for the WISC-R Information subtest are also relevant for the WAIS-R (see Chapter 7).

Digit Span

The Digit Span subtest has two parts: Digits Forward, which contains series ranging in length from three to nine digits, and Digits Backward, which contains series ranging in length from two to eight digits. The examinee listens to a sequence of digits given orally by the examiner and then repeats the digits. There are two sets of digits of each length. Digits Forward is administered first, followed by Digits Backward. On the WAIS-R Digit Span is a regular subtest, whereas on the WISC-R it is supplementary.

All series are scored 2, 1, or 0. On both parts of the subtest, testing is discontinued after failure on both trials of any series. Scaled scores and age-corrected scores are not provided separately for Digits Forward and Digits Backward.

Rationale. The rationale presented for the WISC-R Digit Span subtest applies to the WAIS-R Digit Span subtest (see Chapter 7).

Factor analytic findings. The Digit Span subtest is a fair measure of g (38 percent of its variance may be attributed to g). It has ample subtest specificity across the entire age range to permit specific interpretation of its functions. Digit Span has a high loading on the Freedom from Distractibility factor (*Mdn* loading = .56).

Reliability and correlational highlights. Digit Span is a reliable subtest (r_{xx} = .83). It correlates more highly with Arithmetic (r = .56) and Vocabulary (r = .52) than with the remaining subtests. It has a relatively low correlation with the Full Scale IQ (r = .58), the Verbal Scale IQ (r = .57), and the Performance Scale IQ (r = .50).

Administrative and interpretive considerations. The administrative and interpretive considerations presented for the WISC-R Digit Span subtest are also relevant for the WAIS-R (see Chapter 7).

Vocabulary

The Vocabulary subtest contains 35 words arranged in order of increasing difficulty. Each word is presented orally and in writing, and the examinee is asked to explain aloud its meaning. All examinees start with the fourth word, except those who seem to have poor verbal ability. Each word is scored 2, 1, or 0, and the subtest is discontinued after five consecutive failures.

Rationale. The rationale presented for the WISC-R Vocabulary subtest applies to the WAIS-R Vocabulary subtest (see Chapter 7).

Factor analytic findings. The Vocabulary subtest is the best measure of g in the scale (76 percent of its variance may be attributed to g). The subtest has an adequate amount of subtest specificity across the entire age range and contributes substantially to the Verbal Comprehension factor (*Mdn* loading = .83).

Reliability and correlational highlights.   Vocabulary is the most reliable subtest in the scale ($r_{xx} = .96$). It correlates more highly with Information ($r = .81$) than with any other subtest. It has high correlations with the Full Scale IQ ($r = .81$) and the Verbal Scale IQ ($r = .85$) and a moderate correlation with the Performance Scale IQ ($r = .65$).

Administrative and interpretive considerations.   The administrative and interpretive considerations presented for the WISC-R Vocabulary subtest generally apply to the WAIS-R (see Chapter 7). On the WAIS-R Vocabulary subtest, however, the examinee looks at a word list as the examiner pronounces each word. Also, when the examinee gives a 0- or 1-point definition on the first word, no help is provided by the examiner.

Study carefully the "Sample Responses" section of Appendix A of the WAIS-R manual so that you will know which responses require further inquiry, indicated by "(Q)." The examples indicate that many 0- and 1-point responses should be queried. When a 2-point response is accompanied by a "(Q)," it is the entire response including the elaboration that is worth 2 points.

Arithmetic

The Arithmetic subtest contains 14 problems; 13 are given orally and the other one involves blocks. All examinees start with item 3. All problems are timed, with items 1 through 4 having a time limit of 15 seconds; items 5 through 9, 30 seconds; items 10 through 13, 60 seconds; and item 14, 120 seconds. All items are scored 1 or 0, with up to 2 additional time-bonus points possible on items 10 through 14.

Rationale.   The rationale presented for the WISC-R Arithmetic subtest applies to the WAIS-R Arithmetic subtest (see Chapter 7).

Factor analytic findings.   Arithmetic is a good measure of g (58 percent of its variance may be attributed to g). The subtest has ample subtest specificity to permit interpretation of its functions at ages 20 to 34 years and 45 to 74 years. It has only adequate specificity at ages 18 to 19 years and 35 to 44 years, and it has inadequate specificity at ages 16 and 17 years. Arithmetic has a high loading on the Freedom from Distractibility factor (Mdn loading = .53) and a moderate loading on the Verbal Comprehension factor (Mdn loading = .45).

Reliability and correlational highlights.   Arithmetic is a reliable subtest ($r_{xx} = .84$). It correlates best with Vocabulary ($r = .63$) and Information ($r = .61$). It correlates moderately with the Full Scale IQ ($r = .72$), the Verbal Scale IQ ($r = .70$), and the Performance Scale IQ ($r = .62$).

Administrative and interpretive considerations.   The administrative and interpretive considerations discussed for the WISC-R Arithmetic subtest generally apply to the WAIS-R (see Chapter 7). A booklet is not used to present any of the WAIS-R items to the examinee, however.

Comprehension

The Comprehension subtest contains 16 questions covering a wide range of situations and proverbs. Questions deal with such issues as government operations and laws, health standards, and social mores. All examinees begin the subtest with item 1, and all items are scored 2, 1, or 0. The subtest is discontinued after four consecutive failures.

Rationale.   The rationale presented for the WISC-R Comprehension subtest applies to the WAIS-R Comprehension subtest (see Chapter 7).

Factor analytic findings.   The Comprehension subtest is a good measure of g (61 percent of its variance may be attributed to g). Subtest specificity varies with age. There is ample specificity at ages 45 to 54, adequate specificity at ages 25 to 44 and 65 to 74, and inadequate specificity at ages 16 to 24 and 55 to 64. Consequently, specific interpretation of the subtest's functions is appropriate only at some ages. The Comprehension subtest has a high loading on the Verbal Comprehension factor (Mdn loading = .69).

Reliability and correlational highlights.   Comprehension is a reliable subtest ($r_{xx} = .84$). It correlates more highly with Vocabulary ($r = .74$), Information ($r = .68$), and Similarities ($r = .68$) than with any other subtests. It correlates moderately with the Full Scale IQ ($r = .74$), the Verbal Scale IQ ($r = .76$), and the Performance Scale IQ ($r = .61$).

Administrative and interpretive considerations.   Administrative and interpretive considerations presented for the WISC-R Comprehension subtest are also relevant for the WAIS-R. Study carefully the "Sample Responses" section of Appendix B of the WAIS-R manual so that you will know which responses require further inquiry, indicated by "(Q)." The examples indicate that some 0- and 1-point responses should be queried.

Similarities

The Similarities subtest contains 14 pairs of words; the examinee is asked to explain the similarity between the two words in each pair. All examinees start with the first item. All items are scored 2, 1, or 0, depending on the conceptual level of the response. The subtest is discontinued after four consecutive failures.

Rationale.   The rationale described for the WISC-R Similarities subtest applies to the WAIS-R Similarities subtest (see Chapter 7).

Factor analytic findings.   Similarities is the third-best measure of g in the scale (62 percent of its variance may be attributed to g). The subtest has ample subtest specificity at ages 25 to 34, adequate specificity at ages 18 to 19 and 35 to 74, and inadequate specificity at ages 16 to 17 and 20 to 24. Specific interpretation of the subtest's functions is inappropriate at ages 16 to 17 and 20 to 24. Similarities contributes substantially to the Verbal Comprehension factor (*Mdn* loading = .67).

Reliability and correlational highlights.   Similarities is a reliable subtest (r_{xx} = .84). It correlates best with Vocabulary (r = .72) and Comprehension (r = .68). It correlates moderately with the Full Scale IQ (r = .75), the Verbal Scale IQ (r = .74), and the Performance Scale IQ (r = .64).

Administrative and interpretive considerations.   Most of the administrative and interpretive considerations presented for the WISC-R Similarities subtest apply to the WAIS-R (see Chapter 7). The major difference is that on the WAIS-R all items are scored 2, 1, or 0, whereas on the WISC-R a 2 may be given only on items 5 to 17. Considerable skill is required to score Similarities responses.

Appendix C in the WAIS-R manual merits careful study. First, the general scoring principles, which give the rationale for scores of 2, 1, and 0, should be thoroughly mastered. Second, the sample responses section should be studied carefully so that responses that should be queried, indicated by "(Q)," can be recognized readily.

Picture Completion

The Picture Completion subtest consists of 20 drawings of common objects (such as a door, a boat, and a leaf), each of which lacks a single essential element. The examinee's task is to name or point to the missing portion of the picture. There is a 20-second time limit for each picture. All examinees start with the first item. Each item is scored 1 or 0 (pass-fail), and the subtest is discontinued after five consecutive failures.

Rationale.   The rationale described for the WISC-R Picture Completion subtest applies to the WAIS-R Picture Completion subtest (see Chapter 7).

Factor analytic findings.   The Picture Completion subtest is a fair measure of g (50 percent of its variance may be attributed to g). The subtest has ample specificity at all ages to permit specific interpretation of its functions. Picture Completion contributes substantially to the Perceptual Organization factor at all the age levels except 18 to 19 (*Mdn* loading = .51).

Reliability and correlational highlights.   Picture Completion is a reliable subtest (r_{xx} = .81). It correlates more highly with Vocabulary (r = .55) than with any other subtest. It correlates moderately with the Full Scale IQ (r = .67), the Performance Scale IQ (r = .65), and the Verbal Scale IQ (r = .61).

Administrative and interpretive considerations.   The administrative and interpretive considerations presented for the WISC-R Picture Completion subtest generally apply to the WAIS-R (see Chapter 7). However, whereas on the WISC-R three different guiding statements may be given by the examiner when the examinee gives an incorrect response, on the WAIS-R only one type of guiding statement is permitted (asking for the most important part missing when an unessential missing part is given).

Picture Arrangement

The Picture Arrangement subtest requires the examinee to place a series of pictures in a logical sequence. The 10 series are similar to short comic strips. The individual pictures are placed in a specified disarranged order, and the examinee is asked to rearrange the pictures in the "right" order to tell a story. One set of cards is presented at a time. There is little motor action required, as the pictures must simply be shifted to make a meaningful story.

All examinees start with item 1. The first item has two trials and is scored 2, 1, or 0. For the remaining items (2 to 10), 2 points are given for each correct arrangement completed within the time limit. On items 2, 5, 8, and 9, 1 point is given for an acceptable variation of the correct arrangement. Items 1 to 4 have a 60-second time limit; items 5 to 8, a 90-second time limit; and items 9 and 10, a 120-second time limit.

Rationale.   The rationale presented for the WISC-R Picture Arrangement subtest applies to the WAIS-R Picture Arrangement subtest (see Chapter 7).

Factor analytic findings.   The Picture Arrangement sub test is a fair measure of g (45 percent of its variance may be attributed to g). The subtest has ample specificity at ages 16 to 19, 25 to 64, and 70 to 74 to warrant specific interpretation of its functions at these ages. It has inadequate specificity at ages 20 to 24 and 65 to 69. Picture Arrangement has modest loadings on the Verbal Comprehension (*Mdn* loading = .40), Perceptual Organization (*Mdn* loading = .33), and Freedom from Distractibility (*Mdn* loading = .22) factors. Picture Arrangement cannot be uniquely allocated to any one of the three factors, however.

Reliability and correlational highlights.   Picture Arrangement is relatively reliable (r_{xx} = .74). It correlates more highly with Picture Completion (r = .51) and Vocabulary (r = .51) than with the other subtests. It correlates moderately with the Full Scale IQ (r = .61) and to a lesser degree with the Performance Scale IQ (r = .56) and the Verbal Scale IQ (r = .57).

Administrative and interpretive considerations.   The administrative and interpretive considerations presented for the WISC-R Picture Arrangement subtest generally apply to the WAIS-R (see Chapter 7). However, the bonus points awarded on the WISC-R subtest for speed are not awarded on the WAIS-R subtest.

Block Design

The Block Design subtest contains nine items. The examinee is shown two-dimensional, red-and-white pictures of abstract designs and then must assemble a design that is identical to each picture, using three-dimensional red and white plastic blocks. All examinees start with item 1. On this item only, the examinee is required to reproduce a design from a model constructed by the examiner.

The patterns are arranged in order of increasing difficulty. Four blocks are used for the first five designs, and nine for the last four designs.

All items are timed. The first five items have a time limit of 60 seconds; the last four items have a time limit of 120 seconds. On items 1 and 2, the examinee is given 2 points for successful completion on the first trial or 1 point for successful completion on the second trial. On items 3 to 9, 4 points are given for a correct completion, with up to 3 (items 3 and 4) or 4 (items 5 through 9) additional time-bonus points awarded for quick execution. The subtest is discontinued after three consecutive failures.

Rationale.   The rationale presented for the WISC-R Block Design subtest applies to the WAIS-R Block Design subtest (see Chapter 7).

Factor analytic findings.   The Block Design subtest is the best measure of g among the Performance Scale subtests (53 percent of its variance may be attributed to g). The subtest has either ample or adequate specificity across the entire age range to permit specific interpretation of its functions. The Block Design subtest contributes substantially to the Perceptual Organization factor (*Mdn* loading = .74).

Reliability and correlational highlights.   Block Design is a reliable subtest (r_{xx} = .87). It correlates more highly with Object Assembly (r = .63) than with any other subtest. It correlates moderately with the Full Scale IQ (r = .68), the Performance Scale IQ (r = .70), and the Verbal Scale IQ (r = .61).

Administrative and interpretive considerations.   The administrative and interpretive considerations described for the WISC-R Block Design subtest generally apply to the WAIS-R (see Chapter 7). Timing and bonus points differ on the two subtests.

Object Assembly

In the Object Assembly subtest, the examinee must put jigsaw pieces together to form common objects: a manikin (6 pieces), a profile of a face (7 pieces), a hand (7 pieces), and an elephant (6 pieces). The items are presented one at a time, with the pieces presented in a specified disarranged pattern. Examinees are administered all four items.

All items are timed. The time limit is 120 seconds for the first two items and 180 seconds for the last two items. Up to 3 time-bonus points may be awarded on each item for quick execution. The manikin has a maximum score of 8;

the face, 12; the hand, 10; and the elephant, 11. Points are also awarded for partially correct performances.

Rationale. The rationale presented for the WISC-R Object Assembly subtest applies to the WAIS-R Object Assembly subtest (see Chapter 7).

Factor analytic findings. The Object Assembly subtest is a fair measure of g (40 percent of its variance may be attributed to g). The subtest has ample specificity to permit specific interpretation of its functions only at ages 18 to 19. At all other ages, subtest specificity is inadequate. The Object Assembly subtest has a high loading on the Perceptual Organization factor (*Mdn* loading = .71), which makes it interpretable as a measure of perceptual organization.

Reliability and correlational highlights. Object Assembly is the least reliable of the WAIS-R subtests (r_{xx} = .68). It correlates more highly with the Block Design subtest (r = .63) than with any of the other subtests. Its correlation is relatively low with the Full Scale IQ (r = .57), moderate with the Performance Scale IQ (r = .62), and low with the Verbal Scale IQ (r = .49).

Administrative and interpretive considerations. The administrative and interpretive considerations described for the WISC-R Object Assembly subtest generally apply to the WAIS-R.

Digit Symbol

The Digit Symbol subtest is similar to Coding B on the WISC-R. The subtest requires the copying of symbols that are paired with numbers. The sample (or key) consists of nine boxes, each of which contains one of the numbers 1 through 9 and a symbol. Each test box contains a number in the upper portion and an empty space in the lower portion. In the empty space, the examinee must draw the symbol that was paired with the number in the key. There are seven practice boxes, followed by 93 boxes in the subtest proper.

Both examiner and examinee should use pencils without erasers. It is important that the examinee have a smooth drawing surface. One point is allotted for each correct item. The time limit is 90 seconds; no time-bonus points are awarded.

Rationale. The rationale for the WISC-R Coding subtest applies to the WAIS-R Digit Symbol subtest (see Chapter 7).

Factor analytic findings. The Digit Symbol subtest is a fair measure of g (36 percent of its variance may be attributed to g). It has either ample or adequate specificity across the entire age range to permit specific interpretation of its functions. Digit Symbol has modest loadings on the Verbal Comprehension (*Mdn* loading = .38), Perceptual Organization (*Mdn* loading = .41), and Freedom from Distractibility (*Mdn* loading = .26) factors. Digit Symbol cannot be uniquely allocated to any one of the three factors, however.

Reliability and correlational highlights. Digit Symbol is a reliable subtest (r_{xx} = .82). It correlates more highly with Block Design (r = .47) and Vocabulary (r = .47) than with any other subtests. It has a relatively low correlation with the Full Scale IQ (r = .57), the Performance Scale IQ (r = .52), and the Verbal Scale IQ (r = .54).

Administrative and interpretive considerations. The administrative and interpretive considerations for the WISC-R Coding B subtest generally apply to the WAIS-R Digit Symbol subtest (see Chapter 7).

INTERPRETING THE WAIS-R

Almost all of the material in Chapter 8 on interpreting the WISC-R pertains to the WAIS-R. For example, the successive level approach to test interpretation, profile analysis, Verbal-Performance Scale comparisons, factor score comparisons, and subtest comparisons are essentially the same for both tests. The estimated percentile ranks for subtest scaled scores are shown in Table C-41 in Appendix C. This table also shows suggested qualitative descriptions associated with scaled scores. Table BC-2 on the inside back cover shows the classifications associated with WAIS-R IQs. In Appendix C, Table C-13 summarizes the functions associated with each subtest (substituting Digit Symbol for Coding), Table C-42 presents information about the three scales and factor scores, and Table C-43 gives suggested remediation activities for combinations of Wechsler subtests.

Profile Analysis

As noted above, approaches to profile analysis on the WAIS-R are basically the same as those on the WISC-R (see Chapter 8). The only difference is that different tables in Appendix C must be used.

1. *Comparing Verbal and Performance Scale IQs.* Table C-26 in Appendix C provides the critical values for com-

paring the Verbal and Performance IQs: **12** at the .05 level and **16** at the .01 level at ages 16 to 17, and **10** at the .05 level and **13** at the .01 level for the average of the nine age groups. Verbal-Performance IQ differences are essentially similar in male and female groups in the standardization sample (Matarazzo, Bornstein, McDermott, & Noonan, 1986). This finding means that similar interpretations can be given to the Verbal-Performance profiles of both males and females. Probabilities associated with various Verbal-Performance Scale differences are shown in Table C-32 of Appendix C.

2. *Comparing each Verbal subtest age-corrected scaled score with the mean Verbal age-corrected scaled score.* Table C-27 in Appendix C provides the critical values for comparing Verbal subtests with the mean of the Verbal subtests (all age-corrected scores). They range from 1.8 to 3.0 at the .05 level and from 2.1 to 3.5 at the .01 level for the six Verbal subtests.

3. *Comparing each Performance subtest age-corrected scaled score with the mean Performance age-corrected scaled score.* Table C-27 in Appendix C provides the critical values for comparing Performance subtests with the mean of the Performance subtests (all age-corrected scores). They range from 2.5 to 3.0 at the .05 level and from 3.0 to 4.2 at the .01 level for the five Performance subtests.

4. *Comparing each subtest scaled score with the mean of the 11 age-corrected subtest scaled scores.* Table C-27 in Appendix C provides the critical values for comparing subtests with the mean of all the subtests (all age-corrected scores). They range from 1.9 to 3.5 at the .05 level and from 2.2 to 4.8 at the .01 level for the 11 subtests.

5. *Comparing sets of individual age-corrected subtest scaled scores.* Table C-26 in Appendix C provides the critical values for comparing sets of subtest scores (all age-corrected scores). They range between 2 and 5 at the .05 level and between 3 and 6 at the .01 level. The values in Table C-26 in Appendix C for subtest comparisons are overly liberal (that is, they lead to too many significant differences) when more than one comparison is made. They are most accurate when a priori planned comparisons are made, such as Comprehension versus Picture Arrangement or Digit Span versus Arithmetic. (See Chapter 8 for additional information that can guide interpretations of subtest comparisons.)

Silverstein (1982c) advises that when you make multiple subtest comparisons you first determine the difference between the highest and lowest age-corrected subtest scores. If this difference is 6 or more age-corrected points,

it is significant at least at the .05 level. Differences of 6 or more points between subtests can then be interpreted. If the difference between the highest and lowest subtest score is less than 6 points, multiple comparisons between individual subtests should not be made.

Other Approaches to Profile Analysis

The supplementary approaches to WAIS-R profile analysis described in this section are similar to those discussed for the WISC-R (see Chapter 8).

Base rate differences between each subtest score and an average subtest score in the WAIS-R standardization sample. Table C-31 in Appendix C allows you to see how frequently a particular difference between a subtest score and an average WAIS-R Verbal, Performance, or overall score occurred in the standardization sample. Differences of approximately 3 to 4 points between each subtest score and the respective average Verbal or Performance Scale score were obtained by 5 percent of the standardization sample. *This table should be used only to evaluate differences that have first been found to be reliable.* (See numbers 2, 3, and 4 in the preceding section on profile analysis.)

Base rate Verbal-Performance differences (or probability-of-occurrence approach). Table C-33 in Appendix C presents the empirically observed percentage of individuals in the standardization sample who obtained a given discrepancy between Verbal and Performance Scales. The percentages are shown for five IQ groups and for the total group. For example, 37.8 percent of the individuals in the standardization sample had a 10-point difference between the two IQs.

Comparisons of factor scores. To compare factor scores, you must first convert them to Deviation IQs (see Table C-28 in Appendix C for the conversion table). Table C-26 in Appendix C provides the differences required for significance at the .05 and .01 levels between the three factors (Verbal Comprehension, Perceptual Organization, and Freedom from Distractibility) for ages 16 to 17 and for the average of the nine age groups. Finally, Table C-29 in Appendix C provides the difference scores needed to determine whether any of the individual age-corrected subtest scaled scores that comprise the three factors are significantly different (at the .05 and .01 levels) from the average of all the age-corrected scores that comprise each factor for ages 16 to 17 and for the average of the nine age groups.

As in the WISC-R, factor scores should be compared with other factor scores and not with the Verbal and Performance Scale IQs, to guard against the use of overlapping subtests.

Use of Norm Tables

The norm tables allow each examinee to be compared with his or her age group. The transition point between two normative age groups may affect scores, however, and lead to interpretive problems in some test-retest situations. For example, whereas an examinee aged 19 years, 11 months, 29 days who earns a WAIS-R scaled score total of 100 points receives a Full Scale IQ of 99, the same examinee at 20 years, 0 months receives a Full Scale IQ of 92 for the identical scaled score total. If the same examinee is tested at 19 and 20 years of age, an examiner might be inclined to interpret the drop of 7 points as suggesting a lowering in functioning, when in fact the change is an artifact of the test norms. Such considerations are important to keep in mind when one is evaluating practice effects or conducting psychoeducational reevaluations.

ASSETS OF THE WAIS-R

The WAIS-R is a well-standardized test, with good reliability and validity. It divides the 11 subtests into two sections and provides three IQs—Verbal, Performance, and Full Scale. This procedure is helpful in clinical and psychoeducational work and in the assessment of brain-behavior relationships. The fact that all examinees take a comparable battery of subtests is a valuable feature of the test. Parts of the test also can be administered to examinees limited by sensory impairments (for example, the Verbal Scale to blind individuals or those with motor handicaps; the Performance Scale to deaf individuals).

1. *Good validity.* Concurrent validity data are uniformly positive. WAIS-R IQs correlate significantly with scores from other intelligence tests, measures of academic achievement, and years of formal education. Factor analytic studies indicate that the Full Scale IQ is an excellent measure of *g*, and in most situations the division of the subtests into Verbal and Performance sections is appropriate. Inspection of the age norms for the test indicates that if the Performance Scale subtests are considered as measures of fluid intelligence and the Verbal Scale subtests as measures of crystallized intelligence, then the WAIS-R norms are consistent with predictions based on the Cattell-Horn theory of intelligence.

2. *High reliabilities.* The WAIS-R Full Scale IQ has excellent reliability (average $r_{xx} = .97$). The SE_m's of the IQs on the three scales are consistently less than 5 points. The WAIS-R manual provides reliability data, SE_m's, and intercorrelations of subtest scores for the nine age groups as well as for the average of the nine age groups, permitting evaluation of the test's properties throughout the entire age range covered by the scale. Confidence intervals can be established for IQs for each of the nine age groups (as well as for the average of the nine groups); thus estimates can be made that are applicable to the examinee's specific chronological age group.

3. *Excellent standardization.* The standardization procedures were excellent, sampling four geographic regions, both sexes, white and nonwhite populations, urban and rural residents, and the entire range of socioeconomic classes.

4. *Good administration procedures.* The prescribed procedures for administering the WAIS-R are excellent. Examiners actively probe responses in order to evaluate the breadth of the examinee's knowledge and determine whether the examinee really knows the answer. On items that require two reasons for maximum credit, the examinee is asked for another reason when only one reason is given. These procedures prevent examinees from being penalized for not fully understanding the demands of the question. The emphasis on probing questions and queries is extremely desirable.

5. *Good manual.* The WAIS-R manual is easy to use; it provides clear directions and tables. The examiner's instructions are printed in a different color to facilitate reading of the directions. Helpful suggestions are provided about abbreviations to use in recording responses, such as "Q" for question, "DK" for don't know, "Inc." for incomplete, and "NR" for no response. The test materials are interesting to adolescents and adults.

6. *Helpful scoring criteria.* The criteria for scoring replies have been carefully prepared. The Vocabulary, Comprehension, and Similarities scoring guidelines, for example, give the rationale for the use of 2, 1, and 0 scores and are accompanied by a number of examples that demonstrate the application of the scoring principles. Many typical responses are scored, and those deemed to need further inquiry are indicated by a "(Q)." Studying the scoring sections will aid you not only in scoring responses but also in administering the test.

LIMITATIONS OF THE WAIS-R

Although the WAIS-R is an excellent instrument, some problems exist with the test and the manual.

1. *Limited floor and ceiling.* The range of Full Scale IQs (45 to 150) is insufficient both for moderately to severely retarded persons and for extremely gifted persons. The test is designed so that examinees receive 1 scaled score point on each subtest, even if they give no correct answers. Thus the WAIS-R may not be an appropriate measure for the examinee who earns 0 or 1 raw score point on most subtests.

2. *Nonuniformity of subtest scores.* The range of scaled scores on all subtests is not uniform. At the reference age group (ages 20 to 34) used to obtain scaled scores to calculate IQs, a scaled score of 19 can be earned on only five subtests: Digit Span, Vocabulary, Comprehension, Block Design, and Digit Symbol. The maximum scaled score is 18 on Information, Similarities, and Object Assembly, and 17 on Arithmetic, Picture Completion, and Picture Arrangement. For purposes of profile analysis, the scaled score range is more uniform at ages 16 to 17. At this age group, a scaled score range of 19 can be obtained on nine of the 11 subtests. On the two remaining subtests— Picture Completion and Picture Arrangement—18 is the maximum scaled score.

Nonuniformity is also a problem with the age-corrected subtest scores. The restriction of scores occurs for each of the nine age groups. For example, at ages 45 to 54, scores of 19 can be earned on only six subtests: Digit Span, Vocabulary, Comprehension, Block Design, Object Assembly, and Digit Symbol. At ages 65 to 69, scores of 1 can be obtained on only six subtests: Information, Digit Span, Vocabulary, Comprehension, Object Assembly, and Digit Symbol. The lack of uniformity of available scaled scores and age-corrected scores makes profile analysis more difficult to apply, particularly to the profiles of retarded and gifted examinees. It may be misleading to apply profile techniques uniformly to all subtests for every examinee, because the same number of scaled score points, or age-corrected score points, cannot be obtained on all subtests.

3. *Difficulty of scoring responses.* When responses on the Vocabulary, Comprehension, and Similarities subtests differ from those that appear in the WAIS-R manual, they may be difficult to score. Such difficulties may lead to halo effects in scoring and may contribute to other types of examiner bias. Although mastering the scoring criteria is important for all subtests, it is particularly crucial for these three. Close attention must also be given to the mechanics of scoring.

4. *Lack of normative data for raw scores.* The WAIS-R manual fails to give means, standard deviations, and frequency distributions for the raw scores.

5. *Failure to describe the procedure for establishing*

discontinuance criteria. The WAIS-R manual states that discontinuance criteria were established using data from the standardization sample. The procedure is not described further, however.

TEST YOUR SKILL

The WISC-R Test-Your-Skill Exercises in Chapter 8 also apply to the WAIS-R. You are encouraged to review these exercises.

SUMMARY

1. The revised edition of the Wechsler Adult Intelligence Scale, the WAIS-R, is similar to its 1955 predecessor, with 80 percent of the original items retained. The WAIS-R is applicable to individuals from ages 16-0 to 74-11. Standardization of the scale was excellent, including both white and nonwhite individuals.

2. Reliabilities for the IQs associated with the Verbal, Performance, and Full Scales are extremely high for the standardization sample (average r_{xx} of .97, .93, and .97, respectively), with SE_m's for the Full Scale of about 2.5 IQ points.

3. Practice effects (after a two- to seven-week test-retest interval) for standardization subjects were about 3.3 points on the Verbal Scale, 8.4 points on the Performance Scale, and 6.2 points on the Full Scale.

4. Concurrent and construct validity studies of the WAIS-R have been uniformly positive. The scale correlates significantly with education and with other ability measures. Moreover, the distribution of the age norms is consistent with theory-based expectations, and factor analysis indicates that all 11 subtests measure *g* with a moderate to high degree of success.

5. The WAIS-R tends to provide lower IQs than the WAIS and slightly higher IQs than the WISC-R and Stanford-Binet: Fourth Edition, especially for low-functioning individuals.

6. Higher intercorrelations are observed among the Verbal subtests than among the Performance subtests. Within their respective scales, Vocabulary and Block Design show the highest correlations with the Full Scale IQ (.82 and .67, respectively, at ages 16 to 17).

7. A study of WAIS-R IQs in relation to various stratification variables showed that mean differences between males and females were less than 3 points; the IQs of white subjects were higher than those of black subjects by about 15 points (101.4 vs. 86.8); the mean Full Scale IQ of persons in the highest occupational group was 22 points higher, on average, than that of persons in the lowest occupational group (111.0 vs. 89.0); urban-rural differences and geographic region differences were small; and Full Scale IQs of persons with 16 or more years of education

were, on average, 33 points higher than those of persons with less than 8 years of education.

8. Factor analyses of the WAIS-R usually yield three factors—Verbal Comprehension, Perceptual Organization, and Freedom from Distractibility—but some also report two-factor solutions.

9. The subtests that provide the best measure of *g* are Vocabulary, Information, Similarities, Comprehension, Arithmetic, and Block Design. The remaining subtests are fair measures of *g*.

10. Only some of the subtests have ample subtest specificity at ages 16 to 17 and at other ages throughout the scale. At ages 16 to 17, seven of the subtests have ample or adequate subtest specificity (Information, Digit Span, Vocabulary, Picture Completion, Picture Arrangement, Block Design, Digit Symbol), and four (Arithmetic, Comprehension, Similarities, Object Assembly) have inadequate subtest specificity.

11. Somewhat purer factor scores can be obtained by use of Table C-28 in Appendix C, which converts age-corrected scores into Deviation Quotients as follows: (a) Information, Vocabulary, Comprehension, and Similarities into a Verbal Comprehension Deviation Quotient; (b) Block Design, Object Assembly, and Picture Completion (at every age level except 18 to 19, where the latter subtest should be omitted) into a Perceptual Organization Deviation Quotient; and (c) Digit Span and Arithmetic into a Freedom from Distractibility Deviation Quotient.

12. Although the administrative procedures for the WAIS-R are generally similar to those for the WISC-R, there are some differences. Be sure to use the appropriate procedures for each scale.

13. Table C-30 in Appendix C presents extrapolated IQs for scaled scores that are above those shown in the WAIS-R manual.

14. Numerous WAIS-R short forms have been developed. Tables C-34 through C-40 in Appendix C provide information to assist you in the selection and use of WAIS-R short forms.

15. The rationale and administrative and interpretive considerations for each WAIS-R subtest are similar to those for the respective WISC-R subtests. Consult Chapter 7 for a discussion of these issues.

16. Information is a good measure of *g* and contributes to the Verbal Comprehension factor. Subtest specificity is adequate except at ages 45 to 54. Information is a reliable subtest and correlates highly with Vocabulary.

17. Digit Span is a fair measure of *g*, and contributes to the Freedom from Distractibility factor. Subtest specificity is ample at all ages. Digit Span is a reliable subtest and correlates highly with Arithmetic.

18. Vocabulary is the best measure of *g* in the scale and contributes to the Verbal Comprehension factor. Subtest specificity is adequate at all ages. Vocabulary is the most reliable subtest in the scale and correlates highly with Information.

19. Arithmetic is a good measure of *g* and contributes to the Freedom from Distractibility factor. It has ample or adequate subtest specificity except at ages 16 to 17. Arithmetic is a reliable subtest and correlates best with Vocabulary and Information.

20. Comprehension is a good measure of *g*, and contributes to the Verbal Comprehension factor. Subtest specificity is ample or adequate except at ages 16 to 24 and 55 to 64. Comprehension is a reliable subtest and correlates highly with Vocabulary, Information, and Similarities.

21. Similarities is a good measure of *g* and contributes to the Verbal Comprehension factor. Subtest specificity is ample or adequate except at ages 16 to 17 and 20 to 24. Similarities is a reliable subtest and correlates best with Vocabulary and Comprehension.

22. Picture Completion is a fair measure of *g* and contributes to the Perceptual Organization factor at all ages except 18 to 19. Subtest specificity is ample at all ages. Picture Completion is a reliable subtest and correlates highly with Vocabulary.

23. Picture Arrangement is a fair measure of *g*. Subtest specificity is ample except at ages 20 to 24 and 65 to 69. Picture Arrangement is a reasonably reliable subtest and correlates highly with Picture Completion and Vocabulary.

24. Block Design is a good measure of *g* and contributes to the Perceptual Organization factor. Subtest specificity is ample or adequate at all ages. Block Design is a reliable subtest and correlates highly with Object Assembly.

25. Object Assembly is a fair measure of *g* and contributes to the Perceptual Organization factor. Subtest specificity is ample only at ages 18 to 19. Object Assembly is the least reliable subtest in the scale and correlates highly with Block Design.

26. Digit Symbol is a fair measure of *g*. Subtest specificity is either ample or adequate at all ages. Digit Symbol is a reliable subtest and correlates more highly with Block Design and Vocabulary than with the other subtests.

27. The methods described in Chapter 7 for interpreting the WISC-R also pertain, for the most part, to the WAIS-R.

28. The norm tables should be carefully studied in test-retest situations.

29. The assets of the WAIS-R include its good concurrent validity, high reliabilities, excellent standardization, good administration procedures, good manual, and helpful scoring criteria.

30. Limitations of the WAIS-R include limited floor and ceiling, nonuniformity of subtest scores, difficulty of scoring responses, lack of normative data for raw scores, and failure to describe the procedure for establishing discontinuance criteria.

KEY TERMS, CONCEPTS, AND NAMES

Wechsler-Bellevue Intelligence Scale (p. 220)
WAIS-R standardization (p. 220)
WAIS-R Deviation IQ (p. 220)
WAIS-R scaled scores (p. 220)
Prorating procedure (p. 220)
Scaled score equivalents for age groups (p. 220)
Reliability of the WAIS-R (p. 220)
Standard errors of measurement of the WAIS-R (p. 221)
Stability of the WAIS-R (p. 222)

STUDY QUESTIONS

1. Discuss the following topics with respect to the WAIS-R: standardization, Deviation IQs, scaled score equivalents for age groups, reliability, and validity.

2. Describe WAIS-R factor analytic findings.

3. Discuss some important factors involved in administering the WAIS-R.

4. Discuss WAIS-R short forms. Include a discussion of their values and limitations.

5. Discuss the rationale, factor analytic findings, reliability and correlational highlights, and administrative considerations for each of the following WAIS-R subtests: Information, Digit Span, Vocabulary, Arithmetic, Comprehension, Similarities, Picture Completion, Picture Arrangement, Block Design, Object Assembly, and Digit Symbol.

6. Discuss the intent of profile analysis, methods of profile analysis, and approaches to profile analysis on the WAIS-R.

7. Discuss the assets and limitations of the WAIS-R.

II

STANFORD-BINET INTELLIGENCE SCALE: FOURTH EDITION

All things are engaged in writing their history. The planet, the pebble, goes attended by its shadow. The rolling rock leaves its scratches on the mountain; the river, its channel in the soil; the animal, its bones in the stratum; the fern and leaf, their modest epitaph in the coal. The falling drop makes its sculpture in the sand or the stone. Every act of the man inscribes itself in memories, manners and face. Every object is covered with hints which speak to the intelligent.

—Emerson

The Stanford-Binet Intelligence Scale: Fourth Edition (SB: FE) (Thorndike, Hagen, & Sattler, 1986a) is a battery of 15 subtests that covers an age range of 2 through 23 years (see Figure 11-1 and Exhibit 11-1). The SB: FE uses a point-scale format similar to that of the Wechsler scales. Prior editions of the Stanford-Binet Intelligence Scales, as noted in Chapter 3, used an age-scale format. Some of the major characteristics of the earlier versions of the Binet-Simon Scales and the Stanford-Binet Intelligence Scale are summarized in Table 11-1.

1937 AND 1960 STANFORD-BINET INTELLIGENCE SCALES

1937 Stanford-Binet Scales

In 1937, after 21 years, the 1916 Stanford-Binet Intelligence Scale was revised. Two new forms were designed, Form L and Form M. The 1937 revision was recognized as a

milestone in the progress of the individual testing of intelligence. The scale was better standardized, two forms were made available, and there were more performance tests at the earlier levels. New types of tests were more prevalent at the preschool and adult levels, and more use was made of differential scoring of the same test. Improvements were made in memory tests, in the wording of questions, in year-level assignments, and in the scoring of the Vocabulary test. The scale was extended downward to year level II, with tests appearing at half-year levels between years II and V and upward to the Superior Adult III level. Tests were also provided for year levels XI and XII.

The scales had excellent reliability (ranging from .98 for those with IQs below 70 to .90 for those with IQs above 129) and acceptable validity (*r*'s of .40 to .50 with school success). Factor analytic studies indicated that most of the tests loaded heavily on a common factor, although group factors (for example, verbal, memory, visualization, spatial, and reasoning) were also reported.

The 1937 scales represented a significant improvement

Figure 11-1.   Stanford-Binet Intelligence Scale: Fourth Edition. Courtesy Riverside Publishing Company.

Table 11-1
Some Characteristics of the Binet-Simon and Stanford-Binet Scales from 1905 to 1972

Scale year	Authors	Number of tests	Year levels covered	Modifications made in revisions	Limitations
1905	Binet and Simon	30	Very low grade idiots to upper elementary grades		Poorly standardized ($N = 50$) Inadequate range Tests did not always discriminate No objective method for arriving at a total score
1908	Binet and Simon	59	III to XIII	New tests added Some tests eliminated, especially those at the idiot level Tests grouped according to age commonly passed Mental-age concept introduced	Inadequate standardization ($N = 203$) No credits given for fractions of a year Lower year level tests too easy, higher year level tests too difficult Scoring and administrative procedures inadequate Unequal number of tests at different year levels
1911	Binet and Simon	54	III to Adult	New tests added, some eliminated Credit given for fraction of a year Tests shifted More detailed instructions Adult year level included	Almost same limitations as those noted for 1908 scale; there were no fundamental changes
1916	Terman	90	III to Superior Adult I	New tests added Some tests revised Location changed for some tests Scoring and administrative procedures changed and better organized Alternate tests introduced IQ concept introduced Representative sampling attempted	Poor standardization at extremes Only single form Inadequate standardization ($N = 1,000$ native-born Californian children and 400 adults) Inadequate measure of adult mental capacity Too heavily weighted with verbal and abstract materials Inadequate scoring and administrative procedures at some points Some tests dated by the 1930s Some tests placed at wrong age level Too much credit for rote memory
1937	Terman and Merrill	129	II to Superior Adult III	Better standardization ($N = 3,184$) Two forms (L and M) More performance tests at earlier year levels	Equal variability at all ages not present Sample somewhat higher in socioeconomic level than general population, and more urban than rural subjects included Some tests difficult to score Low ceiling with above-average adolescents
1960	Terman and	142	II to Superior	One form (L-M) which incorporated best tests from Forms L	Too heavily weighted with verbal materials

(Table continues next page)

Table 11-1 (cont.)

Scale year	Authors	Number of tests	Year levels covered	Modifications made in revisions	Limitations
	Merrill		Adult III	and M	Originality and creative abilities not measured
				New group of children used to check changes in test difficulty ($N = 4{,}498$)	Inadequate for very superior students
				Some tests relocated, dropped, or rescored	Abstract verbal tests appeared at too low a level and rote memory tests appeared at too high a level
				Substitution of Deviation IQ for ratio IQ—standard score with $M = 100$ and $SD = 16$	Restandardization procedures not appropriate
				Use of age 18 years as ceiling level rather than 16 years	
				Clarification of scoring principles	
1973	Thorndike	—	—	Restandardized in 1972 ($N = 2{,}100$)	—

over the 1916 scale and were greeted favorably by many reviewers. The scales were improved statistically and had many clinical applications. They were seen as efficient instruments for diagnosing mental retardation and for gaining insights into a child's temperament. Reviewers characterized the 1937 Stanford-Binet as combining the facets of the clinical interview with those of an objective assessment. Dissatisfaction was expressed, however, with the emphasis on verbal material, age-scale format, ceiling procedure, item placements, emphasis on rote memory, administration procedures, incomplete statistical data, use of one score only, inadequate measurement of g, inappropriateness of many items for adults, and applicability of the scale in clinical situations. Despite these criticisms, the 1937 scales were extremely popular, yielding acceptable validity coefficients and serving as the standard for the development of other tests. The scales, although by no means perfect instruments, served as important tools in clinical and educational settings.

1960 Stanford-Binet Scale: Form L-M

In 1960 a new revision appeared. In many ways the 1960 edition was not a genuine revision. The revision was carried out by selecting the best items from Form L and Form M and combining them into a new form. A new standardization group was not obtained; instead, a sample of 4,498 subjects who had taken the scale between 1950 and 1954 was used to check on changes in item difficulty. New material was not introduced, nor were the essential features of the scale changed. With the 1960 revision, only one form was available. Validity data were not presented with

the revision; its validity rested on the fact that the same types of tests were used as in the 1937 scales.

One of the most important developments in Form L-M was the replacement of the 1937 scale's IQ tables, which represented the conventional ratio IQ, with Deviation IQs for ages 2 through 18 years. The Deviation IQ is basically a normalized standard score with a mean of 100 and a standard deviation of 16. It expresses the deviation of the ratio IQ from the mean ratio IQ at each age level. The Deviation IQ controls for the variability in IQ distributions that was found to exist at various levels of the former revisions. A specific IQ at different ages in Form L-M indicates close to the same relative ability or standing regardless of the age of the examinee.

Dissatisfaction was expressed with the manner in which the Deviation IQs were constructed and with the norming sample, however. Additionally, the 1960 scale was criticized for being too heavily weighted with verbal materials, for not measuring creative abilities, and for improper placement of some items. The 1960 revision, however, still produced acceptable validity coefficients and remained one of the standard instruments for the assessment of children's intelligence until the 1980s.

1972 Norms

Revised norms for Form L-M were published in 1973. Except for two minor changes in the test procedures (a more attractive female doll card was used and the word "charcoal" was substituted for "coal"), the tests in the scale and the directions for scoring and administration were the same. The standardization group for the revision consisted

Exhibit 11-1

Stanford-Binet Intelligence Scale: Fourth Edition–Like Items

1. Vocabulary (14 pictures, 32 words)
The task on the first 14 items is to name the pictured object. Words 15 through 46 are both given orally and shown to the examinee; the examinee must define these words.
train   dime   taut   cryptography

2. Bead Memory (42 items)
The task is to reproduce bead patterns by finding them in photographs or placing beads on a stick (see Figure 11-1)

3. Quantitative (40 questions)
The task is to solve quantitative problems.
Match •• (see Figure 11-1).
Count the number of blocks in the picture.
What is the smallest whole number that can be divided evenly by 1, 2, and 3?
How many 12-inch-by-12-inch tiles will be needed to cover a floor that is 6 feet by 6 feet?

4. Memory for Sentences (42 items)
The task is to repeat successively longer sentences.
Say: Small cow.
Say: High clouds appeared on the horizon.
Say: The field of science can aid mankind by discovering many useful things.

5. Pattern Analysis (42 items)
For the first 6 items the task is to complete a form board (see Figure 11-1). For the remaining items the task is to reproduce stimulus designs using two, three, four, six, or nine blocks (see Figure 11-1). An example of a Pattern Analysis design is shown below.

6. Comprehension (42 questions)
The task is to point to body parts (at earlier levels) and to answer questions dealing with social comprehension.
Point to the doll's foot (see Figure 11-1).
Why do we have nurses?
What advantages does an airplane have over a car?
Why do we have a Congress?

7. Absurdities (32 items)
The task is to identify the incongruity in pictures.
Writing with a spoon.
Riding a bicycle that has one wheel missing.
A map of the United States with Florida on the West coast.

8. Memory for Digits
The task is to recall digits correctly.
Digits Forward contains 14 series of digits, 3 to 9 digits in length (Example: 3-9-5).
Digits Reversed contains 12 series of digits, 2 to 7 digits in length (Example: 5-8-9-4).

9. Copying (28 items)
The task is to reproduce designs with blocks (items 1 to 12) or to copy simple and complex geometric designs, such as lines, rectangles, and partial circles, that are shown on cards.

10. Memory for Objects (14 items)
The task is to recall pictured objects in the exact sequence in which they were presented. The examinee points to the pictured items on a card that contains both the stimulus items and distractor items. For example, the examinee is first shown a picture of a knife and a dog and then shown a card containing the pictures of a knife, dog, spoon, cat, and house.

11. Matrices (26 items)
The task is to select the object, design, or letter that best completes the matrix. An example of a Matrices item is shown below.

X	X
X	

• Y A X 11
A B C D E

12. Number Series (26 items)
The task is to predict the next two numbers in a series. To succeed, the examinee must discern the pattern in the series.
5, 4, 3, ___, ___
$\frac{4}{14}, \frac{4}{13}, \frac{4}{12}, \frac{4}{11},$ ___, ___
10, 2, 11, 2, 12, ___, ___

13. Paper Folding and Cutting (18 items)
The task is to select the picture that shows how a folded and cut piece of paper would look unfolded.

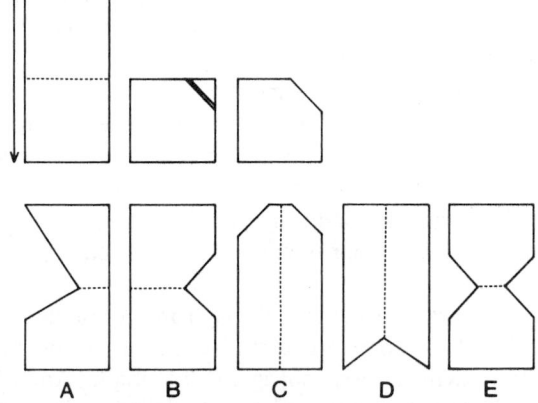

14. Verbal Relations (18 items)
The task is to indicate how the first three items are alike but different from the fourth.

(Exhibit continues next page)

Exhibit 11-1 (cont.)

How are a dog, cow, and pig alike but different from a bird?
How are a car, truck, and motorcycle alike but different from a bicycle?

15. Equation Building (18 items)
The task is to arrange numbers and mathematical signs (+, −, ÷, etc.) into an equation.

4 2 6 + =
¼ 2 7 1 − ÷ =

Note. These items are similar to those on the Stanford-Binet: Fourth Edition, but they are not actually from the test.

---

of a representative sample of 2,100 children, with approximately 100 subjects at each Stanford-Binet year level. A special procedure, based on test scores from the group-administered Cognitive Abilities Tests, was used for stratifying each age sample to ensure proportionate representation of all ability levels. Unlike the 1960 norms, which did not include nonwhites in the standardization group, the 1972 norms contained nonwhites (including black and Spanish-surnamed individuals) and whites. Subjects were, however, excluded from the normative sample if English was not the primary language spoken in the home. The greatest differences in test scores between the 1972 and 1960 norms were found at the preschool level. For a similar performance, the 1972 norms yielded IQs that were about 10 points lower than those given by the 1960 norms. (See Sattler, 1982b, for a comprehensive review of administrative and interpretive procedures for the Stanford-Binet: Form L-M.)

INTRODUCTION TO THE SB: FE

Some continuity is maintained between the SB: FE and prior editions. Item types the editions have in common are vocabulary (both pictures and words), comprehension, picture absurdities, paper folding and cutting, copying, repeating digits, memory for sentences, copying a bead chain from memory, similarities, form-board items, and quantitative items. The SB: FE has some new items of these types and also some new item types (memory for objects, number series, and equation building). Every effort was made to design items with culture-fair content. A panel of ethnic minority reviewers evaluated the items for biased content.

The 15 subtests are not used through all ages of the scale (see Table 11-2). Some are administered only at the preschool and elementary school ages (for example, Absurdities and Copying), whereas others are administered only at the upper year levels (for example, Number Series and Equation Building). Of the 15 subtests, only 6 run throughout the scale—Vocabulary, Comprehension, Pattern Anal-

ysis, Quantitative, Bead Memory, and Memory for Sentences.

A three-level hierarchical model was used to guide the construction of the SB: FE. The model postulates (a) *g* (a general intelligence factor) at the highest level of interpretation; (b) crystallized, fluid, and short-term memory factors at the second level; and (c) more specific factors—such as verbal reasoning, quantitative reasoning, and abstract visual reasoning—at the third level. The specific factors at the third level, plus short-term memory at the second level, form four area scores in the SB: FE. Within each area specific subtests are designated (see Table 11-2); however, the placement of subtests was not based on factor analytic findings. The Composite Score reflects the highest level and is considered to be the best estimate of *g* in the scale.

STANDARDIZATION

The standardization sample consisted of 5,013 individuals in 17 age groups. The number of individuals ranged from 194 in the 18-0 to 23-11 age group to 460 in the 5-0 to 5-11 group. The sample was selected so as to be representative of the U.S. population according to 1980 census data. Stratification variables included geographic region, community size, ethnic group, age, gender, and socioeconomic status. Because the final sample included too many children with high SES backgrounds, weighting procedures were used to make the sample conform to the census data.

COMPOSITE SCORES, STANDARD AGE SCORES, AND TEST-AGE EQUIVALENTS

Raw scores are converted into three types of standard scores: standard age scores (or scaled scores) for the subtests ($M = 50$, $SD = 8$), area scores ($M = 100$, $SD = 16$), and a Composite Score ($M = 100$, $SD = 16$). The Composite Score is similar to the Deviation IQ employed on the Wechsler scales. The Wechsler scales use a

**Table 11-2
Areas, Subtests, and Age Spans for Stanford-Binet:
Fourth Edition**

Designated area	Subtest	Age span
Verbal Reasoning	Vocabulary	2 to 23
	Comprehension	2 to 23
	Absurdities	2 to 14
	Verbal Relations	12 to 23
Abstract/Visual Reasoning	Pattern Analysis	2 to 23
	Copying	2 to 13
	Matrices	7 to 23
	Paper Folding and Cutting	12 to 23
Quantitative Reasoning	Quantitative	2 to 23
	Number Series	7 to 23
	Equation Building	12 to 23
Short-Term Memory	Bead Memory	2 to 23
	Memory for Sentences	2 to 23
	Memory for Digits	7 to 23
	Memory for Objects	7 to 23

standard deviation of 15, however, whereas the SB: FE uses a standard deviation of 16, which is consistent with previous editions of the Stanford-Binet. Raw scores obtained by the examinee on each subtest are first converted into standard age scores within the examinee's own age group through tables in the *Guide for Administering and Scoring the Fourth Edition*. Age groups are divided into 4-month intervals from 2 to 6 years (the one exception is a 3½ month interval at age 2-0-0 to 2-3-15), 6-month intervals from 6 to 12 years, 1-year intervals from 12 to 18 years, and a 6-year interval from 18 to 23-11 years.

The procedure used in the SB: FE allows for the computation of area and Composite Scores when less than the entire battery is administered. Proration or special short form procedures are not needed to calculate area or Composite Scores. After the subtest scaled scores have been obtained, they are entered in a table that provides area standard age scores ($M = 100$, $SD = 16$). The area score can be obtained by use of one or more of the subtest scaled scores that comprise the area.

The area standard scores then can be converted to a Composite Score through use of a table on pages 187 and 188 in the *Guide*. This table is divided into two sections; one part is for ages 2-0-0 to 9-11-15, the other for ages 9-11-16 to 23-11-15. As with the areas scores, the Composite Score can be obtained by use of 1, 2, 3, or 4 area scores.

As you will read shortly, this text advocates the use of factor scores in place of area scores. Consequently, the factor scores will be highlighted throughout the chapter. The area score tables in the *Guide*, however, still must be used to compute the Composite Score and the factor scores.

The *Stanford-Binet: Fourth Edition Technical Manual* provides a table (Table G.1) of test-age equivalents to facilitate interpretation of a child's performance. Chapters 2 and 4 in this text discuss the advantages and disadvantages associated with the use of test-age equivalents.

RELIABILITY

The Composite Score of the SB: FE has excellent reliability. Internal consistency reliabilities for the Composite Score range from .95 to .99 over the 17 age groups. The median Composite Score reliability is .97. (Reliability of the factor scores will be discussed later in this chapter.)

As expected, the reliabilities for the subtests are less satisfactory than those for the Composite Score (see Table 11-3). The median subtest reliabilities range from a low of .73 for Memory for Objects to a high of .94 for Paper Folding and Cutting. Subtest reliabilities differ somewhat according to age group, ranging from a low of .66 for Memory for Objects at age 10 years to a high of .96 for Pattern Analysis at ages 18–23.

Standard Errors of Measurement

The median standard error of measurement (SE_m) in scaled-score points ($M = 100$, $SD = 16$) is 2.8 for the Composite Score (see Table 11-3). For the subtests, the smallest median SE_m's, are associated with Paper Folding and Cutting and Pattern Analysis (2.0 and 2.3 scaled-score points, respectively), and the largest median SE_m's are associated with Memory for Objects and Memory for Digits (4.2 and 3.3 scaled-score points, respectively).

Stability

The stability of the SB: FE was assessed by retesting two groups (57 children with a M age of 5-2 and 55 children with a M age of 8-1) after an interval of two to eight months (Thorndike et al., 1986b). For the 5-year-olds, the stability coefficient was excellent for the Composite Score ($r_{xx} = .91$). Stability coefficients for the eight subtests ranged from .56 for Bead Memory to .78 for Memory for Sentences. For the 8-year-olds, the stability coefficient was again excellent for the Composite Score ($r_{xx} = .90$). Sta-

Table 11-3
Median Reliability Coefficients and Standard Errors of Measurement for Stanford-Binet Intelligence Scale: Fourth Edition Subtests, Factor Scores, and the Composite Score

Subtest, Factor Score, or Composite Score	Median reliability coefficient	Median standard error of measurement
Subtest		
Vocabulary	.87	2.9
Comprehension	.89	2.6
Absurdities	.87	2.9
Verbal Relations	.91	2.4
Pattern Analysis	.92	2.3
Copying	.87	2.9
Matrices	.90	2.5
Paper Folding and Cutting	.94	2.0
Quantitative	.88	2.8
Number Series	.90	2.5
Equation Building	.91	2.4
Bead Memory	.87	2.9
Memory for Sentences	.89	2.6
Memory for Digits	.83	3.3
Memory for Objects	.73	4.2
Factor		
Verbal Comprehension	.95	3.6
Nonverbal Reasoning/Visualization	.96	3.2
Memory	.91	4.8
Composite		
Composite score	.97	2.8

Source: Adapted, in part, from Thorndike et al. (1986b).

bility coefficients for the 12 subtests ranged from .28 for Quantitative to .86 for Comprehension.

In both groups, children obtained *higher* scores on the second testing. The mean Composite Score change was 8.2 points for the 5-year-olds and 6.4 points for the 8-year-olds. For the individual subtests in the 5-year-old sample, mean changes ranged from a low of 1.5 scaled-score points on Vocabulary to a high of 4.3 scaled-score points on Copying. For the individual subtests in the 8-year-old sample, mean changes ranged from a low of 1.2 scaled-score points on Memory for Objects to a high of 3.7 scaled-score points on Pattern Analysis.

The test-retest reliability coefficients indicate that the Composite Score is substantially more reliable than the individual subtest scores. The average change noted for the Composite Score was about half of a standard deviation. Considerable fluctuation in scores was evident on the individual subtests, suggesting that they should not be relied on to provide stable measures of ability.

Precision Range

Table C-44 in Appendix C shows the 68, 85, 90, 95, and 99 percent confidence intervals for the three factor scores — Verbal Comprehension, Nonverbal Memory/Visualization, and Memory — and for the Composite Score for all age groups in the standardization sample. Confidence intervals are not provided for the average of the age groups because the composition of the scale changes at various age levels. Additionally, the confidence intervals change considerably with age. For example, the confidence interval for the Composite Score at the 68 percent level is ± 4 for 2-year-olds and ± 2 for 10-year-olds. Confidence intervals therefore should be reported for the examinee's specific age group.

VALIDITY

The *Technical Manual* for the SB: FE presents several studies investigating the Scale's criterion validity. Comparisons were made with various other tests, including the Stanford-Binet: Form L-M, WISC-R, WPPSI, WAIS-R, and K-ABC, for both normal and exceptional populations. In the 13 studies reported in the manual, correlations between the SB: FE and these criterion measures ranged from a low of .27 to a high of .91 (*Mdn r* = .80). The median *r* of .80 supports the concurrent validity of the SB: FE. The one study with a low correlation was with a gifted sample of 82 7-4-year-old children who were administered both the SB: FE and Form L-M. In 10 of the 13 studies the SB: FE yielded lower mean scores than did the criterion test. In most cases, differences were 5 points or less. In two studies, however, the SB: FE yielded substantially lower scores. Scores of a gifted population were, on the average, 13.7 points lower than Form L-M scores, those of a mentally retarded population were 9.3 points lower than WAIS-R scores. The reasons for these findings are unclear at this time. They could be associated with ceiling or floor effects, item difficulties, better differentiation of abilities, or some combination of these or other factors.

Additional studies have investigated the concurrent validity of the SB: FE. In a sample of 30 normal children (*M* age = 11.3), the SB: FE correlated highly with Form

L-M ($r = .72$) and produced similar overall scores ($M = 114.42$, $SD = 12.31$ on the SB: FE; $M = 113.07$, $SD = 15.18$ on Form L-M) (Hartwig, Sapp, & Clayton, 1987). With a sample of 120 gifted children (M age $= 6.11$), the SB: FE yielded lower overall scores ($M = 122.46$, $SD = 9.17$) than Form L-M ($M = 130.45$, $SD = 11.20$, $r = .64$) (Livesay, 1986).

With a population of 19 special education children aged 7 to 16 years the WISC-R and the SB: FE yielded scores that were essentially similar ($M = 83.63$, $SD = 14.82$ on WISC-R and $M = 83.11$, $SD = 13.30$ on SB: FE, $r = .88$) (Hollinger & Baldwin, 1987). With 32 normal second-grade children (M age $= 7.77$), the SB: FE yielded a mean Composite Score that was 7 points lower than the WISC-R score ($M = 105.53$, $SD = 9.84$ on SB: FE; $M = 112.53$, $SD = 9.42$ on WISC-R) (Rothlisberg, 1987). With 166 gifted children (M age $= 10.33$), the SB: FE and the WISC-R produced similar scores ($M = 121.47$, $SD = 9.72$ on SB: FE, $M = 123.33$, $SD = 9.58$ on WISC-R, $r = .55$) (Livesay, 1986). And with 32 normal college students (M age $= 18.0$), the WAIS-R and the SB: FE yielded similar scores ($M = 103.5$, $SD = 10.9$ on WAIS-R, $M = 100.9$, $SD = 9.1$ on SB: FE, $r = .91$) (Carvajal, Gerber, Hewes, & Weaver, 1987).

The results of the preceding studies suggest that for populations within the average intellectual range, the SB: FE is likely to yield Composite Scores that are similar to those provided by the WISC- R, WAIS-R, and Form L-M. With gifted and mentally retarded populations, however, the SB: FE may yield lower scores than Form L-M and the WAIS-R.

In studies with the WRAT-R, the SB: FE Composite Score has been found to have acceptable validity coefficients. With a sample of 47 emotionally disturbed children (ages 7-5 to 16-1), the correlations were .51 with Reading, .55 with Spelling, and .58 with Arithmetic (Blakeslee, 1987). With 49 emotionally disturbed children (M age $= 13-4$), the correlations were .48 with Reading, .37 with Spelling, and .70 with Arithmetic (Lewis-O'Donnell, 1986).

The results of the preceding studies are based on the administration of the entire battery. It is not known to what extent results would be similar if the complete battery were not administered.

Construct validity was established in a number of ways. First, raw scores increase as a function of age. Second, factor analyses support a number of dimensions of the scale, such as adequate to high g loadings of the subtests and specific factors at various age levels of the scale. Third, all of the subtests correlate moderately to highly positively with the Composite Score.

INTERCORRELATIONS BETWEEN SUBTESTS AND BETWEEN SUBTESTS AND THE COMPOSITE SCORE

Intercorrelations provide information about the relationships of the SB: FE subtests to each other and to the Composite Score. Median intercorrelations between the 15 subtests range from a low of .29 to a high of .73 (Mdn $r = .47$). The *highest* median subtest intercorrelations (.60 and above) are between Vocabulary and Comprehension (.73), Vocabulary and Verbal Relations (.71), Quantitative and Number Series (.67), Matrices and Number Series (.66), Number Series and Equation Building (.64), Vocabulary and Memory for Sentences (.64), Comprehension and Verbal Relations (.63), Vocabulary and Absurdities (.62), Quantitative and Equation Building (.61), Paper Folding and Cutting and Number Series (.61), and Pattern Analysis and Paper Folding and Cutting (.60).

The *lowest* median subtest intercorrelations (less than .40) are between Memory for Objects and Paper Folding and Cutting (.29), Memory for Objects and Equation Building (.30), Memory for Objects and Verbal Relations (.32), Memory for Objects and Absurdities (.33), Memory for Digits and Copying (.33), Memory for Digits and Comprehension (.34), Memory for Digits and Absurdities (.34), Memory for Digits and Pattern Analysis (.35), Memory for Sentences and Paper Folding and Cutting (.35), Memory for Objects and Pattern Analysis (.36), Memory for Digits and Verbal Relations (.36), Memory for Digits and Paper Folding and Cutting (.37), Memory for Objects and Comprehension (.38), and Memory for Sentences and Equation Building (.38).

Median correlations between the subtests and the Composite Score range from .60 to .82 ($Mdn = .74$). Quantitative and Number Series have the *highest* correlation with the Composite Score (both .82), followed by Vocabulary (.81), Matrices (.78), and Comprehension and Verbal Relations (both .76). Memory for Objects has the *lowest* correlation with the Composite Score (.60), followed by Memory for Digits (.64), Copying (.66), Absurdities (.72), and Bead Memory (.72). Thus reasoning and verbal comprehension subtests have the highest correlations with the Composite Score and memory subtests have the lowest correlations.

SB: FE COMPOSITE SCORES AND STRATIFICATION VARIABLES

The relationship between Composite Scores and the demographic characteristics of the standardization sample are shown for three age groups (Table 4.5 in the *Technical Manual*): (a) 2 through 6, (b) 7 through 11, and (c) 12 through 23. Differences between males' and females' mean Composite Scores were less than 2 points. Thus sex differences are not large enough to assume any practical significance on the scale. Mean Composite Scores of white examinees were about 10 to 17 points higher than those of black examinees: 14 points at ages 2 through 6 (104.7 vs. 91.0), 10 points at ages 7 through 11 (102.6 vs. 92.7), and 17 points at ages 12 through 23 (103.5 vs. 86.1). White examinees also obtained higher scores than other ethnic groups, except at ages 7 through 11, where Asian examinees obtained a mean Composite Score of 103.6 and the white examinees a mean Composite Score of 102.6. This difference, however, is not very meaningful. Table 11-4 shows the mean Composite Scores based on the median scores of the three age groups for the various demographic characteristics studied.

Mean Composite Scores show a clear relationship to parental education and parental occupational groups: Composite Scores of children whose parents were college graduates were about 16 points higher, on the average, than those of children whose parents had less than a high school education (110.1 vs. 94.4). Similarly, Composite Scores of children of managerial and professional workers were 14 points higher, on the average, than those of children of operators, fabricators, and others (108.0 vs. 94.0). Community size differences varied depending on the age group in the standardization sample. For example, in the 2 through 6 age group the range was about 5 points (103.4 vs. 98.1). In the 7 through 11 age group, the range was about 12 points—a low of 91.4 for cities with 300,000 to 999,999 versus a high of 103.0 for moderately sized cities (25,000 to 99,999). Finally, in the 12 through 18–23 age group, the range was about 8 points (102.6 for moderately sized cities vs. 94.4 for small towns).

Table 11-4
Relationship of Stanford-Binet Intelligence Scale: Fourth Edition Composite Scores to Sex, Race, Parental Education, Parental Occupation, and Community Size

	Demographic variables	*M*	*SD*
Sex	Males	99.1	16.0
	Females	100.4	15.1
Race	Asian	99.9	15.4
	Black	91.0	13.2
	Hispanic	94.9	13.4
	Native American	94.7	17.7
	White	103.5	15.8
Parental education	1. Less than high school	94.4	14.8
	2. High school graduate	99.0	14.3
	3. 1 to 3 years college	103.4	15.2
	4. College graduate	110.1	14.4
Parental occupational group	1. Managerial/professional	108.0	15.3
	2. Technical/sales	101.5	14.3
	3. Service occupations	93.5	15.7
	4. Farming/forestry	96.0	16.7
	5. Precision production	96.8	16.6
	6. Operators, fabricators, other	94.0	15.0
Community size	1. 1,000,000 or more	98.6	15.8
	2. 300,000 to 999,999	98.5	17.9
	3. 100,000 to 299,999	100.4	14.4
	4. 25,000 to 99,999	103.0	14.1
	5. 2,500 to 24,999	98.1	16.6
	6. less than 2,500	101.0	14.8

Note. These are mean Composite Scores based on the median scores of the three age groups listed in Table 4.5 of the *Technical Manual for the Stanford-Binet: Fourth Edition*.
Source: Adapted from Thorndike et al. (1986b).

FACTOR ANALYSIS

The findings in this section are based on the results obtained from principal components analysis with varimax rotation of the 15 subtests of the SB: FE administered to the standardization sample. It differs from the one presented in the *Technical Manual*. A principal components analysis lends itself to the development of factors that may be useful in guiding interpretations needed for clinical and psychoeducational evaluations. Because subtests in the SB: FE are not continuous throughout the scale and because different subtests are administered at different ages, the factor structure of the scale differs at different ages.

The results of the principal components analysis are summarized in Table 11-5. At ages 2 through 6, a two-factor solution best characterizes the scale: *Verbal Comprehension* and *Nonverbal Reasoning/Visualization*. At ages 7 through 23, a three-factor solution is most appropri-

Table 11-5
Stanford-Binet Intelligence Scale: Fourth Edition Subtest Loadings on Factor A (Verbal Comprehension), Factor B (Nonverbal Reasoning/Visualization), and Factor C (Memory) for Seventeen Age Levels Following Varimax Rotation

	Age level																	
Subtest	*2*	*3*	*4*	*5*	*6*	*7*	*8*	*9*	*10*	*11*	*12*	*13*	*14*	*15*	*16*	*17*	*18ªMdn.*	
Factor A — Verbal Comprehension																		
Vocabulary	75	76	78	73	79	71	77	79	70	81	72	76	79	78	75	78	77	77
Comprehension	66	78	76	82	74	71	79	75	66	68	52	70	68	62	68	46	63	68
Absurdities	53	72	60	59	44	41	50	49	46	51	72	40	49	–	–	–	–	50
Verbal Relations	–	–	–	–	–	–	–	–	–	–	61	53	67	70	75	60	67	67
Pattern Analysis	28	34	29	32	24	17	26	28	18	27	49	27	23	21	26	15	28	27
Copying	13	28	34	28	18	16	27	19	30	29	74	24	–	–	–	–	–	25
Matrices	–	–	–	–	–	10	20	13	18	28	43	37	33	24	38	25	25	25
Paper Folding and Cutting	–	–	–	–	–	–	–	–	–	–	18	22	37	28	31	23	24	24
Quantitative	33	32	42	40	36	40	44	34	41	50	38	52	49	38	56	41	40	41
Number Series	–	–	–	–	–	18	27	23	26	32	33	29	33	25	41	24	28	28
Equation Building	–	–	–	–	–	–	–	–	–	–	01	23	34	38	45	19	22	23
Bead Memory	11	20	36	40	26	31	28	26	31	42	35	40	29	10	29	30	14	29
Memory for Sentences	67	64	56	59	63	60	58	51	64	63	42	69	57	39	51	45	56	58
Memory for Digits	–	–	–	–	–	26	20	21	27	22	17	46	25	15	15	20	32	22
Memory for Objects	–	–	–	–	–	20	16	08	11	28	15	43	17	18	15	25	07	17
Factor B — Nonverbal Reasoning/Visualization																		
Vocabulary	17	29	36	38	27	35	30	32	45	35	36	33	33	33	37	30	38	33
Comprehension	37	32	34	32	25	29	30	26	45	33	47	29	40	45	39	28	27	32
Absurdities	44	33	42	43	43	48	49	49	69	58	27	45	44	–	–	–	–	44
Verbal Relations	–	–	–	–	–	–	–	–	–	–	03	45	32	30	34	37	45	34
Pattern Analysis	64	66	71	71	70	55	72	69	77	64	39	60	76	61	71	51	32	66
Copying	58	70	62	60	53	48	52	52	49	46	-04	32	–	–	–	–	–	52
Matrices	–	–	–	–	–	23	57	63	57	55	47	65	63	64	60	58	65	60
Paper Folding and Cutting	–	–	–	–	–	–	–	–	–	–	25	67	65	71	63	70	65	65
Quantitative	43	63	68	70	64	48	40	43	54	35	49	59	56	58	54	60	47	54
Number Series	–	–	–	–	–	14	57	59	61	48	68	74	61	73	69	69	70	64
Equation Building	–	–	–	–	–	–	–	–	–	–	51	58	42	60	51	73	72	58
Bead Memory	55	65	63	63	63	56	57	42	48	54	33	51	50	36	51	40	38	51
Memory for Sentences	12	26	37	39	63	20	26	15	16	26	24	19	16	13	20	18	19	20
Memory for Digits	–	–	–	–	–	19	24	20	14	25	33	35	25	24	25	26	28	25
Memory for Objects	–	–	–	–	–	19	37	22	30	36	21	31	32	26	19	16	18	24

(Table continues next page)

Table 11-5 (cont.)

Subtest	2	3	4	5	6	7	8	9	10	11	12	13	14	15	16	17	18[a]	Mdn.

Age level

Factor C—Memory

Subtest	2	3	4	5	6	7	8	9	10	11	12	13	14	15	16	17	18[a]	Mdn.
Vocabulary	—	—	—	—	—	22	22	28	29	26	44	24	33	35	32	32	29	29
Comprehension	—	—	—	—	—	26	15	21	21	25	43	20	30	38	21	36	28	26
Absurdities	—	—	—	—	—	25	14	13	04	16	13	42	30	—	—	—	—	15
Verbal Relations	—	—	—	—	—	—	—	—	—	—	12	07	16	17	16	33	15	16
Pattern Analysis	—	—	—	—	—	32	17	22	19	29	14	28	27	27	28	12	29	27
Copying	—	—	—	—	—	26	16	10	22	37	37	82	—	—	—	—	—	26
Matrices	—	—	—	—	—	53	31	37	40	41	29	31	33	37	31	20	25	32
Paper Folding and Cutting	—	—	—	—	—	—	—	—	—	—	15	15	15	14	17	04	17	15
Quantitative	—	—	—	—	—	11	22	29	27	44	40	23	38	49	39	33	40	36
Number Series	—	—	—	—	—	80	28	33	38	52	30	36	43	32	36	42	34	36
Equation Building	—	—	—	—	—	—	—	—	—	—	29	18	29	18	24	27	17	24
Bead Memory	—	—	—	—	—	14	24	37	34	29	45	31	43	43	47	29	49	36
Memory for Sentences	—	—	—	—	—	36	50	61	53	45	67	37	57	65	57	69	64	57
Memory for Digits	—	—	—	—	—	57	81	55	71	71	60	38	64	70	74	64	66	65
Memory for Objects	—	—	—	—	—	42	44	53	58	37	63	30	53	51	54	32	61	52

Note. Decimal points omitted. Factor loadings are for a two-factor solution at ages 2, 3, 4, 5, and 6; three-factor solution at ages 7, 8, 9, 10, 11, 13, 14, 15, and 16; and four-factor solution at ages 12, 17, and 18–23.
[a] Represents ages 18–23.

ate: *Verbal Comprehension, Nonverbal Reasoning/Visualization,* and *Memory.* The grouping of the subtests for factor scores at various age levels is shown in Table 11-8. The rationale is explained further in the section on Factor Scores later in this section.

The Verbal Comprehension factor score measures verbal knowledge and understanding obtained by formal and informal education and reflects the ability to apply verbal skills to new situations. The Nonverbal Reasoning/Visualization factor score reflects the ability to interpret and organize visually perceived material, to perform basic arithmetical operations using visual cues or verbal cues, to visualize patterns, to demonstrate visual-motor skills, and to use reasoning to solve problems. Both reasoning and visualization are key components of this factor. The Memory factor measures the ability to attend or concentrate, or short-term memory, but also may involve sequencing skills.

SB: FE Subtests as Measures of *g*

As shown in Table 11-6, all of the SB: FE subtests are either good or fair measures of *g* (the general intelligence factor). Based on the median of the 17 age levels, the subtests with the *highest* loadings are Vocabulary (.80), Number Series (.79), Quantitative (.77), Comprehension (.75), Matrices (.74), Absurdities (.72), Memory for Sentences (.71), and Pattern Analysis (.70). The subtests with fair *g* loadings are Paper Folding and Cutting (.69), Bead Memory (.68), Verbal Relations (.68), Equation Building (.67), Copying (.61), Memory for Digits (.60), and Memory for Objects (.54). The subtests with high *g* loadings include both verbal and nonverbal subtests.

Subtest Specificity

Subtest specificity refers to the proportion of a subtest's variance that is both reliable (that is, not due to errors of measurement) and distinctive to the subtest. Although individual SB: FE subtests overlap in their measurement properties, many of them possess a relatively high degree of specificity, which justifies interpretation of specific subtest functions (for example, interpreting Verbal Relations as a measure of conceptual thinking) (see Table 11-7). Of the 15 subtests in the scale, 11 have ample or adequate specificity throughout the entire age range covered by the subtests. These subtests are Absurdities, Verbal Relations, Pattern Analysis, Copying, Matrices, Paper Folding and Cutting, Number Series, Equation Building, Bead Memory, Memory for Sentences, and Memory for Digits. The

Table 11-6
Stanford-Binet Intelligence Scale: Fourth Edition Subtests as Measures of _g_

	Good measure of g			Fair measure of g	
Subtest	Median loading of g	Percentage of variance attributable to g	Subtest	Median loading of g	Percentage of variance attributable to g
Vocabulary	.80	64	Paper Folding and Cutting	.69	48
Number Series	.79	62	Bead Memory	.68	46
Quantitative	.77	60	Verbal Relations	.68	46
Comprehension	.75	56	Equation Building	.67	45
Matrices	.74	55	Copying	.61	37
Absurdities	.72	52	Memory for Digits	.60	36
Memory for Sentences	.71	50	Memory for Objects	.54	29
Pattern Analysis	.70	49			

four subtests with inadequate specificity at various ages are Vocabulary, Comprehension, Quantitative, and Memory for Objects.

At ages at which subtests have inadequate specificity, scores should not be interpreted as measuring specific functions, and cautious interpretation is required for subtests falling within the adequate specificity category. These subtests, however, can be interpreted as measuring _g_ and the appropriate factor (Verbal Comprehension, Nonverbal Reasoning/Visualization, or Memory).

Obtaining Factor Scores

Of the 15 subtests in the battery, 12 have been selected as the primary subtests to form the factor scores. The preferred way to obtain the three factor scores is to use the following combination of subtests:

Verbal
Comprehension = (a) Sum of scaled scores on Vocabulary, Comprehension, Absurdities, and Memory for Sentences at ages 2 through 7

Table 11-7
Amount of Specificity in Stanford-Binet: Fourth Edition Subtests

Ample specificity		Adequate specificity		Inadequate specificity	
Subtest	Ages	Subtest	Ages	Subtest	Ages
Vocabulary	2 and 15	Vocabulary	10, 12–13, 16–18	Vocabulary	3–9, 11, 14
Comprehension	2, 7, 10–13, 16–18	Comprehension	3–4, 14–15	Comprehension	5–6, 8–9
Absurdities	2–9, 11–14	Absurdities	10	Quantitative	6, 18
Verbal Relations	12–18	Pattern Analysis	14	Memory for Objects	12
Pattern Analysis	2–13, 15–18	Copying	12		
Copying	2–11, 13	Quantitative	14–16		
Matrices	7–18	Number Series	7, 12–13, 16–18		
Paper Folding and Cutting	12–18	Memory for Sentences	18		
Quantitative	2–5, 7–13, 17	Memory for Digits	10		
Number Series	8–11, 14–15				
Equation Building	12–18				
Bead Memory	all ages				
Memory for Sentences	2–17				
Memory for Digits	7–9, 11–18				
Memory for Objects	7–11, 13–18				

Note. Age 18 includes ages 18 through 23. The procedure described by Kaufman (1975a) was used to evaluate the specificity of the subtests.

     (b) Sum of scaled scores on Vocabulary, Comprehension, and Absurdities at ages 8 through 14

     (c) Sum of scaled scores on Vocabulary, Comprehension, and Verbal Relations at ages 15 through 23

Nonverbal Reasoning/ Visualization = (a) Sum of scaled scores on Pattern Analysis, Copying, Quantitative, and Bead Memory at ages 2 through 11

     (b) Sum of scaled scores on Pattern Analysis, Matrices, Quantitative, and Bead Memory at ages 12 through 23

Memory (not calculated for ages 2–6) = (a) Sum of scaled scores on Memory for Digits and Memory for Objects at age 7

     (b) Sum of scaled scores on Memory for Sentences, Memory for Digits, and Memory for Objects at ages 8 through 23

In addition to the subtests noted above, other subtests can be used to obtain factor scores. For the Verbal Comprehension factor, Verbal Relations can be used at ages 12 through 14. For the Nonverbal Reasoning/Visualization factor, Matrices and Number Series can be used at ages 9 through 11, Number Series and Equation Building at ages 12 through 18–23, and Paper Folding and Cutting at ages 13 through 18–23. Table 11-8 lists the factor scores by age level and subtests, and Exhibit 11-2 shows a worksheet for computing factor scores, together with an example. The factor scores are highly reliable (r_{xx}'s range from .91 to .96, with SE_m's of 3.2 to 4.8; see Table 11-3).

ADMINISTERING THE SB: FE

In the SB: FE items in each subtest are arranged in order of increasing difficulty, with two items of approximately equal difficulty placed at each level. Levels are designated by letters. The levels are used to determine entry and discontinuance points. Figure 11-2 shows the front page of the record booklet. A guide by Delaney and Hopkins (1987) provides useful information for administering the SB: FE.

Adaptive Testing

All examinees are first given the Vocabulary subtest, which is also referred to as the routing test. Performance on this subtest, together with the examinee's chronological age, is used to determine the entry level for all of the other subtests from a routing chart.

The routing subtest and routing chart, however, may not be accurate for mentally retarded children and perhaps other groups. One study (Bissette, 1987) and several field reports have indicated that the entry levels were too high for trainable mentally retarded children. In fact, the entry levels suggested in the *Guide* tend to be above TMR children's ceiling levels on most subtests. Examiners will have to adjust the entry level to make it more applicable to the examinee's probable level of performance.

Basal level and ceiling levels.   The two consecutive levels at which all items are passed (4 items) are termed the *basal level*. The two consecutive levels at which three of the four items or all four items are failed are termed the *ceiling level*. The ceiling level is also the point at which a subtest is discontinued. When a double basal level is obtained, the lower basal level is used in calculating the raw score. When a double ceiling level is obtained, the higher ceiling level is used in obtaining the raw score. These procedures take into account all of the child's actual failures and successes. A complete administration of the SB: FE requires the establishment of one basal level and one ceiling level. In cases where either a basal or a ceiling level is not reached, scores can still be reported, but with the notation "*Estimate*" following the scores.

Chronological age.   The child's chronological age is obtained by subtracting date of birth from date of examination. Chronological age is recorded in years and months, with 16 or more days rounded to the next higher month.

Timing of items.   Of the 15 subtests in the SB: FE, only one—Pattern Analysis—calls for timing of the examinee. (In several subtests the presentation of stimulus items is timed.) In the other subtests, judgment must be used to decide when to proceed to the next item.

Scratch paper.   Scratch paper may be used on the Quantitative, Number Series, and Equation Building subtests. The scratch paper should be collected after the examination.

Table 11-8
Suggested Subtest Combinations for Factor Scores at Various Age Ranges for the Stanford-Binet: Fourth Edition

Factor score	Age	Subtest combination
Verbal Comprehension	2 through 7	Vocabulary Comprehension Absurdities Memory for Sentences
	8 through 14	Vocabulary Comprehension Absurdities
	15 through 18–23	Vocabulary Comprehension Verbal Relations
Nonverbal Reasoning/Visualization	2 through 11	Pattern Analysis Copying Quantitative Bead Memory
	12 through 18–23	Pattern Analysis Matrices Quantitative Bead Memory
Memory	2 through 6	None
	7	Memory for Digits Memory for Objects
	8 through 18–23	Memory for Sentences Memory for Digits Memory for Objects

Note. Other subtests may be added or substituted to obtain factor scores. For the Verbal Comprehension factor, Verbal Relations can be used at ages 12, 13, and 14. For the Nonverbal Reasoning/Visualization factor, (a) Matrices and Number Series can be used at ages 9, 10, and 11; (b) Number Series and Equation Building at ages 12 through 18–23; and (c) Paper Folding and Cutting at ages 13 through 18–23.

Physical Abilities Necessary for the SB: FE

Adequate hearing and language functions are required for verbal subtests, and adequate vision and/or visual-motor ability are required for the nonverbal subtests (see Table 11-9). As discussed in Chapter 6 for the WISC-R, for examinees with physical disabilities, you must attempt to find ways to give the test without, in the process, providing the child with cues to answers. Alternative ways of administering subtests to children younger than 6 or 7 years of age are restricted by the fact that they have limited writing and reading skills. Most of the discussion about adaptive administration of the WISC-R (see page 140) also pertains to the SB: FE.

Short Forms

Various short forms are suggested in the *Guide for Administering and Scoring the Fourth Edition*, including a four-subtest short form composed of Vocabulary, Bead Memory, Quantitative, and Pattern Analysis. Another is a six-subtest short form composed of Vocabulary, Bead Memory, Quantitative, Memory for Sentences, Pattern Analysis, and Comprehension. Both of these short forms contain subtests that are found at all age levels of the scale. Additionally, the six-subtest short form yields estimates of two factor scores: Verbal Comprehension (Vocabulary, Comprehension, and Memory for Sentences) and Nonverbal Reasoning/Visualization (Pattern Analysis, Quantitative, and Bead Memory). When the complete battery is administered, Memory for Sentences is part of the Verbal Comprehension factor at ages 2 through 7 and part of the Memory factor after age 7. Because Memory for Sentences also has high loadings on the Verbal Comprehension factor, it can be used to obtain a Verbal Comprehension factor score when the six-subtest short form is administered at any age. Short forms on the SB: FE have the same advantages and disadvantages as they do on the

Exhibit 11-2

Worksheet for Computing Factor Scores

Examinee's name: _____Jim_____	*Date:* _____Nov. 1, 1987_____
Date of birth: _____Dec. 1, 1980_____	*Examiner's name:* _____Bill Smith_____
Age: _____6-11_____ *Sex:* _____M_____	

VERBAL COMPREHENSION

Ages 2 through 7

SUBTEST	STANDARD SCORE
1 Vocabulary (VR)	40
6 Comprehension (VR)	45
7 Absurdities (VR)	30
4 Memory for Sentences (STM)	43

STEPS

(1) Sum of standard scores on Vocabulary + Comprehension + Absurdities	115
(2) Verbal Reasoning (VR) Area SAS (p. 183 of *Guide* for 3 subtests)	73
(3) Short-Term Memory (STM) Area SAS (multiply the standard score by 2)	86
(4) Sum of (2) + (3)	159
(5) **Verbal Comprehension Factor Score** (p. 187 of *Guide* for 2 area scores)	77

Ages 8 through 14

SUBTEST	STANDARD SCORE
1 Vocabulary (VR)	_____
6 Comprehension (VR)	_____
7 Absurdities (VR)	_____

STEPS

(1) Sum of standard scores on Vocabulary + Comprehension + Absurdities	_____
(2) Verbal Reasoning (VR) Area SAS (p. 183 of *Guide* for 3 subtests)	_____
(3) **Verbal Comprehension Factor Score** (p. 187 or 188 of *Guide* for 1 area score)	_____

Ages 15 through 18–23

SUBTEST	STANDARD SCORE
1 Vocabulary (VR)	_____
6 Comprehension (VR)	_____
14 Verbal Relations (VR)	_____

STEPS

(1) Sum of standard scores on Vocabulary + Comprehension + Verbal Relations	_____
(2) Verbal Reasoning (VR) Area SAS (p. 183 of *Guide* for 3 subtests)	_____

(3) **Verbal Comprehension Factor Score** (p. 188 of *Guide* for 1 area score)   _____

NONVERBAL REASONING/VISUALIZATION

Ages 2 through 11

SUBTEST	STANDARD SCORE
5 Pattern Analysis (A/VR)	33
9 Copying (A/VR)	30
3 Quantitative (QR)	33
2 Bead Memory (STM)	35

STEPS

(1) Sum of standard scores on Pattern Analysis + Copying	63
(2) Abstract/Visual Reasoning (A/VR) Area SAS (p. 184 of *Guide* for 2 subtests)	57
(3) Quantitative Reasoning (QR) Area SAS (multiply the standard score by 2)	66
(4) Short-Term Memory (STM) Area SAS (multiply the standard score by 2)	70
(5) Sum of (2) + (3) + (4)	193
(6) **Nonverbal Reasoning/Visualization Factor Score** (p. 187 or 188 of *Guide* for 3 area scores)	58

Ages 12 through 18–23

SUBTEST	STANDARD SCORE
5 Pattern Analysis (A/VR)	_____
11 Matrices (A/VR)	_____
3 Quantitative (QR)	_____
2 Bead Memory (STM)	_____

STEPS

(1) Sum of standard scores on Pattern Analysis + Matrices	_____
(2) Abstract/Visual Reasoning (A/VR) Area SAS (p. 184 of *Guide* for 2 subtests)	_____
(3) Quantitative Reasoning (QR) Area SAS (multiply the standard score by 2)	_____
(4) Short-Term Memory (STM) Area SAS (multiply the standard score by 2)	_____

(Exhibit continues next page)

Exhibit 11-2 (cont.)

(5) Sum of (2) + (3) + (4)   _____
(6) **Nonverbal Reasoning/Visualization
    Factor Score** (p. 188 of *Guide* for 3
    area scores)   _____

MEMORY

Age 7

SUBTEST	STANDARD SCORE
8 Memory for Digits (STM)	_____
10 Memory for Objects (STM)	_____

STEPS

(1) Sum of standard scores on Memory for
    Digits + Memory for Objects   _____
(2) Short-Term Memory (STM) Area SAS
    (p. 186 of *Guide* for 2 subtests)   _____

(3) **Memory Factor Score** (p. 187 of
    Guide for 1 area score)   _____

Ages 8 through 18–23

SUBTEST	STANDARD SCORE
4 Memory for Sentences (STM)	_____
8 Memory for Digits (STM)	_____
10 Memory for Objects (STM)	_____

STEPS

(1) Sum of standard scores on Memory for
    Sentences + Memory for Digits
    + Memory for Objects   _____
(2) Short-Term Memory (STM) Area SAS
    (p. 186 of *Guide* for 3 subtests)   _____
(3) **Memory Factor Score** (p. 187 or 188
    of *Guide* for 1 area score)   _____

Wechsler scales (see Chapter 6). They should be used primarily for screening purposes.

Content Area Scores

The SB: FE provides four content area scores: Verbal Reasoning, Abstract/Visual Reasoning, Quantitative Reasoning, and Short-Term Memory. Because these area scores are not supported by factor analysis, they should not be used for most interpretive purposes. The four areas must be used, however, to obtain the Composite Score and to obtain the factor scores. The factor scores are preferred for interpretative purposes.

Profile Sheet

After the scale has been scored and factor scores computed, a profile sheet can be used to plot the examinee's scores (see Exhibit 11-3). This profile sheet has entries for the Composite Score, factor scores, and subtest scores. The profile sheet provides a visual picture of the examinee's performance.

Recommended Subtest Battery

Table 11-10 shows the recommended subtest battery for each age level of the SB: FE. The 8-subtest and 10-subtest combinations shown in Table 11-10 were selected on the basis of factor analysis, time considerations, and clinical

and psychoeducational usefulness. At ages 2 through 6, an 8-subtest battery is recommended: the six subtests that run throughout the battery plus Absurdities and Copying. At ages 7 through 11, the 10-subtest contains these eight subtests plus Memory for Digits and Memory for Objects. At age 12, Matrices is substituted for Copying, and at age 15, Verbal Relations is substituted for Absurdities. The routine use of these batteries is recommended for all children. Administration time will be considerably shortened, and the use of a standard battery will facilitate interpretive and placement decisions. The remaining three subtests—Paper Folding and Cutting, Number Series, and Equation Building—can be used for special diagnostic purposes.

SB: FE SUBTESTS

Vocabulary

The Vocabulary subtest contains 46 items divided into a picture vocabulary section (items 1 to 14) and an oral vocabulary section (items 15 to 46). For the picture items, the child is asked to name the picture or give the most pertinent detail of the picture. For the oral vocabulary section, the child is asked to explain orally the meaning of each word. The subtest is administered throughout all ages covered by the scale. Each word is scored 1 or 0.

STANFORD-BINET INTELLIGENCE SCALE

RECORD BOOKLET

Stanford-Binet Intelligence Scale: Fourth Edition

Name _____

_____ Sex _____

Ethnicity   NA   H   B   W/NH   O/AA   PI   Other _____

	YEAR	MONTH	DAY
Date of Testing	_____	_____	_____
Birth Date	_____	_____	_____
Age	_____	_____	_____

School _____

Grade _____

Examiner _____

Father's Occupation: _____

Mother's Occupation: _____

FACTORS AFFECTING TEST PERFORMANCE
Overall Rating of Conditions

Optimal	Good	Average	Detrimental	Seriously detrimental

9-74539

	RAW SCORE	STANDARD AGE SCORE ✳
Verbal Reasoning		
1 Vocabulary	_____	_____
6 Comprehension	_____	_____
7 Absurdities	_____	_____
14 Verbal Relations	_____	_____
Sum of Subtest SAS's		_____
Verbal Reasoning SAS		_____
Abstract/Visual Reasoning		
5 Pattern Analysis	_____	_____
9 Copying	_____	_____
11 Matrices	_____	_____
13 Paper Folding & Cutting	_____	_____
Sum of Subtest SAS's		_____
Abstract/Visual Reasoning SAS		_____
Quantitative Reasoning		
3 Quantitative	_____	_____
12 Number Series	_____	_____
15 Equation Building	_____	_____
Sum of Subtest SAS's		_____
Quantitative Reasoning SAS		_____
Short-Term Memory		
2 Bead Memory	_____	_____
4 Memory For Sentences	_____	_____
8 Memory For Digits	_____	_____
10 Memory For Objects	_____	_____
Sum of Subtest SAS's		_____
Short-Term Memory SAS		_____
Sum of Area SAS's		_____

		COMPOSITE SCORE ✳
Test Composite		
Partial Composite		_____
Partial Composite based on _____		

✳ Be sure that all Standard Age Scores (SAS's) are based on the tables in the *Guide* with the number 9-74502 on the cover.

	1	2	3	4	5	
Attention						
a) Absorbed by task						Easily distracted
Reactions During Test Performance						
a) Normal activity level						Abnormal activity level
b) Initiates activity						Waits to be told
c) Quick to respond						Urging needed
Emotional Independence						
a) Socially confident						Insecure
b) Realistically self-confident						Distrusts own ability
c) Comfortable in adult company						Ill-at-ease
d) Assured						Anxious
Problem-Solving Behavior						
a) Persistent						Gives up easily
b) Reacts to failure realistically						Reacts to failure unrealistically
c) Eager to continue						Seeks to terminate
d) Challenged by hard tasks						Prefers only easy tasks
Independence of Examiner Support						
a) Needs minimum of commendation						Needs constant praise and encouragement
Expressive Language						
a) Excellent articulation						Very poor articulation
Receptive Language						
a) Excellent sound discrimination						Very poor sound discrimination

Was it difficult to establish rapport with this person?

Easy |___|___|___|___|___| Difficult

The Riverside Publishing Company

Robert L. Thorndike
Elizabeth P. Hagen
Jerome M. Sattler

Figure 11-2. Cover page of Stanford-Binet Intelligence Scale: Fourth Edition record booklet. Reprinted with permission of the Riverside Publishing Company from *Stanford-Binet Intelligence Scale: Fourth Edition* by R. L. Thorndike, E. P. Hagen, J. M. Sattler. THE RIVERSIDE PUBLISHING COMPANY, 8420 W. Bryn Mawr Avenue, Chicago, IL 60631. Copyright 1986.

Table 11-9
Physical Abilities Necessary and Adaptable for Stanford-Binet Intelligence Scale: Fourth Edition

Subtest	Vision	Hearing	Oral speech	Arm-hand use
Vocabulary	Xr	Xa	Xa	Xw
Comprehension	Xr	Xa	Xa	Xw
Absurdities	X	Xa	Xa	Xw
Verbal Relations	Xr	Xa	Xa	Xw
Pattern Analysis	X	Xa	–	X
Copying	X	Xa	–	X
Matrices	X	Xa	Xo	Xa
Paper Folding and Cutting	X	Xa	Xo	Xa
Quantitative	X	Xa	Xa	Xw
Number Series	Xa	Xa	Xa	Xw
Equation Building	Xa	Xa	Xa	Xw
Bead Memory	X	Xa	–	X
Memory for Sentences	–	X	Xa	Xw
Memory for Digits	–	X	Xa	Xw
Memory for Objects	X	Xa	Xa	Xw

Note. The code is as follows:

X – This ability is required. Adaptation is not feasible if this function is absent or more than mildly impaired.

Xa – This ability is required for standard administration, but the subtest is adaptable.

Xo – Examinees who are able to speak can say their answers.

Xr – Examinees who are able to read can be shown the questions. If the examinee cannot read, hearing is necessary. If neither the ability to read nor the ability to hear is present, the subtest should not be administered.

Xw – Examinees who are able to write can write their answers.

Rationale. The rationale presented for the WISC-R Vocabulary subtest generally applies to the oral vocabulary section of the SB: FE (see page 151). Formal education is less likely to be an influence for picture vocabulary than for oral vocabulary. Experience is likely to be the major contributing factor to the vocabulary development of preschool children.

The purpose of the picture vocabulary section is to see whether the child correctly identifies a picture by any of its appropriate names. Visual perception is involved, as are verbal retrieval and word recall abilities. In complex pictures, the child must appreciate the main element in the picture. Correct association of word with object, the ability to vocalize the word, and the ability to comprehend the spoken word are all important. These skills represent emergent aspects of language use. The emphasis is on comprehending what the spoken word stands for and not on articulation skills.

Factor analytic findings. The Vocabulary subtest is a good measure of g (64 percent of its variance may be attributed to g). The subtest has ample or adequate specificity at ages 2, 10, 12, 13, 16, 17, and 18–23 to permit specific interpretation of its functions. At other ages,

where its specificity is inadequate, the Vocabulary subtest still can be interpreted as a measure of verbal comprehension. Vocabulary contributes substantially to the Verbal Comprehension factor at all ages (*Mdn* loading = .77).

Reliability and correlational highlights. Vocabulary is a reliable subtest (r_{xx} = .87). It correlates more highly with Comprehension (r = .73) than with any other subtest. It also correlates highly with the Composite Score (r = .81).

Administrative and interpretive considerations. The administrative and interpretive considerations presented for the WISC-R Vocabulary subtest generally apply to the SB: FE Vocabulary subtest (see page 151). On the SB: FE, however, different administrative procedures are used for the picture vocabulary and oral vocabulary sections.

Study carefully the "General Guidelines for Scoring the Vocabulary Test" (Appendix A) in the *Stanford-Binet: Fourth Edition Guide* so that you will know which responses need further inquiry. The examples indicate that many responses should be queried. Unlike the WISC-R, on which vocabulary responses may be scored 2, 1, or 0, the SB: FE uses a 1 or 0 system in an attempt to make

Exhibit 11-3

Profile Sheet for the Stanford-Binet Intelligence Scale: Fourth Edition

Name: _____ Sex: _____ Date of examination: _____

Date of birth: _____ CA: _____ Examiner's name: _____

Percentile rank	Standard score	Summary scores — Verbal Comprehension	Nonverbal Reasoning/Visualization	Memory	Composite Score	Standard score	Verbal Comprehension — Vocabulary	Comprehension	Absurdities	Memory for Sentences	Verbal Relations	Pattern Analysis	Copying	Quantitative	Bead Memory	Matrices	Number Series	Equation Building	Paper Folding and Cutting	Memory for Sentences	Memory for Digits	Memory for Objects	Percentile rank
99+	156	•	•	•	•	78	•	•	•	•	•	•	•	•	•	•	•	•	•	•	•	•	99+
99+	152	•	•	•	•	76	•	•	•	•	•	•	•	•	•	•	•	•	•	•	•	•	99+
99+	148					74																	99+
99+	144	•	•	•	•	72	•	•	•	•	•	•	•	•	•	•	•	•	•	•	•	•	99+
99	140	•	•	•	•	70	•	•	•	•	•	•	•	•	•	•	•	•	•	•	•	•	99
99	136	•	•	•	•	68	•	•	•	•	•	•	•	•	•	•	•	•	•	•	•	•	99
98	132					66																	98
96	128	•	•	•	•	64	•	•	•	•	•	•	•	•	•	•	•	•	•	•	•	•	96
93	124	•	•	•	•	62	•	•	•	•	•	•	•	•	•	•	•	•	•	•	•	•	93
89	120	•	•	•	•	60	•	•	•	•	•	•	•	•	•	•	•	•	•	•	•	•	89
84	116					58																	84
77	112	•	•	•	•	56	•	•	•	•	•	•	•	•	•	•	•	•	•	•	•	•	77
69	108	•	•	•	•	54	•	•	•	•	•	•	•	•	•	•	•	•	•	•	•	•	69
60	104	•	•	•	•	52	•	•	•	•	•	•	•	•	•	•	•	•	•	•	•	•	60
50	100					50																	50
40	96	•	•	•	•	48	•	•	•	•	•	•	•	•	•	•	•	•	•	•	•	•	40
31	92	•	•	•	•	46	•	•	•	•	•	•	•	•	•	•	•	•	•	•	•	•	31
23	88	•	•	•	•	44	•	•	•	•	•	•	•	•	•	•	•	•	•	•	•	•	23
16	84					42																	16
12	80	•	•	•	•	40	•	•	•	•	•	•	•	•	•	•	•	•	•	•	•	•	12
7	76	•	•	•	•	38	•	•	•	•	•	•	•	•	•	•	•	•	•	•	•	•	7
4	72	•	•	•	•	36	•	•	•	•	•	•	•	•	•	•	•	•	•	•	•	•	4
2	68					34																	2
1	64	•	•	•	•	32	•	•	•	•	•	•	•	•	•	•	•	•	•	•	•	•	1
1	60	•	•	•	•	30	•	•	•	•	•	•	•	•	•	•	•	•	•	•	•	•	1
1−	56	•	•	•	•	28	•	•	•	•	•	•	•	•	•	•	•	•	•	•	•	•	1−
1−	52					26																	1−
1−	48	•	•	•	•	24	•	•	•	•	•	•	•	•	•	•	•	•	•	•	•	•	1−
1−	44	•	•	•	•	22	•	•	•	•	•	•	•	•	•	•	•	•	•	•	•	•	1−

Table 11-10
Recommended Subtest Battery for Each Age of the Stanford-Binet: Fourth Edition

Subtest	2	3	4	5	6	7	8	9	10	11	12	13	14	15	16	17	18
1 Vocabulary	•	•	•	•	•	•	•	•	•	•	•	•	•	•	•	•	•
6 Comprehension	•	•	•	•	•	•	•	•	•	•	•	•	•	•	•	•	•
7 Absurdities	•	•	•	•	•	•	•	•	•	•	•	•	•				
14 Verbal Relations														•	•	•	•
5 Pattern Analysis	•	•	•	•	•	•	•	•	•	•	•	•	•	•	•	•	•
9 Copying	•	•	•	•	•	•	•	•	•	•							
11 Matrices											•	•	•	•	•	•	•
13 Paper Folding and Cutting																	
3 Quantitative	•	•	•	•	•	•	•	•	•	•	•	•	•	•	•	•	•
12 Number Series																	
15 Equation Building																	
2 Bead Memory	•	•	•	•	•	•	•	•	•	•	•	•	•	•	•	•	•
4 Memory for Sentences	•	•	•	•	•	•	•	•	•	•	•	•	•	•	•	•	•
8 Memory for Digits						•	•	•	•	•	•	•	•	•	•	•	•
10 Memory for Objects						•	•	•	•	•	•	•	•	•	•	•	•
Number of Subtests	8	8	8	8	8	10	10	10	10	10	10	10	10	10	10	10	10

scoring more objective and less dependent on examiner judgment.

The following suggestions are useful in evaluating a child's performance on the picture vocabulary items (Taylor, 1961, pp. 308–309, with changes):

. . .Note all responses obtained. Does the child find some responses for every picture, or is he or she apt to say, "I do not know"? Does he or she try to find a new word for each picture, or does he or she use the same word several times, successively or at intervals? Does the child seem to grope for the correct word, or does he or she seem to say the first word that comes to his or her lips? Do the errors show associations easily recognizable as such (e.g., *dog* for lamb) or meaningful to those around him (e.g., "*Daddy go*" for car)? Does the child's naming show that he or she tends to perceive pictures in a primitive, diffuse, global way, paying attention to "qualities of the whole" rather than fine details (e.g., *stick* for hammer)?

Are errors the result of a carryover from a previous picture or from other familiar verbal patterns? Carefully observe the child's enunciation; note which of the consonants may be missing or defective. Watch for dropped consonants (*boo-* for book, *fla-* for flag). For children with very poor articulation, note and check with the mother on nuances in sound productions which may mean different words to the child even if only barely perceptible to outsiders. Observe gestures and whether they accompany or replace verbal responses. Are they relevant and meaningful or only incidental? If they are the child's only form of response, do they indicate that he or she is, or is not, familiar with the picture?

The picture vocabulary items can be used for testing-of-limits in the following ways (Taylor, 1961, pp. 309–310, with changes):

. . .GESTURES. The picture material may be used to study more specifically children's ability to express themselves without words. Show the picture of the scissors (or hammer, bat, shovel) and ask, "Show me what it does" or "Show me what we do with it." For children who do not seem to understand language, show by a sample what is wanted of them.

Note: Does the child use varied appropriate gestures, or does he or she tend to use the same gestures with all pictures? Are the child's means of expression mostly manual, facial, or both? Is there any sign that the child indicates objects of the same category in similar ways? Does he or she, for instance, describe animals by their sounds and movements, tools by their use, or point to a book in the room to indicate a book? Observations of a child's use of gestures can be of considerable diagnostic significance with respect to development of communication.

    . . .ALTERNATE NAMING. If the child has designated an object either in words or through gestures, you may ask, "What else could it be?" The child may or may not find a second response, produce a synonym, a better word, or a better gesture.

    . . .POINTING. This picture material may also be used to investigate comprehension of language. Use four pictures at one time. Present the pictures by asking, "Where is the flower, etc.?" The child can indicate by pointing or nodding at the pictures, or in any other way he or she chooses. For a severely handicapped child who is unable to point accurately or to turn his or her head freely, the pictures may be spread far enough apart to avoid equivocal responses, yet near enough so that they all remain in the line of vision.

Note whether the child scans the field for the proper picture or responds haphazardly, pointing first to one, then to another. Does the child point to the correct picture only? Does the child know at least the general area in which it belongs? (Does he or she point to a hammer when asked for a bat, for instance?) Does the child seem to see all the pictures correctly, or does he or she make unexpected errors? Are such errors possibly attributable to sensory difficulties? Check whether a wrong picture is pointed to because of poor perception, eyesight, or hearing. Does the child not *understand* or does he or she not *see* the difference in the looks of a bat and hammer, or *hear* the difference between the words flag and flower?

    . . .Experience shows that, in general, normal children are able to point out all pictures adequately before, or at least at the same age as, they can find names for them. Often one may find children who can point correctly to something long before they are able to name it. It may be important for the clinician to discover whether a child understands more language than he or she is able to express. The procedure is therefore of considerable value in all cases of speech retardation, as well as in those where sensory difficulties are suspected.

These testing-of-limits procedures are excellent for obtaining a more thorough assessment, especially of handicapped children but of other children as well.

Comprehension

The Comprehension subtest contains 42 items, 6 of which require a pointing response (items 1 to 6) and 36 of which require a verbal response (items 7 to 42). The first six items measure knowledge of body parts. The remaining items cover understanding of basic physiological processes and

Courtesy Herman Zielinski.

hygiene, environmental hazards, societal practices, and political and economic activities. The items thus tap the child's comprehension of survival skills, social skills, economic skills, and political skills. The subtest is administered throughout all ages covered by the scale. Items are scored 1 or 0.

Rationale. The rationale presented for the WISC-R Comprehension subtest generally applies to the SB: FE Comprehension subtest (see page 153). Additionally, the pointing items involve some appreciation of the proper location of body parts. Items at the upper level of the subtest involve comprehension of the political and economic process, particularly the role of government in our society. These upper-level items provide insight about individuals' understanding of how their society functions.

Factor analytic findings. The Comprehension subtest is a good measure of *g* (56 percent of its variance may be attributed to *g*). The subtest has ample or adequate specificity to permit specific interpretation of its functions at all ages except 5–6 and 8–9. At the ages where its specificity is inadequate, the Comprehension subtest still can be interpreted as a measure of verbal comprehension. Comprehension contributes substantially to the Verbal Comprehension factor at most ages, except at 17 years where it makes a moderate contribution (*Mdn* loading = .68).

Reliability and correlational highlights. Comprehension is a reliable subtest (r_{xx} = .89). It correlates more highly with Vocabulary than with any other subtest (r = .73). It correlates moderately with the Composite Score (r = .76).

Administrative and interpretive considerations. The administrative and interpretive considerations presented for the WISC-R Comprehension subtest generally apply to the SB: FE Comprehension subtest (see Chapter 7). Study carefully the "General Guidelines for Scoring the Comprehension Test" (Appendix B) in the SB: FE *Guide* so that you will know which responses need further inquiry. The examples indicate that many responses should be queried. Unlike the WISC-R, on which Comprehension responses may be scored 2, 1, or 0, the SB: FE uses only a two-point system—1 or 0.

Absurdities

The Absurdities subtest contains 32 items. Items 1 to 4 are in multiple-choice format and require a pointing response, whereas items 5 to 32 require a verbal response. On the latter items the child is asked to state the essential incongruity in the picture. The subtest is administered from ages 2 to 14. Each item is scored 1 or 0.

Rationale. The Absurdities subtest involves recognizing what is visually depicted in the stimulus picture, appreciating that there may be some incongruity, and determining that incongruity. Success depends, in part, on perception of detail, alertness, concentration, and social understanding. The task is conceptual and involves some understanding of right and wrong. Performance on the multiple-choice items in part reflects the child's ability to delay impulses.

Factor analytic findings. The Absurdities subtest is a good measure of *g* (52 percent of its variance may be attributed to *g*). The subtest has ample or adequate specificity at all of its age levels to permit specific interpretation of its functions. Absurdities contributes either substantially or moderately to the Verbal Comprehension factor at all of its age levels (*Mdn* loading = .50). It also has modest loadings on the Nonverbal Reasoning/Visualization factor (*Mdn* loading = .44).

Reliability and correlational highlights. Absurdities is a reliable subtest (r_{xx} = .87). It correlates more highly with Vocabulary (r = .62) and with Comprehension (r = .59) than with any other subtests. It correlates moderately with the Composite Score (r = .72).

Administrative and interpretive considerations. Items 1 to 4 are easy to score because they are multiple-choice items. Responses to items 5 to 32, however, may be ambiguous. The item book lists typical responses needing inquiry. All responses should be studied so that you know which of them need to be queried and which pass or fail. If an examinee says that nothing is foolish, encourage another response. The factor analytic findings suggest that both verbal and nonverbal processes may be involved in successful performance.

Verbal Relations

The Verbal Relations subtest contains 18 items, each consisting of four words. All four words have something in common, but the first three words also share one characteristic that the fourth word does not have. The examinee must state what is true about the first three words that is not true of the fourth word. The subtest is administered to adolescents and young adults (ages 12 to 18–23).

Rationale. The Verbal Relations subtest involves perceiving the common elements of three terms, bringing these common elements together in a concept, and contrasting the common elements with a fourth term. Because the fourth term is both similar to and different from the first

Courtesy Herman Zielinski.

three terms, the Verbal Relations subtest involves both verbal concept formation and reasoning—the ability to place objects and events together in a meaningful group and then decide how the meaningful group contrasts with a member of another group. Verbal Relations also may involve the ability to view facts from various angles at the same time and coordinate the multiple relationships involved, the ability to test and discard hypothetical situations, and flexibility.

Factor analytic findings. The Verbal Relations subtest is a fair measure of g (46 percent of its variance may be attributed to g). The subtest has ample specificity at all of its age levels to permit specific interpretation of its functions. Verbal Relations contributes substantially to the Verbal Comprehension factor at all of its age levels (*Mdn* loading = .67).

Reliability and correlational highlights. Verbal Relations is a reliable subtest (r_{xx} = .91). It correlates more highly with Vocabulary than with any other subtest (r = .71). It correlates moderately with the Composite Score (r = .76).

Administrative and interpretive considerations. The interpretive suggestions presented for the WISC-R Similarities subtest generally apply to the SB: FE Verbal Relations subtest (see Chapter 7). Verbal Relations, however, requires a different type of conceptualization than does Similarities. Verbal Relations is somewhat more demanding, as it also requires reasoning. Consequently, it is more difficult to determine the precise cause for failure on the Verbal Relations subtest.

Study carefully the "General Guidelines for Scoring the Verbal Relations Test" (Appendix E) in the SB: FE *Guide* so that you will know which responses need further inquiry. Unlike the WISC-R, on which Similarities responses may be scored 2, 1, or 0, the SB: FE uses only a two-point system—1 or 0.

Pattern Analysis

The Pattern Analysis subtest contains 42 items. The first six items require children to place pieces in appropriate recesses on the form board. The remaining items use two-dimensional, black-and-white pictures of abstract designs. On items 7 to 24 a model is constructed by the examiner, and on items 25 to 42 designs are shown on pictures. The number of blocks used varies from 1 block on items 7 to 10 to 9 blocks on items 39 to 42. The subtest is administered throughout the age levels covered by the scale.

Items 7 to 42 are timed. Items 7 to 18 and 25 to 30 are given a maximum of 30 seconds each; items 19 to 24 and 31 to 36, 45 seconds; items 37 and 38, 60 seconds; and items 39 to 42, 90 seconds. Items are scored 1 or 0.

Rationale. The rationale described for the WISC-R Block Design subtest generally appears to apply to most of the items on the Pattern Analysis subtest (see page 159). The form-board items, however, primarily measure visual-motor ability and recognition and manipulation of forms. Additionally, "the form-board items require accurate spatial skills and a sensitivity to form differences, plus an awareness of the match between block outline and the corresponding hole in the form board. The latter becomes crucial when the form board is reversed" (Wilson, 1978b, p. 947).

Factor analytic findings. The Pattern Analysis subtest is a good measure of g (49 percent of its variance may be attributed to g). The subtest has ample or adequate specificity at all age levels to permit specific interpretation of its functions. Pattern Analysis contributes substantially to the Nonverbal Reasoning/Visualization factor at all age levels (*Mdn* loading = .66).

Reliability and correlational highlights. Pattern Analysis is a reliable subtest (r_{xx} = .92). It correlates more highly with Paper Folding and Cutting (r = .60) and Matrices and Number Series (r's = .55) than with any other subtests. It correlates moderately with the Composite Score (r = .74).

Administrative and interpretive considerations. The administrative and interpretive considerations presented for the WISC-R Block Design subtest generally apply to the Pattern Analysis subtest (see Chapter 7). On Pattern Analysis the examiner constructs the model on items 7 through 25, whereas on items 26 through 42 the model is shown via pictures. It is likely that models constructed out of blocks are somewhat easier to reproduce than those shown on pictures. Because this is the only subtest in the battery in which the examinee's performance is timed, be sure to observe whether timing leads to increased anxiety or affects performance in other ways.

Copying

The Copying subtest contains 28 items divided into two sections. In the first section (items 1 to 12), the child reproduces a block design built by the examiner (using 3 or 4 blocks). In the second section (items 13 to 28) the child copies printed line drawings. The drawings range from a straight line to multiple rectangular objects and cubes. The drawings are made directly in the record booklet. The subtest is applicable for ages 2 through 13 years. Items are scored 1 or 0. There is no time limit for the items.

Rationale.   The Copying subtest involves visual-motor ability and eye-hand coordination. Previous experience with pencil and paper may contribute to better performance. Adequate reproduction of the designs requires appropriate fine motor development, perceptual discrimination ability, and ability to integrate perceptual and motor processes. The child must shift attention between the stimulus and the reproduction and monitor his or her performance. Constructing a cube tower involves psychomotor dexterity and sustained goal-oriented activity. The child must retain the instructions in memory and must organize his or her production "to match the examiner's model, with the necessary intermediate steps of comparison and adjustment" (Wilson, 1978b, p. 947).

Factor analytic findings.   The Copying subtest is a fair measure of g (37 percent of its variance may be attributed to g). The subtest has ample or adequate specificity at all of its age levels to permit specific interpretation of its functions. It contributes substantially or moderately to the Nonverbal Reasoning/Visualization factor except at ages 12 and 13 (*Mdn* loading = .52). At age 12 it has a high loading on the Verbal Comprehension factor, and at age 13 it has a modest loading on the Nonverbal Reasoning/ Visualization factor.

Reliability and correlational highlights.   Copying is a reliable subtest (r_{xx} = .87). It correlates more highly with Pattern Analysis than with any other subtest (r = .50). It correlates moderately with the Composite Score (r = .66).

Administrative and interpretive considerations.   The Copying subtest is difficult to score, particularly for items 13 to 28. Each of these designs has up to 10 different special scoring criteria. You will need to study the scoring criteria carefully to become proficient in scoring the Copying subtest (Appendix D in the *Guide*). The guidelines described in Chapter 14 for observing visual-motor performance are also useful for administering and interpreting performance on the Copying subtest.

Matrices

The Matrices subtest contains 26 items. The matrices are made up of either a four-figure configuration (items 1 to 12)

or a nine-figure configuration (items 13 to 26). Items 1 to 12 show pictures of animals, people, or geometric figures; items 13 to 22 show geometric figures only; and items 23 to 26 show letters only. Items 1 to 22 are multiple-choice items, whereas items 23 to 26 require a written response. The examinee selects the best alternative to complete the matrix. In each item, the missing figure has some logical relationship to the other figures. The subtest spans the ages of 7 to 23 years.

Rationale.   The Matrices subtest involves perceptual reasoning ability. Analogic reasoning, attention to detail, and concentration are required for successful performance. Additionally, spatial ability may be involved for some examinees. Experience with part-whole relationships may be helpful, as may a willingness to respond when uncertain.

Factor analytic findings.   The Matrices subtest is a good measure of g (55 percent of its variance may be attributed to g). The subtest has ample subtest specificity at all of its age levels to permit specific interpretation of its functions. It contributes substantially or moderately to the Nonverbal Reasoning/Visualization factor at most of its age levels (*Mdn* loading = .60). The one exception is at age 7, where it has a low loading on the Nonverbal Reasoning/Visualization factor.

Reliability and correlational highlights.   Matrices is a reliable subtest (r_{xx} = .90). It correlates more highly with Number Series (r = .66) than with any other subtest. It correlates moderately with the Composite Score (r = .78).

Administrative and interpretive considerations.   Matrices is simple to score because there is only one correct response for each item. The varied item content suggests that the subtest is not a pure measure of nonverbal or figural reasoning. Both abstract stimuli and meaningful stimuli are used, and the last four items use letters. Impulsive examinees may have difficulty with the tasks because of the detailed nature of the stimuli. The processes involved in solving the items on the Matrices subtest are shown in Table 11-11.

Paper Folding and Cutting

The Paper Folding and Cutting subtest contains 18 items. The examinee first looks at a sequence of drawings showing a piece of paper being folded and cut and then must select the diagram that shows how the folded and cut paper

Table 11-11

Processes Involved in Solving Items on the Matrices Subtest of the Stanford-Binet Intelligence Scale: Fourth Edition

Item	Processes involved in solving items
Sample 1	Find a likeness
Sample 2	Find a likeness
Sample 3	Find a likeness or change shape and shading
Sample 4	Change orientation and shading or change orientation
1	Find a likeness
2	Find a likeness or a like relationship using physical characteristics
3	Find a likeness or a like relationship using size and shape
4	Change size
5	Find a like relationship using size and shape
6	Find a like relationship using physical characteristics
7	Add and/or change orientation
8	Change size, shape, and shading or change size and shading
9	Find a like relationship using size and shape
10	Change size and shading or change size, shape, and shading
11	Find a like relationship using shape and size
12	Find a like relationship using shape and number
13	Find a like relationship using addition and subtraction
14	Find a like relationship using addition and subtraction
15	Find a like relationship using size, color, and orientation
16	Find a like relationship using the number of elements and reversal of color
17	Find a like relationship using subtraction and orientation
18	Find a like relationship using size, color, and orientation
19	Find a like relationship using addition, subtraction, size, color, and shape
20	Find a like relationship using subtraction
21	Find a like relationship using subtraction
22	Find a like relationship using color and orientation
23	Find a like relationship using letter sequence, orientation, and number of elements
24	Find a like relationship using letter sequence, orientation, and number of elements
25	Find a like relationship using letter sequence, orientation, and number of elements
26	Find a like relationship using letter sequence and orientation

Source: Courtesy of Jeannine Feldman.

would look unfolded. (In the early items the examiner makes cuts in a piece of paper, whereas in later items pictures depict where the cuts are made.) Items vary from simple one-fold and one-cut problems to multiple-fold-and-cut snowflake-like designs. The subtest covers ages 12 to 18–23 years.

Rationale. The Paper Folding and Cutting subtest involves visualization, spatial ability, the integration of visual and spatial abilities, and attention to visual clues. Successful performance requires visualization of what the folded and cut paper would look like if the paper were unfolded.

Factor analytic findings. The Paper Folding and Cutting subtest is a fair measure of g (48 percent of its variance may be attributed to g). The subtest has ample subtest specificity at all of its age levels to permit specific interpretation of its functions. It contributes substantially to the Nonverbal Reasoning/Visualization factor at all of its age levels (*Mdn* loading = .65), with the exception of age 12, where it has a low loading on this factor.

Reliability and correlational highlights. Paper Folding and Cutting is a reliable subtest ($r_{xx} = .94$). It correlates more highly with Number Series ($r = .61$) and Pattern Analysis ($r = .60$) than with any other subtests. It correlates moderately with the Composite Score ($r = .74$).

Administrative and interpretive suggestions. Because all items are in a multiple-choice format, scoring is easy on the Paper Folding and Cutting subtest. Observe how the examinee responds to the items. Does he or she understand the instructions? Is he or she perplexed by the task? Does he or she find the task too abstract? Does he or she seem to be challenged by the task? The subtest may be particularly valuable in identifying individuals with excellent visualization skills.

Quantitative

The Quantitative subtest consists of 40 problems that cover a range of quantitative concepts. Early items involve matching and addition primarily; later items involve subtraction, division, multiplication, and algebra. Solutions require an understanding (or use) of ordinality, mathematical language, comparisons, utilization of space, mixing, interest, and logic. The stimulus materials are dice-like blocks for the first 12 items and pictures or word problems for items 13 to 40. Item content varies, including whole numbers, objects, money, fractions, and measurement. Table 11-12 presents the processes, content, and stimulus material for each item on the Quantitative subtest. The subtest spans the entire age range of the scale.

Rationale. The rationale presented for the WISC-R Arithmetic subtest generally applies to the Quantitative subtest of the SB: FE (see page 150). The skills required by the earlier Quantitative items, however, are less likely to be dependent on formal education than are those required for the WISC-R Arithmetic subtest. Items 1 to 3 and 6 to 8 on the Quantitative subtest require the child to make perceptual discriminations and appear to measure nonverbal reasoning ability.

Factor analytic findings. The Quantitative subtest is a good measure of g (60 percent of its variance may be attributed to g). The subtest has ample or adequate subtest specificity at all ages in the scale, except at ages 6 and 18–23, where specificity is inadequate to permit specific interpretation of its functions. The Quantitative subtest contributes moderately or substantially to the Nonverbal Reasoning/Visualization factor at all age levels (*Mdn* loading = .54). It also has modest loadings on the Verbal Comprehension factor (*Mdn* loading = .41).

Reliability and correlational highlights. Quantitative is a reliable subtest (r_{xx} = .88). It correlates more highly with Number Series (r = .67) and Equation Building

(r = .61) than with any other subtests. It correlates highly with the Composite Score (r = .82).

Administrative and interpretive considerations. As on the WISC-R Arithmetic subtest, it is useful to determine the reasons for the child's failures through testing-of-limits procedures. You might say, for example, "Let's try this one again. Tell me how you solved the problem." Failure may be caused by poor knowledge of arithmetical operations, inadequate conceptualization of the problem, temporary inefficiency or anxiety, poor concentration, carelessness, or some combination of factors.

Question: If you take one apple from four apples, how many apples will you have?
Answer: One.

Number Series

The Number Series subtest consists of 26 items. Five to seven numbers are arranged in a logical sequence, and the examinee must indicate (either verbally or in writing) which two numbers would come next in the series. The subtest spans ages 7 to 23 years.

Rationale. The Number Series subtest involves logical reasoning and concentration when using numbers. Examinees must be able to discover the rationale underlying the series. They must come to understand the relationship between sets of numbers and apply this understanding to arrive at a solution. Correct solutions may involve trial-and-error, persistence, and/or flexibility. The subtest measures analogic reasoning with quantitative materials.

Factor analytic findings. The Number Series subtest is a good measure of g (62 percent of its variance may be attributed to g). The subtest has ample or adequate specificity at all of its age levels to permit specific interpretation of its functions. Number Series contributes substantially to the Nonverbal Reasoning/Visualization factor at all of its age levels, with the exception of age 7, where it has a low loading (*Mdn* loading = .64).

Reliability and correlational highlights. Number Series is a reliable subtest (r_{xx} = .90). It correlates more highly with Quantitative (r = .67) and Matrices (r = .66) than with any other subtests. It also correlates highly with the Composite Score (r = .82).

Table 11-12
Analysis of the Quantitative Subtest by Process and Content Variables and Stimulus Material

Item	Process	Content	Stimulus material
1	Matching	Whole numbers	Blocks
2	Matching	Whole numbers	Blocks
3	Matching	Whole numbers	Blocks
4	Counting	Whole numbers	Blocks
5	Counting	Whole numbers	Blocks
6	Matching	Whole numbers	Blocks
7	Matching	Whole numbers	Blocks
8	Matching	Whole numbers	Blocks
9	Addition/counting	Whole numbers	Blocks
10	Addition/counting	Whole numbers	Blocks
11	Addition/counting	Whole numbers	Blocks
12	Ordinality/reasoning	Whole numbers	Blocks
13	Addition/counting	Whole numbers	Picture
14	Subtraction	Whole numbers	Picture
15	Applying concepts	Objects	Picture
16	Measuring	Objects	Picture
17	Division	Objects	Picture
18	Matching	Objects	Picture
19	Division	Whole numbers	Word problem
20	Utilization of space	Objects	Picture
21	Comparing	Objects	Picture
22	Mixing	Whole numbers/money	Word problem
23	Addition	Objects	Picture
24	Comparing	Objects	Picture
25	Division	Whole numbers	Word problem
26	Division	Whole numbers/money	Word problem
27	Division	Whole numbers/money	Word problem
28	Utilization of space	Objects	Word problem
29	Converting numbers	Fractions/decimals	Word problem
30	Mixing	Whole numbers/money	Word problem
31	Multiplication	Whole numbers/money	Word problem
32	Applying mathematical logic	Measurement	Word problem
33	Applying mathematical logic	Measurement	Word problem
34	Applying mathematical logic	Measurement	Word problem
35	Utilization of space	Measurement	Word problem
36	Applying mathematical logic	Money	Word problem
37	Applying mathematical logic	Money	Word problem
38	Applying mathematical logic	Measurement	Word problem
39	Applying mathematical logic	Whole numbers	Word problem
40	Applying mathematical logic	Whole numbers	Word problem

Administrative and interpretive considerations.
Number Series is easy to score. Note how the examinee proceeds to answer the items. Are responses given quickly or slowly? Does the examinee appear confident or anxious? How are failures handled? Does the examinee show flexibility in shifting from ascending to descending series? Are any particular series especially difficult, such as fractions or ones with numbers and letters? How much time is needed to solve the problems?

Equation Building

The Equation Building subtest, used for ages 12 to 18–23, has 18 items. Each item consists of a series of four to five numbers followed by three to four signs. The numbers and signs must be rearranged to make a true number sentence. Paper and pencil can be used for this subtest.

The responses can be given either orally or in writing; the examiner records them directly in the record booklet. Although there is no time limit for this subtest, 2 minutes is the suggested amount of time to allow per item.

Rationale. The Equation Building subtest involves working with relationships among numbers. The subtest involves logic, flexibility, and trial-and-error. The task is to manipulate mathematical signs of operation and numbers so as to form a valid equation. The subtest can be considered to be a type of mathematical anagram.

Factor analytic findings. The Equation Building subtest is a fair measure of g (45 percent of its variance may be attributed to g). The subtest has ample subtest specificity at all of its age levels to permit specific interpretation of its functions. Equation Building contributes substantially or moderately to the Nonverbal Reasoning/Visualization factor at all of its age levels (*Mdn* loading = .58).

Reliability and correlational highlights. Equation Building is a reliable subtest (r_{xx} = .91). It correlates more highly with Number Series (r = .64) and Quantitative (r = .61) than with any other subtests. It correlates moderately with the Composite Score (r = .74).

Administrative and interpretive considerations. Equation Building is relatively easy to score. There are, however, some correct solutions that are not in the scoring guide; these should be given credit. Additional solutions for items on the Equation Building subtest are as follows:

   4. $4 - 1 + 2 = 5$
   8. $3 \times 6 \div 2 = 3 \times 3$
 13. $8 \div 2 \times 1 = 4$
 15. $5 + 4 + 1 = 13 - 3$
 16. $5 - 6 + 9 = 4 \times 2$
     $9 - 2 \times 4 + 5 = 6$

Observe the examinee's reactions to this subtest. How flexible is the examinee? Does he or she enjoy the challenge or find the tasks burdensome? Does the examinee work well with fractions? Does the examinee know how to use parentheses? How is failure handled?

Bead Memory

The Bead Memory subtest, which is administered to all ages, consists of 42 items. Four bead shapes (round, cylin-

drical, cone, and flattened round or saucer-like) in three colors are used for the subtest. On items 1 to 10 a photograph of the beads is used, whereas on items 11 to 42 a plastic base and stick are used. On items 1 to 10 the examiner shows the child one or two beads for 2 or 3 seconds, and the child then must point to the correct bead(s) on the photograph. The order in which the beads are pointed to does not matter on these items.

On items 11 to 42 a photograph is shown of two to eight beads arranged vertically on a stick. After 5 seconds, the photograph is removed and the child must construct the design. For these items, the design must be an exact duplication of the one shown on the photograph. There is no time limit on the Bead Memory subtest.

Rationale. The Bead Memory subtest involves short-term memory for visual stimuli. Form perception and discrimination, spatial relations, and alertness to detail are also involved. Success requires attention and concentration. Additionally, eye-hand coordination is involved in placing the beads on the stick for items 11 to 42.

Factor analytic findings. The Bead Memory subtest is a fair measure of g (46 percent of its variance may be attributed to g). The subtest has ample subtest specificity at all ages to permit specific interpretation of its functions. Bead Memory contributes substantially or moderately to the Nonverbal Reasoning/Visualization factor at all ages (*Mdn* loading = .51). It also contributes moderately to the Memory factor at some ages (*Mdn* loading = .36).

Reliability and correlational highlights. Bead Memory is a reliable subtest (r_{xx} = .87). It correlates more highly with Number Series (r = .54) and Matrices and Quantitative (r's = .52) than with any other subtests. It correlates moderately with the Composite Score (r = .72).

Administrative and interpretive suggestions. The subtest is easy to administer. In order to take the Bead Memory subtest, the child must be able to identify correctly at least three of the four shapes. If the child fails to meet this criterion, the subtest is not administered. Observe how the examinee proceeds. Is tremor present? If so, to what extent does it interfere with the task? What is the tempo of the examinee's manner of responding? Does the examinee verbalize as he or she works? Does the task appear to be enjoyable or burdensome? Does the examinee arrange the shapes correctly but choose the wrong color, or vice versa? When there are failures, how many of the beads are incorrect? What might have caused the failures? How many near successes are there?

Memory for Sentences

The Memory for Sentences subtest consists of 42 items. The subtest spans the entire age range covered by the scale. Each item is read by the examiner and repeated by the child. The child must repeat the sentence exactly to receive credit. The items are scored 1 or 0. The sentences range in complexity and length from simple two-word phrases to statements of 22 words.

Rationale. The Memory for Sentences subtest is a memory test, measuring immediate recall and attention. Short-term auditory memory is involved, which includes attention, concentration, listening comprehension, and auditory processing. Because success may depend on verbal facility, failure may not necessarily reflect poor memory ability. For children 5 years and older, scores may be related primarily to memory ability, but for younger children, scores may reflect verbal knowledge and comprehension rather than immediate recall ability per se.

Factor analytic findings. Memory for Sentences is a good measure of g (50 percent of its variance may be attributed to g). The subtest has ample or adequate specificity at all ages to permit specific interpretation of its functions. Memory for Sentences contributes substantially or moderately to the Verbal Comprehension factor at all ages (Mdn loading = .58) and to the Memory factor at ages 7 through 18–23 (Mdn loading = .57). The factor analytic findings show that Memory for Sentences should be included in the Verbal Comprehension factor at ages 2 through 7 and in the Memory factor at ages 8 through 18–23.

Reliability and correlational highlights. Memory for Sentences is a reliable subtest (r_{xx} = .89). It correlates most highly with Vocabulary (r = .64) and Comprehension (r = .58) and correlates moderately with the Composite Score (r = .73).

Administrative and interpretive considerations. The subtest is easy to administer. The sentences should be read clearly and in a steady voice. Attempt to determine the kinds of errors made by the examinee—omissions, substitutions, additions, changes in words, or changes in order of words. Were any idiosyncratic or peculiar words added? Did errors occur toward the beginning, middle, or end of sentences? Were sentences completely missed, or were only a few errors made in each sentence? The examinee who misses a few words may be revealing minor temporary inefficiencies, whereas the one who cannot recall any words in the sentences may have more serious memory problems.

Memory for Digits

The Memory for Digits subtest is composed of two parts: Digits Forward and Digits Reversed. Each part is administered and scored separately. Each item is presented verbally at a rate of one digit per second. Digits Forward has 14 items. It begins with three digits per item, with one digit being added for each new level up to nine digits. Digits Reversed has 12 items. It begins with two digits and goes up to seven digits per item. The raw score is equal to the sum of the raw scores on Digits Forward and Digits Reversed. The subtest covers ages 7 through 18–23.

Rationale. The rationale presented for the WISC-R Digit Span subtest applies to the SB: FE Memory for Digits subtest (see page 154).

Factor analytic findings. The Memory for Digits subtest is a fair measure of g (36 percent of its variance may be attributed to g). The subtest has ample or adequate specificity at all of its age levels to permit specific interpretation of its functions. Memory for Digits contributes substantially to the Memory factor at all of its ages (Mdn = .65).

Reliability and correlational highlights. Memory for Digits is a reliable subtest (r_{xx} = .83). It correlates more highly with Memory for Sentences (r = .56) and Number Series (r = .52) than with any other subtests. It correlates moderately with the Composite Score (r = .64).

Administrative and interpretive considerations. The administrative and interpretive considerations presented for the WISC-R Digit Span subtest are also relevant for the Memory for Digits subtest.

Memory for Objects

The Memory for Objects subtest, which covers ages 7 through 18–23 years, consists of 14 items. Each card has an illustration of one object. The cards are shown at a rate of one per second. No time limits are placed on the child. After all cards for an item have been shown, the child must pick out the objects shown from a card containing 5 to 12 objects. To receive credit, the child must point to the correct objects in the exact order in which they were

Courtesy Herman Zielinski.

shown. The items are scored 1 or 0. The subtest begins with two stimuli per item and ends with eight stimuli per item.

Rationale. The Memory for Objects subtest is a memory test, measuring immediate recall and attention. Short-term visual memory is involved, which includes attention, concentration, visual comprehension, and visual processing. Because performance may depend on recognition of objects, success may be enhanced by familiarity with objects or by labeling of objects.

Factor analytic findings. The Memory for Objects subtest is a fair measure of g (29 percent of its variance may be attributed to g). The subtest has ample subtest specificity at all of its age levels to permit specific interpretation of its functions, with the exception of age 12, where it has inadequate specificity. Memory for Objects contributes substantially or moderately to the Memory factor at all of its age levels (Mdn loading = .52).

Reliability and correlational highlights. Memory for Objects is a moderately reliable subtest (r_{xx} = .73). It correlates most highly with Memory for Digits and Bead Memory (r's = .44) and correlates moderately with the Composite Score (r = .60).

Administrative and interpretive considerations. The subtest is easy to administer. Look for possible patterns in the errors made by the examinee. Were the correct objects pointed to but in the wrong order? Did errors occur toward the beginning, middle, or end of the series? Was the order completely missed, or were only a few errors made in the order? The examinee who points to the correct objects but in the wrong order or who misses only one or two objects at the end of a long series may have less serious memory problems than one who makes many errors. Observe how the examinee approaches the task. Does he or she name the objects as they are pointed to? Is he or she aware of any errors? How does the examinee react to failures?

INTERPRETING THE SB: FE

Much of the material in Chapter 8 on interpreting the WISC-R pertains to the SB: FE. Profile analysis, the successive level approach to test interpretation, factor-score comparisons, and subtest comparisons are essentially the same for the WISC-R and the SB: FE. You are encouraged to read or review Chapter 8 before reading the rest of this chapter.

The information in Table C-52 in Appendix C can aid in interpreting the SB: FE subtests, as well as in writing reports. It summarizes the abilities thought to be measured by each subtest, background factors that may influence subtest performance, implications of high and low scores, and instructional implications. This table deserves careful study.

The classifications associated with the SB: FE Composite Scores are shown in Table BC-2 on the inside back cover. Table BC-1 on the inside back cover shows the percentile ranks for the Composite Score and for the factor scores. If there are any questions about the validity of the Composite Score, consider to what extent the separate factor scores may have greater validity. Percentile ranks associated with subtest scores are shown in Table C-53 in Appendix C.

Like the Wechsler subtests, the individual SB: FE subtests should not be viewed as a means of determining specific cognitive skills with precision. Rather, subtest scores should be used to generate hypotheses about the child's abilities. The most reliable estimates of specific abilities are derived from the Verbal Comprehension factor, Nonverbal Reasoning/Visualization factor, and Memory factor, not from the individual subtest scores. All hypotheses developed on the basis of performance on the SB: FE must be considered in relation to all other sources of data.

Profile Analysis

Because the SB: FE is essentially a new scale, little evidence is available to help establish the meaning and implications of various test profiles. Research and clinical studies with the scale are needed. Nevertheless, tentative hypotheses about a child's strengths and weaknesses can be formulated on the basis of profile analysis.

As noted previously, the *approaches* to profile analysis for the SB: FE are basically the same as those for the WISC-R (see Chapter 8). The main difference is that different tables in Appendix C must be used.

1. *Comparing Verbal Comprehension, Nonverbal Reasoning/Visualization, and Memory factor scores.* Table C-46 in Appendix C provides the critical values for comparing the Verbal Comprehension, Nonverbal Reasoning/Visualization, and Memory factor scores. The critical values range from 8 to 15 for various comparisons. Because the range is so large, no single critical value is appropriate for all comparisons, either at the .05 level or at the .01 level; rather, the values shown for each age group and comparison should be used. (Probabilities associated with various differences between factor scores are shown in Table C-49 of Appendix C.)

2. *Comparing each Verbal Comprehension factor subtest scaled score with the mean Verbal Comprehension factor scaled score.* Table C-47 in Appendix C provides the critical values for comparing Verbal Comprehension subtests with the mean of the Verbal Comprehension subtests. They range from 5.18 to 6.18 at the .05 level and 6.37 to 7.51 at the .01 level for the subtests that comprise this factor.

3. *Comparing each Nonverbal Reasoning/Visualization factor subtest scaled score with the mean Nonverbal Reasoning/Visualization factor scaled score.* Table C-47 provides the critical values for comparing Nonverbal Reasoning/Visualization subtests with the mean of the Nonverbal Reasoning/Visualization subtests. They range from 5.22 to 6.15 at the .05 level and from 6.35 to 7.42 at the .01 level for the subtests that comprise this factor.

4. *Comparing each Memory factor subtest scaled score with the mean Memory factor scaled score.* Table C-47 provides the critical values for comparing Memory subtests with the mean of the Memory subtests. They range from 5.98 to 7.51 at the .05 level and from 7.34 to 9.73 at the .01 level for the subtests that comprise this factor.

5. *Comparing sets of individual subtest scores.* Table C-45 in Appendix C provides the critical values for comparing sets of subtest scaled scores. They range between 6 and 10 at the .05 level and between 8 and 14 at the .01 level. The values in Table C-45 in Appendix C for subtest comparisons are overly liberal (that is, they lead to too many significant differences) when more than one comparison is made. They are most accurate when a priori planned comparisons are made (such as Memory for Sentences versus Memory for Digits or Pattern Analysis versus Matrices).

Before multiple subtest comparisons are made (that is, more than one set of subtest scores is compared), the difference between the highest and lowest subtest scores should be determined. A difference of 13 scaled-score points between the highest and lowest scaled scores is significant at the .05 level. (This critical difference is for the 12 subtests that comprise the factor scores; excluded are Paper Folding and Cutting, Number Series, and Equation Building. If all 15 subtests are administered, the critical difference between the highest and lowest subtest scores becomes 14.) Differences that are 13 scaled-score points or greater can then be interpreted. If the difference between the highest and lowest subtest scaled scores is less than 13 scaled-score points, multiple comparisons between individual subtest scores should not be made.

Other Approaches to Profile Analysis

The supplementary approaches to SB: FE profile analysis described in this section are similar to those discussed for the WISC-R (see Chapter 8).

Base rate differences between each subtest score used in a factor and an average subtest factor score in the SB: FE standardization sample.   Table C-48 in Appendix C gives the frequencies with which various differences between subtest scores and average SB: FE Verbal Comprehension, Nonverbal Reasoning/Visualization, or Memory scores occurred in the standardization sample. The table shows, for example, that a difference as large as 7.02 points between the scaled score on Vocabulary and the Verbal Comprehension factor average was obtained by 5 percent of the standardization sample at ages 2 through 7. This table should be used only when differences have been found to be statistically significant. (See numbers 2, 3, and 4 in the preceding profile analysis section.) Differences of approximately 5 to 9 points between each subtest score and the respective average Verbal Comprehension or Nonverbal Reasoning/Visualization or Memory factor score were obtained by 5 percent of the standardization sample.

Base rate differences between factor scores (the probability-of-occurrence approach).   Table C-49 in Appendix C presents the percentage of individuals in the standardization group who obtained a given discrepancy between the factor scores. The table, for example, shows that between 25 and 50 percent of the population had a median discrepancy (in either direction) of from 9 to 13 points between Verbal Comprehension and Nonverbal Reasoning/Visualization factor scores.

Ranges for Subtests, Short Forms, Factor Scores, and Composite Score

Table C-51 in Appendix C presents the ranges in standard age scores (or scaled scores) for each subtest, three short forms, three factors, and two Composite Scores in the SB: FE by age level. The discussion that follows summarizes the highlights of Table C-51.

Range of subtests. Unfortunately there are no subtests in the Fourth Edition that provide the full range of scores from ± 3 SD's (or more) from the mean over the entire age range covered by the subtests (see Table 11-13). This non-uniformity of scaled scores complicates the use of profile analysis. Some examples are instructive. (a) Although the Vocabulary subtest provides a ± 3 SD range of scores from ages 3-3-16 to 23-11-15, Bead Memory only provides this range beginning with age 4-3-16. (b) There are no scores on Verbal Relations, Paper Folding and Cutting, or Equation Building that run below -2 SD's from the mean. (c) Pattern Analysis provides a ± 3 SD range of scores only for ages 3-3-16 to 10-5-15.

Profile analysis cannot be applied to subtest scores without consideration of the available score ranges. Statements about differential strengths and weaknesses will not be meaningful unless the available subtest ranges are taken into account. Consequently, Table C-51 in Appendix C should be referred to frequently in evaluating individual profiles.

Subtests that do not have adequate ceilings for the age ranges they cover (at least ± 3 SD's from the mean) are Comprehension (at age 15-11-16 and on), Absurdities (at age 11-11-16 and on), Verbal Relations (at age 17-11-16 and on), Pattern Analysis (at age 10-5-16 and on), Copying (at age 9-11-16 and on), Paper Folding and Cutting (at age 15-11-16 and on), Quantitative (at age 17-11-16 and on), and Number Series (at age 15-11-16 and on).

Subtests that do not have adequate floors for the age ranges they cover (at least -3 SD's from the mean) are Vocabulary (at age 3-3-15 and below), Comprehension (at age 3-3-15 and below), Absurdities (at age 4-3-15 and below), Verbal Relations (at all ages), Pattern Analysis (at age 3-3-15 and below), Copying (at age 3-11-15 and below), Matrices (at age 10-5-15 and below), Paper Folding and Cutting (at all ages), Quantitative (at age 4-11-15 and be-

low), Number Series (at age 11-11-15 and below), Equation Building (at all ages), Bead Memory (at age 4-3-15 and below), Memory for Sentences (at age 3-11-15 and below), Memory for Digits (at age 9-5-15 and below), and Memory for Objects (at age 9-11-15 and below).

Fortunately, five of the six subtests (Vocabulary, Comprehension, Quantitative, Bead Memory, and Memory for Sentences) that cover the entire age range provide a range of scores of ± 2.1 to 3 SD's for ages 4-11-16 to 15-11-15. Table 11-14 shows the ages at which each subtest, three short forms, three factor scores, and two Composite Scores (based on factor scores and full battery) span ± 2.1 to 3 and ± 3.1 to 4 SD's from the mean.

Range for short forms. The ranges for three useful short forms are as follows (see Tables 11-14 and 11-15). The Vocabulary plus Pattern Analysis two-subtest combination allows for the range of scores up to ± 2.1 to 3 SD's from ages 3-3-16 to 17-11-15 only. The ± 3.1 to 4 SD range spans an eight-year range (4-7-16 to 12-11-15).

The Vocabulary, Pattern Analysis, Quantitative, and Bead Memory four-subtest short form allows for the range of scores up to ± 2.1 to 3 SD's from ages 3-7-16 to 23-11-15. The ± 3.1 to 4 SD range is from ages 4-11-16 to 16-11-15.

The Vocabulary, Comprehension, Pattern Analysis, Quantitative, Bead Memory, and Memory for Sentences six-subtest short form allows for the range of scores up to ± 2.1 to 3 SD's from ages 3-3-16 to 23-11-15. The ± 3.1 to 4 SD range is from ages 4-3-16 to 14-11-15.

Range for factor scores. The Verbal Comprehension factor allows for the range of scores up to ± 2.1 to 3 SD's from ages 3-3-16 to 23-11-15. The ± 3.1 to 4 SD range is from ages 4-3-16 to 15-11-15.

The Nonverbal Reasoning/Visualization factor allows for the range of scores up to ± 2.1 to 3 SD's from ages 3-7-16 to 23-11-15. The ± 3.1 to 4 SD range is from 4-11-16 to 16-11-15. The Memory factor allows for the range of scores up to ± 2.1 to 3 SD's from ages 7-11-16 to 23-11-15. The ± 3.1 to 4 SD range is from 8-11-16 to 23-11-15.

Range for Composite Scores. The Composite Score for the factor score battery allows for the range of scores up to ± 2.1 to 3 SD's from 3-3-16 to 23-11-15. The ± 3.1 to 4 SD range is from 4-3-16 to 17-11-15.

The Composite Score for the full battery allows for the range of scores up to ± 2.1 to 3 SD's from ages 3-3-16 to 23-11-15. The ± 3.1 to 4 SD range is from ages 4-3-16 to 23-11-15. These ranges mean that the two Composite Scores on the SB: FE do not have a sufficient floor to classify children as mentally retarded until they reach age

Table 11-13
Subtest Age Ranges in *SD* Units for Stanford-Binet Intelligence Scale: Fourth Edition

Subtest	+4 (82–75)	+3 (74–67)	+2 (66–59)	+1 (58–51)
Vocabulary	2-0-0 to 17-11-15	17-11-16 to 23-11-15	—	—
Comprehension	2-0-0 to 12-11-15	12-11-16 to 15-11-15	15-11-16 to 23-11-15	—
Absurdities	2-0-0 to 9-11-15	9-11-16 to 11-11-15	11-11-16 to 14-11-15	—
Verbal Relations	11-11-16 to 13-11-15	13-11-16 to 17-11-15	17-11-16 to 23-11-15	—
Pattern Analysis	2-0-0 to 8-11-15	8-11-16 to 10-5-15	10-5-16 to 14-11-15	14-11-16 to 23-11-15
Copying	2-0-0 to 7-5-15	7-5-16 to 9-11-15	9-11-16 to 11-11-15	11-11-16 to 13-11-15
Matrices	6-11-16 to 14-11-15	14-11-16 to 23-11-15	—	—
Paper Folding and Cutting	11-11-16 to 13-11-15	13-11-16 to 15-11-15	15-11-16 to 23-11-15	—
Quantitative	2-0-0 to 14-11-15	14-11-16 to 17-11-15	17-11-16 to 23-11-15	—
Number Series	6-11-16 to 12-11-15	12-11-16 to 15-11-15	15-11-16 to 23-11-15	—
Equation Building	9-11-16 to 23-11-15	—	—	—
Bead Memory	2-0-0 to 23-11-15	—	—	—
Memory for Sentences	2-0-0 to 23-11-15	—	—	—
Memory for Digits	6-11-16 to 16-11-15	16-11-16 to 23-11-15	—	—
Memory for Objects	6-11-16 to 10-11-15	10-11-16 to 23-11-15	—	—

3-3-16. In fact, the lowest score a 2-0-0 can receive is 95 on both Composites. The lowest score drops to 87 at 2-3-16, 80 at 2-7-16, 73 at 2-11-16, and 66 at 3-3-16. Thus, at the 2-year-old level, the SB: FE is more suitable for the study of exceptionally gifted children than for the study of mentally retarded children.

A SUCCESSIVE LEVEL APPROACH TO TEST INTERPRETATION

The successive level approach to interpreting the SB: FE is similar to the one described for the Wechsler scales in Chapter 8. The approach is presented again, however, because there are some subtle differences.

I. *The Composite Score.* The Composite Score serves as the first level of interpretation. It provides a global estimate of the child's level of cognitive ability. The child's overall classification is based on the Composite Score (see Table BC-2 on the inside back cover sheets). Converting the Composite Score into a percentile rank (see Table BC-1 on the inside back cover sheets) will help you to interpret this score for persons who may not be familiar with standard scores.

II. *Factor scores.* The second level of interpretation focuses on the absolute level of the three factor scores and the extent to which there are differences between them. (A

discussion of these factors follows this approach to test interpretation.)

III. *Subtest variability within factors.* The third level of interpretation focuses on deviations of the various subtests from the mean of the Verbal Comprehension factor or Nonverbal Reasoning/Visualization factor or Memory factor. Hypotheses about strengths and weaknesses can be developed from these analyses.

IV. *Intersubtest variability.* The fourth level focuses on comparisons between sets of subtests or among clusters of subtests. Although these comparisons are open to the errors associated with multiple comparisons, they are valuable for generating hypotheses. (Table C-53 in Appendix C provides the percentile ranks for subtest scaled scores.)

V. *Intrasubtest variability.* The fifth level of interpretation focuses on the pattern of performance within each individual subtest. Because the items are arranged in order of difficulty, patterns of successes and failures need to be evaluated carefully. For example, a child who passes the first item, fails the next two, passes the next one, fails the next two, passes the next two, and overall passes a total of four items is showing a different pattern from one who passes the first four items and fails the remainder, although both children receive a raw score of 4 points. The child with the markedly uneven pattern may have cognitive or attentional inefficiencies that should be explored further.

VI. *Qualitative analysis.* The sixth level of interpretation focuses on specific item failures and the content of the responses, or qualitative analysis. Inspecting responses to

−1 (50–42)	−2 (41–34)	−3 (33–26)	−4 (25–18)	Subtest
2-0-0 to 2-3-15	2-3-16 to 3-3-15	3-3-16 to 5-11-15	5-11-16 to 23-11-15	Vocabulary
2-0-0 to 2-3-15	2-3-16 to 3-3-15	3-3-16 to 6-5-15	6-5-16 to 23-11-15	Comprehension
2-0-0 to 2-11-15	2-11-16 to 4-3-15	4-3-16 to 6-5-15	6-5-16 to 14-11-15	Absurdities
11-11-16 to 13-11-15	13-11-16 to 23-11-15	—	—	Verbal Relations
2-0-0 to 2-3-15	2-3-16 to 3-3-15	3-3-16 to 5-3-15	5-3-16 to 23-11-15	Pattern Analysis
2-0-0 to 2-11-15	2-11-16 to 3-11-15	3-11-16 to 6-5-15	6-5-16 to 13-11-15	Copying
6-11-16 to 7-11-15	7-11-16 to 10-5-15	10-5-16 to 16-11-15	16-11-16 to 23-11-15	Matrices
11-11-16 to 15-11-15	15-11-16 to 23-11-15	—	—	Paper Folding and Cutting
2-0-0 to 3-7-15	3-7-16 to 4-11-15	4-11-16 to 6-11-15	6-11-16 to 23-11-15	Quantitative
6-11-16 to 8-11-15	8-11-16 to 11-11-15	11-11-16 to 23-11-15	—	Number Series
11-11-16 to 15-11-15	15-11-16 to 23-11-15	—	—	Equation Building
2-0-0 to 3-3-15	3-3-16 to 4-3-15	4-3-16 to 6-5-15	6-5-16 to 23-11-15	Bead Memory
2-0-0 to 2-11-15	2-11-16 to 3-11-15	3-11-16 to 5-11-15	5-11-16 to 23-11-15	Memory for Sentences
—	6-11-16 to 9-5-15	9-5-16 to 17-11-15	17-11-16 to 23-11-15	Memory for Digits
—	6-11-16 to 9-11-15	9-11-16 to 23-11-15	—	Memory for Objects

specific items can aid you in understanding the child's knowledge of specific information, such as how to count coins on the Quantitative subtest or the meaning of specific words on the Vocabulary subtest. Both verbal and nonverbal responses should be evaluated. (Chapter 18 also discusses qualitative aspects of test interpretation.)

COMPARISONS BETWEEN FACTOR SCORES THAT CAN GUIDE INTERPRETATIONS

The evaluation of the SB: FE factor scores depends primarily on the hypotheses made about the individual subtests that comprise the respective factor scores. Some general observations can be made concerning the three factors, however.

Interpretation of Verbal Comprehension, Nonverbal Reasoning/Visualization, and Memory Factors

The Verbal Comprehension factor is dependent on the child's accumulated experience. The items in this factor usually tap into the child's repertoire of verbal knowledge. The questions are presented either verbally or visually, and the responses are given orally. The Verbal Comprehension factor might be considered an index of verbal ability and crystallized intelligence.

The Nonverbal Reasoning/Visualization factor, in contrast, is more dependent on the child's immediate problem-solving ability. The stimuli are nonverbal and are presented visually. Solutions require motor, pointing, or verbal responses. The Nonverbal Reasoning/Visualization factor might be considered an index of nonverbal ability and fluid intelligence.

The Memory factor is dependent on the child's ability to sustain attention. Also involved are short-term memory, encoding ability (including sequencing ability), use of rehearsal strategies, ability to shift mental operations rapidly on symbolic material, and ability to self-monitor. These processes are similar to those described for the Freedom from Distractibility factor on the WISC-R and WAIS-R.

Solving problems that comprise the Verbal Comprehension, Nonverbal Reasoning/Visualization, and Memory factors involves both verbal and nonverbal strategies. Within the Verbal Comprehension factor, Absurdities may involve visualization strategies to a greater extent than do solutions on the other Verbal Comprehension subtests. Within the Nonverbal Reasoning/Visualization factor, Quantitative and Matrices may involve verbal strategies to a greater extent than does Pattern Analysis, Copying, or Bead Memory. Within the Memory factor, Memory for Sentences involves verbal processing to a greater extent than do the other memory subtests.

Table 11-14
Age Ranges That Span ±2.1 to 3 *SD* and ±3.1 to 4 *SD* of the Stanford-Binet Intelligence Scale: Fourth Edition for Subtests, Short Forms, Factors, and Composite Scores

Subtest, short forms, factors, and composite scores	±2.1 to 3 SD	±3.1 to 4 SD
Subtest		
Vocabulary	3-3-16 to 23-11-15	5-11-16 to 17-11-15
Comprehension	3-3-16 to 15-11-15	6-5-16 to 12-11-15
Absurdities	4-3-16 to 11-11-15	6-5-16 to 9-11-15
Verbal Relations	–	–
Pattern Analysis	3-3-16 to 10-5-15	5-3-16 to 8-11-15
Copying	3-11-16 to 9-11-15	6-5-16 to 7-5-15
Matrices	10-5-16 to 23-11-15	–
Paper Folding and Cutting	–	–
Quantitative	4-11-16 to 17-11-15	6-11-16 to 14-11-15
Number Series	11-11-16 to 15-11-15	–
Equation Building	–	–
Bead Memory	4-3-16 to 23-11-15	6-5-16 to 23-11-15
Memory for Sentences	3-11-16 to 23-11-15	5-11-16 to 23-11-15
Memory for Digits	9-5-16 to 23-11-15	–
Memory for Objects	9-11-16 to 23-11-15	–
Short Form		
2-Subtest short form	3-3-16 to 17-11-15	4-7-16 to 12-11-15
4-Subtest short form	3-7-16 to 23-11-15	4-11-16 to 16-11-15
6-Subtest short form	3-3-16 to 23-11-15	4-3-16 to 14-11-15
Factor		
Verbal Comprehension	3-3-16 to 23-11-15	4-3-16 to 15-11-15
Nonverbal Reasoning/Visualization	3-7-16 to 23-11-15	4-11-16 to 16-11-15
Memory	7-11-16 to 23-11-15	8-11-16 to 23-11-15
Composite		
Composite for factor battery	3-3-16 to 23-11-15	4-3-16 to 17-11-15
Composite for full battery	3-3-16 to 23-11-15	4-3-16 to 23-11-15

Note. Subtest short forms are as follows: 2 subtests: Vocabulary and Pattern Analysis; 4 subtests: Vocabulary, Bead Memory, Quantitative, and Pattern Analysis; 6 subtests: Vocabulary, Bead Memory, Quantitative, Memory for Sentences, Pattern Analysis, and Comprehension. See Table 11-8 for subtests that form the factor scores.

Formulating Hypotheses About Factor Score Discrepancies

Significant factor score differences may indicate the following:

- interest patterns
- cognitive style
- psychopathology
- deficiencies or strengths in processing information
- sensory deficiencies
- motivational changes

Which interpretations are pertinent must be decided on the basis of the child's entire performance and clinical history.

Hypotheses about factor score differences should be formulated in relationship to the child's *absolute* Verbal Comprehension, Nonverbal Reasoning/Visualization, and Memory factor scores and only when the differences are significant. Thus, for example, you would not say that a child with a Verbal Comprehension factor score of 140 and a Memory factor score of 120 had a memory deficit. In this case, both verbal comprehension and memory are well developed. Similarly, a child with a Nonverbal Reasoning/ Visualization factor score of 65 and a Memory score of 50 should be viewed as having deficits in both nonverbal and memory areas; the higher Nonverbal Reasoning/Visualization score of 65 should not be considered an absolute strength.

1. *Illustrative Hypotheses for Verbal Comprehension > Nonverbal Reasoning/Visualization*

a. Verbal skills are better developed than performance skills.

b. Auditory-vocal processing skills are better developed than visual discrimination skills.

c. Knowledge acquired through accumulated experience is better developed than immediate problem-solving ability.

d. Practical tasks are more difficult than nonpractical tasks.

e. Performance deficits may exist, including deficits in copying skills.

f. Limitations in visual-motor integration may be influencing performance.

2. *Illustrative Hypotheses for Verbal Comprehension > Memory*

a. Verbal skills are better developed than short-term memory skills.

b. Long-term memory is better developed than short-term memory.

c. Limitations in attention, possibly due to anxiety and distractibility, may be influencing performance.

3. *Illustrative Hypotheses for Nonverbal Reasoning/Visualization > Verbal Comprehension*

a. Performance skills are better developed than verbal skills.

b. Visual-motor discrimination skills are better developed than auditory-vocal processing skills.

c. Immediate problem-solving ability is better developed than knowledge acquired as a result of accumulated experience.

d. Reading skill and performance on academic tasks are not satisfactory.

e. A language deficit may exist.

f. Limitations in auditory conceptual skills and auditory processing skills may be influencing performance.

4. *Illustrative Hypotheses for Nonverbal Reasoning/Visualization > Memory*

a. Nonverbal reasoning skills are better developed than short-term memory skills.

b. Visual-motor discrimination skills are better developed than memory skills.

c. Immediate problem-solving ability is better developed than memory skills.

d. Limitations in attention, possibly due to anxiety and distractibility, may be influencing performance.

5. *Illustrative Hypotheses for Memory > Verbal Comprehension*

a. Short-term memory skills are better developed than verbal skills.

b. Short-term memory is better developed than long-term memory.

c. Encoding ability (such as sequencing ability) is better developed than knowledge acquired as a result of accumulated experience.

d. Reading skill and performance on academic tasks are not satisfactory.

e. A language deficit may exist.

6. *Illustrative Hypotheses for Memory > Nonverbal Reasoning/Visualization*

a. Short-term memory skills are better developed than nonverbal reasoning and visualization skills.

b. Short-term memory skills are better developed than visual-motor discrimination skills.

c. Encoding ability (such as sequencing ability) is better developed than immediate problem-solving ability.

d. Practical tasks are more difficult than nonpractical tasks.

e. Performance deficits may exist, including deficits in copying skills.

f. Limitations in visual-motor integration may be influencing performance.

COMPARISONS BETWEEN SUBTESTS THAT CAN GUIDE INTERPRETATIONS

Once differences between subtest scaled scores have been found to be significant (see Table C-45 in Appendix C), the findings must be translated into meaningful descriptions. Interpreting differences between subtest scores is not an easy matter. The material in this chapter will help you in making interpretations. Table 11-16 charts suggested abilities and factors associated with the 15 SB: FE subtests. You should view the interpretations that follow as hypotheses that may prove to be useful in the evaluation of a child's performance. These hypotheses, however, need to be further investigated through a study of the child's entire test performance and clinical history.

The following list of subtest comparisons does not include all possible comparisons, nor does it reflect all possible interpretations. On the basis of these examples, you should be able to develop other comparisons and formulate other interpretations. *All hypotheses should be treated as tentative. Conclusions derived from profile analysis should never be referred to as definitive findings.* (See Table C-52 in Appendix C for a summary of interpretive rationales and suggested remediation activities for the SB: FE subtests.) *All hypotheses must be developed on the basis of both significant differences between subtest scores and the absolute values of the subtest scores.* Thus scaled

Table 11-15
Short Forms, Factors, and Composite Score Ranges in the Stanford-Binet Intelligence Scale: Fourth Edition

Short forms, factors, and composite scores	+4 (164–149)	+3 (148–133)	+2 (132–117)	+1 (116–101)
Short Form				
2-Subtest short form	2-0-0 to 12-11-15	12-11-16 to 17-11-15	17-11-16 to 23-11-15	–
4-Subtest short form	2-0-0 to 16-11-15	16-11-16 to 23-11-15	–	–
6-Subtest short form	2-0-0 to 15-11-15	15-11-16 to 23-11-15	–	–
Factor				
Verbal Comprehension factor	2-0-0 to 15-11-15	15-11-16 to 23-11-15	–	–
Nonverbal Reasoning/Visualization factor	2-0-0 to 16-11-15	16-11-16 to 23-11-15	–	–
Memory factor	2-0-0 to 23-11-15	–	–	–
Composite				
Composite Score (factor scores)	2-0-0 to 17-11-15	17-11-16 to 23-11-15	–	–
Composite Score (full battery)	2-0-0 to 23-11-15	–	–	–

Note. Subtest short forms are as follows: 2 subtests: Vocabulary and Pattern Analysis; 4 subtests: Vocabulary, Bead Memory, Quantitative, and Pattern Analysis; 6 subtests: Vocabulary, Bead Memory, Quantitative, Memory for Sentences, Pattern Analysis, and Comprehension. See Table 11-8 for subtests that form the factor scores.

scores of 50 or higher never reflect absolute weaknesses, and scaled scores of 49 or lower never reflect absolute strengths.

COMPARING VERBAL COMPREHENSION FACTOR SUBTESTS

1. *Vocabulary (V) and Comprehension (C).* Both subtests involve verbal processing, but in somewhat different contexts.

V > C: High Vocabulary and low Comprehension may suggest inability to use verbal ability and general knowledge fully in life situations and therefore may indicate impaired judgment.

V < C: Low Vocabulary and high Comprehension may suggest limited concept formation, except when conceptualizing ability is applied to solving problems in the social world.

2. *Vocabulary (V) and Verbal Relations (VR).* Both Vocabulary and Verbal Relations measure level of abstract thinking and ability to form concepts, but Verbal Relations is a better measure of these abilities.

VR > V: High Verbal Relations and low Vocabulary may suggest good ability to do abstract thinking but limited ability to understand the meaning of words.

VR < V: Low Verbal Relations and high Vocabulary may suggest difficulty in forming abstract concepts but good ability to understand the meaning of individual words.

3. *Verbal Relations (VR) and Comprehension (C).* Verbal Relations and Comprehension both involve, in part, conceptualizing skills. Verbal Relations usually requires a single word response, whereas Comprehension requires an extended response that interrelates a set of ideas (that is, propositional thinking).

VR > C: High Verbal Relations and low Comprehension may suggest good abstract thinking but difficulty in applying conceptualizing ability to problem solving in the social world. This pattern also may suggest a verbal-expressive deficit involving propositional thinking.

VR < C: Low Verbal Relations and high Comprehension may suggest a deficit in verbal concept formation relative to real-world conceptualizing ability.

4. *Comprehension (C) and Absurdities (A).* Comprehension and Absurdities both reflect social intelligence to some extent. The comparison relates knowledge of social conventions (Comprehension) to the ability to discern incongruities in visually presented material (Absurdities).

A > C: High Absurdities coupled with low Comprehension may suggest keen observational skills, but limited understanding of social conventions.

A < C: Low Absurdities coupled with high Comprehension may suggest an understanding of social conventions but difficulty in using observational skills.

5. *Vocabulary (V) and Memory for Sentences (MS).* Vocabulary and Memory for Sentences both involve verbal processing (particularly from 2 to 7 years of age). Comparing the two subtests may provide an index of the relative

−1 (100–84)	−2 (83–68)	−3 (67–52)	−4 (51–36)	Short forms, factors, and composite scores
				Short Form
2-0-0 to 2-3-15	2-3-16 to 3-3-15	3-3-16 to 4-7-15	4-7-16 to 23-11-15	2-Subtest short form
2-0-0 to 2-7-15	2-7-16 to 3-7-15	3-7-16 to 4-11-15	4-11-16 to 23-11-15	4-Subtest short form
2-0-0 to 2-7-15	2-7-16 to 3-3-15	3-3-16 to 4-3-15	4-3-16 to 23-11-15	6-Subtest short form
				Factor
2-0-0 to 2-3-15	2-3-16 to 3-3-15	3-3-16 to 4-3-15	4-3-16 to 23-11-15	Verbal Comprehension factor
2-0-0 to 2-11-15	2-11-16 to 3-7-15	3-7-16 to 4-11-15	4-11-16 to 23-11-15	Nonverbal Reasoning/Visualization factor
−	6-11-16 to 7-11-15	7-11-16 to 8-11-15	8-11-16 to 23-11-15	Memory factor
				Composite
2-0-0 to 2-7-15	2-7-16 to 3-3-15	3-3-16 to 4-3-15	4-3-16 to 23-11-15	Composite Score (factor scores)
2-0-0 to 2-7-15	2-7-16 to 3-3-15	3-3-16 to 4-3-15	4-3-16 to 23-11-15	Composite Score (full battery)

balance between long-term memory (Vocabulary) and short-term memory (Memory for Sentences).

V > MS: High Vocabulary and low Memory for Sentences may suggest that long-term memory is better developed than short-term memory.

V < MS: Low Vocabulary and high Memory for Sentences may suggest that short-term memory is better developed than long-term memory.

6. *Comprehension (C) and Memory for Sentences (MS).* Both comprehension and Memory for Sentences involve verbal processing (particularly from 2 to 7 years of age). This comparison provides an estimate of verbal reasoning versus short-term verbal memory.

C > MS: High Comprehension and low Memory for Sentences may suggest that verbal reasoning is better developed than short-term verbal memory.

C < MS: Low Comprehension and high Memory for Sentences may suggest that verbal reasoning is not as well developed as short-term verbal memory.

COMPARING NONVERBAL REASONING/ VISUALIZATION FACTOR SUBTESTS

7. *Pattern Analysis (PA) and Copying (CP).* This comparison relates visual-spatial ability to visual-motor ability.

PA > CP: High Pattern Analysis and low Copying may suggest adequate visual-spatial ability but inadequate visual-motor ability.

PA < CP: Low Pattern Analysis and high Copying may suggest inadequate visual-spatial ability but adequate visual-motor ability.

8. *Pattern Analysis (PA) and Matrices (M).* Both Pattern Analysis and Matrices involve nonverbal reasoning ability. In Pattern Analysis, however, the reasoning in-

volves analysis and synthesis, whereas in Matrices the reasoning is more analogic.

PA > M: High Pattern Analysis and low Matrices may suggest adequate analysis and synthesis skills but inadequate analogic reasoning skills.

PA < M: Low Pattern Analysis and high Matrices may suggest inadequate analysis and synthesis skills but adequate analogic reasoning skills.

9. *Pattern Analysis (PA) and Paper Folding and Cutting (PF).* Both Pattern Analysis and Paper Folding and Cutting involve visual-spatial ability, but Paper Folding and Cutting is a purer measure of this ability. In Pattern Analysis a concrete representation of the stimulus is provided, whereas in Paper Folding and Cutting the examinee must discern how the folded and cut paper would look if it were unfolded.

PA > PF: High Pattern Analysis and low Paper Folding and Cutting may suggest that visual-spatial ability is more adequate when the stimulus is concrete than when it is less concrete.

PA < PF: Low Pattern Analysis and high Paper Folding and Cutting may suggest that visual-spatial ability is less adequate when the stimulus is concrete than when it is less concrete.

10. *Pattern Analysis (PA) and Quantitative (Q).* This comparison relates nonverbal spatial reasoning to numerical reasoning.

PA > Q: High Pattern Analysis and low Quantitative may suggest adequate nonverbal spatial reasoning ability but inadequate numerical reasoning ability.

PA < Q: Low Pattern Analysis and high Quantitative may suggest inadequate nonverbal spatial reasoning ability but adequate numerical reasoning ability.

Table 11-16
Suggested Abilities or Factors Associated with the 15 Subtests of the Stanford-Binet Intelligence Scale: Fourth Edition

Vocabulary (V)	Comprehension (C)	Absurdities (A)	Verbal Relations (VR)	Pattern Analysis (PA)	Copying (CP)	Matrices (M)	Paper Folding and Cutting (PF)	Quantitative (Q)	Number Series (NS)	Equation Building (EB)	Bead Memory (BM)	Memory for Sentences (MS)	Memory for Digits (MD)	Memory for Objects (MO)	M	Suggested abilities or factors
		A			CP	M	PF	Q	NS	EB	BM	MS	MD	MO	___	Attention
								Q				MS	MD		___	Auditory memory
		A			CP	M	PF	Q	NS	EB	BM	MS	MD	MO	___	Concentration
V	C	A													___	Cultural opportunities at home
		A						Q			BM	MS	MD	MO	___	Freedom from distractibility
V			VR					Q							___	Long-term memory
				PA		M	PF								___	Nonverbal reasoning
								Q	NS	EB					___	Numerical ability
				PA		M	PF								___	Perceptual organization
						M									___	Perceptual planning ability
				PA	CP						BM				___	Perceptual reproduction
				PA			PF								___	Perceptual synthesis
				PA		M	PF								___	Perception of abstract stimuli
V(P)		A				M								MO	___	Perception of meaningful stimuli
				PA											___	Psychomotor speed
									NS			MS	MD	MO	___	Sequencing
								Q		EB	BM	MS	MD	MO	___	Short-term memory
	C														___	Social judgment
				PA	CP		PF				BM				___	Spatial perception
V	C	A	VR												___	Verbal comprehension
V(P)		A						Q	NS						___	Little verbal expression
V(O)	C		VR												___	Much verbal expression
V			VR												___	Verbal concept formation
	C							Q							___	Long verbal questions
V			VR										MD		___	Short verbal questions
	C	A						Q		EB					___	Verbal reasoning
				PA	CP						BM				___	Visual-motor coordination
							PF				BM			MO	___	Visual memory
				PA											___	Working under time pressure

Note. V(P) = Picture Vocabulary, V(O) = Oral Vocabulary. *M* = mean of the subtest scaled score or factor.

11. *Pattern Analysis (PA) and Bead Memory (BM)*. Pattern Analysis and Bead Memory both involve visual discrimination and spatial relations. In Bead Memory, however, these skills are measured in the context of a short-term visual memory task, whereas in Pattern Analysis the skills are measured using stimuli that remain in view during the task. Additionally, Pattern Analysis has a strong reasoning component, whereas Bead Memory does not.

PA > BM: High Pattern Analysis and low Bead Memory may suggest that visual discrimination and spatial relations skills are adequate when short-term memory is not involved but are inadequate when short-term memory is involved.

PA < BM: Low Pattern Analysis and high Bead Memory may suggest that visual discrimination and spatial relations skills are adequate when short-term memory is involved but are inadequate when short-term memory is not involved.

12. *Quantitative (Q) and Number Series (NS)*. Both Quantitative and Number Series involve numerical reasoning ability, but Number Series is a purer measure of reasoning ability.

Q > NS: High Quantitative and low Number Series may suggest adequate understanding of mathematical concepts but inadequate numerical reasoning ability.

Q < NS: Low Quantitative and high Number Series may suggest inadequate understanding of mathematical concepts but adequate numerical reasoning ability.

13. *Quantitative (Q) and Equation Building (EB)*. Both Quantitative and Equation Building involve numerical reasoning ability, but Equation Building requires more logical reasoning and flexibility in rearranging and manipulating mathematical symbols.

Q > EB: High Quantitative and low Equation Building may suggest adequate understanding of mathematical concepts but inadequate logical reasoning and flexibility in the use of mathematical symbols.

Q < EB: Low Quantitative and high Equation Building may suggest inadequate understanding of mathematical concepts but adequate logical reasoning and flexibility in the use of mathematical symbols.

14. *Number Series (NS) and Equation Building (EB)*. Both Number Series and Equation Building involve numerical reasoning. Equation Building, in addition, involves knowledge of conventional arithmetical operations and flexibility in the use of mathematical symbols.

NS > EB: High Number Series and low Equation Building may suggest adequate numerical and logical reasoning ability but inadequate knowledge of conventional operations and limited flexibility in the use of mathematical symbols.

NS < EB: Low Number Series and high Equation Building may suggest inadequate numerical and logical reasoning ability but adequate knowledge of conventional operations and flexibility in the use of mathematical symbols.

COMPARING MEMORY FACTOR SUBTESTS

15. *Memory for Sentences (MS), Memory for Digits (MD), Memory for Objects (MO), and Bead Memory (BM)*. The Memory for Sentences, Memory for Digits, Memory for Objects, and Bead Memory subtests all involve short-term memory. Differences exist among the four subtests, however, in the stimuli used to elicit responses (meaningful or nonmeaningful) and the processing modality (auditory or visual) (see Figure 11-3). Memory for Sentences involves meaningful stimuli presented in the auditory modality. Memory for Digits involves nonmeaningful stimuli presented in the auditory modality. Memory for Objects involves meaningful stimuli presented in the visual modality. Bead Memory involves nonmeaningful stimuli presented in the visual modality.

The subtests also load on different factors. Bead Memory loads on the Nonverbal Reasoning/Visualization factor, whereas the other three subtests load on the Memory factor. (Memory for Sentences also loads on the Verbal Comprehension factor throughout the scale.) On Bead Memory the stimuli are shown as a group (or presented as a gestalt), whereas on the other subtests the stimuli are presented sequentially.

MS > MD: High Memory for Sentences and low Memory for Digits may suggest adequate short-term memory

	Meaningful memory	Nonmeaningful memory
Auditory memory	Memory for Sentences	Memory for Digits
Visual memory	Memory for Objects	Bead Memory

Figure 11-3.   Classification of four memory subtests on the Stanford-Binet Intelligence Scale: Fourth Edition.

for meaningful material but inadequate short-term memory for nonmeaningful material.

MS < MD: Low Memory for Sentences and high Memory for Digits may suggest inadequate short-term memory for meaningful material but adequate short-term memory for nonmeaningful material.

MS > MO: High Memory for Sentences and low Memory for Objects may suggest that, for meaningful stimuli, short-term auditory memory is adequate but short-term visual memory is inadequate.

MS < MO: Low Memory for Sentences and high Memory for Objects may suggest that, for meaningful stimuli, short-term auditory memory is inadequate but short-term visual memory is adequate.

MD > BM: High Memory for Digits and low Bead Memory may suggest that, for nonmeaningful material, short-term auditory memory is adequate but short-term visual memory is inadequate.

MD < BM: Low Memory for Digits and high Bead Memory may suggest that, for nonmeaningful material, short-term auditory memory is inadequate but short-term visual memory is adequate.

BM > MO: High Bead Memory and low Memory for Objects may suggest that short-term visual memory is adequate for nonmeaningful material but inadequate for meaningful material.

BM < MO: Low Bead Memory and high Memory for Objects may suggest that short-term visual memory is less adequate for nonmeaningful material than for meaningful material.

16. *Memory for Digits — Digits Forward (MD-F) versus Digits Reversed (MD-R).* The two components of Memory for Digits — Digits Forward and Digits Reversed — both involve attention. Digits Reversed, however, involves more complex attentional processes.

MD-F > MD-R: High Digits Forward and low Digits Reversed (differences of 3 or more raw-score points) may indicate that the child did not put forth the extra effort needed to master the more difficult task of recalling digits in reversed sequence. Alternatively, it may indicate good auditory memory but poor short-term visual memory based on auditory information (a very tentative hypothesis).

MD-F < MD-R: Low Digits Forward and high Digits Reversed may indicate that the child sees Digits Reversed as a challenge rather than as a task involving mere repetition of numbers.

17. *Memory for Sentences (MS) and Memory for Objects (MO) versus Memory for Digits (MD) and Bead Memory (BM).* This comparison contrasts subtests that measure short-term memory for meaningful material (Memory for Sentences, Memory for Objects) versus short-term memory for nonmeaningful material (Memory for Digits, Bead Memory) (see Figure 11-3).

MS, MO > MD, BM: High Memory for Sentences and Memory for Objects coupled with low Memory for Digits and Bead Memory may suggest that the examinee has better short-term memory when the material is meaningful than when it is nonmeaningful.

MS, MO < MD, BM: Low Memory for Sentences and Memory for Objects coupled with high Memory for Digits and Bead Memory may suggest that the examinee has better short-term memory when the material is nonmeaningful than when it is meaningful.

18. *Memory for Sentences (MS) and Memory for Digits (MD) versus Memory for Objects (MO) and Bead Memory (BM).* This comparison contrasts short-term auditory memory with short-term visual memory (see Figure 11-3).

MS, MD > MO, BM: High Memory for Sentences and Memory for Digits and low Memory for Objects and Bead Memory may suggest that the examinee's short-term auditory memory is better than his or her short-term visual memory.

MS, MD < MO, BM: Low Memory for Sentences and Memory for Digits and high Memory for Objects and Bead Memory may suggest that the examinee's short-term auditory memory is poorer than his or her short-term visual memory.

19. *Bead Memory (BM) versus Memory for Sentences (MS), Memory for Digits (MD), and Memory for Objects (MO).* This comparison contrasts a subtest that uses simultaneously presented stimuli with those that use sequentially presented stimuli.

BM > MS, MD, MO: High Bead Memory and low Memory for Sentences, Memory for Digits, and Memory for Objects may suggest that the examinee's short-term memory is better when the stimuli are presented simultaneously than when they are presented sequentially.

BM < MS, MD, MO: Low Bead Memory and high Memory for Sentences, Memory for Digits, and Memory for Objects may suggest that the examinee's short-term memory is poorer when the stimuli are presented simultaneously than when they are presented sequentially.

COMPARING VERBAL COMPREHENSION, NONVERBAL REASONING/VISUALIZATION, AND MEMORY FACTOR SUBTESTS

20. *Verbal Relations (VR) and Pattern Analysis (PA).* Verbal Relations and Pattern Analysis both reflect abstract reasoning ability. They both require the abstraction of relations among stimulus items.

VR > PA: High Verbal Relations and low Pattern Analysis may suggest that abstract reasoning ability is better with verbal stimuli than with nonverbal stimuli.

VR < PA: Low Verbal Relations and high Pattern Analysis may suggest that abstract reasoning ability is better with nonverbal stimuli than with verbal stimuli.

21. *Comprehension (C) and Quantitative (Q) versus Vocabulary (V), Verbal Relations (VR), and Memory for Digits (MD).* This comparison contrasts subtests that have relatively long verbal questions (Comprehension and Quantitative) with those that have relatively short verbal questions (Vocabulary, Verbal Relations, Memory for Digits).

C, Q > V, VR, MD: High Comprehension and Quantitative coupled with low Vocabulary, Verbal Relations, and Memory for Digits may suggest that the child performs better when the verbal stimuli are long than when they are short. The child may put forth more effort to attend to verbal material that is of a relatively long duration. The pattern may also reflect the child's ability to benefit from the contextual cues contained in the longer questions.

C, Q < V, VR, MD: Low Comprehension and Quantitative coupled with high Vocabulary, Verbal Relations, and Memory for Digits may suggest that the child performs better when verbal stimuli are short than when they are long. The child may put forth more effort to attend to verbal material that is of a relatively short duration. This pattern also may suggest an auditory processing deficit associated with deriving meaning from spoken language.

22. *Vocabulary (Oral) (V(0)), Comprehension (C), and Verbal Relations (VR) versus Absurdities (A), Quantitative (Q), and Number Series (NS).* This comparison contrasts subtests that require a fair amount of verbal expression (Vocabulary [Oral], Comprehension and Verbal Relations) with those that require relatively little verbal expression (Absurdities, Quantitative, and Number Series).

V(O), C, VR > A, Q, NS: High Vocabulary (Oral), Comprehension, and Verbal Relations coupled with low Absurdities, Quantitative, and Number Series may suggest that the child performs better when the tasks require a fair amount of verbal expression than when they require relatively little. One possibility is that the child may put forth an extra effort in situations that require verbal expression.

V(O), C, VR < A, Q, NS: Low Vocabulary (Oral), Comprehension, and Verbal Relations coupled with high Absurdities, Quantitative, and Number Series suggest that the child performs better when the tasks require relatively little verbal expression. One possibility is that the child may put forth effort only when tasks require minimal verbal effort. Additionally, this pattern may be associated with communication problems or shyness associated with speaking in relatively long sentences.

23. *Absurdities (A) versus Pattern Analysis (PA), Matrices (M), and Paper Folding and Cutting (PF).* This comparison contrasts a subtest that contains relatively meaningful perceptual stimuli (Absurdities) with those that have relatively abstract perceptual stimuli (Pattern Analysis, Matrices, and Paper Folding and Cutting). (Matrices contains some meaningful stimuli as well, but primarily at the younger ages.)

A > PA, M, PF: High Absurdities coupled with low Pattern Analysis, Matrices, and Paper Folding and Cutting may suggest that the child performs better when the visual stimuli are meaningful than when they are abstract or nonmeaningful.

A < PA, M, PF: Low Absurdities coupled with high Pattern Analysis, Matrices, and Paper Folding and Cutting may suggest that the child performs better when the visual stimuli are abstract than when they are concrete.

24. *Vocabulary (V), Verbal Relations (VR), and Quantitative (Q) versus Bead Memory (BM), Memory for Sentences (MS), Memory for Digits (MD), and Memory for Objects (MO).* This comparison contrasts subtests that involve long-term memory (Vocabulary, Verbal Relations, and Quantitative) with those that involve primarily short-term memory (Bead Memory, Memory for Sentences, Memory for Digits, and Memory for Objects).

V, VR, Q > BM, MS, MD, MO: High Vocabulary, Verbal Relations, and Quantitative coupled with low Bead Memory, Memory for Sentences, Memory for Digits, and Memory for Objects may suggest that the examinee performs better on tasks requiring long-term memory than on those requiring short-term memory.

V, VR, Q < BM, MS, MD, MO: Low Vocabulary, Verbal Relations, and Quantitative coupled with high Bead Memory, Memory for Sentences, Memory for Digits, and Memory for Objects may suggest that the examinee performs better on tasks requiring short-term memory than on those requiring long-term memory.

25. *Pattern Analysis (PA), Paper Folding and Cutting (PF), and Bead Memory (BM) versus Quantitative (Q) and Matrices (M).* This is a comparison that distinguishes subtests that may tap spatial visualization processes from subtests with perceptual tasks that do not involve these processes.

PA, PF, BM > Q, M: High Pattern Analysis, Paper Folding and Cutting, and Bead Memory coupled with low Quantitative and Matrices may suggest that the examinee performs better when perceptual tasks require spatial visualization than when the tasks do not.

PA, PF, BM < Q, M: Low Pattern Analysis, Paper Folding and Cutting, and Bead Memory coupled with high Quantitative and Matrices may suggest that the examinee performs more poorly when perceptual tasks require spatial visualization than when they do not.

ADDITIONAL SUGGESTIONS FOR USING AND INTERPRETING THE SB: FE

The following additional suggestions for interpreting the SB: FE apply only in cases where other information is available to confirm the hypothesis. Because the SB: FE is essentially a new test, the suggestions below must be viewed in a tentative manner. They must be confirmed by research investigations as well as clinical experience.

• Some subtests may be less culturally loaded than others. Candidates include Paper Folding and Cutting, Matrices, Pattern Analysis, Number Series, and Bead Memory.

• Some subtests may be especially sensitive to brain damage that affects conceptual processes or visualization or flexibility in rearranging materials. Possible candidates are Pattern Analysis, Matrices, Paper Folding and Cutting, Verbal Relations, and Equation Building. Other subtests may be sensitive to brain damage that affects *short-term memory* (Bead Memory, Memory for Sentences, Memory for Digits, Memory for Objects), *long-term memory* (Vocabulary, Verbal Relations, Quantitative), or *judgment and reasoning* (Comprehension, Absurdities, Matrices).

• The four memory subtests—Bead Memory, Memory for Sentences, Memory for Digits, and Memory for Objects—may prove to be especially helpful in assessment of learning disabled children. These subtests permit comparisons of simultaneous and successive processing, auditory and visual processing, and meaningful and nonmeaningful processing.

• The three numerical ability subtests—Quantitative, Number Series, and Equation Building—provide a powerful measure of quantitative skills. These subtests may be especially useful in counseling students about their mathematical talents.

• Four subtests provide potentially useful information about skills in spatial perception—Pattern Analysis, Copying, Paper Folding and Cutting, and Bead Memory. These subtests may prove to be useful in identifying children with visual-spatial talents.

• The Nonverbal Reasoning/Visualization factor subtests together with the Memory for Objects subtest may be a useful screening tool for measuring the cognitive skills of hearing-impaired children.

• The Vocabulary, Comprehension, Memory for Sentences, Memory for Digits, Verbal Relations, and Number Series subtests may be a useful screening tool for measuring the cognitive skills of visually impaired children.

• The examinee's performance on the Pattern Analysis subtest may provide some clues about how he or she performs under time pressure.

ASSETS OF THE SB: FE

The SB: FE is a well standardized test, with excellent internal-consistency reliability and adequate concurrent validity. Of the 15 subtests in the scale, 12 are recommended for routine use. These 12 subtests form three factors: *Verbal Comprehension* (Vocabulary, Comprehension, Absurdities [at ages 2 through 14], Memory for Sentences [at ages 2 through 7], and Verbal Relations [at ages 15 through 18–23]), *Nonverbal Reasoning/ Visualization* (Pattern Analysis, Copying [at ages 2 through 11], Quantitative, Bead Memory, and Matrices [at ages 12 through 18–23]), and *Memory* (Memory for Sentences [at ages 8 through 18–23], Memory for Digits, and Memory for Objects). The three remaining subtests can be considered as supplementary, to be used for special purposes (Paper Folding and Cutting, Number Series, and Equation Building). The division of the scale into two factors at lower age levels (2 through 6 years) and three factors at elementary and high school years is especially helpful in clinical and psychoeducational work and aids in the assessment of brain-behavior relationships. The following are the assets of the SB: FE:

1. *Good validity*. The SB: FE has adequate concurrent validity, demonstrated by correlations with a variety of ability measures.

2. *High reliabilities*. The internal consistency reliabilities of the Composite Score and factor scores are extremely high (*Mdn* r_{xx}'s range from .91 to .97), with standard errors of measurement of less than 5 points on the Composite and factor scores. Because the *Technical Manual* provides reliability data, standard errors of measurement, and intercorrelations of subtest scores by one-year age intervals as well as median reliabilities, the scale's properties can be evaluated throughout its entire age range. Confidence intervals can be established for the Composite Score for each of the 17 separate age groups, thereby providing estimates that are specifically applicable to each child's chronological age.

3. *Excellent standardization*. The standardization procedures were excellent, with sampling done on the basis of geographical region, community size, ethnic group, age, gender, and socioeconomic status. Weighting procedures

were used to make the sample conform to the 1980 census data.

4. *Good administration procedures.* The prescribed procedures for administering the SB: FE are excellent. Borderline responses are probed, and sample items are provided for many of the subtests.

5. *Adequate administrative guidelines and test materials.* The administrative guidelines are adequate, although somewhat cumbersome. The use of both letters and numbers for items complicates the use of the scale. The test directions, however, are easy to read. The art work and photos are clear, and the materials are well constructed. The easel-format for administering the subtests is a decided advantage. The sample items on many subtests help the examinee understand the task requirements. Finally, the minimal time requirements are an advantage for those examinees who do not perform well under time pressure.

6. *Helpful scoring criteria.* The criteria for scoring the responses have been carefully prepared. The Vocabulary, Comprehension, and Verbal Relations scoring guidelines, for example, detail the rationale for 1 and 0 scores. A number of examples demonstrate the application of the scoring principles. Many typical responses are scored, and those deemed to require further inquiry are placed under a query section.

LIMITATIONS OF THE SB: FE

1. *Lack of a comparable battery throughout the age ranges covered by the scale.* The SB: FE fails to provide a comparable battery of subtests throughout the age ranges covered by the scale. This is a limitation because it means that scores obtained by children at different ages are based on different combinations of subtests. Only six subtests run throughout the entire scale (Vocabulary, Comprehension, Pattern Analysis, Quantitative, Bead Memory, and Memory for Sentences). Two subtests begin at the lowest age levels but stop during the adolescent years (Absurdities and Copying). Four subtests begin at age 7 and run to the upper age level (Matrices, Number Series, Memory for Digits, and Memory for Objects). One subtest begins at age 12 and goes to the upper age level (Equation Building). Only at two ages can a child be given all 15 subtests (ages 12 and 13). The lack of continuity across ages and within subtests makes it difficult to monitor changes in performance on individual subtests and may make it difficult to perform longitudinal studies.

2. *Variable range of scores.* The SB: FE fails to provide the same range of Composite Scores, factor scores, or subtest scores throughout the age levels covered by the scale. For example, Composite Scores of up to 164 can be obtained from ages 2-0-0 to 12-11-15. After this age they begin to drop—at the age of 17-11-16 the highest Composite Score is 149. *This means that even if an examinee answers every item correctly, his or her score will differ by 15 points (about 1 standard deviation) if he or she is tested first at age 12 and again at age 18 years.*

Similarly, a Composite Score as low as 36 cannot be obtained at all age levels. For example, the lowest possible scores at the 2-year level are 95 (2-0-0), 87 (2-3-16), 80 (2-7-16), and 73 (2-11-16). It is only at age level 3-3-16 that a child can obtain a score more than 2 *SD*'s below the mean. This limited floor means that a diagnosis of mental retardation cannot be established through use of the SB: FE for children who are between 2 and 3 years of age.

The nonuniformity of scores also holds for all comparable combinations of subtests, either in factors or otherwise established. Applying profile analysis uniformly to all subtests would be misleading for individual cases because the same number of scaled-score points cannot be obtained on all subtests.

3. *Limited support for four area scores.* Factor analysis does not support the four area scores throughout the age levels of the scale. Thus the routine use of area scores is not recommended. Factor scores are useful in describing the examinee's abilities, however.

4. *Difficulty in scoring responses.* When responses on Verbal Relations, Comprehension, and Vocabulary subtests differ from those that are in the *Guide*, they may be difficult to score. The Copying subtest is also likely to be difficult to score. Such difficulties may lead to halo effects in scoring and contribute to examiner bias.

5. *Difficulty in interpreting norms for subtests that have estimated scaled-score values at some ages.* Figure 2 in the *Guide* lists nine subtests that have estimated standard score values. For example, estimated standard score values are provided for ages 15, 16, and 17 years for the Absurdities subtest. For these years, raw scores can be converted into standard scores. The *Guide* fails to provide any descriptive statistics for these age levels, however. Similarly, it fails to provide descriptive statistics for any of the ages at which the subtest scores are estimated. Therefore it is recommended that subtests be used only for ages at which descriptive statistics are provided.

6. *Lack of description of procedure for establishing cutoff criteria.* Neither the *Guide* nor the *Technical Manual* provides information concerning how the cutoff criteria (the number of items that should be administered before the test is discontinued) were determined (that is, empirically or intuitively).

7. *Overly long administration time.* Because the SB: FE

has only one timed subtest, examinees can take an inordinate amount of time to solve the problems. Even in cases where the child does not take an excessive amount of time to respond, it may take two hours or more to administer the complete battery to an adolescent.

8. *Incorrect entry level points.* The entry level points indicated in the *Guide* may not be appropriate for all children. Therefore, the test may be unnecessarily prolonged and children may be given items that are too difficult at the beginning of the test.

CONCLUDING COMMENT ON THE SB: FE

The SB: FE is a potentially powerful tool for assessment of the cognitive ability of young children, adolescents, and young adults. It has some serious shortcomings, however, that must be recognized. The most serious of these are the lack of a comparable battery throughout the age levels covered by the scale and the nonuniformity of Composite Scores, factor scores, and scaled scores. Users of the scale must be extremely alert to these features of the scale. Profiles and changes in performance cannot be evaluated in a routine manner. In each case attention must be given to the range of scores provided by the scale for the examinee's particular age. Critical decisions must be made with these considerations in mind.

SUMMARY

1. The SB: FE represents a significant departure from former editions, although some continuity is maintained with former editions. The 1937 and 1960 editions of the Stanford-Binet were generally well received, although there were criticisms associated with their emphasis on verbal material, age-scale format, ceiling procedure, item placements, emphasis on rote memory, administrative procedures, inappropriateness for use with adults, and use in clinical situations. The scales produced acceptable validity coefficients, however, and remained popular until the 1980s.

2. Only 6 of the 15 subtests run consecutively throughout the scale.

3. The standardization sample was selected to be representative of the U.S. population based on 1980 census data, but weighting procedures were needed because the sample contained too many children with high SES backgrounds.

4. The SB: FE continues to use $M = 100$ and $SD = 16$ for the Composite Score. For the subtests, $M = 50$ and $SD = 8$ are used.

5. Internal consistency reliabilities are excellent for the Composite Score (*Mdn* $r_{xx} = .97$, *Mdn* $SE_m = 2.8$). Reliabilities

for the subtests are less satisfactory (r_{xx}'s range from .73 to .94). Stability coefficients are satisfactory for the Composite Score ($r_{xx} = .90$), but not for some of the subtests (r_{xx}'s range between .28 and .86).

6. Validity studies comparing the SB: FE with other intelligence tests indicate satisfactory concurrent validity (*Mdn* $r = .80$). SB: FE Composite Scores and IQs on other tests may not be comparable, however, especially in gifted or mentally retarded populations. In these populations the SB: FE has been found to yield lower scores than either the Stanford-Binet: Form L-M or the WAIS-R.

7. Higher intercorrelations are observed among the verbal subtests and nonverbal subtests than among the memory subtests. The memory subtests have low correlations with most other subtests. The subtests with the highest correlations with the Composite Score are Quantitative, Number Series, Vocabulary, Matrices, Comprehension, and Verbal Relations (all above .75).

8. The relationships between SB: FE Composite Scores and demographic characteristics indicate that black children tend to score 10 to 17 points lower than white children. There is about a 14-point difference between children in the highest and lowest socioeconomic status groups (108 vs. 94). Differences associated with gender were minimal, but some meaningful differences were associated with community size.

9. A principal components analysis of the SB: FE supports two factors at ages 2 through 6—Verbal Comprehension and Nonverbal Reasoning/Visualization—and three factors at ages 7 through 23—Verbal Comprehension, Nonverbal Reasoning/Visualization, and Memory. The subtests that comprise these factors differ at different ages.

10. All SB: FE subtests are either good or fair measures of *g*. Those with the highest *g* loadings are Vocabulary, Number Series, Quantitative, Comprehension, and Matrices.

11. Of the 15 subtests in the SB: FE, only Vocabulary, Comprehension, Quantitative, and Memory for Objects have inadequate specificity at some ages.

12. Factor scores are the preferred way to identify meaningful psychological dimensions on the SB: FE. The factor scores are highly reliable.

13. The routing procedure used on the SB: FE may not be applicable to mentally retarded children. Entry level points for these children may have to be considerably lower than those indicated in the record booklet. You should feel free to adjust the entry level when testing a mentally retarded child (and other children as well, if necessary).

14. A complete administration of the SB: FE requires establishing a basal level (two consecutive levels at which both items are passed) and a ceiling level (two consecutive levels at which three or four items are failed).

15. Specific physical abilities are required to take the subtests, but some modifications may be made for physically handicapped children.

16. Short forms discussed in the chapter are available for screening purposes.

17. A profile sheet is useful in plotting the examinee's scores.

It can be used in conjunction with the recommended battery for each age group or with the entire battery.

18. The interpretive rationale, factor analytic findings, reliability and subtest correlations, and administrative considerations for each of the 15 SB: FE subtests are presented in the chapter.

19. The rationale for the WISC-R Vocabulary subtest generally applies to the oral section of the Vocabulary subtest in the SB: FE. For the picture section of the Vocabulary subtest, formal education likely plays a minor role. The subtest is a good measure of g and contributes to the Verbal Comprehension factor. It is a reliable subtest ($r_{xx} = .87$). Scoring requires considerable judgment.

20. The rationale for the WISC-R Comprehension subtest generally applies to the SB: FE Comprehension subtest. The subtest is a good measure of g and contributes to the Verbal Comprehension factor. It is a reliable subtest ($r_{xx} = .89$). Scoring requires considerable judgment.

21. Absurdities measures the ability to isolate the incongruities and absurdities of visual material. Success depends on perception of detail, alertness, concentration, and social understanding. The subtest is a good measure of g and contributes to the Verbal Comprehension factor. It is a reliable subtest ($r_{xx} = .87$) and relatively easy to administer.

22. Verbal Relations measures verbal concept formation and reasoning ability. It is a fair measure of g and contributes to the Verbal Comprehension factor. It is a reliable subtest ($r_{xx} = .91$), but may be somewhat difficult to score.

23. The rationale for the WISC-R Block Design subtest generally applies to most of the items on the Pattern Analysis subtest of the SB: FE. The form-board items, however, primarily measure visual-motor ability and recognition and manipulation of forms. The subtest is a good measure of g and contributes to the Nonverbal Reasoning/Visualization factor. It is a reliable subtest ($r_{xx} = .92$) and is easy to score.

24. The Copying subtest measures visual-motor ability and eye-hand coordination. The subtest is a fair measure of g and contributes to the Nonverbal Reasoning/Visualization factor. It is a reliable subtest ($r_{xx} = .87$). The subtest may be the most difficult of all SB: FE subtests to score.

25. Matrices measures analogic reasoning, attention to detail, and concentration. The subtest is a good measure of g and contributes to the Nonverbal Reasoning/Visualization factor. It is a reliable subtest ($r_{xx} = .90$) and is easy to administer.

26. Paper Folding and Cutting measures visualization, spatial ability, the integration of visual and spatial abilities, and attention to visual cues. The subtest is a fair measure of g and contributes to the Nonverbal Reasoning/Visualization factor. It is a reliable subtest ($r_{xx} = .94$) and is easy to score.

27. The rationale presented for the WISC-R Arithmetic subtest generally applies to the Quantitative subtest, although formal education probably has less influence on performance on the early Quantitative items. The subtest is a good measure of g and contributes to the Nonverbal Reasoning/Visualization factor. It is a reliable subtest ($r_{xx} = .88$) and is easy to score.

28. Number Series measures logical reasoning and concentration when using numbers. The subtest is a good measure of g and contributes to the Nonverbal Reasoning/Visualization factor. It is a reliable subtest ($r_{xx} = .90$) and is easy to score.

29. Equation Building measures logic, flexibility, and trial and error. The subtest is a fair measure of g and contributes to the Nonverbal Reasoning/Visualization factor. It is a reliable subtest ($r_{xx} = .91$) and is relatively easy to score.

30. Bead Memory measures short-term visual memory and involves form perception and discrimination, spatial relations, and alertness to detail. The subtest is a fair measure of g and contributes to the Nonverbal Reasoning/Visualization factor. It is a reliable subtest ($r_{xx} = .87$) and is easy to administer.

31. Memory for Sentences measures short-term auditory memory for meaningful material. The subtest is a good measure of g and contributes to the Verbal Comprehension factor and Memory factor. It is included in the Verbal Comprehension factor at ages 2 through 7 and in the Memory factor at ages 8 through 18–23. It is a reliable subtest ($r_{xx} = .89$) and is easy to administer.

32. The rationale for the WISC-R Digit Span subtest applies to the Memory for Digits subtest. The subtest is a fair measure of g and contributes to the Memory factor. It is a reliable subtest ($r_{xx} = .83$) and is easy to administer.

33. Memory for Objects measures short-term visual memory. The subtest is a fair measure of g and contributes to the Memory factor. It is a moderately reliable subtest ($r_{xx} = .73$) and is easy to administer.

34. Although the same considerations that apply to profile analysis on the WISC-R apply to the SB: FE, more care should be taken in using profile analysis with the SB: FE because it is essentially a new instrument. The proposed interpretive rationales and possible implications of high and low scores are summarized in Table C-52 of Appendix C.

35. The non-uniform scaled-score ranges for subtests, short forms, factor scores, and Composite Scores complicate the use of profile analysis on the SB: FE. Profile analysis must be performed by considering the available score ranges, as shown in Table C-51 in Appendix C.

36. As with the Wechsler scales, a successive level approach to test interpretation is helpful with the SB: FE.

37. The Verbal Comprehension factor is dependent on the examinee's accumulated experience. The Nonverbal Reasoning/Visualization factor is more dependent on the examinee's immediate problem-solving ability. The Memory factor is dependent on the examinee's ability to sustain attention. All three factors involve verbal and nonverbal strategies in the solution of problems.

38. Significant differences between factor scores must be interpreted within the context of the examinee's entire performance and clinical history and always in relationship to the examinee's absolute level of functioning.

39. When the Verbal Comprehension factor score is higher than Nonverbal Reasoning/Visualization and Memory factor scores, auditory processing skills may be better developed than visual processing and memory skills. When the Nonverbal Reasoning/Visualization factor score is higher than Verbal Comprehension and Memory factor scores, nonverbal processing

skills may be better developed than verbal and memory processing skills. When the Memory factor is higher than the Verbal Comprehension and Nonverbal Reasoning/Visualization factor scores, short-term memory skills may be better developed than verbal and nonverbal reasoning skills.

40. Any hypotheses generated from subtest comparisons should be treated as tentative and formulated in relation to the examinee's *absolute* level of scaled scores.

41. Special combinations of subtests in the SB: FE may prove useful in generating interpretive hypotheses.

42. The assets of the SB: FE include its good validity, high reliabilities, excellent standardization, good administration procedures, well-constructed and well-designed materials, and helpful scoring criteria.

43. The limitations of the SB: FE include the lack of a comparable battery throughout the age ranges covered by the scale, variable range of scores, limited support for four area scores, difficulty in scoring some subtests, difficulty in interpreting norms for subtests that have estimated scaled scores at some ages, the manual's failure to describe procedure for establishing cutoff criteria, overly long administration time, and incorrect entry level points.

44. The SB: FE is a potentially powerful tool for the assessment of cognitive ability of young children, adolescents, and young adults. Profile analysis, however, cannot be done in a routine manner—attention must be given to the range of scores available for each subtest and age.

KEY TERMS, CONCEPTS, AND NAMES

STUDY QUESTIONS

1. Discuss the SB: FE. Include in your discussion the following issues: standardization, Composite Score, test-age equivalents, reliability, and validity.

2. Describe and interpret intercorrelations on the SB: FE (a) between subtests and (b) between subtests and the Composite Score.

3. Describe and interpret the SB: FE Composite Scores with respect to the stratification variables used in the standardization sample.

4. Describe and interpret SB: FE factor analytic findings.

5. Discuss SB: FE administrative considerations.

6. Discuss SB: FE short forms.

7. Discuss the rationale, factor analytic findings, reliability and correlational highlights, and administrative considerations for each of the following SB: FE subtests: Vocabulary, Comprehension, Absurdities, Verbal Relations, Pattern Analysis, Copying, Matrices, Paper Folding and Cutting, Quantitative, Number Series, Equation Building, Bead Memory, Memory for Sentences, Memory for Digits, and Memory for Objects.

8. Discuss the intent of profile analysis, methods of profile

analysis, and approaches to profile analysis on the SB: FE. Include in your discussion the effect of score ranges on profile analysis.

9. Discuss how to interpret differences between SB: FE factor scores.

10. Discuss how to interpret differences between SB: FE sub-tests. Cite at least seven subtest comparisons in your presentation.

11. What are some general considerations in interpreting the SB: FE?

12. Discuss the assets and limitations of the SB: FE.

12

ASSESSMENT OF INTELLIGENCE AND INFANT DEVELOPMENT WITH SPECIALIZED MEASURES

An "intelligence quotient" may be of provisional value as a first crude approximation when the mental level of an individual is sought; but whoever imagines that in determining this quantity he has summed up "the" intelligence of an individual once and for all . . . leaves off where psychology should begin.

—William Stern

This chapter covers a selection of specialized instruments for the assessment of cognitive ability. Some of the tests are specialized because they are limited to a specific (a) age range, such as infancy or early childhood, (b) handicapping condition, such as visual impairment or hearing impairment, or (c) area of cognitive ability, such as figural reasoning. Other tests make excellent follow-up tools to more traditional measures. These tests allow you to explore or confirm clinical hypotheses generated by tests that have been more rigorously standardized and cover a wide spectrum of cognitive functioning.

The individually administered tests of intelligence surveyed in this chapter make valuable additions to your fund of assessment techniques; they are especially useful in situations in which it is not feasible or practical to administer the WISC-R, WPPSI, WAIS-R, or Stanford-Binet Intelligence Scale: Fourth Edition. The infant tests discussed in this chapter are best seen as measures of development (or maturational growth) rather than of intelligence. The developmental scores obtained from infant tests, however, do have prognostic value for assessing the cognitive abilities of handicapped infants (see Chapter 4).

The tests described in this chapter can be used for screening, follow-up evaluations, and assessing handicapped as well as normal children. Unlike other standard measures of intelligence, some of these tests require only a simple response such as pointing, eye movements, or a "yes" or "no" sign symbolized by a prearranged signal. In some cases instructions may be pantomimed. The administration of some tests in this chapter (for example, the Slosson Intelligence Test) can be learned relatively quickly and easily, whereas that of other tests (for example, the Bayley Scales) requires considerable training. In any case, considerable skill is needed to establish rapport, recognize signs of psychopathology, and interpret assessment findings.

Although most of the infant and early childhood tests covered in this chapter provide limited material for qualitative analysis, especially those that require only a pointing response, possible reasons for the child's failures and successes should be considered. For example, do failures represent limited cognitive ability or inability to understand the directions? Are they associated with sensory limitations? How reliable and valid are the results?

Critical decisions, such as placement decisions or predictions about future academic or vocational success, normally should not be based solely on any of the tests described in this chapter. Some of the tests covered in the chapter have limited validity and reliability, others have a limited or out-of-date norms, and still others measure only some limited subdomains of ability. Additionally, for individual children large discrepancies have been reported between IQs obtained on some of these tests and those obtained on the WISC-R, even though mean IQs may not be significantly different. The WISC-R, WPPSI, WAIS-R, and Stanford-Binet Intelligence Scale: Fourth Edition are recommended for the assessment of intelligence in preference to these other measures when a child has the necessary physical capacities to respond to the test questions, when the child is of appropriate age to take the test, and when time is not at a premium. Administration of one of the more traditional measures is particularly important when the IQ is to be used for critical decisions. When verbal responses cannot be elicited from the child, when sensory or motor handicaps limit the child's performance, or when time is at a premium and only a screening decision is being made, however, specialized intelligence tests, brief intelligence tests, or brief forms of longer intelligence tests can be useful. (Appendix F presents the highlights of the tests covered in this and other chapters of the book.)

MCCARTHY SCALES OF CHILDREN'S ABILITIES

The McCarthy Scales of Children's Abilities (McCarthy, 1972) is a well standardized and psychometrically sound measure of the cognitive abilities of young children (see Figure 12-1). It is individually administered, covers the age range from 2½ to 8½ years, and takes approximately 45 to 60 minutes to administer, depending on the age of the child. The McCarthy Scales has some unique features valuable for the assessment of young children with learning problems or other exceptionalities (Sattler, 1978). It renders a general measure of intellectual functioning called the General Cognitive Index (GCI), as well as a profile of abilities that includes measures of verbal ability, nonverbal reasoning ability, number aptitude, short-term memory, and coordination. Several items also assess hand dominance.

Tests Contained in the McCarthy Scales

The McCarthy Scales contains the following six scales: Verbal Scale, Perceptual-Performance Scale, Quantitative Scale, Memory Scale, Motor Scale, and General Cognitive Scale. The General Cognitive Scale contains the 15 tests that comprise the Verbal Scale, the Perceptual-Performance Scale, and the Quantitative Scale. The only tests not included in the General Cognitive Scale are three tests that measure gross motor coordination. (Tests in the

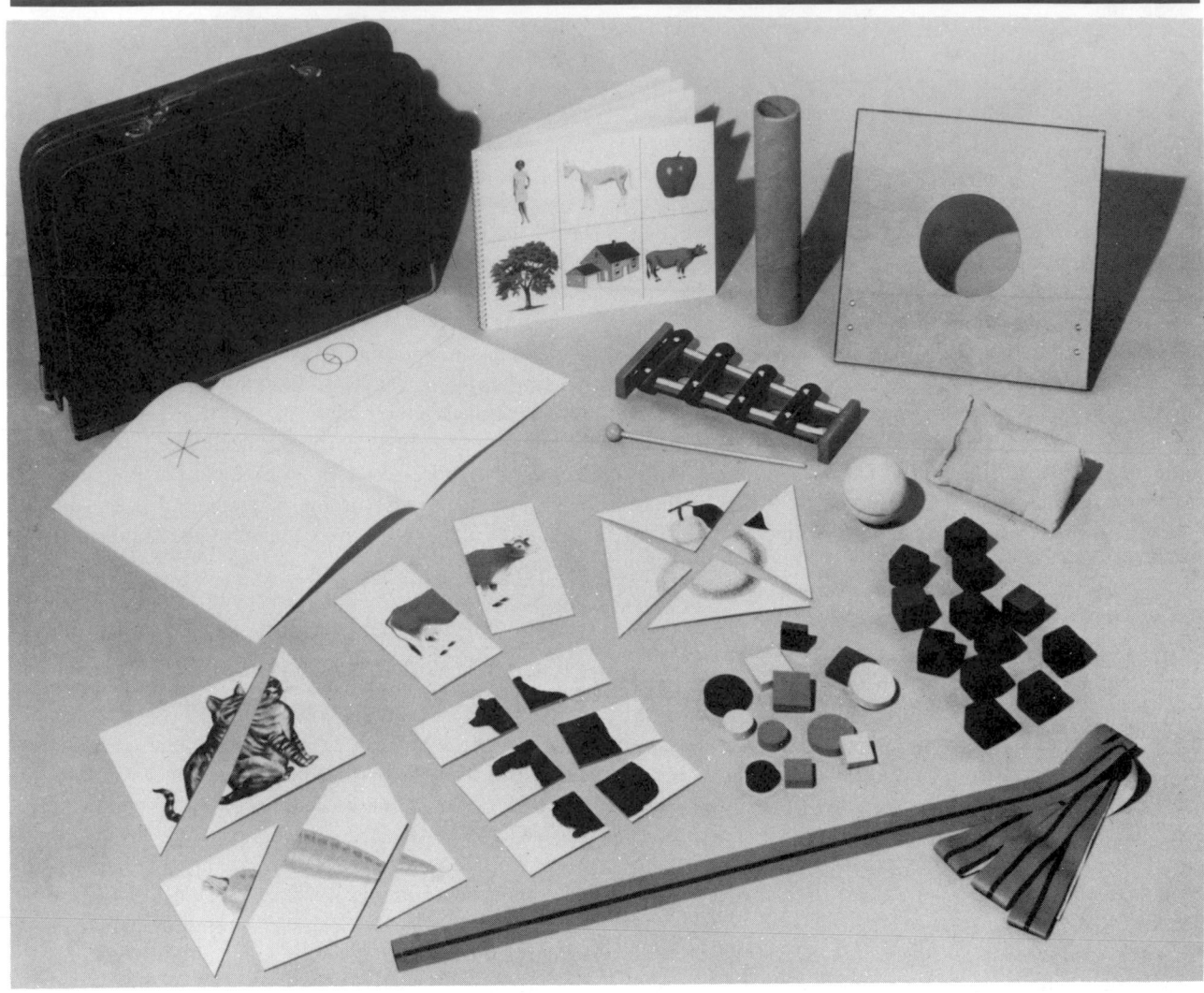

Figure 12-1.   McCarthy Scales of Children's Abilities. Courtesy of The Psychological Corporation.

Memory Scale, as well as the rest of those in the Motor Scale also appear in other scales.) The abilities thought to be measured by the scales and subtests are shown in Table 12-1.

Scores

The five scale indices derived from the McCarthy Scales subtests represent standard scores, with $M = 50$ and $SD = 10$. The overall GCI has $M = 100$ and $SD = 16$. The GCI is an estimate of the child's ability to integrate his or her accumulated knowledge and adapt that knowledge in

order to perform the tasks on the scales. This functional definition of the GCI is strikingly similar to definitions associated with the Intelligence Quotient, a term McCarthy deliberately has avoided. Further evidence suggesting that the two terms were intended to be comparable comes from (a) the descriptive classifications associated with the GCI, which are almost the same as those used for IQs on Wechsler's scales, and (b) the availability of mental ages for the GCI, which can serve as indications of mental competence. For all practical purposes, the definitions and uses proposed for the GCI and the IQ are the same; however, psychometrically these scores are not comparable. This point will be emphasized later in this section.

Table 12-1
Abilities Thought to Be Measured by McCarthy Scales and Subtests

		Verbal Scale *(Ability to understand and process verbal stimuli and to express thoughts)*		
Pictorial Memory	*Word Knowledge*	*Verbal Memory*	*Verbal Fluency*	*Opposite Analogies*
Short-term memory (auditory and visual) Early language development Attention	Verbal concept formation Early Language development Verbal expression (Part II)	Short-term memory (auditory) Verbal comprehension Attention Concentration (Part II) Verbal expression (Part II)	Verbal concept formation Logical classification Creativity (divergent thinking) Verbal expression	Verbal concept formation Early language development Verbal reasoning

			Perceptual-Performance Scale *(Visual-motor coordination and nonverbal reasoning through manipulation of concrete materials)*			
Block Building	*Puzzle Solving*	*Tapping Sequence*	*Right-Left Orientation*[a]	*Draw-A-Design*	*Draw-A-Child*	*Conceptual Grouping*
Visual-motor coordination Spatial relations	Visual perception Nonverbal reasoning Visual-motor coordination Spatial relations	Short-term memory (primarily visual) Visual-motor coordination Attention	Spatial relations Verbal concept formation Nonverbal reasoning Directionality	Visual perception Visual-motor coordination Spatial relations	Nonverbal concept formation Visual-motor coordination Body image	Logical classification Nonverbal reasoning Verbal concept formation

	Quantitative Scale *(Facility in dealing with numbers and understanding of quantitative concepts)*	
Number Questions	*Numerical Memory*	*Counting and Sorting*
Numerical reasoning Computational skills Number facts and concepts Concentration Verbal comprehension	Short-term memory (auditory) Attention Reversibility (Part II)	Rote counting Number concepts Numerical reasoning

		Memory Scale *(Short-term memory across a wide range of visual and auditory stimuli)*	
Pictorial Memory	*Tapping Sequence*	*Verbal Memory*	*Numerical Memory*
Short-term memory (auditory and visual) Early language development Attention	Short-term memory (primarily visual) Visual-motor coordination Attention	Short-term memory (auditory) Verbal comprehension Attention Concentration (Part II) Verbal expression (Part II)	Short-term memory (auditory) Attention Reversibility (Part II)

(Table continues next page)

Table 12-1 (cont.)

Motor Scale (Gross and fine motor coordination)				
Leg Coordination	*Arm Coordination*	*Imitative Action*	*Draw-A-Design*	*Draw-A-Child*
Gross motor coordination Balance	Gross motor coordination Precision of movement	Gross motor coordination Fine motor coordination	Fine motor coordination	Fine motor coordination

General Cognitive Scale[b] (Reasoning, concept formation, and memory when solving verbal and numerical problems and when manipulating concrete materials)

[a] For ages 5 and above.
[b] The 15 separate tests included in the General Cognitive Scale are described in the Verbal, Perceptual-Performance, and Quantitative Scales.
Source: Adapted from Kaufman and Kaufman (1977).

Standardization

The standardization of the McCarthy Scales was excellent, with the sample closely matching the 1970 census data. Stratification variables included age, sex, race, geographic region, father's occupation, and urban-rural residence. A total of 1,032 children between the ages of 2½ and 8½ years were tested; 100 to 106 children, equally divided by sex, were tested for each of the 10 age levels included in the standardization sample. Sex differences in the standardization sample are minimal (Kaufman & Kaufman, 1973).

Reliability

Reliability coefficients, standard errors of measurement, and intercorrelations between the scales are reported for the 10 different age levels in the standardization sample for each of the six scales. The average split-half reliability of the GCI is excellent ($r_{xx} = .93$), and average split-half reliabilities for the other five scales are satisfactory (from .79 to .88). The average standard error of measurement of the GCI is 4 points. The lowest intercorrelations occur between the Motor Scale and the other five scales. Stability of the McCarthy Scales, measured over a retest interval of approximately 30 days for a sample of 125 children, is adequate, with coefficients of .90 for the GCI and of .69 to .89 for the other scale indices. The GCI also has adequate stability over a one-year period for white children ($r_{xx} = .85$; Davis & Slettedahl, 1976) and for Mexican-American children ($r_{xx} = .85$; Valencia, 1983).

Validity

Concurrent validity of the McCarthy Scales is acceptable with the Stanford-Binet: Form L-M, WISC, WISC-R, WPPSI, K-ABC, and Slosson Intelligence Test used as criteria; correlations range from .45 to .91 (*Mdn r* = .75) (Arinoldo, 1982; Bickett, Reuter, & Stancin, 1984; Bondy, Sheslow, Norcross, & Constantino, 1982; Davis, 1975; Davis & Rowland, 1974; Davis & Walker, 1977; Gerken, Hancock, & Wade, 1978; Goh & Youngquist, 1979; Harrison & Wiebe, 1977; Hynd et al., 1980; Krohn & Traxler, 1979; Levenson & Zino, 1979; McCarthy, 1972; Naglieri, 1980a; Naglieri, 1985a; Reilly et al., 1985). Concurrent validity is also acceptable with achievement tests used as criteria (*Mdn r* = .58) (Massoth & Levenson, 1982; Naglieri, 1980b; Naglieri & Harrison, 1982; Sturner, Funk, & Green, 1984).

Although concurrent validity coefficients are satisfactory, large differences have been reported between McCarthy GCIs and Stanford-Binet: Form L-M and WISC-R IQs for samples of preschool children (Gerken et al., 1978), mentally retarded children (Levenson & Zino, 1979), and learning-disabled children (Goh & Youngquist, 1979). With gifted children, means differed by 10 points on the Stanford-Binet: Form L-M (*M* GCI = 105, *M* IQ = 115), but individual discrepancies were as much as 20 to 30 points (with McCarthy GCIs lower than Stanford-Binet: Form L-M IQs). With mentally retarded children, McCarthy GCIs were, on the average, 20 points lower than Stanford-Binet: Form L-M IQs (44 vs. 64). With learning-disabled children, GCIs were lower than WISC-R IQs by 8 to 15 points, on the average. These results suggest that GCIs are not interchangeable with either Sanford-Binet: Form L-M IQs or WISC-R IQs.

Satisfactory predictive validity is indicated by correlations with performances on various achievement tests, including the Metropolitan Achievement Tests, Peabody Individual Assessment Test, Wide Range Achievement Test, and California Achievement Test (*Mdn r* = .66) (Funk, Sturner, & Green, 1986; Harrison, 1981; Massoth, 1985; Reilly et al., 1985; Taylor & Ivimey, 1980).

Construct validity appears to be questionable. Although the standardization data yielded five factors generally throughout the scale—Verbal, Motor, General Cognitive, Memory, and Perceptual-Performance (Kaufman, 1975b)—later studies have not replicated these findings. In a large sample (*N* = 300) of school-aged children 6 to 8½ years old, only three factors were found: General Cognitive, Verbal, and Motor (Keith & Bolen, 1980). With low-functioning children, no general factor was found (Naglieri, Kaufman, & Harrison, 1981). In a sample of 4-year-old children, four factors were found: General, Perceptual-Performance, Verbal, and Motor (Trueman, Lynch, & Branthwaite, 1984). Finally, different factor structures were found for males and females (Purvis & Bolen, 1984; Wiebe & Watkins, 1980).

These findings suggest that caution should be exercised in interpreting the McCarthy Scales in a similar manner for all groups of exceptional children. Additionally, because the five scales are not factorially independent, they should not be interpreted as reflecting distinct abilities. This is especially true of the Quantitative and Memory scales. The failure to find distinct factors in some samples means that profile analysis using all five scales may not always be appropriate. The scales may be better measures of general cognitive abilities than of the specific abilities designated by the names of the scales.

Factor analysis of the McCarthy Scales in samples of black and white children (Kaufman & DiCuio, 1975) and in samples of Mexican-American and white children (Mishra, 1981) indicate that the factor structures are similar in these groups.

Some Useful Administrative and Interpretive Considerations

Confidence intervals and percentile ranks. Confidence intervals for the five scales and the GCI by age level are shown in Table C-54 in Appendix C. Tables BC-1 and BC-2 on the inside back cover can be used to obtain the percentile ranks for GCIs and the classifications associated with the GCIs, respectively.

Short forms. Various short forms have been proposed for the McCarthy Scales. One consists of Puzzle Solving, Word Knowledge, Numerical Memory, Verbal Fluency, Counting and Sorting, and Conceptual Grouping (Kaufman, 1977). Another consists of Counting and Sorting, Pictorial Memory, Number Questions, Verbal Fluency, Numerical Memory, and Tapping Sequence (Taylor, Slocumb, & O'Neill, 1979). Still another consists of Right-Left Orientation, Draw-A-Design, Numerical Memory, Leg Coordination, and Conceptual Grouping (McCarthy, 1978). These short forms should be used only for screening purposes.

Extrapolated GCIs. Extrapolated GCIs above 150 and below 50 are found in a publication by Harrison and Naglieri (1978). These extrapolated GCIs may be used to avoid the floor and ceiling effects, which limit the scale's ability to provide GCIs for gifted or low-functioning mentally handicapped children.

Significant differences for index scores. Table C-55 in Appendix C provides the critical differences required in order for significance to be attributed to a discrepancy between an index and the mean index for each of the five scales. The critical differences are 8 points for the Verbal Index, 9 points for the Perceptual-Performance Index, and 10 points for the Quantitative, Memory, and Motor Indices. One or more of the five scale indices were significantly different from the mean score on 62 percent of the profiles from the standardization sample (Kaufman, 1976a). These results suggest that one should exercise caution in interpreting variability on the McCarthy Scales.

McCarthy suggested that about a 15-point difference is needed in order for a discrepancy between the Verbal and Memory, Perceptual-Performance and Motor, and Quantitative and Memory Scales to be considered "noteworthy." Yet differences as low as 10 points are significant (Ysseldyke & Samuel, 1973). Because significant differences between scale indices vary by as much as 4 scaled-score points at various ages, it is best to use the table presented by Ysseldyke and Samuel (1973) to obtain the significant differences between scales needed at various age levels.

Conversion to scaled scores. Reynolds (1985b) provides tables for converting raw scores to scaled scores

($M = 100$, $SD = 15$) for the Draw-A-Design and Draw-A-Child tests for children from 4 years, 4 months to 8 years, 7 months of age.

Limitations of the McCarthy Scales

Although the McCarthy Scales has many strengths, it also has limitations (cf. Kaufman & Kaufman, 1977).

1. Much clerical work is required to transform scores on the 18 separate tests into indices on the six scales.

2. The failure to include social comprehension and judgment tasks or many abstract problem-solving tasks limits the breadth of the scale.

3. The scale may not be suitable for school-age children because of the cumbersomeness of some of the procedures.

4. The GCI floor of 50 limits the scale's usefulness in assessing the abilities of severely mentally retarded children and 2½-year-olds with below-average cognitive abilities; the low ceilings on many tests limit the scale's usefulness in assessing the abilities of older gifted children.

5. The absence of norms for older children and adolescents limits the utility of the scales in follow-up evaluations.

6. The internal consistency reliabilities for some of the indices are low (below .80).

7. Some of the scales overlap in content, and factor analyses do not support the construct validity of independent scales in all populations.

8. The scales makes no provision for prorating when tests are spoiled or not administered. Thus it is not possible to compute an index for any scale that includes a spoiled or omitted test. [Fortunately, Kaufman and Kaufman (1977) describe proration procedures that permit the estimation of scores in such situations.]

Comment on the McCarthy Scales of Children's Abilities

Because the McCarthy Scales does not provide scores that are equivalent to those provided by the WISC-R, caution should be exercised in using GCIs for placement decisions, especially in the assessment of mentally retarded or gifted children. Is the McCarthy GCI more valid than the WISC-R IQ? Unfortunately, there is insufficient research to answer this question.

According to McCarthy, the individual tests are not sufficiently reliable by themselves to permit meaningful evaluation. The validity of this statement cannot be verified, however, because individual test reliabilities are not

presented. The lack of standard scores for each test by age level limits the diagnostic usefulness of the McCarthy Scales. Additionally, there is limited information about the extent to which the scaled scores can assist in educational or clinical treatment decisions.

In spite of these limitations, the McCarthy Scales of Children's Abilities provides a profile of abilities that may be particularly useful in evaluating young children. The manual is convenient to use, the general guidelines for testing are thorough, the materials are well constructed, and the tasks are likely to appeal to children. The test is useful for assessing the cognitive ability and, to a lesser extent, the motor abilities of young children and therefore deserves serious consideration. (Further information about the McCarthy Scales of Children's Abilities can be obtained in the text by Kaufman and Kaufman, 1977.)

KAUFMAN ASSESSMENT BATTERY FOR CHILDREN

The Kaufman Assessment Battery for Children (K-ABC) (Kaufman & Kaufman, 1983) is a measure of intelligence and achievement designed for children ages 2-6 through 12-5 years. Four scales are included in this multi-subtest battery: Sequential Processing Scale, Simultaneous Processing Scale, Achievement Scale, and Nonverbal Scale. The K-ABC is intended for use in school and clinical settings, with administration time being approximately 45 minutes for preschool children and about 75 minutes for those of school age.

Not all subtests are administered at every age. Only three subtests run throughout the ages covered by the battery: Hand Movements, Gestalt Closure, and Faces and Places. Thus composite scores are derived from different combinations of subtests, depending on the child's age. Of the 16 subtests in the K-ABC, no more than 13 are administered to any one child.

Description of Scales and Subtests

The Sequential and Simultaneous Processing Scales are hypothesized to reflect the child's style of problem solving and information processing. Scores from these two scales are combined to form the Mental Processing Composite, which serves as the measure of intelligence on the K-ABC. The Sequential and Simultaneous Processing Scales were designed to reduce the effects of verbal processing and gender and ethnic bias. In contrast, the Achievement Scale is more heavily loaded with verbal stimuli. The interpretive rationales and implications of high and low K-ABC mental processing and achievement subtest scores are shown in Table C-56 in Appendix C.

Sequential Processing Scale. The Sequential Processing Scale was designed to measure children's abilities to solve problems that require the arrangement of stimuli in sequential or serial order. This scale contains three subtests: Hand Movements, Number Recall, and Word Order. The Hand Movements subtest requires children to reproduce raps on a table using the fist, palm, or side of the hand. On the Number Recall subtest children repeat a series of numbers. On the Word Order subtest children touch or point to a series of silhouettes of objects in the order in which they are named by the examiner. For school-age children, some items also include an interference task.

Simultaneous Processing Scale. The Simultaneous Processing Scale was designed to measure children's abilities to solve spatial, analogic, or organizational problems that require the processing of many stimuli at once. This scale contains seven subtests: Magic Window, Face Recognition, Gestalt Closure, Triangles, Matrix Analogies, Spatial Memory, and Photo Series.

The Magic Window subtest requires the identification of a picture that is passed slowly behind a window so that only part of the picture is visible at any one time. The Face Recognition subtest requires the selection of a photograph of a face previously seen from a group of photographs. On the Gestalt Closure subtest children identify an object or scene in a partially completed drawing (ink blot). On the Triangles subtest children reproduce a design by using several identical rubber triangles. The Matrix Analogies subtest requires selection of the picture or design that best completes a visual analogy. On the Spatial Memory subtest children recall the location of pictures randomly arranged on a page. The Photo Series subtest requires the arrangement of a series of photographs in a meaningful order.

Achievement Scale. The Achievement Scale was designed to assess children's factual knowledge and skills. The subtests on the scale were kept separate from those in the Sequential and Simultaneous Scales in an effort to distinguish between knowledge acquired by exposure to environmental stimulation or educational opportunities and knowledge that results from an integration of sequential and simultaneous processing. This separation appears to be faulty, however, because it artificially distinguishes the ways in which children acquire and process information.

The Achievement Scale contains six subtests: Expressive Vocabulary, Faces and Places, Arithmetic, Riddles, Reading/Decoding, and Reading/Understanding. On the Expressive Vocabulary subtest children name objects pictured in photographs. On the Faces and Places subtest children name fictional characters, famous persons, and well known places. On the Arithmetic subtest children identify numbers, count, compute, and demonstrate other mathematical skills. On the Riddles subtest children name a concrete or abstract verbal concept after having been given several of its characteristics. The Reading/Decoding subtest requires that children identify letters and read and pronounce words. On the Reading/Understanding subtest children read sentences silently and then act out the commands given in the sentences.

Nonverbal Scale. The Nonverbal Scale is not a new scale. It is composed of those subtests from the Sequential and Simultaneous Processing Scales (Face Recognition, Hand Movements, Triangles, Matrix Analogies, Spatial Memory, and Photo Series) that do not require words. The examiner conveys instructions through gestures, and the child responds with movements.

Scores

Raw scores for the global scales are transformed into standard scores with $M = 100$ and $SD = 15$. Subtests, in turn, are converted into scaled scores with $M = 10$ and $SD = 3$. An index of mental ability, called the Mental Processing Composite, is derived only from scores on the Simultaneous and Sequential Processing Scales; the Achievement subtests are not included. The Mental Processing Composite is more heavily weighted with Simultaneous Processing subtests than with Sequential Processing subtests. Chatman, Reynolds, and Willson (1984) provide tables that show levels of interscale and subtest variability and frequencies of significant interscale and intrascale differences on the K-ABC.

Standardization

The standardization of the K-ABC was adequate, with the sample, for the most part, closely matching the 1980 census data. Stratification variables included age, sex, geographic region, socioeconomic status (parental education), race or ethnicity, and community size. A total of 2,000 children between the ages of 2-6 and 12-5 years were tested, with 200 to 300 children, equally divided by sex, at each of nine age levels.

Reliability

Reliability coefficients, standard errors of measurement, and intercorrelations between the scales and between the subtests are reported. Internal consistency reliabilities for the Mental Processing Composite and the Achievement Scale were, on the average, .91 and .93, respectively, for preschool children and .94 and .97, respectively, for school-age children. Average internal consistency reliabilities for the other three scales are satisfactory, ranging from .86 to .93. The Mental Processing Composite has an average standard error of measurement of 4.6 points for preschool children and 3.5 points for school-age children. The highest average intercorrelation is between the Simultaneous and Achievement Scales ($r = .66$) for school-age children, whereas the lowest average intercorrelation is between the Sequential and Simultaneous Processing Scales for preschool children ($r = .41$). Stability of the K-ABC, measured over a retest interval of two to four weeks for three samples of children (Ns of 70 to 92), is adequate, with median coefficients of .88 for the Mental Processing Composite and .95 for the Achievement Scale. Median gain scores were 4.9 points for the Mental Processing Composite and 2.0 points for the Achievement Scale.

Validity

Statistics on various forms of validity are presented in the K-ABC manual. Evidence of construct validity is presented in the form of increases in subtest raw scores with age. Factor analysis supports the organization of the K-ABC into three scales.

Evidence of concurrent validity is presented in the form of correlations of the K-ABC with various individual and group tests of intelligence and achievement. Median correlations between the Mental Processing Composite and the WISC-R or WPPSI are .50 with the Verbal Scale, .65 with the Performance Scale, and .70 with the Full Scale. These medians are based on 13 to 18 samples. With the Stanford-Binet: Form L-M, the median correlation was .63, based on six samples. Median correlations with tests of achievement were .56 for the Mental Processing Composite (based on 12 correlations) and .68 for the Achievement score (based on 13 correlations). Correlations of the K-ABC with various achievement tests administered 6 to 12 months after the K-ABC indicate adequate predictive validity. Median correlations with the total score on the achievement tests were .56 for the Mental Processing Composite and .80 for the Achievement score (based on six samples).

Comment on the K-ABC

Following are are some practical and theoretical issues that need to be considered in connection with the use of the K-ABC for the assessment of intelligence.

1. The use of the term *mental processing* for some subtests and the term *achievement* for others is potentially misleading. Subtests involving vocabulary, arithmetic, and riddles, for example, which are included on the Achievement Scale, require mental processing just as do memory and visual analogy tasks. Similarly, the tasks involving recalling numbers, solving puzzle problems, and recognizing faces measure achievement as well as mental processing. Many of the subtests on the Achievement Scale may measure verbal ability more than achievement (Keith, 1985). In fact, Achievement scores correlate more highly with scores on the WISC-R Verbal Scale than with scores on the Iowa Test of Basic Skills.

2. It is not clear why the Mental Processing Composite places more emphasis on Simultaneous Processing subtests than on Sequential Processing subtests. There is no theoretical justification for this differential weighting.

3. The lack of verbal comprehension or reasoning items on the Mental Processing Composite is a fundamental weakness of the K-ABC. In an attempt to reduce the cultural bias attributed to existing tests and to permit more accurate assessment of exceptional children, authors of the K-ABC eliminated from its principal composite score one of the key components of intellectual ability—namely, tasks that measure verbal skills.

4. The heavy reliance on short-term memory and attention tasks may reduce the effectiveness of the K-ABC in providing a valid measure of cognition for children with attention and short-term recall difficulties.

5. For children ages 2½ to 3 years, only five subtests form the Mental Processing Composite. The number of tests, and hence the types of processes measured, is too limited to provide a complete picture of young children's intellectual or problem-solving ability.

6. There are potential difficulties in using the term *processing* to characterize some of the K-ABC subtests and not others. Subtests on the Achievement Scale involve sequential and simultaneous processing, as do those on the Simultaneous and Sequential Processing Scales. Although the K-ABC authors recognize this fact, the separation is likely to cause some confusion. Additionally, nothing in the K-ABC allows one to determine whether a child's *response* is arrived at through sequential or simultaneous processing modalities. The responses required of a child are just like those he or she would give on other standardized individually administered intelligence tests—for ex-

ample, reciting numbers given in a digit memory task or selecting a card to complete a matrix analogy. In no case does the scoring take into account how the child processes information. Evaluation of the manner in which the child processes information must be inferred from other sources—such as subtest scores, other test scores, observations, or case history information.

7. The terms *simultaneous processing* and *sequential processing* are ambiguous. Do they refer to how information is presented to the child? Do they refer to the form of the response given by the child? Do they refer to certain areas or hemispheres of the brain involved in processing information? Do they refer to specific strategies used by the child—such as labeling, rehearsal, chunking, elaboration, or imagery—in receiving information and in giving a response? Do they reflect executive functions involved in a child's knowing when to stop processing information or when to give a response? Do they mean all of these things and other things as well? These terms are too vague to enable us to understand cognitive processes better. Keith (1985) suggested that the Simultaneous Processing Scale can be interpeted as a measure of *nonverbal reasoning ability*, whereas the Sequential Processing Scale can be thought of as a measure of *verbal memory*, particularly at the 5-year-old level. Additionally, it is important to recognize that each subtest combines elements of more than one processing style.

8. The K-ABC should not be used for the classification of mental retardation over the entire age range covered by the scale. A 2½-year-old child who failed every item on the Sequential and Simultaneous Processing Scale would obtain a Mental Processing Composite of 79. For a 3-year-old this same failure rate would yield a Mental Processing Composite of 70. Even at 4 years of age complete failure would result in a composite score of 60.

9. The K-ABC has a low ceiling that may limit its usefulness in evaluating gifted children. Over half of the subtests on the Simultaneous and Sequential Processing Scales provide maximum scores that are only 2 standard deviations or less above the mean. The Achievement Scale also has a restricted range. The highest scores range from 133 to 144 for 10½- to 12½-year-olds. Any attempt to apply a discrepancy formula to differences between mental processing and achievement of gifted children is likely to yield misleading results. Significant discrepancies result even when adolescent gifted children pass all items on the Mental Processing and Achievement Scales. The K-ABC yields scores that are as much as 13 to 22 points below the WISC-R and Stanford-Binet: Form L-M (for example, $M = 124.5$ vs. 144.3) (McCallum et al., 1984; Van Melis-Wright & Strein, 1986).

10. It is difficult to evaluate the effectiveness of instructional strategies based on a child's K-ABC profile. The studies in the K-ABC manual are few, and their sample sizes were small. One study (Ayres & Cooley, 1986) found that first-grade children who performed better on a sequential learning task obtained higher scores on the Simultaneous Processing Scale than on the Sequential Processing Scale. This result is *contrary* to what would be predicted by the K-ABC. This study failed to support the construct validity of the K-ABC and the proposed remedial instruction strategies offered in the K-ABC manual. Additionally, Goetz and Hall (1984) concluded that the K-ABC does not provide the information needed to develop appropriate educational interventions. Further research is needed to evaluate the validity of the proposed instructional strategies based on K-ABC profiles.

11. There are major sampling problems with the K-ABC standardization sample. Hispanic-Americans were underrepresented by 24 percent, and low-educational-level blacks were underrepresented by 10 percent. Bracken (1985) concluded that adjusting for sampling differences at the uppermost age level produces a difference of approximately 12 points between blacks and whites, in favor of whites. This difference approaches the difference of 1 standard deviation found on other intelligence tests. Thus there is little evidence that the K-ABC significantly reduces differences between blacks and whites.

The K-ABC may prove to be useful in certain situations, particularly when information is needed about nonverbal cognitive abilities. In most cases, however, the K-ABC should not be used as the primary instrument for identifying the intellectual abilities of normal or special children, including the mentally retarded, gifted, or learning disabled. Neither should it be the primary instrument for measuring intelligence in clinical assessments.

DETROIT TESTS OF LEARNING APTITUDE—2

The Detroit Tests of Learning Aptitude (DTLA-2) (Hammill, 1985a) is a multidimensional battery designed to measure intellectual abilities. Separate scores are provided for subtests, composites, and the General Intelligence Quotient. The battery was first published in 1935; a revised manual, based on the 1935 norms, was published in 1967. A need for updated norms and better standardization procedures led to the latest revision.

The DTLA-2 is designed for children 6 through 18 years of age. It takes approximately 50 minutes to 2 hours to administer. There are 11 subtests in the battery: Word Opposites, Sentence Imitation, Oral Directions, Word Sequences, Story Construction, Design Reproduction, Object Sequences, Symbolic Relations, Conceptual Matching, Word Fragments, and Letter Sequences. Seven subtests were retained from the original DTLA, and four new ones were added (Story Construction, Symbolic Relations, Conceptual Matching, and Word Fragments).

The 11 subtests are grouped into eight separate composites, four domains, and one overall composite, as shown in Table 12-2. All 11 subtests are used in calculating the Overall Aptitude Composite. The separate composites include varying numbers of tests. For example, the six subtests that form the Verbal Composite are Word Opposites, Sentence Imitation, Oral Directions, Word Sequences, Story Construction, and Word Fragments. The five subtests that make up the Nonverbal Composite are Design Reproduction, Object Sequences, Symbolic Relations, Conceptual Matching, and Letter Sequences. The composites in turn are grouped into Linguistic, Cognitive, Attentional, and Motoric domains. All 11 subtests are represented within each domain.

Scores

The DTLA-2 yields three types of scores: raw scores, percentile ranks, and standard scores for the subtests ($M = 10$, $SD = 3$), composites ($M = 100$, $SD = 15$), and a General Intelligence Quotient (GIQ) ($M = 100$, $SD = 15$). No age norms are provided for the DTLA-2.

Standardization

The DTLA-2 was standardized on a sample of 1,532 children from 6 to 17 years of age, living in 30 states. The sample closely conformed to the 1980 census data with respect to sex, race, residence, and geographic area. Parental education levels were not matched with the census data, however. The parents of 52 percent of the standardization sample had attended college or received graduate or postgraduate education. Thus the standardization sample appears to have been overly weighted with children whose parents have advanced educational degrees or training.

Reliability

Internal consistency reliability was computed for 300 subjects at six age intervals between 6 and 17 years. Average coefficients ranged from .81 to .95 for the 11 subtests and from .95 to .97 for the eight composite scores.

Test-retest reliability for the General Intelligence Quotient (GIQ) is reported in the manual to be .82 for 33 students retested at an interval of two weeks. Standard errors of measurement ranged from .90 to 1.80 points for the subtests, and 4.00 to 6.70 for the composites. The SE_m for the GIQ is 3.70. A 12-point difference between composite scores is required for significance at the .05 level (Silverstein, 1986c).

Validity

Correlations between the DTLA-2 GIQ and the WISC-R IQ for a sample of 76 referred students were .83 for the Verbal Scale, .70 for the Performance Scale, and .83 for the Full Scale. A .75 correlation was obtained between the DTLA-2 GIQ and the PPVT standard score for a sample of 25 referred children. These are satisfactory concurrent validity indices.

Correlations between raw scores on the 11 subtests and subjects' ages ranged from .42 to .68 (Mdn $r = .54$).

Table 12-2
Domains, Composites, and Subtests of the DTLA-2

Subtest	Linguistic Domain		Cognitive Domain		Attentional Domain		Motoric Domain	
	Verbal Composite	Nonverbal Composite	Conceptual Composite	Structural Composite	Attention-Enhanced Composite	Attention-Reduced Composite	Motor-Enhanced Composite	Motor-Reduced Composite
Word Opposites	X		X			X		X
Sequence Imitation	X		X		X			X
Oral Directions	X		X		X		X	
Word Sequences	X			X	X			X
Story Construction	X		X			X		X
Design Reproduction		X		X	X		X	
Object Sequences		X		X	X		X	
Symbolic Relations		X	X			X		X
Conceptual Matching		X	X			X		X
Word Fragments	X		X			X		X
Letter Sequences		X		X	X		X	

Source: Reprinted, with changes in notation, with permission of the publisher and author from A. B. Silverstein, "Organization and Structure of the Detroit Tests of Learning Aptitude (DTLA-2)," *Educational and Psychological Measurement*, 1986, *46*, p. 1062.

These coefficients support the claim that the subtests' contents are developmental in nature—as children become older, they earn more points. Correlations between the subtests and the GIQ for a sample of 300 children ranged from .44 to .66. Correlations between the DTLA-2 and the SRA Achievement Series for 77 public school students in second, sixth, and eleventh grade were .58, .89, and .93, respectively.

A factor analysis of the DTLA-2, as well as a cluster analysis, failed to support any of the eight DTLA-2 composites (Silverstein, 1986c). The factor analytic results suggest three factors: (a) one composed of Word Opposites, Oral Directions, Story Construction, Design Reproduction, Symbolic Relations, Conceptual Matching, and Word Fragments; (b) a second composed of Sentence Imitation, Word Sequences, and Letter Sequences; and (c) a third composed of Oral Directions, Design Reproduction, Object Sequences, Symbolic Relations, and Letter Sequences. Two tests—Oral Directions and Letter Sequences—load on two factors.

Comment on the Detroit Tests of Learning Aptitude—2

The DTLA-2 has adequate reliability and concurrent validity as a test of cognitive ability. The test is limited in a number of ways, however. First, there are some concerns about the representativeness of the standardization sample. Second, factor analysis does not support the domains proposed by the test. Third, the domain scores are not easily interpretable. For example, what interpretations should be given to scores on the Conceptual and Structural Domains? The DTLA-2 may be useful as a measure of general intelligence, but its separate part scores do not appear to be supported adequately by either factor analysis or cluster analysis.

DETROIT TESTS OF LEARNING APTITUDE—P

The Detroit Tests of Learning Aptitude—P (DTLA-P) (Hammill, 1985b) is an abbreviated version of the DTLA-2. It contains 130 items arranged in developmental order from easiest to most difficult. The test covers an age range from 3 through 9 years. It overlaps with the DTLA-2 at ages 6 through 9 years. Items are administered in a continuous fashion rather than by subtests. Each item in the record booklet, however, is simultaneously classified into four of the eight subtests. The eight subtests included in the DTLA-P are Verbal Aptitude, Nonverbal Aptitude, Conceptual Aptitude, Structural Aptitude, Attention-

Enhanced Aptitude, Attention-Reduced Aptitude, Motor-Enhanced Aptitude, and Motor-Reduced Aptitude. The DTLA-P takes approximately 15 to 45 minutes to administer.

Scores

There are standard scores for the eight subtests and one composite (General Overall Aptitude or GIQ). For all scores, $M = 100$ and $SD = 15$.

Standardization

The DTLA-P was standardized on 1,676 children residing in 36 states. The sample is representative of the U.S. population with regard to sex, residence, race, ethnicity, and geographic area. No information is provided about the socioeconomic status of the sample.

Reliability

Internal consistency reliability for the GIQ is .95, with subtest reliabilities ranging from .89 to .92. Test-retest reliabilities range between .63 and .89 for individual subtests. For the GIQ, they are .85 and .89 in two studies reported in the manual.

Validity

The DTLA-P was correlated with both aptitude and achievement tests. Satisfactory concurrent validity was found between the DTLA-P GIQ and the WISC-R Full Scale ($r = .84$), Verbal Scale ($r = .84$), and Performance Scale ($r = .80$). Correlations between the WISC-R Full Scale and the DTLA-P subtests ranged from .74 to .85. The DTLA-P GIQ was significantly correlated with the Slosson Intelligence Test ($r = .72$) and with the Peabody Picture Vocabulary Test—Revised ($r = .63$). Correlations between the DTLA-P GIQ and various achievement tests ranged from .33 to .66 ($Mdn\ r = .51$).

Intercorrelations among the eight subtests ranged from .78 to .97. Correlations between each subtest and the General Intelligence Quotient ranged from .93 to .97, lending support to the construct validity of the DTLA-P as a measure of g.

Comment on the Detroit Tests of Learning Aptitude—P

The Detroit Tests of Learning Aptitude—P, like the DTLA-2, appears to be a psychometrically sound measure

of cognitive ability. The failure to describe the standardization sample fully detracts from its usefulness, however. Information is needed about the extent to which variance among the subtests warrants interpretation. Consequently, a factor analysis of the DTLA-P would be useful.

EXTENDED MERRILL-PALMER SCALE

The Extended Merrill-Palmer Scale (Ball, Merrifield, & Stott, 1978) is an individually administered test of cognitive ability for children between the ages of 3-0 and 5-11 years. The scale evaluates both the content of thinking (that is, the material that is actually processed by the child) and the process of thinking (that is, the way in which this material is used to form new concepts) in young children. The Extended Scale was based on the 1931 Merrill-Palmer Scale. The new version contains 9 of the original 38 tests, as well as 7 new tests. The tests retained are the three copying tests, the two pyramid building tasks, the pink tower, questions, matching colors (directions), and action-agent (word meaning). All timed tests were excluded from the new edition, as were tests that failed to meet adequate statistical standards or other criteria. The Extended Scale takes approximately 1 hour to administer.

Theoretical Basis of Scale

The Extended Scale is based on Guilford's Structure of Intellect model (see Chapter 3). It assesses two types of thought content (semantic and figural) and two types of thought processes (productive thinking and evaluative). The two content categories and the two process categories are combined to define four dimensions: Semantic Production, Figural Production, Semantic Evaluation, and Figural Evaluation (see Figure 12-2). Semantic Production involves the use of language or other means of communication. Tests in this area tap the availability and flow of ideas. Semantic Evaluation requires judging whether a given action, statement, or configuration fits a given criterion. Figural Production involves producing a variety of responses by using a crayon or pencil or sticks or by describing ink blots. Figural Evaluation requires matching a configuration by using a crayon or pencil or by moving objects.

Tests Contained in the Extended Scale

Each of the 16 tasks presented in the Extended Scale measures one of the four Structure of Intellect dimensions. Within each dimension there are four tasks. Following is a brief description of each task:

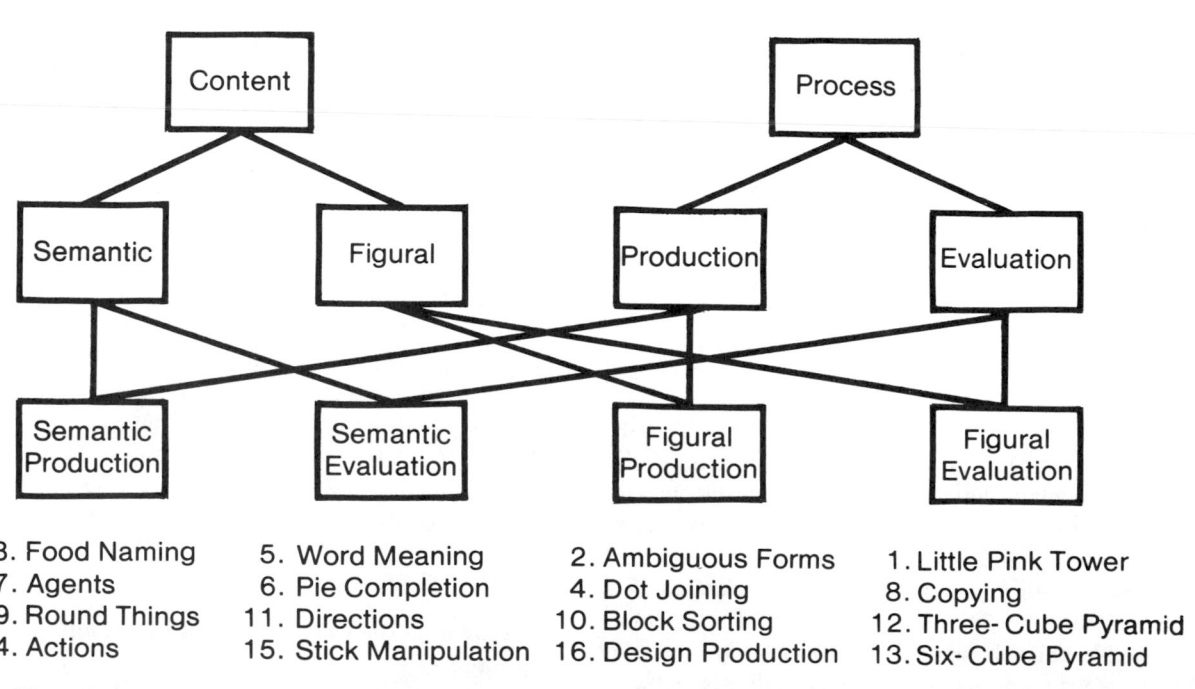

3. Food Naming
7. Agents
9. Round Things
14. Actions

5. Word Meaning
6. Pie Completion
11. Directions
15. Stick Manipulation

2. Ambiguous Forms
4. Dot Joining
10. Block Sorting
16. Design Production

1. Little Pink Tower
8. Copying
12. Three-Cube Pyramid
13. Six-Cube Pyramid

Figure 12-2. Cognitive components of the four dimensions measured on the Extended Merrill-Palmer Scale.

1. Little Pink Tower—building a five-block tower from memory.

2. Ambiguous Forms—naming things seen in ink blots.

3. Food Naming—naming things that people eat.

4. Dot Joining—joining dots.

5. Word Meaning—giving the use or meaning of words.

6. Pie Completion—cutting a pie into parts from the center outward.

7. Agents—naming several agents for each of 10 different actions (for example, "What runs?").

8. Copying—copying a circle, cross, star, and diamond.

9. Round Things—selecting round objects from a visual display.

10. Block Sorting—sorting 16 blocks by color, shape, and size.

11. Directions—following directions, using knowledge of colors and understanding of concepts (for example, "Put the red and green cars inside the blue box").

12. Three-Cube Pyramid—building a pyramid from three blocks.

13. Six-Cube Pyramid—building a pyramid from six blocks.

14. Actions—giving several actions for each of seven different objects.

15. Stick Manipulation—reproducing figures constructed by the examiner.

16. Design Production—making designs with a set of sticks.

Record Form

The Extended Scale record form is useful for administering the test. Each task has its own record form, complete with instructions for the task and space for recording the child's responses. The forms are convenient, making it unnecessary to refer to the manual continuously while administering the test.

Scores

Raw scores are transformed into weighted composite scores for each dimension. Each weighted score is then converted into a percentile range, which is presented on a bar graph. Children are evaluated separately on each dimension on the basis of how they compare to their same-age peer group. Percentile bands are provided by six-month intervals between ages 36 months and 71 months.

Specific percentiles are not given for any score, however, nor is an overall score provided.

Standardization

The Extended Merrill-Palmer Scale was standardized on 1,124 white preschool children from Ohio and New York. Children were selected on the basis of their mothers' educational levels—one-quarter college graduates, one-half high school graduates, and one-quarter with not more than a ninth grade education.

Reliability

Reliability coefficients are presented as part-whole coefficients for the four separate scores by six-month age levels. The median part-whole reliability is .74 (range of .54 to .81). These coefficients are not acceptable as reliability estimates, because the tasks are not parallel forms of the same test. Consequently, the reliability of the Extended Merrill-Palmer Scale is unknown at this time.

Validity

No validity indices are reported in the manual.

Comment on the Extended Merrill-Palmer Scale

The Extended Merrill-Palmer Scale has potential for the assessment of the cognitive ability of preschool children. The scale is deficient in a number of ways, however.

1. The standardization sample was not representative of the country. Minorities were entirely excluded from the norm group, and only an informal method was used to classify the socioeconomic status of the sample.

2. The psychometric properties of the scale are questionable. No information is given about test-retest reliabilities. The part-whole reliabilities are less than .80—in one case as low as .54—and are not appropriate reliability estimates. Additionally, standard errors of measurement are not provided.

3. No validity data are presented in the manual.

4. The percentile bands do not allow for a precise evaluation of a child's performance. In some instances, the range may be as great as 20 percentage points, making it impossible to tell exactly where a child's abilities lie. A child who exceeds 32 percent of the children in the normative group on Figural Production obviously is not as well developed in this skill as one whose score falls at the 52nd percentile. Yet this differentiation cannot be made by

referring to the bar graphs. As a result, it is difficult in some cases to determine whether a child's performance is below average or average.

5. The failure to provide a general estimate of ability limits the scale's usefulness.

6. An extensive scoring guide is not provided. Thus scoring difficulties are likely to arise.

Despite the above difficulties, the Extended Merrill-Palmer Scale deserves consideration as a potential component of the assessment battery. Scores on the four cognitive components provide useful information. The nonverbal scores are useful in assessing language-handicapped children, whereas the verbal scores are useful in assessing motorically handicapped youngsters. Additionally, the scale provides a profile of abilities. Research with the scale is needed.

SLOSSON INTELLIGENCE TEST

The Slosson Intelligence Test (SIT) (Slosson, 1983) is an age-scale test of intelligence designed for persons between 2 and 18 years of age. Two major sources for the items were the Stanford-Binet Intelligence Scale: Forms L and M and the Gesell Institute of Child Development Behavior Inventory. The SIT was originally published in 1963 and was renormed in 1981. Expanded norms were published in 1985 (Jensen & Armstrong, 1985).

For children over 4 years of age, all questions are presented verbally and require spoken responses. There are no time limits. The test takes between 10 and 30 minutes to administer, and scoring is fairly objective.

Scores

MA raw scores are converted into Deviation Quotients ($M = 100$, $SD = 16$). Scores were closely equated with those provided by the Stanford-Binet Intelligence Scale: Form L-M. Prior to the 1981 renorming, the SIT used the ratio IQ.

Standardization

The standardization sample for the 1981 norms contained 1,109 children from 2 years, 3 months to 18 years of age, living in New England. With the exception of age and IQ, no sample demographic characteristics were reported. Consequently, there is no way to determine to what extent the sample was representative of the U.S. population.

Reliability

Reliability coefficients reported in the manual are in the form of parallel-form reliability, with the Stanford-Binet: Form L-M used as the alternate form. A reliability coefficient of .95 was reported. This form of reliability, however, is questionable because Form L-M is not a parallel form of the SIT. Unfortunately, internal consistency and test-retest reliabilities were not reported for the 1981 norm sample.

Validity

Concurrent and predictive validity studies are reported in the manual for the 1963 edition of the SIT only. With the WISC, median coefficients were .75 with the Full Scale, .82 with the Verbal Scale, and .62 with the Performance Scale. With several achievement and ability tests, the median *r* was .55. For gifted children, the 1981 norms average about 5 points *lower* than the 1963 norms (Tomsic & Rankin, 1985). For a small sample of 24 young learning-disabled children, the SIT Deviation IQs were approximately 9 points higher, on the average, than WISC-R Full Scale IQs (Jeffrey & Jeffrey, 1984). The test places heavy emphasis on language skills for children between 2 and 3 years of age; consequently it may not be valid for children in this age group who have delayed language development.

Comment on the Slosson Intelligence Test

The Slosson Intelligence Test may have some merit as a screening device. Advantages include the short administration time and the relative ease with which it can be used by personnel with minimal training in the administration of individual intelligence tests. The SIT has a number of disadvantages, however. First, it is based on Stanford-Binet Form L-M norms that may be out of date. Second, the standardization sample is poorly described. Third, IQs obtained on the SIT are not interchangeable with those obtained on the WISC-R, WPPSI, or Stanford-Binet Intelligence Scale: Fourth Edition. The SIT should not be used as a substitute for the Stanford-Binet: Form L-M or Fourth Edition, WISC-R, or WPPSI to assess mental retardation or giftedness.

RAVEN'S PROGRESSIVE MATRICES

Raven's Progressive Matrices (Raven, Court, & Raven, 1986), originally introduced in 1938, is a nonverbal test of reasoning ability based on figural test stimuli. It can be administered individually or to a group. The test measures the ability to form comparisons, to reason by analogy, and to organize spatial perceptions into systematically related wholes. Raven's Progressive Matrices comes in three different forms: Coloured Progressive Matrices, Standard Progressive Matrices, and Advanced Progressive Matrices (Sets I and II).

The Coloured Progressive Matrices is a 36-item test applicable for children from 5 to 11 years of age. Colors are used in this form to attract and hold the attention of the children. The Standard Progressive Matrices is used primarily for persons from 6 to 17 years of age, although it also can be administered to adults. It contains 60 items presented in five sets, with 12 items per set. The Advanced Progressive Matrices is suitable for older adolescents and adults, particularly for individuals with more than average intellectual ability. There are 12 problems in Set I and 36 problems in Set II.

In each form, the examinee is presented with a matrix-like arrangement of figural symbols and must complete the matrix by selecting the appropriate missing symbol from a group of symbols (see Figure 12-3). In the easier sets, a design is shown, with a piece appearing to have been cut out. In other sets, individual pieces are arranged in either a 2 × 2 or a 3 × 3 matrix. One piece or design is left out of the matrix, and the examinee must select, from a group of six to eight choices, the one that best completes the matrix. Each form takes between 15 and 30 minutes to administer.

Problem-Solving Strategies

The matrices can be solved through use of one of two problem-solving strategies. The rule or principle required to solve each item can either be formulated in verbal terms or be derived from a visual perceptual discovery of the internal structure of the stimulus. In the former case, an analytic approach is used in which logical operations are applied to features contained within the elements of the problem matrix. In the latter case, a Gestalt approach involving visual perception is used to solve problems.

Testing-of-Limits

Testing-of-limits procedures include (a) asking children to describe their approach or strategy while they are solving the problems; (b) asking children to describe the principles or reasons for their solutions after they give their answers; (c) giving children feedback on correct performance, incorrect performance, or both and seeing how the feedback affects their performance; and (d) showing children the correct solution when they fail and seeing how this feedback affects their performance (Carlson & Wiedl, 1979). With third-grade children, such feedback led to higher scores, increased visual search behavior, reduced text anxiety, and more positive evaluations of the testing situation (Bethge, Carlson, & Wiedl, 1982).

Scores

Raw scores are converted into percentile ranks.

Standardization

Numerous normative studies have been done since Raven's Progressive Matrices was originally published. The most recent compendium of North American normative studies was published in 1986 (Raven & Summers, 1986). Included in this compendium are norms for the Coloured Progressive Matrices and the Standard Progressive Matrices.

Norms for the Coloured Progressive Matrices for chil-

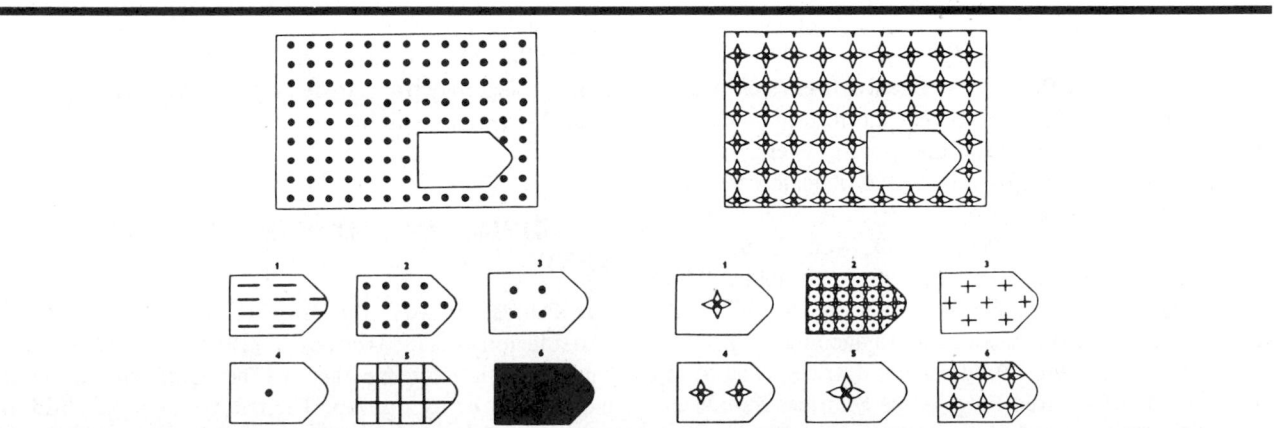

Figure 12-3. Sample Progressive Matrices items. Reprinted by permission of J. C. Raven, Ltd.

dren in the United States aged 5.03 to 11.09 years also are shown in Raven and Summers (1986) (see Table C-57 in Appendix C). Norms collected by various investigators for Mexican-American children and black children also are shown. The United States norms are based on weighting separate samples of children in various areas of the United States. No attempt was made to use a stratified random sampling procedure. Because of the large samples employed in various school districts, however, the norms are probably representative of the school-age population. Norms for the Standard Progressive Matrices are shown for children in the United States from age 6.03 to age 16.08 (see Table C-58 in Appendix C). The Advanced Progressive Matrices has norms for a sample of University of California Berkeley students (see Table C-59 in Appendix C).

Reliability

Split-half reliabilities range from .65 to .94 for the Coloured Progessive Matrices (Raven et al., 1986). For the Standard Progressive Matrices a split-half reliability coefficient of .86 is the best estimate (Raven, Court, & Raven, 1983). Test-retest reliabilities are adequate for each form, ranging from .71 to .93. The lowest reliabilities are for young children (Raven, 1938, 1960, 1965; Raven et al., 1986).

Validity

The three forms have adequate concurrent validity as established by correlations with intelligence tests and achievement tests. Populations studied included white, black, Mexican-American, American Indian, deaf, and mentally retarded children (Raven et al., 1986; Raven & Summers, 1986). Validity coefficients with intelligence tests are in the .50s to .80s; validity coefficients with achievement tests are in the .30s to .60s.

The structure of Raven's Progressive Matrices is not clear. Some research suggests that the test contains primarily a g factor (Inductive or Reasoning), whereas others indicate that it contains two, three, or more factors (Burke, 1958; Carlson & Jensen, 1980; Corman & Budoff, 1974; Dillon, Pohlmann, & Lohman, 1981; Keir, 1949; MacArthur, 1960; MacArthur & Elley, 1963; Rimoldi, 1948; Schmidtke & Schaller, 1980; Wiedl & Carlson, 1976). A single dimension (g) is inadequate to account for performance on the Coloured Progressive Matrices. The three factors for the Coloured Progressive Matrices have been labeled I—Closure and Abstract Reasoning by Analogy (items A_7, A_9, A_{10}, A_{b2}, B_2, B_3, A_{b4}, A_{b5}, A_{b7}, A_{b8}, B_4,

B_6), II—Pattern Completion through Identity and Closure (items B_8, B_9, B_{10}, B_{11}, B_{12}), and III—Simple Pattern Completion (items A_2, A_3, A_4, A_5, B_1) (Carlson & Jensen, 1980).

A two-factor solution appears useful in accounting for performance on the Advanced Progressive Matrices (Dillon et al., 1981). Factor I—Visual-Figural Transformation (items 7, 9, 10, 11, 16, 21, 28, 35) reflects solutions obtained by adding and subtracting patterns. Factor II—Pattern Progression (items 2, 3, 4, 5, 17, 26, 36) reflects solutions obtained by perceiving the progression of a pattern. Factor I may measure the ability to make rapid decisions in situations in which part-whole relationships must be perceived for successful performance, whereas Factor II may be related to mechanical ability, including mental rotations.

Comment on Raven's Progressive Matrices

Raven's Progressive Matrices is a useful measure of nonverbal reasoning ability. The updated norms for the Coloured and Standard Progressive Matrices forms should prove to be of considerable value. Similar comprehensive norms are needed for the Advanced Progressive Matrices. The ease of administration (instructions can be pantomimed) and the limited sensory demands make the test a useful supplementary screening test for children and adults with severe language, auditory, or physical disabilities. In addition, it is useful in testing children who do not speak English or who have limited command of English, as it is a culturally reduced test.

Raven's Progressive Matrices should not be used as a substitute for the Stanford-Binet: Fourth Edition or the Wechsler scales. It provides a measure of intelligence based on figural reasoning only. The test may not provide a valid estimate of cognitive ability for examinees who are not capable of doing figural-reasoning tasks. Supplementing the Raven's Progressive Matrices with an English vocabulary test may prove to be helpful in the assessment of English-speaking children.

GOODENOUGH-HARRIS DRAWING TEST

The Goodenough-Harris Drawing Test (Harris, 1963), also referred to as the Draw-A-Man test, is a brief, nonverbal test of intelligence that can be administered either individually or to a group. The test requires the child to draw a person. Points are given for various body parts drawn by the child. Individual administration is recommended for preschool children and for children tested in clinical settings. The test covers ages 3-0 through 15-11 years, but the preferred ages are 3 to 10 years. The norms are less useful for children older than 10 years.

Purpose of Test

The purpose of the Goodenough-Harris Drawing Test is to measure intellectual maturity — the ability to form concepts of an abstract character. This ability involves perception (discrimination of likenesses and differences), abstraction (classification of objects), and generalization (assigning newly experienced objects to the correct class). Evaluation of the child's drawing of the human figure serves as a way of measuring the complexity of his or her concept formation ability. The human figure is used because it is the most familiar and meaningful figure for the child.

The Draw-A-Man Test is based on Goodenough's (1926) assumption that the intelligence of early school-age children can be estimated from their drawings of the figure of a man. The Harris revision includes a more extensive and objective scoring system, as well as two additional forms: the Draw-A-Woman Test and the Drawing of the Self Test. The latter also can be used as a vehicle for exploring self-concept. The revision also attempts to extend the usefulness of the test through 15-11 years of age.

Suggested Instructions

The following instructions can be used to introduce the test: "I want you to make a picture of a man. Make the very best picture you can; take your time and work very carefully. Try very hard and see what a good picture you can make. Be sure to make the whole man, not just his head and shoulders." Almost identical instructions are given for the drawing of the woman (substituting "woman" for "man" in two places) and the drawing of the self. For the drawing of the self, children are also told: "So take care and make this last one the very best of the three." In individual examinations, any ambiguous aspects of the drawing can be clarified by asking the child to identify the body parts and describe the picture. The three drawings take between 5 and 15 minutes to complete.

Scores

Two different scoring procedures can be used to evaluate the child's drawings of a man and a woman. One procedure is based on the Point Scale, Harris's expanded version of the scale originally proposed by Goodenough (1926). Each

item is rated pass or fail (0 or 1 point) based on the presence or absence of a body part or a specific detail (for example, hair styling). The Draw-A-Man Test has 73 items; Harris added 22 items to Goodenough's original 51 items. The Draw-A-Woman Test has 71 items. Each drawing can be scored in 3 to 4 minutes. A thorough scoring guide is provided in the manual. Exhibit 12-1 summarizes the major scoring guidelines for the Draw-A-Man Test, and Figure 12-4 illustrates the scoring of a sample drawing of a man.

The second procedure is based on a 12-point Quality Scale, with 1 indicating the lowest category and 12 the highest. This rapid scoring procedure is carried out by comparing the child's drawing with 12 model drawings that represent a continuum from least to greatest excellence. For more precision, it is also possible to use a finely graded 23-step Quality Scale, which ranges from .5 to 11.5, in .5 intervals. The Quality Scale was standardized by having

Figure 12-4.   Drawing of a man done by a 12-1-year-old girl. Items credited are 1, 2, 4–6, 9–11, 14, 17, 22, 30, 35, 44–47, 53–55, 63–64. Scaled score = 70.

Exhibit 12-1

Short Scoring Guide for Draw-A-Man Test

1. Head present
2. Neck present
3. Neck, two dimensions
4. Eyes present
5. Eye detail: brow or lashes
6. Eye detail: pupil
7. Eye detail: proportion
8. Eye detail: glance
9. Nose present
10. Nose, two dimensions
11. Mouth present
12. Lips, two dimensions
13. Both nose and lips in two dimensions
14. Both chin and forehead shown
15. Projection of chin shown; chin clearly differentiated from lower lip
16. Line of jaw indicated
17. Bridge of nose
18. Hair I
19. Hair II
20. Hair III
21. Hair IV
22. Ears present
23. Ears present: proportion and position
24. Fingers present
25. Correct number of fingers shown
26. Detail of fingers correct

27. Opposition of thumb shown
28. Hands present
29. Wrist or ankle shown
30. Arms present
31. Shoulders I
32. Shoulders II
33. Arms at side or engaged in activity
34. Elbow joint shown
35. Legs present
36. Hip I (crotch)
37. Hip II
38. Knee joint shown
39. Feet I: any indication
40. Feet II: proportion
41. Feet III: heel
42. Feet IV: perspective
43. Feet V: detail
44. Attachment of arms and legs I
45. Attachment of arms and legs II
46. Trunk present
47. Trunk in proportion, two dimensions
48. Proportion: head I
49. Proportion: head II
50. Proportion: face
51. Proportion: arms I
52. Proportion: arms II
53. Proportion: legs
54. Proportion: limbs in two dimensions

55. Clothing I
56. Clothing II
57. Clothing III
58. Clothing IV
59. Clothing V
60. Profile I
61. Profile II
62. Full face
63. Motor coordination: lines
64. Motor coordination: junctures
65. Superior motor coordination
66. Directed lines and form: head outline
67. Directed lines and form: trunk outline
68. Directed lines and form: arms and legs
69. Directed lines and form: facial features
70. "Sketching" technique
71. "Modeling" technique
72. Arm movement
73. Leg movement

Source: From *Children's Drawings as Measures of Intellectual Maturity*, p. 275, by Dale B. Harris. Copyright © 1963 by Harcourt Brace Jovanovich, Inc. Reprinted by permission of the publisher.

---

judges rate the level of maturity of 240 drawings by children ages 5 through 15 years.

Norms

Norms for the Point Scale are provided separately for boys and girls from age 3 through age 15 in whole-year intervals. Raw scores are converted into standard scores ($M = 100$, $SD = 15$). Norms are also available for the Quality Scale for ages 5 through 15 years. These norms, too, are standard scores ($M = 100$, $SD = 15$). There are no norms for the Drawing of the Self Test.

Standardization

The standardization sample for the Point Scale consisted of 2,975 boys and girls in the United States, selected so as to

be representative of the population as reflected by the 1960 census. Four geographical areas of the country were sampled. Seventy-five children were included at each age level from 5 through 15 years.

Reliability

Studies reviewed by Scott (1981) indicate that the Draw-A-Man Test is reliable (*Mdn* test-retest $r_{xx} = .74$) and provides stable scores. Interrater reliabilities are satisfactory (*Mdn r*'s = .90 for Draw-A-Man and .94 for Draw-A-Woman).

Validity

Studies reviewed by Scott (1981) indicate the Draw-A-Man Test effectively discriminates the performance of children at age levels from 5 through 12 years. The test is a relatively poor predictor of scores on other intelligence tests (M $r = .49$), however. Additionally, correlations with measures of achievement are poor.

Comment on the Goodenough-Harris Drawing Test

The Draw-A-Man Test is an acceptable screening instrument for use as a nonverbal measure of cognitive ability, particularly with children from 5 to 12 years of age. It is most effective in the lower ranges of intelligence (Scott, 1981). There is little justification, however, for the use of the Draw-A-Man Test as a measure of intelligence: the test should never be used for decision-making purposes. Its popularity is related to its nonverbal nature, its adaptability to group administration, and the ease with which it can be integrated into a battery of tests. Of course, none of these reasons should be primary selection criteria for any test.

With ethnic minorities the Draw-A-Man Test is also useful as a screening measure of cognitive ability, because it may not be as culturally loaded as are other tests (Cundick, 1970; Oakland & Dowling, 1983). The child's cultural background may influence test scores, however, for different cultures place varying emphases on body parts and clothing.

Although the standardization sample was excellent, the norms need to be refined into half-year and quarter-year intervals for young children and to be brought up to date. Another needed revision is a modernization of the scoring guidelines for the Draw-A-Woman Test. Many of the criteria for appropriate dress and hairstyling date back to the 1950s.

LEITER INTERNATIONAL PERFORMANCE SCALE

The Leiter International Performance Scale (Leiter, 1948) is a nonverbal test of intelligence used to evaluate children who have sensory or motor deficits or who have difficulty in speaking or reading. Although the scale has also been purported to be a culture-free measure of intelligence, there is no evidence to support this assertion. The scale contains 54 tests arranged in an age-scale format from year II to year XVIII (see Figure 12-5). It takes approximately 30 to 45 minutes to administer.

On the Leiter, the child must arrange a series of blocks by selecting the blocks bearing appropriate symbols or pictures and inserting them into the appropriate recess of a frame used to administer the scale. Items range from pairings of colors, shapes, and objects at early levels to

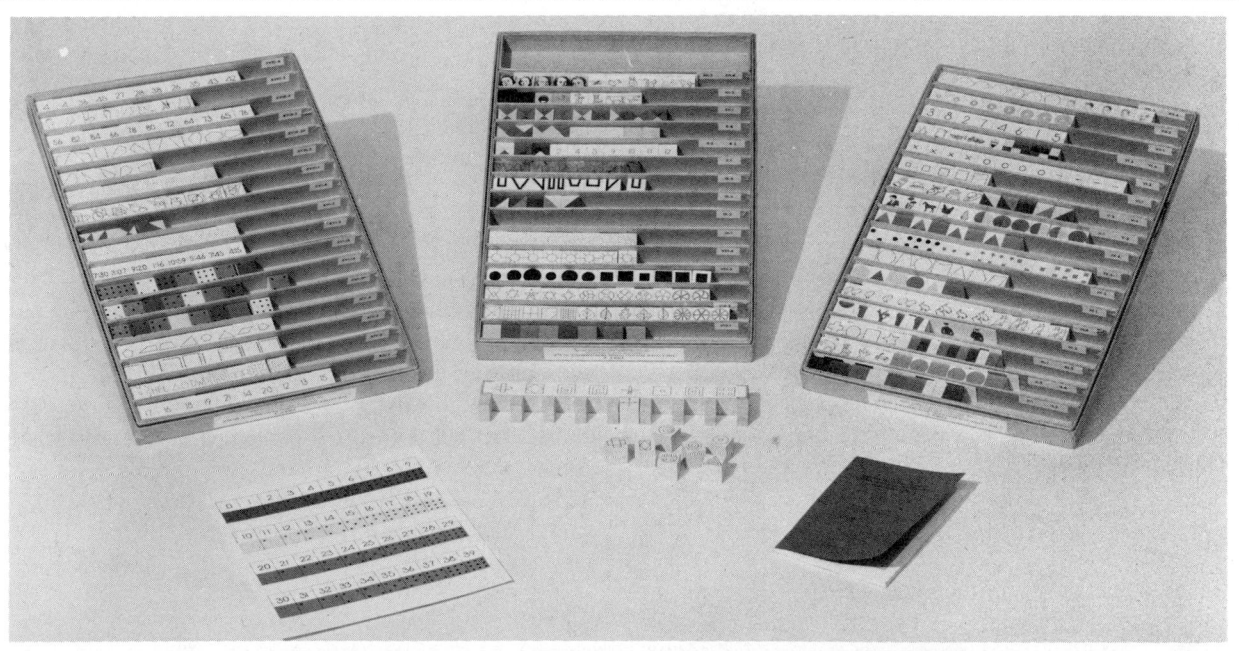

Figure 12-5. Leiter International Performance Scale. Courtesy of C. H. Stoelting Company.

items involving analogies, perceptual patterns, and concepts at the later levels. There is no time limit, and instructions are given in pantomime. The scale generally measures perceptual organization and discrimination ability. At the lowest levels, however, it may measure the ability to learn new material, rather than assess learned material.

The 1948 edition is the latest in a series of revisions. The initial version of the Leiter scale was reported in 1929 in Leiter's master's thesis. In principle, the Leiter is a nonverbal version of the 1937 Stanford-Binet scale, based on the concept of measuring intelligence in terms of developmental age.

Arthur (1949) issued an adapted version of the 1948 revision because she found the norms too high for children between the ages of 3 and 8 years. The Arthur Adaptation covers the age range between 3 and 8 years, with tests from year levels II through XII. However, the 1948 revision of the Leiter and the Arthur Adaptation use exactly the same test materials through year level XII, where the Arthur Adaptation ends.

A Leiter profile that classifies subtests into areas of cognitive ability is available to assist in qualitative analysis (Levine, Allen, Alker, & Fitzgibbons, 1974). Care must be exercised in using the profile, however, because the areas covered by the Leiter are not uniform throughout the age range of the scale.

Scores

The MA obtained on the Leiter is used to obtain an IQ by the ratio method (IQ = 100 × MA/CA).

Standardization

The manual does not describe the standardization sample adequately.

Reliability

The manual does not contain any reliability data. Satisfactory test-retest reliabilities (in the .80s and .90s) have been reported, however, in studies of handicapped children (Black, 1973; Sharp, 1958; Spellacy & Black, 1972) and normal children (Reeve, French, & Hunter, 1983).

Validity

Correlations between the Leiter and several intelligence and ability tests range from .37 to .92 (studies cited by Ratcliffe & Ratcliffe, 1979, plus studies by Bessent, 1950; Bonham, 1974; Mask & Bowen, 1984; Ollendick, Finch, &

Ginn, 1974; Reeve et al., 1983). With the Stanford-Binet: Form L-M or the WISC the correlations are usually in the .70s to .80s. The Leiter has a higher correlation with the WISC Performance Scale than with the Verbal Scale. Although correlations may be high, large differences in IQs between the Leiter and other tests *occasionally* have been reported. For example, in a study (Bonham, 1974) of deaf children, the Leiter yielded a mean IQ that was 17 points *lower* than the WISC Performance IQ (79 vs. 96).

Comment on the Leiter International Performance Scale

The Leiter has a number of limitations, including uneven item difficulty levels, outdated pictures, too few tests at each year level, and use of the ratio IQ. The most serious difficulties are the outdated norms, inadequate standardization, and lack of information about the reliability of the scale. Because the norms underestimate children's intelligence, Leiter (1959) recommended that five points be added to the IQ obtained on the scale. I recommend against use of the Leiter for placement or decision-making purposes.

In spite of its limitations, the Leiter merits consideration as an aid in clinical diagnosis, especially with language-handicapped children who cannot be administered the language parts of the Stanford-Binet: Fourth Edition, WISC-R, WPPSI, or WAIS-R. Although the test may be less culturally loaded than verbal intelligence tests, there is no evidence that it is a culture-fair measure of intelligence.

PICTORIAL TEST OF INTELLIGENCE

The Pictorial Test of Intelligence (PTI) (French, 1964) assesses intelligence of normal and handicapped children between the ages of 3 and 8 years. There are six subtests in the scale: Picture Vocabulary, Form Discrimination, Information and Comprehension, Similarities, Size and Number, and Immediate Recall. The subtests are not timed, and the test takes approximately 45 minutes to administer. The items are presented in multiple-choice format, making scoring a simple procedure. Eye movements can be used to record responses for those children who are not capable of pointing to their choices.

Scores

Raw scores are converted into MA units and then into Deviation IQs (M = 100, SD = 16).

Standardization

The standardization sample consisted of 1,830 children stratified by regional area, community size, and father's occupational level to conform with the 1960 census data. Although race was not used as a stratification variable, children from various races were included in the sample.

Reliability

The PTI manual reports test-retest and internal consistency reliabilities in the high .80s and low .90s. Other studies (Howard & Plant, 1967; Sawyer, 1968), however, reported reliabilities in the .70s and .80s. Test-retest reliabilities have not been as adequate as split-half reliabilities, with the test-retest reliabilities being lowest at age 8 years.

Validity

Correlations with other tests of intelligence range from .42 to .75 (*Mdn r* = .65), whereas with tests of achievement they range from .23 to .79 (*Mdn r* = .56) (Elliott, 1969; French, 1964; Pasewark, Sawyer, Smith, Wasserberger, Dell, Brito, & Lee, 1967). A factor analytic study of the construct validity of the PTI indicated that a general factor best accounts for performance on the test—individual subtests do not assess discrete mental functions (Sawyer, Stanley, & Watson, 1979).

Comment on the Pictorial Test of Intelligence

The Pictorial Test of Intelligence appears to be useful in evaluating children with motor and speech handicaps and in evaluating the learning aptitude of children from 3 to 6 years of age. The norms are dated, however, and there are concerns about the reliability of the scale. The PTI should not be used for any decision-making purposes.

COLUMBIA MENTAL MATURITY SCALE

The Columbia Mental Maturity Scale (CMMS), Third Edition (Burgemeister, Blum, & Lorge, 1972), is an untimed test of reasoning ability. It is useful in evaluating children who have sensory or motor deficits or who have difficulty in speaking; the test does not depend on reading skills. The scale covers an age range from 3 years, 6 months to 9 years, 11 months.

The CMMS contains 92 cards (6 by 19 inches), 50 of which are completely new to the Third Edition. The task is simple—to select the one drawing on each card that is different from the others. Young or deaf children, however, may have difficulty in understanding the concept of pointing to the "one that does not belong." With deaf children who clearly understand the directions, the test can be used for screening purposes.

The CMMS usually takes 15 to 20 minutes to administer, and it is simple to score. The child is required to make perceptual discriminations involving color, shape, size, use, number, missing parts, and symbolic material. Tasks include simple perceptual classifications and abstract manipulation of symbolic concepts. Although the CMMS appears to measure general reasoning ability, it may be more of a test of the ability to form and use concepts than a test of general intelligence.

Scores

Raw scores are converted into age deviation scores ($M = 100$, $SD = 16$), which range from 50 to 150. The standard error of measurement is 5 points for 3½ through 5½ years, and 6 points for 6 through 9½ years. A second score, the Maturity Index, which essentially is an age-equivalent score, can also be obtained. The Maturity Index indicates the standardization age group whose test performance was most similar to that of the child.

Standardization

The standardization sample for the Third Edition consisted of 2,600 children residing in 25 states. The norming procedures were designed to ensure a representative national sample on the variables of geographic region, race, parental occupation, age, and sex, based on the 1960 census data.

Reliability

Test-retest and split-half reliabilities are in the high .80s.

Validity

Correlations with other tests of intelligence generally range from the .30s to .60s, with many in the .50s. Concurrent validity is satisfactory ($r = .74$) with the Stanford-Binet: Form L-M used as the criterion with below-average children (Ritter, Duffey, & Fischman, 1974). Black and white 4- to 5-year-old children obtained similar scores on the CMMS (Ratusnik & Koenigsknecht, 1976). Mexican-American children scored 6 points lower than Anglo-American children (83 vs. 89), however (Melear & Boyle, 1974).

Comment on the Columbia Mental Maturity Scale

The Third Edition of the CMMS is an improved version of the scale. It is a satisfactory nonverbal measure of intelligence. It can be useful in evaluating handicapped children and may be less culturally loaded than other intelligence tests. The scores obtained on the CMMS are not interchangeable with those on the Stanford-Binet Form: L-M, WISC-R, or WPPSI, however.

BLIND LEARNING APTITUDE TEST

The Blind Learning Aptitude Test (BLAT) (Newland, 1971) is a nonverbal cognitive test designed to assess the learning aptitude of blind children from ages 6 to 16 years. Six different types of cognitive functioning are measured on the BLAT: recognition of differences, recognition of similarities, identification of progressions, identification of the missing element in a four-element matrix, completion of a figure, and identification of the missing element in a nine-figure matrix.

The BLAT contains 12 training items and 49 test items. The items are in bas-relief form, consisting of dots and lines similar to those used in Braille but not requiring the fine tactile discrimination needed for Braille reading. Most of the items (86 percent) were adapted from tests such as the Cattell Culture Free Test and Raven's Progressive Matrices. The remaining 14 percent of the items were created specifically for the BLAT. The directions for the BLAT are given verbally, and responses are given by pointing. It takes from 45 to 60 minutes to administer the test.

Scores

Raw scores are converted into learning quotients, which are standard scores ($M = 100$, $SD = 15$).

Standardization

The BLAT was standardized on 760 blind children in residential schools from 12 states and 201 blind children in 55 day schools in 16 cities within those states (total $N = 961$). The sample approximated 1966 U.S. census data with respect to sex, race, and socioeconomic status. Normative data are provided for children from ages 6 to 16 years ($N = 836$), although children up to 20 years of age were included in the standardization sample.

Reliability

Internal consistency reliability is high ($r_{xx} = .93$). Test-retest reliability (seven-month interval) for a sample of 93 children, ages 10 through 16 years, is satisfactory ($r_{xx} = .87$).

Validity

Validity for the BLAT was based on three criteria. First, mean scores showed improved performance with increasing age levels. Second, satisfactory correlations were found between the BLAT and the Hayes-Binet ($r = .74$), another cognitive measure intended for visually handicapped examinees, and the WISC Verbal Scale ($r = .71$). Third, correlations with the Stanford Achievement Test were satisfactory (*Mdn r* = .58, range of *r*'s from .32 to .76).

A factor analysis yielded four factors: a General factor, a Matrix Reasoning factor, an Identification of Similarities and Differences factor, and a Pattern Completion factor.

Comment on the Blind Learning Aptitude Test

The Blind Learning Aptitude Test is a useful supplementary test for evaluating the nonverbal cognitive abilities of blind children. It should be used in conjunction with a verbal test. The test appears to be most useful for children in the elementary grades (ages 6 to 12). When used with children 12 years of age or older, the BLAT loses some of its discriminating power.

HISKEY-NEBRASKA TEST OF LEARNING APTITUDE

The Hiskey-Nebraska Test of Learning Aptitude (H-NTLA) (Hiskey, 1966) is a performance scale for use with children ages 3 to 17 years. There are 12 subtests in the scale: Bead Patterns, Memory for Color, Picture Identification, Picture Association, Paper Folding, Visual Attention Span, Block Patterns, Completion of Drawings, Memory for Digits, Puzzle Blocks, Picture Analogies, and Spatial Reasoning. The subtests involve verbal labeling, categorization, concept formation, and rehearsal.

The H-NTLA can be administered entirely through pantomimed instructions and does not require a verbal response from the examinee. Thus it is useful with children who are deaf, mentally retarded, speech or language handicapped, or bilingual. Alternatively, the H-NTLA may be administered using verbal instructions in cases of mild hearing impairments. The scale takes about 50 minutes to administer.

Scores

Raw scores are converted into a Deviation Learning Quotient (LQ) ($M = 100$, $SD = 16$).

Standardization

The H-NTLA was standardized on 2,153 individuals (1,079 deaf and 1,074 normal hearing) aged 2-6 to 17-5 years. The deaf individuals came mostly from schools for the deaf, but the representativeness of the deaf sample is unknown. The normal-hearing individuals were selected on the basis of the occupational levels of their parents and are representative of the population based on the 1960 U.S. census. No information is given as to the ethnicity of the sample. Norms are provided for both deaf and nonimpaired samples.

Reliability

For the deaf individuals, split-half reliability coefficients were .95 for those 3 to 10 years old and .92 for those 11 to 17 years old. For the nonimpaired individuals, split-half reliability coefficients were .93 for those 3 to 10 years old and .90 for those 11 to 17 years old. A test-retest study of 43 10-year-old hearing-impaired children found relatively high correlations over periods of 1, 3, and 5 years (r's of .79, .85, and .62, respectively) (Watson, 1983). Over one-half the sample had scores that changed by 10 points or more upon retesting, however.

Validity

Correlations between the H-NTLA and other intelligence tests range from .78 to .86, whereas correlations with several achievement scales range from −.09 to .72 (*Mdn r* = .49) for grades 2 through 12. Correlations with teacher ratings range from .06 to .64 (*Mdn r* = .46). In one study (Watson & Goldgar, 1985) the H-NTLA was compared with the WISC-R Performance Scale for a sample of 71 hearing-impaired children. Although the means on the two scales were similar (*M* LQ = 100.21 and *M* IQ = 99.13, *r* = .85), the H-NTLA scores were more variable (*SD*'s of 22.36 and 17.42, respectively) and more often extreme (below 70 or above 119) than the WISC-R Performance Scale scores. In another study (Phelps & Ensor, 1986) the H-NTLA and the WISC-R Performance Scale were found

to have similar means (*M* = 90.41 and 91.90, respectively, *r* = .93) for a sample of 49 prelingual deaf children.

Comment on the Hiskey-Nebraska Test of Learning Aptitude

The Hiskey-Nebraska Test of Learning Aptitude is a nonverbal intelligence test that has been found to be helpful with children with a variety of language handicaps. Reliability and validity are satisfactory. A most important feature of the scale is that it has parallel instructions for administering each subtest to deaf and to normal-hearing children. The norm group, however, is seriously out of date and may not be representative of the hearing-impaired population. The WISC-R Performance Scale appears to be a better measure of the cognitive skills of hearing-impaired children: it is easier to administer than the H-NTLA, takes less time, and has more up-to-date norms for both hearing-impaired and normal-hearing children. (Chapter 20 discusses the assessment of hearing-impaired children.)

PIAGETIAN TESTS

Piagetian tests provide insight into a child's thinking processes. Representative Piagetian tests are shown in Exhibit 12-2 for ages 5 through 11 years. The tests cover the understanding of conservation, logical operations, and seriation. Many other Piagetian tests are available, but these were selected because they require few special materials and can be administered quickly and easily. These tests are informal tests with approximate age norms.

BAYLEY SCALES OF INFANT DEVELOPMENT

The Bayley Scales of Infant Development (Bayley, 1969) is a carefully developed measure of infant development for children from 2 months to 2½ years of age (see Figure 12-6). Two standard scores are provided: a Mental Developmental Index, obtained from the Mental Scale, and a Psychomotor Developmental Index, obtained from the Motor Scale. An Infant Behavior Record rating scale also can be completed.

The Mental Scale contains 163 items arranged by tenths of months (see Table 12-3). Items involve shape discrimination, sustained attention, purposeful manipulation of objects, imitation and comprehension, vocalization, memory, problem solving, and naming objects. The 81 items in

Exhibit 12-2

Examples of Piagetian Tasks

Conservation of Number

This conservation task measures the child's understanding that variations in the configuration of a row of objects do not affect the number of objects.

Materials: Twenty checkers.

Procedure: Present two rows of 10 checkers in one-to-one correspondence. Say: "Do the two rows contain the same numbers of checkers?" If the child says "No," help him or her to understand that both rows have the same number of checkers. Then spread apart the row closest to the child. Say: "Do the rows have the same number, or does one row have more? How do you know?"

Age: 5 to 6 years.

Conservation of Continuous Quantity: Solids

This conservation task measures the child's understanding that changes in the shape of a solid do not change the quantity of that solid.

Materials: Two balls of clay identical in size, shape, and weight.

Procedure: Show the two balls of clay to the child. Say: "Do the two balls have the same amount of clay?" If the child says "No" or if there is any doubt about the child's understanding, encourage the child to make them the same. Then say, "Suppose I roll one of the balls into a hot dog. Will there be as much clay in the hot dog as in the ball? Will they both have the same amount of clay?" After the child answers, roll one of the balls into a sausage shape. Say: "Is there as much clay in the hot dog as in the ball? Do they both have the same amount of clay?" After the child responds, say, "Why did you say that?"

Age: 6 years.

Conservation of Length

This conservation task measures the child's understanding that the comparative length of objects is unaffected by their relative positions.

Materials: Two unsharpened pencils of identical length and color.

Procedure: Place the two pencils in a horizontal position, one directly beneath the other, about 1 inch apart. Say: "Are the two pencils the same length?" After the child agrees that the two pencils are the same length, take the pencil closest to the child and turn it 45 degrees. Say: "Are the two pencils still the same length? Why?"

Age: 6 years.

Conservation of Weight

This conservation task measures the child's understanding that changes in the shape of an object do not cause changes in its weight.

Materials: Two balls of clay, identical in size, shape, and weight.

Procedure: Give the two balls of clay to the child. Say: "Do the two balls weigh the same?" If the child says "No" or if there is any doubt, encourage the child to make them the same. Then say: "Suppose I roll one of the balls into a hot dog. Will the hot dog weigh the same as the balls?" After the child answers, roll one of the balls into a sausage shape. Say: "Do they both weigh the same?" After the child responds, say: "Why is that?"

Age: 6 years.

Seriation: Size

This test of seriation measures the child's understanding that objects can be put in order according to their size.

Materials: Twelve sticks, 10 of which range in length from 9 to 16.2 cm, each being .8 cm longer than the preceding one, one of which is midway between sticks 3 and 4 in length, and one of which is midway between sticks 7 and 8 in length.

Procedure: Place the first 10 sticks before the child in random order, but all in the vertical direction. Say: "Look at these sticks carefully. I want you to put them in order. Put them in order so that the very smallest comes first, and then the next smallest, and then the next smallest, all the way to the biggest. Go ahead."

After the child finishes arranging the set of sticks, give him or her the additional stick that goes between the 7th and 8th stick. Say: "Here's an extra stick. You put it in the right place where it belongs."

After the child inserts the stick, remove it, give the child the second stick, and say: "Here's another stick. Put this stick in the right place where it belongs."

Age: 7 years.

Conservation of Continuous Quantity: Liquids

This conservation test measures the child's understanding that variations in the shape of a container of liquid do not affect the quantity of that liquid.

Materials: Equal quantities of water in two identical large glasses, and three identical empty small glasses.

(Exhibit continues next page)

Exhibit 12-2 (cont.)

Procedure: With the child watching, pour water from one large glass into the three small glasses. Say: "Now I have this one to drink [point to the large glass with water] and you have all three glasses of water to drink. Will you have more to drink, or will I have more to drink? How do you know?"

Age: 8 years.

Additive Classification: Visual

This test of logical operations measures the child's ability to group objects according to a common attribute.

Materials: Four large red squares, four large blue squares, four small red circles, four small blue circles, two white sheets of paper.

Procedure: Place the 16 squares and circles in random order before the child. Say: "Tell me what you see." After the child finishes the description, say: "See these two sheets of paper [point to the sheets of paper]. I want you to put some of the blocks on one sheet and the others on the other sheet. Put those together on each sheet that you think belong together." After the blocks have been placed on the two sheets, remove the blocks and scramble them. Say: "Now put them together on each sheet another way." Repeat this procedure one additional time.

Age: 9 years for three classifications.

Class Inclusion

This test of logical operations measures the child's understanding of the relationship among a group of objects.

Materials: Four white squares, two blue squares, three blue circles.

Procedure: Show the child the objects and say:

1. "Are all the blue ones circles? Why?"
2. "Are all the squares white? Why?"
3. "Are there more circles or more blue things? Why?"
4. "Are there more blue things than there are squares, or the same, or fewer? Why?"

Age: 10 years for questions 1 and 2; after 10 years of age for questions 3 and 4.

Figure 12-6. Bayley Scales of Infant Development. Courtesy of The Psychological Corporation.

Table 12-3
Illustrative Items from the Bayley Scales of Infant Development

Age (in months)	Mental Scale	Motor Scale
2	Visually recognizes mother	Elevates self by arms: prone
4	Turns head to sound of rattle	Balances head
6	Looks for fallen spoon	Sits alone for 30 seconds or more
8	Uncovers toy	Pulls self to standing position
10	Looks at pictures in book	Walks with help
12	Turns pages of book	Walks alone
14	Spontaneously scribbles	Walks sideways
16	Builds tower of 3 cubes	Stands on left foot with help
18	Initiates crayon stroke	Tries to walk on walking board
20	Differentiates scribble from stroke	Walks with one foot on walking board
22	Names 3 pictures	Stands on left foot alone
24	Names 3 objects	Jumps from bottom step
26	Makes train of cubes	Walks down stairs alone: both feet on each step
28	Understands 2 prepositions	Jumps from second step
30	Builds tower of 8 cubes	Walks on tiptoe, 10 feet

the Motor Scale cover gross and fine motor abilities, such as sitting, standing, walking, and grasping. The Bayley takes approximately 45 minutes to administer, although some infants and toddlers may require 75 minutes or more.

The Infant Behavior Record provides a systematic way of assessing and recording observations of a child's behavior during the examination. Ratings cover the following 11 areas: social orientation, cooperativeness, fearfulness, tension, general emotional tone, object orientation, goal directedness, attention span, endurance, activity, and reactivity. Behaviors oriented toward cognitive tasks (for example, goal directedness, attention span, object orientation, and reactivity) have been found to be related to mental scores, whereas behaviors related to social extroversion (for example, social orientation to the examiner, cooperativeness, and emotional tone) have been found to have little predictive power (Matheny, Dolan, & Wilson, 1974).

Scores

Raw scores on the Bayley Scales are converted into a Mental Developmental Index and a Psychomotor Developmental Index, which are normalized standard scores ($M = 100$, $SD = 16$). Extrapolated mental developmental indices (below 50) have been published by Naglieri (1981b).

Standardization

The Bayley was standardized on a representative national sample of 1,262 normal infants and children in 14 age groups, from 2 months to 30 months of age. The stratification variables included geographic area, urban-rural residence, sex, race, and education of head of household.

Reliability

Split-half reliability coefficients for the 14 age groups range from .81 to .93 ($Mdn\ r_{xx} = .88$) on the Mental Scale and from .68 to .92 ($Mdn\ r_{xx} = .84$) on the Motor Scale. Mental Scale reliabilities are fairly consistent throughout the age periods covered by the test. On the Motor Scale, however, reliabilities are lower for the first four months (ages 2 through 5 months) than for later months. Split-half reliability is also satisfactory for black infants on both the Mental and Motor Scales (King & Seegmiller, 1973).

Correlations between the Mental and Motor Scales vary widely for the 14 age groups—from .18 to .75 ($Mdn\ r = .46$). Because the correlations tend to decrease with age, there may be a clearer differentiation between mental and motor skills as the child develops.

Validity

The manual reports a correlation of .57 between the Mental Scale and the Stanford-Binet: Form L-M for a sample of 120 children, ages 24 to 30 months, in the standardization group. Validity coefficients for the younger age groups are not reported.

A factor analysis of the Infant Behavior Record suggests that the items cluster into three categories: Task Orientation (for example, goal directedness and attention span), Test Affect-Extraversion (for example, cooperativeness and fearfulness), and Activity (for example, body motion and energy) (Matheny, 1983). Factor scores obtained for 300 to 400 infants indicated that these aspects of infant behavior are *not* stable during the period from 6 to 24 months of age (Matheny, 1983).

Comment on the Bayley Scales of Infant Development

Administration of the Bayley Scales requires considerable practice and experience. The Bayley Scales is an excellent addition to the area of infant assessment. It is, at present, by far the best measure of infant development and provides valuable information about patterns of early mental development. An example of information in a report based on the Bayley Scales follows.

Helen, a 22-month-old, was extremely reluctant to talk to the examiner and occasionally had to be encouraged by her mother to respond to the examiner's questions. She was greatly interested in the test materials, however, and seemed to try her best on most tasks. She often frowned when tasks were difficult. Only on the last few items did she refuse to continue. Her mother, however, was able to coax her into completing the last few tasks. She was alert and usually interested in the objects in the kit.

Helen obtained a Mental Developmental Index of 111 (75th percentile rank), with a mental age of 24 months. Her best abilities were in discrimination of objects (ball, clock, cup), object constancy (ball under cup), and beginning verbal communication ("here Mommy"). Her Psychomotor Developmental Index was 108 (69th percentile rank), with a psychomotor age of 23 months. Thus she has average motor skills, such as coordination of large muscles (getting up from lying on back, walking on a line), balance (on one foot with help), and fine motor skills (copying a single line). Overall, her current developmental status is well within normal limits.

OTHER INFANT ASSESSMENT MEASURES

In addition to the Bayley Scales, other procedures are available for assessing infants soon after birth and throughout the entire stage of infancy. The Gesell Developmental Schedule (Ilg & Ames, 1965) and the Cattell Infant Intelligence Test (Cattell, 1940) are two such scales. They are not as psychometrically sound as the Bayley Scales, however. The Baby Behavior Questionnaire (3 to 10 months of age) and the Toddler Behavior Questionnaire (11 to 15 months of age) are useful in measuring broad areas of infant temperament and behavior (Hagekull, 1985).

Apgar Score

The neonatal status of a child is often expressed in terms of an Apgar score. An Apgar score is derived by evaluating five factors—heart rate, color, respiration, muscle tone, and reflexes—1 minute after delivery and again 5 minutes after delivery. Each factor is rated on a 3-point scale (with 0 being weakest and 2 being strongest). An extremely low score indicates that the newborn child may have a potential problem.

Rochester Obstetrical Scale

The Rochester Research Obstetrical Scale (Sameroff, 1979) contains 27 items grouped into three scales: a Prenatal Scale, a Delivery Scale, and an Infant Scale. The Apgar items are incorporated into the Delivery Scale. The scale holds promise for evaluating birth process factors that may be related to the child's developmental status.

Neonatal Behavioral Assessment Scale

The Neonatal Behavioral Assessment Scale (Brazelton, 1973) is another useful procedure for evaluating infants during the early months of development. Items on this scale range from the evaluation of neurological reflexes to the evaluation of alertness. Sameroff (1978) provides a detailed review of this scale.

Infant Psychological Development Scale

The Infant Psychological Development Scale (Uzgiris & Hunt, 1975) measures intellectual processes associated with natural stages of development between the ages of 2 weeks and 2 years. It contains eight subscales developed on the basis of Piagetian theory, each measuring the development of a specific ability. The subscales consist of a number of separate ordinal steps, with each step delineating a stage in the development of the ability. The subscales are as follows:

1. Object Permanence (15 steps)
2. Use of Objects as Means (9 steps)
3. Learning and Foresight (5 steps)
4. Development of Schemata (11 steps)
5. Development of an Understanding of Causality (10 steps)
6. Conception of Objects in Space (11 steps)
7. Vocal Imitation (8 steps)
8. Gestural Imitation (5 steps)

In one study (Wachs, 1975) scores on most subscales of the Infant Psychological Development Scale were found to be significantly related to later performance on the Stanford-Binet: Form L-M only if infants were 18 months of age or older at the time of testing. The one exception was Object Permanence. Scores on this subscale obtained at 12, 15, 18, 21, and 24 months of age were significantly related to later Stanford-Binet performance. This subscale also showed the most consistently significant pattern of relationships across all five age levels. The development of object permanence (which involves understanding of what happens to an object or person when out of sight) early in life may play an important role in cognitive development. This finding was essentially supported in a study of severely and profoundly retarded children (Kahn, 1983). Object Permanence and Vocal Imitation were found to be the best predictors of language development in the sample.

The Infant Psychological Development Scale can be used to design developmentally sequenced curriculum programs. A manual by Dunst (1980) provides information on clinical and educational uses of the scale and ways to estimate a developmental age. Evidence of the concurrent validity of the developmental ages was obtained by administering the Bayley Scales to a group of handicapped infants (Heffernan & Black, 1984).

Following is a summary statement in a report based on the Uzgiris-Hunt Scales (Dunst, 1982).

Craig, a developmentally delayed child, was 23 months old when he was administered the Uzgiris-Hunt Scales. He had been diagnosed as having brain damage and he manifested many autistic-like tendencies. Craig showed a variable pattern of performance on the scale, functioning between 2 months (vocal imitation) and 14 months of age (causality and space). His overall Sensorimotor Age was 10 months. His performance suggested an atypical pattern of development.

Comment on Infant Developmental Scales

There is some controversy about whether an age correction should be made for prematurity when infants' and young children's scores on a test of mental development are determined (Siegel, 1979, 1983). An uncorrected score uses the child's actual chronological age, whereas a corrected score takes into account the child's degree of prematurity. The corrected age is obtained by subtracting the child's gestational age from 40 weeks and then subtracting this difference from his or her chronological age. Thus, at 20 weeks after birth, an infant born at a gestational age of 32 weeks would have a corrected age of 12 weeks.

The child's level of functioning may be overestimated by the corrected chronological age or underestimated by the uncorrected chronological age. Siegel's (1983) research suggests that the corrected age has somewhat better pre-

dictive powers during the first year of life, but after 1 year of age both scores have equal predictive ability. Other research (Miller, Dubowitz, & Palmer, 1984), however, indicates that use of the uncorrected chronological age provides a more sensitive indicator of developmental disabilities, particularly after 9 months of age. Thus the issue of whether an age correction should be made has not been fully resolved.

Infant scales provide information about the child's current status, particularly about deviations from normal expected development. An understanding of normal developmental sequences in adaptive, motor, language, and personal-social behavior is helpful in assessing infants and young children. Careful study of Table C-60 in Appendix C, which presents some important developmental milestones, will assist you in attaining this understanding.

PSYCHOLOGICAL EVALUATION

The psychological evaluation in Exhibit 12-3 covers a 7-year longitudinal study of a high-risk child who was born prematurely. Cindy was found to be precocious as an infant. As she grew older, however, her activity level increased and she became more distractible and less attentive. Subsequently, a language disorder was identified, in addition to hyperactivity. It is not known whether Cindy's excessive activity level interfered with her acquisition of language skills or the failure to meet language demands led to her hyperactivity. Some combination of the two is probably the best explanation.

One interesting aspect of this case is the reduction in the Bayley scores between the 6th- and 24th-month evaluations; performance dropped from above average to below average. The discrepancy between IQs on the Leiter (IQ = 92) and the Stanford-Binet: Form L-M (IQ = 67) at 3 years of age was mirrored in the discrepancy between WISC-R Verbal and Performance Scale IQs at 7 years of age. This case illustrates that (a) IQs can change over time, (b) a child with slow language development may obtain an invalid score on a test that requires verbal abilities, (c) different kinds of tasks are needed in order to arrive at a valid clinical diagnosis, (d) with high risk children, in particular, repeated evaluations are essential, and (e) early intervention can help bring a child's abilities from well below average to the average range. Additionally, this case study shows the importance of identifying developmental delays and labeling them as such rather than labeling a very young child as mentally retarded. (Also see Chapter 21 for information about a developmental delay diagnosis.)

Exhibit 12-3

Psychological Evaluation: A Seven Year Follow-up of a High-Risk Child

Name: Cindy
Date of birth: January 1, 1979

Dates of examination: Noted below
Date of report: February 1, 1986

Tests Administered

6-Month Evaluation — 10/13/79 (Adjusted age: 6 months)

Bayley Scales of Infant Development

Mental Developmental Index (MDI): 124
Psychomotor Developmental Index (PDI): 112

12-Month Evaluation — 3/17/80 (Adjusted age: 12 months)

Bayley Scales of Infant Development

Mental Developmental Index (MDI): 103
Psychomotor Developmental Index (PDI): 86

24-Month Evaluation — 4/5/81 (Adjusted age: 24 months)

Bayley Scales of Infant Development

Mental Developmental Index (MDI): 85
Psychomotor Developmental Index (PDI): 87

3-Year Evaluation — 2/21/82 (No age adjustment)

Stanford-Binet Intelligence Scale: Form L-M

Chronological age: 3-2
Mental age: 2-6
Intelligence Quotient: 67 ± 10 at the 95 percent confidence level

Leiter International Performance Scale, Arthur Adaptation

Chronological age: 3-2
Mental age: 2-11
Intelligence Quotient: 92

Peabody Picture Vocabulary Test — Revised

Chronological age: 3-2
Standard score: 79

Vineland Adaptive Behavior Scales

Chronological age: 3-2
Adaptive Behavior Composite: 94 ± 6 at the 95% confidence level, 34th percentile rank

4-Year Evaluation — 4/16/83

Stanford-Binet Intelligence Scale: Form L-M

Chronological age: 4-3
Mental age: 4-5
Intelligence Quotient: 93 ± 10 at the 95 percent confidence level

5-Year Evaluation — 5/14/84

Stanford-Binet Intelligence Scale: Form L-M

Chronological age: 5-4

Mental age: 5-1
Intelligence Quotient: 87 ± 10 at the 95 percent confidence level

7-Year Evaluation — 1/5/86

WISC-R

Chronological age: 7-0

VERBAL SCALE		PERFORMANCE SCALE	
Information	8	Picture Completion	10
Similarities	9	Picture Arrangement	10
Arithmetic	8	Block Design	11
Vocabulary	7	Object Assembly	11
Comprehension	8	Coding	11

Verbal Scale IQ: 87
Performance Scale IQ: 104
Full Scale IQ: 94 ± 7 at the 95 percent confidence level

Bender Visual Motor Gestalt Test

Standard Score: 95; 37th percentile

Developmental Test of Visual-Motor Integration
Standard score: 7; 32nd percentile

(Exhibit continues next page)

Exhibit 12-3 (cont.)

Reason for Referral

Cindy had a difficult neonatal period following a premature birth and is considered to be a "high-risk" child. She has been seen for periodic reevaluations. This report covers evaluations from the age of 6 months through 7 years of age.

Background Information

Cindy's 35-year-old single mother had a normal pregnancy until the 6th month, when an accidental fall caused Cindy to be born 3 months prematurely (28 weeks gestation). Cindy weighed 1,469 grams at birth, had respiratory distress syndrome and jaundice, and was placed in an isolette for 6 weeks. From 2 to 19 months of age she had recurrent hospitalizations (at 2, 12, 14, 15, and 19 months) for pneumonia and bronchitis.

Cindy achieved fairly normal motor milestones—sitting at about 7 months, crawling at 9 months, and walking alone at 17 months. Language abilities were somewhat slow to develop, as she was using only single words at 2 years of age. Normal development would predict three-word sentences by this age. At 3 years, she was nearly completely toilet trained. At the age of about 12 months, her mother noted increasing hyperactivity and attention difficulties. During her second year, Cindy's activity level continued to increase, and she became more distractible, less attentive, and difficult to control. She continues to have attention and concentration difficulties and requires structure and close management of her behavior.

Assessment Results and Clinical Impressions

The Bayley Scales of Infant Development was administered at 9 months of age (adjusted age of 6 months was used to compensate for her 3-month premature birth). She obtained a Mental Developmental Index of 124 (93rd percentile) and a Pyschomotor Developmental Index of 112 (77th percentile). Both scores were above average. No vocalizations were observed during the evaluation.

Prior to the 12-month evaluation, Cindy was hospitalized for one week with pneumonia. Her gross motor functioning deteriorated during the hospitalization, but improved to a normal level again shortly after her return home. The results of the Bayley Scales at 15 months (again, age adjusted) indicated a Mental Developmental Index of 103 (57th percentile) and a Psychomotor Developmental Index of 86 (19th percentile). Both scores were considerably lower than those obtained at 9 months of age. Cindy's mental ability was average, but her motor ability was below average.

During the 27-month evaluation (age adjustment again used), Cindy was extremely active, difficult to test, and occasionally uncooperative. However, the results of the evaluation appeared to be reliable. Bayley scores were 85 (17th percentile) for the Mental Developmental Index and 87 (21st percentile) for the Psychomotor Developmental Index. Both scores were below average. Her mental ability showed a continued

decline, but no change was evident in her motor ability. Although she seemed to have the most difficulty with language tasks, some verbal imitations were observed. Recurrent hospitalizations for pneumonia and bronchitis may have contributed to her slower developmental rate.

At the 3-year evaluation (CA 3-2, not age adjusted), Cindy obtained a Mental Age of 2-6 and an IQ of 67 ± 10 (2nd percentile) on the Stanford-Binet Intelligence Scale: Form L-M. This IQ is classified within the Mentally Retarded classification. The chances that the range of scores from 57 to 77 included her true IQ were about 95 out of 100. Cindy passed all tests at year level II, but failed all tests at year level IV. Language skills were delayed and were more typical of a child aged 2 to 2½ years. Although she was able to identify concrete objects and objects by use, her vocabulary was limited. She also was unable to repeat two digits, responding with the last digit only, and was unable to consistently follow simple commands. Cindy's performance on the Peabody Picture Vocabulary Test—Revised (Standard Score = 79, 8th percentile) generally supported the Stanford-Binet results with respect to a classification of below-average language development.

Cindy's performance was nearly average on tasks requiring visual-motor skills. For example, she could sort buttons by color, reproduce a bridge of blocks, and place beads on a string. Because of the discrepancy between her functioning on tasks requiring visual-motor processing and those requiring language, the Leiter International Performance Scale was administered. On this nonverbal measure of intelligence, she achieved an IQ of 92, which placed her within the normal range of intelligence. Thus nonverbal reasoning ability was within the normal range. Her Vineland Adaptive Behavior Scales score of 94 also was within normal limits for her age, indicating appropriate social and self-help skills.

Because her lowered Stanford-Binet IQ was probably associated with language impairment, it is highly unlikely that her overall level of cognitive functioning was in the mentally retarded range. Her decreased ability to process auditory information and communicate effectively may have been a result of her hyperactivity, or it may have been, in part, a symptom of frustration. It was then recommended that she receive a speech and language evaluation, a hearing test, and a neurological examination.

The neurological evaluation supported a diagnosis of a mild language dysfunction and an attention deficit disorder with hyperactivity. The neurologist believed that medication would not be needed if a suitable educational facility with special speech assistance was obtained for Cindy. Her hearing was found to be within normal limits. The speech and language evaluation indicated a delay of approximately 6-9 months in receptive language and approximately 1 year in expressive language. She had difficulty repeating 2-word sequences, did not understand action verb forms, and could not follow com-

(Exhibit continues next page)

Exhibit 12-3 (cont.)

mands that involved more than one step. Expressive language was limited to 2- or 3-word phrases.

Subsequently, Cindy attended speech therapy twice weekly for a 3- to 4-month period and showed steady gains in speech and language skills. Attention span also improved, although auditorially she continued to be highly distractible. She was placed in a special preschool setting that provided intensive daily speech and language stimulation for children with learning handicaps.

At the time of the 4-year evaluation, Cindy's mother reported a remarkable improvement in her language development and organizational ability. On the Stanford-Binet: Form L-M, she obtained a Mental Age of 4-5 and an IQ of 93 ± 10 (34th percentile). Although she continued to exhibit some residual difficulties related to her language disorder, her speech ability was developing rapidly (speech therapy and special school placement may have contributed to her satisfactory progress). She demonstrated less distractibility, longer attention span, and greater cooperation than she had shown in previous testing sessions. Continued therapy, particularly with regard to auditory processing and speech therapy, was recommended.

Approximately one year later, at the age of 5 years, 4 months, Cindy obtained a Mental Age of 5-1 and an IQ of 87 ± 10 (21st percentile) on the Stanford-Binet: Form L-M. The results were similar to those of her 4-year examination. Although Cindy continued to show better attention for visual or performance tasks, she tended to respond too quickly to verbal items. It was recommended that Cindy be placed in a regular kindergarten program. When she was 6 years of age, her physician recommended that Ritalin be given for a trial period to see if it would have some positive effect on her behavior.

By the time of her 7-year evaluation, Cindy had progressed from a special preschool setting to a regular kindergarten and was attending school in a regular first-grade classroom. She had been given Ritalin twice a day for the past year, and her mother believed that the Ritalin helped to decrease Cindy's hyperactive behavior. Because of difficulty in controlling Cindy's impulsive behavior in her current school setting, her teacher questioned the appropriateness of her classroom placement; it was decided she should be retained in her present regular classroom, however. Cindy continued to need close supervision with respect to her inattentiveness.

On the WISC-R, Cindy obtained a Verbal IQ of 87 (19th percentile), a Performance IQ of 104 (61st percentile), and a Full Scale IQ of 94 ± 7 (34th percentile). Cindy's verbal skills were significantly less developed than her performance skills, although overall she performed within the Average range.

When verbal responses were required during the testing session, Cindy responded with short, concrete answers accompanied by hyperactive behavior and apparent inattention. On the Performance Scale, although she demonstrated good attention and concentration, her responses were quick and, at times, impulsive. Her performance on the Developmental Test of Visual-Motor Integration (standard score = 7, 32nd percentile) appeared much more organized, neat, and controlled than did her drawings on the Bender Visual Motor Gestalt Test. However, on the Bender-Gestalt she obtained a score similar to the one on the Visual-Motor Integration Test (7 errors, standard score of 95, 37th percentile). The errors were primarily distortions of shape (5 of 7), and her designs were poorly organized.

Cindy's difficulties in maintaining attention and concentration, particularly for verbal tasks, might well impede her ability to master new concepts in a regular classroom. She needs time, repetition, and mastery to help her learn. Recommendations include close monitoring of her medication and management of her behavior in the classroom. Based on Cindy's continuing difficulties, a special educational setting where she can be given more structure and individual encouragement to maintain her attention might become necessary in the future. However, this recommendation should only be pursued if she is unable to perform at an adequate level in her current classroom setting.

Summary

In summary, this child, who was born prematurely, showed variability in her test scores during the first 7 years of life. Although her developmental scores during her first year were average to above average, they had dropped to below average by 2 years of age. Her nonverbal skills were superior to her verbal skills when she was 3 years old, and speech and language therapy was instituted. She progressed from a special preschool educational program through a regular first grade, and significant improvements were noted in her language skills. At the age of 7 years, she was functioning in the Average range intellectually, although her verbal abilities continued to be less well developed than her nonverbal abilities. Because of her continuing difficulties in maintaining attention and concentration, especially for verbal tasks, Cindy still requires close supervision and special help in the classroom.

(Signature) _____

Jane T. Jones, MA

Note. The center in which Cindy was evaluated used age-adjusted scores up until the age of 2 years.

SUMMARY

1. The tests reviewed in this chapter are useful in the assessment of handicapped children, children with limited knowledge of English, or young children. They also can serve as screening instruments or as supplements to tests such as the Stanford-Binet: Fourth Edition, WISC-R, WPPSI, and WAIS-R.

2. The McCarthy Scales of Children's Abilities, applicable for children between 2½ and 8½ years of age, contains 18 tests grouped into six scales. It is well standardized and has excellent reliability. Caution is needed in using the General Cognitive Index for placement purposes, however.

3. The Kaufman Assessment Battery for Children is a battery of cognitive and achievement tests designed for children between 2-6 and 12-5 years of age. Although reliability and validity are satisfactory, there are a number of difficulties with the test. These include the failure to include any verbal reasoning or verbal comprehension subtests in the Mental Processing Composite, a limited floor and ceiling, and ambiguity about the terms *simultaneous* and *sequential processing*. Caution is needed in using the test in clinical or psychoeducational assessments.

4. The Detroit Tests of Learning Aptitude – 2 is a multidimensional battery designed to measure intellectual ability in children and adolescents from 6 through 18 years of age. The test has adequate reliability and validity, but the standardization sample is questionable. The total score is the preferred measure because the cluster scores are not supported by factor analysis or cluster analysis.

5. The Detroit Tests of Learning Aptitude – P is an abbreviated form of the DTLA-2, covering an age range from 3 to 9 years. The test has adequate reliability and validity, but adequacy of the standardization sample is as questionable as that of the longer DTLA-2.

6. The Extended Merrill-Palmer Scale covers the age period from 3-0 to 5-11 years. It provides opportunities to evaluate the content and the process of thinking, following Guilford's Structure of Intellect model. Unfortunately, little is known about the validity of the scale. The manual does not provide standard scores for any of the measures. Although the scale has limitations, it does provide assessment information that is not easily obtainable from other instruments.

7. The Slosson Intelligence Test can be used as a screening instrument. It should not be used as a substitute for the Stanford-Binet: Fourth Edition, WISC-R, WPPSI, or WAIS-R. Although the test was restandardized in the 1980s, it was based on Stanford-Binet: Form L-M norms that may be out of date.

8. Raven's Progressive Matrices is a nonverbal test of reasoning ability that comes in three forms. These forms cover individuals from age 5 through adulthood. Recent U.S. norms should prove useful. The test relies too heavily on figural reasoning to be useful for estimating the cognitive ability of some children.

9. The Goodenough-Harris Drawing Test provides a quick estimate of children's ability, particularly for children between the ages of 3 and 10 years. It may have some use in the evaluation of ethnic minority children.

10. The Leiter International Performance Scale is a nonverbal intelligence test that taps perceptual organization and discrimination ability. Its outdated norms and inadequate standardization are major shortcomings. There is no evidence that the test is culture-fair. It may be useful for testing children with language deficiencies, however.

11. The Pictorial Test of Intelligence serves to evaluate the learning aptitude of children, primarily those from 3 to 6 years of age. It is useful in evaluating children with motor or speech handicaps.

12. The Columbia Mental Maturity Scale is a nonverbal test of intelligence designed for children between 3½ and 10 years of age. It requires perceptual discrimination and probably measures the ability to form and use concepts.

13. The Blind Learning Aptitude Test measures nonverbal cognitive ability of blind children from 6 to 16 years. It is a reliable and valid test that should be used in conjunction with a verbal test of cognitive ability.

14. The Hiskey-Nebraska Test of Learning Aptitude is a nonverbal scale designed for children ages 3 to 17 years. It has been used frequently with hearing-impaired children. The test has adequate reliability and validity, but the standardization group is poorly described. The WISC-R Performance Scale appears to be a more appropriate instrument for the assessment of hearing-impaired children.

15. Piagetian tests can supplement norm-referenced tests, providing additional understanding of the child's thinking processes.

16. The Bayley Scales of Infant Development is excellent for assessing infants. It covers the age period from 2 months to 2½ years of age. A Mental Scale, a Motor Scale, and an Infant Behavior Record are provided. It is a well standardized test.

17. Other infant assessment devices include the Gesell Developmental Schedule, the Cattell Infant Intelligence Test, Baby Behavior Questionnaire, Toddler Behavior Questionnaire, Apgar score, Rochester Obstetrical Scale, Neonatal Behavioral Assessment Scale, and the Infant Psychological Development Scale.

18. The issue of whether an age correction should be used in calculating Developmental Quotients and Deviation IQs for premature infants is still unresolved.

KEY TERMS, CONCEPTS, AND NAMES

McCarthy Scales of Children's Abilities (p. 295)
General Cognitive Index (GCI) (p. 295)
Kaufman Assessment Battery for Children (p. 300)
Sequential Processing Scale (K-ABC) (p. 301)
Simultaneous Processing Scale (K-ABC) (p. 301)
Detroit Tests of Learning Aptitude – 2 (p. 303)
Detroit Tests of Learning Aptitude – P (p. 305)
Extended Merrill-Palmer Scale (p. 306)
Slosson Intelligence Test (p. 308)
Raven's Progressive Matrices (p. 308)

Coloured Progressive Matrices (p. 309)
Standard Progressive Matrices (p. 309)
Advanced Progressive Matrices (p. 309)
Goodenough-Harris Drawing Test (p. 310)
Leiter International Performance Scale (p. 313)
Pictorial Test of Intelligence (p. 314)
Columbia Mental Maturity Scale (p. 315)
Blind Learning Aptitude Test (p. 316)
Hiskey-Nebraska Test of Learning Aptitude (p. 316)
Piagetian tests (p. 317)
Bayley Scales of Infant Development (p. 317)
Mental Developmental Index (p. 317)
Psychomotor Developmental Index (p. 317)
Infant Behavior Record (p. 317)
Apgar score (p. 321)
Rochester Obstetrical Scale (p. 321)
Neonatal Behavioral Assessment Scale (p. 321)
Infant Psychological Developmental Scale (p. 321)
Age correction for prematurity (p. 322)

STUDY QUESTIONS

Discuss the assets and limitations of the following tests.
1. The McCarthy Scales of Children's Abilities
2. The Kaufman Assessment Battery for Children
3. The Detroit Tests of Learning Aptitude—2
4. The Detroit Tests of Learning Aptitude—P
5. The Extended Merrill-Palmer Scale
6. The Slosson Intelligence Test
7. Raven's Progressive Matrices
8. The Goodenough-Harris Drawing Test
9. The Leiter International Performance Scale
10. The Pictorial Test of Intelligence
11. The Columbia Mental Maturity Scale
12. The Blind Learning Aptitude Test
13. The Hiskey-Nebraska Test of Learning Aptitude
14. Piagetian tests
15. The Bayley Scales of Infant Development
16. Informal infant assessment measures

ASSESSMENT OF ACADEMIC ACHIEVEMENT AND SPECIAL ABILITIES

Have you ever considered what the mere ability to read means? That it is the key which admits us to the whole world of thought and fancy and imagination? To the company of saint and sage, of the wisest and wittiest at their wisest and wittiest moment? That it enables us to see with the keenest eyes, hear with the finest ears, and listen to the sweetest voices of all time?

—James Russell Lowell

The assessment of academic achievement plays an important role in psychoeducational evaluations, which often are carried out in order to screen for learning disabilities, mental handicaps, or behavior disorders or to identify children for gifted programs or other academic referrals. It plays a lesser role in clinical evaluations. Included in this chapter are tests of reading, arithmetic, spelling, language processing and receptive vocabulary, auditory comprehension, developmental screening, divergent thinking, and the System of Multicultural Pluralistic Assessment, a system that attempts to integrate data obtained from a variety of sources. (Table C-68 provides percentile ranks for tests that have $M = 50$ and $SD = 10$ or 15. Appendix F presents the highlights of the tests covered in this and other chapters of the book.)

The academic achievement tests covered in this chapter are designed for individual administration. The many group-administered tests available for measuring academic achievement and reading skills (such as the California Achievement Test, Iowa Tests of Basic Skills, Metropolitan Achievement Tests, Stanford Achievement Test, Gates-MacGinitie Reading Tests, and Nelson Reading Skills Test) are not reviewed here because the focus of this text is on individual assessment. Nevertheless, these and other group-administered achievement tests at times deserve a place in the psychoeducational battery. They often provide a more thorough sampling of achievement than do individual screening achievement tests.

OBSERVATIONAL GUIDELINES AND ADMINISTRATIVE SUGGESTIONS FOR GIVING TESTS OF ACADEMIC ACHIEVEMENT AND SPECIAL ABILITIES

Observational Guidelines

As is emphasized throughout this text, it is important to carefully observe all aspects of a child's test performance. A thorough evaluation will consider not only whether the answers were right or wrong, but also what types of errors the child made and what type of response style the child used (see Chapter 5). Various guidelines are presented in Chapter 20 for observing and recording reading errors (Tables 20-2 and 20-4), writing style (Table 20-6), and spelling errors (Table 20-7). These guidelines are also applicable to observing a child's performance on tests of achievement. Exhibit 13-1 presents guidelines for observing and analyzing a child's performance on arithmetic tests.

Exhibit 13-1

Guidelines for Analyzing Children's Performance on Arithmetic Tests

1. Does the child use concrete counting aids (fingers, pencil marks, and so forth)?
2. Does the child confuse place values when writing numbers?
3. Does the child line up answers in the correct place?
4. Does the child carry the right number?
5. Does the child confuse arithmetic processes (for example, add when he or she should subtract)?
6. Does the child understand the written instructions?
7. Does the child attend to details?
8. Does the child reverse, invert, or transpose numbers?
9. Does the child use all the working space on the sheet?
10. Can the child easily shift from addition to subtraction problems?
11. Does the child give the same answer to different problems (perseverance)?
12. Does the child exhibit directional confusion by adding columns from left to right?

Guidelines for Administering Informal Reading Inventories

Informal reading inventories, whether prepared commercially or by teachers or clinicians, usually consist of graded word lists, graded passages, and comprehension questions for each passage. The *graded word lists* are used to determine which passages should be administered, to assess sight vocabulary for isolated words, and to provide some information about how the child figures out unknown words. The *graded passages* provide information about the child's understanding of words in context, attention to meaning, and strategies for coping with unfamiliar words. The *comprehension questions* sample the child's understanding at various levels. Children can read the material orally or silently or the examiner can read the material aloud, depending on the particular goal of the assessment.

Informal reading inventories usually allow for classification of four different levels of reading skill. These classifications are useful in selecting an appropriate level of reading material.

1. The *independent level* is the level at which the child can read without assistance.

2. The *instructional level* is the level at which the material is challenging for the child—neither too difficult nor too easy.

3. The *frustration level* is the level at which the child would find it frustrating to try to understand what he or she reads.

4. The *listening capacity*, or *potential*, *level* is the level at which the child is able to understand material that is read aloud to him or her.

In administering informal reading inventories, it is useful to make a tape recording of the child's reading of the passages. You can then listen to the tape later if there is some doubt about the accuracy of your scoring. The recording also enables you to better inform teachers and parents about the nature of a child's reading problems. Whenever there is any doubt about the scoring, the child's responses to comprehension questions should be written out for later review.

Other useful guidelines for administering informal reading inventories include the following:

• Examine the child's performance on all areas of the inventory to determine the highest instructional level permitting independent reading.

• Be attentive to any signs of frustration.

• Ask additional questions about passages when appropriate to gain further information about the child's comprehension.

• Make a list of responses that are as acceptable as the ones provided in the test manual.

Guidelines for Administering Multiple-Choice Picture Tests to Children with Severe Motor Handicaps

A modified procedure can be used to administer multiple-choice picture tests (such as the Peabody Picture Vocabulary Test—Revised) to children with severe speech and motor handicaps. When children cannot speak or point, the following "eyeblink" response procedure can be used:

1. Inform the child about the type of item that you are going to administer.

2. Show the child a sample item, and explain how it will be administered.

3. Tell the child that answers can be given by eyeblinks.

4. Show the child a card. Say the first word, and then say "I want you to tell me which picture shows _____. I'll point to each picture, and you blink your eyes once for no and twice for yes. Is it this one?" Point to the picture in the

Courtesy Herman Zielinski.

upper left-hand corner (as the child views it) and wait for the child's response. Then point to the upper right-hand corner, asking "Is it this one?" After the child responds, proceed to the lower left-hand drawing and then the lower right-hand drawing.

5. Record the answer on the answer sheet.

6. Continue using this same technique until the test is discontinued. To standardize the procedure, you must always point to all four pictures on a card in the prearranged order noted in step 4.

Guidelines for Administering Tests to Hard-of-Hearing Children

A modified procedure can also be used to administer picture tests to hard-of-hearing children who can read. The stimuli are shown individually on 3×5 cards, and the directions are pantomimed, as follows:

1. Point to the word on the sample 3×5 card.

2. Point to each of the pictures on the plate, shaking your head while pointing to the incorrect picture and nodding while pointing to the correct picture.

The child should easily grasp the idea of pointing.

WIDE RANGE ACHIEVEMENT TEST— REVISED

The Wide Range Achievement Test—Revised (WRAT-R) (Jastak & Wilkinson, 1984) is a brief, individually administered achievement test. It contains three subtests: Reading, Spelling, and Arithmetic. The Reading subtest measures the ability to recognize and name letters and pronounce words. The Spelling subtest measures the ability to copy marks resembling letters, write one's name, and write single words from dictation. The Arithmetic subtest measures skills such as counting, reading number symbols, solving oral problems, and performing written computations. The WRAT-R is concerned primarily with mastery of the mechanics of these three subject areas.

The WRAT was originally published in 1936. Revisions appeared in 1946, 1965, 1976, 1978, and 1984. For the 1984 revision, additional arithmetic items were added, as well as some precomputation items; otherwise the items in the revisions since 1965 are essentially the same.

The WRAT-R is divided into two sections: Level I for ages 5-0 to 11-11 and Level II for ages 12-0 to 74-11. The items in each subtest are arranged in ascending order of difficulty. The test is timed and takes approximately 20 to 30 minutes to administer.

Scores

All responses are scored 1 (correct) or 0 (incorrect). Raw scores can be converted into standard scores ($M = 100$, $SD = 15$, range of 46 to 155), T scores, scaled scores ($M = 10$, $SD = 3$), percentile ranks, stanines, and normal curve equivalents. Grade-equivalent scores are also provided for raw scores (beginning, middle, and end of grade for grades 1 and 2; beginning and end of grade for grades 3 through 12).

Standardization

The WRAT-R was standardized on a stratified national sample on the basis of age, sex, race, geographical region, and metropolitan/nonmetropolitan residence. The sample included 5,600 individuals, 200 in each of 28 age groups from 5 years, 0 months to 74 years, 11 months of age. An important stratification variable—socioeconomic status—was not used.

Reliability

Test-retest reliabilities on two samples of children ($N = 148$) who were between 7 and 10 years of age and between 13 and 16 years of age ranged from .94 to .96 for the 7- to 10-year-olds and from .79 to .90 for the 13- to 16-year-olds. The retest interval was not indicated. Arithmetic had the lowest reliability ($r_{xx} = .79$). Unfortunately, there are no reliability coefficients provided for the entire sample and no indices of internal consistency.

Table 13-1 shows the minimum difference required between scores on WRAT-R subtests for one to be considered significantly different from another for ages 7 to 10 and 13 to 16. This table is based on standard scores with $M = 100$ and $SD = 15$. Because the test-retest samples were poorly described, Table 13-1 should be viewed as tentative. Table 13-1 indicates that at the .05 level, a difference of either 8 or 9 standard score points is needed at ages 7 to 10 to conclude that two subtests differ significantly, whereas differences of between 14 and 17 points are needed at ages 13 to 16.

Validity

The construct validity of the WRAT-R is supported by increasing raw scores from age 5 through early adulthood. The manual indicates that correlations between the WRAT

Table 13-1
Significant Differences Between WRAT-R Subtest Scores ($M = 100$, $SD = 15$)

	Age 7-0 to 10-5				Age 13-0 to 16-5			
	Reading Subtest		Spelling Subtest		Reading Subtest		Spelling Subtest	
Subtest	.05	.01	.05	.01	.05	.01	.05	.01
Spelling	8	10	—	—	14	18	—	—
Arithmetic	8	12	9	11	16	22	17	22

Note. See Chapter 8, Exhibit 8-1 for an explanation of the method used to arrive at the required magnitude of differences.

and other achievement and ability tests are in the .60s to .80s. For a sample of adults, WRAT-R scores were found to be lower than WRAT scores by approximately 8 to 11 points (Spruill & Beck, 1986).

Comment on the Wide Range Achievement Test— Revised

The WRAT-R is an extremely popular screening test because it is quick and easy to administer, provides standard scores, and measures the three major achievement areas of word recognition, arithmetic, and spelling. The test does not measure reading comprehension or understanding of complex mathematical problems, however. Additionally, the manual provides no information about the socioeconomic distribution of the standardization sample, and reliability data are meager. Although no information is presented about the validity of the revised edition, research with prior editions indicates that the scale has acceptable validity. These limitations mean that the test should be used in a cautious manner and only for screening—not for diagnostic/placement decisions.

PEABODY INDIVIDUAL ACHIEVEMENT TEST

The Peabody Individual Achievement Test (PIAT) (Dunn & Markwardt, 1970) is an individually administered screening measure of achievement. It takes about 30 to 40 minutes to administer. The PIAT covers mathematics, reading recognition, reading comprehension, spelling, and general information for kindergarten through high school. The Mathematics, Reading Comprehension, and Spelling subtests have a multiple-choice format. The Reading Recognition subtest employs a combination of multiple-choice items and letters or names that the child reads aloud to the examiner. The General Information subtest requires oral answers only. Overall, half of the items use a multiple-choice pointing response format.

The general format of the test, the manual, and the record booklet are superior (Lyman, 1971). Although most of the test requires minimal training to administer, the Spelling and Reading Comprehension subtests require some administrative skill.

PIAT Subtests

A brief description of each subtest follows. The Mathematics subtest ranges from testing early skills of matching, discriminating, and recognizing numerals to measuring understanding of concepts in geometry and trigonometry. The Reading Recognition subtest requires matching letters of the alphabet with identical stimuli, naming individual letters, and reading individual words aloud. The Reading Comprehension subtest contains sentences that children are required to read silently, after which they select the best meaning of the sentence. The Spelling subtest requires the identification of printed letters and the correct spelling of words. The General Information subtest measures general knowledge of science, social studies, fine arts, and sports.

Scores

The PIAT provides grade equivalents, age equivalents, percentile ranks, and standard scores ($M = 100$, $SD = 15$) for the total test and for each of the five subtests.

Standardization

The standardization sample contained 2,889 male and female school children attending regular classrooms in public schools and living in nine geographic divisions in the United States. The sample generally conformed to the 1967 census data. There were approximately 200 children for each of the 13 grade levels, from kindergarten through grade 12.

Reliability

Median test-retest reliabilities, with retest intervals of one month, are .89 for Total Test, .74 for Mathematics, .88 for Reading Recognition, .64 for Reading Comprehension, .65 for Spelling, and .76 for General Information. The median standard error of measurement for the Total Test is 12; for the five subtests, the median standard errors of measurement range from 3.06 to 6.51. Satisfactory test-retest and split-half reliabilities for the scale also have been reported in other studies with samples of Anglo-American, Mexican-American, and handicapped children (Dean, 1977c; Lamanna & Ysseldyke, 1973; Naglieri & Pfeiffer, 1983b; Wilson & Spangler, 1974). Table C-61 in Appendix C shows the differences required for significance when each PIAT subtest score is compared to the mean PIAT score for any individual child.

Validity

The PIAT measures general achievement areas satisfactorily, as noted by concurrent validity studies with various achievement and ability tests in several different populations (Baum, 1975; Bray & Estes, 1975; Burns, Peterson, & Bauer, 1974; Davenport, 1976; Ollendick, Murphy, & Ollendick, 1975; Simpson & Eaves, 1983; Sitlington, 1970; Soethe, 1972; Wetter & French, 1973; Wilson & Spangler, 1974). PIAT scores should not be used interchangeably with WRAT-R scores or with other achievement test scores, however.

Studies of the WISC-R and the PIAT indicate that much overlap exists between the two tests (Bretzing, 1977; Dean, 1977b). The two tests share a verbal-educational factor. The WISC-R is the preferred test, but adding the two PIAT reading subtests to the assessment education battery enables one to obtain an estimate of the child's reading skills.

The PIAT appears to tap two factors (Reynolds, 1979; Wikoff, 1978). One factor, Verbal Comprehension and Reasoning Skills (or Word Recognition), is composed of the two reading subtests and the Spelling subtest. The second factor, Acquired Practical Knowledge (or School-related Knowledge), is composed of the Mathematics and General Information subtests.

Comment on the Peabody Individual Achievement Test

Although the item content for each of the five subtests seems appropriate and there are advantages to having an individually administered achievement test, the PIAT suffers in comparison to its group competitors in two respects: (a) reliability coefficients are somewhat low, and (b) it has no subtests for science, social studies, or study skills (Lyman, 1971). The PIAT is useful for locating a child's general level of achievement, after which a longer, more comprehensive achievement test should be administered. More confidence can be placed in the total score than in the subtest scores.

The multiple-choice pointing format on three of the five subtests makes it possible to obtain an achievement measure for language-impaired children who otherwise might be difficult to examine. Although the high concentration of items at lower levels adds to the discriminating power of the PIAT for children with limited academic skills, the norms need to be extended downward to increase the usefulness of the PIAT for educable mentally retarded children (Burns et al., 1974).

KAUFMAN TEST OF EDUCATIONAL ACHIEVEMENT

The Kaufman Test of Educational Achievement (K-TEA) (Kaufman & Kaufman, 1985) is an untimed, individually administered measure of school achievement for children ages 6 through 18 years. The K-TEA Comprehensive Form contains five subtests: Reading Decoding, Reading Comprehension, Mathematics Applications, Mathematics Computation, and Spelling. Testing time is approximately 1 hour for older children and somewhat less for younger children.

K-TEA Subtests

A brief description of the subtests follows.

The Reading Decoding subtest (60 items) measures the child's ability to identify letters and pronounce phonetic and nonphonetic words. The Reading Comprehension subtest (50 items) measures inferential and literal comprehension of paragraphs of varying lengths. One or two questions about the passage are shown to the examinee, who must respond either by gesture or orally. Items 1 through 8 require a gestural response, whereas items 9 through 50 require an oral response.

The Spelling subtest (50 items) measures spelling ability, using a list of words of increasing difficulty. Each word is both read aloud and used in a sentence. Although examinees generally write the words, those who cannot write can spell the words orally.

The Mathematics Applications subtest (60 items) assesses several arithmetic concepts, particularly as they relate to real-life situations. Questions are presented orally while at the same time the examinee is shown pictures or the questions themselves. The Mathematics Computation subtest (60 items) assesses skills in solving arithmetic word problems spanning the four basic arithmetical operations and complex computational abilities.

The K-TEA provides a systematic approach for evaluating errors on the five subtests. Items on the two mathematics subtests and the Reading Comprehension subtest are classified by the processes or skills they assess. Reading Decoding and Spelling are classified according to the orthographic characteristics (phonemic, morphemic, and syllabic components) of the words.

Scores

All items are scored 1 (correct) or 0 (incorrect). Raw scores are converted into standard scores ($M = 100$, $SD = 15$) for each subtest as well as for the Composite Score. Age-equivalent and grade-equivalent scores are provided for raw scores. Norms are given for both age and grade.

Standardization

The K-TEA was standardized on 1,409 children in the spring normative group and 1,067 children in the fall normative group. The sample was stratified on the basis of grade, sex, geographic region, socioeconomic status, and ethnicity to match U.S. census data for 1983 in four geographic regions.

Reliability

Split-half reliability coefficients for the Battery Composite are high ($M\ r_{xx} = .98$). The individual subtests show equally impressive split-half reliability coefficients ($M\ r_{xx}$'s range from .92 to .95). Test-retest reliability with a sample of 172 students (retest interval from 1 to 35 days) ranged from .83 (Mathematics Computation) to .96 (Spelling and Reading Decoding). An r_{xx} of .97 was reported for the Battery composite. Interrater reliability for the Reading Decoding and Spelling error analysis ranged from .65 to .85.

Validity

Concurrent validity was assessed by correlating the K-TEA with various achievement and ability tests, including the Wide Range Achievement Test, Peabody Individual Achievement Test, K-ABC, Peabody Picture Vocabulary Test – Revised, Stanford Achievement Test, Metropolitan Achievement Test, and Comprehensive Test of Basic Skills. Median coefficients are in the .60s to .80s with appropriate subtest comparisons. Increases in raw scores with grade level constitute evidence of construct validity.

Brief Form

The K-TEA is also available in a brief form that has completely different items. It is intended as a nonoverlapping form that can be administered in approximately 30 minutes. The Brief Form contains three subtests: Reading, Mathematics, and Spelling. Standard scores ($M = 100$, $SD = 15$) are provided for the subtests and the composite. Alternate form reliabilities for the Brief Form (correlations with the Comprehensive Form) range from .80 to .92.

Comment on the Kaufman Test of Educational Achievement

The Kaufman Test of Educational Achievement is a well-normed standardized individual test of educational achievement. It provides reliable and valid scores for the basic achievement areas covered in school and offers a procedure for evaluating examinee errors. This latter feature may cause difficulty for the average examiner, and the reliability and validity of the error analysis procedure are questionable. A breakdown of scores for the ethnic groups included in the standardization sample would be helpful. Overall, the K-TEA appears to be a useful instrument for the assessment of academic skills of children from 6 through 18 years of age.

BASIC ACHIEVEMENT SKILLS INDIVIDUAL SCREENER

The Basic Achievement Skills Individual Screener (BASIS) (The Psychological Corporation, 1983) is an individually administered measure of reading, mathematics, and spelling. An optional writing exercise is also included. The BASIS is designed for use with students in grades 1 through 12, as well as for post–high school use. The test can be administered in approximately 45 to 60 minutes.

BASIS Tests

The Reading Test, which assesses comprehension of graded passages, covers primer through eighth grade levels. The student reads passages aloud and supplies the missing word (or words) in the story (cloze technique). Two readiness subtests measure skills in reading individual words, reading sentences, letter identification, and visual discrimination.

The Mathematics Test contains items that measure addition, subtraction, multiplication, division, and use of fractions, decimals, percents, and exponents. Problems are presented on paper as well as by dictation. A readiness subtest measures understanding of basic number concepts.

The Spelling Test consists of six words at each grade level. The examiner reads the words individually and in a sentence, after which the student writes the word.

The Writing Test requires the student to write for 10 minutes about his or her favorite place.

Scores

Raw scores for the three basic tests are converted into standard scores ($M = 100$, $SD = 15$) as well as a variety of other derived scores, including percentile ranks, stanines, normal curve equivalents, age equivalents, and Rasch scaled scores. Additionally, criterion-referenced information is provided – grade-referenced placement scores – for clusters of test items that reflect the curriculum of specific grades. For the optional writing exercise, a three-point rating scale is used to evaluate the passage—below average, average, and above average. The rating is made by comparing the student's sample to average student papers. One sample is provided in the manual for each of grades 3 to 8, along with reading criteria (ideas, organization, vocabulary, sentence structure, and mechanics).

Grade norms are provided for the beginning and end of each school grade for grades 1 through 8 and for full school grades for grades 9 through 12 and post–high school. ("Beginning" and "full" school grade norms are best used in October of each year.) Percentile rank tables are provided for chronological ages 6 through 18 years. Special tables allow for conversion of percentile ranks to normal curve equivalents, standard scores, and Rasch scaled scores.

Standardization

The BASIS was standardized in the fall of 1982 on a sample of 3,296 students in grades 1 through 12 and a selected post–high school sample. The norm sample was selected on the basis of 1970 educational data with regard to geographic, socioeconomic, and ethnic representation. A total of 66 school systems from 23 states participated in the standardization.

Reliability

Internal consistency reliabilities for grades 1 through post–high school range from .84 to .95 ($Mdn\ r_{xx} = .94$) for the Reading Test, from .85 to .94 ($Mdn\ r_{xx} = .92$) for the Mathematics Test, and from .87 to .96 ($Mdn\ r_{xx} = .94$) for the Spelling Test. Similar high reliability coefficients are reported for age level. Test-retest reliability coefficients for three samples of children in grades 2 ($N = 60$), 5 ($N = 66$), and 8 ($N = 52$) ranged from .74 to .95 ($Mdn\ r_{xx} = .83$) for the three tests, with retest intervals of 2 to 4 weeks.

Validity

The construct validity of the BASIS is partially supported by increasing raw scores from ages 5 through 14. After age 14, however, there is little, if any, increase in raw scores on the three tests. Concurrent validity was evaluated in a number of ways. Correlations between BASIS raw scores and teacher grades range from .29 to .61 ($Mdn\ r = .44$) in grades 2 through 6. With standardized achievement tests, correlations range from .30 to .72 ($Mdn\ r = .63$) in grades

2 through 8. No validity data are reported for students in the standardization sample who were above the eighth grade. The percentage of students whose grade-referenced placement scores agreed with their actual grade placement levels ranged from 43 to 98 percent (Mdn percent agreement = 71 percent); with text level assignment, the percentage of agreement ranged from 54 to 97 percent (Mdn percent agreement = 84 percent). Special correlational studies are reported in the manual for samples of exceptional students. Correlations between the BASIS and various achievement tests ranged between .12 and .90 ($Mdn\ r = .58$).

Comment on the Basic Achievement Skills Individual Screener

The BASIS is a useful screening test for the assessment of reading, arithmetic, and spelling. The test is well standardized. The BASIS, however, has a number of limitations.

1. Scores reach a ceiling after the age of 14 years. Consequently, the test probably cannot identify older students with advanced skills.

2. There are no validity studies for students in high school and for those who have graduated from high school.

3. There are no interrater reliability studies for the Writing Test.

4. Reading comprehension is measured by a specialized cloze procedure, which may not be appropriate for those children who are not able to master the task requirements.

BASIS, consequently, is most useful for children between 6 and 14 years of age and for those children who grasp the cloze procedure. Reliability and validity are acceptable for ages 6 to 14 years. The test should be supplemented with measures of silent reading.

WOODCOCK-JOHNSON PSYCHO-EDUCATIONAL BATTERY

The Woodcock-Johnson Psycho-Educational Battery (Woodcock, 1977) is a comprehensive, individually administered set of 27 tests that assesses three areas of functioning: cognitive ability, achievement, and interest (see Table 13-2). The Tests of Cognitive Ability in Part I are composed of 12 subtests that cover vocabulary, spatial relations, memory, quantitative concepts, and concept formation. The Tests of Achievement in Part II cover 10 achievement areas, including reading, spelling, capitalization, punctuation, and knowledge of science, humanities,

Table 13-2
Subtest and Cluster Structure of the Woodcock-Johnson Psycho-Educational Battery

Part I: Tests of Cognitive Ability	*Part II. Tests of Achievement*
Subtests	**Subtests**
1. Picture Vocabulary	13. Letter-Word Identification
2. Spatial Relations	14. Word Attack
3. Memory for Sentences	15. Passage Comprehension
4. Visual-Auditory Learning	16. Calculation
5. Blending	17. Applied Problems
6. Quantitative Concepts	18. Dictation
7. Visual Matching	19. Proofing
8. Antonyms-Synonyms	20. Science
9. Analysis-Synthesis	21. Social Studies
10. Numbers Reversed	22. Humanities
11. Concept Formation	
12. Analogies	**Clusters (subtests in cluster)**
	Reading (13–15)
Clusters (subtests in cluster)	Mathematics (16–17)
Broad Cognitive—Full Scale (1–12)	Written Language (18–19)
Broad Cognitive—Preschool Scale (1–6)	Knowledge (20–22)
Broad Cognitive—Brief Scale (6–7)	Skills (13, 17–18)
Verbal Ability (1, 8–9)	
Reasoning (8–9, 11–12)	*Part III. Tests of Interest Level*
Perceptual Speed (2, 7)	
Memory (3, 10)	**Subtests**
Reading Aptitude (4–5, 8, 12)	23. Reading Interest
Math Aptitude (7–9, 11)	24. Math Interest
Written Language Aptitude (6–8, 10)	25. Written Language Interest
Knowledge Aptitude (3, 6, 8, 12)	26. Physical Interest
	27. Social Interest
	Clusters (subtests in cluster)
	Scholastic Interest (23–25)
	Nonscholastic Interest (26–27)

and social studies. The Tests of Interest Level in Part III cover five areas: interest in reading, mathematics, language, physical activities, and social activities.

Although the battery covers individuals from 3 years of age through adulthood, not all of the tests are administered at every age. At the preschool level, only 6 of the 12 cognitive ability tests and 5 of the 10 achievement tests are applicable. None of the five interest tests were designed for children below grade three. The entire battery can be administered in approximately 2 hours, with Part I taking about one hour; Part II, 30 to 40 minutes; and Part III, about 15 minutes.

The subtests are arranged in various combinations to form clusters of two or more subtests. The Perceptual Speech cluster contains 2 subtests, whereas the Full Scale cluster contains 12 subtests. The clusters are not independent of one another—the same subtests appear in more than one cluster. The Cognitive Ability subtests are grouped into 11 clusters, the Achievement subtests into 5 clusters, and the Interest Level subtests into 2 clusters.

Scores

On the Cognitive Ability Tests each cluster score can be converted into a percentile rank, which, in turn, can be converted into a standard score ($M = 100$, $SD = 15$ or $M = 50$, $SD = 10$). Grade-level scores are also provided for subtests and cluster scores.

A special score, termed the Relative Performance Index, is provided for the Full Scale, Preschool Scale, and Brief Scale clusters. This index indicates the percent of mastery predicted for an examinee when the reference group performs at a 90 percent level of success. For example, a 50/90 Relative Performance Index indicates that when the reference group shows 90 percent mastery, the examinee is likely to demonstrate only 50 percent mastery.

Two of the Cognitive Ability clusters — Verbal Ability and Reasoning — contain suppressor subtests with negative weights. (Suppressor subtests are subtests given negative weights to remove their influence from a cluster score. The weights are derived from multiple-regression procedures.) The negative weights produce some paradoxical scoring effects, particularly when a child has high or low scores on all of the subtests in a cluster or when the suppressor subtest score is much higher or lower than the scores on principal subtests in the cluster. To deal with these problems, Woodcock (1985) created two alternative clusters — Oral Language (Picture Vocabulary, Antonyms-Synonyms, Analogies) and Broad Reasoning (Analysis-Synthesis, Concept Formation, Analogies), eliminated the suppressor subtests, and equally weighted all subtests in these clusters. Mather and Burch (1986) advocate the use of these new clusters in the assessment of learning-disabled, mentally retarded, and gifted children.

On the Tests of Achievement and Tests of Interest Level, the cluster scores can be converted into percentile ranks and standard scores. Relative Performance Indices are provided for all of the achievement cluster scores, but not for the interest clusters.

The Woodcock-Johnson also provides an Achievement-Aptitude Profile, which is based on a comparison between the Tests of Cognitive Ability (aptitude) and the Tests of Achievement. The profile provides Relative Performance Indices for Reading, Mathematics, Written Language, and Knowledge. These indices are interpreted in the same manner as the Relative Performance Index for the Tests of Cognitive Ability.

Standardization

The battery was standardized on 4,732 persons from 3 through 80 years of age, living in 49 communities across the United States. The sample was carefully chosen to be representative of the population, as reflected by U.S. census data, with respect to gender, race, occupational status, geographical region, and community (urban, nonurban).

Reliability

Reliabilities (split-half or test-retest) range from .57 to .96 for the Cognitive Ability subtests. The Cognitive Ability cluster scores, the Tests of Achievement, and the Tests of Interest Level have reliabilities in the .80s and .90s.

A study (Breen, 1984) of the temporal stability of the Cognitive Ability subtests over 6 months in a sample of 57 learning-disabled children reported satisfactory reliability coefficients for the Full Scale ($r_{xx} = .84$) and Verbal Ability clusters ($r_{xx} = .87$), but unsatisfactory reliability for the Reasoning ($r_{xx} = .45$) and Perceptual Speed ($r_{xx} = .46$) clusters. Breen advised that the Cognitive Ability subtests be used for screening but not for decision-making purposes.

Validity

Several concurrent and predictive coefficients are reported in the manual, with various intelligence, ability, and achievement tests used as the criteria. Coefficients are satisfactory, ranging from the .40s to the .80s. Since the publication of the Woodcock-Johnson, numerous concurrent validity studies have been published. In 19 samples, correlations between the Broad Cognitive Ability Cluster and the WISC-R Full Scale ranged from .62 to .93, with a median $r = .77$ (McGrew, 1986). Other studies cited by McGrew (1986) indicate highly significant correlations between the Broad Cognitive Ability Cluster and measures of reading, mathematics, and language (r's range from .55 to .82).

Factor analyses do not support the validity of either the cognitive or the aptitude clusters. In the standardization sample only two primary factors were found: a Verbal factor and a Nonverbal/Visual-Spatial factor (McGrew, 1985). The Verbal factor was consistent across grades, whereas the Nonverbal/Visual-Spatial factor showed considerable variation. At the third and fifth grades, the Verbal factor accounted for almost 70 percent of the variance, whereas the Nonverbal/Visual-Spatial factor accounted for approximately 30 percent of the variance. Another factor analytic study (McGue, Shinn, & Ysseldyke, 1982) also provided little support for either the cognitive or the aptitude clusters in a sample of fourth-grade learning-disabled children.

In samples of academically handicapped (learning-disabled and educable mentally retarded) children, the Woodcock-Johnson Cognitive Abilities Full Scale yielded scores that were considerably *lower* than those yielded by the WISC-R (12 studies cited by McGrew, 1986, pp. 246–247). The mean difference between the two scales based on the median results from these 12 studies was found to be 9.1 points. These findings indicate that when learning-disabled children are assessed with the Woodcock-Johnson rather than the WISC-R, they are more at risk of being misclassified as non-learning-disabled. Because the significant discrepancy between scores on ability and achievement tests required for classification may not be obtained, use of the Woodcock-Johnson to measure cognitive abilities may result in a denial of educational services (see Chapter 20).

Comment on the Woodcock-Johnson Psycho-Educational Battery

There are some serious questions about the psycho-educational use of the Tests of Cognitive Ability on the Woodcock-Johnson Psycho-Educational Battery.

1. Factor analytic studies do not support the use of the various cluster scores. Additionally, the overlap of subtests in the various clusters means that the clusters are not independent.

2. The use of terms such as *aptitude*, *ability*, and *achievement* is confusing and possibly misleading: all test scores are best thought of as measures of a child's achievements. There is no evidence that the Woodcock-Johnson provides scores that differentially measure aptitude, ability, and achievement.

3. The Tests of Cognitive Ability appear to be heavily weighted in favor of subtests that measure academic achievement skills. The Full Scale cluster may underestimate the cognitive abilities of children with language handicaps. Scores on the Tests of Cognitive Ability, consequently, are not likely to provide the independent measure of ability needed for use in evaluating learning-disabled children. Decisions concerning eligibility are likely to be further clouded by use of the Woodcock-Johnson Cognitive Ability scores in an assessment battery.

4. The classifications provided by the Woodcock-Johnson Tests of Cognitive Ability differ from those obtained on the WISC-R. Cummings (1982) observed that the classifications provided by the Woodcock-Johnson Full Scale cluster change as a function of the examinee's chronological age or grade placement. The nonuniform classifications throughout the age levels covered by the scale are likely to cause confusion when children are reassessed with the scale.

5. In the Cognitive Ability cluster, subtest variability is considerable within the standardization group (Marston & Ysseldyke, 1984). Thus it is difficult to use subtest variability to guide interpretations.

6. The two clusters in the Cognitive Ability Scale with negative weights cause interpretive problems.

The Woodcock-Johnson Psycho-Educational Battery has some unique features not found in other cognitive and achievement tests. As with other scales, the overall cluster scores are more reliable than the subtest scores. Correlations with other tests indicate that both concurrent and predictive validity are adequate. Construct validity is not satisfactory for the Cognitive Ability cluster scores, however. The concerns raised above indicate that the Cognitive Ability Full Scale score should not be used as a replacement for other standardized measures of intelligence such as scores on the Wechsler Scales or Stanford-Binet Intelligence Scale: Fourth Edition. On the other hand, the Tests of Achievement appear to be useful in measuring achievement domains.

NEW SUCHER-ALLRED READING PLACEMENT INVENTORY

The New Sucher-Allred Reading Placement Inventory (Sucher & Allred, 1981), developed in 1968 and revised in 1973 and 1981, is an individually administered reading test that covers levels from primer through ninth grade. It is available in two forms. Both forms have a Word-Recognition Test and an Oral Reading Test. Administration time is approximately 20 minutes.

Word-Recognition Test

The Word-Recognition Test consists of 12 lists of words that cover primary through ninth-grade levels. The test is used to find a starting level for the Oral Reading Test and to determine word recognition achievement. The two lists used for the primer and first reader levels contain 15 words each. The remaining 10 lists contain 20 words each.

The test is begun at a level at which the child is unlikely to make errors. The child is encouraged to read each word quickly. Mispronunciations or hesitations longer than two seconds are recorded as errors. The child's instructional level is designated as the level at which four to eight word-recognition errors occur.

Oral Reading Test

The Oral Reading Test contains 12 reading selections that cover primer through ninth-grade levels. This test is designed to identify three reading levels: the independent level, the instructional level, and the frustration level.

Independent level.   At the independent level the child is able to read without aid and to answer comprehension questions. The performance criteria are 97 percent or better word recognition, 80 percent or better comprehension, few or no head movements, and good phrasing and expression in oral reading. This level is used as a guide in providing the child with appropriate independent reading materials.

Instructional level.   At the instructional level the child is developing new reading skills and vocabulary. Material at this level is challenging but not too difficult. The performance criteria are 92 to 96 percent word recognition, 60 to 79 percent comprehension, few or no head movements, and good phrasing and expression in oral reading. This level is used as a guide in providing the child with appropriate instructional materials.

Frustration level.   At the frustration level the child has difficulty in recognizing words or in comprehending much of what is read. The performance criteria are less than 92 percent word recognition, less than 60 percent comprehension, excessive head movements, finger pointing, labored and slow oral reading, tension, and frequent self-correction. This level is used as a guide to avoid giving the student reading material that is too difficult.

Administering the Oral Reading Test.   The Oral Reading Test is started at the level below the level of the Word-Recognition Test at which the student made four to five errors. The test is terminated when the child reaches the frustration level. Six types of word-recognition errors are scored: mispronunciation, nonpronunciation, omission of a word, insertion of a word, substitution of a word, and repetition of three or more words. Two other types of errors (self-corrections and poor phrasing) are recorded but not scored.

Scores

After the child reads a selection, five comprehension questions are administered. These questions cover the main idea (title), facts, sequence, inference, and critical thinking. A full error, a partial error, or no error is recorded for each question. A full error would be recorded if, for instance, the student did not respond to the question or gave an answer unrelated to the question. A key is provided that indicates the number of errors associated with each reading level.

Standardization Sample, Reliability, and Validity

No information on the test's norms, reliability, or validity is provided. Word frequencies in graded readers were used to

select the words in the Word-Recognition Test. For the Oral Reading Test special formulas were used to determine the readability of each selection.

Comment on the New Sucher-Allred Reading Placement Inventory

The New Sucher-Allred manual is easy to comprehend and the tests are easy to administer; however, there are a number of problems with the inventory.

1. Because no specific data are provided about the standardization sample, reliability, or validity, the psychometric properties of the test cannot be evaluated.
2. The test does not provide an in-depth assessment of reading difficulties.
3. The starting level of the Oral Reading Test may be too high, and no instructions are provided as to what the examiner should do if a child is at the frustration level on the first selection.
4. There are not enough reading selections at any one level to generate a reliable pattern of comprehension errors.
5. No silent reading selections are included. Although oral reading requirements are acceptable for the primary grades, silent reading becomes important at the upper grade levels.

Overall, the New Sucher-Allred may be viewed as a gross, informal measure of a child's reading ability. However, standardization, reliability, and validity data, more complete administrative procedures, and more complete scoring instructions are needed.

CLASSROOM READING INVENTORY

The Classroom Reading Inventory (5th edition, Silvaroli, 1986) is an individually administered, diagnostic reading inventory designed for *screening* students in grades 1 through 12 and adults. It takes approximately 15 minutes to administer. The inventory assists in placing children at their appropriate reading levels, in pinpointing particular reading problems, and in developing appropriate remedial instruction. There are three parts to the inventory: the Graded Word Lists, the Graded Oral Paragraphs, and the Graded Spelling Survey. Four forms are available—two alternate forms for the first through sixth grades, one for junior high school, and one for high school and adult levels.

Graded Word Lists

Each Graded Word List consists of a series of 20 words that the child reads aloud. They allow the examiner to identify specific word recognition errors and estimate a starting level for the Graded Oral Paragraphs.

Graded Oral Paragraphs

The Graded Oral Paragraphs are short selections that the child reads aloud. After the child has read a selection, three types of comprehension questions are asked: (a) factual (for example, "What was the name of the horse in the story?"), (b) vocabulary (for example, "What does the word 'grind' mean?"), and (c) inferential (for example, "Why is sky diving like being in a dream?").

Graded Spelling Survey

The Graded Spelling Survey consists of 10 words for each level from grades 1 through 6. This section of the inventory can be individually or group administered.

Scores

The two major areas in which the Graded Oral Paragraphs provides ratings are word recognition and comprehension. On each of the selections administered, the child's performance in each area is classified as being at one of three levels of proficiency. These results are then used to determine the child's overall independent reading level, instructional reading level, and frustration reading level. The independent level is the grade level at which the child reads comfortably. The instructional level is the one at which the child can read a textbook with a teacher's guidance at a 95 percent accuracy level in word recognition and at a 75 percent or better accuracy level in comprehension. The frustration level is the level beyond the instructional level, where comprehension of concepts and questions is poor.

Scoring the Graded Oral Paragraphs requires considerable judgment, because the list provided in the manual does not cover all possible responses. The Graded Word Lists are scored by calculating the percentage of words correctly read.

In addition to the above scores, a listening capacity level can be obtained. The examiner reads selections orally to determine whether the examinee can understand and discuss what was heard at levels above the instructional level obtained from the Graded Oral Paragraphs. The listening capacity level is the level at which the examinee can comprehend 75 percent of the material read to him or her.

Standardization, Reliability, and Validity

The manual provides no data about the standardization sample, reliability, or validity. Various techniques were used by Silvaroli to obtain readability levels. One study (Johns, 1975), however, does report satisfactory validity for an earlier edition of the Classroom Reading Inventory, with the Gates-MacGinitie Reading Test used as the criterion (correlations between .70 and .80 for a sample of fourth-grade children).

Comment on the Classroom Reading Inventory

The major limitations of the Classroom Reading Inventory are its failure to provide reliability, validity, and normative information. Minor difficulties are that some of a child's deficiencies may go unnoticed because there are only five comprehension questions for each selection, the test does not tap higher-level thinking abilities, and there are no silent reading passages. Overall, the Classroom Reading Inventory may be useful as an *informal* measure to provide information about children's reading levels, word recognition, and reading comprehension abilities.

KEYMATH DIAGNOSTIC ARITHMETIC TEST

The KeyMath Diagnostic Arithmetic Test is an untimed, individually administered diagnostic test that assesses mathematical skills (Connolly, Nachtman, & Pritchett, 1971). It contains 14 subtests classified into the following three major areas: content, operations, and applications. The test is used primarily in the first through sixth grades, but there is no upper limit on clinical or remedial use. The content area measures knowledge of basic mathematical concepts (such as numeration, fractions, geometry, and symbols) that are necessary to perform mathematical operations and to make meaningful mathematical applications. The mathematical operations area covers computational processes (addition, subtraction, multiplication, and division), mental computation, and numerical reasoning. The applications area contains problems involving the use of mathematical processes in everyday life. Administration time is approximately 30 minutes.

Scores

Scores are provided for four diagnostic levels—total test performance, area performance, subtest performance, and item performance. Total test performance is described by a grade-equivalent score. Area performance indicates the child's strengths and weaknesses in content, operations, and applications. Subtest performance describes relative performance on the 14 subtests. The manual provides no information that would allow the user to determine whether there are significant discrepancies between subtest scores. Item performance provides information about the child's performance on each item. Criterion-referenced information is available from an appendix in the manual that gives the behavioral objective of each item in the test.

Standardization

The 1,222 children in the standardization sample ranged in grade level from kindergarten through seventh grade and lived in 21 school districts in eight states. They came from a wide range of urban, suburban, and rural settings and from varied ethnic backgrounds. The sample was weighted to conform to race and community size based on 1970 U.S. census data.

Reliability

The reliability of the KeyMath total score is satisfactory, as evidenced by a median split-half reliability coefficient of .96 for a sample of 934 children in kindergarten through seventh grade. Subtest reliabilities are substantially lower, with median reliabilities ranging from .64 to .84. The median standard error of measurement is 3.3 for the total score and .60 to 1.3 for the subtest scores.

Validity

Validity information about the KeyMath is limited. A correlation of .63 has been reported between the KeyMath and the Metropolitan Achievement Test for a sample of children with learning disabilities (Kratochwill & Demuth, 1976). A factor analysis (Greenstein & Strain, 1977) of the KeyMath with a sample of adolescents with learning disabilities established two factors: Operations and Applications. The content items were assimilated into these two areas.

The KeyMath has been found to be a satisfactory screening instrument for assessing strengths and weaknesses of educable mentally retarded children in general mathematics (Goodstein, Kahn, & Cawley, 1976). Because there are too few items at the middle range of difficulty, however, the test may not provide sufficient diagnostic information to affect programming decisions for children whose difficulties lie in this range. The KeyMath also has been found to discriminate between the performances of learning-disabled and normal children (Greenstein & Strain, 1977).

Comment on the KeyMath Diagnostic Arithmetic Test

The KeyMath test provides useful information that can guide teachers in the selection of appropriate procedures for remediation of arithmetic deficiencies. The broad range and diversity of item content and the absence of reading and writing requirements make the KeyMath attractive for use with exceptional children. There does not appear to be sufficient item coverage to pinpoint deficiencies within specific domains, however. Furthermore, in some domains the item coverage is so uneven across grade levels that passing one additional item is all that differentiates a score at grade level from one below grade level. If these caveats are kept in mind, the KeyMath appears to be a useful addition to the clinician's assessment battery for working with children in the elementary school grades.

SEQUENTIAL ASSESSMENT OF MATHEMATICS INVENTORIES

The Sequential Assessment of Mathematics Inventories (SAMI) (Reisman, 1985) is designed to measure the mathematical ability of children in kindergarten through eighth grade. The SAMI is individually administered in 20 to 60 minutes. It covers the following eight strands of mathematics: Mathematical Language, Ordinality, Number and Notation, Computation, Measurement, Geometric Concepts, Mathematical Applications, and Word Problems. Sample questions are shown in Table 13-3.

Scores

Raw scores for the total test are converted into standard scores ($M = 100$, $SD = 15$), percentile ranks, stanines, normal curve equivalents, and grade equivalents. Standard scores ($M = 10$, $SD = 3$) are also provided for the subtests.

Standardization

The SAMI was standardized on a nationally stratified sample of 1,456 children who came from six states and represented each of the four major regions in the United States.

" I THOUGHT THIS IS WHAT WE HAVE COMPUTERS FOR ! "

Reprinted by permission of the Chicago Tribune–New York News Syndicate, Inc.

Reliability

Test-retest reliability coefficients over a period of six weeks for children in grades 3, 5, and 8 were as follows: r_{xx} = .89, .84, and .78, respectively. Internal consistency reliability coefficients are excellent for the total score (.93 to .98) and satisfactory for all of the subtests, with the exception of Mathematical Language for kindergarten to third grade. (The r_{xx} for Mathematical Language for kindergarten to third grade is .37, whereas the other subtest reliabilities range from .73 to .96.) The standard errors of measurement for the total scores range between 3.9 and 4.6 for the grade levels covered by the scale.

Table 13-3
Sample Items on the Sequential Assessment of Mathematics Inventories (SAMI)

Strand	Problem
Mathematical Language	Point to the picture that has objects that are all similar.
Ordinality	Say the number that comes just before 25.
Number and Notation	Tell the number of chairs at the table.
Computation	752 + 175
Measurement	Point to the tallest building.
Geometric Concepts	Point to the closed figure.
Mathematical Applications	Tell the average of 8, 6, and 3.
Word Problems	Jack bought 6 cars. He gave 5 away. How many does he have left?

Validity

The content validity of the SAMI is satisfactory, as the test samples the essential components of the elementary school mathematics curriculum. Construct validity was established by moderate intercorrelations among the subtests (range of .26 to .74). Criterion-related validity is acceptable, as shown by high correlations between the SAMI and other mathematical achievement tests (r's of .46 to .92).

Comment on the Sequential Assessment of Mathematics Inventories

The Sequential Assessment of Mathematics Inventories is a well standardized test of achievement for elementary grade children. Norm tables based on children's ages in six-month increments would be a valuable addition. Separate subtest norms based on the eight strands of mathematics covered in the SAMI are a useful feature of the scale.

BOEHM TEST OF BASIC CONCEPTS— REVISED

The Boehm Test of Basic Concepts—Revised (BTBC-R) (Boehm, 1986b) is a pictorial multiple-choice test designed to measure knowledge of various concepts (such as direction, amount, and time) that are thought to be necessary for achievement in the first few years of school. An earlier version of the test was published in 1971. The BTBC-R is a screening and teaching instrument and is not intended as a measure of mental ability. The test can be individually or group administered. There are two forms (C and D), each containing 50 picture items arranged in increasing order of difficulty. For each item, the child selects one picture from a set of three, based on a statement read by the examiner. For example, one item is "Look at the trees; mark the tree on the left." Items cover concepts of relative relationships, such as space (next to, farthest), quantity (few, most), and time (always, after).

The revised version of the test contains relatively minor changes. Seven new items were added, four items moved downward, two deleted, and one divided into two items; some artwork also was modified.

The test is intended for use in kindergarten through second grade and takes approximately 30 minutes to administer.

Scores

Raw scores are converted into percentile ranks and normal curve equivalents. Norms are provided by grade level, SES level, and beginning and end of the school year. Tables also show the percentage of children passing each item by grade level, SES level, and beginning and end of the school year.

Standardization

The two forms were administered to children in kindergarten, first, or second grade at the beginning of the school year and at the end of the school year. For Form C, 5,577 children were tested at the beginning of the school year and 5,326 at the end of the school year. School children in 19 cities across the Northeast, Midwest, Southwest, and West participated in the standardization. The overall sample was weighted to match national school enrollment data published in 1978 and 1981 with respect to district size and region.

Children were classified into three socioeconomic levels on the basis of the percentage of children eligible for subsidized lunches in the school. High SES schools had no more than 10 percent of the children eligible for subsidized lunches, middle SES schools had percentages ranging from 11 to 50 percent, and low SES schools had percentages exceeding 50 percent. This is a somewhat crude method of identifying SES.

Reliability

Split-half reliability coefficients for Form C range from .55 to .85 (Mdn r_{xx} = .82). The higher coefficients are generally for the kindergarten children. For Form D, split-half reliability coefficients range from .57 to .87 (Mdn r_{xx} = .82). Test-retest reliabilities for samples of 63 to 111 children, with a retest interval of approximately 1 week, ranged from .75 to .88 (Mdn r_{xx} = .83). Correlations between the two forms are somewhat low (r's of .82, .77, and .65 in kindergarten, grade 1, and grade 2, respectively) in samples of approximately 200 children.

Validity

The manual reports several predictive validity studies for Forms C and D, with sample sizes ranging from 56 to 223 children in kindergarten, grade 1, and grade 2. Criterion tests used included the Comprehensive Test of Basic Skills, California Achievement Test, and Iowa Test of Basic Skills. For Form C, correlations ranged from .38 to .58 (Mdn r = .52). For Form D, they ranged from .43 to .64 (Mdn r = .50). These coefficients indicate that the Boehm-R has satisfactory predictive validity. Face validity of the Boehm-R is good, as items appear to tap understanding of concepts that children need to know for school.

Validity studies with the earlier edition also are useful in evaluating the validity of the revised version, because the two versions are highly similar (r's of .62 and .64 for the two forms) (Boehm, 1986b). These studies report that the Boehm has acceptable concurrent validity (.84 with the PPVT; .21 to .54 with various McCarthy Scales subtests; .74 with the Test of Auditory Comprehension of Language) and acceptable predictive validity (.54 and .72 with Spelling and Language tests of the Stanford Achievement Test; .27 to .72 with the Reading, Listening, Work Analysis, and Mathematics tests of the Cooperative Primary Tests; .54 with the SRA Achievement Test) (Beech, 1981; Herman, Huesing, Levett, & Boehm, 1973; Hutcherson, 1978; Piersel & McAndrews, 1982; Steinbauer & Heller, 1978).

Language comprehension seems to be a key factor underlying the test. The child must interpret the structure and form of the syntax in the verbal statement given by the examiner and identify the pictured stimulus correctly. A factor analysis of the 1971 edition yielded one large factor, which appears to suggest that the Boehm-R measures acquisition of basic verbal concepts rather than acquisition of understanding of specific dimensions such as space, quantity, or time (Piersel & Reynolds, 1981).

Boehm Test of Basic Concepts—Preschool Version

A downward extension of the Boehm-R is also available—the Boehm Test of Basic Concepts—Preschool Version (BTBC-PV) (Boehm, 1986a). The Boehm-Preschool contains 26 relational concepts—such as size (tallest), direction (up), position in space (under), quantity (many), and time (after)—considered necessary for achievement in the beginning years of school. The test is designed for children from 3 to 5 years of age and takes approximately 15 minutes to administer.

Like the Boehm-R, the Boehm-Preschool is a pictorial multiple-choice test in which the child points to one of three pictures, based on a statement read by the examiner. Unlike the Boehm-R, however, the Boehm-Preschool is only individually administered. The 26 concepts are distributed among 52 items. Pictures are clearly drawn and readily identifiable.

Raw scores are converted into percentile ranks or T scores ($M = 50$, $SD = 10$). Norms are provided for five age levels from 3 to 5 years. The standardization group consisted of 433 children drawn from the four major regions of the United States. Sample characteristics closely matched 1980 census data. Parents' educational level was used to determine socioeconomic status. Internal consistency reliabilities are satisfactory—alpha coefficients range from .85 to .91 ($Mdn\ r_{xx} = .87$), and split-half coefficients range from .80 to .87 ($Mdn\ r_{xx} = .86$). Test-retest reliabilities for two samples of children (N's of 44 and 34) retested after an interval of 7 to 10 days were satisfactory (r_{xx}'s of .94 and .87). Concurrent validity was established by correlating the Boehm-Preschool with the Peabody Picture Vocabulary Test—Revised. Correlations were .63 with Form L of the PPVT-R and .57 with Form M. The first correlation was based on a sample of 29 preschool children (M age = 3-10), and the second on a sample of 19 language-delayed children (M age = 4-4).

Comment on the Boehm Test of Basic Concepts— Revised and the Boehm Test of Basic Concepts— Preschool Version

The Boehm-R provides useful information about children's knowledge of certain basic concepts. Poor performance on the Boehm-R may be related to inability to (a) focus on key words in the directions, (b) understand the complex directions, (c) visualize spatially, (d) label or understand word meanings, (e) deal with abstractions, (f) understand negative concepts, or (g) recall sentences adequately in short-term memory (Spector, 1979). Although it is difficult to determine which explanation best accounts for a particular child's failures, an attempt should be made to do so. Children with low Boehm-R scores should be evaluated further, especially to determine their general level of cognitive ability.

A useful addition to the manual would be the provision of standard scores. The Boehm-R appears to have accept-

able validity but only minimally adequate reliability; it should be used with caution. The Boehm-Preschool appears to be a useful downward extension of the test, but more information is needed to evaluate its validity. A particularly noteworthy feature is the testing of each concept twice.

BRACKEN BASIC CONCEPT SCALE

The Bracken Basic Concept Scale (BBCS) (Bracken, 1984) is an individually administered cognitive test designed to assess basic knowledge of general concepts that most children acquire during preschool and early elementary school years. Concepts covered include color, letters, numbers, comparisons, shapes, direction, social/emotional connotations, size, texture, quantity, and time. The BBCS includes a Diagnostic Test covering the entire age range of the scale—from 2-6 to 8-0 years—and a Screening Test appropriate for children from age 5-0 to age 7-0. The Diagnostic Test measures the child's general range of concepts, whereas the Screening Test (which has two alternate forms) is a briefer screening measure.

The Diagnostic Test contains 258 items. The stimuli consist of four pictures on a plate, three of which are distractor items. The child is asked to name or point to the correct picture. Pictures were designed to be familiar to children across a broad range of ethnic and socioeconomic backgrounds. The Diagnostic Test contains 11 subtests (see Table 13-4) and requires approximately 30 minutes to administer. Each form of the Screening Test contains 30 items and takes approximately 10 minutes to administer.

Scores

Standard scores ($M = 100$, $SD = 15$), percentile ranks, normal curve equivalents, and stanines are provided for the Diagnostic Test, based on the entire 11-subtest battery. A School Readiness Composite is also provided; it is based on the first five subtests. This composite serves as a guide for determining a child's mastery of concepts needed to begin school; it is not intended for use as a predictor of scholastic success. Separate standard scores ($M = 10$, $SD = 3$) are provided for subtests 6 through 11. The Screening Test also provides standard scores ($M = 100$, $SD = 15$).

Standardization

The standardization sample for the Diagnostic Test consisted of 1,109 children stratified by geographic region,

Table 13-4
Description of Subtests in the Bracken Basic Concept Scale (BBCS)

	Subtest	Description
I	Colors	Measures child's knowledge of color terms.
II	Letter Identification	Measures child's knowledge of upper- and lower-case letters.
III	Numbers/Counting	Measures child's understanding of the numbers 1 through 9.
IV	Comparisons	Measures child's ability to match objects.
V	Shapes	Measures child's knowledge of shapes.
VI	Direction/Position	Measures child's understanding of relational terms describing location.
VII	Social/Emotional	Measures child's comprehension of terms describing kinship, gender, relative ages, and social appropriateness.
VIII	Size	Measures child's understanding of size.
IX	Texture/Material	Measures child's knowledge of concepts that describe the salient characteristics of an object.
X	Quantity	Measures child's understanding of quantitative concepts.
XI	Time/Sequence	Measures child's understanding of events along a temporal/sequential continuum.

sex, and ethnic background following the 1980 U.S. census figures. For the Screening Test, a standardization sample of 850 children was used.

Reliability

Split-half reliability coefficients are excellent for the Diagnostic Test total score (r_{xx}'s from .94 to .98). They are less satisfactory for the subtests, however (r_{xx}'s from .47 to .96). Alternate-form reliability of the Screening Test is low in some age groups (r's from .71 to .80), as are internal consistency reliabilities (r's from .76 to .80). Correlations between Form A and Form B of the Screening Test and between these forms and the Diagnostic Test are somewhat low (r's from .60 to .64).

Validity

Acceptable validity coefficients are reported with the Boehm Test of Basic Concepts (r's of .78 to .88), the Peabody Picture Vocabulary Test—Revised (r's of .74 to .84), and the Token Test for Children ($r = .68$).

Comment on the Bracken Basic Concept Scale

The Bracken Basic Concept Scale is a well-standardized test that measures mastery of basic concepts learned during preschool and early elementary school years. The overall score on the Diagnostic Test appears to be the most reliable score in the battery. Reliabilities are not as satisfactory for the subtests or the Screening Test. The pictures shown in the BBCS are line drawings; it would have been more interesting for young children to have real-life photographs as test stimuli. A factor analysis would be helpful in identifying the factors measured by the scale.

ILLINOIS TEST OF PSYCHOLINGUISTIC ABILITIES

The Illinois Test of Psycholinguistic Abilities (ITPA) (Kirk, McCarthy, & Kirk, 1968) is designed to assess verbal and nonverbal psycholinguistic ability. It is an individually administered test used with children between 2-4 and 10-3 years of age. There are 12 subtests, two of which are supplementary (see Table 13-5). The test was constructed in accordance with Osgood's (1957) psycholinguistic model.

The test is divided into two levels of organization, the representational level and the automatic level. The *representational level* focuses on language symbols and includes subtests that measure auditory and visual reception, auditory and visual association, and verbal and manual expression. The *automatic level* focuses on highly organized and integrated habitual patterns of retention and retrieval of language. Subtests included in this level are auditory, grammatical, and visual closure; sound blending; and auditory and visual sequential memory. The battery takes about 1 hour to administer.

Scores

The ITPA provides three scores: (a) scaled scores for each subtest, with a mean of 36 and a standard deviation of 6, (b) psycholinguistic ages, and (c) a psycholinguistic quotient. The psycholinguistic quotient is derived by dividing

Table 13-5
Description of Illinois Test of Psycholinguistic Abilities (ITPA) Subtests

Subtest	Description
Auditory Reception	Measures ability to understand spoken words. Example: "Do chairs eat?"
Visual Reception	Measures ability to gain meaning from familiar pictures. Example: Match picture stimulus with picture from same category.
Auditory Association	Measures ability to relate concepts presented orally. Example: Verbal-analogies test (e.g., "Grass is green, sugar is _____."
Visual Association	Measures ability to relate concepts presented visually. Example: Relate a pictorial stimulus to its conceptual counterpart (e.g., bone goes with dog).
Verbal Expression	Measures ability to express concepts verbally. Example: Describe common objects verbally.
Manual Expression	Measures ability to demonstrate knowledge of the use of objects pictured. Example: Express an idea with gestures (e.g., "Show me what to do with a hammer").
Grammatic Closure	Measures ability to use proper grammatical forms to complete statement. Example: "Here is a dog. Here are two _____."
Visual Closure	Measures ability to identify common objects from an incomplete visual presentation. Example: Locating specific objects in a scene filled with distracting stimuli.
Auditory Sequential Memory	Measures ability to reproduce orally a sequence of digits from memory. Example: Repeating digits.
Visual Sequential Memory	Measures ability to reproduce sequences of geometrical forms from memory. Example: Placing geometric shapes in proper sequence from memory.
Auditory Closure	Measures ability to complete a word when only fragments of it are orally presented. Example: "Listen. Tell me who I am talking about. DA / Y. Who is that?"
Sound Blending	Measures ability to synthesize into words syllables spoken at half-second intervals. Example: "What word is D−OG?"

Note. The two supplementary subtests are Auditory Closure and Sound Blending.

psycholinguistic age by chronological age and multiplying by 100. Unfortunately, the psycholinguistic quotient and psycholinguistic ages do not have consistent variances at each age level of the scale.

Standardization

The ITPA was standardized on 962 boys and girls with normal intelligence, ages 2-7 to 10-1 years, living in five predominantly middle-class Midwestern communities. Fathers' occupations closely matched those of the population as reflected in the 1960 U.S. census data.

Reliability

Internal consistency reliabilities range from .67 to .95 for the 10 principal subtests (Paraskevopoulos & Kirk, 1969). Test-retest reliabilities, at 5- to 6-month intervals, range between .28 and .90 for the 10 principal subtests for samples of 4- to 6-year-old children. Other test-retest reliabilities have been reported, ranging from .70 to above .90 for normal children at an interval of 3 months (Wisland & Many, 1967) and .95 for mentally retarded children at an

interval of 1 year (Hubschman, Polizzotto, & Kaliski, 1970). Ysseldyke and Sabatino (1972) published a table that provides the differences between subtest scores significant at the .05 and .01 levels of confidence.

Validity

Newcomer and Hammill (1975) surveyed 28 studies that investigated the concurrent validity of the ITPA, using a variety of achievement tests as criteria. Median subtest correlations ranged from nonsignificant to significant (below .21 to .42), whereas median total score correlations ranged from .30 to .51. Highly significant correlations have been found between the ITPA and various measures of intelligence (Huizinga, 1973; Kirk & Kirk, 1978; Taddonio, 1973).

Factor analytic studies report varied findings (Belford & Blumberg, 1975; Burns & Watson, 1973; Meyers, 1969; Ramanaiah, O'Donnell, & Adams, 1978; Sedlak & Weener, 1973; Wisland & Many, 1969). In general, three major factors have been found: Verbal Comprehension, Vocal-Motor Expression, and Meaningful Figural Comprehension. There is little, if any, evidence that the ITPA measures 10 independent areas.

Comment on the ITPA

The ITPA has been criticized for having an inadequate normative sample, using incorrect reliability procedures, having a middle-class emphasis in speech patterns, and being of limited utility in the design of effective educational remediations (Burns, 1976, 1977; Carroll, 1972; Lumsden, 1978; Waugh, 1978; Wiederholt, 1978). Silverstein (1978) wonders whether the test is anything more than another individual test of general intelligence. However, the test's breakdown of different aspects of linguistic functioning into comprehension (decoding) and production (encoding) appears to be potentially valuable, as does the distinction between input and output channels involved in the communication process. Overall the ITPA appears to have limited use in a psychoeducational assessment battery.

TEST OF AUDITORY COMPREHENSION OF LANGUAGE—REVISED

The Test of Auditory Comprehension of Language—Revised (TACL-R) (Carrow-Woolfolk, 1985) is an individually administered test of auditory comprehension (or receptive language functioning) designed for children between 3-0 and 9-11 years of age. The TACL-R, originally published in 1971, contains three sections—Word Classes and Relations, Grammatical Morphemes, and Elaborated Sentences. Table 13-6 shows the types of items found in each section. For each item the examiner presents a test plate containing three pictures (one is the correct picture and two are contrasting linguistic forms or decoys) and

says a stimulus word or sentence. The examinee is required to point to the correct picture.

Within each section, the items are arranged in order of ascending difficulty. Basal and ceiling rules help to minimize administration time (approximately 5 to 15 minutes) and examinee fatigue. To aid clinicians in analyzing errors, a chart in the manual shows the grammatical structures measured by each item.

TACL-R Subtests

A brief description of each section follows.

Word Classes and Relations contains 40 items composed of nouns, verbs, modifiers, and word relations. The items are thought to measure mastery of vocabulary and concepts needed by children in preschool, kindergarten, and elementary grades.

Grammatical Morphemes contains 40 items composed of short, simple sentences that measure grammatical morphemes, including prepositions, pronouns, noun inflections, verb inflections, noun-verb agreement, and derivational suffixes.

Elaborated Sentences contains 40 items composed of complex sentences that vary on a number of dimensions. Included are sentences with interrogatives; active and passive voice; direct and indirect objects; and coordination, subordination, and embedding of contextual elements.

Scores

The total and section raw scores can be converted into age scores, grade-level scores, T scores, Deviation Quotients ($M = 100$, $SD = 15$), normal curve equivalents, and percentile ranks. Norms are in half-year increments for ages 3 to 6 years and in one-year increments for ages 6 to 9 years.

Table 13-6
Example of Items on the Test of Auditory Comprehension of Language—Revised (TACL-R)

Word Classes and Relations	Grammatical Morphemes	Elaborated Sentences
boy	The cat is on the box.	Who is by the chair?
down	The ball is under the spoon.	She wouldn't ride on the clown's donkey.
a large red ball	Show me the tallest man.	The girl is chased by the dog.
slow	She is pointing at the book.	She couldn't reach it although she was tall.
many	They swim.	Neither the girl nor the boy is running.
old	She would have skipped.	The firefighter the waitress with the black cap served was holding some tea.

Note. These items are similar to those on the TACL-R, but are not actually from the test. The child is asked to point to a picture that relates to the word or words.

Standardization

The standardization sample contained 1,003 children selected to correspond to 1981 U.S. census data. A stratified random sampling procedure was used. Stratification variables included family occupation, ethnic origin, age, sex, community size, and geographical distribution.

Reliability

Split-half reliabilities are presented for each section for the 10 age groups and for the total score. The split-half reliability is .94 for Word Classes and Relations (range of .73 to .95), .94 for Grammatical Morphemes (range of .82 to .95), .95 for Elaborated Sentences (range of .86 to .96), and .97 for the total score (range of .88 to .97). For a sample of 100 children retested three to four weeks following the first administration, test-retest reliabilities were .89 to .91 for the three sections and .95 for the total score.

Validity

Extensive theoretical and logical analysis of language-skill development indicates satisfactory content validity. Construct validity was demonstrated by showing that scores increase with age and that items increase in difficulty from Words and Classes to Elaborated Sentences. Also, the TACL-R discriminates between normal and language-impaired groups.

Concurrent validity appears to be satisfactory, as shown by significant correlations between the TACL-R and tests such as the ITPA (r's of .37 to .73), PPVT ($r = .68$), Sequenced Inventory of Communication Development (r's = .73 and .76), and Stanford-Binet: Form L-M ($r = .55$). Except for the TACL-R/PPVT sample ($N = 168$), however, these correlations are based on extremely small sample sizes (N's of 11 to 21).

Performance on the TACL-R relates to perceptual discrimination skills as well as skills in analyzing the stimulus pictures. Impulsive children may obtain lower scores if they fail to look at each picture carefully. Children with attention difficulties may perform poorly if they fail to attend to the wording of each item. Consequently, scores for some children may not be a reflection of language competency per se.

Comment on the Test of Auditory Comprehension of Language — Revised

The Test of Auditory Comprehension of Language — Revised appears to be a well-standardized test of receptive language functioning. It is well normed. Reliabilities are excellent for the total score, but are less adequate for the section scores at some ages. More information about the validity of the scale is needed, especially about construct validity. For highly distractible children the test may not give an accurate estimate of receptive language functioning. The test also may not be suitable for children who speak in dialects that differ from standard English. The TACL-R must be supplemented with tasks that measure the child's expressive language in order to obtain a well-rounded picture of the child's language ability. The error analysis procedure is helpful in establishing specific language areas in need of improvement. The TACL-R is a useful language assessment instrument.

PEABODY PICTURE VOCABULARY TEST—REVISED

The Peabody Picture Vocabulary Test — Revised (PPVT-R) (Dunn & Dunn, 1981) was originally developed in 1959 and was revised in 1981. It is a nonverbal, multiple-choice test designed to evaluate the hearing vocabulary or receptive knowledge of vocabulary of children and adults. It covers individuals from age 2½ years through adulthood. The test is untimed and requires no reading ability. The physical abilities required of examinees are adequate hearing and the ability to indicate yes or no in some manner. Neither a pointing nor an oral response is essential. Testing time is between 10 and 15 minutes.

Of the 300 items in the 1959 edition, 111 (37 percent) are included in the 1981 edition. Item analysis procedures were used to select new items for the revision. Words were selected so as to include a relatively good balance of nouns, gerunds, and modifiers in 19 content categories. Items favoring one sex were eliminated entirely or counterbalanced by adding items favoring the opposite sex. Words from the earlier edition that were found to be culturally, regionally, or racially biased were not included in the revision. The manual does not, however, describe the basis for item elimination.

The PPVT-R has two forms, L and M, with 175 plates in each form. Each plate contains four pictures. Items are arranged in increasing levels of difficulty. The two forms use different words and pictures. The pictures are clearly drawn, free of fine detail, and pose no figure-ground problems. (A figure-ground problem occurs when the background interferes with the key stimulus or figure of the picture.)

"No, Timmy, not 'I sawed the chair.' It's 'I saw the chair' or 'I have seen the chair.'"

Courtesy Glenn Bernhardt.

Scores

Raw scores are converted into standard scores, with a mean of 100 and standard deviation of 15. The standard scores range from 40 to 160.

Standardization

The normative group was a representative national sample of 4,200 youths, ages 2½ through 18 years, and 828 adults, ages 19 through 40 years, based on the 1970 U.S. census data. Two hundred children, equally divided by sex, were included within each of 21 age groups. These groups were at half-year intervals for ages 2-6 through 6-11 years and at one-year intervals for ages 7 through 18 years. The sample was stratified by sex, geographic region (Northeast, South, Northcentral, and West), occupation of major wage earner, race, and community size.

In the adult sample, four age groups were used: 19 through 24, 25 through 29, 30 through 34, and 35 through 40. The sample was stratified by age, sex, and occupation. (It should be noted that although four geographic regions were sampled, proportionate allocations were not made.)

Adults were tested in a group setting (with the exception of 11 adults who were tested individually) via a slide presentation.

Reliability

Split-half reliability coefficients for ages 2-6 through 18-0 years range from .67 (at the 2-6 year level) to .88 (at the 18 year level) (*Mdn* r_{xx} = .80) on Form L. On Form M they range from .61 (at the 7-0 year level) to .86 (at the 12 year level) (*Mdn* r_{xx} = .81). For the adult sample, Form L has a median split-half reliability coefficient of .82; no split-half reliability coefficient was reported for Form M. The median standard error of measurement for the standard scores is 7 points for Forms L and M, for both children and adults.

Alternate-form reliabilities for a sample of 642 children given both forms in counterbalanced order ranged from .74 to .89 (*Mdn* r_{xx} = .81). In a sample of 962 children given Forms L and M within 9 to 31 days, alternate-form reliabilities ranged from .50 to .89 (*Mdn* r_{xx} = .76). Other studies suggest that the two forms correlate reasonably well (*r*'s between .65 and .89) (Bracken, Prasse, & McCallum, 1984).

Estimates of PPVT-R internal-consistency and alternate-form reliabilities are somewhat lower than desirable, with half of the estimates under .81.

Validity

Numerous studies have correlated the PPVT-R with intelligence and achievement measures, with most studies using the WISC-R. Correlations between the PPVT-R and the WISC-R range from .16 to .86 (*Mdn r* = .68) (Altepeter & Handal, 1985; Breen, 1981; Breen & Siewert, 1983; Davis & Kramer, 1985; Haddad, 1986; Hollinger & Sarvis, 1984; Naglieri, 1982; Naglieri & Yazzie, 1983; Prasse & Bracken, 1981; Worthing et al., 1984; Wright, 1983). These correlations establish the concurrent validity of the PPVT-R as a measure of cognitive ability. The PPVT-R correlates better with the Verbal than with the Performance Scale, however. Additionally, PPVT-R standard scores are not interchangeable with WISC-R standard scores. In many cases, the PPVT-R yields considerably lower scores than does the WISC-R. The PPVT-R also correlates significantly with measures of reading, language, and general achievement (*r*'s from .30 to .63) (Altepeter & Handal, 1985; McLoughlin & Gullo, 1984; Naglieri, 1981a; Naglieri & Pfeiffer, 1983c; Vance, Kitson, & Singer, 1985).

Few items have been found to be culturally biased against ethnic minorities (Argulewicz & Abel, 1984; Reynolds, Willson, & Chatman, 1984). With ethnic minority children, however, the PPVT-R yields standard scores that are much lower than those obtained on the WISC-R. For example, a sample of Navajo Indian children obtained a mean WISC-R Full Scale IQ of 87, whereas their mean PPVT-R standard score was 61 (Naglieri & Yazzie, 1983). Hispanic-American children also achieve lower scores on the PPVT-R than on the McCarthy Scales (see Chapter 19). These studies indicate that using the PPVT-R to evaluate the general cognitive abilities of ethnic minority children may be especially dangerous.

Overall, the studies involving intelligence tests indicate that *PPVT-R scores are not interchangeable with IQs obtained on individually administered intelligence tests for any group of children*. This conclusion raises an intriguing question: What do the PPVT-R and other picture vocabulary tests measure? The answer is not a simple one. The test has been described as measuring language ability, verbal comprehension, vocabulary ability, receptive language, recognition vocabulary, verbal intelligence, vocabulary comprehension, vocabulary usage, comprehension of single words, single-word hearing vocabulary, single-word receptive vocabulary, and intelligence.

One common thread in these descriptions is the involvement of vocabulary. The vocabulary abilities measured, however, encompass both recognition and visual comprehension, because pictures are used together with words. Additionally, perceptual scanning and delay of impulse are involved. The vocabulary tests on the Stanford-Binet: Form L-M and Fourth Edition and on the Wechsler batteries involve retrieval of information to a greater extent than does the PPVT-R. Obviously, receptive (or recognition) vocabulary ability is related to general intelligence, but these constructs are by no means the same. Thus the practice of using the PPVT-R to estimate general intelligence does not appear to be justified. The test is much too limited in its scope, measuring only one facet of a child's ability repertoire.

Comment on the Peabody Picture Vocabulary Test—Revised

The PPVT-R is a vastly improved instrument, especially with regard to standardization. The manual is excellent, providing users with much valuable information. Reliability coefficients (split-half and alternate form) and standard errors of measurement are provided for raw scores and standard scores by age group. A summary of the extensive literature on the reliability and validity of the PPVT also is included in the manual.

The PPVT-R is useful in measuring extensiveness of receptive vocabulary. *It should not be used as a screening device for measuring intellectual level of functioning.* Scores on the PPVT-R are *not* substitutes for IQs obtained on the Stanford-Binet: Fourth Edition or the Wechsler batteries. Additionally, PPVT-R scores should not be considered in isolation from other measures of language ability.

Differences between the scores obtained by language-impaired children on the PPVT-R and on the Leiter International Performance Scale, Columbia Mental Maturity Scale, or Raven's Progressive Matrices may be valuable aids in obtaining an estimate of language deficits. Special care must be taken in examining ethnic minority group children, because they have been found to obtain lower scores on the PPVT-R than on intelligence tests. Their lower PPVT-R scores may in part be a reflection of their verbal and experiential differences.

The PPVT-R uses the designation "standard score" for the derived score, in place of the term "Deviation IQ" used on the PPVT. This change is an important and welcome one, because receptive vocabulary ability measured by a multiple-choice pointing procedure represents only a limited part of the cognitive ability domain.

The PPVT-R, like other picture vocabulary tests, does not provide a general picture of the child's vocabulary knowledge (Muma & Pierce, 1981). First, because only one referent is allowed (or pictured) for each word, there is no opportunity for the child to display knowledge of other possible word-referent relationships; thus the test is a poor measure of referential meanings (e.g., ability to use words in association with particular objects during communication). Second, the PPVT-R does not measure combinational meaning (e.g., ability to combine words into meaningful groups) or intentional meaning (e.g., ability to communicate intentions when speaking). Third, the PPVT-R provides no information about the sequence of language acquisition. Finally, the PPVT-R does not assess the child's word usage; rather, the test uses only an a priori set of words.

DENVER DEVELOPMENTAL SCREENING TEST—REVISED

The Denver Developmental Screening Test—Revised (DDST-R) (Frankenburg, Dodds, Fandal, Kazuk, & Cohrs, 1975) was designed as an aid in identifying delays in the development and behavior of children from birth to 6 years of age. The test is a screening instrument and should not be used as a substitute for a diagnostic evaluation.

The DDST-R provides information about four domains of development: personal-social (23 items), fine motor (30 items), language (21 items), and gross motor (31 items). *Personal-social* items deal with the child's ability to get along with others, to play, and to initiate self-care; *fine motor* items are concerned with the ability to pick up objects and to draw objects; *language* items assess the ability to hear, understand, and use language; and *gross motor* items measure body control, balance, and coordination. The test requires approximately 20 minutes to administer and score.

The 1975 edition differs from the 1967 edition (Frankenburg & Dodds, 1967) in its interpretation of scores. Some scores interpreted as abnormal or questionable in the 1967 edition are classified as questionable or normal in the revised edition. In all other respects, the two editions are the same.

The DDST-R can be used in conjunction with the Revised Denver Prescreening Developmental Questionnaire (R-DPDQ) (Frankenburg, 1986). The R-DPDQ is a parent-answered developmental questionnaire for children from birth to 6 years of age. It covers the same four areas of development as are found on the DDST-R. The items on the R-DPDQ are arranged in chronological order according to the ages at which 90 percent of children in the DDST standardization sample were able to perform them successfully. Failure of a child to master an item signifies a "delay." If the child still has one or more delays on rescreening a month after the initial test, a second-stage screening with the DDST-R is recommended. In one study (Frankenburg, Fandal, & Thornton, 1987), the R-DPDQ was found to have a high level of agreement (84 percent) with the DDST-R in a sample of 1,434 children.

Scores

Only items that are passed are scored. Items are arranged in chronological order within each of the four domains. The order is based on the age at which 90 percent of the children in the normative group passed the item. Although four domains are represented on the test, no separate scores are available for the domains. Profile scores are interpreted as *abnormal*, *questionable*, *normal*, or *untestable* based on the number of passes in each of the four domains of the test.

Standardization

The DDST was standardized on 1,036 children (543 male, 493 female) between the ages of 2 weeks and 6.4 years, living in Denver, Colorado. The sample was closely representative of the racial-ethnic and occupational-group characteristics of the Denver population according to 1960 census data, although stratified random sampling techniques were not used (Frankenburg & Dodds, 1967).

Reliability

DDST test-retest reliability coefficients for 13 age groups over a one-week interval are somewhat low, ranging from .66 to .93 for 186 Colorado children between 1.5 and 49 months of age (Frankenburg, Camp, Van Natta, Demersseman, & Voorhees, 1971). Rates of agreement among four examiners who participated in the standardization ranged from 80 to 95 percent. A test-retest correlation (14 month interval) of .70 was reported in a sample of 106 rural lower socioeconomic status children (Harper & Wacker, 1983).

Validity

The manual claims a high degree of agreement between the DDST normal/abnormal ratings and both Stanford-Binet: Form L-M IQs and Bayley Scales of Infant Development Developmental Quotients. Of a group of 236 children classified as normal or questionable on the basis of DDST scores, it was found that 7 percent of those in the questionable category would have been in the normal category and 3 percent of those in the normal category would have been in the questionable category if the groups had been formed on the basis of a cutoff of 70 on the Stanford-Binet: Form L-M or Bayley Scales. A correlation of .97 was reported between the DDST and the Yale Developmental Examination for 18 children aged 4 to 68 months (Frankenburg & Dodds, 1967). Correlations ranging from .84 to .95 have been reported between the DDST and the Stanford-Binet: Form L-M, Revised Yale Developmental Schedule, and Bayley Scales for 236 normal and mentally retarded children (Frankenburg, Camp, & Van Natta, 1971). Woodcock (1977) reported correlations of .82, .65, and .52 between the DDST and Developmental Indicators for the Assessment of Learning, the Stanford-Binet: Form L-M, and the PPVT, respectively.

Other research raises serious questions about the validity of the DDST. A study of 250 preschool and primary students with the Quick Neurological Screening Test, the DDST, and a neurological examination indicated that the DDST was not an appropriate instrument for neurodevelopmental screening of kindergarten and primary-school-age children (Sterling & Sterling, 1977). The DDST clearly identified only 3 of 18 children diagnosed on the basis of a neurological examination as having significant neurological or neurodevelopmental disorders and flagged only 5 additional children. In a sample of children under 30 months of age, low correlations were obtained (r's from .25 to .52) between the DDST and Bayley Scales, as well as poor agreement in classifications (Appelbaum, 1978).

A study of rural, lower socioeconomic status preschool children ($N = 555$) showed that the DDST failed to identify 66 percent of the children who obtained scores in the mentally retarded range on the Stanford-Binet: Form L-M or WPPSI (Harper & Wacker, 1983). Such misclassifications suggest that children needing assistance may not be appropriately referred solely on the basis of results on the DDST.

Comment on the Denver Developmental Screening Test—Revised and the Revised Denver Prescreening Developmental Questionnaire

Because the DDST-R has several weaknesses, it should be used with caution. First, although the authors of the DDST maintain that the DDST is not an intelligence test, they use an intelligence test to validate their instrument. Second, some research suggests that the DDST-R does not adequately classify children who appear to be at risk based on

intelligence test performance. Finally, because almost half the items are based on parental reports, DDST-R scores are heavily dependent on the accuracy of those reports. The main difficulty with the R-DPDQ is that little is known about its validity or reliability. No manual accompanies the questionnaire. Consequently, the questionnaire must be used with considerable caution.

SYSTEM OF MULTICULTURAL PLURALISTIC ASSESSMENT

The System of Multicultural Pluralistic Assessment (SOMPA) (Mercer, 1979; Mercer & Lewis, 1978) is a battery of measures that incorporates medical, social, and pluralistic information in the assessment of the cognitive, perceptual-motor, and adaptive behavior of black, white, and Hispanic-American children between the ages of 5-0 and 11-11 years. The SOMPA uses nine measures drawn from three assessment models: the medical model, the social system model, and the pluralistic model. It takes approximately 5 hours to administer the entire battery. The SOMPA attempts to provide a comprehensive assessment that will allow educational and placement decisions to be made in a racially or culturally nondiscriminatory fashion. As we shall see, this effort has not been successful—test content was not altered on the WISC-R, bilingualism was not addressed, and national standardization and validation of the procedures for estimating learning potential were ignored.

Medical Model

Six measures are used within the medical model paradigm: Physical Dexterity Tasks, Bender Visual Motor Gestalt Test, Weight by Height, Visual Acuity, Auditory Acuity, and Health History Inventories. This model attempts to answer the question "Is the child a biologically normal individual?" where *normal* is defined as the absence of pathological organic symptoms.

Social System Model

The purpose of the social system model is to evaluate the child's role performance relative to social groups. Because the model is based on a social deviance model, the emphasis is on determining whether a child's behavior in a given situation is normal—that is, conforms to expectations of group members. Abnormal behavior is that which violates these expectations. The measures in the social system model are the WISC-R (the IQs are referred to as School

Functioning Level) and the Adaptive Behavior Inventory for Children (ABIC). (See Chapter 15 for a review of the ABIC.)

Pluralistic Model

The pluralistic model of the SOMPA uses multiple norms to estimate a child's learning potential. The goal is to evaluate the child within the context of his or her own social and cultural group rather than by the standards of the majority culture. Two complementary assumptions are made: (a) all tests are culture-specific and measure learning; and (b) children must be compared with other children from a similar cultural background before any conclusions concerning intelligence can be reached.

Sociocultural Scales and the Estimated Learning Potential (ELP).
The WISC-R is the sole measure in the pluralistic model, and its interpretation is guided by the use of the Sociocultural Scales. The four Sociocultural Scales are Family Size, Family Structure, Socioeconomic Status, and Urban Acculturation. The weighted raw scores on the scales are converted into scaled scores appropriate for the child's ethnic background. Scores from these four scales are plugged into a multiple regression equation in order to transform the standard WISC-R IQ into an *Estimated Learning Potential (ELP) IQ*. This adjustment in WISC-R scores is intended to allow for individual differences in children's sociocultural backgrounds.

Computation of the Estimated Learning Potential (ELP).
The computation of the ELP is not based on any changes in WISC-R items, administrative procedures, or validity data. Children are awarded points *solely* on the basis of their more "marginal" status, based on ratings on the four Sociocultural Scales.

Let us compute an ELP IQ for the hypothetical case of a black child who obtained a Verbal IQ of 70, a Performance IQ of 70, and a Full Scale IQ of 69 on the WISC-R. If this child came from a very large family with an inadequate family structure, low socioeconomic status, and limited urban acculturation (thus obtaining a raw score of 0 on each of the latter three scales), the child would receive ELP IQs of 108 for the Verbal Scale, 102 for the Performance Scale, and 108 for the Full Scale. In this case, *the ELP Full Scale IQ is 39 points higher than the child's actual obtained IQ of 69*. The ELP changes the child's Full Scale IQ from the 2nd percentile to the 70th percentile. As noted previously, the change is based *solely* on the Sociocultural Scales and not on any achievement indices or testing-of-limits procedures. The SOMPA manual provides no evidence that the ELP IQs are valid predictors of children's school performance or of any other performance.

Standardization

The standardization sample of the SOMPA consisted of 2,085 California public school children aged 5-0 to 11-11 years. Three racial ethnic groups were represented in approximately equal numbers: there were 696 black children, 690 Hispanic children, and 699 white children. The children were randomly sampled from pre-selected school districts. No attempt was made to match the U.S. census distribution for California or for the United States.

Comment on the System of Multicultural Pluralistic Assessment

Considerable controversy has arisen about SOMPA. There are concerns about (a) the effectiveness of its tripartite model scheme, (b) pitfalls in ELP-based prediction, (c) the lack of adequate national norms and the lack of representativeness of the norm sample, (d) problems with the ABIC, (e) medical model problems, and (f) Bender-Gestalt norms. The lack of empirical support to validate SOMPA's performance in practical assessment is of particular concern. The Estimated Learning Potential scores that are derived by transforming WISC-R scores according to SOMPA-devised sociocultural norms are the most suspect and controversial aspect of the battery. The effect of sociocultural factors on Bender-Gestalt performance also needs to be considered more fully.

The SOMPA system makes no provision for observing the child in school, for interviewing the teacher, for observing the teacher, for using school grades, or for evaluating the curriculum (Oakland, 1979b). It is regrettable that a system designed to facilitate the assessment of school children entirely ignores school performance and school personnel.

Effectiveness of tripartite model.
Empirical evidence is needed about the relationship between SOMPA medical model measures and school variables (Brown, 1979). It is questionable whether medical model measures should be used at all in making educational decisions. Similarly, little is known about the relationship between the adaptive behavior measure and school achievement. Much more information is needed before we can evaluate the usefulness of the tripartite model for educational planning.

Pitfalls of ELP-based prediction.
The validity of ELPs as predictors of achievement is suspect. First, standard IQs

predict achievement better than do ELPs. Studies indicated that ELPs were no more effective than WISC-R IQs in predicting school-related performance as measured by learning tasks (Johnson & Danley, 1981; Wurtz, Sewell, & Manni, 1985). Additionally, ELPs had lower correlations with measures of achievement than did IQs (Wurtz et al., 1985). With measures of reading and mathematics achievement, ELPs correlate in the high .40s, whereas IQs correlate in the high .60s (Oakland, 1979b; Oakland, 1983a). Mercer's own data show that the sociocultural scales account for less than 15 percent of the variance in WISC-R scores among blacks and Hispanics. Second, there is no evidence that the ELP measures potential ability. Third, the ELPs yielded by SOMPA regression equations for students in Texas do not match those of the California sample (Oakland, 1979b). The contention that SOMPA Sociocultural Scales can equalize educational opportunities for ethnic minority children is not supported.

Thus the use of the ELP for placement or clinical decisions is not warranted. Any use of the ELP violates the widely accepted test standards of the American Psychological Association and Public Law 94-142 (see Chapter 24). Making students ineligible for special education services by reclassifying them based on ELP IQs is not in their best interests.

The ELP IQs also are likely to create misleading expectations among children, parents, and teachers. Children who are led to believe that they can achieve in the society at large, on the basis of predicted scores based on sociocultural norms that do not represent the culture at large, may be placed in situations with which they cannot cope. They may experience disappointment and frustration and come to resent school systems and psychologists who have led them to form such expectations. Conversely, stigmatizing children as having no potential discourages remedial efforts. The use of SOMPA is not recommended, given its inadequate validity. *There is no justification for using the ELP for any clinical or psychoeducational purpose.*

The need for renorming. The California-based SOMPA norms may not apply to other areas of the country. Even within California they may not be appropriate. No information is presented in the manual regarding the socioeconomic distribution of the norm sample; therefore the norm sample may not even be representative of the school-based population of California children. Renorming is essential for SOMPA to have nationwide validity (Brown, 1979; Clarizio, 1979).

Problems with the ABIC. As you will read in Chapter 15, the ABIC's principal strength is that it is a standardized instrument for measuring adaptive behavior. It has certain drawbacks, however, such as items that may discriminate against children of lower socioeconomic classes and norms that may not be applicable nationwide.

Medical model problems. There is no empirical evidence that the medical measures are related to school variables. Until such evidence is presented, these measures should not be used to make educational decisions about children.

Bender-Gestalt norms. The Bender Visual Motor Gestalt Test is included in the SOMPA without provision of any separate ethnic norms. Yet black children made significantly more errors on the Bender-Gestalt than did either white children or Hispanic children, whereas Hispanic children made significantly more errors than did white children at ages 8 and 10 years only (Sattler & Gwynne, 1982a). The use of one set of Bender-Gestalt norms for all ethnic groups does not fit in with the SOMPA's attempt at pluralistic assessment.

Concluding Comment on the System of Multicultural Pluralistic Assessment

The claim that SOMPA can lead to educational decisions that are culturally fair has not been empirically supported. In fact, the use of ELPs in the SOMPA may result in biased educational decisions. Users of the SOMPA must recognize its serious limitations.

INFORMAL ASSESSMENT OF DIVERGENT THINKING

The assessment of divergent thinking provides information about the child's ability to formulate new ideas and produce a variety of responses. Supplementing standardized cognitive measures, which usually assess mainly convergent thinking, with informal measures of divergent thinking may provide additional information about a child's thinking style. These measures may be of special value in the assessment of brain-injured children and ethnic minority children, as well as in the assessment of creativity. Table 13-7 illustrates a variety of informal divergent thinking tasks.

Table 13-7
Examples of Divergent Thinking Tasks

Test	Description	Example
Unusual Uses	Child is asked to identify novel ways to use specific common objects.	Instructions that have been used for the test are as follows (Price-Williams & Ramirez, 1977, p. 7): "Let's see how clever you can be about using things. For instance, if I ask you how many ways an old tire could be used, you might say: fix up an old car, for a swing, to roll around and run with, to cut up for shoe soles, and so on. Now if I asked you: 'How many ways can you use a pebble?' what would you say?" After these instructions are given, ask the child to give uses for a newspaper, a table knife, a coffee cup, a clock, and money. Two scores are obtained: an ideational fluency score (the uses mentioned for all five objects are summed) and an ideational flexibility score (the number of different categories of usage for each object are summed). The following examples illustrate the scoring: A response to newspaper, "To read, to make a mat, and to use as an umbrella," receives a fluency score of 3 and flexibility score of 3. A response to table knife, such as "cut your meat and cut other things" receives a fluency score of 2 and a flexibility score of 1. The two scores also form an efficiency index (ratio of flexibility score to fluency score).
Common Situations	Child is asked to list problems inherent in a common situation.	"Can you list problems that someone might have while walking with a crutch?"
Product Improvement	Child is asked to suggest ways to improve an object.	"Can you think of different ways to improve a toy car so that you would have more fun playing with it?"
Consequences	Child is asked to list the effects of a new and unusual event.	"Just suppose that people no longer needed or wanted automobiles. What would happen? List your ideas and guesses."
Object Naming	Child is asked to list objects that belong to a broad class of objects.	"Can you name objects that cut?"
Differences	Child is asked to suggest ways in which two objects are different.	"Can you list ways in which a spoon and ball are different?"
Similarities	Child is asked to suggest ways in which two objects are alike.	"Can you list ways in which cheese and vegetables are alike?"
Word Arrangements	Child is asked to produce sentences containing specified words.	"Make up a sentence containing the words 'dog' and 'walked.'"
Word Fluency	Child is asked to say words that contain a specified word or letter.	"What words have the /b/ sound in them?"
Possibilities	Child is asked to list objects that can be used to perform a certain task.	"Can you tell me different things that can be used to write with?"
Quick Response	Child is asked to say the first word that he or she can think of in response to words read aloud.	"What is the first word you think of when I say 'run'?"
Associational Fluency	Child is asked to list synonyms for a given word.	"What words mean the same as 'big'?"

(Table continues next page)

Table 13-7 (cont.)

Test	Description	Example
Social Institutions	Child is asked to list two improvements for a social institution.	"Can you tell me two ways that you could improve or change marriage?"
Planning Elaboration	Child is asked to detail the steps needed to make a briefly outlined plan work.	"Your club is planning to have a party. You are in charge of the arrangements. What will you do?"
Ask and Guess	Child is encouraged to ask questions about a particular picture or to guess possible consequences of actions presented in the picture.	"Here is a picture of a boat. What are some questions that you can ask about the picture?"
What Would	Child is asked to think of items that could be improved if changed in a particular way.	"What would taste better if it were sweeter?"
Criteria	Child is asked to tell the criteria that might be used in judging an event or object.	"List reasons why people might like to eat apple pie."
Questions	Child is asked to list questions related to particular words.	"What questions could you ask about the word 'city'?"

Source: The tasks are from Guilford and Hoepfner (1971), Parnes (1966), Torrance (1966), and Torrance and Myers (1970).

COMMENT ON TESTS OF ACHIEVEMENT AND SPECIAL ABILITIES

Screening achievement tests, such as the WRAT-R and the PIAT, measure only a limited aspect of reading ability. For example, a child with exceptional individual word recognition skills may obtain high scores, although his or her ability to read with meaning may be limited. Reading in context is a different skill from recognizing or reading individual words. Reading assessment instruments, such as the New Sucher-Allred Reading Placement Inventory and the Classroom Reading Inventory, are inadequate instruments for classification or placement, but they may have some utility as follow-up tests for exploring specific areas of deficit in order to establish a focus for remediation.

WRAT-R vs. PIAT

In deciding on the relative merits of the Wide Range Achievement Test–Revised versus the Peabody Individual Achievement Test, consider their different formats for measuring ability. The WRAT-R requires expressive skills, whereas the PIAT requires receptive or recognition skills. On the PIAT Reading Comprehension subtest, children who have good visual skills and who are shrewd at guessing may perform at a level above their true reading level. Additionally, the WRAT-R Arithmetic and Spelling subtests require a written response, whereas the PIAT subtests do not. The PIAT arithmetic questions emphasize problem solving and general conceptual development rather than computations, which are emphasized on the WRAT-R.

It is important to use a test of oral reading along with either the PIAT or the WRAT-R to assess oral reading of paragraphs as well as comprehension. A child may perform at normal levels on the WRAT-R or the PIAT (demonstrate normal phonetic-analytic or word-attack skills), but perform poorly when more protracted reading is required. As you become more familiar with these (and similar) instruments, their assets and limitations will become more apparent to you. Always keep in mind that WRAT-R and PIAT scores are not interchangeable.

Pitfalls in Using Limited Ability Measures as General Ability Measures

In school and clinical evaluations, as well as in research studies, it is a poor practice to use a test of a specific ability, such as the Peabody Picture Vocabulary Test–Revised, to estimate a child's overall mental ability. Research studies have found that the researcher tends to engage in an insidious reasoning process (Wheldall & Jeffree, 1974). The researcher transfers a child's raw score into a Vocabulary Age, which is then confused with Verbal Age, which then may be construed to be equivalent to an MA—a measure of general ability. Applying this false logic to the psycho-educational assessment of mentally retarded children is particularly dangerous, because their receptive vocabulary is unlikely to reflect their general levels of ability. Receptive vocabulary may be acquired in a relatively automatic, mechanical way, much as the mechanics of reading can be learned without comprehension. If an individual measure of general mental ability is required, tests in the Wechsler series, the Stanford-Binet: Fourth Edition, or other tests covered in Chapter 12 should be used.

SUMMARY

1. The tests described in this chapter are useful for the assessment of academic achievement, psycholinguistic and receptive vocabulary skills, auditory comprehension, developmental screening, and divergent thinking.

2. In observing children's performance on reading, spelling, and arithmetic tests, attend to the types of errors made by the child as well as the child's successes and failures and response style.

3. Informal reading inventories determine the child's listening level and his or her reading level—independent, instructional, or frustration.

4. An "eyeblink" procedure can be used to administer multiple-choice picture tests (such as the Peabody Picture Vocabulary Test—Revised) to children with severe motor handicaps.

5. With hard-of-hearing children, stimulus words used on vocabulary tests can be printed on cards and instructions pantomimed.

6. The Wide Range Achievement Test—Revised (WRAT-R) provides measures of word recognition, spelling, and arithmetic. The test does not provide for an in-depth study of academic skills, however. Thus it should only be considered as a screening instrument.

7. The Peabody Individual Achievement Test (PIAT) is a screening test measuring mathematics, reading, and spelling ability and general information. Over half of the items have a multiple-choice format. The content of the PIAT overlaps with that of the WISC-R.

8. The Kaufman Test of Educational Achievement (K-TEA) provides measures of reading, mathematics, and spelling ability for children from 6 to 18 years of age. It appears to be a useful measure of achievement.

9. The Basic Achievement Skills Individual Screener (BASIS) provides measures of reading, mathematics, and spelling ability for children from 6 to 18 years of age. The preferred ages, however, are 6 to 14 years. It appears to be a useful measure of achievement.

10. The Woodcock-Johnson Psycho-Educational Battery is an omnibus test that covers cognitive ability, achievement, and interest. Its reliability appears to be satisfactory. The cognitive cluster, however, appears to be heavily weighted in favor of subtests that measure academic skills. Concerns have been voiced about the construct validity of the cluster scores, the fact that the cognitive clusters yield scores that are lower than those yielded by the WISC-R, and the appropriateness of the cognitive cluster for classification purposes. The Tests of Achievement are useful in measuring achievement, however.

11. The New Sucher-Allred Reading Placement Inventory and the Classroom Reading Inventory are useful screening instruments for evaluating children's reading level.

12. The KeyMath Diagnostic Arithmetic Test and the Sequential Assessment of Mathematics Inventories are useful instruments that provide diagnostic information about children's arithmetic skills.

13. The Boehm Test of Basic Concepts—Revised (BTBC-R) measures knowledge of concepts related to space, quantity, and time among children in kindergarten through second grade. A downward version of the scale is available for ages 3 to 5 years, the Boehm Test of Basic Concepts—Preschool Version (BTBC-PV). Both versions measure useful concepts.

14. The Bracken Basic Concept Scale (BBCS) measures knowledge of such concepts as color, letters, numbers, comparisons, shapes, direction, social/emotional connotations, size, texture, quantity, and time, which children generally acquire during preschool and early elementary school years. The overall score is the most reliable measure in the scale.

15. The Illinois Test of Psycholinguistic Abilities (ITPA) provides information about various areas of linguistic functioning. Its usefulness is limited by questions concerning its reliability and validity.

16. The Test of Auditory Comprehension of Language—Revised (TACL-R) measures auditory comprehension in children from 3 to 10 years of age. It contains three sections—Word Classes and Relations, Grammatical Morphemes, and Elaborated Sentences. The total score is the most reliable. More information is needed about its validity.

17. The Peabody Picture Vocabulary Test—Revised (PPVT-R) measures receptive vocabulary ability. The test has a multiple-choice format. It should not be used as a measure of intelligence.

18. The Denver Developmental Screening Test—Revised (DDST-R) attempts to measure developmental delays in children between birth and 6 years of age. Its validity, however, is questionable. The DDST-R can be used in conjunction with a parent-answered questionnaire, the Revised Denver Prescreening Developmental Questionnaire (R-DPDQ). The R-DPDQ, however, must be used with considerable caution, because its validity is unproven.

19. The System of Multicultural Pluralistic Assessment (SOMPA) combines medical, social, ethnic, cognitive, perceptual-motor, and adaptive behavior information. The unique aspect of SOMPA is its attempt to define an estimated

learning potential (ELP) by adjusting WISC-R scores based on family size, family structure, socioeconomic status, and urban acculturation variables. There is no evidence that (a) the ELP measures "potential," (b) the SOMPA makes any additional contribution to the assessment process, or (c) the SOMPA is culturally nondiscriminatory.

20. An assessment of divergent thinking can contribute to the assessment processes.

21. The reading tests covered in this chapter measure limited aspects or reading ability. They serve primarily as screening instruments or for exploring specific areas of deficit.

22. The WRAT-R and PIAT use different formats for measuring ability: the WRAT requires expressive skills, the PIAT, receptive skills. These tests should be supplemented with tests of oral reading.

23. Scores obtained from tests of specific ability should not be used as indices of general ability.

KEY TERMS, CONCEPTS, AND NAMES

Informal reading inventories (p. 329)
Independent reading level (p. 329)
Instructional reading level (p. 330)
Frustration reading level (p. 330)
Listening capacity reading level (p. 330)
Wide Range Achievement Test—Revised (WRAT-R) (p. 331)
Peabody Individual Achievement Test (PIAT) (p. 332)
Kaufman Test of Educational Achievement (K-TEA) (p. 333)
Basic Achievement Skills Individual Screener (BASIS) (p. 334)
Woodcock-Johnson Psycho-Educational Battery (p. 335)
New Sucher-Allred Reading Placement Inventory (p. 338)
Classroom Reading Inventory (p. 339)
KeyMath Diagnostic Arithmetic Test (p. 340)
Sequential Assessment of Mathematics Inventories (SAMI) (p. 341)
Boehm Test of Basic Concepts—Revised (BTBC-R) (p. 342)
Boehm Test of Basic Concepts—Preschool Version (BTBC-PV) (p. 343)
Bracken Basic Concept Scale (BBCS) (p. 344)
Illinois Test of Psycholinguistic Abilities (ITPA) (p. 345)
Test of Auditory Comprehension of Language—Revised (TACL-R) (p. 347)

Peabody Picture Vocabulary Test—Revised (PPVT-R) (p. 348)
Denver Developmental Screening Test—Revised (DDST-R) (p. 351)
Revised Denver Prescreening Developmental Questionnaire (R-DPDQ) (p. 351)
System of Multicultural Pluralistic Assessment (SOMPA) (p. 352)
SOMPA Estimated Learning Potential (ELP) (p. 353)
Divergent thinking (p. 354)

STUDY QUESTIONS

1. Discuss some administrative suggestions and observational guidelines for giving tests of academic achievement and special abilities.

2. Discuss the assets and limitations of
a. the Wide Range Achievement Test—Revised
b. the Peabody Individual Achievement Test
c. the Kaufman Test of Educational Achievement
d. the Basic Achievement Skills Individual Screener
e. the Woodcock-Johnson Psycho-Educational Battery
f. the New Sucher-Allred Reading Placement Inventory
g. the Classroom Reading Inventory
h. the KeyMath Diagnostic Arithmetic Test
i. the Sequential Assessment of Mathematics Inventories
j. the Boehm Test of Basic Concepts—Revised and the Boehm Test of Basic Concepts—Preschool Version
k. the Bracken Basic Concept Scale
l. the Illinois Test of Psycholinguistic Abilities
m. the Test of Auditory Comprehension of Language—Revised
n. the Peabody Picture Vocabulary Test—Revised
o. the Denver Developmental Screening Test—Revised and the Revised Denver Prescreening Developmental Questionnaire
p. the System of Multicultural Pluralistic Assessment

3. Compare and contrast the Wide Range Achievement Test—Revised, Peabody Individual Achievement Test, Kaufman Test of Educational Achievement, and Woodcock-Johnson Psycho-Educational Battery.

4. Compare and contrast the New Sucher-Allred Reading Placement Inventory and the Classroom Reading Inventory.

14

ASSESSMENT OF VISUAL-MOTOR PERCEPTION, AUDITORY PERCEPTION, AND MOTOR PROFICIENCY

What should be remembered is that many less than perfect measures have proven to be useful in psychology. . . .

—Edward F. Zigler

General Guidelines for Administering and Interpreting Visual-Motor Tests

Bender Visual Motor Gestalt Test

Developmental Test of Visual-Motor Integration

Auditory Discrimination Test

Lindamood Auditory Conceptualization Test

Goldman-Fristoe-Woodcock Test of Auditory Discrimination

Bruininks-Oseretsky Test of Motor Proficiency

Comment on Tests of Visual-Motor Perception, Auditory Perception, and Motor Proficiency

Summary

The tests reviewed in this chapter focus on visual-motor perception and integration, visual perception, auditory perception, and motor proficiency. These expressive and receptive functions are an important link in the processing of information, and their measurement is particularly useful in evaluating children with possible learning disabilities or neurological deficits. Tests of visual-motor integration ability, auditory ability, and fine and gross motor ability are useful in determining the intactness of the child's sensory and motor modalities and in developing remediation programs. Perceptual-motor tests, however, are likely to be less appropriate (or perhaps completely inappropriate) for children who have severe visual or motor handicaps. In such cases, the results obtained from perceptual-motor tests must be interpreted with considerable caution.

GENERAL GUIDELINES FOR ADMINISTERING AND INTERPRETING VISUAL-MOTOR TESTS

Observing Performance

In observing a child's performance on visual-motor tests, consider the following:

1. How, and in which hand, does the child hold the pencil?

2. Are the drawings done with extreme care and deliberation or impulsively?

3. Does the child trace the design with a finger before drawing it?

4. Does the child count the dots, loops, or sides of figures, or does he or she draw the designs haphazardly?

5. Does the child glance at the design briefly and then draw from memory?

6. Does the child rotate the card or paper (or both)?

7. Does the child erase frequently? If so, on what figures or parts of figures (for example, curves, angulations, overlapping parts, or open figures)?

8. What part of a design does the child draw first?

9. What direction does the child use to copy the designs? For example, are the designs drawn from top down or bottom up, or from inside out or outside in? Does the direction of movement change from design to design?

10. Does the child use sketching?

11. Is there unusual blocking on any design?

12. How much space does the child use to draw the design (for example, is the drawing approximately the same size as the original or greatly reduced or expanded)?

13. Does the child spend approximately the same amount of time on each design?

14. Does the child recognize errors and correct them?

15. What sort of comments does the child make about the designs?

16. Does he or she express dissatisfaction over poorly executed drawings?

17. Are there signs of fatigue?

18. Did the child need encouragement to complete the drawings?

19. How long did the entire task take? Is this time excessive or unusually short?

Answers to these questions will provide information about the child's style of responding, reaction to frustration, ability to correct errors, and related issues. Consider the child's maturational level, visual-motor integration skills, and medical condition, as well as other factors that may be involved in perceptual-motor functioning. Motivational factors alone might explain the child's performance or contribute to those factors more directly involved with perceptual-motor functioning. The information you obtain from observing the child's performance will complement the more formal evaluation of visual-motor skills and aid you in developing hypotheses to account for the child's performance.

Testing-of-Limits

In testing-of-limits on visual-motor tests, you can ask the child to compare his or her drawing with the model drawing. For example, you might say "Look at your drawing and the one on the card. How are they alike and how are they different?" After exploring the child's response, you can give the child another opportunity to draw one or more of the designs. You might say "Draw this design again. Do your very best." Your inquiries should help you answer such questions as the following: Does the child recognize any differences between his or her drawing and the model? Are the figures drawn correctly when the child is given a second chance? Were the failures due to poor attention to detail, carelessness, impulsiveness, poor organization, fear of completing a difficult task, fatigue, or lack of interest?

Some, but not all, children will be aware of their errors. Those who are aware of their errors still may not be able to correct them. Testing-of-limits procedures may help to pinpoint whether the problem is perceptual, motor, or a matter of perceptual-motor integration. Such procedures also can be used to test hypotheses about the child's performance and to develop recommendations.

Interpreting Performance

Reproducing designs in visual-motor tests probably requires appropriate fine motor development, perceptual discrimination ability, and ability to integrate perceptual and motor processes. Copying designs also involves a shifting of attention between the original design and the copy. Inadequate performance may be a result of misperception (faulty interpretation of input information), execution difficulties (faulty fine motor response output), or integrative or central processing difficulties (faulty memory storage or retrieval systems).

Inadequate visual-motor performance may be associated with maturational delay, limited intellectual stimulation, unfamiliarity with testing situations, or neurological impairment. In evaluating any signs suggestive of visual-motor disturbance, consider (a) the extent of the deviation (for example, does the drawing represent a major or a minor distortion of the model?), (b) the frequency of the types of distortions on one or many designs, (c) the child's degree of awareness that the distortions are present, and (d) the child's ability to correct the deviation.

Sometimes it is possible to discern whether the difficulty lies in the output (motor or expressive functions) or the input (perceptual or receptive functions) process. Generally, if children struggle to reproduce the designs, the difficulty is likely to be motor or expressive, whereas if they draw them quickly and easily but with errors that are not recognized, the difficulty may be perceptual or receptive and not entirely motor. When children cannot see their errors, the trouble may lie in the input mechanisms; when they can acknowledge their errors but cannot correct them, the difficulty may be due to faulty output mechanisms.

Variables that may lead to poor perceptual-motor functioning and thus affect drawings made on visual-motor tests include physiological limitations, sensory deprivation, muscular weakness, and other physical handicapping conditions; physiological disruptions, such as illness, in-

jury, or fatigue; immediate, temporary environmental stress; poor motivation; affective disruptions; intellectual retardation; social or cultural deprivations; and limited experiences (Koppitz, 1975; Palmer, 1983).

Subtle physical handicaps may affect visual-motor performance in many ways. Some children with poor drawings have undetected visual problems, whereas others' difficulties in fine motor control may be the first signs of a disorder such as muscular dystrophy or multiple sclerosis. Hyperactive children may make serious errors on visual-motor tests. Certain medical conditions, such as low birth weight, cerebral palsy, and sickle cell anemia, can interfere with visual-motor performance. Obviously, children with severe visual acuity impairments should not be administered visual-motor tests unless their vision has been sufficiently corrected with glasses.

BENDER VISUAL MOTOR GESTALT TEST

The Bender Visual Motor Gestalt Test (Bender, 1938) is one of the most widely used psychological tests and certainly the most popular of the visual-motor tests. It was developed in 1938 by Lauretta Bender for use as a visual-motor test with adult clinical populations and as a developmental test with children. The test was derived from Gestalt configurations devised by Wertheimer in 1923 to demonstrate principles of Gestalt psychology in relation to perception.

The Bender-Gestalt is an individually administered, paper-and-pencil test that contains nine geometric figures drawn in black (see Figure 14-1) on 4×6 inch white cards. The designs are presented one at a time, and the child is required to copy the designs on a blank sheet of paper. The test serves as a good icebreaker with which to begin the

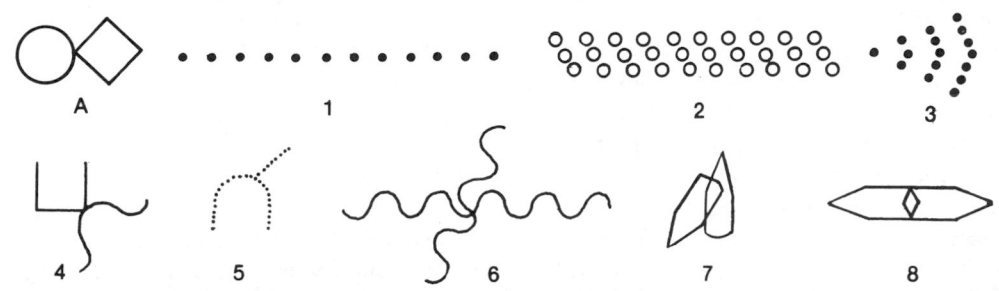

Figure 14-1. Designs on the Bender Visual Motor Gestalt Test.

testing session—the task is innocuous, nonthreatening, interesting, and appealing to children.

Administrative Suggestions

The child should be given a number 2 pencil with an eraser, and an unlined blank sheet of 8½ × 11 inch paper should be placed vertically in front of the child on the table. Extra sheets of paper, usually equal to the number of cards, should be available on the table, along with an extra pencil in case of breakage.

Recommended instructions are as follows:

Place the stack of nine Bender-Gestalt cards face down (card A on the top and card 8 on the bottom) on the table and say:

"I have nine cards here with designs on them for you to copy. [Point to the stack of cards.] Here is the first one. [Turn over the first card.] Now go ahead and make one just like it."

or

"Now I would like you to draw some designs for me. There are nine cards here and each card has a drawing on it. [Point to the stack of cards.] I want you to copy the drawings. Make them the best you can." [Turn over the first card.]

If the child raises any questions, give a noncommital reply such as "Make it look as much like the picture on the card as you can," "Do it the way you think best," or "Do the best job you can."

Present each card individually, beginning with card A and following with cards 1 through 8 in numerical order. (The cards are numbered sequentially in approximate order of difficulty.) Permit the child to erase, but do not allow the use of any mechanical aids such as rulers; the drawings must be done freehand.

The nine designs take approximately 5 minutes to complete. Note any large deviation in the time required to complete the designs. Large time deviations may be suggestive of the child's approach to novel situations. For example, children who require 15 minutes to copy the designs might have a slow, methodical approach to situations, compulsive tendencies, or depressive features, whereas those who finish in less than 2 or 3 minutes might have an impulsive style. A caret (^) should be placed at the top of any paper containing a design that appears to be rotated. The caret will help you recall at a later time the extent of the child's rotations from the visual plane. Finally, note the child's approach to the task (for example, degree of impulsiveness or compulsiveness, ability to cope with frustration, or attitude toward the task).

Variations in Administration

Several variations are commonly used in administering the Bender-Gestalt. Two of the most popular are (a) the tachistoscopic procedure and (b) the memory phase procedure. In the tachistoscopic procedure, each card is shown for 5 seconds. It is then removed, and the child is asked to draw the design from memory. In the memory procedure, the child first completes the standard procedure. After all of the designs have been copied, the child is asked to draw as many of the figures as he or she can remember ("Now draw as many of the designs as you can from memory").

The Bender-Gestalt can also be administered as a group test. Four methods of group administration have been used: (a) presentation of enlarged Bender-Gestalt cards at the front of the room; (b) presentation of special Bender-Gestalt test booklets in which the designs are drawn and the children copy the designs in blank spaces; (c) presentation of the designs by means of an opaque projector, overhead projector, or slide projector; and (d) presentation of individual decks of Bender-Gestalt cards. The most successful method with large numbers of children is the first method, the presentation of enlarged Bender-Gestalt cards. The projector methods have the disadvantages of necessitating special equipment and requiring that the children draw their designs in semi-darkness. Individual decks have been most successful with hyperactive or immature children who require extra attention, although only two or three children should be tested at once. Overall, studies indicate that group administration of the Bender-Gestalt yields reliable protocols comparable to those obtained under individual administration (Koppitz, 1975).

Koppitz Developmental Bender Scoring System

The Koppitz Developmental Bender Scoring System (Koppitz, 1964, 1975) for evaluating the Bender-Gestalt drawings of young children is probably the most popular objective scoring system for the test. It is composed of two parts: (a) developmental scoring and (b) scoring of emotional indicators. The first part has the most relevance for the evaluation of visual-motor perception. There are 30 developmental scoring items, with each item receiving 1 or 0 points, depending on whether an error occurs (see Table 14-1).

A four-category system is used to classify errors: (a) distortion of shape, (b) rotation, (c) integration difficulties, and (d) perseveration. A scoring sheet can be used to record 1 point for each distortion made by the child. The points are summed to obtain a total error score, which is then compared to norms for the child's age. Percentile norms are available for children aged 5-0 through 11-11 years (Koppitz, 1975). Standard scores ($M = 100$, $SD = 15$) are also available in Table C-62 of Appendix C. These scores are most suitable for ages 5-0 through 8-0. Standard scores ($M = 50$, $SD = 15$) are also available for the SOMPA (see Chapter 13) standardization sample (Mercer & Lewis, 1978).

The Koppitz and SOMPA standard score equivalents are not interchangeable (Moore & Zarske, 1984; Sattler & Bowman, 1981). For the same raw score, the two systems may yield standard scores that are as much as 1 standard deviation apart. For example, a raw score of 9 (for an 8-year-old child) is about 1 SD below the mean on the SOMPA norms, and about 2 SD below the mean on the Koppitz norms. Until further validity evidence is available, caution is needed in making any placement decisions based on either set of norms.

Error classifications. The four types of errors in the Koppitz system are as follows:

1. *Distortion of shape* involves destruction of the Gestalt, such as misshapen figures, disproportion between the sizes of the component parts of the figure; substitution of circles or dashes for dots; substitution of distinct angles for curves or total lack of curves where they should exist; extra angles; or missing angles. Distortion of shape is scored for Figures A, 1, 3, 5, 6, 7, and 8, for a possible total error score of 10 points.

2. *Rotation* involves a rotation of the figure or any part thereof by 45 degrees or more. Rotation is scored when the Bender-Gestalt card is rotated, even if it is copied correctly as shown on the rotated card. This error is scored for Figures A, 1, 2, 3, 4, 5, 7, and 8, for a possible total error score of 8 points.

3. *Integration* involves (a) failure to connect properly the two parts of a figure, either by leaving more than ⅛ inch between the parts or causing them to overlap; (b) failure to cross two lines or crossing them in an incorrect place; or (c) omission or addition of rows of dots or

loss of the overall shape in the case of figures composed of dots or circles. Integration difficulties may be scored for Figures A, 2, 3, 4, 5, 6, and 7, for a possible total error score of 9 points.

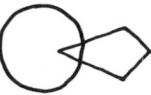

4. *Perseveration* involves increase, continuation, or prolongation of the number of units in the design. It is scored for three of the designs: (a) when there are more

Table 14-1
Classification of Errors in the Koppitz Scoring System for the Bender-Gestalt

Figure		Error
Figure A	1a.	Distortion of shape
	1b.	Distortion of shape (disproportion)
	2.	Rotation
	3.	Integration
Figure 1	4.	Distortion of shape (circles for dots)
	5.	Rotation
	6.	Perseveration
Figure 2	7.	Rotation
	8.	Integration (row added, omitted)
	9.	Perseveration
Figure 3	10.	Distortion of shape (circles for dots)
	11.	Rotation
	12a.	Integration (shape lost)
	12b.	Integration (lines for dots)
Figure 4	13.	Rotation
	14.	Integration
Figure 5	15.	Distortion of shape (circles for dots)
	16.	Rotation
	17a.	Integration (shape lost)
	17b.	Integration (lines for dots)
Figure 6	18a.	Distortion of shape (angles in curves)
	18b.	Distortion of shape (straight line)
	19.	Integration
	20.	Perseveration
Figure 7	21a.	Distortion of shape (disproportion)
	21b.	Distortion of shape (incorrect angles)
	22.	Rotation
	23.	Integration
Figure 8	24.	Distortion of shape (incorrect angles)
	25.	Rotation

Note. See Koppitz (1964) for a description of the complete scoring system.

Cartoon by Tony Hall from *Of Children, An Introduction to Child Development*, Third Edition by Guy R. Lefrancois © 1980 by Wadsworth, Inc., Belmont, California 94002. Reprinted by permission of the publisher.

than 15 dots in a row in Figure 1; (b) when there are more than 14 columns of circles in a row in Figure 2; and (c) when there are 6 or more complete curves in either direction in Figure 6. A total error score of 3 points is possible. This type of perseveration is known as within-card perseveration. There is a second, much rarer type of perseveration called card-to-card perseveration, which occurs when a preceding design or parts of it influence succeeding designs. This type of perseveration is not scored in the Koppitz system.

Emotional indicators. There are 12 emotional indicators in the Koppitz scoring system. These indicators evaluate the child's visual-motor performance qualitatively in regard to emotional stability. Little is known about the validity of these indicators, however.

Standardization. The 1975 Koppitz norms are based on a sample of 975 elementary school children, aged 5-0 to 11-11 years, living in rural areas, small towns, suburbs, and large metropolitan centers in the West, South, and Northeast. The composition of the sample was 86 percent white, 8.5 percent black, 4.5 percent Mexican-American and Puerto Rican, and 1 percent Asian. The sample was not representative of the country, as its geographic distribution

was highly skewed in favor of the Northeast. The socioeconomic characteristics of the sample were not reported.

Reliability. With samples of 19 to 193 children in kindergarten through sixth grade, test-retest reliabilities for the Developmental Scoring System total score range from .50 to .90 (*Mdn* r_{xx} = .77), with intervals ranging from the same day to 8 months (Koppitz, 1975). These reliabilities are not sufficiently high to warrant the making of diagnostic decisions. They do appear adequate for formulating hypotheses about visual-motor ability, however.

Interscorer reliabilities are highly acceptable, ranging from .79 to .99 (*Mdn* r = .91) (Koppitz, 1975). These reliabilities were based on samples of normal and mentally retarded children.

The test-retest reliabilities of the four separate error scores (distortion, rotation, integration, and perseveration) are much lower than those of the total score (r_{xx} = .83 for total score, and r_{xx}'s of .29 to .62 for error scores) (Wallbrown & Fremont, 1980). Therefore, the focus in interpreting the Bender-Gestalt should be on the total score and not on the individual sources of error.

Validity. The validity of the Developmental Scoring System depends on how the test is used. Various types of validity are now considered.

Perceptual-motor development. When used as a test of perceptual-motor development in children, the Bender-

Gestalt appears to have acceptable validity. Copying errors decrease steadily between ages 5 and 9 years, suggesting that the test is sensitive to maturational changes. For children over 8 years of age, however, the Developmental Scoring System distinguishes only those with below-average perceptual-motor development from those with normal development, because most children obtain near-perfect performance after 8 years of age (Koppitz, 1964).

Other measures of visual-motor perception. Concurrent validity for the Developmental Scoring System has been established by correlating it with various tests of visual-motor perception (Koppitz, 1975). Correlations with the Frostig Developmental Test of Visual Perception range from .39 to .56 (*Mdn r* = .47), and correlations with the Developmental Test of Visual-Motor Integration range from .59 to .73 (*Mdn r* = .65) (Breen, 1982; DeMers, Wright & Dappen, 1981; Krauft & Krauft, 1972; Lehman & Breen, 1982; Porter & Binder, 1981; Skeen, Strong, & Book, 1982; Spirito, 1980; Wright & DeMers, 1982).

Measures of intelligence. Correlations with a variety of intelligence tests range from −.19 to −.66, (*Mdn r* = −.48) (Koppitz, 1975). (The negative correlations occur because the Developmental Scoring System yields error scores—*higher* error scores are associated with *lower* intelligence test scores.)

Educational readiness. Studies indicate that the Bender-Gestalt has low to moderate (below −.40) correlations with measures of reading, arithmetic, and school grades for elementary school children (Blaha, Fawaz, & Wallbrown, 1979; Caskey & Larson, 1980; Fuller & Wallbrown, 1983; Koppitz, 1975; Lesiak, 1984; Vance, Fuller, & Lester, 1986). These findings suggest that the relationship between the Bender-Gestalt and academic skills is too weak to warrant the use of the Bender-Gestalt for predicting school achievement for any individual child. Successful academic achievement depends on many factors, including cognitive ability, level of maturity, experience, school atmosphere, pedagogy, perceptual-motor development, motivational variables, and familial factors; perceptual-motor skills, therefore, comprise only one part of the total picture.

The Bender-Gestalt as a Diagnostic Tool

The Bender-Gestalt is frequently used to assess brain damage. Although signs have been proposed for the diagnosis of brain damage and even psychosis, there are no specific pathognomonic signs definitively associated with brain damage or psychosis. *The Bender-Gestalt should never be used alone to make a diagnosis of brain damage or psychosis.* It is a tool for evaluating visual-motor ability, and inadequate visual-motor ability may or may not be reflective of brain damage. For the assessment of brain damage, the Bender-Gestalt should be used in conjunction with a battery of neuropsychological tests (see Chapter 22). The following sections emphasize further cautions that apply to the use of the Bender-Gestalt in evaluating brain damage, mental retardation, psychosis, and various other handicapping conditions.

Brain damage. Some signs that may be associated with brain damage, particularly with children older than 11 years of age, are as follows (Marley, 1982).

1. Sequence confusion—changing directions three or more times (a directional change is noted when the order is different from the expected or logical progression). Example:

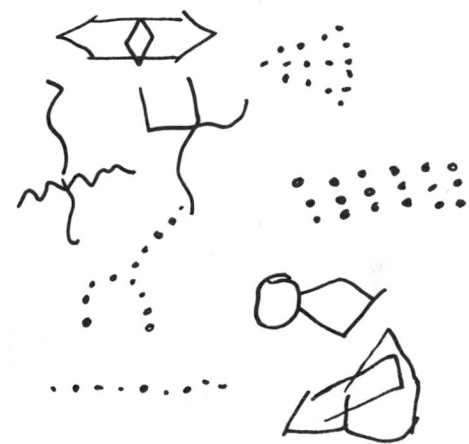

2. Collision—crowding the designs or allowing the end of one design to touch or overlap a part of another design. Example:

3. Superimposition of design—drawing one design (or more) directly on top of another design. Example:

4. Workover—reinforcing a line or lines of a part or whole design. Example:

5. Irregular line quality—drawing irregular lines, particularly when observable tremor is present during the drawing of the lines. Example:

6. Angulation difficulty—drawing a design that shows an increase, decrease, distortion, or omission of the angulation on any figure. Example:

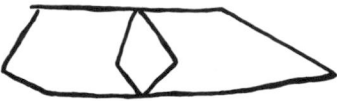

7. Perseveration—redrawing an entire design or a part thereof. Example:

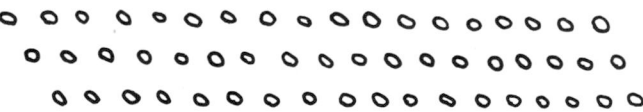

8. Line extension—extending a line or adding lines that were not present in the stimulus figure. Example:

9. Contamination—combining parts of two different Bender-Gestalt figures. Example:

10. Rotation—rotating one or more figures 40 degrees or more from its standard position. Example:

11. Omission—leaving a gap in a figure, reproducing only a part of a figure, separating or fragmenting parts of a design, or omitting some elements of a design. Example:

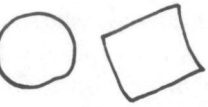

12. Retrogression—substituting solid lines or loops for circles; substituting dashes for dots, dots for circles, or circles for dots; filling in circles; or a mixture of the above. Example:

These signs and those proposed in other systems have questionable validity in the diagnosis of brain damage. First, although there are many different types of brain damage, the Bender-Gestalt only evaluates damage that may interfere with visual discrimination and visual-motor coordination. Second, the proposed signs of brain damage may be found in the drawings of children who are neurologically immature but do not have demonstrable brain damage. (They also may be associated with pathology other than brain damage.) Third, the absence of difficulties does not necessarily rule out the possibility of brain damage. Finally, the presence of visual-motor difficulties is not sufficient reason to diagnose brain injury.

Thus it seems obvious that a diagnosis of brain damage should never be made on the basis of the Bender-Gestalt alone. If, however, several of these signs exist concurrently with behavioral indices of brain damage found using other measures of neurological integrity (see Chapter 22), the possibility of visual-motor impairment can be considered. Assessment information obtained from medical, developmental, educational, psychological, and neuropsychological evaluations would then be needed to confirm whether neurological impairment may be present. (Exhibits 22-2 and 22-5 in Chapter 22 present Bender-Gestalt protocols of brain-injured children.)

Mental retardation.   There are no special Bender-Gestalt signs or diagnostic indicators associated with mental retardation. Bender-Gestalt developmental scores of retarded children tend to be lower than those of non-retarded children, however (Koppitz, 1964). In severe cases, signs similar to those for brain damage may appear, such as line extension, perseveration, omissions, and retrogression (Halpern, 1951; Koppitz, 1975). The presence of one or more of these signs does not imply intellectual retardation or brain damage, however.

Autistic disorder or schizophrenia. There has been no widescale attempt to use the Bender-Gestalt for diagnosing autistic disorder or schizophrenia. Still, a number of diagnostic indicators may be associated with an autistic disorder or schizophrenia, as errors or distortions of the figures may reflect impaired reality testing (the inability to test or explore the nature of one's social and physical environment). Many of the errors found in the Bender-Gestalt reproductions of children with an autistic disorder or schizophrenia are similar to those that occur with brain-damaged children. These include fragmentation, omission or retrogression, collision, and superimposition of design (Halpern, 1951; Stellern, Vasa, & Little, 1976). Errors that are more specific to the reproductions of children with an autistic disorder or schizophrenia include collision, elaboration or bizarre doodling, and scribbling (Halpern, 1951; Stellern et al., 1976).

Again, these signs alone are not sufficient reason to make a diagnosis of autistic disorder or schizophrenia. First, they overlap with indices of brain damage. Second, they may be by-products of temporary states of inefficiency. Finally, a diagnosis of autistic disorder or schizophrenia must be based on many sources of data, not on the Bender-Gestalt exclusively.

Variables related to Bender-Gestalt scores. Studies have investigated various factors associated with Bender-Gestalt performance, including ethnic differences, gender differences, and deafness.

Ethnic differences. Ethnic minority children, especially black children, tend to score lower than white children on the Bender-Gestalt (Koppitz, 1975; Marmorale & Brown, 1977; Sattler & Gwynne, 1982a; Taylor & Partenio, 1984). A number of reasons have been proposed to account for their lower performance, including slower perceptual-motor development, delayed maturation, difficulty in understanding the task requirements, insufficient motivation, limited perceptual-motor experiences, cognitive deficits, and insufficient experience in the use of verbal mediation in solving nonverbal tasks (Greenberg & Alshan, 1974; Vega & Powell, 1970). Which reason or combination of reasons is most important is still open to study.

When IQs are held constant across ethnic groups, the performances of black and white children on the Bender-Gestalt are not significantly different (Zuelzer, Stedman, & Adams, 1976). Consequently, perceptual-motor differences between ethnic groups may be related to differences in level of measured intelligence or to some other variable that may be mediated by level of measured intelligence, such as motivation or task orientation.

There are few differences between the perceptual-motor skills of Mexican-American and Anglo-American children (Zuelzer et al., 1976). American Indian children between 5 and 10 years of age, however, have less well developed visual-motor skills than do Anglo-American children (Price, 1976; Taylor & Thweatt, 1972). By the age of 11 to 12 years, children in the two groups perform at a similar level. Perceptual immaturity and differences in school experiences might account for the group differences at the younger ages. Overall, the Bender-Gestalt appears to be less culturally loaded than are tests of cognitive ability.

Gender differences. Minor sex differences appear on the Bender-Gestalt (Koppitz, 1975). Girls in kindergarten may score slightly higher than boys, but the differences disappear by first grade.

Deafness. Bender-Gestalt scores of deaf children have been found to be lower than those of children with normal hearing (Gilbert & Levee, 1967; Keogh, Vernon, & Smith, 1970). One possible reason for this difference is that deafness has many etiologies that can affect visual-motor ability, including brain damage.

Comment on the Bender-Gestalt

The Bender-Gestalt is useful in an assessment battery for developing hypotheses about the child's perceptual-motor ability. Alone it is not a sufficient basis for making definitive diagnoses. It provides useful indices of the perceptual-motor development of children, particularly those between 5 and 8 years of age, and of perceptual-motor deficits in older children and adults.

Test-Your-Skill Exercises

A series of interpretive statements made about children's Bender-Gestalt drawings are presented in Exhibit 14-1. Critically evaluate each statement and then compare your answers with those shown in Appendix A.

Exhibit 14-1

Test-Your-Skill Exercises for the Bender-Gestalt

Directions: Each statement in this exhibit contains some error. Critically evaluate each statement. Then compare your answers with those found in Appendix A.

Poor Writing

1. "Her perceptual-motor skill fell in her age level."
2. "She drew quickly and carefully during the Bender-Gestalt test, but rarely inspected the cards. She positioned her face very close to each card and was very precise by counting the dots."
3. "The Bender-Gestalt determines whether or not the person is suffering from distortion in the visual-motor process."

Technical Errors

4. "The Bender-Gestalt results are invalid because the Koppitz system does not permit one to score the Bender-Gestalt for a 14-year-old."
5. "On the Bender-Gestalt she had two errors."

Inaccurate or Incomplete Interpretations

6. "All of the errors Tom made on the Bender-Gestalt are significant indicators of brain disorder."
7. "Two figures collided, which possibly indicates some peripheral neurological impairment."
8. "The Bender-Gestalt results suggest good reading ability."
9. "Her small Bender-Gestalt drawings suggest that she was anxious during the test session."

10. "Alice, a 14-year-old, scored a 1 on the Koppitz developmental scoring system for the Bender-Gestalt. Therefore, a slight perceptual-motor problem may exist."
11. "Her completion of the designs in less than 3 minutes may indicate an impulsive style."
12. This statement was written about a 16-year-old: "Bill's performance on the Bender-Gestalt suggests a slightly abnormal level of perceptual-motor maturation."
13. "Karla's generally quiet behavior during testing was supported by indications of passivity in her Bender-Gestalt drawings."
14. "Her use of space on the Bender-Gestalt—constricting and expanding in the same protocol—may indicate ambivalent modes of approach-avoidance behavior and wide mood fluctuations."
15. This statement was written about an 11-year-old girl: "Susan's Bender-Gestalt drawings showed no score, and suggest no obvious personality characteristic."
16. "His methodical sequencing may indicate rigidity in cognitive style."

Inappropriate Recommendations

17. "The existence of emotional indicators on the Bender-Gestalt suggests that Joanne should participate in counseling."
18. "His performance on the Bender-Gestalt indicate that Frank should have visual-motor training to assist in his handwriting skills."

DEVELOPMENTAL TEST OF VISUAL-MOTOR INTEGRATION

The Developmental Test of Visual-Motor Integration (DTVMI) (Beery, 1982) is a perceptual-motor ability test for children aged 4 through 13 years. The DTVMI was originally normed in 1964 and then renormed in 1981. The child is required to copy up to 24 geometric forms, which are arranged in order of increasing difficulty. Testing may be discontinued after three consecutive failures. The test can be either individually or group administered in about 15 minutes. Each design is scored on a pass-fail basis.

Scores

Raw scores are converted into standard scores with $M = 10$, $SD = 3$. Additionally, percentile ranks and age-equivalent scores are provided. Norms are from ages 4-0 through 13-0 and up.

Standardization

The standardization group for the 1981 norms consisted of 3,090 children, ages 2-9 through 19-8. The sample contained children from various ethnic and socioeconomic groups, almost equally divided by sex. No information is provided as to how well the standardization sample represented the population as described by U.S. census data.

Reliability

Reliabilities reported in the manual are based on the 1964 norms. Test-retest reliabilities, with intervals ranging from 2 weeks to 7 months, range from .63 to .92 (*Mdn*

$r_{xx} = .81$), whereas internal consistency reliabilities range from .66 to .93 (Mdn $r_{xx} = .79$). Interrater reliabilities range from .58 to .99 (Mdn $r = .93$).

Validity

Validity studies reported in the manual are based on the 1964 norms. The concurrent validity of the test is satisfactory, based on such criteria as chronological age ($r = .89$), reading achievement ($r = .50$), mental age (r's from .38 to .59), perceptual skill ($r = .80$), and psycholinguistic skills (r's from .20 to .81). In a study of children in kindergarten to third grade, the DTVMI was found to have the following four factors: simple horizontal and vertical lines, open geometric designs, closed geometric designs, and three-dimensional designs (Polubinski, Melamed, & Prinzo, 1986).

Comment on the Developmental Test of Visual-Motor Integration

The Developmental Test of Visual-Motor Integration is useful for measuring visual-motor ability. In spite of the high interrater reliability, however, a large number of subjective scoring judgments are required and substantial scoring disagreements have been found (Snyder, Snyder, & Massong, 1981). The test would benefit from a more adequate description of the standardization sample and from standard errors of measurement for the scores. Many of the interpretive rationales described for the Bender-Gestalt also apply to the Developmental Test of Visual-Motor Integration.

AUDITORY DISCRIMINATION TEST

The Auditory Discrimination Test (ADT) (Reynolds, 1987) was originally published by Wepman in 1958. It is designed to measure children's ability to hear spoken language accurately. The ADT was revised and nationally standardized in the early 1980s and is applicable for children from 4 years, 0 months to 8 years, 11 months of age. The test consists of 40 word-pairs matched for familiarity, length, and phonetic category. Ten of the word-pairs do not differ, whereas 30 word-pairs differ in a single phoneme (initial consonant, final consonant, or medial vowel). The examiner reads each pair, and the child must indicate whether the words are the same or different. The test comes in two forms (1A and 2A). Administration time is approximately 5 to 10 minutes.

Scores

The score is determined on the basis of 30 of the 40 items. The raw score is based on the number of nonidentical pairs correctly identified. Raw scores are converted into T scores ($M = 50$, $SD = 10$), percentile ranks, and a Qualitative Score. The conversion tables are presented in 6-month increments. If the child's score on the "different" items is less than 10, or if the child identifies 7 or more of 10 "same" items as unidentical, the test is considered to be invalid. The Qualitative Score is a rough global index of a child's auditory discrimination ability. It is based on a 5-point scale that ranges from $+2$ (good) to -2 (poor).

Standardization

The standardization sample consisted of 1,885 children stratified on the basis of geographic region, age, sex, ethnic background, parent's occupation, and community size. The sample appears to be representative of the U.S. population.

Reliability

Internal consistency reliabilities for Form 1A range from .57 to .80 (Mdn $r_{xx} = .75$) over the 10 age groups. For Form 2A, they range from .65 to .82 (Mdn $r_{xx} = .79$).

Validity

Various data are presented in an attempt to validate the test. First, the Auditory Discrimination Test scores increase with age level (M at age 4-0 years $= 24.00$ and M at age 8-6 years $= 27.56$). This range, however, is extremely limited. Second, correlations between the ADT and measures of auditory speech and language abilites range from $-.69$ to $+.85$ (Reynolds, 1987). Third, correlations between the ADT and intelligence and achievement tests range from $-.82$ to $+.46$; a median r of .31 has been reported between the ADT and measures of general reading ability (Reynolds, 1987). Finally, first-grade children with known articulatory problems obtained lower scores than those without articulatory problems.

Caution is needed in using the ADT with children who speak nonstandard black English, because the test is not sensitive to their speech patterns (Smith & Brewer, 1983). With these children, as well as with other children who speak a dialect other than standard English, the ADT may be more of a measure of their degree of familiarity with standard-English phonology than of their auditory discrimination ability.

Comment on the Auditory Discrimination Test

Although the renorming of the Auditory Discrimination Test improved the test substantially, problems still remain. First, the range of scores is very narrow and reliabilities are minimally adequate. Second, the ADT fails to sample many auditory discriminations that are important in English. Finally, children may fail some items and yet be able to imitate syllables correctly. The current restandardization suggests that the ADT can serve as a rough screening measure of auditory discrimination for preschool and young elementary school–age children.

LINDAMOOD AUDITORY CONCEPTUALIZATION TEST

The Lindamood Auditory Conceptualization Test (Lindamood & Lindamood, 1979) is an individually administered test designed to evaluate children's ability to (a) discriminate speech sounds and (b) perceive the number and order of sounds within a spoken pattern. The test, designed for use with children in kindergarten through twelfth grade, assists in the identification of auditory perceptual deficiencies. Two alternate forms of the test are available.

The test has two parts. The first part requires discrimination of individual sounds, such as $|g|$ $|b|$ $|v|$, and the second part requires discrimination of longer sound patterns, such as $|op|$ from $|vop|$. The second part entails the identification of omissions, substitutions, shifts, repetitions, and differentiations.

A unique method is used to administer the test. Eighteen blocks, with six different colors, are used by the child to indicate sounds. The child selects a color to represent a sound. For example, if the examiner says "Show me $|g|$ $|g|$," the child is required to pick out any two blocks of the same color to represent this sound.

Before the test formally begins, a pretest is administered to determine whether the child knows the following concepts needed for the test: (a) left and right, (b) first and last, (c) same and different, and (d) counting to four. If the child does not know these concepts, the test cannot be administered. The test takes approximately 20 to 30 minutes to administer, pretest included. An audiotape is available to train examiners to administer the test.

Scores

Each item is scored either pass or fail (1 or 0). The raw scores for each part are multiplied by a constant to obtain a converted score. The total raw scores, by deciles, can be converted into percentile ranks for kindergarten through sixth grade; there are no conversion tables for the higher grades or for converting raw scores on the separate parts to percentile ranks. Recommended minimum scores are provided for kindergarten through twelfth grade, but the test reaches a ceiling after sixth grade. Standard scores are not available.

Standardization

The standardization sample consisted of 660 boys and girls in kindergarten through twelfth grade from a large heterogeneous school district in Monterey, California. The sample included a range of socioeconomic classes, ethnic backgrounds, and linguistic backgrounds. There were 420 children from kindergarten through sixth grade and 240 children from seventh through twelfth grades. The children were selected from groups rated by their teachers as performing well or poorly in school.

Reliability

Alternate-form reliability with a sample of 52 children was high, $r_{xx} = .96$. No information is available about within-grade reliabilities.

Validity

For the standardization sample, correlations between the combined reading and spelling subtests of the Wide Range Achievement Test and the Lindamood Auditory Conceptualization Test range from .66 to .81 (*Mdn r* = .75). For another sample of 52 children, the correlations range from .72 to .78.

Comment on the Lindamood Auditory Conceptualization Test

The Lindamood Auditory Conceptualization Test has several shortcomings. The major problem with the Lindamood Auditory Conceptualization Test is the absence of normative data. The lack of means, standard deviations, and scaled scores prevents an evaluation of the test's psychometric properties. Reliability and validity data are also insufficient.

Another possible problem with the test is that examiners all must have excellent diction skills, because differences among examiners in these skills would contribute to test unreliability. Furthermore, the test cannot be used unless the child has knowledge of certain concepts, thus limiting its use with preschool children. Finally, adequate vision is required.

In spite of its shortcomings, the Lindamood Auditory Conceptualization Test provides a unique method of assessing auditory skills in such areas as sound discrimination, short-term memory, and sequencing (Butler, 1978). The test should be viewed as a screening device, rather than as an instrument that provides a precise estimate of auditory ability.

GOLDMAN-FRISTOE-WOODCOCK TEST OF AUDITORY DISCRIMINATION

The Goldman-Fristoe-Woodcock Test of Auditory Discrimination (Goldman, Fristoe, & Woodcock, 1970) provides standardized measures of speech-sound discrimination ability for children (as young as 4 years of age) and adults. Measures of auditory discrimination are obtained (a) under ideal conditions (Quiet Subtest) and (b) in the presence of controlled background noise (Noise Subtest). Individual words are presented by means of an audiocassette tape. The examinee is required to point to one of four pictures on a plate that best corresponds to the word.

The test has three parts:

1. *Training procedure.* During the training procedure the examinee is familiarized with the pictures and names that are used on the two subtests.

2. *Quiet Subtest.* Individual words are presented in the absence of any noise. This subtest provides a measure of auditory discrimination under ideal conditions.

3. *Noise Subtest.* The words are presented in the presence of distracting "cafeteria" background noise on the tape. This subtest provides a measure of auditory discrimination under conditions similar to those encountered in everyday life.

The Goldman-Fristoe-Woodcock is relatively easy to administer, requiring a minimum of preparation and training. A tape recorder and a set of earphones are needed to monitor what the examinee is hearing. A quiet and adequately lighted testing room is recommended. The test takes approximately 15 minutes to administer.

Scores

The primary method of scoring consists of determining the number of errors made by the examinee. This number is then converted by age level into a standard score ($M = 50$, $SD = 10$) on each subtest. The manual provides a procedure for evaluating errors, such as those made on voiced sound words (those involving use of vocal cords) or unvoiced sound words.

Standardization

The Goldman-Fristoe-Woodcock was standardized on 745 individuals, 3 years to 84 years of age, with varying numbers of individuals (from 6 to 83) at each age level. They resided in three states—Minnesota, New Jersey, and Tennessee. Individuals with moderate or severe hearing losses were excluded from the sample. No information is given about the socioeconomic status or ethnicity of the sample.

Reliability

In the standardization sample the internal consistency (split-half reliability) coefficient is .79 for the Quiet Subtest and .68 for the Noise Subtest. The authors believe that these low reliabilities are a product of the brevity of the test. In a clinical sample of 242 children, ages 4 to 12 years, the split-half reliability coefficients were .87 for the Quiet Subtest and .68 for the Noise Subtest. Test-retest reliability coefficients (interval of two weeks) for a sample of 17 preschool speech-handicapped children were .87 for the Quiet Subtest and .81 for the Noise Subtest.

Validity

The manual reports a variety of validity indices. Point-biserial correlations of .68 and .72 were found between auditory discrimination ability scores and scores on the Quiet Subtest and Noise Subtest, respectively. The two subtests had correlations of .39 for the standardization group and .53 for clinical samples. Correlations with the Stanford-Binet: Form L-M for a sample of 40 culturally disadvantaged preschool children were .60 for the Quiet Subtest and .52 for the Noise Subtest. For a sample of educable mentally retarded children, correlations with the Peabody Picture Vocabulary Test were extremely low: .15 for the Quiet Subtest and .00 for the Noise Subtest. For a sample of 122 kindergarten children, correlations with the Primary Mental Abilities Test were .48 for the Quiet Subtest and .24 for the Noise Subtest. Finally, correlations with the Auditory Attention Span for Related Syllables subtest from the Detroit Tests of Learning Aptitude were .34 for the Quiet Subtest and .20 for the Noise Subtest.

Comment on the Goldman-Fristoe-Woodcock Test of Auditory Discrimination

The psychometric properties of the Goldman-Fristoe-Woodcock are less than adequate. The reliability coefficients are not up to acceptable standards, and the standard errors of measurement are quite large. Furthermore, the test has limited validity. Although the test may be helpful as a crude measure of auditory discrimination, it fails to differentiate adequately among some age groups. For example, an error of 3 results in exactly the same standard score for children ages 11 through 18. It may be, however, that auditory discrimination skills reach a peak at some time during the preadolescent period, so only those who severely deviate from the norm can be reliably diagnosed.

BRUININKS-OSERETSKY TEST OF MOTOR PROFICIENCY

The Bruininks-Oseretsky Test of Motor Proficiency (Bruininks, 1978) is an individually administered test of gross and fine motor functioning of children from 4½ to 14½ years of age. The test contains 46 items grouped into eight subtests (see Table 14-2), four of which measure gross motor skills (subtests 1, 2, 3, and 4); three, fine motor skills (subtests 6, 7, and 8); and one, both gross and fine motor skills (subtest 5). In addition to scores for each subtest, composite scores are obtained for the gross motor subtests, fine motor subtests, and total battery. A short form of 14 items is also available for use as a brief survey of motor proficiency. The complete test takes between 45 and 60 minutes to administer.

The Bruininks-Oseretsky is based on the United States adaptation of the Oseretsky Tests of Motor Proficiency

(Doll, 1946). About 60 percent of the items are new; the remainder are from the Oseretsky Tests of Motor Proficiency. The Bruininks-Oseretsky reflects advances in content, structure, and technical qualities over former versions of the tests.

Scores

The test provides subtest scores ($M = 15$, $SD = 5$), a Gross Motor Composite score, a Fine Motor Composite score, and a Battery Composite score ($M = 50$, $SD = 10$ for all composite scores). For each of these areas, standard scores, percentile ranks, and stanines are available. In addition, age equivalents are available for the subtest scores.

Standardization

The Bruininks-Oseretsky was standardized on 765 boys and girls selected from various schools, day-care centers, nursery schools, and kindergartens in the United States and Canada. A stratified sampling procedure, based on the 1970 U.S. census, was used to select the children. Stratification variables included age, sex, race, community size, and geographic region.

Reliability

Test-retest reliabilities range from .86 to .89 for the Battery Composite, and from .68 to .88 for the Fine and Gross Motor Composites. The Gross Motor Composite yields somewhat higher reliabilities than does the Fine Motor Composite. Average subtest test-retest reliabilities range from .56 to .86. Reliabilities associated with the individual

Table 14-2
Description of Subtests on the Bruininks-Oseretsky Test of Motor Proficiency

Test	Description
1. Running Speed and Agility (one item)	Running speed
2. Balance (eight items)	Static balance and maintaining balance while executing various walking movements
3. Bilateral Coordination (eight items)	Sequential and simultaneous coordination of upper with lower limbs, and upper limbs only
4. Strength (three items)	Arm and shoulder strength, abdominal strength, and leg strength
5. Upper Limb Coordination (nine items)	Visual tracking with movements of arms and hands and precise movements of arms, hands, or fingers
6. Response Speed (one item)	Ability to respond quickly to a moving visual stimulus
7. Visual-Motor Control (eight items)	Ability to coordinate precise hand and visual movements
8. Upper Limb Speed and Dexterity (eight items)	Hand and finger dexterity, hand speed, and arm speed

subtests suggest that extreme caution is needed in using individual subtest scores as a basis for clinical interpretation. Average standard errors of measurement are 4.0 for the Battery Composite, 4.6 for the Gross Motor Composite, and 4.7 for the Fine Motor Composite.

Validity

Construct validity of the Bruininks-Oseretsky was evaluated in terms of (a) the relationship between test scores and chronological age, (b) the internal consistency of the subtests, and (c) the factor structure of the items in each subtest. Product-moment correlations between subtest scores and chronological age for the standardization sample range from .57 to .86 (*Mdn r* = .78). These correlations indicate that there is a close relationship between subtest scores and chronological age. Subtest scores show the expected increase from one age group to the next. Internal consistency measures indicate that the correlations between items and their respective subtest scores are closer than between items and the total test scores.

A factor analysis performed on the standardization sample provides limited support for grouping the items into the various subtests. Five factors were found, with one factor (general motor ability) accounting for approximately 70 percent of the total variance. The remaining factors were specifically associated with the various subtests. Most of the items measuring fine motor ability (14 out of 17) loaded on the general motor ability factor. The fine motor subtests did not cluster together on clearly identifiable factors as did the gross motor subtests.

Comment on the Bruininks-Oseretsky Test of Motor Proficiency

The Bruininks-Oseretsky Test is useful in assessing gross and fine motor skills, developing and evaluating motor training programs, and screening for special purposes. It is a refinement of the previous scale, which has proved to be useful for the clinical evaluation of motor skills. The manual and materials are attractive and well designed. The variety of scores available facilitates the use and interpretation of the results.

COMMENT ON TESTS OF VISUAL-MOTOR PERCEPTION, AUDITORY PERCEPTION, AND MOTOR PROFICIENCY

Although the Bender-Gestalt and the Developmental Test of Visual-Motor Integration are similar tests of visual-

motor integration skills, the scores derived from the two tests are not interchangeable (Breen, 1982; Breen, Carlson, & Lehman, 1985; DeMers et al., 1981; Knoff & Sperling, 1986; Lehman & Breen, 1982; Skeen et al., 1982). For example, in a study of the 1982 DTVMI norms, 11 of 32 comparisons between the DTVMI and Bender-Gestalt revealed differences of at least 18 months (Breen, 1982). The two tests require somewhat different formats. The DTVMI is more structured than the Bender-Gestalt. On the DTVMI the child copies the designs within a designated area on the page, whereas on the Bender-Gestalt the child can draw the designs anywhere on the page with minimal size restraints. The different formats may subtly affect the child's performance.

In addition to the tests covered in this chapter, Appendix F briefly reviews the Purdue Perceptual-Motor Survey, the Developmental Test of Visual Perception, and the Southern California Sensory Integration Tests. These tests are occasionally useful as supplements for the assessment of perceptual and motor functions, but should primarily be used on an informal basis.

Tests of auditory perception need further refinement, because at present they do not correlate highly with one another (Koenke, 1978). They also suffer "from the problem of phonemic irrelevance and insufficient trials" (Locke, 1979, p. 126). Thus results from auditory discrimination tests should be viewed cautiously, subject to verification through a more detailed study of the child's abilities.

SUMMARY

1. The assessment of visual-motor perception and integration, visual perception, auditory perception, and motor proficiency can aid in the evaluation of learning disabilities and neurological deficits.

2. Observation of a child's visual-motor performance complements the more formal scoring procedures and aids in developing hypotheses.

3. Testing-of-limits procedures are useful in pinpointing areas of possible visual-motor deficits.

4. Low performance on tests of visual-motor ability may result from misperception, execution difficulties, or integrative or central processing difficulties.

5. The Bender Visual Motor Gestalt Test is the most popular visual-motor test and has received much study. The Koppitz Developmental Scoring System for the Bender-Gestalt is helpful in evaluating the maturational skills of children, primarily those from 5 through 8 years of age. The major errors studied in the system are distortion of shape, rotation, integration, and perseveration. The reliability of the Developmental Scoring System

is not adequate for the purpose of individual diagnosis. The system has acceptable validity when used to assess perceptual-motor development, but concurrent and predictive validities are too low for predicting school achievement.

6. Possible diagnostic indicators of brain damage on the Bender-Gestalt are as follows: sequence confusion, collision, crowding of designs, superimposition of design, workover, irregular line quality, angulation difficulty, perseveration, line extension, contamination, rotation, omission, and retrogression. These signs, however, also appear in the records of normal children. A diagnosis of brain damage should *never* be made on the basis of the Bender-Gestalt alone. It has not been possible to differentiate accurately Bender-Gestalt indications of immaturity from those of pathology.

7. Black children tend to obtain lower scores on the Bender-Gestalt than do white children, whereas there are relatively few differences between the scores of Mexican-American and Anglo-American children. Sex differences on the Bender-Gestalt are minor.

8. The Developmental Test of Visual Motor Integration is a useful test for measuring visual-motor ability.

9. The Auditory Discrimination Test is useful as a rough screening measure of auditory discrimination for children between 4 and 8 years of age. The test may not be appropriate for ethnic minority children, however.

10. The Lindamood Auditory Conceptualization Test has some shortcomings and limitations, but still can serve as a screening device for assessing auditory skills.

11. The Goldman-Fristoe-Woodcock Test of Auditory Discrimination has poor psychometric properties, but may serve as a crude measure of auditory discrimination.

12. The Bruininks-Oseretsky Test of Motor Proficiency is a useful test for assessing gross and fine motor skills of children ages 4½ to 14½ years.

KEY TERMS, CONCEPTS, AND NAMES

Visual-motor tests as diagnostic tools (p. 360)
Bender Visual Motor Gestalt Test (p. 361)
Bender-Gestalt tachistoscopic procedure (p. 362)
Bender-Gestalt memory phase (p. 362)
Koppitz Developmental Bender Scoring System (p. 362)
Distortion of shape on Bender-Gestalt (p. 363)
Rotation on Bender-Gestalt (p. 363)
Integration difficulties on Bender-Gestalt (p. 363)
Perseveration on Bender-Gestalt (p. 363)
Sequence confusion on Bender-Gestalt (p. 365)
Collision on Bender-Gestalt (p. 365)
Superimposition of design on Bender-Gestalt (p. 365)
Workover on Bender-Gestalt (p. 366)
Irregular line quality on Bender-Gestalt (p. 366)
Angulation difficulty on Bender-Gestalt (p. 366)
Line extension on Bender-Gestalt (p. 366)
Contamination on Bender-Gestalt (p. 366)
Omissions on Bender-Gestalt (p. 366)
Retrogression on Bender-Gestalt (p. 366)
Developmental Test of Visual-Motor Integration (p. 368)
Auditory Discrimination Test (p. 369)
Lindamood Auditory Conceptualization Test (p. 370)
Goldman-Fristoe-Woodcock Test of Auditory Discrimination (p. 371)
Bruininks-Oseretsky Test of Motor Proficiency (p. 372)

STUDY QUESTIONS

1. Discuss how you would go about observing performance on visual-motor tests.

2. Discuss some general factors in administering and interpreting visual-motor tests.

3. Discuss the assets and limitations of

a. the Bender Visual Motor Gestalt Test

b. the Developmental Test of Visual Motor Integration

c. the Auditory Discrimination Test

d. the Lindamood Auditory Conceptualization Test

e. the Goldman-Fristoe-Woodcock Test of Auditory Discrimination

f. the Bruininks-Oseretsky Test of Motor Proficiency

ASSESSMENT OF
ADAPTIVE BEHAVIOR
AND BEHAVIOR PROBLEMS

Talents are best nurtured in solitude: character is best formed in the stormy billows of the world.

—Goethe

This chapter reviews some of the major adaptive behavior scales and behavior checklists currently in use. These instruments are used primarily to generate information that is helpful in making classification, training, and intervention decisions. Adaptive behavior scales play an important role in the assessment of mentally retarded individuals. Behavioral checklists, on the other hand, are used with a wide variety of children with behavioral disorders. Both types of procedures are heavily dependent on the informant's ability to give reliable and valid information.

INTRODUCTION TO ASSESSMENT OF ADAPTIVE BEHAVIOR AND BEHAVIOR PROBLEMS

Definition of Adaptive Behavior

The American Association on Mental Deficiency (AAMD) (Grossman, 1983) defines adaptive behavior as behavior that is effective in meeting the natural and social demands of one's environment. (See Chapter 21 for a discussion of adaptive behavior in relation to the definition of mental retardation.) The assessment of adaptive behavior focuses on two major issues: (a) the degree to which individuals are able to function and maintain themselves independently and (b) the degree to which they meet satisfactorily the culturally imposed demands of personal and social responsibility. Thus adaptive behavior reflects a person's competence in meeting independent needs and the social demands of his or her environment. Definitions of adaptive behavior tend to be imprecise, because there is no way of knowing the environments in which individuals will be required to function. Furthermore, adaptive behavior must be considered within a developmental context: maturation during the preschool years, academic performance during the school years, and social and economic independence beginning in early adulthood. Adaptive behavior includes independent functioning skills, physical development, language development, and academic competencies. No one instrument can measure all of the relevant domains of adaptive behavior.

Applications of Adaptive Behavior Scales and Behavioral Checklists

Well-normed adaptive behavior scales and behavioral checklists (a) identify the examinee's behavioral (and sometimes affective) strengths and deficiencies; (b) provide an objective basis for evaluating the examinee's progress or the results of an intervention program; (c) permit comparison of the examinee's behavior in different situations (for example, at home, school, or hospital ward); (d) facilitate comparison of information from different informants; (e) provide a standardized way of reporting information between and within organizations; and (f) stimulate new intervention programs and research. Some adaptive behavior scales and behavioral checklists also provide schedules of normal development.

Adaptive behavior scales and behavioral checklists provide information about a child or group of children that complements information obtained from other assessment procedures. These instruments permit a study of how each parent views the child's problems, how parents' views compare with teachers' views, and how behavior may change as a result of therapeutic or remedial interventions. They also are helpful in describing clinically relevant dimensions of behavior. When a child's adaptive abilities are evaluated, other features of the child's environment must also be considered, including the child's culture, socioeconomic status, and motivation, as well as parental expectations. Adaptive behavior scores are complex products of a myriad of personal, social, cognitive, and situational variables.

Factors That Contribute to Adaptive Behavior Scores and Behavioral Checklist Ratings

Adaptive behavior scores and behavioral checklist ratings reflect the complex interaction of the characteristics of

• the scale or checklist used (content of items, social desirability of items, scale values, wording of items, standardization sample)
• the child (age, sex, type of disturbance)
• the informant or rater (expectancies, recall ability, openness, comprehension of items, response bias)
• the examiner (sex, ethnicity, traits, status)
• the setting (school, home, playground, hospital, clinic, prison)
• the reasons for the evaluation (screening, diagnosis, placement, program evaluation).

Although on some occasions some characteristics will play a more important role than others, each contributes to the final score or rating. You should be cognizant of these factors and how they may influence the assessment findings.

Types of Behavioral Checklists

There are hundreds of instruments that are useful in obtaining behavioral ratings of children. They can be distinguished by the age group they cover, the setting to which the questions are directed (for example, school or family), and the type of classifications they provide (for example, broad-band syndromes or more differentiated syndromes). The checklists referred to in this chapter are representative of the many behavioral checklists available.

Factor Labels in Behavioral Checklists

An inspection of different behavioral checklists indicates that in various checklists the same factor label covers different behaviors, and, conversely, similar behaviors are given different factor labels. For example, some scales isolate hyperactive behavior, whereas others include hyperactive behavior under a conduct-problem factor.

Some checklists present a small number of broad-band factors (for example, Conduct Problem, Personality Problem, Immaturity), whereas others present a large number of narrow-band factors (for example, Hyperactivity, Withdrawal, Aggression). In general, broad-band factors appear to be more reliable than narrow-band factors. Broad-band factors are valuable for group analyses. They permit the clustering of people into groups on the basis of factor profiles. Narrow-band factors, however, provide valuable information about specific problems that may be of interest to teachers and clinicians, and they can be grouped to provide broad-band factors.

The Informant

The informants who provide the information required for adaptive behavior scales or behavioral checklists may be parents, teachers, mental health workers, aides, nurses, social workers, or occasionally "naive" observers. Informants are required to make judgments about the child's (or adult's) functioning. Because these judgments are subject to bias and distortion, each informant's credibility must be evaluated. Serious doubts about the informant's credibility should result in adaptive behavior estimates' being questioned or even discarded. Informants will reveal their own attitudes toward the examinee and toward the areas of adaptive behavior and social competence being evaluated. These attitudes also should be considered in the overall evaluation. When there are multiple informants, consider to what extent they agree. For example, which behaviors show stability across informants and which behaviors consistently show differences?

Different ratings may mean that (a) the child varies his or her behavior depending on the situation or setting, (b) one or more of the informants is not reliable, (c) the informants have different response styles, or (d) other unknown factors are contributing to the unreliability of the ratings. Level of agreement also may be dependent on the level of stress in the respondents (for example, levels of agreement are generally higher in nondistressed than in distressed families) and on the type of psychopathology manifested by the child (for example, levels of agreement are generally higher for children with a conduct disorder than for those with an anxiety reaction).

Informants may differ as to their familiarity with the child, sensitivity and tolerance for behavior problems, personality, expectations, and willingness to use certain rating scale positions. Raters also may use different frames of reference, depending on whether the children are clinic patients or school children. Additionally, some raters may be influenced by the child's race, socioeconomic status, or appearance and allow these variables to affect their judgments of the child's behavior. In such cases, their judgments are biased and their ratings invalid.

The reliability and validity of ratings may be affected by the specificity of the rating task. Items that require ratings of specific behaviors (for example, "Has the child fought with another child on at least three occasions during the last month?") may yield different coefficients from items that require more global judgments (for example, "Is the child depressed?").

Because parents and teachers are likely to see different aspects of the child, both sources are needed to obtain a comprehensive clinical picture. Parents are better able to rate behaviors that occur primarily at home (eating, sleeping, sibling relations), whereas teachers are more qualified to rate behaviors that occur primarily at school (academic performance, peer relations, attention, following directions). Teacher ratings have the advantage of being based on observations made in a relatively standardized classroom and on direct comparisons with other children of the same developmental level as the referred child (Edelbrock, 1979). Teachers may not be available during summer months, however, and their ratings may rely on limited information when they are made during the first few months of the school year or refer to behaviors that occur outside the classroom. Parent ratings have the advantage of being based on observations of the child's behavior in a variety of situations and over a longer period of time.

Comparison of Adaptive Behavior Scales, Behavioral Checklists, and Direct Observation of Behavior

Behavior problems can be evaluated by direct observation methods (see Chapter 17) as well as by adaptive behavior scales and behavioral checklists. Unfortunately, the three methods may not provide congruent data. Discrepancies occur primarily because the behavior samples are not usually the same for the three methods. Teacher rating scales generally sample a broad range of behaviors, with the incidence of certain behaviors tending to be exaggerated relative to the actual rates of occurrence, whereas direct observation of behavior often focuses on a more limited segment of behavior.

Teacher ratings are also based on contact with the child over a longer period of time than are direct observations. Thus behavioral checklists may capture rare but significant issues missed by time-sampling observations. Because rating scale methods and direct observation methods may be valid for different purposes and because each method provides a different perspective on problem behaviors, both should be used to assess behavior traits.

Criteria Used to Select Adaptive Behavior Scales and Behavioral Checklists

In selecting among the many available adaptive behavior scales and behavioral checklists, consider how applicable each scale or checklist is for the specific assessment or screening task. Important factors to take into account in evaluating adaptive behavior scales and behavioral checklists, include (a) *the reliability and validity of the scale or checklist*; (b) *the reliability of the informants who complete the scale or checklist*; and (c) *the scope*, *structure*, and *clinical utility of the scale or checklist*.

Reliability and validity. Reliability and validity are important features of adaptive behavior scales and behavioral checklists. Careful attention should be given to internal consistency reliability as well as to interrater reliability. The standardization group for the scale should be appropriate for the examinee.

Reliability of informants. Rating scale and checklist methods are subject to many of the same sources of error as are observational methods—halo effects, leniency errors, proximity errors, and social desirability effects (see Chapter 17). Situational factors also may affect informants' ratings. Raters may rate a child as more deviant on the initial assessment and less deviant at the end of treatment simply to please the therapist or teacher. Precautions must be taken to keep such errors from occurring.

Scope. Adaptive behavior scales usually focus on competencies, whereas behavioral checklists usually focus on maladaptive behaviors; however, adaptive behavior scales and behavioral checklists may overlap in their content.

Structure. The structure of adaptive behavior scales and behavioral checklists encompasses the content of the items, domains covered, number of items, number of response alternatives, number of points defined on the rating scale, time period covered by the items, and types of judgments required.

Although there are many adaptive behavior scales and behavioral checklists, most cover only certain types of behaviors; no single instrument covers all areas of behavior. Thus it is important to select an adaptive behavior scale or behavioral checklist with item content and domains appropriate to your purposes. A behavioral checklist designed to evaluate hyperactivity, for example, may not be suitable as a general screening tool or a diagnostic tool, but it will be useful for its intended purpose.

Some scales or checklists have two response alternatives (for example, *yes* or *no*), whereas others may have 3, 5, or 7 alternatives (for example, the 3 response alternatives could be *never*, *seldom*, *often*). Some scales or checklists specify each point on the scale (*very weak*, *weak*, *neither weak nor strong*, *strong*, *very strong*), whereas others specify only the end points (*very weak* to *very strong*). Ratings may be based on no specific time period (for example, rate how aggressive the child is) or on definite time periods (for example, rate how aggressive the child was during the last week).

The diversity of ratings required by some adaptive behavior scales and behavioral checklists is so great that few informants have the ability to judge the child's skills adequately. Some items require the informant to observe behavior in a natural setting, whereas other items require observations in a controlled testing situation. In such cases, more than one informant may be needed to obtain an overall picture of the child's adaptive behavior.

Clinical utility. Adaptive behavior scales and behavioral checklists should have good clinical utility: they should be easy to administer, require relatively little time to complete, and be sensitive to treatment effects.

AAMD ADAPTIVE BEHAVIOR SCALE

The AAMD Adaptive Behavior Scale (ABS) (Nihira, Foster, Shellhaas, & Leland, 1974) is a behavior rating scale for use with mentally retarded, emotionally maladjusted, and developmentally disabled individuals who are institutionalized. It covers an age range from 3 to 69 years. Two types of competencies are assessed: behavioral and affective (see Table 15-1). The scale evaluates the personal and social resources of institutionalized individuals. The 1974

Table 15-1
AAMD Adaptive Behavior Scale Domains

Part I (10 behavior domains)	
I. Independent functioning	C. Other domestic activities
A. Eating	VII. Vocational activity
B. Toilet use	VIII. Self-direction
C. Cleanliness	A. Initiative
D. Appearance	B. Perseverance
E. Care of clothing	C. Leisure time
F. Dressing and undressing	IX. Responsibility
G. Travel	X. Socialization
H. General independent functioning	
II. Physical development	*Part II* (14 domains related to personality and behavior disorders)
A. Sensory development	
B. Motor development	I. Violent and destructive behavior
III. Economic activity	II. Antisocial behavior
A. Money handling and budgeting	III. Rebellious behavior
B. Shopping skills	IV. Untrustworthy behavior
IV. Language development	V. Withdrawal
A. Expression	VI. Stereotyped behavior and odd mannerisms
B. Comprehension	VII. Inappropriate interpersonal manners
C. Social language development	VIII. Unacceptable vocal habits
V. Numbers and time	IX. Unacceptable or eccentric habits
VI. Domestic activity	X. Self-abusive behavior
A. Cleaning	XI. Hyperactive tendencies
B. Kitchen duties	XII. Sexually aberrant behavior
	XIII. Psychological disturbances
	XIV. Use of medications

Source: Reprinted by permission of the publisher and author from C. J. Fogelman (Ed.), *AAMD Adaptive Behavior Scale Manual, 1974 Revision*, pp. 6–7. Copyright 1974, American Association on Mental Deficiency.

version is a revision of the first scale, which was published in 1969.

Part I of the ABS, covering 10 behavioral domains, measures basic survival skills and habits important in the maintenance of personal independence in daily living. Part II, covering 14 domains, focuses primarily on maladaptive behavior related to personality and behavior disorders. Part I is organized along developmental lines; Part II focuses on maladaptive behavior.

The ABS takes approximately 15 to 30 minutes to administer and can be given by persons with minimal training. One of three methods is used to obtain information about the referred individual. In first-person assessment, the informant completes the scale himself or herself; the informant must both be familiar with the individual and have had enough professional training to make appropriate ratings. In the interview method, which is most useful with parents, the interviewer completes the scale based on the information provided by the interviewees. In third-party assessment, information is obtained from more than one informant, including ward attendants, parents, and nurses.

In evaluating the adaptive behavior levels of deaf-blind children, the language development items (Domain IV) of the ABS should be modified to allow credit to be given for alternative methods of communication, such as sign language, Braille, and finger spelling (Suess, Cotten, Gustave, & Sison, 1983) (see Exhibit 15-1). By not permitting credit to be given for alternative forms of communication, a literal interpretation of Domain IV items penalizes many children with severe sensory impairments for their inability to use normal modes of communication; the modifications allow for improved language development scores.

Scores

Raw scores are converted to percentile ranks for the 11 age groups.

Standardization

The ABS was standardized on approximately 4,000 persons residing in 68 facilities for the mentally retarded

━ **Exhibit 15-1** ━━━

Modification of Items for Scoring Alternative Communication Domain IV (Language Development, Items 32–40) of the AAMD Adaptive Behavior Scale

Please indicate individual's primary mode of receptive and expressive communication (e.g., sign language, Braille, fingerspelling, teletouch, etc.)

Receptive: _____

Expressive: _____

A. Expression
(32) Writing and/or Brailling (Circle only one)
(33) Preverbal Expression (No revision of ABS item)
(34) Articulation:
   If Verbal: (check all statements which apply)
   Speech is low, weak, whispered, or difficult to hear.
   Speech is slowed, deliberate, or labored.
   Speech is hurried, accelerated, or pushed.
   Speaks with blocking, halting, or other irregular interruptions.
   (Score is 4 minus number checked)
   If Nonverbal: (check all statements which apply)
   Signing or fingerspelling is indiscriminant or difficult to understand.
   Signing or fingerspelling is slowed, deliberate, or labored.

Signing or fingerspelling is hurried, accelerated, or pushed.
Signs or fingerspells with blocking, halting, or other irregular interruptions.
(Score is 4 minus number checked)
(35) Sentences (Spoken, signed, or fingerspelled)
(36) Word Usage (Spoken, signed, or fingerspelled)

B. Comprehension
(37) Reading (Sight or Braille)
(38) Complex Instruction (Verbal, signed, Brailled, or other form of communication)

C. Social Language Development
(39) Conversation (Spoken, signed, fingerspelled, teletouch or other form of communication)
(40) Miscellaneous Language Development (Spoken, signed, fingerspelled, print-on-palm, Braille, etc.)

Source: Reprinted from J. F. Suess, P. D. Cotten, F. P. Gustave, and P. D. Sison, Jr., "The American Association on Mental Deficiency–Adaptive Behavior Scale: Allowing Credit for Alternative Means of Communication," *American Annals of the Deaf*, 1983, *128*, p. 391. Reprinted by permission of the Conference of Educational Administrators Serving the Deaf and the authors.

━━━

throughout the United States. The norming process did not take into account either intelligence level or level of retardation of the sample.

Reliability

Interrater reliability, as presented in the manual, is acceptable for Part I ($M r = .86$) but not for Part II ($M r = .57$). Isett and Spreat (1979) confirm that Part I has more satisfactory interrater reliability than Part II. Although the manual provides no estimates of test-retest or internal consistency reliabilities, other studies indicate that these reliabilities are satisfactory for Part I but not for Part II (Bean & Roszkowski, 1982; Isett & Spreat, 1979; Salagaras & Nettelback, 1983; Stack, 1984).

Validity

The ABS discriminates between individuals (a) who are classified at different adaptive behavior levels by clinical judgment and (b) who differ as to type of placement within an institution (Nihira et al., 1974). The scale is sensitive to

changes resulting from a rehabilitation program. Additionally, Part I, but not Part II, is sensitive to differences in adaptive and maladaptive behavior in subgroups of mentally retarded children (Salagaras & Nettelback, 1983).

Performance on Part I of the ABS also is related to intelligence. In a study (Roszkowski & Bean, 1980) of 224 institutionalized, mentally retarded individuals, scores on Part I were highly correlated with IQ ($r = .77$); this relationship, however, did not hold for Part II ($r = .22$).

The construct validity of the individual domain scores appears to be questionable. There is increasing evidence that the most useful scores obtained from the ABS are two general scores: an adaptive behavior score (Part I) and a maladaptive behavior score (Part II) (Arndt, 1981; Katz-Garris, Hadley, Garris, & Barnhill, 1980; Roszkowski, 1980; Spreat, 1980). The two general scores, defined as the sum of the scores for each part, are more reliable and valid than any of the individual subscores.

Although the ABS possesses some discriminant validity, serious discrepancies exist between ratings made on the ABS and those obtained by direct observation. Of 400 ratings of adaptive behavior levels across 10 behavior domains in a sample of mentally retarded persons, more than half (56 percent) were found to differ from those obtained by direct observation of the individuals' performance (Millham, Chilcutt, & Atkinson, 1978). These findings suggest that caution is needed in making generalizations from the ABS to actual behavior.

Interpreting the subscales within Part I is difficult, because several measure a wide range of skills within a domain and others only a limited range. Low ceilings on certain subscales also contribute to interpretive difficulties. Reporting raw scores for those subscales with limited ceilings (for example, Physical Development) as well as percentile ranks will help guard against misinterpretations.

The scores in Part II are skewed, with 40 to 50 percent of the standardization group displaying no inappropriate behavior. The skewness results in percentile rank scores that are difficult to interpret. The limited variability of scores also restricts the usefulness of Part II for studies needing pre- and post-measures. Additionally, scoring fails to take into account the severity of the maladaptive behavior. Serious infractions such as rape receive the same score as minor social infractions. Part II also has too few items, making it difficult to detect the individual's progress or change. All these difficulties reduce the validity of Part II.

Comment on the AAMD Adaptive Behavior Scale

The ABS is a clinically useful scale that provides information about important areas of competence for mentally retarded and other institutionalized persons. Practitioners and researchers have found the scale to be helpful, especially in describing individuals' daily living performance and the adequacy of complex social and interpersonal behavior. Despite the useful applications of the ABS, it has some major drawbacks. Its standardization group is limited, as it contained only mentally retarded individuals residing in institutions. Reliability data are limited, and validity has not been sufficiently established. Limited ceilings on some subscales cause interpretive problems. The psychometric soundness of the ABS is questionable.

AAMD ADAPTIVE BEHAVIOR SCALE— SCHOOL EDITION

The AAMD Adaptive Behavior Scale—School Edition (ABS-SE) (Lambert, Windmiller, Tharinger, & Cole, 1981) is a revision of the public school version published in 1975. The ABS-SE is used with children aged 3 years, 3 months to 17 years, 2 months. The ABS-SE aids school personnel in determining the child's adaptive behavior

level and areas of functioning within which remediation may be applied.

The ABS-SE is similar to the ABS, which was constructed for and normed on an institutionalized, mentally retarded population, except that it does not include the domains which are not applicable to behaviors in the school setting (Domestic Activity for Part I, Self-Abusive Behavior and Sexually Aberrant Behavior for Part II). The remainder of the domains in Part I and Part II of the scale are the same as those in the ABS.

It is administered in the same manner as the ABS, taking approximately 30 minutes. Both parents and teachers should complete the ABS-SE in order to generate a more complete record of the child's adaptive behavior.

Scores

The ABS-SE provides five empirically derived factor scores—Personal Self-Sufficiency, Community Self-Sufficiency, Personal-Social Responsibility, Social Adjustment, and Personal Adjustment—as well as a comparison score (or summary score) based on a combination of the first three factor scores. Raw scores are converted into scaled scores with $M = 10$, $SD = 3$. Percentile ranks, but not standard scores, are given for the comparison score. Percentile ranks also are given for the 21 domains in the scale. Separate tables are provided for regular, educable mentally retarded (EMR), and trainable mentally retarded (TMR) pupils.

Standardization

The ABS-SE was standardized on a sample of 6,500 children, ages 3 years, 3 months to 17 years, 2 months, primarily from California. Children in the sample were drawn from classes containing regular, EMR, and TMR children. No information is provided in the manual about the representativeness of the sample.

Reliability

Internal consistency reliabilities (coefficient alpha) are presented for the five factor scores by age level, separately for regular, EMR, and TMR groups. Reliability coefficients are variable. For example, on the Personal Self-Sufficiency factor the lowest reliability is .44 for regular 12-year-old pupils and the highest reliability is .89 for 6-year-old TMR pupils. The Personal Adjustment factor has a reliability coefficient as low as .27. Median reliabilities are as follows: Personal Self-Sufficiency $r_{xx} = .81$, Community Self-Sufficiency $r_{xx} = .89$, Personal-Social Responsibility r_{xx} = .88, Social Adjustment r_{xx} = .94, and Personal Adjustment r_{xx} = .65. No reliability coefficients are presented for the comparison score or for the domain scores. Additionally, no interrater reliability coefficients are reported for any scores. This is an important omission for a scale that is based on information obtained from informants.

Validity

The validity studies reported in the manual are for the most part *not* based on the revised 1981 edition. Therefore, it is difficult to determine precisely to what extent the ABS-SE is a valid instrument. Median correlations between the factor scores and IQ (tests not indicated) were as follows for a sample of 3,737 regular, EMR, and TMR children between 3 and 12 years of age: Personal Self-Sufficiency *Mdn r* = .33, Community Self-Sufficiency *Mdn r* = .67, Personal-Social Responsibility *Mdn r* = .34, Social Adjustment *Mdn r* = −.10, and Personal Adjustment *Mdn r* = −.18. These correlations indicate that IQ is most highly related to Community Self-Sufficiency. The domains in this factor include Economic Activity, Language Development, Numbers and Time, and part of Independent Functioning. There is little relationship between IQ and Social Adjustment or Personal Adjustment. The ABS-SE correctly classified 63 to 85 percent of a sample of students into regular, EMR, and TMR groups. Overall, 74 percent of the children were correctly classified.

Comment on the AAMD Adaptive Behavior Scale—School Edition

The reliability and validity of the ABS-SE are questionable. Reliability coefficients are lower than desirable (below .90) for making critical diagnostic decisions about individual children. Part I of the scale may be inappropriate for children who have physical handicaps, such as deafness, blindness, or orthopedic difficulties; who show evidence of emotional disturbance; or who have not had the opportunity to learn the adaptive behaviors being assessed (Mastenbrook, 1977). The ABS-SE is not recommended for classifying children. It does provide some information about children's adaptive behavior strengths and weaknesses, however.

ADAPTIVE BEHAVIOR INVENTORY FOR CHILDREN

The Adaptive Behavior Inventory for Children (ABIC) (Mercer & Lewis, 1978) contains six scales: Family,

Peers, Community, School, Earner/Consumer, and Self-Maintenance. Items deal with the child's family life, peer relations in school, ability to function in a variety of settings and roles, leisure time activities, and performance of routine household chores. Representative ABIC items are as follows: "How does the child get along with the children in the neighborhood?" "How often does the child become afraid at night because of bad dreams, fear of the dark, or things like that?" "Does the child use a can or bottle opener?" "How often does the child pool his/her money with other children to buy candy, soda, or other things?" Both English and Spanish editions are available.

The ABIC is administered by interviewing the child's principal guardian, usually the mother. The scale contains 242 questions, divided into two sections. Questions in the first section (1 to 35) are asked of all respondents; in the second section only those questions appropriate for the child's age are asked (36 to 242). A scale is discontinued after eight consecutive 0 (never) or N (no opportunity) responses in any combination.

Scores

Each item receives one of five scores: 0 (never), 1 (sometimes), 2 (often), N (no opportunity or not allowed), or DK (don't know). Raw scores are converted into scaled scores by using tables appropriate to the child's age. The scaled-score equivalents for the six scales and for the total score have M = 50 and SD = 15. Standard errors of measurement range from 1.95 to 2.59 for the total score and from 3.83 (Community at age 6 years) to 6.88 (Self-Maintenance at age 8 years) for the six scales.

Standardization

The ABIC was standardized on a sample of 2,085 California public school children 5-0 to 11-11 years of age. The children, randomly chosen from preselected school districts, represent three ethnic groups in approximately equal numbers (696 blacks, 690 Hispanics, and 696 whites).

Reliability

Split-half (odd-even) reliabilities for the scaled scores were calculated for each age level from 5 to 11 years for the entire standardization sample and separately for each ethnic group. Reliabilities for the total score for the complete sample and for each ethnic group were .95 or above. For the individual scales, reliabilities range from .78 (Earner/Consumer at age 5 years) to .92 (Community at ages 10 and

11 years) (*Mdn* r_{xx} = .86). Intercorrelations among the scales range from .66 to .87 (*Mdn r* = .77).

Validity

Correlations between the ABIC and the WISC-R for white and black children in the standardization sample yielded coefficients of .16 with the Verbal Scale, .14 with the Performance Scale, and .17 with the Full Scale IQ. Other studies generally report low correlations between the ABIC and the WISC-R or the California Achievement Test (Oakland, 1983b; Oakland & Feigenbaum, 1980; Sapp, Horton, McElroy, & Ray, 1979; Tebeleff & Oakland, 1977). One study (Vacc & Atwell, 1980), however, reported an *r* of .50 between the ABIC and the WISC-R in a sample of 37 5- to 11-year-old children seen at a developmental evaluation center.

Oakland (1983b) concluded that the ABIC contributes little to the prediction of either reading or mathematics achievement beyond that provided by the WISC-R. His research provided no support for the joint use of the ABIC and the WISC-R to predict achievement. Additionally, IQs from either the WISC-R or the Stanford-Binet: Form L-M were found to be better predictors of learning potential scores in a sample of normal and retarded children than were ABIC scores (Popoff-Walker, 1982).

Studies have also investigated the applicability of the ABIC to different regions of the country. In a study of 146 white, 120 black, 112 Hispanic, and 104 native American Papago children, all living in Arizona, Kazimour and Reschly (1981) reported that significant differences were found among the four ethnic groups, with the native American Papago children obtaining the lowest scores. These findings indicate that the ABIC norms are of questionable value for children living in locations other than California. Children in Texas also obtained scores significantly lower than those reported for the standardization sample (Buckley & Oakland, 1977; Scott, Mastenbrook, & Fisher, 1982).

The manual reports few significant correlations between the ABIC and the four sociocultural scales (Family Size, Family Structure, Socioeconomic Status, and Urban Acculturation) found in the SOMPA. Correlations between the ABIC and the Bender-Gestalt and between the ABIC and Visual Acuity were also low (< .15).

Comment on the Adaptive Behavior Inventory for Children

The principal strength of the ABIC is that it is a standardized instrument that measures role behavior in the home, neighborhood, and community. Six areas of adaptive behavior are measured fairly accurately, making the ABIC a potentially useful instrument for the assessment of adaptive behavior (Oakland, 1979a). Profile analysis is facilitated by the six scaled scores. (See Reynolds, 1985a, for differences required for significance when each ABIC scale is compared to the mean scaled score.)

The ABIC has some serious drawbacks. Some items have a middle-class emphasis that may discriminate against lower-socioeconomic-class children and ethnic minority children. The norms do not appear to be applicable nationwide. Additionally, the ABIC makes no provision for consideration of the child's opportunities to learn adaptive behaviors. The finding that low-income Mexican-American children score lower than other groups on the ABIC (Gridley & Mastenbrook, 1977; Scott et al., 1982) might be associated with their having fewer opportunities and lower parental expectations for acquiring adaptive behavior skills than do other groups of children. The score "no opportunity or not allowed" on the ABIC results in a lowering of the adaptive behavior score without an explanation for the lack of opportunity.

The validity of the ABIC is said to be "judged by its ability to reflect accurately the extent to which the child is meeting the expectations of the members of the social systems covered in the scales . . ." (Mercer, 1979, p. 109). This statement implies that the evaluation of a child's adaptation within each social system rests on knowledge of the expectations that surround the child within that social system. To evaluate a child's adaptation in the community, we should know the expectations that the community has for the child. The ABIC, however, makes no provision for acquiring such information; therefore, the ABIC does not support the evaluation of the child's adaptive behavior against the expectations present in different social systems (Oakland, 1979b).

VINELAND ADAPTIVE BEHAVIOR SCALES

The Vineland Adaptive Behavior Scales (VABS) (Sparrow, Balla, & Cicchetti, 1984) is a revision of the Vineland Social Maturity Scale published by Doll in 1953. The VABS assesses the social competence of handicapped and nonhandicapped individuals from birth through age 19. The VABS requires that a respondent familiar with the behavior of the individual in question answer behavior-oriented questions posed by a trained examiner (interviewer) or complete a questionnaire. There are three versions of the VABS: Survey Form, Expanded Form, and Classroom Edition.

Adaptive behavior—the principal focus of measurement—is defined as the ability to perform daily activities required for personal and social sufficiency. In each version of the scale adaptive behavior is measured in four domains: Communication, Daily Living Skills, Socialization, and Motor Skills. The combination of these four domains forms the Adaptive Behavior Composite. The Survey and Expanded Forms also include a Maladaptive Behavior domain.

Each domain is designed to evaluate various adaptive skills. The Communication domain samples receptive, expressive, and written communication skills. The Daily Living Skills domain evaluates personal living habits, domestic task performance, and behavior in the community. The Socialization domain focuses on interactions with others, including play, use of free time, and responsibility and sensitivity to others. The Motor Skills domain evaluates gross and fine motor coordination. Finally, the Maladaptive Behavior domain deals with undesirable behaviors that may interfere with adaptive behavior. Sample items from each domain are shown in Table 15-2.

The Survey Form contains 297 items administered over a 20- to 60-minute period. The Expanded Form, which takes approximately 60 to 90 minutes to administer, contains 577 items, including the 297 items on the Survey Form. It was constructed to provide a comprehensive measure of adaptive behavior and to aid in designing educational, habilitative, and treatment programs. The Class-

room Edition contains 244 items, designed for children from 3 years, 0 months to 12 years, 11 months of age. It provides an assessment of adaptive behavior in the classroom. This form is designed to be completed by the child's teacher in approximately 20 minutes.

Scores

All three versions of the Vineland have $M = 100$ and $SD = 15$ for the four domain scores and for the Adaptive Behavior Composite. *Unfortunately, the means and SD's vary considerably from age group to age group* (Silverstein, 1986b). These fluctuations mean that (a) both the standard errors of measurement and the bands of error reported in the manual are only rough approximations, (b) critical differences needed to evaluate significant differences among domain scores also may be only rough approximations, and (c) it is difficult to compare individuals across ages or perform longitudinal comparisons for the same individual. Silverstein advises caution in using the VABS standard scores for any of these purposes.

Standardization

The standardization sample for the Survey and Expanded Forms closely matched the population as described by 1980 U.S. census data. The ages of the 3,000 individuals in the sample ranged from newborn to 18 years, 11 months. Stratification variables included sex, race or ethnic group, geographical region, community size, and parents' educational level. Norms are provided from birth to 18 years, 11 months. From birth through 1 year, norms are broken into 1-month increments; from 2 through 5 years, into 2-month increments; from 6 through 8 years, into 3-month increments; and from 9 through 18 years, into 4-month increments. Separate norms also are provided for mentally retarded, emotionally disturbed, and physically handicapped children and adults.

The Classroom Edition had a representative sample of about 3,000 students, ages 3 years, 0 months to 12 years, 11 months, again selected to conform to 1980 U.S. census data, and used the same stratification variables as the other forms.

Reliability

Three measures of reliability were reported in the manual—split-half, test-retest, and interrater reliability. Split-half reliability coefficients for the Survey Form are as follows: For the Communication domain, split-half reliabilities range from .73 to .93 (*Mdn r_{xx}* = .89); for the

Table 15-2
Sample Items from the Vineland Adaptive Behavior Scales

Domain	Sample items
Communication	Turns eyes and head toward sound (age < 1 to 2 years)
	Uses sentences of four or more words (age 2 years)
Daily Living Skills	Uses sharp knife to cut food (age 12 to 15 years)
	Washes own clothes (age 16 to 18+ years)
Socialization	Makes own friends (age 7 to 10 years)
	Has a hobby (age 13 to 14 years)
Motor Skills	Runs with some falling (age 2 years)
	Throws ball (age 5+ years)
Maladaptive Behavior	Has temper tantrums
	Displays behaviors that are self-injurious

Daily Living Skills domain, they range from .83 to .92 (*Mdn* r_{xx} = .90); for the Socialization domain, they range from .78 to .94 (*Mdn* r_{xx} = .86); and for the Motor Skills domain, they range from .70 to .95 (*Mdn* r_{xx} = .83). The Adaptive Behavior Composite split-half reliability coefficients range from .84 to .98 (*Mdn* r_{xx} = .94), and the Maladaptive Behavior domain coefficients range from .77 to .88 (*Mdn* r_{xx} = .86).

Split-half reliability coefficients for the Expanded Form were estimated based on the Survey Form and adjusted by the Spearman-Brown formula. For Communication, estimates of split-half reliabilities range from .84 to .97 (*Mdn* r_{xx} = .94); for Daily Living Skills, they range from .92 to .96 (*Mdn* r_{xx} = .95); for Socialization, they range from .88 to .97 (*Mdn* r_{xx} = .92); and for Motor Skills, they range from .83 to .97 (*Mdn* r_{xx} = .91). The Adaptive Behavior Composite reliability estimates range from .94 to .99 (*Mdn* r_{xx} = .97); estimated split-half reliability coefficients for the Maladaptive Behavior domain are identical to those for the Survey Form.

Test-retest reliability for the Survey Form (2- to 4-week retest interval) are in the .80s and .90s. No test-retest reliabilities were computed for the Expanded Form.

Interrater reliability coefficients for the Survey and Expanded Forms range from .62 to .75.

In the Survey Form, standard errors of measurement range from 3.4 to 8.2 over the four domains, and from 2.2 to 4.9 ($M SE_m$ = 3.6) for the Adaptive Behavior Composite. In the Expanded Form, standard errors of measurement range from 2.4 to 6.2 over the four domains and from 1.5 to 3.6 ($M SE_m$ = 2.6) for the Adaptive Behavior Composite.

Validity

Concurrent validity was established by correlating the Vineland Adaptive Behavior Scales with various tests. An r = .55 was reported with the original Vineland. With normal samples, correlations between the Vineland Adaptive Behavior Composite and several intelligence and ability tests were as follows: r's = .32 and .37 with the K-ABC Mental Processing and Achievement scales, respectively, and r = .28 with the PPVT-R. Correlations with the WISC or WISC-R were .52 for emotionally disturbed children, .70 for visually handicapped children, and .47 for hearing-impaired children; correlations with the Hayes-Binet and Perkins-Binet were .82 and .71, respectively, for visually handicapped children.

The manual reports relationships between the VABS Adaptive Behavior Composite and various demographic variables. Whereas females obtained scores that were 4.5 to 5.0 points higher than those of males, there was less than a 2.5 point difference, on the average, among racial or ethnic groups. Level of parents' education was an important factor, however. Those children whose parents had attended four or more years of college scored on the average 8.3 points higher than did children whose parents had less than a high school education. Regional differences were minor (less than 4.0 points), and community size had virtually no effect.

The manual also provides tables for equating the Adaptive Behavior Composite on the Survey and Expanded Forms with Social Quotients and Deviation Social Quotients from the Vineland Social Maturity Scale and with standard scores on the K-ABC Mental Processing Composite, Achievement Scale, and Nonverbal Scale.

Comment on the Vineland Adaptive Behavior Scales

The Vineland Adaptive Behavior Scales is a potentially useful tool for the assessment of adaptive behavior. Difficulties still exist with the scales, however, despite the care and effort that have gone into the revision. Silverstein's (1986b) analysis seriously questions the norming procedures. The fluctuations in the means and *SD*'s of the standard scores from age group to age group are a problem, particularly with mentally retarded individuals. Of less serious concern are difficulties in framing questions, eliciting appropriate responses, and scoring responses (Oakland & Houchins, 1985). (Some items require knowledge that informants may not possess. For example, in the Communication domain, informants must tell whether the child says at least 100 recognizable words, uses irregular plurals, and prints or writes at least 10 words from memory.) Further research will be needed to evaluate how adequately the VABS assesses adaptive behavior.

SCALES OF INDEPENDENT BEHAVIOR

The Scales of Independent Behavior (SIB) (Bruininks, Woodcock, Weatherman, & Hill, 1984) is an individually administered measure of skills needed to function independently in home, social, and community settings. The SIB can be used from infant to mature adult levels (age 40 years and older). It contains 14 subscales organized into (a) four adaptive behavior skill clusters (Motor, Social Interaction and Communication, Personal Living, and Community Living) and (b) eight problem behavior areas grouped into three maladaptive behavior clusters (Internalized, Asocial, and Externalized) (see Table 15-3). A General

Table 15-3
Scales of Independent Behavior (SIB)

Cluster	Skills/Areas
Adaptive Behavior Skills	
Motor Skills	Gross Motor
	Fine Motor
Social Interaction and	Social Interaction
Communication Skills	Language Comprehension
	Language Expression
Personal Living Skills	Eating
	Toileting
	Dressing
	Personal Self-Care
	Domestic Skills
Community Living Skills	Time and Punctuality
	Money and Value
	Work Skills
	Home/Community Orientation
Problem Behavior Areas	
Internalized Maladaptive	Hurtful to Self
Behavior	Unusual or Repetitive Habits
	Withdrawal or Inattentive
	Behavior
Asocial Maladaptive Behavior	Socially Offensive Behavior
	Uncooperative Behavior
Externalized Maladaptive	Hurtful to Others
Behavior	Destructive to Property
	Disruptive Behavior

Maladaptive Index also can be derived from the eight problem areas. A Broad Independence (Full Scale) cluster score is obtained from the adaptive skill clusters. There is also a 32-item Short Form for persons at any developmental level and an Early Development scale of adaptive behavior for children 2½ years of age and younger or for severely and profoundly handicapped individuals who function developmentally at below the 2½-year level.

The full SIB takes approximately 60 minutes to administer, whereas the Short Form takes about 10 to 15 minutes to administer. Although information about the person's adaptive behavior skills is usually obtained from an informant, in some cases the individual being assessed can provide the information needed to complete the scales.

Scores

For the adaptive behavior skill clusters, items are scored on a 4-point scale: 0 (never or rarely performs the task or activity), 1 (does the task, but not well, or about one-fourth of the time), 2 (does the task fairly well, or about three-fourths of the time), 3 (does the task very well always or almost always). For these clusters, raw scores can be converted into age-equivalent scores, percentile ranks, standard scores ($M = 100$, $SD = 15$), stanines, or normal curve equivalents. Some newer types of scores are also included, such as an instructional range score and an adjusted behavior score associated with the Woodcock-Johnson Broad Cognitive Ability cluster score.

Standardization

The norm sample for the SIB consisted of 1,764 persons. Individuals were chosen on the basis of sex, race, occupational level, occupational status, geographic region, and type of community, in accordance with the 1980 U.S. census data. Norms are included for infant through adult levels. Weighting procedures were used to equate the sample with the census data.

Reliability

For the adaptive behavior area, median split-half reliabilities range from .83 to .96 for the four cluster and full-scale scores. Split-half reliabilities are much lower for the individual subscales—at one age the split-half reliability coefficient is as low as .36 for a subscale. Test-retest reliabilities over a 4-week period in two samples of non-handicapped elementary school children ranged from .71 to .96 for the various adaptive behavior clusters and from .69 to .90 for the problem behavior indices. Interrater agreement correlations were high (in the .90s).

Validity

Construct validity is supported by several types of evidence. First, correlations between SIB adaptive behavior scores and chronological age in groups of nonhandicapped and handicapped persons were high (r's = .68 to .82 in the total sample). Second, the adaptive behavior scores and maladaptive behavior scores of handicapped samples were lower than those of normal samples. Third, intercorrelations between the four adaptive behavior skill clusters ranged from .50 to .80, indicating a moderate degree of overlap in content.

Criterion-related validity was established with satisfactory correlations between the SIB and the Adaptive Behavior Scale—School Edition (r's = .66 to .81 for the cluster and broad independence scores in a sample of 52 10- to 12-year-old children) and the Woodcock-Johnson Broad Cognitive Ability Scores (r's = .66 to .82 for the cluster and broad independence scores in a sample of 326 nonhandicapped children). The SIB Maladaptive Behavior indices and the Quay-Peterson Revised Behavior Problem Checklist Scales show correlations ranging from −.66 to .12. The pattern of correlations between the Quay-Peterson Revised Behavior Problem Checklist indicates satisfactory concurrent validity for the Maladaptive Behavior indices.

Comment on the Scales of Independent Behavior

The Scales of Independent Behavior is useful in assessing adaptive behavior over a wide age range. The myriad of scores complicates the use of the scales, however. Additional research is needed, especially with regard to the validity of the specialized scores. A unique feature of the SIB is that it allows the user to evaluate the examinee's adaptive behavior scores in relationship to the Woodcock-Johnson Broad Cognitive Ability cluster score. Research is needed to evaluate the usefulness of this feature, however, especially in light of questions concerning the validity of the Broad Cognitive Ability cluster score (see Chapter 13).

BATTELLE DEVELOPMENTAL INVENTORY

The Battelle Developmental Inventory (BDI) (Newborg, Stock, & Wnek, 1984) is an untimed, individually administered assessment battery of key developmental skills in children from birth to 8 years of age. The BDI consists of 341 items grouped into five domains: Personal-Social, Adaptive, Motor, Communication, and Cognitive. Items within each domain are clustered into subdomains, or specific skill areas (see Table 15-4). Additionally, there is a Screening Test composed of 96 of the 341 test items. The full BDI takes approximately 60 minutes to administer. The Screening Test takes between 10 and 15 minutes for children under 3 years and between 20 and 30 minutes for children over 3 years.

A description of the five domains follows:

• The Personal-Social domain consists of 85 items that center on the child's ability to engage in meaningful social interactions. Items involve the quality and frequency of the child's interactions with adults, ability to express emotions such as affection or anger, development of self-awareness and personal knowledge, quality of interactions with children of the same age, ability to deal with the environment, and adequacy of social-interpersonal development.

• The Adaptive domain consists of 59 items related to self-help skills and task-related skills. Behaviors that will enable the child to become increasingly independent are stressed. Items relate to visual and auditory attention skills and skills involved in eating, dressing, assuming personal responsibilities, and toileting.

• The Motor domain consists of 82 items assessing gross and fine motor development. Abilities assessed include control over large muscles used in sitting, standing, and transferring objects from one hand to the other; physical coordination; locomotion skills; and fine motor control and visual-motor coordination involved in turning pages, stringing beads, building towers, printing, and other similar activities.

• The Communication domain consists of 59 items assessing receptive and expressive communication skills. The receptive skills involve the ability to discriminate, recognize, and understand sounds, words, nonverbal signs, and gestures. The expressive skills involve the ability to produce and use sounds, words, and gestures in order to relate information to others.

• The Cognitive domain consists of 56 items assessing conceptual skills. Abilities assessed include perceptual discrimination, memory, reasoning and academic skills, and ability to grasp concepts and draw relationships among objects.

Table 15-4
Domains and Subdomains in the Battelle Developmental Inventory

Domain	Subdomains
Personal-Social	Adult Interaction
	Expression of Feelings/Affect
	Self-Concept
	Peer Interaction
	Coping
	Social Role
Adaptive	Attention
	Eating
	Dressing
	Personal Responsibility
	Toileting
Motor	Muscle Control
	Body Coordination
	Locomotion
	Fine Muscle
	Perceptual Motor
Communication	Receptive
	Expressive
Cognitive	Perceptual Discrimination
	Memory
	Reasoning and Academic Skills
	Conceptual Development

Source: J. Newborg, J. R. Stock, and L. Wnek, 1984.

The information needed for each item is collected by one of three methods: (a) a structured test format, (b) interviews with parents, or (c) observations of the child in natural settings. Items can be modified for use with handicapped children. Items are arranged in order of increasing difficulty. They are grouped by 6-month increments from birth to 2 years and 1-year increments from 2 through 8 years.

Scores

Scoring of test items is based on a three-point system: 2 points for behavior meeting the specified criterion, 1 point for behavior attempted but not meeting the specified criterion, and 0 points for behavior failed or not attempted. Raw scores on the BDI are converted into T scores or Deviation Quotients ($M = 100$, $SD = 15$).

Standardization

Stratified quota sampling was used to match the norming sample to 1981 U.S. census data, with the stratification variables being geographical region of the United States, race, and sex. A total of 800 children participated nationally. Although socioeconomic status was not used as a stratification variable, the SES spectrum was wide, but with a middle-class emphasis. The varied test sites controlled, to some extent, the urban/rural and SES characteristics of the sample.

Reliability

Test-retest reliability was determined by retesting 183 children in the norming and clinical samples within one month of their original test. Correlation coefficients were high (r_{xx}'s from .71 to 1.00). Interrater reliability was satisfactory (r's from .70 to 1.00). Internal consistency reliabilities were not reported.

Validity

Content validity is acceptable, as judged by experts who evaluated the item content. Construct validity is also satisfactory, as indicated by high intercorrelations among the subdomains and the increasing percentages of items passed by older children. Additionally, the nonclinical standardization sample obtained higher scores than did a clinical sample.

Correlations between the BDI and the Vineland Social Maturity Scale, Developmental Activities Screening Inventory, Stanford-Binet Intelligence Scale: Form L-M,

WISC-R, and PPVT were significant in most cases. The highest correlations were obtained with the Vineland (r's from .79 to .93). With the WISC-R Full Scale IQ, the *highest* correlations were with the Expressive and Fine Motor subdomains (r's of .79 and .75, respectively), whereas the *lowest* correlations were with the Personal-Social and Cognitive subdomains (r's of .42 and .44, respectively). The low correlation between the Cognitive subdomain and the WISC-R is not easy to explain. Because a factor analysis is not reported for the standardization sample, there is no way of knowing to what extent the domains are independent.

Comment on the Battelle Developmental Inventory

The Battelle Developmental Inventory is a developmental measure useful for obtaining information about important areas of development in young children. It appears to be standardized adequately. More information is needed about its reliability, validity, and factor structure, however. Useful features include the mixture of structured test items with interview and observational data and the provisions for evaluating physically handicapped children. As with some other developmental scales, the results are heavily dependent on the informant's ability to provide accurate information. Exhibit 15-2 is a case study based on the BDI.

T.M.R. SCHOOL COMPETENCY SCALES

The T.M.R. School Competency Scales (Levine, Elzey, Thormahlen, & Cain, 1976) is designed to measure social and personal skills of trainable mentally retarded children in a school setting. The five scales are Perceptual-Motor, Initiative-Responsibility, Cognition, Personal-Social, and Language. There are two separate forms: one for ages 5 to 10 years and one for ages 11 years and over. Each form contains 128 items, 66 of which are the same on the two forms. There are four levels of competence to choose from on each item. The scale is completed by the child's teacher.

Scores

Raw scores are converted into percentile ranks for each subscale and for the total score.

Standardization

The scale was standardized on 302 randomly selected TMR students attending public schools in suburban and urban communities in California.

Exhibit 15-2

Case Study with the Battelle Developmental Inventory

INTRODUCTORY REMARKS

This is a case study of Karen, a 14-month-old female born with Down's syndrome and some weaknesses in her left arm and leg. Domain percentile ranks were as follows: Personal-Social: 1st percentile; Adaptive Behavior: 2nd percentile; Motor: 1st percentile; Communication: 1st percentile; Cognitive: 6th percentile; Total: 1st percentile. Subdomains within each domain showed some variability, especially in the Personal-Social Domain (range of 2nd to 33rd) and the Cognitive Domain (range of 8th to 45th).

CASE STUDY

Personal-Social

In this domain, Karen demonstrates relative strength in self-concept skills; the expression of feelings is weak. Karen displays anticipatory excitement and pleasure in play. She expresses emotion and shows awareness of her own hands. She occasionally responds to her own name and will gaze at herself in a mirror. She shows delays in the areas of adult and peer interaction. Karen is generally aware of others, shows a desire to be picked up and held, explores adult faces, and discriminates between familiar and unfamiliar persons. At this time, she does not initiate social contacts with peers. Karen's overall personal-social skills are at the 6-month level.

Adaptive

In this domain, Karen demonstrates a relative strength in eating skills. She drinks from a cup with help and feeds herself bite-size pieces of food. Dressing skills are mildly delayed. At this time, Karen does not assist when being dressed and undressed. Attention skills are significantly delayed. Karen attends to light and sound and can occupy herself for 10 or more minutes without demanding adult attention. Karen's overall adaptive skills are at the 7-month level.

Motor

In this domain, Karen demonstrates relative strengths in muscle control and perceptual-motor skills. She can stand for 5 to 10 seconds while holding on to a solid object. In addition, she can reach for and touch an object placed before her. At this time, Karen's body coordination, locomotion, and fine-muscle skills are significantly delayed. She can bring her hands together at the midline and bring objects to her mouth. She attempts to bring herself to a standing position and rolls to her side easily. She makes one or two stepping movements when held upright, crawls forward one or two feet, holds on to objects, and attempts to open drawers and cupboard doors. Gross-motor skills are at the 6-month level; fine-motor skills are at the 5-month level. Karen's overall motor skills are developed to the 6-month level.

Communication

Karen's expressive and receptive language skills are significantly delayed compared with those of other children in her age group. Receptive skills are at the 4-month level; expressive skills are at the 8-month level. Overall communication skills are at the 6-month level. Karen responds to sounds and voices outside her field of vision and locates sounds by turning her head. She also vocalizes sounds to express her feelings, produces consonant-vowel sounds such as "baa," and repeats single syllables.

Cognitive

In this domain, Karen demonstrates a relative strength in perceptual discrimination. Karen's memory, reasoning and academic skills, and conceptual development are marginal compared with those of other children in her age group. Karen's overall cognitive development is at the 9-month level. She physically explores her environment, follows auditory and visual stimuli, searches for a removed object, and pulls a string to obtain a toy.

Recommendations

Although Karen continues to show growth in all developmental areas, her progress is a great deal slower than that of other children in her age group. Currently, she is at the level of children half her age as demonstrated by her performance on the BDI. Overall total score places her at the 1st percentile with an age equivalent of 7 months. Total scores for domains are as follows: Personal-Social total score, 6 months; Adaptive total score, 7 months; Motor total score, 6 months; Communication total score, 6 months; and Cognitive total score, 9 months. The following recommendations are made.

1. Placement in an early childhood program.

2. Provide Karen's family with the opportunity to supplement the intervention program goals at home. Children like Karen often have difficulty transferring and generalizing what they learn from one setting to another. Working on similar activities and techniques at home will help expedite transference and generalization.

3. If Karen has particular difficulty attaining a new goal or objective, keep in mind that she will need more time, more examples, and more exposures than other children. Vary the materials and allow several adults to interact with her. Task analysis also may be a useful tool—that is, breaking down a task into small parts and then chaining these parts together. This may appear to be more work but ultimately will be less frustrating and more rewarding for Karen. Use fading and passive shaping when appropriate.

(Exhibit continues next page)

Exhibit 15-2 (cont.)

4. Frequent program reviews are recommended along with continued input from a multidisciplinary team of professionals. Speech and language, occupational, and physical therapy evaluations also are recommended.

Source: Reprinted, with changes in notation, from J. Newborg, J. R. Stock, and L. Wnek (pp. 33, 35), *Battelle Developmental Inventory: Examiner's Manual*, © 1984 by LINC Associates. Published by DLM Teaching Resources, a division of DLM, Inc., Allen, TX 75002.

Reliability

Split-half reliabilities for all age groups were in the high .80s to .90s for the subscales, and in the high .90s for the total score. Subscale and total score intercorrelations for each age group ranged from the high .60s to the low .90s.

Validity

No validity data are presented in the manual.

Comment on the T.M.R. School Competency Scales

Although the T.M.R. Scales has many of the same items as the Cain-Levine Social Competency Scale (Cain, Levine, & Elzey, 1963), the T.M.R. Scales also contains an additional Cognition subscale and an extended age range. The scale has questionable psychometric properties. It may be useful, however, as a rough measure for evaluating the progress of TMR children.

BALTHAZAR SCALES OF ADAPTIVE BEHAVIOR

The Balthazar Scales of Adaptive Behavior (Balthazar, 1976) is designed for the assessment of severely and profoundly mentally retarded institutionalized individuals. It can be used to measure a range of functional abilities and to evaluate the effectiveness of treatment and training programs. The scale is divided into two sections: Scales of Functional Independence and Scales of Social Adaptation (see Table 15-5). In order to complete the scales, the rater both observes the individual directly, over several days if necessary, and obtains information either from the individual or from informants.

Section I, the Scales of Functional Independence, assesses how well an individual can perform basic self-care activities. It contains three scales: Eating Scales, Dressing Scales, and Toileting Scales. The Eating Scales is designed to assess the individual's eating skills. It measures how well individuals can feed themselves, eat finger foods, handle a

spoon and fork, and drink from a glass or cup. There is also a supplementary checklist for evaluating other aspects of eating behavior. The Dressing Scales and Toileting Scales are used to obtain information about self-care. The information about toileting activities is obtained from an informant, usually an aide.

Section II, the Scales of Social Adaptation, provides an objective measure of interpersonal behaviors. The eight scales in the section evaluate the individual's interpersonal adjustment and social interactions. Approximately six observation sessions of 10 minutes each are required to administer the scale.

Scores

Raw scores are converted into percentile ranks.

Standardization

The norms were based on ambulant institutionalized residents at a state training school in Wisconsin. Their ages ranged from 5 to 57 years (*Mdn* = 17 years), and all had IQs below 35. There were 122 subjects tested for the Eating Scales, 200 for the Dressing Scales, 129 for the Toileting Scales, and 288 for the Scales of Social Adaptation. The manual strongly encourages users of the scales to develop their own norms, because the scales are not well standardized.

Reliability

There are no standard reliability coefficients reported for any of the scales. Interrater agreements in scoring the Scales of Functional Independence were high (.94 or higher). Less agreement was found between two raters scoring the Scales of Social Adaptation (42 to 100 percent, *Mdn* = 81 percent agreement).

Validity

The manual presents no validity data. Validity for the scales is assumed to be inherent and limited to the behaviors observed by each rater.

Table 15-5
Illustrations of Items on the Balthazar Scales of Adaptive Behavior

Scales of Functional Independence	*Scales of Social Adaptation*
Eating Scales I. Dependent Feeding: opens mouth voluntarily; removes food from spoon with lips II. Finger Foods: eats finger foods (e.g., bread, fruit, etc.); reaches for finger foods (initiates reaching for food) III. Spoon Usage: eats tray foods with spoon; manipulates spoon with precision; does not stuff mouth IV. Fork Usage: same as spoon usage but with fork V. Drinking: takes liquids from cup; lifts cup off table with one hand to drink **Dressing Scales** Consists of a list of clothing (e.g., shoes, socks, shirt, and pants). Individuals are graded on how well they put on and take off clothing. **Toileting Scales** Consists of a questionnaire used for interviewing. Sample item: "Adjusts clothing appropriately before toileting—For an average 10 times that the individual eliminates, how often does he (she) pull his (her) pants down by himself (herself)?"	1. Unadaptive Self-directed Behaviors: failure to respond to staff or peers; disorderly or nonsocial behavior 2. Unadaptive Interpersonal Behaviors: aggression; withdrawal 3. Adaptive Self-directed Behaviors: generalized, exploratory, recreational activity 4. Adaptive Interpersonal Behaviors: fundamental social behaviors; noncommunication 5. Verbal Communication: verbalization 6. Play Activities: playful contact 7. Response to Instructions: cooperative contact; response to firmly given instructions 8. Checklist: clothing adjustment; drinking; napping on ward

Source: Adapted from Balthazar (1976).

Comment on the Balthazar Scales of Adaptive Behavior

The Balthazar must be completed by a treatment-trainer person or someone closely involved with the individual. Although one of its strongest and most appealing features is the direct observation of behavior, raters are given only limited information about how to use the rating categories. A satisfactory level of rater agreement may be difficult to achieve on the Scales of Social Adaptation.

The Balthazar Scales of Adaptive Behavior attempts to provide a standardized way of monitoring the training and treatment of severely and profoundly mentally retarded individuals living in an institution. The Balthazar provides finely grained measures; they are potentially some of the best tools for their purpose (Meyers, 1978). The scale also appears to be one of the better designed instruments of its type (Proger, 1973). Further research, however, is required before the Balthazar Scales of Adaptive Behavior can be accepted as being better than other adaptive behavior assessment techniques (Silverstein, 1972), and revisions and improvements are needed.

WISCONSIN BEHAVIOR RATING SCALE

The Wisconsin Behavior Rating Scale (WBRS) (Song, Jones, Lippert, Metzgen, Miller, & Borreca, 1984) is an adaptive behavior rating scale designed for profoundly retarded individuals who function developmentally at below the 3-year level. The WBRS contains the following 11 subscales: Gross Motor, Fine Motor, Expressive Communication, Receptive Communication, Play Skills, Socialization, Domestic Activities, Eating, Toileting, Dressing, and Grooming. The WBRS takes approximately 30 minutes to administer.

Scores

Various types of scores are provided on the WBRS. Each item in the scale has a behavioral age. Age-equivalent scores as well as percentile ranks are given for each subscale. The total score also can be converted into a percentile rank.

Standardization

The WBRS was standardized on 325 residents, aged 1 to 72 years, in a Wisconsin center for the developmentally disabled and on 350 nonretarded infants and children, aged 2 weeks to 4.0 years, living in the Madison metropolitan area.

Reliability

Interrater reliabilities (intraclass correlations) for the subscales and the total score range from .83 to .99. Interrater agreements (kappa coefficients) ranged from .60 to .88.

Validity

Concurrent validity is high, as demonstrated by an r of .84 between the WBRS and the Fairview Self-Help Scale and an r of .97 between the WBRS and the Vineland Social Maturity Scale. Construct validity also appears to be satisfactory, as correlations between the subscale scores and chronological age were high for both the community sample ($r = .97$) and the resident sample ($r = .65$). A factor analysis suggests that the scale taps two factors: Cognition and Psychomotor.

Comment on the Wisconsin Behavior Rating Scale

The Wisconsin Behavior Rating Scale is a criterion-referenced and norm-referenced scale useful for the assessment of adaptive behavior of severely and profoundly delayed individuals. A more representative sample and an extension of the age norms would enhance its usefulness. A particularly valuable feature of the WBRS is the provision of a behavioral age for each item in the scale.

EXAMPLES OF BEHAVIORAL CHECKLISTS

Some of the more popular checklists are discussed in detail in this section. See Appendix F for a summary of the principal features associated with the following behavioral checklists: AML Behavior Rating Scale, Child Behavior Checklist, Child Behavior Scale, Classroom Adjustment Ratings Scale, Conners Parent Rating Scale, Conners Teacher Rating Scale, Devereux Adolescent Behavior Rating Scale, Devereux Child Behavior Rating Scale, Devereux Elementary School Behavior Rating Scale, Health Resources Inventory, Kohn Problem Checklist, Kohn Social Competence Scale, Preschool Behavior Questionnaire, Revised Behavior Problem Checklist,

Teacher Behavioral Description Form, Teacher-Child Rating Scale, Teacher's Report Form, and Youth Self-Report. Appendix F also provides information about where each checklist can be obtained.

Child Behavior Checklist

The Child Behavior Checklist has evolved over a 20-year period (Achenbach & Edelbrock, 1986a). It contains a list of behavioral problems and competencies, which are rated by parents or parent-surrogates. The checklist can be self-administered or administered by an interviewer. One version of the Child Behavior Checklist covers ages 4 to 16 years (113 items), and another version covers ages 2 to 3 years (100 items). A three-point scale is used to rate items (0 = not true, 1 = somewhat or sometimes true, 2 = very true or often true). The version for children from 4 to 16 years of age provides separate norms (T scores) for children ages 4 to 5, 6 to 11, and 12 to 16 by sex.

Within each age group, separate scales were developed on the basis of factor analysis. For example, the nine scales for the 6 to 11 age group are as follows: Schizoid or Anxious, Depressed, Uncommunicative, Obsessive-Compulsive, Somatic Complaints, Social Withdrawal, Hyperactive, Aggressive, and Delinquent. For the 4 to 5 age group, there are eight scales: Social Withdrawal, Depressed, Immature, Somatic Complaints, Sex Problems, Schizoid, Aggressive, and Delinquent.

The specific scales, also referred to as specific minor-band factors, are grouped into two broad-band factors: Internalizing and Externalizing. Compared to externalizers, internalizers tend to be brighter, better readers, less egocentric, better able to use adaptive means to cope with stressful situations, better able to adjust in school (fewer conduct problems and less overactivity), and better able to conform to rules (Cohen, Gotlieb, Kershner, & Wehrspann, 1985). The Child Behavior Checklist is well standardized and has adequate reliability and validity. (Also see comments on the Youth Self-Report in Appendix F. This form has many of the same items found on the Child Behavior Checklist. It is a self-administered checklist designed to complement the Child Behavior Checklist.)

Teacher's Report Form

The Teacher's Report Form (Achenbach & Edelbrock, 1986b) is designed to obtain ratings of many of the same problem areas as are covered by the Child Behavior Checklist. It provides a multidimensional profile of empirically derived problem behavior syndromes, plus scales reflecting adaptive behavior and school performance. The 113-item form can be completed by a teacher or a teacher's aide. The three-point scale is the same as that used for the Child Behavior Checklist. Norms (*T* scores) are provided for ages 6 to 11 years and 12 to 16 years, separate by sex. The Teacher's Report Form is well standardized and has adequate reliability and validity.

There are eight scales in the Teacher's Report Form for boys aged 6 to 11 years: Anxious, Social Withdrawal, Unpopular, Self-Destructive, Obsessive-Compulsive, Inattentive, Nervous-Overactive, and Aggressive. The scales are further divided into Internalizing scales (Anxious, Social Withdrawal), Mixed scales (Unpopular, Self-Destructive, Obsessive-Compulsive), and Externalizing scales (Inattentive, Nervous-Overactive, and Aggressive).

For experienced observers, an observation form is also available for noting many of the same behavior problems covered by the Teacher's Report Form. The Direct Observation Form uses four-step rating scales geared to 10-minute samples of behavior. It also has a section for scoring on-task behaviors at 1-minute intervals. More information is needed about the validity and reliability of the Direct Observation Form.

Conners Parent Rating Scale

The Conners Parent Rating Scale (Conners, 1985) is a widely used rating scale that can help identify behavioral problems in children 3 to 17 years of age. Two versions are available: a 93-item version and a 48-item abbreviated version. The 93-item version yields eight factors (Conduct Disorder, Fearful-Anxious, Restless-Disorganized, Learning Problem–Immature, Psychosomatic, Obsessional, Antisocial, and Hyperactive-Immature), whereas the 48-item version yields five factors (Conduct Problem, Learning Problem, Psychosomatic, Impulsive-Hyperactive, and Anxiety). Because sex-by-age normative data are available for the 48-item version, this version will be discussed in this section. The scale itself is shown in Exhibit 15-3.

Symptoms are rated on a 4-point scale (0–3). Raw scores on each factor are transformed into *T* scores ($M = 50$, $SD = 10$). Table C-63 in Appendix C presents the norms for the Conners Parent Rating Scale. *T* scores 2 or more standard deviations above the mean ($T \geq 70$) may indicate problem areas.

Studies indicate that the Conners Parent Rating Scale has adequate reliability and validity (Conners, 1985). Additionally, factor analysis provides support for the five primary factors provided by the scale.

A shortened version of the scale, the Abbreviated Parent Questionnaire, is a useful 10-item scale for follow-up assessment and screening purposes (see Exhibit 15-4). Also referred to as a hyperactivity index, it consists of the most

highly loaded symptoms from the factor scales. Norms for this brief version ($M = 50$, $SD = 10$) for ages 3 to 17 years are shown in Table C-64 in Appendix C.

Conners Teacher Rating Scale

The Conners Teacher Rating Scale (Conners, 1985) is a widely used rating scale that provides measures for identifying a variety of behavioral problems in children 4 to 12 years old. This scale complements the Conners Parent Rating Scale. Various versions of the scale are available, including 28- and 39-item versions. This section describes the 39-item version, because normative data based on a sample of 9,583 Canadian children are available for this version (Trites, Blouin, & Laprade, 1982).

The 39-item version contains 6 factors: Hyperactivity, Conduct Problem, Emotional Overindulgent, Anxious-Passive, Asocial, and Daydream-Attendance Problem. The scale itself is shown in Exhibit 15-5.

As in the Conners Parent Rating Scale, symptoms are rated on a 4-point scale (0 to 3). Raw scores on each factor are transformed into *T* scores ($M = 50$, $SD = 10$). Table C-65 in Appendix C presents the norms for the Conners Teacher Rating Scale. *T* scores 2 or more standard deviations above the mean ($T \geq 70$) may indicate problem areas.

Studies indicate that the Conners Teacher Rating Scale has adequate reliability and validity (Conners, 1985; Epstein & Nieminen, 1983; Schachar, Sandberg, & Rutter, 1986). Additionally, factor analysis provides support for the six primary factors provided by the scale.

A shortened version of the scale, the Abbreviated Teacher Questionnaire, is a useful 10-item scale for follow-up assessment and screening purposes (see Exhibit 15-4). It is the same scale as the Abbreviated Parent Questionnaire. Also referred to as a hyperactivity index, it consists of the most highly loaded symptoms from the factor scales. Norms for this brief version ($M = 50$, $SD = 10$) for ages 3 to 17 years are shown in Table C-66 in Appendix C.

Revised Behavior Problem Checklist

The Revised Behavior Problem Checklist (Quay & Peterson, 1983, 1987) is a revision of the Behavior Problem Checklist originally published in 1979. It uses a 3-point scale (0 = does not constitute a problem, 1 = mild problem, 2 = severe problem) for rating problem behavior traits occurring during childhood and adolescence. The checklist covers ages 6 to 18 years. There are a total of 89 items grouped into six scales: Conduct Disorder, Socialized Aggression, Attention Problems–Immaturity, Anxiety-Withdrawal, Psychotic Behavior, and Motor Ex-

Exhibit 15-3

Conners Parent Rating Scale

PARENT'S QUESTIONNAIRE

Name of child _____   Date _____

Date of birth _____   Name of parent _____

Age _____   Sex _____

Instructions: Please answer all questions. Beside *each* item below, indicate the degree of the problem with a checkmark (✓).

	Not at all	Just a little	Pretty much	Very much
1. Picks at things (nails, fingers, hair, clothing).				
2. Sassy to grown-ups.				
3. Problems with making or keeping friends.				
4. Excitable, impulsive.				
5. Wants to run things.				
6. Sucks or chews (thumb; clothing; blankets).				
7. Cries easily or often.				
8. Carries a chip on his or her shoulder.				
9. Daydreams.				
10. Difficulty in learning.				
11. Restless in the "squirmy" sense.				
12. Fearful (of new situations; new people or places; going to school).				
13. Restless, always up and on the go.				
14. Destructive.				
15. Tells lies or stories that aren't true.				
16. Shy.				
17. Gets into more trouble than others same age.				
18. Speaks differently from others same age (baby talk; stuttering; hard to understand).				
19. Denies mistakes or blames others.				
20. Quarrelsome.				
21. Pouts and sulks.				
22. Steals.				
23. Disobedient or obeys but resentfully.				
24. Worries more than others (about being alone; illness or death).				
25. Fails to finish things.				
26. Feelings easily hurt.				
27. Bullies others.				
28. Unable to stop a repetitive activity.				
29. Cruel.				
30. Childish or immature (wants help he or she shouldn't need; clings; needs constant reassurance).				
31. Distractibility or attention span a problem.				
32. Headaches.				
33. Mood changes quickly and drastically.				
34. Doesn't like or doesn't follow rules or restrictions.				
35. Fights constantly.				
36. Doesn't get along well with brothers or sisters.				

(Exhibit continues next page)

Exhibit 15-3 (cont.)

37. Easily frustrated in efforts.				
38. Disturbs other children.				
39. Basically an unhappy child.				
40. Problems with eating (poor appetite; up between bites).				
41. Stomach aches.				
42. Problems with sleep (can't fall asleep; up too early; up in the night).				
43. Other aches and pains.				
44. Vomiting or nausea.				
45. Feels cheated in family circle.				
46. Boasts and brags.				
47. Lets self be pushed around.				
48. Bowel problems (frequently loose; irregular habits; constipation).				

Note. Scoring is on a 4-point scale: 0 (*not at all*), 1 (*just a little*), 2 (*pretty much*), 3 (*very much*). Table C-63 in Appendix C provides norms for ages 3 to 17 years for the Conners Parent Rating Scale.
Source: Courtesy C. Keith Conners.

cess. Raw scores are converted into T scores ($M = 50$, $SD = 10$).

The checklist is useful for identifying dimensions of deviant behavior. New items, as well as additional scales, have been added in the revision. The Revised Behavior Problem Checklist was constructed on the basis of factor analysis using various clinical samples. Internal consistency reliability, interrater reliability, and test-retest reliability appear to be adequate. Concurrent and construct validity also appear to be adequate.

COMMENT ON ADAPTIVE BEHAVIOR SCALES AND BEHAVIORAL CHECKLISTS

Progress has been made in assessing adaptive behavior and social competence, but further refinements are needed. All of the available scales have been found to have one or more major difficulties. For example, many adaptive behavior scales are normed only on a retarded population. In such cases, norms are limited in that the examinee is being compared with norms that in themselves embody deviance instead of normalcy. In spite of their limitations, each of the adaptive behavior scales reviewed in this chapter can contribute to the assessment of adaptive behavior.

Adaptive behavior scales and behavioral checklists are popular because they are economical, can be administered and scored easily, survey a wide range of behaviors, and can be used to evaluate treatment effects. Difficulties in-clude respondent biases and misperceptions and limited predictive validity data. As with any assessment tool, the strengths and limitations of adaptive behavior scales and behavioral checklists need to be recognized. Although more information is needed about the reliability and validity of adaptive behavior scales and behavioral checklists, they do serve an important function in the assessment process.

SUMMARY

1. Adaptive behavior scales and behavioral checklists provide valuable assessment information.

2. Adaptive behavior refers to behavior that is effective in meeting the natural and social demands of one's environment. This and similar definitions tend to be imprecise. No single instrument measures all of the relevant domains of adaptive behavior. Adaptive behavior should be considered within a developmental context.

3. Well-normed adaptive behavior scales and behavioral checklists serve various purposes. They identify the examinee's behavioral strengths and weaknesses, provide an objective basis for monitoring intervention efforts, permit comparison of the examinee's behavior across situations and informants, facilitate communication between and within organizations, and stimulate new intervention programs and research.

4. Ratings on adaptive behavior scales and behavioral checklists reflect the interaction of the characteristics of the scale or checklist, child, informant or rater, examiner, setting, and reasons for the evaluation.

5. Behavioral checklists can be distinguished by the age

Exhibit 15-4

Conners Abbreviated Parent/Teacher Questionnaire

ABBREVIATED PARENT/TEACHER QUESTIONNAIRE

Name of child _____ Date _____

Date of birth _____ Name of parent/teacher _____

Age _____ Sex _____

Instructions: Please answer all questions. Beside *each* item below, indicate the degree of the problem with a checkmark (✔).

Observation	Degree of activity			
	Not at all	*Just a little*	*Pretty much*	*Very much*
1. Restless or overactive				
2. Excitable, impulsive				
3. Disturbs other children				
4. Fails to finish things he or she starts—short attention span				
5. Constantly fidgeting				
6. Inattentive, easily distracted				
7. Demands must be met immediately—easily frustrated				
8. Cries often and easily				
9. Mood changes quickly and drastically				
10. Temper outbursts, explosive and unpredictable behavior				

Comments: _____

_____

_____

_____

_____

_____

Note. Scoring is on a 4-point scale: 0 (*not at all*), 1 (*just a little*), 2 (*pretty much*), 3 (*very much*). Tables C-64 and C-66 in Appendix C provide norms for ages 3 to 17 years for the Conners Abbreviated Parent Questionnaire and Conners Abbreviated Teacher Questionnaire, respectively.
Source: Courtesy C. Keith Conners.

group covered, the setting to which the questions are directed, and the types of classifications provided.

6. Behavioral checklists differ as to the types of factors covered. The same factor name on different checklists may not measure the same behaviors.

7. The credibility of the informant is a critical factor in evaluating information obtained from adaptive behavior scales and behavioral checklists.

8. The ratings of multiple informants should be compared and contrasted.

9. Many factors may affect informants' judgments on adaptive behavior scales and behavioral checklists. These include their familiarity with the child, sensitivity to and tolerance for behavior problems, personality, expectations, and willingness to use certain scale positions. Another relevant factor is the specificity of the rating task. Some raters may be influenced by the child's race, socioeconomic status, appearance, or psychopathology, in which case their ratings are invalid.

10. Adaptive behavior scales, behavioral checklists, and behavioral observation may not provide congruent data.

11. Before an adaptive behavior scale or behavioral checklist is selected, its properties should be thoroughly evaluated. Factors to consider include the reliability and validity of the checklist or scale, the reliability of the available informants, and the scope, structure, and clinical utility of the scale or checklist.

12. The AAMD Adaptive Behavior Scale (ABS) assesses basic survival skills and maladaptive behaviors of mentally retarded, emotionally maladjusted, and developmentally disabled

Exhibit 15-5

Conners Teacher Rating Scale

TEACHER'S QUESTIONNAIRE

Name of child _____   Date _____

Date of birth _____   Name of teacher _____

Age _____   Sex _____

Instructions: Please answer all questions. Beside *each* item below, indicate the degree of the problem with a checkmark (✔).

Observation	*Not at all*	*Just a little*	*Pretty much*	*Very much*
	Degree of activity			
Classroom Behavior				
1. Constantly fidgeting				
2. Hums and makes other odd noises				
3. Demands must be met immediately—easily frustrated				
4. Coordination poor				
5. Restless or overactive				
6. Excitable, impulsive				
7. Inattentive, easily distracted				
8. Fails to finish things he or she starts—short attention span				
9. Overly sensitive				
10. Overly serious or sad				
11. Daydreams				
12. Sullen or sulky				
13. Cries often and easily				
14. Disturbs other children				
15. Quarrelsome				
16. Mood changes quickly and drastically				
17. Acts "smart"				
18. Destructive				
19. Steals				
20. Lies				
21. Temper outbursts, explosive and unpredictable behavior				
Group Participation				
22. Isolates himself or herself from other children				
23. Appears to be unaccepted by group				
24. Appears to be easily led				
25. No sense of fair play				
26. Appears to lack leadership				
27. Does not get along with opposite sex				
28. Does not get along with same sex				
29. Teases other children or interferes with their activities				
Attitude Toward Authority				
30. Submissive				
31. Defiant				
32. Impudent				
33. Shy				

(Exhibit continues next page)

Exhibit 15-5 (cont.)

Observation	Degree of activity			
	Not at all	Just a little	Pretty much	Very much
34. Fearful				
35. Excessive demands for teacher's attention				
36. Stubborn				
37. Overly anxious to please				
38. Uncooperative				
39. Attendance problem				

Note. Scoring is on a 4-point scale: 0 (*not at all*), 1 (*just a little*), 2 (*pretty much*), 3 (*very much*). Table C-65 in Appendix C provides norms for the Conners Teacher Rating Scale for ages 4 through 12 years.
Source: Courtesy C. Keith Conners.

individuals residing in an institution. It covers an age range from 3 to 69 years. Although the scale has useful features, reliability data are limited and validity has not been sufficiently established.

13. The AAMD Adaptive Behavior Scale—School Edition (ABS-SE) is a modified version of the ABS for use in school with children between the ages of 3 and 17 years. It assesses most of the same behavior domains as the ABS, with the exception of those areas that are not applicable to the school setting. The scale can be used in the evaluation of different kinds of handicapped children. Although the scale has useful features, reliability and validity are questionable.

14. The Adaptive Behavior Inventory for Children is used to assess the behavior of noninstitutionalized school-age children between 5 and 11 years of age in kindergarten through fifth grade. It provides scores for six areas of adaptive behavior: Family, Peers, Community, School, Earner/Consumer, and Self-Maintenance. Although the scale has useful features, there are concerns about item content, norms, and validity.

15. The Vineland Adaptive Behavior Scales is designed to assess the adaptive behavior of handicapped and nonhandicapped individuals from birth to 19 years of age. Adaptive behavior is defined as the ability to perform daily activities required for personal and social sufficiency. Four domains are covered: Communication, Daily Living Skills, Socialization, and Motor Skills. Three forms are available: Survey, Expanded, and Classroom Edition. Although standardization was excellent, concerns have been voiced about the fluctuations in the means and *SD*'s across age groups, especially when the scale is used with mentally retarded individuals.

16. The Scales of Independent Behavior is designed to assess skills needed to function independently in home, school, and community settings in individuals from birth through maturity. Four adaptive skill clusters are covered: Motor, Social Interaction and Communication, Personal Living, and Community Living. Three maladaptive behavior clusters are also measured: Internalized, Asocial, and Externalized. Standardization, reliability, and validity appear to be acceptable. The myriad of scores may cause some difficulty for users, however.

17. The Battelle Developmental Inventory is designed to assess key developmental skills in children from birth to 8 years of age. Five domains are measured: Personal-Social, Adaptive, Motor, Communication, and Cognitive. Subdomains are included within each domain. A screening form is also available. Standardization was excellent. More information is needed about the inventory's reliability and validity.

18. The T.M.R. School Competency Scales uses Perceptual-Motor, Initiative-Responsibility, Cognition, Personal-Social, and Language scales to measure various personal and social skills of trainable mentally retarded school children. Although the scale may have some usefulness, more information is needed about its validity.

19. The Balthazar Scales of Adaptive Behavior contains two separate scales, each dealing with a different area of behavior. The scale is similar to the AAMD-ABS in that Part I assesses basic self-help skills and Part II assesses maladaptive and adaptive coping behaviors. The Balthazar is used for the assessment of ambulant severely and profoundly mentally retarded children and adults, less retarded young children, and emotionally disturbed children. Coverage begins at 5 years of age. Although the Balthazar is potentially useful, more information is needed about its validity.

20. The Wisconsin Behavior Rating Scale is designed for profoundly retarded individuals who function developmentally at below the 3-year level. It contains 11 subscales that cover motor skills, expressive and receptive communication skills, play and socialization, and self-care skills. Although standardization is limited, the scale has some useful features.

21. Numerous behavioral checklists have been published. Five of the more popular ones are the Child Behavior Checklist, Teacher's Report Form, Conners Parent Rating Scale, Conners Teacher Rating Scale, and Revised Behavior Problem Checklist. Each of these scales is well normed and provides standard scores.

22. Although progress has been made in the assessment of adaptive behavior, further refinements are needed. All of the existing scales have some problems.

KEY TERMS, CONCEPTS, AND NAMES

Definition of adaptive behavior (p. 376)
Adaptive behavior scales (p. 376)
Behavioral checklists (p. 376)
Broad-band factors (p. 377)
Narrow-band factors (p. 377)
Informant (p. 377)
Scope of scales and checklists (p. 378)
Structure of scales and checklists (p. 378)
Clinical utility of scales and checklists (p. 378)
AAMD Adaptive Behavior Scale (ABS) (p. 378)
AAMD Adaptive Behavior Scale – School Edition (ABS-SE) (p. 381)
Adaptive Behavior Inventory for Children (ABIC) (p. 382)
Vineland Adaptive Behavior Scales (VABS) (p. 383)
Scales of Independent Behavior (SIB) (p. 385)
Battelle Developmental Inventory (BDI) (p. 387)
T.M.R. School Competency Scales (p. 388)
Balthazar Scales of Adaptive Behavior (p. 390)
Wisconsin Behavior Rating Scale (WBRS) (p. 391)
Child Behavior Checklist (p. 392)
Teacher's Report Form (p. 392)
Conners Parent Rating Scale (p. 393)
Conners Teacher Rating Scale (p. 393)
Revised Behavior Problem Checklist (p. 393)

STUDY QUESTIONS

1. Discuss the assessment of adaptive behavior and behavior problems.
2. Discuss the assets and limitations of
a. the AAMD Adaptive Behavior Scale
b. the AAMD Adaptive Behavior Scale – School Edition
c. the Adaptive Behavior Inventory for Children
d. the Vineland Adaptive Behavior Scales
e. the Scales of Independent Behavior
f. the Battelle Developmental Inventory
g. the T.M.R. School Competency Scales
h. the Balthazar Scales of Adaptive Behavior
i. the Wisconsin Behavior Rating Scale
3. Compare and contrast the following behavioral checklists: Child Behavior Checklist, Teacher's Report Form, Conners Parent Rating Scale, Conners Teacher Rating Scale, and Revised Behavior Problem Checklist.

_16

ASSESSMENT OF BEHAVIOR
BY INTERVIEW METHODS

A question rightly asked is half answered.
—C. G. J. Jacobi

An answer is invariably the parent of a great family of new questions.
—John Steinbeck

Observe what a man does; listen to what he says; how then can you not know what he is.
—Attributed to Confucius

The objective of the clinical assessment interview is similar to that of other assessment procedures: to obtain relevant, reliable, and valid information. In addition, the interview may provide insight into the interviewee's personality, temperament, and lifestyle. The information obtained from the interview, used in conjunction with other assessment results, should help you to arrive at a meaningful picture of the child and to decide on appropriate interventions. Clinical assessment interviewing requires a thorough knowledge of a broad range of psychological principles derived from personality theory, psychopathology, biological basis of behavior, family dynamics, and interpersonal communication. These principles will allow you to evaluate systematically the verbal and nonverbal contents of the interview.

This chapter first discusses the basic components of the interview, the advantages and disadvantages of the interview, and the skills and strategies needed to conduct the interview. It then provides a detailed analysis of the initial interview and post-assessment interview, focusing on children, parents, and teachers. It concludes by considering the reliability and validity of the interview, the confidentiality of interview material, and ways of evaluating your interview techniques. After you have completed this chapter, the major components of the clinical assessment interview should be evident to you. It will take considerable training and supervised experience, however, to master clinical assessment interviewing.

THE CLINICAL ASSESSMENT INTERVIEW VS. A CONVERSATION

The clinical assessment interview, although similar to ordinary conversation, differs in some fundamental respects (Kadushin, 1983).

1. The clinical assessment interview has a definite purpose.

2. The interviewer takes responsibility for directing the interaction and choosing the content.

3. There is a nonreciprocal relationship between the interviewer and interviewee—the interviewer questions, the interviewee answers.

4. The interviewer's behavior is planned and organized.

5. The interviewer is usually obliged to accept the interviewee's request for an interview, although in some settings (for example, schools) and on some occasions children and parents are obliged to come for an interview.

6. The interview requires sustained attention to the interaction.

7. The interview is usually a formally arranged meeting.

8. Unpleasant facts and feelings are not avoided. A premium is placed on making explicit what might be left unstated in ordinary conversation, and the interaction itself may become the focus of the discussion.

Ordinary conversation, in contrast, is more spontaneous, less formal, and more unstructured and may have few, if any, of the characteristics associated with formal interviews. Essentially, the primary difference between the interview and conversation is that the interview involves an interpersonal interaction that has a mutually accepted purpose, with formal, clearly defined roles and a set of norms governing the interaction.

Various purposes are served by the clinical assessment interview. These include establishing trust and rapport, gaining information about behavior and the attitudes underlying the behavior, and giving information about the agency or services. The information you obtain could be instrumental in helping the child, parents, teachers, or other professionals. As an interviewer, you should strive to make the quest for understanding a collaborative effort toward a common goal.

THE CLINICAL ASSESSMENT INTERVIEW VS. THE NONCLINICAL INTERVIEW

The skills needed for clinical assessment interviews are similar in many ways to those needed for nonclinical interviews, such as survey research interviews. There are, however, some major differences between the two types of interviews. In survey research, the interview is usually initiated by the interviewer, with interviewees encouraged to restrict themselves to replying to specific questions posed by the interviewer. Additionally, the consequences of the survey research interview for the interviewee are minimal (Cannell & Kahn, 1968). The issues in nonclinical interviews are usually well focused, with opinions about particular topics being at the forefront. In contrast, in clinical assessment, the interviewee (or family, for example) often initiates the interview, motivated by a desire for relief of symptoms or a desire to change. Regardless of who initiates them, clinical assessment interviews hold significant consequences for the interviewee. Interviewees are encouraged to provide in-depth responses, focusing on personal experiences and behavior.

In addition, in clinical assessment interviews, the apparent reason for the interview, often called the *referral ques-*

tion, may not be the most important issue. It may be that the problems are much more complex than the referral source recognized. Referral questions are the "tickets" into a clinic—there more important issues may emerge that need to be addressed. Thus, identifying the critical problem area becomes a pivotal focus of the clinical assessment interview.

ADVANTAGES AND DISADVANTAGES OF THE INTERVIEW

The interview has a number of distinct advantages as an assessment procedure (Edelbrock & Costello, 1988; Gorden, 1975; Gresham, 1984). It allows you to motivate the interviewee to provide accurate and complete information; be flexible in questioning the interviewee; resolve ambiguous responses; clarify misunderstandings; document the context and chronicity of the interviewee's problem behaviors; obtain the chronology and history of events; evaluate the validity of information by simultaneously observing the interviewee's verbal and nonverbal behaviors; learn about the beliefs, values, and expectations that parents (and other adults) hold regarding their children's behavior; and assess the interviewee's receptivity to various intervention strategies and willingness to follow recommendations. The interview is a flexible assessment procedure that you can direct so as to pursue useful leads or to change focus as needed. You should be guided by the interviewee's verbal responses and nonverbal behavior—such as posture, gestures, facial expressions, and voice inflection. The interview may be the only direct means of obtaining information from some children or parents—particularly those who are illiterate or severely depressed and those who are unwilling to provide information by any other assessment means.

The interview also has some disadvantages as an assessment tool. Reliability and validity are difficult to establish. Interviewees may provide inaccurate information. Interviewees are susceptible to subtle, unintended cues from the interviewer that may lead them to distort their replies. Bias may occur, particularly in cross-cultural interviews. These and other types of difficulties are explored more fully toward the end of this chapter.

THE INTERVIEW AS AN EXCHANGE OF INFORMATION

The interview represents an interpersonal encounter in which there is an exchange of information. Although it is a two-way process, the central purpose of the initial interview is for the interviewer to gather relevant and valid information from the interviewee. A major goal of the post-assessment interview is for the interviewer to present and interpret information and to discuss recommendations. Your goal as an interviewer is to facilitate the flow of this information. In order to communicate clearly, you must modify your habitual patterns of conversation, as well as develop appropriate interviewing skills and strategies. Ensuring that the interviewee obtains clear, relevant, and meaningful communications from you increases the likelihood that you will obtain clear, relevant, and valid information in return.

The uniqueness of each interviewee requires that you be flexible in your procedure. You will have to use good judgment in deciding how much information you can obtain during any one interview, and when it is necessary to schedule subsequent interviews.

INTERVIEWING SKILLS

When you and the interviewee first meet, you will form initial impressions of the interviewee. As the interview progresses, other impressions will be formed and original impressions will be modified by the ebb and flow of the interaction. It is important to attend to possible signs of psychopathology (discussed in a later part of the chapter), as well as signs of competence and strength. In addition, you should be attentive to the feelings invoked in you by the interviewee—such as compassion, pity, attraction, irritation, or discomfort—in order to determine how to regulate the pace of the interview and to gain some appreciation of how the interviewee affects others. In order to form accurate impressions, you must be a skilled listener and observer.

Listening

Much of the art of interviewing lies in the ability to listen creatively and empathically and to probe skillfully beneath the surface of the communication. The ability to *listen* is the key factor in the interview (Benjamin, 1981). Being a good listener means being free of preoccupations and giving the interviewee your full attention. A good listener is attentive not only to *what* is said but also to *how* it is said—the interviewee's tone, expressions, gestures—and to physiological cues, such as pupil dilation, tremors, and blushing. A good listener is aware too of what is *not* said—feelings or facts that are lurking behind what is spoken. This requires use of the "inner ear" as well as the outer one.

Good listening requires that you be attentive not only to the interviewee, but also to yourself. As the interview unfolds, be aware of your own needs, values, and standards. Examine how these may affect your interview techniques and the hypotheses you develop about the interviewee. Do you recognize how your standards may affect the kinds of judgments you make? For example, do you think it is permissible for your adolescent interviewee to be lazy because you were lazy as a 12-year-old? ("Why can't these parents be like my parents and leave her alone?") Are you able to determine the basis for your hypotheses? For example, is your hypothesis that an interviewee is hiding some facts about an issue based on what the child said, the way she looked when she said it, the way she reacted to your questions, or a combination of all of these? Are you self-aware in your communications? ("Why am I speaking more rapidly with this interviewee?") Becoming attuned to your own thoughts, feelings, and actions and learning how to deal with them appropriately during the interview are keys to becoming a competent interviewer.

Observing Voice and Speech

During the interview, observe the interviewee's voice and speech, including the following (cf. Nay, 1979):

- loudness or speech intensity (for example, excessively loud or excessively soft, monotonous)
- pitch of voice (for example, low versus high pitched, monotonous)
- rate of speaking (for example, unusually slow or rapid, monotonous, jerky)
- ease of speech (for example, hesitations or blocking)
- spontaneity (for example, spontaneous or guarded)
- reaction time (for example, slow or quick)
- relevance of speech production (for example, relevant or irrelevant)
- manner of speaking (for example, pedantic, formal or relaxed, or overly familiar)
- marked speech deviations (for example, neologisms, echolalia, clang associations, or word salad)
- organization of speech (for example, organized or disorganized)
- vocabulary (for example, limited or extensive)
- diction (for example, poor or clear)
- voice quality (for example, harsh, hoarse, hypernasal, hyponasal)
- and fluency (for example, repetitions, revisions, incomplete phrases, broken words, prolonged sounds)

When voice or speech deviations occur, try to find out why. Some deviations, such as omitting sounds (saying "ing" for "thing"), substituting sounds (saying "den" for "then"), or distorting sounds, suggest an articulation disorder. Other deviations, such as saying "dad" for "pad" or "run" for "bun," may indicate difficulty in distinguishing sounds. Do the deviations occur with particular content? Do they reflect sensory difficulties or possible brain injury? Do they indicate anxiety or inattention? The accurate interpretation of such behaviors is an essential element of good interviewing.

Observing Nonverbal Behavior

An interviewer must observe the interviewee's broad range of nonverbal behavior and be alert for changes. Four general categories of nonverbal behavior can be delineated:

- motor behavior (mannerisms, level of coordination, and activity level—for example, hyperactivity, hypoactivity, tics, twitches, tremors, clumsiness, agitation, pacing, grimacing, rituals, self-stimulation, rocking movements, stereotypic motion)
- posture and changes therein (for example, slouched, relaxed, rigid, tense, stooped, erect, recumbent)
- facial expressions and their appropriateness to the content of the interview (for example, alert, vacant, bland, scowling, smiling, perplexed, anxious, angry, distressed, sad)
- eye contact (none to continuous)

Some possible meanings of various types of nonverbal behavior are shown in Table 16-1.

Observing Personal Appearance

Notice the interviewee's clothing, hairstyle, and grooming. Is the interviewee's dress neat, disheveled, dowdy, or dirty? By paying careful attention to physical appearance, you may gain clues about the interviewee's attitude toward himself or herself and the group that he or she belongs to or emulates.

Integrating Observations

Mood. Both verbal and nonverbal cues can be used to form impressions of the interviewee's mood and overall emotional tone. Is the tone congruent with the content? For example, does the interviewee seem depressed, anxious, or angry, but give responses that suggest a lack of concern about matters that would trouble other people more deeply? Note the interviewee's activity level and changes in

Table 16-1
Illustrations of the Meaning of Nonverbal Behavior

Nonverbal behavior	Possible meaning
1. Direct eye contact	Readiness or willingness for interpersonal communication, attentiveness
2. Staring at or fixating on a person or object	Confrontive defiance, preoccupation, possible rigidity or anxiety
3. Tight lips (pursed together)	Stress, determination, anger, hostility
4. Shaking head from left to right	Disagreement, disapproval, disbelief
5. Slouching in chair, turned away from interviewer	Sadness, discouragement, resistance to discussion
6. Trembling, fidgety hands	Anxiety, anger
7. Foot-tapping	Impatience, anxiety
8. Whispering	Difficulty in disclosing material
9. Silence	Reluctance to talk, preoccupation
10. Clammy hands, shallow breathing, pupil dilation, paleness, blushing, rashes on neck	Fearfulness, arousal—positive (excitement, interest) or negative (anxiety, embarrassment), drug intoxication

Note. These meanings may not hold for all subcultural groups.
Source: Adapted from Cormier and Cormier (1979).

activity level as the interview proceeds. Observe the appropriateness of the interviewee's affect to content and the themes associated with the affect. Are facial expressions consistent with the communications? Observe nuances in body movements and posture. What do the interviewee's body movements suggest (for example, tension or relaxation)?

Physical and neurological development.   Observing the interviewee's posture, gait, fine and gross motor coordination, speech, and quality and tone of voice will provide you with information about physical and neurological development. In observing motor behavior be especially aware of the possible causes of any abnormalities, including side effects of medication; also, if there are motor problems, consider their frequency and the interviewee's reactions to them. Also watch for any visual or auditory problems (see Chapter 5 for a list of signs). Clues to physical development, particularly with children, can also be obtained by observing the interviewee's height, weight, skin tone, and general appearance.

INTERVIEWING STRATEGIES

Underlying all successful interview strategies is an attempt to communicate clearly and to understand the communications of the interviewee. The interviewing strategies covered in this section apply to clinical assessment interviews with both children and adults. (In order to assess children,

you will also need to interview adults, particularly parents and teachers, to gain information about children.) Practical suggestions are frequently presented, but they are meant only to illustrate some of the many possible means of handling the interview process. In the latter part of the chapter, additional interview strategies are described that focus more directly on the assessment of children and specific ways to identify problem areas.

Establishing Rapport

The success of an interview, like that of any other assessment procedure, depends on the establishment of rapport with the interviewee. Rapport is based on mutual confidence, respect, and acceptance. It is your responsibility to engage the interviewee and bring him or her to see you as a trusting and helping person. Your aim is to create an atmosphere of warmth and acceptance so that interviewees will feel understood and safe and begin to communicate openly without fear of being judged or criticized.

The establishment of rapport can be facilitated by maintaining appropriate eye contact; maintaining a natural, relaxed, and attentive posture; speaking slowly and clearly in a calm, matter-of-fact, friendly, and accepting manner; using a warm and expressive tone; approaching the interviewees' communications in a nonjudgmental manner; and making the interview a joint undertaking. Your verbal responses should take into account not only the interviewees' comments but also the interviewees' verbal and nonverbal behavior. You should not interrupt the interviewees unless it is necessary.

Showing interest. Being interested in the information given by interviewees is crucial to establishing rapport. Interviewees need to sense that you want to understand how they see the world; appreciate their experiences; share in their struggle to recall, organize, and express their experiences; appreciate their difficulties in discussing personal material; and want to reflect accurately their opinions, feelings, and beliefs (Gorden, 1975). Statements that show interest, responsiveness, empathy, sensitivity, appreciation, and recognition should be accompanied by appropriate nonverbal behaviors.

Handling anxiety. Many interviewees experience appreciable anxiety and will need reassurance. Older children may wonder what will happen to them as a result of the assessment. Parents may be anxious to learn about their child's problem and what can be done about it. Anxiety may be expressed through verbal or nonverbal modalities or both. Verbal indices of anxiety include sentence corrections, slips of the tongue, repetitions, stuttering, intruding or incoherent sounds, omissions, and frequent use of "ah." Nonverbal indices include sweating, trembling, fidgeting, restlessness, hand clenching, twitching, scowling, and forced smiling.

When you sense that an interviewee's anxiety is interfering with rapport, encourage him or her to talk about it. Possible leads are as follows (Stevenson, 1974): "Something makes it hard for you to talk about this matter; can you tell me what it is?" or "Are you afraid of what I will think of you?" When all else fails and interviewees are still resistant, it may be necessary to gently point out their responsibility as interviewees: "We have to work together; we can't accomplish very much unless you can tell me more about yourself." By being attentive to their possible distress, you can help interviewees experience what a therapeutic relationship might be like. This knowledge then serves as a valuable starting point for therapeutic interventions, if and when they are needed.

Facilitating communication. Various factors may inhibit or facilitate communication in the interview (see Table 16-2). It is important to be alert to these factors,

Table 16-2
Factors That Inhibit or Facilitate Communication in the Interview

Inhibitors of Communication	*Facilitators of Communication*
1. Competing demands for time—interviewee feels rushed because of other commitments	1. Fulfilling expectations—interviewee will try to conform to the interviewer's expectations communicated by verbal and nonverbal means
2. Etiquette—interviewee believes that a response would be inappropriate	2. Recognition—interviewer tries to give the interviewee sincere recognition (approval, praise, respect) whenever there is an appropriate opportunity
3. Trauma—interviewee experiences pain in reliving unpleasant feelings associated with a crisis experience	3. Need for guidance—interviewee's need for guidance may motivate him or her to volunteer information
4. Forgetting—interviewee is unable to recall some information	4. Empathic understanding—interviewee's desire to be understood and have someone lend a sympathetic ear may facilitate the interview, particularly when the interviewer's empathic attitude is directed toward the objectives of the interview
5. Chronological confusion—interviewee confuses chronological order of his or her experiences	5. Catharsis—the interviewee's need for catharsis (a release from tensions obtained by telling about the source of the tensions and expressing feelings) increases the spontaneity of the interview once an atmosphere of empathic understanding has been established
6. Inferential confusion—interviewee gives inaccurate and confusing information because he or she has made wrong inferences	6. Need for meaning—if the subject of the interview disturbs the interviewee's system of meaning, the interviewee will be strongly motivated to talk it through
7. Preconscious behavior—interviewee is not aware of his or her preconscious behavior	7. Extrinsic rewards—use of extrinsic rewards (motivators other than those directly associated with the interview) may be helpful in obtaining the interviewee's cooperation

Source: Adapted from Gorden (1975).

because you may have some control over many of them during the interview. The goal is to try to minimize the inhibitors and maximize the facilitators of communication.

Using the Interviewee's Natural Spontaneity

In the initial phases of the interview, allow the interviewee's natural spontaneity to set the pace. Some interviewees may inundate you with their innermost feelings and concerns until they almost overwhelm you. When this occurs, you may not be able to grasp everything that is being said to you and you may need to make a mental or written note of the questions to which you may want to return.

Using Appropriate Vocabulary

Use vocabulary that is understood clearly by the interviewee and that does not unintentionally load the question in favor of a particular response (Gorden, 1975). Be sure that your questions are concrete and easily understood. Avoid ambiguous words, psychological jargon, and phrases with double meanings. Avoid repeating the interviewee's slang or imitating idioms that are unnatural to you. An appropriate vocabulary helps to establish an optimal relationship.

Clarifying the Interviewee's Terms

As an interviewer, you are responsible for maintaining effective communication during the interview. Your role, in part, is to clarify potentially ambiguous communications when they occur. For example, if a child says, "I study a little every day," find out what she means by "little." Do not take for granted that your understanding of "little" is the same as hers. Here is another example of how an interviewer (IR) might clarify an ambiguous statement by an interviewee (IE):

IE: When my son was 12 years old, he had a bad attack of nerves.
IR: What do you mean by an "attack of nerves"?

Sometimes an interviewer can help the interviewee clarify and describe an indefinite communication (Stevenson, 1960):

IE: When I was younger I had a nervous breakdown.
IR: Tell me about the nervous breakdown.
IE: I was just nervous then. It was terrible.
IR: Well, can you tell me exactly how you felt?
IE: I was weak all over and I couldn't concentrate. I felt panicky and would go to bed for hours at a time, and. . . .

Terms that may need clarification because of a possible relationship to medical or psychological conditions include *spells*, *blackouts*, *dizziness*, *weakness*, *nervous breakdown*, *nervousness*, *tension*, *anxiety*, *voices in the head*, *peculiar thoughts*, and *strange feelings*. In addition, members of various subcultures may use terms and phrases with which you are unfamiliar, in which case clarification is required. The goal is *not* to reject the interviewee's language, but to understand what the interviewee means by what he or she says.

Formulating Appropriate Questions

Open-ended questions, which may be either broad or narrow, are useful in the interview. *Broad questions* (such as "How can I help you?" or "Tell me about your family") are particularly useful in discovering the interviewee's associations, values, perspectives, and perception of facts, whereas *narrow questions* (such as "What subjects does your son like in school?") are more efficient in eliciting specific information and speed up the interview process. Open-ended questions are often formulated to obtain *clarification* of a response previously given by the interviewee. By formulating open-ended questions, you give interviewees the opportunity to describe events in their own words and thus you gain a better appreciation of their perspective.

Avoid yes-no questions.   Except when specific facts are required (such as whether a child received help for a particular problem before), questions should be formulated so that a simple yes or no will not suffice. For example, instead of asking "Do you like arithmetic?" or "Are your headaches severe?" it is preferable to ask "What do you think about arithmetic?" or "Tell me about your headaches." The first two questions are less desirable because they are leading questions that can be answered by a yes or no, after which the interviewee can remain silent. The last two questions invite a reply that is longer than one word, giving the interviewee an opportunity to answer more freely.

Another disadvantage of yes-no questions is that they may require you to ask additional questions (Darley, 1978). For example, "What illnesses has Bill had?" is a more effective question than "Has Bill been sick much?" because a yes answer to the latter question will need to be followed up with additional questions to obtain needed information. Frame your questions so that there is a good chance of getting the information you want directly. It is a good strategy to get the interviewee to describe a particular disorder or situation as fully as possible. Table 16-3 provides additional examples of yes-no questions and more desirable questions.

Table 16-3
Examples of Yes-No Questions and More Desirable Questions

Yes-no questions	More desirable questions
"Do your parents argue often with you?"	"How do you get along with your parents?"
"Was the pain severe?"	"What was the pain like?" or "Describe the pain."
"Did you miss your father when he left home?"	"How did you feel when your father left home?"
"Are you quick tempered?"	"What is your temper like?"
"Do you like school?"	"How do you feel about school?" or "What things do you like and dislike about school?"
"Do you like sports?"	"What do you do in your free [or spare or leisure] time?"
"Is your mother nice to you?"	"How does your mother treat you?"
"How much time does your father spend with you?"	"What sorts of things do you do with your father?"
"Are your parents sociable?"	"What do your parents do with their friends?"
"Does your father like sports?"	"What does your father like to do?"

Avoid long, multiple questions. Avoid long, multiple questions that allow the interviewee to answer part of the question and avoid the rest: for example, "Tell me about your parents, teacher, and brothers and sisters." Also avoid questions that present one alternative only: for example, "Do you get frustrated when you are tired?" Such questions may result in invalid replies because they are too leading. It is better to ask "When do you get frustrated?" or "How do you feel when you are tired?"

Ask direct questions. State your questions clearly. "Avoid starting a question, then qualifying part of it, then going back and reframing it, ending lamely with an ambiguous set of incoherent ideas for the [interviewee] to sort out" (Darley, 1978, p. 45). For example, instead of asking "How old was your child when you began to teach him habits of—uh, well, letting him know that he should go to the bathroom—you know, control his bladder?" ask "When did you begin Eddie's toilet training?" (Darley, 1978, p. 45).

Use number-of-alternative questions. Questions that present a number of alternatives are a good compromise between open-ended questions and yes-no questions. In talking with a child about a possible class placement, you might ask "Do you believe that it would be better for you to remain in your regular class, or would you like to be placed in a special class?" You could then say "Tell me about your choice." This type of question is not as constraining as a yes-no question, but it is more limiting than the open-ended question. Questions with a number of alternatives are most useful when you want to find out whether something is the case and also to rule out other ways of viewing an issue (Gilmore, 1973).

Use questions properly. Questions can be used improperly. Two improper uses of questioning are random probing and coercive questioning (Gilmore, 1973). *Random probing* occurs when the interviewer does not know what to ask or has undue curiosity about the intimate details of other people's lives. When you understand what information will be useful, you are less likely to resort to random probing. Undue curiosity is inappropriate because it does not further the purposes of the interview.

Coercive questions, which attempt to force the interviewee to see things as the interviewer sees them, also are inappropriate. Some examples are "Don't you think your teacher has some good points?" and "Why do you always find fault with your son?" These types of questions inhibit communication. By trying to understand and accept the interviewee, you can reduce this source of error.

Distinguish between acceptance and endorsement. It is important to appreciate the distinction between accepting the interviewee's communications and endorsing them. *Accepting* the interviewee's communications means that you acknowledge and appreciate his or her point of view. *Endorsing* the interviewee's communications means that you agree that his or her perspective is accurate. When the interviewee relates information about a particular event, try to understand and accept his or her viewpoint but not endorse it. For example, in response to something an interviewee says about an absent third party, it would be appropriate to acknowledge that "you were offended when she did that" but inappropriate to conclude that "that was an awful thing she did to you." Remember, the interviewee may be unintentionally or deliberately misleading. The goal in such situations is to communicate that you appreciate the interviewee's point of view, without necessarily endorsing it.

Avoid embarrassing questions.   Questions should be formulated so that they do not embarrass or offend the interviewee. The question "How many times have you been expelled from school?" would be better phrased as "What difficulties have you had with staying in school?" Or instead of "In what school subjects have you received a failing grade?" you might substitute the question "What school subjects are difficult for you?" In both of these examples the rephrased questions are potentially less embarrassing than the original questions, yet they still solicit the desired information.

Using Structuring Statements

Informing the interviewee about the nature of the interview at the beginning of the session may reduce his or her anxiety and help structure the interview. *Structuring statements* influence the interviewee's behavior by moving the interviewee to the topic at hand and indicating how he or she should proceed (Molyneaux & Lane, 1982). The following examples illustrate two different ways to provide structuring early in an interview.

Example 1.   "The purpose of this interview is to find ways of helping your son Bill. I'm interested in anything you can tell me about him." This type of statement made early in the interview directs the discussion to the subject of the interviewee's son. It acknowledges that the parent is able to give useful information. It enlists the parent's cooperation and gives the parent the option of discussing anything he or she desires about Bill.

Example 2.   "We have about an hour to talk, so perhaps we could begin with your describing the problem as you see it." In this second example the interview is structured within a time limit. The focus is on a problem, and the interviewer assumes that the interviewee will be able to discuss the problem. The statement focuses on the interviewee's perceptions and invites the interviewee to discuss those perceptions.

Structuring statements can be used throughout the interview (Evans, Hearn, Uhleman, & Ivey, 1979). Any time you want to initiate or conclude an interview phase, attain an objective for a given phase of the interview, or provide the interviewee with information about the direction of the interview, the use of structuring statements is appropriate. For example, structuring statements may be useful in

guiding parents to discuss their child's problem rather than their own problems or in controlling excessive elaboration ("Perhaps we can come back to what you are talking about later. But since our time is limited, can you tell me about . . . ?"). Another example: "You indicated that your child has problems in a number of different areas. Perhaps we could talk about each one in detail. How does that sound to you?" When you make structuring statements, try to determine the interviewee's willingness to discuss the material and how much the interviewee agrees with the statement.

Encouraging Appropriate Replies

Various techniques are useful in conveying to the interviewee that you are interested in his or her communications. These techniques, which overlap with probing techniques discussed later, should be used to encourage the interviewee to elaborate on a communication. They include (Stevenson, 1974) nodding the head; giving a prompt such as "uh-huh" and leaning forward expectantly; repeating the last word or phrase of something the interviewee has said in a questioning manner; using gentle urgings, such as "What happened then?" or "Go ahead, you're doing fine" or "I'd like to hear some more about that"; using the interviewee's name frequently; maintaining eye contact; maintaining a friendly attitude, gentle speech, and a kind expression; and expressing signs of understanding and empathy by saying, for example, "I can understand how difficult that must have been for you," "That probably made you feel better," "Surely," or "Naturally." Irrelevant conversation can be discouraged by making a comment such as "This is interesting but perhaps we should get back to [a specific subject]."

Using Probes Effectively

During an interview you may need to obtain more specific information than the interviewee is providing. In such instances it is helpful to probe further. Examples of *probing questions* include the following:

- "Tell me more about that."
- "Is there anything else?"
- "Tell me what you mean by that."
- "Give me some examples."
- "How do you feel about that?"
- "Did that seem to make a difference to you?"
- "Please go on."
- "When you get into an argument with your Mom, what does she do?"
- "What would you do?"

• "You mentioned that you can't sleep at night. What do you do when you can't sleep?"

• "How did you go about toilet training Sally?"

• "Which subjects do you like best?"

• "You mentioned that you like sports. Tell me what kinds of sports you like."

• "You said that you have trouble making friends. What kind of trouble are you having?"

If the interviewee says, for example, that her mother is horrible, you might say "Give me an example of that" or "Horrible? Tell me how" or "Tell me about how she is horrible."

Other types of probing techniques include the following:

• requesting additional information ("When did your son do that?")

• repeating or slightly modifying the original question (IR: What games do you like to play? IE: I like lots of games. IR: I see. What are the names of some of the games you play?)

• echoing the interviewee's last words (IE: Well, I tried to get him to stop hitting other children, but I wasn't successful. IR: You weren't successful?)

• pausing expectantly, with a questioning facial expression

• repeating the interviewee's reply and then pausing

Avoiding leading questions. When you inquire about problem areas, avoid leading questions—questions formulated so as to direct or control a response. Begin with some general questions and then move to more specific ones. For example, in interviewing a teenage problem drinker, you might say "Tell me about your drinking habits." Avoid a question such as "Why do you drink?" both because it is too general and because it may cause the interviewee to think that you are making a moral judgment. You can ask questions such as "When do you drink alcohol?" and "How do you feel after you drink?" and "What thoughts do you have when you *badly* want to drink?" Similarly, instead of asking "Why are you anxious?" you might ask a question such as "What makes you anxious?" or "What do you do when you are anxious?" or "How long does the anxiety last before it goes away?"

Inquiring about emotions. When the interviewee is displaying emotions and you are not sure about their meaning, inquire further. The following questions may be useful (Stevenson, 1960): "What is it about talking about this that makes you anxious?" "What were you thinking about when you were crying just now?" "Tell me what it is about this that makes you angry."

Similarly, when you are interested in what thoughts accompany the interviewee's emotions, you can inquire further with a question like "What do you think about when you are happy?" or "What thoughts do you have when you feel anxious?"

To obtain further information about an incident, you can ask for details by saying something like "What happened then?" or "What did your teacher say?" or "What did you do after the argument was over?" Whatever type of method you use to probe, be sure that the probing questions or comments do not bias the response. They should not direct the interviewee to a particular reply.

Using Reflection and Feedback

By occasionally reflecting and paraphrasing the interviewees' communications, you provide them with valuable feedback, let them know that they are being understood, and help them verbalize other feelings and concerns more clearly. For example, a statement such as "So you felt that you had no one to turn to" conveys that you are attentive. Reflection and feedback also serve another purpose. If your understanding of an interviewee's statement is inaccurate, the interviewee has the opportunity to correct your interpretations.

Reflecting emotions. By reflecting the interviewee's emotions, you not only show understanding but also implicitly give the interviewee permission to experience the emotions. For example, when you see tears in the interviewee's eyes, you might say "I can see that it makes you sad to talk about this" (Stevenson, 1974). Remarks such as this one may help the interviewee experience strong emotions or relive events during the interview. But you must be cautious; otherwise the interviewee may become carried away with his or her feelings or become too threatened by them.

Reflecting content. In reflecting the content of a communication, one paraphrases the main ideas contained in the interviewee's communication without parroting the communication. For example, after a child's lengthy description of an incident at school, a useful statement about the incident might be "You couldn't go back to school after the fight because everybody would look at you." Your summary should restate the main ideas of the communication in an integrated form. Use reflection and feedback only when you believe that these techniques will further the interview process.

Noting discrepancies between verbal and nonverbal communications.   The use of reflection requires particular skill and sensitivity in situations in which you observe marked discrepancies between the interviewee's verbal and nonverbal communications. Incongruency between verbal and nonverbal behaviors suggests that the interviewee may be experiencing conflict. For example, if an interviewee whose words are extremely pleasant, creating a superficial impression that he or she is at ease, is at the same time tapping feet and clasping and unclasping hands, he or she may be revealing discomfort. In some cases, it may be difficult to determine the extent to which the interviewee is aware of possible conflict. When you observe discrepant communications, you will have to judge when to call such discrepancies to the interviewee's attention.

Timing Questions Appropriately

The initial part of the interview should be focused on areas that are not anxiety provoking or extremely sensitive. Premature or poorly timed questions may impede the progress of the interview and discourage disclosure of vital information. Your relationship with the interviewee should guide you in the timing of questions and discussion of sensitive topics. As you and the interviewee develop a more trusting relationship, you will be able to broach topics that you previously avoided. Time your comments and questions so that they are in harmony with the interviewee's flow of thought while at the same time moving toward areas you believe are important to explore. Do not allow the interview to be overly long or to have many lapses. The pace should be rapid enough to retain interest, but slow enough to allow the interviewee to formulate good answers.

Changing Topics

Practice and sensitivity are required to judge when you have exhausted a topic or when you need to change topics. Base your decision on your appraisal of the interviewee and how much shifting you believe he or she can tolerate. Some interviewees are disturbed by sudden shifts, whereas others become bored with a preplanned sequence of topics. As a rule, it is a good idea to move on to another question or topic as soon as the previous question has been answered adequately. Transitional statements are useful in moving the interview to the next topic and help keep the interview going at a steady pace. Examples of transitional statements include "Let's move on to . . ." and "Now I'd like to discuss . . . ."

As the interviewer, you should try to avoid drastic shifts in questioning (Darley, 1978). For example, a question about the child's school grades followed immediately by a question about a family member's illnesses may puzzle the interviewee. Help the interviewee understand what you are trying to learn by providing a transitional explanation: "We've covered Tom's school work pretty thoroughly. Let's now turn to another topic that may relate to his problem."

Darley (1978, p. 47) suggests another case when a transitional statement is useful—namely,

when the [interviewee] has wandered away from the question you asked and has seemingly gotten off the track. You can get someone back on the track without being offensive: respond to what the [interviewee] is telling you, suggest that you may want to get back to that topic later, and hark back to an earlier relevant response. "I can see what you mean and perhaps we can get into that later; you were saying a moment ago that Alan seemed unaware that anything was the matter with his speech. Did he . . . ?"

When the interviewee introduces a relevant new topic, you must decide whether to follow it and risk losing continuity or stay with the previous topic and risk the possibility of losing additional information. In some instances interviewees will change topics as an evasive tactic in an attempt to avoid sensitive but relevant material. In such cases you may want to note the change and return to the original topic later if necessary.

Tolerating Difficult Behavior

If an interviewee shows discomfort by engaging in disruptive play (in the case of a young child) or crying, or behaves in other ways that evoke discomfort in you, do not move in too quickly, stopping the behavior prematurely (Greenspan & Greenspan, 1981). It may be important to allow the interviewee some time to work through the discomfort he or she is displaying. In the process you can learn how the interviewee handles discomfort and the extensiveness of any psychopathology. Dealing with such situations, of course, requires clinical judgment. You do not want to allow a situation to develop in which the interviewee becomes too disorganized or frightened; this would be detrimental to the interviewee and to your relationship. The key is to recognize when the behavior is no longer appropriate. You must develop some tolerance for anxiety-provoking behavior, yet know when to step in to reduce or modify the behavior if it becomes too intense.

Handling Silences

Occasionally conversation may halt. Learn to recognize different kinds of silences. A pause may mean that the interviewee has completed giving information about the topic, needs time to recall more information or consolidate thoughts, senses that he or she has been misunderstood, or feels that a sensitive area has been touched on. Silence may be a sign of mourning or deep reflection over some past tragedy. In such cases, do not feel that you must talk. An empathetic smile or a nod of the head may be all that is needed to indicate that you are waiting for the interviewee to continue. If you do decide to speak, you might say "Where do we go from here?" or "Is there anything else that you want to say?" or "What else is important for me to know?" or "Do you want to just sit and think for a while? That's fine."

When progress of the interview is stifled or when the interviewee is extremely reluctant to continue, be sure to discuss the difficulty with the interviewee. Useful statements to make at these times include the following (Stevenson, 1960):

• "It seems hard for you to talk to me about yourself. Let's talk about that."

• "You seem to be at a loss for words. What are you thinking about right now?"

• "Something seems to be holding you back. Could it have anything to do with your thoughts about me?"

• "I've been wondering if the difficulty you're having in talking comes from your wondering how I'll react to what you tell me."

• "We do not seem to have made much progress. Tell me what we're doing wrong."

• "We're not getting along very well. What do you think is the reason?"

Statements such as these will likely cause the interviewee to respond with renewed interest. If they do not, try to recognize possible sources of irritation or anxiety in the interviewee. An interviewee may be reluctant to talk because of fear of the interviewer, fear of his or her own emotions evoked by a discussion of personal problems, fear of examining himself or herself too closely, or fear about the confidentiality of the interview situation (Stevenson, 1960). You must be sensitive to these fears and be prepared to deal with them. Don't get into an argument with the interviewee in an attempt to get him or her to talk.

If you believe that the silence may be associated with guilt or depression, you might say "I can see that this is something which is very difficult for you to talk about, but it's important that we talk about it sometime. Should we do it now or come back to it later?" Silence can also indicate resistance. When you judge this to be the case, you might want to deal with the resistance by helping the interviewee talk about a meaningful or important topic.

At first, silences may seem to be interminably long, but in time you will learn to appreciate them. Silences can give you some time to think, help to reduce the tempo of an interview that is too intense, or press some interviewees to assume responsibility for what is being discussed (Reisman, 1973). This discussion pertains particularly to older children and adults. For younger children, the implications of silence are discussed in a later section of this chapter (Interviewing Techniques with Children).

Analyzing Information Critically

Carefully evaluate whether the information you obtain meets the objectives of the interview (Gorden, 1975). Interviewees must recognize that their communications are being evaluated and organized into some coherent theme. By conveying an attitude of critical evaluation—interest in precise facts, concern for correct inferences, and desire to establish accurate sequences of events—you show the interviewees that you want to get beneath the surface of the communications and away from vague, superficial, and incomplete responses.

It may be necessary to call attention to apparent inconsistencies, contradictions, or omissions. When you confront the interviewee with discrepancies, do so in a nonthreatening manner and be prepared to explore the interviewee's feelings. Do not use confrontation about discrepancies as a means of punishment or a forum for accusations, judgments, or solutions to problems (Evans et al., 1979). The following excerpt shows how the interviewer called the attention of a 9-year-old boy to a discrepant communication (Reisman, 1973, pp. 60–61, with changes in notation):

IR: You seem to feel very angry.
IE: (Seems to agree, but says nothing.)
IR: Can you tell me why?
IE: The kids at school make fun of me.
IR: Oh, in what way?
IE: They say I don't try in sports, and that I'm no good in baseball.
IR: And this kind of hurts your feelings . . . and makes you feel angry with them.
IE: No, I don't care. They're not my friends so I don't care what they say.
IR: (Pause) Well, I wonder in what ways you would like help.
IE: (Pause) I'd like to have more friends in school.
IR: (Pause) On the one hand, you're saying you don't care about

them, and on the other you're saying you would like them to be your friends.

IE: (Begins to cry quietly) I do want them to be my friends.

Handling Self-Disclosures

Some interviewees may ask you questions about yourself. Be tactful in responding to such questions. If you believe that sharing information will facilitate the interview goals, go ahead. You do not want to allow a situation to develop in which you are doing most of the responding and the interviewee is doing most of the questioning, however. Although some self-disclosure may be helpful, it should generally be kept to a minimum.

Widening the Circle of Inquiry

If you want to widen the circle of inquiry, use the interviewee's communications as a starting point. For example, if a mother reports that her son does not get along with his present teacher, you might ask "You said that your son does not get along with his present teacher; how has he gotten along with his previous teachers?" Then at some later point you might say "Tell me how you feel about his teachers." When the child is the interviewee, you might say "You mentioned your father earlier; what is he like?" Once interviewees begin talking, follow up on areas deemed to be particularly important for the purposes of the evaluation.

Keeping Your Emotions Under Control

During the interview you will react to many things that the interviewee says. You may feel sorrow, disgust, embarrassment, anger, pleasure, or humor. It is not possible or even desirable to suppress these or similar feelings. You should, however, strive to control those emotions which, if displayed, might interfere with the interviewee's communications (Stevenson, 1960). Expressions of anger or disgust, for example, may inhibit the interviewee from talking further about intimate details. Laugh *with* the interviewee, but never at him or her.

Obtaining Useful Leads from Communication Patterns

Useful leads may be provided by various communication patterns in the interview: association of ideas, shifts in conversation, opening and closing sentences, recurrent references, inconsistencies and gaps, and concealed meanings (Garrett, 1982). *Association of ideas* occurs when the

interviewee deviates from the particular topic under discussion and begins to free associate. The free association may provide useful clues about feelings or concerns that were not directly expressed. *Shifts in conversation* may be best understood by examining what the interviewee was saying just before the topic changed. The shifts may provide clues as to what is troubling the interviewee or reveal personal preoccupations. *Opening and closing sentences* may be of special significance. Initial remarks may reveal how the interviewee feels about being interviewed, and closing remarks may reveal what the interview meant to the interviewee. In some cases the initial topic discussed by the interviewee may be one of great importance in his or her life. *Recurrent references* or themes that run throughout the interview may provide clues about the interviewee's major source of concern or significant attitudes. *Inconsistencies and gaps* may be suggestive of guilt, confusion, ambivalence, or avoidance. *Concealed meanings*, which may be revealed by slips of the tongue, rationalizations, or ambivalent questions, may suggest areas that should be explored, either in the first interview or at a later date.

Using Summary Statements

At times during the interview it may be helpful to summarize briefly what the interviewee has said and ask the interviewee to make any needed corrections. Summary statements are useful in obtaining confirmation of your understanding and in integrating what has been communicated to you so far in the interview. "Let me see, as I understand things so far . . . . Is that right? Now let's continue." Summary statements are particularly useful at the end of the interview.

Comment on Interviewing Skills and Strategies

To be successful as an interviewer, you must know yourself, trust your ideas, be willing to make mistakes, and above all have a genuine desire to help the interviewee (Benjamin, 1981). You must be careful not to present yourself as all-knowing; it is important to reveal your humanness to the interviewee. This means being honest with the interviewee and with yourself. For example, by telling the interviewee that you may not have the solution or that solutions may be difficult to find, you emphasize that you are not omnipotent.

The success of the interview also will be determined by your ability to "track" with, or follow the lead of, the interviewees, basing your approach to the interviewee on how the interview unfolds. Some interviewees need much encouragement to talk, whereas others, especially when their communications are superfluous, need to be refocused on relevant material. Always regulate the pace of the interview so that it is in tune with the interviewee's communications.

Listen carefully to what the interviewee says, but do not accept as literal truth everything that he or she says (Stevenson, 1960). Interpret and assess the significance of what the interviewee says in light of the interviewee's values and the attitudes revealed by his or her emotions and other nonverbal behavior. Sometimes emotions are congruent with the interviewee's words and sometimes they are not. *What the interviewee says is important, but how he or she acts and speaks is equally important.* Consequently, you should always attend to both the verbal and the nonverbal communications of the interviewee.

Potential sources of interviewee error are the interviewee's (a) forgetting facts due to the passage of time, (b) withholding or falsifying information, and (c) omitting or distorting facts due to selective recall. You can minimize the first source of error by helping the interviewee recall information through probes for omitted details; the second, by helping the interviewee see that the assessment is important and that you are there to help him or her; and the third, by focusing on highly specific details so as to reduce the interviewee's anxieties.

Potential sources of interviewer error are the interviewer's failure to communicate interest and warmth, uncover the interviewee's anxieties, and recognize that the interviewee's anxieties are being exposed too rapidly. *Failures are more likely to arise from defects in attitude than from technical difficulties* (Stevenson, 1960). Interviewees, as Stevenson observed, are forgiving, except when you show lack of interest or lack of kindness.

During the interview an "inner dialogue" takes place between what you hear from the interviewee and what you hear from yourself. The fruits of this dialogue—your thoughts and reactions—guide your communications. Listening thus involves two simultaneous processes: listening to the interviewee and listening to yourself. The goal is to come to some understanding of the interviewee—how he or she views the problem and how he or she views himself or herself—and eventually to generate some possible solutions to the problems.

In summary, effective interviewing skills involve the following abilities:

• the ability to establish rapport (skills in unobtrusively communicating respect, caring, warmth, and empathic understanding);
• the ability to receive information accurately (skills in listening, observing, and remembering communications given by the interviewee);
• the ability to facilitate communication (skills in using the interviewee's natural spontaneity, using appropriate vocabulary, clarifying the interviewee's terms, formulating appropriate questions, using structuring statements, encouraging appropriate replies, using probes effectively, using reflection and feedback, timing questions appropriately, changing topics, tolerating difficult behavior, handling silences, handling self-disclosures, keeping your emotions under control, and using summary statements);
• the ability to evaluate critically the information received (skills in keeping the objectives of the interview clearly in mind and continually assessing the gap between the information received and that needed to fulfill the objectives of the interview);
• the ability to regulate your own verbal and nonverbal behavior (skills in observing yourself so that you can direct the interviewee toward needed information and motivate him or her to give the needed information)

Developing interviewing skills takes time and practice. Practice with adults and children before actually interviewing clients. Videotape and study yourself conducting interviews. Role play various types of interviews. Observe skilled interviewers and try to get feedback from them and from your peers. These procedures will contribute to your becoming a skilled interviewer.

At this point in the chapter, it may be helpful to do the exercise shown in Table 16-4. It is designed to sharpen your ability to give appropriate responses in the interview.

OVERVIEW OF VARIOUS TYPES OF INTERVIEWS

Interviews serve various purposes. The *initial interview* is designed to obtain information relevant to diagnosis, treatment, remediation, or placement in special programs. In the initial interview parents (and occasionally children) are informed about the assessment process. The initial interview may be part of an assessment process that also includes psychometric testing, or it may be the sole assessment procedure. When psychometric testing is part of the assessment process, the initial interview may precede or be concurrent with the testing. The *post-assessment interview* presents the assessment results to the parents, and in some cases to the child, teacher, or referral source. The *follow-up interview* may measure outcomes of treatment or intervention and gauge the appropriateness of the assessment findings and recommendations. Although the follow-up interview is not discussed in this text, the techniques

Table 16-4
Exercise in Interviewing Skills

Directions: Below are a number of examples of statements made by interviewees, each accompanied by two possible interviewer responses. Select the interviewer response you prefer and give a justification for your selection. (Preferred responses are given in the Comment section at the end of the table.)

EXAMPLES

Example 1
IE: I feel I need affection and can't get any.
IR-1:   Well, we all need affection and you're not alone in this.
IR-2:   What interferes with your getting affection?

Example 2
IE: I'm afraid that I may lose control of myself.
IR-1:   What do you think would happen if you did?
IR-2:   Would that be bad?

Example 3
IE: I was afraid of my parents when I was younger.
IR-1:   What about them made you afraid?
IR-2:   Yes, many young children are afraid of their parents.

Example 4
IE: .   Doctor, I think that I'm going crazy.
IR-1:   Oh, no, you're not. You don't have any symptoms.
IR-2:   Tell me what you mean by crazy.

Example 5
IE: My teacher is mean to me.
IR-1:   Can you give me an example of that?
IR-2:   I'm sorry that he is.

Example 6
IE: My headaches are getting worse and my mother says that she can't stand it much longer.
IR-1:   Does your mother have headaches too?
IR-2:   What does your mother say about your headaches?

Example 7
IE: Yesterday I had a big quarrel with my Dad.
IR-1:   Again?
IR-2:   What happened?

Example 8
IE: I don't think this will help me at all.
IR-1:   Let's talk about that; what do you think is happening?
IR-2:   If you don't cooperate, I'll have to notify the school principal.

Example 9
IE: You look tired.
IR-1:   This headache is killing me.
IR-2:   I've had a touch of sinus congestion, but that won't interfere with our session.

Example 10
IE: I refuse to give in to my mother.
IR-1:   You feel that there is no purpose in doing anything for her.
IR-2:   How can you expect your mother to do anything for you if you don't do anything for her?

Example 11
IE: Well, I liked school a lot. I was on the swim team and had lots of friends. I had a good figure then, too. That was before I gained all this weight. My boyfriend liked me better when I was thin. Then when I was a senior my mother died from cancer. All of my girlfriends got steady boyfriends. That's when I gained weight. Things just weren't the same.
IR-1:   So things were going pretty well for you until your senior year, when many difficult changes occurred?
IR-2:   Tell me about your mother.

Example 12
IE: My marriage was not exactly good. You see, my husband and I used to get into these huge fights, and he'd get really violent. One time, he shoved me so hard I flew through the sliding glass doors. I had to have all kinds of stitches. It was a real mess.
IR-1:   How long were you and your husband married?
IR-2:   That must have been very frightening for you. What kinds of things did you fight about?

COMMENT

Example 1. IR-2's response is preferable. It acknowledges the interviewee's statement and also inquires about possible reasons for not receiving affection. IR-1's response tends to close off the remark, halting further exploration.

Example 2. IR-1's response is preferable. It gives the interviewee room to comment on a range of possible feelings and actions. IR-2's response is less preferable because it is too specific, pointing to the "badness" and loss of control.

(Table continues on next page)

Table 16-4 (cont.)

Example 3. IR1's response is preferable. It opens up the area to further discussion, whereas IR-2's response tends to close the discussion and provide false reassurance.

Example 4. IR-2's response is preferable. It allows the interviewee to say what he or she means by crazy. Although it is reassuring, IR-1's response assumes that the interviewer knows what the interviewee means, and this assumption may not be accurate.

Example 5. IR-1's response is preferable. It leads the interviewee to focus on a specific event and to document the statement. IR-2's response, although somewhat sympathetic, tends to close off discussion and imply endorsement of the interviewee's perception.

Example 6. IR-2's response is preferable. It broaches the subject of the interviewee's relationship with his or her mother, paving the way for other relevant inquiries. IR-1's response is somewhat tangential at this time.

Example 7. IR-2's response is preferable. It asks the interviewee to comment on the quarrel. IR-1's response, which simply recognizes that the quarrel is a recurring event, is not likely to facilitate further discussion.

Example 8. IR-1's response is preferable. It asks the interviewee to explore his or her feelings about the reason for coming for the interview. A punitive response such as IR-2's response should not be used under any circumstances.

Example 9. IR-2's response is preferable. It acknowledges the interviewee's comment but reassures the interviewee that the interviewer is in control. Comments that burden the interviewee with the interviewer's own difficulties, such as IR-1's response, should be avoided.

Example 10. IR-1's response is preferable. It is a reflective probe. Argumentative comments such as IR-2's response should be avoided.

Example 11. IR-1's response is preferable. It acknowledges the interviewee's statements and allows her to comment further on her difficulties. IR-2's response focuses on one specific area. Although it might be valuable to explore this area at another time during the interview, such a focus is premature.

Example 12. IR-2's response is preferable. It is an empathic response, followed by a request for more information about an important area. IR-1's reply is not as responsive to the interviewee's statements. It is a useful information-gathering probe, but seems out of place after these statements.

described in this chapter are useful for follow-up interviews.

INITIAL INTERVIEW: GENERAL CONSIDERATIONS

The interviewer's aims in the initial interview are (a) to obtain accurate information from the interviewee, (b) to describe the assessment procedure to the interviewee, and (c) to form opinions about the interviewee. Initial interviews may involve the child, parents, teacher, and relatives, either individually or together. During the early part of the initial interview, you will form impressions about the interviewee's ability to establish a relationship, general attitude (such as defensive, guarded, suspicious, or hostile), attitude toward answering questions, attitude toward his or her own memory, and need for reassurance. You will also receive a host of other impressions that will be tested and evaluated as the interview progresses. You should obtain as much information as possible during the initial interview, because the client may not be available for a second interview and all the information you can gather will assist you in arriving at a diagnostic impression.

Generating Hypotheses from the Initial Interview

The information obtained in the initial interview is used to generate hypotheses about the child's interpersonal behavior in the natural environment and about factors associated with the child's maladaptive behaviors. In order to develop these hypotheses you will need to identify the problem behaviors, factors associated with these behaviors (such as the antecedents and consequences of the behaviors and the frequency, magnitude, duration, and pervasiveness of the behaviors), and other contributing factors (for example, those associated with the child, parents, school, and environment). When the initial interviews have been completed, you should have useful information about the present problem behaviors, the antecedent contributing conditions, the consequent conditions, the intensity of the problem, and the coping skills of the child, parents, and teacher.

In the following case (Reisman, 1973, pp. 87–88, with a change in notation), the interviewer was able to get to the roots of the problem in the first interview. The interviewer hypothesized that the child's aggressive behavior was due to situational factors rather than to a personality disorder and thus recommended psychotherapy focused on helping the child learn to express feelings in words rather than in actions or looks that could be misunderstood. After three months of therapy, the child was able to return to school.

Ray is a moderately retarded 15-year-old adolescent who was suspended from school for being aggressive and for threatening his teacher. Because of his behavior he was referred for a psycho-logical evaluation.

Ray walked into the interviewer's office wearing a black leather jacket and a surly expression. He glared menacingly but said nothing. The interviewer explained why he was seeing Ray and asked in what way the client wanted things to go. Ray stated that he wished to return to school. As he spoke, it immediately became obvious that he had a severe speech problem. During the interview it was learned that the menacing, surly expression turned out to be a way of putting people off so that Ray would not have to talk, as well as helping Ray to appear in control of a situation when in reality he was afraid. His "aggression" in school came about when his teacher yelled at him for standing up after another student hit him on the back of the head with a pencil. Ray sat down and glared menacingly at the teacher, who became afraid and locked the boy in a closet. When, after a few minutes, the teacher did not release him, Ray became frightened and began yelling to be let out. The teacher could not understand what Ray was saying and was afraid to open the door. In panic, Ray pounded and kicked at the door and knocked it down.

Interviewer-Initiated Interviews

Particularly in school settings and in juvenile detention settings, interviews may be initiated by the psychologist in cases where the child or parent has not specifically sought help for a problem. Whenever the interview is held be-cause you have been asked by the referral source to evalu-ate the child or because your position in the agency re-quires such evaluations, it is important to inform the interviewee simply and directly why you asked him or her to come to see you.

To the parents you might say, for example, "I'm Ms. Grey, the school psychologist. Henry's teacher, Ms. Jones, has told me that he is not doing well in school. I'd like to talk to you about Henry." To a child in a juvenile detention center, you might say "I'm Dr. Brown, a clinical psychol-ogist at the center. I'd like to talk to you about how you got to the center." To a child in school, an appropriate com-ment might be the following: "I'm Dr. Smith, the school psychologist. I understand from Ms. Jones that you are not doing too well in school. I'd like to talk to you about your school work."

THE INITIAL INTERVIEW WITH CHILDREN

Interviews with children will give you information about what they perceive their problems to be, their thoughts and feelings about themselves, and their impressions about their situation and their relationships. How you obtain this information must depend on the developmental level of each child. Young children will likely not respond to stan-dard interview techniques and will need to be encouraged and supported to reveal their thoughts and feelings to you. Interview strategies must be adjusted to the linguistic and conceptual abilities of the child (Bierman, 1983).

The First Meeting

Observations begin when you first meet the parent and child in the waiting room. Notice how they interact.

- Does the parent talk with the child?
- Does the parent yell at or scold the child?
- How does the parent assist the child in taking off his or her jacket (for example, gently or forcefully)?
- Do they sit close together or far apart?
- Does the child cling to the parent?
- What kinds of facial expressions do they have?
- If other siblings are present, is there any obvious difference in the children's appearance and behavior and in the attention given to them by the parent?
- Is the child playing constructively away from the parent?
- Does the child seek the parent's help?
- Does the parent help or ignore the child?
- Do they look relaxed or tense?
- Do they seem preoccupied or estranged?
- Is the family caring and affectionate?
- How does the child make the separation from his or her parents to come with you?

Even a limited period of observation, say 30 seconds, may provide you with useful information about family dynam-ics—how the parent and child communicate and interact and how the family deals with the anxiety-arousing situa-tion of seeing a psychologist.

After your initial observation, introduce yourself to the parent, then pause and give the parent the opportunity to introduce the child to you (Reisman, 1973). If the parent seems to be flustered or embarrassed, turn to the child and introduce yourself: "Hello, I'm Dr. ____. We're going to be talking in my office while your mother waits out here." As Reisman observed, this simple introduction serves four functions. First, it indicates that although the interviewer is a stranger to the child, she or he has some knowledge about the child. Second, it emphasizes (through use of the interviewer's formal title) that the relationship is a profes-sional one. Third, it makes clear that communication is a major activity in which they are to engage. Finally, it tells the child where the parent will be during the meeting, thus helping to alleviate anxiety that the child may have about separation.

Children's Initial Apprehensions

When children are first seen for a psychological evaluation (for example, for evaluation of behavior problems), they are likely to be apprehensive. Typical concerns center on such issues (Swanson, 1970) as medical treatment ("Will I get needles?"), removal from home ("Is this the first step in being 'put away'?"), competency ("Will I have my head examined? How?"), self-concept ("Will they find I am crazy or 'dumb'?"), and being singled out ("Why am I the only one in the family to come?" or "How come the other kids at school don't come?" or "What will I tell my classmates about why I had to leave school today?"). Be prepared to encounter these and other apprehensions. They may not be expressed directly by the child, so watch for signs of their presence. Apprehension may be markedly reduced by a reassuring comment: "Bill, I know how difficult it is for many children to come to a new place and talk with new people."

It also is helpful to determine the child's understanding about the necessity for the evaluation. You might ask "What did your mother tell you about coming to see me?" or "What kind of place did you think this would be?" Any misperceptions should be clarified. If necessary, explain that you do not give shots and that after the session is over the child can go home. Evidence of toys in the room may be reassuring.

Sometimes you may want to inform the child about the reason for the evaluation at the beginning of the interview: "Your parents are concerned about your school work. I'm here to find out how we can help you." By allaying the child's apprehensions through questions and comments, you convey to the child that he or she is being treated "in a professional manner, with decency, safety, and respect" (Swanson, 1970, p. 30).

Preschool Children

Although young children often are not formally interviewed as part of the assessment process, having them talk about themselves is helpful. The interviewing of young children must be guided by the following considerations:

Preschool children conceive of others in simple evaluative and concrete terms. They carve the world into rigid "good" and "bad" categories, and egocentrically consider interpersonal events in terms of the meaning and impact they have on them. They are trapped in the present and must encounter each situation as an isolated incident in which the beliefs and actions of others are unpredictable. Their conceptions of covert variables such as emotions and motives are rudimentary, global, and rigid. Their impressions are greatly biased by immediate and observable events, and they have particular difficulties relating variation in

any one conceptual dimension, attribute, or event to other dimensions simultaneously. Hence, they have difficulty interpreting multiple cues or integrating sequential or inconsistent information. (Bierman, 1983, pp. 230–231)

Additionally, young children are often shy and timid and have difficulty verbalizing their feelings and thoughts. They may confuse temporal and sequential aspects of events and may mix wishful thinking with fact. Finally, they may highlight events that emphasize pleasures and sorrows rather than a broader range of emotions.

If these limitations are kept in mind, talking with young children can provide valuable information about their feelings, interests, and concerns. Murphy (1956, p. x) observed:

Children under five may not be able to express their feelings in words; their language may be full of phrases expressing their wants and descriptions like "Garage man fixes broken bumper," which may reflect some concern about body damage, but such directly expressed remarks as "I was very angry at my mother for not giving me two ice creams" are not within the range of many preschool children. At best a grumbling "Stinky old mommie" attempts to convey the feeling.

Rapport can be established with young children in a number of ways (Yarrow, 1960). One is to play a game with the child or show the child a trick gadget before the interview begins. Another is to visit the child's nursery school or home before the interview. Preschool children who are somewhat familiar with you may be more cooperative in the interview.

With children younger than 5 years of age, the assessment interview may be held in a playroom. Useful materials to have in the playroom are paper, pencils, crayons, paint, paintbrushes, an easel, clay, blocks, balls, dolls, a doll house, puppets, animals, dress-up clothes, and a water supply. Pictures, toys, and stories may help stimulate young children to think and talk about their own immediate concerns. If the interviewer relates his or her ideas, thoughts, and memories in relation to these props, the child may be drawn into an extended discussion.

In observing the child in a free-play setting, pay special attention to characteristics of the child's play, including initiation of play, energy expended, manipulative actions, tempo, body movements, tone, integration, creativity, products, and age-appropriateness. Look for such characteristics as persistence, orderliness, ingenuity, competitiveness, closure, and intensity of play (see Table 16-5). Note the child's general attitude toward play, momentary attitudes toward play, and the relationship of play to other traits and behaviors. Finally, observe shifts and variations in play and observe the child's speech, language, and affect, as well as the content of play.

Table 16-5
Guidelines for Assessing Children's Play

ENTRANCE INTO THE PLAY ROOM

• Does the child go into the playroom easily?
• Does the child ask to hold the mother's or interviewer's hand on the way?
• Does the child approach the toys, or does he or she cling to the mother?

INITIATION OF PLAY ACTIVITIES

• Is the child a quick or slow starter?
• Does the child require help in getting started?
• Does the child need encouragement and approval?
• Is the child able to direct his or her own play?
• Does the child require active and steady guidance?
• Does the child show initiative, resourcefulness, or curiosity?
• Is the child impulsive?
• Does the child initiate many activities but seldom complete them, or does he or she maintain interest in a single activity?

ENERGY EXPENDED IN PLAY

• Does the child work at a fairly even pace, or does he or she use much energy in manipulating the play materials, making body movements, and making verbalizations?
• Does the child seem to pursue an activity to the point of tiring himself or herself?
• Does the child start to work slowly and then gain momentum until the actions are energetic, or does he or she gradually lose momentum?
• Does the child seem listless, lethargic, lacking in vitality?

MANIPULATIVE ACTIONS IN PLAY

• Is the child free or tense in handling the play materials?
• Are movements large and sweeping or small and precise?
• Are movements smooth?
• Are play materials used in conventional or unconventional ways?

TEMPO OF PLAY

• Does the child play rapidly or with deliberation?
• Is the pace of play hurried or leisurely?
• Does the pace of play vary with different activities or is it always about the same?

BODY MOVEMENTS IN PLAY

• Does the child's body seem tense or relaxed?
• Are the child's movements constricted or free?
• Are the child's movements uncertain, jerky, or poorly coordinated?

• Are movements of hands and arms free, incorporating the whole body rhythmically, or are movements rigid, with only parts of the body being used?
• Does the child use the right hand, the left hand, or both hands?

VERBALIZATIONS

• Does the child sing, hum, use nonsense phrases, or use adult phrases as he or she plays?
• Does the child giggle appropriately?
• What is the general tone of the child's voice tones (for example, loud, shrill, excitable, soft, aggressive, tense, enthusiastic, or matter-of-fact)?
• What does the child say?
• What is the purpose of the child's verbalizations, judging from the intonation?

TONE OF PLAY

• What is the general tone of the child's play (for example, angry, satisfied, hostile, impatient)?
• Does the child throw, tear, or destroy play materials?
• Is the child protective of play materials?
• If aggression is present, does it have a goal or is it random?
• Does aggression increase, causing the play to get out of hand and posing a threat of damage to the playroom or interviewer?

INTEGRATION OF PLAY

• Is the play goal-directed or fragmentary?
• Does the play become more integrated over time?
• Does the play have form, or is it haphazard?
• Is the child's attention sustained or fleeting?
• Is the child easily distracted?
• Are there any peculiar elements to the play?

CREATIVITY OF PLAY

• Is the play imaginative or stereotyped?
• Does the child use simple objects for play, or are special toys needed?
• Does the play show elements of improvisation or constriction?

PRODUCTS OF PLAY

• What play materials are preferred?
• What objects are constructed or designs completed during play?
• Do the products have a recognizable form?

(Table continues on next page)

Table 16-5 (cont.)

• How does the child achieve form? • Does the child show interest in the product? • Does the child tell a story about the product? • Does the child show the interviewer and/or parent the product? • Does the child want to save the product? • Does the child want to give the product to someone? • Does the child use the product for protective or aggressive purposes? • Is the child overly concerned with neatness, alignment, or balance of the play materials?	**AGE-APPROPRIATENESS OF PLAY** • Is the play age-appropriate? • Are there changes in the quality of the play? **ATTITUDE TOWARD ADULTS REFLECTED IN PLAY** • Does the child comply with adult requests or do what he or she thinks adults expect of him or her? • Does the child imitate adult manners accurately? • Does the child protect himself or herself from adults? • Does the child attempt to obtain tender responses from adults? • Does the child follow his or her own ideas independently of adults?

Note. These guidelines are not meant to cover all contingencies. They are limited samples of many possible behaviors, included to help sensitize you to the kinds of behaviors that may provide information useful for assessing children.
Source: Goodman and Sours (1967); Hartley, Frank, and Goldenson (1952); Lerner and Murphy (1941).

You might begin the play session by saying to the child (Lerner & Murphy, 1941) "Let's play with the toys. You can play with anything you like." Then as the child plays, record his or her behavior. Answer questions as necessary to keep rapport. For example, if the child asks "What are you writing?" you can say "I'm writing about what you like to do." If the child gives a major lead, pursue it. For example, if the child says "Mommie is mean," you can repeat the phrase in a questioning tone: "Mommie is mean?" If necessary, you can then follow up by asking "How is Mommie mean?" You can also follow up specific play behaviors with questions: for example, "What does Mommie do when you don't eat?" or "What led up to Daddy's spanking the baby?" Ideally, follow-up questions should develop from the child's behaviors. You must decide how to set limits when the child exceeds normal standards, such as by breaking toys or hitting you.

If the mother is present in the playroom, as frequently is the case, you can, in a quiet voice, call certain behaviors to her attention and ask for clarification (Swanson, 1970). "Does he frequently pull his hair at home?" "Is this her natural walk?" "Can he stack blocks at home?" "Is she usually this active?"

Middle-Childhood-Age Children

During middle childhood (5 to 11 years of age), children make great strides in their language and conceptual development (Yarrow, 1960). They use more constructs, provide longer descriptions of other people, make more inferences about other people, and acquire more complete concep-

tions of various social roles (Bierman, 1983). However, children at this age may be reluctant to share their feelings, concerns, and attitudes with adults with whom they are relatively unfamiliar. Competitive board games, such as checkers or Parcheesi, have special appeal for children in this age group and can be used to establish rapport.

Although it usually isn't desirable to structure the interview as a play situation when children are older than 5 years of age, it may be valuable in some cases to have a short period of play observation. Play observation may be particularly helpful with hyperactive children, retarded or low-functioning children, children who have problems handling their own aggression, or children who do not wish to play competitive board games. Use the guidelines presented in Table 16-5 for observing the free play of children. The following case illustrates how valuable clues were obtained by observing the free play of a 7½-year-old boy (Simmons, 1987, p. 18).

John, age 7½, was referred for aggressive behavior at home and at school. He rushed to the playroom the instant he was invited. He quickly took the guns and shot wildly around the room with vivid sound effects and descriptive phrases such as "I got 'em! He's dead!..." He tried to shoot the examiner but was easily persuaded to direct his fire at the targets and the doll figures. As the intensity of his play subsided, he began to talk about his father and of the fun they had fishing, boat riding, and playing ball together last summer.

...John appeared acutely anxious and demonstrated that he handles anxiety by overactivity. He further showed that his behavior can be controlled by mild prohibitions when he acquiesced to the request to shoot inanimate targets rather than the examiner.

He also evidenced inner control by gradually stopping the aggressive play. This contrasts with the behavior of some children, whose aggressive actions tend to snowball in intensity and will cease only with strong external prohibitions.

Adolescent Children

Adolescents have an increasing command of language concepts and have developed the capacity for abstract thinking; their social world, too, is more complex. However, they still may not be able to articulate their feelings clearly or reflect on their experiences, and they tend to be self-conscious. Their willingness to talk will depend on their perception of the interview and the degree of rapport that has been established. Try to help them understand that they have input into the decisions that will be made about them and that it is in their best interest to voice their feelings, desires, and wishes. They need to feel respected and to understand that their opinions are important. Your goal is to enlist their cooperation without undue coercion. This can be accomplished in part by assurances of confidentiality and open, honest communication.

Behaviorally Disordered Children

Behaviorally disordered children may be especially difficult to interview. They may be hesitant to speak and may express overt hostility. Considerable skill is needed to draw them out. Allow sufficient time to establish rapport and to encourage verbalization. Beginning the interview with some area of special interest to the child may help. Since behaviorally disordered children may have a limited attention span, use short questions and reinforce the child's attempts to communicate. You will likely need to provide a great deal of direction and structure for children who are disturbed or confused. The suggestions presented in Chapter 5 for testing behaviorally disordered, autistic, and brain-injured children will also aid you in interviewing, as will the suggestions that follow.

Interviewing Techniques with Children

The most common way to help young children remember, think, and tell you about themselves is to ask them questions. Children will usually answer questions, so asking questions is a good way of directing children and the course of their thinking. Unskilled use of questions, however, may suppress responses. If the interviewer uses a high proportion of questions and relatively few acknowledging or accepting statements (such as "I see," "Oh," or "Really"), children are more likely to answer questions

briefly or give monosyllabic replies. Continual questioning may also inhibit children from seeking information themselves. They may not ask their own questions or volunteer information spontaneously.

In asking questions the interviewer is making demands—he or she is directing the interviewee's attention to memories or ideas that the interviewee might otherwise not have considered.

The compliant listener needs time to think and articulate: such introspection demands considerable skill in self-control and young children require much more time than an adult to inspect their own thoughts and talk about them. An adult's tacit expectations about the pace at which a question-answer exchange will proceed may overestimate what a child can manage. An overly long pause in a conversation can be stressful and the questioner might well be tempted to fill it with a new question or even a suggested answer to his [or her] own previous one, thus further confounding the young child's attempt to think and talk. (Wood, 1982, p. 857)

If you are interested in obtaining only very specific information from children and are confident that they understand the questions, then a direct question-and-answer format may be acceptable (Wood, 1982). However, if you do not know exactly what information you want, if you want children to play an active, constructive role in building up shared knowledge, or if you are not sure that your questions are being understood and responded to accurately (as is often the case with young children), then you should avoid a strict question-and-answer interview format.

General suggestions for conducting interviews were presented in the sections on interviewing skills and strategies. The following list focuses on interview strategies that are particularly useful in establishing rapport with and maintaining the cooperation of a child. (Most of the material in items 2 through 6 and 16 of this section was adapted from Kanfer, Eyberg, & Krahn, 1983.)

1. *Formulate appropriate opening statements.* The opening statement that will be most effective in putting the child at ease will depend on the child's age and behavior and the reason for referral. After introducing yourself and establishing rapport, you might use a statement such as "Your teacher has told me about some of your problems, but I'd like to hear about them from you" or "I understand that you are having trouble at home." To older children, it may be useful to say "What brings you here today?"

2. *Make descriptive comments.* Descriptive comments are those that focus on the child's appearance, behavior, and demeanor. They provide a simple way of giving attention to the child and encouraging the child to continue with

appropriate behavior. An added benefit of descriptive comments is that you can use them to maintain communication with the child while you are formulating other questions. Examples of descriptive comments include "Your shirt is nice," "I see that you are feeding the doll," and "You look cheerful today."

3. *Use reflection.* Reflective statements rephrase what the child has said or done, retaining the essential meaning of the child's communication or behavior. These statements provide clarity and help to organize the child's behavior. For example, in response to the statement "My brother is a brat," you might say "You seem to get upset with your brother."

4. *Give praise frequently.* Praise and support guide the child to talk about areas that you consider important. Younger children will need more praise than older children. Examples of praise are "I appreciate your willingness to tell me about these things" and "Some of these things are hard to talk about, but you are doing fine."

5. *Avoid critical statements.* Criticism is likely to generate emotional reactions—such as anger, hostility, resentment, or frustration—that will interfere with rapport. Examples of critical statements are "You are not trying very hard" and "Stop tearing the paper." When the child is engaging in negative behavior, focus on more appropriate behavior in order to turn the child's attention away from the negative behavior or invoke rules that govern the playroom or office. For example, when a child is throwing blocks say "Let's throw the ball," or when a child is tearing paper that should not be torn say "One of the rules is that you can't tear this paper."

6. *Use simple questions and concrete referents.* Children often respond to standard interview procedures and open-ended questions with sparse and vague replies. By modifying typical interview techniques, you may increase children's responsiveness and elicit more coherent and complete responses. The modifications should be aimed at helping the child to understand and to respond to your questions. This can be accomplished by reducing demands on verbal skills and reducing the complexity of the task—simplifying the questions, adding concrete referents, and simplifying the response required (Bierman, 1983).

Concrete referents may be introduced by having children draw themselves and then list

three things that they really like to do, three things they do not like to do, things they like or do not like about school, things they like or do not like about their families, things that get them into trouble, things that make them mad, and so on. The interviewer can structure a task like this with a cue, such as the following: "What a nice drawing. Now, we're going to do something special with it. I'm going to put some numbers on the side here to help us

tell all about this drawing. For the first list, I need to know three things you like to do." This strategy . . . takes the interviewer's direct (often intimidating) focus off the child and onto the task, and it clarifies the behaviors and responses expected of the child. The interviewer can maintain a very positive and supportive posture, encouraging and praising the child for thinking of things and helping to make the special picture while also providing the child with a channel for expressing hopes, fears, and frustrations.

The clinician can also choose stimuli that reflect situations confronting the child, and then use these to facilitate discussion around problem areas. For a child whose parents were divorced, for example, one might present a picture or doll situation and say, "Here are a mom and dad and a little girl about your age. The mom and dad got divorced." The interviewer can then explore the child's conceptions of divorce with questions such as the following: "What do you think happened?" "What did the mom/dad/ little girl say?" What did the mom/dad/little girl feel?" "What will happen next?" and even "Did that ever happen to you?" "What did you do?" (Bierman, 1983, pp. 233–234).

7. *Formulate questions in the subjunctive mood when necessary.* Hypothetical questions (those formulated in the subjunctive mood) may be useful in getting reticent children to speak. Useful leads that employ a subjunctive mood are "Suppose you were . . . ," "What if you . . . ," and "Let's pretend that . . . ." For example, "Suppose you were to take a friend to your house, and suppose you were going to show your friend some things there, what kinds of things might your friend see?" This type of syntactical structure "allows the child some degree of emotional distance by adding a game-like quality to the question" (Goodman & Sours, 1967, p. 29); for some children, this type of question is preferable to a question such as "What is your house like?"

The following case illustrates the use of hypothetical situations in helping a young girl discuss her feelings toward her mother (Goodman & Sours, 1967, pp. 71–72, with changes in notation).

Sally, an 8-year-old girl referred for outbursts of crying and temper tantrums, seemed resigned to the interview as she came into the office. Her head was bent and her eyes avoided direct contact. Her verbal responses were at first stereotyped. She answered most questions "I don't know," or "because . . . just because," while looking at her feet. She seemed to be struggling to control her feelings. This was most apparent as she spoke of coming to the interview "because my mother says I'm a problem."

Until that point, the interview had been labored, slow, and unproductive. Sally had no inclination to play or to talk spontaneously about herself. The interviewer told her that he once knew "a little girl who did a lot of worrying and felt she couldn't find grown-ups who could understand these worries." Sally made no verbal response but looked directly at the interviewer for a brief moment. Taking the cue, the interviewer went on: "Sometimes this little girl would worry so much that she couldn't eat." "Oh, that's not me," said Sally. "What might you do?" asked the interviewer. Sally started fidgeting with the sash on her dress. The interviewer again asked: "What might you do if the worries get real big?" After further fidgeting and biting her lip, she said: "Nothing." Now more sure of his ground, the interviewer continued: "Well, I sense that you must be pretty worried right now." "How do you know?" she said. "Because you seem to be like this girl—maybe sad and holding back your feelings." Tears rolled down Sally's cheeks. The interviewer then said: "Maybe you can talk a little about what it's like to feel sad." Sally regained her composure, wiped the tears away, and said she would like to play. She then expressed some of the feelings about her mother.

8. *Be tactful.* Questions should be phrased tactfully in order to avoid causing the child anxiety or discomfort. A poorly worded question may lead to discomfort. For example, after a child complained about a teacher, it would be tactless to say "Do you always have trouble with teachers?" You would be more likely to increase the child's responsiveness if you said "Have you found other teachers as upsetting as this one has been for you?" or by simply acknowledging the child's feelings about his or her teacher. Instead of asking "Did you quit school?," which may require an admission of having done so, it is preferable to ask "What was the last grade you completed?"

9. *Use props, crayons, clay, or toys to help young children verbally communicate.* Special skills and techniques are needed to help young children communicate verbally. One method is to use props during the interview—such as having the child talk through the medium of dolls or puppets or carry on a conversation via a toy telephone (Yarrow, 1960). A second method, which may reduce the child's self-consciousness, is to allow the child to use crayons or clay while talking to you. Do not allow the use of crayons or clay to become a convenient escape from talking, however. A third method is to allow young children to express themselves through the use of toys. Observe carefully the child's play—including motor, language, and fantasy elements.

10. *Use special techniques to facilitate the expression of culturally unacceptable responses.* Children, especially those older than 5 years of age, may be reluctant to talk to you about some matters because they believe that their responses are culturally unacceptable (for example, they may not want to portray siblings negatively). The following techniques may prove to be especially useful in facilitating the expression of culturally unacceptable responses (Yarrow, 1960, p. 580, with changes in notation).

a. Suggest in the question that other children might feel the same way. The question may sanction a specific attitude or a general feeling. Examples: "Some boys think they

shouldn't have to take their little brothers along with them when they go out to play. How do you feel about it?" "All of us get mad sometimes when something happens that we don't like. What sorts of things make you feel mad?"

b. Present two alternatives, both of which might be considered acceptable. Example: "If your little brother pulls out all the books from the shelves, do you punish him so that he won't do it again, or do you see that your mother finds out about it?"

c. Choose words that will soften an undesirable response or place the response in a context that might make it more desirable. Example: In the preceding example, use of the phrase "see that your mother finds out about it" instead of "Would you tell your mother on him?" places the response in a more acceptable context.

d. By wording questions in a way that assumes that the child has engaged in this behavior, you can avoid placing the child in the position of having to deny or admit some undesirable behavior. The question "What sorts of things do you and your brother fight about most?" assumes sibling rivalry or quarrels. This technique, however, must be used sensitively to avoid arousing overwhelming guilt feelings.

e. Give the child an opportunity to express a positive response before presenting a question that will require negative or critical evaluations. "What things do you like best about school?... What things aren't so good?"

You may combine these approaches in a question: "There are some things most boys like about school and other things they don't like at all.... What are some of the things you like best... and what are some of the things that aren't so good about school?" These techniques can be extended with specific probes.

Follow-up probes that provide concrete structure are usually more effective in helping children expand their answers to initial questions. For example, a child might respond to the question, "What kinds of things don't you like about school?" with a one-word answer or "I don't know." A structured probe might be: "Well, let's just try to think about one thing first. Tell me one thing you don't like at school." If the child answers simply "math," a structured probe might also be: "What happens in math that you don't like very much?" Or, if that does not work, a choice could be offered: "Well, is it more the work you don't like or the teacher?" These probes are all preferable to options such as "Can you tell me anything else?" This almost invariably receives a negative response. (Bierman, 1983, p. 235)

11. *Clarify an episode of misbehavior by recounting it.* When you want to obtain further information from a child about an episode of misbehavior, ask the child to recount the details of the episode, as illustrated in the following dialogue (Karoly, 1981, p. 102, with changes in notation).

IR: Your teacher tells me that yesterday a bunch of kids in your class "went wild" with paints, throwing them around the room and at other kids.

IE: Yeah.

IR: That really happened?

IE: Yeah. So?

IR: I guess the teacher just doesn't know how to handle kids.

IE: She's okay.

IR: Then what happened?

IE: The kids were bored.

IR: Were you bored?

IE: Yeah, I guess.

IR: Did you enjoy throwing the paints?

IE: What do you mean?

IR: Was it a way to be less bored?

IE: Sure . . . for a while.

IR: Then what happened?

IE: We had to clean the place up. It took all afternoon.

IR: Did you think you would have to clean up?

IE: I don't know.

IR: Was it unfair for her to make you clean up?

IE: The janitor should do it.

IR: But the kids made the mess.

IE: Mrs. Masters [the teacher] is supposed to give us stuff to do.

In this case, the recounting technique brought to light the child's perception that the teacher is responsible for keeping the students occupied at all times. Other assessment techniques—such as classroom observation, teacher interview, or a self-report inventory—are not likely to be as successful as the interview in uncovering the child's attitudes (Karoly, 1981).

12. *Handle children who are minimally communicative by clarifying interview procedures.* Some children may respond to your questions with a yes or no or "I don't know" or "I guess." These responses can be handled with comments like the following (Jennings, 1982, p. 54, with changes): "What I'd like to have you do rather than just saying yes or no is to try to tell me as much as you can about what I ask you." (The modeling of an example may be helpful here.) "You know, I really need you to do more of the talking here if I'm going to get to know you, and one of the ways we could do that is if you would try to talk to me a little more about things rather than just saying yes or no or 'I don't know.'"

On the rare occasion when a child simply refuses to participate in the initial interview, it probably is best to reschedule the interview, as illustrated in the following case (Reisman, 1973).

Suzie, a 7-year-old girl, had refused to attend school. When first seen by the interviewer she was clutching tightly to her mother and refused to accompany the interviewer to his office. When brought to the office by her mother, she began kicking and biting her mother, crying and screaming because her mother wished to go to her own appointment. After the mother left, Suzie retreated to a corner, where she wept angrily, hurling curses at the interviewer, demanding to see her mother, and refusing to cooperate. In such cases it may be best to go along with the child's behavior and allow the behavior to run its course. Attempts should be made to see the child again for another meeting. It may take a few sessions before you obtain the child's trust, acceptance, and cooperation.

13. *Handle avoidance of a topic by discussing it yourself.* If the child is unwilling to talk about a topic, making a statement about the topic or expressing your view about it may stimulate the child (Wood, 1982). Asking a simple question about the topic may also help. Allow time for the child to answer, and give the child a chance to elaborate on his or her initial response. If the response provides relevant information, acknowledge the response ("Hmm," "Yes") or make some relevant remark. If the child stops talking or strays from the topic, ask another question related to what the child has just said, but be sure to intersperse acknowledging or accepting remarks and relevant observations with your questions.

14. *Understand silence.* Because the assessment interview is dependent primarily on verbal communications, a silent child is a challenge. Silence may have a variety of causes—try to determine which one is most applicable. Some children are silent because they resent being at the interview, some are frightened, some may want to talk but don't know what to say, and some prefer to sit quietly and do nothing else (Reisman, 1973). Other possible reasons for silence are discussed in an earlier section of this chapter (Handling Silences). For some children, silence may be comfortable at first but becomes stressful in time. Others may find silence stressful from the beginning but not know how to break it. You must be sensitive to these possibilities and changes in feelings so that you can reduce the child's stress when necessary.

Generally, younger children have more difficulty with silences than older children. Silences may lead to resistance, which in turn can be detrimental to the interview. Therefore, try to keep silences to a minimum with young children.

You may obtain clues about the meaning of the silence by observing the child's nonverbal communications. The child who is angry about coming for the interview will likely begin to talk to you once he or she begins to accept you and understand the purpose of the interview. However, if the child wishes to remain silent, accept this decision, simply pointing out that toys and play materials are available if the child wants to use them. As the silence continues, you can "comment from time to time about the child's enjoyment of the silence, signs of fatigue, or interest, and the approaching end of the meeting" (Reisman, 1973, p. 106). Parallel play with the child may also serve as an indirect way of breaking the child's silence.

15. *Handle resistance and anxiety by giving support and reassurance.* Older children may be reluctant to reveal their feelings and thoughts to a stranger, especially when they are concerned about the reason for and outcome of the evaluation. Try to reduce their anxiety by helping them understand the reasons for the evaluation. The child may express anxiety in various ways—hesitancy in speaking, sadness, hostility, or various indirect expressions (Jennings, 1982).

If you observe that anxiety is present, you may want to help the child express it directly by making a comment such as: "How do you feel about being here today?" or "You look a little nervous about talking to me." You might want to respond to the child's answer with encouragement or support or with a statement that asks for further exploration or acknowledges feelings, depending on the specific circumstances of the interview (Jennings, 1982). One possible response is "Many children feel like you do at the beginning. But in a little while, most feel more at ease. You probably will too." Others include "I'd like to understand why you're so sure that you don't want to talk to me" and "You do seem to feel hesitant about talking with me."

The following suggestions may help minimize anxiety (Yarrow, 1960, pp. 582–583, with changes in notation):

For ethical reasons, as well as from the standpoint of effective motivation, the interviewer should avoid placing the child in a position requiring responses that . . . may arouse guilt feelings. Sometimes one can free a child to admit to knowledge or discuss feelings on which there are . . . taboos and yet avoid or minimize guilt feelings by the form of the question. Matter-of-fact acceptance by the interviewer of everything the child says is the most effective means of avoiding the development of anxiety. If the interview has been essentially nondirective and has not pushed the child to express unacceptable feelings, it is likely that what he [or she] has expressed will not be too disturbing. If taboo areas have been discussed, some provision should be made, either during or following the interview, to reassure the child and to handle any guilt feelings. Assurance of confidentiality can be given if it seems appropriate, and the child can be given an opportunity to express acceptable attitudes on a variety of related topics. Even though the interview [may not be] therapeutically oriented, it may be necessary to help a child achieve some closure on an anxiety-evoking topic that has been opened up in the interview. There is a sensitive line between arousing more anxiety by probing and subtly leading the child to an acceptable resolution.

16. *General suggestions.*

a. Use a simple vocabulary and short sentences tailored to the child's developmental and cognitive level.

b. Be sure that the child understands the questions and that you do not lead the child to give a particular response. Phrase your questions so that the child does not receive any hint that one response is more acceptable than another.

c. Select the questions for your interview on an individual basis, using judgment and discretion and keeping in mind the child's age and developmental level.

d. Be sure that the manner and tone of your voice do not reveal any personal biases.

e. Speak slowly and quietly and try to allow the interview to unfold, using the child's verbalizations and behavior as guides.

f. Use simple terms (for example, *sad* for *depressed*) in exploring affective reactions, and ask the child to give examples of how he or she behaves or how other people behave when emotionally aroused.

g. Assume an accepting and neutral attitude toward the child's communications.

h. Take a more active role with children than with adults and be prepared to change topics if the child becomes distressed.

i. Learn about children's current interests by looking at Saturday morning television programs, talking with parents, visiting toy stores, looking at children's books, and visiting day care centers and schools to observe children in their natural habitat.

Table 16-6 provides examples of less desirable and more desirable questions used in interviewing children. (See Kanfer et al., 1983, for a more detailed discussion of ways to handle problems at each stage of the interview.)

Areas to Cover in the Interview with Children

During the interview try to obtain information about the child's self-perception and perception of parents, siblings, teachers, and other important individuals in his or her life; ability to relate to an unfamiliar adult; ability to discuss relevant information; and interests, thought processes, language, affect, and possible degree of psychopathology. The questions presented in Table 16-7 will aid you in obtaining this information. They are only *sample* questions meant to illustrate the areas most frequently covered in child interviews; they should not be used in a mechanical fashion. Include follow-up and probing questions and reassuring comments as needed.

For children who may enter a psychotherapeutic rela-

Table 16-6
Examples of Less Desirable and More Desirable Questions Used in Interviewing Children

Less desirable questions	More desirable questions
"What things are reinforcing for you?"	"What do you like?"
"Why is your father depressed?"	"What does your father do that makes you think he is sad?"
"When is it that you feel angry and what do you do then?"	"When do you feel angry?" or "What really gets you upset?" followed by "What do you do when you feel angry?" or "How do you act when you get real upset?"
"Where are you most likely to be when you get angry?"	"Where do you get angry?"
"Describe your mom."	"What do you like best about your mom?" "What do you like least about your mom?"
For children younger than 8 years of age:	
"What are your interests and hobbies?"	"What do you do in the afternoons after school?"

Source: Adapted from Kanfer, Eyberg, and Krahn (1983) and La Greca (1983).

tionship after the evaluation, exploration of the following areas may prove valuable (Reisman, 1973):

• the child's understanding of why he or she is at the interview and how he or she feels about it

• what the child believes are the problems and how he or she feels about them (for example, Does the child deny the existence of the problems? Does the child maintain that the problems are incapable of solution?)

• what, if anything, the child intends to do about the problems (for example, Does the child offer reasonable steps for modifying his or her behavior? Does the child intend to take steps to modify the behavior?)

• in what way the child sees the interview as being a help to him or her (for example, Does the child regret being at the interview because it indicates the parents' lack of confidence in his or her ability to change? Is the child willing to cooperate with you and listen to the parents' concerns and their side of the issue?)

For children in a medical setting, coverage of the following areas is especially important (Eyberg, 1985): the child's understanding of why he or she was brought to the hospital or clinic, the child's understanding of the possible treatments under consideration and the child's attitudes toward them, the child's understanding of the cause of his or her medical condition, the child's perceptions of the reactions that family members or friends have about the condition, and the child's expectations about outcome. Coverage of the above areas will help you correct the child's misperceptions, reassure the child, and perhaps increase the child's compliance with the intervention procedures.

In some situations (such as when a therapeutic behavioral intervention is being planned), you may want to inquire about the reinforcers that are important to the child. The sentence-completion technique shown in Table 16-8 is useful on such occasions.

10-24-85 – © 1985 United Feature Syndicate, Inc.

Table 16-7
Example of a Semi-Structured Interview with School-Age Children

Precede the questions below with a preliminary greeting such as the following: "Hi, I'm Dr. Smith. You must be Tom Brown. Come in."

1. Has anyone told you about why you are here today?
2. (If yes) Who?
3. (If yes) What did he [she] tell you?
4. Tell me why *you* think you are here. (If child mentions a problem, explore it in detail.)
5. How old are you?
6. When is your birthday?
7. Your address is . . . ?
8. And your telephone number is . . . ?

School
9. Let's talk about school. What grade are you in?
10. What is your teacher's name?
11. What grades are you getting?
12. What subjects do you like best?
13. And what subjects do you like least?
14. What subjects give you the most trouble?
15. And what subjects give you the least trouble?
16. What activities are you in at school?
17. How do you get along with your classmates?
18. How do you get along with your teachers?
19. Tell me how you spend a usual day at school.

Home
20. Now let's talk about your home. Who lives with you at home?
21. Tell me a little about each of them.
22. What does your father do for work?
23. What does your mother do for work?
24. Tell me what your home is like.
25. Tell me about your room at home.
26. What chores do you do at home?
27. How do you get along with your father?
28. What does he do that you like?
29. What does he do that you don't like?
30. How do you get along with your mother?
31. What does she do that you like?
32. What does she do that you don't like?
33. (Where relevant) How do you get along with your brothers and sisters?
34. What do [does] they [he/she] do that you like?
35. What do [does] they [he/she] do that you don't like?
36. Who handles the discipline at home?
37. Tell me about how they [he/she] handle [handles] it.

Interests
38. Now let's talk about you. What hobbies and interests do you have?
39. What do you do in the afternoons after school?
40. Tell me what you usually do on Saturdays and Sundays.

Friends
41. Tell me about your friends.
42. What do you like to do with your friends?

Mood/Feelings
43. Everybody feels happy at times. What kinds of things make you feel happiest?
44. What are you most likely to get sad about?
45. What do you do when you are sad?
46. Everybody gets angry at times. What kinds of things make you angriest?
47. What do you do when you are angry?

Fears/Worries
48. All children get scared sometimes about some things. What kinds of things make you feel scared?
49. What do you do when you are scared?
50. Tell me what you worry about.
51. Any other things?

Self-Concept
52. What do you like best about yourself?
53. Anything else?
54. What do you like least about yourself?
55. Anything else?
56. Tell me about the best thing that ever happened to you.
57. Tell me about the worst thing that ever happened to you.

Somatic Concerns
58. Do you ever get headaches?
59. (If yes) Tell me about them. [How often? What do you usually do?]
60. Do you get stomach aches?
61. (If yes) Tell me about them. [How often? What do you usually do?]
62. Do you get any other kinds of body pains?
63. (If yes) Tell me about them.

Thought Disorder
64. Do you ever hear things that seem funny or unusual?
65. (If yes) Tell me about them. [How often? How do you feel about them? What do you usually do?]
66. Do you ever see things that seem funny or unreal?
67. (If yes) Tell me about them. [How often? How do you feel about them? What do you usually do?]

Memories/Fantasy
68. What is the first thing you can remember from the time you were a very little baby?
69. Tell me about your dreams.
70. Which dreams come back again?
71. Who are your favorite television characters?
72. Tell me about them.
73. What animals do you like best?

(Table continues on next page)

Table 16-7 (cont.)

74. Tell me about these animals.
75. What animals do you like least?
76. Tell me about these animals.
77. What is your happiest memory?
78. What is your saddest memory?
79. If you could change places with anyone in the whole world, whom would it be?
80. Tell me about that.
81. If you could go anywhere you wanted to right now, where would you go?
82. Tell me about that.
83. If you could have three wishes, what would they be?
84. What things do you think you might need to take with you if you were to go to the moon and stay there for 6 months?

Aspirations

85. What do you plan on doing when you become an adult?
86. Do you think you will have any problem doing that?
87. If you could do anything you wanted when you become an adult, what would it be?

Concluding Questions

88. Do you have anything else that you would like to tell me about yourself?
89. Do you have any questions that you would like to ask me?

FOR ADOLESCENTS

(These questions can be inserted after number 67.)

Heterosexual Relations

1. Do you have any special girlfriend (boyfriend)?
2. (If yes) Tell me about her [him].
3. What kinds of sexual concerns do you have?
4. (If present) Tell me about them.

Drug/Alcohol Use

5. Do your parents drink alcohol?
6. (If yes) Tell me about their drinking. [How much, how frequently, and where?]
7. Do your friends drink alcohol?
8. (If yes) Tell me about their drinking.
9. Do you drink alcohol?
10. (If yes) Tell me about your drinking.
11. Do your parents use drugs?
12. (If yes) Tell me about the drugs they use. [How much, how frequently, and for what reasons?]
13. Do your friends use drugs?
14. (If yes) Tell me about the drugs they use.
15. Do you use drugs?
16. (If yes) Tell me about the drugs you use.

Table 16-8
Mediator-Reinforcer Sentence Completion

Directions: Read all the sentence stems to the child, following up as necessary. Then state all the reinforcers named by the child, and ask the child to rank them in order of their importance.

1. My favorite grown-up [adult] is _____
2. What do you like to do with him [her]? _____
3. The best reward anybody can give me is _____
4. My favorite school subject is _____
5. If I had ten dollars I'd _____
6. My favorite relative in [child's city] is _____
7. When I grow up I want to be a _____
8. The person who punishes me most is _____
9. How does he [she] punish you? _____
10. How effective is the punishment? _____
11. What other punishments does he [she] use? _____
12. Which works best with you? _____
13. The two things I like best to do are _____
14. My favorite adult at school is _____
15. When I do something well, what my mother does is _____
16. I feel terrific when _____
17. The way I get money is _____
18. When I have money, I like to _____
19. When I'm in trouble, my father _____
20. Something I really want is _____
21. If I please my father, what he does is _____
22. If I had a chance, I sure would like to _____
23. The person I would like most to reward me is _____
24. How? _____
25. I will do almost anything to avoid _____
26. The thing I like best to do with my mother is _____
27. The thing I do that bothers my teacher the most is _____
28. The weekend activity or entertainment I enjoy most is ____
29. If I did better at school, I wish my teacher would _____
30. The kind of punishment I hate most is _____
31. I will do almost anything to get _____
32. It sure makes me mad when I can't _____
33. When I'm in trouble, my mother _____
34. My favorite brother or sister is _____
35. The thing I like to do most is _____
36. The only person I will take advice from is _____
37. Not counting my parents, a person I will do almost anything for is _____
38. I hate for my teacher to _____
39. My two favorite TV programs are _____
40. The thing I like best to do with my father is _____

Child's Ranking of Reinforcers

_____
_____
_____
_____

Source: Reprinted, with changes in notation, by permission of the publisher and authors, from R. G. Tharp and R. J. Wetzel, *Behavior Modification in the Natural Environment*, 1969, pp. 225–226. Copyright 1969 by Academic Press, Inc.

Table 16-9
Areas Covered in a Mental Status Interview

APPEARANCE AND BEHAVIOR

• How did the interviewee present himself or herself?
• How did the interviewee look generally? (Note, for example, height, weight, cleanliness, facial appearance, clothes, special adornments, physical handicaps.)
• How did the interviewee act during the interview? (Note, for example, bizarre gestures or actions, repetitive movements, abnormal posture, poor eye contact, inappropriate facial expressions, abnormally slow movements, excessive movements, wildly excited behavior, special mannerisms.)
• Was the interviewee's behavior appropriate for his or her age, education, and vocational status?
• How did the interviewee relate to the interviewer? (For example, was he or she wary, submissive, attentive, friendly, manipulative, approval seeking, excessively conforming, hostile, superficial?)

SPEECH AND COMMUNICATIONS

• How was the general flow of interviewee's speech? (For example, was it rapid, controlled, hesitant, slow, pressured?)
• Does the interviewee have speech impediments?
• How was the general tone and content of the interviewee's speech? (Note, for example, over- or under-productivity of speech, flight of ideas, paucity of ideas, loose associations, clang associations, rambling, circumstantiality, tangentiality, non sequiturs, blocking on certain content, perseveration, irrelevance, vagueness, neologisms, bizarre use of words, incoherence of speech, misleading responses such as answering yes to all questions.)
• What was the relationship between verbal and nonverbal communications?
• Was there congruency in verbal and nonverbal communication?
• What was the relationship between the tone and the content of the communications?
• How interested was the interviewee in communicating?

CONTENT OF THOUGHT

• What did the interviewee discuss? (Note especially content that he or she brought up spontaneously.)
• What were the problem areas?
• Were there any recurrent themes?
• Were there any signs of psychopathology, such as delusions, hallucinations, phobias, obsessions, or compulsions?

SENSORY AND MOTOR FUNCTIONING

• How intact were the interviewee's senses—hearing, sight, touch, and smell?

• How adequate was the interviewee's gross motor coordination?
• How adequate was the interviewee's fine motor coordination?
• Were there signs of motor difficulties such as exaggerated movements, repetitive movements (tics, twitches, tremors), bizarre postures, grimaces, slow movements, or rituals?

COGNITIVE FUNCTIONING

• Was the interviewee oriented as to time, place, and person? (For example, did he or she know time of day, date, place where interview was being conducted, name of city, own name, birthdate?)
• Was the interviewee able to concentrate?
• Was the interviewee alert? (For example, was he or she responsive to changes in the interviewer's questions?)
• How good was the interviewee's memory for immediate, recent, and remote events?
• Did the interviewee's vocabulary and general fund of information reflect his or her occupational and educational background?
• Could the interviewee read, write, and spell appropriately for his or her age group?

EMOTIONAL FUNCTIONING

• What was the general mood of the interviewee? (For example, was he or she sad, elated, indifferent, angry, irritable, changeable, anxious, tense, suspicious, perplexed?)
• Did the interviewee's mood fluctuate or change during the interview?
• How did the interviewee react to the interviewer? (For example, was he or she cold, friendly, cooperative, suspicious, cautious?)
• Was the interviewee's affect appropriate for the speech and content of the communications?
• What did the interviewee say about his or her mood and feelings?
• Was the self-report congruent with the interviewee's behavior during the interview?

INSIGHT AND JUDGMENT

• What is the interviewee's belief about why he or she was coming to the interview?
• Is the belief appropriate and realistic?
• Is the interviewee aware of his or her problem and the concerns of others?
• Does the interviewee have ideas about what caused the problem?
• Does the interviewee have ideas about how the problem could be alleviated?

(Table continues on next page)

Table 16-9 (cont.)

• How good is the interviewee's judgment in carrying out everyday activities?	• Does the interviewee make appropriate use of advice or assistance?
• How does the interviewee solve problems of living — impulsively, independently, responsibly, or through trial and error?	• How much does the interviewee desire help for his or her problems?

Source: Adapted from Crary and Johnson (1975) and Sundberg, Taplin, and Tyler (1983).

Mental Status Interview

As part of the intake interview you may want to conduct a mental status evaluation. Table 16-9 shows the seven areas usually covered in a mental status intake interview. If you do not conduct a formal mental status interview, you should cover the areas described in Table 16-9 in the assessment interview. Some of the questions in Table 16-9 have been mentioned previously in this chapter but are presented here in their most complete form. A brief mental status examination for older children is provided in Table 16-10. All areas, of course, must be interpreted within a developmental framework, using age-appropriate norms.

Psychological Evaluation

Exhibit 16-1 presents a brief report of a 14-year-old adolescent who volunteered to be interviewed. The report includes referral information, behavioral observations, a short case history, and a summary and impressions.

THE INITIAL INTERVIEW WITH PARENTS

The interview with parents is an important part of the multiple-assessment approach with children. Parents have a wealth of knowledge about their child. A well-conducted parental interview will serve as a valuable source of information about the child and family and will lay the groundwork for enlisting parental cooperation with intervention efforts. The interview also serves to establish rapport with the parents, helps to focus the parents' perception of the problem, and aids in formulating a diagnosis (Barkley, 1981a). Where appropriate, siblings and other significant relatives or friends can be interviewed with respect to many of the areas covered in the parental interview, with the same good effects.

Interviews with parents are designed to elicit information about their concerns regarding the child; the child's problems and how they have dealt with the problems in the past; the child's medical, developmental, educational, and social history; the family history; and the parents' expectations for treatment and remediation. When a problem area

Table 16-10
Brief Mental Status Examination for Older Children (and Adults)

1. What is today's date?	16. What is your mother's name?
2. What day is it?	17. When is your birthday?
3. What month is it?	18. Where were you born?
4. What year is it?	19. (If appropriate) When did you finish elementary school?
5. Where are you?	20. (If appropriate) When did you finish high school?
6. What is the name of this city?	21. Say these numbers after me: 6-9-5, 4-3-8-1, 2-9-8-5-7.
7. What is the name of this hospital [or clinic or office]?	22. Say these numbers backwards: 8-3-7, 9-4-6-1, 7-3-2-5-8.
8. What is your name?	23. Say these words after me: pencil, chair, stone, plate.
9. How old are you?	24. What does this saying mean: "A stitch in time saves nine"?
10. What do you do?	25. What does this saying mean: "Too many cooks spoil the broth"?
11. Who is the president of the United States?	26. Read these words: pat, father, setting, intervention.
12. Who was the president before him?	27. Write these words (show same words as in item 26).
13. What are two major news events in the last month?	28. Spell these words: spoon, cover, attitude, procedure.
14. How did you get to this hospital [or clinic or office]?	
15. What is your father's name?	

Note. Questions 1–4, 5–7, and 8–10 test general orientation to time, place, and person, respectively; 11–16 test recent memory; 17–20 test remote memory; 21–23 test immediate memory; 24–25 test insight and judgment; and 26–28 test oral reading, writing, and spelling skills.

■ Exhibit 16-1 ■

Psychological Evaluation: Interview

Name: John
Date of Birth: April 18, 1973
Chronological Age: 14 years
Site of Interview: Beckman House

Interviewer: Jane Roberts
Date of Interview: April 12, 1987
Date of Report: April 16, 1987

Reason for Referral

John volunteered to be interviewed to help the interviewer fulfill a requirement for a psychological assessment course at Blank State University.

Behavioral Observations

John is a 14-year-old, muscular, tan-complexioned, Caucasian male of average height for his age. He had neatly groomed black hair, and he wore a T-shirt, blue jeans, and tennis shoes.

John sat straight in his chair and made frequent eye contact with the interviewer. His voice was low pitched, but not excessively loud or soft. At times he spoke rapidly and slurred his words together. His thoughts were organized, and his vocabulary appropriate for his age. He frequently used slang words such as "nosey-doze" and "booze" when referring to drugs and alcohol.

John's affect was flat and indifferent throughout the interview, except on two occasions: one time when he talked excitedly about his drug use, and another time when he laughed while he described aiming guns at people in a local canyon. After he reported that he had attacked his mother, he was asked what made him threaten her. He turned and faced the wall for about 30 seconds, and then indicated that he had not heard the question. The question was repeated, and he abruptly said he did not remember. John did not discuss why he currently resides at Beckman House, an inpatient treatment center for severely disturbed adolescents.

Interview Findings

John was born in Tennessee. When he was 2 years old, his parents divorced. Shortly afterwards, he was placed in a foster home because his mother could not support him. When John was 7 years old, he was reunited with his mother, and he moved to Albany, New York with her and his 6-year-old sister. John described his relationship with his mother as confused, fluctuating among the roles of husband, brother, and son. However, there apparently has been no incestuous contact.

John attended public schools until the age of 12 years. In sixth grade, he received therapy for a speech impediment. At school, he played with cap guns and wore trench coats and wing-tipped shoes to be different and to attract attention. In addition, he slept during class and talked back to his teachers. His classmates responded by laughing or becoming shocked or scared. John sometimes shot guns in a local canyon with his friends, and he threatened people by aiming his gun at them. John believed he was participating in the Vietnam War while in the canyon.

John said he frequently argued with his mother about staying out late at night and wearing his dirty boots in the house. He and his sister fought over the television and the radio. At age 13, John began drinking alcohol and using cocaine, LSD, and amphetamines. He and his mother argued about his drug use, and she reported him to the police several times. John said he attacked his mother with a machete; this was verified by the director of Beckman House. John subsequently was hospitalized at County Mental Health, El Monte Hospital, and Pinecrest New Alternatives. In October, 1986, John was referred to Beckman House for violent ideation, assault, and drug abuse. John reported that he had a close friend who died at about the time he came to Beckman House. Shortly after arriving, John made a serious suicide attempt by jumping through a plate-glass window. Two months later, his grandfather, with whom he had a close relationship, died. John frequently fantasizes becoming a hero by killing people who are hurting others. He hopes to return home and return to school.

John's records indicate that he was previously diagnosed as having a schizo-affective disorder. His current treatment includes 1500 mg of lithium carbonate for depression, 200 mg of Mellaril as a tranquilizer, and group therapy. Currently, he is functioning well at Beckman House. However, his future remains uncertain.

Summary and Impressions

John is a 14-year-old Caucasian male of muscular build and medium height. At times he spoke rapidly and slurred his words together. John was indifferent throughout the interview, except when he excitedly talked about his drug use and when he laughed while describing aiming guns at people. John's history is filled with instability. His relationships with his mother and sister have been marked with conflict and confused roles. His school adjustment also has been poor. He has had several episodes of violent behavior and has used illegal drugs. He entered several hospitals before coming to Beckman House, where he was referred for violent ideation, assault, and drug abuse. John has also attempted suicide and has fantasies of killing people. He desires to return home and to

(Exhibit continues next page)

Exhibit 16-1 (cont.)

school. John's treatment includes lithium carbonate, Mellaril, and group therapy.

John is an adolescent obsessed with thoughts of violence. His impulse control is weak, and at times he acts out. John displays anger toward others through both verbal and physical means. His suicide attempt suggests that some of his anger may be directed toward himself. It is recommended that his current medication and group therapy continue.

(Signature) _____

Jane Roberts, B.S., Interviewer

---

is disclosed, you should obtain a detailed history of the problem, including a description of the problem, whether prior treatment has been sought, who provided any treatment, and the dates and outcomes of any treatment.

When a child is referred for academic problems, obtain information about the parents' perception of the child's academic problems, whether they work with the child on homework, what they know about the child's reactions to his or her difficulties, their attitude toward academic achievement and toward the school and teacher, their understanding of possible causes of the academic difficulty, what they desire from the school, and their expectations for improvement (Barkley, 1981c). This information can be used in conjunction with the test results to formulate a comprehensive picture of the child's current abilities, behavior, and potential for behavioral change.

After the interview has been completed, evaluate the parents' perceptions of the problem; how their perceptions compare with those of the child and teacher; whether they are more preoccupied with their own problems, failures, and difficulties than with their child's problem; and their resources for overcoming the problem. Did they give a reasonable account of the child's development? Were they open or guarded? Try to determine what the parents wanted from the interview and their openness to change. The questionnaire shown in Table 16-11 is a useful adjunct for obtaining information about the impact of a handicapped child on the family.

Potential Negative Feelings of Parents

It is important to recognize that by the time a school-age child is referred for evaluation, the parents may have already experienced much frustration and anguish. They may have seen other professionals, but still may be seeking a magic solution. They may know that their child has a problem, but may be tired of feeling that they are to blame. You may be the recipient of some suppressed hostility that has developed from prior encounters with the medical and mental health professions. Feelings of inadequacy arising from the parents' inability to work with their child and from their impatience and irritability with their child may produce a loss of self-esteem. Guilt may emerge as a result of these feelings of inadequacy and anger toward the child. In some cases parents may deny that there is a problem, and they may react angrily to being interviewed about a problem that they do not wish to recognize.

Any negative feelings parents have about themselves should be dealt with during their initial contact with you; otherwise these feelings may interfere with the communication process. Give parents an opportunity to talk about their feelings. Help them feel that together you can work to understand and improve the child's behavior and functioning. If necessary, tell them that you are aware of the discomfort they may feel in discussing rather personal topics and that you welcome their questions.

General Guidelines for Use in Interviewing Parents

The initial interview with parents (and other significant adults) is especially important in establishing a positive working relationship; it often sets the tone for future intervention efforts (La Greca, 1983). Take special care to convey respect for parents' feelings and avoid any suggestion that they are to blame for their child's difficulties. Emphasize their constructive and helpful parenting skills rather than their destructive or harmful approaches. Enlist their cooperation in the diagnostic and remediation program; do not be authoritarian. Parents who are hostile may resist your efforts, in which case you may need more than one meeting to gain their cooperation. If possible, make arrangements for both parents to be interviewed. By interviewing both parents you increase both the accuracy of the information and the likelihood of enlisting their cooperation in intervention efforts. Although it is preferable to interview parents together, in some situations individual interviews may be needed, particularly if the parents are hostile to each other.

Useful Interview Formats with Parents

There are several interview formats useful for gathering information from parents. One format is an open-ended

Table 16-11
A Short Form of the Questionnaire on Resources and Stress

This questionnaire deals with your feelings about a child in your family. There are many blanks on the questionnaire. Imagine the child's name filled in on each blank. Give your honest feelings and opinions. Please answer all of the questions, even if they do not seem to apply. If it is difficult to decide between true (T) and false (F), answer in terms of what you or your family feel or do *most* of the time. Sometimes the questions refer to problems your family does not have, but even then they can be answered true or false. Please remember to answer all of the questions.

1. _____ doesn't communicate with others of his/her age group. T F
2. Other members of the family have to do without things because of _____. T F
3. Our family agrees on important matters. T F
4. I worry about what will happen to _____ when I can no longer take care of him/her. T F
5. The constant demands for care for _____ limit growth and development of someone else in our family. T F
6. _____ is limited in the kind of work he/she can do to make a living. T F
7. I have accepted the fact that _____ might have to live out his/her life in some special setting (for example, institution or group home). T F
8. _____ can feed himself/herself. T F
9. I have given up things I have really wanted to do in order to care for _____. T F
10. _____ is able to fit into the family social group. T F
11. Sometimes I avoid taking _____ out in public. T F
12. In the future, our family's social life will suffer because of increased responsibilities and financial stress. T F
13. It bothers me that _____ will always be this way. T F
14. I feel tense whenever I take _____ out in public. T F
15. I can go visit with friends whenever I want. T F
16. Taking _____ on a vacation spoils pleasure for the whole family. T F
17. _____ knows his/her own address. T F
18. The family does as many things together now as we ever did. T F
19. _____ is aware of who he/she is. T F
20. I get upset with the way my life is going. T F
21. Sometimes I feel very embarrassed because of _____. T F
22. _____ doesn't do as much as he/she should be able to do. T F

23. It is difficult to communicate with _____ because he/she has difficulty understanding what is being said to him/her. T F
24. There are many places where we can enjoy ourselves as a family when _____ comes along. T F
25. _____ is overprotected. T F
26. _____ is able to take part in games or sports. T F
27. _____ has too much time on his/her hands. T F
28. I am disappointed that _____ does not lead a normal life. T F
29. Time drags for _____, especially free time. T F
30. _____ can't pay attention for very long. T F
31. It is easy for me to relax. T F
32. I worry about what will be done with _____ when he/she gets older. T F
33. I get almost too tired to enjoy myself. T F
34. One of the things I appreciate about _____ is his/her confidence. T F
35. There is a lot of anger and resentment in our family. T F
36. _____ is able to go to the bathroom alone. T F
37. _____ cannot remember what he/she says from one moment to the next. T F
38. _____ can ride a bus. T F
39. It is easy to communicate with _____. T F
40. The constant demands to care for _____ limit my growth and development. T F
41. _____ accepts himself/herself as a person. T F
42. I feel sad when I think of _____. T F
43. People can't understand what _____ tries to say. T F
44. Caring for _____ puts a strain on me. T F
45. Members of our family get to do the same kinds of things other families do. T F
46. _____ will always be a problem to us. T F
47. _____ is able to express his/her feelings to others. T F
48. _____ has to use a bedpan or a diaper. T F
49. I rarely feel blue. T F
50. I am worried much of the time. T F
51. _____ can walk without help. T F

Note. The 51-item Questionnaire on Resources and Stress, Short Form (QRS-SF), is useful for assessing the resources, coping and adaptation mechanisms, and stress reactions of families with handicapped children. The original form of the QRS was published by Holroyd (1974). Four distinct factors are found on the QRS-SF: Parent and Family Problems, Pessimism, Child Characteristics, and Physical Incapacitation. The QRS-SF has acceptable reliability and validity. Current copyright holder is Clinical Psychology Publishing Company.

Item numbers for the factors and scoring directions are as follows: Factor I, *Parent and Family Problems* (2T, 3F, 5T, 9T, 10F, 12T, 15F, 16T, 18F, 20T, 24F, 31F, 33T, 35T, 40T, 42T, 44T, 45F, 49F, 50T); Factor II, *Pessimism* (4T, 7T, 13T, 22T, 25T, 27T, 28T, 29T, 32T, 46T); Factor III, *Child Characteristics* (1T, 6T, 11T, 14T, 17F, 19F, 21T, 23T, 30T, 34F, 37T, 39F, 41F, 43T, 47F); and Factor IV, *Physical Incapacitation* (8F, 26F, 36F, 38F, 48T, 51F).

Source: Reprinted, with minor changes, with permission of the publisher and authors, from W. N. Friedrich, M. T. Greenberg, and K. Crnic, "A Short-form of the Questionnaire on Resources and Stress," *American Journal of Mental Deficiency*, 1983, *88*, pp. 47-48.

interview to assess what is important to the child's parents, what they hope to accomplish as a result of the evaluation, how they view the problem, and how they view their own role in helping the child. Many of the same content areas shown in Table 16-7 can be covered in the parent interview.

Useful ways to begin the interview or to elicit general information include the following (cf. Lichtenstein & Ireton, 1984):

- "Tell me what brings you here today."
- "How can we help you?"
- "Tell me about your child."
- "Please tell me your concerns about your child."
- "Please tell me what _____ has been doing lately."
- "How well do you think your child is doing?"
- "How do you get along with your child?"

The following excerpt is from an initial interview between a psychologist and a mother who is concerned about her child's school work. The interviewer keeps the conversation moving by making inquiries (Nos. 1 and 5) and reflective comments (Nos. 3 and 7).

IR: Mrs. A, tell me what brings you here today. (1)
IE: It's Billy. His teacher says he can't sit still and he bothers the other children. She's threatening to hold him back in first grade. (2)
IR: And you're worried about him. (3)
IE: Yeah. He gets into trouble because he doesn't finish his work. I know he can do the work, if he wants to. His kindergarten teacher never said anything, but all of a sudden this year his teacher says he's having problems keeping up, especially now that they've started reading. (4)
IR: How does Billy feel about school? (5)
IE: Well, he was really excited about school at first, but now he says he doesn't want to go to school. He complains about the work and he seems cranky when he comes home. Sometimes he puts up a fuss about getting up in the morning and I have to tell him over and over to get moving or he'll be late. (6)
IR: So things are getting harder for both of you. (7)
IE: Yeah. I have to keep after him to finish his homework. He gives up unless I keep after him. (8)

A second format entails having the parents complete a Background Questionnaire before the formal interview (see Table 16-12). This questionnaire (or a similar one) is useful in obtaining a detailed account of the child's developmental, social, medical, and educational history, as well as information about the family. If a Background Questionnaire has been completed, many of the areas described below will not have to be covered in the interview. The questionnaire also can serve as a foundation for the initial interview. You can use the parents' questionnaire responses as discussion leads: for example, "I see that John is having problems at home; would you tell me more about these

problems?" Even when a questionnaire has been completed by the parents, allow them to describe their concerns about the child.

You may prefer to complete the Background Questionnaire jointly with the parents. As you work together you and the parents will become acquainted, and thus the interview may flow more smoothly. However, time constraints or agency policy may not allow you to follow this procedure routinely.

Another format for interviewing involves behavior ratings. Each parent can be asked to fill out a rating scale on which he or she evaluates the child's behavior in a variety of areas, including social, school, and adaptive behavior (see Chapter 15 for a description of such scales). Items requiring further inquiry can be discussed with the parents after the rating scale has been completed.

Obtaining a Case History

If a questionnaire has not been completed, it is necessary to obtain a case history. Like the questionnaire, the case history interview permits you to obtain a detailed chronology of the child's developmental history from the parents. In obtaining a history not only do you gain some perspective on the child's current situation, but you may obtain clues about what interventions have failed to help the child in the past and what might benefit the child in the future. Typical areas covered in a developmental case history are the following (Nay, 1979):

- description of child's birth (including mother's health and use of drugs or cigarettes and pregnancy and birth complications)
- child's developmental history (including important developmental milestones—such as age of sitting, standing, walking, use of functional language, bladder and bowel control, self-help skills, and personal-social relationships)
- child's medical history (including types and dates of injuries, accidents, operations, and significant illnesses, as well as medications the child has received and periods of time during which these medications were taken)
- characteristics of family and family history (including age, ordinal position, sex, occupation, and marital status of family members, as well as significant medical, educational, and psychiatric history of siblings and parents)
- child's interpersonal skills (including child's ability to form friendships and relationships with others, child's play activities, and manner in which child is treated by other children and adults)
- child's educational history (including schools attended, grades, attitude toward schooling, relationships

Table 16-12
Example of a Background Questionnaire Used in a Child Guidance Clinic or School

BACKGROUND QUESTIONNAIRE

FAMILY DATA

Child's name: _____ Today's date: _____

Birthdate: _____ Age: _____ Sex (circle one): Male   Female

Home address: _____ Phone: _____

_____

School: _____ Grade: _____

Person filling out this form (circle one): Mother   Father   Stepmother   Stepfather

    Other (please explain) _____

Mother's name: _____ Age: _____ Education: _____

    Occupation: _____ Phone: Home _____ Business _____

Father's name: _____ Age: _____ Education: _____

    Occupation: _____ Phone: Home _____ Business _____

Stepparent's name: _____ Age: _____ Education: _____

    Occupation: _____ Phone: Home _____ Business _____

Marital status of parents: _____

If parents are separated or divorced, how old was child when the separation occurred? _____

List all people living in household:

Name	*Relationship to Child*	*Age*

If any brothers or sisters are living outside the home, list their names and ages: _____

Primary language spoken in the home: _____

Other languages spoken in the home: _____

PRESENTING PROBLEM

Briefly describe your child's current difficulties: _____

_____

_____

_____

How long has this problem been of concern to you? _____

When was the problem first noticed? _____

(Table continues on next page)

Table 16-12 (cont.)

What seems to help the problem? _____

What seems to make the problem worse? _____

Has the child received evaluation or treatment for the current problem or similar problems? Yes _____ No _____

If yes, when and with whom? _____

Is the child on any medication at this time? Yes _____ No _____

If yes, please note kind of medication: _____

Who referred you here? _____

SOCIAL AND BEHAVIOR CHECKLIST

Place a check next to any behavior or problem that your child currently exhibits.

Check

_____ Has difficulty with speech

_____ Has difficulty with hearing

_____ Has difficulty with language

_____ Has difficulty with vision

_____ Has difficulty with coordination

_____ Prefers to be alone

_____ Does not get along well with brothers and sisters

_____ Is aggressive

_____ Is shy or timid

_____ Is more interested in things (objects) than in people

_____ Engages in behavior that could be dangerous to self or others (describe) _____ _____

_____ Has special fears, habits, or mannerisms (describe) _____ _____

_____ Wets bed

_____ Bites nails

_____ Sucks thumb

Check

_____ Has frequent tantrums

_____ Has frequent nightmares

_____ Has trouble sleeping (describe) _____ _____

_____ Rocks back and forth

_____ Bangs head

_____ Holds breath

_____ Eats poorly

_____ Is stubborn

_____ Has poor bowel control (soils self)

_____ Is much too active

_____ Is clumsy

_____ Has blank spells

_____ Is impulsive

_____ Shows daredevil behavior

_____ Is slow to learn

_____ Gives up easily

_____ Other (describe) _____ _____ _____

EDUCATIONAL HISTORY

Place a check next to any educational problem that your child currently exhibits.

Check

_____ Has difficulty with reading

_____ Has difficulty with arithmetic

_____ Has difficulty with spelling

_____ Has difficulty with writing

Check

_____ Has difficulty with other subjects (please list) ____ _____ _____

_____ Does not like school

(Table continues on next page)

Table 16-12 (cont.)

Is your child in a special education class?   Yes _____   No _____

If yes, what type of class? _____

Has your child been held back in a grade?   Yes _____   No _____

If yes, what grade and why? _____

Has your child ever received special tutoring or therapy in school?   Yes _____   No _____

If yes, please describe: _____

DEVELOPMENTAL HISTORY

During pregnancy, was mother on medication?   Yes _____   No _____

If yes, what kind? _____

During pregnancy, did mother smoke?   Yes _____   No _____

If yes, how many cigarettes each day? _____

During pregnancy, did mother drink alcoholic beverages?   Yes _____   No _____

If yes, what did she drink? _____

Approximately how much alcohol was consumed each day? _____

During pregnancy, did mother use drugs?   Yes _____   No _____

If yes, what kind? _____

Were forceps used during delivery?   Yes _____   No _____

Was a Caesarean section performed?   Yes _____   No _____

If yes, for what reason? _____

Was the child premature?   Yes _____   No _____

If so, by how many months? _____

What was the child's birth weight? _____

Were there any birth defects or complications?   Yes _____   No _____

If yes, please describe: _____

Were there any feeding problems?   Yes _____   No _____

If yes, please describe: _____

Were there any sleeping problems?   Yes _____   No _____

If yes, please describe: _____

As an infant, was the child quiet?   Yes _____   No _____

As an infant, did the child like to be held?   Yes _____   No _____

As an infant, was the child alert?   Yes _____   No _____

Were there any special problems in the growth and development of the child during the first few years?   Yes _____   No _____

If yes, please describe: _____

The following is a list of infant and preschool behaviors. Please indicate the age at which your child first demonstrated each behavior. If you are not certain of the age but have some idea, write the age followed by a question mark. If you don't remember the age at which the behavior occurred, please write a question mark.

(Table continues on next page)

Table 16-12 (cont.)

Behavior	Age		Behavior	Age
Showed response to mother	_____		Put several words together	_____
Rolled over	_____		Dressed self	_____
Sat alone	_____		Became toilet trained	_____
Crawled	_____		Stayed dry at night	_____
Walked alone	_____		Fed self	_____
Babbled	_____		Rode tricycle	_____
Spoke first word	_____			

CHILD'S MEDICAL HISTORY

Place a check next to any illness or condition that your child has had. When you check an item, also note the approximate date (or age) of the illness.

Check	Illness or condition	Date(s) or age(s)	Check	Illness or condition	Date(s) or age(s)
_____	Measles	_____	_____	Dizziness	_____
_____	German measles	_____	_____	Frequent or severe headaches	_____
_____	Mumps	_____	_____	Difficulty concentrating	_____
_____	Chicken pox	_____	_____	Memory problems	_____
_____	Whooping cough	_____	_____	Extreme tiredness or weakness	_____
_____	Diphtheria	_____	_____	Rheumatic fever	_____
_____	Scarlet fever	_____	_____	Epilepsy	_____
_____	Meningitis	_____	_____	Tuberculosis	_____
_____	Encephalitis	_____	_____	Bone or joint disease	_____
_____	High fever	_____	_____	Gonorrhea or syphilis	_____
_____	Convulsions	_____	_____	Anemia	_____
_____	Allergy	_____	_____	Jaundice/hepatitis	_____
_____	Hay fever	_____	_____	Diabetes	_____
_____	Injuries to head	_____	_____	Cancer	_____
_____	Broken bones	_____	_____	High blood pressure	_____
_____	Hospitalizations	_____	_____	Heart disease	_____
_____	Operations	_____	_____	Asthma	_____
_____	Ear problems (disease, infection, injury, or impaired hearing)	_____	_____	Bleeding problems	_____
_____	Visual problems	_____	_____	Eczema or hives	_____
_____	Fainting spells	_____	_____	Suicide attempt	_____
_____	Loss of consciousness	_____	_____	Other _____	_____
_____	Paralysis	_____			

(Table continues on next page)

Table 16-12 (cont.)

FAMILY MEDICAL HISTORY

Place a check next to any illness or condition that any member of the immediate family has had. When you check an item, please note the member's relationship to the child.

Check	Condition	Relationship to child		Check	Condition	Relationship to child
_____	Alcoholism	_____		_____	Nervous or psychological problem	_____
_____	Cancer	_____		_____	Depression	_____
_____	Diabetes	_____		_____	Suicide attempt	_____
_____	Heart trouble	_____		_____	Other _____	_____

OTHER INFORMATION

What are your child's favorite activities?

1. _____ 2. _____ 3. _____

4. _____ 5. _____ 6. _____

What activities would your child like to engage in more often than he/she does at present?

1. _____ 2. _____ 3. _____

What activities does your child like least?

1. _____ 2. _____ 3. _____

Has your child ever been in trouble with the law?   Yes _____   No _____

If yes, please describe briefly: _____

What disciplinary techniques do you usually use when your child behaves inappropriately? Place a check next to each technique that you usually use. There also is space for writing in any other disciplinary techniques that you use.

Check	Disciplinary technique		Check	Disciplinary technique
_____	Ignore problem behavior		_____	Tell child to sit on chair
_____	Scold child		_____	Send child to his or her room
_____	Spank child		_____	Take away some activity or food
_____	Threaten child		_____	Other technique (describe) _____
_____	Reason with child			_____
_____	Redirect child's interest		_____	Don't use any technique

Which disciplinary techniques are usually effective? _____

_____

With what type of problem(s)? _____

_____

Which disciplinary techniques are usually ineffective? _____

_____

With what type of problem(s)? _____

_____

(Table continues on next page)

Table 16-12 (cont.)

What have you found to be the most satisfactory ways of helping your child? _____

_____

What are your child's assets or strengths? _____

_____

Is there any other information that you think may help us in working with your child? _____

_____

_____

_____

Thank you.

with teachers and peers, and special education services received)

• child's sexual behaviors (including relationships with those of the same and opposite sex)

• child's occupational history, if any (including types and dates of employment and attitude toward work and occupational goals)

• description of presenting problem (including a detailed description of the problem, antecedent events, consequences, and how the parents have dealt with the problem)

• parental expectations (including the parents' expectations and goals for treatment of their child and of themselves)

Table 16-13 illustrates questions that can be used to obtain an in-depth case history. A brief semi-structured interview format that can be used with parents of preschool children is illustrated in Table 16-14. It is particularly useful when you want an overview of what the child is doing, for it allows you to obtain information about areas of delayed development, poor adjustment, and parental concerns.

The value of obtaining from a parent a detailed description of the problem, including antecedent events and consequences, is nicely illustrated in the following example (Barkley, 1981b, pp. 149–150, with changes in notation):

IR: How does your child generally behave when there are visitors at your home?

IE: Terrible! He embarrasses me tremendously.

IR: Can you give me some idea of what he does specifically that is bothersome in this situation?

IE: Well, he won't let me talk with the visitors without interrupting our conversation, tugging on me for attention, or annoying the guests by running back and forth in front of us as we talk.

IR: Yes? And what else is he likely to do?

IE: Many times he will fight with his sister or get into something he shouldn't in the kitchen.

IR: How do you usually respond to him when these things happen?

IE: At first I usually try to ignore him. When this doesn't work, I try to reason with him, promise I'll spend time with him after the visitors leave, or try to distract him with something he usually likes to do just to calm him down so I can talk to my guests.

IR: How successfully does that work for you?

IE: Not very well. He may slow down for a few moments, but then he's right back pestering us or his sister, or getting into mischief in the kitchen. I get so frustrated with him by this time. I know what my visitors must be thinking of me not being able to handle my own child.

IR: Yes, I can imagine it's quite distressing. What do you do at this point to handle the situation?

IE: I usually find myself telling him over and over again to stop what he is doing, until I get very angry with him and threaten him with punishment. By now, my visitors are making excuses to leave, and I'm trying to talk with them while yelling at my son.

IR: And then what happens?

IE: Well, I know I shouldn't, but I'll usually grab him and hold him just to slow him down. More often, though, I may threaten to spank him or send him to his room. He usually doesn't listen to me though until I make a move to grab him.

IR: How often does this usually happen when visitors are at your home?

IE: Practically every time; it's frustrating.

IR: I see. How do you feel about your child creating such problems in front of visitors?

IE: I find myself really hating him at times (cries); I know I'm his mother and I shouldn't feel that way, but I'm so angry with him, and nothing seems to work for me. Many of our friends have stopped coming to visit us, and we can't find a babysitter who will stay with him so we can go out. I resent having to

Table 16-13
Example of a Semi-Structured Interview with Parents

Parent's Perception of Problem Behavior
1. By whom were you referred?
2. Please tell me your concerns about _____.
3. Can you describe these concerns a little more?
4. Is there anything else that you are concerned about?
5. Which concerns bother you most?
6. Which one is most pressing to you now?
7. You mentioned that [cite problem] seems to be troubling you most. Let's discuss this problem in more detail.
8. How serious do you consider the problem to be?
9. When was the problem first noticed?
10. How long has the problem been going on?
11. Where does the problem occur?
12. When does the problem occur?
13. How long does the problem behavior last?
14. How often does the problem occur?
15. How many other children in your family also have this problem?
16. How does _____'s problem behavior compare with that of the other children in your family who have the same problem?
17. What happens just before the problem begins?
18. What happens just after the problem appears?
19. What makes the problem worse?
20. What makes the problem better?
21. What do you do when the problem occurs?
22. What attempts have been partially successful?
23. What do you believe caused the problem?
24. Was there any significant event that occurred at the time of onset of the problem (for example, separation or divorce, a move to another city or school, financial problems, hospitalization of a family member)?
25. If so, what was _____'s reaction to the event?
26. How does _____ deal with the problem?
27. How do you deal with the problem?
28. How do family members react to _____'s problem?
29. Has _____ been evaluated or received any help for the problem?
30. (If yes) What type of evaluation or help was received and what progress was made?

Home Environment
31. Tell me what your home is like.
32. Does _____ have his [her] own room?
33. Where does _____ play?

Sibling Relations
34. How does _____ get along with his [her] brothers and sisters?
35. What do they do that _____ likes?
36. What do they do that _____ dislikes?
37. How do they get along when you aren't around?
38. Is it different when you are there?

Peer Relations
39. Does _____ have friends?
40. About how many?
41. What ages?
42. How does _____ get along with his [her] friends?
43. How does he [she] get along with peers of the opposite sex?

Parental Relations
44. How does _____ get along with [each of] you?
45. What does _____ do with [each of] you regularly?
46. What are the good times like with [each of] you?
47. What are the bad times like with [each of] you?
48. Are there other adults present at home?
49. (If yes to question 48) How does _____ get along with them?
50. (If yes to question 48) What are the good times like with each adult?
51. (If yes to question 48) What are the bad times like with each adult?
52. Does _____ listen to what he [she] is told (that is, is _____ compliant)?
53. How do you discipline _____?
54. Which parent is responsible for discipline?
55. Which techniques are effective?
56. Ineffective?
57. What have you found to be the most satisfactory ways of helping your child?

Child's Interests and Hobbies
58. What does _____ like to do in his [her] spare time?
59. What does _____ like to do alone?
60. With friends?
61. With family members?
62. What activities does he [she] like least?

Cognitive Functioning
63. How well does your child learn things?
64. Does _____ seem to understand things that are said to him [her]?
65. Does _____ seem to be quick or slow to catch on?

Academic Functioning
66. How is _____ getting along in school?
67. What does he [she] like best about school?
68. Least?
69. What grades does _____ get?
70. Has any teacher recommended special help?
71. (If yes) Please describe what help, if any, he [she] has received.
72. Does _____ attend a special class?

Biological Functioning
73. Does _____ eat well?

(Table continues on next page)

Table 16-13 (cont.)

74. Sleep well?
75. Does _____ have nightmares or other sleep problems?
76. Does _____ have problems with bowel or bladder control?
77. Has _____ had any medical problems or injuries?

Affective Life
78. What kinds of things make _____ happy?
79. Sad?
80. What does _____ do when he [she] is sad?
81. What kinds of things make _____ angry?
82. What does _____ do when he [she] is angry?
83. What kinds of things make _____ afraid?
84. What does _____ do when he [she] is afraid?
85. What sorts of things does _____ worry about?
86. Think about a lot?
87. Ask questions about?

For Preschoolers or Severely Developmentally Delayed Children
88. How well does _____ dress himself [herself]?
89. Wash?
90. Bathe?
91. Eat?

For a Child Who May Have a Specific Disorder
92. (If you suspect that the child has a specific disorder, you might want to ask about specific symptoms, such as stereotyped behavior or rituals or self-injurious behavior in the case of infantile autism.)

Developmental History—Birth, Infancy and Toddler Periods
93. Tell me about _____'s birth.
94. (If needed) Were there any physical complications at birth? How much did _____ weigh? Were there any birth defects?
95. Tell me about how _____ was as an infant.
96. (If needed) Was _____ satisfied when he [she] was fed? How well did he [she] sleep? Was _____ easily distressed? How readily could _____ be comforted? How well did he [she] adjust to new things or routines? Was he [she] cuddly or rigid? Overactive or underactive? Did he [she] engage in any tantrums? Rocking behavior? Head banging?

97. What was _____'s first year of life like?
98. What was _____ like during his [her] second year of life?
99. When did _____ begin to walk?
100. Talk?
101. Become toilet trained?
102. Were there any problems during his [her] second year of life?
103. What was _____ like as a toddler?
104. How did he [she] get along with other children?
105. Was _____ able to be by himself [herself]?

Additional Questions for Adolescents
106. Is _____ involved in any dating activities?
107. (If yes) What kinds?
108. Are there any restrictions on his [her] dating activities?
109. (If yes) How does he [she] feel about them?
110. What kinds of sexual concerns does _____ have?
111. Are there conflicts with you about sex?
112. Does your child use drugs?
113. Alcohol?
114. Other things to get high?
115. How do you know?
116. (If yes to any of questions 112–114) Tell me about his [her] use.

Questions about Family and Parental Expectations
117. What kinds of serious medical or psychological difficulties have you or members of your family had?
118. Do you see a need for treatment, special education, or special services for _____?
119. What are your expectations for treatment?
120. What are your goals for treatment?
121. Do you desire treatment for your own difficulties?
122. Is there any other information about your child that I should know?

Note. If you want to obtain information about other problems, repeat questions 8 through 30. Any responses given to items on this list can be probed further.

sacrifice what little social life we have. I'm likely to be angry with him the rest of the day.

A case history of a young child will usually be obtained from the parents. However, a case history may be obtained directly from an adolescent child. In such cases it may be of interest to compare information obtained from the ado-

lescent with that obtained from the parents, teachers, or relevant others.

In interviewing parents (or other adults), it is important to have interviewees clarify vague or ambiguous or incomplete statements so that you can obtain a comprehensive and explicit picture of the child's problems, their

Table 16-14
Brief Semi-Structured Screening Interview for Parents of Preschool Children

1. Tell me a little bit about _____.
2. Please tell me what _____ has been doing and learning lately.
3. How well do you think _____ is doing?
4. Do you have any concerns about _____'s health?
5. (If yes) What are your concerns?
6. Are you concerned about _____'s general physical coordination or his [her] ability to run, climb, or do other motor activities?
7. (If yes) What are your concerns?
8. How well does _____ seem to understand things that are said to him [her]?
9. How well does _____ let you know what he [she] needs?
10. Does _____ have any unusual speech behaviors?

11. (If yes to question 10) Tell me what seems to be unusual.
12. (If yes to question 10) Is _____'s speech intelligible?
13. (If yes to question 10) Does _____ speak in sentences?
14. Do you have any concerns about _____'s behavior?
15. (If yes) What are your concerns?
16. (If needed) How well does _____ get along with other children? With adults? With other children in the family? With you and your spouse?
17. How well does _____ feed himself [herself]? Dress himself [herself]? Go to the toilet by himself [herself]?
18. Is there anything else about _____ that you wonder or worry about?
19. Does _____ have any problems that we did not cover?

Note. Probing questions can be used to follow up on problem areas (see, for example, questions 11, 12, and 13).
Source: Adapted from Lichenstein and Ireton (1984).

reactions to the problems, and their concerns. In addition to encouraging them to discuss the various areas covered in the case history, you will need to use follow-up questions to determine the specific conditions that may serve to instigate, maintain, or limit the child's behavior, as well as the parents' resources and motivation to change (Nay, 1979). Also determine in what areas parents agree and disagree about child management. If parents fail to discuss the child, it may be necessary to guide parents to discuss the child's problems rather than their own. If the parents give many irrelevant details, they must be guided back to the topic in as appropriate and gentle a manner as possible. If a second interview is scheduled, it may be useful to ask the parents to keep a record of the occurrences of the problem(s), including where the problematic event occurred, when it occurred, what preceded and what followed it, their reactions to it and their manner of dealing with it, and other individuals involved in it.

Discussing the Assessment Procedure

At some time during the interview with the parents (usually toward the end of the interview), you should discuss the assessment procedure with them. Describe the general features of the tests to be administered, the general assessment procedures, and the type of information obtained from the tests. Inform them about who will have access to the information and how it will be used. If the assessment takes place in school, you may inform them that a report will be available and that they may have a copy. If the assessment is conducted in other settings, however, you may be restricted from revealing the findings unless the child gives permission. (See the section on Confidentiality

of Interview Material and Assessment Findings later in this chapter for further discussion.)

Goals of the Initial Interview with Parents

The goals of the initial clinical assessment interview with parents can be summarized as follows (cf. Mash & Terdal, 1981):

1. to gather information about parental concerns and goals;
2. to assess parental perceptions of the child's problems and strengths;
3. to obtain a case history;
4. to identify problem areas and related antecedent and consequent events;
5. to identify reinforcing events for both child and parents;
6. to assess parents' motivation and resources for change;
7. to obtain informed consent; and
8. to discuss assessment procedures and follow-up contacts.

Major Components of the Initial Interview with Parents

The major components of the initial interview with parents can be outlined as follows:

1. *Greet parents.*
2. *Give your name and professional title.*
3. *Open the interview with an introductory statement.* In child guidance clinics you might begin with a question such as "How can I help you?" In school settings you might

begin with "I understand that your son, John, is having some difficulties in school. I'd like to discuss his difficulties with you and then tell you how we plan to help him." You can then ask parents to discuss their child.

4. *Ask parents about items on the Background Questionnaire.* If the Background Questionnaire has been completed, inspect the questionnaire to determine which items need further inquiry. If the Background Questionnaire has not been completed, ask parents about (a) the child's developmental, medical, educational, and social history, (b) the family's medical and psychiatric history, (c) previous treatments for child, (d) the child's strengths and weaknesses, (e) the child's interests and play activities, and (f) related information.

5. *Review problems.* Review problem areas and ask parents whether they would like to comment further on any area.

6. *Describe the assessment procedure.* Tell parents about the tests that will be administered to the child.

7. *Arrange for a post-assessment interview.* In cases where a number of evaluations are conducted by professionals from varied disciplines, the results are often explained and recommendations made at an interdisciplinary conference that the parents are invited to attend. In other cases, you, as the examiner, may present the results of the interdisciplinary evaluation. If you are conducting the evaluation by yourself (or with a colleague), you can make whatever arrangements are suitable.

8. *Close the interview.* Escort the parents from the room and make appropriate closing remarks, such as "Thank you for coming; in case you have any other questions, here is my phone number" or "Thank you for your cooperation."

The preceding outline does not cover obtaining biographical information. This information is usually obtained by having the parents complete an application form that contains spaces for name, address, phone numbers, teacher's name, grade, family structure, and other important identifying information. The Background Questionnaire shown in Table 16-12 is an example of one such questionnaire. Exhibit 16-2 presents a report of an interview with the mother of a normal 4½-year-old boy.

THE INITIAL INTERVIEW WITH TEACHERS

Many of the same topics are covered in the initial interviews with teachers and parents. The focus, however, is somewhat different in the two interviews. In interviewing a

Courtesy Herman Zielinski.

teacher, you should be concerned not only with the teacher's perception of the problem, the antecedents and consequences of the problem behavior, and what the teacher has done to alleviate the problem, but also with how other children and teachers react to the referred child and how the referred child performs academically at school. Appropriate items from the list of interview questions in Table 16-13 are repeated in Table 16-15 for ease of study. You can also use a teacher-completed rating scale, such as the one shown in Chapter 15, as a basis for further inquiry in the interview.

The following two examples illustrate the kinds of statements you might make in an initial interview with a teacher. The examples also show how the initial interview may be used to develop a plan to obtain further assessment information about the child's problem. (The examples are from Bergan, 1977, pp. 97–99, reprinted, with changes in notation, with permission of the author and publisher.)

CHILD WITH FIRE-SETTING PROBLEM

1. Tell me about Alice's problem in the classroom.

2. What does Alice do when she annoys you?

3. How often during the week does this fire-building occur?

4. You have said that Alice builds fires in the sink of

Exhibit 16-2

Psychological Evaluation—Developmental History

Informant: Helen Blue
Child's Name: Keith Blue
Child's Date of Birth: March 15, 1983
Child's Chronological Age: 4-6

Interviewer: Barbara Smith
Date of Interview: October 16, 1987
Date of Report: October 22, 1987

Reason for Referral

This interview was done to fulfill an assignment for a Blank University psychological assessment course. Helen, the mother of a child enrolled in Blank University's Campus Lab School, volunteered to be interviewed about her child's development.

Behavioral Observations

Helen is a tall, slender, attractive, 39-year-old mother of two children (Debbi, age 13 years, and Keith, age 4½ years). Though Helen started the interview by saying that she did not feel well and had considered canceling the appointment, she was lively, responsive, cooperative, and frequently humorous. Although she was cheerful and appeared to be happy, Helen also seemed tense. She sat quite straight in her chair and frequently clenched her hands. Occasionally, when the content of her conversation was emotion-laden, Helen turned away from the tape recorder. She spoke rapidly, and her movements were sometimes abrupt. Nevertheless, she was articulate and expressed herself clearly, though sometimes in a roundabout way. Helen maintained good eye contact with the interviewer and seemed to speak freely and without hesitation. Thus, the interview findings appear to be accurate.

Interview Findings

According to his mother, Keith is a tall, active, physically strong, and healthy boy. His birth and subsequent development were normal, although he does have exceptional large-muscle coordination for his age. Keith walked before he was 10 months old. At 3 years, 10 months of age he could hit a plastic baseball with a plastic bat and throw and catch a frisbee. His balance is also excellent. He is enrolled in a kindergym class, where he does tumbling and works out on a balance beam.

Keith's mother notes that his small-muscle coordination is less well developed than was his older sister's at the same age. He is, for example, not as adept at writing or drawing as was his sister. His mother added that differences in Keith's large- and small-muscle coordination seem to be related to his preferred activities. Keith's favorite activities are riding his bike and playing ball. At nursery school, he prefers being outside on the playground or building with large blocks over coloring or cutting and pasting. He especially enjoys building with boards, a hammer, and nails.

Keith loves nursery school and is disappointed when he learns that it is the weekend and he cannot go to school for two days. This is in spite of the fact, his mother explained, that most of his friends from last year's class were older and have gone on to kindergarten and he has not yet developed new friendships in this year's class.

Keith was described as a relaxed and easygoing child, yet extremely sensitive to disapproval. He responds to a verbal reprimand with tears, but usually requires no other discipline. On the few occasions when he has had his hand slapped, however, Keith responded not with tears but with anger and defiance. Generally there are no discipline problems with Keith, and the only behavior that worries his mother is his lack of fear. From infancy, he has climbed whatever he could climb. He likes to balance on the edge of the bathtub and walk along ledges where a long fall is possible. He seems, however, to respond reasonably to explanations of the potential danger of such activities.

Keith exhibits compassion and sympathy for those around him. For example, when he notices that people on television are sad, he is sorry. In nursery school, Keith tries to comfort a new girl who cries every day. In addition, he often asks to spend time with his grandfather, who is quite ill. He sits close to his grandfather, with his arm around him, or pats his hand.

Summary and Impressions

In order to fulfill the interviewer's assignment in a psychological assessment course, Helen, the mother of a preschool child, was interviewed about her son's development. Helen was cooperative, cheerful, and articulate. Although she displayed some signs of tension, the tension did not appear to be related to her discussion of Keith, about whom she spoke freely. Keith's birth and development were normal. He is a strong, healthy, and active 4½-year-old boy. His large-muscle coordination is especially good, and his favorite activities are riding a bike and playing ball. Keith enjoys preschool. He is an easygoing child who is sensitive to disapproval and who exhibits sympathy and compassion for others. His fearlessness is of some concern to his mother.

(Signature) _____

Barbara Smith, B.A., Interviewer

Table 16-15
Example of a Semi-Structured Interview with Teacher of the Referred Child

Precede the questions below with an introductory comment such as the following: "I would like to talk with you about [child's name] and his [her] behaviors that bother you most. I'd like to discuss these behaviors, when they occur, how often they occur, and what occurs in your classroom that might influence the behaviors. I also would like to discuss some other matters related to [child's name] that will help us to develop useful interventions."

Teacher's Perception of Problem Behavior
1. Please describe exactly what _____ does that causes you concern.
2. Which behaviors bother you most?
3. Which of these behaviors are most pressing to you now?
4. Which behaviors, in order of most to least pressing, would you like to work on now?
5. Let's look into the first problem in more detail.
6. How serious is the problem?
7. How long has the problem been going on?
8. When does the problem occur?
9. What classroom activity is generally occurring at the time the problem occurs (for example, a lecture, unstructured play, independent work, interaction with you, interaction with other children)?
10. How long does the problem behavior last?
11. How often does the problem occur?
12. How many other children in the class also have this problem?
13. How does the child's problem behavior compare with that of other children in the class who show the same behavior?
14. What happens just before the problem begins?
15. What happens just after the problem appears?
16. What makes the problem worse?
17. What makes the problem better?

Reactions to Problem Behavior
18. What do you do when the problem occurs?
19. What attempts have been partially successful?
20. What do you think is responsible for the problem behavior?
21. What is your reaction to _____ in general?

Relationship with Peers
22. How does _____ get along with other classmates?

23. Does _____ have many friends?
24. Do the children include _____ in their games and activities?
25. How do other children contribute to _____'s problem?
26. What do they do when _____ engages in the problem behavior?
27. How do other children help to reduce the problem?
28. How do other children react to _____ in general?
29. (If relevant) How do other teachers perceive and react to _____?

Academic Performance
30. How does _____ perform in school?
31. Does _____ complete assignments on time?
32. Does _____ have difficulty staying on task?
33. What are _____'s best subjects?
34. What are _____'s poorest subjects?
35. Does _____ perform differently with different teachers?

Child's Strengths
36. What are _____'s strengths?
37. In what situations does _____ display these strengths?
38. How can these strengths be used in helping _____?

View of Child's Family
39. How much contact have you had with _____'s family?
40. How do you feel about _____'s family?

Teacher's Expectations and Suggestions
41. What does _____ like best to do that you find acceptable?
42. What do you consider to be an acceptable level of frequency for the problem behavior?
43. What expectations do you have for _____?
44. What suggestions do you have for remedying the problem?
45. What would you like to see done?

Note. Eleven of the questions in this table were adapted from Witt and Elliott (1983). Questions 6 through 20 can be repeated for additional problem areas.

---

one of the lab tables. She does this about three times a week. Is that right?

5. What is generally going on right before Alice lights a fire in the classroom?

6. What are you usually doing just before Alice lights a fire?

7. What do you do when you discover that Alice has lit a fire?

8. When during the day does this fire-building most often occur?

9. On what days of the week does fire-building usually take place?

10. You have said that Alice usually builds a fire in the sink when your back is turned and you are writing on the blackboard.

11. Afterwards the other kids giggle and laugh and in some cases treat her as though she had really done something great. Is that correct?

12. We need to get a record of Alice's fire-building activities.

13. The record will help us to establish a baseline against which to evaluate the success of our intervention plan.

14. I would suggest that throughout the rest of this week you record on this form the number of times Alice builds a fire.

15. If you have the time to do it, you could also make a note of what happens before and after fire-building.

16. Do these suggestions meet with your approval?

17. We agreed that you would record the number of fires that Alice builds during the rest of this week.

18. You're going to use this form.

19. If you have a chance, you're going to note what happens before and after fire-building.

20. Did I summarize our recording plans accurately?

21. Could we meet Monday or Tuesday of next week?

22. Shall we meet in the teacher's lounge or in your classroom?

23. When could I drop in to see how the data collection is going?

24. I'll give you a call some time this week to see how the data collection is going.

CHILD WITH READING PROBLEM

1. Tell me about Ted.

2. Give me some other examples of Ted's reading difficulties.

3. About how many errors does Ted make during an oral reading session?

4. You said that Ted continually misreads and omits words during oral reading; is that correct?

5. How do you introduce oral reading?

6. How do the other children react when Ted makes errors while reading?

7. What is the sequence of steps that you go through in teaching reading in the oral reading groups?

8. You said that when you call on Ted to read, he volunteers eagerly and that after he has finished, you always go over all of his mistakes with him. You pronounce the words for him and have him say the words correctly. Is that an accurate review of what happens?

9. If you could record the number of errors that Ted makes during reading for the rest of the week, it would help

us to establish a baseline against which we can measure improvement in his reading.

10. You could use this form for recording.

11. And if you have a chance, note the other children's reactions and your own when Ted makes a mistake.

12. Would these plans be okay with you?

13. We said that you would record the number of errors that Ted makes during oral reading on this form for the rest of the week and that if you have the chance, you'll note your own reactions and those of the other children to Ted's mistakes. Is that right?

14. Could we meet Monday or Tuesday of next week?

15. Shall we meet in the teacher's lounge or in your classroom?

16. When could I drop in to see how the data collection is going?

17. I'll give you a call some time this week to see how the data collection is going.

THE INITIAL INTERVIEW WITH THE FAMILY (OR TEACHER/CHILD) TOGETHER

In some situations, such as when a child has a learning problem, you might want to begin the assessment process with a family interview. This procedure has certain advantages (Kinsbourne & Caplan, 1979). First, it informs the child and the parents that you prefer to be open about the problem—you want to include the child in some of the discussions. Second, it allows you to observe how the parents and child interact when discussing the problem areas. It may be a turning point in the child's life when you say to the family "Let's go into my office and discuss why you are here today." The family interview is not a substitute for individual interviews—you should still see the child and each parent separately so that you can observe how the participants behave in both individual and group situations. If you begin the assessment interviewing with a family interview, obtain the child's developmental history from the parents when the child is not present.

Interviews with the child and parents together (or the child and teacher together) provide you with the opportunity to gather valuable information about the problem areas and about family dynamics, communication patterns, and social and cultural values. Family dynamics include how family members view each other in their respective roles, the degree and type of involvement of each member with each other member and with the family as a whole, the extent to which members' behaviors are experienced as annoying by other members, and the degree to which members support and criticize one another,

Table 16-16
Major Questions for a Family Assessment

1. What do parents (and perhaps the referred child and other children) expect from an evaluation?
2. How do they currently explain the child's problems?
3. What are family members' concerns about the child's starting a new program or school?
4. How does each parent see the referred child?
5. How do parents interact with the referred child and siblings?
6. What are the parents' experiences in their families of origin (for example, significant events, individuation, and current relationships)?
7. What is each parent's current level of satisfaction with work and social roles?
8. What roles does each parent have in relation to the referred child?
9. To what degree does parenthood dominate the marital relationship?
10. Do parents use triangulation (focusing on a third person to relieve stress in a dyadic relationship)?
11. To what extent do family members have roles outside the family?
12. What are the support networks within and outside the extended family?
13. To what degree does each member have real input into various decisions?
14. What amount of control can be exerted by various behaviors? (For example, what function does the child's behavior or handicapping condition have in the family?)
15. How are conflict, stress, and crises handled?
16. What are the family rules, especially in relation to responsibilities of each member and topics that can and cannot be discussed?
17. Who enforces the rules and how is this done?
18. What are the consequences of breaking rules?
19. What are the boundaries between the family members and between the family and the outside world?
20. What does each family member see as the family's strengths?
21. What would improve family functioning?
22. How do family members view each other's similarities and differences?
23. What do family members identify as stressors and as annoying or pleasing behaviors in others?
24. How do they react to these behaviors?
25. How do family members perceive the developmental stage of the referred child?
26. How does the child differ from that perception?
27. How does each member deal with the issues of having a disabled or problematic child?

Source: Reprinted, with changes in notation, with permission of the authors and publisher from A. L. Selig and J. Berdie, "Assessing Families with a Developmentally Delayed/Handicapped Child," *Journal of Development and Behavioral Pediatrics*, 1981, 2, pp. 153–154. Copyright 1981 by Williams & Wilkins Co.

induce guilt, and intrude on one another (Wells & Rabiner, 1973). Through family interviews you can determine how the referred child is accepted by the family and how much of an impact the child's difficulties are having on the family, on the parents' relationship, and on other family members. Such interviews also permit evaluation of the family's skill in caring for the referred child and their resources (financial, physical, intellectual, and emotional) for handling possible recommended interventions. Major questions to consider in a family assessment are presented in Table 16-16.

The goals of the family assessment interview are to obtain historical and current details of family life as they pertain to the child's problems and to observe patterns of family interaction. This is accomplished by helping the members discuss issues pertinent to their lives together, encouraging them to interact freely, and helping them describe the conditions that they find most troublesome. Support members who are shy and reticent, encouraging them to give their views. Watching the family interact will help you to develop treatment recommendations and evaluate how changes in individual family members may affect other members and the family as a whole. Recognize, however, that your questions and probes may precipitate potentially painful confrontations among family members; the interview may elicit feelings that had not been previously articulated. When this occurs, you must be prepared to offer support.

Guidelines for Conducting the Family (or Group) Assessment Interview

The following are useful guidelines for conducting the family (or group) assessment interview (cf. Kinston & Loader, 1984):

1. Encourage open discussion among the participants.
2. Make the interview no more stressful than absolutely necessary.
3. Support any participant who is on the "hot seat."

4. Allow the family to defend itself and maintain its status quo without guilt or loss of face.

5. Create a safe and supportive atmosphere so that the participants can interact in a way that they find most comfortable and natural.

6. Accept the family the way it is.

7. Use praise and approval to facilitate the family's acceptance of the interview.

8. Be objective and supportive.

9. Maintain a balance between formality and informality while promoting informality among the participants.

10. Focus the interview on the family.

11. Address questions to the whole group.

12. Encourage the children to participate.

13. Do not provoke the family. (Ask, for example, "How do arguments arise?" rather than "Who is the troublemaker in the family?")

14. Be aware of group dynamics.

Your interest in the family and your ability to see the family's situation from the members' points of view will promote freer discussion of personal and intimate details of their lives.

Phases of the Family Assessment Interview

The family assessment interview has three phases.

Opening phase.   When the family enters the room, note the seating arrangement of the family members and who talks to whom and in what manner. After introducing yourself, you might say "We are all here today to work out the problems you're having as a family. I'd like to hear from each of you about what is going on." Then you might say "Who would like to begin the discussion?" Or, looking at no one in particular, you might say "Would you like to tell me why you are here today?" Encourage reluctant members to speak in the interest of being helpful. Foreclose lengthy or excessive responses by such comments as "We have a lot of ground to cover. Let's hear what Mr. Smith thinks." Be alert to which members talk, in what sequence, at whom they look, and who interrupts, clarifies, registers surprise, disagrees, and engages in other similar behaviors. These behaviors will provide clues about the family's power structure, coalitions, communication patterns, and areas of conflict. It is important to learn about how the family views the referred child's problems.

Middle phase.   After each member has had time (say 15 to 20 minutes) to share his or her views about the presenting problems, you can turn to a discussion of the family

(see questions 10 through 47 in Table 16-17). Be alert especially to nonverbal cues (for example, knowing glances, fidgeting), how the family members talk to each other, their power maneuvers, their provocative behaviors, and their ability to send and receive messages.

In this phase of the interview (or in another phase, if you prefer), you might want to study family interaction patterns by giving the family one or more exercises, such as the following (Baker, Minuchin, Milman, Leibman, & Todd, 1975, pp. 336–337): "Plan a menu for tonight's dinner which you would all enjoy. You are allowed to have one meat dish, two vegetables, one dessert and one drink. Try to include each person's favorite food. Remember that you must agree on the final choice of foods." In addition to revealing the dynamics of role differentiation and conflict resolution, their discussion may reveal such characteristics as overprotectiveness and rigidity as well as language patterns, affective reactions, and communication patterns.

Closing phase.   Toward the end of the interview, you can summarize the salient points of the interview, focusing on those family dynamics most related to the child's problem. After asking the family members to respond to your formulation, give your recommendations, and again ask the members to react. These discussions will help you gauge the family's willingness to change and the members' suitability for treatment.

Table 16-17 provides an example of a semi-structured family assessment interview. It covers the presenting problem as well as issues related to the family's image, perceptions of various members, organization, communication patterns, relationships, activities, conflicts, and decision-making style.

CLOSING THE INITIAL INTERVIEW

The way you end the interview is important, especially when the interviewee is expressing some deeply felt emotion. Try not to end the interview abruptly; you want to leave some time for the interviewee to regain composure before he or she leaves the interview. An interviewee who is in the middle of a communication should be allowed to finish. Gauge the time and, when necessary, provide some indication to the interviewee that the interview will soon be over (say in 5 minutes). When the interviewee recognizes that the interview will soon be over, he or she may begin to move away from the subject at hand and regain composure.

Table 16-17
Example of a Semi-Structured Family Assessment Interview

After introducing yourself, you might lead into the interview by saying, "We are all here today to try to work out the problems you're having as a family. I'd like to hear from everyone about what is going on."

1. Would you like to tell me why you are here today (looking at the family members present)?
2. What do you see as the problem? (Obtain each member's view, if possible.)
3. When did the problem start?
4. How did the problem start?
5. What is the problem like now?
6. How has the problem affected all of you? (Obtain each member's view, if possible.)
7. How have you dealt with the problem? (Obtain each member's view, if possible.)
8. To what degree have your attempts been successful?
9. Have you had any previous professional help? (If yes, inquire further.)
10. What words would you use to describe your family?
11. What's it like when you are all together?
12. What kind of a person is Mr. _____ (looking at the family)?
13. What kind of a person is Mrs. _____ (looking at the family)?
14. What kind of son is _____ (looking at the family)?
15. What kind of daughter is _____ (looking at the family)?
16. (Ask similar questions for other siblings.)
17. Do you agree with the description of yourself given by the other family members? (Obtain a response from each member.)
18. Which parent deals more with the children?
19. Are there any specific jobs for children?
20. Are these arrangements satisfactory or fair?
21. (If not) How could they be better?
22. Do you find it easy to talk with the others in your family? (Explore any difficulties: who is involved and what is the problem.)
23. What's it like when you discuss something together?
24. Who talks the most?
25. The least?
26. Does everybody get a chance to have a say?
27. Do you find you have to be careful with what you say in your family (looking at the family)?
28. Who are the good listeners in your family?
29. Is it helpful to talk things over, or does it seem to be a waste of time?
30. Is it easy to express your feelings in your family?
31. Do you generally know how the others in your family are feeling?
32. How do you tell?
33. How much time do you spend together as a family?
34. What sorts of things do you do together?
35. Who does what with whom?
36. Is this okay with everybody?
37. Who is closest to whom in the family?
38. How are decisions made in your family?
39. Is this satisfactory?
40. What would be preferable?
41. Do you have disagreements in your family?
42. Between whom?
43. What about?
44. What are the disagreements like?
45. What happens?
46. How does it end up?
47. Does it get worked out?
48. What kind of work does Mr. _____ do?
49. What kind of work does Mrs. _____ do?
50. How do you get along with the grandparents (looking at the family)?
51. How might each of you change in order to improve the family situation?
52. Is there anything else that you would like to discuss?

Note. The Family Assessment Interview was prepared by Dr. Peter Loader for the Family Research Programme at Brunel – The University of West London. Work related to the interview schedule was published by Kinston and Loader (1984).
Source: Adapted from Kinston and Loader, unpublished manuscript, 1984.

What you say, of course, will depend on whether you plan to see the interviewee again. If you do not, you might say "You have some deep feelings about. . . . However, our time is about up. I do appreciate your cooperation." If you plan to see the interviewee again, you might say "I can see that this is extremely important to you, and we need to talk about it some more. But our time is just about up for today. We can continue next time." Then arrange for another interview.

The last minutes of the initial interview can be used to give the interviewee an opportunity to ask any remaining questions and to summarize, evaluate, and plan. Useful questions to ask include "Is there anything else you would like to tell me?" and "Is there anything else you think that I should know?" You could also say "I have asked you many questions; are there any questions that you would like to ask me?" A summary statement should attempt to identify the main points of the problem so that the interviewee can confirm or correct that statement; for example, "You be-lieve that Helen's major problem is her inability to read. Emotionally, you see her as being well adjusted. However, her frustration in learning how to read does get her down at times."

Toward the close of the initial interview you might say something like "We met today so that I could learn about Bill. Do you believe that I have most of the important information?" Or you could say "I think we have accom-plished a great deal today. The information you have given me is very helpful. I appreciate your cooperation and look forward to seeing you again after we have completed the evaluation." These statements are not mutually exclusive; they can be used together at the close of the interview. Where relevant, an appointment should be made with the interviewee to discuss the assessment findings and recommendations.

Reward Appropriate Behavior

It may be helpful, especially with children, to acknowl-edge their openness and willingness to share their prob-lems, concerns, hopes, and expectations. Comments such as the following may be appropriate (Jennings, 1982):

- "I appreciate your sharing your concerns with me."
- "It took a lot of courage to talk to me about yourself, your family, and your school."
- "It took a lot of trust to tell me what you just did, and I'm proud of you for doing that."
- "You took this interview seriously, and that makes me feel good."

Acknowledge Your Disappointment with Uncooperative Interviewees

When the interviewee has not been cooperative, you may want to express your concern about the interview: "We didn't get too much accomplished today. Perhaps next time we can cover more ground."

EVALUATING THE INTERVIEW

After you have completed your interviews with the child, parents, and teachers, estimate the extent to which the interviewees were able to report accurately their behav-iors, thoughts, and feelings, as well as events. For exam-ple, how accurate was the teacher in describing the antece-dent and consequent events associated with the problem behavior? How did various factors—intellectual, develop-mental, and situational—interact to affect the interviewees'

replies? These and similar questions should guide you in your evaluation.

Also consider the subjective reactions and feelings the interviewees evoked in you. Did you feel exhausted, frus-trated, indifferent, or satisfied? Do you believe that the interview went well? If not, why not? Do you believe that you came to some understanding of the interviewees? Do you need another interview in order to gain additional information? The answers to these and similar questions are useful because your subjective reactions and feelings about the interviewees are important in the assessment process. They provide some information about how the interviewees function in a structured interpersonal rela-tionship and, together with other sources of information, can aid you in formulating a more complete picture of the child and of the problem.

One of your tasks is to synthesize the information that you have obtained from the various sources. Your synthesis should provide you with information about the child's pre-senting problem (description of problem, antecedent events, and consequences); developmental history (phys-ical, intellectual, emotional, educational, and social devel-opment); current family situation (relationship with par-ents, siblings, relatives); and experiences and behavior at home, at school, and in the community (interests, ac-tivities, hobbies, jobs, relationships with others). When you receive conflicting information, you have to arrive at a picture that you believe is most accurate. Discrepancies can be noted in the report.

The information you have obtained will help you evalu-ate the child's ability to attend and concentrate; tolerate frustration; postpone gratification; cooperate with peers, parents, and teachers; play fair and understand rules; develop a conscience; play constructively; and play alone. Attend carefully to any recent changes in behavior (for example, mood shifts, attentional deficits, memory loss, motor or sensory changes, sleep disturbances, speech abnormalities) or deviations from normal development. Also note any reports of significant delays in reaching developmental milestones.

Other questions you can use in evaluating the interview, developing major themes and impressions, and formulat-ing an appropriate treatment or remediation program in-clude the following (the last 11 questions are from Kanfer & Saslow, 1969):

- What are the child's strengths and weaknesses?
- What are the child's resources for change and for coping with stress?
- Was there any evidence of psychopathology? If so, what was the evidence (for example, non sequiturs, tan-

gential thinking, loose associations, bizarre content, or inappropriate affect)?

• What is your overall impression of the child and the family?

• How valid is the information that you obtained?

• Have you been able to identify the major problem areas?

• Have you cleared up any misconceptions that the interviewees may have had about remediation or treatment possibilities?

• Are the interviewees aware of the clinic's (or school's) policies regarding fees and procedures?

• What would happen if the problem behavior continued without change?

• What would happen if the problem behavior was changed as a result of some intervention?

• What would be the positive *or* adverse effects on the parents (and other significant others) if the child's problem behavior were changed?

• What new problems would successful intervention pose for the child, the parents, and significant others?

• What persons or groups are most effective in controlling the child's behavior problem?

• What reinforcers (for example, social approval, food, money, watching TV, avoidance of punishment) are most effective in controlling the problem behavior?

• Does the problem behavior occur in all or only some settings (for example, child behaves acceptably at school but not at home or vice versa)?

• What consequences have followed from the problem behavior in each setting?

• Has the child acquired some measure of self-control in avoiding situations conducive to performing the problem behavior?

• Can the child match his or her behavior with any spoken intentions to control the problem behavior?

• What conditions or persons seem to help the problem behavior?

SECOND INTERVIEWS

Second interviews, when needed, can begin in a number of different ways (Stevenson, 1960). For example, you might say "How have you been since our last meeting?" or "What's been happening since we last met?" It also may be helpful to say "Last time we had to stop before we covered everything. Perhaps we could continue where we left off." Or you might say "You may have thought of some things that you didn't have a chance to say last time. Let's talk about those things now." If these inquiries are not produc-

tive, you can turn to specific areas of the interviewee's history or current situation that merit further inquiry.

THE POST-ASSESSMENT INTERVIEW WITH CHILDREN

It is desirable to include in the assessment process a post-assessment interview with the child. During this time you can attempt to allay any fears that the child may have about the assessment. You can also check hypotheses generated in the course of testing and probe areas that may need further clarification, such as the child's motivation during the testing. The post-assessment interview can take place immediately after the testing or at some later date. If the assessment results are available, you may want to discuss them with the child, depending on the child's age and other considerations. Adolescents especially may want to be informed about the results of the evaluation.

Children who are able to understand the assessment results benefit from this feedback; they need this information more than anyone else because they make more decisions about themselves than others do about them. For example, many children wrongly estimate their abilities, and a face-to-face conference may give them information needed for self-corrective or esteem-building purposes.

THE POST-ASSESSMENT INTERVIEW WITH PARENTS

The post-assessment interview with parents requires much sensitivity and understanding of feelings, needs, and desires. It is not a matter of simply reciting the results or reading the report. Rather, every effort should be made to enlist the parents' cooperation in working toward an effective treatment or intervention program.

A potentially troubling issue in the post-assessment interview with parents is the confidentiality of the information obtained from the child. Specifically, to what extent does the child have a say in determining what information the parents will receive? Unfortunately, there still are no clear legal guidelines concerning the extent to which information received from children is confidential; the courts and legislatures continue to define the rights of children vis-à-vis their parents. Perhaps because of the unclear legal status of children's rights, professional associations have been hesitant to address this issue clearly in their professional ethics statements. On the one hand, parents are legally and morally responsible for their children. On the other hand, there is an increasing tendency toward protecting the rights of children to make their own decisions, especially when children are able to make competent ones.

If you hold a post-assessment interview with parents of a minor child older than 16 years of age, you should obtain the child's consent to release information. If the child is younger than 16 years of age, obtaining his or her permission is preferable but may not be legally required. Obviously the child's age and ability to give the required permission must be considered, and any release of information must be in accordance with the law of your state. (For further discussion see the section on Confidentiality of the Interview Material and Assessment Findings toward the end of this chapter.)

Guidelines for Conducting the Post-Assessment Interview with Parents

The goals of the post-assessment interview with the parents of an exceptional child are to provide a thorough presentation of the child's learning or emotional problem (description, etiology, severity, and prognosis); plan a specific program geared to the child's needs and capabilities; recognize and deal with the personal problems of the parents as they affect the child or as they are exacerbated by the child's condition; and plan for any future meetings. These goals are accomplished in part by reviewing the presenting problem, reporting and explaining the assessment findings, and discussing your recommendations.

One of the most important parts of the post-assessment interview is to make sure that the parents understand the findings and recommendations, a goal that may not always be easy to accomplish. The guilt some parents experience may interfere with their ability to accept your information and conclusions. Others may be embarrassed to admit that they do not understand what you are saying. Still others may be frustrated at not being able to solve the problem themselves and resent your interference. Be prepared to handle such resistance during the interview.

Tell the parents which problems are major and which are minor. Reading and arithmetic difficulties, for example, may be of major concern, whereas clumsiness may be of minor concern. Focus the interview on the child. Inform the parents that your primary concern is the welfare and happiness of the child and that you want to work with them to achieve this goal. This focus might help to reduce the parents' own personal frustration. It is not that their problems are unimportant, but rather that the present focus should be on the child. Their difficulties and personal concerns can be addressed by another professional or on another occasion. Use simple language, do not lecture, use examples and illustrations, and give the parents something they can do if possible.

Four Phases of the Post-Assessment Interview

The post-assessment interview with parents can be conceptualized as having four phases: the initial phase, the communication of results, discussion of recommendations, and termination.

INITIAL PHASE OF THE POST-ASSESSMENT INTERVIEW

• Make every effort to have both parents present at the interview. Interviewing both parents will enable you to obtain a more objective picture of their reactions and enable the parents to share the responsibilities for carrying out the recommendations.

• Greet parents, giving your name and professional title.

• Establish rapport. Help the parents feel comfortable during the interview and encourage them to talk and to ask questions freely. Recognize the frustration and hardships that they have faced and will be facing. Convey to them that they have something important to contribute to the discussion.

COMMUNICATING THE ASSESSMENT RESULTS

• Summarize the assessment results and their implications as clearly as possible. Inform the parents that you encourage their participation and prepare them for any conflict-arousing information. Use understandable terminology throughout the interview. Give parents the opportunity to ask questions about the findings.

• If the results suggest a handicapping condition, be prepared to deal with a variety of reactions, including anxiety and emotional distress, grief, disbelief, shock, denial, ambivalence, anger, disappointment, guilt, despair, and possibly relief. Some parents may feel cheated because they did not produce a "perfect" being. Others may have feelings of self-deprecation and guilt. Help them express their feelings.

• Present accurate information about the child's handicapping condition and its possible causes. Help the parents understand that handicapped children have the same needs as all children, as well as some unique needs of their own. Stress the child's strengths and potentials, keeping in mind, of course, the nature of the handicap and the limitations associated with it. Parents especially need help in avoiding becoming overwhelmed by their child's disorder.

• Use the diagnostic findings to help the parents give up erroneous ideas and adopt a more realistic approach to the child's problems. Give them copies of the reports and discuss the results obtained. Some diagnoses are easier for parents to relate to than others. A known genetic disorder that has predictable consequences may be easier to discuss than conditions that are not clearcut, such as mental retardation in a very young child. Labels should be used cautiously whenever there is any doubt about the diagnosis.

• Throughout this phase, try to evaluate how the parents feel about the results. You may wish to check the parents' understanding of their child's disorder by saying, "Please tell me in your own words what you understand about your child's condition."

DISCUSSING THE RECOMMENDATIONS

• Try to let the parents formulate a plan of action. Allow some time for them to assimilate the findings. Assist them in planning how much information to give to others, such as siblings, grandparents, friends, and co-workers.

• Present the recommendations and alternatives for consideration, discussing possible courses of action. Try to develop the intervention plans *with* the parents—ask for their opinions about the options. If additional diagnostic procedures are warranted, explain why.

• Give parents the opportunity to ask questions about the recommendations. Recommend instructive reading materials when appropriate. (See Chapter 24 for recommended readings.) Try to evaluate how the parents feel about the recommendations.

• If the parents ask for information about prognosis, as they are likely to do, carefully consider everything you know about the case before offering an opinion. Include appropriate precautions about the tentativeness of any prognosis.

• If you recommend a treatment, be prepared to discuss possible treatment or remediation strategies, length of treatment, and financial costs. If special class placement is needed, describe the benefits of the class and how it will contribute to the child's development. Deal with any concerns that the parents may have in an honest and nondefensive manner. Give parents the opportunity to visit the class (or other facility) and to discuss the program with the teacher (or staff) before they make their final decision.

• Inform parents of their rights and be sure they understand them. In school settings, discuss their rights under Public Law 94-142 (see Chapter 24) and relevant state and local policies.

• Make certain that all vital considerations relevant to a decision are discussed.

TERMINATING THE POST-ASSESSMENT INTERVIEW

• Toward the end of the post-assessment interview with parents, try to gain insight into their understanding and feelings. For example, you could say "We met today so that we could discuss the results of the evaluation. Do you feel that you understand the findings?... How do you feel about the recommendations?"

• Inform the parents that you are available for subsequent meetings, especially if all of the interview goals have not been achieved or if the parents want further discussion. Make it easy for parents to arrange subsequent interviews.

• If parents are unable to accept the results of the evaluation, convey your understanding of their difficulty in accepting the findings and recommendations. Describe referral services and provide them with the names of other agencies or professionals should they desire other opinions.

• Close the interview by giving the parents your business telephone number and inviting them to call if they have further questions. Escort the parents from the room, thank them for their cooperation, and say goodbye.

Questions to Consider in the Post-Assessment Interview with Parents

Some important questions to consider in the post-assessment interview with parents are as follows:

• Do the parents understand the results?
• Do they generally accept the results?
• Do they understand the recommendations?
• Do they generally accept the recommendations?
• What specific areas do they question?
• What kinds of interventions do they desire?
• Do they understand their rights under Public Law 94-142?
• Do they want another evaluation from an independent source?
• What would they consider successful treatment or remediation?
• How willing are they to change their own expectations and behavior?
• Are they willing to be involved in parent training programs or in other skill programs?
• If the child needs to be hospitalized, how frequently do they plan to visit the child?

Exploring Possible Residential Placement of Mentally Retarded Children

In exploring with parents the possibility of placing their child in a residential institution, consider all relevant variables, such as differences among available institutions, the degree and type of retardation, and the family's situation.

Some institutions have excellent training programs, focusing on self-help habit training, motor skills development, and language acquisition programs. Although the residential institution for mentally retarded persons is not in favor, institutions still serve an important role, particularly for the profoundly retarded child.

Understanding the Reactions of Parents of Handicapped Children

Discussing the results of the psychological evaluation with parents of handicapped children requires much tact and skill. For most parents learning that their child is severely handicapped is a traumatic experience. A family's reaction to the diagnosis tends to go through five stages: impact, denial, grief, focusing outward, and closure (Fortier & Wanlass, 1984, see Table 16-18). Your role is to help the parents recognize the problem, formulate a plan, and put the plan into action.

The following interview excerpt illustrates the opening dialogue of a post-assessment interview between a mother and an interviewer who recently tested her 9-year-old son. Notice how the interviewer tries to help the mother accept findings that suggest the child may have academic difficulties (No. 5). Notice, too, how the interviewer relates the child's behavior patterns to the child's level of cognitive and academic performance (Nos. 7 and 9).

IR: As you know Mrs. A., I asked Bill to do a number of different activities, like draw pictures, tell stories, and answer questions. He was cooperative and tried to do everything I asked. But he seems to get frustrated when he can't do something as well as he would like to, and he gives up easily. (1)

IE: Yes, I know. He gives up even when he can do something. He just doesn't try. (2)

IR: Well, in fact, there are many things he can't do yet, no matter how hard he tries. His score on the intelligence test places him at the 10th percentile. This means that he is intellectually behind the majority of other children his age. About 90 out of 100 children score higher. He will learn, but at a much slower pace than other children his age. (3)

IE: So it will take him a while to catch up to the other kids in his class. That's all right, as long as I know he'll be normal. (4)

IR: This may take some time for you to accept. Bill probably will always be behind most children his age. It's going to take him longer to learn to read and to learn some things, and he may never catch up completely. (5)

IE: Oh. (6)

IR: I suspect that he is aware of his limitations. He knows what he can and cannot do. He wants so badly to do well that when he gets frustrated about what he can't do, he tries to distract people by doing something cute, and that often gets him in trouble in school. (7)

IE: Yeah. He's always acting like a clown. He's really funny. (8)

IR: It's his way of keeping others from finding out that he's having difficulty understanding how to do something. (9)

IE: So what can we do to help him? (10)

Various defensive methods, which are all variants of denial, may be used by parents in coping with an unacceptable diagnosis (Cutter & Miller, 1971). One type of denial mechanism used by parents is to state that their child is normal and reject the diagnosis. This type of denial may subject their child to extreme pressure. A second type of denial reaction is to recognize that something is wrong, but hold out for the most acceptable diagnosis. The parent might say "My child is only emotionally disturbed" when in reality the child is brain damaged and functioning in the mentally retarded range. A third denial mechanism is to deny the clinician the opportunity to discuss the child's condition by being overly accepting of the diagnosis: for example, "We know all about the condition and are doing everything possible to accept it, and we do not need any help or suggestions." This mechanism helps the family maintain the status quo rather than consider the implications of the diagnosis.

What parents need most is information to help them understand their child's condition and make appropriate decisions. Help them shift from searching for the cause of the handicap to determining what they can do for the child. Inform them of the limitations of the findings, encourage them to make tentative plans for their child's future, and provide them with factual information regarding community resources, support groups, referral agencies, and institutions. Recommend sources, such as books and pamphlets, that will assist them in learning about their child's handicap.

Different parents will react differently to learning that their child has a handicap. The following case illustrates how two parents within the same family differed in their reactions:

Mr. and Mrs. C. brought their son, 5-year-old Tim, for an evaluation because he seemed to be a slow learner. Testing revealed that Tim was moderately retarded, functioning on the level of about a 3-year-old. The father's initial reaction was overt grief. Stunned by the diagnosis, he cried openly during the initial and later interviews and later became depressed and withdrawn at home. Mrs. C. showed little overt emotion, and questioned the test results because Tim was shy with the examiner. Subsequent to the evaluation, she became highly overprotective of Tim.

After six sessions with the parents, Mr. C. became mobilized and began to actively seek resources. He took Tim to join Special Olympics and signed up as a coach. Mrs. C. became extremely angry with her husband, stating that in so doing he had admitted the child was retarded and had given up hope. Mr. C. felt his wife was denying reality and that her overprotectiveness was prevent-

Table 16-18
Characteristics of Crisis Stages over Five Modalities

Stage	Behavior	Affect	Sensation	Interpersonal relations	Cognition
Impact	Agitation, pacing, fidgeting; or lethargy, moving in slow motion, appearing dazed	Feelings of anxiety or shock	Physiological changes of anxiety or shock: nausea, diarrhea, fainting, muscle tenseness	Seeking support of others, needing to talk; or isolation, withdrawal	Disorientation, confusion, circular thinking
Denial	Shopping for cures or new diagnoses, going through motions of pre-crisis behavior; or selective attention to acceptable data only	Alternating between hope, despair, and avoidance of feelings	Controlled anxiety	Seeking the company of those who support current view of problem and avoiding those who disagree	Disbelief, imagining situations where problem disappears or cure is found, fictionalized explanations, distorted expectations, not hearing
Grief	Sleeplessness, crying, spurts of activity alternating with lethargy, changes in behavior due to care of child	Anger, helplessness, sense of loss, self-pity, self-doubt, sense of isolation, guilt, revival of dormant or unresolved feelings	Anxiety-related physical symptoms, tears, fatigue	Loss of interpersonal warmth	Questioning "how?" and "why?," death wish toward child as possible solution, reliving of prior events that might be "reason for this punishment," thoughts of what it will be like in future
Focusing outward	Information seeking, increased friendliness and contact with others	Relief, confidence	Renewed energy	Talking options over with others, seeking out those who have knowledge	Reconsidering options, increased awareness of reality, formulating plans
Closure	Beginning to meet needs of child and family, returning to pre-crisis behavior where possible	Calm	Relaxed muscles, decrease in physical symptoms	Emergence of family solidarity as work toward new goals begins, increased closeness with similar others	Acceptance of child and situation

Source: Copyrighted (1984) by the National Council on Family Relations, 1910 West County Road B, Suite 147, St. Paul, MN 55113. Reprinted by permission. From L. M. Fortier and R. L. Wanlass, "Family Crisis Following the Diagnosis of a Handicapped Child," *Family Relations,* 1984, *33,* p. 18, with changes in notation.

ing Tim from having many normal daily experiences. She asserted that if she didn't watch his every move, he would surely die—by drowning in the bathtub or other calamities.

Mr. and Mrs. C. reacted in highly different ways to their son's diagnosis, both according to their coping styles and their own needs and fears. As the parents were increasingly able to accept the reactions of the other, and to discuss their own feelings of loss, anger, and depression, they were able to begin working together for Tim's benefit. Mrs. C.'s involvement in a mother's group was an important intervention, where she felt comfortable to express feelings she could not yet expose to her husband. (Miller, 1979, p. 300, with changes in notation)

Parents who "shop around."   When a child is diagnosed as having a serious handicap, such as mental retardation or infantile autism, parents are behaving realistically in seeking a second opinion, given the tremendous impact of the diagnosis. However, some parents of handicapped children "shop around" — that is, they visit a number of different professionals or clinics in order to obtain an acceptable diagnosis. Once the acceptable diagnosis has been obtained, they may look endlessly for new treatments or educational programs to cure the disorder. This shopping behavior is frequently maladaptive. It is costly in time, parental energy, and money. It is disruptive of family life and sometimes involves a family's making long trips or even relocating altogether. It also takes the parents' focus off constructive efforts to work with their child. To prevent or alleviate such behavior, help the parents work through the feelings they experience upon learning about their child's handicap.

Sensitivity to parents' reactions and feelings.   Although the post-assessment interview is designed to share the results of the evaluation with the parent (or other source), it may be necessary to change the focus of the interview if you find that the parent cannot cope well with the recommendations or findings.

The following excerpt from Molyneaux and Lane (1982, pp. 128–129, with changes in notation) is from an interview between a staff worker in a child development clinic and the mother of a 4-year-old developmentally disabled son. How sensitive do you believe the interviewer was?

IR: We are recommending placement of Ronnie in the Developmental Center preschool program. (1)

IE: I won't agree to that. Ronnie is just fine, and you people are making some big deal out of these tests. First the pediatrician, then my in-laws, and now you! (2)

IR: We're all just trying to find out what would be best for Ronnie — to give him the best possible chance to develop. (3)

IE: You act like he's some kind of moron. My husband didn't talk until he was almost 2 years old and there's nothing the matter with him! Taking him around to these places; sitting and waiting until somebody gets good and ready to see us. It's damned annoying! (4)

IR: Well, you had to wait because there are several parts to the tests and different people administer them. (5)

IE: I hope they know more than that pediatrician does. With all the shots and vaccines and vitamins and now these tests — before you know it, there *will* be something the matter with Ronnie! (6)

IR: Mrs. Monner, your son is mentally retarded. There's no doubt about that. But if he's going to get the best possible training, we want to have as much information about his condition as we can. (7)

IE: What do you mean, retarded? That's a terrible thing to say about a little fellow only 4 years old. He's a lot smarter than some of the people we've come across in the last six months! (8)

IR: It's foolish for you to act this way about the situation. People are trying to help and you refuse to face the facts. (9)

IE: Nobody has given me any facts. They're too busy playing God! (10)

In the interview excerpt above, the interviewer failed to deal with the mother's grief, frustration, and defensiveness. Instead, the interviewer almost matter-of-factly related the diagnosis (No. 7) and then went on to berate the parent for not accepting it (No. 9). The interviewer not only failed to prepare the mother for the findings, but also became argumentative. This interview could have been improved by active listening, acceptance of the parent's feelings, and empathic responses.

Understanding the Needs of Parents of Gifted Children

Many of the principles for dealing with parents of handicapped children also apply to parents of gifted children. Both groups of children are "exceptional." Like parents of other exceptional children, parents of gifted children do not simply want information about their child's level of ability. They desire information about their child's social and academic behavior; immediate relevant advice (for example, how to teach the child to do certain things, suggestions for enrichment activities, and information regarding current academic and social progress); and copies of reports written about their child (Dembinski & Mauser, 1978). This information should not be couched in jargon. It should be clear, honest, and realistic and should help parents to obtain a quality education for their child and cope better with their child's needs (see Table 16-19).

Post-Assessment Interview as a Staff Conference

When the post-assessment interview with parents is in the form of a staff conference, the following guidelines complement those presented previously (Greenbaum, 1982, pp. 4–5, with changes in notation and additions):

1. *Prepare for the conference carefully.* Review all case history information, test results, and recommendations.

2. *Set specific goals for the conference.* Prepare goals in advance of the meeting. Be sure that the staff members come to a unified position *before* they see the parents.

3. *Be organized.* Start and end on time, stay on task, and try to follow your agenda. Have each staff member introduce himself or herself. If each staff member is going

Table 16-19
Recommendations by Parents of Gifted Children to Psychologists and Teachers

To psychologists	To teachers
Allow us to ask questions.	Keep us informed about our child's progress or lack of it.
Tell us about all educational alternatives for our special child.	Allow us to ask questions.
Use terminology we understand.	Show us reports on our child and explain them.
Be willing to discuss our child's abilities with his or her teacher.	Allow us to contact you when we need to.
Indicate your recommendations for placement or special programming and explain why you are making them.	Tell us how our child gets along with others in his or her class.
Give us copies of reports and explain them.	Tell us if our child gets into trouble.
Suggest the best means of enrichment at home for our child.	Tell us of any special adjustment problems he or she is having.
Warn us of particular problems we might cause for our child.	Be willing to discuss our child's needs and progress with other professionals involved.
Tell us your impressions as soon as possible.	Tell us whether you think he or she is in the best possible educational setting.
Discuss any special child-rearing practices we should be aware of.	Tell us whether you think our child is progressing at a reasonable rate.
Give us materials to read.	Use terminology we can understand.
Require both parents to discuss their concerns with you.	Give us your impressions of our role in our child's learning process.
Put us in touch with other parents with similar concerns.	Inform us of your most successful techniques in working with our child.
Help us to accept our child as normal.	Require us to attend parent conferences.
Suggest supportive services we might need as a family (counseling, social work, etc.).	Give us suggestions to enrich our child's home life.
Tell us our child's IQ.	Tell us what you expect our child to learn and when.
Tell us how fast we should expect our child to progress.	Give us materials to read.
Give us an opportunity to call for advice—a hot line service.	Show us how to teach things to our child.
	Help us to accept our child as normal.
	Require both parents to discuss their concerns with you.
	Put us in touch with other parents with similar concerns.

Note. Recommendations are listed in rank order from most important to least important.
Source: Adapted from Dembinski and Mauser (1978).

to present his or her findings, be sure that this is done in an organized and orderly fashion.

4. *Appear confident.* Choose your words carefully and maintain your composure. Define in a few words the purpose of the meeting.

5. *Form an alliance with the parents.* Try to get the parents to see themselves as part of the team and work with you in carrying out the recommendations. Allow the parents to address questions to any staff member.

6. *Tune in to the parents' needs.* Try to understand the parents' feelings and reactions and be prepared to switch from the agenda, if necessary, to help the parents work through their special concerns.

7. *Tell it like it is.* Be direct and honest and avoid technical jargon. Include a discussion of Public Law 94-142 as it relates to the child and parents.

8. *Don't be defensive.* Remember that you do not have all the answers. Try not to get involved in power struggles with the parents or staff members.

9. *Individualize the conference.* Focus on material that is relevant and essential to the concerns of the child.

10. *Make a closing statement.* Summarize the findings and decisions, make arrangements for future appointments, and inform the parents about how you can be reached.

Holding a staff conference may not be the best way to conduct a post-assessment interview. Sitting at one end of a table watching six or seven professionals give reports may be an intimidating experience for many parents. An alternative is to have a designated case manager who meets with the parents and summarizes the staff's findings and recommendations, or to have each professional individually meet with the parents.

Comment on the Post-Assessment Interview

The way in which a particular post-assessment interview unfolds will depend on the needs of the parents and on your orientation. In all cases it is important that you show warmth, understanding, and respect. Help parents become less defensive by telling them that you appreciate the effort they are making to help their child. The crucial test of the effectiveness of the post-assessment interview is whether the parents act on the basis of what they have learned.

Erroneous beliefs present before the interview, which have been serving to defend the parents from unpleasant consequences, will probably not be given up after one interview. Consequently, several interviews may be needed. A visit to the home may also be desirable.

In working with families of handicapped children, you must recognize that the family will have considerable influence on the child's ability to deal with the handicap and to profit from therapy. Help the family understand how the child can cope with the handicap so that the family can become part of the rehabilitation team, assisting the rehabilitation staff by working with the child at home. Following are some guidelines for working with parents of handicapped children (Gorham, 1975, pp. 523–524, with changes in notation).

1. Involve the parents as team members every step of the way.

2. Make a realistic management plan part of the assessment process.

3. Be informed about community resources.

4. Write your reports in clear and understandable language.

5. Give copies of the reports to parents.

6. Be sure the parents understand that a diagnosis may change.

7. Help the parents to think of life with their handicapped child in the same terms as life with their other children.

8. Be sure that the parents understand their child's abilities as well as disabilities.

The post-assessment interview represents an important part of the assessment procedure. It can be particularly rewarding, for it allows you to implement in a purposeful way the results of the evaluation. It can also be frustrating and sometimes heartbreaking. Self-understanding, particularly of your attitude toward handicaps and the handicapped, is especially important in working with handicapped children and their parents. Following the guidelines presented in this chapter can alleviate some of the anxieties associated with the communication of test results to parents of exceptional children, as well as to parents of normal children.

Although this section has focused on the post-assessment interview with parents, the procedures discussed are generally applicable to any post-assessment interview — with teachers, physicians, attorneys, or other interested parties.

STRUCTURED CLINICAL INTERVIEWS

The interviewing techniques and guidelines that we have covered so far are appropriate for a variety of assessment situations. In cases where the primary goal is to obtain a psychiatric diagnosis, structured interview formats may prove to be useful because they provide a standardized framework which assists the novice interviewer.

Structured interviews for the assessment of children have been developed only within the last decade. Their aim is to increase the reliability and validity of traditional child diagnostic procedures. Interview schedules have been designed for both parents and children, although some focus on either the parent or the child exclusively. (Most of the material in this section is based on the excellent review by Edelbrock and Costello, 1988.)

Comparison of Semi-Structured and Highly Structured Interview Formats

Two general formats have been developed. One is a *semi-structured interview format*, which provides general and flexible guidelines for conducting the interview and recording information. The other is a *highly structured interview format*, which specifies the exact order, wording, and coding of each question. Semi-structured interview formats are designed for more clinically sophisticated interviewers; these formats permit greater latitude in phrasing questions, pursuing alternative lines of inquiry, and interpreting responses. Highly structured interview formats minimize the role of clinical inference in the interview process and can be used by individuals with minimal training. The ultimate in highly structured interviewing may be computer interviewing (see Exhibit 16-3). Can a machine communicate with interviewees better than other people can? Conclusive answers are not yet available, and much may depend on the client's age and ability. For some situations, however, computer interviewing may be the trend of the future.

Semi-Structured Interview Format

A number of semi-structured interview formats have been presented in this chapter. None should be used in a mechanical fashion. It is important to be attentive to the interviewee's communications and to follow up useful

Exhibit 16-3

Will Computers Replace Interviewers?

Interviewers may soon be obsolete: Computers are now interviewing people.

Techniques and equipment vary. A person seated at a computer keyboard may be asked to type simple responses to questions posed on a video screen, or punch out numbers on a telephone in response to questions asked by a mechanical voice at the other end of a phone line. In many cases, all that's needed is a personal computer capable of storing 256,000 pieces of information and a color videodisplay terminal to heighten appeal.

Limitations

There are limits to what machines can do. They can't win over respondents with social chitchat or explain questions that are misunderstood. Unless the interviewees are good typists, the computers can't solicit lengthy responses. They can't recognize fuzzy or superficial answers and prod respondents to elaborate. They can't ask follow-up questions of interviewees who drop unexpected leads.

Strengths

Backers of computer interviewing say it's the very inanimateness of the machine that gives the method its strength. The computer is unbiased, and it lets the respondent ponder a question as long as necessary without feeling pressured by an interviewer with pencil poised in hand.

Computers, furthermore, put the same question to each respondent in precisely the same way. At the same time, they can be somewhat flexible; responses to questions can trigger new sets of questions tuned to the interests and earlier answers of each interviewee.

The answers don't have to be coded for computer tabulation and analysis; the responses are transcribed automatically on a computer disk. And perhaps most important, people are more willing to disclose sensitive information to an impersonal machine than to other people or a paper questionnaire.

John Greist, a psychiatrist at the University of Wisconsin in Madison, came to that conclusion after interviewing—with computers and trained professionals—a group of people waiting to be treated or waiting for others at a general medical clinic. People, he found, "prefer giving private, personal or sensitive information to a computer rather than a human, be it a nurse, physician or psychotherapist."

For example, when asked about exercise, a nonsensitive area for most people, individuals are equally frank with computers and people, he says. But when it comes to questions about sexual activity, people are more open with the machines, "disclosing more sexual dysfunction to a computer than to well-trained psychiatrists, even of the same sex," Dr. Greist says.

"Computers are perceived as less judgmental," he explains. "We've had all kinds of negative experiences with people." Thus, computer interviews may allow us to gather data faster and obtain more truthful answers.

Source: Adapted from S. Feinstein, "Computers Are Replacing Interviewers for Personnel and Marketing Tasks," *Wall Street Journal*, October 9, 1986, p. 37.

---

leads as they occur during a semi-structured interview. Semi-structured interview formats can also be used to obtain detailed information about specific physical or psychological problems. Illustrations of semi-structured formats for interviewing parents of hearing-impaired children, developmentally handicapped children, and brain-injured children are shown in Chapter 20 (Exhibit 20-10), Chapter 21 (Exhibit 21-5), and Chapter 22 (Exhibit 22-1), respectively.

Highly Structured Interview Format

There are several types of highly structured interview schedules. Some, such as the Interview Schedule for Children (ISC, Kovacs, 1983), Kiddie-SADS (K-SADS, Puig-Antich & Chambers, 1983), and Child Assessment Schedule (Hodges, 1985), have been designed for use with clinically referred children (children seen at a mental

health facility). Others focus on surveying non-referred community populations, such as the Diagnostic Interview Schedule for Children (DISC, Costello, Edelbrock, Dulcan, Kalas, & Klaric, 1984) and the Diagnostic Interview for Children and Adolescents (DICA, Herjamic & Reich, 1982). These latter schedules can also be useful with clinic populations. Interview schedules differ as to the types of information obtained. Most procedures yield information about the presence, absence, severity, onset, and duration of symptoms, but others yield quantitative scores in symptom areas or global indices of psychopathology. Table 16-20 shows some of the types of questions that are included in highly structured psychiatric interview formats.

Comment on Structured Interview Formats

Structured interviews are particularly valuable when all interviewees must be asked the same questions, such as in

Table 16-20
Examples of Questions Used in Structured Psychiatric Interviews

K-SADS-P

Impulsivity
Refers to the child's characteristic pattern of acting before thinking about the consequences. *It does not refer to "bad" actions only* but to a behavioral characteristic spanning all types of behavior independent of moral significance.

Are you the kind of person who tends to get into trouble, or maybe even get hurt, because you rush into doing things without thinking what might happen?

Are you often wrong in school because you answer with the first thing that comes to your mind instead of thinking it over first?

Do you get into trouble in school because you often speak out when you're supposed to be quiet?

Does your teacher often have to tell you what you are supposed to do after the rest of the class has started doing it?

Do you have trouble organizing your work?

Do you often do things on a dare or just because the idea popped into your head or just for the heck of it?

0 No information.
1 Not present.
2 Slight: May occur on occasion when excited (party, etc.), but not typical and no bad consequences.
3 Mild: Definitely present. Acts impulsively at least 3 times a week in at least 2 settings.
4 Moderate: Impulsive in all settings.
5 Severe: Impulsive in all settings and has got into dangerous situations for lack of foresight in a few instances (more than 3 times in a year).
6 Extreme: Very impulsive; it is an almost constant characteristic of child's behavior. Gets into danger at least once a week.

DIAGNOSTIC INTERVIEW SCHEDULE FOR CHILDREN (DISC)

Impulsivity

73. Does your teacher often tell you that you don't listen?   0   2

    (If yes) Does he/she say that to you more than to most kids?   0   1   2

    (If yes) How long has that been happening?

                                                    Months

    (If yes) Have you been like that since you started school?   0   2

74. Does your teacher often tell you that you're not keeping your mind on your work?   0   2

    (If yes) Does he/she say that to you more than to most kids?   0   2

    (If yes) How long has that been happening?

                                                    Months

    (If yes) Have you been like that since you started school?   0   2

76. Sometimes kids rush into things without thinking about what may happen. Do you do that?   0   1   2

    (If yes) Have you always been like that?   0   1   2

    (If yes) How long have you been doing that?

                                                    Months

77. Some kids have trouble organizing their schoolwork. They can't decide what they need. They can't plan what to do first, what to do second. Are you like that?   0   1   2

    (If yes) How long have you been like that?

                                                    Months

78. Do you start your schoolwork and not finish it?   0   1   2

    (If yes) How long has that been happening?

                                                    Months

    (If yes) Have you always had trouble finishing it?   0   2

    (If yes) Is that because you do not know how to do it?   0   1   2

Note. On the K-SADS-P, the interviewer selects a severity rating for each symptom on the schedule, based on the interviewee's answers to questions. In the portion of the schedule shown above, the left-hand column contains questions the interviewer might use to evaluate the interviewee's impulsivity; the right-hand column lists the possible numerical ratings corresponding to various degrees of impulsivity. On the DISC, the interviewer circles 0 for no, 1 for sometimes, and 2 for yes.

Source: K-SADS-P from Puig-Antich and Chambers (1983), p. 68. DISC from Costello et al. (1984), October 1983 version, XV.II, pp. 11–12, with changes in notation.

research studies, or when a specific diagnosis is needed. The standardized format allows for comparisons among interviewees as well as interviewers and helps to ensure that topics are not overlooked. Structured interviews, however, have several disadvantages (Kleinmuntz, 1982, p. 179):

A list of formal questions and topics necessitates a rigidity that often interferes with more relaxed communication. The interview can become an inquisition and consequently may yield little more than minimal answers to the questions. If just enough time is allowed for asking the prescribed questions, opportunities for ferreting out related and pertinent bits of information will be missed. Moreover, with greater structure, the interviewer cannot cover the wide range of topics that could identify problems of which the respondent may be unaware.

Structured psychiatric interviewing of children is relatively new and in the early stages of development. Edelbrock and Costello (1988) concluded that much work is needed before structured psychiatric interview formats can be recommended as assessment and diagnostic tools. I recommend, however, that you study one or more of these structured interviews because they provide useful questions and formats that can be incorporated into the traditional assessment interview.

CROSS-ETHNIC, CROSS-CULTURAL, AND CROSS-CLASS INTERVIEWING

Because the interview takes place within a socio-cultural context, communication difficulties due to ethnic, cultural, or socioeconomic differences between you and the interviewee may arise. Verbal and nonverbal communications may be misinterpreted by either you or the interviewee, particularly if the interviewee speaks in a language or dialect different from your own or if there are subcultural differences in styles of nonverbal communication. Gaze pattern differences, for example, can produce miscues and awkwardness in conversational flow. Many black listeners tend not to look at the speaker when listening, whereas many white listeners tend to look at the speaker. Thus whites may believe that they are not being listened to, and blacks may believe that they are being unduly scrutinized. Such misreading of subcultural communication differences may sustain stereotypic interpersonal judgments.

The following excerpt shows in an amusing manner the misinterpretations that may occur when an interviewer is not familiar with jargon used by an interviewee. It illustrates the danger of making interpretations and diagnoses when one does not fully understand the language used by the interviewee. It is hoped that incidents like this never happen in real life.

IE: I was shooting the breeze with my chick and the pigs came along and took us to jail. But I'm not a bad mother.
(IR quickly jots down, "Fantasies of using a chicken to shoot breezes and association of jail with pigs. Shows inferiority complex, denies being a bad mother. Also shows improper sex identification, as he believes that he is a woman and, in addition, a mother.")

IE: I didn't have on my best rags and they wouldn't let me use a wire to call.
(IR jots, "Claims to wear rags of various quality and believes wires can be used to make phone calls. Definite signs of delusions.")

IE: A T man came down to visit me to talk about Acapulco Gold.
(IR jots, "Bizarre ideation in using letters to identify people and fantasies of having wealth in Mexico. Signs of distorted thinking and grandiosity.")

(*Diagnosis:* Paranoid schizophrenia with delusional material, negative self-images, grandiosity, and improper sex identification. Psychological treatment needed. Prognosis is guarded.)

Symptoms also may be given different interpretations, depending on the individual's group membership. For example, what may be viewed as hypersensitive or paranoid behavior by a middle-class Anglo interviewer may be viewed as reality-oriented coping behavior by a non-Anglo interviewer or interviewee. (The material that follows is generally based on Sattler's 1970, 1973b, and 1977 reviews of cross-ethnic studies.)

Class Differences

Middle-class interviewees, in contrast to lower-class interviewees, tend to assume multiple perspectives in their communications, are careful not to be misunderstood, explore their emotions, and reveal personal information. Middle-class interviewees also tend to be less sensitive to the interviewer's race than lower-class interviewees. These findings should not be generalized to all middle- and lower-class interviewees, as they stem from research on group differences and many exceptions will be found. Each interviewee must be approached as an individual, but with ethnic, cultural, and class memberships taken into consideration.

Nonminority Interviewer with Minority Interviewee

Difficulties in a nonminority interviewer–minority interviewee relationship stem from many sources. Because of racial antagonism, some ethnic minority interviewees may find it difficult to react to nonminority interviewers as individuals, and vice versa. Minority interviewees may view nonminority interviewers with suspicion and distrust, as part of the hostile nonminority world. And because nonminority interviewers have been encouraged through education and training to view prejudice as unacceptable, they may deny or suppress negative reactions toward minority interviewees. When nonminority interviewers begin to feel guilty about their own racial and class identity and allow these feelings to intrude on the relationship, difficulties may arise.

Minority Interviewer with Nonminority Interviewee

Minority interviewers may experience some difficulties in their relationship with nonminority interviewees as a result of the socio-cultural aspects of minority-nonminority interpersonal relations. Conflicts may arise if nonminority interviewees avoid the race issue, depreciate the interviewer, have special admiration for him or her, or view him or her as all forgiving or uncritical. Minority interviewers, on the other hand, may be unsympathetic or punitive because of hostility toward nonminorities, or they may overcompensate by being too permissive (in an effort to deny hostility toward nonminorities or because of over-identification with them). Any and all of these dynamics can affect the interview process.

Minority Interviewer with Minority Interviewee

A minority interviewer of the same ethnic group as the minority interviewee may be in the best position to obtain reliable and valid information. Middle-class minority interviewers, however, may have some difficulties with lower-class minority interviewees. Difficulties arise when the interviewer cannot accept interviewees because of their class or when the interviewer is perceived as being a collaborator with the nonminority community. The minority interviewer walks a very fine line between overidentification and objectivity when interviewing a minority interviewee of the same ethnic background.

Possible Distortions That May Arise in Cross-Ethnic and Cross-Cultural Interviews

Preoccupation and heightened sensitivity to ethnic differences may lead to distortions, guardedness, and evasive-

ness on the part of the interviewee, and to guardedness, failure to probe, defensiveness, and feelings of intimidation on the part of the interviewer. Because responses given by both the interviewee and the interviewer require subtle forms of cognitive activity—such as summarizing one's opinion to oneself, estimating the listener's probable reaction, and then deciding whether or not to convey the opinion accurately to the listener—there is always the potential for opinions, attitudes, and even facts to be distorted.

Do some interviewees replace genuine feelings with a façade of submissiveness, pleasure, impassivity, or humility? Can interviewers be genuine and avoid patronizing? Is any form of social distance between interviewer and interviewee likely to create difficulties with rapport and communication? These and similar questions are a matter of concern in cross-cultural interviews.

Suggestions for Handling Cross-Ethnic, Cross-Cultural, and Cross-Class Interviews

Suggestions for working with members of different ethnic, cultural, and social class groups include studying the culture, language, and traditions of other groups; learning about your own stereotypes and prejudices; seeing the strengths in the coping mechanisms of other groups; appreciating the interviewee's viewpoint and showing a willingness to accept a perspective other than your own; recognizing when group membership differences may be intruding on the communication process; and finding ways to circumvent potential difficulties.

It is important to monitor verbal and nonverbal communications. Do not use words or expressions that may offend the interviewee. Study your nonverbal behavior to see if it changes depending on the ethnicity of the interviewee. For example, if you are a nonminority interviewer and work with both minority and nonminority interviewees, you may find that you are placing yourself further away from the minority interviewees, spending less time with them, or making more speech errors with them. If so, you may be revealing signs of anxiety or avoidance behavior. Videotape your interviews and study them carefully for signs of communication difficulties.

The quality of communications can be improved by establishing trust. In order for trust to develop, the interviewee must perceive that you possess expert knowledge, are a person who can be relied on, and are a person who has good intentions toward him or her. Unless mutual trust can be established, the clinical assessment interview is doomed to failure.

OTHER CONSIDERATIONS RELATED TO INTERVIEWING

External Factors and Atmosphere

The room in which the interview is conducted should be quiet and free from distractions. Interruptions should be held to a minimum, if they cannot be avoided entirely. Telephone interruptions are particularly troublesome. If possible, calls should be held at the switchboard or reception desk or the phone unplugged. If you need to answer the phone, inform the caller that you are busy and will call back. Obviously, you should not be glancing at your mail or eating lunch during the interview. Always begin the interview at the scheduled time. If more time is needed to complete the interview, inform the interviewee. You might say "Mrs. Smith, we have about 5 minutes left. Since we need more time, let's schedule another meeting next Tuesday at the same time, if that is convenient for you."

Recording Information

You can use various procedures to record information. It is difficult, if not impossible, to record every word that the interviewee says, unless you are skilled at shorthand or use a tape recorder. Tape recorders frequently are used during training periods, but less often by skilled clinicians. In taking notes you can paraphrase the interviewee's communications or use various formal or informal shorthand techniques. No matter what method you use to record the interview, inform the interviewee of your need to record.

If you take notes, do not let note-taking interfere with your listening to the interviewee. Do not hide behind your notes ("Let me see my notes about that matter") or use them in a secretive way. Also, be sure to maintain frequent eye contact with the interviewee. If the interviewee speaks too quickly and this interferes with your note-taking, you may say "Please talk more slowly so that I can write down your important ideas." Such a remark, however, may interfere with the flow of conversation. Consequently, make it only when you cannot adjust to the interviewee's tempo.

Scheduling

If you have a heavy interview or assessment schedule, arrange to have some time between sessions to make notes and relax for a few minutes. If there is no break, you may still be thinking of the previous interview while you are conducting the next one.

RELIABILITY AND VALIDITY OF THE INTERVIEW

The interview, like any other assessment technique, must be evaluated for reliability and validity. The reliability of the interview is related to such factors as the following (Mash & Terdal, 1981, p. 46, with changes in notation):

• whether information obtained on one occasion is comparable to information that was or would have been obtained on other occasions from the same interviewee (*test-retest reliability*)
• whether information obtained from the interviewee is comparable to information obtained from another informant—for example, child versus mother (*interobserver agreement*)
• whether the information given by the interviewee is consistent with other information given by the interviewee in the same interview (*internal consistency*)
• whether the information obtained by one interviewer is comparable to that obtained by another interviewer with the same interviewee (*method error*)

Validity of the interview refers to such issues as (Mash & Terdal, 1981, p. 47, italics added) "(1) the extent to which interview information corresponds to that obtained through other methods (*concurrent validity*) and (2) the degree to which interview information predicts either treatment plan or treatment outcome (*predictive validity*)."

The reliability and the validity of interview data are often difficult to evaluate because of the diverse nature of interviews (Bellack & Hersen, 1980). Because the interview yields data in a variety of areas (including demographic information, developmental history, observational impressions, and diagnostic impressions), a number of separate evaluations are required. In addition, because interviews are highly dependent on the specific interviewer, the specific interviewee, the type of interview, and the conditions under which the interview took place, the interaction of these factors with the various interview data must be considered in evaluating the reliability and validity of the data. In spite of all these difficulties, the assessment of reliability and validity is just as important with interview measures as it is with any other type of measure.

Bias Associated with Interviewees

The validity of the information obtained in an interview is dependent on the accuracy of the interviewee's information (Bellack & Hersen, 1980). Interviewees who appear voluntarily for help are likely to provide more accurate information than are individuals who are forced or coerced to come for evaluations. But even the reports of those clients who try to be accurate may be subject to distortion stemming from bias, selective memory, or even evasion. For example, what interviewees say occurred may not be what actually occurred because people tend to interpret their behavior in a manner consistent with the image they have of themselves. Interviewees may have difficulty finding the correct words to describe previous events, or their memories of important developmental milestones may be faulty. When the reliability and the validity of an interview are not satisfactory, information must be sifted and weighed to arrive at a meaningful picture of the child, parents, teachers, and others. Reliability of the material can be checked indirectly by asking questions in different ways or at different times, or by asking two or more interviewees the same questions.

Bias and Errors Associated with Interviewers

The interview is extremely susceptible to interviewer bias. Interviewer bias refers to the interviewer's unintentionally encouraging or discouraging the expression of certain facts or opinions, causing interviewees to distort their communications to please the interviewer. The interviewee's responses can be influenced by the way in which you word a question, your choice of follow-up responses, the tone of voice you use when asking questions and responding to the interviewee's communications, your facial expressions (particularly those associated with responses from the interviewee), your posture, and other verbal and nonverbal means. Interviewer bias may be associated with the way in which you ask questions, probe, or motivate interviewees. In some cases, you may not even recognize that you are sending biasing signals to the interviewee.

Bias can also occur in subtle ways over which you have little control. In cross-ethnic or cross-class situations, as noted earlier, both interviewees and interviewers may distort their replies simply because of racial or class differences. If the interviewee desires help with a particular problem or if the interviewer is aware of the cross-ethnic or cross-class dynamics, less distortion is likely to be present.

During the interview be aware of your own reactions and how your values are communicated to the interviewees. Interviewees will use cues from your verbal and nonverbal behavior to form impressions of you, just as you use cues from these sources to form impressions of them. Your values are communicated during the interview by the types of questions you ask, the comments you make, and your nonverbal behavior. Your nonverbal behavior, as we have seen, also conveys your reactions to the interviewee. Al-

though reactive effects cannot be eliminated, they can be reduced. Clearly identifying your values and objectives and becoming aware of your nonverbal behavior are the first steps in reducing the influence of reactive effects. The most important principle is to be aware *not only of the interviewee's communications and your reactions to them, but also of your own communications and how they may be perceived by the interviewee.*

Other Types of Interviewer Errors

In addition to errors associated with interviewer bias, other types of interviewer errors include recording errors and errors associated with making inferences beyond the obtained data. To reduce recording errors, listen carefully to what the interviewee says and check your notes shortly after the interview is over. If you do not take notes, record (by writing or tape recorder) the information and your impressions as soon as possible after the interview. If there is a lapse in time, important facts and impressions may be forgotten. To reduce errors associated with improper inferences, carefully study all sources of information for corroborating facts.

Comment on the Reliability and Validity of the Interview

In general, the interviewer may introduce errors into the interview process by failing to develop rapport, gather sufficient information to reach valid conclusions, monitor his or her own verbal and nonverbal behavior, interpret accurately the interviewee's verbal and nonverbal behavior, and use good interviewing skills. The validity of an interview can be increased by cross-validating inferences and predictions and by conducting the interview in as objective a manner as possible. In case of any doubts about your findings, make arrangements to have the interviewee interviewed by another interviewer and then compare the results of the two interviews.

You are likely to encounter situations in which you receive conflicting information from different interviewees. Discrepancies may occur between the reports provided by child and parent, teacher and parent, child and teacher, or even two parents. Children and parents agree *least often* about the presence, severity, and duration of the child's symptoms; agreement is higher on overt, easily observable behaviors (such as behavior and conduct problems) than on more covert and private phenomena (such as anxiety, fear, and obsessions) (Edelbrock, Costello, Dulcan, Conover, & Kalas, 1986). Parents are more reliable (r's = .73 to .76) than children (r's = .43 to .71) in reporting a child's symptoms, and children aged 6 to 9 years

(r = .43) are less reliable than children aged 10 to 18 years (r's = .60 to .71) (Edelbrock, Costello, Dulcan, Kalas, & Conover, 1985). Children aged 6 to 9 years do not appear to be reliable informants, except with respect to simple fears. Consequently, the symptoms reported by children under 10 years of age should not be taken at face value. Adolescents' reports are more reliable; their improved cognitive, memory, and language skills enable them to respond more accurately to interview questions that require self-awareness, perspective taking, recall, reasoning ability, and expressive skill. Whenever you get conflicting information from two or more informants, further inquiry may be needed.

CONFIDENTIALITY OF THE INTERVIEW MATERIAL AND ASSESSMENT FINDINGS

The best sources for guidelines on the confidentiality of assessment results are the *Ethical Principles of Psychologists* of the American Psychological Association and the laws of your state. There is a subtle distinction between confidentiality and privileged communication. *Confidentiality* is an ethical practice: the obligation to never reveal information obtained in the assessment (or through any professional relationship) without specific consent from the client. It protects the client from any unauthorized disclosures of information given in confidence to the psychologist. *Privileged communication* is a legal right granted by a state's legal code to psychologists (and others, such as attorneys, clergy, and physicians) that constrains them from disclosing information about a client, without permission, during legal proceedings (check your state law). It protects the client from having his or her confidences revealed in public. Although there are no clear guidelines about confidentiality with respect to the communications of children, a client older than 16 years of age is entitled to the same confidential relationship as is an adult client. This means that test scores and other diagnostic data should not be disclosed to others without the minor's consent.

Exceptions to Confidentiality and Privileged Communication

There are occasions when confidentiality and privileged communication must be suspended (in each case, check your state law):

1. *When there is suspicion of child abuse, you may be legally obliged to report it to the authorities.*

2. *When the interviewee poses a threat to another person, you must consider warning the prospective victim.*

3. *When the interviewee is a minor and poses a threat to himself or herself (for example, the suicidal child), you may be required to notify those responsible for the child.*

These first three exceptions involve the principle that *when there is a clear and imminent danger to another individual or to society or to the child directly, confidentiality may have to be breached.* Accurate predictions of dangerous behavior are extremely rare, however, and studies indicate that mental health professionals tend to vastly overpredict dangerousness (Butcher, Stelmachers, & Maudal, 1983). You must use considerable judgment in determining when a dangerous situation exists.

4. *If you are in private practice, you can release records only with the consent of the parents.*

In schools, clinics, hospitals, prisons, and other agencies, however, agency personnel involved in the case usually have access to the records. Interviewees must be apprised of this fact if they inquire. If a child asks about parental rights to the records, check your state law to determine whether or not you are legally obligated to inform the parents of the assessment results. Parents *do* have the right to obtain a copy of a school psychological report, for they have the right to see any information that is shared with others. However, psychologists need not reveal their private notes to parents so long as the notes have not been revealed to other professionals.

Releasing Information in Cases of Divorce

In cases where parents are divorced, consult the managing custodial parent before you release any information to the other parent. When the custodial parent does not give permission to share the assessment findings with the other parent, check your state law. State law generally indicates that a noncustodial parent *does* have the right to request a psychological evaluation and to receive a report as long as he or she has visitation rights (Overcast, Sales, & Kesler, 1983). If the law is not clear about this matter, check with your state psychological association or your school administrators.

THE CLINICAL ASSESSMENT INTERVIEW VS. THE PSYCHOTHERAPEUTIC INTERVIEW

In reading this chapter on clinical assessment interviewing, you may have wondered how assessment interviewing differs from psychotherapeutic interviewing. Both types of interviews share a number of similarities; there are also important differences.

DIFFERENCES

1. *Goals*. The purpose of the clinical assessment interview is to obtain relevant information in order to make an informed decision about the interviewee (for example, whether there is a problem and what type of treatment may be needed). The clinical assessment interview is not an open-ended, client-centered counseling session—there is an agenda to be covered. The function of the psychotherapeutic interview, in contrast, is to relieve the client's emotional distress, foster insight, and bring about changes in behavior. In this process information will also be collected and treatment strategies formulated.

2. *Direction and structure*. The clinical assessment interview may focus on developmental history, social history, mental status evaluation, or a detailed description of a specific problem. In such cases, a specific set of topics or questions may be covered. In the psychotherapeutic interview, techniques are used to bring about therapeutic goals. The specific direction and structure are dependent on the therapeutic approach.

3. *Contact time*. Although the clinical assessment interview usually covers approximately 50 to 60 minutes, the length of time may vary. In some cases there is no expectation that the interviewer will see the interviewee again. Psychotherapeutic interviews, in contrast, run a specific length of time, and the therapist usually will see the interviewee over a period of weeks, months, or years.

SIMILARITIES

1. *Rapport*. In both types of interviews, it is essential to establish an accepting atmosphere wherein the interviewee feels comfortable in talking about himself or herself. This requires the communication of respect, genuineness, and empathy.

2. *Skills*. Both types of interviews require a knowledge of psychopathology and skills in listening, attending, and reflecting feelings and content.

3. *Goals*. In both types of interviews, affect and content are assessed continuously while information is being gathered.

Clinical assessment interviewing and psychotherapeutic interviewing are not mutually exclusive (see Figure 16-1 for a summary of similarities and differences). If you are conducting a psychotherapeutic interview, you invariably must be alert to the need for continuing assessment strategies and goals. If you are in an assessment mode and the interviewee is so distraught that he or she cannot speak or concentrate, then a more psychotherapeutic strategy may be required.

EVALUATING YOUR INTERVIEW TECHNIQUES

This chapter has presented some general guidelines that should lead to successful assessment interviewing. The guidelines are not meant to be followed rigidly or to cover every possible contingency. Human relationships are

ASSESSMENT INTERVIEW OBJECTIVES	SIMILARITIES	PSYCHOTHERAPEUTIC INTERVIEW OBJECTIVES
1. To obtain relevant information and to arrive at a decision (for example, diagnosis, need for referral, type of treatment or remediation needed)	1. To establish rapport 2. To facilitate communication 3. To communicate respect, genuineness, and empathy	1. To foster behavioral, cognitive, and affective change
2. To cover specific content areas (for example, developmental history, social history, mental status evaluation, analysis of problem behavior) (*focus more on content domain*)	4. To attend, listen, and reflect feelings and content 5. To gather information 6. To allow interviewee to reveal concerns and preoccupations	2. To use approaches geared to therapeutic goals (*focus more on affective domain*)
3. To limit contact—usually to one or two sessions	7. To assess interviewee's verbal and nonverbal communications	3. To maintain contact—usually over a period of weeks, months, or years

Figure 16-1.   Schematic diagram of differences and similarities between assessment interviews and psychotherapeutic interviews.

unique, and a "cookbook" of techniques is neither possible nor desirable. You must be the judge of how, when, and where to use a particular procedure.

It is important, particularly during your training period, to evaluate your interview techniques. One way to conduct a self-evaluation is simply to think about and evaluate the interview shortly after it is completed. Or you can record a number of interviews on either audiotape or videotape and then study the interviews. In reviewing videotapes, evaluate the extent to which you maintained good eye contact, good posture, appropriate gestures, and other appropriate nonverbal behaviors. Both audiotapes and videotapes give you the opportunity to study your diction, speech intensity, and other voice and speech characteristics. In addition, you can analyze carefully the types of verbal interactions that occurred in the interview. Bergan's (1977) classification system will be helpful in this regard. Reviewing your tape recordings with someone who has greater expertise in interviewing can also be beneficial.

The following list of questions provides some general guidelines for evaluating your role in the interview.

SELF-EVALUATION OF THE INTERVIEW

1. Did I handle the opening minutes of the interview adequately?
2. Was my vocabulary appropriate?
3. Did the interviewee have difficulty in understanding my questions?
4. Were my follow-up questions appropriate?
5. Did I follow up all important leads?
6. Did I make any stereotyped comments?
7. Did I use open-ended questions?
8. Did I change topics abruptly?
9. Was I over-controlling?
10. Was I impatient?
11. How was my diction?
12. Was I alert to the interviewee's nonverbal behavior?
13. Was I aware of my own nonverbal behavior?
14. Did I establish and maintain rapport?
15. Was I attentive to the interviewee?
16. Did I daydream or let my mind wander?
17. Did I convey to the interviewee that I wanted to understand him or her?
18. Was I willing to suspend judgment about the interviewee until the interview was over?
19. Were my comments and techniques—such as reflection, praise, and support—successful in motivating the interviewee and in guiding the interviewee to discuss appropriate material?
20. Which techniques, if any, were most successful?
21. How did I handle silences?
22. How did I feel during the silences?
23. How did I handle resistance?
24. How did I handle affective reactions?
25. Was there any material discussed by the interviewee that made me anxious?
26. Did I avoid certain topics?
27. Was I able to take rebuffs without undue anxiety?
28. Was I able to keep my personal needs in the background?
29. Was I able to answer the interviewee's questions?
30. How did I handle personal questions that were asked about me?
31. Did I handle the closing minutes of the interview adequately?
32. Did the interview proceed smoothly?
33. Did the interview accomplish its goals?

If you gave negative answers to any of these questions, try to determine why, when, and where the difficulty occurred and what you can do to improve your interview techniques. For example, if you daydreamed, try to determine why. During what part of the interview did the daydreaming occur? What content was being covered? Did you have other problems with similar content? Was the content of your daydream related to the interviewee's communications in some way? Probing questions should be asked for every technique problem uncovered by your self-evaluation. You may find the interview checklist shown in Table 16-21 helpful in evaluating your interview techniques. It includes some of the questions listed above, but contains additional items as well.

KORCHIN'S OVERVIEW OF THE ASSESSMENT INTERVIEW

Korchin's (1976, pp. 192–193, with changes in notation) overview of the assessment interview provides a fitting end to this chapter. He points out both the virtues and limitations of the assessment interview, and reminds us of how important it is for each interviewer to be fully aware of his or her own role in the interview process.

The interview remains the most basic, most commonly used, and most powerful technique of clinical assessment. Compared to any standardized test, it is an instrument of great flexibility and breadth. It can potentially cover a greater range of information, and as individually relevant themes emerge the course of inquiry can be redirected and refocused. Language and question form can accommodate to the interviewee's communication style; so too the pace, intensity, and duration of the transaction to his or her emotional needs. For most people, the interview is a natural

Table 16-21
Interview Techniques Checklist

Name of Interviewer: _____   Date of Interview: _____
Name of Interviewee: _____   Rater's Name: _____

Rating Key: 1 = excellent demonstration of this skill
              2 = good demonstration of this skill
              3 = fair demonstration of this skill
              4 = poor demonstration of this skill
              5 = very poor demonstration of this skill
              NA = not applicable

Item	*Rating*
1. Created a positive interview climate	1 2 3 4 5 NA
2. Showed respect for and attention to interviewee	1 2 3 4 5 NA
3. Used good diction	1 2 3 4 5 NA
4. Used vocabulary understandable to interviewee	1 2 3 4 5 NA
5. Formulated appropriate general questions	1 2 3 4 5 NA
6. Formulated appropriate open-ended questions	1 2 3 4 5 NA
7. Formulated appropriate follow-up questions	1 2 3 4 5 NA
8. Used appropriate structuring statements	1 2 3 4 5 NA
9. Encouraged appropriate replies	1 2 3 4 5 NA
10. Used probes effectively	1 2 3 4 5 NA
11. Allowed interviewee to express feelings and thoughts in his or her own way	1 2 3 4 5 NA
12. Was alert to interviewee's nonverbal behavior	1 2 3 4 5 NA
13. Conveyed to interviewee a desire to understand him or her	1 2 3 4 5 NA
14. Rephrased questions appropriately	1 2 3 4 5 NA
15. Used reflection appropriately	1 2 3 4 5 NA
16. Used feedback appropriately	1 2 3 4 5 NA
17. Handled minimally communicative interviewee appropriately	1 2 3 4 5 NA
18. Handled interviewee's resistance and anxiety appropriately	1 2 3 4 5 NA
19. Clarified areas of confusion in interviewee's statements	1 2 3 4 5 NA
20. Intervened appropriately when interviewee had difficulty expressing thoughts	1 2 3 4 5 NA
21. Handled rambling communications appropriately	1 2 3 4 5 NA
22. Tolerated difficult behavior in interview	1 2 3 4 5 NA
23. Used props, crayons, clay, or toys appropriately	1 2 3 4 5 NA
24. Timed questions appropriately	1 2 3 4 5 NA
25. Handled silences appropriately	1 2 3 4 5 NA
26. Used periodic summaries appropriately	1 2 3 4 5 NA
27. Made clear transitions	1 2 3 4 5 NA
28. Paced interview appropriately	1 2 3 4 5 NA
29. Maintained appropriate eye contact	1 2 3 4 5 NA
30. Used own nonverbal behavior appropriately	1 2 3 4 5 NA
31. Responded in nonjudgmental manner	1 2 3 4 5 NA
32. Handled interviewee's questions and concerns appropriately	1 2 3 4 5 NA
33. Allowed interviewee to express remaining thoughts and questions at close of interview	1 2 3 4 5 NA
34. Arranged for post-assessment interview	1 2 3 4 5 NA
35. Used appropriate closing statements	1 2 3 4 5 NA
36. Conducted an appropriate interview overall	1 2 3 4 5 NA

37. Comments: _____
_____
_____

situation, for it resembles the conversations of ordinary social life, and, unlike psychological tests, entails no apparatus nor artificial tasks, nor does it as readily suggest the pass/fail evaluation of school testing. As participant-observer, the interviewer both stimulates and records the behavior of the interviewees; though enmeshed in the situation, he or she has control over it. Finally, the interview serves nonassessment purposes vital to the clinical process.

The very strengths of the interview are also its weaknesses, when considered as a method of psychological measurement. Flexibility and breadth allow unreliability and bias. Although there have been many salutary efforts to develop standardized procedures for special purposes, in daily clinical use the lack of standardization, which confounds the psychometrically minded psychologist, also makes possible the desirable properties of the interview. Undoubtedly, assessment interviewing will continue to be a major tool of clinicians; their obligation is to sharpen their understanding of the essential processes involved and of their own contribution to the (in)validity of the resultant findings. Because the clinician is at once stimulus to, observer of, and interpreter of the interviewee's state, the interview is the most difficult of assessment methods.

SUMMARY

1. The clinical assessment interview is an important part of the assessment process. Information obtained from the interview may provide insight into the interviewee's personality, temperament, and lifestyle.

2. Clinical assessment interviews require knowledge of personality theory, psychopathology, family dynamics, and interpersonal communication.

3. In contrast with a conversation, the clinical assessment interview has a definite purpose, requires the interviewer to take responsibility for the interaction, involves a nonreciprocal relationship, is planned, is available to interviewees who request it, requires sustained attention, is a formally arranged meeting, and does not avoid unpleasant facts and feelings.

4. The clinical assessment interview also differs from the nonclinical interview, particularly in that it has more significant consequences for the interviewee.

5. Interviews allow the interviewer to motivate the interviewee, to be flexible in questioning, to resolve ambiguous responses, to clarify misunderstandings, to document the context and chronicity of the interviewee's problem behaviors, to direct the flow of conversation, to use verbal and nonverbal cues to evaluate the validity of the information, to learn about the interviewee's beliefs, and to assess the interviewee's receptivity to recommendations.

6. The reliability and validity of interviews are difficult to establish. Interviews are extremely susceptible to interviewer bias.

7. The ability to *listen* actively is a key factor in conducting the interview.

8. Observation of the interviewee's voice, speech, and nonverbal behavior may provide valuable diagnostic clues.

9. Useful interviewing strategies include establishing rapport, using the interviewee's natural spontaneity, using an appropriate vocabulary, clarifying the interviewee's terms, formulating appropriate questions, using structuring statements, encouraging appropriate replies, using probes effectively, using reflection and feedback, timing questions appropriately, changing topics effectively, tolerating difficult behavior, handling silences effectively, analyzing information critically, handling self-disclosures effectively, widening the circle of inquiry effectively, keeping one's emotions under control, obtaining useful leads from communication patterns, and using summary statements.

10. Successful interviewers know themselves, trust their ideas, acknowledge their mistakes, desire to help people, track with the interviewee, receive information accurately, evaluate critically the information received, and regulate their own verbal and nonverbal behavior.

11. In the initial interview, the interviewer obtains information, describes the assessment procedures, and forms opinions.

12. In interviewing children, it is important to observe the child-parent(s) relationship in the waiting room, recognize children's possible apprehensions, and be aware of how the child's developmental level and type of behavioral disturbance may affect the conduct of the interview.

13. Useful strategies for interviewing children include formulating appropriate opening statements; using descriptive comments; using reflection; giving praise frequently; avoiding critical statements; using open-ended questions; formulating questions in the subjunctive mood when necessary; exercising tact; using props to help young children communicate verbally; using special techniques to facilitate the expression of culturally unacceptable responses; clarifying an episode of misbehavior by recounting it; handling minimally communicative children by clarifying interview procedures; understanding silence; handling resistance and anxiety by giving support and reassurance; using understandable language; participating actively; and helping the child understand the reasons for the interview.

14. Subjects covered in interviews with children include the referral problem, interests, school, peers, family, fears/worries, self-image, mood/feelings, somatic concerns, thought disorders, aspirations, and fantasies. With adolescents, heterosexual relationships, sexual activity, and drug/alcohol use are included in addition.

15. Areas evaluated in a traditional mental status interview should be considered during any interview—the interviewee's appearance and behavior, speech and communications, content of thought, sensory and motor functioning, cognitive functioning, emotional functioning, and insight and judgment.

16. Subjects covered in parent interviews include the referral problem; ways in which the problem has been dealt with; the child's medical, developmental, educational, and social history; family history; prior treatment for the problem; results of past treatment; and expectations and desires about the current evaluation.

17. In interviewing parents, it is important to watch for any negative feelings that parents may have about coming to the interview.

18. Various formats can be used to interview parents. They include the open-ended interview, the Background Questionnaire, and the behavior rating checklist.

19. Subjects covered in teacher interviews include the referral problem, antecedents and consequences of the problem, ways in which the problem has been dealt with, how other children and teachers react to the child and problem, the child's academic performance, the teacher's view of the family, and the teacher's expectations and suggestions.

20. Family interviews provide valuable information about the child's problems, family dynamics, family communication patterns, and family social and cultural values. In addition, they present an opportunity to compare how the child acts in individual and group situations.

21. Useful techniques in family interviewing include encouraging open discussion, supporting members who are on the "hot seat," helping members to express their views, and being a neutral participant.

22. Ending an initial interview requires careful attention to the interviewee's feelings and needs. Gauge the time carefully. Permit the interviewee to ask questions. Summarize, if appropriate, the major concerns expressed by the interviewee. With children especially, acknowledge those who were cooperative and open. Similarly, express your desire that those who were uncooperative will improve during subsequent visits.

23. After the interview has been completed, it is important to evaluate your reactions and feelings and synthesize the information that you have obtained from the various sources. Look for common themes that run through the interview. When discrepancies appear, try to account for them. Look for themes related to the interviewee's strengths and weaknesses, resources for change and for coping with stress, and manifestations of psychopathology.

24. Post-assessment interviews with children allow the interviewer to provide reassurance, to check hypotheses, and to present the findings, depending on the child's age.

25. Conducting the post-assessment interview with parents requires sensitivity to their feelings and needs as well as recognition of older children's right to confidentiality.

26. Goals of the post-assessment interview with parents include thoroughly describing the child's problem, planning a program, dealing with parental problems as they concern the child, and planning for periodic consultation. Strive to ensure that the parents understand the findings and recommendations.

27. In the event that parents are informed that their child has a handicapping condition, the interviewer must be prepared to deal with a variety of parental reactions. Use the findings to help parents give up erroneous ideas and adopt a realistic approach to their child's problems. Encourage the parents to formulate a plan of action. Discuss with the parents all aspects of the treatment plan, including type of treatment, length of treatment, and finan-

cial costs. Inform them of their rights under Public Law 94-142 and of your availability for further discussion.

28. Structured clinical interviews are especially useful when the primary goal of the interview is to obtain a psychiatric diagnosis or when all interviewees must be asked the same set of questions. Semi-structured interviews cover a specific set of topics; they allow for more flexibility than do highly structured interviews.

29. Cross-ethnic, cross-cultural, and cross-class interviews require particular skills. Ethnic, cultural, or class differences between interviewer and interviewee may lead to communication difficulties and to a variety of misinterpretations. Ways to improve cross-ethnic, cross-cultural, and cross-class interviewing include learning about different cultures, learning about one's own stereotypes and prejudices, valuing the coping patterns of other groups, appreciating the perspectives of different groups, recognizing when cultural factors are intruding on the interview process, and finding ways to deal with intrusions. Trust is a key element in cross-ethnic, cross-cultural, and cross-class interviews.

30. Other considerations in interviewing include conducting the interview in a quiet room, recording information unobtrusively, and scheduling breaks between interviews.

31. The reliability and validity of all interview findings should be evaluated. Be careful not to bias the interview through subtle verbal or nonverbal behaviors. Be aware not only of the interviewee's behavior, but of your behavior as well. Try to reduce or eliminate recording errors. Do not make improper inferences. Cross-validate inferences and conduct the interview in an objective manner to increase the validity of your findings.

32. The interviewer is obliged to preserve the confidentiality of the interview material, except when compelled by state law to reveal the findings. Confidentiality is an ethical obligation not to reveal information without the express consent of the interviewee. Privileged communication is a legal right incorporated into a state legal code that requires a psychologist (and designated others) not to disclose information, without the client's permission, during a legal proceeding. However, states may require a psychologist to break confidentiality when there is suspicion of child abuse, when the interviewee poses a threat to another person, or when an interviewee of minor age poses a threat to himself or herself.

33. Clinical assessment interviewing and psychotherapeutic interviewing both involve establishing rapport, facilitating communication, communicating respect, attending, gathering information, and assessing verbal and nonverbal communications. Because the goal of the assessment interview is to arrive at a decision, detailed information is obtained, specific content is covered, and contact is limited to a brief period of time. Because the goal of the psychotherapeutic interview, in contrast, is to foster behavioral, cognitive, and affective change, therapeutic approaches are used and contact is maintained over a period of time.

34. Particularly during training, an interviewer should evalu-

ate his or her interview techniques after completing each interview.

35. The interview holds much potential as an assessment method, but its success is strongly dependent on the interviewer's skills.

KEY TERMS, CONCEPTS, AND NAMES

Referral question (p. 401)
Art of listening (p. 402)
Neologisms (p. 403)
Echolalia (p. 403)
Clang associations (p. 403)
Rapport (p. 404)
Broad questions (p. 406)
Narrow questions (p. 406)
Clarification (p. 406)
Number-of-alternative questions (p. 407)
Random probing (p. 407)
Coercive questioning (p. 407)
Structuring statements (p. 408)
Probing questions (p. 408)
Leading questions (p. 409)
Reflection (p. 409)
Feedback (p. 409)
Timing of questions (p. 410)
Self-disclosure (p. 412)
Association of ideas (p. 412)
Shifts in conversation (p. 412)
Opening and closing sentences (p. 412)
Recurrent references (p. 412)
Inconsistencies and gaps (p. 412)
Concealed meanings (p. 412)
Summary statements (p. 412)
Initial interview (p. 413)
Mental status interview (p. 428)
Post-assessment interview (p. 451)
"Shop around" (p. 456)
Semi-structured interview format (p. 458)
Highly structured interview format (p. 458)
Cross-ethnic, cross-cultural, and cross-class interviews (p. 461)
Test-retest reliability (p. 463)
Interobserver agreement (p. 463)
Internal consistency (p. 463)
Method error (p. 463)
Concurrent validity (p. 463)
Predictive validity (p. 463)
Bias (p. 463)
Confidentiality (p. 465)
Privileged communication (p. 465)
Psychotherapeutic interview (p. 465)

STUDY QUESTIONS

1. How is a clinical assessment interview different from a conversation and from a non-clinical interview?

2. What are some advantages and disadvantages associated with interviews?

3. What are some factors to observe in the interviewee's voice and speech and nonverbal behavior?

4. What are some factors to consider in (a) establishing rapport, (b) formulating appropriate questions, (c) using structuring statements, (d) formulating probing questions, (e) using reflection and feedback, (f) changing topics, (g) tolerating difficult behavior, (h) handling silences, and (i) handling self-disclosures?

5. What are some ways to obtain useful leads from communication patterns?

6. What are some guidelines that can assist you in becoming a skilled interviewer?

7. Discuss the aims of the initial interview and how to generate hypotheses from the initial interview.

8. What are some factors to consider and areas to cover in interviewing children?

9. Discuss eight useful techniques for interviewing children.

10. What are the seven areas evaluated in a mental status interview? Briefly discuss important factors to evaluate in each area.

11. What are some factors to consider in interviewing parents? Include in your discussion various interview formats and areas typically covered in a developmental case history.

12. What are some factors to consider in interviewing teachers?

13. Discuss procedures for interviewing families. Include in your discussion phases of the family assessment interview.

14. Discuss the closing phase of the initial interview.

15. Compare and contrast initial interviews with children, parents, teachers, and families.

16. What factors should be considered in evaluating the information obtained in the interview? Give specific examples in your discussion.

17. Discuss the post-assessment interview with parents. Include in your discussion the four phases of the post-assessment interview.

18. Discuss the possible reactions parents may have upon learning that their child has a handicap.

19. Compare structured clinical interviews with nonstructured clinical interviews.

20. Discuss cross-ethnic, cross-cultural, and cross-class interviewing.

21. Discuss the reliability and validity of the interview.

22. Discuss confidentiality of the interview material.

23. Compare the clinical assessment interview with the psychotherapeutic interview.

24. What factors should you consider in evaluating your interview techniques?

_ 17

ASSESSMENT OF BEHAVIOR BY OBSERVATIONAL METHODS

I assume that some people may find themselves temperamentally more suited to systematic observation than others. But I also assume that anybody can be trained to be a better questioner, a more careful methodologist, a more nuanced paraphraser, a more patient observer, a more subtle student of everyday life, a more complicated person capable of registering more of the complications in the world.

—Karl E. Weick

Observers, then, must be photographers of phenomena; their observations must accurately represent nature. We must observe without any preconceived idea; the observer's mind must be passive, that is, must hold its peace; it listens to nature and writes at nature's dictation.

—Claude Bernard

Observing the behavior of children in natural settings is an important part of the clinical and psychoeducational assessment process. Observations add a personalized idiographic dimension to the assessment process, particularly when they are used in conjunction with objective and projective tests, behavior checklists, questionnaires, interviews, and other assessment procedures. Behavioral observation serves the following valuable functions in the assessment process:

1. It provides a picture of the child's spontaneous behavior in everyday life settings, such as the classroom, playground, home, or hospital ward, or in specially designed settings, such as a clinic playroom.

2. It provides information about the child's interpersonal behavior and learning style.

3. It provides a systematic record of both the child's behaviors and the behaviors of others that can be used for evaluation and intervention planning.

4. It allows for verification of the accuracy of parental and teacher reports regarding the child's behavior.

5. It allows for comparisons between behavior in the test situation and behavior in more naturalistic settings.

6. It is especially useful in the study of young children and developmentally disabled children who may not be easily evaluated by other procedures.

There is almost no limit to the features that can be developed in observational systems. Various levels of analysis can be combined with qualitative and quantitative components of behavior to allow for diversity of features. The procedures may also be uniquely tailored to one child.

The information obtained from the observation of behavior will help you to evaluate the concerns of the referral source, arrive at a diagnosis of the child, provide feedback and suggestions for behavioral change, and monitor the efficacy of various intervention strategies.

Let us look at an example of how behavioral observations can assist in the assessment process. Suppose Bill has been referred to you because of aggressive behavior in class. In addition to carrying out the psychometric assessment and interviews, you decide to visit the classroom a few times to observe Bill and the class. You observe that Bill's aggressive behavior occurs only *after* other children instigate some hostile act directed at him, such as taking away his pencil or kicking his chair. The psychometric and interview data allow you to rule out psychopathology, brain damage, and familial instability. With this information, you can help the teacher understand Bill's behavior. Perhaps simply moving Bill to a part of the room where the children are more supportive might be sufficient to reduce his aggressive behavior. This example shows how observa-

tion of behavior can be used to support and extend the psychometric data so that you obtain a better picture of the child's behavior and can formulate meaningful recommendations.

To be useful scientifically as an assessment procedure, the systematic observation of behavior must have a goal, a focus, limits on the amount of data collected, a standardized recording method, sufficient reliability, and adequate validity. These elements can be achieved by careful attention to the child, the family, the school, the community, and the referral source and by a study of the observational methods covered in this chapter and in other sources.

USING OBSERVATIONAL METHODS

In the systematic observation of behavior, a trained observer watches behavior in natural settings, records or classifies each behavior objectively as it occurs or shortly thereafter, ensures that the obtained data are replicable, and converts the data into quantitative information. Behavioral observations may be used to obtain global impressions, rate and record a variety of behaviors, or focus on specific problematic behaviors (such as aggressive, inattentive, or hyperactive behaviors) identified earlier by means of general observation, interviews, checklists, or reports.

Although the scientific principles on which systematic behavioral observation is based ensure the highest possible degree of accuracy and precision, it is never possible to capture entirely all of the behavior exhibited by a child during a period of observation. Thus judgments must be made about what behavior should be observed and how it should be recorded. *The assumption behind the sampling of behavior is that the behaviors recorded over a period of time will constitute a representative sample of the behaviors under observation in the setting.*

To be a skilled observer, you need the ability to understand behavioral codes, to distinguish one behavior from another, to sustain attention, to be attentive to fine detail, to react quickly, and to summarize behavioral samples verbally. Sensitivity, acuity, and perceptiveness are keys to becoming a skilled observer. This chapter covers the principles of behavioral observation and provides exercises to help you develop skills that you can apply to observing a wide range of human behavior in a multitude of settings.

Defining Observed Behaviors

The behaviors that are to be observed must be defined in objective, clear, and complete terms. Definitions should help the observer to recognize when the behavior is occurring and to distinguish it from other similar behaviors. Some behaviors are easier to define than others. For example, crying—which can be defined as a vocal noise that is loud enough to be heard and does not involve recognizable words—is easier to define than sharing. Workable definitions can be arrived at by focusing on the specific behaviors involved in sharing—such as when the observed child gives a toy or other object to another child, allows another child to sit on the same mat, or gives a piece of candy to another child. Replacing imprecise or vague terms with exact words or descriptions will help to define the behaviors of interest.

Conducting Observations in Sequence

In some situations you may want to begin your observations using global (general) coding categories. This approach would be appropriate, for example, if you were asked to observe a child who was having problems in school. After carefully observing the child's behavior during various classes and times of the day, you might note specific behaviors that you wanted to observe more closely. Further observations would then be directed to the specific behaviors of interest.

When you first observe a child referred for a particular behavioral problem, do not focus exclusively on that problem. At least during the preliminary observation period, try to obtain a complete and thorough record of the child's behavior and of other children's and adults' behavior in the setting. This is important for a number of reasons (Nay, 1979). First, it gives you the opportunity to observe other potentially important behaviors. Second, it places the problem behavior in the context of other behaviors. And, finally, it allows you to evaluate the referred child's behavior in the context of other individuals' behavior in that setting.

Timing Observation Periods

Once you have defined the specific behaviors to be observed, make sure that you select an appropriate observation period, in which the ongoing activity is not incompatible with the target behavior. If, for example, the child is participating in a stand-up spelling bee, it will not be possible to observe and record episodes of inappropriate out-of-seat behavior.

Every effort should be made to observe the referred child at different times during the day and in multiple environments—at home, on the playground, and in various classes. Occasions for sampling behavior should be selected with regard to their representativeness. Failure to obtain a representative sample of behavior will lead to incorrect generalizations.

Attention to Special Occurrences

Even when you are concentrating on specific behaviors, always be attuned to other events that are happening at the time of the observation. Fire drills, substitute teachers, new aides, special events, upcoming holidays, or other children's misbehaviors are a few of the events that may have a direct bearing on the referred child's behavior. Such events should be noted on the observational record.

APPLICABILITY OF OBSERVATIONAL METHODS

Observational methods are particularly useful for (a) studying behaviors that have a relatively high frequency, (b) assessing global behaviors such as aggression, social withdrawal, sociability, and attention, and (c) evaluating a child's progress over time. Systematic observation may not be the method of choice for some behaviors, particularly those that occur infrequently or only in response to some specific stimuli. For example, it may not be possible to observe a child stealing or setting fires, for these behaviors may occur only once every three or four months. For such behaviors, self-monitoring techniques, planned incident procedures (setting up a contrived situation to elicit the specified target behavior—see Exhibit 17-11), or role-play techniques may be preferable.

Ecological Assessment

Assessment by observational methods is particularly valuable in *ecological assessment*, which focuses on the *physical attributes* and the *psychological attributes* of the setting in which behavior occurs. Physical attributes include spatial arrangements, seating arrangements, lighting, and noise, whereas psychological attributes include familial, peer, and teacher relationships. The evaluation of settings is particularly important for answering such questions as "Which classroom is best for this handicapped child?" or "How can the home be modified to improve the child's behavior?" or "What kind of foster home would be best for this child?

An ecological assessment may focus on how changes in one behavior affect other behaviors or how changes in one part of the environment may produce changes in other parts of the environment, in turn affecting the child's behavior. A three-component framework is useful for organizing ecological assessment data (Hiltonsmith & Keller, 1983). The components are *setting appearance and contents*, *setting operation*, and *setting opportunities* (see Table 17-1).

Tests and Interviews

Behavioral observation is conducted on an informal basis during the administration of formal and informal tests and during interviews. Many of the principles discussed in this chapter also apply to these settings. Other guidelines for observing behaviors when administering tests and conducting interviews are presented in various chapters of the text including Chapters 5, 16, 18, and 23.

DESIGNING AN OBSERVATIONAL ASSESSMENT

The key to meaningful descriptions of behavior is the right combination of an observational recording method and an observational coding system. Several recording methods are available, ranging from those geared to describing behavioral sequences to those designed to facilitate observations of only one or a few events. Coding systems specify the categories used in recording the observations. The categories, such as aggressive and passive behavior or on-task and off-task behavior, refer to the behavioral content of the observations. A recording method is usually combined with a coding system in an effort to map the behaviors of interest accurately. In addition to describing the type of behavior being displayed, the coding system is often designed to describe various important dimensions of that behavior (its frequency, duration, intensity, latency) and how the behavior relates to factors in the setting.

The best system for a particular application will depend on the assessment goals. You may want to use a coding system designed by others, combine categories of existing systems, modify existing systems, or design your own system. In selecting or designing a coding system, be guided by the questions you want answered and how the system will help you answer these questions. Existing systems will differ in their range of behaviors and in the level of inference required by the observational categories. If you find a system that is generally useful for your purposes, by all means use it. On some occasions, however, you may have to supplement an existing system with additional categories that have special relevance to a particular case. In such instances, you will need to carefully define the coding categories. Although behaviors representing problem areas will be of prime interest (or targeted), do not hesitate to observe other behaviors that might be relevant.

Table 17-1
A Framework for Organizing Data on Home and School Settings in the Assessment of Children and Families

Data Source

A. *Setting Appearance and Contents* (refers to observable, physical, and generally measurable aspects of the setting)
  1. *Physical features* – spatial layout, arrangement of furniture, and so on.
  2. *Ambient features* – noise level and lighting.
  3. *Setting contents* – presence or absence of television sets, books, interactive board games, computers, and the like.

B. *Setting Operation* (refers to how the setting works, focusing on how people interact with each other, with people in other settings, and with physical aspects of the setting)
  1. *Organizational patterns* – who leads, who follows, and what reinforcers are present in the setting.
  2. *Communication patterns* – who initiates conversation and to whom the conversation is directed.
  3. *Ecological patterns* – how the setting is used by the people in the setting.

C. *Setting Opportunities* (refers to how the setting provides for the needs of the people in the setting)
  1. *Nurturance and sustenance* – how basic needs of the people are met (for example, the needs for food, clothing and shelter).
  2. *Cognitive stimulation* – the degree to which people receive cognitive stimulation.
  3. *Social/emotional stimulation* – the degree to which people receive stimulation for social/emotional growth and development.

Source: Adapted from Hiltonsmith and Keller (1983).

OBSERVATIONAL RECORDING METHODS

Behaviors differ in their frequency, duration, intensity, and latency, as well as their consistency across settings, tasks, and persons. Some behaviors occur frequently, others relatively infrequently. Some have long durations, others short durations. Some are intense, others mild. Some occur immediately after a request, others are delayed. And some are consistent during an episode, whereas others are variable. In designing or selecting your recording method, you should consider the attributes of the target behavior. The attributes of a particular behavior will determine what methods are most likely to ensure that the behavior will be observed and scored.

The observational recording methods particularly useful for clinical and psychoeducational tasks are narrative recording, interval recording, event recording, and ratings recording. The following sections provide information on each of these recording methods, including a description, major uses, design considerations, quantitative data obtained, advantages, disadvantages, examples, and exercises to develop your skill in using the method.

Narrative Recording

The goal of the narrative method is to formulate a rich and comprehensive description of the child's (or group's) natural behavior. Descriptions of behavior can be recorded by trained observers, parents, relatives, or even the child. Narrative recordings are referred to as *anecdotal recordings* when they include anything that seems noteworthy to the observer; a specific time frame is not needed, nor are specific codes or categories. When the observer attempts to record behavior as it occurs, the narrative recording is referred to as a *running record*. Narrative recordings describe events without resorting to quantitative recording procedures.

Molar and molecular descriptions of behavior. The observations recorded in a narrative recording can encompass both molar (broad) and molecular (fine) descriptions of behavior (Barker & Wright, 1954). Molar descriptions focus on actions that reflect the child's behavior as a whole, that are goal directed, and that are within the child's cognitive field. Molecular descriptions are narrower, reflecting subordinate parts of the child's behavior or the setting. For example, in each of the following pairs, the first description is more molar than the second: (a) hurrying to school—raising a foot, (b) eating—chewing, and (c) reciting at school—moving lips.

Barker and Wright (1954, pp. 201–202) provided illustrations of other molar and molecular descriptions:

It is possible to make a record which describes only molar behavior units like the one that follows:

George went berry picking for his mother.

Or one can make a record which includes subordinate molar units like those in italics below:

George *took a basket from the kitchen table* and *walked outdoors* where he *mounted his bicycle* and went to pick berries for his mother.

Finally, one can bring into a record molecular details [as] . . . italicized in the following description:

George, with his *lips quivering*, his *brows knit*, and the *corners of his mouth turned down*, took a basket from the kitchen table, and, with *the fingers of his left hand wound limply around the handle of the basket*, his *shoulders hunched*, his *chin sagging against his chest*, and his *feet dragging*, walked outdoors, where he mounted his bicycle and, with his *head still bent*, went to pick berries for his mother.

Note that molar and submolar details of the *situation*—the mother and the berries, the basket, the bicycle, and the kitchen table—are included in these descriptions. One could add molecular detail to the situation by mentioning, for example, that according to a thermometer on the front porch of the house, the temperature stood at 81.5 degrees.

Consider the first description. It identifies a complete episode. . . . We have suggested that an adequate sample of episodes, so identified, would be useful. It would indeed tell us quite essentially *what* the individuals concerned had been observed to do. We have seen also, however, that a . . . record which did no more than this would be deficient in that it could tell us relatively little about *how* the individuals concerned did what. . . . This is demonstrated by the third example. Thus, we know with some confidence from the quivering lips, the knit brows, and the dragging feet that George went to pick the berries *unwillingly* and *unhappily*. This is one kind of information that we want to put in a . . . record if only because the *hows* of what persons do hold important clues to the meaning for them of their actions and the conditions of their lives.

A continuum of inferential judgments. Narrative observations form a continuum from low inferential judgments (behavioral descriptive statements) to high inferential judgments (behavioral inferential statements). When you record what is directly observable (for example, actions, motor activity, and verbalizations), you are making *low inferential judgments*, whereas when you record inferences based on directly observable behaviors, you are making *high inferential judgments*. Table 17-2 provides examples of these two types of statements. Behavioral descriptive statements relate behaviors as they occur, without explanations beyond the behavior. Behavioral inferential statements go beyond describing behaviors; they are at an integrative or theoretical level. In the early stages of your narrative recording, concentrate on behavioral descriptive statements, keeping interpretive statements to a minimum.

Do not substitute interpretations that generalize *about* behavior for descriptions *of* behavior, but add such interpretations when they point to possibilities of fact that might otherwise be missed. Segregate every interpretation by some such device as indenta-

Table 17-2
Comparison of Behavioral Descriptive Statements and Behavioral Inferential Statements

Behavioral descriptive statements	Behavioral inferential statements
He slams his book on the desk.	He is frustrated.
She hit Helen three times with a stick.	She is angry.
He achieved 100 percent accuracy on his mathematics test.	He is gifted in mathematics.
She says mostly positive things about herself.	She has a good self-concept.

Source: Adapted from Alessi (1980).

tion or bracketing. Straight reporting must be left to stand out. (Wright, 1960, p. 85)

Interpret the recording data only *after* you have had an opportunity to study and make generalizations about the observational findings.

Major uses of narrative recordings. Narrative observations can be conducted in various settings and time periods, providing an in-depth picture of the behavior of a child, group, or teacher. In clinical assessment, narrative recordings are particularly valuable as a precursor to more specific and quantifiable observations. A running account of the child's behavior may provide leads about behavioral and environmental events worthy of further analysis and suggest hypotheses about factors controlling the target behaviors.

The following examples illustrate some situations or settings in which narrative recordings might be used.

Example 1: Observing communication skills. Narrative recording can help you to learn about a child's communication skills (Mattes & Omark, 1984). Observe carefully the child's interactions with others. Notice the child's facial expressions, gestures, and actions *as well as* the body language and actions of others who communicate with the child. Notice how the child initiates interactions and how he or she responds when interactions are initiated by others. Signs suggestive of a communicative disorder include the following:

• The child rarely initiates verbal interactions with others.

• Peers rarely initiate verbal interactions with the child.

• The child does not respond verbally when verbal interactions are initiated by peers.

• The child's communications have little or no effect on the peers.

• The child uses gestures rather than speech to communicate.

• The facial expressions or actions of peers indicate that they may be having difficulty understanding the child's communications.

Example 2: Observing a group. Narrative recordings are also useful when you wish to observe a group. Pay particular attention to the patterns of peer preference or attraction, indifference, antagonism, and influence. The following questions can aid you in your observations of a group of children in a classroom or in other settings:

1. What is the group climate like?
2. What patterns of interaction are evident?
3. Who are the leaders (that is, those who are particularly apt to influence their peers) and who are the followers (that is, those who are particularly susceptible to influence)?
4. What other roles seem to be represented in the group?
5. Which children participate in group activities and which ones are on the fringes?
6. What patterns of relationships do you see? For example, what subgroups are formed?
7. What is the seating arrangement in the room?
8. Which children are accepted by the group and which ones rejected?
9. How does the group react to newcomers?
10. How does the group react when its leaders are absent?
11. How does the group react to different teachers?
12. How does the group react to new situations?

Example 3: Observing a teacher. When assessing a classroom environment, you should observe the teacher's method and style of instruction. Look for the following teaching procedures that may interfere with the children's learning (Rupley & Blair, 1979):

• Seating children in such a way that some children cannot see the materials clearly

• Covering parts of words with fingers while holding up flashcards

• Writing sloppily or so small that children cannot read the words easily

- Using the same reinforcement techniques for all children
- Failing to make certain that all children are looking at the blackboard when it contains information needed for the lesson
- Assuming that all children are paying attention when some are not
- Failing to stop distractions that occur in the classroom

Designing a narrative recording. In designing a narrative recording, you must decide on (a) the number of times you will observe the child, (b) the length of the observation period, (c) the time periods during which the observations will be conducted, (d) the type of narrative recording to be used, (e) the target behaviors to be observed, and (f) the method of recording data.

Frequency, length, and time of observation period. The child's age, the setting, and the reason for the assessment will in part determine the number of times you will need to observe the child, the length of the observation period, and when the observations will be conducted. An observation session may last from 10 to 30 minutes or longer. Try to time your observations so that they will yield representative data; if possible, observe the child on more than one occasion and at different times during the day. The best procedure for collecting representative data is to consult with the referral source (for example, the classroom teacher) about when and where the behavior of concern occurs most frequently and to observe at those times.

Type of narrative recording. For clinical and psychoeducational assessment, anecdotal recordings usually are preferred, although on some occasions other types of narrative recordings may be used. In most cases, there are no restrictions on what is observed. In addition to the behavior of the referred child, fully describe the setting (for example, include a description of the scene, the people in the setting, and the ongoing action). Report everything that the referred child says and does, everything that is said and done to the child, and what other people say and do. Use everyday descriptive language in all of your narratives. The narrative should read like a short story, telling what, when, and how the behavior of concern occurred and what features of the environment served to increase or decrease the behavior.

Target behaviors. In the initial stages of a case referral, you will usually want to include in your narrative recording general impressions of the child and the setting. When it is clearer what the primary behaviors of concern are, you may want to concentrate on preselected behaviors chosen on the basis of interview information, referral information, or behavior identified during formal testing. In such cases, also observe the antecedent and consequent events associated with the behaviors.

Method of recording data. Narrative data can be either written down or recorded on tape. Narrative recording also can be used in conjunction with other recording methods, such as videotaping. You may want to consider using a specially designed anecdotal record form to record specific observations at specified times. This kind of anecdotal recording is generally done when the behaviors of concern occur with a relatively high frequency. Figure 17-1 provides an example of a form that might be used for a classroom observation.

Guidelines for making narrative recordings. The following guidelines will assist you in using the narrative method of observation.

▶

Figure 17-1. Observation protocol based on anecdotal record system—provides for recording of time, behaviors, notes, grouping situations, and teacher reactions. Alessi provided the following description of the anecdotal record protocol and comments about the sample case:

> The top part of the protocol contains identifying information common to any test protocol. Below this is space for noting the reason for referral, classroom activity and rules in effect during the observation period, and a description of the recording procedure used (e.g., 30 second interval). The mid-section of the protocol contains a coding system for noting various behaviors, situations, and teacher reactions during the observation session. The bottom half of the protocol contains 20 blank lines, each one representing either an interval for observation or a time sample frame. These are numbered from 1 to 20 down the left-hand side. Each blank line has a space to record the behavior of the referred and comparison pupils, anecdotal notes on the incident, the grouping situation at that time, and the teacher's reaction to the incident.
>
> The recorded data are summarized at the bottom. In the sample case, the referred pupil was on-task during only 7 of the 20 intervals observed, whereas the comparison pupil was on-task during 17 of the same 20 intervals. Furthermore, the referred pupil's off-task behavior consisted entirely of motor and passive, as opposed to verbal, off-task responses. By contrast, the comparison pupil's off-task behavior was all motor. The teacher gave no attention to either pupil during 17 of 20 intervals observed, and neutral attention during the other three intervals. However, peers attended to the off-task behavior on 6 occasions.

Reprinted, with changes in notation, with permission of the publisher and author from G. J. Alessi, "Behavioral Observation for the School Psychologist: Responsive-Discrepancy Model," *School Psychology Review*, 1980, *9*, pp. 36–37. © National Association of School Psychologists.

Western Michigan University School Psychology Program
CLASSROOM OBSERVATION RECORD PROTOCOL

Pupil: Mary	Comparison: C.J.	Observer: School Psychologist (L.C.)	
Age: 6-10	Age: 6-7	Other Observer: Social Worker	
Grade: 2nd		Class Size: 26	
School: Westwood		Class Type: Regular ed.	
Teacher: Mrs. Kaput		Time Stop: 10:23	
Date: 4/3/87		Time Start: 10:13	
		Total Time: :10	

Reason for observation (What questions do we want to answer?).
To confirm reported discrepancy between Mary's behavior and that of her classroom peers.

Classroom activity and explicit rules in effect at time of observation:
Activity: Math. See notes below for details. Rules: 1. Follow teacher's directions; 2. work quietly; 3. complete work.

Description of observation techniques (interval or time sample and length):
30-second interval for Mary and comparison, 2-minute time sample for class scan check.

Behavior codes:	Grouping codes:	Teacher and peer reaction codes:
T = on task	L = large group	AA = attention to all
V = verbal off task	S = small group	A + = positive attention to pupil
M = motor off task	O = one to one	A − = negative attention to pupil
P = passive off task	I = independent act.	Ao = no attention to pupil
=	F = free time	An = neutral attention to pupil
=	=	=

	Time	Pupil	Comparison	Class scan check	Anecdotal notes on behavior	Grouping	Teacher reaction	Peer reaction
1.	10:13	P	T		Ma not responding to teacher	L	An	Ao
2.		M	T		Standing up—other sitting	L	Ao	A+
3.	10:14	M	T		Te leads Ma back to desk	L	An	Ao
4.		M	T	80%	Standing up	L	Ao	A+
5.	10:15	P	T		Sitting staring at others	L	Ao	A+
6.		T	M		Looking at teacher	S	Ao	Ao
7.	10:16	T	M	76%	Sitting quietly and listening	S	Ao	Ao
8.		T	T		Working at desk	S	Ao	Ao
9.	10:17	P	T		Looking out window	L	Ao	Ao
10.		T	T	83%	Copying math problems	L	Ao	Ao
11.	10:18	P	T		Staring at board	L	Ao	Ao
12.		M	T		On floor getting pencil	L	Ao	Ao
13.	10:19	M	T	80%	On floor getting pencil	L	Ao	A+
14.		M	M		On floor poking other	L	Ao	A+
15.	10:20	P	T		In seat staring	L	Ao	Ao
16.		P	T	88%	In seat staring	L	Ao	Ao
17.	10:21	T	T		Writing math	S	An	Ao
18.		T	T		Writing math	S	Ao	Ao
19.	10:22	M	T	80%	Walking in class	S	Ao	A+
20.		T	T		Writing math	S	Ao	Ao
Summary:		35% (7/20)	85% (17/20)	81%		L = 13; S = 7	Ao = 17; An = 3	Ao = 14; A+ = 6
Reliability = 83%								

479

• Identify the child (or children or adults) engaged in the behavior.

• Clearly identify the behavior of the child (and other children and adults in the setting) and those factors in the situation that affect the behavior.

• Identify the setting and the time of day.

• Consider how the child's environment (including other children, adults, and the physical and spatial determinants) affects the behavior of the child.

• Be alert to both verbal and nonverbal cues generated by the child and others in the child's environment.

• Write down the event (or anecdote) as soon as possible after it occurs.

• Record important verbalizations as precisely as possible, including direct quotations of the child and others, to preserve the flavor of how things were said.

• Preserve the sequence of the episode.

• Be as objective, accurate, and complete as possible.

• Use everyday language to record the behavior.

• Describe rather than interpret the child's behavior.

• Record the reactions of others to the child's behavior.

• Recognize that your initial general impressions may change during the course of the observation.

• Always consider your role in the assessment process, particularly how you are reacting and feeling.

• Do not allow your interest in specific behaviors to keep you from recording general impressions.

• When you interpret the child's behavior after the recordings, try to understand the child's viewpoint rather than impose adult perceptions on the behavior.

• Finally, attempt to integrate all sources of behavioral information, including molar and molecular observations, into a unified and coherent picture of the child's behavior.

Quantitative data in narrative recordings. Although narrative recordings do not involve quantitative recording procedures, the obtained record can be used to obtain quantitative data. For example, you may note the number of times a particular action was performed or the number of times a child spoke. In addition, the information can be coded into various categories (see, for example, Barker & Wright, 1954) and then quantified.

Advantages of narrative recording. Narrative recording

• provides a record of the child's behavior and of general impressions

• maintains the original sequence of events

• provides a means of gathering information and discovering critical behaviors

• serves the function of assessing progress

• provides a record of continuing difficulties

• requires very little equipment

• is valuable as a precursor to more systematic observational procedures

Disadvantages of narrative recording. Narrative recording

• is not well suited to obtaining quantifiable data

• is difficult to validate

• does not fully describe some types of critical behaviors

• produces findings with limited generalizability

• is only as good as the observer

Illustrations of narrative recording. Exhibit 17-1 is a narrative record of a 4½-year-old boy who is busy painting. The record captures the child's mood and contains many qualifying details. Exhibit 17-2 is a four-minute narrative record of a 7-year, 4-month-old boy, beginning at the time he awoke on the morning of a school day. Notice that an attempt was made to record as precisely as possible the mother's statements as well as her voice quality. Similarly, the child's facial expressions, glances, and actions are recorded together with the quality of his behavior.

Exercises for developing narrative recording skills. Some exercises for developing your skills in narrative recording are given in Exhibit 17-3.

Interval Recording

Interval recording (sometimes referred to as *time sampling*, *interval sampling*, or *interval time sampling*) is a recording method that focuses on selected aspects of behavior as they occur within specified intervals of time. The term *sampling* conveys the basic idea of interval recording — you sample behavior rather than recording each and every behavior as it occurs during the observational period. The observational period is divided into brief segments or intervals, usually of 5 to 30 seconds, depending on the length of the observation, during which the observer notes whether a behavior occurs. The presence or absence of the predefined target behaviors in each interval is tallied. Interval recording is especially suitable for controlled observations and laboratory studies.

(Some authors distinguish between time sampling and

Exhibit 17-1

A Narrative Recording

Winky points to the window and with radiant face calls in delight, "It's snowing cherry blossoms! First they are white, then green, then red, red, red! I want to paint!" He goes to the easel and quickly snatches up a smock. Sliding in beside Wayne, he whispers to him caressingly and persuasively, "Wayne, you want blue? I give it to you okay? You give me red because I'm going to make cherries, lots of red cherries!"

After the boys exchanged paint jars, Winky sits erect, and with a sigh of contentment starts quickly but with clean strokes to ease his brush against the edge of the jar. He makes dots all around the outer part of the paper. His tongue licks his upper lip, his eyes shine, his body is quiet but intense. The red dots are big, well-rounded, full of color, and clearly separated. While working, Winky sings to himself, "Red cherries, big, round red cherries!" The first picture completed, he calls the teacher to hang it up to dry. The next picture starts as the first did, dots at the outside edge, but soon filling the whole paper. He uses green too, but the colors do not overlap.

Still singing his little phrase, Winky paints a third and fourth picture, concentrating intently on his work.

The other children pick up his song and Wayne starts to paint blue dots on his paper. Waving his brush, Winky asks, "Wayne, want to try my cherries?" Swiftly and jubilantly he swishes his brush across Wayne's chin. Laughing, he paints dots on his own hands. "My hands are full of cherries," he shouts. He runs into the adjoining room calling excitedly to the children, "My hands are full of cherries!" He strides into the bathroom emphatically to wash his hands. Susie follows him in, calling, "Let's see, Winky." "Ha, I ate them all," he gloats as he shows his washed hands with a sweeping movement. He grabs a toy bottle from the shelf, fills it with water and asks the teacher to put the nipple on. He lies down then on a mattress and contentedly sucks the bottle, his face softly smiling, his eyes big and gazing into space, his whole body limp with satisfaction.

Source: Cohen and Stern (1970, p. 34).

Types of interval recording. There are several different interval recording procedures.

1. In *partial-interval time sampling*, a behavior is recorded (scored) only once regardless of how long it lasts or how many times it occurs in the interval. This is the most popular interval recording method (see Figure 17-2). Particularly useful for behaviors that occur fleetingly, it will reveal the consistency of behavior.

2. In *whole-interval time sampling*, a behavior is scored only when it occurs at the beginning of the interval and lasts throughout the entire interval. This method is particularly useful when you want to know which behaviors (such as out-of-seat behavior) are performed without interruption (or continuously) during an interval.

3. In *point-time interval sampling*, a behavior is scored *only* when it occurs at a specific time (or times) during the interval. Recording a specific behavior if it occurs only during the first 10 seconds of each hour, but not during the remaining 59 minutes and 50 seconds, is an example of point-time sampling. This procedure allows you to observe behavior for brief periods at different times during the day. When the procedure is used with groups of children, a rotational system can be set up in which each child is observed in turn.

4. In *momentary time interval sampling*, a behavior is scored only if it occurs at the moment the interval ends. For example, if the interval is 10 seconds, only behaviors that are observed at the end of the 10-second interval are scored. This procedure can be used for observing groups of children. For five children, a 50-second observation cycle might be set up, with a different one of the five children being observed at the end of each 10-second interval within the 50-second cycle. This variant is useful with behaviors that occur at moderate but steady rates. Examples include tics, hand movements, thumbsucking, frequent stereotypic behavior, and facial expressions.

5. In *variable interoccasion interval time sampling*, only behaviors that occur at preselected random time intervals are scored (that is, the time between occasions of observations is randomly varied). Instead of always recording behaviors during the first minute of each hour (a fixed interval), one might randomly designate a one-minute observation period for each observation hour. Thus for a six-hour observation period, a random one-minute observation schedule might be as follows:

first hour—30th minute to 31st minute
second hour—12th minute to 13th minute
third hour—51st minute to 52nd minute
fourth hour—2nd minute to 3rd minute

interval recording. In this case, *time sampling* is used to refer to a procedure in which brief observations are made at specified times during the day or at random times; it requires that the target behavior have a moderate to high frequency of occurrence. *Interval recording*, in contrast, is used to refer to a procedure in which a specific observational period—for example, 15 or 30 minutes—is divided into a specified number of intervals.)

■ **Exhibit 17-2**

A Narrative Running Record

7:00. Mrs. Birch said with pleasant casualness, "Raymond, wake up." With a little more urgency in her voice she spoke again: "Son, are you going to school today?"

Raymond didn't respond immediately.

He screwed up his face and whimpered a little.

He lay still.

His mother repeated, "Raymond, wake up." This was said pleasantly; the mother was apparently in good spirits and was willing to put up with her son's reluctance.

Raymond whimpered again, and kicked his feet rapidly in protest.

He squirmed around and rolled over crossways on the bed.

His mother removed the covers.

Raymond wore a T-shirt and pajama pants.

He again kicked his feet in protest.

He sat up and rubbed his eyes.

He glanced at me and smiled.

I smiled in return as I continued making notes.

Mrs. Birch took some clothes from the bureau and laid them on the bed next to Raymond. There were a clean pair of socks, a clean pair of shorts, a white T-shirt and a striped T-shirt. Raymond's blue-jean pants were on a chair near the bed. Mrs. Birch continued to stand beside the bed.

7:01. Raymond picked up a sock and began tugging and pulling it on his left foot.

As his mother watched him she said kiddingly, "Can't you get your peepers open?"

Raymond stopped putting on his sock long enough to rub his eyes again. He appeared to be very sleepy.

He said plaintively, "Mommie," and continued mumbling in an unintelligible way something about his undershirt.

7:02. His mother asked, "Do you want to put this undershirt on or do you want to wear the one you have on?"

Raymond sleepily muttered something in reply.

His mother left the room and went into the kitchen.

Raymond struggled out of the T-shirt which he had on.

He put on the clean striped T-shirt more efficiently.

7:03. He pulled on his right sock.

He picked up his left tennis shoe and put it on.

He laced his left shoe with slow deliberation, looking intently at the shoe as he worked steadily until he had it all laced.

7:04. He put on his right shoe.

He laced up his right shoe. Again he worked intently, looking at the shoe as he laced it.

His mother called, "Raymond, do you want an egg for breakfast?" in a pleasant, inquiring tone.

Raymond responded very sleepily, "No." His voice showed no irritation or resentment; he just answered in a matter-of-fact, sleepy way, "No."

Note. Material in italics reflects details of the situation.
Source: Barker and Wright (1966, pp. 15–17).

---

fifth hour — 8th minute to 9th minute
sixth hour — 46th minute to 47th minute

This method is useful when you want to obtain a sample of behavior over an extended period of time and rule out temporal effects.

Major uses of interval recording.   Interval recording is useful for observing behaviors that are overt, that do not have a clearcut beginning and end, and that occur with moderate frequency, such as once every 10 to 15 seconds. Examples include reading, working, sitting, touching objects, roughhousing, conversing appropriately, shouting, screaming, hitting, playing with toys, making noise, smiling, lying down, and thumbsucking.

How to design an interval recording.   In designing an interval recording you must decide on (a) the number of times you will observe the child, (b) the length of the observation period, (c) the time periods during which observations will be conducted, (d) the type of interval recording to be used, (e) the length of the observation interval, (f) the length of the recording interval, if needed, (g) the target behaviors to be observed, and (h) the method of recording data.

Frequency, length, and time of observation period. The child's age, the setting, and the reason for the assessment will determine in part the number of times you will need to observe the child, the length of the observation

---

Exhibit 17-3

Narrative Recording Exercises

Exercise 1

With a co-observer, observe one child on a playground. Make an anecdotal recording for 5 minutes. If the playground is associated with a school, obtain permission from the administration before engaging in this activity.

Compare your record with that of your co-observer. How similar are the two recordings? What did your co-observer include that you did not, and vice versa? Consider the following questions in evaluating your narrative recording.

• How detailed is your recording of the child's behavior? (For example, does the recording provide a visual picture of what was happening?)

• What behaviors might you have missed?

• What led you to record some behaviors and not others?

• How did the setting affect the child's behavior?

• To what extent was the child's behavior representative of that of other children of the same age level?

• What biases, if any, may have affected your observations?

• Were your observations primarily of specific details or of general behaviors?

• What hypotheses did you develop about potential problem behaviors?

• What specific behaviors would you like to observe more carefully at another time?

• How did your presence alter the child's behavior?

• What could you have done to avoid this influence?

• How did your narrative recording contribute to your understanding of the child?

• Which statements in your recording reflect high, medium, and low inferential judgments?

To answer the last question, construct a form with two column headings: (a) statement and (b) inference level (high, medium, low). Select 30 statements from your report—10 from the beginning, 10 from the middle, and 10 from the end. Statements may be complete sentences or sentence fragments. Thus one sentence in your recording may generate one or more statements. Number each statement in your description and place the numbered statement in the first column. Then decide whether the statement reflects a high, medium, or low level of inference. Complete this same form for your co-observer's recording, and have your co-observer do the same for your recording. (Photocopying the two forms *after* the statements are typed but before the classifications are made will facilitate this process.) Table 17-A illustrates how the form would be completed for the first part of the narrative running record shown in Exhibit 17-2. Determine the level of interobserver agreement for each statement by calculating the percentage agreement (number of agreements divided by the number of statements—that is, 30).

Table 17-A
Evaluating the Inference Level of a Narrative Recording

Statement	Inference level (high, medium, low)
1. Mrs. Birch said with pleasant casualness,	Medium
2. "Raymond, wake up."	Low
3. With a little more urgency in her voice she spoke again:	Medium
4. "Son, are you going to school today?"	Low
5. Raymond didn't respond immediately.	Low
6. He screwed up his face	Low
7. and whimpered a little.	Low
8. He lay still.	Low

Write a one- or two-paragraph report describing your observation. Include information about (a) the child (age, sex, physical handicaps, and other relevant characteristics), (b) the physical setting in which the observation took place, (c) the length of time you observed the child, (d) what you observed, (e) the level of agreement with your co-observer, and (f) the implications of the findings (for example, whether the behavior was appropriate or inappropriate).

Exercise 2

With a co-observer, observe a group of children on a playground. Make a narrative running record of the group's behavior for a 5-minute time period. Follow the guidelines given in Exercise 1 for evaluating a recording, but substitute *group* for *child* as the focus of your observation.

Exercise 3

Compare the recordings obtained in Exercises 1 and 2. What are the differences between observing one child and observing a group? What purposes are served by each type of recording? What information do you gain (or lose) in each type of recording? Write up your analysis in a one- or two-paragraph report.

Exercise 4

Narrative recordings can also be used to observe specific types of behavior in various settings. Study the attachment behavior of 1- to 2-year-olds by observing their behavior

(Exhibit continues next page)

Exhibit 17-3 (cont.)

when they are left at a day care center or at a nursery maintained by a church or synagogue during a religious service. Obtain approval from the center, church, or synagogue administration before engaging in this activity.

With a co-observer, make an anecdotal record of (a) one child's behavior at the time his or her parent leaves, (b) the parent's reaction, (c) the caregiver's behavior, (d) the child's response to the caregiver, and (e) the child's behavior after the parent has gone. If your observation takes place in a church or synagogue, also observe the child's and parent's reactions when the parent returns. (You should also observe these reactions at a full-time day care center if you can return at the end of the day.) Conduct the observation for at least a 30- to 60-minute period. If time permits, observe other children, but only one child at a time. Be sure that you and your co-observer agree on the child to be observed. Arrive early. Use the guidelines in Exercise 1 for evaluating your recording.

Referred child: Bill   *Class:* Mrs. Jones
Comparison child: Ted   *Time:* 11:00 to 11:03 A.M.
Date: March 2, 1986

Behavior	Tot.		1	2	3	4	5	6	7	8	9	10	11	12
Passive off-task	5	R	X	O	O	O	O	O	X	X	X	O	O	X
	1	C	O	O	O	O	O	O	O	X	O	O	O	O
Disruptive off-task	1	R	O	O	O	X	O	O	O	O	O	O	O	O
	0	C	O	O	O	O	O	O	O	O	O	O	O	O
On-task	6	R	O	X	X	O	X	X	O	O	O	X	X	O
	11	C	X	X	X	X	X	X	O	X	X	X	X	X

Figure 17-2. Example of a three-minute partial-interval time sample recording. Abbreviations are as follows: R = referred child, C = comparison child, X = behavior observed, O = behavior not observed, Tot. = Total. Each number reflects a 10-second observation period followed by a 5-second pause for recording data. Three types of behavior were recorded: passive off-task behavior, disruptive off-task behavior, and on-task behavior. Bill engaged in off-task behavior in 6 of the 12 intervals; 5 of the off-task behaviors were passive. Thus in 50 percent of the intervals he showed some kind of off-task behavior. In contrast, Ted had only one interval with off-task behavior (passive).

Figure 17-3. General recording protocol. Alessi (1980, p. 36, with changes in notation) provided the following description of the general recording protocol:

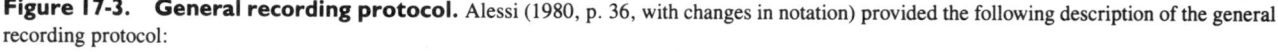

The top half has spaces for identifying information. The bottom half contains spaces down the left side for writing in the behaviors being observed. Across the page are numbers with columns of boxes underneath. Each number can refer to either successive (a) intervals, (b) behavior counts, (c) duration measures, or (d) latency measures. For the interval and behavior measures, data would be recorded with "Xs" (target behavior occurred) or "Os" (target behavior did not occur) in each block. For the duration and latency measures, the actual elapsed time would be entered in the successive boxes (for example, 14″/8″/22″/9″).

Each space for writing in a behavior category has six rows of boxes after it: R = referred student, C = comparison student, T = teacher's reaction, P = peer reaction, G = group reaction, and Sc = Scan check. Two spaces are provided for summarizing the data recorded in the blocks across the first two rows.

Note. The duration recording is entered in the same boxes as the interval data, but it does not refer to any specific intervals. In this example there were four occasions during the session in which the referred child was out of seat and one occasion when the comparison child was out of seat. The duration recording was made independently of the interval recording.

Courtesy of G. J. Alessi and © National Association of School Psychologists.

Western Michigan University
CLASSROOM OBSERVATION RECORD PROTOCOL

Referred (R): _____Chelsea_____   Comparison (C): _____Andrea_____   Observer: _____Psychologist_____

Age: _____8-6_____   Age: _____8-5_____   Other Observer: _____Paraprofessional_____

Grade: _____Third_____   Class Size: _____31_____

School: _____Pine Elementary_____   Class Type: _____regular_____

Teacher: _____Mrs. Graves_____   Time Stop: _____11:16_____

Date: __10__ / __6__ / __87__   Time Start: _____11:09_____
    month   day   year   Total Time _____:7_____

Reason for observation (What questions do we want to answer?):
To observe whether Chelsea's behavior during reading differs from that of another child.

Classroom activity and explicit rules in effect at time of observation:
Activity: Reading. Rules: 1. Work quietly; 2. sit at desks; 3. raise hand for help.

Grouping situation (G):
(circle one)
L = large group   (I) = independent act
S = small group   F = free time
O = one to one

Teacher (T)/peer (P) reaction codes:
AA = attention to all
A+ = positive attention to pupil
A− = negative attention to pupil
Ao = no attention to pupil
An = neutral attention to pupil

Observation recording method:
(a) interval size 15″.
(b) time sample: size ___.
(c) event count
(d) duration
(e) latency

Behaviors*	Tot.		1-15	1-30	1-45	1-60	2-15	2-30	2-45	2-60	3-15	3-30	3-45	3-60	4-15	4-30	4-45	4-60	5-15	5-30	5-45	5-60
Verbal Off-Task	8	R	X	O	O	X	X	O	O	X	X	O	O	X	X	X	O	X				
	2	C	O	X	O	O	X	O	O	O	O	O	O	O	O	O	O	O				
		T	Ao	Ao		Ao	An			Ao	Ao			Ao	An		Ao					
		P																				
		G																				
1		Sc**																				
Motor Off-Task	4	R	X	O	X	O	O	O	O	O	O	O	X	X	O	O	O	O				
	1	C	O	O	O	O	O	O	O	O	O	O	O	O	X	O	O	O				
		T	Ao		Ao							Ao	An	Ao								
		P																				
		G																				
2		Sc																				
Passive Off-Task	1	R	O	O	O	O	O	X	O	O	O	O	O	O	O	O	O	O				
	1	C	O	O	O	O	O	O	O	X	O	O	O	O	O	O	O	O				
		T						Ao	An													
		P																				
		G																				
3		Sc																				
On-Task	3	R	O	X	O	O	O	O	X	O	O	O	O	O	O	X	O					
	11	C	X	O	X	X	O	X	O	X	X	X	X	O	X	X	X					
		T	Ao	An	An	An		Ao			Ao	Ao	An	Ao		Ao	An	Ao				
		P																				
		G																				
4		Sc																				
Out of Seat (duration)	53″	R	14″	8″	22″	9″																
	6″	C	6″																			
		T	A−	A−	An	A−																
		P																				
		G																				
5		Sc																				

Were reliability data collected? (Yes)   No.   If yes, interobserver % agreements = __83__ %.

* Include specific behavior definitions on back, as well as comments (strengths, contextual observations, etc.).   ** Scan check.

period, and when the observations will be conducted. An observation session may last from 10 to 30 minutes or longer. Try to time your observations so that you can observe a representative sample of the target behavior. If possible, observe the child on more than one occasion and at different times during the day.

Length of the observation interval. The length of the observation interval will depend on the target behaviors. The interval length should be geared to the onset and termination of the behaviors under observation. An appropriate interval length will minimize distortion of the behavioral sequences and frequencies. Short intervals are preferable for behaviors that last a short time, such as making excessive noise, pushing other children, mouthing objects, and self-stimulation. Long intervals are useful for behaviors that last a long time, such as arguing excessively, watching an excessive amount of television, or sleeping in the classroom.

Length of the recording interval. A recording interval (an interval in which no observations are made) should always be used whenever the scoring (or recording) will interfere with the ongoing observations. Whenever a recording interval is used, some type of cuing device is needed to signal the onset and offset of the observation and recording intervals. Although various electronic devices may be used, a simple method is to record a tone signaling recording intervals on an audio cassette tape and then listen to the tape via an earjack while observing. Alternatively, a voice on the tape can be used to signal observation and recording intervals. For a 10-second observation interval and 5-second recording interval, the following sequence would be used, with the words "first," "second," and "third" referring to the interval number: "First" (0 seconds), "Record" (10 seconds), "Second" (15 seconds), "Record" (25 seconds), "Third" (30 seconds), "Record" (40 seconds), and so forth. Similar cuing systems can be employed when only observation intervals are used. Whatever the cuing system, it should not interfere with the ongoing observations.

Target behaviors. Target behaviors should be selected on the basis of prior narrative recordings, interview information, referral questions, or test behavior. When a preselected coding system is used (see the section in this chapter on observational coding systems), the target behaviors will be specified in the coding system.

Method of recording data. Data can be recorded with pencil and paper or with electronic recording devices,

such as the Radio Shack PC-2, Sharp PC-1500, Quasar HHC, Panasonic Link, Hewlett-Packard 75, or Epson HX-20. Figure 17-3 shows a standard recording form that can be used with various recording methods and coding systems.

Another approach is to use a system in which the data are automatically graphed as they are recorded. When you finish your observations, you have a ready picture of the child's behavior that can be shared immediately with the referral source. Figure 17-4 shows a self-graphing data recording system in which minutes and days are used as the time intervals. The data collected can also be graphed across days, as shown in Figure 17-5.

When you use interval recording, you may record the score for the behavior(s) either during the interval or immediately afterward. If you record during the interval, there will be no break between intervals; the observation intervals will successive. For a 10-second observation interval, the observation intervals would be as follows:

observation interval and recording (10 seconds)
observation interval and recording (10 seconds)
observation interval and recording (10 seconds)
(sequence continues)

If you record after the interval, the observation intervals will alternate with intervals for recording behavior. For example, the observation period might consist of a series of cycles in which a 10-second observation interval was followed by a 5-second recording interval. A typical sequence would be as follows:

observation interval (10 seconds)
recording interval (5 seconds)
observation interval (10 seconds)
recording interval (5 seconds)
(cycle repeats)

The second method is almost a necessity when you are recording a number of behaviors during an interval, for you must take your eyes away from the child in order to put notations in the appropriate categories. The length of the observation interval—as well as the length of the recording interval, if used—should remain fixed across all observations in order to ensure uniformity of the observations.

To observe the referred child, the teacher, and the class, you might use a sequential procedure in which you observe first the child, then the teacher, and then the class. A 60-second observation period could be divided in the following way:

observe child (1–10 seconds)
observe teacher (11–20 seconds)
observe class (21–30 seconds)

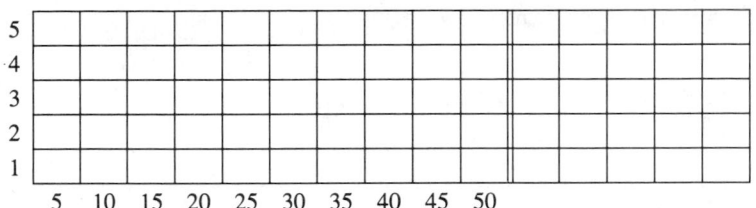

a. Graph paper with series of columns, each five blocks high. Double heavy line marks off 10 columns, for a 50-minute period.

	5	10	15	20	25	30	35	40	45	50					
5	O	O	O												
4	O	O	O												
3	O	O													
2	X	X													
1	X	X	X												

b. Chart after 13 minutes of monitoring pupil's behavior. First two columns are completed, and the third is partially completed. If the pupil behaves appropriately during the next (14th) minute, the observer will mark an "X" in the third column just above the other "X." If the pupil misbehaves, the observer will mark an "O" in that column just under the other two "Os."

	5	10	15	20	25	30	35	40	45	50					
5	O	O	O	O	O	O	O	O	O	O					
4	O	O	O	O	O	O	X	O	X	X					
3	O	O	O	X	O	X	X	X	X	X					
2	X	X	X	X	X	X	X	X	X	X					
1	X	X	X	X	X	X	X	X	X	X					

c. Chart after observer has completed 50-minute period.

Figure 17-4. Self-graphing data recording system. Alessi (1980, pp. 39–40, with changes in notation) provided the following description of the graphing method and commentary on the data shown.

To set up a self-graphing data recording system, start with a piece of graph paper. Mark two heavy lines across the paper so that five blocks are between the lines. You have now a series of columns, all five blocks high. Each block will represent an interval (e.g., minute) of observation time. Mark off the number of 5-block columns needed for the scheduled observation period: a 50-minute period would need 10 columns of 5 blocks, a 30-minute period would need 6 columns, a 45-minute period would need 9 columns, and a 5-minute period would need only one column of 5 blocks. For now let's assume you have scheduled a 50-minute period for your observations, as shown in (a). You have marked off 10 columns on your paper, each five blocks high, for a total of 50 blocks: one block for each minute scheduled.

For each interval (minute) in which the on-task behavior occurs, you will place an "X" in a box. For each interval in which the behavior does not occur, you will place an "O" in a box. Start with the left column and work toward the right. In each column, work from the bottom up with the "Xs," but from the top down with the "O" marks. When the "Xs" and "Os" meet in the middle, the column is filled. Move to the next column to the right and continue: "Xs" from the bottom, "Os" from the top down, until they meet. As you move across the row of 5-block columns, the data recorded will automatically form a graph without any extra effort on your part. With this method, trends in data across the session can be easily identified and shared with school personnel, referral sources, or parents. Focusing on the Xs in (c) shows that the amount of on-task behavior by the pupil is steadily increasing during the observation session (i.e., there are fewer "Xs" in the first columns, and more "Xs" in the later columns).

observe child (31–40 seconds)
observe teacher (41–50 seconds)
observe class (51–60 seconds)
(cycle repeats)

Recording intervals, if needed, can be interspersed with observation periods. The following sequence consists of 7-second observation intervals and 3-second recording intervals:

observe child (1–7 seconds)
record behavior (8–10 seconds)
observe teacher (11–17 seconds)
record behavior (18–20 seconds)

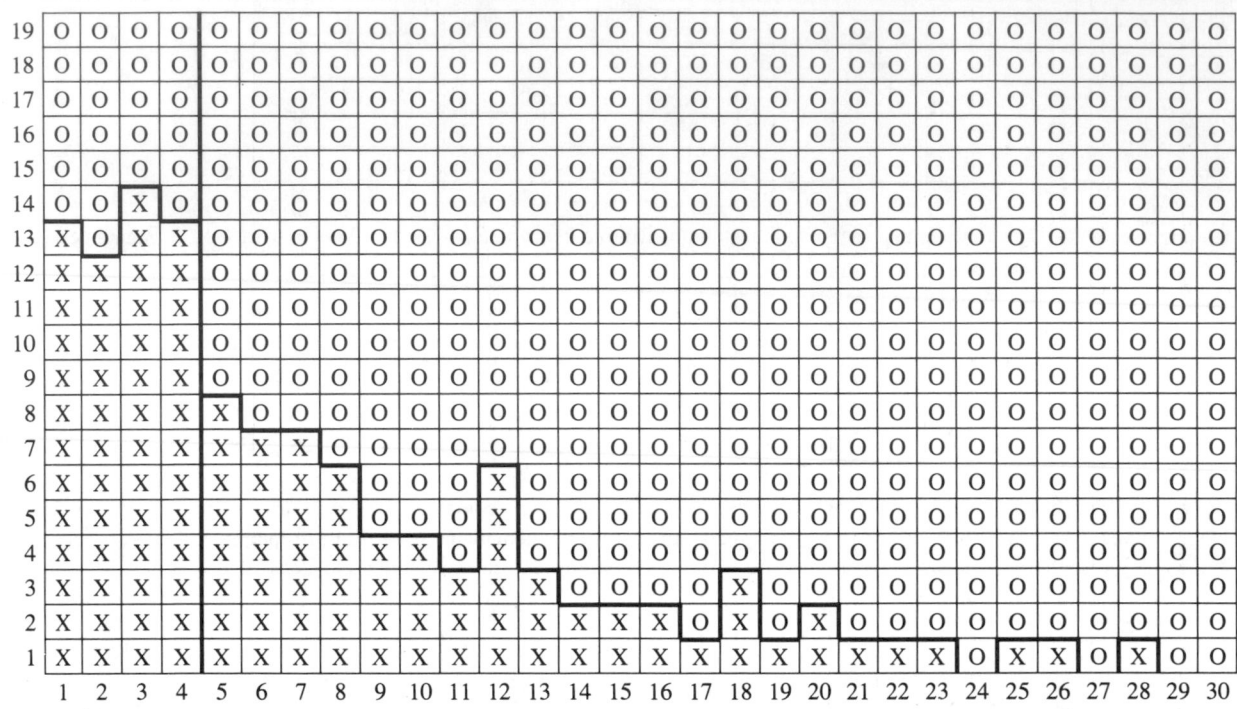

Figure 17-5.   Automatic graphing data collection procedures, with days #1 through #30 across the abcissa and intervals #1 through #19 up the ordinate. The heavy line between days #4 and #5 indicates the beginning of an intervention plan. Intervals with talk-outs are scored with "Xs," and quiet intervals are scored with "Os." By reading from left to right and focusing on the "Xs," you can see a clear downward trend in the number of intervals scored for talking out over the 30-day period (more "Xs" in the earlier columns and fewer "Xs" in the later columns). There is a swift drop in the number of intervals scored for talking out just after the intervention was implemented (day #5), suggesting the effectiveness of this procedure. Reprinted, with changes in notation, with permission of the publisher and author from G. J. Alessi, "Behavioral Observation for the School Psychologist: Responsive-Discrepancy Model," *School Psychology Review*, 1980, *9*, p. 41. © National Association of School Psychologists.

observe class (21–27 seconds)
record behavior (28–30 seconds)
(cycle repeats)

Sequential observation procedures permit great flexibility in recording the behavior of individuals and groups. They also can be used with a variety of behavioral coding systems to fit particular assessment needs.

Quantitative data in interval recording.   The primary piece of quantitative data obtained in interval recording is the frequency count of the number of intervals in which the target behaviors did or did not occur. Note that the frequency count reflects the number of *intervals* in which the behavior occurred, not the number of times the behavior occurred (see Event Recording below).

If information on the intensity of the behavior is desired, an *intensity dimension* can be built into the behavioral code. For example, if you want to record the intensity of hyperactive behavior, you can include codes representing different degrees of intensity (for example, mild, moderate, and extreme hyperactivity).

Advantages of interval recording.   Interval recording (Kazdin, 1981; Nay, 1979)

• may help to define important time-behavior relations
• facilitates checking for interobserver reliability
• helps to ensure that the predefined behaviors are observed under the same conditions each time
• uses time efficiently
• focuses the observer's attention on the child's behavior by structuring the observations
• permits the recording of virtually any behavior
• allows for the collection of a large number of observations in a short period of time

---

Exhibit 17-4

Illustration of Interval Recording in a Classroom

OBSERVING ON-TASK AND OFF-TASK BEHAVIOR

Students and Setting

Three students with attentional problems from a class for the mentally retarded were the focus of the observation. The three children could follow simple instructions and were achieving academically at a first grade level. When assigned an academic task to complete, they were generally off-task, frequently glancing up from assigned work, turning to watch other children, and playing with objects on their desks.

A fourth child was selected as a comparison student. Her teacher reported that she did not have attentional problems.

The observation took place in the classroom during math and spelling periods. There were 13 students in the class. The daily curriculum was aimed at developing basic math, spelling, and phonics skills. Specially prepared materials were constructed for the observation period. These materials would again be used after special training procedures were begun and consisted of sheets of simple one-digit math problems and spelling exercises. During each math session, 140 addition and subtraction problems were given to the children, considerably more than any of them could complete. The spelling exercises required children to copy three- and four-letter words. During each session, the students were asked to copy two pages of spelling words, each containing 16 words.

Coding Categories

The on-task behavior had to meet the following requirements: (a) the children's buttocks had to be touching the seat bottom of the desk and (b) their eyes had to be oriented toward the task materials while (c) they interacted manually with the task materials. Two of the three referred children were observed simultaneously on an alternating basis—that is, every 5 minutes a different pair of children was observed. Thus, during each 30-minute session, each child was observed for a total of 20 minutes. The comparison child was observed separately, once a week for 20 minutes.

A whole-interval rating system was used, with 10-second observation intervals. Any break in eye or manual contact with the task materials or incorrect posturing resulted in that interval's being scored as off-task. Other responses recorded included the percentage of 140 math problems completed, the percentage of attempted math problems correct, the percentage of 350 letters completed, and the percentage of completed words spelled correctly.

Reliability checks were performed twice during each session by a second observer. Reliability for both occurrence and nonoccurrence of on-task behavior was computed on an interval-by-interval basis. The number of agreements was divided by the number of agreements plus disagreements, and the result was multiplied by 100. The reliability of the performance measures was checked by percentage agreement.

Source: Reprinted, with changes in notation, with permission of the publisher and authors from T. L. Whitman, J. W. Scibak, K. M. Butler, R. Richter, and M. R. Johnson, "Improving Classroom Behavior in Mentally Retarded Children Through Correspondence Training," *Journal of Applied Behavior Analysis*, 1982, *15*, pp. 557–558. © Society for the Experimental Analysis of Behavior, Inc.

Disadvantages of interval recording. Interval recording

• provides a somewhat artificial view of the behavior sequence (because the time interval, not the behavioral episode, dictates the recording framework)

• may allow important behaviors related to the problem to be overlooked

• does not provide information about the quality of the behaviors (that is, how the behavior is performed) or about the situation (that is, whether the child was agitated, paying attention, or sleeping while in his or her seat) unless such information is specifically coded into the recording system

• may not reveal the actual frequency or duration of the behavior (for example, one 60-second continuous period of off-task behavior would be recorded as four separate events in a 10-second observation–5-second recording interval system)

• may overestimate the frequency of low-rate behaviors or behaviors of short duration (particularly during point-time sampling) and underestimate the frequency of high-rate behaviors

Illustration of interval recording. Exhibit 17-4 illustrates how interval recording was used to observe on- and off-task behavior of mentally retarded children in a classroom. In addition to the data on on- and off-task behaviors, data were obtained on the number of problems completed and solved. The reliability checks referred to in the illustration are discussed later in this chapter.

▬ **Exhibit 17-5** ▬▬▬▬▬▬▬▬▬▬▬▬▬▬▬▬▬▬▬▬▬▬▬▬▬▬▬▬▬

Interval Recording Exercises

Exercise 1

With a co-observer, observe one child on a playground for 5 minutes. Select a child who appears to be engaged in play with another child. Use a partial-interval time sampling procedure, with 10 seconds for the observation interval and 5 seconds for the recording interval. Use a tape recorder, preferably with earphones, to signal the beginning and end of the observation and recording intervals. Use a two-category coding system: (a) aggressive behavior and (b) nonaggressive behavior. Aggressive behavior is defined in Table 17-11. Mark an X for aggressive behavior and an O for nonaggressive behavior, using the recording protocol shown in Figure 17-3.

After you complete your recording, determine the level of interobserver agreement. Calculate the following interobserver agreement indices: (a) percentage agreement for occurrence of target behavior, (b) percentage agreement for nonoccurrence of target behavior, (c) percentage agreement for both categories, and (d) kappa. Formulas for obtaining these indices are covered toward the end of this chapter.

Consider the following questions in evaluating your interval recording.

• Which behaviors were observed most clearly (that is, most easily classified)?
• To what extent might the time of day have affected the child's behavior?
• To what extent did the behavior setting affect the child's behavior?
• To what extent were the observational categories representative of the child's behavior in those categories?
• What could be done to improve the representativeness of the observations?
• To what extent was the child's behavior representative of that of other children of the same age level?

• Did the coding categories reveal information that might have been missed if only a narrative recording had been used?
• What biases, if any, may have affected your observations?
• How did your presence alter the child's behavior?
• What could you have done to avoid this influence?
• How did your interval recording contribute to your understanding of the child?

Write a one- or two-paragraph report that describes your observation. Include information about (a) the child (age, sex, physical handicaps, and other relevant characteristics), (b) the physical setting in which the observation took place, (c) the length of time you observed the child, (d) the number of intervals in which the target behavior(s) occurred, (e) the level of agreement with your co-observer, (f) any difficulty in determining when the target behavior(s) began and ended, (g) whether the definitions of the target behaviors were satisfactory and suggestions for improving the definitions, and (h) the implications of the findings (for example, whether the behavior was appropriate or inappropriate).

Exercise 2

Follow the steps described in Exercise 1. Using a whole-interval time sampling procedure, observe a different child on the playground. Again choose one who appears to be engaged in play with another child.

Exercise 3

Compare the recordings obtained in Exercises 1 and 2. What are the differences between using a partial-interval and a whole-interval time sampling procedure? Which one gives you a more accurate picture of the child's behaviors? Why? Write up your analysis in a one- or two-paragraph report.

Exercises for developing interval recording skills. Some exercises for developing your skills in interval recording are given in Exhibit 17-5.

Event Recording

In event recording (also referred to as *event sampling*), each instance of a specific behavior or event is recorded as it occurs during the observation period. Like interval recording, event recording *samples behavior*. However, whereas the unit of measure in interval recording is the time interval imposed on the target behavior, the unit of measure in event recording is the behavior itself. The

observer waits for the preselected behavior (the event) to occur and then records it. Like interval recording, event recording is especially useful for controlled observations and laboratory studies.

Major uses of event recording. Event recording provides a continuous temporal record of the observed behaviors and thus is particularly appropriate for measuring discrete responses that have clearly defined beginnings and ends. Examples are spelling a word correctly, completing a problem, making a social response (for example, saying "hello" or sharing a toy), pulling clothing, acting aggressively, getting out of a seat, using profane words, toileting, eating, asking questions, having seizures, making a speech error, or coming late to class.

Event recording is less suitable for high-rate behaviors or for behaviors that vary in duration. For example, hand clapping is a behavior that may occur so frequently that separating each occurrence becomes difficult. Other behaviors that may occur too frequently for event recording include rocking movements; rapid jerks of the head, hands, or legs; running; and tapping objects. An example of a behavior that varies in duration is aggressive interaction with peers; it may be difficult to differentiate between a 5-second and a 5-minute interaction. Other responses that may extend over different periods of time include thumbsucking, reading, and listening.

How to design an event recording.   In designing an event recording you must decide on (a) the number of times you will observe the child, (b) the length of the observation period, (c) the time periods during which observations will be conducted, (d) the target behaviors to be observed, and (e) the method of recording data.

Frequency, length, and time of observation period. The child's age, the setting, and the reason for the assessment will in part determine the number of times you will need to observe the child, the length of the observation period, and when the observations will be conducted. An observation session may last from 10 to 30 minutes or longer. Try to time your observations so that you can observe a representative sample of the target behavior. If possible, observe the child on more than one occasion and at different times during the day.

Target behaviors.   As in interval recording, the selection of target behaviors is based on prior narrative recordings, interview information, referral questions, or test behavior. If you use a predesigned coding system, the target behaviors will be specified in the system (see the next section on Observational Coding Systems). Remember to select behaviors that have an easily discernible beginning and end.

Method of recording data.   Responses can be recorded in various ways, including using a checklist, wrist counter, hand counter, electromechanical counter, or Datamyte Event Recorder or transferring small objects from one pocket to another. For paper-and-pencil recordings, various methods can be used to make tallies. One is the traditional stroke method:

Table 17-3
Two Paper-and-Pencil Methods for Recording Frequency of Behavior

| Behavior | Method | | Frequency of behavior |
	Dot and line	Stroke	
Aggression	⊠	⊮ ||||	9
Cooperation	∴∴	||||	4
Crying	••	||	2

Note. In the dot-and-line method, each dot represents one count and each line represents one count.

Another is the dot-and-line method, which is often used when there is limited space on the protocol:

•1, •• 2, ∴ 3, ∷ 4, ⦂• 5, ⊡ 6, ⊔ 7, ⊓ 8, ⊠ 9, ⊠ 10

Table 17-3 illustrates these tallies.

The general recording protocol shown in Figure 17-3 can also be used for event recording. For behaviors that occur frequently, a combination of event recording and a one-minute interval recording may be the best choice (see Figure 17-6) (Alessi, 1980).

For recording the duration of a behavior, you may use a stopwatch, time clock, wall clock, or some other timing device. Counters can also be used to record both the frequency of an event and its duration. For example, a counter panel that has several keys can be used, with one key assigned to each behavior. You hold the key down for the duration of the behavior, and the panel records the frequency and duration of the behavior on a continuous sheet of paper.

Quantitative data in event recording.   The primary piece of quantitative data obtained in event recording is the frequency count—the number of occurrences of a behavior in a given time period. For example, an event recording might yield the information that "Chris used 10 profane words during a 20-minute observation period." In addition to the frequency of the behavior, several other behavioral dimensions can be measured in event recording, including the rate of the behavior, the duration of the behavior, the intensity of the behavior, and the latency of the behavior. Let us consider each of these dimensions.

1. *Rate of behavior.* The rate at which a behavior occurs during the session is obtained by dividing the number of behaviors by the length of the observation period.

Behaviors	Tot.		1	2	3	4	5	6	7	8	9	10	11	12	13	14	15
Talk-outs by event record	76	R	⊔	⊠	☐	⊘	⊔	L:	⊠		..	::	L:	:	...	.	.
	9	C		::		.		.						.:			
1		T															
Talk-outs by interval record	14	R	X	X	X	X	X	X	X	O	X	X	X	X	X	X	X
	4	C	O	X	O	X	O	X	O	O	O	O	O	X	O	O	O
2		T															

Figure 17-6.   Comparison of event and interval records of observation conducted in 1-minute intervals. Top part shows event data for talking-out behavior within each interval. Bottom part shows same data as scored by the interval-only method. The comparison shows that interval scoring is not as sensitive to the dynamics of the high rate of behavior as is the event-within-interval record. With the event (top) record, one can see a sudden decrease in rate of talking out after minute 7. The interval record is insensitive to this change. Likewise, the discrepancy between the two pupils' data is greater as measured by the actual rate (event) measure; it is underestimated by the interval measure. R = referred pupil, C = control pupil, T = teacher. Reprinted, with changes in notation, with permission of the publisher and author from G. J. Alessi, "Behavioral Observation for the School Psychologist: Responsive-Discrepancy Model," *School Psychology Review*, 1980, *9*, p. 39. © National Association of School Psychologists.

$$\text{Rate of behavior} = \frac{n}{t}$$

where n = number of behaviors
t = length of observation period

For example, if a girl was observed to be out of her seat 40 times during a 10-minute observation period, her rate of behavior would be as follows:

$$\text{Rate of behavior} = \frac{n}{t} = \frac{40}{10 \text{ min.}} = \frac{4}{1}$$

$$= 4 \text{ occurrences per minute}$$

Her rate of out-of-seat behavior was observed to be four times per minute. Rate of behavior is a useful index for noting changes in the child's behavior, especially across observation sessions of different length.

2. *Duration of behavior.* Duration of behavior refers to how long each occurrence of the behavior lasts — the period between the beginning and the end of the behavior. A duration count might be used, for example, to determine the duration of temper tantrums, crying episodes, arguments, verbal tirades, sustained conversations, on-task behavior, out-of-seat behavior, cooperative behavior, thumbsucking, off-task responding, or delays in returning home from school (Gelfand & Hartmann, 1984; Sulzer-Azaroff & Reese, 1982). Unless the behavior is discrete, a duration count will be difficult, if not impossible, to obtain.

In addition to the duration count, there are two other measures of the duration rate of behavior (Cone & Foster, 1982). A percentage duration rate is computed by dividing the total duration of the behavior by the length of the observation period.

$$\text{Percentage duration rate of behavior} = \frac{d}{t} \times 100$$

where d = total duration of behavior
(time spent responding)
t = length of the observation period

An average duration rate per response is computed as follows:

$$\text{Average duration rate of behavior} = \frac{d}{e}$$

where d = total duration of behavior
(time spent responding)
e = number of episodes of the behavior

Example: Suppose a child has two 3-minute tantrums (two episodes) in a 30-minute observation session on Day 1 and six 1-minute tantrums (six episodes) during a 60-minute session on Day 2. The total duration of the tantrums is 6 minutes for both days, but the response patterns differ.

Using the formula for the percentage duration rate of behavior, we have

Day 1:

$$\text{Duration rate of behavior} = \frac{d}{t} \times 100 = \frac{6 \text{ min.}}{30 \text{ min.}} \times 100$$

$$= 20\% \text{ per session}$$

Day 2:

$$\text{Duration rate of behavior} = \frac{d}{t} \times 100 = \frac{6 \text{ min.}}{60 \text{ min.}} \times 100$$

$$= 10\% \text{ per session}$$

Using the formula for the average duration rate of behavior, we have

Day 1:

$$\text{Average duration rate of behavior} = \frac{d}{e} = \frac{6 \text{ min.}}{2}$$

$$= 3 \text{ min. per response}$$

Day 2:

$$\text{Average duration rate of behavior} = \frac{d}{e} = \frac{6 \text{ min.}}{6}$$

$$= 1 \text{ min. per response}$$

The percentage method yields a duration rate of behavior of 20 percent for Day 1 and 10 percent for Day 2, whereas the average method yields an average duration rate of behavior of 3 minutes per response for Day 1 and 1 minute per response for Day 2.

The first method is preferable when you are interested in how much time the child spends in a particular activity relative to other activities, but care little about the duration of individual instances of the behavior. This method masks the duration per response. The second method is useful when you are interested in the average duration of a response, such as when you are assessing the average duration of an appropriate behavior. This method ignores the length of the time interval over which the data are collected (Cone & Foster, 1982). If desired, both duration rates can be reported.

3. *Intensity of behavior.* The intensity of behavior is obtained by dividing the behavior into various degrees of intensity, as in interval recording. For example, if you want to record various intensities of aggressive behavior, you can categorize behaviors as slightly aggressive, moderately aggressive, and severely aggressive. If you are interested in observing a boy whose teacher has reported that he turns in all assignments but complains, you can create three categories, such as "(1) hands in assignment on time with no complaints; (2) hands in assignment late with no complaints; (3) hands in assignment late and complains" (Cone & Foster, 1982, p. 316). In both of these examples, a

separate frequency count would be recorded for each category.

4. *Latency of behavior.* Latency refers to the amount of time that elapses between the initiation of a request (or between an event *known* to produce or facilitate the occurrence of a behavior) and the onset of the behavior; it tells us how long it took the child to begin the behavior. Latency is usually measured by using a stopwatch to determine the time from the initiation of the request to its execution. Latency measures are useful when you need to determine the time it takes a child to begin working after instructions have been given to start, to begin complying with a request, or to get up after an alarm rings (Sulzer-Azaroff & Reese, 1982).

Advantages of event recording. Event recording (Kazdin, 1981; Nay, 1979)

• detects behaviors with low frequency rates, particularly when observations are made by persons who are ordinarily in the setting
• facilitates the study of many different behaviors or events
• uses time and personnel efficiently (especially when observations are made by persons ordinarily in the setting)
• can accommodate many different recording methods
• provides information about changes in behavior over time and about the amount of behavior performed

Disadvantages of event recording. Event recording

• provides a somewhat artificial view of the behavior sequence by separating the present event from conditions in the past that may have led up to it
• does not reveal sequences or temporal patterns unless the time of the response is recorded
• breaks up the continuity of behavior by using limited categories
• is not suited to recording behaviors that are not clearly discrete
• presents difficulties in establishing reliability across multiple observers
• requires observers to maintain an optimal level of attention over long periods of time, because few cues are used and responses may be relatively infrequent
• limits quantification of the *how* and *why* associated with the event, unless this information is also recorded
• makes comparison across sessions difficult if the length of the observation period is not constant

Illustrations of event and duration recording. Figure 17-7 illustrates how event recording can be used to com-

| | *Referred child:* Bill | | *Date:* March 1, 1986 | |
| | *Comparison child:* Ted | | *Class:* Mrs. Jones | |

| | *Time of day* | | | |
Day	9:00 to 9:30	11:00 to 11:30	2:00 to 2:30	*Total* (Bill/Ted)
Monday	4/1	3/0	2/0	9/1
Tuesday	3/0	2/0	0/0	5/0
Wednesday	4/1	4/1	1/0	9/2
Thursday	2/0	2/0	1/1	5/1
Friday	1/0	1/0	0/1	2/1
Total	14/2	12/1	4/2	30/5

Figure 17-7.   Example of event recording of inappropriate talking to another child. This record presents a summary of the observational records for two children: Bill, the referred child, and Ted, the comparison child. The numbers indicate the number of times Bill or Ted spoke with another child inappropriately. Numbers for Bill are to the left of the slash, and numbers for Ted are to the right of the slash. The record indicates that during the 7½ hours of observation, Bill spoke to another child six times more frequently than did Ted. His inappropriate behavior occurred most frequently on Monday and Wednesday and at 9:00–9:30 and 11:00–11:30 A.M. The inappropriate behavior seldom occurred on Friday or at 2:00–2:30 P.M. Further investigation would be needed to determine what factors in the child's environment lead to increases and decreases in the inappropriate behavior. In addition, further observations should be made to determine the stability of the observed behavior pattern.

pare two children's inappropriate talking. Exhibit 17-6 shows how event recording, coupled with a duration count, was used to observe one child's out-of-seat behavior. Notice that a reliability check was performed.

Exercises for developing event recording skills.   Some exercises for developing your skills in event recording are given in Exhibit 17-7.

Ratings Recording

In the rating method, behavior is rated on a scale or checklist, usually at the end of the observation period. Rating scales usually involve a greater degree of observer subjectivity than do the other behavioral recording methods.

Major uses of ratings recording.   Ratings are useful for evaluating the more global aspects of behavior and for quantifying impressions, such as after a psychometric assessment has been completed. The Behavior and Attitude Checklist in Chapter 5 is one such rating procedure. Rating scales are also useful for assessing behaviors or products that are difficult to measure directly. For example, a rating scale that runs from very poor (1) to excellent (7) can be used to rate the legibility of handwriting, quality of arts and crafts products, neatness of a room, or performance style during physical exercises or other activities.

Results based on ratings can be compared with results obtained from more specific observational procedures, such as interval or event recording. Such comparisons reveal the consistency of the results across methods. Ratings are valuable in some assessment situations because they are less costly than other methods in terms of time and personnel resources. Ratings also allow you to consider more subtle and unique clues, to overcome some of the fragmentation associated with behavioral counts, and to evaluate a quality and unity in the child's behavior that is inaccessible to more molecular and objective coding systems. Hence ratings may reveal more subtle aspects of impression formation. The quantitative dimension associated with ratings is sometimes termed "behavior as a whole."

How to design a ratings recording.   In designing a ratings recording you must decide on (a) the number of times you will observe the child, (b) the length of the observation period, (c) the time periods during which the observations will be conducted, (d) the target behaviors to be observed, and (e) the method of recording data.

Frequency, length, and time of observation period. As in the other recording methods, the child's age, the setting, and the reason for the assessment will determine in part the number of times you will need to observe the child, the length of the observation period, and when the observations will be conducted. An observation session may last from 10 to 30 minutes or longer. Try to time the

Exhibit 17-6

Illustration of Event Recording in a Classroom

EVENT AND DURATION RECORDING: OBSERVING OUT-OF-SEAT BEHAVIOR

Student and Setting

Linda, a 9-year-old girl with an IQ of 70, had excessive out-of-seat behavior. She attended a primary level special class for the educable mentally retarded in a public school system. The teacher said that Linda functioned educationally at approximately the first grade level and spent most of the day out of her seat. This behavior interfered with the completion of classroom work and distracted other children. Observations were held Monday through Friday from 9:00 A.M. to 9:20 A.M. during the math period in the child's classroom. The observation was designed so as not to interfere with regular classroom routines.

Coding Category

The observer sat against a wall in the classroom, approximately 10 feet from the child, and observed Linda. One kind of inappropriate response—out-of-seat behavior—was recorded. This behavior was rated as occurring when the child did not have her buttocks in contact with the chair seat and body oriented toward her work. An event recording system was used to count discrete out-of-seat behaviors. In addition, the total duration of each behavior was recorded using a stopwatch that was started and stopped contingent on each behavior. Reliability was assessed by having two observers use the rating system to record Linda's behavior simultaneously but independently. These checks were taken a minimum of two times per session. Observer agreement was calculated by dividing the number of out-of-seat responses scored by the observer with the lower number of responses by the number of out-of-seat responses scored by the observer with the greater number of responses and then multiplying by 100. Duration was calculated in a similar manner.

Source: Adapted from Whitman, Scibak, Butler, Richter, and Johnson (1982).

Method of recording data. Ratings are recorded on a rating scale, usually with five or seven points. Following are some typical setups for rating scales:

Example 1:
Circle the most appropriate number:

1	2	3	4	5
highly co-operative	moderately cooperative	neither co-operative nor un-cooperative	moderately unco-operative	highly un-cooperative

Example 2:
Shares toys (circle one number):

1	2	3	4	5
always	often	occasionally	seldom	never

Example 3:
Place an X on the line that best reflects your rating.

anxious __:__:__:__:__ not anxious

Rating systems can be designed to measure selected antecedents and consequences associated with the target behavior. For example, you might ask "When situation Z occurs, how often does Mike do X?" or "After Mike does X, how often does [other person] react by doing Y?" Rating scales for these questions are shown in Examples 4 and 5 below.

Example 4:
When Mike is asked to read aloud, how often does he throw a temper tantrum? Circle one.

1	2	3	4	5
almost always	frequently	sometimes	infrequently	almost never

Example 5:
After Mike throws a temper tantrum, how often do his peers react by laughing? Circle one.

1	2	3	4	5
almost always	frequently	sometimes	infrequently	almost never

Quantitative data in ratings recording. The prime source of data in ratings is the scale value (or number or score) on the rating scale. A major difficulty associated

---

observation period so that you obtain a representative sample of behavior. If possible, observe the child on more than one occasion and at different times during the day.

Target behaviors. As in interval and event recording, your selection of target behaviors should be based on prior information from narrative recordings, interviews, referral questions, or test behavior.

Exhibit 17-7

Event Recording Exercises

Exercise 1

With a co-observer, observe one child on a playground for 5 minutes. Using an event recording procedure, record each time the child engages in play (as a general category) with another child. Play with another child includes parallel, cooperative, and uncooperative play (see Table E-4 in Appendix E for definitions), but not solitary play. Use the dot-and-line method to record the target behavior.

After you have completed your recording, determine the level of interobserver agreement by calculating percentage agreement (see the section on procedures for assessing reliability toward the end of this chapter). Also calculate the rate of the target behavior.

Consider the following questions in evaluating your event recording.

- Which behaviors were observed most clearly (that is, most easily classified as indicating play)?
- Did the target behavior occur with sufficient frequency to be observed?
- To what extent might the time of day have affected the child's behavior?
- To what extent did the setting affect the child's behavior?
- To what extent was the target behavior representative of the child's behavior during the observation?
- What could be done to improve the representativeness of the observations?
- To what extent was the child's behavior representative of that of other children of the same age level?
- What biases, if any, may have affected your observations?
- How did your presence alter the child's behavior?
- What could you have done to avoid this influence?
- How did your event recording contribute to your understanding of the child?

Write a one- or two-paragraph report that describes your observation. Include information about (a) the child (age, sex, physical handicaps, and other relevant characteristics), (b) the physical setting in which the observation took place, (c) the length of time you observed the child, (d) the frequency of the target behavior, (e) the level of agreement with your co-observer, (f) the difficulty of determining when the target behavior began and ended, (g) whether the definition of the target behavior was satisfactory and suggestions for improving the definition, and (h) the implications of the findings (for example, whether the behavior was appropriate or inappropriate).

Exercise 2

Follow the same general procedure as described in Exercise 1. Now, however, observe three target behaviors: (a) parallel play, (b) cooperative play, and (c) uncooperative play (see Table E-4 in Appendix E for definitions). Calculate the level of interobserver percentage agreement separately for each of the three target behaviors. Calculate the rate of behavior separately for each target behavior. Follow the guidelines in Exercise 1.

Exercise 3

Compare the recordings obtained in Exercises 1 and 2. What are the differences between observing play as a general category, as in Exercise 1, and observing different types of play, as in Exercise 2? What purposes do each type of recording serve? What information do you gain (or lose) with each type of recording? Which recording is more reliable and why? Write up your analysis in a one- or two-paragraph report.

Exercise 4

With a co-observer, observe a child in a preschool for a 30-minute period. Obtain permission from the school administration before beginning this activity. Select a child who appears to be engaging in inappropriate behavior (a target behavior), such as fighting, temper tantrums, disruptive behavior, or uncooperative behavior. Record each time the inappropriate behavior occurs, using the dot-and-line method.

Also observe whether the child's inappropriate behavior receives attention from an adult in the room (a target behavior). This information will provide some indication of the consequences of the behavior. Record each time the child receives attention, using the dot-and-line method. Your recording form should have spaces for recording the frequency of the child's inappropriate behavior and the frequency of the adult's attention.

Calculate the level of interobserver percentage agreement separately for the two target behaviors. Calculate the rate of behavior separately for the two target behaviors. Follow the guidelines in Exercise 1.

Exercise 5

Follow the same general procedure as described in Exercise 1. Now, however, record the *duration* of the child's play with another child. Use a stopwatch or other device to record the elapsed time. Calculate the level of interobserver agreement, the duration rate of behavior, and the average duration rate of behavior.

with ratings is that the assumptions underlying the scale values are not always clear; therefore observers may differ in their interpretation of the scale positions. Providing detailed examples of behaviors associated with each scale point will help observers to apply consistent standards in interpreting scale values. Ratings should always be made shortly after the completion of the observation session. Establishing ratings from memory creates opportunities for distortion and omissions.

Advantages of ratings recording. The ratings method

• is suited to recording many different kinds of behaviors
• can be used to rate the behaviors of many individuals or of a group as a whole
• records subtle aspects of behavior
• generates data in a form suitable for statistical analysis
• uses time efficiently

Disadvantages of ratings recording. The ratings method

• uses scale values which may be based on unclear assumptions
• may have low interrater reliability because of complex or ambiguous terms and scale positions that are interpreted differently by different observers
• is not suited to recording important quantitative information, such as the frequency, duration, or latency of behavior
• is not suited to recording antecedent and consequent events, unless a method for doing so is built into the design of the ratings recording
• may be inaccurate if there is a time delay between the actual behavior and the observer's rating

Illustration of ratings recording. The behavioral rating scale shown in Table 17-4 was developed to assess the presence of distress behaviors (pain and anxiety) in children undergoing a painful medical procedure—bone marrow aspiration treatment for cancer. The scale can be completed at various times during the procedure. The observers do not participate in the treatment procedure; they position themselves so that they are unobtrusive but still have a clear view of the child as he or she lies prone on the treatment table. This scale can also be used for rating children's reactions to other painful medical procedures.

Exercises for developing ratings recording skills. Some exercises for developing your skills in ratings recording are given in Exhibit 17-8.

Table 17-4
Procedure Behavior Checklist

Directions: Rate each behavior using the following 5-point scale.

1	2	3	4	5
very mild	mild	neutral	intense	extremely intense

Circle one number for each behavior.

Behavior		Rating			
1. Muscle tension	1	2	3	4	5
2. Screaming	1	2	3	4	5
3. Crying	1	2	3	4	5
4. Restraint used	1	2	3	4	5
5. Pain verbalized	1	2	3	4	5
6. Anxiety verbalized	1	2	3	4	5
7. Verbal stalling	1	2	3	4	5
8. Physical resistance	1	2	3	4	5

Note. Behaviors are defined as follows: (1) *Muscle tension*—contraction of any observable body part (for example, shuts eyes tight, clenches jaw, stiffens body, clenches fists, or grits teeth); (2) *Screaming*—raises voice or yells with sounds or words; (3) *Crying*—displays tears or sobs; (4) *Restraint used*—is held down by someone or has heavy tape placed across legs onto table; (5) *Pain verbalized*—says "ow," "ouch," or comments about hurting (for example, "You're hurting me"); (6) *Anxiety verbalized*—says "I'm scared" or "I'm afraid"; (7) *Verbal stalling*—verbally expresses desire to delay ("Stop," "I'm not ready," "I want to tell you something," etc.); (8) *Physical resistance*—moves around, will not stay in position, or tries to climb off table.
See Katz, Kellerman, and Siegel (1980) for additional items.
Source: Adapted from LeBaron and Zeltzer (1984).

Interval, Event, and Ratings Recording Methods: Advantages and Special Considerations

Interval, event, and ratings recording methods may not provide the richness of information that narrative recordings do, but they allow you to evaluate systematically specific behaviors of interest, sample a large number of children and a variety of situations, compare children and develop norms, and generalize findings, all within a reasonable period of time.

In both interval and event recording it is relatively easy to tally behaviors, particularly when they are clearly defined and observable. Both methods provide information about behavior during one time period and about changes in the child's behavior over time.

When you wish to obtain information about behavior across time intervals (or temporal patterns of behavioral occurrences), interval recording procedures should be considered. Interval recording can answer a question such as "Did Tom's off-task behavior occur throughout the observation period or just during part of the observational

■ **Exhibit 17-8** ■

Ratings Recording Exercises

Exercise 1

With a co-observer, observe one child on a playground for a period of 5 minutes. After you observe the child, complete the following rating scales.

RATING SCALES

Directions: Place an X in the appropriate space.

1. cooperative ___:___:___:___:___ uncooperative
2. sad   ___:___:___:___:___ happy
3. active   ___:___:___:___:___ inactive
4. coordinated ___:___:___:___:___ uncoordinated
5. aggressive ___:___:___:___:___ passive

After you complete the scales, convert each rating to a number, assigning the number 1 to ratings in the left-most column and the number 5 to ratings in the right-most column. Determine the level of interobserver agreement by calculating (a) the percentage agreement (that is, how many ratings were exactly the same across the five scales) and (b) the product-moment correlation (see Chapter 2).

Consider the following questions in evaluating your ratings recording.

- How did the rating scales guide your observations?
- What additional scales would have been useful?
- To what extent might the time of day have affected the child's behavior?
- To what extent did the setting affect the child's behavior?
- To what extent were the dimensions covered in the scales representative of the child's general behavior?

- What could be done to improve the representativeness of the observations?
- To what extent was the child's behavior representative of that of other children of the same age level?
- Did the scales reveal information that might have been missed with a narrative recording?
- What biases, if any, may have affected your observations?
- How did your presence alter the child's behavior?
- What could you have done to avoid this influence?
- How did your ratings recording contribute to your understanding of the child?

Write a one- or two-paragraph report that describes your observation. Include information about (a) the child (age, sex, physical handicaps, and other relevant characteristics), (b) the physical setting in which the observation took place, (c) the length of time you observed the child, (d) the ratings you made, (e) the level of agreement with your co-observer, (f) the difficulties you had in using the rating scales and suggestions for improving the scales, and (g) the implications of the findings (for example, whether the behavior was appropriate or inappropriate).

Exercise 2

Design your own ratings recording procedure for observing children in some setting. Develop five rating scales different from those used in Exercise 1. With a co-observer, observe one child or a group of children, depending on the specific procedure developed, for a period of 5 minutes. Follow the procedures in Exercise 1 for evaluating your recording.

interval?" Interval recording can be enhanced by making the length of the interval as close as possible to the duration of the behavior. Generally, interval recording provides a sample of behavior adequate for many clinical and psychoeducational purposes, particularly when the concern is whether a behavior occurs. Infrequent momentary behaviors have a reasonable chance of being scored with interval recording if observation sessions are long.

Event recording is somewhat more useful than interval recording when you want a measure of the number of times a behavior is performed. Such a measure is important when either an increase or a decrease in certain behaviors is an intervention goal. Event recording is especially useful when the characteristics of an event or behavior are of interest, such as the frequency of the behavior itself. Event recording, however, is not as useful as interval

recording for behaviors that do not have a discrete beginning and ending.

OBSERVATIONAL CODING SYSTEMS

Observational coding systems are used to categorize behavioral observations. They usually consist of two or more categories that cover a wide range of behaviors, although on occasion a single category may be appropriate. Even a one-category system, however, implicitly contains another category—the nonoccurrence of the target behavior. Thus even though the focus is on one behavior, a one-category coding system used in an interval or event recording method can be conceptualized as having two categories— the presence of the behavior and the absence of it.

Before you use a coding system, you should carefully evaluate the following areas (Nay, 1979): (a) its rationale, (b) the setting(s) in which it is applicable, (c) definitions of the coding categories, (d) description of how behavior is sampled, (e) rules governing the behavior of observers, such as hierarchy of codes, (f) reliability, including types of reliability, overall reliability, and reliability of each coding category, (g) validity, and (h) positive and negative features (including potential problem areas of the coding system).

How to Design an Observational Coding System

In designing an observational coding system, select categories that best meet the assessment, treatment, or research goals. Categories range from those that are primarily *global*, incorporating many different specific behaviors or requiring inferential judgments, to those that are *narrow* or *specific*, focusing on only one or a few behaviors. The two-category system in Table 17-6 contains global behavioral categories: on-task behavior and off-task behavior. In contrast, the 10-category system in Table 17-6 employs narrow categories that relate to specific classroom behaviors.

In selecting (or designing) an observational system, consider the following:

• What questions do you hope to answer with your observational assessment?
• Are you interested in investigating global areas of behavior or just one or a few specific behaviors?
• How many behaviors do you want to observe?
• Are the behaviors you want to observe easily discriminated?

Both global and narrow target behaviors should be defined as completely as possible to help the observer detect behaviors and distinguish one behavior from another. Global categories subsume a host of individual behaviors, whereas narrow categories focus on only one or a few behaviors. When global categories are used, each individual behavior must be classified into one of the global categories.

Use the simplest possible coding system that will answer the questions posed. If your purpose is to obtain a general description of behavior, use global categories. If you are interested in only one or a few behaviors related to the referral question, use a detailed analysis of these behaviors. If you want to examine the relationship between a behavior and its environmental determinants, use a multidimensional system that includes relevant antecedent and consequent events. Finally, if you want to record sequential observational data, use the sequential observational procedures described by Bakeman and Gottman (1986).

Generally, when there are just a few behaviors to be measured, devising an adequate recording system is not difficult. Coding systems that require the observer to make a number of decisions and use many different categories should be avoided because they are difficult to use. Try to memorize the coding system before the formal observation begins, but keep the code definitions handy in case you forget them.

Numerous qualitative observational coding systems have been developed to meet both general and specific needs, including the observation of individual children, groups, and classes in a variety of settings. Observational codes can also cover environmental responses to the child's behavior. Table 17-5 lists observational coding systems that are useful for a variety of purposes. Tables 17-6, 17-7, and 17-8 illustrate coding systems for observing children, teachers, and classrooms. The systems illustrated in these tables require immediate, not retrospective, observation; the observer must observe and record behavior as it occurs, keeping inferences to a minimum.

Examples of Coding Systems for Observing Children's Behavior

Table 17-6 shows several coding systems for observing children's behavior. The *two-category coding system* is one of the simplest systems for observing the behavior of a referred child or group. The information it provides about on-task and off-task behavior is useful particularly when the general climate of a classroom or other facility is the focus of assessment. Distinguishing between the two categories in the system may require some inferential judgments on the part of the observer.

The *three-category system* is a refinement of the two-category system, with off-task behavior divided into passive and disruptive off-task behavior. This refinement is useful for the assessing the passive and active dimensions of inappropriate behavior. These two dimensions are similar to the internalizing (passive) and externalizing (disruptive) dimensions of child behavior found on behavioral checklists. (See Chapter 15 for coverage of behavioral checklists.) This three-category system can be used for individuals as well as for an entire class.

The *four-category system* breaks down the disruptive off-task behavior category into verbal and motor off-task components. This system is useful when information is desired about whether the off-task behavior is verbal, motor, or passive. It is often used for observing individual children in a classroom.

Table 17-5
Some Observational Coding Systems

Authors	Observational system
Achenbach & Edelbrock (1981)	*Child Behavior Checklist—Direct Observation Form*: A 96-item observation form that parallels the parent and teacher versions of the Child Behavior Checklist.
Conger (1984)	*Social Interaction Scoring System*: A group of seven different coding systems emphasizing different aspects of social interactions, including exchanges within families. Codes are for six types of interactions, seven types of emotional affects, and five types of persons.
Dunn, Barker, & Wahler (1981)	*Standardized Observation Codes*: A 29-category coding system (a revision of the Wahler, House, & Stambaugh, 1976, coding system) designed to sample interchanges between a child and the child's adult and peer associates.
Fagot (1984)	*Interactive Behavior Code*: A 51-category behavioral observation code designed to assess a child's play preferences.
Furey & Forehand (1983)	*Daily Child Behavior Checklist*: A 65-item checklist of pleasing and displeasing behaviors that may have occurred in the preceding 24 hours. Parent completes checklist.
Jay & Elliott (1981)	*Observation Scale of Behavioral Distress*: An 11-category observational code for recording anxiety or pain in children undergoing painful medical procedures.
Kirschenbaum, Steffen, & D'Orta (1978)	*Social Competence Classroom Behavioral Observation System*: An 11-category behavioral observation system, including 5 categories of task-irrelevant behavior, 3 categories of task-relevant behavior, and 3 categories of prosocial behavior.
Mash, Terdal, & Anderson (1973)	*Response-Class Matrix*: An observational coding system for recording mother-child interactions, with 7 categories for the mother and 7 categories for the child.
Reid (1978)	*Behavioral Observation Code Used with Families*: A 29-category observational code for recording family interactions.
Roberts, Milich, & Loney (1984)	*Structured Observation of Academic and Play Settings*: A 7-category structured playroom observation procedure for evaluating hyperactivity.

Note. The observational code systems for Furey and Forehand (1983); Kirschenbaum, Steffen, and D'Orta (1978); Mash, Terdal, and Anderson (1973); and Reid (1978) are available in the publications (see the reference section at the end of this text). The other observational systems can be obtained directly from the authors. Their addresses are as follows: Thomas M. Achenbach, University of Vermont, Burlington, VT 05405; Rand D. Conger, College of Home Economics, Iowa State University, Ames, IO 50011; Elizabeth S. Dunn, Child Behavior Institute, University of Tennessee, Knoxville, TN 37996; Beverly I. Fagot, Department of Psychology, University of Oregon, Eugene, OR 97405; Susan M. Jay, Psychosocial Program, Division of Hematology-Oncology, Children's Hospital of Los Angeles, 4650 Sunset Boulevard, Los Angeles, CA 90027; and Mary Ann Roberts, Department of Psychology, University of Iowa, Iowa City, IO 52242.

The *ten-category system* is a more extensive system for observing classroom behavior, with 9 of the 10 categories referring to inappropriate behavior. This and similar systems provide detailed information about a child's actions. The complete system with recording instructions can be found in Appendix E, Table E-1; it is called the Classroom Observation Code: A Modification of the Stony Brook Code. The system is especially useful for recording hyperactive behavior.

Other coding systems are also shown in Appendix E. Table E-2 is a 28-item behavioral observation system for observing the social competence of preschool children; it classifies behavior according to such dimensions as interest, apathy, cooperation, and anger. Table E-3 is a 42-item observation scale for rating autism in real-life settings.

The items are grouped into five areas: sensorimotor responses, social relationships, affectual responses, sensory responses, and language. Table E-4 is a 4-category system for coding children's play.

Coding Systems for Observing Teachers' Behavior

Observational coding systems are also useful for studying the behavior of classroom teachers. The teacher's behavior should be evaluated, because it may affect the referred child's behavior and the classroom climate. The two-, three-, and six-category systems in Table 17-7 provide a record of the teacher's interactions with a specific child or the class as a whole.

Table 17-6
Illustrations of Coding Systems for Observing Children's Behavior

Coding system	*Examples*
I. Two Categories	
1. On-Task Behavior (appropriate behavior for the situation)	Putting hand up when he or she wants to say something, listening while teacher is talking, working quietly at desk, asking teacher for permission to leave desk
2. Off-Task Behavior (inappropriate behavior for the situation)	a. Passive inappropriate actions (for example, staring into space, lack of interest, short attention span, poor concentration, lack of perseverance)
	b. Active inappropriate actions (for example, making noise, hitting, fighting, banging, being out of seat without permission, physical destructiveness, stealing, threatening others, setting fires)
II. Three Categories	
1. On-Task Behavior	See examples under I.1.
2. Passive Off-Task Behavior (passive behavior that is inappropriate but does not disrupt others)	See examples under I.2.a.
3. Disuptive Off-Task Behavior (inappropriate disruptive behavior)	See examples under I.2.b.
III. Four Categories	
1. On-Task Behavior	See examples under I.1.
2. Verbal Off-Task Behavior	Talking out, teasing
3. Motor Off-Task Behavior	Being out of seat, hitting others, throwing objects, playing with objects
4. Passive Off-Task Behavior	Daydreaming, sleeping, sulking
IV. Ten Categories	
1. Interference	Interrupting teacher or student
2. Off-Task	Engaging in other than assigned work
3. Noncompliance	Failing to follow teacher's instructions
4. Minor Motor Movements	Moving buttocks, rocking
5. Gross Motor Movements	Leaving seat, standing without permission
6. Out-of-Chair Behavior	Remaining out of chair for a period of time
7. Physical Aggression	Kicking, hitting
8. Threat or Verbal Aggression	Making threatening gestures, bullying
9. Solicitation of Teacher	Raising hand, calling out to teacher
10. Absence of Behavior	Engaging in no inappropriate behavior as defined by the above categories

Note. The 10-category system is from Abikoff and Gittelman (1985) and can be found in Table E-1 in Appendix E.

Coding Systems for Observing Students, Teachers, and Class

Any of the separate coding systems designed for students and teachers can be combined into one system. Categories also can be added for the entire class.

Table 17-8 illustrates one such combined coding system, which emphasizes appropriate as well as inappropriate behaviors. The 11 categories of student behavior include 6 on-task behaviors, 4 off-task behaviors, and 1 neutral behavior. There are four teacher codes and two class codes.

Table 17-7
Illustrations of Coding Systems for Observing Teachers' Behavior

Coding system	Examples
I. Two Categories	
1. Verbal Approval Responses (comments that follow an on-task behavior)	"Bob, your spelling has improved considerably."
2. Verbal Disapproval Responses (comments that follow an off-task behavior)	"Class, stop making noise."
II. Three Categories	
1. Praise (verbalization indicating that the teacher was pleased with the student's behavior)	"John, your reading was excellent."
2. Prompts (verbalization conveying additional information or directing the student's attention to the task)	"The first step in solving the problem is to divide the sales price by the number of items purchased."
3. Criticism (verbalization indicating that the teacher was displeased with the student's behavior)	"Mary, do not talk during the reading assignment."
III. Six Categories	
1. Academic Approval	"Your score was much improved."
2. Academic Disapproval	"Your study habits are not satisfactory."
3. Social Approval	"I am pleased with your ability to work with Helen."
4. Social Disapproval	"Your relationship with your teammates is poor."
5. Mistake (inappropriate use of one of the above four behaviors)	Informing child that behavior was unsatisfactory when there was no evidence that it was
6. No Approval or Disapproval	Absence of behaviors that could be recorded as approval or disapproval

RECORDING METHOD AND CODING SYSTEM COMBINED

The three examples in this section illustrate how recording methods are combined with coding systems. Exhibit 17-9 shows how event recording is combined with a three-category coding system to examine aggressive behavior on the playground. In Exhibit 17-10 interval recording is combined with a staff-resident interaction coding system to study efforts at habilitation of mentally retarded individuals. The detailed ward coding system allows for an in-depth analysis of staff-resident interactions, whereas the playground coding system focuses on aggressive behaviors only. The playground coding system, of course, can be expanded to include other behavioral categories. Exhibit 17-11 shows how event and ratings recordings can be used in a planned incident procedure to observe preschool children's emotions.

GUIDELINES FOR DESIGNING AN OBSERVATIONAL ASSESSMENT

The following guidelines will assist you in designing a behavioral observation assessment:

• *Design or select a coding system that represents the behaviors of concern.*

• *Select the recording method that best fits the coding system.* (The four major types of recording methods are summarized in Table 17-9.)

• *Use categories sparingly.* Do not overload the coding system with too many categories.

• *Use categories that are easily discriminable.* Clearly define each category, and be sure that the categories can be readily discriminated from each other.

• *Select an appropriate interval length.* Use an interval length that is likely to reveal the duration of the observed behaviors.

• *Select an appropriate length of time for the observations.* Use a duration period that is sufficient to reveal the most salient features of the behavior under observation without taxing your ability to record accurately. Excessively long observations contribute to observer drift and unreliability.

• *Select appropriate observation times and places.* Schedule the observation period so that it coincides with the times of day when the target behavior is most likely to occur. Observational findings are most generalizable when

Table 17-8
Coding System for Observing Students and Teachers in the Classroom

Student Code Summaries

Attending (AT)
The student must be (a) looking at the teacher when the teacher is talking, (b) looking at materials in the classroom that have to do with the lesson, or (c) be engaged in other looking behavior appropriate to the academic situation.

Working (WK)
The student is working on academic material without any overt verbal components either in a group or in individual seatwork situations.

Volunteering (VO)
By verbal or nonverbal means, the student responds to teacher requests by volunteering information of an academic nature.

Reading Aloud (RA)
The student is reading aloud either individually or as a part of a group recitation.

Appropriate Behavior (AB)
This is a broad category used to code appropriate behavior not otherwise specifically defined, including asking or answering questions, raising hand for help, acquiring or passing out materials.

Interaction with Peer about Academic Materials (IP+)
The student is interacting with a peer or peers about academic materials and is not violating classroom rules. Verbal communications between peers, e.g., talking, handing materials, working together on academic materials, etc., were coded IP+.

Interaction with Peer about Nonacademic Materials (IP−)
The student is interacting with a peer about academic materials inappropriate for the period in which the observation occurs (unless this has been approved by the teacher), or about nonacademic material. The interaction may be verbal or nonverbal.

Don't Know (DK)
The child indicates, in either a verbal or nonverbal manner, that he or she does not know the answer.

Inappropriate Locale (IL)
The child, without the teacher's approval, is in a classroom area that is not appropriate for the academic activity that is going on at the time.

Look Around (LA)
The child is looking away from the appropriate academic task at hand.

Inappropriate Behavior (IB)
This is a second broad category used to code inappropriate behaviors not otherwise defined. Illustrations include situations where the child calls out an answer when a question is directed to another student, or interrupts the teacher or another student who is talking.

Teacher Code Summaries

Approval (AP)
The teacher gives a clear verbal, gestural, or physical approval to the student or to the group of which the student is a member.

Disapproval (DI)
The teacher gives a clear verbal, gestural, or physical disapproval of the child's behavior either individually or as part of a group.

No Response (NR)
The teacher does not respond to the student either as a part of the group or individually.

Verbal Interaction (VI)
Verbalizations directed at the child or his or her group which are not approvals or disapprovals. Verbalizations relating to instruction or management.

Class Code Summaries

Appropriate Behavior (AB_g)
The entire class (all students) is engaged in activities that are considered appropriate to the situation as defined by the teacher's rules and the activity at hand.

Inappropriate Behavior (IB)
At least one student in the class is observed engaged in behaviors not considered appropriate according to the teacher's rules and the activity at hand.

Source: Reprinted, with changes in notation, with permission of the publisher and authors from C. R. Greenwood, H. Hops, H. M. Walker, J. J. Guild, J. Stokes, K. R. Young, K. S. Keleman, and M. Willardson, "Standardized Classroom Management Program: Social Validation and Replication Studies in Utah and Oregon," *Journal of Applied Behavior Analysis*, 1979, *12*, p. 240. © Society for the Experimental Analysis of Behavior, Inc.

observations are conducted across multiple environments and on multiple occasions.

• *Design or select an appropriate recording sheet.* Clearly label precoded categories and provide clear spaces for entries.

• *Design a final assessment strategy that is likely to detect the target behaviors of interest, given their typical rate and duration.* To ensure that you meet this goal, conduct extensive general observations *prior* to formulating your specific observational strategy.

■ **Exhibit 17-9** ■

Naturalistic Observation Recording of Children on a Playground: Recording Aggressiveness and Related Behaviors

Coding Categories

Three classes of problem behaviors were observed:

1. *Aggression:* Striking, slapping, tripping, kicking, pushing, or pulling others; "karate" moves ending within 1 foot of another person; doing anything that ends with another child's falling to the ground.

2. *Property abuse:* Taking another person's property without permission; throwing school books, lunches, or anyone else's property; throwing any object at passing or parked cars; digging holes in the ground with one's feet or hands; breaking pencils or pens.

3. *Rule violations:* Resisting or talking back to an aide; climbing more than 1 foot off the ground on a playground structure not meant for climbing; suspending one's self on a playground structure in any position that results in the head's not being 180 degrees above the feet.

The Playground Observation System

The playground was divided into three roughly equivalent "pie slices" based on the existing geography (for example, building corners or edges of playground equipment), which were the responsibility of separate observers. These slices were then halved (again, defined by other permanent structures), and each half was monitored for alternate 15-second periods. Thus an observer attended to only one-sixth of the playground at a time, and only half the playground was observed at any given moment.

Three observers stood in the middle of the playground facing their areas. A tape recording instructed them to start

watching the left-hand portion of their slice, at which time they began recording incidents with the aid of hand counters. After 15 seconds, the tape cued a "switch" to the remaining portion of the observers' area. This continued for 2 minutes, when a "stop" signaled that the cumulative frequency of incidents observed was to be entered on the data sheets. The entire process occurred for 10 iterations (that is, observe left for 15 seconds, observe right for 15 seconds, and back left again, recording the totals every 2 minutes) from 8:20 to 8:40 A.M.

A particular inappropriate incident (for example, kicking) directed at one child by another child was only counted once per 15-second interval. However, more than one incident was scored if one child inflicted several types of aggression on another (for example, one child's hitting and kicking another resulted in two incidents' being counted). If two children assaulted a third individual or one child assaulted two peers, two incidents were scored. The 15-second intervals were arbitrarily considered to be independent; thus, if two children were observed to be wrestling with one another for two intervals, four incidents were recorded.

Reliability

Reliability was determined by having interobserver checks on various days.

Source: Reprinted, with changes in notation, with permission of the publisher and authors from H. A. Murphy, J. M. Hutchison, and J. S. Bailey, "Behavioral School Psychology Goes Outdoors: The Effects of Organized Games in Playground Aggression," *Journal of Applied Behavior Analysis*, 1983, *16*, pp. 30–31. © Society for the Experimental Analysis of Behavior, Inc.

RELIABILITY OF BEHAVIORAL OBSERVATIONS: GENERAL CONSIDERATIONS

Sources of Unreliability

The data obtained from behavioral observations, like those obtained from any other assessment procedure, must be reliable and valid. It is important to establish observer agreement in order to ensure that your observations are replicable and consistent (reliable), which in turn will aid in establishing accuracy (validity). In the observation of behavior, reliability and validity are influenced by the observer; the setting, scales, and instruments; the child; the sample (in observations of a group of children); and the

interactions among all of these sources. Sources of error in the four basic areas are described in Table 17-10. Although most of Table 17-10 requires no explanation, some observer errors and errors associated with the referred child (or group) deserve further comment.

Observer bias. Many errors associated with the personal qualities of the observer are subsumed under the broad category of observer bias. The term *observer bias* is used to refer to any of a number of different errors associated with the personal qualities of the observer. Observer bias encompasses anything an observer does that distorts the recording of behavior—such as form expectations, prefer certain categories or certain scale positions, exer-

Exhibit 17-10

**Naturalistic Observation in an Institution for the Mentally Retarded:
Recording Staff and Residents' Efforts at Habilitation**

Coding Categories

Behaviors of both staff and residents were recorded. The following coding categories were used for staff and resident behaviors:

STAFF BEHAVIORS

1. *No interaction* — no physical or verbal interaction between the staff member and any resident.

2. *Verbal instruction* — through standard language (that is, either vocal or manual communication), staff instructs the resident to perform some activity and offers no physical assistance.

3. *Nonverbal instruction* — through a gesture (not including manual communication), staff instructs the resident to perform some activity and offers no physical assistance.

4. *Verbal instruction with physical assistance* — through standard language (that is, either vocal or manual communication), staff instructs the resident to perform some activity and provides physical assistance (for example, guides resident through a self-dressing task with verbal aid).

5. *Nonverbal instruction with physical assistance* — through a gesture (not including manual communication), staff instructs the resident to perform some activity and provides physical assistance (for example, points to the door and guides resident to move toward the door).

6. *Physical assistance* — without prior verbal or nonverbal instruction, staff physically assists resident (for example, staff helps resident put on his or her shoes).

7. *Social* — staff claps or praises, hugs, etc., resident.

8. *Custodial guidance* — staff physically assists resident in a custodial manner in a non-task situation (for example, ties shoes of resident in order to allow resident to move along quickly with other residents).

RESIDENT BEHAVIORS

1. *On-task* — resident emits a verbal or motoric response to a question, command, instruction, or nonverbal cue (for example, a gesture by the staff), or complies without making an overt response when no overt response is necessary or appropriate (for example, looking at pictures in a book).

2. *Off-task* — in the presence of a cue for responding, resident either does not respond, responds inappropriately, or does not look at relevant task stimuli.

3. *No programming* — nothing is being asked of the resident, being demonstrated to the resident, or being provided for the resident to do.

4. *Self-aggressive* — resident intentionally strikes, bites, slaps, hits, or kicks own body, or causes his or her body to contact with force other objects.

5. *Other aggressive* — resident intentionally strikes at, throws objects at, or verbally threatens others, or in some other way threatens to harm another resident or a staff member.

6. *Self-stimulatory* — resident engages in solitary activity but actively manipulates some object(s), or is engaged in solitary, asocial, repetitive behavior (for example, rocking, headweaving).

Recording Procedure

For 16 days, four observers recorded for 250 minutes per day. Each person observed in one of five locations for about 50 minutes. Then the observer walked to another location and recorded for another 50 minutes. This procedure was followed from about 9:30 to 11:20 A.M. and 1:00 to 3:50 P.M. each day, until each observer had recorded in the five locations. Sites were rotated so that no observer was in one site more than once per day, and so that each site was observed by each person about the same amount of time. Data were recorded at 6-second intervals, with the intervals being signaled through earplugs by a portable tape recorder. At the end of each 6-second interval, the observer marked any response category that had occurred within the 6-second interval.

There were three recording rules other than that of simply marking what had just occurred: (a) After observation of a staff member, something had to be marked. If none of the seven response categories had occurred, the observer marked the no interaction category. (b) After each observation of a resident, on-task, off-task, or no programming had to be marked (the categories of aggression and self-stimulation were to be marked only if they had just occurred). (c) If more than one resident or staff response occurred in the same interval, both could be marked (for example, self-stimulatory and off-task responding).

Reliability

Interobserver agreement was assessed each day by having a second observer randomly assigned to the various recording sites. This produced about 40 hours of reliability assessment. Observations were coordinated through a y-plug from the tape recorder that allowed each observer to hear the beginning of each successive interval. Because something was marked at the end of each 6-second interval and because the observers were 3 meters apart, the observations were quite independent. Interobserver agreement was calculated by dividing the number of intervals in which both observers agreed by the total number of intervals.

Source: Reprinted, with changes in notation, with permission of the publisher and authors from A. C. Repp and L. E. Barton, "Naturalistic Observations of Institutionalized Retarded Persons: A Comparison of Licensure Decisions and Behavioral Observations," *Journal of Applied Behavior Analysis*, 1980, *13*, pp. 335–337. © Society for the Experimental Analysis of Behavior, Inc.

Table 17-9
Observational Recording Methods

Recording method	Types	Applications	Data	Advantages	Disadvantages
Narrative recording Behavior is comprehensively described.	*Anecdotal recording* Anything that appears noteworthy is recorded. *Running record* Observer makes an on-the-spot description of behaviors.	Is useful as a precursor to more specific and quantifiable observations Helps in the development of hypotheses about factors controlling target behaviors Provides an in-depth picture of behavior	No specific quantitative data, although the record can be analyzed for various occurrences of behavior	Provides a record of child's behavior and general impressions Maintains original sequence of events Facilitates discovering critical behaviors and noting of continuing difficulties Requires a minimum of equipment	Is not well suited to obtaining quantifiable data Is costly in terms of time and person power Is difficult to validate Is time consuming May be insensitive to critical behaviors Produces findings with limited generalizing
Interval recording Observational period is divided into brief segments or intervals; observer notes whether a behavior occurs in each interval.	*Partial-interval time sampling* Behavior is scored only once during the interval, regardless of duration or frequency of occurrence. *Whole-interval time sampling* Behavior is scored only when it lasts from the beginning to the end of the interval. *Point-time interval sampling* Behavior is scored only when it occurs at a designated time during the interval. *Momentary time interval sampling* Behavior is scored only when it occurs at the end of the interval.	Is useful for behaviors that are overt or easily observable, that are not clearly discrete, and that occur with reasonable frequency (for example, reading, working, roughhousing, smiling, playing with toys)	Number of intervals in which target behaviors did or did not occur	Defines important time-behavior relationships Facilitates checking interobserver reliability Maintains standard observation conditions in an economical way Enhances attention to specific behaviors Allows for flexibility in recording large numbers of behaviors	Provides somewhat artificial view of behavior sequence May lead observer to overlook important behaviors Usually tells little about quality of behaviors or situation Provides numbers that are usually not related to frequency of behaviors Is not sensitive to very low-frequency behaviors and, in point-time sampling, behaviors of short duration

Variable interoccasion interval time sampling Behavior is scored only when it occurs at designated random time intervals.				
Event recording Each instance of a specific behavior (event) is observed and recorded. *Event* Observer waits for preselected behavior to occur and then records its occurrence. *Duration* Observer determines the amount of time that elapses between the beginning and the end of the behavior. *Intensity* Behavior is divided into various degrees of intensity, and behavior of each degree is recorded separately. *Latency* Observer determines the amount of time that elapses between the initiation of the request and the onset of behavior.	Is useful for behaviors that have clearly defined beginnings and endings, such as spelling words correctly, rocking movements, asking questions, and speech errors	Number of occurrences of the behavior—frequency count Also, in some cases, rate of behavior, duration of behavior (time), intensity of behavior (if built into code), latency of behavior (time)	Facilitates detection of low-frequency behaviors Facilitates study of many different behaviors in an economical and flexible manner Provides information about the frequency with which behavior is performed and changes in behavior over time	Provides artificial view of behavior sequence and breaks up continuity of behavior Is not suited to recording nondiscrete behaviors Presents difficulties in establishing reliability Limits quantification of the hows and whys associated with behavior Makes comparison across sessions difficult if the length of the observation period is not constant
Ratings recording Behavior is observed and then rated on various scales. 5-point scales 7-point scales Other dimensional scales	Is useful for evaluating more global aspects of behavior and for quantifying impressions	Scale value (or number or score) on rating scale	Allows for the recording of many different behaviors in an economical manner Allows for the rating of many individuals and the group as a whole Permits rating of subtle aspects of behavior Facilitates statistical analysis	Uses scale values which may be based on unclear assumptions May have low reliability Does not allow for recording of important quantitative dimensions Does not allow for recording of antecedent and consequent events

━ **Exhibit 17-11** ━━━━━━━━━━━━━━━━━━━━━━━━━━━━━━━━━━

Observing Preschool Children's Reactions to Specially Designed Situations

Zahn-Waxler, McKnew, Cummings, Davenport, and Radke-Yarrow (1984) designed a setting for observing preschool children's reactions to specially created incidents. The referred child, a familiar same-age playmate, parents of the two children, and staff members interact in the setting under various conditions intended to induce conflict, distress, frustration, and enjoyment. Aggressive, altruistic, and other emotions may be revealed.

The room in which the observations are conducted, preferably a living room-kitchenette area, should contain a standard set of toys (for example, rocking horse, ball, pull toy, toy telephone). The following conditions should be established (Zahn-Waxler et al., 1984, p. 237, with changes in notation):

1. *A novel environment.* Initially the children play in the new room, with the mothers watching (5 minutes).

2. *A background climate of affection and sharing.* Two female adults enter the adjoining kitchen. They greet the mothers and children, then cooperate with each other in a warm and friendly fashion while getting coffee for the mothers and juice for the children and straightening up the kitchen (5 minutes).

3. *A neutral context.* There are no experimental interventions (5 minutes).

4. *A background climate of hostility, anger, and rejection.* The two women return and have a verbal argument while washing the dishes. Each accuses the other of not doing her share of work around the building (5 minutes).

5. *A second neutral context* (5 minutes).

6. *A reconciliation.* The adults return, greet each other with affection, and apologize for their unpleasant behavior (2 minutes).

7. *A friend's separation experience.* The mother of the referred child's friend is asked to leave the room (1 minute).

8. *Separation from mother.* The referred child's own mother is called from the room as well (1 minute).

9. *Reunion with the mother.* Both mothers return to the room (4 minutes).

Mothers should be asked not to initiate activities or to interrupt interactions between the children unless something makes them uncomfortable or appears to be dangerous. The above conditions can be modified to suit the specific room arrangements.

Suggested event observational recording codes are as follows (Zahn-Waxler et al., 1984):

1. *Aggression:* actions that have potential for causing physical or psychological harm

a. Interpersonal physical aggression—hitting, kicking, pushing, or throwing things

b. Object struggle—attempts to grab or take another's possession

c. Undirected aggression—acts against the physical environment (for example, banging on walls, throwing things on the floor, kicking toys)

d. Intense aggression—acts that are violent or potentially dangerous

2. *Altruism or empathic intervention*—acts of kindness and caring directed toward others

a. Child helps, cooperates, provides comfort, or sympathizes with other person (for example, by patting or hugging a crying person, kissing a hurt, saying "It's OK" or "Be careful," providing a bottle, sharing toys)

b. Child shares either objects or self (for example, invites others to join in particular play activities).

A suggested scale for rating various forms of emotional expressiveness is as follows:

RATING SCALE

1	2	3	4	5
emotion absent	emotion expressed slightly	emotion expressed somewhat	emotion expressed moderately	emotion expressed frequently

	Rating
a. positive emotion (laughter, smiling, happy excitement expressed facially, vocally, or bodily)	1 2 3 4 5
b. anger (angry yelling, screaming, or facial expressions, impassioned threats or complaints)	1 2 3 4 5
c. distress (crying, crankiness, whining, concerned facial expressions)	1 2 3 4 5
d. emotionality (combined scores for positive emotion, anger, and distress)	1 2 3 4 5

━━━

cise leniency, exercise variable attention, or be influenced by extraneous cues.

Some examples may help to illustrate observer bias. An observer's expectation that the referred child will act ag-

gressively may influence him or her to record marginally aggressive acts as aggressive, when other observers without this expectation would record the same acts as nonaggressive. An extraneous cue in the form of a teacher's

Table 17-10
Sources of Error in Observations of Behavior

Source of error	Type of error
Errors associated with personal qualities of the observer	*Central tendency*—Observer uses the middle category of a rating scale more frequently than the end categories and in the process tends to underestimate intense behaviors and overestimate weak behaviors.
	Leniency or generosity—Observer makes judgments about the referred child that are too favorable.
	Primacy effect—Observer allows first impressions to have a distorting effect on later impressions or judgments.
	Halo effect—Observer makes judgments based on a general impression of the referred child or on his or her most salient characteristic.
	Personal theory—Observer fits the observations to his or her personal theoretical assumptions.
	Personal values—Observer fits the observations to his or her personal expectations, values, and interests.
	Overestimation of traits or behaviors that are barely self-acknowledged—Observer overestimates in the referred child traits and behaviors that he or she barely acknowledges in himself or herself.
	Logical error—Observer makes similar judgments on traits that seem to be logically related.
	Contrast error—On specific traits, observer judges others to be more different from himself or herself than they actually are.
	Proximity error—Observer judges specific traits as similar because the format of the judgments places them close together in time or space.
	Personal effects—Unbeknown to the observer, his or her personal characteristics (such as age, sex, race, and status) affect the referred child's behavior.
	Observer drift—Over time, observer changes criteria (or thresholds) for judging the presence or absence of a behavior because of fatigue or learning or other variables.
	Omission—Observer fails to score a behavior that has occurred.
	Commission—Observer miscodes a behavior.
	Expectancy effects—Observer's expectations influence what he or she records, or observer expects something to happen and communicates these expectations to the child.
	Observer reactivity—Observer changes recording of behavior when he or she is aware of being observed.
	Nonverbal cues—Observer unintentionally furnishes to referred child nonverbal cues that act as reinforcers of certain behaviors.

(Table continues next page)

praising the referred child for having completed a past assignment may lead an observer to record on-task behavior in the interval, even though the referred child was not doing the current class assignment at the time of observation. Observer reactivity (changes in the observer's behavior as a result of situational influences) may occur not only when observers are being observed by another person, but also when they are told that their records will be compared with those of another observer. This knowledge may make them more careful, vigilant, and attentive to details than they ordinarily would be.

Observer drift. When observation continues over a long period of time, observers may show signs of forgetfulness, fatigue, and decreased motivation. For example, an observer may begin with one standard for scoring whispers or brief vocalizations, but over time change that standard. Observer drift may occur even when the observers have agreed on specific definitions of behavior.

Difficulties in coding behavior. Global categories, such as *off-task behavior* or *inappropriate behavior*, require a higher level of inference than do specific categories, such as *hitting* or *out-of-seat behavior*. Reliability may be more difficult to achieve when global categories are used. Although every attempt should be made to define target behaviors precisely, some behaviors may be difficult to categorize. For example, how does one distinguish between a child who is staring into space and one who is thinking about a problem? Thus observational codes require careful judgments on the part of the observer.

Timing of behavior. The timing of events is not as simple as it appears. For example, when exactly does a child's refusal to eat begin and end? The time unit selected by the observer may not reflect an exact mapping of the behavioral event.

Table 17-10 (cont.)

Source of error	Type of error
Errors associated with setting, codes, scales, and instruments	*Unrepresentative behavioral setting* – Observer selects only one setting or only one time period and thereby fails to sample adequately representative behaviors. *Coding complexity* – Observer cannot use codes accurately because there are (a) too many categories in the system, (b) too many categories scored on a given occasion, and/or (c) too many children observed on a given occasion. *Influence of extraneous cues* – Observer is influenced by certain acts in the environment to score the occurrence of a behavior when the behavior is not occurring. *Rating scales* – Observer inappropriately uses broad-category rating scales to classify behaviors and thereby loses fine distinctions. *Mechanical instruments* – Observer fails to check the accuracy of mechanical devices used for recording data (for example, stopwatch or counter).
Errors associated with the referred child (or children)	*Child reactivity* – Referred child's behavior changes as a result of the knowledge that he or she is being observed. *Role selection* – Referred child adopts a particular role as a result of the knowledge that he or she is being observed. *Measurement becomes an agent of change* – Referred child makes a significant change in his or her behavior or attitudes as a result of being measured and observed. *Response set* – Referred child responds in a manner that conforms to cues from the observer. *Behavior drift* – Child's behavior continues, but in a form that drifts outside the range of definitions being used.
Errors associated with the sample (usually large samples or groups)	*Unrepresentative sample* – Observer fails to obtain a representative sample of the population. *Sample instability* – Observer fails to recognize population changes over time, making it difficult to compare present sample's results with those of previous samples. *Unrepresentative data* – Observer fails to recognize geographical and regional differences between samples.

Source: Adapted in part from Fassnacht (1982).

PROCEDURES FOR ASSESSING RELIABILITY

Three useful procedures for estimating the reliability of observational coding are *interobserver reliability or agreement*, *test-retest reliability*, and *internal consistency reliability*. Interobserver reliability is the most important form of reliability for behavioral observations. Without interobserver reliability, the other forms of reliability have little meaning.

Interobserver Reliability or Interobserver Agreement

Estimates of interobserver reliability (or interobserver agreement) are usually based on scores of two or more observers who record the same information while *simultaneously* and *independently* observing the same child or group (Nay, 1979). The data may be in the form of classifications (or nominal scale ratings or categorical judgments)

or interval scale ratings. Once these data have been obtained, an appropriate statistical index of agreement must be selected and calculated. Several procedures are available for measuring interobserver agreement, including correlational coefficients (such as the *product-moment correlation coefficient* and the *intraclass correlation coefficient*) and percentage agreement indices (such as *kappa* and *uncorrected percentage agreement*). These four procedures measure different aspects of interobserver agreement and thus may result in different reliability estimates for the same set of data.

Product-moment correlation coefficient. If you are interested in the pattern of agreement among the observers' ratings, irrespective of the level of agreement, and you have interval data, then the product-moment correlation coefficient is satisfactory (see Chapter 2). The product-moment correlation coefficient is sufficient when you simply want to establish whether one measure is linearly related to some other measure. As an index of agreement between observers, the product-moment correlation coefficient usually is not the method of choice, except with rating scale data.

Intraclass correlation coefficient. When both the pattern of agreement and level of agreement are important and you have an interval scale of measurement, the intraclass correlation coefficient may be used (Fleiss, 1975). The intraclass correlation coefficient takes into account the extent to which all observers mean exactly the same thing by their judgments.

Kappa. When the data form an ordinal scale and you are interested in correcting for chance agreement, kappa is a useful index of agreement (Cohen, 1960, 1968). Kappa takes into consideration both the occurrence and the nonoccurrence of behavior corrected for chance agreement among observers. It is used in situations in which there are no independent criteria or bases for independent expert evaluation. Kappa measures the degree of consensus among observers; it evaluates precision, but does not tell whether the observations are valid. One of the preferred procedures, kappa can be used for multiple observers and multiple categories. Exhibit 17-12 shows the procedure for computing kappa. A microcomputer program is available for computing kappa for multiple observers, multiple categories, and missing data (Oud & Sattler, 1984).

Percentage agreement. When you desire a measure that shows the percentage agreement among two or more observers but are not concerned with correcting for chance agreement, an uncorrected percentage agreement index is useful. Uncorrected percentage agreement, which is simply the percentage of agreement of two or more observers, is particularly susceptible to overestimating agreement when chance agreement is high. Although percentage agreement is not synonymous with reliability, it is useful as a preliminary check of the adequacy of your observational recordings because of its ease of computation and interpretation and its sensitivity to bias and systematic errors. In the material that follows, uncorrected percentage agreement will be referred to as *percentage agreement*.

Interval recording percentage agreement estimates. In interval recording, a number of different percentage agreement methods are used for determining interobserver agreement. Three such methods are (a) overall agreement, (b) agreement on the occurrence of the behavior, and (c) agreement on the nonoccurrence of the behavior. The key difference among the three methods is the specific intervals used to determine the level of interobserver agreement. The data in Figure 17-8 are used to illustrate the three interobserver percentage agreement measures.

1. *Agreement on total observations.* This method of obtaining percentage agreement takes into account the total number of intervals and the occurrence or nonoccurrence of a behavior in each interval. Agreement is defined as both observers' scoring either the occurrence or the nonoccurrence of a behavior in a given interval. The procedure is as follows:

a. Considering all intervals, make two counts, one of the number of intervals in which the observers agreed on the occurrence or nonoccurrence of a behavior and one of the number of intervals in which they disagreed.

b. Divide the number of agreements by the total number of agreements plus disagreements and multiply by 100. The result is the percentage of interobserver agreement for the total number of intervals.

The formula for interobserver percentage agreement for the total number of intervals is as follows:

$$\%A_{\text{IR tot}} = \frac{A_{\text{tot}}}{A_{\text{tot}} + D} \times 100$$

where $\%A_{\text{IR tot}}$ = interval recording percentage agreement for the total number of intervals

A_{tot} = number of intervals in which Observer 1 and Observer 2 *agreed* on whether the behavior occurred or did not occur

D = number of intervals in which Observer 1 and Observer 2 *disagreed* on whether the behavior occurred or did not occur

	1	2	3	4	5	6	7	8	9	10
Observer 1	X	O	X	O	X	O	O	X	O	X
Observer 2	X	O	X	X	X	O	O	O	X	X

X indicates occurrence of behavior, O indicates nonoccurrence of behavior.

Figure 17-8. Raw data for three interobserver percentage agreement measures.

Example: Two observers agreed on whether the target behavior occurred or did not occur in intervals 1, 2, 3, 5, 6, 7, and 10 (seven agreements), but disagreed in intervals 4, 8, and 9 (three disagreements). Therefore there was a 70 percent rate of agreement in scoring the target behavior over the total number of intervals recorded:

$$\%A_{\text{IR tot}} = \frac{A_{\text{tot}}}{A_{\text{tot}} + D} \times 100 = \frac{7}{7+3} \times 100$$
$$= \frac{7}{10} \times 100 = 70\%$$

Exhibit 17-12

Procedures for Computing Kappa (κ)

Kappa (κ) is a useful statistic for measuring interobserver reliability (or interobserver agreement) for categorical data. Kappa indicates the proportion of agreements, corrected for chance agreements. Like correlational coefficients, kappa ranges from +1.00 to −1.00. When kappa is positive, the proportion of observed agreement is *more than* the proportion of chance agreement. When kappa is equal to zero, the proportion of observed agreement *equals* the proportion of chance agreement. When kappa is negative, the proportion of observed agreement is *less than* the proportion of chance agreement.

Let us examine the rationale behind kappa for a hypothetical situation in which two observers scored one child over 100 intervals for the occurrence or nonoccurrence of a behavior. Suppose Observer 1 scored the occurrence of the behavior in 90 intervals and Observer 2 scored the occurrence of the behavior in 80 intervals. In this situation there must be some agreement because of the overlapping of distribution of scores. Figure 17-A shows that for the two observers the lowest possible number of overlapping occurrence intervals

(that is, intervals scored identically by the two observers) is 70. This minimum overlap of 70 intervals occurs when 10 of the occurrence intervals scored by Observer 2 correspond to the 10 nonoccurrence intervals scored by Observer 1. In this case, the correction for chance agreement in the kappa formula is 72 percent. The procedure for obtaining the chance correction is discussed below.

Kappa can be used for multiple categories and multiple raters. Formulas are presented below for computing kappa for (a) two observers and multiple categories and (b) the special case of two observers and two categories (2 × 2 contingency table). Formulas for computing kappa for multiple categories as well as for multiple raters are found in Conger (1980) and Uebersax (1982). Uebersax presents a generalized kappa formula that is also appropriate for handling missing data.

Kappa for Two Observers and Multiple Categories

To introduce the general kappa formula for two observers and multiple categories, let us set up a 3 × 3 contingency table
(Exhibit continues next page)

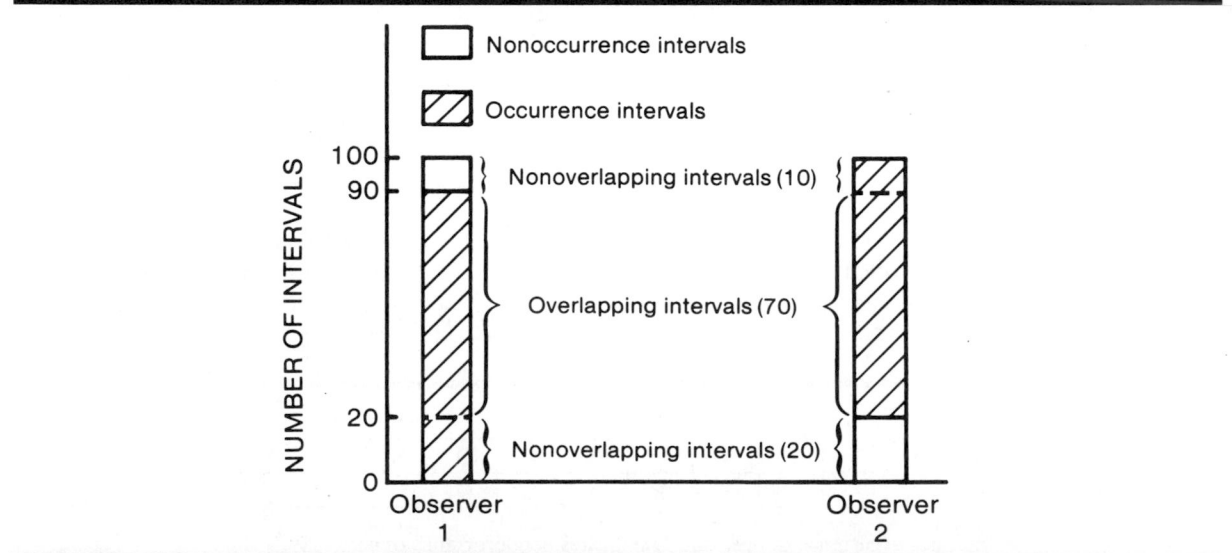

Figure 17-A.   Distribution of occurrence and nonoccurrence intervals scored by two observers.

Exhibit 17-12 (cont.)

representing two observers and three recording categories. The designations for the contingency table are as follows:

Observer 2

		C_1	C_2	C_3	
	C_1	n_{11}	n_{12}	n_{13}	n_{1+}
Observer 1	C_2	n_{21}	n_{22}	n_{23}	n_{2+}
	C_3	n_{31}	n_{32}	n_{33}	n_{3+}
		n_{+1}	n_{+2}	n_{+3}	N

Each cell is designated by two subscripts, one for the row and one for the column (for example, n_{11}, n_{22}, n_{33}). The first subscript refers to the row, the second to the column. Thus n_{23} designates the cell in the second row, third column. The rows and columns correspond to the three different observation categories (C_1, C_2, C_3). The marginal totals for Observer 1 are designated by n_{1+}, n_{2+}, and n_{3+}, and those for Observer 2 are designated by n_{+1}, n_{+2}, and n_{+3}.

The general formula for kappa is

$$\kappa = \frac{p_o - p_c}{1 - p_c}$$

where p_o = the observed proportion of agreement
p_c = the proportion of agreement expected by chance alone

The computational formulas for p_o and p_c are

$$p_o = \frac{\sum_{i=1}^{C} n_{ii}}{N} = \frac{(n_{11} + n_{22} + n_{33} + \cdots + n_{ii})}{N}$$

$$p_c = \frac{\sum_{i=1}^{C} (n_{i+})(n_{+i})}{N^2}$$

$$= \frac{(n_{1+} \times n_{+1}) + (n_{2+} \times n_{+2}) + (n_{3+} \times n_{+3}) + \cdots + (n_{i+} \times n_{+i})}{N^2}$$

where n_{ii} = total number of agreements for the ith category (main diagonal)
n_{i+} = marginal total for Observer 1 on the ith category
n_{+i} = marginal total for Observer 2 on the ith category
N = total number of observation periods (for example, intervals)

Let us apply this formula to some hypothetical data obtained by two observers who scored the same child using three

observation categories over 10 intervals. The three codes used by the two observers were verbal off-task (VO), motor off-task (MO), and on-task (OT). The data were as follows:

Intervals	Observer 1	Observer 2
1	VO	MO
2	VO	VO
3	MO	MO
4	OT	OT
5	OT	OT
6	VO	VO
7	MO	MO
8	MO	VO
9	MO	MO
10	VO	VO

Placing these scores in a 3×3 contingency table gives us the following:

Observer 2

		VO	MO	OT	
	VO	3	1	0	4
Observer 1	MO	1	3	0	4
	OT	0	0	2	2
		4	4	2	10

To calculate kappa, we first obtain p_o and p_c:

$$p_o = \frac{(n_{11} + n_{22} + n_{33} + \cdots + n_{ii})}{N}$$

$$= \frac{3 + 3 + 2}{10} = \frac{8}{10} = .80$$

$$p_c = \frac{(n_{1+} \times n_{+1}) + (n_{2+} \times n_{+2}) + (n_{3+} \times n_{+3}) + \cdots + (n_{i+} \times n_{+i})}{N^2}$$

$$= \frac{(4 \times 4) + (4 \times 4) + (2 \times 2)}{10^2} = \frac{16 + 16 + 4}{100}$$

$$= \frac{36}{100} = .36$$

Then we put the values of p_o and p_c into the formula for kappa:

$$\kappa = \frac{.80 - .36}{1 - .36} = \frac{.44}{.64} = .69$$

(Exhibit continues next page)

Exhibit 17-12 (cont.)

If a straight percentage agreement had been used, the level would have been 80 percent (or what p_o equals). Kappa gives us a coefficient of .69, a somewhat lower level of agreement. A kappa of .70 is considered to indicate an acceptable level of agreement.

Kappa for a 2 × 2 Contingency Table

We now consider kappa for binary ratings, with two observers and two observation categories (for example, occurrence/nonoccurrence or agreement/disagreement in a 2 × 2 contingency table). This is a special case of kappa. The general formula for kappa, as we have seen, is

$$\kappa = \frac{p_o - p_c}{1 - p_c}$$

In a 2 × 2 contingency table, p_o is computed by dividing the two cells in which both observers agree by the total number of observation periods or intervals (N). And p_c is computed by adding the products of the marginal frequencies and then dividing this value by the total number of observation periods or intervals squared.

Thus, for the contingency table

Observer 2

		Occurrence	Non-occurrence	Row total
Observer 1	Occurrence	a	b	$a + b$
	Nonoccurrence	c	d	$c + d$
	Column total	$a + c$	$b + d$	N

$$p_o = \frac{a + d}{N}$$

$$p_c = \frac{(a + b)(a + c) + (c + d)(b + d)}{N^2}$$

where p_o = the observed proportion of agreement
p_c = the proportion of agreement expected by chance alone
N = total number of observation periods

A computationally more convenient formula for computing kappa in a 2 × 2 contingency table is

$$\kappa = \frac{2(ad - bc)}{(a + b)(b + d) + (a + c)(c + d)}$$

where a = the number of intervals in which Observer 1 and Observer 2 scored the behavior as occurring

b = the number of intervals in which Observer 1 scored the behavior as occurring and Observer 2 scored the behavior as not occurring
c = the number of intervals in which Observer 1 scored the behavior as not occurring and Observer 2 scored the behavior as occurring
d = the number of intervals in which Observer 1 and Observer 2 scored the behavior as not occurring

Example: The data for two observers who scored one child over 100 intervals are summarized as follows:

Observer 2

		Occurrence	Non-occurrence	Row total
Observer 1	Occurrence	20	6	26
	Nonoccurrence	2	72	74
	Column total	22	78	100

$$\kappa = \frac{2(ad - bc)}{(a + b)(b + d) + (a + c)(c + d)}$$

$$= \frac{2[(20 \times 72) - (6 \times 2)]}{(26 \times 78) + (22 \times 74)} = \frac{2(1440 - 12)}{2028 + 1628}$$

$$= \frac{2(1428)}{3656} = \frac{2856}{3656} = .78$$

For the above data, p_o, the observed proportion of agreement, is

$$p_o = \frac{a + d}{N} = \frac{20 + 72}{100} = \frac{92}{100} = 92\%$$

and p_c, the proportion of agreement expected by chance alone, is

$$p_c = \frac{(a + b)(a + c) + (c + d)(b + d)}{N^2}$$

$$= \frac{(26 \times 22) + (74 \times 78)}{100^2}$$

$$= \frac{6344}{10,000} = 63\%$$

Again a kappa of .78 is a more conservative estimate of interobserver agreement than the 92 percent agreement rate, uncorrected for chance.

2. *Agreement on occurrence observations.* This method of obtaining percentage agreement takes into consideration only those intervals in which at least one of the two observers recorded the occurrence of a behavior. Agreement is defined as both observers' scoring the occurrence of a behavior in a given interval. This procedure is similar to the one used for total observations, except that only a portion of the intervals is used.

a. Considering only those intervals in which at least one of the two observers recorded the occurrence of a behavior, make two counts — one of the number of intervals in which the observers agreed on the occurrence of a behavior and one of the number of intervals in which the observers disagreed.

b. Divide the number of agreements by the total number of agreements plus disagreements and multiply by 100. The result is the percentage of interobserver agreement for those intervals in which the behavior was scored as occurring.

The formula for interobserver percentage agreement for behavior occurrence is a variant of the one used for overall percentage agreement:

$$\%A_{\text{IR occ}} = \frac{A_{\text{occ}}}{A_{\text{occ}} + D} \times 100$$

where $\%A_{\text{IR occ}}$ = interval recording percentage agreement for intervals in which occurrence of behavior is scored

A_{occ} = number of intervals in which both observers *agreed* that the behavior occurred

D = number of intervals in which the observers *disagreed* on whether the behavior occurred

Example: Two observers agreed that the target behavior occurred in intervals 1, 3, 5, and 10 (four agreements), but only one of the observers scored an occurrence of the behavior in intervals 4, 8, and 9 (three disagreements). Thus there was a 57 percent level of agreement for scoring the target behavior as occurring:

$$\%A_{\text{IR occ}} = \frac{A_{\text{occ}}}{A_{\text{occ}} + D} \times 100 = \frac{4}{4 + 3} \times 100$$

$$= \frac{4}{7} \times 100 = 57\%$$

If neither observer records an instance of an occurrence of a target behavior, a reliability index cannot be calculated for this category.

3. *Agreement on nonoccurrence observations.* This method of obtaining percentage agreement takes into consideration only those intervals in which either one or both observers recorded the nonoccurrence of a behavior. Agreement is defined as both observers' scoring the nonoccurrence of a behavior in a given interval. This procedure is similar to the one described above.

a. Considering only those intervals in which at least one of the two observers recorded the nonoccurrence of a behavior, make two counts — one of the number of intervals in which the observers agreed on the nonoccurrence of a behavior and one of the number of intervals in which observers disagreed.

b. Divide the number of agreements by the total number of agreements plus disagreements and multiply by 100. The result is the percentage of interobserver agreement for those intervals in which the behavior was scored as not occurring.

The formula for interobserver percentage agreement on nonoccurrence of behavior is another variant of the one used for overall percentage agreement:

$$\%A_{\text{IR non}} = \frac{A_{\text{non}}}{A_{\text{non}} + D} \times 100$$

where $\%A_{\text{IR non}}$ = interval recording percentage agreement for intervals in which nonoccurrence of behavior is scored

A_{non} = number of intervals in which both observers *agreed* that the behavior did not occur

D = number of intervals in which the observers *disagreed* on whether the behavior did not occur

Example: Two observers agreed that the target behavior did not occur in intervals 2, 6, and 7 (three agreements). In intervals 4, 8, and 9, however, only one of the observers scored the nonoccurrence of the behavior (three disagreements). Thus the level of agreement was 50 percent for scoring the target behavior as not occurring:

$$\%A_{\text{IR non}} = \frac{A_{\text{non}}}{A_{\text{non}} + D} \times 100 = \frac{3}{3 + 3} \times 100$$

$$= \frac{3}{6} \times 100 = 50\%$$

If neither observer records an instance of a nonoccurrence of a target behavior, an agreement index cannot be calculated for this category.

Comment on interval recording percentage agreement estimates. When observers score a very small proportion of the intervals for the occurrence of a behavior, the most appropriate method may be the second one, which takes into account only those intervals in which an occurrence of the behavior was scored. In these situations, the use of the first procedure (total intervals) might cause some distortion of the rate of agreement.

Example: In a 100-interval observation period, one observer scored the occurrence of the target behavior in three intervals and the other observer scored the occurrence of the behavior in one overlapping interval. Their rate of agreement in scoring the occurrence of the behavior is 33 percent. Use of the total intervals would result in an agreement rate of 98 percent. The 33 percent agreement figure better represents the observers' ability to identify the target behavior when it occurs.

When more than one category is used in an observation system, as is usually the case, a decision must be made about whether to evaluate interobserver agreement for the total observations, for the separate categories, or for both. It is highly recommended that interobserver agreement be computed for each category as well as for the total observations. This approach provides valuable information about where potential difficulties may lie in the observation system or between observers. *A percentage agreement above 80 percent is considered satisfactory.*

When occurrence of a behavior is scored in a large proportion of the intervals, it may be of interest to study the rate of agreement in those intervals in which nonoccurrence of the behavior was scored. In this case the third method can be used. All three methods may be used to report interobserver agreement estimates. Generally, you should choose the index that best answers your question.

In Table 17-11, the three types of percentage agreement measures and kappa are calculated for 10 sets of data. Also included is a column showing chance agreement. It is evident that in some cases the four measures differ greatly. In cases 1, 2, 4, 8, and 10, kappa gives a .00 coefficient, whereas the total percentage agreement measure ranges from 50 to 100 percent. Kappa thus provides a much more conservative index of interobserver agreement. The table also shows that the value of kappa is significantly affected by chance agreement. In example 3 kappa is .66; a change in a single agreement in one interval causes the value of κ to change to .00 in example 4. Therefore it may sometimes be difficult to interpret kappa.

Event recording percentage agreement estimate. In event recording, interobserver percentage agreement can be estimated by dividing the number of occurrences of the event reported by the observer recording the lowest frequency by the number of occurrences reported by the other observer.

The percentage agreement formula for event recording is as follows:

$$\%A_{\text{ER}} = \frac{f_l}{f_h} \times 100$$

where $\%A_{\text{ER}}$ = event recording percentage agreement
   f_l = frequency of observer with the lower event frequency
   f_h = frequency of observer with the higher event frequency

Example: Two observers recorded out-of-seat behavior, the target event. During a 20-minute observation period, one observer recorded 5 occurrences of the behavior and the other observer recorded 8 occurrences. Substitute into the formula as follows:

$$\%A_{\text{ER}} = \frac{f_l}{f_h} \times 100 = \frac{5}{8} \times 100 = 62.5\%$$

There was a 62.5 percent agreement between the two observers in recording the number of occurrences of the target behavior. This level of agreement does not mean that the observers recorded the *same* target behavior, however. It could be that there were 13 occurrences of the target behavior, 5 of which were recorded by one observer and 8 of which were recorded by the other. The level of agreement simply indicates that the ratio of events reported in common was 62.5 percent. Unless specific intervals or times were used in the observational recording procedure, there is no way of knowing whether the two observers recorded the same events.

Duration recording percentage agreement estimates. The interobserver percentage agreement estimate for duration recording is similar to the one used for event recording. The percentage agreement formula for duration recording is as follows:

$$\%A_{\text{DR}} = \frac{t_l}{t_h} \times 100$$

where $\%A_{\text{DR}}$ = duration recording percentage agreement
   t_l = time recorded by observer with the lower time duration
   t_h = time recorded by observer with the higher time duration

Table 17-11
Comparison of Four Different Observer Agreement Formulas for 10 Cases of Data

O_1 / O_2 (O / NO: a, b / c, d)	Chance percentage agreement on occurrence	Occurrence percentage agreement	Nonoccurrence percentage agreement	Total percentage agreement	Kappa
1. 50 0 / 0 0	100	100	—	100	.00
2. 49 1 / 0 0	98	98	0	98	.00
3. 48 1 / 0 1	94	98	50	98	.66
4. 0 1 / 0 49	0	0	98	98	.00
5. 25 0 / 0 25	25	100	100	100	1.00
6. 24 1 / 0 25	24	96	96	98	.96
7. 20 10 / 0 20	24	67	67	80	.62
8. 9 16 / 9 16	18	26	39	50	.00
9. 1 24 / 24 1	25	2	2	4	−.92
10. 14 12 / 13 11	28	36	31	50	.00

Note. See text for computational formulas for each agreement index and kappa. The formula for chance percentage agreement on occurrence is $CO = \frac{(a + b)(a + c)}{N^2}$. In the 2 × 2 table (column one), O_1 = Observer 1, O_2 = Observer 2, O = occurrence, NO = nonoccurrence.

Example: Two observers recorded the target event of a child's staring out the window. One observer clocked an episode at 360 seconds; the other, 365 seconds. Substitute into the formula as follows:

$$\%A_{DR} = \frac{t_l}{t_h} \times 100 = \frac{360}{365} \times 100 = 98\%$$

Thus there was a 98 percent agreement between the two observers in recording the duration of the staring-out-the-window behavior.

Ratings recording percentage agreement estimates. In ratings recording, interobserver percentage agreement can be estimated by determining the extent to which the two observers gave the same rating on each scale.

The percentage agreement formula for ratings recording is as follows:

$$\%A_{RR} = \frac{A_{rr}}{A_{rr} + D} \times 100$$

where $\%A_{RR}$ = ratings recording percentage agreement for the total number of scales

A_{rr} = number of scales in which both observers *agreed* on the rating

D = number of scales in which the observers *disagreed* on the rating

Example: After a 30-minute observation period, two observers completed ten 5-point rating scales. They agreed on ratings for 8 of the 10 scales. Substitute into the formula as follows:

$$\%A_{RR} = \frac{A_{rr}}{A_{rr} + D} \times 100$$

$$= \frac{8}{8 + 2} \times 100 = \frac{8}{10} \times 100 = 80\%$$

Thus there was an 80 percent rate of agreement between the two observers in making their ratings.

In ratings recording, a 7-point scale requires finer judgments than a 3-point scale. Thus the more categories you have in a rating scale, the lower the interobserver percentage agreement is likely to be. Percentage agreement takes into account only the absolute level of agreement—agreement is counted only when both observers give the exact same rating. This agreement procedure does not consider the pattern of ratings. If one observer is consistently one scale position above (or below) the other observer, a disagreement still will be counted for each scale. Consequently, in ratings recording it is also useful to compute a product-moment correlation (or intraclass correlation coefficient) to ascertain the pattern of agreement between the two observers.

Test-Retest Reliability

The consistency of behavior over time and situations is another measure of the reliability of behavioral observations. Every attempt should be made to sample the target behaviors on more than one occasion and in more than one setting. The percentage agreement interval recording formulas can be used to evaluate test-retest reliability. Various correlational procedures can also be used, depending on the scaling of the data.

For example, intraindividual stability can be assessed by correlating the frequency with which each targeted behavior was observed on one occasion with the frequency with which each behavior was observed by the same observer on another occasion. The product-moment correlation coefficient so obtained does not allow you to evaluate which of the behaviors show more or less stability because the correlation is computed across all categories. By scanning the changes from the first to the second observation periods for each category, however, you can obtain some idea of which categories show the most change.

When instability occurs, it may be due to changes in the child, in the setting, in the observer, in the definitions of the behaviors used by the observer, or in the methods used for the observation. Which factor or combination of factors is responsible for the instability must be determined through a careful study of all sources of data and of the procedures used in the observational assessment.

Internal Consistency Reliability

Internal consistency reliability tells us how consistent an assessment instrument is in measuring the same characteristics. One way of obtaining internal consistency estimates is to divide the observation measure into two equal parts (for example, odd- and even-numbered items). Chapter 2 describes various formulas for measuring internal consistency reliability. Factor analysis, discriminant function analysis, and various correlational procedures (depending on the scaling of the data) can also be used to evaluate the internal composition of items in observational coding systems.

VALIDITY OF BEHAVIORAL OBSERVATIONS

The validity of an observational assessment is determined by studying the meaningfulness and relevance of the behavioral measures. Validity refers to the extent to which the procedures are measuring what they are supposed to measure (see Chapter 2). The validity of observational measures, however, is more often assumed than established (Hoge, 1985). If you observed behavior that you wished to classify as hyperactive, for example, you might consider the following questions (Bernstein & Nietzel, 1980):

• In terms of construct validity, do the behaviors coded (for example, fidgeting, out-of-chair movements) constitute a satisfactory and functional definition of hyperactivity?

• In terms of content validity, do the data reflect the nature and degree of hyperactivity shown during the observation?

• In terms of concurrent validity, does the child's behavior under observation accurately reflect his or her reactions in other situations?

• Finally, in terms of predictive validity, do the behaviors coded predict other important criteria?

Answering these questions will not be a simple matter, but only if you can answer them affirmatively can you be fairly certain that you are measuring hyperactivity.

Representativeness and Generalizability of Findings

Two of the major factors affecting the validity of the observational assessment are the *representativeness* and *generalizability* of the findings (Evans, 1983). To what degree does the behavior observed during the time-sampling procedure reflect behavior in the total time period and behavior in other situations to which one wishes to generalize the findings? These questions must be considered in every observational assessment.

Reactivity

Children's behavior under observation may be affected by the knowledge that they are being observed, prior interactions with the observer, or the observer's personal characteristics. This effect is referred to as *reactivity* or the *guinea pig effect*. To minimize reactivity, you should try to conduct your observations as unobtrusively as possible. Ordinarily you should not assume that stable behavior is typical behavior or that the changes you observe would have occurred if you were not present. Children's reactivity to a familiar observer presents a particular threat to the validity of the observational assessment; if the observer is someone the child knows, an independent assessment of the referred child should be carried out by someone not familiar to the child.

You can judge whether reactive effects have occurred by looking for (a) systematic changes in behavior over time, some of which may be related to the presence of the observer, (b) increased variability in behavior, (c) reports from children that they changed their behavior as a result of being observed, and (d) discrepancies between different measures of the same behavior, when measures were obtained under different observation conditions (Haynes & Horn, 1982). Although these indices do not prove conclusively that reactive effects are present, they suggest the possibility that such effects are operating.

Harris and Lahey (1982, p. 536) believe that reactivity is often so powerful that it clouds the observational data: "Unless it has been well-documented that reactivity is not a factor in a given situation, observational data may be taken as a demonstration that a particular behavior is in a [child's] repertoire, but not that it is performed in the absence of observation."

Not everyone agrees, however, that reactivity is necessarily detrimental for observational assessment. Cone and Foster (1982, p. 343), for example, noted that reactivity may pose problems for some research and clinical objectives but not for others.

The important issue seems to be not whether observed individuals react differently under conditions of known observation but rather whether data collected under such conditions are less useful than those collected surreptitiously . . . .

In this vein it is conceivable that reactive data may have even greater utility or social validity than nonreactive data in some circumstances. This could occur when [you wish] to generalize to situations involving similar levels of obtrusive observation. For example, in assessing the adequacy of vocal presentations before audiences, it is probably the case that data obtained from conditions in which the client is aware of being observed will correlate more highly with subsequent real-life presentations. Similarly, it may be the case that relatively reactive heterosocial skills assessment will evidence greater utility than less reactive assessment, given that most heterosocial interactions contain an evaluative component. Removing a significant portion of this component from the assessment process could lead to lower correlations with relevant criteria. As Barker and Wright (1955) pointed out long ago, interaction between an observer and a person observed is important in its own right, not just as a potential confounding element to be uniformly eliminated or controlled.

PROCEDURES FOR REDUCING ERRORS IN OBSERVATION

Reducing Errors in Reliability

A number of procedures can be used to reduce errors in reliability. One method is to study the errors listed in Table 17-10 and then try to avoid them (or limit their occurrence) when you perform behavioral observations. You can reduce or eliminate many of these errors simply by practicing. To eliminate others you may need to further refine your recording procedures and rating scales. Some errors, such as those associated with your personal characteristics (for example, height, weight, skin color, voice) or with the reactions of the referred child, may be difficult to eliminate, but you can minimize their effect simply by being aware of their potential influence.

Reliability can be increased by having clear and precise definitions of behaviors, systematic and precise rules governing the observations, well-trained observers, and observation periods that are not excessively long. Observer drift, although difficult to control, can be reduced by making frequent checks of the recordings, thoroughly training observers beforehand, and having the observers make periodic calibrations during the course of the observation session to check the consistency of their observations. These procedures also serve to reduce many other sources of observer bias.

Errors may also be reduced by gaining an understanding of your decision criteria, such as the degree of certainty you must have in order to report that a behavior did or did not occur, and comparing your decision criteria with those of other observers. Signal detection approaches (derivative measures of which are often referred to as *d'*) can be useful in achieving these goals (Lord, 1985). These approaches focus on an observer's ability to detect stimuli, taking into account the observer's response style. In some cases, using broad categories to classify behavior (such as *on-task* or *off-task*) may be unwise, as these categories do not permit fine distinctions between behaviors. Nevertheless, broad categories can be used when they meet the assessment goals and are methodologically sound.

Comparing Observation Results with a Criterion

During your training, you should regularly compare your results with those of a highly trained observer or with standard criterion recordings. The agreement between an observer's recordings and standard criterion recordings is known as *criterion-related agreement*. Even trained observers should occasionally compare their results with those of another observer or standard criterion recordings to check reliability.

Another method of checking the reliability of your ratings involves videotaping the behavior of a child (or class). After recording your observations in the setting in which the behaviors occur, you then use the videotape to make a second independent recording of the behaviors. The level of agreement between the two recordings is a measure of the reliability of your ratings. This method is generally used only for training purposes, however; because the second observation may be affected by your memory of the first, reliability may be overestimated.

If possible, also compare your observation of the videotape with that of an expert and those of several colleagues. Thoroughly discuss any disagreements and compute estimates of interobserver agreement. Low interobserver percentage agreement may mean that the categories are not clearly defined, that one (or more) of the observers does not understand them, or that other factors are operating to interfere with agreement. You may be able to increase interobserver reliability by practicing observation assessment in environments similar to those in which you will work — observing in the natural settings and/or via videotapes.

An acceptable level of interobserver agreement does not rule out observer error, however. You can have a high level of interobserver agreement and still have observer bias and observer drift if both observers have a similar bias or make similar errors. The level of agreement is even more likely to mask errors when you compare two of your own recordings.

Reducing Reactivity

Although reactivity may be useful in some cases, often you will want to minimize it. To this end, Nay (1979) offers the following suggestions:

• *Become as neutral a stimulus as possible.* Avoid making eye contact with or interacting with the referred child or any other children during the observation period. To provide a rationale for your presence in a classroom, the teacher might say to the class: "Ms. A is here today to see what we do." At the beginning of each school year, make a few short visits to each class so that the children will become used to seeing you visit.

• *Position yourself so that you are away from the ordinary paths of movement in the classroom and yet still have an unobstructed view of the child and setting.* A good position in the classroom is often to the rear or side of the room.

• *Shift your attention from one child to another.* By so doing, you will avoid calling attention to any one individual child.

• *Limit your stimulus value.* Do not dress or act in a manner that attracts attention.

• *Follow all rules, regulations, and informal policies of the school, institution, or family.* Before going into a classroom, institution, or home, review your specific procedures with the teacher, administrative personnel, or parents.

• *Enter the setting when your entrance will be least disruptive of the ongoing behavior.* For classroom observations, enter the classroom before class begins or at break time. If possible, try to be in the setting for a period of time *before* the formal observation begins. If the children or teacher or family have an opportunity to become used to your presence, their behavior may be more natural (that is, less reactive) when the formal observation begins.

These suggestions will help you to become a more natural part of the setting and diminish the children's awareness of your presence. Awareness by itself does not necessarily affect children's behavior (Kazdin, 1979). It is only when the children's awareness of you leads to changes in their behavior that the validity of the observations is diminished. The reason for the assessment may determine how much influence your presence will have on the children's behavior. Children who are told that the results of the assessment may be used to determine their class placement may be more affected by your presence than those who are told that the results will have little or no bearing on their status.

Establishing Informal Norms

Developing informal norms will help you to place the child's behavior in a meaningful context. In a group setting, you might observe the behavior of the referred child and that of one or more peers as well (Alessi, 1980). The behavior of the peer children can then serve as a norm for comparing the behavior of the referred child. The peers should be children of the same age and sex as the referred child who have not been identified as experiencing behavior problems and who are as representative of the total peer group as possible. Another procedure is to establish local norms for the entire class, using the scan check method. The scan check method involves scanning the entire class for, say, 2 seconds every 2 minutes (for a period of 8 to 10 minutes) and recording how many students are off-task. Still another procedure for establishing informal norms is to compare the child's present behavior with his or her past behavior, thereby using the child as his or her own norm.

Obtaining a peer or class rating permits measurement of the relative difference between the frequency with which the referred child engages in a particular behavior and the frequency with which the peer or class does so. A *discrepancy ratio* can be used to summarize the results of peer or class comparisons. The discrepancy ratio is the relative difference between the median level of the referred child's behavior and the median level of the peer's (or class's) behavior. The referred child who is off-task six times per minute while his or her peers are off-task three times per minute could be described as "off-task twice as often as his or her peers."

Here is an example of how informal norms can be obtained (Alessi, 1980). Assume that a teacher referred Robert for his talking-out and out-of-seat behaviors in class. You observe Robert along with Todd, who has not been identified as talking out excessively and is considered an "average" child in this regard. Every few minutes you also scan the class and note how many of the children are talking out or are out of their seats. Your results are as follows:

	Talking-out behavior	Out-of-seat behavior
Robert	20	10
Todd	2	1
Class (%) (6 scans)	3% (1/30)	6% (2/30)

These data suggest that Robert engages in more inappropriate behavior (as defined by the teacher) than does either the comparison child or the class as a whole. If we accept these data as reflecting approximate norms for behavior in this class, we can then conclude that Robert's behavior deviates from the norm. In this example both a comparison child and local class norms provide standards for interpreting the behavior of the referred child. Without these standards, it would be difficult to know the extent to which the behavior of the referred child was deviant.

Developing Sensitivity to Teachers' Needs and Behaviors

Following are a number of problems associated with classroom observations and suggestions for avoiding them (Alessi, 1980).

Problem 1. The observation occurs during a part of the day in which the child does not exhibit the problem behavior or on a day when the child is unusually good.

Suggestion: Confer with the teacher before you schedule your observations.

[Ask the teacher the following questions:] "When do these behaviors occur most often? At what times? Which day or days of the week? During which subjects? When is it best to observe the child to ensure that the behavior can be seen? When is the behavior at its worst? When does it usually occur?" After this information has been gathered, arrange your schedule to observe the child at a prime time. Whenever possible, plan to spread your observation over three or four 10-minute sessions rather than one 30-to-40 minute session. Also spread these shorter sessions across a week or two." (pp. 41–42, with changes in notation)

Problem 2. You cannot obtain a valid sample of behavior because the teacher has trouble staying on a schedule. (This is a variant of problem 1.)

Suggestion: Frequent scheduling problems may indicate that the teacher has a management problem, which may be contributing to the child's problem. Try to help the teacher develop better management skills. If management problems are not resolved, it probably will be difficult to provide a successful intervention for the referred problem.

Problem 3. The referred child fails to behave inappropriately when you are present in the classroom. (This also is a variant of problem 1.)

Suggestion: This is a positive sign in that it indicates that the referred child's inappropriate behavior is under some voluntary control. Inform the teacher of this possibility and work with her or him to establish procedures that will help the child keep the behavior continuously under control, even when the child is not being observed.

Problem 4. The comparison child also has a behavioral problem or, conversely, never engages in the behavior under observation.

Suggestion: This potential difficulty can be controlled by consulting with the teacher about selecting an "average" child or selecting a different comparison child for each 10-minute observation session.

Problem 5. The norm group is inappropriate.

Suggestion: Investigate other classes to see whether the norms in these classrooms are similar to those in the referred child's class. If you find that other classes have more lenient and flexible standards and if you believe that the referred child would benefit from these standards, consider arranging a transfer for the child.

Problem 6. The critical behaviors that should be observed are poorly defined.

Suggestion: Further discussion with the teacher about the child's problems may eliminate this potential source of difficulty.

Problem 7. The child has been referred for reasons other than those given—the teacher has a "hidden agenda" behind the referral.

Suggestion: This may be the most difficult problem to solve. Its solution depends on the teacher's willingness to discuss openly with you her or his feelings and attitudes about the referred child. Teachers may not be aware of their own hidden agendas. Good consultation and interviewing skills (see Chapter 16) are especially important in this situation. Determining the teacher's standards can also be valuable. Some teachers want behaviors to be close to perfection, whereas others allow behavior that borders on being deviant.

General Guidelines for Obtaining Reliable and Valid Observations

The following general guidelines will also assist you in obtaining reliable and valid behavioral observations:

• Understand thoroughly the recording techniques, rating scales, checklists, and mechanical instruments used for the observations. Be sure that the critical behaviors are highly specific and clearly defined.

• Check the accuracy of all mechanical instruments used for the data collection before beginning the observations.

• Train yourself to be a critical observer of behavior.

• Draw samples of behavior from a variety of situations, times, and—particularly when you are observing groups of children or developing norms—children.

• Discover what biases, faults, and weaknesses you have that pertain to the observation of behavior. Develop self-understanding and critical self-evaluation skills.

• Develop a healthy skepticism toward previous reports about the referred child's behavior in order to be as objective as possible.

• Suppress assumptions and speculations about the meaning and implications of the child's behavior while you are recording data.

• When you have finished your observations, consider what factors precipitate and maintain the child's behaviors and how other individuals in the child's setting respond to the behaviors.

• Periodically compare your observations with those of an independent observer who is using the same scoring system.

• Regularly recalibrate your recordings by checking them against standard protocols.

• Keep abreast of research and theory in the field of observation of behavior.

You cannot avoid having beliefs and expectations; what you must avoid is prefiguring everything you will find. Your observations will be affected by the child's behavior, the reasons for the referral, your decision criteria (your willingness to score a behavior as occurring or not occurring), your familiarity with the behavioral observation coding system, the amount of time you spend observing, your experience with exceptional groups of children, your familiarity with the referred child, and other factors. These same factors will affect your co-observer's recordings. An understanding of these factors will help you to obtain more reliable and valid recordings.

CAUTIONS ON THE USE OF OBSERVATIONS

Observational methods, like any other assessment procedure, have their strengths and weaknesses (see Table 17-12). Although time-sampling procedures are extremely useful, there are some disadvantages associated with observing exclusively a single behavior or a few behaviors. First, you may be subtly encouraged to identify behaviors according to how easily they can be observed and recorded. Second, the observation of a limited number of behaviors may complicate detection of other behaviors—either positive or negative—that may reveal important information about the child. Thus when you focus on a single behavior, it is important to remain cognizant of the child's other behaviors as well.

Ethical Considerations in Observing Behavior

The observation of certain behaviors, such as intimate sexual activities, may not be appropriate; in such cases self-reports may be more appropriate. Additionally, socially undesirable behaviors, such as child abuse or excessive punishment, may be difficult to record when the parent or aide is aware of being observed.

Direct observation of behavior is always contraindicated when your presence could lead to undesirable side effects (Cone & Foster, 1982). Going into a work setting to observe an adolescent who has been in a mental hospital could lead the adolescent to be identified, labeled, and socially ostracized, for example. Therefore, always consider any possible unintended harmful consequences associated with your behavioral observations, and be sure to take appropriate steps to avoid such outcomes.

REPORTING BEHAVIORAL OBSERVATIONS

Following is a list of items generally included in a report of observational findings. Not all of the information will be applicable to every situation, of course. Chapter 23 gives further information on including behavioral observations in a report.

1. *Personal data*—child's age, sex, physical handicaps, and other relevant characteristics.
2. *Setting data*—date, time, place, length of observation, setting (including type of room, people, and significant others), recording method, and coding system (or behaviors observed).
3. *Reliability*—including reliability methods, if appropriate.
4. *Validity*.
5. *Intensity*—how much the problem behavior interfered with the child's other activities.
6. *Severity*—the extent to which the problem behavior reflects psychopathology.
7. *Duration*—the length of the problem behavior episode.

Table 17-12
Arguments For and Against the Observation of Behavior

Arguments against the observation of behavior	*Arguments for the observation of behavior*
1. The observer may see an unrepresentative sample of the child's behavioral repertoire.	1. Observation of behavior can yield a representative picture of the natural behavior of a child.
2. The observer may influence the child's behavior in ways that cannot be controlled.	2. Knowledge of a child's behavioral repertoire allows for the formulation of hypotheses about important dimensions of temperament, personality, and interpersonal relations.
3. Observation rooms with one-way screens are an unnatural environment.	3. Exact descriptions of behavior patterns aid in developing treatment and remediation programs.
4. Situational constraints may prevent observations from taking place in situations that could contribute to an understanding of the child.	4. Observation of behavior provides information about the development and adjustment of a child to his or her physical and social surroundings.
5. The norms of society impose constraints on observations, placing great emphasis on the privacy of the child's and family's personal life.	5. Observed behavior may differ from that reported by teachers and parents and by children themselves.
6. Children may feel uneasy when they are observed.	6. Observation of behavior provides information that cannot be gained in other ways from uncooperative children.
7. In classroom observations, teachers may feel intruded upon and insecure, even though it is the child who is being observed.	7. Observation of behavior can yield a more finely differentiated picture of the child's reactions than can broader measures such as test scores or number of right and wrong responses.
8. There are no generally accepted systems of observation.	8. Observation of behavior may yield valid data.
9. Certain observation systems are tied to narrowly focused theories.	9. Observation of behavior can be tailored to the specific concerns of the referral source.
10. Interobserver reliability is a problem.	10. Observation of behavior is important in evaluating and monitoring the progress of treatment and remediation programs.
11. Observation of behavior is a costly method of data collection in terms of personnel, time, and materials.	11. Important psychological concepts, such as attitude, role, and motivation, make most sense when anchored at a behavioral level.
12. Inferential statistics are difficult to apply, particularly because of the need to sample behaviors, times, and situations.	12. Behavior patterns are a basis for making decisions about a child—such as whether a child should be admitted into a treatment program, special home, hospital, or reform school—and for formulating rewards and punishments, and these patterns can best be evaluated through observational methods.

Source: Adapted from Fassnacht (1982).

8. *Frequency*—how often the problem behavior occurred.

9. *Generality*—the number of situations in which the problem behavior occurred.

10. *Norms*—how often the comparison child and the referred child's peer group (or class) engaged in the same behavior.

11. *Antecedents of the problem behavior.*

12. *Consequences of the problem behavior*—for example, how much the problem behavior disrupted the activities of the other children.

13. *Peer group acceptance*—whether the problem behavior was accepted by other children.

14. *Adult acceptance*—whether the problem behavior was accepted by adults.

15. *Additional problem behaviors*—any other problems exhibited by the child.

16. *Positive behaviors*—behaviors that may be useful in designing interventions.

17. *Observation difficulties*—difficulties encountered in conducting the observation (for example, problems in determining onset or termination of response, counting number of responses, defining target responses).

18. *Implications of the findings*—for example, whether the behavior was age appropriate or setting appropriate.

Exhibit 17-13

Psychological Evaluation: Behavioral Observation

Name: Andy Lopez
Date of birth: June 1, 1969
Chronological age: 16-11
Observer: Todd Johnson

Date of observation: May 1, 1986
Date of report: May 6, 1986
Co-observer: Jill Cole

Reason for Referral

Andy was observed at Path Services in order to evaluate his progress in a special training program for mentally retarded adolescents. The observation was conducted to fulfill a requirement for a graduate psychological assessment course at Blank State University.

Description of Client Observed and Setting

Andy was observed for a 1-hour period in a class at Path Services, a vocational training and placement center for mentally retarded individuals. The observation was conducted on May 1, 1986 from 8:30 A.M. to 9:30 A.M.

Andy is a black-haired, olive-complexioned male. He is 16 years, 11 months of age, 5 feet 10 inches tall, and weighs 200 pounds. He wore a blue work shirt, blue work pants, and black calf-high work boots. He looked clean and neatly groomed. Andy was observed during a class lecture on window washing and a window washing activity.

Observational Methods

Narrative, running record, event, interval, and rating observation techniques were used. For the purpose of assessing reliability, two observers simultaneously but independently observed Andy's behavior. During the 10-minute narrative recording, the entire class was observed. For the 5-minute running record, Andy's behavior was observed and recorded.

During the 10-minute event recording, the observers recorded the number of times Andy engaged in the following behaviors: touching a boot with his hand, tapping his foot on the floor, touching his face or head with his hand, yawning, and raising his hand or motioning with it for the purpose of getting another person's attention.

For the interval recording, Andy was observed for three time periods. The first, which lasted for 6 minutes and 40 seconds, consisted of sixteen 15-second observation intervals interspersed with 10-second recording intervals. During this time period, the observers recorded whether or not Andy engaged in any of the following nine behaviors: attending, working, volunteering, reading aloud, displaying other appropriate behavior, interacting with a peer about academic materials, interacting with a peer about nonacademic materials, looking around, and displaying other inappropriate behavior.

The second and third interval recordings each lasted for 4 minutes, and consisted of sixteen 10-second observation intervals interspersed with 5-second recording intervals. The

target behaviors for the second interval recording involved the following behaviors on the part of the teacher with respect to Andy or the entire class: approval, disapproval, no response, and verbal interaction. The target behaviors for the third interval recording were appropriate behavior and inappropriate behavior of the class as a whole.

Andy was observed for approximately 45 minutes while the observers made narrative, running record, event, and interval recordings., An additional 10 minutes of observation time was used for narrative recording of the teacher's behavior in relation to Andy. After all of the observations were finished, the observers completed eight 7-point rating scales: on-task (always–never), verbal off-task (always–never), motor off-task (always–never), passive off-task (always–never), verbalization (clear–unclear), teacher verbal approval responses (frequent–absent), teacher verbal disapproval responses (frequent–absent), and class-appropriate behavior (always–never).

A variety of interobserver agreement indices were calculated from the event, interval, and rating observation data. These included overall percentage of agreement, percentages of agreement on occurrence and nonoccurrence of the behaviors, and kappa. Six reliability indices of the occurrence of particular behaviors could not be calculated because both observers agreed that the behavior never occurred. Fifty-three of the 63 reliability indices calculated were satisfactory (at least 90 percent agreement). The 10 unsatisfactory indices were primarily in areas in which the behavior assessed was not discrete or the observers encountered difficulty with direct observation because their view was restricted. Overall, interrater reliability appears to be satisfactory. The results also appear to be valid.

Observational Findings

Andy engaged in predominantly appropriate class behavior. He did, however, occasionally exhibit inappropriate verbal and passive off-task behaviors. During the first 15 minutes of class, Andy appeared tired, distracted, and restless. He sat in a slouched position, with his buttocks on the edge of the chair, legs outstretched, and upper back against the top of the chairback. He frequently closed his eyes or rubbed them in what looked like an attempt to wake up. He often coughed and yawned. When Andy heard noises or voices outside the classroom, or when someone entered or left, he always turned around to look and he often waved. Andy occasionally bent

(Exhibit continues next page)

Exhibit 17-13 (cont.)

over to untie and retie his boot laces. He frequently rubbed his head or the skin around his mouth and nose; during event recording, he did this at a rate of once every 40 seconds.

Andy demonstrated that his full attention was not on the teacher by asking "Do we have to go outside and clean up?" approximately 2 minutes after the teacher spoke to the class about that same issue. Andy failed to sign in when he entered the room, and the teacher had to tell him to do so approximately 10 minutes into the class period. Upon approaching the sign-in sheet, Andy groped in his pockets for a pen. When he realized he did not have one, he turned toward his classmates and asked in a fairly loud voice if anybody had a pen that he could borrow. On a few occasions, Andy spoke to another class member during the lecture. Despite Andy's inappropriate behavior, he was not disruptive in the classroom.

As the lecture progressed, Andy's boredom and restlessness decreased, and his attentiveness increased. Despite his seeming distractedness, he answered many of the teacher's questions appropriately. First, he eagerly and quickly sat up straight, raised his hand, and then waited for the teacher to call on him. However, on rare occasions he shouted out an answer. After a majority of the class members unsuccessfully guessed answers to a question, Andy answered with conviction, "I know what it is—water is minerals." In response to the teacher's question about what supplies the window-washer needs, Andy quickly said, "squeegee, bucket, spray bottle, and rags—folded." When the teacher subsequently asked what the bucket was used for and why the rags were folded, Andy promptly supplied the correct reasons. When he was not called upon, Andy tended to look disappointed.

Andy exhibited the same eagerness during the window-washing task. He pulled his chair close to the demonstration window, attended to the teacher, and enthusiastically volunteered to perform the task. Andy apparently understood the teacher's instructions, as he washed the window accordingly. He worked diligently and responded well to the teacher's questions. When Andy was done, for example, the teacher said, "Now what are you going to do?" Andy quickly and correctly replied, "Look for streaks." When Andy found spots on the window, he asked the teacher, "Want me to get paper towels?" When the teacher indicated that that was a good idea, Andy promptly retrieved paper towels from the front of the

classroom and wiped the spots off the window. Andy meticulously inspected the window and enthusiastically asked, "How does it look, Tim?" The teacher responded, "Good, I think," and Andy smiled. Andy's verbalizations were always clear and grammatically correct. Although he usually sat off to the side, rather than among his classmates, he appeared to be friendly with them.

The teacher interacted with the students throughout the observation period. Interaction was predominantly verbal—it included lecturing, asking questions, explaining how to wash the window, and commenting on the students' demonstrations. Most of the interaction was instructional; thus approval and disapproval were infrequent. When approval was given, it was more frequently nonverbal (e.g., a smile or a nod of the head) than verbal. Andy appeared content when he was given either verbal or nonverbal approval. When the teacher used disapproval, it was in a firm but gentle manner. Andy did not receive disapproval for any of his actions. Overall, the teacher was patient and had good rapport with the students. Andy and his classmates for the most part were cooperative, respectful, and appropriately behaved. There was, however, a mild air of distractibility and restlessness in the classroom.

Summary and Impressions

This observation was conducted on the morning of May 1, 1986 at Path Services in order to fulfill a course requirement. Andy is a 16-year, 11-month-old male. At the beginning of the class on window washing procedures, Andy appeared to be restless, distracted, and tired. When the teacher began to ask questions, however, Andy became more involved. His attention increased and he eagerly, correctly, and appropriately answered many of the teacher's questions. Andy's verbalizations were always clear and coherent, and he was eager and enthusiastic as he washed windows. He followed instructions and worked diligently and meticulously. Andy's distractibility seemed to be due to an over-alertness to the things happening in his environment. He appeared to be outgoing and amiable. Andy was attracted to both mental and physical stimulation. He seemed to enjoy the recognition he received through successful participation in the class activity.

(Signature)
_____

Todd Johnson, B.A., Observer

PSYCHOLOGICAL EVALUATION

Exhibit 17-13 presents a psychological evaluation of a mentally retarded adolescent who was observed at a vocational training center. The evaluation is a case study involving systematic behavioral observation. The purpose of this case study is to demonstrate the various observational

approaches discussed in this chapter. In practice, observational procedures would typically be chosen judiciously on the basis of the reason for referral, previous psychometric assessment findings, and the frequency, duration, and type of behavior under observation. In most cases only one or two behavioral observational techniques would be used. In the case study five observational techniques are presented to demonstrate the application of each technique and the kinds of results each renders. The report presents a description of the adolescent, a detailed description of the observational methods used (including target behaviors and rating scales), and a statement about reliability and validity. All of the observational findings are then integrated into the report. A short summary, which highlights the observational findings, concludes the evaluation.

SUMMARY

1. The observation of behavior is an important part of the assessment process. It provides information about the child's behavior in everyday settings and about the child's interpersonal behavior and learning style. It serves a variety of evaluation and intervention functions.

2. The assumption underlying the systematic sampling of behavior is that the behaviors recorded over time are representative of the behaviors under observation.

3. Observational methods are useful for studying high-frequency behaviors and global behaviors and for evaluating a child's progress over time. Observational assessment may not be the method of choice for certain kinds of behaviors, particularly those that occur rarely or only under highly specific conditions.

4. The observation of behavior is particularly valuable for an ecological assessment. Ecological assessment focuses on observable aspects of the setting, how the setting works, and how the setting provides for the needs of the persons in it.

5. An observational assessment combines an observational recording method and an observational coding system.

6. Behaviors differ in their attributes. The attributes of the target behaviors should be considered when a recording method is selected.

7. The four principal observation recording methods used in clinical and psychoeducational assessment are narrative, interval, event, and ratings recording.

8. In designing any recording procedure, consider the number of times you will observe the child, the length of the observation period, when the observations will be conducted, the type of recording to be used, the target behaviors under observation (if any), and the method of recording data.

9. Narrative recording focuses on a description of the child's natural behavior. Two forms of narrative recording are anecdotal recordings and running records.

10. Observations can include molar (broad) descriptions of behavior and molecular (fine) descriptions of behavior. Observations also form a continuum from low inferential judgments to high inferential judgments.

11. Narrative recording is particularly valuable as a precursor to more specific observations and as a method for observing groups.

12. In conducting a narrative recording, focus on the child's behavior rather than on making interpretations. Describe the

setting. Be objective, accurate, and thorough in your recording. Recognize your role in the assessment process and how your impressions may influence your observations. The final narrative recording should integrate all sources of information obtained from the observation.

13. Narrative recording maintains the original sequence of events and allows for the discovery of critical behaviors and the noting of continuing difficulties. However, it is time consuming, poses quantification problems, may be insensitive to some types of critical behaviors, and may not provide generalizable findings.

14. Interval recording focuses on selected aspects of behavior as they occur within specified time intervals. Interval recording procedures include partial-interval time sampling (behavior is scored when it occurs any time during any interval), whole-interval time sampling (behavior is scored only when it lasts from the beginning to the end of the interval), point-time interval sampling (behavior is scored only when it occurs at a specific time during the interval), momentary time interval sampling (behavior is scored only when it occurs at the moment the interval ends), and variable interoccasion interval time sampling (behavior is scored only when it occurs at preselected random time intervals).

15. Interval recording is useful for examining easily observable behaviors that are clearly discrete and occur with moderate frequency. A recording interval should be included whenever scoring will interfere with the observations. Sequential recording procedures permit observations of a number of different individuals in a group.

16. The number of intervals in which the target behavior occurs is the primary piece of quantitative data obtained in interval recording.

17. Interval recording provides precise behavioral data within and across observation periods, facilitates checking for reliability, uses standard observation conditions, uses time efficiently, and allows for flexible recordings. However, interval recording provides a somewhat artificial view of the behavior sequence, may overlook important behaviors, provides limited information about the reasons for or quality of the behaviors, may not show the actual frequency or duration of the behavior, and may fail to detect low-rate behaviors.

18. Event recording involves the counting of the number of target behaviors observed during an observation period. It is especially appropriate for measuring discrete responses that have clearly defined beginnings and ends. It is less suitable for high-rate behaviors or for behaviors that vary in duration.

19. The frequency count is the primary piece of quantitative data obtained in event recording. Other behavioral dimensions that can be recorded are the rate, duration, intensity, and latency of behavior.

20. Event recording detects low-rate behaviors, allows for the study of many different behaviors, uses time efficiently, allows for flexible recordings, and provides information about changes in behavior over time and amount of behavior performed. However, event recording provides a somewhat artificial view of the behavior sequence, breaks up the continuity of behavior, provides

limited information about behaviors that are not clearly discrete, presents difficulties in establishing reliability, requires a high level of observer attention, provides limited information about the how and why of behavior, and makes comparisons across sessions difficult if the length of the observation period is not constant.

21. Ratings recording involves using a scale or checklist to rate behavior. It is useful for evaluating the more global aspects of behavior and for quantifying impressions.

22. The scale values on the rating scales constitute the primary quantitative data in ratings recording.

23. Ratings recording can be used for recording many different behaviors of both individuals and groups as a whole. It allows for the observation of subtle aspects of behavior, generates data in a form suitable for statistical analysis, and uses time efficiently. Some disadvantages of ratings recording are that it uses scale values which may be based on unclear assumptions, presents difficulties in achieving satisfactory reliability, and limits the extent to which important quantitative information and antecedent and consequent events are recorded.

24. Observational coding systems cover an entire spectrum of behaviors and include global categories as well as extremely narrow ones. A coding system may be selected from preexisting ones or developed to meet the assessment goals.

25. Guidelines for designing an observational assessment include the following: select or design a coding system that meets the assessment goals, use categories sparingly, use easily discriminable categories, select an appropriate interval length and an appropriate length of time for the observations, select appropriate observation times and places, use an appropriate recording sheet, and design the overall assessment so that the target behaviors are likely to be observed.

26. It is important to obtain reliable and valid observational findings. Sources of error in the observation of behavior include those associated with the personal qualities of the observer and those associated with the setting, codes, scales, and instruments, referred child, and sample.

27. Observer bias is a general term for a variety of errors associated with the personal qualities of the observer.

28. Observer drift refers to the tendency of observers to become less vigilant during the course of the observation.

29. Interobserver reliability can be measured by a variety of procedures that compare one observer's results with those of another observer who simultaneously and independently conducts observations of the same subject.

30. Kappa is favored by many statisticians as an index of agreement that controls for chance agreement. Kappa and percentage agreement may differ for a particular set of data.

31. Percentage agreement is the most popular type of interobserver agreement index. Although it does not take into account chance agreement, it is useful, particularly as a preliminary check on the level of interobserver agreement.

32. In interval recording, it is useful to obtain percentage agreement for the total intervals and for those intervals in which at least one observer recorded the occurrence or nonoccurrence of the behavior.

33. In event recording, interobserver agreement can be obtained by percentage agreement.

34. In ratings recording, percentage agreement can be used to determine the extent to which two observers gave the exact same rating on each scale.

35. Other useful forms of reliability for the observation of behavior are test-retest reliability and internal consistency reliability.

36. The validity of observational findings is more often assumed than established. Every effort should be made to determine the validity of observational findings.

37. Reactivity—defined as changes in the child's behavior as a result of being observed—can threaten the validity of observational findings. In some situations, however, reactivity may not be detrimental to the findings.

38. Errors in observation can be reduced by having clear and precise definitions of behavior, systematic rules governing the observations, well-trained observers, continuous checks on the observers' recordings, and periodic calibrations made by the observer during the course of the observation.

39. As an observer, you can reduce your reactive effects by being as neutral a stimulus in the environment as possible, by positioning yourself in a remote location, by limiting your stimulus value, by following all rules and policies of the setting, and by conducting the observation at the least disruptive times.

40. Additional ways of reducing errors are to establish informal norms, and to develop sensitivity to the teacher's needs when the observations are conducted in a classroom.

41. To ensure that your observations are as reliable and valid as possible, you should understand thoroughly the observational procedures and instruments, check the accuracy of all mechanical instruments, train yourself to become a critical observer of behavior, discover your own biases, develop a healthy skepticism toward previous reports about the referred child's behavior, suppress assumptions about the meaning of the child's behavior while recording your observations, consider what factors precipitate and maintain the child's behaviors, periodically compare your findings with those of another observer, regularly recalibrate your recordings by checking them against standard protocols, and keep abreast of research on the observation of behavior.

42. Be aware of ethical factors that may arise when you observe behavior.

43. In your report of the observational findings, include all important information, such as personal and environmental data; reliability and validity of the observations; intensity, severity, duration, frequency, and generality of the behavior; norms; antecedents and consequences of the behavior; peer group and adult responses to the behavior; additional problem behaviors; positive behaviors; observation difficulties; and implications of findings for the assessment and for intervention planning.

KEY TERMS, CONCEPTS, AND NAMES

Systematic observation of behavior (p. 473)
Ecological assessment (p. 474)
Planned incident procedure (p. 474)
Setting appearance and contents (p. 475)
Setting operation (p. 475)
Setting opportunities (p. 475)
Observational recording method (p. 475)
Observational coding system (p. 475)
Narrative recording (p. 476)
Anecdotal recording (p. 476)
Running record (p. 476)
Molar description (p. 476)
Molecular description (p. 476)
Inferential judgment (p. 476)
Behavioral descriptive statement (p. 476)
Target behavior (p. 478)
Interval recording (p. 480)
Time sampling (p. 480)
Interval sampling (p. 480)
Interval time sampling (p. 480)
Partial-interval time sampling (p. 481)
Whole-interval time sampling (p. 481)
Point-time interval sampling (p. 481)
Momentary time interval sampling (p. 481)
Variable interoccasion interval time sampling (p. 481)
Intensity dimension (p. 488)
Event recording (p. 490)
Event sampling (p. 490)
Frequency count (p. 491)
Rate of behavior (p. 491)
Duration of behavior (p. 492)
Intensity of behavior (p. 493)
Latency of behavior (p. 493)
Ratings recording (p. 494)
On-task behavior (p. 499)
Off-task behavior (p. 499)
Reliability (p. 504)
Observer bias (p. 504)
Central tendency error (p. 509)
Primacy effect error (p. 509)
Halo effect error (p. 509)
Personal theory error (p. 509)
Personal values error (p. 509)
Logical error (p. 509)
Contrast error (p. 509)
Proximity error (p. 509)
Personal effects (p. 509)
Observer drift (p. 509)
Omission (p. 509)
Commission (p. 509)
Observer reactivity (p. 509)
Unrepresentative behavioral setting (p. 510)
Coding complexity (p. 510)
Child reactivity (p. 510)

Role selection (p. 510)
Response set (p. 510)
Unrepresentative sample (p. 510)
Sample instability (p. 510)
Unrepresentative data (p. 510)
Interobserver reliability (p. 510)
Interobserver agreement (p. 510)
Product-moment correlation coefficient (p. 510)
Intraclass correlation coefficient (p. 511)
Kappa (κ) (p. 511)
Uncorrected percentage agreement (p. 511)
Percentage agreement (p. 511)
Agreement of total observations (p. 511)
Agreement of occurrence observations (p. 515)
Agreement of nonoccurrence observations (p. 515)
Test-retest reliability (p. 518)
Internal consistency reliability (p. 518)
Guinea pig effect (p. 519)
Criterion related agreement (p. 520)
Informal norms (p. 521)
Discrepancy ratio (p. 521)

STUDY QUESTIONS

1. What are some of the purposes served by the direct observation of behavior?

2. What is an ecological assessment? Include in your discussion Hiltonsmith and Keller's ecological assessment framework.

3. What are some limitations associated with ecological assessment?

4. Discuss the narrative recording method. Include in your discussion types of narrative recordings, molar and molecular descriptions of behavior, inferential judgments, major uses, design considerations, advantages, and disadvantages.

5. Discuss the interval recording method. Include in your discussion the five different types of interval recording methods, major uses, design considerations, quantitative data, advantages, and disadvantages.

6. Discuss the event recording method. Include in your discussion a description of the method, major uses, design considerations, quantitative data, advantages, and disadvantages.

7. Discuss ratings recording. Include in your discussion a description of the method, major uses, quantitative data, advantages, and disadvantages.

8. Indicate which type of recording method is preferred for observing each of the following and explain why: (a) use of slang words, (b) tics, (c) quality of a story, and (d) the antecedent event preceding an aggressive act.

9. Compare and contrast narrative recording, interval recording, event recording, and ratings recording.

10. What factors should you consider in designing an observational coding system?

11. Discuss factors that may affect the reliability of behavioral observations.

12. Discuss the following four procedures for measuring the level of interobserver agreement: product-moment correlation coefficient, intraclass correlation coefficient, kappa, and percentage agreement.

13. What factors may affect the test-retest reliability of behavioral observations?

14. Discuss some of the factors affecting the validity of behavioral observations.

15. Discuss reactivity in observational recordings. Explain why reactivity may not necessarily be detrimental and discuss ways to reduce reactivity.

16. How would you go about reducing the number of errors that occur in your behavioral observations?

17. Present seven general guidelines for obtaining reliable and valid observations.

18. Discuss the strengths and limitations of observational methods.

19. Present 10 guidelines for reporting behavioral observations.

18

THE ASSESSMENT PROCESS

It is probably unwise to spend much time in attempts to separate off sharply certain qualities of man, such as his intelligence, from such emotional and vocational qualities as his interest in mental activity, carefulness, determination to respond effectively, persistence in his efforts to do so; or from his amount of knowledge; or from his moral or esthetic tastes.

—Edward L. Thorndike

Assessment techniques are used by a professional detective, and the information provided by that detective must be good enough to stand up in the court of life. That is why special techniques are needed, why reliability must be assessed, and why the "ultraviolet lights" provided by your tests and procedures are necessary to see through the clients' shields. But you, again like the detective, are constrained by ethical considerations, and you are not allowed to use the psychological equivalent of the rubber hose, which in part is why you must respect the rights of the client; but of course, for the psychologist respect plays a dual role; you will be more effective as well as more ethical if you give, and thus receive, respect.

—William A. Hillix

The testing by one individual of another human's intellectual, personality, and related characteristics is an invasion of privacy to an extent no less intimate than that involved in an examination carried out on that same individual's person or resources by a physician, attorney, or agent of the Internal Revenue Service.

—Joseph D. Matarazzo

GENERAL ASSESSMENT CONSIDERATIONS

To be an effective assessor, one must know a great deal about tests and about people; be capable of using creative skill, scientific rigor, and caution in developing hypotheses; be flexible enough to modify or reject hypotheses in the light of new data; know the situations about which inferences must be made; and be aware of one's own characteristics as an interpreter of test performance and human behavior.

The multimethod assessment approach advocated in this text synthesizes information obtained from past records and evaluations; interviews with parents, teachers, and the child; observations of the child; and the results of standardized tests, informal tests, and other special procedures. Interviews and behavioral problem checklists are most useful for obtaining personal information; an initial description and classification of behavior; impressions of the child, the child's parents, and the child's teachers; and the child's perception of the problem. Observational procedures are most useful for obtaining information about the child's behavior in environmental settings, peer-group relationships, family relationships, and relationships with teachers and for monitoring progress throughout treatment. Standardized tests are most useful for comparing the child to some norm group and for evaluating changes associated with the handicap, disease process, or remediation efforts. Informal tests are most useful for obtaining information about special abilities or skills that cannot be measured with standardized tests. All of these assessment procedures can be repeated at the termination of the intervention program and at follow-up to evaluate progress and change.

Purposes of Assessment

The purpose of assessment may be screening, diagnosis, counseling and rehabilitation, or progress evaluation. In a *screening assessment*, a relatively brief examination is given to identify children who are eligible for certain programs or who have a disorder in need of remediation or rehabilitation or to determine whether a more comprehensive assessment is needed. In a *diagnostic assessment*, a detailed evaluation of the child's strengths and weaknesses in a variety of areas is undertaken. *Counseling and rehabilitation assessment* is similar to diagnostic assessment except that emphasis is placed on the child's abilities to adjust to and successfully fulfill daily responsibilities; possible responses to treatment and recovery potential are also considered. In a *progress evaluation assessment*, the focus

is on charting the day-to-day or week-to-week progress of the child.

Typical questions addressed in a diagnostic assessment include the following:

1. What is the level of the child's cognitive functioning?
2. If there is a handicap, how has it affected the child's language, motor skills, self-concept, interpersonal relations, and related areas?
3. How is the child performing academically?
4. What is the most appropriate educational program and setting for the child?
5. What realistic goals can be set for the child?
6. How can the school and family deal more effectively with the child's problems or handicaps?

Psychological Assessment and Psychological Testing

Psychological assessment is not synonymous with psychological testing. *Psychological assessment* takes into consideration the unique characteristics and the relevant context of the child who is being assessed. *Psychological testing* is a more limited professional activity that involves the administration and interpretation of one or more psychological tests. *Testing produces findings, whereas assessment gives meaning to the findings within the context of the child's life situation and clinical history.*

Psychological Assessment and Medical Evaluation

A psychological evaluation assesses the child's performance and capabilities and guides the establishment of appropriate intervention programs. Even in cases of brain injury or physical disability, psychological assessment serves valuable functions. A medical evaluation provides information about the etiology of the child's exceptionality, areas of deficit or diminished skill, the need for special environmental adaptations or prosthetic aids, and possible medical treatments. A psychological evaluation complements a medical evaluation by providing information that will help the child to function optimally in everyday life situations.

STEPS IN THE ASSESSMENT PROCESS

The usual steps in the assessment process are as follows (see also Figure 18-1):

1. Review referral information. Check with the referral source—for example, physician, teacher, parents, or court—to clarify any vague information.

2. Obtain information relevant to the child's medical, social, psychological, linguistic, educational, and physical development, including previous psychological evaluations. This information can be obtained from parents, teachers, and others familiar with the child's problem, from medical reports, and from other agencies.

3. Assess the behavior of relevant adults.

4. Observe the child in various settings.

5. Administer an appropriate test battery, selected on the basis of the referral question; the child's age, physical capabilities, language proficiency, and prior test results; and teacher, parental, and medical reports.

6. Interpret the data.

7. Formulate hypotheses.

8. Develop intervention strategies.

9. Write a report, including recommendations.

10. Meet with parents, child (if appropriate), and other concerned individuals to discuss the assessment results and recommendations.

11. Follow up on recommendations and retest.

Working with Relevant Adults

A comprehensive assessment of a child's behavior requires the assessment of relevant adults' behavior as well. Significant adults usually play an important role in the development of the child's behavior. Ideally one should observe how the behavior of parents and teachers affects the child (see Chapter 17). The interview with the parents or teacher should elicit information about how they view the problem, what they have done to alleviate the problem, and their role in maintaining the problem (see Chapter 16). When the test findings do not agree with the parents' or teacher's account of what the child can do, the reasons for the disagreement should be investigated.

Observing the Child's Behavior

During testing, observe the child's ability to participate actively, take initiative, and assume responsibility for responses. On those occasions when you ask a child for further information, observe how he or she complies with the request—for example, whether the original response is rephrased or elaborated. These observations may provide insight into the child's flexibility and willingness to communicate clearly with others. Observations should also be made of how the child approaches the test materials, how the tasks are attempted, and what factors lead to success and failure. Both verbal and nonverbal responses should be observed. (Chapters 5 and 17 provide additional observational guidelines.)

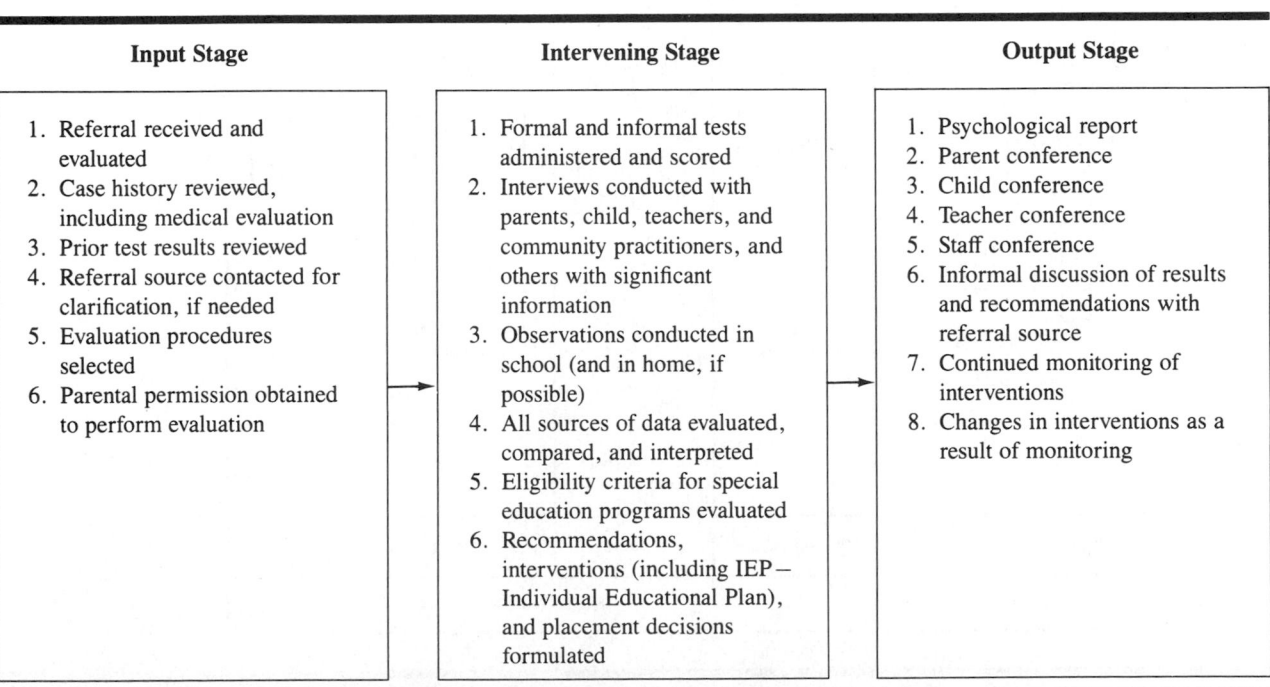

Input Stage	Intervening Stage	Output Stage
1. Referral received and evaluated 2. Case history reviewed, including medical evaluation 3. Prior test results reviewed 4. Referral source contacted for clarification, if needed 5. Evaluation procedures selected 6. Parental permission obtained to perform evaluation	1. Formal and informal tests administered and scored 2. Interviews conducted with parents, child, teachers, and community practitioners, and others with significant information 3. Observations conducted in school (and in home, if possible) 4. All sources of data evaluated, compared, and interpreted 5. Eligibility criteria for special education programs evaluated 6. Recommendations, interventions (including IEP—Individual Educational Plan), and placement decisions formulated	1. Psychological report 2. Parent conference 3. Child conference 4. Teacher conference 5. Staff conference 6. Informal discussion of results and recommendations with referral source 7. Continued monitoring of interventions 8. Changes in interventions as a result of monitoring

Figure 18-1.   **Stages of the assessment process.**

Interpreting the Data

A psychological assessment is a complex activity, as it requires gathering, integrating, organizing, and interpreting the following kinds of data: (a) *developmental* (including information about intelligence, achievement skills, perceptual abilities, social skills, adaptive behavior, and emotional and personality characteristics); (b) *behavioral* (including observations of behavior during the test, at school, and, where feasible, at home); (c) *medical* (including neurological work-up if needed); and (d) *environmental* (including information about the school and family). The information is used to describe the problem, estimate its severity, identify factors related to it, suggest areas for improvement, develop treatment or intervention programs, and determine a prognosis.

The process of interpreting the test results can be conceptualized as a chain with three major links: (a) the test responses, (b) theories through which the responses are integrated and conceptualized, and (c) knowledge of what

to do given this information (for example, recommended interventions). Psychologists working with children must know what is age-appropriate behavior, in order to determine to what extent a child's behavior deviates from the norm.

Factors that influence test scores.   The factors that influence *the output* (the test score) include *the input* (innate factors and factors in the child's background and environment) and *intervening variables* (the factors in the child's personality, situational test demands, and random variation) (see Figure 18-2). The relative importance of the various factors will vary depending on the examinee. An accurate assessment of intelligence and other abilities requires consideration of the factors illustrated in Figure 18-2 plus other factors unique to the examinee.

The influence of innate factors on intelligence test scores has been a matter of concern since the inception of the testing movement. Although we still have no definitive

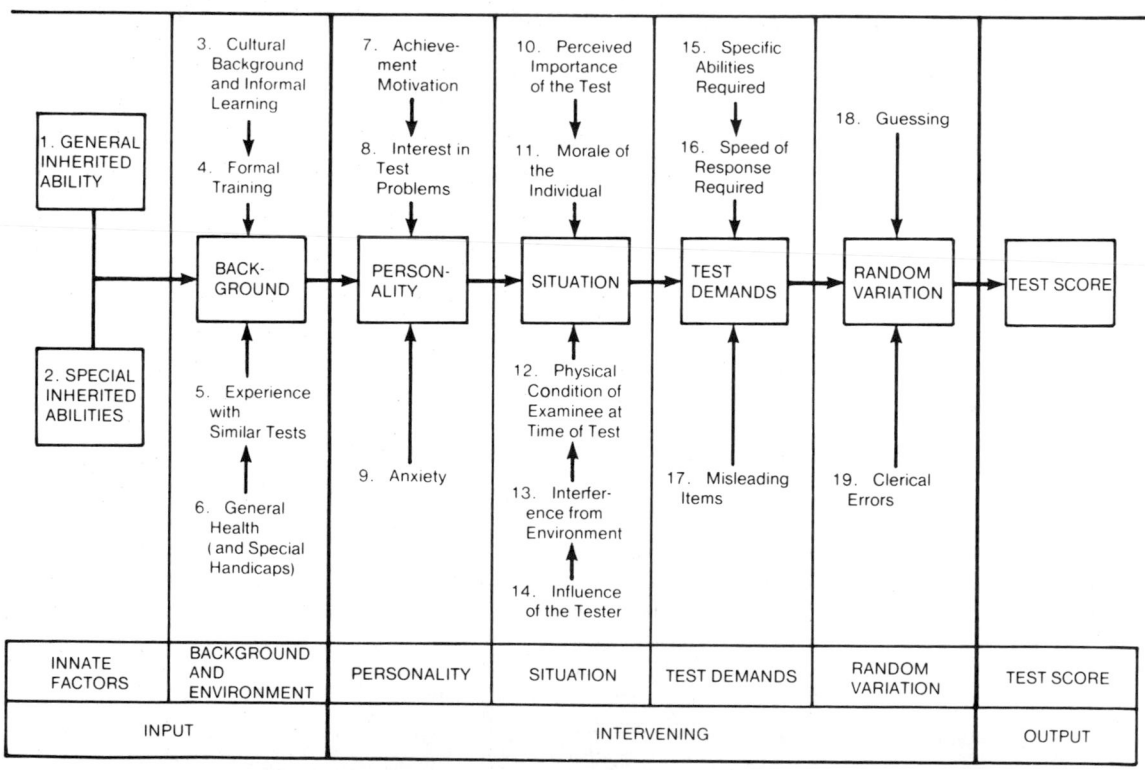

Figure 18-2.   A paradigm for the analysis of influencing variables. Reprinted by permission of the publisher from D. A. Goslin, *The Search for Ability: Standardized Testing in Social Perspective*, p. 130. Copyright 1963, Russell Sage Foundation.

information about the exact contribution of heredity, there is strong evidence that it does make a significant contribution (see Chapter 4). The specific extent to which genetic limitations can be overcome by environmental conditions is not known.

Accounting for failures. Test failures may occur for various reasons. Take the case of a child who fails to stack blocks when asked to do so. Possible causes of this failure include limited hearing, vision, comprehension, or motor capacities; inability to understand the instructions; negativistic behavior; or neurological impairment. Careful analysis of the child's entire performance will be needed to arrive at a likely explanation of the child's failure. Do not simply report the failure without providing an explanation.

Both individual factors (from neuropsychological, physical, experiential, and temperament domains) and environmental factors (from school, home, and peer group) may interact to produce failures (see Figure 18-3). Formal testing will help to evaluate neuropsychological and temperament domains, whereas interviews, observations, and checklists will be useful in assessing experiential and environmental factors.

Problems of generalization. A child's performance in a standard test situation may not reflect how the child would perform if he or she were more comfortable, stimulated or inspired, healthier, or less upset by family anxieties. Tests give information about how the child performs at a specific moment under specific conditions. The overall IQ may not reveal the underlying dynamic trends that are developing in the child. Some children may appear to be slow learners at the time they are assessed, yet they may be storing observations and reflections that may not be revealed until a much later period of their life. They may also have insights that are revealed in ways not adequately measured by standardized test questions. Look for signs of insight or creativity masked or not directly assessed by the objective scores.

Consider the distinction between achievement, in the

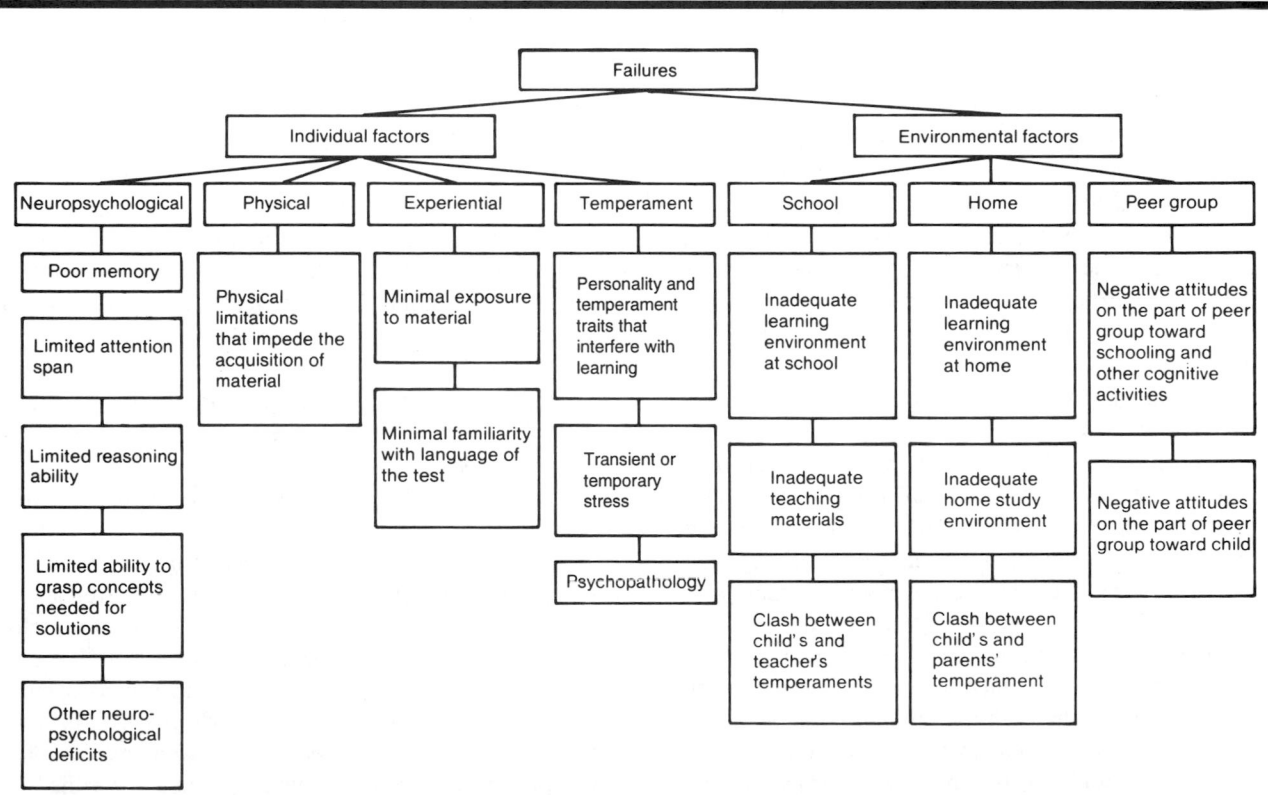

Figure 18-3. Major factors that may account for failures on tests or in school.

restricted sense of level of performance on a given test, and the cumulative achievement that occurs over a much longer span of time (Atkinson, 1974). The child's cumulative achievement reflects the outcome of complex interactions involving ability, motivational dispositions (such as motives, knowledge, beliefs, and conceptions), task requirements, incentives, opportunities in the immediate environment, and other factors that influence the child to engage in various activities. During an individual assessment, these same variables are likely to be operating, although on a more limited basis. The child's intelligence test score must be seen as reflecting not only a level of ability, but also motivation. Unfortunately, there is no simple way to separate out the influence of each component on the final test score. To what extent is the child's level of motivation affecting his or her performance? If motivational differences among children or even in one child over the course of an assessment session are not taken into account, too much emphasis may be placed on the ability component of the test results. Because motivation is not constant among children, a pure ability interpretation of the final test score is inadequate.

Problems in the measurement of psychological processes.   The psychological processes measured by specific tests are not easy to identify. Every test measures a number of different functions. For example, the WISC-R Digit Span subtest, which requires immediate repetition of orally presented sequences of digits, may measure sequencing, short-term memory, and attention as well as motivation, auditory acuity, understanding of task demands, willingness to try, and strategy usage. Which of these are important factors in the child's performance is best determined through the use of relevant assessment devices (Torgesen, 1979).

Specifying the nature of relationships between skills measured on diagnostic tests and classroom performance is difficult (Torgesen, 1979). For example, even though reading-disabled children may perform poorly on tests of short-term sequential memory, it is highly unlikely that they have not learned how to read because they cannot repeat sequences of digits. A more plausible assumption is that the Digit Span subtest taps processes that are important to *both* digit repetition *and* learning to read. This assumption, of course, must be corroborated. Until such evidence is available, it will be difficult to know how test failures are relevant to classroom performance.

Processing difficulties may be related to organic, experiential, learning, and other factors. A failure does not tell us which factor is involved and hence which interventions may be needed. A careful study of the child's entire performance and clinical history must be made to account for any processing difficulties.

Other problems.   Other problems that may compound the difficulty of performing a psychological evaluation include the following:

1. Classification systems are not uniform, and symptoms often fall into more than one diagnostic category.

2. A behavior that is of concern to adults may not be of concern to the child.

3. Because of rapid developmental changes, problems a child has at one age may not be evident at another. A developmental lag rather than psychopathology may be the basis for the problem.

4. Assessment can be time consuming, and sufficient time may not be made available by some parents or school officials.

Formulating Hypotheses

The process of formulating hypotheses starts with a review and analysis of all data sources, including formal and informal assessment results, observations, interviews, clinical history, and prior assessment information. On the basis of this review hypotheses are formulated, and confirming evidence is then sought. Those hypotheses that are supported by only one piece of minor evidence are regarded as very tentative or dropped. Those that are supported by more than one piece of evidence—especially if the supporting data come from more than one source (for example, test results *and* observations)—are retained for further consideration. Evidence that may disconfirm each hypothesis is also sought from the various sources of information. When this process has been completed, those hypotheses that have received support can be advanced. These theories are still hypotheses—that is, tentative and unproved explanations of a complex set of data—but they are ones that can be offered with some degree of confidence.

The examples in Table 18-1 illustrate how *tentative hypotheses* about temperament, personality, and level of ability can be developed from a careful analysis of a child's responses and behavior. The examples indicate that both physical and psychological factors should be considered in attempting to understand a child's performance. As noted above, hypotheses developed from performance on a few items, or from a few test responses, should be verified via other data sources before they are accepted and reported. Judgment always must be used in deciding whether a response reflects the child's habitual style or is a temporary and transient expression. Although you must be careful not to overinterpret every minuscule aspect of the child's performance, there are occasions when hypotheses developed from unique responses may prove to be valuable.

Developing Intervention Strategies

Assessment and treatment are inextricably intertwined. Assessment involves a careful delineation of the child's strengths and weaknesses, a description of the child's temperament and personality, the formulation of a diagnostic label in those cases where it is needed and appropriate, and the development of recommendations.

Traditional forms of psychometric assessment usually do not provide information about the conditions that best facilitate the child's ability to learn—for example, how type of material, rate and modality of presentation, cues, and reinforcements differentially affect learning. Information about these and related factors (see Table 18-2) could help us design more effective intervention programs that might improve the cognitive ability of children. A wedding of experimental and clinical/psychoeducational approaches, which has been in the making for many years, has yet to occur. Until it occurs, we must use the presently available procedures (inferences from performance on standard tests, informal tests, and specialized procedures) to determine which conditions best facilitate the child's ability to learn.

Following Up on Recommendations and Retesting

Effective delivery of services requires close monitoring of recommendations and interventions. Both short- and long-term follow-up are important parts of the psychological assessment process.

Short-term follow-up. Short-term follow-up (within two to six weeks) is strongly recommended, because interventions may prove to be ineffective, either because of changes in the situation or because the interventions were inadequate from the beginning. Other issues requiring additional assessment also may be discovered.

Retesting. Assessment is not a once-and-for-all matter. Children change as a result of development, life experiences, and treatment. An evaluation conducted when the child is 2 years old may have little meaning a year later, except as a basis for comparison. Retesting is an important means of monitoring the child's response to an intervention, the progression of a disease process, or the course and rate of recovery. Repeated assessment is especially important when a clinical intervention procedure—such as medical intervention (for example, chemotherapy or surgery) or a behavioral intervention (for example, a cognitive rehabilitation program)—is used. Repeated assessment is also required when children are placed in special education programs and when preschool children are classified as having a developmental disability.

Unfortunately, the results of repeated evaluations may be difficult to interpret for the following reasons:

1. We cannot easily differentiate those changes that are the result of practice effects (or a retest effect alone) from those that are associated with actual clinical improvement (or changes in adaptive and behavioral functioning). Practice effects refer to changes in performance (usually gains) that result from prior exposure to a task. A higher retest score may be the result of the intervention or learning, or it may be related to prior exposure. For example, is the improvement exhibited by a brain-injured child on retesting related to practice effects or to the child's improved cerebral functioning? Perhaps neurologically impaired children who improve on a retest are showing improved learning ability and not simply a practice effect. (When the change is greater than 1 standard error of measurement, one can be more confident that the score reflects a reliable change.)

2. Practice effects may not occur to the same extent in all populations. The practice effects typically seen among normal (or healthy) children may not occur among mentally retarded children and children with known cerebral dysfunction. Practice effects may also differ as a function of the child's age.

3. Practice effects vary for different types of tasks. For example, practice effects are greater on the Wechsler Performance Scale subtests than on the Verbal Scale subtests. Practice effects may be minimal on finger-tapping and strength-of-grip tests. (See Chapter 22 for a description of these two tests.) Thus the amount of learning indicated by a particular difference between test and retest scores may vary for different tests.

4. The length of time that elapsed between tests affects retest scores. Shorter intervals produce greater practice effects than do longer intervals.

5. The magnitude of the practice effect may vary as a function of the score on the first test. Children whose initial scores were low tend to show more improvement on the retest than do children whose initial scores were high. Such regression-to-the-mean effects occur, in part, because of random factors that vary between the initial test and retest performance.

6. Different tests purporting to measure the same abil-

Table 18-1
Illustrations of How Hypotheses Are Developed from the Child's Test Behavior

Area	*Example*
Behavioral cues	Inability to respond at the moment, rather than lack of knowledge, may be indicated when a child stares blankly ahead and does not respond to one or more questions. Distress, rather than joy, may be indicated by laughter in some emotionally labile children. Aggressiveness may be indicated when a child smashes blocks. Failure to understand directions or feelings of dependency may be seen when the child builds a design directly on the examiner's model. Loss of motivation and interest or a passive-aggressive expression of defiance may be indicated when increasing amounts of time are needed in order for the child to complete the trials on some subtests (such as on pegboards). The expectation is that performance should improve with practice, not get worse. Difficulty in finding a solution, depression, perfectionism, difficulty in making a decision, or a habitual coping style may be revealed by excessive slowness. Impulsiveness (particularly when the solution is not correct) or habitual coping style may be indicated by excessive speed. (Impulsiveness may reflect difficulty in postponing action until the solution has been thought out.) Hypomanic qualities are revealed by an expansive, outpouring, and excited response style. Limited intelligence, shyness or timidity, or deliberate intention to be sure, though slow, may be revealed by failure to answer a question within the allotted period of time.
Quality of verbalization	Artistic talent may be shown by definitions of vocabulary words that are given in highly sensory terms. Obsessive tendencies may be indicated by (a) four or five explanations of courses of action in reply to questions; (b) three, four, or more likenesses in response to the Similarities questions; (c) elaborate and quibbling definitions of Vocabulary words; and (d) overdetailed and doubt-laden responses. Depressive features may be indicated by slow, hesitant, and blocked responses interspersed with self-deprecatory remarks. Paranoid qualities are suggested by querulous, distrustful, and legalistic responses. Dependency may be revealed by answers such as "Ask my mommy" or "Ask my daddy." Hypochondriacal preoccupations may be suggested by constant reference to the body or by responses such as "I should rest." Fearfulness may be revealed by responses such as "They all hurt you." In such cases, the child may be expressing his or her fear that the world is a dangerous place. Exhibitionism may be revealed by responses referring to dress, parties, and ornaments. Aggressiveness may be expressed by responses referring to weapons or battles.
Type of verbalization	Hearing difficulty may be disclosed on memory items by distorting words or numbers, dropping consonants, or omitting prepositions and other connecting words. Misleading results occur when a child with severe speech defects substitutes one word for another simply because the second word is easier to say. For example, the child says *knife* instead of *scissors* to a picture vocabulary card simply because it is easier to say *knife*.
Item content	Boredom may be present when a child passes difficult items but fails easier ones. This type of child may be bored by easy material and stimulated by hard material. Dependency or submissiveness may be indicated by ready and assured responses to routine materials, but anxious, hesitant, and tentative responses to questions that require judgment and evaluation. Compulsive tendencies may be revealed when a child passes tests requiring meticulousness but then fails others because he or she is either more meticulous than the test requires or too inflexible in his or her thinking. A pedantic urge to be accurate may enhance performance on memory tasks. Inhibition and a fear of being incorrect may be shown when a child fails tasks requiring insight and imagination but not other tasks. Difficulty with handling aggression may be indicated when a child becomes disorganized when reading a passage that has aggressive content.

Table 18-2
Some Areas to Consider in Assessing Learning Ability and Developing Intervention Strategies

Area	Questions
Attention	1. Can the child attend to the task long enough to learn it? 2. Are the essential components of the task attended to?
Motivation	3. What motivates the child to learn? 4. Are both intrinsic and extrinsic rewards helpful?
Materials	5. What materials facilitate learning? (For example, does color, shape, or size of materials differentially affect learning?)
Rate	6. Does the rate of presentation affect performance?
Duration	7. What is the optimal duration of presentation of the material?
Modality	8. Which modality best facilitates learning (visual, auditory, tactile, or combinations)?
Content	9. What contents or topics are most meaningful for the child?
Procedures	10. What procedures best facilitate learning (for example, reauditorization, stimulation, modeling, analysis of errors)?
Cueing	11. Do cues facilitate learning? If so, which cues are successful in eliciting correct responses (for example, first phoneme of a word, written presentation, first letter of a word, synonyms, opposites, rhymes, use of error responses)? 12. Is there a hierarchy of cues? 13. Can the child learn to produce his or her own cues? 14. Which type of cue is most effective (verbal, visual, gestural, or combinations)?
Reinforcement	15. How does reinforcement affect performance? 16. Is learning affected by *schedule of reinforcement* (continuous, intermittent, immediate, delayed), *type of reinforcement* (verbal, gestural or token, positive or negative), or *dispenser of reinforcement* (self, clinician, parent)?
Practice/rehearsal	17. Does the child practice or rehearse independently? 18. If the child is distracted from rehearsing, is any part of the material retained?
Patterns of performance	19. Is learning random or consistent? 20. Are there any strategies evident? 21. How rapidly does the child learn?
Level of learning	22. What is the child's level of mastery in the various areas of learning? 23. If a specific behavior cannot be learned, are there alternatives that can be learned? 24. Can alternative communication systems be learned if they are needed?
Retention and transfer	25. Can the child learn new material, retain it, integrate the knowledge, and apply it to new situations?
Analysis of failure	26. What were the sources of difficulty in mastering the material? 27. Was failure caused by the difficulty level of materials; meaningfulness of materials; ineffectiveness of cues, instructions, or examples; or deficits of the child?

Source: Adapted from Chapey (1981, pp. 55–56).

ity, or even the same test at different age levels, may yield scores that are not comparable. If intelligence was measured by Test A on the first occasion and Test B on the second, changes in IQ may be due to differences in the two tests and not to changes in the child. Similarly, a test that covers a wide age range may tap different abilities at different ages. A knowledge of the test instruments and their interrelationships is critical in evaluating the extent to which retest changes are meaningful.

What does it mean to say that there has been improvement *as a result of prior exposure*? Conceivably, any improvement might reflect some degree of learning, given chance fluctuations in scores. But what about children who do not improve on the retest, in spite of the fact that retest changes usually have been found in the population? It may be that these children have a greater skill deficit than those who do show improvement. The distinction between changes in performance associated with practice effects and those associated with actual clinical improvement, particularly in neurologically impaired children, is one that may be difficult to make in practice.

For the results of repeated evaluations to be maximally useful, data are needed on the differential effects of practice in relation to such factors as item content, age, sex, ability level, and illness (type, location, and chronicity). A data base that provided the normative retest changes on various tests with specific normal and clinical populations would be extremely helpful in evaluating practice effects. Any clinical significance attributed to changes in test scores should be corroborated by other assessment and clinical data; validity data would be especially important in this regard. Until such data become available, you should take into account the factors discussed above in evaluating retest changes.

Guidelines for Designing a Clinical and Psychoeducational Assessment

The following guidelines will help you to increase diagnostic precision and develop better intervention plans:

1. *Use a broad spectrum approach to clinical assessment.* Assessment procedures should focus on (a) psychological factors (including cognitive and affective characteristics) and (b) social and interpersonal factors. Additionally, information about somatic factors should be obtained (see Figure 18-4). The interaction of these factors will have profound effects on a child. The more sources (within limits) that are used to sample the child's behavior, the better position you will be in to make firm generalizations about the child and to develop intervention strategies.

A complete individual appraisal, culminating in the development of recommendations, should include consideration of the following areas as they concern the child (see also Table 18-3):

- sensory capabilities (including visual, auditory, and tactile modalities)
- cognition (including intelligence, reading, arithmetic, spelling, written language, oral language, learning ability, and learning style)
- affect and temperament (including attention and activity level)
- motor skills (including both fine and gross motor skills)
- adaptive skills (including self-help skills and knowledge of geographical environment)
- interpersonal skills
- work and study skills
- family, school, neighborhood, friends, and relatives
- strengths, weaknesses, extent of disability or impairment, and resources for change within the child and family
- community resources

2. *Use a variety of assessment procedures to evaluate the child.* No single procedure should be used exclusively, although for some referral questions greater emphasis can be given to one procedure than to another. The use of multiple methods allows you to evaluate the "validity of any one source of information, since information from multiple sources may be systematically compared" (Nay, 1979, p. 283). Observing the child function in natural settings lends ecological validity to the information obtained in the test setting.

3. *Use more than one method to evaluate a particular domain, if feasible.* Errors in the evaluation of a particular domain can be reduced by using more than one assessment tool. For example, two different instruments may be used to measure the child's level of intellectual functioning. Although this may not always be feasible because of time constraints, it should be done whenever possible.

4. *Evaluate the child on more than one occasion.* Assessment across time helps one to determine the stability of the findings. Repeated evaluations may not always be practical, however.

ASSESSMENT IN SCHOOLS

The objectives of the assessment process for children in schools can be stated in the following way: (a) to determine the nature of the learning or behavior problem, (b) to determine the child's strengths and weaknesses in abilities

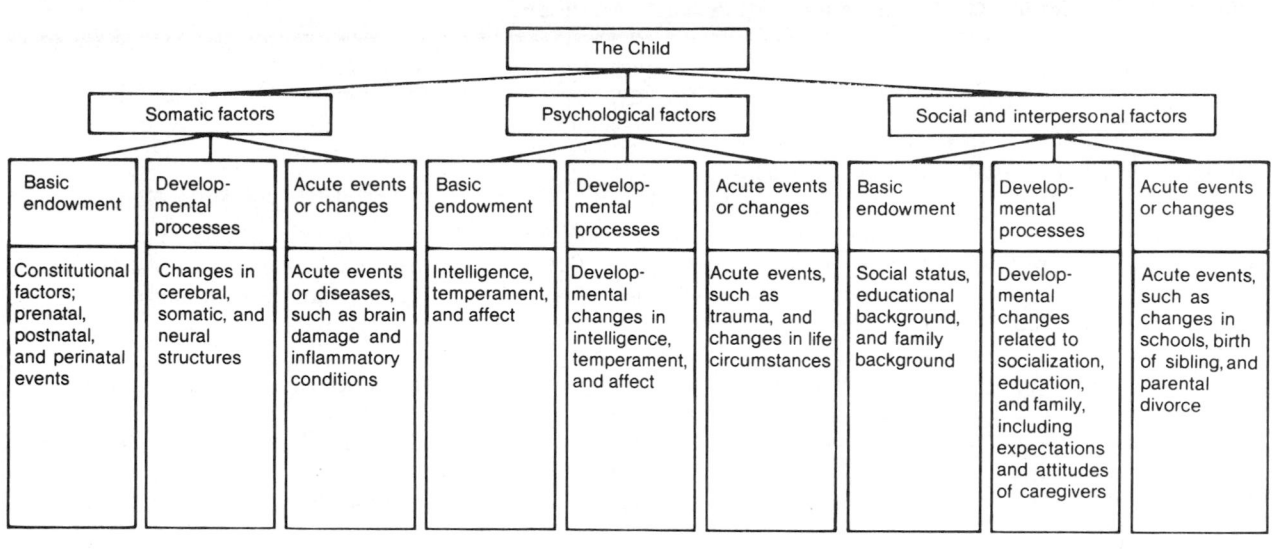

Figure 18-4.   Factors that relate to the child's functioning. Adapted from Spiel, 1981.

related to learning, (c) to evaluate the behavior problem, (d) to develop an educational plan that takes into account the child's abilities and personality, the teacher, and the family, (e) to assess the child's response to intervention efforts, and (f) to recommend modifications in programs and class placements.

Visiting the Classroom

In school settings, the formal assessment should be supplemented with visits to the child's classroom. The characteristics of the particular classroom environment should be observed (see Chapter 17), and intervention strategies tailored to this environment. Classroom visits provide an added benefit—the opportunity to establish rapport with and consult with the teacher. During such visits, you should avoid interfering with regular classroom procedures and try to ensure that the child under study is not stigmatized. Although every effort should be made to reduce the teacher's anxiety about your visit, teachers must understand that their behavior may be part of the problem and that changes in their behavior may be part of the solution. The child's and teacher's behaviors are usually so intertwined that it is almost impossible to examine one without the other.

Writing the Evaluation and Developing Intervention Strategies

Information gained during the evaluation should enable you to describe the positive qualities of the child's functioning, the difficulties he or she faces in mastering problems,

Table 18-3
Variables to Consider in a Clinical and Psychoeducational Assessment

Variable	*Suggested categories or descriptions*
Chronological age	—
Sex	Male, female
Grade level	—
Locale	Rural, small town, suburban, urban
Race/ethnicity	Asian-American, black, Caucasian (not Hispanic), Hispanic, native American, other
Family history	Birth order, number of siblings, parents' marital status, behavioral and emotional adjustment of parents and siblings, family's health history (as pertinent to referral problem), other
Socioeconomic status (SES)	Upper, upper-middle, middle, lower-middle, lower
Language	English, bilingual, non-English (state language)
Educational history	Age-appropriate grade placement, retained in grade, changed schools often, spent most of educational career in special classes
Educational placement	Regular class placement with no special education, regular class placement with special education services, self-contained special education class
Physical and health status	Sensory deficits, physical disabilities, neurological impairment, chronic illness, medications taken, other
Intellectual ability	Individual's repertoire of skills, knowledge, and learning sets
Reading achievement	Ability to recognize and comprehend written symbols
Arithmetic achievement	Ability to perform numerical computations and to know and reason with mathematical concepts
Behavioral and emotional adjustment	Ability to build and maintain satisfactory interpersonal relationships and to display and feel emotions appropriate to the situation
Activity level	Kind and amount of movement displayed during a specific period of time and/or in a specific context (for example, hyperexcitability, acting out, off-task behavior)
Attention	Ability to filter out extraneous stimuli and focus selectively on a task over a period of time (for example, sustained and selective attention, impulsivity, concentration, distractibility)
Auditory perception	Ability to identify, discriminate, interpret, and organize elements of acoustical stimuli (for example, discrimination, blending association, listening comprehension, auditory figure/ground)
Fine motor coordination	Ability to integrate small muscles, usually in conjunction with visual perception (for example, observe handwriting, finger opposition, kinesthetic and tactile discrimination, finger motor speed)
Gross motor coordination	Ability to organize movements of the large muscle groups (for example, observe running, throwing, jumping, hopping, strength, clumsiness)
Memory	Ability to store and retrieve information, regardless of mode of input (for example, short- and long-term memory, visual and auditory memory, sequencing, free recall, incidental learning, rehearsal skills)
Oral language	Ability to comprehend and produce verbal material in the spoken mode (for example, observe semantics, syntax, vocabulary, ability to communicate)
Visual perception	Ability to identify, discriminate, interpret, and organize physical elements of visual stimuli (for example, as indicated by visual acuity, matching, visual-motor integration, figure/ground perception, spatial relations)

Source: Adapted from Keogh, Major-Kingsley, Omori-Gordon, and Reid (1982).

and the quality and style of his or her intellectual and social functioning. It is unlikely, however, that the test results will provide the precise causes of a child's school failure, such as the etiology of specific learning deficits.

The assessment report should not merely enumerate the child's deficits or areas of failure; it should also specify abilities that the child might be able to use to master tasks. By identifying compensatory abilities, you can establish a base for developing intervention strategies. Consideration should be given to what the child *can* do, as well as what the child cannot do.

Diagnosing educational handicaps is a complex and

difficult task. It is often even more difficult, however, to specify with some degree of certainty the procedures needed to ameliorate the child's problems, to create appropriate conditions for learning, and to foster psychological development, social adjustment, and successful participation in the community. Concern with intervention should not tempt us to go beyond the limits of our present knowledge. The results of an assessment do not furnish us with well-validated intervention techniques—developing interventions currently is as much an art as a science.

In spite of the problems associated with developing interventions, you should work with the child's teachers to establish a set of instructional objectives that they can use. These objectives can include determining the tasks that are to be taught, arranging a hierarchy of instructional objectives, eliminating behaviors incompatible with effective instruction, and teaching the tasks most needed by the child.

Assessment—A Continuous Activity

The assessment recommendations are not meant to be the final solution to the child's difficulties. They are starting points for you, as clinician, and for those responsible for the interventions. Assessment should be a continuous activity, with modifications made in the initial intervention plans when the child's needs change or when the plans do not work effectively. All too often, tests are given and recommendations are made and then the psychologist vanishes until the reevaluation years later. Effective consultation requires continuous monitoring of short-term follow-up contacts.

A Recommended Assessment Model for School-Based Referrals

The National Academy of Sciences' Panel on the Selection and Placement of Students in Programs for the Mentally Retarded (Heller, Holtzman, & Messick, 1982) set out to evaluate the placement procedures and quality of services provided to children referred for special education programs. Although the Panel members only addressed problems associated with the placement of children in classes for the mentally retarded, their recommendations are valuable for the assessment of any child who is experiencing academic difficulties.

The Panel recommended that the assessment of referred children be conducted in two phases, as outlined below (from Messick, 1984).

I. A systematic evaluation of the child's learning environment and the nature and quality of the regular instruction received should be conducted.

A. Deficiencies in the learning environment should be ruled out. (If any deficiencies are present, steps should be taken to improve them before the child is referred for an individual assessment.)

1. Is there evidence that the school is using programs and curricula that are effective for children of various ethnic and socioeconomic groups? Standardized achievement test data are one source of evidence.

2. Is there evidence that the students in question have been exposed to the curriculum adequately (for example, few absences or disciplinary exclusions from class)?

3. Is there evidence that the teacher has implemented the curriculum effectively (for example, proper choice of instructional strategies and rewards)? Observational data provided by a school psychologist, consultant, or another teacher are sources of evidence.

B. Documentation should be obtained to show that the child failed to learn under reasonable alternative instructional approaches. (The child should not be referred for individual assessment until reasonable instructional approaches have been tried and have proven fruitless.)

1. Is there objective evidence that the child has not learned what was taught? Criterion-referenced tests tailored directly to the curriculum are one source of evidence.

2. Is there evidence that systematic efforts were used to identify the learning difficulty and to take appropriate corrective instructional actions (for example, introducing remedial approaches, changing curricula, trying a new teacher)? Documentation is needed that alternative procedures were attempted.

II. A comprehensive assessment battery should be administered that includes (a) measures of intellective skills, cognitive skills, and adaptive behavior and (b) procedures to screen for biomedical disorders.

A. Assessment procedures should focus on functional skills for which there exist potentially effective interventions. These skills include *academically relevant skills* (for example, reading, mathematics), *cognitive processing skills* (for example, generalization, self-monitoring), *adaptive and motivational skills* (for example, impulse control, social skills), and *physical skills related to learning* (for example, vision, hearing).

B. The comprehensive battery should include a measure of global intelligence and measures of information-processing skills involved in comprehension, visualization, memory, reasoning, and judgment. These latter measures may be provided by subtests derived from a multisubtest intelligence test or by specialized procedures.

Procedures that measure responsiveness to learning or structured teaching may also prove to be valuable.

C. The comprehensive battery should also include measures that will help to determine whether the child's failure to learn is associated with sensory, motor, or other physical impairments. Limited vision or hearing, psychomotor malfunctions, or hunger may impair a child's classroom performance. Similarly, neurological or endocrine dysfunctions may impede intellectual functioning or lead to behavioral problems. Finally, physical trauma or deprivation may lead to deficits in functioning. In each of these cases corrective treatment may be possible, particularly in the case of sensory, neurological, or endocrine malfunctions.

D. The comprehensive battery should contain measures of adaptive behavior, particularly in the cases of children who are being considered for classes for the mentally retarded. An adaptive behavior measure may help to identify emotional and behavioral deviance, and nonintellective adaptive strengths. Such findings may assist in designing intervention programs aimed at improving practical skills and reducing maladaptive behaviors.

E. Once a child is placed in a special education class, the student's progress should be monitored annually.

Messick (1984) believes that the above procedures will go a long way to ensuring the validity of referral and assessment procedures and the quality of instructional services. A child should be placed in a special education program when there is evidence that effective instruction is being offered in that program and that a regular education class cannot achieve the appropriate educational goals. Retention is justified only when the special education placement is deemed more beneficial than a regular education placement. The Panel's recommendations stress continuous program evaluation and performance monitoring.

ASSESSMENT OF SPEECH AND LANGUAGE

The observation of speech and language is an important part of the assessment process. The assessment of language and speech competency requires many technical skills. Rather than focusing on technical skills, however, this section outlines a basic approach to speech and language assessment and provides some important guideposts.

An Approach to Language and Speech Evaluation

Although there is no single preferred way to evaluate a child's language and speech, the following approach is useful:

1. Interview the referral source to learn about the child's language.

2. Talk with the child, and compare your observations with those of the referral source.

3. Obtain informal language samples (see below).

4. Administer a normative language test—not necessarily to obtain a standard language score, but to document the child's impairments. Normative testing of language must be carefully applied to children of ethnic groups who differ from the norm group. If these children speak nonstandard varieties of English, their language skills may be assessed as being deficient when in fact they are only different.

5. Observe the child interacting with the referring person in order to determine areas of faulty communication.

6. Develop etiological hypotheses after evaluating the degree of language impairment.

Obtaining informal language samples.   Informal language samples can be collected by various means, such as the following:

1. Read a short paragraph to the child and then ask the child to repeat the story. (The story should be one that is readily comprehensible.)

2. Have the child read a short story (one or two paragraphs) and then ask the child to repeat the story. (The story should be one that the child can easily read.)

3. Show a picture to the child, and ask the child to describe the picture. (The picture should show themes that are familiar to the child.)

4. Show a sequence of pictures to the child and ask the child to describe the sequence. (Pictures should show themes that are familiar to the child.)

5. Ask the child to tell you something on a given topic that is well known to him or her.

6. Ask the child to tell you something on a given topic that is somewhat abstract.

These six tasks provide language samples based on oral presentation (task 1), written presentation (task 2), visual nonsequential presentation (task 3), visual sequential presentation (task 4), self-generated concrete content (task 5), and self-generated abstract content (task 6). The tasks are useful for evaluating whether the child shows disturbance of spontaneous speech (or expressive verbal behavior) in the area of repetition, reading, naming objects, or comprehension.

What to Evaluate in a Language Assessment

Language assessment should focus primarily on the child's unique language characteristics, although consideration also should be given to how the child's language ability compares with that of age peers. A thorough analysis of language ability should include an evaluation of the child's (a) consistencies within his or her own language system, (b) strategies and processes used to produce language, (c) language structures, and (d) performance on formal language tests. The assessment of children's language competencies is complicated by our inability to understand fully the stages of normal language acquisition. Because formal language tests fail to measure the context appropriateness of language, every effort should be made to evaluate children's language as it is used in natural contexts.

Language and Speech Deviations

Language difficulties may be related to *syndromes or diseases* (such as infantile autism, brain damage, or hearing impairment), *processing difficulties* (such as limited memory span), or *social or cultural factors* (such as inadequate exposure to English). Exhibit 18-1 covers the definitions, incidence, and etiology of speech disorders. Following are some of the major deviations in language and speech that occur during the preschool and early school years:

1. During the preschool years (3 to 5 years of age), deviations include lack of speech, unintelligible speech, and failure to speak in sentences.

2. At about 5 to 6 years of age, deviations include substitution of easy sounds for difficult ones, consistent dropping of word endings, faulty sentence structure, noticeable nonfluency, and abnormal rhythm, rate, and inflection of speech.

3. By the age of 7 years, deviations can include distortions, omissions, or substitutions of any sounds.

Other signs of difficulties that are not specifically age-related include a delay of more than a year in the appearance of individual speech sounds; use of vowel sounds to the exclusion of almost all other sounds; being embarrassed or disturbed by speech; consistently monotonous, inaudible, or poor-quality voice; consistent use of a pitch inappropriate for the child's age; noticeable hypernasality or lack of nasal resonance; and unusual confusions, reversals, or telegraphic speech (a type of speech in which connectives, prepositions, modifiers, and refinements of language are omitted). When any of the above deviations are observed, the child should be referred for speech evaluation.

A child's utterances may also be evaluated for signs of disturbed content or processing. Indications of disturbed processing include confabulations (for example, bizarre stories loosely connected with the narrative they were supposed to develop), stereotype phrases (repeating a "pet" phrase over and over), misnamings, digression (caused, for example, by accidental associations), mispronunciations, difficulties in the initiation of the narrative (possible articulatory deficit), inability to recognize objects presented in the picture (possible visual deficit), and inability to repeat the story (possible memory deficit). Table 18-4 provides examples of major kinds of language distortions. Severe language distortions may be related to mental disorders or brain damage.

Discrepancies may be observed in a child's language comprehension and production. Some children fail to discriminate the distinctive contrasts in speech reception and yet make the contrasts in production, whereas other children do not produce the contrasts but readily discriminate them. Some children cannot imitate or understand sentences that they can produce, whereas other children can understand what they cannot produce. Evaluate where the difficulties lie—in comprehension or production.

Different factors may affect the ability of children to provide names for things or actions (Williams, 1983). These include (a) linguistic factors associated with the target words (such as how frequently the words appear in written passages and their length), (b) characteristics of the referent stimulus (such as whether it is a real object or a picture of the object), (c) the manner in which response is elicited (such as sentence completion or free recall), and (d) the way in which the naming response is produced (such as single word naming or naming in the context of connected speech).

Questions to Consider About a Child's Language Usage

Language usage is a guide to personality style and to thought processes. The tempo, quality, and content of a child's verbal responses are also important. Answers to the following questions will provide cues about the child's general language style and communication skills.

• Does the child understand what is being said?
• Is gesture understood?
• Are gestures or mime used to communicate?
• Does the child attend to faces or watch lips when people speak?
• Does the child understand oral communications when his or her back is turned to the speaker?

■ Exhibit 18-1 ■━━━

Definitions, Incidence, and Etiology of Speech Disorders

Definitions

Language and speech represent two different but interrelated concepts in communication. *Language*, a system of symbols, is evaluated in terms of its receptive and expressive components. *Receptive language* refers to the symbolic information received and comprehended, primarily through auditory and visual channels. *Expressive language* refers to components such as morphology, syntax, and semantics that are used orally. *Speech*, a motor output system, is the spoken vehicle by which thoughts, expressed symbolically through language, are communicated. Sound is initiated by respiratory air pressures that are interrupted by valving processes in the vocal tract. The valves consist of the vocal folds, the velopharyngeal mechanism, tongue contact with the palate or teeth, and the lips.

The speech system has been divided into four major areas on the basis of a processing classification system: phonation, nasal resonance, articulation, and prosody. *Phonation* is characterized by duration, loudness, pitch, and quality of the sound. *Nasal resonance* refers to vibrations in the nasal cavity that may be perceived as excessive (hypernasality) or insufficient (hyponasality). *Articulation* is related to the production of consonant and vowel sounds in various sequences to form words. *Prosody* is related to the melody, rhythm, and rate of the speech flow.

Incidence

It has been estimated that approximately 10 percent of children exhibit hearing or speech-language disorders. The approximate incidence of all speech disorders is as follows: 5 to 10 percent for phonation, 5 to 10 percent for resonance, 60 to 70 percent for articulation, and 10 to 15 percent for prosody.

Etiology

Five major etiological categories have been suggested: psychosocial, structural, neurological, familial/hereditary, and learning. These categories are not disorder specific, and in many instances they overlap. A *psychosocial* etiology may account for each of the four major speech disorders. In the area of phonation, children with voice disorders may be hoarse from abuse through "yelling" (for example, screamer's nodules). A whiny, hypernasal resonance may be heard in the insecure and overprotected child. Articulation disorders (for example, saying *wabbit* for *rabbit* and *thun* for *sun*) may be caused by emotional problems. Dysfluencies (stuttering) in the speech of the preschool child can be caused by environmental stress factors.

Congenital laryngeal web is an example of a *structural* change that affects the phonation (voice) ability in children. The structural abnormalities of cleft lip and palate can markedly impair resonance and articulation. Prosodic changes are not generally believed to be caused by physical defects.

All four of the speech categories can be affected by a *neurological* etiology. Impairment may vary from congenital minimal brain damage, severe cerebral palsy, and acquired head trauma to infectious diseases, such as meningitis or Reyes syndrome. Children who have sustained neurological damage may experience difficulty in controlling duration, loudness, pitch, or quality. Neurological dysfunction of the soft palate may prevent adequate velopharyngeal closure, which would make a difference in the flow of air through the oral and nasal cavities. Articulatory skills may also be adversely affected by neurological damage (for example, incoordination of tongue, lip, or jaw movement may inhibit precise production of consonant and vowel sounds). Disturbances in the melody, rhythm, and rate of speech (prosody) may be the initial indication of neurological damage. A monotonous, staccato, or highly variable speech flow may be associated with cerebellar or basal ganglia impairment.

Hereditary and *familial* factors may also account for speech disorders. Many cleft lip and cleft palate disorders are familial. Stuttering has long been suspected of having a hereditary or familial origin. Evidence from twin studies suggests that familial articulatory disorders may occur. Transmission of stuttering in families may be explainable by a genetic hypothesis. Many genetic syndromes (for example, Huntington's chorea) are accompanied by a variety of speech disorders involving the categories phonation, resonance, articulation, and prosody.

Speech disorders may result from *learning* from poor speech models in other family members. Speaking with a breathy or nasal voice, for example, can occur if the child mimics an older sibling or parent. Delays in learning proper speech patterns have been noted in some children who come from bilingual homes. Misarticulation, the most common speech problem, may result from the learning of improper sound usage, even in families who use excellent speech. Articulation errors also develop from the learning of inappropriate phonological rules. The etiological basis for the development of misarticulation is largely unknown, and is generally described as a functional articulation disorder.

Source: Reprinted, with changes in notation, with permission of the publisher and authors from W. M. Diedrich and D. B. Carr, "Identification of Speech Disorders," *Journal of Developmental and Behavioral Pediatrics*, 1984, *5*, pp. 38–39. © Williams & Wilkins.

Table 18-4
A Variety of Spoken Language Difficulties or Distortions

Type of difficulty or distortion	Definition
Agrammatism	Omission of syntactical (grammatical, functor, or filler) words.
Anomia	Difficulty in finding the right word (for example, "Well, he, uh, just hurried along" when the child meant to say "ran" or "The thing you put in your mouth" for "spoon").
Blocking	Interruption of a train of speech before a thought or idea has been completed.
Circumstantiality	Pattern of speech that is very indirect, reaching its goal idea belatedly. The child brings in many tedious details and sometimes makes parenthetical remarks.
Clanging	Pattern of speech in which sounds rather than meaningful relationships appear to govern word choice. The intelligibility of the speech is impaired, and redundant words are introduced.
Derailment	Pattern of spontaneous speech in which the speaker goes from the original idea to one that is clearly but obliquely related, or to one that is completely unrelated. Things presented in juxtaposition may lack a meaningful relationship, or the child may shift idiosyncratically from one frame of reference to another. At times, there may be a vague connection between the ideas; at others, none will be apparent.
Distortion of the sounds of language, either in perception or production	Unintelligible speech by a child, usually younger than 8 or 9 years of age.
Distractible speech	Stopping repeatedly in the middle of a sentence or idea and changing the subject in response to a nearby stimulus, such as an object on a desk or the interviewer's clothing or appearance.
Dysarthria	Poor articulation.
Dysprosody	Speech that is unmelodic and dysrhythmic.
Echolalia	Pattern of speech in which the child echoes words or phrases of the interviewer.
Illogicality	Pattern of speech characterized by illogical conclusions.
Incoherence	Speech that is essentially incomprehensible at times.
Loss of goal	Failure to follow a chain of thought through to its natural conclusion. The child begins with a particular subject and then wanders away from it, never to return to it.
Neologisms	New or unconventional words or phrases whose derivation cannot be understood. Neologisms can be created through (a) structural changes, where syllables are scrambled (*helicopter* is produced as *copiheter*); (b) semantic changes, where a word that has similar connotative meanings is used (*pull-ons* for *boots*); and (c) phonological changes, where sounds are exchanged (*brod* for *bread*).
Paragrammatism	Incorrect use of verbs, clauses, or prepositional phrases.
Paraphasia	Substitution of incorrect words for other words (for example, *cow* instead of *spoon* or "The flower is *on* the garden" instead of "The flower is *in* the garden").
Perseveration	Persistent repetition of words, ideas, or subjects. The utterance or idea that is perseverated may be at first meaningful, but its continuation is inappropriate.
Phonemic paraphasia	Recognizable mispronunciation of a word in which sounds or syllables are out of sequence (for example, *psghetti* for *spaghetti*).

(Table continues next page)

Table 18-4 (cont.)

Type of difficulty or distortion	Definition
Poverty of amount of speech	Restriction in the *amount* of spontaneous speech. The replies to questions tend to be brief, concrete, and unelaborated. Unprompted additional information is rarely provided.
Poverty of content of speech	Restriction in the information conveyed by speech. Although long enough, replies convey little information. Language tends to be vague, often overabstract or overconcrete, repetitive, and stereotyped.
Pressure of speech	More spontaneous speech than is considered ordinary or socially customary. Speech is rapid and difficult to interrupt. Some sentences may be left uncompleted because of eagerness to get on to a new idea.
Self-reference	Speech patterns in which the child repeatedly refers the subject under discussion back to himself or herself when someone else is talking.
Stilted speech	Speech that has an excessively stilted or formal quality. It may seem rather quaint or outdated, or it may appear pompous, distant, or overpolite.
Syntactic errors	Unconventional ordering of words (for example, "My house, well, I live in, well, my house, uh, I live in" for "I live in my house").
Tangentiality	Replying to questions or statements in an oblique, tangential, or even irrelevant way (for example, when Bill is asked to pick up the blue notebook, he picks up the blue car and says "car").
Telegraphic speech	Utterances that contain a subject, main verb, and object, but no functor or other "small" words (for example, "I got tricycle" for "I've got a tricycle").
Topical or referential identification problems	Difficulties in selecting the appropriate referent (for example, identifying the appropriate topic) in a conversation (for example, when Ann is asked "Did you put the book on my desk?" she responds "My desk is clean").
Word approximations	Using old words in a new and unconventional way or developing new words by using conventional rules of word formation.

- Is there any speech?
- Are vocalizations normal?
- Is articulation normal?
- What is the usual tempo of the responses? Are they quick or slow?
- What is the output (approximate number of words spoken per minute)?
- What amount of effort is needed to produce speech (for example, do you note any visible struggles, facial grimaces, body posturing, deep breathing, or hard gestures)?
- What is the phrase length (for example, single words or short phrases or complete sentences)?
- Is the speech melodic?
- Does the child take time to consider before responding?
- Is thinking done aloud or is only the final answer given?
- How competent is the child in the use of words and grammar? For example, does the child's language contain objects, actions, and events in a variety of relationships?
- Does the child echo what is said or use words inappropriately?
- Are utterances appropriate for the context?
- Are words used for social communication?
- Are ideas expressed clearly?
- Does the child distinguish between relevant and irrelevant information?
- Does the child verbalize a variety of possibilities and perspectives?
- Are responses self-critical?
- Can the child assume the role or viewpoint of another?
- Are imitation and symbolization used in play?
- Does the child, while playing, respond appropriately to the speaker?
- Do language difficulties, if present, cross reading, writing, and speaking situations?

Examples of a Qualitative Language Analysis

The two illustrations below (Lucas, 1980, p. 125 and p. 130, with changes in notation) show how a qualitative analysis of a child's language may appear in a report. The first description is of a 5-year-old girl, and the second is of a 7-year-old boy.

A qualitative analysis of the language sample utterances revealed the presence of semantic word errors (for example, *vase* for *cup*, *table* for *bed*, *teacher* for *mailman*); neologisms (for example, *pardot* for *parrot*, *lamt* for *lamp* — these could be auditory misperceptions; *an eat with* for *fork*, and *Johnny jump* for *jump rope*); space and time errors (for example, *over* for *next to*, *runs to* for *runs away*, *jumps up* for *stands*); syntactic errors related to semantic problems in organization and sequencing (for example, "The um, girl, um, found, um, the lamp found the girl" and "The teacher, uh, erased, uh the teacher, um erased the teacher").

A qualitative analysis of the language sample indicated several auditory misperceptions (for example, *boin* for *join*, but most of these were unintelligible even though articulation was without error on the word test); some semantic word errors related to parts of pictures or meanings of the story rather than to all of the available information (for example, a chair was described as missing a leg because the boy sitting in the chair obscured the fourth leg, a boy was said to be drowning because he was splashing even though the other pictures related to the story showed the boys playing in the water); and an apparent deficiency in spatio-temporal words and some errors in the terms used (for example, *on* for *in*, *above* for *in front of*). When Jerome showed signs of anxiety, the word finding and verbal perseveration difficulties became evident.

ASSESSMENT OF VISUAL-MOTOR ABILITY

Visual-motor ability is assessed primarily by means of special tests, such as the Bender-Gestalt or the Developmental Test of Visual-Motor Integration (see Chapter 14). Items on intelligence tests and special ability tests may also require visual-motor skills, however. When you administer these items, you should pay particular attention to children's reaction time and to their trial-and-error methods. Signs of visual-motor difficulty include much trial and error, fumbling, tremor, repetition of copying errors, perseveration, rotation, and variable line quality. Visual-motor difficulties may be associated with defects in visual, auditory, or muscular functions, with poor physical condition, with anxiety, or with other conditions.

LEARNING POTENTIAL ASSESSMENT

Learning potential assessment procedures are designed to measure the child's ability to improve performance following a systematic learning experience (Budoff & Hamilton, 1976; Feuerstein, 1979; Guthke, 1982; Hegarty & Lucas, 1978). The child is taught principles that will help him or her to solve a particular problem. For example, the principles that underlie the construction of a particular block pattern on a block design task might be taught. By measuring the child's ability to solve additional block design problems, one obtains an estimate of his or her ability to learn from the teaching and to apply this learning to similar problems. Learning potential assessment focuses on what the child can learn, how readily the child acquires strategies, and whether the strategies are transferable (generalizable). The procedures incorporate mini–learning situations that permit the systematic observation and evaluation of the child's responses to structured teaching.

In a learning potential procedure the child is given progressively more complex tasks, with continual teaching and feedback. The aim is to evaluate the child's ability to acquire and use problem-solving skills. An enrichment program — which stresses the acquisition of learning strategies rather than the acquisition of specific subject-area content — may also be tied to the evaluation procedure.

Three-Step Procedure

A three-step test-train-test sequence usually is followed in a learning potential procedure.

1. *Initial testing.* The child is tested in the standard fashion with test stimuli that are minimally dependent on cultural exposure. The stimuli used may be unfamiliar to the child, particularly when the stimuli are incorporated into the teaching procedure. Nonverbal reasoning tasks frequently are used, such as those found on the Kohs Block Design or Raven's Progressive Matrices.

2. *Teaching of principles.* The child receives instruction in solving the task. Principles include attending to all choices and using analytic skills. Various techniques are used during the training period, including feedback, prompts, and extended teaching with practice in item-solving strategies. Training varies depending on the task. The goal of training is to help the child develop appropriate problem-solving strategies.

3. *Retesting.* The child is retested on the original task or an alternative form of it.

Aims of Learning Potential Assessment

Learning potential assessment aims to evaluate the child's ability to acquire new information and problem-solving strategies. Scores reflect not only the number of correct solutions, but also the number of helping steps needed to solve the problem. In a learning potential assessment, it is necessary to consider such factors as

1. The stimuli used for teaching (for example, spatial-visual and other concept formation tasks, number seria-tion, pictorial series, geometric series, paired-associate learning tasks, or auditory-rote learning tasks);
2. The teaching methods used (for example, feedback linked to each step, open-ended feedback, or social or monetary reinforcement);
3. The extent to which the child knew the correct responses before teaching was started;
4. The extent to which the tasks and activities involved in the test were unfamiliar to the child.

Ideally the child should neither know the correct responses before teaching starts nor be familiar with the test stimuli. If either of these conditions is not met, it will be difficult to evaluate the effectiveness of the assessment because scores will be confounded (that is, they will reflect both present learning *and* prior learning). In practice, these two assumptions may never be fully met.

As a result of training, some children will improve their performance but others will not. Those children who do not learn under one type of teaching strategy may learn more efficiently under another strategy, however. Similarly, those children who perform poorly on some tasks may learn more rapidly on others. Consequently, every learning potential assessment should include a variety of teaching strategies and tasks.

Learning Potential Assessment and Intelligence Assessment

Learning potential assessment differs from traditional intelligence testing in a number of ways (see Table 18-5). Learning potential assessment attempts to measure the *process* of learning rather than the *content* of learning (Hegarty & Lucas, 1978). Traditional intelligence testing focuses on the child's present level of cognitive development (*what* and *how much* has been mastered or learned); learning potential assessment focuses on the child's present learning process (*why* and *how* the material has been mastered). One procedure emphasizes description (intelligence testing); the other, explanation (learning potential assessment).

Table 18-5
Comparison of Traditional Intelligence Testing with Learning Potential Assessment

Intelligence testing	Learning potential assessment
1. Focuses on the content of learning	1. Focuses on the process of learning
2. Attempts to determine what has been learned	2. Attempts to determine why learning takes place
3. Attempts to determine how much of the material has been mastered	3. Attempts to determine how material is mastered
4. Focuses on description of the child's performance	4. Focuses on an explanation of learning
5. Attempts to predict future performance	5. Attempts to prescribe appropriate remedial interventions

Source: Adapted from Hegarty and Lucas (1978).

The two procedures, however, overlap considerably. Both focus on cognitive processes and provide information useful in describing and explaining the child's present level of functioning. A child enters both an intelligence assessment and a learning potential assessment with the same learning history. Both procedures measure current achievement, although in different ways. And although there is not a one-to-one correspondence between intelligence and learning ability (as defined by a learning potential assessment), intelligence is related to the ability to learn. Intelligence and learning ability are complex multi-dimensional concepts, with the former more easily defined and measured than the latter.

Pitfalls in Interpreting the Word "Potential"

The word *potential* in the term *learning potential assessment* may be misleading. A child's potential for learning is based primarily on present (and past) learnings. Because intelligence tests are useful in making judgments about a child's learning potential, attempts to equate learning potential procedures *exclusively* with the measurement of learning potential are wrong. For example, a child with an IQ of 130 has a much higher potential for learning in school than does a child with an IQ of 70. There is no body of evidence indicating that scores on learning potential tests are better indices of future school-related achievement than are scores on intelligence tests (see, for example, Bailey, 1981; Bradley, 1983). Although learning potential procedures are still experimental, their inclusion as additional components of an assessment battery deserves consideration, particularly when the results they furnish are likely to improve understanding of the child and aid in the design of remediation programs.

CLASSIFICATION AND LABELING

Classification systems have two major features (Zigler, 1982). First, they establish rules for placing an individual into a specific class; these rules establish the system's reliability. Second, they provide information about the correlates of class membership — that is, what we know about individuals given a class designation. The robustness of these class correlates establishes the system's validity.

Every description in some sense implies a label. The term *normal range of functioning*, for example, labels some aspect of the child's functioning. Although labels provide a point of reference, they should not be the basis for clinical decisions. Such decisions should be based on the entire assessment results and clinical history.

Arbitrariness of Classification Systems

Classifications such as moderately mentally retarded (for example, IQs of 40 to 54) and mildly mentally retarded (for example, IQs of 55 to 69) are arbitrary cutoffs on a continuum of intelligence test scores. A child with an IQ of 54 is very similar to one with an IQ of 55, even though their classifications are different. Similarly, a child with an IQ of 68 is like a child with an IQ of 70, yet the former child is labeled *mentally retarded*, whereas the latter is not. Although in developing your assessment findings and recommendations, you should be guided by the child's performance and not by a classification system of arbitrary cutoff scores on an intelligence test, you must adhere to a classification system's specific cutoff points and labels when reporting such results (see, for example, Chapter 21).

Self-Fulfilling Prophecy — How Accurate?

It has been alleged that placing a label such as *mentally retarded* on a child initiates a self-fulfilling prophecy. That is, the label is said to induce individuals who come in contact with the labeled child to treat the child in accord with the label, thereby producing a potentially irreversible change in the child's status. Although negative stereotypes are often associated with behavioral deviancy labels and with labels indicating low levels of intellectual function-

ing, research indicates that children's classroom performances are a much more potent force in influencing teachers' expectancies than are labels given to the children (Brophy & Good, 1970; Dusek & O'Connell, 1973; Good & Brophy, 1972; Yoshida & Meyers, 1975).

It seems reasonable that observation of a child's classroom behavior over weeks and months should play the crucial role in the formation of expectancies. When a teacher is told that a new child in the class is mentally retarded, his or her expectations are likely to be generated by the label. These expectations will be modified, however, if the child performs at grade level. The initial impression will be tempered by the child's *actual* classroom performance. Thus although labels often initiate expectations, they hold little power once the observer obtains direct information about the child's functioning. (Teacher expectancies are also discussed in Chapter 19.)

Value of Classification and Labeling

Some clinicians object to diagnosis and classification, maintaining that labels should be avoided because they have a medical, disease-oriented connotation, provide no explanation of the child's difficulties, tell us nothing about the steps necessary for remediation, and lead to a preoccupation with finding the right label rather than focusing on treatment. Diagnosis and classification, however, play crucial roles in the assessment process.

Diagnosis and classification lend organization to the complex and heterogeneous area of exceptionality and aid in the study of etiology, in the development of programs, in the evaluation of the outcomes of intervention programs, in communication with professionals, in problem solving, and in obtaining needed funding. Diagnostic labels are helpful in record keeping, statistical reporting, and the administration of treatment programs and research, help to point out areas in which study is needed, and serve as a rallying point for groups.

Labeling may also have beneficial consequences, such as increasing altruistic behavior and tolerance on the part of those who must deal with deviant behavior (Fernald & Gettys, 1980). For example, a label such as *mental retardation* may elicit more protective, altruistic responses from people than does the label *normal*. For some parents, labels provide closure — a sense of relief that their child's problem is understood — enabling them to view their child in a more favorable light. Without labels, parents (and others) may develop unrealistically high expectancies, which in turn can lead to failure, frustration, and low self-esteem on the part of the child.

Comment on Labeling

We must not allow the above-mentioned advantages to make us complacent about the effects of labeling. Labels do set up expectancies, and such expectancies may influence the observer's behavior, especially when contact with the referred child is limited. In some situations, it is conceivable that the expectations generated by labels could be so powerful as to lead to severe restrictions of the child's opportunities. We know little about the frequency of such occurrences, but even the thought of such a possibility is a potent reminder of the importance of avoiding inappropriate labeling.

THE DSM-III-R AND CLINICAL AND SCHOOL PSYCHOLOGY

The *Diagnostic and Statistical Manual of Mental Disorders (Third Edition—Revised)*, or DSM-III-R (American Psychiatric Association, 1987), represents the most recent diagnostic classification scheme in the field of mental disorders. Classification procedures have been revised in order to achieve greater clarity of diagnostic criteria, redefine major conditions to be consistent with research findings, establish new categories, provide a multiaxial classification system, and provide a definition of mental disorder. In the DSM-III-R a mental disorder is defined in the following way:

Each of the mental disorders is conceptualized as a clinically significant behavioral or psychological syndrome or pattern that occurs in a person and that is associated with present distress (a painful symptom) or disability (impairment in one or more important areas of functioning) or with a significantly increased risk of suffering death, pain, disability, or an important loss of freedom. In addition, this syndrome or pattern must not be merely an expectable response to a particular event, e.g., the death of a loved one. Whatever its original cause, it must currently be considered a manifestation of a behavioral, psychological, or biological dysfunction in the person. Neither deviant behavior, e.g., political, religious, or sexual, nor conflicts that are primarily between the individual and society are mental disorders unless the deviance or conflict is a symptom of a dysfunction in the person, as described above. (p. xxii)

With regard to etiology, the DSM-III-R generally takes an atheoretical approach. That is, the DSM-III-R does not exclusively favor biological, psychosocial, or sociocultural factors as the primary cause of abnormal behavior. Rather, it emphasizes descriptions of mental disorders without resort to theoretical underpinnings.

Although the DSM-III-R is considered to be the definitive guide to psychiatric classification, its psychological and practical utility have been questioned. The reliability and validity of some DSM-III-R categories have not been substantiated, and some syndromes in the DSM-III-R have not been clearly substantiated in empirical studies using multivariate procedures. In spite of these potential problems, the DSM-III-R constitutes a major contribution to psychiatric classification and nomenclature. It attempts to provide more explicit criteria for diagnosing disorders than were found in previous editions.

The multiaxial classification system used in the DSM-III-R has the following five axes:

• Axis I—Clinical Syndromes; Conditions Not Attributable to a Mental Disorder That Are a Focus of Attention or Treatment

• Axis II — Developmental Disorders; Personality Disorders

• Axis III — Physical Disorders and Conditions

• Axis IV — Severity of Psychosocial Stressors

• Axis V — Global Assessment of Functioning

Table 18-6 briefly describes the five axes. The entire classification of mental disorders is contained in Axes I and II. Where applicable, each classification (or code) in the DSM-III-R's Axes I and II is described with the following: essential features (features that are generally required to make the diagnosis and that are always present), associated features (features that are often, but not invariably, present), age at onset, course, impairment, complications, predisposing factors, prevalence, sex ratio, familial pattern, differential diagnosis (how to distinguish the disorder being discussed from similiar disorders), and diagnostic criteria (a listing for each disorder of specific criteria that are needed to make the diagnosis). A brief discussion of each of the five axes follows. You are urged to consult the DSM-III-R for a complete description of the multiaxial classification system.

Axis I

Axis I contains all of the major clinical syndromes, except for developmental and personality disorders. Two other types of codes are also included: one for conditions that are not attributable to a mental disorder but are, nonetheless, a focus of referral or treatment (for example, uncomplicated bereavement or parent-child problem) and the other for unspecified diagnoses, no diagnosis on Axis I or II, or deferred diagnoses. Any classification in the DSM-III-R can be used for children, although some disorders may not be evident in childhood. (Chapter 20 discusses the essential features of the attention-deficit hyperactivity disorder and conduct disorder.)

Axis II

Axis II contains two major classification codes: personality disorders and developmental disorders. The personality disorders classification, which is not listed in Table 18-6, is applied primarily to adults; it is used when there are enduring, maladaptive patterns or traits. Personality disorders may sometimes emanate from a disordered childhood. Three adult personality disorder classifications have childhood counterparts that are represented on Axis I: antisocial personality disorder — conduct disorder; avoidant personality disorder — avoidant disorder of child-

hood or adolescence; and borderline personality disorder — identity disorder.

Within the developmental disorders classification fall mental retardation, pervasive developmental disorders, and specific developmental disorders. Specific categories within the developmental disorders classifications are briefly examined below. (Chapter 21 provides an in-depth discussion of mental retardation, and Chapter 20 discusses pervasive developmental disorders and specific developmental disorders.)

Mental retardation. The diagnosis of mental retardation essentially follows one proposed by the American Association on Mental Deficiency. Three specific criteria are listed. First, intellectual functioning must be significantly subaverage — an IQ of 70 or below is usually required. Second, there must be significant deficits or impairments in adaptive functioning, with the child's age taken into account. Third, onset of the condition must be before 18 years of age.

Although the DSM-III-R recognizes that an individual intelligence test must be used to obtain an IQ, the guidelines fail to note that an IQ of 68 is a more appropriate cutoff for tests that have a standard deviation of 16. Furthermore, the DSM-III-R indicates that a band between IQs of 65 and 75 can be used rather than a specific number. This flexibility was added to the DSM-III-R to allow for a diagnosis of mental retardation when there are significant deficits in adaptive behavior. Conversely, IQs somewhat lower than 70 do not automatically result in a diagnosis of mental retardation when there are no significant deficits in adaptive behavior. The DSM-III-R advocates that, ideally, an adaptive behavior scale be used in conjunction with clinical judgment of general adaptation for the assessment of adaptive behavior.

When an individual beyond 18 years of age develops mental retardation, the classification of dementia, an organic mental disorder, is used. When mental retardation develops before the age of 18 years in a child who previously had normal intelligence, both the mental retardation and the dementia classifications are used.

Pervasive developmental disorders. The two categories under pervasive developmental disorders are autistic disorder and pervasive developmental disorder not otherwise specified. These classifications replace such diagnostic terms as atypical development, symbiotic psychosis, childhood psychosis, and childhood schizophrenia. Autistic disorder also is known as infantile autism.

Table 18-6
DSM-III-R Classifications That Are Most Directly Applicable to Children and Adolescents

Axis I. Disorders Usually First Evident in Infancy, Childhood, or Adolescence

Disruptive Behavior Disorders
  Attention-deficit hyperactivity disorder
  Conduct disorder
    group type
    solitary aggressive type
    undifferentiated type
  Oppositional defiant disorder
Anxiety Disorders of Childhood or Adolescence
  Separation anxiety disorder
  Avoidant disorder of childhood or adolescence
  Overanxious disorder
Eating Disorders
  Anorexia nervosa
  Bulimia nervosa
  Pica
  Rumination disorder of infancy
  Eating disorder not otherwise specified
Gender Identity Disorders
  Gender identity disorder of childhood
  Transsexualism

Gender identity disorder of adolescence or adulthood,
    nontranssexual type
Gender identity disorder not otherwise specified
Tic Disorders
  Tourette's disorder
  Chronic motor or vocal tic disorder
  Transient tic disorder
  Tic disorder not otherwise specified
Elimination Disorders
  Functional encopresis
  Functional enuresis
Speech Disorders Not Elsewhere Classified
  Cluttering
  Stuttering
Other Disorders of Infancy, Childhood, or Adolescence
  Elective mutism
  Identity disorder
  Reactive attachment disorder of infancy or early childhood
  Stereotypy/habit disorder
  Undifferentiated attention-deficit disorder

Axis II. Developmental Disorders

Mental Retardation
  Mild mental retardation
  Moderate mental retardation
  Severe mental retardation
  Profound mental retardation
  Unspecified mental retardation
Pervasive Developmental Disorders
  Autistic disorder
  Pervasive developmental disorder not otherwise specified
Specific Developmental Disorders
  Developmental arithmetic disorder

Developmental expressive writing disorder
Developmental reading disorder
Developmental articulation disorder
Developmental expressive language disorder
Developmental receptive language disorder
Developmental coordination disorder
Specific developmental disorder not otherwise specified
Other Developmental Disorders
  Developmental disorder not otherwise specified

Axis III. Physical Disorders and Conditions

Axis III permits the clinician to indicate any current physical disorder or condition that is potentially relevant to the understanding or treatment of the individual.

Axis IV. Severity of Psychosocial Stressors Scale: Children and Adolescents

		Examples of stressors	
Code	Term	Acute events	Enduring circumstances
1	None	No acute events that may be relevant to the disorder	No enduring circumstances that may be relevant to the disorder
2	Mild	Broke up with boyfriend or girlfriend; change of school	Overcrowded living quarters; family arguments
3	Moderate	Expelled from school; birth of sibling	Chronic disabling illness in parent; chronic parental discord

(Table continues next page)

Table 18-6 (cont.)

		Examples of stressors	
Code	Term	Acute events	Enduring circumstances
4	Severe	Divorce of parents; unwanted pregnancy; arrest	Harsh or rejecting parents; chronic life-threatening illness in parent; multiple foster home placements
5	Extreme	Sexual or physical abuse; death of a parent	Recurrent sexual or physical abuse
6	Catastrophic	Death of both parents	Chronic life-threatening illness
0	Inadequate information, or no change in condition		

Axis V. Global Assessment of Functioning Scale (GAF Scale)

Consider psychological, social, and occupational functioning on a hypothetical continuum of mental health-illness. Do not include impairment in functioning due to physical (or environmental) limitations.

Note: Use intermediate codes when appropriate, e.g., 45, 68, 72.

Code

90 | Absent or minimal symptoms (e.g., mild anxiety before an exam), good functioning in all areas, interested and involved in a
| wide range of activities, socially effective, generally satisfied with life, no more than everyday problems or concerns (e.g., an
81 | occasional argument with family members).

80 | If symptoms are present, they are transient and expectable reactions to psychosocial stressors (e.g., difficulty concentrating
| after family argument); no more than slight impairment in social, occupational, or school functioning (e.g., temporarily
71 | falling behind in school work).

70 | Some mild symptoms (e.g., depressed mood and mild insomnia) OR some difficulty in social, occupational, or school
| functioning (e.g., occasional truancy, or theft within the household), but generally functioning pretty well, has some
61 | meaningful interpersonal relationships.

60 | Moderate symptoms (e.g., flat affect and circumstantial speech, occasional panic attacks) OR moderate difficulty in social,
51 | occupational, or school functioning (e.g., few friends, conflicts with co-workers).

50 | Serious symptoms (e.g., suicidal ideation, severe obsessional rituals, frequent shoplifting) OR any serious impairment in
41 | social, occupational, or school functioning (e.g., no friends, unable to keep a job).

40 | Some impairment in reality testing or communication (e.g., speech is at times illogical, obscure, or irrelevant) OR major
| impairment in several areas, such as work or school, family relations, judgment, thinking, or mood (e.g., depressed man
| avoids friends, neglects family, and is unable to work; child frequently beats up younger children, is defiant at home, and is
31 | failing at school).

30 | Behavior is considerably influenced by delusions or hallucinations OR serious impairment in communication or judgment
| (e.g., sometimes incoherent, acts grossly inappropriately, suicidal preoccupation) OR inability to function in almost all areas
21 | (e.g., stays in bed all day; no job, home, or friends).

20 | Some danger of hurting self or others (e.g., suicide attempts without clear expectation of death, frequently violent, manic
| excitement) OR occasionally fails to maintain minimal personal hygiene (e.g., smears feces) OR gross impairment in
11 | communication (e.g., largely incoherent or mute).

10 | Persistent danger of severely hurting self or others (e.g., recurrent violence) OR persistent inability to maintain minimal
1 | personal hygiene OR serious suicidal act with clear expectation of death.

Source: Axes IV and V reprinted, with a change in notation, by permission of the publisher from the *Diagnostic and Statistical Manual of Mental Disorders (Third Edition—Revised)*, 1987, pp. 11–12. Copyright © American Psychiatric Association. Axes I through III adapted from DSM-III-R.

Specific developmental disorders.   The disorders encoded in Axis II under specific developmental disorders are associated with circumscribed areas of development or learning and behavior that are not caused by another disorder. Consequently, it is necessary to rule out other disorders due to physical or neurologic impairment, pervasive developmental disorders, and deficient educational opportunities before making specific developmental disorders diagnoses. Because children may have associated learning, speech, and motor problems, more than one of the classifications may be used. The diagnostic criteria for each of the specific developmental disorders are shown in Table 18-7.

Children receiving a diagnosis of a developmental arithmetic, writing, or reading disorder must demonstrate skills that are markedly below the expected level, given the child's schooling and level of intelligence. The skills must be measured by individually administered achievement and intelligence tests. A specific developmental disorder classification is *not* used for children who are slow learners.

A developmental articulation disorder diagnosis is used

Table 18-7
Diagnostic Criteria for Specific Developmental Disorders in DSM-III-R

Disorder	Criteria
Developmental Arithmetic Disorder	A. Arithmetic skills, as measured by a standardized, individually administered test, are markedly below the expected level, given the person's schooling and intellectual capacity (as determined by an individually administered IQ test). B. The disturbance in A significantly interferes with academic achievement or activities of daily living requiring arithmetic skills. C. Not due to a defect in visual or hearing acuity or a neurologic disorder.
Developmental Expressive Writing Disorder	A. Writing skills, as measured by a standardized, individually administered test, are markedly below the expected level, given the person's schooling and intellectual capacity (as determined by an individually administered IQ test). B. The disturbance in A significantly interferes with academic achievement or activities of daily living requiring the composition of written texts (spelling words and expressing thoughts in grammatically correct sentences and organized paragraphs). C. Not due to a defect in visual or hearing acuity or a neurologic disorder.
Developmental Reading Disorder	A. Reading achievement, as measured by a standardized, individually administered test, is markedly below the expected level, given the person's schooling and intellectual capacity (as determined by an individually administered IQ test). B. The disturbance in A significantly interferes with academic achievement or activities of daily living requiring reading skills. C. Not due to a defect in visual or hearing acuity or a neurologic disorder.
Developmental Articulation Disorder	A. Consistent failure to use developmentally expected speech sounds. For example, in a three-year-old, failure to articulate p, b, and t, and in a six-year-old, failure to articulate r, sh, th, f, z, and l. B. Not due to a Pervasive Developmental Disorder, Mental Retardation, defect in hearing acuity, disorders of the oral speech mechanism, or a neurologic disorder.
Developmental Expressive Language Disorder	A. The score obtained from a standardized measure of expressive language is substantially below that obtained from a standardized measure of nonverbal intellectual capacity (as determined by an individually administered IQ test). B. The disturbance in A significantly interferes with academic achievement or activities of daily living requiring the expression of verbal (or sign) language. This may be evidenced in severe cases by use of a markedly limited vocabulary, by speaking only in simple sentences, or by speaking only in the present tense. In less severe cases, there may be hesitations or errors in recalling certain words, or errors in the production of long or complex sentences. C. Not due to a Pervasive Developmental Disorder, defect in hearing acuity, or a neurologic disorder (aphasia).

(Table continues next page)

Table 18-7 (cont.)

Disorder	Criteria
Developmental Receptive Language Disorder	A. The score obtained from a standardized measure of receptive language is substantially below that obtained from a standardized measure of nonverbal intellectual capacity (as determined by an individually administered IQ test). B. The disturbance in A significantly interferes with academic achievement or activities of daily living requiring the comprehension of verbal (or sign) language. This may be manifested in more severe cases by an inability to understand simple words or sentences. In less severe cases, there may be difficulty in understanding only certain types of words, such as spatial terms, or an inability to comprehend longer or more complex statements. C. Not due to a Pervasive Developmental Disorder, defect in hearing acuity, or a neurologic disorder (aphasia).
Developmental Coordination Disorder	A. The person's performance in daily activities requiring motor coordination is markedly below the expected level, given the person's chronological age and intellectual capacity. This may be manifested by marked delays in achieving motor milestones (walking, crawling, sitting), dropping things, "clumsiness," poor performance in sports, or poor handwriting. B. The disturbance in A significantly interferes with academic achievement or activities of daily living. C. Not due to a known physical disorder, such as cerebral palsy, hemiplegia, or muscular dystrophy.

Source: Reprinted with permission of the publisher from the *Diagnostic and Statistical Manual of Mental Disorders (Third Edition – Revised)*, 1987, pp. 42–45, 47–49. Copyright © American Psychiatric Association.

when there is a failure to develop consistent articulation of the later-acquired speech sounds, such as *r*, *sh*, *th*, *f*, *z*, and *l*. A developmental expressive language disorder or receptive language disorder diagnosis is used when the child's score on an expressive or receptive language test is substantially below that obtained on a standardized nonverbal measure of intellectual ability. A diagnosis of developmental coordination disorder is made when the child's motor coordination is markedly below the expected level for his or her age and intellectual capacity. The impairment must significantly interfere with academic achievement or activities of daily living. The diagnosis of specific developmental disorder not otherwise specified is used for disorders that do not meet the other criteria, such as aphasia or spelling difficulties.

Axis III

Axis III is used to indicate current physical disorders or conditions (such as diabetes or asthma) that may be relevant to understanding or treating the individual. These conditions are not included in either Axis I or Axis II.

Axis IV and Axis V

Axes IV and V can be used in special clinical and research settings to provide information that supplements the pri-

mary DSM-III-R diagnoses contained in Axes I, II, and III. These last two axes can be especially useful for planning treatments and predicting outcomes.

Axis IV is used to identify and evaluate psychosocial stressors relevant to the assessment and treatment process by means of a 6-point rating scale (see Table 18-6). The rating scale also has a 0 category to allow for a "no information" or "not applicable" rating.

Axis V rates the individual's overall level of psychological, social, and occupational functioning at the time of the evaluation and during the past year. The ratings are made on a 90-point scale (see Table 18-6), which represents a hypothetical continuum of mental health-illness. (Higher ratings indicate better mental health.) Two ratings are made: (a) the level of functioning at the time of the evaluation (current rating) and (b) the highest level of functioning attained in at least a few months during the past year – at least one month during the school year should be included for children and adolescents (past year rating).

Classification with DSM-III-R Axes

Typically, all of the DSM-III-R axes are used in classifying a child or adolescent with a significant disorder. Children with only clinically related problems are generally described using Axes I, II, IV, and V; children with learning and developmental problems are usually described using

◾ Exhibit 18-2 ━━━━━━━━━━━━━━━━━━━━━━━━━━━━━━━━━━━━━

Application of DSM-III-R Multiaxial Diagnosis to Child with a Developmental Disorder

Case History

Mark is a 10-year-old boy who was referred by Child Welfare authorities. Background information reveals that pregnancy and birth were uncomplicated. Developmental milestones were within normal limits. He has experienced the usual childhood illnesses, but has had no serious physical illness. A sister, four years older, is Mark's only sibling in his middle-class family. He has had playmates in the neighborhood and has participated in socialization experiences through his extended family and church.

During the interview, Mark was unresponsive and moved somewhat aimlessly around the room. He made sounds but no identifiable speech. When presented with toys, he seemed to be uninterested in them and did not engage in cooperative play. At times, he sat in his chair staring off in the distance and waved his hands in the air. However, he found it difficult to sit still, moved around the room a great deal, and had to be restrained by the interviewer.

When Mark was 5 years old, his father was burned in an accident at a chemical plant. The father was hospitalized for several weeks, and eventually died from these injuries. When visiting his father, the child would often scream and pull at the bandages covering his father's burns. It was at this point that Mark's mother began to notice "a change" in him.

After his father's death, Mark began exhibiting perseverative speech. For no identifiable reason, he began having "outbursts" of crying and excitability during which he could not be comforted. At times, he would laugh or smile to himself. His mother reported that Mark stopped playing with his toys and would become preoccupied "waving his hands" or "moving his fingers." He began to exhibit head-banging, especially when a change was made in his routine.

Currently, Mark has no language. He continues to have unexplained "temper outbursts" with self-mutilative behavior. He requires careful supervision as he lacks appropriate fear reactions and has also experienced a regression in self-help skills. A pediatric examination revealed no medical problems. Child Welfare authorities are investigating proper placement facilities as his mother reports she can no longer care for the child.

Multiaxial Diagnosis

Axis I: No diagnosis
Axis II: Autistic disorder, with childhood onset; mental retardation, unspecified
Axis III: None
Axis IV: Psychosocial stressors: father's accidental and traumatic death
           Severity: 5 – extreme
Axis V: Current: 10

Discussion

Axis I. No diagnosis would be appropriate on Axis I.

Axis II. The principal diagnosis in this case is autistic disorder, with childhood onset. This child exhibits a gross and sustained impairment in many areas of functioning, especially social relationships, which began after the age of 5 years. If delusions, hallucinations, or marked loosening of associations could be identified, then a diagnosis of schizophrenia would need to be considered.

Although this child is at present untestable, an additional diagnosis of mental retardation would also be given to note the presence of significantly subaverage intellectual functioning and impairment in adaptive functioning.

Axis III. A pediatric exam yielded no relevant physical conditions.

Axis IV. Even though the father's traumatic death occurred five years prior to the present assessment, this event was critical in the onset of the disorder and is mentioned on Axis IV. A coding of Extreme – 5 seems most appropriate. If the father's death were judged to be a catastrophic event, a rating of 6 could be used.

Axis V. Since Mark has functioned at the level demonstrated in the interview during the entire preceding year, a rating of 10 (persistent danger of hurting self or others) seems most appropriate.

Source: Reprinted, with changes in notation and in the multiaxial diagnosis, by permission of the publisher and authors from L. J. Webb, C. C. DiClemente, E. E. Johnstone, J. L. Sanders, and R. A. Perley (Eds.), *DSM-III Training Guide*, pp. 147–148; 155. Copyright 1981, Brunner/Mazel.

Axes II (developmental disorders), III, IV, and V. Exhibit 18-2 illustrates the application of a DSM-III-R multiaxial diagnosis to a child with a developmental disorder.

Comment on the DSM-III-R

The multiaxial classification system used in the DSM-III-R recognizes that children may have disorders that bridge behavioral, cognitive, physical, and developmental dimensions. For example, a child with autism may receive more than one diagnostic code, such as autistic disorder and mental retardation on Axis II and asthma on Axis III, if that condition is present.

Even though DSM-III-R categories are more behaviorally explicit than those in prior systems, judgment is still required of the clinician. Because some of the diagnostic criteria require that a child's symptoms be age-inappropriate, judgment must be used to decide whether a child's behavior is, indeed, deviant. The DSM-III-R does not provide age norms, base rates, or treatment recommendations for any of its classifications.

The DSM-III-R explicitly states that standardized, individually administered reading, arithmetic, and intelligence tests should be used as appropriate to diagnose developmental reading disorder and developmental arithmetic disorder. In addition, individual intelligence test results are required for the diagnosis of mental retardation. Consequently, clinical and school psychologists are best equipped to establish these diagnoses.

The DSM-III-R recognizes that the inclusion of the specific developmental disorders classification is controversial because many children with these disabilities have no "other" signs of psychopathology and the detection and treatment of academic skill disorders take place within the educational system, not within the mental health system. Nevertheless, the inclusion of educationally related difficulties is deemed appropriate because "these conditions . . . conform to the DSM-III-R concept of mental disorder" (p. 40). Children receiving a DSM-III-R diagnosis for these conditions, however, may be stigmatized by a psychiatric label when, in fact, such a label is clearly inappropriate. Similar considerations hold for stuttering and enuresis.

Overall, the DSM-III-R provides a valuable system for classifying individuals who display symptoms of mental disorder. Whether it will lead to improved treatment or better research remains to be seen. Some classifications in the DSM-III-R cannot be made without the specific assistance of psychologists trained to administer and interpret psychological and psychoeducational tests. Thus psychologists and psychoeducational specialists should be thoroughly familiar with the DSM-III-R.

COMMENT ON THE ASSESSMENT PROCESS

Assessment of intelligence and special abilities must be carried out with sensitivity and concern for the child and his or her family. As you perform an assessment, consider the child's expectancies regarding the assessment; how your dress, appearance, ethnicity, and other personal attributes may affect the child (and the child's parents); and how your own expectations, biases, and cultural values will affect the assessment. Be ready to modify your assessment plan in light of new findings that emerge during the assessment.

Tests, interviews, observations, and checklists are behavior sampling tools. Their use in a multidimensional assessment battery will help you to (a) determine the child's strengths and weaknesses, (b) understand the nature, presence, and degree of any handicapping conditions, (c) determine the conditions that inhibit and support the acquisition of appropriate skills, (d) provide baseline information prior to an intervention program, (e) develop useful instructional programs, (f) guide individuals in selecting appropriate educational and vocational programs, (g) monitor changes in the child, and (h) measure the impact of the instructional programs.

The assessment results tell you *what* the child has done at a particular time and place. Knowing *why* the child performed as he or she did requires a careful study of the entire clinical history and assessment results. The results also do not tell you *what* the child might be able to do under a different set of testing conditions. If you want to know what the child is capable of doing under altered testing conditions, testing-of-limits procedures must be employed (see Chapter 5).

Murphy's (1975) insightful suggestions are a fitting conclusion to this chapter on the assessment process. They alert us to the need to discover each child's unique coping strategies:

. . . we need to focus on and better understand the nature of ongoing current coping struggles; how to support them, how to help the child to extract the strength and insight that successive experiences may make available to him [or her]. We need to understand the positive strategic values of withdrawal in certain situations, and be very cautious about talking about a "withdrawn child." Similarly we need to respect and value children's protests, resistances, attempts to change or control situations, and all the other active coping efforts that can give us cues to what the child finds intolerable, unsuitable, boring, distasteful or threatening to his integrity. . . . I am pleading . . . that each clinician, each teacher, use all of the available resources along with his [or her] own fresh look at the child in his [or her] situation in order to discover the meaning of the child's behavior from the child's own point of view. (p. 42)

SUMMARY

1. The multimethod assessment approach synthesizes information from the clinical history, interviews, observations, standardized tests, informal tests, and other special procedures.

2. Psychological testing involves the administration and interpretation of psychological tests, whereas psychological as-

sessment considers the child's unique characteristics, current life situation, and clinical history as well as the results of testing.

3. Various purposes are served by assessment, including screening, diagnosis, counseling and rehabilitation, and progress evaluation.

4. A psychological evaluation can complement a medical evaluation by providing guidelines that can help the child function better in everyday life situations.

5. The steps in the assessment process include reviewing referral information; obtaining information from parents, teachers, and others familiar with the child's problems, as well as from other agencies and physicians; assessing the behavior of relevant adults; observing the child in various settings; selecting and administering a test battery; interpreting data; formulating hypotheses; developing intervention strategies; writing a report; meeting with parents and child; and following up on recommendations and retesting.

6. The test score is influenced by innate, background, and environmental factors as well as by factors in the child's personality, situational test demands, and random variation.

7. In attempting to account for a child's failures, consider all possible factors, including those associated with neuropsychological, physical, experiential, and temperament domains.

8. Test results give information about how a child performed at a specific time under specific conditions. Generalization of findings to other situations may be difficult. Be especially aware of nuances in the child's performance that may suggest special talents.

9. It is difficult to specify the exact function that underlies performance on any given test and the relationship between the skills measured on tests and classroom performance.

10. The difficulty of assessing children is compounded by the fact that (a) classification systems are not uniform, (b) behavioral disorders are not always clear, (c) children undergo rapid developmental changes, and (d) assessment is time consuming.

11. The diagnostic examples presented in the chapter illustrate how hypotheses can be developed from an analysis of the child's responses, performance, and behavior.

12. The assessment of the relationship to learning ability of various factors—such as type of material, rate and modality of presentation, cues, and reinforcements—can contribute to the design of intervention efforts.

13. Assessment and intervention are intertwined, with intervention results providing feedback on the assessment hypotheses. Re-evaluation and follow-up are important parts of the assessment process.

14. The results of repeated evaluations are difficult to interpret because there is no easy way to separate practice effects from actual clinical improvement. Additionally, differential practice effects may occur as a function of the specific population, task, retest interval, initial test score, and specific test.

15. Keys to designing an effective clinical and psychoeducational assessment include (a) using a broad spectrum approach, (b) using a variety of assessment procedures, (c) using multiple

methods to evaluate a particular domain (if possible), and (d) assessing the child on multiple occasions.

16. The assessment process in schools incorporates the general principles of assessment, but focuses more directly on learning and educational intervention. The evaluation should focus on the child's strengths and compensatory abilities as well as on areas of deficiency.

17. Although visits to the classroom may provide valuable information, it is necessary that the teacher approve and support such visits.

18. Assessment should be a continuous activity and interventions should be continually monitored.

19. The Panel on the Selection and Placement of Students in Programs for the Mentally Retarded of the National Academy of Sciences made the following recommendations for the assessment of referred children for special education programs: (a) the child's learning environment and the nature and the quality of the regular instruction received should be evaluated systematically and (b) a comprehensive battery that includes measures of intelligence, cognition, adaptive behavior, and screening procedures to detect biomedical disorders should be administered.

20. A language assessment should include evaluation of the child's consistencies within his or her own language system, strategies and processes used to produce language, language structures, and language distortions. Samples of verbal and nonverbal behavior in a variety of settings should be obtained. Both comprehension and production skills should be evaluated. Language difficulties may be associated with syndromes or diseases, processing difficulties, or social and cultural factors.

21. Some speech and language deviations are associated with developmental periods, whereas others may occur throughout the developmental period. Lack of speech, unintelligible speech, and failure to speak in sentences may be first noticed at about 3 to 5 years of age; substitution of easy sounds for more difficult ones, dropping of word endings, faulty sentence structure, noticeable nonfluency, and abnormal rhythm, rate, and speech inflection are of concern at about 5 to 6 years; and distortions, omissions, and substitutions of any sounds are of concern at about 7 years. Late-appearing speech sounds, being embarrassed by speech, poor voice quality, and telegraphic speech are examples of deviations that are not specifically age related.

22. Visual-motor performance can be observed not only on visual-motor tests, but also on intelligence and special ability tests.

23. In the learning potential assessment strategy, the child is first tested, then given specialized training, then tested again. Learning potential assessment attempts to measure the *process* of learning rather than the content of learning, including why and how the material was mastered. The word *potential* may be misleading because there is little evidence that learning potential assessment measures are better at predicting school-related achievement than are intelligence tests. Learning potential procedures are still in an experimental stage and should not be substituted for intelligence tests in any decision-making activity.

24. Although classification and labeling have potential negative consequences, they serve many useful functions, such as aiding in the study of exceptionality, facilitating communication and record keeping, enhancing others' altruistic behavior and tolerance for deviant behavior, and providing a sense of closure for parents.

25. *The Diagnostic and Statistical Manual of Mental Disorders*, 3rd edition – Revised (DSM-III-R) is the standard system for diagnostic classification of mental disorders. It has a five-level multiaxial classification system: I – clinical syndromes, II – developmental disorders and personality disorders, III – physical disorders and conditions, IV – severity of psychosocial stressors, and V – global assessment of functioning. Clinical and school psychologists are the individuals best equipped to establish the diagnoses of mental retardation and specific developmental disorders.

26. Clinical and psychoeducational assessment must be carried out with concern for the child and his or her family and sensitivity to your role as an examiner in the assessment process. The key to effective assessment is to portray each child's unique ability pattern.

KEY TERMS, CONCEPTS, AND NAMES

Multimethod assessment (p. 532)
Psychological assessment (p. 532)
Psychological testing (p. 532)
Cumulative achievement (p. 536)
Psychological processes (p. 536)
Repeated assessments (p. 537)
Practice effects (p. 537)
Regression-to-the-mean effects (p. 537)
National Academy of Sciences' Panel on the Selection and Placement of Students in Programs for the Mentally Retarded (p. 543)
Language assessment (p. 544)
Receptive language (p. 546)
Expressive language (p. 546)
Speech (p. 546)
Phonation (p. 546)
Nasal resonance (p. 546)
Articulation (p. 546)
Prosody (p. 546)
Dysfluencies (p. 546)
Congenital laryngeal web (p. 546)
Agrammatism (p. 547)
Anomia (p. 547)
Blocking (p. 547)
Circumstantiality (p. 547)
Clanging (p. 547)
Derailment (p. 547)
Distortion of language sounds (p. 547)

Distractible speech (p. 547)
Dysarthria (p. 547)
Dysprosody (p. 547)
Echolalia (p. 547)
Illogicality (p. 547)
Incoherence (p. 547)
Loss of goal (p. 547)
Neologisms (p. 547)
Paragrammatism (p. 547)
Paraphasia (p. 547)
Perseveration (p. 547)
Phonemic paraphasia (p. 547)
Poverty of amount of speech (p. 548)
Poverty of content of speech (p. 548)
Pressure of speech (p. 548)
Self-reference (p. 548)
Stilted speech (p. 548)
Syntactic errors (p. 548)
Tangentiality (p. 548)
Telegraphic speech (p. 548)
Topical or referential identification problems (p. 548)
Word approximations (p. 548)
Learning potential assessment (p. 549)
Mini-learning situations (p. 549)
Classification and labeling (p. 551)
Self-fulfilling prophecy (p. 551)
DSM-III-R (p. 552)

STUDY QUESTIONS

1. Describe and evaluate the multimethod assessment approach.

2. How does psychological assessment differ from psychological testing?

3. Discuss the purposes of assessment.

4. Describe the steps in the assessment process.

5. What are some of the difficulties associated with the assessment of children?

6. Discuss a model that is useful for understanding factors that may influence test scores.

7. What factors should be considered in accounting for failures on a test or assessment procedure?

8. What are some problems in generalizing from a child's test performance to other situations?

9. Discuss the problems involved in the measurement of psychological processes.

10. What difficulties are involved in evaluating the results of repeated assessments?

11. Present at least *seven* illustrations of how hypotheses may be formulated from a child's responses and performance.

12. Discuss the role of assessment of learning ability in developing intervention strategies.

13. Describe some guidelines for designing a clinical and psychoeducational assessment.

14. Discuss the assessment process in schools.

15. Discuss the assessment model for school-based referrals recommended by the Panel on the Selection and Placement of Students in Programs for the Mentally Retarded.

16. What are some developmental considerations in evaluating language and speech deviations?

17. Discuss some important guideposts for observing the child's language and speech.

18. Discuss learning potential assessment.

19. Discuss the pros and cons of classification and labeling.

20. Discuss the implications of the DSM-III-R for the practice of clinical and school psychology.

_ 19

ASSESSMENT OF ETHNIC MINORITY CHILDREN

IQ and achievement tests are nothing but updated versions of the old signs down South that read "For Whites Only."

—Robert L. Williams

Moreover, it is precisely the black students who need IQ tests most of all, for it is precisely with black students that alternative methods of spotting intellectual ability have failed.

—Thomas Sowell

Shared standards are like mortar, holding the multicolored mosaics of civilization together. Good tests, like good laws, embody shared standards.

—Barbara Lerner

Exhibit 19-1

How to Establish Rapport with an Inner-City Child: The Education of a Psychologist

Some years ago, a birthday party for a member of the staff at a well-known psychological clinic played a novel role in the test performance of a black child. Prior to the party this boy, whom we shall call James, had been described on the psychological record as "sullen, surly, slow, unresponsive, apathetic, unimaginative, lacking in inner life." This description was based on his behavior in the clinic interviews and on his performance on a number of psychological measures, including an intelligence test and a personality test. His was not an unusual record; many [minority] children are similarly portrayed.

On the day of the birthday party, James was seated in an adjoining room waiting to go into the clinician's office. It was just after the lunch hour and James had the first afternoon appointment. At the conclusion of the lunch break on this particular day, the staff presented a surprise birthday cake to one of the clinicians, who was black. The beautifully decorated cake was brought in and handed to the clinician by James's clinician, who was white, as were all the other members of the staff. The black clinician was deeply moved by the cake—and the entire surprise. In a moment of great feeling, she warmly embraced the giver of the cake. James inadvertently perceived all this from his vantage point in the outer office. That afternoon he showed amazing alacrity in taking the tests and responding in the interview. He was no longer sullen and dull. On the contrary, he seemed alive and enthusiastic, and he answered questions readily. His psychologist was astonished at the change and in the course of the next few weeks repeated with James the tests on which he had done so poorly. James now showed marked improvement, and the psychologist quickly revised not only James's test appraisal on his clinical record card, but her general personality description of him as well.

The high point of this new, positive relationship came some months later when James confided to the psychologist that she had gotten off on the wrong foot with him on the first day in the first three minutes of contact. The psychologist was taken aback and said, "What do you mean? I was very friendly; I told you my name and asked you yours." He responded, "Yeh,

and I said James Watson and right away you called me Jimmy and you bin callin' me Jimmy ever since. My name is James, 'cept to my very good friends maybe. Even my mother calls me James." Then he went on to tell her how he had changed his opinion of her on the day of the birthday party because of the close relationship he had seen between her and the black psychologist.

This little story illustrates a number of things. First, it shows that the test is a social situation. The testing situation, whether it be a psychological test or any other kind of test for that matter, reflects a relationship between people, a relationship that is often remarkably subtle. And when anything hampers this relationship, the result is likely to show in the test score itself. This can occur on an individual test as well as a group test, an IQ test as well as a personality test, a subject-matter examination as well as a psychological measure.

The story also shows how the behavior evidenced in the clinical situation tends to be seen by the psychologist as indicative of the basic personality of the child. This is frequently done with little awareness of how much this behavior is a product of the particular relationship between the psychologist and the child, and of the testing situation as such. Children from different cultural backgrounds respond very differently to clinical situations and to the idea of being tested or evaluated.

The anecdote also points up the fact that a well-meaning, clinically trained, unprejudiced psychologist can have poor rapport with an inner-city child, not because of deficient psychological technique, but because of limited knowledge about certain cultural attitudes. In this case, the attitude in question is the feeling held by many black people that the informality intended by nicknames signifies a lack of respect when it takes place across cultural lines. This does not suggest that the child himself was aware of this reasoning, but rather than he was simply reflecting his mother's wish that he be called by his full name.

Source: Reprinted, with a change in notation, by permission of the publisher and author from F. Riessman, *The Inner-City Child*, pp. 53–55. Copyright 1976, Harper & Row.

INTRODUCTION

The first two sections of this chapter cover arguments for and against the testing of ethnic minority children. General considerations in ethnic minority testing are then discussed, including the effects of poverty, cultural diversity, response style, bilingualism, racial differences in intelligence, and culture-fair tests. The chapter then focuses on cultural values and styles of black, Hispanic-American, American Indian, and Asian-American ethnic groups. Finally, general recommendations for testing ethnic minority children are presented.

Use of Appropriate Designations

The label *ethnic minority children* is used to designate children who belong to a recognized ethnic group and whose values, customs, patterns of thought, and/or language are significantly different from those of the majority of the society in which they live. The groups from which ethnic minority children come include blacks, Mexican-Americans, American Indians, Puerto Ricans, and Asian-Americans. The use of such labels as "culturally handicapped," "culturally disadvantaged," and "culturally deprived" to designate ethnic minority children has been unfortunate, because these terms have value implications. No one has the right to degrade a subculture because it does not conform to the patterns of the majority group. Different cultural mores and traditions expressed by minority groups may be both healthy and adaptive, for the lifestyles of these groups may differ markedly from those of the majority culture. The extent to which a group is handicapped may depend on the eyes of the beholder. This chapter therefore uses the term *ethnic minority children* instead of alternatives that may have pejorative connotations.

Adopting a Multifactor, Pluralistic Approach

In order to understand cultural groups in our society, it is important to adopt a multifactor, pluralistic approach. Cultural groups may vary with respect to cultural values (stemming in part from cultural shock, discontinuity, or conflict); language and nuances in language style; views of life and death; roles of family members; problem-solving strategies; attitudes toward education, mental health, and mental illness; and stage of acculturation (the group may follow traditional values, accept the dominant group's values, or be at some point between the two). You should adopt a frame of reference that will enable you to understand how particular behaviors make sense within each culture. "Racist thinking is revealed not in recognizing differences as such, but in aligning them along an inferior-superior axis and ascribing them to unchangeable determinants" (Korchin, 1980, pp. 264–265).

Appreciating Cultural Values and Coping Patterns

It is important to develop an appreciation for each ethnic minority's culture, because one or more of the previously named factors may affect the assessment situation. As the incident described in Exhibit 19-1 shows, these factors are powerful forces that shape a child's attitudes toward the assessment situation, including the test materials, the ex-

aminer, and the reasons for the assessment. Ethnic minorities have developed coping patterns that are a response to an environment that has been less than hospitable. It is important to understand how these coping patterns facilitate or hinder children's adjustments to their own subculture, as well as to the culture at large.

Guarding Against Inappropriate Generalizations

Generalizations about a particular minority group may not apply to individual members of that group. Each individual examinee must be evaluated on the basis of his or her own dynamics, family, and subculture. There is no one monolithic black, Hispanic-American, American Indian, or Asian-American subculture, so you should not assume that every minority person experiences his or her ethnicity in the same manner. Research on lower-class members of an ethnic group may not generalize to other socioeconomic classes in that group.

Are Mental Health Services Needed?

Ethnic minorities in the United States face overwhelming problems associated with jobs, physical health, and housing, as well as general oppression and racism. Their mental health is likely to be directly related to these problems. One may ask whether it is even appropriate to look at mental health problems and related assessment questions when these other areas need attention. This is a valid question, and it is not easy to answer. But I believe that, in spite of the injustices and racism rampant in our society, mental health professionals and psychoeducational specialists can improve the lot of ethnic minorities by helping them with their psychological and educational concerns. Like white children, ethnic minority children have mental health problems and learning difficulties and experience trauma associated brain damage. They may perform poorly in school; have learning problems; need vocational guidance; become depressed, suicidal, anxious, fearful, psychotic, or alcoholic; or experience family discord and self-doubts.

Assessment Issues as Part of the Fabric of Society

The issues involved in the assessment of ethnic minority children are complex, because they are woven into the very fabric of society. Assessment results have an impact on children's self-esteem and influence their chances of having a successful life. If tests are detrimental to ethnic minority children, then they must be changed or eliminated. If tests are beneficial to ethnic minority children, however, then their elimination may be a disservice to countless children. Whenever tests are used, you must ensure that the results are employed for the good of the child. The purpose of this chapter is to demonstrate how this goal can be accomplished.

ARGUMENTS AGAINST THE USE OF INTELLIGENCE TESTS IN ASSESSING ETHNIC MINORITY CHILDREN

Many allegations have been made about the inappropriateness of using tests, and in particular intelligence tests, with ethnic minority children. The major arguments are listed below and then are considered in more detail in the following subsections.

• *Intelligence tests have a cultural bias*. Standard intelligence tests have a strong white, Anglo-Saxon, middle-class bias.

• *National norms are inappropriate for minorities*. National norms based primarily on white, middle-class, Anglo-Saxon samples are inappropriate for use with ethnic minority children.

• *Minorities are handicapped in test-taking skills*. Ethnic minority children are handicapped in taking tests because of (a) deficiencies in motivation, test practice, and reading; (b) failure to appreciate the achievement aspects of the test situation; and (c) limited exposure to the culture.

• *The fact that most examiners are white has the effect of depressing the scores of ethnic minority children*. Rapport and communication problems exist between white examiners and ethnic minority children. These problems interfere with the ability of ethnic minority children to respond to the test items.

• *Tests results lead to inadequate and inferior education*. Test results are the main reason why ethnic minority children are segregated into special classes. These classes have inadequate curriculum and provide inferior education. Test results also create negative expectancies in teachers.

Cultural Bias Argument

There are many definitions of test bias, each of which has some value in explaining the properties of tests and their uses. In examining test bias, you should first consider the meaning of a test score. Is a test score an indication of past achievement or of aptitude for future achievement? Many arguments concerning test bias rest on which of these interpretations is considered correct. It is an important

distinction and one that is often made between achievement tests and aptitude tests. This distinction has never been clearly resolved in the case of intelligence tests.

This textbook advocates that intelligence tests and other special ability tests be used as measures of achievement, not as pure measures of aptitude or capacity. Intelligence test scores, representing the interplay of biological factors and environmental factors, reflect past learnings. Low scores obtained by ethnic minority children indicate a need to improve educational systems, not to abandon the tests.

Measures of test bias.   The various criteria used to measure test bias are reviewed in the following paragraphs (obtained from Flaugher, 1978), as are findings of research studies based on these definitions of test bias.

Mean differences.   A test is considered by some to be biased when it yields lower scores for one group than for another. This definition is not acceptable, however, because mean differences are not a legitimate standard for identifying test bias. Because of disparities among various groups in our nation with respect to socioeconomic status and other variables, it would be surprising if intelligence and achievement tests did *not* show mean differences in favor of some groups.

When disparities in socioeconomic status between black and white groups are reduced, IQs become more similar. For example, the IQs of 7-year-old black children were less than 5 points below those of white 7-year-olds when both groups came from the same socioeconomic level, lived in the same city, and had mothers who had gone to the same hospital for prenatal care (Nichols & Anderson, 1973). This 5-point difference between black and white children contrasts with the oft-reported 15-point difference (in favor of white children).

Single-group or differential validity.   Another measure of validity is whether a test is an equally good predictor for two (or more) ethnic groups within the United States. Two related ways of comparing validity coefficients are used to determine whether this form of test bias is present. With the single-group validity approach, test bias is considered to be present when a validity coefficient is significantly different from 0 for one ethnic group but not for another. With the differential validity approach, test bias is considered to be present when there is a significant difference *between* two validity coefficients. The majority of research with ethnic minorities in our country indicates that these forms of test bias are not commonly present. That is, neither single-group validity bias nor differential validity bias is generally found. Although there are instances in which single-group or differential validity has been found, "the fact that they are so elusive, difficult to detect, and debatable is good evidence that they are not very potent phenomena relative to all other possible sources of problems in the interaction of minorities and testing" (Flaugher, 1978, p. 674).

Studies with the WISC-R, Stanford-Binet: Form L-M, PPVT, and Raven's Progressive Matrices indicate that the regression lines for black children, white children, and Hispanic-American children are similar when Wide Range Achievement Test scores and other achievement indices are used as criteria (Bossard, Reynolds, & Gutkin, 1980; Hall, Huppertz, & Levi, 1977; Reschly & Sabers, 1979; Reynolds & Hartlage, 1979). In addition, studies have shown that the concurrent validity of the WISC-R, WISC, and Stanford-Binet: Form L-M with such criteria as the California Achievement Test, Wide Range Achievement Test, Metropolitan Achievement Tests, teacher ratings, Stanford Achievement Test, and California Test of Mental Maturity, is excellent for black, white, Mexican-American, and American Indian children, with median validity coefficients in the .50s (see Table 19-1). These findings support the conclusion that intelligence tests generally are equally good predictors for black, Hispanic-American, and white children.

Differential construct validity. Another way to evaluate the possible bias of intelligence tests is to study the extent to which they measure similar abilities in various ethnic groups. Studies examining the factor structure of the WISC, WISC-R, WPPSI, and McCarthy Scales of Children's Abilities for black, Hispanic-American, and white children indicate that these groups have comparable factor structures (Dean, 1980; Greenberg, Stewart, & Hansche, 1986; Gutkin & Reynolds, 1981; Guy, 1977; Jensen & Reynolds, 1982; Johnston & Bolen, 1984; Kaufman & DiCuio, 1975; Kaufman & Hollenbeck, 1974; Lawlis, Stedman, & Cortner, 1980; Miele, 1979; Reschly, 1978; Semler & Iscoe, 1966; Silverstein, 1973; Vance, Huelsman, & Wherry, 1976; Vance & Wallbrown, 1978). These findings suggest that (a) intelligence tests measure the same abilities in white, black, and Hispanic-American children and (b) the Verbal-Performance distinction in some of these tests is appropriate for the three ethnic groups.

The mean WISC-R subtest scores obtained by black and white children in the standardization sample are shown in Table 19-2. These scores indicate that average scores are similar on both the Verbal and Performance sections of the scale for black children (*M* Verbal scaled score = 8.25 vs. *M* Performance scaled score = 8.18) and for white chil-

Table 19-1
Concurrent Validity—Median Correlations Between Intelligence Tests and Achievement Tests for Anglo-American, Black-American, and Hispanic-American Children

| | Achievement area | | | |
| | Reading | | Arithmetic | |
Ethnic group	Number of studies	Mdn r	Number of studies	Mdn r
Anglo-American	14	.52	12	.54
Black-American	17	.60	11	.58
Hispanic-American	7	.51	7	.53

Note. These median correlations are based on the following studies: Bossard, Reynolds, & Gutkin, 1980; Dean, 1977a, 1979b; Henderson, Butler, & Goffeney, 1969; Henderson, Fay, Lindmann, & Clarkson, 1973; Kennedy, Van de Riet, & White, 1963; Komm, 1978; Oakland, 1980, 1983a; Oakland & Feigenbaum, 1979; Reschly & Reschly, 1979; Reynolds & Gutkin, 1980a; Reynolds & Nigl, 1981; Sewell, 1979; Sewell & Severson, 1974, 1975; Svanum & Bringle, 1982; Weaver, 1968; Weiner & Kaufman, 1979.

dren (*M* Verbal scaled score = 10.33 vs. *M* Performance scaled score = 10.37).

Content bias. Evaluation of content bias focuses on whether the content of particular test items is unfair to some groups of the population. Inspection of standardized

Table 19-2
Mean WISC-R Subtest Scores for Black and White Children in the Standardization Sample

| | Group | |
Subtest	White (N = 1868)	Black (N = 305)
Information	10.4	8.1
Similarities	10.3	7.9
Arithmetic	10.4	8.6
Vocabulary	10.4	7.9
Comprehension	10.4	7.8
Digit Span	10.1	9.2
Picture Completion	10.4	8.1
Picture Arrangement	10.4	8.1
Block Design	10.4	7.7
Object Assembly	10.4	7.9
Coding	10.2	8.9
Mazes	10.4	8.4

Source: Adapted from Gutkin and Reynolds (1981).

intelligence tests reveals few, if any, items that appear to be biased systematically in favor of one group over another. Agreement among the members of a panel of experts as to which items are biased tends to be very low. A useful empirical approach for investigating content bias is to examine item performance statistics group by group to determine the difficulty level of each item. "If a particular item is extraordinarily difficult for minority-group members relative to the difficulty of other items in the same test, then that item is a good candidate for suspicion of this kind of bias" (Flaugher, 1978, p. 675). Studies cited by Flaugher suggest that the elimination of such items from standardized tests makes little if any difference in test scores.

Several different types of internal criteria are available for studying content bias. They include examining differences between groups in (a) the rank order of the percent passing each item, (b) the percent passing adjacent items in the test, (c) the number of persons passing each item when both groups are equated for total score, and (d) the types of item content that discriminate most and least between the two groups (Jensen, 1974a). Applications of these criteria to the intelligence test and ability test performances of black and white children and adults have produced no evidence that differences between blacks and whites are related to cultural bias (Jensen, 1974a; Meyer & Goldstein, 1971; Miele, 1979; Nichols, 1971; Olivier & Barclay, 1967; Sandoval, 1979; Sandoval, Zimmerman, & Woo-Sam, 1983). Tests in these investigations included the Stanford-Binet: Form L-M, WISC-R, PPVT, and Raven's Progressive Matrices.

Miele (1979) reported that the WISC Comprehension item 4 — "What should you do if a child smaller than you begins to fight with you?" — which was singled out by Robert Williams in the CBS documentary "The IQ Myth" as a blatant manifestation of cultural bias, proved to be easier for black children than for white children. It was the 42nd easiest item for 111 black children (M age = 6-1) and the 47th easiest item for 163 white children (M age = 6-2). Sandoval and Miille (1980) reported that neither black, Hispanic-American, nor Anglo-American judges were able to determine accurately which WISC-R items were more difficult for minority students. The ethnic background of the judges made no difference in accuracy of item selection.

Individual intelligence test items have been evaluated by federal judges for biased content (see Chapter 24). Seven WISC and WISC-R items judged to be culturally biased by Judge Grady in the PASE case (Parents in Action on Special Education v. Joseph P. Hannon) were empirically evaluated with a sample of 180 black children and 180 white children attending schools in Chicago. The average age of

the children was 11 ½ years. As Table 19-3 shows, although the largest differences between the two groups were a 9 percent difference on the rubies item and a 4 percent difference on the stomach item, both in favor of white children, none of the differences between the two ethnic groups was statistically significant. The notorious fight item discussed above was passed by 73 percent of the black children and by 71 percent of the white children. These results conclusively demonstrate that an "armchair" inspection of test items cannot reveal which items are more difficult for one ethnic group than for another.

Factors affecting the validity of test results.   Measures of validity can provide statistical evidence that a test does not have an inherent bias against any ethnic minority group. Whether use of a particular test in a particular situation results in discrimination, however, will depend on such factors as the purposes to which the results are put, how the results are interpreted, and how the test is administered.

Uniqueness of the black experience.   One of the main thrusts of the culture-bias argument has been that intelligence tests are not relevant to the experiences of ethnic minority children. Black children, for example, are said to develop unique verbal skills that are neither measured by conventional tests nor accepted by the middle-class-oriented classroom (Williams, 1970). There has been little, if any, research to support this contention. Furthermore, items on intelligence tests represent important aspects of competence in the *common* culture; the items are

Table 19-3
Percent of Black and White Children Passing Seven Items on the WISC Comprehension Subtest Said by Judge Grady to Be Culturally Biased

	Group	
Item	Black (N = 180)	White (N = 180)
Rubies	26%	35%
Stomach	7	11
C.O.D.	1	0
Loaf of bread	74	67
Fight	73	71
Pay bills by check	21	22
Give money to charity	12	12

Note. Mean age of black children was 11.30; mean age of white children was 11.27 years.
Source: Adapted from Koh, Abbatiello, and McLoughlin (1984).

not reflective of purely middle-class values. For a democratic society to endure, these common cultural forms and practices need to be maintained and extended to the culture as a whole—"*cultural apartheid ought not to be encouraged in this society*" (Ebel, 1975, p. 86, italics added).

Ebel (1975, p. 87) also noted:

The bias which accounts for poor test performance by some minority persons is not in the tests so much as it is in the culture, and thus is another problem altogether. So long as the tests under scrutiny truly measure the skills necessary to success in the prevailing culture, minority interests are not well served by blaming "test bias" for poor performance.

The tests we use in education ought to be as free of bias as we can make them. But the extent and seriousness of bias in our current educational tests can be, and probably has been, exaggerated. The "well-known" bias of tests against minority group members seems to be more fanciful than factual.

The argument that intelligence tests are not valid because ethnic minorities have not had the same experiences as white middle-class children becomes difficult to accept when we consider the fact that a population quite far removed from white middle-class America actually does better on nonverbal tests than do American children themselves. The mean scores of children in Japan on many of the Wechsler Performance Scale subtests are higher than those of the American standardization samples (Lynn, 1977). Lynn believes that these findings indicate that tests such as the Wechsler Performance Scale may be much fairer culturally than many critics have been willing to admit.

Humphreys (1973, p. 3) also believes that the cultural differences between blacks and whites may not be as great as some propose:

There is every reason to accept a single biological species for blacks and whites and a high degree of cultural similarity as well. While there are obvious environmental differences, these differences are not as profound as to require different principles in the explanation of black and white behavior. The two groups use a highly similar (if not identical) language, attend similar schools, are exposed to similar curricula, listen to the same radio programs, look at the same commodities, etc. Cultural differences are a question of degree, not of kind.

Selection model. The *selection bias* of a test refers to the extent to which the test has a differential effect on the number of examinees from various groups who enter certain programs (such as special classes, college, or vocational training programs) or are selected for certain jobs. There is little agreement about the best statistical procedure to use to reduce selection bias. Should the same cutoff scores be used for all groups, or should some groups be given extra points? All selection procedures are tied to ethical and social values. Universal acceptance of one set of values will be difficult to achieve.

Validity criteria. A test can only be valid with respect to particular criteria. Criteria vary in such characteristics as importance, reliability, and innovativeness. If the wrong criterion is used to establish validity, the test scores may in fact be biased. For example, a test composed only of verbal items may be valid for selecting people good at speaking or writing about music, but it may not be valid for selecting promising musicians who are talented in producing music. Although the criterion problem is a difficult one, attempts should be made to examine thoroughly the criteria used to validate tests.

Atmosphere. If examinees feel out of place or unwelcome when taking a test, they will not give their best performance. If the examinees' real capacities are inhibited when they are confronted by a test, then the test scores are biased. This type of bias appears to play only a limited role, if any, in most testing situations, however, because examiners take much care to obtain the child's best performance in the individual testing situation.

Overinterpretation. When test users generalize from a limited domain of measurement to a broad range of ability, the issue of bias in the results is legitimately raised. For example, it is a great leap to say that a child "lacks practical judgment" simply because he or she was unable to answer correctly a few problems on a test.

Inappropriateness of National Norms

The argument that national norms are inappropriate for ethnic minority children has led some writers (for example, Mercer, 1976) to advocate establishing pluralistic norms. Those who favor pluralistic norms believe that it is useful to know how a child's performance compares to that of others in his or her own ethnic group. Pluralistic norms are potentially dangerous, however, because they (a) provide a basis for invidious comparisons among different ethnic groups, (b) may lower the expectations of ethnic minority children and reduce their level of aspiration to succeed, (c) may have little relevance outside of the child's specific geographic area, and (d) furnish no information about the complex reasons why some ethnic groups tend to score lower than others on intelligence tests (DeAvila & Havassy, 1974). The renorming of tests to devise pluralistic norms is inappropriate because it does not involve test modifications, nor does it take into account whether the test should be used with ethnic minority children (Bernal, 1972). And the use of pluralistic norms gives rise to new questions — what norms should be used for a child who has a Mexican father and a Hungarian mother?

Some charge that norms for the major individual intelligence tests are based *entirely* on the performance of middle-class whites. This simply is not true. The Stanford-Binet: Form L-M and Fourth Edition, WISC-R, WPPSI, WAIS-R, and McCarthy Scales have all used excellent sampling procedures to obtain their stratified samples for standardization. Ethnic minority children are represented in each of the norm groups in proportion to their representation in the general population.

National norms reflect the performance of the population as a whole. Because they describe the typical performance of our nation's children, they are important as a frame of reference and as a guidepost for decision-making. This is not to say that other norms should not be used. Test results may be interpreted from several frames of reference. But it is important that test users and consumers of test information clearly recognize which norms are being used and why they were selected.

Deficiencies in Test-Taking Skills

Ethnic minority children may be deficient in the ability to employ test-taking skills, choose proper problem-solving strategies, and balance speed and power. They also may exhibit test anxiety. Western culture emphasizes achievement and problem solving, and by the time children begin school, they are usually ready to accept intellectual challenge. Some ethnic minority children may fail to comprehend or accept the achievement aspects of the test situation, however. They may view it as an enjoyable child-adult encounter, rather than as a time to achieve; or, if they recognize the problem-solving aspects of the situation, they may ignore them. For example, American Indian children may not work quickly on timed tests because of a desire *not* to compete with others.

Although ethnic minority children may have an adequate storage and retrieval system to answer questions correctly, they may fail in practice because they have not been exposed to the material (Zigler & Butterfield, 1968). For example, they may respond incorrectly to the question "What is a gown?" because they have never heard the word *gown*. Motivational factors also may affect the performance of some ethnic minority children; they may know what a gown is, but respond with "I don't know" in order to terminate as quickly as possible the unpleasantness of interacting with a strange and demanding adult. Additionally, they may be more wary of adults, more motivated to secure adults' attention and praise, less motivated to be correct for the sake of correctness alone, or more willing to settle for lower levels of achievement success. Therefore, low IQs may be associated with limited exposure to test content or with motivational factors.

There is sufficient evidence that some ethnic minority children have limited test-taking skills. But this is true of some non-ethnic minority children as well. We do not know how pervasive this limitation is among ethnic minority children, or to what degree it lowers their performance on tests. Further research is needed in this area.

Racial Examiner Effects

With black children. The anxiety, insecurity, latent prejudice, and other reactions to contemporary black-white relations that are experienced by white clinicians in their work with black children may be transmitted to the children in a number of ways. Examiners may exhibit paternalism, overidentification, overconcern, excessive sympathy, indulgence, reactive fear, or inhibition. Black children, in turn, may exhibit fear and suspicion, verbal constriction, strained and unnatural reactions, or a facade of stupidity to avoid appearing "uppity." Some may deliberately score low to avoid personal threat; others may view the test as a means for whites, not blacks, to get ahead in society. Although many of these behaviors, patterns, and perceptions are likely to exist and are important phenomena in their own right, there is no way of knowing to what extent they affect black children's test scores (Sattler, 1970, 1973a).

Some psychologists believe that white examiners impair the intelligence test performance of black children. A careful study of the research literature refutes the myth of racial examiner effects, however. In 25 of the 29 published studies dealing with racial examiner effects on individual intelligence tests or other cognitive measures, no significant relationship was found between the race of the examiner and the examinees' scores (Sattler & Gwynne, 1982b). It is apparent that in the overwhelming majority of cases white examiners have not impaired the intelligence test performance of black children.

The result is all the more impressive when one considers the wide range of tests, grade levels, geographic areas, and dates of administration encompassed by these studies. The tests included the WISC, WAIS, WPPSI, Stanford-Binet: Form L-M, PPVT, Draw-A-Man, Iowa Test of Preschool Development, and several other tests of cognitive ability. The grade levels of the children in these studies ranged from preschool through grade twelve. The geographic locations, though largely urban, included Eastern, Midwestern, Southern, and Western cities. The years of publication ranged from 1964 to 1977.

Communication difficulties may be present in interethnic testing situations (see Chapter 16). Because misunderstandings may result in mistrust and sustain stereotypic judgments, every attempt should be made to reduce the likelihood of any misunderstandings. Differences in dialect may be a source of difficulty. Some argue that black children do not clearly understand white examiners, and this causes their scores to be lower than those they obtain when tested by black examiners. Studies, however, have failed to provide any support for this position. Quay (1972, 1974), for example, reported that black children scored no higher when the Stanford-Binet: Form L-M was administered in black dialect (by a black examiner) rather than in standard English. There is increasing evidence that black children are bidialectical in that they have the ability to comprehend black dialect and standard English equally well (Genshaft & Hirt, 1974; Hall, Turner, & Russell, 1973; Harver, 1977; Levy & Cook, 1973).

Although the race of examiners has not been found to affect black children's performance on intelligence tests, examiners cannot be indifferent to the examinee's ethnicity. They must be alert to any nuances in the test situation that suggest an invalid performance. Testing children from different cultures is a demanding task. At times it may be difficult to understand children's responses, and every effort must be used to enlist their best efforts.

With Hispanic-American children. Stereotypes held by the Anglo-American examiner about the Hispanic-American examinee, or by the Hispanic-American examinee about the Anglo-American examiner, may interfere with rapport. The two groups are keenly aware of the differences that divide them, and feelings of resentment — stemming from a mutual lack of understanding — may be present on both sides. Anglos generally do not know much about the customs and values of Hispanic-Americans, nor are they knowledgeable about the conditions that exist in the *barrio* (section of town in which Hispanic-Americans live). The Hispanic-American examinee's language may serve as a cue for group identification, and, like skin color, it may influence the examiner-examinee relationship. Every attempt must be made by examiners to overcome any stereotypes they may have.

The assertion that Anglo-American examiners are not as effective as Hispanic-American examiners in testing Hispanic-American children has not received support. For example, Gerken (1978) reported that neither the examiners' ethnicity (Hispanic-American or Anglo-American) nor their language facility (bilingual or monolingual) significantly affected the IQs obtained by Hispanic-American kindergarten children on the WPPSI or the Leiter International Performance Scale. Morales and George (1976) found that bilingual Hispanic-American first, second, and third graders obtained higher WISC-R Performance IQs when tested by monolingual non-Hispanic examiners than when tested by bilingual Hispanic examiners who gave the test directions in both English and Spanish. The children tested by non-Hispanic examiners also obtained significantly higher scores on the ITPA Grammatical Closure subtest, but not on the Screening Test of Spanish Grammar. These two studies, although limited, do show that Anglo-American examiners do not necessarily impair the test performance of Hispanic-American elementary school children.

Although the studies above provide no support for the assertion that Anglo-American examiners are less effective than Hispanic-American examiners, examiners of both ethnic groups must be aware of stereotyped attitudes toward Hispanic-American children that may interfere with their clinical judgments. For example, a study of teachers' attitudes toward Hispanic-American third and fourth graders who spoke minimally accented, moderately accented, or highly accented English showed that most favorable ratings were given to the minimally accented speakers and least favorable ratings to the highly accented speakers (Carter, 1977). Although Hispanic-American teachers had more favorable attitudes than Anglo-American teachers, both groups had more unfavorable attitudes toward the highly accented speakers. These results suggest that examiners may hold stereotypes about children who have accented speech. Such stereotypes must not be allowed to affect test interpretations and recommendations or to impair the examiner-examinee relationship.

Placement in Inadequate and Inferior Educational Programs

Test results, it is claimed, are used to place black children in special education classes (or tracks), which are considered inadequate and inferior. This argument is based on a number of premises. One premise is that black children who are placed in special classes would achieve at a higher level if they were not removed from the regular class. Tests are held accountable because they are one of the means by which the schools place children in special classes. A second premise is that test results produce negative expectancies in teachers — when teachers learn that black children have low scores, they then begin to treat them as if they will perform at a below-average level.

The role of individual assessments.   Although test results may be one link in the educational chain that leads teachers and school administrators to assign children to special classes or programs, in most cases children are referred for individual assessment only *after* they have performed poorly in school. Most black children, and other children for that matter, are *never* seen for a comprehensive individual assessment. Thus the school performance of ethnic minority children can seldom be linked to the results of individual psychological assessments.

Expectancy effects.   The premise that test results contribute to the development of expectancy effects has some merit. The strength of such expectancy effects must be evaluated, however. The claim that initial negative expectancies produce a self-fulfilling prophecy has little merit. The self-fulfilling prophecy concept received great impetus from the work of Rosenthal and Jacobson (1968), which supposedly demonstrated that children who were characterized as "late bloomers" performed better than other children on ability tests. This study, however, had so many pitfalls that its results cannot be accepted (Snow, 1969; Thorndike, 1968). As Cronbach (1975, pp. 6–7) observed:

In my view, *Pygmalion in the Classroom* merits no consideration as research. The "experimental manipulation" of teacher belief was unbelievably casual—one sheet of paper added to the teacher's in-basket, which apparently moved within seconds to the wastebasket. The technical reviews indicate that the advertised gains of the "magic" children were an artifact of crude experimental design and improper statistical analysis. (No doubt there are expectancy effects in the classroom. The question ought to be whether tests add to bias or instead bring expectations closer to the truth. On that there is no direct evidence.)

Other studies have failed to document this type of self-fulfilling prophecy (or expectancy) effect (Anttonen & Fleming, 1976; Claiborn, 1969; Dusek & O'Connell, 1973; Fielder, Cohen, & Feeney, 1971; Fleming & Anttonen, 1971; Ginsburg, 1970; Gozali & Meyen, 1970). In a meta-analysis of 47 teacher expectation studies, the effect of teacher expectations on pupils' IQ was found to be very small (*M* effect size was .16 of a point for 22 effects) (Smith, 1980). The intellectual growth of children does not appear to be hampered by teachers' knowing the pupils' intelligence test scores. The study of self-fulfilling prophecies in the classroom is quite complex, as it involves teachers' communication of expectations to students, teachers' beliefs about curriculum, the effectiveness of instruction, student motivation, the quality of the teacher-student relationship, and teacher and student individual difference variables (Brophy 1983).

Are special education classes needed?   We must also carefully examine the premise that special education classes for the mentally retarded do not provide the kinds of intervention programs needed by ethnic minority children who are functioning in the mentally retarded range. Do low-functioning ethnic minority children need special programs emphasizing enrichment and verbal stimulation? Do they benefit from the usual type of program designed for the mentally retarded? Definitive answers to these questions are not available. We need to learn a great deal about the differential effectiveness of special programs—such as resource rooms, tutoring, nongraded classes, and learning centers—and traditional programs designed for low-functioning children.

ARGUMENTS FOR THE USE OF INTELLIGENCE TESTS IN ASSESSING ETHNIC MINORITY CHILDREN

Although some of the previous arguments against the use of intelligence tests in the assessment of ethnic minority children deserve consideration, the crucial ones related to culture bias have little, if any, merit. The arguments for the continued use of intelligence tests and other ability tests for assessing ethnic minority children will now be considered.

Useful in Evaluating Present Functioning

Intelligence test scores of ethnic minority children are useful indices of their current cognitive ability. The evidence cited earlier indicates that intelligence tests have little or no cultural bias. They generally have the same properties for ethnic minority children as they do for white children. Tests can provide valuable information about ethnic minority children's cognitive strengths and weaknesses and can help to evaluate change and progress. For example, in cases of brain damage, intelligence and special ability tests help to document the extent of damage (see Chapter 22). Present test results can be compared with past results to evaluate changes as a result of the damage. In cases of psychopathology, tests serve similar purposes.

Doing away with tests would deprive clinicians and educators of vital information needed to assist children. A report sponsored by the American Psychological Association's Board of Scientific Affairs (Cleary, Humphreys, Kendrick, & Wesman, 1975) stressed the importance of evaluation in education: "*Diagnosis, prognosis, prescription, and measurement of outcomes are as important in education as in medicine*" (p. 18, italics added).

Useful in Indicating Future Functioning

Standardized intelligence tests provide good indices of future levels of academic success and performance as defined by the majority culture.

Useful in Obtaining Special Programs

Tests can be useful in obtaining special enrichment programs and services for ethnic minority children as well as other children. Abandoning formal assessment procedures may deprive handicapped ethnic minority children of the opportunity to obtain appropriate attention and services to which they are legally entitled. The problem of poor achievement of black inner-city children is real. It has not been caused by tests. Tests have been helpful in documenting the severity of the educational deficits. As Green (1978, p. 669) noted, "The tests are not bigoted villains but color-blind measuring instruments that have demonstrated a social problem to be solved."

Useful in Evaluating Programs

Tests evaluate the outcomes of school and special programs. They can be used to determine whether children have learned to read or to perform arithmetical operations. Thus tests serve as a means of providing objective evidence of school accountability. "*As such, far from being a part of the problem, tests are an absolutely essential part of the solution*" (Flaugher, 1974, p. 14, italics added). Those calling for the elimination of testing altogether would, in fact, allow the educational system to be released from any accountability at all.

Useful in Revealing Inequalities

By revealing the inequalities of opportunity available to various groups, tests may provide the stimulus for special intervention to facilitate the maximum development of each child's potentialities. Perhaps those in the field of testing now should be less concerned with unbiased predictive validity and more concerned with facilitating equal opportunity.

Useful in Providing an Objective Standard

Tests serve as a corrective device by providing information that cannot be obtained easily or reliably by other means. They give students an alternative means of demonstrating academic ability. Tests also provide a measure that is comparable across schools and across time. Test scores do not depend on the predilections of teachers at a specific school or on a student's interpersonal relationship with teachers. Consequently, tests have helped to prevent educational misplacement of many ethnic minority children.

Ethnic minority groups should favor the use of ability tests; these tests constitute a universal and objective rather than a prejudicial standard of competence and potential. Other selection methods may decrease the opportunities of ethnic minority children. Jensen (1975, p. 67) observed that "objective means of revealing talents stand to benefit talented members of disadvantaged groups the most, since in their cultural circumstances certain talents are more apt to go unrecognized and underdeveloped." Educational tests encourage and reward individual efforts to learn. If tests were abandoned, programs would be difficult to evaluate and educational opportunities might be based more on ancestry and influence and less on aptitude and merit. Decisions on curriculum would be based less on evidence and more on prejudice and caprice.

Comment on the Value of Intelligence Tests

Intelligence tests (and other ability tests) measure the abilities that they were designed to measure with reasonable accuracy for ethnic minority children as well as for children from the dominant culture. Tests have the potential to do much good in our society. Tests assess a child's current intellectual functioning irrespective of race or social status. The consequences of not testing might be to increase bias and discrimination.

GENERAL CONSIDERATIONS IN ETHNIC MINORITY TESTING

The Culture of Poverty and Its Effects on the Test Performance of Ethnic Minority Children

Many members of our nation's ethnic minorities suffer from economic deprivation. Poverty affects maternal health as well as the child's own health and social functioning; both may be related to school failure. Poverty may also affect rate of learning, which in turn influences intelligence and academic success. Figure 19-1 shows the vicious circle uniting various environmental variables with poverty and educational failure. The conditions assaulting inner-city children's central nervous systems include perinatal disease, malnutrition, infection, anemia, and lead poisoning. Blacks also have a considerably higher rate of premature birth and a higher incidence of abnormalities of pregnancy than do whites (Wiener & Milton, 1970).

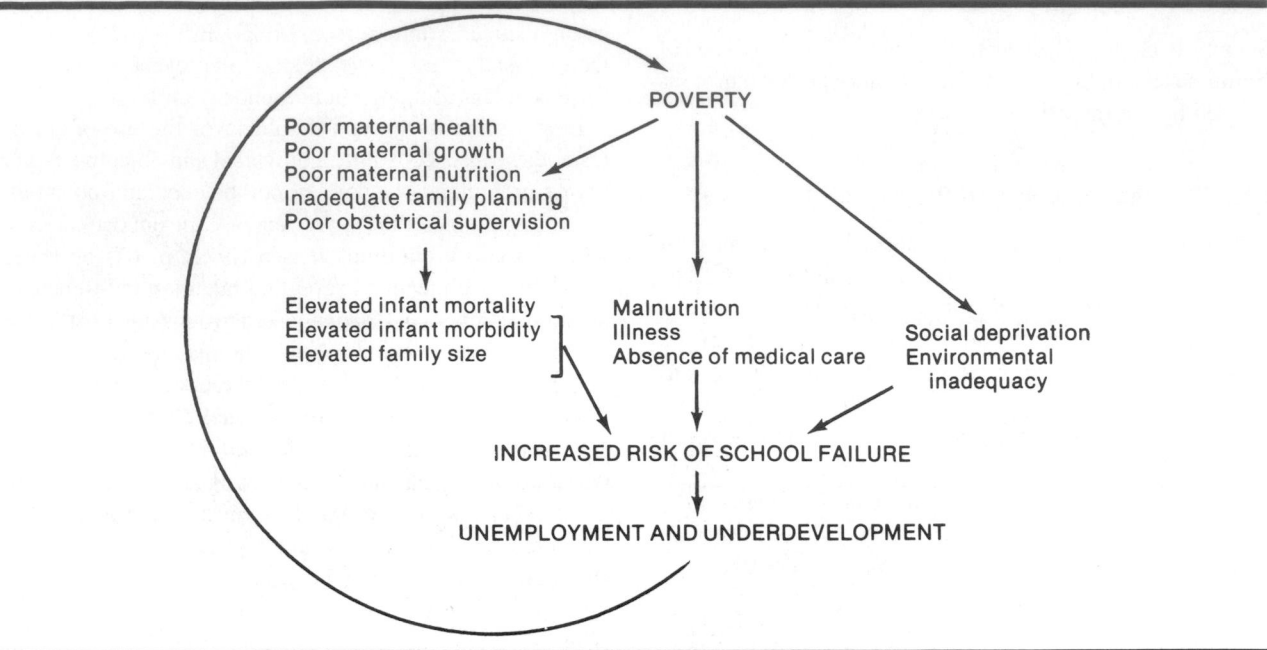

Figure 19-1.   Environmental relationships between poverty and educational failure. Reprinted by permission of the publisher and authors from H. G. Birch and J. D. Gussow, *Disadvantaged Children: Health, Nutrition, and School Failure*, p. 268. Copyright 1970, Grune & Stratton.

Poverty, as such, is neither a necessary nor a sufficient condition to produce intellectual deficits, especially if nutrition and the home cultural environment are adequate. It is only when these and related factors are inadequate that there are likely to be learning deficits. Imagine, for example, what effect poor nutrition and health care, substandard housing, low family income, prevalent family disorganization, anarchic discipline, diminished personal worth, low expectations, frustrated aspirations, and other environmental handicaps may have on the development of adequate intellectual skills. Table 19-4 summarizes some key indications of the culture of poverty.

Elkind's premature structuring and alternate elaboration hypothesis.   Two intriguing concepts—*premature structuring* and *alternate elaboration*—have been offered to account for the lower test scores of low-income and ethnic minority youth. Premature structuring occurs when children "are forced to apply their abilities to practical matters before these abilities are fully realized or elaborated. The effect is to stunt or limit growth" (Elkind, 1973, p. 79). Low-income youth may have to direct their intellectual abilities to practical issues, such as assuming responsibility for their siblings at an early age, and such early application to real-life matters may inhibit the future growth of cognitive skills. Premature structuring is most

likely to occur when children have little or no opportunity to develop their mental abilities.

Alternate elaboration occurs when children develop mental abilities in ways that are different from those of most other children. Some children who live in the inner city acquire a kind of cognitive language that may make it difficult for them to elaborate their abilities "or to learn academic material in a traditional school setting" (Elkind, 1973, p. 81). The following case illustrates how a low-income youth may appear to have limited ability, as assessed by standard tests, but function quite well in his community.

One young man . . . came to the court clinic because he was not going to school and was suspected of pushing dope and of having a couple of girl friends doing "tricks" for him. He was well dressed and smooth talking with a vocabulary rich in the argot of the street and the underworld. He was alternatively amused and annoyed at the test questions, and he did best in arithmetic and worst on the test of general information and vocabulary.

His poor performance on information and vocabulary, however, does not reflect deficiency but rather alternate elaboration. This young man was far from lacking in general information. Indeed, his fund of information in many areas was much greater than mine. The same was true for his vocabulary, which was rich in words not found on intelligence tests. To call this young man deficient in ability would be a gross error. On the contrary, his at

Table 19-4
Some Indications of the Culture of Poverty

Individuals	Community	Family	Feelings and beliefs
Are unemployed or under-employed in a miscellany of unskilled occupations	Housing is poor and crowded.	Families are often female- or mother-centered.	Strong feeling of alienation
Do not own property	Organization is minimal beyond the level of the nuclear and extended family.	Family solidarity is an ideal rarely achieved.	Feeling that existing institutions do not serve interests and needs
Do not belong to labor unions		Childhood is not treated as a specially prolonged and protected stage in the life cycle.	Strong feelings of helplessness
Do not participate in Social Security		Structure is often authoritarian.	Sense of resignation and fatalism
Borrow from local moneylenders			Strong feeling of dependence
Lack food reserves in the home			Feelings of powerlessness
Lack savings			Belief in male superiority
Are chronically short of cash			Martyr complex among women
Are constantly struggling for survival			
Have a low level of education			

Source: Adapted from Kutner (1975).

least average intellectual abilities were elaborated in a subcultural domain that is virtually unknown to the middle-class test maker and user. (Elkind, 1973, p. 80)

Premature structuring and alternate elaboration are possible replacement models for other deficit models that have been proposed to account for the poor test performance of low-income youth. "From a developmental standpoint the mental growth of some low income youth may simply be different in direction and elaboration than that of the offspring of more affluent parents" (Elkind, 1973, p. 81).

Poverty and testing. Formal testing procedures may identify those individuals who cannot compete in our technologically oriented culture. When improperly used, tests can become major instruments for casting out the physically sick, the uneducated, and those with special personal problems. The poor, as a group, are the most vulnerable, and it is *poverty* that is the main shared characteristic of minority groups (Leland, 1971). The adaptive strategies of the poor are not always conducive to good test performance. They may cope poorly with external pressures and experience failure—even in areas where they have some cognitive strengths—because they feel that things often happen to them in spite of themselves and without their participation.

Testing situations may arouse tension and feelings of suspicion in poor children. They may react with aggression or with passivity, but simultaneously may feel that it is important to establish a friendly relationship with the examiner. If they become too preoccupied about their relationship with the examiner, they may fail to give their undivided attention to the test questions. Such strategies leave the poor child ill-equipped to cope with tests. Leland (1971) made the telling observation that when children who perform adequately in their own environment are given a label as a result of testing, the label makes the children visible and begins to create social problems where previously none had existed.

Cumulative deficit hypothesis. The term *cumulative deficit* refers to a progressive decline with age in the measured intelligence or scholastic achievement scores of culturally or socially disadvantaged children relative to those of more advantaged children. The evidence is by no means clear about the extent to which such deficits appear or the ethnic and subcultural groups involved (Cox, 1983). The theory behind cumulative deficit is that children who are deprived of enriching cognitive experiences during their early years are less able to profit from environmental stimulation because of a mismatch between their cognitive schemata and the requirements of the new (or advanced) learning situations. The cumulative deficit theory accords a crucial role to the child's early learning. It is not known, however, to what extent the quality of a child's learning *following* early deprivation can improve cognitive functioning.

Effects of Response Style on Test Scores

Ethnic minority children, as we have seen, may approach the test situation with attitudes and test strategies that differ from those of non–ethnic minority children. Those ethnic minority children who have a tendency not to attempt a response when given a question or to terminate an initial response before completing it are more likely to obtain lower scores than are those who do try to solve the test questions. The scores of those who tend to terminate responses prematurely (giving up with little effort) may be more an index of their "willingness to retrieve information or to problem solve on demand, and less an index of accumulated knowledge and ability" (Moore, 1986, p. 322).

Spontaneous elaboration response style. Moore (1986) describes the importance of a spontaneous elaboration response style:

Children's tendency to spontaneously elaborate on their work responses may be a very important index of their level of involvement in task performance, strategies for problem solving, level of motivation to generate a correct response, and level of adjustment to the standardized test situation. For example, a child may not have learned the dictionary definition of the word "nuisance," but may be familiar with the word from some context. Once the child places the word in an experiential context, the meaning may be inferred and a definition constructed during testing (e.g., "Nuisance, um, that's what my teacher always calls me when I'm acting silly, um, it's something that bothers you, something that disturbs you, like flies; they're a nuisance when we go camping, right?"). The child's elaboration on the definition of a word can serve a number of purposes for the child and tester. First, it can provide feedback to the child on the efficiency with which the problem-solving strategy employed (in this case, association) can be used to generate correct responses to test items, and it can confirm that the tester understands why the child views the construction of the definition of nuisance as correct. The spontaneous extension may also serve as a tension release for the child. In providing the elaboration, especially when generating a response to a demand that challenges the child, the child verifies for him- or herself that based upon his or her understanding of the problem, the response is reasonable and acceptable.

The child's use of spontaneous elaborations on responses indicates to the tester that the child is task focused by virtue of the child's ability and willingness to overtly associate the problem with personal experiences. Such responses also indicate that the child is motivated to provide appropriate responses to the problems that the test poses and is sufficiently relaxed in the test situation to explore different strategies for generating solutions to the problem. (p. 322)

Maternal behaviors and response style. There is some tentative evidence that maternal reactions to response style differ in black and white groups. Black mothers in one study (Moore, 1986) tended to be less supportive than white mothers of child-initiated strategies that did not contribute to problem solutions. Children raised in this environment may believe that "rather than guess at the answer to a challenging question and risk disapproval of adults (such as the tester) for being wrong, it is better to say 'I don't know' or request help from the tester" (Moore, 1986, p. 325). In contrast, the implicit message from white mothers was "It's okay to be wrong as long as you are trying" (Moore, 1986, p. 325).

Perhaps the ethnicity of the child's environment, not just socioeconomic status and maternal education level,

exerts a significant influence on children's styles of responding to standardized intelligence tests and their test achievement. The effects of the ethnic rearing environment appear to be mediated, in part, by mothers through their socialization of affective orientations to impersonal problem-solving situations and the problem-solving strategies they encourage. (Moore, 1986, p. 325)

Bilingualism

Bilingualism generally involves the learning of a second language, although it may involve the learning of two languages simultaneously. Research on second-language learning in children provides no evidence that bilingualism affects general intelligence, although in some individual cases verbal scores may be lowered and performance in English-speaking classrooms may be impeded because of ignorance of words, ideas, and grammatical structures (McLaughlin, 1977).

The effects of bilingualism depend in part on whether children are adding a second language to a well-developed first language or whether a second language is gradually replacing the first language. Hispanic-American children, for example, usually are required to learn English as a second language and then to use this second language in their school work. They continue, however, to use Spanish at home and in the community, in speaking but seldom in reading. Because of this form of bilingualism, many chil-

---

Exhibit 19-2

Informal Assessment of Language Preference

Questions for Teacher

1. What language does _____ use in the classroom?
2. In what language can _____ read?
3. In what language does _____ speak with his (or her) classmates?
4. What language does _____ use on the playground?
5. In what language does _____ write?
6. Overall, how competent is _____ in English?
7. Overall, how competent is _____ in _____ (language)?

Questions for Parents

1. In what language do you speak with _____?
2. In what language does your spouse speak with _____?
3. In what languages do you speak with your spouse?
4. In what language does _____ speak with you?
5. In what language does _____ speak with his (or her) father (mother)?
6. In what language does _____ speak with his (her) sisters and brothers?
7. What language does _____ prefer to speak at school?
8. In what language are the television programs _____ watches?
9. In what language do you read stories to _____?
10. In what language does _____ prefer to be tested?

---

dren fail to develop a sufficient mastery of either language, and learning is more difficult under such conditions.

A number of overlapping informal methods are useful for determining the language preference of children who speak more than one language. First, you may ask the child in which language he or she prefers to be tested. Second, you may observe which language the child uses in the classroom and at home. Third, you may ask the teacher and parent to describe the child's language preference, using questions such as those shown in Exhibit 19-2.

Classifying a child's degree of language proficiency is a difficult task. Although there are a number of formal instruments available for evaluating Spanish-speaking children's language proficiency, few, if any, meet acceptable psychometric standards. Additionally, norms on bilingual assessment instruments are not representative of all groups of Hispanic-American children. Bilingual tests also may show a disparity in how they classify children as to their degree of English proficiency. For example, of a group of first-grade Hispanic-American children, 13 percent were classified as fluent English speakers by the

Bilingual Syntax Measure, 30 percent by the Language Assessment Scales, and 58 percent by the Bilingual Inventory of Natural Language (Ulibarri, Spencer, & Rivas, 1981). Appendix F reviews the Bilingual Syntax Measure, Bilingual Syntax Measure II, Language Assessment Battery, and Language Assessment Scales.

After making an informal and formal assessment of language proficiency, you should classify the child's degree of language proficiency. A useful 5-point classification scale is as follows:

1. Monolingual speaker of a language other than English (speaks the other language exclusively).
2. Predominantly speaks a language other than English (speaks mostly the other language, but also speaks some English).
3. Bilingual (speaks both the other language and English with equal ease).
4. Predominantly speaks English (speaks mostly English, but also speaks some other language).
5. Monolingual speaker of English (speaks English exclusively).

Racial Differences in Intelligence

In 1969 Arthur Jensen published an article in the *Harvard Educational Review* called "How Much Can We Boost IQ and Scholastic Achievement?" which raised a storm of controversy that has yet to be quieted. According to McGuire and Hirsch (1977), this article was responsible for the resurgence of racist thinking in the United States. Others maintain that Jensen's views must not be dismissed lightly (Denniston, 1975; Eysenck, 1971; Herrnstein, 1973; Nichols, 1974). In the ensuing years, Jensen published numerous books and articles defending and elaborating on his position, culminating in his text *Bias in Mental Testing*, published in 1980.

The major points of Jensen's 1969 article were as follows:

1. Intelligence tests measure a highly relevant dimension of general ability.
2. This dimension has a high degree of heritability (about 80 percent).
3. Educational programs have not been effective in bringing about significant changes in this ability.
4. Genetic factors are strongly implicated in the average black-white intelligence difference (about 15 points in favor of whites), although environmental factors still may play a role in accounting for this difference.
5. Teaching methods should be tailored to the child's particular learning skills.

The heritability estimate of .80 for intelligence is based on studies of white persons; consequently it is difficult to know how accurate this estimate is for other racial groups. As noted in Chapter 4, recent advances in genetics suggest that a heritability estimate of around .50 may be more accurate. Heritability estimates based on studies *within* one specific group may have little relevance to an understanding of how genetic variation can account for differences in a trait *between* two or more groups. Consequently, the heritability of IQ differences *between* racial or ethnic groups cannot be estimated at present.

The present consensus is that valid inferences cannot be drawn about genetic differences among races as long as there are relevant systematic differences in cultural patterns and in the psychological environment. These differences influence the development of cognitive skills in complex ways, and no one has succeeded in either estimating or eliminating their effects. Centuries of discrimination have made meaningless the direct comparisons of biological mental ability traits of blacks and whites.

The data from which heritability is established come, in general, from studies of white children attending school or in families in which the value of schooling for a child's future is taken for granted. In general, that environment lacks at least one fundamental feature of the black child's: prejudice, with effects cumulative over generations. The black child is not only exposed to it himself; he is brought up also by parents who are already defeated by it. We have simply no way of estimating the extent of its effect on cognitive development. The direct effect of poverty is the lack of toys and books, and parents with time to talk to the child. The effect must be multiplied in an environment in which hope has been lost. There is no justification for generalizing to this environment from that of the ordinary white child. (Hebb, 1971, p. 736)

Even when social class and economic variables are equated, there are still important differences between ethnic groups in lifestyle and experience.

During the first year or two of life, children exhibit few differences in intellectual functions related to race or social class. At 3 or 4 years of age, however, race and social class differences arise that remain fairly stable during the school years. These findings suggest that "the schools can mostly be exonerated from the charges of creating the black-white difference in average IQ-test performance or of increasing it during the period of school attendance" (Loehlin, Lindzey, & Spuhler, 1975, pp. 156–157). The lower scores of black children may be associated with the increased *g* loading of intelligence test items between 2 and 5 years of age or with certain environmental differences in the black home or community (Jensen, 1975).

The debate about the relative importance of genetic and environmental influences on differences between black and white groups in our country should not obscure the facts that (a) within both the black and the white population there are wide individual variations in genetic potential and (b) there are wide variations in educational opportunity. Furthermore, a heritability hypothesis should not be used as a convenient rationalization for inadequate schooling or for our failure to cope with

the emergence of a growing and self-perpetuating lower class, disproportionately Afro- and Latin-American in its ethnic composition, excluded from the mainstream of American life and alienated from its values, isolated in rural areas and urban ghettos, and dependent for the means of bare survival on an increasingly hostile and resentful majority. (Layzer, 1972, p. 267)

Ethnicity and Patterns of Mental Abilities

An early study (Lesser, Fifer, & Clark, 1965) investigating the organization of mental abilities in various ethnic groups found that patterns of intellectual ability differed in Chinese, Jewish, black, and Puerto Rican children. Chinese children were found to have excellent spatial ability, but were considerably weaker than the other groups in verbal ability. Jewish children's verbal skills were superior to those of the other three groups. Black children were weak in spatial skills and average in verbal ability. The Puerto Rican children's verbal skills were weaker than their other abilities.

Other studies, however, have failed to replicate these findings. Sitkei and Meyers (1969), using a battery of 22 tests, reported that the pattern of abilities of black and white children from the lower and middle socioeconomic classes was essentially similar. Flaugher and Rock (1972) found that a battery of nine cognitive tests given to junior high school students with black, white, Mexican-American, and Asian backgrounds yielded similar patterns of abilities, regardless of the children's ethnic background. Finally, after making an extensive study in which a battery of 10 mental ability and achievement tests was administered to 2,985 Afro-American, Hispanic, Jewish, and Caucasian-gentile high school seniors, Hennessy and Merrifield (1976) reported that there are highly similar structures of mental abilities in the four groups. These findings suggest that intelligence and achievement tests likely measure the same abilities in a variety of ethnic groups.

Development and Use of Culture-Fair Tests for Assessing Ethnic Minority Children

Attempts to develop tests that are culture-fair have not been successful. Williams (1972), for example, developed a

100-item multiple-choice test termed the Black Intelligence Test of Cultural Homogeneity (BITCH), based on items drawn from the black culture. It is a culture-specific test measuring special information about the inner city. Items deal with black slang, which is itself not uniform throughout the country. Two examples are "Boot: (a) cotton farmer, (b) black, (c) Indian, (d) Vietnamese citizen" and "Clean: (a) just out of the bathtub, (b) very well dressed, (c) very religious, and (d) has a great deal" (answers are b for both items). Williams (1972) reported low correlations between the BITCH and the California Achievement Test (Reading, $r = .39$; Language, $r = .33$; and Mathematics, $r = .18$) in a sample of 28 blacks 16 to 18 years old.

Other studies have indicated that the BITCH has questionable validity. One study (Long & Anthony, 1974) showed that a group of 30 black 16-year-old high school students, enrolled in educable mentally retarded classes in Florida, did no better on the BITCH than on the WISC. They scored below the 3rd percentile on the WISC and at the 1st percentile on the BITCH. In another study (Andre, 1976) of 150 seventh graders, both black and white, in a Southeastern urban school system, the black middle-class adolescents obtained higher scores on the BITCH than did the white middle-class adolescents, whereas lower-class whites and blacks obtained the same score. In still another study (Komm, 1978), mean scores obtained on the BITCH by 65 black 13½- to 16½-year-olds in San Francisco were 25 points lower than those obtained by the St. Louis standardization sample ($M = 62$ vs. 87). Furthermore, the WISC-R was found to be a better predictor of achievement as measured by the California Achievement Test than was the BITCH (for example, with Vocabulary, BITCH $r = .47$, WISC-R Full Scale $r = .60$).

The BITCH may be useful for building black pride, but it is not a useful predictor of educational success. The test measures knowledge of black slang, not problem-solving or reasoning abilities. At present, the BITCH does not appear to be useful in the assessment of the cognitive ability of black children.

Tests like the Leiter International Performance Scale and Raven's Progressive Matrices tend to be thought of as culture-fair because they emphasize problems involving pictorial, spatial, or figural content, which many believe may be answered on the basis of experiences that have been more nearly equal across ethnic and racial groups. These tests, however, have been no more successful than special culture-fair tests, such as the Davis-Eells Test of General Intelligence on Problem Solving Ability, the Culture Fair Intelligence Test, and the BITCH, in reducing measured ability differences among ethnic minority groups. Ethnic minorities do not perform any better on supposedly culture-fair tests than on the more conventional tests of intelligence (Arvey, 1972). In fact, black children have as much difficulty on nonverbal tests and on culture-fair tests as they have on verbal tests.

Ethnic minorities may have even less chance of entering educational institutions or of being considered for a job or a training program when culture-fair tests, rather than more traditional tests of cognitive abilities, are used as the selection instruments. The available evidence suggests that culture-fair tests do not show greater validity for ethnic minorities than do more verbally loaded tests, such as the Stanford-Binet: Form L-M or the WISC-R. Culture-fair tests are not the panacea that some believed they would be for the assessment of ethnic minorities.

Probably no test can be created that will entirely eliminate the influence of learning and cultural experiences. The test content and materials, the language in which the questions are phrased, the test directions, the categories for classifying the responses, the scoring criteria, and the validity criteria are all culture bound. In fact, all human experience is affected by the culture, from prenatal development on. As Scarr (1978) observed: "Intelligence tests are not tests of intelligence in some abstract, culture-free way. They are measures of the ability to function intellectually by virtue of knowledge and skills in the culture of which they [are a] sample" (p. 339).

Every test is *culturally loaded* to some extent. Thus it is important to distinguish between a test that is *culturally loaded* and one that is *culturally biased* (Jensen, 1974a). Although, as discussed earlier in the chapter, there is little evidence that individual intelligence tests are culturally biased according to most definitions of bias, tests do vary in their degree of cultural loading. Picture vocabulary tests, such as the PPVT-R, are highly culturally loaded because they use pictorial stimuli that call for specific information associated with a given culture, such as familiarity with the language of the culture and objects representative of the linguistic terms. On the other hand, matrix tests (such as the Raven's Progressive Matrices), digit span memory tests, and maze tests are *culturally reduced* tests, because they are less dependent on exposure to specific language symbols. Even these types of tests have some degree of cultural loading, however—they are neither culture fair nor culture free.

SUBCULTURAL CONSIDERATIONS

Assimilation into the majority culture may be difficult for members of ethnic minority groups because they are physically distinguishable, use a foreign language, and/or have cultural practices that are not always compatible with those of the majority culture. This section briefly reviews material on black American, Hispanic-American, American Indian, and Asian-American groups. Many of the issues discussed also pertain to other ethnic minority groups. Although generalizations about subcultural groups are always suspect and cannot be applied in a blanket way to individual members of a subculture, the information in this section should help you in your work with ethnic minority children and their families.

Black American Children

Blacks in the United States tend to be bicultural, incorporating aspects of mainstream culture and black culture. The roots of black culture in the United States include not only an Africa heritage, but also a survival strategy developed by people required to deal daily with institutional racism and personal discrimination. Black cultural patterns are

also a means of dealing with the bicultural situation of the group, which requires people to learn to live in two worlds, to coordinate the elements of the two traditions borne by the parents, to learn the conventions of two cultures, and to manage the contradictions between them. (Young, 1974, p. 411)

To be black in the United States is to be more than simply a person of black color. The black experience incorporates the collective experiences unique to black Americans, encompassing racism, language, child-rearing practices, role expectations, socioeconomic status, and kinship bonds. To survive in the United States, blacks must be able to size up potentially difficult situations and deal with persons who may be prejudiced against them and perform discriminatory actions. They must be able to interpret conflicting sets of messages and respond to them. Black oriented music, religion, and speech patterns are means by which black children are socialized into black American culture.

Black culture has minimal organization, particularly with regard to status and authority positions (Young, 1974). It is a pragmatic culture. Rather than utilizing specific rule- and value-based behavior, it uses modes, sequences, and styles of behavior that have highly varied content and values. It is a remarkably adaptive culture. The various Afro-American cultures that exist in the United States attempt to retain their self-identity and interpersonal cohesion while constantly responding to the forces exerted by the dominant culture.

Portrait of black culture. Although it is extremely difficult to arrive at a portrait of black culture, Boykin's (1983)

formulation captures some important dimensions. Black Americans have cultural traditions that are based in part on those found in traditional African societies. The African perspective emphasizes (a) spiritualism in the universe; (b) harmony with nature and other people; (c) feelings, expressiveness, and spontaneity; and (d) duty to the group and group property (see Exhibit 19-3). The Euro-American perspective, in contrast, emphasizes (a) materialism; (b) mastery over nature and individualism; (c) control of impulses, self-discipline, and dispassionate reason; and (d) individual rights and private property.

Afro-Americans are then faced with a triple quandary. They are likely to be incompletely socialized in the Euro-American cultural ethos. They typically develop a stylistic repertoire that arises out of their African heritage but is at odds with mainstream ideology. And finally, they are victimized by racial and economic oppression. (Boykin, 1983, p. 350)

The withering effect of racism may lead to major psychiatric problems among black individuals. Family patterns developed in the inner city, which may be adaptive for occupational and economic survival, are likely unsuitable for socializing children to achieve in the middle-class mainstream culture. This quandary is part of the psychological experience of many, if not all, black Americans.

Distrust of the environment. Some black children and their parents have learned to distrust their environment. Distrust develops when they encounter events that place them in an inferior position or that single them out simply because they are black. The tendency to blame criminal behavior on blacks, high unemployment rates, and minimal social or educational opportunities are a few reasons why black families often come to distrust their environment. When distrust exists, it may be difficult to conduct an assessment. Cooperative behavior may be replaced by hostility, and silence substituted for openness. Although you are likely to feel frustrated in such situations, every effort must be made to establish rapport. Changes will likely occur in the attitudes of black clients when they are better able to control their environment and influence the way information about them is used.

"I'd like to think that I'd have my problems no matter what I was, and sometimes I believe it. But sometimes I think it's all because I'm black. I can't be sure. I just don't know. Maybe you could tell me what it really means to be black" (Karon, 1975, p. 165).

Black English. Some black children speak a variant of English that is referred to variously as black English,

Exhibit 19-3

A Portrait of the African Perspective

1. *Spirituality*. Spirituality entails approaching life as though its primary essence were vitalistic rather than mechanistic. It means conducting oneself in a manner consistent with the possibility that the nonobservable and nonmaterial have governing powers in the everyday affairs of people. Permeating all sectors of one's life space is the conviction that greater powers than man are continuously at play. One strives to remain in touch with the greater spiritual essences.

2. *Harmony*. Rather than seeing oneself as distinct from one's environmental surroundings, one sees oneself as, and in turn acts as though one were, inextricably linked to one's surroundings. Rather than striving to partition one's life space into discrete elements, the aim is to blend them together into some kind of organic, harmonious whole. The conviction is that what will happen will happen, mainly because it is supposed to or because it is best that it does. Rather than attempting to maximize one's effort or attain excellence with regard to a single dimension or a relatively narrow range of expertise, one strives to be versatile.

3. *Movement*. Movement is actually a shorthand designation for the interwoven mosaic of movement, music, dance, percussiveness, and rhythm, personified by the musical beat. Music and dancing are ways of engaging life itself and are life-sustaining media, vital to one's psychological health. Also implied is a rhythmic orientation toward life: a complex and multidimensional recurrent pattern that typifies one's personal conduct and self-presentation.

4. *Verve*. This dimension is essentially extracted from the psychological residue of the movement dimension. It connotes a disdain for the routinized, the dull, and the bland, regardless of what ends are served. It implies a propensity for the energetic, the intense, the stimulating, and the lively. It connotes a tendency to attend to several concerns at once and to shift focus among them rather than to focus on a single concern or a series of concerns in a rigidly sequential fashion.

5. *Affect*. Affect implies integration of feelings with thoughts and actions, such that it would be difficult to engage in an activity if one's feelings toward the activity ran counter to such engagement. Also implied is the importance of emotional expressiveness, the affective value of information, and a particular sensitivity to emotional cues given off by others.

6. *Communalism*. Communalism denotes awareness of the interdependence of people. One's orientation is social rather than being directed toward objects. One acts in accordance with the notion that duty to one's social group is more important than individual privileges and rights. Sharing is promoted because it signifies the affirmation of social interconnectedness; self-centeredness and individual greed are disdained.

7. *Expressive individualism*. Expressive individualism refers to the cultivation of a unique or distinctive personality or essence and putting one's own personal brand on an activity, a concern with style more than with being correct or efficient. It implies genuineness and sincerity of self-expression, an emphasis on spontaneity rather than on systematic planning. It is what is being manifested when we witness the gorilla dunk in basketball, or the end-zone touchdown spike/dance in football. It is the expressive essence of the jazz artist or the soul singer. It implies approaching life as though it were an artistic endeavor.

8. *Orality*. Orality refers to the special importance attached to knowledge gained and passed on through word of mouth and the cultivation of oral virtuosity. It implies a special sensitivity to aural modes of communication and a reliance on oral expression to carry meanings and feelings. Words cannot always be interpreted literally, but must be understood in terms of the interpersonal context in which they are uttered. There is a reliance on the call-and-response mode of communication; to be quiet and wait one's turn to speak often implies a lack of interest in what the other is saying. Speaking is construed as a performance and not merely as a vehicle for interacting or communicating information.

9. *Social time perspective*. Commitment to time as a social phenomenon implies construing time primarily in terms of the significant events to be engaged in and not to be rigidly bound to clocks and calendars. It also connotes that behavior is bound to social traditions and customs of the past that serve as guideposts and beacons for future endeavors.

Source: Excerpted from "The Academic Performance of Afro-American Children" by A. Wade Boykin in ACHIEVEMENT AND ACHIEVEMENT MOTIVES edited by Janet T. Spence. Copyright © 1983 W. H. Freeman and Company. Reprinted with permission.

nonstandard black English, or black dialect. Although black English shares many language features with standard English, it has a number of pronunciational and grammatical features that distinguish it from other English language dialects (see Table 19-5). Black English is a fully formed linguistic system in its own right, with its own rules of grammar and pronunciation; it has a rich repertoire of forms and usages. When you encounter children who speak black English, you will have to be extremely alert.

Black English has roots in the oral traditions followed by the African ancestors of black Americans. In many black African groups, the history and traditions of the group were transmitted orally, and the elder who kept this information was a revered member of the community. The value of orality is maintained in black American culture today. Being able to *rap*, *sound*, or *run it down* is a prized oral skill. This holds not just for the street culture, but for every level of black culture. Sources of prestige among inner-city black youth include skill in using language in ritual insults, verbal routines with girls, singing, jokes, and storytelling. Exhibit 19-4 further describes communication patterns within the inner city.

Every effort must be made to communicate with children who speak in black English. In school, some black children may be told that their dialect is "wrong" and standard English dialect is "right." By extension, they may feel that they are inadequate and inferior to other children who speak standard English. These feelings may extend to the testing situation and lead to reticence and even withdrawal. There may not be much you can do to alleviate such feelings immediately, but every effort must be made to be supportive and to encourage the child to do his or her best. You should recognize that those black children who can speak both black English and standard English have a highly developed skill. Black English should not be viewed as inferior.

Black English serves various purposes. It may provide a sense of protection, belonging, and solidarity. It continues to be used because of habit, ease of usage, peer pressure, and group identification. The social distance between black and white Americans also contributes to its maintenance.

An understanding of black English is a necessity for evaluating possible language deficits. Children should be encouraged to speak in their natural language so that valid language samples can be obtained. The results of informal tests should be compared with those obtained from formal tests in order to determine to what extent the child is being penalized for speaking a nonstandard dialect.

Hispanic-American Children

Hispanic-Americans—persons of Spanish-speaking origin in the United States—comprise the fastest growing ethnic minority group in the United States. They currently constitute the second largest ethnic group, after blacks. Approximately 19 million people of Spanish origin live in the United States, roughly 8 percent of the total population. The Hispanic-American populations in the United States are not homogeneous. The major groups are the Mexican-Americans (Chicanos), Puerto Ricans, Cubans, and people from Central and South America.

Mexican-Americans are the largest Hispanic group, with approximately 12 million concentrated in five southwestern states—California, Texas, Arizona, Colorado, and New Mexico. The largest concentration of Mexican-Americans, approximately 40 percent, is in California. One important feature of the Mexican-American population is that the median age is 21.8 years, compared with a

Table 19-5
Some Differences Between Black English and Standard English

Black English		Standard English	
Usage	*Example*	*Usage*	*Example*
1. Uses the verb *got*	The girls got a cat.	1. Uses the verb *have*	The girls have a cat.
2. Omits *is* and *are*	The cat in the wagon.	2. Uses *is* and *are*	The cat is in the wagon.
3. Omits the third person singular ending *-s*	The man ask the boy what to wear.	3. Uses the *-s* verb ending	The man asks the boy what to wear.
4. Omits the *-ed* ending	The dog get chase by the cat.	4. Uses *-ed* ending	The dog is chased by the cat.
5. Uses *do*	The girl do pull the wagon to the boat.	5. Uses *does*	The girl does pull the wagon to the boat.
6. Uses *be* in place of *am*, *is*, and *are*	The big ball be rolling down the hill.	6. Uses *am*, *is*, and *are* in place of *be*	The big ball is rolling down the hill.
7. Uses *he be*, *we be*, and *they be*	They be going home.	7. Uses *he is*, *we are*, and *they are*	They are going home.

Exhibit 19-4

Some of Kochman's Thoughts on Inner-City Black Children's and Adults' Communication Patterns

The Channel of Communication

The prestige norms within the culture of the black inner-city child place a high premium on the ability to use words. The channel through which this ability is promoted and developed and through which recognition is given is oral-aural. Expertise via this channel is more highly regarded and developed in black culture than in white middle-class culture. On the other hand, expertise via the written channel, by virtue of the cultural aesthetic that motivates achievement through this channel, is more highly regarded and more extensively developed in white middle-class culture than in black culture.

The prestige attached to men of words—preachers, storytellers, tellers of toasts and jokes, signifiers, "dozens" players—within the black community is unrivaled. A rich and colorful oral tradition is an integral part of the black cultural aesthetic. (p. 239)

Mechanism of Communication

It is perfectly proper and acceptable in black culture for a black man to approach a black woman whom he does not know and talk to her. This is because there is a mechanism in black culture that permits him to do this. The mechanism is called *rapping*, and both male and female roles are clearly defined within the framework of this initial transaction.... (p. 241)

Correlation of Manipulative Ability with Words and Status

Status on the street is not inherited or conferred but has to be earned. Acquiring status is a prime motivation for the black street youngster. Verbal ability, like the ability to dance, fight, sing, or run, is highly prized in the black community because such ability helps to establish one's "rep." At the same time life on the streets is full of hazards, and control over events is desirable. While one is often secure within one's group, intergroup transactions are often filled with uncertainties. Verbal ability helps the black child maximize control in those contexts, especially expert development of the directive function that permits him to establish control over people through the art of persuasion, manipulation, deception, and a developed sensitivity as to what motivates others. Since status is often achieved by this directive use of words, there is generally a high correlation in black street culture between high status and this kind of ability. (pp. 241–242)

The Communication Network

Peer-group influence on the inner-city child, white or black, occurs earlier and is far more extensive than peer-group influence on the middle-class child. (p. 242)

Audience Dynamics

Black speech events such as rapping to a peer group frequently involve active audience participation. For example, the "call and response" pattern and accompanying rhythms, which may also include handclapping, nodding, and swaying, and which derive from the black church service and the role the audience plays in that event, are often extended to secular speech events such as the first form of rapping.... (p. 244)

Source: Adapted from Kochman (1972).

---

median age of 30 years for the United States population as a whole. This fact suggests that the Mexican-American population can be expected to increase substantially in the next several decades.

Puerto Ricans are the second largest group of Spanish-speaking persons in the United States. The island of Puerto Rico was ceded to the United States in 1898, was a territory until 1948, and then became a commonwealth. Puerto Ricans became citizens of the United States in 1917 with the passage of the Jones Act. There are approximately 2 million Puerto Ricans on the mainland, compared with 3 million inhabiting the island of Puerto Rico. On the mainland, they reside mostly in the Northeast (particularly New York, New Jersey, Connecticut, Pennsylvania, and Massachusetts); a great many also live in Illinois. New York state accounts for about 50 percent of the total Puerto Rican population in the United States. Puerto Ricans are an economically deprived group, being at a great disadvantage with respect to income, employment, and education.

Approximately 1 million Cubans live in southern Florida and other states on the East Coast. There are approximately 4 million other Latin Americans who live in the United States, with the largest numbers coming from the Dominican Republic, Colombia, and Chile.

Most Hispanic-American groups share a similar language and Spanish heritage, but they maintain their autonomy and are clearly distinguishable from one another. It is important to recognize that there are differences among Hispanic-Americans, especially between the lower and middle classes and between those born in the United States and those born in other countries. Some cautious generalizations about the Hispanic-American culture relevant to the assessment situation and mental health services can, however, be helpful.

In evaluating Hispanic-American children, consider such factors as cultural practices, bilingualism, speech, rapport, and test translations. The validity of the test results is likely to be affected by each of these factors, with the impact depending on the child's degree of cultural assimilation.

Hispanic-American vs. Anglo-American values.   Although it is difficult to generalize about cultural groups, Anglo-Americans tend to value efficiency, task-centeredness, and individual accomplishment, whereas Hispanic-Americans tend to value human relations, person-centeredness, and open acceptance of affective temperament. Hispanic-American socialization practices emphasize clear norms, responsibility training, and pressure to conform to adult standards. The traditional values are undergoing change, however, as a result of increased urbanization and higher levels of assimilation. Young Hispanic-Americans believe that people can actively control their fate, that planning for the future brings rewards, that trust can be placed in people other than the family or friends, and that family ties should not hamper a person's individual career. But traditional values still exert a powerful force and must be considered in working with Hispanic-American children and their families.

Hispanic-Americans, caught between two cultures, may experience severe value conflicts. When such conflicts occur, reactions such as rebellion (for example, the desire to be seen as an American and disassociate oneself from the folk culture) or in-group identification (for example, affiliation with the folk culture and hostility toward American values and symbols) may create adjustment difficulties.

Attitudes toward mental health.   Attitudes toward mental health may affect how Hispanic-Americans perceive psychological services. Because Hispanic-American families tend to be more tolerant than Anglo-American families of deviant behavior and to resist hospitalization and possible removal of the child from the family, they tend to underuse organized mental health services. As a group, Hispanic-Americans institutionalize their mentally retarded children at a somewhat lower rate than do Anglo-American families (Dohrenwend & Chin-Shong, 1967; Eyman, Boroskin, & Hostetter, 1977). The strong group and family orientations of Hispanic-Americans may be counterproductive in those educational and psychotherapeutic settings that are predicated on strong individualistic orientations.

Traditional Hispanic-Americans generally prefer to solve emotional problems within a family context. The pride of the Hispanic-American family (manifested, for example, by a family's not wanting to lose face by admitting that a child is handicapped) may make it extremely difficult even to arrange for an evaluation. Other cultural factors also may interfere with the family's acceptance of emotional or physical disability.

When family members recognize a handicap, they may give the handicapped child special treatment, such as excessive sympathy and overindulgence, and place few demands on the child. Special classes may be mistrusted because they are for "sick" or "crazy" children. "How long will it take to make the child well?" is often the most immediate concern. Much care and attention may be needed to help Hispanic-American families accept the need for evaluation and treatment.

Program objectives should be explained so that the family understands them fully. The fact that the welfare of the child is the primary consideration must repeatedly be stressed. The family may need much support. Value conflicts should be resolved to the satisfaction of the family. The family must learn to accept the child's handicap and to be realistic about the disability. Useful approaches to achieving these goals include initiating intervention programs in the home setting, recruiting other Spanish-speaking parents with children in special programs to assist in orienting new Hispanic-American families, and establishing discussion groups for Spanish-speaking parents.

Economic and social difficulties.   Hispanic-Americans share economic and social difficulties, such as poverty, inadequate employment, segregation in housing, inequality before the law, and various kinds of social discrimination. The parents of Hispanic-American children tend to have less education and less income than the average Anglo-American parents.

School performance.   Hispanic-American children have a lower level of scholastic achievement, a higher dropout rate from school, and poorer reading skills than do Anglo-American children. Hispanic-American children have a higher dropout rate and less formal schooling than blacks, with as many as 50 percent of Spanish-speaking students leaving school permanently before they reach tenth grade. Boys may drop out of school to work in order to help support their families, and girls may drop out to help care for younger brothers and sisters.

Many explanations have been offered to account for their poor school performance, including low socioeconomic status, bilingualism, negative attitudes toward school, negative self-image, low aspirations, feelings of external control, cultural values that conflict with those of the Anglo culture, overt prejudice, culturally biased testing, low teacher and community expectations, low quality of schools attended, lack of appreciation in schools for Hispanic cultural heritage, and differences in cognitive style (Kagan & Zahn, 1975). Which, if any, of these explanations are valid is a matter for future research, but some seem more likely to play an important role than others. Several of these factors may be associated with the culture of poverty and not with ethnic cultural patterns per se.

Suggestions for working with Hispanic-American clients. Non-Hispanic-American clinicians must examine their own values and become familiar with Hispanic-American culture if they are to be successful in work with Hispanic-American children. Observing the following guidelines will help:

1. Learn about the Hispanic-American groups with which you plan to work.
2. Call the children by their right names (Hispanic-Americans are often given two last names, one from each parent).
3. Work with the family.
4. If you do not speak Spanish, rely on an interpreter in a family conference rather than on the child to avoid undue strain on the family and distortions.
5. Recognize that in the assessment situation the Anglo-American clinician is the stranger.
6. Be aware of the fact that the child may be an "hijo de crianza" (that is, the child may be being raised by someone other than the parents).

Non-Hispanic-American examiners can become more credible in the eyes of Hispanic-American families by conducting several informal interviews initially and visiting the child's home. Honesty and reliability will prove most effective in altering any anti–mental health opinions of the Hispanic-American family. Those of you who are patient, understanding, competent, and tolerant will be able to diminish hostile feelings and help the family see that the child's welfare is the concern of all involved.

Language difficulties. Linguistically, Hispanic-American children are a heterogeneous group, with wide variations in the degree of mastery of the two languages. Although bilingualism per se usually does not affect intelligence, many Hispanic-American children have difficulty in both languages. Six-year-old Hispanic-American children were found to perform better on English vocabulary

tests, but not on an achievement test, if their parents spoke both English and Spanish in the home rather than Spanish only (Spence, Mishra, & Ghozeil, 1971). Bilingual Hispanic-American high school juniors and seniors were found to have greater difficulty in learning lists of words in Spanish than in English (López & Young, 1974), a result that may be related to the learning history of the children. Because they are expected to learn in English in school, Hispanic-American children are more likely to develop the coding strategies necessary for rapid acquisition of verbal material in English rather than in Spanish.

Because Hispanic-American children often speak Spanish as their primary language, the Anglo-American examiner may have difficulty communicating with the Hispanic-American examinee. Speech patterns of bilingual Hispanic-American children often are a complex mixture of English and Spanish, and the children may never become proficient in speaking either language. Spanish-speaking children may encounter three types of difficulties when they speak their own language. First, because their Spanish vocabulary is limited, they may borrow from a limited English vocabulary to complete expressions begun in Spanish. Second, they may use *pochismos*—English words given Spanish pronunciations and endings. For example, a Spanish speaker may use the word *huachar* (from the English verb "to watch") instead of the correct Spanish verb *mirar*, or the word *chuzar* (from the English verb "to choose") instead of the correct Spanish word *escoger*. Third, they may have difficulties in pronunciation and enunciation.

Test translations. In an attempt to make intelligence tests more appropriate for Spanish-speaking children, test items or directions have been translated into Spanish. Test translations have some inherent difficulties, however.

1. Many concepts either have no equivalent in another language or are difficult to translate without engendering ambiguity. Thus the meaning of important phrases may be lost in translations.
2. Translations are usually made into standard Spanish, with no provision for dialectical or regional variations. The word "kite," for example, may be translated as *cometa, huila, volantin, papalote,* or *chiringa,* depending on the country of origin.
3. The language familiar to Spanish-speaking children may be a combination of two languages ("Pocho," "pidgin," "Spanglish," or "Tex-Mex"), so a monolingual translation may be inappropriate.
4. Some words may have different meanings for Mexican-Americans, Puerto Ricans, Cubans, and other

Hispanic-Americans. For example, *tostón* means a half dollar to a Chicano child, but a squashed section of a fried banana to a Puerto Rican child.

5. The level of difficulty of words may change as a result of translation. For example, the Spanish equivalent of the common English word "pet" is *animál doméstico*, an uncommon word.

6. Translation can alter the meanings of words. For example, seemingly harmless English words may translate into Spanish profanity. *Huevón* is the literal translation of the word "egg," but the Spanish term has more earthy connotations.

The major problem in translations is to ensure that each translated phrase is equivalent to the phrase in the original language. An important rule in translating is that the translator must have a good acquaintance with the language as used by the prospective examinee. No matter how carefully the translation is done, it is likely to be ineffective if the two cultures do not share similar experiences and concepts.

Studies designed to investigate the effect of Spanish translations of intelligence tests and vocabulary tests reveal no consistent trend. The Spanish test version may result in higher, similar, or lower scores than the English version (Bergan & Parra, 1979; Chandler & Plakos, 1969; Chavez, 1982; Eklund & Scott, 1965; Galvan, 1967; Holland, 1960; Keston & Jimenez, 1954; Levandowski, 1975; Myers & Goldstein, 1979; Palmer & Gaffney, 1972; Sattler & Altes, 1984; Sattler, Avila, Houston, & Toney, 1980; Swanson & DeBlassie, 1971; Thomas, 1977). The results of these studies suggest that translations do not guarantee more valid results. In fact, Hispanic school children often have been found to have poorly developed language skills in both English and Spanish.

Heavily weighted *language-based tests* do not appear to provide the most effective way to evaluate Hispanic-American children's cognitive skills. Hispanic-American children reared in a bilingual environment may not have any "native" language. Although Hispanic-American children often learn Spanish in their early years of life, English becomes, in many cases, the predominant mode of communication in their school years.

Reliability and validity of intelligence tests and tests of special abilities with Hispanic-American children. Most research on the individual intelligence test performance of Hispanic-American children has focused on the WISC-R (or WISC). The WISC-R Verbal, Performance, and Full Scale IQs have been found to be reliable and stable for the assessment of bilingual Hispanic-American chil-

dren (Dean, 1977e, 1979b; Elliott, Piersel, Witt, Argulewicz, Gutkin, & Galvin, 1985). The three IQs on the WISC-R also have been found to have predictive validity for Hispanic-American children with respect to such criteria as performance on the Peabody Individual Assessment Test, Wide Range Achievement Test, and Iowa Test of Basic Skills (Dean, 1977a, 1979b; Reynolds & Gutkin, 1980a). In addition, factor analysis of the WISC-R supports its construct validity for Hispanic-American school children who have been referred for psychological testing (Gutkin & Reynolds, 1980).

The Block Design subtest may have the most cross-cultural validity of any of the WISC-R subtests for Hispanic-American children. This subtest has been found to correlate significantly with classroom performance (Morales & George, 1976) and with mathematical ability (Buriel, 1978). Studies almost universally report that Hispanic-American children obtain higher Performance IQs than Verbal IQs (Dean, 1979a; Gerken, 1978; Milne, 1975; Reynolds & Gutkin, 1980a; Swanson & DeBlassie, 1971). This latter finding is probably associated with the language difficulties experienced by Hispanic-American children.

Other individually administered intelligence tests that have been shown to be reliable and valid in the assessment of Hispanic-American children include the McCarthy Scales of Children's Abilities (Laosa, 1984; Valencia & Rothwell, 1984) and Raven's Progressive Matrices (Valencia, 1984).

The Peabody Picture Vocabulary Test—Revised should *never* be used to obtain an estimate of young Hispanic-American children's intelligence. This test is a measure of receptive vocabulary, not of general intelligence. There is no evidence that the PPVT-R provides a valid measure of preschool- and kindergarten-age Hispanic-American children's intelligence.

Results obtained from verbal intelligence tests or special ability tests administered in English to Spanish-speaking children should be considered highly suspect unless the examinee's degree of proficiency in English has been taken into account. Because some Hispanic-American children may be reluctant to reveal their deficiencies in English, they may pretend to understand the instructions. If there is any hint that such may be the case, an interpreter should be employed. Similarly, because some Hispanic-American children have never learned to read in Spanish, it is inappropriate to give every Spanish-speaking child written tests in Spanish. For those who have a poor command of English, a Spanish language test and a nonverbal test—such as Raven's Progressive Matrices, Wechsler Performance Scales, Abstract/Visual Reasoning subtests of the Stanford-Binet: Fourth Edition, nonverbal subtests of the

K-ABC, the Leiter International Performance Scale, or the Draw-A-Man—can be administered to obtain an estimate of cognitive ability. A verbal test in English is useful for estimating the child's proficiency in English.

American Indian Children

According to the 1980 U.S. census, there are about 1.4 million American Indians, constituting about .6 percent of the U.S. population. Because of underestimation, 2 million may be a more accurate estimate of the American Indian population, including Alaskan natives. The term *American Indian* is a broad, almost arbitrary category covering over 500 tribes or Indian groups in the United States. The American Indian identity is complex (Everett, Proctor, & Cartmell, 1983, p. 601):

The search for an Indian identity goes in many directions and is compounded by the immediate difficulty of defining an Indian. There is no single definition of an Indian. Individuals vary in degree of blood and level of acculturation. For some purposes one may be an Indian but not for others, and one may be accepted as an Indian by some individuals but not by others. This search for a definition involves both legal and emotional issues.

The primary identification that American Indians make is with their particular group, such as Navajo, San Juan Pueblo, or Eastern Band Cherokee. Because there is great cultural diversity among American Indian groups, they should not be treated as homogeneous. You must learn about the history and traditions of the particular American Indian communities that you are serving if you are to achieve success.

American Indians are an impoverished group in the United States. Their infant mortality rate is twice as high as that for other American infants (32.2 deaths per 1,000 live births), and after the first 27 days of life, the death rate for Indian infants is four times that for white infants (Farris & Farris, 1976). The outlook for American Indian children in schools is poor, and work opportunities are limited. American Indian school dropout rates are double the national average. The median educational level for American Indians is 9.8 years, in contrast to 12.1 years for the white population. Median educational levels for Indian groups vary from 3 years among some nonurban groups to 11 years or more among some urban and other nonurban groups. Their low scholastic achievement may be related to cultural conflict, motivational differences, and emotional maladjustment, including alienation from self and the community. American Indian children face a future with restricted opportunities, and unless radical changes are made in society's treatment of the Indian, few, if any, significant improvements will occur.

Cultural values. Part of the cultural conflict between Indians and the majority culture involves differences in values. The values of the American Indian child may include (a) a desire for harmony with nature instead of a mastery over nature, (b) an orientation toward the present time rather than a future time, (c) a tendency to explain natural phenomena by mythology and sorcery rather than by science, together with a fear of the supernatural, (d) an aspiration to follow in the ways of old people and to cooperate and maintain the status quo rather than to compete and climb the ladder of success, (e) a preference for anonymity and submissiveness over individuality and aggression, and (f) a desire to satisfy present needs and to share, rather than to work to get ahead and save for the future (Zintz, 1962).

Other culturally based tendencies of American Indians relevant to mental health service delivery include the following (Everett et al., 1983): (a) attaching a great deal of importance to the extended family; (b) using a noncoercive and noninterfering parenting style (allowing children to develop freely); (c) providing children with warmth and support; (d) ignoring or shunning children who misbehave or correcting them quietly or verbally rather than by using physical punishment (although child-rearing patterns vary from traditional to assimilated patterns); (e) respecting individuality by observing a principle of noninterference (direct interventions are antithetical to this principle) while still being sensitive to group values; (f) valuing modesty and humility in the presence of others (for example, not talking about assets or things done well, not readily identifying strengths and assets during an interview); (g) emphasizing giving, sharing, and cooperating (holding a nonmaterialistic view of life and eschewing competition); (h) viewing time in a spatial rather than a linear way (time moves not by the hands of a clock but by natural phenomena, the occurrence of events, the location in space of these events, and the internal feelings of synchronicity); (i) valuing childhood and old age; and (j) attaching importance to religion (belief in a supreme force and deep reverence for nature, with much mysticism—belief in spirits, spells, hexes, anthropomorphism, and reincarnation).

The following case illustrates the importance of understanding cultural differences and avoiding cross-cultural misinterpretations:

This 7-year-old boy was referred by his teacher to a psychologist because of his withdrawn, sullen behavior. This child seldom raised his hand in class and avoided eye contact with teachers. He was also reportedly not as competitive in recess play as the teacher thought he should be. The teacher perceived this behavior as depressed and as a sign of psychological disturbance. Such behaviors were not interpreted within the context of this child's more traditional rearing in a rural area of Oklahoma. Fortunately, the psychologist appreciated the role that culture played in this child's behavior. Although this child was not clinically depressed, he was clearly unhappy about the many demands on him that were inconsistent with his culture. Consultation with the teacher was an important part of the intervention, and changing the teacher's expectations and reactions improved this Indian child's affect and school performance and behavior. (Everett et al., 1983, p. 597)

Cultural conflict poses special problems for American Indian children and their families, particularly upon entering into Anglo schools and during adolescence. In working with American Indians, be aware of the varied styles along the acculturation continuum and the position of the child and family along that continuum.

One cannot for long have one's feet placed in two canoes.
— Iroquois saying

Problems in assessment.   American Indians may approach non-Indian clinicians with apprehension, mistrust, and even hostility (Everett et al., 1983). Such attitudes will be major barriers to an effective assessment and to the delivery of mental health services. Unless trust is established, the assessment results may have little, if any, value.

Communicating with American Indian children and their families may be difficult because there is no universal, traditional Indian language (Everett et al., 1983). Each tribe is likely to have its own language, and within a tribe different dialects may exist. American Indians differ in their command of the English language. "As with any bilingual group, these abilities range from a very articulate command of English to that of a limited receptive vocabulary and little or no expressive vocabulary" (Everett et al., 1983, p. 592).

American Indians' communication styles differ from those found in the Anglo culture (Everett et al., 1983). It is disrespectful for American Indians, but not for Anglo-Americans, to make eye contact. American Indians, but not Anglo-Americans, view a firm handshake as aggressive and disrespectful. American Indians perceive an interviewer's asking of direct questions (as occurs when a social history is being taken) as rude or incompetent, preferring that the interviewer share personal information about himself or herself (self-disclosure); Anglos accept direct interrogation and an impersonal interviewer style. American Indians may be slow in accepting help, may maintain long silences during the interview, and may be sensitive to the timing of discussion topics. Anglos, in contrast, may have little hesitation about accepting help and expressing their concerns and feelings, and they may

be less sensitive to how topics are broached. American Indians may be more sensitive to the clinician's nonverbal behavior than Anglos. Everett et al. (1983) recommend that "Sincerity and patience, although always important, may be especially so when working with traditional American Indians" (p. 594).

Because American Indian children's command of English may be limited, they may have difficulty in understanding test questions. English-speaking examiners, in turn, may experience difficulties in communicating with those Indian children who speak a native language and have limited knowledge of English. Some Indian children may be hesitant to speak or may speak softly, and their responses may be short and lack important details. They may work slowly, attempting to be sure that they make few errors. Some Indian children may be more fearful of making a mistake than are white children.

Studies of intelligence and academic ability.   Studies of the intellectual ability of American Indian children uniformly indicate that they obtain higher scores on performance tests than on verbal tests (McShane & Plas, 1984; Teeter, Moore, & Petersen, 1982). This pattern of achievement may be a reflection of language, cultural, and experiential factors that diverge from those of the norm group. Specifically, American Indian children may have a visual style of learning and limited familiarity with English. The degree of discrepancy between verbal and performance abilities may also be an indication of the degree of acculturation that has taken place. Better performance than verbal skills may be adequate for traditional ways, but inadequate for the requirements of a highly technological society.

American Indian children may obtain WISC-R Performance Scale IQs that are as much as 25 to 30 points higher than their Verbal Scale IQs (McShane & Plas, 1984; Teeter et al., 1982). Similarly, their PPVT-R scores may be much below scores obtained on performance tests (Naglieri & Yazzie, 1983). Thus it is important to examine carefully the IQs generated by different tests. Verbal tests should seldom be used alone to estimate American Indian children's level of cognitive ability. As with Hispanic-American children, the PPVT-R should never be used with young American Indian children to obtain an estimate of intelligence. In addition to the Stanford-Binet: Fourth Edition or Wechsler scales, the Draw-A-Man Test and, on some occasions, other nonverbal tests, such as Raven's Progressive Matrices or the K-ABC, can be used to evaluate the cognitive skills of Indian children. Because American Indian children's visual-spatial abilities are much better developed than their verbal skills, misleading results may be obtained

From M. L. Arkava and M. Snow, *Psychological Tests and Social Work Practice*, 1978, p. 39. Courtesy of Charles C Thomas, Publisher, Springfield, Illinois.

if reliance is placed primarily on the scores provided by verbal tests.

Asian-American Children

Asian-Americans include members of Japanese, Chinese, Philippino, Korean, Asian-Indian, and Vietnamese groups. There are approximately 3,260,000 Asian-Americans living in the United States. Although it is difficult to generalize about such diverse groups, Asian-Americans all face the problems of racism and discrimination. (This section is based on Sue, 1981, and primarily pertains to Chinese and Japanese groups.)

There is a bimodal distribution of wealth among Asian-Americans, with some families living close to poverty and others enjoying economic success. Educationally, Asian-Americans tend to do well in the physical sciences but poorly in subjects requiring mastery of the English language. Like Hispanic-Americans, Asian-Americans tend to underutilize mental health services and may have difficulties in speaking and understanding English.

Importance of the family.   Some Asian-Americans carry on the traditions and customs of their forefathers. One tradition is to view ancestors and elders with great respect. The father is the traditional head of the household, and his authority is unquestioned. Male and female children have different allegiances after they marry: the male to the family in which he was born, the female to the family into which she marries.

Asian-American families tend to be conservative, to resist change, and to stress high achievement. Family roles are rigidly defined. Problems are not confronted directly, and efforts are made to avoid offending others. The restraining of emotions is emphasized, particularly in Chinese culture. The family has great importance, and the reputation of individual family members reflects on the entire family. Techniques such as the induction of guilt, shame, and appeals to obligation are used to keep family members in line.

Problems of assimilation.   Assimilation and acculturation produce conflicts among Asian-Americans. For example, Anglo-Americans tend to view restraint of feelings in a negative light (as being passive and inhibited), which causes confusion in Asian-Americans about how they should behave. The way such conflicts are resolved plays an important role in the adjustment of Asian-Americans. Clashes with the dominant society, such as the internment of Japanese-Americans during World War II, have led to the suppression of self-expression among some Asian-Americans. They have come to value silence and inconspicuousness when dealing with the Anglo-American culture.

Contrasts between Anglo-American and Asian-American character traits.

In comparison with Anglo-Americans, Asian-Americans tend (a) to be more practical in approaching problems; (b) to favor concrete and well-structured ideas that have immediate practical application; (c) to be less autonomous and more dependent, conforming, and obedient to authority; (d) to be more inhibited, reserved, and law abiding; (e) to be more withdrawn from social contacts and responsibilities and to experience social alienation; (f) to emphasize formality in interpersonal relationships; and (g) to view outsiders with suspicion.

Utilization of mental health and psychoeducational services.

The low rates of psychiatric hospitalization and juvenile delinquency among Asian-Americans likely reflect cultural values and not low rates of psychopathology. Public admission of personal problems may be difficult for many Asian-Americans because such admission might bring shame on the family. When mental health problems exist, Asian-Americans tend to express them via physical complaints. In working with children from Asian-American groups, you will need to consider the family and how they view the child's difficulties.

RECOMMENDATIONS FOR ASSESSING ETHNIC MINORITY CHILDREN

Following are some recommendations for assessing ethnic minority children.

Improving the Clinician's Role

• Learn as much as you can about the child's ethnic group and culture, with particular emphasis on the group's preferences. Those of you who are able to help children develop pride in their native language and culture will be making an important contribution to the educational process. The ability to speak Spanish will facilitate the testing of Hispanic-American children with minimal proficiency in English.

• Recognize any stereotypes that you may have about the child's ethnic group and take precautions to ensure that your preconceived images or notions do not interfere with your work.

• Try to understand the ethnic group's viewpoint, and

accept the premise that each child must be given an equal opportunity to achieve to the limits of his or her capacity.

Optimizing the Testing Situation

• Determine the child's preferred language before beginning the formal assessment.

• Make every effort to enlist the child's motivation and interest by helping him or her to feel as comfortable as possible in the assessment situation. You should take as much time as is needed to ensure the child's cooperation. If at all possible, the clinician should be someone who is familiar to the child.

• Choose your tests carefully and use a multimethod assessment approach — never base your findings and recommendations on one test, one score, or one assessment procedure only. Neither a single score nor any small number of scores can provide an adequate picture of the intellectual abilities of a child. A sampling of cognitive abilities is especially important in evaluating the strengths and weaknesses of children from educationally different backgrounds, because there may be more variability in their patterns of abilities than in the patterns of children who are from the dominant culture.

• Use an appropriate balance between formal and less formal assessment techniques. Standardized tests should be supplemented with information obtained from observations and interviews and from narrative self-reports, autobiographic reports, actual work samples, and anecdotal information.

• Use testing-of-limits procedures. It may be helpful to know to what extent children can profit from help and from extra testing procedures.

Using Tests Appropriately

• In testing children who have learned a language other than English in the home, administer a language test in the language spoken by the child *and* a nonlanguage performance scale; never use a nonlanguage test or a language test exclusively. In testing a bilingual child, administer intelligence tests in both languages on the assumption that the ability repertoires in the separate languages will rarely overlap completely. Unfortunately, there are few objective psychometric techniques for accomplishing this goal.

• Never view test scores as an index of the child's personal worth; this is the most pernicious use of tests.

Interpreting Data Appropriately

• Know when to include the child's extended family in

the interviews, in the gathering of clinical material, and in the interpreting of test information.

• Recognize that principles of test interpretation that apply to the non-minority group may not be applicable to all ethnic minority groups.

• Be flexible in your interpretations.

• Know the research findings about how children from specific ethnic groups perform on the tests that you have selected.

• Take into account the degree of acculturation, which will be determined in part by assimilation pressures on the group's ecology and how the pressures are resisted. Recognize that acculturation will take different forms among different ethnic groups and subgroups.

Implementing Effective Interventions

• Focus assessment on discovering ways to help children. The emphasis should be on gaining knowledge about children, improving instruction, and helping children develop their potentialities rather than on screening, classification, and selection. Implementing these (and other) aims may reduce some of the current objections to intelligence and achievement testing.

• Never recommend that children who have a limited command of English be placed in special education classes for the mentally retarded unless the results leave little room for question. You should be extremely wary of identifying children whose native language is not English as mentally retarded when the tests require understanding of English — either in the test items or in the test directions. If nonverbal tests are used, you should be certain that the child understands the test directions, and that the test items do not require familiarity with the English language.

• Before considering special class placement, give careful consideration to test results, adaptive behavior information, classroom performance, medical and family history, and cultural patterns. Although this recommendation applies to all children, it is especially important to follow for children from ethnic minority groups.

Considering Broader Societal Issues

We need to strive to eliminate social inequalities and prejudice from our society. Rather than attack intelligence and other ability tests, we should focus on the environmental problems that have created the intellectual and academic disparities. Improving the quality of education and changing attitudes toward learning in the home may go a long way toward improving test scores and changing attitudes toward testing. As Wesman (1972) observed: "*If tests re-*

veal that the disadvantaged have been deprived of opportunities to learn fundamental concepts, the remedy is to provide those opportunities—not do away with the source of the information" (p. 401, italics added). Additionally, "*The remedy for the ills of society is not to dispense with diagnosis; it is to treat the ills*" (p. 402, italics added).

Tests that will help to evaluate the psychological processes by which children learn need to be developed. Present tests sample primarily what children have already learned. New tests or procedures are needed that will lead to prescriptions for each individual child. Tests developed in the future should be properly constructed and empirically validated on ethnic minority children. These children should be represented in the standardization sample. Tests are needed that can evaluate the thought processes, modes of perceiving, and modes of expression of children from different cultures. These tests should recognize differing cultural contents. The development of culture-specific tests for distinctive cultural groups in the United States may assist in the assessment process. At present, however, there is no evidence that such tests have a sufficient degree of reliability and validity or that they can assist in furthering our understanding of the abilities of ethnic minority children.

Assessments may improve when educational systems become more responsive to the attitudes, perceptions, and behaviors of ethnic minority children. Additionally, parents should be encouraged to become more involved in the educational process and helped to learn more effective ways of reinforcing their child's achievements.

Teachers must understand that the educational difficulties displayed by ethnic minority children represent a difference rather than a deficit in intelligence.

Gains in scholastic aptitude should be encouraged through educational strategies, such as instruction in the use of concepts and the development of verbal problem-solving strategies, training in study habits, and the development of achievement motivation, field independence, reflectivity, and delay of gratification. Ethnic minority children who perform poorly on intelligence and ability tests are still growing intellectually; they need the best educational programming available to increase their academic skills.

COMMENT ON ASSESSMENT OF ETHNIC MINORITY CHILDREN

There are many challenges in assessing children from ethnic minority groups. We know that many ethnic minority children are different from non-minority children, but we are not sure *how* or *why* they are different or *what* these differences may mean with respect to test administration and interpretation.

Intelligence tests deal with only a certain part of the broad spectrum of abilities labeled *intelligence*; they measure primarily problem-solving and abstract abilities. Other indices of intelligent behavior should also be considered (see Chapters 3 and 4). Ethnic minority children must be given the full benefit of a battery of assessment techniques. The evaluation should tap all available sources of information. Intelligence tests, as imperfect as they undoubtedly are, are a first step toward better understanding and measurement of important aspects of human nature.

The most efficacious way of treating scholastic deficiencies may be to develop teaching procedures geared to the individual strengths of each child; tests can help to determine the best kinds of learning approaches.

We need to know . . . the extent to which deficits . . . can be overcome for a given function, in a given person, at a given period of development. Related to these needs are the choice of techniques to use, how long the remediation will take, and the amount the remediation will cost. (Humphreys, 1975, p. 126)

Assuming there is a need to evaluate ethnic minority children, which test or tests can be used? Some minority group members do not appear to accept any of the available standardized intelligence tests. Although educators and psychologists must be responsive to the needs of minority group children, they should not abandon the use of tests in clinical and psychoeducational assessments. The shortcomings of using standardized intelligence tests with ethnic minority children have been discussed in this chapter, and recommendations have been presented that may pave the way for more appropriate uses of tests. I believe that standardized intelligence and special ability tests should be used, but only with recognition of their shortcomings and difficulties when applied to the evaluation of children from ethnic minority groups. Tests should be used if the potential exists for them to contribute to the development of the child. Obviously, tests should never be used when they would physically or emotionally harm any child.

As Cole (1981) noted, "The concern with test bias has arisen out of a broad social concern with equitable treatment of special groups in this society" (p. 1074). In her review of test bias research, Cole offered the following conclusions:

First, we have learned that there is not large-scale, consistent bias against minority groups in the technical validity sense in the major, widely used and widely studied tests. Second, we have learned that the lack of such bias means neither that the use made of the tests is necessarily socially good nor that improvements in the tests cannot be made. Third, we have learned that there are still many subtle aspects of the testing situation that we do not adequately understand and that are promising areas for future research to increase that understanding. However, these areas are not likely to yield results with a direct impact on sociopolitical policy decisions. Finally, and actually foremost, we have learned that whether or not tests are biased, their role is only a small part of the complex social policy issues facing the legislatures, the courts, and the citizenry at large. To pretend that these broader issues are essentially issues of test bias is to be deceived. These policy issues require decisions about values that must be made whether or not tests are involved. (p. 1075)

We can hope that we do not lose sight of the importance of our nation's children and of finding ways to help them reach their potentialities. The elimination of intelligence and special ability tests from the schools of our nation will not contribute to this goal. Decisions made about the use of tests should be based on methodologically sound investigations. The evidence from many divergent studies indicates that individual intelligence tests are not culturally biased. They provide a profile of abilities that can be valid for black, Hispanic-American, American Indian, Asian-American, and other ethnic minority children, as well as for white children.

PSYCHOLOGICAL EVALUATION

A brief report on a Navajo adolescent is shown in Exhibit 19-5. Compare the child's Verbal and Performance scores. Notice how the clinician reported the Verbal Scale IQ.

SUMMARY

1. The term *ethnic minority children* designates children who come from ethnic groups having sociocultural patterns that differ from those of the predominant society. These groups include blacks, Hispanic-Americans, American Indians, and Asian-Americans.

2. A multifactor, pluralistic approach is advocated for understanding cultural groups in our society.

3. The issues surrounding the assessment of ethnic minority children are complex and are woven into the very fabric of our society. Assessment results have an important impact on children, influencing their life chances.

4. Arguments against the use of intelligence tests in assessing ethnic minority children include the following: (a) Tests have a white, Anglo-Saxon, middle-class bias. (b) National norms are inappropriate. (c) Ethnic minority children are deficient in motivation, test practice, reading, and exposure to the culture and, therefore, are handicapped in taking tests. (d) Problems exist in examiner-examinee rapport. (e) Test results lead to the placement

Exhibit 19-5

Psychological Evaluation (Brief Report): A Navajo Adolescent

Name: Mark
Date of birth: Oct. 15, 1974
Chronological age: 13-0

Date of evaluation: Oct. 15, 1987
Date of report: Oct. 18, 1987
Grade: 8th

Tests Administered

Bender-Gestalt

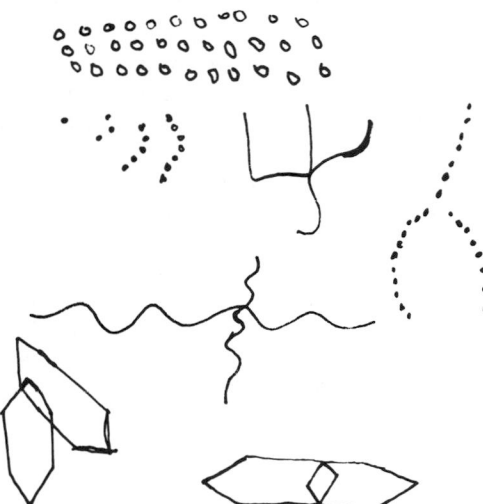

1.	Cat (cat)	10.	(material)
2.	run (run)	11.	(ruin)
3.	arm (arm)	12.	(fashion)
4.	train (train)	13.	(believe)
5.	shout (shout)	14.	(suggestion)
6.	Crect (correct)	15.	(equipment)
7.	circle (circle)	16.	(majority)
8.	heaven (heaven)	17.	(institute)
9.	(educate)	18.	(literature)

WISC-R:

VERBAL SCALE		PERFORMANCE SCALE	
Information	3	Picture Completion	8
Similarities	4	Picture Arrangement	10
Arithmetic	7	Block Design	7
Vocabulary	1	Object Assembly	8
Comprehension	3	Coding	7
Digit Span	9	Mazes	14

Verbal Scale IQ—not valid
Performance Scale IQ = 95 ± 10 at the 95% confidence level
Full Scale IQ—not valid

WRAT—R

	STANDARD SCORE	PERCENTILE
Reading	81	10
Spelling	77	6
Arithmetic	69	2

Discussion

Mark is a 13-0-year-old Navajo Indian whose primary language is Navajo, although he also speaks English. His teachers referred him for possible placement in an educable mentally retarded class. During the evaluation, he seldom spoke, and when he did, it was mostly in short statements. His nonverbal skills are within the Average range (37th percentile), whereas his verbal skills are only at the 1st percentile. Because of his limited English language proficiency, the best estimate of his ability is the Performance Scale IQ. The Verbal and Full Scale IQs are not valid estimates of his cognitive functioning. Academically, his skills are poor, being at or below the 10th percentile in reading, spelling, and arithmetic. Visual-motor development is adequate. Mark needs intensive remedial work, if he is to increase his English language and academic skills. Placement in an educable mentally retarded class is not considered appropriate.

(Signature) _____

Examiner's name

of ethnic minority children in inferior special education classes and create negative expectancies in teachers.

5. Research suggests the following: (a) Studies using both external and internal procedures to evaluate bias indicate that there is little, if any, evidence to support the position that intelligence tests are culturally biased. (b) Although pluralistic norms may have a limited use, national norms are important because they reflect the performance of the population as a whole. (c) Although there is some evidence that ethnic minority children may have reduced motivation to perform on tests, it is not known to what extent this reduced motivation lowers their test scores. (d) There is no evidence that white examiners impair the intelligence test performance of black children. (e) There is insufficient evidence to support claims that special education classes are necessarily harmful or that test results create self-fulfilling prophecies.

6. Arguments for the use of intelligence tests in assessing ethnic minority children include the following: (a) Tests scores are useful in evaluating current functioning. (b) Tests provide predictive indices of future academic success. (c) Tests are instrumental in obtaining special services. (d) Tests serve to evaluate the outcomes of programs. (e) Tests can reveal the inequalities of opportunity available to various groups. (f) Tests provide a universal and objective standard of competence.

7. The culture of poverty may interfere with the development of intelligence. Low-income youth may develop intellectual skills that deviate from those of the majority culture. Premature structuring (attending to practical matters instead of developing intellectual skills) and alternate elaboration (developing mental abilities in ways that differ from those of most other children) are examples of this phenomenon.

8. Evidence on the validity of the cumulative deficit hypothesis—that measured intelligence or scholastic achievement declines progressively with age—is unclear.

9. Ethnic minority children's response styles—such as not attempting to answer a question, giving up easily, or failing to elaborate a response—may lead to lower test scores. Some evidence suggests that maternal reactions to their children's response style differ in black groups and white groups.

10. Jensen's 1969 *Harvard Educational Review* article on racial differences in intelligence was very controversial, particularly with regard to genetic implications. Current viewpoints stress the difficulty in drawing valid inferences about the amount of variance in intelligence attributable to genetic differences among races because of systematic differences in cultural patterns and psychological environments.

11. Research suggests that many ethnic groups have similar ability patterns.

12. So-called culture-fair tests do not provide more valid measures of the cognitive abilities of ethnic minority children than do standard tests. All tests are culturally loaded to some extent.

13. Black Americans have been influenced by traditional African societies, which stress spiritualism in the universe; har-

mony with nature and other people; feelings, expressiveness, and spontaneity; and duty to the group and group property.

14. According to Boykin, black Americans are incompletely socialized in the Euro-American cultural ethos, develop a lifestyle that is at odds with mainstream ideology, and are victims of racial and economic oppression.

15. A biculturation model best explains the behavior of black Americans. This model emphasizes cultural influences that stem from both Afro-American and Euro-American traditions.

16. Hispanic-Americans are the fastest growing ethnic group in the United States. The major subgroups are the Mexican-Americans, Puerto Ricans, Cubans, and people from Central and South America.

17. In assessing Hispanic-American children, consider how (a) cultural practices, bilingualism, speech, rapport, and test translations may affect the findings; (b) attitudes toward mental health may affect the Hispanic-Americans' perceptions of psychological services; and (c) economic and social difficulties may affect their attitudes toward education.

18. Hispanic-Americans tend to value human relations, person-centeredness, and open acceptance of affective temperament, whereas Anglo-Americans tend to value efficiency, task centeredness, and individual accomplishment.

19. Hispanic-American families tend to be more tolerant of deviant behavior than are Anglo-American families. The pride of Hispanic-American families and possible distrust of clinical and psychoeducational services may make it difficult for clinicians to arrange for evaluations and treatment services.

20. Many Hispanic-American families face economic and social difficulties. Those difficulties may contribute to Hispanic-American children's high dropout rate from school.

21. In working with Hispanic-American children, the following guidelines are recommended: learn about Hispanic-American culture, call children by their right names, work with the family, refrain from using the child as an interpreter during a family conference, establish rapport by being sensitive to needs of the family, and be tolerant of living arrangements that differ from those found in the Anglo-American culture.

22. Bilingualism, per se, does not affect general intelligence, although many Hispanic-American children have difficulty in mastering either language.

23. Anglo-American examiners may have difficulty in understanding the speech of some Hispanic-American children.

24. Informal methods are useful in determining the language preference of Hispanic-American children.

25. Translated tests or test directions are fraught with difficulties, such as loss of meaning in the translation, failure to account for dialectical or regional variations, changes in difficulty level, and alteration in the meaning of words. Spanish versions of tests have been found to produce equivocal results; scores may be higher than, similar to, or lower than those on English versions.

26. The WISC-R, but not the PPVT-R, is a reliable and valid measure of the intelligence of Hispanic-American children. Hispanic-American children usually obtain higher Performance

IQs than Verbal IQs, a result that may be related to limited proficiency in English.

27. Assessment procedures must take into account Hispanic-American children's degree of proficiency in English. Nonverbal tests should be emphasized with those children who have a poor command of English.

28. There is great cultural diversity among American Indians. As a group, however, American Indians are impoverished and have a high rate of infant mortality. Their educational level is well below the national norm.

29. An appreciation of American Indian cultural values—such as an emphasis on harmony and present time orientation and a deemphasis on competitive individualism and achievement motivation—will be helpful in working with American Indian children. Awareness of the child's and family's degree of acculturation also will be useful.

30. Assessment problems may arise in the evaluation of American Indian children because of such problems as apprehension and mistrust, as well as differences in language, communication styles (for example, use of eye contact), and work tempo.

31. In evaluating the intellectual skills of American Indian children, emphasis should be placed on scores derived from nonverbal tests, such as those found on the WISC-R Performance Scale.

32. Asian-American is a term applied to a diverse group of cultures, all of which share the brunt of racism and discrimination.

33. Asian-American families, particularly Chinese-American and Japanese-American, tend to stress the importance of obedience and conformity to elders, high achievement, and behaviors that bring honor to the family. Individuality is sacrificed for the welfare of the family.

34. Problems of assimilation and acculturation tend to cause confusion in Asian-Americans about their behavior.

35. The character traits of Asian-Americans include practicality in approaching problems, dependency, conformity, obedience to authority, inhibition, formality in interpersonal relations, and suspiciousness of others.

36. Asian-Americans tend to have low rates of psychiatric hospitalization and juvenile delinquency. These low rates appear to reflect cultural practices rather than extraordinary mental health. Physical complaints are more acceptable than mental health problems. Consideration of the family is especially important in working with children from Asian-American groups.

37. Recommendations for assessing ethnic minority children include improving the clinician's role, optimizing the testing situation, using tests appropriately, developing appropriate interventions, and interpreting data appropriately.

38. The fundamental solution to the problem of testing minority children is to eliminate social inequalities and prejudice from our society. In addition, we must develop tests, validated on ethnic minorities, that better measure the processes by which the children learn and that include items reflective of their culture.

39. Responsible use of tests in the assessment of ethnic minority children (and all other children as well) mandates that the assets as well as the limitations of tests be recognized.

KEY TERMS, CONCEPTS, AND NAMES

Ethnic minority children (p. 564)
Multifactor, pluralistic approach (p. 565)
Cultural bias argument (p. 566)
Mean difference as measure of test bias (p. 566)
Single-group or differential validity (p. 566)
Differential construct validity (p. 567)
Content bias (p. 567)
Selection bias (p. 569)
Use of the wrong criterion for validity (p. 569)
Atmosphere as a source of bias (p. 569)
Overinterpretation (p. 569)
Inappropriateness of national norms argument (p. 569)
Deficiencies in test-taking skills argument (p. 570)
Racial examiner effect argument (p. 570)
Barrio (p. 571)
Inadequate and inferior education argument (p. 571)
Self-fulfilling prophecy (p. 572)
Pygmalion in the Classroom (p. 572)
Useful in evaluating present functioning argument (p. 572)
Useful in indicating future functioning argument (p. 573)
Useful in obtaining special programs argument (p. 573)
Useful in evaluating programs argument (p. 573)
Useful in revealing inequalities argument (p. 573)
Useful in providing an objective standard argument (p. 573)
Culture of poverty (p. 573)
Premature structuring (p. 574)
Alternate elaboration (p. 574)
Cumulative deficit hypothesis (p. 575)
Response style (p. 576)
Spontaneous elaboration response style (p. 576)
Bilingualism (p. 576)
Classifying language preference (p. 577)
Racial differences in intelligence (p. 577)
Ethnicity and patterns of mental abilities (p. 578)
Culture-fair tests (p. 578)
Black Intelligence Test of Cultural Homogeneity (BITCH) (p. 579)
Culturally loaded tests (p. 579)
Culturally reduced tests (p. 579)
Biculturation model (p. 580)
African perspective (p. 580)
Euro-American perspective (p. 580)
Racism (p. 580)
Hispanic-American culture (p. 582)
Speech patterns of Hispanic-American children (p. 585)
Test translations (p. 585)
American Indian culture (p. 587)

STUDY QUESTIONS

1. To whom does the term *ethnic minority children* refer?

2. Critically evaluate the arguments and evidence concerning the use of intelligence tests in assessing ethnic minority children.

3. How does the culture of poverty affect the test performance of ethnic minority children? Include in your discussion Elkind's premature structuring and alternate elaboration hypothesis and the cumulative deficit hypothesis.

4. Discuss how response styles affect test scores.

5. Discuss the controversy over racial differences in intelligence.

6. Discuss the use of culture-fair tests in the assessment of ethnic minority children.

7. Discuss the culture of black Americans as it relates to assessment and mental health services.

8. Discuss the culture of Hispanic-Americans as it relates to assessment and mental health services.

9. Discuss the culture of American Indians as it relates to assessment and mental health services.

10. Discuss the culture of Asian-Americans as it relates to assessment and mental health services.

11. The text presents recommendations for assessing ethnic minority children. Critically evaluate these recommendations.

12. Compare and contrast Anglo-American culture, Afro-American culture, Hispanic-American culture, American Indian culture, and Asian-American culture.

13. How would you go about answering the question "Are intelligence tests biased?"

20

ASSESSMENT OF LEARNING DISABILITIES, ATTENTION-DEFICIT HYPERACTIVITY DISORDER, CONDUCT DISORDER, PERVASIVE DEVELOPMENTAL DISORDERS, AND SENSORY IMPAIRMENTS

The most turbulent, the most restless child has, amidst all his faults, something true, ingenious and natural, which is of infinite value, and merits every respect.
—Felix A. Dupanlowp

Learning Disabilities: An Overview

Reading Disability

Assessment of Learning Disabilities

Attention-Deficit Hyperactivity Disorder: An Overview

Assessment of Attention-Deficit Hyperactivity Disorder

Conduct Disorder: An Overview

Assessment of Conduct Disorder

Nonspecific Behavior Disorders: An Overview

Assessment of Nonspecific Behavior Disorders

Pervasive Developmental Disorders: An Overview

Assessment of Pervasive Developmental Disorders

Assessment of Visually Impaired Children

Assessment of Hearing-Impaired Children

Summary

This chapter reviews a number of childhood exceptionalities: learning disabilities, attention-deficit hyperactivity disorder, conduct disorder, pervasive developmental disorders, and sensory impairments. Background information and assessment considerations are presented for each exceptionality. Effective clinical and psychoeducational assessment rests on a firm foundation of theoretical and empirical knowledge about childhood exceptionalities and psychopathology. This and the following two chapters provide some of this foundation. Texts in the field of child psychopathology and exceptional children should be reviewed for a more in-depth survey of these fields.

LEARNING DISABILITIES: AN OVERVIEW

Learning Disability as Defined by PL 94-142

The term *learning disability* can be used in both a broad and a narrow sense. In the broad sense it refers to learning difficulties that can be associated with any type of factor, including mental retardation, brain injury, sensory difficulties, or emotional disturbance. In the narrow sense in which it is used in this chapter, it refers to the failure, on the part of a child who has adequate intelligence, maturational level, cultural background, and educational experiences, to learn a scholastic skill. The most common learning disability is reading disability. Other learning disabilities are associated with writing, spelling, and arithmetic skills.

The narrower meaning is more explicitly designated by the term *specific learning disability*, defined as follows in Public Law 94-142 (*Federal Register*, December 29, 1977, p. 65083, 121a.5):

"Specific learning disability" means a disorder in one or more of the basic psychological processes involved in understanding or in using language, spoken or written, which may manifest itself in an imperfect ability to listen, think, speak, read, write, spell, or to do mathematical calculations. The term includes such conditions as perceptual handicaps, brain injury, minimal brain dysfunction, dyslexia, and developmental aphasia. The term does not include children who have learning problems which are primarily the result of visual, hearing, or motor handicaps, of mental retardation, of emotional disturbance, or of environmental, cultural, or economic disadvantage.

Public Law 94-142 also indicates that a designation of specific learning disability should be applied only to children who have a severe discrepancy between achievement and intellectual ability in one or more expressive or receptive skills, such as written expression, listening and reading comprehension, or mathematics. (Issues associated with determining whether a learning disability exists are discussed later in this chapter.)

Learning Disability as Defined by the National Joint Committee for Learning Disabilities

The National Joint Committee for Learning Disabilities (NJCLD) formulated a somewhat different definition of learning disabilities (Hammill, Leigh, McNutt, & Larsen, 1981, p. 336, italics deleted):

Learning disabilities is a generic term that refers to a heterogeneous group of disorders manifested by significant difficulties in the acquisition and use of listening, speaking, reading, writing, reasoning or mathematical abilities. These disorders are intrinsic to the individual and presumed to be due to central nervous system dysfunction. Even though a learning disability may occur concomitantly with other handicapping conditions (e.g., sensory impairment, mental retardation, social and emotional disturbance) or environmental influences (e.g., cultural differences, insufficient/inappropriate instruction, psychogenic factors), it is not the direct result of those conditions or influences.

The NJCLD definition emphasizes that the designation *learning disabilities* includes any disorder that may seriously handicap an individual in specific (listed) areas of functioning. The disorder is caused by factors associated with the individual and not with the environment. Presumably, the factors are related to central nervous system dysfunction and are not a *direct* result of other handicapping conditions or environmental deprivation.

Comment on Definitions of Learning Disability

Neither the federal nor the NJCLD definition has met with universal acceptance. Cruickshank (1977), in particular, objects to the inclusion of "adequate intelligence" as a necessary condition for a child to be classified as learning disabled. He conceives of learning disability as a *perceptual processing deficit* that results in a specific learning problem of some sort and involves one or more sensory modalities. Because perceptual processing deficits are not bound by intellectual levels of functioning, he maintains that a learning disability can occur at any intellectual level. Consequently, he considers it illogical to establish an arbitrary cutoff level of, say, an IQ of 80 or higher for defining learning disability. Cruickshank also maintains that children who have learning difficulties due to poor teaching, mother-child separation, and other similar problems should be distinguished from children with learning disabilities that are due to a perceptual processing deficit, which he believes is likely to have a neurological origin.

Various terms used in the federal definition are not clear. For example, "basic psychological processes" are difficult to identify and define. The statement "the term does not include children who have learning problems which are *primarily* [italics added] the result of visual. . ." assumes that clinicians can distinguish primary from secondary causes. But in practice it is often difficult to determine which condition is primary and which is secondary (Berk, 1984). For instance, are the emotional problems of learning-disabled children due to poor achievement, or do children with emotional problems develop learning problems? The term "severe discrepancy" is also open to many different interpretations (see the discussion of discrepancy formulas later in this chapter).

The NJCLD definition, unfortunately, does not markedly improve upon the federal definition of learning disability and guidelines for identification. For example, "significant difficulties" is as unclear as "severe discrepancy"; "due to central nervous system dysfunction" is as difficult to verify as "disorder in one or more basic psychological processes"; and "it is not the direct result of those conditions or influences" is analogous to the exclusion clause in the federal definition (Berk, 1984).

The current federal definition of learning disabilities may exclude children who are physically handicapped from receiving a learning-disabled classification. The definition assumes that when physically handicapped children have learning difficulties, their difficulties are related to physical handicaps and not to information processing difficulties. This assumption is not warranted. The definition of learning disability should be amended so that physically handicapped children are not excluded from learning-disability programs, when such programs are needed to remediate underlying processing difficulties (Padula, 1979).

Etiology of Learning Disability

Five models are useful in understanding etiological factors in learning disability (Aman & Singh, 1983).

• The *difference model* postulates that individual differences in cognitive ability tend to be normally distributed throughout a given population and learning difficulties result from the natural occurrence of poorly developed cognitive skills.

• The *deficit model* postulates that learning difficulties are associated with organic conditions that interfere with learning. These conditions may include mixed cerebral dominance, maldevelopment or disease of the brain, vestibular difficulties, and ocular difficulties.

• The *delay model* postulates that learning difficulties are associated with immaturity in development; eventually, adequate achievement skills probably will develop.

• The *disruption model* postulates that extraneous factors, such as severe anxiety or depression, are disrupting the learning process.

• The *personal-historical model* postulates that the basic skills needed for learning have not been acquired because of environmental factors, such as a failure in the teaching or learning process.

No single model has been shown to explain learning disabilities completely. The models are not mutually exclusive, however; elements of each cause may be associated with other causes. For example, environmental factors and brain damage may be related, as complications of pregnancy are more frequent in groups with lower socioeconomic status. The origins of learning disability appear to be multifactorial.

An Information Processing Model to Account for Some Deficits in Learning-Disabled Children

Information processing approaches to the study of cognition, which are discussed in Chapter 3, are also helpful in the study of learning-disabled children. The four-stage information processing model shown in Figure 20-1 emphasizes the importance of various types of memory in the intervening stages between the reception of information and the output of a response.

The model has a sensory input stage (Stage 1), two intervening processing stages (Stages 2 and 3), and a response output stage (Stage 4). Three memory stores are postulated: a short-term sensory store (in Stage 1), a short-term memory store (in Stages 2 and 3), and a long-term memory store (in Stage 3). Various control processes—such as selective attention, coding, organization, rehearsal, and retrieval—facilitate memory functions and help to regulate the flow of information through the various stages (Hagen, Barclay, & Schwethelm, 1982). The control processes direct the child toward sources of relevant information, arrange material to be remembered in meaningful *chunks*, store information in the short-term memory store, and mediate the transfer of information to the long-term memory store. The stages of the model are discrete; incoming stimuli are transformed, and the transformed (or recoded) stimuli serve as input to subsequent stages.

Basically the process is as follows (Stanovich, 1978, p. 31, with changes in notation):

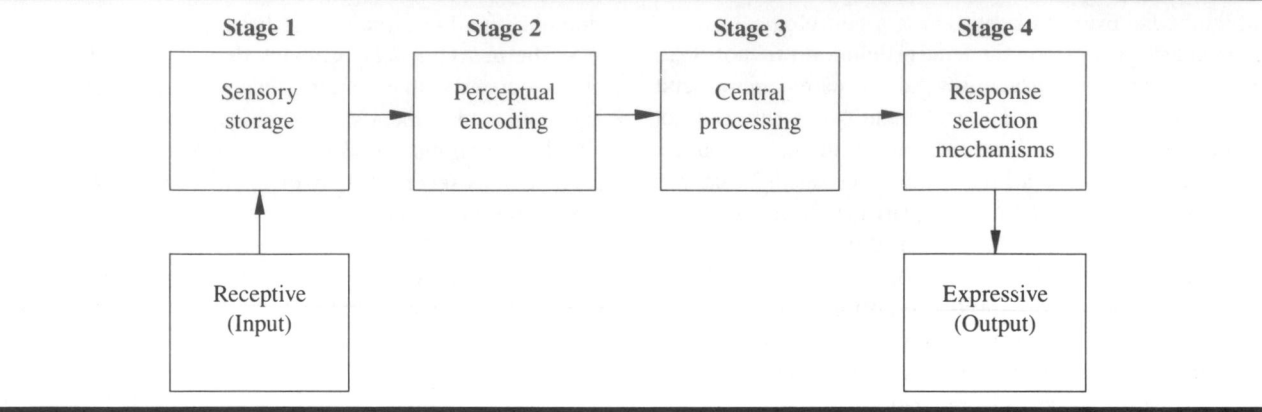

Figure 20-1.   Diagram of a four-stage information processing model. Adapted from Stanovich (1978).

Stage 1. Sensory storage. In this initial stage of processing, the short-term sensory store preserves an intact representation of the incoming information for a brief duration.

Stage 2. Perceptual encoding. In the second stage, the information in the intact representation is encoded into a more permanent representation, probably a name code, which can be held in the short-term memory store. The short-term memory store is a temporary holding area where information is maintained for immediate use or for transfer to the long-term memory store.

Stage 3. Central processing. In the third stage, manipulations of the encoded information and decisions are carried out. For example, the encoded stimulus may be compared with others held in short-term memory, associations of the encoded stimulus may be retrieved from long-term memory, or response codes of the stimulus may be accessed. The long-term memory store has much capacity and is relatively permanent in nature.

Stage 4. Response selection mechanisms. Finally, a response program is selected, based on decisions made in the previous stage.

Deficits Associated with Learning-Disabled Children from an Information Processing Perspective

Learning-disabled children perform poorly on tasks requiring active information processing (Torgesen, 1981). They tend to make little use of such mnemonic aids as labeling, verbal rehearsal, clustering, chunking, and selective attention. They do not attend to or remember central information as well as their normal peers do. Their difficulty in focusing attention may reflect inadequate executive control functions (for example, rules and strategies used to understand, remember, and solve problems, including generalization of strategies and flexible deployment of strategies—see Chapter 3). Those who have a reading disability may also have a deficit in encoding phonological information in long-term memory (Jorm & Share, 1983). The major problem of learning-disabled children may be not so much an inability to attend selectively to materials as an inability to analyze tasks in ways that will result in the best performance strategy. (Difficulty in applying efficient task strategies is not unique to learning-disabled children. Educable mentally retarded and younger normal children also have such difficulties.)

Various explanations have been offered to account for learning-disabled children's inefficient use of actively organized strategies (Torgesen, 1980). One possibility is that learning-disabled children have verbal language processing difficulties, such as difficulty encoding speech. Deficits in memory and attention may in turn be the basis for deficits in verbal encoding and word retrieval and for slow naming. A second possibility is that the development of strategy use is slower in learning-disabled children than in normal children. Because they have only recently acquired basic skills necessary for the execution of a strategy, they have not had time to learn how to apply these skills in a strategic way to facilitate learning (developmental-lag hypothesis). A third possibility is that learning-disabled children come to school unprepared to assume the role of an active, organized learner. Their preschool environment may not have taught them how to participate actively in the teaching-learning process. Each of these hypotheses has merit and should be considered in evaluating a learning-disabled child.

The effects of early failure in school must also be considered. Delayed development of efficient task strategies may be a response, in part, to failure and to the development of a negative self-concept. Learning-disabled children can be taught to use more efficient learning strategies, as described in the next section. Children with effective strategies are likely to discover or make use of the organization present in the material being learned. In contrast, poor learners may have the necessary knowledge and strategies at their disposal, but fail to use them in an effective manner.

Designing Remediation Programs

Instructional programs should be designed to help learning-disabled children acquire problem-solving skills, mnemonic strategies, and good study habits. These strategies should be made part of their repertoire of learning skills through step-by-step instruction and generalization training. Instructional programs must begin with a careful analysis of task functions. Following are some guidelines for designing and evaluating remediation programs (Hagen et al., 1982; Torgesen, 1982a, b):

1. Break large tasks into subtasks and subskills and organize the subtasks into teachable units.

2. Arrange the tasks in a hierarchy from simple skills to more complex ones.

3. Obtain a baseline level of performance before the intervention takes place, using explicit step-by-step instructions to ensure that the child understands what is required.

4. Use performance incentives to increase the rate and consistency with which learning-disabled children apply strategies *already* in their repertoire. Do *not* expect incentives to alter the way learning-disabled children process information.

5. Use orienting procedures to help children retain information or concepts, such as telling children to recall words or pictures by categories.

6. Teach children strategies that will improve their performance, including

• highly specific task strategies that apply to only one type of task;

• mnemonic strategies, such as verbal rehearsal, self-testing, and the generation of meaningful or vivid associations between items to aid retention;

• other school-related strategies, such as strategies for note-taking, planning, and test-taking; and

• broad control processes involved in problem-solving, such as awareness of one's own cognitive processes or reflective problem-solving activities (for example, attacking the problem in an orderly fashion with a question such as "Where do I begin?" or "Is there a problem that needs solving?"), self-monitoring of results ("Does this outcome make sense?" or "What past solution efforts were effective or ineffective?"), and searching for alternative procedures ("What should I try now?").

7. Provide the children with explicit feedback on their performance.

8. Measure the children's performance regularly and compare the results to baseline data, in order to assess the effectiveness of the teaching techniques and materials.

9. Use the results of your assessment as a guide in selecting new teaching techniques and materials.

"Your feelings of insecurity seem to have started when Mary Lou Gurnblatt said, 'Maybe I don't have a learning disability—maybe you have a teaching disability.'"

Courtesy of Tony Saltzman.

READING DISABILITY

Reading is a highly complex process that involves a variety of cognitive functions. These include attention, concentration, ability to form associations within and between sensory modalities, and such overlapping subskills and abilities as phonological awareness, rapid decoding, verbal comprehension, and general intelligence (Stanovich, Cunningham, & Feeman, 1984). *Phonological awareness* (awareness of the sound characteristics of a word) likely underlies the ability to segment and analyze speech, an ability particularly important in decoding unknown words. *Rapid decoding*—the ability to recognize words quickly and automatically—helps the child process information rapidly, thereby freeing the child to attend to comprehending the material rather than to decoding (or recognizing) the words. *Verbal comprehension* is necessary for the child to understand words and word order, a crucial skill underlying reading. And *general intelligence* relates to overall reading skill.

Deficient *semantic* or *syntactic development* will impede the ability to learn to identify whole words, whereas deficient phonological development will impede the development of phonetic decoding skills and code acquisition in general. (Features of words important in the acquisition of reading ability are defined in Table 20-1.)

Reading Disability Defined

Reading disability, or *dyslexia*, is defined as a type of learning disability in which children fail to master basic processes, such as letter recognition and sound blending, despite adequate intelligence and educational opportunities. The definition suggests that the term *reading disability* does not refer to children who are dull, have had poor educational experiences, or have missed schooling. Children in these latter categories may also be poor readers, but they are not considered to have a reading disability.

Subtypes of Reading-Disabled Children

There are three primary subtypes of reading-disabled children: the auditory-linguistic deficit subtype, the visual-spatial deficit subtype, and the mixed deficit subtype (see Table 20-2). Children with *auditory-linguistic deficits* exhibit poor auditory sequential memory span, sound blending and discrimination difficulties, sound confusion, bizarre spelling problems, and sequencing problems. Their primary difficulty is in integrating symbols with sounds; they have little understanding of letter-sound relationships. This subtype of reading disability is the most common one.

Children with *visual-spatial deficits* have poor visual sequential memory, visual discrimination and directional problems, difficulty in spelling words that are phonetically irregular, visual analysis and synthesis difficulties, and spatial problems. Their primary difficulty is in reading words as wholes (perceiving letters and whole words as configurations or gestalts).

Children with *mixed deficits* have problems in both language-related areas and visual-spatial areas.

Table 20-1
Description of Word Features

Category	Description and comment
Graphic	The particular visual patterns of a word that are formed by the unique array of letters that comprise the word (*bad* vs. *dad*). In learning to read, children must store featural information in order to distinguish accurately among printed words.
Orthographic	The internal structural features of a word. These features include structural regularities, such as sequential dependencies (*sta* acceptable, *xtz* unacceptable), and letter-sound correspondences (*at* in *fat*, *cat*, and *rat*). The child who discovers the regularities and redundancies of orthography is developing efficient processing strategies for making fine-grained discriminations among visually similar words (e.g., *fat/rat*, *was/saw*) and reducing the amount of visual information that must be processed in doing so.
Semantic	The particular concept or entity symbolized by a word. Semantic properties are dynamic—they change as a result of the child's experience. It is these properties that make the word a linguistic unit that can be remembered.
Syntactic	The more abstract qualities of a word—those features it has in common with other words by virtue of grammatic rules. Syntactic classes include nouns, verbs, adjectives, and adverbs. Children use syntactic clues to determine whether words make sense in given locations. Implicit knowledge of such markers helps make words memorable.
Phonologic	The particular sound characteristics of words defined by the unique ordering of phonemes that comprise given words.

Source: Adapted from Vellutino and Shub (1982).

Table 20-2
Three Major Subtypes of Reading-Disabled Children

Auditory-linguistic deficits	Visual-spatial deficits	Mixed deficits[a]
Confuses sounds (e.g., *e/i, e/a, p/b, m/n, c/g, d/t*).	Spells phonetically (e.g., *sight*→site, *cemetery*→semetry).	Spells phonetically.
Omits consonants in simple words (e.g., *lent*→let).	Mixes capitals and small letters in spelling (e.g., cAt).	Orientation of letters and words is poor (e.g., reverses both words and letters).
Omits syllables or parts (e.g., *polish*→plish, *ceiling*→cling).	Visualizes the beginning and ending of a word and omits the middle (e.g., *happy*→hapy).	Makes bizarre attempts at spelling (e.g., *circus*→cricksie, *face*→frie).
Mispronounces words (e.g., *chimney*→chimley).	Confuses sequencing of letters (e.g., *guest*→geust, *thistle*→thitsle, *bread*→beard).	Has difficulty in sounding out words and letters.
Uses synonyms (e.g., reads *mother* as mummy).	Guesses at words or says words that look similar or start in the same way (e.g., *surface*→surprise, *transportation*→transparent).	Reading ability is poor.
Omits endings (e.g., *ed, s, ing*).		
Blends sounds poorly when making words (e.g., is slow in sounding out a word and does so letter by letter).	Adds words that are not there, reads through punctuation (hence distorting meaning), and skips lines and loses place when reading.	
Makes bizarre errors—no apparent relationship between the sounds and the letters representing them (e.g., *partial*→transparent, *urchins*→raul).	Usually has a slow rate of perception and reads word by word.	
Reverses letters (e.g., *b/d*) (this category also appears in visual-spatial deficits).	Reverses words or letters (e.g., *b/d, on/no*).	
Visual-perceptual skills are intact.	Auditory-visual skills are intact.	
Verbal IQ is poorer than Performance IQ.	Verbal IQ is better than Performance IQ.	

[a] Combination of the auditory-linguistic and visual-spatial deficit types.
Source: Adapted from Thomson (1982).

The typology described above appears to be the most parsimonious system available for classifying reading-disabled children. Still other subtypes are possible, and not all reading-disabled children will fit clearly into any single subtype or manifest all of the symptoms. These classifications are valuable, however, because they may lead to the development of remediation efforts that are tailored to the specific deficiencies of each reading-disabled child.

Two Syndromes of Acquired Dyslexia: Surface Dyslexia and Phonological Dyslexia

It is important to distinguish between *developmental dyslexia*, failure to develop the ability to read, and *acquired dyslexia*, loss of ability already acquired, usually as a result of brain injury. Two syndromes of acquired dyslexia in children are surface dyslexia and phonological dyslexia (Temple, 1984a, b).

In *surface dyslexia* whole word recognition is impaired (for example, *south* is read as sug, *circuit* as kircute, *bowl* as bowel, *sour* as sowl). Children with surface dyslexia frequently sound words out to obtain their pronunciation and meaning. Short words are processed better than long words. Errors are likely to occur when words with irregular spelling-to-sound patterns are read; homophone confusions are also common (for example, *sail*→*sale*).

In *phonological dyslexia* whole word recognition may be intact, but phonological skills are limited. Children with phonological dyslexia have difficulty sounding words out (for example, *circuit* is read as circle, *bowl* as barrel, *children* as child, *high* as height). Nonwords (nonsense syllables) cause much confusion.

Although both syndromes lead to visual errors, children with surface dyslexia use a phonological route, whereas those with phonological dyslexia use a semantic route. Differentiating between the two syndromes may lead to the development of more precise individualized remedial programs.

Etiology of Reading Disability

The models described earlier in this chapter, in connection with the etiology of learning disabilities in general, also apply to reading disability. Research on possible causes of reading difficulty—including brain damage, maturational lag, genetic factors, right-hemisphere dominance, ocular factors, environmental factors, and behavioral factors—is inconclusive with respect to the etiology of reading disorders (see Table 20-3). Like learning disabilities in general, reading disability is likely to be multifactorial in origin. Much remains to be learned about the mysteries of reading disability.

A Progression of Reading Skills

Learning to read likely involves the successive acquisition of a number of hierarchically organized skills that are finally integrated. The stages in learning to read are as follows (Vernon, 1979):

1. Differentiating and identifying the individual letter shapes or graphemes. This process involves abstracting and generalizing significant features and ignoring irrelevant features.

2. Learning to associate graphemes with appropriate phonemes and breaking whole words down into sounds.

Table 20-3
A Summary of Research Findings on Etiological Components of Reading Disability

Etiological component	Findings
Physiological Factors	
Brain damage	Studies suggest that moderate to severe brain damage is likely associated with reading disability. The degree of association is not strong, however. Many children with mild or subtle neurological damage do not have reading difficulty.
Maturational lag	Studies indicate that children with reading disability display lags on psychological and other behavioral tests. Studies are unclear, however, about whether children with reading disability will catch up to their peers. We do not know whether the lags reflect true maturational delay or are symptoms of a general neurological dysfunction.
Genetic inheritance	Studies in this area have been poorly designed. Therefore, it is difficult to estimate the degree to which genetic factors affect reading disability. It is unclear whether genetic factors affect reading independent of intelligence or whether reading difficulty is part of a more pervasive picture influenced in part by low intelligence.
Cerebral dominance	Studies indicate that few generalizations can be made about the role of cerebral asymmetry in reading disorders. Conceptual and methodological problems plague this area of research.
Ocular factors	Studies indicate that there is little evidence that peripheral ocular factors play an important role in reading disorders.
Nonphysiological Factors	
Environmental causes	Studies indicate that environmental conditions—such as social class, family size, geographical location, child-rearing practices, family history of reading problems, economic disadvantage, school factors, level of parents' education, overcrowding, broken home, and motivational factors—are clearly associated with academic attainment, which depends on reading proficiency. The findings are not proof of a cause-effect relationship, however. Some environmental factors also are associated with genetic influences.
Behavioral factors	Studies clearly indicate that children with specific reading disorders frequently have behavioral and emotional problems, including hyperactivity, inattention, and conduct problems. Although behavioral factors may not necessarily cause reading disorders, they may play a role in sustaining reading difficulties.

Source: Adapted from Aman and Singh (1983).

3. Gradually grasping the variations in grapheme-phoneme association in different word contexts.

4. Sampling the most significant words while scanning a sentence without directly perceiving all of them. One understands the whole sentence by integrating the semantically and syntactically related words into meaningful units of thought.

Children with reading difficulties may be stuck at different stages in the reading process, for reading difficulties may be associated with deficiencies in information processing skills connected with any of these stages. The processes most often affected are analyzing complex perceptual patterns, attending to and extracting their significant characteristic details, organizing these details, and generalizing these organizations conceptually. As reading progresses, these processes are applied to more complex material, and word meanings must be integrated in the reading process. Reading difficulty, then, typically is a form of cognitive deficiency manifested by different individuals at different stages in learning to read.

Research (Siegel & Linder, 1984) suggests that younger learning-disabled children (8 to 9 years of age) have a deficiency in phonological coding, whereas older learning-disabled children (10 to 13 years of age) use a phonemic code but have a more general deficit in short-term memory, particularly in the context of language processing. These findings are important because they suggest that a phonemic code does develop in the short-term memory of learning-disabled children, albeit more slowly.

The following poem illustrates some of the complexities involved in learning how to read English (author unknown):

Our Incredible Language
When the English tongue we speak
Why is "break" not rhymed with "freak?"
Will you tell me why it's true
We say "sew" but likewise "few?"
And the maker of a verse
Cannot cap his "horse" with "worse."
"Beard" sounds not the same as "heard."
"Cord" is different from "word."
Cow is "cow," but low is "low."
"Shoe" is never rhymed with "roe."
Think of "hose" and "dose" and "lose."
And think of "goose" and yet of "choose."
Think of "comb" and "tomb" and "bomb."
"Doll" and "roll" and "home" and "come."
And since "pay" is rhymed with "say,"
Why not "paid" with "said," I pray?

We have "blood" and "food" and "good,"
"Mould" is not pronounced like "could."
Wherefore "done" but "gone" and "lone."
Is there any reason known?
And, in short, it seems to me
Sounds and letters disagree.

Individual Differences in Perceptual-Cognitive Processes Related to Reading Ability

Research on the relationship between perceptual-cognitive processes and reading ability suggests the following (Stanovich, 1985):

1. Deficient eye movement patterns do not appear to cause reading problems.

2. Visual processing abilities—such as iconic memory (brief initial representation of an external stimulus), feature extraction (identification of relevant features of an external stimulus), visual segmentation (isolation of relevant aspects of the visual field)—are at best weakly related to reading fluency.

3. Phonological awareness and phonological coding skills are strongly linked with early acquisition of reading ability.

4. Difficulty in accessing the name code of a symbolic stimulus is only weakly linked to reading deficits.

5. "The ability to recognize words automatically is related to reading skill, but a strong relationship is only present in the early stages of reading acquisition" (Stanovich, 1985, p. 200).

6. "Skilled readers are adept at [using] contextual strategies to facilitate comprehension, but skilled and less skilled readers are equally adept at using context to facilitate word recognition. . . . Poor readers may fail to show contextual effects in situations where their deficient word recognition skills have rendered the context functionally useless" (Stanovich, 1985, p. 193).

7. Short-term memory is related to reading ability. "Poorer readers are less adept at employing the active, planful memorization strategies (e.g., verbal rehearsal, elaboration) known to facilitate memory performance" (Stanovich, 1985, p. 195). Strategy deficiency cannot explain all of the memory difficulties experienced by poor readers, however. Some memory problems may be due to inadequate phonological coding.

8. Less skilled readers have comprehension deficits that are independent of their decoding skills, such as depressed listening comprehension and poor use of general comprehension strategies (for example, inefficient comprehen-

sion monitoring, inefficient manner of approaching text [for example, too much passivity], inefficient text-scanning strategies, less sensitivity to text structure, and less elaborate encoding of text).

Intelligence and Reading Ability

Reading ability is significantly related to intelligence test scores (Stanovich et al., 1984). The correlations increase with age; typical values are in the .30 to .50 range for early elementary grade children, the .45 to .65 range for middle grade children, and the .60 to .75 range for adults. Median correlations between reading scores and scores on the WISC-R (and WISC) and the Stanford-Binet Intelligence Scale: Form L-M are .44 and .46, respectively (Hammill & McNutt, 1981). The verbal portions of these two intelligence tests tap many subskills critical for reading, such as use of real-world knowledge, inferential skills, memory strategies, and vocabulary. Future reading performance is more accurately predicted by current reading achievement scores than by intelligence test scores, however (Stanovich, 1985).

Remediation of Reading Disability

Special instruction, designed in accordance with the guidelines discussed in the previous section, can help reading-disabled children learn to understand the task demands, identify and attend to contextual cues in reading passages, monitor their own reading to determine whether they comprehend the material, and backtrack or scan ahead when comprehension falters (Wong, 1982). A phonics approach should be used in early reading programs. Emphasis early in the program should be on learning the alphabetic code rather than reading for meaning, letter-sound correspondences should be taught together with blending, the initial reading material should be controlled for letter-sound regularity, and skills that help children segment words into phonemes should be stressed (Jorm & Share, 1983).

Hyperlexia

Children who have a precocious ability to recognize written words, beyond what would be expected given their general level of intellectual development, are said to be hyperlexic. Hyperlexic children may have accelerated neurological development that results in a precocious ability to recognize written words as linguistic symbols (Richman & Kitchell, 1981). Hyperlexic children may also demonstrate a delay or disorder in receptive or expressive

language development, however. It is important that parents and teachers not develop unrealistic expectations of these children's educational abilities. Although they have superior word-naming ability, many do not have the commensurate comprehension ability.

ASSESSMENT OF LEARNING DISABILITIES

The assessment of learning-disabled children has three major aims. One is to obtain an estimate of general intelligence in order to determine whether the child has the ability for higher achievement despite past or present performance. A second goal is to determine areas of impaired functioning that may lend themselves to remediation. A third is to find areas of strength that may prove helpful in remediation efforts.

Approaches to Determining Whether a Learning Disability Exists

Establishing whether a child has a learning disability is not a simple task. All relevant factors must be considered. The U.S. Office of Education provided, as part of Public Law 94-142, the following guidelines for determining the existence of a specific learning disability (*Federal Register*, December 29, 1977, p. 65083, 121a.541):

(a) A team may determine that a child has a specific learning disability if:

(1) The child does not achieve commensurate with his or her age and ability levels in one or more of the areas listed in paragraph (a)(2) of this section, when provided with learning experiences appropriate for the child's age and ability levels; and

(2) The team finds that a child has a severe discrepancy between achievement and intellectual ability in one or more of the following areas:

(i) Oral expression;
(ii) Listening comprehension;
(iii) Written expression;
(iv) Basic reading skills;
(v) Reading comprehension;
(vi) Mathematics calculation; or
(vii) Mathematics reasoning.

(b) The team may not identify a child as having a specific learning disability if the severe discrepancy between ability and achievement is primarily the result of:

(1) A visual, hearing, or motor handicap;
(2) Mental retardation;
(3) Emotional disturbance; or
(4) Environmental, cultural or economic disadvantage.

The guidelines, however, *do not indicate how a severe discrepancy between achievement and intellectual ability should be determined.* Although various proposals, described below, have been offered to help clinicians determine whether a child's performance is significantly below expectation for his or her age level and intelligence, these proposals should be viewed simply as helpful guideposts. *In the final analysis, both clinical and psychoeducational factors must be considered in arriving at a diagnosis of learning disability.*

Defining a severe discrepancy. The indicator most frequently used to identify learning disability in children is an ability-achievement discrepancy. Children who are low achievers in school, yet of average or above average intelligence, are candidates for identification based on this criterion. The major classification problem centers on how to define a severe discrepancy between *ability*, usually defined by an intelligence test score, and *achievement*, usually defined by a reading, arithmetic, or spelling test score or by an overall achievement score. (Note, however, that the federal guidelines do not provide for a spelling disability.)

Two other indicators used to classify children as learning-disabled are low achievement (regardless of level of intelligence) and a discrepancy between results of verbal and performance sections of an intelligence test. *These latter two methods, however, are not appropriate.* Low achievement may result from factors that are not related to learning per se. And a Verbal-Performance IQ discrepancy should not be used as the only means of classification, for it does not take into account achievement in school tasks. It is poor practice to use patterns on an intelligence test *exclusively* to arrive at a diagnosis of learning disability.

Academic underachievement has been operationally defined in terms of a deviation from grade level, an expectancy formula, a regression equation, or a difference between standard scores.

1. *Deviation from grade or age level.* Underachievement is most simply defined as a discrepancy between the child's grade-equivalent score on an achievement test and his or her grade placement. For example, a fifth-grade child who obtains a grade-equivalent score that is at the third-grade level would be characterized as being two years below grade placement. Definitions with a constant deviation criterion specify a particular minimum value the discrepancy must have in order to be considered severe. The use of a constant deviation criterion fails to take into account, however, that the same discrepancy means something different at different grade levels. A two-years-

below-grade-level performance reflects a much greater deficit for a fourth grader than for an eighth grader. Consequently, some definitions use a graduated deviation criterion in which the amount of deviation required between grade placement and achievement varies as a function of current grade placement. The discrepancy may be 1 year in first and second grades, 1½ years in third and fourth grades, 2 years in fifth through eighth grades, and 3 years in ninth through twelfth grades.

The deviation-from-grade-level procedure is inadequate, because the grade-equivalent scores that it uses have few acceptable psychometric properties (see Chapter 2). Any procedure that uses differences between a grade-level score on an achievement test and actual grade level or chronological age level or mental age level is fraught with danger.

2. *Expectancy formulas.* Expected grade equivalent, rather than actual grade placement, may be used in the computation of an ability-achievement discrepancy. Expectancy formulas are based on the child's mental age (MA) and chronological age (CA). An example of an expectancy formula is

$$\text{Expected Grade Equivalent} = [(2MA + CA)/3] - 5$$

For example, the Expected Grade Equivalent for a 6-year-old child with an MA of 6 would be

$$\begin{aligned}[(2 \times 6 + 6)/3] - 5 &= [(12 + 6)/3] - 5 \\ &= [(18)/3] - 5 = 6 - 5 \\ &= 1\end{aligned}$$

or 1st grade. One problem with expectancy formulas is that they assume that the correlation between scores on the ability test (where the MA was obtained) and scores on the achievement test (which are predicted) is 1.0, which is rarely the case. Furthermore, such formulas rely heavily on the MA concept, which has serious limitations (see Chapter 2). Any formula that arbitrarily weights mental age or chronological age usually has limited, if any, theoretical support.

3. *Regression equations.* A better method is to use a regression equation to determine expected scores (see Chapter 2). The equation takes into account regression-to-the-mean effects, which occur when the correlation between two measures is less than perfect, and the standard error of measurement of the difference score. The regression-to-the-mean effect means that children who are above average on one measure will tend to be less superior on the other, whereas those who are below average on the

first measure will tend to be less inferior on the second. Use of the most effective regression equation requires knowledge of the correlation between the two tests used in the equation; the correlation should be based on a large representative sample.

4. *Difference between standard scores.* Another procedure is to compare standard scores on two tests. A criterion level for a significant (or meaningful) discrepancy is set, such as a difference of 1 standard deviation between the academic achievement test score and the general ability test score (usually an intelligence test score). This procedure does not take into account the regression of IQ on achievement, however, and, like the expectancy formula, implicitly assumes a near-perfect correlation between ability and achievement. It also requires that each test be based on the same standard score distribution (see Chapter 2). If the standard score distributions are not the same, one of the distributions must be changed to the other's scale, or both distributions can be changed to z scores.

Comment on discrepancy formulas.   The United States Department of Special Education, Special Education Programs Work Group on Measurement Issues in the Assessment of Learning Disabilities (Reynolds, 1984) recommends that regression procedures be used to arrive at a significant discrepancy. Some research (Valus, 1986) suggests, however, that there is a great overlap between comparisons based on regression procedures and those based on standard scores.

As noted above, some learning-disability discrepancy formulas call for a significant discrepancy between an achievement test score and an intelligence test score. Any discrepancy formula that is used without regard to the absolute level of the student's performance may result in serious misclassifications. *A discrepancy formula should never be applied without considering the child's actual scores — that is, the level at which he or she is functioning.* Take the case of a student who obtains an IQ of 150 on the WISC-R and standard scores of 132 on the WRAT-R Reading, Spelling, and Arithmetic subtests. This student is clearly superior in the achievement areas measured by both tests. To call this child learning disabled because of these discrepant scores would be extremely unfortunate. This student is functioning in the 99th percentile rank on both tests. A learning-disability label indicates that a student needs special help to remediate a disability. Clearly, that is not the case in this example.

Discrepancy formulas assume that the tests used to evaluate a child measure independent functions, when actually reading and intelligence tests to some extent measure the same factors. Additionally, the same processing difficulties that reduce achievement test scores may reduce intelligence test scores. Which IQ do we use when there is a large discrepancy between the Verbal and Performance Scale IQs of the Wechsler battery? The use of one scale for one child and another for a different child would mean that the same criteria would not be used in each case, and such a procedure is unacceptable. Formulas also disregard individual ability patterns and the variability that is inherent in growth and development. Formulas should not be used in a mechanical fashion. Diagnostic labeling is a skilled clinical decision-making activity. A formula that uses only two test scores cannot substitute for skilled clinical judgment and a synthesis of all relevant information.

Any method involving the use of tests to classify children must be based on reliable and valid measuring instruments. Unfortunately, different instruments yield different estimates of intelligence and achievement skills. Therefore, clinicians using the same discrepancy formula but different tests are likely to arrive at different classifications. These and similar factors should be considered in arriving at meaningful classifications.

It should be noted that discrepancy formulas fail to identify those learning-disabled children who show no discrepancy between achievement and intelligence test scores. Thus the system overlooks all children who have a learning disability (defined as a deficit in information processing despite average intellectual and sensory ability) that interferes with the overall development of both intellectual and academic achievement skills.

Algozzine and Ysseldyke (1983) believe that there is currently no defensible system for classifying children as learning disabled. Little is known about the distribution of discrepancies in the general population, making the use of any discrepancy procedure problematic. They suggest that low achievement per se be recognized as a problem and appropriate remediation be provided whenever it occurs. Although their position has merit, learning disability still appears to be a useful classification. What is needed is further refinements in theory and classification.

Guidelines for the Assessment of Learning Disabilities

In the assessment of learning-disabled children, it is important to evaluate the following (Barkley, 1981c):

• *developmental-cognitive processes* (for example, verbal-linguistic, visual-spatial-constructional, sequential-analytic, and planning processes);
• *achievement skills* (for example, reading, spelling, mathematics, and written expression);

• *environmental demands* (for example, demands on the child in the school and family);

• *reactions of others* (for example, how the parents, teachers, and peers respond to the child's failures); and

• *interaction effects* (for example, how the above areas interact over time to affect the child's performance and adjustment).

Assessment questions. Useful questions related to assessment of the above-mentioned factors include the following (Barkley, 1981c, pp. 461–462, with changes in notation):

1. What are the nature and the extent of deficits in those cognitive skills that are important to academic achievement? What is the nature of the errors in performance?

2. Can the origin of the learning disability be determined?

3. With what particular tasks in the classroom are the cognitive deficits interfering (such as mathematics, reading, or spelling)?

4. What are the nature and the extent of primary or secondary emotional behaviors that may occur with, or be a reaction to, the learning disability?

5. How are the learning disability and its concomitant behavioral-emotional disorders affecting the child's interactions with and reactions from parents, teachers, and peers? In what setting are these interactional problems most likely to occur?

6. How will the factors at these various levels of analysis interact over time to improve or exacerbate the child's problems?

7. How can the child's remaining cognitive "strengths" be used in habilitating or coping with the existing problems?

8. What resources exist within the family, school, and community that can be used to assist in habilitation?

Assessment battery. The most important tools in the assessment of learning-disabled children are reliable and valid intelligence and achievement tests that assess major content areas such as reading, mathematics, and spelling. Although there is no one standard battery for the assessment of learning disability, many of the tests reviewed in Chapters 6 through 15 are useful. As always, the selection of tests should be based partly on the referral question. Evaluating auditory skills and visual-perceptual processing skills, in addition to intelligence and achievement skills, may be helpful. Ideally, diagnostic procedures should not be conducted outside of the classroom; rather, they should be an ongoing part of the regular classroom

activity—particularly after the psychoeducational evaluation and related studies have been completed.

The assessment of reading-disabled children should focus on the child's skills in reading—such as repertoire of words identified on sight; knowledge of speech sounds, such as vowels, consonants, and blends; comprehension skills; silent reading skills; and oral reading skills—and should incorporate trial remediation procedures.

Learning Disabilities and the WISC-R

Attempts have been made to determine whether various WISC-R (or WISC) patterns—such as Verbal-Performance discrepancy, pattern of subtest scores, and range of subtest scores—can distinguish learning-disabled children from normal children, behavior problem children, and mentally retarded children. Bannatyne (1974) proposed that the WISC subtests be recategorized as follows to aid in evaluating learning-disabled children:

Spatial: Picture Completion, Block Design, and Object Assembly
Conceptual: Comprehension, Similarities, and Vocabulary
Sequential: Arithmetic, Digit Span, and Coding
Acquired Knowledge: Information, Arithmetic, and Vocabulary.

The Spatial category samples the ability to manipulate objects in multidimensional space, either directly or symbolically. The Conceptual category covers abilites related to language development. The Sequential category is the same as the Freedom from Distractibility factor found in WISC-R factor analytic studies; it reflects the ability to retain and use sequences of auditory and memory stimuli in short-term memory storage. The Acquired Knowledge category represents abilities usually learned at school or at home.

Bannatyne's recategorization was based on an inspection of the subtests, not on factor analytic findings. It is simply a heuristic model designed to aid in test interpretation. The pattern proposed to be characteristic of learning disability is Spatial > Conceptual > Sequential.

Unfortunately, attempts to find unique WISC-R patterns among learning-disabled children have not been successful. After an extensive investigation of 94 WISC-R studies with learning-disabled children, Kavale and Forness (1984) reported that no recategorization of WISC-R scores, profiles, factor clusters, or patterns revealed a significant difference between the learning-disabled and normal samples. Even within the learning-disabled group, no regrouping scheme was found to be useful in differential diagnosis.

The failure to find a unique WISC-R pattern for learning-disabled children is not surprising. Learning-disabled children represent a group that is too heterogeneous for one type of WISC-R profile to be typical of all or even most of its members. Thus, for example, the Bannatyne recategorizations have not been successful in differentiating children with visual-perceptual deficits from those with auditory-perceptual deficits (Miller, Stoneburger, & Brecht, 1978) or in differentiating learning-disabled children from (a) normal children with average intelligence (Mueller, Matheson, & Short, 1983), (b) emotionally disturbed or mentally retarded children (Henry & Wittman, 1981), (c) slow learners (Cooley & Lamson, 1983), or (d) other types of exceptional children (Clarizio & Bernard, 1981; Thompson, 1981).

These results strongly suggest that a child's WISC-R profile should not be used to establish a diagnosis of learning disability. Regrouping tests according to the Bannatyne scheme or other schemes does not aid in clinical diagnosis. At present, there is no unique WISC-R profile that is reliably diagnostic of learning disability. The WISC-R should be used to assess the child's intelligence and patterns of cognitive efficiency; it should not be used in the absence of other tests and information to make a differential diagnosis.

Rank order of WISC-R subtests for reading-disabled children.   Trends are emerging from studies that have evaluated the rank order of WISC and WISC-R subtest scores in heterogeneous groups of reading-disabled children. An inspection of 30 studies (Sattler, 1982b) indicates that, based on the average scores of inadequate readers, the subtests rank as follows, from easiest to most difficult:

1. Picture Completion
2. Picture Arrangement
3. Block Design
4. Object Assembly
5. Similarities
6. Comprehension
7. Vocabulary
8. Coding
9. Digit Span
10. Arithmetic
11. Information

The four most difficult subtests form the acronym ACID (Arithmetic, Coding, Information, and Digit Span). In nearly every study that reported Verbal Scale and Performance Scale IQs, Verbal Scale IQs were *lower* than Performance Scale IQs. This discrepancy is consistent with the rank order data, which indicate that the four easiest subtests are Performance Scale subtests. Low scores on Coding may reflect failure to use an effective labeling strategy as a memory aid, which increases the time needed to complete the task.

Factor analysis.   The WISC-R factor structure for learning-disabled children is essentially similar to that for normal children (Blaha & Vance, 1979; Lombard & Riedel, 1978; Naglieri, 1981c; Snow, Cohen, & Holliman, 1985; Sutter & Bishop, 1986a). These results suggest that the ability structure of learning-disabled children, as measured by the WISC-R, is similar to that of normal children.

Informal Assessment

Well-normed standardized tests are not available for all types of school readiness skills, written and oral expression skills, and listening comprehension skills. Informal tests and criterion-referenced tests are valuable in assessing these and related areas. Additionally, the diagnostic process should include a study of the examinee's behavior, classroom work samples, and errors made on both formal and informal tests, as well as factors that facilitate the examinee's learning. This section discusses a number of useful informal assessment procedures in these areas.

Informal assessment of reading skills.   In the evaluation of reading skills, note the extent and type of reading deficit and possible reasons for the deficit. Also note (a) *degree of fluency* (for example, hesitations, smooth transitions), (b) *inflection* (appropriate or inappropriate), (c) *ability to make use of linguistic context in identifying words in sentences*, and (d) *ability to comprehend what is read*.

Recording oral reading errors.   A useful procedure for recording a child's oral reading errors is shown in Table 20-4. After recording the errors, evaluate the types of errors that occurred and how they affected the child's reading (Rupley & Blair, 1979). For example, what types of errors occurred most frequently? Did the omissions change the meaning of the text, occur with any specific types of words, or interfere with the child's ability to respond to comprehension questions? What types of substitutions were most prevalent? Did insertions change the meaning of the text? Was there a pattern to the insertions? Did the mispronunciations occur with a particular type of

Table 20-4
Recording Word-Recognition Miscues and Errors

Miscue	Marking
External assistance	time
Functional attribute	sit on chair
Hesitation	time
Insertion	new time ∧ to
Losing place	lp time
Mispronunciation	door dog
Omission	time (to)
Phonemic substitution	stool spool
Refusal to pronounce	rp time
Repetition	r time
Reversal	time to go
Self-correction	time
Semantic substitution	leap jump
Synonym substitution	big large
Verb substitution	beat heart
Visual misidentification	ball balloon

word, such as names or multisyllabic words? Were any reading errors associated with dialect differences?

Word prediction abilities (or cloze procedures). The way a child uses semantic and syntactic cues to identify words can be studied by administering informal tests of word prediction abilities; these tests are a supplement to standardized reading tests. *Cloze procedures*, illustrated in Table 20-5, require the child to complete various types of sentences. One suggested procedure is to administer six items of each type, but testing should be terminated earlier if the child becomes frustrated. The results from a cloze assessment are useful in developing instructional recommendations.

Phonological awareness. An important subskill in learning how to read is phonological awareness. A child's

degree of phonological awareness can be assessed by tasks such as those illustrated in Exhibits 20-1 and 20-2. In the *strip initial consonant task* (Exhibit 20-1), two words are used on the practice trials and nine additional words are presented on the test trials. In the *phonological oddity task* (Exhibit 20-2), the stimuli are nine sets of four words. Within each set of four words, three begin with a common sound. The child is asked to name the odd word in the set. Measures of phonological awareness are good predictors of the speed with which children acquire reading fluency in the early grades (Stanovich, Cunningham, & Cramer, 1984).

Informal assessment of written expression. Informal assessment of written expression can include the following (State of Iowa, 1981):

- analysis of classroom writing assignments
- comparison of a child's writing assignment with those of a random sample of other children
- analysis of how the child copies letters, words, sentences, and short paragraphs, presented in cursive, printed form, or both, from near-point (placed on the desk) and far-point (placed on the blackboard)
- analysis of how the child writes letters, words, or sentences from dictation (using both uppercase and lowercase cursive or print or both)
- analysis of how the child writes original sentences for 10 different pictures
- analysis of the child's behavior during a writing assignment period

During the test session, you can ask the child to write his or her name, write words and sentences from dictation, and write a story. These tasks will provide some information about the child's writing skills and ability to express ideas in writing.

A useful checklist for evaluating penmanship, spelling, grammar, and ideation is shown in Table 20-6. It can be used to evaluate various types of written work, including stories, poems, letters, reports, and reviews.

The following case illustrates an informal assessment of written expression for a fifth-grade girl, aged 10 years, 11 months (State of Iowa, 1981).

Mary's ability for written expression was evaluated by analyzing five classroom writing assignments completed since the beginning of the school year, comparing the five samples with a random sample of 10 writing assignments from classmates, administering the Capitalization and Punctuation subtests of the Brigance Diagnostic Inventory of Basic Skills, and evaluating her ability to copy short paragraphs (in cursive). Mary made numerous spelling and writing errors on each assignment. High fre-

Table 20-5
Informal Tests of Word Prediction Abilities

Task	Procedure and Examples
Auditory Cloze	
Child is required to complete a spoken sentence or phrase orally with a word that is both semantically and syntactically correct. This is a good beginning task for children, regardless of age, because it defines the prediction abilities necessary for the subsequent tasks.	Orally present the child with an incomplete sentence. Have the child complete the sentence orally. 1. John went to the lake to _____. (fish, swim, relax, etc.) 2. Maria used her money to buy some _____. (candy, clothes, food, etc.) 3. A horse can run very _____. (fast, quickly, slowly, etc.) 4. On a lonely farm in the country lived a man and his _____. (wife, child, donkey, etc.) 5. Mr. Cook was going to the _____ to get some eggs. (store, market, shop, etc.) 6. Ray finished picking up the trash and walked back to the _____. (house, store, barn, etc.)
Auditory Cloze and Initial Grapheme	
Child is presented with a spoken phrase or sentence with a single word omitted and is given the initial grapheme of the missing word. The prediction now involves an added constraint: not only must the response be semantically and syntactically acceptable, but it must also begin with the indicated grapheme. This task, unlike Auditory Cloze, requires familiarity with letters, words, and the reading act.	Orally present the child with an incomplete sentence. Then present the initial letter of the missing word printed on a card. Have the child complete the sentence orally with a word that begins with the grapheme indicated. 1. My kitten drinks m_____. (milk) 2. Today, the mailman brought a l_____. (letter) 3. Sandy put the small rock in his p_____. (pocket, pack) 4. Last night for supper we had potatoes and b_____. (bread, beef, bacon, etc.) 5. The alligator was hiding in the w_____ of the swamp. (water, weeds) 6. When the car stopped, the old man got out and k_____ it. (kicked)
Visual Cloze with Alternatives	
Child selects, from two alternatives, the more appropriate word to complete the written sentence. This task, which assesses use of semantic and syntactic cues, relies heavily on a child's ability to read the target sentence and the alternatives. A child may err on this task even though adequate word prediction ability exists. The chance factor is much higher on this task than on the others.	Present the child with a printed sentence, one part of which is in parentheses (the correct word and an alternative incorrect word). Have the child choose the correct word orally. 1. Sam can hit the (dill/ball). 2. Mary picked some (fingers/flowers) from her garden. 3. An old lady was in her (house/horse). 4. Kim will (come/came) home after the ballgame. 5. Because she was mad, Mom said, "Go to your room and don't come (out/our)." 6. On the way to school Tim stopped to pick up a (life/leaf).
Visual Cloze with Word Supplied Orally	
Child is required to complete orally a written sentence with a word that is both semantically and syntactically correct. Odd responses may be based on a miscue of one of the words in the item, not in a misapplication of semantic and syntactic constraints. Scoring should be based on semantic and syntactic acceptability.	Present the child with a printed sentence with one word omitted. Have the child read the sentence silently and supply an appropriate word orally. Record the child's response. 1. Run as fast as you _____. (can, want, etc.) 2. The baby was very _____. (happy, sad, etc.) 3. At breakfast Max spilled milk all over the _____. (table, floor, kitchen, etc.) 4. A red bird built a nest in the _____. (tree, chimney, etc.) 5. The dog is old but he still _____. (runs, eats, etc.) 6. Every day I eat a big bowl of cereal _____ breakfast. (for, at)

(Table continues next page)

Table 20-5 (cont.)

Task	Procedure and Examples
	Visual Cloze
Child is presented with a written phrase or sentence with a word omitted and is required to write an appropriate word in the space provided. Scoring should be based primarily on semantic and syntactic acceptability.	Present the child with a printed sentence with one word omitted. Have the child print an appropriate word in the blank space. 1. The boy kicked the _____. (ball, dog, car, etc.) 2. One day a _____ ran off the road. (car, bike, motorcycle, etc.) 3. I wanted to see if I could _____ fudge. (make, cook, etc.) 4. The duck flew over the water and soon we could not _____ him. (see, find, etc.) 5. Once upon a time there was a king who was so _____ they called him King Fatso. (fat, big, heavy, etc.) 6. Texas Dan was the best cowboy around and he could _____ a bucking bronco. (ride)
	Visual Cloze with Initial Grapheme
Child is presented with a written sentence with a word omitted and is required to provide an appropriate word using the grapheme shown. Providing the initial grapheme limits the range of acceptable responses. Some children seem to become bound to the grapheme, giving responses that meet the initial grapheme criterion but that do not follow the semantic and syntactic cues.	Present the child with a printed sentence with one word omitted but for the initial letter. Have the child, either orally or in writing, complete the sentence with a word that begins with the grapheme indicated. 1. The girl eats the h_____. (hotdog, hamburger, etc.) 2. Peter named his dog B_____. (Bill, Boy, Ben, etc.) 3. My bike is r_____ and white. (red) 4. Mary didn't want her little brother playing w_____ her toys. (with) 5. Where could I go if I wanted t_____ hide? (to) 6. The artist could draw the most beautiful p_____ of flowers. (picture)

Source: Adapted from Allington (1979). The six items for each procedure were obtained from R. L. Allington, personal communication, April 1982.

quency words were misspelled, sentences were incomplete, and capitalization and punctuation errors were frequent. She mixed cursive and printing style, letter formation was awkward and frequently illegible, and she varied spacing between words. Her sentences were simple sentences, with limited use of adjectives and adverbs, and she wrote only one long paragraph.

Mary's written samples differed from those of her classmates. Her classmates consistently used cursive style; showed lower frequency of capitalization, punctuation, and spelling errors; demonstrated more accurate letter formation and more consistency in spacing; showed more frequent use of adjectives and adverbs; demonstrated the use of paragraph development; and showed use of compound sentences, questions, quotations, and complex sentences.

The two Brigance subtests indicate that Mary knows the correct use of capitalization and punctuation, but does not apply this knowledge when writing (Capitalization subtest = 80 percent accuracy, Punctuation subtest = 70 percent accuracy).

Her copying was laborious. She copied word by word, and with some words, letter by letter, mixing cursive and printing style. Before proceeding to the next copying sample, she elected to use printing. After questioning, Mary said that she did not like to use cursive writing ("I don't know how to make all the letters"). The general appearance (legibility, spacing, and letter formation) of her writing improved significantly when she used printing

only. She is the only student in her class who does not use cursive style.

In summary, Mary demonstrates significant problems in using correct spelling, capitalization, punctuation, and paragraph development in her writing. Her use of complex language structures in writing is considerably more limited than that of her classmates. The quality of her handwriting is below that of her classmates. The results suggest that Mary has a severe disability in writing. Specialized remedial efforts will be needed for her to improve her skills in written expression.

Informal assessment of spelling errors. Table 20-7 provides guidelines for classifying spelling errors. Although many such systems are available, the system illustrated in Table 20-7 is particularly useful in the assessment of children with neurological difficulties.

Paragraph recall. The stories in Exhibit 20-3 can be used to evaluate meaningful memory for a paragraph. The stories are divided into 44, 34, and 37 logical units, respectively. The following instructions may be used: "I am going to read a story. Listen carefully. When I am through, tell me the story." The child is given 1 point for each unit recalled correctly; exact wording is not important.

Strip Initial Consonant Task

Directions: Speak clearly and distinctly and emphasize the key word in each item or example.

Say: "Listen carefully. I am going to say a word. If you take away the first sound of the word I say, you will find a new word. First, I'll show you how to do it: *ball*. If you take away the first sound, the new word is *all*. Now let's try another."

Give Sample Item 1.

Sample Item 1

Say: "Tell me what the new word is when you take away the first sound in *cat*. What is the new word when you take away the first sound?"

If the child succeeds, go to Sample Item 2. If the child fails, say: "If you take away the first sound from the word *cat*, the new word is *at*."

Repeat Sample Item 1. Say: "*Cat*. What is the new word when you take away the first sound?"

If the child succeeds, go to Sample Item 2. If the child fails, say: "If you take away the first sound from the word *cat*, the new word is *at*." Proceed to Sample Item 2.

Sample Item 2

Say: "Let's try another. What is the new word when you take away the first sound from the word *task*?"

If the child succeeds, go to Test Item 1. If the child fails,

say: "If you take away the first sound from the word *task*, the new word is *ask*."

Repeat Sample Item 2. Say: "What is the new word when you take away the first sound from the word *task*?"

If the child succeeds, go to Test Item 1. If the child fails, say: "If you take away the first sound from the word *task*, the new word is *ask*." Proceed to Test Item 1.

Test Items

Give test items 1 through 9. Say the word. Then say: "If you take away the first sound, what is the new word?" If necessary, repeat these instructions before each word is said. Do not correct any answers. Give all nine items.

1. pink
2. man
3. nice
4. win
5. bus
6. pitch
7. car
8. hit
9. pout

Source: Adapted from Stanovich, Cunningham, and Cramer (1984).

Phonological Oddity Task

Directions: Speak clearly and distinctly and emphasize the four key words in each item or example.

Say: "Listen carefully. I am going to say four words. One of the words begins with a sound that is different from the other words. Here is an example. If I say *bag, nine, beach, bike*, the word that begins with a different sound is *nine*. Now you try one."

Give Sample Item 1.

Sample Item 1

Say: "Which word begins with a sound that is different from the other words: *rat, roll, ring, pop*?"

If the child succeeds, go to Sample Item 2. If the child fails, say: "*rat, roll, ring, pop*. The word that has a different beginning sound is *pop*."

Repeat Sample Item 1. Say: "Which word begins with a sound that is different from the other words: *rat, roll, ring, pop*?"

If the child succeeds, go to Sample Item 2. If the child fails, say: "*rat, roll, ring, pop*. The word that has a different beginning sound is *pop*." Go to Sample Item 2.

Sample Item 2

Say: "Let's try another one. Which word has a different beginning sound: *nut, sun, sing, sort*?"

If the child succeeds, go to Test Item 1. If the child fails, say: "*nut, sun, sing, sort*. The word that has a different beginning sound is *nut*."

Repeat Sample Item 2. Say: "Which word has a different beginning sound: *nut, sun, sing, sort*?"

If the child passes, proceed to Test Item 1. If the child fails, say: "*nut, sun, sing, sort*. The word that has a different beginning sound is *nut*." Proceed to Test Item 1.

Test Items

Give test items 1 through 9. Say the four words. Then say: "Which word has a different beginning sound?" If necessary, repeat these instructions before each item. Do not correct any answers. Give all nine items.

1. not no nice *son*
2. ball bite *dog* beet
3. girl *pat* give go
4. *yes* run rose round
5. cap *jar* coat come
6. hand hut *fun* here
7. *cat* tan time ton
8. luck like look *arm*
9. fill fork *ear* fire

Source: Adapted from Stanovich, Cunningham, and Cramer (1984).

Table 20-6
Checklist of Written Expression

Student's Name _____ Grade _____ Examiner _____ Date _____

I. PENMANSHIP
   (1 = it's a mess, 5 = beautiful)
   A. Spacing on the page _____
   B. Spacing of the sentences _____
   C. Spacing of the words _____
   D. Spacing of letters _____
   E. Slant _____
   F. Letter formations _____
   G. Pressure on the paper _____
   H. Pencil grip _____

II. SPELLING
   _____% misspelled
   (Check areas in which the student has problems.)
   A. Miscalled rule _____
   B. Letter insertion _____
   C. Letter omission _____
   D. Letter substitution _____
   E. Phonetic spelling _____
   F. Directional confusion _____
   G. Schwa or *r*-controlled vowels _____
   H. Letter orientation _____
   I. Sequence _____
   J. Other _____

III. GRAMMAR
(TA = too advanced or not appropriate, A = adequately used in the sample, I = skills needed to be introduced to improve writing, R = needs remediation or review)

	TA	A	I	R	Notes
A. Capitalization					
1. Proper noun _____					_____
2. Proper adjective _____					_____
3. First word in a sentence _____					_____
4. First word in a line of verse _____					_____
5. First word in a quotation _____					_____
6. Principal words in a title _____					_____
7. Personal title _____					_____
8. Use of "I" or "O" _____					_____
9. Salutation in a letter _____					_____
10. Complimentary close in a letter _____					_____
11. Other _____					_____
B. Punctuation					
1. Period _____					_____
2. Comma _____					_____
3. Apostrophe _____					_____
4. Quotation marks _____					_____
5. Question mark _____					_____
6. Semicolon _____					_____
7. Exclamation mark _____					_____
8. Colon _____					_____
9. Dash _____					_____
10. Parentheses _____					_____
11. Brackets _____					_____
12. Slash _____					_____
C. Syntax					
1. Parts of speech					
a. Verbs _____					_____
b. Nouns _____					_____
c. Pronouns _____					_____
d. Adjectives _____					_____
e. Adverbs _____					_____
f. Prepositions _____					_____
g. Conjunctions _____					_____
h. Interjections _____					_____

(Table continues next page)

Table 20-6 (cont.)

	TA	A	I	R	Notes
2. Agreement _____					
3. Case _____					
4. Pronoun reference _____					
5. Order/position of words _____					
6. Parallelism _____					
7. Abbreviations/numbers _____					
8. Paragraph _____					
9. Tense _____					

IV. IDEATION
  A. Type of writing
    1. Story _____ 2. Poem _____ 3. Letter _____ 4. Report _____ 5. Review _____
  B. Substance
    1. Naming _____ 2. Description _____ 3. Plot _____ 4. Issue _____
  C. Productivity
    1. Number of words written _____
      a. Acceptable number _____ b. Too few _____
  D. Comprehensibility
    1. Easy to understand _____ 2. Difficult to understand _____ 3. Incomprehensible _____
      a. Perseveration of words _____ b. Perseveration of ideas _____ c. Illogical _____ d. Disorganized _____
  E. Reality
    1. Accurate perception of stimulus or task _____ 2. Inaccurate perception of stimulus or task _____
  F. Style
  (Tallies)
    1. Sentence sense
      a. Completeness
        (1) Complete sentences _____
        (2) Run-on sentences _____
        (3) Sentence fragments _____
      b. Structure
        (1) Simple _____
        (2) Compound _____
        (3) Complex _____
        (4) Compound/complex _____
      c. Types
        (1) Declarative _____
        (2) Interrogative _____
        (3) Imperative _____
        (4) Exclamatory _____
    2. Tone
      a. Intimate _____ b. Friendly _____ c. Impersonal _____
    3. Word choice
    (N = none, F = few, S = some, M = many)
      a. Formality
        (1) Formal _____ (2) Informal _____ (3) Colloquial _____
      b. Complexity
        (1) Simple _____ (2) Multisyllable _____ (3) Contractions _____
      c. Descriptiveness
        (1) Vague _____ (2) Vivid _____ (3) Figures of speech _____
      d. Appropriateness
        (1) Inexact words _____ (2) Superfluous words/repetitions _____ (3) Omissions _____

Source: Reprinted, with changes in notation, with permission of the publisher and author from J. A. Poteet, "Informal Assessment of Written Expressions," *Learning Disability Quarterly*, 1980, *3*(4), pp. 90–92. © Council for Learning Disabilities.

Table 20-7
An Example of a System for Classifying Spelling Errors

Type of error	Target word	Response
1. Reversals (rearranging the proper sequence of letters)	GLASS	GLSSA
2. Substitutions		
a. Vowel	MIRROR	MIRRER
b. Visual (confusion of one letter for another one similar in appearance)	HAIR	HAIK
c. Acoustic (confusion of two letters having the same functional sound)	ERASER	ERACER
d. Visual/acoustic	BROOM	BROON
e. Random (replacement of one letter by another having no apparent relationship)	DRUM	DRUP
3. Omissions	PEPPER	PEPPR
4. Additions (extraneous letters inserted in or tacked on to the end of the word)	COMB	COMBY
a. Duplications	ERASER	ERASSER
b. Plurals (addition of *s* or *es*)	MATCH	MATCHES
5. Major error (a combination of letters bearing little if any resemblance to the target word)	MIRROR	MURYMY
6. Incomplete (no more than the first two letters of a word)	HOLE	HO
7. Wrong word (a different but real word)	HOLE	HOOK
8. Perserveration (repetition of previously presented word)	–	–
9. No response	–	–

Source: Reprinted, with a change in notation, from W. Wapner and H. Gardner (1979), "A Study of Spelling in Aphasia," *Brain and Language, 7,* 370. Copyright 1979 by Academic Press, Inc.

Brief Case Studies of Learning-Disabled Children

Four brief case studies using the WISC-R, the Wide Range Achievement Test—Revised (WRAT-R), and the Bender-Gestalt are shown in Exhibit 20-4.

Psychological Evaluation

Exhibit 20-5 presents a psychological evaluation of a learning-disabled child. This boy appears to have both auditory and visual processing difficulties and would likely be classified as having a mixed type of deficit.

ATTENTION-DEFICIT HYPERACTIVITY DISORDER: AN OVERVIEW

The term proposed by the American Psychiatric Association (1987) in their revised third edition of the *Diagnostic and Statistical Manual of Mental Disorders* (DSM-III-R) for conditions previously referred to as attention-deficit disorder with hyperactivity, hyperkinesis, or minimal brain dysfunction is attention-deficit hyperactivity disorder. The criteria for this condition are shown in Exhibit 20-6.

The DSM-III-R criteria indicate that attention-deficit hyperactivity disorder is a behavioral syndrome marked by inattention, impulsivity, and hyperactivity. Academic underachievement is found in most children with the disorder. Other symptoms that occasionally occur are low self-esteem, mood lability, low tolerance for frustration, and temper outbursts. The disorder becomes most evident when children reach school age and have difficulty meeting the demands of the classroom. Overactivity is a major part of the syndrome in early childhood. The syndrome is more common in boys than in girls, with some estimates of the boy-girl ratio as high as 9:1 (Campbell, 1976).

Etiology of Attention-Deficit Hyperactivity Disorder

The etiology of attention-deficit hyperactivity disorder is unknown. Various theories attribute hyperactivity to a dysfunction of the brain or central nervous system (such as underarousal of the central nervous system), delayed maturation of the central nervous system, genetic variation, metabolic disturbance, emotional disturbance, or an allergic reaction to certain foods, such as those containing artificial coloring and food additives. These factors may occur either alone or in combination. Although brain impairment or dysfunction is a possible etiologic factor, studies indicate that there is no clear correspondence between traditional signs of brain damage (for example, loss of

8

 618 618618618 618618618 618618618618618618618618618618618618618

Exhibit 20-3

Stories for Meaningful Memory Recall

Bozo Story

1) Once there were three 2) thieves 3) named 4) Bozo, 5) Tommy, and 6) Frank. 7) Bozo 8) was their leader. 9) They were good 10) friends and 11) went everywhere 12) together. 13) One night the 14) three of them 15) sneaked 16) through 17) a window 18) into 19) a house 20) on a hill. 21) There were trees 22) around the house. 23) Suddenly a 24) light 25) came on 26) in another 27) room. 28) They quickly 29) climbed 30) out 31) of the window. 32) Bozo and 33) Tommy 34) ran 35) down 36) the hill. 37) The other thief 38) climbed 39) a tree. 40) When a man 41) came 42) to the door of the house, 43) he could see 44) no one.

Airplane Story

1) The airplane 2) was coming in 3) for a landing. 4) It was 5) full 6) of people. 7) Suddenly, 8) the airplane 9) leaned 10) far to 11) the left 12) side. 13) All of the passengers 14) were afraid. 15) The pilot 16) did not know 17) what was wrong 18) so he landed the plane 19) very carefully. 20) As he landed, 21) one wing of the plane 22) scraped 23) the ground. 24) The passengers 25) and the pilot 26) climbed out 27) and looked 28) at the plane. 29) To their surprise 30) a large 31) group 32) of birds 33) was sitting 34) on the wing of the plane.

Linda Story

1) Linda 2) was playing 3) with her new 4) doll 5) in front 6) of her house. 7) Suddenly, 8) she heard 9) a strange 10) sound 11) coming from under 12) the porch. 13) It was the flapping 14) of wings. 15) Linda ran 16) inside 17) the house and 18) grabbed 19) a shoe 20) box 21) from the closet. 22) She found 23) some sheets 24) of paper 25) and cut 26) the paper 27) into pieces 28) and put them 29) in the box. Linda 30) gently 31) picked up 32) the helpless 33) animal 34) and took it 35) with her. 36) Her teacher 37) knew what to do.

Source: Reprinted with permission of E. H. Bacon and D. C. Rubin, unpublished material. These stories were used in research by Bacon and Rubin (1983).

---

coordination, ataxia, paralysis, or reflex abnormalities) and the attention-deficit hyperactivity disorder (Campbell, 1976; Taylor, 1983). Similarly, there is no compelling evidence that hyperactive children are distinguishable from other children on the basis of biochemical or physiological characteristics (McMahon, 1981). Though hyperactive children usually present a similar clinical picture, they may differ greatly with regard to physical and neurological factors, psychological factors, neurophysiological functioning, familial patterns of psychiatric illness, and developmental history.

EEG and Attention-Deficit Hyperactivity Disorder

There is *little* evidence that hyperactive children with abnormal EEGs have poorer intellectual functioning, greater impairment in learning, more severe problems in the classroom or at home, or a poorer prognosis (as measured by response to stimulant medication) than those with normal EEGs (Freeman, 1967; Satterfield, 1973; Satterfield, Cantwell, Saul, & Yusin, 1974). Consequently, it should *not* be assumed that signs of organicity (such as an abnormal EEG) in hyperactive children necessarily indicate a more pathological condition and a poorer prognosis. Because there appears to be no relationship between the presence of an EEG abnormality and psychological test performance, little emphasis should be placed on an abnormal EEG—in the absence of some known brain damage or mental retardation—in the diagnosis or placement of children manifesting the attention-deficit hyperactivity disorder.

Diagnostic Difficulties

Arriving at a diagnosis of attention-deficit hyperactivity disorder is not easy. Restlessness and overactive behavior are common in normal children, especially in boys between 6 and 12 years of age. Some "problem" children are never referred for hyperactive behavior because they have parents who are tolerant of their behavior, teachers who do not perceive their behavior as a problem, or optimal environments that provide structure for their behavior. Conversely, there are essentially normal but active children who are referred for evaluation because of less tolerant environments. Use of a reliable and valid rating scale can be of assistance in making the diagnosis (see Chapter 15). Scores that are 2 *SD*'s above the mean for the child's peer group suggest behavior that is significantly deviant.

Estimates of hyperactivity in clinical populations of children range from 23 percent to 50 percent, depending on the criteria used to define hyperactivity. Hyperactivity appears to account for a large proportion of the problems treated at child mental health clinics. In the school-age population as a whole, estimates of hyperactivity range from 3 percent to 20 percent (Cantwell, 1975).

Hyperactivity in Adolescence

Hyperactive children continue to have difficulties in adolescence, but the manifestations of the disorder appear to

━ **Exhibit 20-4** ━━

Brief Case Studies of Learning-Disabled Children

INTRODUCTORY REMARKS

Children classified as learning disabled usually must have a significant discrepancy between ability, as measured by an intelligence test, and achievement, as measured by a test of academic proficiency. The four children described in this exhibit have a discrepancy of 1 standard deviation or more between at least one of their Wide Range Achievement Test – Revised (WRAT-R) scores and their Full Scale WISC-R IQ. Two children (Cases 3 and 4) had significantly higher WISC-R Performance than Verbal Scale IQs, one child (Case 2) earned a significantly higher Verbal than Performance Scale IQ, and one child (Case 1) had similar Verbal and Performance IQs (see Table 20-A). All four children had some difficulty with immediate memory (low Digit Span scores), and most also had difficulty with arithmetical concentration (low Arithmetic scores). Two children (Cases 2 and 3) also had difficulty with a visual-motor task (low Coding scores). These four WISC-R profiles demonstrate that there is no uniform pattern of variability among the WISC-R profiles of learning-disabled children.

All of the children performed below average in at least two of the areas measured by the WRAT-R. In two instances (Cases 2 and 4), the children had an average WRAT-R score on the Arithmetic subtest. Three of the children (Cases 2, 3, and 4) had subtle visual-motor difficulties, as measured by the Bender-Gestalt and scored by the Koppitz system. Not all children with learning disabilities have visual-motor difficulties, however.

The assessment of learning disabilty requires a more extensive sampling of abilities than can be achieved using just the WISC-R, WRAT-R, and Bender-Gestalt. Other tests are reported in some of the cases. Tests of reading comprehension and auditory processing should also be included in the test battery. Many tests besides those shown in this exhibit can be useful in the assessment of learning disabilities.

The WISC-R profiles and Bender-Gestalts shown in this exhibit belong to children who were identified as having learning problems in school. Children who do not have learning problems could have similar profiles, however. Whether a child has or does not have learning problems depends on many factors, as has been discussed in this chapter. The WISC-R profile should never be used exclusively to diagnose a learning disability.

Case 1

Rocky, a 14-year, 5-month-old male adolescent, was referred because of poor school performance. He expressed a desire to obtain help with reading and spelling and exhibited an excellent sense of humor during the testing sessions. Although his WISC-R Full Scale IQ was in the Average classification, he demonstrated noticeable weaknesses in visual sequencing,

arithmetic reasoning, and fund of information; his strengths were in understanding of social customs, ability to differentiate essential from nonessential visual detail, and planning ability. His performance on the Bender-Gestalt suggests age-appropriate visual-motor skills. On the WRAT-R Rocky scored at the 13th percentile in reading, the 2nd percentile in spelling, and the 2nd percentile in arithmetic. Speech discrimination was adequate in a quiet setting, but inadequate in a noisy setting, as measured by the Goldman-Fristoe-Woodcock Auditory Selective Attention Test. On the Gilmore Oral Reading Test, comprehension was at the seventh grade level. He needs special services to help him with his academic work.

Case 2

Phil, an 8-year, 6-month-old male child, was referred because of reading difficulties and increasing frustration with school. His WISC-R Full Scale IQ of 113 is classified as High Average. His verbal skills are better developed than his nonverbal skills. Phil generally scored less well on those tasks that are affected by attention and concentration. His Bender-Gestalt performance suggested minor perceptual-motor difficulties (21st percentile, standard score = 88). The WRAT-R revealed below-average word recognition ability (16th percentile) and spelling (23rd percentile), but average arithmetic achievement (39th percentile). Except for adequate letter identification ability (43rd percentile), the Woodcock Reading Mastery Test indicated below-average reading mastery (11th to 22nd percentiles). Because of Phil's attention difficulties and academic deficits, it is recommended that he be considered for a learning-disabled children's program.

Case 3

Tom, a 10-year, 11-month-old male, has had longstanding difficulties in mastering academic subjects. He is a likeable child who worked hard on test problems when he felt confident. With school-like tasks, however, he became noticeably distressed and embarrassed. His performance on the WISC-R is classified as Low Average. He has better developed nonverbal than verbal skills, however. His WRAT-R scores were below average (below the 9th percentile) in the three areas measured by the test (word recognition, spelling, and arithmetic). His three errors on the Bender-Gestalt placed him at the lower limits of the average range for his age group (25th percentile, standard score = 90). Educational assistance outside of the regular classroom should be provided.

Case 4

Janet, a 9-year, 5-month-old female, currently is being tutored in reading after repeating the third grade. She was

(Exhibit continues next page)

Exhibit 20-4 (cont.)

referred for testing because of continuing difficulties in spelling and reading. Her WISC-R Full Scale IQ of 99 is classified in the Average range. Her nonverbal skills are better developed than her verbal skills. Although her conceptual reasoning ability was a strength, she had difficulty with expressive language tasks, such as defining words. Her Bender-Gestalt performance was average (standard score 92, 30th percentile). Her WRAT-R scores revealed below-average word recognition (5th percentile) and spelling ability (18th percentile), but average arithmetic skills (47th percentile). On the Silvaroli graded paragraphs, her reading comprehension was at the second-grade level. There was no evidence of hearing difficulties. She should continue to receive special help in language skills.

Table 20-A
Test Scores and Bender-Gestalt Protocols for Four Cases of Learning Disability

Test	Case 1 (male, age 14-5)	Case 2 (male, age 8-6)	Case 3 (male, age 10-11)	Case 4 (female, age 9-5)
WISC-R		*Scaled Score*		
Information	6	15	5	7
Similarities	11	15	7	14
Arithmetic	6	9	7	8
Vocabulary	8	12	5	6
Comprehension	14	15	8	6
Digit Span	8	8	7	11
Picture Completion	14	13	14	13
Picture Arrangement	6	12	13	13
Block Design	9	11	11	8
Object Assembly	12	13	10	12
Coding	9	4	6	12
Mazes	15	—	—	18
		Standard Score		
Verbal Scale IQ	94	119	78	88
Performance Scale IQ	100	104	105	111
Full Scale IQ	96	113	89	99
WRAT-R		*Standard Score*		
Reading	83	85	71	75
Spelling	69	89	71	86
Arithmetic	70	96	79	99

Bender-Gestalt

(Case 1)

(Case 2)

(Case 3)

(Case 4)

Exhibit 20-5

Psychological Evaluation of a Learning-Disabled Child

Name: James
Date of birth: February 27, 1975
Chronological age: 10-9

Dates of evaluation: December 12 and 13, 1985
Date of report: December 20, 1985
Grade: Fourth

Tests Administered

Wechsler Intelligence Scale for Children — Revised (WISC-R):

VERBAL SCALE		PERFORMANCE SCALE	
Information	10	Picture Completion	10
Similarities	6	Picture Arrangement	12
Arithmetic	9	Block Design	10
Vocabulary	10	Object Assembly	11
Comprehension	8	Coding	3
Digit Span	(4)		

Verbal Scale IQ	91
Performance Scale IQ	93
Full Scale IQ	91 ± 5 at 90 percent confidence level

Wide Range Achievement Test — Revised (WRAT-R):

	STANDARD SCORE	PERCENTILE
Reading	65	1
Spelling	62	1
Arithmetic	74	4

1. *go*
2. *cat*
3. *in*
4. *boy*
5. *and*
6. *will*
7. *mrack*
8. *him*
9. *say*
10. *cot*
11. *cook*
12. *lite*
13. *mats*
14. *dast*
15. *rask*
16. *odare*
17. *whach*
18. *nart*
19. *goon*

Lindamood Auditory Conceptualization Test:

Mid–3rd grade level

Woodcock-Johnson Psycho-Educational Battery

	PERCENTILE
Math	10
Reading	0
Written Language	9

Bender Visual Motor Gestalt Test:

Standard score = 82; percentile = 12th (Koppitz scoring system)

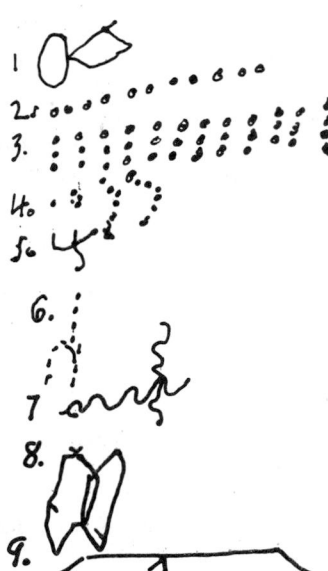

Goodenough-Harris Drawing Test:

Standard score = 70; percentile = 2nd

(Exhibit continues next page)

Exhibit 20-5 (cont.)

Reason for Referral

James was referred for a psychoeducational evaluation by his teacher because he is experiencing academic difficulties in his fourth-grade classroom. Reading and copying tasks are particularly difficult for James, and he becomes easily frustrated when unable to do assigned work.

Background Information

James has a long history of poor achievement in school. During kindergarten, he was certified for speech and language services because of poor articulation and voice quality and weak language development. He has received speech therapy since kindergarten. James was referred for special education evaluation during second grade, but his parents refused to allow him to be evaluated. Instead, they placed him in a local parochial school where he continued to experience academic problems. One year later, James returned to the public schools where he was retained in grade 3. Presently James is in the fourth grade, and his parents are concerned about his school difficulties. They now agree that an evaluation is needed.

Behavioral Observations

James is a large, overweight 10 year, 9 month old boy who was seen for testing on two consecutive days in December 1985. At that time, the frame of his glasses was broken and he had difficulty keeping them straight on his face. Although his speech was not fluent and involved poor tonal quality, it was easily understood.

James approached the tasks in a slow and deliberate manner. He tended to repeat the same word pattern frequently. For instance, during the WISC-R Picture Completion subtest, James stated, "This card is missing _____" for each item. When unable to answer, he definitively stated, "I do not know!" He became defensive when asked to reconsider or extend responses.

During the initial interview, James was unable to give pertinent information about himself, such as his street address, phone number, or year of birth. "I get numbers mixed up," he said. James also stated that because he was unable to write his last name, he would write his first name only on his assignments. He stated that he lives with his parents and two younger siblings on a farm where he helps care for numerous farm animals. His hobbies include fixing bikes and collecting sports cards.

When asked about school, James said that he finds reading, spelling, and copying very hard. Although he answered the examiner's questions, he appeared to be somewhat impatient and defensive. He was restless and fidgety and said that he wanted to get through the test as soon as possible and return to his classroom.

James was observed in his classroom during a social studies lesson involving oral reading and questioning. He did not appear to be following the book and was unable to answer the teacher's questions. James appeared restless, as noted by his continually playing with his hands, a string, and his books. When called upon to read, he struggled through the material with numerous errors and dysfluencies.

Assessment Results and Clinical Impressions

On the WISC-R, James, with a chronological age of 10-9, achieved a Verbal Scale IQ of 91 (27th percentile), a Performance Scale of 93 (32nd percentile), and a Full Scale IQ of 91 ± 5. The chances that the range of scores from 86 to 96 includes his true IQ are about 90 out of 100. His overall performance is classified in the Average range and is ranked at the 27th percentile. These, as well as other test results, appear to be reliable and valid.

Overall, both his verbal and his performance skills are at the lower limits of the Average range. The most striking aspects of his WISC-R profile were his poor attention skills for orally presented numbers and his poor speed and accuracy in learning an unfamiliar visual-motor task. Both of these tasks involve short-term memory and ability to sustain attention. These difficulties likely contribute to his poor school performance.

James also has some difficulties in verbal concept formation. He often responded to questions asking for the similarity of two things with concrete responses. He has an average fund of information, and vocabulary and his visual-organization and planning skills are also average.

The Bender Visual Motor Gestalt Test was administered, and results suggested a moderate deficit in visual perceptual skills based on the Koppitz scoring system. His figure drawing was also poorly executed and incomplete (2nd–3rd percentile).

On the Wide Range Achievement Test—Revised, James earned low scores in all measured areas. On the Reading subtest, he demonstrated a limited sight vocabulary. James was able to identify individual consonant sounds but not vowel sounds. Spelling skills were also extremely weak; James was able to spell 9 words but was not able to analyze words auditorally. On the Arithmetic subtest, he was able to do only addition and subtraction problems that did not involve carrying or borrowing. James also obtained low scores on the Woodcock-Johnson Achievement subtests.

James's ability to analyze how many sounds he had heard and where he had heard same and different sounds within a syllable was very poor (mid–3rd grade level). He could correctly represent the sounds about 75 percent of the time. Integration of auditory and visual-motor modalities was poor.

Summary and Recommendations

James is a 10 year, 9 month old boy who was seen for evaluation in order to assess his eligibility for additional special education services. He currently receives speech therapy. Test results suggest that James has average intellectual ability, but

(Exhibit continues next page)

Exhibit 20-5 (cont.)

deficits in auditory memory, visual perceptual motor production, and abstract verbal reasoning. He has an average fund of information, vocabulary, and visual organization and planning skills. Academic skills are extremely weak, and James is easily frustrated by his awareness of his learning problems.

A significant discrepancy exists between James's potential and achievement as measured by standardized tests and supported by interview and observation, suggesting that he qualifies for special education services as a learning-disabled student. A staff conference should be convened to determine certification and programming. Instruction may best be approached in a multisensory way, as James has weaknesses and strengths in both auditory and visual learning channels. Classroom assignments should be modified so that oral directions are simplified and written assignments minimized. James needs successes to improve his self-confidence and decrease his frustration.

(Signature)
_____

Horace Jones

Exhibit 20-6

Diagnostic Criteria for Attention-Deficit Hyperactivity Disorder in DSM-III-R

Note: Consider a criterion met only if the behavior is considerably more frequent than that of most people of the same mental age.

A. A disturbance of at least six months during which at least eight of the following are present:

(1) often fidgets with hands or feet or squirms in seat (in adolescents, may be limited to subjective feelings of restlessness)

(2) has difficulty remaining seated when required to do so

(3) is easily distracted by extraneous stimuli

(4) has difficulty awaiting turn in games or group situations

(5) often blurts out answers to questions before they have been completed

(6) has difficulty following through on instructions from others (not due to oppositional behavior or failure of comprehension), e.g., fails to finish chores

(7) has difficulty sustaining attention in tasks or play activities

(8) often shifts from one uncompleted activity to another

(9) has difficulty playing quietly

(10) often talks excessively

(11) often interrupts or intrudes on others, e.g., butts into other children's games

(12) often does not seem to listen to what is being said to him or her

(13) often loses things necessary for tasks or activities at school or at home (e.g., toys, pencils, books, assignments)

(14) often engages in physically dangerous activities without considering possible consequences (not for the purpose of thrill-seeking), e.g., runs into street without looking

Note: The above items are listed in descending order of discriminating power based on data from a national field trial of the DSM-III-R criteria for Disruptive Behavior Disorders.

B. Onset before the age of seven.

C. Does not meet the criteria for a Pervasive Developmental Disorder.

Criteria for severity of Attention-deficit Hyperactivity Disorder:

Mild: Few, if any, symptoms in excess of those required to make the diagnosis **and** only minimal or no impairment in school and social functioning.

Moderate: Symptoms or functional impairment intermediate between "mild" and "severe."

Severe: Many symptoms in excess of those required to make the diagnosis **and** significant and pervasive impairment in functioning at home and school and with peers.

Source: Reprinted with permission of the publisher from the _Diagnostic and Statistical Manual of Mental Disorders (Third Edition—Revised)_, 1987, pp. 52–53. Copyright © American Psychiatric Association.

change with age (Campbell, 1976). Although restlessness, distractibility, and poor concentration may diminish, they do remain problems for some adolescents. The major shift appears to be in the emergence of difficulties associated with social behavior and interpersonal relationships. Particularly evident are rebelliousness, antisocial behavior, and low self-esteem. Problems with academic achievement and problem solving remain. Hyperactive adolescents repeat more school grades, perform more poorly in academic subjects, and obtain lower intelligence test scores on group-administered tests than do normal children. Studies of the cognitive style of hyperactive adolescents indicate that, in comparison with normal adolescents, they (a) are more impulsive and field-dependent, (b) are more likely to respond without thinking, and (c) are more easily distracted by incorrect but compelling cues. In the classroom, hyperactive adolescents continue to show problems in attention and concentration, but these problems are less disruptive than in earlier years.

Hyperactivity and Test Performance

Hyperactive children tend to do more poorly than nonhyperactive children on tests of perceptual-motor functioning, measures of sustained attention (especially in situations in which the stimulus is unpredictable), and measures requiring delay of impulse, such as the Matching Familiar Figures Test, which is a visual matching test (Campbell, 1976). In these and other situations, hyperactive children tend to respond more quickly and make more errors than do nonhyperactive children. Possibly their poorer performance reflects problems of attention and impulse control rather than problems of perceptual-motor control. Hyperactive children can be helped in these and

other areas by use of stimulant medication and predictable positive reinforcement (for example, praise) and by training in the use of self-directed verbal commands to remind themselves to slow down and pay attention.

Treatment of Attention-Deficit Hyperactivity Disorder

The most popular treatment for hyperactivity is a psychostimulant medication—most often amphetamines such as dextroamphetamine (Dexedrine) or, more frequently, methylphenidate (Ritalin). Hyperactive children taking stimulant medication often show dramatic behavioral changes, with noticeable improvement in attention and impulse control. Stimulant drugs do much more than simply reduce activity level. They may alter children's activity levels, goal-directedness, mood, personality, concentration, perception, and motor coordination, and changes in these areas, in turn, can affect the children's relationships with their family, school, and peers. It is unlikely, however, that stimulant drugs will improve their skills in language, reading, arithmetic, or other related school subjects. Unfortunately, once the medication is withdrawn, the gains associated with behavioral control often disappear.

The extent to which drugs affect the intelligence test performance of hyperactive (and learning-disabled) children appears to be quite variable. Some studies report improvements in Verbal IQ or Performance IQ, whereas others reveal few or no changes (see Whalen & Henker, 1976, for a review). The major effect of stimulants given to hyperkinetic children appears to be improvement in classroom manageability rather than in academic performance (Barkley & Cunningham, 1979).

The use of psychostimulants markedly improves the

From Washington Star Syndicate, May 9, 1974. Copyright 1974, Universal Press Syndicate. All rights reserved.

performance of hyperactive children on laboratory tasks involving attention, memory, and learning, which require sustained attention and are regulated by an examiner. The findings indicate that broad-gauged cognitive abilities — such as reasoning and problem-solving skills — do not appear to be affected directly by stimulants, whereas more refined skills — such as attentional skills — are enhanced by drugs. Drugs appear to help hyperactive children plan and control their responding.

Approximately 70 percent of hyperactive children respond positively to stimulant medication (Satterfield, Cantwell, & Satterfield, 1974). Methylphenidate does not appear to be particularly useful in the treatment of hyperactivity in preschoolers, although more research is needed about the effects of stimulants on preschool children (Campbell, 1976). When hyperactive children are not responsive to stimulants, alternative forms of therapy should be sought and the medication discontinued. Other treatment approaches include psychoactive drugs (for example, chlorpromazine and imipramine), lithium carbonate, behavior modification, low-sugar diets, megavitamins, avoidance of artificial food additives, exercise, and optometric treatment.

The hyperactive children who respond best to stimulant medication appear to be those who have low central nervous system arousal levels as measured by EEGs, low evoked cortical response, or low skin conductance levels (Satterfield et al., 1974). Stimulant medications may restore both central nervous system arousal levels and inhibitory levels to normal, thereby providing hyperactive children with better controls and permitting a wider range of behaviors. The use of chemotherapy does *not* mean that special services are not needed. Remediation is required for all children who have serious academic deficiencies. Both appropriate educational management and counseling of parents should be used in conjunction with drug management.

The principal aim in treating hyperactive children and other children with similar problems is to help them to focus and sustain their attention and keep impulsive responding under control. A useful method is to teach children to verbalize to themselves effective problem-solving strategies, such as planning ahead, stopping to think, and being careful. Self-verbalizations of these kinds help hyperactive children to bring their behavior under their own control and also make it possible for them to reinforce themselves for employing appropriate strategies. A structured and predictable environment with clear, consistent expectations and immediate feedback can also help in the treatment of hyperactivity.

ASSESSMENT OF ATTENTION-DEFICIT HYPERACTIVITY DISORDER

Many of the considerations involved in the assessment of learning-disabled children hold for those with an attention-deficit hyperactivity disorder. Hyperactive children perform better in an individual test situation than in a group test situation (Minde, Weiss, & Mendelson, 1972). In the individual test situation, examiners can be responsive to lapses in attention, making sure that they have the child's attention before administering the test questions. Group intelligence tests may underestimate the ability level of hyperactive children; consequently, IQs obtained by hyperactive children on group-administered tests must be interpreted cautiously.

The major difficulties of hyperactive children, as we have seen, lie in their inability to focus, sustain, and organize attention and to inhibit impulsive responding. These difficulties are likely to be reflected in their performance on some but not all psychological tests. Their scores on individual intelligence tests may be more variable than those of normal children. Lower scores may be obtained on the Bender-Gestalt, Bruininks-Oseretsky Test of Motor Proficiency, Developmental Test of Visual Perception, and Draw-A-Man. No particular patterns of scores (for example, Verbal-Performance discrepancies or lower abstract reasoning scores) on the WISC-R or on other intelligence tests have been found to be associated with hyperactivity, however.

In addition to standard intelligence and ability tests, three procedures have been found to be especially useful in discriminating hyperactive from normal children. These are the (a) Porteus Maze Test (Porteus, 1959), a measure of planning and organization; (b) Jumbled Numbers Game, a measure of sustained attention and sequencing (numbers from 1 to 18, printed on one of three colored backgrounds, are randomly arranged on a large black cardboard — the child's task is to say the numbers in order and, with each count, name the color of the background on which the number is printed); and (c) Bobo punching doll, a measure of frustration tolerance and aggressive behavior. (See Homatidis & Konstantareas, 1981, for administration and scoring guidelines.)

An important cue in evaluating hyperkinesis is the child's performance on cognitive tasks that require concentrated effort over a period of time. Because attentional factors probably permeate these tasks, children with hyperkinesis may do more poorly on them. Useful behavioral rating scales that can be completed by teachers and parents are shown in Chapter 15.

CONDUCT DISORDER: AN OVERVIEW

According to the DSM-III-R (American Psychiatric Association, 1987, p. 53), the essential feature of the conduct disorder classification "is a persistent pattern of conduct in which the basic rights of others and major age-appropriate societal norms or rules are violated. The behavior pattern typically is present in the home, at school, with peers, and in the community." The diagnostic criteria for the conduct disorder classification are shown in Exhibit 20-7.

IQs of children with a conduct disorder (or delinquents) average about 8 points lower than those of nondelinquents; this relationship appears to be independent of the effects of socioeconomic status (Moffitt, Gabrielli, Mednick, & Schulsinger, 1981). Among delinquents, there are more of low average and fewer of superior intelligence. Although the reasons for these findings are not clear, it may be that bright delinquents are more apt to escape detection, commit fewer delinquent acts, or are less likely to be prosecuted.

Overall, studies indicate that bright delinquents share the same criminological, educational, and social characteristics as the great majority of other delinquents. However, they are less frequently encountered in the juvenile court system, are treated more leniently by the courts, and are more often presented to the courts as emotionally disturbed (Gath & Tennent, 1972). Their comparative rarity may be a result of differential immunity given to them because of higher social class and higher intelligence. Interestingly, the school performance of highly intelligent delinquents is less satisfactory than that of nondelinquents.

Evidence is inconclusive about how the intelligence level of delinquents is related to their responsiveness to treatment. Rate of recidivism does not appear to be related to intelligence level (Tennent & Gath, 1975).

Delinquents may have less adequate neuropsychological abilities than nondelinquents, as shown by their poor performance on neuropsychological tests (Berman & Siegal, 1976; Yeudall, 1979). An intriguing hypothesis is that some individuals may become delinquent as a consequence of consistent failures caused by deficits in adaptive abilities that are needed for success in our society.

ASSESSMENT OF CONDUCT DISORDER

A battery of psychological tests should be used in the assessment of children who may have a conduct disorder. The battery should be similar to the one used in the assessment of learning disabilities, including measures of

---

Exhibit 20-7

Diagnostic Criteria for Conduct Disorder in DSM-III-R

A. A disturbance of conduct lasting at least six months, during which at least three of the following have been present:

   (1) has stolen without confrontation of a victim on more than one occasion (including forgery)

   (2) has run away from home overnight at least twice while living in parental or parental surrogate home (or once without returning)

   (3) often lies (other than to avoid physical or sexual abuse)

   (4) has deliberately engaged in fire-setting

   (5) is often truant from school (for older person, absent from work)

   (6) has broken into someone else's house, building, or car

   (7) has deliberately destroyed others' property (other than by fire-setting)

   (8) has been physically cruel to animals

   (9) has forced someone into sexual activity with him or her

   (10) has used a weapon in more than one fight

   (11) often initiates physical fights

   (12) has stolen with confrontation of a victim (e.g., mugging, purse-snatching, extortion, armed robbery)

   (13) has been physically cruel to people

Note: The above items are listed in descending order of discriminating power based on data from a national field trial of the DSM-III-R criteria for Disruptive Behavior Disorders.

B. If 18 or older, does not meet criteria for Antisocial Personality Disorder.

Criteria for severity of Conduct Disorder:

Mild: Few if any conduct problems in excess of those required to make the diagnosis, **and** conduct problems cause only minor harm to others.

Moderate: Number of conduct problems and effect on others intermediate between "mild" and "severe."

Severe: Many conduct problems in excess of those required to make the diagnosis, **or** conduct problems cause considerable harm to others, e.g., serious physical injury to victims, extensive vandalism or theft, prolonged absence from home.

Source: Reprinted with permission of the publisher from the *Diagnostic and Statistical Manual of Mental Disorders (Third Edition—Revised)*, 1987, p. 55. Copyright © American Psychiatric Association.

intelligence, personality, visual-motor ability, and academic achievement. Interviews, observations, and behavioral checklists are also valuable.

The evidence is strong that delinquents, on the average, obtain higher Wechsler Performance IQs than Verbal IQs (for example, Hays, Solway, & Schreiner, 1978; Hubble & Groff, 1981b; and Saccuzzo & Lewandowski, 1976). Consequently, the perceptual organization abilities of delinquents are likely to be better developed than their verbal comprehension abilities. *But the fact that a Verbal-Performance discrepancy is likely to appear in delinquent children does not mean that this pattern can be used as a diagnostic sign of delinquency.* Many normal and exceptional children also show this form of discrepancy. The discrepancy may have no diagnostic relevance, especially when it is not statistically significant. It may simply be a reflection of poor education, reading disability, bilingualism, cognitive style, or some other factor. Perhaps the Performance > Verbal pattern is a reflection of the learning handicaps that are a relatively frequent concomitant of delinquency, rather than of delinquency itself.

Administering the WISC-R provides an opportunity to obtain many insights about the child from the pattern of subtest scores and from the content of the responses. Chapter 8 provides examples of how interpretations can be developed from a careful analysis of a child's WISC-R performance, particularly for a child with a conduct disorder.

NONSPECIFIC BEHAVIOR DISORDERS: AN OVERVIEW

This section briefly covers nonspecific behavior disorders, surveying some findings related to gender differences and intelligence. There is no category in the DSM-III-R corresponding to nonspecific behavior disorders. Rather, this discussion reflects surveys of children with a variety of behavior problems. This material also is pertinent to children with attention-deficit hyperactivity disorder or a conduct disorder.

In a comprehensive review of research on sex differences in childhood behavior disorders, males were found to outnumber females in every major category (Eme, 1979). Consequently, the male child appears to be more at risk for maladjustment than the female child. Culturally

"His Freudian therapist says he has Oedipal conflicts, his Rogerian therapist says he has trouble with self-actualization, his Eriksonian therapist says he has identity-diffusion, and I say he is a brat!"

Courtesy of Ford Button.

determined role expectations and biological differences are two possible explanations for these findings. Beginning with adolescence and continuing into adulthood, a different pattern emerges: females outnumber males in neurotic disorders and affective psychotic disorders, while males continue to outnumber females in personality and gender identity disorders, and no sex differences emerge in schizophrenic disorders.

In a study (Stone, 1981) of a public elementary school population of approximately 25,000 children, teachers were asked to complete a modified form of the Behavior Problem Checklist. Children at lower IQ levels were rated as having more behavior problems than children at the average and upper IQ levels. As Table 20-8 shows, fourth-grade children with IQs below 70 were rated as having five times as many conduct problems and four times as many personality problems as those with IQs above 130. Children with IQs below 70 were rated as having three times as many conduct problems and over twice as many personality problems as children with average IQs. Similar trends were noted for sixth-grade children.

ASSESSMENT OF NONSPECIFIC BEHAVIOR DISORDERS

During an examination children may exhibit attitudes suggestive of a behavior disorder, including irritability and suspiciousness, restlessness, lack of spontaneity, variable mood, apathy, cynicism, regarding the test as "kid stuff,"

Table 20-8
Mean Number of Conduct and Personality Problems by Intellectual Level

IQ category	Fourth-graders		Sixth-graders	
	N conduct problems	N personality problems	N conduct problems	N personality problems
Below 70	10.6	6.2	13.9	7.3
70–79	11.0	6.6	12.4	7.5
80–89	9.5	5.7	10.5	6.4
90–99	6.0	3.9	7.6	5.0
100–109	3.7	2.6	4.4	3.2
110–119	2.2	1.7	3.4	2.5
120–129	2.1	1.5	3.2	2.3
130 and up	2.0	1.4	2.6	1.7

Source: Reprinted with permission of the publisher and author from F. B. Stone, "Behavior Problems of Elementary-School Children," in *Journal of Abnormal Child Psychology*, 9, p. 415, copyright 1981 by Plenum Publishing Corporation.

euphoria, and dysphoria. Language difficulties suggestive of a behavior disorder include speech difficulty, rambling, blocking, circumstantiality, clang associations, circumlocution, confabulation, overelaboration, and self-reference (see Chapter 18). Behaviors suggestive of anxiety include restlessness; apprehensiveness; impaired attention and concentration; bodily expressions indicating discomfort (for example, tics, nailbiting, fidgeting, and coughing); difficulty in finding words; impulsively blurting out unfinished, unchecked, or inappropriate replies; and fumbling about for adequate formulations.

The WISC-R is a reliable and stable instrument for evaluating children with behavior disorders (Dean, 1977d). Unfortunately, there are no WISC-R patterns that can distinguish reliably between children with various behavior disorders, although children with some behavior disorders may exhibit greater variability of scores (see, for example, Clarizio & Veres, 1983; Hale & Landino, 1981; Hamm & Evans, 1978; Morris, Evans, & Pearson, 1978). Factor analytic studies of the WISC-R indicate that there are no qualitative differences in the structure of intellectual abilities of normal children and those with behavior disorders (DeHorn & Klinge, 1978; Petersen & Hart, 1979).

PERVASIVE DEVELOPMENTAL DISORDERS: AN OVERVIEW

Pervasive developmental disorders is a broad classification of severe and pervasive disorders affecting children's social skills and language, attention, perception, reality testing, and motor activity. Multiple areas of functioning are affected. The children so diagnosed display severe qualitative abnormalities that are not normal for any developmental stage. There are two classifications within this DSM-III-R category: autistic disorder and pervasive developmental disorder not otherwise specified. The diagnostic criteria for the autistic disorder classification are shown in Exhibit 20-8. (Schizophrenia, which is distinguished from the autistic disorder by the presence of hallucinations and delusions, is not discussed in the text because it is a diagnosis given primarily to older adolescents and adults.)

Autistic Disorder

Children with an autistic disorder (formally classified as infantile autism) have a severe behavioral disorder that usually appears before 3 years of age. Autistic children may show poor response to sensory stimuli such as sound or light, may not recognize their parents, and may lack

At least eight of the following sixteen items are present, these to include at least two items from A, one from B, and one from C.

Note: Consider a criterion to be met *only* if the behavior is abnormal for the person's developmental level.

A. Qualitative impairment in reciprocal social interaction as manifested by the following:

(The examples within parentheses are arranged so that those first mentioned are more likely to apply to younger or more handicapped, and the later ones, to older or less handicapped, persons with this disorder.)

(1) marked lack of awareness of the existence or feelings of others (e.g., treats a person as if he or she were a piece of furniture; does not notice another person's distress; apparently has no concept of the need of others for privacy)

(2) no or abnormal seeking of comfort at times of distress (e.g., does not come for comfort even when ill, hurt, or tired; seeks comfort in a stereotyped way, e.g., says "cheese, cheese, cheese" whenever hurt)

(3) no or impaired imitation (e.g., does not wave bye-bye; does not copy mother's domestic activities; mechanical imitation of others' actions out of context)

(4) no or abnormal social play (e.g., does not actively participate in simple games; prefers solitary play activities; involves other children in play only as "mechanical aids")

(5) gross impairment in ability to make peer friendships (e.g., no interest in making peer friendships; despite interest in making friends, demonstrates lack of understanding of conventions of social interaction, for example, reads phone book to uninterested peer)

B. Qualitative impairment in verbal and nonverbal communication, and in imaginative activity, as manifested by the following:

(The numbered items are arranged so that those first listed are more likely to apply to younger or more handicapped, and the later ones, to older or less handicapped, persons with this disorder.)

(1) no mode of communication, such as communicative babbling, facial expression, gesture, mime, or spoken language

(2) markedly abnormal nonverbal communication, as in the use of eye-to-eye gaze, facial expression, body posture, or gestures to initiate or modulate social interaction (e.g., does not anticipate being held, stiffens when held, does not look at the person or smile when making a social approach, does not greet parents or visitors, has a fixed stare in social situations)

(3) absence of imaginative activity, such as playacting of adult roles, fantasy characters, or animals; lack of interest in stories about imaginary events

(4) marked abnormalities in the production of speech, including volume, pitch, stress, rate, rhythm, and intonation (e.g., monotonous tone, questionlike melody, or high pitch)

(5) marked abnormalities in the form or content of speech, including stereotyped and repetitive use of speech (e.g., immediate echolalia or mechanical repetition of television commercial); use of "you" when "I" is meant (e.g., using "You want cookie?" to mean "I want a cookie"); idiosyncratic use of words or phrases (e.g., "Go on green riding" to mean "I want to go on the swing"); or frequent irrelevant remarks (e.g., starts talking about train schedules during a conversation about sports)

(6) marked impairment in the ability to initiate or sustain a conversation with others, despite adequate speech (e.g., indulging in lengthy monologues on one subject regardless of interjections from others)

C. Markedly restricted repertoire of activities and interests, as manifested by the following:

(1) stereotyped body movements, e.g., hand-flicking or -twisting, spinning, head-banging, complex whole-body movements

(2) persistent preoccupation with parts of objects (e.g., sniffing or smelling objects, repetitive feeling of texture of materials, spinning wheels of toy cars) or attachment to unusual objects (e.g., insists on carrying around a piece of string)

(3) marked distress over changes in trivial aspects of environment, e.g., when a vase is moved from usual position

(4) unreasonable insistence on following routines in precise detail, e.g., insisting that exactly the same route always be followed when shopping

(5) markedly restricted range of interest and a preoccupation with one narrow interest, e.g., interested only in lining up objects, in amassing facts about meteorology, or in pretending to be a fantasy character.

D. Onset during infancy or childhood.

Specify if childhood onset (after 36 months of age).

Source: Reprinted with permission of the publisher from the *Diagnostic and Statistical Manual of Mental Disorders (Third Edition — Revised)*, 1987, pp. 38–39. Copyright © American Psychiatric Association.

interest in the environment. Some children appear distressed for long periods of time and cry continuously; others appear apathetic. Feeding and sleeping may be erratic and unpredictable. In time, the child may show obsessional features, aloofness and lack of interest in people, language disturbances, and retarded intellectual functioning.

Autistic children may have remarkable visual-spatial skills. They may notice minute details, react to very small changes in their surroundings, and spot missing objects. These skills, which enable them to locate things when others have given up searching, may be present even in autistic children who are retarded in other areas of functioning.

The autistic disorder can be behaviorally defined as a specific syndrome that is manifested at birth or shortly thereafter. The various symptoms associated with an autistic disorder appear to be expressive of an underlying neuropathophysiological process that affects developmental rate, perception, language, cognition, intelligence, and social relationships. Prognosis is guarded, as almost all children manifest severe symptomatology throughout their lives. In the following case, which traces the course of language, cognitive, and social development in an autistic child, we find the simultaneous presence of remarkable talents and profound deficits.

James was the third of four children, born following an uncomplicated pregnancy and labor. His health during the first 3 months of life was good, but shortly thereafter his mother expressed concern because of his sensitivities to light and sound, his failure to make an anticipatory response to being picked up, his fluctuating moods between inconsolable crying and extreme passiveness, and his failure to look at her when she fed him. She reported that he preferred lying in his crib, staring at the mobile, to being held or played with. Because his motor milestones appeared at the appropriate times, James' pediatrician reassured his mother that his development was fine. However, by age 16 months, James had not begun to babble or say single words, and spent most of his time in a corner repetitively moving toy cars back and forth. At 20 months, other symptoms emerged: he developed unusual hand movements and body postures; his obliviousness to people increased; he reacted to even the most subtle interruption in his routine or other changes in the world with extreme disorganization and panic; he developed a fascination with light switches and with studying tiny bits of paper and twigs.

At 4 years, James had not yet begun to speak socially to others, but could identify by name many numbers and all of the letters of the alphabet. He was able to execute the most graceful maneuvers, spinning in circles about a room without touching a piece of furniture. At other times, he appeared clumsy and uncoordinated. He persisted in lining up objects in the most complex patterns, but could never use objects appropriately. His parents complained about how difficult it was to buy birthday and Christmas gifts that could replace the tiny bits of paper and pieces of string he preferred. At about the age of 4½ years, he began to echo long and complicated sentences, some of which his mother reported he may have heard days or even weeks before. He was able to complete puzzles designed for 8- and 9-year-olds quickly, but was unable to reproduce a line or circle.

At about age 5, James made his first spontaneous statement. His mother reported that he had been looking at the sky and said, "It looks like a flower." He did not speak again for 8 months, but then began talking in full sentences. Most often, the content was concerned with numbers—he would read encyclopedias and report to whomever would listen that a certain river was 1,000 miles long and had 200 tributaries. When he met strangers, he mechanically introduced himself without ever establishing eye contact, and then rushed on to ask what the person's birthday, anniversary, and social security number were, often appearing not to pause long enough to get the answers. Years later, upon remeeting the person, he was able to recite back these facts.

James was remarkably talented musically, and could sing the lyrics to popular tunes and TV commercials. While he could read well, he was unable to abstract from written information, to draw inferences or make conclusions. At age 9, he remained socially distant, although he had learned many of the rules for social situations. He received superior scores on the WISC Object Assembly, Picture Completion, and Block Design subtests, but very low scores on the Comprehension, Similarities, and Information subtests. (Caparulo & Cohen, 1977, pp. 623–624, with changes in notation)

Etiology of autistic disorder.　Various explanations have been offered to account for the etiology of autistic disorder. One view is that autistic disorder is a disorder of the central nervous system that manifests itself in impaired comprehension and use of language. The cause of the cognitive deficit, however, remains unknown. Brain damage may be present in some cases, whereas in others developmental or genetic factors may be implicated. Autism may also involve a dysfunction of the complex circuitry providing the central connections of the vestibular system to the cerebellum and the brain stem. This proposal attempts to account for the strange sensorimotor behavior observed in autistic children (for example, spontaneous spinning and flicking of objects, flapping and oscillating of extremities, and whirling and rocking of the body).

There is substantial evidence that autism is probably not related to the psychological characteristics of autistic children's parents (Koegel, Schreibman, O'Neill, & Burke, 1983). When stress is found in parents of autistic children, it is likely to be highly situational. Findings such as these support a neurophysiological and biological basis for the disorder.

Intelligence and autistic disorder. In the past, IQs obtained from autistic children were often considered to be invalid. The hope was that with the right treatment, intellectual ability would develop to a normal level. Unfortunately, however, therapy with autistic children has not resulted in significantly improved levels of intellectual performance.

Research on autistic children's intellectual functioning points to several important findings.

1. As many as three-fourths of autistic children obtain IQs that are in the mentally retarded range of functioning (DeMyer, 1976; DeMyer, Barton, & Norton, 1972; Hingtgen & Bryson, 1972; Rutter, 1974, 1978; Rutter & Bartak, 1971).

2. The IQs obtained by autistic children have the same properties as do those obtained by other children (DeMyer, Barton, Alpern, Kimberlin, Allen, Yang, & Steele, 1974; Lotter, 1967; Rutter & Lockyer, 1967). Thus, for example, (a) IQs show moderate stability throughout childhood and adolescence (test-retest correlations for periods of 2 to 15 years ranged from .63 to .90), especially if the children are tested after 5 years of age, and (b) IQs are a reasonable predictor of later educational attainments.

3. The IQs of autistic children fail to change markedly even after their social responsiveness greatly improves. Poor motivation, consequently, does not appear to account for autistic children's below-average performance on intelligence tests.

4. Initially untestable autistic children later have been found to perform in a manner similar to that of severely retarded children (Bartak & Rutter, 1971, 1973; DeMyer et al., 1974; Gittelman & Birch, 1967; Lockyer & Rutter, 1969; Rutter & Bartak, 1973). In addition, those who appear to be untestable may be testable when given items representing sufficiently low mental age levels.

5. Autistic children who have adequate conversational speech or adequate social relationships obtain higher IQs than do other autistic children (DeMyer et al., 1974).

6. The fact that autistic children have relatively good visual-spatial and memory abilities but poor sequencing and language skills suggests a specific cognitive defect involving the use of language.

The above findings strongly suggest that autistic children with low IQs function like other children with low IQs. Therefore, do not dismiss the IQs obtained by autistic children as being a result of some easily reversible temporary impairment.

Treatment and prognosis of autistic disorder. Autistic children can be helped if the following guidelines are kept in mind (Gallagher & Wiegerink, 1976, p. 329):

1. Autistic children are educable.

2. Their unique learning characteristics are related to basic cognitive deficits in information processing.

3. Such deficits can be compensated for, in part, by carefully structured educational programs with specified developmental learning sequences and enhanced reinforcing stimuli.

4. Structured educational programs should begin early in life, with the parental figure as the primary teacher.

5. Providing educational programs for autistic children is feasible and in the long run is less costly than institutional care.

6. The provision of appropriate educational programs for autistic children is not a manifestation of public generosity but rather a reflection of the fact that these children, too, have a clear right to an appropriate education.

The goal of treatment is to develop better social and language skills in children who have cognitive handicaps. Programs should be tailored to the unique needs of each individual child. Teaching of sign language is useful in improving communication.

Autistic children face extreme interpersonal, behavioral, intellectual, and neurological difficulties when they reach adolescence and early adulthood (DeMyer, Barton, DeMyer, Norton, Allen, & Steele, 1973; Lotter, 1974, 1978; Rutter, 1970, 1974). In adolescence and adulthood, a majority of autistic individuals (about 60 percent) remain severely handicapped and are unable to lead an independent life; about 15 percent make a good social adjustment, holding a job and getting along in society; and about 25 percent have an intermediate outcome, with some degree of independence and only minor problems in behavior (Rutter, 1977). Even those with a good social adjustment have interpersonal difficulties and display oddities of behavior. When language does develop, it tends to be concrete, repetitive, literal, and automatic. A substantial minority of autistic children develop epilepsy during adolescence, especially those who are severely retarded.

Research findings involving autistic children support the following conclusions with regard to prognosis.

• There is substantial evidence that the IQs of autistic children in early childhood are excellent predictors of their later educational attainments and social adjustment. Autistic children with IQs below 50 have a very poor prognosis, whereas approximately half of those with IQs above 70 show a good adjustment in adolescence and adult life (Rutter, 1977).

• Level of language development is another important prognostic factor. A good outcome is more likely if language comprehension is not severely impaired in the preschool years or if the child has useful speech by the age of 5 years.

• Other prognostic factors include the severity of the behavioral disturbance in early childhood, the variety of play patterns, the type of schooling, and the nature of family interactions. Prognosis is better with less severe behavioral disturbance, with some constructive play, with good schooling, with a harmonious family, and with normal EEGs.

ASSESSMENT OF PERVASIVE DEVELOPMENTAL DISORDERS

A thorough assessment of children who may have an autistic disorder or pervasive developmental disorder not otherwise specified requires an evaluation of language, intelligence, neurological status, adaptive behavior, and familial factors, as well as the interrelationships of these separate factors. During the evaluation, attention should be given to the child's language, affect, interpersonal relations, and perceptual-motor performance. Any extreme deviations should raise questions about the possible presence of impaired ability. In making a clinical diagnosis it is important to consider current symptomatology, developmental changes in the symptoms (if any), intellectual level and language, and familial psychopathology.

Speech and Language of Children with an Autistic Disorder

Children with an autistic disorder may show delayed acquisition of speech. Some are suspected of having a hearing deficit because they do not respond to sounds. The most common characteristic of children with an autistic disorder is echolalia, either immediate or delayed. During the assessment a variety of language distortions may be revealed. These include echoing, circumlocution, rambling, fragmentation, irrelevant speech, bizarreness,

neologisms, blocking, automatic phrases, confabulation, circumstantiality, clang association, over elaboration, self-reference, confusion or omission of pronouns and connecting words, and mixtures of concrete and abstract words. Many of these terms are defined in Table 18-4 in Chapter 18.

Observations of the Behavior of Children with Autistic Disorder

Observing the toy play of children suspected of having an autistic disorder can provide useful information. Their toy play may show fewer combinational, appropriate, constructive, and functional uses; more restricted repertoires of toy play; longer latencies in approaching toys; and more repetitive manipulations of toys and their own bodies. Be alert to these and other aspects of the toy play of children. (Chapter 16 provides additional information about play interviews.) Behavioral observations also can be obtained from informants through the use of adaptive behavior scales or behavioral checklists, such as those covered in Chapter 15.

The Childhood Autism Rating Scale (Schopler, Reichler, DeVellis, & Daly, 1980) evaluates 15 dimensions of behavior (see Table 20-9). It can be completed after the diagnostic evaluation and its results incorporated into the psychological report. The scale can be used to rate autistic and other children in a variety of situations.

The Ritvo-Freeman Real Life Rating Scale is also useful in the diagnosis of infantile autism (Freeman, Ritvo, Yokota, & Ritvo, 1986). It appears to be a reliable and valid measure that can be used by both professionals and nonprofessionals. There are five parts, measuring sensorimotor functions, social relationships, affectual responses, sensory responses, and language. The scale is reproduced in Table E-3 in Appendix E.

The Autism Screening Instrument for Educational Planning (Krug, Arick, & Almond, 1980) is a battery of five procedures useful in evaluating autistic children. The procedures are Autism Behavior Checklist, Sample of Vocal Behavior, Interaction Assessment, Educational Assessment of Functional Skills, and Prognosis of Learning Rate. Scores and percentile ranks are provided for each procedure.

Intelligence Test Performance

There is no one pattern of performance on intelligence tests that is diagnostic of an autistic disorder. Some autistic

Table 20-9
Childhood Autism Rating Scale (CARS)

Scale	Rating			
	1 *Age appropriate*	*2* *Mildly abnormal*	*3* *Moderately abnormal*	*4* *Severely abnormal*
I. Relationships with people	Age-appropriate degrees of shyness, guardedness, negativeness	Some lack of eye contact; some negativism or avoidance; excessive shyness; some lack of responsiveness to the examiner	Considerable aloofness; intensive intrusion may be necessary to get a response, contact is not normally initiated by child	Intense aloofness, avoidance, obliviousness; child seldom responds to examiner; only the most intensive intervention produces a response
II. Imitation (verbal and motoric)	Age-appropriate imitation (both verbally and motorically)	Child imitates most of the time; occasionally prodding may be required or imitation may be delayed	Child imitates only part of the time; great persistence is required on the part of the examiner	Child seldom, if ever, imitates either verbally or motorically
III. Affect	Age- and situation-appropriate affective responses—child shows pleasure, displeasure, and interest through changes in facial expression, posture, and manner	Some lack of appropriate responsiveness to changes in affective stimuli; affect may be somewhat inhibited or excessive	Definite signs of inappropriate affect; reactions are quite inhibited or excessive or are often unrelated to the stimulus	Extremely rigid perseveration of affect; responses are seldom appropriate to the situation and are extremely resistant to modification by the examiner
IV. Use of body	Age-appropriate use and awareness of body	Minimal peculiarities in body use and awareness—some stereotyped movements, clumsiness and lack of coordination	Moderate signs of dysfunction—peculiar finger or body posturing, examination of body, self-directed aggression, rocking, spinning, finger-wiggling, toe-walking	Extreme or pervasive occurrence of functions listed in third column
V. Relation to non-human objects	Age-appropriate interest in, use of, and exploration of objects	Mild lack of interest in materials or mildly age-inappropriate use of materials—infantile mouthing of objects, banging of materials, fascination with materials that squeak, turning lights on and off	Significant lack of interest in most objects or some peculiar and obvious preoccupation with repetitive use of objects—e.g., picking at objects with fingernails, spinning wheels, becoming fascinated with one small part	Severely inappropriate interest in, use of, and exploration of objects—extreme or pervasive occurrence of those functions listed in third column; child is very difficult to distract

(Table continues next page)

Table 20-9 (cont.)

	Rating			
Scale	1 Age appropriate	2 Mildly abnormal	3 Moderately abnormal	4 Severely abnormal
VI. Adaptation to environmental change	Age-appropriate responses to change	Some evidence of resistance to environmental changes—staying with an object or activity or persisting in same response pattern; child can be distracted	Active resistance to change in activities, with signs of irritability and frustration; child is difficult to distract when intervention is attempted	Severe reactions to change that are extremely resistant to modification; child may engage in a tantrum if change is insisted upon
VII. Visual responsiveness	Age-appropriate visual responses used in an integrated way with other sensory systems	Child must be reminded occasionally to look at materials; some preoccupation with mirror image; some avoidance of eye contact; some staring into space; some fascination with lights	Child must be reminded frequently to look at what he or she is doing, likes to look at shiny objects, makes little eye contact even when forced, looks "through" people, frequently stares into space	Pervasive visual avoidance of objects and people; bizarre use of visual cues
VIII. Auditory responsiveness	Age-appropriate auditory responses used in an integrated way with other sensory systems	Some lack of response to auditory stimuli or to particular sounds; responses may be delayed; stimuli may occasionally have to be repeated; child is hypersensitive to or distracted by extraneous noises	Inconsistent responses to auditory stimuli; stimuli may have to be repeated several times before child responds; child is hypersensitive to certain sounds (e.g., very easily startled, covers ears)	Pervasive auditory avoidance, regardless of type of stimulus, or extreme hypersensitivity
IX. Near receptor responsiveness	Normal response to pain, appropriate to intensity; normal tactual and olfactory exploration, but not to the exclusion of other forms of exploration	Some lack of appropriate response to pain or evidence of mild preoccupation with tactual exploration, smelling, tasting, etc.; some infantile mouthing of objects	Moderate lack of appropriate response to pain or evidence of moderate preoccupation with tactual exploration, smelling, tasting, etc.	Excessive preoccupation with tactual exploration (mouthing, licking, feeling, or rubbing) for sensory rather than functional experience; pain may be either ignored completely or grossly overreacted to
X. Anxiety reaction	Age- and situation-appropriate reactions—reactions are not prolonged	Mild anxiety reactions	Moderate anxiety reactions	Severe anxiety reactions—child may not settle down during the entire session or may be obviously fearful, withdrawn, etc.

(Table continues next page)

Table 20-9 (cont.)

	Rating			
Scale	1 Age appropriate	2 Mildly abnormal	3 Moderately abnormal	4 Severely abnormal
XI. Verbal communication	Age-appropriate speech	Overall retardation of speech; most speech is meaningful, but it may include remnants of echolalia	Absence of speech or a mixture of some meaningful speech with some inappropriate speech (e.g., echolalia, jargon)	Severely abnormal speech; virtual absence of intelligible words or peculiar and bizarre use of more recognizable language
XII. Nonverbal communication	Age-appropriate nonverbal communication	Overall retardation of nonverbal communication; communication may consist of simple or vague responses, such as pointing to or reaching for what is wanted	Absence of nonverbal communication—child does not use or respond to nonverbal communication	Peculiar, bizarre, and generally incomprehensible nonverbal communication
XIII. Activity level (motility patterns)	Normal activity level—child is neither hyperactive nor hypoactive	Child is mildly restless or is somewhat slow to move about, but generally can be controlled; activity level interferes only slightly with performance	Child is quite active and hard to restrain, with a driven quality to activity, or quite inactive and slow-moving; examiner must either exert control frequently or exert a great effort to get a response	Extremely abnormal activity level—child is either driven or apathetic; child is very difficult to manage or to get to respond to anything; almost constant control by an adult is required
XIV. Intellecual functioning	Normal intellectual functioning—no evidence of retardation	Mildly abnormal intellectual functioning—skills appear fairly evenly retarded across all assessed areas	Moderately abnormal intellectual functioning—some skills appear retarded and others are at or very near age level (hints of potential)	Severely abnormal intellectual functioning—some skills appear retarded and others are above age level or are unusual
XV. General impression	No autism	Minimal or mild autism	Moderate signs of autism	Maximum or extreme signs of autism

Note. This table is a condensed tabular presentation of the Childhood Autism Rating Scale, which is described in the unpublished appendix that accompanies Schopler, Reichler, DeVellis, and Daly (1980). See Schopler, Reichler, and Renner (1986) for a more current version of the CARS. Permission to reprint this condensed version of the CARS was given by E. Schopler.

children differ little in performance from normal children, whereas others show considerable unevenness in functioning. In some cases, administering performance tests may be the only way to obtain an estimate of the child's intelligence level. Likely choices are the Leiter International Performance Scale and performance subtests from the WISC-R, WPPSI, Stanford-Binet Intelligence Scale:

Fourth Edition, and K-ABC. There may also be some indications of illogical thinking. Extreme variability in subtest scores cannot be used as a diagnostic sign.

Many tests require linguistic skill and sustained attention, two abilities that children with an autistic disorder may lack. Their failure to perform adequately on some tests may therefore reflect deficiencies in these areas rather than more general cognitive deficiencies. Research has shown that when the linguistic and attentional requirements for solution of Piagetian tasks were eliminated, children with an autistic disorder (ages 4 to 9 years) performed at levels comparable to those of normal children (Lancy & Goldstein, 1982).

Psychological Evaluation

Exhibit 20-9 presents a psychological evaluation of a child who probably would be classified as having a pervasive developmental disorder not otherwise specified.

ASSESSMENT OF VISUALLY IMPAIRED CHILDREN

The two major sensory impairments are blindness and deafness. Children with these handicaps not only are restricted in their activities, but also are limited in their opportunities for social, cultural, and intellectual stimulation. These limitations may affect the development of intelligence and other abilities. (Suggestions for testing children with sensory impairments are presented in Chapter 5.)

Types of Visual Impairment

Types of visual dysfunction include the following (Du-Bose, 1979a):

- refractive errors in the form of myopia (nearsightedness) or hyperopia (farsightedness) — the most common cause of eye problems,
- astigmatism (distorted or blurred vision),
- amblyopia (lazy eye),
- strabismus (failure of the eyes to focus properly on the same points, leading to a squint, cross-eye, or wall-eye),
- cataract (cloudy condition in the lens of the eye),
- glaucoma (increased pressure within the globe of the eye),
- retinitis pigmentosa (an inherited disease caused by changes in the retina that may result in night blindness and tunnel vision),
- retinal detachment (separation of the inner layer of the retina from its outer layer), and
- macular degeneration (degeneration of a small area in the retina).

Early Development

An investigation of the first two years of gross motor development of infants blind from birth revealed that, although adequate neuromuscular maturation was demonstrated, there was a considerable delay in self-initiated mobility (Adelson & Fraiberg, 1974). Perhaps this prolonged period of immobility during the first year of life of blind infants lessens their ability to explore independently and to discover by themselves the objective rules that govern things and events in the external world. An intervention program carried out by Adelson and Fraiberg, which focused on human relationships, adaptive hand behavior, and coordination of tactile and auditory schemas, was partially successful in increasing the mobility of the youngsters.

Suppes (1974, p. 149) pointed out:

Educating blind children is a difficult task because the normal mode of taking in information is heavily dependent on the printed word. The cognitive deficits present in blind children may simply be due to the relatively simple fact of not having an alternative input channel that can match the rate of visual processing, and thus they are "information poor," deprived in the quantitative sense of the amount of information transmitted to them.

Visual Impairment and Intelligence

Blind children usually obtain a mean IQ in the normal range, but their distribution of scores tends to be bimodal: there are more superior as well as more inferior children in the blind group than in the normal group (Crowell, 1957). Studies using the WISC-R Verbal Scale indicate that blind children are likely to perform best on the Digit Span subtest, poorest on the Similarities subtest, and slightly better on the Comprehension subtest (Gilbert & Rubin, 1965; Hopkins & McGuire, 1966; Tillman, 1967a; Tillman & Bashaw, 1968; Tillman & Osborne, 1969). These results suggest that blind children have well-developed rote memory capacities but are less adequate in conceptual thinking and social comprehension. Because of the variability in subtest scores, it is important to examine both the Verbal Scale IQ and the individual subtest scores. It is possible that the Verbal Scale IQ may not provide as adequate a measure as some of the individual subtests do (Tillman & Bashaw, 1968).

Studies of the WISC Verbal Scale with blind children report satisfactory reliability (Tillman, 1973). Much less is known about the validity of the WISC (and the WISC-R) for blind children, however.

The WISC Verbal Scale and the Hayes-Binet (a special form of the Stanford-Binet: Form L-M that is used with

Exhibit 20-9

Psychological Evaluation: Pervasive Developmental Disorder Not Otherwise Specified

Name: Mark
Date of birth: January 11, 1980
Chronological age: 7-1

Date of examination: February 9, 1987
Date of report: February 13, 1987
Grade: 2nd

Reason for Referral

Mark was referred for psychological reevaluation by the Center for the Developmentally Disabled, where he has been followed since his initial evaluation when he was 4 years, 8 months old.

Tests Administered

Wechsler Intelligence Scale for Children—Revised:

VERBAL SCALE		PERFORMANCE SCALE	
Information	6	Picture Completion	8
Similarities	9	Picture Arrangement	1
Arithmetic	6	Block Design	1
Vocabulary	2	Object Assembly	11
Comprehension	4	Coding	6

Verbal Scale IQ = 72
Performance Scale IQ = 70
Full Scale IQ = 69 ± 3 at the 68 percent confidence level

Vineland Adaptive Behavior Scales:

Adaptive Behavior Composite = 90 ± 6 at the 95 percent confidence level

Bender Visual Motor Gestalt Test:

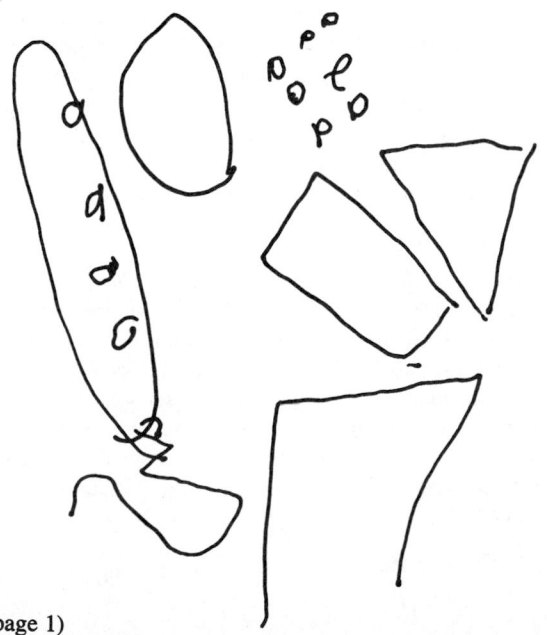

(page 1)

(page 2)

History

Mark was initially evaluated in 1984 because the day care center he was attending reported that his fine motor coordination appeared to be delayed. The results of the initial evaluation not only confirmed the center's suspicion, but also revealed a Borderline range of intelligence (IQ of 79 on the Stanford-Binet Intelligence Scale: Form L-M), accompanied by some depression and inappropriate affect. Expressive and receptive speech and language were delayed; Mark spoke in short incomplete sentences, often marked by neologisms and jargon. There was no suggestion of a hearing loss, nor were there any positive neurological signs.

In both the first and second grades Mark has experienced problems with comprehension, especially in arithmetic. His parents are concerned, because their son is unable to answer many of his teacher's questions. His language has improved somewhat since the first evaluation, however. Mark has been having nightmares several times weekly and frequently wets his bed. In addition, he often refuses to obey his parents and teachers and has frequent aggressive temper tantrums. He has only one friend, whom he sees only on a limited basis.

(Exhibit continues next page)

Exhibit 20-9 (cont.)

Mark is a tall, attractive boy. He appeared sullen and negative at first, resisting entrance to the testing room and failing to answer questions. When he did respond, there were long hesitations between questions and responses as he appeared to ponder one single aspect or word in the question. Thus, his responses were unrelated to the questions, and his thought processes appeared to be fragmented and illogical. Periodic neologisms, frequent associative responses, and often bizarre responses were observed. For example, when asked to define a "hat," Mark said, "A hat makes brains." When asked what to do if he cut his finger, he replied, "If you cut your finger you should break your hand; iron it on."

Sometimes Mark acted silly and laughed hysterically when he played with a series of words or neologisms that he had created. Echoing the examiner's words or rhyming them endlessly caused peals of laughter. Often he could not focus on the essential elements of a task. He would become absorbed in irrelevant details, such as the difference in color of the fronts and backs of puzzle pieces, exclaiming, "I feel much better on the pink side."

His behavior also shifted rapidly and unpredictably from aggression to affection. For example, Mark pummeled, strangled, and swore at a stuffed bear in the room and shortly thereafter began to stroke the bear affectionately and hug it while whispering into its ear. Similarly, frequent verbal aggressive outbursts ("You stupid big mouth") were followed by friendly exchanges.

When Mark was presented with verbal items that he initially failed to understand, he became anxious and angry and yelled at the examiner, "You stupid big mouth." When asked about this frequent remark, Mark said a big mouth is a monster. He then trailed off into illogical associative thoughts, forgetting his initial statement. Mark often seemed preoccupied during testing. Several times it seemed as though he was trying to shut out auditory stimulation by closing his eyes or covering his face with his hands, showing a confusion in modalities. Throughout the test session, Mark seemed most comfortable when provided with gentle but firm structure. He became most anxious and disturbed when he was presented with an unstructured task.

Test Results

Mark, with a chronological age of 7-1, achieved a Verbal IQ of 72, a Performance IQ of 70, and a Full Scale IQ of 69 ± 3 on the WISC-R. This places him in the Mentally Retarded range. The chances that the range of scores from 66 to 72 includes his true IQ are about 68 out of 100. His level of functioning exceeds that of 2 percent of the children in the standardization group, a group that is roughly representative of the United States population.

Much variability was evident in his WISC-R performance. He ranged from extremely inadequate performance in areas requiring word knowledge, interpretation of social situations, and spatial visualization (all within the 1st percentile) to average performance in verbal concept formation (37th percentile) and perceptual organization (63rd percentile). Within subtests, he often missed easy items and passed more difficult ones later. The often bizarre content and the extreme variability of scores suggests that there is impairment in his cognitive functioning.

On the Vineland Adaptive Behavior Scales, Mark obtained an Adaptive Behavior Composite of 90 ± 6 at the 95 percent confidence level. He is able to bathe with assistance, go to school unattended, and print simple words. He cannot tell time or comb his hair, however. His visual-motor coordination, as measured by the Bender-Gestalt, was at the 4th percentile (Koppitz norms), indicating a serious delay in the development of these skills. His errors included collision, rotation, fragmentation, distortion of shape, and expansion.

In a free play situation, Mark continued to evidence loose thinking. While playing with a puppet, he excitedly described how a live pig went inside the skin of another pig. Although he was vague about himself and his relationships, unable to answer such questions as what grade he was in and where he lived, he talked lucidly and in detail about the book *The Wizard of Oz.*

Clinical Impressions

Mark, who is functioning in the Mentally Retarded range, shows numerous social adjustment difficulties. Unevenness in development is apparent, with gross immaturities characterized by atypical and bizarre behavior. He is experiencing significant learning difficulties in a regular second-grade class. Throughout the test session there were indications of a marked behavior disorder and expressions of an aggressive and disorganized nature. Mark relates poorly to others and is extremely sensitive to minimal pressure, either becoming verbally aggressive or attempting to screen out sounds by covering his eyes. Mark's intellectual deficits, coupled with marked behavioral and thought disturbances, suggest a diagnosis of pervasive developmental disorder not otherwise specified, which should be confirmed by psychiatric evaluation.

Recommendations

In view of the present test results and observations, it is recommended that Mark be referred for a psychiatric evaluation. EEG and neurological exams should be conducted to rule out organicity. Based on the results of this and previous evaluations, modifications in the regular school setting need to be explored to meet Mark's needs. Placement in an emotionally disturbed classroom should be considered. Psychotherapy for Mark and counseling for his parents are also suggested.

(Signature)_____

Examiner

blind children) have been compared in various samples of blind children. In one sample of children who were between 9 and 15 years of age, the two scales were highly correlated ($r = .86$), but WISC IQs ($M = 110$) were about 8 points lower than Hayes-Binet IQs ($M = 118$) (Hopkins & McGuire, 1966). These results were essentially confirmed in another study (Hopkins & McGuire, 1967). The two scales were also found to yield similar IQs in a study of children between the ages of 6 and 14 years (M's of 78 and 75 for the Verbal Scale and Hayes-Binet, respectively) (Gilbert & Rubin, 1965) and in a study of young children ($r = .94$, M's of 98 and 99 for the Verbal Scale and Hayes-Binet, respectively) (Lewis, 1957). The Hayes-Binet has been found to be somewhat more valid than the WISC when teachers' ratings were used as the criterion (r's of .51 and .37, respectively) (Denton, 1954).

These studies indicate that the WISC and the Hayes-Binet cannot be considered to be interchangeable for blind children with above-average ability. For blind children with average or below-average ability, the scales appear to yield more comparable IQs. Additional study is needed of the relationship between intelligence test scores and academic achievement in blind children.

Other instruments available for testing visually handicapped children are the Perkins-Binet Tests of Intelligence for the Blind (Davis, 1980) and the Blind Learning Aptitude Test (Newland, 1971). Genshaft and Ward (1982) reviewed the Perkins-Binet and made suggestions for its administration. The Blind Learning Aptitude Test is reviewed in Chapter 12.

ASSESSMENT OF HEARING-IMPAIRED CHILDREN

Developing competence in a standard natural language is of critical importance for hearing-impaired children. An important instructional goal is to teach hearing-impaired children to produce speech sounds similar to those produced by normally hearing English-speaking persons. Their ability to develop a language generally varies directly with the magnitude of their hearing loss. Although deaf children follow a normal pattern of vocalizations (for example, babbling, crying, and cooing) until about 6 to 9 months of age, their ability to communicate orally decreases after this time.

Types of Hearing Loss

There are three general types of hearing loss. A *conductive hearing loss* results from problems associated with the outer or middle ear, which prevent clear transmission of sound waves to the inner ear. These problems may be due to impounded wax, foreign objects (such as beans or candy), inflammation in the middle ear, excess fluid in the Eustachian tube, or infection of the Eustachian tube and are amenable to medical treatment or amplification. A *sensorineural loss* results from defects in the inner ear caused by damage to the auditory nerve; correction may not be possible. A *mixed hearing loss* results when both a conductive loss and a sensorineural loss are present; amplification may help, but some problems often remain.

Causes of Hearing Impairment

The two major causes of hearing impairment in children are genetic or chromosomal abnormalities and disease or trauma (DuBose, 1979b). Hearing impairment may result from viral infections (such as maternal rubella), meningitis, and serous otitis media (a blockage of the Eustachian tube that forces the middle ear to become partially closed); from drugs, taken either by the mother or by the child (impairment is usually reversible once the drug is discontinued); and from physical injuries (for example, blows to the head and injury to bones in the ear), infections from the throat and nasal passages, prolonged exposure to high-intensity sounds, blood incompatibility, and birth complications.

As many as one-third of school-age hearing-impaired children may have learning or behavior problems that cannot be attributed solely to their hearing loss (Jensema & Mullins, 1974). Consequently, the distribution of intelligence in hearing-impaired children may be bimodal, with the multiply handicapped forming one group and the nonmultiply handicapped forming the other (Sullivan, 1982).

Early Development

Deaf children who have an early, severe hearing loss may not have the lateral specialization of the brain for language that characterizes the hearing population (Kelly & Tomlinson-Keasey, 1977). Without the auditory processing of speech, the left hemisphere may not develop a specialization for language. Instead, deaf children are likely to process cognitive information with right hemisphere structures (that is, with visual codes rather than with language-oriented auditory codes). Although this type of research is only in its rudimentary stages, it holds promise for a better understanding of the cognitive processing of deaf children.

The greatest single handicap associated with hearing loss during the prelingual years is the barrier to learning language (Gerken, 1979). Hearing impairment impedes the normal acquisition of both receptive and expressive language skills. It has been estimated that a normal 4-year-old child has a working vocabulary of between 2,000 and 3,000 words, whereas a prelingually deaf child of this age has fewer than 25 words (Meadow, 1968). This latter estimate may not hold for a deaf child of deaf parents who has been exposed to education programs as an infant; such exposure expands a child's vocabulary. Hearing-impaired children also have syntactical deficiencies in the use of language. Because the normal sequence of language mastery is impeded, difficulties arise in acquiring reading, writing, and spelling skills.

Social Maturity

Deaf children are generally behind their hearing peers in social maturity (Meadow, 1975). Within the deaf population, social maturity appears to be dependent on at least two factors. First, deaf children with adequate communication skills are likely to be more socially mature than those with poor communication skills. Second, deaf children of deaf parents are likely to be more socially mature than deaf children of hearing parents. The delayed language acquisition experienced by most deaf children probably leads to more limited opportunities for social interaction, which, in turn, may cause frustration for both children and parents. Generally, deaf children appear to have more adjustment problems than hearing children.

Intelligence Test Scores

Deaf children usually obtain scores within the normal range on nonverbal intelligence tests, although their mean scores are somewhat lower than those of hearing children (Meadow, 1975). For example, a national sample of 1,228 deaf children obtained a mean IQ of 95.70 on the WISC-R Performance Scale (Sisco & Anderson, 1978). The subtests, from easiest to most difficult, were Object Assembly ($M = 10.32$), Mazes ($M = 10.03$), Picture Completion ($M = 9.51$), Block Design ($M = 9.48$), Picture Arrangement ($M = 8.71$), and Coding ($M = 8.03$). In contrast, the general level of academic achievement of deaf children was much below that which would be expected from their performance on intelligence tests. Reading achievement especially was below the expected level. The limited access to language stimulation is perhaps the key to why deaf children perform poorly on reading tests and on verbal intelligence tests. *Verbal tests are useful in testing the verbal language abilities of hearing-impaired children, but not their level of cognitive functioning.*

The number of low IQs is also disproportionately higher among hard-of-hearing children than among normal children. One explanation for this finding is that the etiologies of profound hearing loss are also associated with other neurological impairments that frequently interfere with cognitive processes. For example, diseases or conditions such as maternal rubella, purulent meningitis of early onset, premature birth, and tuberculous meningitis may lead to mental retardation as well as to deafness.

The Performance Scale of the WISC-R is a reliable and valid instrument for the assessment of deaf children (Hirshoren, Hurley, & Kavale, 1979; Hirshoren, Kavale, Hurley, & Hunt, 1977; Hurley, Hirshoren, Hunt, & Kavale, 1979). *The Verbal Scale and other verbal tests are inappropriate for measuring the intelligence of deaf children.* A comparison of the Verbal IQ with the Performance IQ, however, can provide an estimate of the degree to which a deaf child has mastered verbal concepts.

The WISC-R Performance Scale has the same factor structure in deaf and hearing groups (Braden, 1985). There is no evidence that intelligence, as measured by the WISC-R, differs qualitatively in deaf and hearing groups. Additionally, the internal validity, construct validity, and criterion validity of the WISC-R Performance Scale are essentially the same for deaf children as for hearing children, and the norms presented in the WISC-R manual are valid for the assessment of deaf children.

A study of the sensorimotor development of 16 deaf children 23 to 38 months of age, using the Infant Psychological Development Scale, showed that the children were progressing normally except in the area of vocal imitation, where the deaf children performed below age expectation (Best & Roberts, 1976). The six scales showing normal development were Object Permanence, Objects as Means, Schemas, Causality, Objects in Space, and Motor Imitation (see Chapter 12). The Infant Psychological Development Scale is easily adapted for use with deaf children, because it requires little or no language for administration.

Other Assessment Techniques and Considerations

Exhibit 20-10 shows a semi-structured interview format that can be used with parents of a hearing-impaired child. It should be used in conjunction with the interview questions shown in Chapter 16, to obtain information about the developmental history of the child.

For older children and adults, the Hearing Performance Inventory—a 158-item self-report inventory—can be used to assess how the person with a hearing problem experiences difficulties in everyday listening (Giolas, Owens, Lamb, & Schubert, 1979). The six areas of the inventory

Exhibit 20-10

Example of a Semi-Structured Interview with Parents of a Hearing-Impaired Child

1. When was the hearing loss first suspected?
2. Describe the behavior that caused concern.
3. What action has been taken to determine whether a hearing loss exists?
4. Have other professionals been consulted?
5. (If yes) What were their conclusions and what advice did they give you about management of the child?
6. Do other persons in the family have hearing losses?
7. (If yes) Tell me about their losses.
8. Describe _____'s speech and language development.
9. At what ages did _____ begin to use words [pause], phrases [pause], sentences?
10. Is _____'s speech intelligible?
11. How does _____ communicate her (his) needs to others (gestures, speech)?
12. How do others communicate with _____?
13. Does _____ respond to loud sounds [pause], soft sounds [pause], vibrations?
14. Can _____ understand what is said to her (him) without gestures [pause], with gestures?
15. Does _____ watch the face of the speaker?
16. Are there words that _____ seems to understand that she (he) cannot say?
17. Has _____ ever worn a hearing aid?
(If yes, ask the following questions.)
18. Who recommended it?
19. What model is the hearing aid and who is the manufacturer?
20. When was it purchased?
21. Has it been satisfactory?
22. Describe _____'s reactions to the hearing aid.
23. In which ear does _____ wear it?
24. How consistently?

Note. See Table 16-13 in Chapter 16 for questions concerning developmental, medical, social, and educational history.
Source: Adapted from C. V. Anderson and J. M. Davis (1979).

are understanding speech, intensity, response to auditory failure, social, personal, and occupational. Following are examples of items in the six categories (the entire inventory is reproduced in the Giolas et al. publication):

1. You are in a fairly quiet room. Can you carry on a conversation with a woman in another room if her voice is loud enough for you?
2. Can you hear an airplane in the sky when others around you can hear it?
3. You are in a restaurant. When you miss something important that the waitress/waiter said, do you ask for it to be repeated?
4. You are talking with five or six friends. When you miss something important that was said, do you ask the person talking to repeat it?
5. Does your hearing problem discourage you from going to the movies?
6. Does your hearing problem interfere with your getting a job easily?

Assessing Hard-of-Hearing Children Whose Primary Language Is Not English

Assessing hard-of-hearing children whose primary language is not English is even a more formidable task than assessing native English speaking hard-of-hearing children because of problems associated with the use of two languages. In devising an appropriate assessment strategy for such children, consider (a) the languages understood and spoken by the child, including sign language, and the degree of proficiency in each area; (b) the languages spoken at home, including sign language; (c) the child's degree of hearing loss; and (d) the modality preferred by the child for receptive purposes and for expressive purposes.

Improving Competencies

To improve the performance of hearing-impaired children, it may be useful to employ multisensory experiences, emphasizing the auditory dimension in conjunction with a good oral technique or focusing on transformation within a single mode. For example, "Sesame Street" (Children's Television Workshop) often transforms multiple visuals of an object into the word for that object. In addition, the stimuli provided for visual and auditory processing should be as diverse as possible. Deaf children who develop good communication skills are likely to be those who have been exposed to both oral and manual training at an early age. Early intervention programs with deaf children should focus on vocal imitation, communication abilities, and curriculum materials that teach social interaction concepts.

SUMMARY

1. Specific learning disability is a term used to refer to children who have difficulty mastering one or more basic scholastic skills, but who have adequate intelligence, maturational level, and cultural background.

2. Current definitions of learning disability are difficult to operationalize.

3. Five models are useful in understanding the etiology of learning disability: the difference model, the deficit model, the delay model, the disruption model, and the personal-historical model. Each model has some merit in explaining learning disability, and they are not mutually exclusive. The etiology of learning disability is likely multifactorial.

4. Information processing models may be helpful in understanding learning disability. One model postulates four stages: sensory storage, perceptual encoding, central processing, and response selection mechanisms. The stages of the model are discrete; incoming stimuli are transformed, and the transformed stimuli serve as input into subsequent stages.

5. Tasks that require the active processing of information are difficult for learning-disabled children. Specifically, such children tend to make little use of such mnemonic aids as labeling, verbal rehearsal, clustering, chunking, and selective attention. These difficulties may in part account for their deficits in verbal encoding and word retrieval. Inadequate executive control functions—that is, difficulty in applying efficient task strategies—may be a key element in their attention problems.

6. Remediation programs should be designed to help learning-disabled children acquire problem-solving skills, mnemonic strategies, and good study habits.

7. Reading involves such factors as attention, concentration, ability to form associations within and between sensory modalities, phonological awareness, rapid decoding, verbal comprehension, and general intelligence.

8. Reading disability, or dyslexia, is best defined as a syndrome of learning disability in which children with adequate intelligence and educational opportunities fail to master basic processes, such as letter recognition and sound blending.

9. The three primary subtypes of reading disability are auditory-linguistic deficits, visual-spatial deficits, and mixed deficits. Children with auditory-linguistic deficits have difficulty integrating symbols with their sounds. Children with visual-spatial deficits have difficulty reading words as a whole. Those with mixed deficits have difficulty in both language-related and visual-spatial areas. The majority of children with reading disability have auditory-linguistic deficits.

10. Two syndromes of acquired dyslexia are surface dyslexia and phonological dyslexia. In surface dyslexia, whole word recognition is impaired, particularly for words with irregular spelling-to-sound patterns. In phonological dyslexia, whole word recognition is somewhat intact, but words cannot be sounded out without difficulty.

11. The etiology of reading disability is not clear. The causes of reading disability may be multifactorial. Causes that have been postulated include brain damage, maturational lag, genetic factors, right-hemisphere dominance, ocular factors, environmental factors, and behavioral factors.

12. The process of learning to read includes (a) differentiating and identifying individual letter shapes or graphemes, (b) learning to associate graphemes with appropriate phonemes and breaking down whole words into sounds, (c) grasping the variations that can occur in grapheme-phoneme association in differ-

ent word contexts, and (d) sampling the most significant words in a sentence without directly perceiving all of the words. At each step in learning to read, children may experience difficulty.

13. Younger learning-disabled children are likely to have a deficiency in phonological coding, whereas older learning-disabled children use a phonemic code but have a more general deficit in short-term memory, particularly in the context of language processing.

14. The perceptual-cognitive processes *least* related to reading are eye movement patterns, visual processing abilities, and accessing the name code of a symbolic stimulus. Those *most* related to reading are phonological awareness and coding skills, contextual strategies that facilitate comprehension, short-term memory, listening comprehension, and general comprehension strategies.

15. Developmental dyslexia refers to a failure to develop the ability to read. Acquired dyslexia refers to the loss of ability previously acquired.

16. Reading ability and intelligence are significantly related. Median correlations between reading ability and scores on the WISC-R and the Stanford-Binet: Form L-M are .44 and .46, respectively. The correlations between reading ability and intelligence rise from a low of .30 to .50 in the elementary grades to a high of .60 to .75 for adults.

17. Reading-disabled children should be helped to develop efficient reading strategies. These include understanding task demands, identifying and attending to important aspects of reading passages, monitoring their reading to determine their comprehension level, and backtracking or scanning ahead when comprehension falters.

18. Children who have a precocious ability to recognize words, beyond what would be expected given their general level of intellectual ability, are said to be hyperlexic.

19. The assessment of learning-disabled children focuses on obtaining an estimate of general intelligence, determining areas of impaired functioning, and finding strengths that may prove helpful in remediation efforts.

20. As outlined in Public Law (PL) 94-142, the key indicator of a specific learning disability is a severe discrepancy between achievement and intellectual ability in one or more of the following areas: oral expression, listening comprehension, written expression, basic reading skills, reading comprehension, mathematical calculation, or mathematical reasoning. The discrepancy cannot be a result of sensory handicaps, mental retardation, emotional disturbance, or environmental, cultural, or economic disadvantage. The guidelines of PL 94-142, however, do not indicate how a severe discrepancy should be determined. Clinical and psychoeducational considerations must come together in a diagnosis of learning disability.

21. At least four means are available for evaluating a discrepancy between ability and achievement. These involve deviation from grade or age level, expectancy formulas, regression equations, and standard score comparisons. Regression procedures are highly recommended, but there is some evidence that the easier standard score comparison procedure highly overlaps with

the regression equation procedure. Discrepancy procedures must take into account the child's *absolute* level of functioning. Discrepancy procedures have various shortcomings that should be considered whenever they are used.

22. In assessing learning-disabled children, it is important to evaluate developmental-cognitive processes, achievement skills, environmental demands, reactions of others, and the interaction of these factors over time.

23. Although there is no single preferred battery of tests for the assessment of learning disability, an intelligence test, an achievement test, and a visual-motor test usually should be included. Evaluation of auditory skills and visual-perceptual processing skills is also helpful, as are trial teaching procedures and classroom observations.

24. There is no WISC-R pattern that is reliably diagnostic of learning disability or reading disability. On the average, however, the four most difficult WISC-R subtests for reading-disabled children are Arithmetic, Coding, Information, and Digit Span. (The acronym ACID is a mnemonic for remembering this cluster.)

25. Informal assessment of academic and learning skills may include the evaluation of oral reading errors, word prediction abilities, phonological awareness, written expression, spelling errors, and paragraph recall.

26. The key behavioral features of the attention-deficit hyperactivity disorder are hyperactivity, impulsivity, distractibility, excitability, and short attention span. The syndrome is much more common in boys than in girls. It is not always easy to differentiate restlessness and overactive behavior from hyperactive behavior.

27. The etiology of attention-deficit hyperactivity disorder is unknown. Many different theories have been proposed to account for hyperactivity, including minimal brain damage, delayed maturation, genetic variation, metabolic disturbance, emotional disturbance, and allergic reaction to certain foods.

28. Hyperactive children tend to do more poorly than nonhyperactive children on tests of perceptual-motor functioning, measures of sustained attention, and measures requiring delay of impulse.

29. Psychostimulant medications such as Ritalin and Dexedrine are frequently used in the treatment of hyperactive children. These medications improve attention and impulse control but not broad-gauged cognitive abilities.

30. Individual intelligence tests are the preferred instruments for the assessment of children with an attention-deficit disorder. There are no specific patterns on the WISC-R that are associated with hyperactivity. Three assessment procedures have been found to be especially useful in differentiating hyperactive from normal children: the Porteus Maze Test, Jumbled Numbers Game, and Bobo punching doll.

31. Delinquent children, on the average, obtain IQs that are about 8 points lower than those of nondelinquents. The comparative rarity of delinquents with superior intelligence may be a result of differential immunity given to them by the courts.

32. Delinquents, on the average, obtain higher Performance than Verbal IQs. The discrepancy may be more reflective of learning difficulties than of delinquency per se.

33. Males outnumber females in every major category of childhood behavior disorder.

34. Fourth and sixth graders with low IQs have been found to have significantly more conduct and personality problems than those with average or superior ability.

35. During the assessment, indicators of behavior disorder can be observed in children's attitudes (for example, irritability and suspiciousness), language (for example, speech difficulties and rambling), and bodily expressions (for example, tics and nail biting).

36. The WISC-R cannot reliably distinguish among various groups of behaviorally disturbed children.

37. Autistic disorder usually appears between birth and 3 years of age. The primary symptoms include pervasive lack of responsiveness to other people, gross deficits in language development, deviant language, and bizarre responses to the environment. An absence of delusions, hallucinations, loosening of associations, and incoherence distinguishes autistic disorder from schizophrenia.

38. A neuropathophysiological process appears to be responsible for autistic disorder. The prognosis is guarded.

39. Evidence suggests that autistic disorder is probably not related to the psychological characteristics of autistic children's parents.

40. Almost 75 percent of autistic children obtain IQs that are in the mentally retarded range of functioning. IQs obtained by autistic children are as valid as those obtained by normal children.

41. The treatment of children with autistic disorder should begin early in life, with the parental figures as the primary teachers. Stress should be given to improving social and language skills.

42. The most favorable prognostic indicators in autistic children are (a) IQs over 70, (b) useful speech by 5 years of age, (c) infrequent and mild pathology, (d) ability to attend school, (e) appropriate use of play material, and (f) normal EEGs.

43. The assessment of children with autistic disorders requires an evaluation of language, intelligence, neurological status, adaptive behavior, and familial factors. Children with these disorders may show delayed acquisition of speech, and some are suspected of having a hearing deficit. Echolalia is a frequent symptom of children with autistic disorders. Close attention should be paid to any indications of language distortions. Important information can be obtained by observing the toy play of autistic children. Useful instruments include the Childhood Autism Rating Scale, the Ritvo-Freeman Real Life Rating Scale, and the Autism Screening Instrument for Educational Planning. Intelligence tests and adaptive behavior scales are also valuable tools in the assessment battery.

44. Vision may be affected by various impairments, including refractive errors, astigmatism, and other conditions that affect the lens of the eye or retina.

45. The average intelligence level of blind children is in the

normal range, but their distribution of scores tends to be bimodal, with more superior as well as more inferior scores. Although the WISC-R Verbal Scale and the Hayes-Binet are not interchangeable, they both appear to be reliable instruments for the assessment of the intelligence of blind children.

46. The three general types of hearing loss are a conductive hearing loss (problems with the outer or middle ear prevent clear transmission of sound waves to the inner ear), a sensorineural loss (defects in the inner ear caused by damage to the auditory nerve interfere with the transmission of auditory messages), and a mixed hearing loss (when both a conductive loss and a sensorineural loss are present).

47. The two main causes of hearing impairment in children are (a) genetic or chromosomal abnormalities and (b) disease or trauma. As many as one third of school-age hearing-impaired children may be multiply handicapped.

48. The greatest handicap faced by hearing-impaired children is the barrier to learning language.

49. On nonverbal tests, deaf children obtain scores that fall within the normal range of intelligence, although their mean WISC-R IQ in one study with a large sample was toward the lower limits of the Average range (M IQ = 95.70). The number of children with low IQs is disproportionately higher among hard-of-hearing children than among normal children.

50. Only performance tests should be used to arrive at an estimate of the intelligence level of hearing-impaired children. One such test is the WISC-R Performance Scale, which is a reliable and valid instrument for the assessment of deaf children.

51. Assessing hard-of-hearing children whose primary language is not English is a formidable task.

52. Multisensory experiences can be used to improve the competencies of hearing-impaired children.

KEY TERMS, CONCEPTS, AND NAMES

Learning disability (p. 598)
Specific learning disability (p. 598)
Perceptual processing deficit (p. 598)
Difference model (p. 599)
Deficit model (p. 599)
Delay model (p. 599)
Disruption model (p. 599)
Personal-historical model (p. 599)
Four-stage information processing model (p. 599)
Short-term sensory store (p. 599)
Short-term memory store (p. 599)
Long-term memory store (p. 599)
Sensory storage (p. 600)
Perceptual encoding (p. 600)
Central processing (p. 600)
Response selection mechanisms (p. 600)
Executive control functions (p. 600)
Verbal encoding (p. 600)

Phonological awareness (p. 602)
Rapid decoding (p. 602)
Graphic feature of a word (p. 602)
Orthographic feature of a word (p. 602)
Semantic feature of a word (p. 602)
Syntactic feature of a word (p. 602)
Phonologic feature of a word (p. 602)
Dyslexia (p. 602)
Auditory-linguistic deficit (p. 602)
Visual-spatial deficit (p. 602)
Mixed deficit (p. 602)
Developmental dyslexia (p. 603)
Acquired dyslexia (p. 603)
Surface dyslexia (p. 603)
Phonological dyslexia (p. 603)
Reading disability (p. 604)
Hyperlexia (p. 606)
Ability-achievement discrepancy (p. 607)
Deviation from grade level or age level (p. 607)
Expectancy formulas (p. 607)
Regression equations (p. 607)
Standard score comparisons (p. 608)
Bannatyne recategorization of the WISC-R (p. 609)
Bannatyne WISC-R spatial category (p. 609)
Bannatyne WISC-R conceptual category (p. 609)
Bannatyne WISC-R sequential category (p. 609)
Bannatyne WISC-R acquired knowledge category (p. 609)
Word prediction abilities (p. 611)
Cloze procedures (p. 611)
Strip initial consonant task (p. 611)
Phonological oddity task (p. 611)
Attention-deficit hyperactivity disorder (p. 617)
Psychostimulant medication (p. 624)
Amphetamines (p. 624)
Methylphenidate (p. 624)
Ritalin (p. 624)
Dextroamphetamine (p. 624)
Dexedrine (p. 624)
Porteus Maze Test (p. 625)
Jumbled Numbers Game (p. 625)
Bobo punching doll (p. 625)
Conduct disorder (p. 626)
Pervasive developmental disorders (p. 628)
Autistic disorder (p. 628)
Pervasive developmental disorder not otherwise specified (p. 628)
Echolalia (p. 629)
Childhood Autism Rating Scale (p. 632)
Ritvo-Freeman Real Life Rating Scale (p. 632)
Autism Screening Instrument for Educational Planning (p. 632)
Refractive errors (p. 636)
Myopia (p. 636)
Hyperopia (p. 636)
Astigmatism (p. 636)

STUDY QUESTIONS

1. Discuss learning disabilities. Include in your discussion (a) definitions of PL 94-142 and the NJCLD, and a critical evaluation of these definitions, (b) the etiology of learning disability, (c) an information processing model to account for some deficits in learning-disabled children, and (d) the type of remediation program that may be helpful for learning-disabled children.

2. Discuss reading disability. Include in your discussion (a) the cognitive functions involved in reading, (b) subtypes of reading disability, (c) syndromes of dyslexia, (d) the etiology of reading disability, (e) stages of learning to read, (f) information processing deficiencies associated with reading, (g) developmen-tal aspects of reading disability, (h) individual differences in perceptual-cognitive processes related to reading, (i) intelligence and reading ability, and (j) remediation of reading disability.

3. Discuss assessment considerations in evaluating learning-disabled children. Include in your discussion the guidelines offered in PL 94-142, procedures for arriving at a discrepancy, general assessment guidelines, an assessment battery, the use of the WISC-R, and informal assessment procedures.

4. Discuss the attention-deficit hyperactivity disorder. Include in your discussion its essential features, associated features, etiology, treatment, and assessment approaches.

5. Discuss behavior disorders. Include in your discussion types of behavior disorders according to the DSM-III-R, sex differences in behavior disorders, behavior problems and level of intelligence, delinquency and level of intelligence, and assessment considerations, including the use of the WISC-R.

6. Discuss the autistic disorder syndrome. Include in your discussion the main features of the syndrome, etiological considerations, relationship with level of intelligence, treatment and prognosis, and assessment considerations.

7. Discuss the assessment of visually impaired children. Include in your discussion types of impairments, developmental considerations, levels of intelligence, and assessment considerations.

8. Discuss the assessment of hearing-impaired children. Include in your discussion types of impairments, developmental considerations, levels of intelligence, and assessment considerations.

21

ASSESSMENT OF MENTAL RETARDATION AND GIFTEDNESS

Some measure of genius is the rightful inheritance of every man.

—Alfred North Whitehead

A great society not only searches out excellence but rewards it when it is found.

—Anonymous

ASSESSMENT OF MENTALLY RETARDED CHILDREN

Definition of Mental Retardation

The term *mental retardation* describes a heterogeneous group of conditions characterized by low or very low intelligence and deficits in adaptive behavior. The most widely used definition of mental retardation is the one proposed by the American Association on Mental Deficiency (AAMD) (Grossman, 1983, p. 11):

Mental retardation refers to significantly subaverage general intellectual functioning existing concurrently with deficits in adaptive behavior, and manifested during the developmental period.

This definition refers to a level of behavioral performance without reference to etiology. The key terms in the definition bear closer inspection.

• *Significantly subaverage* refers to performance that is 2 or more standard deviations below the population mean.

• *General intellectual functioning* refers to performance on a standardized intelligence test that measures, as far as is possible, general cognitive ability rather than one limited facet of ability, such as receptive vocabulary or spatial-analytic skills.

• *Adaptive behavior* refers to the effectiveness with which individuals meet the standards of personal independence and social responsibility expected of individuals of their age and cultural group. Deficits in adaptive behavior are evaluated according to developmental age. During infancy and early childhood, adaptive behavior deficits are evaluated in relationship to sensorimotor skills, communication skills, self-help skills, and socialization skills. During childhood and early adolescence, the focus is on the application of (a) basic academic skills in daily life activities, (b) appropriate reasoning and judgment in interacting with the environment, and (c) social skills. During late adolescence and adult life, adaptive behavior centers on vocational and social responsibilities and performances.

• *The developmental period* is regarded as the period between birth and about 18 years of age.

The AAMD definition indicates that two criteria—level of intelligence and level of adaptive behavior—must be considered jointly in arriving at a diagnosis. Only when an individual falls into the retarded category with respect to *both* intellectual functioning *and* adaptive behavior functioning is a diagnosis of mental retardation appropriate.

Intelligence is assessed through objective measurement; adaptive behavior is assessed clinically or by means of an objective scale.

The AAMD definition has several implications. First, the assessment must focus on a description of *present behavior*; prediction of later intelligence is a separate process and one fraught with many difficulties. Second, the contribution of individually administered intelligence tests is specifically recognized. Third, the diagnosis is tied to the developmental process, with behavioral descriptions anchored to the individual's own age level. Fourth, a diagnosis of mental retardation does not rule out the coexistence of other forms of childhood disorders. Fifth, the definition avoids the implication that mental retardation is irreversible. Finally, a diagnosis of mental retardation is inappropriate when an individual is adequately meeting the demands of his or her environment.

The definition proposed by the AAMD, which is similar to the one in the DSM III-R, is not without its critics (see, for example, Zigler, Balla, & Hodapp, 1984; Zigler & Farber, 1985). The critics believe that social adaptation is an elusive concept that is difficult to define and measure; thus mental retardation should be conceptualized in terms of actual cognitive functioning and defined solely in terms of performance on an intelligence test (more than 2 *SD* below the mean). Under such a system, if a child fell in this range, a statement of etiology (familial or organic) would also be presented. These arguments have much merit, but until the AAMD standards are changed, we must adhere to current, nationally recommended definitions, which include the assessment of adaptive behavior. The AAMD definition remains the standard in the field.

Classification of Mental Retardation

The AAMD classification of mental retardation contains four categories—mild, moderate, severe, and profound—based on levels of intelligence in conjunction with the classification of adaptive behavior (see Table 21-1). In using the AAMD classification system, remember that the level of retardation arrived at by an intelligence test is dependent on the standard deviation (*SD*) of the test. For example, if the −2 *SD* criterion is used, then the IQ just below the −2 *SD* point is 69 for the WISC-R, WPPSI, and WAIS-R, but 67 for the Stanford-Binet. The cutoff points are different because the Wechsler scales have an *SD* of 15, whereas the Stanford-Binet (Fourth Edition and Form L-M) has an *SD* of 16. Still other cutoff points may be appropriate for other instruments, depending on the *SD* of the test. Although the Wechsler scales and the Stanford-Binet have been standardized so that the *SD*'s are the same throughout the ages covered by the scales, such may not be the case for other instruments. Each test must be carefully evaluated before it is used in the assessment of mental retardation.

Table 21-2 shows a classification system for adaptive behavior that parallels the classification system for measured intelligence. The system coordinates developmental stages and level of retardation, emphasizing sensorimotor skills, language and communication, learning, degree of self-sufficiency, and vocational potential. A child's adaptive behavior classification may differ from his or her intelligence classification. For instance, an individual may receive a *mildly* retarded adaptive behavior classification, but a *moderately* retarded intelligence classification.

The assessment of intelligence is a much more precise procedure than is the assessment of adaptive behavior. The Stanford-Binet and Wechsler scales are well normed instruments, with excellent reliability and validity. Their respective normative groups are relatively up to date. In contrast, there are few nationally standardized instruments available for the assessment of adaptive behavior during the developmental period that meet acceptable psychometric standards. Instruments such as the AAMD Adaptive Behavior Scale and the Vineland Adaptive Behavior Scales can assist in the assessment of adaptive behavior, but they are highly dependent on the reliability of the informant. The informant's ability to observe and report reliably the child's skills, behavior, and temperament will determine the accuracy of the adaptive behavior ratings. In contrast, it is the child who actually performs on the intelligence test; no intermediary is necessary. In the final analysis, present guidelines suggest that a diagnosis of mental retardation must rest in part on clinical judgment — all relevant factors must be considered.

Etiology of Mental Retardation

Etiologically, mental retardation falls into two broad groupings — familial and organic.

1. The *familial group* encompasses most mildly mentally retarded persons, in the IQ range of 50 to 69. The familially retarded are primarily individuals in the lower portion of the normal distribution of intelligence; their performance reflects normal intellectual variability. The variability is likely to be the result of normal polygenic variation — that is, the combined action of many genes. Performance in this range can also be associated with (a) pathological factors that interfere with brain functioning (such as subclinical organic damage that has yet to be discovered) or (b) the combined effect of below-average heredity and a markedly below-average environment. The familially retarded tend to come from low socioeconomic status (SES) groups.

Familially retarded children tend to exhibit the following behaviors (Zigler & Balla, 1981): (a) they are more responsive to social reinforcement than their non-retarded peers; (b) their expectancy of success is low, whereas their expectancy of failure is high; (c) they perform better on a variety of tasks when the reward is tangible; and (d) they are outer directed (for example, they are sensitive to cues provided by adults and are highly imitative). These behaviors are likely the result of motivational and emotional differences between the experiential histories of retarded and average children.

The familially retarded do not often come to the attention of the professional community as adults. One plausible explanation for this finding is that intellectual limitation is more obvious in school settings than in employment settings, where there is less need for certain cognitive

Table 21-1
Classification of Mental Retardation

Level of mental retardation	Educational equivalent description	Range in standard deviation value	Range in IQ for Stanford-Binet: Form L-M and Fourth Edition[a]	Range in IQ for WISC-R, WPPSI, and WAIS-R[a]	Approximate mental age at adulthood	Approximate percent of the population	Approximate percent of retarded persons
Mild	Educable	−2.01 to −3.00	67–52	69–55	8-3 to 10-9	2.7	89.0
Moderate	Trainable	−3.01 to −4.00	51–36	54–40	5-7 to 8-2	0.2	6.0
Severe	Trainable (dependent)	−4.01 to −5.00	35–20	39–25	3-2 to 5-6	0.1	3.5
Profound	Custodial (life support)	< −5.00	< 20	< 25	< 3-2	0.05	1.5

[a] The IQs shown for the severe and profound levels for the Stanford-Binet and Wechsler tests are extrapolated.

Table 21-2
Levels of Adaptive Behavior for the Mentally Retarded

Level	Preschool age: birth to 5 years	School age: 6 to 21 years	Adult: over 21 years
Mild retardation	Can develop social and communication skills; minimal retardation in sensorimotor areas; rarely distinguished from normal until later age.	Can learn academic skills to approximately 6th grade level by late teens. Cannot learn general high school subjects. Needs special education, particularly at secondary school age levels.	Capable of social and vocational adequacy with proper education and training. Frequently needs guidance when under serious social or economic stress.
Moderate retardation	Can talk or learn to communicate; poor social awareness; fair motor development; may profit from self-help; can be managed with moderate supervision.	Can learn functional academic skills to approximately 4th grade level by late teens if given special education.	Capable of self-maintenance in unskilled or semi-skilled occupations; needs supervision and guidance when under mild social or economic stress.
Severe retardation	Poor motor development; speech is minimal; generally unable to profit from training in self-help; little or no communication skills.	Can talk or learn to communicate; can be trained in elemental health habits; cannot learn functional academic skills; profits from systematic habit training.	Can contribute partially to self-support under complete supervision; can develop self-protection skills to a minimal useful level in controlled environment.
Profound retardation	Gross retardation; minimal capacity for functioning in sensorimotor areas; needs nursing care.	Some motor development present; cannot profit from training in self-help; needs total care.	Some motor and speech development; totally incapable of self-maintenance; needs complete care and supervision.

Note. States may differ in their definitions of these levels.
Source: Reprinted, with a change in notation, by permission of the publisher and authors from W. Sloan and J. W. Birch, "A Rationale for Degrees of Retardation," *American Journal of Mental Deficiency*, *60*, p. 262. Copyright 1955, American Association on Mental Deficiency.

skills. A second possibility is that mildly retarded persons gradually acquire many adaptive skills. Finally, some of these individuals may improve in intellectual ability in adolescence and in early adult years.

2. The *organic* group includes primarily the more severely mentally retarded, in the IQ range below 50, although organic etiologies are seen in some milder forms of mental retardation as well. The etiology of the organic type of mental retardation may be associated with a genetic component linked to single gene effects, chromosomal abnormalities, or brain damage. Organically mentally retarded children usually have severe and often diffuse brain damage or malformations, commonly originating during the prenatal period. They show a severe lag in behavioral development, sometimes accompanied by an abnormal appearance. Identification of the more severe forms of retardation is relatively easy because the children fail to

reach normal motor and language developmental milestones.

Most mentally retarded children (85 percent) have mild forms of mental retardation, with etiologies associated with social, cultural, psychological, or perhaps genetic factors. The remaining 15 percent of retarded children have moderate to severe deficits, such as microcephaly, Down's syndrome (mongolism), phenylketonuria, and cerebral dysfunction; these have primarily organic etiologies.

A study of 17,432 white and 19,419 black children in the National Institute of Neurological and Communicative Disorders and Stroke Collaborative Perinatal Project (Nichols, 1984) provided excellent support for the two-group theory of mental retardation in the white population. Specifically, mildly retarded white children had more affected relatives than did the severely retarded, consistent with the two-group theory of mental retardation. In the black population, however, differences in family patterns between the mildly and severely retarded were less clear, with most of the retardation appearing to be of the familial type.

Prevalence Rates of Mental Retardation as a Function of the Relationship Between Measured Intelligence and Adaptive Behavior

The AAMD's definition of mental retardation requires that a child be below the population average by at least 2 standard deviations on a measure of intelligence and a measure of adaptive behavior. Because intelligence and adaptive behavior are not perfectly correlated, children who fall below -2 SD on an intelligence test may have adaptive behavior skills that do not fall into this range. Thus the number of children classified as mentally retarded is likely to be lower when the two criteria are used than when a single criterion is applied. As can be seen in Table 21-3, hypothetical prevalence rates decrease markedly as one moves from a correlation of 1.00 (reflecting the hypothetical case in which all children whose intelligence test scores fell in the retarded range also had adaptive behavior scores in this range) to a correlation of .00 (Silverstein, 1973). Nationwide estimated prevalence rates, using -2 SD as the cutting score on each measure, range from 120,000 to over 5,400,000, depending on the correlation assumed between the two measures.

Table 21-3
Hypothetical Prevalence Rates of Mental Retardation per 1,000 Population and Hypothetical Nationwide Prevalence Using -2 Standard Deviation Cutting Score for Estimates of the Population Correlation Between Measured Intelligence and Adaptive Behavior

Correlation	Hypothetical prevalence rate per 1,000	Hypothetical nationwide prevalence
.00	.5	120,000
.20	1.4	336,000
.40	2.9	696,000
.60	5.5	1,320,000
.80	9.8	2,352,000
1.00	22.8	5,472,000

Note. These data are based on an assumed population of 240,000,000. Estimates in the third column provided by Silverstein in a personal communication in 1987.
Source: Adapted from Silverstein (1973).

In one study (Mastenbrook, 1978) of 300 children who obtained WISC-R IQs between 50 and 70, less than 35 percent had adaptive behavior scores that also were lower than 2 standard deviations below the mean. Consequently, the joint use of both criteria—IQ and adaptive behavior—for the classification of mental retardation eliminated 65 percent of those who would have been so classified through the exclusive use of the IQ criterion. Similar findings have been reported by Childs (1982). Children receiving a mental retardation classification on the basis of both criteria are likely to be more impaired than those classified solely on the basis of their IQs.

Some General Considerations in Understanding Mental Retardation

Mental retardation is not a disease; rather, it is a symptom of a wide variety of conditions that may interfere with the normal development of the brain, and intellectual impairment is a functional expression of the interference. As with normal children, there is considerable variability in the personality and behavior of children considered to be retarded. Having a low IQ is not synonymous with being passive, acquiescent, or helpless. In an impressive series of experiments, Braginsky and Braginsky (1971) demonstrated that mentally retarded children have the interpersonal awareness and manipulative skills necessary to control, to some extent, their own fates. In one of the experiments, for example, the children were able to appear either slow or bright on the Quick Test, depending on which strategy was appropriate to satisfy their personal goals.

In all periods of their lives, mentally retarded children are more vulnerable to the development of maladaptive behavior than are normal children. They may also exhibit symptoms of mental illness and have emotional disorders similar to those that occur among children of normal intelligence.

The field of mental retardation is a complex one to study. Generalizations about cognitive processes and personality are as difficult to make in the field of mental retardation as in any other field of psychology.

Importance of chronological age. Chronological age (CA) exerts control over many of an individual's traits and should be considered in evaluating mentally retarded individuals. Although chronological age per se may have little impact on intelligence test performance, it does affect less cognitively demanding social behaviors and interests (Zigler et al., 1984). For example, a 25-year-old retarded person with a mental age of 7 should be expected to catch a bus and go downtown, an activity that one would be hesitant to expect of a 7-year-old with average intelligence. Behaviors such as skating at age 7, dating at age 17, and being married and working at age 25 are also tied to chronological age. Behaviors that are CA-sensitive should be carefully considered in formulating recommendations for mentally retarded persons. Retarded individuals are highly motivated to perform age-appropriate tasks when they have the necessary intellectual abilities.

Heterogeneity among the children labeled mentally retarded. Children labeled mentally retarded may show a great heterogeneity of performance. Although two children who obtain IQs of 67 may both be described as mentally retarded, one who is a slow learner is obviously far different from one who exhibits no language or self-help skills. Among those who function in the Educable Mentally Retarded (EMR) range, there are differences in form perception, clerical speed, spatial ability, and dexterity (Watkins, 1980). The label *mental retardation* should not blind us to the fact that mentally retarded children differ among themselves, just as do children in any other group. The brief case studies in Exhibit 21-1 illustrate the heterogeneity of four children diagnosed as mentally retarded.

Developmental issues in cognitive and social adaptation. The cognitive development and social adaptation skills of mentally retarded children, obtained from research investigations, are highlighted in Exhibit 21-2. Many of the issues dealt with in the exhibit are discussed in this and other chapters of the text.

Mental Retardation and Intelligence Testing

As early as the first decade of the twentieth century, the National Education Association was concerned with the proper use of intelligence tests in the study of mentally retarded children. A committee of the association formulated a policy concerning the use of tests that is as appropriate today as it was when it was first issued:

Tests of mental deficiency are chiefly useful in the hands of the skilled experimenter. No sets of tests have been devised which will give a categorical answer as to the mental status of any individual. In nearly every instance in which they are used, they need to be interpreted. (Bruner, Barnes, & Dearborn, 1909, p. 905)

The committee noted that the tests proposed by DeSanctis and by Binet and Simon were of considerable value as tests of general capacity. Today, the testing of intelligence is still

one of the important functions of schools and of institutions for the mentally retarded.

The Stanford-Binet Intelligence Scale: Fourth Edition appears to be a useful instrument in the assessment of mental retardation. Additional research is needed to determine its validity for this population, however. The Wechsler scales (WISC-R, WPPSI, and WAIS-R) are also popular instruments for the evaluation of mild mental retardation. The Stanford-Binet: Fourth Edition has a somewhat lower floor than the Wechsler scales, but not at all age levels. Neither the Stanford-Binet: Fourth Edition nor the Wechsler batteries was designed for the assessment of severely and profoundly retarded children.

Stability of the IQ. Mentally retarded persons tend to show less change in IQ when retested than do persons who are not mentally retarded (Silverstein, 1982b). This generalization, however, is in part dependent on the time interval between tests and on the types of tests used for each evaluation. When the interval between testings is short and when the same test is administered each time, IQs are likely to be more similar (see Chapters 2 and 4).

Goal in evaluating mentally retarded children. The assessment principles discussed throughout this text apply to mentally retarded children as well as to children of normal intelligence. The relative strengths of mentally retarded children should be evaluated, as well as their weaknesses. Important goals in evaluating mentally retarded children are to understand why they do not function socially, if that is their problem, and to determine their assets and limitations so that remedial action can be taken. The intelligence test plays a crucial role in the evaluation of a mentally retarded child. Consequently, the utmost care and attention must be exercised in the testing of children suspected of functioning in the mentally retarded range. In such cases, there must be no doubt about the reliability and validity of the obtained IQ.

The following case demonstrates the value of using repeated testing to follow the course of treatment of a child with phenylketonuria (PKU). When the child was taken off his diet, his IQ declined. On reinstatement of the diet, his IQ partially recovered.

Roger's early development was delayed, as noted, for example, by his being unable to sit unsupported at the age of 9 months. At 13 months he had infantile spasms and received a diagnosis of phenylketonuria (PKU). Treatment with a low phenylalanine (PA) diet stopped the spasms and improved his development. Over the next 7 years his blood PA level was well maintained and development and growth were normal. He attended regular classes, but received special help. Because of his overactive behavior and persistently abnormal EEGs, he was treated with medication from the age of 4 years.

At 8 years of age, WISC-R IQs were in the 90's (Verbal IQ = 90, Performance IQ = 96, Full Scale IQ = 92). He was then started on a normal diet. Four months later he became lethargic and moody, and his school work deteriorated. His

parents attributed these problems to a change in classrooms. Because of their dissatisfaction, they moved him to a new school. During this time he consumed large amounts of protein. He developed a tremor of his hands and exaggerated knee reflexes. Testing showed a marked decrease in intellectual functioning (Verbal IQ = 71, Performance IQ = 79, Full Scale IQ = 72).

A strict low PA diet was reintroduced, and within a few weeks

---

Exhibit 21-1

Brief Case Studies of Mentally Retarded Children

Introductory Remarks

Although children classified as mentally retarded all have IQs that are 2 or more standard deviations below the mean of the standardization sample, considerable variation may be evident in their test profiles. You will find substantial differences in the test performances of the four children described below, all of whom were diagnosed as mentally retarded (see Table 21-A). In some cases the range of WISC-R subtest scores is limited (1 to 6), whereas in others it is extensive (1 to 12). In addition, the children have different strengths and weaknesses. On the Bender-Gestalt, there is variation in the types of errors and in the number of errors (from 3 to 11 on the Koppitz system). Wide Range Achievement Test—Revised (WRAT-R) profiles, however, are similar—at the 5th percentile or lower in the three achievement areas assessed. Adaptive behavior estimates are lower than average in each case. In assessing mentally retarded children, it is important to remember that they may have unique patterns of strengths and weaknesses.

Case 1

Jerry, a 9-year, 8-month-old male, was evaluated for possible placement in a class for the mentally retarded. He was cooperative during the evaluation and performed in a slow, cautious manner. His WISC-R Full Scale IQ was in the Mentally Retarded range. His WRAT-R scores in reading, spelling, and arithmetic were at the 1st percentile. His 11 errors on the Bender-Gestalt, which place him at the 1st percentile (standard score = 38) according to the Koppitz norms, indicate considerable perceptual-motor difficulty. Estimates of adaptive behavior place him at a much younger age level. A special education program should be considered.

Case 2

Colleen, a 13-year, 3-month-old female, was seen for a re-evaluation of her present level of functioning. She is currently in an educable mentally retarded class. Although she was cooperative during testing, she displayed some excitability and immaturity. Language and communication difficulties were also noted. Her WISC-R Full Scale IQ was in the Mentally Retarded range. On the WRAT-R, all scores were at

the 1st percentile. She obtained an Adaptive Behavior Composite score of 67 (1st percentile rank) on the Vineland Adaptive Behavior Scales. The Bender-Gestalt results place her in the 8½- to 9-year age range. Further evaluation is needed to assess her speech and language difficulties. It is recommended that she continue in her current class placement.

Case 3

Lisa, a 16-year, 2-month-old female, was referred for testing because of academic difficulties. In prior years, she repeated two grades; currently she is in the 8th grade. Her WISC-R Full Scale IQ was in the Mentally Retarded range. She performed well below average on all tasks. On the WRAT-R, she also obtained scores that were below average (Reading, 1st percentile; Arithmetic, 5th percentile; Spelling, 3rd percentile). She obtained an Adaptive Behavior Composite score of 68 (2nd percentile rank) on the Vineland Adaptive Behavior Scales. Her performance on the Bender-Gestalt placed her well below age level according to the Koppitz norms (an age of 6½ to 7 years was indicated), suggesting some perceptual-motor deficits. It is recommended she be placed in a class for the developmentally handicapped.

Case 4

Donald, a 10-year, 0-month-old male with a history of neurological impairment (microcephaly), was referred for evaluation for class placement. His WISC-R Full Scale IQ was in the Mentally Retarded range. He scored well below average on all tasks. His scores on the WRAT-R were consistently low (Reading, 1st percentile; Spelling, 4th percentile; Arithmetic, 2nd percentile), as were his scores on the Woodcock Reading Mastery Tests, which placed his reading skills at the first grade level. His Bender-Gestalt performance, which places him below age level (at the 1st percentile, standard score = 44) according to the Koppitz norms, indicates deficits in perceptual-motor ability. He obtained an Adaptive Behavior Composite score of 61 (1st percentile rank) on the Vineland Adaptive Behavior Scales. It is recommended that Donald be placed in an Educable Mentally Retarded class.

(Exhibit continues next page)

Exhibit 21-1 (cont.)

Table 21-A
Test Scores and Bender-Gestalt Protocols for Four Cases of Mental Retardation

Test	Case 1 (male, age 9-8)	Case 2 (female, age 13-3)	Case 3 (female, age 16-2)	Case 4 (male, age 10-0)
WISC-R		Scaled Score		
Information	4	1	4	2
Similarities	5	1	5	4
Arithmetic	5	4	2	2
Vocabulary	4	1	4	3
Comprehension	8	1	4	1
Digit Span	—	1	5	2
Picture Completion	9	5	5	6
Picture Arrangement	1	3	3	2
Block Design	1	7	5	1
Object Assembly	3	12	1	6
Coding	4	8	6	4
Mazes	—	—	—	—
		Deviation IQ		
Verbal IQ	70	47	62	52
Performance IQ	58	80	61	60
Full Scale IQ	62	61	58	52
WRAT-R		Standard Score		
Reading	61	68	67	64
Spelling	46	66	71	73
Arithmetic	48	67	75	68

Bender-Gestalt

(Case 1)

(Case 2)

(Case 4)

(Case 3)

■ **Exhibit 21-2** ■

Mental Retardation: Developmental Issues in Cognitive and Social Adaptation

Learning and Cognition

1. The principles governing the acquisition, maintenance, and extinction of simple responses and basic memory functions are the same for retarded and nonretarded children, with the exception of those who have significant neurological impairment.

2. Mental age exerts a powerful influence on many aspects of learning and cognition.

3. Noncognitive factors affect learning and thinking. (Noncognitive factors include temperament or personality, motivation, and sensory and motor capacities.)

4. Retarded children's intellectual deficiencies are related more closely to higher-order cognitive processes than to subordinate processes. (Higher-order cognitive processes include efficient problem-solving strategies, generalization, and abstraction. Subordinate cognitive processes include attention, rehearsal, ability to inhibit responses, and discrimination of elements of a problem.)

5. Even with cognitive training and supportive environments, retarded children continue to differ from nonretarded children. (No combination of sophisticated prosthetic aids, instructional approaches, and supportive social environments has made retarded children function the same as normal children.)

In sum, retarded children's behavior is similar in many ways to that of normal children, especially younger children of like mental ages. The disparity between retarded children's mental and chronological ages often creates an atypical pattern of life experiences relative to those of nonretarded children. These life experiences sometimes contribute to added noncognitive differences between normal and retarded children. Noncognitive factors such as motivation and self-concept sometimes further reduce the cognitive performance of retarded people. This result argues for the type of "relativistic appraisal" of intelligence advocated by Wechsler and is consistent with the view that mental retardation represents nonoptimal functioning in many domains.

The Social Ecology of Retarded Children's Lives

1. The quality of environments cannot be judged without reference to the specific characteristics and needs of the children in those environments. (Adjustment is best facilitated when there is a match between environmental expectations and children's abilities.)

2. It is important to consider a child's mental or developmental age when evaluating his or her social environment. (Caretaker's behavior may be a direct function of the child's capabilities—such as mental age or level of productive speech; consequently, the child's social environment must be judged in relationship to the child's age, condition, and functional abilities.)

3. Environmental variables account for much of the behavior of retarded children. (Environmental variables are highly correlated with behavioral patterns, and social behavior is modifiable by altering environmental conditions.)

4. To assess the impact of environmental variables, the child's total social repertoire and behavior in many situations should be considered.

In sum, retarded children show a variety of deficits and delays in their social development relative to normal children of the same chronological ages. Relative to normal children of the same mental ages, retarded children show fewer social differences. At least some of the differences are due to a mismatch between retarded children's social and learning environments and their cognitive capabilities. Theoretically, successful social adaptation is influenced by many personal qualities, such as self-confidence, physical attractiveness, communication style, consideration of others, willingness to change, and so forth. Many of these attributes can be modified by a combination of environmental manipulations, direct instruction, and provision of prosthetic aids.

Source: Adapted from Landesman-Dwyer and Butterfield (1983). Most of the statements in this exhibit are direct quotes from the authors (pp. 492–493, 495, 498–499, 502–504, 507).

the tremor disappeared and his behavior and school progress gradually improved. At age 10 years, 3 months his verbal ability was still somewhat below his previous test scores but performance ability had recovered (Verbal IQ = 79, Performance IQ = 92, Full Scale IQ = 83). (Lobascher & Cavanagh, 1980, pp. 258–259, with changes in notation)

Mentally retarded and normal children of similar mental age. The mental age (MA) obtained from a test of intelligence may be used as a rough index of a mentally

retarded child's cognitive deficiency at a given point in time. Children of different chronological ages who obtain the same mental age on a test have reached similar levels of intellectual development. There may be differences, however, in the qualitative aspects of their intellectual functioning. The younger children (viewed as being bright) have reached the same level of functioning as the older children (viewed as being less able) at an earlier age.

Studies have shown that on Piagetian tests nonorganically impaired mentally retarded children, but not organically impaired mentally retarded children, use reasoning processes similar to those used by their normal mental-age counterparts (Weisz & Yeates, 1981). Thus a developmental-lag hypothesis best accounts for differences between nonorganically impaired mentally retarded children and normal children. The hypothesis states that non-organically impaired mentally retarded children pass through a normal sequence of cognitive developmental stages, but their rate of progress through the sequence is relatively slow and the upper limit of cognitive development is relatively low. Organically impaired mentally retarded children, in contrast, may show performance anomalies in specific kinds of reasoning and problem-solving tasks. Therefore, the developmental-lag hypothesis may not be appropriate to account for their performance.

Using the WISC-R for the assessment of mental retardation. The WISC-R is a reliable and valid instrument for assessing mild levels of mental retardation. There is no evidence that the WISC-R can reliably differentiate brain-injured from non–brain-injured mentally retarded children, however.

Factor analytic studies indicate that the factor structure of the WISC-R is similar for mentally retarded children and normal children, although some minor differences emerge (Vance & Wallbrown, 1977; Vance, Wallbrown, & Fremont, 1978; Van Hagen & Kaufman, 1975). For example, the Freedom from Distractibility factor (Arithmetic, Digit Span, and Coding) is less stable for retarded children than for normal children. In general, however, the factor analytic studies suggest that there may be no qualitative differences in the structure of intelligence for normal and mentally retarded children.

The relative difficulty of WISC-R subtests for mentally retarded children, from easiest to hardest, is as follows (Mueller, Dash, Matheson, & Short, 1984): (1) Picture Completion, (2) Object Assembly, (3) Comprehension, (4) Block Design, (5.5) Coding, (5.5) Picture Arrangement, (7) Arithmetic, (8) Vocabulary, (9) Similarities, and (10) Information. As a group, mentally retarded children tend to score *lowest*, relative to their own mean performance, on Information, Similarities, and Vocabulary—subtests that form the Verbal Comprehension factor—and *highest* on Picture Completion and Object Assembly—subtests that load on the Perceptual Organization factor.

WISC-R test results should be used in conjunction with other test results, interviews, observations, and case history information to assess the mentally retarded child's abilities.

Development of Recommendations for Educational Programming

Recommendations as to appropriate educational programs for mentally retarded children should be based on the results of a battery of tests. The battery should include an intelligence test, an achievement test, an adaptive behavior scale, and one or more special ability tests.

Educational programs must be geared to the ages of children and to their levels of functioning. Preschool and school-aged children functioning in the mild range of retardation can benefit from programs offered in regular schools—either in special education programs or, when appropriate, in regular classes. (See Chapter 24 for a discussion of mainstreaming.) Much, too, can be done to help those families that are not able to take advantage of opportunities to help their children develop properly. Intervention strategies for such families include providing financial aid, better housing, preschool education for the children, further education for the parents, and effective family planning.

Questions to consider in formulating recommendations. After the assessment has been completed, consider the following questions in formulating the report and developing recommendations:

1. Do the results indicate that the child should be classified as mentally retarded?
2. Is the child eligible for special services?
3. What is the least restrictive program that will facilitate the child's cognitive development (see Chapter 24)?
4. Is mainstreaming a viable option, or is the child so handicapped that a special class is necessary (see Chapter 24)?
5. Which social and interpersonal skills are adequately developed, and which ones need remediation?
6. What skills could the child use for productive employment (for older children)?
7. What type of sheltered workshop would be most beneficial for job training (for older children)?
8. Can the individual live independently, or will special facilities be needed (for example, transition group home, community-based home, or residential setting)?

Placement of children. You must evaluate the test results and other data very carefully before recommending that a child be placed in a class for the mentally retarded. Psychologists, it has been alleged, are primarily responsible for assigning children to classes for the mentally retarded. Yet, a study of large metropolitan school districts showed that in 43 percent of the cases psychologists *failed* to confirm teachers' judgments of children who were referred for possible placement in mentally retarded classes (Ashurst & Meyers, 1973). Thus the referrals to school psychologists may have prevented the incorrect placement of many children in classes for the mentally retarded. The study also showed that neither the ethnicity nor the sex of children had any relation to the frequency of placement in special classes. The team's placement decisions appeared to have been made on the basis of the child's needs, rather than on the basis of test results per se.

Educational programs should be attempted, regardless of the specific IQ attained by a child. If retarded children are to be helped to reach their potential, test scores must not be used as a basis for prohibiting a child from participating in programs that can be stimulating. Many children whose test scores fall into the mentally retarded range can develop into self-sufficient and productive citizens as adults.

Ten current themes.   Current efforts focus on integrating mentally retarded persons into society, recognizing their rights for individualization, and providing opportunities for growth and development. Current themes include the following:

1. An emphasis on the similarities between retarded and nonretarded people rather than on their differences.
2. A recognition that retarded people can improve their level of functioning if they are given a proper opportunity.
3. A questioning of the concept of mental retardation.
4. A de-emphasis on labeling.
5. Increased individualization.
6. Expansion of legal rights for the mentally retarded.
7. An increased tolerance of deviance.
8. A recognition that some mental retardation arises out of conditions in society.
9. An emphasis on prevention.
10. Planning and coordination of services.

Distinguishing Between Mental Retardation and Developmental Delay

When mental retardation is suspected, another diagnosis that should be considered is *developmental delay*, especially with infants or preschool-aged children. A diagnosis of mental retardation should be made only in cases that clearly involve significantly below average general intellectual functioning as well as significant deficits in adaptive behavior.

There are three reasons for distinguishing between mental retardation and developmental delay during infancy and the preschool years (Fotheringhan, 1983). First, although

a child may meet the criteria for a diagnosis of mental retardation, the measure of intelligence may not be reliable—with infants it reflects primarily developmental progress (see Chapter 12). When examinees are young, repeated assessments over time are required to ensure a definitive diagnosis and to check for changes in the rate of development. Second, other conditions may mimic mental retardation. For example, aphasia or cerebral palsy may reduce a young child's ability to communicate, thus making the assessment of intellectual ability difficult. Third, there may be home circumstances that, if altered, might significantly increase the child's adaptive functioning beyond the retarded range.

When a child shows impaired functioning and a diagnosis of mental retardation cannot be reliably made, a tentative diagnosis of developmental delay may be appropriate. A diagnosis of developmental delay alerts readers of the psychological report to the possibility that (a) the basis for the cognitive deficit is ambiguous; (b) the deficiency may be transitory; (c) the reduced functioning in adaptive behavior may not be sufficient to warrant a diagnosis of mental retardation; or (d) the problems in adaptive behavior may be temporary. In contrast, a diagnosis of mental retardation implies a significant general reduction in cognitive ability and adaptive behavior determined on the basis of reliable and valid assessment findings.

Assessment of Severely and Profoundly Retarded Children

Severely and profoundly mentally retarded individuals often have severe physical defects (for example, impaired vision, hearing, and motor coordination), difficulty in attaining an upright posture, difficulty in interacting with the environment, undeveloped speech, lack of feeding and toileting skills, and difficulty in guarding against physical dangers. The care required by severely and profoundly retarded children can be burdensome on the family.

Profoundly retarded children, in particular, have a high incidence of devastating motoric, sensory, and physical handicaps. Their mortality rate is high. Compared to severely retarded children, they tend to have a higher incidence of delayed puberty, institutionalization, seizures, enuresis, poor communication, pica (a strong craving to eat nonnutritive objects, such as paint, gravel, or hair), self-biting, fecal smearing, mutism, echopraxia (a tendency toward automatic imitation of the movements and gestures of others), lack of self-recognition, rumination, abnormal EEGs, encopresis (involuntary defecation not due to a local organic defect or illness), lack of socialization skills, and high pain thresholds (Switzky, Haywood, & Rotatori, 1982).

In spite of the seemingly overwhelming burdens, the moderately and severely retarded can lead productive lives. As noted in Exhibit 21-3, with proper training many retarded individuals are able to maintain gainful employment.

As a result of Public Law 94-142 and the movement toward deinstitutionalization, more children with severe handicaps are being served in public schools and community agencies. Children who were previously unserved are now receiving services, and fewer children are being placed in residential facilities. Additionally, severely handicapped children now tend to be in school for a greater number of years and, thus, require more triennial assessments (see Chapter 24).

Institutionalized mentally retarded and level of intelligence. In individuals who are institutionalized for mental retardation, there is often a direct relationship between level of intelligence and both physical handicaps and behavior. In a study (Ross, 1972) of over 11,000 individuals residing in institutions for the mentally retarded, higher levels of intelligence were found to be associated with fewer physical handicaps, greater self-help skills, and fewer behavior problems. Thus the level of measured intelligence should be considered in developing programs for institutionalized mentally retarded individuals.

Guidelines for working with the severely and profoundly retarded. Popovich and Laham (1982) and Somerton and Myers (1976) developed excellent guidelines for working with moderately, severely, and profoundly retarded individuals in such areas as self-help skills, motor development, eye-hand coordination, language development, and socialization. Kiernan and Jones (1977) presented a criterion-referenced battery designed to aid in the assessment of profoundly handicapped children. It covers 12 different areas of functioning, including self-help skills, communication, perceptual problem solving, and play.

Problems with standardized tests and scales. Techniques for assessing the achievement of severely and profoundly handicapped children must be conceptually different from traditional approaches used with nonhandicapped children. Standardized norm-referenced tests are of limited use in the assessment of severely and profoundly handicapped children. These children may have difficulty in following the instructions, administrative procedures may be too inflexible to permit them to display their knowledge by unconventional means, and the small number of items at the extreme ranges of ability may restrict the sampling of their abilities. Extrapolated test scores are not appropriate for individual diagnosis because their reliability is unknown. Norm-referenced tests are also relatively insensitive to the developmental changes that occur in severely and profoundly handicapped children (White & Haring, 1978). Simply to maintain their relative standing, severely or profoundly handicapped children would need to develop their abilities as rapidly as normal children, which is highly unlikely. Thus raw scores may be preferred over standard scores for evaluating the progress of severely and profoundly handicapped children.

Criterion-referenced tests, which usually follow standard curriculum guidelines, may not be appropriate for severely and profoundly handicapped children, because these children are rarely candidates for instruction in the school's standard curriculum. These tests may fail to take into account the children's handicapping condition, as the standardization groups for most criterion-referenced tests are composed of normal children (White & Haring, 1978). Also, criterion-referenced tests do not provide information about what children must do to become successful. Although severely and profoundly handicapped children may obtain low scores on criterion-referenced tests, their skills may enable them to function successfully. For example, some children with limited vocabulary may still be able to make their needs known. In other cases, handicapped children may need to develop proficiency in a specific skill to overcome a disability, as in the case of deaf children who must develop skills needed for signing.

The use of normal developmental scales with severely and profoundly handicapped children is also fraught with problems (White & Haring, 1978). These scales fail to take into account the limited opportunities that severely and profoundly handicapped children have to develop and refine concepts—their development does not proceed like that of normal young children. If normal developmental models are used as the basis for curriculum planning, it is important to identify carefully those points in the sequence where alternative developmental sequences might be necessary or preferred.

Although standardized norm-referenced, criterion-referenced, and developmentally based tests and scales have potentially serious shortcomings, they still have a role to play in the assessment of severely and profoundly retarded youngsters. Mental ages, test ages, and developmental ages from these scales provide useful indices which place the child's performance at an approximate developmental level. Individual items provide information about what the child can and cannot accomplish. The most

■ **Exhibit 21-3** ■

Moderately and Severely Mentally Retarded May Have More Capabilities Than Is Commonly Thought

The older man can print his name only if you print it first. The younger man can do nothing more demanding intellectually than tell time. But together they have made a once-filthy shopping mall in Jersey City, N.J., spotless.

Faced with shortages of reliable unskilled labor, major employers say they are expanding efforts to hire the retarded.

More surprisingly, many companies are taking on the more seriously retarded, workers once thought unemployable in competitive jobs. Of 2,000 people whom the Association for Retarded Citizens placed in full-pay-and-benefits jobs last year, nearly 400 were "moderately" or even "severely" retarded, says Catherine Neman, the national director of employment projects at the nonprofit service group. "Two years ago, practically everyone placed was 'mildly' retarded."

The difference can be crucial. While achievement levels vary, mildly retarded adults typically can read at an elementary level. But many moderately retarded people can recognize only a few words by sight and can write only their names.

If they are placed in the right job and thoroughly trained, the retarded are effective and motivated workers.

But training the more seriously retarded takes patience and ingenuity. At the Young Adults Institute in New York, a new program takes about six months to train a moderately retarded adult to clean offices. "Five years ago, the general perception was that a person in this category couldn't be competitively employed," says Joel M. Levy, the executive director of the institute.

For restaurant-busman jobs, the agency may spend 10 days teaching how to set silverware. First, the trainee places silverware on a paper place mat that has a knife, fork, and spoon each outlined in its proper place. Later, the place mats have only one or two utensils drawn in, and the trainee must figure out what is missing. Eventually, the trainee places silver on a blank place mat—over and over again, until this becomes a habit.

Even with less retarded workers, the agency helps organize jobs into fixed routines. In a Manhattan office building, employment-training specialist Brenda Kantarian establishes a route for cleaning hallways. Then she accompanies a new worker on the job, full-time, for several days.

It works. "If I stick to the route, I don't get confused," says Julio Gerena, 22, industriously sweeping cigarette butts from a floor he keeps immaculate.

Employers have developed numerous techniques to solve work problems. To help workers sort out laundry, Marriott sometimes uses different-colored bins for various sizes of sheets and towels.

The Association for Retarded Citizens even placed a Mary-land woman with an IQ under 30 in a job, cleaning offices. It equipped her with a Walkman-like device that plays music. Periodically, a voice interrupts the music to ask if she has emptied the waste basket and ashtrays and to remind her to move on to the next office. Elsewhere, McDonald's Corp. assigns a woman with an IQ of 36 to spend all day making french fries—a task she could grasp even though it involves 47 steps.

Agencies that provide special training for the retarded often offer long-term follow-up. The Association for Retarded Citizens spent three weeks teaching a New Jersey man with an IQ of 28 how to pack bags at a supermarket. "Every few months, we get a call that David is once again putting the bread at the bottom and the milk on top," says M. Joseph Sebian. "So we send a job coach to work side by side with him for two or three days, and he gets back in the right habits."

Agencies figure it is well worth the effort. At age 32, the supermarket bagger has spent 25 years in an institution, and he had a vocabulary of 10 words when he started the supermarket job. "Now he speaks in short sentences and is doing a very conscientious job," Mr. Sebian says.

The worker now lives in the equivalent of a foster home, gets to work in a county-run van for the disabled and elderly, earns $3.85 an hour and has advanced to packing two bags at a time. "Most people get bored in jobs like that, but David will be there forever; there is no absenteeism problem whatever," Mr. Sebian says.

Mr. Sebian says about 80 percent of his office's matches of retarded workers and jobs prove successful. When a placement fails, the office seeks a different job for the worker. Some workers now earning the $3.35-hourly minimum wage, or more, before were earning less than 50 cents an hour in sheltered workshops.

Many employers say they are hiring the mentally disabled because of their dependability and willingness to stay on the job.

In a Washington, D.C., department-store chain, one retarded worker has been washing pots and pans in its kitchen for six years. "Normally, we would have a turnover of two or three a year in that job," says Fred M. Thompson, the company's manager of personnel and community services. Retarded workers "don't get bored as quickly," he says, adding, "We don't yet know the full potential of a retarded person."

important point to recognize in using standardized instruments is that you must not equate the child's failure "*to move toward normality with failure to develop functionally useful skills or to progress in any meaningful way at all*" (White & Haring, 1978, p. 170, italics added).

Suggested assessment procedures for use with severely and profoundly retarded children. Informal assessment procedures and functional assessment procedures are particularly useful in the assessment of children with severe handicaps. Whatever assessment procedures are used, it is important to determine whether failures are due to physical disabilities, motivational deficits, or knowledge deficits. The procedures discussed below are designed to determine how environmental factors can be arranged to improve the functioning of severely handicapped children. What is assessed is directly linked to what is to be taught (Strain, Sainto, & Maheady, 1984). Functional assessment procedures also focus on children's knowledge of survival skills—for example, their ability to ask directions, to identify police officers, to make change, and to recognize monetary values. The procedures discussed in this section can be used to supplement traditional assessment instruments.

Task analysis. Task analysis procedures focus on which components of a skill have been mastered and which have not. After subdividing a skill into component parts (task analysis), one assesses the number of steps in the task that the child can perform independently. For example, washing hands can be subdivided into 22 specific steps (see Exhibit 21-4). If you wanted to evaluate Bridgette's ability to wash her hands, you might say "Bridgette, show me how you would wash your hands" and then observe how adequately she performed the task. If she had difficulty, you could determine the appropriate entry level skill with which to begin instruction. Resources for learning about task-analysis procedures include Wehman (1979) and Van Etten, Arkell, and Van Etten (1980).

Systematic observation and controlled teaching trials. Various strategies can be implemented to determine which elements of a child's behavior interfere with instruction, how these interfering elements can be reduced, and what motivates the child to attend and respond. Ideally one should assess behavior in all settings in which the child is expected to function (for example, school, home, bus, and a sheltered workshop). Daily functional needs of the child can be observed by teachers as well as by parents. In some cases it may be necessary to evaluate the child's skills over an extended period of time.

Exhibit 21-4

Task Analysis for Washing Hands

Component Skills

1. Comes to front of sink (soap bar on sink).
2. Directs hand toward water faucet handle (cold, then hot).
3. Touches water faucet handle.
4. Grasps water faucet handle.
5. Turns on water.
6. Discriminates for adequate temperature (not too hot or cold).
7. Wets hands under running water.
8. Removes hands from water.
9. Directs hand toward soap dish.
10. Touches soap.
11. Picks up soap.
12. Rubs soap between hands.
13. Puts soap back into soap dish.
14. Rubs palms of hands together (creating lather).
15. Rubs back of right hand.
16. Rubs back of left hand.
17. Places hands under running water.
18. Rinses all soap off hands.
19. Turns off running water.
20. Gets towel.
21. Dries hands.
22. Puts down towel.

Source: Van Etten, Arkell, and Van Etten, 1980, p. 178.

The following examples illustrate how observation and controlled teaching trials might be implemented:

1. Assess the behavior patterns that interfere with instruction—such as self-stimulating behavior, attention difficulties, or destructive behavior—and the conditions under which they occur through observation or controlled teaching trials (Strain et al., 1984).

2. Determine which motivational mechanism supports the deviant behavior—such as desire to (a) obtain positive reinforcement, (b) terminate an unpleasant task, or (c) obtain sensory feedback—and then use this information to develop remediation procedures (Strain et al., 1984). Preferences for either visual or auditory stimulation can be determined by asking teachers or parents to identify children's preferences.

Generally, the school environment is not well suited for assessing the learning needs of severely developmentally delayed children. For instance, the home-living skills needed by severely retarded children for daily functioning *cannot* be readily evaluated in the classroom (Hawkins & Hawkins, 1981). Classroom observation will not reveal how adequately the child uses the bathtub, the refrigerator, or a stove; how the child spends leisure time; or whether the child discriminates edible from inedible items at home. On the other hand, appropriate judgments can be made about how the child functions in the cafeteria, locates the bathroom, interacts with schoolmates, places forms on a formboard, or performs other school-related activities.

Various procedures can be used to evaluate the daily living skills of severely retarded children at home (Hawkins & Hawkins, 1981). First, parents can be instructed to keep a daily diary or checklist (or both) for a week at a time, observing their child's daily activities and performance systematically and noting skills needing development. Role playing and other procedures can help parents learn good observation and recording skills.

Second, daily communication between home and school can be used by parents and teacher to keep abreast of the effect of changes in teaching methods and home procedures on the child's behavior.

Third, teachers (or psychologists) can make systematic observations in the home and community. This is important because parents may fail to observe some important behaviors or environmental contingencies.

Finally, stimuli in the school environment can be made to approximate those of the home environment. Closely matching eating utensils, toys, clothing items, and other stimuli to those found at home will facilitate the assessment process.

Informal assessment of communicative competence.   The assessment of communicative competence in severely and profoundly retarded children with standardized, nationally normed language and cognitive instruments is problematic. Informal assessment may prove more useful. A key question is "How does the child communicate his or her needs?" Observation can be supplemented with interactions designed to elicit certain reactions. For example, a toy may be withheld from the child and the child's reaction noted. Parents, teachers, and others involved in caretaking roles can be interviewed. Questions such as "How does _____ request food?" or "How does _____ request help?" or "How does _____ request to go to the bathroom?" may provide useful information about the child's means of communication. (Chapter 18 describes other procedures useful in assessing communicative competence.)

The assessment of communicative functions has a number of goals (Schuler & Goetz, 1981). The first goal is to identify how the child communicates various needs—for example, how the child obtains the attention of others, makes food needs known, makes interaction needs known, or requests information. Are these needs communicated by crying, tantrums, grunts, facial expressions, gestures, stereotyped speech, rituals, signs or other symbols, appropriate speech, or other means? Which means are used for which communicative functions? The assessment focuses on the range and differential frequency of communicative needs and the means by which these needs are expressed.

A second goal is to evaluate how the child uses speech and language to achieve communicative ends. Traditional methods of analyzing speech and language can be used for this type of evaluation (see Chapter 18). A key question is "Are language skills equivalent to communicative skills?" Some children may have adequate language skills but fail to use them appropriately to communicate.

A third goal is to evaluate the child's cognitive functioning. For children with severe communication problems, assessment tasks should not require speech output or be presented in a verbal format. For some children, tasks should not require self-motivation or complex motor responses. Nonverbal tasks may be especially useful for assessing the cognitive competence of children with severe communicative problems. Such tasks are found, for example, on the Stanford-Binet Intelligence Scale: Fourth Edition, the WISC-R, the WPPSI, and the K-ABC.

The above procedures will generate a profile of speech and language abilities, with particular emphasis on the extent to which speech, language, communication, and cognitive skills are differentially developed. Whenever norm-referenced tests appear to be appropriate, however, their use is highly recommended.

Adaptive behavior questionnaires, checklists, and interviews.   The adaptive behavior questionnaires and developmental checklists described in Chapter 15 can be useful in the assessment of severely and profoundly retarded children. The semi-structured interview format shown in Exhibit 21-5 is also useful for obtaining information about severely handicapped children's language and speech comprehension and production; nonverbal communication; responses to sensory stimuli; movement, gait, and posture; social and emotional responses; resistance to change; play; immaturity; special skills; self-care; sleeping patterns; school activities; and domestic and practical skills. The questions can be answered by the parent or another adult caretaker. Exhibit 21-5 can be used in conjunction with Table 16-13 in Chapter 16, which can assist in obtaining a developmental history. Exhibit 21-6 presents a psychological evaluation of a severely retarded 6-year-old girl. This evaluation illustrates how two different instruments are useful in obtaining normative information about a variety of skill domains.

Criterion-referenced instruments.   The cues that help a child perform a task—such as a prior model, physical prompts, or extensive feedback to maintain attention to the task—are important to determine. Standardized or criterion-referenced instruments (for example, the Learning Accomplishment Profile, the Uniform Performance Assessment System, and the Brigance Inventory of Basic Skills) can be used to determine where instruction should begin for various skill domains. Various cues then can be administered to determine which ones facilitate learning.

A recommended graduated assessment procedure is as follows (Strain et al., 1984, p. 185):

Step 1: Every other item on the instrument(s) is presented according to the test manual (minimal or no level of assistance).

Step 2: Each item (on a per item basis) not performed successfully at Step 1 is reintroduced with a model of the correct response provided.

Step 3: Each item not performed successfully at Step 2 is reintroduced with a model and a partial physical prompt (e.g., moving a child's hand part-way toward a correct choice; partially scooting out a chair given the command, "Stand-up"; moving a child's hand to his [or her] facial area given the command, "Show me your nose").

Step 4: Each item not performed successfully at Step 3 is reintroduced with a model and a full physical prompt (e.g., examiner has his [or her] hand over child's when fitting a puzzle piece; examiner lifts a child from chair given the command, "Stand-up").

Step 5: Steps 1 through 4 are repeated with the examiner providing an identifiably effective reinforcer(s) for general attention to the tasks at hand.

With the most severely handicapped children, this process, applied to language, motor, social, self-care, and cognitive skills, requires 6 to 8 hours. It is recommended that a single assessment period be no more than 20 minutes long, although two or three 20-minute sessions may be held per day.

Problems of misdiagnosis.   The consequences of failure to recognize the effects of a hearing loss on a child's intellectual functioning are tragically illustrated in the case of *Donald Snow* v. *the State of New York* (see Exhibit 21-7). In this case, the State of New York was found negligent in its evaluation procedures.

Psychological Evaluation

The psychological evaluation in Exhibit 21-8 illustrates the application of a multimethod approach to the assessment of a mentally retarded 8-year-old child. The findings obtained from the various assessment procedures complement one another in providing a picture of the child's current level of performance. Ted, the child described in the evaluation, appears to be familially retarded.

ASSESSMENT OF GIFTED CHILDREN

Attributes associated with the term *giftedness* include achievement of outstanding prominence in an area, extremely high IQ (above 130), excellence in art or music, and high scores on tests of creativity. An early definition of gifted and talented children offered by the U.S. Office of Education is as follows (Marland, 1972, p. 10):

Gifted and talented children are those identified by professionally qualified persons who by virtue of outstanding abilities are capable of high performance. These are children who require differentiated educational programs and services beyond those normally provided by the regular program in order to realize their contribution to self and society.

Children capable of high performance include those with demonstrated achievement and/or potential ability in any of the following areas.

1. General intellectual ability
2. Specific academic aptitude
3. Creative or productive thinking
4. Leadership ability
5. Visual and performing arts
6. Psychomotor ability [this category was later dropped from the criteria]

A more recent federal definition of gifted and talented children is as follows:

For the purposes of this part, the term "gifted and talented children" means children and, whenever applicable, youth, who are identified at the preschool, elementary, or secondary level as possessing demonstrated or potential abilities that give evidence of high performance capability in areas such as intellectual, creative, specific academic, or leadership ability, or in the performing and visual arts, and who by reason thereof, require services or activities not ordinarily provided by the school. (Gifted and Talented Children's Education Act of 1978, Section 902)

Essentially, the term *gifted* is used to describe children with exceptionally high IQs, those who have creative talents, and those who are high on both dimensions. It is estimated that this definition applies to approximately 3 to 5 percent of the population.

■ **Exhibit 21-5** ■■■■■■■■■■■■■■■■■■■■■■■■■■■■

Example of Semi-Structured Interview with Parents of Developmentally Disabled Children

Language

1. Does _____ respond to his (her) own name?
2. Does _____ point to a familiar object when asked?
3. Does _____ obey very simple instructions such as "Give me your cup"?
4. Do you ever send _____ out of the room to get one object?
5. Could _____ be sent out for two or three things?
6. Can _____ follow a sequence of commands, such as "First do this, then this, then this"?
7. Can _____ understand the past tense [pause], future tense [pause], present tense?
8. Does _____ have any problems with words such as *under* or *in* or *above*?
9. Does _____ understand better if instructions are sung to a tune instead of spoken?
10. Does _____ talk? (If no, go to question 11. If yes, go to question 16.)
11. Does _____ make any noises?
12. Does _____ babble like a baby?
13. Do _____'s noises have a conversational sound?
14. Do any of _____'s noises have a definite meaning?
15. How does _____ get things he (she) wants? (Go to question 50.)
16. Do _____'s words make sense or are they just parrot-like echoing?
17. Does _____ name any objects or people when asked?
18. Does _____ name some things spontaneously?
19. Does _____ join two words together?
20. Does _____ make longer phrases but skip the small linking words?
21. Does _____ make complete sentences?
22. Does _____ use the past tense [pause], present tense [pause], future tense?
23. How clearly does _____ speak?
24. Can _____ be understood by people who know him (her) well [pause] and by strangers?
25. Does _____ use intonation to aid expression, such as raising his (her) voice in asking questions, in showing puzzlement, in showing hesitation?
26. Does _____ control the loudness and pitch of his (her) voice?
27. Does _____ ever use a special voice, different from his (her) usual one?
28. Does _____ immediately repeat words or phrases spoken by other people in a parrot-like meaningless way?
29. Does _____ repeat words or phrases used by other people some time after he (she) has heard them?
30. Does _____ talk to himself (herself) using these repeated phrases?

31. Does _____ confuse pronouns—for example, saying *you* when he (she) means *I*?
32. Does _____ use words and phrases in a rigid, stereotyped way?
33. Does _____ confuse the sequence of letters in words—for example, saying *diccifult* for *difficult*?
34. Does _____ confuse the sequence of words in sentences—for example, saying "Take park to dog"?
35. Does _____ confuse words that are opposites, such as *on* and *off* or *yes* and *no*?
36. Does _____ confuse words that are usually paired, such as *sock* and *shoe* or *Mom* and *Dad*?
37. Does _____ hesitate and search for words when talking spontaneously?
38. Does _____ spontaneously talk about things that have happened to him (her)? (If yes, go to question 39. If no, go to question 42.)
39. How often does he (she) do this?
40. How much detail does _____ give?
41. Does _____ tend to repeat the same things or tell of new things as they happen?
42. Does _____ ever engage in a conversation? (If yes, go to question 43. If no, go to question 50.)
43. Are his (her) contributions stereotyped and repetitious, or can he (she) converse freely and change the subject appropriately?
44. Does he (she) converse about things outside his (her) own immediate experience?
45. Does _____ ask questions?
46. Are these limited to his (her) own needs, or does he (she) ask questions because of curiosity?
47. Does he (she) ask questions about things outside his (her) own personal experience?
48. Are his (her) questions repetitive and stereotyped, or do his (her) questions show a creative developing interest?
49. Does he (she) talk to, or otherwise communicate with, children of his (her) own age?

Nonverbal Communication

50. Does _____ know he (she) is going out when he (she) sees his (her) coat?
51. Does _____ understand pointing and beckoning?
52. Does _____ respond to a simple mime, such as a finger on the lips to mean quiet?
53. Does _____ respond to complex mime, such as pretending to eat, drink, or brush hair?
54. Can _____'s behavior be controlled by his (her) teacher's facial expressions, such as smiles or frowns?
55. Do these have to be exaggerated for _____ to respond?

(Exhibit continues next page)

Exhibit 21-5 (cont.)

56. Does _____ understand that a nod or a shake of the head means yes or no?
57. Does _____ have a range of facial expressions?
58. (If yes) Tell me about them.
59. Does _____ nod or shake his (her) head, clearly meaning yes or no?
60. Does he (she) use other gestures such as "thumbs up" to indicate success or approval?

Responses to Sensory Stimuli

61. Does _____ ignore some sounds?
62. Do some sounds distress _____?
63. Do some sounds fascinate _____?
64. How does _____ react to lights [pause] and shiny objects?
65. Does _____ twist and flick his (her) hands or objects near his (her) eyes?
66. Does _____ like to watch things spin?
67. Does _____ seem to concentrate on one aspect of an object and ignore the rest?
68. Does _____ seem to concentrate on one aspect of a person and ignore the rest?
69. Does _____ seem to identify things and people by their outline rather than by the details of appearance?
70. Does _____ ignore pain [pause], heat [pause], or cold [pause], or is _____ oversensitive to pain?
71. Does _____ deliberately injure himself (herself) in any way?
72. Does _____ especially enjoy rapid movement toys, such as swings or slides?
73. Does _____ spin himself (herself) round?
74. (If yes) Does _____ become giddy when he (she) does this?
75. Does _____ show any stereotyped movements, such as rocking?
76. Does _____ tend to explore objects and people through touch [pause], taste [pause], or smell?

Movement, Gait, Posture

77. How does _____ walk (such as with swinging arms, walking on tip toe, looking odd and awkward or looking graceful)?
78. Is _____ dextrous or clumsy in fine finger movements?
79. Is _____'s posture odd or awkward in any way?
80. Can _____ copy other people's movements?
81. Does _____ wave good-bye?
82. Does _____ clap?
83. (If yes to 80, 81, or 82) Are these movements easy, or are they stiff and awkward?
84. How easily does he (she) learn gymnastic exercises, dances, or miming games?
85. Does he (she) confuse up/down, back/front, right/left when trying to imitate others?
86. How does he (she) behave when excited?

87. Does the excitement produce movements of his (her) whole body, including face, arms, and legs?

Social Responses

88. Who are the people that _____ could recognize and respond to if he (she) met them in an unfamiliar context (such as parents, teachers, friends, neighbors)?
89. How does _____ respond to gentle touches [pause], to cuddling [pause], to rough-and-tumble games?
90. How does _____ respond to social approaches without physical contact?
91. Is _____ affectionate?
92. How does _____ react to children of his (her) own age?
93. Does _____ have any friends of his (her) own age?
94. How does _____ make eye contact?
95. Does _____ have a blank, unfocused stare?
96. Does _____ avoid making eye contact at all?
97. Does _____ give brief flashing glances only?
98. Does _____ stare too long at times?
99. Is _____'s eye contact better with people he (she) knows than with strangers?

Emotional Responses

100. Does _____ have any special fears?
101. Does _____ seem unaware and unafraid of some real dangers?
102. Does _____ sometimes laugh or seem very distressed for no reason at all?
103. Does _____ show any response to other people's feelings; for example, would _____ be sympathetic if someone had an accident, or would _____ be aware if someone felt miserable or ill?

Resistance to Change and Attachment to Objects and Routines

104. How does _____ respond to changes in the daily routine?
105. Does _____ insist upon exact repetition of some or all of the daily program, such as taking the same route on the daily walk or having everyone at the same place at the table?
106. Does _____ carry out rituals of his (her) own, such as tapping on a chair before sitting down or touching everything on the table before eating?
107. Does _____ arrange objects in special ways, such as in long lines or patterns?
108. Does _____ replace things in the exact position from which they came, down to the smallest detail?
109. Is _____ attached to particular objects that must accompany him (her) everywhere?
110. How does _____ react if the object is lost?

(Exhibit continues next page)

Exhibit 21-5 (cont.)

111. Does _____ collect any type of object in what seems to be a completely purposeless way, such as leaves, boxes of detergent, or pieces of rubber?
112. Does _____ have an obsessive, repetitive, uncreative, stereotyped interest in certain subjects, such as the planets, electricity, or bodily functions?
113. Does _____ engage in repetitive and stereotyped play, such as continually manipulating the same objects in the same way, playing the same record again and again, re-doing the same puzzle repeatedly, or performing the same series of physical actions for hours at a time?

Play and Amusements

114. What sorts of games does _____ play?
115. How well can _____ handle objects and constructional toys?
116. Does _____ roll things along the floor?
117. How many blocks can _____ use to build a tower?
118. Can _____ use screw toys?
119. Can _____ do in-set puzzles or real jigsaw puzzles?
120. (If yes) How many pieces?
121. Does _____ make things with constructional toys?
122. Can _____ follow the printed diagrams with, for example, Legos or Tinker Toys?
123. Does _____ perform imitative play?
124. Does _____ engage in imaginative play?
125. Does _____ copy his (her) mother in domestic tasks?
126. Does _____ use real objects for their correct purpose?
127. Does _____ play with cars or trains as if they were real, such as by putting cars into a garage or moving trains?
128. Does _____ play with toy animals or dolls or tea sets as if they were real?
129. Does _____ kiss the toy animals and dolls, put them to bed, hold tea parties for them, or play school with them?
130. Does _____ pretend to be a cowboy (cowgirl), policeman (policewoman), or doctor, acting out an imaginary game?
131. Does _____ engage in imaginative play with other children, such as doctor and nurse, mother and father, or cowboys and Indians?
132. Does _____ take an active part, or is he (she) always passive and not contributing to the play fantasy?
133. Does _____ join in cooperative play that does not need fantasy, such as tag, hide-and-seek, ball games, and table games?
134. What types of outings does _____ enjoy?
135. What does _____ watch on television?
136. Is _____ interested in stories read aloud?
137. Does _____ enjoy listening to music?
138. Can _____ sing in tune?
139. Can _____ play any instrument?

Difficult or Socially Immature Behavior

140. Does _____ run away or wander?
141. Is _____ destructive?
142. Does _____ scream frequently or for long periods, or have temper tantrums?
143. Is _____ aggressive to adults [pause] or to children?
144. How does _____ behave in public?
145. For example, does _____ grab things in shops, scream in the street, make naive remarks, or feel people's clothing, hair, or skin?
146. Does _____ tend to be less active than other children, or is he (she) overactive?
147. Does _____ resist whatever you try to do for him (her)?
148. Does _____ automatically say no to any suggestion?

Special Skills

149. Does _____ have any special skills in dismantling, assembling, or manipulating mechanical or electrical objects?
150. Does _____ have any outstanding musical skill?
151. Does _____ have absolute pitch?
152. Can _____ do lengthy calculations in his (her) head?
153. Does _____ remember verbal material unusually well, such as poems, songs, lists of names, or details of a subject that especially interests him (her)?
154. Does _____ notice if any object, however small or unimportant, is moved from its usual position?
155. Does _____ seem to recognize routes and places with unusual accuracy?
156. Does _____ remember details of maps with unusual accuracy?
157. Does _____ remember numerical material unusually well, such as multiplication tables, the dates of events, days on which dates fall, or train timetables?

Self-Care

158. Can _____ walk without help?
159. (If yes) Can _____ run as well as other children of his (her) age?
160. Can _____ walk upstairs without help?
161. Can _____ walk downstairs without help?
162. Is _____ able to climb with agility?
163. Can _____ pedal a tricycle or a bicycle?
164. Does _____ have to be fed or can he (she) feed himself (herself) with his (her) fingers, a spoon, a spoon and a fork, or a knife and a fork?
165. Can _____ help himself (herself) to food when at the table?
166. Can _____ cut a slice of bread from a loaf?
167. How good are _____'s table manners?
168. Are there any problems with chewing?

(Exhibit continues next page)

Exhibit 21-5 (cont.)

169. Does _____ dribble?
170. Does _____ eat only one type of food exclusively?
171. Does _____ suck or swallow inedible objects?
172. Can _____ wash and dry his (her) hands?
173. Can _____ bathe himself (herself) without help?
174. Is _____ aware when his (her) hands or face is dirty?
175. Can _____ put on any of his (her) garments by himself (herself)?
176. Can _____ button his (her) shirt?
177. Can _____ tie his (her) shoes?
178. Can _____ undress himself (herself)?
179. Can _____ unbutton his (her) shirt?
180. Can _____ untie his (her) shoes?
181. Can _____ brush and comb his (her) own hair?
182. Can _____ brush his (her) own teeth?
183. Is _____ concerned if his (her) clothes are dirty or untidy?
184. What stage has _____ reached in his (her) toilet training in the daytime?
185. Does _____ stay dry at night?
186. Can _____ get objects that he (she) wants for himself (herself)?
187. Does _____ look for things that are hidden?
188. Does _____ climb on a chair to reach things?
189. Can _____ open doors?
190. Can _____ open locks?
191. Is _____ aware of dangers, such as from hot things or sharp things?
192. Is _____ aware of the danger of heights or of deep water?
193. Is _____ aware that traffic is dangerous?
194. Does _____ know how to cross a road safely?
195. How much does _____ have to be supervised?
196. Is _____ allowed to go alone into another room [pause], into the street [pause], in the neighborhood [pause], farther away?
197. Could _____ travel on a bus or train alone?

Sleep

198. At what time does _____ go to sleep?
199. At what times does _____ get up?
200. Is _____'s sleep disturbed?
201. (If yes) Tell me about it.

School

202. Does _____ go to school?
203. (If yes) How is _____ doing in school?
204. Can _____ recognize objects in pictures?
205. Does _____ read?
206. Is _____ able to write?
207. Can _____ do arithmetic?
208. (If yes) Tell me about _____'s skills.
209. Can _____ tell time?
210. Does _____ know the days of the week?
211. Does _____ know the months of the year?
212. Does _____ know dates?
213. Can _____ draw?
214. What other subjects does _____ study in school?
215. (If subjects named) Tell me about how _____ is doing in these subjects.

Domestic and Practical Skills

216. Does _____ help set the table?
217. Clean the table?
218. Does _____ straighten up his (her) room?
219. Wash his (her) clothes?
220. Use a vacuum cleaner?
221. Help with shopping?
222. Help prepare food?
223. Cook?
224. Knit or sew?
225. Do woodwork?
226. Do any other craft work?

Other Problems

227. Does _____ have any problems that we didn't discuss?

Source: Adapted from L. Wing, "Assessment: The Role of the Teacher" in M. P. Everard (Ed.), *An Approach to Teaching Autistic Children*, pp. 18–29. Copyright 1976 by Pergamon Press. Permission to adapt the material in this exhibit was obtained from the publisher and the author.

Table 21-4 shows expected prevalency rates, based solely on IQ, for scores at 0 to 6 standard deviations above the mean. The table shows, for example, that approximately 2 in 100 individuals have IQs of 130 or above, whereas only approximately 3 in 100,000 individuals have IQs of 160 or higher.

The terms *giftedness* and *talent* are subtly different (Gagné, 1985). Giftedness refers to distinctly above-average competence in intellectual, creative, socio-emotional, or sensorimotor ability. In contrast, talent re-fers to distinctly above-average competence in one or more fields of human performance, such as the fine arts or the performing arts. Individuals who are gifted may not necessarily be talented. Motivation is a catalyst in transforming giftedness into talent.

Identifying Gifted Children

There is no one best system for identifying gifted children. Any means of identification is in part dependent on the

Exhibit 21-6

Psychological Evaluation of a Severely Retarded Child

Name: Betty
Date of birth: July 6, 1980
Chronological age: 6-0

Date of examination: July 7, 1986
Date of report: July 8, 1986

Test Results

Bayley Scales of Infant Development:

Mental age = 18 months

Wisconsin Behavior Rating Scale:

Behavioral age = 16.9 months

Reason for Referral

Betty is a 6-year-old girl with short brown hair and crossed eyes who was referred by the Upland County School and Social Services for a behavioral and intellectual evaluation. Behavior problems include sleep disturbances, reluctance to give up the bottle, self-abuse, self-stimulatory behavior, and tantrums whenever her routine is changed. Betty currently attends school half days in the afternoon. She is inflexible about routines at home and school.

Background, Assessment Results, and Clinical Impressions

Betty is ambulatory. She can walk up and down stairs, but cannot jump or run. When walking she likes to trail her hand along walls, as if blind. Betty has impaired but usable vision, with many of her behaviors resembling those of a visually impaired child. She will not wear her glasses.

Betty can turn pages of books and magazines, but does not yet scribble with crayon or pencil. She will play on a swing, look at picture books, whistle songs, and play simple ball rolling games with some interaction. She enjoys mirror play and interaction with some adults and seeks affection, but doesn't yet share or take turns.

Betty has many specific food likes, dislikes, and behaviors. She will bite, chew, and finger-feed, but will not drink from a cup or use a spoon. These latter skills, however, appear to be within reach of her maturational and developmental level.

Betty is beginning to indicate when she is wet or needs changing, but she refuses to sit on a commode. She generally stays dry at night. Night time is a problem, as Betty frequently gets up and roams the house. She is generally quiet, and she may get a snack and then return to bed. She frequently sleeps until noon. A full-day school program might be helpful in changing her sleep schedule.

Betty is, for the most part, nonverbal, although she uses a few words meaningfully and follows simple directions. She does not form sentences, use prepositions, or use words to identify pictures.

Because Betty did not want to accompany me to the testing room, I had to carry her after she stiffened out in protest. She did not want to hold hands while walking or accept physical pats as reinforcers. Once in the room, she sat willingly for the Bayley toylike materials, and even clapped her hands in excitement several times. She pushed away those materials (e.g., crayons) that did not interest her. Betty's Bayley Mental Age of 18 months suggests that she currently functions in the moderate to severe range of retardation. She had some success as high as 21 months (completed a puzzle board). She was, however, unable to name or point to pictured objects, to make a two-word sentence, to mend a broken doll, or generally to use words to make her needs known. Betty's best Bayley performances were in completing puzzles and placing pegs rather than in verbal areas.

On the Wisconsin Behavior Rating Scale she earned a behavioral age of 16.9 months, a score similar to the one she obtained on the Bayley. Subscale age-equivalent scores ranged from 7 months (Grooming) to 30 months (Dressing). Other subscale scores were Gross Motor—18 months; Fine Motor—13 months; Expressive Language—13 months; Receptive Language—13 months; Play Skills—18 months; Socialization—13 months; Domestic Activity—7 months; Eating—9 months; and Toileting—24 months.

Summary and Recommendations

Betty functions in the moderate to severe range of mental retardation. Her skills are at a preacademic level, with significant delays in all areas, especially receptive and expressive langauge and self-feeding. Betty walks without support up and down stairs, but cannot jump or run. She will not wear her glasses. Her prescription should be checked, and she should be rewarded for wearing her glasses. Betty engages in self-stimulatory behavior. She is essentially nonverbal, making very small gains. Screaming outbursts still occur, but teachers report mild improvement. Toileting and feeding skills need improvement. Increased toileting control appears to be a reasonable goal within the next 6 months.

Inclusion in a full-time education program appears possible, with great potential benefits to the parents. Her extreme need to maintain control remains a major hindrance to learning. Favorable signs for learning include the occasional joy she shows upon achieving success in toileting and feeding, her increased willingness to play with cuddly toys (fuzzy bear), and her increased acceptance of cuddling from parents and teachers. In order for an educational program to succeed, adults will have to gain more control of her behavior by identifying reinforcers for which she would like to work.

(Signature)
_____

Alex Brill, Examiner

■ Exhibit 21-7 ■

Donald Snow v. The State of New York

In 1973, at the age of 11 years, Donald Snow filed a medical malpractice suit against the State of New York, claiming that he was misdiagnosed as being mentally retarded when in fact he was only deaf.

In 1964, at the age of 2½, Donald was placed in a home for mental defectives after his parents were informed by a family physician that he was retarded. At that time he obtained an IQ of 44 (test not indicated) and was diagnosed as mentally retarded with an unknown etiology.

In 1965 he was transferred to Willowbrook State School. A physical examination revealed that his hearing was questionable. He was administered the Kuhlmann Test of Mental Development and obtained an IQ of 24. The school concluded that he "was functioning at the Imbecile level of intellect and was not suitable for the Willowbrook training and education program."

Six years passed before he was reevaluated. In 1971 he was administered the Hiskey-Nebraska Test of Learning Aptitude, which resulted in an IQ of 57.

In 1972, at the age of 10, Donald was transferred to another state school. Testing on the Leiter International Performance Scale resulted in an IQ of 102 (mental age of 10-6), whereas testing on the Wechsler Intelligence Scale for Children yielded an IQ of 75. He obtained a Social Quotient of 70 on the Vineland Social Maturity Scale. In 1973 testing on the Leiter resulted in an IQ of 76.

Donald was again tested on the WISC in 1973, 1976, and 1977 and obtained IQs of 90, 93, and 85, respectively. Based on these results, Donald's parents were advised that he was functioning at a normal level and Donald was enrolled at a school for the deaf.

In 1982 Judge Edward J. Amann, Jr. of the New York State Court of Claims, who tried the case without a jury, ruled that New York State was negligent in misdiagnosing Donald as mentally retarded. This misdiagnosis was further com-

pounded by the fact that the child was not reevaluated for six years. The judge noted that the New York State Mental Hygiene Law requires that suitable tests be used for the assessment of hearing-impaired children and that steps be taken to remedy the hearing impairment. New York State not only failed to evaluate Donald adequately, but also failed to reevaluate him. This failure occurred despite his teachers' recommendations that he be reevaluated. Even though New York State failed to prescribe a hearing aid, the judge ruled that the State was not negligent in this area because it followed accepted medical practice.

Citing the case of *Hoffman* v. *Board of Education of the City of New York*, the State argued that Donald not only had failed to prove educational malpractice, but could not maintain an action for educational malpractice. (See Exhibit 1-1 in Chapter 1 for a discussion of the case of *Hoffman* v. *Board of Education of the City of New York*.) Judge Amann noted that the case differed from *Hoffman* in several ways. The two most important differences were that (a) the *Hoffman* case involved educational malpractice whereas the *Snow* case involved medical malpractice, and (b) in the *Snow* case there was a clear violation of a section of the Mental Hygiene Law that a suitable test must be provided for individuals with speaking or hearing problems.

At the age of 19, Donald Snow was awarded $2.5 million. He had spent nearly nine years of his life in facilities for the mentally retarded when in fact he was only deaf. In December 1984 the New York Court of Appeals upheld the verdict, ruling that awards may be granted when medical malpractice has educational consequences.

Source: This review is based on the Decision of Judge Edward J. Amann, Jr., State of New York, Court of Claims, No. 60758, dated January 11, 1982.

goals of the program. A program that emphasizes cognitive skills needs different identification procedures from one focusing on art or music. Identification procedures may include the use of standardized tests, parent and teacher reports, direct observation of the child's behavior, and review of the child's creative work (Jackson, 1980). The most effective means of identification combines the results from several procedures, such as IQ, achievement, and behavioral-checklist data.

A sequential identification system for gifted children might begin with parent and teacher nominations, followed by group testing and then individual testing. Exhibits 21-9

and 21-10 show a parent information form and a teacher nomination form, respectively, that can be used to assist in the selection process. The Scales for Rating the Behavioral Characteristics (Renzulli, Smith, White, Callahan, & Hartman, 1976) is a commercially available scale.

No system of identification of gifted children is perfect; the task is a time-consuming one. The following questions should be considered in designing an identification system (Jackson, 1980, p. 64, with changes in notation):

1. Does the standard test component of the identification system include measures of a child's abilities in each area relevant to the content and goals of the program?

Exhibit 21-8

Psychological Evaluation: A Mentally Retarded Child

Name: Ted
Date of birth: April 16, 1979
Chronological age: 8-2

Date of examination: June 15, 1987
Date of report: June 17, 1987
Grade: 1st

Assessment Procedures

Wechsler Intelligence Scale for Children—Revised (scaled scores):

VERBAL SCALE		PERFORMANCE SCALE	
Information	6	Picture Completion	7
Similarities	1	Picture Arrangement	3
Arithmetic	3	Block Design	2
Vocabulary	5	Object Assembly	6
Comprehension	4	Coding	6
Digit Span	5	Mazes	4

Verbal Scale IQ = 60
Performance Scale IQ = 67
Full Scale IQ = 60 ± 6 at 95 percent confidence level

Vineland Adaptive Behavior Scales:

Adaptive Behavior Composite = 65 ± 8 at the 95 percent confidence level

Peabody Picture Vocabulary Test (PPVT-R) (Form L):

Standard score = 76

Draw-A-Person (G-H Scoring):

Time: 3′ 14″
Standard score = 71

Auditory Discrimination Test—Form 1A (2nd ed.):

Standard score = 35, percentile = 7th.

Bender-Gestalt:

Time: 8′ 31″
Koppitz score: standard score = 77, percentile = 6th.

Wide Range Achievement Test—Revised (WRAT-R):

	STANDARD SCORE	PERCENTILE
Reading	77	6th
Arithmetic	70	2nd
Spelling	67	1st

Peabody Individual Achievement Test (PIAT):

	STANDARD SCORE	PERCENTILE
Mathematics	82	12th
Reading Recognition	74	4th
Reading Comprehension	68	1st
Spelling	84	14th
General Information	72	3rd

(Parent interview, teacher interview by phone, informal information, play activities, and trial teaching were also used in the assessment.)

Reason for Referral

Ted was referred by his pediatrician, who wished to obtain an estimate of the child's level of mental development.

Background Information

Ted is the third child from an intact family of four children. Ted's older brother (age 14) and sister (age 12) as well as his younger brother (age 6) are described by the mother as good students. Both parents agreed that during his early development Ted was always a healthy, happy child who was easy to care for and manage, although he seemed to lag consistently a year or more behind his brothers and sister in language acquisition, toilet training, self-help, and play activities.

(Exhibit continues next page)

Exhibit 2I-8 (cont.)

The parents appeared to be open and honest with each other and strongly committed to family activities such as church, sports, camping, and fishing. Both parents have completed high school and specialized vocational training. Ted's mother is an office manager, a position she has held for 16 years. The father is employed as a machinist in a local aircraft plant where he has a history of steady, stable employment since the beginning of the marriage.

The parents reported that they had waited until Ted was 6 years of age to enroll him in a public school kindergarten on the advice of their pediatrician, who had expressed concern over Ted's slowness to develop, his lack of readiness, and his general immaturity. The pediatrician was concerned that Ted not be subjected to academic pressure before he was mature enough to cope with the school curriculum.

Kindergarten was a pleasant, stimulating experience for Ted. School records indicated not only that he was cooperative, friendly, and willing to share, but also that he showed significant improvement in fine and gross motor skills, listening skills, cooperative play, oral language, and ability to follow simple directions. It was noted, however, that because Ted scored low on a reading readiness test, difficulty with first grade work was predicted.

In the first grade he fell further and further behind the other children until mid-year, when he was the only student still working on readiness skills. Despite daily two-hour tutoring sessions for the remainder of first grade, Ted did not show much progress. A major concern of his teacher was Ted's emerging pattern of withdrawal, isolation, and daydreaming, which the teacher attributed to negative self-concept because other children were already reading.

Behavioral Observations

Ted is a big, sturdy, handsome child who comes across as pleasant and very gregarious. He was intrigued by the possibilities of game-like activities, eager to talk about his own experiences, and full of questions (for example, where did I live and where did I get the picture books in the testing kit). Although he seemed genuinely interested in this lively social give-and-take, he also seemed to use the conversational tactics to avoid the inevitable: having to deal with questions and school-related tasks.

During formal testing it was often difficult to hold his interest and attention. Faced with even minimal challenge, he began changing the subject, wiggling in his chair, and, in some instances, simply putting his head down on the desk and refusing to respond. Given constant individual encouragement, as well as some rewards (for example, "Just one more thing and you can take a recess"), he managed to complete four half-hour work sessions. It was interesting, and perhaps significant, that his span of attention and energy level increased immediately when the tasks were sufficiently simple and structured to offer an opportunity for success.

Assessment Results and Clinical Impressions

The results of the assessment suggest that Ted is currently functioning within the mild range of retardation in measured intelligence. This finding is suggested by data from interviews and observations, as well as a consistent pattern of scores from standardized tests of intelligence, adaptive behavior, perceptual development (auditory and visual), and academic achievement.

First, the WISC-R Full Scale IQ of 60 ± 6 is at the 1st percentile rank and is classified in the Mentally Retarded range. The chances that the range of scores from 54 to 66 includes his true IQ are about 95 out of 100. Other scores, including the WISC-R Verbal and Performance IQs, Draw-A-Person IQ, and PPVT-R receptive vocabulary score, are all below average. The fact that Ted consistently scored below average on a wide range of different ability-type tasks provides strong support for inferring mild mental retardation. The test results appear to be reliable and valid.

Second, the background data provided by the parents and school officials are consistent with the ability estimates reported. Specifically, both parents agreed that Ted was much slower than their other three children in many areas.

Third, the observations of the kindergarten and first grade teachers indicate that Ted's response to classroom instruction is much slower than that of his age mates, despite a positive attitude and a sincere effort to learn. His first grade teacher observed that "Ted seems to have reached a plateau. He can't go from letters to words and he can't go any further with his counting."

Finally, Ted comes from a stable, child-centered home that has provided adequate stimulation for intellectual development.

The pattern summarized above indicates a mild degree of retardation in academic aptitude or general intelligence (the ability to master the academic aspects of the school curriculum). In terms of age level, it appears that Ted's overall level of cognitive, social, and perceptual development falls around 6-0 years. For example, age-equivalent scores on the WISC-R and on the communication, daily living skills, and socialization domains of the Vineland Adaptive Behavior Scales are at this level. Instructionally, a realistic expectancy for academic work would be for Ted to respond somewhat like an average 5½- to 6-year-old child. Ted's performance on the Bender-Gestalt indicates that his visual-motor perception is less well developed than that of others his age and is congruent with the mental age suggested above. Similarly, scores on the Auditory Discrimination Test suggest difficulties in discriminating between common speech sounds and a short attention span for auditory material, which is congruent with the overall developmental level of the average 5½- to 6-year-old child.

Analysis of performance on the WRAT-R and PIAT, along

(Exhibit continues next page)

Exhibit 21-8 (cont.)

with the observations of the first grade teacher and examining psychologist, suggests that Ted's level of academic (readiness) skills is comparable to that of the average student beginning first grade (6-0 to 6-6). During the assessment Ted demonstrated the following skills: (a) repeated letters of the alphabet in correct sequence and named all letters of the alphabet in isolation; (b) wrote capital letters (manuscript) in correct sequence; (c) counted meaningfully through 29; (d) wrote the numerals in correct sequence through 39; (e) recognized and named the colors red, white, orange, yellow, black, green, brown, blue, pink, and gray; (f) sequenced objects by height and size; and (g) described what was happening in pictures. This information, as well as most of the achievement test scores, suggests that Ted's overall level of academic (readiness) skills is somewhat higher than the overall level of perceptual-cognitive development.

Recommendations

1. The parents should seriously consider enrolling Ted in the class for the educably mentally handicapped children in the neighborhood public school. However, there are several regular class activities that he should be able to benefit from, such as physical education, music, and art. Consistent participation in regular classroom activities is of critical importance for Ted if he is to continue developing and enhancing his already adequate social skills.

2. Ted's tendency to withdraw and daydream may be counteracted by having him respond actively in the classroom (for example, answer a question, collect papers, or draw a picture). Verbal praise and nonverbal reinforcement (for example, smile, happy face, or pat on shoulder) should be used to reinforce Ted for raising his hand and volunteering to participate in class at appropriate times.

3. Special attention should be given to helping Ted learn to pay closer attention to verbal directions—such as by having him repeat directions. Further, the teacher should take care to establish eye contact, physical contact, and physical proximity to help Ted focus and sustain his attention on verbal directions.

4. Activities designed to help Ted improve his oral comprehension should include listening to high-interest simple stories, songs, and rhymes. At the conclusion of each activity, Ted should be asked elementary questions about the story, song, or rhyme.

5. A pictorial approach can be used effectively to help expand Ted's vocabulary and expressive skills.

6. Overlearning (initial thorough learning, relearning, and consistent review and practice) may enable Ted to retain newly learned skills.

7. Improvement in arithmetic skills is probable if the work assignments center around money values and making change and are broken down into small segments ensuring frequent successes.

8. An inductive approach should be used to help Ted learn abstract verbal concepts such as same, different, and opposite. Probably the best way to teach these concepts is to use pictures to provide Ted with a large number of examples.

9. It would probably be unwise to discontinue efforts to teach Ted to read, even though his overall level of perceptual-cognitive development is substantially below the level we ordinarily think of as being necessary for the initiation of formal reading instruction. Ted is highly motivated to read, and his teacher believes that he is becoming discouraged and starting to develop a negative self-concept because of his inability to learn words. If reading instruction is terminated, Ted may feel that he is being rejected and removed from the parochial school because he has not been successful in learning to read. In view of Ted's high motivation, giving Ted some reading instruction in the special class or allowing him to join a first grade class working at the appropriate level is desirable to forestall further feelings of failure and rejection. In addition, continuance of his tutoring sessions at his original school seems advisable.

(Signature) _____

Examiner's Name

2. Are all of the measures that are included relevant to the program?

3. Are the standard tests known to yield reliable and valid estimates of abilities for children who are likely to perform at levels far beyond those expected for their age group?

4. Does the system include consideration of information about a child's everyday behavior collected from parents or others who know the child well?

5. Are those who are a part of the identification process trained to consider all aspects of the available information, such as the adequacy of the test session or special features of the child's background?

6. Are all components of the identification system appropriate for use with children from the cultural groups represented by the applicants?

7. Can a child qualify for the program despite a low score on an individual component of the identification battery if performance is very strong on other components?

8. Can the identification process be accomplished with the time, staff, and funds available?

Table 21-4
Expected Occurrence of IQs at or Above Each Standard Deviation Above the Mean

Standard deviation above the mean	IQ		Approximate expected occurrence
	SD = 15	SD = 16	
0	100	100	50 in 100
1	115	116	16 in 100
2	130	132	2 in 100
3	145	147	1 in 1,000
4	160	162	3 in 100,000
5	175	177	3 in 10,000,000
6	190	192	1 in 1,000,000,000

Identifying gifted children is a challenging activity. Although teacher nomination of gifted children is used more extensively than any other approach, it is successful in identifying gifted children only about 45 percent of the time (Gear, 1976). Group intelligence tests are about as successful as teacher nomination in identifying gifted children. They tend to yield lower IQs than individually ad-ministered intelligence tests, however, and may underestimate the attainment of many bright students.

To increase their effectiveness as raters, teachers should be given (a) adequate preparation for making judgments (for example, an explanation of the purposes of the identification process and an explicit definition of giftedness) and (b) adequate tools for expressing judgments (for example, well-standardized scales) (Hoge & Cudmore, 1986). Teacher judgments should then be used in combination with other assessment tools.

The single best method available for the identification of children with superior cognitive abilities is a standardized, individually administered test of intelligence, such as the Stanford-Binet Intelligence Scale: Fourth Edition or those in the Wechsler series. Zigler and Farber (1985) state that a specific IQ level is currently the most adequate index of giftedness. Reliable assessment of concepts—such as creativity, task commitment, and talent—that may be associated with giftedness is difficult to attain.

Determining academic skills. In addition to administering an individual test of intelligence, it is important to determine gifted children's abilities in various academic areas. Because not all gifted children are equally talented

---

Exhibit 21-9

Parent Information Form

SAN DIEGO CITY SCHOOLS
EDUCATIONAL SERVICES DIVISION
GIFTED AND TALENTED EDUCATION

(date) _____

Dear Parent/Guardian:

Your child has been recommended for evaluation to determine eligibility for the Gifted and Talented Education program. Students selected for this program possess a capacity for excellence far beyond that of other students of the same age.

These students' extraordinary capacities require special services and programs. Various enrichment activities supplement the regular school program and are provided in a number of different learning situations. Because information supplied by the parent can frequently be helpful in the evaluation of a student's ability, we request that you complete the form printed on the back of this page.

Before your child may be evaluated individually, written parent consent is required. Please indicate your decision by signing the form as indicated on the back of this page. Questions concerning the program may be directed to the principal of your child's school.

Sincerely,

Gifted and Talented Education Review Committee

(Exhibit continues next page)

Exhibit 21-9 (cont.)

Parent Information Form

Date _____

Child's name _____

            (last)   (first)   (MI)

Phone: Home _____

Address _____

Mother's work phone _____

_____

Father's work phone _____

            (zip)

Birth date _____ Sex _____ School _____ Grade _____ Room number _____

1. *Schools attended by child*   *Grade*   *Dates attended*

   _____ _____ _____

   _____ _____ _____

2. Names and ages of brothers and sisters: _____

   _____

3. Language(s) spoken in the home: _____

4. Describe your child's attitude toward school: _____

   _____

5. List any special interest, talents, and skills your child may have: _____

   _____

6. How does your child spend spare time? _____

   _____

7. What special lessons, training, or learning opportunities has your child had outside of school? _____

   _____

8. What other things would you like us to know that would assist us in planning a program for your child? _____

Name of person
completing this form _____

Relationship
to student _____

Parent Permission for Testing

_____ I give my permission for screening and/or evaluation.

_____ I do not give my permission for screening and/or evaluation.

_____
(Signature of parent/guardian)

Source: Reprinted with permission of the San Diego City Schools, Educational Services Division, Gifted and Talented Education, 1986.

in all academic areas, special ability tests should be used to supplement intelligence tests. Some gifted children may have exceptional talent in mathematics or the language arts, whereas others may have specific learning disabilities that interfere with their ability to realize their potentials—as noted in the case below. Once gifted children have been

identified, it is important that they receive increased educational opportunities.

Paul, aged 13 years, 2 months, was referred because of a severe spelling disability (1st percentile on the Stanford Achievement Test). His teachers indicated that his specific deficits in spelling

Exhibit 21-10

Teacher Nomination Form

SAN DIEGO CITY SCHOOLS
EDUCATIONAL SERVICES DIVISION
GIFTED AND TALENTED EDUCATION

Teacher Nomination Form

Date _____

Student name _____
(last)   (first)   (MI)

Ethnic code _____

Birth date _____ Sex _____ School _____ Grade _____ Room number _____

Guide for Identification of Prospective GATE Children

Please rate (name) _____ on each of the following characteristics. This is a five-point scale with the lower end of the scale (#1) indicating lower than average performance and the upper end (#5) indicating excellent or exemplary performance. Place a checkmark (✔) in the appropriate space opposite each item.

	1	2	3	4	5
I. PERSONAL					
1. Curious; asks many questions	—	—	—	—	—
2. Self-motivated; requires little external direction or encouragement	—	—	—	—	—
3. Likes to organize people and structure activities	—	—	—	—	—
4. Generates many ideas, questions, and suggestions	—	—	—	—	—
5. Flexible; adapts readily to new situations	—	—	—	—	—
6. Impatient with routine tasks	—	—	—	—	—
II. EXPRESSION					
7. Vocabulary beyond chronological age or grade level	—	—	—	—	—
8. Advanced skill in written expression	—	—	—	—	—
9. Proficiency in oral expression	—	—	—	—	—
III. THOUGHT PROCESSES					
10. Quick and accurate recall of factual information	—	—	—	—	—
11. A storehouse of information on a variety of topics	—	—	—	—	—
12. Readily recalls visual information	—	—	—	—	—
13. Readily recalls auditory information	—	—	—	—	—
14. Generalizes learning from one experience to another	—	—	—	—	—
15. Finds differences and similarities in events	—	—	—	—	—
16. Understands concepts without extensive concrete examples	—	—	—	—	—
17. Can establish relationships between seemingly unrelated concepts and ideas	—	—	—	—	—
18. Is insightful about cause and effect relationships	—	—	—	—	—
IV. PRODUCTION AND OUTPUT					
19. Displays a great deal of imagination	—	—	—	—	—
20. Manipulates ideas (i.e., makes changes and elaborates upon them)	—	—	—	—	—
21. Concerned with improving or adapting objects and systems	—	—	—	—	—
22. Capable of intense concentration on tasks of interest to her/him	—	—	—	—	—
23. Does not give up easily when confronted with a challenge; shows determination in achieving goals	—	—	—	—	—
24. Offers unique, clever responses to questions	—	—	—	—	—
25. Resourceful, knows where to find answers	—	—	—	—	—
V. ACHIEVEMENT					
26. High performance (grades) in a particular subject, e.g., math, language arts, science, other _____	—	—	—	—	—
27. Achieves at a high educational level	—	—	—	—	—

(Exhibit continues next page)

Exhibit 21-10 (cont.)

VI.   LEADERSHIP

    28. Has strong communication skills; gets ideas across effectively   __ __ __ __ __

    29. Assumes leadership role easily   __ __ __ __ __

    30. Facilitates and directs efforts   __ __ __ __ __

VII.   OTHER CHARACTERISTICS

    31. Dominates situations   __ __ __ __ __

    32. Expressive of thoughts and opinions   __ __ __ __ __

    33. Compulsive about work and work habits; strives for perfection   __ __ __ __ __

    34. Becomes involved in task, loses awareness of time   __ __ __ __ __

    35. Persistent in pursuing discussion beyond cutoff point   __ __ __ __ __

    36. Appears inattentive, withdrawn (daydreams)   __ __ __ __ __

Prepared by _____   Recommended? Yes _____ No _____
            (Teacher)

Reviewed by_____   Recommended? Yes _____ No _____
            (Administrator/designee)

Source: Reprinted with permission of the San Diego City Schools, Educational Services Division, Gifted and Talented Education, 1986.

---

and writing were interfering with his academic performance. Other achievement scores indicated average to above-average reading skills (44th to 88th percentiles) and average to above-average arithmetic skills (54th to 94th percentiles). Reading comprehension scores were better than word recognition scores. On the WISC-R he obtained a Verbal IQ of 135, a Performance IQ of 127, and a Full Scale IQ of 134. The results suggested that Paul is a gifted youngster with a specific learning disability.

Gifted groups that are difficult to identify.   There are subgroups of gifted children who are difficult to identify (Whitmore, 1985). One group is gifted *underachievers* who are reading at an average or below-average level and who are unmotivated, immature, or passive-aggressive. Indications of their giftedness may be obtained from observations that suggest superior oral language; excellent memory, comprehension, and general knowledge; analytical and creative problem-solving abilities; advanced interests; and evidence of originality and creativity.

A second difficult-to-identify group is those gifted children who are *physically or neurologically handicapped.* Children in this group may have difficulty in reading, writing, and spelling; poor perceptual-motor skills; poor attention; poor oral communication skills; aggressive-disruptive behavior; withdrawn behavior; and developmental delays. Indications of giftedness are similar to those mentioned above, except that some physically or neurologically handicapped children may not have superior oral language. In addition, these children may show a drive to communicate through alternative modes and a drive to know and master material.

A third group of difficult-to-identify children is those gifted children who are *culturally different.* They may exhibit language difficulties, interests that deviate from those of the dominant culture, a low level of participation in class activities, and disruptive behavior. In addition, they may meet with negative stereotyped expectations (for example, laziness, slowness, lack of diligence, and tendency toward delinquency). Indications of giftedness are similar to those noted for the first group, except that culturally different children may not display superior oral language skills.

Gifted Preschoolers

Extraordinary preschool children tend to be more precocious in memory than in general intelligence, reading achievement, or spatial reasoning. Of a group of 53 such preschoolers studied by Roedell (1980a), about 30 percent were precocious in memory, whereas only 5 to 13 percent were precocious in general intelligence, reading, or spatial reasoning. Examples of children who met the criterion of extraordinarily precocious performance were (a) a 3-year-old child with a Stanford-Binet Intelligence Scale: Form L-M IQ of 164 and (b) a 4-year-old child who read at the fourth grade level. The following case provides a profile of a remarkably gifted preschool girl (Roedell, 1980a):

This preschool girl obtained an estimated Stanford-Binet Intelligence Scale: Form L-M IQ of 177. Her highest performance was on verbal reasoning items; she showed less extraordinary spatial reasoning skills. Although she was not remarkably proficient in map-making or design-copying, she read at the fourth grade level by the age of 4 years. Her favorite books at that time were *The Little House* series by Laura Ingalls Wilder. She also enjoyed making up elaborate fantasy dramas involving several characters and complicated plots. Her everyday language skills also were excellent.

The academic abilities of gifted preschoolers show an extreme diversity in skill patterns (Roedell, 1980a). The early acquisition of advanced academic skills may not necessarily be related to level of intelligence. Some preschool children with IQs above 160 have not mastered reading or arithmetic, whereas others with IQs of 116 are fluent readers by the age of 3 years. Gifted preschool children may show highly differentiated abilities in various cognitive areas, such as highly developed spatial reasoning abilities and vocabularies, exceptional memory ability, unusual mathematical skills, or early reading skills. Young children who are exceptionally adept in one area are not necessarily advanced in other areas—"intraindividual differences among abilities are the rule, not the exception" (Robinson, 1981, p. 72). For example, children with extraordinary spatial reasoning ability may have only moderately advanced verbal skills; those who have remarkable skills in memory may be ordinary in other respects. It is *highly unlikely*, however, that children who are extraordinary in one area of mental functioning will be average or below average in all other areas of functioning.

The following sketch describes some personality and adjustment patterns of gifted preschoolers.

Gifted children show a wide range of personality characteristics and levels of social maturity. While children with moderately advanced intellectual abilities often show good overall adjustment, children with extremely advanced intellectual skills may have more difficulty. Adjustment problems may, in some cases, result from the uneven development that occurs when intellectual capabilities far outstrip the child's levels of physical or social development. Children with advanced intellectual skills sometimes tend to show advanced understanding of social situations and to be better able to judge other people's feelings. Intellectually advanced preschoolers, however, may need guided social experience to help them make use of their advanced social understanding. (Roedell, 1980a, p. 26)

Identifying Preschool Gifted Children

The procedures used to identify preschool gifted children are similar to those used with school-age children. Some additional considerations are warranted, however. The competencies of gifted preschoolers are best assessed with a battery of tests that includes measures of spatial-perceptual reasoning skills (for example, Block Design and Mazes), short-term memory, mathematics, reading ability, and general intellectual ability. [The presentation in this section is primarily based on Jackson's (1980) excellent chapter on the identification of gifted performance in young children.]

Assessment of intellectual skills. A number of techniques are available for obtaining information about the *upper limits* of a preschool child's intellectual ability. If a child obtains scores at the highest level on one or more WPPSI subtests, similar WISC-R subtests can be administered, even though the WISC-R was not standardized on preschool children. In such cases, the child's performance can be interpreted in terms of test-age equivalent norms. For example, a 4-year-old who obtains a raw score of 30 on the WISC-R Block Design subtest may be said to be at an 11-2-year-old level.

The WPPSI and WISC-R can also be used for obtaining estimates of the ability of children younger than 4 years of age. The test-age equivalents that accompany each subtest also are helpful for this purpose. Other useful instruments are the Stanford-Binet Intelligence Scale: Fourth Edition and K-ABC.

For children between 2 and 3 years of age, Jackson recommends using the Seguin Form Board (Stutsman, 1931) to estimate spatial reasoning ability. The WPPSI Block Design and Mazes subtests are good for children 3½ years old and older, but because they require precise motor skills these subtests are too sophisticated for younger children.

Although it is somewhat unreliable for preschoolers because of its sensitivity to anxiety and inattentiveness, the Numerical Memory subtest of the McCarthy Scales of Children's Abilities can be used as a screening measure of short-term memory. High Numerical Memory scores may indicate a superior capacity to absorb new experiences. The entire McCarthy Scales of Children's Abilities may not be a suitable instrument for identifying intellectually gifted preschoolers, however. Jackson (1980) reported that McCarthy General Cognitive Indexes for a group of gifted preschool children were considerably lower than their Stanford-Binet Intelligence Scale: Form L-M and WPPSI IQs. In addition, the children often refused to respond to the Verbal Memory, Part II, items that required them to retell a short story that the examiner had recited. Group tests of general intelligence should not be used with preschool children because the children usually are not sufficiently attentive, compliant, and persistent in a group situation. Exhibit 21-11 illustrates the kind of difference that may exist between the McCarthy GCI and scores on other standardized tests; it describes a preschool child who showed remarkable progress in a special preschool program.

Exhibit 21-11

Case Study of Bruce: A Child with Advanced Intellectual Abilities

INTRODUCTION

Following is a longitudinal case study of a gifted child who was initially tested at the age of 3 years. At that time he also entered a preschool program. The case illustrates a number of important principles related to testing and assessment. First, it shows that different tests purportedly measuring the same ability (in this case, general intelligence) may yield different results. Second, it shows that the same test may yield different scores on different occasions. Third, it shows how scores on some parts of tests may be particularly influenced by the child's motivation and interest (note Bruce's WPPSI Vocabulary and Animal house scores). Fourth, it shows that a young child's interests may change. Fifth, it points out the value of parental and teacher reports and observations conducted outside the testing session in obtaining an in-depth picture of the child. Other comments are presented in the report below.

CASE STUDY

Background

Bruce participated in a project designed to identify young gifted children. When Bruce was 3 years old, his mother reported that he seemed advanced, relative to other children his age, in his ability to grasp concepts and memorize new information. He had learned to read from watching the television programs "Sesame Street" and "The Electric Company" and was reading at about the first grade level.

Bruce's mother, who has a B.A. degree, had herself begun reading before entering kindergarten. His father, a business executive with an M.S. degree, had also been described as exceptionally intelligent. Both parents reported that they spent a great deal of time with Bruce and with his younger sister, who is also quite advanced in her intellectual development.

Parent Information

Bruce's mother had kept a detailed record of his early development in a baby book. According to her records, Bruce talked in 3–4 word sentences by age 12 months and showed an interest in letters and numbers while still in his playpen. By age 14 months he could recite numbers to 10; by 18 months he could recite numbers to 30 and recite the full alphabet. At this age he was also able to recognize and name all capital letters. At 19 months he recognized the words *Safeway*, *Bruce*, *momma*, and *Colgate*. On his second birthday, he could sound out and read many words, count to 50, spell many words, and recite his address and phone number. He did somersaults and wrote some letters and numbers.

When Bruce was about 3 years old, his mother described him as having a "categorized mind—once interested in some-

thing he becomes obsessed with it." A major obsession during his preschool years was anything to do with cars and trucks.

Test Results

Bruce was tested repeatedly from age 3 to age 6. The test results are summarized below:

Stanford-Binet: Form L-M

CA	3-0	4-8	5-3	6-0	
MA	4-5	7-6	8-3	10-0	
IQ	127	152	152	159+	(linear extrapolation 163)

McCarthy Scales of Children's Abilities:

Chronological age = 3-4

SCALE	SCALE INDEX
Verbal	51
Perceptual-performance	58
Quantitative	75
General Cognitive Index	116
Memory	58
Motor	37

Wechsler Preschool and Primary Scale of Intelligence (WPPSI):

Chronological age = 4-0

VERBAL SCALE	SCALED SCORE
Information	19
Vocabulary	6
Arithmetic	19
Similarities	17
Comprehension	12
Sentences	18

PERFORMANCE SCALE	
Animal House	7
Picture Completion	16
Mazes	18
Geometric Design	19
Block Design	18

Verbal Scale IQ	129
Performance Scale IQ	138
Full Scale IQ	137

(Exhibit continues next page)

Exhibit 21-11 (cont.)

Peabody Individual Achievement Test (PIAT)
(grade equivalents):

| | AGE AT ADMINISTRATION | | | | |
SUBTEST	4-0	4-6	5-1	5-8	6-0
Mathematics	1.7	1.9	2.5	3.3	7.4
Reading Recognition	3.5	4.4	4.4	5.8	6.6
Reading Comprehension	3.6	2.7	5.0	5.3	4.7
Spelling	3.2	3.0	4.1	5.6	4.9
General Information	–	1.6	3.7	3.6	4.1
Total	2.5	2.6	3.8	4.3	5.1

On the Peabody Individual Achievement Test (PIAT), grade-equivalent scores are reported instead of the more generally accepted percentile ranks, because no percentile norms are available for the performance of a pre-kindergarten child on this test and because Bruce's performance on the later PIAT tests was consistently above the percentile scale limits for kindergarten and first grade.

The Stanford-Binet: Form L-M results indicate that Bruce was consistently in the superior to very superior range. The most significant change was between the first (age 3-0, IQ = 127) and the second (age 4-8, IQ = 152) testing. During his first Stanford-Binet test, he was anxious and did not give long verbal responses. He was cooperative on the other Stanford-Binet tests, but at the 6-0 year testing he also was anxious about being correct.

When he was administered the McCarthy Scales at 3 years, 4 months of age, he was uncooperative. He refused to answer questions on many subtests, and a second testing session was needed. However, he refused to draw a child at both testing sessions. His General Cognitive Index was in the Above Average range.

At the age of 4 years, 0 months, his WPPSI performance was in the Superior range. However, his Vocabulary and Animal House subtest scores were below average, a result that could not be easily explained. The examiner noted that Bruce was simply not interested in the tasks on these two subtests.

On the PIAT he was consistently above average on all tests administered from 4-0 to 6-0 years of age. At the age of 6-0 years, he earned grade-equivalents above 4.0 in all areas. His highest score was in Mathematics, in which he earned a grade equivalent of 7.4. These are superior achievements given that the average grade equivalent at 6 years of age is 1.0.

Social-Emotional and Motor Development

During Bruce's first year at the preschool, when he was 3 years old, his teacher was concerned about his frequent tantrums, his tendency to play alone rather than with other children, and an awkwardness in his running and climbing. He habitually held one of his hands at a stiff, awkward angle, and he had periods when he would stand tensely still, trembling all over. Over time, however, all of these behavior patterns changed.

By his kindergarten year, Bruce was described as cooper-

ative and affectionate in his relationships with his classmates. His teacher reported that he made great progress during that year in the area of self-control. His large and small motor skills were described as good to excellent, and nothing in his motor behavior was noted as a problem. After Bruce's first grade year in a public school program for gifted children, his mother reported that he was generally well liked by his peers, although he was still sometimes impatient and verbally aggressive when angry or frustrated.

Academic Achievements in Kindergarten

A detailed report prepared by Bruce's teacher at the end of his kindergarten year includes many examples of his advanced academic abilities:

Bruce worked equation sheets of addition, subtraction, and multiplication, ones I created and those in the second grade Lippincott math book. These were initially challenging to him, but he mastered them quickly. . . .

Bruce often chose alphabet books and number books to read. He said that he didn't enjoy reading very much, but that he knew most words. This fact was borne out in his classroom behavior. He was more interested in words than ideas. . . .

Bruce was fantastic at mapping. He was the only child who could find his locker on a map of the hall and the lockers of all the other children. He could locate points by coordinates on maps and follow directions. . . .

Bruce wrote a book, "All About Apples," which took approximately two hours to write. In it he outlined all the possible uses of apples that he could imagine, including descriptions of foods that might accompany apple foods. The composition was clear and the tone was entertaining. . . .

Bruce's attention span was extremely long. He would often come back to projects two or three days in a row. . . .

Comment

Bruce's case history illustrates several important things. One striking feature of this history is the richness and predictive validity of the information his parents gave us about his very early intellectual accomplishments. Bruce's classroom and test performance at 5 and 6 years are more consistent with the early parental reports and our own informal observations of his early behavior than with his initial intelligence test scores.

Another point evident in this history is that, as a child of preschool age, Bruce was not as advanced in social-emotional and motor development as in intellectual development. Bruce needed educational programs that could cope with *both* precocious academic skills and 3-year-old tantrums.

Finally, the pattern of skills observed at 2, 3, and 4 years of age did not provide an obvious prediction of his later interest

(Exhibit continues next page)

Exhibit 21-11 (cont.)

and ability patterns. The most salient aspect of Bruce's performance at age 3 years was his reading ability; by age 6, his greatest interest and ability were in mathematics and his reading comprehension scores had leveled off. There was, however, continuity in Bruce's interest in solving perceptual-logical problems.

Note. This case study was prepared by Nancy Ewald Jackson from records of a longitudinal study of children with advanced intellectual abilities. The study was directed by the late Halbert B. Robinson, principal investigator, and Nancy Ewald Jackson and Wendy Conklin Roedell, associate investigators. The study was supported by grants from the Spencer Foundation. Parts of the case study (Introduction and Test Result sections) were edited and written by Jerome M. Sattler.

Assessment of achievement skills.   Skills in reading and mathematics should be considered when young children are screened for special programs. Some preschool children read at extraordinarily advanced levels, even though their IQs are in the normal range. The Peabody Individual Assessment Test, the Woodcock-Johnson Psycho-Educational Battery, the Kaufman Test of Educational Achievement, and the Basic Achievement Skills Individual Screener are useful for evaluating these areas in preschool children. Additional tools for assessing mathematical skills include items from the Stanford-Binet Intelligence Scale: Fourth Edition, the WPPSI, the KeyMath Diagnostic Arithmetic Test, and the Sequential Assessment of Mathematics Inventories.

Other identification procedures.   Measures of divergent thinking are useful in identifying gifted preschool children (see Chapter 13), as are questionnaires administered to parents and teachers (see Exhibits 21-9 and 21-10). Excellent observational guidelines for identifying young gifted children appear in Exhibit 21-12.

To supplement objective tests and questionnaires, parents can keep a diary or write out a detailed report of their child's activities, skills, and interests. An example of such a report follows:

By the age of two, Alice could identify all colors, including shades, count to ten, had begun "spelling" road signs by naming the letters, could identify all letters of the alphabet by name, and spoke in sentences of up to ten words, using all basic parts of speech. She now (at 28 months) speaks in sentences of up to 16 words and uses complex sentence structures; for example, this morning she has said, "I'm trying to figure out where I left my dancing shoes," and, "I want to take a look at this story to see what kinds of boys and girls it has in it.". . . Alice has memorized most of *Birds: A Guide to the Most Familiar American Birds* and recognizes the common ones we see frequently; at the zoo she identified the kingfisher, bald eagle, vultures, and owls from having seen them in the book and was indignant over the lack of a purple martin and a tufted titmouse. . . . Alice got her first books when she was six months old, and they immediately became her primary interest. She now has over a hundred books and has learned most of them by heart. (Jackson, 1980, p. 59)

Educating Gifted Children

Gifted children should receive education at a level commensurate with their abilities and interests. In some cases, this means exposing children to programs several levels above those their age mates are receiving. The simplest way to do this is by placing academically advanced children in existing classes at more advanced grade levels. *The*

10-9-81 — © 1981 United Feature Syndicate, Inc.

Exhibit 21-12

Observational Guidelines for Identifying Young Gifted Children

1. Notice when a child uses advanced vocabulary correctly or when a child asks about a new word heard in a story or lesson and then practices that word.

2. Notice when a child uses metaphors or analogies. For example, a child might say that moss on a tree is like an old man's beard, thus going beyond the simple perception of moss.

3. Notice when a child spontaneously makes up songs or stories, particularly when these elaborate on new experiences or when they involve "playing" with the pronunciation of words, rhymes, rhythms, and the like.

4. Notice when a child makes interesting shapes or patterns with small blocks, large blocks, pounding board shapes, playdough, or drawing materials. Notice if a child attempts to copy a pattern or if the pattern created is symmetrical. Notice also elaborate or unusual artwork in any media. Notice the process children go through as they plan their work.

5. Notice when a child appears to modify his or her language for less mature children. For example, a child might appropriately shorten sentences, use less sophisticated words, and change his or her pitch when speaking to very young children.

6. Notice when a child displays skill in putting together new or difficult puzzles, particularly if she or he examines the shape of puzzle pieces and seems to know where to place them without trial and error.

7. Notice when a child says or does something that indicates a sense of humor. For example, a child might pretend that the characteristics of one thing belong to another, as in a dog meowing.

8. Notice when a child expresses an understanding of abstract or complex concepts such as death, time, or electricity.

9. Notice when a child masters a new skill, a new concept, song, or rhyme with unusual speed or when a child demonstrates a competence that has been presented in a lesson some time previously. For example, a child might independently use construction paper to assemble a witch, copying a technique demonstrated by a teacher some weeks earlier.

10. Notice when a child seems capable of locating him or herself in the environment. For example, does the child seem to know where everything is in the room and in the school building? When on a walk, can he or she tell how to get back to the school? Does the child maneuver his or her tricycle skillfully around the yard and seem to know when a space is too small to drive through? Does she or he understand how to keep out of the way of the swing?

11. Notice when children use language for a real exchange of ideas and information among themselves.

12. Notice when a child becomes totally absorbed in one kind of knowledge. For example, a boy or girl might spend all of his or her free time with cars and trucks, draw only cars and trucks, want to read books about cars and trucks, and talk knowledgeably about different types of cars and trucks.

13. Notice when a child displays great interest or skill in ordering and grouping items. For example, a child might create block constructions that are systematically organized by shape, sort toy vehicles by size and type, or spontaneously arrange pegboard pieces to form a rainbow-ordered color series.

14. Notice when a child takes apart and reassembles things with unusual skill.

15. Notice if a child identifies left or right, both in relation to his or her own body and the body of another person, or if she or he understands how to move to the left or right.

16. Notice when a child remembers and makes mental connections between past and present experiences. For instance, a child might spontaneously apply a principle learned in a group time about mammals to another lesson, weeks later, concerned with dinosaurs.

17. Notice when a child behaves in a way that indicates sensitivity to the needs or feelings of another child or adult. For example, a girl or boy might spontaneously help another child who had fallen or might move out of the way of another child without being asked.

18. Notice when a child is able to carry out complex instructions to do several things in succession or when a boy or girl is able to absorb several new concepts in a single session.

19. Notice when a child is unusually attentive to features of the classroom environment. For instance, a youngster might frequently be the first to notice a small change in the arrangement of the room, a teacher's new hairstyle, or a different picture on the wall.

20. Notice when a child uses verbal skills to handle conflict or to influence other children's behavior. For example, a child might use verbal skills to initiate a toy exchange, to decide peer group activities, or to exercise general leadership.

principle is placement according to competence (Robinson, 1980). Following this procedure ensures many children the right to an appropriate education. Arguments that acceleration will be harmful to children have proven to be without foundation. The following case illustrates the application of the principle to a mathematically gifted adolescent.

C-B is one of the brightest students identified by Julian C. Stanley's "Mathematically Precocious Youth" talent search project. In December, 1975, a month after his tenth birthday, C-B took the SAT in a regular administration and scored 600 Verbal and 680 Mathematical; a year later he raised these scores to 710 and 750, respectively. A variety of intelligence test scores indicated an IQ of about 200. A Chinese-American youngster whose father is a professor of physics and whose mother has a master's degree in psychology, C-B has two younger siblings who are also very bright. He attended a private school in Baltimore, where he was given special opportunities.

It was discovered that, although C-B had only taken first-year high-school algebra (as a fifth grader), he had acquired by age 11 the subject matter of algebra II, algebra III, and plane geometry. Trigonometry took him a few weeks to learn, as did analytic geometry. At age 12, while his father was doing research using the linear accelerator at Stanford University, C-B completed his high school career in Palo Alto while simultaneously taking a demanding calculus course at Stanford. In the fall of 1978, when he was still 12 years old, C-B entered Johns Hopkins with sophomore standing. He had been accepted at Harvard and Cal Tech as well. He received his baccalaureate in May 1981, at age 15, with a major in physics. (Robinson, 1980, pp. 11–12, with changes in notation)

Schools must be flexible in order to provide gifted and talented students with programs that match their abilities (Robinson, 1980). This can be done, for the most part, with classes that are already available in the educational system. Although no grade-placement system can provide the perfect match for talented students, such a system has the best chance of meeting the educational needs of gifted and talented youngsters.

Terman's Study of the Gifted

One of the most extensive longitudinal investigations of children (Terman, 1925; Terman & Oden, 1959) studied a sample of 1,528 gifted children (857 males and 671 females) from the time they were approximately 11 years of age. (The children's IQs on the Stanford-Binet Intelligence Scale: 1916 Form ranged from 135 to 200, and their IQs on group tests were 135 and above.) Physicians rated the children as physically superior to a group of unselected children. On tests of achievement, their performance was superior to that of other children in such areas as reading, arithmetical reasoning, and information, but not as superior in computation and spelling. They were also more interested in abstract subjects (literature, debating, dramatics, and history) and somewhat less interested in practical subjects (penmanship, manual training, drawing, and painting).

Teachers rated these gifted children as above the mean of the control group on intellectual, volitional, emotional, aesthetic, moral, physical, and social traits. Only in one area, mechanical ingenuity, were the gifted children rated slightly below the control group.

On follow-up in middle age (Terman & Oden, 1959), members of the gifted group were found to have more education, higher incomes, more desirable and prestigious occupations, more entries in *Who's Who*, better physical and mental health, a lower suicide rate, a lower mortality rate, a lower divorce rate, and brighter spouses and children than a random sample of the population. The follow-up demonstrates that IQs do relate to accomplishments outside of school. As Brody and Brody (1976, p. 109) observed: "It is doubtful that the attempt to select children scoring in the top 1% of any other single characteristic would be as predictive of future accomplishment."

A similar, but less extensive, study was carried out in England with a sample of 55 English boys and girls, ages 8 to 12 years, with WISC Verbal IQs above 140 (Lovell & Shields, 1967). Teachers rated the children *outstandingly high* in general intelligence and desire to know; *very high* in originality, desire to excel, truthfulness, common sense, will power, perseverance, and conscientiousness; *rather high* in prudence and forethought, self-confidence, and sense of humor; and *close to the average* in traits such as freedom from vanity and egotism. Sex differences were few. The mean ratings given by the British teachers to these children were very close to those given by American teachers to the children in Terman's sample over 40 years earlier. A correlation of .90 was found between the rank orders of traits in the two studies. Thus, despite changes over time and between countries in education and in life generally, teachers in the United States in the 1920s and in England in the 1960s rated the gifted child in very similar ways. The results also indicated that tests of creativity did not measure any intellectual functions that were independent of those measured by the WISC or by tests of logical thought.

Creativity and Intelligence

Like intelligence, *creativity*, is a loosely defined, broad, and multifaceted concept. The relationship between creativity and intelligence is complex, complicated by problems of measurement and definition. The distinct but overlapping sets of influences in creativity and intelligence are explained by Amabile (1983) as follows. At low levels of intelligence, creativity is minimal, whereas at high levels of intelligence, all levels of creativity may be found. This suggests that intelligence is a component of creativity—a necessary but not sufficient contributing factor. Some minimum level of intelligence is likely required for creative performance. Traditional intelligence tests, however, are not likely to assess components necessary for creativity, such as intrinsic motivation for a task or personality dispositions conducive to deep levels of concentration. This information will be difficult to obtain from any standardized test.

The major attributes associated with creativity can be grouped into three areas (Rossman & Horn, 1972): *abilities* (intelligence, originality, flexibility, fluency, memory, sensitivity to problems, and perceptual receptivity), *motives* (need for achievement, striving for novelty, striving to test self [risk-taking], and preference for complexity), and *temperament traits* (independence of judgment, tendency to dominate, attitudinal openness, lack of anxiety, affective or aesthetic sensitivity, and playfulness). Different theorists emphasize one or more of the three areas. For example, Guilford (1967) stresses the ability area, maintaining that divergent thinking is the *sine qua non* of creative potential. Roe (1953) suggests that creativity is primarily the outcome of motivation, whereas Cattell and Drevdahl (1955) emphasize temperament or style in accounting for creative behaviors. It is useful to think of creativity and intelligence as the outgrowths of distinct (although overlapping) sets of influences.

A portrait of the creative person follows:

Despite differences in age, cultural background, area of operation or eminence, a particular constellation of psychological traits emerges consistently in the creative individual, and forms a recognizable schema of the creative personality. This schema indicates that creative persons are distinguished more by interests, attitudes, and drives, than by intellectual abilities. . . .

The cognitive capacities that appear to be most frequently associated with the creative are an above-average intelligence and the effective use of this intelligence, the ability to produce unusual and appropriate ideas, an exceptional retention and more ready availability of life experiences, ideational fluency and the ability to synthesize remote or disparate ideas, discriminative observation, and a general cognitive flexibility.

In the realm of personality, a clearly differentiating factor that characterizes the creative is the relative absence of impulse and imagery control by means of repression. . . .

Although the creative appears to be subject to considerable psychic turbulence, empirical evidence has shown no basis for a significant and demonstrated relationship between psychopathology and creativity. . . .

Independence in attitudes and social behavior emerges with striking consistency as relevant to creativity. Possessed of an individualistic rather than a sociocentric orientation, the creative [individual] is not concerned with social activities, nor preoccupied with the opinion others have of him [or her]. . . .

Though the evidence can hardly be called overwhelming, it does seem to indicate that the creator is endowed with strong, intrinsic motivation, involving a degree of resoluteness and egotism that sustains him [or her] in his [or her] work. . . .

In brief, the roots of creativity do not seem to lie in convergent or divergent thinking, but rather . . . in the personality and motivational aspects of character. (Dellas & Gaier, 1970, pp. 67–68)

Identifying Creativity

Measures of creativity that emphasize divergent thinking (for example, Guilford-type tests that measure unusual uses, consequences, and problem situations) correlate only very modestly with tests of intelligence (between .25 and .30). Tests of creativity correlate just as little with each other as they do with measures of intelligence, however. What little common variance they have may be accounted for by *g*, the general intelligence factor. Some tests of creativity may possibly measure cognitive abilities that are not reliably distinguished from intelligence, whereas others measure attributes that are different from those measured on intelligence tests.

Construct validity is difficult to attain for tests of creativity. Creativity tests often assess a narrow range of abilities; hence it is inappropriate to label a particular test score as generally indicative of creativity. For example, on the Torrance Tests of Creative Thinking, the heavy influence of verbal fluency on the originality scores restricts the meaning of originality.

Scoring procedures of many creativity tests are basically subjective, relying on the test constructor's criteria rather than more meaningful criteria such as novelty, appropriateness, or satisfyingness. Although many creativity tests do measure abilities and dispositions that are probably important for creative performance, "it is inappropriate to label their results as directly indicative of some global quality that can be called creativity . . . such judgments can ultimately only be subjective" (Amabile, 1983, p. 26).

Although there are numerous procedures for identifying creativity—including teacher and peer nominations, judgments of products, divergent thinking measures (see Chapter 13), biographical characteristics, attitudes and interests, personality traits, and creative achievements—the simplest and most straightforward method is the last:

an inventory of creative achievements and activities (Hocevar, 1981). Examples of creative achievements and activities include placing first, second, or third in a science contest; exhibiting or performing a work of art; publishing poems, stories, or articles in a newspaper; inventing a patentable or useful device; and acting in plays. Exhibit 21-13 is a useful checklist for rating creative traits in children.

Suggestions for Maintaining and Enhancing Creativity in Children

Following are some suggestions for encouraging creativity in children (Amabile, 1983).

1. *Create a stimulating teaching environment.* Teaching should take place in environments that are perceptively and cognitively stimulating, and children should be taught

---

Exhibit 21-13

Checklist for Identifying Creative Children

Child's name: _____   Rater: _____

Sex: _____   Date: _____

Grade: _____   Class: _____

Rating scale:

1	2	3	4	5
Not present	Minimally present	Somewhat present	Moderately present	Strongly present

Trait	Rating (circle one number)	Trait	Rating (circle one number)
1. Ability to concentrate	1 2 3 4 5	20. Inventiveness	1 2 3 4 5
2. Ability to defer judgment	1 2 3 4 5	21. Lack of tolerance for boredom	1 2 3 4 5
3. Above average IQ	1 2 3 4 5	22. Need for supportive climate	1 2 3 4 5
4. Adaptability	1 2 3 4 5	23. Nonconformism	1 2 3 4 5
5. Aesthetic appreciation	1 2 3 4 5	24. Openness to experience	1 2 3 4 5
6. Attraction to the complex and mysterious	1 2 3 4 5	25. Playfulness	1 2 3 4 5
7. Curiosity	1 2 3 4 5	26. Willingness to take risks	1 2 3 4 5
8. Delight in beauty of theory	1 2 3 4 5	27. Self-confidence	1 2 3 4 5
9. Delight in invention for its own sake	1 2 3 4 5	28. Sense of identity as originator	1 2 3 4 5
10. Desire to share products and ideas	1 2 3 4 5	29. Sense of mission	1 2 3 4 5
11. Eagerness to resolve disorder	1 2 3 4 5	30. Sensitivity	1 2 3 4 5
12. Extensive knowledge background	1 2 3 4 5	31. Ability to see that solutions generate new problems	1 2 3 4 5
13. Flexibility	1 2 3 4 5	32. Spontaneity	1 2 3 4 5
14. Good memory, attention to detail	1 2 3 4 5	33. Commitment to task	1 2 3 4 5
15. High energy level, enthusiasm	1 2 3 4 5	34. Tolerance for ambiguity and conflict	1 2 3 4 5
16. Humor (perhaps bizarre)	1 2 3 4 5	35. Willingness to face social ostracism	1 2 3 4 5
17. Imagination, insight	1 2 3 4 5	36. Willingness to daydream and fantasize	1 2 3 4 5
18. Independence	1 2 3 4 5		
19. Internal locus of control and evaluation	1 2 3 4 5		

Source: Traits obtained from Ford and Ford (1981).

to scan the environment for cues that might be relevant to problem solving. When children show special aptitudes, they should be provided with special teachers, special materials, and the time and freedom to develop their talents.

2. *Use teaching methods that will enhance creativity.* Children should be trained to identify and use the positive aspects of their own work and the work of others. Teachers should be enthusiastic and encouraging, and they should especially nurture creative processes in children who may be nonconforming and unpredictable.

3. *Diminish peer influences for conformity.* Highly talented children may benefit from being taught in special classes. The creativity of all children will be increased if they can be taught to resist peer pressure to conform.

4. *Be aware of dangers of formal education.* Although in most domains formal education is essential for high levels of creativity, an excessively extended formal education can be detrimental, particularly if it leads to over-reliance on established ways of thinking.

5. *Use appropriate socialization experiences.* Parents should display low levels of authoritarianism and avoid overly close affectional bonds that might lead to smothering of their children. Parents should also show respect for and confidence in their children, providing secure affection but at the same time allowing their children some independence from parental evaluation. Children should be exposed to models of creative achievement and encouraged to go beyond the observed modeled behavior. The capacity for creative behavior can be enriched and elevated by exposing children to cultural diversity throughout their development—through travel and other means.

6. *Encourage appropriate work attitudes.* Children should be encouraged to see the enjoyable aspects of their work, the inherent satisfaction in engaging in work activities, and the pleasure of watching their own work unfold. In addition, they should be encouraged to eliminate the strict dichotomy between work and play.

7. *Minimize control.* Children should be allowed as much choice as possible in their activities. They should have the freedom to decide on problems to attack, materials to use, methods of approach, and subgoals. Children should be taught to be self-observant and to engage in self-evaluation in order to limit dependence on external evaluation. High levels of self-determination and self-control should be encouraged. Teachers should allow some time in the classroom for individualized and self-directed learning in an informal atmosphere.

8. *Use rewards sparingly.* Rewards should be limited, especially if they are given explicitly as payment for some activity. Unusually high rewards, however, given as bonuses for performance, may enhance creativity.

9. *Stimulate interest level.* The above recommendations assume that children have a high initial level of intrinsic interest in their work. When a high initial level of intrinsic interest is not present, efforts should be made to enhance the child's interest. In such cases, it may be necessary to offer a reward to encourage the child to engage in the activity. As interest develops, rewards can be withdrawn or be made less salient. At both home and school, reinforcements should be tailored to the individual child's level of interest and ability.

SUMMARY

1. The most widely used definition of mental retardation is as follows: "Mental retardation refers to significantly subaverage general intellectual functioning existing concurrently with deficits in adaptive behavior and manifested during the developmental period." This definition implies that the diagnosis is only a description of present behavior, acknowledges the contribution of intelligence tests, ties diagnosis to the developmental process, and minimizes problems of differential diagnosis.

2. The definition of mental retardation specifies that two criteria—level of intelligence and level of adaptive behavior—must be used in arriving at a diagnosis of mental retardation. Adaptive behavior is more difficult to assess than intelligence.

3. Four levels of mental retardation are identified— mild, moderate, severe, and profound. In order for an individual to be diagnosed as mentally retarded, his or her score on the intelligence test used in the evaluation must fall 2 or more standard deviations below the mean score.

4. There are two broad groupings of mental retardation: familial and organic. The familial type encompasses most of the milder forms of mental retardation, reflecting primarily normal polygenic variation. The organic type encompasses the more severe forms of mental retardation as well as some milder forms; it is associated with genetic or chromosomal defects or brain damage.

5. Estimated prevalence rates for mental retardation, using a $-2\ SD$ cutoff point, range from 120,000 to 5,472,000, depending on the correlation assumed between adaptive behavior and intelligence. The higher the correlation assumed between adaptive behavior and intelligence, the larger the estimated prevalence rate.

6. Mentally retarded children are more vulnerable than normal children to the development of maladaptive behavior.

7. A child's chronological age should be considered in the evaluation because it is related to social behavior and interests.

8. There are large and meaningful differences among individuals labeled "mentally retarded."

9. The most popular intelligence tests for evaluating mental retardation are the Stanford-Binet Intelligence Scale and the Wechsler scales. Neither the Stanford-Binet: Fourth Edition nor the Wechsler scales is appropriate for the assessment of severely and profoundly retarded children, however.

10. Mentally retarded individuals tend to have more stable IQs over time than do individuals who are not mentally retarded.

11. Intelligence tests play an extremely important role in the assessment of mental retardation. Therefore every attempt must be made to ensure the reliability and validity of the test results.

12. On Piagetian tests nonorganically impaired mentally retarded children use reasoning processes that are similar to those used by their normal mental age peers; organically impaired retardates do not. A developmental-lag hypothesis best accounts for the findings with respect to the nonorganically impaired mentally retarded. This hypothesis states that these children pass through a normal sequence of cognitive developmental stages, but their rate of progress through the sequence is relatively slow and they have a relatively low upper limit of development.

13. The WISC-R is a popular, useful, and valid instrument for the assessment of mild levels of mental retardation. The WISC-R cannot reliably differentiate brain-injured from non-brain-injured mentally retarded, however. The WISC-R factor structure is similar for normal and mentally retarded children, although some minor differences have been found. Picture Completion and Object Assembly appear to be somewhat less difficult than Arithmetic, Vocabulary, Similarities, and Information for mentally retarded children.

14. Every attempt should be made to provide the best educational programming available for mentally retarded children. A battery of tests should be used for assessment. Children at the moderate, severe, and profound levels of retardation can benefit from educational training.

15. Recommendations as to the child's eligibility for special programs and the programs that might be most effective should be based on a careful study of the results of the evaluation. Older mentally retarded children may need sheltered workshop training.

16. Psychologists often do not confirm teachers' judgments that children referred for testing are in need of special education.

17. Current efforts focus on ways to integrate mentally retarded individuals into society.

18. A diagnosis of developmental delay is appropriate when mental retardation is suspected, but the results are not definitive.

19. As a result of Public Law 94-142 and the movement toward deinstitutionalization, more severely and profoundly retarded children are being educated in public schools. These children have not only limited intellectual ability, but also severe motoric, sensory, and physical handicaps. Moderately and severely retarded people can lead productive lives.

20. Among institutionalized mentally retarded individuals, those with higher levels of intelligence are likely to have fewer physical handicaps, greater self-help skills, and fewer behavior problems than those with lower levels of intelligence.

21. Norm-referenced, criterion-referenced, and developmentally based tests and scales are somewhat limited in their ability to assess severely and profoundly handicapped children. These scales often fail to sample the children's abilities and are somewhat inflexible in their procedures. They are relatively insensitive to the developmental changes that occur in severely and profoundly handicapped children. In spite of these shortcomings, standardized tests and scales provide useful age-equivalent scores and information about what the child can and cannot accomplish.

22. In addition to standardized tests and scales, other assessment procedures used with severely and profoundly retarded children include informal assessment procedures and functional assessment procedures. Among these procedures are task analysis; systematic observation and controlled teaching trials; informal assessment of communicative competence; adaptive behavior questionnaires, checklists, and interviews; and criterion-referenced instruments.

23. Children who fall into the gifted classification may have exceptionally high IQs (over 130), creative talents, or both.

24. *Giftedness* refers to distinctly above-average competence in one or more ability domains, whereas *talent* refers to distinctly above-average competence in one or more fields of human performance.

25. In general, the most effective means of identifying gifted children is one that combines intelligence, achievement, and behavioral-checklist data. Teacher judgments are useful in the identification process. The single best method for identifying children with superior cognitive abilities is a standardized individually administered test of intelligence.

26. Intelligence tests should be supplemented with achievement tests in the assessment of gifted children.

27. Gifted children who are difficult to identify include underachievers, those who are physically or neurologically handicapped, and the culturally different.

28. Gifted preschoolers are more often precocious in memory than in other cognitive domains. There is extreme diversity in the academic skills acquired by gifted preschoolers.

29. A battery of tests that includes both intellectual and academic tasks should be used to assess the competencies of gifted preschoolers. Age-equivalent scores for preschoolers can be obtained from tests that have been standardized on older children. Group tests of intelligence should not be used to assess preschool children.

30. Measures of divergent thinking are useful in assessing gifted children.

31. The key principle in educating gifted children is placement according to competence.

32. Gifted children not only are brighter than the general population of children, but also tend to perform better in school, be better adjusted, and have better physical health. In later life, they tend to make many contributions to society.

33. *Creativity* is a difficult concept to define. The primary determinants of creativity are abilities (intelligence and origi-

nality), motives (need for achievement and striving for novelty), and temperament traits (independence of judgment and tendency to dominate). Some minimum level of intelligence is likely required for creative performance.

34. Measures of divergent thinking correlate only moderately with tests of intelligence (between .25 and .30) and other tests of creativity.

35. Obtaining inventories of creative achievement from individuals is an excellent way of identifying creative talent.

36. Creativity can be enhanced and maintained in children by creating a stimulating teaching environment, using effective teaching methods, diminishing peer influences for conformity, reducing formal education, providing appropriate socialization experiences, encouraging appropriate work attitudes, minimizing control, using rewards sparingly, and stimulating interest level.

KEY TERMS, CONCEPTS, AND NAMES

American Association on Mental Deficiency (AAMD) (p. 647)
Mental retardation (p. 647)
Significantly subaverage (p. 647)
Adaptive behavior (p. 647)
Developmental period (p. 647)
Mild retardation (p. 648)
Moderate retardation (p. 648)
Severe retardation (p. 648)
Profound retardation (p. 648)
Educable mentally retarded (p. 648)
Trainable mentally retarded (p. 648)
Trainable (dependent) mentally retarded (p. 648)
Custodial (life support) mentally retarded (p. 648)
Familial retardation (p. 648)
Organic retardation (p. 649)
Stability of IQ among the mentally retarded (p. 651)
Developmental-lag hypothesis (p. 655)
Developmental delay (p. 656)
Deinstitutionalization (p. 657)
Task analysis (p. 659)
Controlled teaching trials (p. 659)
Communicative competence (p. 660)
Donald Snow v. *The State of New York* (pp. 661, 667)

Giftedness (p. 661)
Talent (p. 665)
Identifying gifted children (p. 665)
Underachievers (p. 674)
Placement according to competence (p. 680)
Terman's study of the gifted (p. 680)
Creativity and intelligence (p. 680)
Attributes associated with creativity (p. 681)
Identifying creativity (p. 681)
Enhancing creativity (p. 682)

STUDY QUESTIONS

1. Define mental retardation and discuss the implications of the definition and related classification issues.

2. Discuss the etiology of mental retardation.

3. How are prevalence rates for mental retardation a function of the relationship between measured intelligence and adaptive behavior?

4. What are some general considerations in understanding mental retardation? Include in your discussion the importance of chronological age, heterogeneity among children labeled mentally retarded, and developmental issues in cognitive and social adaptation.

5. Discuss the role of intelligence testing in the assessment of mental retardation. Include such issues as stability of the IQ, goals of the assessment, similarities and differences between mentally retarded and normal children of similar mental ages, and the use of the WISC-R.

6. Discuss educational programming and consultation with the mentally retarded.

7. Discuss the assessment of severely and profoundly mentally retarded children. Include in your discussion problems with standardized tests and scales and examples of alternative assessment procedures.

8. Discuss the assessment of gifted children. Include in your discussion definitions of gifted, means of identification, difficult-to-identify groups, preschool gifted children, educational placement, and Terman's study of the gifted.

9. Discuss the concept of creativity. Include in your discussion attributes associated with creativity, means of identification, and ways to enhance and maintain creativity in children.

22

ASSESSMENT OF BRAIN DAMAGE

I prefer to think of man's humanity as vested in his bodily structure and function, not least, in the activities of his brain.

—Oliver L. Zangwill

What Is Brain Damage?

Comparison of Neurological and Neuropsychological Approaches

Neurological Examination

Neuropsychological Evaluation

Lateralization of Cognitive, Perceptual, and Motor Activities

Aphasia in Children

Prognosis for Brain-Damaged Children

Aspects of a Neuropsychological Assessment

The Clinical History

Behavioral Observations

Neuropsychological Test Batteries for Children

Wechsler Scales as Part of a Neuropsychological Test Battery

Other Procedures Useful in the Assessment of Brain Damage in Children

Evaluating Assessment Results

Developing Intervention Procedures for Brain-Damaged Children

Report Writing

Psychological Evaluation

Summary

This chapter provides an *introduction* to the area of neuropsychological assessment. The word *introduction* is stressed because neuropsychological assessments require specialized training that is beyond the scope of an introductory assessment course. Nevertheless, the material in this chapter will help you gain an appreciation of issues in neuropsychological assessment, including the use of both formal and informal tests and the qualitative analysis of an individual's performance. Those behaviors on intelligence tests, visual-motor tests, and other achievement and special ability tests that may be suggestive of possible brain dysfunction are highlighted. Much still remains to be learned about the study of brain functioning and, particularly, brain-behavior relationships.

WHAT IS BRAIN DAMAGE?

Brain damage refers to any structural (anatomical) or physiological change of a pathological nature in the tissue of the brain.

Causes of Brain Damage

The causes of cerebral dysfunction in children must be considered in relation to developmental periods.

Prenatal environmental factors. Brain damage can be sustained as a result of prenatal environmental factors. These factors include severe maternal malnutrition; maternal ingestion of alcohol, drugs, or toxic substances (such as lead, asbestos, chlorines, fluorides, nickel, and mercury); maternal infections due to viruses or bacteria (for example, rubella, syphilis, and other sexually transmitted diseases); and radiation.

Perinatal factors. Various conditions associated with birth may lead to brain damage. These include prematurity, physical trauma, asphyxia, hypoglycemia, infection (meningitis, encephalitis), kernicterus (a condition involving widespread destructive changes in the red blood cells), and maternal sensitization (such as Rh incompatibility).

Postnatal factors. During the postnatal period, abnormalities of the nervous system may appear as a result of abnormal fetal development or environmental factors. Conditions causing abnormal fetal development include hydrocephaly, endocrine dysfunctions (such as hypothyroidism and Tay-Sachs disease), and metabolic disorders (such as PKU and galactosemia). The metabolic disorders, often a result of hereditary dysfunctions, are associated with deficient production of particular enzymes. Environmental factors that may lead to brain damage include poor nutrition (for example, iodine deficiency, protein deficiency, or vitamin A, B_6, B_{12}, or D deficiency), trauma (such as that resulting from automobile accidents, falls, or child abuse), infection (including scarlet fever, rabies, Rocky Mountain spotted fever, and encephalomyelitis), radiation, drug abuse, and ingestion of toxic substances (such as lead, arsenic, or mercury).

Types of Brain Damage

Brain insults may produce focal lesions or diffuse effects. Focal lesions are limited to fairly specific sites; they may be associated with small tumors, strokes, or trauma that penetrates the skull. Diffuse effects usually result from such brain insults as degenerative diseases, metabolic disorders, oxygen deficits, drug abuse, or trauma that does not penetrate the skull.

Head injuries may be open or closed. With *open head injuries* there may be skull fracture and tearing or penetration of the dura mater by skull depression, extensive local laceration with associated complications of intracranial hematoma (disruption of blood vessels), venous sinus involvement, and infection. These types of injuries frequently have focal effects. The fracture of the skull may absorb much of the shock of the impact and allow the brain to swell and compress against the skull with no resulting damage. The extensiveness of damage to subcortical regions may be difficult to ascertain, however.

With *closed head injuries* generalized symptoms may occur as a result of skull deformation, shearing injuries (portions of tissue sliding over other portions of tissue), and generalized cerebrovascular congestion. Laceration at various locations (including those opposite the point of impact) may also occur, secondary to impact on cerebral tissue. Closed head injuries are more likely to lead to progressively greater pathology than are open head injuries because of degenerative processes. Loss of consciousness and amnesia are two important clinical signs frequently associated with traumatic brain injury.

Cognitive, affective, and behavioral dysfunctions are somewhat specific and limited with focal lesions, but more generalized with diffuse brain damage. Brain damage may produce a general deterioration in all aspects of functioning; differential effects, depending on such variables as the location, extent, and type of injury and the age of the individual; highly specific effects in certain locations; or no observable effects at all. The focus of this chapter is on traumatic brain injury, because it is the most common cause of brain dysfunction in young children and adolescents. Infants and toddlers are especially vulnerable to damage associated with falls or with collisions against the dashboard or windshield of an automobile.

COMPARISON OF NEUROLOGICAL AND NEUROPSYCHOLOGICAL APPROACHES

Although the goal of both the neurological and the neuropsychological examination is to assess brain damage accurately, the former focuses primarily on the intactness of lower level functions (for example, motor system and reflexes), whereas the latter deals more extensively with higher level cognitive processes (for example, language and memory). Consequently, the neuropsychological examination probably is more sensitive to higher level cognitive dysfunction than is the neurological examination.

A standard neurological examination—coupled with an EEG and other ancillary diagnostic studies—usually is effective in establishing the presence and locus of intracranial disease or damage. These procedures are by no means perfect diagnostic tools, however. The neuropsychological evaluation—although it does not permit definitive diagnosis (that is, specification of a specific etiology)—can aid in establishing a diagnosis of brain dysfunction. Moreover, whether or not there is clear evidence of brain damage from other neurodiagnostic procedures, the neuropsychological evaluation can be useful in defining the nature and the severity of specific defects in higher (cognitive) and lower (motor and perceptual) cerebral functions. In cases where findings are equivocal or where there is brain disease or trauma early in life, the effects of the underlying acute or chronic cerebral damage may not be readily apparent. These effects, however, may manifest themselves through slightly defective performance on different psychological tests or through marked impairment in selected performances on certain tests.

Increased diagnostic precision in medicine should result in a shift in emphasis in neuropsychological assessment (Costa, 1983). Less emphasis will be placed on identification of the etiology and locus of the disease process, and more on the behavioral consequences of neurologically related disorders and the intervention techniques needed for remediation. Some questions a neuropsychological assessment might seek to answer would be the following:

"What type of education program should this child receive this year, next year, or ever?" and "Is the child a good candidate for a visualization-memory training group?"

The assessment of brain damage should be a joint venture of the neurologist and the neuropsychologist. It is a complex and exacting task requiring extensive specialized professional knowledge and cooperation.

NEUROLOGICAL EXAMINATION

A neurological examination includes a clinical history, a brief mental status examination, and a study of cranial nerves, motor functions (including tone, strength, and reflexes), coordination, sensory functions, and gait. Several laboratory procedures may augment the neurological examination, including CT scans (computerized tomography), PET scans (positron emission tomography), MRI scans (magnetic resonance imaging), EEGs (electroencephalograms), skull x-rays, spinal taps, and cerebral angiograms. A brief description of the scanning and radiography methods follows.

CT is an imaging technique in which an array of detectors is used to collect information from an x-ray beam that has passed through a portion of the brain (or another body part). The beam is rotated to produce the equivalent of a "slice" through the area of interest. A computer reconstructs the internal structure from the information collected and displays it on a screen. CT scans are useful in locating tumors and hemorrhages.

PET is a scanning method that produces a cross-sectional image of radioactivity following intravenous injection of a radioactive substance. PET scans provide anatomical information and information about cerebrovascular membrane permeability. The information generated is similar to that produced by CT scans, but PET scans more precisely measure blood flow and metabolism in specific regions of the brain.

MRI provides a two-dimensional color intensity plot of a cross-sectional slice of any part of the body. The plot is a magnetic resonance image of the anatomy at the cross section. MRI is nonevasive and involves no harmful radiation. The advantages of MRI scans over CT scans include the ability to show better contrasts on soft tissue, a feature that makes it particularly suitable for the investigation of tumors, edema, or tissue pathology.

EEGs are recordings of the potentials of the skull generated by currents emanating spontaneously from nerve cells of the brain.

Cerebral angiograms are radiographic recordings of internal structures of the vascular system of the brain.

They are produced by action of x-rays or gamma rays on a specially sensitive film after injection of contrast material (for example, iodinated compounds) into the arterial blood system.

Neurological Signs

Neurological signs suggestive of brain damage are referred to as hard or soft. The *hard signs* are those that are fairly definitive indicators of cerebral dysfunction (for example, abnormalities in reflexes, cranial nerves, and motor organization; asymmetrical failures in sensory and motor responses) and are usually correlated with other independent evidence of brain damage, such as that obtained from CT scans or EEGs.

The *soft*, or *equivocal*, *signs* are associated with more complex behaviors, including mental activities, coordination, and sensation. Representative soft signs are poor balance; impaired fine motor coordination; clumsiness; slight reflex asymmetries; choreiform (irregular, jerky) limb movements; inability to perform rapid alternating movement of hands and feet in a smooth, fluent, and rhythmic fashion (dysdiadochokinesia); inability to detect predisplayed symbols traced on the palmar surface when blindfolded (dysgraphesthesia); inability to identify three-dimensional objects in the outstretched hand when blindfolded (astereognosis); awkwardness, impaired auditory integration, atypical sleep patterns; and visual-motor difficulties. Useful procedures for assessing soft signs are shown in Table 22-1.

The term *soft signs* is applied to behavioral and motor indicators that may not have any systematic relationship to demonstrated neuropathology, but may be suggestive of neurological impairment, immaturity of development, or a continuum of dysfunction. Age norms are necessary for soft signs if they are to be interpreted correctly. (Denckla, 1985, provides norms for various soft signs.)

NEUROPSYCHOLOGICAL EVALUATION

A neuropsychological evaluation complements a neurological examination. It may include measures of sensory perceptual functions (tactile, visual, and auditory modalities), motor functions relating to speed and strength, psychomotor problem solving, language and communication skills, and other cognitive and intellectual skills. Neuropsychological evaluations provide a profile of cognitive, sensorimotor, and affective domains. They are useful in differentiating brain-damaged children from those who are not brain damaged; localizing hemispheric involvement; differentiating static from rapidly growing lesions (particularly with serial evaluations); evaluating the effects of progressive diseases of the central nervous system on adaptive abilities (for example, documenting rate and quality of change with the passage of time); differentiating behavioral disturbances associated with brain damage from those that occur in the absence of cerebral dysfunction; planning for rehabilitation; and providing objective data for research.

Neuropsychological evaluations may also be of assistance in evaluating children who have reading or other academic problems, learning disabilities, and minimal brain dysfunction. Neuropsychological tests provide objective behavioral information about the individual's adaptive functioning and base-line measures for serially evaluating the course of various neuropathological processes and the effects of different therapeutic programs on cerebral functions.

The aim of the neuropsychological evaluation is to draw inferences about the organic integrity of the cerebral hemispheres as well as to specify the adaptive strengths and weaknesses of the child. An adequate assessment of brain-behavior relationships requires the use of a variety of tests, as no single test can adequately assess the behavioral effects of widely variable cerebral lesions. Psychological correlates of brain functions can best be understood by eliciting a more complete sample of brain-related behavior than is elicited with any single test.

Clinical neuropsychology also makes other contributions to the diagnostic process. In cases of civil liability suits involving head injuries, a neuropsychological examination provides objective measures of adaptive deficits (Schwartz, 1987). Neuropsychological assessment increases our understanding of the psychological effects of brain damage and, more generally, of brain-behavior relations. A battery of neuropsychological tests provides a comprehensive, objective, and quantified series of measures useful in assessing initial and later effects of various neuropathological conditions, neurosurgical procedures, and drug therapies.

LATERALIZATION OF COGNITIVE, PERCEPTUAL, AND MOTOR ACTIVITIES

Lateralization refers to the specialization of the hemispheres of the cerebral cortex in various cognitive, perceptual, and motor or sensory activities. In general, the sensorimotor activities are predominantly mediated by the

Table 22-1
Examples of "Soft" Neurological Signs of Defects

Sign	Tests or symptoms
Poor coordination	*Tests:* Finger-to-nose, heel-to-knee (eyes open and closed), finger pursuit, rapid individual finger movements, rapid alternating movements, tying shoes, using buttons and zippers, writing, picking up small objects. *Symptoms:* dysmetria (abnormal difficulty in positioning a limb), ataxia (poor muscle control resulting from cerebellar difficulty in positioning a limb), dysdiadochokinesia (difficulty in executing rapid alternating movements)
Abnormal gait	*Tests:* Walking, running, walking on toes, walking on heels, hopping
Impaired position sense	*Tests:* Passive movement of great toe (child is asked to give direction of movement in at least five trials), location of finger in space (examiner places one of child's index fingers in space, and child is asked, with eyes closed, to touch it with the other index finger)
Astereognosis	*Tests:* Identify by touch, with eyes closed, a bottle cap, nickel, button, key, marble, ¾-inch block (the symptom is reflected by an inability to recognize the objects)
Nystagmus	*Symptoms:* Jerky eye movements when looking ahead, on directed horizontal or vertical gaze, or in one eye when the other is covered
Strabismus	*Symptoms:* Unilateral or bilateral esotropia (deviation of visual axis toward that of the other eye) or exotropia (deviation of visual axis away from that of the other eye), alternating internal strabismus (a convergent deviation of the eye that affects each eye alternately), alternating external strabismus (a divergent deviation of the eye that affects each eye alternately), other impaired extraocular movements
Abnormal reflexes	*Symptoms:* Hypoactive, hyperactive, or asymmetrical biceps, triceps, ankle, or knee jerk, with sustained ankle clonus (at least six rapid contractions of the triceps surae muscle); abnormal plantar response
Mirror movements	*Tests:* Examinee performs rapid thumb-forefinger apposition on one hand — examiner checks whether movements occurred on the other hand
Other abnormal movements	*Symptoms:* Fasciculation (quick involuntary contraction of muscle), myoclonus (quick nonrhythmic repetitive contrations of muscle, usually associated with limb movement), spontaneous tremor (including tremor present at rest), intention tremor (tremor elicited by attempted voluntary activity), athetosis (slow, worm-like writhing, spasmodic and repetitive movements affecting peripheral muscle of limbs and face), chorea (rapid involuntary jerks of trunk, head, face, or extremities), dystonia (involuntary fluctuations of tone and muscle spasms of the neck, trunk, and proximal musculature of the limbs), ballismus (large-scale, violent flinging movements involving major portions of a limb), tic (repeated stereotyped movement resembling voluntary movements), other unclassified abnormal or unwanted movements
Abnormal tactile finger recognition	*Tests:* Identify finger lightly touched, with fingers out of sight (each of the 10 fingers)

Source: Adapted from Nichols and Chen (1981).

side of the brain contralateral to (pertaining to the side opposite) the peripheral location examined. Consequently, a right cerebral hemisphere lesion may result in weakness or insensitivity on the left side of the body, whereas a left cerebral hemisphere lesion may produce deficits on the right side of the body. (Subcortical damage may produce deficits on the same side of the body as the damage.) Procedures for examining lateralized differences in lower level functions include motor functioning tests (measuring such factors as finger tapping rate, strength of grip, and motor dexterity), bilateral simultaneous stimulation (touching both sides of the body simultaneously), dichotic listening, and standard neurological techniques for assessing tactile, visual, and auditory senses.

Hemispheric Higher Level Functions

The two hemispheres also appear to be specialized with respect to certain higher level cognitive and perceptual processes.

Among nearly all right-handed individuals and about two-thirds of left-handed individuals, the left hemisphere is primarily responsible for verbal functions (including discrimination of verbal sounds, verbal sequencing, verbal learning and memory, and language comprehension), speech, spelling, reading, writing, and certain kinds of arithmetic.

The right hemisphere specializes in nonverbal, perceptual, and spatial functions, including spatial visualization, visual learning and memory, complex visual-motor organization, and nonverbal sequencing.

Left hemisphere processing has been characterized as analytic, sequential, serial, and differential, whereas right hemisphere processing is considered holistic, gestalt-like, parallel, and integrative. For simple tasks, nonverbal stimuli can be processed holistically by either hemisphere. The right hemisphere is clearly inferior to the left in expressive functions of speech and writing, but is less deficient in language comprehension. A more detailed listing of functions attributed to the left and right cerebral hemispheres appears in Table 22-2.

Some of the specialized functions of the cerebral hemispheres include the following. The *frontal lobes* are associated with planning, initiation, and modulation of behavior and expressive verbal fluency; the *temporal lobes* with auditory perception, auditory comprehension, learning/memory, and cross-modal integration; the *parietal lobes*

Table 22-2
Brain Functions Attributed to the Left and Right Cerebral Hemispheres

Left cerebral hemisphere	Right cerebral hemisphere
Expressive speech	Spatial orientation
Receptive language	Simple language comprehension
Language (general)	Nonverbal ideation
Complex motor functions	Picture and pattern sense
Vigilance	Performance-like functions
Paired-associate learning	Spatial integration
Liaison to consciousness	Creative associative thinking
Ideation	Facial recognition
Conceptual similarities	Sound (environmental)
Temporal analysis	recognition
Analysis of detail	Nonverbal paired-associate
Arithmetic	thinking
Writing	Tactile perception
Calculation	Gestalt perception
Finger naming	Logographic (pictograph)
Right-left orientation	processing
Sequential processing	Intuitive problem solving
	Humorous thinking
	Simultaneous processing

Source: Adapted from Berent (1981).

with somatosensory functions and visual-spatial ability; and the *occipital lobes* with visual perception and the semantic connotations of visual objects (that is, verbal associations or verbal encodings given to visual objects).

Development of Lateralization

The development of lateralization appears to be a gradual process, evidenced in psychomotor development by the replacement of bilateral movements with unilateral movements. The process begins in infancy and may continue throughout the developmental period. The degree of lateralization appears to be related to the skill level of the task being performed, with manual activities requiring high skill becoming increasingly lateralized and those requiring low skill remaining less lateralized (Miller, 1982). Similarly, lower levels of language development, such as involuntary primitive speech responses, are probably organized bilaterally; intermediate levels of language development, such as comprehension, are probably partially lateralized; and the highest levels of language, such as propositional speech, are likely specialized in the left hemisphere.

A review of research (Hahn, 1987) covering studies of dichotic listening, tachistoscopic viewing, electroencephalography, haptic identification, and somatosensory discrimination in normal children from infancy through childhood indicated that linguistic functions are localized in the left hemisphere at birth for children of both sexes. Functions lateralized in the right hemisphere, however, are less straightforward—certain abilities are lateralized at birth, whereas others become lateralized with age. For example, the right hemisphere appears to be specialized at birth in processing nonlinguistic stimuli, whereas developmental changes likely occur in the right hemisphere's ability to process spatial information. Research on cerebral lateralization in childhood is an ongoing activity.

Comment on Lateralization

Lateral specialization cannot always be clearly established. For example, the role of lateralization is less clear for visuoconstructional skills than for language skills. On memory tasks that allow stimuli to be encoded either verbally or perceptually (such as those involving figures that are easily recognizable and have familiar names), the specific process used by an individual often cannot be specified, and therefore it is difficult to make inferences about whether the tasks involve cerebral lateralization. Although the evidence for lateralized cerebral specialization is strong, young children show language disorders even when they have right-sided lesions (Hécaen, 1983). Perhaps there is less cerebral specialization with respect to language in young children than in adults. Additionally, even though language and speech appear to be lateralized at birth, there are complex changes in the direction and strength of hemispheric specialization as development proceeds (Lewkowicz & Turkewitz, 1982).

Once language develops, the left hemisphere appears to be dominant for language for most individuals; only some potential for language functions is present in the right hemisphere. Language disorders in children, as in adults, are associated more frequently with left-hemisphere damage than with right-hemisphere damage. Although there may be some recovery of function mediated by the right hemisphere, deficits may continue to exist, particularly in syntactic, reading, and writing skills (Moscovitch, 1981).

It appears that a primary function of the right hemisphere is to act as a concrete spatial synthesizer, allowing information to be perceived as a meaningful gestalt. "It does not have the analytic skills that are required to process linguistic input phonetically or to decode complex syntax" (Moscovitch, 1981, p. 47). The right hemisphere does, however, support communication. Impairments of the right hemisphere may interfere with communication, conceptual skills, memory, and other cognitive functions, especially when a task requires the integration of multiple sources of information or comprehension of nonliteral language, such as metaphor or sarcasm. Additionally, the right hemisphere is thought to be important in prosody, or the affective aspect of language. It gives emotional expression to speech and may be important for evaluating the emotional content of the speech of others.

APHASIA IN CHILDREN

Childhood aphasia is a central nervous system dysfunction manifested through disorders in the perception, production, and symbolic utilization of language. Three subgroups of aphasia are *congenital aphasia*, a language dysfunction marked by an almost complete failure to acquire language; *developmental aphasia*, a less pervasive cognitive and developmental impairment in which language is late in onset and fails to develop fully; and *acquired aphasia*, a language dysfunction resulting from brain injury following normal language development. The subgroups differ from one another mainly in the severity and age of onset of the same basic language dysfunction.

Major Forms of Aphasia

Aphasia may involve expressive components, receptive components, or both. Individuals with receptive aphasic disturbances also have expressive deficits, but those with expressive disturbances may not necessarily have receptive problems. *Expressive aphasia* is defined as impaired ability to use spoken or written language. A subcategory of expressive aphasia is *agraphia*, the loss or impairment of the ability to express language in written or printed form. *Receptive aphasia* is defined as impaired ability to understand spoken or written language. *Auditory aphasia* refers to the loss or impairment of the ability to comprehend the meaning of spoken words, and *alexia* refers to the loss or impairment of the ability to comprehend written or printed language despite adequate vision and intelligence.

Brain injury may also manifest itself in two other symbolic deficits broadly classified as aphasic disturbances: *agnosia*, which involves failure to recognize or understand the significance of sensory stimuli, or defects of imagination, and *apraxia*, which is a disturbance of the execution of learned movements that is not due to motor or sensory defects, poor comprehension, or intellectual deterioration. Procedures used to evaluate aphasia, agnosia, and apraxia are illustrated in Table 22-3 and Table 22-6.

Differential Effects of Aphasia in Younger and Older Children

In children under the age of 10, aphasia is usually characterized by a severe reduction in spontaneous speech (Satz & Bullard-Bates, 1981). The pattern is generally initial mutism, followed by limited speech, hesitations, dysarthria (imperfect articulation of speech caused by disturbances of muscular control resulting from damage to the central or peripheral nervous system), and impoverished communications. Paraphasias (substitutions of incorrect and unintended words or sounds for correct ones—*chair* for *table*, *jail* for *hospital*, *trable* for *table*) are rare. Errors may include omission of crucial words, errors in word choice, and disturbances of word order. Children may be unable to comprehend purely verbal commands unless they are accompanied by gestures.

Young aphasic children are usually alert, attentive, and intent on communicating their thoughts and reactions. After the age of 10, a more mixed pattern resembling that of adults emerges, with an increased frequency of disorders involving speech. The prognosis is more favorable for childhood aphasia than for adult aphasia, with spontaneous recovery occurring in the majority of cases. Recovery may be incomplete, however; serious cognitive and academic sequelae may be found, as well as some language deficits.

The following case describes the course of recovery in

Table 22-3
Illustration of Procedures Used in Testing for Aphasia, Agnosia, and Apraxia

Area	Procedure
Aphasia	
Visual-verbal comprehension	Ask child to read a sentence from the newspaper and explain its meaning. If child is unable to talk, print instructions and determine whether the child can carry them out.
Motor speech	Ask child to imitate several different sounds and phrases: "la-la," "me-me," "this is a good book," and others of increasing difficulty. Note abnormal word usage in conversation.
Automatic speech	Ask child to repeat one or two series that the child has learned in the past, such as the days of the week or the months of the year.
Volitional speech	Determine whether child can answer questions relevantly.
Writing	Have child write (a) his or her name and address, (b) a simple sentence, (c) one word, with eyes closed, and then (d) the name of an object that is shown to the child, with eyes open.
Agnosia	
Sound recognition	Ask child to identify familiar sounds, with eyes closed.
Auditory-verbal comprehension	Determine whether child can answer questions and carry out instructions.
Recognition of body parts and sidedness	Determine whether child knows left from right and recognizes body parts.
Visual object recognition	Ask child to identify familiar objects such as a pen or wristwatch.
Apraxia	
Performance of skilled motor acts	Determine whether child can complete motor acts, such as drinking from a cup, closing a safety pin, or using common tools.

an aphasic patient (Levin, 1981, p. 444, with changes in notation):

A 17-year-old student was involved in a motor vehicle accident in which she received a closed head injury. Although she obeyed commands on the day of admission, delayed neurological deterioration was reflected by the post-admission development of a right hemiparesis and progressive aphasia. Three days postinjury a partial left temporal lobectomy was performed with evacuation of an intracerebral hematoma. The patient remained confused for a month after injury, but exhibited gradual improvement of receptive language. Administration of an aphasia battery 2 months after injury disclosed findings consistent with an anomic aphasia. There were frequent errors of circumlocution (for example, an *island* was defined as *a place where you fish* and a *triangle* was described as *the thing you use when you play pool*), and semantic approximation (for example, the trunk of an elephant was described as a nose). Approximately one year after the injury the patient's recovery of language was complete, with the exception of a subtle residual anomic disturbance that was evident only under formal detailed testing conditions.

PROGNOSIS FOR BRAIN-DAMAGED CHILDREN

The prognosis for children who have experienced brain injury depends on the age at which the child incurs the injury, the location and extent of the brain damage, and the occurrence of post-traumatic complications, such as seizures. Certain types of difficulties resulting from brain injury, such as hemiplegias (paralysis on one side of the body) and visual field defects, may show little or no improvement after many years, whereas sensorimotor functions tend to be recovered earlier and more completely. Mental processes may be recovered gradually even years after the initial insult. These processes are of a more complex order than sensory or motor processes and are not as circumscribed or anatomically restricted. *Recoverability of intellectual functions is less certain with severe trauma, early damage, fronto-temporal area damage, and post-traumatic epilepsy.* Rate of recovery is most rapid in the months immediately following injury. The extent of intellectual impairment generally is related to the severity of the head injury.

Differential Effects of Brain Damage in Young Children and Adults

The effects of brain damage in young children are different from those in adults because the young child's brain is still developing. When an adult sustains brain injury, there may be a loss or dissolution of previously acquired functions, manifested in impairment of language, memory, social relations, or general intelligence. In contrast, when a child sustains brain injury, there may be interference with development rather than a striking loss of function. If the interference is global, mental retardation may be the result; if it is region-specific, specific difficulties may result, such as with speech or with recognition of shapes.

Acquired brain damage tends to produce less specific dysfunctions in young children than in adults. Because cortical specialization has not yet been completed, damage to the immature brain is likely to affect the development of the whole brain rather than produce localized abnormalities. In young children brain damage may have more than a simple depressing effect on their ability structures; it may alter the basic pattern of ability development. Large unilateral injuries in infants tend to produce a more widespread deficit in intellectual functions than do similar injuries in adults.

Brain damage in children can be better understood by considering the principles of behavior development and the relationship between neural structures and behavior (Shaheen, 1984). The first five years of life constitute the period of greatest cortical development. The progress of myelination in various anatomical regions affects behavioral development. Conceivably, the type of behavioral difficulties that occur could be related to the neurostructural components that are undergoing the most rapid development at the time of the brain injury. Diffuse brain injuries during the second year of life, for example, may affect the development of speech and language, whereas similar injuries during the third year of life may affect spatial-symbolic manipulations.

Older children who incur brain damage — particularly those above the age of 11 or 12 — show a more mixed pattern of deficits, with deficits being similar to those found in adult patients. This is true to some extent of all children above 5 years of age, especially if speech has developed. Classical neurological patterns may be shown, such as verbal disorders associated with left hemisphere lesions and nonverbal or visuospatial disorders associated with right hemisphere lesions.

Cerebral Plasticity

Cerebral plasticity refers to the ability of one part of the brain to take over functions impaired by lesions in another part of the brain. This process operates primarily between birth and 4 or 5 years of age. Changes in the functional organization of the central nervous system (or reorganization) may enable the child to recover functions. The assumption that the brain possesses such plasticity has been questioned, however. Are the effects of early brain injuries more or less severe than those of later brain injuries?

Although there are no simple answers to this question, there is increasing evidence that young children are no less, and perhaps even more, vulnerable at times than are adults to the deleterious effects of diffuse brain injury on memory and cognition (Bruno, 1986; Levin, Eisenberg, Wigg, & Kobayashi, 1982). One possible explanation is that it is during its phase of most rapid development that the immature brain is most vulnerable to damage from such conditions as encephalitis, meningitis, and therapeutic irradiation of the brain. Consequently, injuries sustained after a long period of normal development may interfere less with intellectual functioning than do those that occur early in development (Eiser, 1981).

Overall, studies of patients with hemispherectomies (resection of an entire cerebral hemisphere) in infancy, childhood, and adulthood, as well as related research, indicate that there is insufficient evidence to support the assumption of plasticity (St. James-Roberts, 1981). In other words, there is little reason to believe that young children recover better than older children. Instead, recovery is variable within each age group. Perhaps even more important than age or hemisphere damaged are variables associated with the child's congenital makeup and experiential history and the type of brain damage. Research findings support neither a plasticity hypothesis nor a critical period hypothesis (that certain functions can be developed only at specific times in development). Changes in cognitive development after brain damage may best be viewed as involving cumulative interactions among etiological, recovery period, and experiential variables.

Questions of compensation and plasticity make prognosis much more precarious with children than with adults, as does the fact that many areas tested in adults — such as language and speech — cannot be tested in young children who have developed only rudimentary skills. Additionally, study is needed not only of the degree of recovery following brain damage but also of the child's ability to learn and relearn cognitive skills.

ASPECTS OF A NEUROPSYCHOLOGICAL ASSESSMENT

A wide spectrum of psychological deficits, varying in nature and degree, accompany brain injury in children. Although a neuropsychological assessment may not establish the specific nature, site, and extent of an underlying brain lesion, it can accurately determine the sensory, motor, and mental deficits that may be present. Neuropsychological assessment batteries provide information about verbal and nonverbal intellectual abilities and perceptual-motor abilities, including vocabulary, comprehension, concept formation, memory, perception, and motor skills. This information complements the overall IQ, which by itself is often insufficient for evaluating the effects of brain lesions on specific mental processes. In all cases, test scores should be based on age-appropriate norms, although raw scores can be used to study the child's performance over time.

Repeated psychological testing (or serial testing), where needed, is an excellent means of monitoring the evolving clinical picture for possible mental changes in the course of the disease process. Serial testing charts the rate of recovery or decline following surgery, follows the course of any degenerative process, and aids in educational, vocational, and rehabilitational decisions. The updated information about the child's progress can help the family, teachers, and others responsible for the child's welfare determine what can realistically be expected of the child. A neuropsychological assessment may also help in estimating the probable course of development and progress in school and in formulating intervention procedures. All sources of information should be considered in the neuropsychological assessment, including the clinical history, behavioral observations, current test results, previous test results (where available), and the neurological evaluation.

THE CLINICAL HISTORY

Clinical Assessment Interview with Parents

The clinical history should focus on the child's development (see Chapter 16). The history should begin with events surrounding the birth process (prenatal, perinatal, and postnatal). Prematurity, Rh incompatibility, difficult labor, and a low Apgar score (a score derived from assessment of the neonate's heart rate, respiratory effort, muscle tone, cry, and color; see Chapter 12) are relevant factors. Particular emphasis should be given to events that may have etiological importance for brain damage. These include prolonged high fevers; injuries to the head; use of anesthetics during surgery; poisoning associated with foods, chemicals, or medications; occasions of prolonged nausea and vomiting not related to common illnesses; and changes in energy expenditure.

If the child suffered any injury to the head, you should inquire about the location of the injury, whether the child lost consciousness and for how long, whether medical attention was available, what the child's behavior was like both immediately and for several days following the injury, sleep disturbances, complaints of pain, and whether there were any delayed personality changes. In evaluating a child's progress following brain injury, it is useful to ask a parent or other informant the questions shown in Exhibit 22-1. They cover various areas, including motor, sensory-kinesthetic, affective, and cognitive functioning; content, form, and practical use of language; changes in consciousness; social-personality characteristics; and the informant's personal reactions to the child's injury. With slight modifications, the questions can be used directly with older brain-injured children and adults who are able to communicate.

Also inquire about recent changes in the child's lifestyle, level of functioning, and emotional stability. For example, instability, irritability, or lethargy may precede other symptoms of a brain tumor, whereas a progressive decline in academic functioning may be an early sign of degenerative brain disease. Sudden and inadequately explained changes in behavior are likely to be associated with acute, as opposed to chronic, brain disorders.

Clinical Assessment Interview with the Child

In interviewing the child, obtain information about his or her general orientation to the present time, place, and person; memory; changes in behavior; and other related issues (see Tables 16-9 and 16-10 in Chapter 16). With older children (or with parents acting as informants), begin with open-ended questions and proceed to more specific questions as the interview proceeds. Be sure to conduct the interview in a nonthreatening and casual manner.

Elicit information about the child's chief complaint (What does the child see as the major problem?), and try to obtain a clear understanding of the onset and progression of symptoms. With older children, determine such facts as

■ **Exhibit 22-1** ▬▬▬▬▬▬▬▬▬▬▬▬▬▬▬▬▬▬▬▬▬▬▬▬

Semi-Structured Interview Format for Use with Parents of Brain-Injured Children

You might start the interview by saying "I'd like to talk with you about how your child is getting along now." If the parent responds with a "yes" to any question, inquire further. You might say, for example, "Tell me more about that" or "Please describe his [or her] behavior in more detail." The questions can be rephrased or altered in any manner deemed appropriate. *In evaluating responses, take into consideration the child's age and the capabilities that were present before the brain injury.* See Chapter 16 for information about interview techniques.

Motor

1. Is _____ more hyperactive now than before the injury?
2. Is _____ more awkward now? For example, does he (or she) seem clumsy or bump into things?
3. Is his (or her) handwriting poorer now?
4. Printing?
5. Drawing?
6. Does _____ have a rigid posture?
7. Does _____ have more speech difficulties?
8. Does _____ seem to repeat movements?
9. Does _____ complain of numbness or loss of sensation?
10. Does _____ have difficulty copying gestures?
11. Does _____ have difficulty standing?
12. Walking?
13. Running?
14. Balancing?

Sensory/Kinesthetic

15. Does _____ have a short attention span? For example, does he (or she) often request that you repeat information?
16. Does _____ have difficulty comprehending or following directions?
17. Is _____ distractible?
18. Does _____ reverse or scramble what he (or she) hears?
19. Does _____ confuse words and sounds and their meanings?
20. Has there been a change in _____'s vision?
21. Does _____ reverse words, letters, or numbers when reading?
22. Does _____ have difficulty with depth perception?
23. Does _____ have difficulty in recognizing objects?
24. Does _____ have difficulty in building or constructing things?
25. Does _____ report smelling odd odors?
26. Has _____ experienced blurred or double vision? (If appropriate, add "even with glasses on.")
27. Do lights disturb _____?
28. Does _____ experience light flashes?
29. Has there been a change in _____'s hearing?
30. Does _____ experience ringing sounds?
31. Is _____ unusually sensitive to sound?
32. Does _____ hear music as noise?
33. Has _____ experienced any change in taste?
34. In smell?
35. Have any of _____'s favorite odors become unpleasant and then pleasant again?
36. Does _____ report being dizzy?
37. Has _____ recently fainted?
38. Does _____ have to hold on to things to keep from falling?
39. Does _____ experience tingling sensations in the fingertips or toes?
40. Numbness?
41. Has there been any disturbance in _____'s ability to make turns or put his (or her) arms into the correct sleeve?

Affective

42. Does _____ easily lose control of his (or her) emotions?
43. Does _____'s mood change easily?
44. Does _____ become angry without cause?
45. Is _____ irritable?
46. Does _____ talk too much or too little?
47. Is _____ anxious?
48. Is _____ listless and depressed?
49. Has _____ become more hostile?
50. Aggressive?
51. Uncooperative?
52. Negative?
53. Does _____ lie?
54. Steal?
55. How does _____ feel about himself (or herself)?
56. Have there been any changes in his (or her) personality?
57. Is _____ concerned about his (or her) body?
58. Is _____ compulsive?
59. Does _____ deny that he (or she) has any problems?
60. Does _____ feel insecure or weak or uncertain of himself (or herself)?

Cognitive

61. Does _____ have difficulty with memory?
62. (If yes) In general? With specific events? With material that he (or she) just learned? With material that he (or she) learned a while ago?
63. Does _____ understand what is read to him (or her)?
64. Has there been any change in _____'s understanding of what he (or she) reads?
65. Has there been a general decline in _____'s overall intellectual ability?

(Exhibit continues next page)

Exhibit 22-1 (cont.)

66. In judgment?
67. In planning?
68. In ability to combine things?
69. Does _____ have problems with language?
70. Has there been any change in _____'s ability to recognize numbers, letters, or musical notations?
71. Has there been any change in _____'s writing?
72. Arithmetic skills?
73. Does _____ recognize numbers when written or spoken?
74. Can _____ do mental calculations?
75. Does _____ deal with problems more concretely?
76. Does he (or she) have difficulty in changing from one activity to another?

(If there have been changes in the child's language, you can use the following questions to inquire about language content, language form, and practical use of language.)

Language Content

77. Can _____ define words?
78. Can _____ name objects that are shown to him (or her)?
79. Can _____ complete an open-ended sentence such as "The sky is _____"?
80. Can _____ count?
81. Name the days of the week?
82. Can _____ recognize an appropriate word when it is offered to him (or her)? For example, if he (or she) was holding an orange and could not name it and you said *orange*, would he (or she) recognize that you had said the correct name?
83. Can _____ repeat names?
84. Can _____ follow changes in the topics of conversation? For instance, if you were talking about baseball and you switched to talking about what you were having for dinner, could he (or she) follow that?
85. Can _____ understand what you say?

Language Form

86. Can _____ construct phrases and sentences?
87. Can _____ use a variety of sentence types, such as simple sentences and questions?
88. Does _____ use articles (such as *a*), prepositions (such as *of*), pronouns (such as *me*), and conjunctions (such as *and*)?
89. Does _____ use word endings to make words possessive ('s), plural (-s), and past tense (-ed or -t)? For example, would he (or she) say "Mary's parents walked"?
90. Is _____ aware of language errors when he (or she) makes them?

Practical Use of Language

91. Does _____ use the telephone?
92. Does _____ answer the telephone when it rings?

93. Does _____ look up telephone numbers in the directory?
94. Is _____ able to remember some telephone numbers?
95. Does _____ read the newspaper?
96. How has this changed since the brain injury?
97. Does _____ read magazines?
98. How has this changed since the brain injury?
99. Does _____ watch television?
100. How has this changed since the brain injury?
101. Does _____ go shopping?
102. How has this changed since the brain injury?
103. Does _____ handle money on his (or her) own?
104. How has this changed since the brain injury?
105. Does _____ visit friends?
106. How has this changed since the brain injury?
107. Does _____ talk about the past?
108. How has this changed since the brain injury?
109. Does _____ talk about the future?
110. How has this changed since the brain injury?
111. When _____ speaks, is what he (or she) says appropriate to each situation? That is, does what he (or she) says match the situation?
112. Can _____ deal with difficulties in talking with others? For example, when others stop talking, can he (or she) respond and keep the conversation going?
113. How often do people in your family talk to _____?
114. How has this changed since the brain injury?
115. How often does _____ talk to others?
116. How has this changed since the brain injury?
117. When would you say that _____ does the most talking?
118. Why?
119. Where is the best place for _____ to talk?
120. Does _____ have more or less opportunity to talk now than before the brain injury?
121. How has _____'s desire to talk changed since the brain injury?
122. Does _____ ever argue?
123. (If yes) About what?
124. Is _____ able to give directions?
125. Does _____ complain?
126. (If yes) About what?

Changes in Consciousness

127. Does _____ appear to be disoriented? For example, does he (or she) get lost easily or have trouble finding his (or her) way around?
128. Has _____ experienced blackouts, during which he (or she) is unable to hear when someone talks to him (or her) or is unable to respond?
129. Does _____ experience feelings that he (or she) is losing his (or her) body?
130. Has _____ reported strange feelings, such as a feeling that some unknown danger is about to happen?

(Exhibit continues next page)

Exhibit 22-1 (cont.)

131. Has _____ been doing things that he (or she) is unaware of?
132. Has _____ started out doing one thing and then found himself (or herself) doing something else?
133. Has _____ reported that he (or she) feels that the size of his (or her) hands or feet or head is changing?

Personal Reactions

134. Since _____'s brain injury, do you lose patience with him (or her) more often?
135. Since _____'s brain injury, have you limited your social activities?
136. Since _____'s brain injury, does he (or she) expect you to spend more time with him (or her)?
137. Since _____'s brain injury, do friends who typically visited you at home still do so?
138. Since _____'s brain injury, do you find it more difficult to concentrate on your work?
139. Has _____'s brain injury affected your physical health?
140. Has _____'s brain injury affected your emotional health?

141. Since _____'s brain injury, do you find that you are more protective of him (or her)?

General

142. How do you aid _____ in understanding and producing speech?
143. What could you change around your home so that _____ would enjoy talking more?
144. What sorts of things do you talk about with _____?
145. How has this changed since the brain injury?
146. If a stranger were to visit _____, how would you prepare the stranger for the visit?
147. If I were coming to live in your home, what would you tell me it is like to live with _____ since the brain injury?

Note. The first 133 questions, with minor changes in wording (for example, "do you" for "does _____") can be used to interview children and adults directly.
Source: Adapted, in part, from Chapey (1981) and Small (1980).

---

the date the problem was first noticed, how the symptoms developed, what aggravates and diminishes the symptoms, what type of help has been received, and what the child's current level of functioning is.

The following symptoms may be of special neurological significance and are worthy of specific inquiry during the interview (Adams & Jenkins, 1981, pp. 272–273, with changes in notation):

1. headaches and times of day they occur
2. alteration in consciousness
3. abnormal movements (tremors, jerking, tics)
4. seizures
5. disturbances in vision
6. disturbances in perception, especially olfactory hallucinations
7. pain and paresthesias (abnormal sensations)
8. muscle weakness, stiffness, or paralysis
9. vertigo with or without nausea or vomiting
10. difficulty in auditory perception and/or the presence of tinnitus (ringing in the ears)
11. difficulty in the use of language (expression and comprehension)
12. bowel, bladder, or genital dysfunction
13. confusion, decreased intellectual efficiency, or memory difficulties
14. changes in mood or emotional regulation

During the interview be alert to the child's level of consciousness, language, memory, intellectual and cognitive functioning, and sensorimotor functioning. The developmental history (see Tables 16-12 and 16-13 in Chapter 16) may provide etiological clues about the examinee's symptomatology. If the child has not been seen for a neurological workup and you find symptoms suggestive of organic dysfunction—particularly complaints of memory deficits, seizures, headaches, *or* unusual behavioral symptoms, such as deterioration of academic performance, reversion to an immature pattern of social and emotional behavior, and conversion reactions (for example, loss of function of limbs or reduction in visual acuity)—refer the child for a pediatric neurological examination.

BEHAVIORAL OBSERVATIONS

During the psychological evaluation, the child may exhibit behavior patterns suggestive of brain damage. Table 22-4 lists a number of such patterns. You would be well advised to develop an awareness of these behavior patterns, if only to rule them out; the earlier brain injury is detected, the better the possibilities for rehabilitation. Also review Table 18-4 in Chapter 18, which lists a variety of language difficulties, many of which may be shown by brain-damaged patients.

Table 22-4
Possible Signs and Symptoms of Brain Damage Observed During the Neuropsychological Evaluation

Motor	Sensory	Affective	Cognitive	Social/Personality
Hyperkinesis (constant movement, inability to sit still; fingering, touching, and mouthing objects; voluble and uninhibited speech)	Short attention span (e.g., difficulty in retaining and recalling information or words)	Reduced frustration threshold	Some intellectual deficit	Interpersonal difficulties (e.g., hostile, aggressive, uncooperative)
Awkwardness in locomotion (clumsiness, bumping into things, atypical arm swing, incoordination, tremors, involuntary movements, asymmetry of facial musculature and expressive gestures while talking)	Poor concentration (e.g., difficulty in comprehending or following directions, difficulty in performing a sequence of tasks in the order given)	Emotional lability (e.g., mood shifts, impulsivity, irritability, aggressiveness, tearfulness, loss of control of emotions, inappropriate laughter)	Impaired judgment	Immaturity (e.g., may regress to more childlike forms of behavior)
Awkwardness in skilled movement (poor printing, writing, and drawing)	Distractibility	Talking too much or too little	Conceptual difficulties (e.g., in abstracting, planning, organizing, anticipating, analyzing and synthesizing, and integrating)	Negativism
Impaired copying of geometric designs	Perceptual difficulty (e.g., closure difficulty, visual-motor disturbances, use of fingers to trace visual shapes, turning materials around)	Anxiety (occasional panic reactions)	Specific learning deficit (in reading, writing, spelling, or arithmetic)	Antisocial behavior (lying, stealing, truancy, sexual offenses)
Postural rigidity	Difficulty in matching objects or symbols with verbal stimuli	Problems in self-regulation (e.g., overactivity or underactivity)	Language difficulties (e.g., malapropisms, imprecise synonyms, truncated sentences, mispronunciations, circumstantiality)	Disturbed self-concept
Speech difficulties (e.g., slow speech)	Reversal or scrambling of what is heard	Depression or flat affect	Attraction to minute details	Disturbed body concept or body image
Mixed left-right dominance	Confusing words and sounds and their meanings		Impaired right-left orientation	Changes in personality (e.g., a previously fastidious child has become unkempt and careless)
Repetitive movements	Difficulty in reading		Perseveration	Hypochondriacal preoccupations
Perseveration	Word, letter, number reversals		Concrete, rigid, and inflexible thinking	Compulsive tendencies
Numbness and loss of sensation	Confusing letters		Difficulty in shifting from one activity to another	Denial (e.g., a child may deny that he or she has any problems)
Difficulty in crossing limbs across center of body	Difficulty with depth perception		Memory difficulty (recent, remote, or both; visual, auditory, or both)	Indications of insecurity (e.g., expressions of weakness, uncertainty, and inadequacy in dealing with test materials)
Difficulty in copying gestures	Difficulty in recognizing objects		Disorientation (e.g., gets lost easily, is disoriented in familiar settings)	Impaired social judgment
	Difficulty in building or constructing things			
	Unusual episodic sensory experiences (e.g., odd odors or vision of lights)			

During the evaluation, consider the extent to which (a) special techniques are needed to secure the child's attention, (b) instructions have to be repeated before the child does what is asked, and (c) extraneous activity has to be prevented. Be especially alert for behaviors indicative of motor restlessness. Hyperactivity (or any other behavioral sign), however, should *never* be taken by itself as indicative of cerebral damage or dysfunction.

NEUROPSYCHOLOGICAL TEST BATTERIES FOR CHILDREN

Halstead-Reitan Neuropsychological Test Battery for Older Children and Reitan-Indiana Neuropsychological Test Battery for Children

Two batteries for evaluating children suspected of having brain damage are the Halstead-Reitan Neuropsychological Test Battery for Older Children, designed for children between 9 and 14 years of age, and the Reitan-Indiana Neuropsychological Test Battery for Children, designed for children between 5 and 8 years of age (Reitan & Davison, 1974; Reitan & Wolfson, 1985; Selz, 1981). Both batteries contain cognitive and perceptual-motor tests, some of which also appear in the adult battery and some of which were especially designed for young children. (See Table 22-5 for a description of the batteries.) Table 22-6 shows the Reitan-Indiana Aphasia Screening Test, and Figure 22-1 shows the stimulus figures for the test. The complete Halstead battery also includes an intelligence test.

Information about the reliability and validity of the Halstead-Reitan and Reitan-Indiana children's batteries is scarce, and norms are extremely limited. Therefore, their usefulness depends on the clinical sophistication of the examiner. (Norms for the adult version are available for 15- through 17-year-old children, in a publication by Fromm-Auch & Yeudal, 1983.) In one study (Selz & Reitan, 1979), the Halstead-Reitan Neuropsychological Test Battery for Older Children, together with some additional tests, was found to classify children, ages 9 to 14 years, into one of three groups (normal, learning-disabled, and brain-damaged) with 73 percent accuracy. A short screening battery drawn from the Halstead-Reitan battery was found to be useful in differentiating brain-damaged children from controls (Reitan & Herring, 1985).

Performance on the Halstead-Reitan Neuropsychological Test Battery for Older Children is not independent of level of intellectual functioning. A study (Seidenberg, Giordani, Berent, & Boll, 1983) of 121 9- to 14-year-old children with documented seizure disorders indicated that those with higher WISC-R IQs had better Halstead-Reitan scores on 6 of 14 tests. Tests most related to intelligence were those dealing with problem solving, language, and auditory-perceptual analysis (Category Test, TPT Location, Speech Perception Test, Seashore Rhythm Test, Trail Making Test B, and Aphasia Screening Test). Tests least related to intelligence were those of simple motor functions and right-left hand differences. Thus differences in intellectual ability were most evident in tasks requiring problem solving and mental efficiency. The results emphasize the importance of considering the child's IQ in interpreting performance on the Halstead-Reitan Neuropsychological Battery for Older Children.

Luria-Nebraska Neuropsychological Battery: Children's Revision

The Luria-Nebraska Neuropsychological Battery: Children's Revision (LNNB-C) is designed to assess a broad range of neuropsychological functions in children 8 to 12 years of age (Golden, 1987). It can be considered a downward extension of the adult version, although items are not necessarily interpreted in the same manner on the two tests. The LNNB-C is designed to assess cognitive deficits and aid in planning rehabilitation programs.

The LNNB-C is individually administered. It contains 149 items grouped into 11 clinical scales (see Table 22-7) and two optional scales. Additionally, the items are regrouped into three summary scales and 11 factor scales. The *clinical scales* are designed to assess sensorimotor, perceptual, and cognitive abilities. The *summary scales* provide information for discriminating between brain-injured and normal children. The *factor scales* are said to be helpful in assessing specific neuropsychological functions, although they must be interpreted cautiously. The LNNB-C takes approximately 2½ hours to administer to a brain-damaged child.

Scoring. All items are scored 0, 1, or 2. A score of 0 indicates normal functioning, 1 indicates weak evidence of brain dysfunction, and 2 indicates strong evidence of brain dysfunction. Note that higher raw scores indicate a *poorer* response. Raw scores are transformed into T scores ($M = 50$, $SD = 10$). Higher T scores indicate poorer performance. A qualitative scoring system can be used to evaluate items on which errors occurred. The system has 57 individual categories, such as attention difficulties, fatigue, jargon, perseveration, sequence errors, and tremors.

Table 22-5
Description of the Halstead-Reitan Neuropsychological Test Battery for Older Children and the Reitan-Indiana Neuropsychological Test Battery for Children

Test	Description
Category Test[a]	Measures concept formation; requires child to find a reason (or rule) for comparing or sorting objects.
Tactual Performance Test[a]	Measures somatosensory and sensorimotor ability; requires child, while blindfolded, to place blocks in appropriate recess using dominant hand alone, nondominant hand alone, and both hands.
Finger Tapping Test[a]	Measures fine motor speed; requires child to press and release a lever like a telegraph key as fast as possible.
Aphasia Screening Test[a]	Measures expressive and receptive language functions and laterality; requires child to name common objects, spell, identify numbers and letters, read, write, calculate, understand spoken language, identify body parts, and differentiate between right and left.
Matching Pictures Test[b]	Measures perceptual recognition; requires child to match figures at the top of a page with figures at the bottom of the page.
Individual Performance Test[b]	
Matching Figures	Measures perception; requires child to match different complex figures.
Star	Measures visual-motor ability; requires child to copy a star.
Matching Vs	Measures perception; requires child to match "Vs."
Concentric Squares	Measures visual-motor ability; requires child to copy a series of concentric squares.
Marching Test[b]	Measures gross motor control; requires child to (a) connect a series of circles with a crayon in a given order with right hand alone and with left hand alone and (b) reproduce examiner's finger and arm movements.
Progressive Figures Test[b]	Measures flexibility and abstraction; requires child to connect several figures, each consisting of a small shape contained within a large shape.
Color Form Test[b]	Measures flexibility and abstraction; requires child to connect color shapes, first by color and then by shape.
Target Test[b]	Measures memory for figures; requires child to reproduce a visually presented pattern after a three-second delay.
Rhythm Test[c]	Measures alertness, sustained attention, and auditory perception; requires child to indicate whether two rhythms are the same or different.
Speech Sounds Perception Test[c]	Measures auditory perception and auditory-visual integration; requires child to indicate, after listening to a word on tape, which of four spellings represents the word.
Trail Making Test (Parts A and B)[c]	Measures appreciation of symbolic significance of numbers and letters, scanning ability, flexibility, and speed; requires child to connect circles that are numbered.
Sensory Imperception[c]	Measures sensory-perceptual ability; requires child to perceive bilateral simultaneous sensory stimulation for tactile, auditory, and visual modalities in separate tests.
Tactile Finger Recognition[c]	Measures sensory-perceptual ability; requires child, while blindfolded, to recognize which finger is touched.
Fingertip Number Writing[c]	Measures sensory-perceptual ability; requires child, while blindfolded, to recognize numbers written on fingertips.
Tactile Form Recognition[c]	Measures sensory-perceptual ability; requires child to identify various coins through touch alone with each hand separately.
Strength of Grip[c]	Measures motor strength of upper extremities; requires child to use Smedley Hand Dynamometer with preferred hand and nonpreferred hand.

Note. The WISC-R (or WAIS-R) is often administered as part of the complete battery.
[a] This test appears both on the Halstead-Reitan Neuropsychological Test Battery for Older Children and on the Reitan-Indiana Neuropsychological Test Battery for Children.
[b] This test appears only on the Reitan-Indiana Neuropsychological Test Battery for Children.
[c] This test appears only on the Halstead-Reitan Neuropsychological Test Battery for Older Children.

Table 22-6
Instructions for the Reitan-Indiana Aphasia Screening Test

Task	Instructions
1. Copy *Square*	*First, draw this* (point to the square) *on your paper. I want you to do it without lifting your pencil from the paper. Make it about this same size* (pointing to the square).
2. Name *square*	*What is that shape called?* (or) *What is the name for that figure?*
3. Spell *square*	*Would you spell that word for me?*
4. Copy *cross*	*Draw this* (point to the cross) *on your paper. Go around the outside like this* (quickly draw a finger-line around the edge of the stimulus figure) *until you get back to where you started. Make it about the same size* (point to the cross).
5. Name *cross*	*What is that shape called?*
6. Spell *cross*	*Would you spell the name of it?*
7. Copy *triangle*	*Now I want you to draw this figure.* (Point to the triangle.)
8. Name *triangle*	*What would you call that figure?*
9. Spell *triangle*	*Would you spell the name of it for me?*
10. Name *baby*	*What is this?* (Show item 10.)
11. Write *clock*	*Now I am going to show you another picture but do NOT tell me the name of it. I don't want you to say anything out loud. Just WRITE the name of the picture on your paper.* (Show item 11.)
12. Name *fork*	*What is this?* (Show item 12.)
13. Read *7 six 2*	*I want you to read this.* (Show item 13.)
14. Read *M G W*	*Read this.* (Show item 14.)
15. Reading I	*Now I want you to read this.* (Show item 15.)
16. Reading II	*Can you read this?* (Show item 16.)
17. Repeat *triangle*	*Now I am going to say some words. I want you to listen carefully and say them after me as carefully as you can. Say this word: "triangle."*
18. Repeat *Massachusetts*	*The next one is a little harder but do your best. Say this word: "Massachusetts."*
19. Repeat *Methodist Episcopal*	*Now repeat this one: "Methodist Episcopal."*
20. Write *square*	*Don't say this word out loud.* (Point to the stimulus word "*square.*") *Just write it on your paper.*
21. Read *seven*	*Would you read this word?* (Show item 21.)
21A. Repeat *seven*	Remove the stimulus card and say: *Now, I want you to say this after me: "seven."*
22. Repeat-explain *He shouted the warning*	*I am going to say something that I want you to say after me, so listen carefully: "He shouted the warning." Now you say it. Tell me in your own words what that means.*
23. Write *He shouted the warning*	*Now I want you to write that sentence on the paper.*
24. Compute *85 − 27 =*	*Here is an arithmetic problem. Copy it down on your paper any way you like and try to work it out.* (Show item 24.)
25. Compute *17 × 3 =*	*Now do this one in your head. Write down only the answer.*
26. Name *key*	*What is this?* (Show item 26.)
27. Demonstrate use of *key*	(Still presenting the picture of the key:) *If you had one of these in your hand, show me how you would use it.*
28. Draw *key*	*Now I want you to draw a picture that looks just like this* (pointing to the picture of the key). *Try to make your key look enough like this one* (still pointing to the picture of the key) *so that I would know it was the same key from your drawing. Make it about the same size.*
29. Read	*Would you read this?* (Show item 29.)
30. Place *left hand to right ear*	*Now, would you do what it said?* Be sure to note any false starts or even mild expressions of confusions.
31. Place *left hand to left elbow*	*Now I want you to put your left hand to your left elbow.*

Note. See Figure 22-1 for stimulus figures. The Reitan-Indiana Aphasia Screening Test is part of the Reitan-Indiana Neuropsychological Test Battery for Children. Considerable clinical experience is needed to administer and interpret the test as well as the battery. Two books that can assist you in interpreting the battery are *Aphasia and Sensory-Perceptual Deficits in Adults* by Reitan (1984) and *Aphasia and Sensory-Perceptual Deficits in Children* by Reitan (1985). Additionally, Reitan and Wolfson's (1985) *Halstead-Reitan Neuropsychological Test Battery: Theory and Clinical Interpretation* is an excellent source for information on how to integrate the findings of the Reitan-Indiana Aphasia Screening Test with the rest of the results of the Halstead-Reitan Neuropsychological Test Battery for a complete neuropsychological assessment. Separate kits for adults and children, which include the appropriate book, recording forms, and test booklet, are available from the Neuropsychology Press, 1338 E. Edison Street, Tucson, AZ 85719.
Source: Reprinted, with changes in notation, with permission of the publisher and authors from R. M. Reitan and D. Wolfson, *The Halstead-Reitan Neuropsychological Test Battery* (Tucson, AZ: Neuropsychology Press, 1985), pp. 75–78. Copyright 1985 by Neuropsychology Press.

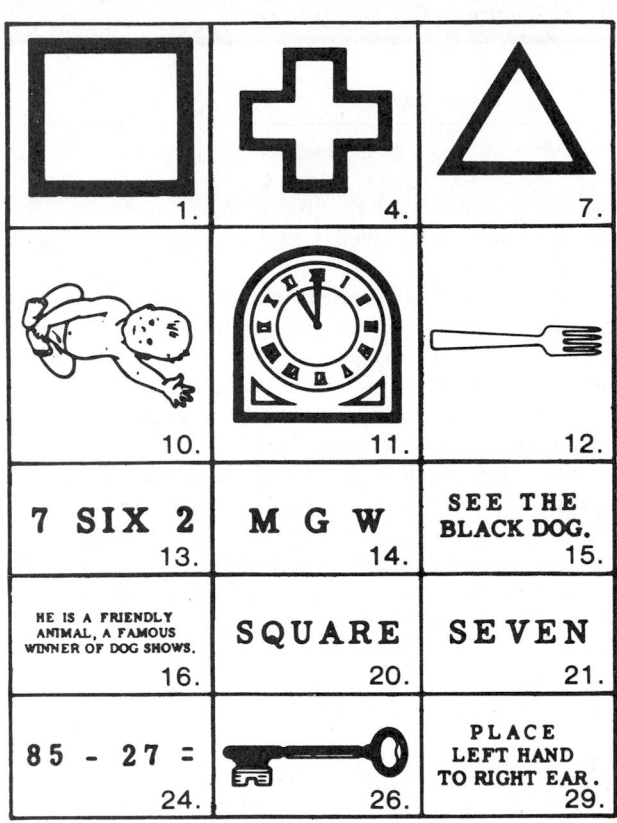

Figure 22-1. Stimulus figures for the Reitan-Indiana Aphasia Screeening Test (Table 22-6). Reprinted with permission of the publisher and authors from R. M. Reitan and D. Wolfson, *The Halstead-Reitan Neuropsychological Test Battery* (Tucson, AZ: Neuropsychology Press, 1985), p. 74. Copyright 1985 by Neuropsychology Press.

Standardization sample. The normal group in the standardization sample consisted of 125 children (65 females, 60 males) between 8 and 12 years of age. An additional sample of 719 children, many of whom were handicapped, was used in the development and validation of the scales. Unfortunately, demographic information is scarce, and no information is given about the representativeness of the normal group.

Reliability. Internal consistency reliability coefficients, based on 714 children (240 nonimpaired, 474 impaired), range from .67 to .90 (*Mdn* r_{xx} = .82) for the 11 clinical scales. Reliability coefficients are much higher for the brain-damaged group than for the nonimpaired group. Golden (1987) attributes this difference to the restriction in the range of scores in the nonhandicapped group—children in this group made few errors. Reliabilities are somewhat

low in the learning-disabled group as well. Other studies cited in the manual suggest adequate reliability for clinical samples. Standard errors of measurement are provided for both the nonimpaired sample (SE_m's from 1.2 to 3.2) and the impaired sample (SE_m's from 1.4 to 3.6). Internal consistency reliability coefficients for the summary scales are similar to those for the clinical scales.

Validity. The manual cites a number of studies that appear to support the construct validity and criterion-related validity of the LNNB-C. For example, the LNNB-C was found to discriminate significantly between brain-damaged and non–brain-damaged children. Classification of normal and brain-damaged groups is far from perfect, however. In one study the LNNB-C classified 91 percent of the normative sample accurately but only 65 percent of the brain-damaged sample. The accuracy with which subjects are classified as nonimpaired or brain damaged is very dependent on the number of scales used in the classification and the critical level of the cutoff scores.

Comment on the LNNB-C. Overall, the LNNB-C may be a useful addition to the field of neuropsychological assessment; however, more research is needed to evaluate its contribution. Caution is needed in using the scale because the manual fails to describe adequately the standardization sample and reliability is less than adequate. Each scale likely measures a heterogeneous group of skills, making interpretation difficult. Additionally, the difficulties associated with the adult version of the scale also pertain to the children's version (see, for example, Delis & Kaplan, 1983; Stambrook, 1983; Stanley & Howe, 1983). Finally, it is not clear whether the LNNB-C makes a distinct assessment contribution, or whether a battery composed of the WISC-R, WRAT-R, and other special ability tests would serve the same purpose.

Contributions to Neuropsychological Assessment Battery

The Contributions to Neuropsychological Assessment Battery (Benton, Hamsher, Varney, & Spreen, 1983) contains 12 individual tests designed to measure orientation, learning, perception, and motor ability. Five of the tests have norms for children (see Table 22-8). Although reliability data are not provided in the manual for any of the tests, the tests have a long history of use in the field of neuropsychological assessment and should prove to be useful in the assessment process.

Table 22-7
Clinical Scales of the Luria-Nebraska Neuropsychological Battery: Children's Revision (LNNB-C)

Scale	Number of items	Description
C1: Motor Functions	34	Measures various motor functions, such as motor speed, kinesthetic movement, coordination, construction skills, motor imitation skills, and verbal control of simple motor behaviors; requires child to perform various motor movements.
C2: Rhythm	8	Measures auditory perception; requires child to hum, sing, report number of beeps heard, and reproduce a series by tapping.
C3: Tactile Functions	16	Measures various aspects of tactile sensitivity; requires child to report cutaneous sensation, to discriminate the point of a pin, to discriminate pressure differentials, to report direction of pressure, to recognize various objects, to discriminate a number written on wrist, and to recognize objects placed in hand.
C4: Visual Functions	7	Measures perceptual skills without involving motor movements; requires child to recognize objects visually and to detect spatial positions of objects.
C5: Receptive Speech	18	Measures ability to understand spoken speech; requires child to repeat sounds and letters, discriminate phonemic sounds, comprehend words, understand simple sentences, and understand logical grammatical structures.
C6: Expressive Speech	21	Measures fluency and articulatory speech skills; requires child to repeat spoken sounds and words, pronounce sounds and words that are read, repeat sentences from memory, count, and engage in spontaneous speech.
C7: Writing	7	Measures ability to communicate in writing; requires child to spell, copy letters and syllables, and write from dictation.
C8: Reading	7	Measures ability to read; requires child to read letters, syllables, words, phrases, and sentences.
C9: Arithmetic	9	Measures arithmetical ability; requires child to write and read numbers; tell which number is larger; perform simple multiplication, addition, and subtraction; and count backwards.
C10: Memory	8	Measures verbal and nonverbal memory; requires child to recall orally presented words, pictures, visually presented words, and a meaningful paragraph.
C11: Intellectual Processes	14	Measures complex reasoning and problem-solving skills; requires child to describe and put pictures in a meaningful order, to indicate what is foolish about a picture, to interpret a story, to define words, to identify the similarity and difference between two things, and to answer arithmetical reasoning problems.

Note. The Optional Scales are Spelling and Motor Writing; the Summary Scales group items into Pathognomonic, Left Sensorimotor, and Right Sensorimotor Scales; the Factor Scales group items into Academic Achievement, Integrative Functions, Spatial-Based Movement, Motor Speed and Accuracy, Drawing Quality, Drawing Speed, Rhythm Perception and Production, Tactile Sensations, Receptive Language, Expressive Language, and Word and Phrase Repetition Scales.
Source: Adapted from Golden (1987).

WECHSLER SCALES AS PART OF A NEUROPSYCHOLOGICAL TEST BATTERY

The Wechsler scales serve as a cornerstone of most neuropsychological test batteries. They provide a standardized series of tasks for evaluating the cognitive and visual-motor skills of brain-injured children and adults. At any age, brain damage can impair the ability to learn, to solve unfamiliar problems, and to abstract. The Wechsler scales are sensitive measures of brain damage because they assess these and other abilities extremely well (see Chapters 6 through 10).

There is no single pattern of scores that is revealing of brain damage. Some brain-injured children show extreme variability in their WISC-R subtest scores, exhibiting as much as a 30-point difference between their Verbal and Performance Scale IQs, whereas other children display little difference. Subtest scores may range from considerably above average to below average. Even when brain-damaged children perform in the average range, they may show specific difficulties, such as deficits in attention. *An*

Table 22-8
Description of Tests with Children's Norms in the Contributions to Neuropsychological Assessment Battery

Test	Description
Facial Recognition	Measures sensory-perceptual ability; requires child to identify and discriminate photographs of unfamiliar human faces (norms from 6 to 14 years).
Judgment of Line Orientation	Measures spatial perception and orientation; requires child to select from a stimulus array a line that points in the same direction as the stimulus line (norms from 7 to 14 years).
Tactile Form Perception	Measures nonverbal tactile discrimination and recognition; requires child to touch concealed geometric figures made of fine-grade sandpaper and then to visually identify the figures on a card containing ink-line drawings of the figures (norms from 8 to 14 years).
Finger Localization	Measures sensory-perceptual ability; requires child to identify fingers touched when hand is visible and not visible (norms from 3 to 12 years).
Three-Dimensional Block Construction	Measures visuoconstructive ability; requires child to construct an exact replica of three block models (a pyramid, an 8-block four-level construction, a 15-block four-level construction) (norms from 6 to 12 years).

Note. The total battery consists of 12 tests: Temporal Orientation, Right-Left Orientation, Serial Digit Learning, Facial Recognition, Judgment of Line Orientation, Visual Form Discrimination, Pantomime Recognition, Tactile Form Perception, Finger Localization, Phoneme Discrimination, Three-Dimensional Block Construction, and Motor Impersistence.
Source: Benton, Hamsher, Varney, and Spreen (1983).

overall reduction in level of intelligence is a key finding in some cases of brain damage.

Intelligence tests permit the study not only of patterns of test performance but also of numerous qualitative indices related to cognitive efficiency and control. Indices related to brain injury include perseveration, confusion, conceptual and reasoning difficulties, and visual-motor difficulties. Some of these difficulties may reflect compensatory adjustments associated with brain damage, whereas others are a more direct expression of the injury. Qualitative indices should be interpreted in relation to other test indices.

Wechsler Verbal-Performance Scale Discrepancies

Attempts to use WISC-R Verbal-Performance Scale discrepancies to distinguish between right- and left-sided lesions have not been successful consistently. Studies (Aram & Ekelman, 1986; Aram, Ekelman, Rose, & Whitaker, 1985; Hynd, Obrzut, & Obrzut, 1981) report highly variable relationships between lateralized brain damage in children, WISC-R Verbal and Performance IQs, and age of onset of lesion. The relationship between the laterality of the lesion and Verbal-Performance IQs is tenuous. Even in adults, discrepancies between Verbal and Performance IQs do not occur regularly enough in patients with either right or left hemisphere damage to be clinically reliable (Bornstein, 1983; Kljajic & Berry, 1984; Larrabee, 1986; Lezak, 1983).

The preceding findings do not mean that the Verbal-

Performance IQ relationship is of no importance in the assessment of neurobehavioral deficit. The relationship still provides important information about the behavioral consequences of brain damage for individual patients, particularly when the Wechsler scales are used in conjunction with tests of sensorimotor, language, and visual-spatial ability.

In cases where brain damage has been documented (by history, CT scan, PET scan , MRI scan, or surgery), the Wechsler scales may be used to assess the cognitive sequelae of the neurological disorder and to identify adaptive deficits requiring more detailed analysis. *If the Verbal IQ is 12 or more points lower than the Performance IQ*, you should consider the possibility of language impairment. Carefully analyze the patient's verbal responses to questions on the Comprehension, Similarities, and Vocabulary subtests. Specialized tests of naming, verbal fluency, and language comprehension may be needed if word finding difficulties, paraphasias, or inability to grasp the intent of the instructions or questions is observed. A careful analysis of responses to the Arithmetic and Digit Span subtests will provide information about the examinee's ability to attend, concentrate, and deal effectively with numerical stimuli. Poor scores in these areas may suggest the need for additional procedures to evaluate the extent of impairment.

If the Performance IQ is 12 or more points below the Verbal IQ, you should consider the possibility of impaired visual-spatial, constructional, or perceptual organization skills. An examination of the quantitative and qualitative features of performance on the Block Design, Object Assembly, and Picture Arrangement subtests may reveal a need for further assessment focusing on graphomotor, spatial, and visual scanning abilities.

Even discrepancies of 15 or more points on the Wechsler scales cannot be considered pathognomonic of brain injury, because approximately 20 percent of normal children in the WISC-R standardization group (see Table C-9 in Appendix C) and 18 percent of normal adults in the WAIS-R standardization group (see Table C-33 in Appendix C) had differences of this or greater magnitude. A large Verbal-Performance IQ discrepancy is not evidence of brain damage; rather, it is an index of test performance that should be used to generate hypotheses for further investigation via a consideration of individual subtest scores, qualitative features of subtest performance, behavioral observations, and additional neuropsychological and neurological assessment procedures.

The interpretation of Verbal-Performance IQ differences in each individual case is a highly skilled professional undertaking. (See Chapter 8 for further discussion.) Be careful not to overinterpret any given discrepancy, and be prepared to supplement the Wechsler scales with other specialized measures to complete the neuropsychological evaluation.

Wechsler Subtest Interpretation

Detailed descriptions of each WISC-R subtest are provided in Chapter 7. Much of this material has neuropsychological implications. The interpretive suggestions discussed here apply to developing and testing clinical hypotheses; they are not meant to be diagnostic rules. All hypotheses formulated about subtest scores (and all Wechsler scores) should be integrated with hypotheses developed on the basis of qualitative features of the examinee's performance, the results of specialized neuropsychological measures, the clinical history, and the neurological evaluation.

• Performance on Information, Vocabulary, and Comprehension is considered to be least affected by brain damage, except in cases of aphasia. Scores on these subtests may provide an estimate of the patient's premorbid level of functioning, particularly for older adolescents and adults.

• Similarities may reveal difficulties with verbal abstraction. In some cases, brain-damaged patients may show extremely concrete reasoning—"Orange and banana are not alike because one is long and one is round."

• Digit Span may reveal attention problems. Additionally, large differences between Digits Forward and Digits Backward (differences of 3 or more digits correctly recalled) may be suggestive of a loss of flexibility or of impaired attention in particularly demanding situations.

• Arithmetic is a good subtest for evaluating attention and concentration as well as cognitive reasoning processes. When testing-of-limits procedures are used on this subtest, valuable information may be obtained about writing skills, sequencing, and mastery of basic arithmetical processes.

• Picture Completion is sometimes sensitive to visual difficulties. Responses such as "nothing is missing" may be given when a patient's visual field is restricted. Patients with visual agnosia may completely misidentify the stimulus picture, whereas those with expressive language difficulties may give an incorrect verbal response while simultaneously correctly pointing to the missing part.

• Picture Arrangement is sensitive to disturbances in serial ordering or sequencing. Some brain-injured patients may leave the cards in the order in which they were set out or only minimally move the cards. This behavior may indicate marked attentional deficits or other cognitive impairment. (For example, failure to understand the task may be indicative of severe perseveration or very impaired conceptual skills.)

• Block Design is a sensitive neuropsychological test that may reveal visual-spatial difficulties. Observe carefully the examinee's performance. Notice whether he or she has difficulty in bringing the parts together to form a whole. Are fumbling or angulation difficulties present? Are the reproductions grossly inaccurate? Breaks in a 2×2 or 3×3 block configuration may be particularly suggestive of visual-spatial difficulties. Low Block Design scores may indicate constructional apraxia in the context of brain damage.

• Object Assembly also may reveal visual organization problems. Notice which items were passed and which ones were failed. Did the items require appreciation of contour and edge alignment for success (for example, the hand and elephant items on the WAIS-R) or did they require appreciation of internal details and contour (for example, the WAIS-R profile item)? What kind of test-taking strategies did the examinee use? Can the examinee say what the object is supposed to be even though he or she is unable to assemble the pieces accurately?

• Coding or Digit Symbol may reveal information about sequencing, speed, visual-motor functioning, new learning, and other related processes. Observe carefully the examinee's performance. Note, for example, whether perseveration, rotation of figures, extreme caution, or slowness is present.

As noted in Chapter 18, performance on intelligence tests (and other tests as well) is likely to be multidetermined. For example, the written responses to the WISC-R Coding subtest are the end product of the integration of visual, perceptual, oculomotor (pertaining to eye movements), fine manual motor, and mental functions. Disturbances in any or all of these functions may result in poor performance. Consequently, in order to establish which factor or combination of factors accounts for the deficit, you need to rule out separately the defects in each of the possible component areas related to performance on the subtest.

Testing-of-Limits Procedures

On occasion, it may be helpful to use testing-of-limits procedures to evaluate the adequacy of various sensory and response modalities. For example, on the Digit Span subtest the child's spoken responses can be compared with his or her written responses in order to determine which response modality is more adequate. A child also might be asked to draw a circle from an oral request only and then to copy a circle from a stimulus figure. A brain-injured child with word retrieval difficulties may not be able to recall a word, but when given a choice of words may respond correctly. For example, to a question about who discovered America, the child may not give the right answer; however, when given four choices (Lincoln, Roosevelt, Columbus, Michelangelo), the child may pick the correct one.

Comment on Individual Intelligence Tests

The effects of brain damage may be general—a global reduction in intelligence—or specific—impairment of selective areas of cognitive functioning. Because of this variability, there are no patterns on the WISC-R (such as Verbal-Performance discrepancies, subtest patterns, or specific subtest scores) that reliably differentiate brain-damaged children from emotionally disturbed children, normal children, or both. Brain-damaged children often obtain lower IQs than normal children. *Perhaps the best single index of the presence of brain damage is lower than expected total scores (for age, education, socioeconomic status, and related factors) derived from a test or a battery of tests.*

Exhibit 22-2 presents four brief case studies of brain-damaged children. In each case, the WISC-R, the WRAT-R, and the Bender-Gestalt are featured.

OTHER PROCEDURES USEFUL IN THE ASSESSMENT OF BRAIN DAMAGE IN CHILDREN

Determination of Lateral Preference

A child's lateral preference must be established in order to interpret norms for procedures that compare right and left side performance. The expectation is that there will be a 10 percent superiority in the preferred (or mostly utilized) side.

With young children, lateral preference can be measured through performance tasks. You can ask the child to (a) pick up and throw a ball to you, (b) point to your nose, (c) pick up a crayon and draw a circle, and (d) touch his or her own nose with a finger. With children over the age of 8 years, ask the following questions (Roszkowski, Snelbecker, & Sacks, 1981):

• "Which hand do you use to throw a ball?" (or "hammer with" for children 11 years of age and older)
• "Which hand do you use to draw?"
• "Which hand do you use to write with?"

Their responses can be classified as follows: 0 = never performed, 1 = always left, 2 = usually left, 3 = both equally, 4 = usually right, 5 = always right. Higher scores are associated with a right-hand preference (that is, a left hemisphere dominance).

Bender-Gestalt Test

Performance on the Bender-Gestalt may reveal visual-motor difficulties that may be associated with brain damage (see Chapter 14). The Bender-Gestalt can also be administered first as a memory test and then as a copying test, so as to test different mental functions—short-term visual memory and visual perception—that involve the same modalities in perception and task execution.

Revised Visual Retention Test

The Revised Visual Retention Test (Benton, 1963) assesses visual memory, visual perception, and visuoconstructive abilities. It has three forms, with 10 designs in each form. The child is required to copy the designs directly and to draw them from memory. The test is scored by counting the number of correct responses or the number of errors. The Revised Visual Retention Test is similar to the Bender-Gestalt, but contains more complex stimuli. Detailed norms have been developed by Rice (1972).

■ Exhibit 22-2 ■

Brief Case Studies of Brain-Damaged Children

Introductory Remarks

Of the four brain-damaged children whose cases are presented in this exhibit (see Table 22-A), two sustained damage due to automobile accidents (Cases 2 and 3) and the other two sustained damage at birth (Cases 1 and 4). Three of the four children have Full Scale WISC-R IQs that are below average (Cases 1, 3, and 4), whereas one child has average ability (Case 2). Differences are evident in the pattern of Verbal-Performance discrepancies. For example, the Verbal IQ is significantly higher than the Performance IQ in Cases 1 and 4, but the reverse pattern is seen in Case 2. In Case 3, the Verbal-Performance discrepancy is minimal. Notice that each child has a different pattern of subtest variability, with subtest score ranges of 1 to 10, 6 to 16, 3 to 13, and 1 to 11, respectively. Block Design is low in some cases, but in others it is high. Coding is low in each of the four cases.

WRAT-R scores are generally within the same percentile range as the WISC-R Full Scale IQs, but there are exceptions. For example, in Case 2 the Verbal Scale IQ is 91, but the WRAT-R reading standard score is 122, a clear strength. In Case 4, the Verbal Scale IQ is 98, but the WRAT-R Spelling standard score is 72, a clear weakness. These WRAT-R scores could not have been predicted on the basis of either the children's Verbal Scale IQs or their Full Scale IQs.

Three of the four children have difficulty in visual-motor coordination, as measured by the Bender-Gestalt (Cases 1, 3, and 4), with Case 3 having the most difficulty. The specific pattern of test scores in each case may be related partially to the location of damage within the cerebral hemispheres. The cases demonstrate the variability in test scores that can occur in children diagnosed as brain damaged.

Case 1

Kim, an 8-year, 10-month-old female, has had an inoperable lesion in the right cerebral hemisphere since birth. She occasionally has seizures that are partially controlled by phenobarbital. She is enrolled in a learning disability class where she also receives speech therapy. During testing, she was friendly and cooperative, eager to achieve, and willing to attempt all of the tasks presented. Her WISC-R Full Scale IQ is classified in the Borderline range of intellectual functioning. Her achievement scores are all low, at or below the 3rd percentile. When she read, some reversals of letters occurred. Her 10 errors on the Bender-Gestalt place her at the 1st percentile (Koppitz standard score = 58) and indicate considerable perceptual-motor difficulties. She will need continued individualized instruction.

Case 2

Shawn, at the age of 9 years, 11 months, sustained a severe closed head injury when he was hit by an automobile. He suffered damage to the left frontal and anterior temporal lobes and began to exhibit continued right hemiparesis and memory difficulties. Although he was an above-average student before the accident, he now receives remedial instruction in reading and English composition. A psychological evaluation was administered when he was 11 years, 5 months old. His WISC-R IQ was classified in the Average range, but there was considerable variability in his subtest scores (range from 6 to 16). Although he had difficulty in finding appropriate words with which to express himself, his WRAT-R scores reflected word recognition skills at the 86th percentile. Spelling and arithmetic skills were at the 37th percentile. His two errors on the Bender-Gestalt reflect performance that is within the average range (at the 34th percentile, Koppitz standard score = 94). A follow-up evaluation when he was 14-9 years old showed significant improvement in the performance area (Performance IQ = 126), but little improvement in the verbal area (Verbal IQ = 94); his Full Scale IQ was 107.

Case 3

Amanda is a left-handed female who was struck by an automobile when she was 12 years, 0 months old. She sustained a closed head injury, with loss of consciousness, left-frontal laceration and hematoma, and right hemiparesis. A neuropsychological examination administered 7 weeks after the injury indicated residual right hemiparesis and expressive language difficulties. Her WISC-R Full Scale IQ was in the Borderline range of intellectual functioning. Both verbal and nonverbal memory deficits were present. On the WRAT-R, her word recognition skills were at the 12th percentile, spelling skills at the 5th percentile, and arithmetic skills at the 2nd percentile. She made 9 errors on the Bender-Gestalt, indicating serious perceptual-motor difficulties. A follow-up WISC-R administered one year after the accident indicated that Amanda was still functioning in the Borderline range (Verbal IQ = 77, Performance IQ = 72, Full Scale IQ = 72). Special class placement was recommended.

Case 4

Henry is a 13-year, 5-month-old male who has suffered from convulsions since 1 year of age. He has been taking phenobarbital and Dilantin to control his seizures and is currently enrolled in a program for the educationally handicapped. Although his Full Scale IQ is classified as being in the Low Average range of intellectual functioning, his Verbal IQ was significantly higher than his Performance IQ. His performance on the Bender-Gestalt suggests difficulties in visual-motor coordination. His Wide Range Achievement Test—Revised scores are below the 10th percentile. Results from projective testing indicated the existence of suppressed anger

(Exhibit continues next page)

Exhibit 22-2 (cont.)

and depression. It was recommended that he receive continued remediation for his visual-perceptual problems and be seen in therapy to resolve emotional difficulties secondary to his organic deficits.

Table 22-A
Test Scores and Bender-Gestalt Protocols for Four Cases of Brain Damage

Test	Case 1 (female, age 8-10)	Case 2 (male, age 11-5)	Case 3 (female, age 12-2)	Case 4 (male, age 13-5)
WISC-R		*Scaled Score*		
Information	9	9	6	11
Similarities	10	11	9	11
Arithmetic	6	11	7	5
Vocabulary	8	6	4	12
Comprehension	8	6	7	10
Digit Span	9	10	4	3
Picture Completion	4	13	5	9
Picture Arrangement	5	9	5	8
Block Design	1	16	13	6
Object Assembly	5	9	7	6
Coding	4	7	3	1
Mazes	3	9	—	6
		Standard Score		
Verbal Scale IQ	88	91	79	98
Performance Scale IQ	60	105	77	73
Full Scale IQ	72	97	76	85
WRAT-R		*Standard Score*		
Reading	71	122	82	80
Spelling	79	97	75	72
Arithmetic	68	97	70	58

Bender-Gestalt

(Case 1)

(Case 2)

(Case 3)

(Case 4)

Bruininks-Oseretsky Test of Motor Proficiency

The Bruininks-Oseretsky Test of Motor Proficiency (see Chapter 14) may contribute to the assessment of neurological dysfunction because it reliably measures fine and gross motor functions.

Purdue Pegboard

The Purdue Pegboard test provides measures of sensorimotor functions, particularly fine motor coordination, that are essentially independent of educational achievement. In the first three parts of the test, the child places pegs in a pegboard with the preferred hand, with the nonpreferred hand, and with both hands for 30-second periods. In the fourth part of the test, the child forms "assemblies" consisting of a peg, a washer, a collar, and another washer. The test is a quick, simple instrument that has value for predicting the presence and laterality of cerebral lesions. Norms are available for preschool children aged 2-6 through 5-11 (Wilson, Iacoviello, Wilson, & Risucci, 1982) and for school-age children aged 5-0 through 16-11 years (Gardner, 1979).

Tests such as the Purdue Pegboard may reveal performance deficits indicating neurological dysfunction in children (or adults) who have well-developed intellectual capacities but who are only slightly impaired. These tests also permit comparison of lower level functions with higher level cognitive functions and provide information about lateralized or bilateral deficits.

Test of Right-Left Discrimination

A useful procedure for obtaining information about the child's understanding of right and left is shown in Exhibit 22-3. The results must be interpreted in relation to the child's age.

Finger Localization Test

Another procedure for evaluating soft signs of brain injury is the Finger Localization Test (see Table 22-9). Again, the results of this test must be considered in relation to the child's age.

Verbal Fluency Tests

Tests of verbal fluency are useful in assessing word-finding ability in brain-damaged children. Verbal fluency can be defined as the ability to retrieve words that belong to a

---

Exhibit 22-3

Right-Left Discrimination Test

1. Raise your right hand.
2. Touch your left ear.
3. Point to your right eye.
4. Raise your left hand.
5. Show me your right leg.
6. Show me your left leg.
7. Point to your left ear with your right hand.
8. Point to the wall on your right.
9. Examiner touches the child's left hand: "Which hand is this?"
10. Examiner touches his or her own right eye: "Which eye is this?"
11. Examiner touches his or her own right hand: "Which hand is this?"
12. Examiner touches his or her own left ear: "Which ear is this?"
13. With the child's eyes closed, the examiner touches the child's left ear: "Which ear is this?"
14. Examiner touches his or her own left hand: "Which hand is this?"
15. Examiner touches his or her own left eye: "Which eye is this?"
16. Examiner touches child's right hand: "Which hand is this?"

Scoring: One point for each correct response.

Source: Adapted from Belmont and Birch (1965) and from Croxen and Lytton (1971).

---

specified category in a given time period. Factors associated with verbal fluency include the ability to accumulate and store items and to access the stored information within a limited amount of time. The two different types of verbal fluency tests shown in Table 22-10 require different kinds of semantic processing. The Animal-Naming Test requires retrieval from a narrowly defined category, with words being accessed according to their meaning; this task involves a semantic factor. In contrast, the Controlled Word Association Test (naming as many words as possible that begin with a certain letter) requires retrieval from different logical categories, with word meanings becoming irrelevant or being suppressed; this task involves a symbolic factor. When both tests are given, comparisons can be made between semantic and symbolic word-finding abilities. If individuals cannot speak, responses can be written. The child's age and intelligence must be taken into account in evaluating the results of verbal fluency tests.

Table 22-9
Finger Localization Test

Subtest	Instructions
I. Visual Subtest	Ask the child to extend his or her arm with the palm of the hand up. With the child's hand visible to him or her, ask the child to localize single fingers that have been tactually stimulated. Give 10 stimulations to each hand. Touch each finger twice in a randomized order. Maximum Score = 20.
II. Tactual Subtest	Ask the child to extend his or her arm with the palm of the hand up. Use a card as a shield to prevent the child from seeing his or her hand. With the child's hand hidden from his or her view, ask the child to localize single fingers that have been tactually stimulated. Give 10 stimulations to each hand. Touch each finger twice in a randomized order. Maximum Score = 20.
III. Tactual Pairs Subtest	This subtest is like the Tactual Subtest, but the child localizes two fingers that have been tactually stimulated simultaneously. Give 10 stimulations to each hand. Touch every possible combination on each hand. Maximum Score = 20.

Scoring: One point for each correct response. For the Tactual Pairs Subtest, a misidentification of either one or both of the fingers is counted as a single error. Maximum Score = 60.

Note. In administering the three subtests in the Finger Localization Test, two numbered diagrams of a right and left hand are shown to the child. The child "localizes" by indicating the finger touched by pointing to it on the diagram, or by indicating its number, or by naming it. A paperclip may be used to touch the child's fingertips.
Source: Adapted from Benton (1959) and from Croxen and Lytton (1971).

Measures of Volitional Movements

Useful procedures for measuring two forms of developmental apraxia—isolated volitional oral movement and sequential volitional oral movement—are shown in Table 22-11. A comparison of the child's performance on the two tasks will provide information about the child's nonverbal sequencing ability. Again, the child's age must be considered in evaluating performance on these tasks.

Picture Naming

Dysnomia, or difficulty in naming objects, can be measured through use of the WISC-R Picture Completion subtest. The following procedure may be used to screen for dysnomia among children who may have language impairments or aphasia. The examiner points to a part of a picture on the Picture Completion subtest and says, "What is this called?" The parts of the pictures pointed to and the

Table 22-10
Verbal Fluency Tests

Test	Directions
1. Naming Animals	"Give the names of as many animals as you can think of. Begin." Allow 60 seconds.
2. Controlled Word Association Test	"Give as many words as you can think of that begin with the letter *F*. Do not give names of persons—like Frank or Florence—or names of states or cities—like Florida or Fresno—or other proper names. Begin." Allow 60 seconds. Then say "Now give as many words as you can think of that begin with the letter *A*. Again do not give proper names. Begin." Allow 60 seconds. Then say "Now give as many words as you can think of that begin with the letter *S*. Again do not give proper names. Begin." Allow 60 seconds.

Scoring: One point for each correct response. Do not count repetitions, proper nouns, or different forms of the same word.

Note. Verbal fluency tests can be administered in either an oral or a written format. For children younger than 7 or 8 years of age, the written format generally is not appropriate. With older children, it may be valuable occasionally to compare oral and written performances on the same test. The directions above are for the oral version. For the written version, substitute the word *write* for *give*.

Table 22-11
Measures of Developmental Apraxia

Name: _____   Examiner's name: _____

Age: _____   Date: _____

Sex: _____

Isolated Volitional Oral Movements Task

Task	Score
1. Stick out your tongue	_____
2. Whistle	_____
3. Yawn	_____
4. Try to touch the tip of your nose with your tongue	_____
5. Show me how you would lick an ice cream cone	_____
6. Show me how you would kiss someone	_____
7. Show me how your teeth chatter when you are cold	_____
8. Open and close your mouth as if you were chewing	_____
9. Puff or blow	_____
10. Clear your throat	_____
TOTAL	_____

Scoring Key:

Response	Observed Behavior	Score
Correct	Accurate performance immediately following oral command	2
Correct-Cued	Accurate performance immediately following demonstration of behavior	1
Correct-Delayed	Accurate performance preceded by protracted pauses, during which unsuccessful movements may be present	1
Partial	Some important part of gesture is lacking—though the rest is performed correctly	0
Perseveration	Gestures elicited by preceding items performed	0
Irrelevant	Some other incorrect oral performance (including speech sounds) is produced	0
Nil	No oral performance is produced	0

Sequenced Volitional Oral Movements Task

Task	Trials			
	1st	2nd	3rd	4th
1. Blow and then try to touch the tip of your nose with your tongue	—	—	—	—
2. Show me how you lick ice cream and then whistle	—	—	—	—
3. Show how you would kiss someone and then clear your throat	—	—	—	—
4. Stick out your tongue and then show how you would kiss someone and then whistle	—	—	—	—
5. Show how you would lick ice cream and then show how your teeth chatter when you are cold and then yawn	—	—	—	—
6. Clear your throat and then show how you would chew and then blow	—	—	—	—
TOTAL	—	—	—	—

Scoring Key: Each item must be complete and in the sequence presented. 1st trial—Correct, 4; 2nd trial—Correct, 3; 3rd trial—Correct, 2; 4th trial—Correct, 1; Incorrect after 4th trial, 0. Testing for each sequence is terminated immediately after the child exhibits a correct response.

Source: Reprinted, with a change in notation, with permission from the publisher and author from C. L. Prichard, M. E. Tekieli, and J. M. Kozup, "Developmental Apraxia: Diagnostic Considerations," *Journal of Communication Disorders*, 1979, *12*, pp. 342–343. Copyright 1979, by the Elsevier Science Publishing Co., Inc.

correct responses are shown in Table 22-12. Similar procedures can be followed with the WAIS-R and WPPSI Picture Completion subtests.

Raven's Progressive Matrices

Raven's Progressive Matrices test provides an estimate of nonverbal cognitive ability. Examinees who perform more poorly on Raven's Progressive Matrices (see Chapter 12) than on verbal intelligence tests and who are suspected of having brain damage may have nonverbal reasoning difficulties. They may be able to concentrate on only one aspect of the stimulus array and thus may be unable to integrate the necessary spatial relationships to arrive at a correct response. In such cases, the score on Raven's Progressive Matrices should not be used as an indication of general intelligence.

The strategies needed to solve Raven's Progressive Matrices are not unique to either hemisphere (Zaidel, Zaidel, & Sperry, 1981). For example, the matrices may be solved either with an analytic strategy — sampling one element at a time — or a synthetic strategy — grouping patterns into larger units or wholes. Consequently, lateralization of injury should not be assessed on the basis of performance on Raven's Progressive Matrices.

Table 22-12
WISC-R Picture Completion Stimulus Cards for Assessing Dysnomia

	Stimulus card	Examiner points to	Correct response
1.	Card 1	tooth	teeth, tooth
2.	Card 3	ear	ear
3.	Card 4	fingernail	fingernail
4.	Card 5	whiskers	whiskers
5.	Card 6	doll	doll; baby
6.	Card 8	leg	leg; foot
7.	Card 9	step	step
8.	Card 10	knob	knob
9.	Card 13	hinge	hinge
10.	Card 14	diamond	diamond
11.	Card 15	sock	sock, socks
12.	Card 20	notch	notch; slit; slot
13.	Card 21	hoof	hoof
14.	Card 22	thermometer	thermometer
15.	Card 23	shadow	shadow
16.	Card 24	cord	cord; wire

Source: Adapted from Schiller, DeSimone, Gross, Hoey, McGuire, Smith, and Torres (1982).

Token Test

The Token Test for Children (DiSimoni, 1978) is useful as a screening test of receptive language (auditory comprehension) for children between the ages of 3-0 and 12-5. Other versions are available for older adolescents and adults (De Renzi, 1980; De Renzi & Faglioni, 1978). The test requires children to manipulate tokens in response to commands given by the examiner, such as "Touch the red circle." The commands vary in length and syntactic complexity. The 20 tokens vary along the dimensions of color, shape, and size. The Token Test is a sensitive measure for identifying mild receptive disturbances in aphasic children who have passed other auditory tests. Although the test is only a screening device because its psychometric properties are not well established, it appears to be a useful instrument for the assessment of receptive aphasia.

Reporter's Test

The Reporter's Test is a useful screening test for examining expressive language (De Renzi & Ferrari, 1978). The examiner performs various actions on the array of 20 tokens used in the Token Test. The examinee is required to report the performance verbally so as to enable a hypothetical third person to replicate the actions. For example, if the examiner touches the large yellow square, the examinee must state the relevant information so that the action can be performed by the imaginary third person ("Touch the large yellow square"). The examinee must produce a connected sequence of words, the choice and order of which is determined in advance. Research suggests that the Reporter's Test provides useful information for assessing expressive language (Feldman, 1984; Hall & Jordan, 1985; Jordan & Hall, 1985). The Reporter's Test complements the Token Test; it should be administered *after* the Token Test.

Other Informal Procedures for Assessment of Aphasia

In addition to the Token Test, Reporter's Test, word fluency procedures, and procedures for evaluating dysnomia, the following informal procedures can be used to assess aphasic disturbances (Spreen & Risser, 1981):

• evaluation of spontaneous or conversational speech
• evaluation of ability to repeat digits, simple words, multisyllabic words, and complex sentences
• evaluation of receptive language and praxis (You can say, for example, "Here are three papers: a big one, a middle-sized one, and a little one. Take the biggest one,

rumple it up, and throw it on the ground. Give me the middle-sized one. Put the smallest one in your pocket." For the child with major motor impairment, it will be necessary to restrict the examination to questions that can be answered yes or no.)

• evaluation of word-finding ability (You can, for example, ask for the names of common objects, such as the child's clothing and body parts, both with and without prompting.)

• evaluation of the ability to read

• evaluation of the ability to write (You can start with the child's own name and proceed to dictated and spontaneous writing, saying, for example, "Describe your school.")

Spreen and Risser (1981) provide an excellent review of tests for aphasia, many of which are useful with adolescents.

Norms for Neuropsychological Tests

Normative data for 12 neuropsychological tests, stratified for age and sex (ages 15 through 40 years), are useful in work with late adolescents and adults (Yeudall, Fromm, Reddon, & Stefanyk, 1986). The tests are Language Modalities Test for Aphasia, Memory-for-Designs, Raven's Coloured Progressive Matrices, Symbol-Gestalt, Minute Estimation, Controlled Word Association, Written Word Fluency, Purdue Pegboard, Williams Clinical Memory, Symbol Digit Modalities, L. J. Tactile Recognition, and Wisconsin Card Sorting.

EVALUATING ASSESSMENT RESULTS

A comprehensive neuropsychological evaluation may reveal disturbances in motor, sensory, affective, cognitive, social, temperament, and personality domains. For example, intellectual deficits may be revealed by a global reduction of IQ or by reduced efficiency in specific performance areas or verbal areas. During the early stages of brain damage, subtle forms of behavioral change may occur that mimic psychiatric disorders. Brain damage itself may play a major role in predisposing children to severe forms of psychopathology as well as to subtle changes in personality. Brain damage may also exacerbate a premorbid subclinical psychiatric condition. Psychiatric disorders are seen more frequently in children with brain damage to the higher cortical (or subcortical) centers (that is, above the brain stem) than in those with chronic physical handicaps not associated with brain pathology.

Inferential Methods of Test Analysis

Several inferential methods are used to analyze the data obtained from a neuropsychological test battery.

1. *The level of performance approach* compares the child's test scores with cutoff points established on the basis of the normative sample to distinguish brain-damaged children from normal children.

2. *The pattern of performance approach* considers the relationships among the child's performances on a group of tests in an effort to discover specific combinations of strengths and deficits that may relate to a possible lesion or to outcome criteria.

3. *The pathognomonic signs of brain damage approach* focuses on signs of pathology in the child's test performance (for example, aphasic or apractic disturbances, visual field defects, or severe memory disturbances) and on neurological tests (for example, electroencephalographic abnormalities).

4. *The comparison of performance on the two sides of the body approach* attempts to determine (usually through tests of sensory or motor functioning) lateralization of deficits — the relative efficiency of the right versus the left side of the body.

The findings resulting from each method should be compared to arrive at a diagnostic impression; no one method should be used exclusively.

Factors to Consider in Evaluating the Behavioral Effects of Brain Damage

The following factors are important in the evaluation of the behavioral effects of brain damage:

1. Age of child when injury occurred
2. Present age of child
3. Sex of child
4. Lateralization of injury (right or left hemisphere)
5. Location of injury within the hemisphere
6. Type of injury
7. Duration of lesion (acute vs. chronic)
8. Rate of onset of disease
9. State of disease process (such as evolving vs. resolving or static vs. progressive)
10. Diaschisis (a lesion in one part of the brain indirectly affecting other parts of the brain)
11. Time interval between damage and testing
12. Condition of child at the time of testing, apart from brain damage (such as associated physical and emotional problems, drug regimen, and level of cooperation and motivation)

13. Premorbid (before-damage) condition of the child
14. Home and school environments in which the child functions

These factors interact to produce highly complex behavioral effects. Because of the complexity of the interactions, similar forms of brain damage do not always produce the same behavioral effects, nor do behavioral differences among brain-damaged children always relate directly to the severity of the damage or to premorbid personality characteristics. To complicate matters further, some individuals with brain damage are able to compensate for deficits and may not show markedly impaired performance on psychological tests. Conversely, because complex human behavior is multidetermined (for example, by the integrity of the brain, emotions, and motivational factors), impaired performance on psychological tests does not necessarily mean that brain damage is present.

Recent findings in neuroanatomy and physiology suggest "that the brain is an interactive system whose two hemispheres participate conjointly in the production of behavior, and that damage in one component inevitably affects other components" (Sergent, 1984, p. 99). Thus even in the case of unilateral brain damage, changes in brain-behavior functioning must be understood in the context of the whole system. Each case must be thoroughly studied in order to identify the factors responsible for the particular behavioral effects.

Diagnosis

Because particular test scores or behavior patterns may be related either to psychogenic (pertaining to conditions that have no clearcut organic foundations) or to organic factors, it is essential to investigate thoroughly the child's entire performance and clinical history before inferring from any pattern that brain damage may be present. For example, low test scores may be related to motivational difficulties, anxiety, educational deficits, physical handicaps (such as impaired hearing or vision), cultural factors, developmental delays, or cerebral impairment. This means that you cannot rely on level of performance alone as a key diagnostic sign to evaluate brain damage; other factors also must be considered.

There are several situations in which there may be positive neurological findings without observable behavioral correlations. One is where cerebral dysfunction affects only specific deep reflexes or superficial reflexes. A second is where lesions involve the cranial nerves or other subcortical structures only. A third is where transient epi-

leptiform activity (brain waves that resemble those of an epileptic disorder but are not associated with any clinically directly observable indication of seizures) is noted on the EEG. The insensitivity of neuropsychological tests must also be considered. In other cases, however, psychological tests may reveal marked impairment in some areas of functioning, even though the neurological examination indicates intact functioning.

Diagnostic difficulties arise for a number of reasons. First, with evolving cerebral lesions there may be an interval when pathological processes in various parts of the brain develop without affecting the specific functions tapped by either neurological or neuropsychological examinations. Second, early in the pathological development, compensation for deficits may mask clinical manifestations of progressive dysfunction. Third, it is often difficult to distinguish brain-damaged children with vague complaints—such as loss of memory, dizziness, and irritability—from children with similar symptoms who have no identifiable cerebral lesion. Finally, brain damage incurred at an early age may not become evident for several years because of the nature and course of development of some higher level cognitive functions.

Children with a hearing deficit, mild mental retardation (without brain damage), autistic disorder, emotional instability, or delayed speech may display symptoms similar to those of brain-injured children, thus making a differential diagnosis difficult. For example, the emotionally disturbed behavior of the brain-injured aphasic child, which may stem from the frustrating inability to communicate and understand language, may be difficult to differentiate from that of the emotionally disturbed child who does not have brain damage. Children with aphasia share with autistic children abnormal responses to sounds, delay in language acquisition, and articulation difficulties. They usually do not manifest the perceptual or motor disturbances characteristic of autistic children, however. Furthermore, aphasic children can relate to others through nonverbal gestures and expressions; they are sensitive to gestures and expressions of others; they can learn to point toward desired objects; and they show communicative intent and emotion when they acquire speech.

A careful synthesis of the obtained findings should, however, enable you to make judgments about a child's performance in the following areas (Rie, Rie, Stewart, & Ambuel, 1976):

• *integrating-synthesizing skills*—ability to organize, combine, and restructure data in order to arrive at a correct solution or conclusion
• *degree of perseveration*—extent to which the child

continues to use a verbal or motor response when it has ceased to be relevant

• *ability to make conceptual shifts*—ability to change focus from one concept or idea to another, to alter the boundaries or limits of an idea, and to avoid continued preoccupation with a thought that is no longer relevant

• *degree of concrete thinking*—extent to which the child focuses unduly on immediately present stimuli, is unable to think abstractly or to generalize relative to age expectations, and interprets statements in an excessively literal way

• *word recall ability*—ability to select and use words with reasonable fluency, to recall words immediately in a brief interchange, and to use words to convey adequately the desired meanings

• *degree of word misuse*—extent to which the child selects words that are incorrect but have some irrelevant or tangential relation to the word intended

The more problems revealed in these and other areas, the greater the likelihood of cognitive dysfunction suggestive of brain damage. Application of this principle, however, must be tempered by consideration of the extent to which the environment may have contributed to the development of any cognitive, perceptual-motor, or behavioral deficits. Environmental considerations are important, especially in work with children coming from adverse environments. In such cases, some judgment must be made concerning the extent to which the environment may have contributed to their poor performance. If the environment looms large as a possible contributing factor to the child's poor performance, then considerable caution should be exercised in making a diagnosis of brain dysfunction.

Qualitative approaches to test interpretation together with testing-of-limits approaches are primarily good for generating (not proving) hypotheses. These approaches are not standardized and do not have norms or validated rules for interpretation. They require more experience and caution than do interpretations more closely tied to research findings. You must take care not to confuse an interesting hypothesis based on qualitative analysis with a finding that has received substantial empirical support. Nevertheless, qualitative analysis and testing-of-limits are important components of the assessment process.

DEVELOPING INTERVENTION PROCEDURES FOR BRAIN-DAMAGED CHILDREN

Brain-damaged children may differ from normal children not only in their capacity to learn but also in their approach to learning. Deficits in abstract thinking, flexibility of thought, and memory are likely to persist following brain damage. Rehabilitation needs to be directed to these areas as well as to sensory and motor deficits. In designing a rehabilitation program, consider the areas and sources of deficits, the child's present level of functioning (such as competencies and impairments), the interactions between emotional and neurological problems, the child's behavior patterns in natural settings (such as in school), and the child's environment (for example, the family's strengths and how to develop environmental supports).

The following procedures are recommended for teaching brain-damaged children:

1. Do not "overload" the child with information.
2. Present information in a controlled and manageable fashion.
3. Determine the optimum level for reception of information for each child individually.
4. Use repetition and practice to consolidate previously learned material.
5. Keep choices to a minimum on learning tasks.

Behavioral deficits may require remediation strategies that address the source of the deficit. For example, a reading disability may be the result of (a) faulty learning (or education) in a child who is otherwise normal or (b) an acquired structural or biochemical anomaly of the brain. For treatment purposes, it is important to determine which of these is the cause of the reading disability. Even with such diagnostic knowledge, however, appropriate treatment programs are difficult to design. There are gaps in our knowledge about relationships between conditions of the central nervous system and appropriate treatment techniques, and even between patterns of adaptive functioning and treatment alternatives. Educational programs are best designed by considering how to make use of the child's strengths.

REPORT WRITING

Detailed guidelines for report writing are presented in Chapter 23. There may be occasions, however, when you will want to use a standardized format for reporting assessment results. One general form, which can be modified to suit the needs of the examiner, is shown in Exhibit 22-4. The worksheet outlines the various procedures used in the evaluation, with appropriate spaces for recording the findings. Some items simply call for a checkmark (for example, tests administered) or a number (IQ or percentile

Exhibit 22-4

Neuropsychological Report Writing Worksheet for School-Aged Children

WORKSHEET

Instructions: Insert applicable information in the spaces. Cross out inapplicable phrases.

Reason for Referral

_____ is a _____ year old male/female who was born on _____. He/she was referred for a neuropsychological evaluation after a _____ on _____.

Tests Administered

The following records, tests, and assessment procedures were used [check appropriate ones]:

1. School records
2. Medical records
3. Interview with parents
4. Interview with child
5. Wechsler Intelligence Scale for Children – Revised
6. Wechsler Adult Intelligence Scale – Revised
7. Stanford-Binet: Fourth Edition
8. Bender-Gestalt
9. Revised Visual Retention Test
10. Wide Range Achievement Test – Revised
11. Halstead-Reitan Neuropsychological Test Battery for Older Children
12. Reitan-Indiana Neuropsychological Test Battery for Children
13. Luria-Nebraska Neuropsychological Battery: Children's Revision
14. Contributions to Neuropsychological Assessment Battery
15. Bruininks-Oseretsky Test of Motor Proficiency
16. Purdue Pegboard
17. Token Test for Children
18. Reporter's Test
19. Progressive Matrices
20. Informal tests
21. Other tests: _____
_____
_____

History

The child has noticed/parents have reported the following problems since the accident/onset of symptoms:

1. _____
2. _____
3. _____

4. _____
5. _____
6. _____
7. _____

These problems appear to be improving/getting worse/ remaining the same.

The child is in the _____ grade and was performing at a satisfactory/unsatisfactory level before the injury/onset of symptoms. There were/were no previous head injuries. Behavioral problems were/were not present before the brain injury. [If present, describe the behavioral problems: The child had difficulties in _____
_____.]

Birth was normal/abnormal. [If abnormal, describe what was abnormal. _____
_____.]

Developmental milestones were satisfactory/delayed. [If delayed, describe what milestones were delayed. _____
_____.]

Behavioral Observations

When seen for testing, _____ was/was not alert and well oriented. There were/were not any difficulties observed during the evaluation. [If present, describe the difficulties: These difficulties included _____
_____
_____.]

Intellectual Functioning

The child achieved a Verbal Scale IQ of _____ (_____ percentile), a Performance Scale IQ of _____ (_____ percentile), and a Full Scale IQ of _____ ± _____ on the Wechsler Intelligence Scale for Children – Revised/Wechsler Adult Intelligence Scale – Revised. His/her overall score suggests that current intellectual functioning falls within the _____ range and at the _____ percentile. The chances that the range of scores from _____ to _____ includes his/her true IQ are about _____ out of 100. The results appear to be reliable/not reliable.

The Full Scale IQ appears/does not appear to reflect the child's level of functioning before the injury. This estimate is based on parental and teacher reports/prior psychological tests. Thus, there is/is no evidence of a general loss of intel-

(Exhibit continues next page)

Exhibit 22-4 (cont.)

lectual functioning. [If present, describe the estimated loss:

The loss appears to be of approximately _____ IQ points.]

Marked intellectual impairments were/were not noted on the subtests of the WISC-R/WAIS-R. There was/was no evidence of clinically significant scaled score deviations. [If present, describe which subtest scores deviated significantly

from the mean of each scale: Weaknesses were shown in __

_____

_____ .

Strengths were shown in _____

_____ .]

Higher cognitive functions (comprehension, abstract thinking, problem solving) appeared to be generally intact/ impaired.

Educational Achievement

Reading skills are at the _____ grade level and at the _____ percentile (standard score of _____); spelling skills at the _____ grade level and at the _____ percentile (standard score of _____); and arithmetic skills at the _____ grade level and at the _____ percentile (standard score of _____) as measured by the _____ .
These standardized achievement scores are relatively consistent/discrepant with _____'s level of scholastic attainment before the injury. There is/is no evidence of a learning disability. [If present, describe the learning disability: The learning disability involves the child's reading,/ spelling,/arithmetic, with difficulties in _____

_____

_____ .]

Motor Functioning

_____ demonstrated consistent right/left hand dominance. Gross motor coordination was intact/impaired. Fine motor coordination was adequate/impaired. [Additional comments: _____

_____ .]

Auditory Perceptual Functioning

Auditory perceptual functioning was intact/impaired. _____ had no/had difficulty in differentiating between pairs of words. [Additional comments: _____

_____ .]

Tactile Perceptual Functioning

Tactile perceptual functioning was relatively intact/impaired. There were no/some errors indicating finger agnosia, no/

some errors in graphaesthesia, and no/some errors in stereognosis. [Additional comments: _____

_____

_____ .]

Visuo-Spatial Functioning

Visuo-spatial functioning appeared to be adequate/impaired. Visuomotor speed was adequate/impaired. [Additional comments: _____

_____

_____ .]

Language Ability

Language ability was intact/impaired with respect to reading, writing, listening, and talking. There was no/was evidence of dysarthria. Motor aspects of speech were intact/impaired, as there was no/was evidence of disturbance in articulation and repetition. Comprehension of speech was adequate/inadequate and thus not indicative/indicative of a receptive disorder. Word finding fluency was intact/impaired and thus not indicative/indicative of an expressive disorder. There was/ was no evidence of a reading disability. Writing ability was adequate/impaired and thus not indicative/indicative of dysgraphia. [Additional comments: _____

_____

_____ .]

Memory Processes

_____'s immediate memory was intact/impaired. Recent memory, including the ability to learn both new verbal and visual information, was adequate/impaired. Remote memory was satisfactory/impaired. There was no/was evidence of an impairment of concentration or attention. [Additional comments: _____

_____ .]

Behavior

Parental reports indicate that _____ has satisfactory/ unsatisfactory behavior patterns. [If unsatisfactory, include additional comments here: They report that _____

_____ .]

School reports indicate that his/her behavior in school is satisfactory/unsatisfactory. [If unsatisfactory, include additional comments here: His/her teacher(s) reports that _____

_____

_____ .]

(Exhibit continues next page)

rank), whereas others require detailed comments (for example, behavioral observations). The final report can be typed directly from the worksheet.

PSYCHOLOGICAL EVALUATION

Exhibit 22-5 presents a neuropsychological evaluation of a 10-year-old boy who was referred for evaluation of behavior problems at home and school. Although his WISC-R Full Scale IQ of 68 is classified in the Mentally Retarded range, there was an 18-point discrepancy between the Verbal and Performance IQs, in favor of the Performance IQ. This discrepancy suggests a differential pattern of strengths and weaknesses. Additionally, there was considerable variability in the WISC-R subtest scores. On the Wide Range Achievement Test—Revised, he performed at a slightly higher level. His Bender-Gestalt performance was marked by perseveration on all of the figures.

Because neuropsychological test data were highly suggestive of neurological impairment, he was referred for neurological examination. The neurologist reported that the child had an abnormal EEG consistent with the presence of a seizure disorder. The electroencephalographic report was as follows: "Abnormal EEG with epileptogenic focus at the left frontal region, together with generalized seizure discharges throughout the recording. This EEG would be compatible with partial seizure or generalized seizures." This case is an excellent example of (a) the way a psychological assessment can detect a cognitive deficit consistent with a probable neurological disorder and (b) the importance of referring questionable cases for further evaluation.

SUMMARY

1. Brain damage refers to a structural or physiological change of a pathological nature in the neural tissue of the brain. Brain damage may result from prenatal, perinatal, or postnatal factors. Prenatal factors are most often associated with maternal exposure to alcohol, drugs, toxic chemicals, infections, and radiation. Perinatal factors include prematurity, physical trauma, asphyxia, and infection. Postnatal factors include metabolic disorders, endocrine disorders, poor nutrition, trauma, infection, pesticides, drug abuse, and ingestion of metals.

2. Brain injury may result in focal lesions (lesions limited to fairly specific sites) or diffuse effects. Open head injuries often have focal effects. Closed head injuries may lead to progressively greater pathology than open head injuries because of degenerative processes.

3. The neurological examination is primarily concerned with the intactness of lower level functions (such as reflexes), whereas the neuropsychological evaluation focuses on higher level cognitive processes. Neuropsychological assessment plays an important role in the evaluation of the behavioral consequences of brain damage and in the development of the intervention techniques needed for remediation.

4. A neurological examination includes a clinical history, a brief mental status examination, and a study of cranial nerves, motor functions, coordination, sensory functions, and gait. Laboratory procedures—such as CT, PET, and MRI scans; EEGs; skull x-rays; spinal taps; and cerebral angiograms—complement the neurological examination.

5. The hard signs (such as pathological reflexes) observed on a neurological examination are fairly definitive indicators of brain damage, whereas the soft signs (such as visual-motor difficulties) are less consistently associated with brain damage.

6. A neuropsychological examination complements the neurological examination. It includes measures of sensory perceptual functions, motor functions, psychomotor problem solving, language and communication skills, and other cognitive and intellectual skills. Neuropsychological evaluations serve many purposes, providing objective information about the individual's adaptive functioning and base-line measures for evaluating the course of neuropathological processes, recovery from illness or other insults to the brain, and the effects of different therapeutic programs on cerebral functions. Several tests are needed to evaluate brain-behavior relationships.

7. Many cognitive, perceptual, and motor activities are specialized within the left and right hemispheres. The hemisphere controlling sensory or motor functions is usually contralateral to the side involved in the activity. The left hemisphere, which typically is most important in mediating verbal functions, uses analytic, sequential, serial, and differential processing. The right

■ **Exhibit 22-5** ■

Neuropsychological Evaluation

Name: Jeff
Date of birth: March 9, 1977
Chronological age: 10-0

Date of examination: March 31, 1987
Date of report: April 10, 1987
Grade: 3rd

Tests Administered

Wechsler Intelligence Scale for Children — Revised (WISC-R):

VERBAL SCALE		PERFORMANCE SCALE	
Information	5	Picture Completion	7
Similarities	1	Picture Arrangement	9
Arithmetic	1	Block Design	2
Vocabulary	3	Object Assembly	8
Comprehension	8	Coding	8
Digit Span	5	Mazes	8

Verbal Scale IQ = 60
Performance Scale IQ = 78
Full Scale IQ = 68 ± 6 at the 95% confidence level

Bender-Gestalt:

13 errors

(page 1)

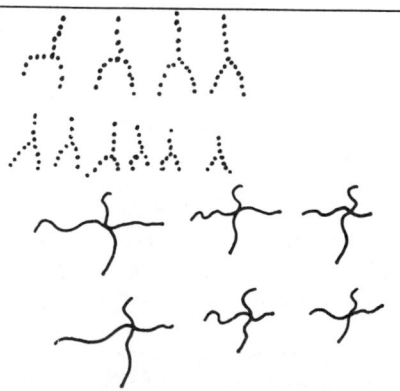

(page 2)

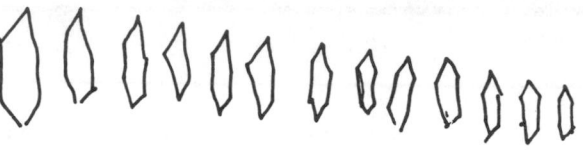

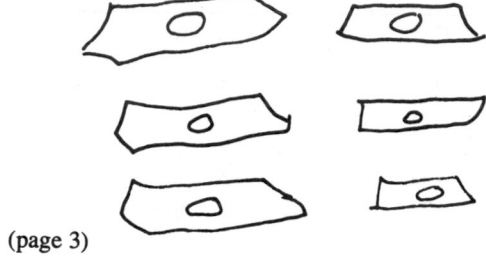

(page 3)

Wide Range Achievement Test — Revised (WRAT-R):

	STANDARD SCORE	PERCENTILE	GRADE LEVEL
Reading	86	18	3.4
Spelling	83	13	3.3
Arithmetic	80	9	3.1

Halstead-Reitan Neuropsychological Test Battery for Older Children (selected subtests)

Luria-Nebraska Neuropsychological Battery: Children's Revision

STANDARD T SCORES	
Motor	83
Rhythm	64
Tactile	79
Visual	62
Receptive Speech	67
Expressive Speech	89
Writing	91
Reading	61
Math	89
Memory	77
Intelligence	67

Reason for Referral

Jeff was referred for testing because of behavior difficulties both at school and at home.

(Exhibit continues next page)

Exhibit 22-5 (cont.)

Background Information

Jeff, a 10-year, 0-month-old black male, has a history of aggressive acting-out behavior in school. His mother described him as "always on the go, biting his fingernails, and pulling his hair." His appetite tends to be poor, but he sleeps well and is generally healthy. Past medical history indicated that he has had a number of respiratory ailments, but no significant medical problems or injuries. He is performing below average in all of his school subjects.

Behavioral Observations

Jeff is a thin child, who appeared somewhat younger than his age. He was generally cooperative, but quiet throughout the testing session. Although he became somewhat restless toward the end of the session, this was not a significant factor in his test performance.

Assessment Results and Clinical Impressions

With a chronological age of 10-0, Jeff obtained a Verbal Scale IQ of 60, a Performance Scale IQ of 78, and a Full Scale IQ of 68 ± 6 on the WISC-R. His overall performance is classified in the Mentally Retarded range and is ranked at the 2nd percentile. This means that he exceeds only 2% of the children in the standardization group, which was roughly representative of the population of the United States. His effort and motivation were adequate. Therefore, the results appear to provide a reliable and valid estimate of his current level of functioning.

Jeff demonstrated considerably more facility and potential in working with nonverbal than with verbal tasks. In the verbal area, he exhibited numerous deficiencies, with the exception of minimally adequate knowledge of social customs. Significant deficits were observed in verbal and arithmetic reasoning. In contrast, his performance on nonverbal tasks was somewhat better, in the borderline range, except for a weakness in visual-motor spatial ability.

On the Wide Range Achievement Test — Revised, Jeff's performance was somewhat stronger than would be expected from his WISC-R verbal scores. His percentile ranks were as follows: 18th in reading, 13th in spelling, and 9th in arithmetic.

On the Bender-Gestalt, Jeff exhibited an unusual and pronounced form of perseveration. He drew each design at least 8 to 15 times. He also exhibited rotation and integration errors. Overall, his performance placed him in the 5- to 5½-year range (standard score of 12, 1st percentile), according to the Koppitz Developmental Scoring System. He exhibited extreme difficulty on the Halstead-Reitan Trail Making subtest, which taps abilities in visual tracking, planning, and sequencing. He was found to be right dominant with respect to eyes, hands, and feet. However, he exhibited an unexpected nondominant hand (left hand) advantage in his strength of grip. On the Luria-Nebraska he had elevated scores in 8 of the 11 areas. The elevated scores, which are suggestive of neurological dysfunction, were on the following scales: Motor, Tactile, Receptive Speech, Expressive Speech, Writing, Math, Memory, and Intelligence.

Although the overall WISC-R results suggest that Jeff is functioning in the mild range of mental retardation, specific deficits were noted that contribute to his low functioning. Neuropsychological test data suggest a pattern that may be reflective of significant cortical dysfunctioning. Deficits were noted in verbal skills, motor and tactile skills, expressive skills, writing skills, math skills, memory skills, and integration skills. In spite of these numerous difficulties, Jeff has acquired a third-grade proficiency in recognizing words, spelling, and arithmetic.

Recommendations

A neurological examination is highly recommended because the results strongly point to the possibility of neurological impairment. Jeff should be provided resource room assistance for his learning deficits. He needs assistance in learning to focus and organize in a more appropriate manner and to complete tasks and assignments. Emphasis should be placed on reducing impulsivity and perseveration, possibly simply by requiring that Jeff wait a few seconds before answering questions and rewarding immediately his first correct response. He should be encouraged to express himself verbally, both at home and at school. Abstract verbal reasoning skill development should be emphasized, perhaps using picture books or a scrapbook to classify objects by function or size, with a discussion included to encourage verbal expression. Jeff's visual-motor perceptual skills might be improved by the use of fun activities, such as dot-to-dot, bead-stringing, pegboard, maze, or paper-folding exercises.

It is also suggested that Jeff's mother receive counseling in positive parenting and be given information on how to deal with a child with possible neurological difficulties and definite academic deficits of the type Jeff is experiencing. The information given to the mother, of course, will depend in part on the results of the neurological evaluation. Jeff's progress should be monitored through close contact with the mother. A reevaluation within one year is recommended.

(Signature) _____

Examiner's name

hemisphere, which typically is most important in many nonverbal (especially spatial) cognitive functions, uses holistic, gestalt-like, parallel, and integrative processing. Some specialization of function can be detected as early as the first year of life—namely, linguistic functions are usually localized in the left hemisphere at birth for most children of both sexes.

8. The cerebral lobes have different functions. The frontal lobes are associated with planning and expressive verbal behavior, the temporal lobes with auditory perception and cross-modal integration, the parietal lobes with somatosensory functions and visual-spatial ability, and the occipital lobes with visual perception and the semantic connotations of visual objects.

9. There may be less specialization in the cerebral hemispheres for language in young children than in adults.

10. Childhood aphasia refers to disorders in the comprehension and production of language that may accompany brain damage. Three subgroups of childhood aphasia may be delineated: congenital aphasia (marked by failure to acquire language), developmental aphasia (a less pervasive impairment characterized by failure of normal language to develop), and acquired aphasia (dysfunction resulting from brain injury following normal language development).

11. Aphasia may involve expressive and receptive functions. Specific forms of aphasia may involve cognitive, perceptual, or motor functions. In all aphasias, the deficit usually involves the use or interpretation of language or language-related symbols.

12. In children below 10 years of age, aphasia is usually characterized by a severe reduction in spontaneous speech. Children older than 10 years of age have a more mixed pattern of language deficits resembling that of adults. Recovery from aphasia typically is more likely for children than for adults, but other more general cognitive deficits may remain.

13. The prognosis for brain-damaged children is dependent on the severity of damage, the child's age when injured, the location and extent of brain damage, the occurrence of complications following damage, and other factors. The poorest prognosis is associated with severe trauma, early damage, fronto-temporal area damage, and post-traumatic epilepsy.

14. Brain damage in children differs from brain damage in adults in several important respects. With adults, there may be a loss of or interference with previously acquired functions; with children, there may be interference with development. Major localized lesions are less common in children than in adults. There is evidence that some children who sustain brain damage at an early age have more deficits than those who sustain damage at a later age. The older the child, the more likely it is that the deficits associated with brain damage will be similar to those observed in adults.

15. Cerebral plasticity, which refers to the ability of one part of the brain to take over functions impaired by lesions in another part of the brain, operates primarily during the first 4 or 5 years of life. There is increasing evidence, however, that early brain injuries may interfere with development. Because there is a great deal of variability among children, generalizations about recoverability of functions cannot be made easily. The behavioral

consequences of early brain damage depend on genetic factors, type of injury, how the impaired neural tissue affects the course of development, age at injury, and intervening experiential influences.

16. In the clinical assessment interview with parents, it is important to obtain a detailed developmental and clinical history. Detailed inquiry should be made about events related to the brain injury. Be particularly cognizant of changes in the child's lifestyle.

17. In the clinical assessment interview with children, a mental status evaluation should be conducted. With older children, obtain their perception of the events surrounding the brain damage. Detailed inquiry should be made about any symptoms that may have special neurological significance, such as headaches, alteration in consciousness, abnormal movements, seizures, disturbances in perception, and motor or language difficulties.

18. During the evaluation be alert to any abnormal behavior possibly suggestive of brain damage. Evidence may be revealed in motor, sensory, affective, cognitive, and social/personality spheres. Possible signs include hyperkinesis, short attention span, lability of mood, intellectual deficits, interpersonal difficulties, and disturbed self-concept.

19. Findings from the assessment of brain-damaged children indicate that, in some but not all cases, there may be a lowering of intelligence and impairments in perceptual, motor, and perceptual-motor areas. There are no intelligence test patterns that reliably differentiate brain-damaged children from emotionally disturbed or normal children.

20. Widely used neuropsychological test batteries include the Halstead-Reitan Neuropsychological Test Battery for Older Children, Reitan-Indiana Neuropsychological Test Battery for Children, Luria-Nebraska Neuropsychological Battery: Children's Revision, and Contributions to Neuropsychological Assessment Battery.

21. The Wechsler scales serve as an important component of a neuropsychological assessment. The three IQs, pattern of subtest performance, and qualitative indices should be evaluated. Although there is no one pattern of scores indicative of brain damage, an overall reduction in level of intelligence may be a key finding in some cases. There appears to be no predictable relationship in children between the laterality of the cerebral lesion and Verbal-Performance IQ discrepancies. Verbal-Performance discrepancies, as well as scores on individual subtests, may be useful in developing hypotheses, however.

22. Examples of other procedures useful in the assessment of brain damage in children include measures of lateral preference, the Bender-Gestalt, the Revised Visual Retention Test, the Bruininks-Oseretsky Test of Motor Proficiency, the Purdue Pegboard, tests of right-left discrimination, the Finger Localization Test, verbal fluency tests, measures of volitional movements, picture naming, Raven's Progressive Matrices, the Token Test, the Reporter's Test, and informal assessment of aphasic disturbances.

23. A neuropsychological evaluation may reveal disturbances

in motor, sensory, affective, cognitive, social, temperament, and personality domains. Brain damage may play a major role in predisposing children to severe forms of psychopathology as well as to subtle changes in personality.

24. Several inferential methods are used to interpret the results of a neuropsychological evaluation, including (a) analysis of level of performance, (b) analysis of pattern of performance, (c) analysis of pathognomonic signs, and (d) comparison of performance on the two sides of the body.

25. Several factors should be considered in evaluating the behavioral effects of brain damage. These include (a) child's age at the time of the injury, child's age at the time of the evaluation, and child's sex; (b) lateralization, location, and type of injury; (c) duration of lesion; (d) rate of onset of disease and state of disease process; (e) diaschises effects; (f) time interval between injury and testing; (g) associated physical and health problems; (h) premorbid condition; and (i) home and school environments.

26. Similar forms of brain damage do not always produce the same behavioral effects, nor do behavioral differences among brain-damaged children always relate directly to the severity of the brain damage.

27. There is no one-to-one relationship between brain damage and specific behavioral change. Moreover, some symptoms of brain injury mimic psychiatric symptoms. Differentiating brain-injured from non-brain-injured children is not easy. Although aphasic children share language disturbances with autistic children, they are better at relating to others.

28. A consideration of all the neuropsychological assessment results should allow you to evaluate the child's integrating-synthesizing skills, degree of perseveration, ability to make conceptual shifts, degree of concrete thinking, word recall ability, and degree of word misuse. Cognitive dysfunctions in these areas may be associated with brain damage.

29. Teaching and remediation strategies should be individually tailored to the needs of each brain-damaged child.

KEY TERMS, CONCEPTS, AND NAMES

Brain damage (p. 687)
Prenatal factors (p. 687)
Perinatal factors (p. 687)
Postnatal factors (p. 687)
Focal lesions (p. 687)
Open head injuries (p. 687)
Closed head injuries (p. 687)
Neurological examination (p. 688)
CT scans (p. 688)
PET scans (p. 688)
MRI scans (p. 688)
EEGs (p. 688)
Cerebral angiograms (p. 688)
Hard neurological signs (p. 689)
Soft neurological signs (p. 689)
Choreiform limb movements (p. 689)

Neuropsychological evaluation (p. 689)
Lateralization (p. 689)
Dysdiadochokinesia (p. 690)
Dysgraphesthesia (p. 690)
Astereognosis (p. 690)
Nystagmus (p. 690)
Strabismus (p. 690)
Mirror movements (p. 690)
Hemispheric functions (p. 690)
Four cerebral lobes (p. 691)
Childhood aphasia (p. 692)
Congenital aphasia (p. 692)
Developmental aphasia (p. 692)
Acquired aphasia (p. 692)
Expressive aphasia (p. 692)
Receptive aphasia (p. 692)
Auditory aphasia (p. 692)
Alexia (p. 692)
Agraphia (p. 692)
Agnosia (p. 692)
Apraxia (p. 692)
Paraphasia (p. 692)
Cerebral plasticity (p. 694)
Critical period hypothesis (p. 694)
Halstead-Reitan Neuropsychological Test Battery for Older Children (p. 700)
Reitan-Indiana Neuropsychological Test Battery for Children (p. 700)
Luria-Nebraska Neuropsychological Battery: Children's Revision (p. 700)
Contributions to Neuropsychological Assessment Battery (p. 703)
Wechsler scales (p. 704)
Lateral preference (p. 707)
Bender-Gestalt Test (p. 707)
Revised Visual Retention Test (p. 707)
Bruininks-Oseretsky Test of Motor Proficiency (p. 710)
Purdue Pegboard (p. 710)
Right-left discrimination (p. 710)
Finger Localization Test (p. 710)
Verbal fluency tests (p. 710)
Measures of volitional movements (p. 711)
Picture naming procedure (p. 711)
Dysnomia (p. 711)
Raven's Progressive Matrices (p. 713)
Token Test (p. 713)
Reporter's Test (p. 713)
Informal procedures for assessing aphasia (p. 713)
Inferential methods of test analysis (p. 714)
Level of performance (p. 714)
Pattern of performance (p. 714)
Pathognomonic signs of brain impairment (p. 714)
Comparison of performance on two sides of body (p. 714)
Integrating-synthesizing skills (p. 715)
Degree of perseveration (p. 715)

Ability to make conceptual shifts (p. 716)
Concrete thinking (p. 716)
Word recall ability (p. 716)
Word misuse (p. 716)
Intervention procedures (p. 716)

STUDY QUESTIONS

1. Discuss the causes of brain damage from a developmental perspective.

2. What are some important factors to consider in evaluating the behavioral effects of brain damage?

3. Compare and contrast the neurological examination and the neuropsychological evaluation.

4. Discuss some of the issues surrounding the lateralization of cognitive, perceptual, and motor activities in children.

5. Discuss aphasia in children.

6. Discuss the prognosis for brain-damaged children. Include the concept of cerebral plasticity in your discussion.

7. How does a clinical assessment interview contribute to the neuropsychological assessment?

8. What types of disturbances associated with brain damage may be revealed on the neuropsychological evaluation?

9. Describe the inferential methods used to analyze the findings from a neuropsychological assessment.

10. What are some of the difficulties in diagnosing brain damage and in differentiating brain damage from other types of disturbances?

11. Discuss intervention procedures for brain-damaged children.

12. Discuss the place of neuropsychological test batteries in the assessment process.

13. Discuss the role of the Wechsler batteries in the assessment of brain damage in children.

14. Describe assessment procedures—other than neuropsychological test batteries and the Wechsler batteries—useful in the assessment of brain damage in children.

23

REPORT WRITING

Writing is, for most, laborious and slow. The mind travels faster than the pen; consequently, writing becomes a question of learning to make occasional wing shots, bringing down the bird of thought as it flashes by. A writer is a gunner, sometimes roaming the countryside hoping to scare something up. Like other gunners, he must cultivate patience; he may have to work many covers to bring down one partridge.
—William Strunk, Jr., and E. B. White

In our Victorian dislike of the practice of calling a spade a bloody shovel, it is not necessary to go to the opposite extreme of calling it an agricultural implement.
—Robert W. Seton-Watson

The difference between the right word and the almost right word is the difference between lightning and a lightning bug.
—Mark Twain

If it is possible to cut a word out, always cut it out.
—George Orwell

Don't write merely to be understood. Write so that you cannot possibly be misunderstood.
—Robert Louis Stevenson

The psychological assessment is complete only after the results have been shared with the referral source. Although such communication may be accomplished in a variety of formal and informal ways, the traditional medium for presenting the assessment results is the psychological report. The preparation and writing of the report are integral parts of the assessment effort. A child who is assessed deserves to have a report that clearly and concisely expresses your findings and recommendations. The referral source deserves similar consideration. A well-written psychological report may influence readers for years to come. Therefore, it deserves much care and consideration.

You should evaluate the content and organization of the report just as carefully as you conducted the assessment. A good clinical or psychoeducational report does not merely report test scores. It brings together test scores, behavioral observations, other assessment findings, case history material, and significant temperament and personality variables in the context of the child's behavior during the assessment process. In short, the report presents what you have learned about the child in a way that shows respect for his or her individuality. This respect for individuality should permeate the entire assessment process: the child should be viewed as an individual and not simply as a stimulus for gathering statistics.

In formulating and constructing your report, you must take into consideration the circumstances under which the testing took place, the limited opportunities for observation and interaction, and the behavioral bases for the judgments made in the report. Specific examples should be used to illustrate not only qualitative characteristics of the child's performance, but also clinical interpretations. Recommendations should be made with an appreciation of the needs and values of the child, the family, the school, society, and yourself.

A clinical or psychoeducational report serves a number of purposes, including the following:

1. It provides accurate assessment-related information to the referral source and other concerned parties.

2. It provides a source of information for testing clinical hypotheses and for conducting program evaluation and research.

3. It serves as an archive of historical, interview, psychometric, observational, and other information, as well as of current remediation and treatment plans.

4. It may serve as a legal document.

Although you should strive for objectivity and accuracy in writing an assessment report, it is important to recognize that no report can be completely objective. Every report has elements of subjectivity—others might interpret even the test findings differently. *You* choose which words to use to describe the child, which behaviors to highlight, which elements of the history to cite, and which sequence to follow in presenting the findings. Recognizing that your personal viewpoints are part of any report may help to reduce the influence of any biased or prejudiced views that you may have.

The psychological report should be written as soon as possible after the evaluation has been completed, to ensure that important details are not forgotten. The referral source needs a prompt reply. Unfortunately, in clinical and school settings there is often a delay between the time a child is referred and the initiation of the psychological evaluation. You, as the psychologist, should not contribute to further delay by neglecting to write up the report promptly.

SUGGESTED REPORT OUTLINE

A typical report will have the following sections:

1. Identifying Information
2. Reason for Referral
3. Background Information
4. Behavioral Observations
5. Assessment Results and Clinical Impressions
6. Recommendations
7. Summary
8. Signature

Identifying Information

The first part of the report presents relevant identifying information. Include, as a minimum, the following:

- child's name
- date of examination
- date of birth
- chronological age
- date of report
- grade
- examiner's name
- names of tests administered
- names of other assessment procedures

You may also want to include the child's sex, teacher's name, and parents' names.

Reason for Referral

The second section of the report usually consists of a brief summary of the referral source's questions regarding the child. Since the reason for the referral often guides you in selecting appropriate assessment instruments, citing it helps to shed light on why certain tests were administered and the thrust of the subsequent inquiry.

The following information may be covered in the referral section:

- name and position of the referral source
- why the referral source wants the child to be assessed
- specific questions the referral source has about the child
- a brief summary of the specific behaviors or symptoms that led to the referral
- to whom the child was referred

Background Information

The information in the Background Information section may come from interviews with the child, parents, and teacher(s); the child's educational file; and past psychological and medical reports. Acknowledge the sources of the information and report relevant dates.

The following information may be included in the Background Information section:

- child's age
- grade in school
- educational history
- present level of academic functioning
- previous interventions and outcomes regarding the referral question
- current family situation
- family constellation
- relevant family history, including pertinent information on parents' occupations, education, individual views on discipline and on the child's responsibilities, and involvement with the child
- significant health history
- developmental history, including events in the child's life that may have a bearing on his or her psychological or educational problems
- social interactions and peer relationships
- prior test results
- teachers' observations of child's behavior and attitudes
- parents' observations of child's behavior and attitudes

In reviewing past test results, consider the following questions:

- What were the major findings?
- What was the diagnostic impression?

- What were the examiner's impressions of the child's parents and other important adults?
- Were the parents cooperative and concerned?
- What recommendations were made?
- If implemented, were they effective?
- What follow-ups were conducted?

In your summary of the results of the past evaluations, note how the referral problem has changed since the prior evaluations, pointing out what progress has been made and which recommendations were effective.

The sample Background Information section that follows provides information on the child's life that may help the reader to understand his current level of functioning. The child was admitted to a psychiatric hospital on an emergency basis because of bizarre, unpredictable, and out-of-control behavior. His mother reported that he had been talking to himself, with possible delusions and hallucinations.

Henry, a 12-year, 9-month-old adolescent, is the youngest of five children. He lives with his mother, who has been married three times. He last saw his father when he was 5 months old and just beginning to crawl. He first walked alone at 15 months and achieved bowel control at 2 years of age. However, bladder control was never achieved, and he remains enuretic at the present time.

He attended a Head Start Program at the age of 4 years, but was referred to a child guidance clinic because of behavioral problems. He received a diagnosis of hyperactivity at this time. When Henry was 5 years old, his maternal grandmother died of a stroke, and Henry became extremely depressed. His mother noted that shortly afterwards Henry told her that he knew in advance that his grandmother was going to die; he claimed that he had psychic abilities.

At 6 years of age, Henry attempted suicide by throwing himself in front of a car after his mother had been hospitalized for hypertension; however, he was not seriously injured. Henry told her that he believed that she was going to die and he wanted to die, too. This attempted suicide resulted in Henry's referral to County Mental Health where he was treated for the suicide attempt and also for hyperactivity and enuresis.

When Henry was 9 years old, his youngest sister attempted suicide by drug overdose. Henry was upset for several months. At the age of 10 years, he was expelled from school for alleged sexually inappropriate behavior, including touching other children's genitalia. He was subsequently transferred to another school, where he currently attends special education classes. Academically, he has always performed poorly.

According to Henry's mother, their relationship has always been close, although recently he has become "difficult to get along with." She described Henry as a social isolate—having no friends and preferring to spend his time alone or with her only. He has had no serious medical problems.

Behavioral Observations

One of the challenges in writing a report is to communicate what is observed during the assessment. A good report carefully describes the child's behavior as observed during the evaluation, interviews, and any observations conducted in classroom, home, or hospital settings. A description of behavior helps the reader to understand what you consider to be important features of the child's behavior. It also lends some objectivity to the psychological report by providing the reader with information about what the child did that led you to form specific impressions. Behavioral observations may also help to account for the child's test scores (for example, did the child fail an item due to poor ability, difficulty in understanding the directions, lack of effort, or insufficient time?). Finally, behavioral descriptions may suggest methods for remediation.

The goal in writing behavioral observations is to clearly describe and interpret the child's behaviors within the context of the setting in which they are observed. Although statements that describe the child's behavior should be distinguished clearly from statements that interpret behavior, both should be included. (See Chapter 5 for guidelines on observing behavior in assessment situations, and see Chapter 17 for a discussion of the skills involved in observing behavior and the various instruments available for recording observations.) In making inferences from observations, be sure to keep in mind that conclusions based on the samples of behavior obtained in the test situation may not generalize to behavior outside of the test situation. Because the test situation is a relatively narrow and, to some degree, artificial situation, it is necessary to evaluate the behaviors obtained in the test situation in light of the entire case study.

Following is a list of topics that may be addressed in the Behavioral Observations section of the report:

- physical appearance
- reactions to test session and to you
- general behavior
- typical mode of relating to you
- language style
- general response style
- response to failures
- response to successes
- response to encouragement
- activity level
- attitude toward self
- attitude toward you and the testing process
- visual-motor ability
- unusual habits, mannerisms, or verbalizations
- your reaction to child

Examples of material that may appear in the Behavioral Observations section follow.

EXAMPLE 1

William is an attractive 5-year, 2-month-old child with blond hair and brown eyes. He is a friendly and animated little boy and appeared quite eager to begin the test. He was curious about the examiner's manual and the contents of the test kit, continuously glancing into the kit. Although he squirmed in his seat, exhausting nearly every position possible while remaining on his chair, William maintained a high degree of interest throughout the test. He was attentive and followed directions well, and excellent rapport was established.

EXAMPLE 2

Regina is an attractive 16½-year-old adolescent whose makeup and hairstyle make her look somewhat older than her chronological age. She appeared anxious and somewhat depressed throughout the evaluation. Her wide-eyed look and clenched hands underscored her anxiety and tension and suggested fearfulness. Although Regina seemed able to relax somewhat when talking with the examiner, she was extremely tense during the more formal evaluation procedures. During some tasks, she made numerous self-deprecating remarks, such as "I can't do this" and "I'm terrible at that." She also responded with "I don't know" rather than attempting to answer more difficult questions. Despite Regina's tension and anxiety, she occasionally smiled and laughed appropriately.

EXAMPLE 3

Karl is a bright eyed, amiable, 6-year, 3-month-old child of above average height. He was eager to begin the test and immediately took a seat when asked to do so. Initially, he chatted easily with the examiner and seemed ready for the test to begin. He became somewhat shy after the introductory conversation was terminated, although he did not display any hesitance until the actual testing began. His attitude of confidence and self-composure seemed to deteriorate, and he became compliant, bordering on deferential. Initially, his answers to questions were whispered, whether or not he knew they were correct. It appeared that he was afraid to respond in the event that the examiner might disapprove of his answers. He was concerned about and sensitive to the examiner's opinion of his responses, and frequently asked, "Was that OK?" or "Is that right?"

Karl was quite disappointed when he knew that he could not answer a test question correctly. Even when gently encouraged to tell exactly what he meant, he continued to use the same words or added, "I don't know." On tasks that he perceived to be too difficult, he did not persevere and simply shrugged his shoulders.

Karl appeared to relax somewhat as the test progressed. When he realized that the examiner was not in any way critical of responses, he gave his answers in a normal voice and became more assertive. Karl was given a short break because of his restlessness, after which he seemed considerably more relaxed and comfortable.

EXAMPLE 4

Frank, a 17-year, 4-month-old adolescent, avoided eye contact with the examiner, and at times seemed to have difficulty finding the right words to express himself. He showed some signs of anxiety, such as heavy breathing, sniffling a great deal, mumbling, and short, quick movements with his hands and head. On some of the test items he seemed to guess impulsively. He would occasionally answer incorrectly, then say quietly, "No, wait," and then give the correct answer. The tests that were timed seemed to generate more anxiety and guessing than the untimed tests.

Assessment Results and Clinical Impressions

The Assessment Results and Clinical Impressions section consolidates the assessment information generated from a variety of sources and provides a comprehensive picture of the assessment findings. Topics should include test reliability and validity, assessment findings, precision range, and clinical and diagnostic impressions.

Reliability and validity. Assessment findings should not be reported or interpreted unless, in your opinion, they are a valid indication of the child's ability or behavior. Any concerns that an assessment finding may not be a reliable or valid indicator of the child's ability or behavior should be stated clearly along with the reasons for your concern, at the beginning of the Results portion of the report.

You should evaluate the reliability and validity of each assessment instrument *before* you administer any test or instrument by carefully reading the test manuals and studying other literature on the assessment procedure that does not appear in the manual. After the test is administered, you should evaluate the reliability and validity of the test again, looking for any factors that might make the results questionable. Reliability may be affected by numerous factors, including test length, guessing, and variations in the test instructions or test setting. Validity may be affected by a variety of test-related and situation-related factors that may temporarily impair a child's performance. Because validity is affected by reliability, an unreliable performance cannot be considered to be a valid one. (See Chapter 2 for further discussion of factors that may affect test reliability and validity.)

In reporting assessment results that you believe are valid (in which case they must be reliable), you might say "The results of the present testing appear to be valid because Jim's motivation and attention were good throughout testing." An appropriate way of reporting test results that have questionable validity might be "The intelligence test findings may not be valid and may underestimate Rebecca's abilities because she was ill on the day of the testing."

Assessment findings. Test scores should not simply be reported; the data should be integrated and interpreted. Included in the assessment findings might be the following:

- child's chronological age and mental age (if the Stanford-Binet: Form L-M is used)
- factors that may have affected the results of particular tests
- names of tests
- test scores, including IQs and other standard scores
- Verbal and Performance IQs if the WPPSI, WISC-R, or WAIS-R is used
- classification of IQ
- percentile ranks of test scores
- description of the child's strengths and weaknesses, as reflected by the scores and significant differences between the subtest scores and total test score
- comparison of verbal and nonverbal skills
- academic skills (if relevant)
- content of responses
- signs suggestive of psychopathology
- signs suggestive of exceptionality, such as creativity, giftedness, or learning disability
- interrelationships among test findings
- interrelationships among all sources of data
- implications of assessment findings
- diagnostic impressions

Precision range. Whenever you report an IQ, give a precision range for that IQ. The precision range is a function of both the standard error of measurement and the confidence level: the greater the confidence level or the lower the reliability of the test, the wider the precision range. Precision ranges for various intelligence tests are provided in Appendix C.

Suppose that Joe, a 6-year-old child, obtained a Full Scale IQ of 100 on the WISC-R, and you wish to use the 68 percent level of precision. Table C-1 in Appendix C shows that for this precision level and age, the appropriate confidence interval is 3. The recommended way of reporting the IQ using this precision range is as follows:

Joe obtained an IQ of 100 ± 3 on the Wechsler Intelligence Scale for Children—Revised. The chances that the range of scores from 97 to 103 includes his true IQ are about 68 out of 100.

If another confidence level is selected, the range and probability statement will change. For example, the recommended ways of expressing the 85 and 99 percent levels for Joe are as follows:

Joe obtained an IQ of 100 $\pm$ 5 on the Wechsler Intelligence Scale for Children – Revised. The chances that the range of scores from 95 to 105 includes his true IQ are about 85 out of 100.

Joe obtained an IQ of 100 $\pm$ 9 on the Wechsler Intelligence Scale for Children – Revised. The chances that the range of scores from 91 to 109 includes his true IQ are about 99 out of 100.

As the confidence level in the preceding examples increased from 68 out of 100 to 99 out of 100, the precision range went from $\pm$ 3 to $\pm$ 9. As the confidence level decreases, the width of the range for the true IQ also decreases.

Clinical and diagnostic impressions. When you develop hypotheses about a child's performance, consider all sources of information, including the child's test scores; the child's attitude, background, and temperament; testing of limits; observations; interviews with teachers, parents, and the child; and other background information. Consistent findings from several sources provide you with a firmer ground for making interpretations. Use extreme caution in making any interpretations or diagnostic formulations when the data are not consistent. Inconsistent data pose questions that should be explored. In any case, *never make diagnostic statements on the basis of insufficient data.*

Organizing the Assessment Results and Clinical Impressions section. You may choose to organize the assessment results on a test-by-test basis, a domain-by-domain basis, or a combined test-by-test and domain-by-domain basis. This decision usually is based on the nature of the referral question and which approach will provide the most clarity for the reader. A typical report based on the more common test-by-test organization includes a separate paragraph describing the results of each test – intelligence, visual-motor, achievement, personality, and so on. The topic sentence of the paragraph highlights the main result of each test. A summary paragraph at the end of the section then integrates the main findings.

A typical report based on domain-by-domain organization includes a separate paragraph for each domain of interest – such as intelligence, achievement, and adaptive behavior. Each paragraph reports the information obtained from the different assessment procedures that is relevant to interpreting the child's functioning in that domain. Topic sentences generally summarize the clinician's interpretation of the child's functioning in that domain and are followed by a report of the data that led to the interpretation. For example, a report on a learning disabled child might include a paragraph on achievement skills starting with the sentence "Beth has significant reading and arithmetical difficulties." The rest of the paragraph would then report supporting data from the achievement tests, appropriate subtests from an intelligence test, informal observation, and teacher and parental reports.

A variant of the domain-by-domain organization is to organize the findings into areas of specific ability, such as comprehension, reasoning, memory, motor ability, spatial ability, and perceptual ability. In each area discussion might cover verbal and nonverbal components (where appropriate), expressive and receptive functions, and indices of psychopathology.

Novice report writers may find test-by-test organization somewhat easier to use than the domain-by-domain style. Whichever style you choose, be sure all of the assessment findings are synthesized and presented clearly.

Recommendations

Recommendations are an important part of a psychological evaluation. They should be based on the child's overall level of performance, the child's pattern of strengths and weaknesses, and the implications of this pattern for remediation, class placement, treatment, or rehabilitation. The intent is not so much to look for a "cure" or "label" as to offer a flexible approach for interventions and appropriate placements.

Recommendations should describe realistic and practical intervention goals and treatment strategies. Questions to consider in developing the recommendations include the following:

• How representative are the present test results? Can they be generalized?

• Were all relevant factors considered in arriving at the recommendations, including previous and present test results, interpersonal behavior, discrepancies in performance, parental reports, teacher reports, medical evaluations, school grades, and the child's self-reports?

• What type of intervention program is needed (for example, behavioral, academic, or counseling)?

• What are some possible goals of the program?

• How can the child's strengths be used in the remediation?

• How might the child's weaknesses be remediated?

• How might family members become involved in the treatment plan?

• Are the recommendations feasible given the child's present classroom and home situation?

• What community and school resources are available or necessary to carry out the recommendations? Who is willing to be involved in implementing these recommendations?

• Are the recommendations written in a clear and understandable fashion and are they sufficiently detailed that they can be easily implemented?

• Is there a need for evaluation in other areas?

• Are follow-up evaluations necessary? If so, when and by whom?

In a survey of teachers' ratings of school psychological reports, Rucker (1967a) found that the most important factor in the utility of a report was the quality of the recommendations. Recommendations to teachers should increase the teacher's understanding of the child's problems and, where possible, include suggestions for curriculum changes. Educational or other kinds of programs may be recommended for the child, with the focus and goals of the program specifically described. Information about what the child's aptitudes and skills in various subject areas are and how any strengths may be used, the child's style of problem solving, and situational conditions that affect the child's learning and performance should be noted. The child's temperament, attitudes, and motivation should be considered in choosing methods of remediation. Specific suggestions for stimulating and enhancing the child's psychological growth and development also may be given. Recommendations should enable the reader to design a program suitable to the child's unique needs and level of functioning and should help both teacher and parents to approach the child in a new way. Any need for retesting or further evaluation should be covered in the recommendations.

It may be helpful to list the specific recommendations in order of priority. The highest priority recommendations should address the referral question in some way.

Involving children, parents, and teachers.   An important aim in making recommendations (and carrying out the assessment process as a whole) is to try to find ways to help children help themselves and to involve teachers and parents directly in any educational and therapeutic effort. The emphasis is on the child, on the child's situation, and on identifying avenues for growth and enrichment. The child's active involvement in influencing his or her own life should be encouraged. Suggestions for change should be practical, concrete, individualized, and based on sound educational and psychological practice.

Using caution in making long-range predictions.
Making predictions about further levels of attainment is

difficult and risky. Predictions are potentially damaging to the child because the reader of the report may be lulled into thinking that a course of development is fixed or unchangeable. Tyler (1965, p.71) cautioned:

Those responsible for the guidance of children need to realize that a single intelligence test can never be used as a basis for a definite judgment about what a child will be able to do several years later. Each new decision, at successive stages of development, calls for a recheck.

Therefore, although it is important to indicate the child's present level of functioning and to make suggestions about what can be expected of him or her, statements dealing with performance in the distant future must be made cautiously, if at all.

The recommendations should be written so that the reader recognizes clearly your degree of confidence in any predictions. Cite test data or behavioral data when needed to help the reader better understand the recommendations. Recommendations should individualize the report, highlighting the major findings and their implications for intervention.

Summary

A summary, which reviews and integrates the test findings, is optional. In addition to being repetitious and unnecessarily lengthening the report, a summary may detract from the report by giving readers the idea that they can ignore the main body of the report. Ideally, the report itself should be precise, compact, and to the point. In settings where a summary is expected (such as medical settings), however, it should be included in the report.

When you write a summary, limit it to one or two short paragraphs. Consider incorporating rephrased topic sentences from each part of the report. *Do not include any new material in the summary.*

The summary might include:

• reason for referral and most pertinent background information and behavioral observations
  • assessment results
  • validity of assessment results
  • classification of scores
  • child's strengths and weaknesses
  • child's verbal and nonverbal abilities
  • interrelationships among test scores
  • special features of the child's performance
  • diagnostic impressions
  • general recommendations

Signature

Your name and professional title or capacity should be typewritten at the end of the report, and your signature placed above your typewritten name.

Comment on Report Outline

The preceding report outline is meant to serve as a guide — there is no fixed, unalterable way to organize a report. The way you organize a report depends on your preference, which may be governed partly by the users of the report. The organization of the report should be logical and convey the assessment findings, interpretations, and recommendations as clearly as possible. In some cases, you may want to place the Recommendations section after the summary rather than before it. The summary would then focus on the assessment results and on related information — not on the recommendations.

ORGANIZING THE ASSESSMENT FINDINGS

> **Principle 1. Organize assessment findings by detecting common themes through and across procedures, integrating the main findings, and using a theoretical focus.**

For many students making sense out of the myriad assessment results is initially a burdensome and puzzling task. Some findings appear to be clear-cut, others murky. Occasionally different instruments purporting to measure the same ability will give different results. Although there is no one best method for integrating the data, you can facilitate the interpretive task by using a consistent strategy and keeping clear goals in mind. (Ideally the goal of the psychological assessment is to obtain a comprehensive view of the child and his or her life situation. Often, however, the assessment is designed to serve the narrower focus of addressing a more circumscribed referral question.) With experience, you will find that the clinical decision-making process will become less burdensome and more challenging and stimulating.

Before you begin to organize the report, it is helpful to reach some kind of general understanding of all the available information by considering the following questions:

- What are the reasons for testing and for the referral?
- What are the major findings that you wish to report?
- How do the present results compare with the previous ones?
- What are the major themes that you wish to develop?
- What are the major recommendations that you wish to present?
- How has the assessment helped to answer the referral question?
- What questions remain unanswered?
- What is the background of the persons for whom the report will be written?

Once you have a general understanding of the information, you are ready to undertake the following four-step process of organizing assessment findings.

Detect Common Themes

The first step is to detect the common themes and trends that run through each of the individual assessment procedures. Common themes can be detected by analyzing the findings obtained from each assessment procedure using the following guidelines:

- What are the consistent themes? (For example, do the results suggest below-average functioning in all achievement areas?)
- How important are the divergent findings?
- Are there minor or major deviations from the themes?
- What do the themes suggest to you about the child's present problems, strengths, weaknesses, coping mechanisms, and possibilities for remediation or change?
- How do significant others fit in? (For example, do all anxiety attacks occur when the mother is present?)
- What are some of the important environmental contingencies? (For example, does the child have trouble eating in the cafeteria but not at home?)

The second step is to detect the common themes and trends that run across the assessment procedures. Use the same guidelines as shown in the first step. Themes related to the child's intellectual, social, emotional, or perceptual-motor development may be revealed by looking at consistencies in performance, patterns of errors and successes on various tests, major discrepancies among scores, responses to the testing of limits, observations of learning style, and interview material obtained from parents, child, and teachers. For example, all the test data related to perceptual-motor functioning could be correlated with observational findings, or all indications of distractibility found on separate tests, during observations, and on parent and teacher reports could be compared.

Integrate Main Findings

The third step, initiated during the course of detecting common themes, *is to integrate and interpret the main findings and themes*. Earlier in this chapter, various formats for organizing the Assessment Results and Clinical Impressions section of a report were described, including test-by-test, domain-by-domain, and combined organizational formats. Regardless of what format you choose, bring together findings that relate to common themes. For example, if a diagnosis of learning disability appears probable, discuss the findings that support this clinical impression. Or if the findings suggest the presence of neurological dysfunction, describe the pertinent facts that led you to this clinical impression.

Show how the child's abilities are interrelated, rather than dissecting intellectual ability or personality into many components. To illustrate the interplay of abilities, use expressions signaling comparison and contrast, such as *however, but, on the one hand, on the other hand*, or *in comparison with*. An integrated picture of the child's abilities will result.

Be sure that you do not omit important data that diverge from the main theme or themes in an effort to give a consistent and integrated account of the child's abilities. Discrepancies (or variability) in performance or behavior are useful in guiding predictions, inferences, and recommendations. Suppose, for example, that there is a general pattern of memory difficulty, but not a consistent one. This variability should be noted and taken into account in arriving at a diagnostic formulation. It may be that the child has sufficient memory in some areas, which can be capitalized on in a rehabilitation program. Lack of consistency may suggest that some of the child's successes or failures were partially due to factors present during the examination—such as fatigue, anxiety, or lack of interest. This information may also shed light on the child's available resources.

Be aware of two potential sources of error in integrating findings (Nay, 1979). One source of error is forming hypotheses prematurely, which leads one to ignore findings that conflict with the initial conceptualization. A second source of error is overgeneralizing based on limited findings. It is inappropriate to draw conclusions about a child's school behavior within or across days from a limited sampling of behavior in school, or to generalize to other settings on the basis of samples of behavior in the testing situation alone.

Use a Theoretical Focus

The fourth step is to integrate the material on the basis of a theoretical focus or an eclectic theoretical approach. If

possible, use a theoretical position that not only sheds light on the child's behavior, but also offers some strategies for remediation and treatment. In many cases it may be useful to interpret findings from more than one theoretical position. Following are some issues on which psychological reports commonly focus:

• the environmental contingencies related to the problem behavior
• the child's and parents' view of themselves, others, and the environment
• the child's and parents' attitudes and beliefs
• the historical antecedent events
• the medical history and present medical condition of the child

Although not every case will require an in-depth study of each of these areas, they should always be considered.

DECIDING WHAT MATERIAL TO INCLUDE

> **Principle 2. Include in the report relevant material and delete potentially damaging material.**

In deciding what to include in the report, consider whether the material will be relevant, have an impact on the reader, do justice to the child, and augment the reader's knowledge of the child with regard to the questions at hand. Omit information that does not contribute to a clear understanding of the test findings, interpretations, conclusions, and recommendations. You must use good judgment and discretion in deciding whether to include certain material in the report because there are no fixed rules.

No matter how interesting or true it is, any information that does not contribute to an understanding of the referral question and to the clinical and psychoeducational evaluation is irrelevant and consequently should be left out of the report. The value of each statement should be weighed; statements should not be made simply to fill up space. Critically evaluate how the information will contribute to an understanding of the child's performance. If a controversial sentence is left in the report, its relevance should be made very clear and supporting data presented.

In general, it is desirable to include in the report a mix of general implications, specific behavioral illustrations, and some testing details. This blend will help the reader understand how you arrived at your conclusions and interpretations.

What information does the reader really need? The reader needs material that helps to describe the child's uniqueness, relates to the referral questions, and reflects the child's unusual behaviors and attitudes. Should information about the father's sex life, for example, be included in a report about a child who was referred for learning problems? In most cases, such information is not germane to the evaluation. In exceptional cases where such information has a direct bearing on the problem, think carefully about the most professional way to phrase the information so that it does not become simply an item of interesting gossip.

When is it worthwhile to note in a report the child's handedness or grooming? Information on the child's handedness may be useful if there is a possibility that mixed dominance exists. A discussion of the child's grooming may be helpful if it contributes to an understanding of the child's self-concept, attitudes, or family environment (for example, parental care and guidance). In other cases, neither handedness nor grooming will be of importance.

Focus on the Presence of a Behavior

Focusing on the *presence* of a behavior rather than on its absence will help to promote clarity. You can cite an almost infinite number of adjectives that did *not* characterize the child's behavior (for example, not sad, not anxious, not impulsive), but such citations are not very illuminating. Instead, emphasize how the child actually performed. Occasionally you may be asked to comment about a specific problem or symptom. In such cases, you would include a statement about the problem or symptom, even if it did not occur.

Exclude Damaging Material

Exclude from the report, if possible, any information that is potentially harmful or damaging to the child (Drake & Bardon, 1978), such as "Susan has been overheard saying she dislikes one of her teachers." If you must convey such information, do it orally to an appropriate member of the staff, with the firm understanding that the information will not become part of the child's official record.

MAKING GENERALIZATIONS

> **Principle 3.** Use all relevant sources of information about the child—including reliable and valid test results, behavioral observations, individual test responses, interview data, and the case history—in generating hypotheses, formulating interpretations, and arriving at recommendations. Avoid undue generalizations.

Conclusions and generalizations about the child should follow logically from the information presented in the report. Base generalizations on reliable and sufficient data. Avoid the temptation to infer strengths or weaknesses from success or failure on one test, or to assume that a behavior demonstrated in one setting occurs in another setting. For example, do not assume that a child who is hyperactive in the classroom is also hyperactive at home. Consider all relevant sources of information, and make generalizations only when you have a clear, consistent pattern of successes or failures. Do not assume definite cause-and-effect relationships without supporting data.

Cite supporting data for any generalizations you make, particularly if the generalization has important consequences for the child's future. For example, a statement that Johnny needs special education might be supported by stating that "Johnny's academic achievement is significantly below that of his age peers as demonstrated by his performance on the reading and mathematics sections of the Wide Range Achievement Test—Revised, whereas his intellectual skills, as estimated by the WISC-R, are in the average range."

CONVEYING THE DEGREE OF CERTAINTY OF THE STATEMENTS

> **Principle 4.** Be definitive in your writing when the findings are clear; be cautious in your writing when the findings are problematic.

Phrases and words such as *probably, it appears, perhaps,* and *it seems* are often used in reports when the writer is not completely sure about his or her conclusions, inferences, or predictions. When definitive data are available, however, present them confidently. For example, you might write: "The child's current intellectual abilities are classified in the Superior range. The chances that the range of scores from 130 to 140 includes her true IQ are about 68 in 100." Do not use multiple qualifiers, such as "It *appears* as though he has a *tendency* toward *sometimes* saying the wrong thing."

The degree of certainty you convey should relate to the adequacy of your information—the more current, reliable, complete, and valid your information, the higher your degree of certainty. It should also relate to the type of data—observed data (what a child actually *did* on a test) have a higher degree of certainty than inferred conclusions (what he or she *may* be able to do under other conditions or in the future). For example, you usually are certain that the child has brown eyes or that the child obtained an IQ of 110. You are only reasonably sure that the range from 100 to 120 includes the child's true IQ. You are less sure that the child will improve his or her performance if transferred to another teacher.

Be definitive when the test findings are clear. For example, when the difference between the WISC-R Verbal and Performance IQs is significant or when two subtest scores differ significantly, you can say that one skill, as measured by the scale or subtest, is better developed than the other. There is no need to hedge with such terms as *appears to be* or *may be better than*. Similarly, when the Verbal Scale is 25 points higher than the Performance Scale, a term stronger than *somewhat* is needed, such as *considerably higher* or *much better developed*. A difference of 25 points is almost twice as great as that needed for these IQs to be significantly different.

USING ILLUSTRATIONS TO SUPPORT INFERENCES AND CONCLUSIONS

> **Principle 5. Use behavioral referents to enhance the report's readability.**

Inferences and conclusions are based on many different factors, including the quality of the interaction between you and the child, the child's scores and responses, previous test results, and the case history. Although you usually should avoid citing raw data or the processes that you used to arrive at inferences and conclusions, it is a good idea to add carefully selected examples of the child's performance that illustrate your conclusions. For exam-

ple, if you say that the child gave overly elaborate responses, provide an example. In some cases you may need to paraphrase the specific test question to help the reader understand the child's response.

Specific examples are particularly valuable in cases where conclusions are phrased in rather technical terms. A statement that a child has poor sequential planning ability may not mean much to a teacher. However, if you back it up with the comment that the child is "unable to recall more than two digits in the proper sequence or place pictures in their proper sequence," the teacher can identify specifically where the problem lies and provide direct remediation by focusing on tasks that might help the child to overcome the deficit.

Sources should be given for any examples that you did not obtain personally. Attributions such as "his mother reported," "according to his classroom teacher," or "according to the report prepared by the school psychologist" lend credence to the information.

ANCHORING THE REPORT TO THE INTELLIGENCE LEVEL

> **Principle 6. In most cases, consider the overall IQ as the best estimate of the child's intelligence.**

When the goal of the evaluation is to estimate the child's intelligence, primary emphasis should be given to the child's general level of intellectual functioning, with the obtained IQ serving as the anchor point. A child with an IQ of 130 should appear superior intellectually in the report, whereas one with an IQ of 70 should appear limited intellectually.

When you discuss intellectual strengths or weaknesses, keep in mind the overall IQ. The overall IQ should also be considered when you evaluate the child's behavior and performance on achievement tests, visual-motor perception tests, adaptive behavior tests, and other tests. On the Wechsler scales, for example, the Full Scale IQ is almost always the best estimate of intelligence because it is based on the child's entire test performance. Of lesser importance are the Verbal and Performance IQs, followed in importance by the individual subtest scaled scores. In only a few instances (such as with certain ethnic minority groups or with handicapped children) is the Verbal or Performance IQ the most representative index of cognitive ability.

REPORTING AND INTERPRETING TEST RESULTS

> **Principle 7. Interpret the meaning and implications of a child's scores, rather than simply citing test names and scores.**

Test results may appear in a report in the form of either test-oriented statements, which present technical data such as standard scores and age equivalents, or child-oriented statements, in which the data are used to describe the child's abilities. The statement "John correctly defined 12 vocabulary words, which resulted in a scaled score of 8" is test-oriented, whereas such statements as "John's vocabulary ability is average" and "John's vocabulary ability is age appropriate" are more child-oriented. Regardless of where you focus, try to ensure that the data you report describe the child. You want to show, for example, how one child with an IQ of 100 differs from another child with the same IQ. In so doing, you fulfill one of the primary objectives of the report: portraying the child's unique pattern and style of performance.

Statements of the child's test scores should always be followed by a discussion of the cognitive abilities reflected by the scores. A mere listing of scores leaves interpretation up to the reader, whose competencies in test interpretation are unknown to you. Be sure that your interpretations are well grounded in common clinical usage, research findings, or test rationales. Any speculations should be clearly labeled as such.

Describe the functions believed to underlie performance on each scale or subtest. Otherwise readers may assume that the scale or subtest measures only whatever abilities the name suggests.

When a child gets different scores on two subtests that appear to measure the same ability, do not say that a particular ability is both "strong" and "weak." Instead, try to synthesize the test findings so as to present a coherent picture of the child's abilities. Discuss the implications and possible reasons for the variable subtest or test pattern.

Be sure to describe the implications of a child's test performance completely. A statement such as "there was a noteworthy difference between Bill's ability to do arithmetical problems and recall numbers" should be followed with an explanation of why the difference was noteworthy.

Intelligence test scores should seldom be interpreted as indicating strengths or weaknesses in specific academic areas, such as reading or spelling. To assess these and similar skill areas, use specific achievement tests.

Test scores, or patterns of test scores, do not assess a child's performance in all domains, but simply provide some indication or estimate of the child's current level of performance within a particular domain, such as intelligence or achievement. Statements about the child's capacity for learning and future performance should be made cautiously, after much consideration has been given to all sources of assessment data.

INTERPRETING IQ CLASSIFICATIONS

> **Principle 8. Obtain the classification of IQs and other test scores from the numerical ranges given in the test manuals.**

Tests usually provide some system by which to classify scores. Follow the specified classification system strictly, labeling scores according to the manual. If you believe that a classification does not accurately reflect the examinee's status, state this concern in the report when you discuss the reliability and validity of the findings.

The Wechsler scales use seven different classifications to describe various IQ ranges. The classification Average, for example, designates IQs from 90 through 109. These classifications should be used carefully. For example, be sure not to describe an IQ of 110, which is in the Above Average classification, as falling into the Average range.

Use only the obtained IQ to arrive at a classification, regardless of the range of IQs established by the confidence range. For example, rather than saying that a child's current level of intellectual functioning, based on an IQ of 123 ± 9, is classified in the High Average, Superior, and Very Superior ranges, say that it is classified in the Superior range. (Note that this wording focuses on the child's intelligence rather than the test and on the fact that the IQ represents the child's *current ability level*, a level that may or may not change.)

INTERPRETING DEVIATION IQS AND SCALED SCORES

> **Principle 9. Use percentile ranks whenever possible to describe a child's scores because they will be easily understood by most readers of reports.**

Percentile ranks provide a way of communicating technical findings to readers of the report. Deviation IQs and other types of composite standard scores may be converted to percentile ranks (see, for example, Table BC-1 on the inside back cover). However, when two tests use different standard score systems, the same standard scores will represent different percentile ranks, except at the mean and extremes of the distribution. For example, on the WISC-R (*SD* = 15) a Full Scale IQ of 115 corresponds to the 84th percentile rank, whereas on the Stanford-Binet: Fourth Edition (*SD* = 16) a composite score of 115 corresponds to the 83rd percentile rank. Scaled subtest scores on the Wechsler scales (and on other tests) can also be converted to percentile ranks (see Table C-41 in Appendix C).

Age-equivalent scores can be used to supplement percentile ranks, or they can be used alone when percentile ranks are not available. Standard scores that fall below the 25th percentile or above the 75th percentile can be referred to as indicating weaknesses or strengths, respectively, relative to the child's age peers. In conferences with parents or others, be sure to clarify the difference between percentile ranks and percentage correct. The fact that a child's standard score is at the 84th percentile rank does not mean that the child answered correctly 84 percent of the problems; rather, it means that 84 percent of the norm group scored below that child's standard score.

INTERPRETING SUBTEST SCORES

> **Principle 10. Interpret subtest scores using both a normative comparison and an intraindividual comparison. Be sure that it is clear which comparison you are discussing at any particular point.**

Scores on the Wechsler scales (and on other tests) can be analyzed relative to the child's (a) age group and (b) unique pattern of scores. In the former case only the norm group is considered (an interindividual comparison with age peers), whereas in the latter the child's own pattern of scores is considered (an intraindividual comparison).

Comparison with Norm Group Only

On the Wechsler scales, relative to the child's age peers, scaled scores of 13 (84th percentile rank) or higher reflect strengths, scaled scores of 7 (16th percentile rank) or lower reflect weaknesses, and scaled scores of between 8 (25th percentile rank) and 12 (75 percentile rank) reflect average ability. If all scores are 8 or above, the child has no

weaknesses relative to his or her age peers. If all scores are 7 or below, the child has no strengths *relative to his or her age peers*. However, he or she may have cognitive strengths or weaknesses in areas *not* measured by the test.

Intraindividual Comparison

When scaled scores are used to evaluate the child's unique pattern of scores, phrases such as "reflects a better developed ability" or "relatively more developed" can be used for those scores that are clearly *higher* than the child's other scores, and phrases such as "reflects a less developed ability" or "relatively less developed" can be used for those scores that are clearly *lower* than the child's other scores. It is best to avoid associating the term "weakness" with any scores that are 8 or higher and to avoid associating the term "strength" with any scores that are 7 or lower. For example, if a child has nine subtest scaled scores that are below 4 and one subtest scaled score of 7, you could say that the scaled score of 7, which is at the 16th percentile, reflects a "better developed ability relative to the child's other abilities." (In this example, all of the scores reflect weaknesses relative to the child's age peers.) If a child has nine subtest scaled scores that are above 16 and one subtest scaled score of 10, you could say that the score of 10, which is at the 50th percentile, reflects a "less well developed ability relative to the child's other abilities." (In this example, all of the scores are average or above average relative to the child's age peers.)

All strengths or weaknesses are relative to some standard: either to the performance of the child's age peers or to the child's own pattern of abilities. Be sure that the reader clearly knows which standard you are referring to when you discuss the child's performance.

INTERPRETING DIFFERENCES BETWEEN STANDARD SCORES

> **Principle 11. Interpret a standard score on a test or a part of a test as being higher or lower than a standard score on another test or another part of the same test only when an appropriate level of significance is reached (usually the .05 level or less).**

Most intelligence tests, academic achievement tests, and special ability tests yield standard scores. In order to determine whether scores from two tests or subtests within the same test are significantly different for an individual child, the standard scores must be on a common metric — that is, a scale with the same mean and standard deviation. If the scales are different, they must be transformed. The z score transformation described in Table 2-4 in Chapter 2 is such a transformation. After the scores have been transformed, the procedure described in Exhibit 8-1 in Chapter 8 can be used to determine whether the two scores differ significantly.

Tables C-2, C-15, and C-26 in Appendix C present the exact figures that reflect significant differences between Wechsler IQs on the WISC-R, WPPSI, and WAIS-R, respectively. Before you can say that the Verbal IQ is higher or lower than the Performance IQ (that it reflects a more or less well developed ability), the difference between the two IQs must be statistically significant.

Even when there is a significant difference between the Verbal and Performance Scales, do not routinely recommend that further investigation is needed. Significant differences may simply reflect the child's unique cognitive style. Recommend further investigation only on the basis of the entire evaluation and other sources of relevant information.

INTERPRETING VARIABILITY

Principle 12. Interpret the implications of subtest or test variability with extreme caution, making use of all available sources of information.

Variability in subtest scores may reflect the child's cognitive style, or it may be related to other factors such as motivation, bilingualism, ethnic background, psychopathology, temporary inefficiency, or cognitive disturbance. For example, brain damage or depression may depress all subtests or test scores uniformly or only selected subtests or tests. Brain damage may also increase variability of subtest or test scores. In any event, do not assume that variability in scores always reveals something diagnostically important about the child's functioning, indicates lack of persistence, or suggests better potential. The appropriate explanation of intersubtest (or test) variability should be sought by reviewing the entire test performance, behavioral observations, and background information.

INTERPRETING EXTRAPOLATED SCORES

Principle 13. Use with caution any scores obtained by extrapolation.

The validity of test scores is diminished to some degree when they are obtained by extrapolation (the extension of norms to scores not actually obtained in the standardization sample). If a score is extremely high or extremely low, one option is to report the score as falling above or falling below the highest or lowest scores given in the norms (for example, "above an IQ of 154" or "below an IQ of 55"). Another option is to report the extrapolated scores, followed by the term "estimated."

MAKING DIAGNOSES

Principle 14. Refrain from making diagnoses about psychopathology or educational diagnoses solely on the basis of test scores; consider all sources of information.

After the interpretations of test scores and other behavioral data have been completed, a diagnosis can be made. A diagnosis is based on all relevant sources of information about a child and his or her environment. Hypotheses about possible psychopathology or educational deficiencies based on test results should be considered in conjunction with clinical interviews, observations, background data, behavior scale profiles, and other sources of information.

Following are two examples of inappropriate statements in a Wechsler report.

• "The low Performance IQ and the high Verbal IQ indicate brain damage."

• "His low scores on Arithmetic, Coding, and Digit Span indicate that he has a learning disability and poor reading ability."

The first statement is inappropriate because a discrepancy between the Verbal and Performance IQs by itself should *never* be considered indicative of brain damage. First of all, this discrepancy is only one of many possible indicators of brain dysfunction: some individuals with brain damage may have a high Performance IQ and a low Verbal IQ. More important, discrepancies between Verbal and Performance IQs may have nothing to do with brain damage. Many normal children have this pattern.

The second statement is inappropriate because scores on the WISC-R should *never* be used by themselves to establish a diagnosis of educational disability. To make a diagnosis of learning disability or reading disability, you need scores on an intelligence test, achievement test, and other tests as well. Furthermore, in the case of mental retardation, where level of intelligence plays an important role, it is inappropriate to make a diagnosis based on the IQ alone; adaptive behavior must be evaluated together with level of intelligence.

COMMUNICATING EFFECTIVELY

> **Principle 15. Communicate clearly and eliminate unnecessary technical material to enhance the report's readability.**

Good writing is essential in clearly communicating the test findings, interpretations, and recommendations. Your ideas should be presented in a logical and orderly sequence, with smooth transitions from thought to thought. Clear communication will be impeded if sentences are arranged in an awkward manner, if words are unfamiliar, or if the report is excessively wordy or contains irrelevant material. Table 23-1 provides useful stylistic and grammatical guidelines.

Use Clear Statements

Statements in the report should leave no room for misinterpretation. Make all statements in the report as direct and concrete as possible so that the reader knows exactly what you mean; abstract ideas and terms may be unclear and misleading. Behavioral descriptions are preferable to general statements. For example, "Johnny refused to be tested and ran away from the office in tears" is better than "Johnny is a negative child who shows hostility toward those who wish to help him." (If the latter statement were based only on the observation that the child ran away from the office in tears, it would be unacceptable on the grounds that it was an undue generalization.)

Use Transition Words

Continuity is achieved through the appropriate use of transition words. Some transition devices are time links (*then, next, after, while, since*), cause-effect links (*therefore, consequently, as a result*), addition links (*in addition, moreover, furthermore, similarly*), and contrast links (*however, but, conversely, nevertheless, although, whereas*). Although the transition word *while* is often used in informal writing and conversation to refer to connections other than time (for example, *while* is used when *whereas* is meant), it is recommended that only the original meaning of this word be used in scientific and professional writing (American Psychological Association, 1983).

Use Unambiguous Terms

The terms used to describe a child's performance should be clear and accurate.

Most terms fall on a continuum. In order to accurately describe a child's behavior, you need to select the term in the proper position on the continuum. Was the child *anxious, eager, uninterested,* or *depressed*? Did the child *walk, stomp, prance, saunter,* or *race* around the room?

Make sure that you use terms correctly. Do not say that *mental ability* was better than *nonverbal ability* because *mental ability* includes both verbal and nonverbal cognitive abilities. Be extremely careful not to say that a child *lacks* an ability when you mean that the child's ability is *weak.* Also, do not say that there was *no significance* to be found in the scores. The term *significance* can be used either in a technical sense (with respect to statistically significant differences between scores) or in defining importance. All scores are significant in the sense of being important because they tell you something about the child's performance. If statistical significance is being described, make sure that is clear to the reader.

Use of colloquial expressions with surplus meaning (for example, *gang* for peer group), informal meanings of terms (for example, *feel* for *think* or *believe*), and terms of approximation (for example, *quite a few* or *lots* for a specific number) may be misleading because such terms may be interpreted in various ways by different readers. By using such terms to describe your observations and interpretations, you weaken your presentation. It is acceptable, of course, to use these terms in a direct quotation of what the examinee or interviewee said.

When you use synonyms to avoid repetition of terms, choose your words carefully so that you do not unintentionally suggest a subtle difference between terms. The use of pronouns can reduce repetitions without creating ambiguity.

Table 23-1
Some Prescriptions for Good Report Writing

Prescription	Symptom	Cure
1. *Use language that is specific rather than general, definite rather than vague, concrete rather than abstract.*	"The child appeared to be mentally retarded."	"Tom obtained an IQ of 62 ± 5 on the Wechsler Intelligence Scale for Children—Revised. This level of intelligence falls within the Mentally Retarded range."
2. *Make the verb of a sentence agree with the subject.* Singular verb forms must be used with singular subjects and plural verb forms with plural subjects.	"All of the students in the class was able to answer the question but Joey."	"All of the students in the class except Joey were able to answer the question."
	"Lisa's grades are below average, but is an accurate reflection of her abilities."	"Lisa's grades are below average, but appear to be an accurate reflection of her abilities."
3. *Avoid unnecessary shifts in number, tense, subject, voice, or point of view.*	"When he heard about his grade he complains."	"When he heard about his grade he complained."
	"Tom was born in California, but New York was his home in later years."	"Tom was born in California, but lived in New York in later years."
4. *Avoid sentence fragments.* Fragments often occur when syntax becomes overly complicated.	"Not being sure of himself, several items which should have been easy for him, though he said they were difficult."	"Not being sure of himself, James said that several items were difficult, even though they should have been easy for him."
5. *Avoid redundancies and superfluous material.*	"His confidence was congruent with his abilities, and although he realized he was intelligent, he did not appear to undervalue it or overvalue it, but rather seemed to accept it without evaluating it."	"He displayed a great deal of confidence in his abilities."
	"He did not appear to be anxious or concerned but was willing to try to succeed within his normal pattern of motivation."	"His motivation was satisfactory."
	"The client complained of numbness and loss of feeling."	"The client complained of numbness."
	"The client was excited and agitated."	"The client was agitated."
	"The client is doing well without problems."	"The client is doing well."
6. *Make the participial phrase at the beginning of a sentence refer to the grammatical subject.* The first sentence to the right is puzzling. Who administered the Vineland Scale? Who was enuretic?	"Administering the Vineland Adaptive Behavior Scales, the mother admitted that enuresis was still a problem."	"Replying to questions on the Vineland Adaptive Behavior Scales, the mother said that the child was enuretic."
	"Analyzing the results of the two tests, the scores indicated below average functioning."	"The results of the two tests indicated below average functioning."
	"After climbing the mountain, the view was nice."	"After climbing the mountain we saw a nice view."
7. *Use verb forms rather than noun forms of words whenever possible.* Using verb forms puts life into reports and helps to shorten sentences.	"The principal suggested the implementation of a point system for the improvement of Ricky's playground behavior."	"The principal suggested using a point system to improve Ricky's playground behavior."
	"Authorization for the absence was given by the teacher."	"The teacher authorized the absence."
	"The child is negligent in the details of her work."	"The child neglects her work."

(Table continues on next page)

Table 23-1 (cont.)

Prescription	Symptom	Cure
8. *Do not overuse the passive voice.* Although use of the passive voice is acceptable, overusing it can make a report sound dull. To change a sentence from passive to active voice, make the actor the subject of the sentence.	"The previous testing was completed during her former hospitalization."	"Bonnie underwent assessment during her hospital stay earlier this year."
9. *Provide adequate transitions.* Each sentence in a report should follow logically from the prior one. The first sentence in a paragraph should usually prepare the reader for what follows.	"Richard is above average on memory items. He failed a memory test at a level below his chronological age."	"Richard's memory ability is above average relative to that of his age peers, even though he failed a memory test at a level below his chronological age."
10. *Keep related sentence elements together, and keep unrelated elements apart.* Express new thoughts in new sentences.	"Mrs. James has not attended any teacher conferences this year, and she has been married four times."	"Mrs. James has not attended any teacher conferences this year. She has been married four times."
11. *Express coordinate ideas in similar form.* Elements that are parallel in thought should be parallel in form. The content, not the style, should protect the clinic report from monotony.	"The patient sat alone at 6 months. At 8 months crawling began. Walking was noted at 12 months."	"The patient sat alone at 6 months, crawled at 8 months, and walked at 12 months."
	"The recommendations are to learn a phonics approach and attending an individualized reading class."	"The recommendations are to learn a phonics approach and to attend an individualized reading class."
12. *Combine or restructure sentences to avoid repeating the same word, phrase, or idea.* Consecutive sentences with the same subject, or ones that describe the same process, often require revision.	"Jim's mother said that he had been in an automobile accident last year. His mother also told me that Jim has had memory difficulties since the accident."	"Jim's mother said that he has had memory difficulties since his automobile accident last year."
	"Hyperactivity characterized Jim's behavior. He was hyperactive in class and hyperactive on the playground, and he was also hyperactive in the test session."	"Jim was constantly in motion in the classroom, on the playground, and during the test session."
13. *Do not use too many prepositional phrases in one sentence.*	"The teacher reported that John slept poorly the night before the test session, which resulted in his being too tired to stay awake in class."	"The teacher reported that John slept poorly the night before the test and was too tired to stay awake in class."
14. *In formal writing, do not end sentences with a preposition.*	"Eric could not decide which hand he wanted to do the block design with."	"Eric could not decide with which hand to complete the block design."
15. *Omit needless words and phrases. Make every word count.* Words that duplicate information contained in an adjective or verb or that detract from the subject or major point of the sentence should be cut out.	"the question as to whether"	"whether"
	"whether or not"	"whether"
	"he is a man who"	"he"
	"call your attention to the fact that"	"remind you (notify you)"
	"due to the fact that"	"because"
	"in order to"	"to"
	"for the purposes of"	"to" or "so" or "for"
	"in the event that"	"if"
	"in an effort to"	"to"
	"by means of"	"with"
	"in connection with"	"with"

(Table continues on next page)

Table 23-1 (cont.)

Prescription	Symptom	Cure
	"for the length of time that"	"while"
	"with the result that"	"so"
	"is supportive of"	"supports"
	"to be of great benefit"	"beneficial"
	"in such a state that"	"so" or "such"
	"pertains to the problem of"	"concerns"
	"at this point in time"	"now"
	"am (or are) in agreement with"	"agree"
	"insofar as"	"so"
	"with reference to"	"regarding"
	"many in number"	"many"
	"round in shape"	"round"
	"audible to the ear"	"audible"
	"tasted bitter to the tongue"	"tasted bitter"
	"second time in my life"	"second time"
	"quickly with haste"	"quickly"
	"there were several members of the family who said"	"several family members said"
	"they were both alike"	"they were alike"
	"four different teachers said"	"four teachers said"
	"absolutely essential"	"essential"
	"one and the same"	"the same"
	"in close proximity"	"in proximity" or "close"
	"period of time"	"time"
	"the reason is"	"because"
	"summarize briefly"	"summarize"
	"Although it cannot be definitely established, it is quite probable that the patient, in all likelihood, is suffering some degree of aphasia."	"The patient is probably aphasic."
	"The client was positioned in bed in such a way that the left leg could not be moved sideways or bend at the knee."	"The client's left leg was immobilized."
16. *Avoid misplaced modifiers.* Misplaced modifiers add to confusion and occasionally create unintended humor in the report. Be sure that modifiers qualify the appropriate elements in the sentence. Modifiers should be placed (a) close to the words they modify and (b) away from words that they might mistakenly be taken to modify.	"In response to my instructions, Erin picked up the ball and walked around the room with his left hand."	"In response to my instructions, Erin picked up the ball with his left hand, then walked around the room."
	"Dr. Jones instructed the patient while in the hospital to watch his diet carefully."	"While visiting her patient in the hospital, Dr. Jones told him to watch his diet carefully."
17. *Avoid the use of qualifiers.* Rather, very, little, pretty—these are the leeches that infest the pond of prose, sucking the blood of words.	"The patient was very attentive."	"The patient was attentive."
	"She was a pretty good student."	"She was a good student" *or* "She was a mediocre student" *or* "She had a grade point average of 3.4."
	"a pretty important rule"	"an important rule"

(Table continues on next page)

Table 23-1 (cont.)

Prescription	Symptom	Cure
18. *Use words correctly.* Misused words reflect unfavorably on the writer and discredit the report. Two commonly misused words are *affect* and *effect*.	"The behavior modification approach used by the teacher seems to have had a favorable affect on Edward."	"The behavior modification approach used by the teacher seems to have had a favorable effect on Edward" *or* "The behavior modification approach used by the teacher seemed to affect Edward favorably."
19. *Avoid fancy words.* The line between the fancy and the plain is sometimes alarmingly fine. The wise report writer will avoid an elaborate word when a simple one will suffice. The clinic report must not become a two-page exhibition of the writer's professional vocabulary. The best report writers use vocabulary true to their own experience.	"The patient exhibited apparent partial paralysis of motor units of the superior sinistral fibres of the genioglossus resulting in insufficient lingual approximation of the palatoalveolar regions. A condition of insufficient frenulum development was noted, producing not only sigmatic distortion but also obvious ankyloglossia."	"The patient was tongue-tied."
20. *Do not take shortcuts at the expense of clarity.* Acronyms should be avoided unless they will be understood by all readers. (Even sophisticated readers appreciate having test names written out initially.)	"The PPVT-R, VABS, and WISC-R were administered."	"The following tests were administered: Peabody Picture Vocabulary Test—Revised (PPVT-R), Vineland Adaptive Behavior Scales (VABS), and Wechsler Intelligence Scale for Children—Revised (WISC-R)."
21. *Capitalize proper names of tests.*	"In a previous assessment, he was given the bender and the motor-free test."	"In a previous assessment, he was given the Bender Visual Motor Gestalt Test and the Motor-Free Visual Perception Test."
22. *Avoid the use of contractions in a report.* Report writing is a mode of formal writing, and words that might be spoken informally as contractions should be spelled out in the report. An exception is a contraction within quotation marks.	"Jim couldn't pronounce many of the vocabulary words." "Joanne's mother said that Joanne can't sit still for 5 minutes."	"Jim could not pronounce many of the vocabulary words." "Joanne's mother told the examiner, 'Joanne can't sit still for 5 minutes.'"
23. *Put statements in positive form. Make definite assertions. Avoid tame, colorless, hesitating, noncommittal language.* Consciously or unconsciously, the reader is dissatisfied with being told only what is not; he or she wishes to be told what is as well.	"The child did not know his colors." "The patient did not have good motor control."	"The child did not name the colors of the red and blue blocks. However, he did separate the blocks by color and matched them to other red and blue objects in the room." "The patient stacked two blocks, but was unable to stack three blocks."
24. *Do not affect a breezy manner.* Be professional, avoid pet ideas and phrases, and cultivate a natural rather than a flippant style of writing.	"Would you believe, Ma and Pa had a fuss right in the middle of the interview over when the child began to walk."	"The child's parents disagreed as to when the child had first walked."

(Table continues on next page)

Table 23-1 (cont.)

Prescription	Symptom	Cure
25. *Do not overstate.* If you overstate, the reader will be instantly on guard, and everything that preceded your overstatement, as well as everything that follows it, will be suspect in his or her mind.	"There is no tension in the home." "The client is absolutely brilliant."	"Bill's father reported no tension in the home." "The client scored 141 on the Stanford-Binet Intelligence Scale: Fourth Edition, presented an all 'A' report card, and was voted 'most intelligent' by the high school faculty."

Source: Adapted from Bates (1985), Gearheart and Willenberg (1980), Kolin and Kolin (1980), and Moore (1969).

Avoid Technical Terms

Keeping technical descriptions to a minimum will enhance a report's readability. Strive to describe and interpret a child's performance using common expressions. The inclusion of technical jargon and technical information in the report is unnecessary and may be counterproductive. Technical jargon may confuse the lay reader and it may communicate to other professionals meanings different from those you intended to convey. Surveys have found that psychologists, teachers, and psychiatrists do not always agree on the interpretation of psychological terminology (Cuadra & Albaugh, 1956; Grayson & Tolman, 1950; Rucker, 1967b; Shively & Smith, 1969).

Refer to technical details only in exceptional cases. A report on the testing of a foreign-born child, for instance, might note that the Stanford-Binet: Fourth Edition, WISC-R, and WPPSI were standardized on children in the United States. Do not include general historical or technical information about any tests. For example, do not mention that Terman and Merrill revised the Stanford-Binet in 1937, that the WISC-R is a derivative of the adult form of the Wechsler, or that the standard deviation of the McCarthy General Cognitive Index is 16.

The reader does not need to know about the procedures that you used in interpreting the child's performance or about the specific steps that you used to arrive at the interpretations. Discussion of the statistical methods used to arrive at the conclusions presented in the report will unnecessarily confuse most readers. References to standard deviations, raw scores, significance levels, scatter, and most other technical concepts should be left out of the report. Focus instead on the implications of the findings, such as how they reflect the child's strengths and weaknesses.

It *is* important to identify the scoring system and norms that were used for a particular test, if more than one

scoring system or set of norms is available for that test. For example, because there are at least two scoring systems used with the Bender-Gestalt, including the Koppitz system and the Hutt system, the report should identify which one was used.

Avoid Confusing and Inappropriate Devices

Some writers use devices found in creative writing in order to inject excitement into their prose. However, devices such as shifts in topic, tense, or mood, surprising or ambiguous statements, or lengthy analogies may confuse the reader of the clinical report and should be avoided (cf., American Psychological Association, 1983). Creative embellishment within the context of a clinical report can also backfire on the writer: it appears nonprofessional and may cast shadows on the writer's credibility as a professional clinician.

Language that attracts undue attention to itself may distract readers and diminish the focus of the ideas being presented. Examples of inappropriate linguistic devices include heavy alliteration, rhyming, poetic expressions, and clichés. Metaphors should be used with care, and mixed metaphors should be avoided. (For example, do not use "She tends to get on bandwagons, go off in all directions, and end up clear out in left field" for "she is impetuous.") Use figurative or colorful expressions (like "tired as a dog") sparingly to avoid sounding labored or unnatural.

Avoid Apologetic Statements

Do not undermine your message by making excuses either for the test or for the child's test performance. Report, without apology, the results of the evaluation in as objective a manner as possible.

ELIMINATING BIASED WORDING

> **Principle 16. Eliminate biased terms from the report.**

The report should avoid implications of bias. Removing bias may be difficult, however, because biased language is well established in our culture. The use of *man* to denote *humanity* and the use of *he* as a generic pronoun are common examples of biased terminology. These terms may convey an implicit message to the reader that women are not included in the reference or that females are of secondary importance. Sentences should be rephrased to eliminate the use of gender-referenced nouns, pronouns, and adjectives to refer to people in general.

Implications of bias may also arise from the use of nonparallel terms. *Woman* and *husband*, for example, are not parallel, and using them together may imply differences in the roles of women and men. The terms *husband* and *wife* are parallel as are *man* and *woman* (cf., American Psychological Association, 1983). Guard against using any expressions and clichés that imply inappropriate roles or inequalities between men and women.

Members of ethnic groups should be referred to with nouns and adjectives that are acceptable given (a) the current social trends, (b) the preferences of members of the group being referred to, and (c) the preferences of the readers of the report. You should consider carefully whether ethnic designations are even relevant to the report. For example, reporting that a child's teacher is Hispanic or black may be important if you are discussing the child's responses to the teacher, but not if the teacher is merely being cited as an informant about the child. Generally the ethnicity of the subjects of the report is useful information for the reader.

Look for any signs of stereotypes or prejudice in your writing. For example, do not assume that welfare clients have limited intellectual ability or that fat people are happy. Do not make inferences about the child's family or friends based on knowledge of the child's social class or ethnic group. Irrelevant, negative evaluations of ethnic groups may occur if you compare one group (usually your own group) with another. There is rarely, if ever, any need to make evaluative statements regarding ethnic groups or members of these groups in a report.

WRITING A CONCISE REPORT

> **Principle 17. Write a report that is concise but yet presents your findings and recommendations adequately.**

Too much elaboration or tangential discussion in a report may obscure your most important points and ideas. To ensure conciseness, evaluate all your material with respect to its relevance to the ideas you wish to present. It may be helpful to outline in advance the ideas and points you want to convey.

Overly Long Reports

Many reports are too long because they contain redundancies and circumlocutions (like, *a generally pervasive mood* or *feeling unsettled* for *depression*). Evasiveness about a point may also result in needless discussion. The substitution of a euphemistic phrase or jargon for a familiar term is another major cause of excessively lengthy reports (like *weight beyond the norms of a typical child* for *overweight*) (American Psychological Association, 1983).

Length of Sentences

The length of sentences is an important factor in readability. A lot of short, choppy sentences may make the text sound disjointed and dull, but many long, complicated sentences may render the text difficult to follow. Varying the sentence length is one effective way of capturing and maintaining the reader's interest and aiding comprehension. When long sentences are needed to communicate a difficult concept, the simplest words and sentence construction should be used.

Length of Paragraphs

The length of paragraphs in a report is another factor in readability. Although the requirement that every paragraph contain a cohesive and unifying thought may make a single-sentence paragraph necessary in some situations, single-sentence paragraphs often sound abrupt. On the other hand, long paragraphs may require the reader to strain to recognize the unifying themes and ideas. A rule of thumb is that a paragraph that runs longer than one double-spaced typescript page probably strains the reader's attention span (American Psychological Association, 1983). Such a paragraph should be broken down and reorganized.

Sufficient Depth

A report should be long enough that major findings, interpretations, conclusions, and recommendations are presented adequately. Although another psychologist may have no difficulty in understanding a brief account, the child's parents, teachers, physicians, and counselors may have difficulty in comprehending a report written without adequate explanations and illustrations, as well as headings delineating the major areas of discussion.

ATTENDING TO THE TECHNICAL ASPECTS OF REPORT WRITING

> **Principle 18. Attend carefully to grammatical and stylistic points in your writing.**

Conventional grammatical rules must be followed in writing psychological reports. A good general reference source for technical writing is the American Psychological Assocation's (1983) *Publication Manual*. For specific reference questions it may be necessary to consult a dictionary or a grammar text. The following grammatical, stylistic, and structural aspects of report writing merit special emphasis and discussion.

Abbreviations

Abbreviations generally should not be used in a report. Terms such as *etc.* can be misleading and should be used only on rare occasions. Technical abbreviations such as IQ, MA, and CA may be used, however, because they are accepted terms that pertain to intelligence testing. These three terms are always capitalized and are written without periods. *Examiner* and *examinee* should not be abbreviated because the reader may not understand the meaning of the abbreviations. Although it is permissible to abbreviate the names of commonly used tests (for example, WISC-R, WAIS-R), the first time they appear the names should be spelled out completely and followed immediately by the accepted abbreviation in parentheses.

Capitalization

Capitalize the first letter of each major word in a test name, as in *Digit Span*. Capitalization helps to distinguish a reference to a particular test or subtest, such as the WISC-R Vocabulary subtest, from a reference to the skill being measured, such as vocabulary. Capitalize the first letter of the child's IQ classification as an attention-getting device, as in *Average classification*.

The names of general areas of intelligence, such as language skills or visual-motor abilities, usually are not capitalized because they do not correspond to specific tests in the examination. The terms *examiner* and *examinee* should not be capitalized.

Hyphens

The rules for hyphenation are complex. It is helpful to consult a dictionary or other sources, such as *The Chicago Manual of Style* published by the University of Chicago Press (1982). A term such as *7-year-old* is usually hyphenated, both as a noun (the 7-year-old) and as a compound adjective (a 7-year-old child).

Punctuation

Effective punctuation supports the meaning of the text, contributing to continuity of thought in a report. Punctuation cues the reader to the relationship between ideas, as well as to the normal pauses and inflections that help to emphasize the main ideas and concepts. The overuse or underuse of punctuation may obscure the meaning of your communication and confuse the reader.

The problem of positioning punctuation marks with respect to quotation marks arises often in the writing of psychological reports. A period or comma is always placed *before* the closing quotation mark, even when the quotation marks enclose only a single word. For example, Mark's mother said that "Mark reported to her that he 'talked quietly' in class, but she did not believe him." Mark also has a favorite word, "maple." A colon or semicolon is placed *after* the closing quotation mark. Similarly, a question mark is placed *after* the closing quotation mark, unless it is part of the quoted material.

Tense

The major problem writers encounter with tenses is determining when to use the past tense and when to use the present tense. In discussing a child's level of intelligence, it is preferable to use the present tense: "The child is currently functioning in the Average range of intelligence." If the past tense had been used in the preceding sentence, it would sound as if the child were deceased or no longer average at the time the report was written. In general, enduring traits existing at the time the report is written, such as ethnicity, intelligence, sex, and physical characteristics, should be referred to in the present tense: "John is a muscular, overweight adolescent who was cooperative on the examination." Test behavior, in contrast, is described in the past tense, because the behavior was displayed on a specific past occasion.

Spacing

When a report is to be sent to an agency, single spacing should be used. During your training, however, double space your reports to allow for corrections and for the supervisor's comments.

DEVELOPING STRATEGIES TO IMPROVE WRITING STYLE

> **Principle 19. Develop appropriate strategies to improve your writing, such as using an outline and rereading your rough draft.**

Writers tend to develop particular writing strategies that suit their needs and style. Two effective ways of improving the quality of your psychological reports are writing from an outline and putting aside the first draft for later rereading and editing.

Using an Outline

Writing from an outline helps you to maintain the logic of the report because main ideas and subordinate concepts are identified from the outset (American Psychological Association, 1983). An outline may also aid you in writing more precisely and ensure that all pertinent data are included. The report outline shown earlier in the chapter and illustrated throughout this text may be used as the basis for a more detailed report outline.

Rereading Your Rough Draft

Examine the draft for errors and ways to enhance the clarity of the material. Be sure that all findings, interpretations, and recommendations are clearly presented; revise sections that are vague or ambiguous. Strive to write a succinct report that deals with relevant issues and avoids undue generalization and speculation. Consider whether the report can be understood by an intelligent layperson.

The following questions may help you to assess the quality of your presentation:

- Are the identifying data correct? Be sure to check the accuracy of the child's name, date of birth, chronological age, sex, date of examination, your name, and date of report.
- Is the referral question stated clearly and succinctly?
- Does the background material contain relevant historical data, such as prior test results and recommendations (if available), developmental history, and family history?
- Do the behavioral observations enable the reader to form a clear impression of the child?
- Is there a statement about the validity of the test findings?
- Are the test scores, percentile ranks, and other test-related data correct?
- Are the confidence range and classification of the IQ presented?
- Are the findings clearly organized, succinct, and integrated?
- Does the report answer the referral question(s)?
- Are the present results compared with past results and any discrepancies noted and discussed?
- Are themes about the child's functioning clearly delineated?
- Are the results and observations backed up with illustrative examples and descriptions?
- Are any doubts about the findings or conclusions stated clearly?
- Does the report indicate which questions remain unanswered or answered incompletely?
- Are clinical impressions clearly stated?
- Do the recommendations clearly follow from the assessment findings?
- Are the recommendations clear and practical?
- Are speculations clearly labeled as such?
- Is the writing style professional and grammatically correct?
- Is the report free of jargon?
- Is the report free of ambiguities?

When the report has been typed, proofread it carefully. Look for spelling errors, grammatical errors, and omitted phrases or other typing errors. Major revisions will be needed less often as you gain experience, but careful proofreading will always be needed. The preceding strategies may require you to invest more time in a report than you had anticipated, but these strategies will result in greater accuracy, thoroughness, and clearer communication.

Studying Table 23-2 will help you to avoid some of the common pitfalls in report writing. Under each category are examples of sentences that fail to meet acceptable

Table 23-2
Common Pitfalls in Report Writing

Pitfall	Example	Comment
Inappropriate Generalizations	"Nancy was weak in numerical reasoning, as evidenced by her missing one easy item on the Arithmetic test."	Reference to one item is not sufficient justification for concluding that a child is weak in numerical reasoning. It is hazardous to generalize from one failure or from one success only.
	"The examinee is small for his age and may feel a need to achieve."	Without additional information these two thoughts are unrelated—a non sequitur. If the only bit of data available to you about the child's achievement needs is that he is small, do not make this interpretation.
	"On the basis of his Full Scale IQ of 107, it is predicted that Mark will do at least average work in school and that he will excel in athletics."	This sentence contains two inappropriate generalizations. First, the 107 IQ indicates that Mark is *capable* of performing at a normal level in school; it does not mean that he *will* perform at that level. Second, a statement about athletics cannot be made on the basis of a child's performance on an intelligence test.
	"Charles demonstrated good attention span, which indicates that he is free from anxiety."	Satisfactory performance on the Digit Span or Sentences subtests, for example, does not indicate that the child is free from anxiety. The most that can be said is that anxiety did not appear to affect the child's performance in a particular area.
	"Mrs. Jones's rejection of Susan has led to her lying and stealing in school."	Supporting information is needed here. For example, "Responses on the projective test suggest that Susan's lying and stealing may be related to feelings of maternal rejection" (Drake & Bardon, 1978).
	"Johnny's educational skills are poor."	Again, supporting information is needed, such as "Johnny's test scores on the X achievement test are at the 13th percentile on national norms for reading comprehension and the 16th percentile for arithmetic calculation" (Drake & Bardon, 1978).
Ambiguous Statements	"It is possible that his performance may reflect the lack of proper emotional orientation that is necessary for meaningful and emotionally relevant action."	The concept "meaningful and emotionally relevant action" is ambiguous and needs clarification. In addition, it would help if illustrations of the child's behavior were added.
	"Joe lacks language ability."	*Lacks* may mean either *is deficient in* or *shows a complete absence of.* The examiner most likely does not mean that there is a complete absence of language ability; rather, he or she desires to convey that the child is *below average* or *inadequate* or *retarded* or *slow.* The latter terms convey more precisely the level at which the child is functioning. For example, you might note that the child is below average in language ability or that language functioning level is approximately two years below chronological age. In a case where the child does *lack* a particular skill, a sentence such as "Joe cannot write, speak, or understand the speech of others" conveys this information.
Vague Statements	"It is recommended that additional information be gathered in regard to her background and her achievement."	In and of itself, this recommendation is acceptable. However, the statement should be more specific so that the reader knows *what* information is needed and *why* it is needed.

(Table continues on next page)

Table 23-2 (cont.)

Pitfall	Example	Comment
		What do you hope to learn from the additional information? What purpose will it serve? Do you wish to see the child for further evaluation after the additional information is obtained? Recommendations should incorporate, if possible, the rationale used in their formulation.
	"Bobby shows indications of strength in numerical reasoning and in nonverbal reasoning, and on tests dealing with nonmeaningful memory. Other areas of strength include. . . ."	These are tantalizing sentences because the reader is not given information concerning the child's absolute strength. It would be helpful to know how strong the child was in these areas and in what ways the strengths were shown. Referring to a percentile rank (or ranks) would help describe the child's strengths in relative terms.
	"Mary is unable to concentrate."	It would be helpful to use supporting information or behavioral descriptions. For example, "Classroom observation and the teacher's report indicated that Mary seldom completes assigned work and usually does not attend to a specific task for longer than 2 minutes" (Drake & Bardon, 1978).
	"Joan demonstrates no progress beyond the preprimer level in reading."	Supporting information or behavioral descriptions would be useful. For example, "Joan's classroom teacher reports that Joan is unable to identify 60 percent of the words in the primer reading book used by the class" (Drake & Bardon, 1978).
Unnecessary Technical Terms and Information	"His attention to detail should be strengthened, as indicated by his performance on the Magic Window subtest."	A subtest name is likely to have little, if any, meaning to the reader. If you refer to a specific test, illustrate the activities required by the test.
	"When she reached the ceiling level, she became more restless and serious."	The term *ceiling level* may not be understood by the reader. You could say instead "When the more difficult levels of the test were reached, she . . . ." If you use the term *ceiling level*, add "the level at which all or most tests were failed" in parentheses.
	"The child was particularly strong in memory-span tests."	Instead of saying "strong in memory-span tests," describe the child's abilities. For example, "The child has a good memory span." Discuss the child's abilities rather than noting the test names.
Abstract Statements	"It is recommended that Joey be tested again after a 3-year period to ascertain whether maturation will result in an improved operational level."	This is a highly abstract way of saying "Retesting in 3 years is recommended to evaluate Joey's developmental status."
	"His seemingly conscious withdrawal from conversation coupled with an outwardly stoic nature yielded an impression of social impoverishment."	*Conscious withdrawal*, *stoic nature*, and *social impoverishment* are complex concepts. Reticence and a suggested stoical nature may not indicate social impoverishment. The child, boxed in stoicism, wrapped and tied in conscious withdrawal, and labeled as socially impoverished, is defenselessly delivered to the reader. Rephrasing may achieve clarity and avoid misinterpretation. The child's behavior could be described as follows: "He showed little emotion during the test."

(Table continues on next page)

Table 23-2 (cont.)

Pitfall	Example	Comment
Overly Cautious Statements	"The Intelligence Quotient of 120 on the WISC-R would seem to indicate a High Average to Superior range of functioning."	An IQ of 120 is in the Superior classification, according to the WISC-R manual. There is no need to hedge. A better statement would be "The Intelligence Quotient of 120 indicates that Mary's performance is in the Superior range as assessed by the WISC-R."
	"Jim obtained an IQ of approximately 86."	The IQ obtained on any one occasion is an estimate of intelligence and, as stressed in this text, should be accompanied by a statement of precision (standard error). The examination does, however, permit the calculation of a score that is a specific, exact number. Therefore, in the sentence above, the word "approximately" should be eliminated, and a precision range should be used instead (for example, 86 ± 5).
Inexact Interpretations and Statements	"Her physical appearance suggested no behavioral problems."	Rarely will a child's physical appearance denote a behavioral problem. Additionally, this is an example of stating positive information in the negative. Suggestion: "Her appearance was quite ordinary. She was dressed in a loosely fitting sweater and skirt. Her height and weight are normal for her age."
	"Bill achieved an IQ of 112. He has just begun kindergarten and needs to develop listening skills and an approach to solving problems."	It is difficult to imagine how the child could have achieved an IQ of 112 without having developed *some* listening and problem-solving skills. The examiner failed to use a transition to indicate that the two sentences were unrelated. If other information leads you to conclude that a child, for example, is more active or impulsive than the average child his or her age, clearly indicate this in the report. Always consider what the appropriate normative behavior is for the child's developmental stage.
	"Bill's only weakness was shown by his score of 10 on the Arithmetic subtest."	This sentence was based on the child's obtaining WISC-R scaled scores of 13 or more on all of the subtests, with the exception of a 10 on Arithmetic. The interpretation is incorrect because a scaled score of 10 represents average functioning. This child had no significant weaknesses in relation to the standardization group. His score on the Arithmetic subtest does indicate that he is not as well developed in arithmetical skills as he is in other areas of the test.
Undocumented Statements	"Billy has uncontrolled temper tantrums."	The source for such a statement should be cited. For example, "According to Billy's classroom teacher, he cries and stomps his feet when she denies him a privilege. All methods tried by the teacher to prevent these tantrums have proved unsuccessful" (Drake & Bardon, 1978).
	"The father is an alcoholic."	Either a source should be cited for this statement or the statement should be eliminated. For example, "The father stated that he is an alcoholic and a member of AA" (Drake & Bardon, 1978). Be very careful about accepting such information from sources other than the person involved.

(Table continues on next page)

Table 23-2 (cont.)

Pitfall	Example	Comment
Disjointed Statements	"Jay has excellent conceptual thinking. Another average ability is memory."	The second sentence does not follow from the first. The reader is first told about an *excellent* ability and then without any warning is informed about an *average* abililty. A more meaningful and positive way to combine this information would be "Jay has average memory ability but excellent conceptual thinking ability." The implications of these findings then could be discussed.
	"Katie's reading comprehension is average, her arithmetic skills are below average, and her Full Scale IQ is in the Average range."	This sentence fails to integrate the data. Katie's reading and arithmetic skills should be understood in relation to her overall IQ. A better way of presenting this information would be "Katie's reading comprehension skills are average, which is consistent with her obtained IQ. Her arithmetic skills, however, are below average."
Apologetic Statements	"Jill gave the impression of enjoying herself, and at the same time was willing to try to meet the challenge of the seemingly never-ending questions of the examiner."	To whom did the questions seem never-ending? Do not apologize for the examination techniques: apologetic statements tend to indirectly belittle your professional status and may diminish the value of the report.
	"The examiner is sorry that Jim achieved an IQ of only 85."	The terms *sorry* and *only* reflect the examiner's personal feelings. If other information led you to expect the child to perform at a higher level of functioning, note the expectation and the relevant information. Include in the report any doubts about how representative the results are. The use of the term *only* leaves the reader wondering why it was included. Your personal values should not be imposed or projected on either the children or the readers.
Value-Laden Statements	"Joe appeared disheveled and dirty at times, which may be accounted for by the fact that his family is on welfare."	It is improper to assume that Joe appears disheveled and dirty simply because his family lives on a limited income. This statement shows the writer's prejudices about people who receive aid. The problem here could be corrected by making separate statements about Joe's appearance and family income, without assuming a relationship between them.
	"Eileen did much better than expected in social comprehension items, given the fact that she lives in an impoverished neighborhood."	The assumptions here reveal the writer's prejudices. First, the writer labeled the neighborhood as *impoverished*. A more effective way of presenting information about the child's living conditions would be to describe what was observed in the neighborhood rather than simply labeling it. However, reference to a lower class neighborhood may be suitable. Second, the writer has made the assumption that poor living conditions lead to lower scores in social comprehension, which is probably an erroneous assumption. Finally, the writer made a value-laden judgment that the child did much better than expected without presenting a reasonable explanation for this interpretation. The child's specific level of performance on the social comprehension tasks should, of course, be presented.
Irrelevant Statements	"Jeffrey's mother has been seen leaving the house at odd hours."	If this statement is potentially relevant, cite the source, use the qualifier *reportedly*, or convey the information verbally to the referral source (Drake & Bardon, 1978).

(Table continues on next page)

Table 23-2 (cont.)

Pitfall	Example	Comment
	"Beverly was sexually molested when a child."	If this statement is potentially relevant, cite the source, use the qualifier *reportedly*, or convey the information verbally to the referral source (Drake & Bardon, 1978).
	"At one time she wanted to use my pencil and draw a picture, but I explained to her that she had to wait until we were finished. After the test she drew a quick picture and took it with her."	Unless they illustrate a point, these statements should not be included. Otherwise, wondering why material was included may distract the reader.
	"John told me that he walks to school and that he likes television."	Without other relevant details, this information is not useful. However, if the child's walking to school reflects recovery from an illness or emerging independence, then this information should be included with a commentary.

standards of communication. Try to figure out the error in the sentence before you read the *Comment* column.

You can also improve your report writing skills by studying the content and style of reports written by other psychologists. Exhibit 23-1 presents a detailed analysis of a psychological report based on a battery approach, to help you understand the component parts of a report. It may also be helpful to read (or review) other reports that are shown throughout this book. All psychological evaluations are listed in the List of Exhibits at the beginning of this text.

PROBLEMS WITH REPORTS

Psychological reports have received their share of criticism (Affleck & Strider, 1971; Garfield, Heine, & Leventhal, 1954; Hartlage & Merck, 1971; Lacey & Ross, 1964; Moore, Boblitt, & Wildman, 1968; Olive, 1972; Smyth & Reznikoff, 1971; Tallent, 1963; Tallent & Reiss, 1959a, 1959b, 1959c). The studies on reports evaluated those written by psychologists in schools, clinics, and hospitals. Problems included lack of supporting data or behavioral referents, poor expression (for example, use of clichés and jargon, loose use of terms, and vagueness), poor organization, inconsistencies, incorrect use of theory, poor differentiation between test data and other data, failure to answer the referral problem, and excessive length and irrelevance.

In a study in which elementary school teachers rated reports written by school psychologists (Rucker, 1967a), *negatively* rated reports were described as:

• being too brief
• lacking form and organization
• failing to explain results or leaving results out
• having vague or brief recommendations
• failing to answer referral questions
• providing unrealistic suggestions for the classroom teacher

In contrast, the *positively* rated reports were described as:

• being understandable
• being enjoyable to read
• providing motivation to follow the suggestions
• having excellent interpretations of the test results
• explaining the results to naive readers
• showing how the problem came about
• answering specific referral questions
• providing recommendations that could be implemented in the classroom without singling out the child
• conveying that the teacher had asked relevant questions that deserved careful answers.

An evaluative questionnaire, such as the one shown in Table 23-3, can be used to obtain feedback from teachers about the usefulness of your psychological reports. In addition to helping you to identify strengths and weaknesses in your written communications, the questionnaire, which can be completed on a case-by-case basis, will allow you to learn about different needs that exist among various referral sources, such as regular classroom teachers, special education teachers, counselors, and speech therapists; clarify your role; and establish realistic expectations on the part of the referral sources about the kinds of information that can be obtained from the assessment process.

Exhibit 23-1

Analysis of and Line-by-Line Commentary on a Psychological Evaluation of a Boy with a Learning Problem

INTRODUCTORY REMARKS

Shown on the following pages is a case study of a 9-year-old boy who is experiencing difficulty at home and at school. This case provides a good example of how several sources — including parental interview, test scores, teacher consultation, and behavioral observations — may be used to develop hypotheses about a child's skills and to make recommendations. This well-organized report shows how recommendations can be addressed to the problem areas identified by the test results.

ANALYSIS OF THE REPORT

Identifying Data

Important identifying data about Bill appear at the beginning of the report. In an actual report, Bill's first and last name would be included.

Tests Administered

The section on tests administered is included in this exhibit (and in other exhibits in this text) to provide you with the original test data; it is optional in actual reports. A listing of the test names might be sufficient for an actual report. You may also cite the child's test scores in the assessment results section. Although copies of the child's handwriting, spelling, drawings, and other raw data are included in this exhibit for teaching purposes, they are seldom included in the actual reports.

Reason for Referral

The referral section gives the reason that Bill was referred and who initiated the referral.

Background Information

Background information is helpful because it sets the stage for understanding Bill's life situation and his relationship with others. The two paragraphs in this section deal with relevant educational and family information and medical history.

Behavioral Observations

The report notes the ease with which Bill became comfortable, because level of anxiety can affect test performance. The examiner also describes verbal difficulties observed in informal conversation. Reporting these difficulties may help the reader to isolate possible problem areas, become more alert to the implications of the test results, and consider possible explanations for this behavior. Anecdotal information about Bill's style of problem solving and dealing with frustration tends to complete Bill's profile and leads smoothly into the test data that follow.

Assessment Results and Clinical Impressions

The most notable characteristic of Bill's WISC-R scores is the 27-point discrepancy between his Verbal and Performance Scale IQs. Table C-2 in Appendix C shows that this difference is significant at the .01 level. Thus the Verbal/Performance difference reflects a difference that cannot be attributed to chance. The examiner also determined whether the Verbal and Performance subtests differed significantly from their respective means. Each mean was calculated: Verbal Scale subtest $M = 6.2$, Performance Scale subtest $M = 10.8$. The obtained differences between the subtests and their respective scale means were compared with the differences listed in Table C-3 of Appendix C. None of the Verbal subtests was found to differ significantly from the Verbal subtests' mean. However, the score for Coding was significantly lower ($p < .01$) than the mean scaled score for the Performance subtests. The examiner also determined standard scores, confidence levels, and significant interindividual and intraindividual subtest differences before writing the Assessment Results and Clinical Impressions section.

The individual subtest scores suggest that Bill's strengths lie in spatial reasoning ability and perceptual integration. Weaknesses were noted in auditory processing skills — that is, short-term auditory memory (low Digit Span score) and psychomotor speed (low Coding score). Verbal subtest scores were consistently below average.

Bill's responses were somewhat confused regarding temporal relationships and weight concepts.

Bill's Draw-A-Man performance was compared with his WISC-R IQ.

Bill's Wide Range Achievement Test — Revised scores were then discussed. The examiner pointed out areas of difficulty. Hypotheses about the sources of these difficulties were offered, together with evidence to support the hypotheses.

The Vineland Adaptive Behavior Scales suggested some social immaturity. The examiner suggested that Bill's social immaturity might be related to the limits placed on his freedom of movement and on his responsibilities.

Bill's performance on the Bender-Gestalt was well within normal limits.

Classroom observations, although based on a limited sample of behavior, corroborated the formal assessment results. Bill appears to have difficulty attending to reading assignments.

Recommendations

The Recommendations section lists specific steps for remediation that could be implemented by the family or school

(Exhibit continues next page)

Exhibit 23-I (cont.)

staff, or by Bill himself. These suggestions include emphasizing language skill development through speech and language therapy, using areas of strength to build skills, and personal counseling for the family. The first recommendation is directed to the referral question regarding academic placement. The second recommendation focuses on Bill's general needs. The third recommendation shows how Bill's strengths could be used in new programs. The fourth recommendation focuses on family involvement. Although the initial referral did not address family stress, information brought up during the test session suggested to the examiner that this area was also important. The last recommendation focuses on Bill's social immaturity.

Summary

The summary provides a concise wrapup of the report and its findings. It introduces no new information, but consolidates the report into a few easily read sentences. It highlights central issues of the report.

THE REPORT WITH LINE-BY-LINE COMMENTARY

Name: Bill
Date of Birth: April 10, 1976
Chronological age: 9-8

Date of examination: December 12, 1985
Date of report: December 15, 1985
Grade: Second

Tests Administered

Wechsler Intelligence Scale for Children—Revised

VERBAL SCALE		PERFORMANCE SCALE	
Information	4	Picture Completion	13
Similarities	7	Picture Arrangement	9
Arithmetic	6	Block Design	12
Vocabulary	8	Object Assembly	14
Comprehension	7	Coding	6
Digit Span	5		

Verbal Scale IQ = 78
Performance Scale IQ = 105
Full Scale IQ = 89 ± 6 at the 95% confidence level

Wide Range Achievement Test—Revised

	STANDARD SCORE	PERCENTILE
Reading	67	1
Spelling	61	9
Arithmetic	80	9

1. N (in)
2. ojow (go)
3. cat (cat)
4. boe (boy)
5. ohb (and)
6. woll (will)
7. maek (make)
8. humo (him)
9. sae (say)
10. kut (rut)
11. kuk (cook)
12. lork (light)
13. mast (must)
14. dust (dress)
15. rech (reach)

Vineland Adaptive Behavior Scales (Survey Form):

Adaptive Behavior Composite = 76 ± 11 at the 95% confidence level, 5th percentile

Draw-A-Man:

Standard score = 99
Percentile = 47th

Bender-Gestalt:

Standard score = 81
Percentile = 10th

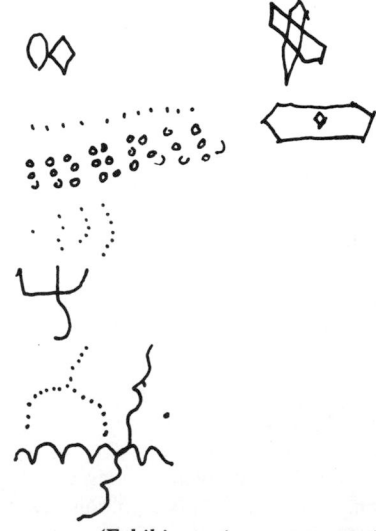

(Exhibit continues next page)

Exhibit 23-I (cont.)

Reason for Referral

1 Bill was referred by his teacher because of learning	1–3 who was referred and reason
2 problems at school, particularly in reading, spelling,	
3 and language arts.	

Background Information

4 Bill, a 9-year, 8-month-old boy, is being retained in the	4–5 current age and grade level
5 second grade, having also repeated the first. A recent	5 educational history
6 parental divorce, the death of a grandfather, and the	5–8 current family stress
7 return home of Bill's two older brothers have made for	
8 a tumultuous home setting. Bill's mother seems to be	8–10 mother's response to stress
9 trying to deal with these numerous areas of frustration	
10 and tension.	
11 Besides his two older brothers, Bill has a 13-year-	11–12 family constellation and relationship with siblings
12 old sister with whom he is close. He appears to be in	12–14 health history
13 good health, and no serious childhood illnesses were	
14 reported. His mother recalled that some of Bill's motor	14–15 developmental history
15 and speech milestones were delayed.	

Behavioral Observations

16 Bill, who arrived with his mother, initially seemed shy	16 who came to session
17 with the examiner. Nevertheless, he willingly came	16–17 initial relations with examiner
18 with the examiner and, except for occasionally laugh-	17–19 overall level of cooperativeness
19 ing anxiously, seemed relatively at ease. Bill tended to	19–21 mode of relating during test
20 be chatty, with a somewhat disconnected conversa-	
21 tional style. Numerous sound substitutions and omis-	21–31 language problems and examples
22 sions (such as *vorsed* for *divorced* and *skies* for *dis-*	
23 *guised*) and syntax errors (often in tenses as well as	
24 subject-verb agreement) were noted in his spon-	
25 taneous speech. He also displayed some word retrieval	
26 difficulties, such as labeling dresser knobs as *holes*;	
27 auditory discrimination difficulties, such as defining	
28 *contagious* as *cage*; and difficulty repeating short sen-	
29 tences (such as rendering the statement "How many	
30 things make a dozen?" as "How much make a	
31 bunch?").	
32 Bill's work style tended to be slow and cautious, and	32 general response style
33 he seemed to want to avoid all errors. Although gener-	33 response to errors
34 ally cooperative, he sometimes gave up when tasks	33–35 response to frustration
35 became difficult, but persisted with mild verbal en-	35–36 response to encouragement
36 couragement. Overall, his level of activity was age	36–37 activity level
37 appropriate and he reacted appropriately to success	37–38 response to successes and failures
38 and failure.	

Assessment Results and Clinical Impressions

39 On the WISC-R, Bill, with a chronological age of 9–8,	39 WISC-R named, chronological age
40 achieved a Verbal Scale IQ of 78 (8th percentile), a	40 Verbal Scale IQ
41 Performance Scale IQ of 105 (63rd percentile), and a	41 Performance Scale IQ
42 Full Scale IQ of 89 ± 6. The chances that the range of	42 Full Scale IQ
43 scores from 83 to 95 includes his true IQ are about 95	42–44 confidence limits
44 out of 100. His overall performance is classified in the	44–45 intellectual classification
45 Below Average range and is ranked at the 24th percen-	45–46 percentile rank
46 tile. These, as well as other test results, appear to be	46–47 test's reliability and validity
47 reliable and valid.	

(Exhibit continues next page)

Exhibit 23-1 (cont.)

48 A significant difference of 27 points was noted	48–51 Verbal/Performance Scale discrepancy noted and
49 between Bill's Verbal and Performance Scale IQs.	described
50 Functioning was borderline in verbal areas and aver-	
51 age in performance areas. Bill has strengths in the	51–52 strengths
52 areas of spatial reasoning and perceptual integration.	
53 His weaknesses are in short-term auditory memory,	53–54 weaknesses
54 psychomotor speed, and fund of general information.	
55 Qualitatively, many of Bill's verbal responses on the	55–56 qualitative responses on the WISC-R and language
56 WISC-R were confused and unusual. For example, he	difficulties
57 named the days of the week when asked for the sea-	56–58 confusion of temporal relationships
58 sons of the year and responded to the question "How	58–59 conceptual difficulties
59 many pounds make a ton?" with "Elephant." In gen-	59–61 summary of verbal difficulties
60 eral, his answers tended to be concrete and poorly	
61 organized, with a loose run-on sentence structure.	
62 On the Goodenough-Harris Draw-A-Man test, a	62–64 Draw-A-Man test results
63 screening measure of mental ability, Bill scored at the	
64 47th percentile. This result is somewhat higher than	64–66 comparison of Draw-A-Man and WISC-R
65 the percentile rank associated with his Full Scale	
66 WISC-R IQ.	
67 On the Wide Range Achievement Test—Revised,	67–69 percentile rank on WRAT-R reading and spelling
68 Bill's reading ability (that is, word recognition) and	
69 spelling both rank at the 1st percentile. Although he	69–72 strengths and weaknesses in spelling
70 knows numerous spelling rules, he has considerable	
71 difficulty in employing them appropriately. For exam-	
72 ple, he spelled the word *boy* as *b-o-e*. His reading does	72–75 phonetic difficulties
73 not reflect an effective use of phonetic skills. For	
74 example, he read the word *red* for *run* and said *get* for	
75 *big*. He can identify letters reliably. In attempting to	75 ability to identify letters
76 read words, he tends to fractionate each phonetic	75–78 reading style
77 unit and then is often unable to integrate the units	
78 effectively.	
79 Arithmetical skills are at the 9th percentile. Al-	79 arithmetic score
80 though he seems to have mastered simple addition and	79–81 arithmetic strengths
81 subtraction skills including borrowing and carrying,	
82 he has difficulty with age-appropriate arithmetic	82–83 arithmetic weaknesses
83 tasks.	
84 It is not surprising that a young man who has diffi-	84–88 further comments on Bill's achievement scores
85 culty in auditory discrimination (for example, saying	
86 *masic* for *magic* and *gammel* for *gamble*) and verbal	
87 sequencing also has difficulty spelling and reading	
88 phonetically. For example, he was unable to sequence	88–92 examples of information deficits
89 all the sounds when asked the name of his school.	
90 Other common information that he seemed unable to	
91 give included his own address, his brother's age, and	
92 labels for familial relationships, such as uncle.	
93 On the Vineland Adaptive Behavior Scales, with	93 Vineland Adaptive Behavior Scales
94 Bill's mother as informant, Bill obtained an Adaptive	94 informant described
95 Behavior Composite of 76 ± 11, which suggests	94–97 score on Vineland presented and interpreted
96 adaptive functioning at the 5th percentile. This indi-	
97 cates that his adaptive level is moderately low. Bill's	97–102 home environment as it relates to social maturity
98 freedom and responsibility are limited at home, as his	
99 mother does not allow him to leave the yard. His	
100 chores at home are few, and his mother still helps him	

(Exhibit continues next page)

Exhibit 23-1 (cont.)

101 with many self-care activities, including combing his	
102 hair.	
103 His performance on the Bender-Gestalt suggested	103–106 Bender-Gestalt results
104 perceptual-motor difficulties (standard score = 81,	
105 10th percentile). His level of perceptual-motor matu-	
106 ration is close to that of a 7½- to 8-year-old child.	
107 Bill was also observed in his classroom for approxi-	107–122 observations in classroom
108 mately 50 minutes from 9:30 to 10:20 a.m. on De-	
109 cember 11, 1985. The class was engaged in a reading	
110 assignment for the first part of the period and in an	
111 arithmetic assignment for the second part of the pe-	
112 riod. During the entire time Bill never raised his hand	
113 to answer a question. He often looked around the	
114 room, stared out the window, and played with his	
115 pencil. Only one other child was similarly distracted.	
116 When asked by his teacher to read, he was unable to	
117 sound out words correctly. However, he did answer a	
118 simple arithmetic problem correctly. During the ob-	
119 servation period he did not talk with any classmates.	
120 His teacher was understanding of his reading difficulty	
121 and complimented him on his correct arithmetic	
122 response.	

Recommendations

123 Bill qualifies for placement in a program for the learn-	123–126 diagnostic impression
124 ing disabled. He is experiencing considerable diffi-	
125 culty in a traditional school setting because of lan-	
126 guage processing difficulties. The following recom-	126–127 recommendations introduced
127 mendations are offered:	
128 1. Because of Bill's identified weakness in language	128–131 kind of program needed
129 skills, an individualized program of special educa-	
130 tion with particular emphasis on language and lan-	
131 guage-related skills is recommended. The program	131–133 possible goals of program
132 should emphasize reading and writing skills to im-	
133 prove Bill's two areas of academic weakness.	
134 2. Speech and language therapy integrated with the	134–135 additional specific language program
135 special education curriculum would be desirable.	
136 3. Bill's nonverbal spatial strengths should be used in	136–139 how strengths might be used
137 the remediation program. For example, reading	
138 materials related to building models might be	
139 appropriate.	
140 4. Bill's mother could use guidance to help sort out	140–141 goal of involving mother
141 and resolve personal as well as family stress. Some	141–147 specific issues for mother to resolve
142 possible areas on which she might focus would	
143 include encouraging communication among fam-	
144 ily members, dealing with hostilities felt toward	
145 her husband and older children, learning how to	
146 cope with being a single parent, and helping her	
147 children deal with the issue of the divorce.	
148 5. Bill's mother should be encouraged to help Bill	148–151 additional area for remediation
149 develop more independent behaviors. A program	
150 emphasizing social skills and supervised by his	
151 teacher should be considered.	

(Exhibit continues next page)

Exhibit 23-I (cont.)

Summary

152	Bill, who is 9–8 years old, was referred because of	152–153	name, age, reason for referral
153	educational difficulties. Medical history was normal,	153–154	medical history
154	but there were some developmental delays. His coop-	154–156	reliability and validity
155	erative behavior and other factors suggest that the		
156	testing results are reliable and valid. Bill showed un-	156–159	comparison of strengths and weaknesses
157	usually diverse strengths and weaknesses across intel-		
158	lectual areas, with verbal abilities at a below-average		
159	level and performance abilities at an average level.		
160	Overall, he obtained a WISC-R Full Scale IQ of	160–161	WISC-R score and percentile rank
161	89 ± 6, which is at the 24th percentile and in the	161–162	WISC-R classification
162	Below Average range. He has made little progress in	162–164	school achievement
163	developing skills in spelling, word recognition, and		
164	arithmetic, despite repeating first and second grades.		
165	These deficits are probably manifestations of his lan-	165–166	language processing
166	guage processing difficulties. Socially, Bill acts like a	166–167	social behavior
167	child younger than his age. He evidences charac-	167–168	diagnostic impression
168	teristics of a learning disability. Recommendations are	168–173	recommendations
169	that he be provided with a special education program		
170	focusing on language and speech therapy. In addition,		
171	his family should be offered the opportunity to partici-		
172	pate in counseling to help them resolve their problems		
173	in the home.		
174	(Signature of Examiner) _____	174	examiner's signature
175	Examiner's name	175	examiner's name typed

CONCLUDING COMMENTS ON REPORT WRITING

The overall goal of report writing is to *use clear and precise language to write a well-integrated and logical report that is meaningful to the reader and relevant to the child and his or her problems.* In formulating the report, be open to all sources of data, possible implications of the data, and possible interventions. Work through this material carefully and logically. Recognize whether your statements are based on observations or inferences. Be cognizant of the theoretical model of intelligence, personality, and behavior that you are using. Clearly acknowledge inconclusive findings and do not rationalize or dismiss uncertain or incongruous findings. Finally, avoid premature closure by keeping an open mind about the case referral until you are ready to turn in the final draft.

You can help the reader master the information by formulating a report that is engaging, presents the findings clearly and succinctly, and is specific about the help needed by the child. Avoid having a report become an assessment of the reader's ability to understand your language. The following guidelines will help you to achieve these goals.

• Make your presentation straightforward and objective.

• Edit the report carefully to make certain that spelling, grammar, and punctuation are accurate.

• Watch your semantics – avoid overused or nebulous words, colloquial or pet expressions, and stereotyped phrases.

• Avoid writing a report that is so bland that it might represent anyone. Instead, try to describe a unique, specific child.

• Make the report *tight.*

• Avoid using the report as a place to display your learning or to parade a large vocabulary.

• Stay close to the data until you wish to draw your observations together to make some interpretations.

Report writing is a process of refining ideas, establishing clarity of expression, and using expertise in decision making. The ability to write a clear and meaningful report is highly valued. The psychologist, through the psychological report, contributes to the educational and treatment process, a process that involves other professionals who

Table 23-3
Evaluation Form for Psychological Reports

We are attempting to determine how well our reports meet the needs of persons who request a psychological assessment for a student. This questionnaire is designed to provide us with information about the extent to which this report provides the information which you requested. Your feedback is very important in helping us improve the quality of our service. The first nine items can be answered by checking the appropriate response to each question. The other questions are designed so you can provide feedback about different aspects of the report.

1. To what extent does this report provide an adequate answer to the referral question(s)?

   _____ adequate   _____ partially adequate   _____ inadequate

2. To what extent does this report provide you with new information or insights about the student?

   _____ very helpful   _____ somewhat helpful   _____ not helpful

3. To what extent does this report confirm the insights that you already had about the student?

   _____ very much   _____ somewhat   _____ none

4. To what extent are the information and insights provided in this report helpful to you in developing new ideas of your own about working with the student?

   _____ very helpful   _____ somewhat helpful   _____ not helpful

5. To what extent does this report provide useful recommendations about instructional strategies that may be appropriate for this student?

   _____ very useful   _____ somewhat useful   _____ not useful   _____ none provided

6. To what extent does this report provide helpful recommendations for dealing with the student's behavior?

   _____ very helpful   _____ somewhat helpful   _____ not useful   _____ none provided

7. To what extent do the recommendations in this report reflect an understanding of classroom procedures?

   _____ good understanding   _____ some understanding   _____ poor understanding

8. What is your overall evaluation of the usefulness of this report?

   _____ highly useful   _____ somewhat useful   _____ not useful

9. What type of information did you request when you referred this student for a psychological evaluation?

   ___ eligibility for special education services   ___ suggestions for classroom teaching

   ___ information to increase your understanding of the student   ___ other (please specify) _____

10. What, if any, additional information should have been included in this report?

11. What, if any, technical terms were unclear to you?

12. What, if any, information and/or insights from the report are useful in improving your work with this student?

13. What, if any, of the recommendations will you be implementing in your work with this student?

14. What, if any, suggestions can you provide to help the examining psychologist improve the quality of his/her written reports?

15. Please indicate your position and grade level (if appropriate):

   ___ teacher (grade level _____)   ___ special education teacher (specialty area _____)

   ___ counselor (level _____)   ___ administrator/supervisor (level or area _____)

   ___ speech and language clinician (level _____)   ___ other (please specify) _____

Note. Items 4 through 7 in the questionnaire pertain to remediation and program development and may not be applicable to reports that deal only with classification and placement decisions.

Source: Reprinted with permission of the publisher and authors, from R. L. Ownby and F. H. Wallbrown, "Evaluating School Psychological Reports, Part I: A Procedure for Systematic Feedback," *Psychology in the Schools*, 1983, *20*, p. 44.

are also working toward the goal of enhancing and developing the child's potential.

TEST YOUR SKILL

Exhibit 23-2 presents a series of exercises designed to test your report writing and interpretation skills. In each item there is some inadequacy of description or interpretation. After you have finished evaluating the sentences check your answers with those in Appendix A.

SUMMARY

1. The psychological report is a key part of the assessment process. The report conveys your findings, interpretations, and recommendations and serves as a record of the examinee's performance. It deserves careful preparation.

2. Strive for objectivity and accuracy in the report, but recognize that all reports have elements of subjectivity, including those deriving from your value system.

3. Write the report as soon as possible after the evaluation.

4. The psychological evaluation usually includes eight areas: Identifying Information, Reason for Referral, Background Information, Behavioral Observations, Assessment Results and Clinical Impressions, Recommendations, Summary, and Signature.

5. The Reason for Referral section summarizes the concerns of the referral source.

6. The Background Information section provides relevant material about the child's developmental history and current family and educational situation.

7. The Behavioral Observations section provides a careful description of the child's behavior during testing and attempts to capture the child's unique style.

8. The Assessment Results and Clinical Impressions section synthesizes the major findings. It should include a precision range for the IQ when intelligence is tested.

9. The Recommendations section is developed on the basis of all available information. Specificity is important in making recommendations. Long-range predictions should be made cautiously, if at all, and the wording should convey their speculative nature.

10. The summary presents a concise picture of the findings and recommendations. It generally includes one or more major findings (or points) from each section.

11. To organize your report, look for common themes and trends in the test findings, behavioral observations, and case history. The findings should be integrated in part by use of theoretical perspectives. Note any meaningful deviations from the trends or themes.

12. Use judgment and discretion in deciding what to include in the report and what material to emphasize. Be guided in part by the referral question(s).

13. Generalizations should only be made from reliable findings that form a consistent and clear picture.

14. Intepretations of the child's performance should take into account all available sources of information.

15. The degree of certainty you express in statements should depend on the type of data you are discussing.

16. Illustrations can be used effectively to support inferences and conclusions. Carefully selected examples of the examinee's performance are especially helpful to the reader.

17. In most cases the discussion of the examinee's intellectual ability should be anchored to the overall IQ.

18. Test manuals should be used to obtain the appropriate IQ classification.

19. Percentile ranks are useful in conveying the child's level of functioning.

20. Differences between standard scores should be interpreted only when they are statistically significant.

21. Interpreting the variability of subtest scores requires considerable skill. Consider all information that may be relevant to understanding the pattern of scores.

22. Extrapolated scores must be used with caution.

23. Diagnostic formulations and recommendations should not be based solely on test scores—all available information should be synthesized.

24. Strive for clear, logical, and precise writing and avoid technical terms.

25. Eliminate biased language (or implications of bias) from reports.

26. Strive to write a concise report.

27. Attend to grammar, spelling, and punctuation, and proofread.

28. To improve your writing, develop strategies such as using an outline and rereading your rough draft.

29. Surveys have found that a number of psychologists working in a variety of settings write reports that fail to communicate clearly. Problems center on organization, terminology, content, style, and recommendations.

KEY TERMS, CONCEPTS, AND NAMES

Report outline (p. 726)
Precision range (p. 729)
Test-by-test comparison (p. 730)
Domain-by-domain comparison (p. 730)
Test-oriented statements (p. 736)
Child-oriented statements (p. 736)
IQ classifications (p. 736)
Percentile ranks (p. 736)
Differences between standard scores (p. 737)
Variability (p. 738)
Extrapolated scores (p. 738)
Diagnoses (p. 738)

Exhibit 23-2

Test-Your-Skill Exercises for General Test Interpretation and Report Writing

Read each item to determine where it is inadequate. Check your evaluation with the comments in Appendix A.

Poor Writing

1. An academic weakness for Keith is in arithmetic computation. His spelling ability is below average. Word recognition was also poor.
2. She appears to have rather good academic skills, since she scored in the 99th percentile on the Peabody Individual Achievement Test.
3. Linda was a little tired by the time we reached the last test items.
4. Michelle was easily distracted, which is understandable since it was close to lunchtime.
5. When discussing the future, it became apparent that John's parents have unusually high expectations.
6. Ted appeared to be curious about his environment.
7. It was very difficult to identify the disparate characteristics of her abilities which distinguished her strengths from her weaknesses on all of the subtests comprising the five McCarthy subscale indices.
8. His ability to differentiate essential details contained many inexactitudes and superficial descriptions.
9. The child's drawings were accurate, and without errors within the tolerance guidelines for acceptable designs.
10. Informing her parents as to Connie's abilities and exploring the possibility of an inconsistency between their expectations of her and the time spent with their child.
11. Vocational counseling is recommended to further evaluate the relationship between Henry's anxiety, vision, and goal of becoming a corporate pilot in addition to consideration of other option's for earning a living in the future.
12. She scored an IQ score of 111.
13. Helen's definitions of words were not always clear, concise, and direct. On one definition item she answered it in terms of baseball.
14. Ann has shown scores of average intelligence with a lack of intellectual maturity.
15. This testing with a young adult just flew by in terms of time, because the subject either answered, or did the tasks quickly and directed without any hitch.
16. He does not demonstrate good pencil control at the automatic level yet.
17. He tapped his foot nervously on the floor.
18. In comparison, his interpretation of social situations was below average.
19. This subject is a small girl with a pleasant disposition and rapport.
20. The client frequently said, "I don't know".
21. Rick's attention and concentration throughout testing was excellent.

22. In view of the ideal testing conditions, the results of the test seem to be valid in terms of administration and the subject's participation.
23. She currently shares an apartment with several other students which she doesn't get along with.
24. His level of functioning exceeds that of 95 percent of the children in the standardization group.
25. She errored in all tasks.
26. The results to some extent have to be discounted, or strictly speaking not be considering valid, if one wants to use rigid criteria in this instance.
27. Although quite verbal, this 9-year-old girl did not exhibit the egocentric babbling of a less mature child.
28. The following comment was made for a 6-year-old child: "She has limited ability in manipulating her environment."
29. Fred appears to be a youngster with a good vocabulary, but ironically he did not do as well as the examiner expected.
30. The following sentence was written for a child with an IQ of 73: "Some consideration of not allowing Tom to do less than his potential should be kept in mind."
31. In line with speed, competitiveness was apparent when he would ask questions about how his times compared to others.
32. Beth's overreaction to criticism very often leads to a type of perseveration that impacts following behaviors until success is again achieved.
33. He generally raced through items with which he was most adept, while malingering over those items with which he was less familiar.
34. Considering his sister reportedly having hearing problems and himself reporting occasional hearing difficulties, this may have interfered with his performance.
35. She prioritizes working fast.

Inaccurate, Incomplete, or Irrelevant Statements

36. Her rigid approach to the Block Design task may indicate covert feelings of inadequacy.
37. Since there is no evidence of Oedipal conflict in Gunnar's behavior, he must have completely repressed it.
38. Her average visual-motor coordination is an indication of field dependence and left-hemisphere processing.
39. Bill is considered a troublemaker and this may be due to good social judgment and grasp of social conventionality.
40. His sometimes wandering attention may have contributed to his scatter of subtest scores.
41. It appears that Terry has well-developed learning skills by the fact that he picked up learning and performance sets quickly.

(Exhibit continues next page)

Exhibit 23-2 (cont.)

42. Her IQ of 134 predicts excellent success in school.
43. Jeff could not even write his own name.
44. Joey never pays attention in class.
45. Ted is in excellent health, but does have food allergies. Some researchers have posited an association between learning disabilities and allergies.
46. Lower scores were found on items that probably reflect natural endowment as opposed to early educational environment.
47. "John had severe perceptual and verbal expression problems." This sentence was then followed by a discussion of arithmetic skills.
48. Because he performed at the same level in all aspects of the test, he is probably well adjusted in school.
49. Items that reflect John's ability to learn were not high.
50. On the basis of his IQ of 107, there would be no mismatch between his level of intelligence and the kind of instruction he would receive in the regular classroom.
51. James told the examiner that his mother frequently invited different men over to the house.
52. Because of Tim's level of anxiety, it is likely that the results may be somewhat lower than his true level of functioning but are believed to be not sufficiently altered to give an invalid picture of his present level of functioning.
53. It must be noted, however, that because Steve is a minority student, the low score of 68 on this intelligence test cannot be used as a valid input toward a nonbiased assessment of this youngster.
54. The results of this test herein should be seen in the context of the "practice effect," since Helen has done (practiced) this test more than once already.

Inappropriate Abbreviations

55. His score places him in the 92%ile.
56. Most of our LDs are resourced, but Mark is in self-contained because he's both LD and EMH.

Inappropriate Value Judgments

57. Hector's mother is on welfare, so it's no wonder he often comes to school dirty or hungry.
58. Although her parents are concerned about her and try to aid her in any way possible, their own lack of education and verbal abilities has an effect on the child's learning process.
59. Based on family size and income, she has been subject to too little cultural and social enrichment.
60. John's teacher believes that the family is on welfare, which would account for John's torn clothing and tattered appearance at times.
61. Richard's obnoxious mannerisms tend to irritate adults.

Inappropriate Recommendations

62. A speech pathologist should conduct an evaluation to look at auditory questions raised by her test performance.
63. Any kind of remediation that she is involved in should emphasize socially related reinforcement. Her test performance shows that she understands and acts to a large degree based on her social perceptions.
64. He should receive direct help (counseling) with hypothesized emotional issues.
65. Periodic general evaluations are recommended.

Transition words (p. 739)
Biased language (p. 745)
Pitfalls in report writing (p. 748)

STUDY QUESTIONS

1. What purposes do psychological reports serve?
2. What information is included in each of the following sections of a report: Background Information, Behavioral Observations, Assessment Results and Clinical Impressions, Recommendations, and Summary?
3. Compare and contrast the various sections of a psychological report.
4. What strategies can you use to organize the assessment findings?
5. What guidelines should you use to decide which material to include in the report?
6. What are some guidelines for making generalizations, interpretations, and diagnoses?
7. What are some important factors to consider in communicating your findings?
8. How can you eliminate biased language in the report?
9. Describe some useful strategies for writing reports.
10. Develop a checklist for evaluating the quality of a psychological report.
11. What are some typical problems that readers encounter in psychological reports?
12. Discuss seven common pitfalls in report writing.

_24

ISSUES IN CONSULTATION

Why can we not look at our social problems in different ways? We continue to provide old answers, rather than search for new questions. Shall we continue to ask what is "wrong" with the child, but neglect to ask what is wrong with his world? Shall we ask what makes people poor, but not what makes people rich? Shall we inquire as to why the child fails the school, and not why the school fails the child? Shall we ask how a child is different, but fail to consider how he is alike? New questions may require that we look at things differently— perhaps to proceed in directions in which we do not have the resolve to go.

—Alfred Baumeister and John R. Muma

It is easy for critics to produce logical arguments against testing children. Mislabeling, of course, can deny a child educational opportunities and damage the self-image of the child. Yet most such arguments remain at the abstract level. The exceptions are a few well-publicized cases. What we do not hear about are the thousands of cases in which well-trained professional psychologists, working with caring teachers and loving parents, quietly identify the sources of children's frustrations and place them in an environment in which growth and success, not frustration, become the norm. We also do not hear about the other thousands of cases in which children remain frustrated because well-meaning teachers and parents fail or refuse to have a child tested because they "don't believe in testing." It is the psychological equivalent of refusing to take a child to a doctor because you "don't believe in doctors." Psychologists, like physicians, sometimes make mistakes; but it is a much bigger mistake to regard errors as the norm, and behave as though Binet, Simon, Terman, and Wechsler and all the other great names in the assessment field had never been born, and as though psychologists had no expertise to offer in this field.

—William A. Hillix

Your role as a psychologist does not end with the testing of the child and the writing of a report. As a result of the information provided in the report, decisions will be made and actions will be taken. You may be called on to present your findings at a case conference, to confer with individual teachers and other school personnel, to meet with the child and parents, or to consult with other professionals. In these ways the findings of the psychological evaluation become "alive," enabling you to contribute to the decision-making process.

To be effective as a consultant, you should know as intimately as possible the situations in which change is to take place. If the consultation occurs in a school setting, you should have a harmonious working relationship with the school personnel and knowledge of the child's classroom and classroom behavior; additionally, continuous interactions and feedback are desirable. If you are working in the larger community, you should have information about the available agencies, centers, workshops, and inpatient facilities. You should know what treatments are offered at the various facilities and their effectiveness in helping children.

ETHICAL STANDARDS OF PSYCHOLOGISTS

The Ethical Standards of Psychologists of the American Psychological Association (1981) should serve as guidelines for your work as a consultant. A careful study of the standards will enable you to understand some of the responsibilities associated with your professional role.

Some of the highlights of the standards, with respect to assessment, are as follows:

1. Psychologists must recognize that their recommendations may alter the lives of others and be aware of their social responsibilities.

2. Psychologists must recognize their own competencies and the limitations of their techniques.

3. Public statements made about diagnostic services must be accurate and objective.

4. Psychologists must protect the confidentiality of the information obtained in the course of the evaluation. The only exceptions are when consent is given by the client (or guardian) to release the information, when you are working with other professionals within an agency, or when failure to release information would violate the law.

5. Before beginning an assessment, psychologists should make sure that clients clearly understand the financial costs connected with the assessment.

6. Clients have a right to have access to their test results and should be provided with the basis for the conclusions and recommendations.

7. Security of tests and test results must be maintained.

8. Doubts concerning the reliability or validity of the test results should be clearly stated in the report.

9. Research on assessment must take into consideration the dignity and welfare of the subjects participating in the research project.

A study of professional malpractice claims (Wright, 1981) indicates that they often relate to psychological evaluations. Complaints include allegations of wrongful use or misuse of tests, wrongful use of derived data, misinterpretation of tests or interviews, invasion of privacy, and violation of confidence. To reduce professional liability, Wright suggests that the psychologist fully inform the client about the purpose of the evaluation, the results of the evaluation (including findings and recommendations), the variety of uses to which the results may be put, and the various individuals who may see the report. Additionally, tests should be administered in standardized fashion, and specific and detailed notes should be made concerning the interview and the examination. Obviously, some of the above recommendations do not apply to young children. All of the recommendations can be carried out with adolescents, however. In most cases, except when the examinee is a self-referred adolescent over 18 years of age, the child's parents should be informed of the purpose of the evaluation, the results, and the individuals who may see the report.

CONSULTATION IN THE SCHOOLS

Consultation in schools involves working with children, teachers, other school personnel, and parents. The parents are a crucial part of the equation. Their support (or lack thereof) will greatly influence remediation efforts. You must be able to communicate with the parents, as well as the teacher and the child.

Although our focus here is on consultation with teachers and parents of handicapped children, you may also be consulting with teachers and parents of normal and gifted children. Many of the principles discussed in this chapter apply to these consultations as well.

Orientation of School Psychologists

If you work in schools as a psychologist, you should be a *school* psychologist, emphasizing the learning process, particularly as it relates to formal education. This role contrasts with that of the psychometrician, who focuses on test results, and that of the clinical psychologist, who focuses on psychopathology. The school psychologist's view must encompass more than just the tests and the child. The school environment, the teacher, and the educational program are all important elements of the learning matrix, as are the child's individual dynamics and the home environment. School psychologists, then, must aim to facilitate children's learning in the school setting; to apply psychological research theory and technology to the solution of school-related problems; and to assist teachers, parents, administrators, and other school personnel.

Functions of School Psychologists

The professional functions of school psychologists include assessment, intervention and counseling, consultation, research and evaluation, and administration. Administration refers to the effective coordination of resources to promote the development of all pupils. School psychologists are called upon to assist not only in their traditional roles as diagnosticians, but also as learning specialists, capable of determining the learning environment and procedures that will best facilitate the child's learning. In order to function

successfully as a consultant to schools, you must know about the structure, function, and effectiveness of regular and special education classes, resource rooms, and regular classes for handicapped, exceptional, and normal children. Some children may require a trial period in a special education program or a regular day class before you can determine which is the most beneficial learning environment. Children may also benefit from combinations of regular and special classes, along with the services of resource specialists (for example, reading specialists, speech specialists, and counselors), special tutors, and peer counselors. The poem in Exhibit 24-1 vividly captures the work of the school psychologist.

Role of the Psychological Evaluation in School Consultation

Teachers refer children for psychological evaluation primarily for learning-related problems, emotional problems, or attention-related problems. Because many school psychologists spend a large part of their time performing diagnostic work, they have been called the "gatekeepers" for special education. School psychologists, as part of a multidisciplinary team, play a vital role in determining who will be placed in special classes. Assessment informa-

---

Exhibit 24-1

Ode to a School Psychologist

Tick tock	Give a WISC-R	Try a contract	Attend a workshop	*Source:* Reprinted with permission of the publisher and author from C. A. Rapinz, "Ode to a School Psychologist," in *Ohio School Psychologist*, 1982, 28(1), p. 16.
goes the clock	then a WRAT	make a chart	read a book	
keep on going	add a Bender	behavior mod's	give phone messages	
never stop	after that	a useful art	a second look	
test test	Draw A Person	chart the goals	create a handout	
score score	read a word	check learning style	run a group	
have a conference	say the numbers	make proper notes	have P.P.S. meeting	
always more	as they're heard	in child's file	attempt to recoup	
meet with teacher				
meet with dad	Catch the kid	Place in L.D.	THEN . . .!!!	
meet with mother	being good	discrepancy needed		
teacher glad	learn to listen	place in I.I.	Tick tock	
write write	as you should	Vineland completed	goes the clock	
read sign	be firm kind	place in S.B.H.	keep on going	
keep the paperwork	and consistent	behavior treated	never stop . . .	
in line	don't give up	in any case		
here a conference	be insistent	I.E.P. needed		
there a test				
consultation				
for the rest				

tion should be used to find the least restrictive placement that will best facilitate the child's education; assessment should not be simply a matter of arriving at a diagnostic label.

The psychological evaluation serves various important functions. The major objectives include classification, description of learning style, class placement, and development of remediation, management, and teaching strategies. If you are to carry out these functions, you will need to have knowledge of (a) psychological and psychoeducational assessment instruments, (b) child psychopathology and exceptionality, (c) behavioral and educational interventions, (d) Public Law 94-142 and other pertinent laws, and (e) the special needs of transitional pupils who are being transferred from special education to regular education.

The purpose of consultation is to help teachers find solutions to pupil problems. The emphasis should be on translating the results of the assessment directly into programming activities. The psychological report and follow-up consultations should help teachers (a) modify their behavior, (b) deal more effectively with the child, parents, and other teachers and school personnel, (c) plan new teaching strategies or curriculum changes, and (d) develop a framework within which they can view changes in children over time. These goals can be met in part by helping teachers to clarify the nature of the problem, determine interventions that have been tried (both successful and unsuccessful ones), and find possible alternatives. Ongoing consultation is required to determine whether recommendations must be modified on the basis of the child's response (or lack thereof).

Illustrations of Recommendations Made by School Psychologists

Teachers want school psychologists to be concerned not only with diagnosis, but also with intervention. Thus you will need to identify sources of interference in the educational process, understand the dynamics of those sources, and recommend appropriate intervention or remediation strategies.

Recommendations made by the multidisciplinary team of which the school psychologist is a part may include the following:

• placement of the child in special programs or special classes, or with special teachers;
• remedial techniques that could facilitate the child's learning;

• changes in curriculum, subject matter presentation, or learning atmosphere;
• behavior management programs that teachers or parents could implement to help the child in social, emotional, and educational spheres;
• counseling or therapy by a school counselor or psychologist, or at an outside agency; and
• assistance with academic activities at home.

Unfortunately, teachers are not likely to follow recommendations that require great effort; they are more likely to do so, however, when follow-up contacts are made. Recommendations should always take into consideration the assets and limitations of the classroom and the resources available in the school, home, and community.

Techniques for Working with Parents and Teachers

Parents and teachers need to feel comfortable expressing their needs, problems, and desires to you. Show them respect and understanding. *Recognize that it will be the teacher and parents who will have to continue to work with the child after the evaluation is completed.* Obtain the teacher's support for the recommended prescriptive teaching program; if you do not, diagnostic testing will become a meaningless procedure that will not benefit the child, teacher, or school. If you sense that the parents or teachers feel threatened, modify your techniques in order to resolve these feelings. Focus on ways to help parents and teachers become more sensitive in their relationship with the child.

Help to translate the teacher's strengths into potential actions, and design the interventions so that they are congruent with the teacher's conception of his or her role. Additional guidelines for working with teachers are as follows (Handler, Gerston, & Handler, 1965):

• Work with the teacher to define the problem behaviors.
• Describe the assessment strategy to the teacher.
• Pool your information with the teacher's information.
• Prepare a plan for the teacher that takes into account his or her capabilities and limitations and those of the school and home.
• Supplement the written report with an oral report.
• Explore with the teacher the ways in which the personnel and the resources of the school and community may be used advantageously.
• Relieve the teacher of inappropriately assumed responsibility for the child's behavior.

• Help the teacher understand that immediate results may not be forthcoming.

• Encourage the teacher to adopt a variety of methods in dealing with students, stressing the use of flexible procedures.

• Remain available for future consultation.

Teachers are in a key position to identify handicapped children. As observers of children's performance in the classroom, they are also in an excellent position to help in developing remediation strategies. In many cases, teachers may have sufficient information to develop appropriate educational programs themselves, once they have been given assessment information on the child's strengths, weaknesses, and exceptionalities.

PUBLIC LAW 94-142: THE EDUCATION FOR ALL HANDICAPPED CHILDREN ACT OF 1975

Public Law 94-142, the Education for All Handicapped Children Act of 1975, has important implications for the practice of psychology in the schools and other settings. The law was designed to ensure the right to education for all persons, including handicapped children. It incorporates many of the ethical principles discussed previously. Educational programming for the handicapped is a key provision of the law. The law establishes safeguards for the evaluation and placement of children; makes its provisions applicable to private as well as public schools; requires the identification of children presently unserved; requires the elimination of architectural barriers; requires that the education of handicapped children be in the least restrictive environment (for example, within a regular class as much as possible); calls for the development of individual educational programs (IEPs); gives parents the right to have access to records and participate in the development of educational objectives; requires nondiscriminatory assessment procedures; and requires confidentiality of information.

Testing and Evaluation Procedures

Public Law 94-142 stipulates that state and local educational agencies shall ensure, at a minimum, that:

(a) Tests and other evaluation materials:
(1) Are provided and administered in the child's native language or other mode of communication, unless it is clearly not feasible to do so;

(2) Have been validated for the specific purpose for which they are used;
(3) Are administered by trained personnel in conformance with the instructions provided by their producer.
(b) Tests and other evaluation materials include those tailored to assess specific areas of educational need and not merely those which are designed to provide a single general intelligence quotient;
(c) Tests are selected and administered so as best to ensure that when a test is administered to a child with impaired sensory, manual or speaking skills, the test results accurately reflect the child's aptitude or achievement level or whatever other factors the test purports to measure, rather than reflecting the child's impaired sensory, manual, or speaking skills (except where those skills are the factors which the test purports to measure);
(d) No single procedure is used as the sole criterion for determining an appropriate educational program for a child; and
(e) The evaluation is made by a multidisciplinary team or group of persons, including at least one teacher or other specialist with knowledge in the area of suspected disability.
(f) The child is assessed in all areas related to the suspected disability, including, where appropriate, health, vision, hearing, social and emotional status, general intelligence, academic performance, communicative status, and motor abilities. (*Federal Register*, August 23, 1977, Vol. 42, No. 163, pp. 42496–42497, 121a.532)

In addition,

testing and evaluation materials and procedures used for the purposes of evaluation and placement of handicapped children must be selected and administered so as not to be racially or culturally discriminatory. (*Federal Register*, August 23, 1977, Vol. 42, No. 163, p. 42496, 121a.530)

Development of an Individualized Educational Program (IEP)

An IEP is a plan designed to help a handicapped child achieve particular educational goals. It is a team effort, bringing together the skills and resources of the educational staff. Each word in the term "individualized educational program" has a particular meaning: *individualized* means that the program is directed toward the unique needs of a specific child; *educational* means that the program is directed to learning activities; and *program* refers to specific and clearly formulated goals and means to reach those goals.

Components of the IEP.   The IEP is a statement of the expectations the educational staff has for the handicapped child. The basic components of an IEP are as follows:

1. A description of the child's present level of educational performance.

2. Annual instructional objectives (or long-range goals) that specify the educational performance to be achieved by the end of the school year. These are concrete statements of what the student will be able to do. The objectives should be realistic — the student should be able to accomplish them in a nine-month period. Examples of some long-term goals are to increase reading level from the first-grade to the second-grade level, to improve spelling, to improve practical and applied arithmetical skills, and to improve social interactions with peers. Exhibit 24-2 is an example of an IEP checklist.

In arriving at instructional objectives, you should consider program content, conditions in which the learning takes place, and the proposed level of performance. It is also important to consider the child's learning style, rate of learning, need for structure, and favored sense modalities. The written goals and objectives serve a number of purposes: they provide for accountability; they motivate students; they facilitate teacher-parent communication; and they focus attention on learning activities.

3. Short-term instructional objectives. These objectives are similar to long-term instructional objectives, but they focus on specific functions that can be achieved in a short time, such as buttoning and unbuttoning a coat, identifying vowel sounds, walking 10 feet, using complete sentences, and making appropriate social responses to peers. These goals usually correspond to manageable units of instruction.

4. A description of the specific educational services needed by the child. All special services required to meet the unique needs of the child should be specified, including the appropriate type of physical education. All special instructional media and materials that will be needed should also be listed.

5. The date when special services will begin and the anticipated length of time that services will be given.

6. The extent to which the child will participate in regular education programs. (Every attempt must be made to place the handicapped child in the least restrictive educational alternative.)

7. A justification for the type of educational placement that the child will have.

8. A list of the individuals who are responsible for implementation of the IEP.

9. The objective criteria, evaluation procedures, and schedules for determining whether the instructional objectives are being achieved. According to PL 94-142, the IEP should be reviewed at least once a year and revised if

necessary. Parents, teacher, and an administrator should be present at the review meeting. This review meeting usually takes place at the end of the school year, but can also occur when a student transfers to another school district, when there is a change in placement, or on the anniversary of the child's original placement.

The annual review serves a number of functions: plans, procedures, and outcomes are reviewed and evaluated; difficulties with the plan are identified; reasons for any difficulties are sought; new goals and procedures are formulated; and feedback is provided to those responsible for the plan and for its implementation.

Notifying parents.   When an individual assessment is planned, the parents should receive written notice of their child's referral in ordinary wording and in the primary language used in the home. The procedures described below should then be followed to ensure that the parents' "informed consent" is obtained.

The parents should be invited to attend a meeting with staff personnel. The following items should be discussed at the meeting or, if the parents are unable to appear, presented in writing or through documented telephone calls or a home visit: (a) the nature of the problem; (b) assessment needs and procedures, including any anticipated referrals of records; (c) all tests, records, and information-gathering procedures to be used; (d) possible uses of information gathered; and (e) due process, procedural safeguards, confidentiality, and parent access to records. The following items should be sought from parents at the meeting, or in some other manner if no meeting is held: written consent for you to perform the assessment; written consent for you to obtain and share information; information on languages used in the home; and parental perceptions of the child's problem, adaptive behavior, and resources.

Parents are expected to take an active role in the IEP meeting:

The IEP meeting serves as a communication vehicle between parents and school personnel, and enables them as equal participants to jointly decide what the child's needs are, what services will be provided to meet those needs, and what the anticipated outcomes will be. (*Federal Register*, January 19, 1981, p. 5462)

In some cases, however, the "equal participant" expectation may not be realistic. Many parents prefer to *receive* information, rather than to contribute actively. Encouraging parents to share their perceptions may enable them to take a more active role.

Comment on IEPs.   The development of IEPs is by no means an easy task. The statements contained in the IEP

Exhibit 24-2

IEP Checklist

Toledo Public Schools

INITIAL IEP

PSYCHOLOGICAL SERVICES

Student's Name _____

Annual Goals and Short-Term Instruction Objectives (IO)

Please indicate with a ＼ the goals and objectives selected at the IEP conference. The mastery level criterion for each IO is 90% unless otherwise specified. IO's will be evaluated by teacher post test or observation. Additional goals should be written as needed. The classroom teacher will indicate with a ／ when goals are mastered.

Key ＼ objective selected Date goals and objectives were selected _____
　　✕ objective mastered Date goals and objectives were reviewed _____

Goals for Learning Disabled students should focus on those area(s) of discrepancy which established eligibility. Goals for Developmentally Handicapped students must include both academics and social emotional (adaptive behavior) goals.

☐ **INCREASE PERFORMANCE IN READINESS ACTIVITIES.**
☐ Recognize following colors ☐ Red ☐ Blue ☐ Green ☐ Yellow ☐ Orange ☐ Purple ☐ Brown ☐ Black ☐ Pink ☐ Gray
☐ Visually discriminate like and different symbols.
☐ Follow left to right sequence.
☐ Copy following shapes ☐ Circle ☐ Plus sign ☐ Square ☐ Triangle ☐ Diamond
☐ Draw-A-Person with detail.
☐ Identify _____ of 19 body parts. (See Brigance record booklet for specific body parts)
☐ Comprehend _____ of 20 directional and prepositional concepts. (see Brigance record booklet for specific concepts)
☐ Give following personal data verbally ☐ Name ☐ Age ☐ Address ☐ Phone number ☐ Birthday ☐ Brothers ☐ Sisters ☐ Parents
☐ Count by rote to _____
☐ Recite alphabet to _____
☐ Read numerals 1 - 10.
☐ Understand numerals 1 - 10.
☐ Recognize following lower case letters _____
☐ Recognize following upper case letters _____
☐ Write following dictated lower case letters _____
☐ Write following dictated upper case letters _____
☐ Write first and last name.
☐ Write numbers in sequence to _____

ACADEMIC FUNCTIONING

☐ **INCREASE PERFORMANCE IN BASIC READING SKILLS.**
☐ Increase reading readiness skills (See readiness goals and objectives).
☐ Increase performance in word recognition _____ of 250 Brigance basic sight words. (See Brigance record booklet for specific words)
☐ Increase performance in following phonetic word analysis (word attack skills).
☐ Initial consonants (☐ auditorily ☐ visually) ☐ ending sounds (☐ Auditorily ☐ visually) ☐ naming vowels ☐ short vowel sounds ☐ long vowel sounds
☐ Initial clusters (☐ auditorily ☐ visually)
☐ Verbal blends (digraphs) ☐ diphthongs ☐ Root words and affixes. (See Brigance record book for specifics)
☐ Improve reading rate.
☐ _____
☐ _____
☐ **INCREASE PERFORMANCE IN READING COMPREHENSION.**
☐ Improve Brigance oral reading comprehension skill level from _____ to _____.
☐ Improve following passage comprehension skills ☐ sequential order ☐ locating information ☐ paraphrasing ☐ inferences ☐ conclusions ☐ cause and effect ☐ mood ☐ main idea
☐ _____
☐ _____
☐ **INCREASE PERFORMANCE IN MATHEMATICS CALCULATION.**
☐ Perform precomputational mathematical operations (See readiness goals and objectives).
☐ Know following ordinal numbers ☐ first ☐ second ☐ third ☐ fourth ☐ fifth ☐ sixth ☐ seventh ☐ eighth
☐ Demonstrate knowledge of following math symbols ☐ + ☐ - ☐ × ☐ - ☐ $ ☐ ¢
☐ Know addition combinations (addition facts) thru 10
☐ Demonstrate knowledge of following place values ☐ 1 ☐ 10 ☐ 100 ☐ 500 ☐ 1000
☐ Perform addition mathematical operations _____ digits with _____ renamings
☐ Know subtraction combinations (subtraction facts) thru 10

☐ Perform subtraction mathematical operations _____ digits with _____ renamings
☐ Know multiplication combinations (multiplication facts) thru 10
☐ Perform multiplication operations _____ digits x _____ digits _____ with carrying.
☐ Know division combinations (division facts) thru 10.
☐ Perform division mathematical operations _____ digits by _____ digits with remainder.
☐ Perform following mathematical operations with fractions. ☐ Addition ☐ Subtraction ☐ Multiplication ☐ Division ☐ Conversion (☐ lower term ☐ higher term ☐ other ___)
☐ Perform following mathematical operations with decimals. ☐ Addition ☐ Subtraction ☐ Multiplication ☐ Division
☐ Other math goals added by IEP team _____
☐ _____
☐ **INCREASE PERFORMANCE IN MATHEMATICS REASONING.**
☐ Read following numbers ☐ 1 thru 10 ☐ 11 thru 19 ☐ 20 thru 100
☐ Understanding following concepts ☐ more than ☐ less than ☐ large ☐ small ☐ shorter ☐ taller
☐ Name fractional parts when shown pictorial representation
☐ Name following coins and currency ☐ penny ☐ nickel ☐ dime ☐ quarter ☐ half dollar ☐ dollar
☐ State value of following coins ☐ penny ☐ nickel ☐ dime ☐ quarter ☐ half dollar ☐ dollar
☐ State following coin relationships ☐ penny ☐ nickel ☐ dime ☐ quarter ☐ half dollar ☐ dollar
☐ Make change for less than ☐ one dollar ☐ ten dollars
☐ Perform time operations — tell time to ☐ hour ☐ 1/2 hour ☐ 15 minutes ☐ minutes
☐ Perform calendar operations ☐ Name day, month, seasons in order ☐ Relationship of calendar units
☐ Perform following measurement operations ☐ Ruler ☐ Liquid ☐ Weight ☐ Thermometer
☐ Perform following metric measurement operations ☐ Ruler ☐ Liquid ☐ Weight ☐ Thermometer
☐ Identify equivalents ☐ linear ☐ liquid
☐ Other math reasoning goals and objectives _____
☐ **IMPROVE ORAL EXPRESSION**
☐ Increase prespeech ☐ affective expression ☐ prespeech nonverbal expression
☐ Increase following spoken vocabulary skills. ☐ Verbalize picture names ☐ Number of spoken words ☐ sequence
☐ Improve oral grammar and syntax (correct verb forms with noun).
☐ Improve following verbal fluency skills ☐ Repeating sequence of _____ ☐ Intonation ☐ Rate ☐ Clarity
☐ Improve signing skills
☐ Care for auditory equipment
☐ Participate in class discussions
☐ _____
☐ _____
☐ **INCREASE LISTENING COMPREHENSION SKILLS**
☐ Improve auditory discrimination
☐ Improve following listening and attending skills. ☐ Name object by auditory description
☐ Recall following details of paragraph read at ☐ Grade Level ☐ Sequential Order ☐ inference ☐ conclusions ☐ cause and effect ☐ mood ☐ main idea
☐ Follow _____ part verbal directions
☐ Categorize ☐ Objects ☐ Ideas with common characteristics
☐ _____
☐ _____
☐ **IMPROVE WRITTEN EXPRESSION SKILLS.**
☐ Improve following spelling skills ☐ Improve word recall ☐ Use basic phonics skills in spelling ☐ Use spelling correctly in other subjects
☐ Improve following handwriting skills ☐ writing manuscript letters (☐ lower case ☐ upper case) ☐ writing cursive letters (☐ lower case ☐ upper case) ☐ decrease reversals of following letters _____ ☐ spacing ☐ paper position ☐ copy from board

(Exhibit continues next page)

Exhibit 24-2 (cont.)

☐ Write following personal data information ☐ name ☐ address ☐ age ☐ phone ☐ birthdate ☐ school ☐ grade ☐ teacher ☐ signature

☐ Increase following capitalization skills ☐ beginning of sentence ☐ names of people ☐ days of week ☐ months ☐ special days ☐ streets ☐ cities ☐ states ☐ countries ☐ titles of peoples ☐ books

☐ Increase following sentence writing skills ☐ Differentiate between sentence & phrase ☐ identify and use different kinds of sentences ☐ parts of speech ☐ subject and predicate

☐ write a simple sentence.

☐ Increase paragraph writing skills.

☐ Increase following letter writing skills ☐ personal ☐ business ☐ social

☐ Improve following punctuation skills ☐ period ☐ question mark ☐ commas ☐ exclamation point ☐ quotation marks ☐ apostrophe

☐ Improve written expression content.

☐ _____

☐ _____

PHYSICAL FUNCTIONING

☐ **IMPROVE FOLLOWING FINE MOTOR SKILLS DEVELOPMENT**

☐ Increase using both hands ☐ Increase tracking skills ☐ Increase grasping skills

☐ Increase bilateral hand use skills

☐ Increase manipulation skills ☐ Increase cutting, pasting and painting skills

☐ _____

☐ _____

☐ **IMPROVE FOLLOWING GROSS MOTOR SKILLS**

☐ Increase following pre-ambulatory developmental skills ☐ sitting ☐ walking

☐ Increase crawling skills.

☐ Increase standing and walking skills.

☐ Increase following advanced locomotion skills ☐ running ☐ jumping ☐ using stairs ☐ climbing

☐ Increase balancing and gymnastics skills.

☐ Increase following coordination skills ☐ throwing ball ☐ catch ball ☐ ride tricycle ☐ bicycle

☐ Increase skills in exercise and dance.

☐ Increase skills in wheelchair use.

☐ Increase skills in games and sports.

☐ Increase skills in moving about ☐ school environment ☐ community ☐ outside community

☐ Increase skills in using public transportation.

☐ _____

☐ _____

SOCIAL EMOTIONAL FUNCTIONING

☐ **INCREASE SOCIALIZATION SKILLS**

☐ Increase abilities in expressing and recognizing feelings.

☐ Increase assertiveness skills.

☐ Increase following appropriate interpersonal relationship skills with peers and adults.

☐ Initiate social communication ☐ cooperative interaction ☐ belong to group ☐ dating.

☐ **Increase Following Play and Leisure Time Skills** ☐ play with toys ☐ play with others ☐ make believe activities ☐ share and cooperate ☐ watch TV ☐ follow game rules ☐ play games ☐ begin group activities ☐ hobbies extra curricular activities ☐ go places with friends independently

☐ **Increase Following Coping Skills** ☐ follow rules ☐ begin politeness ☐ use manners in conversation ☐ be responsible for time ☐ be sensitive to others ☐ use table manners ☐ control impulses ☐ apologize ☐ borrowing and returning ☐ make and keep appointments ☐ emergency procedures

☐ **Decrease Following Maladaptive Behaviors** _____

_____

☐ **IMPROVE STUDY SKILLS.**

☐ Develop organization and study skills necessary for completion of course work.

☐ Increase monitoring and general copying skills.

☐ Develop note-taking skills.

☐ Develop out-lining skills.

☐ Pass regular classes.

☐ Complete assignments ☐ classroom ☐ homework

☐ Improve following reference skills ☐ alphabetical order ☐ dictionary use ☐ reference books ☐ parts of a book ☐ location ☐ purpose ☐ library skills

☐ _____

☐ _____

☐ **INCREASE VOCATIONAL SKILLS.**

☐ Increase following pre-vocational job skills.

☐ Improve job attitudes.

☐ Improve job identification skills.

☐ Improve job selection skills.

☐ Improve job search skills.

☐ Demonstrate knowledge of job rules and regulation.

☐ Improve on-the-job performance.

☐ _____

☐ _____

☐ **IMPROVE DOMESTIC AND COMMUNITY LIVING SKILLS.**

☐ Increase skills in food planning, preparation and serving.

☐ Increase skills in clothing selection and preparation.

☐ Increase skills in housing selection.

☐ Increase skills in home furnishing and crafts.

☐ Increase telephone skills.

☐ Increase knowledge of leisure and recreation.

☐ Increase knowledge of family planning and development.

☐ Increase mobility and transportation.

☐ Increase following money management skills ☐ budgeting ☐ use of checkbook ☐ use of savings account ☐ finance charge.

☐ _____

☐ _____

☐ **INCREASE PERSONAL DAILY LIVING SKILLS**

☐ Increase following dressing/undressing skills ☐ remove clothing ☐ fasten fasteners ☐ put on shoes ☐ put on clothing ☐ wear clothing ☐ appropriate for weather

☐ Increase following feeding/eating skills ☐ eating ☐ drinking ☐ using tablewear

☐ Increase toileting skills

☐ Increase following personal hygiene skills ☐ bathe with assistance ☐ brush teeth ☐ wash hands and face ☐ care for nose ☐ bathe without assistance ☐ care for hair ☐ care for fingernails

☐ _____

☐ _____

☐ **OTHER GOALS/SHORT-TERM OBJECTIVES/COMMENTS:**

☐ _____

☐ _____

☐ _____

☐ _____

☐ _____

☐ _____

☐ _____

☐ _____

☐ _____

Source: Reprinted with permission of the Toledo Public Schools.

are "plans"; they are not foolproof prescriptions. Although they represent the best thinking of the educational staff and the child's parents—developed on the basis of assessment information, available resources, and staff discussions—they must be monitored continually. They should be viewed as guideposts, not as fixed and unchangeable strategies and goals. If the goals and objectives set forth in the IEP are not met, school personnel are not held accountable (*Federal Register*, January 19, 1981, p. 5462).

"Oscar, I do not consider 'beating some sense into their stubborn little heads' an acceptable behavioral objective."

Courtesy of *Phi Delta Kappan* and the artist, Bardulf Ueland.

Parents' Right to an Independent Educational Evaluation

One provision of PL 94-142 allows parents to obtain an independent educational evaluation of their child if they disagree with the evaluation performed at the local educational agency. The evaluation is paid for by the school district only upon the recommendation of a hearing officer, however. If the parents initiate the independent educational evaluation, the results must be considered and evaluated by the state and local educational agency, but the agency is not obliged to comply with the results and recommendations of the external evaluation.

If parents reject the placement decisions of the educational staff, they are entitled under the due process clause of PL 94-142 to seek another decision. Alternative procedures available to parents include (from least to most

formal): informal discussions in the mediation stage, hearings/arbitration, and formal legal proceedings at the court level. In order to participate adequately in these hearings, psychologists have to develop forensic skills. (See the section on challenges of being an expert witness toward the end of this chapter.)

Periodic Evaluations

Reevaluation of the child must be conducted at least every three years, or more frequently if conditions warrant it. Reevaluations serve three major purposes: (a) to evaluate whether the child continues to be eligible for a special class placement according to the placement criteria, (b) to evaluate progress made in the special class placement, and (c) to identify new areas for instruction within regular and special education programs and develop new intervention plans to meet the needs identified. Reevaluations thus are an important means of checking periodically to ensure that a child is not misplaced in a special education program and of evaluating program progress and making recommendations for future educational programming.

Parents' Right to Examine Records

Parents have the right to inspect and review any information in their child's file. A request by parents to have a copy of their child's test protocols poses a difficult problem. Giving them a copy of the test protocol breaches test security (by making test items public) and violates copyright law. If the protocol is withheld, parents are being denied a copy of their child's educational records. The Division of School Psychology (Division 16) of the American Psychological Association provides the following guidelines for handling such requests (Martin, 1985, p. 9, with changes in notation):

Some of the legal constraints impinging on this issue are discussed in a policy letter (dated Jan. 9, 1979) from the Bureau for Education of the Handicapped (BEH). This policy letter was in response to a question raised by a school district regarding parents' right to assessment information as outlined in PL 94-142. The BEH response made several important points:

(1) The provisions for parents' rights to information outlined in part B of PL 94-142 are essentially identical to regulations from the Family Education Rights and Privacy Act. This act considers test protocols to be educational records, and states that they must be accessible to parents.

(2) This mandate is met if the school district allows parents to examine and discuss the protocols under school supervision.

(3) If this procedure were followed, schools and other agencies would *not* be required to provide copies of protocols to parents.

(4) However, an agency must give test protocols to parents if (a) the parents cannot come to school during a 45-day period after a request has been made to review the records if the reasons for not coming during this period are serious illness, extended travel, or related reasons, and if parents request copies of their child's protocol, or (b) if the parents or agency request a due process hearing in which the test protocols will be introduced by either party as evidence at the hearing.

For circumstances other than those that legally require that copies of protocols be forwarded to parents, the following procedure is suggested by Division 16 Ethics Committee. The procedure is designed to meet the applicable ethical standards when parental requests for test protocols are made.

(1) Parents should be made aware of their rights to all information in their child's educational records including information included on test protocols.

(2) Parents should be given the right to inspect test protocols. This might include discussion of examples of test items and responses to these items. This inspection should be done under the supervision of the school psychologist who administered the assessment procedure, or other responsible, appropriately trained personnel.

(3) Parents should not be given photocopies of completed protocols or copies of blank protocols, nor should they be allowed to copy word-for-word extended portions of test protocols.

(4) If parents request copies of protocols they should be made aware of the ethical obligation of the psychologist to maintain test security.

Least Restrictive Environment

The least restrictive environment provision of PL 94-142 is often referred to as *mainstreaming*—the placement of handicapped children into regular classes. Although mainstreaming has been of major concern to educators for decades, it has received special attention since the passage of PL 94-142. The aim of the provision is to provide for each individual child the environment that maximizes rehabilitation efforts and has the highest probability of remedying academic deficits.

Figure 24-1 shows a continuum of educational services from least restrictive to most restrictive. At the top of the hierarchy is the regular classroom (least restrictive); at the bottom is an institutional setting (most restrictive). The tapered design depicts the fact that there are usually fewer children in the more restrictive specialized programs. The most specialized facilities are likely to be needed by the fewest children.

Awareness of relative merits of alternative educational programs.   Public Law 94-142 requires the psychoeducational team to be aware of the relative merits of alternative educational programs. For example, when must a residen-

tial facility be recommended over a special education class for a severely handicapped child? Answers will depend on what facilities and programs are available in the public school system, private school system, and mental health system; the personnel in such programs; the types of children currently enrolled in such programs; and the efficacy of the educational and treatment programs (Franzoni & Jones, 1981). Conflicts may arise over the "ideal" placement *versus* the "least restrictive environment" placement *versus* a placement based on the legal and fiscal responsibilities of the public school district. Parents may lobby schools for special placements for their handicapped children:

Many school psychologists have witnessed increasing numbers of determined parents accompanied by legal advisers demanding payment for residential private school placement, the cost of which ranged from $20,000 or more annually per child. Plaintiffs argued convincingly that the recommended treatment facility "best" met the needs of the child. In some instances, family conflict issues were involved or related medical services were indicated. Requested programs appeared to involve total service provisions rather than appropriate educational opportunities mandated by law . . . .

The involvement of school psychologists in cases demanding unwarranted public funds for private school placement serves as one reminder that PL 94-142, although well intended, has invited distorted interpretations and associated abuses. (Franzoni & Jones, 1981, pp. 358-359)

Pressures toward mainstreaming.   Advocates of mainstreaming believe that it removes stigmas, enhances the social status of exceptional children, facilitates modeling of appropriate behavior by handicapped children, provides a more stimulating and competitive environment, offers more flexible cost-effective service, and is more acceptable to the public and, in particular, to minority groups. The pressure for mainstreaming stems, in part, from the idea that it affords handicapped children more opportunity to be in contact with nonhandicapped peers and in the process be exposed to "normal" role models. The concern of the courts "with protecting the civil rights of handicapped children and special educators' advocacy of the philosophy of normalization. . . are in the forefront of current efforts to alter traditional special-education practices" (Gottlieb, 1981, p. 115).

How to evaluate the effectiveness of mainstreaming. Research on mainstreaming should be conducted with several concerns in mind (Gottlieb, 1981):

• Appropriate instructional strategies should be identified.

• The effects of mainstreaming programs should be studied longitudinally.

• The characteristics of "successfully" mainstreamed educably mentally handicapped pupils should be determined.

• The efficacy of mainstreaming children singly or in groups should be studied.

• The effects of the presence of handicapped children on the academic and social performance of nonhandicapped classmates should be determined.

• The costs of educating handicapped children in self-contained versus mainstreamed classrooms should be evaluated.

• The type of inservice training needed to provide regular and special educators with the skills necessary to educate handicapped children in the mainstream should be determined.

• Future mainstreaming programs should be reconceptualized as the composition of classes changes.

• The usefulness of paraprofessionals in mainstreamed classes should be evaluated.

• Those characteristics of handicapped children which are the best predictors of academic and social adjustment in the mainstream should be determined.

Evaluating the progress of mainstreamed children. It is important to monitor the special child's placement in a regular class. Exhibit 24-3 provides a list of questions that can be used to obtain information from teachers, parents, and the child about the child's progress in academic, behav-

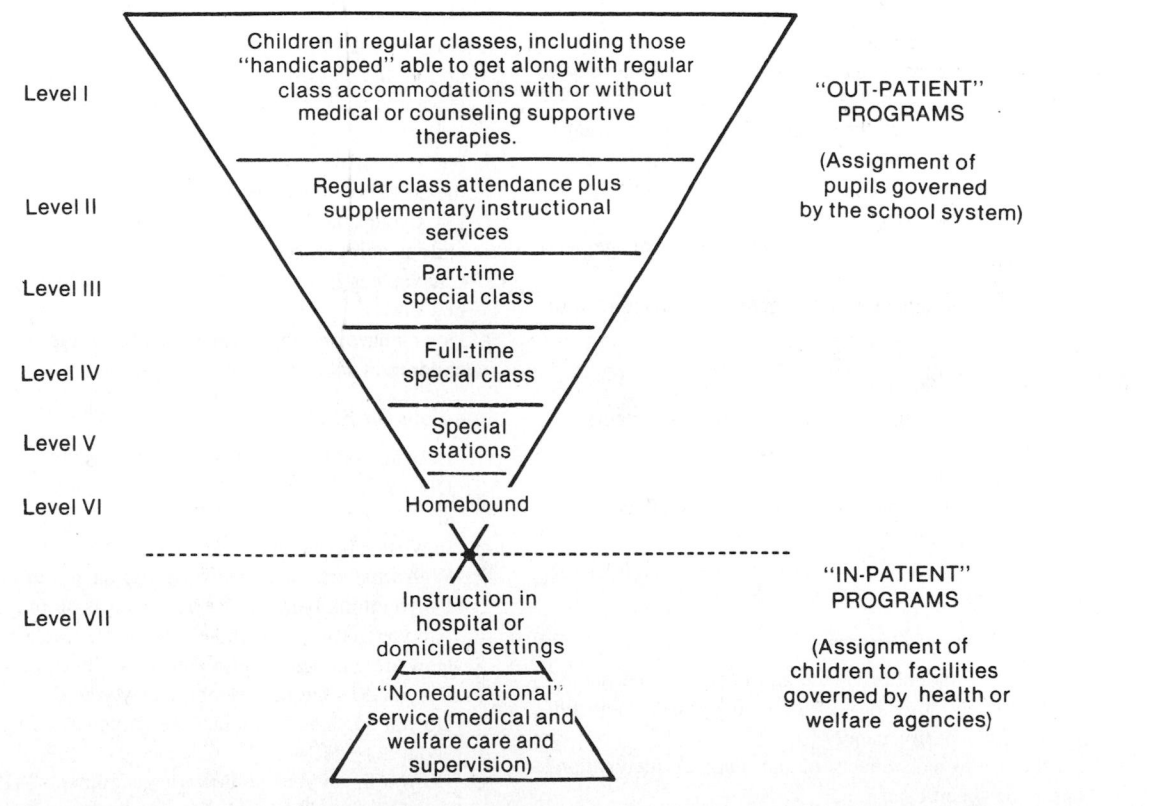

Figure 24-1. The cascade system of special education service. The tapered design indicates the considerable difference in the number of children involved at the different levels and calls attention to the fact that the system serves as a diagnostic filter. The most specialized facilities are likely to be needed by the fewest children on a long-term basis. This organizational model can be applied to development of special education services for all types of disability. Reprinted with permission of the publisher and author from E. Deno, "Special Education as Developmental Capital," *Exceptional Children*, 37, p. 235. Copyright 1970, Council for Exceptional Children.

Exhibit 24-3

Evaluating the Progress of Mainstreamed Students

Questions for Teachers

Academic Achievement

1. Briefly describe the student's academic achievement.
2. In what academic areas does the student excel?
3. With what academic areas does the student have difficulty?
4. What approaches and materials have been successful with the student?
5. What approaches and materials have not been successful with the student?
6. Are academic modifications and adaptations that were discussed prior to the student's placement being implemented? How are these adaptations working?
7. Does the student complete classwork, homework, or other assigned projects?
8. Was the student academically ready for entry into your class?

Behavioral Abilities

1. Briefly describe the student's behavioral progress.
2. In what behavioral areas does the student demonstrate proficiency? (Please be specific.)
3. With what behavioral areas does the student experience difficulty? (Please be specific.)
4. Describe the student's study skills and work habits.
5. How do you discipline the student?
6. How does the student react to your classroom management system?
7. Was the student behaviorally prepared for entry into your class?

Social-Emotional Adjustment

1. How does the student get along with his or her peers?
2. In what school clubs or extracurricular activities does the student participate?
3. How do you think the new placement is affecting the student's self-concept?
4. Was the student socially and emotionally ready for entry into your class?

Medical and Physical Concerns

1. How are the student's hygiene and health-related habits?
2. Are the student's prostheses functioning properly and aiding his or her performance?
3. Are there any side effects of the student's medication? (Please be specific.)
4. What, if any, architectural barriers exist in the classroom?

Supplementary Support Services

1. Are you and the student receiving the necessary services from ancillary support personnel?

2. How is the communication system among school personnel functioning?
3. To what extent have the student's parents been involved in the mainstreaming?
4. How is the communication system with the student's parents functioning?

General Satisfaction

1. Are you satisfied with the student's progress in your class?
2. What solutions would you suggest to remediate identified problem areas?
3. What school-wide mainstreaming policies would you like to see retained or revised?

Questions for Parents

1. How do you feel about your child's being placed in a new class?
2. How do you think your child feels about the new class?
3. How is your child handling the work in the new class?
4. How well is your child getting along with the other children in the class?
5. Have you noticed any changes in your child since he (or she) has been in the new class?
6. Are you satisfied with your role in helping your child get the best class placement?
7. Does your child's teacher or counselor tell you how your child is doing in school?
8. Can you suggest any ways to help your child adjust to the new class?
9. Do you have any suggestions about how the school places children in special or regular classes?

Questions for Students

1. How do you feel about your new class?
2. Did you understand why you were placed in your new class?
3. In what school subjects are you doing well?
4. With what school subjects are you having difficulty?
5. Do you think being in the new class is helping you?
6. Are you getting enough help from the teachers?
7. How are you behaving in your new classroom?
8. Do you do what the teacher asks you to do?
9. Do you finish all your class assignments? (If not, tell me about it.)
10. Do you finish your homework assignments? (If not, tell me about it.)
11. How do you get along with the other children in your class?

(Exhibit continues next page)

Exhibit 24-3 (cont.)

12. Are you in a school club or sport? (If yes or no, tell me about it.)
13. Can you think of any ways to help you get used to your new class?
14. Were you ready to go into your new class?

15. What do you like about this new class?
16. What don't you like about the new program?

Source: Reprinted, with changes in notation, with permission of the publisher and author from S. J. Salend, "Mainstreaming: Sharpening Up Follow-up," *Academic Therapy, 18,* pp. 300–303. Copyright 1983.

ioral, social, and emotional areas. Many of the questions in Exhibit 24-3 are also useful in evaluating the progress of special (and normal) children in a variety of other settings.

Research on mainstreaming. Research on mainstreaming is extremely difficult to evaluate, often because studies are poorly designed. Because the findings are equivocal (Greenwood, 1985), it is difficult to determine which setting is most appropriate for a specific exceptional population. *It may be that the key to a favorable outcome is instructional effectiveness and not simply the specific setting or placement.* Mainstreaming does not necessarily lead to social acceptance—handicapped students may be more accepted in self-contained homogeneous classrooms than in regular classrooms.

Parents report a high level of satisfaction with program options, but there is not an unequivocal preference for mainstream placements (Greenwood, 1985). Regular classroom teachers generally favor mainstreaming less than either their special education counterparts or non-teaching lay persons (Greenwood, 1985). *Knowledge of the regular classroom teacher's expectations and standards may be the critical factor in making satisfactory placements.* The psychologist needs to use this knowledge as a starting point for investigating a case referral thoroughly, however, and should not consider the teacher's expectations for placement or other programming as an obligation that must be fulfilled. Such decisions should be made by multidisciplinary teams based on all of the assessment information collected in the case.

Studies on mainstreaming mentally retarded children indicate that it benefits mentally retarded children neither academically nor socially in comparison with self-contained classes (Gottlieb, Alter, & Gottlieb, 1983). Little is known about the characteristics of regular classes into which mentally retarded children should be mainstreamed. Additionally, little is known

about how to decide which children are to be mainstreamed and into which classes they should be mainstreamed. Until these two questions—at the very least—can be answered, discussions of the virtues or evils of mainstreaming cannot progress beyond the realm of speculation. (Gottlieb et al., 1983, p. 75)

Finally,

the most significant research on mainstreaming is yet to come: How does mainstreaming affect a handicapped person's functioning in the adult world after graduation? Social competence should be the ultimate criterion for monitoring the effectiveness of mainstreaming. (Zigler & Muenchow, 1979, p. 995)

Comment on mainstreaming. Mainstreaming involves far more than simply placing handicapped children in regular classrooms. The simple placement of handicapped children in mainstream settings is not likely to bring about desired outcomes (Greenwood, 1985). Placement must be complemented by procedures designed to support the development of desired changes in such settings. *Handicapped children will be benefited by the effective implementation of instructional strategies—not by the setting alone.* Unless the IEP can be carried out effectively, it will be of little use. Regular class teachers need special assistance in developing programs and modifying the standard curriculum to accommodate exceptional children's learning styles.

Some say that the least restrictive environment provision of PL 94-142 "may be viewed as restricting the rights of children to be different or to have special needs" (Silverman, 1979, p. 63). Behaviorally disturbed children, as well as seriously physically handicapped children, may need special long-term help in special class settings. This additional help should not be prematurely discontinued with the first signs of improvement, as it is in some cases. Seriously behaviorally disturbed children may not be able to function in regular classes. In some cases, the least restrictive environment for many handicapped children may be self-contained special classes, with integration occurring in nonacademic subjects.

The social as well as the educational needs of handicapped children must be considered. Integrating the social needs of these children with those of regular class children will require special effort. Mainstreaming does not guarantee that the handicapped child will be accepted by other children. Normal children's negative stereotypes and reactions toward handicapping conditions must be modified. Bringing about changes in attitudes of teachers and non-handicapped students toward handicapped children will be of crucial importance.

The physical environment also must be considered. Efforts must be made to design environments so as to best accommodate the handicapped child. Behavior settings must also be designed (or altered) to maximize the child-environment fit.

The success with which handicapped children are placed in regular classrooms will depend on the acceptance and consideration of teachers, administrators, parents, and children. In the final analysis, the attitude of the people involved is the crucial factor. In determining appropriate placements, the child's educational needs, and not the type of handicap, should be of primary concern. *Do not forget that the slow learner placed either in a regular class or in a special education class still has a learning problem that must be remediated.*

Comment on PL 94-142

The inclusion of procedural safeguards in PL 94-142 is an attempt to promote fair classification. It recognizes that school placement decisions are consequential to the student and family and are not to be undertaken lightly or arbitrarily. Schools are held accountable for the accuracy of their classification and the appropriateness of the recommended program. School personnel are obliged to specify the basis upon which they classify children and must demonstrate that programs are likely to benefit the child. Before a child is assigned to a special program, the school should inform the parents and child, explain the proposed action, and describe available alternatives. It is imperative that the parents and child not be coerced or intimidated into accepting the school's decision. Some parents do not understand placement procedures and special education programs. The educational team must take care to express decisions about eligibility, placement, program goals, and the review process in clear, jargon-free language, using concepts understandable to parents.

Perhaps the weakest aspect of PL 94-142 is its failure to define clearly what is meant by racially or culturally non-discriminatory procedures. The law does not specify any acceptable procedures and yet uses such concepts as "significantly subaverage general intellectual functioning" in its definition of mental retardation. This and other statements suggest that PL 94-142 recognizes the importance of

standardized tests in the assessment process. Another serious shortcoming of PL 94-142 is the lack of guidance concerning ways of determining the child's *native language*. When ethnic minority children speak more than one language, it is extremely difficult to determine whether they have a single "native language."

Two surveys have shed light on how PL 94-142 affects psychologists and teachers. A national survey in 1979–80 focused on the impact of PL 94-142 on the practice of school psychology (Goldwasser, Meyers, Christenson, & Graden, 1983). The 856 psychologists who responded reported that the legislation had had remarkably little impact on the evaluation procedures used or on the role of school psychologists. Some changes have occurred, however. These include increases in teamwork, work with handicapped children, and paperwork. Although most respondents served on evaluation (91 percent) or pupil placement (84 percent) teams, less than 50 percent were involved in the IEP process, follow-up consultations, or direct intervention procedures. Interestingly, a large percentage of the respondents infrequently (31 percent) or never (9 percent) developed IEPs for the children they tested. The survey also revealed that the respondents spent 70 percent of their time in testing and related diagnostic activities, 20 percent in consultation, and 10 percent in providing direct interventions to children. Most of the time (71 percent) was spent with handicapped children.

Another survey (Dreibelbis, 1981) evaluated attitudes of over 500 Pennsylvania special education teachers toward PL 94-142. Although the teachers believed that their pupils were being evaluated accurately, the information they received from psychological reports often was of limited help in preparing IEPs. The teachers liked the IEP format but were dissatisfied with the fact that the IEP content was similar for many students and the content of a given child's IEP did not change significantly from year to year. The IEP conference with parents was another problem area. Parents seldom actively took part in designing the IEP, and many did not adequately understand the provisions of PL 94-142. Although the teachers generally were favorable toward PL 94-142, a majority believed that the law had not ended inadequate education of the handicapped, inappropriate classifications, or inappropriate educational programs.

Overall, PL 94-142 represents an attempt by the federal government to ensure that handicapped children receive a meaningful education. The law, however, will not end inadequate education of the handicapped, inappropriate classifications, or inappropriate educational programs. The ultimate measure of the usefulness of PL 94-142 is the quality of the education received by each handicapped child.

THE FAMILY EDUCATIONAL RIGHTS AND PRIVACY ACT OF 1974

In an effort to eliminate some of the abuses associated with data gathering and personal files, the U.S. Congress passed the Family Educational Rights and Privacy Act of 1974, commonly known as the "Buckley Amendment." Some of the highlights of the act are as follows:

1. Parents have access to official educational records of their children.

2. Parental consent must be obtained for release of records to other agencies.

3. These rights transfer to public school pupils at the age of 18 years and to other students, regardless of age, upon entering post-secondary educational institutions.

4. Schools must provide a hearing, when requested by parents or students, in which records may be challenged.

5. Schools have the responsibility to inform parents of their right of access to the records.

6. Failure to follow these guidelines may result in removal of federal funding for the school.

A survey in New Jersey (Zampardi, 1978) reported that as a result of the Family Educational Rights and Privacy Act school psychologists have changed their procedures in the following ways: shortened reports and reduced their technicality, increased the use of private files and memory aids, omitted highly personal or legally sensitive information regarding parents or students from files, increased oral communication with other professionals, and changed methods of reporting IQs. These changes were reported by over two-thirds of the psychologists surveyed. The frequency of use of conventional tests remained generally unchanged. It appears that some unintended consequences have arisen from the Buckley Amendment.

The effects of the Buckley Amendment have been both positive and negative. On the positive side, the open records policy has led to closer relationships with parents, a reduction in the number of conjectural and speculative statements in psychological reports, a reduction in labeling, and greater attention to the writing of psychological reports. On the negative side, the policy has led to more paperwork, constricted and diluted reports, concern about lawsuits, and concern about the ability of parents to understand the report.

PUBLIC LAW 99-457: THE EDUCATION OF THE HANDICAPPED ACT AMENDMENTS OF 1986

Public Law 99-457, passed in 1986, amends the Education of the Handicapped Act (Public Law 94-142) to (a) authorize an early intervention program for handicapped infants and toddlers and their families and (b) extend all the rights and protections of Public Law 94-142 to handicapped children ages 3 through 5 years beginning in the school year 1990-91. The reasons for the amendments regarding handicapped infants and toddlers are as follows:

Sec. 671. (a) FINDINGS. – The Congress finds that there is an urgent and substantial need –

(1) to enhance the development of handicapped infants and toddlers and to minimize their potential for developmental delay,

(2) to reduce the educational costs to our society, including our Nation's schools, by minimizing the need for special education and related services after handicapped infants and toddlers reach school age,

(3) to minimize the likelihood of institutionalization of handicapped individuals and maximize the potential for their independent living in society, and

(4) to enhance the capacity of families to meet the special needs of their infants and toddlers with handicaps.

(b) POLICY. – It is therefore the policy of the United States to provide financial assistance to States –

(1) to develop and implement a statewide, comprehensive, coordinated, multidisciplinary, interagency program of early intervention services for handicapped infants and toddlers and their families,

(2) to facilitate the coordination of payment for early intervention services from Federal, State, local, and private sources (including public and private insurance coverage), and

(3) to enhance its capacity to provide quality early intervention services and expand and improve existing early intervention services being provided to handicapped infants, toddlers, and their families.

DEFINITIONS

Sec. 672. As used in this part

(1) The term 'handicapped infants and toddlers' means individuals from birth to age 2, inclusive, who need early intervention services because they –

(A) are experiencing developmental delays, as measured by appropriate diagnostic instruments and procedures in one or more of the following areas: Cognitive development, physical development, language and speech development, psychosocial development, or self-help skills, or

(B) have a diagnosed physical or mental condition which has a high probability of resulting in developmental delay. Such term may also include, at a State's discretion, individuals from birth to age 2, inclusive, who are at risk of having substantial developmental delays if early intervention services are not provided.

(2) 'Early intervention services' are developmental services which—

(A) are provided under public supervision,

(B) are provided at no cost except where Federal or State law provides for a system of payment by families, including a schedule of sliding fees,

(C) are designed to meet a handicapped infant's or toddler's developmental needs in any one or more of the following areas:

(i) physical development,

(ii) cognitive development,

(iii) language and speech development,

(iv) psycho-social development, or

(v) self-help skills,

(D) meet the standards of the State, including the requirements of this part,

(E) include—

(i) family training, counseling, and home visits,

(ii) special instruction,

(iii) speech pathology and audiology,

(iv) occupational therapy,

(v) physical therapy,

(vi) psychological services,

(vii) case management services,

(viii) medical services only for diagnostic or evaluation purposes,

(ix) early identification, screening, and assessment services, and

(x) health services necessary to enable the infant or toddler to benefit from the other early intervention services,

(F) are provided by qualified personnel, including—

(i) special educators,

(ii) speech and language pathologists, and audiologists,

(iii) occupational therapists,

(iv) physical therapists,

(v) psychologists,

(vi) social workers,

(vii) nurses, and

(viii) nutritionists, and

(G) are provided in conformity with an individualized family service plan. (100 STAT 1145–1147)

The act establishes a state grant program to provide early intervention services for handicapped infants, toddlers, and preschoolers. The act will provide handicapped infants and toddlers and their families with an assessment of their unique needs and an individualized family service plan to meet these needs. The individualized family service plan, which will be evaluated once a year, will include a statement of the child's present level of development, the family's strengths and weaknesses, the major outcomes that can be expected, specific services to be provided, the dates of initiation and the duration of these services, and the name of the child's case manager.

ASSESSMENT PROCEDURES AND SPECIAL EDUCATION ON TRIAL

Over the past 20 years, the procedures used by schools to place children in special education programs have been evaluated by the courts of our nation. Two principal issues have surfaced. (See Table 24-1 for a summary of the outcomes of various lawsuits.)

One issue is the rights of children, regardless of the degree of handicap, to receive a free and appropriate education. The courts have clearly ruled that handicapped children are entitled to such rights.

The second issue is the overrepresentation of ethnic minority children in classes for the educable mentally retarded. Associated with this issue are the related matters of the assessment techniques used to certify placement in special education programs and the value and role of special education. It has been argued that (a) ethnic minorities are overrepresented in classes for the educable mentally retarded, (b) special education represents a dead end and provides substandard educational programs, (c) intelligence tests are biased, (d) pupils with limited facility in English have been inappropriately administered tests requiring extensive facility in English, and (e) a full range of assessment techniques has not been used in arriving at placement decisions. Implied in these arguments is the contention that the children were denied equal protection under the Fourteenth Amendment of the Constitution. In many of the cases that have come before the judiciary, both parties have signed consent agreements, which have attempted to rectify procedures that were unfair to ethnic minorities. In addition, provisions of PL 94-142 have sought to protect the rights of ethnic minority children.

Larry P. v. Riles

In *Larry P.* v. *Riles*, a federal court found the California State Department of Education to be in violation of Title VI of the Civil Rights Act of 1964, the Rehabilitation Act of 1973, and PL 94-142. In October 1979, Judge Robert Peckham ruled that standardized intelligence tests "are racially and culturally biased, have a discriminatory impact against black children, and have not been validated for the purpose of essentially permanent placements of black children into educationally dead-end, isolated, and stigmatizing classes for the so-called educable mentally retarded."

In January 1984, the U.S. Ninth Circuit Court of Appeals upheld, by a 2-1 margin, Judge Peckham's ruling in the *Larry P.* v. *Riles* case. Judge William B. Enright, the dissenter, noted that proper placement in EMR (educable mentally retarded) classes is a benefit, not a stigmatic dead-end assignment; that before the tests in question can

Table 24-1
Representative Court Cases Involving Assessment and Placement of Ethnic Minority Children and Handicapped Children in Special Education Classes

Case	Decision
Hobson v. *Hansen* — 269 F. Supp. 401 (D.D.C. 1967)	A U.S. district court invalidated the District of Columbia school system's educational tracking practices. Special classes, however, were permissible as long as testing procedures were rigorous and retesting was frequent.
Diana v. *State Board of Education* — C-70 37 RFT (N.D. Cal. 1970)	A U.S. federal court in California invalidated testing procedures that were used to evaluate Mexican-American children for placement in special education classes. The school system agreed that linguistically different children would be tested both in their primary language and in English, that primarily nonverbal tests would be used for the assessment of these children's cognitive skills, and that an interpreter would be used if a bilingual examiner was not available.
Pennsylvania Association for Retarded Children v. *Commonwealth of Pennsylvania* — 343 F. Supp. 279 (E.D. PA 1972)	A U.S. federal court in Pennsylvania ratified a consent agreement assuring that retarded children would have the right to publicly supported schooling appropriate to their needs. Extensive remedial education programs were then instituted for those retarded children previously denied an education.
Wyatt v. *Stickney* — 344 F. Supp. 387 (M.D. Ala. 1972)	An Alabama federal court ruled that children in a state institution for the mentally retarded have a constitutional right to treatment.
Guadalupe v. *Tempe Elementary School District* — Stipulation and Order (January 24, 1972)	A U.S. district court in Arizona agreed to a stipulated agreement that children could not be placed in educable mentally retarded classes unless they scored lower than 2 standard deviations below the population mean on an approved IQ test administered in the child's own language. It was also stipulated that other assessment procedures must be used in addition to intelligence tests and that parental permission must be obtained for such placements.
Mattie T. v. *Holladay* — No. DC-75-31-S (1979)	A U.S. district court in Mississippi approved a consent decree stipulating that (a) classification and placement procedures for special education must be evaluated by outside experts, (b) a remedy must be devised to solve the problem of large numbers of black children in classes for the mentally retarded, and (c) all misclassified children are to be identified and given compensatory education through tutoring or vocational training, even beyond the age of 21.
Larry P. v. *Riles* — No. C-71-2270 RFP (1979) and No. 80-4027 DC No. CV 71-2270 in the United States Court of Appeals for the Ninth Circuit (1984)	A U.S. federal district court in California ruled that standardized intelligence tests are culturally biased and cannot be used in the assessment of black children for possible placement in educable mentally retarded classes. The court further stipulated that the proportion of black children in classes for the educable mentally retarded must closely match their proportion in the population. The Ninth Circuit Court of Appeals upheld the district court's verdict.
Parents in Action on Special Education v. *Joseph P. Hannon* — No. 74 C 3586 (N.D. Ill. 1980)	A U.S. federal district court in Illinois ruled that the WISC, WISC-R, and Stanford-Binet are not racially or culturally biased. Furthermore, when these tests are used in conjunction with other procedures, they do not discriminate against black children in the Chicago public schools. The court believed that the school system was complying with federally mandated criteria for determining an appropriate educational program for a child. The court, which heard from some of the same witnesses who testified for the plaintiffs in the *Larry P.* case, noted that in the *Larry P.* case the judge failed to undertake a detailed examination of the items on the intelligence tests. Without such an examination, the court believed, the issue of cultural bias could not be properly evaluated.
Georgia State Conference of Branches of NAACP v. *State of Georgia* — Eleventh Circuit Court of Appeals, No. 84-8771 (October 29, 1985) and *Marshall* v. *Georgia*, U.S. District Court for the Southern District of Georgia, CV 482-233, June 28, 1984; Amended August 24, 1984	A U.S. court of appeals for the Eleventh District ruled that the State of Georgia did not discriminate against black children by placing them in disproportionate numbers in classes for low achievers or by using standard assessment procedures for the evaluation and placement of black children in special education programs for the educable mentally retarded. The Eleventh Circuit Court of Appeals affirmed a lower U.S. district court's ruling in favor of the State of Georgia.

be labeled as discriminatory, there must be evidence that intelligence tests resulted in improper placement in the EMR program and no such evidence was presented; that the widely recognized IQ tests employed by the defendants have long been hailed for their ability to correct the exact abuse complained of in this case — misevaluations and misplacement; and that educators have long recognized that subjective evaluation, uncorroborated by objective criteria, carries enormous potential for abuse and misplacements based on the personal or cultural values of the evaluator. Judge Enright also noted that the court's decision was striking down the only objective criteria for placement.

In June 1986, the U.S. Circuit Court of Appeals issued an amended decision that reaffirmed the district court's finding of violation of federal statutory law, but *reversed* the finding of violations of the equal protection clause of the Fourteenth Amendment of the Constitution. In September 1986, the California State Department of Education issued a directive to implement further the federal court's decision. The directive stated that individually administered intelligence tests were not to be used for the assessment of any black child referred for special education services. Although the original case dealt with placement decisions for EMR classes only, the new stipulation covers *all* special education placements in the public schools.

Parents in Action on Special Education v. Joseph P. Hannon

In *Parents in Action on Special Education* v. *Joseph P. Hannon*, a federal court ruled that intelligence tests are not culturally biased against black children. This court stipulated that, when used with other criteria in the assessment process, intelligence tests comply with federal guidelines concerning the use of nondiscriminatory procedures. Judge John Grady noted: "There is no evidence in this record that such misassessments as do occur are the result of racial bias in test items or in any aspect of the assessment process currently in use in the Chicago public school system." He found that the defendants were complying with federal guidelines.

Georgia Conferences of NAACP v. Georgia

In *Georgia Conferences of NAACP* v. *Georgia*, the NAACP alleged that the State of Georgia discriminated against black children by using evaluation procedures that resulted in their overrepresentation in classes for the educable mentally retarded. Their complaints paralleled those

in the *Larry P.* v. *Riles* case. Both the trial court and the Eleventh Circuit Court of Appeals rejected the claims of the NAACP. The courts noted that there was no evidence of differential treatment of black and white students. Overrepresentation of black children in classes for the mentally retarded by itself was not sufficient to prove discrimination.

Comment on Assessment Procedures and Special Education on Trial

Three federal courts and two federal appeals courts have now been involved in cases involving overrepresentation of black children in classes for the educable mentally retarded. In all of these cases, individual intelligence tests, a key diagnostic tool in the placement process, have been characterized by the plaintiffs as being culturally biased and therefore inappropriate for the assessment of black children. Courts in California agreed with this characterization, whereas courts in Illinois and Georgia did not. Obviously, further judicial rulings will be needed to resolve the thorny issues involved in the placement of minority children in special education classes. As some jurists noted in *Daniel Hoffman* v. *The Board of Education of the City of New York* (see Chapter 1), the courts may not be the appropriate place to resolve complex issues concerning the fairness of tests and appropriate educational procedures.

COURT INTERPRETATIONS OF PL 94-142 AND RELATED LEGAL DECISIONS

State and federal courts, as well as the Supreme Court, have heard cases dealing with the provisions of PL 94-142 and related educational matters. This section reviews outcomes of some important cases.

Board of Education v. Rowley

The U.S. Supreme Court in June 1982 ruled in *Board of Education* v. *Rowley* (80-1002) that school boards are *not* required to provide services that will enable handicapped children to realize their *full potential*. By a vote of 6 to 3, the justices decided that PL 94-142 only requires that handicapped children's education be sufficient to enable them to achieve passing marks and advance from grade to grade.

Amy Rowley, a 10-year-old deaf girl, wanted a sign-language interpreter in her classroom, but school officials said it would be too costly and unnecessary. The majority of the U.S. Supreme Court agreed with the school board, noting that Congress did not mean to give handicapped children "strict equality of opportunity" with other students. A minority of the justices disagreed. They said that the new law was designed to

eliminate the effects of [a] handicap, at least to the extent that the child will be given an equal opportunity to learn, if that is reasonably possible. Amy Rowley, without a sign language interpreter, comprehends less than half of what is said in the classroom—less than half of what normal children comprehend. . . . This is hardly an equal opportunity to learn, even if Amy makes passing grades.

Bales v. *Clark*

In a similar case tried in Virginia in 1981, Judge Dortch Warriner of the Eighth U.S. Circuit Court of Appeals ruled that a deaf child could be educated in local public schools even though she would get a better education in a state school for the deaf (*Bales* v. *Clark*, Oct. 16, 1981, Civ A. 80-0568-R, 523 Fed. Supp. p. 1366). Evelyn Ann Bales, a 13-year-old girl, sustained head injuries in an automobile accident in 1977. After two years of rehabilitation, her parents wanted her to attend a private school for handicapped children that was located some distance from their home. The school, however, recommended a public special education center closer to her home school district. Judge Warriner ruled that

neither they nor any other parents have the right under the law to write a prescription for an ideal education for their child and to have the prescription filled at public expense. The law requires an appropriate free education. Efforts to build this requirement into something more will threaten the substantial gains already made in the education of the handicapped.

The judge concluded: "No language in state or federal law can properly be read as mandating that costs may not be considered in determining what education is appropriate for a child—handicapped or nonhandicapped." Factors such as the differences in travel costs to the two schools "must be considered in determining the appropriateness of the schools," he said.

In the above case the parents had also requested reimbursement for summer tutoring that they had obtained for their daughter. Judge Warriner ruled that the child is "not entitled to year-round schooling without showing an irreparable loss of progress during summer months," and no such loss had been demonstrated in this case.

Rettig v. *Kent School District*

A federal appeals court supported a school district's refusal to provide a 16-year-old autistic adolescent with summer classes and year-round therapy in *Rettig* v. *Kent School District* (Vol. 94-FDR-12). Judge Robert Krupansky of the Sixth Circuit Court of Appeals based his decision in part on the *Board of Education* v. *Rowley* case. He wrote that states must use procedures that are "reasonably calculated" to enable a handicapped child to receive educational benefits, and the school was deemed to be using such procedures.

Doe v. *Board of Education of Montgomery County*

In a case similar to *Hoffman* v. *Board of Education* (see Exhibit 1-1 in Chapter 1), the Maryland Court of Appeals ruled that parents do not have the right to sue a board of education. In *Doe* v. *Board of Education of Montgomery County* (Md. Ct. App; 12/22/82) (51 LW 2410), the court ruled that courts are not the proper place to test the validity of an educational decision to place a student in a special education class. Permitting such suits would allow parents to file suits questioning the propriety of all procedures used in the education of children.

The case involved a diagnostic dispute between a school psychologist and a physician. On the basis of a psychological evaluation, the psychologist concluded that the child was brain damaged, functioning at the retarded or borderline intellectual level, and in need of special education. The parents had the child examined by a physician who concluded that the child was dyslexic, rather than brain damaged, and recommended a regular class placement. When the child was not retested and was retained in the special education program, the parents sued for damages.

CONSULTATION WITH PARENTS

Earlier sections of this chapter covered parental rights under PL 94-142 and The Family Education Rights and Privacy Act. This section briefly discusses some issues involved in working with parents of exceptional children and parents of minority children. (Techniques for interviewing parents and presenting assessment information are discussed in Chapter 16.)

In working with parents who have a handicapped or special child, always consider how the handicap affects the entire family. The family's, as well as the child's, attitudes, feelings, and reactions will have an impact on how the child copes with his or her handicap. Help the parents see their child's assets as well as limitations. Emphasize the active role that they and their child can play in coping with the disability. Help them to understand that the disability is only one aspect of their child's life, and that difficulties should be dealt with, not avoided. This positive, coping framework contrasts with a succumbing framework that focuses on the negative impact of disability. Details of each framework are shown in Table 24-2.

Negative reactions of parents to their behaviorally disturbed children may be a response to their child's behavior rather than a major cause of the behavior. Interaction conflicts are a two-way process: children affect parents and

parents affect children. Consequently, bidirectional effects in family interactions should always be examined.

Parents of Mentally Retarded Children

Parents of mentally retarded children do not simply "adjust" to their child's retardation. They experience periodic sorrow, especially at various important developmental milestones. Following are some examples of parental reactions to raising a mentally retarded child (Wikler, Wasow, & Hatfield, 1981, p. 69):

- "Perhaps disappointing would be a better word than sorrow. I firmly believe we did have many peaks and

Table 24-2
Characteristics of the Coping-Succumbing Frameworks

Coping	Succumbing
1. The emphasis is on what the person *can do*.	1. The emphasis is on what the person *cannot* do.
2. Areas of life in which the person can participate are seen as worthwhile.	2. Little weight is given to the areas of life in which the person can participate.
3. The person is perceived as playing an *active role* in molding his or her life constructively.	3. The person is seen as *passive*, as a *victim* of misfortune.
4. The accomplishments of the person are appreciated in terms of his or her benefits to the person and others (asset evaluation) and not devalued because they fall short of some irrelevant standard.[a]	4. The person's accomplishments are minimized by highlighting his or her shortcomings (comparative-status evaluation, usually measured in terms of "normal" standards).[a]
5. The negative aspects of the person's life, such as the pain that is suffered or difficulties that exist, are felt to be manageable. They are limited because satisfactory aspects of the person's life are recognized.	5. The negative aspects of the person's life, such as the pain that is suffered or difficulties that exist, are kept in the forefront of attention. They are emphasized and exaggerated and even seen to usurp all of life (spread).
6. Managing difficulties means reducing limitations through changes in the social and physical environment as well as in the person. Examples are: a. eliminating barriers b. environmental accommodations c. medical procedures d. prostheses and other assistive devices e. learning new skills	6. Prevention and cure are the only valid solutions to the problem of disability.
7. Managing difficulties *also* means *living on satisfactory terms* with one's limitations (although the disability may be regarded as a nuisance and sometimes a burden). This involves important *value changes*.	7. The only way to live with the disability is to resign oneself or to act as if the disability did not exist.
8. The fact that individuals with disabilities can live meaningful lives is indicated by their participation in valued activities and by their sharing in the satisfactions of living.	8. The person with a disability is pitied and his or her life essentially devaluated.

[a] The coping framework does not preclude instances where the nature of the situation requires that people be ranked on a given dimension (as in competitive activities such as sports and merit examinations), but it does preclude instances where comparative-status evaluation is actually irrelevant to the situation.
Source: Reprinted with permission of the publisher and author from B. A. Wright, *Physical Disability—A Psychosocial Approach* (2nd ed.) (New York: Harper & Row, 1983), p. 195.

valleys. There is sadness, but many joyous and funny moments too."

• "When I first realized my son was lagging, I felt very guilty and wondered if I had somehow caused it. Then I began to tell myself that I'm too inept to cope with a retarded child, all the while I was coping with him."

• "I find each new crisis or situation has to be dealt with, and I always pray our family has enough strength and courage to work through them. So far we have been able to keep the peace, but it isn't easy."

These and similar reactions suggest that families of retarded children may need continued services throughout the life span of the retarded individual.

Parents of Autistic Children

An autistic disorder is one of the most baffling childhood behavior disorders (see Chapter 20). The parents and family of the autistic child must deal with problems and feelings unique to their situation. They need professional help in understanding the problem. (This section is based on Morgan, 1984.)

First, give parents a realistic and cautious interpretation of autism, presenting the child as a unique individual with a special set of problems. Parents may have misconceptions about the disorder, perhaps stemming from a stereotypic image of autism derived from television or magazine articles. Help them recognize that symptoms such as bizarre responses to the environment, insistence on sameness, attachments to objects, and deficient and unusual language are part of the syndrome of an autistic disorder.

Second, help parents to understand their child's level of functioning in cognitive and adaptive areas and possibilities for improvement. Often they want to believe that cognitive impairment is only temporary, and that the child will return to normal when behavioral and emotional problems are resolved. Parents should be cautioned that isolated abilities—such as early motor development or good rote memory—should not be equated with general intelligence. Convey to the parents their child's strengths and weaknesses, using age-equivalent scores where appropriate. By interpreting the child's relative skills, you may help parents feel less threatened, and as a result they may become more receptive to your suggestions.

Third, assure parents that they are not responsible for the child's refusal to interact with the world. Parents of autistic children often blame themselves for their child's condition, because autism often appears to be social and emotional in nature. A prime feature of autism, one that distinguishes it from other disorders, is the child's inability to form affectionate relationships. This is most disturbing to parents. Their feelings of guilt can best be dealt with by presenting them with factual information about the diagnosis and causes of autism. Knowing that they did not cause their child's disorder enables parents to move past their guilt and participate in treatment programs.

Fourth, be prepared to deal with other parental reactions, such as anger and denial, that may occur when they learn that their child is handicapped (see Chapter 16).

Fifth, phrase statements about prognosis cautiously. Most cases of autism are severe and long term. Parents can play an active role in intervention programs, however.

Finally, be prepared to work with the autistic child's siblings in order to help them understand their brother's or sister's disorder. Families who gain an understanding of an autistic disorder will be in a better position to accept and help the autistic child in their home.

Parents of Gifted Children

Parents of children who are being evaluated for special programs for the gifted need to be informed that the procedures for the identification of intelligence, creativity, and related skills reflect the limitations of available assessment instruments. When a child is *not* accepted for a gifted program, inform the parents that the child's performance at that particular time does not meet the specified entrance requirements and fully explain the findings. Understand the parents' disappointment. Make every effort to ensure that nonacceptance into the program does not have an enduring negative effect on their perceptions of their child. Retesting in the future should be recommended for any child whose performance was slightly below the level needed for acceptance into the program.

Parents of Minority Children

Ethnic minority parents, particularly those who are first-generation immigrants, may feel estranged from schools and mental health facilities. They may be unfamiliar with school, clinic, or hospital procedures for filling out forms or validating documents. Those who are undocumented aliens may feel especially vulnerable, living in constant fear of deportation. Because of this fear, families may refrain from seeking help. If you are working in an institution, consider the family's cultural values in designing rehabilitation services for the child. Help the parents understand that in the institution opportunities will be provided for their child to participate in activities relevant to their culture, and be sure that such opportunities are provided. You will need extra patience to cope with language barriers and cultural differences, interpret laws and regulations, and adjust to differences in values.

Sources of Information for Parents of Handicapped Children

Exhibit 24-4 provides a list of books and pamphlets that can assist parents in coping with their handicapped child. Also included in the list is a bibliography of resources recommended for children.

Courtesy Herman Zielinski.

CONSULTATION IN PEDIATRIC MEDICAL SETTINGS

The psychologist practicing in a pediatric medical setting, such as a hospital or medical clinic, will face situations, goals, and problems different from those experienced by

the school psychologist. (This section is based on Roberts, 1986.) In a medical setting, where the pediatrician has little free time and pediatrician/patient contact is brief, psychological consultation is equally brief and psychological interventions are short term.

In contrast to school psychologists, who may have lengthy interactions with teachers, pediatric psychologists must learn to be quick and brief in their dealings with physicians. A "hallway consultation," focusing on only the most pertinent assessment and intervention issues, may be completed in several minutes. Similarly, pediatricians want brief, terse reports that focus on only the most pertinent aspects of the case.

The medical setting also differs from the school setting in that behavioral techniques, crisis intervention procedures, and relatively brief assessment procedures are used more frequently than long-term interventions and extensive test batteries. The pediatric psychologist receives referrals for problems such as medical noncompliance, failure to thrive, adjustment to severe burns, and terminal illness. The considerable volume of data that would be generated by an extensive test battery may be of limited use given the immediacy of the reason for referral.

Faced with a traditional medical setting power hierarchy, the psychologist must walk a fine line. The physician, who is high on the hierarchy, must be respected, but at the same time the psychologist must maintain his or her personal and professional dignity. In some cases turf issues may arise, where a physician believes that the psychologist has invaded his or her professional territory. For example, if psychological techniques are successful in treating encopresis (voluntary or involuntary passage of feces in inappropriate places), a physician may feel that this success reflects negatively on his or her own professional reputation. Such problems can best be handled through communication. The psychologist must maintain contact with the referring physician, using tact, diplomacy, and, above all, professional competence to build rapport.

Pediatric psychologists may provide consulting services in a number of ways. They may work as independent consultants on the same cases as, but not with, physicians. In this instance, each professional is concerned with a different aspect of the case. Psychologists can also provide indirect consultation, where the client is not seen. This might take the form of a phone call, an on-the-spot consultation, or a presentation of a seminar or staff training. The ideal situation, however, is a collaborative one, where pediatrician and psychologist work together with shared responsibility and decision-making. This is most likely to occur in special units or institutions using a team approach.

Exhibit 24-4

General Sources of Information for Parents of Handicapped Children and for Children

Books for Parents

Aspar, V., & Beck, J. (1972). *Is my baby all right?* New York: Pocket Books. (*M*)

Ayrault, E. V. (1971). *Helping the handicapped teenager mature*. New York: Association Press. (A guide to common problems. This book includes directories of rehabilitation services, camps, colleges, and universities accepting the physically handicapped.) (*M*)

Blank, J. P. (1976). *Nineteen steps up the mountain: The story of the DeBolt family*. New York: Lippincott. (The awesome and inspiring account of the efforts of one couple who have successfully raised a number of severely handicapped youngsters.) (*L*)

Brown, H. (1976). *Yesterday's child*. New York: New American Library. (A mother writes openly about the emotions and realities she faced in raising her multiply handicapped daughter.) (*M*)

Brutten, M., Richardson, S., & Mangel, C. (1973). *Something's wrong with my child*. New York: Harcourt Brace Jovanovich. (Practical information on various aspects of raising a child with learning disabilities.) (*M*)

Burks, H. F. (1978). *School and homework together*. Huntington Beach, CA: Arden Press. (This manual contains numerous practical suggestions on a variety of topics, most of which directly concern handicapped students. Most ideas can be implemented both in the classroom and at home.) (*L*)

Cruickshank, W. M. (1977). *Learning disabilities in home, school, and community*. New York: Syracuse University Press. (This is an extremely comprehensive book on the subject of learning disabilities for parents, as well as teachers and other professionals, by a leading figure in the field.) (*R*)

Featherstone, H. A. (1980). *A difference in the family: Living with a disabled child*. New York: Basic Books. (A parent writes about her profoundly handicapped child and her experiences with other parents who have similar problems.) (*M*)

Finnie, N. R. (1975). *Handling the young cerebral palsied child at home*. New York: Dutton. (*M*)

Grabow, B. W. (1978). *Your child has a learning disability . . . What is it? A guide for parents and teachers*. Chicago: National Easter Seal Society for Crippled Children and Adults. (This inexpensive booklet provides parents and teachers with basic information concerning the nature of learning disabilities, as well as practical tips for coping with the problem.) (*L*)

Greenfield, J. (1973). *A child called Noah*. New York: Warner Paperback. (A father writes of the family's experiences in coping with their autistic son.) (*M*)

Guide to resources for parents of the handicapped child.

(1978). In *Yearbook of special education*. Chicago: Marquis Academic Media. (This is an excellent resource list for parents, including annotations of books, self-help resources, and miscellaneous materials.) (*L*)

Heisler, V. A. (1972). *A handicapped child in the family: A guide for parents*. New York: Grune & Stratton. (A handicapped professional author frankly and perceptively discusses what it means to be the parent of a handicapped child.) (*M*)

Henderson, M., & Synhorst, D. (1975). *Care of the infant with myelomeningocele and hydrocephalus: A guide for parents*. Iowa City: University of Iowa Press. (*M*)

Kronick, D. (Compiler). (1970). *They too can succeed: A practical guide for parents of learning disabled children*. San Rafael, CA: Academic Therapy Publications. (This is a collection of articles written for parents of learning disabled children. The book covers a wide variety of topics related to child management and offers practical ways for parents to help their children overcome learning problems.) (*L*)

Kronick, D. (1975). *What about me? The L.D. adolescent*. San Rafael, CA: Academic Therapy Publications. (This book is about learning disabled adolescents and the particular problems experienced by them, their parents, teachers, and other professionals working with them. It is particularly sensitive to the questions of parents and to questions the developing adolescent asks about himself or herself.) (*R*)

Lowenfeld, B. (1971). *Our blind children*. Springfield, IL: Thomas. (Written primarily for parents of blind children, this is a comprehensive treatment of the situation from birth through adolescence. It provides helpful suggestions for parents on a variety of topics of concern.) (*L*)

Mantle, M. (1985). *Some just clap their hands: Raising a handicapped child*. New York: Adama Books. (This account of raising handicapped children is based on interviews and case histories. Its three parts include discovering the handicap, coping with it, and placement outside the home.)

Massie, R., & Massie, S. (1975). *Journey*. New York: Knopf. (The authors write of their son's chronic, debilitating disease, hemophilia, and have much to say to families of children with other handicapping conditions.) (*M*)

McNamara, J., & McNamara, B. (1977). *The special child handbook*. New York: Hawthorn. (The authors have directed their book toward parents of exceptional children. They cover practical information on topics such as helpful organizations and agencies, communicating with doctors, and selecting appropriate schools.) (*L*)

(Exhibit continues next page)

Exhibit 24-4 (cont.)

Osman, B. B. (1979). *Learning disabilities: A family affair*. New York: Random House. (The book briefly covers the diagnostic process and then focuses on parents' feelings, on acceptance of their child, and on behavior at home, at school, and with friends. Clinical case examples are used liberally, making reading easier.) (*R*)

Osman, B. B. (1982). *No one to play with: The social side of learning disabilities*. New York: Random House. (This book deals sensitively with the social dilemmas of the learning disabled child and how the learning problems and sensory and attention deficits cause social problems. Case examples offer helpful, concrete suggestions for facilitating social and emotional development. The book also includes helpful lists of legal resources, college programs, and state support groups.) (*R*)

Parent's Campaign for Handicapped Children and Youth. *Closer Look*. Box 1492, Washington, DC 20013. (Published by an organization for parents that is sponsored by the U.S. Department of Education, this extremely informative newsletter is appropriate for professionals as well as for handicapped people and their parents. *Closer Look* and other publications of the organization are free.) (*L*)

Park, C. C. (1983). *The siege: The first eight years of an autistic child: With an epilogue, 15 years later*. London: Hutchinson. (A mother writes sensitively about raising her autistic daughter.) (*M*)

Schimmel, D., & Fischer, L. (1977). *The rights of parents in the education of their children*. National Committee for Citizens in Education, Suite 410, Wilde Lake Village Green, Columbia, MD 21044. (Although this book was not written especially for parents of handicapped children, it does cover many legal questions that apply. One chapter is devoted to special education.) (*L*)

Schoonover, R. J. (1983). *Handbook for parents of children with learning disabilities*. Danville, IL: Interstate Printers and Publishers. (This is a short, concise, and easy-to-read book, packed with useful information for parents of learning disabled children.) (*R*)

Scott, E. P., Jan, J. E., & Freeman, R. D. (1977). *Can't your child see? A guide for parents and professionals*. Baltimore: University Park Press. (This is a general guide for parents of visually handicapped children. It covers various aspects of blindness and offers suggestions for parents and professionals.) (*L*)

Spradley, T. S., & Spradley, J. P. (1978). *Deaf like me*. New York: Random House. (This is the true account of a family's experiences with their deaf daughter, including their search for an appropriate education. The authors advocate a total communication approach to language development.) (*L*)

Stevens, S. H. (1980). *The learning-disabled child: Ways that parents can help*. Winston-Salem, NC: John F. Blair. (This book contains much useful information, especially on what teachers can offer learning disabled youngsters and their parents. It also provides helpful guidelines for parents

regarding management of homework, teacher-parent conferences, tutoring, and how to obtain appropriate professional help.) (*R*)

Strauss, S. (1975). *Is it well with the child? A parent's guide to raising a mentally handicapped child*. New York: Doubleday. (A professional writer tells of her own experiences as the parent of a mentally handicapped child and gives general advice for parents and professionals.) (*M*)

Turnbull, A., & Turnbull, H. (1978). *Parents speak out: Views from the other side of the two way mirror*. Columbus, OH: Charles Merrill. (Insights from professional parents of handicapped children.) (*M*)

Ulrich, S. (with Wolf, A. W. M.). (1972). *Elizabeth*. Ann Arbor: University of Michigan Press. (A mother describes the first five years of her blind child's life and provides many useful ideas for home care.) (*M*)

Wallbrown, J. D., & Wallbrown, F. H. (1981). *So your child has a learning problem, now what?* Brandon, VT: Clinical Psychology Publications. (This book is helpful in understanding the nature and diagnosis of learning disabilities and how parents and teachers can help the learning disabled child. It is recommended primarily to parents who have a child with auditory processing problems.) (*R*)

Weiss, M. S., & Weiss, H. G. (1976). *Home is a learning place: A parent's guide to learning disabilities*. Boston: Little, Brown. (This is a practical volume that explains the many ramifications of learning disabilities and offers advice to parents concerning ways they can help their children.) (*L*)

West, P. (1970). *Words for a deaf daughter*. New York: Harper & Row. (Novelist-poet-critic tells the story of his deaf and brain-damaged daughter.) (*M*)

White, R. (1972). *Be not afraid*. New York: The Dial Press. (A father chronicles his family's experiences for 14 years following the diagnosis of epilepsy in his 8-year-old son.) (*M*)

Books for Children

Campanella, R. (1959). *It's good to be alive*. Boston: Little, Brown. (The well-known baseball star tells of his life after being paralyzed as a result of an automobile accident.) (*Youth*) (*M*)

Fassler, J. (1975). *Howie helps himself*. Chicago: Albert Whitman & Co. (This book is appropriate to share with a child in a wheelchair who may be pleased to read a book about another child who is disabled.) (*Primary*) (*G*)

Gilson, J. (1980). *Do bananas chew gum?* New York: Lothrop, Lee & Shepard. (This is a fictional story about a sixth-grade boy with a learning disability, whose thoughts and feelings about himself are sensitively presented.) (*Youth*) (*R*)

(Exhibit continues next page)

Exhibit 24-4 (cont.)

Gordon, S. (1975). *Living fully: A guide for young people with a handicap, their parents, their teachers and professionals*. New York: John Day. (This special educator has a no-nonsense and compassionate approach to disabled kids.) (*Youth*) (*M*)

Griese, A. A. (1969). *At the mouth of the luckiest river*. New York: Crowell. (Tatlek, the hero, is an Athabascan Indian child in Alaska who has an orthopedic handicap but deals with this difference in natural, pragmatic fashion.) (*Elementary*) (*M*)

Harries, J. (1981). *They triumphed over their handicaps*. New York: Franklin Watts. (This book is a profile of six disabled people who have achieved in sports, music, and careers. Among the more famous disabled individuals included in the book are Ray Charles, a blind musician; Kathy Miller, who, although physically handicapped, went on to win the International Valor in Sports Award for her running; Ted Kennedy, Jr., who skis, swims, and scuba dives in spite of having had one leg amputated; and finally Kitty O'Neil, who, after becoming deaf in childhood and then discovering she had cancer at age 25, became the women's 1964 10-meter diving champion. The reader learns about the inspirational experiences in each of the individual's lives and how the handicap was overcome.) (*Elementary* and *Intermediate*) (*G*)

Hayes, M. L. (1974). *The tuned-in, turned-on book about learning problems*. Novato, CA: Academic Therapy Publications. (This book will give learning disabled children a better understanding of their problems and will help them develop some coping skills.) (*Youth*) (*R*)

Hickok, L. A. (1958). *The story of Helen Keller*. New York: Grosset & Dunlap. (A biography of the accomplished and famous blind and deaf woman.) (*Elementary* and *Intermediate*) (*M*)

Kellogg, M. (1968). *Tell me that you love me Junie Moon*. New York: Farrar, Straus, & Giroux. (A group of "rejects" leave the rehabilitation institution and learn to live and love in the world.) (*Youth*) (*M*)

Krents, H. (1972). *To race the wind*. New York: G. P. Pulnarus. (An autobiography of an undaunted blind young man, both moving and humorous.) (*Youth*) (*M*)

Ominsky, E. (1977). *Jon O. A special boy*. Englewood Cliffs, NJ: Prentice-Hall. (Photographs and text describe the life of a young boy with Down's syndrome.) (*Preschool* and *Primary*) (*M*)

Peterson, J. W. (1977). *I have a sister, my sister is deaf*. New York: Harper & Row. (This book is a realistic portrait of an independent and happy child who happens to be deaf.) (*Primary*) (*G*)

Pevsner, S. (1977). *Keep stompin' till the music stops*. New York: Clarion Books. (This is a fictional story of a 12-year-old who has a learning disability. The story is generally upbeat and the vocabulary and humor are fairly sophisticated.) (*Youth*) (*R*)

Robinson, V. (1966). *David in silence*. Philadelphia: Lippincott. (A deaf boy in industrial Birmingham, England has many adventures, and his thoughts and feelings are sensitively chronicled in this story.) (*Intermediate* and *Youth*) (*M*)

Sobol, H. L. (1977). *My brother Steven is retarded*. New York: Macmillan. (The photographs and text tell a poignant and sensitive story from the perspective of a younger sister.) (*Elementary*) (*M*)

Southall, I. (1968). *Let the balloon go*. New York: St. Martin's Press. (This compelling story portrays an intelligent, imaginative Australian boy with cerebral palsy as he learns to assert himself and overcome the expectations of family and peers.) (*Elementary* and *Intermediate*) (*M*)

Warfield, F. (1957). *Keep listening*. New York: Viking Press. (The author tells of her struggles as a hard-of-hearing adolescent.) (*Youth*) (*M*)

Wolf, B. (1974). *Don't feel sorry for Paul*. Philadelphia: Lippincott. (This book is a photo-journalistic documentary about a child who wears a prosthesis. It will inspire children, disabled or not, to work hard to accomplish what they want even if the odds seem to be against them.) (*Elementary* and *Intermediate*) (*G*)

White, P. (1978). *Janet at school*. New York: Crowell. (Text and photographs portray appealing 5-year-old Janet, who has spina bifida, in many school experiences.) (*Preschool* and *Primary*) (*M*)

Note. Preschool level — Books that can be read aloud to children ages 2 to 5, usually with pictures that also tell the story. *Primary level* — Books that can be read aloud or by beginning readers, of interest to kindergarten through third graders, usually illustrated. *Elementary level* — Books on a third- to eighth-grade level of interest and reading. *Intermediate level* — Books on approximately a seventh- through ninth-grade reading level. *Youth* — Books of interest to those of high school age (and often to adults), with a relatively uncomplicated literary style. Some youth books may be of interest to younger readers.

Abbreviations for sources of entries are as follows: *G* (Grossman, 1983), *L* (Lombana, 1982), *M* (Mullins, 1983), and *R* (Reed, 1985). *Source:* Portions reprinted with permission of the publishers and authors from J. H. Lombana, *Guidance for Handicapped Students* (Springfield, IL: Charles C Thomas, 1982), pp. 382–384; and J. B. Mullins, "The uses of bibliotherapy in counseling families confronted with handicaps," in M. Seligam (Ed.), *The Family with a Handicapped Child: Understanding and Treatment* (San Diego: Grune & Stratton, 1983), pp. 257–259. Other references from Grossman (1983), Reed (1985), and the author of this text.

CONSULTATION IN COURTS AND IN CORRECTIONAL SETTINGS

The forensic application of psychological tests—the use of tests in the legal system or court setting—is one of the most challenging areas of consultation. Psychological testing may be used in pretrial competency hearings, court trials, dispositional and sentencing hearings, criminal investigations, civil court procedures, and Social Security Administration hearings. Psychological testing is important and valuable in forensic matters. It informs the court about the individual's current level of functioning, providing information that cannot readily be obtained through interviewing the individual.

The following case illustrates the use of testing in a pretrial competency hearing (Weitz, 1976, pp. 6–7):

[A] criminal matter in which psychological testing proved to be highly significant involved a 17-year-old male, who was accused of murdering a 42-year-old prostitute, when he allegedly fought with her about her fee for services rendered. Following his arrest, the young man signed a confession. I [Weitz] was brought into this case by his defense counsel and subsequently examined the defendant while he was detained at the County Jail. The testing revealed an intelligence classification of "mental defective" on the basis of the Wechsler Scale. The projective techniques confirmed the low level mental acuity. The Gray Standardized Oral Reading Paragraphs indicated that he was a nonreader. In my pretrial testimony, wherein I presented my report, I referred to some of the questions and answers in the confession-which the defendant signed:

Question: "Is this a true and voluntary statement made of your own free will?"
Answer: "Yes."
Question: "Can you read and write?"
Answer: "Yes."
Question: "After given an opportunity to read this statement, will you sign it?"
Answer: "Yes."

It quickly became obvious to the court that the defendant could not have read nor was he able to understand the contents of the confession which he signed. The presiding judge declared the confession to be null and void and set the defendant free. During the course of my study, the defendant admitted to me that he was forced to sign the confession out of fear after having been beaten severely with a rubber hose. Ironically, within a few weeks after he was released, the police apprehended two men who proved to be the murderers.

Ethical Concerns of the Court Psychologist

The demands placed on psychologists who work in courts or in correctional settings create a number of unique moral and ethical issues. These issues are also relevant to the work of psychologists employed in other agencies or in private practice. (The following analysis is based on Riscalla, 1971.)

The duties of court psychologists include making recommendations as to an individual's competency to stand trial, whether a juvenile should remain with his or her family, and whether an offender should receive probation or be incarcerated. Psychologists must decide to what extent protecting the offender's rights may conflict with the rights of the community and with the psychologists' employment by the court. Their duties place them in a captive adversary role—they may be called upon to support a particular position that is held either by the prosecutor or by the offender. They should recognize their own feelings about their role, as well as their attitudes toward certain offenses, and should consider how their moral standards will affect their relationship with the offender and with the court.

Court psychologists may perceive their role in a number of ways. One is that of the *anti-establishment psychologist* who takes sides with the offender by rationalizing the offense on the basis of personality dynamics or adverse environmental conditions. A second is that of the *punitive, self-righteous psychologist* who aims to protect the rights of society and thus words reports so that the court may take punitive action against the offender. A third is that of the *uninvolved psychologist* who is afraid of authority and preserves his or her neutrality at any price. The fourth and proper role, according to Riscalla, is that of the *psychologist who recognizes his or her captive adversary role* and yet tries to limit it, insofar as that is possible, by illuminating issues and pointing out constructive alternatives that might lead to solutions.

Discussing Results with Clients

Psychologists must recognize that in their role as representatives of the court they may be viewed with suspicion and hostility by clients. Sharing the results of the evaluation with the offender *before* the report is written may help to reduce suspiciousness and increase rapport, increase the accuracy of the report, make the recommendations more realistic, and give the client insight into his or her behavior. Clients who do not wish to participate in the evaluation should have their wishes granted.

Clients, their representatives, or other interested authorized individuals should be permitted to discuss the report with the psychologist and to examine it, if necessary, prior to its submission to legal authorities. This and the other procedures discussed will help psychologists working in court settings to serve their clients better, to write more understandable reports, and to make the assessment procedure more relevant and meaningful.

CHALLENGES OF BEING AN EXPERT WITNESS

Psychologists, psychoeducational specialists, and clinicians are occasionally called upon to testify at special hearings conducted in schools, agencies, or courts. Testifying as an expert witness can be a frustrating experience, especially in court or court-like settings. The structure of the courtroom is radically different from that of the staff conference room or classroom. The witness in court is expected to answer many questions with a simple one-word response. "Isn't it true that . . ." is a form that questions often take, and little opportunity is afforded to qualify responses. The courtroom is a place for decision-making—not a place to debate or solve complex issues.

When you testify at fair hearings in schools, as required by PL 94-142, expect to answer questions about your professional background, credentials, and experience; the amount of contact you have had with the child; the history of the child's difficulties; the procedures used to evaluate the child, including their rationale, reliability, validity, and bias; the test findings, interpretations, and conclusions drawn from the findings; and the recommendations. Many of these questions can be answered by referring to the psychological report. An expert witness can and should rely on notes or other materials for information that cannot be readily recalled. "Refreshing recollection" is both an acceptable and the most accurate means of providing information to the court.

The following list of suggestions may help you better prepare for those occasions when you testify as an expert witness (Fineman, 1983; Sattler, 1982c):

1. Be sure that each evaluation meets acceptable standards of reliability and validity. Any modification of standard procedures should be noted. Remember that test scores are *estimates* of performance, and that these estimates were obtained under a given set of circumstances.

2. Keep detailed records of all contacts with students, parents, and teachers, and date every observation, conference, and evaluation.

3. Be thoroughly prepared. It may be helpful to outline your major points and to support these points with data. Generally you need to know exactly what information you included in the report and to be able to support your decision to include that information. Be prepared to

experience some anxiety. You can minimize your anxiety, however, by being well prepared and having adequate notes. Never allow yourself to be rushed. Recognize that any notes you refer to in the courtroom must be made available to all parties upon request. Good judgment is imperative in deciding what notes to use in the courtroom.

4. Dress in conservative fashion.

5. Speak slowly, clearly, and loudly enough to be heard. Maintain eye contact with the attorney or hearing officer who is asking questions.

6. Be prepared to have your credentials carefully reviewed and your expertise questioned. During the cross-examination, the opposing attorney is likely to question your credentials and credibility. The attorney may ask you about your education, if you do not have a doctoral degree ("Isn't it true that a Ph.D. degree is the accepted degree for the practice of psychology?"); the amount of time that you spent with the child ("Do you mean that you spent only two hours testing the child?"); the amount and kind of testing that was done ("Do you think that you know the child well enough to make a recommendation on the basis of four tests?"); the reliability and validity of the tests used in the evaluation ("Isn't it true that tests are culturally biased?" or "Tell me about the reliability and validity of the WISC-R"); and the type of recommendations that you made ("How can you be sure that the child needs a classroom for learning-disabled children rather than a special tutor?").

7. Recognize that the opposing lawyers may do anything within the legal limits of courtroom procedure to impeach your testimony.

8. Recognize that court hearings are based on the adversary process. In this context there are few absolute "truths"; the result often depends on which party presents a more convincing case.

9. Do not talk informally with any of the opposing lawyers or witnesses, unless you are prepared to face a cross-examination about such discussions.

10. Do not introduce newspaper reports or conversations with others as the basis for formulating your opinions.

11. Expect to review with your lawyer (if he or she so recommends) a detailed list of possible questions and to prepare answers to them.

12. Be prepared to have statements in reports, articles, or books taken out of context.

13. Listen carefully to what is asked and make your responses to the point, brief, and jargon-free.

14. Report your findings impartially, and be honest at all times. Admit your weaknesses simply and directly. Be prepared to discuss test norms, and avoid undue generalizations in your interpretations.

15. Ask for clarification when you do not understand a question.

16. Try not to be defensive. It is permissible to rely on your professional opinion as adequate reason for taking certain actions or forming certain opinions.

17. Take time to think prior to responding to a question.

18. Do not invoke the opinions of other experts; you are the expert.

19. Keep abreast of your local, state, and federal guidelines regarding psychological evaluations and placement procedures.

When you participate as an expert witness, you should expect the unexpected. No matter how well you have prepared, the opposing attorney is likely to come up with novel ways to impeach your testimony. The better prepared you are, the better able you will be to present the best case possible and to deal with the stress of a most difficult professional situation. Exhibit 24-5 illustrates questions that were asked of a psychologist at a fair hearing trial.

The world's most widely used computer language:

USE OF COMPUTERS IN PSYCHOLOGICAL ASSESSMENT

Because of their ability to process large volumes of information, computers one day may greatly facilitate the performance of clinical tasks, such as writing psychological reports and administering tests. However, the use of computers in psychological assessment, particularly ability testing, is still in the experimental stage.

At present, computerized reports are used to assist clinicians in generating hypotheses about the examinee. Test data is inputted, and the computer program outputs hypotheses based on the data. (Exhibit 24-6 illustrates a computer-generated report for the WISC-R, based solely on test scores and age.) After placing the computer's hypotheses in the context of all available assessment information obtained from other test results, observation, the clinical history, school records, and the interview, the clinician formulates interpretations and recommendations based on the unique configuration of assessment data. Anyone using computerized reports should recognize their limitations. Computerized reports are usually based on only one, two, or three tests; they usually do not take into account either the examinee's unique clinical history or the complete assessment results (Matarazzo, 1986). Thus computerized reports cannot replace clinical judgment. Also, clinicians are still responsible for communicating the results from computerized reports in a nontechnical manner to clients. As with any assessment procedure, validity must be established for each type of report.

The use of computers for psychological assessment poses a number of potential difficulties. In the hands of an untrained psychologist, an unvalidated computerized test report could be harmful to the examinee (Matarazzo, 1986). If the psychologist and the unwary examinee accept as accurate an invalid computer printout, decisions about the examinee may be affected adversely. Who is liable for any harm caused? The answer is uncertain—it could be the manufacturer of the software or the interpreter of the results (Hartman, 1986). No legal precedents have yet been set. Product-liability disclaimers do not protect the manufacturer or the psychologist. Consequently, clinicians need to be trained in the limitations and uses of computerized test reports.

Computer-administered tests are only effective with examinees who understand how to use the computer keyboard. If the examinee is left unattended, there is no way to evaluate the extent to which he or she understands each question. It is *unlikely* that either young children or examinees who are severely disturbed will be able to take computer-administered tests. Even in the case of able examinees, however, research is needed to examine the validity of computerized test administration.

New challenges await professionals who use computers in their clinical work—many new legal, ethical, clinical, professional, and philosophical issues are raised by computer-generated reports and assessment procedures. At present, the new technology is not without its problems.

This exhibit illustrates the kinds of questions that may be asked at a fair hearing. The questions in this exhibit were asked of a school psychologist who testified at a fair hearing trial on an appropriate educational placement for a child. The parents wanted a residential school placement, whereas the school district was satisfied with the child's progress in a special education program. Because of space limitations, the psychologist's testimony is not reproduced. In addition, some minor editorial changes have been made. Although each case involves unique issues and concerns, the school psychologist's testimony generally involves issues related to the use and interpretation of tests, development of the IEP, and placement recommendations. All names shown in the exhibit are fictitious.

Direct Examination

Please tell us your name.

By whom are you employed?

In what capacity?

What is your formal educational background?

How long have you been employed as a school psychologist?

Have you had any other educational experience?

Did you have occasion to test a child by the name of John Smith?

Do you know when you first tested him?

What types of tests did you give him?

Did you prepare a report in reference to that?

Is this the report (District's Exhibit 1) you drew up as a result of the tests you gave John?

Does this report indicate how he performed on the WRAT test?

And what does it indicate as far as his level on the WRAT test?

What is the PIAT?

And is there any correlation between the results that one would get by giving the WRAT and giving the PIAT?

All right. So in your opinion, as far as school psychologists are concerned, they are pretty comparable as far as their results are concerned?

I'd like to direct your attention to Exhibit 1, the psychological report. Would you examine it please? What are his PIAT scores?

Now tell us about his intelligence test scores.

Do you have any reason to believe that the scores set forth in Exhibit 1 are anything other than factual?

Now, did you participate in the development of the IEP for John which was used during the period of time that he was in the special education program at Roosevelt Elementary School?

And did you have occasion to monitor that program as it was being administered?

And did you formulate an opinion as to whether or not John was successful in that program?

In other words, he appeared to be happy during the periods — during the days that you visited the classroom.

Do you know who the teacher was?

Did the teacher ever indicate to you that the program that John was enrolled in, that she was teaching him, that that was an inappropriate program for him?

Now, did either Mr. or Mrs. Smith at any time request of you that a new IEP be written?

Do you know what grades John was receiving in school?

Did his teacher, Mrs. Blank, ever make any comments to you about how John was doing in class?

And were those comments made on one occasion or on more than one occasion?

Now approximately how many times would you say you had occasion to discuss John's performance with Mrs. Blank?

And none of those times did she bring up the fact that he was not doing well? [*Hearing officer:* Was that a no? I'll ask you to speak up.]

Now did you ever have occasion to receive any communications from either Mr. or Mrs. Smith indicating that John was not doing well in the special classes during the period of time he was in that class?

[*Parents' attorney:* I'm going to object. That's a very leading question. We haven't established whether she had any conversations with them, and now we've led her into the answer. I think the question should be better framed, particularly since the district is represented by counsel.

Hearing officer: Sustained.]

Did you ever have any conversations during the period of time that John was involved in the special education class with Mrs. Smith?

Was Mrs. Smith present when the IEP was written for John that was in force and effect when he was in Mrs. Blank's class?

Did Mrs. Blank ever give you any reason to believe that the grades she put on her report cards were not reflective of the actual progress of the students under her care?

Did anything ever come to your attention that the IEP was inappropriate?

Do you believe that the IEP is appropriate?

Do you believe John's class placement represents a least restrictive environment?

Cross Examination

What year did you become employed by this district?

At that time, what was your degree that you held?

Where were you assigned in 1985?

And what was your job with regard to those four schools?

How many IEP committees did you sit on last year?

How many schools were you assigned to last year?

(Exhibit continues next page)

Exhibit 24-5 (cont.)

And in those four schools you worked only with the special education children?

When a child is referred to you, what does that mean?

Okay. So the referrals to you are for purposes of making a recommendation with regard to the placement of the child?

So you do evaluations, such as the one you did on John Smith?

And who makes the referral to you?

Do you know what the total population at Roosevelt Elementary School is?

Now, your job is to all students, not just special education students?

Now, of the 500 students at Roosevelt, how many of them were in special education classes?

How many students were in special education classes at the three other schools that you were assigned to?

How often would you visit Roosevelt Elementary School?

[*School's attorney:* It's irrelevant and immaterial how often she'd do it. How often she visited John Smith is relevant. How often she did her job generally is irrelevant and immaterial.

Hearing officer: Give me an offer of proof.

Parents' attorney: Yeah. I mean, I think I'm entitled to inquire. She's just testified that based on her observations of John Smith she's able to determine a great deal. I think we have a perfect right, and the total right, to go into what her duties are, what she was expected to do, how often she was expected to do it, and so on, to show whether or not she could, in fact, give the opinions that she's given. He put her on as an expert to say all of these things. We have a right to know what the background is, at least to that, and indeed, to find out whether it's reasonable to assume that one could be so certain about something under those conditions.

School's attorney: I think the question could be asked how many times did she see John Smith, how many times did she talk to the teacher, that's all relevant. What she did with all these other students and other times is irrelevant and immaterial.

Hearing officer: I'll overrule your objection, I'll allow you to go on, but I would like for it to be brief.]

And when you would go to Roosevelt Elementary School, what would you do?

Now, you have been shown your report, District's Exhibit 1, can you tell me how long it took you to conduct that examination?

And how long did it take you to prepare the report?

So you spent about five hours total on it?

Is that pretty standard, the amount of time you spend on a report and examination?

How many children would you typically test in a week?

In the month of November, when you tested in 1985, when you tested John, do you recall how many other students you tested that week?

But, generally, the maximum number of children you would test on any given day at any given school is two?

On the days that you test two students, are you able to spend any time in any of the classrooms?

What does one of your typical days look like?

When does your school day end?

Between 2:35 and 5:00 p.m. what do you normally do?

When did you visit John Smith's classroom?

How much time do you think you spent that day in the class?

What happened when you went into the classroom?

Did you talk with John?

Was it in front of the other children or did you take him out?

Did you always go at the same time of the day to the classroom?

Other than these 10- or 15-minute visits, did you ever spend any time in that classroom watching John Smith perform in the classroom?

Did you ever see him during the lunch period?

Showing you your report, it indicates that on November 8, 1985 you administered something called the WRAT, is that correct?

What do those initials stand for?

And it indicates that your reading score that you obtained was a 5.4, is that correct?

What does that mean?

What is the reading score obtained on the PIAT?

Now, as between the WRAT and the PIAT, is the reading recognition test for each of those tests given in the same manner?

Now can you describe for us the kind of work of John's that you saw?

And you've never seen John in the group instructional setting?

And you've never seen John in the lunch room situation, is that correct?

Did you ever see John before school, walking into the school, on the playground before school?

Did you ever see him in the physical education program?

Did you ever speak to his physical education teacher about him?

What's the longest conversation you had with John between November 8, 1985 and May 8, 1986?

Could you tell us when that 5-minute conversation occurred?

Do you remember whether it was at the beginning of the period he was in the classroom, or towards the end?

Do you know if progress charts were maintained on John?

Did you see charts for any of the students in the class John Smith was enrolled in?

[*School's attorney:* Again, it assumes a fact not in evidence; it assumes that their IEPs required charts to be kept.

Parents' attorney: All I'm asking is if she saw a chart for any student.

School's attorney: It assumes that there were charts.

Parents' attorney: It doesn't assume that at all.

(Exhibit continues next page)

Exhibit 24-5 (cont.)

School's attorney: It sure does. It assumes that there were charts.

Parents' attorney: It doesn't.

Hearing officer: Overruled, go ahead.]

Did you see a chart for any other student in the class?

Did you ever develop a behavior modification plan for John Smith?

In the IEP it indicates under placement data the type of disability. How was it arrived at?

Do you have an opinion whether the special education program that he was placed in was still appropriate in May 1986?

I have no further questions.

Redirect Examination

[At this point the school's attorney has the opportunity to ask a few questions.]

Have you ever administered eight tests in one week?

Now, are the PIAT scores recognized as accurate indications of a student's achievement in the field of school psychology?

Now, this morning on cross examination you said you went into John Smith's classroom three or four times. Did you mean three or four times per month, or three or four times during the entire time he was in there?

[*Editorial note:* The parents' request for residential placement was denied.]

CONCLUDING COMMENT

This text has been dedicated to the principle that tests of intelligence and special abilities, interviews, observations, and informal tests provide the cornerstones for the consultation process. These cornerstones help us to identify the observable manifestations of childhood disorders and, when linked with our knowledge of child development and child psychopathology, form the foundation for assessment decisions. Objective measurements help us make independent judgments about a child's level of functioning that are useful in determining the extent of psychopathology and in communicating with other professionals. Knowledge gained about the behavioral concomitants of psychological and physical illness constitutes an important contribution to the study of children. Ideally, each clinical and psychoeducational assessment should be a learning opportunity for both the psychologist and the child. A knowledgeable and responsible use of intelligence and special ability tests, and of other assessment procedures, will be of value to the child, to those responsible for his or her care and education, and, ultimately, to society as a whole.

SUMMARY

1. The consultant role requires a knowledge of the situations in which change is to take place.

2. You must know the ethical standards of your profession. With respect to assessment, the standards indicate that the effects of recommendations must be kept in mind, limitations of tests must be recognized, confidentiality must be protected, clients must have access to their test results, and any doubts about the reliability or validity of results must be stated in the report.

3. Psychologists who work in schools help children learn, solve school-related problems, and help school personnel. Their functions include assessment, intervention, consultation, research and evaluation, and administration.

4. The objectives of psychological evaluation in schools include classification, description of learning style, class placement, and development of remediation, management, and teaching strategies. The aim is to help teachers find solutions to pupil problems.

5. Recommendations made by school psychologists as part of the multidisciplinary team include special placements, remedial techniques, curriculum changes, behavior management programs, counseling or therapy, and assistance at home.

6. The teacher and the parents will continue to be responsible for the child's education after the evaluation is completed. Your recommendations should help them in their efforts.

7. Public Law 94-142 has many implications for the assessment of children, particularly in the school setting but also in the community. The law is designed to protect the rights of children and parents and to ensure education for all handicapped children. It incorporates many of the ethical principles of the American Psychological Association. It mandates, for example, that (a) consideration be given to the child's native language, (b) only valid tests be used for the assessment, (c) more than one assessment technique be used, (d) the child's physical handicaps be considered, (e) all relevant factors be considered in the evaluation, (f) a team approach be used, (g) the assessment procedures not be racially or culturally discriminatory, (h) an individualized educational program be designed, (i) parents have the right to an independent evaluation, (j) re-evaluations be performed at least every three years, (k) parents have the right to examine their child's records, and (l) the child be placed in the least restrictive educational environment. Two serious shortcomings of PL 94-142 are its failure to specify clearly (a) what is meant by "racially and culturally nondiscriminatory procedures" and (b) how "native language" can be determined.

Exhibit 24-6

The Psychological Corporation WISC-R Interpretive Report

```
Kane                                                                  Page 1

                WISC-R Microcomputer-Assisted Interpretive Report

CLIENT: Stephen Kane                 SEX: Male          DATE OF TEST: 01-12-85
SCHOOL: Murray Elem.                 GRADE: 3           DATE OF BIRTH: 03-06-76
EXAMINER: Dr. Leslie K. Anderson                        AGE: 8 yrs 10 mos 6 days

REASON FOR TESTING:
Stephen was referred by his teacher because of suspected learning
disabilities.
=============================================================================
                          DESCRIPTIVE INFORMATION
=============================================================================
                  SUM OF                   PERCENTILE
    SCALE      SCALED SCORES      IQ          RANK      CLASSIFICATION
-----------------------------------------------------------------------------
VERBAL              73           128          97
PERFORMANCE         49            98          45
FULL SCALE         122           116          86         High Average
-----------------------------------------------------------------------------
```

SUBTEST	RAW SCORE	SCALED SCORE	PERCENTILE RANK
Information	17	15	95
Similarities	14	13	84
Arithmetic	11	11	63
Vocabulary	35	15	95
Comprehension	26	19	99
(Digit Span)	(10)	(10)	(50)
Picture Completion	17	11	63
Picture Arrangement	31	14	91
Block Design	12	8	25
Object Assembly	18	10	50
Coding	25	6	9
(Mazes)	(—)	(—)	(—)

```
-----------------------------------------------------------------------------
       NOTE:   Subtests in parentheses are supplementary subtests.
-----------------------------------------------------------------------------
                                       PERCENTILES
SUBTEST                     1  2  5  9 16 25 37 50 63 75 84 91 95 98 99

Information           .  .  .  .  .  .  .  .  .  .  .  X  .  .  .
Similarities          .  .  .  .  .  .  .  .  .  X  .  .  .  .  .
Arithmetic            .  .  .  .  .  .  .  X  .  .  .  .  .  .  .
Vocabulary            .  .  .  .  .  .  .  .  .  .  .  X  .  .  .
Comprehension         .  .  .  .  .  .  .  .  .  .  .  .  .  .  X
Digit Span            .  .  .  .  .  .  .  X  .  .  .  .  .  .  .
Picture Completion    .  .  .  .  .  .  .  X  .  .  .  .  .  .  .
Picture Arrangement   .  .  .  .  .  .  .  .  .  .  X  .  .  .  .
Block Design          .  .  .  .  .  X  .  .  .  .  .  .  .  .  .
Object Assembly       .  .  .  .  .  .  .  X  .  .  .  .  .  .  .
Coding                .  .  .  .  X  .  .  .  .  .  .  .  .  .  .
Mazes                 .  .  .  . N O T  A D M I N I S T E R E D  . . . .
-----------------------------------------------------------------------------
              1  2  3  4  5  6  7  8  9 10 11 12 13 14 15 16 17 18 19
                               SCALED SCORES
```

(Exhibit continues next page)

Exhibit 24-6 (cont.)

Kane   Page 2

===
                        STATISTICAL INFORMATION
===
CONFIDENCE INTERVALS
The 95% confidence interval for the Full Scale IQ is 110 to 121. These are
reasonable limits of the range within which Stephen's "true" Full Scale
IQ lies.

The 95% confidence interval for the Verbal IQ is 119 to 133, and for the
Performance IQ it is 89 to 107.

DIFFERENCE BETWEEN VERBAL AND PERFORMANCE IQS
The Verbal IQ exceeds the Performance IQ by 30 points, a difference that is
statistically significant at the .05 level. Differences of this size
or greater were found in only 2% of the children in the WISC-R
standardization sample.

DEVIATION OF SUBTEST SCORES FROM THE SUBJECT'S OWN MEAN SCORE, BY SCALE

SUBTEST	SCALED SCORE	DEVIATION FROM MEAN SCALED SCORE	SIGNIFICANCE AT .05 LEVEL
Information	15	1.17	no
Similarities	13	−0.83	no
Arithmetic	11	−2.83	no
Vocabulary	15	1.17	no
Comprehension	19	5.17	yes
(Digit Span)	10	−3.83	yes

        MEAN VERBAL SCALED SCORE = 13.83

Picture Completion	11	1.20	no
Picture Arrangement	14	4.20	yes
Block Design	8	−1.80	no
Object Assembly	10	0.20	no
Coding	6	−3.80	yes
(Mazes)	(--)	(--)	(--)

        MEAN PERFORMANCE SCALED SCORE = 9.80

   NOTE: A positive deviation from the mean indicates that the subtest
   score is higher than the mean. A negative deviation from the mean
   indicates that the subtest score is lower than the mean. The two
   supplementary subtests are listed in parentheses.

(Exhibit continues next page)

Exhibit 24-6 (cont.)

Kane   Page 3

```
==========================================================================
                        ADDITIONAL INFORMATION
==========================================================================
Stephen's previous tests yielded high scores, yet his grades have been
consistently low.
```

```
==========================================================================
                        INTERPRETIVE INFORMATION
==========================================================================
     Stephen's Full Scale IQ of 116 falls at the 86th percentile in
comparison with children of his age, and places Stephen in the
High Average classification.  This IQ provides an assessment
of general intelligence and scholastic aptitude.

     Stephen obtained a Verbal IQ of 128, which falls at the 97th
percentile.  This IQ provides an indication of his verbal comprehension,
which includes the ability to reason with words, to learn verbal material,
and to process verbal information.

     Stephen's Performance IQ of 98 falls at the 45th percentile.
This IQ contributes an understanding of his perceptual organization,
which includes nonverbal reasoning, the ability to employ visual images
in thinking, and the ability to process visual material efficiently.

     As noted earlier, the Verbal IQ is significantly higher than the
Performance IQ.  Furthermore, the size of the difference is not common
in samples of normal children, and efforts should be made to uncover
reasons for this difference.  Possible interpretations of the
difference include the following:

     1. Expressive language skills are better developed than
        nonverbal skills.

     2. Auditory processing is better developed than visual
        processing.

     3. Academic opportunities and interests may be a factor.


These possibilities are not necessarily the only ones.  None should
be accepted as applying to Stephen unless supported by independent
evidence such as the results of other tests, behavioral
observations, and background information.
```

(Exhibit continues next page)

Exhibit 24-6 (cont.)

Kane   Page 4

     Because the Verbal and Performance IQs differ considerably,
Stephen's Full Scale IQ appears to summarize diverse abilities.

     Only one of the scores contributing to the Verbal IQ differed sig-
nificantly from Stephen's average verbal score. Therefore the
Verbal IQ is probably a good indication of his abilities in this area.

     Two of the scores contributing to Stephen's Performance IQ differed
significantly from his average performance score. Therefore, Stephen's
Performance IQ is an average of diverse abilities and may not be as easily
interpretable as otherwise.

     The relatively low scores on the Arithmetic, Digit Span, and Coding
subtests may be associated with distractibility, short attention or memory
span, poor concentration, or lack of facility in handling numbers, in
comparison with others of Stephen's ability.

     The score on the Comprehension subtest suggests good practical judgment
and common-sense reasoning in comparison with the other verbal abilities
measured by the WISC-R. Such scores imply the effective use of one's
knowledge.

     The score on Picture Arrangement may reflect any of several
relative strengths -- for example, the ability to appraise a total
situation that is shown in segments, to anticipate the consequences
of social actions, and to distinguish essential from unimportant details.

```
*****************************************************************************
*                                                                          *
*     This report is based only on the subject's WISC-R scores and age.    *
* Other information about the individual must be considered when interpreting *
* results.                                                                 *
*                                                                          *
*****************************************************************************
```

8. The IEP (individualized educational program) includes a description of the child's present level of educational performance, annual instructional objectives, short-term instructional objectives, specific educational services needed by the child, the date when special services will begin and their anticipated duration, the extent to which the child will participate in regular education programs, a justification for the placement, a list of individuals responsible for implementation, and procedures for evaluating instructional objectives. IEPs are plans that must be monitored continually.

9. Instructional effectiveness, and not the specific setting, may be the key to successful mainstreaming. For mentally retarded children, mainstreaming has not been more effective than self-contained classes in improving academic or social performance.

10. The Family Educational Rights and Privacy Act of 1974 established that parents must have access to their children's records and that parents must be consulted before these records are released to other agencies. It has been found that psychologists have modified their reports in response to this law.

11. Public Law 99-457, the Education of the Handicapped Act Amendments of 1986, authorizes early intervention programs for handicapped infants, toddlers, and their families and extends the protection of Public Law 94-142 to handicapped children aged 3 to 5 beginning in the school year 1990–91.

12. Ethnic minorities have gone to the courts to challenge assessment procedures that have resulted in an apparent over-representation of ethnic minorities in educable mentally retarded classes. Most cases have been settled by consent agreements. In three cases, however, federal courts have ruled on the placement of black children in educable mentally retarded classes. In *Larry P.* v. *Riles*, a federal judge banned the use of intelligence tests in the assessment of black children. This verdict was generally upheld by the Ninth Circuit Court of Appeals. In *Parents in Action on Special Education* v. *Hannon*, a federal judge ruled that intelligence tests are *not* culturally biased. In *Georgia Conference of NAACP* v. *Georgia*, a federal court ruled that the State of Georgia did not treat black and white students differentially in special education placements. The Eleventh Court of Appeals affirmed the trial court's ruling. Further judicial rulings will be needed to resolve the issues involved in the assessment and placement of minority children in special classes.

13. The U.S. Supreme Court and other federal courts generally have supported local school districts' decisions regarding appropriate educational opportunities for handicapped children.

14. When you consult with parents of exceptional children, understand that each developmental stage may bring about a new crisis. Parents of autistic children must be given a realistic and cautious interpretation of autism. Parents of children who are not accepted into gifted programs need special understanding. Your work with parents of minority children may be hampered by language barriers, cultural differences, problems in interpreting laws and regulations, and clashes of values. Considerable patience and understanding are needed to work effectively with minority families.

15. Books on coping with handicapped children and books containing personal accounts by handicapped individuals can aid both parents and children in adjusting to the child's handicap.

16. In pediatric medical settings psychologists need to be quick and brief in dealing with physicians, who usually want terse reports that focus on only the most pertinent aspects of the case. Turf issues that arise must be handled diplomatically and professionally.

17. An important area of assessment involves the forensic application of psychological tests. Psychologists working in the courts should recognize their captive adversary role and try to limit it by developing constructive alternatives.

18. Testifying as an expert witness requires much preparation; the experience may be a taxing one.

19. Computerized reports must be used with extreme caution, and only as an aid to generate hypotheses.

20. The proper use and application of intelligence and special ability tests, and of other assessment procedures, can be of benefit to both the child and society as a whole.

KEY TERMS, CONCEPTS, AND NAMES

STUDY QUESTIONS

1. Discuss ethical standards related to assessment.

2. Discuss consultation in the schools.

3. Discuss PL 94-142 as it relates to assessment. Include in your discussion (a) testing and evaluation procedures, (b) IEPs, (c) parents' rights, and (d) least restrictive environment.

4. Discuss PL 99-457 as it amends PL 94-142.

5. Discuss the Family Educational Rights and Privacy Act of 1974.

6. Discuss recent court cases concerning assessment procedures and special education.

7. Discuss court interpretations of PL 94-142 and related legal decisions.

8. Discuss consultation with parents.

9. Discuss consultation in courts and in correctional settings.

10. Discuss the challenges of being an expert witness.

11. Discuss the use of computers in psychological assessment.

APPENDIX A

ANSWERS TO TEST-YOUR-SKILL EXERCISES

CHAPTER 8: TEST-YOUR-SKILL EXERCISES FOR THE WISC-R

Unnecessary Technical Information

1. This information is too technical to present in a report. Furthermore, the sentence does not give the direction of the difference. The primary focus should be on differences between each subtest and the mean of the Verbal or Performance Scale. The intersubtest comparisons of interest should be made only after comparisons with the mean of each scale have been made. Also, it is not necessary to present significance levels.

2. Stress what the child did do, not what he or she did not do. The latter information serves no useful purpose in a report; it should be deleted.

3. It is not necessary to say in the report that 10 is average and 19 is the ceiling. This technical information about the test is not informative. Suggestion: "Bill's social reasoning and verbal comprehension are well developed."

4. Delete this sentence from the report unless there is some special significance to the pattern of missed items. If there is, discuss the significance of the pattern.

5. This sentence neither indicates direction nor gives interpretation of the difference. If the Object Assembly score were 12 and the mean Performance Scale score were 8, you could say "Her attention to detail and perceptual organization skills are relatively strong in comparison with other performance skills."

6. Reference to "5 points" is potentially misleading. The reader does not know whether the 5 points refers to a raw score or a standard score. This sentence should be written to convey the child's knowledge of what is required on the Similarities subtest. If his score is below average (scaled score of 7) and below his Verbal Scale mean, you could say "Bill's ability for conceptual thinking is less well developed (at the 16th percentile) than are his other verbal skills."

7. This sentence fails to communicate useful information.

Unless it serves to make some important point, do not include such information.

8. This sentence provides unnecessary technical information about test structure ("optional subtest") and test procedures ("not used in computing the IQ"). It should be deleted from the report.

9. This statement provides technical information that communicates little to the average reader. Providing percentile equivalents of scaled scores is a preferred way of reporting this information.

10. It is not necessary to report the total scaled score; rather, cite the IQs obtained on the Verbal, Performance, and Full Scales.

11. Standard deviation is a technical concept and should not be used in the report. The scaled scores should be interpreted rather than cited. Suggestion: "His range of knowledge is above average."

12. Most readers will not understand the reference to Bannatyne's recategorization system. Also, citing a prorated IQ of 127 may cause confusion. The reader does not know how this IQ compares with the Full Scale IQ. Delete this sentence, substituting a more useful interpretation of the test scores.

13. "Freedom from Distractibility" is a technical term that may not be understood by most readers of the report. Suggestion: "Frank had difficulties with attention and concentration."

14. This is a poorly written sentence. It presents technical information not needed in the report, but more importantly, it fails to communicate useful information. It tells neither which ability is better developed nor whether the abilities measured by these subtests are well or poorly developed. Assuming that her Comprehension score was significantly higher than her Vocabulary score, a suggested sentence is "In the verbal area, Glenda's social reasoning ability is better developed than her word knowledge."

15. This sentence fails to present useful information. The reader does not know whether these scores reflect strengths or weaknesses. It is not necessary to describe the exact relationships

among the subtest scores. Suggestion: "Her sequencing and visual memory abilities are weaker than her spatial and perceptual organization abilities."

16. It is not necessary to cite the probability level (too technical). It is preferable simply to say something like "John's Verbal IQ was significantly higher (or lower) than his Performance IQ." Also, the example fails to indicate whether the Verbal IQ was higher or lower than the Performance IQ.

17. It is not necessary to report the mean score.

18. This sentence will have little meaning to the average reader. If all scores are between 9 and 11 on the Verbal Scale subtests, you could say "On verbal tasks, his performance was consistently within the Average range."

Poor Writing

19. The IQ achieved by a child is a specific number. You do not have to say "approximately 98." The notion of "approximately" is handled by the confidence interval or precision range. Suggestion: "He obtained a Full Scale IQ of 98 ± 6 on the WISC-R. This score is in the Average classification."

20. It is redundant to say "when compared to other children of her chronological age group." Including this phrase every time a child's ability is discussed would unnecessarily lengthen the report. The phrase should simply be deleted.

21. This sentence is poorly constructed and redundant in places. Suggestion: "She has average attention and concentration skills."

22. This sentence is awkward. One way of expressing the difference between the two scales is as follows: "The 37-point difference between the Verbal and Performance Scales, in favor of the Performance Scale, indicates that visual nonverbal skills are better developed than auditory processing skills." Other possible interpretations are discussed in Chapter 8.

23. This sentence is too colloquial. Suggestion: "All of his Verbal scores were in the Average range."

24. This sentence is confusing and vague. Recommendations should be as clear and concise as possible. Suggestion: "To increase his mathematics skills, John's regular classroom teacher might make math more meaningful by incorporating it into daily activities. For example, he could be shown how to use mathematics to learn how to buy groceries and to make a budget."

25. The term "respectable" is not appropriate for describing a test score. It implies that some scores are "not respectable." Also, the reference to a score of 7, without some explanation, is not informative for the lay reader. Suggestion: "All of Mary's abilities appear to be developed at an average level, with the exception of short-term memory for digits, which is relatively weak."

26. Both WISC-R Verbal and Performance Scales measure "mental" abilities. The writer may have meant to say "verbal" instead of "mental."

27. The term "statistical factors" is too general, and the phrase "tenor of his performance" is vague. The recommended way to express the precision range is as follows: "Joe obtained an IQ of 123 ± 6. The chances that the range of scores from 117 to 129 includes his true IQ are about 95 out of 100."

28. "Conception of his environment" is a vague phrase. Suggestion: "Jim's nonverbal abilities are well developed."

29. This sentence is poorly written. It is not clear why there is a "thus." Did the child dismantle the design before allowing the examiner to record her performance? Suggestion: "She behaved impulsively when reproducing block designs, dismantling the designs, whether correct or not, as soon as they were completed."

30. This sentence is too tentative, because the scores are definitely in the Average range. Suggestion: "Her verbal subtest scores are in the Average range."

31. The wording of these sentences is awkward and is likely to confuse most readers. Also, the first sentence is grammatically incorrect because the subject of the sentence ("accuracy") takes a singular verb ("was," not "were"). Suggestion: "On many subtests he failed easy items but passed more difficult ones."

32. This sentence is awkwardly written. Suggestion: "He showed outstanding ability in a task requiring alertness to details."

33. This sentence is poorly written. The wording "appears to be a significance" is incorrect; the sentence should say "a significant difference at the .05 level of confidence." It is not necessary to state probability levels in the report, however. Assuming that the score on Block Design was significantly higher than the score on Object Assembly, the sentence could read: "On performance tasks, her deductive reasoning ability is stronger than her inductive reasoning ability."

34. The correct word is "peak," not "peek." Furthermore, this information, by itself, is not informative. Was the Comprehension score above average, average, or below average? Was it significantly different from the other scores? Assuming that the Comprehension score of 10 was significantly above the mean of the Verbal subtests, the sentence could read "The area in which she showed the strongest verbal ability is social reasoning and judgment (at the 50th percentile)."

35. The score itself is not retarded, although it may reflect a weakness or poorly developed skill. If the score on Object Assembly is low, it is preferable to say "Her spatial visualization skills are not well developed, as indicated by her weak performance in completing puzzle items."

Technical Errors

36. Scaled scores of 9 or higher on any of the Wechsler subtests do not indicate "poor" ability. A scaled score of 9 is only one-third of a standard deviation below the mean scaled score of 10; it is within the Average range.

37. Prorated IQs that refer to clusters of subtest scores should not be cited in the report. These additional IQs are likely to confuse the reader, and little is known about their validity. It is sufficient to report three IQs (Full Scale, Verbal Scale, and Performance Scale). In addition, do not refer to esoteric areas, such as Sequencing I and Sequencing II.

38. The WISC-R does not use mental ages, but it provides

test-age equivalents for the 12 subtests. These test ages should be used cautiously.

39. This statement is not accurate because it focuses on some of the subtests, rather than on the Full Scale, to characterize the child's overall level of ability. Furthermore, "standard deviations" is a technical term and should not be included in the report.

40. It is not necessary to put in the report the technical information contained in this sentence (that is, ". . . approaches significance at the 5% level . . ."). Because the 10-point difference is not significant, it is not appropriate to infer that verbal development is better than nonverbal development. This inference should only be made when there is a significant discrepancy between the Verbal and Performance Scale IQs.

41. A Full Scale IQ of 109 receives an Average classification, not an Above Average classification. Suggestion: "Her Full Scale IQ of 109 ± 6 is classified in the Average range on this test." If there is reason to suspect a higher level of functioning than the test scores indicate, discuss your concerns.

42. This range from 6 (9th percentile) to 16 (98th percentile) indicates both strengths and weaknesses. Do not say that this range indicates only good performance.

43. It is preferable to report percentiles for individual subtests. Classification labels should be used only for the Full Scale and occasionally, if desired, for the Verbal and Performance Scales. Suggestion: "Her scores on the WISC-R ranged from the 5th to the 91st percentile."

44. It is not appropriate to conclude that a subtest may be "spoiled" or invalid because the score is lower than the score on another subtest. A subtest is spoiled when it is improperly administered or when the child does not attend to the task, not when a child's score on it is low. Focus on the implications of the findings (strengths and weaknesses) rather than on the procedures used to arrive at the implications. Any interpretations of the discrepancy between the two subtest scores should relate to characteristics of the child. For example, "Although his visual perception and attention to detail skills are strong, his application of these skills to social situations is less well developed."

45. Although a precision range is attached to the IQ (for example, ± 9), cite only one classification for the obtained IQ. In this case, an IQ of 114 falls into the High Average classification. Presenting more than one classification is confusing.

46. There are no weaknesses in this profile. The sentence might be rephrased to reflect relative strengths and weaknesses. Suggestion: "All of his scores were above average. However, there was some variability, which reflects strengths and weaknesses relative to his own level of functioning." This statement should be followed with a discussion of the child's relative strengths and weaknesses.

47. This sentence mixes up scaled scores and IQs. It is better to report IQs for all three of the scales. For example, "Bill achieved a Verbal Scale IQ of 118, a Performance Scale IQ of 114, and a Full Scale IQ of 118." Then add a precision range.

48. Classifications should be used primarily for the Full Scale IQ. On some occasions, classifications can also be used for the Verbal and Performance Scale IQs, but they should never be used

for subtest scores. A verbal label, such as "considerably below average" or "represents a weakness," can be used to describe a scaled score of 3. Or you might say "Her knowledge of factual information is limited and at the 1st percentile rank."

49. Although this statement is literally correct, it does not belong in the report because the four-point difference is not significant. Suggestion: "Her verbal and nonverbal skills are not significantly different from each other, being at the 68th and 77th percentiles, respectively."

Inaccurate or Incomplete Interpretations

50. This hypothesis is interesting, but it should be supported by more information before it is offered in the report. A low Information score may result from a variety of factors, such as limited schooling, few interests, and inadequate stimulation.

51. There is little, if any, basis for making this interpretation. Nothing in the response appears to warrant an interpretation of aggression.

52. This type of sentence does not aid in describing the child's strengths and weaknesses. Try to describe the pattern of scores in reference to strengths, weaknesses, and average abilities. Suggestion: "In comparison with his overall average verbal ability, his verbal comprehension is a strength (84th percentile rank), whereas his difficulty in performing mental arithmetic is a weakness (9th percentile rank)."

53. This is an inappropriate way to interpret subtest scores. Reading proficiency should be evaluated by a reading test, not by an intelligence test. Reading involves many different skills, and only a reliable and valid reading test should be used to evaluate reading proficiency. Intelligence tests can assist in evaluating some cognitive skills of children; however, no single test can be used to evaluate every type of cognitive and perceptual-motor skill. In interpreting subtest scores, discuss the abilities that appear to be associated with the subtests.

54. It is interesting to attempt to use patterns of intelligence-test scores for developing hypotheses about personality style. Verbal-Performance discrepancies alone, however, should not be used to substantiate such hypotheses. Discrepancy scores should be used in conjunction with other test scores and behavior to develop hypotheses. Furthermore, a 10-point discrepancy is within the realm of chance on the WISC-R and, as such, is not a significant difference that requires additional comment.

55. There is little, if any, research to support this interpretation. Remember, you only have a sample of the child's performance in a limited, controlled, and formal encounter. You do not know whether the level of energy displayed during the test can be sustained outside of the examination setting.

56. There are many possible reasons why changes may occur in the test scores; therefore it is potentially misleading to offer only two of these reasons. Differences in test scores may be associated with, for example, maturational changes, growth spurts, changes in item content, motivation, situational variables, or environmental changes. Unless you know which reasons are most probable, it is better not to offer any. What is most important

is to try to determine which IQ (and test performance) is the most reliable and valid, and to try to account for the changed performance.

57. Describing the subtest profile or configuration is far less meaningful than describing what the profile may mean. Suggestion: "Mary performed better on tasks that reflect long-term memory and school learning than on short-term auditory memory tasks."

58. Although this statement is literally correct, it fails to inform the reader of the possible implications of this profile. Suggestion: "Helen's verbal comprehension skills are better developed than her perceptual organization skills."

59. "Lack of" is a strong statement. A scaled score of 8, although slightly below average, reflects a level of ability that still enables a child to function adequately in many situations. It is incorrect to interpret a scaled score of 8 as indicating a "lack of social judgment." If Comprehension was the child's relatively weakest area and if the responses were immature, a better way to state these findings would be to say "Her social judgment is relatively weak (at the 25th percentile), as indicated by her immature responses to questions relating to social situations."

60. Many children are persistent and still fail items. There is more involved in success on the Object Assembly items than mere persistence. Persistence may help a child in solving various tasks, but unless it is coupled with adequate cognitive ability, the child's performance is not likely to be successful. Suggestion: "In completing puzzle items, Bill was persistent and worked quickly and accurately. His high score in this area reflects his strong abilities in understanding spatial relationships and in perceptual organization."

61. *Intelligence test scores in and of themselves should never be used as a basis for establishing a learning disability designation.* Many factors, especially a discrepancy between estimates of intelligence and achievement, must be taken into account in arriving at a classification of learning disability. Suggestion: "The 15-point discrepancy between Mary's Verbal and Performance Scale IQs indicates that her verbal abilities are better developed than her nonverbal abilities." (See Chapter 20 for a discussion of learning disability.)

62. This interpretation is problematical. A child may have consistently low or consistently high scores for various reasons. Some depressed children have uniformly low test scores; some gifted children have uniformly high test scores. In the latter case, the test may not have an adequate ceiling. Test results provide information about *current functioning*, not *capacity*. It is better not to use the term "capacity" in a report. This sentence should be deleted.

63. A score of 12 is above average. To say that it is his lowest score is potentially misleading. Citing the scaled score without interpretation or explanation is not informative. Suggestion: "His alertness to details is above average, but it is not as well developed as his other abilities."

64. Hearing ability is required by all of the subtests, unless sign language or pantomime instructions are used. Digit Span appears to measure attention span and other abilities; it is not primarily a measure of hearing. Suggestion: "Jim's auditory attention span and short-term memory for digits are weak."

65. There is no one-to-one correlation between verbal knowledge, as revealed by high Verbal subtest scores, and expressive skills. There are many bright individuals who have expressive difficulties (for example, in writing or in speech). This statement should be supported by observation of the examinee's behavior.

66. The WISC-R provides information about cognitive functioning; it does not provide *direct* information about school performance. It is risky to apply labels such as "slow learner" or "low average student" based solely on the WISC-R (or on any other intelligence test). Suggestion: "His scores indicate that he is functioning in the Low Average range."

67. A scaled score of 10 is in the Average range and should not be considered "poor." The sentence should be rewritten. Suggestion: "She has excellent concept formation skills but average rote memory ability."

68. The explanation offered for the child's Verbal-Performance discrepancy is interesting but probably incorrect. The items on the WISC-R Performance Scale call for cognitive skills primarily. Although visual-motor skills are necessary for some items, they are not the major determinant of success on the Performance items. Indeed, if the writer's reasoning were correct, there would be no way for children who were maturationally average to obtain superior nonverbal scores. Additionally, scaled scores are normed in reference to children of the same age as the child being tested; therefore lower scores indicate abilities that are less well developed than those of other children of the same age.

69. Comprehension, like all of the other WISC-R subtests, is a test of cognition. Practical judgment is probably measured by the subtest. There is no way to evaluate the extent to which the subtest taps social adaptation or self-direction, however. Also, the concept of self-direction is somewhat vague.

70. Intrasubtest variability indicates an uneven pattern of performance. It is a great leap, and likely an improper one, to infer "lack of persistence" solely on the basis of intrasubtest variability. Furthermore, "intrasubtest scatter" is a technical concept that is better left out of the report. Suggestion: "There were many failures on easy items and successes on more difficult ones." Then offer an interpretation of this pattern.

71. These "weaknesses" are relative and should be labeled as such. A second problem is that the connection between these two sentences is ambiguous; the two sentences should be tied together with a transitional phrase. Suggestion: "Unlike his overall level of performance, which is high, Bill's visual-motor coordination and spatial orientation are average."

72. The Performance Scale measures more than attentional skill. If the writer is referring to one particular Performance Scale subtest, this subtest should be specifically mentioned.

73. This interpretation is misleading. Verbal subtests do not simply require automatic responding; they also require judgment, problem solving, conceptualization, and attention. This

sentence also contains vague terminology ("automatic responding").

74. Mentioning subtest names is not informative. It is better to discuss the abilities tapped by the subtests than to simply name the subtests. Suggestion: "His strongest abilities in relation to his other skills are in short-term auditory memory and processing and short-term visual memory."

75. This interpretation has little, if any, basis from either a clinical or research perspective. It should be deleted from the report.

76. This interpretation includes a number of inaccuracies. First, because each WISC-R Performance subtest requires somewhat different cognitive skills, it may be stretching the point to say that similar skills are measured by all of the Performance Scale subtests. Second, the hypothesis that the child may not have applied the same effort to all of the subtests should be based on observational data, not on subtest scores alone. Third, it is highly unlikely that visual acuity problems are responsible for this pattern of scores. Fourth, because most of the subtest scores are not significantly different from one another, it is preferable not to imply that there are meaningful differences in the pattern of subtest scores, with the exception of Block Design, which is higher than Picture Arrangement and Object Assembly. Suggestion: "Her nonverbal skills, such as visual perception, spatial orientation, nonverbal reasoning, attention to detail, and visualizing a whole from its parts, range from the 16th to 50th percentile."

77. This sentence, although literally correct, does not give sufficient emphasis to the 29-point Verbal/Performance discrepancy. Suggestion: "Monica's verbal skills (97th percentile) are significantly better developed than her performance skills (50th percentile)."

78. This sentence fails to present the child's level of performance. Also, the term "significance," as used here, is vague. The sentence should be deleted, and a discussion of the child's test performance substituted.

79. The writer is referring to the Freedom from Distractibility factor. This factor—like all factors, scales, and subtests—measures both strengths and weaknesses. The sentence reads as if the factor only measured weaknesses. Also, this sentence should convey how the child performed on this factor. Suggestion: "John has poor attention and concentration and has difficulty in screening out distracting influences."

80. All areas of an intelligence test are related to some degree to the individual's life experiences, social-educational exposure, and learning. It is misleading to single out one area. Furthermore, most readers are unfamiliar with a reference to the "area of acquired knowledge." The writer should describe the skills tapped by these subtests. Suggestion: "Jim is average in his range of information, arithmetical ability, and word knowledge."

81. This interpretation is problematical. This child does not "lack" verbal abilities. Her scores suggest that some abilities are better developed than others. Her good performance in school should not be attributed to compensation for average verbal

skills. The logic of this inference is not clear. Suggestion: "Her performance abilities are significantly better developed than her verbal abilities." This statement can be followed with an analysis of the specific pattern of scores.

82. The Performance Scale does not measure fine or gross motor skills, as is implied in this statement. Rather, it measures cognitive skills and visual-motor coordination and integration. It is the integration of cognitive and motor skills that is required for success on many Performance Scale items. Suggestion: "Frank's excellent nonverbal cognitive skills (98th percentile rank) are considerably better developed than are his verbal cognitive skills (39th percentile rank)."

83. Low functioning on the Coding subtest may be associated with several factors. The basis for the interpretation should be described in the report. Also, the interpretation fails to discuss the underlying abilities measured by the Coding subtest.

84. This is not a clear description of the task. Coding requires the child to use a key or to learn a key. The symbols may be meaningful to some children. The statement, as written, makes it sound as if the child were required to do something actively—attach a symbol to a number, when in fact the symbol-number association (or combination) is given in the subtest. A preferred way to describe Coding A would be to say "The Coding task is a psychomotor task that requires the child to copy rapidly simple figures associated with different shapes." A preferred way to describe Coding B would be to say "The Coding task is a psychomotor task that requires the child to copy rapidly symbols associated with numbers."

85. "Trying hard" does not seem to be sufficient for obtaining success on the subtests. Some children may try hard and still not succeed. In describing this child's efforts, focus on the behavior without referring to test scores. Say, for example, "She appeared hard-working while taking the test."

Inappropriate Recommendations

86. If this recommendation were made each time there was a significant difference between a child's verbal and performance skills, thousands of hours of perhaps needless testing would take place. A significant difference simply means that the difference between the scores is not a chance difference. It does not mean that there is a problem. Some individuals have a varied pattern of skills; this pattern does not necessarily call for further investigation, unless other factors are present. The recommendation should tell the reader why further investigation is needed—what might be learned in a further investigation that could be helpful to the child.

87. There are two problems with this sentence. First, using the term "scatter" without explanation may mislead readers. It is preferable to use the word "variability." Second, the sentence raises the question of the reason for a referral to a neurologist. It is inappropriate to recommend a neurological evaluation simply on the basis of variability of scores. A neurological examination is a costly procedure. There should be some pathognomonic

signs suggestive of brain damage (see Chapter 22) in the test findings, observations, or case history before this recommendation is made.

CHAPTER 9: TEST-YOUR-SKILL EXERCISES FOR THE WPPSI

1. These interpretations are inaccurate. Block Design and Geometric Design subtests do not assess moral judgment or ability to analyze school situations. Suggestion: "Tom has above-average visual perception, nonverbal reasoning, and fine motor abilities."

2. A label (such as "slow learner") should never be applied to a child based on one subtest score. Suggestion: "Her perceptual-motor skills were weak."

3. None of these subtest scores is significantly different from the mean of the Performance Scale ($M = 13.2$); therefore this interpretation is erroneous. Furthermore, even if Block Design and Animal House scores were significantly lower than the mean Performance Scale score, it is unlikely that "visual acuity problems" would be the reason for the low scores. Visual acuity is also required for the other Performance Scale subtests in which the child performed adequately.

CHAPTER 14: TEST-YOUR-SKILL EXERCISES FOR THE BENDER-GESTALT

Poor Writing

1. This sentence is awkward. Suggestion: "Her perceptual-motor skills appear to be adequate for her age level."

2. This description is confusing. If she rarely inspected the cards, how could she have been very precise by counting the dots?

3. This is an awkward way of describing the abilities required by the Bender-Gestalt. A better way to describe the child's performance on the Bender-Gestalt is as follows: "On the Bender-Gestalt, which is a measure of visual-motor ability, the child's performance was in the normal range (at the 55th percentile)."

Technical Errors

4. "Invalid" means that the test instrument does not measure what it purports to measure—the validity of the Bender-Gestalt cannot be criticized based on the absence of norms for 14-year-olds in the Koppitz scoring system. Additionally, it is possible to interpret the Bender-Gestalt even though the Koppitz norms are not used. There are other scoring systems, and the drawings can be evaluated for visual-motor difficulties using the Koppitz framework.

5. This sentence fails to give the name of the scoring system or the standard score and percentile rank associated with the two errors. A list of the number of errors is of limited, if any, use. Suggestion: "Using the Koppitz Developmental Scoring System, her standard score on the Bender-Gestalt was _____, placing her at the _____ percentile for her age."

Inaccurate Interpretations

6. This statement is potentially misleading. Errors on the Bender-Gestalt may have no relationship to brain damage. They may simply be indicators of maturational difficulties, developmental delays, perceptual difficulties, integration difficulties, and so forth. Do not suggest a possible brain disorder on the basis of Bender-Gestalt errors. All relevant test results and the clinical history must be taken into account.

7. Do not interpret collision as indicating "peripheral neurological impairment." This interpretation is not supported by research. Collision may be due to poor planning, carelessness, impulsiveness, or other factors; it may have nothing to do with peripheral neurological impairment. As noted in the previous example, a statement indicating possible neurological impairment should never be made solely on the basis of Bender-Gestalt performance.

8. Results from the Bender-Gestalt should not be used to assess reading ability. Reading ability should be evaluated by a valid reading test.

9. Small Bender-Gestalt drawings may have nothing to do with anxiety. Small drawings simply may reflect an individual response style.

10. The Koppitz norms are primarily applicable for ages 5 through 8, and somewhat applicable for ages 9, 10, and 11 years. Although the norms do not apply after 11 years, the method of analyzing errors is applicable for any age. One minor error at any age is not likely to reflect a perceptual problem.

11. Drawing or copying rapidly is not necessarily an indication of impulsivity. Although completing designs rapidly is a possible indication of impulsivity, the quality of performance is also important in determining impulsivity. The examiner should look for corroborating signs of impulsivity.

12. The term "abnormal" is a powerful one that may be misinterpreted. Do not use it unless there is clear evidence of severe perceptual-motor difficulties. It is preferable to describe the performance as reflecting perceptual-motor difficulties. Suggestion: "Bill's performance on the Bender-Gestalt suggests that he has some perceptual-motor difficulties." This statement should be followed by a discussion of the aspects of the child's performance that led to this conclusion.

13. There is little, if any, research to indicate that the Bender-Gestalt provides valid indices of "passivity" in children. Therefore this inference should be deleted from the report.

14. Variable use of space may simply indicate difficulty in organization, subtle loss of efficiency of judgment or planning, or some other type of difficulty. This pattern may have little to do with personality or mood.

15. This is a poor way of saying that her performance was

excellent or that no errors were made. Also, the interpretation is misleading because the reader is led to believe that (a) the test measures personality rather than perceptual-motor skills and (b) the child has "no personality." Suggestion: "Susan's visual-motor perceptual ability is appropriate for her age."

16. Being methodical could also indicate a well organized and careful style. The hypothesis given is fraught with problems and should be deleted. It is permissible, however, to say that the child approached the task in a careful and methodical manner.

Inappropriate Recommendations

17. Emotional indicators on the Bender-Gestalt are not well supported by research. The clinical history, observations, interview, and other test results should be considered in evaluating the child's affective reactions. The Bender-Gestalt alone should never be used to make a recommendation for counseling.

18. This recommendation is vague because it does not specify what type of visual-motor training is needed. Furthermore, the Bender-Gestalt does not assess handwriting skills, so this recommendation is inappropriate.

CHAPTER 23: TEST-YOUR-SKILL EXERCISES FOR GENERAL TEST INTERPRETATION AND REPORT WRITING

Poor Writing

1. These sentences would read more smoothly if they were expressed in a more conversational manner. Suggestion: "Keith's academic weaknesses are in arithmetic computation, spelling, and word recognition."

2. These findings should be presented in a more definitive and confident manner. Suggestion: "She scored in the 99th percentile overall on the Peabody Individual Achievement Test, indicating that she possesses strong academic skills."

3. Qualifiers such as "little" should not be used. Suggestion: "Linda appeared tired and became distracted toward the end of the testing." If desired, the specific behaviors that led to this statement can then be listed.

4. The examiner seems to be excusing the child's behavior. The information should be reported more objectively. Suggestion: "Michelle became distracted about an hour after the testing began. She frequently stood up to look out the window and asked the examiner when she would be excused."

5. This sentence is ambiguous because the subject of the sentence is not clear. We do not know who was discussing the future—John or his parents—or what kind of expectations the parents have. Suggestion: "In discussing plans for his future, John said that his parents expect him to attend college and to pursue a professional career."

6. The word "environment" should be clarified. Does it refer to the child's immediate environment (that is, the testing room and building) or to the larger environment? Suggestion: "Ted appeared to be curious about his immediate environment, asking the examiner several questions about objects in the examination room."

7. The examiner may be trying to convey that the child's abilities were equally developed, but the sentence is difficult to follow. Suggestion: "All of her McCarthy scores were at an average level."

8. This sentence is awkward. Suggestion: "He had difficulty distinguishing between essential and nonessential details."

9. The last part of the sentence is awkward and does not provide useful information. Suggestion: "Her drawings were accurate."

10. This is not only an incomplete sentence—it is an *unclear* incomplete sentence. Suggestion: "Connie's parents should be informed of the results and helped to accept the findings."

11. This sentence is poorly written. We do not know what the word "between" refers to because three things are mentioned. The word "vision" is mentioned without any qualifier. The word "options" is not a possesive and requires no apostrophe. The entire sentence is awkward. Suggestion: "Vocational counseling is recommended to help Henry reevaluate his goal of becoming a corporate pilot, in view of his poor vision and high level of anxiety."

12. This sentence has two problems. First, referring to "IQ" as a score is redundant. Second, the source of the IQ should be specified. A better way to express this finding would be to say "She obtained a WISC-R IQ of 111," and then present a confidence interval and other descriptive information.

13. The second sentence is vague. The reader has no way of knowing why this illustration was included, or what was unusual about the response. The statement should be clarified.

14. The two ideas in this sentence appear to be in conflict with each other. Although the term "intellectual maturity" is imprecise, average intelligence would seem to be suggestive of intellectual maturity.

15. This sentence is poorly written. The colloquial expressions "just flew by in terms of time" and "without any hitch" are not appropriate. The expression "did the tasks quickly and directed" is not clear. Suggestion: "John was cooperative, well motivated, and showed a quick response pattern."

16. This statement is confusing because it is not clear to what "automatic level" refers. A possible restatement: "John's fine motor control is poorly developed, as can be seen by his inability to write legibly."

17. A term such as "rapidly" is preferable to the word "nervously," which is too subjective.

18. This sentence is not clear because we do not know what comparison the writer has in mind.

19. This sentence is awkward. Suggestion: "The child is a small girl who has a pleasant disposition. Rapport was easily established."

20. The final quotation marks should be placed *after* the period.

21. Attention and concentration are *two* separate processes. Consequently, the sentence needs the verb "were."

22. This sentence is awkward. Most of the last part of the sentence is not needed. Suggestion: "In view of the ideal testing conditions, the results are considered to be valid."

23. The word "which" is not the correct pronoun for "other students." The proper pronoun is "whom" (with whom). Also, prepositions such as "with" generally should not appear at the end of a sentence.

24. The correct term is "standardization group," not standardized group.

25. "Error" is a noun and should not be used as a verb. Even if "errored" were changed to "made errors," the sentence still would not communicate adequately. Most children will make errors as they reach the ceiling level on a test. The emphasis should be not simply on the fact that a child makes errors, but on the overall performance, on specific noteworthy items, and on what the errors might reveal.

26. This sentence has many problems, including a spelling error (exten*d* for extent) and garbled writing. If the test results are suspect, say so. Suggestion: "The results cannot be considered valid" or "The results are not valid." An explanation of why the results are not valid should follow.

27. Observations of behavior should concentrate on what the child did, not on what was not done. Why does the writer choose to focus on the "egocentric babbling of a less mature child"? Why does the sentence begin with "although"? Suggestion: "Jane used mature language in her conversation."

28. "Manipulating" has a number of connotations, one of which is "to manage or influence by artful or devious skill." Presumably the writer did not have this meaning in mind. The sentence should be clarified.

29. This is a teasing sentence. First, in what way does the child "appear" to have a good vocabulary? Second, why was it ironic that he performed below the examiner's expectation? Was the examiner's expectation based on objective data or just a hunch? Third, how far below the expected level did his performance fall?

30. This sentence is poorly written. Suggestion: "Every effort should be made to encourage Tom to work at a level commensurate with his abilities."

31. The opening clause "in line with speed" is confusing and should be deleted from the sentence. Asking about how others performed may not necessarily indicate competitiveness. It could also indicate concern about one's own performance. Suggestion: "He appeared to be concerned with his speed and test performance; several times he asked how his speed of performance compared with others'."

32. The sentence has several problems. First, the word "impacts" is not used properly. Second, the phrase "type of perseveration" is vague. Third, the failure to cite specific behaviors leaves the reader with little information. The writer should describe the child's reaction to criticism and how the child's reaction affected her performance.

33. "Malingering," which means pretending to be ill, is used incorrectly in this sentence. "Lingering" was probably intended.

34. This sentence is poorly written. The style is awkward, and the logic is not clear. What does the child's sister's hearing difficulties have to do with his hearing difficulties? Were there any indications during the test of hearing difficulties? If so, they should be described and the test results interpreted accordingly.

35. The word "prioritizes" is jargon. The sentence should be rewritten, and the basis for the comment given. For example: "Speed of performance appeared to be important to her, as she asked how fast she was working and seemed to enjoy being timed."

Inaccurate, Incomplete, or Irrelevant Statements

36. The interpretation of a rigid approach to solving a cognitive task (for example, Block Design) as a possible indication of feelings of inadequacy is a precarious one. Obtain additional information from other sources before making this type of interpretation.

37. The interpretation may or may not have merit, depending on one's theoretical orientation. It is better to avoid making such interpretations, however, especially when they are based on the *absence* of data.

38. There is no evidence in the literature to back up these two interpretations. This statement should be omitted from the report.

39. "Troublemaker" implies a value judgment. Whenever such a label is used, the source of the label should be cited, as well as the basis for it. Also, it is far from reasonable to assume that good social judgment and grasp of social conventionality might cause a child to become what might be described as a troublemaker.

40. "Scatter" is a technical concept and may be misunderstood by lay readers. It is better to use the term "differences" (for example, "contributed to the marked differences between his subtest scores").

41. The phrase "learning and performance sets" is not clear. A comment on learning skills should be based on observable performance, and the observations should be presented. Standard psychometric test scores do not allow definitive statements to be made about the rate of learning new skills. In addition, "by the fact that" is a colloquial and awkward expression.

42. This is an interesting statement. The examiner goes out on a limb, making a statement about future performance on the basis of the IQ alone. The IQ should be used primarily to evaluate current abilities and performance, not to predict future performance. There are many factors (for example, intelligence, motivation, and study habits) that affect school performance, and intelligence is only one of them. However, you might state, "Her IQ of 134 indicates that she possesses the cognitive ability to excel in school." The failure of such a child to excel in school suggests the need to look for factors other than intelligence that could be inhibiting her academic achievement.

43. This statement has two problems. First, rather than simply implying that the child should be able to write his name at this age, it should specifically say so. Second, it should include positive statements about what the child can do. Suggestion: "Although he was not able to write his name when asked, Jeff was able to write all the letters of the alphabet."

44. This statement may be an overgeneralization about Joey's attention in class. Suggestion: "Joey's ability to attend to his work in class is limited. For the two hours during which he was observed, Joey attended to his assignments 20 percent of the time."

45. There is much controversy about the relationship between learning disabilities and food allergies. Therefore the second sentence should be deleted. The writer might recommend that Ted be referred to a physician, if he is not already under treatment.

46. It is difficult (if not impossible) to separate out items that reflect only natural endowment from those that reflect only educational or experiential opportunities. Because *all* items require some degree of natural endowment together with exposure to the environment, it is misleading to write that some items reflect natural endowment.

47. This description is incomplete because it fails to indicate (a) the type of perceptual problem (for example, visual or auditory or both), (b) the type of verbal expression problem (for example, written word or spoken word or both), and (c) how the problems were manifested in the test situation. A statement such as this one should be preceded or followed by a discussion of the examiner's observations that led to the conclusion.

48. Performing at the same level on all parts of a test does not necessarily mean that the child is well adjusted in school. Adjustment in school depends on much more than minimal variability of test scores. Performance at the same level on the various areas of a test simply means that the child is not showing variability in the cognitive areas measured by the test.

49. All items on intelligence tests in one way or another reflect the child's ability to learn. Therefore it is misleading to imply that only specific items reflect learning ability. Items differ in the extent to which they tap old vs. new learning (or content vs. process, or crystallized vs. fluid abilities), but all items to some extent reflect learning ability.

50. This statement may or may not be true. Children with learning disabilities or with emotional, physical, or sensory disabilities may have average (or above average) scores on an intelligence test. The regular classroom may not be suitable for these children. It is improper to conclude, solely on the basis of an IQ, that a regular classroom is the appropriate learning environment. Consider performance on other types of tests, classroom behavior, and the case history before deciding on an appropriate classroom placement recommendation.

51. This information is unlikely to add to the understanding of the child or test results, and it is potentially damaging to the child. Omit it or replace it by a statement that may give some insight about the child's feelings. For example, "James expressed resentment about frequent male visitors to his house."

52. This long, awkward sentence fails to address the issue of validity. Consequently, the reader is left in doubt about the validity of the test results. If you believe that the results are not valid, clearly say so in the report. For example: "Tim's level of anxiety was high during the test, which probably invalidated these test results."

53. This conclusion may be faulty. Minority status of the examinee is not a sufficient basis for concluding that the test results are biased. Was the child's native language English? Did the nonverbal scores match the verbal scores? Were the achievement test scores similar to scores on the intelligence test? All relevant information must be considered in arriving at a decision concerning the validity of the test results, and this information should be discussed in the report.

54. The writer needs to specify the effect to which he or she is referring. "Practice effects" is a vague term. The sentence seems to imply that the results are not valid because they may overestimate the examinee's abilities. Suggestion: "Helen was familiar with the test items because she has been tested on this instrument before. Therefore, the results may overestimate her level of functioning."

Inappropriate Abbreviations

55. The word "percentile" should be written out.

56. Many readers will not know these abbreviations. They are best left out or, if they are needed, described fully. Suggestion: "Mark is in a classroom for children with learning problems."

Inappropriate Value Judgments

57. This statement reveals the writer's prejudice. It has no place in the report. A description of the child's appearance and behavior, however, may be appropriate. Suggestion: "Hector often says that he is hungry and asks his teacher for food. The teacher reports that he sometimes seems to need a bath."

58. This type of interpretation should only be made when there is sufficient evidence. Has the clinician observed the family? If so, a statement of the observed behavior should be included and then a possible interpretation of the implications of this behavior offered. The report could say, for example, "In a meeting with the family, I observed that little verbal interaction takes place between Joanne and her parents. Perhaps this pattern has hindered the development of Joanne's verbal skills." It is important to recognize that parents with limited education and limited verbal abilities may have children who excel on intelligence tests.

59. The writer's prejudice or stereotypes may be showing in this sentence. No such interpretation should be made simply on the basis of family size and income. Large families with low income may provide adequate cultural and social enrichment. To ascertain whether the child's family has or has not provided cultural and social enrichment, it is important to interview the parents or visit the home.

60. This statement is based on hearsay and should be verified. It may be best to omit the reference to the family's source of income.

61. This statement represents a value judgment, because the behavior in question may not necessarily be irritating to all adults. Suggestion: "Richard's mannerisms tended to irritate me" or "Richard's snorting, popping of gum, and wriggling in his chair were irritating" or "Richard's teachers report that he has unpleasant mannerisms that are irritating."

Inappropriate Recommendations

62. The "auditory questions" raised by the evaluation should be described more fully. For example: "It is recommended that she be evaluated further by a speech pathologist to obtain more information about her apparent difficulties in auditory attention and memory."

63. Complex ideas are being expressed in these two sentences. The writer's recommendation may be a good one, but it needs clarification. The type of remediation required by the child needs to be stated precisely. Also, the child's test performance must have involved factors that were not related to social perceptions, and these factors should be included in the discussion of the child's test performance.

64. In addition to being awkwardly written, this recommendation for treatment is not backed by sufficient evidence that treatment is needed. Always present such evidence when making a recommendation. For example: "He may benefit from counseling to help him accept the difficult family situation that he described during the test session."

65. Further examination should not be recommended routinely without sufficient justification. If periodic examinations are recommended, present the justification for the recommendation.

APPENDIX B

PUBLISHERS OF TESTS REVIEWED

T. M. Achenbach, University Associates in Psychiatry, One South Prospect St., Burlington, Vermont 05401.

American Association on Mental Deficiency, 5201 Connecticut Ave., N.W., Washington, D.C. 20015.

American Guidance Service, Inc., Publishers' Building, Circle Pines, Minnesota 55014.

American Orthopsychiatric Association, Inc., 1790 Broadway, New York, New York 10019.

Bobbs-Merrill Co., Inc., 4300 West 62nd St., Indianapolis, Indiana 46268.

William C. Brown Co., Publisher, 2460 Kerper Blvd., Dubuque, Iowa 52001.

California Test Bureau/McGraw-Hill, Del Monte Research Park, Monterey, California 93940.

Consulting Psychologists Press, Inc., 577 College Ave., Palo Alto, California 94306.

Denver Developmental Materials, Inc., P.O. Box 20037, Denver, Colorado 80220.

The Devereux Foundation Press, 19 South Waterloo Rd., Devon, Pennsylvania 19333.

DLM Teaching Resources, One DLM Park, Allen, Texas 75002.

Economy Company, Box 25308, 1901 North Walnut, Oklahoma City, Oklahoma 73125.

Grune and Stratton, Inc., 111 Fifth Ave., New York, New York 10003.

Marshall S. Hiskey, 5640 Baldwin, Lincoln, Nebraska 68507.

Jastak Associates, Inc., 1526 Gilpin Ave., Wilmington, Delaware 19806.

Language Research Associates, Inc., 175 East Delaware Pl., Chicago, Illinois 60611.

Linguametrics Group, P.O. Box 454, Corta Madera, California 94925.

Charles E. Merrill Publishing Co., 1300 Alum Creek Dr., Columbus, Ohio 43216.

Modern Curriculum Press, 13900 Prospect Rd., Cleveland, Ohio 44316.

Neuropsychology Press, 1338 E. Edison St., Tucson, Arizona 85719.

Pro-Ed, 5341 Industrial Oaks Blvd., Austin, Texas 78735.

The Psychological Corporation, P.O. Box 9954, San Antonio, Texas 78204.

Psychological Test Specialists, Box 1441, Missoula, Montana 59801.

Herbert C. Quay, University of Miami, P.O. Box 248074, Coral Gables, Florida 33124.

The Riverside Publishing Co., 3 O'Hare Towers, 8420 Bryn Mawr Ave., Chicago, Illinois 60631.

Science Research Associates, 155 North Wacker Dr., Chicago, Illinois 60606.

Slosson Educational Publications, Inc., P.O. Box 28052, East Aurora, New York 14052.

Stoelting Company, 1350 South Kostner Ave., Chicago, Illinois 60623.

University of Illinois Press, Urbana, Illinois 61801.

Western Psychological Services, 12031 Wilshire Blvd., Los Angeles, California 90025.

APPENDIX C

MISCELLANEOUS TABLES

See the Contents, p. xv, for a complete listing of tables in Appendix C.

Table C-1
Confidence Intervals for WISC-R Scales

Age level	Scale	Confidence level				
		68%	85%	90%	95%	99%
6½ (6-0-0 through 6-11-30)	Verbal Scale IQ	± 4	± 6	± 7	± 8	± 11
	Performance Scale IQ	± 5	± 7	± 8	± 9	± 12
	Full Scale IQ	± 3	± 5	± 6	± 7	± 9
7½ (7-0-0 through 7-11-30)	Verbal Scale IQ	± 4	± 6	± 7	± 8	± 10
	Performance Scale IQ	± 5	± 7	± 8	± 9	± 12
	Full Scale IQ	± 3	± 5	± 6	± 7	± 9
8½ (8-0-0 through 8-11-30)	Verbal Scale IQ	± 4	± 6	± 6	± 8	± 10
	Performance Scale IQ	± 4	± 6	± 7	± 9	± 12
	Full Scale IQ	± 3	± 5	± 5	± 6	± 8
9½ (9-0-0 through 9-11-30)	Verbal Scale IQ	± 4	± 5	± 6	± 7	± 10
	Performance Scale IQ	± 4	± 6	± 7	± 9	± 12
	Full Scale IQ	± 3	± 5	± 5	± 6	± 8

(Table continues next page)

Table C-I (cont.)

Age level	Scale	Confidence level				
		68%	85%	90%	95%	99%
10½ (10-0-0 through 10-11-30)	Verbal Scale IQ	± 4	± 5	± 6	± 7	± 9
	Performance Scale IQ	± 5	± 7	± 8	± 9	± 12
	Full Scale IQ	± 3	± 5	± 5	± 6	± 8
11½ (11-0-0 through 11-11-30)	Verbal Scale IQ	± 3	± 5	± 6	± 7	± 9
	Performance Scale IQ	± 4	± 6	± 7	± 9	± 11
	Full Scale IQ	± 3	± 4	± 5	± 6	± 8
12½ (12-0-0 through 12-11-30)	Verbal Scale IQ	± 3	± 5	± 5	± 6	± 8
	Performance Scale IQ	± 5	± 7	± 8	± 9	± 12
	Full Scale IQ	± 3	± 4	± 5	± 6	± 8
13½ (13-0-0 through 13-11-30)	Verbal Scale IQ	± 3	± 5	± 6	± 7	± 9
	Performance Scale IQ	± 5	± 7	± 8	± 10	± 13
	Full Scale IQ	± 3	± 5	± 5	± 6	± 8
14½ (14-0-0 through 14-11-30)	Verbal Scale IQ	± 3	± 5	± 6	± 7	± 9
	Performance Scale IQ	± 5	± 7	± 8	± 9	± 12
	Full Scale IQ	± 3	± 5	± 5	± 6	± 8
15½ (15-0-0 through 15-11-30)	Verbal Scale IQ	± 3	± 5	± 6	± 7	± 9
	Performance Scale IQ	± 5	± 7	± 8	± 9	± 12
	Full Scale IQ	± 3	± 5	± 5	± 6	± 8
16½ (16-0-0 through 16-11-30)	Verbal Scale IQ	± 4	± 5	± 6	± 7	± 9
	Performance Scale IQ	± 5	± 7	± 8	± 9	± 12
	Full Scale IQ	± 3	± 5	± 5	± 6	± 8
Average	Verbal Scale IQ	± 4	± 5	± 6	± 7	± 9
	Performance Scale IQ	± 5	± 7	± 8	± 9	± 12
	Full Scale IQ	± 3	± 5	± 5	± 6	± 8

Note. Chapter 2 describes the procedure for computing confidence intervals. For the WISC-R Full Scale IQ, the confidence intervals are obtained by the following procedure: (a) The appropriate SE_m for the child's age is located in Table 10 of the WISC-R manual. For a 6-year-old child, $SE_m = 3.41$. (b) This SE_m is multiplied by the respective z value in order to obtain the confidence intervals for the desired level. At the 68 percent confidence level the SE_m is multiplied by 1 ($1 \times 3.4 = 3$). At the 99 percent level the SE_m is multiplied by 2.58 ($2.58 \times 3.41 = 9$).

The procedure used to arrive at the confidence intervals in this table has been questioned by some psychometrists (for example, Dudek, 1979; Knight, 1983). They argue that confidence limits should be based on the predicted value of the true score, not the obtained score, and that a different formula should be used to obtain the SE_m. Table L-2 in Appendix L provides confidence intervals based on the predicted true score for the WISC-R and the other Wechsler scales.

Table C-2
Significant Differences Between WISC-R Scaled Scores, IQs, and Factor Scores (.05/.01 significance levels)

	I	S	A	V	C	DS	PC	PA	BD	OA	CO
S	4/5										
A	4/5	4/5									
V	3/4	3/5	4/5								
C	4/5	4/5	4/5	4/5							
DS	4/5	4/5	4/5	4/5	4/5						
PC	4/5	4/5	4/5	4/5	4/5	4/5					
PA	4/5	4/5	4/5	4/5	4/5	4/5	4/6				
BD	3/4	3/5	4/5	3/4	4/5	4/5	4/5	4/5			
OA	4/5	4/6	4/6	4/5	4/6	4/6	4/6	5/6	4/5		
CO	4/5	4/5	4/6	4/5	4/6	4/6	4/6	4/6	4/5	5/6	
M	4/5	4/6	4/6	4/5	4/6	4/6	4/6	5/6	4/5	5/6	5/6

Boxed values:

	PC	PA
PSIQ		VSIQ 12/15

	BD	OA	CO	PA
POIQ			VCIQ 12/16	
FDIQ			13/18	POIQ 14/19

Note. Abbreviations: I = Information; S = Similarities; A = Arithmetic; V = Vocabulary; C = Comprehension; DS = Digit Span; PC = Picture Completion; PA = Picture Arrangement; BD = Block Design; OA = Object Assembly; CO = Coding; M = Mazes; VSIQ = Verbal Scale IQ; PSIQ = Performance Scale IQ; VCIQ = Verbal Comprehension IQ; POIQ = Perceptual Organization IQ; FDIQ = Freedom from Distractibility IQ.

Sample reading: A difference of 4 points between scaled scores on the Information and Similarities subtests is significant at the 5 percent level; a difference of 5 points is significant at the 1 percent level. The first small box shows that a 12-point difference between the Verbal Scale IQ and Performance Scale IQ is needed for the 5 percent level, and a 15-point difference is needed for the 1 percent level.

The values in this table for the subtest comparisons are overly liberal when more than one comparison is made for a subtest. They are more accurate when a priori planned comparisons are made, such as Information vs. Comprehension or Digit Span vs. Arithmetic. The values in this table are based on the average of the 11 age groups.

See Chapter 8, Exhibit 8-1 for an explanation of the method used to arrive at magnitude of differences.

See Table C-4 in the Appendix for the procedure used to obtain the Deviation IQs for the Verbal Comprehension, Perceptual Organization, and Freedom from Distractibility factors.

Standard errors of measurement for WISC-R factor Deviation IQs obtained from Gutkin (1979).

Table C-3
Differences Required for Significance When Each WISC-R Subtest Scaled Score Is Compared to the Mean Scaled Score for Any Individual Child

Subtest	Mean of 5 Verbal Scale subtests[a]		Mean of 6 Verbal Scale subtests		Mean of 5 Performance Scale subtests[b]		Mean of 6 Performance Scale subtests	
	.05	.01	.05	.01	.05	.01	.05	.01
Information	2.81	3.37	2.94	3.50	—	—	—	—
Similarities	3.07	3.68	3.22	3.84	—	—	—	—
Arithmetic	3.14	3.76	3.30	3.93	—	—	—	—
Vocabulary	2.74	3.29	2.86	3.41	—	—	—	—
Comprehension	3.15	3.78	3.32	3.95	—	—	—	—
Digit Span	—	—	3.42	4.07	—	—	—	—
Picture Completion	—	—	—	—	3.38	4.06	3.55	4.22
Picture Arrangement	—	—	—	—	3.59	4.31	3.78	4.50
Block Design	—	—	—	—	2.92	3.50	3.03	3.61
Object Assembly	—	—	—	—	3.82	4.58	4.03	4.80
Coding	—	—	—	—	3.70	4.43	3.89	4.64
Mazes	—	—	—	—	—	—	4.03	4.80

(Table continues next page)

Table C-3 (cont.)

Subtest	Mean of 10 Subtests[c]		Mean of 11 Subtests[b]		Mean of 11 Subtests[a]		Mean of 12 Subtests	
	.05	.01	.05	.01	.05	.01	.05	.01
Information	3.25	3.80	3.29	3.85	3.30	3.86	3.34	3.89
Similarities	3.60	4.21	3.65	4.27	3.66	4.28	3.71	4.32
Arithmetic	3.69	4.32	3.75	4.38	3.76	4.39	3.81	4.44
Vocabulary	3.15	3.69	3.19	3.73	3.20	3.74	3.24	3.78
Comprehension	3.71	4.35	3.77	4.41	3.78	4.42	3.83	4.47
Digit Span	–	–	3.89	4.55	–	–	3.96	4.61
Picture Completion	3.86	4.52	3.92	4.58	3.93	4.59	3.98	4.64
Picture Arrangement	4.14	4.85	4.21	4.92	4.22	4.93	4.28	4.99
Block Design	3.20	3.75	3.24	3.79	3.25	3.80	3.29	3.83
Object Assembly	4.45	5.22	4.53	5.30	4.54	5.31	4.61	5.37
Coding	4.29	5.02	4.36	5.10	4.37	5.10	4.43	5.17
Mazes	–	–	–	–	4.54	5.31	4.61	5.37

Note. Table C-3 shows the minimum deviations from an individual's average subtest scaled score that are significant at the .05 and .01 levels.

The following formula, obtained from Davis (1959), was used to compute the deviations from average that are significant at the desired significance levels: $D = CR \times SE_{m((T/m) - Z_i)}$, where D is the deviation from average, CR is the critical ratio desired, and $SE_{m((T/m) - Z_i)}$ is the standard error of measurement of the difference between an average subtest scaled score and any one of the subtest scaled scores that entered into the average. The standard error of measurement can be obtained by the following formula:

$$SE_{m((T/m) - Z_i)} = \sqrt{\frac{SE_{mT}^2}{m^2} + \left(\frac{m-2}{m}\right)SE_{mZ_i}^2}$$

where SE_{mT}^2 is the sum of the squared standard errors of measurement of the m subtests, m is the number of subtests included in the average, T/m is the average of the subtest scaled scores, and $SE_{mZ_i}^2$ is the squared standard error of measurement of any one of the subtest scaled scores. The critical ratio for the 5 percent level ranges from 2.58 to 2.87, and that for the 1 percent level from 3.09 to 3.34, depending on the number of subtests. These critical ratios were obtained by use of the Bonferroni inequality, which controls the familywise error rate at .05 (or .01) by setting the error rate per comparison at .05/m (or .01/m).

The following example illustrates the procedure. We will determine the minimum deviation required for a child's score on the WISC-R Information subtest to be significantly different from his or her average score on the five standard Verbal Scale subtests (Information, Similarities, Arithmetic, Vocabulary, and Comprehension) at the 95 percent level of confidence. We calculate SE_{mT}^2 by first squaring and then summing the appropriate average standard errors of measurement for each of the five subtests. These standard errors of measurement appear in Table 10 of the WISC-R manual:

$$SE_{mT}^2 = (1.19)^2 + (1.34)^2 + (1.38)^2 + (1.15)^2 + (1.39)^2 = 8.37$$

We determine $SE_{mZ_i}^2$ by squaring the average standard error of measurement of the subtest of interest, the Information subtest:

$$SE_{mZ_i}^2 = (1.19)^2 = 1.4161$$

The number of subtests, m, equals 5.
Substituting these values into the formula yields the following:

$$SE_{m((T/m) - Z_i)} = \sqrt{\frac{8.37}{(5)^2} + \left(\frac{5-2}{5}\right)1.4161} = 1.087$$

The value, 1.087, is then multiplied by the appropriate z value for the 95 percent confidence level to obtain the minimum significant deviation (D). The z value is 2.58 using the Bonferroni correction (.05/5 = .01).

$$D = 2.58 \times 1.087 = 2.81$$

[a] Digit Span excluded
[b] Mazes excluded
[c] Digit Span and Mazes excluded
Source: The figures in the table courtesy of A. B. Silverstein.

Table C-4
Estimated WISC-R Deviation IQs for Verbal Comprehension, Perceptual Organization, and Freedom from Distractibility Factors

Sum of scaled scores	Estimated Deviation IQ			Sum of scaled scores	Estimated Deviation IQ		
	Verbal Comprehension[a]	Perceptual Organization[b]	Freedom from Distractibility[c]		Verbal Comprehension[a]	Perceptual Organization[b]	Freedom from Distractibility[c]
3	—	—	41	40	100	100	122
4	47	42	43	41	101	102	124
5	49	44	45	42	103	103	126
6	50	46	47	43	104	105	129
7	51	47	49	44	106	106	131
8	53	49	52	45	107	108	133
9	54	50	54	46	109	110	135
10	56	52	56	47	110	111	137
11	57	54	58	48	112	113	140
12	59	55	60	49	113	114	142
13	60	57	63	50	115	116	144
14	62	58	65	51	116	118	146
15	63	60	67	52	118	119	148
16	65	62	69	53	119	121	151
17	66	63	71	54	121	122	153
18	68	65	74	55	122	124	155
19	69	66	76	56	124	126	157
20	71	68	78	57	125	127	159
21	72	70	80	58	126	129	—
22	74	71	82	59	128	130	—
23	75	73	85	60	129	132	—
24	76	74	87	61	131	134	—
25	78	76	89	62	132	135	—
26	79	78	91	63	134	137	—
27	81	79	93	64	135	138	—
28	82	81	96	65	137	140	—
29	84	82	98	66	138	142	—
30	85	84	100	67	140	143	—
31	87	86	102	68	141	145	—
32	88	87	104	69	143	146	—
33	90	88	107	70	144	148	—
34	91	90	109	71	146	150	—
35	93	92	111	72	147	151	—
36	94	94	113	73	149	153	—
37	96	95	115	74	150	154	—
38	97	97	118	75	151	156	—
39	99	98	120	76	153	158	—

Note. The formulas used to compute the Deviation Quotients, using subtest scaled scores, are as follows:

Verbal Comprehension Deviation Quotient = 1.47 (Information + Similarities + Vocabulary + Comprehension) + 41.2.
Perceptual Organization Deviation Quotient = 1.60 (Picture Completion + Picture Arrangement + Block Design + Object Assembly) + 36.0.
Freedom from Distractibility Deviation Quotient = 2.2 (Arithmetic + Digit Span + Coding) + 34.

[a] Verbal Comprehension subtests are Information, Similarities, Vocabulary, and Comprehension.
[b] Perceptual Organization subtests are Picture Completion, Picture Arrangement, Block Design, and Object Assembly.
[c] Freedom from Distractibility subtests are Arithmetic, Digit Span, and Coding.
Source: First two columns adapted from Gutkin (1978).

Table C-5
Differences Required for Significance When Each WISC-R Subtest Scaled Score Is Compared to the Respective Mean Factor Scaled Score for Any Individual Child

Subtest	Mean of Verbal Comprehension subtests[a]		Mean of Perceptual Organization subtests[b]		Mean of Freedom from Distractibility subtests[c]	
	.05	.01	.05	.01	.05	.01
Information	2.62	3.20	—	—	—	—
Similarities	2.82	3.44	—	—	—	—
Arithmetic	—	—	—	—	2.80	3.43
Vocabulary	2.58	3.12	—	—	—	—
Comprehension	2.93	3.54	—	—	—	—
Digit Span	—	—	—	—	2.85	3.50
Picture Completion	—	—	3.15	3.81	—	—
Picture Arrangement	—	—	3.35	4.05	—	—
Block Design	—	—	2.78	3.36	—	—
Object Assembly	—	—	3.52	4.26	—	—
Coding	—	—	—	—	3.04	3.72
Mazes	—	—	—	—	—	—

Note. Table C-5 shows the minimum deviations from an individual's mean factor scaled score that are significant at the .05 and .01 levels. See Note in Table C-3 for an explanation of how differences were obtained. The following Bonferroni corrections were used: .05 = 2.500, .01 = 3.025 for Verbal Comprehension and Perceptual Organization, .05 = 2.39, .01 = 2.93 for Freedom from Distractibility.

[a] Verbal Comprehension subtests are Information, Similarities, Vocabulary, and Comprehension.

[b] Perceptual Organization subtests are Picture Completion, Picture Arrangement, Block Design, and Object Assembly.

[c] Freedom from Distractibility subtests are Arithmetic, Digit Span, and Coding.

Table C-6
Extrapolated IQ Equivalents of Sums of Scaled Scores for WISC-R

	Verbal		Performance		Full Scale[a]	
	Sum of scaled scores	IQ	Sum of scaled scores	IQ	Sum of scaled scores	IQ
	5	44	5	39	10	36
	•	•	6	41	11	37
	•	•	7	42	12	38
	•	•	8	44	13	39
	94	155	•	•	14	39
	95	157	•	•	•	•
			•	•	•	•
			91	156	•	•
			92	158	185	161
			93	159	186	162
			94	160	187	163
			95	162	188	163
					189	164
					190	165

Note. WISC-R regression equations:

$$\text{Verbal IQ} = 37.3513 + 1.2552 \text{ (scaled score)}$$
$$\text{Performance IQ} = 32.6814 + 1.3580 \text{ (scaled score)}$$
$$\text{Full Scale IQ} = 29.3456 + .7124 \text{ (scaled score)}$$

[a] Wechsler recommends that a Full Scale IQ not be calculated unless raw scores greater than 0 are obtained on at least *three* Verbal and *three* Performance Scale subtests.

Table C-7
Estimates of the Differences Obtained by Various Percentages of the WISC-R Standardization Sample When Each WISC-R Subtest Scaled Score Is Compared to the Mean Scaled Score for Any Individual Child

Subtest	Verbal average				Performance average				Overall average			
	10%	5%	2%	1%	10%	5%	2%	1%	10%	5%	2%	1%
Information	2.9	3.4	4.1	4.5					3.3	3.9	4.7	5.2
Similarities	3.0	3.6	4.2	4.7					3.3	3.9	4.7	5.2
Arithmetic	3.3	4.0	4.7	5.2					3.7	4.4	5.2	5.7
Vocabulary	2.6	3.2	3.7	4.1					3.2	3.8	4.5	4.9
Comprehension	3.2	3.9	4.6	5.1					3.5	4.2	5.0	5.5
Digit Span	4.0	4.8	5.7	6.3					4.3	5.1	6.0	6.7
Picture Completion					3.5	4.2	5.0	5.5	3.8	4.5	5.4	5.9
Picture Arrangement					3.6	4.3	5.1	5.7	3.9	4.6	5.5	6.0
Block Design					3.0	3.6	4.2	4.7	3.3	3.9	4.7	5.2
Object Assembly					3.3	3.9	4.7	5.2	3.8	4.5	5.4	5.9
Coding					4.3	5.1	6.0	6.7	4.4	5.2	6.2	6.9
Mazes					3.8	4.5	5.4	6.0	4.2	5.1	6.0	6.6

Source: Reprinted with permission of the publisher and author from A. B. Silverstein, "Pattern Analysis: The Question of Abnormality." *Journal of Consulting and Clinical Psychology*, 1984, *52*, p. 938. Copyright 1984 by the American Psychological Association.

Table C-8
Probability of Obtaining Designated Differences Between Individual WISC-R Verbal and Performance IQs

Probability of obtaining given or greater discrepancy by chance	Age level											
	6½	7½	8½	9½	10½	11½	12½	13½	14½	15½	16½	Av.[a]
.50	4.32	4.32	4.08	3.99	4.08	3.81	3.83	4.16	4.02	4.09	4.02	4.06
.25	7.20	7.20	6.80	6.66	6.80	6.34	6.38	6.93	6.71	6.82	6.70	6.77
.20	8.01	8.01	7.57	7.41	7.57	7.06	7.10	7.71	7.47	7.59	7.45	7.54
.10	10.33	10.33	9.76	9.55	9.75	9.10	9.15	9.94	9.62	9.78	9.61	9.72
.05	12.27	12.27	11.59	11.35	11.59	10.81	10.87	11.81	11.43	11.62	11.41	11.54
.02	14.59	14.59	13.78	13.49	13.77	12.85	12.93	14.04	13.59	13.81	13.57	13.72
.01	16.16	16.15	15.26	14.93	15.25	14.23	14.31	15.54	15.05	15.29	15.02	15.19
.001	20.66	20.66	19.51	19.10	19.51	18.20	18.31	19.88	19.25	19.56	19.22	19.43

Note. Table C-8 is entered in the column appropriate to the examinee's age. The discrepancy that is just less than the discrepancy obtained by the examinee is located. The entry in the same row, first column, gives the probability of obtaining a given or greater discrepancy by chance. For example, the hypothesis that a 6½-year-old examinee obtained a Verbal-Performance discrepancy of 17 by chance can be rejected at the .01 level of significance. Table C-8 is two-tailed. See Chapter 8, Exhibit 8-1 for an explanation of the method used to arrive at magnitude of differences.
[a] Av. = Average of 11 age groups.

Table C-9
Percentage of Population Obtaining Discrepancies Between WISC-R Verbal and Performance IQs

Percentage obtaining given or greater discrepancy in either direction	Age level												Percentage obtaining given or greater discrepancy in a specific direction
	6½	7½	8½	9½	10½	11½	12½	13½	14½	15½	16½	Av.[a]	
50	8.66	8.53	8.78	7.74	8.41	8.02	7.61	8.78	8.28	9.26	8.41	8.41	25
25	14.43	14.22	14.64	12.91	14.01	13.36	12.68	14.64	13.80	15.43	14.01	14.01	12.5
20	16.06	15.83	16.29	14.37	15.60	14.87	14.11	16.29	15.36	17.17	15.60	15.60	10
10	20.71	20.41	21.00	18.52	20.11	19.17	18.19	21.00	19.80	22.13	20.11	20.11	5
5	24.60	24.24	24.95	22.00	23.88	22.77	21.00	24.95	23.52	26.30	23.88	23.88	2.5
2	29.24	28.82	29.66	26.15	28.39	27.07	25.68	29.66	27.96	31.26	28.39	28.39	1
1	32.38	31.91	32.84	28.96	31.44	29.97	28.44	32.84	30.96	34.61	31.44	31.44	.5
.1	41.41	40.82	42.00	37.04	40.21	38.34	36.37	42.00	39.60	44.27	40.21	40.21	.05

Note. Table C-9 is entered in the column appropriate to the examinee's age. The discrepancy that is just less than the discrepancy obtained by the examinee is located. The entry in the same row, first column, gives the percentage of the standardization population obtaining discrepancies as large as or larger than the located discrepancy. For example, a 6½-year-old examinee with a Verbal-Performance discrepancy of 14 on the WISC-R will be found in between 25 and 50 percent of the standardization population.

The method used to compute the discrepancy between the Verbal and Performance Scale IQs that reflects the percentage of the population obtaining the discrepancy is as follows: Discrepancy $= \sigma_1 z \sqrt{2 - 2r_{xy}}$. The first term is the standard deviation of the test, the second is the selected z value, and the last is the correlation between the two scales. For example, for a 6½-year-old child the discrepancy between the WISC-R Verbal and Performance Scale IQs that represents 5 percent of the population is $15(1.96)\sqrt{2 - 2(.65)} = 24.60$.
[a] Av. = Average of 11 age groups.

Table C-10
Validity Coefficients of Proposed WISC-R Short Forms

Dyad			Triad				Tetrad					Pentad					
Short form		*r*	Short form			*r*	Short form				*r*	Short form					*r*
V	BD	.906	S	V	BD	.931	I	V	C	BD	.947	S	A	V	PA	OA	.963
I	BD	.888	I	V	BD	.929	S	V	PA	BD	.947	S	A	V	PA	BD	.962
S	BD	.885	I	C	BD	.928	I	C	PC	BD	.945	S	A	V	BD	OA	.960
C	BD	.878	I	S	BD	.925	S	A	V	OA	.944	I	C	PC	BD	CO	.960
V	OA	.878	V	C	BD	.924	I	V	PA	BD	.944	I	V	PC	BD	CO	.960
V	PC	.868	S	C	BD	.921	I	S	C	BD	.944	S	A	C	PA	OA	.960
S	V	.864	S	V	OA	.919	I	C	PA	BD	.944	I	S	C	PA	BD	.960
I	S	.860	V	PA	BD	.919	I	S	PA	BD	.943	I	V	C	PC	BD	.959
I	PC	.858	A	V	OA	.919	S	V	PC	BD	.943	A	V	C	BD	OA	.959
I	V	.857	V	PC	BD	.919	S	V	BD	OA	.943	A	V	C	PA	BD	.958

Note. Abbreviations: I = Information; S = Similarities; A = Arithmetic; V = Vocabulary; C = Comprehension; PC = Picture Completion; PA = Picture Arrangement; BD = Block Design; OA = Object Assembly; CO = Coding.

The following formula, obtained from Q. McNemar (*Journal of Clinical and Consulting Psychology*, 1974, *42*, 145-146), was used to compute the part-whole correlations:

$$r = \frac{k + \Sigma\Sigma r_{hj}}{\sqrt{n + 2\Sigma r_{ij}}\sqrt{k + 2\Sigma r_{gh}}}$$

where $\Sigma\Sigma r_{hj}$ is the sum of the correlations between each of the k subtests and all the other subtests, n is the total number of subtests, Σr_{ij} is the sum of the correlations between each of the n subtests, and Σr_{gh} is the sum of the intercorrelations of the k subtests. The term $\sqrt{n + 2\Sigma r_{ij}}$ becomes a constant for all computations. The formula was applied to the average subtest intercorrelations for the 11 age groups that composed the standardization sample ($N = 2200$) to determine the correlations with the Full Scale of all possible short forms of two, three, four, and five subtests. The average subtest intercorrelations are based on the 10 standard subtests (Digit Span and Mazes are omitted). The standard errors of estimate for the best dyad, triad, tetrad, and pentad are 6.34, 5.48, 4.82, and 4.04 IQ points, respectively.

Table C-11
Yudin's Abbreviated Procedure for the WISC-R as Modified by Silverstein

Subtest	Items administered	Multiply score by
Information	Every 3rd	3
Similarities	Odd only	2
Arithmetic	Odd only	2
Vocabulary	Every 3rd	3
Comprehension	Odd only	2
Picture Completion	Every 3rd	3
Picture Arrangement	Odd only	2
Block Design	Odd only	2
Object Assembly	Odd only	2
Coding	All items	1

Source: Adapted from Silverstein (1968a).

Table C-12
WISC-R Structure of Intellect Classifications

Item	SOI abbreviation	SOI classification	Description
		Information	
Items 1 to 3	MMU	Memory for Semantic Units	The ability to remember isolated ideas or word meanings
Items 4, 5	MMR	Memory for Semantic Relations	The ability to remember meaningful connections between items of verbal information
Items 6, 11, 25, 28	CMU	Cognition of Semantic Units	The ability to comprehend the meaning of words or ideas
Items 7, 8, 10	MMS	Memory for Semantic Systems	The ability to remember meaningfully ordered verbal information
Item 9	EMR	Evaluation of Semantic Relations	The ablity to make choices among semantic relationships based on the similarity and consistency of the meanings
	MMR	Memory for Semantic Relations	The ability to remember meaningful connections between items of verbal information
Items 12, 13, 17	MMR	Memory for Semantic Relations	The ability to remember meaningful connections between items of verbal information
	NMR	Convergent Production of Semantic Relations	The ability to produce a word or idea that conforms to specific relationship requirements
Items 14, 18	MMR	Memory for Semantic Relations	The ability to remember meaningful connections between items of verbal information
Item 15	CMU	Cognition of Semantic Units	The ability to comprehend the meaning of words or ideas
	MMS	Memory for Semantic Systems	The ability to remember meaningfully ordered verbal information
Items 16, 22	MMI	Memory for Semantic Implications	The ability to remember arbitrary connections between pairs of meaningful elements of information
Item 17	MMR	Memory for Semantic Relations	The ability to remember meaningful connections between items of verbal information
	NMR	Convergent Production of Semantic Relations	The ability to produce a word or idea that conforms to specific relationship requirements
Item 19	MFS	Memory for Figural Systems	The ability to remember spatial order or placement of given visual information or to remember auditory complexes of rhythm or melody
Item 20	MSS	Memory for Symbolic Systems	The ability to remember the order of symbolic information
	CMU	Cognition of Semantic Units	The ability to comprehend the meaning of words or ideas

(Table continues next page)

Table C-12 (cont.)

Item	SOI abbreviation	SOI classification	Description
Items 21, 23, 29	NMU	Convergent Production of Semantic Units	The ability to converge on the appropriate name, or summarizing word, for any given information
Item 24	EMR	Evaluation of Semantic Relations	The ablity to make choices among semantic relationships based on the similarity and consistency of the meanings
Item 26	MMR	Memory for Semantic Relations	The ability to remember meaningful connections between items of verbal information
	NMI	Convergent Production of Semantic Implications	The ability to deduce meaningful information implicit in the given information
Item 27	MMU	Memory for Semantic Units	The ability to remember isolated ideas or word meanings
	NMU	Convergent Production of Semantic Units	The ability to converge on the appropriate name, or summarizing word, for any given information
Item 30	CMU	Cognition of Semantic Units	The ability to comprehend the meaning of words or ideas
	MMR	Memory for Semantic Relations	The ability to remember meaningful connections between items of verbal information

Similarities

Item	SOI abbreviation	SOI classification	Description
Items 1 to 15	CMR	Cognition of Semantic Relations	The ability to see relations between ideas or meanings of words
	CMT	Cognition of Semantic Transformations	The ability to see potential changes of interpretations of objects and situations
Item 16	CSR	Cognition of Symbolic Relations	The ability to see relations between items of symbolic information
Item 17	CMR	Cognition of Semantic Relations	The ability to see relations between ideas or meanings of words
	CMT	Cognition of Semantic Transformations	The ability to see potential changes of interpretations of objects and situations

Arithmetic

Item	SOI abbreviation	SOI classification	Description
Every item	MSI	Memory for Symbolic Implications	The ability to remember arbitrary connections between symbols
	CMS	Cognition of Semantic Systems	The ability to comprehend relatively complex ideas

Vocabulary

Item	SOI abbreviation	SOI classification	Description
Every Item	CMU	Cognition of Semantic Units	The ability to comprehend the meaning of words or ideas

Comprehension

Item	SOI abbreviation	SOI classification	Description
Every item	EMI	Evaluation of Semantic Implications	The ability to judge the adequacy of a meaningful deduction

Digit Span

Item	SOI abbreviation	SOI classification	Description
Every item	MSS	Memory for Symbolic Systems	The ability to remember the order of symbolic information

(Table continues next page)

Table C-12 (cont.)

Item	SOI abbreviation	SOI classification	Description
		Picture Completion	
Every item	CFU	Cognition of Figural Units	The ability to perceive or recognize figural entities
	EFS	Evaluation of Figural Systems	The ability to evaluate a system of figural units that have been grouped in some manner
Item 14 (also)	MSS	Memory for Symbolic Systems	The ability to remember the order of symbolic information
		Picture Arrangement	
Every item	EMR	Evaluation of Semantic Relations	The ablity to make choices among semantic relationships based on the similarity and consistency of the meanings
	NMS	Convergent Production of Semantic Systems	The ability to order information into a verbally meaningful sequence
		Block Design	
Every item	CFR	Cognition of Figural Relations	The ability to recognize figural relations between forms
	EFR	Evaluation of Figural Relations	The ability to choose a form based on the evaluation of what the relations are between the figures or forms in the sequence
		Object Assembly	
Every item	CFS	Cognition of Figural Systems	The ability to comprehend arrangements and positions of visual objects in space
	CFT	Cognition of Figural Transformations	The ability to visualize how a given figure or object will appear after given changes, such as unfolding or rotation
	EFR	Evaluation of Figural Relations	The ability to choose a form based on the evaluation of what the relations are between the figures or forms in the sequence
		Coding A	
Entire subtest	NFU	Convergent Production of Figural Units	The ability to reproduce correctly a form
	EFU	Evaluation of Figural Units	The ability to judge units of figural information as being similar or different
		Coding B	
Entire subtest	NSU	Convergent Production of Symbolic Units	Factorial meaning has not been described
	ESU	Evaluation of Symbolic Units	The ability to make rapid decisions regarding the identification of letter or number sets
		Mazes	
Every item	CFI	Cognition of Figural Implications	The ability to foresee the consequences involved in figural problems

Note. Templates and SOI profile forms as well as five workbooks to accompany prescriptions based on SOI templates are available from the SOI Institute, 343 Richmond, El Segundo, CA 90245.
Source: WISC-R SOI designations obtained from M. Meeker at the SOI Institute.

Table C-13
Interpretive Rationales, Implications of High and Low Scores, and Instructional Implications for Wechsler Subtests

Ability[a]	Background factors	Possible implications of high scores	Possible implications of low scores	Instructional implications
Information				
Verbal comprehension Range of knowledge Long-term memory	Natural endowment Richness of early environment Extent of schooling Cultural predilections Interests	Good range of factual knowledge Good range of information Possession of knowledge associated with the cultural and educational environment Good memory Enriched background Alertness and interest in the environment Intellectual ambitiousness Intellectual curiosity Urge to collect knowledge	Poor range of factual knowledge Poor range of information Poor memory Hostility to a school-type task Tendency to give up easily Foreign background Low achievement orientation Impoverished background	Stress factual material by having child read newspaper articles, discuss current events, and do memory exercises Use other enrichment activities, including calendar activities, science and social studies information, and projects involving animals and their function in society
Similarities				
Verbal comprehension Verbal concept formation Abstract and concrete reasoning abilities Capacity for associative thinking Ability to separate essential from nonessential details Long-term memory	A minimum of cultural opportunities Interests and reading patterns	Good conceptual thinking Good ability to see relationships Good ability to use logical and abstract thinking Good ability to discriminate fundamental from superficial relationships Good ability to select and verbalize appropriate relationships between two objects or concepts Flexibility of thought processes	Poor conceptual thinking Difficulty in seeing relationships Difficulty in selecting and verbalizing appropriate relationships between two objects or concepts Overly concrete mode of thinking Rigidity of thought processes Negativism	Focus on recognition of differences and likenesses in shapes, textures, and daily surroundings Stress language development, synonyms and antonyms, and exercises involving abstract words, classifications, and generalizations
Arithmetic				
Freedom from distractibility[b] and verbal comprehension	Opportunity to acquire fundamental arithmetical	Facility in mental arithmetic Good ability to apply reasoning skills in	Inadequate ability in mental arithmetic Poor concentration Distractibility	Develop arithmetical skills Develop concentration skills

(Table continues next page)

Table C-13 (cont.)

Ability[a]	Background factors	Possible implications of high scores	Possible implications of low scores	Instructional implications
Numerical reasoning ability Mental computation Application of basic arithmetical processes Concentration Attention Short-term memory Long-term memory	processes	the solution of mathematical problems Good ability to apply arithmetical skills in personal and social problem-solving situations Good concentration Good ability to focus attention Good ability to engage in complex thought patterns (for upper-level items, particularly) Teacher-oriented student	Anxiety over a school-like task Blocking toward mathematical tasks Poor school achievement (perhaps associated with rebellion against authority or with cultural background) Anxiety (e.g., worry over personal problems)	Use concrete objects to introduce concepts Drill in basic skills Develop interesting and "real" problems to solve

Vocabulary

Ability[a]	Background factors	Possible implications of high scores	Possible implications of low scores	Instructional implications
Verbal comprehension Language development Learning ability Fund of information Richness of ideas Memory Concept formation Long-term memory	Education Cultural opportunities	Good word knowledge Good verbal comprehension Good verbal skills and language development Good family or cultural background Good schooling Good ability to conceptualize Intellectual striving	Poor word knowledge Poor verbal comprehension Poor verbal skills and language development Limited educational or family background Difficulty in verbalization Foreign language background Verbalization not encouraged in culture	Develop a working vocabulary Encourage child to discuss experiences, ask questions, and make a dictionary Use other verbal enrichment exercises, including Scrabble, analogy, and other word games

Comprehension

Ability[a]	Background factors	Possible implications of high scores	Possible implications of low scores	Instructional implications
Verbal comprehension Social judgment Common sense Use of practical knowledge and judgment in social situations Knowledge of conventional standards of	Extensiveness of cultural opportunities Ability to evaluate and use past experience Development of conscience or moral sense	Good social judgment and common sense Good ability to recognize social demands when practical judgment and common sense are necessary Knowledge of rules of conventional	Poor social judgment Failure to take personal responsibility (e.g., overdependency, immaturity, limited involvement with others) Overly concrete thinking	Help child understand social mores, customs, and societal activities, such as how other children react to things, how the government works, and how banks operate

(Table continues next page)

Table C-13 (cont.)

Ability[a]	Background factors	Possible implications of high scores	Possible implications of low scores	Instructional implications
behavior Ability to evaluate past experience Moral and ethical judgment		behavior Good ability to organize knowledge Social maturity Ability to verbalize well Wide experience	Difficulty in expressing ideas verbally Doubt-laden individual Creative individual looking for unusual solutions Foreign-born with differing life experiences	Discuss the actions of others to help children develop awareness of social relationships and what is expected of them in terms of the behavior of others Role-play situations, such as reporting fires, calling police, and obtaining help for plumbing problems
Digit Span				
Freedom from distractibility[b] Short-term memory Rote memory Immediate auditory memory Attention Concentration Auditory sequencing	Ability to passively receive stimuli	Good rote memory Good immediate recall ability Ability to attend well in a testing situation Good ability to attend to auditory stimuli	Anxiety Inattention Distractibility A possible learning deficit Difficulty in auditory sequencing	Emphasize listening skills by using sequencing activities, reading a short story and asking child to recall details, and seeing whether child can follow directions Use short and simple directions and repeat when necessary Use other memory exercises and memory games
Picture Completion				
Perceptual organization Ability to differentiate essential from nonessential details Identification of familiar objects (visual recognition) Concentration on visually perceived material	Experiences Alertness to environment	Good perception and concentration Good alertness to details Ability to establish a learning set quickly Good ability to differentiate between essential and nonessential details	Anxiety affecting concentration and attention Preoccupation with irrelevant details Negativism ("nothing is missing") Limited interest in the environment Depression Reality distortion	Focus on visual learning techniques stressing individual parts that make up the whole Use perceptual activities that focus on recognizing objects, describing objects, and attention to details

(Table continues next page)

Table C-13 (cont.)

Ability[a]	Background factors	Possible implications of high scores	Possible implications of low scores	Instructional implications
Reasoning Visual organization Visual perception (closure) Visual long-term memory		Interest in the environment		(e.g., maps and art work) Improve scanning techniques aimed at identifying missing elements in pictures

Picture Arrangement

Ability[a]	Background factors	Possible implications of high scores	Possible implications of low scores	Instructional implications
Perceptual organization Planning ability Interpretation of social situations Nonverbal reasoning ability Attention to details Alertness Visual sequencing Common sense Anticipation of consequences Recognition of plot	A minimum of cultural opportunities	Planning ability Ability to anticipate in a meaningful way what results might be expected from various acts of behavior Alertness to detail Forethought Good ability to detect sequences Good ability to synthesize parts into intelligible wholes	Difficulty with visual organization (sequencing) Difficulty in anticipating events and their consequences Difficulty in seeing cause-and-effect relationships Inattentiveness Anxiety Failure to use cues	Focus on cause-and-effect relationships, logical sequential presentations, and part-whole relationships Use story completion exercises Discuss alternative behaviors and endings in stories and events

Block Design

Ability[a]	Background factors	Possible implications of high scores	Possible implications of low scores	Instructional implications
Perceptual organization Visual-motor coordination Spatial visualization Abstract conceptualizing ability Analysis and synthesis Nonverbal reasoning	Rate of motor activity Color vision	Good visual-motor-spatial integration Good conceptualizing ability Good spatial orientation in conjunction with speed, accuracy, and persistence Good analyzing and synthesizing ability Speed and accuracy in sizing up a problem Good hand-eye coordination Good nonverbal reasoning ability Good trial-and-error methods	Poor visual-motor-spatial integration Visual-perceptual problems Poor spatial orientation Poor nonverbal reasoning	Use puzzles, blocks, spatial-visual tasks, perceptual tasks involving breaking down an object and building it up again, and art work with geometric forms and flannel board Focus on part-to-whole relationships and working with a model or key

(Table continues next page)

Table C-13 (cont.)

Ability[a]	Background factors	Possible implications of high scores	Possible implications of low scores	Instructional implications
		Object Assembly		
Perceptual organization Visual-motor coordination Ability to synthesize concrete parts into meaningful wholes Spatial relations	Rate of motor activity Familiarity with figures Capacity to persist at a task Experience with part-whole relationships Working for an unknown goal	Good visual-motor coordination Good ability to visualize a whole from its parts Ability to perceive a whole, with critical understanding of the relationships of the individual parts Successful trial and error Experience in assembling puzzles Persistence	Visual-motor difficulties Visual-perceptual problems Poor planning ability Difficulty in perceiving a whole Minimal experience with construction tasks Limited interest in assembly tasks Limited persistence	Develop perceptual and psychomotor skills through guided practice in assembling parts into familiar configurations Encourage trial-and-error activities Reinforce persistence Work with puzzles and activities centering on recognition of missing body parts Employ construction, cutting, and pasting activities Focus on interpretation of wholes from minimal cues
		Coding		
Freedom from distractibility[b] Visual-motor coordination or dexterity Speed of mental operation Psychomotor speed Short-term memory Visual recall Attentional skills Symbol-associative skills	Rate of motor activity Motivation	Visual-motor dexterity Good concentration Sustained energy or persistence Ability to learn new material associatively and reproduce it with speed and accuracy Good motivation or desire for achievement	Visual-motor coordination difficulties Distractibility Visual defects Poor pencil control Disinterest in a school-like task Excessive concern for detail in reproducing symbols exactly Lethargy	Use visual-motor learning exercises, such as having child develop a code for matching geometric figures and numbers, learn Morse Code, and work on tracing activities
		Mazes		
Perceptual organization Planning ability Foresight Visual-motor control Eye-hand coordination Attention and	Visual-motor organization Ability to delay action	Good perceptual organization Planning efficiency Speed and accuracy Good ability to follow instructions Nonimpulsivity Good sustained	Poor visual-motor organization Poor planning efficiency Difficulty in delaying action Impulsivity Poor sustained	Focus on planning skills, directionality, visual discrimination, and other paper-and-pencil activities emphasizing

(Table continues next page)

Table C-13 (cont.)

Ability[a]	Background factors	Possible implications of high scores	Possible implications of low scores	Instructional implications
concentration		attention	attention	planning and anticipation Help child evaluate responses prior to emitting them

Note. Select the appropriate implication(s) based on the entire test protocol and background information. Also see Table C-24 for the WPPSI-R.
[a] The first entry under "Ability" is based on factor analytic findings. Other entries are derived from clinical and psychoeducational hypotheses.
[b] Freedom from Distractibility for WISC-R Arithmetic, Digit Span, and Coding; Verbal Comprehension for WISC-III Arithmetic and Digit Span; Processing Speed for WISC-III Coding.
Source: Adapted, in part, from Blatt and Allison (1968), Freeman (1962), Glasser and Zimmerman (1967), Kaufman (1975a), Rapaport, Gill, and Schafer (1968), and Searls (1975).

Table C-14
Confidence Intervals for WPPSI Scales

Age level	Scale	Confidence level				
		68%	85%	90%	95%	99%
4 (3-10-16 through 4-2-29)	Verbal Scale IQ	± 4	± 5	± 6	± 7	± 9
	Performance Scale IQ	± 4	± 6	± 7	± 9	± 11
	Full Scale IQ	± 3	± 4	± 5	± 6	± 8
4½ (4-3-0 through 4-8-29)	Verbal Scale IQ	± 4	± 5	± 6	± 7	± 9
	Performance Scale IQ	± 4	± 6	± 7	± 8	± 10
	Full Scale IQ	± 3	± 4	± 5	± 6	± 8
5 (4-9-0 through 5-2-29)	Verbal Scale IQ	± 4	± 5	± 6	± 7	± 9
	Performance Scale IQ	± 4	± 5	± 6	± 7	± 10
	Full Scale IQ	± 3	± 4	± 5	± 6	± 7
5½ (5-3-0 through 5-8-29)	Verbal Scale IQ	± 3	± 5	± 6	± 7	± 9
	Performance Scale IQ	± 3	± 5	± 6	± 7	± 9
	Full Scale IQ	± 3	± 4	± 4	± 5	± 7
6 (5-9-0 through 6-2-29)	Verbal Scale IQ	± 3	± 5	± 6	± 7	± 9
	Performance Scale IQ	± 3	± 5	± 6	± 7	± 9
	Full Scale IQ	± 3	± 4	± 4	± 5	± 7
6½ (6-3-0 through 6-7-15)	Verbal Scale IQ	± 4	± 5	± 6	± 7	± 10
	Performance Scale IQ	± 4	± 6	± 7	± 8	± 10
	Full Scale IQ	± 3	± 4	± 5	± 6	± 8

Note. See Table C-1 for an explanation of method used to obtain confidence intervals.

Table C-15
Significant Differences Between WPPSI Scaled Scores and Between IQs (.05/.01 significance levels)

	I	V	A	S	C	Se	AH	PC	M	GD
V	3/5									
A	4/5	3/5								
S	4/5	3/4	3/5							
C	4/5	3/5	4/5	4/5						
Se	3/5	3/4	3/4	3/4	3/5					
AH	4/5	4/5	4/5	4/5	4/5	4/5				
PC	4/5	3/4	3/5	3/5	4/5	3/4	4/5			
M	3/4	3/4	3/4	3/4	3/4	3/4	4/5	3/4		
GD	4/5	3/5	4/5	3/5	4/5	3/4	4/5	3/5	3/4	
BD	4/5	3/5	4/5	3/5	4/5	3/4	4/5	3/5	3/4	4/5

	VSIQ
PSIQ	11/14

Note. Abbreviations: I = Information; V = Vocabulary; A = Arithmetic; S = Similarities; C = Comprehension; Se = Sentences; AH = Animal House; PC = Picture Completion; M = Mazes; GD = Geometric Design; BD = Block Design; VSIQ = Verbal Scale IQ; PSIQ = Performance Scale IQ.

Sample reading: A difference of 3 points between scaled scores on the Information and Vocabulary subtests is significant at the 5 percent level; a difference of 5 points is significant at the 1 percent level. The small box shows that an 11-point difference between the Verbal Scale IQ and Performance Scale IQ is needed for the 5 percent level, and a 14-point difference is needed for the 1 percent level. The Sentences subtest was not included in computation of significant differences for the Verbal Scale.

The values in this table for the subtest comparisons are overly liberal when more than one comparison is made. They are more accurate when a priori planned comparisons are made, such as Information vs. Vocabulary or Similarities vs. Comprehension. The values in this table are based on the average of the six age groups.

See Chapter 8, Exhibit 8-1 for an explanation of the method used to obtain magnitude of differences.

Table C-16
Differences Required for Significance When Each WPPSI Subtest Scaled Score Is Compared to the Mean Scaled Score for Any Individual Child

Subtest	Mean of 5 Verbal scale subtests[a]		Mean of 6 Verbal scale subtests		Mean of 5 Performance scale subtests		Mean of 10 Subtests[a]		Mean of 11 Subtests	
	.05	.01	.05	.01	.05	.01	.05	.01	.05	.01
Information	3.05	3.66	3.19	3.80	—	—	3.55	4.16	3.61	4.22
Vocabulary	2.83	3.39	2.94	3.50	—	—	3.25	3.80	3.29	3.85
Arithmetic	2.86	3.43	2.98	3.55	—	—	3.29	3.86	3.34	3.91
Similarities	2.90	3.48	3.02	3.60	—	—	3.34	3.91	3.39	3.96
Comprehension	3.02	3.62	3.15	3.76	—	—	3.51	4.11	3.56	4.16
Sentences	—	—	2.89	3.44	—	—	—	—	3.22	3.76
Animal House	—	—	—	—	3.26	3.91	3.84	4.50	3.90	4.56
Picture Completion	—	—	—	—	2.81	3.37	3.22	3.78	3.27	3.82
Mazes	—	—	—	—	2.61	3.13	2.94	3.45	2.98	3.48
Geometric Design	—	—	—	—	2.96	3.55	3.43	4.02	3.49	4.08
Block Design	—	—	—	—	2.91	3.49	3.36	3.94	3.41	3.99

Note. Table C-16 shows the minimum deviations from an individual's average subtest scaled score that are significant at the .05 and .01 levels. See the Note in Table C-3 for an explanation of how the deviations were obtained.
[a] Sentences subtest excluded
Source: The figures in the table courtesy of A.B. Silverstein.

Table C-17
Extrapolated IQ Equivalents of Scaled Scores for WPPSI

Verbal		Performance		Full Scale			
Sum of scaled scores	IQ	Sum of scaled scores	IQ	Sum of scaled scores	IQ	Sum of scaled scores	IQ
5	45	5	39	10	35	•	•
•	•	6	40	11	36	178	156
•	•	7	41	12	37	179	157
•	•	8	43	13	38	180	157
95	156	•	•	14	38	181	158
		•	•	15	39	182	159
		•	•	16	40	183	160
		92	157	17	40	184	160
		93	158	18	41	185	161
		94	160	19	42	186	162
		95	161	20	43	187	162
				21	43	188	163
				22	44	189	164
				•	•	190	165
				•	•		

Note. WPPSI regression equations:

$$\text{Verbal IQ} = 38.3946 + 1.2366 \text{ (scaled score)}$$
$$\text{Performance IQ} = 31.7940 + 1.3624 \text{ (scaled score)}$$
$$\text{Full Scale IQ} = 28.17 + .72 \text{ (scaled score)}$$

Source: IQs of 156 and above reprinted by permission of the publishers and author from A. B. Silverstein, "WISC and WPPSI IQs for the Gifted," *Psychological Reports*, 1968, *22*, p. 1168. Copyright 1968 Psychological Reports. IQs of 45 and below reprinted by permission of the publishers and author from A. B. Silverstein, "WPPSI IQs for the Mentally Retarded," *American Journal of Mental Deficiency, 73*, p. 446. Copyright 1968, American Association on Mental Deficiency.

Table C-18
Estimates of the Differences Obtained by Various Percentages of the WPPSI Standardization Sample When Each WPPSI Subtest Scaled Score Is Compared to the Mean Scaled Score for Any Individual Child

Subtest	Verbal average				Performance average				Overall average			
	10%	5%	2%	1%	10%	5%	2%	1%	10%	5%	2%	1%
Information	2.9	3.4	4.1	4.5					3.2	3.8	4.5	5.0
Vocabulary	3.2	3.8	4.5	5.0					3.5	4.1	4.9	5.4
Arithmetic	3.2	3.9	4.6	5.1					3.3	3.9	4.6	5.1
Similarities	3.3	3.9	4.6	5.1					3.7	4.4	5.2	5.8
Comprehension	3.0	3.5	4.2	4.6					3.4	4.0	4.8	5.3
Sentences	3.3	3.9	4.6	5.1					3.6	4.3	5.1	5.7
Animal House					3.6	4.3	5.1	5.6	3.9	4.7	5.5	6.1
Picture Completion					3.4	4.1	4.8	5.3	3.7	4.4	5.2	5.7
Mazes					3.3	4.0	4.7	5.2	3.9	4.6	5.5	6.1
Geometric Design					3.2	3.9	4.6	5.1	3.8	4.5	5.3	5.9
Block Design					3.3	3.9	4.7	5.2	3.6	4.3	5.2	5.7

Source: Reprinted with permission of the publisher and author from A. B. Silverstein, "Pattern Analysis: The Question of Abnormality." *Journal of Consulting and Clinical Psychology*, 1984, *52*, p. 937. Copyright 1984 by the American Psychological Association.

Table C-19
Probability of Obtaining Designated Differences Between Individual WPPSI Verbal and Performance IQs

Probability of obtaining given or greater discrepancy by chance	Age level					
	4	4½	5	5½	6	6½
.50	3.8	3.7	3.5	3.3	3.3	3.7
.25	6.6	6.2	6.0	5.6	5.6	6.2
.20	7.3	6.9	6.7	6.2	6.2	7.0
.10	9.4	8.9	8.6	8.0	8.0	8.9
.05	11.2	10.6	10.3	9.5	9.5	10.7
.02	13.3	12.6	12.2	11.3	11.3	12.6
.01	14.7	13.9	13.5	12.5	12.5	14.0
.001	18.8	17.9	17.3	16.1	16.0	17.9

Note. Table C-19 is entered in the column appropriate to the examinee's age. The discrepancy that is just less than the discrepancy obtained by the examinee is located. The entry in the same row, first column, gives the probability of obtaining a given or greater discrepancy by chance. For example, the hypothesis that a 4-year-old examinee obtained a Verbal-Performance discrepancy of 17 by chance can be rejected at the .01 level of significance. Table C-19 is two-tailed. See Chapter 8, Exhibit 8-1 for an explanation of the method used to arrive at magnitude of differences.

Table C-20
Percentage of Population Obtaining Discrepancies Between WPPSI Verbal and Performance IQs

Percentage obtaining given or greater discrepancy in either direction	Age level						Percentage obtaining given or greater discrepancy in a specific direction
	4	4½	5	5½	6	6½	
50	8.1	8.6	8.7	8.2	7.7	8.8	25
25	13.8	14.7	14.8	14.0	13.1	15.0	12.5
20	15.4	16.3	16.5	15.6	14.7	16.8	10
10	19.7	21.0	21.2	20.0	18.8	21.5	5
5	23.5	25.0	25.3	23.9	22.4	25.6	2.5
2	27.9	29.6	30.0	28.3	26.6	30.4	1
1	30.9	32.8	33.2	31.4	29.4	33.7	.5
.1	39.6	42.0	42.6	40.2	37.7	43.2	.05

Note. Table C-20 is entered in the column appropriate to the examinee's age. The discrepancy that is just less than the one obtained by the examinee is located. The entry in the same row, first column, gives the percentage of the standardization population obtaining discrepancies as large or larger than the located discrepancy. For example, a 4-year-old examinee with a Verbal-Performance discrepancy of 15 will be found in between 20 and 25 percent of the standardization population. See Table C-9 for an explanation of the method used to arrive at magnitude of differences.

Table C-21
Validity Coefficients of Proposed WPPSI Short Forms

Dyad			Triad				Tetrad					Pentad					
Short form		r	Short form			r	Short form				r	Short form					r
I	BD	.835	I	A	PC	.878	I	V	GD	BD	.906	V	A	S	PC	GD	.923
I	GD	.833	I	A	MA	.878	I	C	MA	BD	.904	I	A	C	PC	MA	.923
I	A	.830	A	C	PC	.877	V	A	PC	GD	.904	V	A	C	PC	GD	.923
V	A	.828	I	V	GD	.877	A	C	PC	GD	.904	I	V	A	PC	GD	.922
I	MA	.828	V	A	PC	.876	I	C	GD	BD	.904	I	A	C	PC	GD	.922
A	PC	.828	V	A	GD	.876	I	A	PC	GD	.904	I	A	S	PC	GD	.922
I	PC	.823	V	A	MA	.875	I	V	A	MA	.903	I	V	A	MA	BD	.921
A	C	.822	A	C	MA	.875	I	A	C	MA	.903	I	V	A	MA	GD	.921
V	BD	.822	I	V	BD	.875	A	C	PC	MA	.903	V	A	C	PC	MA	.921
V	GD	.820	I	C	GD	.875	I	V	MA	BD	.903	V	A	C	MA	BD	.921

Note. Abbreviations: I = Information; V = Vocabulary; A = Arithmetic; S = Similarities; C = Comprehension; PC = Picture Completion; MA = Mazes; GD = Geometric Design; BD = Block Design.
Source: Reprinted by permission of the publisher and author from A. B. Silverstein, "Reappraisal of the Validity of the WAIS, WISC, and WPPSI Short Forms," *Journal of Consulting and Clinical Psychology*, 1970, *34*, p. 13. Copyright 1970 by the American Psychological Association.

Table C-22
Yudin's Abbreviated Procedure for the WPPSI as Modified by Silverstein

Subtest	Item used	Multiply score by
Information	Every 3rd	3
Vocabulary	Every 3rd	3
Arithmetic	Odd only	2
Similarities	Odd only	2
Comprehension	Odd only	2
Animal House	Unchanged	1
Picture Completion	Every 3rd	3
Mazes	Odd only	2
Geometric Design	Odd only	2
Block Design	Odd only	2

Source: Adapted from Silverstein (1968a).

Table C-23
WPPSI Structure of Intellect Classifications

Item	SOI abbreviation	SOI classification	Description
Information			
Items 1, 2, 3, 6	MMU	Memory for Semantic Units	The ability to remember isolated ideas or word meanings
Items 4, 5, 8, 14	MMR	Memory for Semantic Relations	The ability to remember meaningful connections between items of verbal information
	EMR	Evaluation of Semantic Relations	The ability to make choices among semantic relationships based on the similarity and consistency of the meanings
Items 7, 12, 20, 21	CMU	Cognition of Semantic Units	The ability to comprehend the meaning of words or ideas
Item 9	MMR	Memory for Semantic Relations	The ability to remember meaningful connections between items of verbal information
	CMU	Cognition of Semantic Units	The ability to comprehend the meaning of words or ideas
Item 10	MFU	Memory for Figural Units	The ability to remember given figural objects
	CFS	Cognition of Figural Systems	The ability to comprehend arrangements and positions of visual objects in space
Item 11	EFU	Evaluation of Figural Units	The ability to judge units of figural information as being similar or different
Item 13	CFR	Cognition of Figural Relations	The ability to recognize figural relations between forms
	MMU	Memory for Semantic Units	The ability to remember isolated ideas or word meanings
Items 15, 17, 19	EMR	Evaluation of Semantic Relations	The ability to make choices among semantic relationships based on the similarity and consistency of the meanings
Items 16, 18, 22	MSS	Memory for Symbolic Systems	The ability to remember the order of symbolic information
Item 23	MMR	Memory for Semantic Relations	The ability to remember meaningful connections between items of verbal information
Vocabulary			
Every item	CMU	Cognition of Semantic Units	The ability to comprehend the meaning of words or ideas
Arithmetic			
Items 1 to 4	EFR	Evaluation of Figural Relations	The ability to choose a form based on the evaluation of what the relations are between the figures or forms in the sequence
Items 5 to 8	MSU	Memory for Symbolic Units	The ability to remember isolated items of symbolic information, such as syllables and words
Items 9 to 20	MSI	Memory for Symbolic Implications	The ability to remember arbitrary connections between symbols
	CMS	Cognition of Semantic Systems	The ability to comprehend relatively complex ideas

(Table continues next page)

Table C-23 (cont.)

Item	SOI abbreviation	SOI classification	Description
Similarities			
Items 1 to 5	EMR	Evaluation of Semantic Relations	The ability to make choices among semantic relationships based on the similarity and consistency of the meanings
	NMS	Convergent Production of Semantic Systems	The ability to order information into a verbally meaningful sequence
Items 6, 8, 10	EMR	Evaluation of Semantic Relations	The ability to make choices among semantic relationships based on the similarity and consistency of the meanings
	CMT	Cognition of Semantic Transformations	The ability to see potential changes of interpretations of objects and situations
Items 7, 9	NMS	Convergent Production of Semantic Systems	The ability to order information into a verbally meaningful sequence
	EMR	Evaluation of Semantic Relations	The ability to make choices among semantic relationships based on the similarity and consistency of the meanings
Items 11 to 16	CMT	Cognition of Semantic Transformations	The ability to see potential changes of interpretations of objects and situations
Comprehension			
Every item	EMI	Evaluation of Semantic Implications	The ability to judge the adequacy of a meaningful deduction
Sentences			
Every item	MMS	Memory for Semantic Systems	The ability to remember ordered verbal information
Animal House			
Every Item	NFU	Convergent Production of Figural Units	The ability to reproduce correctly a form
	EFU	Evaluation of Figural Units	The ability to judge units of figural information as being similar or different
Picture Completion			
Every item	CFU	Cognition of Figural Units	The ability to perceive or recognize figural entities
	EFS	Evaluation of Figural Systems	The ability to evaluate a system of figural units that have been grouped in some manner
Mazes			
Every item	CFI	Cognition of Figural Implications	The ability to foresee the consequences involved in figural problems
Geometric Design			
Every item	NFU	Convergent Production of Figural Units	The ability to reproduce correctly a form
Block Design			
Every item	CFR	Cognition of Figural Relations	The ability to recognize figural relations between forms

(Table continues next page)

Table C-23 (cont.)

Item	SOI abbreviation	SOI classification	Description
	EFR	Evaluation of Figural Relations	The ability to choose a form based on the evaluation of what the relations are between the figures or forms in the sequence
	NFR	Convergent Production of Figural Relations	The ability to reproduce correct relationships between forms

Note. Templates and SOI profile forms as well as five workbooks and modules for training with accompanying prescriptions based on SOI templates are available from the SOI Institute, 343 Richmond, El Segundo, CA 90245.
Source: WPPSI SOI designations obtained from M. Meeker at the SOI Institute.

Table C-24
Interpretive Rationales and Implications of High and Low Scores for WPPSI-R and WPPSI Subtests

Ability[a]	Background factors	Possible implications of high scores	Possible implications of low scores
Information			
Verbal comprehension	Natural endowment	Good range of information	Poor range of information
Range of knowledge	Richness of early	Good memory	Poor memory
Long-term memory	environment	Enriched background	Tendency to give up easily
	Extent of pre-schooling	Alertness and interest in the	Foreign background
	Cultural predilections	environment	Low achievement orientation
	Interests	Intellectual ambitiousness	
		Intellectual curiosity	
		Urge to collect knowledge	
Vocabulary			
Verbal comprehension	Education	Good verbal comprehension	Poor verbal comprehension
Language development	Cultural opportunities	Good family or cultural	Limited educational or
Learning ability		background	family background
Fund of information		Good pre-schooling	Difficulty in verbalization
Richness of ideas		Good ability to	Foreign language
Memory		conceptualize	background
Concept formation		Intellectual striving	Verbalization not encouraged
Expressive ability			in culture
Verbal fluency			
Word knowledge			
Arithmetic			
Verbal comprehension	Opportunity to acquire	Facility in mental arithmetic	Inadequate ability in mental
Numerical reasoning ability	fundamental arithmetical	Good concentration	arithmetic
Mental computation	processes	Good ability to focus	Poor concentration
Application of basic		attention	Distractibility
arithmetical processes			Blocking toward
Concentration			mathematical tasks

(Table continues next page)

Table C-24 (cont.)

Ability[a]	Background factors	Possible implications of high scores	Possible implications of low scores
Attention Short-term memory Long-term memory Nonverbal reasoning ability Quantitative concepts			

		Similarities	
Verbal comprehension Logical thinking (items 1–10) Verbal concept formation (items 11–16) Abstract and concrete reasoning abilities Capacity for associative thinking (items 11–16) Ability to separate essential from nonessential details Long-term memory Reasoning by analogy	A minimum of cultural opportunities Interests	Good conceptual thinking (e.g., ability to select and verbalize appropriate relationships between two objects or concepts) Flexibility of thought processes	Poor conceptual thinking (e.g., difficulty in selecting and verbalizing appropriate relationships between two objects or concepts) Overly concrete mode of thinking Rigidity of thought processes Negativism

		Comprehension	
Verbal comprehension Social judgment Linguistic skill Logical reasoning Common sense Use of practical knowledge and judgment in social situations Knowledge of conventional standards of behavior Ability to evaluate past experience Moral and ethical judgment	Extensiveness of cultural opportunities Ability to evaluate and use past experience Development of conscience or moral sense	Good social judgment Knowledge of rules of conventional behavior Good ability to organize knowledge Social maturity Ability to verbalize well Wide experience	Poor social judgment Failure to take personal responsibility (e.g., overdependency, immaturity, limited involvement with others) Overly concrete thinking Difficulty in expressing ideas verbally

		Sentences	
Verbal comprehension Short-term memory Rote memory Immediate auditory memory Attention Concentration Auditory sequencing Verbal facility	Ability to passively receive stimuli	Good rote memory Good immediate recall ability Ability to attend well in a testing situation	Anxiety Inattention Distractibility Difficulty in auditory sequencing

(Table continues next page)

Table C-24 (cont.)

Ability[a]	*Background factors*	*Possible implications of high scores*	*Possible implications of low scores*
		Animal House	

Perceptual organization
Attention
Goal awareness
Concentration
Finger and manual dexterity
Learning ability
	Rate of motor activity	Visual-motor dexterity
		Good concentration
		Sustained energy or
		  persistence
		Ability to learn new material
		  associatively and
		  reproduce it with speed
		  and accuracy
		Good motivation or desire
		  for achievement
			Visual-motor coordination
			  difficulties
			Distractibility
			Visual defects
			Lethargy

		Picture Completion	

Perceptual organization
Ability to differentiate
  essential from
  nonessential details
Identification of familiar
  objects (visual
  recognition)
Concentration on visually
  perceived material
Alertness to detail
Reasoning
Visual organization
Visual perception (closure)
Visual long-term memory
	Experiences
	Alertness to environment
		Good perception and
		  concentration
		Good alertness to details
		Ability to establish a
		  learning set quickly
			Anxiety affecting
			  concentration and
			  attention
			Preoccupation with
			  irrelevant details
			Negativism ("nothing is
			  missing")

		Mazes	

Perceptual organization
Planning ability
Foresight
Visual-motor control
	Visual-motor organization	Good perceptual
		  organization
		Planning efficiency
		Speed and accuracy
		Good ability to follow
		  instructions
			Poor visual-motor
			  organization
			Poor planning efficiency
			Difficulty in delaying action

		Block Design	

Perceptual organization
Visual-motor coordination
Spatial visualization
Abstract conceptualizing
  ability
Analysis and synthesis
	Rate of motor activity
	Color vision
		Good visual-motor-spatial
		  integration
		Good conceptualizing ability
		Good analyzing and
		  synthesizing ability
		Speed and accuracy in sizing
		  up a problem
		Good hand-eye coordination
		Good nonverbal reasoning
		  ability
		Good trial-and-error
		  methods
			Poor visual-motor-spatial
			  integration
			Visual-perceptual problems

(Table continues next page)

Table C-24 (cont.)

Ability[a]	Background factors	Possible implications of high scores	Possible implications of low scores
Geometric Design			
Perceptual organization Perceptual-motor ability Visual-motor organization	Motor ability	Good perceptual-motor ability Good eye-hand coordination	Poor perceptual-motor ability Poor eye-hand coordination Developmental immaturity
Object Assembly			
Perceptual organization Visual-motor coordination Ability to synthesize concrete parts into meaningful wholes Spatial relations	Rate of motor activity Familiarity with figures Capacity to persist at a task Experience with part-whole relationships Working for an unknown goal	Good visual-motor coordination Good ability to visualize a whole from its parts Ability to perceive a whole, with critical understanding of the relationships of the individual parts Successful trial and error Experience in assembling puzzles Persistence	Visual-motor difficulties Visual-perceptual problems Poor planning ability Difficulty in perceiving a whole Minimal experience with construction tasks Limited interest in assembly tasks Limited persistence

Note. For each individual examinee, select the appropriate implication (or implications) listed in the columns only after careful consideration of the entire test protocol and background information.

[a] The first entry under "Ability" is based on factor analytic findings. The other entries in this column are derived from clinical and educational interpretations of the subtest functions.

Source: Adapted, in part, from Blatt and Allison (1968), Freeman (1962), Glasser and Zimmerman (1967), Herman (1968), Kaufman (1975a), Rapaport, Gill, and Schafer (1968), Searls (1975), and Wechsler (1967).

Table C-25
Confidence Intervals for WAIS-R Scales

Age level	Scale	Confidence level				
		68%	85%	90%	95%	99%
16–17	Verbal Scale IQ	± 3	± 5	± 5	± 7	± 9
	Performance Scale IQ	± 5	± 8	± 9	± 10	± 13
	Full Scale IQ	± 3	± 4	± 5	± 6	± 8
18–19	Verbal Scale IQ	± 3	± 4	± 5	± 6	± 7
	Performance Scale IQ	± 5	± 7	± 8	± 9	± 12
	Full Scale IQ	± 3	± 4	± 5	± 6	± 8
20–24	Verbal Scale IQ	± 3	± 4	± 5	± 6	± 8
	Performance Scale IQ	± 4	± 6	± 7	± 8	± 11
	Full Scale IQ	± 3	± 4	± 4	± 5	± 7
25–34	Verbal Scale IQ	± 3	± 4	± 4	± 5	± 7
	Performance Scale IQ	± 4	± 6	± 6	± 8	± 10
	Full Scale IQ	± 2	± 3	± 4	± 4	± 6
35–44	Verbal Scale IQ	± 3	± 4	± 4	± 5	± 7
	Performance Scale IQ	± 4	± 5	± 6	± 7	± 10
	Full Scale IQ	± 2	± 3	± 4	± 4	± 6
45–54	Verbal Scale IQ	± 3	± 4	± 4	± 5	± 7
	Performance Scale IQ	± 4	± 5	± 6	± 7	± 10
	Full Scale IQ	± 3	± 4	± 4	± 5	± 7
55–64	Verbal Scale IQ	± 3	± 4	± 4	± 5	± 7
	Performance Scale IQ	± 4	± 6	± 6	± 8	± 10
	Full Scale IQ	± 3	± 4	± 4	± 5	± 7
65–69	Verbal Scale IQ	± 3	± 4	± 4	± 5	± 7
	Performance Scale IQ	± 4	± 5	± 6	± 7	± 10
	Full Scale IQ	± 2	± 3	± 4	± 4	± 6
70–74	Verbal Scale IQ	± 3	± 4	± 4	± 5	± 6
	Performance Scale IQ	± 4	± 6	± 7	± 8	± 10
	Full Scale IQ	± 2	± 4	± 4	± 5	± 6
Average	Verbal Scale IQ	± 3	± 4	± 4	± 5	± 7
	Performance Scale IQ	± 4	± 6	± 7	± 8	± 10
	Full Scale IQ	± 3	± 4	± 4	± 5	± 7

Note. See the Note in Table C-1 in Appendix C for an explanation of the method used to arrive at the confidence intervals.

Table C-26
Significant Differences Between WAIS-R Scaled Scores, IQs, and Factor Scores at Ages 16 to 17 and for the Average of the Nine Age Groups (.05/.01 significance levels)

	I	D	V	A	C	S	PC	PA	BD	OA
Ages 16–17										
D	3/4									
V	2/3	3/4								
A	3/4	4/5	3/3							
C	3/4	4/5	2/3	3/4						
S	3/4	4/5	3/4	3/5	3/5					
PC	3/4	4/5	3/4	4/5	4/5	4/5				
PA	3/4	4/5	3/4	4/5	4/5	4/5	4/5			
BD	3/3	3/4	2/3	3/4	3/4	3/4	3/4	3/5		
OA	4/5	5/6	4/5	4/6	4/6	5/6	5/6	5/6	4/6	
DS	3/5	4/5	3/4	4/5	4/5	4/5	4/5	4/5	4/5	5/6

Ages 16–17 factor scores:

	VIQ		VCIQ	POIQ
PIQ	12/16	POIQ	13/17	
		FDIQ	14/18	17/22

	I	D	V	A	C	S	PC	PA	BD	OA
Average of 9 age groups										
D	3/4									
V	2/3	3/4								
A	3/4	3/4	3/3							
C	3/4	3/4	3/3	3/4						
S	3/4	3/5	3/4	3/4	3/4					
PC	3/4	3/5	3/4	3/4	3/4	3/5				
PA	3/4	4/5	3/4	4/5	4/5	4/5	4/5			
BD	3/3	3/4	2/3	3/4	3/4	3/4	3/4	3/4		
OA	4/5	4/5	3/4	4/5	4/5	4/5	4/5	4/5	4/5	
DS	3/4	4/5	3/4	3/4	3/5	3/5	3/5	4/5	3/4	4/5

Average of 9 age groups factor scores:

	VIQ		VCIQ[a]	POIQ[a]
PIQ	10/13	POIQ	11/14	
		FDIQ	11/15	13/17

Note. Abbreviations: I = Information; D = Digit Span; V = Vocabulary; A = Arithmetic; C = Comprehension; S = Similarities; PC = Picture Completion; PA = Picture Arrangement; BD = Block Design; OA = Object Assembly; DS = Digit Symbol; VIQ = Verbal IQ; PIQ = Performance IQ; VCIQ = Verbal Comprehension IQ; POIQ = Perceptual Organization IQ; FDIQ = Freedom from Distractibility IQ.

Sample reading: A difference of 3 points between scaled scores on the Information and Digit Span subtests is significant at the 5 percent level; a difference of 4 points is significant at the 1 percent level.

The values in this table for the subtest comparisons are overly liberal when more than one comparison is made for a subtest. They are more accurate when a priori planned comparisons are made, such as Information vs. Comprehension or Digit Span vs. Arithmetic.

See Chapter 8, Exhibit 8-1 for an explanation of the method used to arrive at magnitude of differences. See Table C-28 for a description of the factor scores.

[a] For ages 18–19, significant differences between the factor scores are as follows:

	VCIQ	POIQ
POIQ	12/16	
FDIQ	12/16	15/20

Table C-27
Differences Required for Significance When Each WAIS-R Age-Corrected Subtest Scaled Score Is Compared to the Mean Age-Corrected Scaled Score for Any Individual Examinee

Subtest	Mean of 6 Verbal Scale subtests .05	.01	Mean of 5 Performance Scale subtests .05	.01	Mean of 11 Full Scale subtests .05	.01
Information	2.33	2.78	—	—	2.59	3.07
Digit Span	2.91	3.47	—	—	3.31	3.92
Vocabulary	1.77	2.11	—	—	1.87	2.21
Arithmetic	2.73	3.26	—	—	3.09	3.66
Comprehension	2.85	3.40	—	—	3.24	3.84
Similarities	2.93	3.49	—	—	3.34	3.95
Picture Completion	—	—	2.92	3.49	3.36	3.98
Picture Arrangement	—	—	3.19	3.83	3.75	4.44
Block Design	—	—	2.47	2.96	2.71	3.21
Object Assembly	—	—	3.43	4.10	4.08	4.83
Digit Symbol	—	—	2.94	3.53	3.41	4.04

Note. Table C-27 shows the minimum deviations from an individual's mean subtest scaled score that are significant at the .05 and .01 levels. See the Note in Table C-3 for an explanation of how the deviations were obtained.

Table C-28
Estimated WAIS-R Deviation IQs for Verbal Comprehension, Perceptual Organization, and Freedom from Distractibility at Selected Ages and for the Average of Nine Age Groups Using Age-Corrected Scores

Sum of aged-scaled scores	Verbal Comprehension 16–17	Av.	Perceptual Organization 16–17	18–19	Av.	Freedom from Distractibility 16–17	Av.	Sum of aged-scaled scores	Verbal Comprehension 16–17	Av.	Perceptual Organization 16–17	18–19	Av.	Freedom from Distractibility 16–17	Av.
2	–	–	–	–	–	49	49	40	100	100	122	–	121	–	–
3	–	–	–	52	–	52	51	41	101	101	124	–	123	–	–
4	–	–	46	55	49	55	54	42	103	103	126	–	125	–	–
5	51	51	48	58	51	58	57	43	104	104	128	–	127	–	–
6	52	52	51	61	53	60	60	44	106	106	129	–	129	–	–
7	54	54	53	64	55	63	63	45	107	107	132	–	131	–	–
8	55	55	55	66	57	66	65	46	108	108	135	–	133	–	–
9	57	57	57	69	59	69	68	47	110	110	137	–	135	–	–
10	58	58	59	72	61	72	71	48	111	111	139	–	137	–	–
11	59	59	61	75	63	75	74	49	113	113	141	–	139	–	–
12	61	61	63	78	65	78	77	50	114	114	143	–	141	–	–
13	62	62	65	80	67	81	79	51	115	115	145	–	143	–	–
14	64	64	67	83	69	82	82	52	117	117	147	–	145	–	–
15	65	65	69	86	70	86	85	53	118	118	148	–	147	–	–

(Table continues next page)

Table C-28 (cont.)

16	66	66	72	89	73	89	88	54	120	120	151	—	149	—	—
17	68	68	74	92	75	92	91	55	121	121	153	—	151	—	—
18	69	69	76	94	77	95	93	56	122	122	156	—	153	—	—
19	71	71	78	97	79	98	96	57	124	124	—	—	—	—	—
20	72	72	80	100	81	101	99	58	125	125	—	—	—	—	—
21	73	73	82	103	83	104	102	59	127	127	—	—	—	—	—
22	75	75	84	106	85	107	105	60	128	128	—	—	—	—	—
23	76	76	86	108	87	110	107	61	129	129	—	—	—	—	—
24	78	78	88	111	89	113	110	62	131	131	—	—	—	—	—
25	79	79	90	114	90	115	113	63	132	132	—	—	—	—	—
26	80	80	93	117	93	118	116	64	134	134	—	—	—	—	—
27	82	82	95	120	95	121	119	65	135	135	—	—	—	—	—
28	83	83	97	122	97	124	121	66	136	136	—	—	—	—	—
29	85	85	99	125	99	127	124	67	138	138	—	—	—	—	—
30	86	86	101	128	101	130	127	68	139	139	—	—	—	—	—
31	87	87	103	131	103	133	130	69	141	141	—	—	—	—	—
32	89	89	105	134	105	136	133	70	142	142	—	—	—	—	—
33	90	90	107	136	107	137	135	71	143	143	—	—	—	—	—
34	92	92	109	139	109	142	138	72	145	145	—	—	—	—	—
35	93	93	111	142	110	144	141	73	146	146	—	—	—	—	—
36	94	94	114	145	113	147	144	74	148	148	—	—	—	—	—
37	96	96	116	148	115	150	147	75	149	149	—	—	—	—	—
38	97	97	118	150	117	153	149	76	150	150	—	—	—	—	—
39	99	99	120	—	119	—	—								

Note. Verbal Comprehension = Information, Vocabulary, Comprehension, Similarities; Perceptual Organization for all ages except 18–19 = Picture Completion, Block Design, Object Assembly; Perceptual Organization for ages 18–19 = Block Design and Object Assembly; Freedom from Distractibility = Digit Span, Arithmetic; Av. = Average of the nine age groups.

The formulas used to compute the Deviation Quotients, using age-corrected subtest scores, are as follows for ages 16–17:

Verbal Comprehension Deviation Quotient = $1.4 \times$ (Information, Vocabulary, Comprehension, Similarities) + 44
Perceptual Organization Deviation Quotient = $2.1 \times$ (Block Design, Object Assembly, Picture Completion) + 38
Freedom from Distractibility Deviation Quotient = $2.9 \times$ (Digit Span, Arithmetic) + 43

The formula used to compute the Deviation Quotient, using age-corrected subtest scores, is as follows for ages 18–19:

Perceptual Organization Deviation quotient = $2.8 \times$ (Block Design, Object Assembly) + 44

The formulas used to compute the Deviation Quotients, using age-corrected subtest scores, are as follows for the average of the nine age groups:

Verbal Comprehension Deviation Quotient = $1.4 \times$ (Information, Vocabulary, Comprehension, Similarities) + 44
Perceptual Organization Deviation Quotient = $2.0 \times$ (Block Design, Object Assembly, Picture Completion) + 41
Freedom from Distractibility Deviation Quotient = $2.8 \times$ (Digit Span, Arithmetic) + 43

The SE_m's for the three factors are as follows:

Verbal Comprehension: SE_m = 3.00 for ages 16–17 and SE_m = 3.00 for the average of the nine age groups.
Perceptual Organization: SE_m = 5.81 for ages 16–17 and SE_m = 4.74 for the average of the nine age groups.
Freedom from Distractibility: SE_m = 6.54 for ages 16–17 and SE_m = 4.97 for the average of the nine age groups.

Table C-29
Differences Required for Significance When Each WAIS-R Subtest Age-Corrected Scaled Score Is Compared to the Respective Mean Factor Age-Corrected Scaled Score for Any Individual Examinee

Subtest	Mean of Verbal Comprehension subtests[a]						Mean of Perceptual Organization subtests[b]						Mean of Freedom from Distractibility subtests[c]					
	Ages 16–17		Ages 18–19		Average		Ages 16–17		Ages 18–19		Average		Ages 16–17		Ages 18–19		Average	
	.05	.01	.05	.01	.05	.01	.05	.01	.05	.01	.05	.01	.05	.01	.05	.01	.05	.01
Information	1.94	2.34	1.92	2.31	2.09	2.52	—	—	—	—	—	—	—	—	—	—	—	—
Digit Span	—	—	—	—	—	—	—	—	—	—	—	—	2.10	2.63	2.05	2.57	1.88	2.36
Vocabulary	1.52	1.83	1.50	1.81	1.68	2.03	—	—	—	—	—	—	—	—	—	—	—	—
Arithmetic	—	—	—	—	—	—	—	—	—	—	—	—	2.10	2.63	2.05	2.57	1.88	2.36
Comprehension	2.40	2.90	2.37	2.86	2.48	3.00	—	—	—	—	—	—	—	—	—	—	—	—
Similarities	2.60	3.14	2.32	2.81	2.54	3.07	—	—	—	—	—	—	—	—	—	—	—	—
Picture Completion	—	—	—	—	—	—	2.85	3.50	—	—	2.47	3.03	—	—	—	—	—	—
Picture Arrangement	—	—	—	—	—	—	—	—	—	—	—	—	—	—	—	—	—	—
Block Design	—	—	—	—	—	—	2.45	3.01	2.05	2.58	2.22	2.73	—	—	—	—	—	—
Object Assembly	—	—	—	—	—	—	3.34	4.11	2.05	2.58	2.76	3.40	—	—	—	—	—	—
Digit Symbol	—	—	—	—	—	—	—	—	—	—	—	—	—	—	—	—	—	—

Note. Table C-29 shows the minimum deviations from an individual's mean factor scaled score that are significant at the .05 and .01 levels. See the Note in Table C-3 for an explanation of how differences were obtained. Bonferroni corrections were used.

[a] Verbal Comprehension subtests are Information, Vocabulary, Comprehension, and Similarities.

[b] Perceptual Organization subtests are Picture Completion, Block Design, and Object Assembly for ages 16–17 and average; subtests are Block Design and Object Assembly for ages 18–19.

[c] Freedom from Distractibility subtests are Arithmetic and Digit Span.

Table C-30
Extrapolated WAIS-R IQ Equivalents of Sums of Scaled Scores (Not Age-Corrected) for Verbal Scale, Performance Scale, and Full Scale

	Verbal Scale								
Sum of scaled scores	Age								
	16–17	18–19	20–24	25–34	35–44	45–54	55–64	65–69	70–74
110	172	169	163	161	162	163	163	165	166
109	171	168	162	160	161	162	162	163	165
108	170	166	161	159	160	161	161	162	164
107	169	165	160	158	159	160	160	161	162
106	168	164	159	157	158	159	159	160	161
105	167	163	158	156	157	158	158	159	160
104	166	162	157	154	155	157	157	158	159
103	164	161	155	153	154	155	156	157	158
102	163	160	154	152	153	154	155	156	157
101	162	159	153	151	152	153	154	155	156
100	161	157	152	—	151	152	153	154	155
99	160	156	151	—	—	151	152	153	154
98	159	155	—	—	—	—	151	152	153
97	158	154	—	—	—	—	—	151	152
96	156	153	—	—	—	—	—	—	151
95	155	152	—	—	—	—	—	—	—
94	154	151	—	—	—	—	—	—	—
93	153	—	—	—	—	—	—	—	—
92	152	—	—	—	—	—	—	—	—
91	151	—	—	—	—	—	—	—	—

	Performance Scale								
Sum of scaled scores	Age								
	16–17	18–19	20–24	25–34	35–44	45–54	55–64	65–69	70–74
90	167	163	157	159	162	165	173	184	192
89	165	162	155	158	160	164	172	182	190
88	164	161	154	157	159	162	170	181	189
87	163	159	153	155	158	161	169	179	187
86	161	158	151	154	156	160	168	178	186
85	160	156	—	153	155	159	166	176	184
84	158	155	—	151	154	157	165	175	183
83	157	154	—	—	153	156	164	174	181
82	156	152	—	—	151	155	162	172	180
81	154	151	—	—	—	153	161	171	178
80	153	—	—	—	—	152	160	169	177
79	152	—	—	—	—	151	158	168	175
78	—	—	—	—	—	—	157	166	173
77	—	—	—	—	—	—	156	165	172
76	—	—	—	—	—	—	154	163	170
75	—	—	—	—	—	—	153	162	169
74	—	—	—	—	—	—	152	160	167
73	—	—	—	—	—	—	—	159	166
72	—	—	—	—	—	—	—	158	164

(Table continues next page)

Table C-30 (cont.)

Performance Scale

Sum of scaled scores	Age								
	16–17	18–19	20–24	25–34	35–44	45–54	55–64	65–69	70–74
71	—	—	—	—	—	—	—	156	163
70	—	—	—	—	—	—	—	155	161
69	—	—	—	—	—	—	—	153	160
68	—	—	—	—	—	—	—	152	158
67	—	—	—	—	—	—	—	—	156
66	—	—	—	—	—	—	—	—	155
65	—	—	—	—	—	—	—	—	153
64	—	—	—	—	—	—	—	—	152

Full Scale

Sum of scaled scores	Age								
	16–17	18–19	20–24	25–34	35–44	45–54	55–64	65–69	70–74
200	174	172	166	165	167	169	173	178	183
199	174	171	165	165	166	168	172	178	183
198	173	171	165	164	166	168	171	177	182
197	172	170	164	163	165	167	171	176	181
196	172	169	163	163	164	167	170	176	181
195	171	169	163	162	164	166	169	175	180
194	170	168	162	161	163	165	169	174	179
193	169	167	162	161	163	165	168	174	179
192	169	167	161	160	162	164	167	173	178
191	168	166	160	160	161	163	167	172	177
190	167	165	160	159	161	163	166	172	176
189	167	165	159	158	160	162	166	171	176
188	166	164	158	158	159	161	165	170	175
187	165	163	158	157	159	161	164	170	174
186	165	163	157	156	158	160	164	169	174
185	164	162	156	156	157	159	163	168	173
184	163	161	156	155	157	159	162	167	172
183	163	161	155	154	156	158	162	167	172
182	162	160	154	154	156	158	161	166	171
181	161	159	154	153	155	157	160	165	170
180	161	159	153	152	154	156	160	165	169
179	160	158	152	152	154	156	159	164	169
178	159	157	152	151	153	155	158	163	168
177	159	157	151	150	152	154	158	163	167
176	158	156	150	—	152	154	157	162	167
175	157	155	—	—	151	153	156	161	166
174	157	155	—	—	150	152	156	161	165
173	156	154	—	—	—	152	155	160	165
172	155	153	—	—	—	151	154	159	164
171	155	153	—	—	—	150	154	159	163
170	154	152	—	—	—	—	153	158	162
169	153	151	—	—	—	—	152	157	162

(Table continues next page)

Table C-30 (cont.)

| | *Full Scale* | | | | | | | | |
| | | | | | *Age* | | | | |
Sum of scaled scores	*16–17*	*18–19*	*20–24*	*25–34*	*35–44*	*45–54*	*55–64*	*65–69*	*70–74*
168	153	151	–	–	–	–	152	157	161
167	152	–	–	–	–	–	151	156	160
166	151	–	–	–	–	–	150	155	160
165	151	–	–	–	–	–	–	155	159
164	–	–	–	–	–	–	–	154	158
163	–	–	–	–	–	–	–	153	158
162	–	–	–	–	–	–	–	153	157
161	–	–	–	–	–	–	–	152	156
160	–	–	–	–	–	–	–	151	155
159	–	–	–	–	–	–	–	150	155
158	–	–	–	–	–	–	–	–	154
157	–	–	–	–	–	–	–	–	153
156	–	–	–	–	–	–	–	–	153
155	–	–	–	–	–	–	–	–	152
154	–	–	–	–	–	–	–	–	151
153	–	–	–	–	–	–	–	–	151

Note. WAIS-R regression equations for the Verbal Scale are as follows:

16–17: Verbal Scale IQ = 47.0969 + 1.1386 (scaled score)
18–19: Verbal Scale IQ = 45.2039 + 1.1221 (scaled score)
20–24: Verbal Scale IQ = 43.4291 + 1.0879 (scaled score)
25–34: Verbal Scale IQ = 39.8336 + 1.1022 (scaled score)
35–44: Verbal Scale IQ = 42.9675 + 1.0816 (scaled score)
45–54: Verbal Scale IQ = 44.5330 + 1.0715 (scaled score)
55–64: Verbal Scale IQ = 45.5278 + 1.0723 (scaled score)
65–69: Verbal Scale IQ = 46.5225 + 1.0731 (scaled score)
70–74: Verbal Scale IQ = 47.5171 + 1.0739 (scaled score)

WAIS-R regression equations for the Performance Scale are as follows:

16–17: Performance Scale IQ = 41.8642 + 1.3888 (scaled score)
18–19: Performance Scale IQ = 41.0293 + 1.3581 (scaled score)
20–24: Performance Scale IQ = 40.4008 + 1.2911 (scaled score)
25–34: Performance Scale IQ = 43.4307 + 1.2857 (scaled score)
35–44: Performance Scale IQ = 47.5354 + 1.2666 (scaled score)
45–54: Performance Scale IQ = 50.5086 + 1.2709 (scaled score)
55–64: Performance Scale IQ = 52.1149 + 1.3432 (scaled score)
65–69: Performance Scale IQ = 52.4798 + 1.4589 (scaled score)
70–74: Performance Scale IQ = 53.0145 + 1.5437 (scaled score)

WAIS-R regression equations for the Full Scale are as follows:

16–17: Full Scale IQ = 38.7060 + .6776 (scaled score)
18–19: Full Scale IQ = 37.2474 + .6742 (scaled score)
20–24: Full Scale IQ = 36.0737 + .6500 (scaled score)
25–34: Full Scale IQ = 36.1322 + .6460 (scaled score)
35–44: Full Scale IQ = 39.6791 + .6366 (scaled score)
45–54: Full Scale IQ = 40.6129 + .6424 (scaled score)
55–64: Full Scale IQ = 41.9824 + .6536 (scaled score)
65–69: Full Scale IQ = 42.7008 + .6781 (scaled score)
70–74: Full Scale IQ = 43.4488 + .7000 (scaled score)

Table C-31
Estimates of the Differences Obtained by Various Percentages of the WAIS-R Standardization Sample When Each WAIS-R Age-Corrected Subtest Score Is Compared to the Mean Age-Corrected Scaled Score for Any Individual Examinee

Subtest	Verbal average				Performance average				Overall average			
	10%	5%	2%	1%	10%	5%	2%	1%	10%	5%	2%	1%
Information	2.6	3.1	3.7	4.0					3.0	3.5	4.2	4.7
Digit Span	3.6	4.3	5.1	5.7					3.8	4.5	5.3	5.9
Vocabulary	2.2	2.7	3.2	3.5					2.7	3.3	3.9	4.3
Arithmetic	3.0	3.6	4.3	4.7					3.2	3.8	4.5	5.0
Comprehension	2.7	3.3	3.9	4.3					3.1	3.7	4.3	4.8
Similarities	2.8	3.4	4.0	4.4					3.0	3.6	4.3	4.7
Picture Completion					3.1	3.7	4.4	4.8	3.4	4.1	4.8	5.3
Picture Arrangement					3.4	4.1	4.8	5.4	3.6	4.3	5.1	5.7
Block Design					2.9	3.5	4.1	4.5	3.3	3.9	4.7	5.2
Object Assembly					3.2	3.8	4.5	5.0	3.8	4.5	5.4	6.0
Digit Symbol					3.6	4.3	5.1	5.6	3.8	4.5	5.4	5.9

Source: Reprinted with permission of the publisher and author from A. B. Silverstein, "Pattern Analysis: The Question of Abnormality." *Journal of Consulting and Clinical Psychology*, 1984, *52*, p. 938. Copyright 1984 by the American Psychological Association.

Table C-32
Probability of Obtaining Designated Differences Between Individual WAIS-R Verbal and Performance IQs

Probability of obtaining given or greater discrepancy by chance	Age level									
	16–17	18–19	20–24	25–34	35–44	45–54	55–64	65–69	70–74	Av.[a]
.50	4.18	3.80	3.49	3.20	3.12	3.06	3.16	3.14	3.22	3.38
.25	7.06	6.43	5.89	5.42	5.28	5.18	5.35	5.31	5.45	5.71
.20	7.92	7.21	6.61	6.08	5.92	5.81	6.00	5.96	6.12	6.40
.10	10.13	9.23	8.46	7.77	7.57	7.43	7.68	7.62	7.83	8.19
.05	12.04	10.96	10.05	9.23	9.00	8.82	9.12	9.05	9.30	9.73
.02	14.31	13.03	11.94	10.97	10.69	10.49	10.84	10.76	11.05	11.57
.01	15.85	14.43	13.23	12.15	11.84	11.62	12.00	11.91	12.24	12.81
.001	20.27	18.46	16.92	15.54	15.15	14.86	15.35	15.24	15.65	16.38

Note. The table is entered in the column appropriate to the examinee's age. The discrepancy that is just less than the discrepancy obtained by the examinee is located. The entry in the same row, first column, gives the probability of obtaining a given or greater discrepancy by chance. For example, the hypothesis that a 16-year-old examinee obtained a Verbal-Performance discrepancy of 16 by chance can be rejected at the .01 level of significance. This table is two-tailed. See Chapter 8, Exhibit 8-1 for an explanation of the method used to arrive at magnitude of differences.
[a] Av. = Average of nine age groups.

Table C-33
Percentage of Cases in the WAIS-R Standardization Sample with Differences Between Verbal (V) and Performance (P) IQs of Different Magnitudes

WAIS-R Full Scale IQ	N	10 + Points			13 + Points			15 + Points			22 + Points		
		V > P	P > V	Total	V > P	P > V	Total	V > P	P > V	Total	V > P	P > V	Total
120 and above	177	26.0	21.5	47.5	20.3	14.1	34.5	15.8	9.6	25.4	6.2	3.4	9.6
110-119	312	24.4	20.2	44.6	17.9	13.5	31.4	14.1	10.6	24.7	4.2	2.6	6.7
90-109	924	19.5	21.4	40.9	11.4	14.1	25.4	8.3	10.8	19.2	3.6	3.7	7.3
80-89	302	11.6	16.2	27.8	7.6	9.3	16.9	4.3	5.3	9.6	0.7	0.7	1.3
79 and below	165	8.5	7.3	15.8	2.4	4.2	6.7	0.6	1.8	2.4	0.0	0.0	0.0
Total group	1880	18.7	19.1	37.8	11.9	12.3	24.3	8.7	9.0	17.7	3.1	2.7	5.8

Source: Reprinted with permission of the publisher and authors from J.D. Matarrazo and D. O. Herman, "Clinical Uses of the WAIS-R: Base Rates of Differences Between VIQ and PIQ in the WAIS-R Standardization Sample," in *Handbook of Intelligence: Theories, Measurements, and Applications*, edited by B. B. Wolman. New York: John Wiley, 1985, p. 923.

Table C-34
Validity Coefficients of Proposed WAIS-R Short Forms

Dyad		Triad				Tetrad					Pentad					
Short form	r	Short form			r	Short form				r	Short form					r
V	BD	.90	V	S	BD	.92	V	A	S	BD	.94	V	A	S	PC	BD	.95
V	A	.88	V	C	BD	.92	V	A	PC	BD	.93	V	A	C	PC	BD	.95
I	BD	.88	V	A	BD	.92	V	A	C	BD	.93	D	V	S	PC	BD	.95
V	PC	.88	I	V	BD	.92	V	S	PC	BD	.93	D	V	C	PC	BD	.95
C	BD	.87	I	S	BD	.92	V	C	PC	BD	.93	I	D	V	PC	BD	.94
V	S	.87	V	A	PC	.92	I	V	PC	BD	.93	I	V	A	PC	BD	.94
S	BD	.87	V	PC	BD	.92	D	V	S	BD	.93	I	D	S	PC	BD	.94
A	S	.87	I	C	BD	.91	I	A	S	BD	.93	I	D	C	PC	BD	.94
V	OA	.86	V	PA	BD	.91	V	A	S	PC	.93	V	A	S	BD	DS	.94
V	C	.86	V	A	S	.91	V	C	BD	DS	.93	V	A	S	PA	BD	.94

Note. Abbreviations: I = Information; D = Digit Span; V = Vocabulary; A = Arithmetic; C = Comprehension; S = Similarities; PC = Picture Completion; PA = Picture Arrangement; BD = Block Design; OA = Object Assembly; DS = Digit Symbol.

The following formula was used to compute the part-whole correlations:

$$r_c = \frac{\Sigma r_{hh} + \Sigma\Sigma r_{hj}}{\sqrt{n + 2\Sigma r_{ij}}\sqrt{k + 2\Sigma r_{gh}}}$$

where Σr_{hh} is the sum of the reliabilities of the k subtests, Σr_{hj} is the sum of the correlations between each of the k subtests and all the other subtests, n is the total number of the subtests, Σr_{ij} is the sum of the correlations between each of the n subtests, k is the number of subtests in the short form, and Σr_{gh} is the sum of the intercorrelations of the k subtests. The term $\sqrt{n + 2\Sigma r_{ij}}$ becomes a constant for all computations. The formula was applied to the average subtest intercorrelations for the nine age groups that composed the standardization sample ($N = 1880$) to determine the correlations with the Full Scale of all possible short forms of two, three, four, and five subtests. The average subtest intercorrelations are based on the 11 standard subtests.

Table C-35
Satz and Mogel's/Yudin's Abbreviated Procedure for the WAIS-R

Subtest	Items used	Multiply score by
Information	Every 3rd	3
Digit Span	All items	1
Vocabulary	Every 3rd	3
Arithmetic	Odd only	2
Comprehension	Odd only	2
Similarities	Odd only	2
Picture Completion	Every 3rd	3
Picture Arrangement	Odd only	2
Block Design	Odd only	2
Object Assembly	Odd only	2
Digit Symbol	All items	1

Table C-36
Constants for Converting Wechsler Composite Scores into Deviation Quotients

2 Subtests			3 Subtests			4 Subtests			5 Subtests		
Σr_{jk}	a	b	Σr_{jk}	a	b	Σr_{jk}	a	b	Σr_{jk}	a	b
.78–.92	2.6	48	2.16–2.58	1.8	46	3.95–4.85	1.4	44	6.96–8.83	1.1	45
.66–.77	2.7	46	1.79–2.15	1.9	43	3.21–3.94	1.5	40	5.50–6.95	1.2	40
.54–.65	2.8	44	1.48–1.78	2.0	40	2.60–3.20	1.6	36	4.36–5.49	1.3	35
.44–.53	2.9	42	1.21–1.47	2.1	37	2.09–2.59	1.7	32	3.45–4.35	1.4	30
.35–.43	3.0	40	.97–1.20	2.2	34	1.66–2.08	1.8	28	2.71–3.44	1.5	25
.26–.34	3.1	38	.77–.96	2.3	31	1.29–1.65	1.9	24	2.10–2.70	1.6	20
.19–.25	3.2	36	.59–.76	2.4	28	.98–1.28	2.0	20	1.59–2.09	1.7	15

Source: Reprinted by permission of the publisher and authors from A. Tellegen and P. F. Briggs, "Old Wine in New Skins: Grouping Wechsler Subtests into New Scales," *Journal of Consulting Psychology*, 1967, *31*, p. 504. Copyright 1967 by the American Psychological Association.

Table C-37
Estimated WISC-R, WPPSI, and WAIS-R Full Scale IQ Equivalents for Sum of Scaled Scores on Vocabulary and Block Design

Vocabulary plus Block Design scaled score[a]	Estimated WISC-R Full Scale IQ	Estimated WPPSI Full Scale IQ	Estimated WAIS-R Full Scale IQ		
			Age group		
			16–17 25–44 65–74	18–24	45–64
1	45	43	—	—	—
2	48	46	50	46	48
3	51	49	52	49	51
4	54	52	55	52	54
5	56	55	58	55	57
6	59	58	61	58	59
7	62	61	64	61	62
8	65	64	66	64	65
9	68	67	69	67	68
10	71	70	72	70	71
11	74	73	75	73	74
12	77	76	78	76	77
13	80	79	80	79	80
14	83	82	83	82	83
15	85	85	86	85	86
16	88	88	89	88	88
17	91	91	92	91	91
18	94	94	94	94	94
19	97	97	97	97	97
20	100	100	100	100	100
21	103	103	103	103	103
22	106	106	106	106	106
23	109	109	108	109	109
24	112	112	111	112	112
25	115	115	114	115	115
26	117	118	117	118	117
27	120	121	120	121	120
28	123	123	122	124	123
29	126	126	125	127	126
30	129	129	128	130	129
31	132	132	131	133	132
32	135	135	134	136	135
33	138	138	136	139	138
34	141	141	139	142	141
35	144	143	142	145	144
36	146	147	145	148	146
37	149	150	148	151	149
38	152	153	150	154	152
39	155	156	—	—	—
40	158	159	—	—	—

[a] Use age-corrected scaled scores for the WAIS-R.

Source: The estimated WAIS-R Full Scale IQ equivalents are reprinted with permission of the publisher and authors from B. H. Brooker and J. J. Cyr, "Tables for Clinicians to Use to Convert WAIS-R Short Forms," *Journal of Clinical Psychology*, 1986, *42*, p. 983. Copyright 1986 by the Clinical Psychology Publishing Company.

Table C-38
Estimated WAIS-R Full Scale IQ Equivalents of Sum of Age-Corrected Scores on Vocabulary, Block Design, and Information

Sum of age-scaled scores	Age group 16–17 25–54 65–74	18–24 55–64	Sum of age-scaled scores	Age group 16–17 25–54 65–74	18–24 55–64	Sum of age-scaled scores	Age group 16–17 25–54 65–74	18–24 55–64
3	49	46	22	85	84	40	119	120
4	51	48	23	87	86	41	121	122
5	53	50	24	89	88	42	123	124
6	54	52	25	91	90	43	125	126
7	56	54	26	92	92	44	127	128
8	58	56	27	94	94	45	129	130
9	60	58	28	96	96	46	130	132
10	62	60	29	98	98	47	132	134
11	64	62	30	100	100	48	134	136
12	66	64	31	102	102	49	136	138
13	68	66	32	104	104	50	138	140
14	70	68	33	106	106	51	140	142
15	72	70	34	108	108	52	142	144
16	73	72	35	110	110	53	144	146
17	75	74	36	111	112	54	146	148
18	77	76	37	113	114	55	148	150
19	79	78	38	115	116	56	149	152
20	81	80	39	117	118	57	151	154
21	83	82						

Source: Reprinted with permission of the publisher and authors from B. H. Brooker and J. J. Cyr, "Tables for Clinicians to Use to Convert WAIS-R Short Forms," *Journal of Clinical Psychology*, 1986, *42*, pp. 983–984. Copyright 1986 by the Clinical Psychology Publishing Company.

Table C-39
Estimated WAIS-R Full Scale IQ Equivalents of Sum of Age-Corrected Scores on Vocabulary, Block Design, Arithmetic, and Similarities

Sum of age-scaled scores	Age group 16–19 25–74	Age group 20–24	Sum of age-scaled scores	Age group 16–19 25–74	Age group 20–24	Sum of age-scaled scores	Age group 16–19 25–74	Age group 20–24
4	46	42	29	84	82	53	120	121
5	48	44	30	85	84	54	121	122
6	49	46	31	87	86	55	123	124
7	51	47	32	88	87	56	124	126
8	52	49	33	90	89	57	126	127
9	54	50	34	91	90	58	127	129
10	55	52	35	93	92	59	129	130
11	57	54	36	94	94	60	130	132
12	58	55	37	96	95	61	132	134
13	60	57	38	97	97	62	133	135
14	61	58	39	99	98	63	135	137
15	63	59	40	100	100	64	136	138
16	64	62	41	102	102	65	138	140
17	66	63	42	103	103	66	139	142
18	67	65	43	105	105	67	141	143
19	69	66	44	106	106	68	142	145
20	70	68	45	108	109	69	144	146
21	72	70	46	109	110	70	145	148
22	73	71	47	111	111	71	147	150
23	75	73	48	112	113	72	148	151
24	76	74	49	114	114	73	150	153
25	78	76	50	115	116	74	151	154
26	79	78	51	117	118	75	153	156
27	81	79	52	118	119	76	154	158
28	82	81						

Source: Reprinted with permission of the publisher and authors from B. H. Brooker and J. J. Cyr, "Tables for Clinicians to Use to Convert WAIS-R Short Forms," *Journal of Clinical Psychology*, 1986, *42*, pp. 984–985. Copyright 1986 by the Clinical Psychology Publishing Company.

Table C-40
Estimated WAIS-R Full Scale IQ Equivalents of Sum of Age-Corrected Scores on Information, Arithmetic, Picture Completion, and Block Design

Sum of four scaled scores	Estimated Full Scale IQ	Sum of four scaled scores	Estimated Full Scale IQ	Sum of four scaled scores	Estimated Full Scale IQ
4	51	29	85	54	118
5	52	30	86	55	119
6	54	31	88	56	121
7	55	32	89	57	122
8	56	33	90	58	123
9	58	34	92	59	125
10	59	35	93	60	126
11	61	36	95	61	128
12	62	37	96	62	129
13	63	38	97	63	130
14	65	39	98	64	132
15	66	40	99	65	133
16	67	41	100	66	134
17	69	42	102	67	136
18	70	43	103	68	137
19	71	44	104	69	138
20	73	45	106	70	140
21	74	46	107	71	141
22	76	47	108	72	142
23	77	48	110	73	144
24	78	49	111	74	145
25	80	50	113	75	147
26	81	51	114	76	148
27	82	52	115		
28	84	53	117		

Source: Reprinted with permission of the publisher and authors from C. R. Reynolds, V. L. Willson, and P. L. Clark, "A Four-Test Short Form of the WAIS-R for Clinical Screening," *Clinical Neuropsychology*, 1983, *5*, p. 114. Copyright 1983 by Melnic Press.

Table C-41
Percentile Ranks and Suggested Qualitative Descriptions for Scaled Scores on the Wechsler Scales

Scaled score	Percentile rank		Qualitative descriptions
19	99		Exceptional strength
			or
18	99		Very well developed
			or
17	99		Superior
		Strength or Above average	or
16	98		Excellent
15	95		Strength
			or
14	91		Well developed
			or
			Above average
13	84		or
			Good
12	75		
11	63		
10	50	Average	Average
9	37		
8	25		
7	16		Weakness
			or
			Poorly developed
6	9		or
			Below average
5	5		or
		Weakness or Below average	Poor
4	2		Exceptional weakness
			or
3	1		Very poorly developed
			or
2	1		Far below average
			or
1	1		Very poor

Table C-42
Interpretive Rationales, Implications of High and Low Scores, and Instructional Implications for Wechsler Scales and Factor Scores

Ability	Background factors	Possible implications of high-scores	Possible implications of low scores	Instructional implications
Full Scale				
General intelligence Scholastic aptitude Academic aptitude Readiness to master a school curriculum	Natural endowment Richness of early environment Extent of schooling Cultural opportunities Interests Rate of motor activity Persistence Visual-motor organization Alertness	Good general intelligence Good scholastic aptitude Readiness to master a school curriculum	Poor general intelligence Poor scholastic aptitude Not ready to master school curriculum	Focus on language development activities Focus on visual learning activities Develop concept formation skills Reinforce persistence
Verbal Scale or Verbal Comprehension Factor				
Verbal comprehension Application of verbal skills and information to the solution of new problems Verbal ability Ability to process verbal information Ability to think with words	Natural endowment Richness of early environment Extent of schooling Cultural opportunities Interests	Good verbal comprehension Good scholastic aptitude Possession of knowledge of the cultural milieu Good concept formation Readiness to master school curriculum Achievement orientation	Poor verbal comprehension Poor scholastic aptitude Inadequate understanding of the cultural milieu Poor concept formation Bilingual background Foreign background Not ready to master school curriculum Poor achievement orientation	Stress language development activities Use verbal enrichment activities Focus on current events Use exercises involving concept formation

(Table continues next page)

Table C-42 (cont.)

Ability	Background factors	Possible implications of high-scores	Possible implications of low scores	Instructional implications
Performance Scale or Perceptual Organization Factor				
Perceptual organization Ability to think in terms of visual images and manipulate them with fluency, flexibility, and relative speed Ability to interpret or organize visually perceived material against a time limit Nonverbal ability Ability to form relatively abstract concepts and relationships without the use of words	Natural endowment Rate of motor activity Persistence Visual-motor organization Alertness Cultural opportunities Interests	Good perceptual organization Good alertness to detail Good nonverbal reasoning ability Good persistence Good ability to work quickly and efficiently Good spatial ability	Poor perceptual organization Poor alertness to detail Poor nonverbal reasoning ability Limited persistence Poor ability to work quickly and efficiently Poor spatial ability	Focus on visual learning activities Focus on part-whole relationships Use spatial-visual tasks Encourage trial-and-error activities Reinforce persistence Focus on visual planning activities Improve scanning techniques
Freedom from Distractibility				
Ability to sustain attention Short-term memory Numerical ability Encoding ability Ability to use rehearsal strategies Ability to shift mental operations on symbolic material Ability to self-monitor	Natural endowment Ability to passively receive stimuli	Good ability to sustain attention Good short-term memory Good numerical ability Good encoding ability Good use of rehearsal strategies Good ability to shift mental operations on symbolic material Good ability to self-monitor	Difficulty in sustaining attention Distractibility Anxiety Short-term retention deficits Encoding difficulties Poor rehearsal strategies Difficulty in rapidly shifting mental operations on symbolic material Inadequate self-monitoring skills	Develop attention skills Develop concentration skills Focus on small, meaningful units of instruction

Source: The first column adapted, in part, from Cohen (1959) and Wallbrown (1979).

Table C-43
Suggested Remediation Activities for Combinations of Wechsler Subtests

Subtests	Ability	Activities
Information, Vocabulary, and Comprehension	General knowledge and verbal fluency	(1) Review basic concepts, such as days of the week, months, time, distances, and directions; (2) have children report major current events by referring to pictures and articles from magazines and newspapers; (3) teach similarities and differences of designs, topography, transportation, etc.; (4) have children make a scrapbook of pictures of animals, buildings, etc.; (5) introduce words, dictionary work, abstract words; (6) have children repeat simple stories; (7) have children explain how story characters are feeling and thinking.
Similarities and Vocabulary	Verbal conceptual	(1) Use show-and-tell games; (2) have children make a scrapbook of classifications, such as of animals, vehicles, and utensils; (3) have children match abstract concepts; (4) have children find commonality in dissimilar objects; (5) review basic concepts such as days of the week, months, time, directions, and distances.
Digit Span, Arithmetic, Picture Completion, and Picture Arrangement	Attention and concentration	(1) Have children arrange cards in a meaningful sequence; (2) have children learn telephone number, address, etc.; (3) use spelling word games; (4) use memory games; (5) have children learn days of week, months of year; (6) use mathematical word problems; (7) use dot-to-dot exercises; (8) have children describe details in pictures; (9) use tracing activities; (10) use Tinker Toys.
Block Design and Object Assembly	Spatial-visual	(1) Have children identify common objects and discuss details; (2) use guessing games involving description of a person, place, or thing; (3) have children match letters, shapes, numbers, etc.; (4) use jigsaw puzzles; (5) use block-building activities.
Coding, Digit Symbol, Block Design, Object Assembly, Animal House, and Mazes	Visual-motor	(1) Use paper-folding activities; (2) use finger-painting activities; (3) use dot-to-dot exercises; (4) use scissor-cutting exercises; (5) use sky-writing exercises; (6) have children string beads in patterns; (7) use pegboard designs; (8) use puzzles (large jigsaw pieces); (9) have children solve a maze; (10) have children follow a moving object with coordinated eye movements; (11) use tracing exercises (e.g., trace hand, geometric forms, and letters); (12) have children make large circles and lines on chalkboard; (13) have children copy from patterns; (14) have children draw from memory.

Table C-44
Confidence Intervals for the Stanford-Binet Intelligence Scale: Fourth Edition

Age level	Factor and Composite Score	68%	85%	90%	95%	99%
2 (2-0-0 through 2-11-15)	Verbal Comprehension Factor Score	± 4	± 6	± 6	± 8	± 10
	Nonverbal Reasoning/Visualization Factor Score	± 6	± 8	± 9	± 11	± 14
	Memory Factor Score	—	—	—	—	—
	Composite Score	± 4	± 5	± 6	± 7	± 9
3 (2-11-16 through 3-11-15)	Verbal Comprehension Factor Score	± 4	± 6	± 6	± 7	± 9
	Nonverbal Reasoning/Visualization Factor Score	± 4	± 6	± 6	± 8	± 10
	Memory Factor Score	—	—	—	—	—
	Composite Score	± 3	± 5	± 5	± 6	± 8
4 (3-11-16 through 4-11-15)	Verbal Comprehension Factor Score	± 4	± 5	± 6	± 7	± 9
	Nonverbal Reasoning/Visualization Factor Score	± 4	± 5	± 6	± 7	± 9
	Memory Factor Score	—	—	—	—	—
	Composite Score	± 3	± 4	± 5	± 5	± 7
5 (4-11-16 through 5-11-15)	Verbal Comprehension Factor Score	± 4	± 5	± 6	± 7	± 9
	Nonverbal Reasoning/Visualization Factor Score	± 3	± 5	± 5	± 6	± 8
	Memory Factor Score	—	—	—	—	—
	Composite Score	± 3	± 4	± 5	± 5	± 7
6 (5-11-16 through 6-11-15)	Verbal Comprehension Factor Score	± 5	± 7	± 7	± 9	± 12
	Nonverbal Reasoning/Visualization Factor Score	± 4	± 6	± 6	± 8	± 10
	Memory Factor Score	—	—	—	—	—
	Composite Score	± 3	± 5	± 5	± 6	± 8
7 (6-11-16 through 7-11-15)	Verbal Comprehension Factor Score	± 5	± 7	± 7	± 9	± 12
	Nonverbal Reasoning/Visualization Factor Score	± 4	± 6	± 7	± 8	± 11
	Memory Factor Score	± 6	± 9	± 10	± 12	± 15
	Composite Score	± 3	± 4	± 5	± 5	± 7
8 (7-11-16 through 8-11-15)	Verbal Comprehension Factor Score	± 5	± 7	± 7	± 9	± 12
	Nonverbal Reasoning/Visualization Factor Score	± 4	± 6	± 6	± 8	± 10
	Memory Factor Score	± 5	± 7	± 8	± 9	± 12
	Composite Score	± 3	± 4	± 5	± 5	± 7
9 (8-11-16 through 9-11-15)	Verbal Comprehension Factor Score	± 4	± 5	± 6	± 7	± 9
	Nonverbal Reasoning/Visualization Factor Score	± 4	± 6	± 6	± 8	± 10
	Memory Factor Score	± 5	± 8	± 9	± 10	± 14
	Composite Score	± 3	± 4	± 5	± 5	± 7
10 (9-11-16 through 10-11-15)	Verbal Comprehension Factor Score	± 4	± 5	± 6	± 7	± 9
	Nonverbal Reasoning/Visualization Factor Score	± 3	± 5	± 5	± 6	± 8
	Memory Factor Score	± 5	± 7	± 8	± 10	± 13
	Composite Score	± 2	± 3	± 4	± 5	± 6
11 (10-11-16 through 11-11-15)	Verbal Comprehension Factor Score	± 4	± 5	± 6	± 7	± 9
	Nonverbal Reasoning/Visualization Factor Score	± 3	± 5	± 5	± 6	± 8
	Memory Factor Score	± 4	± 5	± 6	± 7	± 9
	Composite Score	± 2	± 3	± 4	± 5	± 6
12 (11-11-16 through 12-11-15)	Verbal Comprehension Factor Score	± 3	± 5	± 5	± 6	± 8
	Nonverbal Reasoning/Visualization Factor Score	± 3	± 5	± 5	± 6	± 8
	Memory Factor Score	± 5	± 7	± 8	± 10	± 13
	Composite Score	± 2	± 3	± 4	± 5	± 6

(Table continues next page)

Table C-44 (cont.)

Age level	Factor and Composite Score	Confidence level				
		68%	85%	90%	95%	99%
13	Verbal Comprehension Factor Score	± 3	± 5	± 5	± 6	± 8
(12-11-16	Nonverbal Reasoning/Visualization Factor Score	± 3	± 4	± 5	± 5	± 7
through	Memory Factor Score	± 5	± 7	± 7	± 9	± 12
13-11-15)	Composite Score	± 2	± 2	± 3	± 3	± 4
14	Verbal Comprehension Factor Score	± 3	± 5	± 5	± 6	± 8
(13-11-16	Nonverbal Reasoning/Visualization Factor Score	± 3	± 5	± 5	± 6	± 8
through	Memory Factor Score	± 5	± 7	± 8	± 9	± 12
14-11-15)	Composite Score	± 2	± 2	± 4	± 5	± 6
15	Verbal Comprehension Factor Score	± 3	± 5	± 5	± 6	± 8
(14-11-16	Nonverbal Reasoning/Visualization Factor Score	± 3	± 4	± 5	± 5	± 7
through	Memory Factor Score	± 5	± 7	± 8	± 9	± 12
15-11-15)	Composite Score	± 2	± 2	± 4	± 5	± 6
16	Verbal Comprehension Factor Score	± 3	± 5	± 5	± 6	± 8
(15-11-16	Nonverbal Reasoning/Visualization Factor Score	± 3	± 4	± 5	± 5	± 7
through	Memory Factor Score	± 5	± 7	± 8	± 9	± 12
16-11-15)	Composite Score	± 2	± 2	± 4	± 5	± 6
17	Verbal Comprehension Factor Score	± 3	± 4	± 5	± 5	± 7
(16-11-16	Nonverbal Reasoning/Visualization Factor Score	± 3	± 4	± 5	± 5	± 7
through	Memory Factor Score	± 4	± 6	± 7	± 8	± 11
17-11-15)	Composite Score	± 2	± 2	± 3	± 3	± 4
18–23	Verbal Comprehension Factor Score	± 3	± 4	± 5	± 5	± 7
(17-11-16	Nonverbal Reasoning/Visualization Factor Score	± 2	± 3	± 4	± 4	± 6
through	Memory Factor Score	± 4	± 6	± 6	± 8	± 10
23-11-15)	Composite Score	± 2	± 2	± 3	± 3	± 4

Table C-45
Significant Differences Between Stanford-Binet Intelligence Scale: Fourth Edition
Subtest Scaled Scores (.05/.01 significance levels)

	V	C	A	VR	PA	CP	M	PF	Q	NS	EB	BM	MS	MD
C	8/10													
A	8/11	8/10												
VR	7/10	7/9	6/8											
PA	7/10	7/9	7/10	7/9										
CP	8/11	8/10	8/11	6/8	7/10									
M	8/10	8/10	8/10	7/9	7/9	8/10								
PF	7/9	7/9	7/9	6/8	6/8	7/9	6/8							
Q	8/10	8/10	8/10	7/10	7/9	8/10	7/10	7/9						
NS	8/10	8/10	8/10	7/9	7/9	8/10	7/9	6/8	7/10					
EB	7/8	7/10	7/10	7/9	7/9	6/8	7/9	6/8	7/10	7/9				
BM	8/11	8/11	8/11	7/10	7/10	8/11	8/10	7/9	8/10	8/10	7/10			
MS	8/10	7/9	8/10	7/9	7/9	8/10	7/9	6/8	7/10	7/9	7/9	8/10		
MD	9/11	8/11	8/11	8/11	8/10	9/11	8/11	8/10	8/11	8/11	8/11	9/11	8/11	
MO	10/13	10/13	10/13	9/12	9/12	10/13	10/13	9/12	10/13	10/13	9/12	10/13	10/13	10/14

Note. Abbreviations: V = Vocabulary; C = Comprehension; A = Absurdities; VR = Verbal Relations; PA = Pattern Analysis; CP = Copying; M = Matrices; PF = Paper Folding and Cutting; Q = Quantitative; NS = Number Series; EB = Equation Building; BM = Bead Memory; MS = Memory for Sentences; MD = Memory for Digits; MO = Memory for Objects.

Table C-46
Significant Differences Between Factor Scores on the Stanford-Binet Intelligence Scale: Fourth Edition (.05/.01 significance levels)

Factor scores	Age																				
	2	3	4	5	6	7	8	9	10	11	12	13	14	15	16	17	18-23
Verbal Comprehension vs. Nonverbal Reasoning/ Visualization	13/18	10/14	10/13	9/12	12/15	12/16	12/15	10/14	9/12	9/12	9/12	8/11	9/12	8/11	8/11	8/10	9/12
Verbal Comprehension vs. Memory	—	—	—	—	—	15/19	13/17	13/17	12/16	10/13	12/15	11/14	11/15	11/15	11/15	10/14	9/12
Nonverbal Reasoning/ Visualization vs. Memory	—	—	—	—	—	14/19	12/16	13/17	12/15	9/12	12/15	10/14	11/15	11/14	11/14	10/13	11/14

Note. See Table 11-8 for subtests comprising each factor.

861

Table C-47
Differences Required for Significance When Each Stanford-Binet Intelligence Scale: Fourth Edition Subtest Scaled Score Is Compared to the Respective Mean Factor Scaled Score for Any Individual Child

	Verbal Comprehension					
	2 through 7		8 through 14		15 through 18–23	
Subtest	.05	.01	.05	.01	.05	.01
Vocabulary	6.18	7.51	5.57	6.84	5.57	6.84
Comprehension	5.74	6.99	5.18	6.37	5.18	6.37
Absurdities	6.18	7.51	5.57	6.84	—	—
Memory for Sentences	5.74	6.99	—	—	—	—
Verbal Relations	—	—	—	—	5.26	6.46

	Nonverbal Reasoning/Visualization			
	2 through 11		12 through 18–23	
Subtest	.05	.01	.05	.01
Pattern Analysis	5.30	6.44	5.22	6.35
Copying	6.15	7.41	—	—
Quantitative	6.02	7.33	5.95	7.24
Bead Memory	6.15	7.41	6.10	7.42
Matrices	—	—	5.50	6.69

	Memory			
	7		8 through 18–23	
Subtest	.05	.01	.05	.01
Memory for Sentences	—	—	5.98	7.34
Memory for Digits	5.98	7.50	6.60	8.11
Memory for Objects	5.98	7.50	7.51	9.73

Note. See the Note in Table C-3 for an explanation of how differences were obtained.

Table C-48
Estimates of the Differences Obtained by Various Percentages of the Stanford-Binet Intelligence Scale: Fourth Edition Standardization Sample Between Each Subtest Score and an Average Subtest Score

| | Verbal Comprehension average | | | | | | | | | | | |
| | 2 through 7 | | | | 8 through 14 | | | | 15 through 18–23 | | | |
Subtest	10%	5%	2%	1%	10%	5%	2%	1%	10%	5%	2%	1%
Vocabulary	5.90	7.02	8.34	9.24	6.24	7.41	8.81	9.75	4.75	5.64	6.71	7.43
Comprehension	6.47	7.68	9.13	10.11	6.19	7.35	8.74	9.68	5.12	6.08	7.22	8.00
Absurdities	7.92	9.41	11.18	12.38	6.98	8.29	9.86	10.91	—	—	—	—
Verbal Relations	—	—	—	—	—	—	—	—	4.36	5.17	6.15	6.81
Memory for Sentences	7.92	9.41	11.18	12.38	—	—	—	—	—	—	—	—

| | Nonverbal Reasoning/Visualization average | | | | | | | |
| | 2 through 11 | | | | 12 through 18–23 | | | |
Subtest	10%	5%	2%	1%	10%	5%	2%	1%
Pattern Analysis	7.92	9.41	11.18	12.38	7.80	9.27	11.02	12.20
Copying	8.55	10.15	12.07	13.36	—	—	—	—
Quantitative	8.13	9.66	11.49	12.72	7.59	9.02	10.72	11.87
Bead Memory	8.13	9.66	11.49	12.72	7.80	9.27	11.02	12.20
Matrices	—	—	—	—	7.80	9.27	11.02	12.20

| | Memory average | | | | | | | | | | | |
| | 2 through 6 | | | | 7 | | | | 8 through 18–23 | | | |
Subtest	10%	5%	2%	1%	10%	5%	2%	1%	10%	5%	2%	1%
Memory for Digits	—	—	—	—	6.98	8.29	9.86	10.91	7.34	8.72	10.37	11.48
Memory for Objects	—	—	—	—	6.98	8.29	9.86	10.91	8.45	10.04	11.93	13.21
Memory for Sentences	—	—	—	—	—	—	—	—	7.52	8.94	10.62	11.76

Note. The following formula was used to compute the estimated differences (Silverstein, 1984):

$$SD_{Da} = 8\sqrt{1 + \bar{G} - 2\bar{T}_a}$$

where SD_{Da} is the standard deviation of the difference for subtest a; 8 is the standard deviation of the scaled scores on each of the subtests; $\bar{G}$ is the mean of all the elements in the matrix (including the diagonal); and $\bar{T}_a$ is the mean of the elements in row or column a of the matrix (again including the diagonal). This formula is applied to the matrix of subtest intercorrelations, with 1s in the main diagonal. SD_{Da} is multiplied by the respective z value to estimate how large a difference was obtained by 10, 5, 2, or 1 percent of the standardization sample.

Table C-49
Probability of Obtaining Designated Differences Between Stanford-Binet Intelligence Scale: Fourth Edition Factor Scores

Verbal Comprehension vs. Nonverbal Reasoning/Visualization

Probability of obtaining given or greater discrepancy by chance	\	\	\	\	\	Ages	\	\	\	\	\	\	\	\	\	\	\
	2	3	4	5	6	7	8	9	10	11	12	13	14	15	16	17	18-23
.50	4.62	3.61	3.44	3.26	4.07	4.22	4.07	3.61	3.26	3.26	3.08	2.88	3.08	2.88	2.88	2.67	3.26
.25	7.81	6.11	5.82	5.52	6.89	7.13	6.89	6.11	5.52	5.52	5.21	4.86	5.21	4.86	4.86	4.51	5.52
.20	8.76	6.85	6.53	6.19	7.73	8.00	7.73	6.85	6.19	6.19	5.84	5.46	5.84	5.46	5.46	5.06	6.19
.10	11.20	8.76	8.35	7.92	9.88	10.23	9.88	8.76	7.92	7.92	7.47	6.98	7.47	6.98	6.98	6.47	7.92
.05	13.31	10.41	9.92	9.41	11.74	12.15	11.74	10.41	9.41	9.41	8.88	8.29	8.88	8.29	8.29	7.68	9.41
.02	15.82	12.37	11.79	11.18	13.96	14.45	13.96	12.37	11.18	11.18	10.55	9.86	10.55	9.86	9.86	9.13	11.18
.01	17.52	13.70	13.05	12.38	15.45	16.00	15.45	13.70	12.38	12.38	11.69	10.91	11.69	10.91	10.91	10.11	12.38
.001	22.41	17.52	16.70	15.84	19.77	20.46	19.77	17.52	15.84	15.84	14.95	13.96	14.95	13.96	13.96	12.94	15.84

Verbal Comprehension vs. Memory

Probability	7	8	9	10	11	12	13	14	15	16	17	18-23
.50	5.11	4.49	4.35	4.22	3.44	4.07	3.77	3.92	3.92	3.92	3.61	3.26
.25	8.64	7.59	7.36	7.13	5.82	6.89	6.38	6.64	6.64	6.64	6.11	5.52
.20	9.69	8.51	8.26	8.00	6.53	7.73	7.16	7.44	7.44	7.44	6.85	6.19
.10	12.39	10.89	10.56	10.23	8.35	9.88	9.16	9.52	9.52	9.52	8.76	7.92
.05	14.72	12.94	12.54	12.15	9.92	11.74	10.88	11.31	11.31	11.31	10.41	9.41
.02	17.50	15.38	14.91	14.45	11.79	13.96	12.93	13.44	13.44	13.44	12.37	11.18
.01	19.38	17.03	16.50	16.00	13.05	15.45	14.32	14.89	14.89	14.89	13.70	12.38
.001	24.78	21.78	21.12	20.46	16.70	19.77	18.32	19.04	19.04	19.04	17.52	15.84

Nonverbal Reasoning/Visualization vs. Memory

Probability	7	8	9	10	11	12	13	14	15	16	17	18-23
.50	4.98	4.22	4.49	4.07	3.26	4.01	3.61	3.92	3.73	3.77	3.44	3.77
.25	8.43	7.13	7.59	6.89	5.52	6.79	6.11	6.64	6.31	6.37	5.82	6.37
.20	9.46	8.00	8.51	7.73	6.19	7.61	6.85	7.44	7.08	7.15	6.53	7.15
.10	12.09	10.23	10.89	9.88	7.92	9.74	8.76	9.52	9.06	9.14	8.35	9.14
.05	14.37	12.15	12.94	11.74	9.41	11.56	10.41	11.31	10.76	10.86	9.92	10.86
.02	17.08	14.45	15.38	13.96	11.18	13.75	12.37	13.44	12.79	12.91	11.79	12.91
.01	18.91	16.00	17.03	15.45	12.38	15.22	13.70	14.89	14.16	14.29	13.05	14.29
.001	24.19	20.46	21.78	19.77	15.84	19.47	17.52	19.04	18.12	18.28	16.70	18.28

Table C-50
Percentage of Population Obtaining Discrepancies Between Stanford-Binet Intelligence Scale: Fourth Edition Factor Scores

Percentage obtaining given or greater discrepancy in either direction	2	3	4	5	6	7	8	9	10	11	12	13	14	15	16	17	18–23	Mdn	Percentage obtaining given or greater discrepancy in a specific direction
																	Age level		
Verbal Comprehension vs. Nonverbal Reasoning/Visualization																			
50	10.66	9.73	8.29	8.14	9.73	9.11	8.70	9.23	7.54	7.69	7.85	7.54	7.38	8.70	7.54	7.85	7.38	8.14	25
25	18.03	16.46	14.02	13.77	16.46	15.40	14.72	15.62	12.75	13.01	13.27	12.75	12.48	14.72	12.75	13.27	12.48	13.77	12.5
20	20.23	18.46	15.73	15.44	18.46	17.27	16.51	17.52	14.31	14.59	14.89	14.31	14.00	16.51	14.31	14.89	14.00	15.44	10
10	25.87	23.61	20.11	19.75	23.61	22.09	21.12	22.41	18.30	18.66	19.04	18.30	17.90	21.12	18.30	19.04	17.90	19.75	5
5	30.73	28.05	23.89	23.46	28.05	26.24	25.09	26.62	21.74	22.17	22.62	21.74	21.27	25.09	21.74	22.62	21.27	23.46	2.5
2	36.53	33.34	28.40	27.89	33.34	31.20	29.82	31.64	25.84	26.35	26.89	25.84	25.28	29.82	25.84	26.89	25.28	27.89	1
1	40.45	36.92	31.45	30.88	36.92	34.55	33.02	35.04	28.61	29.18	29.77	28.61	27.99	33.02	28.61	29.77	27.99	30.88	.5
.1	51.74	47.22	40.23	39.50	47.22	44.19	42.24	44.81	36.60	37.32	38.08	36.60	35.81	42.24	36.60	38.08	35.81	39.50	.05
Verbal Comprehension vs. Memory																			
50						10.88	9.73	10.44	9.85	8.70	9.11	8.43	8.70	9.73	10.09	8.00	8.84	9.42	25
25						18.40	16.46	17.65	16.66	14.72	15.40	14.25	14.72	16.46	17.07	13.52	14.95	15.93	12.5
20						20.64	18.46	19.80	18.69	16.51	17.27	15.98	16.51	18.46	19.14	15.17	16.77	17.87	10
10						26.40	23.61	25.33	23.91	21.12	22.09	20.44	21.12	23.61	24.49	19.40	21.45	22.85	5
5						31.36	28.05	30.09	28.40	25.09	26.24	24.28	25.09	28.05	29.09	23.05	25.48	27.15	2.5
2						37.28	33.34	35.77	33.76	29.82	31.20	28.87	29.82	33.34	34.58	27.40	30.29	32.27	1
1						41.28	36.92	39.60	37.38	33.02	34.55	31.97	33.02	36.92	38.29	30.34	33.54	35.74	.5
.1						52.80	47.22	50.66	47.82	42.24	44.19	40.89	42.24	47.22	48.97	38.81	42.90	45.71	.05
Nonverbal Reasoning vs. Memory																			
50						11.41	9.73	10.55	9.67	8.14	8.70	8.43	8.70	9.23	8.97	8.84	8.14	8.91	25
25						19.30	16.46	17.84	16.86	13.77	14.72	14.25	14.72	15.62	15.17	14.95	13.77	15.06	12.5
20						21.65	18.46	20.01	18.91	15.44	16.51	15.98	16.51	17.52	17.02	16.77	15.44	16.90	10
10						27.69	23.61	25.59	24.19	19.75	21.12	20.44	21.12	22.41	21.76	21.45	19.75	21.61	5
5						32.89	28.05	30.40	28.73	23.46	25.09	24.28	25.09	26.62	25.85	25.48	23.46	25.67	2.5
2						39.10	33.34	36.14	34.16	27.89	29.82	28.87	29.82	31.64	30.73	30.29	27.89	30.51	1
1						43.29	36.92	40.01	37.82	30.88	33.02	31.97	33.02	35.04	34.03	33.54	30.88	33.79	.5
.1						55.37	47.22	51.18	48.38	39.50	42.24	40.89	42.24	44.81	43.53	42.90	39.50	43.22	.05

Note. Table C-50 is entered in the column appropriate to the examinee's age. The discrepancy that is just less than the discrepancy obtained by the examinee is located. The entry in the same row, first column, gives the percentage of the standardization population obtaining discrepancies as large as or larger than the located discrepancy. For example, a 2-year-old examinee with a Verbal Comprehension–Nonverbal Reasoning/Visualization discrepancy of 30 in either direction in the Stanford-Binet Intelligence Scale: Fourth Edition will be found in between 5 and 10 percent of the standardization population.

Table C-51
Ranges of Standard Scores on the Stanford-Binet Intelligence Scale: Fourth Edition for Subtests, Short Forms, Factor Scores, and Composite Score

Age

Subtests, Short Forms, Factor Scores, and Composite Score	2-0-0 L	2-0-0 H	2-3-16 L	2-3-16 H	2-7-16 L	2-7-16 H	2-11-16 L	2-11-16 H	3-3-16 L	3-3-16 H	3-7-16 L	3-7-16 H	3-11-16 L	3-11-16 H	4-3-16 L	4-3-16 H	4-7-16 L	4-7-16 H	4-11-16 L	4-11-16 H	5-3-16 L	5-3-16 H	5-7-16 L	5-7-16 H	5-11-16 L	5-11-16 H	6-5-16 L	6-5-16 H	6-11-16 L	6-11-16 H
Vocabulary	42	82	40	82	38	82	35	82	33	82	32	82	30	82	29	82	28	82	28	82	27	82	26	82	25	82	24	82	23	82
Comprehension	40	82	38	82	36	82	34	82	32	82	31	82	30	82	29	82	29	82	28	82	28	82	27	82	26	82	25	82	24	82
Absurdities	49	82	46	82	43	82	40	82	37	82	36	82	34	82	33	82	32	82	31	82	30	82	29	82	27	82	25	82	22	82
Verbal Relations	–	–	–	–	–	–	–	–	–	–	–	–	–	–	–	–	–	–	–	–	–	–	–	–	–	–	–	–	–	–
Pattern Analysis	44	82	41	82	38	82	36	82	33	82	31	82	30	82	28	82	27	82	26	82	25	82	24	82	23	82	23	82	22	82
Copying	48	82	45	82	42	82	40	82	37	82	35	82	33	82	31	82	30	82	29	82	28	82	27	82	26	82	24	80	23	77
Matrices	–	–	–	–	–	–	–	–	–	–	–	–	–	–	–	–	–	–	–	–	–	–	–	–	–	–	–	–	45	82
Paper Folding & Cutting	–	–	–	–	–	–	–	–	–	–	–	–	–	–	–	–	–	–	–	–	–	–	–	–	–	–	–	–	–	–
Quantitative	52	82	50	82	47	82	45	82	42	82	40	82	38	82	36	82	34	82	32	82	30	82	29	82	28	82	27	82	25	82
Number Series	–	–	–	–	–	–	–	–	–	–	–	–	–	–	–	–	–	–	–	–	–	–	–	–	–	–	–	–	46	82
Equation Building	–	–	–	–	–	–	–	–	–	–	–	–	–	–	–	–	–	–	–	–	–	–	–	–	–	–	–	–	–	–
Bead Memory	53	82	50	82	46	82	43	82	39	82	36	82	34	82	31	82	30	82	29	82	28	82	27	82	26	82	25	82	24	82
Memory for Sentences	48	82	45	82	42	82	40	82	37	82	34	82	32	82	29	82	28	82	28	82	27	82	26	82	25	82	24	82	23	82
Memory for Digits	–	–	–	–	–	–	–	–	–	–	–	–	–	–	–	–	–	–	–	–	–	–	–	–	–	–	–	–	37	82
Memory for Objects	–	–	–	–	–	–	–	–	–	–	–	–	–	–	–	–	–	–	–	–	–	–	–	–	–	–	–	–	38	82
Two Subtest Short Form	84	164	79	164	73	164	68	164	62	164	59	164	55	164	52	164	50	164	49	164	46	164	44	164	42	164	41	164	39	164
Four Subtest Short Form	94	164	89	164	81	164	75	164	68	164	64	164	59	164	55	164	52	164	49	164	46	164	44	164	41	164	40	164	37	164
Six Subtest Short Form	92	164	86	164	78	164	72	164	65	164	60	164	56	164	51	164	48	164	46	164	43	164	40	164	38	164	36	164	36	164
Verbal Comprehension	90	164	83	164	77	164	71	164	65	164	60	164	56	164	51	164	50	164	49	164	47	164	44	164	41	164	39	164	36	164
Nonverbal Reasoning/Visualization	100	164	94	164	86	164	80	164	72	164	66	164	61	164	56	164	53	164	49	164	46	164	44	164	41	164	39	164	36	164
Memory	–	–	–	–	–	–	–	–	–	–	–	–	–	–	–	–	–	–	–	–	–	–	–	–	–	–	–	–	71	164
Composite – Factor	95	164	87	164	80	164	73	164	66	164	60	164	55	164	50	164	47	164	44	164	41	164	39	164	36	164	36	164	36	164
Composite – Full	95	164	87	164	80	164	73	164	66	164	60	164	55	164	50	164	47	164	44	164	41	164	39	164	36	164	36	164	43	164

(Table continues next page)

Table C-51 (cont.)

Subtests, Short Forms, Factor Scores, and Composite Score	7-5-16 L	7-5-16 H	7-11-16 L	7-11-16 H	8-5-16 L	8-5-16 H	8-11-16 L	8-11-16 H	9-5-16 L	9-5-16 H	9-11-16 L	9-11-16 H	10-5-16 L	10-5-16 H	10-11-16 L	10-11-16 H	11-11-16 L	11-11-16 H	12-11-16 L	12-11-16 H	13-11-16 L	13-11-16 H	14-11-16 L	14-11-16 H	15-11-16 L	15-11-16 H	16-11-16 L	16-11-16 H	17-11-16 L	17-11-16 H
Vocabulary	22	82	21	82	21	82	20	82	20	82	19	82	19	82	18	82	18	82	18	82	18	82	18	82	18	80	18	77	18	72
Comprehension	23	82	22	82	21	82	20	82	19	82	18	82	18	81	18	75	18	75	18	73	18	72	18	69	18	65	18	63	18	60
Absurdities	20	82	18	80	18	79	18	77	18	75	18	74	18	72	18	66	18	66	18	63	18	60	18	58	18	55	18	52	—	—
Verbal Relations	—	—	—	—	—	—	—	—	—	—	—	—	—	—	45	78	45	78	44	76	41	73	39	70	38	68	38	67	38	66
Pattern Analysis	21	81	20	79	19	77	19	74	18	71	18	68	18	66	18	63	18	63	18	61	18	59	18	57	18	57	18	57	18	57
Copying	22	74	22	73	21	71	21	69	21	67	20	64	19	62	18	57	18	57	18	55	—	—	—	—	—	—	—	—	—	—
Matrices	43	82	41	82	39	82	37	82	36	82	34	82	33	82	32	80	30	78	29	76	28	75	27	74	26	73	25	71	24	68
Paper Folding & Cutting	—	—	—	—	—	—	—	—	—	—	—	—	—	—	—	—	47	78	45	75	43	70	42	67	41	66	40	65	40	65
Quantitative	24	82	22	82	21	82	20	82	20	82	19	82	18	82	18	78	18	78	18	76	18	75	18	74	18	71	18	69	18	66
Number Series	45	82	44	82	42	82	40	82	39	82	37	82	36	81	35	75	33	75	32	70	31	68	31	67	30	66	29	65	28	64
Equation Building	—	—	—	—	—	—	—	—	—	—	—	—	—	—	47	82	47	82	46	82	44	80	43	80	41	78	41	78	39	76
Bead Memory	23	82	22	82	21	82	20	82	19	82	18	82	18	82	18	82	18	82	18	82	18	82	18	82	18	80	18	76	18	76
Memory for Sentences	22	82	21	82	21	82	20	82	20	82	20	82	20	82	18	82	18	82	18	82	18	82	18	82	18	82	18	80	18	76
Memory for Digits	36	82	35	82	34	82	34	82	33	82	32	82	32	82	31	82	30	82	29	80	28	79	27	77	26	75	26	72	25	71
Memory for Objects	38	82	37	82	37	82	35	82	35	81	33	80	33	78	32	72	31	72	30	72	29	71	28	70	28	70	28	69	27	69
Two Subtest Short Form	36	164	36	164	36	164	36	163	36	159	36	154	36	152	36	150	36	149	36	147	36	144	36	142	36	140	36	137	36	131
Four Subtest Short Form	36	164	36	164	36	164	36	164	36	164	36	164	36	164	36	160	36	160	36	157	36	156	36	154	36	150	36	145	36	140
Six Subtest Short Form	36	164	36	164	36	164	36	164	36	164	36	164	36	164	36	159	36	159	36	156	36	154	36	152	36	148	36	145	36	142
Verbal Comprehension	36	164	36	164	36	164	36	164	36	164	36	164	36	164	36	155	36	155	36	152	36	149	43	154	42	148	42	143	42	136
Nonverbal Reasoning/ Visualization	36	164	36	164	36	164	36	164	36	164	36	164	36	160	36	162	36	162	36	159	36	157	36	155	36	151	36	145	36	142
Memory	70	164	53	164	52	164	49	164	48	164	46	164	46	164	43	164	41	164	39	164	38	164	36	164	36	164	36	159	36	155
Composite—Factor	36	164	36	164	36	164	36	164	36	164	36	164	36	164	36	163	36	163	36	160	36	157	36	157	36	153	36	150	36	145
Composite—Full	39	164	37	164	36	164	36	164	36	164	36	164	36	164	36	164	38	164	37	163	38	159	38	160	37	157	36	159	36	149

Note. Standard scores for subtests are based on $M = 50$, $SD = 8$. Standard scores for short forms and composites are based on $M = 100$, $SD = 16$. Short forms are composed of the following subtests:

(a) 2 subtest short form: Vocabulary and Pattern Analysis

(b) 4 subtest short form: Vocabulary, Pattern Analysis, Quantitative, and Bead Memory

(c) 6 subtest short form: Vocabulary, Comprehension, Pattern Analysis, Quantitative, Bead Memory, and Memory for Sentences

Composite—Factor refers to composite based on factor scores; Composite—Full refers to composite score based on full battery, using nonextrapolated scores. See Table 11-8 for the subtests that comprise the factor scores.

Table C-52
Interpretive Rationales, Implications of High and Low Scores, and Instructional Implications for Stanford-Binet Intelligence Scale: Fourth Edition Subtests

Ability	Background factors	Possible implications of high scores	Possible implications of low scores	Instructional implications
Vocabulary				
Verbal retrieval Word-finding ability Recall and verbal identification by recognition of familiar objects (PV) Perceptions (PV) Verbal comprehension Language development Learning ability Fund of information Richness of ideas Memory Concept formation Long-term memory	Language stimulation Environmental stimulation Alertness to environment Educational experiences Interests	Good word knowledge Good verbal comprehension Good verbal skills and language development Good family or cultural background Good schooling Good ability to conceptualize Intellectual striving	Poor word knowledge Poor verbal comprehension Poor verbal skills and language development Limited educational or family background Difficulty in verbalization Foreign language background Verbalization not encouraged in culture	Develop a working vocabulary Encourage child to discuss experiences, ask questions, and make a dictionary Use other verbal enrichment exercises, including Scrabble, analogy, and other word games
Comprehension				
Verbal comprehension Social judgment Common sense Use of practical knowledge and judgment in social situations Knowledge of conventional standards of behavior Ability to evaluate past experience Moral and ethical judgment Reasoning Ability to evaluate situations and give a pertinent response	Extensiveness of cultural opportunities Ability to evaluate and use past experience Development of conscience or moral sense	Good social judgment and common sense Good ability to recognize social demands when practical judgment and common sense are necessary Knowledge of rules of conventional behavior Good ability to organize knowledge Social maturity Good ability to verbalize well Wide experience	Poor social judgment Failure to take personal responsibility (e.g., overdependency, immaturity, limited involvement with others) Overly concrete thinking Difficulty in expressing ideas verbally Creative individual looking for unusual solutions	Help child understand social mores, customs, and societal activities, such as how other children react to things, how the government works, and how banks operate Discuss the actions of others to help children develop an awareness of social relationships and what is expected of them in terms of the behavior of others Role-play situations, such as reporting fires, calling police, and obtaining help for plumbing problems

(Table continues next page)

Table C-52 (cont.)

Ability	Background factors	Possible implications of high scores	Possible implications of low scores	Instructional implications
Absurdities				
Verbal comprehension Social intelligence Ability to isolate incongruities and absurdities in visual material Attention Concentration	Richness of early environment Interests Cultural opportunities	Good verbal comprehension Good ability to isolate incongruities and absurdities in visual material Good attention Good social intelligence	Poor verbal comprehension Poor ability to isolate incongruities and absurdities in visual material Distractibility Poor concentration Poor social intelligence	Emphasize how things are organized Focus on visual learning techniques stressing cause-and-effect relationships
Verbal Relations				
Verbal comprehension Verbal concept formation Conceptual thinking Abstract and concrete reasoning abilities Capacity for associative thinking Ability to separate essential from nonessential details Long-term memory Verbal reasoning Classification Flexible thinking Ability to view facts from various angles at the same time and coordinate the multiple relationships involved Ability to test and discard hypothetical situations Flexibility and factual knowledge Ability to discriminate on an abstract or ideational level Verbally mediated abstract thinking Receptive and expressive vocabulary General fund of information Verbal retrieval and word-finding ability	Cognitive response style (reflective/ impulsive) Concentration Cognitive flexibility Tolerance for frustration Cultural opportunities Extent of reading Language stimulation Environmental stimulation Educational experiences Interests	Good conceptual thinking Good ability to see relationships Good ability to use logical and abstract thinking Good ability to discriminate fundamental from superficial relationships Good ability to select and verbalize appropriate relationships between two objects or concepts Flexibility of thought processes Good verbal reasoning	Poor conceptual thinking Difficulty in seeing relationships Difficulty in selecting and verbalizing appropriate relationships between two objects or concepts Overly concrete mode of thinking Rigidity of thought processes Negativism Poor verbal reasoning	Focus on recognition of differences and likenesses in shapes, textures, and daily surroundings Stress language development, synonyms and antonyms, and exercises involving abstract words, classifications, and generalizations

(Table continues next page)

Table C-52 (cont.)

Ability	Background factors	Possible implications of high scores	Possible implications of low scores	Instructional implications
Pattern Analysis				
Nonverbal reasoning Visual-motor coordination Visual-spatial ability Abstract conceptualization ability Analysis and synthesis Visual discrimination Visual imagery Visual processing Nonverbal conceptual ability	Attention Concentration Cognitive style Problem-solving strategies Anxiety	Good visual-motor-spatial integration Good conceptualizing ability Good spatial orientation in conjunction with speed, accuracy, and persistence Good analyzing and synthesizing ability Speed and accuracy in sizing up a problem Good eye-hand coordination Good nonverbal reasoning ability Good trial-and-error methods	Poor visual-motor-spatial integration Visual-perceptual problems Poor spatial orientation	Use puzzles, blocks, spatial-visual tasks, perceptual tasks involving breaking down an object and building it up again, and art work with geometric forms and flannel board Focus on part-to-whole relationships and working with a model or key
Copying				
Visual-motor ability Eye-hand coordination Fine motor coordination Perceptual discrimination Integration of perceptual and motor processes	Motor ability Experiences	Good visual-motor ability Good eye-hand coordination Good fine motor coordination Good perceptual discrimination Good integration of perceptual and motor processes Good maturation	Poor visual-motor ability Poor eye-hand coordination Poor fine motor coordination Poor perceptual discrmination Poor integration of perceptual and motor processes Maturational delay	Use pencils and crayons to develop fine motor skills Use tracing activities with a variety of shapes and designs
Matrices				
Perceptual reasoning ability Analogic reasoning Attention to visual detail Concentration Simultaneous processing	Experience with part-whole relationships Willingness to respond when uncertain	Good perceptual ability Good analogic reasoning ability Good attention to visual detail Good concentration	Poor perceptual ability Difficulty with analogic reasoning Poor attention to visual detail Poor concentration	Focus on part-whole relations Develop understanding of sequencing and ordering of events Use patterns to demonstrate how component parts are related

(Table continues next page)

Table C-52 (cont.)

Ability	Background factors	Possible implications of high scores	Possible implications of low scores	Instructional implications
Paper Folding and Cutting				
Perceptual organization Visualization Spatial ability Visual-spatial ability Attention to visual cues	Familiarity with figures	Good visualization Good spatial orientation Good conceptualizing ability	Poor visualization Poor spatial orientation Poor conceptualizing ability	Develop visualization skills through use of blocks, geometric figures, and other forms Focus on analyzing how objects are viewed from various perspectives Work with paper cuttings, analyzing how forms look when unfolded
Quantitative				
Numerical reasoning ability Mental computation Application of basic arithmetical processes Concentration Attention Short-term memory Long-term memory Perception Understanding of mathematical concepts, symbols, and vocabulary Acquired knowledge General fund of information	Educational experiences Environmental stimulation Alertness to environment Interests Opportunities to acquire fundamental arithmetical processes	Facility in mental arithmetic Good ability to apply reasoning skills in the solution of mathematical problems Good ability to apply arithmetical skills in personal and social problem-solving situations Good concentration Good ability to focus attention Good ability to engage in complex thought patterns (for upper-level items, particularly) Teacher-oriented student	Inadequate ability in mental arithmetic Poor concentration Distractibility Anxiety over a school-like task Blocking toward mathematical tasks Poor school achievement (perhaps associated with rebellion against authority or with cultural background) Anxiety (e.g., worry over personal problems)	Develop arithmetical skills Develop concentration skills Use concrete objects to introduce concepts Drill in basic arithmetical skills Develop interesting "real" problems to solve
Number Series				
Numerical reasoning Logical reasoning Concentration	Education Cultural opportunities	Good numerical reasoning ability Good logical reasoning ability Good concentration	Poor numerical reasoning ability Poor logical reasoning ability Poor concentration	Develop logical reasoning skills

(Table continues next page)

Table C-52 (cont.)

Ability	Background factors	Possible implications of high scores	Possible implications of low scores	Instructional implications
Equation Building				
Knowledge of numbers Knowledge of conventional arithmetical operations Flexibility in rearranging and manipulating materials Numerical reasoning Logical reasoning Application of basic arithmetical processes Concentration Willingness to engage in trial and error	Education Cultural opportunities	Good knowledge of numbers Good knowledge of conventional arithmetical operations Good ability to rearrange and manipulate arithmetical materials Good numerical reasoning ability Good logical reasoning ability Good concentration	Poor knowledge of numbers Poor knowledge of conventional arithmetical operations Poor ability to rearrange and manipulate arithmetical materials Poor numerical reasoning ability Poor logical reasoning ability Poor concentration	Develop number skills Help child understand basic arithmetical operations Stress relationship between numbers Use a weighing scale to show how numbers can be equated or balanced
Bead Memory				
Short-term visual memory Rote memory Form perception and discrimination Alertness to detail Ability to perceive spatial relations Attention Concentration Simultaneous processing Fluid ability Eye-hand coordination	Ability to receive stimuli passively	Good rote memory Good immediate recall ability Ability to attend well in a testing situation Good ability to attend to visual stimuli	Anxiety Inattention Distractibility Poor visual memory	Emphasize looking skills by showing pictures and asking child to recall details of pictures Help child learn to discriminate features of objects Ask child to arrange different geometric designs in order and then recall the order Use other memory exercises and games
Memory for Sentences				
Short-term auditory memory Immediate recall of verbal information Rote memory Familiarity with words Auditory acuity Attention Concentration Listening comprehension Sequential processing Auditory processing Fluid ability	Ability to receive stimuli passively Cultural opportunities	Good rote memory Good immediate recall ability Good ability to attend well in a testing situation	Anxiety Inattention Distractibility A possible learning deficit Difficulty in auditory sequencing	Emphasize listening skills by reading sentences of increasing length and asking child to recall details Give directions of increasing complexity and have child follow them Use other memory exercises and games

(Table continues next page)

Table C-52 (cont.)

Ability	Background factors	Possible implications of high scores	Possible implications of low scores	Instructional implications
Memory for Digits				
Freedom from distractibility Short-term memory Rote memory Immediate auditory memory Attention Concentration Auditory sequencing Visualization Perceptual reorganization ability Fluid ability	Ability to receive stimuli passively	Good rote memory Good immediate recall ability Ability to attend well in a testing situation Good ability to attend to auditory stimuli Good learning strategies (rehearsal, chunking/grouping)	Anxiety Inattention Distractibility A possible learning deficit Difficulty in auditory sequencing Poor learning strategies (rehearsal, chunking/grouping)	Emphasize listening skills by using sequencing activities, reading a short story and asking child to recall details, and having child follow directions Use short and simple directions and repeat when necessary Use other memory exercises and memory games
Memory for Objects				
Short-term visual memory Rote memory Immediate visual memory Alertness to detail Attention Concentration Successive processing	Ability to receive stimuli passively	Good rote memory Good immediate recall ability Good ability to attend to visual stimuli Ability to attend well in a testing situation	Anxiety Inattention Distractibility A possible learning deficit Difficulty in visual sequencing	Emphasize looking skills by showing pictures and asking child to recall details Help child learn to discriminate features of objects Ask child to arrange pictures in order and then recall order Use other memory exercises and games

Note. PV = Picture Vocabulary.

Table C-53
Percentile Ranks for Standard Scores for Subtests on the Stanford-Binet Intelligence Scale: Fourth Edition

Standard score	Percentile rank	Standard score	Percentile rank	Standard score	Percentile rank
82	99.99	60	89	38	7
81	99.99	59	87	37	5
80	99.99	58	84	36	4
79	99.98	57	81	35	3
78	99.98	56	77	34	2
77	99.97	55	73	33	2
76	99.94	54	69	32	1
75	99.91	53	64	31	.89
74	99.87	52	60	30	.62
73	99.79	51	55	29	.44
72	99.70	50	50	28	.30
71	99.56	49	45	27	.21
70	99.38	48	40	26	.13
69	99.11	47	36	25	.09
68	99	46	31	24	.06
67	98	45	27	23	.03
66	98	44	23	22	.02
65	97	43	19	21	.02
64	96	42	16	20	.01
63	95	41	13	19	.01
62	93	40	11	18	.01
61	91	39	9		

Note. $M = 50$, $SD = 8$.

Table C-54
Confidence Intervals for the McCarthy Scales

Age level	Scale	Confidence level				
		68%	85%	90%	95%	99%
2½ (2-4-16 through 2-8-29)	Verbal	± 3	± 5	± 7	± 6	± 8
	Perceptual-Performance	± 5	± 7	± 8	± 9	± 12
	Quantitative	± 5	± 7	± 8	± 10	± 13
	General Cognitive	± 4	± 6	± 7	± 8	± 11
	Memory	± 5	± 7	± 8	± 9	± 12
	Motor	± 4	± 6	± 7	± 8	± 10
3 (2-9-0 through 3-2-29)	Verbal	± 3	± 5	± 5	± 6	± 8
	Perceptual-Performance	± 4	± 5	± 6	± 7	± 9
	Quantitative	± 4	± 6	± 7	± 8	± 11
	General Cognitive	± 4	± 5	± 6	± 7	± 10
	Memory	± 5	± 7	± 8	± 10	± 13
	Motor	± 4	± 6	± 7	± 8	± 11
3½ (3-3-0 through 3-8-29)	Verbal	± 3	± 4	± 5	± 5	± 7
	Perceptual-Performance	± 3	± 5	± 5	± 6	± 8
	Quantitative	± 4	± 6	± 7	± 8	± 11
	General Cognitive	± 3	± 5	± 6	± 7	± 9
	Memory	± 4	± 6	± 7	± 8	± 11
	Motor	± 4	± 6	± 7	± 8	± 11
4 (3-9-0 through 4-2-29)	Verbal	± 3	± 5	± 5	± 6	± 8
	Perceptual-Performance	± 4	± 5	± 6	± 7	± 9
	Quantitative	± 5	± 8	± 9	± 10	± 14
	General Cognitive	± 5	± 7	± 8	± 9	± 12
	Memory	± 4	± 6	± 7	± 8	± 10
	Motor	± 5	± 7	± 8	± 9	± 12
4½ (4-3-0 through 4-8-29)	Verbal	± 4	± 5	± 6	± 7	± 9
	Perceptual-Performance	± 3	± 5	± 5	± 6	± 9
	Quantitative	± 5	± 7	± 8	± 9	± 12
	General Cognitive	± 4	± 5	± 6	± 7	± 10
	Memory	± 5	± 7	± 8	± 10	± 13
	Motor	± 4	± 6	± 7	± 8	± 11
5 (4-9-0 through 5-2-29)	Verbal	± 4	± 5	± 6	± 7	± 9
	Perceptual-Performance	± 4	± 5	± 6	± 7	± 10
	Quantitative	± 4	± 5	± 6	± 7	± 10
	General Cognitive	± 4	± 6	± 7	± 8	± 10
	Memory	± 5	± 7	± 8	± 10	± 13
	Motor	± 4	± 6	± 7	± 8	± 11
5½ (5-3-0 through 5-11-29)	Verbal	± 4	± 5	± 6	± 7	± 9
	Perceptual-Performance	± 4	± 6	± 6	± 8	± 10
	Quantitative	± 4	± 5	± 6	± 7	± 10
	General Cognitive	± 4	± 6	± 7	± 8	± 11
	Memory	± 5	± 8	± 9	± 10	± 14
	Motor	± 4	± 6	± 7	± 9	± 12

(Table continues next page)

Table C-54 (cont.)

Age level	Scale	Confidence level				
		68%	85%	90%	95%	99%
6½ (6-0-0 through 6-11-29)	Verbal	± 4	± 6	± 6	± 8	± 10
	Perceptual-Performance	± 5	± 7	± 8	± 9	± 12
	Quantitative	± 4	± 6	± 7	± 8	± 11
	General Cognitive	± 5	± 7	± 8	± 10	± 13
	Memory	± 4	± 6	± 7	± 8	± 10
	Motor	± 6	± 8	± 9	± 11	± 14
7½ (7-0-0 through 7-11-29)	Verbal	± 3	± 5	± 5	± 6	± 9
	Perceptual-Performance	± 4	± 6	± 7	± 8	± 11
	Quantitative	± 4	± 6	± 7	± 8	± 11
	General Cognitive	± 4	± 6	± 6	± 8	± 10
	Memory	± 4	± 6	± 7	± 8	± 10
	Motor	± 5	± 7	± 8	± 10	± 13
8½ (8-0-0 through 8-11-29)	Verbal	± 4	± 5	± 6	± 7	± 10
	Perceptual-Performance	± 5	± 7	± 8	± 10	± 13
	Quantitative	± 4	± 6	± 7	± 8	± 11
	General Cognitive	± 4	± 6	± 7	± 9	± 12
	Memory	± 4	± 6	± 7	± 8	± 11
	Motor	± 6	± 9	± 10	± 12	± 16
Average	Verbal	± 3	± 5	± 6	± 7	± 9
	Perceptual-Performance	± 4	± 6	± 7	± 8	± 10
	Quantitative	± 4	± 6	± 7	± 8	± 11
	General Cognitive	± 4	± 6	± 7	± 8	± 11
	Memory	± 4	± 6	± 7	± 9	± 12
	Motor	± 5	± 7	± 8	± 9	± 12

Note. See Table C-1 for an explanation of the method used to arrive at confidence intervals.

Table C-55
Differences Required for Significance When Each McCarthy Scale Index Is Compared to the Mean Scale Index for Any Individual Child

Index	.05	.01
Verbal	8.36	9.97
Perceptual Performance	9.34	11.16
Quantitative	9.87	11.78
Memory	10.22	12.20
Motor	10.57	12.62

Note. See the Note in Table C-3 for an explanation of how the deviations were obtained.

Table C-56
Interpretive Rationales and Implications of High and Low Scores for K-ABC Mental Processing and Achievement Subtests

Ages	Ability	Background factors	Possible implications of high scores	Possible implications of low scores
		Hand Movements		
2-6 through 12-5 years	Sequential processing and simultaneous processing Fluid ability Perceptual organization Short-term visual memory Spatial ability Visual-motor coordination	Experience with visual-motor integration tasks	Good attention span Good concentration	Inattention Poor concentration Distractibility Perseveration Anxiety Visual-motor coordination difficulty
		Number Recall		
2-6 through 12-5 years	Sequential processing Fluid ability Short-term auditory memory	Ability to receive stimuli passively	Good rote memory Good immediate recall ability Ability to attend well in a testing situation Good ability to attend to auditory stimuli	Anxiety Inattention Distractibility A possible learning deficit Difficulty in auditory sequencing
		Gestalt Closure		
2-6 through 12-5 years	Simultaneous processing Attention to visual detail Perceptual organization and closure Ability to convert abstract stimuli into a concrete object	Alertness to environment Willingness to respond when uncertain	Good attention to visual detail Good concentration Good perceptual organization and closure Good reasoning	Inattention Distractibility Poor perceptual organization and closure Poor reasoning
		Triangles		
4-0 through 12-5 years	Simultaneous processing Nonverbal concept formation Spatial visualization Perceptual organization Analysis and synthesis Visual-motor coordination	Rate of motor activity	Good visual-motor-spatial integration Good conceptualizing ability Good spatial orientation in conjunction with speed, accuracy, and persistence Good analyzing and synthesizing ability	Poor visual-motor-spatial integration Visual-perceptual problems Poor spatial orientation Poor nonverbal reasoning ability
		Word Order		
4-0 through 12-5 years	Sequential processing Fluid ability Short-term auditory memory	Cultural opportunities	Good concentration Good attention span	Distractibility Inattention Anxiety

(Table continues next page)

Table C-56 (cont.)

Ages	Ability	Background factors	Possible implications of high scores	Possible implications of low scores
		Magic Window		
2-6 through 4-11 years	Simultaneous processing Attention to visual detail Short-term visual memory	Cultural opportunities	Good attention span Good concentration	Inattention Distractibility Impulsivity
		Face Recognition		
2-6 through 4-11 years	Simultaneous processing Attention to visual detail Short-term visual memory	Ability to receive stimuli passively	Good attention span Good concentration	Inattention Distractibility Impulsivity
		Matrix Analogies		
5-0 through 12-5 years	Simultaneous processing Analogic thinking Attention to visual detail Perceptual reasoning ability	Experience with part-whole relationships Willingness to respond when uncertain	Good analogic thinking Good attention to visual detail Good perceptual reasoning ability	Poor analogic thinking Poor attention to visual detail Poor perceptual reasoning ability
		Spatial Memory		
5-0 through 12-5 years	Simultaneous processing Immediate recall in a spatial context	Experience with developing strategies for solving problems	Good concentration Good attention span	Poor concentration Inattention Distractibility Anxiety
		Photo Series		
6-0 through 12-5 years	Simultaneous processing Nonverbal reasoning ability Planning ability Alertness Visual sequencing Attention to details Perceptual organization	A minimum of cultural opportunities	Good planning ability Alertness to detail Good ability to synthesize parts into an intelligible whole Good attention span Concentration	Difficulty with visual organization (sequencing) Difficulty in anticipating events Inattention Poor concentration Impulsivity
		Expressive Vocabulary		
2-6 through 4-11 years	Language ability Word knowledge Long-term memory Recall and verbal identification by recognition of familiar objects	Cultural opportunities	Good knowledge of words Good verbal skills Good family or cultural background	Poor knowledge of words Poor verbal skills Limited educational or family background

(Table continues next page)

Table C-56 (cont.)

Ages	Ability	Background factors	Possible implications of high scores	Possible implications of low scores
Faces and Places				
2-6 through 12-5 years	Range of knowledge Long-term memory	Cultural opportunities	Good range of specific knowledge Possession of knowledge associated with cultural and educational environment Good memory	Poor range of specific knowledge Poor memory Foreign background
Arithmetic				
3-0 through 12-5 years	Numerical reasoning ability Mental computation Application of basic arithmetical processes Concentration Attention Memory	Opportunity to acquire fundamental arithmetic processes	Facility in mental arithmetic Good reasoning skill in mathematical problems Good concentration Good ability to focus attention Teacher-oriented student	Inadequate ability in mental arithmetic Poor concentration Distractibility Anxiety over a school-like task Blocking toward mathematical tasks Poor school achievement Anxiety
Riddles				
3-0 through 12-5 years	Verbal reasoning Integration of sequentially presented auditory stimuli	Cultural opportunities	Good verbal reasoning ability Good ability to integrate sequentially presented auditory stimuli Good concentration Good attention span	Poor verbal reasoning ability Difficulty in integrating sequentially presented auditory stimuli Poor concentration Inattention
Reading/Decoding				
5-0 through 12-5 years	Reading skills Long-term memory	Cultural opportunities Education	Good reading skills Good long-term memory	Poor reading skills Poor long-term memory
Reading/Understanding				
7-0 through 12-5 years	Reading comprehension Ability to integrate auditory information with a motor response	Richness of early environment Cultural opportunities Education Motor ability	Good reading comprehension Good auditory-motor integration of meaningful information Good attention span	Poor reading comprehension Poor auditory-motor integration of meaningful information Inattention

Note. This table is based in part on Kaufman and Kaufman (1983). See Kaufman and Kaufman for a more complete discussion of each of the K-ABC subtests.

Table C-57
Norms for the Coloured Progressive Matrices

Total score	Age (in years)												
	5½ 5.03 to 5.08	6 5.09 to 6.02	6½ 6.03 to 6.08	7 6.09 to 7.02	7½ 7.03 to 7.08	8 7.09 to 8.02	8½ 8.03 to 8.08	9 8.09 to 9.02	9½ 9.03 to 9.08	10 9.09 to 10.02	10½ 10.03 to 10.08	11 10.09 to 11.02	11½ 11.03 to 11.09
35							99	97	95	95	94	94	88
34						98	97	95	93	93	90	89	75
33					98	96	95	93	90	89	83	77	65
32				99	96	94	93	90	85	78	75	64	57
31				97	94	92	90	85	76	65	66	56	50
30			99	95	92	90	85	76	67	60	57	50	44
29			97	93	90	86	76	67	60	55	50	44	39
28			95	91	87	81	68	60	55	50	44	39	34
27		98	93	90	83	75	63	55	50	45	40	34	29
26		96	92	87	79	69	58	50	45	40	35	30	25
25	98	94	90	84	75	64	54	45	39	35	30	25	21
24	96	92	87	80	70	59	50	39	34	30	25	21	17
23	94	90	84	75	65	54	45	34	30	25	21	17	14
22	93	87	80	70	60	50	41	29	25	21	17	14	12
21	90	83	75	65	55	45	36	25	21	17	14	12	10
20	87	79	70	60	50	41	30	21	17	14	12	10	8
19	83	75	65	55	45	36	24	17	14	12	10	8	6
18	79	70	60	50	41	31	20	14	12	10	8	6	5
17	75	66	55	45	37	25	15	12	10	8	6	5	4
16	70	61	50	39	31	18	12	10	8	6	5	4	2
15	66	56	44	33	24	13	10	8	6	5	4	2	
14	62	50	36	24	16	10	8	6	5	4	2		
13	56	39	25	15	10	7	6	5	4	2			
12	48	26	15	10	7	5	5	4	2				
11	31	17	10	7	5	3	4	2					
10	16	10	7	5	3	1	2						
9	10	6	5	3	1								
8	6	3	3	1									
7	2	1											
6	1												

Note. These are smoothed norms for U.S. children.

Source: Reprinted with permission of the authors and publisher from J. C. Raven and B. Summers, *Manual for Raven's Progressive Matrices and Vocabulary Scales—Research Supplement No. 3*, 1986, p. 36. London: H. K. Lewis & Co.

Table C-58
Norms for the Standard Progressive Matrices

Age (in years)

Total score	6½ (6.03–6.08)	7 (6.09–7.02)	7½ (7.03–7.08)	8 (7.09–8.02)	8½ (8.03–8.08)	9 (8.09–9.02)	9½ (9.03–9.08)	10 (9.09–10.02)	10½ (10.03–10.08)	11 (10.09–11.02)	11½ (11.03–11.08)	12 (11.09–12.02)	12½ (12.03–12.08)	13 (12.09–13.02)	13½ (13.03–13.08)	14 (13.09–14.02)	14½ (14.03–14.08)	15 (14.09–15.02)	15½ (15.03–15.08)	16 (15.09–16.02)	16½ (16.03–16.08)
60																					99
59																				99	98
58																			99	97	95
57																		99	97	95	90
56																	99	97	94	93	85
55																99	97	95	92	90	80
54															99	98	95	93	90	87	75
53														99	98	96	93	92	86	82	70
52													99	97	96	94	92	90	81	75	65
51												99	97	95	94	92	90	87	75	69	59
50											99	98	96	94	92	90	87	82	68	64	54
49										99	97	96	94	92	90	86	82	74	63	59	50
48									99	98	95	94	92	90	86	81	75	67	58	54	46
47								99	97	96	94	92	90	86	81	75	68	62	54	50	43
46							99	97	96	94	92	90	86	81	75	70	63	57	50	47	39
45						99	97	96	94	92	90	86	81	75	70	65	58	53	46	43	35
44					99	97	96	94	92	90	86	81	75	70	65	61	54	50	42	39	31
43				99	98	96	94	92	90	86	81	75	70	65	61	57	50	46	39	36	25
42				98	97	94	92	90	86	81	75	70	65	61	57	53	46	42	35	31	18
41				97	95	92	90	87	81	75	70	65	61	57	53	50	42	39	31	25	15
40				96	94	90	87	83	79	70	65	61	57	53	50	46	38	35	24	18	13
39			99	95	92	87	83	79	75	65	61	57	53	50	46	42	34	31	18	15	11
38			98	94	90	83	79	75	70	61	57	53	50	46	43	38	30	24	15	13	10
37			97	92	87	79	75	70	64	57	53	50	46	43	38	34	24	17	12	12	9
36		99	95	90	83	75	70	64	59	53	50	46	42	39	34	30	19	14	11	10	8
35		97	93	87	79	70	66	59	54	50	46	42	38	34	30	24	16	13	10	9	7
34	99	96	91	84	75	67	61	54	50	46	42	38	34	24	24	19	13	11	9	8	6
33	98	95	89	81	71	63	57	50	46	42	37	34	25	18	19	16	11	10	8	7	6
32	97	94	87	78	68	60	53	46	40	37	33	25	18	15	16	13	10	9	7	6	5
31	96	91	85	75	65	56	50	41	35	31	24	18	14	12	13	11	9	8	6	6	5
30	95	89	82	72	61	53	43	37	31	25	18	14	12	12	11	10	7	6	6	5	4

(Table continues next page)

881

Table C-58 (cont.)

										Age (in years)											
Total score	6½ 6.03 to 6.08	7 6.09 to 7.02	7½ 7.03 to 7.08	8 7.09 to 8.02	8½ 8.03 to 8.08	9 8.09 to 9.02	9½ 9.03 to 9.08	10 9.09 to 10.02	10½ 10.03 to 10.08	11 10.09 to 11.02	11½ 11.03 to 11.08	12 11.09 to 12.02	12½ 12.03 to 12.08	13 12.09 to 13.02	13½ 13.03 to 13.08	14 13.09 to 14.02	14½ 14.03 to 14.08	15 14.09 to 15.02	15½ 15.03 to 15.08	16 15.09 to 16.02	16½ 16.03 to 16.08
29	93	87	78	69	58	50	40	34	28	22	15	12	11	9	8	7	6	5	5	4	2
28	91	85	75	65	56	47	37	31	25	19	14	11	10	8	7	6	5	4	4	3	1
27	89	82	71	62	53	44	34	28	22	16	12	10	9	7	6	5	4	3	2	1	
26	87	78	68	59	50	41	31	25	19	14	11	9	8	6	5	4	3	2	1		
25	85	75	65	56	47	38	28	22	17	13	10	8	7	6	4	3	2	1			
24	83	72	62	53	44	35	25	19	15	11	9	7	6	5	3	2	1				
23	81	69	59	50	42	32	22	17	13	10	8	6	6	4	2	1					
22	78	66	56	47	39	29	19	15	11	9	7	6	5	3	1						
21	75	63	53	44	36	25	17	13	10	8	6	5	4	2							
20	72	60	50	41	32	20	15	11	8	7	6	4	3	1							
19	69	57	46	38	29	17	13	10	7	6	5	3	2								
18	66	53	43	34	25	14	11	8	6	5	4	2	1								
17	62	49	39	30	20	11	10	7	5	4	3	1									
16	59	45	35	24	15	10	8	6	4	3	2										
15	55	40	30	18	13	8	7	5	3	2	1										
14	49	33	24	13	10	7	6	4	2	1											
13	39	25	18	10	8	6	5	3	1												
12	26	18	13	8	6	5	4	2													
11	18	13	10	6	5	4	3	1													
10	14	10	7	5	4	3	2														
9	10	7	5	4	3	2	1														
8	7	5	4	3	2	1															
7	5	4	3	2	1																
6	4	3	2	1																	
5	3	2	1																		
4	2	1																			
3	1																				

Note. These are smoothed norms for U.S. children.

Source: Reprinted with permission of the authors and publisher from J. C. Raven and B. Summers, *Manual for Raven's Progressive Matrices and Vocabulary Scales – Research Supplement No. 3,* 1986, p. 15. London: H. K. Lewis & Co.

Table C-59
Norms for the Advanced Progressive Matrices

Total score	Percentile rank	Total score	Percentile rank
13	1	26	43
15	3	27	52
17	4	28	57
18	6	29	65
19	7	30	74
20	11	31	81
21	14	32	86
22	18	33	89
23	24	34	93
24	29	35	98
25	37	36	100

Note. Based on 300 students at the University of California, Berkeley.
Source: Adapted from Paul (1985).

Table C-60
Landmarks of Normal Behavior Development

Age	Motor behavior	Adaptive behavior	Language	Personal and social behavior
Under 4 weeks	Makes alternating crawling movements Moves head laterally when placed in prone position	Responds to sound of rattle and bell Regards moving objects momentarily	Small, throaty, un-differentiated noises	Quiets when picked up Impassive face
4 weeks	Tonic neck reflex positions predominate Hands fisted Head sags but can hold head erect for a few seconds	Follows moving objects to the midline Shows no interest and drops objects immediately	Beginning vocalization, such as cooing, gurgling, and grunting	Regards face and diminishes activity Responds to speech
16 weeks	Symmetrical postures predominate Holds head balanced Head lifted 90 degrees when prone on forearm	Follows a slowly moving object well Arms activate on sight of dangling object	Laughs aloud Sustained cooing and gurgling	Spontaneous social smile Aware of strange situations
28 weeks	Sits steadily, leaning forward on hands Bounces actively when placed in standing position	One-hand approach and grasp of toy Bangs and shakes rattle Transfers toys	Vocalizes "m-m-m" when crying Makes vowel sounds, such as "ah, ah"	Takes feet to mouth Pats mirror image

(Table continues next page)

Table C-60 (cont.)

Age	Motor behavior	Adaptive behavior	Language	Personal and social behavior
40 weeks	Sits alone with good coordination Creeps Pulls self to standing position	Matches two objects at midline Attempts to imitate scribble	Says "da-da" or equivalent Responds to name or nickname	Responds to social play, such as "pat-a-cake" and "peek-a-boo" Feeds self cracker and holds own bottle
52 weeks	Walks with one hand held. Stands alone briefly	Releases cube in cup Tries tower of 2 cubes	Uses expressive jargon Gives a toy on request	Cooperates in dressing "Plays" ball
15 months	Toddles Creeps upstairs	--	Says 3 to 5 words meaningfully Pats pictures in books Shows shoes on request	Points or vocalizes wants Throws objects in play or refusal
18 months	Walks, seldom falls Hurls ball Walks upstairs with one hand held	Builds a tower of 3 or 4 cubes Scribbles spontaneously and imitates a writing stroke	Says 10 words, including name Identifies one common object on picture card Names ball and carries out two directions, for example "put on table" and "give to mother"	Feeds self in part, spills Pulls toy on string Carries or hugs a special toy, such as a doll
2 years	Runs well, no falling Kicks large ball Goes upstairs and downstairs alone	Builds a tower of 6 or 7 cubes Aligns cubes, imitating train Imitates vertical and circular strokes	Uses 3-word sentences Carries out four simple directions	Pulls on simple garment Domestic mimicry Refers to self by name
3 years	Rides tricycle Jumps from bottom steps Alternates feet going upstairs	Builds a tower of 9 or 10 cubes Imitates a 3-cube bridge Copies a circle	Gives sex and full name Uses plurals Describes what is happening in a picture book	Puts on shoes Unbuttons buttons Feeds self well Understands taking turns
4 years	Walks downstairs one step per tread Stands on one foot for 4 to 8 seconds	Copies a cross Repeats 4 digits Counts 3 objects with correct pointing	Names colors, at least one correctly Understands five prepositional directives—"on," "under," "in," "in back of" or "in front of," and "beside"	Washes and dries own face Brushes teeth Plays cooperatively with other children
5 years	Skips, using feet alternatively Usually has complete sphincter control	Copies a square Draws a recognizable man with a head, body, limbs Counts 10 objects accurately	Names the primary colors Names coins: pennies, nickels, dimes Asks meanings of words	Dresses and undresses self Prints a few letters Plays competitive exercise games

Source: Reprinted, with a change in notation, with permission of the publisher and author from S. Chess, "Health Responses, Developmental Disturbances, and Stress or Reactive Disorders: I: Infancy and Childhood." In A. M. Freedman and H. I. Kaplan (Eds.), *Comprehensive Textbook of Psychiatry*, p. 1362, Copyright 1967, Williams & Wilkins, 1967.

Table C-61
Differences Required for Significance When Each Peabody Individual Achievement Test (PIAT) Subtest Is Compared to the Mean Score for Any Individual Child

Subtest	.05	.01
Mathematics	17.66	21.19
Reading Recognition	13.32	15.98
Reading Comprehension	20.04	24.04
Spelling	19.81	23.76
General Information	17.15	20.58

Note. See the Note in Table C-3 for an explanation of how the deviations were obtained.
Source: Adapted from Silverstein (1981).

Table C-62
Standard Scores for the Koppitz Developmental Scoring System

Errors	Chronological age												
	5-0 to 5-5	5-6 to 5-11	6-0 to 6-5	6-6 to 6-11	7-0 to 7-5	7-6 to 7-11	8-0 to 8-5	8-6 to 8-11	9-0 to 9-5	9-6 to 9-11	10-0 to 10-5	10-6 to 10-11	11-0 to 11-11
0	160	143	139	131	126	125	125	118	119	116	115	115	115
1	155	138	135	127	122	119	119	112	112	109	107	107	104
2	150	134	130	122	117	114	113	106	105	102	99	98	94
3	146	130	125	118	113	109	107	100	99	95	91	90	83
4	141	125	121	114	108	103	101	94	92	88	83	82	72
5	137	121	116	109	104	98	95	88	85	81	76	73	61
6	132	116	112	105	99	92	89	82	78	74	68	65	51
7	128	112	107	101	95	87	83	76	71	66	60	57	
8	123	108	103	97	90	82	77	70	65	59	52		
9	119	103	98	92	85	76	71	64	58	52			
10	114	99	94	88	81	71	65	58	51	45			
11	110	94	89	84	76	66	59	52					
12	105	90	85	79	72	60	53	46					
13	100	85	80	75	67	55	47						
14	96	81	75	71	63	50							
15	91	77	71	67	58								
16	87	72	66	62	54								
17	82	68	62	58	49								
18	78	63	57	54	45								
19	73	59	53	49									
20	69	55	48	45									
21	64	50											
22	60	46											
23	55												

Note. These standard scores ($M = 100$, $SD = 15$) are based on a linear transformation of the data obtained from E. M. Koppitz's (1975) 1974 normative sample. Standard scores are useful primarily from 5 to 8 years of age. After the age of 8 years, the low ceiling and the skewed distribution of developmental scores make standard scores not too meaningful.

Table C-63
Norms for Conners Parent Rating Scale (48-Item Form)

Total score	Male					Female				
	Age (in years)					Age (in years)				
	3–5	6–8	9–11	12–14	15–17	3–5	6–8	9–11	12–14	15–17
Conduct Problem										
0	36	38	36	38	39	36	35	39	40	39
1	40	41	39	41	42	40	40	42	43	43
2	43	44	43	44	45	43	44	46	47	46
3	46	47	46	47	48	47	49	49	50	50
4	49	50	49	50	51	50	53	53	53	54
5	52	53	53	53	54	54	58	56	56	58
6	56	56	56	56	56	57	62	60	59	62
7	59	59	59	59	59	61	67	63	62	65
8	62	63	62	62	62	65	71	67	65	69
9	65	66	66	65	65	68	76	70	68	73
10	68	69	69	69	68	72	80	74	72	77
11	72	72	72	72	71	75	84	77	75	80
12	75	75	76	75	73	79	89	81	78	84
13	78	78	79	78	76	82	93	84	81	88
14	81	81	82	81	79	86	98	88	84	92
15	84	84	85	84	82	90	102	91	87	96
16	88	88	89	87	85	93	107	94	90	99
17	91	91	92	90	88	97	111	98	93	103
18	94	94	95	93	90	100	116	101	97	107
19	97	97	99	96	93	104	120	105	100	111
20	101	100	102	99	96	107	125	108	103	115
21	104	103	105	102	99	111	129	112	106	118
22	107	106	108	105	102	115	134	115	109	122
23	110	109	112	108	105	118	138	119	112	126
24	113	113	115	111	108	122	143	122	115	130
Learning Problem										
0	35	36	38	38	39	39	38	39	40	41
1	42	41	43	43	43	44	45	45	46	47
2	50	47	47	47	48	48	51	52	51	54
3	58	52	52	52	52	52	58	58	57	61
4	65	58	57	56	57	57	64	65	62	67
5	73	64	62	60	61	61	71	72	68	74
6	80	69	67	65	66	65	78	78	74	80
7	88	75	71	69	71	70	84	85	79	87
8	95	80	76	74	75	74	91	91	85	93
9	103	86	81	78	80	79	97	98	90	100
10	111	91	86	82	84	83	104	104	96	107
11	118	97	91	87	89	87	111	111	101	113
12	126	102	95	91	93	92	117	118	107	120

(Table continues next page)

Table C-63 (cont.)

Total score	Male					Female				
	Age (in years)					Age (in years)				
	3–5	6–8	9–11	12–14	15–17	3–5	6–8	9–11	12–14	15–17
Psychosomatic										
0	45	44	43	45	45	44	43	44	42	42
1	62	55	53	51	55	59	52	53	51	52
2	79	66	62	56	64	74	61	62	60	62
3	95	77	72	62	74	88	71	71	69	72
4	112	88	82	68	83	103	80	80	78	82
5	129	99	91	73	93	118	89	89	86	92
6	145	110	101	79	103	132	99	98	95	102
7	162	120	110	85	112	147	108	106	104	112
8	179	131	120	90	122	162	117	115	113	122
9	195	142	130	96	132	176	126	124	122	132
10	212	153	139	102	141	191	136	133	131	142
11	229	164	149	108	151	206	145	142	140	152
12	245	175	158	113	160	221	154	151	149	162
Impulsive–Hyperactive										
0	34	35	35	35	36	35	34	36	37	39
1	38	39	39	39	41	38	38	41	41	44
2	42	43	43	44	46	42	42	45	46	48
3	46	47	47	49	51	45	47	49	51	53
4	50	51	51	53	56	48	51	53	55	57
5	54	55	56	58	61	51	55	58	60	62
6	58	60	60	63	66	55	59	62	64	66
7	61	64	64	67	71	58	64	66	69	71
8	65	68	68	72	75	61	68	70	73	75
9	69	72	72	76	80	64	72	75	78	80
10	73	76	76	81	85	68	76	79	82	85
11	77	80	81	86	90	71	81	83	87	89
12	81	85	85	90	95	74	85	87	91	94
Anxiety										
0	39	40	41	40	40	41	41	41	40	40
1	43	45	46	44	44	46	45	46	45	45
2	47	50	52	49	48	50	49	50	49	50
3	51	55	57	53	53	54	53	55	54	55
4	55	60	62	57	57	58	57	59	59	59
5	60	65	68	61	61	63	60	63	63	64
6	64	69	73	66	66	67	64	68	68	69
7	68	74	78	70	70	71	68	72	73	73
8	72	79	84	74	74	75	72	76	78	78
9	76	84	89	78	79	79	75	81	82	83
10	80	89	94	83	83	84	79	85	87	88
11	84	94	100	87	87	88	83	90	92	92
12	88	99	105	91	92	92	87	94	96	97

Note. Norms are in T scores ($M = 50$, $SD = 10$). Item numbers for the five factor scores are as follows: Conduct Problem (2, 8, 14, 19, 20, 27, 35, 39); Learning Problem (10, 25, 31, 37); Psychosomatic (32, 41, 43, 44); Impulsive-Hyperactive (4, 5, 11, 13); and Anxiety (12, 16, 24, 47). The Hyperactivity Index can be obtained from items 4, 7, 11, 13, 14, 25, 31, 33, 37, and 38 and norms on page 888 used.
Source: Courtesy C. Keith Conners.

Table C-64
Norms for Conners Abbreviated Parent Questionnaire

Total score	Male Age (in years)					Female Age (in years)				
	3–5	6–8	9–11	12–14	15–17	3–5	6–8	9–11	12–14	15–17
0	32	35	35	36	38	36	33	35	36	38
1	35	37	37	38	40	38	36	38	39	41
2	37	39	40	41	42	40	39	41	41	44
3	40	42	42	43	45	41	42	44	44	46
4	42	44	44	45	47	43	45	46	47	49
5	45	46	46	47	50	45	47	49	50	52
.6	47	48	49	50	52	47	50	52	53	55
7	50	50	51	52	55	49	53	55	56	58
8	52	52	53	54	57	50	56	58	59	61
9	55	55	55	56	60	52	59	61	62	64
10	57	57	58	58	62	54	62	64	65	67
11	60	59	60	61	64	56	65	67	68	70
12	62	61	62	63	67	58	67	70	71	73
13	65	63	65	65	69	59	70	73	74	76
14	67	65	67	67	72	61	73	76	77	79
15	70	68	69	70	74	63	76	79	80	82
16	72	70	71	72	77	65	79	82	83	85
17	75	72	74	74	79	66	82	85	86	88
18	77	74	76	76	81	68	85	88	89	91
19	80	76	78	78	84	70	87	91	91	94
20	82	78	80	81	86	72	90	94	94	96
21	85	81	83	83	89	74	93	96	97	99
22	87	83	85	85	91	75	96	99	100	102
23	90	85	87	87	94	77	99	102	103	105
24	92	87	90	90	96	79	102	105	106	108
25	95	89	92	92	99	81	105	108	109	111
26	97	92	94	94	101	83	107	111	112	114
27	100	94	96	96	103	84	110	114	115	117
28	102	96	99	98	106	86	113	117	118	120
29	105	98	101	101	108	88	116	120	121	123
30	107	100	103	103	111	90	119	123	124	126

Note. Norms are in T scores ($M = 50$, $SD = 10$).
Source: Courtesy C. Keith Conners.

Table C-65
Norms for Conners Teacher Rating Scale (39-Item Form)

Total score	Male Age (in years) 4	5	6	7	8	9	10	11	12	Female Age (in years) 4	5	6	7	8	9	10	11	12
									Hyperactivity									
0	40	40	39	39	39	39	39	40	38	41	42	42	42	41	42	42	43	41
1	41	41	40	40	40	40	40	41	39	43	43	43	44	43	43	43	44	42
2	42	42	41	41	41	41	41	42	40	44	44	44	45	44	44	45	45	43
3	43	43	42	42	42	42	42	43	41	46	46	45	46	45	45	46	46	44
4	44	44	43	43	43	43	43	44	42	47	47	46	47	46	47	47	48	45
5	45	45	43	44	44	44	44	45	42	48	48	47	49	47	48	48	49	46
6	46	46	44	45	45	45	45	46	43	50	50	49	50	48	49	50	50	47
7	47	47	45	46	46	45	46	47	44	51	51	50	51	50	50	51	51	48
8	48	48	46	47	47	46	47	48	45	52	52	51	52	51	51	52	53	50
9	49	49	47	48	48	47	48	49	46	54	54	52	54	52	52	53	54	51
10	50	50	48	49	49	48	49	50	46	55	55	53	55	53	54	55	55	52
11	51	51	49	50	50	49	50	51	47	56	56	54	56	54	55	56	56	53
12	52	52	50	51	51	50	51	52	48	58	57	55	57	56	56	57	57	54
13	53	53	51	52	52	51	52	53	49	59	59	56	59	57	57	58	59	55
14	54	54	51	53	53	52	53	54	50	60	60	57	60	58	58	60	60	56
15	55	55	52	54	54	53	54	55	51	62	61	58	61	59	60	61	61	57
16	56	56	53	55	55	54	55	56	51	63	63	59	62	60	61	62	62	58
17	57	57	54	56	56	55	56	57	52	64	64	60	64	62	62	63	64	59
18	58	58	55	57	57	56	57	58	53	66	65	61	65	63	63	65	65	60
19	60	59	56	58	58	57	58	59	54	67	67	62	66	64	64	66	66	61
20	61	60	57	59	59	58	59	60	55	69	68	63	67	65	66	67	67	62
21	62	61	58	59	60	59	60	61	55	70	69	64	69	66	67	68	69	63
22	63	62	59	60	60	60	62	61	56	71	71	65	70	67	68	70	70	64
23	64	63	59	61	61	61	63	62	57	73	72	66	71	69	69	71	71	65
24	65	64	60	62	62	62	64	63	58	74	73	67	72	70	70	72	72	66
25	66	65	61	63	63	63	65	64	59	75	74	68	74	71	72	73	73	67
26	67	66	62	64	64	64	66	65	59	77	76	69	75	72	73	75	75	68
27	68	67	63	65	65	65	67	66	60	78	77	70	76	73	74	76	76	69
28	69	68	64	66	66	66	68	67	61	79	78	71	77	75	75	77	77	70
29	70	69	65	67	67	67	69	68	62	81	80	72	79	76	76	78	78	71
30	71	70	66	68	68	67	70	69	63	82	81	73	80	77	77	80	80	72
31	72	71	67	69	69	68	71	70	63	83	82	74	81	78	79	81	81	73
32	73	72	67	70	70	69	72	71	64	85	84	75	82	79	80	82	82	74
33	74	73	68	71	71	70	73	72	65	86	85	76	84	80	81	83	83	75
34	75	74	69	72	72	71	74	73	66	87	86	77	85	82	82	85	85	76
35	76	75	70	73	73	72	75	74	67	89	88	78	86	83	83	86	86	77
36	77	76	71	74	74	73	76	75	67	90	89	79	87	84	85	87	87	78
37	78	77	72	75	75	74	77	76	68	91	90	80	89	85	86	88	88	79
38	79	78	73	76	76	75	78	77	69	93	92	81	90	86	87	90	89	80
39	80	79	74	77	77	76	79	78	70	94	93	82	91	88	88	91	91	81
40	81	80	75	78	78	77	80	79	71	96	94	83	92	89	89	92	92	82
41	83	81	75	79	79	78	81	80	71	97	95	84	94	90	91	93	93	83
42	84	82	76	80	80	79	82	81	72	98	97	85	95	91	92	95	94	84
43	85	83	77	81	81	80	83	82	73	100	98	86	96	92	93	96	96	85
44	86	84	78	82	82	81	84	83	74	101	99	87	97	94	94	97	97	86

(Table continues next page)

Table C-65 (cont.)

Total score	Male									Female								
	Age (in years)									Age (in years)								
	4	5	6	7	8	9	10	11	12	4	5	6	7	8	9	10	11	12
45	87	85	79	83	83	82	85	84	75	102	101	88	99	95	95	98	98	87
46	88	86	80	84	84	83	86	85	76	104	102	89	100	96	97	100	99	88
47	89	87	81	85	84	84	87	86	76	105	103	90	101	97	98	101	101	89
48	90	88	82	86	85	85	88	87	77	106	105	91	102	98	99	102	102	90
49	91	89	83	87	86	86	89	88	78	108	106	92	104	99	100	103	103	91
50	92	90	83	87	87	87	90	89	79	109	107	93	105	101	101	105	104	92
51	93	91	84	88	88	88	91	90	80	110	109	94	106	102	102	106	105	93

Conduct Disorder

Total score	Male									Female								
	4	5	6	7	8	9	10	11	12	4	5	6	7	8	9	10	11	12
0	43	44	44	43	43	43	43	43	42	44	45	45	45	44	45	45	45	44
1	45	45	45	45	45	45	45	45	43	46	47	47	48	47	47	47	47	46
2	46	47	47	46	46	46	46	46	44	48	49	49	50	49	49	50	49	47
3	48	49	48	48	48	48	48	48	45	50	52	51	52	51	51	52	51	49
4	49	50	50	50	50	49	49	49	47	52	54	53	54	53	52	54	53	50
5	51	52	51	51	51	51	51	51	48	54	56	55	57	55	54	56	55	51
6	52	54	53	53	53	52	53	52	49	56	59	57	59	57	56	58	56	53
7	54	56	54	55	55	54	54	54	50	58	61	59	61	60	58	60	58	54
8	55	57	56	56	56	55	56	55	51	60	63	61	64	62	60	62	60	55
9	57	59	57	58	58	57	57	57	52	62	66	63	66	64	62	64	62	57
10	59	61	59	59	60	58	59	58	53	64	68	65	68	66	64	66	64	58
11	60	62	60	61	61	60	60	60	55	65	70	67	70	68	66	69	66	59
12	62	64	62	63	63	61	62	61	56	67	72	69	73	71	68	71	68	61
13	63	66	63	64	65	63	64	63	57	69	75	71	75	73	70	73	69	62
14	65	67	65	66	66	65	65	64	58	71	77	73	77	75	72	75	71	63
15	66	69	66	67	68	66	67	66	59	73	79	75	79	77	74	77	73	65
16	68	71	68	69	70	68	68	67	60	75	82	77	82	79	76	79	75	66
17	69	72	69	71	71	69	70	69	61	77	84	79	84	81	78	81	77	68
18	71	74	71	72	73	71	71	70	63	79	86	81	86	84	80	83	79	69
19	72	76	72	74	75	72	73	72	64	81	89	83	89	86	82	85	81	70
20	74	77	74	76	76	74	75	73	65	83	91	85	91	88	83	88	83	72
21	76	79	75	77	78	75	76	75	66	85	93	87	93	90	85	90	84	73
22	77	81	77	79	80	77	78	76	67	87	96	89	95	92	87	92	86	74
23	79	82	78	80	81	78	79	77	68	89	98	91	98	95	89	94	88	76
24	80	84	80	82	83	80	81	79	70	90	100	93	100	97	91	96	90	77
25	82	86	81	84	85	81	82	80	71	92	102	95	102	99	93	98	92	78
26	83	87	83	85	86	83	84	82	72	94	105	97	105	101	95	100	94	80
27	85	89	84	87	88	84	86	83	73	96	107	99	107	103	97	102	96	81
28	86	91	86	88	90	86	87	85	74	98	109	101	109	105	99	104	97	82
29	88	92	87	90	91	88	89	86	75	100	112	103	111	108	101	107	99	84
30	89	94	89	92	93	89	90	88	76	102	114	105	114	110	103	109	101	85
31	91	96	90	93	95	91	92	89	78	104	116	107	116	112	105	111	103	86
32	93	97	92	95	96	92	93	91	79	106	119	109	118	114	107	113	105	88
33	94	99	93	97	98	94	95	92	80	108	121	111	121	116	109	115	107	89
34	96	101	95	98	100	95	97	94	81	110	123	113	123	119	111	117	109	91
35	97	102	96	100	101	97	98	95	82	112	126	115	125	121	113	119	110	92
36	99	104	98	101	103	98	100	97	83	114	128	117	127	123	114	121	112	93
37	100	106	99	103	105	100	101	98	85	116	130	119	130	125	116	123	114	95
38	102	107	100	105	106	101	103	100	86	117	132	121	132	127	118	126	116	96
39	103	109	102	106	108	103	104	101	87	119	135	123	134	129	120	128	118	97

(Table continues next page)

Table C-65 (cont.)

Total score	Male									Female								
	Age (in years)									Age (in years)								
	4	5	6	7	8	9	10	11	12	4	5	6	7	8	9	10	11	12
Emotional Overindulgent																		
0	41	43	42	43	42	43	42	43	41	42	43	43	43	43	43	43	43	42
1	44	45	45	45	45	45	45	45	43	45	45	45	46	46	45	46	46	44
2	47	48	47	48	47	48	47	48	45	47	48	48	49	48	48	49	50	46
3	49	50	50	50	50	50	50	50	47	49	50	51	53	51	51	52	53	49
4	52	52	52	53	53	52	52	53	49	52	53	54	56	54	53	55	56	51
5	54	55	55	55	55	55	55	55	52	54	55	57	59	57	56	59	59	53
6	57	57	58	58	58	57	57	58	54	56	58	59	62	60	58	62	62	55
7	59	60	60	61	60	59	60	60	56	59	60	62	65	63	61	65	65	57
8	62	62	63	63	63	61	62	63	58	61	63	65	68	66	64	68	68	59
9	65	64	65	66	66	64	65	65	60	64	65	68	71	69	66	71	71	61
10	67	67	68	68	68	66	67	68	62	66	68	71	74	72	69	74	74	63
11	70	69	70	71	71	68	70	70	64	68	70	73	77	75	72	77	77	65
12	72	72	73	73	74	71	72	73	66	71	73	76	80	77	74	80	80	67
13	75	74	76	76	76	73	75	75	68	73	75	79	83	80	77	83	83	69
14	77	76	78	78	79	75	77	78	70	76	78	82	86	83	79	86	86	71
15	80	79	81	81	81	78	80	80	72	78	80	84	89	86	82	89	90	73
16	83	81	83	83	84	80	82	83	74	80	83	87	92	89	85	92	93	76
17	85	84	86	86	87	82	85	85	76	83	85	90	95	92	87	95	96	78
18	88	86	88	88	89	85	88	87	78	85	88	93	98	95	90	98	99	80
19	90	88	91	91	92	87	90	90	81	87	91	96	101	98	93	101	102	82
20	93	91	94	93	94	89	93	92	83	90	93	98	104	101	95	104	105	84
21	96	93	96	96	97	92	95	95	85	92	96	101	107	104	98	107	108	86
22	98	96	99	98	100	94	98	97	87	95	98	104	110	106	100	110	111	88
23	101	98	101	101	102	96	100	100	89	97	101	107	114	109	103	113	114	90
24	103	100	104	103	105	98	103	102	91	99	103	109	117	112	106	116	117	92
Anxious–Passive																		
0	39	39	38	39	39	38	37	39	37	38	39	38	40	39	38	37	39	38
1	42	42	41	42	42	41	41	42	40	41	42	41	43	42	41	40	42	40
2	45	45	43	45	45	44	44	45	43	44	45	44	46	45	43	43	46	43
3	48	48	46	48	48	47	47	49	46	47	47	47	49	48	46	46	49	45
4	51	51	49	51	51	50	50	52	49	49	50	49	51	51	49	49	52	48
5	53	54	52	54	54	53	54	55	53	52	53	52	54	54	52	52	55	50
6	56	56	54	57	57	56	57	59	56	55	55	55	57	57	55	55	58	53
7	59	59	57	60	61	59	60	62	59	57	58	57	60	60	58	58	61	55
8	62	62	60	63	64	62	63	65	62	60	61	60	63	63	60	61	64	58
9	65	65	62	66	67	65	66	69	65	63	64	63	66	66	63	64	67	61
10	67	68	65	69	70	68	70	72	68	66	66	66	69	69	66	67	70	63
11	70	71	68	72	73	70	73	75	71	68	69	68	72	72	69	71	73	66
12	73	74	70	75	76	73	76	79	74	71	72	71	75	75	72	74	76	68
13	76	77	73	78	79	76	79	82	77	74	74	74	78	78	75	77	79	71
14	79	80	76	81	82	79	82	85	80	76	77	77	81	81	77	80	82	73
15	81	83	79	84	85	82	86	88	83	79	80	79	84	84	80	83	85	76
16	84	85	81	87	88	85	89	92	86	82	82	82	87	87	83	86	88	78
17	87	88	84	90	91	88	92	95	89	85	85	85	90	90	86	89	91	81
18	90	91	87	93	94	91	95	98	92	87	88	87	93	93	89	92	94	84

(Table continues next page)

Table C-65 (cont.)

Total score	Male Age (in years)									Female Age (in years)								
	4	5	6	7	8	9	10	11	12	4	5	6	7	8	9	10	11	12
Asocial																		
0	43	44	44	44	43	43	43	44	42	44	44	45	45	44	44	44	45	38
1	47	49	48	49	47	48	47	48	45	48	50	50	50	48	49	49	49	43
2	50	53	53	54	51	52	51	51	49	52	55	54	55	52	53	53	53	49
3	54	58	57	59	55	56	55	55	52	56	60	59	60	56	58	57	58	54
4	58	62	61	63	59	60	59	59	55	60	65	63	66	59	62	62	62	60
5	62	67	65	68	63	64	63	63	59	64	70	68	71	63	67	66	66	65
6	65	71	69	73	67	68	67	67	62	68	75	72	76	67	72	71	71	71
7	69	75	73	78	70	72	72	71	65	72	81	77	81	71	76	75	75	76
8	73	80	77	82	74	76	76	75	68	77	86	82	86	75	81	80	79	82
9	77	84	81	87	78	80	80	79	72	81	91	86	91	78	86	84	84	87
10	81	89	86	92	82	84	84	83	75	85	96	91	97	82	90	89	88	93
11	84	93	90	97	86	89	88	87	78	89	101	95	102	86	95	93	92	98
12	88	98	94	102	90	93	92	91	82	93	106	100	107	90	99	98	97	104
13	92	102	98	106	94	97	96	95	85	97	111	105	112	94	104	102	101	109
14	96	107	102	111	98	101	100	99	88	101	117	109	117	97	109	106	105	115
15	99	111	106	116	101	105	104	103	91	105	122	114	122	101	113	111	109	120
Daydream – Attendance Problem																		
0	41	41	40	41	41	40	41	41	39	43	43	43	43	42	42	42	43	41
1	47	47	45	46	46	45	46	46	43	48	49	48	49	47	48	48	48	45
2	53	52	49	51	51	50	51	51	47	54	54	52	55	53	55	54	54	49
3	58	58	54	56	56	55	56	56	51	60	60	57	61	58	61	60	60	53
4	64	63	59	61	60	60	61	61	56	66	66	62	67	64	68	66	65	58
5	70	69	63	66	65	64	66	66	60	72	72	67	73	69	74	71	71	62
6	76	74	68	71	70	69	71	71	64	78	77	72	79	75	80	77	77	66
7	82	80	72	76	75	74	76	75	68	84	83	77	85	80	87	83	83	70
8	88	85	77	81	80	79	81	80	72	90	89	82	91	86	93	89	88	74
9	94	91	81	87	85	84	86	85	76	96	94	87	97	91	99	95	94	78
10	100	96	86	92	90	89	91	90	80	102	100	92	102	97	106	101	100	82
11	105	102	91	97	95	93	96	95	85	108	106	97	108	102	112	106	105	86
12	111	107	95	102	100	98	101	100	89	114	112	102	114	108	119	112	111	90

Note. Norms are in *T* scores (*M* = 50, *SD* = 10). Item numbers for the six factor scores are as follows: Hyperactivity (1, 2, 3, 4, 5, 6, 7, 8, 11, 14, 15, 17, 24, 29, 32, 35, 38); Conduct Disorder (15, 16, 17, 18, 19, 20, 21, 25, 29, 31, 32, 36, 38); Emotional Overindulgent (3, 9, 10, 12, 13, 16, 21, 36); Anxious-Passive (24, 26, 30, 33, 34, 37); Asocial (22, 23, 25, 27, 28); and Daydream-Attendance Problem (8, 11, 22, 39). The Hyperactivity Index can be obtained from items 1, 3, 5, 6, 7, 8, 13, 14, 16, and 21 and norms on page 893 used.
Source: Courtesy C. Keith Conners.

Table C-66
Norms for Conners Abbreviated Teacher Questionnaire

Total score	Male					Female				
	Age (in years)					Age (in years)				
	3–5	6–8	9–11	12–14	15–17	3–5	6–8	9–11	12–14	15–17
0	42	40	40	40	41	39	42	42	43	44
1	43	42	41	42	43	40	44	44	47	46
2	44	44	43	44	45	42	46	46	51	47
3	45	45	44	47	48	43	49	48	55	49
4	46	47	46	49	50	45	51	50	59	51
5	47	49	47	51	52	46	53	53	63	52
6	48	50	49	54	54	48	55	55	68	54
7	49	52	50	56	56	49	58	57	72	55
8	50	54	52	58	59	51	60	59	76	57
9	51	55	54	61	61	52	62	61	79	59
10	52	57	55	63	63	54	64	63	84	60
11	53	59	57	65	65	55	66	65	88	62
12	54	60	58	68	68	57	69	67	93	64
13	55	62	60	70	70	58	71	69	97	65
14	56	63	61	72	72	60	73	71	101	67
15	57	65	63	75	74	61	75	73	105	68
16	58	67	64	77	76	63	78	75	109	70
17	59	68	66	79	79	64	80	78	113	72
18	60	70	67	82	81	66	82	80	117	73
19	61	72	69	84	83	67	84	82	122	75
20	62	73	70	86	85	69	86	84	126	76
21	63	75	72	89	88	70	89	86	130	79
22	64	77	74	91	90	72	91	88	134	80
23	66	78	75	93	92	73	93	90	138	81
24	67	80	77	96	94	75	95	92	143	83
25	68	81	78	98	96	76	98	94	147	85
26	69	33	80	100	99	78	100	96	151	86
27	70	85	81	103	101	79	102	98	155	88
28	71	86	83	105	103	81	104	100	159	89
29	72	88	84	107	105	82	106	103	163	90
30	73	90	86	110	108	84	109	105	168	93

Note. Norms are in T scores ($M = 50$, $SD = 10$).
Source: Courtesy C. Keith Conners.

Table C-67
Definitions of Categories in the Structure of Intellect

Operations

Major kinds of intellectual activities or processes; things that the organism does with the raw materials of information, information being defined as "that which the organism discriminates."

C   *Cognition.* Immediate discovery, awareness, rediscovery, or recognition of information in various forms; comprehension or understanding.

M   *Memory.* Retention or storage, with some degree of availability, of information in the same form it was committed to storage and in response to the same cues in connection with which it was learned.

D   *Divergent Production.* Generation of information from given information, where the emphasis is on variety and quantity of output from the same source. Likely to involve what has been called *transfer*. This operation is most clearly involved in aptitudes of creative potential.

N   *coNvergent Production.* Generation of information from given information, where the emphasis is on achieving unique or conventionally accepted best outcomes. It is likely that the given (cue) information fully determines the response.

E   *Evaluation.* Reaching decisions or making judgments concerning criterion satisfaction (correctness, suitability, adequacy, desirability, etc.) of information.

Contents

Broad classes or types of information discriminable by the organism.

F   *Figural.* Information in concrete form, as perceived or as recalled; possibly in the form of images. The term "figural" minimally implies figure-ground perceptual organization. Visual spatial information is figural. Different sense modalities may be involved; e.g., visual kinesthetic.

S   *Symbolic.* Information in the form of denotative signs, having no significance in and of themselves, such as letters, numbers, musical notations, codes, and words, when meanings and form are not considered.

M   *seMantic.* Information in the form of meanings to which words commonly become attached, hence most notable in verbal communication but not identical with words. Meaningful pictures also often convey semantic information.

B   *Behavioral.* Information, essentially non-verbal, involved in human interactions where the attitudes, needs, desires, moods, intentions, perceptions, thoughts, etc., of other people and of ourselves are involved.

Products

The organization that information takes in the organism's processing of it.

U   *Units.* Relatively segregated or circumscribed items of information having "thing" character. May be close to Gestalt psychology's "figure on a ground."

C   *Classes.* Conceptions underlying sets of items of information grouped by virtue of their common properties.

R   *Relations.* Connections between items of information based on variables or points of contact that apply to them. Relational connections are more meaningful and definable than implications.

S   *Systems.* Organized or structured aggregates of items of information; complexes of interrelated or interacting parts.

T   *Transformations.* Changes of various kinds (redefinition, shifts, or modification) of existing information or in its function.

I   *Implications.* Extrapolations of information, in the form of expectancies, predictions, known or suspected antecedents, concomitants, or consequences. The connection between the given information and that extrapolated is more general and less definable than a relational connection.

Source: Reprinted by permission of the publisher and author from M. N. Meeker, *The Structure of Intellect*, pp. 195–196. Copyright 1969, Charles E. Merrill.

Table C-68
Percentile Ranks for Standard Scores with a Mean of 50 and Standard Deviation of 10 or 15

Standard score	SD 10	SD 15	Standard score	SD 10	SD 15	Standard score	SD 10	SD 15	Standard score	SD 10	SD 15
95	99.99	99.87	72	99	93	49	46	47	26	1	5
94	99.99	99.83	71	98	92	48	42	45	25	1	5
93	99.99	99.79	70	98	91	47	38	42	24	.47	4
92	99.99	99.74	69	97	90	46	34	39	23	.35	4
91	99.99	99.69	68	96	88	45	31	37	22	.26	3
90	99.99	99.62	67	96	87	44	27	34	21	.19	3
89	99.99	99.53	66	95	86	43	24	32	20	.13	2
88	99.99	99	65	93	84	42	21	30	19	.10	2
87	99.99	99	64	92	82	41	18	27	18	.07	2
86	99.98	99	63	90	81	40	16	25	17	.05	1
85	99.98	99	62	88	79	39	14	23	16	.03	1
84	99.97	99	61	86	77	38	12	21	15	.02	1
83	99.95	99	60	84	75	37	10	19	14	.02	1
82	99.93	98	59	82	73	36	8	18	13	.01	1
81	99.90	98	58	79	70	35	7	16	12	.01	1
80	99.87	98	57	76	68	34	5	14	11	—	.47
79	99.81	97	56	73	66	33	4	13	10	—	.38
78	99.74	97	55	69	63	32	4	12	9	—	.31
77	99.65	96	54	66	61	31	3	10	8	—	.26
76	99.53	96	53	62	58	30	2	9	7	—	.21
75	99	95	52	58	55	29	2	8	6	—	.17
74	99	95	51	54	53	28	1	7	5	—	.13
73	99	94	50	50	50	27	1	6			

_ APPENDIX D _____

MODIFIED INSTRUCTIONS FOR ADMINISTERING THE WISC-R AND WISC-III PERFORMANCE SCALE SUBTESTS TO DEAF CHILDREN

PANTOMIME INSTRUCTIONS

Picture Completion

Show child Card 2 from Wechsler Intelligence Scale for Children (WISC) (Wechsler, 1949). This item depicts a table with three legs. Count legs by pointing to each with index finger. Hold up three fingers, then point to missing leg by tracing its designated outline with index finger. Hold up four fingers. Summarize directions by counting each leg with index finger, holding up three fingers, pointing to missing area, and holding up four fingers.

Present age-appropriate initial item from WISC-R Picture Completion booklet. Point to child, point to picture (not to missing part), and point to child again.

Follow instructions in WISC-R manual regarding failure and discontinuation procedures. If child fails to indicate missing part on Cards 1 and 2 within 20 seconds, point to missing part.

Picture Arrangement

Place sample item (SCALE) in front of child in numerical order indicated in WISC-R manual. Point to pictures in general. Arrange pictures in correct order. Point to Picture A and hold up one finger, point to Picture B and hold up two fingers, and point to Picture C and hold up three fingers, thereby designating first, second, and third. Rearrange pictures in original administration order. Point to series in general sweeping motion, and then point to child.

Present age-appropriate initial item from WISC-R Picture Arrangement subtest. Point to series in general sweeping motion, and then point to child. If child does not respond or does not arrange the cards in the correct order for Item 1 (FIGHT) and/or Item 2 (PICNIC), arrange the cards in the correct sequence. Then point to each card, designating first, second, and third. Allow child to look at correct sequence for about 10 seconds, and then put the cards in their original numerical order. Point to series in general sweeping motion, and then point to child. If child fails to arrange Item 3 (FIRE) and/or Item 4 (PLANK) in the correct sequence, put the cards in their original numerical order. Take Card "F" or "W" from the array and place it below the other three cards. Point to it and hold up one finger. Then point to remaining cards in general sweeping motion, and point to child.

In Items 5 to 12, arrange cards in numerical sequence, point to cards in general sweeping motion, and point to child.

Follow instructions in WISC-R manual regarding timing and discontinuation procedures.

Block Design

Design 1. Place four blocks in front of child and turn each block to show the different sides. Point to each different side of each block during this demonstration. Arrange the four blocks into Design 1. Give child four other blocks. Point to child, point to child's blocks, and point to model. If child fails, assemble child's blocks to match modeled design. Point to child's blocks and point to model. Scramble child's blocks. Point to child, point to child's blocks, and point to model.

Design 2. Assemble Design 2 behind a screen. Present model to child in completed form. Point to child, point to child's blocks, and point to model. If child fails on first trial, follow procedure given for Design 1.

Reprinted, with changes in notation, with permission of the author from P. M. Sullivan, *A Comparison of Administration Modifications on the WISC-R Performance Scale with Different Categories of Deaf Children*, unpublished doctoral dissertation, University of Iowa, 1978.

Design 3. Display card depicting Design 3. Assemble blocks into Design 3 in full view of child. Point to card and point to blocks. Scramble the blocks. Point to child, point to child's blocks, and point to card. If child fails on first trial, repeat above administration procedure. If child is 8 or older and subtest begins with this item, follow procedure for designating color patterns and similarities of blocks given at the beginning of section on Design 1.

Designs 4 to 11. Display card showing each respective design. Point to child, point to blocks, and point to card.

Follow instructions in WISC-R manual regarding timing and discontinuation procedures.

Object Assembly

Arrange the pieces of sample item (APPLE) behind shield. Expose array and assemble pieces together. Rearrange pieces in original presentation sequence. Point to child and point to array. If child does not respond, repeat above procedure. Correct any errors.

Items 1 to 4. Arrange pieces behind shield. Expose array, point to child, and point to pieces. Correct errors on Item 1 only.

Follow instructions in WISC-R manual for timing and scoring.

Coding

Coding A. Point to star, circle, triangle, cross, and box in general sweeping motion. Point to each mark in each geometric form individually. Point to blank sample items and fill in the first circle. Give child pencil, point to child, and point to remaining sample items. Stop child after completion of last sample item. Point to subtest items in general sweeping motions for each row. Point to child and point to first item. If child discontinues work after completing first row, point to next row. Follow timing instructions in the WISC-R manual.

Coding B. Point to numbered boxes in general sweeping motion. Then point to each number and its respective symbol individually in the entire array. Point to blank sample items and fill in the first one. Give child pencil, point to child, and point to remaining sample items. Stop child after completion of last sample item. Point to subtest items in general sweeping motion for each row. Point to child and point to first item. If child discontinues work after completing first row, point to next row. Follow timing instructions in WISC-R manual.

Mazes

Give child booklet. Point to sample item. Point to figure in center of maze and to opening that leads to exit. Demonstrate sample item. On reaching opening to outside of center, pause, and, without lifting the pencil, point to blind alley. Then point to correct route and finish the tracing.

Items 1 to 9. Point to center of maze, to exit opening, and to child. Follow discontinuation procedure in WISC-R manual. If child does not begin work in center of maze, stop work, place pencil in center of maze, and point for child to continue.

Follow timing and scoring instructions in WISC-R manual.

MURPHY-NEUHAUS-REED-SULLIVAN INSTRUCTIONS

Picture Completion

This modification is based on Neuhaus (1967).

Materials. Three pictures are drawn on 3½″ × 3½″ white cardboard squares. Each item shows a picture with a missing detail on one side accompanied by the same picture with the missing detail filled in on the other side. The three constructed sample items include a picture of an arrow with the tip missing on one side and drawn in on the other, a picture of an elephant with the trunk missing on one side and drawn in on the other, and a picture of a doll with an arm missing on one side and drawn in on the other side.

Procedure. Present Sample Item 1 (ARROW). Show side with missing detail first, turn picture over and show side with completed detail. Point to completed detail. Repeat procedure above. Present Sample Item 2 (ELEPHANT) and Sample Item 3 (DOLL) in the manner given above.

Present age-appropriate initial item from WISC-R Picture Completion booklet. Follow instructions in WISC-R manual regarding failure and discontinuance procedures. If child fails to indicate missing part on Cards 1 and 2 within 20 seconds, point to missing detail.

Picture Arrangement

This modification is based on Reed (1970).

Materials. One set of three 3½″ × 3½″ white cardboard square cards with the numeral 1 printed on one card, the numeral 2 on one card, and the numeral 3 on one card.

One set of three 3½″ × 3½″ white cardboard square cards with the letter A printed on one card, the letter B on one card, and the letter C on one card. Use the sample item (SCALE) from the WISC-R Picture Arrangement subtest.

Procedure. Present Sample Item 1 (NUMBERS) in order 2, 3, 1 from child's left to right. Arrange cards in correct numerical sequence. Allow child to view for 10 seconds. Rearrange cards in original administration order. Motion child to arrange cards by pointing to them in general sweeping motion. If child does not respond or arranges cards incorrectly, arrange cards in their correct sequence. Then rearrange cards in original administration order and motion child to arrange cards. Follow same procedure for Sample Item 2 (LETTERS) and sample item (SCALE) from WISC-R Picture Arrangement subtest.

Items 1 to 4. Present age-appropriate initial item from WISC-R Picture Arrangement subtest. If child does not respond or does not arrange cards in the correct order for Item 1 (FIGHT) and/or Item 2 (PICNIC), arrange the cards in the correct sequence. Allow child to look at correct sequence for about 10 seconds and then rearrange cards in their original numerical order. Motion to child to rearrange cards. If child fails to arrange Item 3 (FIRE) and/or Item 4 (PLANK) in correct sequence, put cards in their original numerical order. Take Card "F" or "W" from the array and place it below the other three cards. Motion for child to complete arrangement by pointing to remaining cards in general sweeping motion.

Items 5 to 12. Arrange cards in numerical sequence and motion for child to complete arrangement by pointing to sequence in general sweeping motion.

Follow instructions in WISC-R manual regarding discontinuance and timing procedures.

Block Design

This modification is based on Murphy (1957).

Materials.   One white strip of cardboard 4″ × 1″ on which the instructions "Make one like this" are printed.

Procedure.   *Design 1.* Set out four blocks in single line with red color on top. Point to each block in sequence. Repeat this procedure with white and red/white sides aligned in top position of sequence. Arrange the four blocks into Design 1, taking care to use both hands in the process. Give child four other blocks. Give child written instructions. Motion for child to make pattern by pointing to model and to child's blocks. If child fails, assemble child's blocks to match modeled design. Scramble child's blocks and point to instructions, to model, and to child's blocks.

Design 2. Assemble Design 2 behind a screen. Present model to child in completed form. Give child written instructions. Motion for child to complete pattern by pointing to model and to child's blocks. If child fails on Design 2, follow procedure given for Design 1.

Design 3. Display card depicting Design 3 in full view of child, taking care to use both hands in the process. Scramble the blocks. Give child written instructions. Motion for child to construct pattern by pointing to card and to child's blocks. If child fails on first trial, repeat above administration procedure. If child is 8 or older and subtest begins with this item, follow procedure for designating color patterns and similarities of blocks given at the beginning of section on Design 1.

Designs 4 to 11. Display card showing each respective design. Point to written instructions. Motion for child to construct pattern by pointing to card and to child's blocks.

Follow timing, scoring, and discontinuance instructions in WISC-R manual.

Object Assembly

This modification is based on Neuhaus (1967).

Materials.   Three pictures drawn on 3½″ × 3½″ white cardboard squares. These pictures consist of an apple, a girl, and a horse.

Procedure.   Arrange the pieces of sample item (APPLE) behind shield. Expose array and place Picture 1 (APPLE) beside it. Point to picture. Assemble pieces together.

Items 1 and 2. Arrange pieces behind shield. Expose array and place picture of GIRL or HORSE beside it. Point to picture. Motion child to assemble pieces together by pointing to pieces in general sweeping motion. Correct errors on *Item 1 only*. Time and score as in WISC-R manual.

Items 3 and 4. Arrange pieces behind shield. Expose array. Motion child to assemble pieces together by pointing to pieces in general sweeping motion. Time and score as shown in WISC-R manual.

Coding

This modification is based on Murphy (1957).

Materials.   Coding protocol from Wechsler Intelligence Scale for Children (WISC) (Wechsler, 1949). One white strip of cardboard 4″ × 1″ on which the instructions "Do this quickly" are printed.

Procedure.   The same procedure will be followed for Coding A and B. Sit next to child and fill out sample items on WISC Coding protocol. Point to each geometric form or number and its respective symbol with pencil before filling in the first three sample items. Work quickly on remaining four sample items and do not point to components of code. Give child WISC-R Coding protocol and point to each geometric form or number and its respective symbol with pencil. Give child pencil and point to sample items. When child has completed sample items, point to subtest items with pencil in general sweeping motions for each row. Place written instructions beside protocol and point to them. If child ceases work after completion of Row 1, redirect attention to Row 2 by pointing to first item in row. Time and score as in WISC-R manual.

Mazes

This modification is based on Sullivan (1978).

Materials.   Mazes protocol from Wechsler Intelligence Scale for Children (WISC) (Wechsler, 1949). One white strip of cardboard 4″ × 1″ on which the instructions "Start in the middle. Find your way out." are written.

Procedure.   Sit next to child and point to sample maze on WISC protocol. Place written directions beside protocol and point to them. Demonstrate sample item. Give child Mazes protocol from WISC-R. Place written directions beside protocol and point to them. Give child pencil and point to center of sample maze.

Items 1 to 9. Point to written directions and to center of each maze. Follow discontinuance procedure in WISC-R manual. If child does not begin work in center of maze, stop work, place pencil in center, and motion for child to continue.

Follow timing and scoring instructions in WISC-R manual.

For Sattler's pantomime instructions for Symbol Search, see Appendix M.

APPENDIX E

OBSERVATION CODING SYSTEMS

Table E-1
Classroom Observation Code: A Modification of the Stony Brook Code

GENERAL INSTRUCTIONS FOR UTILIZING BEHAVIORAL OBSERVATIONS CODING SYSTEM IN THE CLASSROOM

1. This observation coding system is used to record behaviors that occur during structured didactic teaching and/or during periods of independent work under teacher supervision. Behaviors that occur during free play periods, snack time, etc., are not recorded. In addition, observers should not code behaviors in the following situations: a) whenever the child is out of seat at the teacher's request to hand out or collect materials, read in front of the class, work at the blackboard, or wait in line to have work checked; b) whenever the child receives individualized instruction from the teacher; c) whenever there is no assigned task, including instances in which a child is not required to initiate a new task after completion of assigned work; and d) whenever the teacher leaves the room.

2. Observers must be aware of the specific task assigned to the child and must note the particular class activity on the observation sheet. In addition, observers must be familiar with the general rules in each classroom. These rules, obtained from the teacher, are used as guidelines for employing this coding system. For example, a child who leaves his or her seat to sharpen a pencil without asking the teacher will be scored as "Gross Motor-Standing" (*GMs*) only if this behavior requires teacher permission. (*See* attached form: Observer Data Sheet—Classroom Rules.)

3. When a behavior category is observed, *circle* the respective symbol on the coding sheet. If no behavior category is observed, then code "Absence of Behavior" (*AB*); one should slash this particular symbol.

4. In coding a particular category, it is essential that the observer be familiar with the *timing requirements* of each of the behavior categories. That is, non-timed behaviors are coded as soon as they occur within a 15-second interval, with only the first occurrence noted. Timed categories are coded only if the child engages in the behavior for *more* than 15 consecutive seconds. For example, a child is scored as "Off-Task" in interval 2 if the behavior began in interval 1 and continued uninterrupted throughout interval 2. Continue coding the behavior in subsequent intervals as long as the behavior continues, uninterrupted, throughout these intervals. Each box on the observation coding sheet corresponds to a 15-second interval.

5. Any time the child leaves the room for more than one full interval without permission, those interval boxes on the coding sheet should be crossed out. (*See* "Non-Compliance" and "Off-Task" for further details.)

6. Each coding sheet is divided into two 4-minute blocks. Observe each child for a total of 16 minutes, alternating 4-minute observations on each child.

I. Interference—Symbol: *I*

Purpose: This category is intended to detect any verbal or physical behaviors or noises that are disturbing to others; the purpose here is to detect a discrete and distinct behavior that does not necessarily persist.

Timing: This category is coded as a Discrete, Non-Timed Behavior.

Description:

A. Interruption of the teacher or another student during a lesson or quiet work period.

(Table continues next page)

Table E-1 (cont.)

Examples:

1. Calling out during a lesson when the teacher or another student has the floor (includes ooh's and ahh's when raising hand).

2. Initiating discussion with another child during a work period.

Note:

1. "Interference" is coded immediately within the interval in which it first occurs.

2. If the child initiates a conversation that overlaps two intervals, code *I* only in the first interval.

3. If conversation stops and then starts anew in the next interval, code that interval as *I* if conversation is initiated by the target child.

4. In most classrooms a child is scored as *I* if he or she calls out an answer to the teacher's question. However, *I* is *not* coded in classrooms where calling out answers is permitted.

5. If the child engages in a conversation overlapping two intervals that is initiated by *another* child, do *not* code *I* in *either* interval.

6. Do *not* score the child as *I* if there is *uncertainty* as to whether the child initiated conversation or is only responding to another child.

7. Do *not* score the child as *I* if there is any *uncertainty* as to whether or not a sound (e.g., "ooh") was made by the child.

B. Production of Sounds

Examples:

1. Vocalizations: e.g., screams, whistles, calls across room. Include operant coughs, sneezes, or loud yawns.

2. The child makes noises other than vocalization through the use of materials available: slamming or banging objects, tapping ruler, foot tapping, hand clapping, etc.

Note: Do not code *I* if a sound is made accidentally (e.g., the child drops a book, knocks over a chair, etc.).

C. Annoying Behavior: This behavior refers to non-verbal interruption. The child interrupts *another child* during a teacher-directed or independent work lesson.

Examples:

1. Tapping lightly or making gentle physical movements or gestures toward another child.

2. Sitting on another's desk when that child is present at the desk.

3. Moving or lifting another's desk when the owner is present.

D. Clowning: The following behaviors are to be coded as *I*.
Examples:

1. Mimicking the teacher or another child.

2. Kicking an object across the floor.

3. Engaging in or organizing games and other inappropriate activities during a work period (e.g., playing kickball in the class, throwing and catching a ball).

4. Showing off his or her own work when not called on by the teacher.

5. Making animal imitations.

6. Calling out a wildly inappropriate answer or making an obviously inappropriate public statement.

7. Shooting paper clips, airplanes, spitballs, etc. (If aimed at someone, this behavior is coded as "Aggression," *A*.)

8. Standing on a desk, chair, or table when not requested to do so by the teacher, or in any other inappropriate situation.

9. Posturing (child acts to characterize an action, an object, or another person).

10. Dancing in the classroom.

11. Play-acting.

12. Making mock threats — if this does not occur in a clowning situation, then it is coded instead as "Threat or Verbal Aggression" (*AC*).

Note: If clowning involving vigorous gross motor movements (e.g., running, dancing) occurs while the child is out of chair, then code both *I* and "Gross Motor-Vigorous" (*GMv*).

II. Off-Task — Symbol: *X*

Purpose: This category is intended to monitor behaviors where the child, *after initiating* the appropriate task-relevant behavior, attends to stimuli other than the assigned work.

Timing: This category is coded as a Timed Behavior.

Description:

A. Manipulation and/or attending to objects, people, or parts of the body to the *total exclusion* of the task for one full interval following the interval in which the behavior began.

Examples:

1. The child plays with a pencil for one full interval after the interval in which the behavior was initially seen, without visual orientation toward the assigned task.

2. The child engages in extended conversation when he or she is supposed to be working.

3. The child does a task other than the assigned one (e.g., reads a different book). It is therefore essential that the observer be aware of the classroom situation and the specific assigned task.

Note:

1. When the child is doing something under the desk or where the observer can't see and is not attending to the task, assume the behavior is inappropriate and code *X*.

2. If the teacher is conducting a lesson at the blackboard, such that the task requires the child to *look at* the teacher or the board, score the child as *X* if he or she does *not* look at the teacher and/or the board *at any time* during the interval after the interval in which he or she first looked away.

3. If the teacher or another student is lecturing, reading a story, issuing instructions, etc., such that the child's task is to *listen* to the speaker, then code *X* if the child, by *his or her behavior*, indicates that he or she is not listening (e.g., head down

(Table continues next page)

Table E-I (cont.)

on desk, doodling in book, looking in book, etc.). Do *not* code *X* if the child *looks at* the speaker at any time during the interval.

4. Do *not* code *X* if the child shows any visual orientation to the task. Do *not* code *X* if there is uncertainty as to his or her visual orientation.

5. Do *not* code *X* if the child, by *his or her behavior*, indicates that he or she is listening (e.g., the child looks at the speaker, the child makes a verbal statement related to the speaker's subject matter).

6. Do *not* code *X* if the child plays with or manipulates an object while attending to the task.

B. Code as *X* those instances when the child is allowed to leave his or her seat (e.g., to throw refuse away) but remains away from the seat for more than five consecutive intervals following the interval in which he or she first left the seat.

Example:

Leaves Seat	Out of Seat	Out of Seat	Out of Seat	Out of Seat	Out of Seat	Out of Seat
1	2	3	4	5	6	7

Interval 7 is coded as *X* and "Out-of-Chair" (*OC*). Continue coding *X* and *OC* as long as the child remains away from his or her desk. If the child engages in task-relevant behavior while out of seat (e.g., attends to a teacher lesson), then stop coding *X* but continue coding *OC*.

Note:

1. If after initiating the task the child leaves the classroom for more than one full interval without permission, code *X* and indicate that the child is out of the room by crossing out the interval box. Continue coding *X* as long as the child remains out of the room.

2. Do *not* code *X* if the child stops working and there is *uncertainty* as to whether he or she has *completed* the task. However, put a dot above the interval in which there is uncertainty. If the teacher then confirms that the child was off-task (e.g., she says: "Why aren't you working?"), then go back and code these "dotted" intervals as *X*. If the teacher gives no indication, do not code *X*.

3. Do *not* code *X* in any interval that has been coded as "Solicitation" (*S*).

III. Non-Compliance — Symbol: *NC*

Purpose: This category is intended to monitor behaviors that reflect a failure on the part of the child to follow teacher instructions.

Timing: This category is coded as a Timed Behavior.

Description: The child fails to *initiate* appropriate behavior in response to a command or request from the teacher. It is to be distinguished from "Off-Task" (*X*), which is coded when the child, *after initiating* task-relevant behavior, ceases this task-relevant behavior.

Example: After a command has been given by the teacher (e.g., "Copy the words on the board into your notebook"), the child has one full interval after the interval in which the command was given to initiate the request. If the child has not complied, begin coding *NC* and continue coding *NC* for each full interval in which the child fails to initiate the task.

Note:

1. When the teacher gives a specific command, write "T.C." *above* the interval box in which the teacher *finished* giving the command.

2. If the child indicates that he or she is *carrying out* the teacher's command (e.g., the child looks for his or her notebook), then allow the child *five* full intervals to comply. If after this time period he or she has not initiated task-relevant behavior (e.g., copying words), then begin coding *NC*.

3. If before initiating the task the child leaves the classroom for more than one full interval without permission, code *NC* and cross out the interval box. Continue coding *NC* as long as the child remains out of the room.

4. The teacher will often issue *commands* that are *not task-related*, but are instead related to the *handling of materials* (e.g., "Put down your pencils," "Put away your book"). If the child has not complied by the end of the first full interval following the interval in which the command was given, then code that interval as *NC*. Do *not* continue coding *NC*. If the teacher repeats the same commands, then note "*T.C.*" and begin to time the child to see if he or she complies.

5. A teacher may issue more than one command (e.g., "Put down your pencils and look at the board"). The child should *not* be scored as *NC* if he or she looks at the board but does not put down his or her pencil. Therefore, do not code *NC* if the child follows the more salient, task-related aspect of the teacher's command. The child should be scored as *NC* if he or she does *not* follow the more salient command, i.e., "look at the board."

6. The teacher will often tell the class to take out a textbook and begin working independently on a particular page. Do *not* code *NC* if the child begins working in the book on the wrong page.

7. A child may not have a book in school or may be unable to find it. Give the child *five* full intervals to attempt to find the appropriate materials. If at the end of this time interval the child has not informed the teacher that he or she doesn't have the book (homework, crayons, etc.), then begin coding *NC* until he or she notifies the teacher.

Situations arise in the classroom which make it difficult to decide whether a child is noncompliant or off-task. The following guidelines should be useful in clarifying some of these situations.

8. During a classroom lesson the teacher will often issue commands that are *specific to the ongoing lesson*. In these instances, a child who had been working on the lesson but did not follow the new command should be scored as *X* rather than *NC*.

For example, during a math lesson, the children have been

(Table continues next page)

Table E-I (cont.)

working in their math workbooks. They have been following the teacher's directions and have worked on specific math examples. The teacher tells them to "Do example 10." The child has been working all along but does not do example 10. If the required time interval elapses and the child has not begun work on this example, he or she should be scored as *X*.

9. The following situations should be coded as *NC* and not "Off-Task" (*X*). During a classroom lesson, the teacher issues a command such that the children are expected to work on or direct their attention to a task different from the one on which they had been working.

For example, during a math lesson, the children have been working in their math *workbooks*. The teacher now shifts the focus of the math lesson and instructs the children to work on set theory using *colored blocks*. If the child does *not* follow these instructions within the required time interval, he or she should be scored as *NC*.

IV. Minor Motor Movement — Symbol: *MM*

Purpose: There are two aspects to this category, both of which are intended to monitor behaviors of the child that are indicative of restlessness and fidgeting.

Timing: This category is coded as a Discrete, Non-Timed Behavior.

Description: Minor motor movements refer to *buttock movements* and *rocking movements* of the child when he or she is in the seat and/or to buttock movements while he or she is in *non-erect* positions while out of seat.

A. The child engages in in-seat movements such that there is an *observable* movement of the lower buttock(s) — i.e., that part of the buttock(s) that is in contact with the seat of the chair.

Examples: The following pertain to movements of one or both buttocks.

1. Sliding in seat.
2. Twisting, turning, wiggling, etc. — coded only when accompanied by buttock movement.
3. Lifting one or both buttocks off the seat.
4. Buttock movements while kneeling or squatting in seat.

B. The child produces *rocking* movements of his or her body and/or chair. Body rocking movements are defined as *repetitive* movements (at least two complete back and forth movements) where the child moves from the waist up in a back and forth manner.

Movements of the chair are also coded as *MM* when the child lifts two chair legs off the floor.

Note:

1. Do *not* code *MM* if the child makes *just one* forward leaning movement or *just one* backward leaning movement. However, if this movement is accompanied by an observable buttock movement, then *MM* should be coded.

2. Code as *MM any* movement which takes the child from a

seated position into a kneeling, squatting, or crouching position, either in or out of the seat.

3. If the child is kneeling in or out of his or her seat, or *leaning* over a desk or table, then code as *MM* any observable movements of the lower and/or upper buttocks — i.e., that area from the upper thigh to the hip.

4. If the child goes from a standing to a kneeling or squatting position, code this as *MM*.

5. Do *not* code *MM* if the *physical* set-up is such that the child *must* move in order to work on a task. There are *two* specific situations where minor motor movements should not be coded.

(a) The position of the child's desk requires that he or she *must* move in order to work on a task (e.g., the child faces the side of the room and the blackboard is in front). In this situation, the child *must* move his or her buttocks in order to copy from the board.

(b) While working on a task that requires his or her visual attention (e.g., copying from the board, watching the teacher), the child's view is obstructed, thereby requiring him or her to move in order to maintain visual contact.

6. Do *not* code *MM* if the child moves from a standing or kneeling position to a sitting position in the chair.

V. Gross Motor Behavior

Purpose: There are two aspects of this category which are intended to monitor motor activity that results in the child's leaving his or her seat and/or engaging in vigorous motor activity.

Timing: This category is coded as a Discrete, Non-Timed Behavior.

A. Gross Motor-Standing — Symbol: *GMs*

Description: *GMs* refers to motor activity that results in the child's *leaving* his or her seat and *standing* on one or both legs (on the floor, chair, or desk) in an erect or semi-erect position such that the child's body from the waist up is *at least* at a 135 degree angle with the floor.

Note:

1. Do *not* code *GMs* when the child has *permission*, specific or implied, to leave his or her seat (e.g., to sharpen a pencil, throw refuse away, get materials, go to the board, go to the teacher's desk, etc.) If the child leaves his or her seat without permission, then code *GMs*.

2. Do *not* code *GMs* if the *physical* set-up is such that the child *must* move in order to work on a task. For example, while working on a task that requires his or her visual attention (e.g., copying from the board, watching a demonstration), the child's view is *obstructed*, thereby requiring him or her to stand up in order to maintain visual contact.

If there is *uncertainty* as to whether or not the child had to stand up, then code *GMs*.

B. Gross Motor-Vigorous — Symbol: *GMv*

Description: This is coded when the child engages in vigorous

(Table continues next page)

Table E-I (cont.)

motor activity *while not seated at his or her desk*, or when the child *leaves* his or her seat in a sudden, abrupt, or impulsive manner.

Examples:
1. Jumping up out of seat
2. Running away from seat
3. Running in the classroom
4. Crawling across the floor
5. Twirling
6. Acrobatics
7. Swinging between two seats or desks

VI. Out-of-Chair Behavior – Symbol: *OC*

Purpose: This category is intended to monitor extended out-of-seat behavior.

Timing: This category is coded as a Timed Behavior.

Description: The child remains out of chair for one full interval after the interval in which he or she first left the seat.

Note:

1. "Out-of-Chair" is coded for each complete interval that the child remains out of a chair, irrespective of whether the child is standing, sitting, or kneeling on the floor or roaming around the classroom.

2. If while being coded as *OC* the child kneels or squats (out-of-chair) or sits on the floor, then code this movement as "Minor Motor Movement" (*MM*) and continue to code *OC*. Any buttock movements that occur while the child is seated on the floor are coded as *MM*. "Out-of-chair" is discontinued only when a child sits or kneels in a chair – be it his or her own or someone else's.

3. If the child is out of a chair getting materials, sharpening a pencil, getting a drink of water, throwing refuse away, etc. (when these are *permitted* behaviors), then allow the child a maximum of five full intervals after the interval in which he or she first left the seat to complete this task. After these five intervals, if the child is still out of chair, then begin coding *OC*. If the child is *not working* during this period, then also score him or her as "Off-Task" (*X*).

4. If less than five intervals have elapsed and the child has obtained his or her goal (e.g., gotten his book, thrown away refuse, etc.), then allow him or her one full interval to return to his or her seat. If at the end of that interval he or she has not returned to the seat, then code that interval as *OC*.

5. It is essential to be familiar with those classroom rules regarding leaving seat with and without permission.

VII. Physical Aggression – Symbol: *A*

Purpose: This category is intended to measure physical aggression directed at another person, or destruction of other's property. This behavior is coded regardless of the accuracy of the intended assault.

Timing: This category is coded as a Discrete, Non-Timed Behavior.

Description:

A. The child makes a forceful movement directed at another person, either directly or by utilizing a material object as an extention of the hand.

Examples:
1. Blocking someone with arms or body, tripping, kicking, or hitting another person.
2. Throwing objects at another person.
3. Pinching, biting.

Note:

1. In all of the above examples, even if the child misses his or her goal, the behavior should be coded as *A*.

2. Code *A* even when the physical aggression is initiated by another child and the target child defends himself or herself. However, this should be noted on the coding sheet.

B. Destruction of other's materials or possessions, or school property.

Examples:
1. Tearing or crumpling other's work.
2. Breaking crayons, pencils, or pens of others.
3. Misusing other's books (ripping out pages, writing in them, etc.).
4. Writing on another child or on another child's work.
5. Writing on a school desk.
6. Writing in a school textbook.

Note:

1. Code *A* even if the owner of the material is not at his or her desk.

2. If the child engages in *continuous* destructive behavior (e.g., writes on a desk or in a school textbook for several consecutive intervals), then code *A* only in the first interval in which the behavior occurs. If the child *interrupts* this destructive behavior and then returns to it, then code *A* anew.

C. Grabbing material in a sudden manner.

Examples:
1. The child grabs a book out of the hands of another child.
2. The child grabs his or her own material from another child. Exclude casually taking material out of another's hand.

VIII. Threat or Verbal Aggression – Symbol: to Children = *AC*, to Teacher = *AT*

Purpose: This category is intended to monitor verbalizations or physical gestures of children that are abusive or threatening.

Timing: This category is coded as a Discrete, Non-Timed Behavior.

Description:

A. The child uses abusive language and gestures to children (*AC*) or to teacher (*AT*).

(Table continues next page)

Table E-I (cont.)

Examples:
1. The child curses at another; says "shut up" to another.
2. The child sticks out his tongue at another; makes a threatening gesture; etc.
3. The child threatens others.
4. The child teases others; criticizes others.
5. The child bullies others.

B. When asked to do something by the teacher, the child directly states, "No I won't, I am not going to do that." This should be coded as "Interference" (*I*) and *AT*. Do *not* code "Solicitation" (*S*).

C. The child answers the teacher back when a reply is *not* acceptable.

Example: The teacher states, "We are not going outside today." The child calls back in a defiant manner, "Why not? I want to."

IX. Solicitation of Teacher — Symbol: *S*

Purpose: This category monitors behaviors directed toward the teacher. It is important to note that this behavior is *target-child initiated*.

Timing: This category is coded as a Discrete, Non-Timed Behavior.

Description:

A. Behaviors directed at obtaining the teacher's attention.

Examples:
1. Leaving seat and going up to the teacher. [This would be coded as *S* and "Gross Motor-Standing (*GMs*); if the child speaks to the teacher, "Interference" (*I*) is also coded.]
2. Raising hand.
3. Calling out to the teacher.

Note:
1. These behaviors are coded as *S* whether or not the teacher recognizes the child.
2. When a child calls out to the teacher by mentioning the teacher's name, or directs a question or statement specifically to the teacher while the teacher is attending to another child or addressing the class, then the behavior is coded as both *S* and "Interference" (*I*).
3. If the child says "ooh," "ahh," etc., while raising his or her hand in response to a teacher's question, code this as "Interference" (*I*) but *not S*.
4. If the observation begins while a teacher-child interaction is taking place, assume that the teacher initiated the interaction and do *not* code *S*.
5. If the child raises his or her hand in order to solicit the teacher and keeps the hand raised for more than one interval, *S* is coded *only* in the first interval in which the behavior occurred.
6. "Solicitation" and "Interference" (*I*) are coded if the child calls out an answer to the teacher when another child has the floor.
7. "Solicitation" is *not* coded if the child raises his or her hand in response to a teacher's question.
8. "Solicitation" is *not* coded if the child calls out in response to a teacher's question. In most classrooms, the child is scored as "Interference" (*I*) if he or she calls out an answer to a teacher's question.

X. Absence of Behavior — Symbol: *AB*

If no inappropriate behaviors as defined by the above categories occur in an interval, then code *AB*.

Classroom Observation Code
Observer Data Sheet

\# _____ **Child A:** _____ **Seat:** _____
B: _____ **Seat:** _____
School: _____ **Teacher:** _____ **Room #:** _____

Classroom Rules:
1. Must a child always raise his or her hand before asking or answering questions?
   a) During a teacher-conducted lesson _____
   b) During independent work _____
   c) Comments _____

2. May a child engage in conversation with other children?
   a) During a teacher-conducted lesson _____
   b) During independent work _____
   c) Comments _____

(Table continues next page)

Table E-I (cont.)

3. Must a child work after completion of assigned task? _____
   a) On what? _____
   b) Can this be done out of his or her assigned seat? _____

4. May a child leave the room without permission? _____

5. May a child leave his or her seat without permisison to:
   a) sharpen a pencil _____   e) get materials _____
   b) throw refuse away _____   f) stand while working _____
   c) get a drink _____   g) other _____
   d) speak to the teacher _____

6. Other class rules: _____

Classroom Observation Code
Scoring Sheet

Observer _____ Date _____ Time _____

Source: Reprinted, with changes in notation, with permission of the authors from H. Abikoff and R. Gittelman, "Classroom Observation Code: A Modification of the Stony Brook Code," *Psychopharmacology Bulletin,* 1985, *21,* pp. 901–909.

Table E-2
Social Competence Observation Schedule

Category	Description
Interacting with Peers	
1. Passively accepts aggression or domination from peer	Child allows another to boss, push, hit, or grab things from him or her without retaliation of any kind
2. Communicates in a positive way with peer	Child shows natural communication with peers—appears at ease and comfortable in the situation
3. Is involved in cooperative activity with peer	Child voluntarily becomes involved with one or more children in an activity not required by the teacher
4. Shows successful leadership activity	Child initiates activity and makes suggestions that are followed by peers
5. Bosses or bullies peer—verbal	Child tells others what or what not to do, commands others
6. Exhibits physical aggression against peer	Child engages in aggression involving actual physical contact
Interacting with Teacher	
7. Clings to teacher	Child constantly stays by teacher's side or, for example, holds on to teacher's hand or clothes
8. Tenses or withdraws in response to teacher's approach	Child tenses body or moves farther away when approached by teacher
9. Communicates feelings to teacher in positive way	Child makes a positive statement to the teacher that is not a suggestion related to classroom activities
10. Volunteers ideas or suggestions to teacher	Child makes suggestions or gives ideas during formal, teacher-directed classroom activities
11. Seeks attention of teacher while latter is interacting with another child	Child calls out to teacher, grabs teacher's arm, or performs similar actions when teacher is involved with another child
12. Exhibits physical aggression toward teacher	Child hits, kicks, or bites teacher
13. Seeks teacher attention—negative	Child uses inappropriate behavior to seek teacher's attention
14. Follows teacher request for help	Child follows teacher's directions willingly and immediately
15. Follows teacher suggestion regarding play activity	Child accepts and follows teacher's ideas or suggestions during informal, free activity
16. Exhibits other cooperative interactions with teacher	—
Child Is Alone	
17. Quietly listens to peer or teacher	Child is attentive to teacher while latter is giving instruction, reading a story, or performing a similar activity
18. Daydreams, stares into space, has blank look	Child has tuned out what is happening in the classroom, is unaware of what is going on, and looks sad
19. Puts things away carefully	—
20. Appears alone, confused, and bewildered	Child's face registers confusion; child appears not to understand or know how to organize or carry out an activity
21. Cries or screams—frightened	Child cries or screams from some emotion other than, for example, anger or humiliation
22. Wanders aimlessly	—
23. Engages in task in positive manner	Child is actively involved in carrying out task sanctioned by teacher; he or she is concentrating, alert, and interested
24. Engages in task in negative manner	Child resists instructions, destroys an object, or engages in similar negative behaviors
25. Throws temper tantrum	Child screams, kicks
26. Exhibits inappropriate verbal activity	Child expresses anger or frustration through words or gestures
27. Exhibits inappropriate gross motor activity	Child runs around room, throws objects, jumps, or performs similar inappropriate gross motor activity
28. Exhibits other isolated negative behavior	—

Note. Item numbers for the factor scores are as follows: Factor I (Interest-Participation vs. Apathy-Withdrawal) (1, 2, 4, 7, 8, 9, 10, 17, 18, 19, 20, 21, 22, 28); Factor II (Cooperation-Compliance vs. Anger-Defiance) (3, 5, 6, 11, 12, 13, 14, 15, 16, 23, 24, 25, 26, 27). The following items are scored in a negative direction: 1, 5, 6, 7, 8 11, 12, 13, 18, 20, 21, 22, 24, 25, 26, 27, 28.
   This schedule was designed to parallel the two teacher-judgment measures developed by Martin Kohn (the Social Competence Scales and the Problem Checklist). For additional information about the schedule, see Ali Khan and R. D. Hoge, "A Teacher-Judgment Measure of Social Competence: Validity Data," *Journal of Consulting and Clinical Psychology*, 1983, *51*, 809–814.
Source: Reprinted, with changes in notation, by permission of R. D. Hoge.

Table E-3
A Scale for Rating Symptoms of Patients with the Syndrome of Autism in Real-Life Settings

INSTRUCTIONS FOR THE RITVO-FREEMAN REAL LIFE RATING SCALE

A. Observation setting. Patient is to be observed in the same setting, at the same time of day, and on the same day of the week, for 30 min. each time. Notes may be made by the observer. The data sheet is completed at the end of each 30-min. observation session.

B. Coding the frequency of behaviors. Each behavior is rated on the following scale:

0 = *Never* demonstrates the target behavior
1 = *Rarely* — target behavior is seen only 1-3 times
2 = *Frequently* — target behavior is seen 4 or more times
3 = *Almost always* — target behavior is seen almost constantly throughout observation period.

C. Obtaining interobserver agreement. Raters should review definitions and observe and score patients together on at least 3 separate occasions or until they reach 80% agreement.

D. Scoring. A mean score for each scale (sensory-motor, social, affect, sensory, and language) is determined by adding the individual ratings (0 to 3) for each behavior in the scale and dividing by the number of behaviors on that scale. A mathematical sign correction to subtract normal behavior must be made as follows:

Scale I. *Sensory-Motor:* No mathematical corrections are necessary.

Scale II. *Social:* Behavior 1 (appropriate response to interaction), behavior 2 (appropriate response to events in the environment), and behavior 3 (initiates appropriate interaction) scores are subtracted from the other behaviors before the mean is computed.

Scale III. *Affect:* No mathematical changes are necessary.

Scale IV. *Sensory:* Behavior 1 (uses objects appropriately) is subtracted from the other behaviors before the mean is computed.

Scale V. *Language:* Behaviors 1 (communicative use of language), 2 (initiates communication with gestures), and 3 (initiates appropriate verbal communication) are subtracted from the other behaviors before the mean is computed.

E. Charting. A simple graph showing the means of each scale can be made to compare baseline and subsequent time periods. (See the Ritvo-Freeman Real Life Rating Scale at the end of this table for a form that can be used to summarize the ratings obtained on the scale.)

RITVO-FREEMAN REAL LIFE RATING SCALE TARGET BEHAVIORS AND DEFINITIONS

Scale I. Sensory-Motor Scale

1. *Whirls.* Sits or stands in one place and spins himself or herself around.

2. *Flaps arms, hands, fingers.* Moves arms, hands, and/or fingers in an up-down, side-to-side, or circular motion at least two times. He or she may utilize one or both arms and hands, one or all fingers during this activity. Fingers may be wiggled individually or in unison. He or she may flap arms, hands, and/or fingers in front of, to the side of, or behind body. Frequently the child will engage in this behavior in front of eyes, in which case "Watches motion of own hands or objects" is noted in addition.

3. *Pacing.* Walks, skips, or runs in a repetitive course.

4. *Bangs head, hits self.* Three types of behaviors are included here:

(1) Hits head or any part of his or her body with own hand or object.
(2) Strikes head against another object or person such as wall, table, floor, etc.
(3) Hits any part of his or her body.

5. *Rocks head or body.* Sits or stands in one place and moves his or her body and/or head in a back-and-forth, side-to-side, or circular motion at least two times.

6. *Toe walks.* Child stands or walks on balls of feet or toes.

7. *Other.* Any other idiosyncratic motor behavior. Specify the behavior.

Scale II. Social-Relationship to People Scale

1. *Appropriate response to interaction attempt.* Refers to gestures, facial reactions, and posture.

2. *Appropriate response to activities and events in the environment.* This encompasses a broad number of responses. Some examples are shows interest in conversation around him or her, responds appropriately to noises (such as a siren, shout, object's being dropped).

3. *Initiates appropriate physical interaction with others.* Any appropriate affectionate or play interactions.

4. *Ignores or withdraws from interaction attempt.* Ignores or withdraws from approach or attempt to initiate interaction. This may be seen as the following: appears to be oblivious to the interaction attempt, showing no facial, physical, or verbal reactions.

5. *Physically provokes or disturbs others.* Hits, pokes, kicks, bites, pushes, pinches other children or adults. Include also attempts at aggression (e.g., child swings fist to hit another person, but misses) and token aggression.

6. *Changes activities.* Interrupts obvious normal sequences for no apparent reason (suddenly runs to door, darts to a wall).

7. *Genital manipulation.* Touches or rubs genital area or breasts using hands, fingers, or another objects, such as a toy, eating utensil, or the like. Child also may rub against other people or objects (e.g., rug, wall, chair).

8. *Isolates self from the group.* Sits, stands, wanders, or runs away from the group. Or may remain with the group, but not

(Table continues next page)

Table E-3 (cont.)

actively participate or show interest in the group's activities or conversation. Does not seek out others for conversation or gestural interaction. Also usually seen at these times are behaviors from the sensory-motor, affectual response, and sensory response categories (noncommunication, vocalizations, noncommunicative use of immediate or delayed echolalia, hallucinatory or delusionary behavior). These should be noted in the appropriate categories.

9. *Responds to hugs/being held by rigidity.* Body becomes rigid and stiff in response to a hug or being held. Does not extend arms to the person initiating the holding-hugging behavior.

Scale III. Affectual Response Scale

1. *Abrupt affectual changes.* Suddenly begins to cry, laugh, giggle, or smile without any apparent reasons or stimulus from the immediate environment.

2. *Grimaces.* Funny or strange facial expressions or movements. This may be seen while staring into a mirror.

3. *Temper outbursts, explosive and unpredictable behavior.* Anger directed or expressed by body movement.

4. *Cries.*

5. *Other.* Any other idiosyncratic affectual behaviors observed.

Scale IV. Sensory Response Scale

1. *Uses objects and toys appropriately.* Uses objects in the manner in which they were intended. This includes eating utensils.

2. *Agitated by loud/sudden noises.*

3. *Whirls or spins objects.*

4. *Rubs surfaces.* Uses hand, fingers, or any other part of his or her body to rub against another person or object. May be a repetitive act.

5. *Agitated by new activities or environment.* Cries, becomes agitated or upset when given a new activity or as a result of a change in the environment or change to a new environment.

6. *Watches motion of own hands or objects.* Includes finger wiggling.

7. *Repetitive behavior (stereotypic actions).* Repeats some behavior at least two times. Examples are waving objects, tapping objects, repeatedly putting food in mouth and then spitting it out, picking up napkin and dropping it again.

8. *Sniffs self or objects.* Smells any part of his or her body, other people, or objects.

9. *Lines up objects.* Lines up, orders, or arranges 2 or more objects, such as toys, food, or furniture.

10. *Visual detail scrutiny.* Scrutinizes small details, i.e., looks at objects in front of eyes.

11. *Destructive to objects.* Throws, hits, bangs, kicks, and bites objects or toys.

12. *Repetitive vocalizations.* Makes same sound at least two times—e.g., clicking of teeth.

13. *Stares.* Stares into space for at least 5 seconds.

14. *Covers eyes, ears.* Covers eye(s) and/or ear(s) with his or her hand or object.

15. *Flicks objects.* Uses fingers to flick repetitively.

16. *Other.* Any idiosyncratic sensory response—specify behavior.

Scale V. Language Scale

1. *Communicative use of language.* Speech directed to other people. Included here is labeling of objects.

2. *Initiates or responds to communication using gestures.* Two behaviors constitute this category:
(a) Starts up an appropriate verbal exchange.
(b) Verbally lets needs or desires be known. For example: "I have to go to the bathroom."

3. *Noncommunicative use of delayed echolalia.* Says words, phrases, and sentences heard in the past, with little or no relationship to current situation.

4. *Immediate echolalia.* Repeats words or phrases after hearing them. May repeat a question in part or whole instead of answering.

5. *Delusions.* Verbalized nonrational (psychotic) ideation.

6. *Auditory hallucinations.* Appears to be hearing things that are not there.

7. *Visual hallucinations.* Appears to be seeing things that are not there.

8. *Noncommunicative vocalizations.* Makes single vowel (aaaa) or consonant (mmm) sounds or combines vowels and consonants in a nonrepetitive pattern (ba na da go). Nondirected screaming and screeching is included here.

9. *No or brief response to communication attempts.* Answers briefly or not at all when others attempt conversation.

(Table continues next page)

Table E-3 (cont.)

RITVO-FREEMAN REAL LIFE RATING SCALE

ID: ___0011___
Visit: ___0015___
Date: ___05/14/84___

Child's name: _____Eddie R._____

Description & time of setting: _____Classroom_____

People present: _____BJ, AKY, AMR_____

Never = 0; Rarely = 1; Frequently = 2; Almost always = 3

Scale I: Sensory Motor Behaviors

1. Whirls	2
2. Flaps	3
3. Pacing	0
4. Bangs/hits self	0
5. Rocks	2
6. Toe walks	0
7. Other	0
Sum I:	7
Mean:	1.0

Scale II: Social Relationship to People

*1. Appro. resp. to interaction attempt	2
*2. Appro. resp. to activities in envir.	1
*3. Initiates appro. physical interaction	0
4. Ignores interaction attempt	1
5. Disturbs others	0
6. Changes activities	3
7. Genital manipulation	0
8. Isolates self	2
9. Resp. to hugs/being held by rigidity	0
Sum II:	3
Mean:	.33

Scale III: Affectual Reactions

1. Abrupt change	2
2. Grimaces	1
3. Temper outbursts/unpred.	0
4. Cries	0
5. Other	0
Sum III:	3
Mean:	.6

Scale IV: Sensory Responses

*1. Uses objects appro.	2
2. Agitated by noises	0
3. Whirls/spins objects	3
4. Rubs surfaces	0
5. Agitated by new activity	0
6. Watches motion hand/obj.	2
7. Repetitive/stereotypic	3
8. Sniffs self or objects	1
9. Lines up objects	1
10. Visual detail/scrutiny	2
11. Destructive to objects	0
12. Repetitive vocalizations	3
13. Stares	3
14. Covers ears or eyes	2
15. Flicks	0
16. Other	0
Sum IV:	18
Mean:	1.13

Scale V: Language

*1. Communicative use of language	0
*2. Initiates or resp. to communication	1
*3. Initiates appro. verbal communication	0
4. Noncommunicative use of d. echolalia	1
5. Immediate echolalia	2
6. Delusions	0
7. Auditory hallucination	0
8. Visual hallucination	0
9. Noncommunicative vocalizations	3
10. No or brief resp. to comm. attempts	3
Sum V:	8
Mean:	.8

Overall Scale:
Sum:

I __1.00__ II __0.33__ III __0.60__ IV __1.13__ V __0.80__ ÷ 5 = __0.77__

*Score of behavior is subtracted from others before the mean is computed.
(*Note:* Sum = sum of means.)

Source: Reprinted, with changes in notation, with permission of the publisher and authors from B. J. Freeman, E. R. Ritvo, A. Yokota, and A. Ritvo, "A Scale for Rating Symptoms of Patients with the Syndrome of Autism in Real Life Settings," *Journal of the American Academy of Child Psychiatry*, 1986, 25, pp. 131–136. © American Academy of Child and Adolescent Psychiatry.

Table E-4
Coding System for Observing Children's Play

Category	Definition
1. SP = Solitary play	Child plays by himself or herself
a. SMP = Simple manipulation play	Child performs simple object manipulations. Examples: mouthing, waving, banging, throwing, and exploring with fingers
b. RP = Relational play	Child combines two or more objects in a nonfunctional manner. Examples: touching or banging two objects together, stacking objects, and using one object as a container to hold another object
c. FP = Functional play	Child makes appropriate use of an object or conventional association of two or more objects. Examples: self-directed acts—combing one's hair; doll-directed acts—giving doll a bath; other-directed acts—holding a telephone receiver to the mother's ear; and object-directed acts—placing the top on a teapot or putting an animal in a cage
d. SYP = Symbolic play	Child differentiates objects and actions, showing ability to represent and transform objects internally in thought, fully independent of overt actions. Examples: substitution play (using one object as if it were a different object)—using a teacup as a telephone; agent play (using a doll as an independent agent of action)—propping a bottle in a doll's arms as if it could feed itself; and imaginary play (creating objects or people that have no physical representation in the immediate environment)—making pouring sounds as imaginary tea is being poured from a teapot into a cup
2. PP = Parallel play	Child plays in close proximity to another child, but each is working on his or her own task
3. CP = Cooperative play	Child works with another child on a common task
4. UP = Uncooperative play	Child fails to work cooperatively with another child on a common task

Note. The four subcategories under Solitary play describe a developmental progression of play from 6 to 24 months of age; the subcategories are from Ungerer and Sigman (1981).

APPENDIX F

HIGHLIGHTS OF ASSESSMENT MEASURES

Table F-1
Classification of Assessment Instruments by Age and Type of Measure

Instrument	Age				Type of measure													
	Infant	Preschool	School age	Adult	Achievement	Adaptive behavior	Auditory discrimination	Behavior checklist	Bilingual	Infant and developmental	Intelligence – nonverbal	Intelligence – verbal & nonverbal	Motor/motor dexterity	Neuropsychological	Omnibus	Psycholinguistic	Receptive vocabulary	Visual motor
AAMD Adaptive Behavior Scale[a]	X	X	X	X		X												
AAMD Adaptive Behavior Scale – School Edition		X	X			X												
Abbreviated Parent/Teacher Questionnaire		X	X					X										
Adaptive Behavior Inventory for Children			X			X												
AML Behavior Rating Scale			X					X										
Auditory Discrimination Test		X	X				X											
Balthazar Scales of Adaptive Behavior[a]			X	X		X												
Basic Achievement Skills Individual Screener			X		X													
Battelle Developmental Inventory	X	X	X			X												
Bayley Scales of Infant Development	X									X								
Bender Visual Motor Gestalt Test			X															X
Bilingual Syntax Measure and Bilingual Syntax Measure II			X						X									
Blind Learning Aptitude Test[b]			X								X							
Boehm Test of Basic Concepts – Preschool Version		X			X													
Boehm Test of Basic Concepts – Revised			X		X													

(Table continues next page)

Table F-I (cont.)

Instrument	Infant	Preschool	School age	Adult	Achievement	Adaptive behavior	Auditory discrimination	Behavior checklist	Bilingual	Infant and developmental	Intelligence—nonverbal	Intelligence—verbal & nonverbal	Motor/motor dexterity	Neuropsychological	Omnibus	Psycholinguistic	Receptive vocabulary	Visual motor
Bracken Basic Concept Scale		X	X		X													
Bruininks-Oseretsky Test of Motor Proficiency		X	X										X					
Child Behavior Checklist		X	X					X										
Child Behavior Scale			X					X										
Classroom Adjustment Ratings Scale			X					X										
Classroom Reading Inventory			X		X													
Columbia Mental Maturity Scale		X	X								X							
Conners Parent Rating Scale		X	X					X										
Conners Teacher Rating Scale		X	X					X										
Denver Developmental Screening Test—Revised	X	X	X							X								
Detroit Tests of Learning Aptitude—P		X	X									X						
Detroit Tests of Learning Aptitude—2			X									X						
Developmental Test of Visual-Motor Integration		X	X															X
Developmental Test of Visual Perception		X	X															X
Devereux Adolescent Behavior Rating Scale			X					X										
Devereux Child Behavior Rating Scale			X					X										
Devereux Elementary School Behavior Rating Scale			X					X										
Extended Merrill-Palmer Scale		X	X									X						
Goldman-Fristoe-Woodcock Test of Auditory Discrimination		X	X	X			X											
Goodenough-Harris Drawing Test		X	X								X							
Halstead-Reitan Neuropsychological Test Battery for Older Children			X											X				
Health Resources Inventory			X					X										
Hiskey-Nebraska Test of Learning Aptitude		X	X								X							
Illinois Test of Psycholinguistic Abilities, Revised Edition		X	X													X		
Infant Psychological Developmental Scale	X									X								
Kaufman Assessment Battery for Children		X	X									X						
Kaufman Test of Educational Achievement			X		X													
KeyMath Diagnostic Arithmetic Test			X		X													
Kohn Problem Checklist		X	X					X										
Kohn Social Competence Scale		X	X					X										
Language Assessment Battery			X						X									
Language Assessment Scales			X	X					X									
Leiter International Performance Scale		X	X	X							X							
Lindamood Auditory Conceptualization Test			X				X											

(Table continues next page)

Table F-1 (cont.)

Instrument	Infant	Preschool	School age	Adult	Achievement	Adaptive behavior	Auditory discrimination	Behavior checklist	Bilingual	Infant and developmental	Intelligence—nonverbal	Intelligence—verbal & nonverbal	Motor/motor dexterity	Neuropsychological	Omnibus	Psycholinguistic	Receptive vocabulary	Visual motor
			Age									*Type of measure*						
Luria-Nebraska Neuropsychological Battery: Children's Revision			X											X				
McCarthy Scales of Children's Abilities		X	X									X						
New Sucher-Allred Reading Placement Inventory			X		X													
Peabody Individual Achievement Test			X		X													
Peabody Picture Vocabulary Test—Revised		X	X	X													X	
Pictorial Test of Intelligence		X	X								X							
Preschool Behavior Questionnaire		X						X										
Purdue Pegboard		X	X	X									X					
Purdue Perceptual-Motor Survey			X															X
Raven's Progressive Matrices			X	X							X							
Reitan-Indiana Neuropsychological Test Battery for Children			X											X				
Revised Behavior Problem Checklist			X					X										
Revised Denver Prescreening Developmental Questionnaire	X	X	X							X								
Revised Visual Retention Test			X	X														X
Scales of Independent Behavior	X	X	X	X		X												
Sequential Assessment of Mathematics Inventories			X		X													
Slosson Intelligence Test		X	X									X						
Southern California Sensory Integration Tests		X	X											X				
Stanford-Binet Intelligence Scale: Fourth Edition		X	X	X								X						
System of Multicultural Pluralistic Assessment			X												X			
Teacher Behavioral Description Form			X					X										
Teacher-Child Rating Scale			X					X										
Teacher's Report Form			X					X										
Test of Auditory Comprehension of Language—Revised		X	X														X	
T.M.R. School Competency Scales[a]			X	X		X												
Token Test for Children		X	X													X		
Vineland Adaptive Behavior Scales	X	X	X	X		X												
Wechsler Adult Intelligence Scale—Revised			X	X								X						
Wechsler Intelligence Scale for Children—Revised			X									X						
Wechsler Preschool and Primary Scale of Intelligence		X	X									X						
Wide Range Achievement Test—Revised			X	X	X													
Wisconsin Behavior Rating Scale[a]	X	X				X												
Woodcock-Johnson Psycho-Educational Battery		X	X	X											X			
Youth Self-Report			X					X										

[a] Designed for mentally retarded individuals.
[b] Designed for blind individuals.

Table F-2
Characteristics of Assessment Measures

Title, author, and publisher	Description	Norms/reliability/validity	Comment
AAMD Adaptive Behavior Scale (ABS) (Nihira, Foster, Shellhaas, & Leland, 1974), American Association on Mental Deficiency	Behavior rating scale for use with institutionalized mentally retarded, emotionally maladjusted, and developmentally disabled individuals. Assesses basic survival skills and maladaptive behaviors. Provides percentile ranks. For ages 3-0 to 69 years. Takes approximately 15 to 30 minutes to administer.	Norms are based on institutionalized mentally retarded and are adequate for this population. Interrater reliability is satisfactory for survival skill domains but not for maladaptive behavior domains. More information is needed about its validity.	A somewhat useful scale for evaluating competencies of institutionalized mentally retarded individuals and other institutionalized individuals. Respondent is attendant, parent, or teacher.
AAMD Adaptive Behavior Scale—School Edition (ABS-SE) (Lambert, Windmiller, Tharinger, & Cole, 1981), CTB/McGraw-Hill	Behavior rating scale for use with elementary school children. Similar to ABS, except that some ABS domains have been eliminated. Provides standard scores ($M = 10$, $SD = 3$). For ages 3-3 to 17-2 years. Takes approximately 15 to 30 minutes to administer.	Norm group is not adequately described. Reliability and validity are questionable.	May be useful as an informal measure of adaptive behavior competencies of school children. However, scores should not be used to classify children.
Abbreviated Parent/Teacher Questionnaire (Conners, 1985)[a]	Ten-item behavior checklist developed from the Conners Parent Rating Scale. Provides T scores ($M = 50$, $SD = 10$). For ages 3 to 17 years. Takes approximately 2 minutes to administer.	Norm group, reliability, and validity are adequate.	A useful quick screening scale for assessing behavior problems of children. Respondent is parent or teacher.
Adaptive Behavior Inventory for Children (ABIC) (Mercer & Lewis, 1978), The Psychological Corporation	Behavior rating scale that measures six areas of adaptive behavior: family, peers, community, school, earner/consumer, and self-maintenance. Provides scaled scores for each area and a total score ($M = 50$, $SD = 15$). For ages 5-0 to 11-11 years. Takes approximately 30 minutes to administer.	Norm group is limited. Reliability is satisfactory. More information is needed about its validity.	A somewhat useful instrument for evaluating competencies of mentally retarded elementary school children. Respondent is parent.
AML Behavior Rating Scale (Cowen, Trost, Lorion, Dorr, Izzo, & Isaacson, 1975)[b]	Brief 11-item behavior checklist. Contains three measures: acting-out, shyness-timidity-withdrawal, and learning disability. Provides raw scores. For primary grade children. Takes approximately 2 minutes to administer.	Norm group is limited. More information is needed about its reliability and validity.	A somewhat useful screening scale for evaluating behavior problems of elementary school children. Respondent is teacher.

(Table continues next page)

Table F-2 (cont.)

Title, author, and publisher	Description	Norms/reliability/validity	Comment
Auditory Discrimination Test (ADT) (Reynolds, 1987), Western Psychological Services	Contains 40 word pairs matched for familiarity, length, and phonetic category. Provides T scores ($M = 50$, $SD = 100$). For ages 4-0 to 8-11 years. Takes approximately 5 to 10 minutes to administer.	Norm group is adequate. Reliability and validity minimally satisfactory.	Serves as a rough screening measure of auditory discrimination ability.
Balthazar Scales of Adaptive Behavior (Balthazar, 1976), Consulting Psychologists Press	Behavior rating scale for use with severely and profoundly mentally retarded individuals. Assesses functional independence and social adaptations. Provides percentile ranks. For ages 5 years to adult. Takes approximately 90 minutes to administer.	Norms are limited. More information is needed about its reliability and validity.	A somewhat useful instrument for informal measurement of the competencies of institutionalized mentally retarded individuals. Respondent is attendant.
Basic Achievement Skills Individual Screener (BASIS) (The Psychological Corporation, 1983), The Psychological Corporation	Contains Reading, Mathematics, and Spelling Tests and an optional Writing Test. Provides standard scores ($M = 100$, $SD = 15$). For ages 6 to 18, but preferred ages are 6 to 14. Takes approximately 45 to 60 minutes to administer.	Norm group is generally representative of the population. Reliability and validity are acceptable for ages 6 to 14 years.	A somewhat useful screening instrument of academic skills.
Battelle Developmental Inventory (BDI) (Newborg, Stock, & Wnek, 1984), DLM Teaching Resources	Developmental inventory that measures development in five areas: personal-social, adaptive, motor, communication, and cognitive. Provides standard scores ($M = 100$, $SD = 15$). For ages newborn to 8 years. Takes approximately 10 to 30 minutes to administer.	Norm group is adequate. More information is needed about its reliability and validity.	A somewhat useful instrument for measuring important areas of development in young children. Respondent is parent.
Bayley Scales of Infant Development (Bayley, 1969), The Psychological Corporation	Measures infant mental and motor development. Provides standard scores ($M = 100$, $SD = 16$). For ages 2 months to 2-6 years. Takes approximately 45 to 75 minutes to administer.	Norm group is excellent. Reliability and validity are satisfactory.	The best measure of infant development available.
Bender Visual Motor Gestalt Test (Bender, 1938), American Orthopsychiatric Association	Consists of nine cards with geometric designs that child copies. Provides standard scores ($M = 100$, $SD = 15$) in the Developmental Bender Scoring System. For ages 5-0 to 11-11 in Developmental Bender Scoring System. Takes approximately 5 minutes to administer.	Norm group is limited for Developmental Bender Scoring System. Reliability is minimally satisfactory. Validity is satisfactory when the test is used as a measure of perceptual-motor development.	Useful in evaluating visual-motor abilities.

916

Test	Description	Technical	Comment
Bilingual Syntax Measure and Bilingual Syntax Measure II (Burt, Dulay, & Hernandez, 1976, 1978), The Psychological Corporation	Consists of questions about pictures, designed to elicit responses incorporating syntactic structures (e.g., plurals, reflexives, and subjunctives) in Spanish and English. Provides a level of proficiency on a 5-point (or 6-point) scale. For kindergarten through sixth grade. Takes approximately 25 to 30 minutes to administer each form.	No norms. Reliability and validity are limited.	Measures limited aspect of language proficiency. Serves as a rough screening measure.
Blind Learning Aptitude Test (BLAT) (Newland, 1971), University of Illinois Press	Measures learning aptitude of blind children by assessing recognition of differences and similarities, identification of progressions and missing elements, and ability to complete a figure. Items are in a bas-relief format. Provides standard scores ($M = 100$, $SD = 15$). For ages 6 to 16 years. Takes approximately 45 to 60 minutes to administer.	Norm group, reliability, and validity are satisfactory.	Serves as supplementary test for evaluating the nonverbal cognitive abilities of blind children. Should be used in conjunction with a verbal test. Appears to be most useful for ages 6 to 12 years.
Boehm Test of Basic Concepts–Preschool Version (BTBC-PV) (Boehm, 1986a), The Psychological Corporation	A pictorial multiple-choice test that measures knowledge of various concepts (size, direction, position in space, quantity, and time) considered necessary for achievement in the beginning school years. Provides percentile ranks and T scores. For ages 3 to 5 years. Takes approximately 15 minutes to administer.	Norms and reliability are satisfactory. More information is needed about its validity.	A somewhat useful supplementary measure of basic concepts.
Boehm Test of Basic Concepts–Revised (BTBC-R) (Boehm, 1986b), The Psychological Corporation	A pictorial multiple-choice test that measures knowledge of various concepts (direction, amount, and time) considered necessary for school achievement. Provides percentile ranks. For children in kindergarten through second grade. Takes approximately 30 minutes to administer.	Norms are satisfactory. Reliability is minimally satisfactory. Validity is satisfactory.	A somewhat useful supplementary measure of basic concepts.

(Table continues next page)

Table F-2 (cont.)

Title, author, and publisher	Description	Norms/reliability/validity	Comment
Bracken Basic Concept Scale (BBCS) (Bracken, 1984), The Psychological Corporation	A pictorial multiple-choice battery that measures knowledge of various concepts: color, letter identification, numbers, comparisons, shapes, direction, social/emotional connotation, size, textures, quantity, and time. Battery has 11 subtests. Provides subtest standard scores ($M = 10$, $SD = 3$) and composite score ($M = 100$, $SD = 15$). For ages 2½ to 8 years. Takes approximately 30 minutes to administer.	Norms are excellent. Reliability and validity are excellent for composite score but less satisfactory for subtest scores.	A useful supplementary measure of basic concepts.
Bruininks-Oseretsky Test of Motor Proficiency (Bruininks, 1978), American Guidance Service	Measures gross and fine motor skills with eight subtests. Provides subtest standard scores ($M = 15$, $SD = 5$) and a composite score ($M = 50$, $SD = 10$). For ages 4-6 to 14-6 years. Takes approximately 45 to 60 minutes to administer.	Norm group is excellent. Reliability is satisfactory for Battery Composite score, less satisfactory for Fine and Gross Composites, and unsatisfactory for individual subtests. More information is needed about its validity.	Useful in the assessment of gross and fine motor skills.
Child Behavior Checklist (Achenbach & Edelbrock, 1986a), Author	Behavior checklist that provides a profile of behavioral deviancy (eight or nine scales) and social competence (three scales). Provides standard scores ($M = 50$, $SD = 10$). For ages 4-0 to 16-0 years and ages 2 to 3 years. Takes approximately 30 to 40 minutes to administer.	Norm group, reliability, and validity are satisfactory.	A useful checklist for evaluating behavior problems of children. Based on factor analytic findings. Respondent is parent.
Child Behavior Scale (Lahey, Stempniak, Robinson, & Tyroler, 1978)[c]	Behavior checklist with 110 items and four scales: Conduct Problems, Learning Disabilities, Anxiety-Withdrawal, and Hyperactivity. Provides raw scores. For fourth through eighth grade. Takes approximately 20 minutes to administer.	Norm group is limited. No information is provided about reliability. Validity is adequate.	A somewhat useful screening instrument for evaluating behavior problems of elementary school children. Respondent is teacher.
Classroom Adjustment Ratings Scale (CARS) (Lorion, Cowen, & Caldwell, 1975)[b]	Behavior checklist with 41 items and three scales: Learning Problems, Acting-Out, and Shy-Anxious. Provides raw scores. For first through third grade. Takes approximately 5 to 10 minutes to administer.	Norms are limited. No reliability information is provided. Validity is adequate.	A somewhat useful screening instrument for evaluating behavior problems of young elementary school children. Respondent is teacher.

918

Instrument	Description	Standardization	Comments
Classroom Reading Inventory (Silvaroli, 1986), William C. Brown Co.	Measures word reading, paragraph reading, and spelling. Error scores are converted to reading levels. For first through twelfth grade. Takes approximately 15 minutes to administer.	No information is reported in the manual about norm group, reliability, or validity.	A useful informal screening instrument. Provides information about reading levels, word recognition, and reading comprehension. Psychometric properties are unproven.
Columbia Mental Maturity Scale (CMMS) (Burgemeister, Blum, & Lorge, 1972), The Psychological Corporation	Measures general reasoning ability. Provides standard scores ($M = 100$, $SD = 16$). For ages 3-6 to 9-11 years. Takes approximately 15 to 20 minutes to administer.	Norms are excellent. Reliability and validity are satisfactory.	Serves as a supplementary nonverbal measure of intelligence. May be less culturally loaded than other intelligence tests.
Conners Parent Rating Scale (Conners, 1985)[a]	Behavior checklist with 48 items that has five factors covering behavior problems. Provides T scores ($M = 50$, $SD = 10$). For ages 3 to 17 years. Takes approximately 20 minutes to administer.	Norm group, reliability, and validity are adequate.	A useful screening scale for evaluating behavior problems of children. Respondent is parent.
Conners Teacher Rating Scale (Conners, 1985)[a]	Behavior checklist with 39 items that has six factors covering behavior problems. Provides T scores ($M = 50$, $SD = 10$). For ages 4 through 12 years. Takes approximately 10 to 15 minutes to administer.	Norm group, reliability, and validity are adequate.	A useful screening instrument for evaluating behavior problems of children. Respondent is teacher.
Denver Developmental Screening Test–Revised (DDST-R) (Frankenburg, Dodds, Fandal, Kazuk, & Cohrs, 1975), Denver Developmental Materials	Provides information about personal-social, fine motor, language, and gross motor areas. Basic score is a pass. For ages newborn to 6 years. Takes approximately 20 minutes to administer.	Norm group is limited. More information is needed about its reliability and validity.	A screening instrument with marginal psychometric properties. Caution is needed in using it for classification purposes.
Detroit Tests of Learning Aptitude–P (DTLA-P) (Hammill, 1985b), Pro-Ed	An abbreviated 8-subtest version of the DTLA-2. Provides subtest and standard scores and a composite score ($M = 100$, $SD = 15$). For ages 3 through 9 years. Takes approximately 15 to 45 minutes to administer.	Norm group is generally satisfactory. Reliability and validity are satisfactory.	A useful screening measure of general cognitive ability.

(Table continues next page)

Table F-2 (cont.)

Title, author, and publisher	Description	Norms/reliability/validity	Comment
Detroit Tests of Learning Aptitude–2 (DTLA-2) (Hammill, 1985a), Pro-Ed	A multidimensional battery of 11 subtests designed to measure various cognitive skills. Provides subtest standard scores ($M = 10$, $SD = 3$) and a composite score ($M = 100$, $SD = 15$). For ages 6 through 18. Takes approximately 1 to 2 hours to administer.	Norm sample appears to be overly weighted with families who have advanced educational degrees or training. Reliability and concurrent validity are adequate.	Useful as a measure of general intellectual ability, but separate part scores are not supported by either factor analysis or cluster analysis.
Developmental Test of Visual-Motor Integration (VMI) (Beery, 1982), Modern Curriculum Press	Consists of 24 geometric designs that child copies. Provides standard scores ($M = 10$, $SD = 3$). For ages 4-0 to 13 years. Takes approximately 10 minutes to administer.	Limited information is provided about norm group. Reliability is satisfactory, but more information is needed about the validity of the revised norms.	A useful test for evaluating children's visual-motor abilities.
Developmental Test of Visual Perception (DTVP) (Frostig, Maslow, Lefever, & Whittlesey, 1964), Consulting Psychologists Press	Contains five subtests: Eye-Hand Coordination, Figure-Ground Perception, Form Constancy, Position in Space, and Perception of Spatial Relations. Provides a Perceptual Quotient ($Mdn = 100$, $SD = 16$) and perceptual age equivalents. For ages 3-0 to 9-0 years. Takes approximately 40 minutes to administer.	Norm group is not satisfactory. Reliability of Perceptual Quotient is low. Reliabilities of subtests are unsatisfactory. Validity is minimally adequate for Perceptual Quotient.	Serves as an informal screening instrument for evaluating visual perception. Should not be used to measure reading readiness or to predict reading skill.
Devereux Adolescent Behavior Rating Scale (Spivack, Haimes, & Spotts, 1967), The Devereux Foundation	Behavior checklist with 84 items. Provides a profile of behavior problem areas (12 behavior factors and 3 clusters). Provides standard scores for each scale ($M = 0$, $SD = 1$). For ages 13-0 to 18-0. Takes approximately 10 to 15 minutes to administer.	Norms are limited. Reliability is poor. Validity is satisfactory.	A somewhat useful scale for evaluating behavior problems of adolescents. Respondent is attendant or teacher.
Devereux Child Behavior Rating Scale (Spivack & Spotts, 1966), The Devereux Foundation	Behavior checklist with 97 items. Provides a profile of behavior competencies (10 factors) and behavior control (seven factors). Provides standard scores for each scale ($M = 0$, $SD = 1$). For ages 8-0 to 12-0 years. Takes approximately 15 to 20 minutes to administer.	Norms are limited. Reliability and validity are satisfactory.	A somewhat useful scale for evaluating behavior problems of elementary school children. Respondent is attendant or parent.

Test	Description	Norms/Reliability/Validity	Comments
Devereux Elementary School Behavior Rating Scale (Spivack & Swift, 1967), The Devereux Foundation	Behavior checklist with 47 items. Provides a profile of behavior problem areas (10 behavior competence factors and seven behavior control factors). Provides standard scores ($M = 0$, $SD = 1$). For kindergarten through sixth grade. Takes approximately 5 to 10 minutes to administer.	Norms are limited. Reliability and validity are satisfactory.	A somewhat useful scale for evaluating behavior problems of elementary school children. Respondent is teacher.
Extended Merrill-Palmer Scale (Ball, Merrifield, & Stott, 1978), Stoelting Co.	Sixteen verbal and nonverbal tests grouped into four dimensions: Semantic Production, Figural Production, Semantic Evaluation, and Figural Evaluation. Provides percentile bands. For ages 3-0 to 5-11 years. Takes approximately 1 hour to administer.	Norms are not representative of the country. Reliability and validity are inadequate.	Test has a unique way of organizing abilities, but it does not provide an overall score or a precise way of evaluating a child's cognitive performance.
Goldman-Fristoe-Woodcock Test of Auditory Discrimination (Goldman, Fristoe, & Woodcock, 1970), American Guidance Service	Measures auditory discrimination under quiet and noisy conditions. Provides standard scores ($M = 50$, $SD = 10$). For ages 4 years through adult. Takes approximately 10 to 15 minutes to administer.	Norm group is limited. Reliability is poor. More information is needed about its validity.	A crude measure of auditory discrimination. Its psychometric properties are poor.
Goodenough-Harris Drawing Test (Draw-A-Man) (Harris, 1963), The Psychological Corporation	Brief nonverbal test of intelligence based on child's drawing of a man, woman, and/or self. Provides standard scores ($M = 100$, $SD = 15$). For ages 3-0 to 15-11 years. Takes approximately 5 to 15 minutes to administer.	Norms may be dated. Reliability is somewhat poor, but validity is satisfactory.	A somewhat useful supplementary screening instrument for measuring cognitive ability. May be less culturally loaded than other ability tests.
Halstead-Reitan Neuropsychological Test Battery for Older Children (Reitan & Wolfson, 1985), Neuropsychology Press	A battery of cognitive and perceptual-motor tests used primarily as a clinical procedure. For ages 9 to 14 years. Takes approximately 4 to 6 hours to administer.	Norms are limited. Little is known about the reliability and validity of the battery.	A somewhat useful battery for the assessment of brain damage.
Health Resources Inventory (Gesten, 1976)[d]	Behavior checklist with 54 items that measure five areas of competence: Good Student, Gutsy, Peer Sociability, Rules, and Frustration Tolerance. Scored on a 5-point scale. For first through sixth grades. Takes approximately 5 to 10 minutes to administer.	Norm group is limited. Reliability and validity are satisfactory.	A somewhat useful screening scale for evaluating behavior competencies of elementary school children. Respondent is teacher.

(Table continues next page)

Table F-2 (cont.)

Title, author, and publisher	Description	Norms/reliability/validity	Comment
Hiskey-Nebraska Test of Learning Aptitude (H-NTLA) (Hiskey, 1966), Author	A nonverbal measure of intelligence containing 12 subtests that involve verbal labeling, categorization, concept formation, and rehearsal. Can be administered entirely through pantomimed instructions. Provides standard scores ($M = 100$, $SD = 16$). For ages 3 to 17 years. Takes approximately 50 minutes to administer.	Norm sample contained deaf and non-hearing-impaired children. Norm group is satisfactory for non-hearing-impaired sample, but representativeness of the deaf sample is unknown. Reliability and validity are satisfactory.	Out-of-date norms and questions about the representativeness of the norm sample of this test make the WISC-R Performance Scale a better choice for testing hearing-impaired children.
Illinois Test of Psycholinguistic Abilities, Revised Edition (ITPA) (Kirk, McCarthy, & Kirk, 1968), University of Illinois Press	Contains 12 subtests that measure various facets of language ability. Provides scaled scores ($M = 36$, $SD = 6$). Ratio method is used to compute a psycholinguistic age. For ages 2-4 to 10-3 years. Takes approximately 1 hour to administer.	Norm group is limited. Reliability and validity are satisfactory.	Many of its subtests are similar to those that appear on intelligence tests. Has limited usefulness in the assessment battery.
Infant Psychological Developmental Scale (Uzgiris & Hunt, 1975)e	Contains eight subscales based on Piagetian theory. Score for each subscale is the highest number scored on that scale. For ages 2 weeks to 2 years. Takes approximately 40 to 60 minutes to administer.	Norm group is limited. Reliability is satisfactory. More information is needed about its validity.	A useful addition to the area of infant assessment.
Kaufman Assessment Battery for Children (K-ABC) (Kaufman & Kaufman, 1983), American Guidance Service	Designed to assess intelligence and achievement. Provides subtest standard scores ($M = 10$, $SD = 3$) and composite scores ($M = 100$, $SD = 15$). For ages 2-6 to 12-5 years. Takes about 45 to 75 minutes to administer.	Norm group is generally satisfactory, but ethnic minorities were not proportionally represented. Reliability and validity are satisfactory.	Its main limitation is that it fails to include measures of verbal cognitive processes in the composite score. May be useful when a nonverbal measure of ability is needed.
Kaufman Test of Educational Achievement (K-TEA) (Kaufman & Kaufman, 1985), American Guidance Service	Contains Reading Decoding, Reading Comprehension, Mathematics Applications, Mathematics Computation, and Spelling subtests. Provides standard scores ($M = 100$, $SD = 15$). For ages 6 to 18 years. Takes approximately 40 to 60 minutes to administer.	Norm group is excellent. Reliability and validity are good.	Useful as a screening measure of achievement.

Test	Description	Norms, Reliability, and Validity	Comments
KeyMath Diagnostic Arithmetic Test (Connolly, Nachtman, & Pritchett, 1971), American Guidance Service	Contains 14 subtests that measure three areas of arithmetic ability: content, function, and applications. Grade equivalents are available. For first through sixth grade. Takes approximately 30 minutes to administer.	Norm group is excellent. Reliability and validity are satisfactory.	Useful for assessing the arithmetical ability of elementary school children.
Kohn Problem Checklist (Kohn, 1986a), The Psychological Corporation	Behavior checklist with 49 items and two dimensions: Apathy-Withdrawal and Anger-Defiance. Provides standard scores ($M = 0$, $SD = 100$). For ages 3-0 to 6-0 years. Takes approximately 10 to 15 minutes to administer.	Norms are limited. Reliability is poor. Validity is satisfactory.	A somewhat useful screening scale for evaluating behavior problems of preschool children. Respondent is teacher.
Kohn Social Competence Scale (Kohn, 1986b), The Psychological Corporation	Behavior checklist with 64 or 73 items and two dimensions: Interest-Participation vs. Apathy-Withdrawal and Cooperation-Compliance vs. Anger-Defiance. Provides standard scores ($M = 0$, $SD = 100$). For ages 3-0 to 6-0 years. Takes approximately 10 to 15 minutes to administer.	Norms are limited. Reliability is poor. Validity is satisfactory.	A somewhat useful screening scale for evaluating the social competence of preschool children. Respondent is teacher.
Language Assessment Battery (New York City Board of Education, 1977), Riverside Publishing Co.	Designed to assess reading, writing, listening comprehension, and speaking in English and in Spanish for children in kindergarten through twelfth grade. Contains three levels. Provides percentiles and stanines by grade level. Takes approximately 10 to 40 minutes to administer.	Norms are not representative of the country. Reliability is satisfactory. No validity information is available.	Measures limited aspects of language proficiency. Serves as a rough screening measure.
Language Assessment Scales (DeAvila & Duncan, 1977), Linguametrics Group	Measures four areas of language in English and in Spanish: phonemic, referential, syntactical, and pragmatic. No standard scores are available. For ages kindergarten through fifth grade and up. Takes approximately 30 minutes to administer.	Norms are poorly described and extremely limited. Reliability is limited for some measures. Validity is limited. Scores show no appreciable change as a function of age.	Measures limited aspects of language proficiency. Serves as a rough screening measure.

(Table continues next page)

Table F-2 (cont.)

Title, author, and publisher	Description	Norms/reliability/validity	Comment
Leiter International Performance Scale (LIPS) (Leiter, 1948), Stoelting Co.	Measures intelligence by means of nonverbal items. Uses age-scale format. Provides IQs by the ratio method. For ages 2 years to adult. Takes approximately 30 to 45 minutes to administer.	Norm group is poorly described. Reliability and validity are satisfactory.	Norms are outdated and standardization is inadequate. Serves as a supplementary measure of intelligence. May be less culturally loaded than other intelligence tests.
Lindamood Auditory Conceptualization Test (LACT) (Lindamood & Lindamood, 1979), DLM Teaching Resources	Requires discrimination of individual sounds and long sound patterns. Provides percentile ranks. For kindergarten through sixth grade primarily. Takes approximately 20 to 30 minutes to administer.	Norm group is limited. More information is needed to evaluate its reliability and validity.	Serves as a screening device for the assessment of auditory ability.
Luria-Nebraska Neuropsychological Battery: Children's Revision (LNNB-C) (Golden, 1987), Western Psychological Services	A battery of 11 clinical scales and 2 optional scales that assess sensorimotor, perceptual, and cognitive abilities. Provides standard scores ($M = 50$, $SD = 10$). For ages 8 to 12 years. Takes approximately 2½ hours to administer.	Norm group is limited. Reliability is less than adequate. More research is needed to evaluate its validity.	A somewhat useful scale for the assessment of brain damage.
McCarthy Scales of Children's Abilities (McCarthy, 1972), The Psychological Corporation	Eighteen tests grouped into six scales: Verbal, Perceptual-Performance, Quantitative, Memory, Motor, and General Cognitive. Provides a General Cognitive Index (GCI) ($M = 100$, $SD = 16$). For ages 2-6 to 8-6 years. Takes approximately 1 hour to administer.	Norms, reliability, and validity are excellent.	A useful test. Provision of a profile of abilities is one of its advantages. Scores may not be interchangeable with those on other intelligence tests.
New Sucher-Allred Reading Placement Inventory (Sucher & Allred, 1981), The Economy Company	Contains a Word-Recognition Test and an Oral Reading Test which are used to identify levels of reading proficiency. Provides approximate reading levels. For primary grades through ninth grade. Takes approximately 20 minutes to administer.	No information is reported about norm group, reliability, or validity.	A somewhat useful informal screening measure of reading skill. Psychometric properties are unproven.
Peabody Individual Achievement Test (PIAT) (Dunn & Markwardt, 1970), American Guidance Service	Contains Mathematics, Reading Recognition, Reading Comprehension, Spelling, and General Information subtests. Standard scores are provided ($M = 100$, $SD = 15$). For kindergarten through high school. Takes approximately 30 to 40 minutes to administer.	Norm group is excellent. Reliability and validity are excellent for total score but less satisfactory for subtests.	A brief, limited screening measure of academic skills. The multiple-choice format of some subtests makes test useful for some handicapped children.

Test	Description	Technical Evaluation	Comments
Peabody Picture Vocabulary Test—Revised (PPVT-R) (Dunn & Dunn, 1981), American Guidance Service	A nonverbal, multiple-choice test that measures receptive vocabulary. Provides standard scores ($M = 100$, $SD = 15$). For ages 2–6 to adult. Takes approximately 10 to 15 minutes to administer.	Norm group is excellent. Reliability is marginally satisfactory. Validity is satisfactory.	Useful as a screening device for measuring extensiveness of vocabulary, particularly for children with expressive difficulties. Should not be used to measure intelligence.
Pictorial Test of Intelligence (PTI) (French, 1964), Riverside Publishing Co.	Contains six subtests: Picture Vocabulary, Form Discrimination, Information and Comprehension, Similarities, Size and Number, and Immediate Recall. Provides standard scores ($M = 100$, $SD = 16$). For ages 3–0 to 8–0 years. Takes approximately 45 minutes to administer.	Norms are excellent. Reliability and validity are satisfactory.	Serves as a supplementary nonverbal measure of learning aptitude for young children with motor and speech handicaps.
Preschool Behavior Questionnaire (Behar & Stringfield, 1974)[f]	Behavior checklist with 30 items and three scales: Hostile-Aggressive, Anxious, and Hyperactive-Distractible. Percentiles are available for the three scales and for the total score. For preschool children. Takes approximately 5 to 10 minutes to administer	Norms are limited. Reliability is satisfactory. More information is needed about its validity.	A somewhat useful screening device for evaluating behavior problems of preschool children. Respondent is teacher or parent.
Purdue Pegboard (Tiffin, 1948), Science Research Associates	A manual dexterity task that measures fine motor coordination. Gardner (1979) and Wilson et al. (1982) provide percentile norms. For ages 2–6 years to adult. Takes approximately 2 minutes to administer.	Norms are limited. Reliability and validity are satisfactory.	A useful measure of fine motor coordination and laterality.
Purdue Perceptual-Motor Survey (Roach & Kephart, 1966), The Psychological Corporation	Consists of 22 items divided into areas of laterality, perceptual-motor matching, and directionality. Provides ordinal scaled scores based on qualitative judgments. For second through fourth grade. Takes approximately 10 to 15 minutes to administer.	Norm group is poor. More information is needed about its reliability and validity.	A supplementary informal method for evaluating perceptual and motor behavior.
Raven's Progressive Matrices (Raven, 1938, 1960, 1965), The Psychological Corporation	Three different forms measuring nonverbal reasoning ability. Provides percentile ranks. For ages 6 years to adult. Takes approximately 15 to 30 minutes to administer.	Current norms are for U.S. children. Reliability and validity are satisfactory.	A useful supplementary measure of nonverbal reasoning ability. May be less culturally loaded than other intelligence tests.

(Table continues next page)

Table F-2 (cont.)

Title, author, and publisher	Description	Norms/reliability/validity	Comment
Reitan-Indiana Neuropsychological Test Battery for Children (Reitan & Wolfson, 1985), Neuropsychology Press	A battery of cognitive and perceptual-motor tests used primarily as a clinical procedure. For ages 5 to 8 years. Takes approximately 4 to 6 hours to administer.	Norms are limited. Little is known about the reliability and validity of the battery.	A somewhat useful battery for the assessment of brain damage.
Revised Behavior Problem Checklist (Quay & Peterson, 1983), Author	Behavior checklist with 89 items and six scales: Conduct Disorder, Socialization-Aggression, Attention Problems–Immaturity, Anxiety-Withdrawal, Psychotic Behavior, and Motor Excess. Provides T scores ($M = 50$, $SD = 10$). For ages 6 to 18 years. Takes approximately 20 minutes to administer.	Norm group, reliability, and validity are satisfactory	A useful scale for evaluating behavior problems of children. Based on a theoretical model of deviancy. Respondent is teacher or parent.
Revised Denver Prescreening Developmental Questionnaire (Frankenburg, 1986), Denver Developmental Materials	Provides information about personal-social, fine motor, language, and gross motor areas. Scores are "pass" or "delay." For ages newborn to 6 years. Takes approximately 20 minutes to administer.	No information is reported about norm group, reliability, or validity.	A screening instrument that may prove to be useful in identifying preschool children with delayed development. However, until information is available about its reliability and validity, it must be used with considerable caution. Respondent is parent or guardian.
Revised Visual Retention Test (Benton, 1963), The Psychological Corporation	Consists of three forms, each with 10 geometric designs which the child both copies directly and draws from memory. Provides standard scores ($M = 100$, $SD = 15$) (see Rice, 1972). For ages 5 to 11 years and older. Takes approximately 10 to 15 minutes to administer.	Norms are limited. More information is needed about its reliability and validity.	A somewhat useful test for evaluating memory for visual-motor reproductions.
Scales of Independent Behavior (SIB) (Bruininks, Woodcock, Weatherman, & Hill, 1984), DLM Teaching Resources	Behavior rating scale that measures four areas of adaptive behavior (motor, social interaction and communication, personal living, and community living) and three areas of maladaptive behavior (internalized, asocial, and externalized). Provides standard scores ($M = 100$, $SD = 15$). For ages newborn to adult. Takes approximately 1 hour to administer.	Norm group is excellent. Reliability and validity are adequate for cluster and full scales but less adequate for subscales.	A useful scale for assessing adaptive behavior over a wide age range. Respondent is attendant, parent, or teacher.

Test	Description	Evaluation	Comments
Sequential Assessment of Mathematics Inventories (SAMI) (Reisman, 1985), The Psychological Corporation	Contains eight subtests that measure various areas of mathematical ability: mathematical language, ordinality, number and notation, computation, measurement, geometric concepts, mathematical applications, and word problems. Provides standard scores for subtests and total score ($M = 100$, $SD = 15$). For ages 5 to 13 years. Takes from 20 to 60 minutes to administer.	Norm group is excellent. Reliability and validity are satisfactory for total scores but less satisfactory for subtest scores.	Useful for assessing the arithmetical ability of elementary school children.
Slosson Intelligence Test (SIT) (Slosson, 1983), Slosson Educational Publications	Contains items similar to those on the Gessell and Stanford-Binet: Form L-M. Provides standard scores ($M = 100$, $SD = 16$). For ages 2 to 18 years. Takes approximately 10 to 30 minutes to administer.	Norm group is poorly described. Reliability coefficient is based on Stanford-Binet: Form L-M. No information is reported about validity of revised norms.	Serves as a screening device, but norm group may not be satisfactory.
Southern California Sensory Integration Tests (Ayres, 1972), Western Psychological Services	Contains 17 tests that measure four areas of perceptual and perceptual-motor functioning: form and space perception, postural and bilateral integration, tactile perception, and motor skills. Provides standard scores ($M = 0$, $SD = 1$). For ages 4 to 8 years. Takes approximately 75 to 90 minutes to administer.	Norm group is limited. Reliabilities are poor. No validity data are reported in the manual.	A rough informal screening guide for those knowledgeable about perceptual and perceptual-motor areas. Psychometric properties are poor.
Stanford-Binet Intelligence Scale: Fourth Edition (Thorndike, Hagen, & Sattler, 1986a), Riverside Publishing Co.	Fifteen subtests grouped into Verbal Comprehension, Nonverbal Reasoning/Visualization, and Memory factors. Provides subtest standard scores ($M = 50$, $SD = 8$) and composite standard scores ($M = 100$, $SD = 16$). For ages 2-0 to 23 years. Takes approximately 2 to 2½ hours to administer complete battery.	Norms, reliability, and validity are excellent.	One of the best intelligence tests available. However, profile analysis must be used with considerable caution because of the uneven range of standard scores.
System of Multicultural Pluralistic Assessment (SOMPA) (Mercer & Lewis, 1978), The Psychological Corporation	Incorporates medical, social, and pluralistic information in the assessment of cognitive, perceptual-motor, and adaptive behavior. Provides standard scores for some measures ($M = 50$, $SD = 15$) and an estimated learning potential (ELP). For ages 5-0 to 11-11 years. Takes approximately 5 hours to administer.	Norm group is limited. Reliability is generally satisfactory. Validity of the ELP has not been established.	There is no evidence that SOMPA provides nonbiased assessment measures. The use of the ELP for any clinical or psychoeducational purpose is not justified.

(Table continues next page)

927

Table F-2 (cont.)

Title, author, and publisher	Description	Norms/reliability/validity	Comment
Teacher Behavioral Description Form (Seidman, Linney, Rappaport, Herzberger, Kramer, & Alden, 1979)g	Behavior checklist with 23 items and three scales: Anxiety–Withdrawal, Attention Getting–Aggressive, and "Ideal" Student Behavior. Has 3-point rating scale. For first and second grades. Takes approximately 5 to 10 minutes to administer.	Norm group is limited. Reliability is poor. Validity is satisfactory.	A somewhat useful screening instrument for evaluating behavior problems of young elementary school children. Respondent is teacher.
Teacher-Child Rating Scale (T-CRS) (Hightower, Work, Cowen, Lotyczewski, Spinell, Guare, & Rohrbeck, 1986), Author	Behavior checklist with 38 items and seven scales: Acting Out, Shy-Anxious, Learning, Frustration Tolerance/Behavioral Limits, Assertive Social Skills, Task-Orientation/Educational Performance, and Peer Social Skills. Provides percentile ranks. For kindergarten to sixth grade. Takes approximately 10 minutes to administer.	Norm group is limited. Reliability and validity are good.	A useful screening instrument for evaluating behavior problems and social skill areas. Respondent is teacher.
Teacher's Report Form (Achenbach & Edelbrock, 1986b)	Behavior checklist with 113 items that provides a profile of behavioral deviancy (eight or nine scales) and adaptive functioning (four scales). Provides standard scores ($M = 50$, $SD = 10$) for ages 6 to 16 years. Takes approximately 30 minutes to administer.	Norm group, reliability, and validity are satisfactory.	A useful checklist for evaluating behavior problems of children. Based on factor analytic findings. Respondent is teacher.
Test of Auditory Comprehension of Language–Revised (TACL-R) (Carrow-Woolfolk, 1985), DLM Teaching Resources	A pictorial multiple-choice language test with three sections: Word Classes and Relations, Grammatical Morphemes, and Elaborated Sentences. Provides standard scores ($M = 100$, $SD = 15$). For ages 3-0 to 9-11 years. Takes approximately 5 to 15 minutes to administer.	Norms and reliability are excellent. More information is needed about its validity.	A somewhat useful screening measure of auditory comprehension.
T.M.R. School Competency Scales (Levine, Elzey, Thormahlen, & Cain, 1976), Consulting Psychologists Press	Behavior rating scale for use with trainable mentally retarded in a school setting. Measures perceptual-motor, initiative-responsibility, cognition, personal-social, and language areas. Provides percentile ranks. For ages 5 years and over. Takes approximately 20 to 30 minutes to administer.	Norm group is limited. Reliability is satisfactory. No information is given about validity.	Usefulness is limited because manual fails to provide any validity data. Respondent is teacher.

928

Test	Description	Technical Adequacy	Comments
Token Test for Children (DiSimoni, 1978), DLM Teaching Resources	Employs auditory commands that require child to manipulate tokens varying along three dimensions—color, shape, and size. Provides standard scores ($M = 500$, $SD = 5$). For ages 3-0 to 12-5 years and older. Takes approximately 10 to 15 minutes to administer.	Norms are limited. More information is needed about its reliability and validity.	A somewhat useful screening measure of auditory comprehension, especially helpful in identifying mild receptive disturbances in aphasic individuals.
Vineland Adaptive Behavior Scales (VABS) (Sparrow, Balla, & Cicchetti, 1984), American Guidance Service	Behavior rating scale that measures four areas of adaptive behavior (communication, daily living skills, socialization, and motor skills) and one general area of maladaptive behavior. Provides standard scores ($M = 100$, $SD = 15$). For ages newborn to adult. Takes approximately 60 to 90 minutes to administer.	Norm group is excellent, but questions have been raised about the norming procedures. Reliability and validity are excellent for overall score but less adequate for individual domain scores.	A somewhat useful scale for assessing adaptive behavior over a wide age range. Questions about norming procedures reduce its usefulness. Expanded and classroom versions are available. Respondent is attendant, parent, or teacher.
Wechsler Adult Intelligence Scale—Revised (WAIS-R) (Wechsler, 1981), The Psychological Corporation	Eleven subtests grouped into a Verbal Scale and a Performance Scale. Provides subtest standard scores ($M = 10$, $SD = 3$) and Deviation IQs ($M = 100$, $SD = 15$). For ages 16-0 to 74-11. Takes approximately 1 hour to administer.	Norms, reliability, and validity are excellent.	One of the best intelligence tests available.
Wechsler Intelligence Scale for Children—Revised (WISC-R) (Wechsler, 1974), The Psychological Corporation	Twelve subtests grouped into a Verbal Scale and a Performance Scale. Provides subtest standard scores ($M = 10$, $SD = 3$) and Deviation IQs ($M = 100$, $SD = 15$). For ages 6-0 to 16-11 years. Takes approximately 1 hour to administer.	Norms, reliability, and validity are excellent.	One of the best intelligence tests available.
Wechsler Preschool and Primary Scale of Intelligence (WPPSI) (Wechsler, 1967), The Psychological Corporation	Eleven subtests grouped into a Verbal Scale and a Performance Scale. Provides subtest standard scores ($M = 10$, $SD = 3$) and Deviation IQs ($M = 100$, $SD = 15$). For ages 4-0 to 6-6 years. Takes approximately 1 hour to administer	Norms, reliability, and validity are excellent.	One of the best intelligence tests available.
Wide Range Achievement Test—Revised (WRAT-R) (Jastak & Wilkinson, 1984), Jastak Associates	Contains Reading, Spelling, and Arithmetic subtests. Provides subtest standard scores ($M = 100$, $SD = 15$). For ages 5-0 to 74-11 years. Takes approximately 20 to 30 minutes to administer.	Norm group is generally representative of the population. Reliability and validity are satisfactory.	A brief, limited screening instrument of academic skills.

(Table continues next page)

Table F-2 (cont.)

Title, author, and publisher	Description	Norms/reliability/validity	Comment
Wisconsin Behavior Rating Scale (WBRS) (Song, Jones, Lippert, Metzgen, Miller, & Borreca, 1984), Author	Behavior rating scale for use with institutionalized mentally retarded. Assesses basic survival skills in 11 areas. Provides percentile ranks and age-equivalent scores. For individuals functioning at a developmental level of 3 years or below. Takes approximately 30 minutes to administer.	Norm group is limited. Reliability is ~quate. Validity is good.	A somewhat useful scale for assessing adaptive behavior in institutionalized mentally retarded individuals.
Woodcock-Johnson Psycho-Educational Battery (Woodcock, 1977), DLM Teaching Resources	Contains 27 tests that cover assessment of cognitive ability, achievement, and interest. Not all areas are tested at every age. Provides standard scores ($M = 100$, $SD = 15$). For ages 3 years to adult. Takes approximately 2 hours to administer.	Norm group is excellent. Reliability is satisfactory. Concurrent validity, but not construct validity, is satisfactory.	Cognitive ability scores may not be interchangeable with WISC-R IQs for learning-disabled children. Its achievement subtests appear to be more satisfactory than its cognitive ability subtests.
Youth Self-Report (Achenbach & Edelbrock, 1986a), Author	Self-report behavior checklist with 112 items, many of which are found on the Child Behavior Checklist. Contains two competence scales and seven problem scales. Provides T scores ($M = 50$, $SD = 10$). For ages 11 to 18 years. Takes approximately 30 minutes to administer.	Norm group and reliability are satisfactory. More information is needed about its validity.	A somewhat useful scale for evaluating the problems of adolescent children.

Note. Appendix B lists addresses of the test publishers.
a Checklist is reproduced in Chapter 15.
b Scale is reproduced in journal publication.
c Child Behavior Scale can be obtained from Benjamin B. Lahey, Department of Psychology, University of Georgia, Athens, GA 30601.
d Health Resources Inventory can be obtained from Ellis L. Gesten, Psychology Department, University of South Florida, Fowler Ave., Tampa, FL 33620.
e All the information needed to administer the scale is contained in Uzgiris and Hunt (1975).
f Preschool Behavior Questionnaire can be obtained from Lenore B. Behar, Division of MH/MR/SAS, State Department of Human Resources, 325 N. Salisbury St., Raleigh, NC 27611.
g Teacher Behavioral Description Form can be obtained from Edward Seidman, Bank Street College of Education, 601 W. 112 St., New York, NY 10025.

REFERENCES

Abikoff, H., & Gittelman, R. (1985). Classroom observation code: A modification of the Stony Brook Code. *Psychopharmacology Bulletin, 21*, 901–909.

Achenbach, T. M., & Edelbrock, C. S. (1981). Behavioral problems and competencies reported by parents of normal and disturbed children aged four through sixteen. *Monographs of the Society for Research in Child Development, 46*, (1, Serial No. 188).

Achenbach, T. M., & Edelbrock, C. S. (1986a). *Child Behavior Checklist* and *Youth Self-Report*. Burlington, VT: Author.

Achenbach, T. M., & Edelbrock, C. S. (1986b). *Teacher's Report Form*. Burlington, VT: Author.

Adams, R. L., & Jenkins, R. L. (1981). Basic principles of the neuropsychological examination. In C. E. Walker (Ed.), *Clinical practice of psychology: A guide for mental health professionals* (pp. 244–292). New York: Pergamon Press.

Adelson, E., & Fraiberg, S. (1974). Gross motor development in infants blind from birth. *Child Development, 45*, 114–126.

Affleck, D. C., & Strider, F. D. (1971). Contribution of psychological reports to patient management. *Journal of Consulting and Clinical Psychology, 37*, 177–179.

Alessi, G. J. (1980). Behavioral observation for the school psychologist: Responsive-discrepancy model. *School Psychology Review, 9*, 31–45.

Algozzine, B., & Ysseldyke, J. E. (1981). An analysis of difference score reliabilities on three measures with a sample of low achieving youngsters. *Psychology in the Schools, 18*, 133–138.

Algozzine, B., & Ysseldyke, J. E. (1983). Learning disabilities as a subset of school failure: The oversophistication of a concept. *Exceptional Children, 50*, 242–246.

Ali, F., & Costello, J. (1971). Modification of the Peabody Picture Vocabulary Test. *Developmental Psychology, 5*, 86–91.

Allington, R. L. (1979). Diagnosis of reading disability: Word prediction ability tests. *Academic Therapy, 14*, 267–274.

Altepeter, T., & Handal, P. J. (1985). A factor analytic investigation of the use of the PPVT-R as a measure of general achievement. *Journal of Clinical Psychology, 41*, 540–543.

Altepeter, T., & Handal, P. J. (1986). Use of the PPVT-R for intellectual screening with school-aged children: A caution. *Journal of Psychoeducational Assessment, 4*, 145–154.

Amabile, T. M. (1983). *The social psychology of creativity*. New York: Springer-Verlag.

Aman, M. G., & Singh, N. N. (1983). Specific reading disorders: Concepts of etiology reconsidered. In K. D. Gadow & I. Bialer (Eds.), *Advances in learning and behavioral disabilities* (Vol. 2, pp. 1–47). Greenwich, CT: JAI Press.

American Psychiatric Association. (1987). *Diagnostic and statistical manual of mental disorders* (3rd ed. – revised). Washington, DC: Author.

American Psychological Association. (1981). Ethical principles of psychologists. *American Psychologist, 36*, 633–638.

American Psychological Association. (1983). *Publication manual of the American Psychological Association* (3rd ed.). Washington, DC: Author.

American Psychological Association. (1985). *Standards for educational and psychological testing*. Washington, DC: Author.

Anderson, C. V., & Davis, J. M. (1979). Supplementary case history outline: Hearing loss. In F. L. Darley & D. C. Spriestersbach (Eds.), *Diagnostic methods in speech pathology* (2nd ed., pp. 73–77). New York: Harper & Row.

Andre, J. (1976). Bicultural socialization and the measurement of intelligence. *Dissertation Abstracts International, 36*, 3675B-3676B. (University Microfilms No. 75–29,904)

Anthony, J. J. (1973). A comparison of Wechsler Preschool and Primary Scale of Intelligence and Stanford-Binet Intelligence Scale scores for disadvantaged preschool children. *Psychology in the Schools, 10*, 297–299.

Anttonen, R. G., & Fleming, E. S. (1976). Standardized test information: Does it make a difference in black student performance. *Journal of Educational Research, 70*, 26–31.

Appelbaum, A. S. (1978). Validity of the Revised Denver Developmental Screening Test for referred and nonreferred samples. *Psychological Reports, 43*, 227–233.

Appelbaum, A. S., & Tuma, J. M. (1982). The relationship of the WISC-R to academic achievement in a clinical population. *Journal of Clinical Psychology, 38*, 401–405.

Aram, D. M., & Ekelman, B. L. (1986). Cognitive profiles of children with early onset unilateral lesions. *Developmental Neuropsychology, 2*, 155–172.

Aram, D. M., Ekelman, B. L., Rose, D. F., & Whitaker, H. A. (1985). Verbal and cognitive sequelae following unilateral lesions acquired in early childhood. *Journal of Clinical and Experimental Neuropsychology, 7*, 55–78.

Argulewicz, E. N., & Abel, R. R. (1984). Internal evidence of bias in the PPVT-R for Anglo-American and Mexican-American children. *Journal of School Psychology, 22*, 299–303.

Arinoldo, C. G. (1982). Concurrent validity of McCarthy's Scales. *Perceptual and Motor Skills, 54*, 1343–1346.

Arndt, S. (1981). A general measure of adaptive behavior. *American Journal of Mental Deficiency, 85*, 554–556.

Arthur, G. (1949). The Arthur Adaptation of the Leiter International Performance Scale. *Journal of Clinical Psychology, 5*, 345–349.

Arvey, R. D. (1972). Some comments on culture fair tests. *Personnel Psychology, 25*, 433–448.

Ashurst, D. I., & Meyers, C. E. (1973). Social system and clinical model in school identification of the educable retarded.

In R. K. Eyman, C. E. Meyers, & G. Tarjan (Eds.), *Sociobehavioral studies in mental retardation. Monographs of the American Association on Mental Deficiency, 1*, 150–163.

Atkinson, J. W. (1974). Motivational determinants of intellective performance and cumulative achievement. In J. W. Atkinson & J. O. Raynor (Eds.), *Motivation and achievement* (pp. 389–410). New York: Wiley.

Atkinson, L., & Cyr, J. J. (1984). Factor analysis of the WAIS-R: Psychiatric and standardization samples. *Journal of Consulting and Clinical Psychology, 52*, 714–716.

Auffrey, J., & Robertson, M. (1972). Case history information and examiner experience as determinants of scoring validity on Wechsler intelligence   sts. *Proceedings of the 80th Annual Convention of the American Psychological Association, 7*, 553–554.

Austin, J. J., & Carpenter, P. (1970, September). The use of the WPPSI in early identification of mental retardation and preschool special education. In R. S. Morrow (Chair), *Diagnostic and educational application of the Wechsler Preschool and Primary Scale of Intelligence (WPPSI)*. Symposium presented at the meeting of the American Psychological Association, Miami.

Ausubel, D. P., Novak, J. D., & Hanesian, H. (1978). *Educational psychology: A cognitive view* (2nd ed.). New York: Holt, Rinehart and Winston.

Ausubel, D. P., & Sullivan, E. V. (1970). *Theory and problems of child development* (2nd ed.). New York: Grune & Stratton.

Ayres, A. J. (1972). *Sensory integration and learning disorders*. Los Angeles: Western Psychological Services.

Ayres, R. R., & Cooley, E. J. (1986). Sequential versus simultaneous processing on the K-ABC: Validity in predicting learning success. *Journal of Psychoeducational Assessment, 4*, 211–220.

Babad, E. Y., Mann, M., & Mar-Hayim, M. (1975). Bias in scoring the WISC subtests. *Journal of Consulting and Clinical Psychology, 43*, 268.

Bach, L. C. (1968). *A comparison of selected psychological tests used with trainable mentally retarded children. Dissertation Abstracts, 29*, 2990-A. (University Microfilms, No. 69–3111)

Back, R., & Dana, R. H. (1977). Examiner sex bias and Wechsler Intelligence Scale for Children scores. *Journal of Consulting and Clinical Psychology, 45*, 500.

Bacon, E. H., & Rubin, D. C. (1983). Story recall by mentally retarded children. *Psychological Reports, 53*, 791–796.

Badian, N. A. (1984). Can the WPPSI be of aid in identifying young children at risk for reading disability. *Journal of Learning Disabilities, 17*, 583–587.

Bailey, D. B., Jr. (1981). Investigation of learning measures as screening procedures with kindergartners. *Psychology in the Schools, 18*, 489–495.

Bakeman, R., & Gottman, J. M. (1986). *Observing interaction*. New York: Cambridge University Press.

Baker, A. F. (1983). Psychological assessment of autistic children. *Clinical Psychology Review, 3*, 41–59.

Baker, L., Minuchin, S., Milman, L., Leibman, R., & Todd, T.

(1975). Psychosomatic aspects of juvenile diabetes mellitus: A progress report. In Z. Laron (Ed.), *Modern problems in pediatrics (Vol. 12): Diabetes in juveniles: Medical and rehabilitation aspects* (pp. 332–343). New York: Karger.

Ball, R. S., Merrifield, P., & Stott, L. H. (1978). *Extended Merrill-Palmer Scale*. Chicago: Stoelting.

Balthazar, E. E. (1976). *Balthazar Scales of Adaptive Behavior*. Palo Alto, CA: Consulting Psychologists Press.

Bannatyne, A. (1974). Diagnosis: A note on recategorization of the WISC scaled scores. *Journal of Learning Disabilities, 7*, 272–273.

Barclay, A. G., & Yater, A. C. (1969). Comparative study of the Wechsler Preschool and Primary Scale of Intelligence and the Stanford-Binet Intelligence Scale, Form L-M, among culturally deprived children. *Journal of Consulting and Clinical Psychology, 33*, 257.

Barker, R. G., & Wright, H. F. (1954). *Midwest and its children: The psychological ecology of an American town*. Evanston, IL: Peterson.

Barker, R. G., & Wright, H. F. (1966). *One boy's day: A specimen record of behavior*. New York: Archon Books.

Barkley, R. A. (1981a). *Hyperactive children: A handbook for diagnosis and treatment*. New York: Guilford Press.

Barkley, R. A. (1981b). Hyperactivity. In E. Mash & L. Terdal (Eds.), *Behavioral assessment of childhood disorders* (pp. 127–184). New York: Guilford Press.

Barkley, R. A. (1981c). Learning disabilities. In E. Mash & L. Terdal (Eds.), *Behavioral assessment of childhood disorders* (pp. 441–482). New York: Guilford Press.

Barkley, R. A., & Cunningham, C. E. (1979). The effects of methylphenidate on the mother-child interactions of hyperactive children. *Archives of General Psychiatry, 36*, 201–208.

Barron, R. C. (1971). A comparison of patterns of intellectual and psycho-linguistic abilities among first graders with average and very low reading ability. *Dissertation Abstracts International, 32*, 1817B. (University Microfilms No. 71–22,182)

Bartak, L., & Rutter, M. (1971). Educational treatment of autistic children. In M. Rutter (Ed.). *Infantile autism: Concepts, characteristics and treatment* (pp. 258–280). London: Churchill Livingstone.

Bartak, L., & Rutter, M. (1973). Special educational treatment of autistic children: A comparative study—I: Design of study and characteristics of units. *Journal of Childhood Psychology and Psychiatry and Allied Disciplines, 14*, 161–179.

Bates, J. D. (1985). *Writing with precision* (rev. ed.). Washington, DC: Acropolis Books.

Bat-Haee, M. A., Mehyrar, A. H., & Sabharwal, V. (1972). The correlation between Piaget's conservation of quantity tasks and three measures of intelligence in a select group of children in Iran. *Journal of Psychology, 80*, 197–201.

Baum, D. D. (1975). A comparison of the WRAT and the PIAT with learning disability children. *Educational and Psychological Measurement, 35*, 487–493.

Bauman, M. K. (1974). Blind and partially sighted. In M. V.

Wisland (Ed.). *Psychoeducational diagnosis of exceptional children* (pp. 159–189). Springfield, IL: Charles C Thomas.

Bayley, N. (1969). *Bayley Scales of Infant Development: Birth to two years*. San Antonio: The Psychological Corporation.

Bean, A. G., & Roszkowski, M. J. (1982). Item-domain relationships in the adaptive behavior scale (ABS). *Applied Research in Mental Retardation*, *3*, 359–367.

Beck, N. C., Horwitz, E., Seidenberg, M., Parker, J., & Frank, R. (1985). WAIS-R factor structure in psychiatric and general medical patients. *Journal of Consulting and Clinical Psychology*, *53*, 402–405.

Beech, M. C. (1981). Concurrent validity of the Boehm Test of Basic Concepts. *Learning Disability Quarterly*, *4*, 53–60.

Beery, K. E. (1982). *Revised administration, scoring, and teaching manual for the Developmental Test of Visual-Motor Integration*. Cleveland, OH: Modern Curriculum Press.

Behar, L., & Stringfield, S. (1974). A behavior rating scale for the preschool child. *Developmental Psychology*, *10*, 601–610.

Belford, B., & Blumberg, H. M. (1975). Factor analytic study of the Revised Illinois Test of Psycholinguistic Abilities (ITPA). *Perceptual and Motor Skills*, *40*, 153–154.

Bellack, A. S., & Hersen, M. (1980). *Introduction to clinical psychology*. New York: Oxford University Press.

Belmont, L., & Birch, H. G. (1965). Lateral dominance, lateral awareness, and reading disability. *Child Development*, *36*, 57–71.

Bender, L. (1938). A Visual Motor Gestalt Test and its clinical use. *American Orthopsychiatric Association Research Monograph*, No. 3.

Bender, L. (1970). The life course of schizophrenic children. *Biological Psychiatry*, *2*, 165–172.

Benjamin, A. (1981). *The helping interview* (3rd ed.). Boston: Houghton Mifflin.

Bennett, D. K. (1970). The tester and intelligence testing: An examination of protocol interpretation. *Dissertation Abstracts International*, *31*, 2095-A. (University Microfilms No. 70–20,142)

Bennett, R. E. (1982). The use of grade and age equivalent scores in educational assessment. *Diagnostique*, *7*, 139–146.

Benton, A. L. (1959). *Right-left discrimination and finger localization*. New York: Hoeber-Harper.

Benton, A. L. (1963). *Benton Visual Retention Test* (rev. ed.). San Antonio: The Psychological Corporation.

Benton, A. L., Hamsher, K. DeS., Varney, N. R., & Spreen, O. (1983). *Contributions to neuropsychological assessment: A clinical manual*. New York: Oxford University Press.

Berent, S. (1981). Lateralization of brain function. In S. B. Filskov & T. J. Boll (Eds.), *Handbook of clinical neuropsychology* (pp. 74–101). New York: Wiley.

Bergan, A., McManis, D. L., & Melchert, P. A. (1971). Effects of social and token reinforcement on WISC Block Design performance. *Perceptual and Motor Skills*, *32*, 871–880.

Bergan, J. R. (1977). *Behavioral consultation*. Columbus, OH: Charles E. Merrill.

Bergan, J. R., & Parra, E. B. (1979). Variations in IQ testing and instruction and the letter learning and achievement of Anglo and bilingual Mexican-American children. *Journal of Educational Psychology*, *71*, 819–826.

Berk, R. A. (1981). What's wrong with using grade-equivalent scores to identify LD children? *Academic Therapy*, *17*, 133–140.

Berk, R. A. (1984). *Screening and diagnosis of children with learning disabilities*. Springfield, IL: Charles C Thomas.

Berman, A., & Siegal, A. (1976). A neuropsychological approach to the etiology, prevention, and treatment of juvenile delinquency. In A. Davids (Ed.), *Child personality and psychopathology: Current topics* (Vol. 3, pp. 259–294). New York: Wiley.

Bernal, E. M., Jr. (1972, February). *Assessing assessment instruments: A Chicano perspective*. Paper prepared for the Regional Training Program to Serve the Bilingual/Bicultural Exceptional Child, Montal Educational Associates, Sacramento, CA.

Bernstein, D. A., & Nietzel, M. T. (1980). *Introduction to clinical psychology*. New York: McGraw-Hill.

Bessent, T. E. (1950). A note on the validity of the Leiter International Performance Scale. *Journal of Consulting Psychology*, *14*, 234.

Best, B., & Roberts, G. (1976). Early cognitive development in hearing impaired children. *American Annals of the Deaf*, *121*, 560–564.

Bethge, H. J., Carlson, J. S., & Wiedl, K. H. (1982). The effects of dynamic assessment procedures on Raven Matrices performance, visual search behavior, test anxiety and test orientation. *Intelligence*, *6*, 89–97.

Bickett, L., Reuter, J., & Stancin, T. (1984). The use of the McCarthy Scales of Children's Abilities to assess moderately mentally retarded children. *Psychology in the Schools*, *21*, 305–312.

Bierman, K. L. (1983). Cognitive development and clinical interviews with children. In B. B. Lahey & A. E. Kazdin (Ed.), *Advances in clinical child psychology* (Vol. 6, pp. 217–250). New York: Plenum.

Binet, A., & Simon, T. (1905). Méthodes nouvelles pour le diagnostic du niveau intéllectuel des anormaux. *L'Année Psychologique*, *11*, 191–244.

Binet, A., & Simon, T. (1916). *The development of intelligence in children* (E. S. Kit, trans.). Baltimore: Williams & Wilkins.

Birch, H. G., & Gussow, J. D. (1970). *Disadvantaged children: Health, nutrition and school failure*. New York: Grune & Stratton.

Bishop, D., & Butterworth, G. E. (1979). A longitudinal study using the WPPSI and WISC-R with an English sample. *British Journal of Educational Psychology*, *49*, 156–168.

Bissette, D. C. (1987). *Area score patterning of the Stanford-Binet (4th Edition) with trainable mentally retarded students*. Unpublished manuscript, Biola University, Rosemead School of Psychology, La Mirada, CA.

Black, F. W. (1973). Neurological dysfunction and reading disorders. *Journal of Learning Disabilities*, *6*, 313–316.

Blaha, J., Fawaz, N., & Wallbrown, F. H. (1979). Information processing components of Koppitz errors on the Bender Visual-Motor Gestalt Test. *Journal of Clinical Psychology*, *35*, 784–790.

Blaha, J., & Vance, H. (1979). The hierarchical factor structure of the WISC-R for learning disabled children. *Learning Disability Quarterly*, *2*(4), 71–75.

Blaha, J., & Wallbrown, F. H. (1982). Hierarchical factor structure of the Wechsler Adult Intelligence Scale–Revised. *Journal of Consulting and Clinical Psychology*, *50*, 652–660.

Blakeslee, D. E. (1987). *Psychometric properties, subtest patterning and concurrent validity of the Stanford-Binet Intelligence Scale, Fourth Edition with emotionally disturbed children (public school setting)*. Unpublished doctoral dissertation, Biola University, La Mirada, CA.

Blatt, S. J., & Allison, J. (1968). The intelligence test in personality assessment. In A. I. Rabin (Ed.), *Projective techniques in personality assessment* (pp. 421–460). New York: Springer.

Boehm, A. E. (1986a). *Boehm Test of Basic Concepts–Preschool Version*. San Antonio: The Psychological Corporation.

Boehm, A. E. (1986b). *Boehm Test of Basic Concepts–Revised*. San Antonio: The Psychological Corporation.

Bondy, A. S., Sheslow, D., Norcross, J. C., & Constantino, R. (1982). Comparison of Slosson and McCarthy Scales for minority pre-school children. *Perceptual and Motor Skills*, *54*, 356–358.

Bonham, S. J., Jr. (1974). Predicting achievement for deaf children. *Psychological Service Center Journal*, *14*, 35–44.

Boring, E. G. (1950). *A history of experimental psychology* (2nd ed.). New York: Appleton-Century-Crofts.

Borkowski, J. G. (1985). Signs of intelligence: Strategy generalization and metacognition. In S. R. Yussen (Ed.), *The growth of reflection in children* (pp. 105–144). Orlando, FL: Academic Press.

Bornstein, R. A. (1983). Verbal IQ-Performance IQ discrepancies on the Wechsler Adult Intelligence Scale–Revised in patients with unilateral or bilateral cerebral dysfunction. *Journal of Consulting and Clinical Psychology*, *51*, 779–780.

Bossard, M. D., Reynolds, C. R., & Gutkin, T. B. (1980). A regression analysis of test bias on the Stanford-Binet Intelligence Scale. *Journal of Clinical Child Psychology*, *9*, 52–54.

Bouchard, T. J., Jr. (1984). [Review of frames of the mind: The theory of multiple intelligence]. *American Journal of Orthopsychiatry*, *54*, 506–508.

Bouchard, T. J., Jr., & McGue, M. (1981). Familial studies of intelligence: A review. *Science*, *212*, 1055–1058.

Bouchard, T. J., Jr., & Segal, N. L. (1985). Environment and IQ. In B. B. Wolman (Ed.), *Handbook of intelligence: Theories, measurements, and applications* (pp. 391–464). New York: Wiley.

Boykin, A. W. (1983). The academic performance of Afro-American children. In J. T. Spence (Ed.), *Achievement and achievement motives: Psychological and sociological approaches* (pp. 321–371). San Francisco: W. H. Freeman.

Bracken, B. A. (1984). *Bracken Basic Concept Scale*. San Antonio: The Psychological Corporation.

Bracken, B. A. (1985). A critical review of the Kaufman Assessment Battery for Children (K-ABC). *School Psychology Review*, *14*, 21–36.

Bracken, B. A., Prasse, D. P., & Breen, M. J. (1984). Concurrent validity of the Woodcock-Johnson Psycho-Educational Battery with regular and learning-disabled students. *Journal of School Psychology*, *22*, 185–192.

Bracken, B. A., Prasse, D. P., & McCallum, R. S. (1984). Peabody Picture Vocabulary Test–Revised: An appraisal and review. *School Psychology Review*, *13*, 49–60.

Bradbury, P. J., Wright, S. D., Walker, C. E., & Ross, J. M. (1975). Performance on the WISC as a function of sex of *E*, sex of *S*, and age of *S*. *Journal of Psychology*, *90*, 51–55.

Braden, J. P. (1985). Futile gestures: A reply to Courtney, Hayes, Couch, and Frick regarding pantomimed administration of the WISC-R performance scale. *Journal of Psychoeducational Assessment*, *3*, 181–185.

Braden, J. P., & Paquin, M. M. (1985). A comparison of the WISC-R and WAIS-R Performance Scales in deaf adolescents. *Journal of Psychoeducational Assessment*, *3*, 285–290.

Bradley, F. O., Hanna, G. S., & Lucas, B. A. (1980). The reliability of scoring the WISC-R. *Journal of Consulting and Clinical Psychology*, *48*, 530–531.

Bradley, T. B. (1983). Remediation of cognitive deficits: A critical appraisal of the Feuerstein model. *Journal of Mental Deficiency Research*, *27*, 79–92.

Bradley-Johnson, S., Graham, D. P., & Johnson, C. M. (1986). Token reinforcement on WISC-R performance for white, low-socioeconomic, upper and lower elementary-school-age students. *Journal of School Psychology*, *24*, 73–79.

Bradley-Johnson, S., Johnson, C. M., Shanahan, R. H., Rickert, V. I., & Tardona, D. R. (1984). Effects of token reinforcement on WISC-R performance of black and white, low socioeconomic second graders. *Behavioral Assessment*, *6*, 365–373.

Braginsky, D. D., & Braginsky, B. M. (1971). *Hansels and Gretels; studies of children in institutions for the mentally retarded*. New York: Holt, Rinehart and Winston.

Brannigan, G. G., Calnen, T., Loprete, L. J., & Rosenberg, L. A. (1976). A comparison of WISC and WISC-R scoring criteria for Comprehension, Similarities, and Vocabulary responses. *Journal of Clinical Psychology*, *32*, 94.

Brannigan, G. G., Rosenberg, L. A., Loprete, L. J., & Calnen, T. (1977). Scoring of WISC-R Comprehension, Similarities, and Vocabulary responses by experienced and inexperienced judges. *Psychology in the Schools*, *14*, 430.

Bray, N. M., & Estes, R. E. (1975). A comparison of the PIAT, CAT, and WRAT scores and teacher ratings with learning disabled children. *Journal of Learning Disabilities*, *8*, 519–523.

Brazelton, T. B. (1973). *Neonatal Behavioral Assessment Scale*. Philadelphia: J. B. Lippincott.

Breen, M. J. (1981). Comparison of the Wechsler Intelligence

Scale for Children — Revised and the Peabody Picture Vocabulary Test — Revised for a referred population. *Psychological Reports*, *49*, 717–718.

Breen, M. J. (1982). Comparison of educationally handicapped students' scores on the Revised Developmental Test of Visual-Motor Integration and Bender-Gestalt. *Perceptual and Motor Skills*, *54*, 1227–1230.

Breen, M. J. (1984). The temporal stability of the Woodcock-Johnson Tests of Cognitive Ability for elementary-aged learning disabled children. *Journal of Psychoeducational Assessment*, *2*, 257–261.

Breen, M. J., Carlson, M., & Lehman, J. (1985). The Revised Developmental Test of Visual-Motor Integration: Its relation to the VMI, WISC-R, and Bender Gestalt for a group of elementary aged learning disabled students. *Journal of Learning Disabilities*, *18*, 136–138.

Breen, M. J., & Siewert, J. C. (1983). Comparison of the Peabody Picture Vocabulary Test — Revised and the Wechsler Intelligence Scale for Children — Revised for learning-disabled and referred students. *Journal of Psychoeducational Assessment*, *1*, 95–99.

Bretzing, B. H. (1977, September). *IQ and achievement tests: Is there a difference?* Paper presented at the meeting of the American Psychological Association, San Francisco.

Breuning, S. E., & Zella, W. F. (1978). Effects of individualized incentives on norm-referenced IQ test performance of high school students in special education classes. *Journal of School Psychology*, *16*, 220–226.

Brittain, M. (1969). The WPPSI: A Midlands study. *British Journal of Educational Psychology*, *39*, 14–17.

Brody, E. B., & Brody, N. (1976). *Intelligence: Nature, determinants, and consequences*. New York: Academic Press.

Broman, S. H., & Nichols, P. L. (1975, September). *Early mental development, social class, and school-age IQ*. Paper presented at the meeting of the American Psychological Association, Chicago.

Brooker, B. H., & Cyr, J. J. (1986). Tables for clinicians to use to convert WAIS-R short forms. *Journal of Clinical Psychology*, *42*, 982–986.

Brooks, R. (1979). Psychoeducational assessment: A broader perspective. *Professional Psychology*, *10*, 708–722.

Brooks-Gunn, J., & Lewis, M. (1983). Screening and diagnosing handicapped infants. *Topics in Early Childhood Special Education*, *3*, 14–28.

Brophy, J. E. (1983). Research on the self-fulfilling prophecy and teacher expectations. *Journal of Educational Psychology*, *75*, 631–661.

Brophy, J. E., & Good, T. L. (1970). Teachers' communication of differential expectations for children's classroom performance: Some behavioral data. *Journal of Educational Psychology*, *61*, 365–374.

Brown, A. L., & French, L. A. (1979). The zone of potential development: Implications for intelligence testing in the year 2000. *Intelligence*, *3*, 255–273.

Brown, F. (1979). The SOMPA: A system of measuring potential abilities? *School Psychology Digest*, *8*, 37–46.

Bruininks, R. H. (1978). *Bruininks-Oseretsky Test of Motor Proficiency*. Circle Pines, MN: American Guidance Service.

Bruininks, R. H., Woodcock, R. W., Weatherman, R. F., & Hill, B. K. (1984). *Scales of Independent Behavior* (SIB). Allen, TX: DLM Teaching Resources.

Bruner, F. G., Barnes, E., & Dearborn, W. F. (1909). Report of committee on books and tests pertaining to the study of exceptional and mentally deficient children. *Proceedings of the National Education Association*, *47*, 901–914.

Bruno, J. P. (1986). Age-dependent effects of brain damage: The Kennard principle revisited [Review of *Early brain damage*, Vols. 1–2]. *Contemporary Psychology*, *31*, 274.

Buckley, K. J., & Oakland, T. D. (1977, August). *Contrasting localized norms for Mexican-American children on the ABIC*. Paper presented at the meeting of the American Psychological Association, San Francisco.

Budoff, M., & Hamilton, J. L. (1976). Optimizing test performance of moderately and severely mentally retarded adolescents and adults. *American Journal of Mental Deficiency*, *81*, 49–57.

Burgemeister, B. B. (1962). *Psychological techniques in neurological diagnosis*. New York: Harper & Row.

Burgemeister, B. B., Blum, L. H., & Lorge, I. (1972). *Columbia Mental Maturity Scale* (3rd ed.). San Antonio: The Psychological Corporation.

Buriel, R. (1978). Relationship of three field-dependence measures to the reading and math achievement of Anglo American and Mexican American children. *Journal of Educational Psychology*, *70*, 167–174.

Burke, H. R. (1958). Raven's Progressive Matrices: A review and critical evaluation. *Journal of Genetic Psychology*, *93*, 199–228.

Burns, E. (1976). Effects of restricted sampling on ITPA scaled scores. *American Journal of Mental Deficiency*, *80*, 394–400.

Burns, E. (1977). The effects of skewness on the interpretation of ITPA scaled scores. *Journal of School Psychology*, *15*, 219–224.

Burns, E., Peterson, D., & Bauer, L. (1974). The concurrent validity of the Peabody Individual Achievement Test. *Training School Bulletin*, *70*, 221–223.

Burns, G. W., & Watson, B. L. (1973). Factor analysis of the revised ITPA with underachieving children. *Journal of Learning Disabilities*, *6*, 371–376.

Burt, M. K., Dulay, H. C., & Hernandez, C. E. (1976). *Bilingual Syntax Measure technical handbook*. San Antonio: The Psychological Corporation.

Burt, M. K., Dulay, H. C., & Hernandez, C. E. (1978). *Bilingual Syntax Measure II manual: English edition*. San Antonio: The Psychological Corporation.

Busch, J. C., & Osborne, W. L. (1976). Significant vs meaningful differences in the effects of tangible reinforcement on intelligence test achievement and reliability of TMR subjects. *Psychology in the Schools*, *13*, 219–225.

Butcher, J. N., Stelmachers, Z. T., & Maudal, G. R. (1983). Crisis intervention and emergency psychotherapy. In I. B. Weiner (Ed.), *Clinical methods in psychology* (2nd ed., pp. 572–633). New York: Wiley.

Butler, B. V., & Engel, R. (1969). Mental and motor scores at eight months in relation to neonatal photic responses. *Developmental Medicine and Child Neurology, 11,* 77–82.

Butler, K. G. (1978). Review of the Lindamood Auditory Conceptualization Test. In O. K. Buros (Ed.), *The eighth mental measurements yearbook* (pp. 1464–1465). Highland Park, NJ: Gryphon Press.

Cain, L. F., Levine, S., & Elzey, F. F. (1963). *Cain-Levine Social Competency Scale.* Palo Alto, CA: Consulting Psychologists Press.

Campbell, S. B. (1976). Hyperactivity: Course and treatment. In A. Davids (Ed.), *Child personality and psychopathology: Current topics* (Vol. 3, pp. 201–236). New York: Wiley.

Campione, J. C., & Brown, A. L. (1978). Toward a theory of intelligence: Contributions from research with retarded children. *Intelligence, 2,* 279–304.

Cannell, C. F., & Kahn, R. L. (1968). Interviewing. In G. Lindzey & E. Aronson (Eds.), *The handbook of social psychology,* (2nd ed., Vol. 2, pp. 526–595). Reading, MA: Addison-Wesley.

Cantwell, D. P. (Ed.). (1975). *The hyperactive child: Diagnosis, management, current research.* New York: Spectrum.

Caparulo, B. K., & Cohen, D. J. (1977). Cognitive structures, language, and emerging social competence in autistic and aphasic children. *Journal of the American Academy of Child Psychiatry, 16,* 620–645.

Carlson, J. S., & Jensen, C. M. (1980). The factorial structure of the Raven Coloured Progressive Matrices Test: A reanalysis. *Educational and Psychological Measurement, 40,* 1111–1116.

Carlson, J. S., Jensen, C. M., & Widaman, K. F. (1983). Reaction time, intelligence, and attention. *Intelligence, 7,* 329–344.

Carlson, J. S., & Wiedl, K. H. (1979). Toward a differential testing approach: Testing-the-limits employing the Raven Matrices. *Intelligence, 3,* 323–344.

Carlson, L. C., & Reynolds, C. R. (1981). Factor structure and specific variance of the WPPSI subtests at six age levels. *Psychology in the Schools, 18,* 48–54.

Carlson, L. C., Reynolds, C. R., & Gutkin, T. B. (1983). Consistency of the factorial validity of the WISC-R for upper and lower SES groups. *Journal of School Psychology, 21,* 319–326.

Carroll, J. B. (1972). Review of Illinois Test of Psycholinguistic Abilities. In O. K. Buros (Ed.), *The seventh mental measurements yearbook* (pp. 819–823). Highland Park, NJ: Gryphon Press.

Carroll, J. B., & Horn, J. L. (1981). On the scientific basis of ability testing. *American Psychologist, 36,* 1012–1020.

Carrow-Woolfolk, E. (1985). *Test for Auditory Comprehension of Language* (rev. ed.). Allen, TX: DLM Teaching Resources.

Carter, R. B. (1977). A study of attitudes: Mexican American and Anglo American elementary teachers' judgments of Mexican American bilingual children's speech. *Dissertation Abstracts International, 37,* 4941A–4942A. (University Microfilms No. 77–1502)

Carvajal, H., Gerber, J., Hewes, P., & Weaver, K. A. (1987). Correlations between scores on Stanford-Binet IV and Wechsler Adult Intelligence Scale – Revised. *Psychological Reports, 61,* 83–86.

Carvajal, H., & Weyand, K. (1986). Relationships between scores on Stanford-Binet IV and Wechsler Intelligence Scale for Children – Revised. *Psychological Reports, 59,* 963–966.

Caskey, W. E., Jr., & Larson, G. L. (1980). Scores on group and individually administered Bender-Gestalt Test and Otis-Lennon IQs of kindergarten children. *Perceptual and Motor Skills, 50,* 387–390.

Cattell, P. (1937). Stanford-Binet IQ variations. *School and Society, 45,* 615–618.

Cattell, P. (1940). *Cattell Infant Intelligence Scale.* San Antonio: The Psychological Corporation.

Cattell, R. B. (1963). Theory of fluid and crystalized intelligence: A critical experiment. *Journal of Educational Psychology, 54,* 1–22.

Cattell, R. B., & Drevdahl, J. E. (1955). A comparison of the personality profile (16 P.F.) of eminent researchers with that of eminent teachers and administrators, and of the general population. *British Journal of Psychology, 46,* 248–261.

Chandler, J. T., & Plakos, J. (1969). Spanish-speaking pupils classified as educable mentally retarded. *Integrated Education, 7,* 28–33.

Chapey, R. (1981). The assessment of language disorders in adults. In R. Chapey (Ed.), *Language intervention strategies in adult aphasia* (pp. 31–84). Baltimore: Williams & Wilkins.

Chastain, R. L., & Reynolds, C. R. (1984, August). *An analysis of WAIS-R performance by sample stratification variables used during standardization.* Paper presented at the annual convention of the American Psychological Association, Toronto, Canada. (Ed 249 409)

Chatman, S. P., Reynolds, C. R., & Willson, V. L. (1984). Multiple indexes of test scatter on the Kaufman Assessment Battery for Children. *Journal of Learning Disabilities, 17,* 523–531.

Chavez, E. L. (1982). Analysis of a Spanish translation of the Peabody Picture Vocabulary Test. *Perceptual and Motor Skills, 54,* 1335–1338.

Chess, S. (1967). Healthy responses, developmental disturbances, and stress or reactive disorders. I: Infancy and childhood. In A. M. Freedman & H. I. Kaplan (Eds.), *Comprehensive textbook of psychiatry* (pp. 1358–1366). Baltimore: Williams & Wilkins.

Childs, R. E. (1982). A study of the adaptive behavior of retarded children and the resultant effects of this use in the diagnosis of mental retardation. *Education and Training of the Mentally Retarded, 17,* 109–113.

Cieutat, V. J. (1965). Examiner differences with the Stanford-Binet IQ. *Perceptual and Motor Skills, 20,* 317–318.

Cieutat, V. J., & Flick, G. L. (1967). Examiner differences among Stanford-Binet items. *Psychological Reports, 21,* 613–622.

Claiborn, W. L. (1969). Expectancy effects in the classroom: A failure to replicate. *Journal of Educational Psychology, 60,* 377–383.

Clampit, M. K., Adair, J., & Strenio, J. (1983). Frequency of discrepancies between deviation quotients on the WISC-R: A table for clinicians. *Journal of Consulting and Clinical Psychology, 51,* 795–796.

Clarizio, H. F. (1979). Commentary on Mercer's rejoinder to Clarizio. *School Psychology Digest, 8,* 207–209.

Clarizio, H. F., & Bernard, R. (1981). Recategorized WISC-R scores of learning disabled children and differential diagnosis. *Psychology in the Schools, 18,* 5–12.

Clarizio, H. F., & Veres, V. (1983). WISC-R patterns of emotionally impaired and diagnostic utility. *Psychology in the Schools, 20,* 409–414.

Clarizio, H. F., & Veres, V. (1984). A short-form version of the WISC-R for the learning disabled. *Psychology in the Schools, 21,* 154–157.

Cleary, T. A., Humphreys, L. G., Kendrick, S. A., & Wesman, A. G. (1975). Educational uses of tests with disadvantaged students. *American Psychologist, 30,* 15–41.

Clingman, J., & Fowler, R. L. (1975). The effects of contingent and noncontingent rewards on the I.Q. scores of children of above-average intelligence. *Journal of Applied Behavior Analysis, 8,* 90.

Cohen, D. H., & Stern, V. (1970). *Observing and recording the behavior of young children.* New York: Teachers College Press.

Cohen, E. (1950). Is there examiner bias on the Wechsler-Bellevue? *Proceedings of Oklahoma Academy of Science, 31,* 150–153.

Cohen, E. (1965). Examiner differences with individual intelligence tests. *Perceptual and Motor Skills, 20,* 1324.

Cohen, J. (1959). The factorial structure of the WISC at ages 7-6, 10-6, and 13-6. *Journal of Consulting Psychology, 23,* 285–299.

Cohen, J. (1960). A coefficient of agreement for nominal scales. *Educational and Psychological Measurement, 20,* 37–46.

Cohen, J. (1968). Weighted kappa: Nominal scale agreement with provision for scaled disagreement or partial credit. *Psychological Bulletin, 70,* 213–220.

Cohen, L. (1970). The effects of material and non-material reinforcement upon performance of the WISC Block Design subtest by children of different social classes: A follow-up study. *Psychology, 7*(4), 41–47.

Cohen, N. J., Gotlieb, H., Kershner, J., & Wehrspann, W. (1985). Concurrent validity of the internalizing and externalizing profile patterns of the Achenbach Child Behavior Checklist. *Journal of Consulting and Clinical Psychology, 53,* 724–728.

Cole, N. S. (1981). Bias in testing. *American Psychologist, 36,* 1067–1077.

Coleman, M. C., & Harmer, W. R. (1985). The WISC-R and Woodcock-Johnson Tests of Cognitive Ability: A comparative study. *Psychology in the Schools, 22,* 127–132.

Cone, J. D., & Foster, S. L. (1982). Direct observation in clinical psychology. In P. C. Kendall & J. N. Butcher (Eds.), *Handbook of research methods in clinical psychology* (pp. 311–354). New York: Wiley.

Conger, A. J. (1980). Integration and generalization of kappas for multiple raters. *Psychological Bulletin, 88,* 322–328.

Conger, R. D. (1984). *Social Interaction Scoring System.* Unpublished manuscript, Iowa State University, Ames, IA.

Conners, C. K. (1985). *The Conners Rating Scales: Instruments for the assessment of childhood psychopathology.* Unpublished manuscript, Children's Hospital National Medical Center, Washington, DC.

Connolly, A. J., Nachtman, W., & Pritchett, E. M. (1971). *The KeyMath Diagnostic Arithmetic Test.* Circle Pines, MN: American Guidance Service.

Cook, L. C. (1973). The effects of verbal and monetary feedback on the WISC scores of lower-SES Spanish American and lower- and middle-SES Anglo students. *Dissertation Abstracts International, 34,* 1693A–1694A. (University Microfilms No. 73-23,317)

Cooley, E., & Lamson, F. (1983). *A comparison of intellectually average and below average children with learning problems.* Paper presented at the meeting of the Western Psychological Association, San Francisco, CA.

Corey, M. T. (1970, September). The WPPSI as a school admissions tool for young children. In R. S. Morrow (Chair), *Diagnostic and educational application of the Wechsler Preschool and Primary Scale of Intelligence* (WPPSI). Symposium presented at the meeting of the American Psychological Association, Miami.

Corman, L., & Budoff, M. (1974). Factor structures of Spanish-speaking and non-Spanish-speaking children on Raven's Progressive Matrices. *Educational and Psychological Measurement, 34,* 977–981.

Cormier, W. H., & Cormier, L. S. (1979). *Interviewing strategies for helpers: A guide to assessment, treatment, and evaluation.* Monterey, CA: Brooks/Cole.

Costa, L. (1983). Clinical neuropsychology: A discipline in evolution. *Journal of Clinical Neuropsychology, 5,* 1–11.

Costello, A. J., Edelbrock, C., Dulcan, M. K., Kalas, R., & Klaric, S. H. (1984). *Development and testing of the NIMH diagnostic interview schedule for children in a clinic population.* Final report (Contract #RFP-DB-81-0027). Center for Epidemiologic Studies, NIMH, Rockville, MD.

Cowen, E. L., Trost, M. A., Lorion, R. P., Dorr, D., Izzo, L. D., & Isaacson, R. V. (1975). *New ways in school mental health: Early detection and prevention of school maladaptation.* New York: Human Sciences Press.

Cox, T. (1983). Cumulative deficit in culturally disadvantaged children. *British Journal of Educational Psychology, 53,* 317–326.

Craig, R. J. (1969). An illustration of the Wechsler Picture Arrangement subtest as a thematic technique. *Journal of Projective Techniques and Personality Assessment, 33,* 286–289.

Crary, W. G., & Johnson, C. W. (1975). Mental status examination. In C. W. Johnson, J. R. Snibbe, & L. A. Evans (Eds.), *Basic psychopathology: A programmed text* (pp. 50–89). New York: Spectrum.

Croake, J. W., Keller, J. F., & Catlin, N. (1973). WPPSI, Rutgers, Goodenough, Goodenough-Harris I.Q.'s for lower socioeconomic, black, preschool children. *Psychology, 10*(2), 58–65.

Crockett, B. K., Rardin, M. W., & Pasewark, R. A. (1975). Relationship between WPPSI and Stanford-Binet IQs and subsequent WISC IQs in Headstart children. *Journal of Consulting and Clinical Psychology, 43,* 922.

Crockett, B. K., Rardin, M. W., & Pasewark, R. A. (1976). Relationship of WPPSI and subsequent Metropolitan Achievement Test scores in Head-Start children. *Psychology in the Schools, 13,* 19–20.

Crofoot, M. J., & Bennett, T. S. (1980). A comparison of three screening tests and the WISC-R in special education evaluations. *Psychology in the Schools, 17,* 474–478.

Cronbach, L. J. (1975). Five decades of public controversy over mental testing. *American Psychologist, 30,* 1–14.

Crowell, D. H. (1957). Sensory defects. In C. M. Louttit (Ed.), *Clinical psychology of exceptional children* (3rd ed., pp. 425–491). New York: Harper.

Crowell, D. H., & Crowell, D. C. (1954). Intelligence test reliability for cerebral palsied children. *Journal of Consulting Psychology, 18,* 276.

Croxen, M. E., & Lytton, H. (1971). Reading disability and difficulties in finger localization and right-left discrimination. *Developmental Psychology, 5,* 256–262.

Cruickshank, W. M. (1977). Myths and realities in learning disabilities. *Journal of Learning Disabilities, 10,* 51–58.

Cuadra, C. A., & Albaugh, W. P. (1956). Sources of ambiguity in psychological reports. *Journal of Clinical Psychology, 12,* 109–115.

Cuenot, R. G., & Darbes, A. (1982). A comparison of interscorer agreement for the Comprehension, Similarities, and Vocabulary subtests of the WISC and WISC-R. *Educational and Psychological Measurement, 42,* 417–421.

Cummings, J. A. (1982). Interpreting functioning levels: Woodcock-Johnson Psycho-Educational Battery. *Psychological Reports, 50,* 1167–1171.

Cundick, B. P. (1970). Measures of intelligence on Southwest Indian students. *Journal of Social Psychology, 81,* 151–156.

Curr, W., & Gourlay, N. (1956). Differences between testers in Terman-Merrill testing. *British Journal of Statistical Psychology, 9,* 75–81.

Cutter, A. V., & Miller, E. A. (1971). The interpretive and summing up process with parents during and after diagnostic studies of children. In R. L. Noland (Ed.), *Counseling parents*

of the ill and the handicapped (pp. 62–77). Springfield, IL: Charles C Thomas.

Dangel, H. L. (1972). Biasing effect of pretest referral information on WISC scores of mentally retarded children. *American Journal of Mental Deficiency, 77,* 354–359.

Darley, F. L. (1978). A philosophy of appraisal and diagnosis. In F. L. Darley & D. C. Spriestersbach (Eds.), *Diagnostic methods in speech pathology* (pp. 1–60). New York: Harper & Row.

Das, J. P. (1972). Patterns of cognitive ability in nonretarded and retarded children. *American Journal of Mental Deficiency, 77,* 6–12.

Das, J. P. (1973). Cultural deprivation and cognitive competence. In N. R. Ellis (Ed.), *International review of research in mental retardation* (Vol. 6, pp. 1–53). New York: Academic Press.

Das, J. P., Kirby, J., & Jarman, R. F. (1975). Simultaneous and successive syntheses: An alternative model for cognitive abilities. *Psychological Bulletin, 82,* 87–103.

Das, J. P., & Molloy, G. N. (1975). Varieties of simultaneous and successive processing in children. *Journal of Educational Psychology, 67,* 213–220.

Davenport, B. M. (1976). A comparison of the Peabody Individual Achievement Test, the Metropolitan Achievement Test, and the Otis-Lennon Mental Ability Test. *Psychology in the Schools, 13,* 291–297.

Davis, C. (1980). *Perkins-Binet Tests of Intelligence for the Blind.* Watertown, MA: Perkins School for the Blind.

Davis, E. E. (1975). Concurrent validity of the McCarthy Scales of Children's Abilities. *Measurement and Evaluation in Guidance, 8,* 101–104.

Davis, E. E., & Rowland, T. (1974). A replacement for the venerable Stanford-Binet? *Journal of Clinical Psychology, 30,* 517–521.

Davis, E. E., Slettedahl, R. W. (1976). Stability of the McCarthy Scales over a 1-year period. *Journal of Clinical Psychology, 32,* 798–800.

Davis, E. E., & Walker, C. (1977). McCarthy Scales and WISC-R. *Perceptual and Motor Skills, 44,* 966.

Davis, F. B. (1959). Interpretation of differences among averages and individual test scores. *Journal of Educational Psychology, 50,* 162–170.

Davis, F. B. (1971). The measurement of mental capability through evoked potential recording. *Educational Records and Research Bulletin, 1,* 1–171.

Davis, S. E., & Kramer, J. J. (1985). Comparison of the PPVT-R and WISC-R: A validation study with second-grade students. *Psychology in the Schools, 22,* 265–268.

Davis, W. E., Peacock, W., Fitzpatrick, P., & Mulhern, M. (1969). Examiner differences, prior failure, and subjects' WAIS Arithmetic scores. *Journal of Clinical Psychology, 25,* 178–180.

Dean, R. S. (1977a). Analysis of the PIAT with Anglo and Mexican-American children. *Journal of School Psychology, 15,* 329–333.

Dean, R. S. (1977b). Canonical analysis of a jangle fallacy. *Multivariate Experimental Clinical Research*, *3*, 17–20.

Dean, R. S. (1977c). Internal consistency of the PIAT with Mexican-American children. *Psychology in the Schools*, *14*, 167–168.

Dean, R. S. (1977d). Patterns of emotional disturbance on the WISC-R. *Journal of Clinical Psychology*, *33*, 486–490.

Dean, R. S. (1977e). Reliability of the WISC-R with Mexican-American children. *Journal of School Psychology*, *15*, 267–268.

Dean, R. S. (1977f). The validity and reliability of abbreviated versions of the WISC-R. *Educational and Psychological Measurement*, *37*, 1111–1116.

Dean, R. S. (1979a). Distinguishing patterns for Mexican-American children on the WISC-R. *Journal of Clinical Psychology*, *35*, 790–794.

Dean, R. S. (1979b). Predictive validity of the WISC-R with Mexican-American children. *Journal of School Psychology*, *17*, 55–58.

Dean, R. S. (1980). Factor structure of the WISC-R with Anglos and Mexican Americans. *Journal of School Psychology*, *18*, 234–239.

DeAvila, E. A., & Duncan, S. E. (1977). *Language Assessment Scales* (2nd ed.). Corte Madera, CA: Linguametrics Group.

DeAvila, E. A., & Havassy, B. (1974). The testing of minority children: A neo-Piagetian approach. *Today's Education*, *63*(4), 72–75.

DeHorn, A., & Klinge, V. (1978). Correlations and factor analysis of the WISC-R and the Peabody Picture Vocabulary Test for an adolescent psychiatric sample. *Journal of Consulting and Clinical Psychology*, *46*, 1160–1161.

Delany, E., & Hopkins, T. (1987). *Examiner's handbook: An expanded guide for Fourth Edition users*. Chicago: Riverside Publishing.

Delis, D. C., & Kaplan, E. (1983). Hazards of a standardized neuropsychological test with low content validity: Comment on the Luria-Nebraska Neuropsychological Battery. *Journal of Consulting and Clinical Psychology*, *51*, 396–398.

Dellas, M., & Gaier, E. (1970). Identification of creativity: The individual. *Psychological Bulletin*, *73*, 55–73.

Dembinski, R. J., & Mauser, A. J. (1978). Parents of the gifted: Perceptions of psychologists and teachers. *Journal for the Education of the Gifted*, *1*, 5–14.

DeMers, S. T., Wright, D., & Dappen, L. (1981). Comparison of scores on two visual-motor tests for children referred for learning or adjustment difficulties. *Perceptual and Motor Skills*, *53*, 863–867.

DeMyer, M. K. (1976). The nature of the neuropsychological disability in autistic children. In E. Schopler & R. J. Reichler (Eds.), *Psychopathology and child development: Research and treatment* (pp. 93–114). New York: Plenum.

DeMyer, M. K., Barton, S., Alpern, G. D., Kimberlin, C., Allen, J., Yang, E., & Steele, R. (1974). The measured intelligence of autistic children. *Journal of Autism and Childhood Schizophrenia*, *4*, 42–60.

DeMyer, M. K., Barton, S., DeMyer, W. E., Norton, J. A., Allen, J., & Steele, R. (1973). Prognosis in autism: A follow-up study. *Journal of Autism and Childhood Schizophrenia*, *3*, 199–246.

DeMyer, M. K., Barton, S., & Norton, J. A. (1972). A comparison of adaptive, verbal, and motor profiles of psychotic and non-psychotic subnormal children. *Journal of Autism and Childhood Schizophrenia*, *2*, 359–377.

Denckla, M. B. (1985). Revised neurological examination for subtle signs (1985). *Psychopharmacology Bulletin*, *21*, 773–789.

Denniston, C. (1975). Accounting for differences in mean IQ [Review of *Educability and group differences* by A. R. Jensen]. *Science*, *187*, 161–162.

Deno, E. (1970). Special education as developmental capital. *Exceptional Children*, *37*, 229–237.

Denton, L. R. (1954, December). Intelligence test performance and personality differences in a group of visually handicapped children. *Bulletin of the Maritime Psychological Association*, pp. 47–50.

De Renzi, E. (1980). The Token Test and the Reporter's Test: A measure of verbal input and a measure of verbal output. In M. T. Sarno & O. Hook (Eds.), *Aphasia: Assessment and treatment* (pp. 158–169). New York: Masson Publishing.

De Renzi, E., & Faglioni, P. (1978). Normative data and screening power of a shortened version of the Token Test. *Cortex*, *14*, 41–49.

De Renzi, E., & Ferrari, C. (1978). The Reporter's Test: A sensitive test to detect expressive disturbances in aphasics. *Cortex*, *14*, 279–293.

Deutsch, M., Fishman, J. A., Kogan, L., North, R., & Whiteman, M. (1964). Guidelines for testing minority group children. *Journal of Social Issues*, *20*(2), 129–145.

Diedrich, W. M., & Carr, D. B. (1984). Identification of speech disorders. *Journal of Developmental & Behavioral Pediatrics*, *5*, 38–41.

Dillon, R. F., Pohlmann, J. T., & Lohman, D. F. (1981). A factor analysis of Raven's Advanced Progressive Matrices freed of difficulty factors. *Educational and Psychological Measurement*, *41*, 1295–1302.

Di Lorenzo, L. T., & Nagler, E. (1968). Examiner differences on the Stanford-Binet. *Psychological Reports*, *22*, 443–447.

Dirks, J. (1982). The effect of a commercial game on children's Block Design scores on the WISC-R IQ test. *Intelligence*, *6*, 109–123.

Dirks, J., Wessels, K., Quarfoth, J., & Quenon, B. (1980). Can short-form WISC-R IQ tests identify children with high Full Scale IQ? *Psychology in the Schools*, *17*, 40–46.

DiSimoni, F. G. (1978). *Token Test for Children*. Allen, TX: DLM Teaching Resources.

Dlugokinski, E., Weiss, S., & Johnston, S. (1976). Preschoolers at risk: Social, emotional and cognitive considerations. *Psychology in the Schools*, *13*, 134–139.

Dodwell, P. C. (1961). Children's understanding of number concepts: Characteristics of an individual and of a group test. *Canadian Journal of Psychology, 15*, 29–36.

Dohrenwend, B. P., & Chin-Shong, E. (1967). Social status and attitudes toward psychological disorder: The problem of tolerance of deviance. *American Sociological Review, 32*, 417–433.

Dokecki, P. R., Frede, M. C., & Gautney, D. B. (1969). Criterion, construct, and predictive validities of the Wechsler Preschool and Primary Scale of Intelligence. *Proceedings of the 77th Annual Convention of the American Psychological Association, 4*, 505–506.

Doll, E. A. (1946). *The Oseretsky Tests of Motor Proficiency: A translation from the Portuguese adaption*. Minneapolis: Educational Test Bureau.

Donahue, D., & Sattler, J. M. (1971). Personality variables affecting WAIS scores. *Journal of Consulting and Clinical Psychology, 36*, 441.

Drake, E. A., & Bardon, J. I. (1978). Confidentiality and interagency communication: Effect of the Buckley Amendment. *Hospital and Community Psychiatry, 29*, 312–315.

Dreibelbis, R. M. (1981). Views of Pennsylvania teachers on P.L. 94-142. *Phi Delta Kappan, 63*, 212.

Du Bois, P. H. (1970). *A history of psychological testing*. Boston: Allyn and Bacon.

Du Bois, P. H. (1972). Increase in educational opportunity through measurement. *Proceedings of the 1971 Invitational Conference on Testing Problems*. Princeton, NJ: Educational Testing Service.

DuBose, R. F. (1979a). Working with sensorily impaired children (Part I): Visual impairments. In S. G. Garwood (Ed.), *Educating young handicapped children: A developmental approach* (pp. 323–359). Germantown, MD: Aspen Systems.

DuBose, R. F. (1979b). Working with sensorily impaired children (Part II): Hearing impairments. In S. G. Garwood (Ed.), *Educating young handicapped children: A developmental approach* (pp. 361–398). Germantown, MD: Aspen Systems.

Dudek, F. J. (1979). The continuing misinterpretation of the standard error of measurement. *Psychological Bulletin, 86*, 335–337.

Dudek, S. Z., Lester, E. P., Goldberg, J. S., & Dyer, G. B. (1969). Relationship of Piaget measures to standard intelligence and motor scales. *Perceptual and Motor Skills, 28*, 351–362.

Dunn, E. S., Barker, M. L., & Wahler, R. G. (1981, September). *Standardized Observation Codes*. Unpublished manuscript.

Dunn, L. M., & Dunn, L. M. (1981). *Peabody Picture Vocabulary Test—Revised*. Circle Pines, MN: American Guidance Service.

Dunn, L. M., & Markwardt, F. C., Jr. (1970). *Peabody Individual Achievement Test*. Circle Pines, MN: American Guidance Service.

Dunst, C. J. (1980). *A clinical and educational manual for use with the Uzgiris and Hunt Scales of Infant Psychological Development*. Baltimore: University Park Press.

Dunst, C. J. (1982). The clinical utility of Piagetian-based scales of infant development. *Infant Mental Health Journal, 3*, 259–275.

Dusek, J. B., & O'Connell, E. J. (1973). Teacher expectancy effects on the achievement test performance of elementary school children. *Journal of Educational Psychology, 65*, 371–377.

Ebel, R. L. (1971). Criterion-referenced measurements: Limitations. *School Review, 79*, 282–288.

Ebel, R. L. (1975). Educational tests: Valid? Biased? Useful? *Phi Delta Kappan, 57*, 83–89.

Edelbrock, C. S. (1979). Empirical classification of children's behavior disorders: Progress based on parent and teacher ratings. *School Psychology Digest, 8*, 355–369.

Edelbrock, C. S. (1983). Problems and issues in using rating scales to assess child personality and psychopathology. *School Psychology Review, 12*, 293–299.

Edelbrock, C. S. (1984). Developmental considerations. In T. H. Ollendick & M. Hersen (Eds.), *Child behavioral assessment: Principles and procedures* (pp. 20–37). New York: Pergamon Press.

Edelbrock, C., & Costello, A. J. (1988). Structured psychiatric interviews for children. In M. Rutter, A. H. Tuma, & I. Lann (Eds.), *Assessment diagnosis in child psychopathology* (pp. 87–112). New York: Guilford Press.

Edelbrock, C. S., Costello, A. J., Dulcan, M. K., Conover, N. C., & Kalas, R. (1986). Parent-child agreement on child psychiatric symptoms assessed via structured interview. *Journal of Child Psychology and Psychiatry, 27*, 181–190.

Edelbrock, C. S., Costello, A. J., Dulcan, M. K., Kalas, R., & Conover, N. C. (1985). Age differences in the reliability of the psychiatric interview of the child. *Child Development, 56*, 265–275.

Edinger, J. D., Shipley, R. H., Watkins, C. E., Jr., & Hammett, E. B. (1985). Validity of the Wonderlic Personnel Test as a brief IQ measure in psychiatric patients. *Journal of Consulting and Clinical Psychology, 53*, 937–939.

Edlund, C. V. (1972). The effect on the behavior of children, as reflected in the IQ scores, when reinforced after each correct response. *Journal of Applied Behavior Analysis, 5*, 317–319.

Edwards, B. T., & Klein, M. (1984). Comparison of the WAIS and the WAIS-R with Ss of high intelligence. *Journal of Clinical Psychology, 40*, 300–302.

Egeland, B. (1967). Influence of examiner and examinee anxiety on WISC performance. *Psychological Reports, 21*, 409–414.

Egeland, B. (1969). Examiner expectancy: Effects on the scoring of the WISC. *Psychology in the Schools, 6*, 313–315.

Eiser, C. (1981). Psychological sequelae of brain tumours in childhood: A retrospective study. *British Journal of Clinical Psychology, 20*, 35–38.

Eklund, S., & Scott, M. (1965). Effects of bilingual instructions on test responses of Latin American children. *Psychology in the Schools, 2*, 280–282.

Ekren, U. W. (1962). *The effect of experimenter knowledge of a subject's scholastic standing on the performance of a reasoning task*. Unpublished master's thesis, Marquette University.

Elkind, D. (1961). Children's discovery of the conservation of mass, weight, and volume: Piaget replication study II. *Journal of Genetic Psychology, 98,* 219–227.

Elkind, D. (1973). Border-line retardation in low and middle income adolescents. In R. M. Allen, A. D. Cortazzo, & R. P. Toister (Eds.), *Theories of cognitive development: Implications for the mentally retarded* (pp. 57–85). Coral Gables, FL: University of Miami Press.

Elkind, D. (1974). *Children and adolescents: Interpretive essays on Jean Piaget* (2nd ed.). New York: Oxford University Press.

Elkind, D. (1979). The figurative and the operative in Piagetian psychology. In M. H. Bornstein & W. Kesson (Eds.), *Psychological development from infancy* (pp. 225–250). Hillsdale, NJ: Erlbaum.

Elkind, D. (1981). *Children and adolescents: Interpretive essays on Jean Piaget* (3rd ed.). New York: Oxford University Press.

Elliott, R. N., Jr. (1969). Comparative study of the Pictorial Test of Intelligence and the Peabody Picture Vocabulary Test. *Psychological Reports, 25,* 528–530.

Elliott, S. N., Piersel, W. C., Witt, J. C., Argulewicz, E. N., Gutkin, T. B., & Galvin, G. A. (1985). Three-year stability of WISC-R IQs for handicapped children from three racial/ethnic groups. *Journal of Psychoeducational Assessment, 3,* 233–244.

Eme, R. F. (1979). Sex differences in childhood psychopathology: A review. *Psychological Bulletin, 86,* 574–595.

Emerick, L. L., & Hatten, J. T. (1974). *Diagnosis and evaluation in speech pathology.* Englewood Cliffs, NJ: Prentice-Hall.

Engel, R., & Fay, W. H. (1972). Visual evoked responses at birth, verbal scores at three years, and IQ at four years. *Developmental Medicine and Child Neurology, 14,* 283–289.

Engel, R., & Henderson, N. B. (1973). Visual evoked responses and IQ scores at school age. *Developmental Medicine and Child Neurology, 15,* 136–145.

Epstein, M. H., & Nieminen, G. S. (1983). Reliability of the Conners Abbreviated Teacher Rating Scale across raters and across time: Use with learning disabled students. *School Psychology Review, 12,* 337–339.

Erikson, R. V. (1967). Abbreviated form of the WISC: A re-evaluation. *Journal of Consulting Psychology, 31,* 641.

Estabrook, G. E. (1984). A canonical correlation analysis of the Wechsler Intelligence Scale for Children—Revised and the Woodcock-Johnson Tests of Cognitive Ability in a sample referred for suspected learning disabilities. *Journal of Educational Psychology, 76,* 1170–1177.

Estes, W. K. (1974). Learning theory and intelligence. *American Psychologist, 29,* 740–749.

Evans, D., Hearn, M., Uhleman, M. R., & Ivey, A. E. (1979). *Essential interviewing: A programmed approach to effective communication.* Monterey, CA: Brooks/Cole.

Evans, I. M. (1983). Behavioral assessment. In C. E. Walker (Ed.), *The handbook of clinical psychology: Theory, research and practice* (pp. 391–419). Homewood, IL: Dow Jones-Irwin.

Evans, R. G. (1985). Accuracy of the Satz-Mogel procedure in estimating WAIS-R IQs that are in the normal range. *Journal of Clinical Psychology, 41,* 100–103.

Everett, F., Proctor, N., & Cartmell, B. (1983). Providing psychological services to American Indian children and families. *Professional Psychology: Research and Practice, 14,* 588–603.

Exner, J. E., Jr. (1966). Variations in WISC performances as influenced by differences in pretest rapport. *Journal of General Psychology, 74,* 299–306.

Eyberg, S. M. (1985). Behavioral assessment: Advancing methodology in pediatric psychology. *Journal of Pediatric Psychology, 10,* 123–139.

Eyman, R. K., Boroskin, A., & Hostetter, S. (1977). Use of alternative living plans for developmentally disabled children by minority parents. *Mental Retardation, 15*(1), 21–23.

Eysenck, H. J. (1967). Intelligence assessment: A theoretical and experimental approach. *British Journal of Educational Psychology, 37,* 81–98.

Eysenck, H. J. (1971). *The IQ argument: Race, intelligence and education.* New York: Library Press.

Fagan, J. F. (1984a). The intelligent infant: Theoretical implications. *Intelligence, 8,* 1–9.

Fagan, J. F. (1984b). The relationship of novelty preferences during infancy to later intelligence and later recognition memory. *Intelligence, 8,* 339–346.

Fagan, J. F., Broughton, E., Allen, M., Clark, B., & Emerson, P. (1969). Comparison of the Binet and WPPSI with lower-class five-year-olds. *Journal of Consulting and Clinical Psychology, 33,* 607–609.

Fagan, J. F., & Singer, L. T. (1983). Infant recognition memory as a measure of intelligence. *Advances in Infancy Research, 2,* 31–78.

Fagot, B. I. (1984). The consequence of problem behavior in toddler children. *Journal of Abnormal Child Psychology, 12,* 385–395.

Farris, C. E., & Farris, L. S. (1976). Indian children: The struggle for survival. *Social Work, 21,* 386–389.

Fassnacht, G. (1982). *Theory and practice of observing behavior.* New York: Academic Press.

Faulstich, M., McAnulty, D., Gresham, F., Veitia, M., Moore, J., Bernard, B., Waggoner, C., & Howell, R. (1986). Factor structure of the WAIS-R for an incarcerated population. *Journal of Clinical Psychology, 42,* 369–371.

Feinstein, S. (1986). Computers are replacing interviewers for personnel and marketing tasks. *Wall Street Journal,* October 9, 1986, p. 37.

Feldman, J. A. (1984). *Performance of learning disabled and normal children on three versions of the Token Test.* Unpublished master's thesis, San Diego State University, San Diego, CA.

Fell, L., & Fell, S. S. (1982). Effectiveness of WISC-R short-forms in screening gifted children. *Psychological Reports, 51,* 1017–1018.

Fernald, C. D., & Gettys, L. (1980). Diagnostic labels and

perceptions of children's behavior. *Journal of Clinical Child Psychology, 9*, 229–233.

Feuerstein, R. (1979). *The dynamic assessment of retarded performers: The learning potential assessment device, theory, instruments, and techniques.* Baltimore: University Park Press.

Fielder, W. R., Cohen, R. D., & Feeney, S. (1971). An attempt to replicate the teacher expectancy effect. *Psychological Reports, 29*, 1223–1228.

Finch, A. J., Jr., Kendall, P. C., Spirito, A., Entin, A., Montgomery, L. E., & Schwartz, D. J. (1979). Short form and factor analytic studies of the WISC-R with behavior problem children. *Journal of Abnormal Child Psychology, 7*, 337–344.

Fineman, C. A. (1983, August). *Preparing school psychologists to testify at due process hearings.* Paper presented at the 1983 Annual Convention of the American Psychological Association, Anaheim, CA.

Finkle, L. J., Hanson, D. P., & Hostetler, S. K. (1983). The assessment of profoundly handicapped children. *School Psychology Review, 12*, 75–81.

Fischbein, S. (1980). IQ and social class. *Intelligence, 4*, 51–64.

Fiscus, E. D. (1975). The effects of pre-test information on school psychologists' scoring of the Wechsler Intelligence Scale for Children. *Dissertation Abstracts International, 36*, 1387A. (University Microfilms No. 75–19,435)

Fishler, K., Graliker, B. V., & Koch, R. (1965). The predictability of intelligence with Gesell Developmental Scales in mentally retarded infants and young children. *American Journal of Mental Deficiency, 69*, 515–525.

Fishman, M. A., & Palkes, H. S. (1974). The validity of psychometric testing in children with congenital malformations of the central nervous system. *Developmental Medicine and Child Neurology, 16*, 180–185.

Flaugher, R. L. (1974). Some points of confusion in discussing the testing of black students. In L. P. Miller (Ed.), *The testing of black students: A symposium* (pp. 11–16). Englewood Cliffs, NJ: Prentice-Hall.

Flaugher, R. L. (1978). The many definitions of test bias. *American Psychologist, 33*, 671–679.

Flaugher, R. L., & Rock, D. A. (1972). Patterns of ability factors among four ethnic groups. *Proceedings of the 80th Annual Convention of the American Psychological Association, 7*, 27–28.

Fleiss, J. L. (1975). Measuring agreement between two judges on the presence or absence of a trait. *Biometrics, 31*, 651–659.

Fleming, E. S., & Anttonen, R. G. (1971). Teacher expectancy or My Fair Lady. *American Educational Research Journal, 8*, 241–252.

Flumen, A. L., & Flumen, L. B. (1979). WISCOS and WPPSICLES. *Journal of School Psychology, 17*, 82–85.

Fogelman, C. J. (Ed.). (1974). *AAMD Adaptive Behavior Scale Manual, 1974 Revision.* Washington, DC: American Association on Mental Deficiency.

Ford, B. G., & Ford, R. D. (1981). Identifying creative potential in handicapped children. *Exceptional Children, 48*, 115–122.

Fortier, L. M., & Wanlass, R. L. (1984). Family crisis following the diagnosis of a handicapped child. *Family Relations, 33*, 13–24.

Fotheringhan, J. B. (1983). Mental retardation and developmental delay. In K. D. Paget & B. A. Bracken (Eds.), *The psychoeducational assessment of preschool children* (pp. 207–223). New York: Grune & Stratton.

Fowles, G. P., & Tunick, R. H. (1986). WAIS-R and Shipley estimated IQ correlations. *Journal of Clinical Psychology, 42*, 647–649.

Frankenburg, W. K. (1986). *Revised Denver Prescreening Developmental Questionnaire.* Denver: Denver Developmental Materials.

Frankenburg, W. K., Camp, B. W., & Van Natta, P. A. (1971). Validity of the Denver Developmental Screening Test. *Child Development, 42*, 475–485.

Frankenburg, W. K., Camp, B. W., Van Natta, P. A., Demersseman, J. A., & Voorhees, S. F. (1971). Reliability and stability of the Denver Developmental Screening Test. *Child Development, 42*, 1315–1325.

Frankenburg, W. K., & Dodds, J. B. (1967). The Denver Developmental Screening Test. *Journal of Pediatrics, 71*, 181–191.

Frankenburg, W. K., Dodds, J. B., Fandal, A. W., Kazuk, E., & Cohrs, M. (1975). *Denver Developmental Screening Test* (rev. ed.). Denver: Denver Developmental Materials.

Frankenburg, W. K., Fandal, A. W., & Thornton, S. M. (1987). Revision of Denver Prescreening Developmental Questionnaire. *Journal of Pediatrics, 110*, 653–657.

Franklin, M. R., Jr., Stillman, P. L., Burpeau, M. Y., & Sabers, D. L. (1982). Examiner error in intelligence testing: Are you a source? *Psychology in the Schools, 19*, 563–569.

Franzoni, J. B., & Jones, R. W. (1981). Implications for school psychologists: The challenge of Public Law 94–142. *Professional Psychology, 12*, 356–362.

Frederiksen, N. (1986). Toward a broader conception of human intelligence. *American Psychologist, 41*, 445–452.

Freeman, B. J., Ritvo, E. R., Yokota, A., & Ritvo, A. (1986). A scale for rating symptoms of patients with the syndrome of autism in real life settings. *Journal of the American Academy of Child Psychiatry, 25*, 130–136.

Freeman, F. S. (1955). *Theory and practice of psychological testing.* New York: Holt.

Freeman, F. S. (1962). *Theory and practice of psychological testing* (3rd ed.). New York: Holt, Rinehart and Winston.

Freeman, R. D. (1967). Special education and the electroencephalogram: Marriage of convenience. *Journal of Special Education, 2*, 61–73.

French, J. L. (1964). *Manual: Pictorial Test of Intelligence.* Chicago: Riverside Publishing.

Friedrich, W. N., Greenberg, M. T., & Crnic, K. (1983). A short-form of the Questionnaire on Resources and Stress. *American Journal of Mental Deficiency, 88*, 41–48.

Fromm-Auch, D., & Yeudall, L. T. (1983). Normative data for the Halstead-Reitan neuropsychological tests. *Journal of Clinical Neuropsychology, 5*, 221–238.

Frostig, M., Maslow, P., Lefever, D. W., & Whittlesey, J. R. B. (1964). The Marianne Frostig Developmental Test of Visual Perception, 1963 standardization. *Perceptual and Motor Skills, 19,* 463–499.

Fuchs, D., & Fuchs, L. S. (1986). Test procedure bias: A meta-analysis of examiner familiarity effects. *Review of Educational Research, 56,* 243–262.

Fuller, G. B., & Wallbrown, F. H. (1983). Comparison of the Minnesota Percepto-Diagnostic test and Bender-Gestalt: Relationship with achievement criteria. *Journal of Clinical Psychology, 39,* 985–988.

Funk, S. G., Sturner, R. A., & Green, J. A. (1986). Preschool prediction of early school performance: Relationship of McCarthy Scales of Children's Abilities prior to school entry to achievement in kindergarten, first, and second grades. *Journal of School Psychology, 24,* 181–194.

Furey, W., & Forehand, R. (1983). The Daily Child Behavior Checklist. *Journal of Behavioral Assessment, 5,* 83–95.

Gagné, F. (1985). Giftedness and talent: Reexamining a reexamination of the definitions. *Gifted Child Quarterly, 29,* 103–112.

Galbraith, G., Ott, J., & Johnson, C. M. (1986). The effects of token reinforcement on WISC-R performance of low-socioeconomic Hispanic second-graders. *Behavioral Assessment, 8,* 191–194.

Galdieri, A. A., Barcikowski, R. S., & Witmer, J. M. (1972). The effect of verbal approval upon the performance of middle- and lower-class third-grade children on the WISC. *Psychology in the Schools, 9,* 404–408.

Gallagher, J. J., & Wiegerink, R. (1976). Educational strategies for the autistic child. In E. Schopler & R. J. Reichler (Eds.), *Psychopathology and child development: Research and treatment* (pp. 319–330). New York: Plenum.

Galvan, R. R. (1967). Bilingualism as it relates to intelligence test scores and school achievement among culturally deprived Spanish-American children. *Dissertation Abstracts, 28,* 3021-A. (University Microfilms No. 68–1131)

Gardner, H. (1983). *Frames of mind: The theory of multiple intelligences.* New York: Basic Books.

Gardner, R. A. (1979). *The objective diagnosis of minimal brain dysfunction.* Cresskill, NJ: Creative Therapeutics.

Gardner, R. A. (1981). Digits forward and digits backward as two separate tests: Normative data on 1567 school children. *Journal of Clinical Child Psychology, 10,* 131–135.

Garfield, S. L., Heine, R. W., & Leventhal, M. (1954). An evaluation of psychological reports in a clinical setting. *Journal of Consulting Psychology, 18,* 281–286.

Garrett, A. M. (1982). *Interviewing: Its principles and methods* (3rd ed.). New York: Family Service Association of America.

Gath, D., & Tennent, G. (1972). High intelligence and delinquency: A review. *British Journal of Criminology, 12,* 174–181.

Gayton, W. F., Wilson, W. T., & Bernstein, S. (1970). An evaluation of an abbreviated form of the WISC. *Journal of Clinical Psychology, 26,* 466–468.

Gear, G. H. (1976). Accuracy of teacher judgment in identifying intellectually gifted children: A review of the literature. *Gifted Child Quarterly, 20,* 478–490.

Gearheart, B. R., & Willenberg, E. P. (1980). *Application of pupil assessment information* (3rd ed.). Denver: Love Publishing.

Gelfand, D. M., & Hartmann, D. P. (1984). *Child behavior analysis and therapy* (2nd ed.). New York: Pergamon Press.

Genshaft, J. L., & Hirt, M. (1974). Language differences between black children and white children. *Developmental Psychology, 10,* 451–456.

Genshaft, J. L., & Ward, M. E. (1982). A review of the Perkins-Binet Tests of Intelligence for the Blind with suggestions for administration. *School Psychology Review, 11,* 338–341.

Gerken, K. C. (1978). Performance of Mexican American children on intelligence tests. *Exceptional Children, 44,* 438–443.

Gerken, K. C. (1979). Assessment of high risk preschoolers and children and adolescents with low incident handicapping conditions. In G. D. Phye & D. J. Reschly (Eds.), *School psychology: Perspectives and issues* (pp. 157–190). New York: Academic Press.

Gerken, K. C., Hancock, K. A., & Wade, T. H. (1978). A comparison of the Stanford-Binet Intelligence Scale and the McCarthy Scales of Children's Abilities with preschool children. *Psychology in the Schools, 15,* 468–472.

Gesten, E. L. (1976). A Health Resources Inventory: The development of a measure of the personal and social competence of primary-grade children. *Journal of Consulting and Clinical Psychology, 44,* 775–786.

Ghiselli, E. E., Campbell, J. P., & Zedeck, S. (1981). *Measurement theory for the behavioral sciences.* San Francisco: W. H. Freeman.

Gilandas, A., Touyz, S., Beumont, P. J. V., & Greenberg, H. P. (1984). *Handbook of neuropsychological assessment.* Orlando, FL: Grune & Stratton.

Gilbert, J. G., & Levee, R. F. (1967). Performances of deaf and normally-hearing children on the Bender-Gestalt and the Archimedes Spiral Tests. *Perceptual and Motor Skills, 24,* 1059–1066.

Gilbert, J. G., & Rubin, E. J. (1965). Evaluating the intellect of blind children. *New Outlook for the Blind, 59,* 238–240.

Gillingham, W. H. (1970). An investigation of examiner influence on Wechsler Intelligence Scale for Children scores. *Dissertation Abstracts International, 31,* 2178-A. (University Microfilms No. 70-20,458)

Gilmore, S. K. (1973). *The counselor-in-training.* New York: Appleton-Century-Crofts.

Ginsburg, R. E. (1970). An examination of the relationship between teacher expectancies and students' performance on a test of intellectual functioning. *Dissertation Abstracts International, 31,* 3337-A. (University Microfilms No. 71-922)

Giolas, T. G., Owens, E., Lamb, S. H., & Schubert, E. D. (1979). Hearing Performance Inventory. *Journal of Speech and Hearing Disorders, 44,* 169–195.

Gittleman, M., & Birch, H. G. (1967). Childhood schizophrenia: Intellect, neurologic status, perinatal risk, prognosis, and family pathology. *Archives of General Psychiatry, 17,* 16–25.

Glass, A. (1982, August). Factor analyses of the WAIS-R. In D. Herman (Chair), *WAIS-R factor structures and patterns of performance in various groups.* Symposium presented at the meeting of the American Psychological Association, Washington, DC.

Glasser, A. J., & Zimmerman, I. L. (1967). *Clinical interpretations of the Wechsler Intelligence Scale for Children.* New York: Grune & Stratton.

Goddard, H. H. (1908). The Binet and Simon tests of intellectual capacity. *Training School, 5,* 3–9.

Goddard, H. H. (1910). A measuring scale of intelligence. *Training School, 6,* 146–155.

Goetz, E. T., & Hall, R. J. (1984). Evaluation of the Kaufman Assessment Battery for Children from an information-processing perspective. *Journal of Special Education, 18,* 281–296.

Goh, D. S. (1978). *New method in the design of intelligence test short forms—the WISC-R example.* Paper presented at the meeting of the American Psychological Association, Toronto, Canada.

Goh, D. S., & Lund, J. M. (1977). Verbal reinforcement, socioeconomic status, and intelligence test performance of preschool children. *Perceptual and Motor Skills, 44,* 1011–1014.

Goh, D. S., & Youngquist, J. A. (1979). A comparison of the McCarthy Scales of Children's Abilities and the WISC-R. *Journal of Learning Disabilities, 12,* 344–348.

Golden, C. J. (1987). *Luria-Nebraska Neuropsychological Battery: Children's Revision.* Los Angeles: Western Psychological Services.

Goldman, R., Fristoe, M., & Woodcock, R. W. (1970). *Goldman-Fristoe-Woodcock Test of Auditory Discrimination.* Circle Pines, MN: American Guidance Service.

Goldschmid, M. L. (1967). Different types of conservation and nonconservation and their relation to age, sex, I.Q., M.A., and vocabulary. *Child Development, 38,* 1229–1246.

Goldwasser, E., Meyers, J., Christenson, S., & Graden, J. (1983). The impact of PL 94-142 on the practice of school psychology: A national survey. *Psychology in the Schools, 20,* 153–165.

Good, T. L., & Brophy, J. E. (1972). Behavioral expression of teacher attitudes. *Journal of Educational Psychology, 63,* 617–624.

Goodenough, F. L. (1926). *Measurement of intelligence by drawings.* New York: World Book.

Goodman, J. D., & Sours, J. A. (1967). *The child mental status examination.* New York: Basic Books.

Goodstein, H. A., Kahn, H., & Cawley, J. F. (1976). The achievement of educable mentally retarded children on the KeyMath Diagnostic Arithmetic Test. *Journal of Special Education, 10,* 61–70.

Gorden, R. L. (1975). *Interviewing: Strategy, techniques and tactics* (rev. ed.). Homewood, IL: Dorsey.

Gorham, K. A. (1975). A lost generation of parents. *Exceptional Children, 41,* 521–525.

Goslin, D. A. (1963). *The search for ability: Standardized testing in social perspective.* New York: Russell Sage Foundation.

Gottfried, A. W., & Brody, N. (1975). Interrelationships between and correlates of psychometric and Piagetian scales of sensorimotor intelligence. *Developmental Psychology, 11,* 379–387.

Gottlieb, J. (1981). Mainstreaming: Fulfilling the promise? *American Journal of Mental Deficiency, 86,* 115–126.

Gottlieb, J., Alter, M., & Gottlieb, B. W. (1983). Mainstreaming mentally retarded children. In J. L. Matson & J. A. Mulick (Eds.), *Handbook of mental retardation* (pp. 67–77). New York: Pergamon Press.

Gozali, J., & Meyen, E. L. (1970). The influence of the teacher expectancy phenomenon on the academic performances of educable mentally retarded pupils in special classes. *Journal of Special Education, 4,* 417–424.

Grace, W. C. (1986). Equivalence of the WISC-R and WAIS-R in delinquent males. *Journal of Psychoeducational Assessment, 4,* 257–262.

Graham, G. A. (1971). The effects of material and social incentives on the performance on intelligence test tasks by lower class and middle class Negro preschool children. *Dissertation Abstracts International, 31,* 4311-B. (University Microfilms No. 70-27,072)

Grayson, H. M., & Tolman, R. S. (1950). A semantic study of concepts of clinical psychologists and psychiatrists. *Journal of Abnormal and Social Psychology, 45,* 216–231.

Green, B. F., Jr. (1978). In defense of measurement. *American Psychologist, 33,* 664–670.

Green, B. F., Jr. (1981). A primer of testing. *American Psychologist, 36,* 1001–1011.

Green, F. (1960–1962). The examiner as a possible source of constant error in intelligence testing. In R. L. Cromwell (Ed.), *Abstracts of Peabody studies in mental retardation* (Vol. 2). Nashville: George Peabody College for Teachers. (Abstract No. 36)

Greenbaum, A. (1982). Conducting effective parent conferences. *Communique, 10*(6), 4–5.

Greenberg, J. W., & Alshan, L. M. (1974). Perceptual-motor functioning and school achievement in lower-class black children. *Perceptual and Motor Skills, 38,* 60–62.

Greenberg, R. D., Stewart, K. J., & Hansche, W. J. (1986). Factor analysis of the WISC-R for white and black children evaluated for gifted placement. *Journal of Psychoeducational Assessment, 4,* 123–130.

Greenspan, S. I., & Greenspan, N. T. (1981). *The clinical interview of the child.* New York: McGraw-Hill.

Greenstein, J., & Strain, P. S. (1977). The utility of the KeyMath Diagnostic Arithmetic Test for adolescent learning disabled students. *Psychology in the Schools, 14,* 275–282.

Greenwood, C. R. (1985). Settings or setting events as treatment in special education? *Advances in Development and Behavioral Pediatrics, 6,* 205–239.

Greenwood, C. R., Hops, H., Walker, H. M., Guild, J. J., Stokes, J., Young, K. R., Keleman, K. S., & Willardson, M. (1979). Standardized classroom management program: Social validation and replication studies in Utah and Oregon. *Journal of Applied Behavior Analysis*, *12*, 235–253.

Gregg, N., & Hoy, C. (1985). A comparison of the WAIS-R and the Woodcock-Johnson tests of cognitive ability with learning-disabled college students. *Journal of Psychoeducational Assessment*, *3*, 267–274.

Gresham, F. M. (1984). Behavioral interviews in school psychology: Issues in psychometric adequacy and research. *School Psychology Review*, *13*, 17–25.

Gridley, G., & Mastenbrook, J. L. (1977, September). ABIC, sociocultural, IQ, and achievement. In M. Kaplan (Chair), *Research on Mercer and Lewis' Adaptive Behavior Inventory for Children (ABIC)*. Symposium presented at the meeting of the American Psychological Association, San Francisco.

Griesel, R. D., & Bartel, P. R. (1976). The visual evoked response in relation to measures of intelligence and development in a group of four-year-old children. *South African Journal of Psychology*, *6*, 33–42.

Groff, M., & Hubble, L. M. (1982). WISC-R factor structures of younger and older youth with low IQs. *Journal of Consulting and Clinical Psychology*, *50*, 148–149.

Grossman, C. S. (1983). Children's books: Developing positive attitudes by and toward the handicapped. *Clinical Pediatrics*, *23*, 448–463.

Grossman, F. D. (1978). The effect of an examinee's reported academic achievement and/or physical condition on examiners' scoring of the WISC-R Verbal IQ. *Dissertation Abstracts International*, *38*, 4091A. (University Microfilms No. 77-28,462)

Grossman, F. M. (1985). Interpreting clinically derived WISC-R subtest groupings: A statistical approach. *Journal of Psychoeducational Assessment*, *3*, 89–96.

Grossman, F. M., & Johnson, K. M. (1982). WISC-R factor scores as predictors of WRAT performance: A multivariate analysis. *Psychology in the Schools*, *19*, 465–468.

Grossman, H. J. (Ed.). (1983). *Classification in mental retardation*. Washington, DC: American Association on Mental Deficiency.

Grunau, R. V. E., Purves, S. J., McBurney, A. K., & Low, M. D. (1981). Identifying academic aptitude in adolescent children by psychological testing and EEG spectral analysis. *Neuropsychologia*, *19*, 79–86.

Guilford, J. P. (1967). *The nature of human intelligence*. New York: McGraw-Hill.

Guilford, J. P., & Hoepfner, R. (1971). *The analysis of intelligence*. New York: McGraw-Hill.

Gustafsson, J. E. (1984). A unifying model for the structure of intellectual abilities. *Intelligence*, *8*, 179–203.

Guthke, J. (1982). The learning test concept—an alternative to the traditional static intelligence test. *German Journal of Psychology*, *6*, 306–324.

Gutkin, T. B. (1978). Some useful statistics for the interpretation of the WISC-R. *Journal of Consulting and Clinical Psychology*, *46*, 1561–1563.

Gutkin, T. B. (1979). The WISC-R Verbal Comprehension, Perceptual Organization, and Freedom from Distractability Deviation Quotients: Data for practitioners. *Psychology in the Schools*, *16*, 359–360.

Gutkin, T. B., & Reynolds, C. R. (1980). Factorial similarity of the WISC-R for Anglos and Chicanos referred for psychological services. *Journal of School Psychology*, *18*, 34–39.

Gutkin, T. B., & Reynolds, C. R. (1981). Factorial similarity of the WISC-R for white and black children from the standardization sample. *Journal of Educational Psychology*, *73*, 227–231.

Gutkin, T. B., Reynolds, C. R., & Galvin, G. A. (1984). Factor analysis of the Wechsler Adult Intelligence Scale—Revised (WAIS-R): An examination of the standardization sample. *Journal of School Psychology*, *22*, 83–93.

Guy, D. P. (1977). Issues in the unbiased assessment of intelligence. *School Psychology Digest*, *6* (3), 14–23.

Haddad, F. A. (1986). Comparison of the WISC-R, PPVT-R, and PPVT for learning disabled children. *Psychological Reports*, *58*, 659–662.

Hagekull, B. (1985). The Baby and Toddler Behavior Questionnaires: Empirical studies and conceptual considerations. *Scandinavian Journal of Psychology*, *26*, 110–122.

Hagen, J. W., Barclay, C. R., & Schwethelm, B. (1982). Cognitive development of the learning-disabled child. In N. R. Ellis (Ed.), *International review of research in mental retardation* (Vol. 11, pp. 1–41). New York: Academic Press.

Hagin, R. A., Silver, A. A., & Corwin, C. G. (1971). Clinical-diagnostic use of the WPPSI in predicting learning disabilities in grade 1. *Journal of Special Education*, *5*, 221–232.

Hahn, W. K. (1987). Cerebral lateralization of function: From infancy through childhood. *Psychological Bulletin*, *101*, 376–392.

Hale, R. L., & Landino, S. A. (1981). Utility of WISC-R subtest analysis in discriminating among groups of conduct problem, withdrawn, mixed, and nonproblem boys. *Journal of Consulting and Clinical Psychology*, *49*, 91–95.

Hall, P. K., & Jordan, L. S. (1985). The Token and Reporter's Test: Use with 123 language-disordered students. *Language, Speech, and Hearing Services in Schools*, *16*, 244–255.

Hall, V. C., Huppertz, J. W., & Levi, A. (1977). Attention and achievement exhibited by middle- and lower-class black and white elementary school boys. *Journal of Educational Psychology*, *69*, 115–120.

Hall, V. C., Turner, R. R., & Russell, W. (1973). Ability of children from four subcultures and two grade levels to imitate and comprehend crucial aspects of standard English: A test of the different language explanation. *Journal of Educational Psychology*, *64*, 147–158.

Halpern, F. (1951). The Bender Visual Motor Gestalt Test. In H. H. Anderson & G. L. Anderson (Eds.), *An introduction to projective techniques* (pp. 324–340). New York: Prentice Hall.

Hamm, H. A., & Evans, J. G. (1978). WISC-R subtests patterns of severely emotionally disturbed students. *Psychology in the Schools, 15*, 188–190.

Hammill, D. D. (1985a). *Detroit Tests of Learning Aptitude – 2.* Austin, TX: Pro-Ed.

Hammill, D. D. (1985b). *Detroit Tests of Learning Aptitude – P.* Austin, TX: Pro-Ed.

Hammill, D. D., Leigh, J. E., McNutt, G., & Larsen, S. C. (1981). A new definition of learning disabilities. *Learning Disability Quarterly, 4*, 336–342.

Hammill, D. D., & McNutt, G. (1981). *Correlates of reading.* Austin, TX: Pro-Ed.

Handler, L., Gerston, A., & Handler, B. (1965). Suggestions for improved psychologist-teacher communication. *Psychology in the Schools, 2*, 77–81.

Hanson, R. A. (1975). Consistency and stability of home environmental measures related to IQ. *Child Development, 46*, 470–480.

Harper, D. C., & Wacker, D. P. (1983). The efficiency of the Denver Developmental Screening Test with rural disadvantaged preschool children. *Journal of Pediatric Psychology, 8*, 273–283.

Harris, D. B. (1963). *Children's drawings as measures of intellectual maturity: A revision and extension of the Goodenough Draw-a-Man Test.* New York: Harcourt, Brace & World.

Harris, F. C., & Lahey, B. B. (1982). Subject reactivity in direct observational assessment: A review and critical analysis. *Clinical Psychology Review, 2*, 523–538.

Harrison, K. A., & Wiebe, M. J. (1977). Correlational study of McCarthy, WISC, and Stanford-Binet scales. *Perceptual and Motor Skills, 44*, 63–68.

Harrison, P. L. (1981). Mercer's Adaptive Behavior Inventory, the McCarthy Scales, and dental development as predictors of first-grade achievement. *Journal of Educational Psychology, 73*, 78–82.

Harrison, P. L., & Naglieri, J. A. (1978). Extrapolated General Cognitive Indexes on the McCarthy Scales for gifted and mentally retarded children. *Psychological Reports, 43*, 1291–1296.

Hartlage, L. C., & Merck, K. H. (1971). Increasing the relevance of psychological reports. *Journal of Clinical Psychology, 27*, 459–460.

Hartley, R. E., Frank, L. K., & Goldenson, R. M. (1952). *Understanding children's play.* New York: Columbia University Press.

Hartman, D. E. (1986). Artificial intelligence or artificial psychologist? Conceptual issues in clinical microcomputer use. *Professional Psychology: Research and Practice, 17*, 528–534.

Hartwig, S. S., Sapp, G. L., & Clayton, G. A. (1987). Comparison of the Stanford-Binet Intelligence Scale: Form L-M and the Stanford-Binet Intelligence Scale Fourth Edition. *Psychological Reports, 60*, 1215–1218.

Harver, J. R. (1977). Influence of presentation dialect and orthographic form on reading performance of black inner-city children. *Educational Research Quarterly, 2*, 9–16.

Hawkins, R. P., & Hawkins, K. K. (1981). Parental observations on the education of severely retarded children: Can it be done in the classroom? *Analysis and Intervention in Developmental Disabilities, 1*, 13–22.

Hawthorne, L. W., Speer, S. K., & Buccellato, L. (1983). Appropriateness of the Wechsler Preschool and Primary Scale of Intelligence for gifted children. *Journal of Consulting and Clinical Psychology, 51*, 463–464.

Haynes, J. P., & Howard, R. C. (1986). Stability of WISC-R scores in a juvenile forensic sample. *Journal of Clinical Psychology, 42*, 534–537.

Haynes, J. P., & Atkinson, D. (1983). Validity of two WPPSI short forms in outpatient clinic settings. *Journal of Clinical Psychology, 39*, 961–964.

Haynes, J. P., & Atkinson, D. (1984). Factor structure of the WPPSI in mental health clinic settings. *Journal of Clinical Psychology, 40*, 805–808.

Haynes, S. N., & Horn, W. F. (1982). Reactivity in behavioral observation: A review. *Behavioral Assessment, 4*, 369–385.

Hays, J. R., Solway, K. S., & Schreiner, D. (1978). Intellectual characteristics of juvenile murderers versus status offenders. *Psychological Reports, 43*, 80–82.

Hebb, D. O. (1971). Whose confusion? *American Psychologist, 26*, 736.

Hécaen, H. (1983). Acquired aphasia in children: Revisited. *Neuropsychologia, 21*, 581–587.

Heffernan, L., & Black, F. W. (1984). Use of the Uzgiris and Hunt Scales with handicapped infants: Concurrent validity of the Dunst age norms. *Journal of Psychoeducational Assessment, 2*, 159–168.

Hegarty, S., & Lucas, D. (1978). *Ability to learn? The pursuit of culture-fair assessment.* Windsor Banks, England: NFER Publishing Co.

Heil, J., Barclay, A. G., & Endres, J. M. B. (1978). A factor analytic study of WPPSI scores of educationally deprived and normal children. *Psychological Reports, 42*, 727–730.

Heinemann, A. W., Harper, R. G., Friedman, L. C., & Whitney, J. (1985). The relative utility of the Shipley-Hartford Scale: Prediction of WAIS-R IQ. *Journal of Clinical Psychology, 41*, 547–551.

Heller, K. A., Holtzman, W. H., & Messick, S. (Eds.). (1982). *Placing children in special education: A strategy for equity.* Washington, DC: National Academy Press.

Henderson, N. B., Butler, B. V., & Goffeney, B. (1969). Effectiveness of the WISC and Bender-Gestalt Test in predicting arithmetic and reading achievement for white and nonwhite children. *Journal of Clinical Psychology, 25*, 268–271.

Henderson, N. B., & Engel, R. (1974). Neonatal visual evoked potentials as predictors of psychoeducational tests at age seven. *Developmental Psychology, 10*, 269–276.

Henderson, N. B., Fay, W. H., Lindemann, S. J., & Clarkson, Q. D. (1973). Will the IQ test ban decrease the effectiveness of reading prediction? *Journal of Educational Psychology, 65*, 345–355.

Henderson, R. W., & Rankin, R. J. (1973). WPPSI reliability

and predictive validity with disadvantaged Mexican-American children. *Journal of School Psychology, 11*, 16–20.

Hennessy, J. J., & Merrifield, P. R. (1976). A comparison of the factor structures of mental abilities in four ethnic groups. *Journal of Educational Psychology, 68*, 754–759.

Henry, S. A., & Wittman, R. D. (1981). Diagnostic implications of Bannatynes' recategorized WISC-R scores for identifying learning disabled children. *Journal of Learning Disabilities, 14*, 517–520.

Herjanic, B., & Reich, W. (1982). Development of a structured psychiatric interview for children: Agreement between child and parent on individual symptoms. *Journal of Abnormal Child Psychology, 10*, 307–324.

Herman, D. O. (1968). A study of sex differences on the Wechsler Preschool and Primary Scale of Intelligence. *Proceedings of the 76th Annual Convention of the American Psychological Association, 3*, 455–456.

Herman, D. O., Huesing, P. D., Levett, C. A., & Boehm, A. E. (1973). *A follow-up study of the BTBC standardization sample: Correlation with later measures of achievement*. Unpublished paper, The Psychological Corp.

Herrell, J. M., & Golland, J. H. (1969). Should WISC subjects explain Picture Arrangement stories? *Journal of Consulting and Clinical Psychology, 33*, 761–762.

Herrnstein, R. J. (1973). *I.Q. in the meritocracy*. Boston: Little, Brown.

Hersh, J. B. (1971). Effects of referral information on testers. *Journal of Consulting and Clinical Psychology, 37*, 116–122.

Hightower, A. D., Work, W. C., Cowen, E. L., Lotyczewski, B. S., Spinell, A. P., Guare, J. C., & Rohrbeck, C. A. (1986). The Teacher-Child Rating Scale: A brief objective measure of elementary children's school problem behaviors and competencies. *School Psychology Review, 15*, 393–409.

Hiltonsmith, R. W., Hayman, P. M., & Kleinman, P. (1984). Predicting WAIS-R scores from the Revised Beta for low functioning minority group offenders. *Journal of Clinical Psychology, 40*, 1063–1066.

Hiltonsmith, R. W., & Keller, H. R. (1983). What happened to the setting in person-setting assessment? *Professional Psychology: Research and Practice, 14*, 419–434.

Hingtgen, J. N., & Bryson, C. Q. (1972). Recent developments in the study of early childhood psychoses: Infantile autism, childhood schizophrenia, and related disorders. *Schizophrenia Bulletin*, 8–54.

Hirshoren, A., Hurley, O. L., & Kavale, K. (1979). Psychometric characteristics of the WISC-R Performance Scale with deaf children. *Journal of Speech and Hearing Disorders, 44*, 73–79.

Hirshoren, A., Kavale, K., Hurley, O. L., & Hunt, J. T. (1977). The reliability of the WISC-R Performance Scale with deaf children. *Psychology in the Schools, 14*, 412–415.

Hiskey, M. S. (1966). *Manual for the Hiskey-Nebraska Test of Learning Aptitude*. Lincoln, NE: Union College Press.

Hobby, K. L. (1980). *WISC-R split-half short form manual*. Los Angeles: Western Psychological Services.

Hocevar, D. (1981). Measurement of creativity: Review and critique. *Journal of Personality Assessment, 45*, 450–464.

Hodges, K. (1982). Factor structure of the WISC-R for a psychiatric sample. *Journal of Consulting and Clinical Psychology, 50*, 141–142.

Hodges, K. (1985). *Manual for the Child Assessment Schedule (CAS)*. Unpublished manuscript, University of Missouri, Columbia.

Hoge, R. D. (1985). The validity of direct observation measures of pupil classroom behavior. *Review of Educational Research, 55*, 469–483.

Hoge, R. D., & Cudmore, L. A. (1986). The use of teacher-judgment measures in the identification of gifted pupils. *Teaching and Teacher Education, 2*, 181–196.

Holland, W. R. (1960). Language barrier as an educational problem of Spanish-speaking children. *Exceptional Children, 27*, 42–50.

Hollinger, C. L., & Baldwin, C. (1987). *Comparing the Stanford-Binet, Fourth Edition with the WISC-R among exceptional children*. Unpublished manuscript, Cleveland State University.

Hollinger, C. L., & Sarvis, P. H. (1984). Interpretation of the PPVT-R: A pure measure of verbal comprehension? *Psychology in the Schools, 21*, 34–41.

Holroyd, J. (1974). The Questionnaire on Resources and Stress: An instrument to measure family response to a handicapped family member. *Journal of Community Psychology, 2*, 92–94.

Homatidis, S., & Konstantareas, M. M. (1981). Assessment of hyperactivity: Isolating measures of high discriminant ability. *Journal of Consulting and Clinical Psychology, 49*, 533–541.

Hoover, H. D. (1984). The most appropriate scores for measuring educational development in the elementary schools: GE's. *Educational Measurement: Issues & Practice, 3*, 8–14.

Hopkins, K. D., & McGuire, L. (1966). Mental measurement of the blind: The validity of the Wechsler Intelligence Scale for Children. *International Journal for the Education of the Blind, 15*, 65–73.

Hopkins, K. D., & McGuire, L. (1967). IQ constancy and the blind child. *International Journal for the Education of the Blind, 16*, 113–114.

Horn, J. L. (1967). Intelligence—why it grows, why it declines. *Trans-action, 5*, 23–31.

Horn, J. L. (1968). Organization of abilities and the development of intelligence. *Psychological Review, 75*, 242–259.

Horn, J. L. (1978a). Human ability systems. In P. B. Baltes (Ed.), *Life-span development and behavior* (Vol. 1, pp. 211–256). New York: Academic Press.

Horn, J. L. (1978b). The nature and development of intellectual abilities. In R. T. Osborne, C. E. Noble, & N. Weyl (Eds.), *Human variation: The biopsychology of age, race, and sex* (pp. 107–136). New York: Academic Press.

Horn, J. L. (1979). Trends in the measurement of intelligence. *Intelligence, 3*, 229–239.

Horn, J. L. (1985). Remodeling old models of intelligence. In B. Wolman (Ed.), *Handbook of intelligence* (pp. 267–300). New York: Wiley.

Horn, J. L., & Cattell, R. B. (1967). Age differences in fluid and crystallized intelligence. *Acta Psychologica, 26,* 107–129.

Horn, J. L., & Knapp, J. R. (1973). On the subjective character of the empirical base of Guilford's structure-of-intellect model. *Psychological Bulletin, 80,* 33–43.

Howard, J. L., & Plant, W. T. (1967). Psychometric evaluation of an Operation Headstart program. *Journal of Genetic Psychology, 111,* 281–288.

Hubble, L. M., & Groff, M. (1981a). Factor analysis of WISC-R scores of male delinquents referred for evaluation. *Journal of Consulting and Clinical Psychology, 49,* 738–739.

Hubble, L. M., & Groff, M. (1981b). Magnitude and direction of WISC-R Verbal-Performance IQ discrepancies among adjudicated male delinquents. *Journal of Youth and Adolescence, 10,* 179–184.

Huberty, T. J., & Koller, J. R. (1984). WISC-R test ages as predictors of achievement. *Educational & Psychological Research, 4,* 73–79.

Hubschman, E., Polizzotto, E. A., & Kaliski, M. S. (1970). Performance of institutionalized retardates on the PPVT and two editions of the ITPA. *American Journal of Mental Deficiency, 74,* 579–580.

Hudson, L. (1972). The context of the debate. In K. Richardson, D. Spears, & M. Richards (Eds.), *Race and intelligence: The fallacies behind the race-IQ controversy* (pp. 10–16). Baltimore: Penguin Books.

Huizinga, R. J. (1973). The relationship of the ITPA to the Stanford-Binet Form L-M and the WISC. *Journal of Learning Disabilities, 6,* 451–456.

Hulme, C., & Turnbull, J. (1983). Intelligence and inspection time in normal and mentally retarded subjects. *British Journal of Psychology, 74,* 365–370.

Humphreys, L. G. (1971). Theory of intelligence. In R. Cancro (Ed.), *Intelligence: Genetic and environmental influences* (pp. 31–42). New York: Grune & Stratton.

Humphreys, L. G. (1973). Statistical definitions of test validity for minority groups. *Journal of Applied Psychology, 58,* 1–4.

Humphreys, L. G. (1975). Race and sex differences and their implications for educational and occupational equality. In M. L. Maehr & W. M. Stallings (Eds.), *Culture, child and school* (pp. 124–141). Belmont, CA: Brooks/Cole.

Humphreys, L. G. (1979). The construct of general intelligence. *Intelligence, 3,* 105–120.

Humphreys, L. G. (1985). General intelligence: An integration of factor, test, and simplex theory. In B. B. Wolman (Ed.), *Handbook of intelligence: Theories, measurements, and applications* (pp. 201–224). New York: Wiley.

Humphreys, L. G., & Parsons, C. K. (1979). Piagetian tasks measure intelligence and intelligence tests assess cognitive development: A reanalysis. *Intelligence, 3,* 369–382.

Humphreys, L. G., Parsons, C. K., & Park, R. K. (1979). Dimensions involved in differences among school means of cognitive measures. *Journal of Educational Measurement, 16,* 63–76.

Hunt, E., & Pellegrino, J. (1985). Using interactive computing to expand intelligence testing: A critique and prospectus. *Intelligence, 9,* 207–236.

Hurley, O. L., Hirshoren, A., Hunt, J. T., & Kavale, K. (1979). Predictive validity of two mental ability tests with black deaf children. *Journal of Negro Education, 48,* 14–19.

Hutcherson, R. (1978). Correlating the Boehm and PPVT. *Academic Therapy, 13,* 285–288.

Hutton, J. B., & Davenport, M. A. (1985). The WISC-R as a predictor of Woodcock-Johnson Achievement Cluster Scores for learning-disabled students. *Journal of Clinical Psychology, 41,* 410–413.

Hynd, G. W., Obrzut, J. E., & Obrzut, A. (1981). Are lateral and perceptual asymmetries related to WISC-R and achievement test performance in normal and learning-disabled children? *Journal of Consulting and Clinical Psychology, 49,* 977–979.

Hynd, G. W., Quackenbush, R., Kramer, R., Connor, R., & Weed, W. (1980). Concurrent validity of the McCarthy Scales of Children's Ability with Native American primary-grade children. *Measurement and Evaluation in Guidance, 13,* 29–34.

Ilg, F. L., & Ames, L. B. (1965). *School readiness: Behavior tests used at the Gesell Institute.* New York: Harper & Row.

Illingworth, R. S., & Birch, L. B. (1959). The diagnosis of mental retardation in infancy. A follow-up study. *Archives of Disease in Childhood, 34,* 269–273.

Isett, R. D., & Spreat, S. (1979). Test-retest and interrater reliabilities of the AAMD Adaptive Behavior Scale. *American Journal of Mental Deficiency, 84,* 93–95.

Jackson, A. M., Farley, G. K., Zimet, S. G., & Gottman, J. M. (1979). Optimizing the WISC-R test performance of low- and high-impulsive emotionally disturbed children. *Journal of Learning Disabilities, 12,* 622–625.

Jackson, N. E. (1980). Identification of gifted performance in young children. In W. C. Roedell, N. E. Jackson, & H. B. Robinson (Eds.), *Gifted young children* (pp. 27–65). New York: Teachers College Press.

Jarman, R. F., & Das, J. P. (1977). Simultaneous and successive syntheses and intelligence. *Intelligence, 1,* 151–169.

Jastak, S., & Wilkinson, G. S. (1984). *Wide Range Achievement Test—Revised.* Wilmington, DE: Jastak Associates.

Jay, S. M., & Elliott, C. (1981). *Observation Scale of Behavioral Distress.* Unpublished manuscript, Children's Hospital of Los Angeles.

Jeffrey, T. B., & Jeffrey, L. K. (1984). Validity of the Slosson Intelligence Test with young learning disabled children. *Psychological Reports, 54,* 97–98.

Jenkins, J. J., & Paterson, D. G. (Eds.). (1961). *Studies in individual differences.* New York: Appleton-Century-Crofts.

Jennings, R. L. (1982). *Handbook for basic considerations in interviewing children.* Unpublished manuscript. Counseling and Assessment Service, Independence, IA.

Jensema, C., & Mullins, J. (1974). Onset, cause, and additional handicaps in hearing impaired children. *American Annals of the Deaf, 119,* 701–705.

Jensen, A. R. (1969). How much can we boost IQ and scholastic achievement? *Harvard Educational Review*, *39*, 1–123.

Jensen, A. R. (1970). A theory of primary and secondary familial mental retardation. In N. R. Ellis (Ed.), *International review of research in mental retardation* (Vol. 4, pp. 33–105). New York: Academic Press.

Jensen, A. R. (1974a). How biased are culture-loaded tests? *Genetic Psychology Monographs*, *90*, 185–244.

Jensen, A. R. (1974b). Review of T. Dobzhansky, *Genetic diversity and human equality. Perspectives in Biology and Medicine*, *17*, 430–434.

Jensen, A. R. (1975). The price of inequality. *Oxford Review of Education*, *1*, 59–71.

Jensen, A. R. (1979a). g: Outmoded theory or unconquered frontier? *Creative Science and Technology*, *11*, 16–29.

Jensen, A. R. (1979b). The nature of intelligence and its relation to learning. *Journal of Research and Development in Education*, *12*(2), 79–95.

Jensen, A. R. (1980). *Bias in mental testing*. New York: The Free Press.

Jensen, A. R., & Osborne, R. T. (1979). *Forward and backward digit span interaction with race and IQ: A longitudinal developmental comparison*. Berkeley: University of California. (ERIC Document Reproduction Service No. ED 173 384)

Jensen, A. R., & Reynolds, C. R. (1982). Race, social class and ability patterns on the WISC-R. *Personality and Individual Differences*, *3*, 423–438.

Jensen, D. R., & Engel, R. (1971). Statistical procedures for relating dichotomous responses to maturation and EEG measurements. *Electroencephalography and Clinical Neurophysiology*, *30*, 437–443.

Jensen, J. A., & Armstrong, R. J. (1985). *Slosson Intelligence Test (SIT) for children and adults: Expanded norms tables application and development*. East Aurora, NY: Slosson Educational Publications.

Jinks, J. L., & Fulker, D. W. (1970). Comparison of the biometrical genetical, MAVA, and classical approaches to the analysis of human behavior. *Psychological Bulletin*, *73*, 311–349.

John, E. R., Ahn, H., Prichep, L., Trepetin, M., Brown, D., & Kaye, H. (1980). Developmental equations for the electroencephalogram. *Science*, *210*, 1255–1258.

Johns, J. L. (1975). Can teachers use standardized reading tests to determine students' instructional levels? *Illinois School Research*, *11*(3), 29–35.

Johnson, C. M., Bradley-Johnson, S., McCarthy, R., & Jamie, M. (1984). Token reinforcement during WISC-R administration II. Effects on mildly retarded, black students. *Applied Research in Mental Retardation*, *5*, 43–53.

Johnson, D. L., & Danley, W. (1981). Validity: Comparison of the WISC-R and SOMPA Estimated Learning Potential scores. *Psychological Reports*, *49*, 123–131.

Johnson, R. C., McClearn, G. E., Yuen, S., Nagoshi, C. T., Ahern, F. M., & Cole, R. E. (1985). Galton's data a century later. *American Psychologist*, *40*, 875–892.

Johnston, W. T., & Bolen, L. M. (1984). A comparison of the factor structure of the WISC-R for blacks and whites. *Psychology in the Schools*, *21*, 42–44.

Jordan, J. S. (1932). Reliability of Stanford-Binet intelligence quotients derived by student examiners. *Journal of Educational Research*, *26*, 295–301.

Jordan, L. S., & Hall, P. K. (1985). The Token and Reporter's Tests using two scoring conventions: A normative study with 286 grade and junior high students. *Language, Speech, and Hearing Services in Schools*, *16*, 227–243.

Jorm, A. F., & Share, D. L. (1983). Phonological recording and reading acquisition. *Applied Psycholinguistics*, *4*, 103–147.

Kadushin, A. (1983). *The social work interview* (2nd. ed.). New York: Columbia University Press.

Kagan, S., & Zahn, G. L. (1975). Field dependence and the school achievement gap between Anglo-American and Mexican-American children. *Journal of Educational Psychology*, *67*, 643–650.

Kahn, J. V. (1983). Sensorimotor period and adaptive behavior development of severely and profoundly mentally retarded children. *American Journal of Mental Deficiency*, *88*, 69–75.

Kanfer, F. H., & Saslow, G. (1969). Behavioral diagnosis. In C. M. Franks (Ed.), *Behavior therapy: Appraisal and status* (pp. 430–437). New York: McGraw-Hill.

Kanfer, R., Eyberg, S. M., & Krahn, G. L. (1983). Interviewing strategies in child assessment. In C. E. Walker & M. C. Roberts (Eds.), *Handbook of clinical child psychology* (pp. 95–108). New York: Wiley.

Kaplan, H. B. (1985). A comparison of the Vane Kindergarten Test with the WPPSI and a measure of self-control. *Psychology in the Schools*, *22*, 277–282.

Karnes, F. A., & Brown, K. E. (1981). A short form of the WISC-R for gifted students. *Psychology in the Schools*, *18*, 169–173.

Karoly, P. (1981). Self-management problems in children. In E. J. Mash & L. G. Terdal (Eds.), *Behavioral assessment of childhood disorders* (pp. 79–126). New York: Guilford Press.

Karon, B. P. (1975). *Black scars: A rigorous investigation of the effects of discrimination*. New York: Springer.

Kaspar, J. C., Throne, F. M., & Schulman, J. L. (1968). A study of the inter-judge reliability in scoring the responses of a group of mentally retarded boys to three WISC subscales. *Educational and Psychological Measurement*, *28*, 469–477.

Katz, E. R., Kellerman, J., & Siegel, S. E. (1980). Behavioral distress in children with cancer undergoing medical procedures: Developmental considerations. *Journal of Consulting and Clinical Psychology*, *48*, 356–365.

Katz-Garris, L., Hadley, T. J., Garris, R. P., & Barnhill, B. (1980). A factor analytic study of the Adaptive Behavior Scale. *Psychological Reports*, *47*, 807–814.

Kaufman, A. S. (1972a). A short form of the Wechsler Preschool and Primary Scale of Intelligence. *Journal of Consulting and Clinical Psychology*, *39*, 361–369.

Kaufman, A. S. (1972b). Piaget and Gesell: A psychometric

analysis of tests built from their tasks. *Child Development*, *42*, 1341–1360.

Kaufman, A. S. (1973a). Comparison of the performance of matched groups of black children and white children on the Wechsler Preschool and Primary Scale of Intelligence. *Journal of Consulting and Clinical Psychology*, *41*, 186–191.

Kaufman, A. S. (1973b). Comparison of the WPPSI, Stanford-Binet, and McCarthy Scales as predictors of first-grade achievement. *Perceptual and Motor Skills*, *36*, 67–73.

Kaufman, A. S. (1973c). The relationship of WPPSI IQs to SES and other background variables. *Journal of Clinical Psychology*, *29*, 354–357.

Kaufman, A. S. (1975a). Factor analysis of the WISC-R at 11 age levels between 6½ and 16½ years. *Journal of Consulting and Clinical Psychology*, *43*, 135–147.

Kaufman, A. S. (1975b). Factor structure of the McCarthy Scales at five age levels between 2½ and 8½. *Educational and Psychological Measurement*, *35*, 641–656.

Kaufman, A. S. (1976a). Do normal children have "flat" ability profiles? *Psychology in the Schools*, *13*, 284–285.

Kaufman, A. S. (1976b). A four-test short form of the WISC-R. *Contemporary Educational Psychology*, *1*, 180–196.

Kaufman, A. S. (1976c). A new approach to the interpretation of test scatter on the WISC-R. *Journal of Learning Disabilities*, *9*, 160–168.

Kaufman, A. S. (1976d). Verbal-performance IQ discrepancies on the WISC-R. *Journal of Consulting and Clinical Psychology*, *44*, 739–744.

Kaufman, A. S. (1977). A McCarthy short form for rapid screening of preschool, kindergarten, and first-grade children. *Contemporary Educational Psychology*, *2*, 149–157.

Kaufman, A. S. (1979a). *Intelligent testing with the WISC-R*. New York: Wiley-Interscience.

Kaufman, A. S. (1979b). The role of speed on WISC-R performance across the age range. *Journal of Consulting and Clinical Psychology*, *47*, 595–597.

Kaufman, A. S. (1979c). WISC-R research: Implications for interpretation. *School Psychology Digest*, *8*, 5–27.

Kaufman, A. S., & DiCuio, R. F. (1975). Separate factor analyses of the McCarthy Scales for groups of black and white children. *Journal of School Psychology*, *13*, 10–18.

Kaufman, A. S., & Doppelt, J. E. (1976). Analysis of WISC-R standardization data in terms of the stratification variables. *Child Development*, *47*, 165–171.

Kaufman, A. S., & Hollenbeck, G. P. (1974). Comparative structure of the WPPSI for blacks and whites. *Journal of Clinical Psychology*, *30*, 316–319.

Kaufman, A. S., & Kaufman, N. L. (1973). Sex differences on the McCarthy Scales of Children's Abilities. *Journal of Clinical Psychology*, *29*, 362–365.

Kaufman, A. S., & Kaufman, N. L. (1977). *Clinical evaluation of young children with the McCarthy Scales*. New York: Grune & Stratton.

Kaufman, A. S., & Kaufman, N. L. (1983). *K-ABC: Kaufman*

Assessment Battery for Children. Circle Pines, MN: American Guidance Service.

Kaufman, A. S., & Kaufman, N. L. (1985). *Kaufman Test of Educational Achievement*. Circle Pines, MN: American Guidance Service.

Kavajecz, L. G. (1969). A study of results on the Wechsler Preschool and Primary Scale of Intelligence of inadequate readers. *Dissertation Abstracts International*, *30*, 4143-A. (University Microfilms No. 70-7135)

Kavale, K. A., & Forness, S. R. (1984). A meta-analysis of the validity of Wechsler Scale profiles and recategorizations: Patterns or parodies? *Learning Disability Quarterly*, *7*, 136–156.

Kazdin, A. E. (1979). Unobtrusive measures in behavioral assessment. *Journal of Applied Behavior Analysis*, *12*, 713–724.

Kazdin, A. E. (1981). Behavioral observation. In M. Hersen & A. S. Bellack (Eds.), *Behavioral assessment: A practical handbook* (2nd ed., pp. 101–124). New York: Pergamon Press.

Kazimour, K. K., & Reschly, D. J. (1981). Investigation of the norms and concurrent validity for the Adaptive Behavior Inventory for Children (ABIC). *American Journal of Mental Deficiency*, *85*, 512–520.

Keasey, C. T., & Charles, D. C. (1967). Conservation of substance in normal and mentally retarded children. *Journal of Genetic Psychology*, *111*, 271–279.

Keating, D. P. (1975). Precocious cognitive development at the level of formal operations. *Child Development*, *46*, 276–280.

Keir, G. (1949). The Progressive Matrices as applied to school children. *British Journal of Psychology, Statistical Section*, *2*, 140–150.

Keith, T. Z. (1985). Questioning the K-ABC: What does it measure? *School Psychology Review*, *14*, 9–20.

Keith, T. Z., & Bolen, L. M. (1980). Factor structure of the McCarthy Scales for children experiencing problems in school. *Psychology in the Schools*, *17*, 320–326.

Kelly, M. P., Montgomery, M. L., Felleman, E. S., & Webb, W. W. (1984). Wechsler Adult Intelligence Scale and Wechsler Adult Intelligence Scale – Revised in a neurologically impaired population. *Journal of Clinical Psychology*, *40*, 788–791.

Kelly, R. R., & Tomlinson-Keasey, C. (1977). Hemispheric laterality of deaf children for processing words and pictures visually presented to the hemifields. *American Annals of the Deaf*, *122*, 525–533.

Kennedy, L. P., & Elder, S. T. (1982). WISC-R: An abbreviated version. *Journal of Clinical Psychology*, *38*, 174–178.

Kennedy, W. A., Van de Riet, V., & White, J. C., Jr. (1963). A normative sample of intelligence and achievement of Negro elementary school children in the southeastern United States. *Monographs of the Society for Research in Child Development*, *28*(6), 1–112.

Keogh, B. K., & Kopp, C. B. (1978). From assessment to intervention: An elusive bridge. In F. D. Minifie & L. L. Lloyd (Eds.), *Communicative and cognitive abilities – early behav-*

ioral assessment (pp. 523–547). Baltimore: University Park Press.

Keogh, B. K., Major-Kingsley, S., Omori-Gordon, H., & Reid, H. P. (1982). *A system of marker variables for the field of learning disabilities*. Syracuse, NY: Syracuse University Press.

Keogh, B. K., Vernon, M., & Smith, C. E. (1970). Deafness and visuo-motor function. *Journal of Special Education*, *4*, 41–47.

Keston, M. J., & Jimenez, C. (1954). A study of the performance on English and Spanish editions of the Stanford-Binet Intelligence Test by Spanish American children. *Journal of Genetic Psychology*, *85*, 263–269.

Khan, N. A., & Hoge, R. D. (1983). A teacher-judgment measure of social competence: Validity data. *Journal of Consulting and Clinical Psychology*, *51*, 809–814.

Kieffer, D. A., & Goh, D. S. (1981). The effect of individually contracted incentives on intelligence test performance of middle- and low-SES children. *Journal of Clinical Psychology*, *37*, 175–179.

Kiernan, C., & Jones, M. (1977). *Behavior assessment battery*. Atlantic Highlands, NJ: Humanities.

King, J. D., & Smith, R. A. (1972). Abbreviated forms of the Wechsler Preschool and Primary Scale of Intelligence for a kindergarten population. *Psychological Reports*, *30*, 539–542.

King, W. L., & Seegmiller, B. (1973). Performance of 14- to 22-month-old black, firstborn male infants on two tests of cognitive development: The Bayley Scales and the Infant Psychological Development Scale. *Developmental Psychology*, *8*, 317–326.

Kinsbourne, M., & Caplan, P. J. (1979). *Children's learning and attention problems*. Boston: Little, Brown.

Kinston, W., & Loader, P. (1984). Eliciting whole-family interaction with a standardized clinical interview. *Journal of Family Therapy*, *6*, 347–363.

Kirk, S. A., & Kirk, W. D. (1978). Uses and abuses of the ITPA. *Journal of Speech and Hearing Disorders*, *43*, 58–75.

Kirk, S. A., McCarthy, J. J., & Kirk, W. D. (1968). *The Illinois Test of Psycholinguistic Abilities*. Urbana: University of Illinois Press.

Kirk, W. D. (1974). *Aids and precautions in administering the Illinois Test of Psycholinguistic Abilities*. Urbana: University of Illinois Press.

Kirschenbaum, D. S., Steffen, J. J., & D'Orta, C. (1978). An easily mastered Social Competence Classroom Behavioral Observation System. *Behavioral Analysis and Modification*, *2*, 314–322.

Kitson, D. L., & Vance, H. B. (1982). Relationship of the Wechsler Intelligence Scale for Children—Revised and the Wide-Range Achievement Test for a selected sample of young children. *Psychological Reports*, *50*, 981–982.

Klanderman, J., Devine, J., & Mollner, C. (1985). The K-ABC: A construct validity study with the WISC-R and Stanford-Binet. *Journal of Clinical Psychology*, *41*, 273–281.

Klapper, Z. S., & Birch, H. G. (1966). The relation of childhood characteristics to outcome in young adults with cerebral palsy. *Developmental Medicine and Child Neurology*, *8*, 645–656.

Kleinmuntz, D. (1982). *Personality and psychological assessment*. New York: St. Martin's Press.

Klett, W. G., Watson, C. G., & Hoffman, P. T. (1986). The Henmon-Nelson and Slosson tests as predictors of WAIS-R IQ. *Journal of Clinical Psychology*, *42*, 343–347.

Kling, J. O., & Kupersmith, A. (1984, May). *Henmon-Nelson and Quick Test IQ scores and WAIS-R Full Scale IQ scores in a general psychiatric population*. Paper presented at the annual convention of the Midwestern Psychological Association, Chicago.

Kljajic, I., & Berry, D. (1984). Brain syndrome and WAIS PIQ VIQ difference scores corrected for test artifact. *Journal of Clinical Psychology*, *40*, 271–277.

Klugman, S. F. (1944). The effect of money incentive versus praise upon the reliability and obtained scores of the Revised Stanford-Binet test. *Journal of General Psychology*, *30*, 255–269.

Knight, R. G. (1983). On interpreting the several standard errors of the WAIS-R: Some further tables. *Journal of Consulting and Clinical Psychology*, *51*, 671–673.

Knobloch, H., & Pasamanick, B. (1960). Environmental factors affecting human development before and after birth. *Pediatrics*, *26*, 210–218.

Knoff, H. M., & Sperling, B. L. (1986). Gifted children and visual-motor development: A comparison of Bender-Gestalt and VMI test performance. *Psychology in the Schools*, *23*, 247–251.

Kochman, T. (1972). Black American speech events and a language program for the classroom. In C. B. Cazden, V. P. John, & D. Hymes (Eds.), *Functions of language in the classroom* (pp. 211–261). New York: Teachers College Press.

Koegel, R. L., Schreibman, L., O'Neill, R. E., & Burke, J. C. (1983). The personality and family-interaction characteristics of parents of autistic children. *Journal of Consulting and Clinical Psychology*, *51*, 683–692.

Koenke, K. (1978). A comparison of three auditory discrimination-perception tests. *Academic Therapy*, *13*, 463–468.

Kogan, K. L. (1957). Repeated psychometric evaluations of preschool children with cerebral palsy. *Pediatrics*, *19*, 619–621.

Koh, T., Abbatiello, A., & McLoughlin, C. S. (1984). Cultural bias in WISC subtest items: A response to Judge Grady's suggestion in relation to the *PASE* case. *School Psychology Review*, *13*, 89–94.

Kohn, M. (1986a). *Kohn Problem Checklist*. San Antonio: The Psychological Corporation.

Kohn, M. (1986b). *Kohn Social Competence Scale*. San Antonio: The Psychological Corporation.

Kolin, P. C., & Kolin, J. L. (1980). *Professional writing for nurses in education, practice, and research*. St. Louis: Mosby.

Komm, R. A. (1978). A comparison of the Black Intelligence Test of Cultural Homogeneity with the Wechsler Intelligence Scale for Children (Revised), as measured by a conventional achievement test within a black population at different social class levels. *Dissertation Abstracts International, 39,* 6031A-6032A. (University Microfilms No. 79–05059)

Koppitz, E. M. (1964). *The Bender Gestalt Test for young children.* New York: Grune & Stratton.

Koppitz, E. M. (1975). *The Bender Gestalt Test for young children* (Vol. 2): *Research and application, 1963–1973.* New York: Grune & Stratton.

Korchin, S. J. (1976). *Modern clinical psychology.* New York: Basic Books.

Korchin, S. J. (1980). Clinical psychology and minority problems. *American Psychologist, 35,* 262–269.

Kovacs, M. (1983). *The interview schedule for children (ISC).* Unpublished interview schedule, Department of Psychiatry, University of Pittsburgh.

Kratochwill, T. R., & Demuth, D. M. (1976). An examination of the predictive validity of the KeyMath Diagnostic Arithmetic Test and the Wide Range Achievement Test in exceptional children. *Psychology in the Schools, 13,* 404–406.

Krauft, V. R., & Krauft, C. C. (1972). Structured vs. unstructured visual-motor tests for educable retarded children. *Perceptual and Motor Skills, 34,* 691–694.

Krebs, E. G. (1969). The Wechsler Preschool and Primary Scale of Intelligence and prediction of reading achievement in first grade. *Dissertation Abstracts International, 30,* 4279-A. (University Microfilms, No. 70–3361)

Krohn, E. J., & Traxler, A. J. (1979). Relationship of the McCarthy Scales of Children's Abilities to other measures of preschool cognitive, motor, and perceptual development. *Perceptual and Motor Skills, 49,* 783–790.

Krug, D. A., Arick, J. R., & Almond, P. J. (1980). *Autism Screening Instrument for Educational Planning.* Portland, OR: ASIEP Educational Company.

Kutner, N. G. (1975). The poor vs. the non-poor: An ethnic and metropolitan-nonmetropolitan comparison. *Sociological Quarterly, 16,* 250–263.

Lacey, H. M., & Ross, A. O. (1964). Multidisciplinary views on psychological reports in child guidance clinics. *Journal of Clinical Psychology, 20,* 522–526.

LaCrosse, J. E. (1964). *Examiner reliability on the Stanford-Binet Intelligence Scale (Form L-M) in a design employing white and Negro examiners and subjects.* Unpublished master's thesis, University of North Carolina.

La Greca, A. M. (1983). Interviewing and behavioral observations. In C. E. Walker & M. C. Roberts (Eds.), *Handbook of clinical child psychology* (pp. 109–131). New York: Wiley.

Lahey, B. B., Stempniak, M., Robinson, E. J., & Tyroler, M. J. (1978). Hyperactivity and learning disabilities as independent dimensions of child behavior problems. *Journal of Abnormal Psychology, 87,* 333–340.

Lamanna, J. A., & Ysseldyke, J. E. (1973). Reliability of the Peabody Individual Achievement Test with first-grade children. *Psychology in the Schools, 10,* 437–439.

Lambert, N. M., Windmiller, M., Tharinger, D., & Cole, L. J. (1981). *AAMD Adaptive Behavior Scale – School Edition.* Monterey, CA: CTB/McGraw-Hill.

Lancy, D. F., & Goldstein, G. I. (1982). The use of nonverbal Piagetian tasks to assess the cognitive development of autistic children. *Child Development, 53,* 1233–1241.

Landesman-Dwyer, S., & Butterfield, E. C. (1983). Mental retardation: Developmental issues in cognitive and social adaptation. In M. Lewis (Ed.), *Origins of intelligence: Infancy and early childhood* (2nd ed., pp. 479–519). New York: Plenum.

Landis, D. (1972). Review of the Purdue Perceptual-Motor Survey. In O. K. Buros (Ed.), *The seventh mental measurements yearbook* (pp. 1284–1285). Highland Park, NJ: Gryphon Press.

Laosa, L. M. (1984). Ethnic, socioeconomic, and home language influences upon early performance on measures of abilities. *Journal of Educational Psychology, 76,* 1178–1198.

Larrabee, G. J. (1986). Another look at VIQ-PIQ scores and unilateral brain damage. *International Journal of Neuroscience, 29,* 141–148.

Larrabee, L. L., & Kleinsasser, L. D. (1967). *The effect of experimenter bias on WISC performance.* Unpublished manuscript, Psychological Associates, St. Louis.

Lawlis, G. F., Stedman, J. M., & Cortner, R. H. (1980). Factor analysis of the WISC-R for a sample of bilingual Mexican-Americans. *Journal of Clinical Child Psychology, 9,* 57–58.

Lawson, J. S., & Inglis, J. (1983). A laterality index of cognitive impairment after hemispheric damage: A measure derived from a principal-components analysis of the Wechsler Adult Intelligence Scale. *Journal of Consulting and Clinical Psychology, 51,* 832–840.

Layzer, D. (1972). Science or superstition? (A physical scientist looks at the IQ controversy.) *Cognition, 1,* 265–299.

LeBaron, S., & Zeltzer, L. (1984). Assessment of acute pain and anxiety in children and adolescents by self-reports, observer reports, and a behavior checklist. *Journal of Consulting and Clinical Psychology, 52,* 729–738.

Lehman, J., & Breen, M. J. (1982). A comparative analysis of the Bender-Gestalt and Beery-Buktenica Tests of Visual-Motor Integration as a function of grade level for regular education students. *Psychology in the Schools, 19,* 52–54.

Leiter, R. G. (1948). *Leiter International Performance Scale.* Chicago: Stoelting Co.

Leiter, R. G. (1959). Part I of the manual for the 1948 Revision of the Leiter International Performance Scale: Evidence of the reliability and validity of the Leiter tests. *Psychological Service Center Journal, 11,* 1–72.

Leland, H. (1971, September). Testing the disadvantaged. In W. C. Rhodes (Chair), *Use and misuse of standardized intelligence tests in psychological and educational research and practice.* Symposium presented at the meeting of the American Psychological Association, Washington, DC.

Lerner, E., & Murphy, L. B. (1941). Methods for the study of personality in young children. *Monographs of the Society for Research in Child Development, 6*(4, Serial No. 30).

Lesiak, J. (1984). The Bender Visual Motor Gestalt Test: Implications for the diagnosis and prediction of reading achievement. *Journal of School Psychology, 22,* 391–405.

Lesser, G. S., Fifer, G., & Clark, D. H. (1965). Mental abilities of children from different social-class and cultural groups. *Monographs of the Society for Research in Child Development, 30*(4, Whole No. 102).

Lester, E. P., Muir, R., & Dudek, S. Z. (1970). Cognitive structure and achievement in the young child. *Canadian Psychiatric Association Journal, 15,* 279–287.

Levandowski, B. (1975). The difference in intelligence test scores of bilingual students on an English version of the intelligence test as compared to a Spanish version of the test. *Illinois School Research, 11*(3), 47–51.

Levenson, R. L., Jr., & Zino, T. C. (1979). II. Assessment of cognitive deficiency with the McCarthy Scales and Stanford-Binet: A correlational analysis. *Perceptual and Motor Skills, 48,* 291–295.

Levin, H. S. (1981). Assessment in closed head injury. In M. T. Sarno (Ed.), *Acquired aphasia* (pp. 427–463). New York: Academic Press.

Levin, H. S., Eisenberg, H. M., Wigg, N. R., & Kobayashi, K. (1982). Memory and intellectual ability after head injury in children and adolescents. *Neurosurgery, 11,* 668–673.

Levine, M. N., Allen, R. M., Alker, L. N., & Fitzgibbons, W. (1974). *Clinical profile form for the Leiter International Performance Scale.* Chicago: Stoelting.

Levine, S., Elzey, F. F., Thormahlen, P., & Cain, L. F. (1976). *Manual for the T.M.R. School Competency Scales.* Palo Alto, CA: Consulting Psychologists Press.

Levy, B. B., & Cook, H. (1973). Dialect proficiency and auditory comprehension in standard and black nonstandard English. *Journal of Speech and Hearing Research, 16,* 642–649.

Lewis, L. L. (1957). The relation of measured mental ability to school marks and academic survival in the Texas School for the Blind. *International Journal for the Education of the Blind, 6,* 56–60.

Lewis, M. L., & Johnson, J. J. (1985). Comparison of WAIS and WAIS-R IQs from two equivalent college populations. *Journal of Psychoeducational Assessment, 3,* 55–60.

Lewis-O'Donnell, M. (1986). *A comparison study of the performance of inpatient emotionally disturbed non-psychotic children and the standardization sample using the Stanford-Binet (Fourth Edition).* Unpublished doctoral dissertation, Biola University, La Mirada, CA.

Lewkowicz, D. J., & Turkewitz, G. (1982). Influence of hemispheric specialization in sensory processing on reaching in infants: Age and gender related effects. *Developmental Psychology, 18,* 301–308.

Lezak, M. D. (1983). *Neuropsychological assessment* (2nd ed.). New York: Oxford University Press.

Lichtenstein, R., & Ireton, H. (1984). *Preschool screening: Identifying young children with developmental and educational problems.* Orlando, FL: Grune & Stratton.

Lichtman, M. V. (1969). Intelligence, creativity, and language: An examination of the interrelationships of three variables among preschool, disadvantaged Negro children. *Dissertation Abstracts International, 31,* 1625-A. (University Microfilms, No. 70–13,956)

Lindamood, C., & Lindamood, P. (1979). *Lindamood Auditory Conceptualization Test* (rev. ed.). Allen, TX: DLM Teaching Resources.

Linden, K. W., & Linden, J. D. (1968). *Modern mental measurement: A historical perspective.* Boston: Houghton Mifflin.

Lippold, S., & Claiborn, J. M. (1983). Comparison of the Wechsler Adult Intelligence Scale and the Wechsler Adult Intelligence Scale – Revised. *Journal of Consulting and Clinical Psychology, 51,* 315.

Livesay, K. K. (1986, October). *Comparisons of the Stanford-Binet: Fourth Edition to the S-B L-M and WISC-R with gifted referrals.* Paper presented at the annual conference of the Florida Association of School Psychologists, Jacksonville, FL.

Lobascher, M. E., & Cavanagh, N. P. (1980). Patterns of intellectual change in the dementing school child. *Child: Care, Health and Development, 6,* 225–265.

Locke, J. L. (1979). Review of the Auditory Discrimination Test. In F. L. Darley (Ed.), *Evaluation of appraisal techniques in speech and language pathology* (pp. 124–127). Reading, MA: Addison-Wesley.

Lockyer, L., & Rutter, M. (1969). A five- to fifteen-year follow-up study of infantile psychosis. III: Psychological aspects. *British Journal of Psychiatry, 115,* 865–882.

Loehlin, J. C., Lindzey, G., & Spuhler, J. N. (1975). *Race differences in intelligence.* San Francisco: W. H. Freeman.

Lombana, J. H. (1982). *Guidance for handicapped students.* Springfield, IL: Charles C Thomas.

Lombard, T. J., & Riedel, R. G. (1978). An analysis of the factor structure of the WISC-R and the effect of color on the Coding subtest. *Psychology in the Schools, 15,* 176–179.

Long, P. A., & Anthony, J. J. (1974). The measurement of mental retardation by a culture-specific test. *Psychology in the Schools, 11,* 310–312.

Longstreth, L. E. (1984). Jensen's reaction-time investigations of intelligence: A critique. *Intelligence, 8,* 139–160.

Longstreth, L. E., Davis, B., Carter, L., Flint, D., Owen, J., Rickert, M., & Taylor, E. (1981). Separation of home intellectual environment and maternal IQ as determinants of child IQ. *Developmental Psychology, 17,* 532–541.

López, M., & Young, R. K. (1974). The linguistic interdependence of bilinguals. *Journal of Experimental Psychology, 102,* 981–983.

Lord, C., & Baker, A. F. (1977). Communicating with autistic children. *Journal of Pediatric Psychology, 2,* 181–186.

Lord, R. G. (1985). Accuracy in behavioral measurement: An alternative definition based on raters' cognitive schema and signal detection theory. *Journal of Applied Psychology, 70,* 66–71.

Lorion, R. P., Cowen, E. L., & Caldwell, R. (1975). Normative and parametric analyses of school maladjustment. *American Journal of Community Psychology, 3,* 291–301.

Lotter, V. (1967). Epidemiology of autistic conditions in young children. II. Some characteristics of the parents and children. *Social Psychiatry*, *1*, 163–173.

Lotter, V. (1974). Factors related to outcome in autistic children. *Journal of Autism and Childhood Schizophrenia*, *4*, 263–277.

Lotter, V. (1978). Follow-up studies. In M. Rutter & E. Schopler (Eds.), *Autism: A reappraisal of concepts and treatment* (pp. 475–495). New York: Plenum.

Lovell, K., & Shields, J. B. (1967). Some aspects of a study of the gifted child. *British Journal of Educational Psychology*, *37*, 201–208.

Lubinski, R. (1981). Environmental language intervention. In R. Chapey (Ed.), *Language intervention strategies in adult aphasia* (pp. 223–245). Baltimore: Williams & Wilkins.

Lucas, E. V. (1980). *Semantic and pragmatic language disorders*. Rockville, MD: Aspen.

Lumsden, J. (1978). Review of the Illinois Test of Psycholinguistic Abilities, revised edition. In O. K. Buros (Ed.), *The eighth mental measurements yearbook* (pp. 578–580). Highland Park, NJ: Gryphon Press.

Luria, A. R. (1966a). *Higher cortical functions in man*. New York: Basic Books.

Luria, A. R. (1966b). *Human brain and psychological processes*. New York: Harper & Row.

Lyle, J. G., & Johnson, E. G. (1973). Analysis of WISC Coding: 3. Writing and copying speed, and motivation. *Perceptual and Motor Skills*, *36*, 211–214.

Lyman, H. B. (1971). Review of the Peabody Individual Achievement Test. *Journal of Educational Measurement*, *8*, 137–138.

Lynn, R. (1977). The intelligence of the Japanese. *Bulletin of the British Psychological Society*, *30*, 69–72.

MacArthur, R. S. (1960). The Coloured Progressive Matrices as a measure of general intelligence ability for Edmonton grade III boys. *Alberta Journal of Educational Research*, *6*, 67–75.

MacArthur, R. S., & Elley, W. B. (1963). The reduction of socioeconomic bias in intelligence testing. *British Journal of Educational Psychology*, *33*, 107–119.

Maccoby, E. E., & Jacklin, C. N. (1974). *The psychology of sex differences*. Stanford, CA: Stanford University Press.

Madden, T. M. (1974). A note on the administration and scoring of the WISC Mazes subtest. *Psychology in the Schools*, *11*, 143–146.

Mahan, T. W., Jr. (1963). Diagnostic consistency and prediction: A note on graduate student skills. *Personnel and Guidance Journal*, *42*, 364–367.

Margolis, R. B., Taylor, J. M., & Greenlief, C. L. (1986). A cross-validation of two short forms of the WAIS-R in a geriatric sample suspected of dementia. *Journal of Clinical Psychology*, *42*, 145–146.

Marjoribanks, K. (1972). Environment, social class, and mental abilities. *Journal of Educational Psychology*, *63*, 103–109.

Marland, S. P., Jr. (1972). *Education of the gifted and talented: Report to the Congress of the United States by the Commis-* *sioner of Education*. Washington, DC: U.S. Government Printing Office.

Marley, M. L. (1982). *Organic brain pathology and the Bender-Gestalt Test: A differential diagnostic scoring system*. New York: Grune & Stratton.

Marmorale, A. M., & Brown, F. (1977). Bender-Gestalt performance of Puerto Rican, white, and Negro children. *Journal of Clinical Psychology*, *33*, 224–228.

Marshall, W., Hess, A. K., & Lair, C. V. (1978). The WISC-R and WRAT as indicators of arithmetic achievement in juvenile delinquents. *Perceptual and Motor Skills*, *47*, 408–410.

Marston, D., & Ysseldyke, J. (1984). Concerns in interpreting subtest scatter on the tests of cognitive ability from the Woodcock-Johnson Psycho-Educational Battery. *Journal of Learning Disabilities*, *17*, 588–591.

Martin, R. P. (1985). Ethics column. *The School Psychologist*, *39*(4), 9.

Mash, E. J., & Terdal, L. G. (1981). Behavioral assessment of childhood disturbance. In E. J. Mash and L. G. Terdal (Eds.), *Behavioral assessment of childhood disorders* (pp. 3–76). New York: Guilford Press.

Mash, E. J., Terdal, L. G., & Anderson, K. (1973). The response-class matrix: A procedure for recording parent-child interactions. *Journal of Consulting and Clinical Psychology*, *40*, 163–164.

Mask, N., & Bowen, C. E. (1984). Comparison of the WISC-R and the Leiter International Performance Scale with average and above-average students. *Journal of Clinical Psychology*, *40*, 303–305.

Masling, J. M. (1959). The effects of warm and cold interaction on the administration and scoring of an intelligence test. *Journal of Consulting Psychology*, *23*, 336–341.

Massey, J. O. (1964). *WISC scoring criteria*. Palo Alto, CA: Consulting Psychologists Press.

Massey, J. O., Sattler, J. M., & Andres, J. R. (1978). *WISC-R scoring criteria*. Palo Alto, CA: Consulting Psychologists Press.

Massoth, N. A. (1985). The McCarthy Scales of Children's Abilities as a predictor of achievement: A five-year follow-up. *Psychology in the Schools*, *22*, 10–13.

Massoth, N. A., & Levenson, R. L., Jr. (1982). The McCarthy Scales of Children's Abilities as a predictor of reading readiness and reading achievement. *Psychology in the Schools*, *19*, 293–296.

Mastenbrook, J. (1977, September). *Analysis of the content of Adaptive Behavior and two instruments*. Paper presented at the meeting of the American Psychological Association, San Francisco.

Mastenbrook, J. (1978). Future directions in adaptive behavior assessment: Environmental adaptation measure. In A. T. Fisher (Chair), *Impact of adaptive behavior: ABIC and the environmental adaptation measure*. Symposium presented at the meeting of the American Psychological Association, Toronto, Canada.

Matarazzo, J. D. (1986). Computerized clinical psychological test interpretations: Unvalidated plus all mean and no sigma. *American Psychologist*, *41*, 14–24.

Matarazzo, J. D., Bornstein, R. A., McDermott, P. A., & Noonan, J. V. (1986). Verbal IQ vs. Performance IQ difference scores in males and females from the WAIS-R standardization sample. *Journal of Clinical Psychology*, *42*, 965–974.

Matarazzo, J. D., & Herman, D. O. (1984a). Base rate data for the WAIS-R: Test-retest stability and VIQ-PIQ differences. *Journal of Clinical Neuropsychology*, *6*, 351–366.

Matarazzo, J. D., & Herman, D. O. (1984b). Relationship of education and IQ in the standardization sample. *Journal of Consulting and Clinical Psychology*, *52*, 631–634.

Matarazzo, J. D., & Herman, D. O. (1985). Clinical uses of the WAIS-R: Base rates of differences between VIQ and PIQ in the WAIS-R standardization sample. In B. B. Wolman (Ed.), *Handbook of intelligence: Theories, measurements and applications* (pp. 899–932). New York: Wiley.

Matheny, A. P., Jr. (1983). A longitudinal twin study of stability of components from Bayley's Infant Behavior Record. *Child Development*, *54*, 356–360.

Matheny, A. P., Jr., Dolan, A. B., & Wilson, R. S. (1974). Bayley's Infant Behavior Record: Relations between behaviors and mental test scores. *Developmental Psychology*, *10*, 696–702.

Mather, N., & Burch, M. (1986). An examination of Woodcock-Johnson suppressor effects with learning-disabled and gifted subjects. *Journal of Psychoeducational Assessment*, *4*, 45–51.

Mattes, L. J., & Omark, D. R. (1984). *Speech and language assessment for the bilingual handicapped*. San Diego: College-Hill Press.

Maxwell, J. K., & Wise, F. (1984). PPVT IQ validity in adults: A measure of vocabulary, not of intelligence. *Journal of Clinical Psychology*, *40*, 1048–1053.

McCall, R. B. (1977). Childhood IQ's as predictors of adult educational and occupational status. *Science*, *197*, 482–483.

McCall, R. B. (1979). The development of intellectual functioning in infancy and the prediction of later I.Q. In J. D. Osofsky (Ed.), *Handbook of infant development* (pp. 707–741). New York: Wiley.

McCall, R. B., Appelbaum, M. I., & Hogarty, P. S. (1973). Developmental changes in mental performance. *Monographs of the Society for Research in Child Development*, *38*(3) (Serial No. 150), 1–83.

McCallum, R. S., Karnes, F. A., & Edwards, R. P. (1984). The test of choice for assessment of gifted children: A comparison of the K-ABC, WISC-R, and Stanford-Binet. *Journal of Psychoeducational Assessment*, *2*, 57–63.

McCarthy, D. A. (1972). *Manual for the McCarthy Scales of Children's Abilities*. San Antonio: The Psychological Corporation.

McCarthy, D. A. (1978). *McCarthy Screening Test (MST)*. San Antonio: The Psychological Corporation.

McConnell, R. E. (1930). The origin of mental tests. *Education*, *50*, 464–473.

McGee, M. G. (1982). Spatial abilities: The influence of genetic factors. In M. Potegal (Ed.), *Spatial abilities: Development and physiological foundations* (pp. 199–222). New York: Academic Press.

McGrew, K. S. (1983). Comparison of the WISC-R and Woodcock-Johnson tests of cognitive ability. *Journal of School Psychology*, *21*, 271–276.

McGrew, K. S. (1985). Investigation of the Verbal/Nonverbal structure of the Woodcock-Johnson: Implications for subtest interpretation and comparisons with the Wechsler Scales. *Journal of Psychoeducational Assessment*, *3*, 65–71.

McGrew, K. S. (1986). *Clinical interpretation of the Woodcock-Johnson Tests of Cognitive Ability*. Orlando, FL: Grune & Stratton.

McGue, M., Shinn, M., & Ysseldyke, J. (1982). Use of cluster scores on the Woodcock-Johnson Psycho-Educational Battery with learning disabled students. *Learning Disability Quarterly*, *5*, 274–287.

McGuire, T. R., & Hirsch, J. (1977). General intelligence (g) and heritability (H^2, h^2). In I. C. Uzgiris & F. Weizmann (Eds.), *The structuring of experience* (pp. 25–72). New York: Plenum Press.

McLaughlin, B. (1977). Second-language learning in children. *Psychological Bulletin*, *84*, 438–459.

McLoughlin, C. S., & Gullo, D. F. (1984). Comparison of three formal methods of preschool language assessment. *Language, Speech, & Hearing Services in Schools*, *15*, 146–153.

McMahon, R. C. (1981). Biological factors in childhood hyperkinesis: A review of genetic and biochemical hypotheses. *Journal of Clinical Psychology*, *37*, 12–21.

McMahon, R. C., Kunce, J. T. (1981). A comparison of the factor structure of the WISC and WISC-R in normal and exceptional groups. *Journal of Clinical Psychology*, *37*, 408–410.

McNamara, J. R., Porterfield, C. L., & Miller, L. E. (1969). The relationship of the Wechsler Preschool and Primary Scale of Intelligence with the Coloured Progressive Matrices (1956) and the Bender Gestalt Test. *Journal of Clinical Psychology*, *25*, 65–68.

McNemar, Q. (1942). *The revision of the Stanford-Binet Scale*. Boston: Houghton Mifflin.

McNemar, Q. (1974). Correction to a correction. *Journal of Consulting and Clinical Psychology*, *42*, 145–146.

McShane, D. A., & Plas, J. M. (1984). The cognitive functioning of American Indian children: Moving from the WISC to the WISC-R. *School Psychology Review*, *13*, 61–73.

Meacham, F. R. (1984). *A comparative study of the WISC-R and WAIS-R performance IQ scores of 16-year-old hearing impaired students in a residential program*. Unpublished doctoral dissertation, University of Alabama, Tuscaloosa, AL.

Meadow, K. P. (1968). Early manual communication in relation to the deaf child's intellectual, social, and communicative functioning. *American Annals of the Deaf*, *113*, 29–41.

Meadow, K. P. (1975). The development of deaf children. In E. M. Hetherington (Ed.), *Review of child development research* (Vol. 5, pp. 441–508). Chicago: University of Chicago Press.

Meeker, M. N. (1969). *The structure of intellect*. Columbus, OH: Charles E. Merrill.

Melear, J., & Boyle, J. (1974). The relationship of the Columbia Mental Maturity Scale to the WISC with reference to low achieving Anglo and Spanish bilingual children. *Colorado Journal of Educational Research*, *14*, 8–10.

Mercer, J. R. (1976). Pluralistic diagnosis in the evaluation of Black and Chicano children: A procedure for taking sociocultural variables into account in clinical assessment. In C. A. Hernandez, M. J. Haug, & N. N. Wagner (Eds.), *Chicanos: Social and psychological perspectives* (2nd ed., pp. 183–195). St. Louis: Mosby.

Mercer, J. R. (1979). *System of Multicultural Pluralistic Assessment technical manual*. San Antonio: The Psychological Corporation.

Mercer, J. R., & Lewis, J. F. (1978). *System of Multicultural Pluralistic Assessment*. San Antonio: The Psychological Corporation.

Mercy, J. A., & Steelman, L. C. (1982). Familial influence on the intellectual attainment of children. *American Sociological Review*, *47*, 532–542.

Messick, S. (1980). Test validity and the ethics of assessment. *American Psychologist*, *35*, 1012–1027.

Messick, S. (1984). Assessment in context: Appraising student performance in relation to instructional quality. *Educational Researcher*, *13*(3), 3–8.

Meyer, W. J., & Goldstein, D. (1971). Performance characteristics of middle-class and lower-class preschool children on the Stanford-Binet, 1960 Revision. (ERIC Document Reproduction Service No. ED 044 429)

Meyers, C. E. (1969). What the ITPA measures: A synthesis of factor studies of the 1961 edition. *Educational and Psychological Measurement*, *29*, 867–876.

Meyers, C. E. (1978). Review of the Balthazar Scales of Adaptive Behavior. In O. K. Buros (Ed.), *The eighth mental measurements yearbook* (pp. 696–698). Highland Park, NJ: Gryphon Press.

Miele, F. (1979). Cultural bias in the WISC. *Intelligence*, *3*, 149–164.

Miller, C. A. (1982). Degree of lateralization as a hierarchy of manual and cognitive levels. *Neuropsychologia*, *20*, 155–162.

Miller, C. K., & Chansky, N. M. (1972). Psychologists' scoring of WISC protocols. *Psychology in the Schools*, *9*, 144–152.

Miller, C. K., Chansky, N. M., & Gredler, G. R. (1970). Rater agreement on WISC protocols. *Psychology in the Schools*, *7*, 190–193.

Miller, G., Dubowitz, L. M. S., & Palmer, P. (1984). Follow-up of pre-term infants: Is correction of the developmental quotient for prematurity helpful? *Early Human Development*, *9*, 137–144.

Miller, J. F. (1981). *Assessing language production in children*. Austin, TX: Pro-Ed.

Miller, M., Stoneburger, R. L., & Brecht, R. D. (1978). WISC subtest patterns as discriminators of perceptual disability. *Journal of Learning Disabilities*, *11*, 449–452.

Miller, N. B. (1979). Parents of children with neurological disorders: Concerns and counseling. *Journal of Pediatric Psychology*, *4*, 297–306.

Miller, R. A. (1974). Social milieu and the effects of reinforcement on I.Q. tests. *Dissertation Abstracts International*, *35*, 517B–518B. (University Microfilms No. 74–15,373)

Millham, J., Chilcutt, J., & Atkinson, B. L. (1978). Comparability of naturalistic and controlled observation assessment of adaptive behavior. *American Journal of Mental Deficiency*, *83*, 52–59.

Milne, N. D. M. (1975). Relationships among scores obtained on the Wechsler Intelligence Scale for Children, Columbia Mental Maturity Scale and Leiter International Performance Scale by Mexican-American children. *Dissertation Abstracts International*, *35*, 6516A. (University Microfilms No. 75–9073)

Minde, K., Weiss, G., & Mendelson, N. (1972). A 5-year follow-up study of 91 hyperactive school children. *Journal of the American Academy of Child Psychiatry*, *11*, 595–610.

Mishra, S. P. (1981). Factor analysis of the McCarthy Scales for groups of white and Mexican-American children. *Journal of School Psychology*, *19*, 178–182.

Mishra, S. P. (1983). Effects of examiners' prior knowledge of subjects' ethnicity and intelligence on the scoring of responses to the Stanford-Binet Scale. *Psychology in the Schools*, *20*, 133–136.

Mishra, S. P., & Brown, K. H. (1983). The comparability of WAIS and WAIS-R IQs and subtest scores. *Journal of Clinical Psychology*, *39*, 754–757.

Mitchell, J. V., Jr. (Ed.). (1985). *The ninth mental measurements yearbook* (Vols. 1–2). Lincoln, NE: The Buros Institute of Mental Measurements of the University of Nebraska–Lincoln.

Mitchell, R. E., Grandy, T. G., & Lupo, J. V. (1986). Comparison of the WAIS and the WAIS-R in the upper ranges of IQ. *Professional Psychology: Research and Practice*, *17*, 82–83.

Moffitt, T. E., Gabrielli, W. F., Mednick, S. A., & Schulsinger, F. (1981). Socioeconomic status, IQ, and delinquency. *Journal of Abnormal Psychology*, *90*, 152–156.

Molyneaux, D., & Lane, V. W. (1982). *Effective interviewing: Techniques and analysis*. Boston: Allyn and Bacon.

Moore, C. H., Boblitt, W. E., & Wildman, R. W. (1968). Psychiatric impressions of psychological reports. *Journal of Clinical Psychology*, *24*, 373–376.

Moore, C. L., & Zarske, J. A. (1984). Comparison of Native American Navajo Bender-Gestalt performance with Koppitz and SOMPA norms. *Psychology in the Schools*, *21*, 148–153.

Moore, E. G. J. (1986). Family socialization and the IQ test performance of traditionally and transracially adopted black children. *Developmental Psychology*, *22*, 317–326.

Moore, M. V. (1969). Pathological writing. *Asha*, *11*, 535–538.

Morales, E. S., & George, C. (1976, September). *Examiner effects in the testing of Mexican-American children*. Paper presented at the meeting of the American Psychological Association, Washington, DC.

Moran, J. D. III, McCullers, J. C., & Fabes, R. A. (1984). Developmental analysis of the effects of reward on selected Wechsler subscales. *American Journal of Psychology*, *97*, 205–214.

Morgan, S. B. (1984). Helping parents understand the diagnosis of autism. *Developmental and Behavioral Pediatrics*, *5*, 78–85.

Morris, J. D., Evans, J. G., & Pearson, D. R. (1978). The WISC-R subtest profile of a sample of severely emotionally disturbed children. *Psychological Reports*, *42*, 319–325.

Morris, J. D., Martin, R. A., Johnson, E., Birch, M. C., & Thompson, D. (1978). Subtest order and WISC-R scores of a sample of educable mentally retarded subjects. *Psychological Reports*, *43*, 383–386.

Morsbach, G., McGoldrick, G., & Younger, J. (1978). Inter-scorer reliability of the Geometric Design subtest of the WPPSI. *Journal of Behavioural Science*, *2*, 279–284.

Moscovitch, M. (1981). Right-hemisphere language. *Topics in Language Disorders*, *1*(4), 41–61.

Mueller, H. H., Dash, U. N., Matheson, D. W., & Short, R. H. (1984). WISC-R subtest patterning of below average, average, and above average IQ children: A meta-analysis. *Alberta Journal of Educational Research*, *30*, 68–85.

Mueller, H. H., Matheson, D. W., & Short, R. H. (1983). Bannatyne-recategorized WISC-R patterns of mentally retarded, learning disabled, normal, and intellectually superior children: A meta-analysis. *Mental Retardation and Learning Disability Bulletin*, *11*, 60–78.

Mullins, J. B. (1983). The uses of bibliotherapy in counseling families confronted with handicaps. In M. Seligman (Ed.), *The family with a handicapped child: Understanding and treatment* (pp. 235–259). New York: Grune & Stratton.

Muma, J. R., & Pierce, S. (1981). Language intervention: Data or evidence? *Topics in Learning and Learning Disabilities*, *1*(2), 1–11.

Murphy, H. A., Hutchison, J. M., & Bailey, J. S. (1983). Behavioral school psychology goes outdoors: The effects of organized games on playground aggression. *Journal of Applied Behavior Analysis*, *16*, 29–35.

Murphy, K. P. (1957). Tests of abilities and attainments. In A. W. G. Ewing (Ed.), *Educational guidance and the deaf child* (pp. 213–251). Manchester: Manchester University Press.

Murphy, L. B. (1956). *Personality in young children* (Vol. 1). New York: Basic Books.

Murphy, L. B. (1975). The stranglehold of norms on the individual child. In M. D. Cohen (Ed.), *Testing and evaluation: New views* (pp. 39–44). Washington, DC: Association for Childhood Education International. (ERIC Document Reproduction Service No. ED 109 143)

Myers, B., & Goldstein, D. (1979). Cognitive development in bilingual and monolingual lower-class children. *Psychology in the Schools*, *16*, 137–142.

Naglieri, J. A. (1980a). Comparison of McCarthy General Cognitive Index and WISC-R IQ for educable mentally retarded,

learning disabled, and normal children. *Psychological Reports*, *47*, 591–596.

Naglieri, J. A. (1980b). McCarthy and WISC-R correlations with WRAT Achievement Scores. *Perceptual and Motor Skills*, *51*, 392–394.

Naglieri, J. A. (1981a). Concurrent validity of the Revised Peabody Picture Vocabulary Test. *Psychology in the Schools*, *18*, 286–289.

Naglieri, J. A. (1981b). Extrapolated developmental indices for the Bayley Scales of Infant Development. *American Journal of Mental Deficiency*, *85*, 548–550.

Naglieri, J. A. (1981c). Factor structure of the WISC-R for children identified as learning disabled. *Psychological Reports*, *49*, 891–895.

Naglieri, J. A. (1982). Use of the WISC-R and PPVT-R with mentally retarded children. *Journal of Clinical Psychology*, *38*, 635–637.

Naglieri, J. A. (1984). Concurrent and predictive validity of the Kaufman Assessment Battery for children with a Navajo sample. *Journal of School Psychology*, *22*, 373–379.

Naglieri, J. A. (1985a). Normal children's performance on the McCarthy Scales, Kaufman Assessment Battery, and Peabody Individual Achievement Test. *Journal of Psychoeducational Assessment*, *3*, 123–129.

Naglieri, J. A. (1985b). Use of the WISC-R and K-ABC with learning disabled, borderline mentally retarded, and normal children. *Psychology in the Schools*, *22*, 133–141.

Naglieri, J. A., & Anderson, D. F. (1985). Comparison of the WISC-R and K-ABC with gifted students. *Journal of Psychoeducational Assessment*, *3*, 175–179.

Naglieri, J. A., & Haddad, F. A. (1984). Learning disabled children's performance on the Kaufman Assessment Battery for Children: A concurrent validity study. *Journal of Psychoeducational Assessment*, *2*, 49–56.

Naglieri, J. A., & Harrison, P. L. (1982). McCarthy scales, McCarthy Screening Test, and Kaufman's McCarthy short form correlations with the Peabody Individual Achievement Test. *Psychology in the Schools*, *19*, 149–155.

Naglieri, J. A., Kaufman, A. S., & Harrison, P. L. (1981). Factor structure of the McCarthy Scales for school-age children with low GCIs. *Journal of School Psychology*, *19*, 226–232.

Naglieri, J. A., & Pfeiffer, S. I. (1983a). Reliability and stability of the WISC-R for children with below average IQs. *Educational & Psychological Research*, *3*, 203–208.

Naglieri, J. A., & Pfeiffer, S. I. (1983b). Stability and concurrent validity of the Peabody Individual Achievement Test. *Psychological Reports*, *52*, 672–674.

Naglieri, J. A., & Pfeiffer, S. I. (1983c). Stability, concurrent and predictive validity of the PPVT-R. *Journal of Clinical Psychology*, *39*, 965–967.

Naglieri, J. A., & Yazzie, C. (1983). Comparison of the WISC-R and PPVT-R with Navajo children. *Journal of Clinical Psychology*, *39*, 598–600.

Nay, W. R. (1979). *Multimethod clinical assessment*. New York: Gardner Press.

Nettelbeck, T. (1985). Inspection time and mild mental retardation. In N. R. Ellis & N. W. Bray (Eds.), *International review of research in mental retardation* (Vol. 13, pp. 109–141). Orlando, FL: Academic Press.

Neuhaus, M. (1967). Modifications in the administration of the WISC Performance subtests for children with profound hearing losses. *Exceptional Children*, *33*, 573–574.

Newborg, J., Stock, J. R., & Wnek, L. (1984). *Battelle Developmental Inventory*. Allen, TX: DLM Teaching Resources.

Newcomer, P. L., & Hammill, D. D. (1975). ITPA and academic achievement: A survey. *Reading Teacher*, *28*, 731–741.

Newland, T. E. (1971). *Blind Learning Aptitude Test*. Champaign, IL: University of Illinois Press.

New York City Board of Education (1977). *Language Assessment Battery*. Chicago: Riverside Publishing.

Nichols, P. L. (1971). The effects of heredity and environment on intelligence test performance in 4 and 7 year white and Negro sibling pairs. *Dissertation Abstracts International*, *32*, 101B–102B. (University Microfilms No. 71–81,874)

Nichols, P. L. (1984). Familial mental retardation. *Behavior Genetics*, *14*, 161–170.

Nichols, P. L., & Anderson, V. E. (1973). Intellectual performance, race, and socioeconomic status. *Social Biology*, *20*, 367–374.

Nichols, P. L., & Chen, T. C. (1981). *Minimal brain dysfunction: A prospective study*. Hillsdale, NJ: Lawrence Erlbaum.

Nichols, R. C. (1959). The effect of ego involvement and success experience on intelligence test results. *Journal of Consulting Psychology*, *23*, 92.

Nichols, R. C. (1974). Review of *Genetics and education* by A. R. Jensen. *Educational Studies*, *5*, 35–38.

Nihira, K., Foster, R., Shellhaas, M., & Leland, H. (1974). *AAMD Adaptive Behavior Scale* (rev. ed.). Washington, DC: American Association on Mental Deficiency.

Nitko, A. J. (1980). Distinguishing the many varieties of criterion-referenced tests. *Review of Educational Research*, *50*, 461–485.

Oakland, T. D. (1979a). Research on the ABIC and ELP: A revisit to an old topic. *School Psychology Digest*, *8*, 209–213.

Oakland, T. D. (1979b). Research on the Adaptive Behavior Inventory for Children and the Estimated Learning Potential. *School Psychology Digest*, *8*, 63–70.

Oakland, T. D. (1980). An evaluation of the ABIC, pluralistic norms, and estimated learning potential. *Journal of School Psychology*, *18*, 3–11.

Oakland, T. D. (1983a). Concurrent and predictive validity estimates for the WISC-R IQs and ELPs by racial-ethnic and SES groups. *School Psychology Review*, *12*, 57–61.

Oakland, T. D. (1983b). Joint use of adaptive behavior and IQ to predict achievement. *Journal of Consulting and Clinical Psychology*, *51*, 298–301.

Oakland, T. D., & Dowling, L. (1983). The Draw-a-Person test: Validity properties for nonbiased assessment. *Learning Disability Quarterly*, *6*, 526–534.

Oakland, T. D., & Feigenbaum, D. (1979). Multiple sources of test bias on the WISC-R and Bender-Gestalt Test. *Journal of Consulting and Clinical Psychology*, *47*, 968–974.

Oakland, T. D., & Feigenbaum, D. (1980). Comparisons of the psychometric characteristics of the Adaptive Behavior Inventory for Children for different subgroups of children. *Journal of School Psychology*, *18*, 307–316.

Oakland, T. D., & Houchins, S. (1985). Testing the test: A review of the Vineland Adaptive Behavior Scales, Survey Form. *Journal of Counseling and Development*, *63*, 585–586.

Oakland, T. D., King, J. D., White, L. A., & Eckman, R. (1971). A comparison of performance on the WPPSI, WISC, and SB with preschool children: Companion studies. *Journal of School Psychology*, *9*, 144–149.

Oakland, T. D., Lee, S. W., & Axelrad, K. M. (1975). Examiner differences on actual WISC protocols. *Journal of School Psychology*, *13*, 227–233.

Obrzut, A., Obrzut, J. E., & Shaw, D. (1984). Construct validity of the Kaufman Assessment Battery for Children with learning disabled and mentally retarded. *Psychology in the Schools*, *21*, 417–424.

O'Grady, K. E. (1983). A confirmatory maximum likelihood factor analysis of the WAIS-R. *Journal of Consulting and Clinical Psychology*, *51*, 826–831.

Olive, H. (1972). Psychoanalysts' opinions of psychologists' reports: 1952 and 1970. *Journal of Clinical Psychology*, *28*, 50–54.

Olivier, K., & Barclay, A. G. (1967). Stanford-Binet and Goodenough-Harris Test performances of Head Start children. *Psychological Reports*, *20*, 1175–1179.

Ollendick, D. G., Murphy, M. J., & Ollendick, T. H. (1975). Peabody Individual Achievement Test: Concurrent validity with juvenile delinquents. *Psychological Reports*, *37*, 935–938.

Ollendick, T. H., Finch, A. J., Jr., & Ginn, F. W. (1974). Comparison of Peabody, Leiter, WISC, and academic achievement scores among emotionally disturbed children. *Journal of Abnormal Child Psychology*, *2*, 47–51.

O'Neill, A. M. (1981). ". . . On the other foot." *Journal of School Psychology*, *19*, 71–72.

Orpet, R. E., Yoshida, R. K., & Meyers, C. E. (1976). The psychometric nature of Piaget's conservation of liquid for ages six and seven. *Journal of Genetic Psychology*, *129*, 151–160.

Osgood, C. E. (1957). Motivational dynamics of language behavior. In *Nebraska symposium on motivation* (Vol. 5, pp. 348–424). Lincoln: University of Nebraska Press.

Oud, J. H., & Sattler, J. M. (1984). Generalized kappa coefficient: A microsoft BASIC program. *Behavior Research Methods, Instruments, & Computers*, *16*, 481.

Overcast, T. D., Sales, B. D., & Kesler, J. A. (1983). Psychological evaluation of children at the request of noncustodial parents. *Psychotherapy in Private Practice*, *1*, 65–74.

Ownby, R. L., & Matthews, C. G. (1985). On the meaning of the

WISC-R third factor: Relations to selected neuropsychological measures. *Journal of Consulting and Clinical Psychology*, *53*, 531–534.

Ownby, R. L., & Wallbrown, F. H. (1983). Evaluating school psychological reports, Part I: A procedure for systematic feedback. *Psychology in the Schools*, *20*, 41–45.

Padula, W. V. (1979). A point of discrimination—Public Law 94-142. *Journal of Learning Disabilities*, *12*, 682–683.

Palmer, J. O. (1983). *The psychological assessment of children* (2nd ed.). New York: Wiley.

Palmer, M., & Gaffney, P. D. (1972). Effects of administration of the WISC in Spanish and English and relationship of social class to performance. *Psychology in the Schools*, *9*, 61–64.

Paramesh, C. R. (1982). Relationship between Quick Test and WISC-R and reading ability as used in a juvenile setting. *Perceptual and Motor Skills*, *55*, 881–882.

Paraskevopoulos, J., & Kirk, S. A. (1969). *The development and psychometric characteristics of the revised Illinois Test of Psycholinguistic Abilities*. Urbana: University of Illinois Press.

Parker, K. (1983). Factor analysis of the WAIS-R at nine age levels between 16 and 74 years. *Journal of Consulting and Clinical Psychology*, *51*, 302–308.

Parnes, S. (1966). *Workshop for creative problem solving institutes and courses*. Buffalo, NY: Creative Educational Foundation.

Pasewark, R. A., Rardin, M. W., & Grice, J. E., Jr. (1971). Relationship of the Wechsler Preschool and Primary Scale of Intelligence and the Stanford-Binet (L-M) in lower class children. *Journal of School Psychology*, *9*, 43–50.

Pasewark, R. A., Sawyer, R. N., Smith, E. A., Wasserberger, M., Dell, D., Brito, H., & Lee, R. (1967). Concurrent validity of the French Pictorial Test of Intelligence. *Journal of Educational Research*, *61*, 179–183.

Pasewark, R. A., Scherr, S. S., & Sawyer, R. N. (1974). Correlations of scores on the Vane Kindergarten, Wechsler Preschool and Primary Scale of Intelligence and Metropolitan Reading Readiness Tests. *Perceptual and Motor Skills*, *38*, 518.

Paul, S. M. (1985). The Advanced Raven's Progressive Matrices: Normative data for an American university population and an examination of the relationship with Spearman's *g*. *Journal of Experimental Education*, *54*, 95–100.

Pedersen, D. M., Shinedling, M. M., & Johnson, D. L. (1968). Effects of sex of examiner and subject on children's quantitative test performance. *Journal of Personality and Social Psychology*, *10*, 251–254.

Perry, N. W., Jr., McCoy, J. G., Cunningham, W. R., Falgout, J. C., & Street, W. J. (1976). Multivariate visual evoked response correlates of intelligence. *Psychophysiology*, *13*, 323–329.

Petersen, C. R., & Hart, D. H. (1979). Factor structure of the WISC-R for a clinic-referred population and specific subgroups. *Journal of Consulting and Clinical Psychology*, *47*, 643–645.

Peterson, J. (1925). *Early conceptions and tests of intelligence*. Yonkers-on-Hudson, NY: World Book.

Phares, E. J. (1984). *Clinical psychology: Concepts, methods, and profession* (rev. ed.). Homewood, IL: Dorsey Press.

Phelps, L., & Ensor, A. (1986). Concurrent validity of the WISC-R using deaf norms and the Hiskey-Nebraska. *Psychology in the Schools*, *23*, 138–141.

Phelps, L., Rosso, M., & Falasco, S. L. (1985). Multiple regression data using the WISC-R and the Woodcock-Johnson tests of cognitive ability. *Psychology in the Schools*, *22*, 46–49.

Piersel, W. C., Brody, G., & Kratochwill, T. R. (1977). A further examination of motivational influences on disadvantaged minority group children's intelligence test performance. *Child Development*, *48*, 1142–1145.

Piersel, W. C., & McAndrews, T. (1982). Concept acquisition and school progress: An examination of the Boehm Test of Basic Concepts. *Psychological Reports*, *50*, 783–786.

Piersel, W. C., & Reynolds, C. R. (1981). Factorial validity of item classification on the Boehm Test of Basic Concepts (BTBC), Forms A and B. *Educational and Psychological Measurement*, *41*, 579–583.

Plant, W. T. (1967). Cited by D. Wechsler, *Manual for the Wechsler Preschool and Primary Scale of Intelligence* (p. 34). San Antonio: The Psychological Corporation.

Plant, W. T., & Southern, M. L. (1968). First grade reading achievement predicted from WPPSI and other scores obtained 18 months earlier. *Proceedings of the 76th Annual Convention of the American Psychological Association*, *3*, 593–594.

Plomin, R., & DeFries, J. C. (1980). Genetics and intelligence: Recent data. *Intelligence*, *4*, 15–24.

Plumb, G. R., & Charles, D. C. (1955). Scoring difficulty of Wechsler Comprehension responses. *Journal of Educational Psychology*, *46*, 179–183.

Polubinski, J., Melamed, L. E., & Prinzo, O. V. (1986). Factor structure evidence for developmental levels of perceptual processing on the Developmental Test of Visual-Motor Integration. *Psychology in the Schools*, *23*, 337–341.

Pommer, L. T. (1986). Seriously emotionally disturbed children's performance on the Kaufman Assessment Battery for Children: A concurrent validity study. *Journal of Psychoeducational Assessment*, *4*, 155–162.

Popoff-Walker, L. E. (1982). IQ, SES, adaptive behavior, and performance on a learning potential measure. *Journal of School Psychology*, *20*, 222–231.

Popovich, D., & Laham, S. L. (Eds.). (1982). *The adaptive behavior curriculum: Prescriptive behavior analyses for moderately, severely, and profoundly handicapped students* (Vol. 1). Baltimore: Paul H. Brookes.

Portenier, L. G. (1942). Psychological factors in testing and training the cerebral palsied. *Physiotherapy Review*, *22*, 301–303.

Porter, G. L., & Binder, D. M. (1981). A pilot study of visual-motor development inter-test reliability: The Beery Developmental Test of Visual-Motor Integration and the Bender Visual

Motor Gesalt Test. *Journal of Learning Disabilities*, *14*, 124–127.

Porteus, S. D. (1959). *The Maze Test and clinical psychology*. Palo Alto, CA: Pacific Books.

Post, J. M. (1970). The effects of vocalization on the ability of third grade students to complete selected performance subtests from the Wechsler Intelligence Scale for Children. *Dissertation Abstracts International*, *31*, 1579-A. (University Microfilms No. 70–19,602)

Poteet, J. A. (1980). Informal assessment of written expression. *Learning Disability Quarterly*, *3*(4), 88–98.

Prasse, D. P., & Bracken, B. A. (1981). Comparison of the PPVT-R and WISC-R with urban educable mentally retarded students. *Psychology in the Schools*, *18*, 174–177.

Price, T. L. (1976). Sioux children's Koppitz scores on the Bender-Gestalt given by white or native American examiners. *Perceptual and Motor Skills*, *43*, 1223–1226.

Price-Williams, D. R., & Ramirez, M., III. (1977). Divergent thinking, cultural differences, and bilingualism. *Journal of Social Psychology*, *103*, 3–11.

Prichard, C. L., Tekieli, M. E., & Kozup, J. M. (1979). Developmental apraxia: Diagnostic considerations. *Journal of Communication Disorders*, *12*, 337–348.

Prifitera, A., & Ryan, J. J. (1983). WAIS-R/WAIS comparisons in a clinical sample. *Clinical Neuropsychology*, *5*, 97–99.

Prizant, B. M., & Duchan, J. F. (1981). The functions of immediate echolalia in autistic children. *Journal of Speech and Hearing Disorders*, *46*, 241–249.

Proger, B. B. (1973). Review of the Balthazar Scales of Adaptive Behavior. *Journal of Special Education*, *7*, 95–101.

Prosser, N. S., & Crawford, V. B. (1971). Relationship of scores on the Wechsler Preschool and Primary Scale of Intelligence and the Stanford-Binet Intelligence Scale Form LM. *Journal of School Psychology*, *9*, 278–283.

The Psychological Corporation. (1983). *Basic Achievement Skills Individual Screener*. San Antonio: Author.

Puig-Antich, J., & Chambers, W. J. (1983). *Schedule for Affective Disorders and Schizophrenia for School-Aged Children*. Unpublished interview schedule, Western Psychiatric Institute and Clinic, Pittsburgh.

Purvis, M. A., & Bolen, L. M. (1984). Factor structure of the McCarthy Scales for males and females. *Journal of Clinical Psychology*, *40*, 108–114.

Quay, H. C., & Peterson, D. R. (1983). *Revised Behavior Problem Checklist*. Coral Gables, FL: Author. (University of Miami)

Quay, H. C., & Peterson, D. R. (1987). *Manual for the Revised Behavior Problem Checklist*. Coral Gables, FL: Author. (University of Miami)

Quay, L. C. (1971). Language dialect, reinforcement, and the intelligence-test performance of Negro children. *Child Development*, *42*, 5–15.

Quay, L. C. (1972). Negro dialect and Binet performance in severely disadvantaged black four-year-olds. *Child Development*, *43*, 245–250.

Quay, L. C. (1974). Language dialect, age, and intelligence-test performance in disadvantaged black children. *Child Development*, *45*, 463–468.

Quereshi, M. Y. (1968). Intelligence test scores as a function of sex of experimenter and sex of subject. *Journal of Psychology*, *69*, 277–284.

Quereshi, M. Y., & McIntire, D. H. (1984). The comparability of the WISC, WISC-R and WPPSI. *Journal of Clinical Psychology*, *40*, 1036–1043.

Rabourn, R. E. (1983). The Wechsler Adult Intelligence Scale (WAIS) and the WAIS–Revised: A comparison and a caution. *Professional Psychology: Research and Practice*, *14*, 357–361.

Ramanaiah, N. V., & Adams, M. L. (1979). Confirmatory factor analysis of the WAIS and the WPPSI. *Psychological Reports*, *45*, 351–355.

Ramanaiah, N. V., O'Donnell, J. P., & Adams, M. L. (1978). A test of the theoretical model of the Revised Illinois Test of Psycholinguistic Abilities. *Applied Psychological Measurement*, *2*, 519–525.

Ramey, C. T., Bryant, D. M., & Suarez, T. M. (1985). Preschool compensatory education and the modifiability of intelligence: A critical review. In D. K. Detterman (Ed.), *Current topics in human intelligence (Vol. 1) — research methodology* (pp. 247–296). Norwood, NJ: Ablex Publishing Corporation.

Ramirez, D. N. (1978). *College of the Desert guide: Education of handicapped adults*. Palm Desert, CA: College of the Desert.

Rapaport, D., Gill, M. M., & Schafer, R. (1968). *Diagnostic psychological testing* (rev. ed.). New York: International Universities Press.

Rappaport, N. B., & McAnulty, D. P. (1985). The effect of accented speech on the scoring of ambiguous WISC-R responses by prejudiced and nonprejudiced raters. *Journal of Psychoeducational Assessment*, *3*, 275–283.

Rasbury, W. C., Falgout, J. C., & Perry, N. W., Jr. (1978). A Yudin-type short form of the WISC-R: Two aspects of validation. *Journal of Clinical Psychology*, *34*, 120–126.

Rasbury, W. C., McCoy, J. G., & Perry, N. W., Jr. (1977). Relations of scores on WPPSI and WISC-R at a one-year interval. *Perceptual and Motor Skills*, *44*, 695–698.

Ratcliffe, K. J., & Ratcliffe, M. W. (1979). The Leiter scales: A review of validity findings. *American Annals of the Deaf*, *124*, 38–44.

Ratusnik, D. L., & Koenigsknecht, R. A. (1976). Cross-cultural item analysis of the Columbia Mental Maturity Scale: Potential application by the language clinician. *Language, Speech, and Hearing Services in Schools*, *7*, 186–190.

Raven, J. C. (1938). *Progressive Matrices*. London: Lewis.

Raven, J. C. (1960). *Guide to using the Standard Progressive Matrices*. London: Lewis.

Raven, J. C. (1965). *The Coloured Progressive Matrices Test*. London: Lewis.

Raven, J. C., Court, J. H., & Raven, J. (1983). *Manual for Raven's Progressive Matrices and Vocabulary Scales (Section*

3) — *Standard Progressive Matrices (1983 edition)*. London: Lewis.

Raven, J. C., Court, J. H., & Raven, J. (1986). *Manual for Raven's Progressive Matrices and Vocabulary Scales (Section 2 — Coloured Progressive Matrices (1986 edition, with U.S. norms)*. London: Lewis.

Raven, J. C., & Summers, B. (1986). *Manual for Raven's Progressive Matrices and Vocabulary Scales — research supplement no. 3*. London: Lewis.

Reed, M. (1970). Deaf and partially hearing children. In P. Mittler (Ed.), *The psychological assessment of mental and physical handicaps* (pp. 403–441). London: Methuen.

Reed, M. (1985). Books for parents and children on learning disabilities. *Journal of Clinical Child Psychology*, *14*, 257–263.

Reeve, R. R., French, J. L., & Hunter, M. (1983). A validation of the Leiter International Performance Scale with kindergarten children. *Journal of Consulting and Clinical Psychology*, *51*, 458–459.

Reid, J. B. (1978). *A social learning approach to family intervention: Observations in the home setting* (Vol. 2). Eugene, OR: Castalia Publishing.

Reid, W. B., Moore, D., & Alexander, D. (1968). Abbreviated form of the WISC for use with brain-damaged and mentally retarded children. *Journal of Consulting and Clinical Psychology*, *32*, 236.

Reilly, T. P., Drudge, O. W., Rosen, J. C., Loew, D. E., & Fischer, M. (1985). Concurrent and predictive validity of the WISC-R, McCarthy Scales, Woodcock-Johnson, and academic achievement. *Psychology in the Schools*, *22*, 380–382.

Reisman, F. K. (1985). *Sequential Assessment of Mathematics Inventories*. San Antonio: The Psychological Corporation.

Reisman, J. M. (1973). *Principles of psychotherapy with children*. New York: Wiley.

Reitan, R. M., & Davison, L. A. (Eds.). (1974). *Clinical neuropsychology: Current status and applications*. Washington, DC: V. H. Winston & Sons.

Reitan, R. M., & Herring, S. (1985). A short screening device for identification of cerebral dysfunction in children. *Journal of Clinical Psychology*, *41*, 643–650.

Reitan, R. M., & Wolfson, D. (1985). *The Halstead-Reitan Neuropsychological Test Battery*. Tucson: Neuropsychology Press.

Rellas, A. J. (1969). The use of the Wechsler Preschool and Primary Scale (WPPSI) in the early identification of gifted students. *California Journal of Educational Research*, *20*, 117–119.

Renzulli, J. S., Smith, L. H., White, A. J., Callahan, C. M., & Hartman, R. K. (1976). *Scales for Rating the Behavioral Characteristics of Superior Students*. Wethersfield, CT: Creative Learning Press.

Repp, A. C., & Barton, L. E. (1980). Naturalistic observations of institutionalized retarded persons: A comparison of licensure decisions and behavioral observations. *Journal of Applied Behavior Analysis*, *13*, 333–341.

Reschly, D. J. (1978). WISC-R factor structures among Anglos, blacks, Chicanos, and native-American Papagos. *Journal of Consulting and Clinical Psychology*, *46*, 417–422.

Reschly, D. J., & Reschly, J. E. (1979). Validity of WISC-R factor scores in predicting achievement and attention for four sociocultural groups. *Journal of School Psychology*, *17*, 355–361.

Reschly, D. J., & Sabers, D. L. (1979). Analysis of test bias in four groups with the regression definition. *Journal of Educational Measurement*, *16*, 1–9.

Resnick, L. B. (1979). The future of IQ testing in education. *Intelligence*, *3*, 241–253.

Retzlaff, P., Slicner, N., & Gibertini, M. (1986). Predicting WAIS-R scores from the Shipley Institute of Living Scale in a homogeneous sample. *Journal of Clinical Psychology*, *42*, 357–359.

Reynolds, C. R. (1979). Factor structure of the Peabody Individual Achievement Test at five grade levels between grades one and 12. *Journal of School Psychology*, *17*, 270–274.

Reynolds, C. R. (1984). Critical measurement issues in learning disabilities. *Journal of Special Education*, *18*, 451–476.

Reynolds, C. R. (1985a). Evaluating subscale performance on the Adaptive Behavior Inventory for Children. *Psychology in the Schools*, *22*, 14–18.

Reynolds, C. R. (1985b). Standard score tables for the McCarthy Drawing Tests. *Psychology in the Schools*, *22*, 117–121.

Reynolds, C. R., & Gutkin, T. B. (1980a). A regression analysis of test bias on the WISC-R for Anglos and Chicanos referred for psychological services. *Journal of Abnormal Child Psychology*, *8*, 237–243.

Reynolds, C. R., & Gutkin, T. B. (1980b). Stability of the WISC-R factor structure across sex at two age levels. *Journal of Clinical Psychology*, *36*, 775–777.

Reynolds, C. R., & Gutkin, T. B. (1981). A multivariate comparison of the intellectual performance of black and white children matched on four demographic variables. *Personality and Individual Differences*, *2*, 175–180.

Reynolds, C. R., & Hartlage, L. (1979). Comparison of WISC and WISC-R regression lines for academic prediction with black and with white referred children. *Journal of Consulting and Clinical Psychology*, *47*, 589–591.

Reynolds, C. R., & Nigl, A. J. (1981). A regression analysis of differential validity in intellectual assessment for black and for white inner city children. *Journal of Clinical Child Psychology*, *10*, 176–179.

Reynolds, C. R., & Piersel, W. C. (1983). Multiple aspects of bias on the Boehm Test of Basic Concepts (Forms A & B) for white and for Mexican-American children. *Journal of Psychoeducational Assessment*, *1*, 135–142.

Reynolds, C. R., Willson, V. L., & Chatman, S. P. (1984). Item bias on the 1981 revision of the Peabody Picture Vocabulary Test using a new method of detecting bias. *Journal of Psychoeducational Assessment*, *2*, 219–224.

Reynolds, C. R., Willson, V. L., & Clark, P. L. (1983). A four-test short form of the WAIS-R for clinical screening. *Clinical Neuropsychology*, *5*, 111–116.

Reynolds, C. R., Wright, D., & Dappen, L. (1981). A comparison of the criterion-related validity (academic achievement) of the WPPSI and the WISC-R. *Psychology in the Schools*, *18*, 20–23.

Reynolds, W. M. (1987). *Auditory Discrimination Test* (2nd ed.). Los Angeles: Western Psychological Services.

Rhodes, L. E., Dustman, R. E., & Beck, E. C. (1969). The visual evoked response: A comparison of bright and dull children. *Electroencephalography and Clinical Neurophysiology*, *27*, 364–372.

Rice, J. A. (1972, September). *Benton's Visual Retention Test: New age, scale scores, and percentile norms for children*. Paper presented at the meeting of the American Psychological Association, Honolulu.

Richards, H. C., Fowler, P. C., Berent, S., & Boll, T. J. (1980). Comparison of WISC-R factor patterns for younger and older epileptic children. *Journal of Clinical Neuropsychology*, *2*, 333–341.

Richards, J. T. (1968). The effectiveness of the Wechsler Preschool and Primary Scale of Intelligence in the identification of mentally retarded children. *Dissertation Abstracts*, *29*, 3880-A. (University Microfilms No. 60–4019)

Richards, J. T. (1970). Internal consistency of the WPPSI with the mentally retarded. *American Journal of Mental Deficiency*, *74*, 581–582.

Richman, L. C., & Kitchell, M. M. (1981). Hyperlexia as a variant of developmental language disorder. *Brain and Language*, *12*, 203–212.

Ricklefs, R. (1986, October 21). Faced with shortages of unskilled labor, employers hire more retarded workers. *Wall Street Journal*, p. 39.

Rie, H. E., Rie, E. D., Stewart, S., & Ambuel, J. P. (1976). Effects of methylphenidate on underachieving children. *Journal of Consulting and Clinical Psychology*, *44*, 250–260.

Riessman, F. (1976). *The inner-city child*. New York: Harper & Row.

Rimoldi, H. J. (1948). A note on Raven's Progressive Matrices Test. *Educational and Psychological Measurement*, *8*, 347–352.

Riscalla, L. M. (1971, September). The captive psychologist and the captive patient: The dilemma and alternatives. In S. L. Brodsky (Chair), *Shared results and open files with the client: Professional irresponsibility or effective involvement?* Symposium presented at the meeting of the American Psychological Association, Washington, DC.

Ritter, D., Duffey, J., & Fischman, R. (1974). Comparability of Columbia Mental Maturity Scale and Stanford-Binet, Form L-M, estimates of intelligence. *Psychological Reports*, *34*, 174.

Roach, E. G., & Kephart, N. C. (1966). *The Purdue Perceptual-Motor Survey*. San Antonio: The Psychological Corporation.

Robb, G. P., Bernardoni, L. C., & Johnson, R. W. (1972).

Assessment of individual mental ability. Scranton, PA: Intext Educational.

Roberts, M. A., Milich, R., & Loney, J. (1984). *Structured Observation of Academic and Play Settings (SOAPS)*. Unpublished manuscript, University of Iowa, Iowa City.

Roberts, M. C. (1986). *Pediatric psychology: Psychological interventions and strategies for pediatric problems*. New York: Pergamon.

Robinson, H. B. (1980, November). *A case for radical acceleration: Programs of the Johns Hopkins University and the University of Washington*. Paper presented at the meeting of the 1980 Symposium of the Study of Mathematically Precocious Youth, Baltimore.

Robinson, H. B. (1981). The uncommonly bright child. In M. Lewis & L. A. Rosenblum (Eds.), *The uncommon child: Genesis of behavior* (Vol. 3, pp. 57–81). New York: Plenum Press.

Robinson, N., & Harris, S. R. (1980). *Tricks of the trade: Testing infants and preschoolers*. Unpublished manuscript, University of Washington, Child Development and Mental Retardation Center.

Roe, A. (1953). *The making of a scientist*. New York: Dodd, Mead.

Roedell, W. C. (1980a). Characteristics of gifted young children. In W. C. Roedell, N. E. Jackson, & H. B. Robinson (Eds.), *Gifted young children* (pp. 7–26). New York: Teachers College Press.

Roedell, W. C. (1980b). Programs for gifted young children. In W. C. Roedell, N. E. Jackson, & H. B. Robinson (Eds.), *Gifted young children* (pp. 66–89). New York: Teachers College Press.

Rogers, D. L., & Osborne, D. (1984). Comparison of the WAIS and WAIS-R at different ages in a clinical population. *Psychological Reports*, *54*, 951–956.

Rogers, S. J. (1977). Characteristics of the cognitive development of profoundly retarded children. *Child Development*, *48*, 837–843.

Rosenthal, R. (1966). *Experimenter effects in behavioral research*. New York: Appleton-Century-Crofts.

Rosenthal, R., & Jacobson, L. (1968). *Pygmalion in the classroom*. New York: Holt, Rinehart and Winston.

Ross, R. T. (1972). Behavioral correlates of levels of intelligence. *American Journal of Mental Deficiency*, *76*, 545–549.

Rossman, B. B., & Horn, J. L. (1972). Cognitive, motivational and temperamental indicants of creativity and intelligence. *Journal of Educational Measurement*, *9*, 265–286.

Rosso, M., Falasco, S. L., & Koller, J. R. (1984). Investigations into the relationship of the PPVT-R and the WISC-R with incarcerated delinquents. *Journal of Clinical Psychology*, *40*, 588–591.

Roszkowski, M. J. (1980). Concurrent validity of the Adaptive Behavior Scale as assessed by the Vineland Social Maturity Scale. *American Journal of Mental Deficiency*, *85*, 86–89.

Roszkowski, M. J., & Bean, A. G. (1980). The Adaptive Behavior Scale (ABS) and IQ: How much unshared variance is there? *Psychology in the Schools, 17,* 452–459.

Roszkowski, M. J., Snelbecker, G. E., & Sacks, R. (1981). Children's, adolescents', and adults' reports of hand preference: Homogeneity and discriminating power of selected tasks. *Journal of Clinical Neuropsychology, 3,* 199–213.

Roth, D. L., Hughes, C. W., Monkowski, P. G., & Crosson, B. (1984). Investigation of validity of WAIS-R short forms for patients suspected to have brain impairment. *Journal of Consulting and Clinical Psychology, 52,* 722–723.

Rothlisberg, B. A. (1987). Comparing the Stanford-Binet: Fourth Edition to the WISC-R: A concurrent validity study. *Journal of School Psychology, 25,* 193–196.

Rothman, C. (1974). Differential vulnerability of WISC subtests to tester effects. *Psychology in the Schools, 11,* 300–302.

Rubin, H. H., Goldman, J. J., & Rosenfeld, J. G. (1985). A comparison of WISC-R and WAIS-R IQs in a mentally retarded residential population. *Psychology in the Schools, 22,* 392–397.

Ruchalla, E., Schalt, E., & Vogel, F. (1985). Relations between mental performance and reaction time: New aspects of an old problem. *Intelligence, 9,* 189–205.

Rucker, C. N. (1967a). Report writing in school psychology: A critical investigation. *Journal of School Psychology, 5,* 101–108.

Rucker, C. N. (1967b). Technical language in the school psychologist's report. *Psychology in the Schools, 4,* 146–150.

Rupley, W. H., & Blair, T. R. (1979). *Reading diagnosis and remediation: A primer for classroom and clinic.* Chicago: Rand McNally.

Ruschival, M. L., & Way, J. G. (1971). The WPPSI and the Stanford-Binet: A validity and reliability study using gifted preschool children. *Journal of Consulting and Clinical Psychology, 37,* 163.

Rust, J. O., & Lose, B. D. (1980). Screening for giftedness with the Slosson and the Scale for Rating Behavioral Characteristics of Superior Students. *Psychology in the Schools, 17,* 446–451.

Rutter, M. (1970). Autistic children: Infancy to adulthood. *Seminars in Psychiatry, 2,* 435–450.

Rutter, M. (1974). The development of infantile autism. *Psychological Medicine, 4,* 147–163.

Rutter, M. (1977). Infantile autism and other child psychoses. In M. Rutter & L. Hersov (Eds.), *Child psychiatry: Modern approaches* (pp. 717–747). Oxford: Blackwell Scientific.

Rutter, M. (1978). Diagnosis and definition. In M. Rutter & E. Schopler (Eds.), *Autism: A reappraisal of concepts and treatment* (pp. 139–161). New York: Plenum.

Rutter, M., & Bartak, L. (1971). Causes of infantile autism: Some considerations from recent research. *Journal of Autism and Childhood Schizophrenia, 1,* 20–32.

Rutter, M., & Bartak, L. (1973). Special educational treatment of autistic children: A comparative study: II. Follow-up findings and implications for services. *Journal of Child Psychology and Psychiatry and Allied Disciplines, 14,* 241–270.

Rutter, M., Greenfeld, D., & Lockyer, L. (1967). A five to fifteen year follow-up study of infantile psychosis: II. Social and behavioural outcome. *British Journal of Psychiatry, 113,* 1183–1199.

Rutter, M., & Lockyer, L. (1967). A five to fifteen year follow-up study of infantile psychosis: I. Description of sample. *British Journal of Psychiatry, 113,* 1169–1182.

Ryan, J. J. (1985). Application of a WAIS-R short form with neurological patients: Validity and correlational findings. *Journal of Psychoeducational Assessment, 3,* 61–64.

Ryan, J. J., Georgemiller, R. J., Geisser, M. E., & Randall, D. M. (1985). Test-retest stability of the WAIS-R in a clinical sample. *Journal of Clinical Psychology, 41,* 552–556.

Ryan, J. J., Larsen, J., & Prifitera, A. (1983). Validity of two- and four-subtest short forms of the WAIS-R in a psychiatric sample. *Journal of Consulting and Clinical Psychology, 51,* 460.

Ryan, J. J., Prifitera, A., & Larsen, J. (1982). Reliability of the WAIS-R with a mixed patient sample. *Perceptual and Motor Skills, 55,* 1277–1278.

Ryan, J. J., Prifitera, A., & Powers, L. (1983). Scoring reliability on the WAIS-R. *Journal of Consulting and Clinical Psychology, 51,* 149–150.

Ryan, J. J., Prifitera, A., & Rosenberg, S. J. (1983). Interrelationships between and factor structures of the WAIS-R and WAIS in a neuropsychological battery. *International Journal of Neuroscience, 21,* 191–196.

Ryan, J. J., & Rosenberg, S. J. (1983). Relationship between the WAIS-R and Wide Range Achievement Test in a sample of mixed patients. *Perceptual and Motor Skills, 56,* 623–626.

Ryan, J. J., Rosenberg, S. J., & DeWolfe, A. S. (1984). Generalization of the WAIS-R factor structure with a vocational rehabilitation sample. *Journal of Consulting and Clinical Psychology, 52,* 311–312.

Ryan, J. J., Rosenberg, S. J., & Heilbronner, R. L. (1984). Comparative relationships of the Wechsler Adult Intelligence Scale—Revised (WAIS-R) and the Wechsler Adult Intelligence Scale (WAIS) to the Wechsler Memory Scale (WMS). *Journal of Behavioral Assessment, 6,* 37–43.

Ryan, J. J., & Schneider, J. A. (1986). Factor analysis of the Wechsler Adult Intelligence Scale—Revised (WAIS-R) in a brain-damaged sample. *Journal of Clinical Psychology, 42,* 962–964.

Saccuzzo, D. P., & Lewandowski, D. G. (1976). The WISC as a diagnostic tool. *Journal of Clinical Psychology, 32,* 115–124.

Saigh, P. A. (1981a). The effects of positive examiner verbal comments on the total WISC-R performance of institutionalized EMR students. *Journal of School Psychology, 19,* 86–91.

Saigh, P. A. (1981b). The validity of the WISC-R examiner verbal praise procedure as a concurrent predictor of the academic achievement of intellectually superior students. *Journal of Clinical Psychology, 37,* 647–649.

Saigh, P. A., & Payne, D. A. (1976). The influence of examiner verbal comments on WISC performances of EMR students. *Journal of School Psychology, 14,* 342–345.

Salagaras, S., & Nettelbeck, T. (1983). Adaptive behavior of mentally retarded adolescents attending school. *American Journal of Mental Deficiency, 88*, 57–68.

Salend, S. J. (1983). Mainstreaming: Sharpening up follow-up. *Academic Therapy, 18*, 299–304.

Salend, S. J. (1984). Selecting and evaluating educational assessment instruments. *Pointer, 28*, 20–22.

Sameroff, A. J. (Ed.). (1978). Organization and stability of newborn behavior: A commentary on the Brazelton Neonatal Behavior Assessment Scale. *Monographs of the Society of Research in Child Development, 43*, (5–6, Serial No. 177).

Sameroff, A. J. (1979). The etiology of cognitive competence: A systems perspective. In R. B. Kearsley & I. E. Sigel (Eds.), *Infants at risk: Assessment of cognitive functioning* (pp. 115–152). Hillsdale, NJ: Lawrence Erlbaum.

Sandoval, J. (1979). The WISC-R and internal evidence of test bias with minority groups. *Journal of Consulting and Clinical Psychology, 47*, 919–927.

Sandoval, J., & Miille, M. P. W. (1980). Accuracy of judgments of WISC-R item difficulty for minority groups. *Journal of Consulting and Clinical Psychology, 48*, 249–253.

Sandoval, J., Zimmerman, I. L., & Woo-Sam, J. M. (1983). Cultural differences on WISC-R verbal items. *Journal of School Psychology, 21*, 49–55.

Sapp, G. L., Horton, W., McElroy, K., & Ray, P. (1979, April). An analysis of ABIC score patterns of selected Alabama school children. In *Proceedings of the National Association of School Psychologists/California Association of School Psychologists and Psychometrists*. San Diego.

Satterfield, J. H. (1973). EEG issues in children with minimal brain dysfunction. *Seminars in Psychiatry, 5*, 35–46.

Satterfield, J. H., Cantwell, D. P., & Satterfield, B. T. (1974). Pathophysiology of the hyperactive child syndrome. *Archives of General Psychiatry, 31*, 839–844.

Satterfield, J. H., Cantwell, D. P., Saul, R. E., & Yusin, A. (1974). Intelligence, academic achievement, and EEG abnormalities in hyperactive children. *American Journal of Psychiatry, 131*, 391–395.

Satterly, D. (1981). *Assessment in schools*. Oxford, England: Blackwell.

Sattler, J. M. (1966). Comments on Cieutat's "Examiner differences with the Stanford-Binet IQ." *Perceptual and Motor Skills, 22*, 612–614.

Sattler, J. M. (1969). Effects of cues and examiner influence on two Wechsler subtests. *Journal of Consulting and Clinical Psychology, 33*, 716–721.

Sattler, J. M. (1970). Racial "experimenter effects" in experimentation, testing, interviewing, and psychotherapy. *Psychological Bulletin, 73*, 137–160.

Sattler, J. M. (1973a). Examiners' scoring style, accuracy, ability, and personality scores. *Journal of Clinical Psychology, 29*, 38–39.

Sattler, J. M. (1973b). Racial experimenter effects. In K. S. Miller & R. M. Dreger (Eds.), *Comparative studies of blacks and whites in the United States* (pp. 8–32). New York: Seminar Press.

Sattler, J. M. (1976). Scoring difficulty of the WPPSI Geometric Design subtest. *Journal of School Psychology, 14*, 230–234.

Sattler, J. M. (1977). The effects of therapist-client racial similarity. In A. S. Gurman & A. M. Razin (Eds.), *Effective psychotherapy: A handbook of research* (pp. 252–290). Elmsford: NY: Pergamon Press.

Sattler, J. M. (1978). Review of McCarthy Scales of Children's Abilities. In O. K. Buros (Ed.), *The eighth mental measurements yearbook* (pp. 311–313). Highland Park, NJ: Gryphon Press.

Sattler, J. M. (1982a). Age effects on Wechsler Adult Intelligence Scale–Revised tests. *Journal of Consulting and Clinical Psychology, 50*, 785–786.

Sattler, J. M. (1982b). *Assessment of children's intelligence and special abilities* (2nd ed.). Boston: Allyn and Bacon.

Sattler, J. M. (1982c). The psychologist in court: Personal reflections of one expert witness in the case of *Larry P. et al.* v. *Wilson Riles, et al. School Psychology Review, 11*, 306–318.

Sattler, J. M., & Altes, L. M. (1984). Performance of bilingual and monolingual Hispanic children on the Peabody Picture Vocabulary Test–Revised and the McCarthy Perceptual Performance Scale. *Psychology in the Schools, 21*, 313–316.

Sattler, J. M., Andres, J. R., Squire, L. S., Wisely, R., & Maloy, C. F. (1978). Examiner scoring of ambiguous WISC-R responses. *Psychology in the Schools, 15*, 486–489.

Sattler, J. M., Avila, V., Houston, W. B., & Toney, D. H. (1980). Performance of bilingual Mexican American children on Spanish and English versions of the Peabody Picture Vocabulary Test. *Journal of Consulting and Clinical Psychology, 46*, 782–784.

Sattler, J. M., & Bowman, G. E. (1981). A comparison between the Koppitz and SOMPA norms for the Koppitz Developmental Bender-Gestalt Scoring System. *School Psychology Review, 10*, 396–397.

Sattler, J. M., & Gwynne, J. (1982a). Ethnicity and Bender Visual Motor Gestalt Test performance. *Journal of School Psychology, 20*, 69–71.

Sattler, J. M., & Gwynne, J. (1982b). White examiners generally do not impede the intelligence test performance of black children: To debunk a myth. *Journal of Consulting and Clinical Psychology, 50*, 196–208.

Sattler, J. M., Hillix, W. A., & Neher, L. A. (1970). Halo effect in examiner scoring of intelligence test responses. *Journal of Consulting and Clinical Psychology, 34*, 172–176.

Sattler, J. M., & Kuncik, T. M. (1976). Ethnicity, socioeconomic status, and pattern of WISC scores as variables that affect psychologists' estimates of "effective intelligence." *Journal of Clinical Psychology, 32*, 362–366.

Sattler, J. M., & Martin, S. (1971). Anxious and nonanxious examiner roles on two WISC subtests. *Psychology in the Schools, 8*, 347–349.

Sattler, J. M., Polifka, J. C., Polifka, S., & Hilsen, D. E. (1984).

A longitudinal study of the WISC-R and WAIS-R with special education students. *Psychology in the Schools*, *21*, 294–295.

Sattler, J. M., & Ryan, J. J. (1973a). Scoring agreement on the Stanford-Binet. *Journal of Clinical Psychology*, *29*, 35–38.

Sattler, J. M., & Ryan, J. J. (1973b). Who should determine the scoring of WISC Vocabulary responses? *Journal of Clinical Psychology*, *29*, 50–54.

Sattler, J. M., & Squire, L. S. (1982). Scoring difficulty of the McCarthy Scales of Children's Abilities. *School Psychology Review*, *11*, 83–88.

Sattler, J. M., Squire, L. S., & Andres, J. R. (1977). Scoring discrepancies between the WISC-R Manual and two scoring guides. *Journal of Clinical Psychology*, *33*, 1058–1059.

Sattler, J. M., & Theye, F. (1967). Procedural, situational, and interpersonal variables in individual intelligence testing. *Psychological Bulletin*, *68*, 347–360.

Sattler, J. M., & Winget, B. M. (1970). Intelligence testing procedures as affected by expectancy and IQ. *Journal of Clinical Psychology*, *26*, 446–448.

Sattler, J. M., Winget, B. M., & Roth, R. J. (1969). Scoring difficulty of WAIS and WISC Comprehension, Similarities, and Vocabulary responses. *Journal of Clinical Psychology*, *25*, 175–177.

Satz, P., & Bullard-Bates, C. (1981). Acquired aphasia in children. In M. T. Sarno (Ed.), *Acquired aphasia* (pp. 399–426). New York: Academic Press.

Satz, P., & Mogel, S. (1962). An abbreviation of the WAIS for clinical use. *Journal of Clinical Psychology*, *18*, 77–79.

Satz, P., Van de Riet, H., & Mogel, S. (1967). An abbreviation of the WISC for clinical use. *Journal of Consulting Psychology*, *31*, 108.

Saunders, B. T., & Vitro, F. T. (1971). Examiner expectancy and bias as a function of the referral process in cognitive assessment. *Psychology in the Schools*, *8*, 168–171.

Sawyer, R. N. (1968). An investigation of the reliability of the French Pictorial Test of Intelligence. *Journal of Educational Research*, *61*, 211–214.

Sawyer, R. N., Stanley, G. E., & Watson, T. E. (1979). A factor analytic study of the construct validity of the Pictorial Test of Intelligence. *Educational and Psychological Measurement*, *39*, 613–623.

Scarr, S. (1978). From evolution to Larry P., or what shall we do about IQ tests? *Intelligence*, *2*, 325–342.

Schachar, R., Sandberg, S., & Rutter, M. (1986). Agreement between teachers' ratings and observations of hyperactivity, inattentiveness, and defiance. *Journal of Abnormal Child Psychology*, *14*, 331–345.

Schachter, F. F., & Apgar, V. (1958). Comparison of preschool Stanford-Binet and school-age WISC IQs. *Journal of Educational Psychology*, *49*, 320–323.

Schiller, J. J., DeSimone, J. R., Gross, R., Hoey, J. A., McGuire, J. P., Smith, E. A., & Torres, P. A. (1982). A screening instrument for the assessment of dysnomia of children. *Clinical Neuropsychology*, *4*, 22–25.

Schmidtke, A., & Schaller, S. (1980). Comparative study of factor structure of Raven's Coloured Progressive Matrices. *Perceptual and Motor Skills*, *51*, 1244–1246.

Schmits, D. W., & Beckenbaugh, L. (1979, March). *A comparison of WPPSI and McCarthy scores in a preschool population*. Paper presented at the meeting of the National Association of School Psychologists/California Association of School Psychologists and Psychometrists, San Diego.

Schooler, D. L., Beebe, M. C., & Koepke, T. (1978). Factor analysis of WISC-R scores for children identified as learning disabled, educable mentally impaired, and emotionally impaired. *Psychology in the Schools*, *15*, 478–485.

Schopler, E., Reichler, R. J., DeVellis, R. F., & Daly, K. (1980). Toward objective classification of childhood autism: Childhood Autism Rating Scale (CARS). *Journal of Autism & Developmental Disorders*, *10*, 91–103.

Schopler, E., Reichler, R. J., & Renner, B. R. (1986). *The Childhood Autism Rating Scale (CARS)*. New York: Irvington.

Schroeder, H. E., & Kleinsasser, L. D. (1972). Examiner bias: A determinant of children's verbal behavior on the WISC. *Journal of Consulting and Clinical Psychology*, *39*, 451–454.

Schuler, A. L., & Goetz, L. (1981). The assessment of severe language disabilities: Communicative and cognitive considerations. *Analysis and Intervention in Developmental Disabilities*, *1*, 333–346.

Schwartz, M. L. (1966). The scoring of WAIS Comprehension responses by experienced and inexperienced judges. *Journal of Clinical Psychology*, *22*, 425–427.

Schwartz, M. L. (1987). Limitations on neuropsychological testimony by the Florida Appellate decisions: Action, reaction, and counteraction. *Clinical Neuropsychologist*, *1*, 51–60.

Schwartz, R. H., & Flanigan, P. J. (1971). Evaluation of examiner bias in intelligence testing. *American Journal of Mental Deficiency*, *76*, 262–265.

Schwebel, A. I., & Bernstein, A. J. (1970). The effects of impulsivity on the performance of lower-class children on four WISC subtests. *American Journal of Orthopsychiatry*, *40*, 629–636.

Scott, L. H. (1981). Measuring intelligence with the Goodenough-Harris Drawing Test. *Psychological Bulletin*, *89*, 483–505.

Scott, L. S., Mastenbrook, J. L., & Fisher, A. T. (1982). Adaptive behavior inventory for children: The need for local norms. *Journal of School Psychology*, *20*, 39–44.

Scottish Council for Research in Education. (1967). *The Scottish standardization of the Wechsler Intelligence Scale for Children*. London: University of London Press.

Searls, E. F. (1975). *How to use WISC scores in reading diagnosis*. Newark, DE: International Reading Association.

Seashore, H. G., Wesman, A. G., & Doppelt, J. E. (1950). The standardization of the Wechsler Intelligence Scale for Children. *Journal of Consulting Psychology*, *14*, 99–110.

Sedlak, R. A., & Weener, P. (1973). Review of research on the Illinois Test of Psycholinguistic Abilities. In L. Mann & D. A. Sabatino (Eds.), *The first review of special education* (Vol. 1, pp. 113–164). Philadelphia: JSE Press.

Seidenberg, M., Giordani, B., Berent, S., & Boll, T. J. (1983). IQ level and performance on the Halstead-Reitan Neuropsychological Test Battery for Older Children. *Journal of Consulting and Clinical Psychology*, *51*, 406–413.

Seidman, E., Linney, J. A., Rappaport, J., Herzberger, S., Kramer, J., & Alden, L. (1979). Assessment of classroom behavior: A multiattribute, multisource approach to instrument development and validation. *Journal of Educational Psychology*, *71*, 451–464.

Selig, A. L., & Berdie, J. (1981). Assessing families with a developmentally delayed/handicapped child. *Journal of Development and Behavioral Pediatrics*, *2*, 151–154.

Selz, M. (1981). Halstead-Reitan Neuropsychological Test Battery for Children. In G. W. Hynd & J. E. Obrzut (Eds.), *Neuropsychological assessment and the school-age child: Issues and procedures* (pp. 195–235). New York: Grune & Stratton.

Selz, M., & Reitan, R. M. (1979). Neuropsychological test performance of normal, learning-disabled, and brain damaged older children. *Journal of Nervous and Mental Disease*, *167*, 298–302.

Semler, I. J., & Iscoe, I. (1966). Structure of intelligence in Negro and white children. *Journal of Educational Psychology*, *57*, 326–336.

Sergent, J. (1984). Inferences from unilateral brain damage about normal hemispheric functions in visual pattern recognition. *Psychological Bulletin*, *96*, 99–115.

Sewell, T. E. (1977). A comparison of the WPPSI and Stanford-Binet Intelligence Scale (1972) among lower SES black children. *Psychology in the Schools*, *14*, 158–161.

Sewell, T. E. (1979). Intelligence and learning tasks as predictors of scholastic achievement in black and white first-grade children. *Journal of School Psychology*, *17*, 325–332.

Sewell, T. E., & Severson, R. A. (1974). Learning ability and intelligence as cognitive predictors of achievement in first-grade black children. *Journal of Educational Psychology*, *66*, 948–955.

Sewell, T. E., & Severson, R. A. (1975). Intelligence and achievement in first-grade black children. *Journal of Consulting and Clinical Psychology*, *43*, 112.

Shaheen, S. J. (1984). Neuromaturation and behavior development: The case of childhood lead poisoning. *Developmental Psychology*, *20*, 542–550.

Sharp, H. C. (1958). A note on the reliability of the Leiter International Performance Scale 1948 Revision. *Journal of Consulting Psychology*, *22*, 320.

Sharp, S. E. (1898). Individual psychology: A study in psychological method. *American Journal of Psychology*, *10*, 329–391.

Sherman, M., Chinsky, J. M., & Maffeo, P. (1974). Wechsler Preschool and Primary Scale of Intelligence Animal House as a measure of learning and motor abilities. *Journal of Consulting and Clinical Psychology*, *42*, 470.

Shiek, D. A., & Miller, J. E. (1978). Validity generalization of the WISC-R factor structure with 10½-year-old children. *Journal of Consulting and Clinical Psychology*, *46*, 583.

Shively, J. J., & Smith, A. E. (1969). Understanding the psychological report. *Psychology in the Schools*, *6*, 272–273.

Shontz, F. C. (1977). Six principles relating disability and psychological adjustment. *Rehabilitation Psychology*, *24*, 207–210.

Shouksmith, G. (1970). *Intelligence, creativity and cognitive style*. New York: Wiley.

Siegel, L. S. (1979). Infant perceptual, cognitive, and motor behaviours as predictors of subsequent cognitive and language development. *Canadian Journal of Psychology*, *33*, 382–395.

Siegel, L. S. (1983). Correction for prematurity and its consequences for the assessment of the very low birth weight infant. *Child Development*, *54*, 1176–1188.

Siegel, L. S., & Linder, B. A. (1984). Short-term memory processes in children with reading and arithmetic learning disabilities. *Developmental Psychology*, *20*, 200–207.

Siegler, R. S., & Richards, D. D. (1982). The development of intelligence. In R. J. Sternberg (Ed.), *Handbook of human intelligence* (pp. 897–971). Cambridge, England: Cambridge University Press.

Silvaroli, N. J. (1986). *Classroom Reading Inventory* (5th ed.). Dubuque, IA: Wm. C. Brown.

Silverman, M. (1979). Beyond the mainstream: The special needs of the chronic child patient. *American Journal of Orthopsychiatry*, *49*, 62–68.

Silverstein, A. B. (1968a). Validity of a new approach to the design of WAIS, WISC, and WPPSI short forms. *Journal of Consulting and Clinical Psychology*, *32*, 478–479.

Silverstein, A. B. (1968b). WISC and WPPSI IQs for the gifted. *Psychological Reports*, *22*, 1168.

Silverstein, A. B. (1968c). WPPSI IQs for the mentally retarded. *American Journal of Mental Deficiency*, *73*, 446.

Silverstein, A. B. (1970). Reappraisal of the validity of the WAIS, WISC, and WPPSI short forms. *Journal of Consulting and Clinical Psychology*, *34*, 12–14.

Silverstein, A. B. (1972). Review of the Balthazar Scales of Adaptive Behavior. *American Journal of Mental Deficiency*, *77*, 361.

Silverstein, A. B. (1973). Note on prevalence. *American Journal of Mental Deficiency*, *77*, 380–382.

Silverstein, A. B. (1978). Note on the construct validity of the ITPA. *Psychology in the Schools*, *15*, 371–372.

Silverstein, A. B. (1981). Pattern analysis on the PIAT. *Psychology in the Schools*, *18*, 13–14.

Silverstein, A. B. (1982a). Factor structure of the Wechsler Adult Intelligence Scale—Revised. *Journal of Consulting and Clinical Psychology*, *50*, 661–664.

Silverstein, A. B. (1982b). Note on the constancy of the IQ. *American Journal of Mental Deficiency*, *87*, 227–228.

Silverstein, A. B. (1982c). Pattern analysis as simultaneous statistical inference. *Journal of Consulting and Clinical Psychology*, *50*, 234–240.

Silverstein, A. B. (1982d). Validity of Satz-Mogel-Yudin-type short forms. *Journal of Consulting and Clinical Psychology*, *50*, 20–21.

Silverstein, A. B. (1984). Pattern analysis: The question of abnormality. *Journal of Consulting and Clinical Psychology*, *52*, 936–939.

Silverstein, A. B. (1985a). A formula for the standard error of estimate of deviation quotients on short forms of Wechsler's Scales. *Journal of Clinical Psychology*, *41*, 408–409.

Silverstein, A. B. (1985b). Two- and four-subtest short forms of the WAIS-R: A closer look at validity and reliability. *Journal of Clinical Psychology*, *41*, 95–97.

Silverstein, A. B. (1986a). Cluster analysis of the Wechsler Preschool and Primary Scale of Intelligence. *Journal of Psychoeducational Assessment*, *4*, 83–86.

Silverstein, A. B. (1986b). Nonstandard standard scores on the Vineland Adaptive Behavior Scales: A cautionary note. *American Journal of Mental Deficiency*, *91*, 1–4.

Silverstein, A. B. (1986c). Organization and structure of the Detroit Tests of Learning Aptitude (DTLA-2). *Educational and Psychological Measurement*, *46*, 1061–1066.

Simmons, J. E. (1987). *Psychiatric examination of children* (4th ed.). Philadelphia: Lea and Febiger.

Simon, C. L., & Clopton, J. R. (1984). Comparison of WAIS and WAIS-R scores of mildly and moderately mentally retarded adults. *American Journal of Mental Deficiency*, *89*, 301–303.

Simon, W. E. (1969). Expectancy effects in the scoring of vocabulary items: A study of scorer bias. *Journal of Educational Measurement*, *6*, 159–164.

Simpson, R. G., & Eaves, R. C. (1983). The concurrent validity of the Woodcock Reading Mastery Tests relative to the Peabody Individual Achievement Test among retarded adolescents. *Educational & Psychological Measurement*, *43*, 275–281.

Sisco, F. H., & Anderson, R. J. (1978). Current findings regarding the performance of deaf children on the WISC-R. *American Annals of the Deaf*, *123*, 115–121.

Sitkei, E. G., & Meyers, C. E. (1969). Comparative structure of intellect in middle- and lower-class four-year-olds of two ethnic groups. *Developmental Psychology*, *1*, 592–604.

Sitlington, P. L. (1970). *Validity of the Peabody Individual Achievement Test with educable mentally retarded adolescents*. Unpublished master's thesis, University of Hawaii.

Skeen, J. A., Strong, V. N., & Book, R. M. (1982). Comparison of learning disabled children's performance on Bender Visual-Motor Gestalt Test and Beery's Developmental Test of Visual-Motor Integration. *Perceptual and Motor Skills*, *55*, 1257–1258.

Sloan, W., & Birch, J. W. (1955). A rationale for degrees of retardation. *American Journal of Mental Deficiency*, *60*, 258–264.

Slosson, R. L. (1983). *Slosson Intelligence Test (SIT) and Oral Reading Test (SORT) for children and adults*. East Aurora, NY: Slosson Educational Publications.

Small, L. (1980). *Neuropsychodiagnosis in psychotherapy* (rev. ed.). NY: Brunner/Mazel.

Small, L. (1982). *The minimal brain dysfunctions: Diagnosis and treatment*. New York: Free Press.

Smith, A. L., & Brewer, L. M. (1983). Linguistic analysis of the Wepman Auditory Discrimination Test and the appropriateness of its use with black-English speaking children. *Learning Disability Quarterly*, *6*, 513–516.

Smith, H. W., & May, W. T. (1967). Individual differences among inexperienced psychological examiners. *Psychological Reports*, *20*, 759–762.

Smith, H. W., May, W. T., & Lebovitz, L. (1966). Testing experience and Stanford-Binet scores. *Journal of Educational Measurement*, *3*, 229–233.

Smith, M. L. (1980). Meta-analysis of research on teacher expectations. *Evaluation in Education*, *4*, 53–55.

Smith, R. S. (1983). A comparison study of the Wechsler Adult Intelligence Scale and the Wechsler Adult Intelligence Scale—Revised in a college population. *Journal of Consulting and Clinical Psychology*, *51*, 414–419.

Smith, T. C., & Smith, B. L. (1986). The relationship between the WISC-R and WRAT-R for a sample of rural referred children. *Psychology in the Schools*, *23*, 252–254.

Smyth, R., & Reznikoff, M. (1971). Attitudes of psychiatrists toward the usefulness of psychodiagnostic reports. *Professional Psychology*, *2*, 283–288.

Sneed, G. A. (1976). An investigation of examiner bias, teacher referral reports, and socioeconomic status with the WISC-R. *Dissertation Abstracts International*, *36*, 4367A. (University Microfilms No. 75-29,943)

Snow, J. H., Cohen, M., & Holliman, W. B. (1985). Learning disability subgroups using cluster analysis of the WISC-R. *Journal of Psychoeducational Assessment*, *3*, 391–397.

Snow, R. E. (1969). Unfinished Pygmalion [Review of *Pygmalion in the classroom*]. *Contemporary Psychology*, *14*, 197–199.

Snow, R. E. (1978). Theory and method for research on aptitude processes. *Intelligence*, *2*, 225–278.

Snyder, P. P., Snyder, R. T., & Massong, S. F. (1981). The Visual-Motor Integration Test: High interjudge reliability, high potential for diagnostic error. *Psychology in the Schools*, *18*, 55–59.

Snyderman, M., & Rothman, S. (1987). Survey of expert opinion on intelligence and aptitude testing. *American Psychologist*, *42*, 137–144.

Soethe, J. W. (1972). Concurrent validity of the Peabody Individual Achievement Test. *Journal of Learning Disabilities*, *5*, 560–562.

Somerton, M. E., & Myers, D. G. (1976). Educational programming for the severely and profoundly mentally retarded. In N. G. Haring & L. J. Brown (Eds.), *Teaching the severely handicapped* (Vol. 1, pp. 111–154). New York: Grune & Stratton.

Song, A., Jones, S., Lippert, J., Metzgen, K., Miller, J., & Borreca, C. (1984). Wisconsin Behavior Rating Scale: Measure of adaptive behavior for the developmental levels of 0 to 3 years. *American Journal of Mental Deficiency, 88,* 401–410.

Sparrow, S. S., Balla, D. A., & Cicchetti, D. V. (1984). *Vineland Adaptive Behavior Scales.* Circle Pines, MN: American Guidance Service.

Spearman, C. E. (1923). *The nature of intelligence and the principles of cognition.* London: Macmillan.

Spearman, C. E. (1927). *The abilities of man.* New York: Macmillan.

Spector, C. C. (1979). The Boehm Test of Basic Concepts: Exploring the test results for cognitive deficits. *Journal of Learning Disabilities, 12,* 564–567.

Spellacy, F., & Black, F. W. (1972). Intelligence assessment of language-impaired children by means of two nonverbal tests. *Journal of Clinical Psychology, 28,* 357–358.

Spence, A. G., Mishra, S. P., & Ghozeil, S. (1971). Home language and performance on standardized tests. *Elementary School Journal, 71,* 309–313.

Spiel, W. (1981). Some critical comments on a systematic approach to diagnosis: Contribution to a documentation and classification system in child neuropsychiatry. *Acta Paedopsychiatrica, 47,* 269–278.

Spirito, A. (1980). Scores on Bender-Gestalt and Developmental Test of Visual-Motor Integration of learning-disabled children. *Perceptual and Motor Skills, 50,* 1214.

Spivack, G., Haimes, P. E., & Spotts, J. (1967). *Devereux Adolescent Behavior Rating Scale Manual.* Devon, PA: Devereux Foundation.

Spivack, G., Spotts, J. (1966). *Devereux Child Behavior Rating Scale Manual.* Devon, PA: Devereux Foundation.

Spivack, G., & Swift, M. (1967). *Devereux Elementary School Behavior Rating Scale Manual.* Devon, PA: Devereux Foundation.

Spreat, S. (1980). The Adaptive Behavior Scale: A study of criterion validity. *American Journal of Mental Deficiency, 85,* 61–68.

Spreen, O., & Risser, A. (1981). Assessment of aphasia. In M. T. Sarno (Ed.), *Acquired aphasia* (pp. 67–127). New York: Academic Press.

Spruill, J., & Beck, B. (1986). Relationship between the WRAT and WRAT-R. *Psychology in the Schools, 23,* 357–360.

Stack, J. G. (1984). Interrater reliabilities of the adaptive behavior scale with environmental effects controlled. *American Journal of Mental Deficiency, 88,* 396–400.

Stambrook, M. (1983). The Luria-Nebraska Neuropsychological Battery: A promise that may be partly fulfilled. *Journal of Clinical Neuropsychology, 5,* 247–269.

Stankov, L. (1983). Attention and intelligence. *Journal of Educational Psychology, 75,* 471–490.

Stanley, B., & Howe, J. G. (1983). Identification of multiple sclerosis using double discrimination scales derived from the Luria-Nebraska Neuropsychological Battery: An attempt at cross-validation. *Journal of Consulting and Clinical Psychology, 51,* 420–423.

Stanovich, K. E. (1978). Information processing in mentally retarded individuals. *International Review of Research in Mental Retardation, 9,* 29–60.

Stanovich, K. E. (1985). Cognitive determinants of reading in mentally retarded individuals. *International Review of Research in Mental Retardation, 13,* 181–214.

Stanovich, K. E., Cunningham, A. E., & Cramer, B. B. (1984). Assessing phonological awareness in kindergarten children: Issues of task comparability. *Journal of Experimental Child Psychology, 38,* 175–190.

Stanovich, K. E., Cunningham, A. E., & Feeman, D. J. (1984). Intelligence, cognitive skills, and early reading progress. *Reading Research Quarterly, 19,* 278–303.

State of Iowa, Department of Public Instruction. (1981). *The identification of pupils with learning disabilities.* Des Moines, IA: Author.

Steinbauer, E., & Heller, M. S. (1978). The Boehm Test of Basic Concepts as a predictor of academic achievement in grades 2 and 3. *Psychology in the Schools, 15,* 357–360.

Stellern, J., Vasa, S. F., & Little, J. (1976). *Introduction to diagnostic-prescriptive teaching & programming.* Glen Ridge, NJ: Exceptional Press.

Sterling, H. M., & Sterling, P. J. (1977). Experiences with the QNST. *Academic Therapy, 12,* 339–342.

Stern, W. (1914). *The psychological methods of testing intelligence.* Baltimore: Warwick & York.

Sternberg, R. J. (1986). *Intelligence applied: Understanding and increasing your intellectual skills.* San Diego: Harcourt Brace Jovanovich.

Stevenson, I. (1960). *Medical history-taking.* New York: Paul B. Hoeber.

Stevenson, I. (1974). The psychiatric interview. In S. Arieti (Ed.), *American handbook of psychiatry* (2nd ed., Vol. 1, pp. 1138–1156). New York: Basic Books.

Stewart, K. J., & Moely, B. E. (1983). The WISC-R third factor: What does it mean? *Journal of Consulting and Clinical Psychology, 51,* 940–941.

St. James-Roberts, I. (1981). A reinterpretation of hemispherectomy data without functional plasticity of the brain. *Brain and Language, 13,* 31–53.

Stoddard, G. D. (1943). *The meaning of intelligence.* New York: Macmillan.

Stone, F. B. (1981). Behavior problems of elementary-school children. *Journal of Abnormal Child Psychology, 9,* 407–418.

Strain, P. S., Sainto, D. M., & Maheady, L. (1984). Toward a functional assessment of severely handicapped learners. *Educational Psychologist, 19,* 180–187.

Sturner, R. A., Funk, S. G., & Green, J. A. (1984). Predicting kindergarten school performance using the McCarthy Scales of Children's Abilities. *Journal of Pediatric Psychology, 9,* 495–503.

Stutsman, R. (1931). *Mental measurement of preschool children.* Yonkers-on-Hudson, NY: World Book.

Sucher, F., & Allred, R. A. (1981). *New Sucher-Allred Reading Placement Inventory.* Oklahoma City: The Economy Company.

Sue, D. W. (1981). *Counseling the culturally different: Theory & practice*. New York: Wiley.

Suess, J. F., Cotten, P. D., Gustave, F. P., & Sison, P. D., Jr. (1983). The American Association on Mental Deficiency—Adaptive Behavior Scale: Allowing credit for alternative means of communication. *American Annals of the Deaf, 128,* 390–393.

Sullivan, P. M. (1978). *A comparison of administration modifications on the WISC-R Performance Scale with different categories of deaf children.* Unpublished doctoral dissertation, University of Iowa.

Sullivan, P. M. (1982). Administration modifications on the WISC-R Performance scale with different categories of deaf children. *American Annals of the Deaf, 127,* 780–788.

Sulzer-Azaroff, B., & Reese, E. P. (1982). *Applying behavioral analysis: A program for developing professional competence.* New York: Holt, Rinehart and Winston.

Sundberg, N. D., Taplin, J. R., & Tyler, L. E. (1983). *Introduction to clinical psychology: Perspectives, issues, and contributions to human service.* Englewood Cliffs, NJ: Prentice-Hall.

Suppes, P. (1974). A survey of cognition in handicapped children. *Review of Educational Research, 44,* 145–176.

Sutter, E. G., & Bishop, P. C. (1986a). Factor structure of the WISC-R and ITPA for learning-disabled, emotionally disturbed, and control children. *Journal of Clinical Psychology, 42,* 975–978.

Sutter, E. G., & Bishop, P. C. (1986b). Further investigation of the correlations among the WISC-R, PIAT, and DAM. *Psychology in the Schools, 23,* 365–367.

Sutton, G. W., Koller, J. R., & Christian, B. T. (1982). The Stanford-Binet mental age and the WISC-R test age: A comparison study. *Psychology in the Schools, 19,* 287–289.

Svanum, S., & Bringle, R. G. (1982). Race, social class, and predictive bias: An evaluation using the WISC, WRAT, and teacher ratings. *Intelligence, 6,* 275–286.

Swanson, E. N., & DeBlassie, R. (1971). Interpreter effects on the WISC performance of first grade Mexican-American children. *Measurement and Evaluation in Guidance, 4,* 172–175.

Swanson, F. L. (1970). *Psychotherapists and children: A procedural guide.* New York: Pitman.

Swanson, H. L. (1985). Assessing learning disabled children's intellectual performance: An information processing perspective. In K. D. Gadow (Ed.), *Advances in learning and behavioral disabilities* (Vol. 4, pp. 225–272). Greenwich, CT: JAI Press.

Sweet, R. C., & Ringness, T. A. (1971). Variations in the intelligence test performance of referred boys of differing racial and socioeconomic backgrounds as a function of feedback or monetary reinforcement. *Journal of School Psychology, 9,* 399–409.

Swerdlik, M. E., & Schweitzer, J. (1978). A comparison of factor structures of the WISC and WISC-R. *Psychology in the Schools, 15,* 166–172.

Switzky, H. N., Haywood, H. C., & Rotatori, A. F. (1982). Who are the severely and profoundly mentally retarded? *Education and Training of the Mentally Retarded, 17,* 268–272.

Taddonio, R. O. (1973). Correlation of Leiter and the visual subtests of the Illinois Test of Psycholinguistic Abilities with deaf elementary school children. *Journal of School Psychology, 11,* 30–35.

Tallent, N. (1963). *Clinical psychological consultation.* Englewood Cliffs, NJ: Prentice-Hall.

Tallent, N., & Reiss, W. J. (1959a). Multidisciplinary views on the preparation of written clinical psychological reports: I. Spontaneous suggestions for content. *Journal of Clinical Psychology, 15,* 218–221.

Tallent, N., & Reiss, W. J. (1959b). II. Acceptability of certain common content variables and styles of expression. *Journal of Clinical Psychology, 15,* 273–274.

Tallent, N., & Reiss, W. J. (1959c). III. The trouble with psychological reports. *Journal of Clinical Psychology, 15,* 444–446.

Taylor, E. M. (1961). *Psychological appraisal of children with cerebral defects.* Cambridge, MA: Harvard University Press.

Taylor, H. D., & Thweatt, R. C. (1972). Cross-cultural developmental performance of Navajo children on the Bender-Gestalt Test. *Perceptual and Motor Skills, 35,* 307–309.

Taylor, H. G. (1983). MBD: Meanings and misconceptions. *Journal of Clinical Neuropsychology, 5,* 271–287.

Taylor, R. L., & Ivimey, J. K. (1980). Predicting academic achievement: Preliminary analysis of the McCarthy Scales. *Psychological Reports, 46,* 1232.

Taylor, R. L., & Partenio, I. (1984). Ethnic differences on the Bender-Gestalt: Relative effects of measured intelligence. *Journal of Consulting and Clinical Psychology, 52,* 784–788.

Taylor, R. L., Slocumb, P. R., & O'Neill, J. (1979). A short form of the McCarthy Scales of Children's Abilities: Methodological and clinical applications. *Psychology in the Schools, 16,* 347–350.

Tebeleff, M., & Oakland, T. D. (1977, August). *Relationships between the ABIC, WISC-R and achievement.* Paper presented at the annual meeting of the American Psychological Association, San Francisco.

Teeter, A., Moore, C. L., & Petersen, J. D. (1982). WISC-R Verbal and Performance abilities of native American students referred for school learning problems. *Psychology in the Schools, 19,* 39–44.

Teglasi, H., & Freeman, R. W. (1983). Rapport pitfalls of beginning testers. *Journal of School Psychology, 21,* 229–240.

Tellegen, A., & Briggs, P. F. (1967). Old wine in new skins: Grouping Wechsler subtests into new scales. *Journal of Consulting Psychology, 31,* 499–506.

Temple, C. M. (1984a). New approaches to the developmental dyslexias. *Advances in Neurology, 42,* 223–232.

Temple, C. M. (1984b). Surface dyslexia in a child with epilepsy. *Neuropsychologia, 22,* 569–576.

Tennent, G., & Gath, D. (1975). Bright delinquents: A three-year follow-up study. *British Journal of Criminology, 15,* 386–390.

Terman, L. M. (1911). The Binet-Simon Scale for measuring

intelligence: Impressions gained by its application. *Psychological Clinic*, 5, 199–206.

Terman, L. M. (1916). *The measurement of intelligence*. Boston: Houghton Mifflin.

Terman, L. M. (1921). A symposium. Intelligence and its measurement. *Journal of Educational Psychology*, 12, 127–133.

Terman, L. M. (1925). *Genetic studies of genius* (Vol. 1). Stanford, CA: Stanford University Press.

Terman, L. M., & Childs, H. G. (1912). A tentative revision and extension of the Binet-Simon Measuring Scale of Intelligence. *Journal of Educational Psychology*, 3, 61–74, 133–143, 198–208, 277–289.

Terman, L. M., & Merrill, M. A. (1960). *Stanford-Binet Intelligence Scale*. Boston: Houghton Mifflin.

Terman, L. M., & Oden, M. H. (1959). *The gifted group at midlife*. Stanford, CA: Stanford University Press.

Terrell, F., Taylor, J., & Terrell, S. L. (1978). Effects of type of social reinforcement on the intelligence test performance of lower-class black children. *Journal of Consulting and Clinical Psychology*, 46, 1538–1539.

Terrell, F., Terrell, S. L., & Taylor, J. (1981). Effects of type of reinforcement on the intelligence test performance of retarded black children. *Psychology in the Schools*, 18, 225–227.

Tew, B. J., & Laurence, K. M. (1983). The relationship between spina bifida children's intelligence test scores on school entry and at school leaving: A preliminary report. *Child: Care, Health and Development*, 9, 13–17.

Tharp, R. G., & Wetzel, R. J. (1969). *Behavior modification in the natural environment*. New York: Academic Press.

Thomas, A., Hertzig, M. E., Dryman, I., & Fernandez, P. (1971). Examiner effect in IQ testing of Puerto Rican working-class children. *American Journal of Orthopsychiatry*, 41, 809–821.

Thomas, P. J. (1977). Administration of a dialectical Spanish version and standard English version of the Peabody Picture Vocabulary Test. *Psychological Reports*, 40, 747–750.

Thompson, A. P., Howard, D., & Anderson, J. (1986). Two- and four-subtest short forms of the WAIS-R: Validity in a psychiatric sample. *Canadian Journal of Behavioural Science*, 18, 287–293.

Thompson, P. L., & Brassard, M. R. (1984). Validity of the Woodcock-Johnson Tests of Cognitive Ability: A comparison with the WISC-R in LD and normal elementary students. *Journal of School Psychology*, 22, 201–208.

Thompson, R. J., Jr. (1981). The diagnostic utility of Bannatyne's recategorized WISC-R scores with children referred to a developmental evaluation center. *Psychology in the Schools*, 18, 43–47.

Thomson, M. E. (1982). The assessment of children with specific reading difficulties (dyslexia) using the British Ability Scales. *British Journal of Psychology*, 73, 461–478.

Thorndike, E. L. (1927). *The measurement of intelligence*. New York: Bureau of Publications, Teachers College, Columbia University.

Thorndike, R. L. (1968). [Review of R. Rosenthal and L. Jacobson, *Pygmalion in the classroom*]. *American Educational Research Journal*, 5, 708–711.

Thorndike, R. L., & Hagen, E. P. (1977). *Measurement and evaluation in psychology and education* (4th ed.). New York: Wiley.

Thorndike, R. L., Hagen, E. P., & Sattler, J. M. (1986a). *Guide for administering and scoring, the Stanford-Binet Intelligence Scale: Fourth Edition*. Chicago: Riverside Publishing.

Thorndike, R. L., Hagen, E. P., & Sattler, J. M. (1986b). *Technical manual, Stanford-Binet Intelligence Scale: Fourth Edition*. Chicago: Riverside Publishing.

Thurstone, L. L. (1938). Primary mental abilities. *Psychometric Monographs*, No. 1.

Tiber, N., & Kennedy, W. A. (1964). The effects of incentives on the intelligence test performance of different social groups. *Journal of Consulting Psychology*, 28, 187.

Tiffin, J. (1948). *Manual for the Purdue Pegboard*. Chicago: Science Research Associates.

Tillman, M. H. (1967a). The performance of blind and sighted children on the Wechsler Intelligence Scale for Children: Study I. *International Journal for the Education of the Blind*, 16, 65–74.

Tillman, M. H. (1967b). The performances of blind and sighted children on the Wechsler Intelligence Scale for Children: Study II. *International Journal for the Education of the Blind*, 16, 106–112.

Tillman, M. H. (1973). Intelligence scales for the blind: A review with implications for research. *Journal of School Psychology*, 11, 80–87.

Tillman, M. H., & Bashaw, W. L. (1968). Multivariate analysis of the WISC scales for blind and sighted children. *Psychological Reports*, 23, 523–526.

Tillman, M. H., & Osborne, R. T. (1969). The performance of blind and sighted children on the Wechsler Intelligence Scale for Children: Interaction effects. *Education of the Visually Handicapped*, 1, 1–4.

Tomsic, M., & Rankin, R. J. (1985). Selecting gifted children with the Slosson Intelligence Test: 1981 vs. 1961 norms. *Psychology in the Schools*, 22, 102–103.

Torgesen, J. K. (1979). What shall we do with psychological processes? *Journal of Learning Disabilities*, 12, 514–521.

Torgesen, J. K. (1980). Conceptual and educational implications of the use of efficient task strategies by learning disabled children. *Journal of Learning Disabilities*, 13, 364–371.

Torgesen, J. K. (1981). The relationship between memory and attention in learning disabilities. *Exceptional Education Quarterly*, 2(3), 51–59.

Torgesen, J. K. (1982a). The learning disabled child as an inactive learner: Educational implications. *Topics in Learning and Learning Disabilities*, 2(1), 45–52.

Torgesen, J. K. (1982b). The study of short-term memory in learning disabled children: Goals, methods, and conclusions. In K. D. Gadow & I. Bialer (Eds.), *Advances in learning and behavioral disabilities* (Vol. 1, pp. 117–149). Greenwich, CT: JAI Press.

Torrance, E. P. (1966). *Torrance Tests of Creative Thinking*. Princeton, NJ: Personnel Press.

Torrance, E. P., & Myers, R. E. (1970). *Creative learning and teaching*. New York: Dodd, Mead.

Tramill, J. L., Tramill, J. K., Thornthwaite, R., & Anderson, F. (1981). Investigations into the relationships of the WRAT, the PIAT, the SORT, and the WISC-R in low-functioning referrals. *Psychology in the Schools, 18*, 149–153.

Trites, R. L., Blouin, A. G. A., & Laprade, K. (1982). Factor analysis of the Conners Teacher Rating Scale based on a large normative sample. *Journal of Consulting and Clinical Psychology, 50*, 615–623.

Trueman, M., Lynch, A., & Branthwaite, A. (1984). A factor analytic study of the McCarthy Scales of Children's Abilities. *British Journal of Educational Psychology, 54*, 331–335.

Tsushima, W. T., & Stoddard, V. M. (1986). Predictive validity of a short-form WPPSI with prekindergarten children: A 3-year follow-up study. *Journal of Clinical Psychology, 42*, 526–527.

Tuddenham, R. D. (1962). The nature and measurement of intelligence. In L. J. Postman (Ed.), *Psychology in the making* (pp. 469–525). New York: Knopf.

Tufano, L. G. (1976). The effect of effort and performance reinforcement on WISC-R IQ scores of black and white EMR boys. *Dissertation Abstracts International, 36*, 5961A. (University Microfilms No. 76–6455)

Turnbull, W. W. (1979). Intelligence testing in the year 2000. *Intelligence, 3*, 275–282.

Tyler, L. E. (1965). *The psychology of human differences* (3rd ed.). New York: Appleton-Century-Crofts.

Uebersax, J. S. (1982–83). A design-independent method for measuring the reliability of psychiatric diagnosis. *Journal of Psychiatric Research, 17*, 335–342.

Ulibarri, D. M., Spencer, M. L., & Rivas, G. A. (1981). Language of proficiency and academic achievement: A study of language proficiency tests and their relationship to school ratings as predictors of academic achievement. *National Association for Bilingual Education (NABE) Journal, 5*, 47–80.

Ungerer, J. A., & Sigman, M. (1981). Symbolic play and language comprehension in autistic children. *Journal of the American Academy of Child Psychiatry, 20*, 318–337.

University of Chicago Press. (1982). *The Chicago manual of style* (13th ed.). Chicago: Author.

Urbach, P. (1974). Progress and degeneration in the "IQ debate." *British Journal of the Philosophy of Science, 25*, 99–135, 235–259.

Urbina, S. P., Golden, C. J., & Ariel, R. N. (1982). WAIS/WAIS-R: Initial comparisons. *Clinical Neuropsychology, 4*, 145–146.

Uzgiris, I. C., & Hunt, J. McV. (1975). *Assessment in infancy: Ordinal scales of psychological development*. Urbana: University of Illinois Press.

Vacc, N. A., & Atwell, B. (1980). Relationship of the Adaptive Behavior Inventory for Children and intelligence. *Psychological Reports, 47*, 402.

Valencia, R. R. (1983). Stability of the McCarthy Scales of Children's Abilities over a one-year period for Mexican-American children. *Psychology in the Schools, 20*, 29–34.

Valencia, R. R. (1984). Reliability of the Raven Coloured Progressive Matrices for Anglo and for Mexican-American children. *Psychology in the Schools, 21*, 49–52.

Valencia, R. R., & Rothwell, J. G. (1984). Concurrent validity of the WPPSI with Mexican-American preschool children. *Educational & Psychological Measurement, 44*, 955–961.

Valus, A. (1986). Achievement-potential discrepancy status of students in LD programs. *Learning Disability Quarterly, 9*, 200–205.

Vance, H. B., Fuller, G. B., & Lester, M. L. (1986). A comparison of the Minnesota Perceptual Diagnostic Test Revised and the Bender Gestalt. *Journal of Learning Disabilities, 19*, 211–214.

Vance, H. B., Huelsman, C. B., Jr., & Wherry, R. J. (1976). The hierarchical factor structure of the Wechsler Intelligence Scale for Children as it relates to disadvantaged white and black children. *Journal of General Psychology, 95*, 287–293.

Vance, H. B., Kitson, D., & Singer, M. G. (1985). Relationship between the standard scores of Peabody Picture Vocabulary Test—Revised and Wide Range Achievement Test. *Journal of Clinical Psychology, 41*, 691–693.

Vance, H. B., & Wallbrown, F. H. (1977). Hierarchical factor structure of the WISC-R for referred children and adolescents. *Psychological Reports, 41*, 699–702.

Vance, H. B., & Wallbrown, F. H. (1978). The structure of intelligence for black children: A hierarchical approach. *Psychological Record, 28*, 31–39.

Vance, H. B., Wallbrown, F. H., & Fremont, T. S. (1978). The abilities of retarded students: Further evidence concerning the stimulus trace factor. *Journal of Psychology, 100*, 77–82.

Vandenberg, S. G., & Volger, G. P. (1985). Genetic determinants of intelligence. In B. B. Wolman (Ed.), *Handbook of intelligence: Theories, measurements, and applications* (pp. 3–57). New York: Wiley.

VanderVeer, B., & Schweid, E. (1974). Infant assessment: Stability of mental functioning in young retarded children. *American Journal of Mental Deficiency, 79*, 1–4.

Van Etten, G., Arkell, C., & Van Etten, C. (1980). *The severely and profoundly handicapped: Programs, methods, and materials*. St. Louis: C. V. Mosby.

Van Hagen, J., & Kaufman, A. S. (1975). Factor analysis of the WISC-R for a group of mentally retarded children and adolescents. *Journal of Consulting and Clinical Psychology, 43*, 661–667.

Van Melis-Wright, M., & Strein, W. (1986). Materials review: A comparison of the K-ABC global scales and the Stanford-Binet with young gifted children. *Topics in Early Childhood Special Education, 6*, 88–91.

Vega, M., & Powell, A. (1970). The effects of practice on Bender Gestalt performance of culturally disadvantaged children. *Florida Journal of Educational Research, 12*, 45–49.

Vellutino, F. R., & Shub, M. J. (1982). Assessment of disorders in formal school language: Disorders in reading. *Topics in Language Disorders*, 2(4), 20–33.

Vernon, M. C. (1974). Deaf and hard of hearing. In M. V. Wisland (Ed.), *Psychoeducational diagnosis of exceptional children* (pp. 190–212). Springfield, IL: Charles C Thomas.

Vernon, M. C., & Brown, D. W. (1964). A guide to psychological tests and testing procedures in the evaluation of deaf and hard-of-hearing children. *Journal of Speech and Hearing Disorders*, 29, 414–423.

Vernon, P. A. (1983). Speed of information processing and general intelligence. *Intelligence*, 7, 53–70.

Vernon, P. E. (1950). *The structure of human abilities*. New York: Wiley.

Vernon, P. E. (1965). Ability factors and environmental influences. *American Psychologist*, 20, 723–733.

Vernon, P. E. (1979). *Intelligence: Heredity and environment*. San Francisco: W. H. Freeman.

Wachs, T. D. (1975). Relation of infants' performance on Piaget scales between twelve and twenty-four months and their Stanford-Binet performance at thirty-one months. *Child Development*, 46, 929–935.

Wahler, R. G., House, A. E., & Stambaugh, E. E. (1976). *Ecological assessment of child problem behavior: A clinical package for home, school, and institutional settings*. New York: Pergamon Press.

Walker, R. E., Hunt, W. A., & Schwartz, M. L. (1965). The difficulty of WAIS Comprehension scoring. *Journal of Clinical Psychology*, 21, 427–429.

Wallbrown, F. H. (1979, March). *A factor analytic framework for the clinical interpretation of the WISC-R*. Paper presented at the meeting of the National Association of School Psychologists/California Association of School Psychologists/Psychometrists, San Diego.

Wallbrown, F. H., Blaha, J., Wallbrown, J. D., & Engin, A. W. (1975). The hierarchical factor structure of the Wechsler Intelligence Scale for Children—Revised. *Journal of Psychology*, 89, 223–235.

Wallbrown, F. H., Blaha, J., & Wherry, R. J. (1973). The hierarchical factor structure of the Wechsler Preschool and Primary Scale of Intelligence. *Journal of Consulting and Clinical Psychology*, 41, 356–362.

Wallbrown, F. H., & Fremont, T. S. (1980). The stability of Koppitz scores on the Bender-Gestalt for reading disabled children. *Psychology in the Schools*, 17, 181–184.

Wapner, W., & Gardner, H. (1979). A study of spelling aphasia. *Brain and Language*, 7, 363–374.

Warner, M. H. (1983). *Practice effects, test-retest reliability and comparability of WAIS and WAIS-R: Issues in the assessment of cognitive recovery in detoxified alcoholics*. Unpublished doctoral dissertation, University of Georgia, Athens, GA.

Wasik, B. H., & Wasik, J. L. (1976). Patterns of conservation acquisition and the relationship of conservation to intelligence for children of low income. *Perceptual and Motor Skills*, 43, 1147–1154.

Wasik, J. L., & Wasik, B. H. (1970). A note on use of the WPPSI

in evaluating intervention programs. *Measurement and Evaluation in Guidance*, 3, 54–56.

Watkins, M. W. (1980). Intellectual and special aptitudes of tenth grade EMH students. *Education and Training of the Mentally Retarded*, 15, 139–142.

Watson, B. U. (1983). Test-retest stability of the Hiskey-Nebraska Test of Learning Aptitude in a sample of hearing-impaired children and adolescents. *Journal of Speech & Hearing Disorders*, 48, 145–149.

Watson, B. U., & Goldgar, D. E. (1985). A note on the use of the Hiskey-Nebraska Test of Learning Aptitude with deaf children. *Language, Speech, and Hearing Services in the Schools*, 16, 53–57.

Waugh, R. P. (1978). The I.T.P.A.: Ballast or bonanza for the school psychologist. *Journal of School Psychology*, 13, 201–208.

Weaver, A. S. (1968). The prediction of first grade reading achievement in culturally disadvantaged children. *Dissertation Abstracts*, 28, 3789A. (University Microfilms No. 68–2,887)

Webb, L. J., DiClemente, C. C., Johnstone, E. E., Sanders, J. L., & Perley, R. A. (Eds.). (1981). *DSM-III training guide*. New York: Brunner/Mazel.

Wechsler, D. (1939). *The measurement of adult intelligence*. Baltimore: Williams & Wilkins.

Wechsler, D. (1949). *Manual for the Wechsler Intelligence Scale for Children*. San Antonio: The Psychological Corporation.

Wechsler, D. (1955). *Manual for the Wechsler Adult Intelligence Scale*. San Antonio: The Psychological Corporation.

Wechsler, D. (1958). *The measurement and appraisal of adult intelligence* (4th ed.). Baltimore: Williams & Wilkins.

Wechsler, D. (1967). *Manual for the Wechsler Preschool and Primary Scale of Intelligence*. San Antonio: The Psychological Corporation.

Wechsler, D. (1974). *Manual for the Wechsler Intelligence Scale for Children—Revised*. San Antonio: The Psychological Corporation.

Wechsler, D. (1981). *Manual for the Wechsler Adult Intelligence Scale—Revised*. San Antonio: The Psychological Corporation.

Wehman, P. (1979). *Curriculum design for the severely and profoundly handicapped*. New York: Human Sciences Press.

Weiner, S. G., & Kaufman, A. S. (1979). WISC-R vs. WISC for black children suspected of learning or behavioral disorders. *Journal of Learning Disabilities*, 12, 100–105.

Weisz, J. R., & Yeates, K. O. (1981). Cognitive development in retarded and nonretarded persons: Piagetian tests of the similar structure hypothesis. *Psychological Bulletin*, 90, 153–178.

Weitz, R. (1976, September). Forensic applications of psychological testing. In L. W. Field (Chair), *Contribution of psychological testing to clinical practice*. Symposium presented at the meeting of the American Psychological Association, Washington, DC.

Wells, C. F., & Rabiner, E. L. (1973). The conjoint family

diagnostic interview and the family index of tension. *Family Process*, *12*, 127–144.

Werner, E. E., Honzik, M. P., & Smith, R. S. (1968). Prediction of intelligence and achievement at ten years from twenty months pediatric and psychologic examinations. *Child Development*, *39*, 1063–1075.

Wesman, A. G. (1968). Intelligent testing. *American Psychologist*, *23*, 267–274.

Wesman, A. G. (1972). Symposium: Tests and counseling: I. Testing and counseling: Fact and fancy. *Measurement and Evaluation in Guidance*, *5*, 397–402.

Wetter, J., & French, R. W. (1973). Comparison of the Peabody Individual Achievement Test and the Wide Range Achievement Test in a learning disability clinic. *Psychology in the Schools*, *10*, 285–286.

Whalen, C. K., & Henker, B. (1976). Psychostimulants and children: A review and analysis. *Psychological Bulletin*, *83*, 1113–1130.

Wheldall, K., & Jeffree, D. (1974). Criticisms regarding the use of the E.P.V.T. in subnormality research. *British Journal of Disorders of Communication*, *9*, 140–143.

White, D. R., & Jacobs, E. (1979). The prediction of first-grade reading achievement from WPPSI scores of preschool children. *Psychology in the Schools*, *16*, 189–192.

White, O. R., & Haring, N. G. (1978). Evaluating educational programs serving the severely and profoundly handicapped. In N. G. Haring & D. D. Bricker (Eds.), *Teaching the severely handicapped* (Vol. 3, pp. 153–200). Seattle: American Association for the Education of the Severely/Profoundly Handicapped.

White, T. H. (1979). Correlations among the WISC-R, PIAT, and DAM. *Psychology in the Schools*, *16*, 497–501.

Whitman, T. L., Scibak, J. W., Butler, K. M., Richter, R., & Johnson, M. R. (1982). Improving classroom behavior in mentally retarded children through correspondence training. *Journal of Applied Behavior Analysis*, *15*, 545–564.

Whitmore, J. (1985). New challenges to common identification practices. In J. Freeman (Ed.), *The psychology of gifted children: Perspectives on development and education* (pp. 93–113). New York: Wiley.

Whyte, J., Curry, C., & Hale, D. (1985). Inspection time and intelligence in dyslexic children. *Journal of Child Psychology and Psychiatry*, *26*, 423–428.

Wiebe, M. J., & Watkins, E. O. (1980). Factor analysis of the McCarthy Scales of Children's Abilities on preschool children. *Journal of School Psychology*, *18*, 154–162.

Wiederholt, J. L. (1978). Review of the Illinois Test of Psycholinguistic Abilities, revised edition. In O. K. Buros (Ed.), *The eighth mental measurements yearbook* (pp. 580–583). Highland Park, NJ: Gryphon Press.

Wiedl, K. H., & Carlson, J. S. (1976). The factorial structure of the Raven Coloured Progressive Matrices Test. *Educational and Psychological Measurement*, *36*, 409–413.

Wiener, G., & Milton, T. (1970). Demographic correlates of low birth weight. *American Journal of Epidemiology*, *91*, 260–272.

Wikler, L., Wasow, M., & Hatfield, E. (1981). Chronic sorrow revisited: Parent vs. professional depiction of the adjustment of parents of mentally retarded children. *American Journal of Orthopsychiatry*, *51*, 63–70.

Wikoff, R. L. (1978). Correlational and factor analysis of the Peabody Individual Achievement Test and the WISC-R. *Journal of Consulting and Clinical Psychology*, *46*, 322–325.

Willerman, L., & Fiedler, M. F. (1977). Intellectually precocious preschool children: Early development and later intellectual accomplishments. *Journal of Genetic Psychology*, *131*, 13–20.

Williams, R. L. (1970). From dehumanization to black intellectual genocide: A rejoinder. *Clinical Child Psychology Newsletter*, *9*, 6–7.

Williams, R. L. (1972, September). *The BITCH-100: A culture-specific test*. Paper presented at the meeting of the American Psychological Association, Honolulu, Hawaii.

Williams, S. E. (1983). Factors influencing naming performance in aphasia: A review of the literature. *Journal of Communication Disorders*, *16*, 357–372.

Willis, J., & Shibata, B. (1978). A comparison of tangible reinforcement and feedback effects on the WPPSI IQ scores of nursery school children. *Education and Treatment of Children*, *1*, 31–45.

Wilson, B. C., Iacoviello, J. M., Wilson, J. J., & Risucci, D. (1982). Purdue Pegboard performance of normal preschool children. *Journal of Clinical Neuropsychology*, *4*, 19–26.

Wilson, J. D., & Spangler, P. F. (1974). The Peabody Individual Achievement Test as a clinical tool. *Journal of Learning Disabilities*, *7*, 384–387.

Wilson, R. S. (1975). Twins: Patterns of cognitive development as measured on the Wechsler Preschool and Primary Scale of Intelligence. *Developmental Psychology*, *11*, 126–134.

Wilson, R. S. (1978a). Sensorimotor and cognitive development. In F. D. Minifie & L. L. Lloyd (Eds.), *Communicative and cognitive abilities—early behavioral assessment* (pp. 135–149). Baltimore: University Park Press.

Wilson, R. S. (1978b). Synchronies in mental development: An epigenetic perspective. *Science*, *202*, 939–948.

Wilson, R. S. (1983). The Louisville Twin Study: Developmental synchronies in behavior. *Child Development*, *54*, 298–316.

Wing, L. (1976). Assessment: The role of the teacher. In M. P. Everard (Ed.), *An approach to teaching autistic children* (pp. 15–30). New York: Pergamon Press.

Wisland, M. V., & Many, W. A. (1967). A study of the stability of the Illinois Test of Psycholinguistic Abilities. *Educational and Psychological Measurement*, *27*, 367–370.

Wisland, M. V., & Many, W. A. (1969). A factorial study of the Illinois Test of Psycholinguistic Abilities with children having above average intelligence. *Educational and Psychological Measurement*, *29*, 367–376.

Wissler, C. (1901). The correlation of mental and physical tests. *Psychological Review*, *3* (Monograph Supplement 16).

Witt, J. C., & Elliott, S. N. (1983). Assessment in behavioral consultation: The initial interview. *School Psychology Review*, *12*, 42–49.

Wolf, R. (1966). The measurement of environments. In A. Anastasi (Ed.), *Testing problems in perspective* (pp. 491–503). Washington, DC: American Council on Education.

Wolf, T. H. (1969). The emergence of Binet's conceptions and measurement of intelligence: A case history of the creative process. Part II. *Journal of the History of the Behavioral Sciences*, *5*, 207–237.

Wong, B. Y. (1982). Understanding learning disabled students' reading problems: Contributions from cognitive psychology. *Topics in Learning and Learning Disabilities*, *1*(4), 43–50.

Wood, D. J. (1982). Talking to young children. *Developmental Medicine & Child Neurology*, *24*, 856–859.

Woodcock, R. W. (1977). *Woodcock-Johnson Psycho-Educational Battery: Technical report*. Allen, TX: DLM Teaching Resources.

Woodcock, R. W. (1985). *Oral Language and Broad Reasoning Clusters for the Woodcock-Johnson Psycho-Educational Battery*. Assessment Service Bulletin No. 2. Allen, TX: DLM Teaching Resources.

Worthing, R. J., Phye, G. D., & Nunn, G. D. (1984). Equivalence and concurrent validity of PPVT-R forms L and M for school-age children with special needs. *Psychology in the Schools*, *21*, 296–299.

Wright, B. A. P. (1983). *Physical disability—A psychosocial approach* (2nd ed.). New York: Harper & Row.

Wright, D. (1983). Effectiveness of the PPVT-R for screening gifted students. *Psychology in the Schools*, *20*, 25–26.

Wright, D., & DeMers, S. T. (1982). Comparison of the relationship between two measures of visual-motor coordination and academic achievement. *Psychology in the Schools*, *19*, 473-477.

Wright, H. F. (1960). Observational child study. In P. H. Mussen (Ed.), *Handbook of research methods in child development* (pp. 71–139). New York: Wiley.

Wright, R. H. (1981). Psychologists and professional liability (malpractice) insurance: A retrospective review. *American Psychologist*, *36*, 1485–1493.

Wrightstone, J. W. (1941). *A supplementary guide for scoring the Revised Stanford-Binet Intelligence Scale, Form L*. New York: Board of Education.

Wurtz, R. G., Sewell, T. E., & Manni, J. L. (1985). The relationship of estimated learning potential to performance on a learning task and achievement. *Psychology in the Schools*, *22*, 293–302.

Yarrow, L. J. (1960). Interviewing children. In P. H. Mussen (Ed.), *Handbook of research methods in child development* (pp. 561–602). New York: Wiley.

Yater, A. C., Barclay, A. G., & Leskosky, R. (1971). Goodenough-Harris Drawing Test and WPPSI performance of disadvantaged preschool children. *Perceptual and Motor Skills*, *33*, 967–970.

Yerkes, R. M. (1917). The Binet versus the point scale method of measuring intelligence. *Journal of Applied Psychology*, *1*, 111–122.

Yeudall, L. T. (1979, February). *Neuropsychological concomitants of persistent criminal behavior*. Paper presented at the annual meeting of the Ontario Psychological Association, Toronto, Canada.

Yeudall, L. T., Fromm, D., Reddon, J. R., & Stefanyk, W. O. (1986). Normative data stratified by age and sex for 12 neuropsychological tests. *Journal of Clinical Psychology*, *42*, 918–946.

Young, R. M., Bradley-Johnson, S., & Johnson, C. M. (1982). Immediate and delayed reinforcement on WISC-R performance for mentally retarded students. *Applied Research in Mental Retardation*, *3*, 13–20.

Young, V. H. (1974). A black American socialization pattern. *American Ethnologist*, *1*, 405–413.

Yoshida, R. K., & Meyers, C. E. (1975). Effects of labeling as educable mentally retarded on teachers' expectancies for change in a student's performance. *Journal of Educational Psychology*, *67*, 521–527.

Ysseldyke, J. E., & Sabatino, D. A. (1972). Identification of statistically significant differences between scaled scores and psycholinguistic ages on the ITPA. *Psychology in the Schools*, *9*, 309–313.

Ysseldyke, J. E., & Samuel, S. (1973). Identification of diagnostic strengths and weaknesses on the McCarthy Scales of Children's Abilities. *Psychology in the Schools*, *10*, 304–315.

Yudin, L. W. (1966). An abbreviated form of the WISC for use with emotionally disturbed children. *Journal of Consulting Psychology*, *30*, 272–275.

Yule, W., Berger, M., Butler, S., Newham, V., & Tizard, J. (1969). The WPPSI: An empirical evaluation with a British sample. *British Journal of Educational Psychology*, *39*, 1–13.

Yule, W., Gold, R. D., & Busch, C. (1982). Long-term predictive validity of the WPPSI: An 11-year follow-up study. *Personality and Individual Differences*, *3*, 65–71.

Zachary, R. A., Crumpton, E., & Spiegel, D. E. (1985). Estimating WAIS-R IQ from the Shipley Institute of Living Scale. *Journal of Clinical Psychology*, *41*, 532–540.

Zahn-Waxler, C., McKnew, D. H., Cummings, E. M., Davenport, Y. B., & Radke-Yarrow, M. (1984). Problem behaviors and peer interactions of young children with a manic-depressive parent. *American Journal of Psychiatry*, *141*, 236–240.

Zaidel, E., Zaidel, D. W., & Sperry, R. W. (1981). Left and right intelligence: Case studies of Raven's Progressive Matrices following brain bisection and hemidecortication. *Cortex*, *17*, 167–186.

Zajonc, R. B. (1976). Family configuration and intelligence. *Science*, *192*, 227–236.

Zampardi, M. G. (1978). *School psychologists' opinions and practices regarding the Buckley amendment*. Paper presented at the meeting of the American Psychological Association, Toronto, Canada.

Zigler, E. (1982, August). *On the definition and classification of mental retardation*. Paper presented at the meeting of the American Psychological Association, Washington, DC.

Zigler, E., & Balla, D. (1981). Recent issues in developmental approach to mental retardation. In M. P. Friedman, J. P. Das, & N. O'Connor (Eds.), *Intelligence and learning* (pp. 25–38). New York: Plenum.

Zigler, E., Balla, D., & Hodapp, R. (1984). On the definition and classification of mental retardation. *American Journal of Mental Deficiency, 89*, 215–230.

Zigler, E., & Butterfield, E. C. (1968). Motivational aspects of changes in IQ test performances of culturally deprived nursery school children. *Child Development, 39*, 1–14.

Zigler, E., & Farber, E. A. (1985). Commonalities between the intellectual extremes: Giftedness and mental retardation. In F. D. Horowitz & M. O'Brien (Eds.), *The gifted and talented: Developmental perspectives* (pp. 387–408). Washington, DC: American Psychological Association.

Zigler, E., & Muenchow, S. (1979). Mainstreaming: The proof is in the implementation. *American Psychologist, 34*, 993–996.

Zimmerman, I. L., Covin, T. M., & Woo-Sam, J. M. (1986). A longitudinal comparison of the WISC-R and WAIS-R. *Psychology in the Schools, 23*, 148–151.

Zimmerman, I. L., & Woo-Sam, J. M. (1970). The utility of the Wechsler Preschool and Primary Scale of Intelligence in the public school. *Journal of Clinical Psychology, 26*, 472.

Zimmerman, I. L., & Woo-Sam, J. M. (1985). Clinical applications. In B. B. Wolman (Ed.), *Handbook of intelligence: Theories, measurements, and applications* (pp. 873–898). New York: Wiley.

Zins, J. E., & Barnett, D. W. (1984). A validity study of the K-ABC, the WISC-R, and the Stanford-Binet with nonreferred children. *Journal of School Psychology, 22*, 369–371.

Zintz, M. V. (1962). Problems of classroom adjustment of Indian children in public elementary schools in the Southwest. *Science Education, 46*, 261–269.

Zuelzer, M. B., Stedman, J. M., & Adams, R. (1976). Bender Gestalt scores in first-grade children as related to ethnocultural background, socioeconomic class, and sex factors. *Journal of Consulting and Clinical Psychology, 44*, 875.

_ APPENDIX G

WECHSLER PRESCHOOL AND PRIMARY SCALE OF INTELLIGENCE— REVISED (WPPSI-R)

Thought once awakened does not slumber.
—Thomas Carlyle

This appendix describes the latest version of the Wechsler Preschool and Primary Scale of Intelligence—Revised (WPPSI-R) [D. Wechsler (1989), *Wechsler Preschool and Primary Scale of Intelligence—Revised* (San Antonio: The Psychological Corporation)]. The test is one of the major instruments for assessing the cognitive ability of young children. The content of this appendix is based primarily on the WPPSI-R manual, a factor analysis for each age level of the scale, and research based on the prior edition of the test. The appendix should be read in conjunction with Appendixes J and K on the WISC-III and Chapter 8 on the WISC-R. Because the WISC-R (WISC-III) and the WPPSI-R are so similar, psychometric, clinical, and psychoeducational approaches used on the WISC-R (WISC-III) can also be applied to the WPPSI-R. However, because the WPPSI (and the WPPSI-R) has not been as widely used or researched as the WISC-R (WISC-III), more caution is needed in interpreting test findings and in generating hypotheses about the implications of children's performance on the WPPSI-R.

The WPPSI-R (see Figure G-1) was published 22 years after the original version. The length of time between revisions is somewhat long, but it is comparable to that for the other Wechsler scales. The WPPSI-R is more elaborate than its predecessor. It has a more extensive age range (from 3 years, 0 months to 7 years, 3 months) and one additional subtest (Object Assembly). The new age range is approximately two years wider than that of the original WPPSI—one year downward and one year upward. Unfortunately, the WPPSI-R is not completely distinct from the WISC-III; some items overlap with those on four WISC-III subtests (Picture Completion, Mazes, Vocabulary, and Information). As noted later in the appendix, this overlap is a limitation in the retesting of children. It would have been preferable to have the scale completely distinct from the other Wechsler scales.

The WPPSI-R contains 12 subtests (see Exhibit G-1), 6 in the Performance Scale and 6 in the Verbal Scale. Five of the six subtests in each scale are designated as the standard subtests. They are Object Assembly, Geometric Design, Block Design, Mazes, and Picture Completion in the Performance Scale and Information, Comprehension, Arithmetic, Vocabulary, and Similarities in the Verbal Scale. The optional subtests are Animal Pegs in the Performance Scale and Sentences in the Verbal Scale. Nine of the 12 subtests are similar to those in the WISC-III (Object Assembly, Block Design, Mazes, Picture Completion, Information, Comprehension, Arithmetic, Vocabulary, and

Figure G-1.   Wechsler Preschool and Primary Scale of Intelligence—Revised. From the *Wechsler Preschool and Primary Scale of Intelligence—Revised.* Copyright © 1989 by The Psychological Corporation. Reproduced by permission. All rights reserved.

Exhibit G-1

WPPSI-R–Like Items

Object Assembly (6 items)

There are two types of tasks: (a) placing pieces into a form board and (b) assembling jigsaw puzzles. An example of an Object Assembly item is shown below.

Geometric Design (16 items)

The task for the first seven items is to select the matching design from four choices. The task for the last nine items is to copy a geometric design shown on a printed card. The designs include a circle, square, triangle, and diamond.

Block Design (14 designs)

The task is to reproduce designs using three or four blocks.

Mazes (11 mazes)

The task is to complete a series of mazes.

Picture Completion (28 items)

The task is to identify the essential missing part of the picture.
A picture of a doll without a leg.
A picture of a rabbit without an ear.
A picture of a car without a wheel.

Animal Pegs

The task is to place appropriate colored pegs in the corresponding holes on a board. The colored pegs are matched with four different animals. The Animal Pegs task is shown in the photograph of the WPPSI-R (see Figure G-1).

Information (27 items)

Point to the picture that shows the one you cut with.
How many legs does a cat have?
In what kind of store do we buy meat?
How many pennies make a dime?

Comprehension (15 items)

Why do you need to take a bath?
Why do we have farms?
What makes a sailboat move?

Arithmetic (23 items)

A card with squares of different sizes is placed in front of child. Examiner says, "Here are some squares. Which one is the biggest? Point to it."
Bill had one penny and his mother gave him one more. How many pennies does he now have?
Judy had 4 books. She lost 1. How many books does she have left?
Jimmy had 7 bananas and he bought 8 more. How many bananas does he have altogether?

Vocabulary (25 items)

Examiner shows child a picture of a dog and says, "What is this?"
What is a boot?
What does "nice" mean?
What does "annoy" mean?

Similarities (20 items)

Examiner shows child a picture of objects that go together and says, "Look at these pictures. They're all alike—they all go together. Now look at these pictures. Which one is like these?"
You can read a book and you can also read a _____.
In what way are a quarter and a dollar alike?
In what way are a cow and a pig alike?

Sentences (12 items)

The task is to repeat sentences given orally by the examiner.
Birds fly.
Ted eats apples in the morning.
The children like to visit the city every Saturday during the summer.

Similarities), and three are unique to the WPPSI-R (Sentences, Animal Pegs, and Geometric Design). Essentially, the WPPSI-R can be considered a downward extension of the WISC-R (WISC-III), except at 6 to 7¼ years, where the two tests overlap.

STANDARDIZATION

The WPPSI-R was standardized on 1,700 children, 100 boys and 100 girls in each of eight age groups from 3 to 7 years and one group of 50 boys and 50 girls from 7 years,

0 months to 7 years, 3 months. The 1986 U.S. census data were used to select representative children for the normative sample. White children and nonwhite children were included in the sample, based on the ratios found in the census for four geographical regions in the United States (Northeast, North Central, South, and West).

DEVIATION IQS, SCALED SCORES, AND TEST-AGE EQUIVALENTS

The WPPSI-R, like the WISC-III and the WAIS-R, employs the Deviation IQ ($M = 100$, $SD = 15$) for the Verbal, Performance, and Full Scale IQs, and scaled scores ($M = 10$, $SD = 3$) for the 12 individual subtests. The IQs are obtained by comparing the examinee's scores with the scores earned by a representative sample of his or her own age group. A raw score is first obtained on each subtest and then converted to a scaled score within the examinee's own age group through use of a table in the WPPSI-R manual (Table 25, pages 170–186). Age groups are divided into 16 three-month intervals from 2-11-16 (years, months, days) to 6-11-15 and 1 four-month interval from 6-11-16 to 7-3-15.

The table in the WPPSI-R manual used to obtain IQs (Table 27, pages 188–189) is based on the 10 standard subtests. The two optional subtests are excluded from the calculation of the IQ unless a subtest is spoiled or not given. When a subtest is excluded on the Performance Scale, Animal Pegs is substituted, and when one is excluded on the Verbal Scale, Sentences is substituted. When an optional subtest is substituted for a standard subtest, little is known about the reliability and validity of the IQs generated by the altered combination of subtests because neither optional subtest was used in the construction of the tables used to generate the IQs.

Prorating Procedure

When fewer than 10 subtests are administered, IQs can be computed either by prorating or by a special short-form procedure designed to estimate the Performance, Verbal, and Full Scale IQs. Although the WPPSI-R manual provides a table (Table 26, page 187) for prorating the scores when four of the subtests are administered in each scale, it is advisable to compute IQs by using the procedure described later in this chapter whenever fewer than 10 subtests are administered. The special short-form procedure takes into account the intercorrelations between the specific subtests administered for each age of the child; prorating does not take this factor into account.

Test-Age Equivalents

The WPPSI-R manual provides a table of test-age equivalents (Table 28, page 190) to facilitate interpretation of a child's performance. The test ages were arrived at for each age level by obtaining the raw score corresponding to a scaled score of 10. Because a scaled score of 10 represents the mean, the test-age equivalents of the raw scores shown in Table 28 can be understood as reflecting the average score for each particular age group. The assets and limitations associated with test-age equivalents are discussed on pages 20–21 and pages 75–76 of this text.

RELIABILITY

The WPPSI-R Performance, Verbal, and Full Scale IQs have excellent reliability in eight of the nine age groups covered by the test. From ages 3 through 6½ years, the reliabilities for each of the three IQs range from .90 to .97; this range is excellent. However, at age 7 years the reliability coefficients for the Performance and Verbal Scale IQs ($r_{xx} = .85$ and .86, respectively) are less satisfactory than that for the Full Scale IQ ($r_{xx} = .90$). The WPPSI-R manual attributes the lower reliability coefficients at the 7-year level to ceiling effects, but provides no research evidence to support this hypothesis. (Ceiling effects exist when a test has too few items at the upper levels to measure reliably the ability of bright children.) Across the nine age groups, the average internal consistency reliabilities are .92 for the Performance Scale IQ, .95 for the Verbal Scale IQ, and .96 for the Full Scale IQ (see Table G-1).

Subtest Reliabilities

The reliabilities for the subtests are lower than those for the three scales (see Table G-1). The average subtest reliabilities range from a low of .63 for Object Assembly to a high of .86 for Similarities. For the nine age groups, median reliabilities are highest for ages 3, 3½, 4, 4½, and 5 ($Mdn\ r_{xx}$'s range from .830 to .870), followed by age 6 ($Mdn\ r_{xx} = .780$), age 5½ ($Mdn\ r_{xx} = .775$), age 6½ ($Mdn\ r_{xx} = .745$), and age 7 ($Mdn\ r_{xx} = .660$). The lowest subtest reliabilities are found at age 7 (see Table G-2).

Standard Errors of Measurement

The average standard errors of measurement (SE_m) in IQ points are 3.00 for the Full Scale, 4.24 for the Performance Scale, and 3.35 for the Verbal Scale (see Table G-1).

Table G-1
Average Reliability Coefficients and Standard Errors of Measurement for WPPSI-R Subtests and Scales

Subtest or scale	Average reliability coefficient	Average standard error of measurement
Object Assembly	.63	1.82
Geometric Design	.79	1.37
Block Design	.85	1.16
Mazes	.77	1.44
Picture Completion	.85	1.16
Animal Pegs	.66	1.75
Information	.84	1.20
Comprehension	.83	1.24
Arithmetic	.80	1.34
Vocabulary	.84	1.20
Similarities	.86	1.12
Sentences	.82	1.27
Performance IQ	.92	4.24
Verbal IQ	.95	3.35
Full Scale IQ	.96	3.00

Note. Reliability coefficients for all subtests except Animal Pegs are split-half coefficients corrected by the Spearman-Brown formula. For Animal Pegs the reliability coefficient is a test-retest coefficient.
Source: Adapted from Wechsler (1989).

Table G-2
Median Subtest Reliabilities at Nine Age Groups and at the Average of the Nine Age Groups on the WPPSI-R

Age	Range	Median
3	.63–.90	.850
3½	.63–.89	.845
4	.66–.89	.870
4½	.56–.93	.840
5	.59–.86	.830
5½	.57–.86	.775
6	.66–.86	.780
6½	.66–.83	.745
7	.54–.86	.660
Average	.63–.86	.825

Thus, as with all of the Wechsler scales, more confidence can be placed in an IQ based on the Full Scale than in one based on either the Performance or Verbal Scale alone.

The average standard errors of measurement for the subtests in scaled-score points range from 1.16 to 1.82 for the Performance Scale subtests and from 1.12 to 1.34 for the

Verbal Scale subtests. Within the Performance Scale, Block Design and Picture Completion have the smallest SE_m (1.16 for both). Within the Verbal Scale, Similarities, Information, and Vocabulary have the smallest SE_m (1.12, 1.20, and 1.20, respectively).

Test-Retest Reliablity

When the WPPSI-R was readministered to 175 children in the standardization group after a period of approximately 3 to 7 weeks ($M = 4$ weeks), average increases of 6.3, 2.8, and 5.1 IQ points (which were all significant at $p < .001$) were found on the Performance, Verbal, and Full Scales, respectively (see Table G-3) (Wechsler, 1989). Respective

Table G-3
Test-Retest WPPSI-R IQs for 175 Children at Two Age Groups—3 Through 4-11 and 5 Through 7¼ Years of Age

Scale	First testing		Second testing		
	Mean IQ	SD	Mean IQ	SD	Change[a]
Performance IQ	101.8	14.4	108.1	16.6	+ 6.3
Verbal IQ	101.4	14.7	104.2	16.3	+ 2.8
Full Scale IQ	101.7	14.4	106.8	16.6	+ 5.1

[a] All mean change scores are significant at $p < .001$.
Source: Adapted from Wechsler (1989).

test-retest correlations were .87, .89, and .91 for the Performance, Verbal, and Full Scales. The changes in subtest scaled scores, which were probably related to practice effects, were as follows: Object Assembly, +1.2; Geometric Design, 0; Block Design, +1.3; Mazes, +1.0; Picture Completion, +.9; Animal Pegs, +.7; Information, +.4; Comprehension, +.4; Arithmetic, +.4; Vocabulary, −.2; Similarities, +.9; and Sentences, +.4.

The preceding changes, which ranged from −.2 (Vocabulary) to +1.3 (Block Design), were significant for 10 of the 12 subtests. The two exceptions were Geometric Design, where there was no change, and Vocabulary, where the change was extremely small. Generally, subtests on the Performance Scale showed greater practice effects (M change = .85) than did subtests on the Verbal Scale (M change = .45). (Differences in test–retest change scores for the three scales and 12 subtests were evaluated by using a t test for differences between correlated means.)

Precision Range

Table H-1 in Appendix H shows the confidence intervals for the 68, 85, 90, 95, and 99 percent levels for the WPPSI-R Performance, Verbal, and Full Scale IQs by age level. The precision ranges (or confidence intervals) on the WPPSI-R are generally similar throughout the nine age groups. For the Full Scale IQ, they range between 6 and 8 points at the 95 percent confidence level. The precision ranges are narrower for the Full and Verbal Scale IQs than for the Performance Scale IQ and narrower at ages 3 to 5 than at ages 5½ to 7. *The child's specific age group should be used to obtain the most accurate confidence interval.* For further discussion of precision ranges and how to report them, see pages 28–29 and 729–730.

VALIDITY

Although approximately 42 percent of the items on the WPPSI-R are new, much of the research on the validity of the WPPSI probably is pertinent to the WPPSI-R. Studies related to the validity of the WPPSI, reviewed on pages 195–198 of this text, indicate that it has adequate construct, concurrent, and predictive validity for many different types of normal and handicapped children in the age range from 4 to 6½ years.

Concurrent Validity

Because the WPPSI-R is a newly published test, little is known about how valid it is over its entire age range, except for the few studies reported in the WPPSI-R manual. These studies are summarized in Table G-4 and are discussed below.

1. *WPPSI-R and WPPSI.* Full Scale IQs on the WPPSI-R were found to be about *8 points lower*, on the average, than those on the WPPSI in a sample of 144 children between the ages of 48 and 79 months. Similarly, IQs on the Performance Scale and Verbal Scale were lower on the WPPSI-R than on the WPPSI by about 9 and 5 IQ points, respectively, on the average.

For the 11 subtests in common, correlations ranged from a low of .58 for Mazes to a high of .79 for Sentences (*Mdn r* = .69). Correlations between subtests on the Perfor-

Table G-4
Summary of Concurrent Validity Studies Reported in WPPSI-R Manual

Study	N	Age range	Test-retest interval	Scale	Test WPPSI-R	Test	D^a	r
1	144	48–79 mos. (*M* = unknown)	3–5 weeks		WPPSI-R	WPPSI		
				Performance				
				M	102.8	112.2	− 9.4	.82
				SD	15.9	15.7	−	−
				Verbal				
				M	104.0	109.1	− 5.1	.85
				SD	15.9	16.9	−	−
				Full Scale				
				M	103.9	111.6	− 8.3	.87
				SD	16.2	16.3	−	−
2	50	72–86 mos. (*M* = 79 mos.)	3–30 days (*M* = 19 days)		WPPSI-R	WISC-R		
				Performance				
				M	99.8	108.7	− 8.9	.71
				SD	13.1	12.3	−	−
				Verbal				
				M	106.9	111.6	− 4.7	.77
				SD	11.3	15.3	−	−
				Full Scale				
				M	103.8	111.3	− 7.5	.85
				SD	11.6	11.7	−	−

(Table continues next page)

Table G-4 (cont.)

Study	N	Age range	Test-retest interval	Scale	Test		D^a	r
3	115	4-0 to 7-2 yrs. (M = 5-10)	1–90 days (M = 16.7 days)	Performance	WPPSI-R	Stanford-Binet −4th Ed.		
				M	104.8	—	—	.56
				SD	13.2	—	—	—
				Verbal				
				M	104.1	—	—	.73
				SD	15.1	—	—	—
				Full Scale				
				M	105.3	107.2[b]	− 1.9	.74
				SD	14.0	12.8	—	—
4	93	4–6 yrs. (M = 62.5 mos.)	7–21 days (M = 14 days)	Performance	WPPSI-R	McCarthy Scales		
				M	101.2	—	—	—
				SD	14.4	—	—	.66
				Verbal				
				M	103.3	—	—	.77
				SD	12.9	—	—	—
				Full Scale				
				M	102.4	104.8[c]	− 2.4	.81
				SD	13.5	14.3	—	—
5	59	37–76 mos. (M = 61 mos.)	5–14 days (M = 9.5 days)	Performance	WPPSI-R	K-ABC		
				M	100.4	—	—	.41
				SD	13.5	—	—	—
				Verbal				
				M	94.4	—	—	.42
				SD	12.5	—	—	—
				Full Scale				
				M	96.8	103.1[d]	− 6.3	.49
				SD	12.6	13.1	—	—

[a]Difference.
[b]Using Composite Score.
[c]Using General Cognitive Index.
[d]Using Mental Processing Composite.

mance Scale were slightly lower (range of .58 to .74, *Mdn r* = .64) than those on the Verbal Scale (range of .59 to .79, *Mdn r* = .69). These somewhat low correlations suggest that the subtests in common on the WPPSI-R and the WPPSI do not share a close degree of correspondence. It is not clear why the correlations between the subtests on the two tests were not higher.

2. *WPPSI-R and WISC-R*. In another sample of 50 children, ages 72 to 86 months, the WPPSI-R yielded *lower* Full Scale IQs than the WISC-R by about *8 points*, on the average. Performance Scale IQs on the WPPSI-R were lower by about 9 points and Verbal Scale IQs were lower by about 5 points, on the average, than the respective WISC-R IQs.

3. *WPPSI-R and Stanford-Binet Intelligence Scale — 4th Edition*. In a sample of 115 children between 4-0 and 7-2 years, IQs were found to be *similar* on the WPPSI-R and Stanford-Binet Intelligence Scale — 4th Edition. The mean

Full Scale IQ on the WPPSI-R was about 2 points lower than the mean Composite Score on the Stanford-Binet—4th Edition.

4. *WPPSI-R and McCarthy Scales of Children's Abilities.* The WPPSI-R yielded scores that were *similar* to those on the McCarthy Scales of Children's Abilities in a sample of 93 children, ages 4 to 6 years. The mean WPPSI-R Full Scale IQ was about 2 points lower than the mean General Cognitive Index on the McCarthy Scales.

5. *WPPSI-R and K-ABC.* The WPPSI-R yielded lower IQs than did the K-ABC in a sample of 59 children ages 37 to 76 months. The mean WPPSI-R Full Scale IQ was about *6 points lower* than the mean K-ABC Mental Composite.

Construct Validity

The principal components analysis cited later in this appendix, as well as the factor analyses cited in the WPPSI-R manual, indicates that the test measures adequately two factors that correspond to the Verbal and Performance Scales of the test. In addition, the test provides a fair measure of general intelligence. Thus, there is support for the construct validity of the WPPSI-R.

Comment on the Validity of the WPPSI-R

The validity studies in the WPPSI-R manual suggest that the WPPSI-R has adequate concurrent and construct validity. This conclusion, however, may not pertain to all ages covered by the test, particularly ages 36 to 48 months, which are new to the revision. Because only one of the studies cited in the WPPSI-R manual sampled this age period, much additional research is needed to investigate the validity of the WPPSI-R at the earliest age levels of the test. It also would be helpful to have additional studies for children who are 7 years old, because this age group is new to the test, and for children between 4 and 6½ years as well.

The WPPSI-R and the WISC-R should not be considered parallel forms. The study cited above suggests that children tested first with the WPPSI-R and then with the WISC-R will probably show an increase of about 8 IQ points, on the average. (This generalization may not hold for handicapped or exceptional children, particularly for those at the lower or upper levels of the IQ distribution.) This increase in WISC-R scores may have *nothing* to do with any intervening events resulting in changes in the child or in the child's environment and *likely is associated with the two different sets of norms.* Almost 15 years separate the standardization of the two instruments, and

any differences in scores may be *solely* a function of the different standardization samples. It is also possible that the WPPSI-R is a more difficult test than the WISC-R. Changes greater than 8 points may reflect genuine changes in performance, however.

Similarly, children first tested with the WISC-R (say at the age of 6 years) and then retested with the WPPSI-R (say at the age of 7 years) may show a *decrease* in scores of up to 8 points, on the average. Again, this decrease should be understood solely as a function of the different instruments, and not attributed to decrements in the intellectual ability of the children. Decreases beyond 8 points may suggest decrements in performance, however.

The other concurrent validity studies cited in the WPPSI-R manual suggest that the WPPSI-R yields IQs that are similar to those of the Stanford-Binet Intelligence Scale—4th Edition and McCarthy Scales of Children's Abilities for children in the normal range of functioning. The comparability of the WPPSI-R and Stanford-Binet—4th Edition and WPPSI-R and McCarthy Scales needs further study in samples of exceptional children. The WPPSI-R yielded IQs that were not comparable to those on the K-ABC. Scores on the K-ABC were generally about 6 points higher than those on the WPPSI-R. Again, the relationship between the two tests needs to be studied in samples of exceptional children and additional samples of normal children.

INTERCORRELATIONS BETWEEN SUBTESTS AND SCALES

Intercorrelations between subtests and scales permit us to observe the degree of relationship between various parts of the WPPSI-R. Average intercorrelations between the 12 subtests range from a low of .25 (Object Assembly and Sentences) to a high of .66 (Information and Comprehension). The median intercorrelation is .41. The six *highest* subtest average intercorrelations are between Information and Comprehension (.66), Information and Vocabulary (.60), Comprehension and Vocabulary (.60), Information and Arithmetic (.59), Information and Similarities (.57), and Information and Sentences (.55). The seven *lowest* subtest average intercorrelations (seven are listed instead of six because of ties) are between Mazes and Sentences (.24), Object Assembly and Sentences (.25), Geometric Design and Vocabulary (.26), Object Assembly and Comprehension (.26), Mazes and Comprehension (.26), Mazes and Vocabulary (.26), and Animal Pegs and Vocabulary (.26). The Verbal subtests have higher intercorrelations than the Performance subtests. The lowest correlations are found between the subtests of the two different scales.

FACTOR ANALYSIS

A principal components analysis with varimax rotation was performed on the standardization data. (See pages 31–34 of this text for a brief explanation of factor analysis.) Two principal factors were found at all age levels, with the exception of age 7, where a three-factor solution was also appropriate. (In the three-factor solution Mazes and Animal Pegs were the only subtests that had loadings above .40 on the third factor.) The two-factor solution best ex-

plains the WPPSI-R throughout all of its age levels. The Verbal factor (or Verbal Comprehension) is best represented at all ages by the six subtests in the Verbal Scale: Comprehension, Information, Vocabulary, Sentences, Similarities, and Arithmetic. The Performance factor (or Perceptual Organization) is best represented at most ages by five of the six subtests in the Performance Scale: Block Design, Geometric Design, Object Assembly, Mazes, and Animal Pegs (see Table G-5).

Picture Completion does not consistently load on the Performance factor at all ages. It has higher loadings on the Verbal than Performance factor at age 3 and loads well on both the Verbal and Performance factors at ages 3½, 4, 4½, 6½, and 7. It clearly loads on the Performance factor *only* at ages 5, 5½, and 6. For all ages combined, Picture

Table G-5
Factor Loadings of WPPSI-R Subtests for Nine Age Groups and the Average Following Varimax Rotation

Subtest	\multicolumn{10}{c}{Age group}
	3	3½	4	4½	5	5½	6	6½	7	Av.
\multicolumn{11}{c}{**Factor A — Verbal**}
Object Assembly	21	15	08	12	23	13	06	30	02	14
Geometric Design	38	29	22	19	−03	17	20	16	09	18
Block Design	12	22	34	26	45	23	18	39	15	26
Mazes	25	15	26	23	13	−04	24	06	13	15
Picture Completion	63	55	49	53	32	22	22	41	41	41
Animal Pegs	18	19	30	28	41	26	15	24	24	24
Information	83	79	81	77	80	73	78	79	70	78
Comprehension	80	87	85	84	80	77	79	75	75	81
Arithmetic	59	69	70	63	62	52	64	65	66	62
Vocabulary	79	79	77	83	81	79	78	82	70	79
Similarities	73	72	78	74	72	75	68	71	65	72
Sentences	72	77	71	76	73	75	76	61	73	74
\multicolumn{11}{c}{**Factor B — Performance**}
Object Assembly	70	68	75	76	64	66	76	68	77	72
Geometric Design	69	75	75	77	80	67	65	72	55	72
Block Design	69	77	74	76	65	80	78	72	78	75
Mazes	69	69	63	63	79	73	69	75	50	69
Picture Completion	37	53	55	56	65	62	66	55	44	57
Animal Pegs	52	58	64	65	38	50	48	31	36	52
Information	32	33	34	37	25	22	28	26	30	31
Comprehension	21	20	19	21	07	10	04	13	08	16
Arithmetic	43	39	38	44	50	54	40	36	30	44
Vocabulary	13	13	18	16	08	17	21	18	26	17
Similarities	25	30	24	28	29	20	30	25	−05	26
Sentences	22	13	27	19	22	13	13	29	16	19

Note. Av. = Average. Decimal points omitted. Factors based on principal components analysis.

Completion has a substantial loading on *both* the Verbal and Performance factors, but somewhat higher loadings on the Performance factor. At 3 years, a purer measure of the Performance factor can be obtained by using only Object Assembly, Geometric Design, Block Design, and Mazes (and also adding Animal Pegs if desired).

WPPSI-R Subtests as Measures of *g*

The extent to which the WPPSI-R subtests measure general intelligence or *g* can be determined by examining the loadings on the first unrotated factor in the principal component analysis. Overall, the WPPSI-R is a fair measure of *g*, with 45 percent of its variance attributed to *g*. Higher *g* loadings are found at ages 3 to 5 (average loadings range from 45 to 50 percent) than at ages 5 to 7 (average loadings range from 34 to 44 percent), with age 7 having the *lowest* *g* loadings (average loading is 34 percent).

With respect to the measurement of *g*, the WPPSI-R subtests form two clusters: (a) Information, Arithmetic, Comprehension, Similarities, and Vocabulary are *good measures of g*, and (b) Picture Completion, Block Design, Sentences, Geometric Design, Object Assembly, Mazes, and Animal Pegs are *fair measures of g* (see Table G-6). The subtests in the Verbal Scale have higher *g* loadings than those in the Performance Scale. In the Verbal Scale, Information has the *highest* loading, whereas in the Performance Scale, Picture Completion and Block Design have the *highest* loadings. Any of the five standard Verbal sub-

tests may serve as a good measure of *g*. Although none of the Performance subtests are good measures of *g*, Block Design and Picture Completion, with 47 percent of their variance attributed to *g*, could be used if nonverbal measures of *g* are needed.

At each age level, the Verbal subtests have, on the average, consistently higher *g* loadings than do the Performance subtests. The consistency of this finding is striking. There are only two age levels at which any Verbal subtest contributes less than 40 percent to the measurement of *g*: at age 6, Comprehension (38 percent), and at age 7, Similarities (26 percent). Block Design is a fair-to-good measure of *g* at each of the nine age levels. Picture Completion is a fair-to-good measure of *g* at every age level of the test.

WPPSI-R Subtest Specificity

Subtest specificity refers to the proportion of a subtest's variance that is both reliable (that is, not due to errors of measurement) and distinctive to the subtest (see pages 32–34 of this text for further information about subtest specificity). Although the individual subtests on the WPPSI-R overlap in their measurement properties (that is, the majority of reliable variance for most subtests is common factor variance), most possess sufficient specificity at some age levels to justify interpretation of specific subtest functions (see Table G-7).

Throughout the entire age range covered by the WPPSI-R, Picture Completion is the only subtest that has *ample*

Table G-6
WPPSI-R Subtests as Measures of *g*

	Good measure of *g*			Fair measure of *g*		
Subtest	Average loading of *g*	Proportion of variance attributed to *g* (%)		Subtest	Average loading of *g*	Proportion of variance attributed to *g* (%)
Information	.79	63		Picture Completion	.69	47
Arithmetic	.76	57		Block Design	.68	47
Comprehension	.72	52		Sentences	.68	46
Similarities	.72	51		Geometric Design	.61	37
Vocabulary	.71	51		Object Assembly	.57	33
				Mazes	.56	32
				Animal Pegs	.52	27

Note. Following were the criteria used to classify subtests as good, fair, or poor measures of *g*: *good*—variance attributed to *g* was approximately 50 percent or higher; *fair*—variance attributed to *g* was between 26 percent and 49 percent; *poor*—variance attributed to *g* was between 0 percent and 25 percent. The proportion of variance attributed to *g* was based on a five-place decimal number.

Table G-7
Amount of Specificity in WPPSI-R Subtests

WPPSI-R subtest	Ages with ample specificity	Ages with adequate specificity	Ages with inadequate specificity
Object Assembly	–	–	3–7, Av.
Geometric Design	6, 7	3–3½, 4½, Av.	4, 5–5½, 6½
Block Design	3	3½–5, 6, 7, Av.	5½, 6½
Mazes	3–4½, 6, 7, Av.	–	5–5½, 6½
Picture Completion	3–7, Av.	–	
Animal Pegs	3, 5, 6–7, Av.	–	3½–4½, 5½
Information	–	3½, 4½	3, 4, 5–7, Av.
Comprehension	–	3, 5–5½	3½–4½, 6–7, Av.
Arithmetic	3, 5½, 6½	3½, 4½, 6, Av.	4, 5, 7
Vocabulary	4	3, 5–5½, Av.	3½, 4½, 6–7
Similarities	3–3½, 4½–6, Av.	4	6½–7
Sentences	3–4	4½–5, Av.	5½–7

Note. Av. = average of the nine age groups. Kaufman's (1975a) rule of thumb was used to classify the amount of specificity in each subtest. Subtests with *ample specificity* have specific variance that (a) reflects 25 percent or more of the subtest's total variance *and* (b) exceeds the subtest's error variance. Subtests with *adequate specificity* have specific variance that (a) reflects between 15 to 24 percent of the subtest's total variance *and* (b) exceeds the subtest's error variance. Subtests with *inadequate specificity* have specific variance that is either (a) less than 15 percent of the subtest's total variance *or* (b) equal to or less than the subtest's error variance.

specificity and Object Assembly is the only subtest that has *inadequate specificity*. Each of the 10 other subtests shows a unique pattern of specificity—that is, the ages at which each one has ample, adequate, or inadequate specificity differ. More subtests have inadequate specificity at ages 4, 5½, 6½, and 7 than at the other ages, however.

Subtests with inadequate specificity should not be interpreted as measuring specific functions, and cautious interpretation is required for those subtests falling within the adequate specificity category. Subtests with inadequate specifity, however, still can be interpreted as measuring *g* (see Table G-6) and the appropriate principal factor (Verbal or Performance) (see Table G-5).

Factor Analysis of the WPPSI-R Compared to the WISC-R

The factor structure of the WPPSI-R is generally similar to that of the WISC-R, particularly in regard to the Verbal (or Verbal Comprehension) factor and Performance (or Perceptual Organization) factor. The primary difference between WPPSI-R and WISC-R factor structures is that a Freedom from Distractibility factor emerges on the WISC-R but not on the WPPSI-R. Conceivably, sustained directed attention, partly measured by the Freedom from Distractibility factor, is a part of every subtest at younger age levels and emerges as a separate factor only at some-

what older age levels. Alternatively, it may be that the Freedom from Distractibility factor does not emerge on the WPPSI-R because the test does not include either Digit Span or Coding; these two subtests, along with Arithmetic, generally defined Freedom from Distractibility on the WISC-R.

IQ RANGES AND SUBTEST SCALED-SCORE RANGES

Information about the range of IQs available at each age level of the test will help you (a) to determine whether the WPPSI-R is an appropriate instrument for evaluating children at the extreme ranges of intelligence and (b) to monitor children's performance over time. Knowing about the available range of subtest scaled scores at each age level of the test will help in profile analysis. This section of the chapter discusses the range of IQs and subtest scaled scores in the WPPSI-R and provides guidelines for evaluating IQs and subtest scaled scores that are at the extremes of the range.

IQ Ranges

The range of Full Scale IQs from 41 to 160, as shown in Table 26 of the WPPSI-R manual, cannot be obtained at every age level of the test. When the rule of thumb recommended in the WPPSI-R manual for computing IQs is followed—that IQs be computed only when the child has a minimum of three raw scores of 1 on the Performance Scale and three raw scores of 1 on the Verbal Scale—it is not until 5¾ years that a Full Scale IQ of 41 can be obtained (six raw scores of 1 and four raw scores of 0). The lowest Full Scale IQ possible at 3 years, for example, is 65, which is barely below two standard deviations from the mean (see Table G-8). (The lower limits of the ranges shown in Table

Table G-8
Performance, Verbal, and Full Scale IQ Ranges by Three-Month Age Intervals on the WPPSI-R

Age[a]	Performance Scale	Verbal Scale	Full Scale
3	66–160	71–160	65–160
3¼	62–160	67–160	61–160
3½	60–160	66–160	59–160
3¾	56–160	63–160	56–160
4	52–160	58–160	51–160
4¼	49–160	54–160	47–160
4½	48–160	54–160	46–160
4¾	47–160	53–160	45–160
5	47–160	48–160	43–160
5¼	45–160	48–160	42–160
5½	45–160	47–160	42–160
5¾	45–160	46–160	41–160
6	45–160	46–160	41–160
6¼	45–160	46–160	41–160
6½	45–156	46–157	41–160
6¾	45–156	46–152	41–160
7	45–156	46–152	41–160

Note. Age 7 represents a four-month interval. Ranges were obtained by using data from Table 25, "Scaled Score Equivalents of Raw Scores," and Table 27, "IQ Equivalents of Sums of Scaled Scores," in the WPPSI-R manual. Ranges based on the 10 standard subtests using the suggested criterion in the WPPSI-R manual that examinees must have three raw scores of at least 1 on the Performance Scale and three raw scores of at least 1 on the Verbal Scale in order for an IQ to be computed. The lower limits of the IQ range represent the lowest IQs that can be obtained. Other combinations of successes and failures will produce slightly higher IQs at the lower limits of the range.
[a] In years.

G-8 may vary depending on the combination of subtests for which raw-score points are earned.) The lowest possible Performance Scale IQ at 3 years is 66 and the lowest possible Verbal Scale IQ is 71 (three scores of 1 point and two scores of 0 points on each scale). Because the lower limit of IQs provided by the WPPSI-R is not consistent throughout the scale, monitoring changes in the perfor-

mance of children functioning more than two standard deviations below the mean of the test will be difficult.

IQs at the lower limits. The following example illustrates the IQs given to a 3-year-old child who has raw scores of 1 on the Object Assembly, Geometric Design, Block Design, Information, Arithmetic, and Vocabulary subtests and raw scores of 0 on each of the four remaining subtests. Six 1-point raw scores will yield a Performance Scale IQ of 66 (22 scaled-score points), a Verbal Scale IQ of 71 (26 scaled-score points), and a Full Scale IQ of 65 (48 scaled-score points). This example demonstrates that the WPPSI-R may not provide precise IQs for children who are functioning two or more standard deviations below the mean of the test. Research is needed to determine the validity of the WPPSI-R for mild and moderately mentally retarded children. If a child fails all or most of the items on the WPPSI-R, it is advisable to administer a test that may provide a more accurate estimate of the child's ability.

Another example illustrates how the restricted range of IQs at the earliest year levels of the test may seriously affect the interpretation of a child's performance. A 3-year-old boy obtains a Full Scale IQ of 65, and when retested at 5¼ years, he obtains a Full Scale IQ of 41. The 24-point drop between the first and second examinations may be purely an artifact of the IQs available at each age level of the test. As previously noted, at the earliest year levels of the test, the floor is much higher than at the later year levels—that is, the lowest IQs cannot be obtained at the early ages. *Thus, in the case of low-functioning children, when the results of two (or more) examinations given two (or more) years apart are compared, there is simply no way of knowing whether there was a serious decrement in the children's performance.* In the preceding example (and in similar cases), it would be best to assume that no decrement in mental ability occurred during the interval between the two examinations.

IQs at the upper limits. In contrast to the restricted and variable range of IQs at the lower limits of the WPPSI-R, the upper limit of the WPPSI-R IQ range—a Full Scale IQ of 160—can be obtained at every age level of the test. On the one hand, the uniform ceiling is a definite advantage in follow-up evaluations of children who are functioning three or four standard deviations above the mean. On the other hand, the uniform ceiling also represents a low ceiling level for extremely bright 3-year-olds who answer every item correctly. For example, if every item of the test were answered correctly by both a 3-year-old and a 7-year-old, both children would obtain the exact same IQ of 160. It is quite likely that the 3-year-old is brighter than the 7-year-old, but this is not reflected in his or her score.

The failure of the WPPSI-R to differentiate between the brightest of the 3-year-olds and the brightest of the 7-year-olds happens in part because at the 3-year level (and at adjacent ages) several raw scores at the upper limits of each subtest are awarded the *exact* same scaled score of 19. For example, raw scores from 21 to 47 on the Vocabulary subtest are given a scaled score of 19, as are raw scores from 24 to 42 on the Block Design subtest. The failure of the WPPSI-R to differentiate among young children who are functioning more than four standard deviations above the mean is not a major criticism of the scale, however. None of the leading measures of cognitive ability have a range of IQs greater than that of the WPPSI-R.

Although the ceiling level on the Full Scale is uniform throughout the WPPSI-R, the ceiling level on the Performance and Verbal Scales is somewhat less uniform (see Table G-8). The highest Performance IQ available at ages 6½ through 7 is 156, whereas the highest Verbal IQ available at age 6½ is 157 and at ages 6¾ and 7 is 152. These somewhat restricted ranges at the upper ages should not cause too much of a problem in interpreting IQs on the Performance and Verbal Scales.

Subtest Scaled-Score Ranges

The major problem with the scaled-score ranges occurs at the first year level of the test, where points are awarded to children who fail every item. For example, children who fail every item on Geometric Design, Mazes, Picture Completion, Information, Comprehension, Similarities, or Sentences are given 5 or 6 scaled-score points (see Table G-9). At 3 years, Object Assembly is the only subtest on which a scaled score of 1 can be obtained. This problem is related to the limited floor discussed previously. For example, 3-year-old children receive up to 43 scaled-score points even when they fail every item on the 10 standard subtests; the corresponding IQ is 62. It is also noteworthy that at none of the 17 separate age groups listed in Table 25, "Scaled Score Equivalents of Raw Scores," of the WPPSI-R manual (pages 170–186) is it possible to obtain the entire range of scaled-score points from 1 to 19 on all subtests.

The WPPSI-R manual, as noted before, advises that IQs not be computed (as was done in the previous example) unless children obtain at least one success on three Verbal and on three Performance subtests. Research is needed, however, to determine the validity of this recommendation.

Table G-9
Subtest Scaled-Score Ranges by Three-Month Age Intervals on the WPPSI-R

	Subtest											
Age[a]	OA	GD	BD	MA	PC	AP	I	C	A	V	S	Se
3	1–19	5–19	4–19	5–19	5–19	2–19	5–19	6–19	3–19	3–19	6–19	5–19
3¼	1–19	4–19	4–19	4–19	4–19	1–19	4–19	6–19	3–19	2–19	5–19	4–19
3½	1–19	4–19	4–19	3–19	4–19	1–19	4–19	5–19	3–19	2–19	5–19	3–19
3¾	1–19	3–19	3–19	2–19	3–19	1–19	3–19	5–19	2–19	2–19	4–19	3–19
4	1–19	2–19	3–19	1–19	2–19	1–19	2–19	4–19	1–19	2–19	3–19	3–19
4¼	1–19	1–19	3–19	1–19	1–19	1–19	2–19	3–19	1–19	1–19	3–19	2–19
4½	1–19	1–19	3–19	1–19	1–19	1–19	2–19	3–19	1–19	1–19	3–19	2–19
4¾	1–19	1–18	2–19	1–19	1–19	1–19	1–19	3–19	1–19	1–19	2–19	2–19
5	1–19	1–18	1–19	1–19	1–19	1–19	1–19	2–19	1–19	1–19	2–19	1–19
5¼	1–19	1–17	1–19	1–19	1–19	1–19	1–19	2–19	1–19	1–19	2–19	1–19
5½	1–18	1–17	1–19	1–19	1–19	1–19	1–19	2–18	1–19	1–19	1–19	1–19
5¾	1–18	1–17	1–19	1–19	1–19	1–19	1–19	1–18	1–19	1–19	1–19	1–19
6	1–17	1–17	1–19	1–19	1–19	1–19	1–19	1–18	1–19	1–19	1–19	1–19
6¼	1–17	1–17	1–19	1–19	1–19	1–19	1–19	1–18	1–18	1–19	1–18	1–19
6½	1–16	1–16	1–18	1–18	1–19	1–19	1–18	1–17	1–17	1–19	1–18	1–19
6¾	1–16	1–16	1–18	1–18	1–18	1–19	1–17	1–17	1–16	1–19	1–17	1–19
7	1–16	1–16	1–18	1–18	1–18	1–19	1–17	1–17	1–16	1–19	1–17	1–17

Note. Abbreviations: OA = Object Assembly, GD = Geometric Design, BD = Block Design, MA = Mazes, PC = Picture Completion, AP = Animal Pegs, I = Information, C = Comprehension, A = Arithmetic, V = Vocabulary, S = Similarities, Se = Sentences. Age 7 represents a four-month interval. Ranges based on Table 25, "Scaled Score Equivalents of Raw Scores," in WPPSI-R manual.
[a] In years.

It should be considered as tentative because the WPPSI-R manual fails to indicate the basis for it. We don't know, for example, whether IQs derived from four (or five) raw scores of 1 are reliable and valid. In addition, we need to know more about the reliability and validity of IQs obtained using the rule of thumb given in the WPPSI-R manual.

A minor problem occurs at the upper limits of the last two years of the test. At age 7, for example, it is possible to obtain 19 scaled-score points on only two of the subtests— Animal Pegs and Vocabulary. In addition, at age 7, there is a low ceiling (scaled score of 16) on three subtests: Object Assembly, Geometric Design, and Arithmetic. Finally, on some subtests the ceiling level of 19 scaled-score points is reached midway through the age range (for example, at age 4½ for Geometric Design and at age 5¼ for Object Assembly and Comprehension), after which the ceiling level goes down.

The failure to have a uniform scaled-score range throughout all age levels of the test means that profile analysis cannot be performed in a routine manner, particularly at the lower and upper limits of the scaled-score range. *Therefore, in interpreting children's profiles, you must take into account the range of scaled scores available for that child's specific age.*

NORMATIVE CHANGES ON ANIMAL PEGS

Because Animal Pegs is the only subtest that has exactly the same number of items, scoring procedure, and time limits in the WPPSI and in the WPPSI-R, it is of interest to see how the norms have changed over the 22-year period between the publication of the original and revised versions of the test. At ages 4 through 6½, where the two forms overlap, children, in most cases, must earn more raw-score points on the WPPSI-R than on the WPPSI to obtain the same scaled score. The changes range from −1 to 17 raw-score points (*Mdn* change = 4 raw-score points).

Changes Related to Age and Ability Level

The normative changes on the Animal Pegs subtest tend to be related to both age and ability level. *The groups usually most affected by the changes are (a) children between 4 and 4½ years with above-average ability (for example, with scaled scores above 10) and (b) children between 4¾ and 6½ years with below-average ability (for example, with scaled scores below 10). These groups, in most cases,*

need to be more proficient (in either speed, accuracy, or some combination of the two) to maintain the same relative position on the WPPSI-R that they had on the WPPSI. In contrast, 4-year-olds with below-average ability and 5- to 6½-year-olds with above-average ability have not changed appreciably (see Table G-10). Overall, changes are greatest at age 4 (*Mdn* change = 7 raw-score points) and smallest at age 6½ (*Mdn* change = 1 raw-score point) (see Table G-11).

Table G-10
Median Additional Raw-Score Points Needed on WPPSI-R Animal Pegs to Obtain Same Scaled Score as on WPPSI at Younger and Upper Ages for Low and High Scaled-Score Ranges

Scaled-score range	Ages		
	4–4½	4¾–5¾	6–6½
1–9	1	8	6
11–19	8	3	1

Table G-11
Additional Points Needed on WPPSI-R Animal Pegs to Obtain Same Scaled Score as on WPPSI at Ages 4, 5¼, and 6½ Years

Scaled score	Age			
	4	5¼	6½	Mdn[a]
1	0	0	0	0
4	1	7	17	7
7	2	13	1	9
10	7	7	1	7
13	11	3	0	3
16	9	3	0	3
19	13	5	2	5
Mdn[b]	7	4	1	4

Note. Based on Table 25 in the WPPSI-R manual and Table 21 in the WPPSI manual. The raw scores shown in the table are at the lower limits of the range of raw scores for each scaled score. Animal Pegs is called Animal House on the WPPSI.
[a] Over 11 age intervals from 4 through 6½ years.
[b] Over the range of scaled scores from 1 through 19.

These trends are examined in more detail in Table G-11, which shows the additional raw-score points needed for seven representative scaled scores at ages 4, 5¼, and 6½ years. A 4-year-old child needs, for example, 13 more raw-score points on the WPPSI-R than on the WPPSI to earn a scaled score of 19. Translated into time requirements, this means that to earn the highest scaled score, a 4-year-old with a perfect performance must work 1 minute *faster* on the WPPSI-R than on the WPPSI (30″ on the WPPSI-R and 1′30″ on the WPPSI). Another way to understand the changes on Animal Pegs is to note, for example, that a 4-year-old with a raw score of 52 earns a scaled score of 19 on the WPPSI, but a scaled score of only 15 on the WPPSI-R. For a 6½-year-old child, a raw score of 15 earns a scaled score of 4 on the WPPSI, but a scaled score of only 1 on the WPPSI-R. These are some of the most dramatic normative changes on the Animal Pegs subtest.

Accounting for Normative Changes on Animal Pegs

It is not easy to account for the normative changes that have taken place on the Animal Pegs subtest. Perhaps during the years between the initial standardization and the revision, young children have had better nutrition or increased exposure to manipulative experiences at preschool or at home. The normative changes also may be due to unknown differences in the WPPSI-R and WPPSI standardization groups.

Examining the changes in relation to both age and ability level suggests that changes have been minimal for younger children with below-average ability. However, during the years between the original test and the revision, school-aged children with below-average ability appear to have become more proficient in the skills measured by the Animal Pegs subtest. On the original norms, the school-age children with above-average ability were already near or at the ceiling level, and therefore few changes could be expected in their performance. Overall, the data indicate that children must be more proficient on the WPPSI-R than on the WPPSI Animal Pegs subtest to maintain their same relative position.

COMPARISON OF THE WPPSI-R AND WPPSI

Although similar to its predecessor, the WPPSI-R differs from it in some important ways.

1. As previously noted, the age range is greater for the revision. On the WPPSI the age range was from 4 to 6½, whereas on the WPPSI-R it goes from 3 to 7¼ years. To increase the range, 91 new items were added, and the total number of items expanded from 182 to 217.

2. The revision contains a new subtest, Object Assembly, which makes the WPPSI-R more similar to the WISC-R.

3. The Animal House subtest has been renamed Animal Pegs and made an optional subtest, and the retest (Animal House Retest) is not included in the revision.

4. Full-color art is included in some of the pictorial materials in the revision.

5. Scoring guidelines and administrative procedures for some subtests have been modified in the revision.

6. Speed (coupled with correct performance) is awarded additional bonus points on the Block Design subtest in the revision.

7. Reliability coefficients for the Performance, Verbal, and Full Scales differ somewhat in the two tests. On the WPPSI reliability coefficients for the IQs on the three scales were .90 or above at all ages, whereas on the WPPSI-R reliability coefficients for the Performance and Verbal Scale IQs are in the .80s at the 7-year level and in the .90s at other age levels.

8. The WPPSI-R is more of a test of speed than the WPPSI was, because Object Assembly and Block Design have bonus points for speed.

9. At the upper age levels of the test, the WPPSI-R covers a more extensive IQ range than does the WPPSI — 41 to 160 instead of 45 to 155.

Examiners familiar with the WPPSI should study carefully the administrative and scoring procedures on the WPPSI-R. Although many of the procedures are the same for both tests, some modifications have been made and these new procedures must be mastered.

ADMINISTERING THE WPPSI-R

The general administrative suggestions described for the WISC-III (see pages 1051–1067 of this text) are also appropriate for the WPPSI-R. In addition, the two scales have common problems in administration and scoring. Because many subtest names are the same in both scales, care must be taken not to substitute WISC-III directions for WPPSI-R directions or vice versa. The suggestions shown in Exhibit G-2, which supplement those given in other parts of this appendix, and the checklist shown in Exhibit G-3 should help you learn to administer the WPPSI-R. You can review the checklist before you administer the test, complete it as you review a videotape of your test administration, and have another student complete it as he or she observes you administer the test (in person or on videotape). Your course instructor (or teaching assistant) may also use the checklist. Figure G-2 shows the cover of the WPPSI-R record form.

Exhibit G-2

Administering the WPPSI-R

1. Complete the top of the record form.
2. Using date of testing and date of birth, calculate the chronological age (CA) and put it in the box provided. On the WPPSI-R, CA must be stated in years, months, and days.
3. Administer the subtests in the order presented in the manual, except in rare circumstances. Do not change the wording on any subtest. Read the directions exactly as shown in the manual. Do not ad lib.
4. Start with the appropriate item on each subtest and follow discontinuance criteria. You must know correct scoring criteria *before* you give the test.
5. Write out all responses completely and legibly. Do not use unusual abbreviations. Record time accurately.
6. Question all ambiguous or unscorable responses, writing a (Q) after each questioned response.
7. Be patient when working with children in the WPPSI-R age group. Several breaks may be needed during the testing.
8. On Comprehension, if a child only gives one reason to Question 11, request a second reason.
9. Carefully score each protocol, recheck the scoring, and transfer subtest scores to the front of the record form under Raw Score. If you have failed to question a response when you should have and the response is obviously not a 0 response, give the child the most appropriate score.
10. If a subtest was spoiled, write *spoiled* by the subtest total score and on the front of the record form where the raw and scaled scores appear. If for some reason a subtest was not administered, write *NA* in the margin in the record form next to the subtest name and on the front of the record form.
11. Transform raw scores into scaled scores by using Table 25 on pages 170–186 of the WPPSI-R manual. Be sure to use the page of the table that is appropriate for the child's age and the correct row and column for each transformation.
12. Base the Performance Score on the total of the scaled scores on the five standard Performance Scale subtests. Base the Verbal Score on the total of the scaled scores on the five standard Verbal Scale subtests. Do not use Ani-

mal Pegs to compute the Performance Score unless you substitute it for another Performance subtest. Similarly, do not use Sentences to compute the Verbal Score unless you substitute it for another Verbal subtest. Add the Performance Score and the Verbal Score together to get the Full Scale Score.
13. If fewer than five subtests were administered in the Performance section or fewer than five subtests in the Verbal section, use the Tellegen and Briggs short-form procedure described on page 138 of this text to compute the IQ.
14. Obtain the IQs from Table 27 in the WPPSI-R manual. Be sure to use the correct section of the table for each of the three IQs—page 188 for the Performance and Verbal IQs and page 189 for the Full Scale IQ. Record the IQs. Next, recheck all of your work. If the IQ was obtained by use of a short form, write *SF* beside the appropriate IQ.
15. Look up the confidence intervals for the Full Scale IQ, Performance Scale IQ, and Verbal Scale IQ in Table H-1 in Appendix H. Normally, the confidence intervals are not used with the Performance or Verbal IQs unless these were the only IQs reported.
16. Look up the percentile rank and classification for each of the IQs in Tables BC-1 and BC-2 on the inside back cover of this text.
17. If desired, use the material on page 190 (Table 28) of the WPPSI-R manual to obtain test-age equivalents. They can be placed (in parentheses) in the right-hand margin of the cover page of the record form next to the scaled score. For test-age equivalents above those in the table, use the highest test-age equivalent and a plus sign. For test-age equivalents below those in the table, use the lowest test-age equivalent and a minus sign.
18. In summary, be sure to read directions verbatim, pronounce words clearly, query at the appropriate times, start with the appropriate item, discontinue at the proper place, place items properly before the child, use correct timing, and follow the specific guidelines in the manual for administering the test.

Source: Adapted and revised from material written by M. L. Lewis for the WPPSI. Courtesy of M. L. Lewis.

■ **Exhibit G-3**

Administrative Checklist for the WPPSI-R

ADMINISTRATIVE CHECKLIST FOR THE WPPSI-R

Name of examiner: _____   *Date:* _____

Name of examinee: _____   *Name of observer:* _____

(Note. *If an item is not applicable, mark NA next to the item.*)

Object Assembly   *Circle One*

1. Reads directions verbatim   Yes   No
2. Reads directions clearly   Yes   No
3. Administers all items   Yes   No
4. Uses shield correctly   Yes   No
5. Presents puzzles with pieces arranged
   properly   Yes   No
6. Records time accurately   Yes   No
7. Gives appropriate prompt once only if child
   dawdles on items 1 and 2   Yes   No
8. Demonstrates correct arrangement if child
   fails item 1   Yes   No
9. Does not demonstrate correct arrangement
   on items 2 through 6 if child fails these
   items   Yes   No
10. Gives no prompts on items 3–6   Yes   No
11. Discontinues at proper place   Yes   No

Comments: _____

_____

Information

1. Reads items verbatim   Yes   No
2. Reads items clearly   Yes   No
3. Queries at appropriate times   Yes   No
4. Demonstrates the correct answer if child fails
   item 1   Yes   No
5. Does not demonstrate correct answer if child
   fails on items 2–27   Yes   No
6. Discontinues at proper place   Yes   No

Comments: _____

_____

Geometric Design

1. Reads directions verbatim   Yes   No
2. Reads directions clearly   Yes   No
3. Uses prompts appropriately for items 1–7   Yes   No
4. Gives correct answer to item 1 if child fails
   item   Yes   No
5. Does not give correct answer on items 2–16
   if child fails these items   Yes   No

6. Uses black-lead primary pencils with
   erasers   Yes   No
7. Uses sheet of cardboard or other firm,
   smooth surface for items 8–16 if table top is
   not smooth   Yes   No
8. Folds sheets correctly on items 8–16   Yes   No
9. Queries appropriately   Yes   No
10. Discontinues at proper place   Yes   No

Comments: _____

_____

Comprehension

1. Reads items verbatim   Yes   No
2. Reads items clearly   Yes   No
3. Queries at appropriate times   Yes   No
4. Asks for a second response on item 11 if
   child gives only 1 answer   Yes   No
5. Gives correct answers to items 1 and 2 if
   child gives a 0- or 1-point response   Yes   No
6. Does not give correct answers to items 3–15
   if child fails or does not give a 2-point
   response   Yes   No
7. Discontinues at proper place   Yes   No

Comments: _____

_____

Block Design

1. Reads directions verbatim   Yes   No
2. Reads directions clearly   Yes   No
3. Starts at appropriate item   Yes   No
4. Places blocks and cards properly   Yes   No
5. Provides demonstration and an explanation
   when administering items 1–3 and item 6 on
   first trial   Yes   No
6. Provides demonstration without explanation
   when administering items 4, 5, and 7–14 on
   first trial   Yes   No
7. Provides demonstration and an explanation
   when administering items 6, 8, and 10–14 on
   second trial   Yes   No

(Exhibit continues next page)

Exhibit G-3 (cont.)

Circle One

8. Provides demonstration without explanation when administering items 1–5, 7, and 9 on second trial   Yes   No
9. Discontinues at proper place   Yes   No

Comments: _____

_____

Arithmetic

1. Reads items verbatim   Yes   No
2. Reads items clearly   Yes   No
3. Starts with appropriate item   Yes   No
4. Uses correct timing   Yes   No
5. On items 1–11 proceeds to next item if child shows no sign of responding after 10 or 15 seconds   Yes   No
6. Asks for clarification when two responses are given   Yes   No
7. Gives credit when child answers correctly by holding up fingers only   Yes   No
8. Gives no credit when child holds up correct number of fingers but gives incorrect verbal response   Yes   No
9. Probes on item 11 if child leaves incorrect number of blocks   Yes   No
10. Probes on item 14 if child says "one"   Yes   No
11. Places items properly   Yes   No
12. Discontinues at proper place   Yes   No

Comments: _____

_____

Mazes

1. Reads directions verbatim   Yes   No
2. Reads directions clearly   Yes   No
3. Uses red-lead pencil   Yes   No
4. Gives child black-lead primary pencils without erasers   Yes   No
5. Starts with appropriate item   Yes   No
6. Exposes sheet properly   Yes   No
7. Gives correct demonstration   Yes   No
8. Provides "cautions" correctly   Yes   No
9. Uses correct timing   Yes   No
10. Discontinues at proper place   Yes   No

Comments: _____

_____

Vocabulary

1. Reads directions verbatim   Yes   No
2. Reads directions clearly   Yes   No

3. Pronounces words clearly   Yes   No
4. Queries at appropriate times   Yes   No
5. Gives correct answer for item 1 if child misses item   Yes   No
6. Does not give correct answers for items 2–25 if child misses items   Yes   No
7. Discontinues at proper place   Yes   No

Comments: _____

_____

Picture Completion

1. Reads directions verbatim   Yes   No
2. Reads directions clearly   Yes   No
3. Reads words clearly   Yes   No
4. Starts with appropriate item   Yes   No
5. Places booklet properly   Yes   No
6. Gives child at least 15 seconds to respond to items 1 and 2   Yes   No
7. Gives child at least 30 seconds to respond to items 2–28   Yes   No
8. Gives child correct answers for items 1–4 if child gives incorrect answers   Yes   No
9. Gives the prompt "Yes, but what is missing?" no more than twice for items 4–28   Yes   No
10. Gives the prompt "A part is missing in the picture. What is it that is missing?" no more than twice for items 4–28   Yes   No
11. Inquires correctly on items 16, 17, 22, and 28 when certain responses are given   Yes   No
12. Discontinues at proper place   Yes   No

Comments: _____

_____

Similarities

1. Reads directions verbatim   Yes   No
2. Reads directions clearly   Yes   No
3. Reads items verbatim and clearly   Yes   No
4. Queries at appropriate times   Yes   No
5. Gives child correct answers for items 1, 7, 13, and 14 if child gives incorrect answers   Yes   No
6. Does not give correct answers for items 2–6, 8–12, and 15–20 if child gives incorrect answers   Yes   No
7. Gives an example of a 2-point response if child gives a 1-point response to item 13   Yes   No

(Exhibit continues next page)

Exhibit G-3 (cont.)

	Circle One	
8. Queries at appropriate times	Yes	No
9. Discontinues at proper place	Yes	No

Comments: _____

_____

Animal Pegs

1. Reads directions verbatim	Yes	No
2. Reads directions clearly	Yes	No
3. Demonstrates tasks clearly	Yes	No
4. Uses correct timing	Yes	No
5. Gives correct prompt or caution when child hesitates after completing first row	Yes	No
6. Gives correct prompt or caution when child loses the sense of the task	Yes	No
7. Gives correct prompt or caution no more than twice when child selects pegs of one color and completes that color before starting another	Yes	No
8. Gives correct prompt or caution when child removes pegs after finishing one row and starts over again	Yes	No

Comments: _____

_____

Sentences

1. Reads directions verbatim	Yes	No
2. Reads directions clearly	Yes	No
3. Reads items verbatim	Yes	No
4. Reads items clearly	Yes	No
5. Starts with correct item	Yes	No
6. Gives correct answers if child fails items 1, 2, and 6	Yes	No
7. Does not give correct answers to items 3–5 and 7–12 if child fails any of these items	Yes	No
8. Discontinues at proper place	Yes	No

Comments: _____

_____

Overall Assessment of Test Administration

Circle one:

Excellent   Above Average   Average   Poor   Failing

Overall strengths: _____

Overall weaknesses: _____

Other comments: _____

_____

Physical Abilities Necessary for the WPPSI-R

The physical abilities children need to take the WPPSI-R are, for the most part, the same as those required for the WISC-III (see Table I-15 on page 1073). Adequate visual-motor skills, in particular, are needed to handle the Performance Scale materials. Alternative ways of adminstering the WPPSI-R items are limited because young children who cannot speak usually will not be able to write their answers, and those who cannot hear usually will not be able to read the questions. The specific suggestions for administering the WISC-III to handicapped children also are useful for the WPPSI-R (see pages 1072–1074). This material should be carefully reviewed before the WPPSI-R is administered to physically handicapped children.

Testing-of-Limits on the WPPSI-R

The general testing-of-limits suggestions presented in Chapter 5 (see pages 110–112) are also useful with the WPPSI-R.

WPPSI-R Short Forms

Short forms of the WPPSI-R have the same advantages and disadvantages as those of the WISC-III (see page 1071). *Of crucial importance is that short forms never be used for classification or selection purposes.* A short form may be useful for screening or research studies, however. The information in Table H-6 in Appendix H can aid you in the selection of a short form. This table, based on the average of the total standardization group, shows the best WPPSI-R short forms for combinations of two, three, four, and five subtests. Because the short forms of a given length are, for all practical purposes, mutually interchangeable, clinical or other considerations can be used to select the short form. Estimated WPPSI-R Full Scale IQ equivalents for the 10 best short-form dyads, triads, and tetrads are shown in Tables H-7, H-8, and H-9 in Appendix H, respectively.

An inspection of the coefficients in Table H-6 indicates that the four- and five-subtest combinations yield the highest reliability coefficients (.927 and above) and validity coefficients (.910 and above). Consequently, if time per-

RECORD FORM

Name _____   Parent's Name _____

Address _____

School _____   Grade _____

Place of Testing _____   Examiner _____

Age _____   Sex _____   Handedness _____

	Year	Month	Day
Date Tested			
Date of Birth			
Age			

Performance Tests	Raw Score	Scaled Score
Object Assembly		
Geometric Design *		
Block Design		
Mazes		
Picture Completion		
(Animal Pegs)	( )	( )

Total Performance Tests [ ]

Verbal Tests	Raw Score	Scaled Score
Information		
Comprehension		
Arithmetic		
Vocabulary		
Similarities		
(Sentences)	( )	( )

Total Verbal Tests [ ]

	Scaled Score	IQ
Performance Score		
Verbal Score		
Full Scale Score		

WPPSI-R PROFILE

Clinicians who wish to draw a profile should first transfer the child's *scaled scores* to the row of boxes below. Then mark an X on the dot corresponding to the scaled score for each test, and draw a line connecting the X's.*

Performance Tests — Object Assembly, Geometric Design, Block Design, Mazes, Picture Completion, (Animal Pegs)

Verbal Tests — Information, Comprehension, Arithmetic, Vocabulary, Similarities, (Sentences)

Scaled Score [ ][ ][ ][ ][ ][ ]   Scaled Score [ ][ ][ ][ ][ ][ ]   Scaled Score

19 18 17 16 15 14 13 12 11 10 9 8 7 6 5 4 3 2 1

*See the Manual for a discussion of the significance of differences between scores on the tests.

Ψ THE PSYCHOLOGICAL CORPORATION
HARCOURT BRACE JOVANOVICH, INC.

Figure G-2.   Cover page of WPPSI-R record form. From the *Wechsler Preschool and Primary Scale of Intelligence—Revised.* Copyright © 1989 by The Psychological Corporation. Reproduced by permission. All rights reserved.

mits, a four- or five-subtest combination is preferable to a two- or three-subtest combination. In addition, if a purer estimate of verbal and performance abilities is needed, the short form chosen should not include Picture Completion because it does not load primarily on the Performance factor at all ages. If the goal is simply to select a general cognitive screening measure, however, Picture Completion can be used because it is a good measure of cognitive functioning. Because Sentences and Animal Pegs were not used in arriving at the IQ scores shown in the manual, these subtests are not recommended for use in a short form.

Another short-form procedure, initially developed by Yudin (1966) and modified by Silverstein (1968a), can be applied to the WPPSI-R. The procedure uses either every second or every third item in each of the 10 standard subtests (see Table G-12). Once again, Animal Pegs and Sentences are excluded from this short form because they were omitted in establishing the IQ table.

Table G-12
Yudin's Abbreviated Procedure for the WPPSI-R as Modified by Silverstein

Subtest	Item used	Multiply score by
Object Assembly	Odd only	2
Geometric Design	Odd only	2
Block Design	Odd only	2
Mazes	Odd only	2
Picture Completion	Every 3rd	3
Information	Every 3rd	3
Comprehension	Odd only	2
Arithmetic	Odd only	2
Vocabulary	Every 3rd	3
Similarities	Odd only	2

Note. Procedure for Object Assembly provided by text author.
Source: Adapted from Silverstein (1968a).

Choosing Between the WPPSI-R and the WISC-R

The WPPSI-R overlaps with the WISC-R from 6-0-0 to 7-3-15 years. Consequently, a decision must be made about which form to use for these ages. The WPPSI-R manual recommends that the WISC-R be administered to children with average or above-average ability who also have average communication ability, whereas it recommends the WPPSI-R for children who are below average in either of these areas. However, the WPPSI-R manual does not pre-

sent any empirical evidence to support this recommendation. As noted on page 139 of this text, the choice of a test should depend on the validity of the inferences that can be made from it. To this end, research is needed with samples of both normal and exceptional children to investigate which test is more valid at the overlapping ages.

The test with the lowest standard error of measurement also would be preferred. Again, it is difficult to compare the WPPSI-R and the WISC-R at the overlapping ages because standard errors of measurement are not given at ages 6 and 7 for the WISC-R. At age 6½, where standard errors of measurement are available for both tests, they are highly similar for the Performance, Verbal, and Full Scale IQs. Although direct comparisons cannot be made for age 7, the standard errors of measurement provided at ages 6½ and 7½ of the WISC-R and at age 7 of the WPPSI-R suggest that the WISC-R provides lower standard errors of measurement than does the WPPSI-R.

Still another useful criterion is which test provides the more reliable and valid estimate of intelligence at different levels of intelligence. Because neither reliability nor validity coeffients are provided in either manual for different levels of intelligence, it is impossible to evaluate this criterion. However, the WPPSI-R provides a more thorough sampling of ability than does the WISC-R in the overlapping age range, because more WPPSI-R than WISC-R items must be administered in order to obtain the same scaled score. For example, on the WPPSI-R Information subtest 16 raw-score points correspond to a scaled score of 5, whereas on the WISC-R Information subtest 2 raw-score points result in this same scaled score. Similarly, for a scaled score of 10 on the Information subtest, the WPPSI-R requires a raw score of 21 points, whereas the WISC-R requires a raw score of 5 points. Similar relationships exist for the other subtests common to both forms.

Research is needed to determine at what ages the greater sampling of ability on the WPPSI-R results in more reliable and valid scores. As noted previously, the WISC-R may have a lower standard error of measurement than the WPPSI-R at age 7, even though the WPPSI-R provides a greater sampling of ability. (Pages 1071–1072 discuss choosing between the WPPSI-R and WISC-III.)

WPPSI-R SUBTESTS

This section describes the 12 WPPSI-R subtests. Included is a brief discussion of each subtest, its rationale, factor analytic findings, reliability and correlational highlights, and administrative and interpretive considerations. Reliabilities above .80 are preferred for clinical and psychoeducational tasks, and reliabilities at or above .90 are preferred for decision-making tasks. Subtests with reliabilities between .70 and .79 are *relatively reliable*; between .60 and .69, *marginally reliable*; and below .60, *unreliable*.

Object Assembly

The Object Assembly subtest requires children to place rectangular pieces in their appropriate recess in a frame (item 1 – three pieces) or put jigsaw pieces together to form common objects – a flower (item 2 – four pieces in a frame), a car (item 3 – three pieces), a teddy bear (item 4 – four pieces), a face (item 5 – five pieces), and a dog (item 6 – four pieces). There is no sample item. On each item, the pieces are laid out in a specified disarranged pattern. All children start with the first item, and the subtest is discontinued after three consecutive failures in which children receive a score of 0. Object Assembly is new to the WPPSI-R.

All items are timed. Items 1 through 4 are given 120 seconds, and items 5 and 6, 150 seconds. A perfect performance is given 3 points for the rectangles, teddy bear, and dog; 2 points for the car; and 5 points for the face. Bonuses of up to 3 points are awarded for speed and accuracy on items 3 through 6. With the bonus points, the face item has a maximum score of 8; the teddy bear and dog, 6; and the car, 5. Points also are given for partially correct solutions, depending on the number of pieces placed correctly.

Rationale. The rationale presented for the WISC-III Object Assembly subtest appears to apply to the WPPSI-R Object Assembly subtest (see page 1099). However, there are some subtle differences in the items on the two scales. One is that the first WPPSI-R Object Assembly item is a form-board item and does not require the child to make a meaningful picture; in contrast, there are no form-board items on the WISC-III. A second is that the WISC-III items have more pieces than the WPPSI-R items. And a third is that one WISC-III item has a longer time limit (180 seconds) than any on the WPPSI-R.

Factor analytic findings. The Object Assembly subtest overall is a fair measure of *g* (33 percent of its variance may be attributed to *g* – range of 22 to 44 percent in the nine age groups). The subtest contributes substantially to the Performance factor (*Mdn* loading = .70). Subtest specificity is inadequate at every age level and at the average of the nine age groups.

Reliability and correlational highlights. Object Assembly overall has a marginal level of reliability (r_{xx} = .63). Reliability coefficients are *below* .70 at seven of the nine age groups; the two exceptions are at ages 4 and 6, where the reliability coefficients are both equal to .70. The subtest correlates more highly with Block Design (r = .52) than with any other subtest. It has low correlations with the Full Scale (r = .50), Performance Scale (r = .56), and Verbal Scale (r = .37).

Administrative and interpretive considerations. The administrative and interpretive considerations presented for the WISC-III Object Assembly subtest (pages 1099–1100) are also relevant for the WPPSI-R Object Assembly subtest. It is especially important to observe the time limits on each item and to record precisely the elapsed time because additional bonus points are awarded for quick execution on the last four items. Profile analysis should take into account that the full range of scaled scores from 1 to 19 is available only at ages 3 to 5¼ years (see Table G-9).

Geometric Design

The Geometric Design subtest has two parts; in the first children must make visual discriminations, and in the second they copy designs. The subtest contains 16 items. Items 1 through 7 require visual recognition and discrimination, whereas items 8 through 16 require visual-motor coordination. Of the 16 items, 10 are new and 6 are either unchanged or slightly modified from the WPPSI. There is no time limit. Items 1 to 7 are given either 0 or 1 point; items 8 through 16 are given 0, 3, 4, 6, 8, or 12 points.

All children begin the subtest with the first item. Special attention must be given to the discontinuance procedures. There are two distinct discontinuance procedures – one for Part 1 (items 1 through 7) and one for Part 2 (items 8 through 16). Part 1 is discontinued after three consecutive failures. Part 2 is then administered, which begins with item 8 (the first drawing item). Part 2 (and the entire subtest) is discontinued after two consecutive failures. Thus, it is important to remember that Part 2 is always administered, even when Part 1 has been discontinued.

Rationale. The first part of the Geometric Design subtest (items 1 through 7) involves perceptual recognition and discrimination ability. The child must match a target figure with one of the four figures below it. Because attention probably is involved, impulsive children who make quick, careless choices may perform poorly, especially if they fail to scan all four choices.

The second part of the subtest (items 8 through 16) involves perceptual and visual-motor ability, visual construction, and eye-hand coordination. Previous experience with paper and pencil may help the child succeed. Adequate reproduction of the designs requires appropriate fine motor development, perceptual discrimination ability, and ability to integrate perceptual and motor processes. The child must shift attention between the stimulus and the reproduction and monitor his or her performance.

It is not known to what extent perceptual recognition and discrimination abilities are forerunners of visual-motor skills. It may be that there are two (or more) distinct processes measured by the two different parts of the Geometric Design subtest; research will be needed to investigate this hypothesis.

Low scores may indicate lags in the developmental process. Even some bright young children may have difficulty obtaining high scores, because the motor ability needed for successful performance (the ability to grasp a pencil appropriately, make contact with paper, and draw appropriate lines) is associated in part with maturational processes that may be independent of the development of cognitive processes.

Factor analytic findings. The Geometric Design subtest overall is a fair measure of g (37 percent of its variance may be attributed to g – range of 15 to 53 percent in the nine age groups). The subtest contributes substantially to the Performance factor (*Mdn* loading = .72). Subtest specificity is either ample or adequate at five of the ages and at the average of the nine age groups, and inadequate at ages 4, 5, 5½, and 6½.

Reliability and correlational highlights. Geometric Design overall is a relatively reliable subtest (r_{xx} = .79). Reliability coefficients are *above* .70 at eight of the nine age groups; the one exception is at age 7, where the reliability coefficient is .68. It correlates more highly with Block Design (r = .49) than with any other subtest. It has low correlations with the Full Scale (r = .54), Performance Scale (r = .58), and Verbal Scale (r = .41).

Administrative and interpretive considerations. The WPPSI-R manual presents detailed guidelines for scoring designs 8 through 16, which will require careful study. Although previous research indicated that the WPPSI Geometric Design subtest was difficult to score (e.g., Morsbach, McGoldrick, & Younger, 1978; Sattler, 1976), research described in the WPPSI-R manual suggests that the new scoring rules have improved the scoring accuracy of

examiners. Additional research will be needed to determine whether the revised scoring criteria have improved scorer reliability with other samples of examiners.

The special copyrighted blank paper obtained from the test publisher for the administration of the Geometric Design subtest is not necessary. You need only cut a sheet of paper in half, writing on each sheet the number of the design and "top" and "bottom" relative to the child's frame of reference. Give the child a *new* half sheet of paper for each drawing so that there is no possible distraction from any other drawing made on the paper.

Profile analysis should take into account that the full range of scaled scores from 1 to 19 is available only at ages 4¼ to 4½ years (see Table G-9).

Block Design

The Block Design subtest requires children to reproduce designs using flat, two-colored blocks. The subtest contains 14 items, 8 of which are new to the WPPSI-R and 6 of which are unchanged or slightly modified. The child is shown a model constructed by the examiner for the first seven items and designs for the last seven items. Children younger than 6 years of age begin with item 1, whereas children 6 years of age and older begin with item 6. The subtest is discontinued after three consecutive failures. An item is considered failed only when *both* trials are failed.

All of the items are timed. The first six items are given a maximum of 30 seconds; the seventh, 45 seconds; and the eighth through fourteenth, 75 seconds. Items 8 to 14 receive time-bonus credits. On the first seven items, 2 points are given for successful performance on the first trial, 1 point for successful performance on the second trial, and 0 points when both trials are failed. On the last seven items, scores range from 0 (failure) to 4 points, with 3 or 4 points awarded for speed (for example, 4 points are awarded on item 8 if it is completed in 15 seconds or less).

Rationale. The rationale described for the WISC-III Block Design subtest appears to apply to the WPPSI-R Block Design subtest (see page 1097).

Factor analytic findings. The Block Design subtest overall is a fair measure of g (47 percent of its variance may be attributed to g – range of 26 to 58 percent in the nine age groups). The subtest contributes substantially to the Performance factor (*Mdn* loading = .76). Subtest specificity is adequate or ample at most ages and at the average of the nine age groups, with the exception of ages 5½ and 6½, where it is inadequate.

Reliability and correlational highlights. Block Design overall is a reliable subtest ($r_{xx} = .85$). Reliability coefficients are *above* .70 at every age group. It correlates more highly with Picture Completion ($r = .46$), Arithmetic ($r = .46$), and Mazes ($r = .45$) than with any of the other subtests. It correlates moderately with the Full Scale ($r = .62$) and the Performance Scale ($r = .64$) and to a lesser degree with the Verbal Scale ($r = .48$).

Administrative and interpretive considerations. The administrative and interpretive considerations described for the WISC-III Block Design subtest generally apply to the WPPSI-R Block Design subtest (see page 1098). Profile analysis should take into account that the full range of scaled scores from 1 to 19 is available only at ages 5 to 6¼ years (see Table G-9).

Mazes

The Mazes subtest requires children to solve paper-and-pencil mazes that differ in level of complexity. The subtest consists of 11 mazes, 8 of which are unchanged or modified from the WPPSI and 3 of which are new. Seven of the mazes are very similar to those on the WISC-III. Mazes 1 through 4 are horizontal mazes, and mazes 5 through 11 are box mazes. Mazes is a standard subtest in the WPPSI-R, whereas in the WISC-III it is an optional one. Children below the age of 5 years start with maze 1A; those 5 years of age and older start with maze 3A. The subtest is timed and discontinued after two consecutive failures. On the first four items, an item is considered as failed when *both* trials are failed.

Rationale. The rationale described for the WISC-III Mazes subtest appears to apply to the WPPSI-R Mazes subtest (see page 1102).

Factor analytic findings. The Mazes subtest overall is a fair measure of *g* (32 percent of its variance may be attributed to *g*—range of 16 to 41 percent in the nine age groups). The subtest contributes substantially to the Performance factor (*Mdn* loading = .69). Subtest specificity is ample at most ages and at the average of the nine age groups, except at ages 5, 5½, and 6½, where it is inadequate.

Reliability and correlational highlights. Mazes overall is a relatively reliable subtest ($r_{xx} = .77$). Reliability coefficients are above .70 at eight of the nine age groups; the one exception is at age 7, where the reliability coefficient is .65. It correlates more highly with Block Design ($r = .45$) and Geometric Design ($r = .43$) than with any of the other subtests. It has low correlations with the Full Scale ($r = .50$), Performance Scale ($r = .54$), and Verbal Scale ($r = .38$).

Administrative and interpretive considerations. Although the administrative and interpretive considerations described for the WISC-III Mazes subtest generally apply to the WPPSI-R Mazes subtest (see pages 1102–1103), the administrative procedures differ in timing, scoring, and other details. For example, on the WPPSI-R each of the first seven mazes is allowed a maximum of 45 seconds; maze 8, 60 seconds; maze 9, 75 seconds; and mazes 10 and 11, 135 seconds. These time limits differ from those on the WISC-III. Therefore, you must be sure to use the procedures appropriate for the test being administered. Allow children to finish each maze (especially if they want to or are about to complete it), regardless of the errors made, because interruptions may generate anxiety and confusion and leave them with a sense of failure.

Scoring the Mazes subtest requires considerable judgment. You must become familiar with special terms, such as "blind alley," "clear crossing of a wall," "overshoot," "false exit," and "false start," which designate specific features of the mazes or of the child's performance. Likewise, you must be careful to point out these features of the subtest to the child in the sample item.

Study the child's failures carefully. Note whether there is a pattern to the child's failures, or whether there are signs of tremor or other visual-motor difficulties. When the entire test is finished, you might want to return to the Mazes subtest to inquire into the child's performance on any mazes of interest. For example, you can ask "Why did you go that way?"

A careful evaluation of the failures that occur on the Mazes subtest may prove to be useful. Two examples are shown in Figure G-3. In example 1, the girl failed to complete the maze, but made no errors as far as her performance went. In example 2, the boy entered a blind alley, thereby making an error. In the first case one wonders why the girl stopped short before reaching the goal. Perhaps her perseverance is limited, perhaps she takes things for granted and hopes that others will understand her, or perhaps she is easily distracted. In contrast, the second performance may be that of an impulsive boy who works well until he is about to complete a task and then is unable to do so correctly. These analyses are, of course, only tentative, subject to modification after study of the child's performance on the entire subtest and other subtests

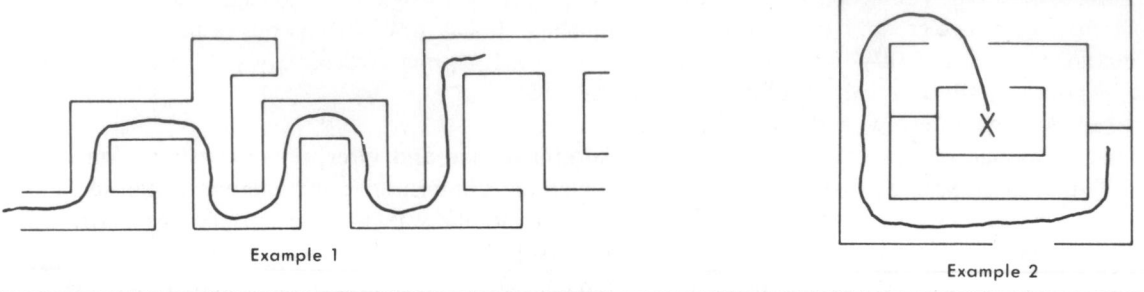

Example 1   Example 2

Figure G-3.   Two examples of failures on the Mazes subtest. From the *Wechsler Preschool and Primary Scale of Intelligence – Revised.*
Copyright © 1989 by The Psychological Corporation. Reproduced by permission. All rights reserved.

on the test, as well as of other sources of data.

Profile analysis should take into account that the full range of scaled scores from 1 to 19 is available only at ages 4 to 6¼ years (see Table G-9).

Picture Completion

The Picture Completion subtest requires children to identify the single most important missing element in 28 drawings of common objects, such as a doll, car, and jacket. The subtest contains 12 new items, but 5 of the 28 items are also found on the WISC-III. The child's task is to discover and name or point to the essential missing portion of the incompletely drawn picture. Although there is no exact time limit for each item, items 1 and 2 are allowed a minimum of 15 seconds, and items 3 through 28, 30 seconds. Children younger than 5 years start with the sample item, and those 5 years and older start with item 3. The subtest is discontinued after five consecutive failures.

Rationale.   The rationale described for the WISC-III Picture Completion subtest appears to hold for the WPPSI-R Picture Completion subtest (see page 1092).

Factor analytic findings.   The Picture Completion subtest overall is a fair measure of *g* (47 percent of its variance may be attributed to *g*—range of 34 to 58 percent in the nine age groups). The subtest has a high loading on the Performance factor (*Mdn* loading = .55) *and* on the Verbal factor (*Mdn* loading = .41). These results suggest that verbal reasoning may help children to detect the missing part of the pictures. Subtest specificity is ample at all ages and at the average of the nine age groups.

Reliability and correlational highlights.   Picture Completion overall is a reliable subtest (r_{xx} = .85). Reliability

coefficients are *above* .70 at all of the age groups. It correlates more highly with Information (r = .47), Block Design (r = .46), and Arithmetic (r = .45) than with any of the other subtests. It correlates moderately with the Full Scale (r = .61) and to a lesser degree with the Performance (r = .54) and Verbal (r = .54) Scales.

Administrative and interpretive considerations.   The administrative and interpretive considerations discussed for the WISC-III Picture Completion subtest generally apply to the WPPSI-R Picture Completion subtest (see pages 1092–1093). The major exception concerns the time limits. Unlike the WISC-III Picture Completion subtest, which allows a maximum of 20 seconds per card, the WPPSI-R Picture Completion subtest has no *absolute* time limits. For qualitative analysis, however, you might want to record the amount of time taken by children to make each response.

Children may have difficulty in identifying the missing part of some pictures because the way in which they are drawn may be confusing (for example, the face item and the suit jacket item).

Profile analysis should take into account that the full range of scaled scores from 1 to 19 is available only at ages 4¼ to 6½ years (see Table G-9).

Animal Pegs

The Animal Pegs subtest, a substitute for the WISC-R Coding subtest, requires children to place colored pegs in holes on a board according to a key at the top of the board. In the original WPPSI, the subtest was called Animal House and was one of the five standard subtests on the Performance Scale; in the WPPSI-R, it is called Animal Pegs and is optional. The subtest essentially remains the same as it was on the WPPSI, with only minor changes in artwork. However, on the WPPSI-R there are no norms provided for a retest on Animal Pegs as there were on the WPPSI, where the retest (and norms) was referred to as "Animal House Retest."

Animal Pegs is a liberally timed subtest (maximum time of 5 minutes) in which a premium is placed on speed. A perfect score in 9 seconds or less is credited with 70 raw-score points, whereas one obtained in 5 minutes is credited with 12 raw-score points.

Rationale.   Animal Pegs requires the child to associate signs with symbols. Memory, attention span, goal awareness, concentration, finger and manual dexterity, and learning ability may all be involved in the child's performance. Research with the WPPSI Animal House subtest indicated that it correlated significantly with a measure of learning ($r = .71$) and a measure of motor skill ($r = -.69$) in a sample of 36 children 5 to 6 years old (Sherman, Chinsky, & Maffeo, 1974). (The negative correlation resulted from the association of *lower* motor skill scores, which reflected faster reaction times, with *higher* Animal House scores.) The combination of learning *and* motor scores led to a better prediction of Animal House scores than did the learning scores by themselves. This research suggests that performance on the Animal House (or Animal Pegs) subtest involves both motor and learning abilities.

Factor analytic findings.   The Animal Pegs subtest is a fair measure of g (27 percent of its variance may be attributed to g—range of 15 to 41 percent in the nine age groups). The subtest has a high loading on the Performance factor (*Mdn* loading = .50). It has ample specificity at five ages and at the average of the nine age groups, and inadequate specificity at four ages (3½, 4, 4½, and 5½).

Reliability and correlational highlights.   Animal Pegs has a marginal level of test-retest reliability ($r_{xx} = .66$). In addition, little is known about its reliability at each specific age level of the test. The only test-retest reliability coefficient reported in the WPPSI-R manual is based on a combined sample of 175 children who were in two age groups: 36 to 59 months and 60 to 87 months of age. Unfortunately, separate test-retest reliability coefficients were not given for each age group. (All tables requiring the use of reliability coefficients in Appendixes G and H of this text use a reliability coefficient of .66 for Animal Pegs.) Animal Pegs correlates more highly with Block Design ($r = .37$) than it does with any other subtest. It has low

correlations with the Full Scale ($r = .45$), Performance Scale ($r = .43$), and Verbal Scale ($r = .37$).

Administrative and interpretive considerations.   Note whether the child is right- or left-handed before administering the subtest. This information is helpful not only in guiding the placement of the box of pegs, but also for clinical purposes. Children should be encouraged to use the hand they prefer. As on all timed subtests, do not stop timing once the subtest has begun. If the subtest is spoiled, do not score it. (This is true, of course, for any subtest that is spoiled.) Because Animal Pegs is an optional subtest, it does not have to be administered. And if it is administered as the sixth Performance Scale subtest, it is not used in calculating the IQ. However, if time permits, the subtest should be administered because it provides potentially useful information about important developmental skills.

Profile analysis should take into account that the full range of scaled scores from 1 to 19 is available at nearly all ages of the test—from 3¼ to 7 years (see Table G-9).

Information

The Information subtest requires children to answer a broad range of questions dealing with factual information. The subtest contains 27 questions, 3 of which are exactly the same as in the WISC-III and one of which is essentially the same. Ten new items have been added to the subtest. Most questions require the child to give a simply stated fact or facts.

All children begin the subtest with the first item. Items 1 through 6 use pictures as stimuli and require either a pointing or verbal response. Items 7 through 27 are given orally and require a verbal response. All items are scored 1 or 0 (pass-fail). The subtest is untimed and discontinued after five consecutive failures.

Rationale.   The rationale presented for the WISC-III Information subtest appears to apply to the WPPSI-R Information subtest (see pages 1080–1081). The WPPSI-R questions, however, appear to assess that part of the child's knowledge of the environment that is gained from experiences rather than from education, especially formal education.

Factor analytic findings.   The Information subtest overall is the best measure of g in the test (63 percent of its variance may be attributed to g—range of 47 to 74 percent in the nine age groups). The subtest contributes substantially to the Verbal factor (*Mdn* loading = .79). Specificity is adequate at ages 3½ and 4½ and inadequate at the other ages and at the average of the nine age groups.

Reliability and correlational highlights. Information overall is a reliable subtest ($r_{xx} = .84$). Reliability coefficients are above .70 at eight of the nine age groups; the one exception is at age 7, where the reliability coefficient is .62. It correlates more highly with Comprehension ($r = .66$) than with any other subtest. It correlates moderately with the Full Scale ($r = .71$) and the Verbal Scale ($r = .75$) and to a lesser degree with the Performance Scale ($r = .52$).

Administrative and interpretive considerations. The administrative and interpretive considerations presented for the WISC-III Information subtest are also relevant for the WPPSI-R Information subtest (see pages 1081–1082). Some WPPSI-R items require special scoring considerations. For example, the sample answers to question 12 in the WPPSI-R manual do not mention grooming products that come in plastic bottles, such as shampoo or liquid soap. Because the term "etc." appears in the scoring criteria, it seems logical to assume that credit should be given for responses that mention such substances and any other substances that come in plastic bottles. Likewise, the scoring criteria for question 14 do not include "planet," yet a planet shines in the sky at night. It is recommended that credit be given for "planet," "comet," and other astronomical terms. Finally, the suggested answers for question 13 do not mention that acceptable answers should include the names of any mammals because all mammals produce milk when feeding their newly born offspring. Therefore, credit should be given for any mammal named.

Profile analysis should take into account that the full range of scaled scores from 1 to 19 is available only at ages 4¾ to 6¼ years (see Table G-9).

Question: What do you call a baby goat?
Answer: Matilda would be a nice name.

Comprehension

The Comprehension subtest requires children to explain situations, actions, or activities that relate to events with which most young children would be familiar. The subtest contains 15 questions, 10 of which are new. None of the items overlap with those in the WISC-III. Several content areas are covered, including health and hygiene, environmental concerns, interpersonal relations, and societal conventions. Items are scored 2, 1, or 0. All children start with item 1. The subtest is untimed and discontinued after four consecutive failures.

Rationale. The rationale presented for the WISC-III Comprehension subtest appears to apply generally to the WPPSI–R Comprehension subtest (see page 1088). Linguistic skill and logical reasoning, however, may play a more important role on the WPPSI-R Comprehension subtest than on the WISC-III Comprehension subtest.

Factor analytic findings. The Comprehension subtest overall is a good measure of g (52 percent of its variance may be attributed to g—range of 38 to 64 percent in the nine age groups). The subtest contributes substantially to the Verbal factor (*Mdn* loading = .80). Specificity is adequate at ages 3, 5, and 5½, and inadequate at the other ages and at the average of the nine age groups.

Reliability and correlational highlights. Comprehension overall is a reliable subtest ($r_{xx} = .83$). Reliability coefficients are above .70 at eight of the nine age groups; the one exception is at age 7, where the reliability coefficient is .59. It correlates more highly with Information ($r = .66$) and Vocabulary ($r = .60$) than with any of the other subtests. It correlates moderately with the Full Scale ($r = .61$) and the Verbal Scale ($r = .70$) and to a lesser degree with the Performance Scale ($r = .41$).

Administrative and interpretive considerations. The administrative and interpretive considerations discussed for the WISC-III Comprehension subtest generally apply to the WPPSI-R Comprehension subtest (see pages 1088–1089). Because Comprehension responses are occasionally difficult to score, judgment is needed to arrive at appropriate scores. As in all decisions on the scoring of WPPSI-R (and WISC-III and WAIS-R) responses, the content of the response, not the quality of the verbalization, should be considered.

Profile analysis should take into account that the full range of scaled scores from 1 to 19 is available at *none* of the age levels in the test (see Table G-9).

Arithmetic

The Arithmetic subtest requires children to demonstrate their understanding of concepts that may be precursors to numerical reasoning and to show their knowledge of numerical concepts. The subtest contains 23 problems, 2 of which are also on the WISC-III. Eight new items have been added to the subtest. For the first 7 items, the stimuli are presented via pictures; for the next 3 items, via blocks; and for the last 13 items, via oral questions. Pointing responses are required on the first 7 items and oral responses on the last 16 items.

The subtest is started with item 1 for children under 6 years and with item 8 for children 6 years of age and older. The first 11 problems have no time limit, but the last 12 items have a 30-second time limit. Each item is scored 1 or 0, and the subtest is discontinued after five consecutive failures.

The problems on the Arithmetic subtest reflect various skills. Problems 1 through 7 entail perceptual judgments involving the concepts of biggest, tallest, longest, more, most, shortest, and same. Problems 8 through 10 require direct counting of concrete quantities. Problems 11 through 23 involve simple addition or subtraction, although simple division or multiplication also can be used. Problems 12 to 23 are arithmetical reasoning problems presented orally by the examiner.

Rationale.　The rationale described for the WISC-III Arithmetic subtest appears to apply generally to the WPPSI-R Arithmetic subtest (see page 1084). The skills required for the WPPSI-R Arithmetic subtest, however, are likely to be less dependent on formal education than are those required for the WISC-III Arithmetic subtest. The first seven WPPSI-R questions, which require the child to make comparisons and perceptual discriminations, appear to measure nonverbal reasoning ability; these seven problems use quantitative concepts without involving the explicit use of numbers.

Factor analytic findings.　The Arithmetic subtest overall is a good measure of g (57 percent of its variance may be attributed to g—range of 50 to 63 percent in the nine age groups). The subtest has a substantial loading on the Verbal factor (*Mdn* loading = .64) and a moderate loading on the Performance factor (*Mdn* loading = .40). Its loading on the Performance factor may be accounted for by the fact that some items employ pictures of sets of objects that must be visually analyzed, after which verbal comparisons may be made. Specificity is either ample or adequate at six age groups and at the average of the nine age groups, and inadequate at ages 4, 5, and 7.

Reliability and correlational highlights.　Arithmetic overall is a reliable subtest (r_{xx} = .80). Reliability coefficients are above .70 at eight of the nine age groups; the one exception is at age 7, where the reliability coefficient is .66. It correlates more highly with Information (r = .59) than with any other subtest. It correlates moderately with the Full Scale (r = .67) and with the Verbal Scale (r = .63) and to a lesser degree with the Performance Scale (r = .55).

Administrative and interpretive considerations.　The administrative and interpretive considerations discussed for the WISC-III Arithmetic subtest generally apply to the WPPSI-R Arithmetic subtest (see pages 1084–1085). Scoring is for the most part easy—1 or 0 points. The time taken by the child to solve each problem should be recorded. On problems 12 through 23, correct answers given after the time limit has expired should also be noted, but of course not credited in the formal scoring.

Profile analysis should take into account that the full range of scores from 1 to 19 is available only at ages 4 to 6 years (see Table G-9).

Vocabulary

The Vocabulary subtest requires children to identify pictured stimuli on the early items and to define words on the later items. The subtest contains 25 words, 4 of which also appear on the WISC-III. Ten new items have been added to the subtest. On items 1 through 3 the child is asked to give the correct name of a pictured object, whereas on items 4 through 25 the child is asked to explain orally the meaning of each word. The first three items are scored 1 or 0, whereas the remainder of the items are scored 2, 1, or 0, depending on the conceptual level of the response. The subtest is untimed, and discontinued after five consecutive failures starting with item 4.

Rationale.　The rationale presented for the WISC-III Vocabulary subtest generally applies to the WPPSI-R Vocabulary subtest (see page 1086). Formal education, however, is less likely to be an influence in vocabulary development for preschool children than for older children. Experiences at home and in the community are likely to be the major contributing factor to the vocabulary development of preschool children.

Factor analytic findings.　The Vocabulary subtest overall is a good measure of g (51 percent of its variance may be attributed to g—range of 46 to 56 percent in the nine age groups). The subtest contributes substantially to the Verbal factor (*Mdn* loading = .79). Specificity is ample or adequate at four ages and at the average of the nine age groups, and inadequate at ages 3½, 4½, 6, 6½, and 7.

Reliability and correlational highlights.　Vocabulary overall is a reliable subtest (r_{xx} = .84). Reliability coefficients are above .70 at all age groups. It correlates more highly with Information (r = .60) and Comprehension (r = .60) than with any of the other subtests. It correlates moderately with the Full Scale ($r = .61$) and with the Verbal Scale ($r = .68$) and to a lesser degree with the Performance Scale ($r = .42$).

Administrative and interpretive considerations. All children start the subtest with the first word. This procedure differs from the one used for the WISC-III, where the starting word depends on the child's age. The general administrative and interpretive guidelines presented for the WISC-III Vocabulary subtest should be followed for the WPPSI-R Vocabulary subtest (see pages 1086–1087). Scoring requires considerable judgment, especially because the WPPSI-R manual provides too few sample responses.

The second Vocabulary item is contaminated by a procedure used on a previous subtest. The second Vocabulary picture is *exactly* the same as one of the pictures used on the second Arithmetic item. On Arithmetic, which is administered *before* Vocabulary, *the examiner tells the name of the picture to the child*. Consequently, success on the second Vocabulary item may be a function of short-term memory rather than of vocabulary ability.

Profile analysis should take into account that the full range of scaled scores from 1 to 19 is available from ages 4¼ to 7 years (see Table G-9).

Similarities

The WPPSI-R Similarities subtest requires children to answer questions about how objects or concepts are alike and to give verbal analogies. Responses may involve perceptual reasoning (and, perhaps, even verbal reasoning) on the early items, and verbal reasoning or conceptual thinking on the later items. The subtest consists of 20 questions, one of which is found on the WISC-III. Eleven new items have been added to the subtest.

Items 1 through 6 require the child to point to the object that is similar to the target object in the pictured array. Items 7 through 12 require a response to simple analogies presented orally by the examiner. Items 13 through 20 require a conceptual reasoning type of response and are similar to those found in the WISC-III.

Items 1 through 12 are scored 1 or 0 (pass-fail), and items 13 through 20 are scored 2, 1, or 0, depending on the conceptual level of the response. The subtest is untimed and discontinued after three consecutive failures on items 1 through 6 or after five consecutive failures on items 7 through 20. All children begin with item 1.

Rationale. The rationale described for the WISC-III Similarities subtest generally applies to the WPPSI-R Similarities subtest for the conceptual reasoning items (items 13 through 20, see page 1082). Items 1 through 6, however, appear to measure reasoning based on classification involving perceptual elements. And items 7 through 12 involve primarily simple analogic reasoning, but, as noted below, may be solved by other means as well.

Because over half of the items are either perceptual reasoning or simple analogic thinking items, the subtest may be measuring logical thinking (or even vocabulary ability in some cases), rather than verbal concept formation, especially at the earlier levels of the subtest (that is, below 5 years of age). In fact, on items 7 through 12 children may not even have to attend to the first half of the statement in order to get the item correct. For example, children need only attend to the second half of item 8 ("... you also ride in a _____") to get the right answer. Thus, it is not known to what extent the simple analogy items are a forerunner of conceptual reasoning and to what extent they reflect vocabulary ability or verbal reasoning skills.

Factor analytic findings. The Similarities subtest overall is a good measure of g (51 percent of its variance may be attributed to g—range of 26 to 57 percent in the nine age groups). The subtest contributes substantially to the Verbal factor (*Mdn* loading $= .72$). Specificity is either ample or adequate at most ages and at the average of the nine age groups, except at ages 6½ and 7, where it is inadequate.

Reliability and correlational highlights. Similarities overall is a reliable subtest ($r_{xx} = .86$). Reliability coefficients are above .70 at eight of the nine age groups; the one exception is at age 7, where the reliability coefficient is .54. It correlates more highly with Information ($r = .57$) than with any other subtest. It correlates moderately with the Full Scale ($r = .62$) and with the Verbal Scale ($r = .65$) and to a lesser degree with the Performance Scale ($r = .45$).

Administrative and interpretive considerations. The administrative and interpretive considerations discussed for the WISC-III Similarities subtest generally apply to the WPPSI-R Similarities subtest (see pages 1082–1083). Scoring procedures, however, differ. Because responses to the first 12 items are scored 1 or 0, few scoring problems should be encountered on these items. As in the WISC-III, however, the items dealing with similarities (13 through 20) are difficult to score. Scoring guidelines should be studied carefully.

Profile analysis should take into account that the full

range of scaled scores from 1 to 19 is available only at ages 5½ to 6 years (see Table G-9).

Sentences

The Sentences subtest requires children to repeat verbatim sentences given orally by the examiner. The subtest is an optional subtest and contains 12 sentences, ranging from 2 to 18 words. Three new items have been added to the subtest. When it is administered as a sixth Verbal Scale subtest, the subtest is not used in calculating the IQ. Items receive from 0 to 5 points, depending on the length of the sentence and the number of errors made. Errors in reproducing the sentences include omissions, transpositions, additions, and substitutions of words. Children younger than 5 years of age start with sentence 1; those older than 5 years of age start with sentence 6. The subtest is untimed, and it is discontinued after scores of 0 are obtained on three consecutive items.

Rationale.   The Sentences subtest is a memory subtest, measuring immediate recall and attention. Short-term auditory memory is involved, which includes attention, concentration, listening comprehension, and auditory processing. Because success may depend on verbal facility, failure may not necessarily reflect poor memory ability. For children 5 years and older, scores may be related primarily to memory ability, but for children younger than 5 years, scores may reflect verbal knowledge and comprehension, rather than immediate recall ability per se.

Factor analytic findings.   The Sentences subtest overall is a fair measure of g (46 percent of its variance may be attributed to g—range of 40 to 52 percent in the nine age groups). The subtest contributes substantially to the Verbal factor (*Mdn* loading = .72). Specificity is either ample or adequate at five ages and at the average of the nine age groups, and inadequate at ages 5½, 6, 6½, and 7.

Reliability and correlational highlights.   Sentences overall is a reliable subtest (r_{xx} = .82). Reliability coefficients are above .70 at all age groups. It correlates more highly with Information (r = .55) than with any other subtest. It correlates moderately with the Full Scale (r = .59) and with the Verbal Scale (r = .65) and to a lesser degree with the Performance Scale (r = .41).

Administrative and interpretive considerations. Scoring responses on the Sentences subtest requires careful attention to the different types of errors. The quality of the child's responses should also be evaluated. For exam-

ple, note (a) if any idiosyncratic or peculiar words were added; (b) if errors were made primarily at the beginning, middle, or end of sentences; and (c) if sentences were partially or completely missed. Missing a few words suggests minor inefficiencies, whereas missing all or most of the words may be indicative of more serious memory problems.

Profile analysis should take into account that the full range of scaled scores from 1 to 19 is available only at ages 5 to 6¾ years (see Table G-9).

INTERPRETING THE WPPSI-R

Most of the material in Chapter 8 (see pages 166–190) on the WISC-R also pertains to the WPPSI-R. The methods of interpretation—such as the successive-level approach, profile analysis, Performance/Verbal Scale comparisons, and subtest comparisons—are essentially the same for both the WISC-R (and WISC-III) and the WPPSI-R.

The information in Table C-24 in Appendix C (pages 836–839) can aid you in interpreting the WPPSI-R subtests, as well as in writing reports. It summarizes the abilities thought to be measured by the 12 WPPSI-R subtests. It deserves careful study. A summary of the interpretive rationales for the Full Scale, Verbal Scale, and Performance Scale of the Wechsler batteries can be found in Table C-42 (pages 856–857). Suggested remediation activities for combinations of Wechsler subtests can be found in Table C-43 (page 858).

The classifications associated with WPPSI-R IQs are shown in Table BC-2 on the inside back cover. Table BC-1 on the inside back cover shows the percentile ranks for the WPPSI-R Full Scale, Performance Scale, and Verbal Scale IQs. Percentile ranks associated with subtest scaled scores are shown in Table C-41 in Appendix C (page 855). The WPPSI Structure of Intellect classifications, many of which pertain to the WPPSI-R, can be obtained from Table C-23 in Appendix C (pages 834–836).

The individual subtests should not be viewed as a means of determining specific cognitive skills with precision. Rather, subtest scores should be used as a means of generating hypotheses about the child's abilities. The most reliable estimates of *specific abilities* are derived from the Performance Scale IQ (performance or perceptual organization abilities) and the Verbal Scale IQ (verbal or verbal comprehension abilities), not from individual subtest scores. In fact, of the 108 separate reliability coefficients for the 12 subtests at the nine age groups of the test, 60 are at .80 or above and of these only 3 are at .90 or above—

Information at ages 3 and 4½ years and Picture Completion at age 4½ years. The remaining 48 reliability coefficients are below .80 and are not sufficiently reliable for decision-making or classification purposes (see Table 9 on page 128 of the WPPSI-R manual).

Because there is a great deal of overlap between the WPPSI-R and the WISC-III, especially for the nine subtest types that they share, much of the information in this text on the WISC-III is pertinent to the WPPSI-R. You are encouraged to read Appendix J (pages 1079–1103), which discusses the WISC-III subtests, before reading the rest of this appendix.

Profile Analysis

Because profile analysis on the WPPSI-R is similar to that on the WISC-R, the material in Chapter 8 (pages 165–180) describing WISC-R profile analysis should be reviewed before a WPPSI-R profile analysis is undertaken. Although much less is known about profile analysis on the WPPSI-R than on other Wechsler scales, the procedures can still be useful in generating hypotheses about a child's strengths and weaknesses.

The five approaches to profile analysis on the WPPSI-R that follow are essentially the same as those described for the WISC-R (see pages 166–171). One difference, however, is that the tables in Appendix H must be used instead of those in Appendix C. Another difference is that the critical values in the tables are based on the child's specific age group instead of on an average value. A third difference is that factor scores are not included in profile analysis on the WPPSI-R because the Performance and Verbal Scales adequately describe the organization of the test.

1. *Comparing Performance and Verbal Scale IQs*. Table H-2 in Appendix H provides the critical values for comparing the Performance and Verbal IQs for the nine age groups of the WPPSI-R. The critical values for each age, as shown in Table H-2, are as follows (.05/.01 significance level):

- 10/13 at ages 3 through 4½
- 11/14 at age 5
- 12/15 at age 5½
- 11/14 at age 6
- 12/16 at age 6½
- 16/21 at age 7

These values indicate that an average critical value based on the entire group would be misleading. Therefore, the values for the child's specific age group should be used in evaluating differences between the child's Performance and Verbal IQs. (Probabilities associated with various differences between the Performance and Verbal Scale are shown in Table H-4 in Appendix H.)

2. *Comparing each Performance subtest scaled score to the mean Performance scaled score*. Table H-3 in Appendix H provides the critical values for each of the nine age groups of the WPPSI-R. Typical values for 3-year-old children for the five standard Performance subtests, for example, range from 2.65 to 3.96 at the .05 level and from 3.16 to 4.72 at the .01 level.

3. *Comparing each Verbal subtest scaled score to the mean Verbal scaled score*. Table H-3 in Appendix H provides the critical values for each of the nine age groups of the WPPSI-R. Typical values for 3-year-old children on the five standard Verbal subtests, for example, range from 2.30 to 3.10 at the .05 level and from 2.75 to 3.70 at the .01 level. These values are lower than those on the Performance Scale.

4. *Comparing each subtest scaled score to the mean subtest scaled score*. Table H-3 in Appendix H provides the critical values for each of the nine age groups in the WPPSI-R for 10, 11, and 12 subtests. For a 3-year-old, for example, they range from 2.62 to 4.72 at the .05 level and from 3.05 to 5.49 at the .01 level for the 10 standard subtests.

5. *Comparing sets of individual subtest scores*. Table H-2 in Appendix H provides the critical values for comparing sets of subtests for each of the nine age groups of the WPPSI-R. They range from 3 to 6 at the .05 level and from 4 to 7 at the .01 level. The values in Table H-2 are overly liberal (that is, lead to too many significant differences) when more than one comparison is made. They are most accurate when a priori planned comparisons are made, such as Comprehension versus Information or Block Design versus Object Assembly. Additional information for making comparisons between subtests can be found on pages 174–179.

Silverstein (personal communication, February 1990) advises determining the difference between the highest and lowest subtest scores before making multiple comparisons. If this difference is 6 scaled-score points or more, a significant difference at the .05 level is indicated. Differences between subtests that are 6 scaled-score points or greater can then be interpreted. If the difference between the highest and lowest subtest scaled scores is less than 6 scaled-score points, multiple comparisons between individual subtest scores should not be made. (The *Note* to Table H-2 in Appendix H shows the formula used to compute the significant difference. The formula considers the average standard error of measurement for each of the 12 subtests and the studentized range statistic.)

Two other tables will assist you in profile analysis. Table 14 (page 136) in the WPPSI-R manual presents the frequencies with which various differences between a child's score on each subtest and his or her average WPPSI-R Verbal, Performance, or overall score occurred in the standardization sample. This table should be used only for differences that first have been shown to be reliable. (See numbers 2, 3, and 4 in the Profile Analysis section above.)

Table H-5 in Appendix H presents the percentage of children in the standardization group who obtained a given discrepancy between the Verbal and Performance Scales. This table shows, for example, that between 25 and 50 percent of the population in each WPPSI-R age group had a 10-point difference (in either direction) between the two IQs.

ASSETS OF THE WPPSI-R

The WPPSI-R is a well-standardized test, with good reliability and validity. It has 12 subtests divided into two sections and provides three IQs—Performance, Verbal, and Full Scale. This is helpful in clinical and psychoeducational work. Parts of the test also can be administered to children limited by sensory impairments (for example, the Verbal Scale to blind children and the Performance Scale to deaf children).

1. *Excellent standardization.* The standardization procedures were excellent, sampling four geographical regions, both sexes, white children and nonwhite children, and the entire socioeconomic status range. The standardization group well represents the nation as a whole for the age groups covered by the test.

2. *Excellent overall psychometric properties.* The WPPSI-R has excellent reliability for the three IQs generated by the scale, with the minor exception at 7 years, where the Performance and Verbal IQs have reliabilities below .90. The few studies available suggest that the WPPSI-R has adequate concurrent and construct validity, although more research is needed to evaluate the validity of the test, especially at its first and last year levels.

3. *Useful diagnostic information.* The WPPSI-R provides diagnostic information useful for the assessment of cognitive abilities of preschool and early elementary-school age children who are functioning within two standard deviations from the mean. In addition, the test is useful for mildly mentally retarded children who are between 4 and 7 years of age and for moderately mentally retarded children who are between 5 and 7 years of age. It also furnishes data likely to be helpful in planning special school programs, perhaps tapping important developmental or maturational factors needed for school success in the lower grades.

4. *Good administrative procedures.* The prescribed procedures for administering the WPPSI-R are excellent. Examiners actively probe responses in order to evaluate the breadth of the child's knowledge and determine whether the child really knows the answers. The emphasis on probing questions and queries is extremely desirable.

5. *Good manual.* The WPPSI-R manual is easy to use; it provides clear directions and tables. The examiner's instructions are printed in a different color to facilitate reading of the directions. Helpful suggestions are provided about abbreviations to use in recording reponses.

6. *High interest level.* Most children should enjoy taking the test; the mixture of performance and verbal items, as well as the varied test materials, should maintain their interest.

LIMITATIONS OF THE WPPSI-R

Although the WPPSI-R is generally an excellent instrument, some problems exist.

1. *Low reliability of individual subtests.* Reliability coefficients for the individual subtests are lower than .80 at some ages. In these cases, the scores may not be dependable. In addition, during the standardization of the scale, test–retest scores for the Animal Pegs subtest were not obtained at each age level of the test. Because the WPPSI-R manual presents only *one* test-retest reliability coefficient for Animal Pegs, the same reliability coefficient had to be used, both by the test publisher and by the text author, to generate the standard errors of measurement and other statistical information for each age level of the test; the accuracy of these estimates is unknown.

2. *Limited floor.* The WPPSI-R is limited by the absence of an adequate floor—that is, it does not clearly differentiate abilities at the lower end of the scale. IQ equivalents of the scores range from 41 to 160, but the lower limit of this range is reached only at 5¼ years.

3. *Nonuniformity of subtest scores.* Because the range of scaled scores on all subtests is not uniform, there are problems in profile analysis, particularly at the lower and upper limits of the scaled-score range.

4. *Long administration time.* Administration time may be too long for some children, although fatigue should not often be a problem for older children. Little is known about how 3- to 4-year-olds will be able to maintain attention on the test. With younger children or with handi-

capped children, two test sessions may be needed. When this procedure is followed, there is no way of determining whether the break between testing sessions affects a child's scores, because the procedure differs from that used in standardizing the scale. Empirical data would be helpful in clarifying the effect of two test sessions on test scores.

5. *Possible difficulties in scoring responses.* Work with the WPPSI suggests that some subtests will be difficult to score. These subtests include the Geometric Design, Vocabulary, Similarities, and Comprehension subtests. The WPPSI-R manual cites a study in which there was high agreement in the scores given to these subtests (and the Mazes subtest as well) by independent examiners. These results are encouraging, but need to be replicated. Consultation with colleagues is recommended when responses are difficult to score.

6. *Problems for some minority children and for children who do not place a premium on speed.* The long administration time, demands for concentration and attention, and need to clarify answers may make some children uncomfortable, particularly those minority children who are unaccustomed to prolonged or intense periods of problem-solving activity. In addition, the test may penalize children who (a) are from a minority group that does not place a premium on speed (see Chapter 19) or (b) work in a slow, deliberate, and thoughtful manner.

7. *Overlap with the WISC-III.* The WPPSI-R and the WISC-III have at least 23 overlapping items, primarily on the Picture Completion, Mazes, Vocabulary, and Information subtests. This overlap is unfortunate for at least two reasons. First, it means that the WPPSI-R and the WISC-III are not independent parallel forms at the overlapping age levels (6 to 7¼ years). Second, it means that children tested with the WPPSI-R and then with the WISC-III (or vice versa) have an advantage on the second test because of practice effects. On the next revision of either test, the overlapping items should be replaced with completely different items.

PSYCHOLOGICAL EVALUATION

The psychological evaluation in Exhibit 9-3 (pages 216–217) illustrates the application of the WPPSI to evaluation of a developmentally immature child and should be helpful in understanding the WPPSI-R as well. The report summarizes information obtained from parents and from a kindergarten teacher and cites both qualitative and quantitative information obtained during the evaluation. Profile analysis is used to develop some assessment information,

and recommendations are based on the test results and background information.

TEST YOUR SKILL

The WISC-R Test-Your-Skill Exercises on pages 187–189 also pertain to the WPPSI-R. If you have not reviewed these exercises recently, you are encouraged to do so now. In addition, three exercises that pertain only to the WPPSI-R follow. In each exercise, there is some inadequacy of description or interpretation. Analyze the mistakes, then check your answers with those shown on page 806 (referred to as "Chapter 9: Test-Your-Skill Exercises for the WPPSI").

1. "Tom's excellent performance on Block Design and Geometric Design suggests that he has good ability in analyzing school situations and has high moral judgment."

2. "The Geometric Design subtest presented problems for her and she fell in the slow learning category."

3. The following interpretation was given to these WPPSI-R Performance Scale scores: Object Assembly, 12; Picture Completion, 15; Mazes, 13; Geometric Design, 14; and Block Design, 12. "While her two lowest scores on the Performance Scale were above average, they may suggest some visual acuity problems."

SUMMARY

1. The WPPSI-R, designed to be used with children between 3 and 7¼ years of age, follows the basic format of the WISC-R (WISC-III), providing Performance, Verbal, and Full Scales IQs.

2. The WPPSI-R contains 12 subtests: Object Assembly, Geometric Design, Block Design, Mazes, Picture Completion, Animal Pegs, Information, Comprehension, Arithmetic, Vocabulary, Similarities, and Sentences. Three of the subtests—Sentences, Animal Pegs, and Geometric Design—do not appear in the WISC-III. Object Assembly is new to the WPPSI-R; it did not appear in the WPPSI.

3. The standardization sample was representative of the 1986 U.S. population and included 1,700 children living in four geographical regions in the United States.

4. Like the other Wechsler scales, the WPPSI-R employs Deviation IQs ($M = 100$, $SD = 15$) for the Performance, Verbal, and Full Scale IQs. Similarly, scaled scores ($M = 10$, $SD = 3$) are provided for each subtest. When fewer than 10 subtests are administered, this text recommends the use of a special short-form procedure to obtain the IQs.

5. The WPPSI-R has excellent reliability for the three IQs (average reliabilities range from .92 to .96), except at age 7,

where the reliabilities for the Performance and Verbal Scale IQs are below .90. The reliabilities for the subtests are less satisfactory (average reliabilities range from .66 to .86) than those for the three scales. The Performance Scale generally shows greater practice effects than does the Verbal Scale.

6. Because the WPPSI-R is a new revision, little is known about its validity, especially for exceptional children. Studies of the prior version indicate that it should have adequate concurrent and predictive validity.

7. Studies cited in the WPPSI-R manual, using such criteria as the WISC-R, Stanford-Binet Intelligence Scale—4th Edition, McCarthy Scales of Children's Abilities, and K-ABC, suggest that the test has good concurrent validity for normal children.

8. Construct validity is adequate as established by factor analytic studies.

9. Little is known about the validity of the WPPSI-R at ages 3 and 7, the two new age levels of the test.

10. Research cited in the WPPSI-R manual indicates that the WPPSI-R and WISC-R cannot be considered parallel forms, because the WISC-R yields IQs that are, on the average, 8 points *higher* than those of the WPPSI-R.

11. Factor analysis indicates that all of the 12 WPPSI-R subtests are either good or fair measures of g. Subtest specificity varies throughout the age levels of the test. A Freedom from Distractibility factor does not emerge on the WPPSI-R.

12. The range of Full Scale IQs from 41 to 160 cannot be obtained until 5¾ years. At 3 years the lowest Full Scale IQ that can be obtained is 65. The lack of a uniform floor at all ages of the WPPSI-R will impede the monitoring of changes in the performance of low-functioning children.

13. The range of subtest scaled scores from 1 to 19 cannot be obtained on any subtest at every age level of the WPPSI-R. Profile analysis, consequently, must take into account the non-uniform scaled-score range, especially at the lower and upper limits of the range.

14. Generally, children must be more proficient on the WPPSI-R Animal Pegs subtest than on the WPPSI to maintain their same relative position. Changes are greatest for the 4- and 4½-year-olds with above-average ability and for the 4¾- to 6½-year-olds with below-average ability.

15. Changes from the WPPSI to the WPPSI-R include extending the age range (changed from 4 to 6½ to 3 to 7¼), adding the Object Assembly subtest, renaming Animal House as Animal Pegs and making it an optional subtest, eliminating retest norms for Animal Pegs, modifying scoring guidelines and administrative procedures, placing a greater emphasis on speed in scoring, and increasing the IQ range to from 41 to 160 at the upper ages of the test.

16. The administrative considerations that apply to the WISC-III generally apply to the WPPSI-R. Because the WPPSI-R is used with a younger age group than is the WISC-III, there are some problems in adapting the subtests to alternative sensory modalities for children with sensory or motor handicaps.

17. Table H-6 in Appendix H shows the best short-form combinations of two, three, four, and five WPPSI-R subtests, and

Tables H-7, H-8, and H-9 show the IQs for the sum of the scaled scores for the 10 best combinations of two-, three-, and four-subtest short forms.

18. Research is needed to determine whether the WPPSI-R or the WISC-R is more valid at the overlapping ages of 6 to 7¼ years.

19. The interpretive rationale, factor analytic findings, reliability and subtest correlations, and administrative and interpretive considerations for each of the WPPSI-R subtests are presented in the chapter. The proposed interpretive rationales and possible implications of high and low scores are summarized in Table C-24 in Appendix C.

20. The rationale for the WISC-III Object Assembly subtest probably applies to the WPPSI-R Object Assembly subtest. The subtest is a fair measure of g, but it contributes to the Performance factor. Its subtest specificity is inadequate at every age, and reliability is marginal (r_{xx} = .63). Administrative procedures differ somewhat from those in the WISC-III.

21. Geometric Design is considered to measure perceptual recognition and discrimination in younger children and visual-motor ability, visual construction, and eye-hand coordination in older children. It is a fair measure of g and contributes to the Performance factor. Subtest specificity is ample or adequate at five of the nine age groups, and reliability is relatively good (r_{xx} = .79). Although improvements have been made in the scoring procedure, the subtest still may be difficult to score.

22. The rationale for the WISC-III Block Design subtest probably applies to the WPPSI-R Block Design subtest. The subtest is a fair measure of g and contributes to the Performance factor. Subtest specificity is ample or adequate at seven of the nine age groups, and reliability is good (r_{xx} = .85). The subtest requires skill to administer.

23. The rationale for the WISC-III Mazes subtest probably applies to the WPPSI-R Mazes subtest. The subtest is a fair measure of g, but it contributes to the Performance factor. Subtest specificity is ample at six of the nine age groups, and reliability is relatively good (r_{xx} = .77). Scoring requires considerable judgment. Administrative procedures differ from those used on the WISC-III.

24. The rationale for the WISC-III Picture Completion subtest probably applies to the WPPSI-R Picture Completion subtest. The subtest is a fair measure of g and contributes to both the Performance and Verbal factors. Subtest specificity is ample at all ages, and reliability is good (r_{xx} = .85). Administration is relatively easy.

25. Animal Pegs is an optional subtest on the WPPSI-R. It is believed to measure memory, attention span, goal awareness, concentration, and finger and manual dexterity. It is a fair measure of g, but it contributes to the Performance factor. Subtest specificity is ample at five of the nine groups, and reliability is marginal (r_{xx} = .66). Administration is relatively easy.

26. The rationale for the WISC-III Information subtest probably applies to the WPPSI-R Information subtest, although WPPSI-R questions may be related more to the child's experiences than to formal education. The subtest is overall the best

measure of g in the scale and contributes to the Verbal factor. Subtest specificity is adequate at only two of the nine age groups, and reliability is good ($r_{xx} = .84$). Judgment is required in scoring responses.

27. The rationale for the WISC-III Comprehension subtest probably applies to the WPPSI-R Comprehension subtest, although linguistic skill and logical reasoning may play a more significant role on the WPPSI-R. The subtest is a good measure of g and contributes to the Verbal factor. Subtest specificity is adequate at three of the nine age groups, and reliability is good ($r_{xx} = .83$). Scoring requires considerable judgment.

28. The rationale for the WISC-III Arithmetic subtest probably applies to the WPPSI-R Arithmetic subtest, although formal education probably has less influence on the WPPSI-R. The subtest is a good measure of g and contributes to both the Verbal *and* Performance factors. Subtest specificity is ample or adequate at six of the nine age groups, and reliability is good ($r_{xx} = .83$). Scoring is easy.

29. The rationale for the WISC-III Vocabulary subtest probably applies to the WPPSI-R Vocabulary subtest, although formal education probably has less influence on the WPPSI-R. The subtest is a good measure of g and contributes to the Verbal factor. Subtest specificity is ample or adequate at four of the nine age groups, and reliability is good ($r_{xx} = .84$). Scoring requires considerable judgment.

30. The WPPSI-R Similarities subtest appears to measure logical thinking to a greater extent than does the WISC-III Similarities subtest, especially at the early ages. The subtest is a good measure of g and contributes to the Verbal factor. Subtest specificity is ample or adequate at seven of the nine age groups, and reliability is good ($r_{xx} = .86$). Judgment is required in scoring the last eight items.

31. Sentences is an optional subtest on the WPPSI-R. It is a memory test, measuring immediate recall and attention. The subtest is a fair measure of g and contributes to the Verbal factor. Subtest specificity is ample or adequate at five of the nine age groups, and reliability is good ($r_{xx} = .82$). Scoring requires considerable skill.

32. Although the same considerations that apply to profile analysis on the WISC-R apply to profile analysis on the WPPSI-R, more care should be taken in using profile analysis with the WPPSI-R because less is known about the scale.

33. Although the WPPSI-R has some limitations—such as long administration time, inadequate floor, and difficult scoring on some subtests—it is, overall, a well-standardized, carefully developed instrument that is a valuable tool for the assessment of young children's intelligence.

KEY TERMS, CONCEPTS, AND NAMES

WPPSI-R standardization (p. 978)
WPPSI-R reliability (p. 979)
WPPSI-R validity (p. 981)
WPPSI-R factor analysis (p. 984)
WPPSI-R subtest specificity (p. 985)
Testing-of-limits (p. 994)
WPPSI-R short forms (p. 994)
Yudin's WPPSI-R short form (p. 996)
WPPSI-R Object Assembly (p. 997)
WPPSI-R Geometric Design (p. 997)
WPPSI-R Block Design (p. 998)
WPPSI-R Mazes (p. 999)
WPPSI-R Picture Completion (p. 1000)
WPPSI-R Animal Pegs (p. 1000)
WPPSI-R Information (p. 1001)
WPPSI-R Comprehension (p. 1002)
WPPSI-R Arithmetic (p. 1002)
WPPSI-R Vocabulary (p. 1003)
WPPSI-R Similarities (p. 1004)
WPPSI-R Sentences (p. 1005)
Profile analysis (p. 1006)

STUDY QUESTIONS

1. Describe the WPPSI-R and then discuss its standardization, reliability, and validity.

2. Describe WPPSI-R factor analytic findings.

3. Discuss some general administrative considerations for the WPPSI-R.

4. Discuss WPPSI-R short forms.

5. Discuss the rationale, factor analytic findings, reliability and correlational highlights, and administrative and interpretive considerations for each of the following WPPSI-R Performance Scale subtests: Object Assembly, Geometric Design, Block Design, Mazes, Picture Completion, and Animal Pegs.

6. Discuss the rationale, factor analytic findings, reliability and correlational highlights, and administrative and interpretive considerations for each of the following WPPSI-R Verbal Scale subtests: Information, Comprehension, Arithmetic, Vocabulary, Similarities, and Sentences.

7. Briefly describe profile analysis on the WPPSI-R.

8. Discuss the assets and limitations of the WPPSI-R.

_ APPENDIX H _____

TABLES FOR THE WPPSI-R

See also Table C-23, "WPPSI Structure of Intellect Classifications (page 834); Table C-24, "Interpretive Rationales and Implications of High and Low Scores for WPPSI-R and WPPSI Subtests" (page 836): Table C-41, "Percentile Ranks and Suggested Qualitative Descriptions for Scaled Scores on the WISC-R, WPPSI-R, WPPSI, and WAIS-R" (page 855); Table C-42, "Interpretive Rationales, Implications of High and Low Scores, and Instructional Implications for Wechsler Scales and Factor Scores" (page 856); and Table C-43, "Suggested Remediation Activities for Combinations of Wechsler Subtests" (page 858).

Table H-1
Confidence Intervals for WPPSI-R Scales

Age level	Scale	Confidence level				
		68%	85%	90%	95%	99%
3 (2-11-16 through 3-5-15)	Performance Scale IQ	± 4	± 6	± 7	± 8	± 10
	Verbal Scale IQ	± 3	± 5	± 5	± 6	± 8
	Full Scale IQ	± 3	± 4	± 5	± 6	± 7
3½ (3-5-16 through 3-11-15)	Performance Scale IQ	± 4	± 6	± 7	± 8	± 10
	Verbal Scale IQ	± 3	± 5	± 5	± 6	± 8
	Full Scale IQ	± 3	± 4	± 5	± 6	± 7
4 (3-11-16 through 4-5-15)	Performance Scale IQ	± 4	± 6	± 7	± 8	± 11
	Verbal Scale IQ	± 3	± 4	± 5	± 6	± 8
	Full Scale IQ	± 3	± 4	± 5	± 6	± 7
4½ (4-5-16 through 4-11-15)	Performance Scale IQ	± 4	± 6	± 7	± 8	± 11
	Verbal Scale IQ	± 3	± 5	± 5	± 6	± 8
	Full Scale IQ	± 3	± 4	± 5	± 6	± 8
5 (4-11-16 through 5-5-15)	Performance Scale IQ	± 4	± 6	± 7	± 9	± 11
	Verbal Scale IQ	± 3	± 5	± 5	± 7	± 9
	Full Scale IQ	± 3	± 4	± 5	± 6	± 8
5½ (5-5-16 through 5-11-15)	Performance Scale IQ	± 5	± 7	± 8	± 9	± 12
	Verbal Scale IQ	± 4	± 5	± 6	± 7	± 9
	Full Scale IQ	± 3	± 5	± 5	± 6	± 8
6 (5-11-16 through 6-5-15)	Performance Scale IQ	± 4	± 6	± 7	± 9	± 11
	Verbal Scale IQ	± 4	± 5	± 6	± 7	± 10
	Full Scale	± 3	± 5	± 5	± 6	± 8
6½ (6-5-16 through 6-11-15)	Performance Scale IQ	± 5	± 7	± 8	± 9	± 12
	Verbal Scale IQ	± 4	± 6	± 7	± 8	± 10
	Full Scale IQ	± 3	± 5	± 7	± 7	± 9
7 (6-11-16 through 7-3-15)	Performance Scale IQ	± 5	± 7	± 8	± 10	± 13
	Verbal Scale IQ	± 5	± 7	± 8	± 10	± 13
	Full Scale IQ	± 4	± 6	± 6	± 8	± 10

Note. See the Note in Table C-1, page 813, for an explanation of method used to obtain confidence intervals.

Table H-2
Significant Differences Between Scaled Scores and Between IQs at Each of the Nine Age Levels of the WPPSI-R (.05/.01 significance levels)

Age level		OA	GD	BD	MA	PC	AP	I	C	A	V	S
3	GD	4/6	—									
(2-11-16	BD	4/6	3/4	—								
through	MA	4/6	3/4	3/4	—							
3-5-15)	PC	4/5	3/4	3/4	3/4	—						
	AP	5/7	4/5	4/6	4/5	4/5	—					
	I	4/5	3/4	3/4	3/4	3/4	4/5	—				
	C	4/5	3/4	3/4	3/4	3/4	4/5	3/4	—			
	A	5/6	4/5	4/5	4/5	3/4	4/6	3/4	3/5	—		
	V	4/6	3/4	3/4	3/4	3/4	4/5	3/4	3/4	4/5	—	
	S	4/5	3/4	3/4	3/4	3/4	4/5	3/4	3/4	3/5	3/4	—
	Se	4/5	3/4	3/4	3/4	3/4	4/5	3/4	3/4	3/5	3/4	3/4

VSIQ / PSIQ 10/13

Age level		OA	GD	BD	MA	PC	AP	I	C	A	V	S
3½	GD	4/6	—									
(3-5-16	BD	4/6	3/4	—								
through	MA	4/6	3/4	3/5	—							
3-11-15)	PC	4/5	3/4	3/4	3/4	—						
	AP	5/7	4/5	4/5	4/6	4/5	—					
	I	4/5	3/4	3/4	3/4	3/4	4/5	—				
	C	4/5	3/4	3/4	3/4	3/4	4/5	3/4	—			
	A	4/6	3/5	3/5	4/5	3/4	4/6	3/4	3/4	—		
	V	4/6	3/4	3/4	3/5	3/4	4/5	3/4	3/4	3/5	—	
	S	4/5	3/4	3/4	3/4	3/4	4/5	3/4	3/4	3/4	3/4	—
	Se	4/6	3/4	3/4	3/4	3/4	4/5	3/4	3/4	3/5	3/4	3/4

VSIQ / PSIQ 10/13

Age level		OA	GD	BD	MA	PC	AP	I	C	A	V	S
4	GD	4/5	—									
(3-11-16	BD	4/5	3/4	—								
through	MA	4/6	4/5	4/5	—							
4-5-15)	PC	4/5	3/4	3/4	4/5	—						
	AP	5/6	4/6	4/5	5/6	4/5	—					
	I	4/5	3/4	3/4	4/5	3/4	4/5	—				
	C	4/5	3/4	3/4	4/5	3/4	4/5	3/4	—			
	A	4/5	4/5	3/4	4/5	3/4	4/6	3/4	3/4	—		
	V	4/5	3/4	3/4	4/5	3/4	4/5	3/4	3/4	3/4	—	
	S	4/5	3/4	3/4	4/5	3/4	4/5	3/4	3/4	3/4	3/4	—
	Se	4/5	3/4	3/4	4/5	3/4	4/5	3/4	3/4	3/4	3/4	3/4

VSIQ / PSIQ 10/13

Age level		OA	GD	BD	MA	PC	AP	I	C	A	V	S
4½	GD	5/6	—									
(4-5-16	BD	4/6	3/4	—								
through	MA	5/6	4/5	4/5	—							
4-11-15)	PC	4/6	3/4	3/3	3/4	—						
	AP	5/7	4/5	4/5	5/6	4/5	—					
	I	4/6	3/4	3/4	3/5	2/3	4/5	—				
	C	4/6	3/4	3/4	4/5	3/3	4/5	3/4	—			
	A	5/6	3/5	3/4	4/5	3/4	4/6	3/4	3/4	—		
	V	5/6	3/4	3/4	4/5	3/4	4/6	3/4	3/4	4/5	—	
	S	4/6	3/4	3/4	4/5	2/3	4/5	3/4	3/4	3/4	3/4	—
	Se	5/6	3/4	3/4	4/5	3/4	4/6	3/4	3/4	4/5	3/5	3/4

VSIQ / PSIQ 10/13

(*Table continues next page*)

Table H-2 (cont.)

Age level		OA	GD	BD	MA	PC	AP	I	C	A	V	S
5	GD	5/6	—									
(4-11-16	BD	4/6	4/5	—								
through	MA	5/6	4/5	4/5	—							
5-5-15)	PC	4/6	4/5	3/4	4/5	—						
	AP	5/7	4/6	4/5	4/6	4/5	—					
	I	4/6	4/5	3/4	4/5	3/4	4/5	—				
	C	4/6	4/5	3/4	4/5	3/4	4/5	3/4	—			
	A	5/6	4/5	3/5	4/5	3/5	4/6	4/5	3/5	—		
	V	4/6	4/5	3/4	4/5	3/4	4/5	3/4	3/4	3/5	—	
	S	4/6	4/5	3/4	4/5	3/4	4/5	3/4	3/4	3/5	3/4	—
	Se	5/6	4/5	3/4	4/5	3/4	4/6	3/5	3/4	4/5	3/4	3/4

VSIQ PSIQ 11/14

Age level		OA	GD	BD	MA	PC	AP	I	C	A	V	S
5½	GD	5/7	—									
(5-5-16	BD	5/6	4/5	—								
through	MA	5/6	4/6	4/6	—							
5-11-15)	PC	5/6	4/5	4/5	4/5	—						
	AP	5/7	5/6	4/6	4/6	4/6	—					
	I	5/6	4/6	4/5	4/5	4/5	5/6	—				
	C	5/6	4/5	4/5	4/5	4/5	4/6	4/6	—			
	A	5/6	4/5	4/5	4/5	4/5	4/6	4/6	4/5	—		
	V	4/6	4/5	3/5	4/5	3/4	4/5	4/5	3/4	3/4	—	
	S	4/6	4/5	3/5	4/5	3/4	4/5	4/5	3/4	3/4	3/4	—
	Se	5/6	4/6	4/6	4/5	4/5	4/6	4/5	4/5	4/5	4/5	4/5

VSIQ PSIQ 12/15

Age level		OA	GD	BD	MA	PC	AP	I	C	A	V	S
6	GD	4/6	—									
(5-11-16	BD	4/5	4/5	—								
through	MA	4/6	4/5	4/5	—							
6-5-15)	PC	4/6	4/5	4/5	4/5	—						
	AP	5/6	4/6	4/5	4/6	4/6	—					
	I	4/6	4/5	4/5	4/5	4/5	5/6	—				
	C	4/6	4/5	4/5	4/5	4/5	4/6	4/5	—			
	A	4/5	4/5	4/5	4/5	4/5	4/6	4/5	4/5	—		
	V	4/5	4/5	3/5	4/5	4/5	4/6	4/5	4/5	4/5	—	
	S	4/5	4/5	3/4	3/5	4/5	4/5	4/5	4/5	3/5	3/4	—
	Se	4/6	4/5	4/5	4/5	4/5	4/6	4/5	4/5	4/5	4/5	4/5

VSIQ PSIQ 11/14

Age level		OA	GD	BD	MA	PC	AP	I	C	A	V	S
6½	GD	5/6	—									
(6-5-16	BD	4/6	4/5	—								
through	MA	5/6	4/6	4/5	—							
6-11-15)	PC	4/6	4/6	4/5	4/5	—						
	AP	5/6	5/6	4/6	5/6	5/6	—					
	I	4/6	4/5	4/5	4/5	4/5	4/6	—				
	C	5/6	4/6	4/5	4/6	4/6	5/6	4/5	—			
	A	4/6	4/5	4/5	4/5	4/5	4/6	4/5	4/5	—		
	V	4/5	4/5	3/5	4/5	4/5	4/6	4/5	4/5	4/5	—	
	S	4/6	4/6	4/5	4/5	4/5	4/6	4/5	4/6	4/5	4/5	—
	Se	5/6	4/6	4/5	4/6	4/6	5/6	4/5	4/6	4/5	4/5	4/6

VSIQ PSIQ 12/16

(*Table continues next page*)

Table H-2 (cont.)

Age level		OA	GD	BD	MA	PC	AP	I	C	A	V	S
7	GD	5/7	—									
(6-11-16	BD	5/6	4/5	—								
through	MA	5/7	5/6	4/5	—							
7-3-15)	PC	5/7	5/6	4/5	5/6	—						
	AP	5/7	5/6	4/5	5/6	5/6	—					
	I	5/7	5/6	4/6	5/7	5/6	5/7	—				
	C	5/7	5/7	4/6	5/7	5/6	5/7	5/7	—			
	A	5/7	5/6	4/5	5/6	5/6	5/6	5/7	5/7	—		
	V	5/7	4/6	4/5	5/6	4/6	5/6	5/6	5/6	5/6	—	
	S	6/7	5/7	5/6	5/7	5/7	5/7	5/7	5/7	5/7	5/7	—
	Se	5/6	4/6	4/5	5/6	4/6	4/6	5/6	5/6	4/6	4/5	5/6

VSIQ
PSIQ 16/21

Note. Abbreviations: OA = Object Assembly, GD = Geometric Design, BD = Block Design, MA = Mazes, PC = Picture Completion, AP = Animal Pegs, I = Information, C = Comprehension, A = Arithmetic, V = Vocabulary, S = Similarities, Se = Sentences.

Sample reading: At age 3, a difference of 4 points between scaled scores on the Object Assembly and Geometric Design subtests is significant at the 5 percent level; a difference of 6 points is significant at the 1 percent level. The small box shows that at age 3 years a 10-point difference between the Performance Scale IQ and Verbal Scale IQ is needed for the 5 percent level, and a 13-point difference is needed for the 1 percent level.

The values in this table for the subtest comparisons are overly liberal when more than one comparison is made. They are more accurate when a priori planned comparisons are made, such as Object Assembly vs. Block Design or Information vs. Vocabulary.

See Chapter 8, Exhibit 8-1, page 168, for an explanation of the method used to arrive at magnitude of differences.

Silverstein (personal communication, February 1990) suggests that the following formula be used to obtain the value of the significant difference at the .05 level between the highest and lowest subtest scores on the profile that allows for making individual subtest comparisons:

$$D = q\sqrt{\Sigma SEM^2/k}$$

where D is the significant difference, q is the critical value of the studentized range statistic, SEM is the standard error of measurement of a particular subtest, and k is the number of subtests. For the WPPSI-R, the q value is 4.62 for 12 and ∞ degrees of freedom and k is 12. The sum of the SEM^2 for the 12 subtests is $3.31 + 1.88 + 1.35 + 2.07 + 1.35 + 3.06 + 1.44 + 1.54 + 1.80 + 1.44 + 1.25 + 1.61 = 22.10$. $D = 4.62 \times \sqrt{22.10/12} = 4.62 \times \sqrt{1.8417} = 4.62 \times 1.3571 = 6$. Thus, a difference of 6 points between the highest and lowest subtest scaled scores represents a significant difference at the .05 level.

Table H-3
Differences Required for Significance When Each Subtest Scaled Score Is Compared to the Mean Scaled Score for Any Individual Child at Each of the Nine Age Levels of the WPPSI-R

Age level	Subtest	Mean of 5 Performance Scale subtests[a]		Mean of 6 Performance Scale subtests		Mean of 5 Verbal Scale subtests[b]		Mean of 6 Verbal Scale subtests	
		.05	.01	.05	.01	.05	.01	.05	.01
3 (2-11-16 through 3-5-15)	Object Assembly	3.96	4.72	4.12	4.92	—	—	—	—
	Geometric Design	2.85	3.40	2.93	3.50	—	—	—	—
	Block Design	2.91	3.47	3.00	3.58	—	—	—	—
	Mazes	2.78	3.32	2.86	3.42	—	—	—	—
	Picture Completion	2.65	3.16	2.72	3.24	—	—	—	—
	Animal Pegs	—	—	3.97	4.74	—	—	—	—
	Information	—	—	—	—	2.30	2.75	2.37	2.82
	Comprehension	—	—	—	—	2.45	2.93	2.54	3.02
	Arithmetic	—	—	—	—	3.10	3.70	3.26	3.88
	Vocabulary	—	—	—	—	2.66	3.18	2.78	3.30
	Similarities	—	—	—	—	2.45	2.93	2.54	3.02
	Sentences	—	—	—	—	—	—	2.57	3.02

	Subtest	Mean of 10 subtests[a,b]		Mean of 11 subtests[a]		Mean of 11 subtests[b]		Mean of 12 subtests	
		.05	.01	.05	.01	.05	.01	.05	.01
	Object Assembly	4.72	5.49	5.22	5.60	4.80	5.58	4.90	5.68
	Geometric Design	3.21	3.73	3.55	3.80	3.25	3.78	3.32	3.85
	Block Design	3.30	3.84	3.65	3.91	3.34	3.89	3.41	3.95
	Mazes	3.12	3.63	3.45	3.70	3.16	3.67	3.22	3.74
	Picture Completion	2.93	3.41	3.24	3.47	2.97	3.45	3.02	3.51
	Animal Pegs	—	—	5.02	5.38	—	—	4.70	5.46
	Information	2.62	3.05	2.90	3.11	2.65	3.08	2.70	3.13
	Comprehension	2.83	3.30	3.13	3.36	2.87	3.33	2.92	3.39
	Arithmetic	3.70	4.31	4.10	4.39	3.76	4.37	3.83	4.45
	Vocabulary	3.12	3.63	3.45	3.70	3.16	3.67	3.22	3.74
	Similarities	2.83	3.30	3.13	3.36	2.87	3.33	2.92	3.39
	Sentences	—	—	—	—	2.87	3.33	2.92	3.39

(Table continues next page)

Table H-3 (cont.)

Age level	Subtest	Mean of 5 Performance Scale subtests[a]		Mean of 6 Performance Scale subtests		Mean of 5 Verbal Scale subtests[b]		Mean of 6 Verbal Scale subtests	
		.05	.01	.05	.01	.05	.01	.05	.01
3½ (3-5-16 through 3-11-15)	Object Assembly	3.95	4.72	4.21	5.01	—	—	—	—
	Geometric Design	2.71	3.23	2.85	3.39	—	—	—	—
	Block Design	2.77	3.31	2.92	3.48	—	—	—	—
	Mazes	3.02	3.61	3.20	3.80	—	—	—	—
	Picture Completion	2.50	2.99	2.62	3.12	—	—	—	—
	Animal Pegs	—	—	4.06	4.83	—	—	—	—
	Information	—	—	—	—	2.37	2.83	2.46	2.93
	Comprehension	—	—	—	—	2.45	2.92	2.55	3.03
	Arithmetic	—	—	—	—	2.98	3.55	3.13	3.73
	Vocabulary	—	—	—	—	2.73	3.25	2.86	3.40
	Similarities	—	—	—	—	2.37	2.83	2.46	2.93
	Sentences	—	—	—	—	—	—	2.71	3.22

	Subtest	Mean of 10 subtests[a,b]		Mean of 11 subtests[a]		Mean of 11 subtests[b]		Mean of 12 subtests	
		.05	.01	.05	.01	.05	.01	.05	.01
	Object Assembly	4.71	5.48	4.81	5.59	4.80	5.58	4.89	5.68
	Geometric Design	3.02	3.52	3.08	3.58	3.07	3.56	3.12	3.62
	Block Design	3.12	3.63	3.18	3.69	3.16	3.67	3.22	3.74
	Mazes	3.46	4.03	3.53	4.11	3.52	4.09	3.58	4.16
	Picture Completion	2.73	3.17	2.78	3.23	2.76	3.21	2.81	3.26
	Animal Pegs	—	—	4.63	5.37	—	—	4.70	5.46
	Information	2.73	3.17	2.78	3.23	2.76	3.21	2.81	3.26
	Comprehension	2.83	3.29	2.89	3.35	2.86	3.33	2.92	3.39
	Arithmetic	3.54	4.12	3.62	4.20	3.60	4.18	3.67	4.26
	Vocabulary	3.21	3.73	3.27	3.80	3.25	3.78	3.31	3.85
	Similarities	2.73	3.17	2.78	3.23	2.76	3.21	2.81	3.26
	Sentences	—	—	—	—	3.07	3.56	3.12	3.62

(*Table continues next page*)

Table H-3 (cont.)

Age level	Subtest	Mean of 5 Performance Scale subtests[a]		Mean of 6 Performance Scale subtests		Mean of 5 Verbal Scale subtests[b]		Mean of 6 Verbal Scale subtests	
		.05	.01	.05	.01	.05	.01	.05	.01
4 (3-11-16 through 4-5-15)	Object Assembly	3.63	4.34	3.86	4.59	—	—	—	—
	Geometric Design	3.10	3.70	3.27	3.89	—	—	—	—
	Block Design	2.66	3.18	2.79	3.32	—	—	—	—
	Mazes	3.38	4.03	3.58	4.26	—	—	—	—
	Picture Completion	2.66	3.18	2.79	3.32	—	—	—	—
	Animal Pegs	—	—	4.07	4.84	—	—	—	—
	Information	—	—	—	—	2.44	2.92	2.54	3.02
	Comprehension	—	—	—	—	2.52	3.00	2.62	3.11
	Arithmetic	—	—	—	—	2.97	3.55	3.13	3.72
	Vocabulary	—	—	—	—	2.52	3.00	2.62	3.11
	Similarities	—	—	—	—	2.37	2.83	2.45	2.92
	Sentences	—	—	—	—	—	—	2.54	3.02

	Subtest	Mean of 10 subtests[a,b]		Mean of 11 subtests[a]		Mean of 11 subtests[b]		Mean of 12 subtests	
		.05	.01	.05	.01	.05	.01	.05	.01
	Object Assembly	4.27	4.97	4.36	5.07	4.35	5.05	4.43	5.14
	Geometric Design	3.55	4.13	3.62	4.21	3.60	4.18	3.67	4.26
	Block Design	2.93	3.41	2.99	3.48	2.97	3.45	3.02	3.51
	Mazes	3.93	4.57	4.01	4.66	3.99	4.64	4.07	4.72
	Picture Completion	2.93	3.41	2.99	3.48	2.97	3.45	3.02	3.51
	Animal Pegs	—	—	4.63	5.38	—	—	4.70	5.46
	Information	2.83	3.30	2.89	3.36	2.87	3.33	2.92	3.39
	Comprehension	2.93	3.41	2.99	3.48	2.97	3.45	3.02	3.51
	Arithmetic	3.55	4.13	3.62	4.21	3.60	4.18	3.67	4.26
	Vocabulary	2.93	3.41	2.99	3.48	2.97	3.45	3.02	3.51
	Similarities	2.73	3.18	2.79	3.24	2.76	3.21	2.81	3.26
	Sentences	—	—	—	—	2.87	3.33	2.92	3.39

(*Table continues next page*)

Table H-3 (cont.)

Age level	Subtest	Mean of 5 Performance Scale subtests[a]		Mean of 6 Performance Scale subtests		Mean of 5 Verbal Scale subtests[b]		Mean of 6 Verbal Scale subtests	
		.05	.01	.05	.01	.05	.01	.05	.01
4½ (4-5-16 through 4-11-15)	Object Assembly	4.28	5.10	4.56	5.42	–	–	–	–
	Geometric Design	2.80	3.35	2.94	3.50	–	–	–	–
	Block Design	2.60	3.11	2.72	3.24	–	–	–	–
	Mazes	3.38	4.04	3.58	4.26	–	–	–	–
	Picture Completion	2.23	2.67	2.31	2.74	–	–	–	–
	Animal Pegs	–	–	4.07	4.85	–	–	–	–
	Information	–	–	–	–	2.29	2.79	2.38	2.83
	Comprehension	–	–	–	–	2.44	2.97	2.55	3.04
	Arithmetic	–	–	–	–	2.91	3.54	3.07	3.66
	Vocabulary	–	–	–	–	2.79	3.39	2.93	3.49
	Similarities	–	–	–	–	2.37	2.88	2.47	2.94
	Sentences	–	–	–	–	–	–	2.93	3.49

	Subtest	Mean of 10 subtests[a,b]		Mean of 11 subtests[a]		Mean of 11 subtests[b]		Mean of 12 subtests	
		.05	.01	.05	.01	.05	.01	.05	.01
	Object Assembly	5.12	5.96	5.23	6.08	5.22	6.07	5.32	6.18
	Geometric Design	3.12	3.63	3.19	3.70	3.17	3.68	3.23	3.74
	Block Design	2.84	3.30	2.89	3.36	2.87	3.34	2.93	3.39
	Mazes	3.93	4.57	4.01	4.66	4.00	4.65	4.07	4.73
	Picture Completion	2.28	2.65	2.32	2.70	2.30	2.67	2.34	2.71
	Animal Pegs	–	–	4.63	5.38	–	–	4.71	5.46
	Information	2.63	3.06	2.68	3.11	2.66	3.09	2.71	3.14
	Comprehension	2.84	3.30	2.89	3.36	2.87	3.34	2.93	3.39
	Arithmetic	3.47	4.04	3.54	4.11	3.52	4.09	3.59	4.16
	Vocabulary	3.30	3.84	3.67	3.91	3.35	3.89	3.41	3.96
	Similarities	2.73	3.18	2.79	3.24	2.77	3.22	2.82	3.27
	Sentences	–	–	–	–	3.35	3.89	3.41	3.96

(Table continues next page)

Table H-3 (cont.)

Age level	Subtest	Mean of 5 Performance Scale subtests[a]		Mean of 6 Performance Scale subtests		Mean of 5 Verbal Scale subtests[b]		Mean of 6 Verbal Scale subtests	
		.05	.01	.05	.01	.05	.01	.05	.01
5 (4-11-16 through 5-5-15)	Object Assembly	4.19	3.36	4.45	5.29	—	—	—	—
	Geometric Design	3.38	3.92	3.56	4.23	—	—	—	—
	Block Design	2.79	3.21	2.91	3.46	—	—	—	—
	Mazes	3.32	3.86	3.50	4.16	—	—	—	—
	Picture Completion	2.79	3.21	2.91	3.46	—	—	—	—
	Animal Pegs	—	—	4.10	4.88	—	—	—	—
	Information	—	—	—	—	2.76	3.30	2.89	3.44
	Comprehension	—	—	—	—	2.63	3.14	2.75	3.27
	Arithmetic	—	—	—	—	3.01	3.60	3.17	3.77
	Vocabulary	—	—	—	—	2.70	3.22	2.82	3.36
	Similarities	—	—	—	—	2.63	3.14	2.75	3.27
	Sentences	—	—	—	—	—	—	3.04	3.61

	Subtest	Mean of 10 subtests[a,b]		Mean of 11 subtests[a]		Mean of 11 subtests[b]		Mean of 12 subtests	
		.05	.01	.05	.01	.05	.01	.05	.01
	Object Assembly	4.97	5.78	5.07	5.89	5.06	5.88	5.16	5.98
	Geometric Design	3.88	4.51	3.95	4.59	3.94	4.58	4.01	4.66
	Block Design	3.06	3.56	3.11	3.62	3.10	3.60	3.15	3.65
	Mazes	3.80	4.43	3.88	4.51	3.86	4.49	3.93	4.57
	Picture Completion	3.06	3.56	3.11	3.62	3.10	3.60	3.15	3.65
	Animal Pegs	—	—	4.64	5.40	—	—	4.72	5.48
	Information	3.24	3.77	3.30	3.83	3.28	3.82	3.34	3.88
	Comprehension	3.06	3.56	3.11	3.62	3.10	3.60	3.15	3.65
	Arithmetic	3.57	4.16	3.64	4.23	3.63	4.21	3.69	4.28
	Vocabulary	3.15	3.66	3.21	3.73	3.19	3.71	3.25	3.77
	Similarities	3.06	3.56	3.11	3.62	3.10	3.60	3.15	3.65
	Sentences	—	—	—	—	3.46	4.02	3.52	4.08

(Table continues next page)

Table H-3 (cont.)

Age level	Subtest	Mean of 5 Performance Scale subtests[a]		Mean of 6 Performance Scale subtests		Mean of 5 Verbal Scale subtests[b]		Mean of 6 Verbal Scale subtests	
		.05	.01	.05	.01	.05	.01	.05	.01
5½ (5-5-16 through 5-11-15)	Object Assembly	4.32	5.16	4.57	5.44	—	—	—	—
	Geometric Design	3.69	4.41	3.88	4.61	—	—	—	—
	Block Design	3.28	3.92	3.42	4.07	—	—	—	—
	Mazes	3.44	4.11	3.60	4.28	—	—	—	—
	Picture Completion	3.05	3.64	3.62	3.77	—	—	—	—
	Animal Pegs	—	—	4.14	4.92	—	—	—	—
	Information	—	—	—	—	3.40	4.06	3.59	4.27
	Comprehension	—	—	—	—	3.01	3.59	3.16	3.75
	Arithmetic	—	—	—	—	3.01	3.59	3.16	3.75
	Vocabulary	—	—	—	—	2.69	3.21	2.81	3.34
	Similarities	—	—	—	—	2.69	3.21	2.81	3.34
	Sentences	—	—	—	—	—	—	3.47	4.13

	Subtest	Mean of 10 subtests[a,b]		Mean of 11 subtests[a]		Mean of 11 subtests[b]		Mean of 12 subtests	
		.05	.01	.05	.01	.05	.01	.05	.01
	Object Assembly	5.10	5.94	5.21	6.05	5.20	6.04	5.29	6.14
	Geometric Design	4.25	4.95	4.33	5.04	4.33	5.03	4.40	5.11
	Block Design	3.68	4.28	3.75	4.35	3.74	4.34	3.80	4.41
	Mazes	3.91	4.54	3.98	4.62	3.97	4.61	4.04	4.68
	Picture Completion	3.36	3.91	3.41	3.97	3.41	3.96	3.46	4.01
	Animal Pegs	—	—	4.66	5.42	—	—	4.74	5.50
	Information	4.05	4.71	4.12	4.79	4.12	4.78	4.19	4.86
	Comprehension	3.52	4.10	3.58	4.16	3.58	4.15	3.63	4.22
	Arithmetic	3.52	4.10	3.58	4.16	3.58	4.15	3.63	4.22
	Vocabulary	3.09	3.60	3.14	3.65	3.13	3.64	3.18	3.69
	Similarities	3.09	3.60	3.14	3.65	3.13	3.64	3.18	3.69
	Sentences	—	—	—	—	3.97	4.61	4.04	4.68

(*Table continues next page*)

Table H-3 (cont.)

Age level	Subtest	Mean of 5 Performance Scale subtests[a]		Mean of 6 Performance Scale subtests		Mean of 5 Verbal Scale subtests[b]		Mean of 6 Verbal Scale subtests	
		.05	.01	.05	.01	.05	.01	.05	.01
6	Object Assembly	3.67	4.38	3.89	4.62	—	—	—	—
(5-11-16	Geometric Design	3.26	3.89	3.43	4.08	—	—	—	—
through	Block Design	2.91	3.47	3.04	3.62	—	—	—	—
6-5-15)	Mazes	3.20	3.82	3.37	4.01	—	—	—	—
	Picture Completion	3.37	4.02	3.55	4.22	—	—	—	—
	Animal Pegs	—	—	4.10	4.87	—	—	—	—
	Information	—	—	—	—	3.37	4.03	3.55	4.22
	Comprehension	—	—	—	—	3.27	3.90	3.43	4.08
	Arithmetic	—	—	—	—	3.10	3.70	3.24	3.85
	Vocabulary	—	—	—	—	2.98	3.55	3.11	3.70
	Similarities	—	—	—	—	2.73	3.25	2.82	3.36
	Sentences	—	—	—	—	—	—	3.37	4.00

	Subtest	Mean of 10 subtests[a,b]		Mean of 11 subtests[a]		Mean of 11 subtests[b]		Mean of 12 subtests	
		.05	.01	.05	.01	.05	.01	.05	.01
	Object Assembly	4.31	5.01	4.39	5.10	4.38	5.10	4.46	5.18
	Geometric Design	3.74	4.36	3.81	4.43	3.80	4.42	3.87	4.49
	Block Design	3.26	3.79	3.31	3.85	3.30	3.84	3.36	3.89
	Mazes	3.67	4.27	3.74	4.34	3.73	4.33	3.79	4.40
	Picture Completion	3.89	4.53	3.97	4.61	3.96	4.60	4.03	4.67
	Animal Pegs	—	—	4.66	5.41	—	—	4.73	5.49
	Information	3.97	4.61	4.04	4.70	4.03	4.69	4.10	4.76
	Comprehension	3.82	4.44	3.89	4.52	3.88	4.51	3.95	4.58
	Arithmetic	3.59	4.18	3.66	4.25	3.65	4.24	3.71	4.30
	Vocabulary	3.43	3.99	3.49	4.05	3.48	4.04	3.54	4.10
	Similarities	3.08	3.58	3.13	3.64	3.12	3.62	3.17	3.68
	Sentences	—	—	—	—	3.80	4.42	3.87	4.49

(*Table continues next page*)

Table H-3 (cont.)

Age level	Subtest	Mean of 5 Performance Scale subtests[a]		Mean of 6 Performance Scale subtests		Mean of 5 Verbal Scale subtests[b]		Mean of 6 Verbal Scale subtests	
		.05	.01	.05	.01	.05	.01	.05	.01
6½ (6-5-16 through 6-11-15)	Object Assembly	3.87	4.62	4.08	4.85	—	—	—	—
	Geometric Design	3.63	4.33	3.82	4.54	—	—	—	—
	Block Design	3.10	3.70	3.22	3.83	—	—	—	—
	Mazes	3.53	4.21	3.71	4.41	—	—	—	—
	Picture Completion	3.48	4.15	3.65	4.34	—	—	—	—
	Animal Pegs	—	—	4.13	4.91	—	—	—	—
	Information	—	—	—	—	3.06	3.66	3.21	3.81
	Comprehension	—	—	—	—	3.55	4.24	3.75	4.46
	Arithmetic	—	—	—	—	3.06	3.66	3.21	3.81
	Vocabulary	—	—	—	—	2.95	3.52	3.07	3.66
	Similarities	—	—	—	—	3.35	3.99	3.52	4.18
	Sentences	—	—	—	—	—	—	3.69	4.39

	Subtest	Mean of 10 subtests[a,b]		Mean of 11 subtests[a]		Mean of 11 subtests[b]		Mean of 12 subtests	
		.05	.01	.05	.01	.05	.01	.05	.01
	Object Assembly	4.52	5.26	4.61	5.35	4.60	5.35	4.68	5.43
	Geometric Design	4.20	4.88	4.27	4.96	4.27	4.96	4.34	5.04
	Block Design	3.45	4.02	3.51	4.08	3.50	4.07	3.56	4.13
	Mazes	4.06	4.72	4.13	4.80	4.13	4.79	4.19	4.87
	Picture Completion	3.99	4.64	4.06	4.72	4.05	4.71	4.12	4.78
	Animal Pegs	—	—	4.67	5.43	—	—	4.75	5.51
	Information	3.53	4.11	3.59	4.18	3.59	4.17	3.64	4.23
	Comprehension	4.20	4.88	4.27	4.96	4.27	4.96	4.34	5.04
	Arithmetic	3.53	4.11	3.59	4.18	3.59	4.17	3.64	4.23
	Vocabulary	3.37	3.92	3.42	3.98	3.42	3.97	3.47	4.03
	Similarities	3.92	4.56	3.98	4.63	3.98	4.62	4.04	4.69
	Sentences	—	—	—	—	4.20	4.88	4.27	4.95

(Table continues next page)

Table H-3 (cont.)

Age level	Subtest	Mean of 5 Performance Scale subtests[a]		Mean of 6 Performance Scale subtests		Mean of 5 Verbal Scale subtests[b]		Mean of 6 Verbal Scale subtests	
		.05	.01	.05	.01	.05	.01	.05	.01
7 (6-11-16 through 7-3-15)	Object Assembly	4.50	5.37	4.75	5.65	—	—	—	—
	Geometric Design	3.90	4.66	4.08	4.86	—	—	—	—
	Block Design	2.96	3.53	3.02	3.60	—	—	—	—
	Mazes	4.04	4.82	4.23	5.04	—	—	—	—
	Picture Completion	3.71	4.43	3.87	4.61	—	—	—	—
	Animal Pegs	—	—	4.18	4.98	—	—	—	—
	Information	—	—	—	—	4.25	5.08	4.42	5.26
	Comprehension	—	—	—	—	4.38	5.23	4.56	5.42
	Arithmetic	—	—	—	—	4.08	4.87	4.23	5.03
	Vocabulary	—	—	—	—	3.71	4.43	3.81	4.53
	Similarities	—	—	—	—	4.58	5.47	4.78	5.69
	Sentences	—	—	—	—	—	—	3.70	4.40

Subtest	Mean of 10 subtests[a,b]		Mean of 11 subtests[a]		Mean of 11 subtests[b]		Mean of 12 subtests	
	.05	.01	.05	.01	.05	.01	.05	.01
Object Assembly	5.34	6.22	5.44	6.32	5.43	6.31	5.52	6.40
Geometric Design	4.54	5.28	4.61	5.36	4.60	5.35	4.67	5.42
Block Design	3.22	3.75	3.25	3.78	3.24	3.76	3.27	3.79
Mazes	4.72	5.50	4.80	5.58	4.79	5.57	4.87	5.65
Picture Completion	4.28	4.98	4.34	5.05	4.34	5.04	4.40	5.10
Animal Pegs	—	—	4.74	5.50	—	—	4.80	5.57
Information	4.90	5.70	4.98	5.79	4.98	5.78	5.05	5.86
Comprehension	5.07	5.90	5.16	5.99	5.15	5.99	5.23	6.07
Arithmetic	4.66	5.43	4.74	5.50	4.73	5.50	4.80	5.57
Vocabulary	4.15	4.83	4.21	4.89	4.20	4.88	4.26	4.94
Similarities	5.34	6.22	5.44	6.32	5.43	6.31	5.52	6.40
Sentences	—	—	—	—	4.05	4.71	4.11	4.77

Note. Table H-3 shows the minimum deviations from an individual's average subtest scaled score that are significant at the .05 and .01 levels. See the Note in Table C-3 for an explanation of how the deviations were obtained.
[a] Animal Pegs excluded.
[b] Sentences excluded.

Table H-4
Probability of Obtaining Designated Differences Between Individual WPPSI-R Performance and Verbal IQs

Probability of obtaining given or greater discrepancy by chance	Age level									
	3	3½	4	4½	5	5½	6	6½	7	Av.[a]
.50	3.43	3.56	3.56	3.56	3.68	4.08	3.82	4.21	3.68	5.49
.25	6.03	6.03	6.03	6.03	6.22	6.90	6.45	7.11	6.22	9.29
.20	6.71	6.71	6.71	6.71	6.92	7.68	7.18	7.92	6.92	10.34
.10	8.65	8.65	8.65	8.65	8.92	9.90	9.26	10.20	8.92	13.33
.05	10.27	10.27	10.27	10.27	10.60	11.76	11.00	12.12	10.60	15.83
.02	12.21	12.21	12.21	12.21	12.60	13.98	13.07	14.41	12.60	18.82
.01	13.52	13.52	13.52	13.52	13.95	15.48	14.48	15.96	13.95	20.84
.001	17.30	17.30	17.30	17.30	17.84	19.80	18.51	20.41	17.84	26.66

Note. To use Table H-4: Find the column appropriate to the examinee's age. Locate the discrepancy that is *just less* than the discrepancy obtained by the examinee. The first column in that same row gives the probability of obtaining the given (or a greater) discrepancy by chance. For example, the hypothesis that a 3-year-old examinee obtained a Performance-Verbal discrepancy of 14 by chance can be rejected at the .01 level of significance. Table H-4 is two-tailed. See Chapter 8, Exhibit 8-1, page 168, for an explanation of the method used to arrive at magnitude of differences.
[a]Av. = Average of the nine age groups.

Table H-5
Percentage of Population Obtaining Discrepancies Between WPPSI-R Performance and Verbal IQs

Percentage obtaining given or greater discrepancy in either direction	Age level										Percentage obtaining given or greater discrepancy in a specific direction
	3	3½	4	4½	5	5½	6	6½	7	Av.[a]	
50	8.41	8.90	8.78	8.78	9.82	10.45	10.14	9.14	10.76	9.37	25
25	14.01	14.84	14.64	14.64	16.36	17.42	16.90	15.23	17.93	15.62	12.5
20	15.60	16.52	16.29	16.29	18.21	19.39	18.81	16.96	19.95	17.39	10
10	20.11	21.29	21.00	21.00	23.48	25.00	24.25	21.86	25.72	22.41	5
5	23.88	25.29	24.95	24.95	27.89	29.69	28.81	25.97	30.55	26.62	2.5
2	28.39	30.07	29.66	29.66	33.16	35.30	34.24	30.87	36.32	31.65	1
1	31.44	33.29	32.84	32.84	36.71	39.09	37.92	34.18	40.22	35.04	.5
.1	39.85	42.19	41.62	41.62	46.53	49.54	48.06	43.32	50.97	44.42	.05

Note. To use Table H-5: Find the column appropriate to the examinee's age. Locate the discrepancy that is *just less* than the one obtained by the examinee. The first column in the same row gives the percentage of the standardization population obtaining discrepancies as large or larger than the located discrepancy. For example, a 3-year-old examinee with a Performance-Verbal discrepancy of 15 will be found in between 20 and 25 percent of the standardization population. See Table C-9 for an explanation of the method used to arrive at magnitude of differences.
[a]Av. = Average of the nine age groups.

Table H-6
Reliability and Validity Coefficients of Proposed WPPSI-R Short Forms

Dyad			Triad				Tetrad				Pentad				
Short form	r_{tt}	r	Short form		r_{tt}	r	Short form			r_{tt}	r	Short form				r_{tt}	r

Short form	r_{tt}	r	Short form		r_{tt}	r	Short form			r_{tt}	r	Short form				r_{tt}	r
BD I	.890	.859	BD I S		.921	.894	BD PC I S			.936	.914	BD PC I A S				.945	.929
PC I	.895	.837	BD I A		.914	.892	BD PC I Se			.930	.914	BD PC I A Se				.941	.929
BD C	.881	.835	BD PC I		.919	.888	BD PC I A			.932	.914	BD PC I A V				.943	.929
I A	.887	.835	BD I V		.918	.887	BD I A S			.934	.913	GD BD I V S				.940	.928
BD S	.894	.829	BD I Se		.912	.835	BD PC I C			.933	.912	BD PC C A S				.942	.927
GD I	.865	.826	BD A V		.909	.883	BD PC C A			.927	.911	GD BD I C S				.939	.927
BD V	.886	.826	BD I C		.918	.882	GD BD I V			.924	.911	BD PC I C A				.943	.927
BD A	.880	.824	BD C A		.908	.881	BD PC I V			.934	.911	GD BD I A V				.937	.927
PC A	.879	.822	BD PC C		.912	.881	BD I A V			.932	.910	BD PC I S Se				.944	.927
I S	.904	.820	PC I A		.915	.881	GD BD I S			.927	.910	GD BD PC I C				.938	.927

Note. Abbreviations: BD = Block Design, GD = Geometric Design, PC = Picture Completion, I = Information, C = Comprehension, A = Arithmetic, V = Vocabulary, S = Similarities, Se = Sentences.

It is recommended that short-form combinations involving Animal Pegs or Sentences not be used because these two subtests were not used in the construction of the IQ tables. The best two-subtest short-form combination for screening children who have severe hearing problems is Block Design and Picture Completion ($r_{tt} = .897$ and $r = .793$) followed by Geometric Design and Block Design ($r_{tt} = .879$ and $r = .746$). For screening children with severe visual deficits, any of the short-form combinations shown in the table involving subtests in the Verbal Scale can be used, such as Information and Arithmetic or Information and Similarities. Tables H-7, H-8, and H-9 provide estimated IQs associated with the ten best dyads, triads, and tetrads.

This table was constructed using a computer program developed by L. Atkinson and G. Yoshida (1989), "A BASIC Program for Determining Reliability and Validity of Subtest Combination Short Forms," *Educational and Psychological Measurement, 49*, 141-143. The program is based on formulas provided by Tellegen and Briggs (1967).

Table H-7
Estimated WPPSI-R Full Scale IQ Equivalents for Sum of Scaled Scores for Ten Best Short-Form Dyads

Sum of scaled scores	Combination				Sum of scaled scores	Combination			
	BD+C	BD+A PC+A PC+I	I+A I+S	BD+V BD+I BD+S GD+I		BD+C	BD+A PC+A PC+I	I+A I+S	BD+V BD+I BD+S GD+I
1	41	45	47	43	21	103	103	103	103
2	44	48	50	46	22	106	106	106	106
3	47	51	52	49	23	109	109	108	109
4	50	54	55	52	24	112	112	111	112
5	54	57	58	55	25	116	115	114	115
6	57	59	61	58	26	119	117	117	118
7	60	62	64	61	27	122	120	120	121
8	63	65	66	64	28	125	123	122	124
9	66	68	69	67	29	128	126	125	127
10	69	71	72	70	30	131	129	128	130
11	72	74	75	73	31	134	132	131	133
12	75	77	78	76	32	137	135	134	136
13	78	80	80	79	33	140	138	136	139
14	81	83	83	82	34	143	141	139	142
15	85	86	86	85	35	147	144	142	145
16	88	88	89	88	36	150	146	145	148
17	91	91	92	91	37	153	149	148	151
18	94	94	94	94	38	156	152	150	154
19	97	97	97	97	39	159	155	153	157
20	100	100	100	100	40	162	158	156	160

Note. Abbreviations: BD = Block Design, C = Comprehension, A = Arithmetic, PC = Picture Completion, I = Information, S = Similarities, V = Vocabulary, GD = Geometric Design.

Reliability and validity coefficients associated with each short-form combination are shown in Table H-6. See Exhibit 6-3, page 138, for an explanation of the procedure used to obtain the estimated IQs.

Table H-8
Estimated WPPSI-R Full Scale IQ Equivalents for Sum of Scaled Scores for Ten Best Short-Form Triads

Sum of scaled scores	Combination BD+ I +S BD+ I +A BD+PC+I BD+ I +V BD+ I +Se BD+ A +V BD+ I +C BD+ C +A	BD+PC+C	PC+I+A	Sum of scaled scores	Combination BD+ I +S BD+ I +A BD+PC+I BD+ I +V BD+ I +Se BD+ A +V BD+ I +C BD+ C +A	BD+PC+C	PC+I+A
1	39	36	42	31	102	102	102
2	41	38	44	32	104	104	104
3	43	41	46	33	106	107	106
4	45	43	48	34	108	109	108
5	48	45	50	35	111	111	110
6	50	47	52	36	113	113	112
7	52	49	54	37	115	115	114
8	54	52	56	38	117	118	116
9	56	54	58	39	119	120	118
10	58	56	60	40	121	122	120
11	60	58	62	41	123	124	122
12	62	60	64	42	125	126	124
13	64	63	66	43	127	129	126
14	66	65	68	44	129	131	128
15	69	67	70	45	132	133	130
16	71	69	72	46	134	135	132
17	73	71	74	47	136	137	134
18	75	74	76	48	138	140	136
19	77	76	78	49	140	142	138
20	79	78	80	50	142	144	140
21	81	80	82	51	144	146	142
22	83	82	84	52	146	148	144
23	85	85	86	53	148	151	146
24	87	87	88	54	150	153	148
25	90	89	90	55	153	155	150
26	92	91	92	56	155	157	152
27	94	93	94	57	157	159	154
28	96	96	96	58	159	162	156
29	98	98	98	59	161	164	158
30	100	100	100	60	163	166	160

Note. Abbreviations: BD = Block Design, I = Information, S = Similarities, A = Arithmetic, PC = Picture Completion, V = Vocabulary, Se = Sentences, C = Comprehension.

Reliability and validity coefficients associated with each short-form combination are shown in Table H-6. See Exhibit 6-3, page 138, for an explanation of the procedure used to obtain the estimated IQs.

Table H-9
Estimated WPPSI-R Full Scale IQ Equivalents for Sum of Scaled Scores for Ten Best Short-Form Tetrads

Sum of scaled scores	*Combination* BD+PC+I+S BD+PC+I+Se GD+BD+I+V GD+BD+I+S	*Combination* BD+PC+I +A BD+ I +A+S BD+PC+I +C BD+PC+C+A BD+PC+I +V BD+ I +A+V	Sum of scaled scores	*Combination* BD+PC+I+S BD+PC+I+Se GD+BD+I+V GD+BD+I+S	*Combination* BD+PC+I +A BD+ I +A+S BD+PC+I +C BD+PC+C+A BD+PC+I +V BD+ I +A+V
1	34	38	39	98	98
2	35	39	40	100	100
3	37	41	41	102	102
4	39	42	42	103	103
5	41	44	43	105	105
6	42	46	44	107	106
7	44	47	45	109	108
8	46	49	46	110	110
9	47	50	47	112	111
10	49	52	48	114	113
11	51	54	49	115	114
12	52	55	50	117	116
13	54	57	51	119	118
14	56	58	52	120	119
15	58	60	53	122	121
16	59	62	54	124	122
17	61	63	55	126	124
18	63	65	56	127	126
19	64	66	57	129	127
20	66	68	58	131	129
21	68	70	59	132	130
22	69	71	60	134	132
23	71	73	61	136	134
24	73	74	62	137	135
25	75	76	63	139	137
26	76	78	64	141	138
27	78	79	65	143	140
28	80	81	66	144	142
29	81	82	67	146	143
30	83	84	68	148	145
31	85	86	69	149	146
32	86	87	70	151	148
33	88	89	71	153	150
34	90	90	72	154	151
35	92	92	73	156	153
36	93	94	74	158	154
37	95	95	75	160	156
38	97	97	76	161	158

Note. Abbreviations: BD = Block Design, PC = Picture Completion, I = Information, S = Similarities, Se = Sentences, GD = Geometric Design, V = Vocabulary, A = Arithmetic, C = Comprehension.

Reliability and validity coefficients associated with each short-form combination are shown in Table H-6. See Exhibit 6-3, page 138, for an explanation of the procedure used to obtain the estimated IQs.

_ APPENDIX I

WECHSLER INTELLIGENCE SCALE FOR CHILDREN—III (WISC-III): DESCRIPTION

Mind is the great lever of all things; human thought is the process by which human ends are ultimately answered.

—Daniel Webster

This chapter describes the Wechsler Intelligence Scale for Children—Third Edition (WISC-III), the latest version of the Wechsler scales for children ages 6 through 16 years (Wechsler, 1991[R][1]; see Figure I-1). The Psychological Corporation published the WISC-III in 1991, 17 years after the previous edition of the test, called the WISC-R (Wechsler, 1974). The primary reason for revising the test was to update the norms. Wechsler developed the earliest version of this test, known as the WISC (Wechsler, 1949), as a downward extension of the adult intelligence test, the Wechsler-Bellevue Intelligence Scale. To make the original adult scale more suitable for children, Wechsler added easier items to the beginnings of the subtests.

The WISC-III contains 13 subtests, 6 in the Verbal Scale and 7 in the Performance Scale. Five subtests in each scale are designated as standard subtests. In the Verbal Scale they are Information, Similarities, Arithmetic, Vocabu-

---

[1] References followed by an [R] are cited in this appendix; all other references are cited in the Reference section.

lary, and Comprehension. In the Performance Scale they are Picture Completion, Coding, Picture Arrangement, Block Design, and Object Assembly. The remaining three subtests—Digit Span in the Verbal Scale and Symbol Search and Mazes in the Performance Scale—are supplementary. Exhibit I-1 shows items similar to those on the WISC-III. About 73 percent of the WISC-R items are retained in the WISC-III (not including the Coding subtest), either in the original or slightly modified form. Symbol Search is a new subtest.

STANDARDIZATION

The WISC-III was standardized on 2,200 children, 100 boys and 100 girls in each of 11 age groups from 6 through 16 years. The sample was stratified on age, race/ethnicity, geographic region, and parent education (used as a measure of socioeconomic status). For race/ethnic membership, children were classified as White, Black, Hispanic, or Other (composed of Native American, Eskimo, Aleut,

Figure I-I. Wechsler Intelligence Scale for Children—III. Courtesy of The Psychological Corporation.

■ Exhibit I-I

WISC-III–Like Items

Information (30 questions)

How many legs do you have?
What must you do to make water freeze?
Who discovered the North Pole?
What is the capital of France?

Similarities (19 questions)

In what way are pencil and crayon alike?
In what way are tea and coffee alike?
In what way are inch and mile alike?
In what way are binoculars and microscope alike?

Arithmetic (24 questions)

If I have one piece of candy and get another one, how many
   pieces will I have?
At 12 cents each, how much will 4 bars of soap cost?
If a suit sells for ½ of the regular price, what is the cost of a
   $120 suit?

Vocabulary (30 words)

ball   summer   poem   obstreperous

Comprehension (18 questions)

Why do we wear shoes?
What is the thing to do if you see someone dropping his
   packages?
In what two ways is a lamp better than a candle?
Why are we tried by a jury of our peers?

Digit Span (15 items; 8 in Digits Forward, 7 in Digits Backward)

The task is to repeat digits presented by the examiner in a
forward direction in one part (2 to 9 digits in length; example:
1-8) and in a backward direction in the other part (2 to 8 digits
in length; example: 6-4-9).

Picture Completion (30 items)

The task is to identify the essential missing part of the picture,
such as (a) a car without a wheel, (b) a dog without a leg, and
(c) a telephone without numbers on the dial (see below).

Courtesy of The Psychological Corporation.

Coding (59 items in Coding A and 119 items in Coding B)

The task is to copy symbols from a key (see below).

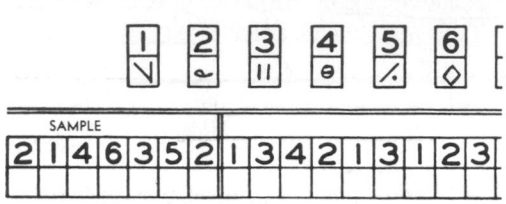

Courtesy of The Psychological Corporation.

Picture Arrangement (14 items)

The task is to arrange a series of pictures into a meaningful
sequence (see below).

Courtesy of The Psychological Corporation.

Block Design (12 items)

The task is to reproduce stimulus designs using four or nine
blocks (see below).

Object Assembly (5 items)

The task is to arrange pieces into a meaningful object (see
below).

Courtesy of The Psychological Corporation.

(Exhibit continues next page)

Exhibit I-I (cont.)

Symbol Search (45 items in Part A and 45 items in Part B)

The task is to decide whether a stimulus figure (a symbol) appears in an array (see below).

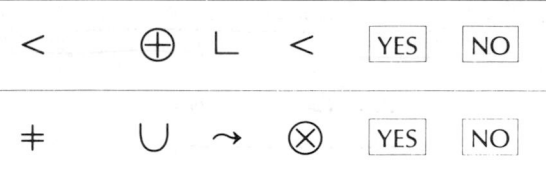

Courtesy of The Psychological Corporation.

Mazes (10 items)

The task is to complete a series of mazes (see below).

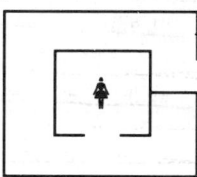

Courtesy of The Psychological Corporation.

Note. The questions resemble those that appear on the WISC-III but are not actually from the test, except for the sample items shown for Symbol Search and Mazes. Appendix J describes each subtest in more detail.

Asian, and Pacific Islander categories). The four geographical regions sampled were Northeast, North Central, South, and West. Within each age group, children were selected so that they matched as closely as possible the proportions found in the 1988 U.S. census data according to race/ethnicity, geographic region, and parent education.

Table I-I shows the educational status and geographic location by race/ethnic group of the standardization sam-ple. Parents in the White and Other classifications had the most education — 51.5 percent of the White group and 57.2 percent of the Other group had some college education, whereas 27.9 percent of the Black group and 19.9 percent of the Hispanic group had some college education. The majority of the White and Black samples came from the North Central and South regions, whereas the majority of the Hispanic and Other samples came from the South and

Table I-I
Demographic Characteristics of WISC-III Standardization Sample: Education and Geographic Region by Race/Ethnic Group

Demographic variable	Race/ethnic group (percent)			
	White	*Black*	*Hispanic*	*Other*[a]
Amount of education				
Eight years or less	1.6	7.1	30.0	5.7
Some high school	8.6	22.7	23.6	8.6
High school graduate	38.4	42.2	26.4	28.6
Some college	29.4	18.8	14.5	22.9
College graduate	22.1	9.1	5.4	34.3
Total	100.1	99.9	99.9	100.1
Geographic region				
Northeast	20.5	12.3	9.1	17.1
North Central	31.2	20.8	6.4	14.3
South	30.0	60.4	43.6	20.0
West	18.3	6.5	40.9	48.6
Total	100.0	100.0	100.0	100.0

Note. Race/ethnic distribution in total group was as follows: White = 70.1%, Black = 15.4%, Hispanic = 11.0%, Other = 3.5%.
[a] Other represents the following groups: Native American, Eskimo, Aleut, Asian, and Pacific Islander.
Source: Adapted from Wechsler (1991[R]).

West. The race/ethnic proportions in the sample were 70.1 percent White, 15.4 percent Black, 11.0 percent Hispanic, and 3.5 percent Other.

Tables 2.2 through 2.5 in the WISC-III manual (pages 23 to 26) indicate that parent education level was stratified within race, that race was stratified within geographic region, and that these variables match the census data with remarkable accuracy. The WISC-III sampling procedure is notably superior to that used on the WISC-R, which stratified race by White v. Non-white categories only. In addition, actual cases were used, without weighting for any demographic variable, to obtain the normative data. This sampling methodology was excellent.

DEVIATION IQS, SCALED SCORES, AND TEST-AGE EQUIVALENTS

The WISC-III, like the WPPSI-R and WAIS-R, uses the Deviation IQ ($M = 100$, $SD = 15$) for the Verbal, Performance, and Full Scale IQs and scaled scores ($M = 10$, $SD = 3$) for the 13 individual subtests. An IQ is computed by comparing the examinee's scores with the scores earned by a representative sample of his or her age group. After each subtest is scored, raw scores are converted to scaled scores within the examinee's own age group through use of Table A.1 in the WISC-III manual (pages 217–249). Age groups are divided into four-month intervals between 6-0-0 (years, months, days) and 16-11-30.

The table in the WISC-III manual used to obtain IQs (Table A.4, pages 253–254) is based on the 10 standard subtests. The three supplementary subtests are *excluded* from the calculation of the IQ unless a standard subtest is either spoiled or not given. When a supplementary subtest is substituted for a standard subtest, little is known about the reliability and validity of the IQs generated by the altered combination of subtests, because none of the supplementary subtests were used in the construction of the tables used to generate IQs. In fact, there is no information at all in the WISC-III manual about what happens to the reliability and validity of the test when supplementary subtests are used to compute the IQ. There is one statement in the manual (page 5), however, that says that when a supplementary subtest was substituted for a standard subtest, mean changes ranged from .1 to .3 point. Nevertheless, be cautious when using supplementary subtests to compute an IQ.

The WISC-III manual provides guidelines for use of the three supplementary subtests. These guidelines, in part, state that Digit Span may substitute for any Verbal subtest, Mazes may substitute for any Performance subtest, and

Symbol Search may substitute for Coding *only*. Unfortunately, the manual fails to discuss the manner in which these recommendations were reached. Why is it improper to substitute both Mazes and Symbol Search for other Performance subtests? It would have been helpful if The Psychological Corporation cited research findings to support its recommendations. [According to Aurelio Prifitera from The Psychological Corporation, this rule was designed to prevent the Performance IQ from being too heavily weighted with subtests that have relatively low *g* loadings (personal communication, January 1992).]

Prorating Procedure

When fewer than 10 subtests are administered, you can compute IQs either by prorating or by using a special short-form procedure designed to estimate the Verbal, Performance, and Full Scale IQs. Although the WISC-III manual provides a table (Table A.8, page 258) for prorating sums of scaled scores when you administer four subtests in each scale, I recommend that you use the Tellegen and Briggs (1967) procedure described in Exhibit I-4 in this chapter. The Tellegen and Briggs procedure considers the intercorrelations between the specific subtests administered to the child; prorating does not take this factor into account.

Test-Age Equivalents

When David Wechsler first developed the WISC, he believed that the mental-age concept was potentially misleading and therefore decided not to use it in calculating IQs. (See pages 20–21 and 75–76 for criticisms associated with the mental-age concept.) Wechsler rejected the notion that mental age represents an absolute level of mental capacity or that the same mental age in different children represents identical intelligence levels. Soon after the initial publication of the WISC, however, he recognized that mental-age or test-age equivalents (the average age associated with a score on a subtest) would be useful. Therefore, in subsequent publications of the WISC, WISC-R, and WISC-III, test-age equivalents are provided (see Table A.9, page 259 in the WISC-III manual). Test-age equivalents are essentially mental age (MA) scores.

Test ages are obtained directly from the raw scores on each subtest. Because a scaled score of 10 represents the mean, the test-age equivalents of the raw scores shown in Table A.9 of the WISC-III manual can be understood as reflecting the average score for each particular age group. To obtain an *average* test-age equivalent, sum the individual subtest age equivalents and divide the sum by the number of subtests you added. To obtain a *median* test age, rank order test ages from high to low and locate the middle-most test age.

The WISC-III test-age equivalent scores can be compared with mental-age or test-age scores from other tests. They also can be used to help parents, teachers, and other individuals better understand the child's level of functioning. Research with the WISC-R suggests that test ages have adequate validity, based on high correlations with the Stanford-Binet: Form L-M mental age *(r* = .88) (Sutton, Koller, & Christian, 1982) and the Peabody Individual Achievement Test *(r* = .82) (Huberty & Koller, 1984). Similar studies are needed with the WISC-III.

Table I-2
Average Internal Consistency Reliability Coefficients, Test-Retest Reliability Coefficients, and Standard Errors of Measurement for WISC-III Subtests and Scales

Subtest or scale	Average internal consistency r_{xx}	Average test-retest r_{tt}	Average SE_m
Information	.84	.85	1.23
Similarities	.81	.81	1.30
Arithmetic	.78	.74	1.41
Vocabulary	.87	.89	1.08
Comprehension	.77	.73	1.45
Digit Span	.85	.73	1.17
Picture Completion	.77	.81	1.44
Coding	.79	.77	1.42
Picture Arrangement	.76	.64	1.48
Block Design	.87	.77	1.11
Object Assembly	.69	.66	1.67
Symbol Search	.76	.74	1.48
Mazes	.70	.57	1.64
Verbal Scale IQ	.95	.94	3.53
Performance Scale IQ	.91	.87	4.54
Full Scale IQ	.96	.94	3.20

Note. Reliabilities for 11 of the 13 subtests (except Coding and Symbol Search) are split-half correlations. For Coding and Symbol Search, the reliability coefficients are test-retest coefficients obtained on a sample of about 60 children in six different age groups (retest interval not given in WISC-III manual). Verbal, Performance, and Full Scale reliability coefficients are based on a formula for computing the reliability of a composite group of tests. Digit Span, Mazes, and Symbol Search were not included in calculating the reliability coefficients for the Verbal, Performance, and Full Scale IQs.
Source: Adapted from Wechsler (1991[R]).

RELIABILITY

The WISC-III has outstanding reliability. The three scales have internal consistency reliability coefficients of .89 or above over the entire age range covered in the standardization group. Average internal consistency reliability coefficients, based on the 11 age groups, are .96 for the Full Scale IQ, .95 for the Verbal Scale IQ, and .91 for the Performance Scale IQ (see Table I-2). The reliability coefficients for ages 6 to 16 years range from .94 to .97 for the Full Scale IQ, .92 to .96 for the Verbal Scale IQ, and .89 to .94 for the Performance Scale IQ. The lowest reliability coefficient is at 14 years for the Performance Scale IQ.

Subtest Reliabilities

The internal consistency reliabilities for the subtests are lower than those for the three scales (see Table I-2). The average subtest internal consistency reliabilities range from a low of .69 for Object Assembly to a high of .87 for Vocabulary and Block Design. For the 11 age groups, median subtest reliabilities range from .76 at 13 years to .83 at 8 years (see Table I-3). Thus there are no sharp differences in subtest internal consistency reliabilities as a function of age.

Standard Errors of Measurement

The average standard errors of measurement (SE_m) in IQ points are 3.20 for the Full Scale, 3.53 for the Verbal Scale, and 4.54 for the Performance Scale (see Table I-2). Thus,

Table I-3
Range and Median Internal Consistency Reliabilities of WISC-III Subtests at 11 Age Groups

Age	Range of r_{xx}	Median r_{xx}
6	.69–.82	.79
7	.65–.84	.77
8	.65–.88	.83
9	.66–.85	.80
10	.69–.89	.79
11	.65–.88	.79
12	.66–.89	.81
13	.70–.90	.76
14	.60–.91	.77
15	.61–.92	.82
16	.67–.90	.82
Average	.69–.87	.78

Source: Adapted from Wechsler (1991[R]).

as with all Wechsler scales, you can place more confidence in IQs based on the Full Scale than in those based on either the Verbal or the Performance Scale. In addition, you can place more confidence in IQs obtained from the Verbal Scale than in those obtained from the Performance Scale.

The average standard errors of measurement for the subtests in scaled-score points range from 1.08 to 1.45 for the Verbal Scale subtests and from 1.11 to 1.67 for the Performance Scale subtests. Within the Verbal Scale, Vocabulary has the smallest SE_m (1.08), and Comprehension, the largest SE_m (1.45). Within the Performance Scale, Block Design has the smallest SE_m (1.11), and Object Assembly, the largest SE_m (1.67).

Test-Retest Reliability

In the standardization sample, the stability of the WISC-III was assessed by having 353 children from six age groups (6, 7, 10, 11, 14, 15 years) retested after an interval ranging from 12 to 63 days (Mdn = 23 days; Wechsler, 1991[R]). The six age groups were then combined to form three age groups for statistical analysis (6–7, 10–11, 14–15 years). In the three age groups, the stability coefficients were, respectively, .92, .95, and .94 for the Full Scale IQ; .90, .94, and .94 for the Verbal Scale IQ; and .86, .88, and .87 for the Performance Scale IQ. Thus, the WISC-III provides stable IQs for the Full Scale and Verbal Scale, but somewhat less stable IQs for the Performance Scale.

The stability coefficients for the subtests ranged from a low of .54 for Mazes at 14–15 years to a high of .93 for Vocabulary at these same ages. Average test-retest reliabilities for the subtests ranged from .57 for Mazes to .89 for Vocabulary (see Table I-2). As expected, internal consistency reliabilities are somewhat higher than average test-retest reliabilities (Mdn r_{xx} = .78 versus Mdn r_{tt} = .74).

Changes in IQs. Table I-4 shows the mean test-retest IQs and standard deviations for the Verbal, Performance, and Full Scales for the three combined age groups. On the average, from the first to the second testing, the Full Scale IQ increased by 7.0 to 8.4 points, the Verbal Scale IQ by 1.7 to 3.3 points, and the Performance Scale IQ by 11.5 to 13.5 points. These increases, which likely result from practice effects, are therefore 4 to 6 times greater for the Performance Scale than for the Verbal Scale. Statistical tests that I performed indicated that all retest gains were significantly greater than chance. Studies will be needed to evaluate the stability of the WISC-III with other samples of children and over longer periods. Studies with the WISC-R (Haynes & Howard, 1986; Naglieri & Pfeiffer, 1983a) reported relatively stable IQs over a two-year interval (mean Verbal, Performance, and Full Scale IQ changes were less than 3 points).

The following may help to explain, in part, why there are greater gains on retest on the Performance subtests than on the Verbal subtests (Kaufman, 1990[R]). When children

Table I-4
Test-Retest WISC-III IQs for Three Groups of Children

| Age | Scale | First testing | | Second testing | | Change |
		Mean IQ	SD	Mean IQ	SD	
6–7	Verbal	100.8	12.7	102.5	12.3	+ 1.7*
(N = 111)	Performance	102.7	14.8	114.2	17.6	+11.5**
	Full	101.6	13.0	108.6	14.3	+ 7.0**
10–11	Verbal	100.3	13.7	102.2	13.8	+ 1.9**
(N = 119)	Performance	99.0	13.1	112.0	15.2	+13.0**
	Full	99.6	13.1	107.3	14.4	+ 7.7**
14–15	Verbal	99.4	13.8	102.7	14.5	+ 3.3**
(N = 123)	Performance	99.6	15.3	112.1	16.7	+12.5**
	Full	99.2	14.5	107.6	15.5	+ 8.4**

Note. Test-retest intervals ranged from 12 to 63 days, with a median retest interval of 23 days. Table I-5 shows the *t*-test formula used to evaluate the mean changes.
   * $p < .01$.
** $p < .001$.
Source: Reprinted, with a change in notation, with permission from the publisher, from *WISC-III Manual* (Wechsler, 1991[R]), pages 170–172, copyright by The Psychological Corporation 1991.

are administered the Performance subtests on a second occasion, they may be able to recall the types of items they were given as well as the strategies they used on the tasks. Initially, the Performance subtests are more novel than the Verbal subtests, but this novelty diminishes on retesting. On retest, the Performance items become less novel, and perhaps more a test of long-term memory and ability to apply learning sets than a test of "adaptability and flexibility when faced with new problem-solving situations" (Kaufman, 1990[R], p. 205).

The large retest gains on the Performance Scale are of major concern when you readminister the WISC-III to children after a period of 2 to 9 weeks. For longer periods of time, however, gains on retest are likely to be lower because practice effects tend to diminish over time. The gains for the short time period were over $\frac{2}{3}$ of a standard deviation on the Performance Scale and about $\frac{1}{2}$ of a standard deviation on the Full Scale, on the average. This means that children are likely to do much better on a second administration of the WISC-III, especially on the Performance Scale. The gain may have nothing to do with their increased ability per se and may simply reflect exposure to the test materials (or practice effects).

Research is needed to determine how much children improve on retest over a longer period of time. Until such research is available, *you should carefully consider whether you want to use the WISC-III for repeated evaluations, especially if you plan to use the results obtained on the retest for placement, eligibility, or diagnostic decisions.* If you decide not to use the WISC-III for a reevaluation when you have given it on a prior occasion, consider using another individually administered well-standardized test of cognitive ability for the reexamination.

Changes in subtest scores. Table I-5 shows the changes in subtest scaled scores from the first to the second testing. The largest gains were for Picture Arrangement (increases of 2.7 to 3.3 scaled-score points), and the smallest gains were for Vocabulary (increases of 0 to .2 scaled-score point) and Comprehension (increases of 0 to .5 scaled-score point). In 34 of the 39 *t* tests that I conducted to evaluate changes in subtest scores, the changes were significantly greater than chance. It is difficult to know why Picture Arrangement scores were higher by almost 1 standard deviation on retest, especially since its internal consistency reliability coefficient is at the median reliability of the Performance subtests. Perhaps, aided by the color of the pictures, the children retained a clear memory of the story elements of the pictures. On the second testing they then may have been able to solve the arrangements more quickly and accurately and gain bonus points.

Table I-5
Test-Retest Gains on WISC-III Subtests for Three Groups of Children

Subtest	Ages		
	6–7 (N = 111)	10–11 (N = 119)	14–15 (N = 123)
Information	.4*	.3*	.7***
Similarities	.5**	.7***	1.2***
Arithmetic	.1	.4*	.4*
Vocabulary	0	.2	.2*
Comprehension	.5*	0	.3
Digit Span	.6**	.7***	.9***
Picture Completion	1.2***	2.0***	2.1***
Coding	1.8***	2.2***	1.9***
Picture Arrangement	3.3***	2.9***	2.7***
Block Design	.9***	1.2***	1.0***
Object Assembly	1.5***	1.5***	1.7***
Symbol Search	1.8***	1.4***	1.4***
Mazes	1.1***	1.0***	1.0***

Note. Test-retest intervals range from 12 to 63 days, with a median retest interval of 23 days. The *t* test used to evaluate the mean changes on each subtest employed a repeated measures formula:

$$t = \frac{M_1 - M_2}{\sqrt{\left(\frac{SD_1}{\sqrt{N_1}}\right)^2 + \left(\frac{SD_2}{\sqrt{N_2}}\right)^2 - 2r_{12}\left(\frac{SD_1}{\sqrt{N_1}}\right)\left(\frac{SD_2}{\sqrt{N_2}}\right)}}$$

* $p < .05$.
** $p < .01$.
*** $p < .001$.
Source: Means and standard deviations obtained from Wechsler (1991[R]), pages 170–172.

The relationship between the gain scores on the subtests and the internal consistency reliabilities of the subtests also is helpful in evaluating the gain scores (personal communication, Leslie Atkinson, January 1992). The moderately negative relationship that was found between these variables (Spearman rank-order correlation of $-.50, p < .05$, one-tailed test) suggests that practice effects acted on error variance in such a way as to increase scores on the subtests in inverse proportion to their reliability—there was a tendency for the more reliable subtests to have somewhat smaller gain scores.

Confidence Intervals

This text provides two types of confidence intervals. The first type is based solely on the child's obtained score (or IQ) and uses the conventional standard error of measurement. The second type is based on the estimated true score (soon to be discussed) and the standard error of measurement associated with the estimated true score (also referred to as the *standard error of estimation*). The WISC-III manual, in contrast, provides confidence intervals based on the estimated true score only. The following guidelines will help you to select which type of confidence interval to use.

Although confidence intervals can be used for every score obtained by the child, I recommend that you use them primarily for the Full Scale IQ because it is this score that is usually used to make diagnostic and classification decisions. *Individuals who use the test findings need to know that the primary score used to make decisions about the child is not perfectly accurate because it has some inherent measurement error.* Consequently, it is important to give confidence intervals when you report the test results.

Confidence interval for obtained score without reference to the estimated true score. When the confidence interval is based solely on the obtained score, without reference to the estimated true score, the standard error of measurement for obtained scores is used. The formula for obtaining the standard error of measurement (also shown in Chapter 2, page 28) is as follows:

$$SE_m = SD\sqrt{1 - r_{xx}}$$

Confidence intervals associated with the 68, 85, 90, 95, and 99 percent levels of confidence can be obtained by multiplying the standard error of measurement by the appropriate z value (namely, 1.00, 1.44, 1.65, 1.96, and 2.58, respectively). (See pages 28 and 29 for further discussion of confidence intervals using the conventional method.)

Glutting, McDermott, and Stanley (1987[R]) pointed out that if you want to answer the question "What is the best measure of an examinee's *current* functioning in the performance area assessed by a specific test?" (p. 613), then the proper score to interpret is the obtained score, without recourse to the estimated true score. They base their recommendation on the following line of reasoning:

The obtained score is the proper score to interpret . . . because the question pertains exclusively to a single examinee on a given test at a particular point in time. Moreover, long-standing conventions in clinical practice, contemporary social policy, and law require that psychologists use obtained scores for diagnostic and classificatory decisions. . . .

In instances where a single examinee is tested alone, and not as a member of an explicit group, the expected error of measurement (in the statistical sense) is zero because the examinee's score

is the mean of the group ($N = 1$) and the obtained score "regresses" toward this mean because of error of measurement. For the lone-tested individual, confidence limits must be constructed around the obtained score by using the standard error of measurement procedure. . . . The standard error of measurement is a *personal* statistic that, theoretically, is computable for a single examinee and independent of a test's reliability and mean. It yields confidence limits that are applicable when the psychologist does not know to which specific subgroup of the general population the examinee belongs. In diagnostic classification, because one cannot presume to know beforehand the resultant assignment of an examinee to a specific clinical or exceptional subgroup, psychologists are compelled to use scores and confidence limits that are personally focused. (pp. 612–613)

Table L-1 in Appendix L shows the confidence intervals, by age, for the Verbal, Performance, and Full Scale WISC-III IQs based on the obtained score and the conventional standard error of measurement—that is, without recourse to the estimated true score or the standard error of estimation. Use of the child's specific age group allows you to obtain the most accurate confidence interval.

Confidence limits for obtained scores with reference to the estimated true score. Glutting et al. (1987[R]) also pointed out that if you are interested in answering the question "What is the best *long-run* (stable) measure of an examinee's functioning in the performance area assessed by a specific test *relative to other examinees in a particular reference group*?" (p. 612), then the proper score to interpret is the estimated true score. They go on to note that

the "reference group" could include all examinees in the standardization sample for the test, or some independent clinical subgroup of those examinees (e.g., the gifted or mentally retarded), or examinees comprising subsets similar to the examinee in age, sex, score level, and other relevant characteristics. In this situation, the estimated true score . . . is the appropriate score for interpretation, as it considers the mean and reliability for the specific reference group in question and corrects for mean regression on that basis. (p. 613)

Table L-2 in Appendix L shows the confidence intervals, by age, for the WISC-III Full Scale, Verbal, and Performance IQs based on the estimated true score and the appropriate standard error of measurement. The confidence intervals in Table L-2, as noted below, are applied to the obtained score just as they are in Table L-1. You can also use this table for the WPPSI-R and WAIS-R, and for any test with $M = 100$ and $SD = 15$ that has a reliability coefficient of .85 to .98. The formula used to obtain the estimated true score is as follows:

$$T = r_{xx}X + (1 - r_{xx})\overline{X}$$

where T = estimated true score

r_{xx} = reliability of the test

X = obtained score

$\overline{X}$ = mean of test.

The formula used to obtain the standard error of estimation (SE_E) is as follows:

$$SE_E = r_{xx}SE_m$$

where SE_E = standard error of estimation (or standard error of measurement of the true score)

r_{xx} = reliability of the test

SE_m = standard error of measurement of the test.

Thus the estimated true score for an obtained WISC-III Full Scale IQ of 60 (where r_{xx} = .96) would be T = .96(60) + .04(100) = 57.60 + 4 = 62. And the standard error of estimation would be SE_E = .96(3.20) = 3.07.

Because the confidence intervals are centered around the estimated true score, the intervals become asymmetrical when applied to the obtained score. The asymmetry is greatest for values farthest from the mean because regression to the mean is greater at the extremes of the distribution than at the center of the distribution. In fact, for scores at the mean, there is no asymmetry at all—the confidence intervals are equal around the mean (see Figure I-2, Section L). The procedure used to obtain the confidence intervals in Table L-2 is the same as that used in the construction of the confidence intervals in the WISC-III manual.

To use Table L-2 in Appendix L, follow this procedure. First, use the chart at the beginning of the table to find which section of the table represents the examinee's age, the appropriate test (WISC-III, WPPSI-R, or WAIS-R), and the appropriate scale (that is, Full Scale, Verbal Scale, or Performance Scale). Then select one confidence level from the columns labeled 68%, 85%, 90%, 95%, and

K. WISC-III—Verbal Scale—Ages 10, 11, 12, 14, 16, and Average; WISC-III—Full Scale—Ages 6, 9, 11, 13, and 14; WPPSI-R—Performance Scale—Age 5; WPPSI-R—Verbal Scale—Average; WPPSI-R—Full Scale—Ages 5½, 6, and 6½; WAIS-R—Verbal Scale—Ages 16–17 (r_{xx} = .95)

68%			85%			90%			95%			99%		
IQ	L	U	IQ	L	U	IQ	L	U	IQ	L	U	IQ	L	U
40–46	0	6	40–41	− 2	8	40–44	− 2	8	40–45	− 3	9	40–45	− 5	11
47–53	− 1	6	42–58	− 2	7	45–55	− 3	8	46–54	− 4	9	46–54	− 6	11

L. WISC-III—Verbal Scale—Ages 8 and 15; WISC-III—Full Scale—Ages 8, 10, 12, 16, and Average; WPPSI-R—Performance Scale—Ages 3, 3½, 4, and 4½; WPPSI-R—Full Scale—Age 5 and Average; WAIS-R—Verbal Scale—Ages 18–19 and 20–24; WAIS-R—Full Scale—Ages 16–17 and 18–19 (r_{xx} = .96)

68%			85%			90%			95%			99%		
IQ	L	U	IQ	L	U	IQ	L	U	IQ	L	U	IQ	L	U
91–109	− 3	3	92–108	− 4	4	94–106	− 5	5	97–103	− 6	6	99–101	− 7	7
110–115	− 3	2	109–116	− 5	4	107–118	− 5	4	104–121	− 6	5	102–123	− 8	7

M. WISC-III—Full Scale—Age 15; WPPSI-R—Full Scale—Ages 3, 3½, 4, and 4½; WAIS-R—Verbal Scale—Ages 25–34, 35–44, 45–54, 55–64, 65–69, 70–74, and Average; WAIS-R—Full Scale—Ages 20–24, 45–54, 55–64, 70–74, and Average (r_{xx} = .97)

68%			85%			90%			95%			99%		
IQ	L	U	IQ	L	U	IQ	L	U	IQ	L	U	IQ	L	U
133–134	− 4	2	130–137	− 5	3	144–155	− 6	3	148–152	− 6	3	101–133	− 7	6
135–160	− 4	1	138–160	− 5	2	156–160	− 6	2	153–160	− 7	3	134–160	− 8	5

Figure I-2. Part of Table L-2 in Appendix L showing WISC-III confidence intervals based on the estimated true score.

99%. The absolute values in the table under the appropriate confidence level will allow you to calculate the lower (L) and upper (U) limits of the confidence interval for the obtained IQ. If the sign is *positive* before the absolute value (no sign precedes the value and the + sign is understood), *add* the absolute value to the obtained IQ. If the sign is *negative* before the absolute value (a − sign precedes the absolute value), *subtract* the absolute value from the obtained IQ. In most cases, the lower limits are found by subtracting an absolute value from the obtained IQ, and the upper limits are found by adding an absolute value to the obtained IQ.

Here are three examples of how to calculate the confidence intervals.

1. To calculate the confidence interval for a 6-year-old child who obtains a WISC-III Full Scale IQ of 46, see Table L-2, Section K, in Appendix L. Section K shows that the absolute values for the lower and upper limits of the confidence interval are 0 and 6 at the 68 percent confidence level, respectively. (Figure I-2 shows the parts of Table L-2 that relate to the three examples in this section.) Because both signs are positive, you can obtain the lower and upper limits of the confidence interval by adding these absolute values to the obtained IQ. The resulting confidence interval is 46 to 52 (lower limit is 46 + 0 = 46; upper limit is 46 + 6 = 52).

2. For a 10-year-old child who obtains a WISC-III Full Scale IQ of 100, see Table L-2, Section L, in Appendix L. Section L shows that the absolute values at the 90 percent confidence level are 5 (preceded by a − sign) and 5 (preceded by a + sign) for the lower and upper limits of the confidence interval, respectively (see Figure I-2). To find the lower limit, subtract the absolute value in the column labeled "L" from the obtained IQ (100 − 5 = 95). To find the upper limit, add the absolute value in the column labeled "U" to the obtained IQ (100 + 5 = 105). Thus the confidence interval is 95 to 105.

3. For a 15-year-old child who obtains a WISC-III Full Scale IQ of 155, see Table L-2, Section M, in Appendix L. At the 99 percent confidence level, Section M shows that the appropriate absolute values are 8 (preceded by a − sign) and 5 (preceded by a + sign) for the lower and upper limits of the confidence interval, respectively (see Figure I-2). To find the lower limit, subtract the absolute value in the column labeled "L" from the obtained IQ (155 − 8 = 147). To find the upper limit, add the absolute value in the column labeled "U" to the obtained IQ (155 + 5 = 160). The confidence interval then is 147 to 160.

Note that although the values for the confidence intervals are obtained for the estimated true score, they are applied to the obtained score. Also note that the estimated true score is not given in the report. It is used only to generate the confidence interval.

Table L-2 in Appendix L is based on the child's age and not on average values for the total sample; this is in contrast to the WISC-III manual, where the confidence intervals are based on the total sample. *Use of the child's specific age group allows you to obtain the most accurate confidence interval.*

Comment on confidence intervals.   In clinical and psychoeducational assessments, questions usually center on how the child is functioning at the time of the referral. Therefore, I recommend that you use the confidence interval based on the child's obtained score, without recourse to the child's estimated true score. If you follow this recommendation, use the confidence intervals for the obtained score and the conventional standard error of measurement—Table L-1 in Appendix L; the WISC-III manual does not provide a similar table. However, when you want to provide information about how the child might perform over a longer period of time in relation to a specific reference group, then use the confidence interval based on the estimated true score—Table L-2 in Appendix L. Again, the confidence intervals shown in Table L-2 are more appropriate than those shown in the WISC-III manual because they are based on the child's specific age.

VALIDITY

Because the WISC-III is a newly published test, little is known about its validity, aside from the studies reported in the WISC-III manual. Although approximately 27 percent of the items on the WISC-III are new, much of the research on the validity of the WISC-R probably applies to the WISC-III. Studies related to the validity of the WISC-R, reviewed on pages 123–125 of this text, indicate that the WISC-R has adequate construct, concurrent, and predictive validity for many different types of normal and handicapped children in the age range covered by the test. Let us now look at the studies reported in the WISC-III manual.

Concurrent Validity

The concurrent validity studies cited below of the WISC-III with the WISC-R, WAIS-R, and WPPSI-R do not allow us to determine with precision how WISC-III IQs compare with those on the other Wechsler tests. This is because the WISC-III was administered in counterbalanced order with another Wechsler test (that is, the two test administrations were alternated). The resulting scores on the second test are thus confounded by practice effects—the second test was influenced by the child's exposure to the first test. In order to know whether scores on two tests differ, we need to have data from independent test administrations. In the studies reported in the WISC-III manual, the independent test data would be from the first test administration *only*; however, these data were not reported. Therefore, you must interpret cautiously the tables in the WISC-III manual that show the means and standard deviations for the WISC-III and other Wechsler tests (that is, Tables 6.8, 6.10, and 6.12); all mean scores in these tables are based on the average of the two orders of administration. The means in these tables are probably a bit higher because of practice effects.

1. *WISC-III and WISC-R.* Two studies are reported in the WISC-III manual regarding concurrent validity between the WISC-III and WISC-R. In the first study, a sample of 206 normal children between the ages of 6 and 16 years (*Mdn* = 11 years) were administered the WISC-III and WISC-R in counterbalanced order. The interval between the two tests ranged from 12 to 70 days (*Mdn* = 21 days). The correlations were .90 for the Verbal Scale, .81 for the Performance Scale, and .89 for the Full Scale.

Full Scale IQs on the WISC-III were 5.3 points *lower*, on the average, than those on the WISC-R (WISC-III *M* IQ = 102.9, *SD* = 14.7; WISC-R *M* IQ = 108.2, *SD* = 15.1). Similarly, IQs on the Verbal Scale and Performance Scale were *lower* on the WISC-III than on the WISC-R by 2.4 and 7.4 points, respectively, on the average. These results agree with previous findings that individuals almost invariably score lower on newer tests than on older ones (Flynn, 1984[R], 1987[R]).

For the 12 subtests that the WISC-III and the WISC-R have in common, correlations ranged from a low of .42 for Picture Arrangement to a high of .80 for Information (*Mdn r* = .685). Correlations between subtests on the Verbal Scale were slightly higher (range of .67 to .80, *Mdn r* = .725) than those on the Performance Scale (range of .42 to .76, *Mdn r* = .575). This pattern suggests that the Verbal subtests on the WISC-III and WISC-R have more in common than do the Performance subtests. It is not clear why the correlations between the subtests on the two tests were not higher, given that approximately 73 percent of the items are the same on both tests.

In the second study, a sample of 104 children, composed primarily of children with learning difficulties, reading difficulties, or attention deficit hyperactivity disorders, were administered the WISC-III and WISC-R in counterbalanced order. The correlations were .86 for the Verbal

Scale, .73 for the Performance Scale, and .86 for the Full Scale. Full Scale IQs on the WISC-III were 5.9 points *lower*, on the average, than those on the WISC-R. Similarly, IQs on the Verbal and Performance Scales were *lower* on the WISC-III than on the WISC-R by 5.4 and 5.1 points, respectively, on the average.

2. *WISC-III and WAIS-R.* Because the WISC-III and WAIS-R overlap at ages 16 to 17 years, it is important to know the relationship between the two tests for this age group. In a sample of 189 16-year-old normal adolescents, the WISC-III and WAIS-R were administered in counterbalanced order. The interval between the two tests ranged from 12 to 70 days (*Mdn* = 21 days). The correlations were .90 for the Verbal Scale, .80 for the Performance Scale, and .86 for the Full Scale.

Full Scale IQs on the WISC-III were 3.9 points *lower*, on the average, than those on the WAIS-R (WISC-III *M* IQ = 101.4, *SD* = 15; WAIS-R *M* IQ = 105.3, *SD* = 14.9). Similarly, IQs on the Verbal and Performance Scales were *lower* on the WISC-III than on the WAIS-R by 1.5 and 5.9 points, respectively, on the average.

For the 11 subtests that the WISC-III and the WAIS-R have in common, correlations ranged from a low of .35 for Picture Arrangement to a high of .85 for Vocabulary (*Mdn r* = .67). Correlations between subtests on the Verbal Scale were higher (range of .51 to .85, *Mdn r* = .72) than those on the Performance Scale (range of .35 to .79, *Mdn r* = .52). This pattern, like that for the WISC-III and WISC-R, suggests that WISC-III and WAIS-R Verbal subtests have more in common than do the Performance subtests.

3. *WISC-III and WPPSI-R.* Because the WISC-III overlaps with the WPPSI-R in the age range of 6 to 7-3 years, it is important to know the relationship between the two tests for this age group. The WISC-III and WPPSI-R were administered in counterbalanced order to 188 normal 6-year-old children. The interval between the two tests ranged from 12 to 62 days (*Mdn* = 21 days). The correlations were .85 for the Verbal Scale, .73 for the Performance Scale, and .85 for the Full Scale. These correlations are somewhat inflated because the two tests have as many as 35 items in common.

Full Scale IQs on the WISC-III were 4.0 points *higher* than those on the WPPSI-R. Similarly, IQs on the Verbal and Performance Scales were *higher* on the WISC-III than on the WPPSI-R by 1.9 and 5.9 points, respectively.

4. *WISC-III and other measures of ability and achievement.* Table I-6 summarizes correlations between the WISC-III and seven different measures of ability or achievement. The WISC-III Full Scale correlates highly with the Total Index of the Otis-Lennon School Ability Test

Table I-6

Summary of WISC-III Criterion Validity Studies Cited in the WISC-III Manual

	WISC-III		
Criterion	Verbal Scale	Performance Scale	Full Scale
Otis-Lennon School Ability Test			
Verbal Index	.69	.59	.73
Nonverbal Index	.44	.59	.58
Total Index	.64	.65	.73
Differential Ability Scales			
Verbal	.87	.31	.71
Nonverbal	.58	.78	.81
Spatial	.66	.82	.86
General Conceptual	.82	.80	.92
Basic Number	.55	.34	.54
Spelling	.54	.29	.51
Word Reading	.54	.41	.58
Wide Range Achievement Test—Revised			
Reading	.62	.29	.53
Spelling	.41	.11	.28
Arithmetic	.61	.40	.58
Halstead-Reitan Neuro-psychological Battery			
Tactual Performance Test—Memory	.19	.45	.37
Finger Tapping	−.40	−.37	−.45
Benton Revised Visual Retention Test	.15	.47	.37
Group-administered achievement tests[a]			
Total	.74	.57	.74
Reading	.70	.43	.66
Mathematics	.63	.58	.68
Written Language	.56	.46	.57
School grades			
GPA	.42	.39	.47
Mathematics	.35	.35	.41
English	.36	.31	.40
Reading	.44	.39	.48
Spelling	.28	.32	.36

Note. The WISC-III manual presents means, standard deviations, and other statistical information about the studies in this table.
[a] See the WISC-III manual for a description of these tests.
Source: Adapted from Wechsler (1991[R]).

($r = .73$) and with the General Conceptual Ability score of the Differential Ability Scales ($r = .92$). Correlations between the WISC-III Full Scale and the Wide Range Achievement Test—Revised (WRAT-R) and the Differential Ability Scales achievement tests are for the most part in the .50s. The one exception is the .28 correlation between the WISC-III Full Scale and WRAT-R Spelling. Correlations between the WISC-III Full Scale and the reading, mathematics, and written language sections of group-administered achievement tests are in the high .50s and .60s. Correlations between the WISC-III Full Scale and measures of visual-motor speed or copying are usually in the .30s to .40s. Finally, correlations between the WISC-III Full Scale and school grades are in the .30s and .40s.

Predictive Validity

Two predictive validity studies are reported in the WISC-III manual. In the first study, the WISC-III was compared with the WISC-R, which had been administered about 13 months earlier (range of 5 to 20 months) to a sample of 23 gifted children (ages and IQs not reported). Full Scale IQs on the WISC-III were 4.9 points *lower*, on the average, than those on the WISC-R. Similarly, IQs on the Verbal and Performance Scales were *lower* on the WISC-III than on the WISC-R by 5.8 and 1.1 points, respectively, on the average.

In the second study, the WISC-III was compared with the WISC-R, which had been administered about 26 months earlier (range of 14 to 37 months), on the average, to a sample of 28 mentally retarded children (ages and IQs not reported). Full Scale IQs on the WISC-III were 8.9 points *lower*, on the average, than those on the WISC-R. Similarly, IQs on the Verbal Scale and Performance Scale were *lower* on the WISC-III than on the WISC-R by 8.9 and 6.8 points, respectively.

The results of these two predictive validity studies with small samples of exceptional children suggest, if replicated, that children will obtain *lower* scores on the WISC-III than on the WISC-R. In fact, after a 2-year interval, mentally retarded children may obtain Full Scale IQs on the WISC-III that are approximately 9 *points lower* than those they obtained on the WISC-R. Similarly, after a 1-year interval, gifted children may obtain Full Scale IQs on the WISC-III that are about 5 *points lower* than those they had on the WISC-R. You should not consider decrements of these magnitudes to reflect meaningful changes in the child's ability. Rather, interpret the changes simply as scores on two different tests that, although highly similar, have different norms. Nevertheless, large differences between scores on the WISC-III and the WISC-R may reflect meaningful changes in the child's ability.

Construct Validity

The maximum-likelihood factor analysis and the principal components analysis cited later in this chapter, as well as the factor analyses cited in the WISC-III manual, indicate that the test adequately measures two factors that correspond to the Verbal and Performance Scales of the test. In addition, the test provides a fair measure of general intelligence. Thus, there is support for the construct validity of the WISC-III.

Comment on the Validity of the WISC-III

The validity studies in the WISC-III manual suggest that the WISC-III has adequate concurrent and construct validity. The validity coefficients reported in the WISC-III manual are similar to those reported for the WISC-R. Thus, there is every reason to believe that studies using such criteria as other intelligence tests, achievement tests, and school grades will find the WISC-III to be a valid instrument.

You should not consider either the WISC-III and WAIS-R or the WISC-III and WPPSI-R to be parallel forms in the overlapping age groups. The WISC-III yields *lower* Full Scale IQs than the WAIS-R by about 4 points and *higher* Full Scale IQs than the WPPSI-R by about 4 points. We do not know to what extent these generalizations hold for handicapped children or exceptional children, and particularly for children at the lower or upper levels of the IQ distribution.

If you administer either the WAIS-R or the WPPSI-R *after* the WISC-III (or vice versa), small changes on the second test may have nothing to do with any intervening events in the child's life. Rather, the changes are likely to be associated with errors of measurement, different norm groups, or practice effects. For example, almost 11 years separate the standardization of the WISC-III and WAIS-R, and 2 years separate the standardization of the WISC-III and WPPSI-R. We do not know why the WISC-III yields *higher* IQs than the WPPSI-R and *lower* IQs than the WAIS-R.

Investigators need to replicate and extend all results reported in the WISC-III manual to different samples of children. Investigators also need to study how the WISC-III compares to the Stanford-Binet Intelligence Scale–4th Edition, K-ABC, and other individually administered measures of intellectual ability and to study how handicapped or exceptional children perform on the WISC-III.

INTERCORRELATIONS BETWEEN SUBTESTS AND SCALES

Inspection of the intercorrelations between WISC-III subtests and scales (see Table C.12, page 281 in the WISC-III manual) indicates that in the total group, correlations between the 13 subtests range from a low of .14 (Mazes and Digit Span) to a high of .70 (Vocabulary and Information; *Mdn r* = .355). The six highest subtest average intercorrelations are between Vocabulary and Information (.70), Vocabulary and Similarities (.69), Similarities and Information (.66), Comprehension and Vocabulary (.64), Comprehension and Similarities (.59), and Arithmetic and Information (.57). The seven lowest subtest average intercorrelations are between Mazes and Digit Span (.14), Mazes and Coding (.15), Mazes and Vocabulary (.17), Mazes and Comprehension (.17), Mazes and Similarities (.18), Mazes and Information (.18), and Coding and Picture Completion (.18). (Seven are given instead of six because of tied ranks.)

In the total group, the Verbal Scale subtests correlate more highly with each other (*Mdn r* = .55) than do the Performance Scale subtests (*Mdn r* = .33). Average correlations between the Verbal Scale subtests and the Verbal Scale range from .42 to .78 (*Mdn r* = .72); those between the Performance Scale subtests and the Performance Scale range from .32 to .65 (*Mdn r* = .45). Thus, the Verbal subtests have more in common with each other than do the Performance subtests (see Table I-7).

Average correlations between the 13 individual subtests and the Full Scale range from .31 to .74 (*Mdn r* = .58). Vocabulary has the highest correlation with the Full Scale (.74), followed by Information (.72), Similarities (.72), Block Design (.66), Arithmetic (.65), Comprehension (.64), Picture Completion (.58), Object Assembly (.58), Symbol Search (.56), Picture Arrangement (.52), Digit Span (.43), Coding (.33), and Mazes (.31). These findings indicate that the five standard Verbal subtests plus Block Design correlate more highly with the Full Scale than do the other subtests (see Table I-7). Vocabulary has the highest correlation with the Verbal Scale (.78), and Block Design has the highest correlation with the Performance Scale (.65).

Table I-7
Average Correlations Between WISC-III Subtests and Scales

Subtest	Verbal Scale	Performance Scale	Full Scale
Information	.75	.55	.72
Similarities	.75	.55	.72
Arithmetic	.62	.54	.65
Vocabulary	.78	.56	.74
Comprehension	.67	.49	.64
Digit Span	.42	.35	.43
Picture Completion	.52	.54	.58
Coding	.29	.32	.33
Picture Arrangement	.45	.49	.52
Block Design	.57	.65	.66
Object Assembly	.48	.60	.58
Symbol Search	.44	.58	.56
Mazes	.23	.35	.31

Source: Adapted from Wechsler (1991[R]), Table C.12 (page 281).

WISC-III AND PARENT EDUCATION

Table I-8 shows the relationship between WISC-III IQs and level of parent education reported in a study by Granier and O'Donnell (1991[R]). Their sample consisted of 1,194 children, ages 6 through 16 years, who were part of the WISC-III standardization group. Children whose parents had a college education had higher IQs (*M* IQ = 106.01) than children whose parents had a ninth grade education or less (*M* IQ = 86.38), a difference of about 20 points. These findings are similar to those found on the WISC-R

Table I-8
Relationship Between Parent Education Level and WISC-III IQs

Parent education level	Verbal IQ	Performance IQ	Full Scale IQ
Less than 9th grade	85.60	89.80	86.38
9th through 11th grade	91.63	94.04	92.10
High school diploma	97.82	98.33	97.72
Some college	100.84	100.92	100.82
College graduate	106.03	105.17	106.01

Source: Reprinted with permission of the authors, M. Granier and L. O'Donnell (1991[R]), *Children's WISC-III scores: Impact of parent education and home environment.* Copyright 1991 by The Psychological Corporation.

(see pages 126 and 128 of this text) even though parent occupation—instead of parent education—was used on the WISC-R as a stratification variable.

FACTOR ANALYSIS

I performed a maximum-likelihood factor analysis of the standardization group for each age group and for the total sample for 2, 3, and 4 factor solutions using BMDP4M (version 1990). The results suggested that a three-factor model best characterizes the WISC-III (see Table I-9). These factors may be labeled Verbal Comprehension, Perceptual Organization, and Processing Speed. The three factors account for 25, 16, and 10 percent of the variance, respectively. Thus the Processing Speed factor accounts for less variance than do the Verbal Comprehension and Perceptual Organization factors.

The term *Verbal Comprehension* describes the hypothesized ability underlying the factor for both item content (verbal) and mental process (comprehension). This factor appears to measure a variable common to most of the Verbal Scale subtests. For the total sample, Vocabulary, Information, Comprehension, and Similarities have the highest loadings on the Verbal Comprehension factor, followed by Arithmetic, which has a moderate loading, and Digit Span, which has a minimal loading. Three Performance Scale subtests—Picture Completion, Picture Arrangement, and Block Design—also have minimal loadings on the Verbal Comprehension factor. It may be that verbal processing is involved in successful performance on Picture Completion and Picture Arrangement and that the high *g* loadings associated with Block Design (see below) explain its correlation with Verbal Comprehension. It also may be that these three Performance Scale subtests, together with the Verbal Scale subtests, are highly related to a more general cognitive factor.

The term *Perceptual Organization* describes the hypothesized ability underlying the factor for both item content (perceptual) and mental process (organization). This factor appears to measure a variable common to several of the Performance Scale subtests. For the total sample, Block Design and Object Assembly have high loadings on the Perceptual Organization factor, followed by Picture Completion, which has a moderate loading, and Mazes, Picture Arrangement, and Symbol Search, which have minimal loadings.

The term *Processing Speed* describes the hypothesized ability underlying the factor for both item content (perceptual processing) and mental process (speed). This factor appears to reflect the ability to employ a high degree of

Table I-9
Factor Loadings of WISC-III Subtests for 11 Age Groups Following Maximum-Likelihood Factor Analysis (Varimax Rotation)

Subtest	6	7	8	9	10	11	12	13	14	15	16	Av.[a]
						Age						
Factor A – Verbal Comprehension												
Information	70	72	77	70	74	69	79	79	74	82	82	75
Similarities	76	66	79	77	80	70	74	68	75	73	77	75
Arithmetic	59	41	56	46	63	35	58	46	64	51	58	55
Vocabulary	65	75	76	87	88	79	84	82	87	81	83	82
Comprehension	58	72	70	60	69	63	73	65	71	58	70	68
Digit Span	50	29	36	31	38	24	24	25	36	36	28	34
Picture Completion	37	22	38	43	48	42	36	30	47	51	36	39
Coding	00	06	12	16	16	13	14	13	16	13	07	13
Picture Arrangement	41	33	40	25	36	34	32	27	34	44	37	34
Block Design	46	19	38	33	28	22	36	29	42	35	45	33
Object Assembly	28	25	23	37	30	29	27	18	11	35	33	28
Symbol Search	32	23	34	21	27	20	20	08	25	29	20	23
Mazes	22	04	20	02	07	02	08	15	01	14	00	09
Factor B – Perceptual Organization												
Information	18	29	33	30	22	24	34	30	34	30	21	29
Similarities	23	26	33	31	19	29	30	37	18	31	28	30
Arithmetic	35	21	43	34	25	28	27	43	30	49	31	37
Vocabulary	31	20	34	14	13	22	19	28	15	27	17	22
Comprehension	19	08	22	15	19	22	25	17	07	41	12	19
Digit Span	24	25	23	12	19	19	22	18	11	38	20	22
Picture Completion	55	55	54	45	39	54	54	60	49	55	58	53
Coding	21	15	12	10	11	37	09	00	09	21	04	12
Picture Arrangement	40	29	20	29	34	40	38	33	48	40	33	36
Block Design	53	71	60	73	86	73	74	77	58	76	62	73
Object Assembly	71	65	78	60	66	59	77	61	73	62	64	67
Symbol Search	17	26	37	26	29	54	31	31	27	40	35	35
Mazes	43	32	32	28	50	23	34	39	20	44	48	36
Factor C – Processing Speed												
Information	18	21	18	22	14	27	08	07	09	12	10	11
Similarities	04	30	09	10	10	31	17	14	17	09	09	10
Arithmetic	20	48	27	32	12	89	21	28	14	15	36	23
Vocabulary	09	21	16	15	23	23	17	16	08	33	14	16
Comprehension	10	07	16	18	19	22	21	27	19	31	19	19
Digit Span	11	26	25	22	22	44	19	38	13	13	35	22
Picture Completion	17	14	07	18	10	09	08	04	07	04	02	09
Coding	45	42	93	76	92	14	77	90	62	94	74	74
Picture Arrangement	24	46	23	35	27	-09	26	26	14	19	29	25
Block Design	29	30	21	15	12	26	20	32	26	23	29	19
Object Assembly	20	19	16	09	12	14	18	22	26	22	19	15
Symbol Search	93	67	54	75	53	13	61	56	71	48	77	62
Mazes	25	19	19	13	14	09	08	03	23	19	13	14

Note. Decimal points omitted.
[a] Av. = average of 11 age groups.

concentration and attention in processing information rapidly by scanning an array. For the total sample, Coding and Symbol Search have high loadings on the Processing Speed factor.

The factor analytic results give strong empirical support to interpretation of the Verbal and Performance IQs as separately functioning entities in the WISC-III. *The factor structure of the WISC-III closely agrees with the actual organization of the subtests.*

Factor Analytic Findings Related to Age

Although the findings of the maximum-likelihood factor analysis suggest that a three-factor model best characterizes the WISC-III, the model is somewhat weak at ages 6 and 15 years, where only two factors emerged using as a criterion eigenvalues of 1 or above. (Eigenvalues refer to the proportion of variance that a given factor can account for; it is a mathematical value obtained from the factor analysis.) In addition, the third factor, Processing Speed, is usually represented by Coding and Symbol Search, but not at all ages. For example, Arithmetic and Digit Span largely represent the third factor at 11 years, and Symbol Search, Arithmetic, Picture Arrangement, and Coding primarily represent the third factor at 7 years. However, for the entire group, Coding and Symbol Search, as noted previously, have substantial loadings on Processing Speed.

Three of the Performance subtests—Picture Completion, Picture Arrangement, and Block Design—correlate (.30 or above) with the Verbal Comprehension factor at almost every age. However, it is difficult to explain why the pattern of correlations was not consistent at all ages. For example, Block Design loaded on Verbal Comprehension at only 7 of the 11 ages. Similarly, Picture Completion loaded on the Verbal Comprehension factor at all ages, except for age 7 years. Another way to look at the findings is to note that 8, 9, or 10 subtests load on Verbal Comprehension at 9 of the 11 ages and at the average of the 11 age groups. Why these specific nine ages? The pattern of factor loadings may simply be a function of measurement error and may not be a reflection of any underlying developmental trends.

Several Verbal subtests also load (.30 or above) on the Perceptual Organization factor. These usually include Arithmetic, Similarities, and Information. Again, the fact that all subtests are related to *g* may explain these correlations. At 4 of the 11 ages, 8 or more subtests load on Perceptual Organization.

The two Verbal subtests that also load (.30 or above) on Processing Speed at some ages are Arithmetic and Digit Span. Arithmetic involves a speed factor to some extent,

but not Digit Span. However, Arithmetic, Digit Span, Coding, and Symbol Search do have in common the need for attention and concentration, perhaps to a greater extent than do the other subtests. Overall, however, Arithmetic and Digit Span do not make a substantial contribution to the Processing Speed factor. Table I-10 summarizes the major trends of the maximum-likelihood factor analysis by age level.

Comment on Maximum-Likelihood Factor Analysis

The findings of the maximum-likelihood factor analysis reported in this text differ from those reported in the WISC-III manual. The Psychological Corporation also performed a maximum-likelihood factor analysis, but used four age-group clusters (6–7, 8–10, 11–13, and 14–16 years) instead of the 11 separate age groups for the analysis. Consequently, the WISC-III manual reports no factor analytic data for the 11 individual age groups. The WISC-III manual suggests that a four-factor model best describes the WISC-III. The fourth factor is the Freedom from Distractibility factor composed of Arithmetic and Digit Span.

I believe that the four-factor model is inappropriate. I also conducted a maximum-likelihood factor analysis using a four-factor solution, as noted earlier, for each separate age group. At each age group and for the total sample, the eigenvalues were below 1 for the fourth factor. But even more telling was the finding that the so-called Freedom from Distractibility factor did not emerge in 4 of the 11 age groups. At ages 6, 8, 10, and 16 years, the loadings on Arithmetic and Digit Span for the proposed Freedom from Distractibility factor were as follows: age 6: .17 and .15, respectively; age 8: .01 and −.22, respectively; age 10: .16 and −.09, respectively; age 16: .20 and .09, respectively. When a subtest has a loading below .30 on a factor, it suggests that the subtest fails to make a contribution to that factor. A principal components analysis provided essentially similar findings. A four-factor solution never emerged in the principal components analysis. These results suggest that the Freedom from Distractibility factor on the WISC-III should be disregarded until there is further evidence to support its use. If you do choose to interpret the Freedom from Distractibility factor as recommended in the WISC-III manual, do so with caution because of the relative weakness of this factor.

WISC-III Manual Cautions for Factor Score Interpretations

The WISC-III manual on page 210 makes a curious state-

Table 1-10

Summary of Major Trends of Maximum-Likelihood Factor Analysis by Age Level and for the Average of the Total Sample on WISC-III

Age	Number of factors	Subtests with loadings of .30 or higher on Verbal Comprehension	Subtests with loadings of .30 or higher on Perceptual Organization	Subtests with loadings of .30 or higher on Processing Speed
6	3[a]	All 6 Verbal subtests, PC, PA, BD, SS	PC, PA, BD, OA, MA, A, V	CD, SS
7	3	I, S, A, V, C, PA	PC, BD, OA, MA	S, A, CD, PA, BD, SS
8	3	All 6 Verbal subtests, PC, PA, BD, SS	PC, BD, OA, SS, MA, I, S, A, V	CD, SS
9	3	All 6 Verbal subtests, PC, BD, OA	PC, BD, OA, I, S, A	A, CD, PA, SS
10	3	All 6 Verbal subtests, PC, PA, OA	PC, PA, BD, OA, MA	CD, SS
11	3	I, S, A, V, C, PC, PA	PC, CD, PA, BD, OA, SS	S, A, DS
12	3	I, S, A, V, C, PC, PA, BD	PC, PA, BD, OA, SS, MA, I, S	CD, SS
13	3	I, S, A, V, C, PC	PC, PA, BD, OA, SS, MA, I, S, A	DS, CD, BD, SS
14	3	All 6 Verbal subtests, PC, PA, BD	PC, PA, BD, OA, I, A	CD, SS
15	3[a]	All 6 Verbal subtests, PC, PA, BD, OA	PC, PA, BD, OA, SS, MA, I, S, A, C, DS	V, C, CD, SS
16	3	I, S, A, V, C, PC, PA, BD, OA	PC, PA, BD, OA, SS, MA, A	A, DS, CD, SS
Av.	3	All 6 Verbal subtests, PC, PA, BD	PC, PA, BD, OA, SS, MA, S, A	CD, SS

Note. Abbreviations: I = Information, S = Similarities, A = Arithmetic, V = Vocabulary, C = Comprehension, DS = Digit Span, PC = Picture Completion, CD = Coding, PA = Picture Arrangement, BD = Block Design, OA = Object Assembly, SS = Symbol Search, MA = Mazes, Av. = Average of 11 age groups.
[a] The eigenvalue for the third factor is less then 1.00 at age 6 years (namely, .87) and at age 15 years (namely, .86). This means that the third factor is weak at these two ages.

ment about the Processing Speed and Freedom from Distractibility factor scores. The statement (italicized below) was made in the context of a study of 38 gifted children who were administered the WISC-III. The children obtained higher scores on the Verbal Comprehension, Perceptual Organization, and Freedom from Distractibility factors than on the Processing Speed factor (*M*s = 126.9, 125.8, 123.0, and 110.2, respectively). These findings were interpreted to mean that

The Freedom from Distractibility and the Processing Speed scales are not as highly related to general intellectual ability as the Verbal Comprehension and Perceptual Organization scales. *Scores on these scales can be expected to vary independently of FSIQ* [Full Scale IQ] *scores* [italics added]. This finding empha-

sizes the reason that the index scores are not referred to as IQ scores. (Wechsler, 1991[R], p. 210)

The statement that "Scores on these scales can be expected to vary independently of FSIQ scores" is misleading. First, the WISC-III manual did not present any data to support this assertion, except for the means on each factor score. In fact, the mean on the Freedom from Distractibility factor was almost as high as the means on the Verbal Comprehension and Perceptual Organization factors. Second, the subtests that make up the third and fourth factors cited in the WISC-III manual all correlate significantly with the Full Scale (Symbol Search *r* = .56, *p* < .001; Coding *r* = .33, *p* < .001; Arithmetic *r* = .65, *p* < .001; Digit Span *r* = .43, *p* < .001; all correlations based on the total group). In some cases, these subtests have as high or higher a correlation with the Full Scale than do other subtests. For example, the correlations between Picture Completion and Picture Arrangement with the Full Scale are .58 and .52, respectively. Furthermore, Arithmetic, Digit Span, and Symbol Search are either good or fair measures of g. Until further data are available, I believe that it is misleading to say that Processing Speed and Freedom from Distractibility scores "vary independently of FSIQ scores."

(In a telephone conversation on November 4, 1991 with Aurelio Prifitera, who was the Project Director in The Psychological Corporation for the WISC-III, Dr. Prifitera indicated that they included this statement in the WISC-III manual to emphasize that examiners should never use the Freedom from Distractibility or Processing Speed factor scores as independent estimates of a child's Full Scale IQ. I agree fully with this recommendation.)

WISC-III Subtests as Measure of g

Examination of the loadings on the first unrotated factor—in either a principal components analysis or a factor analysis—allows us to determine the extent to which the WISC-III subtests measure general intelligence, or g. In this section the results are based on a principal components analysis. Overall, the WISC-III is a fair measure of g, with 43 percent of its variance attributed to g.

The WISC-III subtests form three clusters with respect to the measurement of g: (a) Vocabulary, Information, Similarities, Block Design, Arithmetic, and Comprehension are good measures of g; (b) Object Assembly, Picture Completion, Symbol Search, Picture Arrangement, and Digit Span are fair measures of g; and (c) Coding and Mazes are poor measures of g (see Table I-11). The subtests

in the Verbal Scale have higher g loadings than those in the Performance Scale (52 percent, on the average, for the Verbal subtests; 36 percent, on the average, for the Performance subtests). Highest loadings are for Vocabulary, Information, and Similarities in the Verbal Scale and Block Design, Object Assembly, and Picture Completion in the Performance Scale. Any of the five standard Verbal subtests may serve as a good measure of g, but only Block Design in the Performance Scale may serve as a good measure of g.

Subtest Specificity

Subtest specificity refers to the proportion of a subtest's variance that is both reliable (that is, not due to measurement errors) and distinctive to the subtest (see pages 32–34 of this text for further information about subtest specificity). Although the individual subtests on the WISC-III overlap in their measurement properties (that is, the majority of the reliable variance for most subtests is common factor variance), many possess sufficient specificity at some ages to justify interpretation of specific subtest functions (see Table I-12).

Throughout the age range covered by the WISC-III, Digit Span, Picture Arrangement, and Block Design have ample specificity. In addition, Picture Completion, Coding, and Mazes have ample specificity at 10 of the 11 age levels. Each of the seven remaining subtests shows a unique pattern of specificity—that is, the ages at which each has ample, adequate, or inadequate specificity differ. Similarities, Arithmetic, Comprehension, and Object Assembly have inadequate specificity for at least five ages.

Subtests with inadequate specificity should not be interpreted as measuring specific functions. These subtests, however, can be interpreted as (a) good, fair, or poor

Table I-11

WISC-III Subtests as Measures of g

Good measure of g			Fair measure of g			Poor measure of g		
Subtest	Average loading of g	Proportion of variance attributed to g (%)	Subtest	Average loading of g	Proportion of variance attributed to g (%)	Subtest	Average loading of g	Proportion of variance attributed to g (%)
Vocabulary	.79	62	Object Assembly	.66	44	Coding	.44	20
Information	.78	61	Picture Completion	.66	44	Mazes	.37	13
Similarities	.78	60	Symbol Search	.62	38			
Block Design	.74	56	Picture Arrangement	.60	36			
Arithmetic	.74	54	Digit Span	.51	26			
Comprehension	.70	50						

Table I-12
Amount of Specificity in WISC-III Subtests for II Ages and Average

Subtest	Ages with ample specificity	Ages with adequate specificity	Ages with inadequate specificity
Information	11, Av.	8–10, 12–16	6–7
Similarities	6, 14	11–12, 15–16, Av.	7–10, 13
Arithmetic	6–7, 10, 13, 15, Av.	16	8–9, 11–12, 14
Vocabulary	6, 11	7–8, 12–16, Av.	9–10
Comprehension	6, 8–11, Av.	12	7, 13–16
Digit Span	6–16, Av.	—	—
Picture Completion	6–11, 13–16, Av.	—	12
Coding	6–7, 9–16, Av.	—	8
Picture Arrangement	6–16, Av.	—	—
Block Design	6–16, Av.	—	—
Object Assembly	9, 13, 15	6	7–8, 10–12, 14, 16, Av.
Symbol Search	7, 10–16, Av.	—	6, 8–9
Mazes	6–14, 16, Av.	—	15

Note. Av. = average of the 11 age groups. Kaufman's (1975a) rule of thumb was used to classify the amount of specificity in each subtest. Subtests with ample specificity have specific variance that (a) reflects 25 percent or more of the subtest's total variance (100%) and (b) exceeds the subtest's error variance. Subtests with adequate specificity have specific variance that (a) reflects between 15 and 24 percent of the subtest's total variance and (b) exceeds the subtest's error variance. Subtests with inadequate specificity have specific variance that either (a) is less than 15 percent of the subtest's total variance or (b) is equal to or less than the subtest's error variance.

Specific variance is obtained by subtracting the squared multiple correlation (from the maximum-likelihood factor analysis with varimax rotation) from the subtest's reliability (r_{xx} − SMC) (A. Silverstein, personal communication, October 1991). Error variance is obtained by subtracting the subtest's reliability from 1.00 ($1 - r_{xx}$).

measures of g (see Table I-11) and (b) representing a specific factor (that is, Verbal Comprehension, Perceptual Organization, or Processing Speed; see Table I-9), where appropriate.

You should also determine which subtest scaled scores are significantly different from the mean of their scale and, in some cases, from one another, and analyze performance on all relevant subtests before drawing any conclusions about unusual ability or weakness; we refer to this as *profile analysis.* (See Chapter 8 and Appendix K for a discussion of profile analysis.) For example, low scores on Coding and Symbol Search and average or high scores on the other subtests may indicate that the child is having difficulty processing information rapidly. However, high scores on Coding and low scores on Symbol Search do not suggest difficulty in processing information rapidly; the picture is mixed.

Factor Scores

You can also obtain factor scores from the WISC-III and thereby identify meaningful psychological dimensions. The Verbal Comprehension factor score measures verbal knowledge and understanding obtained through both informal and formal education and reflects the application of verbal skills to new situations. The Perceptual Organization factor score, a nonverbal score, reflects the ability to interpret and organize visually perceived material within a time limit. The Processing Speed factor score measures the ability to process visually perceived nonverbal information quickly. Concentration and rapid eye-hand coordination may be important components of the Processing Speed factor.

There are at least three different ways of obtaining factor scores:

1. *Three-factor model focusing on subtests with high loadings on each factor.* The results of the three-factor maximum-likelihood factor analysis suggest that the following combinations would be most robust in forming factor scores:

Verbal
Comprehension = Sum of scaled scores on Information, Similarities, Vocabulary, and Comprehension

Perceptual
Organization = Sum of scaled scores on Picture Completion, Block Design, and Object Assembly

Processing
Speed   = Sum of scaled scores on Coding
               and Symbol Search

2. *Three-factor model focusing on subtests often said to reflect the two principal factors plus the new factor.* The results of the maximum-likelihood factor analysis provide only weak support for using the same three factors as noted in number 1, with the addition of Picture Arrangement as a fourth subtest in the Perceptual Organization factor. Perceptual Organization is weaker if Picture Arrangement is included because Picture Arrangement has a .36 loading on Perceptual Organization and a .34 loading on Verbal Comprehension. Picture Arrangement, therefore, is not a pure measure of Perceptual Organization, nor does it have a substantial loading on the factor.

3. *Four-factor model as noted in the WISC-III manual.* Based on the results of a four-factor maximum-likelihood factor analysis, the WISC-III manual proposes that the subtests be divided into four factors, as noted previously. This model is similar to that described in number 2, with the addition of Arithmetic and Digit Span to form the Freedom from Distractibility factor. However, the four-factor model needs further empirical support before I can recommend it.

Use of any of the above combinations ensures against subtests' overlapping in any factors. If you decide to follow the procedure recommended in this text, use the following tables to convert the sum of scaled scores into WISC-III Deviation Quotients:

• Table A.5 (page 255) in the WISC-III manual for Verbal Comprehension (Information, Similarities, Vocabulary, and Comprehension)
• Table A.7 (page 257) in the WISC-III manual for Processing Speed (Coding and Symbol Search)
• Table L-13 in Appendix L for Perceptual Organization (Picture Completion, Block Design, and Object Assembly)

If you decide to use Picture Arrangement as part of the Perceptual Organization factor, use Table A.6 (page 256) in the WISC-III manual to obtain the Deviation Quotients. *Do not report factor scores in a psychological report—use them only for evaluating the child's strengths and weaknesses and for generating hypotheses about the child's abilities.*

RANGE OF SUBTEST SCALED SCORES

The WISC-III provides a range of scaled scores from 1 to 19. However, this range is not possible for all subtests at all ages of the test. For example, there are minor problems with scaled-score ranges at 6 years and at 11 through 16 years. At 6 years, children receive 2 scaled-score points credit on four subtests—Information, Similarities, Picture Arrangement, and Block Design—*even though they fail all items on these subtests.* At 7 years and afterward, however, children receive only 1 scaled-score point if they fail all items on these four subtests.

After the age of 11 years, the ceiling level drops for one or more subtests; however, the drop is no more than 2 scaled-score points. Table I-13 shows the maximum possible scaled scores for each subtest by age. The failure to have the same maximum scaled score at the upper limits (that is, a scaled score of 19) throughout the test primarily

Table I-13
Maximum WISC-III Subtest Scaled Scores by Age

Subtest	Maximum scaled score	Age (in years)
Information	19	6 to 14
	18	15
	17	16
Similarities	19	6 to 16
Arithmetic	19	6 to 15
	18	16
Vocabulary	19	6 to 16
Comprehension	19	6 to 15
	18	16
Digit Span	19	6 to 16
Picture Completion	19	6 to 13
	18	14 to 15
	17	16
Coding	19	6 to 16
Picture Arrangement	19	6 to 16
Block Design	19	6 to 15
	18	16
Object Assembly	19	6 to 15
	18	16
Symbol Search	19	6 to 15
	18	16
Mazes	19	6 to 10
	18	11 to 12
	17	13 to 16

affects how you interpret the profiles of bright children aged 14 years and older. (When Mazes is included, there are difficulties in interpreting the profiles of bright children ages 11 through 16 years.)

You can apply profile analysis techniques appropriately at all ages for five subtests only – Similarities, Vocabulary, Digit Span, Coding, and Picture Arrangement. For older gifted children, you can apply profile analysis uniformly only when all scaled scores are 17 or below. *Applying profile analysis uniformly to all subtests would be misleading in some individual cases because the child cannot obtain the same number of scaled-score points on all subtests.* However, the failure to have the same scaled-score range at all age levels and for all subtests is usually only a minor difficulty because all subtests have a scaled-score range of 1 to 17.

RANGE OF FULL SCALE IQs

The range of Full Scale IQs from 40 to 160 on the WISC-III is insufficient for both severely retarded children and extremely gifted children. This range also is not available at some ages of the test. For example, the highest possible IQ that adolescents who are aged 16-8 years can get is 154; the lowest possible IQ that children who are 6-0 years old can get is 46. The test is designed so that every child receives at least 10 scaled-score points for giving *no* correct answers to any subtest. In fact, 6-year-old children receive 14 scaled-score points even when they fail every item.

The Psychological Corporation recognized that awarding scaled-score points for no successes might be a problem. They therefore recommended that examiners compute IQs on each scale only when the child obtains a raw score greater than 0 on at least three subtests on each scale. Similarly, they recommended that examiners compute a Full Scale IQ only when the child obtains raw scores greater than 0 on three Verbal *and* on three Performance subtests. This is a rule of thumb, rather than an empirically based recommendation, but it does have merit. However, validity data are needed to show that this rule of thumb or other procedures are or are not valid for computing IQs. The WISC-III manual provides no validity data to support this recommendation.

If we follow The Psychological Corporation's recommended procedure, what is the lowest possible IQ that a 6-year-old child can receive? If the child obtained raw scores of 1 on the Information, Similarities, Comprehension, Picture Completion, Picture Arrangement, and Block Design subtests and a raw score of 0 on each of the remaining four subtests, the resulting IQs would be as

follows: Verbal Scale IQ = 58 (13 scaled-score points), Performance Scale IQ = 55 (13 scaled-score points), and Full Scale IQ = 53 (26 scaled-score points). Six 1-point successes thus yield an IQ of 53. Therefore, the WISC-III may not provide precise IQs for young children who are functioning at two or more standard deviations below the mean of the scale. The WISC-III does not appear to sample a sufficient range of cognitive abilities for low-functioning children. If a child fails all or most of the items on the WISC-III, consider giving another test that may give you a more accurate estimate of the child's ability.

COMPARISON OF THE WISC-III AND WISC-R

Although similar to its predecessor, the WISC-III differs from the WISC-R in some important ways.

1. As previously noted, the revision contains a new supplementary subtest, Symbol Search.

2. The Freedom from Distractibility factor does not emerge as a strong factor, if at all. In fact, Coding now unites with Symbol Search to form a new factor called *Processing Speed*.

3. Full-color illustrations are used in the revision.

4. Scoring guidelines and administrative procedures for most subtests have been modified in the revision. For example, changes have been made in the order in which the subtests are administered, order of items, starting points, discontinuance criteria, and allotment of bonus points.

5. Speed (coupled with correct performance) is awarded bonus points on the last six Arithmetic subtest items in the WISC-III.

6. The number of items has been increased on Similarties, Arithmetic, Comprehension, Digit Span, Picture Completion, Coding, Picture Arrangement, Object Assembly, and Mazes and decreased on Vocabulary; the number of items on Information remains the same. Table I-14 highlights the changes in the WISC-III.

ADMINISTERING THE WISC-III

The general procedures discussed in Chapter 5 for administering psychological tests should help you administer the WISC-III. However, you must master the special procedures developed for the WISC-III, whether or not you are familiar with the WISC-R. You must be careful not to confuse procedures for the WISC-R, WPPSI-R, or WAIS-R with those for the WISC-III – some subtests with the

Table I-14
Highlights of Changes in WISC-III

Area or subtest	Changes from WISC-R	Area or subtest	Changes from WISC-R
Age range	No change.	Types of scores	Provides IQs ($M = 100$, $SD = 15$) for Verbal, Performance, and Full Scales; Index Scores ($M = 100$, $SD = 15$) for four factor scores; percentile ranks for IQs and Index Scores; and test-age equivalents of raw scores. WISC-R provided IQs for Verbal, Performance, and Full Scales and test-age equivalents of raw scores only.
Standardization	1988 census data used.		
Number of subtests	13 instead of 12.		
Number of items	Number of items increased on most subtests.		
Reliability	Reliability coefficients similar to those on WISC-R.		
Validity	Validity seems to be similar to WISC-R.		
Scoring examples	Somewhat expanded and placed with subtest proper instead of in appendixes in back of manual.	Confidence intervals	Confidence intervals presented in manual based on estimated true score method. No confidence intervals presented in the WISC-R manual.
General administrative changes	Order of administering subtests changed, item order changed on some subtests, starting points changed on some subtests, samples added on some subtests, discontinuance criteria changed on some subtests, bonus-point allotment changed on some subtests. Manual has a built-in stand.	Factor structure	Manual proposes a four-factor model (Verbal Comprehension, Perceptual Organization, Freedom from Distractibility, Processing Speed) which differs from the three factors found on the WISC-R. However, the four-factor model, as noted in this chapter, is questionable.
Computation of IQ	No change (stipulates, as does the WISC-R, that 3 Verbal and 3 Performance subtests must have raw scores greater than 0).	g loading	About the same as on the WISC-R (average loading of g is 43 percent on WISC-III and 42 percent on WISC-R).
Intelligence classification	Uses "intellectually deficient" instead of "mental retardation" to classify IQs below 70.	Art work	Color used instead of black and white on all pictures throughout the test, all pictures enlarged, and art work has a more contemporary appearance.
Record Form	Front cover changed to include places for calculating factor scores, confidence intervals, and percentile ranks; Coding Response Sheet is a separate pullout sheet in Record Form. More space provided for writing responses on Information, Similarities, Vocabulary, and Comprehension subtests. More space provided on Coding Response Sheet between the key and the stimulus items. Full page provided for recording behavioral observations.	Test-retest changes	Retest changes 3 points greater on WISC-III Performance Scale than on WISC-R Performance Scale (approximately 13 vs. 10 IQ points).
		Ceiling and floor level of IQ	Range of Full Scale IQs is from 40 to 160 on both tests, but this range is not available at all ages on either test.
		Ages at which scaled scores of 1 to 19 are available	More subtests have a range of 1 to 19 scaled-score points on WISC-III than on WISC-R.

(Table continues next page)

Table 1-14 (cont.)

Area or subtest	Changes from WISC-R	Area or subtest	Changes from WISC-R
Information	Same number of items (30), with 21 unchanged or slightly reworded, 2 substantially changed, and 7 new items. Starting point item now counted in reverse sequence.	Picture Completion (cont.)	Two additional starting points added for a total of 4 points. Discontinuance rule changed from 4 to 5 consecutive failures.
Similarities	Contains 19 instead of 17 items, with 13 unchanged or slightly reworded and 6 new items. Sample item used. Scoring criteria and sample responses are directly following each item rather than in an appendix.	Coding	Contains 59 items on Coding A, instead of 45, and 119 items on Coding B, instead of 93; additional rows added and additional items added in rows on both parts of the subtest. Symbols enlarged slightly. Black no. 2 pencil required instead of red pencil. Recording form now part of Record Form.
Arithmetic	Contains 24 instead of 18 items, with 14 slightly reworded and 10 new items. Starting point item now counted in reverse sequence. Minor changes in scoring and administration. Bonus points given for speed on items 19 to 24.	Picture Arrangement	Contains 14 instead of 12 items, with 7 slightly redrawn, sample item redrawn, and all pictures in color. Slight changes in starting points. Changes in scoring procedure for alternative arrangements and bonus-point allotment.
Vocabulary	Contains 30 instead of 32 items, with 19 items the same and 11 new items. Starting point item counted in reverse sequence. Discontinuance rule changed from 5 to 4 consecutive failures. Scoring criteria and sample responses are directly following each item rather than in an appendix.	Block Design	Contains 12 instead of 11 items, with 10 items exactly the same and 2 new items added (one easy and one difficult). Changes in bonus-point allotment. Minor administrative changes.
Comprehension	Contains 18 instead of 17 items, with 12 items unchanged or slightly reworded and 6 new items. Eight items (instead of nine) require two responses for full credit. Discontinuance rule changed from 4 to 3 consecutive failures. Scoring criteria and sample responses are directly following each item rather than in an appendix.	Object Assembly	Contains 5 instead of 4 items, with 4 items slightly redrawn and 1 new item; sample item included as in WISC-R. Additional juncture for scoring Face item added. Layout shield is now freestanding. Changes in bonus-point allotment.
Digit Span	Contains 15 instead of 14 sets of digits, with one 2-digit set added to Digits Forward.	Symbol Search	New optional subtest with two levels, with each level containing 45 items.
Picture Completion	Contains 30 items instead of 26, with 17 slightly modified and 13 new items. All pictures enlarged and in color. Sample item added.	Mazes	Contains 10 instead of 9 mazes, with the new maze at the difficult end of the series. Overall design of the mazes is unchanged, although each is slightly larger. Minor administrative changes, including changes in maximum number of errors and elimination of need for red-lead pencil.

same name have different instructions and time limits. Appendix I presents guidelines that will help you administer the WISC-III subtests; they supplement those in the WISC-III manual. Appendix D presents special procedures for administering the WISC-R (and WISC-III) Performance subtests to deaf children. Some general administrative issues are discussed below. Finally, the suggestions in Exhibit I-2 and the checklist shown in Exhibit I-3 should also help you learn to administer the WISC-III.

Study the instructions in the WISC-III manual and become familiar with the test materials before you give the test. Although the Verbal subtests are generally easier to administer than the Performance subtests, they are more difficult to score. You will find a stopwatch (or a wristwatch with a digital timer) helpful, if not essential, for administering the timed WISC-III subtests.

The Record Form (see Figure I-3) should be clearly and accurately completed; record all responses relevant to the test and testing situation *verbatim.* You also need to check all calculations carefully, as well as the conversion of raw scores to scaled scores and of scaled scores to IQs. In converting the raw scores to scaled scores, be aware that the order of subtests on the front of the Record Form is not the same as the order of subtests in Table A.1 (pages 217–249) in the WISC-III manual. The order of subtests on the Record Form is the order in which the subtests are administered, whereas the order of subtests in Table A.1 is by scale—the six Verbal subtests in the upper half of the table and the seven Performance subtests in the lower half of the table. Be sure to use the appropriate columns in Table A.1 for converting raw scores to scaled scores. For example, to convert a raw score on Picture Completion (the first subtest administered) to a scaled score, you must use the columns in the lower half of Table A.1 ("Performance Subtests"), which show the raw scores for the Picture Completion subtest and their corresponding scaled scores. Calculate the child's chronological age with care. If you master the administrative procedures early in your testing career, you will be better able to move ahead and focus on learning how to interpret the test results.

General Problems in Administering the WISC-III

Here are some problems that have been observed when examiners administered the Wechsler tests.

1. Reading questions too quickly or too slowly.
2. Not enunciating clearly.
3. Leaving unessential materials on the table.
4. Not recording all responses.
5. Calculating chronological age incorrectly.

6. Not adhering to guidelines for giving help.
7. Not adhering to directions.
8. Ignoring proper time limits.
9. Not questioning ambiguous or vague responses.
10. Not crediting all responses.
11. Not following starting rule.
12. Not following discontinuance rule.
13. Making errors in converting raw scores to scaled scores.
14. Prorating incorrectly.
15. Giving time-bonus credits incorrectly.
16. Using inappropriate norms.
17. Not giving a score of 0 to an incorrect response.
18. Adding raw scores incorrectly.
19. Adding scaled scores incorrectly.
20. Not checking all Coding subtest responses.
21. Failing to credit items not administered below the starting point.
22. Giving credit to items passed above the discontinuance point.
23. Not giving credit to items missed below the starting point.
24. Not scoring a subtest.
25. Converting scaled scores to IQs incorrectly.
26. Including a supplementary subtest, in addition to the five standard subtests in each scale, to compute an IQ.
27. Using both Coding and Symbol Search to compute an IQ.

One study (Slate & Chick, 1989) found that the most common scoring errors on the WISC-R were the Vocabulary, Comprehension, and Similarities subtests. The major scoring errors were in assigning 2 points to a 1-point response or 1 point to a 0-point response. Other errors found in the student examiners' test administrations were failing to question responses, failing to record responses verbatim, failing to establish the correct starting points and discontinuance points, and failing to add scores properly. Scoring errors may be due to the examiner's receiving poor instructional preparation; ambiguity in the scoring criteria presented in the test manual; carelessness on the part of the examiner; factors in the examiner-examinee relationship; the examiner's personal stress or fatigue; and the examiner's becoming bored with testing (Slate & Hunnicutt, 1988[R]).

To avoid scoring and administration errors, carefully review how you administer and score each subtest. During the test assign tentative scores, and always rescore each item after you finish administering the entire test. If you are unsure of how to score a response while testing, and the item is involved in establishing a starting point (also re-

WISC-III™
Wechsler Intelligence Scale for Children–Third Edition

Name _____ Sex _____

School _____ Grade _____

Examiner _____ Handedness _____

Subtests	Raw Scores	Scaled Scores					
Picture Completion							
Information							
Coding							
Similarities							
Picture Arrangement							
Arithmetic							
Block Design							
Vocabulary							
Object Assembly							
Comprehension							
(Symbol Search)		( )					
(Digit Span)	( )						
(Mazes)		( )					
Sum of Scaled Scores		Verbal	Perfor.	VC	PO	FD	PS
		Full Scale Score		OPTIONAL			

	Year	Month	Day
Date Tested			
Date of Birth			
Age			

	Score	IQ/Index	%ile	___% Confidence Interval
Verbal				–
Performance				–
Full Scale				–
VC				–
PO				–
FD				–
PS				–

Subtest Scores

	Verbal						Performance						
	Inf	Sim	Ari	Voc	Com	DS	PC	Cd	PA	BD	OA	SS	Mz
19	•	•	•	•	•	•	•	•	•	•	•	•	•
18	•	•	•	•	•	•	•	•	•	•	•	•	•
17	•	•	•	•	•	•	•	•	•	•	•	•	•
16	•	•	•	•	•	•	•	•	•	•	•	•	•
15	•	•	•	•	•	•	•	•	•	•	•	•	•
14	•	•	•	•	•	•	•	•	•	•	•	•	•
13	•	•	•	•	•	•	•	•	•	•	•	•	•
12	•	•	•	•	•	•	•	•	•	•	•	•	•
11	•	•	•	•	•	•	•	•	•	•	•	•	•
10	•	•	•	•	•	•	•	•	•	•	•	•	•
9	•	•	•	•	•	•	•	•	•	•	•	•	•
8	•	•	•	•	•	•	•	•	•	•	•	•	•
7	•	•	•	•	•	•	•	•	•	•	•	•	•
6	•	•	•	•	•	•	•	•	•	•	•	•	•
5	•	•	•	•	•	•	•	•	•	•	•	•	•
4	•	•	•	•	•	•	•	•	•	•	•	•	•
3	•	•	•	•	•	•	•	•	•	•	•	•	•
2	•	•	•	•	•	•	•	•	•	•	•	•	•
1	•	•	•	•	•	•	•	•	•	•	•	•	•

IQ Scores   Index Scores (Optional)

VIQ	PIQ	FSIQ	VCI	POI	FDI	PSI

160
150
140
130
120
110
100
90
80
70
60
50
40

09-980004

Figure I-3.   Cover page of WISC-III Record Form. Copyright © 1971, 1974, 1991 by The Psychological Corporation, San Antonio, TX. All Rights Reserved.

1055

■ **Exhibit I-2** ■

Supplementary Instructions for Administering the WISC-III

1. Study and practice administering the test before you give it to a child to fulfill a class assignment.

2. Organize your test materials before the child comes into the room. Make sure that all test materials—including stimulus booklets, blocks, cards, puzzle pieces, Record Form, stop watch, and pencils—are in the kit. Arrange the Picture Arrangement cards in numerical sequence. Have extra blank paper to make notes if needed.

3. Complete the top of the Record Form (examinee's name, sex, school, grade, examiner, and handedness).

4. Enter the date tested and date of birth, calculate the chronological age (CA), and put it in the box provided. Months are considered to have 30 days for testing purposes. Check the chronological age by adding the chronological age to the date of birth to obtain the date of testing.

5. Administer the subtests in the order presented in the manual, except in rare circumstances. Do not change the wording on any subtest. Read the directions exactly as shown in the manual. Do not ad lib.

6. Start with the appropriate item on each subtest and follow discontinuance criteria. You must know the scoring criteria *before* you give the test.

7. Write down verbatim all of the child's responses that are pertinent to the test, testing situation, or referral question or are otherwise helpful in understanding the child. Write clearly and do not use unusual abbreviations. Record time accurately in the spaces provided in the Record Form.

8. Question all ambiguous or unscorable responses, writing a (Q) after each questioned response. Question all responses when a (Q) follows the response in the WISC-III manual.

9. Introduce the test by saying something like "We will be doing lots of different things today. Some will be easy and some will be hard. I'd like you to do the best you can. OK?" Make eye contact with the child from time to time, and use the child's first name when possible. Watch for signs that the child needs a break (for example, a stretch, a drink, or a trip to the bathroom). Between subtests say something like "Now we'll do something different." At the end of the test, thank the child for coming and for being cooperative (if appropriate).

10. On Information item 8, if the child first says "5," ask "How many counting the weekend?" If the child then says "2," ask "How many altogether, all week?"

11. On Arithmetic, you may repeat an item only once.

12. On Comprehension, the Record Form is marked with an asterisk next to those items that require you to ask for a second response.

13. On Digits Forward and Digits Backward, always administer both trials of each series. Read the digits at the rate of one per second and at an even pace—that is, no chunking—and drop your voice inflection slightly on the last digit in the sequence.

14. On Picture Completion, place the Stimulus Booklet flat on the table close to the child. Note that the time limit is 20 seconds. If you are not sure whether the child's verbal response is correct, say "Show me where you mean." You must know the cautions (top of page 61 in the WISC-III manual) and when to use them. On item 29, give credit to "rib" or "spoke" (personal communication, Lawrence Weiss, The Psychological Corporation, September 1991). Although the letters are missing on the buttons of the telephone (item 23), The Psychological Corporation advised that you not give credit to a response mentioning this omission because it is an unessential missing part (personal communication, Lawrence Weiss, The Psychological Corporation, January 1992). If this is the first unessential missing part mentioned by the child, say "Yes, but what is the most important part that is missing?" The child can turn the pages of the test booklet if you are sure that he or she will allow you to set the pace.

15. On Picture Arrangement, when you are doing the sample, move each card down to a new row rather than shifting the cards within their original row. Place the cards at least 3 or 4 inches away from the edge of the table.

16. On Block Design, when you demonstrate the samples, put them together slowly. Be careful not to cover the blocks with your hand; the child needs to see what you are doing. Make the designs so that they are in the appropriate direction for the child. This means that you will be making the designs upside down. Don't make a design right side up and then turn the whole thing around to face the child.

17. On Symbol Search, only items that have been attempted within 120 seconds are counted as correct or incorrect (personal communication, Lawrence Weiss, The Psychological Corporation, January 1992).

18. To facilitate the scoring of the Coding subtest, write at the end of each row of the Coding scoring template the cumulative total number of symbols up to and including that row. For the Coding A template, the numbers that should be written at the ends of rows 1 through 8, respectively, are 3, 11, 19, 27, 35, 43, 51, and 59. On the Coding B template, the cumulative totals are 14, 35, 56, 77, 98, and 119; these numbers should be written at the ends of the first through sixth rows. After you write the numbers, laminate the template to prolong its life (cf. Danielson, 1991). (In January 1992, Aurelio Prifitera, from The Psychological Corporation, informed me that the second printing of the templates will include these numbers.)

19. On subtests that receive bonus points for speed, make

(Exhibit continues next page)

Exhibit I-2 (cont.)

sure that the score you circle on the Record Form corresponds to the time taken by the child to complete the item. In no case give bonus points for 0-point answers.

20. Keep materials, other than those needed for the test, off the table (for example, soda cans, pocketbook, and keys).

21. Carefully score each protocol and recheck your scoring. If you failed to question a response when you should have and the response is obviously not a 0 response, give the child the most appropriate score based on the child's actual response.

22. If a subtest was spoiled, write *spoiled* by the subtest total score and on the front cover of the Record Form next to the name of the subtest. If the subtest was not administered, write *NA* in the margin of the Record Form next to the subtest name and on the front of the Record Form.

23. Add the raw scores for each subtest carefully. Make sure that you give credit for items not administered below the starting-point items. Be sure to add correctly the points associated with the circled numbers on the Record Form for all subtests that have bonus points.

24. Transfer subtest scores to the front of the Record Form under Raw Scores. After transferring all raw scores to the front page of the Record Form, check to see that the raw scores on the front page match those noted inside the Record Form for each subtest.

25. Transform raw scores into scaled scores by using Table A.1 on pages 217 to 249 of the WISC-III manual. Be sure to use the page of Table A.1 that is appropriate for the child's age and the correct row and column for each transformation.

26. Add the scaled scores for the five standard Verbal subtests to compute the sum of the scaled scores. Do not use Digit Span to compute the Verbal score unless you have substituted it for another Verbal subtest. Add the scaled scores for the five standard Performance subtests. Do not include Symbol Search or Mazes to compute the Performance score unless you have substituted Symbol Search for Coding or Mazes for another Performance subtest. You can include both Mazes and Symbol Search to compute the Performance score if you have substituted Symbol Search for Coding and Mazes for some other Performance subtest. Sum the Verbal and the Performance subtest scaled scores to obtain the sum for the Full Scale. Recheck all of your additions.

27. Convert the sums of scaled scores for the Verbal, Performance, and Full Scales by use of the appropriate conversion tables in Appendix A (pages 251 to 254) in the WISC-III manual. Use Table A.2 for the Verbal Scale, Table A.3 for the Performance Scale, and Table A.4 for the Full Scale. Be sure to use the correct table for the appropriate scale. Record the IQs on the front of the Record Form.

28. Recheck all of your work. If the IQ was obtained by use

of a short form, write *SF* beside the appropriate IQ. If IQs were prorated, write *PRO* beside each appropriate IQ.

29. If fewer than five subtests were administered in the Verbal section or fewer than five subtests in the Performance section, use the Tellegen and Briggs short-form procedure described on page 138 of this text to compute the IQ. This procedure is the most reliable one for prorating IQs. You can also consult Table L-12, L-13, L-14, or L-15. These tables provide estimated Full Scale Deviation Quotients for several combinations of short forms based on the Tellegen and Briggs procedure.

30. Make a profile of the examinee's scaled scores on the front of the Record Form by plotting the scores on the graph provided.

31. Look up the confidence intervals for the Full Scale IQ, Verbal Scale IQ, and Performance Scale IQ in Table L-1 or L-2 in Appendix L of this text. Use Table L-1, unless you are making a long-term prediction; in that case use Table L-2. All confidence intervals in Tables L-1 and L-2 are based on the examinee's exact age group as well as on the total sample. Normally, the confidence intervals are not used with the Verbal or Performance IQs, unless these are the only IQs reported. Write the confidence intervals on the front cover of the Record Form in the space provided.

32. Look up the percentile rank and classification for each of the IQs in Tables BC-1 and BC-2 on the inside back cover of this text. You can also use Tables A.2, A.3, and A.4 (pages 251 to 254) in the WISC-III manual for the percentile ranks and Table 2.8 (page 32 in the WISC-III manual) for classifications.

33. If you want to obtain test-age equivalents, use Table A.9 on page 259 of the WISC-III manual. They can be placed (in parentheses) in the right margin of the box that contains the scaled scores. For test-age equivalents *above* those in the table, use the highest test-age equivalent and a plus sign. For test-age equivalents *below* those in the table, use the lowest test-age equivalent and a minus sign.

34. If you want to, you can enter the factor scores on the front cover of the Record Form. The Deviation Quotients associated with the factor scores advocated in this text can be obtained from Tables A.5 and A.7 in the WISC-III manual for Verbal Comprehension and Processing Speed, respectively, and from Table L-13 in Appendix L for Perceptual Organization.

35. In summary, read the directions verbatim, pronounce words clearly, query at the appropriate times, start with the appropriate item, discontinue at the proper place, place items properly before the child, use correct timing, and follow the specific guidelines in the manual for administering the test.

■ Exhibit I-3

Administrative Checklist for the WISC-III

ADMINISTRATIVE CHECKLIST FOR THE WISC-III

Name of examiner: _____   *Date:* _____

Name of examinee: _____   *Name of observer:* _____

(Note. *If an item is not applicable, mark NA to the left of the number.*)

Picture Completion   *Circle One*

1. Reads directions verbatim   Yes   No
2. Reads directions clearly   Yes   No
3. Pronounces words in queries clearly   Yes   No
4. Starts with appropriate item   Yes   No
5. Places booklet flat on table, close to child   Yes   No
6. Begins timing after last word of instructions   Yes   No
7. Gives a maximum of 20 seconds on each item   Yes   No
8. Gives correct answer for sample item and items 1 and 2 if child fails these items   Yes   No
9. Does not give correct answer on items 3–30   Yes   No
10. Gives the prompt "Yes, but what's missing?" no more than one time   Yes   No
11. Gives the prompt "A part is missing in the picture. What is it that is missing?" no more than one time   Yes   No
12. Gives the prompt "Yes, but what is the most important part that is missing" no more than one time   Yes   No
13. Inquires correctly on items 6, 13, 21, 23, 26, and 28 when certain responses are given   Yes   No
14. Gives credit to correct responses made after the prompt   Yes   No
15. Administers items in reverse order, when the first or second item administered is failed, to children ages 8 to 16 until they pass two consecutive items   Yes   No
16. Gives credit to items not administered when those items precede two consecutive successes   Yes   No
17. Gives credit for a correct oral or pointing response   Yes   No
18. Gives 1 point credit for each correct response   Yes   No
19. Gives no credit for correct responses given after time limit   Yes   No
20. Records 0 or 1 point for each item   Yes   No
21. Discontinues subtest after 5 consecutive failures   Yes   No

Picture Completion (cont.)   *Circle One*

22. Adds points correctly   Yes   No

Comments: _____

_____

Information

1. Reads directions verbatim   Yes   No
2. Reads directions clearly   Yes   No
3. Reads items verbatim and clearly   Yes   No
4. Starts with appropriate item   Yes   No
5. Gives sufficient time for child to respond to each question   Yes   No
6. Gives correct answer for item 1 if child fails item   Yes   No
7. Does not give correct answer for items 2–30   Yes   No
8. Says "Explain what you mean" or "Tell me more about it" for responses that are not clear   Yes   No
9. Gives prompts when the child's response suggests that the child has misheard or misunderstood the exact meaning of the question   Yes   No
10. Repeats question if child says he (she) does not understand it   Yes   No
11. Inquires correctly on items 4, 8, 16, 18, 19, 21, 24, 26, 28, 29, 30 when certain responses are given   Yes   No
12. Gives credit to correct responses made after the prompt (or inquiry)   Yes   No
13. Administers items in reverse order, when the first or second item administered is failed, to children ages 8 to 16 until they pass two consecutive items   Yes   No
14. Does not ask leading questions or spell words   Yes   No
15. Gives credit to items not administered when those items precede two consecutive successes   Yes   No
16. Gives 1 point credit for each correct response   Yes   No

(Exhibit continues next page)

Exhibit I-3 (cont.)

Information (cont.)   *Circle One*

17. Records 0 or 1 point for each item   Yes   No
18. Discontinues subtest after 5 consecutive
    failures   Yes   No
19. Adds points correctly   Yes   No

Comments: _____

_____

Coding

1. Reads directions verbatim   Yes   No
2. Reads directions clearly   Yes   No
3. Correctly selects either Coding A or B   Yes   No
4. Provides two no. 2 graphite pencils
   without erasers   Yes   No
5. Removes Coding Response Sheet from the
   Record Form   Yes   No
6. Provides a smooth work surface   Yes   No
7. Provides extra Coding Response Sheet for
   left-handed children   Yes   No
8. Points to the key while reading the first
   part of the instructions   Yes   No
9. Points to the proper forms (e.g., star, ball,
   triangle, circle, box with two lines) while
   reading instructions   Yes   No
10. Follows directions in manual for pointing
    to sample items while reading directions Yes   No
11. Praises child's successes on each sample
    item by saying "yes" or "right"   Yes   No
12. Corrects child's mistakes on sample items Yes   No
13. Does not begin subtest until child clearly
    understands the task   Yes   No
14. Gives proper instructions after child
    completes the sample items and
    understands the task   Yes   No
15. Provides proper caution the first time child
    omits item or does only one type: "Do
    them in order. Don't skip any." Then points
    to the next item and says "Do this one
    next."   Yes   No
16. Gives caution about omitting or skipping
    item only one time   Yes   No
17. Reminds child to continue until told to stop
    (when needed)   Yes   No
18. Does not time the sample items   Yes   No
19. Begins timing immediately after
    completing instructions   Yes   No
20. Allows 120 seconds   Yes   No
21. Records time accurately   Yes   No
22. Uses scoring stencil to score subtest   Yes   No

Coding (cont.)   *Circle One*

23. Places a mark through each incorrect box Yes   No
24. Adds number of correct boxes or subtracts
    number of incorrect boxes from number
    attempted   Yes   No
25. Gives time-bonus credits appropriately on
    Coding A   Yes   No
26. Gives no time-bonus credits on Coding B Yes   No
27. Records correct number of items   Yes   No

Comments: _____

_____

Similarities

1. Reads directions verbatim   Yes   No
2. Reads directions clearly   Yes   No
3. Reads items verbatim and clearly   Yes   No
4. Begins with sample item and then item 1,
   regardless of child's age   Yes   No
5. Gives sufficient time for child to respond to
   each question   Yes   No
6. Gives correct answer for items 1 and 2 if
   child fails items   Yes   No
7. Does not give correct answer for items
   3–19   Yes   No
8. Gives an example of a 2-point response
   if a 1-point response is given on item 6 or
   item 7   Yes   No
9. Queries every response followed in the
   WISC-III manual by a (Q), even if it is a
   0-point response   Yes   No
10. Queries vague responses   Yes   No
11. Says "Explain what you mean" or "Tell me
    more about it" and no other statement to
    query a response   Yes   No
12. Does not query a clearcut response,
    especially one that is not followed in the
    WISC-III manual by a (Q)   Yes   No
13. Asks "Now which one is it?" each time a
    child's response contains both a correct and
    an incorrect answer   Yes   No
14. Gives 1 point credit for each correct
    response to items 1–5   Yes   No
15. Gives 1 or 2 points credit for each correct
    response to items 6–19   Yes   No
16. Records 0, 1, or 2 points as appropriate Yes   No
17. Discontinues after 4 consecutive failures Yes   No
18. Adds points correctly   Yes   No

Comments: _____

_____

(Exhibit continues next page)

Exhibit I-3 (cont.)

Picture Arrangement	Circle One		Arithmetic	Circle One	
1. Reads directions verbatim	Yes	No	1. Reads items verbatim	Yes	No
2. Reads directions clearly	Yes	No	2. Reads items clearly	Yes	No
3. Gives sample item to all children and then item 1 to children aged 6–8 or item 3 to children aged 9–16	Yes	No	3. Starts with appropriate item	Yes	No
			4. Places booklet properly in front of child for items 1–5 and for items 19–24	Yes	No
4. Has cards arranged in numerical sequence and places all cards in correct numerical order from child's left to child's right	Yes	No	5. Uses correct timing	Yes	No
			6. Gives correct answer for items 1 and 2 if child fails items	Yes	No
5. Rearranges sample item in correct order by moving cards one at a time to a new row and then points to each card as story is told	Yes	No	7. Does not give correct answer for items 3–24	Yes	No
			8. Explains the concept of "cover up" without using card for demonstration if child does not understand it on item 3	Yes	No
6. Allows child 10 seconds to look at correct arrangement on sample item	Yes	No	9. Does not allow child to use pencil and paper	Yes	No
7. Begins timing after last word of instructions	Yes	No	10. Allows child to use a finger to "write" on the table	Yes	No
8. Records time in the Record Form	Yes	No			
9. Stops timing when child is obviously finished with each arrangement	Yes	No	11. Administers items in reverse order, when the first or second item administered is failed, to children ages 7 to 16 until they pass two consecutive items	Yes	No
10. Gives a second trial when child fails first trial on items 1–2	Yes	No			
11. Does not give a second trial on items 1–2 when child passes first trial	Yes	No	12. Reads items 19–24 aloud to children who have visual problems or reading difficulties	Yes	No
12. Does not give a second trial on items 4–14	Yes	No	13. Records the exact amount of time taken to solve each problem	Yes	No
13. Uses correct time limits	Yes	No			
14. Gives 2 points credit for each correct response given to items 1 and 2 on first trial or 1 point credit for each correct response given on second trial	Yes	No	14. Begins timing immediately after each problem has been read	Yes	No
			15. Repeats a problem only once	Yes	No
15. Administers items 1 and 2 in that sequence if children between ages 9 and 16 fail item 3	Yes	No	16. Records time from the ending of the first reading of problem to when the response is made, even when problem is read again	Yes	No
16. Allows child to continue working on arrangement after time limit has expired when child is nearing completion of task	Yes	No	17. Asks child to select one of two responses when it is not clear which response is the final choice by saying "You said _____ and you said _____. Which one do you mean?"	Yes	No
17. Records the exact amount of time taken to solve item	Yes	No			
18. Records child's exact arrangement (in letters) in Record Form	Yes	No	18. Gives no credit for correct responses given after time limit	Yes	No
19. Gives correct number of points credit, including time-bonus credit, for items 3–14	Yes	No	19. Gives 1 point credit for each correct response on items 1–18	Yes	No
20. Gives no time-bonus credit to WODAHS arrangement for item 14	Yes	No	20. Gives 2 points credit for each correct response given between 1 and 10 seconds on items 19–24	Yes	No
21. Discontinues after 3 consecutive failures	Yes	No	21. Gives credit for correct numerical quantity even when unit is not given	Yes	No
22. Adds points correctly	Yes	No			
			22. Gives credit when child spontaneously corrects an incorrect response within time limit	Yes	No
Comments: _____			23. Records 0, 1, or 2 points as appropriate	Yes	No
_____					

(Exhibit continues next page)

Exhibit I-3 (cont.)

Arithmetic (cont.)	Circle One
24. Discontinues after 3 consecutive failures	Yes No
25. Adds points correctly	Yes No

Comments: _____

_____

Block Design

	Circle One
1. Reads directions verbatim	Yes No
2. Reads directions clearly	Yes No
3. Turns blocks slowly to show different sides as instructions are read	Yes No
4. Starts with appropriate item	Yes No
5. Places blocks and cards properly	Yes No
6. Constructs model or places Stimulus Booklet approximately 7 inches from the child's edge of the table	Yes No
7. Places model or Stimulus Booklet somewhat to the left of the child's midline for right-handed children and somewhat to the right of midline for left-handed children	Yes No
8. Constructs designs 1 and 2 properly	Yes No
9. Presents pictures in the Stimulus Book with the unbound edge toward the child	Yes No
10. Lays out blocks so that different colored surfaces face up on different blocks	Yes No
11. Lays out blocks so that only one block has a red-and-white side facing up for the two- and four-block designs and only two blocks have a red-and-white side facing up for the nine-block designs	Yes No
12. Scrambles blocks between designs	Yes No
13. Begins timing after the last word of instructions	Yes No
14. Records time in the Record Form	Yes No
15. Uses correct time limits	Yes No
16. Stops timing when child is obviously finished with design (except for items 1–3)	Yes No
17. Allows child to continue working on design after time limit when child is nearing completion of task	Yes No
18. Gives a second trial when child fails first trial on items 1–3	Yes No
19. Does not give second trial on items 4–9	Yes No
20. Uses the correct number of blocks for each item	Yes No
21. Says "But, you see, the blocks go this way" and corrects the child's design the first time child rotates a design	Yes No
22. Gives instructions about need to correct a rotated design only once during the test	Yes No

Block Design (cont.)	Circle One
23. Uses the appropriate instructions for item 3 depending on whether the child started the subtest with item 1 or 3	Yes No
24. Gives 2 points when child gets items 1–3 correct on the first trial	Yes No
25. Gives 1 point when child gets items 1–3 correct on the second trial	Yes No
26. Gives correct number of points, including time-bonus credits, for items 4–12	Yes No
27. Gives no credit for correct responses given after time limit	Yes No
28. Circles on the Record Form a Y (Yes) or N (No) for each item	Yes No
29. Stops child on items 1–3 when time limit has expired on first trial and gives second trial	Yes No
30. Records the exact amount of time taken to solve each item	Yes No
31. Administers items 1 and 2 in normal sequence, when the first or second trial of item 3 is failed, to children ages 8 to 16	Yes No
32. Begins the directions for item 1 by assembling the model when child fails either the first or the second trial of item 3	Yes No
33. Records 0–7 points as appropriate	Yes No
34. Discontinues subtest after 2 consecutive failures	Yes No
35. Adds points correctly	Yes No

Comments: _____

_____

Vocabulary

	Circle One
1. Reads directions verbatim	Yes No
2. Reads directions clearly	Yes No
3. Pronounces words clearly	Yes No
4. Starts with appropriate item	Yes No
5. Gives sufficient time for child to respond to each word	Yes No
6. Queries every response followed in the WISC-III manual by a (Q), even if it is a 0-point response	Yes No
7. Queries vague responses	Yes No
8. Does not query a clearcut response, especially one that is not followed in the WISC-III manual by a (Q)	Yes No
9. Gives the 2-point answer for item 1 if child gives a 0- or 1-point response	Yes No
10. Does not give correct answers for items 2–30 if child misses items	Yes No
11. Does not give credit to a pointing response	Yes No

(Exhibit continues next page)

Exhibit I-3 (cont.)

Vocabulary (cont.)   *Circle One*

12.	Uses "Listen carefully" prompt for misheard words	Yes No
13.	Does not spell any words	Yes No
14.	Gives credit to items not administered when those items precede perfect (2 point) scores on the first two items administered to children ages 9 to 16	Yes No
15.	Administers items in reverse order, when the child fails or gives a 1-point response to first or second item administered, to children ages 9 to 16 until they obtain perfect (2 point) scores on two consecutive items	Yes No
16.	Inquires about vague responses, regionalisms, or slang responses	Yes No
17.	Gives 1 or 2 points credit for each correct response	Yes No
18.	Records 0, 1, or 2 points as appropriate	Yes No
19.	Discontinues after 4 consecutive failures	Yes No
20.	Adds points correctly	Yes No

Comments: _____

_____

Object Assembly

1.	Reads directions verbatim	Yes No
2.	Reads directions clearly	Yes No
3.	Starts with sample item	Yes No
4.	Administers all items	Yes No
5.	Uses shield correctly	Yes No
6.	Presents puzzles with pieces arranged properly	Yes No
7.	Begins timing immediately after last word of instructions	Yes No
8.	Stops timing when child is obviously through	Yes No
9.	Records time accurately	Yes No
10.	Records number of junctures correctly completed within time limit	Yes No
11.	Gives no credit for correct responses given after time limit	Yes No
12.	Gives 10-second exposure after assembling sample item (apple)	Yes No
13.	Demonstrates correct arrangement on item 1 (girl) if child's assembly is incomplete	Yes No
14.	Does not demonstrate correct arrangement on items 2–5 even if child's arrangements are incomplete	Yes No
15.	Does not give name of object for items 3–5	Yes No
16.	Records 0–10 points as appropriate	Yes No
17.	Gives proper time-bonus credit	Yes No

Object Assembly (cont.)   *Circle One*

18.	Adds points correctly	Yes No

Comments: _____

_____

Comprehension

1.	Reads items verbatim	Yes No
2.	Reads items clearly	Yes No
3.	Begins with item 1 for all children	Yes No
4.	Repeats question if child has difficulty remembering it or has not responded after 10–15 seconds	Yes No
5.	Encourages a hesitant child to speak	Yes No
6.	Queries every response followed in the WISC-III manual by a (Q), even if it is a 0-point response	Yes No
7.	Queries vague responses	Yes No
8.	Does not query a clearcut response, especially one that is not followed in the WISC-III manual by a (Q)	Yes No
9.	Gives a few 2-point answers to item 1 if child gives a 0- or 1-point response	Yes No
10.	Does not give correct answers to items 2–18 if child fails or does not give a 2-point response	Yes No
11.	Prompts for second response on items 2, 6, 7, 11, 12, 15, 17, and 18, and only when first response is right	Yes No
12.	Prompts for a second response only *once* per designated item	Yes No
13.	Records 0, 1, or 2 points as appropriate	Yes No
14.	Discontinues after 3 consecutive failures	Yes No
15.	Adds points correctly	Yes No

Comments: _____

_____

Symbol Search

1.	Reads directions verbatim	Yes No
2.	Reads directions clearly	Yes No
3.	Correctly selects either Part A or Part B	Yes No
4.	Provides two no. 2 graphite pencils without erasers	Yes No
5.	Proceeds with test items only when child understands the task	Yes No
6.	Points from child's left to right when giving instructions for sample item	Yes No
7.	Offers praise such as "Yes" or "Right" when child marks the correct answer for the two practice items	Yes No

(Exhibit continues next page)

Exhibit I-3 (cont.)

Symbol Search (cont.)   *Circle One*

8. Gives correct instructions when child fails practice item   Yes No
9. Opens booklet to page 2 after child completes practice items   Yes No
10. Points to correct part of booklet as instructions are read for subtest items   Yes No
11. Turns page briefly to show child third page of items   Yes No
12. Begins timing after completing instructions   Yes No
13. Reminds child, if needed, to go in order and to continue the task until told to stop   Yes No
14. Discontinues after 120 seconds   Yes No
15. Places a mark through each incorrect item   Yes No
16. Records number of correct and incorrect items properly   Yes No
17. Obtains score by subtracting number of incorrect from number of correct items attempted   Yes No

Comments: _____

_____

Digit Span

1. Begins with item 1   Yes No
2. Reads directions verbatim   Yes No
3. Reads directions clearly   Yes No
4. Administers both trials of each item   Yes No
5. Pronounces digits singly, distinctly, at the rate of one digit per second, and without chunking digits   Yes No
6. Drops voice inflection slightly on last digit Yes No
7. Pauses after each sequence to allow child to respond   Yes No
8. Gives sample item for Digits Backward   Yes No
9. Gives child the correct answer to sample item if child fails item on Digits Backward   Yes No
10. Gives both trials of each item for Digits Forward and for Digits Backward   Yes No
11. Discontinues Digits Forward after failure on both trials of any item and then gives Digits Backward   Yes No
12. Discontinues Digits Backward after failure on both trials of any item   Yes No
13. Gives 1 point for each trial passed   Yes No
14. Records successes and failures in Record Form   Yes No
15. Adds points correctly   Yes No

Comments: _____

_____

Mazes   *Circle One*

1. Reads directions verbatim   Yes No
2. Reads directions clearly   Yes No
3. Begins with appropriate item   Yes No
4. Provides two no. 2 graphite pencils without erasers   Yes No
5. Exposes sheet properly (with arrow pointed toward examiner)   Yes No
6. Folds Mazes Response Booklet so that only one page is exposed   Yes No
7. Provides a smooth work surface   Yes No
8. Demonstrates the correct solution if child fails Maze 1   Yes No
9. Demonstrates the correct solution if child fails Maze 2   Yes No
10. Gives credit for all preceding items if child aged 8–16 obtains a perfect score on Maze 4   Yes No
11. Administers Mazes 1–3 in normal sequence if child aged 8–16 obtains partial credit on Maze 4   Yes No
12. Demonstrates sample maze and administers Mazes 1–3 in normal sequence if child aged 8–16 fails Maze 4   Yes No
13. Begins timing after last word of instructions   Yes No
14. Records number of errors in the appropriate column in Record Form   Yes No
15. Uses "pencil point on paper" caution appropriately   Yes No
16. Uses "begins outside center of box" caution appropriately   Yes No
17. Uses "begins at the exit" caution appropriately   Yes No
18. Uses "don't stop" caution appropriately   Yes No
19. Uses "not allowed to start over" caution appropriately   Yes No
20. Uses "not completely clear the exit" caution appropriately   Yes No
21. Does examiner portion of sample appropriately   Yes No
22. Points to boy or girl figure in each maze as instructions are read   Yes No
23. Uses correct timing for each maze   Yes No
24. Records time accurately   Yes No
25. Discontinues after 2 consecutive failures   Yes No
26. Adds points correctly   Yes No

Comments: _____

_____

(Exhibit continues next page)

Exhibit I-3 (cont.)

Other Aspects of Test Administration	Circle One
1. Establishes rapport	Yes No
2. Is well organized	Yes No
3. Has all needed materials in kit	Yes No
4. Has extra paper and pencils	Yes No
5. Makes smooth transition from subtest to subtest	Yes No
6. Provides support between subtests as needed	Yes No
7. Focuses child's attention on tasks	Yes No
8. Handles mild behavior problems appropriately	Yes No
9. Makes the test experience positive	Yes No

Front Page of Record Form

	Circle One
1. Transfers raw scores to front page of Record Form for each subtest correctly	Yes No
2. Converts raw scores to scaled scores for each subtest correctly	Yes No
3. Adds scaled scores correctly for Verbal Scale	Yes No
4. Adds scaled scores correctly for Performance Scale	Yes No
5. Adds scaled scores correctly for Full Scale	Yes No
6. Converts sum of scaled scores in Verbal Scale to IQ correctly	Yes No

Front Page of Record Form (cont.)

	Circle One
7. Converts sum of scaled scores in Performance Scale to IQ correctly	Yes No
8. Converts sum of scaled scores in Full Scale to IQ correctly	Yes No
9. Completes profile of subtest scores correctly	Yes No
10. Completes identifying information section on front of Record Form correctly; assumes that all months have 30 days for purposes of calculating the chronological age; does not round up age (for example, 8 years–2 months–28 days is not rounded to 8 years, 3 months)	Yes No
11. Writes child's name, date, and examiner's name on Coding sheet and on Symbol Search and Mazes forms, if given	Yes No

Overall Assessment of Test Administration

Circle one: Excellent   Good   Average   Poor   Failing

Overall strengths: _____

Overall weaknesses: _____

Other comments: _____

_____

ferred to as a *basal level*) or discontinuance point (also referred to as a *ceiling level*), always err on the side of safety: *It is better to administer an item that may (or may not) be critical to a starting point or discontinuance point than to invalidate the subtest!*

If possible, make a videotape of your test administration and have a fellow student review it with you. Be alert to possible sources of error—both covert and overt—in your test administration and take appropriate steps to prevent these errors from occurring. Also check the Record Form to be sure that it is completed accurately. And, again, have a fellow student review the Record Form with you. In many training programs, your instructor or teaching assistant will give you feedback about your testing techniques. The key to proper test administration is to follow standard test procedures and to be an objective, but sensitive and supportive, examiner.

Following are some examples of how examiners were not sensitive to the child's needs or how they influenced the child's performance inappropriately (from Teglasi & Freeman, 1983, pp. 232–234, 239, with changes in wording and comments by me).

Example 1. Before administering the WISC-III, the examiner discussed with the child issues connected with the child's stealing. Later, when questioned on the Comprehension subtest about finding someone's wallet, the child looked distressed, but the examiner did not recognize the distress. *Comment.* Be sensitive to nonverbal cues as well as verbal ones. An alert examiner would have said something like "Now, this question has nothing to do with our previous discussion. This is one of the questions I ask everyone." An even more sensitive examiner may have waited to discuss the potentially emotionally arousing "stealing" issue until *after* the test was completed. You should always consider how any discussion may affect rapport.

Example 2. The examiner wanted to say something supportive to the examinee after the Digit Span subtest. *Examiner:* "Are you aware that you have a very good memory?" (Child obtained a low score on Digit Span.) *Child:* "No, I have a lousy one. I forget things all the time." *Comment.* Be sure that any reinforcing comments you make are congruent with the examinee's performance and given at appropriate times.

Example 3. The examiner watched a 10-year-old assemble the horse on the Object Assembly subtest, leaving one piece out. When the child said "finished," the examiner pointed to the extra piece. The child quickly corrected the error and was given full credit. *Comment.* Do not give nonverbal cues, such as the one in the example. They are not part of the standard procedure, and their use may invalidate the test results.

Example 4. Only when the child's arrangement on the Picture Arrangement subtest was correct did the examiner ask "finished?" If the child was still checking an incorrect sequence, the examiner was silent. The child soon caught on. *Comment.* Do not give verbal cues that may alert examinees to how well they are doing.

Example 5. The examiner, noting that a child had misplaced only one block in a complicated design on the Block Design subtest, said, "Be sure to check your answer." *Comment.* Do not ad lib directions, especially when your comments may help the examinee obtain higher scores. Stay as close to the directions in the manual as possible.

Subtest Sequence

Administer the subtests in the order specified in the manual unless you have a compelling reason to use another order. For example, a compelling reason might be giving a child who is extremely bored or frustrated a different subtest or a subtest of his or her choice to motivate him or her. Another reason might be giving a child with a sensory handicap selected subtests. Using the standard sequence of administration provides you with a baseline for evaluating children whom you will test in the future; it also represents an order comparable to that given by other examiners. Following the specified order in the WISC-III manual, which alternates nonverbal and verbal subtests, also may help to maintain the child's interest in the tasks.

The WISC-III manual states that "Picture Completion provides an engaging, nonthreatening task" (p. 14). However, for children who have difficulty with perceptual discrimination, Picture Completion may be neither engaging nor nonthreatening. Similarly, children with test anxiety may feel anxious when they start the test, regardless of what the first subtest is. Therefore, you must always carefully attend to the child's behavior, especially at the beginning of the test session. Do not assume that the order of the subtests will automatically reduce children's anxiety level or help them to feel relaxed. We need research to learn about how the order of administering the subtests affects children's anxiety level.

Scoring WISC-III Responses

You may find it difficult to score some responses on the Similarities, Vocabulary, and Comprehension subtests, especially those that are ambiguous. To become a skilled examiner, study carefully the scoring criteria, scoring guidelines, and scoring examples in the WISC-III manual. Although the WISC-III manual provides detailed scoring guidelines for each subtest, the sample responses in the manual simply cannot cover all possible responses that children will give. For this reason, you will have to use judgment in scoring responses.

Some examiners are more lenient than others in giving credit, and at times even the same examiners may not consistently adhere to their own relative standards. Thus, for example, they may be strict on some occasions and lenient on others. Studies have reported dramatic differences in the scoring standards of examiners. For example, in one study, 99 school psychologists gave IQs ranging from 63 to 117 to the *same* WISC protocol (Massey, 1964). In other studies with graduate-student examiners (Miller et al., 1970) and with members of the American Psychological Association (Miller & Chansky, 1972), examiners differed by as much as 17 points in scoring the same WISC protocol.

Starting-Point Scoring Rule

Occasionally, you may have doubts about whether the child passed items at the starting point. (The starting-point items are those that the child must pass before you continue with the subtest.) When this happens, you will need to administer earlier items in the subtest. The WISC-III manual does not provide any guidance in how to score items that the examinee fails *below* the starting point. The WISC-R manual, however, did provide such guidance: *If subsequent scoring of the items indicates that the early items were administered unnecessarily, give the child full credit for these items even if he or she earned only partial or no credit* (cf. Wechsler, 1974, page 59). I recommend that you follow the same procedure on the WISC-III. (Lawrence Weiss from The Psychological Corporation fully supports this recommendation; personal communication, October 1991.) This means that when the child fails one or more items *below* the starting point (or receives partial credit), give *full credit* to these items if further checking indicates that, in fact, the child correctly answered the items at the starting point. This rule usually applies to children aged 7 years and older because they may have starting points above the first item on certain subtests.

Here is an example of the starting-point scoring rule. You administer items 5 and 6 on the Information subtest to an 8-year-old child and are uncertain of how to score the responses. You then administer items 4 and 3, which the child clearly fails, and then items 2 and 1, which the child clearly passes. You follow this procedure because the directions for the subtest state that the child must pass two consecutive items before you administer the rest of the subtest. Because the child passed items 1 and 2, you continue giving the subtest with item 7. After the examination, you decide that the child did indeed pass items 5 and 6. The starting-point scoring rule requires that you give the child full credit for items 3 and 4, even though he or she failed them, because these two items are *below* the starting-point items 5 and 6, which the child passed.

The starting-point scoring rule favors the child by ensuring that you do not penalize him or her for failing items that, as it turned out, need not have been administered. The starting-point scoring rule is an attempt to maintain standardized scoring procedures.

Discontinuance-Point Scoring Rule

The discontinuance-point scoring rule applies to situations in which you have doubts about whether the child failed the items at the discontinuance point and you then administer additional items in the subtest (see page 43 of the WISC-III manual). (The discontinuance-point items are those that the child must fail before you discontinue the subtest.) The discontinuance-point scoring rule is as follows: *If subsequent scoring of the items indicates that the additional items were administered unnecessarily, do not give the child credit for items that he or she passed after the discontinuance point.*

Here is an example of the discontinuance-point scoring rule. You administer the first 15 words of the Vocabulary subtest, but are uncertain of how to score the child's responses to words 11 through 14. You then administer additional words. The child knows words 15 and 16 but not words 17 to 21. You therefore discontinue the subtest after word 21. After the test is over, you check your scoring and decide that the child's answers were wrong on words 11 to 14. The discontinuance-point scoring rule requires that you *not* give the child credit for words 15 and 16, even though the definitions were correct, because these words occur *after* you should have discontinued the subtest.

In contrast to the starting-point scoring rule, the discontinuance-point scoring rule does not favor the child. This scoring rule prevents the child from receiving credit on items that, as it turned out, need not have been administered. This rule constitutes another attempt to maintain standardized scoring procedures.

Repetition of Items

When a child says "I don't know," you must decide whether the response means that the child doesn't know the answer or that the child doesn't want to answer the question. If you decide that it is a motivational issue, encourage the child to attempt an answer. If necessary, repeat the question or ask it again at some later point—especially if the child says "I don't know" to an easy question. Better yet, the first time a child says "I don't know," say something like "I want you to try your hardest on each of these. Try your best to answer each question." Give the child credit if he or she answers the question correctly. However, never repeat items on Digit Span.

Use of Probing Questions and Queries

The sample response sections of the WISC-III manual indicate that you need to query certain responses. However, you will also need to query responses that are not shown in the manual. For example, negativistic or mistrustful responses, such as the following, can be acknowledged and then probed. If a child responded to the Comprehension question dealing with freedom of speech with "Freedom of speech is relative so that at times it is improper when it incites people," you could say "Well, try to give some answers that other people think are reasonable." You will have to be alert to recognize responses needing these kinds of probes. You will also need to probe verbal responses that are incomplete, indefinite, or vague. Ask additional questions (that is, use queries or probes) when you are unsure of how to score a response; however, do not ask additional questions to elicit a higher quality response from the child unless the WISC-III manual so indicates. For responses in the WISC-III manual followed by a "Q" in black, the examinee must give the response shown after the "Q" in order to get the appropriate credit. Consequently, the entire response—that is, the initial response plus the response to the query—receives the appropriate credit.

Spoiled Responses

An explicit scoring rule on the WISC-III is that you give a score of 0 to a spoiled response (see pages 50–51 in the WISC-III manual). A spoiled response is one that initially was partially right, but was spoiled by the child's incorrect elaboration on his or her initial response. For example, a child who says that *clock* means "Goes ticktock," and then says "It's the engine on a motorcycle," in response to a probe, has spoiled his or her response. This elaboration reveals the child's misconception about the meaning of the word *clock*.

Modifying Standard Procedures

Research with the WISC-R indicated that children are likely to obtain higher scores on some subtests when they are encouraged to talk about their problem-solving procedures, think about their answers before responding, explain their picture arrangements, or solve problems after receiving a series of cues (Herrell & Golland, 1969; Post, 1970; Sattler, 1969; Schwebel & Bernstein, 1970). We would expect similar results on the WISC-III. If you use such modifications, employ them only *after* the standard administration. Modifications may be helpful in clinical assessment of the child's potential for learning, but they may invalidate the scores if they are used during the standard administration.

Potential Administrative Problems on Arithmetic and Picture Arrangement

There can be subtle administration problems on the Arithmetic and Picture Arrangement subtests that may never arise, but are worth noting. On the Arithmetic subtest, children are requested to read problems 19 through 24. Because timing begins when children finish reading each of these problems, slow readers have more time to solve the problems than fast readers. Some children also may intentionally slow their reading in order to solve the problems before timing begins. What effect reading speed has on the speed of solving the problems is unknown. Because bonus points are awarded for speed on Arithmetic items 19 through 24, differences in reading speed and in problem-solving strategies may affect children's scores.

Another potential problem with Arithmetic is that some children may feel anxious when they read the problems aloud. If children do feel anxious, we do not know how their anxiety will affect their ability to solve the problems. And finally, there seems to be a subtle difference in administration when the examiner reads items 19 through 24 aloud to children who cannot read and when children read the problems aloud by themselves. In the former case, memory plays an important role because the children cannot "see" the questions. In the latter case, memory plays a smaller role because the children see the problems during the entire time that they work on them.

On Picture Arrangement, not all children receive the same type of help. All children start with the sample item,

which includes the story elements in the directions. Young children (6 to 8 years) are then administered items 1 and 2 and again are told the story elements as part of the directions. Older children (9 to 16 years), in contrast, are not given any story elements when they begin item 3. We do not know to what extent hearing the story elements on items 1 and 2 helps children on later items.

SHORT FORMS OF THE WISC-III

Examiners may use short forms of the WISC-III and other Wechsler scales as *screening devices* (when the short form may be followed by administering the remaining subtests), *for research purposes* (to describe the intellectual level of a group), and *for a quick check on a child's intellectual status* (and only when the IQ is peripheral to the referral question) (Silverstein, 1990b[R]). Ideally, you should select a short form based on such criteria as acceptable reliability and validity, the power of the short form to answer the referral question and provide clinically useful information, the examinee's physical capabilities, and the amount of time available for administering the test.

Researchers often evaluate the validity of short forms by correlating the short-form IQ with the Full Scale IQ, evaluating mean differences between the two IQs, and determining the extent of agreement in the intelligence classifications provided by the two IQs. Silverstein (1985a) argued, however, that these three criteria are not useful. First, it is virtually certain that there will be high correlations between short-form and Full Scale IQs. Second, with sufficiently large samples, a significant difference between long and short IQs is likely to occur, making this criterion nearly meaningless. Third, it is virtually certain that the short-form and Full Scale IQs will yield different classifications. [Goh (1978), for example, found that short-form WISC-R IQs misclassified 45 percent of a group of 142 children.] In light of the findings, Silverstein suggested that examiners use other considerations to determine the appropriateness of a short form. *If you must obtain a specific classification for a clinical or psychoeducational purpose, do not use a short form.*

Selecting the Short Form

Table L-11 in Appendix L shows the 10 best short-form combinations of two, three, four, and five WISC-III subtests. To obtain the reliability and validity coefficients shown in Table L-11, I used the standardization data and the Tellegen and Briggs (1967) procedure, which takes into account the reliabilities of the subtests used in the short form. (Exhibit I-4 shows the formulas used to compute the reliability and validity of the short-form combinations.) An inspection of the coefficients in Table L-11 indicates that all of the four- and five-subtest short-form combinations have reliability coefficients of .93 or higher. Even the three-subtest short-form combinations have reliabilities of .92 to .93. However, 6 of the 10 two-subtest short-form combinations have reliabilities below .90. Therefore, for the combinations shown in Table L-11, the more subtests used in the short form, the higher the reliability will be of the estimated IQ.

Because the reliabilities and validities of the various short forms are high, clinical considerations should also guide you in selecting the short form. For example, if you want to use a four-subtest short form, consider selecting a combination of two Verbal and two Performance Scale subtests, to obtain some representation of both verbal and performance skills in the short form.

An examinee's physical capabilities may also guide you in selecting a short form. Examinees with marked visual impairment or severe motor dysfunction of the upper extremities will have difficulty with Performance Scale tasks. In such cases, the Verbal Scale (or Verbal factor) serves as a useful short form. For hearing-impaired examinees, the Performance Scale (or Performance factor) alone is a useful short form. Administer these short forms by using the child's preferred mode of communication and supplement your evaluation by using other tests designed to accommodate the special physical abilities of the child (see Chapter 12).

Converting Short-Form Scores into Deviation Quotients

After you administer the short form, you will need to convert the child's scaled scores to a Full Scale IQ estimate. Simple prorating and regression procedures are not applicable in this case because they do not deal adequately with the problem of subtest reliability (Tellegen & Briggs, 1967). The more acceptable procedure is to transform the short-form scores into the familiar Wechsler-type Deviation Quotient, which has a mean of 100 and a standard deviation of 15. Exhibit I-4 shows the procedure for converting the short-form scores into a Deviation Quotient. This procedure holds for all Wechsler tests. Although this approach does not eliminate the many problems associated with short forms, it is statistically appropriate.

I used the Tellegen and Briggs (1967) procedure to obtain estimated WISC-III Deviation Quotients for the 10 best short-form dyads, triads, tetrads, and pentads (see Tables L-12, L-13, L-14, and L-15 in Appendix L, respectively).

The notes in Tables L-12, L-13, and L-14 also describe other short-form combinations, some of which are useful for screening hearing-impaired children.

Yudin's Abbreviated Procedure

In the Yudin (1966) WISC short-form procedure, which also applies to the WISC-III, you administer every other item on most subtests. Table C-11 of Appendix C describes the specific procedure, as modified by Silverstein (1968a). After the test is administered, scaled scores and IQs are obtained from the manual in the usual way. The Yudin procedure differs from other short-form procedures in that it uses all of the standard subtests. Its advantages are that you administer a representative sample of items, can apply profile analysis, and use about 56 percent of the items.

Although the Yudin procedure has satisfactory reliability (Reid, Moore, & Alexander, 1968; Yudin, 1966), it has shortcomings. These include a moderate loss of validity and reliability, less reliable profile data, and IQs that differ from those obtained on the Full Scale (Dean, 1977f; Erikson, 1967; Finch, Kendall, Spirito, Entin, Montgomery, & Schwartz, 1979; Gayton, Wilson, & Bernstein, 1970; Goh, 1978; Rasbury, Falgout, & Perry, 1978; Satz, Van de Riet, & Mogel, 1967; Tellegen & Briggs, 1967). Silverstein (1990a[R]) reported, for example, that the Yudin procedure yields a reliability coefficient of .905 for the WISC-R Full Scale IQ, whereas the best four-subtest short-form combination yields a reliability coefficient of .942. Silverstein concluded that "reducing the number of items within subtests rather than the number of subtests exacts a steep price in reliability" (p. 196). Consider carefully the assets and liabilities of the Yudin abbreviated procedure before you use it.

Hobby (1980) described a WISC-R short-form procedure, which you also can use with the WISC-III, in which you administer only odd items on most subtests. It is similar to the Yudin procedure, but has more specific basal and ceiling procedures and correction factors.

A major problem with reduced-item short forms that has not been addressed in the research literature is that they represent a violent departure from the standard administration (personal communication, Leslie Atkinson, January 1992). Because half of the items are excluded, the difficulty slope of the items increases much more rapidly than under standard conditions, while the opportunity for practice decreases equally rapidly. Research to date has involved administering the entire scale and generating validity coefficients for the relevant half. This situation is different from simply administering half of the items. For these reasons,

■ **Exhibit I-4**

Obtaining Deviation Quotients for Wechsler Short Forms

Computing the Deviation Quotient of the Short Form

The following formula is used to compute the Deviation Quotient for a short form:

$$\text{Deviation Quotient} = (15/S_c)(X_c - M_c) + 100$$

where
$S_c = S_s\sqrt{n + 2\Sigma r_{jk}}$ (standard deviation of composite score)

X_c = composite score (sum of subtest scaled scores in the short form)

M_c = normative mean, which is equal to $10n$

S_s = subtest standard deviation, which is equal to 3

n = number of component subtests

Σr_{jk} = sum of the correlations between component subtests.

This equation considers the number of subtests in the short form, the correlations between the subtests, and the total scaled-score points obtained on the short form.

A more straightforward computational formula for obtaining the Deviation Quotient is as follows:

$$\text{Deviation Quotient} = (\text{composite score} \times a) + b$$

where
$a = 15/S_c$
$b = 100 - n(150)/S_c$.

Table C-36 in Appendix C (page 850) can be used in obtaining the appropriate a and b constants. In using Table C-36, first select the heading corresponding to the number of subtests in the short form. The first column under each heading is Σr_{jk}. This term represents the sum of the correlations between the subtests making up the composite score. To obtain Σr_{jk}, use the WISC-III correlation table of the group closest in age to the examinee (Tables C.1 through C.12 on pages 270 through 281 of the WISC-III manual). With two subtests in the short form, only one correlation is needed. With three subtests in the short form, three correlations are summed (1 with 2, 1 with 3, and 2 with 3). With four subtests in the short form, six correlations are summed (1 with 2, 1 with 3, 1 with 4, 2 with 3, 2 with 4, and 3 with 4). With five subtests in the short form, 10 correlations are summed (1 with 2, 1 with 3, 1 with 4, 1 with 5, 2 with 3, 2 with 4, 2 with 5, 3 with 4, 3 with 5, and 4 with 5). After Σr_{jk} is calculated, the values for the two constants are obtained under the appropriate heading.

The procedure used to obtain the Deviation Quotient can be summarized as follows:

1. Sum the scaled scores of the subtests in the short form to obtain the composite score.
2. Sum the correlations between the subtests to obtain Σr_{jk}.
3. Find the appropriate a and b constants in Table C-36 in Appendix C (page 850) after Σr_{jk} has been obtained.
4. Compute the Deviation Quotient by using the composite score and the a and b constants.

Example: A three-subtest short form composed of the Arithmetic, Vocabulary, and Block Design subtests is administered to a 6-year-old child. The child obtains scaled scores of 7, 12, and 13 on the three subtests. The four steps are as follows:

1. The three scaled scores are summed to yield a composite score of 32.
2. The correlations between the three subtests are obtained from Table C.1 (page 270) of the WISC-III manual (Arithmetic and Vocabulary, .50; Arithmetic and Block Design, .51; Vocabulary and Block Design, .53). These are summed to yield 1.54 (Σr_{jk}).
3. The appropriate row in Table C-36 in Appendix C is the third one under the heading "3 Subtests." The values for the constants a and b are 2.0 and 40, respectively.
4. The formula

$$\text{Deviation Quotient} = (\text{composite score} \times a) + b$$

is used to obtain a Deviation Quotient of 104 $[(32 \times 2.0) + 40]$.

Computing the Reliability Coefficient of the Short Form

The following formula is used to obtain the reliability of the short form:

$$r_{ss} = \frac{\Sigma r_{ii} + 2\Sigma r_{ij}}{k + \Sigma 2r_{ij}}$$

where
r_{ss} = reliability of the short form
r_{ii} = reliability of subtest i
r_{ij} = correlation between any subtests i and j
k = number of component subtests.

Example: The reliability of the two-subtest combination of Vocabulary and Block Design is calculated in the following way, given r_{ii} (Vocabulary) = .87, r_{ii} (Block Design) = .87, and r_{ij} (Vocabulary and Block Design) = .46.

$$r_{ss} = \frac{1.74 + .92}{2 + .92} = \frac{2.66}{2.92} = .91$$

(Exhibit continues next page)

Exhibit I-4 (cont.)

Computing the Validity Coefficient of the Short Form

The following formula is used to obtain the validity of the short form:

$$r'_{pw} = \frac{\Sigma\Sigma r_{jl}}{\sqrt{k + 2\,\Sigma r_{ij}}\ \sqrt{t + 2\,\Sigma r_{lm}}}$$

where r'_{pw} = modified coefficient of correlation between the composite part and the composite whole

r_{jl} = correlation between any subtest j included in the part and any subtest l included in the whole, where any included correlation between a subtest and itself is represented by its reliability coefficient

r_{ij} = correlation between subtests i and j

r_{lm} = correlation between subtests l and m

k = number of component subtests

t = number of subtests included in the whole

To obtain $\Sigma\Sigma r_{jl}$, total the following three sums: (a) the sum of the reliabilities of the component subtests, (b) twice the sum of the intercorrelations among the component subtests ($2\Sigma r_{ij}$), and (c) the sum of the intercorrelations between any component subtest and any noncomponent subtest.

Example: The validity of the two-subtest combination of Vocabulary and Block Design is calculated in the following way, given r_{ii} (Vocabulary) = .87, r_{ii} (Block Design) = .87, and r_{ij} (Vocabulary and Block Design) = .46. In this example, all 13 WISC-III subtests are used. In other cases, only the 10 standard subtests may be used.

$$r'_{pw} = \frac{1.74 + .92 + 9.74}{\sqrt{2 + 2(.46)}\ \sqrt{13 + 2(28.91)}}$$

$$= \frac{12.40}{(1.71)(8.42)} = \frac{12.40}{14.40} = .86$$

Source: Adapted from Tellegen & Briggs (1967).

Atkinson recommended that reduced-item short forms not be used.

Vocabulary and Block Design Short Form

A popular screening short form consists of Vocabulary and Block Design. These two subtests have excellent reliability, correlate highly with the Full Scale over a wide age range, and are good measures of *g*. You can use Table L-12 in Appendix L to convert the sum of scaled scores on these two subtests directly to an estimated Deviation Quotient.

Information, Vocabulary, Picture Completion, and Block Design

This short-form combination, which contains two Verbal subtests and two Performance subtests, has high reliability (r_{tt} = .935). It takes longer to administer than the Vocabulary and Block Design short form, but provides more clinical and diagnostic information. You can use Table L-14 in Appendix L to convert the sum of scaled scores on these four subtests directly to an estimated Deviation Quotient.

Other Useful Short Forms

Other short forms discussed in the literature for the WISC-R, which you can also use for the WISC-III, are Similarities and Vocabulary (Fell & Fell, 1982); Similarities and Object Assembly (Fell & Fell, 1982); Similarities, Vocabulary, and Block Design (Karnes & Brown,

1981); Similarities, Vocabulary, Block Design, and Object Assembly (Karnes & Brown, 1981); Similarities, Vocabulary, Block Design, and Picture Completion (Clarizio & Veres, 1984); Similarities, Object Assembly, and Vocabulary (Dirks, Wessels, Quarforth, & Quenon, 1980); Information, Comprehension, Block Design, Picture Arrangement, and Coding (Kennedy & Elder, 1982); and Arithmetic, Vocabulary, Picture Arrangement, and Block Design (Kaufman, 1976b).

If you want to give a short form that you can administer quickly and score relatively easily, consider the following combinations (reliabilities shown in parentheses): two subtests—Information and Picture Completion (r_{xx} = .87); three subtests—Information, Similarities, and Picture Completion (r_{xx} = .91); four subtests—Information, Similarities, Picture Completion, and Object Assembly (r_{xx} = .91). These short forms, although they do not fall into the 10-best combinations, are effective as screening tools and have in their favor, as noted earlier, quick administration with a minimum of scoring problems. The four subtests have relatively high correlations with the Full Scale (*r*'s of .72, .72, .58, and .56, respectively). You can use Tables L-12, L-13, and L-14, respectively, to convert the sum of scaled scores on these combinations directly to an estimated Deviation Quotient. The footnotes at the bottom of these tables indicate which columns to use for these short-form combinations.

A word of caution is in order, however. Even though the Information and Picture Completion short form is more convenient in terms of time and scoring than Vocabulary and Block Design, you do not get any information about how the child copes with a less-structured task (Vocabulary) or uses problem-solving strategies (Block Design) when you use this short form. For the extra time involved, you will get more valuable clinical information by using Vocabulary and Block Design in a two-subtest short form (or in a longer short-form combination). I recommend that you consider using Vocabulary and Block Design in a short form if you need to use one.

Comment on Short Forms of the WISC-III (and Short Forms of Other Tests as Well)

Short forms save time and are useful screening devices, but they have many disadvantages. First, you usually obtain less stable IQs with short forms than you do with the full battery of subtests. Second, you lose information about cognitive patterning (that is, the pattern of strengths and weaknesses and the pattern of variability among subtest scores). Third, you lose the opportunity to observe the examinee's problem-solving methods over a range of situations. Fourth, you lose information about nonverbal ability when you administer short forms composed of Verbal subtests only, and you lose information about verbal ability when you administer short forms composed of Performance subtests only. Finally, the internal consistency reliability of the IQ is diminished when you eliminate subtests.

If you are thinking about using a short form, weigh the time saved against the validity lost. In addition, consider what kind of decision you will make on the basis of the short-form scores. The most efficient testing strategy for a particular situation will depend, in part, on the goal of the evaluation — whether it is for a general assessment of intelligence, classification, selection, or screening.

Even when you administer all of the subtests, the IQ you obtain on any intelligence tests is merely an *estimate* of the abilities possessed by a child. When you use a small number of subtests, the estimate may be far less adequate than that provided by the Full Scale. *Additionally, educational and clinical situations call for more, rather than less, extensive cognitive evaluation. Consequently, the Full Scale should be administered to maximize the diagnostic information you can obtain and to minimize placement errors. I encourage you to administer the Full Scale, unless there is some compelling reason to administer a short form.* Included among these reasons would be situations in which the child was ready to quit testing or the physical capabilities of the examinee made some of the subtests inappropriate. *I do not recommend short forms for any placement, educational, or clinical decision-making purpose.*

CHOOSING BETWEEN THE WISC-III AND THE WPPSI-R AND BETWEEN THE WISC-III AND THE WAIS-R

The WISC-III overlaps with the WPPSI-R for ages 6-0-0 to 7-3-15 and with the WAIS-R for ages 16-0-0 to 16-11-30. The overlap in ages between the WISC-III and the WPPSI-R and between the WISC-III and the WAIS-R is especially helpful in retest situations. For example, you can retest a child first administered the WISC-III at age 6 years with the WPPSI-R at any time during the next 15 months. Similarly, you can retest a 16-year-old adolescent who initially was given the WAIS-R with the WISC-III up until his or her seventeenth birthday. However, because the WISC-III and the WPPSI-R share many items in common, the two tests are not truly independent instruments.

In the overlapping age ranges, Atkinson (personal communication, January 1992) compared the WISC-III with the WPPSI-R and the WISC-III with the WAIS-R on several criteria, including mean subtest reliability, Full Scale reliability, mean subtest floor, mean subtest ceiling, item gradients (refers to number of items needed to reach the mean and the relationship of raw score points to scaled-score points), Full Scale floor, and Full Scale ceiling. His recommendations are discussed below.

WISC-III vs. WPPSI-R

Age considerations should be taken into account in evaluating the choice of either the WISC-III or WPPSI-R.

a. For *ages 6-0 to 6-11*, the WISC-III and WPPSI-R are comparable in all respects, except for measures of item gradients. Item gradient statistics suggest the following:

- *the WPPSI-R is a better choice for children with below-average ability*
- *the WISC-III is a better choice for children with above-average ability*
- *either test is adequate for children with average ability*

b. For *ages 7-0 to 7-3*, the WISC-III has superior subtest reliabilities, higher subtest ceilings, and better item gradients both above and below the mean. In other respects the two tests are comparable. Therefore,

- *the WISC-III is a better choice for all children at 7-0 to 7-3*

The following example illustrates how you can obtain a more thorough sampling on the WPPSI-R than on the WISC-III for a 6-year-old child with below-average ability. To obtain a scaled score of 5 on Information, a 6-year-child needs a raw score of 16 on the WPPSI-R, but only a raw score of 2 on the WISC-III.

Atkinson's recommendations are summarized in the following chart:

Recommendations for Selecting WISC-III or WPPSI-R

	Ability level		
Ages	Below average	Average	Above average
6-0 to 6-11	WPPSI-R	either test	WISC-III
7-0 to 7-3	WISC-III	WISC-III	WISC-III

These recommendations differ somewhat from those presented in the WISC-III manual. The WISC-III manual (page 8) recommends that in the overlapping ages you use the WISC-III for children with average or above-average ability and the WPPSI-R for children with below-average ability. I suggest that you follow Atkinson's recommendations.

WISC-III vs. WAIS-R

For ages 16-0 to 16-11, the WISC-III, in comparison to the WAIS-R, has better subtest reliabilities, lower subtest floors, better item gradients below the mean, a lower Full Scale IQ floor, and a higher Full Scale IQ ceiling. Therefore, Atkinson noted that

- the WISC-III is a better choice than the WAIS-R

Atkinson's recommendations are summarized in the following chart:

Recommendations for Selecting WISC-III or WAIS-R

	Ability level		
Ages	Below average	Average	Above average
16-0 to 16-11	WISC-III	WISC-III	WISC-III

The following example illustrates how you can obtain a more thorough sampling on the WISC-III than on the WAIS-R for a 16-year-, 8-month-old adolescent with below-average ability. On Information, to obtain a scaled score of 5, the adolescent needs a raw score of 14 on the WISC-III but only a raw score of 4 on the WAIS-R.

This recommendation differs from that presented in the WISC-III manual. The WISC-III manual recommends that you use the WISC-III for adolescents with below-average ability, but makes no recommendation for adolescents with

average or above-average ability. I suggest that you follow Atkinson's recommendations.

Comment on Choosing the WISC-III or WPPSI-R and WISC-III or WAIS-R

The previous recommendations were based on internal psychometric data. The issue of validity still needs to be addressed. In the final analysis, the choice of a test in the overlapping ages should depend on the validity of the inferences that you can make from scores on it. To this end, validity studies that compare the WISC-III with the WPPSI-R and the WISC-III with the WAIS-R in their overlapping age ranges, using samples of both normal and exceptional children, would be helpful.

ADMINISTERING THE WECHSLER TESTS TO HANDICAPPED CHILDREN

For handicapped children, you will need to evaluate the child's sensory-motor abilities before you administer one of the Wechsler tests. If you find that the child has a visual, hearing, or motor problem that may interfere with his or her ability to take one or more subtests, do not administer those subtests.

Table I-15 shows the physical abilities that an examinee needs to take a Wechsler test. Obviously, if you give the directions orally, the child must be able to hear what you say. On most of the Performance subtests, the child must be able to see the items and use his or her hands to solve the problems.

If you want to administer a Wechsler test to a child with a physical disability, you will need to administer the subtests without providing cues to the child. If your modifications go beyond simply permitting the child to respond in a different manner or using alternative procedures to present the items, the results may be invalid.

Verbal Scale Subtests

You can administer all of the Verbal Scale subtests orally to a child who can hear. If the child cannot hear but can read, you can type the Information, Comprehension, Similarities, and Vocabulary questions on cards and show the cards to the child one at a time. However, visually presenting the Arithmetic and Digit Span items poses more difficulties because of the time limits involved in the Arithmetic subtest and because visual presentation of the items seems drastically different from oral presentation, especially with Digit Span items. Therefore, you may have to omit Digit

Table I-I5
Physical Abilities Necessary and Adaptable for Subtests on the Wechsler Scales

Subtest	Physical ability			
	Vision	Hearing	Oral speech	Arm-hand use
Information	S	A	A	W
Comprehension	S	A	A	W
Arithmetic	S	A	A	W
Similarities	S	A	A	W
Vocabulary	S	A	A	W
Digit Span	N	R	A	W
Picture Completion	R	A	O	P or W
Coding, Digit Symbol	R	A	N	R
Picture Arrangement	R	A	O	A
Block Design	R	A	N	R
Object Assembly	R	A	N	R
Symbol Search	R	A	O	P or W
Mazes	R	A	N	R
Sentences	S	A	A	W
Animal Pegs	R	A	O	A
Geometric Design	R	A	N	R

Note. The code is as follows:

A—This ability is required for standard administration, but the subtest is adaptable.

N—This ability is not required.

O—Examinees who are able to speak can say their answers.

P—Examinees who are able to point can point to their answers.

R—This ability is required. Adaptation is not feasible if this function is absent or more than mildly impaired.

S—Examinees who are able to read can be shown the questions. If the examinee cannot read, hearing is necessary. If neither the ability to read nor the ability to hear is present, the subtest should not be administered.

W—Examinees who are able to write can write their answers.

Span when you test deaf children. If the child cannot respond orally, you can accept written replies (or those typed on a typewriter or computer) to any of the Verbal Scale subtests.

Performance Scale Subtests

Adaptations of the Performance Scale subtests center on the child's method of responding. You can give the Picture Completion subtest only to a child who has adequate vision and who can describe the missing part either orally or in writing (or typed on a typewriter or computer) or by pointing to it. You cannot easily adapt Block Design, Object Assembly, Coding, Digit Symbol (WAIS-R), Mazes, Animal Pegs (WPPSI-R), and Geometric Design (WPPSI-R) for a child whose arm-hand use is severely impaired. However, you can adapt the Picture Arrangement subtest for a child who has an arm-hand impairment. In this case, ask the child to tell you in what order he or she wants you to arrange the cards. This can be done orally or

by writing or typing. You can adapt Symbol Search by pointing to each item and having the child say (or type) whether the symbol is or is not in the array. Appendixes D and M provide detailed instructions for administering the Performance Scale subtests to a deaf child.

Advantages of Two Separate Scales

The division of the Wechsler subtests into Verbal and Performance Scales is helpful in testing handicapped children. You can administer the Verbal Scale to a blind child or to a child with severe motor handicaps. And you can administer the Performance Scale to a hearing-impaired child or to a child who has little or no speech. If you also administer the Verbal Scale to a hearing-impaired child, you can compare the child's performance on the Verbal and Performance Scales to evaluate the child's verbal deficit. *However, in such cases do not include the Verbal Scale in the computation of the IQ; only use the Performance Scale as the best estimate of the hearing-impaired child's intellectual ability.*

Unknown Effects of Modifications

Without empirical findings, there is no way of knowing how the suggested modifications affect the reliability and validity of the scores. Yet, when you cannot use standard procedures because handicaps prevent the child from comprehending the instructions or manipulating the materials, you may need to use such modifications. *When you use modifications, consider the resulting score only as an approximate estimate of the score that the child might obtain under standardized procedures.*

Timed Subtests

A study of the WISC-R indicated that speed of correct response on the WISC-R Picture Arrangement, Block Design, and Object Assembly subtests significantly relates to children's chronological age and to their problem-solving ability (Kaufman, 1979b). Older children solve the tasks more quickly than younger children, and those who solve the problems quickly also tend to solve more problems than those who solve them slowly. Because speed plays only a limited role in enabling children below 10 years of age to earn bonus points, it is reasonable to administer these subtests to 6- to 10-year-old orthopedically handicapped children who are able to manipulate the materials; you will not unduly penalize these children for failure to earn bonus points (Kaufman, 1979b). These findings likely hold for the WISC-III, although we need research before we can accept them without question.

ASSETS OF THE WISC-III

The WISC-III is a well-standardized test, with excellent reliability and adequate concurrent and construct validity. The 13 subtests are divided into a Verbal and Performance section, and the test provides a Verbal, Performance, and Full Scale IQ. The division into a Verbal and Performance section is especially helpful in clinical and psychoeducational work and aids in the assessment of brain-behavior relationships. A valuable feature of the test is that all children take a comparable battery of subtests. For children with sensory impairments, the Verbal Scale can be administered to blind children and the Performance Scale to deaf children. The following are assets of the WISC-III:

1. *Excellent standardization.* The standardization procedures were excellent, sampling four geographical regions, both sexes, White, Black, Hispanic, and other children, and the entire socioeconomic status range. The standardization group well represents the nation as a whole for the age groups covered by the test.

2. *Excellent overall psychometric properties.* The WISC-III has excellent reliability for the IQs generated by the Verbal, Performance, and Full Scales. The few studies available suggest that the WISC-III has adequate concurrent and construct validity, although we need more research to evaluate the validity of the latest edition of the test.

3. *Useful diagnostic information.* The WISC-III provides diagnostic information useful for the assessment of cognitive abilities of elementary- and high-school age children who are functioning within four standard deviations from the mean ($\pm 4\ SD$). It also furnishes data likely to be helpful in planning special school programs, perhaps tapping important developmental or maturational factors needed for school success, especially in the lower grades.

4. *Good administration procedures.* The procedures described in the WISC-III manual for administering the test are excellent. The examiner actively probes the child's responses to evaluate the breadth of the child's knowledge and determine whether the child really knows the answer. On items that require two reasons for maximum credit, examiners ask the child for another reason when he or she gives only one reason. These procedures ensure that the test does not penalize the child for failing to understand the demands of the questions. The emphasis on probing questions and queries is extremely desirable.

5. *Good manual and interesting test materials.* The WISC-III manual is easy to use; it provides clear directions and tables. Examiners are aided by instructions printed in a color that differs from that of other text material. The manual provides helpful abbreviations for recording the child's responses, such as "P" for Pass, "F" for Fail, "Q" for Query, "DK" for Don't Know, "NR" for No Response, "Inc." for Incomplete, and "R" for Rotation. The test materials are also interesting to children.

6. *Helpful scoring criteria.* Wechsler and The Psychological Corporation carefully prepared the criteria for scoring responses. The Similarities and Vocabulary scoring guidelines, for example, detail the rationale for 2-, 1-, and 0-point scores. Several examples demonstrate the application of the scoring principles. The scoring guidelines present several examples, and those thought to need further inquiry are indicated by a "Q."

7. *Extensive research and clinical literature.* There is a vast amount of research and case material on the WISC-R that you can use to interpret the WISC-III. However, the composition of the WISC-III differs from that of the WISC-R, particularly with regard to factor structure and subtest specificity. These differences mean that the interpretations used for the WISC-R may not always apply to the WISC-III. We also need research to evaluate the validity of hypotheses derived from the WISC-III.

LIMITATIONS OF THE WISC-III

Although the WISC-III is overall an excellent instrument, some problems do exist.

1. *Limited floor and ceiling.* The test is not applicable for severely retarded or extremely gifted children.

2. *Low reliability of individual subtests.* Reliability coefficients for the individual subtests are lower than .80 at most ages. In these cases, the scores may not be dependable. In addition, during the standardization of the scale, The Psychological Corporation did not obtain test-retest scores for the Coding and Symbol Search subtests for each age level of the test; therefore, we do not know the accuracy of the reliability estimates (based on adjacent ages) for the ages at which the two subtests were not readministered.

3. *Nonuniformity of subtest scaled scores.* Because the range of scaled scores on all subtests is less than 19 at some of the older ages, there may be some minor problems in profile analysis at the upper extremes of scores. All subtests, however, do have a range of 1 to 17 for all ages.

4. *Difficulty in interpreting norms when you substitute a supplementary subtest for a regular subtest.* With the norms based on only the 10 standard subtests, you have no way of knowing precisely what the scores mean when you substitute one of the supplementary subtests (Digit Span, Mazes, or Symbol Search) for a regular subtest. Make a substitution of this kind, therefore, only in unusual circumstances and label the results "tentative" when you report the scores.

5. *Possible difficulties in scoring responses.* Work with the WISC-R suggests that Similarities, Vocabulary, and Comprehension may be difficult to score. The WISC-III manual cites a study in which there was high agreement among examiners in the scores they gave to these subtests (and to the Mazes subtest as well). These results are encouraging, but researchers need to replicate them. I recommend that you consult colleagues when you are having trouble scoring responses.

6. *Large practice effects on the Performance Scale.* The large practice effects on the Performance Scale, close to 1 standard deviation, suggest that the WISC-III may give misleading scores in retest situations. This is especially so when the retest interval is less than 9 weeks. This means that the WISC-III may not be useful to gauge change and progress in children retested within a short time. (See pages 537 and 540 for further discussion of practice effects.) Carefully consider whether you want to use the WISC-III for a retest when you have previously given the test and what the retest results may mean if you use the test.

7. *Lack of independence.* At least 23 items overlap on the WISC-III and WPPSI-R, primarily on the Information, Vocabulary, Picture Completion, and Mazes subtests. This overlap is unfortunate for at least two reasons. First, it means that the WISC-III and WPPSI-R are not independent parallel forms at the overlapping age levels (6-0 to 7-3 years). Second, it means that children tested with the WPPSI-R and then with the WISC-III (or vice versa) have an advantage on the second test because of practice effects. On the next revision of either test, The Psychological Corporation should ensure that there are no overlapping items on the two tests.

8. *Problems for children who do not place a premium on speed.* Because many of the subtests place a premium on speed (all Performance Scale subtests and Arithmetic), the test may penalize children who are from a minority group that does not place a premium on speed (see Chapter 19) or any children who work in a slow, deliberate, and thoughtful manner.

9. *Poor quality of some test materials.* Danielson (1991) pointed out that the Coding and Symbol Search templates are poorly constructed and may rip and disintegrate quickly. He also noted that

the puzzle pieces included in the WISC-III Object Assembly subtest are of much lighter construction than are those in the WISC-R and have a tendency to be jarred apart as additional pieces are added to each puzzle. Care should therefore be taken when dealing with highly compulsive children who may spend an inordinate amount of time trying to make sure that all of the edges touch one another. It is also very unclear why the horse in this subtest is gray on both sides. Certainly, this has to increase degree of confusion and the assembly time for children who inadvertently turn one of the pieces over. One of the features on the WISC-R Object Assembly subtest was that the front and back of each piece was clearly a different color. (p. 23)

CONCLUDING COMMENT ON THE WISC-III

The WISC-III will likely be well received by those who use tests to evaluate children's intellectual ability. It has excellent standardization, reliability, and concurrent and construct validity, and much care has been taken to provide useful administrative and scoring guidelines. The manual is excellent, and much thought has gone into the revision. A valuable addition to the manual would have been data about the standard errors of measurement of IQ scores on the Verbal, Performance, and Full Scales at IQ levels of 70, 100, and 130 (if not others). The WISC-III will likely serve as a valuable instrument in the assessment of children's intelligence for many years to come.

THINKING THROUGH THE ISSUES

Although the Wechsler tests were by no means unique when they were developed, they did make a substantial impact on the assessment field. Why do you think the Wechsler tests were so successful as clinical assessment instruments?

The Wechsler tests do not provide interchangeable scores. What problems do you foresee in using different Wechsler tests with children in the overlapping ages where either of the two tests is appropriate?

Here are some other issues that you might want to consider. In what cases would you want to use the WISC-III factor scores? What explanation do you have as to why the WISC-III Verbal Scale subtests are better measures of *g* than the Performance Scale subtests? What can you do to develop proper WISC-III administrative techniques? When do you think WISC-III short forms would be appropriate to use? How would the limitations of the WISC-III affect its clinical usefulness?

Question: What letter comes after T?
Answer: Well, that's easy; V.

SUMMARY

1. The Psychological Corporation published the WISC-III in 1991, 17 years after the former edition, the WISC-R. The WISC-III is similar to its predecessor, with 73 percent of the items retained, plus the original Coding subtest, which was slightly modified. Symbol Search, a supplementary subtest, is new. The WISC-III is applicable to children from 6-0-0 to 16-11-30 years of age. Standardization of the scale was excellent and included White, Black, Hispanic, and other children.

2. The WISC-III provides Deviation IQs for the Verbal, Performance, and Full Scales ($M = 100$, $SD = 15$) and standard scores for the 13 subtests ($M = 10$, $SD = 3$).

3. Although Wechsler objected to the use of mental ages in the calculation of IQs, the WISC-III manual includes a table of test-age equivalents for the scaled scores; these are essentially mental-age scores.

4. The internal consistency reliabilities of the Verbal, Performance, and Full Scales are excellent (average r_{xx} of .95, .91, and .96, respectively). Subtest internal consistency reliabilities range from .69 to .87, and test-retest reliabilities range from .57 to .89. Reliabilities for the three scales are higher than those for the individual subtests.

5. Standard errors of measurement are 3.53 for the Verbal Scale, 4.54 for the Performance Scale, and 3.20 for the Full Scale. Most confidence can be placed in the Full Scale, followed by the Verbal Scale and then the Performance Scale.

6. Shifts in IQ due to practice effects (after approximately a three-week interval) were about 8 IQ points higher on the Full Scale, 2 IQ points higher on the Verbal Scale, and 12 IQ points higher on the Performance Scale.

7. Confidence intervals based on the obtained score and its standard error of measurement should be used when you want to describe the measurement error associated with a child's current functioning. Confidence intervals based on the estimated true score and its standard error of estimation should be used when you want to describe the measurement error associated with the best long-term measure of the child's functioning relative to other children in a particular group. The former method produces symmetrical confidence intervals around the obtained score; the latter method produces asymmetrical confidence intervals around the obtained score. The asymmetry is most pronounced for IQs furthest from the mean.

8. Studies in the WISC-III manual suggest that the WISC-III has acceptable concurrent, criterion, and construct validity. Median correlations with measures of achievement and school grades range from the upper .30s to the low .70s. Correlations with the WISC-R, WPPSI-R, and WAIS-R are in the .70s to .90s for the Verbal, Performance, and Full Scale IQs.

9. Based on the limited studies reported in the WISC-III Manual, the WISC-III tends to provide *lower* IQs than does the WISC-R by about 5 to 9 points, *lower* IQs than the WAIS-R by about 4 points, and *higher* IQs than the WPPSI-R by about 4 points. The various Wechsler scales do not appear to provide interchangeable IQs.

10. The Verbal Scale subtests correlate more highly with each other (*Mdn r* = .55) than do the Performance Scale subtests (*Mdn r* = .33). Correlations between the Verbal subtests and the Verbal Scale (*Mdn r* = .72) are higher than those between the Performance subtests and the Performance Scale (*Mdn r* = .45). The Verbal subtests also have higher correlations with the Full Scale (*Mdn r* = .68) than do the Performance subtests (*Mdn r* = .56).

11. A factor analysis of the WISC-III standardization data indicated that three factors account for the test's structure: Verbal Comprehension, Perceptual Organization, and Processing Speed. The best measures of *g* are Vocabulary, Information, Similarities, Arithmetic, Comprehension, and Block Design.

12. Because several WISC-III subtests have an adequate degree of subtest specificity, interpretation of profiles of subtest scores generally is on firm ground.

13. You can use the Deviation IQs associated with the Verbal and Performance Scale IQs as factor scores. You can obtain somewhat purer factor scores by using (a) Information, Similarities, Vocabulary, and Comprehension for Verbal Comprehension; (b) Picture Completion, Block Design, and Object Assembly for Perceptual Organization; and (c) Coding and Symbol Search for Processing Speed.

14. The subtest scaled-score range is from 1 to 19, but not at all ages. After 11 years, the ceiling level ranges from 17 to 19 scaled-score points, depending on the subtest and age.

15. The WISC-III does not adequately assess the cognitive ability of children who are either severely retarded or exceptionally gifted. Although the WISC-III manual shows a range of Full Scale IQs from 40 to 160, the range of the test is more limited at some ages.

16. The WISC-III differs from the WISC-R in both major and minor ways. The most noticeable changes are the addition of a new subtest (Symbol Search), a new factor (Processing Speed) in place of the Freedom from Distractibility factor, and full color illustrations for all pictures. New items have been added or changed on every subtest, and numerous administrative changes have been made.

17. Developing proper administrative procedures early in your testing career is an important step in becoming a competent clinician.

18. Beginning examiners tend to make administrative errors. These include failing to follow the scoring rules, to complete the Record Form properly, to adhere to directions, to probe ambiguous responses, and to follow starting point and discontinuance procedures.

19. Follow the standard order of administering the subtests in all but the most exceptional circumstances.

20. To ensure that scoring is standardized at the starting and discontinuance points, credit any items failed below the starting-point items when the child passes the starting-point items and do not credit any items passed above the discontinuance-point items when the child fails the discontinuance-point items.

21. The WISC-III requires the use of many probing questions and queries. Give spoiled responses a score of 0.

22. Certain modifications in test procedures have been found to increase children's scores on the WISC-R. Similar modifications probably will affect WISC-III scores. Use such modifications only *after* the standard administration.

23. Scoring WISC-III Similarities, Vocabulary, and Comprehension subtests requires considerable skill. A careful study of the scoring criteria can help to reduce scoring errors.

24. Short forms of the WISC-III, although practical, have serious disadvantages. Short-form IQs may be less stable, impede profile analysis, and result in misclassifications. Do not use short forms for any placement, education, or clinical decision-making purpose. If you need to use a short form for screening purposes, follow the procedures advocated by Tellegen and Briggs to determine Deviation IQs. Table L-11 in Appendix L shows the best short-form combinations of two, three, four, and five WISC-III subtests. Appendixes L-12, L-13, L-14, and L-15 show the estimated IQs associated with these short-form combinations. The best two-subtest short-form combination is Vocabulary and Block Design.

25. Although you can view the WISC-III and the WPPSI-R as alternative forms for children aged 6-0 to 7-3 years, the two tests are not independent because many items overlap. You can give both the WISC-III and the WAIS-R to adolescents aged 16-0 to 16-11 years. I recommend that for children aged 6-0 to 6-11 you give the WPPSI-R to those with below-average ability, the WISC-III to those with above-average ability, and either test to children with average ability. For *all* children aged 7-0 to 7-3, give the WISC-III. I recommend that you give the WISC-III to *all* adolescents aged 16-0 to 16-11.

26. Children must be able to hear to take most WISC-III (and WPPSI-R and WAIS-R) Verbal subtests, although they may use vision as a substitute modality for some subtests. Arm-hand use is a prerequisite for most of the Performance subtests, although some adaptations are possible. Testing handicapped children is facilitated by the arrangement of subtests into a Verbal Scale and a Performance Scale. You usually will need to use special procedures, described in Appendixes D and M, to administer the Performance Scale to deaf children.

27. The assets of the WISC-III include its excellent standardization, excellent reliability, and good validity; usefulness as a diagnostic instrument; good administrative procedures; good manual and interesting test materials; helpful scoring criteria; and extensive research and clinical literature with the prior edition.

28. The limitations of the WISC-III include limited range of IQs (40 to 160), low reliability of individual subtests, nonuniformity of scaled scores, difficulty in interpreting norms when you substitute a supplementary subtest for a standard subtest, difficulty in scoring some subtests, large practice effects for the Performance Scale subtests, overlap of items with the WPPSI-R, problems for children who do not place a premium on speed, and quality of some test materials.

29. Overall, the WISC-III represents a major contribution to the field of intelligence testing of children. It serves as an important instrument for this purpose.

KEY TERMS, CONCEPTS, AND NAMES

STUDY QUESTIONS

1. Discuss the WISC-III. Include in your discussion the following issues: standardization, Deviation IQs, test-age equivalents, reliability, and validity.

2. Discuss two procedures for developing confidence intervals.

3. Describe and interpret the intercorrelations between WISC-III subtests and scales.

4. Describe and interpret WISC-III factor analytic findings.

5. Discuss WISC-III administrative considerations.

6. Discuss WISC-III short forms, including their values and limitations.

7. For overlapping ages, how would you go about choosing between the WISC-III and the WPPSI-R, and between the WISC-III and the WAIS-R?

8. Identify the most important factors to consider in administering the WISC-III (and other Wechsler tests) to handicapped children.

9. Discuss the assets and limitations of the WISC-III.

REFERENCES

Danielson, G. I. (1991). An initial reaction to the WISC-III. *Communiqué, 20*(4), 23.

Flynn, J. R. (1984). The mean IQ of Americans: Massive gains 1932 to 1978. *Psychological Bulletin, 95*, 29–51.

Flynn, J. R. (1987). Massive IQ gains in 14 nations: What IQ tests really measure. *Psychological Bulletin, 101*, 192–212.

Glutting, J. J., McDermott, P. A., & Stanley, J. C. (1987). Resolving differences among methods of establishing confidence limits for test scores. *Educational and Psychological Measurement, 45*, 607–614.

Granier, M. J., & O'Donnell, L. (1991). Children's WISC-III scores: Impact of parent education and home environment. Paper presented at a poster session of the 99th Annual Convention of the American Psychological Association, San Francisco, CA.

Kaufman, A. S. (1990). *Assessing adolescent and adult intelligence.* Needham, MA: Allyn and Bacon.

Silverstein, A. B. (1990a). Notes on the reliability of Wechsler short forms. *Journal of Clinical Psychology, 46*, 194–196.

Silverstein, A. B. (1990b). Short forms of individual intelligence tests. *Psychological Assessment: A Journal of Consulting and Clinical Psychology, 2*, 3–11.

Slate, J. R., & Chick, D. (1989). WISC-R examiner errors: Cause for concern. *Psychology in the Schools, 26*, 78–84.

Slate, J. R., & Hunnicutt, L. C., Jr. (1988). Examiner errors on the Wechsler Scales. *Journal of Psychoeducational Assessment, 6*, 280–288.

Wechsler, D. (1991). *Manual for the Wechsler Intelligence Scale for Children – Third Edition.* San Antonio: The Psychological Corporation.

_ APPENDIX J

WISC-III SUBTESTS

Order and simplification are the first steps toward the mastery of a subject—the actual enemy is the unknown.
—Thomas Mann

This appendix provides information that will help you administer, score, and interpret the 13 WISC-III subtests. It gives the rationale, factor analytic findings, reliability and correlational highlights, administrative suggestions, and interpretive suggestions for each subtest. The factor analytic findings and reliability and correlational data discussed in this appendix are based on the WISC-III standardization sample (as presented in the WISC-III manual). (See Appendix I for information about the factor analysis.) Reliabilities for the Coding and Symbol Search subtests are test-retest correlations, whereas those for the remaining 11 subtests are split-half correlations corrected by the Spearman-Brown formula.

For the 12 subtests that are common to both the WISC-III and WISC-R, Table C-13 in Appendix C summarizes those abilities measured by each subtest, background factors influencing performance, implications of high and low scores, and instructional suggestions to improve a child's abilities. Table L-16 in Appendix L summarizes similar information for the WISC-III Symbol Search subtest. Therefore, both Table C-13 and Table L-16 are useful references for report writing and deserve careful study. If you are interested in the WISC-III Structure-of-Intellect classifications for the Arithmetic, Vocabulary, Comprehension, Digit Span, Picture Completion, Picture Arrangement, Block Design, Object Assembly, Coding, and Mazes subtests, see Table C-12 in Appendix C (page 822); these classifications are based on Guilford's model of intelligence (see Chapter 3). When you consider the abilities measured by the subtests, recognize that all of the subtests require the child to pay attention, to hear, to listen, to understand directions, and to retain these directions in mind while solving problems.

Many of the WISC-III subtests have enough subtest specificity at most ages (see Table I-12 in Appendix I) to provide reliable estimates of specific abilities, or at least to permit development of hypotheses about the underlying cognitive functions that may be measured by a subtest. The subtests that have sufficient specificity at most ages are Information, Similarities, Vocabulary, Digit Span, Picture Completion, Picture Arrangement, Block Design, Symbol Search, and Mazes. The other subtests have ample or adequate specificity only at a few ages.

Combinations of subtests provide the best estimates of specific abilities. For example, the Verbal Scale IQ, derived from a combination of five subtests, yields more accurate data about a child's verbal skills than does a single subtest, such as Vocabulary. Similarly, Coding and Symbol Search together provide more information about speed of processing than does either subtest alone.

For each subtest, this chapter poses questions to help you observe and interpret the child's performance. The answers to these questions will serve as a database for testing any clinical hypotheses you may form. After the test is administered, you will often have questions about the child's performance. For example, you may have questions about the quality of the child's responses, the pattern of failures, or how close to a solution the child was. By recording the child's performance carefully, you will be in a better position to answer any such questions that arise later.

This appendix provides suggestions for testing-of-limits for several of the WISC-III subtests. Testing-of-limits should be done *after* you administer the entire test following standard procedures. Testing-of-limits is useful for several purposes, including following up leads about the child's functioning obtained during the standard administration, testing clinical hypotheses, and evaluating how the child performs when he or she receives additional cues.

This appendix, unlike the WISC-III manual, uses the term "mental retardation" instead of the term "intellectual deficiency" to describe children who may be significantly below average in their intellectual ability. "Mental retardation" is the term used in *DSM III-R* and by the American Association on Mental Retardation. Consequently, I believe that "mental retardation" is the preferred term for describing children who are functioning two or more standard deviations below the mean. Let us now turn to a discussion of each of the 13 WISC-III subtests.

INFORMATION

The Information subtest requires the child to answer a broad range of questions dealing with factual information. The subtest contains 30 questions. Included are questions about names of objects, dates, a literary figure, and historical and geographical facts. The child's age determines which item is used to start testing. Children 6 to 7 years old (and older children suspected of mental retardation) start with item 1, 8 to 10 years old with item 5, 11 to 13 years old with item 8, and 14 to 16 years old with item 11. All items are scored 1 or 0 (pass-fail). The subtest is not timed and is discontinued after five consecutive failures.

Children can usually answer the questions correctly with a brief, simply stated fact. They need only demonstrate that they know specific facts; they need not find relationships between these facts.

Rationale

The amount of knowledge a child possesses may depend on his or her natural endowment, the extent of his or her education (both formal and informal), and his or her cultural opportunities and predilections. In general, the Information subtest samples the knowledge that average children with average opportunities should be able to acquire through normal home and school experiences. The child's responses and comments provide clues about the child's general range of information, alertness to the environment, social or cultural background, and attitudes toward school and school-like tasks (for example, the child may say "Those questions are hard, just like my teacher asks").

You should not necessarily interpret high scores as indications of mental efficiency and competence. Children may have acquired isolated facts but not know how to use them appropriately or effectively. However, intellectual drive may contribute to higher scores. Successful performance on the Information subtest requires memory for habitual, overlearned material (that is, information that the child has likely been exposed to over and over), especially in older children. Thus Information provides clues about the child's ability to store and retrieve old data.

Factor Analytic Findings

The Information subtest is the second-best measure of g in the test (61 percent of its variance may be attributed to g — range of 50 to 69 percent in the 11 age groups). The subtest contributes substantially to the Verbal Comprehension factor (Average loading = .75). Specificity is either ample or adequate at 9 of the 11 ages; at ages 6 and 7 it is inadequate.

Reliability and Correlational Highlights

Information is a reliable subtest (r_{xx} = .84), with reliability coefficients above .70 at each of the 11 age groups (range of .73 to .88). The subtest correlates more highly with Vocabulary (r = .70) and Similarities (r = .66) than with other subtests. It correlates moderately with both the Full Scale (r = .72) and the Verbal Scale (r = .75) and to a lesser degree with the Performance Scale (r = .55).

Administrative Suggestions

The Information subtest is easy to administer. The questions are simple and direct. Scoring is usually straightforward: a correct response receives 1 point and an incorrect response, 0. If the child gives two or more answers to a question, ask the child to choose the best answer. Answers should be recorded verbatim. Encourage a child who is hesitant to respond or guess or take a chance. Give the child credit if he or she answers Information questions correctly at any time during the entire test.

Interpretive Suggestions

Note the quality of a child's answers.

• Is the child thinking the questions through or simply guessing?
• Does the child give answers confidently or hesitantly?
• Does the child give peculiar responses? If so, what does your inquiry reveal?
• Are the child's answers imprecise and roundabout? Difficulty in giving precise answers, such as "When it is hot" for *summer* or "When it is cold" for *winter*, may suggest word-retrieval difficulties.
• Are the child's answers wordy? Overly long responses or responses filled with extraneous information may suggest an obsessive-compulsive orientation — a child with this orientation sometimes feels compelled to prove how much he or she knows. Alternatively, excessive responses may simply reflect the child's desire to impress you. The child's entire test protocol, plus other relevant information, should be considered in interpreting such behavior.
• Does the child seem to be inhibited in making responses? Inability to recall an answer may suggest that the question is associated with conflict-laden material. For example, a child may not be able to recall the number of legs on a dog because of a traumatic experience with dogs.

Examine the pattern of successes and failures. Failures on easy items coupled with successes on more difficult ones may suggest poor motivation, anxiety, temporary inefficiency, boredom, or an environment that has not been consistent. Alternatively, this pattern may indicate a problem with retrieval of information from long-term memory. When you suspect such a problem, analyze the content of the failed items — do they deal with numerical information, history, science, or geography? Content analysis may provide clues about the child's interests or areas that you might want to inquire about after you complete the test.

If you think the child may have word-retrieval problems, you can use a multiple-choice testing-of-limits procedure (Holmes, 1988[R][1]). This procedure may help you differentiate deficits associated with word retrieval from those associated with lack of knowledge. After you complete the test, go back to the item (or items) for which the child seemed to have difficulty in retrieving the correct answer. Then give the child three choices. For example, for item 13 you might say "Was he a king or an explorer or a writer?"

---

[1] References followed by an [R] are cited in this appendix; all other references are cited in the Reference section.

Be sure to vary randomly the position of the correct answer in the series (that is, sometimes put the correct answer as the first choice, sometimes second, and sometimes third). If the child answers the multiple-choice questions correctly but not the open-ended questions, you may infer that he or she has a word-finding difficulty and not a lack of knowledge.

The range of scaled scores from 1 to 19 at ages 6-0 to 13-11 years aids in profile analysis for children in this age range. However, profile analysis is somewhat hindered at ages 14-0 to 15-11 years and 16-0 to 16-11 years, where the scaled scores range from 1 to 18 and 1 to 17, respectively.

Question: What are the four seasons?
Answer: Football, basketball, baseball, and hockey.

SIMILARITIES

The Similarities subtest requires the child to answer questions about how objects or concepts are alike. The subtest contains 19 pairs of words; the child must state the similarity between the two items in each pair. All children start with the sample item and then are administered the first item. The first five items are scored 1 or 0 (pass-fail), and items 6 through 19 are scored 2, 1, or 0, depending on the conceptual quality of the response. The subtest is not timed and is discontinued after four consecutive failures.

Rationale

On the Similarities subtest, in addition to perceiving the common elements of the paired terms, the child must bring these common elements together in a concept to answer the questions. Thus the Similarities subtest may measure verbal concept formation—the ability to place objects and events together into a meaningful group or groups. To do this, the child may need to organize, abstract, and find relationships that are not at first obvious. Although concept formation can be a voluntary, effortful process, it can also reflect well-automatized verbal conventions (Rapaport, Gill, & Schafer, 1968). Performance on the Similarities subtest may be related to cultural opportunities and interest patterns. Memory may also be involved. Success initially depends on the child's ability to comprehend the meaning of the task.

Factor Analytic Findings

The Similarities subtest is the third-best measure of g in the test (60 percent of its variance may be attributed to g—range of 52 to 65 percent in the 11 age groups). The subtest contributes substantially to the Verbal Comprehension factor (Average loading = .75) and to a limited extent to the Perceptual Organization factor (Average loading = .30). Specificity is either ample or adequate at 6 ages (6, 11, 12, 14, 15, 16); at 5 ages (7, 8, 9, 10, 13) it is inadequate.

Reliability and Correlational Highlights

Similarities is a reliable subtest (r_{xx} = .81), with reliability coefficients above .70 at each of the 11 age groups (range of .77 to .84). The subtest correlates most highly with Vocabulary (r = .69) and Information (r = .66). It correlates moderately with the Full Scale (r = .72) and the Verbal Scale (r = .75) and to a lesser degree with the Performance Scale (r = .55).

Administrative Suggestions

Note whether the child understands the task. On items 1 and 2, give the child the correct response if he or she fails to provide an acceptable response to these items. If a child states that he or she does not know the answer, encourage the child to try to answer the question, but do not press him or her unreasonably. When a child gives multiple acceptable responses to an item, score his or her best response. When a child gives both a correct and an incorrect response to an item, say "Now which one is it?" Base your score on the answer to this question. If the child gives a 1-point answer to item 6 or 7, tell the child the 2-point answer; this is done to help the child give 2-point responses on later items.

Responses to the first five questions are generally easy to score, but you will find the scoring of items 6 to 19 more difficult. On these items (6–19), a conceptual response, such as a general classification, receives a score of 2; a more concrete response, such as a specific property of the item, receives a score of 1; and an incorrect response receives a score of 0.

A careful study of the scoring guide in the WISC-III manual will help you become more proficient in scoring Similarities responses. Study carefully the sample responses that follow each item. These sample responses also list responses that you need to probe [as shown by a "(Q)"]. Also master the general scoring principles, which elucidate the rationale for 2, 1, and 0 scores (see page 84 in the WISC-III manual).

If research with the WISC-R holds for the WISC-III, many Similarities responses are likely to be difficult to score. For example, when a group of 110 psychologists and graduate students scored WISC-R Similarities, Vocabulary, and Comprehension subtest responses, the raters achieved a level of 80 percent agreement in scoring for only 51 percent of the ambiguous Similarities responses (95 out of 187 responses) (Sattler, Andres, Squire, Wisely, & Maloy, 1978). In practice, however, it is unlikely that any one protocol would include many ambiguous responses. Scoring difficulties arise in part from the relatively few examples in the manual and the difficulty of establishing precise criteria that apply to all responses, including idiosyncratic ones.

Interpretive Suggestions

You may gain insight into the logical character of the child's thinking processes by studying his or her responses to the items on the Similarities subtest. Observe the child's typical level of conceptualization throughout the subtest. Are the child's answers on a concrete, functional, or abstract level? Concrete answers typically refer to qualities of the objects (or stimuli) that can be seen or touched (apple-banana: "Both have a skin"). Functional answers typically concern a function or use of the objects (apple-banana: "You eat them"). Finally, abstract answers typically refer to a more universal property or to a common classification of the objects (apple-banana: "Both are fruits").

You can tell, in part, whether the child's response style is concrete, functional, or abstract by the numbers of 0-, 1-, and 2-point responses. Responses that are scored 0 or 1 point suggest a more concrete and functional conceptualization style, whereas 2-point responses suggest an abstract conceptualization style. However, a 2-point response does not necessarily reflect abstract thinking ability. It may simply be an overlearned response. For example, there may be a difference between the 2-point response "Both fruits" for apple-banana and the 2-point response "Artistic expressions" for painting-statue. The former, even though it receives 2 points, may be an overlearned response, whereas the latter may reflect a more abstract level of conceptual ability. Furthermore, if the child earns 1 point on a number of items, the child may have a good breadth of knowledge but not depth. If the child generally earns 2 points for each correct response but responds correctly to only a few items, the child may have a good depth of knowledge but less breadth.

Also note whether the child gives *overinclusive responses*. Overinclusive responses are those that are so general that many objects are included in the concept. For example, the reply "Both contain molecules" to a question asking for the similarity between an apple and a banana is overinclusive because it does not delimit the particular characteristics of these two objects. Overinclusive responses may be a subtle indication of disturbed thinking.

Observe how the child handles any frustration induced by the subtest questions. When the child has difficulty answering the questions, does he or she become negativistic and uncooperative, or does the child still try to answer the questions? A child who responds with "They are not alike" may be displaying negativism, avoidance of the task demands, suspiciousness, or a coping mechanism or may just not know the answer. To determine which of these may account for the child's response, compare the child's style of responding to the Similarities questions with his or her style on other subtests.

The range of scaled scores from 1 to 19 at all ages aids in profile analysis.

Question: In what way are an orange and a pear alike?
Answer: Both give me hives.

ARITHMETIC

The Arithmetic subtest requires the child to answer simple to complex problems involving arithmetical concepts and numerical reasoning. The subtest contains 24 problems, with 5 presented on picture cards, 13 presented orally, and 6 presented in written form. The first five and the last six Arithmetic items are in the Stimulus Booklet, which also contains the Picture Completion and Block Design stimuli. Many of the arithmetic problems are similar to those commonly encountered by children in school, although the child cannot use paper and pencil to solve the problems.

Children 6 years old (and older children suspected of mental retardation) start with item 1, 7 to 8 years old with item 6, 9 to 12 years old with item 12, and 13 to 16 years old with item 14. All items are timed, with items 1 to 17 having a 30-second time limit; item 18, a 45-second time limit; and items 19 to 24, a 75-second time limit. Items 1 to 18 are scored 1 or 0 and do not have time-bonus points. Items 19 to 24 are scored 2, 1, or 0 (a score of 2 includes a 1-point bonus for answering the item correctly within the first 10 seconds). The subtest is discontinued after three consecutive failures.

Arithmetic subtest problems test various skills. Problems 1 and 2 require direct counting of discrete objects.

Reprinted with special permission of North America Syndicate, Inc.

Problems 3, 4, and 5 require subtraction using objects as the stimuli. Problems 6 and 17 require simple division. Problems 7 through 14 and problem 16 require simple addition or subtraction. Problem 15 involves multiplication (or addition). Problems 18 through 24 require the use of automatized number facts and subtle mathematical reasoning operations, such as identifying relevant relationships at a glance, understanding task requirements, and understanding probability.

Rationale

The problems on the Arithmetic subtest require the child to follow verbal directions, concentrate on selected parts of questions, and use numerical operations. The child must have knowledge of addition, subtraction, multiplication, and/or division operations, depending on the problem. The emphasis of the problems is not on mathematical knowledge per se, but on mental computation and concentration. Concentration is especially important for the more complex problems.

The Arithmetic subtest measures numerical reasoning—the ability to solve arithmetical problems. It requires the use of noncognitive functions (concentration and attention) in conjunction with cognitive functions (knowledge of numerical operations). Success on the subtest is influenced by education, interests, fluctuations of attention, and transient emotional reactions such as anxiety. Like the Vocabulary and Information subtests, Arithmetic taps memory and prior learning; however, it also requires concentration and the active application of select skills to new and unique situations (Blatt & Allison, 1968).

Information-processing strategies as well as mathematical skills may underlie performance on the Arithmetic subtest (Stewart & Moely, 1983). These strategies may include rehearsal (in order to remember the information presented in the task) and recognition of an appropriate response (in order to change incorrect patterns or strategies). The mathematical skills include the ability to comprehend and integrate verbal information presented in a mathematical context, together with numerical ability.

Factor Analytic Findings

The Arithmetic subtest is a good measure of g (54 percent of its variance may be attributed to g—range of 47 to 61 percent in the 11 age groups). The subtest contributes moderately to the Verbal Comprehension factor (Average loading = .55) and to a limited extent to the Perceptual Organization factor (Average loading = .37). Specificity is either ample or adequate at 6 ages (6, 7, 10, 13, 15, 16); at 5 ages (8, 9, 11, 12, 14 years) it is inadequate.

Reliability and Correlational Highlights

Arithmetic is a relatively reliable subtest (r_{xx} = .78), with reliability coefficients above .70 at each of the 11 age groups (range of .71 to .82). The subtest correlates more highly with Information (r = .57) and Similarities (r = .55) than with the other subtests. It correlates moderately with the Full Scale (r = .65) and Verbal Scale (r = .62) and to a lesser degree with the Performance Scale (r = .54).

Administrative Suggestions

You may need to be especially reassuring to a child who is anxious about his or her arithmetical skills. Although the child is not permitted to use pencil and paper to solve the problems, writing with fingers is permitted. If a child seems to be on the verge of solving a problem and the time limit has been reached, give the child additional time to complete the problem. This will give you information about the child's ability to solve the problem. Even though the child receives no credit for a correct response made after the time limit, record the response and the amount of time the child took to respond.

Interpretive Suggestions

Observe the child's reactions to the items.

- Is the child anxious?
- What approach does the child use to solve problems?
- Does the child show temporary inefficiencies?
- Does the child recognize failures?
- Does the child attempt to correct perceived errors?
- Does the child ask to have questions repeated?

After you complete the standard administration, you might want to learn about the reasons for the child's failure by asking the child about his or her performance. You might say, for example, "Let's try this one again. Tell me how you solved the problem." If necessary, you can tell the child that he or she can think out loud. This may help you see how the child went about solving the problem. Failure may be caused, for example, by poor knowledge of arithmetical operations, inadequate conceptualization of the problem, temporary inefficiency or anxiety, poor concentration, or carelessness.

Allowing the child to use paper and pencil is another testing-of-limits procedure that may help you find out whether the child has poor arithmetical knowledge or attention and concentration difficulties. If the child can solve the problems with pencil and paper, the failure is not associated with lack of arithmetical knowledge; the errors may be associated with attention or concentration difficulties that inhibit mental computation. If the child fails the items in both situations, the failures more likely reflect difficulties with arithmetical knowledge, although attention and concentration difficulties may be interfering with the child's ability to solve written arithmetic problems. Inspect the written work to see whether the child misaligns numbers, sequences computational steps incorrectly, or has poor mastery of basic arithmetical operations. If the child misaligns numbers while working, spatial difficulties may be indicated.

The information you obtain from testing-of-limits may help you to differentiate between failures due to temporary inefficiency and those due to limited knowledge. Successful delayed performance, for example, may indicate temporary inefficiency or a slow, painstaking approach to problem solving. During testing-of-limits, note whether the child passes or fails the items. Of course, do not give the child credit on the test for answering any items correctly during testing-of-limits.

The range of scaled scores from 1 to 19 at ages 6-0 to 15-11 years aids in profile analysis. However, from 16-0 to 16-11 years, profile analysis is somewhat hindered because the scaled scores range from only 1 to 18.

Question:	If I cut a pear in thirds, how many pieces will I have?
Answer:	One.
Question:	(Testing-of-limits) Are you sure I will have only one piece?
Answer:	Yes, and I will have the other two pieces.

DRABBLE reprinted by permission of UFS, Inc.

VOCABULARY

The Vocabulary subtest requires the child to listen as the examiner reads words aloud and then to define the words. The subtest contains 30 words arranged in order of increasing difficulty. The child is asked to explain the meaning of each word (for example, "What is a _____?" or "What does _____ mean?"). Children 6 to 8 years old (and older children suspected of mental retardation) start with item 1, 9 to 10 years old with item 3, 11 to 13 years old with item 5, and 14 to 16 years old with item 7. All items are scored 2, 1, or 0. The subtest is not timed, and it is discontinued after four consecutive failures.

Rationale

The Vocabulary subtest, a test of word knowledge, may tap cognition-related factors—including the child's learning ability, fund of information, richness of ideas, memory, concept formation, and language development—that may be closely related to his or her experiences and educational environments. Because the number of words known by a child correlates with his or her ability to learn and to accumulate information, the subtest provides an excellent estimate of intellectual ability. Performance on the subtest is stable over time and relatively resistant to neurological deficit and psychological disturbance (Blatt & Allison, 1968). Scores on Vocabulary therefore provide a useful index of the child's general mental ability.

Factor Analytic Findings

The Vocabulary subtest is the best measure of g in the test (62 percent of its variance may be attributed to g—range of 51 to 71 percent in the 11 age groups). The subtest contributes substantially to the Verbal Comprehension factor (Average loading = .82). Specificity is either ample or adequate at 9 of the 11 age groups; at ages 9 and 10 it is inadequate.

Reliability and Correlational Highlights

Vocabulary is the most reliable subtest (r_{xx} = .87) in the Verbal Scale. Reliability coefficients are above .70 in each of the 11 age groups (range of .79 to .91). It correlates more highly with Information (r = .70), Similarities (r = .69), and Comprehension (r = .64) than with the other subtests. It correlates moderately with the Full Scale (r = .74) and

the Verbal Scale (r = .78) and to a lesser degree with the Performance Scale (r = .56).

Administrative Suggestions

Be sure to pronounce each word clearly and correctly. Be especially careful about how you pronounce the words, because you are not allowed to show the words to the child or to spell them. When you suspect that the child has not heard a word correctly, have the child repeat it to you. If the child heard the word incorrectly, say the word again. Carefully record the child's definitions.

The scoring system (2, 1, or 0 for all items) considers the quality of the response. Award 2 points for good synonyms, major uses, or general classifications, and award one point for vague responses, less pertinent synonyms, or minor uses. Do not consider the child's elegance of expression in scoring the response.

Vocabulary is one of the more difficult subtests to score, and it may not always be easy to implement the scoring criteria in the WISC-III manual. In the study by Sattler et al. (1978), 80 percent of the raters gave the same score to only 38 percent of 352 ambiguous WISC-R Vocabulary responses. Probing borderline responses and studying carefully the scoring guidelines in the WISC-III manual will help you resolve some of the scoring problems that arise as you give the subtest. Do the best job possible with the guidelines given in the WISC-III manual. Consulting with a colleague may be helpful in scoring ambiguous responses.

When young children (or older children who may be mentally retarded) give a 0- or 1-point response to the first word of the Vocabulary subtest, tell them the 2-point answer. Use this procedure, which is designed to encourage 2-point responses, only on the first item.

Probe responses that suggest regionalisms or slang (for example, "Give me another meaning for _____"). The scoring guidelines following each item in the WISC-III manual list many responses that you should query [as shown by a "(Q)"]; study these guidelines carefully so that you can recognize responses that need to be probed.

The nature of the response should determine whether the inquiry occurs during or after the standard administration. For example, if the answer clearly defines a homonym of the test item, repeat the question by saying "What else does _____ mean?" However, if the response is possibly indicative of a thought disorder, delay probing until you have completed the test. During the testing-of-limits phase, you might say "To the word _____ you said _____. Tell me more about your answer."

Interpretive Suggestions

The following guidelines are useful for observing and evaluating Vocabulary responses (Taylor, 1961).

• Write down all of the child's responses, whether they are correct or not.

• Note whether the child is definitely familiar with the word or only vaguely familiar with it. If the child explains a word, is the explanation precise and brief, roundabout, or vague and lengthy? Are the child's responses objective, or do they relate to personal experiences?

• Note whether the child confuses the word with another one that sounds like it. If the child does not know the meaning of a word, does he or she guess? Does the child readily say "I don't know" and shake off further demands, or does the child pause, ponder, or think aloud about the item?

• If you show the child the words during testing-of-limits, note whether seeing the printed word helps the child.

• Watch for possible hearing difficulties by listening carefully to how the child repeats words. Has the child heard the words correctly or with some distortion?

• Note how the child expresses himself or herself. Does the child find it easy or difficult to say what he or she means? Does the child have mechanical difficulties pronouncing words properly? Does the child seem uncertain about how best to express what he or she thinks? Does the child use gestures to illustrate his or her statements or even depend on them exclusively?

• Note also the content of definitions. Are the words chosen synonyms for the stimulus word (thief: "A burglar"), or do they describe an action (thief: "Takes stuff")? Does the child describe some particular feature of the object (donkey: "It has four legs"), or does the child try to fit it into some category (donkey: "A living creature that is kept in a barn")?

• Note any emotional overtones or reference to personal experiences (alphabet: "I hate to write").

The child's responses to the Vocabulary subtest may reveal something about his or her language skills, background, cultural milieu, social development, life experiences, responses to frustration, and thought processes. See if you can determine the basis for incorrect responses. It is important to distinguish among guesses, clang associations (that is, responses that appear to be based on the sound of the stimulus word rather than on its meaning), idiosyncratic associations, and bizarre associations. Whenever a child gives peculiar responses, mispronounces words, or has peculiar inflections, inquire further. You can occasionally see language disturbances in the word definitions of children with schizophrenia or with other severe forms of mental disorder.

The range of scaled scores from 1 to 19 at all ages aids in profile analysis.

Question: What is a chisel?
Answer: When you are cold you get the chisels.
(Flumen & Flumen, 1979)

PEANUTS reprinted by permission of UFS, Inc.

COMPREHENSION

The Comprehension subtest requires the child to explain situations, actions, or activities that relate to events familiar to most children. The questions cover several content areas, including knowledge of one's body, interpersonal relations, and social mores. The subtest contains 18 questions. All children start with the first item. All items are scored 2, 1, or 0. The subtest is not timed, and it is discontinued after three consecutive failures.

Rationale

On the Comprehension subtest, the child must understand given situations and provide answers to specific problems. Success depends on the child's possession of practical information, plus an ability to draw on previous experiences. Responses may reflect the child's knowledge of conventional standards of behavior, extensiveness of cultural opportunities, and level of development of conscience or moral sense. Success suggests that the child has social judgment, common sense, and a grasp of social conventionality. These characteristics imply an ability to use facts in a pertinent, meaningful, and emotionally appropriate manner. Success is based on the ability to verbalize acceptable actions, as well.

Factor Analytic Findings

The Comprehension subtest is a good measure of g (50 percent of its variance may be attributed to g — range of 35 to 63 percent in the 11 age groups). The subtest contributes substantially to the Verbal Comprehension factor (Average loading = .68). Specificity is adequate at 6 of the 11 age groups (6, 8, 9, 10, 11, 12); at 5 ages (7, 13, 14, 15, 16) it is inadequate.

Reliability and Correlational Highlights

Comprehension is a reasonably reliable subtest ($r_{xx} = .77$), with reliability coefficients above .70 at all ages (range of .72 to .85 in the 11 age groups). The subtest correlates more highly with Vocabulary ($r = .64$), Similarities ($r = .59$), and Information ($r = .56$) than with the other subtests. It correlates moderately with the Full Scale ($r = .64$) and the Verbal Scale ($r = .67$) and to a lesser degree with the Performance Scale ($r = .49$).

Administrative Suggestions

The Comprehension subtest is difficult to score because children may give responses that differ from those provided in the manual. In the Sattler et al. (1978) study, 80 percent of the raters gave the same score to only 49 of the 187 ambiguous WISC-R Comprehension responses.

On the first item, tell the child the correct 2-point response if the child gives a less adequate response (that is, a response scored 1 or 0). This procedure is meant to encourage the child to give 2-point responses and is allowed only on the first item. On the eight items (2, 6, 7, 11, 12, 15, 17, and 18) that require two ideas for full credit (2 points), ask the child for a second idea when he or she gives only one correct idea, so that you do not penalize the child automatically for not giving two reasons. However, on the other items, for which an adequate one-idea answer receives 2 points, do not probe obvious 1-point responses in an attempt to improve the child's score.

The most complete or best response receives a score of 2; a less adequate response, 1; and an incorrect response, 0. Carefully study the examples following each item in the manual so that you will know which response types need further inquiry [these are labeled "(Q)"]. The examples indicate that you should query many 0- and 1-point responses. If, in response to your query, the child alters his or her response, score the response given to your query rather than the initial response. Additional queries offer you an opportunity to evaluate more thoroughly the extensiveness of the child's knowledge.

When a child gives unusual responses, ask him or her to explain the responses. Although your inquiry may give you insight into what the child is thinking, do not routinely inquire after every response. You can conduct an extensive inquiry as part of testing-of-limits *after* you complete the test. Record the child's responses verbatim during the initial presentation of the items and during the inquiry phase so that you have a complete record with which to evaluate the responses.

Interpretive Suggestions

Responses to the Comprehension questions may provide valuable information about the child's personality style, ethical values, and social and cultural background. Unlike the Information questions, which usually elicit precise answers, the Comprehension questions may elicit more complex and idiosyncratic replies. Because the questions involve judgment of social situations, answers may reflect the child's attitudes. Some responses reveal understanding *and* acceptance of social mores, whereas others reveal understanding *but not* acceptance of social mores. A child may know the right answers but not practice them. Some children may maintain that they do not have to abide by social conventions, believing that such matters do not pertain to them personally.

A child's replies can reveal initiative, self-reliance, independence, self-confidence, helplessness, indecisiveness, inflexibility, and other traits. For example, a child with a dependent personality style may say that he or she would seek help from his or her mother or others when faced with problem situations. Replies to question 8, which asks the child what should be done if a much smaller child starts a fight with him or her, may reveal independence, manipulative tendencies, naïve perceptions of problems, cooperative solutions, hostility, or aggression (Robb, Bernardoni, & Johnson, 1972).

Note *how* the child responds to the questions (Taylor, 1961):

• Do the child's failures indicate misunderstanding of the meaning of a word or the implications of a particular phrase?

• Does the child give complete answers or just part of a phrase?

• Does the child respond to the entire question or only to a part of it?

• Does the child seem to be objective, seeing various possibilities and choosing the best way?

• Is the child indecisive—unable to come to firm answers?

• Are the child's responses too quick, indicating failure to consider the questions in their entirety?

• Does the child recognize when his or her answers are sufficient?

Because Comprehension requires considerable verbal expression, the subtest may be sensitive to mild language impairments and to disordered thought processes. Be alert to language deficits (such as word-finding difficulties), circumstantial or tangential speech, or other expressive difficulties.

The range of scaled scores from 1 to 19 at ages 6-0 to 15-11 years aids in profile analysis. However, at 16-0 to 16-11 years, profile analysis is somewhat hindered because the scaled scores range only from 1 to 18.

Question: Why should children who are sick stay home?
 Answer: To take their antibionics.
                            (Flumen & Flumen, 1979)

DIGIT SPAN

The Digit Span subtest, a supplementary subtest, requires the child to repeat a series of digits given orally by the examiner. The subtest has two parts: Digits Forward, which contains series ranging in length from two to nine digits, and Digits Backward, which contains series ranging in length from two to eight digits. There are two series of digits for each sequence length. Digits Forward is administered first, followed by Digits Backward. The subtest is untimed.

Digit Span is not used in the computation of the IQ when the five standard Verbal Scale subtests are administered. All children start with the first trial of Digits Forward, and with the sample item of Digits Backward after Digits Forward is completed. All items are scored 2, 1, or 0. On both Digits Forward and Digits Backward, the subtest is discontinued when the child fails both trials on any one item.

Although Digit Span is a supplementary subtest, administering it may give you useful diagnostic information. Considering the small investment of time and energy required to give it, I recommend that you administer Digit Span routinely.

Rationale

Digit Span is a measure of the child's short-term auditory memory and attention. Performance may be affected by the child's ability to relax, as a child who is calm and relaxed may achieve a higher score on the subtest than one who is excessively anxious. The task assesses the child's ability to retain several elements that have no logical relationship to one another. Because the child must recall auditory information and repeat the information orally in proper sequence, the task also involves sequencing.

Digits Forward primarily involves rote learning and memory, whereas Digits Backward requires transformation of the stimulus input prior to responding. Not only must the child hold the mental image of the numerical sequence longer (usually) than in the Digits Forward sequence, but he or she must also manipulate the sequence before restating it. High scores on Digits Backward may indicate flexibility, good tolerance for stress, and excellent concentration. Digits Backward involves more complex cognitive processing than does Digits Forward and has higher loadings on *g* than does Digits Forward (Jensen & Osborne, 1979).

Because of differences between the two tasks, it is useful to consider Digits Forward and Digits Backward separately. Digits Forward appears to involve primarily sequential processing, whereas Digits Backward appears to involve both planning ability and sequential processing. Additionally, Digits Backward may involve the ability to form mental images and the ability to scan an internal visual display formed from an auditory stimulus. However, more research is needed to support the hypothesis about the role of visualization in Digits Backward performance.

Factor Analytic Findings

The Digit Span subtest is a fair measure of g (26 percent of its variance may be attributed to g—range of 18 to 35 percent in the 11 age groups). The subtest contributes minimally to the Verbal Comprehension factor (Average loading = .34). Specificity is ample at all ages.

Reliability and Correlational Highlights

Digit Span is a reliable subtest ($r_{xx} = .85$), with reliability coefficients above .70 at each age (range of .79 to .91 in the 11 age groups). The subtest correlates more highly with Arithmetic ($r = .43$) than with any other subtest. It has a low correlation with the Full Scale ($r = .43$), Verbal Scale ($r = .42$), and Performance Scale ($r = .35$).

Administrative Suggestions

Be sure that the child cannot see the digits in the manual or on the Record Form. Read the digits clearly at the rate of one per second, and drop your inflection on the last digit in the series. Practice reading speed with a stopwatch. Never repeat any of the digits on either trial of a series during the subtest proper.

Always administer both trials of each series. Give the child credit for each trial that he or she passes. On Digits Backward, if the child passes the sample two-digit series (on either the first or the second trial), proceed to the two-digit series in the subtest proper. If the child fails the sample series, read the specific directions in the manual that explain how the series should be repeated. Whenever there is any doubt about the child's auditory acuity, an audiological examination should be requested. Because this subtest contains no cues (that is, you only present several random series of digits), hard-of-hearing examinees may be especially prone to failure.

You can record the number of digits correctly recalled in each series by placing in the Record Form either a mark designating a correct answer above each digit correctly recalled or a mark designating an incorrect answer on each digit missed. An even better procedure is to record the exact sequence given by the child in the available space. A

good record can help you evaluate the child's performance. A child who consistently misses the last digit in the first series and then successfully completes the second series differs from one who fails to recall any of the digits in the first series but successfully completes the second. Similarly, a child who responds to the sequence 3-4-1-7 with "3-1-4-7" is quite different from the child who says "9-8-5-6."

The scoring system does not distinguish among failure patterns. For example, a child who misses one digit in the eight-digit sequence obtains the same score as a child who misses all eight digits, even though the second child's performance is more inefficient than the first child's performance—perhaps because the second child had lapses in attention associated with anxiety or other factors.

Interpretive Suggestions

Observe whether the child's failures involve leaving out one or more digits, transposing digits, interjecting incorrect digits, producing more digits than were given, or giving a series of digits in numerical order (for example, 6-7-8-9). The child who recalls the correct digits but in an incorrect sequence is more likely to have a deficit in auditory sequential memory than in auditory memory. The child who fails the first trial but passes the second trial may be displaying a learning-to-learn pattern or a need for a warm-up to achieve success.

Consider the following questions:

• Is the child's performance effortless, or does the child seem to use much concentration?

• Does the child view the task as interesting, boring, or difficult?

• Does the child notice his or her errors, or does the child think that his or her answers are always correct?

• Does the child understand the difference between Digits Backward and Digits Forward?

• Are the errors the child makes on Digits Backward similar to or different from those he or she made on Digits Forward?

• As the Digits Backward series proceeds, does the child become stimulated and encouraged or tense, anxious, and frustrated?

• Does the child do much better on Digits Forward than on Digits Backward? (If so, the child may be overwhelmed by the more complex operations required on Digits Backward.)

• Does the child make more errors on Digits Forward than on Digits Backward? (This may mean that the child sees Digits Backward as more of a challenge and therefore

Table J-1
Median Number of Digits Recalled on Digits Forward and Digits Backward by Age

Age	Median Forward	Backward
6	5	3
7	5	3
8	5	3
9	6	4
10	6	4
11	6	4
12	6	4
13	6	4
14	6	5
15	7	5
16	7	5
All ages	6	4

Note. There were 200 children at each age level.
Source: Adapted from Wechsler (1991[R]), Table B.6 (page 267).

mobilizes more of his or her resources – for example, giving added concentration and attention – to cope with Digits Backward.)

The child may use various methods to recall the digits. For example, the child may simply repeat what he or she has heard; visualize the digits; say the digits to himself or herself; use a finger to write the digits; or group the digits. Some grouping techniques introduce meaning into the task so separate digits become numbers grouped into hundreds, tens, or other units (for example, 3-1-7 becomes three hundred seventeen). If the child uses grouping, the function underlying the task may be changed from one of attention to one of concentration. After you complete the subtest, you might ask the child how he or she went about remembering the numbers. If you do, record the child's response.

The WISC-III manual does not provide separate scaled scores for Digits Forward and Digits Backward. However, there are two useful tables in the WISC-III manual that show how the standardization group performed on Digits Forward and on Digits Backward. Table B.6 (page 267 of the WISC-III manual) shows the longest Digits Forward span and the longest Digits Backward span recalled by children. Across all age groups, children had a median Digits Forward span of 6 (range of 5 to 7) and a median Digits Backward span of 4 (range of 3 to 5) (see Table J-1).

Table B.7 (page 268 of the WISC-III manual) shows the extent to which children recalled more digits forward than backwards and vice versa. In all age groups and in the total sample, children recalled more digits forward than backward (*Mdn* difference = 2 at 10 of the 11 age groups and in the total sample, except at age 15, where *Mdn* difference = 1). Thus, raw score differences of 3 points (or more) between Digits Forward and Digits Backward may be considered noteworthy. The percentage of children in the standardization group who recalled more digits backward than forward was less than 4 percent in the total group, about 1 percent at 6 to 8 years, less than 3 percent at 9 to 11 years, between 4 and 6 percent at 12 to 14 years, 10.5 percent at 15 years, and 9 percent at 16 years (see Table J-2).

The range of scaled scores from 1 to 19 at all ages aids in profile analysis.

Question: Now I am going to say some more numbers, but this time when I stop I want you to say them backwards. For example, if I said "8-4-6-5-9-1-7," what would you say?
Answer: I'd say "You've got to be kidding!"
(Adapted from Flumen & Flumen, 1979)

Table J-2
Percentage of Children in Standardization Group Who Recalled More Digits Backward than Digits Forward by Age

Age	Percent
6	1.0
7	1.0
8	.5
9	1.5
10	2.5
11	2.5
12	4.0
13	4.0
14	6.0
15	10.5
16	9.0
All ages	3.8

Note. There were 200 children at each age level.
Source: Adapted from Wechsler (1991[R]), Table B.7 (page 268).

PICTURE COMPLETION

The Picture Completion subtest requires the child to identify the single most important missing detail in 30 drawings of common objects, animals, or people, such as a box, cat, and face. The child's task is to name or point to the essential missing portion of the incomplete picture within the 20-second time limit. The pictures are shown one at a time.

All children start with the sample item. Children 6 to 7 years old (and older children suspected of mental retardation) are then given item 1; 8 to 9 years old, item 5; 10 to 13 years old, item 7; and 14 to 16 years old, item 11. All items are scored 1 or 0 (pass-fail). The subtest is discontinued after five consecutive failures.

Rationale

On the Picture Completion subtest, the child must recognize the object depicted, appreciate its incompleteness, and determine the missing part. It is a test of visual discrimination—the ability to differentiate essential from nonessential details. Picture Completion requires concentration, reasoning (or visual alertness), visual organization, and long-term visual memory (as the items require the child to have stored information about the complete figure).

Picture Completion may also measure perceptual and conceptual abilities involved in visual recognition and identification of familiar objects. Perception, cognition, judgment, and delay of impulse all may influence performance. The time limit on the subtest places additional demands on the child. The richness of the child's life experiences also may affect his or her performance on the subtest.

Factor Analytic Findings

The Picture Completion subtest is a fair measure of g (44 percent of its variance may be attributed to g—range of 32 to 47 percent in the 11 age groups). The subtest contributes moderately to the Perceptual Organization factor (Average loading = .53) and to a lesser extent to the Verbal Comprehension factor (Average loading = .39). These results suggest that verbal reasoning may help children to detect the missing part of the pictures. Subtest specificity is either ample or adequate at 10 of the 11 age groups; at age 12 it is inadequate.

Reliability and Correlational Highlights

Picture Completion is a relatively reliable subtest ($r_{xx} = .77$), with reliability coefficients *above* .70 at all age groups (range of .72 to .84 in the 11 age groups). The subtest correlates more highly with Block Design ($r = .52$), Object Assembly ($r = .49$), and Information ($r = .47$) than with the other subtests. It has low correlations with the Full Scale ($r = .58$), Performance Scale ($r = .54$), and Verbal Scale ($r = .52$).

Administrative Suggestions

Picture Completion is easy to administer. Simply leave the booklet flat on the table and turn the cards over to show each consecutive picture. If the child has speech difficulties, such as those that occur in aphasia, you can administer the subtest by having the child point to the place where the part is missing.

The child should be aware that he or she is being timed, because it is important for the child to realize that speed is expected. Usually, allowing the child to see the stopwatch is all that is necessary. However, you should not tell the child that he or she is being timed.

The WISC-III manual indicates that, if necessary, you may give each of three guiding statements *once* to help the child understand the requirements of this subtest: (a) If the child names the object pictured, ask the child what is missing in the picture. (b) If the child names a part that is not on the card, ask the child what part *in* the picture is missing. (c) If the child mentions a nonessential missing part, ask the child for the most important part that is missing.

On five items (6, 13, 21, 23, 28), ask the child to point to the missing part on the card if he or she gives an ambiguous response. In other cases as well, whenever there is any doubt about the child's verbal or pointing response, ask the child for clarification.

Interpretive Suggestions

As you administer the subtest, consider the following:

• Does the child understand the task?

• Does the child say anything that comes to mind, or does the child search for the right answer?

• When the child fails, does he or she find fault with himself or herself or with the picture?

• What is the child's rate of response—for example, quick and impulsive, or slow and deliberate?

• Is the child fearful of making an error, hesitant, or suspicious?

• Is the child aware of being timed? If so, does the timing make the child anxious or prompt the child to change the pace of his or her responding?

• Does the child give roundabout definitions of parts (sometimes referred to as *circumlocutions*)? [Such responses may suggest word-retrieval difficulties. For example, to item 1 (correct response is "Ear"), a roundabout response would be "The thing you hear with."]

• Does the child point excessively? A child who points excessively or responds with circumlocutions may have word-finding problems (*dysnomia*).

If the child's performance leaves any doubt about his or her visual skills, request a visual examination.

Observe whether perseveration occurs. A child displays perseveration, for example, when he or she says "Ear" for each picture portraying an animal (pictures 1, 3, 5). "Ear" is the correct answer for picture 1, but not for the subsequent pictures depicting animals.

Comparing Picture Completion scores with those on Block Design and Object Assembly may help you distinguish between visuospatial difficulties and visual-motor difficulties. Picture Completion is the only task on the WISC-III Performance Scale that does not have a motor component.

Record each incorrect response verbatim as well as the time the child takes to make the response. The child who usually responds in less than five seconds may be more impulsive, more confident, and, if correct, brighter than the child who takes more time. A child who responds correctly *after* the time limit (for which he or she does not receive credit) may be brighter than the child who fails the item even with additional time. Because the pass-fail scoring makes no provision for such qualitative factors, carefully evaluate individual variations in each case and discuss these qualitative factors in the report. Delayed correct responses may suggest temporary inefficiency, depression, or simply a slow and diligent approach, whereas extremely quick but incorrect responses may reflect impulsivity.

After you administer the subtest, you can inquire about the child's perceptions of the task: "How did you go about coming up with the answer?" or "How did you decide when to give an answer?" Query any peculiar answers. The child's behavior during this subtest may provide insight into how the child reacts to time pressure. As a testing-of-limits procedure, you can ask the child to look again at those pictures that he or she missed. You might say "Look at this picture again. Before, you said that _____ was missing. That's not the part that's missing. Look for something else." In some cases, you may ask the child to name the picture, especially when he or she missed many items.

The range of scaled scores from 1 to 19 at ages 6-0 to 13-11 years aids in profile analysis. However, profile analysis is somewhat hindered at ages 14-0 to 15-11 years and 16-0 to 16-11 years, where the scaled scores range from 1 to 18 and 1 to 17, respectively.

Question: What are 2, 4, and 6?
Answer: That's easy; CBS, NBC, and ABC.

CODING

The Coding subtest requires that the child copy symbols paired with other symbols. The subtest consists of two separate and distinct parts. Each part uses a sample, or key. In Coding A, the sample (or key) consists of five shapes—star, circle, triangle, cross, and square. Within each sample shape, there is a special mark (a vertical line, two horizontal lines, a horizontal line, a circle, and two vertical lines, respectively). The child must place within each test shape (which is empty) the mark that is within the sample shape. There are 5 practice shapes, followed by 59 shapes in the subtest proper.

In Coding B, the sample (or key) consists of boxes containing one of the numbers 1 through 9 in the upper part and a symbol in the lower part. Each number is paired with a different symbol. The test stimuli are boxes containing a number in the upper part and an empty box in the lower part. The child must write in the empty box the symbol that is paired with the number in the sample. There are 7 practice boxes, followed by 119 boxes in the subtest proper. The time limit for each Coding task is 120 seconds.

Coding A is given to children under 8 years of age, and Coding B is given to children 8 years of age and older. On Coding A, 1 point is given for each correct item, and up to 6 additional time-bonus points are given for a perfect score. On Coding B, 1 point is given for each correct item, but there are no time-bonus points.

Rationale

Coding taps the child's ability to learn an unfamiliar task. The subtest involves speed and accuracy of visual-motor coordination, attentional skills, visual scanning and tracking (repeated visual scanning between the code key and answer spaces), short-term memory or new learning (paired-associate learning of an unfamiliar code), cognitive flexibility (in shifting rapidly from one pair to another), handwriting speed, and, possibly, motivation. The subtest also involves speed of mental operation (psychomotor speed) and, to some extent, visual acuity. Success depends not only on comprehending the task, but also on using pencil and paper skillfully. The subtest is sensitive to visuoperceptual difficulties.

Coding B may also involve a verbal-encoding process if the child attaches verbal descriptions to the symbols. For example, a child may label a "+" symbol as a "plus sign" or "cross" and the "V" symbol as the letter "V." A child may improve his or her performance when he or she uses verbal labels to recode the symbols. Consequently, Coding B can also be described as measuring the ability to learn combinations of symbols and shapes and the ability to make associations quickly and accurately. Coding A can also involve a verbal-encoding process, but to a lesser degree. Coding A and Coding B thus may involve separate information-processing modes.

The speed and accuracy with which the child performs the task are a measure of the child's intellectual ability.

At each step in the task the [child] must inspect the next digit, go to the proper location in the table, code the information distinguishing the symbol found, and carry this information in short-term memory long enough to reproduce the symbol in the proper answer box. (Estes, 1974, p. 745)

Coding thus can be conceptualized as an information-processing task involving the discrimination and memory of visual pattern symbols.

Factor Analytic Findings

The Coding subtest is a poor measure of g (20 percent of its variance may be attributed to g — range of 10 to 30 percent in the 11 age groups). The subtest contributes substantially to the Processing Speed factor (Average loading = .74). Specificity is ample at 10 of the 11 age groups; at age 8 it is inadequate.

Reliability and Correlational Highlights

Coding is a relatively reliable subtest (r_{xx} = .79). Reliability coefficients are above .70 at 6 ages (6, 7, 10, 11, 14, 15) reported in the WISC-III manual (range of .70 to .90 in the 6 age groups). Unfortunately, there are no reliability coefficients shown in the WISC-III manual for 5 age groups (8, 9, 12, 13, 16) because no children were retested at these ages. The subtest correlates more highly with Symbol Search (r = .53) than with any other subtest. It has a low

correlation with the Full Scale (r = .33), Performance Scale (r = .32), and Verbal Scale (r = .29).

Administrative Suggestions

The Coding subtest items are located in the Record Form. Administer the subtest on a smooth drawing surface, and tear the page out of the Record Form. Be sure to put the child's name, the date, and your name at the top of the Coding Response Sheet to identify it if it is misplaced. You and the child should each use a no. 2 graphite pencil without an eraser.

A child with visual defects or specific motor disabilities may be penalized on this subtest. Generally, do not give the subtest to a child with either of these disabilities. If you give it, do not count it in the final score.

A left-handed child also may be penalized on the Coding subtest. If the way the child writes causes the child to cover the sample immediately above the line of writing, the child will have to lift his or her hand repeatedly during the task to view the key. If the child is left handed, the WISC-III manual suggests that you place an extra Coding Response Sheet to the right of the child's sheet and have the child work with the separate key both during the sample items and during the subtest proper.

Interpretive Suggestions

Useful observational guidelines are as follows:

• Is the child impulsive or meticulous?
• Does the child display tremor?
• Does the child's speed increase or decrease as he or she proceeds?
• Are the child's symbol marks well executed, barely recognizable, or wrong?
• Do the child's symbol marks show any distortions?
• If the child's symbols marks do show distortions, do the distortions appear only once, occasionally, or each time the child draws the symbol mark? How many different symbols are distorted?
• Does the child draw the same symbol over and over again even though the numbers change (perseveration)?
• Is the child being penalized for lack of speed, for inaccuracy, or for both?
• Does the child understand the task?
• Does the child understand and proceed correctly after you give an explanation?

• Are the child's failures due to inadequate form perception or to poor attention?

• Does the child check each symbol with the sample, or does he or she seem to remember the symbols?

• Does the child recheck every symbol before moving on to the next one?

• Does the child pick out one number only and skip the others?

• Does the child work smoothly, or does he or she seem confused at times?

• Is the child aware of any errors?

• Do the child's errors occur in some regular manner?

• How does the child react to making errors?

• Is the child persistent?

• Does the child need repeated urging?

• Is the child bored with the task?

Answers to the above questions will provide information about the child's attention span, method of working, and other behaviors. An increase in speed, coupled with correct copying of symbols, suggests that the child is adjusting to the task well. A decrease in speed, coupled with incorrect copying of symbols, suggests that the child may be showing fatigue.

Coding is particularly useful for evaluating the child's attention when you suspect attentional difficulties, such as in cases of learning disability or after a head injury. If other tests indicate that the child has adequate response speed and visual acuity, then poor scores on Coding are likely to be associated with attentional deficits and not visuoperceptual difficulties per se. A slow and deliberate approach may suggest depressive features.

Distortion of forms may mean that the child has difficulties with perceptual functioning. Ask the child about any symbol that is peculiarly written to find out whether it has some symbolic meaning to him or her.

Perseveration may suggest neurological difficulties that should be investigated further.

Boredom might be present with a bright child who does not appear to be challenged by the task.

The range of scaled scores from 1 to 19 at all ages aids in profile analysis.

Question: What is celebrated on Thanksgiving Day?
Answer: My cousin's birthday.

PICTURE ARRANGEMENT

The Picture Arrangement subtest requires the child to place a series of pictures in logical order. The subtest contains 14 series, or items, similar to short comic strips. Individual cards, each containing a picture, are placed in a specified disarranged order, and the child is asked to rearrange the pictures in the "right" order to tell a story that makes sense. The number of pictures per set ranges from three to six. One set of cards is given at a time to the child. Each item is timed, with 45 seconds for items 1 to 11 and 60 seconds for items 12 to 14. The only motor action required is for the child to change the position of the pictures.

All children are started with the sample item, after which children 6 to 8 years old (and older children suspected of mental retardation) are given item 1 and children 9 to 16 years are given item 3. There are two trials for items 1 and 2. Items 1 and 2 are scored 2, 1, or 0. Items 3 to 14 are scored 5, 4, 3, 2, or 0, with 2 points for the correct arrangement and up to 3 additional time-bonus points for quick execution. An alternative arrangement on item 14 receives 1 point only, with no time-bonus points. The subtest is discontinued after three consecutive failures.

Rationale

The Picture Arrangement subtest measures the child's ability to comprehend and evaluate a situation. To accomplish the task, the child must grasp the general idea of a story. Although a child may sometimes use trial-and-error experimentation on the subtest, the child usually needs to appraise the total situation depicted in the cards in order to succeed.

The subtest may be viewed as a measure of nonverbal reasoning that involves planning ability, anticipation, visual organization, and temporal sequencing. The subtest measures the ability to anticipate the consequences of initial acts or situations, as well as the ability to interpret social situations. Some children may generate covert, analytical, verbal descriptions of alternative story sequences to guide them in arranging the stimulus cards. In such cases, the subtest may measure verbal sequencing processes as well. The capacity to anticipate, judge, and understand the possible antecedents and consequences of events is important in lending meaningful continuity to everyday experiences (Blatt & Allison, 1968).

Factor Analytic Findings

The Picture Arrangement subtest is a fair measure of *g* (36 percent of its variance may be attributed to *g* — range of 23 to 46 percent in the 11 age groups). The subtest contributes minimally both to the Perceptual Organization factor (Average loading = .36) and to the Verbal Comprehension factor (Average loading = .34). Specificity is ample at all ages.

Reliability and Correlational Highlights

Picture Arrangement is a relatively reliable subtest (r_{xx} = .76), with reliability coefficients of .70 or above at all the ages (range of .70 to .84 in the 11 age groups). The subtest correlates more highly with Block Design (r = .41), Information (r = .40), Vocabulary (r = .40), and Similarities (r = .39) than with other subtests. It has a relatively low correlation with the Full Scale (r = .52), Performance Scale (r = .49), and Verbal Scale (r = .45).

Administrative Suggestions

Arrange the Picture Arrangement items from the child's left to right in the order given in the manual. As you present the demonstration items to the child (that is, the sample item and trial 2 of items 1 and 2), be sure not to cover the pictures with your hand inadvertently — the child should be able to see all the pictures and follow your movements when you are rearranging the pictures. Record the child's Picture Arrangement sequence as soon as you pick up the cards. Coach the child (as indicated in the WISC-III manual) if he or she fails either item 1 or item 2.

The child can earn bonus points for speed on items 3 through 14. To help the child understand the importance of speed, encourage him or her to work quickly. If the child does not tell you when he or she is finished, ask him or her. When the child is perfectionistic, tell the child that the cards do not have to be perfectly straight (or aligned), so that the child does not lose time-bonus points for his or her neatness.

Interpretive Suggestions

The Picture Arrangement subtest gives you the opportunity to observe how the child approaches performance tasks involving planning ability.

• Does the child examine the cards, come to some decision, and then reassess his or her decision while he or she arranges the cards (Taylor, 1961)?

• Does the child proceed quickly without stopping to reconsider his or her decision?

• Are the child's failures due to lack of understanding of the task? (For example, does the child leave the pictures in their original order?)

• What errors does the child make? (For example, are cards placed in a perfunctory or random manner, or is one card always moved to the same position?)

• Is the child persistent, discouraged, impulsive, or rigid?

• What types of trial-and-error patterns does the child use?

• How does the child's approach to the Picture Arrangement items compare with his or her approach to the Block Design and Object Assembly items?

• Does the child employ the same patterns consistently in searching for solutions?

• If the child does not employ the same patterns, what might account for the differences?

• How do task content, fatigue, and mood changes influence the child's approach to the items?

• If you coach the child on trial 2 of items 1 and 2, does the coaching help the child grasp the point of the arrangement, story, or task requirements (cf. Zimmerman & Woo-Sam, 1985)?

It may be useful to ask the child to explain or describe his or her arrangements. If you do so, *wait until you have finished administering the entire test in order to follow standard procedures*. Select items that you think may help you understand the child's thought patterns better. You may want to focus on items that the child failed. However, you can also use items that the child passed, because even correct arrangements do not necessarily mean that the child interpreted the series correctly. Because the last two items attempted are likely to be the most complex for the child, you can select them if you have no other specific choices. Arrange the Picture Arrangement cards for each item separately, in the order given by the child. Then ask the child to "Tell what is happening in the pictures" or to "Make up a story" or to "Tell what the pictures show."

Consider the following in evaluating the stories:

• Are the child's stories logical, fanciful, confused, or bizarre?

• Are the child's stories creative or conventional?

• Does the child reveal any attitudes in the stories, such as self-oriented or socially oriented themes?

• Are the child's incorrect arrangements a consequence of incorrect perceptions of details in the pictures or of failure to consider some details?

• Does the child consider all the relationships in the pictures?

• Are the child's sequences *correct* but the point of the stories not grasped?

• Are the child's sequences *incorrect* but the point of the story grasped?

Useful testing-of-limits procedures include giving the child additional time to complete the arrangement and giving the child cues on items that he or she missed. The latter can be done by placing the first card before the child and saying "Here is the first picture. What goes next?" If one card does not help the child, place the second correct card next to the first one and say "What picture goes next?" In some cases you may need to arrange even more cards to help the child. The child who solves the problems with cues may have more ability than the child who fails in spite of additional guidance. *Introduce graded help only after you have completed the standard examination because such help during testing can raise Picture Arrangement scores* (Sattler, 1969). You may also ask the child to arrange the stories in an alternative sequence.

The range of scaled scores from 1 to 19 at all ages aids in profile analysis.

Question: What is a nuisance?
Answer: My little brother.
(Flumen & Flumen, 1979)

BLOCK DESIGN

The Block Design subtest requires the child to reproduce designs using three-dimensional blocks with a red surface, a white surface, and a surface that is cut diagonally into half red and half white. The subtest contains 12 items. The child uses blocks to assemble a design identical to a model constructed by the examiner (items 1 and 2) or to a two-dimensional, red-and-white picture (items 3 through 12). Children 6 to 7 years old (and older children suspected of mental retardation) start with item 1 and children 8 to 16 years old with item 3. The patterns are arranged in order of increasing difficulty. Two blocks are used for the first design, four blocks for designs 2 to 9, and nine blocks for designs 10 through 12.

All items are timed. Item 1 has a maximum of 30 seconds; items 2 to 5, 45 seconds; items 6 to 9, 75 seconds; and items 10 to 12, 120 seconds. Items 1 to 3 are scored 2, 1,

or 0. Items 4 to 12 are scored 7, 6, 5, 4, or 0, with 4 points for a correct completion and up to 3 additional time-bonus points for quick execution. The subtest is discontinued after two consecutive failures.

Rationale

On the Block Design subtest, the child must perceive and analyze forms by breaking down a whole (the design) into its component parts and then assembling the components into the identical design. This process is referred to as analysis and synthesis. To succeed, the child must use visual organization and visual-motor coordination. Success also involves the application of logic and reasoning to spatial relationship problems. Consequently, Block Design can be considered to be a nonverbal concept formation task requiring perceptual organization, spatial visualization, and abstract conceptualization. It can also be viewed as a constructional task involving spatial relations and figure-ground separation.

A child's performance on Block Design may be affected by his or her rate of motor activity, as well as vision. Do not interpret inadequate performance as direct evidence of inadequate visual form and pattern perception, because the ability to discriminate block designs (that is, to perceive the designs accurately at a recognition level) may be intact even though the ability to reproduce them is impaired. Scores on Picture Completion may help you determine the proper explanation.

Factor Analytic Findings

The Block Design subtest is the best measure of g among the Performance Scale subtests, and it is the fourth-best measure of g in the test (56 percent of its variance may be attributed to g—range of 46 to 64 percent in the 11 age groups). The subtest contributes substantially to the Perceptual Organization factor (Average loading = .73) and to a lesser extent to the Verbal Comprehension factor (Average loading = .33). Specificity is ample at all ages.

Reliability and Correlational Highlights

Block Design is a reliable subtest (r_{xx} = .87), with reliability coefficients above .70 at all ages (range of .77 to .92 in the 11 age groups). The subtest correlates more highly with Object Assembly (r = .61), Picture Completion (r = .52), and Arithmetic (r = .52) than with the other subtests. It correlates moderately with the Full Scale (r = .66) and the Performance Scale (r = .65) and to a lesser degree with the Verbal Scale (r = .57). It correlates more highly with the Verbal Scale than do the other subtests on the Performance Scale.

Administrative Suggestions

Be sure that the area you use to arrange the blocks is clear of other blocks and materials. Construct the design for item 1 by laying out the two blocks from the child's left to right. Construct design 2 by completing, from the child's left to right, the first row (that is, the top row of the design from the child's perspective) and then the second row. Be careful that your hand does not block the child's view. Scramble the blocks before you administer each new design and place before the child the exact number of blocks needed for the item.

Instruct the child to tell you when he or she has completed items 1, 2, 3, 10, 11, and 12, if you have any doubt about when the child is finished. In such cases, say "Tell me when you have finished." Give this instruction routinely on items 4 through 9, as indicated in the WISC-III manual, but also give it on the other items as needed.

Interpretive Suggestions

Block Design is an excellent subtest for observing the child's problem-solving approach. Consider the following issues:

• Is the child hasty and impulsive or deliberate and careful?
• Does the child slowly and methodically check each block with the design?
• Does the child give up easily or become frustrated when faced with possible failure, or does the child persist and keep on working even after he or she reaches the time limit?
• Does the child use only one kind of approach, or does the child alter his or her approach as the need arises?
• Does the child use a slow approach or a rapid trial-and-error approach?
• Does the child study the designs first?
• Does the child appear to have a plan when executing the items?
• Does the child construct the design in units of blocks, or does the child work in a piecemeal fashion?
• Does the child understand the principle of using individual blocks to construct the designs?
• Does the child express concerns about differences between blocks?

• Does the child say that his or her designs are correct when, in fact, they are not?
• Is the child able to succeed even on the more complex block designs (for example, those requiring nine blocks)?

Excessive fumbling or failure to check the pattern suggests anxiety. Visuoperceptual difficulties may be indicated if the child twists his or her body to improve his or her perspective on the design or if the child leaves space between the blocks in the assembled design. Try to differentiate between excessive cautiousness as a personality style and excessive slowness as a possible indication of depression or boredom.

Conduct testing-of-limits *after* you have administered the entire test. Research has shown that children benefit from receiving cues during the standard administration of the Block Design subtest (Sattler, 1969). A useful testing-of-limits procedure is to select one (or more) design(s) that the child failed. Show the child the Block Design card (or assembled design). As you give the directions, place one row or block in its correct position. Say "Let's try some of these again. I'm going to put together some of the blocks. I will make the top row [or arrange the first block]. Now you go ahead and finish it. Now make one like this. Tell me when you have finished." If the child still fails, arrange additional blocks. Record the amount of help the child needs to reproduce the designs accurately. A child who needs many cues may have weaker spatial reasoning ability than a child who needs few cues. In some cases, the additional cues may not help the child reproduce the designs.

The range of scaled scores from 1 to 19 at ages 6-0 to 15-11 years aids in profile analysis. However, at 16-0 to 16-11 years, profile analysis is somewhat hindered because scaled scores range only from 1 to 18.

Cautionary note. Prior experience with the commercial game Trac 4, which uses block design patterns, increased bright 10-year-old children's WISC-R Block Design scores by about 3 scaled-score points (Dirks, 1982). However, scores did not increase on the other subtests. These results, which likely apply to the WISC-III, suggest that you should avoid using the Block Design subtest in short forms if children have played Trac 4, because the scores are likely to be inflated. Standard IQs may also be slightly inflated on the WISC-III if children have played this game.

Question: In what direction does the sun rise?
Answer: Near Kansas City.

OBJECT ASSEMBLY

The Object Assembly subtest requires the child to put jigsaw pieces together to form common objects: a girl (seven pieces), a car (seven pieces), a horse (six pieces), a ball (six pieces), and a face (nine pieces). There is one sample item: an apple (four pieces). Items are given one at a time, and the pieces are presented in the specified disarranged pattern indicated in the WISC-III manual. Every item is administered to all children, beginning with the sample item and continuing with items 1 through 5.

All items are timed. The first item has a maximum of 120 seconds; the next two items, 150 seconds each; and the last two items, 180 seconds each. For perfect performance, the scores are 6 points for the girl, 5 points each for the car and the horse, and 7 points each for the ball and the face. Bonuses of up to 3 points are given for quick performance. The girl, car, and horse items each have a maximum score of 8, and the ball and face items, 10. Points are also given for partially correct assemblies on all items.

Rationale

The Object Assembly subtest is mainly a test of the child's skill at synthesis — putting things together to form familiar objects. It requires visual-motor coordination, with motor activity guided by visual perception and sensorimotor feedback. Object Assembly is also a test of visual organizational ability, for visual organization is needed to produce an object out of parts that may not be immediately recognizable. To solve the jigsaw puzzles, the child must be able to grasp an entire pattern by anticipating the relationships among its individual parts. The tasks require some constructive ability as well as perceptual skill — the child must recognize individual parts and place them correctly in the incomplete figure. Performance may also be related to rate and precision of motor activity; persistence, especially when much trial and error is required; and long-term visual memory (having stored information about the object to be formed).

Factor Analytic Findings

The Object Assembly subtest is a fair measure of g (44 percent of its variance may be attributed to g — range of 46 to 64 percent in the 11 age groups). The subtest contributes substantially to the Perceptual Organization factor (Average loading = .67). Specificity is ample or adequate at 4 of the 11 age groups (6, 9, 13, 15); at 7 age groups (7, 8, 10, 11, 12, 14, 16) it is inadequate.

Reliability and Correlational Highlights

Object Assembly is a marginally reliable subtest (r_{xx} = .69), with reliability coefficients above .70 in only 5 of the 11 age groups (6, 9, 13, 15, 16) and between .60 and .69 in the other age groups (range of .60 to .76 over the 11 age groups). The subtest correlates more highly with Block Design (r = .61) than with any other subtest. It has a somewhat low correlation with the Full Scale (r = .58), a moderate correlation with the Performance Scale (r = .60), and a low correlation with the Verbal Scale (r = .48).

Administrative Suggestions

Make sure that the child does not see the pages of the WISC-III manual that contain pictures of the correctly assembled objects. You can use the Object Assembly Layout Shield, not only to set up the individual puzzle parts, but to shield the manual as well. Place the pieces close to the child so that the child does not have to waste time reaching for them. As in other subtests, you may have to ask the child to tell you when he or she is finished — "Tell me when you have finished." You may need to give this instruction on items 2 through 5 because the directions in the WISC-III manual do not include it. Do not give any cues to the child that indicate approval or disapproval of his or her performance.

Because all items are given to all children, young school-aged children may experience some frustration on Object Assembly. If so, it would be useful to investigate what effects a discontinuance criterion would have on Object Assembly. Would it reduce young children's anxiety level without affecting the reliability and validity of the subtest? This, of course, is a proposal for research. The subtest should still be administered following the exact procedures stated in the WISC-III manual.

Interpretive Suggestions

Object Assembly is an especially good subtest for observing the child's thinking and work habits. Some children envision the complete object almost from the start and either recognize the relations of the individual parts to the whole or have an imperfect understanding of the relations between the parts and the whole. Others merely try to fit the pieces together by trial-and-error methods. Still others may have initial failure, followed by trial and error and then sudden insight and recognition of the object.

Observe how the child responds to errors and how the child handles frustration.

• Does the child demand to know what the object is before he or she constructs it, or insist that pieces are missing, or say that the object doesn't make sense (Zimmerman & Woo-Sam, 1985)?

• If the child has low scores, are they due to temporary inefficiency, such as reversal of two parts, which results in loss of time-bonus credits?

• Does the child spend a long time with one piece, trying to position it in an incorrect location? (If so, this behavior may indicate anxiety or rigidity.)

After you administer the subtest, ask the child about any constructions that may be peculiar or unusual (such as pieces placed on top of each other). You can use testing-of-limits procedures similar to those described for the Picture Arrangement and Block Design subtests *after* you have administered the entire test. For example, you can introduce a series of graduated cues, such as placing one or more pieces in the correct location. Note the amount of help the child needs to complete the task successfully. The child who needs only a few cues to complete the object may have underlying perceptual organization skills not evident during the standard administration of the subtest and may have better perceptual organization skills than the child who needs many cues.

Another testing-of-limits approach is to ask the child to visualize the object in his or her mind before you lay out the puzzle pieces. For example, say "Think of how a horse looks" and give the child the horse item. See if this instruction helps the child to assemble the puzzle.

The range of scaled scores from 1 to 19 at ages 6-0 to 15-11 years aids in profile analysis. However, at ages 16-0 to 16-11 years, profile analysis is somewhat hindered because scaled scores range only from 1 to 18.

Question: What is gasoline?
 Answer: To put on the thing what takes your temperature so it don't hurt you.
(Flumen & Flumen, 1979)

SYMBOL SEARCH

The Symbol Search subtest, a supplementary subtest, requires the child to look at a symbol (or symbols) and then decide whether the symbol(s) is(are) present in an array of symbols. Symbol Search is not used in the computation of the IQ when the five standard Performance Scale subtests are administered. The subtest consists of two separate parts. Part A is administered to children 6 to 7-11 years old, and Part B to children between 8 and 16 years old.

In Part A there is one target symbol and three symbols in the array. The child is told to draw a slash (/) through the box labeled YES if the target symbol is also in the array. If the target symbol is not in the array, the child should draw a slash (/) through the box labeled NO. The target symbols usually are nonsense shapes and designs, as are the symbols in the array. There are 2 demonstration (sample) items and 2 practice items. Part A contains 45 items in addition to the 2 sample and 2 practice items.

In Part B there are two target symbols and five symbols in the array. As in Part A, the child is told to draw a slash (/) through the box labeled YES if either of the target symbols is also in the array. If neither one of the target symbols is in the array, the child should draw a slash (/) through the box labeled NO. The target symbols, like those in Part A, are usually nonsense shapes and designs, as are the symbols in the array. There are 2 demonstration (sample) items and 2 practice items. Part B contains 45 items in addition to the 2 sample and 2 practice items. Some of the symbols in Part A and Part B are the same. Each part has a time limit of 120 seconds.

The score on each part is the number of correct items minus the number of incorrect items. There are no time-bonus credits on either Part A or Part B.

Rationale

On the Symbol Search subtest, the child looks at a stimulus figure (target stimulus), scans an array, and decides whether the stimulus figure appears in the array. The task involves perceptual discrimination, speed and accuracy, attention and concentration, short-term memory, and cognitive flexibility (in shifting rapidly from one array to the next). Visual-motor coordination plays a role, albeit minor, because the only motor movement is that of drawing a slash. Part B is more complex than Part A because there are two target stimulus figures instead of one (as in Part A) and five symbols in the array instead of three (as in Part A).

Most of the symbols used in the Symbol Search subtest will be difficult to encode verbally. However, some symbols may be verbally encoded if children attach verbal descriptions to them. These include, for example, ± (plus or minus), L (L shape), > (greater than sign), ∩ (inverted U), and ⊢ (a T on its side). Research is needed to learn whether children verbally encode these or other symbols and whether the encoding affects their performance.

As in the Coding subtest, the speed and accuracy with which the child performs the task are a measure of the child's intellectual ability. For each item, the child must inspect the target stimulus, go to the array, look at the array items and determine whether the target stimulus is present, and then mark the appropriate box (YES or NO) once he or she makes the decision. You can thus conceptualize Symbol Search as a task involving visual discrimination and visuoperceptual scanning.

Factor Analytic Findings

The Symbol Search subtest is a fair measure of g (38 percent of its variance may be attributed to g — range of 27 to 48 percent in the 11 age groups). The subtest contributes substantially to the Processing Speed factor (Average loading = .62) and to a lesser degree to the Perceptual Organization factor (Average loading = . 35). Subtest specificity is ample at 8 of the 11 age groups (7, 10, 11, 12, 13, 14, 15, 16); at 3 ages (6, 8, 9) it is inadequate.

Reliability and Correlational Highlights

Symbol Search is a relatively reliable subtest (r_{xx} = .76), with reliability coefficients above .70 at 5 of the 6 age groups reported (7, 10, 11, 14, 15); the one exception is at age 6, where the reliability coefficient is .69 (range of .69 to .82 in the 6 age groups). As with Coding, reliability coefficients are not given for 5 age groups (8, 9, 12, 13, 16) because no children were retested at these ages. The subtest correlates more highly with Coding (r = .53) than with any of the other subtests. It has low correlations with the Full Scale (r = .56), Performance Scale (r = .58), and Verbal Scale (r = .44).

Administrative Suggestions

The Symbol Search subtest is in a separate booklet (WISC-III Symbol Search Response Booklet). You and the child should each use a no. 2 graphite pencil without an eraser. Write the child's name, the date, and your name in the space provided on the Symbol Search Response Booklet. Administer the subtest on a smooth drawing surface.

A child with visual defects or specific motor disabilities may be penalized on this subtest. Generally, do not give the subtest to a child with either of these handicaps. If you do give it to a child with these handicaps, do not count it in the final score, even when it replaces a standard Performance Scale subtest. Other types of children also may be penalized on this subtest, including those who are unable to make quick decisions; those who respond slowly and care-

fully; those who are compulsive and need to constantly check the stimulus figure(s) against those in the array; and those who are impulsive and fail to check the array figures against the stimulus figure(s).

Observe the child's work methods. Tell the child who stops working after the first line to "Continue on the next line." Tell the child who fails to turn the page to "Go to the next page." Count these instructions as part of the 2-minute time limit. If the child skips lines, tell him or her to do the lines in order.

Interpretive Suggestions

Useful observational guidelines are as follows:

• Does the child carefully check the target symbol with those in the array?
• Does the child draw the slash (/) mark slowly or quickly?
• Does the child respond impulsively?
• Is the child penalized for working slowly?
• Does the child make many errors?
• Does the child understand the task?
• Does the child work smoothly, or does he or she seem confused at times?
• Does the child seem to be aware of any errors?

Answers to the above questions may provide valuable information about attention, persistence, impulsive tendencies, compulsive tendencies, and depressive features. It will be of interest to compare children who obtain the same score in different ways. For example, two children may get a score of 10, but one child has 10 correct responses and zero errors and the other child has 20 correct responses and 10 errors. These two children likely have different styles of working. The first child may be a careful and diligent worker, but unwilling (or unable) to work quickly, whereas the second child may be a quick worker, but rather careless and impulsive.

After the test is over, for children who make many errors, you may want to go over each item on which an error occurred. You can point to an item on which an error occurred and say "Tell me about your answer" or "Tell me about why you marked a 'No' (or 'Yes')."

Compare the child's response style on Symbol Search with that on other subtests. If there are differences, try to determine what might account for them. Consider, for example, the nature of the tasks, the child's motivation, the child's scores on all tasks, and when the tasks were administered — that is, at the beginning, middle, or end of the examination.

The range of scaled scores from 1 to 19 at ages 6–0 to

15–11 years aids in profile analysis. However, at ages 16–0 to 16–11 years, profile analysis is somewhat hindered because scaled scores range only from 1 to 18.

Question: In what way are a computer and TV alike?
Answer: They both go on the blink when you need them.

MAZES

The Mazes subtest, a supplementary subtest, requires the child to solve paper-and-pencil mazes that differ in level of complexity. Mazes is not used in the computation of the IQ when the five standard Performance Scale subtests are administered. Mazes consists of 1 sample problem and 10 problems in the subtest proper. The child is asked to draw a line from the center of each maze to the outside without crossing any of the lines that indicate walls. Each maze is presented separately. Children 6 to 7 years (and older children suspected of mental retardation) start with the sample maze followed by item 1, whereas children 8 to 16 years start with item 4.

All items are timed. The first four mazes are given a maximum of 30 seconds each; the fifth maze, 45 seconds; the sixth maze, 60 seconds; the seventh and eighth mazes, 120 seconds; and the ninth and tenth mazes, 150 seconds. The number of errors made determines the child's score. Scores range from 0 to 5 points, with mazes 1 to 6 having a maximum score of 2; maze 7, a maximum score of 3; mazes 8 and 9, a maximum score of 4; and maze 10, a maximum score of 5. The subtest is discontinued after two consecutive failures. Although you do not have to administer Mazes routinely, administering it to children who are either language-impaired or from a different culture, in particular, may give you useful information.

Rationale

To complete the Mazes subtest successfully, the child must (a) attend to the directions, which include locating a route from the entrance to the exit, avoiding blind alleys, crossing no lines, and holding the pencil on the paper, and (b) execute the task, which involves remembering and following the directions, displaying visual-motor coordination, and resisting the disruptive effect of an implied need for speed (Madden, 1974). The Mazes subtest appears to measure the child's planning ability and perceptual organizational ability—that is, the ability to follow a visual pattern. To succeed, a child must have visual-motor control combined with speed and accuracy.

Factor Analytic Findings

The Mazes subtest is the poorest measure of g in the test (13 percent of its variance may be attributed to g—range of 5 to 30 percent in the 11 age groups). The subtest contributes minimally to the Perceptual Organization factor (Average loading = .36). Subtest specificity is ample at 10 of the 11 age groups; at age 15 it is inadequate.

Reliability and Correlational Highlights

Mazes is a relatively reliable subtest (r_{xx} = .70), with reliability coefficients above .70 in 6 of the 11 age groups (6, 7, 8, 10, 13, 14) and between .61 and .68 in the other 5 age groups (9, 11, 12, 15, 16; range of .61 to .80 in the 11 age groups). The subtest correlates more highly with Block Design (r = .31) than with any other subtest. It has a low correlation with the Full Scale (r = .31), Performance Scale (r = .35), and Verbal Scale (r = .23).

Administrative Suggestions

The Mazes subtest is in a separate booklet (WISC-III Mazes Response Booklet). Administer the subtest on a smooth drawing surface. Use a no. 2 graphite pencil without an eraser to demonstrate the sample item, and give a no. 2 pencil without an eraser to the child. Write the child's name, the date, and your name in the space provided on the Mazes Response Booklet.

When a child makes certain errors, give the child the cues described in the WISC-III manual. The first time these errors occur, tell the child that he or she has made an error and give the child the appropriate cue. The cues are designed to help the child, especially if he or she does not fully understand what to do. A table in the WISC-III manual (page 159) shows how to score the child's performance. The sample responses that illustrate the scoring criteria should be carefully studied (see pages 160–164 in the WISC-III manual).

In the first printing of the WISC-III manual, there is an incorrect direction on page 157 for maze 3. The sentence says, "If the child completes the maze within the time limit with no more than one error, proceed to Maze 4." *Disregard this direction because it conflicts with the discontinuance rule.* The discontinuance rule states that Mazes should be discontinued after two consecutive failures. Therefore, you should proceed to maze 4 if the child passes maze 1 and maze 2, regardless of the number of errors he or she makes on maze 3. (On October 28, 1991 I notified The Psychological Corporation of this error. Lawrence Weiss acknowledged that the sentence is incorrect in the manual and that it will be changed in the next printing.)

Interpretive Suggestions

Consider the following questions as you observe the child's performance.

- Does the child understand the task?
- Does the child study the mazes extensively and plan a route before proceeding?
- Does the child show signs of tremor, difficulty in controlling the pencil, or difficulty in drawing uniform lines?
- Does the child solve the mazes correctly after the time limit has expired?
- Does the child cross lines?
- If the child crosses lines, is this tendency related to poor visual-motor coordination or to impulsivity?
- Does the child say anything that suggests anxiety (for example, "The little boy is trapped in the center of the maze")?

These observations (and the overall success rate) will give you information about the child's motor planning, speed, execution, impulsivity, and sustained attention.

The range of scaled scores from 1 to 19 at ages 6-0 to 10-11 years aids in profile analysis. However, profile analysis is somewhat hindered at 11-0 to 12-11 years and 13-0 to 16-11 years, where the scaled scores range from 1 to 18 and 1 to 17, respectively.

Question: Listen, say just what I say: "Eating too much cake and ice cream can give you a stomach ache."

Answer: So you have to take an Alka Seltzer, right?
(Adapted from Flumen & Flumen, 1979)

THINKING THROUGH THE ISSUES

In evaluating the 13 WISC-III subtests, consider the following: Which WISC-III subtests are the most reliable? In what ways do the WISC-III subtests share common properties, and in what ways do they differ? What other kinds of subtests would you like to see incorporated in the WISC-III? Why?

If you were evaluating a child who had both language and motor impairments, which WISC-III subtests would be most useful? Which ones might be least useful? Why?

SUMMARY

1. Information measures the child's available information acquired as a result of native ability and early cultural experience. Memory is an important aspect of performance on the subtest. The subtest is the second-best measure of g and contributes to the Verbal Comprehension factor. Subtest specificity is ample or adequate at most ages. Information is a reliable subtest ($r_{xx} = .84$). It is easy to administer and score.

2. Similarities measures verbal concept formation. The subtest is the third-best measure of g. Subtest specificity is ample or adequate at 6 of the 11 ages. Similarities is a reliable subtest ($r_{xx} = .81$). It is easy to administer but difficult to score.

3. Arithmetic measures numerical reasoning ability. The subtest is a good measure of g and contributes to the Verbal Comprehension factor and the Perceptual Organization factor. Subtest specificity is ample or adequate at 6 of the 11 ages. Arithmetic is a reasonably reliable subtest ($r_{xx} = .78$). It is easy to administer and score.

4. Vocabulary measures language development, learning ability, and fund of information. The subtest is an excellent measure of g and contributes to the Verbal Comprehension factor. Subtest specificity is adequate at 9 of the 11 ages. Vocabulary is a reliable subtest ($r_{xx} = .87$). It is relatively easy to administer but difficult to score.

5. Comprehension measures social judgment: the ability to use facts in a pertinent, meaningful, and emotionally appropriate manner. The subtest is a good measure of g and contributes to the Verbal Comprehension factor. Subtest specificity is adequate at 6 of the 11 ages. Comprehension is a relatively reliable subtest ($r_{xx} = .77$). It is easy to administer but difficult to score.

6. Digit Span is a supplementary subtest that measures short-term memory and attention. The subtest is a fair measure of g and contributes to the Verbal Comprehension factor. Subtest specificity is ample at all ages. Digit Span is a reliable subtest ($r_{xx} = .85$). It is easy to administer and score. Administer it routinely, even though it is not used to compute the IQ when the five standard Verbal subtests are administered.

7. Picture Completion measures the ability to differentiate essential from nonessential details. It requires concentration, visual organization, and visual memory. The subtest is a fair measure of g. It contributes to the Perceptual Organization factor and to the Verbal Comprehension factor. Subtest specificity is ample or adequate at 10 of the 11 ages. Picture Completion is a reasonably reliable subtest ($r_{xx} = .77$). It is easy to administer and relatively easy to score.

8. Coding measures visual-motor coordination, speed of mental operation, and short-term memory. The subtest is a poor measure of g and contributes to the Processing Speed factor.

Subtest specificity is adequate at 10 of the 11 ages. Coding is a relatively reliable subtest ($r_{xx} = .79$). It is easy to administer and score.

9. Picture Arrangement measures nonverbal reasoning ability. It may be viewed as a measure of planning ability—that is, the ability to comprehend and evaluate a total situation. The subtest is a fair measure of g and contributes to the Perceptual Organization factor and to the Verbal Comprehension factor. Subtest specificity is ample at all ages. Picture Arrangement is a relatively reliable subtest ($r_{xx} = .76$). It is easy to administer and score.

10. Block Design measures spatial visualization ability and nonverbal concept formation. The subtest is the best measure of g among the Performance Scale subtests. It contributes to the Perceptual Organization factor and to the Verbal Comprehension factor. Subtest specificity is ample at all ages. Block Design is a reliable subtest ($r_{xx} = .87$). It is somewhat difficult to administer but easy to score.

11. Object Assembly measures visual organizational ability. The subtest is a fair measure of g and contributes to the Perceptual Organization factor. Specificity is ample or adequate at 4 of the 11 ages. Object Assembly is a marginally reliable subtest ($r_{xx} = .69$). It is somewhat difficult to administer but relatively easy to score.

12. Symbol Search is a supplementary subtest that measures visual discrimination and visuoperceptual scanning. The subtest is a fair measure of g and contributes to the Processing Speed factor and to the Perceptual Organization factor. Subtest specificity is ample at 8 of the 11 ages. Symbol Search is a relatively reliable subtest ($r_{xx} = .76$). It is easy to administer and score.

13. Mazes is a supplementary subtest that measures planning ability and perceptual organization. The subtest is the poorest measure of g in the test and contributes to the Perceptual Organization factor. Subtest specificity is ample at 10 of the 11 ages. Mazes is a relatively reliable subtest ($r_{xx} = .70$). It is easy to administer but difficult to score.

KEY TERMS, CONCEPTS, AND NAMES

WISC-III Information (p. 1080)
WISC-III Similarities (p. 1082)
WISC-III Arithmetic (p. 1083)
WISC-III Vocabulary (p. 1086)
WISC-III Comprehension (p. 1088)
WISC-III Digit Span (p. 1089)
WISC-III Picture Completion (p. 1092)
WISC-III Coding (p. 1093)
WISC-III Picture Arrangement (p. 1095)
WISC-III Block Design (p. 1097)
WISC-III Object Assembly (p. 1099)
WISC-III Symbol Search (p. 1100)
WISC-III Mazes (p. 1102)

STUDY QUESTION

Discuss the rationale, factor analytic findings, reliability and correlational highlights, and administrative and interpretive considerations for each of the following WISC-III subtests: Information, Similarities, Arithmetic, Vocabulary, Comprehension, Digit Span, Picture Completion, Coding, Picture Arrangement, Block Design, Object Assembly, Symbol Search, and Mazes.

REFERENCES

Holmes, J. M. (1988). Testing. In R. G. Rudel, *Assessment of developmental learning disorders* (pp. 166–201). New York: Basic Books.

Wechsler, D. (1991). *Manual for the Wechsler Intelligence Scale for Children—Third Edition*. San Antonio: The Psychological Corporation.

APPENDIX K

INTERPRETING THE WISC-III

The gifts of nature are infinite in their variety, and mind differs from mind almost as much as body from body.
—Quintilian

Appendix K presents guidelines for interpreting the WISC-III and for writing reports. *The appendix must be used in conjunction with Chapters 8 and 23, because these chapters present more detailed guidelines for interpreting all of the Wechsler tests and for writing reports.* Because the methods of interpreting the WISC-III—such as the successive level approach, profile analysis, Performance/Verbal Scale comparisons, and subtest comparisons—are essentially the same for both the WISC-R and the WISC-III, study carefully the contents of Chapter 8 that pertain to these issues. Appendix K complements these chapters by focusing on the WISC-III. Appendix K also includes a training exercise designed to sharpen your report writing skills (Exhibit K-3) and two illustrative reports (Exhibits K-1 and K-4).

Appendix L contains tables specifically designed to help you interpret the WISC-III. Other tables that can assist you in interpreting the WISC-III and in writing reports are as follows: Table C-13 (page 824), which summarizes the abilities thought to be measured by 12 of the WISC-III subtests (with some minor exceptions, as noted in the footnote to the table; Table L-16 in Appendix L presents similar information for Symbol Search); Table C-42 (pages 856–857), which summarizes the interpretive rationales for the Full Scale, Verbal Scale, and Performance Scale of the Wechsler batteries; and Table C-43 (page 858), which presents activities to improve children's skills based on Wechsler subtests.

On the inside back cover of this text, Table BC-2 shows the classifications associated with WISC-III IQs, and Table BC-1 shows the percentile ranks for the WISC-III Full Scale, Performance Scale, and Verbal Scale IQs. Percentile ranks for the three IQs also can be obtained directly from the WISC-III manual in Tables A.2, A.3, and A.4 (pages 251–254). Table C-41 in Appendix C (page 855) shows the percentile ranks associated with subtest scaled scores. Table C-12 in Appendix C (page 822), which gives the Structure of Intellect classifications for the subtests on the WISC-R, also can be used for the following WISC-III subtests: Arithmetic, Vocabulary, Comprehension, Digit Span, Picture Completion, Picture Arrangement, Block Design, Object Assembly, Coding, and Mazes.

PROFILE ANALYSIS

The seven primary approaches to profile analysis of the WISC-III described below are essentially the same as those described for the WISC-R (see pages 166–171). However, there are some differences.

First, for profile analysis you should use the tables in Appendix L, which cover the WISC-III, instead of those in Appendix C, which cover the WISC-R.

Second, the critical values in Appendix L for the WISC-III are based on the child's specific age group rather than an average value (as in the WISC-R).

Third, factor scores on the WISC-III (see Appendix I) differ from those on the WISC-R (see Chapter 6) in the following ways: Although the Verbal Comprehension factor is the same on both tests (Information, Similarities, Vocabulary, and Comprehension), the Perceptual Organization factor is not (Picture Completion, Block Design, and Object Assembly on the WISC-III and Picture Completion, Block Design, Object Assembly, and Picture Arrangement on the WISC-R). In addition, the WISC-III has a Processing Speed factor (composed of Coding and Symbol Search) that is not present on the WISC-R, and the WISC-R has a Freedom from Distractibility factor (Arithmetic, Digit Span, and Coding) that is not present on the WISC-III. On the WISC-III, Arithmetic, Digit Span, Picture Arrangement, and Mazes are not included in a factor score.

Let us now examine the seven primary approaches to profile analysis.

1. *Comparing Verbal and Performance Scale IQs.* Table L-3 in Appendix L provides the critical values for comparing the Verbal and Performance IQs for the 11 age groups of the WISC-III. These values range from 10 to 13 at the .05 level and from 13 to 17 at the .01 level. Thus, an average critical value based on the entire standardization group would be misleading. Therefore, use the values for the child's specific age group to evaluate differences between the child's Verbal and Performance IQs. (Table L-7 in Appendix L shows the probabilities associated with various differences between the WISC-III Verbal and Performance Scale IQs.)

2. *Comparing each Verbal subtest scaled score to the mean Verbal scaled score.* Table L-4 in Appendix L provides the critical values for each of the 11 age groups of the WISC-III. Typical values for 6-year-old children on the five standard Verbal subtests, for example, range from 3.01 to 3.51 at the .05 level and from 3.60 to 4.20 at the .01 level.

3. *Comparing each Performance subtest scaled score to the mean Performance scaled score.* Table L-4 in Appendix L provides the critical values for each of the 11 age groups of the WISC-III. Typical values for 6-year-old children for the five standard Performance subtests, for example, range from 3.03 to 3.62 at the .05 level and from 3.62 to 4.34 at the .01 level.

4. *Comparing each subtest scaled score to the mean subtest scaled score.* Table L-4 in Appendix L provides the

critical values for each of the 11 age groups in the WISC-III for 10, 11, 12, and 13 subtests. Typical values for 6-year-old children for the 10 standard subtests, for example, range from 3.43 to 4.25 at the .05 level and from 4.02 to 4.97 at the .01 level. This approach to profile analysis tends to be used less often than Methods 2 and 3.

5. *Comparing pairs of individual subtest scores.* Table L-3 in Appendix L provides the critical values for comparing pairs of subtest scores for each of the 11 age groups of the WISC-III. They range from 3 to 5 at the .05 level and from 4 to 7 at the .01 level. The values in Table L-3 are overly liberal (that is, lead to too many significant differences) when you make more than one comparison. They are most accurate when you make a priori planned comparisons, such as Comprehension versus Information or Block Design versus Object Assembly. Pages 174 to 179 provide additional information about making comparisons between subtests.

Before making multiple comparisons, determine the difference between the highest and lowest subtest scores. If this difference is 6 scaled-score points or more, a significant difference at the .05 level is indicated. You can then interpret differences between subtests that are 6 scaled-score points or greater. If the difference between the highest and lowest subtest scaled scores is less than 6 scaled-score points, do not make multiple comparisons between individual subtest scores. (The *Note* to Table H-2 in Appendix H shows the formula used to compute the significant difference. The formula considers the average standard error of measurement for each of the 13 subtests and the studentized range statistic.)

6. *Comparing the Verbal Comprehension, Perceptual Organization, and Processing Speed factor scores.* Table L-3 in Appendix L presents the differences between sets of Verbal Comprehension, Perceptual Organization, and Processing Speed factor scores (in the form of Deviation IQs) needed to reach the .05 and .01 significance levels. (Table L-10 in Appendix L shows the probabilities associated with various differences between WISC-III factor score Deviation Quotients.)

7. *Comparing subtest scaled scores in each factor with their respective factor scores.* Table L-5 in Appendix L provides the critical values for the total WISC-III sample for the Verbal Comprehension, Perceptual Organization, and Processing Speed factors. Typical values for Verbal Comprehension range from 2.48 to 2.99 at the 5 percent level and 3.00 to 3.62 at the 1 percent level. For Perceptual Organization, they range from 2.60 to 3.12 at the 5 percent level and from 3.19 to 3.82 at the 1 percent level. For Processing Speed, they are 2.30 at the 5 percent level and 2.88 at the 1 percent level. The procedure used for this method is similar to that used in Methods 2 and 3 described above.

Supplementary approaches to profile analysis (referred to as *base rate approaches*) examine the kinds of variability found in the normative group, allowing features of an individual child's profile to be compared with those of the normative group. The three base rate approaches described below can be used for examining different kinds of variability.

Base Rate Subtest Scaled-Score Ranges

A descriptive statistic that provides information about the variability, or spread, of a child's subtest scores (also referred to as *scatter*) is the *range* (see Chapter 2, page 15). The scaled-score range indicates the distance between the two most extreme scaled scores in a child's profile. It is obtained by subtracting the lowest scaled score from the highest scaled score. Thus, in a profile where the highest scaled score is 14 and the lowest scaled score is 5, the range is 9 (14 − 5 = 9).

In the standardization group, the median scaled-score range was 7 points for the 10 standard subtests on the Full Scale, 4 points for the 5 standard subtests on the Verbal Scale, and 6 points for the 5 standard subtests on the Performance Scale (see Table B.5, page 266 in the WISC-III manual). The scaled-score range is not a very helpful measure of variability because it is difficult to interpret and little research is available to guide its interpretation. It deals with only 2 scores and therefore fails to take into account the variability among all 10 (or 11, 12, or 13) subtest scores. The range index should not be discarded, however, because it provides base rate information about what occurred in the standardization sample.

Base Rate Verbal-Performance Differences (The Probability-of-Occurrence Approach)

Determining how frequently a Verbal-Performance IQ difference of a given magnitude occurred in the standardization sample is referred to as the probability-of-occurrence approach. The frequencies with which several Verbal-Performance discrepancies are estimated to have occurred in the normative standardization sample are given in the expectancy table in Table L-8 of Appendix L. The table shows, for example, that a 10-point difference in either direction between the Verbal and Performance IQs was estimated to occur among 25 to 50 percent of the children in each age group of the standardization sample. Table L-10 in Appendix L presents a similar table — but only for the total group — for the Deviation Quotients associated with the Verbal Comprehension, Perceptual Organization, and Processing Speed factor scores.

For the total sample, Table B.2 in the WISC-III manual (page 262) shows the actual cumulative percentages of the total standardization sample that obtained various Verbal-Performance IQ discrepancies. (Table B.2 also shows similar information for the factor scores as proposed in the WISC-III manual.) The mean discrepancy was 10.0, and the median discrepancy was 8.0. Twenty-five percent of the sample had a discrepancy of 14 points or higher, and 75 percent of the sample had a discrepancy of 4 points or higher.

Base Rate Differences Between Each Subtest Scaled Score and an Average Subtest Scaled Score in the WISC-III Standardization Sample

Table L-6 in Appendix L gives the estimated frequencies with which various differences occurred in the standardization sample between a child's scaled score on each subtest and his or her average WISC-III Verbal, Performance, or overall scaled score. The table shows, for example, that a difference of 3.12 points between the scaled score on Information and the Verbal Scale average, composed of the five standard subtests, was obtained by 5 percent of the standardization sample. Use this table only for differences that have first been shown to be reliable. (See Methods 2, 3, and 4 above.) Differences of approximately 2.94 to 4.96 points between each subtest scaled score and the respective average Verbal Scale or Performance Scale score were obtained by 5 percent of the standardization sample.

GUIDELINES FOR INTERPRETING AND COMMUNICATING WISC-III FINDINGS IN THE PSYCHOLOGICAL REPORT

The guidelines in this section, used with other material in this appendix and with Appendixes I and J and Chapters 8 and 23, will help you interpret the WISC-III (and other intelligence tests) and write better reports. This section somewhat overlaps with the material in Chapter 23, but any redundancy is intended to emphasize some of the more subtle principles of test interpretation and report writing.

Interpreting Individual Subtests

Scores on individual subtests should not be used as a means of describing specific cognitive skills with precision;

rather, they should be used to generate hypotheses about the child's abilities. You can derive the most reliable estimates of *specific abilities* from the Verbal Scale IQ (verbal or verbal comprehension abilities) and the Performance Scale IQ (performance, perceptual organization, or nonverbal abilities), not from individual subtest scores. Factor scores also provide more reliable information about abilities than do individual subtest scores. In fact, of the 133 separate reliability coefficients for the 13 subtests at the 11 age groups of the test, less than half (65) are .80 or above. Of these, only 7 are .90 or above—Vocabulary at ages 14 and 15, Digit Span at age 15, and Block Design at ages 13, 14, 15, and 16. The remaining 68 reliability coefficients are below .80 and are not sufficiently reliable for decision-making or classification purposes (see Table 5.1 on page 166 of the WISC-III manual). However, reliability coefficients of .70 or above are useful for generating hypotheses.

Integrating Quantitative and Qualitative Aspects of Performance

In interpreting the child's overall performance, look at the level of performance, quality of performance, relationship between level of performance and quality of performance, and problem-solving strategies used by the child to reach a solution (Holmes, 1988[R][1]).

• Level of performance refers to whether the child's scores reflect strengths, weaknesses, or average ability.

• Quality of performance depends on such factors as the child's language, affect, level of attention, and approach to the tasks (for example, systematic or unsystematic), as well as the examiner-examinee interactions.

• Problem-solving strategies refer to such things as the child's verbalizations to himself or herself and whether the child checked solutions, repeated key elements of problems, recognized when the solutions were correct or incorrect, found alternative ways of solving problems, and formulated plans to solve problems.

You may sometimes observe that the examinee has difficulty completing tasks. For example, tasks requiring speed and quick execution, such as Coding or Symbol Search, may be taxing for depressed children. Although depressed children's performance on these tasks may not reflect their level of cognitive ability, the tasks are still valuable because

---

[1] References followed by an [R] are cited at the end of this appendix; all other references are cited in the Reference section.

they provide information not readily obtained from interviews or observations conducted in natural settings. Coding, for example, gives you clues about the child's ability to follow a complex set of instructions, visual scanning processes, and learning ability. And Symbol Search gives you clues about visual scanning and the ability to shift rapidly. You may not want to report a score for these tasks for children who are depressed, but you can use such results to develop hypotheses to guide your clinical judgments.

Here is an illustration of how quantitative and qualitative information were woven into a report, along with a discussion of the profile. The report, only parts of which are shown below, is based on the administration of a WISC-III to a 16-year-, 11-month-old female. Her scores were as follows: Information 12, Similarities 12, Arithmetic 8, Vocabulary, 10, Comprehension 9, Digit Span 6, Picture Completion 9, Coding 11, Picture Arrangement 5, Block Design 9, Object Assembly 9, Verbal IQ 101, Performance IQ 91, and Full Scale IQ 94.

...Her short-term sequential memory is relatively less well developed than her overall verbal skills. The subtest measuring short-term auditory memory involves repeating a sequence of digits from immediate memory. Her weakness in short-term auditory sequential memory may be due to temporary inefficiency caused by anxiety or inattention. However, it is important to note that neither anxiety nor inattention appeared to affect her performance on other subtests adversely. It is more likely that her weakness in short-term auditory memory for digit sequences indicated difficulty forming in memory an adequate mental image of the correct digit sequence. Helen was often able to recall the correct digits but in the wrong sequence, indicating specific weakness in auditory sequential memory rather than in general auditory memory.

... Her visual sequencing ability is relatively less well developed than her other nonverbal skills. Her average attention to visual detail, coupled with her below average visual sequencing ability, indicates that although her perception of visual details is adequate, her ability to organize and sequence these details is poor. Moreover, it is important to note that both her verbal and her nonverbal weaknesses lie in her sequencing ability in different domains—auditory sequencing and visual sequencing. This may indicate an inefficiency in her general sequential processing abilities, although further testing would be needed to substantiate this hypothesis. It is unclear how her weakness in auditory and visual sequencing has affected her academic performance at school; this needs to be investigated. However, her overall average verbal and nonverbal skills indicate that she has the ability to perform adequately in school.

Steps in Analyzing a Wechsler Protocol

Here are some steps that you may find useful in analyzing a Wechsler protocol. They are by no means the only ones you

should consider, but they do cover several important areas that will help you interpret a child's performance.

1. Evaluate the reliability of the test scores.
2. Evaluate the validity of the test scores.
3. Look at the Full Scale IQ and its percentile rank and evaluate the implications of this score.
4. Look at the Verbal Scale IQ and its percentile rank and evaluate the implications of this score.
5. Look at the Performance Scale IQ and its percentile rank and evaluate the implications of this score.
6. Determine whether there is a significant discrepancy between the Verbal and Performance IQs. If there is, which IQ is higher? What is the base rate for the discrepancy? What are the implications of the discrepancy?
7. Determine whether there are any significant discrepancies between subtest scores and the means of their respective scaled scores. If there is a significant discrepancy, is the subtest score lower or higher than the mean? What is the base rate for the discrepancy? What are the implications of the discrepancy? Note the absolute level of each subtest score that differs significantly from its respective mean score.
8. Are there any subtest scores that differ significantly? If so, which ones are they? What are the implications of each discrepancy? Note which subtest score is higher or lower than the other and the absolute level of each score.
9. Consider the child's factor scores. Are there any significant discrepancies among the factor scores? If so, which factor scores differ significantly? Note which factor score is higher or lower than the others and the absolute level of each score. Do any of the subtest scores on a factor differ significantly from the mean factor score? If so, is the subtest score lower or higher than the mean? What are the base rates for the discrepancies? What are the implications of any significant discrepancies?
10. Were there any qualitative features of the child's performance that were especially noteworthy? Is so, what were they? What are the implications of these features by themselves and in relation to the test scores?

Guideline 1. Describe carefully the behaviors you observe. Make inferences about underlying traits or processes only with extreme caution, if at all.

Discussion of Guideline 1

It is tempting to interpret and explain an examinee's behavior. However, be extremely cautious in making interpretations based on a limited sample of behavior. You should, of course, describe the child's behavior in the report. And when you have information that you believe supports an interpretation, go ahead and make it.

Examples of Statements That Do Not Meet Guideline 1

1. "Jean was careless and erratic when she was sure she could perform a task." This statement is questionable because we don't know how the examiner knew that the child "was *sure* she could perform a task." Suggestion: "Jean was careless and erratic on nonverbal tasks. However, on verbal tasks she was more systematic and organized and seemed to be more confident."

2. "From the start, Derek had a tendency either to repeat questions to himself or to ask the examiner to repeat the questions for him. This appeared to be an attempt by Derek to structure or clarify the questions for himself." This behavior pattern may mean one or more things. It could reflect the examinee's attempt to structure the question, but it is not clear how repeating the question helped him to clarify it. It could also be a means of controlling the situation, or it could suggest inattention. In addition, the behavior may reflect a way of holding on, a delay reaction, a need for additional support, or a coping pattern associated with a possible hearing deficit. Examine the entire performance to arrive at the best interpretation. Suggestion: Leave out the second sentence unless other information supports one or more of the above interpretations or some other interpretation.

3. "As the test progressed, he had a tendency to sit with his arms folded or to pick at and scratch his arm when answering questions. Though at first these behaviors made John seem less interested, it appears that he was compensating for his lowered self-confidence." This interpretation seems to have little merit. In what way does folding and scratching arms reflect compensation for lowered self-confidence? Could these actions simply be a habit or a response to frustration? Suggestion: Keep the first sentence and eliminate the second one. Then describe what comments the examinee made about his performance, if any, and note how cooperative he was.

4. "She responded impulsively on the verbal subtests. On the nonverbal subtests, she was more attentive and careful. This behavior may simply reflect an impulsive personality." This interpretation may or may not be correct.

Performing impulsively on one part of the test but not on the other may *not* be an indication of an impulsive personality. Perhaps there are tendencies in this direction, but the generalization may be inappropriate. You should also consider whether there was anything about the verbal items that led her to respond impulsively. Suggestion: Keep the first two sentences and eliminate the third one. Then describe her scores on the verbal and nonverbal parts of the test.

5. "Harry's statements about his inadequacies resulted in an increase in feelings of inferiority and self-deprecating behavior, as demonstrated by an increase in nervous laughter and by impulsive answers." This inference is conjectural. It implies a cause-and-effect relationship between verbal expressions and behavior. There is no way of knowing what the examinee's statements led to. Suggestion: Limit the statements to a description of his verbalizations and behavior. For example, "On difficult items, Harry answered impulsively, laughed anxiously, and made self-deprecatory remarks."

6. "Rachel also showed a tendency to ignore specific directions by giving information that was not asked for. For example, in the Picture Completion subtest, she tended to say what was in the picture rather than what was missing." The examinee's way of responding to the task may have been her way of coping with a difficult situation rather than a case of "ignoring" directions. Suggestion: "On a task requiring her to give the missing details of pictures, Rachel tended to say what was in the picture rather than what was missing." Then state how she performed on the subtest.

7. "The inconsistency in her performance during certain periods of time may have been due to her medical diagnosis of hyperactivity." This statement has at least two difficulties. First, the term *inconsistency* is unclear. It could be a description of her behavior (qualitative information) or a description of her test scores (quantitative information). Second, a diagnosis can't cause an inconsistency. Suggestion: Describe the inconsistency clearly. Note whether it was in behavior, test performance, or both; where it occurred (that is, on what subtests or items); and when it occurred (that is, during the early, middle, or later part of the test session). After you describe the inconsistency, you might want to point out that the inconsistency and her hyperactivity may be related.

8. "On the performance tasks, he seemed to be hampered by the inability to manipulate the pieces easily." This description is ambiguous because *manipulate* can refer to motor dexterity or to the cognitive operations required by the task (for example, planning and organizing). Note that in the following suggested sentence an inference is made ("seemed to be frustrated") that is supported by a reference to the examinee's behavior. Suggestion (assuming these

behaviors were noted): "When assembling puzzle-like pieces, he seemed to be frustrated, slamming pieces down when he could not complete the object correctly."

9. The following interpretation was based on a Verbal IQ of 98: "Her anxious laughter and quick replies of 'I don't know' seem to suggest that overall Mary was less comfortable with verbal tasks than with nonverbal tasks. Whether it is a deficiency of skills in verbal interactions that causes the anxiousness and subsequent poor performance or whether it is the anxiousness that causes a subsequent deficiency in verbal skills is unknown." It is helpful to tie together observations and subtest scores. However, the second sentence is misleading because the examinee does not have a *deficiency* in verbal skills—she obtained an average score. The statement about causality is unnecessary because it is almost impossible to know what is cause and what is effect simply on the basis of performance on an intelligence test. In addition, the expression *verbal interactions* is ambiguous. Suggestion: Leave the second sentence out of the report.

10. The following statement was based on average IQs on the three scales: "Her quick performance on both verbal and nonverbal tasks seemed to lower her scores." This statement may be correct, but it is also possible that even with additional time the examinee would have failed the items or that the examinee worked quickly in order to avoid frustration. Suggestion: "She responded quickly, and often incorrectly, on both verbal and nonverbal tasks. However, it is not known to what extent her performance would have improved if she had taken more time before answering the questions."

> **Guideline 2. Provide clear descriptions of abilities thought to be measured by the subtests, and use factor loadings, if you want to, to guide your interpretations of the subtests.**

Discussion of Guideline 2

Clinical lore has given us several possibilities for describing or interpreting the abilities measured by the WISC-III subtests. These abilities are summarized in Table C-13 on page 824. You will have to decide which description best characterizes the child's performance. Whichever one (or ones) you choose, describe the child's ability clearly. The factor analytic findings also can guide your interpretations. For example, although the WISC-III subtests are grouped into Verbal and Performance Scales, factor analytic findings suggest that Coding and Symbol Search are best interpreted as measuring sustained attention and the ability to process nonmeaningful information rapidly. This would seem to be a more appropriate interpretation than referring to Coding or Symbol Search simply as measures of performance ability.

When you describe the functions thought to be measured by a subtest, try to be as specific as possible. For example, if you are writing about Digit Span, identify the type of short-term memory being evaluated (auditory) and the type of content (nonmeaningful). Furthermore, recognize that every subtest provides only a *sampling* of abilities—no one subtest samples the entire ability domain. Subtests such as Arithmetic, for example, do not measure the entire range of mathematical ability. In fact, the Arithmetic subtest may not reliably and systematically measure skills involving addition, subtraction, multiplication, and division. To measure these skills, select a test that is specifically designed to do so, such as the Key Math Diagnostic Arithmetic Test (see page 340).

Profiles can be analyzed from two frames of reference. In one method, you compare the examinee's scores to the norm group; we refer to this as an *interindividual comparison*. In the other method, you compare the examinee's scores to his or her own unique profile; we refer to this as an *intraindividual comparison* (see below). In either case, you will always be using the scaled scores based on the norm group. Let us now focus on the interindividual approach to profile analysis.

Interindividual comparison. The simplest way to approach a profile is to evaluate the scores in reference to the norm group. The following three categories will be useful for describing the subtest scaled scores:

Scaled score	Description
1 to 7	Weakness or below average
8 to 12	Average
13 to 19	Strength or above average

You can also add to your description the percentiles associated with each qualitative description of the subtest function. The percentiles (or percentile ranks) provide a more precise description of the child's level of functioning (see Table C-41, page 855).

Here are some illustrations of how to describe scaled scores:

• "She has strengths in abstract reasoning (91st percentile) and word knowledge (84th percentile)."

• "His weaknesses are in spatial visualization organization (5th percentile) and sustained attention for auditory information (9th percentile)."

• "She has average ability in . . ., all between the 25th and 75th percentiles. . . ."

• "His abilities are above average (in the 84th to 98th percentiles) in . . . ."

Other statements useful in describing profiles are as follows. These statements were based on Verbal scaled scores of 7 to 12:

• "His verbal skills range from below average to average."

• "Within the verbal domain, his skills range from below average to average. His range of knowledge, concept formation, . . . are all average for his age." The key phrase "are all average for his age" reflects a comparison with the norm group.

You can also use a finer gradation—five categories instead of three—to describe the subtest scaled scores. The five categories are as follows:

Scaled score	Description
1 to 4	Exceptional weakness or very poorly developed or far below average or very poor
5 to 7	Weakness or poorly developed or below average or poor
8 to 12	Average
13 to 15	Strength or well developed or above average or good
16 to 19	Exceptional strength or very well developed or superior or excellent

Either the three- or the five-level category system can be used to describe subtest scaled scores, depending on your preferences or the preferences of your instructor. For different reports, you may prefer different systems. As you study the qualitative descriptions of the subtest scaled scores, *notice that scaled scores of 8 or above are never described as weaknesses and scaled scores of 7 or below are never described as strengths*.

Intraindividual comparison.   When you evaluate the profile from the vantage point of the examinee's own specific pattern of abilities, you are making an *intraindividual comparison* (or using an *ipsative* approach). The focus is on describing areas that are better or more poorly developed for the specific examinee. As noted above, the absolute values of the scaled scores are still used to guide you in the way you describe the examinee's performance. That is,

scores of 13 to 19 are always strengths; 8 to 12, average; and 1 to 7, weaknesses.

• This statement was based on Verbal scaled scores of 3 to 7: "Relative to her own level of verbal ability, her social comprehension is her best developed ability, but still at a below-average level (16th percentile)." The key phrase "relative to her own level of verbal ability" reflects a comparison based on the examinee's individual profile. Note, however, that the absolute values of the scaled scores are still used for an intraindividual profile analysis. Her scaled score of 7 does not indicate a strength, even if it is the highest score in the profile. Also note that in this example the phrase "but still at a below-average level" helps the reader understand that, although social comprehension is the examinee's best ability, it is still at a level that is below average for her peer group.

• This statement was based on scaled scores of 7 to 15 over the 10 standard subtests and a Full Scale IQ of 113: "Within his overall above-average level of functioning, his command of word knowledge is a considerable strength (95th percentile)." The key phrase "within his overall above-average level of functioning" prepares the reader for some comment related to the child's individual profile.

Abilities common to more than one subtest. Descriptions of abilities that apply to more than one subtest, such as verbal comprehension, must be carefully used. For example, if a child has a scaled score of 13 on Vocabulary, you must also consider the child's scores on the other subtests that measure verbal comprehension (Information, Comprehension, Similarities) before you say that the child has a strength in verbal comprehension. For example, if this same child obtained a scaled score of 7 on Information, do not say that verbal comprehension is a strength. Instead use a phrase that refers to Vocabulary but not Information. The same guideline holds for the subtests that measure perceptual organization (Picture Completion, Block Design, Object Assembly) and for those that measure the ability to sustain attention (Coding and Symbol Search).

Examples of Statements That Do Not Meet Guideline 2

1. The following statement was based on a Picture Completion scaled score of 7: "She displayed a weakness in her ability to perceive significant features." The phrase "to perceive significant features" is vague. Suggestion: "She displayed a weakness in her ability to perceive missing details of pictures."

2. The following statement was based on a Picture Arrangement scaled score of 9: "She was average in her ability to anticipate and sequence cause-and-effect social interactions." The phrase "ability to anticipate and sequence cause-and-effect social interactions" is difficult to follow. Suggestion: "Her ability to anticipate in a meaningful way the results that might be expected from various acts of behavior is average (37th percentile)."

3. "His average score in Arithmetic suggests that he has no difficulties in mathematics." This generalization is too broad. Suggestion: "His numerical reasoning ability is average."

4. The following statement was based on a scaled score of 10 on Digit Span: "Short-term memory is adequate." Although this description is satisfactory, it could be more precise. Suggestion: "Short-term auditory memory for nonmeaningful material is average (50th percentile)."

5. "He is average in number reasoning." *Numerical reasoning* is the preferred terminology.

6. "Her WISC-III performance suggests that Helen likes and does well in spelling." There is little, if any, information obtained from the WISC-III that would support this statement.

7. The following statement was based on Profile 2.7 in Table K-1: "Henry showed a strength on a test of perceptual organization." The statement as such is accurate for the Object Assembly subtest, but it fails to consider that Picture Completion and Block Design also measure perceptual organization. Scores on Picture Completion and Block Design were average and not above average. Suggestion: "Henry showed a strength in his ability to synthesize concrete parts into meaningful wholes."

8. The following statement was based on a Similarities scaled score of 6: "She has difficulties in forming verbal concepts that pertain to creativity." There is no way of knowing to what extent Similarities involves creativity. There may be some relationship, but I am not aware of data that support this interpretation. Suggestion: "She has difficulties in forming verbal concepts."

9. The child obtained a Digit Span score of 15, which was the highest score in the profile: "His highest scaled score was on Digit Span, which is a verbal task." Although this statement is technically accurate, it can be improved in two ways. First, instead of listing the name of the subtest, describe what the subtest may measure. Second, use a qualitative description for a scaled score of 15. Suggestion: "His attention span is well developed, as noted by his ability to recall digits."

10. "Jill has ability in the area of perceptual-motor organization, but is less able in numerical reasoning." This sentence doesn't tell the reader about the child's level of performance. The terms "has ability" and "less able" are vague. Suggestion: "Jill's strength is in the area of perceptual-motor organization (84th percentile). She is at an average level in numerical reasoning (50th percentile)."

Table K-1
WISC-III Profiles Cited in Examples in Guidelines

Subtest	Profile						
	2.7	3.3	3.9	4.1	4.7	5.0	8.8
Information	—	9	—	8	15	6	7
Similarities	—	10	—	4	14	5	12
Arithmetic	—	14	—	7	13	3	12
Vocabulary	—	9	—	9	14	6	9
Comprehension	—	10	—	8	13	7	10
Digit Span	—	12	—	7	9	8	12
Picture Completion	8	12	16	6	16	5	10
Coding	9	15	13	9	13	10	14
Picture Arrangement	7	13	14	11	14	5	7
Block Design	9	9	12	6	12	5	14
Object Assembly	13	8	13	7	13	4	10
Symbol Search	—	—	—	—	—	—	—
Mazes	—	—	16	—	16	—	—
Verbal IQ	—	102	—	84	123	74	100
Performance IQ	—	110	—	86	125	74	107
Full Scale IQ	—	106	—	84	126	72	104

Guideline 3. Relate inferences based on subtest scores or IQs to the cognitive processes measured (or thought to be measured) by the subtests and scales.

Discussion of Guideline 3

Although every effort should be made to discuss the implications of the child's test performance, stay close to the cognitive operations measured by the subtests or scales. If you have information about the child's achievements in school, case history information, behavioral observations, and other test data, you will be in a better position to make generalizations about your findings.

Generalizations about how examinees will perform in school, on a job, or in other settings based solely or primarily on the results of an intelligence test must be made with caution. Although scores on intelligence tests correlate significantly with school grades, the correlations tend to run in the .30s and .40s (see Appendix I, page 1042). These correlations mean that intelligence test scores account for only 10 to 20 percent of the variance in school grades. We simply do not know what specific Wechsler scores (or scores on other intelligence tests) are needed in order to do average, above-average, or superior work in school. We also do not know with certainty what scores should be considered deficits. For example, should an IQ of 80 be considered a deficit? If this score is adequate for the examinee to achieve his or her goals, it may not be a deficit.

Other types of generalizations also should be made with caution. For example, the statement "His strengths in immediate auditory memory, numerical reasoning, and visual-motor spatial integration will help him in his understanding of historical events and their link with today's society" may or may not be accurate. Because there is limited, if any, indication in the literature of a relationship between these skills and the understanding of historical events, it is better not to make this type of inference.

How do we discuss the results of an evaluation when they differ from our expectations of how the examinee should have performed? For example, if an examinee obtains an IQ of 150, but is making grades of C, D, and F in school, do we say that the intelligence test scores are invalid? Or is it better to say that the examinee's poor school performance is probably associated not with cognitive difficulties but with other factors? Conversely, if an examinee with an IQ of 80 achieves a B or A average in school, do we say that the IQ is inconsistent with the examinee's school grades? Grading practices are highly variable, and grades also depend on course content, subject matter, and student effort. Unless you have information about grading practices, course content, curriculum, and the child's study habits, be careful about the inferences you make about the relationship between test scores and school grades. When you discuss the examinee's occupational goals or academic performance or potential, consider the examinee's IQ as well as motivation, temperament, interpersonal skills, and other characteristics that may be needed for successful performance.

Recommendations that intelligence test scores could be improved by having the examinee engage in certain activities should be based on research findings or at least on relevant clinical or psychoeducational theories. For example, there is little, if any, evidence that participating in sports aids an examinee in developing the motor coordination needed for successful performance on intelligence tests, as athletics primarily involves gross motor skills. How will involvement in sports improve such nonverbal cognitive skills as eye-hand coordination (Coding) and manipulating materials in an analytic manner (Block Design and Object Assembly)? It is doubtful that participation in athletics leads to better developed nonverbal cognitive skills, as measured by the Performance Scale subtests of the Wechsler tests.

Always use the absolute level of the scaled scores to guide your analysis. Scaled scores of 13 to 19 always indicate strengths—they are in the 84th to 99th percentile rank. For example, if there is one scaled score of 13 in a profile, it still represents a strength, even if the other scores are all 18 or 19. You don't want to imply that a scaled score of 13 indicates limited ability or a weakness or deficit. *It is the absolute score, not a comparison with any other scores, that is used to determine the examinee's level of ability in the areas measured by the subtest or test.* However, in a profile that ranges from 13 to 19, you can identify the scaled score of 13 as a strength that is less well developed than the examinee's other strengths.

Be careful when you discuss cause-and-effect relationships. For example, did the examinee do well in an area because he or she likes the area, or does the examinee like the area because he or she does well in it? In some cases examinees may like an area that they do not do well in or dislike an area that they do well in. Also, to what extent does the examinee's level of performance relate to what happens in the family? Research does suggest that what is emphasized in the home is related to children's cognitive development, but the relationship is far from perfect (see Chapter 4). Therefore, a statement such as "His high nonverbal skills are related to the emphasis on sports in his family" may or may not be accurate. In addition, as noted above, the motor skills involved in sports are not the same as those involved in the performance subtests of the Wechsler tests or other individually administered tests of intelligence.

Examples of Statements That Do Not Meet Guideline 3

Here are examples of questionable inferences made on the basis of test scores:

1. "Dean performed in the low average range. His cognitive deficits during this examination are inconsistent with his reported B average in school." The terms *deficits* and *inconsistent* may not be appropriate, as noted previously. Suggestion: Leave out the terms *deficit* and *inconsistent*, but comment on the examinee's test performance and report that the examinee has above-average school performance.

2. "She demonstrated below-average performance in visual discrimination tasks and nonverbal reasoning tasks. Despite these skills, she exhibited average performance in analyzing and synthesizing nonverbal information." Why are the words "despite these skills" used to begin the second sentence? Does the writer mean to say "In contrast with these below-average skills, her skills..."? The writer seems to imply that visual discrimination skills and nonverbal reasoning skills may also be involved in analyzing and synthesizing nonverbal information. This implication may be appropriate, but it is not adequately developed in the presentation.

3. The following interpretations were based on Profile 3.3 in Table K-1 (page 1113) for a 16-year-, 0-month-old female: "Helen demonstrated abilities overall in the Average range, with strengths in nonverbal social intelligence, numerical reasoning, and symbol association skills. Her performance indicates that she may have trouble with her studies at school." The second sentence does not follow from the first one. Why should average overall ability and skills in specific areas lead to a prediction that the examinee may have trouble in school? It is risky to make such predictions based on a profile of subtest scores that has no absolute weakness and is in the Average range for the Verbal, Performance, and Full Scales.

4. "Debbie's career goals appear to be realistic, based on her IQ of 110." This statement would be more accurate if the examinee also had other characteristics needed for successful performance in a specific career. Suggestion: "Based on her IQ of 110 and her overall motivation and enthusiasm for...."

5. "The low concentration and attention scores may indicate that Jane's inability to ignore distractions (i.e., nervousness, examiner's note taking, etc.) is indicative of a tendency to give up when items get more difficult (i.e., saying 'I don't know' quickly before thinking about an appropriate response to a test item)." This is a confusing sentence. It is not clear how nervousness is related to an inability to ignore distractions. Saying "I don't know" quickly may have been realistic. If not, what factors suggested to the examiner that the examinee had the ability to solve the problems?

6. "Low scores on Information and Arithmetic may indicate weakness in the ability to assimilate given material and then provide a solution for the designated problem." This description attempts to combine functions thought to be involved in the Information and Arithmetic subtests. However, it is not clear how a low score on Information or Arithmetic (or on both) suggests a "weakness in the ability to assimilate given material and then provide a solution for the designated problem." Suggestion: "Her range of factual information and her ability in mental arithmetic are below average."

7. "By comparing some specific subtests within and between Performance and Verbal test categories, Joan achieved high Similarities standard scores and low Comprehension scores." The examinee's subtest scores are independent of any comparisons made with other subtest scores. For example, a score of 13 on Similarities is a strength in and of itself, whether it is higher or lower than another subtest score. The statement is also ungrammatical (for example, the examiner, not Joan, compared the subtests). Suggestion. "Joan has well-developed abstract

thinking ability but poorly developed ability to apply conceptualizing skills to solve problems in the social world."

8. "Her low score on the Arithmetic subtest may be due to her dislike of and disinterest in school mathematics classes." Cause-and-effect relationships are difficult to tease out without more information. It may be that she dislikes mathematics because she is not good at it.

9. The following statements were based on Profile 3.9 in Table K-1 (page 1113) for a girl who was 9 years, 6 months old: "At most activities requiring visual perception, Kirsten would excel, but when the motor aspect is introduced, she is in the average range. Physical activities may improve her motor coordination, bringing it to the same level as her other nonverbal skills." These statements are tenuous at best and provide the reader with potentially misleading information. First, five of the six Performance subtest scores are above average, and one subtest (Block Design) is at the upper end of the average range. Most of the Performance subtests involve motor coordination to some extent. Therefore, the statement "when the motor aspect is introduced, she is in the average range" is incorrect. The next statement, "Physical activities may improve her motor coordination . . . ," is conjectural. Second, all nonverbal skills are at the 75th percentile rank or higher. Thus, it is difficult to foresee how continuation of sports would improve her motor coordination in cognitive tasks. It would be better to emphasize the child's excellent nonverbal skills.

10. The following statement was based on an Information scaled score of 13 and a Comprehension scaled score of 16 for a 13-year-old girl: "Virginia achieved a lower score in her range of knowledge than in her ability to use social judgment, which suggests limited factual knowledge." This statement is misleading. A standard score of 13 indicates above-average ability. The fact that one subtest score is lower than another score does not mean that the lower score reflects limited ability. In this case, Information is not significantly lower than Comprehension (see Table L-3 in Appendix L). Suggestion: "Virginia's range of knowledge and ability to use social judgment are above average."

Guideline 4. Describe the profile in a clear and unambiguous manner. State that two or more abilities reflect different levels of skill only when the scores are significantly different.

Discussion of Guideline 4

Consider all of the information you have in describing the test profile. Choose carefully the words you use to describe the child's performance. Subtests and scales overlap in their measurement properties; consequently, be careful not to make statements that are contradictory. Guideline 2 suggested terms that you can use to describe subtest scores.

Before you say that two abilities are different (or higher/lower or better/more poorly developed), be sure that the scores representing these abilities are *significantly* different. For example, you don't want to say "She may favor verbal expressive tasks that allow her to work at her own pace over more structured time-dependent tasks" when the examinee has a Verbal IQ of 106, a Performance IQ of 104, and a Full Scale IQ of 107. Because the Verbal and Performance IQs are about the same, there is little justification for making this inference. Similarly, you don't want to say "His verbal skills are slightly more well developed than his nonverbal skills" for a Verbal IQ of 83 and a Performance IQ of 82. When two (or more) scores are not significantly different, no inference should be made that one score is slightly better (or poorer) than the other one.

When the Verbal IQ is significantly higher than the Performance IQ, however, you can describe the difference with confidence. For example, for a Verbal IQ of 116 and a Performance IQ of 94, you can say "Her verbal comprehension skills (84th percentile) are better developed than her perceptual organizational skills (34th percentile)" rather than "Her verbal comprehension skills *may be* better developed . . . ."

Your report should clearly indicate when you are describing the examinee's own unique profile.

When you describe the examinee's scores, compare subtest scores, or compare the Verbal and Performance IQs, always give the level at which the scores fall and the direction of the differences between the scores. Thus, for example, the statement "She demonstrated a significant difference between Block Design and Object Assembly" is not informative *because it gives neither the level of the scores (average, above average, or below average) nor the direction of the difference (which score was higher or lower than the other).*

Examples of Statements That Do Not Meet Guideline 4

1. The following statements were based on Profile 4.1 in Table K-1 (page 1113) for a 15-year-old male: "Jim's verbal and nonverbal skills are similarly developed and range from average to well below average. His vocabulary

ability is better developed than his social comprehension." Because the Vocabulary scaled score is not significantly higher than the Comprehension scaled score (9 vs. 8), this statement is misleading.

2. "Her average nonverbal and verbal skills varied in a range from average to above-average ability, with particular strengths and weaknesses in certain tasks." This is a confusing sentence. If all scores are average or above average, how can there be any weaknesses, since we define weaknesses to be skills that are below average (for example, scaled scores of 7 or lower)? Suggestion: Eliminate the last part of the sentence, beginning with "with particular strengths," or use other ways to describe the pattern of scores.

3. "Within Ginny's Verbal IQ, scores ranged from average to very superior." The phrase "within Ginny's Verbal IQ" is awkward and perhaps misleading. The Verbal IQ is one score, although we derive it from several subtest scores. Better: "Ginny's verbal skills range from average to superior."

4. "By comparing the standard scores based on her age group, she demonstrated a significant difference on arithmetic and digit span. High scores on these sub-tests may indicate a strength within the realm of visual-perceptual motor skills." The two sentences fail to give either the direction of the differences or the level at which the scores fall. In addition, subtest names are usually capitalized, and the word *subtests* is usually written without a hyphen. You do not have to put in the report how you proceeded to arrive at your statements. It is preferable to leave out the entire phrase "by comparing the standard scores based on her age group." Finally, the sentence is ungrammatical because the examinee didn't compare the standard scores.

5. The following statement was based on a Picture Completion score of 7 and a Block Design score of 12: "There is a marked difference between her visual perception and her visual-motor-spatial coordination." This statement is misleading because Block Design also involves visual perception. Suggestion: "Her attention to visual details is below average, whereas her spatial visualization ability is average."

6. "Within Becky's scores, a marked difference in ability was found between her Very Superior ability in abstract and concrete reasoning and her Low Average ability in spatial visualization." This is a confusing sentence. Part of the problem is that the opening phrase, "within Becky's scores," is immediately followed by a statement about ability levels. A better way might be to say "Her abstract reasoning ability is excellent, whereas her spatial visualization skills are less well developed but still within the lower limits of the average range." The qualita-

tive descriptions "Very Superior" and "Low Average," if used, should begin with lowercase letters. Capitalize qualitative descriptions only when you refer to the classifications associated with the Full Scale, Verbal Scale, and Performance Scale IQs.

7. The following statements were based on Profile 4.7 in Table K-1 (page 1113): "Jamie has one relative weakness in short-term memory. Within her other verbal scores, short-term memory is significantly less developed than her other scores. Her attention is less developed than her concentration. If, in class, Jamie's teacher asked her for some information just presented in class, Jamie probably would have been concentrating, but her average development in attention and short-term memory might cause her to forget the material."

This is a confusing paragraph. A scaled score of 9 is average and should not be considered weak. In addition, this child has excellent attention skills as noted by her performance on the other subtests. She shows somewhat less developed ability in nonmeaningful immediate auditory memory. I believe that it is inappropriate to speculate that the examinee would forget material presented in a class. In fact, with her outstanding ability, I would think that her recall ability was excellent. Do not stress any score in isolation from the total picture. The writing is also poor. It is incorrect to say that "Within her other verbal scores, short-term memory is . . . ." Finally, stating that "her average development in attention and short-term memory might cause her to forget the material" implies a cause-and-effect relationship that may be difficult to establish.

8. The following statement was based on a Block Design score of 7 and a Picture Completion score of 12: "Her performance on a spatial visual task was inconsistent with her performance on a task measuring alertness to details." This statement may lead the reader to believe that the two tasks should have yielded similar scores. It is preferable to refer to an examinee's scores in terms of strengths and weaknesses and the possible implications of the differences. Suggestion: "Her performance suggests that she has average nonspatial visual perceptual ability but below-average spatial visualization ability."

9. The following statement was written for Performance subtest scores ranging from 6 to 13: "In nonverbal areas Harry displayed uniformly developed skills." This statement is incorrect because this range of 7 scaled-score points (from below average to above average) indicates strengths as well as weaknesses.

10. "There is a 9-point difference between his Verbal and Performance IQs, which suggests that his nonverbal abilities are better developed than his verbal abilities." A 9-point difference is not significant, and thus the interpreta-

tion is incorrect. (See Table L-3 in Appendix L for required differences between the Verbal and Performance IQs at the .05 and .01 levels for the WISC-III.)

Guideline 5. Make recommendations carefully, using all available sources of information.

Discussion of Guideline 5

Recommendations are a valuable part of the report. However, if your assessment is for a class exercise and without a referral question, it may be difficult to arrive at meaningful recommendations. Try to develop one or more ideas that you believe may be appropriate. You want to be on relatively firm ground when you make predictions or recommendations. And you don't want to make statements that are potentially misleading.

Here is an example of recommendations made on the basis of Profile 5.0 in Table K-1 (page 1113):

It appears that Frida will have difficulty processing information, in either an auditory or a visual format, in the classroom. She will need to have material presented to her in a simplified manner in order for her to process, retain, and understand concepts. She would also benefit from lessons designed to help her understand logical and sequential cause-and-effect relationships. Frida's overall performance suggests that she can learn; however, the learning environment should be concrete and repetitive, with many examples provided.

Examples of Statements That Do Not Meet Guideline 5

1. "Information regarding his academic performance is needed to determine the need for intervention in his areas of average ability." This is a confusing recommendation. Why would intervention be needed in areas of average ability?

2. This statement was made on the basis of a Verbal IQ of 108, Performance IQ of 102, and Full Scale IQ of 104: "Jim shows sufficient aptitude to attain advanced degrees, and I recommend that he be considered for a gifted program." This statement is misleading. First, an IQ of 104 may not be sufficient to allow a child to go on to graduate school. I would hesitate to go out on a limb to make such a prediction. Second, it is doubtful that a child with an IQ of 104 would be allowed into a gifted program unless the child

had special strengths in academic performance or other areas that would qualify him or her for the program.

3. The following statement was based on a Verbal IQ of 102, Performance IQ of 96, Full Scale IQ of 101, and Picture Completion score of 7: "Her visual perception skills may affect her duties as a camp counselor." With overall scores average, it is doubtful that a relatively low Picture Completion score would affect the examinee's work as a camp counselor. Predictions about success in occupations based solely on a single subtest score must be made with extreme caution, if at all.

4. "I believe that Jill's nervous behavior exhibited during the Verbal scale test administration was too profound to discount. It is recommended that this correlation between nervousness and verbal performance be considered before any definitive assessment is made." The examiner is concerned about the examinee's level of anxiety, but the recommendation is vague. What does the examiner mean by "before any definitive assessment is made"? Why use the term *correlation*? Why is her "nervous behavior...too profound to discount"? The recommendation should emphasize that the severity of the examinee's anxiety level needs to be further investigated. Did her level of anxiety affect the reliability of the test results? In addition, there are some minor stylistic problems. "Scale" should be capitalized and "test" is superfluous after "scale."

5. "Rachel wants to major in international business. It is recommended that she go into this area. Her strength in social judgment should be useful in international business because of the different cultures and protocols a person must use." This hypothesis is on shaky ground. A high score on the Comprehension subtest suggests good social reasoning, but it is highly culture bound. The social reasoning skills measured by the subtest therefore may not generalize to different cultures. Also, the term *protocols* is vague. Finally, what does it mean to say that she "must use" different cultures?

Guideline 6.   Describe and use statistical concepts in an appropriate manner, check all calculations carefully, and report the reliability and validity of the test results as accurately as possible.

Discussion of Guideline 6

There are preferred ways to describe and use statistical concepts such as percentile rank, probability level, range, and so forth. Here are suggested ways of describing several statistical concepts:

• Percentile rank: "Her Full Scale IQ is at the 55th percentile." (This is preferable to "She is 55% better than other children.")

• Probability level: "The chances that the range of scores from 106 to 120 includes his true IQ are about 95 out of 100." (This is preferable to "There is a 95–100% probability that his true IQ falls between 106 and 120." The use of "100%" is questionable in the latter statement, and it depicts an improper conceptualization of probability levels.)

• Range or classification: "Her overall performance is in the High Average range." (Use the range or classification primarily for the Full Scale IQ and on occasion for the Verbal and Performance IQ. This is preferable to "Her Vocabulary ability is in the Superior classification.")

• Reliability and validity: "The present measure of her level of intellectual functioning appears to be reliable and valid. She was cooperative, motivated, and appeared to do her best." (This is preferable to "On the basis of her consistency, the current results appear to be reliable and valid." An examinee may be consistent, but the scores may still be invalid.)

Examples of Statements That Do Not Meet Guideline 6

1. "Her fatigue and boredom during the latter portions of the test need to be considered in relation to her overall score. Although I don't believe that the test was invalid as a result of Patricia's behavior, I do think it may have influenced her abstract reasoning score somewhat. I would like to see her retested on this one task." The examiner is expressing some doubt about the validity of the test results. If you include an invalid subtest score in calculating the Full Scale IQ, then the Full Scale IQ is invalid as well. I would either eliminate the invalid subtest score when calculating the Full Scale IQ and Verbal Scale IQ (in this case) or point out that these scores also are not valid.

2. "The verbal scores may be an underestimation of his verbal ability because English is his second language. . . . The test results appear to be reliable and valid." These two sentences are contradictory. If part of the test appears to underestimate an examinee's ability, the test results cannot be valid.

3. "She enjoyed the performance subtests; hence, the results should be reliable." I do not think that "enjoyment" is a sufficient reason to conclude that the entire test results are reliable. Additional observations about her performance would be helpful.

4. "Jill was randomly referred for testing by her teacher." It is possible, but highly unlikely, that the teacher randomly referred the child for testing. The statement would be correct if all of the pupils' names were put in a hat and the teacher drew one name randomly or if the teacher used a table of random numbers to select a child for testing.

5. "Her range of knowledge is poor. This was demonstrated in her inability to identify Columbus or name three oceans." Poor knowledge is reflected in an examinee's low scores, not in missing one or two items on any particular subtest. A better example of her poor range of knowledge would be helpful.

> **Guideline 7. Use words that have a low probability of being misinterpreted, that are nontechnical, and that convey as clearly as possible the examinee's performance.**

Discussion of Guideline 7

This guideline and the one that follows address writing style. Guideline 7 focuses on the use of individual words (or word combinations), and Guideline 8 focuses more on the mechanics of writing. Your writing should be as accurate as possible. You want the reader to comprehend the report with a minimal amount of effort. However, you also want to make sure that your statements are clear and that readers will not misinterpret them. Whenever you detect some potential problem in your writing, revise your work so that the problem is solved.

Examples of Statements That Do Not Meet Guideline 7

1. "His performance is a submaximal representation of his intellectual ability." The word *submaximal* is a poor choice. "His scores may underestimate his ability" would be better.

2. "Further support for the inference that Karl is detail oriented may be seen in his mazes." Instead of "in his mazes," it is preferable to say "in his performance on the Mazes subtest." This sentence should be followed by one that explains the "detail orientation."

3. "Helen was unable to let go of a task and referred back to it during the next task, either to correct her previous answer or to contaminate her current answer with the

previous one." This is an interesting and important observation, but the term *contaminate* may be somewhat difficult for the reader to understand; *spoil* or *confuse* might be a good substitute. A statement describing the possible implications of this performance would also be helpful, especially if the behavior occurred frequently during the examination.

4. "There is no reason to question the cultural validity of the WISC-III." *Cultural validity* is not a commonly accepted term. In addition, some psychologists do question the validity of intelligence tests for use with ethnic minority children (see Chapter 19).

5. "He had a tendency to elicit heavy sighs and become visibly frustrated when he was having difficulty with an item." The writer likely means "emit heavy sighs" and not "elicit heavy sighs."

6. "No evidence of abnormality on her verbal or perceptual skills was found in this testing." The term *abnormality* is likely to be confusing to most readers and potentially misleading. If you do use it, indicate what you mean by *abnormality*.

7. "Jane's IQ is an average of diverse abilities which make direct interpretation difficult." This statement is likely to be confusing to most readers. Although the statement is accurate, the profile of scores for a particular examinee can be interpreted. Despite the fact that the Full Scale IQ represents several different subscores, it is still used as a basis for classifying examinees in such areas as mental retardation, giftedness, and learning disability.

8. "The experimenter observed a significant difference between Jane's Perceptual Organizational factor score and Processing Speed factor score. A significant difference was also found between her Verbal Comprehension and Processing Speed factor scores." The first problem with these statements is that the preferred term is *examiner*, not *experimenter*. A second problem is that it may not be very informative for the average reader to read about factor scores by name. Suggestion: "Her verbal skills and perceptual organizational skills are better developed than her attention and concentration skills involving scanning and rapid eye-hand coordination." You can then point out the percentile ranks associated with each of these factor scores or use a qualitative description representing the level of her scores—such as average, above average, or below average.

9. "She also exhibited weaknesses in the Information and Arithmetic standard scores." The emphasis should be on abilities, not on scores per se. The scores are neither weak nor strong; rather, they are high or low. Abilities are weak or strong, or average or normal. You usually do not need to discuss in the report the type of scores (standard scores, raw scores, or age scores) that you are using as the basis for your statements.

10. "Within the subtests of information, arithmetic, and comprehension versus vocabulary, similarities, and digit span, Joan demonstrated a significantly decreased ability in analyzing long verbal questions versus short verbal questions." This is an awkward sentence. The reader is likely to be confused about the use of the terms *within* and *versus*. You don't need to mention the subtest names, but if you do, capitalize them. Also, what meaning may be attached to the difference between the examinee's performance on long and short verbal questions?

DRABBLE reprinted by permission of UFS, Inc.

> **Guideline 8.** Write clearly, cut words where possible, follow all rules of grammar and punctuation, use a consistent style, make clear transitions between different ideas or topics, and give examples of the examinee's abilities and behavior. Do not include, however, information that seems to have little or no value.

Discussion of Guideline 8

Technical and professional writing should leave little room for misinterpretation. Check carefully that the entire report is clearly written. Transition statements are valuable in a report. The reader expects a smooth flow between topics. When you plan to change topics, prepare the reader for the change. Lastly, judicious examples of the examinee's behavior will help the reader understand the assessment findings better.

Examples of Statements That Do Not Meet Guideline 8

1. "His general performance would be described as being within the Average range." The words "would be described" are unnecessary. Suggestion: "His general performance is within the Average range."

2. "Jim was administered the WISC-III and Bender-Gestalt to provide training experience for students in the graduate assessment course at Blank University." It is not clear from the sentence whether the training experience was for Jim, who also could be a student in the assessment class, or for the examiner.

3. "Phil constantly kept finding things in a drawer of the desk he was being tested at to play with throughout the testing period, ie. paperclips, rubberbands, pens, etc." This is an awkward sentence. There are also punctuation mistakes, such as a period missing after the "i" in *i.e.* and a comma missing after the *i.e.* Suggestion: "Throughout the testing period, Phil played with paperclips, rubberbands, and pens that he found in the desk drawer."

4. "Virginia's behavior during the nonverbal subtests seemed to be more confident and less anxious." The sentence needs a reference point—a person has to be more confident and less anxious than she was in some other situation. In addition, grammatically speaking, "behavior" cannot be more confident or less anxious; only Virginia can. Behavior is a manifestation of the person. Suggestion: "Virginia was more confident and less anxious during the

nonverbal portion than during the verbal portion of the test."

5. "He often seemed bored during nonverbal items and often rested his head on his hand, slumped back in his chair, or laid his face down on the table. He displayed more interest in nonverbal items than in verbal items." These two sentences seem to be contradictory. If he was bored with nonverbal items, how could he display more interest in them than in verbal items? The examiner may have meant to write "bored during verbal items" but wrote "nonverbal items" instead. Careful proofreading will help to eliminate such errors.

6. The following statement was written in a report about an 8-year-old with a Verbal IQ of 92, a Performance IQ of 112, and a Full Scale IQ of 101: "Within a single subtest, his behavior and even speech seemed to deteriorate as the problems got successively more difficult." This statement has several problems. First, does the writer mean every subtest on the test, just one subtest, or a few subtests? Second, in what way did the examinee's behavior deteriorate? The word *deteriorate* carries connotations of severe impairment and must be used with caution. Third, in order to obtain average IQs, the examinee must have been able to perform adequately on several of the subtests. Consequently, whatever "deterioration" occurred must have been shortlived because he was able to perform on succeeding subtests.

7. "Gina's behavior during this assessment demonstrated her social intelligence." Without more information, there is no way to know what the word *behavior* refers to. In what way would an examinee's behavior demonstrate social intelligence? The writer may be referring to the examinee's performance on the Comprehension subtest, but this is not clear from the sentence.

8. The following statement was based on Profile 8.8 in Table K-1 (page 1113): "Her lack of reflection may prove to be problematic." This sentence contains two problems. First, does the writer really mean *lack of* reflection? If the examinee *lacked* reflection, how could she perform in the Average range, especially considering that tasks such as Similarities may require reflection, as may other WISC-III subtests? Second, the term *problematic* is not very meaningful. The writer likely means that the examinee's impulsiveness may lead to difficulties when she is faced with problem-solving situations.

9. "The most striking observation was the contrast between his level of interest and motivation during a visual-motor nonverbal task and during a task involving verbal conceptual reasoning. Before answering questions involving arithmetical reasoning, he looked at the examiner in disbelief." The second sentence doesn't follow from the

first sentence. The second sentence should explain the contrast in level of interest and motivation between the two tasks. Instead, a new task is described, and the description does not seem to be related to the prior sentence.

10. "At times, she would lose concentration and perform with less care than usual." This description would benefit from examples of the child's performance. Suggestion: "During the arithmetic items and during the items involving block designs, her concentration seemed to diminish and she became careless."

SUGGESTIONS FOR DESCRIBING WISC-III SCALES AND SUBTESTS TO PARENTS AND THE REFERRAL SOURCE AND IN THE REPORT

Following are summaries of some of the essential features of the three WISC-III scales and 13 subtests. The information can be used to discuss the results with parents and the referral source, as well as in the writing of your report. (Appendix J provides more information about each subtest.)

Full Scale

The Full Scale IQ is usually considered to be the best measure of cognitive ability in the test. It is considered to measure such abilities as general intelligence, scholastic aptitude, and readiness to master a school curriculum. The child's Full Scale IQ may be affected by his or her motivation, interests, cultural opportunities, natural endowment, neurological integrity, attention span, ability to process verbal information (particularly on the verbal subtests), and ability to process visual information (particularly on the performance subtests).

Verbal Scale

The Verbal Scale IQ is a measure of verbal comprehension. This includes the application of verbal skills and information to the solution of new problems, ability to process verbal information, and ability to think with words. The Verbal Scale thus provides information about language processing, reasoning, attention, and verbal learning and memory. The child's Verbal Scale IQ may be affected by his or her motivation, interests, cultural opportunities, natural endowment, neurological integrity, attention span, and ability to process verbal information.

Performance Scale

The Performance Scale IQ is a measure of perceptual organization. This includes the ability to think in visual images and to manipulate these images with fluency and relative speed, to reason without the use of words (in some cases), and to interpret visual material quickly. The Performance Scale thus provides information about visual processing, planning and organizational ability, attention, and nonverbal learning and memory. The child's Performance Scale IQ may be affected by his or her motivation, interests, cultural opportunities, natural endowment, neurological integrity, attention span, and ability to process visual information.

Information

The Information subtest provides a measure of how much general factual knowledge the child has absorbed from his or her environment. The child is asked to answer a series of questions that cover a range of material on several subjects. The subtest provides valuable information about the child's range of factual knowledge and long-term memory. Performance may be influenced by cultural opportunities, outside

interests, richness of early environment, reading, and school learning.

Similarities

The Similarities subtest provides a measure of the child's ability to select and verbalize appropriate relationships between two objects or concepts. The child is asked to say in what way two things are alike. A response indicating an abstract classification receives more credit than a response indicating a concrete classification. The subtest provides valuable information about the child's verbal concept formation and long-term memory. Performance may be influenced by cultural opportunities, interests, reading habits, and school learning.

Arithmetic

The Arithmetic subtest provides a measure of the child's facility in mental arithmetic. The child is asked to solve several different types of arithmetic problems involving addition, subtraction, multiplication, division, and problem solving. The subtest provides valuable information about the child's numerical reasoning ability, concentration, attention, short-term memory, and long-term memory. Performance may be influenced by the child's attitude toward school and by level of anxiety.

Vocabulary

The Vocabulary subtest provides a measure of the child's word knowledge. The child is asked to define individual words of increasing difficulty. The subtest provides valuable information about the child's verbal skills, language development, and long-term memory. Performance may be influenced by cultural opportunities, education, reading habits, and familiarity with English.

Comprehension

The Comprehension subtest provides a measure of the child's social judgment and common sense. The child is asked to answer questions dealing with various problem situations that, in part, involve interpersonal relations and social mores. The subtest provides valuable information about the child's knowledge of conventional standards of behavior. Performance may be influenced by cultural opportunities, ability to evaluate and draw from past experiences, and moral sense.

Digit Span

The Digit Span subtest provides a measure of the child's short-term memory. The child is asked to repeat a series of digits given orally by the examiner. The child must repeat the series as given by the examiner on one part and say the series in the reverse order on the other part. The subtest provides valuable information about the child's rote memory, attention, and concentration. Performance may be influenced by level of anxiety.

Picture Completion

The Picture Completion subtest provides a measure of the child's ability to differentiate essential from nonessential details. The child is shown pictures of objects from everyday life. The child is asked to indicate what important single part is missing from each picture. The subtest provides valuable information about the child's ability to concentrate on visually perceived material and alertness to details. Performance may be influenced by cultural experiences and alertness to the environment.

Coding

The Coding subtest provides a measure of the child's ability to learn a code rapidly. The child is asked to look at a key that shows several symbols paired with other symbols. Then the child is shown one part of the pair and is asked to fill in the matching symbol in the blank space. The subtest provides valuable information about the child's speed and accuracy of eye-hand coordination, short-term memory, and attentional skills. Performance may be influenced by rate of motor activity and by motivation.

Picture Arrangement

The Picture Arrangement subtest provides a measure of the child's ability to comprehend and evaluate social situations. The child is given pictures in a mixed-up order and is asked to rearrange them in a logical sequence. The pictures are similar to those used in short comic strips. The subtest provides valuable information about the child's ability to attend to details, alertness, planning ability, and visual sequencing. Performance may be influenced by cultural opportunities.

Block Design

The Block Design subtest provides a measure of the child's spatial visualization and nonverbal reasoning ability. The child is required to use blocks to assemble a design that is identical to one made by the examiner or one pictured on a card. The subtest provides valuable information about the child's ability to analyze and synthesize visuospatial material and about the child's visual-motor coordination. Performance may be influenced by rate of motor activity and by degree of color vision.

Object Assembly

The Object Assembly subtest provides a measure of the child's ability to synthesize concrete parts into meaningful wholes and of the child's visual-motor coordination. The child is asked to assemble jigsaw pieces correctly to form common objects. The subtest provides valuable information about the child's ability to visualize a whole from its parts, organizational ability, sense of spatial relations, and visual-motor coordination. Performance is influenced by rate of motor activity, persistence, and experience with part-whole relationships.

Symbol Search

The Symbol Search subtest provides a measure of the child's visual discrimination and visual-perceptual scanning ability. The child looks first at the target symbol(s) and then at another group of symbols that may or may not contain the target symbol(s). The child is asked to indicate whether or not a target symbol is in the group of symbols. The subtest provides valuable information about the child's perceptual discrimination, speed and accuracy, attention and concentration, and short-term memory. Performance may be influenced by rate of motor activity and motivation and perhaps by cognitive flexibility (that is, the ability to shift between the target symbol and the other group of symbols as the target symbol and group of symbols change for each item).

Mazes

The Mazes subtest provides a measure of the child's planning ability and the perceptual organizational ability involved in following a visual pattern. The child is shown a series of mazes of increasing difficulty and is requested to draw a continuous line that shows the way out of a maze without running into a blocked passage. The subtest provides valuable information about planning ability, foresight, visual-motor control, and attention and concentration. Performance may be influenced by visual-motor organization ability and ability to delay actions.

PSYCHOLOGICAL EVALUATION

The psychological evaluation in Exhibit 8-2 (pages 183–187), which illustrates the application of the WISC-R

to a 7-year-, 4-month-old child, should help you understand the WISC-III as well. The report cites both qualitative and quantitative information obtained during the evaluation. Profile analysis is used to develop some assessment information, and recommendations are based on the test results and background information.

Exhibit K-1 presents an illustrative report based on the WISC-III. It gives a good description of the child's behavior during the evaluation. It discusses the difference between the child's Verbal and Performance IQs and briefly describes each subtest. It also provides recommendations for further testing.

After you complete the first draft of your report, use the checklist shown in Exhibit K-2 to help you evaluate whether you have included all the pertinent details. The checklist also may be used by your course instructor.

TEST YOUR SKILL

The WISC-R Test-Your-Skill Exercises on pages 187–189 also pertain to the WISC-III, and you are encouraged to do those exercises. Here is another exercise, designed to help you develop the skills needed to write a psychological evaluation based on the WISC-III. There are three parts to the exercise. First, read the WISC-III report in Exhibit K-3, disregarding the superscript numbers. Then read the report in Exhibit K-3 again, focusing on the superscript numbers and the words, phrases, or information associated with each superscript number. Your task is to find the problem, such as an error in punctuation, style, spelling, quantitative information, or interpretation. Record your comments on a sheet of paper, using the numbers 1 to 81. Second, check your comments with those in the Comment section following the report in Exhibit K-3. Third, after reviewing the comments, read and study the suggested report in Exhibit K-4.

THINKING THROUGH THE ISSUES

How does profile analysis help you to evaluate a child's WISC-III performance? How do the various forms of profile analysis complement each other? What are the problems associated with profile analysis?

How can an understanding of base rates help you in interpreting the WISC-III?

How might an evaluation of qualitative factors associated with the child's performance help you better understand the child's quantitative performance?

How will you decide whether or not to include certain kinds of information in the report?

"You're saved! I found a split infinitive in the burglary statutes!"

From the Wall Street Journal — Permission, Cartoon Features Syndicate.

What kinds of data would you like to have before making generalizations about a child's performance?

What steps could you take to improve your report writing skills?

The Verbal and Performance Scale IQs are important features of the WISC-III. How might a child function with a Verbal IQ of 120 and a Performance IQ of 80? How might another child function with a Verbal IQ of 80 and a Performance IQ of 120?

How might the WISC-III be improved?

What problems do you foresee in explaining the results of a psychological evaluation to a parent and to the referral source?

Based on the WISC-III, what would you say to a parent who asked, "What is my child's potential?"

Sign on Faculty Office Door:
COMMITTEE TO STAMP OUT AND ELIMINATE
REDUNDANCY COMMITTEE

SUMMARY

1. Profile analysis on the WISC-III is similar to that on the WISC-R.

2. The primary approaches to profile analysis include comparing Verbal and Performance Scale IQs, comparing Verbal and Performance subtest scaled scores with the mean scores on the respective scales, comparing pairs of individual subtest scaled scores, comparing factor scores, and comparing subtest scaled scores with the average factor score on each factor.

3. Other approaches to profile analysis, based on frequency of occurrence in the population, include an evaluation of subtest scaled-score ranges, deviations of subtest scores from the child's own average, and Verbal-Performance Scale differences.

4. In interpreting the child's performance, look at the child's level of performance, the child's quality of performance, the relationship between level and quality of performance, and the problem-solving strategies used by the child to reach a solution.

5. You may still obtain valuable leads about how the child processes information even when the child has difficulty completing a task.

6. Describe carefully the behaviors you observe. Make inferences about underlying traits or processes with extreme caution, if at all.

7. Provide clear descriptions of abilities thought to be measured by the subtests, and use factor loadings to guide your interpretations of the subtests.

8. Relate inferences based on subtest scores or IQs to the cognitive processes measured (or thought to be measured) by the subtests and scales.

9. Describe the profile in a clear and unambiguous manner. State that two or more abilities reflect different levels of skill only when the scores are significantly different. Indicate clearly whether you are comparing the child's performance to the normative group or whether you are using the scores to describe the child's own profile.

10. Make recommendations carefully, using all available sources of information.

11. Describe and use statistical concepts in an appropriate manner, check all calculations carefully, and report the reliability and validity of the test results as accurately as possible.

12. Use words that have a low probability of being misinterpreted, that are nontechnical, and that convey as clearly as possible the examinee's performance.

13. Write clearly, cut words where possible, follow all rules of grammar and punctuation, use a consistent style, make clear transitions between different ideas or topics, and give examples of the examinee's abilities and behavior. Do not include, however, information that seems to have little or no value.

14. Knowledge of the essential features of the Wechsler scales and subtests presented in this chapter (and in other chapters of the text) will help in your work with parents and the referral source, and when you write reports.

KEY TERMS, CONCEPTS, AND NAMES

Primary methods of profile analysis (p. 1106)
Base rate subtest scaled-score ranges (p. 1107)
Base rate Verbal-Performance differences (or the probability-of-occurrence approach) (p. 1107)
Level of performance (p. 1108)
Quality of performance (p. 1108)
Problem-solving strategies (p. 1108)

■ **Exhibit K-1** ━━

Psychological Evaluation of a Boy with a Reading Problem

Name of examinee: Bill
Date of birth: April 21, 1984
Chronological age: 7-8
Grade: First

Date of examination: Jan. 15, 1992
Date of report: Jan. 20, 1992
Name of examiner: Phyllis Brown

Test Administered

Wechsler Intelligence Scale for Children — III (WISC-III):

VERBAL SCALE		PERFORMANCE SCALE	
Information	10	Picture Completion	14
Similarities	11	Coding	14
Arithmetic	9	Picture Arrangement	10
Vocabulary	7	Block Design	10
Comprehension	9	Object Assembly	10
Digit Span	7	Mazes	15

Verbal Scale IQ = 95
Performance Scale IQ = 111
Full Scale IQ = 103 ± 7 at the 95% confidence level

Reason for Referral

Bill volunteered to take the WISC-III in order for the examiner to obtain experience in administering the test.

Background Information

Bill, a 7-year-, 8-month-old boy, is currently in the first grade. His mother told me that he is experiencing reading difficulties. He states that his favorite subjects in school are spelling and math and that he likes to "work hard." Outside of school he enjoys building things with Legos.

Behavioral Observations

Bill was pleasant, cooperative, and motivated throughout the testing session. He conversed comfortably with me at the beginning of the session and between subtests. He told me that he was having problems learning to read. During both verbal and nonverbal tasks, he occasionally became fidgety and restless, moving back and forth in the chair, sitting on his knees, and laying his head down on the table. This restless behavior occurred more frequently toward the end of subtests (as the items became more difficult) and as the session progressed. However, despite his restlessness, Bill generally remained attentive and on task throughout the session. Bill was cooperative, put away the puzzle pieces in their boxes, and turned the pages of a subtest booklet when I asked him to do so. When frustrated, Bill occasionally asked me for help and exclaimed, "That's hard!" or "Can't do this!"

Bill's articulation was often poor, and he was occasionally difficult to understand. He often answered in the form of a question, as if unsure of his responses. During the verbal subtests that assessed social comprehension and language development, Bill frequently gave long answers, or several answers to the same question, some correct and some incorrect.

During two nonverbal subtests, one requiring visual sequencing and another requiring visual-spatial analytic and synthetic abilities, Bill proceeded quickly and systematically when the items were simple. However, as they became more difficult, he proceeded more slowly, often hesitating, and changing his mind about where to place the cards or blocks. Bill appeared particularly to enjoy puzzles and tasks involving making designs with blocks, and he was disappointed when these tasks were over. In fact, when the puzzle completion task was over, he was eager to go back and try to complete a puzzle that he could not do earlier.

Assessment Results and Clinical Impressions

With a chronological age of 7-8, Bill achieved a Verbal Scale IQ of 95 (37th percentile), a Performance Scale IQ of 111 (79th percentile), and a Full Scale IQ of 103 ± 7 on the WISC-III. His overall performance is classified in the Average range and is ranked at the 55th percentile. The chances that the range of scores from 96 to 110 includes his true IQ are about 95 out of 100. The present measure of his intellectual functioning appears to be reliable and valid because of his cooperativeness, willingness to try, and background characteristics.

There is a 16-point difference between Bill's Verbal and Performance IQs, which indicates that his nonverbal skills are better developed than his verbal skills. This difference may reflect a predominantly nonverbal cognitive style or greater interest and motivation during nonverbal than verbal tasks. As previously mentioned, he liked nonverbal tasks involving puzzles and creating designs with blocks. He also mentioned that he enjoyed building with Legos, a nonverbal spatially oriented activity.

In the verbal domain, his skills range from below average to average. His range of factual knowledge, logical and abstract reasoning, numerical reasoning, and social comprehension are all average for his age. However, his word knowledge and immediate auditory memory are below average for his age. His word knowledge is less well developed than his overall verbal skills. Within the nonverbal domain, his ability to analyze and synthesize visual-spatial material, his visual sequencing ability, and his ability to synthesize concrete parts

(Exhibit continues next page)

Exhibit K-I (cont.)

into meaningful wholes are average for his age. His ability to differentiate essential from nonessential details, speed and accuracy of eye-hand coordination, and visual-motor control are excellent for his age.

Bill's weakness in word knowledge may be related to his reading difficulties. Because of his reading problems, he may be acquiring verbal skills and word knowledge at a slower rate than is typical for children of his age. On the other hand, his weak word knowledge may be contributing in some way to his reading difficulties, though this is unclear. Further testing would be needed to determine the relationship between his poor word knowledge and his reading difficulties. Furthermore, the poor articulation he exhibited throughout the testing session could be related to his poor word knowledge.

His below-average word knowledge and his excellent psychomotor speed and visual-motor control indicate that Bill performs better on tasks having visual-motor components rather than language components. He performs especially well on tasks requiring visual-motor speed and precision. His excellent ability to differentiate essential from nonessential details, coupled with his poor language development, indicates that his ability to recognize and perceive details of objects visually is better developed than his ability to describe objects verbally.

His overall average verbal skills indicate that he has the ability to perform adequately in school subjects requiring verbal skills, but the reason for his reading difficulties remains unclear. Additional testing is needed to assess the nature of his reading problems. Furthermore, Bill's nonverbal skills are well developed for his age, and thus he has the ability to perform well in subjects with nonverbal components.

Recommendations

It is recommended that further testing be conducted to assess the nature of his reading difficulties. Bill may also benefit from exercises in articulation and verbalization of words and from exercises aimed at enhancing his word knowledge. It would be good to capitalize on his affinity for visual-spatial activities by providing him with picture books, objects, puzzles, and other construction activities. During these activities he should be encouraged to describe and explain his actions.

Summary

Although Bill, who is 7 years, 8 months old, was occasionally fidgety and restless during the test, he remained attentive, on task, friendly, and cooperative throughout the session. His articulation was somewhat poor, and he occasionally was difficult to understand. He appeared to enjoy particularly tasks involving puzzles and creating designs with blocks. Bill achieved an IQ of 103 ± 7 on the WISC-III. This IQ is at the 55th percentile and in the Average range. The chances that the range of scores from 96 to 110 includes his true IQ are about 95 out of 100. The test results appear to give a reliable and valid estimate of his present level of intellectual functioning. His nonverbal skills are better developed than his verbal skills. Within the verbal domain, most skills are average, except for word knowledge and immediate auditory memory, which are below average for his age. Within the nonverbal domain, he shows strengths in differentiating essential from nonessential details, speed and accuracy of eye-hand coordination, and visual-motor control, and he shows average ability in analyzing and synthesizing visual-spatial material, visual sequencing, and synthesizing concrete parts into meaningful wholes. It is unclear how his reading difficulties are related to his poor language development and vice versa. Further testing is needed to assess his reading difficulties. Remedial activities should capitalize on his affinity for visual-spatial materials.

Phyllis Brown, B.A., Examiner

STUDY QUESTIONS

1. Discuss profile analysis on the WISC-III.

2. What are some important guidelines for interpreting and communicating WISC-III findings in the psychological report?

3. How would you go about describing each of the following parts of the WISC-III to a parent: Full Scale, Verbal Scale, Performance Scale, Information, Similarities, Arithmetic, Vocabulary, Comprehension, Digit Span, Picture Completion, Coding, Picture Arrangement, Block Design, Object Assembly, Symbol Search, and Mazes?

REFERENCE

Holmes, J. M. (1988). Testing. In R. G. Rudel, *Assessment of developmental learning disorders* (pp. 166–201). New York: Basic Books.

■ Exhibit K-2 ■

Checklist for Accuracy and Completeness of an Intelligence Test Report

Student's name _____   *Report number:* _____
Examinee's name: _____   *Date of report:* _____

Directions: Use this checklist to evaluate the accuracy and completeness of an intelligence test report. Place a checkmark in the box after you check the item in the report. Write "NA" next to items that are not applicable.

☐ 1. *Report Title*
　　2. *Identifying Data*
☐　　a. Examinee's name
☐　　b. Date of birth
☐　　c. Age
☐　　d. Grade
☐　　e. Date of examination
☐　　f. Date of report
☐　　g. Examiner's name
☐ 3. *Name of Test Administered*
☐ 4. *Reason for Referral*
☐ 5. *Background Information*
　　6. *Behavioral Observations*
☐　　a. Attitude toward examiner
☐　　b. Attitude toward test situation
☐　　c. Attitude toward self
☐　　d. Work habits
☐　　e. Reaction to successes
☐　　f. Reaction to failures
☐　　g. Speech
☐　　h. Vocabulary
☐　　i. Visual-motor abilities
☐　　j. Motor abilities
　　7. *Test Results and Impressions*
☐　　a. Verbal IQ (based on 5 standard subtests when 6 subtests given)
☐　　b. Performance IQ (based on 5 standard subtests when 6 or 7 subtests given)

☐　　c. Full Scale IQ
☐　　d. Percentile rank for Verbal IQ
☐　　e. Percentile rank for Performance IQ
☐　　f. Percentile rank for Full Scale IQ
☐　　g. Range designation of Full Scale IQ
☐　　h. Confidence interval for Full Scale IQ
☐　　i. Statement describing confidence interval
☐　　j. Statement about reliability of test results
☐　　k. Statement about validity of test results
☐　　l. Statements about a skill described by a percentile rank or qualitative statement (such as strength, weakness, average, above average, or below average)
☐　　m. Statements comparing one skill with another skill based on significant differences between scores on which skills were based
☐　　n. Interpretations based on substantial data
☐　　o. Clear recommendations
　　8. *Summary and End Matter*
☐　　a. Summary short (about one paragraph)
☐　　b. At least one statement included from each section of the report in the Summary
☐　　c. Examiner's name typewritten at end of report
☐　　d. Examiner's signature included at end of report
　　9. *Technical Qualities*
☐　　a. Report free of spelling errors
☐　　b. Report free of grammatical errors

■ Exhibit K-3

Psychological Evaluation Illustrating Several Problems That May Occur in Writing a WISC-III Report

Name of examinee: Jane Doe
Date of birth: November 12, 1975
Chronological age: 16-8
Grade: High school junior

Date of examination: August, 1992[1]
Date of report: August, 1992[1]
Name of examiner: Alan K. Smith

Test Administered

Wechler Intelligence Scale for Children – III (WISC-III)[2]

VERBAL SCALE		PERFORMANCE SCALE	
Information	7	Picture Completion	9
Similarities	13	Coding	10
Arithmetic	7	Picture Arrangement	10
Vocabulary	11	Block Design	14
Comprehension	11	Object Assembly	13
Digit Span	10		

Verbal Scale IQ = 99
Performance Scale IQ = 108
Full Scale IQ = 104 ± 6 (range of 97 to 110 at the 95% confidence level[3])

Reason for Referral

Jane agreed to act as a subject for a course in psychological assessment at CSU.[4]

Background Information

Jane is a sixteen[5]-year-, 9-month[6]-old white female in her junior year at Blank High School. She is enrolled in a pre-college curriculum and plans to go to college. She would like to become an Elementary School Teacher.[7] One practice of Janes that was mentioned during the interview was her involvement in a flag corp group.[8] The examiner had previously explained to Jane that she could not be shown her test results.[9] No further background information was obtained.

Behavioral Observations

Jane was[10] a sixteen[5]-year-, 9-month[6]-old high school student[11] whose language and behavior appear appropriate to her age and the situation. The most prominent features about Jane were that[12] she was cheerful and cooperative while under observation and insecure during the testing situation.[13] She giggled frequently, especially before answering questions and when she was frustrated.[14] Her answers were often preceded by the word "Um", followed by disclaimers such as "I don't know", "I think", and "I'm no good".[15] These responses suggested some anxiety and nervousness.[16] She seemed more comfortable with the demands of material[17] that required visual attention, physical manipulation, and knowledge organization.[18] Consequently, some variability was apparent during subtests.[19]

Her answers were succinct on the initial portions of some subtests and wordy on the latter portion.[20] Her answers were extensive throughout other subtests.[21] She was not consistently methodical in her approach to problem solving[22] and occasionally acted in a haphazard fashion.[23] Her hands are[10] involved in a washing-like motion.[24] Related to the examiner in an approval-seeking manner.[25] She mimicked the examiner exactly during Digits Forward,[26] including timed delay.[27]On a vocabulary test,[28] she unsurely gave[29] multiple responses when a single answer would have sufficed.

Assessment Results and Clinical Impressions

On the WISC-III Jane achieved a Verbal IQ of 99 (47th percentile, which places her in the average range),[30] a Performance IQ of 108 (70th percentile, which places her in the above average range),[30] and a combined full scale[31] IQ of 104 + 6[32] (61st percentile, which places her in the average range[33] of intellectual functioning). The Verbal IQ is near the mean, whereas the Performance IQ is 2/3 standard deviation above the mean.[34] The chances that the range of scores from 98 to 100[35] includes her true IQ are about 95 out of 100. Jane's voluntary participation suggests that the results represent a reliable[36] and valid estimate of her current level of intellectual functioning.

Janes[37] overall functioning is in the average range,[33] although with notable disparity between her verbal[38] and performance[38] IQs.[39] Her nonverbal skills are uniformly well developed,[40] but her verbal skills show considerably more variability.[41] Her verbal skills range from a low average to a superior classification,[42] whereas her nonverbal skills range from an average to superior classification.[42] Her Verbal Scale scores demonstrate accumulated experience[43] and indicate average performance in verbal skills and language development.[44]

On the six verbal subtests, Jane performed at or above the mean of the standardization sample one-half of the time (Similarities, Comprehension[45] and Digit Span).[46] Her performance on Information and Arithmetic subtests indicated the most notable skill deficits, with performance for each found to be one standard deviation below the mean of the norming sample.[47] Her scaled scores ($M = 10$, $SD = 3$)[48] on Arithmetic and Information were significantly lower than her own Verbal Scale mean score ($p < .05$ and $p < .01$, respectively).[49] Information is the second best measure of g among

(Exhibit continues next page)

Exhibit K-3 (cont.)

the Verbal Scale subtests.[50] Her performance on Information was anemic[51] and erratic[52] and at the Low Average range;[53] she sometimes answered more difficult items correctly and missed easier ones. On Arithmetic, she responded quickly to items involving simple calculations, but did not take time in responding to more difficult items.[54] Her verbal abilities are extremely diverse and do not fall within the Average range of performance; to characterize her verbal abilities as such would be in error.[55]

Within the non-verbal[56] performance[57] area, her perceptual organizational ability, attention to detail, and visual-motor coordination ability and speed are all well developed.[58] She assembled puzzles quickly in an object assembly task, scoring in the 75th percentile.[59] Her analytic and synthetic abilities, nonverbal reasoning ability, and sequencing are superior[60] as assessed by her performance on the Block Design subtest.[61] Block Design is the best measure of general intelligence (*g*) among the Performance Scale subtests.[62]

Her low fund of general information suggests that Jane has not been exposed to the kinds of information that average adolescents acquire through normal home and school experiences.[63] Her low arithmetical reasoning scores suggest that Jane was having difficulty sustaining attention, since this subtest is about halfway to the end of the test.[64] Her good social comprehension score suggests that her social skills are better developed than her other intellectual skills.[65] Overall, her intellectual level of functioning suggests that she will do well in her last two years of high school.[66] She appears to be a happy and goal oriented[67] girl,[68] and increased focus can be expected to add definition to her goals with time and increased high school experience.[69]

Summary

Jane, a healthy[70] 16-year-, 8-month-old high school student, volunteered to be examined for a demonstration of the WISC-III at a training clinic[71] at CSU.[72] Her test results seem to be reliable and valid.[73] She obtained a WISC-III Full Scale IQ of 104 ± 6, which is in the 51st percentile[74] and in the Average range. She was better overall in performance tasks (70th percentile) than in verbal tasks (47th percentile).[75] She has an uneven pattern of scores, as noted above.[76] She has strengths in three tasks and weaknesses in two others.[77] She should do well in her last two years of high school, but may not have been exposed to the kinds of information that other adolescents have been exposed to.[78] She appears to know where many of her improficiencies[79] lie and may often simply be fulfilling a "self-fulfilling prophecy."[80]

A.K.S.[81]

COMMENTS ON THE PSYCHOLOGICAL EVALUATION

Note: The numbers below refer to the superscripts in the Psychological Evaluation.

1. The day should be included.
2. *Wechler* is a misspelling; it should be *Wechsler*.
3. The confidence interval is incorrect. It should be 98 to 110.
4. The name of the school should be spelled out completely. It is preferable not to use abbreviations, except for the name of the test. Under "Test Administered," the first use of the abbreviation follows the full name of the test.
5. Age is usually written in Arabic numerals.
6. The correct age is 16-8, not 16-9.
7. The first letter of each word in the phrase "elementary school teacher" should not be capitalized.
8. This sentence is awkward and contains a punctuation and a spelling error. *Janes* should have an apostrophe (Jane's), and *corp* should have an "s" (corps). The words "during the interview" are not appropriate. A formal interview was not conducted, and a test session should not be characterized as an interview. The sentence could be rewritten as follows: "Jane mentioned that she is a member of the flag corps at Blank High School."
9. Is this sentence needed in the report? It does provide some information about the testing session but doesn't contribute much to our understanding of the examinee. It would be better to delete it.
10. Use the *present tense* to describe the examinee's more enduring characteristics ("Jane is a 16-year-, 8-month-old") and the *past tense* to describe the examinee's behavior, dress, mood, and so forth during the examination ("She *was* cheerful"; "Her hands *were*...").
11. This information is in the Background Information section and therefore need not be repeated.
12. The first eight words ("The...that") are superfluous and should be deleted.
13. The phrases "while under observation" and "during the testing situation" imply two different periods of the examination. Isn't the examinee under observation throughout the examination? It is not clear when the examinee was cheerful and when she was insecure. Additionally, the words *the* and *situation* can be deleted in the phrase "insecure during the testing situation."
14. It would help if the writer indicated when the examinee giggled — on easy or difficult items, on verbal or nonverbal items.
15. The quotation mark *follows* the comma or period.
16. The words "and nervousness" are redundant.
17. The words "the demands of" are not needed.

(Exhibit continues next page)

Exhibit K-3 (cont.)

18. A comparative clause that begins with *than* is needed. "She was more comfortable with X *than* with Y." Additionally, the term *knowledge organization* is vague.

19. This sentence is vague because we don't know to what *variability* refers. For example, does it refer to behavior, test scores, affect, or something else? The variability should be clearly described.

20. The specific subtests should be mentioned.

21. Again, this sentence is vague because we don't know on what subtests (or subtest portions) she gave extensive answers.

22. It would be more helpful if her approach to problem solving were described.

23. *Haphazard* is a strong term and has negative clinical connotations. The examinee's specific behaviors should be mentioned, and an appropriate term used to describe these behaviors.

24. This sentence does not provide enough information to the reader, and it almost implies a Lady Macbeth syndrome. When were her hands making a washing-like motion—throughout the test or only on specific items? On what type of items were the hand movements observed?

25. This is not a complete sentence. Complete sentences should always be used in the body of the report. The statement also would benefit from a description of the behaviors associated with her "approval-seeking manner."

26. Most lay readers will not know what *Digits Forward* refers to; instead describe the task.

27. *Timed delay* is vague.

28. The 13 subtests are usually referred to as *subtests*, not tests. The word *test* should be used to describe a complete test, such as the WISC-III or the Detroit Test of Learning Aptitude.

29. "Unsurely gave" is an awkward expression; it should be revised.

30. It is best to use a classification category only for the Full Scale IQ. A report with more than one classification may confuse readers. The classification is also wrong.

31. The first letter of *full* and of *scale* should be capitalized (Full Scale).

32. The minus sign ($-$) is missing in the confidence interval; it should be ± 6.

33. The first letter in *average* should be capitalized when the term designates a range.

34. This is technical information and is not needed in the report.

35. The confidence interval is incorrect. It should be 98 to 110.

36. Is voluntary participation a sufficient reason for concluding that the examinee's performance was reliable? Examinees can volunteer and still not try. The focus should be on the examinee's behavior and not on the reason for the examination, although that may play a role in certain cases.

37. *Janes* should be written with an apostrophe after the *e* (Jane's).

38. The initial letter in *verbal* and in *performance* should be capitalized when these terms refer to IQs or scales.

39. If the difference between the Verbal and Performance Scale IQs is not significant, report that both areas are developed at a similar level. The wording in this sentence is misleading.

40. Her scaled scores of 9 and 10 indicate average ability; thus the term *well developed* may be misleading. Additionally, the term *uniformly* is misleading because the scaled scores ranged from 9 to 15 on the Performance Scale.

41. The verbal scores range from 7 to 13 (6 points), and the performance scores range from 9 to 14 (5 points). Therefore, it is incorrect to say that the verbal scores show considerably more variability.

42. Subtest scaled scores should not be referred to as representing ranges or classifications such as *high average*. Terms such as *strength* (*above average*, *well developed*) or *weakness* (*below average*, *poorly developed*) are preferred (see Guideline 2 in this chapter). Additionally, using percentile ranks will help you to discuss subtest scores and the Verbal, Performance, and Full Scale IQs.

43. Both the Verbal Scale and the Performance Scale reflect accumulated experience; consequently, this phrase should be either eliminated or revised.

44. It is not clear how language development differs from verbal skills. Isn't language development a part of verbal development?

45. A comma would be helpful after the word *Comprehension*.

46. This statement is not accurate. Her Vocabulary score is also at or above the mean of the standardization group. Additionally, the statement is too technical and should be rewritten.

47. The sentence should be rewritten. This statement, although literally correct, is awkwardly written and too technical. Many readers may not know what the phrase "one standard deviation below the mean of the norming sample" refers to; it should be deleted.

48. It is not necessary to give the mean and standard deviation of the scaled scores.

49. The probability levels should not be included in a report.

50. This information is too technical and should be deleted.

51. *Anemic* is not the correct word in this context.

52. Use *variable* instead of *erratic*.

53. Individual subtest scores should not be classified into formal ranges or classifications (see number 42).

54. Instead of saying "but did not take time in responding to more difficult items," the examiner should describe how Jane responded to the more difficult items.

55. The logic of this sentence is unclear. The examinee's Verbal IQ is 99, which is clearly an average score. Consequently, it would be more appropriate to characterize her overall verbal skills as being average.

(Exhibit continues next page)

Exhibit K-3 (cont.)

56. A hyphen is not needed in *non-verbal* (nonverbal).

57. The word *performance* is redundant.

58. The phrases "attention to detail" and "visual-motor coordination ability and speed" likely pertain to the Picture Completion and Coding subtests, respectively. On these two subtests her scores were average: 9 and 10, respectively. Therefore, the sentence gives misleading information (that is, "are all well developed").

59. First, this sentence contains one error: the percentile rank should be 84th, not 75th, because the scaled score on Object Assembly is 13. Table C-41 on page 855 shows the percentile ranks for scaled scores. Second, the sentence can be rephrased to provide more meaningful information. The implications of her performance should be discussed rather than the specific tasks required by the subtest. For example, to describe her performance on Object Assembly, you could say "Her ability to arrange material under time pressure was excellent."

60. Block Design does not measure sequencing ability.

61. The remainder of the sentence ("as assessed by her performance on the Block Design subtest") is not needed.

62. This information is too technical and should be deleted.

63. There usually is no way of corroborating this hypothesis with the limited information obtained during an evaluation. Consequently, in this case this sentence should be deleted.

64. This is a puzzling inference, especially when you consider that some of her best scores were on Object Assembly and Block Design, which were administered during the second half of the test.

65. Comprehension, like all of the WISC-III subtests, is a measure of cognition. This subtest, therefore, likely measures social judgment and not social skills.

66. A Full Scale IQ of 104 probably indicates that the examinee has the ability to do at least average work in high school. However, because many other factors besides intelligence affect school grades, this statement should be rewritten (for example, "...she has the ability to complete high school").

67. Use a hyphen in *goal oriented* when it modifies a noun (goal-oriented student).

68. *Student* is preferable to *girl*.

69. The last half of this sentence is poorly written; it should be rewritten.

70. Because the term *healthy* was not mentioned in the body of the report, it should not be introduced in the summary. Additionally, unless you have information about the examinee's health, do not make statements about it.

71. The words *training clinic* were not mentioned previously and therefore should not be introduced for the first time in the summary. Additionally, the examinee was tested as part of a course requirement and not at a training clinic.

72. The summary should stand alone. Consequently, it is preferable not to use abbreviations, except for acronyms that are widely known and accepted (for example, *WISC-III*).

73. "Seem to be" is a vague phrase. Be more definite when discussing reliability and validity, if at all possible.

74. The correct percentile rank is 61st.

75. Because the Verbal and Performance IQs are not significantly different, this statement is misleading.

76. The summary should repeat the major findings and not refer readers to the body of the report.

77. This sentence is vague.

78. This is a speculative inference and should be deleted.

79. *Improficiencies* is not a word.

80. The concept of a "self-fulfilling prophecy" was not developed in the report proper and is likely to confuse the reader, especially as it comes at the end of the summary.

81. The examiner's full name should be typewritten in this space, followed by his or her degree (e.g., B.A., M.A., Ph.D.) and the word *Examiner*.

Exhibit K-4

Suggested Psychological Evaluation for Report in Exhibit K-3

Name of examinee: Jane Doe
Date of birth: November 12, 1975
Chronological age: 16-8
Grade: High school junior

Date of examination: August 2, 1992
Date of report: August 15, 1992
Name of examiner: Alan K. Smith

Test Administered

Wechsler Intelligence Scale for Children — III (WISC-III)

Reason for Referral

Jane agreed to be tested in order for the examiner to gain experience in administering the test.

Background Information

Jane is a 16-year-, 8-month-old white female in her junior year at Blank High School. She is enrolled in a precollege curriculum and plans to attend college when she graduates. She lives at home with her parents and is a member of a flag corps at high school. No other information was obtained at the time of evaluation.

Behavioral Observations

Jane is of average height for her age, slightly overweight, and right handed. She was comfortably dressed in jeans and an oversized tee shirt. Her blond hair was pulled back in a ponytail.

Jane was friendly and cooperative throughout the evaluation. However, she initially seemed anxious about being tested and frequently giggled, particularly when she was unsure of an answer. She was often tentative in her responses to verbal items, frequently saying "I think" or "I'm no good at that" when she had difficulty with an item. She often raised her voice at the end of her answers in a questioning way, as though seeking direction or reassurance from the examiner. Her behavior suggested that she has limited self-confidence in her verbal abilities. On nonverbal tasks, Jane worked quickly and calmly. Her attempts to solve problems were initially somewhat unsystematic. As the difficulty of a task increased, however, she became more methodical in her approach, organizing materials, such as blocks, one by one to complete the task. Jane stated that she was more confident about her performance on nonverbal tasks than on verbal tasks.

Assessment Results and Clinical Impressions

Jane, at a chronological age of 16-8 years, achieved a Verbal Scale IQ of 99 (47th percentile), a Performance Scale IQ of 108 (70th percentile), and a Full Scale IQ of 104 ± 6 on the WISC-III. Her overall performance is classified in the Average range and is ranked in the 61st percentile. The chances that the range of scores from 98 to 110 includes her true IQ are about 95 out of 100. The present measure of her level of intellectual functioning appears to be reliable and valid because of her cooperativeness, willingness to try, and background characteristics.

Jane's overall verbal and nonverbal skills are at an average level of development. Within the verbal area, however, both weaknesses and strengths were exhibited in relation to her peer group. Her range of factual information and her numerical reasoning ability are weaknesses; both of them are at the 16th percentile. In contrast, her verbal concept formation is a strength (at the 84th percentile). Her average verbal abilities are in immediate auditory memory (50th percentile), word knowledge (63rd percentile), and social comprehension (63rd percentile).

Within the nonverbal area, she had two strengths and no weaknesses in relation to her peer group. Visual-motor spatial integration and coordination are strengths. She can analyze and synthesize effectively with spatial-visual material (91st percentile) and is well able to synthesize concrete parts into a meaningful whole (84th percentile). Her average nonverbal abilities are in differentiating essential from nonessential details (37th percentile), visual sequencing (50th percentile), and psychomotor speed (50th percentile).

Jane's overall average intellectual skills suggest that she possesses the ability to complete high school. However, she will likely have to work hard at some of her subjects. Her strengths lie in conceptual reasoning, both in verbal and in nonverbal areas. However, weaknesses in factual knowledge and in processing arithmetical concepts are likely to hamper her ability to master some course work.

Jane appears to be aware of her strengths in nonverbal skills but may be less aware of her strong verbal reasoning ability. Furthermore, her anxiety and low self-confidence on verbal tasks may interfere with her concentration, particularly on school-like tasks.

Recommendations

Jane may benefit from feedback regarding both her strengths and her weaknesses, with particular emphasis on her strong reasoning skills. Information regarding her academic performance would be helpful in determining whether any intervention is needed.

(Exhibit continues next page)

Exhibit K-4 (cont.)

Summary

Jane, a 16-year-, 8-month-old junior in high school, agreed to be tested in order for the examiner to gain testing experience. She obtained a Verbal IQ of 99, a Performance IQ of 108, and a Full Scale IQ of 104 ± 6 on the WISC-III. Her Full Scale IQ is in the Average range and at the 61st percentile. The chances that the range of scores from 98 to 110 includes her true IQ are about 95 out of 100. The present results appear to give a reliable and valid estimate of her present level of intellectual functioning. Overall, Jane's verbal and nonverbal skills are developed at an average level. She has, however, strengths in both verbal and nonverbal conceptual reasoning and in visualizing a whole from its parts. Her weaknesses are associated with her range of information and facility in mental arithmetic. Although she likely has the ability to complete high school, she may have difficulties in some course work.

Alan K. Smith, B.A., Examiner

APPENDIX L

TABLES FOR THE WISC-III
(AND OTHER WECHSLER SCALES)

See also Table C-12, "WISC-R Structure of Intellect Classifications" (page 821); Table C-13, "Interpretive Rationales, Implications of High and Low Scores, and Instructional Implications for WISC-R Subtests" (page 824); Table C-41, "Percentile Ranks and Suggested Qualitative Descriptions for the Wechsler Scales" (page 855); Table C-42, "Interpretive Rationales, Implications of High and Low Scores, and Instructional Implications for Wechsler Scales and Factor Scores" (page 856); and Table C-43, "Suggested Remediation Activities for Combinations of Wechsler Subtests."

Table L-I
Confidence Intervals for WISC-III Scales Based on Obtained Score Only

Age level	Scale	Confidence level				
		68%	85%	90%	95%	99%
6	Verbal Scale IQ	± 4	± 6	± 7	± 8	± 10
(6-0-0 through	Performance Scale IQ	± 5	± 6	± 7	± 9	± 12
6-11-30)	Full Scale IQ	± 3	± 5	± 6	± 7	± 9
7	Verbal Scale IQ	± 4	± 6	± 7	± 8	± 11
(7-0-0 through	Performance Scale IQ	± 5	± 7	± 8	± 9	± 12
7-11-30)	Full Scale IQ	± 4	± 5	± 6	± 7	± 9
8	Verbal Scale IQ	± 3	± 4	± 5	± 6	± 8
(8-0-0 through	Performance Scale IQ	± 5	± 7	± 8	± 9	± 12
8-11-30)	Full Scale IQ	± 3	± 4	± 5	± 6	± 8
9	Verbal Scale IQ	± 4	± 6	± 7	± 8	± 10
(9-0-0 through	Performance Scale IQ	± 5	± 6	± 7	± 9	± 12
9-11-30)	Full Scale IQ	± 3	± 5	± 6	± 7	± 9
10	Verbal Scale IQ	± 3	± 5	± 6	± 7	± 9
(10-0-0 through	Performance Scale IQ	± 5	± 6	± 7	± 9	± 12
10-11-30)	Full Scale IQ	± 3	± 4	± 5	± 6	± 8
11	Verbal Scale IQ	± 3	± 5	± 6	± 7	± 9
(11-0-0 through	Performance Scale IQ	± 5	± 7	± 8	± 9	± 12
11-11-30)	Full Scale IQ	± 3	± 5	± 6	± 7	± 9
12	Verbal Scale IQ	± 3	± 5	± 6	± 7	± 9
(12-0-0 through	Performance Scale IQ	± 5	± 6	± 7	± 9	± 12
12-11-30)	Full Scale IQ	± 3	± 4	± 5	± 6	± 8
13	Verbal Scale IQ	± 4	± 5	± 6	± 7	± 9
(13-0-0 through	Performance Scale IQ	± 5	± 7	± 8	± 9	± 12
13-11-30)	Full Scale IQ	± 3	± 5	± 6	± 7	± 9
14	Verbal Scale IQ	± 3	± 5	± 6	± 7	± 9
(14-0-0 through	Performance Scale IQ	± 5	± 7	± 8	± 10	± 13
14-11-30)	Full Scale IQ	± 3	± 5	± 6	± 7	± 9
15	Verbal Scale IQ	± 3	± 4	± 5	± 6	± 8
(15-0-0 through	Performance Scale IQ	± 4	± 5	± 6	± 7	± 9
15-11-30)	Full Scale IQ	± 3	± 4	± 4	± 5	± 7
16	Verbal Scale IQ	± 3	± 5	± 6	± 7	± 9
(16-0-0 through	Performance Scale IQ	± 4	± 6	± 7	± 8	± 11
16-11-30)	Full Scale IQ	± 3	± 4	± 5	± 6	± 8
Average	Verbal Scale IQ	± 4	± 5	± 6	± 7	± 9
	Performance Scale IQ	± 5	± 7	± 7	± 9	± 12
	Full Scale IQ	± 3	± 5	± 5	± 6	± 8

Note. See Table C-1 (page 813) for an explanation of the method used to obtain confidence intervals. Confidence intervals in Table L-1 were obtained by using the appropriate SE_m located in Table 5.2 (page 168) in the WISC-III manual.

Table L-2
Confidence Intervals for Wechsler Scales (and Other Tests) Based on Estimated True Score

Use the following chart to locate the section of Table L-2 that shows confidence intervals based on estimated true scores for Wechsler scales.

WISC-III

Examinee's age	Verbal Scale	Performance Scale	Full Scale
6 (6-0-0 to 6-11-30)	I	G	K
7 (7-0-0 to 7-11-30)	H	F	J
8 (8-0-0 to 8-11-30)	L	F	L
9 (9-0-0 to 9-11-30)	I	G	K
10 (10-0-0 to 10-11-30)	K	G	L
11 (11-0-0 to 11-11-30)	K	F	K
12 (12-0-0 to 12-11-30)	K	G	L
13 (13-0-0 to 13-11-30)	J	F	K
14 (14-0-0 to 14-11-30)	K	E	K
15 (15-0-0 to 15-11-30)	L	J	M
16 (16-0-0 to 16-11-30)	K	H	L
Average	K	G	L

WPPSI-R

Examinee's age	Verbal Scale	Performance Scale	Full Scale
3 (3-0-0 to 3-5-15)	I	L	M
3½ (3-5-16 to 3-11-15)	I	L	M
4 (3-11-16 to 4-5-15)	I	L	M
4½ (4-5-16 to 4-11-15)	I	L	M
5 (4-11-16 to 5-5-15)	H	K	L
5½ (5-5-16 to 5-11-15)	F	J	K
6 (5-11-16 to 6-5-15)	H	J	K
6½ (6-5-16 to 6-11-15)	F	I	K
7 (6-11-16 to 7-3-15)	A	B	F
Average	K	H	L

WAIS-R

Examinee's age	Verbal Scale	Performance Scale	Full Scale
16–17	K	D	L
18–19	L	F	L
20–24	L	H	M
25–34	M	J	N
35–44	M	J	N
45–54	M	J	M
55–64	M	I	M
65–69	M	J	N
70–74	M	H	M
Average	M	I	M

(Table continues next page)

Table L-2 (cont.)

A. WPPSI-R – Verbal Scale – Age 7 ($r_{xx} = .85$)

68%			85%			90%			95%			99%		
IQ	L	U	IQ	L	U	IQ	L	U	IQ	L	U	IQ	L	U
40–42	4	14	40–42	2	16	40–42	1	17	40–41	− 1	19	40–41	− 4	22
43	4	13	43–44	1	16	43–44	0	17	42–45	− 1	18	42–45	− 4	21
44–49	3	13	45–49	1	15	45–49	0	16	46–47	− 2	18	46–48	− 5	21
50	3	12	50	0	15	50	− 1	16	48–52	− 2	17	49–51	− 5	20
51–56	2	12	51–55	0	14	51–55	− 1	15	53–54	− 3	17	52–54	− 6	20
57	2	11	56–57	− 1	14	56–57	− 2	15	55–58	− 3	16	55–58	− 6	19
58–62	1	11	58–62	− 1	13	58–62	− 2	14	59–61	− 4	16	59–61	− 7	19
63	1	10	63–64	− 2	13	63–64	− 3	14	62–65	− 4	15	62–65	− 7	18
64–69	0	10	65–69	− 2	12	65–69	− 3	13	66–67	− 5	15	66–68	− 8	18
70	0	9	70	− 3	12	70	− 4	13	68–72	− 5	14	69–71	− 8	17
71–76	− 1	9	71–75	− 3	11	71–75	− 4	12	73–74	− 6	14	72–74	− 9	17
77	− 1	8	76–77	− 4	11	76–77	− 5	12	75–78	− 6	13	75–78	− 9	16
78–82	− 2	8	78–82	− 4	10	78–82	− 5	11	79–81	− 7	13	79–81	−10	16
83	− 2	7	83–84	− 5	10	83–84	− 6	11	82–85	− 7	12	82–85	−10	15
84–89	− 3	7	85–89	− 5	9	85–89	− 6	10	86–87	− 8	12	86–88	−11	15
90	− 3	6	90	− 6	9	90	− 7	10	88–92	− 8	11	89–91	−11	14
91–96	− 4	6	91–95	− 6	8	91–95	− 7	9	93–94	− 9	11	92–94	−12	14
97	− 4	5	96–97	− 7	8	96–97	− 8	9	95–98	− 9	10	95–98	−12	13
98–102	− 5	5	98–102	− 7	7	98–102	− 8	8	99–101	−10	10	99–101	−13	13
103	− 5	4	103–104	− 8	7	103–104	− 9	8	102–105	−10	9	102–105	−13	12
104–109	− 6	4	105–109	− 8	6	105–109	− 9	7	106–107	−11	9	106–108	−14	12
110	− 6	3	110	− 9	6	110	−10	7	108–112	−11	8	109–111	−14	11
111–116	− 7	3	111–115	− 9	5	111–115	−10	6	113–114	−12	8	112–114	−15	11
117	− 7	2	116–117	−10	5	116–117	−11	6	115–118	−12	7	115–118	−15	10
118–122	− 8	2	118–122	−10	4	118–122	−11	5	119–121	−13	7	119–121	−16	10
123	− 8	1	123–124	−11	4	123–124	−12	5	122–125	−13	6	122–125	−16	9
124–129	− 9	1	125–129	−11	3	125–129	−12	4	126–127	−14	6	126–128	−17	9
130	− 9	0	130	−12	3	130	−13	4	128–132	−14	5	129–131	−17	8
131–136	−10	0	131–135	−12	2	131–135	−13	3	133–134	−15	5	132–134	−18	8
137	−10	−1	136–137	−13	2	136–137	−14	3	135–138	−15	4	135–138	−18	7
138–142	−11	−1	138–142	−13	1	138–142	−14	2	139–141	−16	4	139–141	−19	7
143	−11	−2	143–144	−14	1	143–144	−15	2	142–145	−16	3	142–145	−19	6
144–149	−12	−2	145–149	−14	0	145–149	−15	1	146–147	−17	3	146–148	−20	6
150	−12	−3	150	−15	0	150	−16	1	148–152	−17	2	149–151	−20	5
151–156	−13	−3	151–155	−15	−1	151–155	−16	0	153–154	−18	2	152–154	−21	5
157	−13	−4	156–157	−16	−1	156–157	−17	0	155–158	−18	1	155–158	−21	4
158–160	−14	−4	158–160	−16	−2	158–160	−17	−1	159–160	−19	1	159–160	−22	4

(Table continues next page)

Table L-2 (cont.)

B. WPPSI-R — Performance Scale — Age 7 ($r_{xx} = .86$)

68%			85%			90%			95%			99%		
IQ	L	U	IQ	L	U	IQ	L	U	IQ	L	U	IQ	L	U
40	4	13	40–46	1	15	40–46	0	16	40–42	− 1	18	40–42	− 4	21
41–45	3	13	47–53	0	14	47–53	− 1	15	43	− 1	17	43	− 4	20
46–47	3	12	54–60	− 1	13	54–60	− 2	14	44–49	− 2	17	44–49	− 5	20
48–52	2	12	61	− 1	12	61–67	− 3	13	50	− 2	16	50	− 5	19
53–54	2	11	62–67	− 2	12	68	− 3	12	51–56	− 3	16	51–56	− 6	19
55–59	1	11	68	− 2	11	69–74	− 4	12	57	− 3	15	57	− 6	18
60–61	1	10	69–74	− 3	11	75	− 4	11	58–64	− 4	15	58–63	− 7	18
62–66	0	10	75	− 3	10	76–81	− 5	11	65–71	− 5	14	64	− 7	17
67–69	0	9	76–81	− 4	10	82	− 5	10	72–78	− 6	13	65–71	− 8	17
70–73	− 1	9	82	− 4	9	83–89	− 6	10	79–85	− 7	12	72–78	− 9	16
74–76	− 1	8	83–88	− 5	9	90–96	− 7	9	86–92	− 8	11	79–85	−10	15
77–80	− 2	8	89	− 5	8	97–103	− 8	8	93	− 8	10	86	−10	14
81–83	− 2	7	90–96	− 6	8	104–110	− 9	7	94–99	− 9	10	87–92	−11	14
84–88	− 3	7	97–103	− 7	7	111–117	−10	6	100	− 9	9	93	−11	13
89–90	− 3	6	104–110	− 8	6	118	−10	5	101–106	−10	9	94–99	−12	13
91–95	− 4	6	111	− 8	5	119–124	−11	5	107	−10	8	100	−12	12
96–97	− 4	5	112–117	− 9	5	125	−11	4	108–114	−11	8	101–106	−13	12
98–102	− 5	5	118	− 9	4	126–131	−12	4	115–121	−12	7	107	−13	11
103–104	− 5	4	119–124	−10	4	132	−12	3	122–128	−13	6	108–113	−14	11
105–109	− 6	4	125	−10	3	133–139	−13	3	129–135	−14	5	114	−14	10
110–111	− 6	3	126–131	−11	3	140–146	−14	2	136–142	−15	4	115–121	−15	10
112–116	− 7	3	132	−11	2	147–153	−15	1	143	−15	3	122–128	−16	9
117–119	− 7	2	133–138	−12	2	154–160	−16	0	144–149	−16	3	129–135	−17	8
120–123	− 8	2	139	−12	1				150	−16	2	136	−17	7
124–126	− 8	1	140–146	−13	1				151–156	−17	2	137–142	−18	7
127–130	− 9	1	147–153	−14	0				157	−17	1	143	−18	6
131–133	− 9	0	154–160	−15	−1				158–160	−18	1	144–149	−19	6
134–138	−10	0										150	−19	5
139–140	−10	−1										151–156	−20	5
141–145	−11	−1										157	−20	4
146–147	−11	−2										158–160	−21	4
148–152	−12	−2												
153–154	−12	−3												
155–159	−13	−3												
160	−13	−4												

(Table continues next page)

Table L-2 (cont.)

C. No Wechsler Scale ($r_{xx} = .87$)

68%			85%			90%			95%			99%		
IQ	L	U	IQ	L	U	IQ	L	U	IQ	L	U	IQ	L	U
40	3	13	40	1	15	40	0	16	40	− 1	17	40–41	− 4	20
41–44	3	12	41–44	1	14	41–44	0	15	41–44	− 2	17	42–43	− 5	20
45–47	2	12	45–48	0	14	45–48	− 1	15	45–48	− 2	16	44–48	− 5	19
48–52	2	11	49–51	0	13	49–51	− 1	14	49–51	− 3	16	49–51	− 6	19
53–55	1	11	52–55	− 1	13	52–55	− 2	14	52–55	− 3	15	52–56	− 6	18
56–59	1	10	56–59	− 1	12	56–59	− 2	13	56–59	− 4	15	57–58	− 7	18
60–63	0	10	60–63	− 2	12	60–63	− 3	13	60–63	− 4	14	59–64	− 7	17
64–67	0	9	64–67	− 2	11	64–67	− 3	12	64–67	− 5	14	65–66	− 8	17
68–70	− 1	9	68–71	− 3	11	68–71	− 4	12	68–71	− 5	13	67–72	− 8	16
71–75	− 1	8	72–74	− 3	10	72–74	− 4	11	72–74	− 6	13	73–74	− 9	16
76–78	− 2	8	75–79	− 4	10	75–78	− 5	11	75–79	− 6	12	75–79	− 9	15
79–83	− 2	7	80–82	− 4	9	79–82	− 5	10	80–82	− 7	12	80–81	−10	15
84–86	− 3	7	83–86	− 5	9	83–86	− 6	10	83–86	− 7	11	82–87	−10	14
87–90	− 3	6	87–90	− 5	8	87–90	− 6	9	87–90	− 8	11	88–89	−11	14
91–93	− 4	6	91–94	− 6	8	91–94	− 7	9	91–94	− 8	10	90–95	−11	13
94–98	− 4	5	95–97	− 6	7	95–97	− 7	8	95–97	− 9	10	96–97	−12	13
99–101	− 5	5	98–102	− 7	7	98–102	− 8	8	98–102	− 9	9	98–102	−12	12
102–106	− 5	4	103–105	− 7	6	103–105	− 8	7	103–105	−10	9	103–104	−13	12
107–109	− 6	4	106–109	− 8	6	106–109	− 9	7	106–109	−10	8	105–110	−13	11
110–113	− 6	3	110–113	− 8	5	110–113	− 9	6	110–113	−11	8	111–112	−14	11
114–116	− 7	3	114–117	− 9	5	114–117	−10	6	114–117	−11	7	113–118	−14	10
117–121	− 7	2	118–120	− 9	4	118–121	−10	5	118–120	−12	7	119–120	−15	10
122–124	− 8	2	121–125	−10	4	122–125	−11	5	121–125	−12	6	121–125	−15	9
125–129	− 8	1	126–128	−10	3	126–128	−11	4	126–128	−13	6	126–127	−16	9
130–132	− 9	1	129–132	−11	3	129–132	−12	4	129–132	−13	5	128–133	−16	8
133–136	− 9	0	133–136	−11	2	133–136	−12	3	133–136	−14	5	134–135	−17	8
137–140	−10	0	137–140	−12	2	137–140	−13	3	137–140	−14	4	136–141	−17	7
141–144	−10	−1	141–144	−12	1	141–144	−13	2	141–144	−15	4	142–143	−18	7
145–147	−11	−1	145–148	−13	1	145–148	−14	2	145–148	−15	3	144–148	−18	6
148–152	−11	−2	149–151	−13	0	149–151	−14	1	149–151	−16	3	149–151	−19	6
153–155	−12	−2	152–155	−14	0	152–155	−15	1	152–155	−16	2	152–156	−19	5
156–159	−12	−3	156–159	−14	−1	156–159	−15	0	156–159	−17	2	157–158	−20	5
160	−13	−3	160	−15	−1	160	−16	0	160	−17	1	159–160	−20	4

(Table continues next page)

Table L-2 (cont.)

D. WAIS-R — Performance Scale — Ages 16–17 (r_{xx} = .88)

68%			85%			90%			95%			99%		
IQ	L	U	IQ	L	U	IQ	L	U	IQ	L	U	IQ	L	U
40–41	3	12	40	1	14	40–41	0	15	40–45	− 2	16	40–44	− 5	19
42	2	12	41–42	0	14	42	− 1	15	46	− 2	15	45–47	− 5	18
43–49	2	11	43–49	0	13	43–49	− 1	14	47–53	− 3	15	48–52	− 6	18
50	1	11	50	− 1	13	50	− 2	14	54	− 3	14	53–55	− 6	17
51–57	1	10	51–57	− 1	12	51–57	− 2	13	55–62	− 4	14	56–60	− 7	17
58	0	10	58–59	− 2	12	58	− 3	13	63–70	− 5	13	61–64	− 7	16
59–66	0	9	60–65	− 2	11	59–66	− 3	12	71	− 5	12	65–69	− 8	16
67	− 1	9	66–67	− 3	11	67	− 4	12	72–78	− 6	12	70–72	− 8	15
68–74	− 1	8	68–74	− 3	10	68–74	− 4	11	79	− 6	11	73–77	− 9	15
75	− 2	8	75	− 4	10	75	− 5	11	80–87	− 7	11	78–80	− 9	14
76–82	− 2	7	76–82	− 4	9	76–82	− 5	10	88–95	− 8	10	81–85	−10	14
83	− 3	7	83–84	− 5	9	83	− 6	10	96	− 8	9	86–89	−10	13
84–91	− 3	6	85–90	− 5	8	84–91	− 6	9	97–103	− 9	9	90–94	−11	13
92	− 4	6	91–92	− 6	8	92	− 7	9	104	− 9	8	95–97	−11	12
93–99	− 4	5	93–99	− 6	7	93–99	− 7	8	105–112	−10	8	98–102	−12	12
100	− 5	5	100	− 7	7	100	− 8	8	113–120	−11	7	103–105	−12	11
101–107	− 5	4	101–107	− 7	6	101–107	− 8	7	121	−11	6	106–110	−13	11
108	− 6	4	108–109	− 8	6	108	− 9	7	122–128	−12	6	111–114	−13	10
109–116	− 6	3	110–115	− 8	5	109–116	− 9	6	129	−12	5	115–119	−14	10
117	− 7	3	116–117	− 9	5	117	−10	6	130–137	−13	5	120–122	−14	9
118–124	− 7	2	118–124	− 9	4	118–124	−10	5	138–145	−14	4	123–127	−15	9
125	− 8	2	125	−10	4	125	−11	5	146	−14	3	128–130	−15	8
126–132	− 8	1	126–132	−10	3	126–132	−11	4	147–153	−15	3	131–135	−16	8
133	− 9	1	133–134	−11	3	133	−12	4	154	−15	2	136–139	−16	7
134–141	− 9	0	135–140	−11	2	134–141	−12	3	155–160	−16	2	140–144	−17	7
142	−10	0	141–142	−12	2	142	−13	3				145–147	−17	6
143–149	−10	−1	143–149	−12	1	143–149	−13	2				148–152	−18	6
150	−11	−1	150	−13	1	150	−14	2				153–155	−18	5
151–157	−11	−2	151–157	−13	0	151–157	−14	1				156–160	−19	5
158	−12	−2	158–159	−14	0	158	−15	1						
159–160	−12	−3	160	−14	−1	159–160	−15	0						

(Table continues next page)

Table L-2 (cont.)

E. WISC-III—Performance Scale—Age 14 ($r_{xx} = .89$)

68%			85%			90%			95%			99%		
IQ	L	U	IQ	L	U	IQ	L	U	IQ	L	U	IQ	L	U
40–44	2	11	40–44	0	13	40–43	−1	14	40–43	−2	15	40–44	−5	18
45–46	2	10	45–46	0	12	44–47	−1	13	44–47	−3	15	45–46	−5	17
47–53	1	10	47–53	−1	12	48–52	−2	13	48–52	−3	14	47–53	−6	17
54–55	1	9	54–55	−1	11	53–56	−2	12	53–56	−4	14	54–55	−6	16
56–62	0	9	56–62	−2	11	57–61	−3	12	57–62	−4	13	56–62	−7	16
63–64	0	8	63–64	−2	10	62–65	−3	11	63–65	−5	13	63–64	−7	15
65–72	−1	8	65–71	−3	10	66–70	−4	11	66–71	−5	12	65–72	−8	15
73	−1	7	72–73	−3	9	71–74	−4	10	72–74	−6	12	73	−8	14
74–81	−2	7	74–80	−4	9	75–80	−5	10	75–80	−6	11	74–81	−9	14
82	−2	6	81–82	−4	8	81–83	−5	9	81–83	−7	11	82	−9	13
83–90	−3	6	83–89	−5	8	84–89	−6	9	84–89	−7	10	83–90	−10	13
91	−3	5	90–92	−5	7	90–92	−6	8	90–92	−8	10	91	−10	12
92–99	−4	5	93–98	−6	7	93–98	−7	8	93–98	−8	9	92–99	−11	12
100	−4	4	99–101	−6	6	99–101	−7	7	99–101	−9	9	100	−11	11
101–108	−5	4	102–107	−7	6	102–107	−8	7	102–107	−9	8	101–108	−12	11
109	−5	3	108–110	−7	5	108–110	−8	6	108–110	−10	8	109	−12	10
110–117	−6	3	111–117	−8	5	111–116	−9	6	111–116	−10	7	110–117	−13	10
118	−6	2	118–119	−8	4	117–119	−9	5	117–119	−11	7	118	−13	9
119–126	−7	2	120–126	−9	4	120–125	−10	5	120–125	−11	6	119–126	−14	9
127	−7	1	127–128	−9	3	126–129	−10	4	126–128	−12	6	127	−14	8
128–135	−8	1	129–135	−10	3	130–134	−11	4	129–134	−12	5	128–135	−15	8
136–137	−8	0	136–137	−10	2	135–138	−11	3	135–137	−13	5	136–137	−15	7
138–144	−9	0	138–144	−11	2	139–143	−12	3	138–143	−13	4	138–144	−16	7
145–146	−9	−1	145–146	−11	1	144–147	−12	2	144–147	−14	4	145–146	−16	6
147–153	−10	−1	147–153	−12	1	148–152	−13	2	148–152	−14	3	147–153	−17	6
154–155	−10	−2	154–155	−12	0	153–156	−13	1	153–156	−15	3	154–155	−17	5
156–160	−11	−2	156–160	−13	0	157–160	−14	1	157–160	−15	2	156–160	−18	5

(Table continues next page)

Table L-2 (cont.)

F. WISC-III – Performance Scale – Ages 7, 8, 11, and 13; WPPSI-R – Verbal Scale – Ages 5½ and 6½; WPPSI-R – Full Scale – Age 7; WAIS-R – Performance Scale – Ages 18–19 ($r_{xx} = .90$)

68%			85%			90%			95%			99%		
IQ	L	U	IQ	L	U	IQ	L	U	IQ	L	U	IQ	L	U
40–42	2	10	40–43	0	12	40–44	− 1	13	40–41	− 2	14	40–44	− 5	17
43–47	1	10	44–46	− 1	12	45	− 2	13	42–48	− 3	14	45	− 6	17
48–52	1	9	47–53	− 1	11	46–54	− 2	12	49–51	− 3	13	46–54	− 6	16
53–57	0	9	54–56	− 2	11	55	− 3	12	52–58	− 4	13	55	− 7	16
58–62	0	8	57–63	− 2	10	56–64	− 3	11	59–61	− 4	12	56–64	− 7	15
63–67	− 1	8	64–66	− 3	10	65	− 4	11	62–68	− 5	12	65	− 8	15
68–72	− 1	7	67–73	− 3	9	66–74	− 4	10	69–71	− 5	11	66–74	− 8	14
73–77	− 2	7	74–76	− 4	9	75	− 5	10	72–78	− 6	11	75	− 9	14
78–82	− 2	6	77–83	− 4	8	76–84	− 5	9	79–81	− 6	10	76–84	− 9	13
83–87	− 3	6	84–86	− 5	8	85	− 6	9	82–88	− 7	10	85	−10	13
88–92	− 3	5	87–93	− 5	7	86–94	− 6	8	89–91	− 7	9	86–94	−10	12
93–97	− 4	5	94–96	− 6	7	95	− 7	8	92–98	− 8	9	95	−11	12
98–102	− 4	4	97–103	− 6	6	96–104	− 7	7	99–101	− 8	8	96–104	−11	11
103–107	− 5	4	104–106	− 7	6	105	− 8	7	102–108	− 9	8	105	−12	11
108–112	− 5	3	107–113	− 7	5	106–114	− 8	6	109–111	− 9	7	106–114	−12	10
113–117	− 6	3	114–116	− 8	5	115	− 9	6	112–118	−10	7	115	−13	10
118–122	− 6	2	117–123	− 8	4	116–124	− 9	5	119–121	−10	6	116–124	−13	9
123–127	− 7	2	124–126	− 9	4	125	−10	5	122–128	−11	6	125	−14	9
128–132	− 7	1	127–133	− 9	3	126–134	−10	4	129–131	−11	5	126–134	−14	8
133–137	− 8	1	134–136	−10	3	135	−11	4	132–138	−12	5	135	−15	8
138–142	− 8	0	137–143	−10	2	136–144	−11	3	139–141	−12	4	136–144	−15	7
143–147	− 9	0	144–146	−11	2	145	−12	3	142–148	−13	4	145	−16	7
148–152	− 9	−1	147–153	−11	1	146–154	−12	2	149–151	−13	3	146–154	−16	6
153–157	−10	−1	154–156	−12	1	155	−13	2	152–158	−14	3	155	−17	6
158–160	−10	−2	157–160	−12	0	156–160	−13	1	159–160	−14	2	156–160	−17	5

(Table continues next page)

Table L-2 (cont.)

G. WISC-III – Performance Scale – Ages 6, 9, 10, 12, and Average ($r_{xx} = .91$)

68%			85%			90%			95%			99%		
IQ	L	U	IQ	L	U	IQ	L	U	IQ	L	U	IQ	L	U
40–48	1	9	40	0	11	40–41	− 1	12	40–49	− 3	13	40–43	− 5	16
49–51	0	9	41–48	− 1	11	42–47	− 2	12	50	− 4	13	44–45	− 6	16
52–60	0	8	49–51	− 1	10	48–52	− 2	11	51–60	− 4	12	46–54	− 6	15
61–62	− 1	8	52–59	− 2	10	53–58	− 3	11	61	− 5	12	55–56	− 7	15
63–71	− 1	7	60–62	− 2	9	59–63	− 3	10	62–71	− 5	11	57–65	− 7	14
72–73	− 2	7	63–71	− 3	9	64–69	− 4	10	72	− 6	11	66–67	− 8	14
74–82	− 2	6	72–73	− 3	8	70–74	− 4	9	73–83	− 6	10	68–77	− 8	13
83–84	− 3	6	74–82	− 4	8	75–80	− 5	9	84–94	− 7	9	78	− 9	13
85–93	− 3	5	83–84	− 4	7	81–86	− 5	8	95–105	− 8	8	79–88	− 9	12
94–95	− 4	5	85–93	− 5	7	87–91	− 6	8	106–116	− 9	7	89	−10	12
96–104	− 4	4	94–95	− 5	6	92–97	− 6	7	117–127	−10	6	90–99	−10	11
105–106	− 5	4	96–104	− 6	6	98–102	− 7	7	128	−11	6	100	−11	11
107–115	− 5	3	105–106	− 6	5	103–108	− 7	6	129–138	−11	5	101–110	−11	10
116–117	− 6	3	107–115	− 7	5	109–113	− 8	6	139	−12	5	111	−12	10
118–126	− 6	2	116–117	− 7	4	114–119	− 8	5	140–149	−12	4	112–121	−12	9
127–128	− 7	2	118–126	− 8	4	120–125	− 9	5	150	−13	4	122	−13	9
129–137	− 7	1	127–128	− 8	3	126–130	− 9	4	151–160	−13	3	123–132	−13	8
138–139	− 8	1	129–137	− 9	3	131–136	−10	4				133–134	−14	8
140–148	− 8	0	138–140	− 9	2	137–141	−10	3				135–143	−14	7
149–151	− 9	0	141–148	−10	2	142–147	−11	3				144–145	−15	7
152–160	− 9	−1	149–151	−10	1	148–152	−11	2				146–154	−15	6
			152–159	−11	1	153–158	−12	2				155–156	−16	6
			160	−11	0	159–160	−12	1				157–160	−16	5

(Table continues next page)

Table L-2 (cont.)

H. WISC-III – Verbal Scale – Age 7; WISC-III – Performance Scale – Age 16; WPPSI-R – Verbal Scale – Ages 5 and 6; WPPSI-R – Performance Scale – Average; WAIS-R – Performance Scale – Ages 20–24 and 70–74 ($r_{xx} = .92$)

68%			85%			90%			95%			99%		
IQ	L	U	IQ	L	U	IQ	L	U	IQ	L	U	IQ	L	U
40–42	1	9	40–48	− 1	10	40–49	− 2	11	40–48	− 3	12	40–42	− 5	15
43–44	1	8	49–51	− 2	10	50	− 2	10	49–51	− 4	12	43–44	− 6	15
45–55	0	8	52–60	− 2	9	51–61	− 3	10	52–60	− 4	11	45–55	− 6	14
56–57	0	7	61–64	− 3	9	62–63	− 3	9	61–64	− 5	11	56–57	− 7	14
58–67	− 1	7	65–73	− 3	8	64–74	− 4	9	65–73	− 5	10	58–67	− 7	13
68–69	− 1	6	74–76	− 4	8	75	− 4	8	74–76	− 6	10	68–69	− 8	13
70–80	− 2	6	77–85	− 4	7	76–86	− 5	8	77–85	− 6	9	70–80	− 8	12
81–82	− 2	5	86–89	− 5	7	87–88	− 5	7	86–89	− 7	9	81–82	− 9	12
83–92	− 3	5	90–98	− 5	6	89–99	− 6	7	90–98	− 7	8	83–92	− 9	11
93–94	− 3	4	99–101	− 6	6	100	− 6	6	99–101	− 8	8	93–94	−10	11
95–105	− 4	4	102–110	− 6	5	101–111	− 7	6	102–110	− 8	7	95–105	−10	10
106–107	− 4	3	111–114	− 7	5	112–113	− 7	5	111–114	− 9	7	106–107	−11	10
108–117	− 5	3	115–123	− 7	4	114–124	− 8	5	115–123	− 9	6	108–117	−11	9
118–119	− 5	2	124–126	− 8	4	125	− 8	4	124–126	−10	6	118–119	−12	9
120–130	− 6	2	127–135	− 8	3	126–136	− 9	4	127–135	−10	5	120–130	−12	8
131–132	− 6	1	136–139	− 9	3	137–138	− 9	3	136–139	−11	5	131–132	−13	8
133–142	− 7	1	140–148	− 9	2	139–149	−10	3	140–148	−11	4	133–142	−13	7
143–144	− 7	0	149–151	−10	2	150	−10	2	149–151	−12	4	143–144	−14	7
145–155	− 8	0	152–160	−10	1	151–160	−11	2	152–160	−12	3	145–155	−14	6
156–157	− 8	−1										156–157	−15	6
158–160	− 9	−1										158–160	−15	5

(Table continues next page)

Table L-2 (cont.)

I. WISC-III—Verbal Scale—Ages 6 and 9; WPPSI-R—Verbal Scale—Ages 3, 3½, 4, and 4½; WPPSI-R—Performance Scale—Age 6½; WAIS-R—Performance Scale—Ages 55–64 and Average ($r_{xx}=.93$)

68%			85%			90%			95%			99%		
IQ	L	U	IQ	L	U	IQ	L	U	IQ	L	U	IQ	L	U
40	1	8	40	− 1	10	40–48	− 2	10	40–46	− 3	11	40–42	− 5	14
41–45	0	8	41–45	− 1	9	49–51	− 3	10	47–53	− 4	11	43	− 6	14
46–54	0	7	46–54	− 2	9	52–63	− 3	9	54–60	− 4	10	44–56	− 6	13
55–59	− 1	7	55–59	− 2	8	64–65	− 4	9	61–67	− 5	10	57	− 7	13
60–68	− 1	6	60–68	− 3	8	66–77	− 4	8	68–75	− 5	9	58–71	− 7	12
69–74	− 2	6	69–74	− 3	7	78–79	− 5	8	76–81	− 6	9	72–85	− 8	11
75–82	− 2	5	75–83	− 4	7	80–91	− 5	7	82–89	− 6	8	86	− 9	11
83–88	− 3	5	84–88	− 4	6	92–94	− 6	7	90–96	− 7	8	87–99	− 9	10
89–97	− 3	4	89–97	− 5	6	95–105	− 6	6	97–103	− 7	7	100	−10	10
98–102	− 4	4	98–102	− 5	5	106–108	− 7	6	104–110	− 8	7	101–113	−10	9
103–111	− 4	3	103–111	− 6	5	109–120	− 7	5	111–118	− 8	6	114	−11	9
112–117	− 5	3	112–116	− 6	4	121–122	− 8	5	119–124	− 9	6	115–128	−11	8
118–125	− 5	2	117–125	− 7	4	123–134	− 8	4	125–132	− 9	5	129–142	−12	7
126–131	− 6	2	126–131	− 7	3	135–136	− 9	4	133–139	−10	5	143	−13	7
132–140	− 6	1	132–140	− 8	3	137–148	− 9	3	140–146	−10	4	144–156	−13	6
141–145	− 7	1	141–145	− 8	2	149–151	−10	3	147–153	−11	4	157	−14	6
146–154	− 7	0	146–154	− 9	2	152–160	−10	2	154–160	−11	3	158–160	−14	5
155–159	− 8	0	155–159	− 9	1									
160	− 8	−1	160	−10	1									

J. WISC-III—Verbal Scale—Age 13; WISC-III—Performance Scale—Age 15; WISC-III—Full Scale—Age 7; WPPSI-R—Performance Scale—Ages 5½ and 6; WAIS-R—Performance Scale—Ages 25–34, 35–44, 45–54, and 65–69 ($r_{xx} = .94$)

68%			85%			90%			95%			99%		
IQ	L	U	IQ	L	U	IQ	L	U	IQ	L	U	IQ	L	U
40–49	0	7	40–41	− 1	9	40–46	− 2	9	40–45	− 3	10	40	− 5	13
50	0	6	42	− 1	8	47–53	− 3	9	46–54	− 4	10	41–43	− 5	12
51–65	− 1	6	43–57	− 2	8	54–63	− 3	8	55–62	− 4	9	44–56	− 6	12
66–67	− 1	5	58	− 2	7	64–69	− 4	8	63–71	− 5	9	57–59	− 6	11
68–82	− 2	5	59–74	− 3	7	70–80	− 4	7	72–78	− 5	8	60–73	− 7	11
83–84	− 2	4	75	− 3	6	81–86	− 5	7	79–87	− 6	8	74–76	− 7	10
85–99	− 3	4	76–91	− 4	6	87–96	− 5	6	88–95	− 6	7	77–90	− 8	10
100	− 3	3	92	− 4	5	97–103	− 6	6	96–104	− 7	7	91–93	− 8	9
101–115	− 4	3	93–107	− 5	5	104–113	− 6	5	105–112	− 7	6	94–106	− 9	9
116–117	− 4	2	108	− 5	4	114–119	− 7	5	113–121	− 8	6	107–109	− 9	8
118–132	− 5	2	109–124	− 6	4	120–130	− 7	4	122–128	− 8	5	110–123	−10	8
133–134	− 5	1	125	− 6	3	131–136	− 8	4	129–137	− 9	5	124–126	−10	7
135–149	− 6	1	126–141	− 7	3	137–146	− 8	3	138–145	− 9	4	127–140	−11	7
150	− 6	0	142	− 7	2	147–153	− 9	3	146–154	−10	4	141–143	−11	6
151–160	− 7	0	143–157	− 8	2	154–160	− 9	2	155–160	−10	3	144–156	−12	6
			158	− 8	1							157–159	−12	5
			159–160	− 9	1							160	−13	5

(Table continues next page)

Table L-2 (cont.)

K. WISC-III – Verbal Scale – Ages 10, 11, 12, 14, 16, and Average; WISC-III – Full Scale – Ages 6, 9, 11, 13, and 14; WPPSI-R – Performance Scale – Age 5; WPPSI-R – Verbal Scale – Average; WPPSI-R – Full Scale – Ages 5½, 6, and 6½; WAIS-R – Verbal Scale – Ages 16–17 ($r_{xx} = .95$)

68%			85%			90%			95%			99%		
IQ	L	U	IQ	L	U	IQ	L	U	IQ	L	U	IQ	L	U
40–46	0	6	40–41	− 2	8	40–44	− 2	8	40–45	− 3	9	40–45	− 5	11
47–53	− 1	6	42–58	− 2	7	45–55	− 3	8	46–54	− 4	9	46–54	− 6	11
54–66	− 1	5	59–61	− 3	7	56–64	− 3	7	55–65	− 4	8	55–65	− 6	10
67–73	− 2	5	62–78	− 3	6	65–75	− 4	7	66–74	− 5	8	66–74	− 7	10
74–86	− 2	4	79–81	− 4	6	76–84	− 4	6	75–85	− 5	7	75–85	− 7	9
87–93	− 3	4	82–98	− 4	5	85–95	− 5	6	86–94	− 6	7	86–94	− 8	9
94–106	− 3	3	99–101	− 5	5	96–104	− 5	5	95–105	− 6	6	95–105	− 8	8
107–113	− 4	3	102–118	− 5	4	105–115	− 6	5	106–114	− 7	6	106–114	− 9	8
114–126	− 4	2	119–121	− 6	4	116–124	− 6	4	115–125	− 7	5	115–125	− 9	7
127–133	− 5	2	122–138	− 6	3	125–135	− 7	4	126–134	− 8	5	126–134	−10	7
134–146	− 5	1	139–141	− 7	3	136–144	− 7	3	135–145	− 8	4	135–145	−10	6
147–153	− 6	1	142–158	− 7	2	145–155	− 8	3	146–154	− 9	4	146–154	−11	6
154–160	− 6	0	159–160	− 8	2	156–160	− 8	2	155–160	− 9	3	155–160	−11	5

L. WISC-III – Verbal Scale – Ages 8 and 15; WISC-III – Full Scale – Ages 8, 10, 12, 16, and Average; WPPSI-R – Performance Scale – Ages 3, 3½, 4, and 4½; WPPSI-R – Full Scale – Age 5 and Average; WAIS-R – Verbal Scale – Ages 18–19 and 20–24; WAIS-R – Full Scale – Ages 16–17 and 18–19 ($r_{xx} = .96$)

68%			85%			90%			95%			99%		
IQ	L	U	IQ	L	U	IQ	L	U	IQ	L	U	IQ	L	U
40	0	5	40–41	− 2	7	40–43	− 2	7	40–46	− 3	8	40–48	− 5	10
41–59	− 1	5	42–58	− 2	6	44–56	− 3	7	47–53	− 4	8	49–51	− 5	9
60–65	− 1	4	59–66	− 3	6	57–68	− 3	6	54–71	− 4	7	52–73	− 6	9
66–84	− 2	4	67–83	− 3	5	69–81	− 4	6	72–78	− 5	7	74–76	− 6	8
85–90	− 2	3	84–91	− 4	5	82–93	− 4	5	79–96	− 5	6	77–98	− 7	8
91–109	− 3	3	92–108	− 4	4	94–106	− 5	5	97–103	− 6	6	99–101	− 7	7
110–115	− 3	2	109–116	− 5	4	107–118	− 5	4	104–121	− 6	5	102–123	− 8	7
116–134	− 4	2	117–133	− 5	3	119–131	− 6	4	122–128	− 7	5	124–126	− 8	6
135–140	− 4	1	134–141	− 6	3	132–143	− 6	3	129–146	− 7	4	127–148	− 9	6
141–159	− 5	1	142–158	− 6	2	144–156	− 7	3	147–153	− 8	4	149–151	− 9	5
160	− 5	0	159–160	− 7	2	157–160	− 7	2	154–160	− 8	3	152–160	−10	5

(Table continues next page)

Table L-2 (cont.)

M. WISC-III – Full Scale – Age 15; WPPSI-R – Full Scale – Ages 3, 3½, 4, and 4½; WAIS-R – Verbal Scale – Ages 25–34, 35–44, 45–54, 55–64, 65–69, 70–74, and Average; WAIS-R – Full Scale – Ages 20–24, 45–54, 55–64, 70–74, and Average ($r_{xx} = .97$)

68%			85%			90%			95%			99%		
IQ	L	U	IQ	L	U	IQ	L	U	IQ	L	U	IQ	L	U
40–65	− 1	4	40–62	− 2	5	40–44	− 2	6	40–47	− 3	7	40–66	− 5	8
66–67	− 2	4	63–70	− 3	5	45–55	− 3	6	48–52	− 3	6	67–99	− 6	7
68–99	− 2	3	71–95	− 3	4	56–78	− 3	5	53–81	− 4	6	100	− 7	7
100	− 3	3	96–104	− 4	4	79–88	− 4	5	82–85	− 4	5	101–133	− 7	6
101–132	− 3	2	105–129	− 4	3	89–111	− 4	4	86–114	− 5	5	134–160	− 8	5
133–134	− 4	2	130–137	− 5	3	112–121	− 5	4	115–118	− 5	4			
135–160	− 4	1	138–160	− 5	2	122–144	− 5	3	119–147	− 6	4			
						145–155	− 6	3	148–152	− 6	3			
						156–160	− 6	2	153–160	− 7	3			

N. WAIS-R – Full Scale – Ages 25–34, and 35–44 ($r_{xx} = .98$)

68%			85%			90%			95%			99%		
IQ	L	U	IQ	L	U	IQ	L	U	IQ	L	U	IQ	L	U
40–71	− 1	3	40–74	− 2	4	40–46	− 2	5	40–71	− 3	5	40–43	− 4	7
72–78	− 2	3	75	− 2	3	47–53	− 2	4	72–78	− 4	5	44–56	− 4	6
79–121	− 2	2	76–124	− 3	3	54–96	− 3	4	79–121	− 4	4	57–93	− 5	6
122–128	− 3	2	125	− 3	2	97–103	− 3	3	122–128	− 5	4	94–106	− 5	5
129–160	− 3	1	126–160	− 4	2	104–146	− 4	3	129–160	− 5	3	107–143	− 6	5
						147–153	− 4	2				144–156	− 6	4
						154–160	− 5	2				157–160	− 7	4

Note. Abbreviations: L = Lower limit of confidence interval, U = Upper limit of confidence interval. The values in the table, when added to the obtained IQ (in the first column), will form the confidence interval. For example, for a 7-year-old the confidence interval for an obtained IQ of 40 at the 99% confidence level for the WPPSI-R Verbal Scale (see Section A) is 36 to 62 (40 − 4 = 36; 40 + 22 = 62).

The confidence intervals in Table L-2 can be used for any test having the reliability coefficient shown in each section of the table (r_{xx} range of .85 to .98) and a standard score distribution with $M = 100$ and $SD = 15$.

See page 1038 for an explanation of how confidence intervals were computed.

Table L-3
Significant Differences Between Scaled Scores, Between IQs, and Between Factor Deviation Quotients (DQs) at Each of the 11 Age Levels of the WISC-III (.05/.01 significance levels)

Age level		I	S	A	V	C	DS	PC	CD	PA	BD	OA	SS
6	S	4/6	–										
(6-0-0	A	4/6	4/5	–									
through	V	4/6	4/5	4/5	–								
6-11-30)	C	5/6	4/6	4/6	4/5	–							
	DS	4/6	4/5	4/5	4/5	4/6	–						
	PC	5/6	4/5	4/5	4/5	4/6	4/5	–					
	CD	5/6	4/6	4/6	4/5	5/6	4/6	4/6	–				
	PA	4/6	4/5	4/5	4/5	4/5	4/5	4/5	4/5	–			
	BD	4/6	4/5	4/5	4/5	4/5	4/5	4/5	4/5	4/5	–		
	OA	5/6	4/6	4/6	4/6	5/6	5/6	5/6	5/6	4/6	4/6	–	
	SS	5/6	5/6	5/6	5/6	5/6	5/6	5/6	5/6	5/6	5/6	5/6	–
	MA	4/6	4/5	4/5	4/5	4/6	4/5	4/5	4/6	4/5	4/5	5/6	5/6

Age 6 — IQ: PSIQ | VSIQ 12/16. DQ: VCDQ PSDQ | PODQ 14/18 17/22 | PSDQ 16/21

Age level		I	S	A	V	C	DS	PC	CD	PA	BD	OA	SS
7	S	4/6	–										
(7-0-0	A	5/6	5/6	–									
through	V	4/6	4/6	4/6	–								
7-11-30)	C	5/6	5/6	5/6	5/6	–							
	DS	4/5	4/5	4/6	4/5	4/6	–						
	PC	4/5	4/5	4/5	4/5	4/6	4/5	–					
	CD	5/6	5/6	5/6	5/6	5/6	5/6	4/6	–				
	PA	4/5	4/5	4/5	4/5	4/6	4/5	4/5	4/6	–			
	BD	4/6	4/6	5/6	4/6	5/6	4/5	4/5	5/6	4/5	–		
	OA	5/6	5/6	5/6	5/6	5/7	5/6	5/6	5/7	5/6	5/6	–	
	SS	4/6	4/6	5/6	4/6	5/6	4/5	4/5	5/6	4/5	4/6	5/6	–
	MA	4/6	4/6	5/6	4/5	5/6	4/5	4/5	5/6	4/5	4/6	5/6	4/6

Age 7 — IQ: PSIQ | VSIQ 13/17. DQ: VCDQ PSDQ | PODQ 14/18 17/22 | PSDQ 16/21

Age level		I	S	A	V	C	DS	PC	CD	PA	BD	OA	SS
8	S	4/5	–										
(8-0-0	A	4/5	4/5	–									
through	V	3/4	4/4	4/5	–								
8-11-30)	C	4/5	4/5	4/5	3/4	–							
	DS	4/5	4/5	4/5	4/4	4/5	–						
	PC	4/5	4/5	4/5	4/5	4/5	4/5	–					
	CD	4/5	4/5	4/6	4/5	4/5	4/5	4/5					
	PA	4/5	4/6	5/6	4/5	4/5	4/6	4/6	5/6	–			
	BD	4/5	4/5	4/5	4/5	4/5	4/5	4/5	4/5	4/6	–		
	OA	5/6	5/6	5/6	4/6	5/6	5/6	5/6	5/6	5/7	5/6	–	
	SS	4/5	4/6	5/6	4/5	4/5	4/6	4/6	5/6	5/6	4/6	5/7	–
	MA	4/5	4/5	4/6	4/5	4/5	4/5	4/5	4/6	5/6	4/5	5/6	5/6

Age 8 — IQ: PSIQ | VSIQ 11/15. DQ: VCDQ PSDQ | PODQ 12/16 16/21 | PSDQ 14/18

(Table continues next page)

Table L-3 (cont.)

Age level		I	S	A	V	C	DS	PC	CD	PA	BD	OA	SS
9	S	4/5	—										
(9-0-0	A	4/6	5/6	—									
through	V	4/5	4/5	4/6	—								
9-11-30)	C	4/6	4/6	5/6	4/6	—							
	DS	4/5	4/5	4/6	4/5	4/6	—						
	PC	4/5	4/5	5/6	4/5	4/6	4/5	—					
	CD	4/5	4/5	5/6	4/5	4/6	4/5	4/5	—				
	PA	4/6	4/6	5/6	4/6	5/6	4/6	4/6	5/6	—			
	BD	4/5	4/5	4/6	4/5	4/5	4/5	4/5	4/5	4/5	—		
	OA	4/6	4/6	5/6	4/5	5/6	4/5	4/6	4/6	5/6	4/5	—	
	SS	4/6	4/6	5/6	4/6	5/6	4/6	4/6	5/6	5/6	4/5	5/6	—
	MA	5/6	5/6	5/7	5/6	5/6	5/6	5/6	5/6	5/7	5/6	5/6	5/7

PSIQ VSIQ 12/16 | PODQ VCDQ 13/16 PSDQ 15/20 | PSDQ 14/19

Age level		I	S	A	V	C	DS	PC	CD	PA	BD	OA	SS
10	S	4/5	—										
(10-0-0	A	4/5	4/5	—									
through	V	4/5	4/5	4/5	—								
10-11-30)	C	4/5	4/5	4/5	4/5	—							
	DS	4/5	4/5	4/5	4/4	4/5	—						
	PC	4/6	4/6	4/6	4/5	4/6	4/5	—					
	CD	4/5	4/5	4/5	4/5	4/5	4/5	4/6	—				
	PA	4/6	4/6	4/6	4/5	4/6	4/5	5/6	4/6	—			
	BD	4/5	4/5	4/5	3/4	4/5	3/4	4/5	4/5	4/5	—		
	OA	5/6	5/6	5/6	4/5	5/6	4/6	5/6	5/6	5/6	4/5	—	
	SS	4/6	4/6	5/6	4/5	5/6	4/6	5/6	5/6	5/6	4/5	5/6	—
	MA	4/6	4/6	5/6	4/5	5/6	4/6	5/6	5/6	5/6	4/5	5/6	5/6

PSIQ VSIQ 11/15 | PODQ VCDQ 13/16 PSDQ 16/21 | PSDQ 14/19

Age level		I	S	A	V	C	DS	PC	CD	PA	BD	OA	SS
11	S	4/5	—										
(11-0-0	A	4/5	4/5	—									
through	V	3/4	4/5	4/5	—								
11-11-30)	C	4/5	4/5	4/6	4/5	—							
	DS	4/5	4/5	4/5	4/4	4/5	—						
	PC	4/5	4/5	4/6	4/5	4/6	4/5	—					
	CD	4/5	4/5	4/5	4/5	4/5	4/5	4/5	—				
	PA	4/6	4/6	5/6	4/5	5/6	4/6	5/6	4/6	—			
	BD	4/5	4/5	4/5	4/4	4/5	4/5	4/5	4/5	4/6	—		
	OA	5/6	5/6	5/6	4/6	5/6	5/6	5/6	5/6	5/7	5/6	—	
	SS	4/5	4/5	4/5	4/5	4/6	4/5	4/6	4/5	5/6	4/5	5/6	—
	MA	4/6	5/6	5/6	4/6	5/6	4/6	5/6	5/6	5/6	4/6	5/7	5/6

PSIQ VSIQ 12/15 | PODQ VCDQ 13/17 PSDQ 15/20 | PSDQ 13/17

Age level		I	S	A	V	C	DS	PC	CD	PA	BD	OA	SS
12	S	4/5	—										
(12-0-0	A	4/5	4/5	—									
through	V	3/4	3/4	4/5	—								
12-11-30)	C	4/5	4/5	4/6	4/5	—							
	DS	4/5	4/5	4/5	3/4	4/5	—						
	PC	4/5	4/6	5/6	4/5	4/6	4/5	—					
	CD	4/5	4/5	4/6	4/5	4/5	4/5	4/6	—				
	PA	4/5	4/5	4/6	4/5	4/5	4/5	5/6	4/5	—			
	BD	4/4	4/5	4/5	3/4	4/5	3/4	4/5	4/5	4/5	—		
	OA	4/6	4/6	5/6	4/5	5/6	4/6	5/6	5/6	5/6	4/6	—	
	SS	4/5	4/5	4/6	4/5	4/5	4/5	5/6	4/5	4/5	4/5	5/6	—
	MA	5/6	5/6	5/6	4/6	5/6	4/6	5/7	5/6	5/6	4/6	5/7	5/6

PSIQ VSIQ 11/15 | PODQ VCDQ 12/16 PSDQ 15/19 | PSDQ 13/17

(Table continues next page)

Table L-3 (cont.)

Age level		I	S	A	V	C	DS	PC	CD	PA	BD	OA	SS
13	S	4/5	—										
(13-0-0	A	4/5	4/6	—									
through	V	3/4	4/5	4/5	—								
13-11-30)	C	4/5	5/6	4/6	4/5	—							
	DS	4/4	4/5	4/5	3/4	4/5	—						
	PC	4/5	5/6	4/6	4/5	5/6	4/5	—					
	CD	4/6	5/6	5/6	4/5	5/6	4/5	5/6	—				
	PA	4/5	5/6	4/5	4/5	5/6	4/5	5/6	5/6	—			
	BD	3/4	4/5	4/5	3/4	4/5	3/4	4/5	4/5	4/5	—		
	OA	4/5	5/6	4/6	4/5	5/6	4/5	5/6	5/6	5/6	4/5	—	
	SS	4/5	5/6	4/6	4/5	5/6	4/5	5/6	5/6	5/6	4/5	5/6	—
	MA	4/6	5/6	5/6	4/5	5/6	4/5	5/6	5/6	5/6	4/5	5/6	5/6

Age 13: PSIQ 12/16 VSIQ; PODQ 13/16 VCDQ PSDQ 16/21; PSDQ 15/20

Age level		I	S	A	V	C	DS	PC	CD	PA	BD	OA	SS
14	S	4/5	—										
(14-0-0	A	4/5	4/5	—									
through	V	3/4	3/4	4/5	—								
14-11-30)	C	4/5	4/5	4/6	4/5	—							
	DS	4/5	4/5	4/5	3/4	4/5	—						
	PC	4/5	4/6	5/6	4/5	5/6	4/6	—					
	CD	4/5	4/6	5/6	4/5	5/6	4/6	5/6	—				
	PA	4/5	4/5	4/6	4/5	4/6	4/5	5/6	5/6	—			
	BD	3/4	3/4	4/5	3/4	4/5	3/4	4/5	4/5	4/5	—		
	OA	5/6	5/6	5/7	5/6	5/7	5/6	5/7	5/7	5/7	5/6	—	
	SS	4/5	4/5	4/6	4/5	5/6	4/5	5/6	5/6	4/6	4/5	5/7	—
	MA	4/5	4/6	5/6	4/5	5/6	4/6	5/6	5/6	5/6	4/5	5/7	5/6

Age 14: PSIQ 12/16 VSIQ; PODQ 13/17 VCDQ PSDQ 17/22; PSDQ 15/19

Age level		I	S	A	V	C	DS	PC	CD	PA	BD	OA	SS
15	S	4/5	—										
(15-0-0	A	4/5	4/5	—									
through	V	3/4	4/5	4/5	—								
15-11-30)	C	4/5	4/5	4/5	4/5	—							
	DS	3/4	4/5	4/5	3/4	4/5	—						
	PC	4/5	4/5	4/5	3/4	4/5	3/4	—					
	CD	3/4	4/5	4/5	3/4	4/5	3/4	4/4	—				
	PA	4/5	4/6	4/6	4/5	4/6	4/5	4/6	4/5	—			
	BD	3/4	3/4	3/4	3/4	4/4	3/4	3/4	3/4	4/5	—		
	OA	4/5	4/5	4/5	4/5	4/6	4/5	4/5	4/5	5/6	4/5	—	
	SS	4/5	4/5	4/5	3/4	4/5	3/4	4/5	4/4	4/6	3/4	4/5	—
	MA	5/6	5/6	5/6	4/6	5/6	4/6	5/6	5/6	5/7	-4/6	5/7	5/6

Age 15: PSIQ 10/13 VSIQ; PODQ 11/14 VCDQ PSDQ 13/16; PSDQ 11/15

Age level		I	S	A	V	C	DS	PC	CD	PA	BD	OA	SS
16	S	4/4	—										
(16-0-0	A	4/5	4/5	—									
through	V	3/4	3/4	4/5	—								
16-11-30)	C	4/5	4/5	4/6	4/5	—							
	DS	3/4	3/4	4/5	3/4	4/5	—						
	PC	4/5	4/5	4/5	4/5	5/6	4/5	—					
	CD	3/4	3/4	4/4	3/4	4/5	3/4	4/5	—				
	PA	4/5	4/5	4/6	4/5	5/6	4/5	5/6	4/5	—			
	BD	3/4	3/4	4/4	3/4	4/5	3/4	4/5	3/4	4/5	—		
	OA	4/5	4/6	4/6	4/5	5/6	4/5	5/6	4/5	5/6	4/5	—	
	SS	4/5	4/5	4/5	4/5	4/6	4/5	4/5	4/4	4/6	4/4	4/6	—
	MA	4/6	5/6	5/6	4/6	5/6	4/6	5/6	4/5	5/6	4/5	5/6	5/6

Age 16: PSIQ 11/14 VSIQ; PODQ 12/16 VCDQ PSDQ 13/17; PSDQ 12/15

(Table continues next page)

Table L-3 (cont.)

Age level		I	S	A	V	C	DS	PC	CD	PA	BD	OA	SS
Average	S	4/5	–										
	A	4/5	4/5	–									
	V	4/5	4/5	4/5	–								
	C	4/5	4/5	4/6	4/5	–							
	DS	4/5	4/5	4/5	4/5	4/5	–						
	PC	4/5	4/5	4/6	4/5	4/6	4/5	–					
	CD	4/5	4/5	4/6	4/5	4/6	4/5	4/6	–				
	PA	4/5	4/5	4/6	4/5	4/6	4/5	4/6	4/6	–			
	BD	4/5	4/5	4/5	3/4	4/5	4/5	4/5	4/5	4/5	–		
	OA	4/6	5/6	5/6	4/6	5/6	4/6	5/6	5/6	5/6	4/6	–	
	SS	4/5	4/5	4/6	4/5	4/6	4/5	4/6	4/6	5/6	4/5	5/6	–
	MA	4/6	5/6	5/6	4/5	5/6	4/6	5/6	5/6	5/6	4/6	5/6	5/6

Boxed values:

		VSIQ	
PSIQ	**12/15**		

		VCDQ	**PSDQ**
PODQ	**13/17**		**16/21**
PSDQ	**15/20**		

Note. Abbreviations: I = Information; S = Similarities; A = Arithmetic; V = Vocabulary; C = Comprehension; DS = Digit Span; PC = Picture Completion; CD = Coding; PA = Picture Arrangement; BD = Block Design; OA = Object Assembly; SS = Symbol Search; MA = Mazes; VSIQ = Verbal Scale IQ; PSIQ = Performance Scale IQ; VCDQ = Verbal Comprehension Deviation Quotient; PODQ = Perceptual Organization Deviation Quotient; PSDQ = Processing Speed Deviation Quotient.

The factor scores are composed of the following subtests: Verbal Comprehension: Information, Similarities, Vocabulary, and Comprehension; Perceptual Organization: Picture Completion, Block Design, and Object Assembly; Processing Speed: Coding and Symbol Search.

Sample reading: At the 6-0-0 year level, a difference of 4 points between scaled scores on the Information and Similarities subtests is significant at the 5 percent level; a difference of 6 points is significant at the 1 percent level. The first small box shows that a 12-point difference between the Verbal Scale IQ and the Performance Scale IQ is needed for the 5 percent level, and a 16-point difference is needed for the 1 percent level. The second small box shows that a difference of 14 points is needed between the Verbal Comprehension Deviation Quotient and the Perceptual Organization Deviation Quotient at the 5 percent level, and a difference of 18 points is needed at the 1 percent level.

The values in this table for the subtest comparisons are overly liberal when more than one comparison is made for a subtest. They are more accurate when a priori planned comparisons are made, such as Information vs. Comprehension or Digit Span vs. Arithmetic.

All values in this table have been rounded up to the next higher number.

See Chapter 8, Exhibit 8-1 (page 168) for an explanation of the method used to arrive at magnitude of differences.

See Exhibit I-4 in Appendix I for the procedure used to obtain the reliability coefficients for the factor scores.

Table L-4
Differences Required for Significance When Each Subtest Scaled Score Is Compared to the Mean Subtest Scaled Score for Any Individual Child at Each of the 11 Age Levels of the WISC-III

Age 6-0-0 through 6-11-30

Subtest	Mean of 4 subtests[a]		Mean of 5 subtests[b]		Mean of 6 subtests[c]		Mean of 6 subtests		Mean of 7 subtests		Mean of 10 subtests	
	.05	.01	.05	.01	.05	.01	.05	.01	.05	.01	.05	.01
Information	3.27	3.96	3.51	4.20	3.64	4.38	—	—	—	—	4.11	4.82
Similarities	2.91	3.52	3.07	3.68	3.16	3.80	—	—	—	—	3.52	4.12
Arithmetic	—	—	3.07	3.68	3.16	3.80	—	—	—	—	3.52	4.12
Vocabulary	2.86	3.46	3.01	3.60	3.09	3.72	—	—	—	—	3.43	4.02
Comprehension	3.19	3.85	3.40	4.07	3.52	4.24	—	—	—	—	3.97	4.65
Digit Span	—	—	—	—	3.28	3.95	—	—	—	—	—	—
Picture Completion	3.04	3.67	3.25	3.90	3.38	4.07	3.35	4.03	3.52	4.18	3.75	4.39
Coding	—	—	3.42	4.09	3.56	4.28	3.53	4.25	3.71	4.40	3.97	4.65
Picture Arrangement	2.85	3.44	3.03	3.62	3.13	3.76	3.10	3.73	3.25	3.85	3.43	4.02
Block Design	2.85	3.44	3.03	3.62	3.13	3.76	3.10	3.73	3.25	3.85	3.43	4.02
Object Assembly	3.35	4.05	3.62	4.34	3.78	4.55	3.76	4.52	3.96	4.69	4.25	4.97
Symbol Search	—	—	—	—	3.89	4.68	—	—	4.07	4.83	—	—
Mazes	—	—	—	—	—	—	3.23	3.88	3.39	4.02	—	—

Subtest	Mean of 11 subtests		Mean of 11 subtests		Mean of 11 subtests		Mean of 12 subtests		Mean of 12 subtests		Mean of 13 subtests	
	.05	.01	.05	.01	.05	.01	.05	.01	.05	.01	.05	.01
Information	4.18	4.89	4.19	4.90	4.18	4.89	4.25	5.11	4.25	5.10	4.43	5.00
Similarities	3.57	4.17	3.58	4.18	3.57	4.17	3.62	4.36	3.62	4.35	3.77	4.25
Arithmetic	3.57	4.17	3.58	4.18	3.57	4.17	3.62	4.36	3.62	4.35	3.77	4.25
Vocabulary	3.48	4.07	3.49	4.08	3.48	4.07	3.54	4.25	3.53	4.24	3.68	4.15
Comprehension	4.04	4.72	4.04	4.73	4.04	4.72	4.10	4.93	4.10	4.93	4.28	4.82
Digit Span	3.73	4.36	—	—	—	—	3.79	4.56	3.78	4.55	3.95	4.45
Picture Completion	3.81	4.45	3.82	4.46	3.81	4.45	3.87	4.65	3.86	4.65	4.03	4.55
Coding	4.04	4.72	4.04	4.73	4.04	4.72	4.10	4.93	4.10	4.93	4.28	4.82
Picture Arrangement	3.48	4.07	3.49	4.08	3.48	4.07	3.54	4.25	3.53	4.24	3.68	4.15
Block Design	3.48	4.07	3.49	4.08	3.48	4.07	3.54	4.25	3.53	4.24	3.68	4.15
Object Assembly	4.32	5.05	4.33	5.06	4.32	5.05	4.39	5.28	4.39	5.28	4.58	5.17
Symbol Search	—	—	4.46	5.22	—	—	4.53	5.45	—	—	4.73	5.33
Mazes	—	—	—	—	3.65	4.27	—	—	3.70	4.45	3.86	4.35

(Table continues next page)

Table L-4 (cont.)

	Age 7-0-0 through 7-11-30											
	Mean of 4 subtests[a]		Mean of 5 subtests[b]		Mean of 6 subtests[c]		Mean of 6 subtests		Mean of 7 subtests		Mean of 10 subtests	
Subtest	.05	.01	.05	.01	.05	.01	.05	.01	.05	.01	.05	.01
Information	3.18	3.84	3.40	4.07	3.50	4.21	—	—	—	—	3.92	4.59
Similarities	3.14	3.79	3.35	4.01	3.44	4.14	—	—	—	—	3.85	4.50
Arithmetic	—	—	3.56	4.26	3.67	4.41	—	—	—	—	4.13	4.84
Vocabulary	3.05	3.68	3.24	3.88	3.32	3.99	—	—	—	—	3.70	4.33
Comprehension	3.35	4.05	3.61	4.32	3.72	4.48	—	—	—	—	4.20	4.92
Digit Span	—	—	—	—	3.19	3.84	—	—	—	—	—	—
Picture Completion	2.77	3.34	2.94	3.52	3.00	3.61	2.99	3.60	3.11	3.68	3.29	3.85
Coding	—	—	3.70	4.43	3.84	4.61	3.83	4.61	4.02	4.77	4.33	5.07
Picture Arrangement	2.77	3.34	2.94	3.52	3.00	3.61	2.99	3.60	3.11	3.68	3.29	3.85
Block Design	3.10	3.75	3.34	4.00	3.44	4.14	3.44	4.14	3.59	4.26	3.85	4.50
Object Assembly	3.61	4.36	3.93	4.71	4.09	4.92	4.09	4.92	4.30	5.10	4.65	5.44
Symbol Search	—	—	—	—	3.50	4.21	—	—	3.66	4.34	—	—
Mazes	—	—	—	—	—	—	3.38	4.06	3.53	4.18	—	—

	Mean of 11 subtests		Mean of 11 subtests		Mean of 11 subtests		Mean of 12 subtests		Mean of 12 subtests		Mean of 13 subtests	
Subtest	.05	.01	.05	.01	.05	.01	.05	.01	.05	.01	.05	.01
Information	3.98	4.65	3.98	4.65	3.98	4.65	4.04	4.85	4.04	4.85	4.21	4.74
Similarities	3.90	4.56	3.91	4.57	3.91	4.57	3.96	4.76	3.96	4.76	4.12	4.65
Arithmetic	4.20	4.91	4.20	4.91	4.20	4.91	4.26	5.12	4.26	5.12	4.44	5.01
Vocabulary	3.75	4.38	3.75	4.39	3.75	4.38	3.80	4.57	3.80	4.57	3.96	4.46
Comprehension	4.27	4.99	4.27	4.99	4.27	4.99	4.33	5.21	4.33	5.21	4.52	5.09
Digit Span	3.59	4.19	—	—	—	—	3.63	4.37	3.63	4.37	3.78	4.26
Picture Completion	3.33	3.89	3.33	3.90	3.33	3.89	3.37	4.05	3.37	4.05	3.50	3.95
Coding	4.40	5.15	4.41	5.15	4.41	5.15	4.47	5.38	4.47	5.38	4.66	5.26
Picture Arrangement	3.33	3.89	3.33	3.90	3.33	3.89	3.37	4.05	3.37	4.05	3.50	3.95
Block Design	3.90	4.56	3.91	4.57	3.91	4.57	3.96	4.76	3.96	4.76	4.12	4.65
Object Assembly	4.73	5.53	4.73	5.53	4.73	5.53	4.81	5.78	4.80	5.78	5.01	5.65
Symbol Search	—	—	3.98	4.65	—	—	4.04	4.85	—	—	4.21	4.74
Mazes	—	—	—	—	3.83	4.48	—	—	3.88	4.66	4.04	4.56

(Table continues next page)

Table L-4 (cont.)

Subtest	Mean of 4 subtests[a]		Mean of 5 subtests[b]		Mean of 6 subtests[c]		Mean of 6 subtests		Mean of 7 subtests		Mean of 10 subtests	
	.05	.01	.05	.01	.05	.01	.05	.01	.05	.01	.05	.01
Information	2.44	2.94	2.63	3.15	2.71	3.26	–	–	–	–	3.06	3.59
Similarities	2.55	3.08	2.76	3.31	2.86	3.44	–	–	–	–	3.24	3.80
Arithmetic	–	–	3.13	3.75	3.26	3.92	–	–	–	–	3.73	4.37
Vocabulary	2.32	2.80	2.49	2.98	2.55	3.07	–	–	–	–	2.87	3.36
Comprehension	2.49	3.01	2.70	3.23	2.78	3.35	–	–	–	–	3.15	3.69
Digit Span	–	–	–	–	2.86	3.44	–	–	–	–	–	–
Picture Completion	2.97	3.59	3.12	3.74	3.21	3.86	3.20	3.85	3.34	3.96	3.50	4.09
Coding	–	–	3.29	3.94	3.40	4.09	3.39	4.07	3.54	4.20	3.73	4.37
Picture Arrangement	3.37	4.07	3.60	4.31	3.74	4.50	3.73	4.49	3.91	4.64	4.16	4.88
Block Design	2.87	3.47	3.00	3.60	3.08	3.71	3.07	3.69	3.19	3.79	3.33	3.90
Object Assembly	3.65	4.41	3.93	4.71	4.10	4.94	4.10	4.93	4.31	5.11	4.62	5.41
Symbol Search	–	–	–	–	3.74	4.50	–	–	3.91	4.64	–	–
Mazes	–	–	–	–	–	–	3.50	4.22	3.67	4.35	–	–

Subtest	Mean of 11 subtests		Mean of 11 subtests		Mean of 11 subtests		Mean of 12 subtests		Mean of 12 subtests		Mean of 13 subtests	
	.05	.01	.05	.01	.05	.01	.05	.01	.05	.01	.05	.01
Information	3.10	3.62	3.11	3.64	3.11	3.63	3.15	3.78	3.14	3.78	3.28	3.69
Similarities	3.29	3.84	3.30	3.85	3.29	3.85	3.34	4.01	3.33	4.01	3.48	3.92
Arithmetic	3.79	4.43	3.80	4.44	3.80	4.44	3.85	4.63	3.85	4.63	4.02	4.53
Vocabulary	2.90	3.39	2.91	3.41	2.91	3.40	2.94	3.54	2.94	3.54	3.06	3.45
Comprehension	3.19	3.73	3.21	3.75	3.20	3.74	3.24	3.90	3.24	3.90	3.38	3.81
Digit Span	3.29	3.84	–	–	–	–	3.34	4.01	3.33	4.01	3.48	3.92
Picture Completion	3.55	4.15	3.56	4.16	3.55	4.15	3.60	4.33	3.60	4.33	3.76	4.24
Coding	3.79	4.43	3.80	4.44	3.80	4.44	3.85	4.63	3.85	4.63	4.02	4.53
Picture Arrangement	4.23	4.95	4.24	4.96	4.24	4.96	4.31	5.18	4.31	5.18	4.49	5.07
Block Design	3.38	3.95	3.39	3.96	3.38	3.95	3.43	4.12	3.43	4.12	3.57	4.03
Object Assembly	4.70	5.49	4.71	5.50	4.70	5.50	4.78	5.75	4.78	5.75	4.99	5.63
Symbol Search	–	–	4.24	4.96	–	–	4.31	5.18	–	–	4.49	5.07
Mazes	–	–	–	–	3.95	4.62	–	–	4.01	4.82	4.18	4.72

(Table continues next page)

Table L-4 (cont.)

Age 9-0-0 through 9-11-30

Subtest	*Mean of 4 subtests*[a] .05	.01	*Mean of 5 subtests*[b] .05	.01	*Mean of 6 subtests*[c] .05	.01	*Mean of 6 subtests* .05	.01	*Mean of 7 subtests* .05	.01	*Mean of 10 subtests* .05	.01
Information	2.87	3.47	3.08	3.69	3.16	3.80	–	–	–	–	3.52	4.12
Similarities	2.92	3.53	3.14	3.76	3.22	3.88	–	–	–	–	3.60	4.21
Arithmetic	–	–	3.62	4.34	3.75	4.51	–	–	–	–	4.25	4.98
Vocabulary	2.82	3.41	3.03	3.62	3.09	3.72	–	–	–	–	3.44	4.02
Comprehension	3.20	3.86	3.47	4.15	3.58	4.31	–	–	–	–	4.04	4.74
Digit Span	–	–	–	–	3.09	3.72	–	–	–	–	–	–
Picture Completion	2.95	3.57	3.13	3.75	3.24	3.90	3.26	3.92	3.40	4.04	3.60	4.21
Coding	–	–	3.25	3.89	3.37	4.05	3.38	4.07	3.54	4.20	3.75	4.39
Picture Arrangement	3.31	4.00	3.56	4.27	3.71	4.47	3.73	4.48	3.91	4.64	4.18	4.90
Block Design	2.70	3.27	2.83	3.39	2.91	3.50	2.93	3.52	3.04	3.61	3.18	3.72
Object Assembly	3.18	3.84	3.41	4.08	3.55	4.27	3.56	4.28	3.73	4.42	3.97	4.65
Symbol Search	–	–	–	–	3.71	4.47	–	–	3.91	4.64	–	–
Mazes	–	–	–	–	–	–	4.04	4.86	4.25	5.05	–	–

Subtest	*Mean of 11 subtests* .05	.01	*Mean of 11 subtests* .05	.01	*Mean of 11 subtests* .05	.01	*Mean of 12 subtests* .05	.01	*Mean of 12 subtests* .05	.01	*Mean of 13 subtests* .05	.01
Information	3.57	4.17	3.58	4.18	3.58	4.19	3.62	4.35	3.63	4.36	3.78	4.26
Similarities	3.65	4.27	3.66	4.28	3.66	4.28	3.71	4.46	3.71	4.46	3.87	4.36
Arithmetic	4.32	5.05	4.33	5.06	4.33	5.06	4.39	5.28	4.40	5.28	4.59	5.17
Vocabulary	3.48	4.07	3.49	4.08	3.50	4.09	3.54	4.25	3.54	4.26	3.69	4.16
Comprehension	4.11	4.80	4.12	4.81	4.12	4.82	4.18	5.02	4.18	5.02	4.36	4.92
Digit Span	3.48	4.07	–	–	–	–	3.54	4.25	3.54	4.26	3.69	4.16
Picture Completion	3.65	4.27	3.66	4.28	3.66	4.28	3.71	4.46	3.71	4.46	3.87	4.36
Coding	3.81	4.45	3.82	4.46	3.82	4.47	3.87	4.65	3.87	4.66	4.04	4.55
Picture Arrangement	4.25	4.97	4.26	4.98	4.26	4.98	4.32	5.20	4.33	5.20	4.51	5.09
Block Design	3.22	3.76	3.23	3.77	3.23	3.78	3.26	3.92	3.27	3.93	3.40	3.84
Object Assembly	4.04	4.72	4.04	4.73	4.05	4.73	4.10	4.93	4.11	4.94	4.28	4.83
Symbol Search	–	–	4.26	4.98	–	–	4.32	5.20	–	–	4.51	5.09
Mazes	–	–	–	–	4.66	5.45	–	–	4.73	5.69	4.94	5.57

(Table continues next page)

Table L-4 (cont.)

	Age 10-0-0 through 10-11-30											
	Mean of 4 subtests[a]		Mean of 5 subtests[b]		Mean of 6 subtests[c]		Mean of 6 subtests		Mean of 7 subtests		Mean of 10 subtests	
Subtest	.05	.01	.05	.01	.05	.01	.05	.01	.05	.01	.05	.01
Information	2.74	3.31	2.94	3.52	3.03	3.64	—	—	—	—	3.42	4.00
Similarities	2.74	3.31	2.94	3.52	3.03	3.64	—	—	—	—	3.42	4.00
Arithmetic	—	—	3.12	3.73	3.22	3.88	—	—	—	—	3.66	4.29
Vocabulary	2.41	2.91	2.54	3.05	2.59	3.12	—	—	—	—	2.88	3.37
Comprehension	2.89	3.49	3.12	3.73	3.22	3.88	—	—	—	—	3.66	4.29
Digit Span	—	—	—	—	2.89	3.48	—	—	—	—	—	—
Picture Completion	3.26	3.94	3.48	4.17	3.62	4.35	3.62	4.36	3.80	4.50	4.03	4.72
Coding	—	—	3.27	3.92	3.38	4.07	3.39	4.08	3.54	4.20	3.74	4.38
Picture Arrangement	3.26	3.94	3.48	4.17	3.62	4.35	3.62	4.36	3.80	4.50	4.03	4.72
Block Design	2.53	3.06	2.59	3.11	2.64	3.17	2.64	3.18	2.73	3.23	2.78	3.25
Object Assembly	3.47	4.19	3.73	4.47	3.89	4.68	3.89	4.68	4.09	4.85	4.37	5.12
Symbol Search	—	—	—	—	3.73	4.48	—	—	3.92	4.64	—	—
Mazes	—	—	—	—	—	—	3.84	4.62	4.03	4.78	—	—
	Mean of 11 subtests		Mean of 11 subtests		Mean of 11 subtests		Mean of 12 subtests		Mean of 12 subtests		Mean of 13 subtests	
Subtest	.05	.01	.05	.01	.05	.01	.05	.01	.05	.01	.05	.01
Information	3.47	4.05	3.48	4.07	3.48	4.07	3.52	4.23	3.52	4.24	3.67	4.14
Similarities	3.47	4.05	3.48	4.07	3.48	4.07	3.52	4.23	3.52	4.24	3.67	4.14
Arithmetic	3.72	4.34	3.73	4.35	3.73	4.36	3.78	4.54	3.78	4.54	3.94	4.44
Vocabulary	2.91	3.40	2.92	3.41	2.92	3.42	2.95	3.55	2.95	3.55	3.07	3.46
Comprehension	3.72	4.34	3.73	4.35	3.73	4.36	3.78	4.54	3.78	4.54	3.94	4.44
Digit Span	3.29	3.85	—	—	—	—	3.34	4.02	3.34	4.02	3.48	3.93
Picture Completion	4.10	4.79	4.10	4.80	4.11	4.80	4.17	5.01	4.17	5.01	4.35	4.90
Coding	3.79	4.44	3.80	4.45	3.81	4.45	3.86	4.64	3.86	4.64	4.03	4.54
Picture Arrangement	4.10	4.79	4.10	4.80	4.11	4.80	4.17	5.01	4.17	5.01	4.35	4.90
Block Design	2.80	3.28	2.82	3.29	2.82	3.30	2.84	3.42	2.84	3.42	2.96	3.34
Object Assembly	4.44	5.19	4.45	5.20	4.45	5.21	4.52	5.43	4.52	5.44	4.72	5.32
Symbol Search	—	—	4.25	4.96	—	—	4.31	5.18	—	—	4.50	5.08
Mazes	—	—	—	—	4.39	5.13	—	—	4.45	5.35	4.65	5.24

(Table continues next page)

Table L-4 (cont.)

	Mean of 4 subtests[a]		Mean of 5 subtests[b]		Mean of 6 subtests[c]		Mean of 6 subtests		Mean of 7 subtests		Mean of 10 subtests	
Subtest	.05	.01	.05	.01	.05	.01	.05	.01	.05	.01	.05	.01
Information	2.58	3.11	2.75	3.29	2.82	3.39	—	—	—	—	3.17	3.71
Similarities	2.74	3.31	2.94	3.52	3.03	3.64	—	—	—	—	3.43	4.01
Arithmetic	—	—	3.12	3.73	3.22	3.88	—	—	—	—	3.67	4.29
Vocabulary	2.41	2.91	2.54	3.05	2.59	3.12	—	—	—	—	2.89	3.38
Comprehension	3.03	3.66	3.28	3.93	3.41	4.10	—	—	—	—	3.89	4.56
Digit Span	—	—	—	—	2.89	3.48	—	—	—	—	—	—
Picture Completion	3.23	3.90	3.40	4.07	3.50	4.21	3.53	4.24	3.67	4.36	3.89	4.56
Coding	—	—	3.07	3.68	3.13	3.77	3.16	3.80	3.27	3.88	3.43	4.01
Picture Arrangement	3.48	4.21	3.71	4.44	3.84	4.61	3.86	4.64	4.04	4.79	4.31	5.05
Block Design	2.86	3.46	2.95	3.53	3.00	3.61	3.03	3.64	3.13	3.71	3.26	3.81
Object Assembly	3.68	4.44	3.94	4.72	4.09	4.92	4.12	4.95	4.32	5.12	4.63	5.42
Symbol Search	—	—	—	—	3.32	4.00	—	—	3.48	4.13	—	—
Mazes	—	—	—	—	—	—	3.96	4.77	4.15	4.92	—	—

	Mean of 11 subtests		Mean of 11 subtests		Mean of 11 subtests		Mean of 12 subtests		Mean of 12 subtests		Mean of 13 subtests	
Subtest	.05	.01	.05	.01	.05	.01	.05	.01	.05	.01	.05	.01
Information	3.21	3.75	3.21	3.75	3.22	3.77	3.25	3.91	3.26	3.92	3.39	3.82
Similarities	3.47	4.06	3.48	4.07	3.49	4.08	3.52	4.23	3.53	4.24	3.68	4.14
Arithmetic	3.72	4.35	3.73	4.35	3.73	4.37	3.78	4.54	3.78	4.55	3.94	4.44
Vocabulary	2.92	3.41	2.92	3.41	2.93	3.43	2.95	3.55	2.96	3.56	3.07	3.47
Comprehension	3.95	4.62	3.96	4.63	3.97	4.64	4.01	4.83	4.02	4.83	4.19	4.73
Digit Span	3.30	3.86	—	—	—	—	3.34	4.02	3.35	4.03	3.49	3.93
Picture Completion	3.95	4.62	3.96	4.63	3.97	4.64	4.01	4.83	4.02	4.83	4.19	4.73
Coding	3.47	4.06	3.48	4.07	3.49	4.08	3.52	4.23	3.53	4.24	3.68	4.14
Picture Arrangement	4.38	5.12	4.38	5.13	4.39	5.13	4.45	5.35	4.46	5.36	4.65	5.24
Block Design	3.30	3.86	3.30	3.86	3.31	3.87	3.34	4.02	3.35	4.03	3.49	3.93
Object Assembly	4.71	5.50	4.71	5.51	4.72	5.52	4.79	5.75	4.79	5.76	5.00	5.64
Symbol Search	—	—	3.73	4.35	—	—	3.78	4.54	—	—	3.94	4.44
Mazes	—	—	—	—	4.52	5.29	—	—	4.59	5.52	4.79	5.40

(Table continues next page)

Table L-4 (cont.)

	Mean of 4 subtests[a]		Mean of 5 subtests[b]		Mean of 6 subtests[c]		Mean of 6 subtests		Mean of 7 subtests		Mean of 10 subtests	
Subtest	.05	.01	.05	.01	.05	.01	.05	.01	.05	.01	.05	.01
Information	2.52	3.05	2.73	3.27	2.80	3.37	—	—	—	—	3.15	3.69
Similarities	2.58	3.11	2.80	3.35	2.87	3.45	—	—	—	—	3.24	3.80
Arithmetic	—	—	3.38	4.05	3.51	4.22	—	—	—	—	4.02	4.71
Vocabulary	2.29	2.76	2.46	2.94	2.49	3.00	—	—	—	—	2.77	3.24
Comprehension	2.74	3.31	2.99	3.58	3.08	3.70	—	—	—	—	3.50	4.09
Digit Span	—	—	—	—	2.65	3.19	—	—	—	—	—	—
Picture Completion	3.34	4.04	3.57	4.28	3.70	4.45	3.73	4.49	3.90	4.63	4.16	4.87
Coding	—	—	3.03	3.62	3.10	3.73	3.14	3.77	3.25	3.86	3.41	4.00
Picture Arrangement	3.03	3.67	3.20	3.83	3.29	3.96	3.33	4.00	3.46	4.11	3.65	4.28
Block Design	2.64	3.19	2.71	3.25	2.75	3.31	2.79	3.36	2.88	3.41	2.97	3.47
Object Assembly	3.51	4.24	3.77	4.51	3.92	4.71	3.95	4.75	4.14	4.90	4.43	5.18
Symbol Search	—	—	—	—	3.29	3.96	—	—	3.46	4.11	—	—
Mazes	—	—	—	—	—	—	4.05	4.87	4.25	5.04	—	—

	Mean of 11 subtests		Mean of 11 subtests		Mean of 11 subtests		Mean of 12 subtests		Mean of 12 subtests		Mean of 13 subtests	
Subtest	.05	.01	.05	.01	.05	.01	.05	.01	.05	.01	.05	.01
Information	3.19	3.73	3.20	3.74	3.21	3.75	3.24	3.89	3.25	3.90	3.38	3.81
Similarities	3.28	3.84	3.29	3.85	3.30	3.86	3.33	4.00	3.34	4.01	3.48	3.92
Arithmetic	4.09	4.78	4.09	4.79	4.10	4.80	4.15	4.99	4.16	5.00	4.34	4.89
Vocabulary	2.79	3.27	2.80	3.28	2.82	3.29	2.83	3.40	2.84	3.41	2.95	3.33
Comprehension	3.54	4.14	3.55	4.15	3.56	4.16	3.60	4.32	3.61	4.33	3.76	4.24
Digit Span	3.00	3.51	—	—	—	—	3.04	3.65	3.05	3.67	3.17	3.58
Picture Completion	4.23	4.95	4.24	4.95	4.25	4.96	4.30	5.17	4.31	5.18	4.49	5.07
Coding	3.46	4.04	3.47	4.05	3.48	4.06	3.51	4.22	3.52	4.23	3.67	4.13
Picture Arrangement	3.71	4.33	3.71	4.34	3.72	4.35	3.76	4.53	3.77	4.54	3.93	4.43
Block Design	3.00	3.51	3.01	3.51	3.02	3.53	3.04	3.65	3.05	3.67	3.17	3.58
Object Assembly	4.50	5.26	4.51	5.27	4.52	5.28	4.58	5.50	4.59	5.51	4.79	5.40
Symbol Search	—	—	3.71	4.34	—	—	3.76	4.53	—	—	3.93	4.43
Mazes	—	—	—	—	4.65	5.43	—	—	4.72	5.67	4.93	5.55

(Table continues next page)

Table L-4 (cont.)

Subtest	Mean of 4 subtests[a]		Mean of 5 subtests[b]		Mean of 6 subtests[c]		Mean of 6 subtests		Mean of 7 subtests		Mean of 10 subtests	
	.05	.01	.05	.01	.05	.01	.05	.01	.05	.01	.05	.01
Information	2.65	3.20	2.78	3.33	2.83	3.41	—	—	—	—	3.17	3.71
Similarities	3.18	3.84	3.42	4.10	3.54	4.26	—	—	—	—	4.04	4.73
Arithmetic	—	—	3.03	3.63	3.11	3.74	—	—	—	—	3.51	4.11
Vocabulary	2.42	2.93	2.51	3.01	2.53	3.04	—	—	—	—	2.79	3.27
Comprehension	3.22	3.89	3.47	4.16	3.60	4.33	—	—	—	—	4.11	4.81
Digit Span	—	—	—	—	2.68	3.23	—	—	—	—	—	—
Picture Completion	3.31	3.99	3.59	4.30	3.72	4.48	3.73	4.49	3.91	4.64	4.18	4.89
Coding	—	—	3.69	4.41	3.83	4.61	3.84	4.62	4.03	4.78	4.31	5.05
Picture Arrangement	3.13	3.78	3.38	4.05	3.50	4.21	3.51	4.22	3.67	4.35	3.90	4.56
Block Design	2.42	2.93	2.53	3.03	2.55	3.07	2.57	3.09	2.63	3.12	2.69	3.14
Object Assembly	3.18	3.84	3.43	4.11	3.55	4.28	3.57	4.29	3.73	4.42	3.97	4.65
Symbol Search	—	—	—	—	3.55	4.28	—	—	3.73	4.42	—	—
Mazes	—	—	—	—	—	—	3.84	4.62	4.03	4.78	—	—

Subtest	Mean of 11 subtests		Mean of 11 subtests		Mean of 11 subtests		Mean of 12 subtests		Mean of 12 subtests		Mean of 13 subtests	
	.05	.01	.05	.01	.05	.01	.05	.01	.05	.01	.05	.01
Information	3.21	3.75	3.22	3.76	3.22	3.77	3.25	3.91	3.25	3.91	3.39	3.82
Similarities	4.10	4.79	4.11	4.80	4.11	4.81	4.17	5.01	4.17	5.01	4.35	4.90
Arithmetic	3.56	4.16	3.57	4.17	3.57	4.17	3.61	4.34	3.61	4.35	3.77	4.25
Vocabulary	2.81	3.29	2.82	3.30	2.83	3.31	2.85	3.42	2.85	3.43	2.96	3.34
Comprehension	4.17	4.88	4.18	4.89	4.18	4.89	4.24	5.10	4.24	5.10	4.43	4.99
Digit Span	3.01	3.52	—	—	—	—	3.06	3.67	3.06	3.68	3.18	3.59
Picture Completion	4.24	4.96	4.25	4.97	4.25	4.97	4.31	5.18	4.32	5.19	4.50	5.08
Coding	4.38	5.12	4.39	5.13	4.39	5.13	4.45	5.35	4.46	5.36	4.65	5.24
Picture Arrangement	3.95	4.62	3.96	4.63	3.97	4.64	4.02	4.83	4.02	4.83	4.19	4.73
Block Design	2.70	3.16	2.72	3.18	2.72	3.18	2.73	3.29	2.74	3.29	2.85	3.21
Object Assembly	4.03	4.71	4.04	4.72	4.04	4.72	4.09	4.92	4.10	4.92	4.27	4.82
Symbol Search	—	—	4.04	4.72	—	—	4.09	4.92	—	—	4.27	4.82
Mazes	—	—	—	—	4.39	5.13	—	—	4.46	5.36	4.65	5.24

(Table continues next page)

Table L-4 (cont.)

	Age 14-0-0 through 14-11-30											
	Mean of 4 subtests[a]		Mean of 5 subtests[b]		Mean of 6 subtests[c]		Mean of 6 subtests		Mean of 7 subtests		Mean of 10 subtests	
Subtest	.05	.01	.05	.01	.05	.01	.05	.01	.05	.01	.05	.01
Information	2.42	2.92	2.59	3.10	2.65	3.19	—	—	—	—	2.99	3.50
Similarities	2.58	3.12	2.79	3.34	2.87	3.46	—	—	—	—	3.26	3.82
Arithmetic	—	—	3.21	3.84	3.33	4.01	—	—	—	—	3.82	4.47
Vocabulary	2.17	2.62	2.30	2.75	2.32	2.80	—	—	—	—	2.58	3.02
Comprehension	2.99	3.61	3.27	3.91	3.40	4.09	—	—	—	—	3.90	4.56
Digit Span	—	—	—	—	2.87	3.46	—	—	—	—	—	—
Picture Completion	3.38	4.08	3.63	4.35	3.75	4.51	3.76	4.53	3.93	4.67	4.18	4.89
Coding	—	—	3.73	4.47	3.86	4.64	3.87	4.66	4.05	4.80	4.31	5.05
Picture Arrangement	3.11	3.76	3.32	3.98	3.41	4.10	3.42	4.12	3.56	4.22	3.75	4.39
Block Design	2.52	3.04	2.59	3.10	2.59	3.12	2.61	3.14	2.67	3.16	2.69	3.14
Object Assembly	3.84	4.64	4.18	5.01	4.36	5.24	4.37	5.25	4.59	5.44	4.93	5.77
Symbol Search	—	—	—	—	3.59	4.31	—	—	3.75	4.45	—	—
Mazes	—	—	—	—	—	—	3.87	4.66	4.05	4.80	—	—
	Mean of 11 subtests		Mean of 11 subtests		Mean of 11 subtests		Mean of 12 subtests		Mean of 12 subtests		Mean of 13 subtests	
Subtest	.05	.01	.05	.01	.05	.01	.05	.01	.05	.01	.05	.01
Information	3.02	3.53	3.03	3.54	3.03	3.54	3.06	3.68	3.06	3.68	3.18	3.59
Similarities	3.30	3.86	3.31	3.87	3.31	3.87	3.35	4.02	3.35	4.03	3.49	3.93
Arithmetic	3.88	4.53	3.89	4.54	3.89	4.55	3.94	4.74	3.94	4.74	4.11	4.64
Vocabulary	2.59	3.03	2.60	3.05	2.61	3.05	2.62	3.15	2.63	3.16	2.73	3.08
Comprehension	3.95	4.62	3.96	4.63	3.97	4.64	4.02	4.83	4.02	4.83	4.19	4.73
Digit Span	3.30	3.86	—	—	—	—	3.35	4.02	3.35	4.03	3.49	3.93
Picture Completion	4.24	4.96	4.25	4.97	4.25	4.97	4.31	5.19	4.32	5.19	4.50	5.08
Coding	4.38	5.12	4.39	5.13	4.39	5.13	4.46	5.36	4.46	5.36	4.65	5.25
Picture Arrangement	3.80	4.44	3.81	4.45	3.81	4.46	3.86	4.64	3.86	4.65	4.03	4.54
Block Design	2.71	3.16	2.72	3.18	2.72	3.18	2.74	3.29	2.74	3.30	2.85	3.21
Object Assembly	5.01	5.86	5.02	5.87	5.02	5.87	5.10	6.13	5.10	6.14	5.33	6.01
Symbol Search	—	—	4.04	4.72	—	—	4.09	4.92	—	—	4.27	4.82
Mazes	—	—	—	—	4.39	5.13	—	—	4.46	5.36	4.65	5.25

(Table continues next page)

Table L-4 (cont.)

	Age 15-0-0 through 15-11-30											
	Mean of 4 subtests[a]		Mean of 5 subtests[b]		Mean of 6 subtests[c]		Mean of 6 subtests		Mean of 7 subtests		Mean of 10 subtests	
Subtest	.05	.01	.05	.01	.05	.01	.05	.01	.05	.01	.05	.01
Information	2.34	2.83	2.49	2.98	2.53	3.04	—	—	—	—	2.83	3.31
Similarities	2.73	3.30	2.95	3.54	3.04	3.66	—	—	—	—	3.46	4.05
Arithmetic	—	—	2.95	3.54	3.04	3.66	—	—	—	—	3.46	4.05
Vocabulary	2.15	2.60	2.26	2.71	2.28	2.74	—	—	—	—	2.51	2.94
Comprehension	2.78	3.36	3.01	3.61	3.11	3.74	—	—	—	—	3.54	4.15
Digit Span	—	—	—	—	2.28	2.74	—	—	—	—	—	—
Picture Completion	2.79	3.37	2.92	3.50	3.02	3.64	3.08	3.71	3.21	3.80	3.38	3.96
Coding	—	—	2.38	2.85	2.42	2.92	2.50	3.00	2.56	3.04	2.62	3.07
Picture Arrangement	3.21	3.88	3.43	4.11	3.58	4.31	3.63	4.37	3.80	4.51	4.07	4.76
Block Design	2.23	2.69	2.23	2.67	2.25	2.71	2.33	2.80	2.37	2.82	2.39	2.80
Object Assembly	3.08	3.71	3.27	3.92	3.41	4.10	3.46	4.16	3.62	4.29	3.85	4.51
Symbol Search	—	—	—	—	3.02	3.64	—	—	3.21	3.80	—	—
Mazes	—	—	—	—	—	—	4.25	5.12	4.48	5.31	—	—
	Mean of 11 subtests		Mean of 11 subtests		Mean of 11 subtests		Mean of 12 subtests		Mean of 12 subtests		Mean of 13 subtests	
Subtest	.05	.01	.05	.01	.05	.01	.05	.01	.05	.01	.05	.01
Information	2.86	3.34	2.87	3.35	2.89	3.38	2.90	3.49	2.92	3.51	3.04	3.42
Similarities	3.51	4.11	3.52	4.11	3.54	4.14	3.57	4.29	3.58	4.31	3.73	4.21
Arithmetic	3.51	4.11	3.52	4.11	3.54	4.14	3.57	4.29	3.58	4.31	3.73	4.21
Vocabulary	2.53	2.96	2.54	2.97	2.56	3.00	2.56	3.08	2.58	3.10	2.68	3.02
Comprehension	3.60	4.20	3.60	4.21	3.62	4.23	3.65	4.39	3.67	4.41	3.82	4.31
Digit Span	2.53	2.96	—	—	—	—	2.56	3.08	2.58	3.10	2.68	3.02
Picture Completion	3.43	4.01	3.43	4.01	3.45	4.04	3.48	4.18	3.50	4.20	3.64	4.11
Coding	2.64	3.09	2.65	3.10	2.68	3.13	2.68	3.22	2.70	3.24	2.80	3.16
Picture Arrangement	4.13	4.83	4.14	4.84	4.16	4.86	4.20	5.05	4.22	5.07	4.40	4.96
Block Design	2.41	2.82	2.42	2.83	2.45	2.86	2.44	2.93	2.46	2.96	2.55	2.88
Object Assembly	3.91	4.57	3.92	4.58	3.93	4.60	3.98	4.78	3.99	4.80	4.16	4.69
Symbol Search	—	—	3.43	4.01	—	—	3.48	4.18	—	—	3.64	4.11
Mazes	—	—	—	—	4.94	5.77	—	—	5.02	6.03	5.24	5.91

(Table continues next page)

Table L-4 (cont.)

	Age 16-0-0 through 16-11-30											
	Mean of 4 subtests[a]		Mean of 5 subtests[b]		Mean of 6 subtests[c]		Mean of 6 subtests		Mean of 7 subtests		Mean of 10 subtests	
Subtest	.05	.01	.05	.01	.05	.01	.05	.01	.05	.01	.05	.01
Information	2.39	2.88	2.52	3.01	2.55	3.07	—	—	—	—	2.85	3.34
Similarities	2.61	3.15	2.79	3.34	2.86	3.44	—	—	—	—	3.23	3.78
Arithmetic	—	—	2.91	3.49	3.00	3.60	—	—	—	—	3.40	3.98
Vocabulary	2.33	2.81	2.44	2.93	2.47	2.97	—	—	—	—	2.75	3.22
Comprehension	3.15	3.80	3.42	4.10	3.56	4.28	—	—	—	—	4.08	4.78
Digit Span	—	—	—	—	2.47	2.97	—	—	—	—	—	—
Picture Completion	3.20	3.86	3.38	4.04	3.50	4.21	3.54	4.25	3.69	4.38	3.94	4.61
Coding	—	—	2.45	2.94	2.47	2.97	2.52	3.04	2.58	3.06	2.65	3.10
Picture Arrangement	3.29	3.97	3.48	4.17	3.61	4.35	3.65	4.39	3.82	4.53	4.08	4.78
Block Design	2.45	2.96	2.45	2.94	2.47	2.97	2.52	3.04	2.58	3.06	2.65	3.10
Object Assembly	3.37	4.07	3.58	4.29	3.73	4.48	3.76	4.52	3.94	4.67	4.22	4.94
Symbol Search	—	—	—	—	3.06	3.69	—	—	3.22	3.82	—	—
Mazes	—	—	—	—	—	—	3.97	4.78	4.17	4.94	—	—
	Mean of 11 subtests		Mean of 11 subtests		Mean of 11 subtests		Mean of 12 subtests		Mean of 12 subtests		Mean of 13 subtests	
Subtest	.05	.01	.05	.01	.05	.01	.05	.01	.05	.01	.05	.01
Information	2.88	3.37	2.89	3.38	2.90	3.40	2.92	3.51	2.93	3.52	3.05	3.44
Similarities	3.27	3.82	3.27	3.83	3.29	3.84	3.31	3.98	3.33	4.00	3.46	3.90
Arithmetic	3.44	4.03	3.45	4.03	3.46	4.05	3.50	4.20	3.51	4.22	3.65	4.12
Vocabulary	2.78	3.25	2.78	3.25	2.80	3.27	2.81	3.38	2.82	3.39	2.93	3.31
Comprehension	4.15	4.85	4.15	4.86	4.16	4.87	4.22	5.07	4.23	5.08	4.41	4.97
Digit Span	2.78	3.25	—	—	—	—	2.81	3.38	2.82	3.39	2.93	3.31
Picture Completion	4.00	4.68	4.01	4.69	4.02	4.70	4.07	4.89	4.08	4.90	4.25	4.79
Coding	2.67	3.12	2.68	3.13	2.69	3.15	2.70	3.24	2.71	3.26	2.82	3.18
Picture Arrangement	4.15	4.85	4.15	4.86	4.16	4.87	4.22	5.07	4.23	5.08	4.41	4.97
Block Design	2.67	3.12	2.68	3.13	2.69	3.15	2.70	3.24	2.71	3.26	2.82	3.18
Object Assembly	4.29	5.01	4.29	5.02	4.30	5.03	4.36	5.24	4.37	5.25	4.56	5.14
Symbol Search	—	—	3.45	4.03	—	—	3.50	4.20	—	—	3.65	4.12
Mazes	—	—	—	—	4.57	5.35	—	—	4.64	5.58	4.85	5.46

(Table continues next page)

Table L-4 (cont.)

<table>
<thead>
<tr><th></th><th colspan="12">Average</th></tr>
<tr><th></th><th colspan="2">Mean of 4 subtests[a]</th><th colspan="2">Mean of 5 subtests[b]</th><th colspan="2">Mean of 6 subtests[c]</th><th colspan="2">Mean of 6 subtests</th><th colspan="2">Mean of 7 subtests</th><th colspan="2">Mean of 10 subtests</th></tr>
<tr><th>Subtest</th><th>.05</th><th>.01</th><th>.05</th><th>.01</th><th>.05</th><th>.01</th><th>.05</th><th>.01</th><th>.05</th><th>.01</th><th>.05</th><th>.01</th></tr>
</thead>
<tbody>
<tr><td>Information</td><td>2.65</td><td>3.20</td><td>2.82</td><td>3.38</td><td>2.89</td><td>3.48</td><td>—</td><td>—</td><td>—</td><td>—</td><td>3.25</td><td>3.80</td></tr>
<tr><td>Similarities</td><td>2.80</td><td>3.38</td><td>3.01</td><td>3.60</td><td>3.10</td><td>3.73</td><td>—</td><td>—</td><td>—</td><td>—</td><td>3.50</td><td>4.10</td></tr>
<tr><td>Arithmetic</td><td>—</td><td>—</td><td>3.18</td><td>3.81</td><td>3.29</td><td>3.96</td><td>—</td><td>—</td><td>—</td><td>—</td><td>3.74</td><td>4.38</td></tr>
<tr><td>Vocabulary</td><td>2.48</td><td>3.00</td><td>2.63</td><td>3.15</td><td>2.67</td><td>3.22</td><td>—</td><td>—</td><td>—</td><td>—</td><td>2.97</td><td>3.48</td></tr>
<tr><td>Comprehension</td><td>2.99</td><td>3.62</td><td>3.24</td><td>3.88</td><td>3.35</td><td>4.03</td><td>—</td><td>—</td><td>—</td><td>—</td><td>3.81</td><td>4.46</td></tr>
<tr><td>Digit Span</td><td>—</td><td>—</td><td>—</td><td>—</td><td>2.82</td><td>3.40</td><td>—</td><td>—</td><td>—</td><td>—</td><td>—</td><td>—</td></tr>
<tr><td>Picture Completion</td><td>3.11</td><td>3.76</td><td>3.31</td><td>3.96</td><td>3.42</td><td>4.12</td><td>3.44</td><td>4.14</td><td>3.59</td><td>4.26</td><td>3.81</td><td>4.46</td></tr>
<tr><td>Coding</td><td>—</td><td>—</td><td>3.20</td><td>3.83</td><td>3.30</td><td>3.97</td><td>3.32</td><td>3.99</td><td>3.46</td><td>4.10</td><td>3.66</td><td>4.29</td></tr>
<tr><td>Picture Arrangement</td><td>3.15</td><td>3.81</td><td>3.36</td><td>4.03</td><td>3.48</td><td>4.19</td><td>3.50</td><td>4.21</td><td>3.66</td><td>4.34</td><td>3.89</td><td>4.55</td></tr>
<tr><td>Block Design</td><td>2.62</td><td>3.16</td><td>2.71</td><td>3.25</td><td>2.76</td><td>3.32</td><td>2.78</td><td>3.35</td><td>2.87</td><td>3.41</td><td>2.97</td><td>3.48</td></tr>
<tr><td>Object Assembly</td><td>3.45</td><td>4.17</td><td>3.72</td><td>4.45</td><td>3.87</td><td>4.66</td><td>3.88</td><td>4.67</td><td>4.08</td><td>4.84</td><td>4.37</td><td>5.11</td></tr>
<tr><td>Symbol Search</td><td>—</td><td>—</td><td>—</td><td>—</td><td>3.48</td><td>4.19</td><td>—</td><td>—</td><td>3.66</td><td>4.34</td><td>—</td><td>—</td></tr>
<tr><td>Mazes</td><td>—</td><td>—</td><td>—</td><td>—</td><td>—</td><td>—</td><td>3.83</td><td>4.61</td><td>4.02</td><td>4.77</td><td>—</td><td>—</td></tr>
</tbody>
</table>

<table>
<thead>
<tr><th></th><th colspan="2">Mean of 11 subtests</th><th colspan="2">Mean of 11 subtests</th><th colspan="2">Mean of 11 subtests</th><th colspan="2">Mean of 12 subtests</th><th colspan="2">Mean of 12 subtests</th><th colspan="2">Mean of 13 subtests</th></tr>
<tr><th>Subtest</th><th>.05</th><th>.01</th><th>.05</th><th>.01</th><th>.05</th><th>.01</th><th>.05</th><th>.01</th><th>.05</th><th>.01</th><th>.05</th><th>.01</th></tr>
</thead>
<tbody>
<tr><td>Information</td><td>3.29</td><td>3.85</td><td>3.30</td><td>3.86</td><td>3.30</td><td>3.86</td><td>3.34</td><td>4.01</td><td>3.34</td><td>4.02</td><td>3.48</td><td>3.92</td></tr>
<tr><td>Similarities</td><td>3.55</td><td>4.15</td><td>3.56</td><td>4.16</td><td>3.56</td><td>4.17</td><td>3.60</td><td>4.33</td><td>3.61</td><td>4.34</td><td>3.76</td><td>4.24</td></tr>
<tr><td>Arithmetic</td><td>3.79</td><td>4.43</td><td>3.80</td><td>4.44</td><td>3.80</td><td>4.45</td><td>3.85</td><td>4.63</td><td>3.86</td><td>4.64</td><td>4.02</td><td>4.53</td></tr>
<tr><td>Vocabulary</td><td>3.01</td><td>3.51</td><td>3.02</td><td>3.53</td><td>3.02</td><td>3.53</td><td>3.05</td><td>3.66</td><td>3.05</td><td>3.67</td><td>3.18</td><td>3.58</td></tr>
<tr><td>Comprehension</td><td>3.87</td><td>4.52</td><td>3.88</td><td>4.53</td><td>3.88</td><td>4.54</td><td>3.93</td><td>4.73</td><td>3.94</td><td>4.73</td><td>4.10</td><td>4.63</td></tr>
<tr><td>Digit Span</td><td>3.20</td><td>3.74</td><td>—</td><td>—</td><td>—</td><td>—</td><td>3.24</td><td>3.90</td><td>3.25</td><td>3.91</td><td>3.38</td><td>3.81</td></tr>
<tr><td>Picture Completion</td><td>3.87</td><td>4.52</td><td>3.88</td><td>4.53</td><td>3.88</td><td>4.54</td><td>3.93</td><td>4.73</td><td>3.94</td><td>4.73</td><td>4.10</td><td>4.63</td></tr>
<tr><td>Coding</td><td>3.71</td><td>4.34</td><td>3.72</td><td>4.35</td><td>3.73</td><td>4.36</td><td>3.77</td><td>4.53</td><td>3.78</td><td>4.54</td><td>3.94</td><td>4.44</td></tr>
<tr><td>Picture Arrangement</td><td>3.95</td><td>4.61</td><td>3.95</td><td>4.62</td><td>3.96</td><td>4.63</td><td>4.01</td><td>4.82</td><td>4.01</td><td>4.83</td><td>4.19</td><td>4.72</td></tr>
<tr><td>Block Design</td><td>3.01</td><td>3.51</td><td>3.02</td><td>3.53</td><td>3.02</td><td>3.53</td><td>3.05</td><td>3.66</td><td>3.05</td><td>3.67</td><td>3.18</td><td>3.58</td></tr>
<tr><td>Object Assembly</td><td>4.44</td><td>5.19</td><td>4.45</td><td>5.20</td><td>4.45</td><td>5.20</td><td>4.52</td><td>5.43</td><td>4.52</td><td>5.43</td><td>4.72</td><td>5.32</td></tr>
<tr><td>Symbol Search</td><td>—</td><td>—</td><td>3.95</td><td>4.62</td><td>—</td><td>—</td><td>4.01</td><td>4.82</td><td>—</td><td>—</td><td>4.19</td><td>4.72</td></tr>
<tr><td>Mazes</td><td>—</td><td>—</td><td>—</td><td>—</td><td>4.38</td><td>5.13</td><td>—</td><td>—</td><td>4.45</td><td>5.35</td><td>4.65</td><td>5.24</td></tr>
</tbody>
</table>

Note. Table L-4 shows the minimum deviations from an individual's average subtest scaled score that are significant at the .05 and .01 levels. See the note in Table C-3 (page 815) for an explanation of the method used to obtain the deviations.

[a] In this column, the entries for Information, Similarities, Vocabulary, and Comprehension are compared to the mean of these four subtests. Similarly, the entries for Picture Completion, Picture Arrangement, Block Design, and Object Assembly are compared to the mean of these four subtests.

[b] In this column, the entries for Information, Similarities, Arithmetic, Vocabulary, and Comprehension are compared to the mean of these five subtests. Similarly, the entries for Picture Completion, Coding, Picture Arrangement, Block Design, and Object Assembly are compared to the mean of these five subtests.

[c] In this column, the entries for Information, Similarities, Arithmetic, Vocabulary, Comprehension, and Digit Span are compared to the mean of these six subtests. Similarly, the entries for Picture Completion, Coding, Picture Arrangement, Block Design, Object Assembly, and Symbol Search are compared to the mean of these six subtests.

Table L-5
Differences Required for Significance When Each WISC-III Subtest Scaled Score Is Compared to the Respective Mean Factor Scaled Score for Any Individual Child

Subtest	Mean of Verbal Comprehension subtests		Mean of Perceptual Organization subtests		Mean of Processing Speed subtests	
	.05	.01	.05	.01	.05	.01
Information	2.69	3.26	—	—	—	—
Similarities	2.79	3.38	—	—	—	—
Arithmetic	—	—	—	—	—	—
Vocabulary	2.48	3.01	—	—	—	—
Comprehension	3.02	3.65	—	—	—	—
Digit Span	—	—	—	—	—	—
Picture Completion	—	—	2.80	3.43	—	—
Coding	—	—	—	—	2.30	2.88
Picture Arrangement	—	—	—	—	—	—
Block Design	—	—	2.49	3.05	—	—
Object Assembly	—	—	3.03	3.71	—	—
Symbol Search	—	—	—	—	2.30	2.88
Mazes	—	—	—	—	—	—

Note. Table L-5 shows the minimum deviations from an individual's mean factor scaled score that are significant at the .05 and .01 levels. See Note in Table C-3 (page 815) in Appendix C for an explanation of how differences were obtained. The following Bonferroni corrections were used: .05 = 2.500, .01 = 3.025 for Verbal Comprehension; .05 = 2.39, .01 = 2.93 for Perceptual Organization; .05 = 2.24, .01 = 2.81 for Processing Speed. The values in this table are based on the total sample.

Table L-6
Estimates of the Differences Obtained by Various Percentages of the WISC-III Standardization Sample When Each WISC-III Subtest Scaled Score is Compared to the Mean Scaled Score for Any Individual Child

Subtest	Verbal average (5 subtests)				Verbal average (6 subtests)							
	10%	5%	2%	1%	10%	5%	2%	1%				
Information	2.62	3.12	3.70	4.10	2.80	3.33	3.96	4.39				
Similarities	2.62	3.12	3.70	4.10	2.80	3.33	3.96	4.39				
Arithmetic	3.23	3.84	4.57	5.06	3.17	3.76	4.47	4.95				
Vocabulary	2.48	2.94	3.50	3.87	2.66	3.16	3.75	4.15				
Comprehension	3.02	3.59	4.26	4.72	3.17	3.76	4.47	4.95				
Digit Span	—	—	—	—	4.08	4.84	5.76	6.37				

Subtest	Performance average (5 subtests)				Performance average (6 subtests)				Performance average (6 subtests)			
	10%	5%	2%	1%	10%	5%	2%	1%	10%	5%	2%	1%
Picture Completion	3.42	4.06	4.82	5.34	3.58	4.25	5.06	5.60	3.53	4.19	4.99	5.52
Coding	4.17	4.96	5.89	6.53	4.01	4.76	5.66	6.27	4.24	5.04	5.99	6.63
Picture Arrangement	3.60	4.27	5.08	5.62	3.70	4.39	5.22	5.78	3.70	4.39	5.22	5.78
Block Design	3.04	3.61	4.29	4.75	3.14	3.72	4.43	4.90	3.14	3.72	4.43	4.90
Object Assembly	3.18	3.78	4.50	4.98	3.35	3.98	4.73	5.24	3.28	3.90	4.64	5.13
Symbol Search	—	—	—	—	3.40	4.04	4.80	5.31	—	—	—	—
Mazes	—	—	—	—	—	—	—	—	4.14	4.92	5.85	6.48

Subtest	Full Scale average (10 subtests)				Full Scale average (11 subtests)				Full Scale average (11 subtests)			
	10%	5%	2%	1%	10%	5%	2%	1%	10%	5%	2%	1%
Information	3.10	3.68	4.38	4.85	3.15	3.74	4.45	4.93	3.20	3.80	4.52	5.01
Similarities	3.12	3.70	4.40	4.88	3.17	3.76	4.47	4.95	3.22	3.82	4.52	5.03
Arithmetic	3.42	4.06	4.82	5.34	3.37	4.00	4.75	5.26	3.43	4.08	4.85	5.37
Vocabulary	3.04	3.61	4.29	4.75	3.09	3.67	4.36	4.82	3.14	3.72	4.43	4.90
Comprehension	3.47	4.12	4.89	5.42	3.50	4.16	4.94	5.47	3.51	4.17	4.96	5.50
Digit Span	—	—	—	—	4.22	5.02	5.96	6.60	—	—	—	—
Picture Completion	3.65	4.33	5.15	5.70	3.70	4.39	5.22	5.78	3.70	4.39	5.22	5.78
Coding	4.57	5.43	6.45	7.15	4.54	5.39	6.41	7.10	4.44	5.27	6.27	6.94
Picture Arrangement	3.89	4.63	5.50	6.09	3.94	4.68	5.57	6.17	3.91	4.65	5.52	6.11
Block Design	3.33	3.96	4.71	5.21	3.37	4.00	4.75	5.26	3.33	3.96	4.71	5.21
Object Assembly	3.66	4.35	5.17	5.73	3.71	4.41	5.24	5.81	3.68	4.37	5.20	5.75
Symbol Search	—	—	—	—	—	—	—	—	3.81	4.53	5.38	5.96
Mazes	—	—	—	—	—	—	—	—	—	—	—	—

(Table continues next page)

Table L-6 (cont.)

Subtest	Full Scale average (11 subtests)				Full Scale average (12 subtests)				Full Scale average (12 subtests)			
	10%	5%	2%	1%	10%	5%	2%	1%	10%	5%	2%	1%
Information	3.20	3.80	4.52	5.01	3.23	3.84	4.57	5.06	3.23	3.84	4.57	5.06
Similarities	3.22	3.82	4.54	5.03	3.23	3.84	4.57	5.06	3.25	3.86	4.59	5.08
Arithmetic	3.45	4.10	4.87	5.39	3.38	4.02	4.78	5.29	3.42	4.06	4.82	5.34
Vocabulary	3.15	3.74	4.45	4.93	3.17	3.76	4.47	4.95	3.18	3.78	4.50	4.98
Comprehension	3.53	4.19	4.99	5.52	3.55	4.21	5.01	5.55	3.56	4.23	5.03	5.57
Digit Span	—	—	—	—	4.24	5.04	5.99	6.63	4.24	5.04	5.99	6.63
Picture Completion	3.66	4.35	5.17	5.73	3.73	4.43	5.27	5.83	3.71	4.41	5.24	5.80
Coding	4.54	5.39	6.41	7.10	4.42	5.25	6.24	6.91	4.52	5.37	6.38	7.07
Picture Arrangement	3.89	4.63	5.50	6.09	3.94	4.68	5.57	6.17	3.94	4.68	5.57	6.17
Block Design	3.32	3.94	4.68	5.19	3.37	4.00	4.57	5.26	3.37	4.00	4.75	5.26
Object Assembly	3.65	4.33	5.15	5.70	3.71	4.41	5.24	5.80	3.68	4.37	5.20	5.75
Symbol Search	—	—	—	—	3.81	4.53	5.38	5.96	—	—	—	—
Mazes	4.64	5.51	6.55	7.25	—	—	—	—	4.64	5.51	6.55	7.25

Subtest	Full Scale average (13 subtests)			
	10%	5%	2%	1%
Information	3.30	3.92	4.66	5.16
Similarities	3.32	3.94	4.68	5.19
Arithmetic	3.43	4.08	4.85	5.37
Vocabulary	3.25	3.86	4.59	5.08
Comprehension	3.56	4.23	5.03	5.57
Digit Span	4.26	5.06	6.01	6.66
Picture Completion	3.73	4.43	5.27	5.83
Coding	4.41	5.23	6.22	6.89
Picture Arrangement	3.94	4.68	5.57	6.17
Block Design	3.35	3.98	4.73	5.24
Object Assembly	3.70	4.39	5.22	5.78
Symbol Search	3.81	4.53	5.38	5.96
Mazes	4.64	5.51	6.55	7.25

Note. The formula used to obtain the values in this table was obtained from Silverstein (1984):

$$SD_{Da} = 3\sqrt{1 + \overline{G} - 2\,\overline{T}_a}$$

where SD_{Da} is the standard deviation of the difference for subtest a, 3 is the standard deviation of the scaled scores on each of the subtests, $\overline{G}$ is the mean of all the elements in the matrix (including the diagonal), and $\overline{T}_a$ is the mean of the elements in row or column a of the matrix (again including the diagonal).

Table L-7
Estimates of the Probability of Obtaining Designated Differences Between Individual WISC-III Verbal and Performance IQs by Chance

Probability of obtaining given or greater discrepancy by chance	Age level											
	6	7	8	9	10	11	12	13	14	15	16	Av.[a]
.50	4.02	4.26	3.76	4.02	3.76	3.89	3.76	4.02	4.02	3.18	3.62	3.76
.25	6.90	7.32	6.45	6.90	6.45	6.68	6.45	6.90	6.90	5.45	6.22	6.45
.20	7.68	8.15	7.18	7.68	7.18	7.44	7.18	7.68	7.68	6.07	6.92	7.18
.10	9.90	10.50	9.26	9.90	9.26	9.59	9.26	9.90	9.90	7.83	8.92	9.26
.05	11.76	12.47	11.00	11.76	11.00	11.39	11.00	11.76	11.76	9.30	10.60	11.00
.02	13.98	14.83	13.08	13.98	13.08	13.54	13.08	13.98	13.98	11.05	12.60	13.08
.01	15.48	16.42	14.48	15.48	14.48	14.99	14.48	15.48	15.48	12.24	13.95	14.48
.001	19.74	20.94	18.47	19.74	18.47	19.11	18.47	19.74	19.74	15.61	17.79	18.47

Note. Table L-7 is entered in the column appropriate to the examinee's age. The discrepancy that is just less than the discrepancy obtained by the examinee is located. The entry in the first column in the same row gives the probability of obtaining a given or greater discrepancy by chance. For example, the hypothesis that a 6-year-old examinee obtained a Verbal-Performance discrepancy of 17 by chance can be rejected at the .01 level of significance. Table L-7 is two-tailed. See Chapter 8, Exhibit 8-1 (page 168) for an explanation of the method used to arrive at magnitude of differences.
[a] Av. = Average of 11 age groups.

Table L-8
Estimates of the Percentage of the Population Obtaining Discrepancies Between WISC-III Verbal and Performance IQs

Percentage obtaining given or greater discrepancy in either direction	Age level												Percentage obtaining given or greater discrepancy in a specific direction
	6	7	8	9	10	11	12	13	14	15	16	Av.[a]	
50	8.41	9.32	7.78	8.16	8.65	8.76	8.29	8.53	8.76	6.96	8.29	8.29	25
25	14.43	16.00	13.36	14.01	14.84	15.04	14.22	14.64	15.04	11.95	14.22	14.22	12.5
20	16.06	17.81	14.87	15.60	16.52	16.74	15.83	16.29	16.74	13.30	15.83	15.83	10
10	20.71	22.95	19.17	20.11	21.29	21.58	20.41	21.00	21.58	17.15	20.41	20.41	5
5	24.60	27.26	22.77	23.88	25.29	25.63	24.24	24.95	25.63	20.37	24.24	24.24	2.5
2	29.24	32.41	27.07	28.39	30.07	30.47	28.82	29.66	30.47	24.21	28.82	28.82	1
1	32.38	35.89	29.98	31.44	33.29	33.74	31.91	32.84	33.74	26.81	31.91	31.91	.5
.1	41.29	45.77	38.23	40.09	42.45	43.02	40.70	41.87	43.02	34.19	40.70	40.70	.05

Note. Table L-8 is entered in the column appropriate to the examinee's age. The discrepancy that is just less than the discrepancy obtained by the examinee is located. The entry in the first column in the same row gives the percentage of the standardization population obtaining discrepancies as large as or larger than the located discrepancy. For example, a 6-year-old examinee with a Verbal-Performance discrepancy of 14 on the WISC-III will be found in between 25 and 50 percent of the standardization population. However, a Verbal-Performance discrepancy of 14 in one direction only (that is, Verbal > Performance *or* Performance > Verbal) will be found in between 12.5 and 25 percent of the standardization population.

The method used to compute the discrepancy between the Verbal and Performance Scale IQs that reflects the percentage of the population obtaining the discrepancy is as follows: Discrepancy $= \sigma_1 z \sqrt{2 - 2r_{xy}}$. The first term is the standard deviation of the test, the second is the selected z value, and the last is the correlation between the two scales. For example, for a 6-year-old child, the discrepancy between the WISC-III Verbal and Performance Scale IQs that represents 5 percent of the population is $15(1.96)\sqrt{2 - 2(.65)} = 24.60$.
[a] Av. = Average of 11 age groups.

Table L-9

Estimates of the Probability of Obtaining Designated Differences Between Individual WISC-III Factor Score Deviation Quotients (DQs) by Chance

Probability of obtaining given or greater discrepancy by chance	Verbal Comprehension DQ vs. Perceptual Organization DQ	Verbal Comprehension DQ vs. Processing Speed DQ	Perceptual Organization DQ vs. Processing Speed DQ
.50	4.12	4.88	5.34
.25	7.07	8.38	9.16
.20	7.87	9.33	10.20
.10	10.14	12.02	13.14
.05	12.05	14.28	15.61
.02	14.32	16.98	18.56
.01	15.86	18.80	20.55
.001	20.23	23.97	26.21

Note. The values in Table L-9 are based on the total group. The discrepancy that is just less than the discrepancy obtained by the examinee is located. The entry in the first column in the same row gives the probability of obtaining a given or greater discrepancy by chance. For example, the hypothesis that an examinee obtained a Verbal Comprehension–Perceptual Organization discrepancy of 12 by chance can be rejected at the .10 level of significance. Table L-9 is two-tailed. See Chapter 8, Exhibit 8-1 (page 168) for an explanation of the method used to arrive at the magnitude of differences.

Table L-10

Estimates of the Percentage of the Population Obtaining Discrepancies Between WISC-III Factor Deviation Quotients (DQs)

Percentage obtaining given or greater discrepancy in either direction	Verbal Comprehension DQ vs. Perceptual Organization DQ	Verbal Comprehension DQ vs. Processing Speed DQ	Perceptual Organization DQ vs. Processing Speed DQ	Percentage obtaining given or greater discrepancy in a specific direction
50	8.94	11.13	10.79	25
25	15.34	19.11	18.52	12.5
20	17.08	21.27	20.62	10
10	22.01	27.42	26.58	5
5	26.15	32.57	31.57	2.5
2	31.09	38.72	37.53	1
1	34.42	42.87	41.56	.5
.1	43.90	54.67	53.00	.05

Note. The procedure used to calculate the values in this table is similar to that used by Clampitt, Adair, & Strenio (1983). The z values used were as follows: $z = .67$ for 50%, $z = 1.15$ for 25%, $z = 1.28$ for 20%, $z = 1.65$ for 10%, $z = 1.96$ for 5%, $z = 2.33$ for 2%, $z = 2.58$ for 1%, $z = 3.29$ for .1%. Values in this table are based on the total group.

Verbal Comprehension subtests are Information, Similarities, Vocabulary, and Comprehension. Perceptual Organization subtests are Picture Completion, Block Design, and Object Assembly. Processing Speed subtests are Coding and Symbol Search.

Table L-II
Reliability and Validity Coefficients of Proposed WISC-III Short Forms

Dyad				Triad					Tetrad						Pentad						
Short form		r_{tt}	r	Short form			r_{tt}	r	Short form				r_{tt}	r	Short form					r_{tt}	r
I	V	.915	.803	I	V	BD	.933	.881	I	S	V	BD	.944	.886	I	S	A	V	BD	.949	.899
V	BD	.911	.862	I	S	V	.932	.829	I	A	V	BD	.939	.895	I	S	V	C	BD	.949	.889
S	V	.905	.802	S	V	BD	.928	.878	I	S	V	C	.939	.839	I	S	V	DS	BD	.948	.899
I	BD	.902	.848	I	V	DS	.924	.827	I	V	DS	BD	.939	.890	I	S	V	PC	BD	.947	.898
V	DS	.896	.764	I	V	C	.924	.821	I	S	A	V	.939	.860	I	A	V	DS	BD	.945	.899
I	S	.895	.802	I	S	BD	.923	.874	I	S	V	DS	.938	.852	I	S	A	V	C	.945	.867
DS	BD	.894	.760	I	A	V	.923	.847	I	V	C	BD	.938	.885	I	S	A	V	DS	.945	.872
S	BD	.893	.842	V	DS	BD	.922	.864	S	A	V	BD	.936	.895	I	A	V	C	BD	.945	.901
V	C	.890	.777	A	V	BD	.921	.884	I	V	PC	BD	.936	.889	I	S	V	PA	BD	.944	.902
A	V	.886	.825	S	V	C	.920	.816	S	V	C	BD	.935	.881	I	S	V	C	DS	.944	.863

Note. Abbreviations: I = Information, V = Vocabulary, BD = Block Design, S = Similarities, DS = Digit Span, A = Arithmetic, PC = Picture Completion, PA = Picture Arrangement, SS = Symbol Search, C = Comprehension.

It is recommended that short-form combinations involving Digit Span or Symbol Search not be used because these two subtests were not used in the construction of the IQ tables.

For screening children who have severe hearing problems, the best two-subtest short-form combinations are Picture Completion and Block Design (r_{tt} = .882, r = .777), followed by Block Design and Symbol Search (r_{tt} = .872, r = .784) and Picture Arrangement and Block Design (r_{tt} = .869, r = .777); the best three-subtest short-form combinations are Coding, Block Design, and Symbol Search (r_{tt} = .895, r = .765); Picture Completion, Block Design, and Symbol Search (r_{tt} = .893, r = .830); Picture Completion, Picture Arrangement, and Block Design (r_{tt} = .893, r = .817); and Picture Completion, Block Design, and Object Assembly (r_{tt} = .893, r = .794).

For screening children with severe visual deficits, any of the short-form combinations shown in the table involving subtests in the Verbal Scale can be used, such as Information and Vocabulary or Similarities and Vocabulary.

Tables L-12, L-13, L-14, and L-15 provide estimated Deviation Quotients associated with the ten best dyads, triads, tetrads, and pentads, respectively.

This table was constructed using a computer program developed by L. Atkinson and G. Yoshida (1989), "A BASIC Program for Determining Reliability and Validity of Subtest Combination Short Forms," *Educational and Psychological Measurement, 49*, 141–143. The program is based on formulas provided by Tellegen and Briggs (1967).

Table L-12
Estimated WISC-III Full Scale Deviation Quotients for Sum of Scaled Scores for Ten Best Short-Form Dyads

	Combination				Combination		
Sum of scaled scores	Col. 1[a] V + DS DS + BD	Col. 2[b] V + BD I + BD S + BD	Col. 3 I + V S + V I + S V + C A + V	Sum of scaled scores	Col. 1[a] V + DS DS + BD	Col. 2[b] V + BD I + BD S + BD	Col. 3 I + V S + V I + S V + C A + V
				20	100	100	100
				21	103	103	103
2	45	48	51	22	106	106	105
3	48	51	54	23	109	109	108
4	51	54	57	24	112	112	111
5	54	56	59	25	115	115	114
6	57	59	62	26	118	117	116
7	60	62	65	27	121	120	119
8	63	65	67	28	124	123	122
9	67	68	70	29	127	126	124
10	70	71	73	30	130	129	127
11	73	74	76	31	133	132	130
12	76	77	78	32	137	135	133
13	79	80	81	33	140	138	135
14	82	83	84	34	143	141	138
15	85	85	86	35	146	144	141
16	88	88	89	36	149	146	143
17	91	91	92	37	152	149	146
18	94	94	95	38	155	152	149
19	97	97	97				

Note. Abbreviations: V = Vocabulary, DS = Digit Span, BD = Block Design, I = Information, S = Similarities, CD = Coding, SS = Symbol Search, C = Comprehension, A = Arithmetic, PC = Picture Completion, PA = Picture Arrangement.

Reliability and validity coefficients associated with each short-form combination for the ten best dyads are shown in Table L-11. See Exhibit I-4 in Appendix I for an explanation of the procedure used to obtain the estimated Deviation Quotients.

[a] This column can also be used for the PC + BD combination and for the PA + BD combination useful for screening hard-of-hearing children.
[b] This column can also be used for the BD + SS combination useful for screening hard-of-hearing children and for the I + PC combination useful for a rapid screening.

Table L-13
Estimated WISC-III Full Scale Deviation Quotients for Sum of Scaled Scores for Ten Best Short-Form Triads and Perceptual Organization Factor Score

Sum of scaled scores	Combination				Sum of scaled scores	Combination			
	Col. 1[a]	Col. 2[b]	Col. 3	Col. 4		Col. 1[a]	Col. 2[b]	Col. 3	Col. 4
	V+DS+BD	I+V+DS	I + V +BD / S + V +BD / I + S +BD / A + V +BD / PC+BD+OA[c]	I+S+V / I+V+C / I+A+C / S+V+C		V+DS+BD	I+V+DS	I + V +BD / S + V +BD / I + S +BD / A + V +BD / PC+BD+OA[c]	I+S+V / I+V+C / I+A+C / S+V+C
3	41	44	46	48	30	100	100	100	100
4	43	46	48	49	31	102	102	102	102
5	45	48	50	51	32	104	104	104	104
6	48	50	52	53	33	107	106	106	106
7	50	52	54	55	34	109	108	108	108
8	52	54	56	57	35	111	110	110	110
9	54	56	58	59	36	113	112	112	112
					37	115	115	114	114
					38	117	117	116	116
					39	120	119	118	117
10	56	58	60	61	40	122	121	120	119
11	59	60	62	63	41	124	123	122	121
12	61	63	64	65	42	126	125	124	123
13	63	65	66	67	43	128	127	126	125
14	65	67	68	69	44	131	129	128	127
15	67	69	70	71	45	133	131	130	129
16	69	71	72	73	46	135	133	132	131
17	72	73	74	75	47	137	135	134	133
18	74	75	76	77	48	139	137	136	135
19	76	77	78	79	49	141	140	138	137
20	78	79	80	81	50	144	142	140	139
21	80	81	82	83	51	146	144	142	141
22	83	83	84	84	52	148	146	144	143
23	85	85	86	86	53	150	148	146	145
24	87	88	88	88	54	152	150	148	147
25	89	90	90	90	55	155	152	150	149
26	91	92	92	92	56	157	154	152	151
27	93	94	94	94	57	159	156	154	152
28	96	96	96	96	58	161	158	156	154
29	98	98	98	98					

Note. Abbreviations: V = Vocabulary, DS = Digit Span, BD = Block Design, I = Information, S = Similarities, A = Arithmetic, PC = Picture Completion, OA = Object Assembly, C = Comprehension, CD = Coding, SS = Symbol Search, PA = Picture Arrangement.

Reliability and validity coefficients associated with each short-form combination for the ten best triads are shown in Table L-11. See Exhibit I-4 in Appendix I for an explanation of the procedure used to obtain the estimated Deviation Quotients.

[a] This column can also be used for the CD + BD + SS combination useful for screening hard-of-hearing children.

[b] This column can also be used for the PC + BD + SS combination and for the PC + PA + BD combination useful for screening hard-of-hearing children.

[c] The Perceptual Organization factor score is formed by PC + BD + OA. This combination is also useful for screening hard-of-hearing children.

Table L-14
Estimated WISC-III Full Scale Deviation Quotients for Sum of Scaled Scores for Ten Best Short-Form Tetrads

	Combination			Combination	
	Col. 1[a]	Col. 2		Col. 1[a]	Col. 2
Sum of scaled scores	$I+V+DS+BD$ $I+S+V+DS$ $I+V+PC+BD$	$I+S+V+BD$ $I+A+V+BD$ $I+S+V+C$ $I+S+A+V$ $I+V+C+BD$ $S+A+V+BD$ $S+V+C+BD$	Sum of scaled scores	$I+V+DS+BD$ $I+S+V+DS$ $I+V+PC+BD$	$I+S+V+BD$ $I+A+V+BD$ $I+S+V+C^b$ $I+S+A+V$ $I+V+C+BD$ $S+A+V+BD$ $S+V+C+BD$
			40	100	100
			41	102	102
			42	103	103
			43	105	105
4	44	45	44	106	106
5	45	46	45	108	108
6	47	48	46	109	109
7	48	49	47	111	111
8	50	51	48	113	112
9	51	52	49	114	114
10	53	54	50	116	115
11	55	55	51	117	117
12	56	57	52	119	118
13	58	58	53	120	120
14	59	60	54	122	122
15	61	61	55	124	123
16	62	63	56	125	125
17	64	65	57	127	126
18	65	66	58	128	128
19	67	68	59	130	129
20	69	69	60	131	131
21	70	71	61	133	132
22	72	72	62	135	134
23	73	74	63	136	135
24	75	75	64	138	137
25	76	77	65	139	139
26	78	78	66	141	140
27	80	80	67	142	142
28	81	82	68	144	143
29	83	83	69	145	145

(Table continues next page)

Table L-14 (cont.)

Sum of scaled scores	Combination		Sum of scaled scores	Combination	
	Col. 1[a]	Col. 2		Col. 1[a]	Col. 2
	$I+V+DS+BD$ $I+S+V+DS$ $I+V+PC+BD$	$I+S+V+BD$ $I+A+V+BD$ $I+S+V+C$ $I+S+A+V$ $I+V+C+BD$ $S+A+V+BD$ $S+V+C+BD$		$I+V+DS+BD$ $I+S+V+DS$ $I+V+PC+BD$	$I+S+V+BD$ $I+A+V+BD$ $I+S+V+C^b$ $I+S+A+V$ $I+V+C+BD$ $S+A+V+BD$ $S+V+C+BD$
30	84	85	70	147	146
31	86	86	71	149	148
32	87	88	72	150	149
33	89	89	73	152	151
34	91	91	74	153	152
35	92	92	75	155	154
36	94	94	76	156	155
37	95	95			
38	97	97			
39	98	98			

Note. Abbreviations: I = Information, V = Vocabulary, DS = Digit Span, BD = Block Design, S = Similarities, PC = Picture Completion, A = Arithmetic, C = Comprehension, PA = Picture Arrangement, OA = Object Assembly.

Reliability and validity coefficients associated with each short-form combination for the ten best tetrads are shown in Table L-11. See Exhibit I-4 in Appendix I for an explanation of the procedure used to obtain the estimated Deviation Quotients.

[a] This column can be used to estimate the Deviation Quotients for the PC + PA + BD + OA combination.

[b] This short-form combination represents the Verbal Comprehension factor score. See Table A.5 (page 255) in the WISC-III manual for Deviation Quotients for this short-form combination. The method used by The Psychological Corporation (discussed on pages 30 and 31 of the WISC-III manual) differs from that used in constructing this table. Their weighting and smoothing procedures may account for the difference in their values and the values in this table.

Table L-I5
Estimated WISC-III Full Scale Deviation Quotients for Sum of Scaled Scores for Ten Best Short-Form Pentads

| | Combination | | | Combination | |
| | Col. 1 | Col. 2 | | Col. 1 | Col. 2 |
Sum of scaled scores	$I+S+A+V+BD$ $I+S+A+V+C$	$I+S+V+C+BD$ $I+S+V+DS+BD$ $I+S+V+PC+BD$ $I+A+V+DS+BD$ $I+S+A+V+DS$ $I+A+V+C+BD$ $I+S+V+PA+BD$ $I+S+V+C+DS$	Sum of scaled scores	$I+S+A+V+BD$ $I+S+A+V+C$	$I+S+V+C+BD$ $I+S+V+DS+BD$ $I+S+V+PC+BD$ $I+A+V+DS+BD$ $I+S+A+V+DS$ $I+A+V+C+BD$ $I+S+V+PA+BD$ $I+S+V+C+DS$
			30	75	74
			31	76	76
			32	78	77
			33	79	78
			34	80	80
5	44	43	35	81	81
6	46	44	36	83	82
7	47	45	37	84	83
8	48	46	38	85	85
9	49	48	39	86	86
10	50	49	40	88	87
11	52	50	41	89	89
12	53	51	42	90	90
13	54	53	43	91	91
14	55	54	44	93	92
15	57	55	45	94	94
16	58	57	46	95	95
17	59	58	47	96	96
18	60	59	48	98	97
19	62	60	49	99	99
20	63	62	50	100	100
21	64	63	51	101	101
22	65	64	52	102	103
23	67	66	53	104	104
24	68	67	54	105	105
25	69	68	55	106	106
26	70	69	56	107	108
27	72	71	57	109	109
28	73	72	58	110	110
29	74	73	59	111	111

(Table continues next page)

Table L-15 (cont.)

| Sum of scaled scores | Combination | | Sum of scaled scores | Combination | |
	Col. 1 $I+S+A+V+BD$ $I+S+A+V+C$	Col. 2 $I+S+V+C+BD$ $I+S+V+DS+BD$ $I+S+V+PC+BD$ $I+A+V+DS+BD$ $I+S+A+V+DS$ $I+A+V+C+BD$ $I+S+V+PA+BD$ $I+S+V+C+DS$		Col. 1 $I+S+A+V+BD$ $I+S+A+V+C$	Col. 2 $I+S+V+C+BD$ $I+S+V+DS+BD$ $I+S+V+PC+BD$ $I+A+V+DS+BD$ $I+S+A+V+DS$ $I+A+V+C+BD$ $I+S+V+PA+BD$ $I+S+V+C+DS$
60	112	113	80	137	138
61	114	114	81	138	140
62	115	115	82	140	141
63	116	117	83	141	142
64	117	118	84	142	143
65	119	119	85	143	145
66	120	120	86	145	146
67	121	122	87	146	147
68	122	123	88	147	149
69	124	124	89	148	150
70	125	126	90	150	151
71	126	127	91	151	152
72	127	128	92	152	154
73	128	129	93	153	155
74	130	131	94	154	156
75	131	132			
76	132	133			
77	133	134			
78	135	136			
79	136	137			

Note. Abbreviations: I = Information, S = Similarities, A = Arithmetic, V = Vocabulary, BD = Block Design, C = Comprehension, DS = Digit Span, PC = Picture Completion, PA = Picture Arrangement.

Reliability and validity coefficients associated with each short-form combination for the ten best pentads are shown in Table L-11. See Exhibit I-4 in Appendix I for an explanation of the procedure used to obtain the estimated Deviation Quotients.

Table L-16
Interpretive Rationale, Implications of High and Low Scores, and Instructional Implications for the WISC-III Symbol Search Subtest

Ability	Background factors	Possible implications of high scores	Possible implications of low scores	Instructional implications
		Symbol Search		
Processing speed	Rate of motor activity	Good processing speed	Poor processing speed	Use visual-motor scanning exercises, such as having child look at two or more objects and decide if they are the same or different
Perceptual discrimination	Motivation	Good perceptual discrimination ability	Poor perceptual discrimination ability	
Speed of mental operation				
Psychomotor speed		Good attention and concentration	Distractibility	
Attention and concentration skills		Sustained energy or persistence	Visual defects	
Short-term memory		Good motivation or desire for achievement	Lethargy	
Visual-motor coordination			Poor motivation	
Cognitive flexibility				

MODIFIED INSTRUCTIONS FOR ADMINISTERING THE WISC-III SYMBOL SEARCH SUBTEST TO DEAF CHILDREN

The WISC-III materials plus an instruction sheet prepared by the examiner are needed.

PROCEDURE FOR SYMBOL SEARCH A (FOR CHILDREN AGES 6–7)

The instructions cover the sample items, practice items, and subtest items.

Sample Items

With the Symbol Search Response Booklet before the child, move your finger in a sweeping motion, from the child's left to right, across the entire row of the first sample item in Part A. Then point to the single target symbol in the first column. Next point to the first symbol in the search group. Then catch the child's eye and shake your head "no" to indicate that the first search symbol does not match the target symbol. You must make sure the child is looking at you each time you shake your head "yes" or "no" or when you nod your head for any other purpose.

Repeat this procedure two more times. Point to the single target symbol and then to the second search symbol. Shake your head "no." Again point to the single target symbol and then to the third search symbol. This time shake your head "yes" to indicate that the search symbol matches the target symbol. With a no. 2 pencil, mark a slash in the "YES" box.

For the second sample item in Part A, generally follow the same procedure. However, for this item shake your head "no" for each search symbol. After demonstrating the third search symbol, mark a slash in the "NO" box.

Practice Items

Give the child a no. 2 pencil. Point to the first row of the practice items and move your finger in a sweeping motion, from the child's left to right, along the entire first row. Nod your head to indicate to the child to begin. If the child places a slash mark in the "YES" box, nod your head to indicate "good" and go to the second practice item.

If the child marks "NO" on the first practice item, point to the target symbol and then to the second search symbol. Shake your head to indicate "yes." Then immediately place a slash through the "YES" box. Do not demonstrate the third symbol.

Point to the second practice item and, by nodding your head, encourage the child to do it. If the child marks "NO," nod your head to indicate "good" and proceed to the regular subtest items (see below). If the child marks "YES," correct the child. Point to the target symbol and each of the three search symbols in turn, shaking your head to indicate "no" each time. Then place a slash through the "NO" box.

Do not go on to the regular subtest items until the child understands the task. You may have to erase your marks and the child's marks and ask the child to do the sample and/or practice items again.

Subtest Items

When the child understands the task, open the Symbol Search Booklet to the second page and fold the page over. If the child can read, hand him or her the instruction sheet. This sheet should contain the information beginning in the last paragraph on page 146 and ending with the fifth line on page 147 of the WISC-III manual ("When . . . questions?"). Only copy the material in color. After the child has read the directions, point to the first row to indicate that the child should begin the task.

If the child cannot read, run your finger down the entire second page. Next turn the booklet to the third page, and again run your finger down the entire page. Then turn to the fourth page, and again run your finger down the entire page. After showing the child the three pages of items, turn back to the second page of the booklet. Point to the pencil and then to the first row of the second page, then run your finger down the page, and then nod your head to indicate to the child to begin.

If a child ceases to work after completing the first row, redirect the child's attention to the second row by pointing to the entire second row in a sweeping motion and encourage the child to continue. If a child stops at the end of the second page, turn the booklet to the third page and encourage the child to continue. If the child stops at the end of the third page, turn the booklet to the fourth page and encourage the child to continue. Allow 120 seconds.

PROCEDURE FOR SYMBOL SEARCH B (FOR CHILDREN AGES 8–16)

The instructions cover the sample items, practice items, and subtest items.

Sample Items

With the Symbol Search Response Booklet before the child, move your finger in a sweeping motion, from the child's left to right, across the entire row of the first sample item in Part B. Then point to the two target symbols in the first column. Next point to the first symbol in the search group. Then catch the child's eye and shake your head "yes" to indicate that the first search symbol matches the target symbol. With a no. 2 pencil, immediately mark a slash in the "YES" box. You must make sure the child is looking at you each time you shake your head "yes" or "no" or when you nod your head for any other purpose. Go to the second sample item, without demonstrating the remaining symbols in the first sample item.

For the second sample item in Part B, point to the two target symbols and then to the first search symbol. Shake your head "no" to indicate that the search symbol does not match either of the target symbols. Repeat this procedure four more times. In each case point to the two target symbols and then to the search symbol. Shake your head "no" each time. After the last search symbol, make a slash in the "NO" box.

Practice Items

Give the child a no. 2 pencil. Point to the first row of the practice items and move your finger in a sweeping motion, from the child's left to right, along the entire first row. Nod your head to indicate to the child to begin. If the child places a slash mark in the "YES" box, nod your head to indicate "good" and go to the second practice item.

If the child marks "NO" on the first practice item, correct the child. Point to the two target symbols and then to the *second* search symbol. Shake your head to indicate "yes." Then immediately place a slash through the "YES" box. Do not demonstrate the remaining three symbols. Go to the second practice item.

Point to the second practice item and, by nodding your head, encourage the child to do it. If the child marks "NO," nod your head to indicate "good" and proceed to the regular subtest items (see below). If the child marks "YES," correct the child. Point to the two target symbols and each of the five search symbols in turn, shaking your head to indicate "no" each time. Then place a slash through the "NO" box.

Do not go on to the regular subtest items until the child understands the task. You may have to erase your marks and the child's marks and ask the child to do the sample and/or practice items again.

Subtest Items

When the child understands the task, open the Symbol Search Booklet to the sixth page and fold it over. If the child can read, hand him or her the instruction sheet. This sheet should contain the information beginning in the last paragraph on page 146 and ending with the fifth line on page 147 of the WISC-III manual ("When . . . questions?"). Only copy the material in color. After the child has read the directions, point to the first row to indicate that the child should begin the task.

If the child cannot read, run your finger down the entire sixth page. Next turn the booklet to the seventh page, and again run your finger down the entire page. Then turn to the eighth page, and again run your finger down the entire page. After showing the child the three pages of items, turn back to the sixth page of the booklet. Point to the pencil and then to the first row of the sixth page, then run your finger down the page, and then nod your head to indicate to the child to begin.

If a child ceases to work after completing the first row, redirect the child's attention to the second row by pointing to the entire second row in a sweeping motion and encourage the child to continue. If a child stops at the end of the sixth page, turn the booklet to the seventh page. If the child stops at the end of the seventh page, turn the booklet to the eighth page. Allow 120 seconds.

NAME INDEX

_ SUBJECT INDEX

Table BC-1
Percentile Ranks for Deviation IQs and Composite Scores

IQ	Percentile rank		IQ	Percentile rank		IQ	Percentile rank	
	Wechsler Scales (SD = 15)	Stanford-Binet, McCarthy (SD = 16)		Wechsler Scales (SD = 15)	Stanford-Binet, McCarthy (SD = 16)		Wechsler Scales (SD = 15)	Stanford-Binet, McCarthy (SD = 16)
155	99.99	99.97	118	88	87	81	10	12
154	99.98	99.96	117	87	86	80	9	11
153	99.98	99.95	116	86	84	79	8	9
152	99.97	99.94	115	84	83	78	7	8
151	99.97	99.93	114	82	81	77	6	8
150	99.96	99.91	113	81	79	76	5	7
149	99.95	99.89	112	79	77	75	5	6
148	99.93	99.87	111	77	75	74	4	5
147	99.91	99.83	110	75	73	73	4	5
146	99.89	99.80	109	73	71	72	3	4
145	99.87	99.75	108	70	69	71	3	4
144	99.83	99.70	107	68	67	70	2	3
143	99.79	99.64	106	66	65	69	2	3
142	99.74	99.57	105	63	62	68	2	2
141	99.69	99	104	61	60	67	1	2
140	99.62	99	103	58	57	66	1	2
139	99.53	99	102	55	55	65	1	1
138	99	99	101	53	52	64	1	1
137	99	99	100	50	50	63	1	1
136	99	99	99	47	48	62	1	1
135	99	99	98	45	45	61	.47	1
134	99	98	97	42	43	60	.38	1
133	99	98	96	39	40	59	.31	1
132	98	98	95	37	38	58	.26	.43
131	98	97	94	34	35	57	.21	.36
130	98	97	93	32	33	56	.17	.30
129	97	96	92	30	31	55	.13	.25
128	97	96	91	27	29	54	.11	.20
127	96	95	90	25	27	53	.09	.17
126	96	95	89	23	25	52	.07	.13
125	95	94	88	21	23	51	.05	.11
124	95	93	87	19	21	50	.04	.09
123	94	92	86	18	19	49	.03	.07
122	93	92	85	16	17	48	.03	.06
121	92	91	84	14	16	47	.02	.05
120	91	89	83	13	14	46	.02	.04
119	90	88	82	12	13	45	.01	.03

Note. This table can be used to convert standard scores on any test with a mean of 100 and a standard deviation of 15 or 16 to percentile ranks.